D1289661

Literature

Grade 11

The GREAT GATSBY

F. SCOTT FITZGERALD

COMMON CORE EDITION

Typeset in *The Sans* from LucasFonts.

Acknowledgments appear at the back of the book, following the Index of Titles and Authors.

ART CREDITS

COVER, TITLE PAGE

Front Cover, Title Page: (tl) The Granger Collection, New York; (tr) Alamy/Royalty Free; (cr) The Granger Collection, New York; (bc) Getty Images; (bcr) The Granger Collection, New York; (c) Dave G. Houser/Corbis; (bl) Ken Kinzie/HMH Publishers.

Back Cover: (t) The Laughing Philosopher (1887), George C. Cox. Photograph. © Museum of the City of New York/Bridgeman Art Library; (c) David Zimmerman/Corbis; (cr) Corbis; (bl) BrandX Pictures/Alamy Images.

FM9: © Getty Images

FM39: © Age Fotostock America, Inc.

Art Credits are continued at the back of the book, following the Acknowledgments.

Printed in the U.S.A.

ISBN: 978-0-547-61841-8

3 4 5 6 7 8 9 10 0868 20 19 18 17 16 15 14 13 12 11

4500292649 B C D E F G

HOLT McDOUGAL

Literature

Grade 11

Janet Allen
Arthur N. Applebee
Jim Burke
Douglas Carnine
Yvette Jackson
Carol Jago
Robert T. Jiménez
Judith A. Langer
Robert J. Marzano
Mary Lou McCloskey
Donna M. Ogle
Carol Booth Olson
Lydia Stack
Carol Ann Tomlinson

Special Contributor: Kylene Beers

HOLT McDOUGAL

HOUGHTON MIFFLIN HARCOURT

SENIOR PROGRAM CONSULTANTS

JANET ALLEN Reading and Literacy Specialist; creator of the popular "It's Never Too Late"/"Reading for Life" Institutes. Dr. Allen is an internationally known consultant who specializes in literacy work with at-risk students. Her publications include *Tools for Content Literacy; It's Never Too Late: Leading Adolescents to Lifelong Learning; Yellow Brick Roads: Shared and Guided Paths to Independent Reading; Words, Words, Words: Teaching Vocabulary in Grades 4–12;* and *Testing 1, 2, 3 . . . Bridging Best Practice and High-Stakes Assessments.* Dr. Allen was a high school reading and English teacher for more than 20 years.

ARTHUR N. APPLEBEE Leading Professor, School of Education at the University at Albany, State University of New York; Director of the Center on English Learning and Achievement. During his varied career, Dr. Applebee has been both a researcher and a teacher, working in institutional settings with children with severe learning problems, in public schools, as a staff member of the National Council of Teachers of English, and in professional education. He was elected to the International Reading Hall of Fame and has received, among other honors, the David H. Russell Award for Distinguished Research in the Teaching of English.

JIM BURKE Lecturer and Author; Teacher of English at Burlingame High School, Burlingame, California. Mr. Burke is a popular presenter at educational conferences across the country and is the author of numerous books for teachers, including *School Smarts: The Four Cs of Academic Success; The English Teacher's Companion; Reading Reminders; Writing Reminders;* and *ACCESSing School: Teaching Struggling Readers to Achieve Academic and Personal Success.* He is the recipient of NCTE's Exemplary English Leadership Award and was inducted into the California Reading Association's Hall of Fame.

DOUGLAS CARNINE Professor of Education at the University of Oregon; Director of the Western Region Reading First Technical Assistance Center. Dr. Carnine is nationally known for his focus on research-based practices in education, especially curriculum designs that prepare instructors of K–12 students. He has received the Lifetime Achievement Award from the Council for Exceptional Children and the Ersted Award for outstanding teaching at the University of Oregon. Dr. Carnine frequently consults on educational policy with government groups, businesses, communities, and teacher unions.

YVETTE JACKSON Executive Director of the National Urban Alliance for Effective Education. Nationally recognized for her work in assessing the learning potential of underachieving urban students, Dr. Jackson is also a presenter for the Harvard Principal Center and is a member of the Differentiation Faculty of the Association for Supervision and Curriculum Development. Dr. Jackson's research focuses on literacy, gifted education, and cognitive mediation theory. She designed the Comprehensive Education Plan for the New York City Public Schools and has served as their Director of Gifted Programs.

CAROL JAGO Teacher of English with thirty-two years of experience at Santa Monica High School in California; Author and nationally known Lecturer; and Past President of the National Council of Teachers of English. With varied experience in standards assessment and secondary education, Ms. Jago is the author of numerous books on education and is active with the California Association of Teachers of English, editing its scholarly journal *California English* since 1996. Ms. Jago also served on the planning committee for the 2009 NAEP Framework and the 2011 NAEP Writing Framework.

ROBERT T. JIMÉNEZ Professor of Language, Literacy, and Culture at Vanderbilt University. Dr. Jiménez's research focuses on the language and literacy practices of Latino students. A former bilingual education teacher, he is now conducting research on how written language is thought about and used in contemporary Mexico. Dr. Jiménez has received several research and teaching honors, including two Fulbright awards from the Council for the International Exchange of Scholars and the Albert J. Harris Award from the International Reading Association.

JUDITH A. LANGER Distinguished Professor at the University at Albany, State University of New York; Director of the Center on English Learning and Achievement; Director of the Albany Institute for Research in Education. An internationally known scholar in English language arts education, Dr. Langer specializes in developing teaching approaches that can enrich and improve what gets done on a daily basis in classrooms. Her publications include *Getting to Excellent: How to Create Better Schools* and *Effective Literacy Instruction: Building Successful Reading and Writing Programs.*

ROBERT J. MARZANO Senior Scholar at Mid-Continent Research for Education and Learning (McREL); Associate Professor at Cardinal Stritch University in Milwaukee, Wisconsin; President of Marzano & Associates. An internationally known researcher, trainer, and speaker, Dr. Marzano has developed programs that translate research and theory into practical tools for K–12 teachers and administrators. He has written extensively on such topics as reading and writing instruction, thinking skills, school effectiveness, assessment, and standards implementation.

DONNA M. OGLE Professor of Reading and Language at National-Louis University in Chicago, Illinois; Past President of the International Reading Association. Creator of the well-known KWL strategy, Dr. Ogle has directed many staff development projects translating theory and research into school practice in middle and secondary schools throughout the United States and has served as a consultant on literacy projects worldwide. Her extensive international experience includes coordinating the Reading and Writing for Critical Thinking Project in Eastern Europe, developing integrated curriculum for a USAID Afghan Education Project, and speaking and consulting on projects in several Latin American countries and in Asia.

CAROL BOOTH OLSON Senior Lecturer in the Department of Education at the University of California, Irvine; Director of the UCI site of the National Writing Project. Dr. Olson writes and lectures extensively on the reading/writing connection, critical thinking through writing, interactive strategies for teaching writing, and the use of multicultural literature with students of culturally diverse backgrounds. She has received many awards, including the California Association of Teachers of English Award of Merit, the Outstanding California Education Research Award, and the UC Irvine Excellence in Teaching Award.

CAROL ANN TOMLINSON Professor of Educational Research, Foundations, and Policy at the University of Virginia; Co-Director of the University's Institutes on Academic Diversity. An internationally known expert on differentiated instruction, Dr. Tomlinson helps teachers and administrators develop effective methods of teaching academically diverse learners. She was a teacher of middle and high school English for 22 years prior to teaching at the University of Virginia. Her books on differentiated instruction have been translated into eight languages.

SPECIAL CONTRIBUTOR:

KYLENE BEERS Special Consultant; Former Middle School Teacher; nationally known Lecturer and Author on reading and literacy; and former President of the National Council of Teachers of English. Dr. Beers is the nationally known author of *When Kids Can't Read: What Teachers Can Do* and co-editor of *Adolescent Literacy: Turning Promise into Practice,* as well as articles in the *Journal of Adolescent and Adult Literacy.* Former editor of *Voices from the Middle,* she is the 2001 recipient of NCTE's Richard W. Halley Award, given for outstanding contributions to middle-school literacy.

ENGLISH LEARNER SPECIALISTS

MARY LOU McCLOSKEY Past President of Teachers of English to Speakers of Other Languages (TESOL); Director of Teacher Development and Curriculum Design for Educo in Atlanta, Georgia. Dr. McCloskey is a former teacher in multilingual and multicultural classrooms. She has worked with teachers, teacher educators, and departments of education around the world on teaching English as a second and foreign language. She is author of *On Our Way to English, Voices in Literature, Integrating English,* and *Visions: Language, Literature, Content.* Her awards include the Le Moyne College Ignatian Award for Professional Achievement and the TESOL D. Scott Enright Service Award.

LYDIA STACK International ESL consultant. Her areas of expertise are English language teaching strategies, ESL standards for students and teachers, and curriculum writing. Her teaching experience includes 25 years as an elementary and high school ESL teacher. She is a past president of TESOL. Her awards include the James E. Alatis Award for Service to TESOL (2003) and the San Francisco STAR Teacher Award (1989). Her publications include *On Our Way to English; Wordways: Games for Language Learning;* and *Visions: Language, Literature, Content.*

CURRICULUM SPECIALIST

WILLIAM L. McBRIDE Curriculum Specialist. Dr. McBride is a nationally known speaker, educator, and author who now trains teachers in instructional methodologies. A former reading specialist, English teacher, and social studies teacher, he holds a Masters in Reading and a Ph.D. in Curriculum and Instruction from the University of North Carolina at Chapel Hill. Dr. McBride has contributed to the development of textbook series in language arts, social studies, science, and vocabulary. He is also known for his novel *Entertaining an Elephant,* which tells the story of a burned-out teacher who becomes re-inspired with both his profession and his life.

MEDIA SPECIALISTS

DAVID M. CONSIDINE Professor of Instructional Technology and Media Studies at Appalachian State University in North Carolina. Dr. Considine has served as a media literacy consultant to the U.S. government and to the media industry, including Discovery Communications and Cable in the Classroom. He has also conducted media literacy workshops and training for county and state health departments across the United States. Among his many publications are *Visual Messages: Integrating Imagery into Instruction,* and *Imagine That: Developing Critical Viewing and Thinking Through Children's Literature.*

LARKIN PAULUZZI Teacher and Media Specialist; trainer for the New Jersey Writing Project. Ms. Pauluzzi puts her extensive classroom experience to use in developing teacher-friendly curriculum materials and workshops in many different areas, including media literacy. She has led media literacy training workshops in several districts throughout Texas, guiding teachers in the meaningful and practical uses of media in the classroom. Ms. Pauluzzi has taught students at all levels, from Title I Reading to AP English IV. She also spearheads a technology club at her school, working with students to produce media and technology to serve both the school and the community.

LISA K. SCHEFFLER Teacher and Media Specialist. Ms. Scheffler has designed and taught media literacy and video production curriculum, in addition to teaching language arts and speech. Using her knowledge of mass communication theory, coupled with real classroom experience, she has developed ready-to-use materials that help teachers incorporate media literacy into their curricula. She has taught film and television studies at the University of North Texas and has served as a contributing writer for the Texas Education Agency's statewide viewing and representing curriculum.

TEACHER ADVISORS

These are some of the many educators from across the country who played a crucial role in the development of the tables of contents, the lesson design, and other key components of this program:

Virginia L. Alford, MacArthur High School, San Antonio, Texas

Yvonne L. Allen, Shaker Heights High School, Shaker Heights, Ohio

Dave T. Anderson, Hinsdale South High School, Darien, Illinois

Kacy Colleen Anglim, Portland Public Schools District, Portland, Oregon

Jordana Benone, North High School, Torrance, California

Patricia Blood, Howell High School, Farmingdale, New Jersey

Marjorie Bloom, Eau Gallie High School, Melbourne, Florida

Edward J. Blotzer, Wilkinsburg Junior/Senior High School, Wilkinsburg, Pennsylvania

Stephen D. Bournes, Evanston Township High School, Evanston, Illinois

Barbara M. Bowling, Mt. Tabor High School, Winston-Salem, North Carolina

Kiala Boykin-Givehand, Duval County Public Schools, Jacksonville, Florida

Laura L. Brown, Adlai Stevenson High School, Lincolnshire, Illinois

Cynthia Burke, Yavneh Academy, Dallas, Texas

Hoppy Chandler, San Diego City Schools, San Diego, California

Gary Chmielewski, St. Benedict High School, Chicago, Illinois

Delorse Cole-Stewart, Milwaukee Public Schools, Milwaukee, Wisconsin

Kathy Dahlgren, Skokie, Illinois

Diana Dilger, Rosa Parks Middle School, Dixmoor, Illinois

L. Calvin Dillon, Gaither High School, Tampa, Florida

Dori Dolata, Rufus King High School, Milwaukee, Wisconsin

Jon Epstein, Marietta High School, Marietta, Georgia

Helen Ervin, Fort Bend Independent School District, Sugar Land, Texas

Sue Friedman, Buffalo Grove High School, Buffalo Grove, Illinois

Chris Gee, Bel Air High School, El Paso, Texas

Paula Grasel, The Horizon Center, Gainesville, Georgia

Rochelle L. Greene-Brady, Kenwood Academy, Chicago, Illinois

Christopher Guarraia, Centreville High School, Clifton, Virginia

Michele M. Hettinger, Niles West High School, Skokie, Illinois

Elizabeth Holcomb, Forest Hill High School, Jackson, Mississippi

Jim Horan, Hinsdale Central High School, Hinsdale, Illinois

James Paul Hunter, Oak Park-River Forest High School, Oak Park, Illinois

Susan P. Kelly, Director of Curriculum, Island Trees School District, Levittown, New York

Beverley A. Lanier, Varina High School, Richmond, Virginia

Pat Laws, Charlotte-Mecklenburg Schools, Charlotte, North Carolina

Diana R. Martinez, Treviño School of Communications & Fine Arts, Laredo, Texas

Natalie Martinez, Stephen F. Austin High School, Houston, Texas

Elizabeth Matarazzo, Ysleta High School, El Paso, Texas

Carol M. McDonald, J. Frank Dobie High School, Houston, Texas

Amy Millikan, Consultant, Chicago, Illinois

Eileen Murphy, Walter Payton Preparatory High School, Chicago, Illinois

Lisa Omark, New Haven Public Schools, New Haven, Connecticut

Kaine Osburn, Wheeling High School, Wheeling, Illinois

Andrea J. Phillips, Terry Sanford High School, Fayetteville, North Carolina

Cathy Reilly, Sayreville Public Schools, Sayreville, New Jersey

Mark D. Simon, Neuqua Valley High School, Naperville, Illinois

Scott Snow, Seguin High School, Arlington, Texas

Jane W. Speidel, Brevard County Schools, Viera, Florida

Cheryl E. Sullivan, Lisle Community School District, Lisle, Illinois

Anita Usmiani, Hamilton Township Public Schools, Hamilton Square, New Jersey

Linda Valdez, Oxnard Union High School District, Oxnard, California

Nancy Walker, Longview High School, Longview, Texas

Kurt Weiler, New Trier High School, Winnetka, Illinois

Elizabeth Whittaker, Larkin High School, Elgin, Illinois

Linda S. Williams, Woodlawn High School, Baltimore, Maryland

John R. Williamson, Fort Thomas Independent Schools, Fort Thomas, Kentucky

Anna N. Winters, Simeon High School, Chicago, Illinois

Tonora D. Wyckoff, North Shore Senior High School, Houston, Texas

Karen Zajac, Glenbard South High School, Glen Ellyn, Illinois

Cynthia Zimmerman, Mose Vines Preparatory High School, Chicago, Illinois

Lynda Zimmerman, El Camino High School, South San Francisco, California

Ruth E. Zurich, Brown Deer High School, Brown Deer, Wisconsin

COMMON
CORE

OVERVIEW
Student Edition

LESSONS WITH EMBEDDED COMMON CORE INSTRUCTION

COMMON CORE

Look for the Common Core symbol throughout the book. It highlights targeted objectives to help you succeed in mastering the knowledge and skills you will need for college or for a career.

CONTENTS IN BRIEF

Online at

Log in to learn more at thinkcentral.com, where you can access most program resources in one convenient location.

LITERATURE AND READING CENTER

- Author Biographies
- *PowerNotes* Presentations
- Professional Audio Recordings of Selections
- Graphic Organizers
- Analysis Frames
- NovelWise

WRITING AND GRAMMAR CENTER

- Interactive Student Models*
- Interactive Graphic Organizers*
- Interactive Revision Lessons*
- *GrammarNotes* Presentations and Practice

**also available on WriteSmart CD-ROM*

VOCABULARY CENTER

- *WordSharp* Interactive Vocabulary Tutor
- Vocabulary Practice Copy Masters

MEDIA AND TECHNOLOGY CENTER

- MediaScope: Media Literacy Instruction
- Digital Storytelling
- Speaking and Listening Support

RESEARCH CENTER

- Writing and Research in a Digital Age
- Citation Guide

Assessment Center

- Program Assessments
- Level Up Online Tutorials
- Online Essay Scoring

MORE TECHNOLOGY

Student One Stop

Access an electronic version of your textbook, complete with selection audio and worksheets.

MediaSmart DVD-ROM

Sharpen your critical viewing and analysis skills with these in-depth interactive media studies.

An Emerging Nation
EARLY AMERICAN WRITING
1600–1800

Exploration and the Early Settlers

The Puritan Tradition

Writers of the Revolution

Vocabulary Strategies

Celebrating the Individual
AMERICAN ROMANTICISM
1800–1855

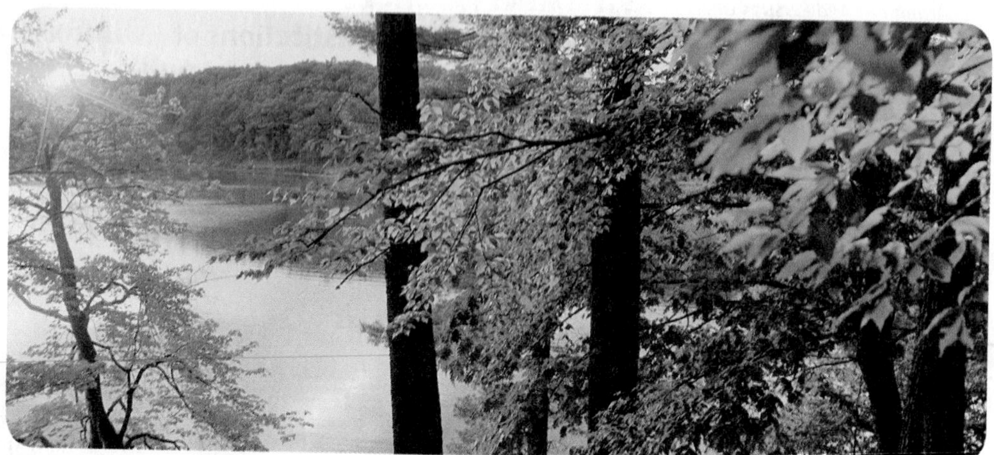

The Fireside Poets

The Transcendentalists

American Gothic

Vocabulary Strategies

An Age of Transition FROM ROMANTICISM TO REALISM

1855–1870

STANDARDS FOCUS

Literature of the Civil War

Capturing the American Landscape

REGIONALISM AND NATURALISM

1870–1910

A Changing Awareness

THE HARLEM RENAISSANCE AND MODERNISM

1910–1940

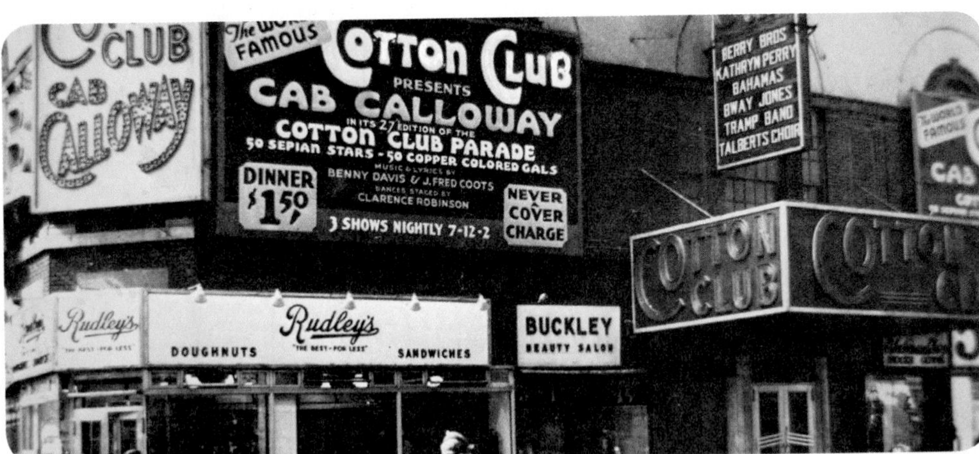

Journalism as Literature

Vocabulary Strategies

New Perspectives
CONTEMPORARY LITERATURE
1940–PRESENT

Investigation and Discovery
THE POWER OF RESEARCH

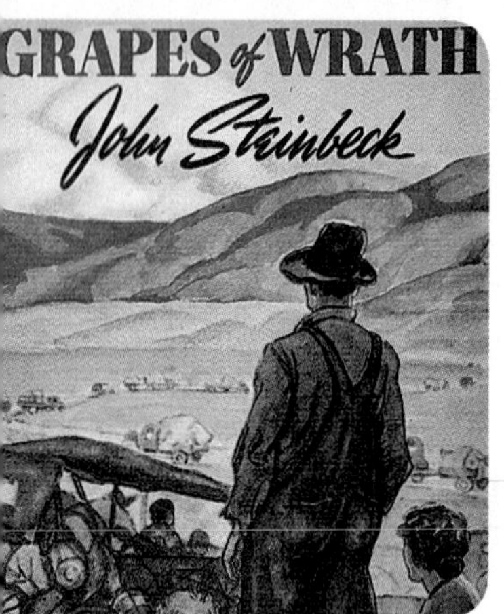

STANDARDS FOCUS
Use Reference Materials and Technology, Evaluate Sources

Use Reference Materials and Technology, Evaluate Sources

FICTION

SHORT STORIES

NOVEL EXCERPTS

FOLK LITERATURE

POETRY

DRAMA

NONFICTION

APHORISMS

AUTOBIOGRAPHY/MEMOIR

ESSAYS

HISTORICAL DOCUMENTS

HISTORICAL NARRATIVES

Features

TEXT ANALYSIS WORKSHOPS

WRITING WORKSHOPS

WriteSmart CD-ROM

SPEAKING AND LISTENING WORKSHOPS

TECHNOLOGY WORKSHOPS

WRAP-UPS

WRITING TO SYNTHESIZE

WRITING TO EVALUATE

WRITING TO ANALYZE

WRITING TO PERSUADE

WRITING TO REFLECT

WRITING TO COMPARE

MEDIA STUDIES

MediaSmart DVD-ROM

VOCABULARY STRATEGIES

GRAMMAR AND STYLE

STUDENT GUIDE TO ACADEMIC SUCCESS

STUDENT GUIDE

The Common Core for Uncommon Achievement

Carol Jago

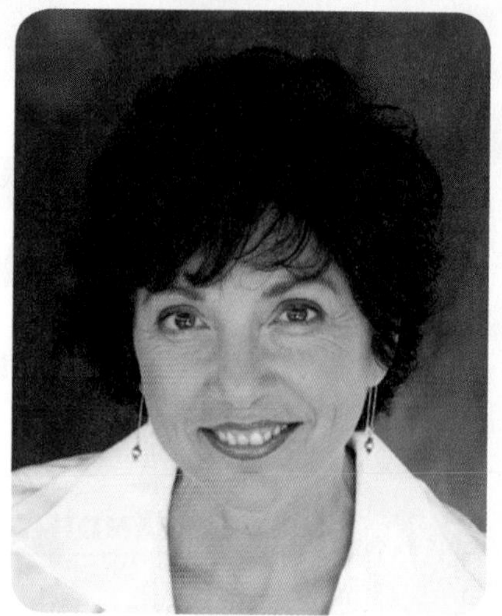

"If you don't know where you are going, any road will get you there." – Lewis Carroll

The Common Core State Standards make clear where students are going. They describe what today's children need to know and be able to do to thrive in post-secondary education and the workplace. By focusing on results — the destination — rather than on the how — the means of transportation — the Common Core allows for a variety of teaching methods and many different classroom approaches. The challenge for teachers is to turn the daily journey towards this destination into an intellectual adventure.

One way to think about the Common Core is as a kind of GPS device to situate curriculum. While some students may choose the road less traveled, the objective is fixed. When students become lost through a wrong turn, teachers recalculate the route, providing a calm and confident voice that guides all students to academic achievement and deep literacy.

Shared Responsibility for Students' Literacy Development

The Common Core State Standards insist that the responsibility for helping students achieve literacy is not the sole responsibility of the English teacher. The introduction states clearly that, "instruction in reading, writing, speaking, listening, and language (should) be a shared responsibility within the school" (4). Citing NAEP Reading assessment test specification guidelines, the Common Core recommends that 55% of what students read in grade 8 and 70% in grade 12 should be informational text. These percentages are not meant to reflect the balance of reading materials in English class alone but rather the totality of what students should be reading across the curriculum in history/social studies, science, and technical subjects as well as in English. Given the type of reading that will be required of students in college and of graduates in the workplace, this distribution is both relevant and practical.

Understanding of Other Perspectives and Cultures

The Common Core also makes clear the importance of literature in the education of America's children. "Through reading great classic and contemporary works of literature representative of a variety of periods, cultures, and worldviews, students can vicariously inhabit worlds and have experiences much different from their own" (7). Reading literature demands that readers look inward, examine their beliefs in light of new information, consider the world through different eyes, take time for reflection. Such reading is a key to student learning.

The Purpose of Exemplar Texts

To describe the quality and complexity of the works students should read at each grade level, the Common Core offers lists of "exemplar texts." While some may choose to treat the texts on these lists as required reading, such usage would represent a misunderstanding of their purpose. "The choices should serve as useful guideposts in helping educators select texts of similar complexity, quality, and range for their own classrooms. They expressly do not represent a partial or complete reading list" (Appendix B, 2). The poems, stories, novels, and nonfiction that appear on the Common Core lists are intended as models for guiding — not dictating — text selection.

The Difference Between Persuasion and Argument

The Common Core writing standards describe the types and purposes for writing that students need to master. You will find extended definitions of argument, informative/explanatory writing, and narrative writing in Appendix A. Of particular note is the distinction the Common Core draws between persuasion and argument. "When writing to persuade, writers employ a variety of persuasive strategies. One common strategy is an appeal to the credibility, character, or authority of the writer (or speaker). A logical argument, on the other hand, convinces the audience because of the perceived merit and reasonableness of the claims and proofs offered rather than either the emotions the writing evokes in the audience or the character or credentials of the writer" (24). Because of its importance for college and workplace readiness, argument holds a special place in the Common Core writing standards.

One way to think about the Common Core is as a kind of GPS device . . .

Complex Literary and Informational Texts

Throughout the Common Core document you will notice the anchor standard, "Read and comprehend complex literary and informational texts independently and proficiently." It isn't enough for students to read with a teacher by their side. They need to be able, often with a little help from their friends or from the habits of mind they learned from their teachers, to read for themselves. They need to be able, like Huck Finn, to head out for the territory on their own. Such a journey requires confidence in one's ability to navigate uncharted waters and to overcome challenges their teachers can't foresee or even imagine. As we guide students on the academic adventure that is high school, let us never forget that the path we tread is the path to intellectual freedom.

WORKS CITED

Common Core State Standards for English Language Arts and History/Social Studies, Science, & Technical Subjects. 2010.

Appendix B. Common Core State Standards for English Language Arts and History/Social Studies, Science, & Technical Subjects. 2010.

Carol Jago has taught middle and high school for over 30 years and was a member of the Common Core Initiative feedback team. She serves as Past President of the National Council of Teachers of English.

Understanding the Common Core State Standards

What are the English Language Arts Common Core State Standards?

The Common Core State Standards for English Language Arts indicate what you should know and be able to do by the end of your grade level. These understandings and skills will help you be better prepared for future classes, college courses, and a career. For this reason, the standards for each strand in English Language Arts (such as reading informational text or writing) directly relate to the College and Career Readiness Anchor Standards for each strand. The Anchor Standards broadly outline the understandings and skills you should learn by the end of high school so that you are well-prepared for college or for a career.

How do I learn the English Language Arts Common Core State Standards?

Your textbook is closely aligned to the English Language Arts Common Core State Standards. Every time you learn a concept or practice a skill, you are working on mastery of one of the standards. Each unit, each selection, and each workshop in your textbook connects to one or more of the standards for English Language Arts listed on the following pages.

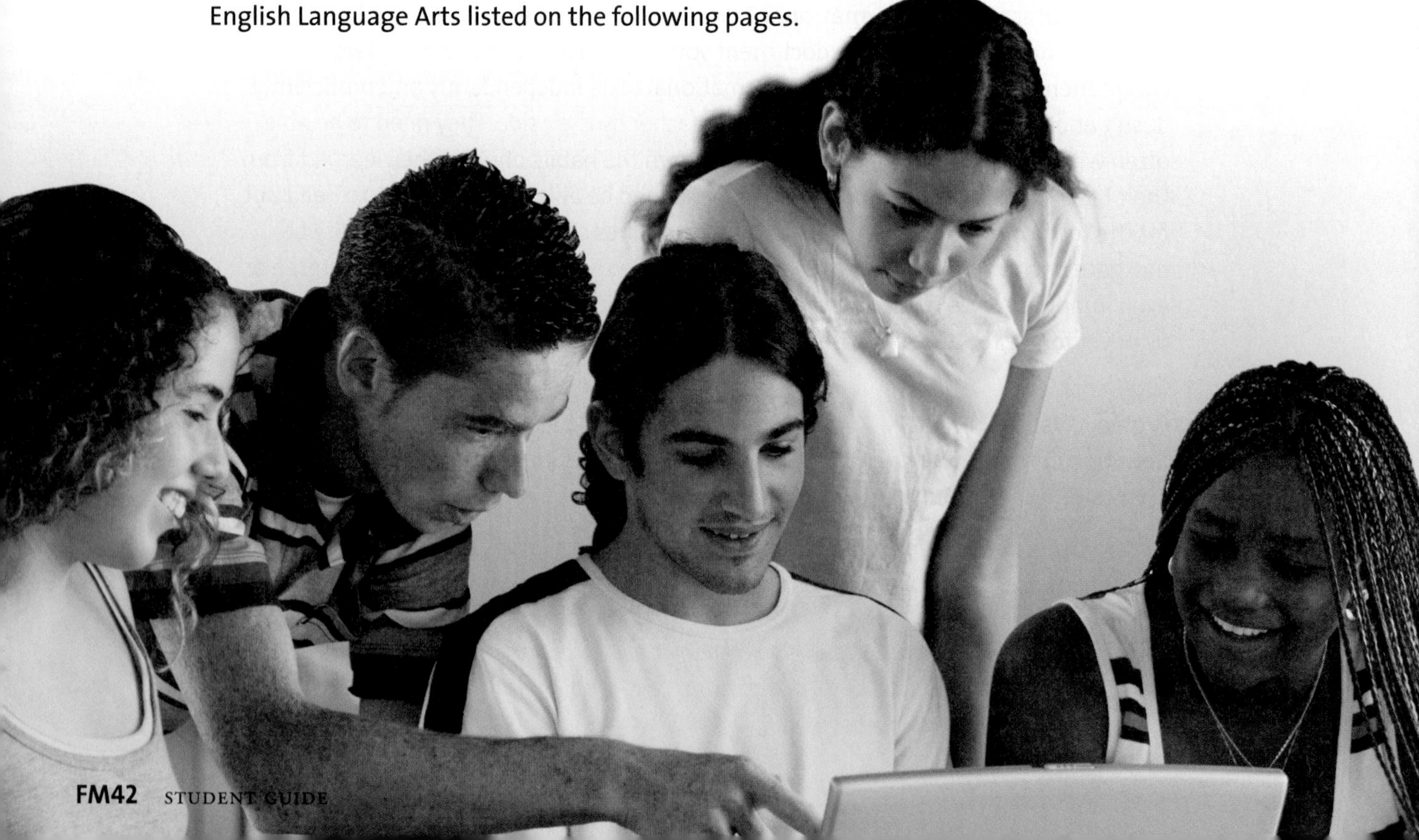

The English Language Arts Common Core State Standards are divided into five strands: Reading Literature, Reading Informational Text, Writing, Speaking and Listening, and Language.

Reading Literature (RL)

This strand concerns the literary texts you will read at this grade level: stories, drama, and poetry. The Common Core State Standards stress that you should read a range of texts of increasing complexity as you progress through high school.

Reading Informational Text (RI)

Informational text includes a broad range of literary nonfiction, including exposition, argument, and functional text, such as personal essays, speeches, opinion pieces, memoirs, and historical and technical accounts. The Common Core State Standards stress that you will also read a range of informational texts of increasing complexity as you progress from grade to grade.

Writing (W)

The Writing strand focuses on your generating three types of texts: arguments, informative or explanatory texts, and narratives, as well as using the writing process and technology to develop and share your writing. The Common Core State Standards also emphasize research and specify that you should write routinely for both short and extended time frames.

Speaking and Listening (SL)

The Common Core State Standards focus on comprehending information presented in a variety of media and formats, on participating in collaborative discussions, and on presenting knowledge and ideas clearly.

Language (L)

The standards in the Language strand address the conventions of Standard English grammar, usage, and mechanics; knowledge of language; and vocabulary acquisition and use.

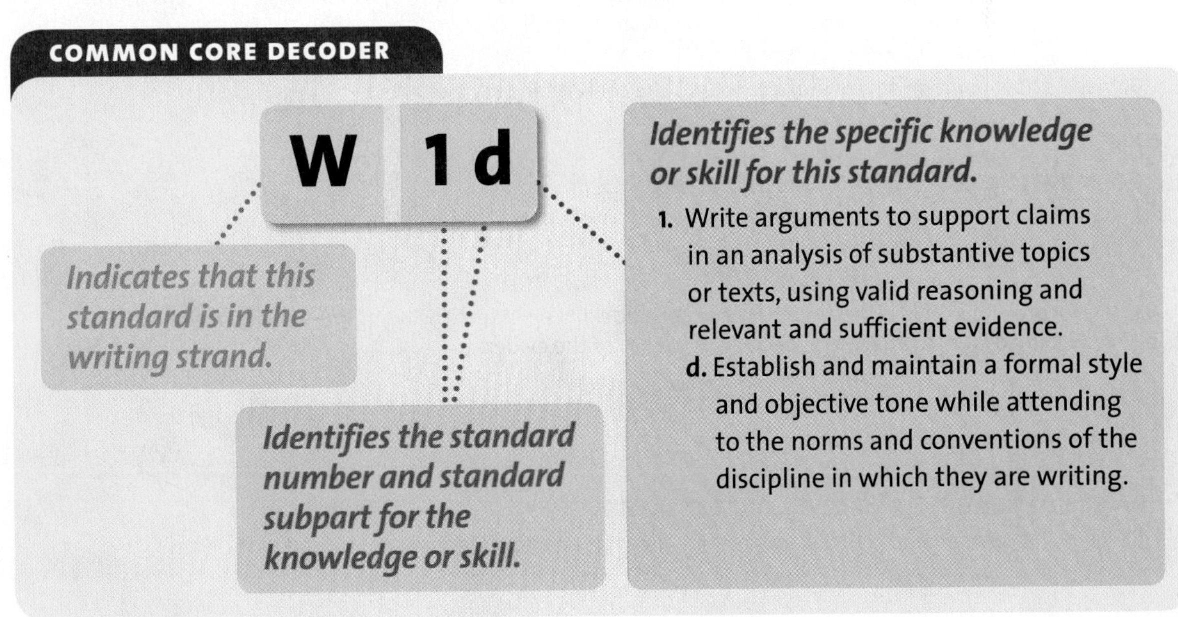

COMMON CORE DECODER
W 1 d
Indicates that this standard is in the writing strand.
Identifies the standard number and standard subpart for the knowledge or skill.
Identifies the specific knowledge or skill for this standard.
1. Write arguments to support claims in an analysis of substantive topics or texts, using valid reasoning and relevant and sufficient evidence.
d. Establish and maintain a formal style and objective tone while attending to the norms and conventions of the discipline in which they are writing.

English Language Arts Common Core State Standards

Listed below are the English Language Arts Common Core State Standards that you are required to master by the end of grade 11. We have provided a summary of the concepts you will learn on your way to mastering each standard. The CCR anchor standards and high school grade-specific standards for each strand work together to define college and career readiness expectations—the former providing broad standards, the latter providing additional specificity.

College and Career Readiness Anchor Standards for Reading

COMMON CORE STATE STANDARDS

KEY IDEAS AND DETAILS

1. Read closely to determine what the text says explicitly and to make logical inferences from it; cite specific textual evidence when writing or speaking to support conclusions drawn from the text.
2. Determine central ideas or themes of a text and analyze their development; summarize the key supporting details and ideas.
3. Analyze how and why individuals, events, and ideas develop and interact over the course of a text.

CRAFT AND STRUCTURE

4. Interpret words and phrases as they are used in a text, including determining technical, connotative, and figurative meanings, and analyze how specific word choices shape meaning or tone.
5. Analyze the structure of texts, including how specific sentences, paragraphs, and larger portions of the text (e.g., a section, chapter, scene, or stanza) relate to each other and the whole.
6. Assess how point of view or purpose shapes the content and style of a text.

INTEGRATION OF KNOWLEDGE AND IDEAS

7. Integrate and evaluate content presented in diverse formats and media, including visually and quantitatively, as well as in words.
8. Delineate and evaluate the argument and specific claims in a text, including the validity of the reasoning as well as the relevance and sufficiency of the evidence.
9. Analyze how two or more texts address similar themes or topics in order to build knowledge or to compare the approaches the authors take.

RANGE OF READING AND LEVEL OF TEXT COMPLEXITY

10. Read and comprehend complex literary and informational texts independently and proficiently.

Reading Standards for Literature, Grades 11–12 Students

The College and Career Readiness Anchor Standards for Reading apply to both literature and informational text.

COMMON CORE STATE STANDARD	WHAT IT MEANS TO YOU
KEY IDEAS AND DETAILS	
1. Cite strong and thorough textual evidence to support analysis of what the text says explicitly as well as inferences drawn from the text, including determining where the text leaves matters uncertain.	You will use strong evidence from a text to support your analysis of its central ideas—both those that are stated directly and those that are suggested—and to show where the text leaves matters uncertain.
2. Determine two or more themes or central ideas of a text and analyze their development over the course of the text, including how they interact and build on one another to produce a complex account; provide an objective summary of the text.	You will analyze the development of at least two of a text's key ideas and themes by showing how they progress and interact throughout the text. You will also summarize the text as a whole without adding your own ideas or opinions.
3. Analyze the impact of the author's choices regarding how to develop and relate elements of a story or drama (e.g., where a story is set, how the action is ordered, how the characters are introduced and developed).	You will analyze the author's choices related to setting, plot structure, and characterization in a story or drama.
CRAFT AND STRUCTURE	
4. Determine the meaning of words and phrases as they are used in the text, including figurative and connotative meanings; analyze the impact of specific word choices on meaning and tone, including words with multiple meanings or language that is particularly fresh, engaging, or beautiful. (Include Shakespeare as well as other authors.)	You will analyze specific words and phrases in the text to determine both their figurative and connotative meanings, as well as how they contribute to the text's tone and meaning as a whole. You will also consider multiple-meaning words and vivid language.
5. Analyze how an author's choices concerning how to structure specific parts of a text (e.g., the choice of where to begin or end a story, the choice to provide a comedic or tragic resolution) contribute to its overall structure and meaning as well as its aesthetic impact.	You will analyze the ways in which the author has chosen to structure and order the text and determine how those choices shape the text's meaning and affect the reader.
6. Analyze a case in which grasping a point of view requires distinguishing what is directly stated in a text from what is really meant (e.g., satire, sarcasm, irony, or understatement).	You will understand a point of view in which what is really meant is different from what is said or stated.
INTEGRATION OF KNOWLEDGE AND IDEAS	
7. Analyze multiple interpretations of a story, drama, or poem (e.g., recorded or live production of a play or recorded novel or poetry), evaluating how each version interprets the source text. (Include at least one play by Shakespeare and one play by an American dramatist.)	You will compare and contrast multiple interpretations of a story, drama, or poem, and analyze how each draws from and uses the source text.
8. (Not applicable to literature)	

Reading Standards for Literature, Grades 11–12 Students, continued

COMMON CORE STATE STANDARD	WHAT IT MEANS TO YOU
9. Demonstrate knowledge of eighteenth-, nineteenth- and early-twentieth-century foundational works of American literature, including how two or more texts from the same period treat similar themes or topics.	You will analyze, compare, and contrast important eighteenth-, nineteenth-, and early-twentieth-century works of American literature.
RANGE OF READING AND LEVEL OF TEXT COMPLEXITY	
10. By the end of grade 11, read and comprehend literature, including stories, dramas, and poems, in the grades 11–12 CCR text complexity band proficiently, with scaffolding as needed at the high end of the range.	You will read and understand grade-level appropriate literary texts by the end of grade 11.

Spotlight on Common Core

RL 9 Demonstrate knowledge of eighteenth-century foundational works of American literature, including how two or more texts from the same period treat similar themes or topics.

Literature: Understanding Themes or Topics in Foundational Works

Foundational works focus on major events and ideas that have shaped American culture. For example, the creation of the United States in the late eighteenth century inspired many writers to portray freedom as an essential American value.

To demonstrate how two or more foundational works from the same period treat similar themes or topics, you can follow these steps:

1. Read each text to determine the theme or topic it addresses; then, note any common, or shared, themes or topics.
2. Identify specific details within each text about the shared themes or topics.
3. Identify specific details across texts to compare and contrast how they treat the shared themes or topics.

Throughout this book, you will be asked to determine how different texts from the same time period treat similar themes or topics. Study the following example:

Phillis Wheatley (c. 1753–1784), born in Africa, was kidnapped and sold into slavery as a child, but later became a free woman. She is recognized as the first published African-American poet. Philip Freneau (1752–1832), born in New York City, was a poet and newspaper editor. A friend of James Madison and Thomas Jefferson, he wrote extensively in favor of American independence from England. Read the following excerpts from poems by Phillis Wheatley and Philip Freneau. Then answer the questions that follow the poems.

from To the Right Honorable William, Earl of Dartmouth,
His Majesty's Principal Secretary of State for North America, etc.
by Phillis Wheatley

Should you, my lord, while you peruse my song,
Wonder from whence my love of *Freedom* sprung,
Whence flow these wishes for the common good,
By feeling hearts alone best understood,

I, young in life, by seeming cruel fate
Was snatch'd from *Afric's* fancy'd happy seat:
What pangs excruciating must molest,
What sorrows labor in my parent's breast?
Steel'd was that soul and by no misery mov'd
That from a father seiz'd his babe belov'd:
Such, such my case. And can I then but pray
Others may never feel tyrannic sway?

(*1773*)

from On Mr. Paine's *Rights of Man*
by Philip Freneau

Without a king, we till the smiling plain;
Without a king, we trace the unbounded sea,
And traffic round the globe, through each degree;
Each foreign clime our honored flag reveres,
Which asks no monarch, to support the STARS:
Without a *king*, the laws maintain their sway,
While honor bids each generous heart obey.
Be ours the task the ambitious to restrain,
And this great lesson teach—that kings are vain;
That warring realms to certain ruin haste,
That kings subsist by war, and wars are waste:
So shall our nation, formed on Virtue's plan,
Remain the guardian of the Rights of Man,
A vast Republic, famed through every clime,
Without a king, to see the end of time.

(*1791*)

1. How does Wheatley describe freedom? Cite specific evidence in the text.
2. How does Freneau describe freedom? Cite specific evidence in the text.
3. What are the similarities and differences in the way these poems praise freedom?

LEARN HOW **Understanding Themes or Topics in Foundational Works** The questions that follow ask you to compare and contrast how two poems treat the same topic—freedom. To do this, gather specific examples from each poem, such as the **diction**, or choice of words, and **rhetorical devices** each writer uses to discuss this topic. Focus on one poem at a time. Notice how you must look carefully at both poems first in order to answer the third question. Here are three examples of how to respond to the questions.

1. How does Wheatley describe freedom in her poem? Cite specific evidence in the text.

Wheatley provides an autobiographical story that explains how her "love of Freedom" sprang from her loss of freedom. Wheatley's diction emphasizes the pain she and her parents experienced when she was kidnapped into slavery. "Snatch'd from Afric's fancy'd, happy seat," she asks the reader to imagine her parents' "pangs excruciating" and "sorrows." She explicitly equates slavery with cruel oppression ("tyrannic sway"), the opposite of the freedom she loves.

controlling idea, or thesis, for the answer

quotations from the text to support the thesis

2. How does Freneau describe freedom in his poem? Cite specific evidence in the text.

Using the plural pronoun "we" to address readers, Freneau outlines the nature of American freedom. He repeats the phrase "without a king" four times to introduce positive examples of the freedom Americans experience now that they are no longer ruled by a monarchy. Freneau uses negative diction, calling kings "vain" and describing how they "subsist by war, and wars are waste." In contrast, he describes America in glowing terms: "Formed on Virtue's plain," it is "the guardian of the Rights of Man."

controlling idea, or thesis, for the answer

quotations from the text to support the thesis

3. What are the similarities and differences in the way these poems praise freedom?

Wheatley and Freneau both love freedom. Both poems contrast what life is like with and without it. However, Wheatley's poem is more autobiographical. Wheatley describes her personal loss of freedom as a slave as the source of her love of freedom. Freneau describes the sense of freedom America enjoys after rejecting government by a monarchy. He provides a general overview of American political life as if speaking for the entire nation.

similarities between poems

differences between the poets' views on freedom

As you study various eighteenth-, nineteenth-, and early twentieth-century foundational works of American literature, focus on exploring how they treat similar themes or topics. Doing so will add to your understanding of the works of that particular period, as well as of later periods.

Reading Standards for Informational Text, Grades 11–12 Students

COMMON CORE STATE STANDARD	WHAT IT MEANS TO YOU
KEY IDEAS AND DETAILS	
1. Cite strong and thorough textual evidence to support analysis of what the text says explicitly as well as inferences drawn from the text, including determining where the text leaves matters uncertain.	You will use details and information from the text to support your analysis of its central ideas—both those that are stated directly and those that are suggested—and to show where the text leaves matters uncertain.
2. Determine two or more central ideas of a text and analyze their development over the course of the text, including how they interact and build on one another to provide a complex analysis; provide an objective summary of the text.	You will analyze the development of at least two of a text's key ideas by showing how they progress and interact throughout the text. You will also summarize the text as a whole without adding your own ideas or opinions.
3. Analyze a complex set of ideas or sequence of events and explain how specific individuals, ideas, or events interact and develop over the course of the text.	You will analyze the specific interactions among a set of ideas, individuals, or a sequence of events in a text.
CRAFT AND STRUCTURE	
4. Determine the meaning of words and phrases as they are used in a text, including figurative, connotative, and technical meanings; analyze how an author uses and refines the meaning of a key term or terms over the course of a text (e.g., how Madison defines *faction* in *Federalist* No. 10).	You will analyze specific words and phrases in the text to determine their figurative, connotative, and technical meanings, as well as to uncover how an author uses them throughout a text.
5. Analyze and evaluate the effectiveness of the structure an author uses in his or her exposition or argument, including whether the structure makes points clear, convincing, and engaging.	You will examine a text's structure and evaluate whether it makes the author's claims clear, convincing, and interesting.
6. Determine an author's point of view or purpose in a text in which the rhetoric is particularly effective, analyzing how style and content contribute to the power, persuasiveness, or beauty of the text.	You will understand the author's purpose and perspective on a topic and analyze how the author uses language to affect the reader.
INTEGRATION OF KNOWLEDGE AND IDEAS	
7. Integrate and evaluate multiple sources of information presented in different media or formats (e.g., visually, quantitatively) as well as in words in order to address a question or solve a problem.	You will integrate multiple and varied sources of information to address a question or solve a problem.
8. Delineate and evaluate the reasoning in seminal U.S. texts, including the application of constitutional principles and use of legal reasoning (e.g., in U.S. Supreme Court majority opinions and dissents) and the premises, purposes, and arguments in works of public advocacy (e.g., *The Federalist*, presidential addresses).	You will analyze the reasoning and underlying principles of important historical U.S. texts for their support of the principles of democracy.

Reading Standards for Informational Text, Grades 11–12 Students, continued

COMMON CORE STATE STANDARD	WHAT IT MEANS TO YOU
9. Analyze seventeenth-, eighteenth-, and nineteenth-century foundational U.S. documents of historical and literary significance (including The Declaration of Independence, the Preamble to the Constitution, the Bill of Rights, and Lincoln's Second Inaugural Address) for their themes, purposes, and rhetorical features.	You will read and analyze important eighteenth-, nineteenth-, and early-twentieth-century documents pertaining to American history to determine their themes, purposes, and use of language.
RANGE OF READING AND LEVEL OF TEXT COMPLEXITY	
10. By the end of grade 11, read and comprehend literary nonfiction in the grades 11–CCR text complexity band proficiently, with scaffolding as needed at the high end of the range.	You will demonstrate the ability to read and understand grade-level appropriate literary nonfiction texts by the end of grade 11.

Spotlight on Common Core

RI 9 Analyze seventeenth-, eighteenth-, and nineteenth-century foundational U.S. documents of historical and literary significance (including The Declaration of Independence, the Preamble to the Constitution, the Bill of Rights, and Lincoln's Second Inaugural Address) for their themes, purposes, and rhetorical features.

Informational Text: Analyzing Significant U.S. Documents

The Common Core State Standards ask you to analyze significant literary and historical U.S. documents for their **themes, purposes, and rhetorical features, or devices**. You can do this by following these steps:

1. Identify the **purpose** of the document by determining why the document was written.
2. Identify the **theme** of the document by identifying the message its author conveys.
3. Identify **rhetorical features, or devices**, the author uses to convey the theme and to accomplish the document's purpose.

Throughout this book, you will be asked to analyze these aspects of significant U.S. historical and literary documents from various time periods. As you study the following examples, think about their purposes, themes, and use of rhetorical devices.

LEARN HOW **Analyzing Audience and Author's Purpose** First, you need to identify the audience for the document. Then, identify the author's purpose for writing it for this audience.

An author usually writes for one or more purposes: to inform or explain, to tell a real or imagined story, or to develop an argument that will support the author's claims about a topic or a text. For example, the purpose of a news report is to inform viewers about important events, while the purpose of a political speech is to make an argument that will persuade listeners to accept the speaker's claims. Consider the purpose for which the document is written. Then, **summarize**, or briefly restate, this purpose in your own words in no more than a few sentences. Here are two examples of how to respond to questions about audience and purpose of historical documents.

from The Declaration of Independence, 1776

When, in the course of human events, it becomes necessary for one people to dissolve the political bands which have connected them with another, and to assume, among the powers of the earth, the separate and equal station to which the laws of nature and of nature's God entitle them, a decent respect to the opinions of mankind requires that they should declare the causes which impel them to the separation.

Preamble to the United States Constitution, 1787

We the people of the United States, in order to form a more perfect union, establish justice, insure domestic tranquility, provide for the common defense, promote the general welfare, and secure the blessings of liberty to ourselves and our posterity, do ordain and establish this Constitution for the United States of America.

1. Who is the audience for each document?

The Declaration of Independence was written to George III (the British king), to the world, and to the people of the American colonies. The U.S. Constitution was written to the people of the United States.

2. What is the purpose of each document?

The purpose of the Declaration of Independence was to tell the world why the colonies wanted to declare their independence by separating from England. The Preamble to the U.S. Constitution, a short introduction to the document, was written to explain the principles that would guide our nation so it would be lawful, peaceful, safe, and prosperous for years to come.

The Common Core State Standards also ask you to consider the **themes** in significant U.S. historical documents. Read the following discussion to see how you can analyze themes in these kinds of documents.

LEARN HOW Analyzing Theme The **theme** of a document is the message its author wishes to convey to its intended audience. You may need to **infer**, or make logical assumptions, about the theme based on a variety of elements, such as the author's choice of words. On the next page, read Amendment VI of the U.S. Constitution, the document that established the essential laws of the United States. How would you summarize the most important idea in Amendment VI? As you did with purpose and audience, state this theme briefly in your own words.

Amendment VI, ratified by Congress 1791

In all criminal prosecutions, the accused shall enjoy the right to a speedy and public trial, by an impartial jury of the State and district wherein the crime shall have been committed; which district shall have been previously ascertained by law, and to be informed of the nature and cause of the accusation; to be confronted with the witnesses against him; to have compulsory process for obtaining witnesses in his favor, and to have the assistance of counsel for his defense.

1. Who is the audience for and what is the purpose of this document?

The audience for Amendment VI is the nation as a whole and anyone else who reads the Bill of Rights. The purpose of the document is to inform the audience about how anyone charged with a crime is tried in the U.S.

2. What is the theme of Amendment VI?

The theme of Amendment VI is the right of every American to receive timely, fair, and just treatment under the law if he or she is accused of a crime. There are several phrases, such as "the accused shall enjoy the right to a speedy and public trial by an impartial jury," that highlight the legal rights of "the accused."

The authors of our important historical documents wrote masterfully and powerfully, employing a range of **rhetorical features, or devices**, to convey their messages to their audiences. The Common Core State Standards also require you to analyze the rhetorical devices incorporated into these significant documents. The following discussion will explain how you can analyze a text to determine its rhetorical features.

LEARN HOW Analyzing Rhetorical Features **Rhetorical features, or devices**, fulfill the author's purpose by vividly conveying the document's theme. Before you can understand a document's rhetorical devices, you need to identify the author's purpose and theme. Rhetorical devices may include any of the following:

- repetition of words or phrases, such as parallel grammatical structures, to create emphasis and unity
- analogies, to make a comparison to illustrate an idea
- word choice, to appeal to the audience's emotions or reason

Notice how Abraham Lincoln uses rhetorical devices in his Second Inaugural Address.

Background Abraham Lincoln gave the following speech for his inauguration as President of the U.S. for a second term in 1865. With the Civil War (1861–1865) nearing an end, the nation reeled from four years of brutal conflict and bloodshed. In the first paragraph, Lincoln recounts how the war started. In the second, he discusses what the nation should do now.

from Abraham Lincoln's *Second Inaugural Address*, 1865

On the occasion corresponding to this four years ago all thoughts were anxiously directed to an impending civil war. All dreaded it, all sought to avert it. While the inaugural address was being delivered from this place, devoted altogether to *saving* the Union without war, insurgent agents were in the city seeking to *destroy* it without war—seeking to dissolve the Union and divide effects by negotiation. Both parties deprecated war, but one of them would *make* war rather than let the nation survive, and the other would *accept* war rather than let it perish, and the war came. . . .

With malice toward none, with charity for all, with firmness in the right as God gives us to see the right, let us strive on to finish the work we are in, to bind up the nation's wounds, to care for him who shall have borne the battle and for his widow and his orphan, to do all which may achieve and cherish a just and lasting peace among ourselves and with all nations.

1. Who is the audience for Lincoln's speech? What is the purpose of the speech?

Lincoln's audience is the people of the United States. Lincoln speaks to the entire country in order to argue that the nation must come together and heal.

2. What is the theme of Lincoln's speech?

The theme of the speech is the need for the country to unite in order to heal and to move forward to a "just and lasting peace among ourselves and with all nations."

3. What rhetorical devices does Lincoln use in this speech?

Lincoln uses repetition and language that appeals to the audience's emotions to achieve his purpose and convey his theme in this speech. In the first paragraph, he explains how the war began. He repeats the word "war" seven times like a drumbeat, to emphasize that the war was inevitable.

In the second paragraph, Lincoln uses repetition again, but for a very different reason. First, he repeats prepositional phrases: "with charity toward all, with malice for none, with firmness in the right. . ." Then he repeats infinitive phrases: "to finish the work we are in, to bind up the nation's wounds, to care for him who shall have borne the battle. . ." These parallel phrases, which mirror each other, also mirror the sense of unity and purpose Lincoln hopes to inspire in the American people. Instead of reminding his audience of the inevitability of the war, Lincoln propels them toward taking positive action to preserve peace.

In addition, Lincoln uses language that appeals to his audience's emotions, addressing them as "us" to bind them to him and to each other. He asks them to join forces to care for vulnerable Americans who have suffered in wartime: "to care for him who shall have borne the battle and for his widow and his orphan."

As you read historical documents in this book, be sure to consider their audience, purpose, theme, and rhetorical features. Focusing on these items will enrich your reading of these documents so important for our nation.

College and Career Readiness Anchor Standards for Writing

COMMON CORE STATE STANDARDS

TEXT TYPES AND PURPOSES

1. Write arguments to support claims in an analysis of substantive topics or texts, using valid reasoning and relevant and sufficient evidence.
2. Write informative/explanatory texts to examine and convey complex ideas and information clearly and accurately through the effective selection, organization, and analysis of content.
3. Write narratives to develop real or imagined experiences or events using effective technique, well-chosen details, and well-structured event sequences.

PRODUCTION AND DISTRIBUTION OF WRITING

4. Produce clear and coherent writing in which the development, organization, and style are appropriate to task, purpose, and audience.
5. Develop and strengthen writing as needed by planning, revising, editing, rewriting, or trying a new approach.
6. Use technology, including the Internet, to produce and publish writing and to interact and collaborate with others.

RESEARCH TO BUILD AND PRESENT KNOWLEDGE

7. Conduct short as well as more sustained research projects based on focused questions, demonstrating understanding of the subject under investigation.
8. Gather relevant information from multiple print and digital sources, assess the credibility and accuracy of each source, and integrate the information while avoiding plagiarism.
9. Draw evidence from literary or informational texts to support analysis, reflection, and research.

RANGE OF WRITING

10. Write routinely over extended time frames (time for research, reflection, and revision) and shorter time frames (a single sitting or a day or two) for a range of tasks, purposes, and audiences.

Writing Standards, Grades 11–12 Students

COMMON CORE STATE STANDARD	WHAT IT MEANS TO YOU
TEXT TYPES AND PURPOSES	
1. Write arguments to support claims in an analysis of substantive topics or texts, using valid reasoning and relevant and sufficient evidence.	You will write and develop arguments with strong evidence and valid reasoning that include
a. Introduce precise, knowledgeable claim(s), establish the significance of the claim(s), distinguish the claim(s) from alternate or opposing claims, and create an organization that logically sequences claim(s), counterclaims, reasons, and evidence.	**a.** a clear organization of precise claims and counterclaims
b. Develop claim(s) and counterclaims fairly and thoroughly, supplying the most relevant evidence for each while pointing out the strengths and limitations of both in a manner that anticipates the audience's knowledge level, concerns, values, and possible biases.	**b.** relevant and unbiased support for claims that incorporates audience considerations
c. Use words, phrases, and clauses as well as varied syntax to link the major sections of the text, create cohesion, and clarify the relationships between claim(s) and reasons, between reasons and evidence, and between claim(s) and counterclaims.	**c.** use of transitional words, phrases, and clauses and varied sentence structures to link information and clarify relationships
d. Establish and maintain a formal style and objective tone while attending to the norms and conventions of the discipline in which they are writing.	**d.** a tone and style that is appropriate and that adheres to the conventions, or expectations, of the discipline
e. Provide a concluding statement or section that follows from and supports the argument presented.	**e.** a strong concluding statement or section that summarizes the evidence presented
2. Write informative/explanatory texts to examine and convey complex ideas, concepts, and information clearly and accurately through the effective selection, organization, and analysis of content.	You will write clear, well-organized, and thoughtful informative and explanatory texts with
a. Introduce a topic; organize complex ideas, concepts, and information so that each new element builds on that which precedes it to create a unified whole; include formatting (e.g., headings), graphics (e.g., figures, tables), and multimedia when useful to aiding comprehension.	**a.** a clear introduction and an organization that builds on each successive idea, including formats, headings, graphic organizers (when appropriate), and multimedia
b. Develop the topic thoroughly by selecting the most significant and relevant facts, extended definitions, concrete details, quotations, or other information and examples appropriate to the audience's knowledge of the topic.	**b.** a sufficient variety of support and background information
c. Use appropriate and varied transitions and syntax to link the major sections of the text, create cohesion, and clarify the relationships among complex ideas and concepts.	**c.** appropriate and varied transitions and sentence structures

Writing Standards, Grades 11–12 Students, continued

COMMON CORE STATE STANDARD	WHAT IT MEANS TO YOU
TEXT TYPES AND PURPOSES	
d. Use precise language, domain-specific vocabulary, and techniques such as metaphor, simile, and analogy to manage the complexity of the topic.	**d.** precise language, relevant vocabulary, and the use of comparisons to express complex ideas
e. Establish and maintain a formal style and objective tone while attending to the norms and conventions of the discipline in which they are writing.	**e.** an appropriate tone and style that adheres to the conventions, or expectations, of the discipline
f. Provide a concluding statement or section that follows from and supports the information or explanation presented (e.g., articulating implications or the significance of the topic).	**f.** a strong concluding statement or section that logically relates to the information presented in the text and that restates the importance or relevance of the topic
3. Write narratives to develop real or imagined experiences or events using effective technique, well-chosen details, and well-structured event sequences.	You will write clear, well-structured, detailed narrative texts that
a. Engage and orient the reader by setting out a problem, situation, or observation and its significance, establishing one or multiple point(s) of view, and introducing a narrator and/or characters; create a smooth progression of experiences or events.	**a.** draw your readers in with a clear topic, well-developed point(s) of view, a well-developed narrator and characters, and an interesting progression of events or ideas
b. Use narrative techniques, such as dialogue, pacing, description, reflection, and multiple plot lines, to develop experiences, events, and/or characters.	**b.** use a range of literary techniques to develop and expand on events and/or characters
c. Use a variety of techniques to sequence events so that they build on one another to create a coherent whole and build toward a particular tone and outcome (e.g., a sense of mystery, suspense, growth, or resolution).	**c.** have a coherent sequence and structure that create the appropriate tone and ending for readers
d. Use precise words and phrases, telling details, and sensory language to convey a vivid picture of the experiences, events, setting, and/or characters.	**d.** use precise words, sensory details, and language in order to keep readers interested
e. Provide a conclusion that follows from and reflects on what is experienced, observed, or resolved over the course of the narrative.	**e.** have a strong and logical conclusion that reflects on the topic
PRODUCTION AND DISTRIBUTION OF WRITING	
4. Produce clear and coherent writing in which the development, organization, and style are appropriate to task, purpose, and audience.	You will produce writing that is appropriate to the task, purpose, and audience for whom you are writing.
5. Develop and strengthen writing as needed by planning, revising, editing, rewriting, or trying a new approach, focusing on addressing what is most significant for a specific purpose and audience.	You will revise and refine your writing, using a variety of strategies, to address what is most important for your purpose and audience.
6. Use technology, including the Internet, to produce, publish, and update individual or shared writing products in response to ongoing feedback, including new arguments or information.	You will use technology to share your writing, provide links to other relevant information, and to update your information as needed.

Writing Standards, Grades 11–12 Students, continued

COMMON CORE STATE STANDARD	WHAT IT MEANS TO YOU
RESEARCH TO BUILD AND PRESENT KNOWLEDGE **7.** Conduct short as well as more sustained research projects to answer a question (including a self-generated question) or solve a problem; narrow or broaden the inquiry when appropriate; synthesize multiple sources on the subject, demonstrating understanding of the subject under investigation.	You will engage in short and more complex research tasks that include answering a question or solving a problem by using multiple sources. Your understanding of the subject will be evident in the product you develop.
8. Gather relevant information from multiple authoritative print and digital sources, using advanced searches effectively; assess the strengths and limitations of each source in terms of the task, purpose, and audience; integrate information into the text selectively to maintain the flow of ideas, avoiding plagiarism and overreliance on any one source and following a standard format for citation.	You will effectively conduct searches to gather information from a variety of print and digital sources and will evaluate each source in terms of the goal of your research. You will appropriately cite your sources of information and will follow a standard format for citation, such as the MLA or APA guidelines.
9. Draw evidence from literary or informational texts to support analysis, reflection, and research.	You will paraphrase, summarize, quote, and cite primary and secondary sources, using both literary and informational texts, to support your analysis, reflection, and research, for purposes including
a. Apply *grades 11–12 Reading standards* to literature (e.g., "Demonstrate knowledge of eighteenth-, nineteenth- and early-twentieth-century foundational works of American literature, including how two or more texts from the same period treat similar themes or topics").	**a.** written analysis of themes, author's choices, or point of view in American literature
b. Apply *grades 11–12 Reading standards* to literary nonfiction (e.g., "Delineate and evaluate the reasoning in seminal U.S. texts, including the application of constitutional principles and use of legal reasoning [e.g., in U.S. Supreme Court Case majority opinions and dissents] and the premises, purposes, and arguments in works of public advocacy [e.g., *The Federalist*, presidential addresses]").	**b.** written analysis of central ideas, text structure, word choice, point of view, or reasoning in American literary nonfiction
RANGE OF WRITING **10.** Write routinely over extended time frames (time for research, reflection, and revision) and shorter time frames (a single sitting or a day or two) for a range of tasks, purposes, and audiences.	You will write a variety of texts for different purposes and audiences over both short and extended periods of time.

Spotlight on Common Core

W 4 Produce clear and coherent writing in which the development, organization, and style are appropriate to task, purpose, and audience.
W 10 Write routinely over extended time frames (time for research, reflection, and revision) and shorter time frames (a single sitting or a day or two) for a range of tasks, purposes, and audiences.

Writing: Maintaining Clarity and Coherence

The Common Core State Standards focus on your ability to communicate clearly and coherently, so your readers can follow and understand what you have written.

Before you begin writing, answer some specific questions to determine and plan your writing process. Pre-planning helps you define your project and establish a realistic timeframe for it. If your project is ill-defined or if you do not allow enough time for a smooth writing process, the clarity and coherence of your writing will inevitably suffer.

For example, what are you writing? A cover letter takes less time to write than a long essay or procedural text. However, all these documents require you to do some research. Then, you will need to allow for time to draft, revise, and proofread what you have written.

It is also wise to plan for the unexpected. Include a little more time than you think you need in case you have unpredictable scheduling conflicts, need to start over and try a new approach to your topic, or do some extra research.

LEARN HOW Planning Your Writing Process Study the chart below. It provides some additional questions that you can ask yourself before you begin writing. It will help you plan your writing process and produce your best work.

Planning Your Writing Process	
Question	Examples
What is my final product?	• *An argumentative essay* • *A cover letter* • *A research paper*
What is my topic?	• *The importance of arts education* • *An application for an internship* • *Key themes in Zora Neale Hurston's Their Eyes Were Watching God*
What is my purpose, or reason, for writing?	• *To convince others to support arts education* • *To be hired for a summer internship* • *To analyze and explain a literary text*
Who is my audience?	• *Other students in class* • *A hiring manager* • *My English teacher*
How much time do I have? Am I writing over a short or extended period of time?	• *A week* • *A day* • *A month*

Once you understand your task, purpose, audience, and timeframe, you can plan your writing process. For example, you can decide how much time you should spend researching your topic based on your purpose and due date. You might try drafting a schedule, using a calendar and what you already know about how much time to allow for each step in the writing process.

LEARN HOW Using Writing Strategies Having crafted a writing plan, you can concentrate on producing clear and coherent writing. The **Writing Workshops** in this book provide several strategies to help you write effectively. Study the chart below, which provides examples of some of these strategies. The highlighted text in the right column reflects the bold-faced points in the left column.

Writing Strategies	
DEVELOPMENT	**WHAT DOES IT LOOK LIKE?**
• Include a memorable introduction and concluding statement or section. • Utilize a **controlling idea or thesis statement**. • Introduce sufficient facts, definitions, **concrete details, quotations**, and other examples that are appropriate to the audience's knowledge of the topic.	*Many schools around the nation face drastic budget cuts. One of the first areas to suffer has been arts education. John Berman, a local school board member, recently summed up many people's opinion: "What good are the arts when students need to be trained for real jobs?" This is an understandable objection, but it overlooks what we will lose if we eliminate arts education. Several students at Jefferson High School asserted that they would have dropped out of school if they had not been in music classes. Arts education is essential to our schools.*
ORGANIZATION	**WHAT DOES IT LOOK LIKE?**
• Establish a **logical organization** that makes sense for the purpose and audience. • Provide graphics, use formatting, or other text features to help aid comprehension, if necessary. • Use organizational patterns, such as cause-and-effect, definitions, or **compare-contrast** to help readers understand the relationship between ideas. • Include words, phrases, and clauses that link sections of text and **create cohesion**, or flow. • Organize complex ideas, concepts, and information to **make important connections and distinctions**.	*Zora Neale Hurston's Their Eyes Were Watching God includes three key themes:* • *the relationship of language and power* • *the construction of female identity* • *the use of dialect* *First, I will compare and contrast Janie Crawford's relationship to language with Jody's, and then with other characters, such as the gossiping townspeople. This comparison-contrast reveals that a character's sense of self is often mirrored in that character's complex relationship to language.*
LANGUAGE AND STYLE	**WHAT DOES IT LOOK LIKE?**
• Maintain an **appropriate style and tone,** such as formal and objective for academic or business writing. • Use **precise language and telling details.** • Exhibit a strong command of grammar, usage, capitalization, punctuation.	*I am applying for a summer internship as a junior photographer with The Paterson Times. I have been lead photographer on my high school newspaper for the past two years. One of my photographs won the Jimson Prize for best high school news photograph. I want to become a professional photographer, but I need to develop my skills further in a professional newspaper environment.* *The Paterson Times is famous for its award-winning photojournalism. An opportunity to work with your world-class photographers this summer would be an invaluable educational opportunity for me.*

Authors combine different strategies to maintain clarity and coherence in their writing. They apply these strategies to texts of varied lengths, purposes, and complexity. Be sure to notice these strategies as you analyze texts throughout this book, and be sure to use them to improve your own writing.

College and Career Readiness Anchor Standards for Speaking and Listening

COMMON CORE STATE STANDARDS

COMPREHENSION AND COLLABORATION

1. Prepare for and participate effectively in a range of conversations and collaborations with diverse partners, building on others' ideas and expressing their own clearly and persuasively.
2. Integrate and evaluate information presented in diverse media and formats, including visually, quantitatively, and orally.
3. Evaluate a speaker's point of view, reasoning, and use of evidence and rhetoric.

PRESENTATION OF KNOWLEDGE AND IDEAS

4. Present information, findings, and supporting evidence such that listeners can follow the line of reasoning and the organization, development, and style are appropriate to task, purpose, and audience.
5. Make strategic use of digital media and visual displays of data to express information and enhance understanding of presentations.
6. Adapt speech to a variety of contexts and communicative tasks, demonstrating command of formal English when indicated or appropriate.

Speaking and Listening Standards, Grades 11–12 Students

COMMON CORE STATE STANDARD	WHAT IT MEANS TO YOU
COMPREHENSION AND COLLABORATION	
1. Initiate and participate effectively in a range of collaborative discussions (one-on-one, in groups, and teacher-led) with diverse partners on grades 11–12 topics, texts, and issues, building on others' ideas and expressing their own clearly and persuasively.	You will actively participate in a variety of discussions in which you
a. Come to discussions prepared, having read and researched material under study; explicitly draw on that preparation by referring to evidence from texts and other research on the topic or issue to stimulate a thoughtful, well-reasoned exchange of ideas.	**a.** have read any relevant material beforehand and have come to the discussion prepared with background research
b. Work with peers to promote civil, democratic discussions and decision-making, set clear goals and deadlines, and establish individual roles as needed.	**b.** work with others to establish goals, processes, and roles within the group in order to have reasonable discussions
c. Propel conversations by posing and responding to questions that probe reasoning and evidence; ensure a hearing for a full range of positions on a topic or issue; clarify, verify, or challenge ideas and conclusions; and promote divergent and creative perspectives.	**c.** ask and respond to questions, encourage a range of positions, and relate the current topic to other relevant information and perspectives
d. Respond thoughtfully to diverse perspectives; synthesize comments, claims, and evidence made on all sides of an issue; resolve contradictions when possible; and determine what additional information or research is required to deepen the investigation or complete the task.	**d.** respond to different perspectives, summarize points of agreement or disagreement when needed, help to resolve unclear points, and set out a plan for additional research as needed

Speaking and Listening Standards, Grades 11–12 Students, continued

COMMON CORE STATE STANDARD	WHAT IT MEANS TO YOU
2. Integrate multiple sources of information presented in diverse formats and media (e.g., visually, quantitatively, orally) in order to make informed decisions and solve problems, evaluating the credibility and accuracy of each source and noting any discrepancies among the data.	You will integrate multiple and varied sources of information, assessing the credibility and accuracy of each source to aid the group-discussion process.
3. Evaluate a speaker's point of view, reasoning, and use of evidence and rhetoric, assessing the stance, premises, links among ideas, word choice, points of emphasis, and tone used.	You will evaluate a speaker's argument and analyze the nature of the speaker's reasoning or evidence.
PRESENTATION OF KNOWLEDGE AND IDEAS	
4. Present information, findings, and supporting evidence, conveying a clear and distinct perspective, such that listeners can follow the line of reasoning, alternative or opposing perspectives are addressed, and the organization, development, substance, and style are appropriate to purpose, audience, and a range of formal and informal tasks.	You will organize and present information, evidence, and your perspective to your listeners in a logical sequence and style that are appropriate to your task, purpose, and audience.
5. Make strategic use of digital media (e.g., textual, graphical, audio, visual, and interactive elements) in presentations to enhance understanding of findings, reasoning, and evidence and to add interest.	You will use digital media to enhance understanding and to add interest to your presentations.
6. Adapt speech to a variety of contexts and tasks, demonstrating a command of formal English when indicated or appropriate.	You will adapt the formality of your speech appropriately, depending on its context and purpose.

Spotlight on Common Core

SL 1b Work with peers to promote civil, democratic discussions and decision-making, set clear goals and deadlines, and establish individual roles as needed.

Speaking and Listening: Interacting Constructively in Discussions

The Common Core State Standards emphasize the importance of working constructively with your peers in group discussions. These discussions provide an opportunity for you to learn from each other by actively sharing opinions and ideas in order to answer a question, solve a problem, or reach consensus. A productive group discussion follows a democratic model. All the participants should feel that their voices are heard, even if they have strong differences of opinion.

Before you begin your group discussion, assign roles to group members to help streamline it. You will need:

1. a **chairperson**, or facilitator, who keeps the group focused on its goal or purpose, participates in the discussion and keeps it on track, and helps resolve conflicts
2. a **recorder** who takes notes on the discussion and summarizes suggestions and decisions
3. a **timekeeper** who keeps the discussion on schedule

Then, answer these questions:

1. What is the goal or purpose of the discussion? In other words, what should this discussion accomplish?
2. How much time does the group have for the discussion?
3. What rules will guide the discussion?

LEARN HOW Interacting in Discussions Review the discussion's purpose and timeframe to focus the group's attention. Establish rules for the discussion to ensure that it will be productive. In order to thrive, a discussion requires a civil atmosphere that encourages the flow of ideas.

- Everyone in the group should feel they have the right to speak, but not to interrupt each other. The rest of the group needs to listen actively to what each person says until it is another person's turn to speak. If time is short, consider establishing a reasonable limit on how long each participant may speak. The timekeeper can monitor the time.
- A peer discussion should inspire a lively argument, not an angry showdown.

Nothing kills the free exchange of ideas faster than someone who stubbornly or aggressively dominates a discussion. As a result, others in the group may not have the opportunity to speak, or may even feel bullied into agreeing with the speaker. If this appears to be happening, the chairperson should quickly step in to politely remind participants to maintain a civil and respectful tone.

Active listening is the process of receiving, interpreting, evaluating, and responding to a message. It is as important as expressing your own ideas clearly and articulately.

- Fully focus your attention on what your peers say. Even if you disagree with what is being said, continue to listen respectfully. The chairperson should remind members of the group to do this if the discussion becomes too heated.
- When it's your turn, first summarize, or restate, the previous speaker's position briefly in your own words to verify that you have understood him or her. Ask the previous speaker clarifying questions if needed or refer to the recorder for further verification.
- State your own views in an articulate, thoughtful way.
- Respond to any questions about or challenges to your point of view calmly.
- Be willing to support your views, but also keep an open mind about considering new ideas.

Constructive disagreements are essential to any group discussion. Without disagreements, people are not challenged by new ideas or contrasting viewpoints and cannot grow. If there is a difference of opinion, participants should speak calmly, ask questions respectfully, and remain open-minded. Nor must all disagreements be resolved. Participants can respectfully agree to disagree. When disagreements arise:

- Participants should not aggressively interrupt or talk over one another.
- Participants must present reasons or evidence to support their positions. If you say you like or dislike an idea, you must say why you do. It is not enough to simply say you agree or disagree.
- Seek common ground. See if participants who disagree with each other can compromise or agree on part of the issue.
- Watch the time. You may not be able to come to a full agreement, but disagreements can spiral out of control. If it does not look as if agreement or compromise can be reached, participants need to agree to disagree and move on.

Spotlight on Common Core

Speaking and Listening: Encouraging Fruitful Discussion

COMMON CORE

SL 1c Propel conversations by posing and responding to questions that probe reasoning and evidence; ensure a hearing for a full range of positions on a topic or issue; clarify, verify, or challenge ideas and conclusions; and promote divergent and creative perspectives.

To encourage a fruitful, wide-ranging discussion, it is important to ask questions, as well as state opinions, that expand, or build upon, that discussion.

- Ask open-ended questions that do not have a yes or no answer.
  Closed: *Did America win the Revolutionary War?*
  Open-Ended: *Why did America win the Revolutionary War?*
- Play devil's advocate by offering an opposing viewpoint.
- Ask for additional examples or other forms of evidence to support a point.
- Combine different arguments to form a new option.

LEARN HOW **Encouraging Discussion** In the following discussion, students are debating whether people are essentially good—that is, can we trust most people to do the right thing?

EFFECTIVE BEHAVIOR	WHAT IT LOOKS LIKE
Support others' contributions.	*Alejandro believes that people are essentially good: we should trust others to do the right thing. He mentions examples of courageous behavior by ordinary people during natural disasters. Genna listens attentively to Alejandro. She has just come from a discussion of slavery in America in her social studies class. She wonders how people can believe in freedom, but enslave others at the same time.*
State your own views thoughtfully.	*When Alejandro finishes speaking, Genna restates his points to make sure she understands his perspective. She comments, "I understand Alejandro's position because I, too, want to believe that people are essentially good. But there are many examples from history of people treating others with cruelty by exploiting them for their own gain. Americans believed in freedom, yet some kept slaves. How is it possible to be essentially good, but then do terrible things?"*
Summarize agreements and disagreements.	*Li speaks next. He summarizes Alejandro's and Genna's opposing views, and then offers an alternative. "It may look like there is a contradiction here. Either people are essentially good or they are not. But what if there is another way of looking at this? What if people are neither one nor the other, but capable of being both?"*
Justify your views or consider new ones.	*Alejandro considers what Li has said. He prepares to offer more evidence that people are essentially good, and extends his argument to respond to Genna's point as well. Perhaps outside forces may affect essential goodness and turn people toward negative thoughts or actions. He decides to mention this when his turn comes up again.* *Li's point makes Genna think, too. She makes a note to ask the group, "If what Li says is true, how do we learn how to make those choices? What makes some people choose to do good, while others choose to do terrible things? And are there times when people may not really have a choice?" Her question will also expand the discussion.*

Alejandro shares his opinion, supporting it with evidence. Genna disagrees with Alejandro but still listens carefully.

Genna verifies that she understands Alejandro's point. Then, she offers another viewpoint, supporting it with an example.

By combining both arguments, Li creates an alternative view of the issue. This expands the discussion.

Alejandro and Genna consider Li's point. Li's alternative offers an opportunity to delve into the original question and expand their own arguments.

Throughout this book you will have opportunities to contribute to a variety of group discussions. Be sure to contribute effectively by understanding and modeling appropriate attitudes and behaviors. When you learn how to contribute effectively to group discussions, your voice is more likely to be heard, and your views are more likely to be understood. And your discussion will accomplish something positive for everyone.

College and Career Readiness Anchor Standards for Language

COMMON CORE STATE STANDARDS

CONVENTIONS OF STANDARD ENGLISH

1. Demonstrate command of the conventions of standard English grammar and usage when writing or speaking.

2. Demonstrate command of the conventions of standard English capitalization, punctuation, and spelling when writing.

KNOWLEDGE OF LANGUAGE

3. Apply knowledge of language to understand how language functions in different contexts, to make effective choices for meaning or style, and to comprehend more fully when reading or listening.

VOCABULARY ACQUISITION AND USE

4. Determine or clarify the meaning of unknown and multiple-meaning words and phrases by using context clues, analyzing meaningful word parts, and consulting general and specialized reference materials, as appropriate.

5. Demonstrate understanding of word relationships and nuances in word meanings.

6. Acquire and use accurately a range of general academic and domain-specific words and phrases sufficient for reading, writing, speaking, and listening at the college and career readiness level; demonstrate independence in gathering vocabulary knowledge when considering a word or phrase important to comprehension or expression.

Language Standards, Grades 11–12 Students

COMMON CORE STATE STANDARD	WHAT IT MEANS TO YOU
CONVENTIONS OF STANDARD ENGLISH	
1. Demonstrate command of the conventions of standard English grammar and usage when writing or speaking.	You will correctly use the conventions of English grammar and usage, including
a. Apply the understanding that usage is a matter of convention, can change over time, and is sometimes contested.	**a.** demonstrating that usage follows accepted standards and can change or be contested
b. Resolve issues of complex or contested usage, consulting references (e.g., *Merriam-Webster's Dictionary of English Usage, Garner's Modern American Usage*) as needed.	**b.** using references to resolve disagreements or uncertainty about usage
2. Demonstrate command of the conventions of standard English capitalization, punctuation, and spelling when writing.	You will correctly use the conventions of standard English capitalization, punctuation, and spelling, including
a. Observe hyphenation conventions.	**a.** hyphens
b. Spell correctly.	**b.** spelling
KNOWLEDGE OF LANGUAGE	
3. Apply knowledge of language to understand how language functions in different contexts, to make effective choices for meaning or style, and to comprehend more fully when reading or listening.	You will apply your knowledge of language in different contexts to guide choices in your own writing and speaking by
a. Vary syntax for effect, consulting references (e.g., Tufte's *Artful Sentences*) for guidance as needed; apply an understanding of syntax to the study of complex texts when reading.	**a.** using appropriate references for guidance to vary your syntax and to understand syntax in complex texts
VOCABULARY ACQUISITION AND USE	
4. Determine or clarify the meaning of unknown and multiple-meaning words and phrases based on grades 11–12 reading and content, choosing flexibly from a range of strategies.	You will understand the meaning of grade-level appropriate words and phrases by
a. Use context (e.g., the overall meaning of a sentence, paragraph, or text; a word's position or function in a sentence) as a clue to the meaning of a word or phrase.	**a.** using context clues
b. Identify and correctly use patterns of word changes that indicate different meanings or parts of speech (e.g., *conceive, conception, conceivable*).	**b.** applying various forms of words according to meaning or part of speech
c. Consult general and specialized reference materials (e.g., dictionaries, glossaries, thesauruses), both print and digital, to find the pronunciation of a word or determine or clarify its precise meaning, its part of speech, its etymology, or its standard usage.	**c.** using reference materials to determine and clarify word meaning, part of speech, etymology, and standard usage
d. Verify the preliminary determination of the meaning of a word or phrase (e.g., by checking the inferred meaning in context or in a dictionary).	**d.** inferring and verifying the meanings of words in context

Language Standards, Grades 11–12 Students, continued

COMMON CORE STATE STANDARD	WHAT IT MEANS TO YOU
5. Demonstrate understanding of figurative language, word relationships, and nuances in word meanings. **a.** Interpret figures of speech (e.g., hyperbole, paradox) in context and analyze their role in the text. **b.** Analyze nuances in the meaning of words with similar denotations.	You will understand figurative language, word relationships, and slight differences in word meanings by **a.** interpreting figures of speech in context **b.** analyzing slight differences in the meanings of similar words
6. Acquire and use accurately general academic and domain-specific words and phrases, sufficient for reading, writing, speaking, and listening at the college and career readiness level; demonstrate independence in gathering vocabulary knowledge when considering a word or phrase important to comprehension or expression.	You will develop and use a range of vocabulary at the college and career readiness level and will demonstrate that you can successfully acquire new vocabulary independently.

Spotlight on Common Core

L 1a Apply the understanding that usage is a matter of convention, can change over time, and is sometimes contested. **L 1b** Resolve issues of complex or contested usage, consulting references (e.g., *Merriam-Webster's Dictionary of English Usage, Garner's Modern American Usage*) as needed.

Language: Understanding and Resolving Preferred Usage

When you understand correct usage, you recognize the accepted rules, or conventions, about words. Some words are incorrect (*ain't*) under any circumstances in academic or business contexts. Other words may be used informally, but are not acceptable for formal writing (*okay*). Still others look similar, but are actually different parts of speech (*loose* and *lose*). Even professional writers are sometimes unsure which word is the correct choice. *A lot* or *alot? Toward* or *towards? Affect* or *effect?*

Language changes over time, and inevitably, so does usage, often in response to changes in cultural beliefs. The word *mankind* has recently fallen out of favor. Writers once used this term to refer to all human beings. However, because it is a term that excludes women as human beings, it is now considered inappropriate. Writers should avoid using this term in favor of more neutral, inclusive words such as *humans, human beings*, or *people*.

LEARN HOW **Understanding Usage** *Lose* and *loose* or *fewer* and *less* are examples of words that frequently confuse writers because they look or sound alike or have similar meanings. You may consult a dictionary of English usage to learn how to use these words correctly. Here are some examples of commonly confused words. See page R79 of this book for an extended list.

Words	Definitions	Examples
lose/loose	***Lose*** means "to misplace or fail to find." ***Loose*** means "free, not restrained."	I hope we don't **lose** any of the horses in the pasture. Who turned the horses **loose?**
less/fewer	***Less*** refers to bulk quantity. ***Fewer*** refers to the number of separate, countable units.	We have **less** literature and **fewer** selections in this year's curriculum.

In some cases, the English language is so changeable that even experts do not fully agree about correct usage. For example, many experts believe that the words *and, also,* or *but* should never be used to begin a sentence. But a clear majority of a group of usage experts polled by *The American Heritage Dictionary* thought that it is acceptable to begin sentences with these words. Many respected publications, such as *The New York Times,* often use *and, also,* and *but* to begin sentences. The important point to remember is that what is considered acceptable usage can change, because language and our attitudes about it evolve over time.

LEARN HOW **Using References to Resolve Usage** You may encounter instances of usage that are complex or that you suspect may be contested. When in doubt about how to use a word, it is better to consult an authoritative reference book than make an uneducated guess. Authoritative reference books gather current findings of language experts about correct usage. Dependable reference books include *Merriam-Webster's Dictionary of English Usage, Garner's Modern American Usage,* and *The American Heritage Book of English Usage.* As in a dictionary, words are arranged alphabetically in these reference works. In some cases, even language experts may not agree on correct usage, but they usually have a preference or majority opinion about it. Make sure you read the information in the reference book carefully to determine if this is the case. Your safest bet as a writer is to go with a word's preferred usage, particularly if you are writing in a school or business context.

A common dilemma is identifying the correct form of a word. In some cases, you will find that one form is clearly correct, while the other is not. In other cases, the answer is not as clear or may even be disputed. Here are some examples.

1. Which version is correct: *alot* or *a lot?*

- In my heart, I knew my sister cared about me *alot.*
- In my heart, I knew my sister cared about me *a lot.*

According to *Merriam-Webster's Dictionary of English Usage, alot* is never correct. *A lot* is the only correct form. The second sentence is correct.

2. Which version is correct: *toward* or *towards?*

- Jamie held out her hand in greeting *toward* Kaylee.
- Jamie held out her hand in greeting *towards* Kaylee.

Experts consider the two words to be interchangeable; however, *toward* is more commonly used in American English, while *towards* is used in British English. The first sentence is the better choice for students writing in American English.

In addition, some words look so similar that it is hard to know which one to use in what context.

3. Which is the correct word to use: *affect* or *effect*?

- Emily Dickinson's poems had a profound ***affect/effect*** on generations of poets.
- Emily Dickinson's poems have profoundly ***affected/effected*** generations of poets.

According to usage experts, *effect* is a noun (the result of something) and *affect* is a verb (to cause something to happen). The word's role in the sentence as a noun or verb tells you which version to use. In the first sentence, *effect* is correct because it is used as a noun. In the second sentence, *affected* is correct because it is used as a verb.

4. Finally, *impact* is a word whose correct usage has changed over time. Is it correct to use it today as a noun or a verb?

- The *impact* of the American Revolution was felt around the world. (used as a noun)
- The health of the economy *impacts* all Americans. (used as a verb)

Experts often struggle with this question. In the past, using *impact* as a noun, not as a verb, was the sole correct usage. However, experts admit that in the past decade, *impact* appears so frequently as a verb that they no longer consider its use as such to be incorrect. However, they still prefer that *impact* be used sparingly as a verb, if at all.

As you write, be sure to employ correct usage. When in doubt, consult an authoritative reference source for information about preferred usage.

Spotlight on Common Core

L 3a Vary syntax for effect, consulting references (e.g., Tufte's *Artful Sentences*) for guidance as needed; apply an understanding of syntax to the study of complex texts when reading.

Language: Varying Syntax for Effect

Syntax is the arrangement of words in phrases, clauses, and sentences. Writers want to engage their readers, but repeatedly using the same wording or sentence structure drains prose of vitality and interest. Varying syntax is the best way to create a more dynamic, engaging verbal rhythm, or flow, in your writing. Varying syntax also allows you to emphasize certain ideas or parts of a sentence to dramatic effect or to include additional information. Here are two strategies you can use to vary syntax:

1. Vary sentence structure by rearranging or adding words to individual sentences or combining multiple sentences.
2. Vary sentence lengths within paragraphs by alternating long and short sentences.

LEARN HOW **Varying Syntax** Varying words, phrases, and clauses in a sentence or across sentences may create a more dynamic rhythm. As you vary syntax, however, remember that your writing must remain appropriate to your task, purpose, and audience. Each sentence must be clear and coherent. For additional options about how to vary syntax, you may consult a reference (such as Virginia Tufte's *Artful Sentences: Syntax as Style*).

Here are some examples of how to revise sentence structure to vary syntax. Note how each revision changes the effect of these sentences on the reader.

The painting sold at auction. There was fierce bidding. It set a world record.

Revision to Vary Syntax	**Effect**
The painting sold at auction after fierce bidding that set a world record.	Improved rhythm
Setting a world record, the painting sold at auction after fierce bidding.	Improved rhythm; emphasizes world record; more dramatic
After fierce bidding, the painting sold at auction, setting a world record.	Improved rhythm; emphasizes fierce bidding; more dramatic
Against expectations, the painting sold at auction after fierce bidding, and set a world record.	Improved rhythm; more dramatic; adds information

You may also vary syntax for emphasis by varying sentence length. Read the paragraph below from "Letter from Birmingham Jail" by Martin Luther King, Jr.

> . . . Let us consider a more concrete example of just and unjust laws. An unjust law is a code that a numerical or power majority group compels a minority group to obey but does not make binding on itself. This is *difference* made legal. By the same token, a just law is a code that a majority compels a minority to follow and that it is willing to follow itself. This is *sameness* made legal.

The two longest sentences in the paragraph explain unjust and just laws. King follows each long sentence with a dramatic short sentence: unjust laws do not consider people as equals ("This is *difference* made legal"), while just laws do ("This is *sameness* made legal"). These short sentences convey King's strong belief in his ideas and emphasize the contrast he makes between just and unjust laws.

In your own writing, be sure to vary syntax to affect your readers. As you analyze the texts in this book, notice how authors vary syntax to affect you as a reader.

Exploring American Literature

INTRODUCING THE ESSENTIALS

- Text Analysis Workshop
- Academic Vocabulary Workshop
- Writing Process Workshop

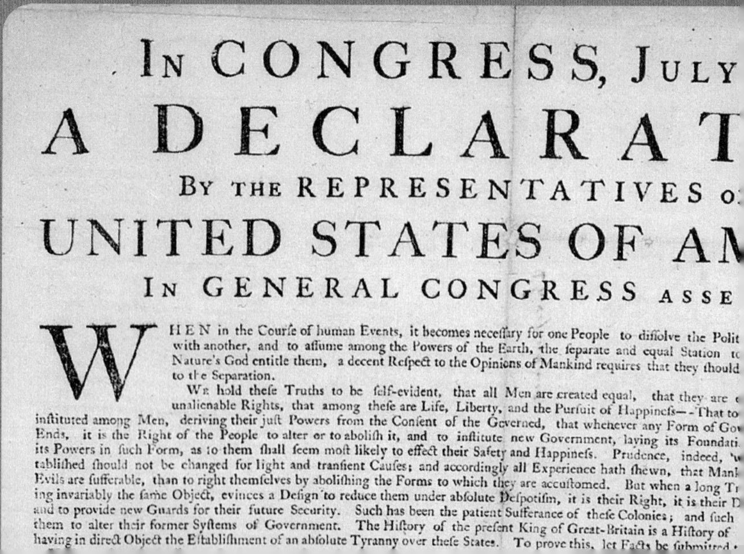

IN CONGRESS, JULY

A DECLARAT

BY THE REPRESENTATIVES O

UNITED STATES OF AM

IN GENERAL CONGRESS ASSE

WHEN in the Courſe of human Events, it becomes neceſſary for one People to diſſolve the Polit
with another, and to aſſume among the Powers of the Earth, the ſeparate and equal Station to
Nature's God entitle them, a decent Reſpect to the Opinions of Mankind requires that they ſhould
to the Separation.

WE hold theſe Truths to be ſelf-evident, that all Men are created equal, that they are
unalienable Rights, that among theſe are Life, Liberty, and the Purſuit of Happineſs—That to
inſtituted among Men, deriving their juſt Powers from the Conſent of the Governed, that whenever any Form of Gov
Ends, it is the Right of the People to alter or to aboliſh it, and to inſtitute new Government, laying its Foundati
its Powers in ſuch Form, as to them ſhall ſeem moſt likely to effect their Safety and Happineſs. Prudence, indeed, w
tabliſhed ſhould not be changed for light and tranſient Cauſes; and accordingly all Experience hath ſhewn, that Mank
Evils are ſufferable, than to right themſelves by aboliſhing the Forms to which they are accuſtomed. But when a long Tr
ing invariably the ſame Object, evinces a Deſign to reduce them under abſolute Deſpotiſm, it is their Right, it is their D
and to provide new Guards for their future Security. Such has been the patient Sufferance of theſe Colonies; and ſuch
them to alter their former Syſtems of Government. The Hiſtory of the preſent King of Great-Britain is a Hiſtory of
having in direct Object the Eſtabliſhment of an abſolute Tyranny over theſe States. To prove this, let Facts be ſubmitted

Insights and Perspectives

America's literature comes from all of us and belongs to everyone. It began with the lore of the Native Americans, then appeared in the journals of settlers, the letters of Civil War soldiers, and the tales of Mark Twain. Fast forward another century, and it lives in the books of John Steinbeck and shines from the poems of Gwendolyn Brooks.

Why does American literature matter? Not only does it keep us connected to the past, but it also gives us insights into the events and issues that challenge the nation today. The literature in this book can help you . . .

Explore BIG IDEAS

Why do we explore new horizons? What is the American dream? Today's generations aren't the first to grapple with questions about freedom, progress, exploration, and injustice. Some ideas and issues are timeless, as you'll discover when you read the dramatic accounts of early explorers and F. Scott Fitzgerald's fiction.

Build CULTURAL LITERACY

There are some questions that all Americans should be able to answer. In the area of American literature, such questions include: Who was Mark Twain? Why was *The Crucible* a work of great courage? By reading American literature, you become aware of the pioneering authors and literary milestones that are a part of the American heritage.

Connect HISTORY *and Literature*

Whether it's the Gettysburg Address or the poetry of the Harlem Renaissance, all works of American literature are products of the events and ideas that inspired their authors. By examining history and literature together, you can gain a deeper understanding of how the country changed over the centuries and what makes its people unique.

Appreciate a LEGACY

Trailblazers in their times, Margaret Fuller and Martin Luther King Jr. fought for equal rights—a fight that still continues. Learning about the great writers, thinkers, and ideas of the past helps you better appreciate how we all continue to build on what we learned from them.

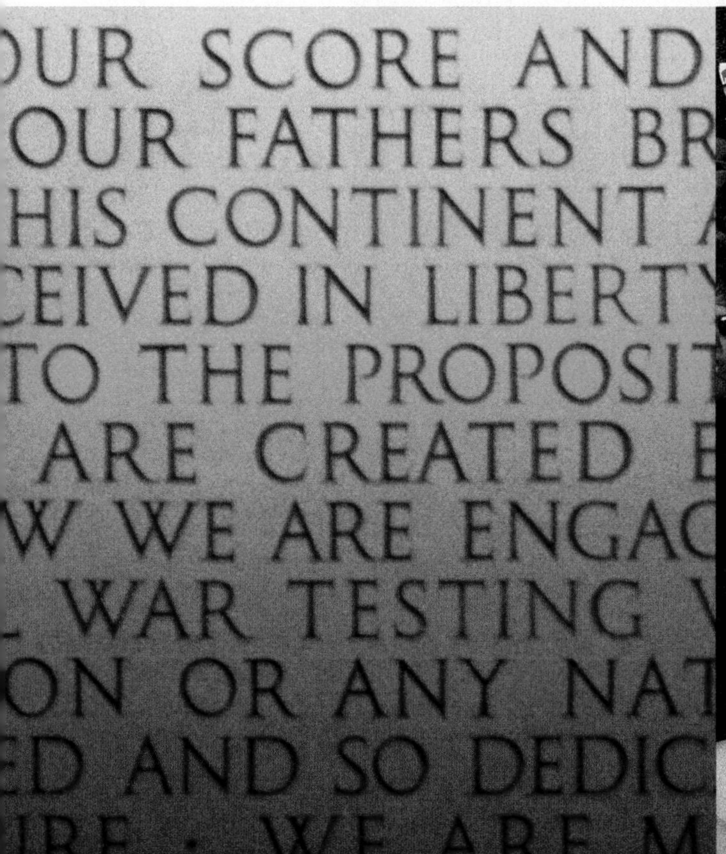

Text Analysis Workshop

Literature and Nonfiction in Context

The growth of the Internet, the discovery of a new medical treatment, a declaration of war, a decision of the Supreme Court—consider how events like these affect your attitudes, your outlook, your politics. They shape the attitudes of writers as well, who then express their ideas in stories, poems, speeches, blogs, and public documents. In the same way, the writing of every time period reflects its unique historical context. By reading it, you can transport yourself back through time and gain perspective on people and events you could never otherwise experience.

COMMON CORE

Included in this workshop:
RL 1, RL 3, RL 9, RI 9, L 3, L 4a, L 4c

LITERARY MOVEMENTS IN CONTEXT

NATIVE AMERICAN EXPERIENCE 1200 B.C.–1600	PURITAN AGE/ COLONIAL PERIOD 1600–1700	REVOLUTIONARY PERIOD/AGE OF REASON 1750–1800	ROMANTICISM/ AMERICAN GOTHIC 1800–1855	TRANSCENDENTALISM 1840–1860
• Sioux • Okanogan • Iroquois • Kiowa	• William Bradford • Anne Bradstreet • Edward Taylor	• Ben Franklin • Thomas Jefferson • Thomas Paine	• Henry Wadsworth Longfellow • Edgar Allan Poe	• Ralph Waldo Emerson • Henry David Thoreau • Margaret Fuller

1200 B.C.–1600 Native American cultures flourish. **1492** Christopher Columbus lands in the Bahamas.	**1607** British settlers establish colony in Jamestown, Virginia. **1692** Witch trials take place in Salem, Massachussetts.	**1776** American colonies declare independence. **1788** U.S. Constitution is ratified.	**1803** Louisiana Purchase doubles the country's size. **1808** United States bans slave trade. **1812** War of 1812 spurs Industrial Revolution.	**1846** Mexican-American War begins. **1848** Gold discoveries in California lead to first gold rush. **1857** Supreme Court's Dred Scott decision denies slaves basic rights.

Literary Movements

Think about how certain types of music reflect the times in which they were written. Some folk songs, for example, can remind listeners of an earlier time of protest. Similarly, the literature of each historical period has a unique flavor. Subject matter, style, form, and attitude all combine to create a **literary movement,** such as **realism** or **regionalism.** While not all writers fit neatly into specific categories, it is still helpful to know the major movements that have defined the nation's literature. By studying these movements in context, you can see not only the overlap between them, but also better appreciate the writers and works from particular time periods.

REALISM
1855–1900

- Stephen Crane
- Ambrose Bierce

1861–1865 North and South fight in Civil War.

1865 13th Amendment abolishes slavery.

1879 Thomas Edison invents the light bulb.

REGIONALISM/ NATURALISM
1870–1910

- Mark Twain
- Willa Cather
- Jack London

1889 Oklahoma is opened for settlement, triggering a land rush.

1903 Wright brothers achieve first airplane flight.

MODERNISM
1910–1945

- T. S. Eliot
- Ernest Hemingway
- Ezra Pound

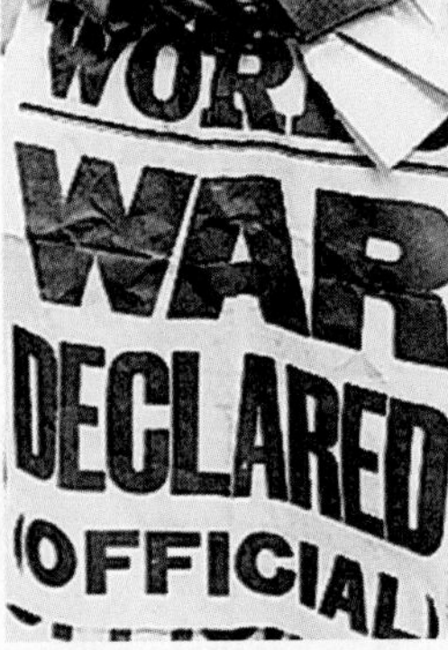

1917 United States enters World War I.

1920 19th Amendment is passed, giving women the right to vote.

HARLEM RENAISSANCE
1920–1930

- Langston Hughes
- Zora Neale Hurston
- Countee Cullen

1919 Race riots erupt in 25 American cities.

1929 The Wall Street stock market crashes and the Great Depression begins.

CONTEMPORARY LITERATURE
1940–PRESENT

- Kurt Vonnegut Jr.
- John Steinbeck
- Rita Dove
- Amy Tan

1941 Attack on Pearl Harbor brings U.S. into World War II.

1965 U.S. enters Vietnam War.

2001 Terrorists attack U.S. cities.

2009 Barack Obama becomes first African American U.S. president.

Using Critical Lenses

Have you ever looked through a prism or camera lens and seen the world in an entirely new way? Critical lenses, or viewpoints from which to consider something, can affect your perception—and your reading—in a similar manner. They allow you to notice details you might otherwise have missed, and can lead you to unexpected insights about a writer and his or her work. Use the following lenses, as well as others you might develop, to see beyond your own personal perspective.

THE LENSES	QUESTIONS TO ASK	
LITERARY LENS **The literary lens is the one you're used to using with literature. It focuses your attention on the author's style and on such elements as plot, setting, character, and theme.**	• What is unique about this author's style? • How do the plot, characters, and setting help to communicate the author's message? • How are language and imagery used to support the themes?	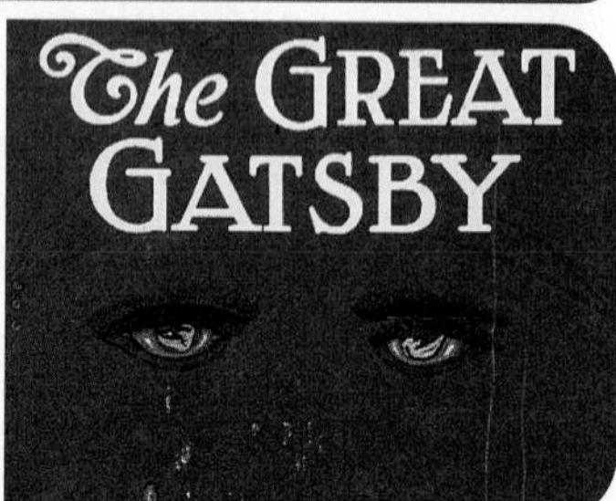
HISTORICAL AND CULTURAL LENSES **Historical and cultural lenses help you consider how elements of history and culture may have influenced the author and the writing.**	• What was going on in the country at the time this work was written? • What attitudes, trends, and priorities characterized the times? • How are those events and attitudes, and the author's reactions to them, reflected in the writing?	
BIOGRAPHICAL LENS **The biographical lens draws you into the arena of an author's personal life. By considering a writer's heritage, experiences, and economic circumstances, you are able to "read into" a piece of literature with far more insight.**	• What were some key events and people in the author's life? • What were his or her social and economic circumstances? • Did culture and heritage play a strong role in shaping the author's attitudes?	
OTHER LENSES **• psychological** **• social** **• political** **• philosophical/moral**	• What motivations might be influencing a character's behavior? (psychological) • Are the characters' choices, behavior, and actions ethical and honest? (philosophical/moral)	

MODEL: CRITICAL LENSES

The Great Gatsby is a novel set in the 1920s. World War I had just ended, and the country was embarking on a time of great self-indulgence, eager to forget what it had just experienced. In this scene, the narrator describes an outing with his friendly but mysterious neighbor, Jay Gatsby. Read the passage twice—with and without lenses.

from

The Great Gatsby

Novel by **F. Scott Fitzgerald**

At nine o'clock, one morning late in July, Gatsby's gorgeous car lurched up the rocky drive to my door and gave out a burst of melody from its three-noted horn. It was the first time he had called on me, though I had gone to two of his parties, mounted in his hydroplane, and, at his urgent invitation, made frequent use of his beach.

"Good morning, old sport. You're having lunch with me today and I thought we'd ride up together."

He was balancing himself on the running board of his car with that resourcefulness of movement that is so peculiarly American—that comes, I suppose, with the absence of lifting work or rigid sitting in youth and, even more, with the formless grace of our nervous, sporadic games. This quality was continually breaking through his punctilious manner in the shape of restlessness. He was never quite still; there was always a tapping foot somewhere or the impatient opening and closing of a hand.

He saw me looking with admiration at his car.

"It's pretty, isn't it, old sport!" He jumped off to give me a better view. "Haven't you ever seen it before?"

I'd seen it. Everybody had seen it. It was a rich cream color, bright with nickel, swollen here and there in its monstrous length with triumphant hat-boxes and supper-boxes and tool-boxes, and terraced with a labyrinth of wind-shields that mirrored a dozen suns. Sitting down behind many layers of glass in a sort of green leather conservatory, we started to town.

I had talked with him perhaps half a dozen times in the past month and found, to my disappointment, that he had little to say. So my first impression, that he was a person of some undefined consequence, had gradually faded and he had become simply the proprietor of an elaborate road-house next door.

And then came that disconcerting ride. We hadn't reached West Egg Village before Gatsby began leaving his elegant sentences unfinished and slapping himself indecisively on the knee of his caramel-colored suit.

"Look here, old sport," he broke out surprisingly, "what's your opinion of me, anyhow?"

Close Read

1. **Literary Lens** What do the details in lines 1–5 tell you about Gatsby and his relationship with the narrator?

2. **Cultural Lens** Reread the boxed text. What is the narrator's attitude toward Americans of this time period? What reality might this attitude be reflecting?

3. **Psychological Lens** Private cars were not common in the 1920s. Why might Gatsby not only want to own a car, but also insist on such a luxurious one?

A little overwhelmed, I began the generalized evasions which that question deserves.

"Well, I'm going to tell you something about my life," he interrupted. "I don't want you to get a wrong idea of me from all these stories you hear."

So he was aware of the bizarre accusations that flavored conversation in his halls.

"I'll tell you God's truth." His right hand suddenly ordered divine retribution to stand by. "I am the son of some wealthy people in the Middle West—all dead now. I was brought up in America but educated at Oxford, because all my ancestors have been educated there for many years. It is a family tradition."

He looked at me sideways—and I knew why Jordan Baker had believed he was lying. He hurried the phrase "educated at Oxford," or swallowed it, or choked on it, as though it had bothered him before. And with this doubt, his whole statement fell to pieces, and I wondered if there wasn't something a little sinister about him, after all.

"What part of the Middle West?" I inquired casually.

"San Francisco."

"I see."

Close Read

4. **Cultural Lens** What "facts" about himself and his background does Gatsby provide? What does this tell you about the cultural values of the time?

5. **Literary Lens** What techniques has Fitzgerald used in this excerpt to create the intriguing character of Jay Gatsby?

Now read the biographical information about F. Scott Fitzgerald and answer the questions. Refer back to the excerpt from *The Great Gatsby* as needed.

F. Scott Fitzgerald

Born in 1896 of southern and Irish heritage, Francis Scott Key Fitzgerald began writing in his early teens. Encouraged by a mentor at school, Fitzgerald pursued his dream of becoming a writer, quickly neglecting his studies in the process. He served in the army during World War I, and convinced he was going to die, dashed off an autobiographical novel. A few years—and several revisions—later, he sold his novel, titled *Tender Is the Night,* and became an overnight success. One week after the novel's publication, Fitzgerald married a southern belle, Zelda Sayre. He and his wife embarked on a flamboyant, high-spending life, although their extravagance and Zelda's illnesses kept Fitzgerald constantly in debt. Fitzgerald died in 1940, impoverished, after spending his lifetime in pursuit of wealth and privilege.

Close Read

1. **Biographical Lens** How might Fitzgerald's own experiences have influenced his characterization of Gatsby?

2. **Biographical Lens** What similarities do you see between Fitzgerald's and Gatsby's values? What was Fitzgerald's attitude toward these values? Why do you think so?

Literature and Nonfiction Strategies

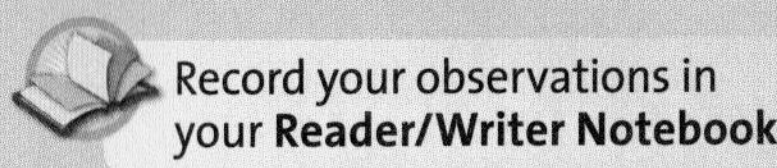

Record your observations in your **Reader/Writer Notebook.**

❶ Understand Context

Texts of all types are shaped by different cultural and historical contexts. In addition to essays and memoirs, American nonfiction includes primary sources, such as historical accounts, letters, and journals. To understand context as you read these texts, ask yourself the following questions:

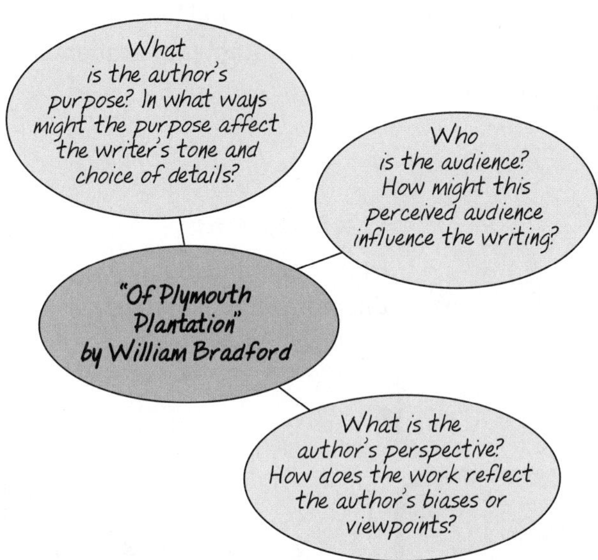

What is the author's purpose? In what ways might the purpose affect the writer's tone and choice of details?
Who is the audience? How might this perceived audience influence the writing?

What is the author's perspective? How does the work reflect the author's biases or viewpoints?

❷ Clarify Meaning

When you read American literature and nonfiction, you will encounter unfamiliar language and difficult sentence structures. Use these strategies and tips to help unlock the meaning of challenging texts.

- **Break Down Sentences** Break down complicated sentences by first locating the sentence's main subject and verb. Then, identify objects, modifiers, and phrases. Try restating the sentences more simply, rearranging word order if necessary.
- **Use Context Clues** A word's context—the words and sentences that surround it—often gives clues to the word's meaning. Dialects, for example, have their own rules of grammar and pronunciation, which you can figure out from context clues.
- **Consult References** When you encounter an unfamiliar word or allusion, check the vocabulary definitions and footnotes provided in this book or look the word up in a print or digital reference source.

❸ Ask Your Own Questions

An important part of analyzing texts is knowing what questions to ask as you read. What should you look for when you read a story, a drama, or a news article? To make your reading more meaningful, it's also important to ask the questions *you* wonder about so that you connect what you read to yourself and the world around you. The following features of your textbook will help you ask the right questions and read with your own questions in mind.

Where to Look	What You'll Find
Text Analysis Workshops (throughout every unit) ▶	Models and **Close Read** questions
Side notes and discussion questions ▶	Questions (throughout and following each selection) that focus on text analysis
Analysis Frames THINK central Go to thinkcentral.com. KEYWORD: HML11-9 ▶	Guided questions for analyzing different types of texts

Academic Vocabulary Workshop

COMMON CORE

Included in this workshop:
L 4a–c, L 6

What Is Academic Vocabulary?

If you are lucky enough, or have studied hard enough, to speak two languages—English and Spanish, for example—you are bilingual. Being bilingual may mean that you use one language at home and another at school or with friends. In a sense, though, we are all bilingual: With family and friends, we use informal and conversational language, but in school, we rely on **academic vocabulary,** the language used to talk and write about school subject matter. Just as we can learn the vocabulary of everyday English, Spanish, or Cantonese, we can learn academic vocabulary.

Criteria, interpret, perspective—you may encounter academic vocabulary words such as these in all subject areas, including science, math, social studies, and language arts. Understanding and using these words correctly will help you to be successful in school and on assessments. This web shows examples of academic vocabulary words in different subject areas.

SOCIAL STUDIES
Describe the effects of a global **conflict.**

LANGUAGE ARTS
Find an example from Chapter 12 that **illustrates** the novel's theme.

U.S. HISTORY
From Hoover's **perspective,** the nation was on the verge of prosperity.

ACADEMIC VOCABULARY
The language that you use to think, talk, and write about different subject areas you are studying

BIOLOGY
Male crickets use their chirps to **establish** a pecking order.

GEOMETRY
Construct and **justify** a statement about the triangle in figure A.

PHYSICAL SCIENCE
Newtonian physics are **adequate** to describe most of the visible world.

Use the following chart to become familiar with some of the academic vocabulary terms in this book. As you read, look for the activities labeled "Academic Vocabulary in Writing" and "Academic Vocabulary in Speaking." These activities provide opportunities to use academic language in your writing and discussions.

Word	Definition	Example
adequate	enough to meet a need; sufficient	Make sure to take detailed notes during the research phase so that you have **adequate** evidence to support your assertions.
apparent	obvious; seeming, especially without deeper examination	The dictator's **apparent** irrationality later proved a shrewd strategy of self-preservation.
confine	to keep within bounds; limit	Walt Whitman refused to **confine** his verse to strict conventions of rhyme and meter.
conflict	to be in opposition; differ; a disagreement or battle	How did the language of the U. S. Constitution **conflict** with reality for women and African Americans?
construct	to create by systematically arranging ideas or terms	**Construct** a response to your audience's potential objections.
economic	relating to the production and exchange of goods and services; efficient	As the recession eases, **economic** activity will increase.
establish	to set up or cause to happen	Only after her death was Emily Dickinson's reputation as one of the premier American poets **established.**
justify	to show or claim to be just or right; vindicate	In the body of your argument, **justify** your claim with evidence and logical reasoning.
illustrate	to clarify, or make clear, with examples	Which diagram correctly **illustrates** the geometric theorem above?
interpret	to explain the meaning or significance of something	Many critics **interpret** Arthur Miller's *The Crucible* as an attack on McCarthyism.
maintain	to preserve or keep up; to declare to be true	To **maintain** air pressure as temperature drops, decrease the volume of the balloon.
perspective	particular way of looking at something; point of view	The park ranger studied the hunter's observations about wolf behavior from a biological **perspective.**
qualitative	measuring the quality, or essential nature, or something	A **qualitative** analysis of the after-school program's success should include interviews with participants.
reinforce	to strengthen something by adding extra support	The images of women in fashion magazines tend to **reinforce** society's unrealistic standards of beauty.

Academic Vocabulary in Action

The terms below are examples of commonly used academic vocabulary. Knowing the meaning of these terms is essential for completing the activities and lessons in this book as well as mastering test items.

perspective *(noun)*

Defining the Word

Perspective is a particular way of looking at something; it is your (or someone else's) point of view. In history class, you may read primary sources that reflect the perspectives of different parties in the same historical period. In literature class, you may read a novel narrated from the perspective of several different characters.

Subject Area & Item or Event	Perspective 1	Perspective 2
U.S. History: Civil War	a letter by Robert E. Lee to his son: Southerners are victims of northern aggression.	a speech by Abraham Lincoln (Gettysburg Address): The Union will continue to fight for freedom and democracy.

Using the Word

Practice using the word *perspective*.

- Using a chart like the one shown, identify items or events in two different subject areas that reflect different perspectives.
- Identify two perspectives on the same item or event. You may describe or sketch the two perspectives.

economic *(adjective)*

Defining the Word

Economic is the adjective form of *economy*—the system of production, distribution, and consumption and exchange of goods and services in a country, area, or period of time. It can also be used as an adjectival form of *economics*—the social science devoted to analyzing economies. Finally, *economic* can refer to the wise, sparing use of resources or language.

Using the Word

Understanding a word's root can help you understand other words with the same root. The root of *economic* and other words beginning with *eco-* is the Greek *oikos*, meaning "house." *Economy* originally referred to household management.

Word	Definition	Sentence
ecology	the connection between organisms and their environment	The ecology of the creek was damaged by fertilizer from bordering lawns.

- In a chart like the one shown, jot down all the words you can think of that begin with or contain *eco*.
- Write down your understanding of the word's meaning, and check your definition in a dictionary.
- Use the word in a sentence.

Strategies That Work: Vocabulary

Record new vocabulary words in your **Reader/Writer Notebook.**

❶ Analyze Roots in Technical Vocabulary

Some academic language is specific to particular content areas. Many of these technical words contain Greek or Latin roots. Understanding the root of a technical word can help you figure out the word's meaning. Keep a list of the roots that occur in technical words. You can remember the meaning of the root by including non-technical words in the list.

arthro (joint)	**cens (opinion)**	**petr (rock)**
arthritis	censorship	petrify
arthropod	censure	petroglyph
arthroscopy	consensus	petrochemical

You probably know that arthritis causes joint pain. This knowledge can help you remember that *arthro* comes from the Greek word for "joint," which in turn can help you understand other words containing that root.

❷ Use Context Clues

A way to recognize unfamiliar words as you read is to use context clues. When you see an unfamiliar word, look not only at its root but at the context—the words, phrases, or sentences that surround that word. Context can give you clues to the word's meaning, as in the following example:

> The President sought consensus among his advisors before taking action, although his decision sometimes ran counter to the majority opinion.

You can tell that *consensus* means "majority opinion." The clue word *although* links *consensus* to *majority opinion* by clarifying that the president did not always follow it.

❸ Use Language References

If neither roots nor context clues help you figure out an unfamiliar word, consult a print or digital language reference. A dictionary will provide most words' meanings, pronunciations, parts of speech, and origins.

Some technical or foreign expressions may be found only in specialized dictionaries, such as medical dictionaries or dictionaries of foreign terms. These may be available in your library, either in print, online, or both. Glossaries may be found at the back of technical manuals and textbooks, including this one.

> **xenophobe** (zĕn ə-fōb, zē nə-) *n.*: a person unduly fearful or contemptuous of that which is foreign, especially of people from foreign countries.

For a complete list of terms in this book, see the **Glossary of Academic Vocabulary in English & Spanish** *on pages R129–R130.*

Writing Process Workshop

Expressing Ideas in Writing

Writing is a powerful tool. It can help you clarify concepts, explore opinions, and add something new to the world of ideas. That is what every writer represented in this book knew, and it's what you will discover as well. Through effective writing, you can formulate your own interpretations, challenge assumptions, and even shape others' perceptions in the process.

COMMON CORE

Included in this workshop:
W 4, W 5, SL 1b–d, L 1, L 2, L 3

Consider Your Options

Are you crafting an impassioned editorial for your school newspaper, writing a personal statement for a college application, or responding to a posting on your friend's blog? Start any writing exploration by clarifying three critical considerations—your **purpose, audience,** and **format** of your writing.

PURPOSE

Why am I writing?
- to entertain
- to inform or explain
- to argue or persuade
- to describe
- to reflect
- to inspire or motivate

AUDIENCE

Who are my readers?
- classmates
- teacher
- friends
- community members
- potential employer
- customer service department
- college admissions office
- Web community

FORMAT

Which format will best suit my purpose and audience?
- analytical essay
- letter
- poem
- research paper
- news article
- blog entry
- summary
- wiki
- short story
- proposal
- speech
- critique
- podcast

Continue with the Process

As you complete the **Writing Workshops** in this book, you'll discover the process that works best for you. Use this model as a guide.

THE WRITING PROCESS

PLANNING/PREWRITING

What will you write? To begin, use one of the prewriting strategies listed on page 17. Be sure to keep your **purpose** and **audience** in mind as you refine your topic.

Depending on your **format** and your **purpose,** you also might formulate your **controlling idea** or **claim** and develop ideas to support your main points.

WHAT DOES IT LOOK LIKE?

Sojourner Truth	Both	Sandra Cisneros
• 18th-century black slave • abused by white owners • not given same freedoms as black men	• social minorities • defy society's expectations • describe their own lives	• 20th-century Latina • left home as an unmarried woman • treated differently from brothers

DRAFTING

In a first draft, you'll move beyond your early plan to develop your ideas. An informal piece, such as a blog, allows you to start writing with no set plan—that is, to **draft to discover.** For a more formal assignment, such as an analytical essay or a research paper, you'll want to **draft from an outline.** In both cases, remember that you may need to do several drafts before you're satisfied with how you've expressed your ideas.

WHAT DOES IT LOOK LIKE?

I. Sojourner Truth and Sandra Cisneros
   A. Different cultural heritages and time periods
   B. Similar struggles over women's social inequality
II. Sojourner Truth
   A. Suffered unequal treatment of enslaved people
   B. Summarized in her 1867 speech
III. Sandra Cisneros
   A. Experienced biased attitudes

REVISING

To strengthen your draft, evaluate its development, organization, and style. Check your draft using a **rubric**, or ask a peer for suggestions. If your draft doesn't fit your purpose or audience, you may need to rewrite some sections or try a new approach.

ASK A PEER READER

- Have I communicated my main idea effectively?
- Where should I add more details or evidence?
- Where could I strengthen my word choice?
- Do my ideas flow smoothly? If not, where can I make improvements?

EDITING AND PUBLISHING

Edit your draft to correct any errors in the conventions of grammar, usage, and mechanics. Then **publish** your work in a way that suits your purpose, audience, and format.

WHAT DOES IT LOOK LIKE?

Born centuries apart, Sojourner Truth and Sandra Cisneros both suffered socail discrimination. Their writings, years apart reflect society's attitude toward women and the authors strength in defying those attitudes.

Scoring Rubric

Score	COMMON CORE TRAITS
6	• **Development** Includes a meaningful, engaging introduction; thoroughly develops the topic with well-chosen, relevant, and sufficient evidence; ends powerfully • **Organization** Logically organizes complex ideas, concepts, and information; uses appropriate and varied transitions to create cohesion and clarify relationships among ideas • **Language** Uses precise language in imaginative ways; maintains an appropriate style and tone for the audience and purpose; shows a strong command of conventions
5	• **Development** Has an engaging introduction; develops the topic with relevant, well-chosen evidence; has an effective concluding section • **Organization** Logically organizes ideas, concepts, and information; uses appropriate transitions to create cohesion and clarify relationships • **Language** Effectively uses precise language; maintains an appropriate style and tone for the audience and purpose; has a few errors in conventions
4	• **Development** Has an introduction, but it could be more engaging; lacks sufficient support for one or two ideas; has an adequate, though routine, concluding section • **Organization** Is logically organized, with one or two exceptions; could use a few more transitions to clarify the relationships among ideas • **Language** Includes some vague word choices; has one or two lapses in style and tone; includes a few distracting errors in conventions
3	• **Development** Has both an introduction and conclusion, but they are superficial or uninteresting; includes some unsupported ideas or irrelevant evidence • **Organization** Has some flaws in organization; needs more transitions • **Language** Uses words correctly, though language is unimaginative; has frequent lapses in style and tone; has some critical errors in conventions
2	• **Development** Has an unfocused, uninteresting introduction; does not develop most ideas; ends abruptly • **Organization** Has an illogical organization; lacks transitions throughout • **Language** Uses vague language and misuses some words; lapses into an inappropriate style and tone in many places; contains many distracting errors in conventions
1	• **Development** Lacks an introduction, development, and a concluding section • **Organization** Has no discernible organization; lacks transitions or uses inappropriate ones • **Language** Uses many words incorrectly; employs an inappropriate style and tone for the audience and purpose; has major problems with conventions

Strategies That Work: Writing

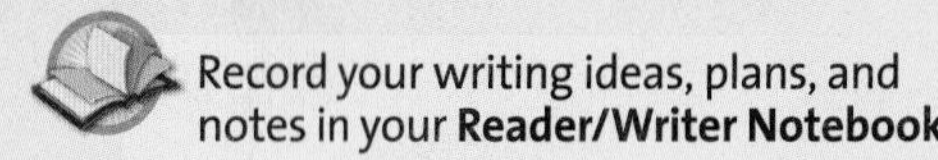
Record your writing ideas, plans, and notes in your **Reader/Writer Notebook.**

1 Use Prewriting Strategies

Unleash your ideas using one or more of these strategies:

- **Brainstorm with others.** Generate topic ideas with a group of classmates.
- **Freewrite.** Write continuously for ten minutes, recording any ideas that pop into your head.
- **Use the news.** Stay current on scientific discoveries, controversial issues, and newsworthy events. Your next topic could be "ripped from the headlines."
- **Get visual.** Use a graphic organizer, such as a cluster diagram or a story map, to get your ideas flowing.
- **Write from a prompt.** Consult the prompts in the **Writing Workshops.**

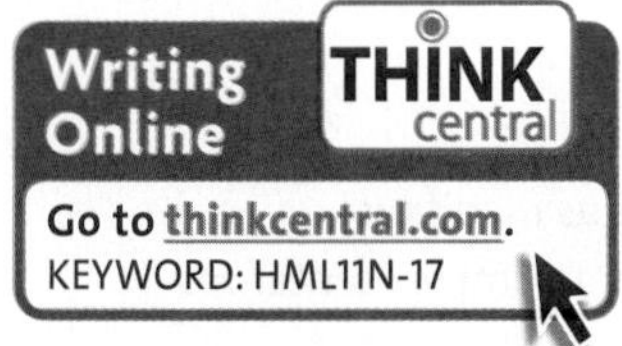

2 Enlist a Peer Reader

Often, peer readers can identify problems that you have overlooked or can't see. Consider the following guidelines:

When You're the Writer	When You're the Reader
• Make sure your peer reader knows your purpose and audience. • Clarify the kind of feedback you want to receive. Should your reader evaluate your ideas, organization, word choice, or all of the above? • Be open to the possibility of rewriting passages that aren't working or rethinking your approach based on your reader's feedback.	• Be respectful and positive in your feedback, noting both strong and weak parts of the writing. • Ask questions to clarify what the writer intends, and answer questions honestly and specifically. • Respond thoughtfully to the writer's ideas. If you are uncertain about a change you are suggesting, help the writer determine whether to consult a reference source or gather more information.

Think About Purpose and Audience

Keep your purpose and audience in mind throughout every stage of the writing process. These two considerations should guide every decision you make, from the organization of your ideas to your choice of words. Ask yourself questions like the ones on the notebook.

Questions To Ask

- What is my purpose? What do I want my audience to know, do, or believe after reading my work?
- What information should I include to help my audience understand my topic? How can I make that information clear and coherent for my readers?
- What level of language should I use to communicate my meaning to this audience in this context? Formal? Conversational? Technical?
- What bias, or point of view, might my audience have about my topic?

COMMON CORE

Preview Unit Goals

TEXT ANALYSIS	• Analyze historical context; analyze cultural characteristics • Identify characteristics of creation myth, trickster tale, folk tale, memoir, historical narrative, drama, and autobiography • Analyze historically important speeches, public documents, and letters • Analyze themes; analyze author's purpose; analyze characters • Analyze diction and tone; analyze imagery and figurative language • Analyze and evaluate elements of an argument • Analyze persuasive techniques and rhetorical devices • Analyze and evaluate primary sources • Analyze various structural patterns • Synthesize ideas and connect texts
READING	• Develop strategies for reading older texts • Develop comprehension monitoring skills
WRITING AND LANGUAGE	• Create a multimedia presentation • Write an argumentative essay • Use prepositional phrases and adverb clauses as modifiers • Understand and use compound and compound-complex sentences
SPEAKING AND LISTENING	• Deliver an argumentative speech • Analyze how media messages influence cultural values and stereotypes • Evaluate film techniques; evaluate multiple interpretations of a play
VOCABULARY	• Determine the meaning of multiple-meaning words • Understand and use specialized vocabulary
ACADEMIC VOCABULARY	• document • illustrate • interpret • promote • reveal
MEDIA AND VIEWING	• Analyze how words, images, graphics, and sounds impact meaning • Evaluate how media messages reflect cultural views • Evaluate the interactions of different techniques used in media

Find It Online!

Go to thinkcentral.com for the interactive version of this unit.

Early American Writing

1600–1800

Mourning Dove

AN EMERGING NATION

- The Native American Experience
- Exploration and the Early Settlers
- The Puritan Tradition
- Writers of the Revolution

Great Stories on Film

Examine how media stereotypes shaped society's attitudes toward Native Americans. Page 66

Questions of the Times

DISCUSS With your whole class or in small groups, discuss these questions. Keep them in mind as you read the selections in this unit and consider how early American writers tried to answer them.

Who owns the LAND?

For thousands of years, Native Americans regarded themselves as caretakers, not owners, of the land. The Europeans who began arriving in North America, however, saw things differently. They laid claim to the land and aggressively defended it from Native Americans—and from one another. In the end, the British claim overpowered all others. Yet the question remains: What entitles people to claim land as their own?

What makes an EXPLORER?

America's early explorers traveled for many reasons: to gain glory for themselves or for their countries, to find gold or other riches, to discover new routes for travel and trade. Yet none of these motivators alone seems enough to make the uncertainties of exploration—unknown destinations, unknown rewards, unknown dangers—worth the risk. What is it that causes people to seek out the unknown?

COMMON CORE

RL 9 Demonstrate knowledge of eighteenth-century foundational works of American literature, including how two or more texts from the same period treat similar themes or topics. **RI 9** Analyze documents of historical and literary significance for their themes, purposes, and rhetorical features.

Are people basically GOOD?

Puritan settlers believed that human beings were sinful creatures doomed to a fiery eternity unless saved by the grace of God. Yet others who came to North America celebrated the powers of reason and proclaimed the goodness and intrinsic worth of humans. Are people destined always to struggle against their basest instincts? Or are they fundamentally good—and capable of becoming even better?

Who has the right to RULE?

For centuries, European kings and queens had ruled because it was believed that they had a God-given right to do so. But in the Age of Enlightenment, people began to question basic assumptions about government. In America, a popular uprising put a new kind of government to the test: democracy. With this experiment, the young American nation was asking: Who really has the right to rule?

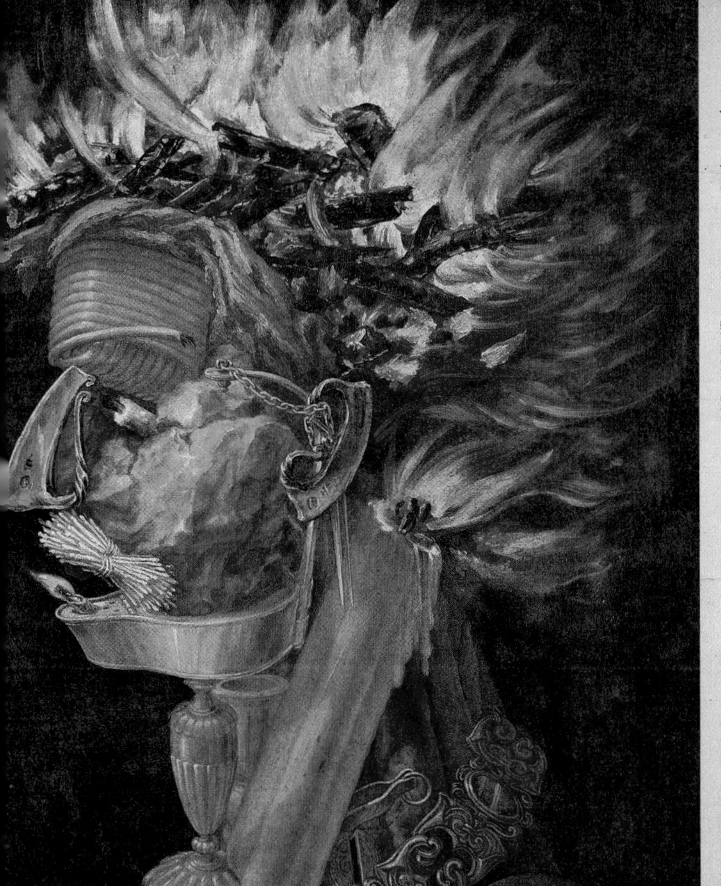

IN CONGRESS, JULY 4, 1776.

A DECLARATION

BY THE REPRESENTATIVES OF THE

UNITED STATES OF AMERICA,

IN GENERAL CONGRESS ASSEMBLED.

WHEN in the Courſe of human Events, it becomes neceſſary for one People to diſſolve the Political Bands which have connected them with another, and to aſſume among the Powers of the Earth, the ſeparate and equal Station to which the Laws of Nature and of Nature's God entitle them, a decent Reſpect to the Opinions of Mankind requires that they ſhould declare the cauſes which impel them to the Separation.

WE hold theſe Truths to be ſelf-evident, that all Men are created equal, that they are endowed by their Creator with certain unalienable Rights, that among theſe are Life, Liberty, and the Purſuit of Happineſs——That to ſecure theſe Rights, Governments are inſtituted among Men, deriving their juſt Powers from the Conſent of the Governed, that whenever any Form of Government becomes deſtructive of theſe Ends, it is the Right of the People to alter or to aboliſh it, and to inſtitute new Government, laying its Foundation on ſuch Principles, and organizing its Powers in ſuch Form, as to them ſhall ſeem moſt likely to effect their Safety and Happineſs. Prudence, indeed, will dictate that Governments long eſtabliſhed ſhould not be changed for light and tranſient Cauſes; and accordingly all Experience hath ſhewn, that Mankind are more diſpoſed to ſuffer, while Evils are ſufferable, than to right themſelves by aboliſhing the Forms to which they are accuſtomed. But when a long Train of Abuſes and Uſurpations, purſuing invariably the ſame Object, evinces a Deſign to reduce them under abſolute Deſpotiſm, it is their Right, it is their Duty, to throw off ſuch Government, and to provide new Guards for their future Security. Such has been the patient Sufferance of theſe Colonies; and ſuch is now the Neceſſity which conſtrains them to alter their former Syſtems of Government. The Hiſtory of the preſent King of Great-Britain is a Hiſtory of repeated Injuries and Uſurpations, all having in direct Object the Eſtabliſhment of an abſolute Tyranny over theſe States. To prove this, let Facts be ſubmitted to a candid World.

HE has refuſed his Aſſent to Laws, the moſt wholeſome and neceſſary for the public Good.

HE has forbidden his Governors to paſs Laws of immediate and preſſing Importance, unleſs ſuſpended in their Operation till his Aſſent ſhould be obtained; and when ſo ſuſpended, he has utterly neglected to attend to them.

HE has refuſed to paſs other Laws for the Accommodation of large Diſtricts of People, unleſs thoſe People would relinquiſh the Right of Repreſentation in the Legiſlature, a Right ineſtimable to them, and formidable to Tyrants only.

HE has called together Legiſlative Bodies at Places unuſual, uncomfortable, and diſtant from the Depoſitory of their public Records, for the ſole Purpoſe of fatiguing them into Compliance with his Meaſures.

HE has diſſolved Repreſentative Houſes repeatedly, for oppoſing with manly Firmneſs his Invaſions on the Rights of the People.

HE has refuſed for a long Time, after ſuch Diſſolutions, to cauſe others to be elected; whereby the Legiſlative Powers, incapable of Annihilation, have returned to the People at large for their exerciſe; the State remaining in the mean time expoſed to all the Dangers of Invaſion from without, and Convulſions within.

HE has endeavoured to prevent the Population of theſe States; for that Purpoſe obſtructing the Laws for Naturalization of Foreigners; refuſing to paſs others to encourage their Migrations hither, and raiſing the Conditions of new Appropriations of Lands.

HE has obſtructed the Adminiſtration of Juſtice, by refuſing his Aſſent to Laws for eſtabliſhing Judiciary Powers.

HE has made Judges dependent on his Will alone, for the Tenure of their Offices, and the Amount and Payment of their Salaries.

HE has erected a Multitude of new Offices, and ſent hither Swarms of Officers to harraſs our People, and eat out their Subſtance.

HE has kept among us, in Times of Peace, Standing Armies, without the conſent of our Legiſlatures.

HE has affected to render the Military independent of and ſuperior to the Civil Power.

HE has combined with others to ſubject us to a Juriſdiction foreign to our Conſtitution, and unacknowledged by our Laws; giving his Aſſent to their Acts of pretended Legiſlation:

FOR quartering large Bodies of Armed Troops among us:

FOR protecting them, by a mock Trial, from Puniſhment for any Murders which they ſhould commit on the Inhabitants of theſe States:

FOR cutting off our Trade with all Parts of the World:

FOR impoſing Taxes on us without our Conſent:

FOR depriving us, in many Caſes, of the Benefits of Trial by Jury:

FOR tranſporting us beyond Seas to be tried for pretended Offences:

FOR aboliſhing the free Syſtem of Engliſh Laws in a neighbouring Province, eſtabliſhing therein an arbitrary Government, and enlarging its Boundaries, ſo as to render it at once an Example and fit Inſtrument for introducing the ſame abſolute Rule into theſe Colonies:

FOR taking away our Charters, aboliſhing our moſt valuable Laws, and altering fundamentally the Forms of our Governments:

FOR ſuſpending our own Legiſlatures, and declaring themſelves inveſted with Power to legiſlate for us in all Caſes whatſoever.

HE has abdicated Government here, by declaring us out of his Protection and waging War againſt us.

HE has plundered our Seas, ravaged our Coaſts, burnt our Towns, and deſtroyed the Lives of our People.

HE is, at this Time, tranſporting large Armies of foreign Mercenaries to compleat the Works of Death, Deſolation, and Tyranny, already begun with circumſtances of Cruelty and Perfidy, ſcarcely paralleled in the moſt barbarous Ages, and totally unworthy the Head of a civilized Nation.

HE has conſtrained our fellow Citizens taken Captive on the high Seas to bear Arms againſt their Country, to become the Executioners of their Friends and Brethren, or to fall themſelves by their Hands.

HE has excited domeſtic Inſurrections amongſt us, and has endeavoured to bring on the Inhabitants of our Frontiers, the mercileſs Indian Savages, whoſe known Rule of Warfare, is an undiſtinguiſhed Deſtruction, of all Ages, Sexes and Conditions.

IN every ſtage of theſe Oppreſſions we have Petitioned for Redreſs in the moſt humble Terms: Our repeated Petitions have been anſwered only by repeated Injury. A Prince, whoſe Character is thus marked by every act which may define a Tyrant, is unfit to be the Ruler of a free People.

Early American Writing
1600–1800

An Emerging Nation

For many people, early America was an experiment in hope. Explorers seeking adventure, settlers searching for religious freedom, colonists building communities, revolutionaries designing a new government—all embraced their challenges with a sense of faith and purpose. Writers of the day recorded and interpreted the extraordinary experiences of these ordinary people. They and their fellow colonists imagined and created an entirely new country and unique way of life.

Early American Writing: Historical Context

Early American literature captures a nation in its infancy. From the first interactions between Native Americans and Europeans to the stirring cries of the Revolutionary War, writers chronicled the tensions and the triumphs of the day.

COMMON CORE

RL 9 Demonstrate knowledge of eighteenth-century foundational works of American literature, including how two or more texts from the same period treat similar themes or topics. **RI 9** Analyze documents of historical and literary significance for their themes, purposes, and rhetorical features.

The Meeting of Two Worlds

Explorers and early settlers forged a life for themselves in America that was completely foreign to what they had known in their home countries. In fact, so extraordinary were their experiences that the earliest American writers concentrated mainly on describing and trying to make sense out of their challenging new environment and the unfamiliar people with whom they shared it. In diaries, letters, and reports back home, they recorded a historical turning point: when the world of the Europeans first intersected with that of the Native Americans.

Unknown to Europeans, people had been living in the Americas for at least tens of thousands of years, adapting to its diverse environments, forming communities, establishing trading networks, and building working cities. Millions of people lived in the Americas on the eve of the arrival of the Europeans—as many as lived in Europe at the time.

The earliest writers chronicled how the Europeans and Native Americans viewed one another and the North American land. In 1634, for example, **William Wood** of Massachusetts Bay Colony noted that the Native Americans "took the first ship they saw for a walking island, the mast to be a tree, the sail white clouds." **William Bradford,** governor of Plymouth Plantation, in turn described North America as "a hideous and desolate wilderness, full of wild beasts and wild men." The land, however, was neither desolate nor hideous, and the Native Americans were usually cooperative—at least until they began to be forced off their land by European colonists.

TAKING NOTES

Outlining As you read this introduction, use an outline to record the main ideas about the characteristics and the literature of the period. You can use article headings, boldfaced terms, and the information in these boxes as starting points. (See page R49 in the **Handbook** for more help with outlining.)

Early American Writing
I. Historical Context
A. The Meeting of Two Worlds
1. Early writers described land and people.
2. Native Americans had well-established communities when Europeans arrived.
3. Writers chronicled Native American and European views of one another.
B. From Colony to Country

From Colony to Country

The first permanent colony was established at **Jamestown** in 1607. By 1733, English colonies stretched all along the Atlantic coast. Once rooted in North American soil, the colonies became increasingly self-reliant and practiced local self-rule.

LOYALTY TO ENGLAND The first colonists thought of themselves as English subjects, even though they did not have representatives in the British parliament. They supported England economically by exporting raw materials to the homeland and importing Britain's manufactured goods.

Britain, in turn, protected its territory. It sent soldiers to fight during the **French and Indian War** (1759–1763), when France allied with a

The Mayflower in Plymouth Harbor, (1882), William Formby Halsall. © Pilgrim Hall Museum, Plymouth, Massachusetts.

number of Native American groups to drive the British out of North America. After many defeats, England brought in new military leaders and made its own alliance with Native Americans—the powerful Iroquois. After a long and costly war, the victorious Great Britain claimed all of North America east of the Mississippi River.

A BREAK WITH ENGLAND When Great Britain tried to tax the colonists to recover some of the money spent on the war, however, it ended up losing far more than its war costs. Fired by cries of "No taxation without representation," the colonists protested British control—in both fiery words and bold actions. With each new act of British "tyranny," writers for colonial newspapers and pamphlets stirred the hearts and minds of the colonists to support independence.

The colonies declared themselves to be "free and independent" in 1776 and fought and defeated one of the greatest military powers on earth to turn their declaration into a reality. The remarkable minds of **Benjamin Franklin, Thomas Jefferson,** and other colonial thinkers put timeless words to this experiment in the form of the **Declaration of Independence** and the **Constitution of the United States.** When the Constitution was approved in 1788, the United States of America was born.

British parliament imposed the Stamp Act and the Tea Act to gain revenue from the colonies. Instead, these acts incited revolt. The Boston Tea Party was but one of many skirmishes leading to the Revolutionary War.

Cultural Influences

Religion was the most influential cultural force on writers of this period. Puritan values and beliefs directed people's everyday lives as well as the formation of an American society.

Puritan Beliefs

Many of the settlers in the 1600s were Puritans. **Puritans** were a group of English Protestants who had sought to "purify" the Church of England and return to simpler ways of worshiping. Their efforts had been most unwelcome in England, however, and many left the country for America to escape persecution.

Puritan settlers believed themselves chosen by God to create a new order in America. **John Winthrop,** for example, wrote in 1630 that "we must consider that we shall be as a City upon a hill. The eyes of all people are upon us." Puritans' values directed every aspect of their lives. They saw human struggle with sin as a daily mission and believed, above all else, that the Bible would help them through the torments of human weakness. Although they felt that humans were essentially sinful, they believed that some, the "elect," would be spared from eternal punishment by God's grace.

Hard work, thrift, and responsibility were therefore seen as morally good, a sign that God was working within. The thriving settlements and financial success that grew from these qualities were thought to be a mark of God's approval. However, Puritanism had a dark side as well. Puritans tended to be inflexible in their religious faith and intolerant of viewpoints other than their own. In one famous case, the Salem witchcraft trials, a whole community fell victim to the hysteria of the witch-hunt, ending with more than 20 people dead by execution.

Ideas of the Age

In the 1700s, both Enlightenment ideals and Puritan values contributed to the country's thirst for independence.

The Enlightenment

In the 1700s, there was a burst of intellectual energy taking place in Europe that came to be known as the **Enlightenment**. Enlightenment thinkers had begun to question previously accepted truths about who should hold the power in government. Their thinking pointed the way to a government by the people—one in which people consent to government limitations in exchange for the government's protection of their basic rights and liberties.

American colonists adapted these Enlightenment ideals to their own environment. The political writings of **Benjamin Franklin, Thomas Paine,** and **Thomas Jefferson** shaped the **American Enlightenment** and began to eclipse even the most brilliant European thought. Enlightenment ideals prompted action and gave colonists a philosophical footing for their revolution. "I know not what course others may take," **Patrick Henry** thundered to the delegates at the second Virginia Convention in 1775, "but as for me, give me liberty, or give me death!"

A Voice from the Times

We hold these truths to be self-evident, that all men are created equal, that they are endowed by their Creator with certain unalienable Rights, that among these are Life, Liberty, and the pursuit of Happiness.

—Thomas Jefferson
from the Declaration of Independence

The Great Awakening

At the same time, many people began to worry that Puritan values were being lost. Preachers such as **Jonathan Edwards** called for people to rededicate themselves to the original Puritan vision, and a new wave of religious enthusiasm began to rise. This movement, called the **First Great Awakening,** united colonists who were in other ways diverse. Across the colonies, people began to feel joined in the belief that a higher power was helping Americans set a new standard for an ethical life.

While the Enlightenment and the Great Awakening emphasized opposing aspects of human experience—reason and emotionalism, respectively—they had similar consequences. Both caused people to question traditional authority, eventually leading colonists to break from Britain's control and embrace democracy.

Early American Literature

Early American writing is as varied as early Americans themselves. Native Americans, explorers, settlers, and revolutionaries all contributed their own perspectives to our knowledge of this literary period.

The Native American Experience

When the Europeans arrived, there were more than 300 different Native American cultures in North America with strongly differing customs and about 200 different languages spoken. Yet wherever they lived—in the smoky longhouses of the Northeastern woodlands, the well-defended cliff dwellings of the desert Southwest, the cedar-scented lodges of the Pacific Northwest—one activity was common to all: storytelling.

The Native North American cultures did not have a written language. Instead, a group's history, legends, and myths were entrusted to memory and faithfully passed from generation to generation through **oral tradition.** In the words of one Native American holy woman, "When you write things down you don't have to remember them. But for us it is different. . . . [A]ll that we are, all that we have ever been, all the great names of our heroes and their songs and deeds are alive within each of us. . . living in our blood."

For Your Notes

NATIVE AMERICANS

- were culturally diverse
- had an oral tradition
- had many different genres of spoken literature
- explored common themes, such as a reverence for nature and the worship of many gods

Analyze Visuals
This modern depiction of a Haida creation story shows the Raven (a popular cultural hero in many Native American myths and legends) opening a shell to release the first humans into the world. What relationship between humans and the natural world does this sculpture suggest?

Raven and the First Men (1980), Bill Reid. Yellow cedar. University of British Columbia Museum of Anthropology, Vancouver, Canada.

LITERARY STYLE The forms of Native American oral literature are rich and varied. Creation stories, ways to explain how the universe and humans came into being, can be found in every Native American culture. Other forms include legendary histories tracing the migration of peoples or the deeds of great leaders, fairy tales, lyrics, chants, children's songs, healing songs, and dream visions.

Tragically, much of this literature did not survive after so many Native Americans fell to European diseases. Some groups lost as many as 90 percent of their people, all of whom had a share in preserving the traditional stories. The surviving works, however, show that diverse Native American groups explored common themes in their spoken literature, including a reverence for nature and the worship of many gods.

Exploration and the Early Settlers

While Native American literature offers us a glimpse into the ways and values of America's indigenous peoples, much of our understanding of pre-colonial America comes from the first-person accounts of its early explorers, settlers, and colonists. The journals, diaries, letters, logs, and historical narratives of those first Europeans to view the American landscape describe in vivid detail its many sights and wonders, as well as its dangers and challenges.

THE EXPLORERS The first of these writings were the journals and letters of **Christopher Columbus,** which recounted his four voyages to the Americas begun in 1492. Columbus's adventures opened the door to a century of Spanish expeditions in the Americas. Incapable of visualizing the historical significance of his travels, however, he died disappointed, convinced that he had barely missed the cities of gold described by Marco Polo. His fascinating journals provide a vivid record of the most significant journeys of his time.

Just over 50 years later came *La Relación.* This report by **Álvar Núñez Cabeza de Vaca,** one of the four survivors of the 600-man Narváez expedition, chronicled his eight years of wandering through Florida, Texas, and Mexico. In it he describes the landscape and people he encountered, as well as animals that were new to Europeans. The French and Dutch also sent explorers such as **Samuel de Champlain,** the "Father of New France," who in the early 1600s wrote vivid accounts of New England and the Iroquois.

EARLY SETTLERS The early English settlers described their difficult and amazing new lives in letters, reports, and chronicles to friends and family back home. Their writings helped people in England imagine what life might be like in America. One of the most influential writings was *A Brief and True Report of the New Found Land of Virginia,* by **Thomas Harriot,** which faithfully captured the area's natural resources, the ways of life of the Native Americans, and the potential for building a successful colony. It was published in 1588 and was accompanied by illustrations that helped thousands upon thousands of English readers form their first clear picture of North America.

For Your Notes

EXPLORERS

- Columbus's journals chronicle his four voyages to the Americas.
- Cabeza de Vaca's *La Relación* tells of his failed expedition.
- Samuel de Champlain wrote accounts of New England and the Iroquois.

EARLY SETTLERS

- Settlers described the new land for those still in Europe.
- Accounts helped English readers visualize North America.

COLONISTS

- Writers focused on the story of the new settlements and their larger purpose.
- Equiano, an enslaved African, described his unjust treatment.

A modern reconstruction of the original Jamestown, Virginia, settlement

COLONIAL HISTORIES As the colonies took root, writing began to focus less on pure description and more on the story of the growth of the colonies. In contrast to the carefully accurate Harriot, for example, **Captain John Smith** wrote sometimes-embroidered accounts of the history of Virginia and New England. By force of his vivid and engaging writing, he created an enduring record of life in the early colonies and an intriguing self-portrait of a man proud of his great deeds and eager to gain recognition. His accounts were also instrumental in attracting settlers to Virginia, thus ensuring the eventual success of that colony.

Other writers who documented the history of the New England settlements wrote in a plainer style and with a more serious purpose. **William Bradford,** longtime governor of Plymouth, and **John Winthrop Sr.,** who served as governor of Massachusetts, reflected upon what they saw as their role in God's plan for a better society. But not all who wrote narrative histories saw the colonists' efforts as following God's plan. **Olaudah Equiano** described his harsh capture from his African home and the brutal and "un-Christian" treatment he received as a slave in the West Indies.

A Voice from the Times

So as there died sometimes two or three of a day . . . , that of one hundred and odd persons, scarce fifty remained.

—**William Bradford**
from *Of Plymouth Plantation*

The Puritan Tradition

Puritan writers had their own purposes for recording history. They believed writing should be useful, a tool to help readers understand the Bible and guide them in their daily lives. For this reason, logic, clarity, and order were more prized in writing than beauty or adornment. One Puritan compared adorned writing to stained-glass windows. "The paint upon the glass may feed the fancy, but the room is not well lighted by it." Using a familiar, down-to-earth metaphor such as this to make a deeper point is a common feature of Puritan writing. The direct, powerful, plain language of much of American literature owes a debt to the Puritans.

For Your Notes

PURITAN WRITERS

- believed writing should be useful and clear
- wrote histories, sermons, scientific works, and essays
- delivered sermons contrasting good and evil
- wrote poems with religious themes

SERMONS AND OTHER WRITINGS The works of Puritan writers, such as **Cotton Mather** and **Jonathan Edwards,** include histories of the colonies and fiery sermons on the dangers of sinful ways. Along with histories and sermons, Cotton Mather chronicled the disturbing Salem witch trials, where 20 people were condemned to death in an atmosphere of mass hysteria. He also wrote about scientific matters, including inoculation for smallpox.

A Voice from the Times

I made seeking salvation the main business of my life.

—Jonathan Edwards

Like Mather, Jonathan Edwards wrote on a variety of subjects, including the flying (or ballooning) spiders he had observed as a boy. His account of these spiders is considered the first natural history essay on that subject. A spider makes another, very different kind of appearance in Edwards's best-known work, his sermon "Sinners in the Hands of an Angry God." In that sermon he warns his listeners that God "holds you over the pit of hell, much as one holds a spider, or some loathsome insect over the fire."

Imagine the scene when Edwards first delivered this sermon: the congregation quaking in fear from Edwards's vivid descriptions of hellfire and a vengeful god. "Sinners in the Hands of an Angry God," while perhaps more fiery than most, is typical of the Puritan sermon. Melodramatic contrasts between good and evil, vivid imagery, powerful language, and strong moral lessons characterized this form of literature.

PURITAN POETRY Most Puritan writers composed "plain" sermons, histories, and treatises, but poetry was the means of expression for others. In fact, the first book issued in the North American colonies was the the *Bay Psalm Book* in 1640, in which the Bible's psalms were rewritten to fit the rhythms of familiar Puritan hymns.

Puritan poets such as **Anne Bradstreet** and **Edward Taylor** viewed poetry primarily as a means of exploring the relationship between the individual and God. Bradstreet's poems reflect her wide learning, deep faith, and love for her husband and children. They also provide insight into the position of women in the male-dominated Puritan society. Her book of poetry, *The Tenth Muse Lately Sprung Up in America* (1650), was the first work by a North American woman to be published. Minister Edward Taylor, possibly considered the best-known Puritan poet, wrote most of his poems as aids for his meditations. His poetry, like much Puritan writing, uses vivid images from nature and from everyday life as a way to help readers grasp the spiritual world beyond.

Evangelical preacher George Whitefield was a key figure in the revival movement of America's "Great Awakening."

Writers of the Revolution

It is curious to consider now, but some of the most famous figures of the American Revolution lived at the same time as Puritans such as Jonathan Edwards. As products of the Enlightenment, however, revolutionary writers focused their energies on matters of government rather than religion.

PAMPHLETS AND PROPAGANDA Many of the gifted minds of this period were drawn to political writing as the effort to launch a grand experiment in government took shape in North America. The most important outlet for the spread of these political writings was the pamphlet. Between 1763 and 1783, about two thousand pamphlets were published. These inexpensive "little books" became the fuel of the revolution, reaching thousands of people quickly and stirring debate and action in response to growing discontent with British rule.

Through these pamphlets the words that would define the American cause against Great Britain became the currency of the day, and the debate about independence grew louder and louder. One such pamphlet, *Common Sense,* by **Thomas Paine,** helped propel the colonists to revolution. Though

▶ *For Your Notes*

WRITERS OF THE REVOLUTION

- expressed the ideas of the Enlightenment
- concentrated on political writing
- used pamphlets to spread ideas
- focused on natural law and human rights
- played a key role in the creation of a new nation

Soldier of the Revolution (1876), George Willoughby Maynard. Oil on canvas, 51″ × 39″. Photo © Christie's Images Ltd.

A Voice from the Times

These are the times that try men's souls: The summer soldier and the sunshine patriot will, in this crisis, shrink from the service of his country; but he that stands it NOW, *deserves the love and thanks of man and woman.*

—Thomas Paine
from *The Crisis*

expressing the views of the rational Enlightenment, Paine also agreed with the Puritan belief that America had a special destiny to be a model to the rest of the world. At the end of his stirring essay, he says that freedom had been hunted down around the globe and calls on America to "receive the fugitive," to give freedom a home, and to welcome people from around the world to its free society.

WRITING THAT LAUNCHED A NATION **Thomas Jefferson** also wrote pamphlets, but his great contribution to American government, literature, and the cause of freedom throughout the world is the **Declaration of Independence,** in which he eloquently articulated the **natural law** that would govern America. This natural law is the idea that people are born with rights and freedoms and that it is the function of government to protect those freedoms.

Eleven years later, after the Revolutionary War had ended, delegates from all but one state gathered at the Philadelphia State House—in the same room in which the Declaration of Independence had been signed—in order to discuss forming a new government. The delegates included many outstanding leaders of the time, such as **Benjamin Franklin, Alexander Hamilton,** and **George Washington.** Four months later, they emerged with perhaps the country's most important piece of writing: the **Constitution of the United States of America.** Although Washington said at the time, "I do not expect the Constitution to last for more than 20 years," it was indeed flexible enough to last through the centuries to come.

VOICES OF THE PEOPLE Statesmen were not the only ones to contribute to the discussion of the day, however. In that age of political writing, even poetry sometimes examined political and social themes. Among the finest is the work of former slave **Phillis Wheatley.** In her poems and letters, Wheatley wrote of the "natural rights" of African-Americans and pointed out the discrepancy between the colonists' "cry for freedom" and their enslavement of fellow human beings.

Another voice calling for the rights of all citizens was **Abigail Adams,** whose husband John became the nation's second president. In letters written while the couple was apart, Adams encouraged her husband to include the rights of women in the nation's founding documents.

Wheatley, Adams, and other women writers join the Native Americans, colonists, Puritans, and patriots who came before them to give us an understanding of the dreams and values that shaped our nation. All contributed their voices and ideals to building this "city upon a hill."

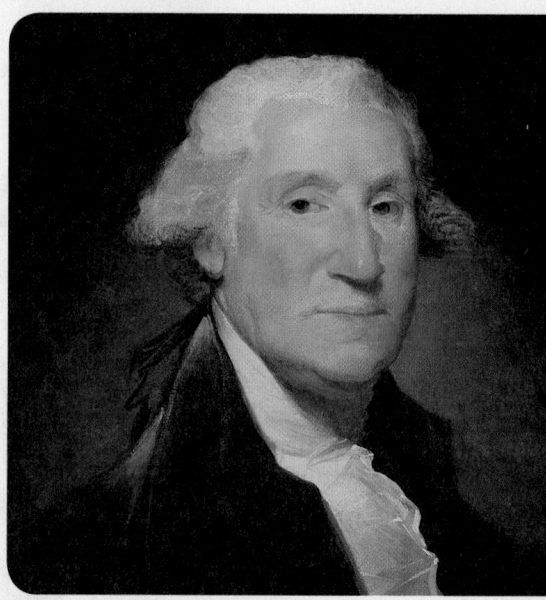

THE ARTISTS' GALLERY

The "Father of American Portraiture"

Many colonial artists earned their livings with portraits, which were in high demand. Gilbert Stuart was among the best of colonial portrait painters. Because he painted the likenesses of virtually all the notable men and women of the period (including the first five American presidents), he earned himself the moniker "The Father of American Portraiture" by his contemporaries.

Painting the President One of Stuart's favorite subjects was the first president of the United States, George Washington. His 104 likenesses of Washington inform the image most of us have of our first president. In fact, one of his paintings became the basis for the one-dollar bill.

Stuart was known to chat with his subjects as they sat for his paintings. By entertaining them during the long hours of posing, he hoped to capture an unguarded, fresh expression on their faces. The serious George Washington, however, found Stuart's chat annoying. The artist says of Washington, "An apathy seemed to seize him, and a vacuity spread over his countenance, most appalling to paint." Nevertheless, in *George Washington (Vaughan portrait),* 1795, shown here, Stuart was able to capture Washington's imposing presence by placing his head high in the design and adding a crimson glow around it.

Connecting Literature, History, and Culture

Early American writing reflects the growing pains of a new nation but also reveals much about trends occurring elsewhere in the world. Use this timeline and the questions on page 33 to find connections between literature, history, and culture.

AMERICAN LITERARY MILESTONES

1600

1624 John Smith publishes *The General History of Virginia.*

1630 William Bradford describes his journey across the Atlantic and pilgrims' settlement in *Of Plymouth Plantation.*

1640 *Bay Psalm Book* is the first book to be printed in America. ▶

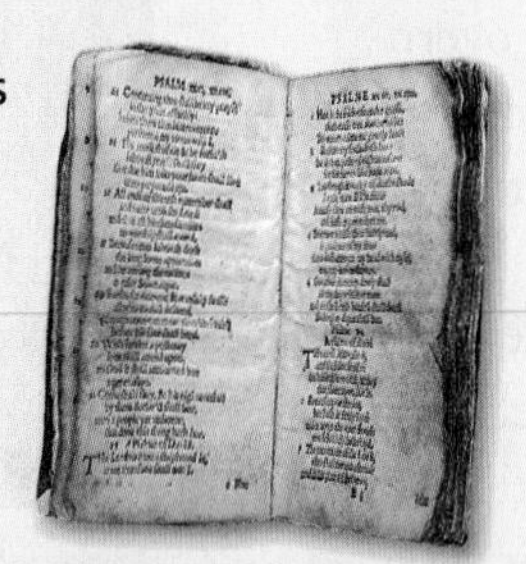

1650

1650 Anne Bradstreet's poems, collected as *The Tenth Muse Lately Sprung Up in America,* are published in London.

1682 Mary Rowlandson publishes *The Sovereignty and Goodness of God,* an account of her captivity at the hands of Algonquian Indians.

1693 Cotton Mather publishes *The Wonders of the Invisible World* in defense of the Salem witch trials.

HISTORICAL CONTEXT

1600

1607 The first permanent English settlement is founded in Jamestown, Virginia.

1619 The first enslaved Africans arrive in North America at Jamestown.

1620 The *Mayflower* pilgrims establish the Massachusetts Bay Colony at Plymouth. ▶

1635 North America's first public school is founded in Boston.

1650

1676 The Puritans' victory in King Philip's War ends Native American resistance in New England colonies.

1682 William Penn founds the colony of Pennsylvania.

1688 Quakers voice opposition to slavery.

1692 Salem witch trials show atmosphere of mass hysteria. ▶

WORLD CULTURE AND EVENTS

1600

1615 Inquisition condemns Italian scientist Galileo Galilei for supporting Copernicus's theory.

1616 Shakespeare dies.

1632 Indian emperor Shah Jahan begins construction of Taj Mahal. ▶

1650

1652 Dutch found Cape Town on the southern tip of South Africa.

1687 Isaac Newton publishes *Philosophiae naturalis principia mathematica,* considered to be the most important work of the Scientific Revolution.

1694 Japanese poet Matsuo Bashō, known for revitalizing the haiku form, dies.

MAKING CONNECTIONS

- Religion played a central role in America during this period. What works written at this time might support this observation?
- While American writers of this period worked mostly in nonfiction and poetry, groundbreaking novels were being written elsewhere in the world. Name one.
- The Revolutionary War was a defining event in American history. What other country held a bloody revolution during this period?

COMMON CORE

RI 7 Integrate and evaluate multiple sources of information presented in different media or formats as well as in words in order to address a question or solve a problem.

1700

1704 The *Boston Newsletter,* the first American newspaper, is established. ▶

The Boston News-Letter.
Published by Authority.

1722 Benjamin Franklin uses humor to criticize the Puritan establishment in his first published work, *The Dogood Papers.*

1741 Jonathan Edwards delivers a sermon called "Sinners in the Hands of an Angry God." The sermon typifies the religious movement known as the Great Awakening.

1750

1774 Abigail Adams writes first entry in what is published as *Familiar Letters of John Adams and His Wife, Abigail.*

1776 Thomas Paine's widely read pamphlet *Common Sense* passionately argues the case for independence.

1776 George Washington invites Phillis Wheatley to visit after receiving from her a poem and letter.

1789 Olaudah Equiano's *The Interesting Narrative of . . . Olaudah Equiano* details harsh treatment of captive Africans. ▶

1700

1720 The colonial population reaches about a half million; Boston's population is about 12,000.

1739 The religious revival known as the Great Awakening (1739–1742) begins.

1744 The six nations of the Iroquois Confederation (whose tribe-mark is shown here) cede Ohio Valley territory north of the Ohio River to Britain. ▶

1750

1773 The Boston Tea Party marks a violent rejection of Britain's taxation policies. The Revolutionary War begins two years later. ▶

1776 July 4: Second Continental Congress adopts the Declaration of Independence.

1781 British defeat at Yorktown ends the American Revolution.

1787 U.S. Constitution is approved.

1700

1721 Johann Sebastian Bach composes the *Brandenburg Concertos.*

1725 Peter the Great, czar of Russia, dies.

1726 Jonathan Swift publishes *Gulliver's Travels.* ▶

1750

1752 Calcutta's population reaches 120,000.

1762 Catherine the Great, an "enlightened despot," becomes empress of Russia.

1784 The Indian sacred text the *Bhagavad-Gita* is translated into English for the first time.

1789 Storming of the Bastille incites the French Revolution.

1791 The classic Chinese novel *Dream of the Red Chamber* is published.

The Legacy of the Era

An American Work Ethic

COMMON CORE

W 7 Conduct short research projects to answer a question; narrow the inquiry; synthesize multiple sources, demonstrating understanding of the subject. **SL 1** Initiate and participate effectively in a range of collaborative discussions, building on others' ideas and expressing their own clearly and persuasively.

Shunning frivolous pleasures that would distract them from thoughts of God, Puritans instead trained their energy on hard, useful work. That hard work often led to material success, which was in turn seen as a sign of God's favor. Many Americans today also believe in the intrinsic value of hard work—as well as the idea that hard work leads to financial success.

DISCUSS With your class, discuss whether work in and of itself is something to value. What does work provide? In your opinion, does work indeed lead to success? What other factors might be involved?

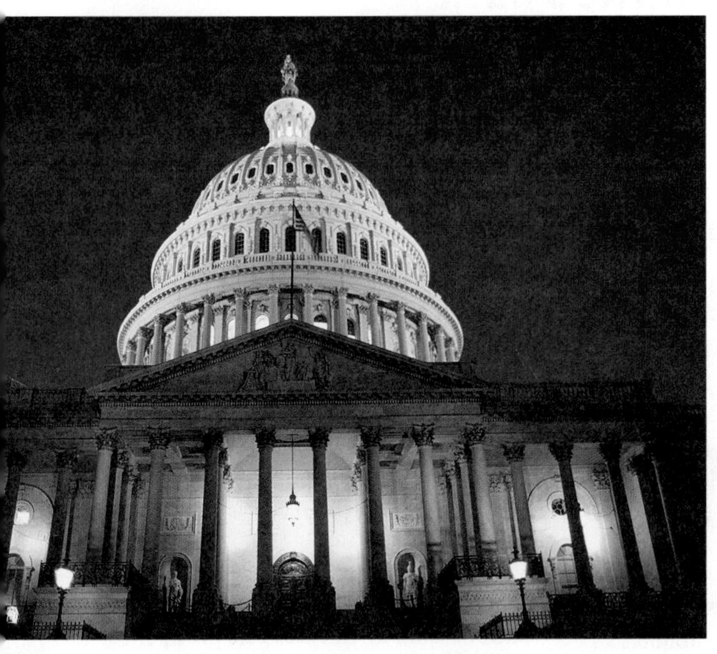

Government by the People

Democracy is surely the most significant legacy of the early American period. Reacting against the monarchy they had left behind and embracing Enlightenment ideals, the framers of the Constitution ensured that governmental power would be shared by the people. The people would elect representatives to carry out their will, and a system of checks and balances would ensure that no one person could rule over all. More than two centuries later, the system still stands.

TAKE ACTION Contact your local representative or senator and ask for support on a current issue that affects you. For example, you may wish to discuss the condition of your local parks or the lack of an after-school center in your area. Contact information can be found at www.congress.org.

The Power of Political Writing

During the early American period, political writing served as an agent for change. Thomas Paine's *Common Sense,* for example, furthered the case for American independence. Later, when the army suffered several brutal defeats and many soldiers were deserting, Paine wrote a series of articles called *The Crisis.* These articles inspired greater public support for the war and convinced many soldiers to reenlist. Today, political writers of all stripes are working in nearly every form—hardcover, softcover, editorial, blog, newsmagazine—to influence our current political landscape.

WRITE AND DISCUSS Catalog the political writing you encounter over the course of one week. Make a list that includes the formats, the topics covered, and your response to each. Then, with a small group, discuss the issues that are motivating today's political writers. Are these writers changing the public debate, or merely recording it?

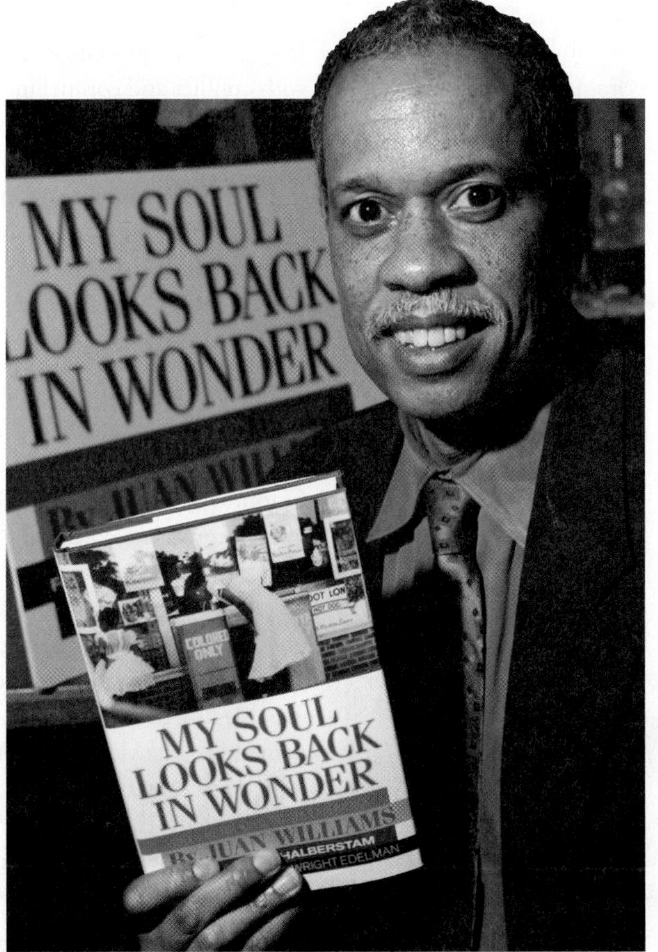

Journalist Juan Williams

The World on the Turtle's Back

Iroquois Creation Myth

COMMON CORE

RL 1 Cite textual evidence to support analysis of what the text says explicitly as well as inferences drawn from the text, including determining where the text leaves matters uncertain. **RL 2** Determine two or more themes or central ideas of a text and analyze their development over the course of the text, including how they interact and build on one another to produce a complex account; provide an objective summary of the text.

DID YOU KNOW?

- Both the U.S. Constitution and the founding charter of the United Nations are based on ideas found in the Iroquois constitution, known as "The Great Binding Law."
- Iroquois women had many more rights than colonial American women.
- More than 50,000 Iroquois live in the United States today.

Background

The totem, or tribal symbol, of the Iroquois

"The World on the Turtle's Back" is an Iroquois (ĭr′ə-kwoi′) creation story filled with conflict and compelling characters. The Iroquois passed down this story from one generation to the next by telling it in elaborate performances. In the 1800s, David Cusick, an Iroquois author, recorded one version of the story in print. Today, more than 25 written versions of the story exist.

The Power of Unity The term *Iroquois* refers to six separate Native American groups—the Seneca, Cayuga, Oneida, Onondaga, Mohawk, and Tuscarora. Five of these groups—all but the Tuscarora—once resided in what is now New York State. They continually waged war with one another, putting themselves at risk of attack from neighboring Algonquin tribes. Troubled by the bloodshed, a Huron named Deganawidah (də-gä′nə-wē′-də) joined forces with an Onondaga chief named Hiawatha (hī′ə-wŏth′ə) to end the fighting. Sometime between 1570 and 1600, they formed the Iroquois League, a confederacy empowered to negotiate treaties with foreign nations and to resolve conflicts among the five nations. In 1722, the Tuscarora, from North Carolina, joined the league. For the next 175 to 200 years, the Iroquois managed to dominate other Native American groups and to remain free of both British and French rule.

The Iroquois Way of Life The league's effectiveness stemmed in part from the nations' shared culture. The groups spoke similar languages, held similar beliefs, and followed similar ways of life. They lived in longhouses made of pole frames covered with elm bark, and they built fences around their villages for protection. Up to 50 people occupied each longhouse, and 300 to 600 people lived in each village. Villages were governed by a chief or chiefs, who received advice from a council of adult males. Groups of women gathered wild fruits and nuts and cultivated corn, beans, and squash. In addition to waging war, the men traded, hunted, fished, and built the longhouses.

The Iroquois Through Time During the American Revolution, the Iroquois nations disagreed about whether to support the rebelling colonists or Great Britain. This dispute severely weakened the Iroquois League. Today, the league shows renewed vigor as it fights for environmental protection and increased recognition by the U.S. government.

Author Online THINK central

Go to thinkcentral.com. KEYWORD: HML11-36

TEXT ANALYSIS: CREATION MYTHS

A **myth** is a traditional story, usually involving supernatural beings or events, that explains how some aspect of human nature or the natural world came to be. A **creation myth** is a specific kind of myth that typically

- describes how the universe, the earth, and life began
- explains the workings of the natural world
- supports and validates social customs and values

As you read "The World on the Turtle's Back," note the supernatural explanations it offers of the world's origin. Think about how this myth serves the functions listed here.

READING STRATEGY: READING FOLK LITERATURE

You're probably already familiar with different types of **folk literature**, which includes folk tales, myths, fables, and legends passed orally from one generation to the next. The creation myth you are about to read is another example of folk literature. Using the following strategies as you read will help you not only understand and appreciate the myth's **themes** but also glean information about the culture it comes from:

- Read the myth aloud, or imagine a storyteller's voice as you read silently.
- Note mysteries of nature and details about creation that the myth explains.
- Make inferences about the social values or customs taught through the characters and situations.
- Look for details that reveal other aspects of Iroquois culture.

As you read, use a chart like the one shown to record your notes and observations about the three kinds of information you find in this myth.

Details About Creation/Nature	*Social Values or Customs*	*Other Cultural Details*
Before the earth was created, humans and animals "of the kind that are around us now" did not exist.		

Complete the activities in your **Reader/Writer Notebook**.

How do we make SENSE *of our world?*

Since the beginning of time, people of all cultures have gathered to discuss one of life's biggest questions: how was the world created? The Iroquois creation myth you're about to read offers one answer to this question about the origin of the world.

DISCUSS What different accounts of creation—biblical narratives, scientific theories, or stories from other cultures, for example—have you heard or read? With a small group of classmates, summarize as many of these accounts as you know.

The World on the Turtle's Back

Iroquois

In the beginning there was no world, no land, no creatures of the kind that are around us now, and there were no men. But there was a great ocean which occupied space as far as anyone could see. Above the ocean was a great void of air. And in the air there lived the birds of the sea; in the ocean lived the fish and the creatures of the deep. Far above this unpeopled world, there was a Sky-World. Here lived gods who were like people—like Iroquois.

In the Sky-World there was a man who had a wife, and the wife was expecting a child. The woman became hungry for all kinds of strange delicacies, as women do when they are with child. She kept her husband busy almost to distraction finding delicious things for her to eat.

In the middle of the Sky-World there grew a Great Tree which was not like any of the trees that we know. It was tremendous; it had grown there forever. It had enormous roots that spread out from the floor of the Sky-World. And on its branches there were many different kinds of leaves and different kinds of fruits and flowers. The tree was not supposed to be marked or mutilated by any of the beings who dwelt in the Sky-World. It was a sacred tree that stood at the center of the universe. **A**

The woman decided that she wanted some bark from one of the roots of the Great Tree—perhaps as a food or as a medicine, we don't know. She told her husband this. He didn't like the idea. He knew it was wrong. But she insisted, and he gave in. So he dug a hole among the roots of this great sky tree, and he bared some of its roots. But the floor of the Sky-World wasn't very thick, and he broke a hole through it. He was terrified, for he had never expected to find empty space underneath the world.

Analyze Visuals ▶
Examine the painting on page 39. How does the artist use light and color to emphasize the division between the Sky-World and the void below it?

A CREATION MYTHS
So far, how is this myth similar to and different from other accounts of creation you've heard or read? Explain your answer, citing details.

Sky Woman (1936), Ernest Smith. Courtesy of the Rochester Museum and Science Center, Rochester, New York.

But his wife was filled with curiosity. He wouldn't get any of the roots for her, so she set out to do it herself. She bent over and she looked down, and she saw the ocean far below. She leaned down and stuck her head through the hole and looked all around. No one knows just what happened next. Some say she slipped. Some say that her husband, fed up with all the demands she had made on him, pushed her.

So she fell through the hole. As she fell, she frantically grabbed at its edges, but her hands slipped. However, between her fingers there clung bits of things that were growing on the floor of the Sky-World and bits of the root tips of the Great Tree. And so she began to fall toward the great ocean far below.

The birds of the sea saw the woman falling, and they immediately consulted with each other as to what they could do to help her. Flying wingtip to wingtip they made a great feathery raft in the sky to support her, and thus they broke her fall. But of course it was not possible for them to carry the woman very long. Some of the other birds of the sky flew down to the surface of the ocean and called up the ocean creatures to see what they could do to help. The great sea turtle came and agreed to receive her on his back. The birds placed her gently on the shell of the turtle, and now the turtle floated about on the huge ocean with the woman safely on his back.

The beings up in the Sky-World paid no attention to this. They knew what was happening, but they chose to ignore it.

When the woman recovered from her shock and terror, she looked around her. All that she could see were the birds and the sea creatures and the sky and the ocean.

And the woman said to herself that she would die. But the creatures of the sea came to her and said that they would try to help her and asked her what they could do. She told them that if they could find some soil, she could plant the roots stuck between her fingers, and from them plants would grow. The sea animals said perhaps there was dirt at the bottom of the ocean, but no one had ever been down there so they could not be sure.

If there was dirt at the bottom of the ocean, it was far, far below the surface in the cold deeps. But the animals said they would try to get some. One by one the diving birds and animals tried and failed. They went to the limits of their endurance, but they could not get to the bottom of the ocean. Finally, the muskrat said he would try. He dived and disappeared. All the creatures waited, holding their breath, but he did not return. After a long time, his little body floated up to the surface of the ocean, a tiny crumb of earth clutched in his paw. He seemed to be dead. They pulled him up on the turtle's back and they sang and prayed over him and breathed air into his mouth, and finally, he stirred. Thus it was the muskrat, the Earth-Diver, who brought from the bottom of the ocean the soil from which the earth was to grow. **B**

The woman took the tiny clod of dirt and placed it on the middle of the great sea turtle's back. Then the woman began to walk in a circle around it, moving in the direction that the sun goes. The earth began to grow. When the earth was big

Language Coach

Meanings of idioms. "Fed up with" in line 28 is an idiom, an expression that means something different than the literal meaning of the words. "Fed up with" means "wearied or tired of" (to the point of losing patience or control). Use this idiom to explain in your own words why the husband may have pushed his wife.

B FOLK LITERATURE
Reread lines 46–62 and consider the role that "all the creatures" play in this myth. What does this suggest about the Iroquois' attitude toward animals?

enough, she planted the roots she had clutched between her fingers when she fell from the Sky-World. Thus the plants grew on the earth.

To keep the earth growing, the woman walked as the sun goes, moving in the direction that the people still move in the dance rituals. She gathered roots and plants to eat and built herself a little hut. After a while, the woman's time came, and she was delivered of a daughter. The woman and her daughter kept walking in a circle around the earth, so that the earth and plants would continue to grow. They lived on the plants and roots they gathered. The girl grew up with her mother, cut off forever from the Sky-World above, knowing only the birds and the creatures of the sea, seeing no other beings like herself.

One day, when the girl had grown to womanhood, a man appeared. No one knows for sure who this man was. He had something to do with the gods above. Perhaps he was the West Wind. As the girl looked at him, she was filled with terror, and amazement, and warmth, and she fainted dead away. As she lay on the ground, the man reached into his quiver, and he took out two arrows, one sharp and one blunt, and he laid them across the body of the girl, and quietly went away.

When the girl awoke from her faint, she and her mother continued to walk around the earth. After a while, they knew that the girl was to bear a child. They did not know it, but the girl was to bear twins.

Within the girl's body, the twins began to argue and quarrel with one another. There could be no peace between them. As the time approached for them to be born, the twins fought about their birth. The right-handed twin wanted to be born in the normal way, as all children are born. But the left-handed twin said no. He said he saw light in another direction, and said he would be born that way. The right-handed twin beseeched him not to, saying that he would kill their mother. But the left-handed twin was stubborn. He went in the direction where he saw light. But he could not be born through his mother's mouth or her nose. He was born through her left armpit, and killed her. And meanwhile, the right-handed twin was born in the normal way, as all children are born. **C**

The twins met in the world outside, and the right-handed twin accused his brother of murdering their mother. But the grandmother told them to stop their quarreling. They buried their mother. And from her grave grew the plants which the people still use. From her head grew the corn, the beans, and the squash—"our supporters, the three sisters."[1] And from her heart grew the sacred tobacco, which the people still use in the ceremonies and by whose upward-floating smoke they send thanks. The women call her "our mother," and they dance and sing in the rituals so that the corn, the beans, and the squash may grow to feed the people.

But the conflict of the twins did not end at the grave of their mother. And, strangely enough, the grandmother favored the left-handed twin.

The right-handed twin was angry, and he grew more angry as he thought how his brother had killed their mother. The right-handed twin was the one who did everything just as he should. He said what he meant, and he meant what he said.

COMMON CORE RL 2

C CREATION MYTHS
Mythic stories often include the miraculous birth of a child. In the *Star Wars* movies, the hero Luke Skywalker and his twin sister Leia are born when their mother dies during childbirth. The miraculous birth of the *Star Wars* twins is kept a secret from others in the story, but the Iroquois rely on this element of the text structure to show how their world was created. What else might the birth of the twins represent here?

1. **the three sisters:** Corn, beans, and squash—the Iroquois' staple food crops—were grown together. The bean vines climbed and were supported by the corn stalks; squash, which spread across the ground and kept weeds from growing, was planted around the bean plants.

He always told the truth, and he always tried to accomplish what seemed to be right and reasonable. The left-handed twin never said what he meant or meant what he said. He always lied, and he always did things backward. You could never tell what he was trying to do because he always made it look as if he were doing the opposite. He was the devious one. **D**

These two brothers, as they grew up, represented two ways of the world which are in all people. The Indians did not call these the right and the wrong. They called them the straight mind and the crooked mind, the upright man and the devious man, the right and the left.

The twins had creative powers. They took clay and modeled it into animals, and they gave these animals life. And in this they contended with one another. The right-handed twin made the deer, and the left-handed twin made the mountain lion which kills the deer. But the right-handed twin knew there would always be more deer than mountain lions. And he made another animal. He made the ground squirrel. The left-handed twin saw that the mountain lion could not get to the ground squirrel, who digs a hole, so he made the weasel. And although the weasel can go into the ground squirrel's hole and kill him, there are lots of ground squirrels and not so many weasels. Next the right-handed twin decided he would make an animal that the weasel could not kill, so he made the porcupine. But the left-handed twin made the bear, who flips the porcupine over on his back and tears out his belly.

And the right-handed twin made berries and fruits of other kinds for his creatures to live on. The left-handed twin made briars and poison ivy, and the poisonous plants like the baneberry and the dogberry, and the suicide root with which people kill themselves when they go out of their minds. And the left-handed twin made medicines, for good and for evil, for doctoring and for witchcraft.

And finally, the right-handed twin made man. The people do not know just how much the left-handed twin had to do with making man. Man was made of clay, like pottery, and baked in the fire. . . .

The world the twins made was a balanced and orderly world, and this was good. The plant-eating animals created by the right-handed twin would eat up all the vegetation if their number was not kept down by the meat-eating animals, which the left-handed twin created. But if these carnivorous animals ate too many other animals, then they would starve, for they would run out of meat. So the right- and the left-handed twins built balance into the world.

As the twins became men full grown, they still contested with one another. No one had won, and no one had lost. And they knew that the conflict was becoming sharper and sharper, and one of them would have to vanquish the other.

And so they came to the duel. They started with gambling. They took a wooden bowl, and in it they put wild plum pits. One side of the pits was burned black, and by tossing the pits in the bowl and betting on how these would fall, they gambled against one another, as the people still do in the New Year's

D FOLK LITERATURE
Reread lines 95–112. Which twin is characterized as being more admirable? What does this characterization tell you about Iroquois values?

Language Coach

Word Definitions
Look at the word *doctoring* in line 133. Many people know the term *doctor*, but *doctoring* or *to doctor* might be unfamiliar. *Doctoring* here means "healing." What clues from the text help you guess the meaning of *doctoring*?

Detail of *Sky Woman* (1936), Ernest Smith. Courtesy of the Rochester Museum and Science Center, Rochester, New York.

rites.[2] All through the morning they gambled at this game, and all through the afternoon, and the sun went down. And when the sun went down, the game was done, and neither one had won.

So they went on to battle one another at the lacrosse[3] game. And they contested all day, and the sun went down, and the game was done. And neither had won.

And now they battled with clubs, and they fought all day, and the sun went down, and the fight was done. But neither had won. E

And they went from one duel to another to see which one would succumb. Each one knew in his deepest mind that there was something, somewhere, that would vanquish the other. But what was it? Where to find it?

Each knew somewhere in his mind what it was that was his own weak point. They talked about this as they contested in these duels, day after day, and somehow the deep mind of each entered into the other. And the deep mind of the right-handed twin lied to his brother, and the deep mind of the left-handed twin told the truth.

On the last day of the duel, as they stood, they at last knew how the right-handed twin was to kill his brother. Each selected his weapon. The left-handed twin chose a mere stick that would do him no good. But the right-handed twin

E FOLK LITERATURE
Reread lines 146–156. Note in your chart the information about Iroquois customs and rituals you learn from these lines.

2. **New Year's rites:** various ceremonies to get ready for the New Year. They often included community confession of sins, the replenishing of hearths in the homes, and sacred dances, as well as the gambling ritual.

3. **lacrosse:** a game of Native American origin wherein participants on two teams use long-handled sticks with webbed pouches to maneuver a ball into the opposing team's goal.

picked out the deer antler, and with one touch he destroyed his brother. And the left-handed twin died, but he died and he didn't die. The right-handed twin picked up the body and cast it off the edge of the earth. And some place below the world, the left-handed twin still lives and reigns.

When the sun rises from the east and travels in a huge arc along the sky dome, which rests like a great upside-down cup on the saucer of the earth, the people are in the daylight realm of the right-handed twin. But when the sun slips down in the west at nightfall and the dome lifts to let it escape at the western rim, the people are again in the domain of the left-handed twin—the fearful realm of night.

Having killed his brother, the right-handed twin returned home to his grandmother. And she met him in anger. She threw the food out of the cabin onto the ground and said that he was a murderer, for he had killed his brother. He grew angry and told her she had always helped his brother, who had killed their mother. In his anger, he grabbed her by the throat and cut her head off. Her body he threw into the ocean, and her head, into the sky. There, "Our Grandmother, the Moon" still keeps watch at night over the realm of her favorite grandson. F

The right-handed twin has many names. One of them is Sapling. It means smooth, young, green and fresh and innocent, straightforward, straight-growing, soft and pliable, teachable and trainable. These are the old ways of describing him. But since he has gone away, he has other names. He is called "He Holds Up the Skies," "Master of Life," and "Great Creator."

The left-handed twin also has many names. One of them is Flint. He is called the devious one, the one covered with boils. Old Warty. He is stubborn. He is thought of as being dark in color.

These two beings rule the world and keep an eye on the affairs of men. The right-handed twin, the Master of Life, lives in the Sky-World. He is content with the world he helped to create and with his favorite creatures, the humans. The scent of sacred tobacco rising from the earth comes gloriously to his nostrils.

In the world below lives the left-handed twin. He knows the world of men, and he finds contentment in it. He hears the sounds of warfare and torture, and he finds them good.

In the daytime, the people have rituals which honor the right-handed twin. Through the daytime rituals, they thank the Master of Life. In the nighttime, the people dance and sing for the left-handed twin.

F CREATION MYTHS
The transformation of a character is a common element of mythology, often used to explain natural phenomena. Consider the natural feature explained in lines 172–183. How does this myth explain the fact that the moon is visible mainly at night?

THEME AND GENRE
The right-handed twin is also called "the Master of Life." Many works of mythic literature are built around the idea of a good hero overcoming obstacles and eventually achieving a reward. The 2001 film *Shrek* uses some of the elements of mythic literature to illustrate the struggle of a character who must overcome the problems of an ogre to gain his reward. How would you relate the idea of a good hero who overcomes obstacles to a recent film you've seen?

Comprehension

1. **Recall** How do the animals help the woman who fell from the sky?
2. **Recall** What roles do the grandmother and her daughter play in the earth's creation?
3. **Summarize** What is the outcome of the battles between the twins?

COMMON CORE

RL 1 Cite textual evidence to support analysis of what the text says explicitly as well as inferences drawn from the text, including determining where the text leaves matters uncertain. **RL 2** Determine two or more themes or central ideas of a text and analyze their development over the course of the text, including how they interact and build on one another to produce a complex account; provide an objective summary of the text.

Text Analysis

4. **Compare and Contrast** How does this myth compare with the accounts of the world's origin you summarized before you read? Use a Venn diagram to record the differences and similarities between "The World on the Turtle's Back" and one of the accounts you discussed.

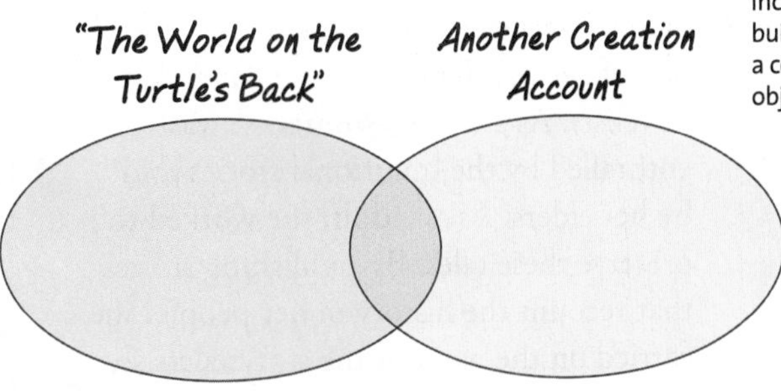

5. **Analyze a Creation Myth** Reread lines 105–112. Summarize the differences between the right-handed twin and the left-handed twin. Why do you think the Iroquois honor both twins? What elements of human nature are explained by "The World on the Turtle's Back"?
6. **Draw Conclusions from Folk Literature** Folk literature often transmits central ideas about a people's culture and way of life. Review the details you noted in your chart as you read. From this myth, what did you learn about the Iroquois'
   - attitude toward nature?
   - view of their gods?
   - important food, games, and rituals?
   - beliefs about good and evil?

Text Criticism

7. **Critical Interpretations** Creation stories often serve many purposes. According to Larry Evers and Paul Pavich, scholars of Native American literature, such stories "remind the people of who and what they are, why they are in this particular place, and how they should continue to live here." Do you think that "The World on the Turtle's Back" fulfills these functions? Explain, citing evidence from the text to support your interpretation.

How do we make **SENSE** *of our world?*

How did the Iroquois make sense of their surroundings? Why might this story have been important to them?

Coyote and the Buffalo

Folk Tale Retold by Mourning Dove

COMMON CORE

RL 1 Cite textual evidence to support analysis of what the text says explicitly as well as inferences drawn from the text, including determining where the text leaves matters uncertain. **RL 3** Analyze the impact of the author's choices regarding how to develop and relate elements of a story. **RL 5** Analyze how an author's choices concerning how to structure specific parts of a text contribute to its overall structure and meaning as well as its aesthetic impact.

DID YOU KNOW?

Mourning Dove . . .

- was born in a canoe while her mother was crossing a river in Idaho.
- learned to read English by poring over melodramatic dime-store novels.
- was the first woman ever elected to the Colville tribal council.

Meet the Author

Mourning Dove c. 1885–1936

Mourning Dove is the pen name of Christine Quintasket (kwən-tăs'kət), who triumphed over adversity to become one of the first female Native American novelists. As a child, Quintasket was enthralled by the traditional stories told by her elders. As an adult, she worked to preserve these tales. By publishing stories that recount the history of her people, she carried on the work of the storytellers she so admired.

Determined to Write Quintasket grew up on the Colville Reservation in Washington State with her mother, the daughter of a Colville chief, and her father, an Okanogan. When Quintasket was 14, her mother died, leaving her to run the household and help raise her younger siblings. Despite her many responsibilities, Quintasket pushed herself to learn to write in English. She later attended secretarial school to learn how to type and business school to hone her grammar and writing skills. She drafted a novel in 1912 but put it away for several years until she met Lucullus McWhorter, a Native American–rights activist, who offered to edit it.

Battling Stereotypes Published in 1927, Mourning Dove's novel, *Cogewea, the Half-Blood,* is credited with breaking down the stereotype of Native Americans as stoic, or unfeeling. "It is all wrong, this saying that Indians do not feel as deeply as whites," the author asserted. "We do feel, and by and by some of us are going to make our feelings appreciated, and then will the true Indian character be revealed."

Chronicling Her Culture After *Cogewea* was published, Mourning Dove began to record traditional stories of the Okanogan and other Colville tribes. A migrant worker, she picked fruit ten hours a day but managed to do her writing at night. *Coyote Stories,* from which "Coyote and the Buffalo" is taken, was published in 1933. "Coyote and the Buffalo" is a folk tale once told by Okanogan storytellers in Salish, their native language. Mourning Dove's retelling includes Salish words and place names. This story and others like it help keep the Okanogan culture alive today.

Mourning Dove's Legacy In addition to preserving her people's culture, Mourning Dove worked hard to promote their welfare. She fought for their rights in court, started organizations supporting Native American crafts, and paved the way for female participation on tribal councils. Worn down by chronic illness and fatigue, the writer and activist died in 1936.

Author Online THINK central

Go to thinkcentral.com. KEYWORD: HML11-46

TEXT ANALYSIS: TRICKSTER TALES

You already know that a folk tale is a simple story passed orally from one generation to the next. **The trickster tale** is a type of folk tale that features an animal or human character who typically engages in deceit, violence, and magic. Often, trickster tales are mythic, explaining how some aspect of human nature or the natural world came to be. The opening lines of "Coyote and the Buffalo" announce what this trickster tale will explain.

No buffalo ever lived in the Swah-netk'-qhu *country. That was Coyote's fault.*

Tricksters are **archetypal characters**—character types that can be found in literary works from different cultures throughout the ages. As incurable practical jokers, with universal appeal, they appear frequently in American literature and film—from the coyote of Native American myths to the tricksters of 20th-century animated cartoons and beyond. As you read this tale, notice how Coyote's character is developed. He demonstrates the trickster's contradictory qualities of being foolish yet clever, greedy yet helpful, and immoral yet moral. In addition, Coyote is given the human characteristic of speech. The first words out of his mouth further clarify his character type:

"Now I will have some fun," Coyote remarked. "I will have revenge for the times Buffalo made me run."

READING STRATEGY: PREDICT

Tricksters are often schemers or scoundrels—they don't usually act as other characters do. Using your background knowledge of this character's contradictory qualities, as well as text clues, can help you **predict** upcoming story events. As you read, use a chart like the one shown to record Coyote's key traits and unusual behavior. Pause occasionally to predict what will happen next.

Coyote's Traits and Behavior	*My Predictions*
Coyote is "foolish and greedy"; it is his fault there are no buffalo in Swah-netk'-qhu country.	*This story will reveal that Coyote did something reckless or unwise to scare away the buffalo.*

Complete the activities in your **Reader/Writer Notebook**.

Why do we root for the "BAD GUY"?

Wherever they go, they ignore the rules. They stir up trouble. And yet we admire and love them despite—or maybe because of—their bad behavior. Many societies have famous villains or trickster figures, who both infuriate and inspire the people around them.

QUICKWRITE Think about movies or books in which the villain is more compelling than the hero. What qualities does such a villain typically display? Which of these traits contribute most to his or her appeal? Record your responses in a short paragraph.

Coyote and the Buffalo

Retold by Mourning Dove

BACKGROUND "Coyote and the Buffalo" is one of many traditional stories featuring the Animal People, a race of supernatural beings believed by the Okanogan to have been the first inhabitants of the world. The Animal People had magical powers and could alter their shapes. When human beings appeared on the earth, the Animal People were changed into different animal species. Coyote, one of the most important Animal People, is thought to have made the world habitable for humans by killing monsters and bringing fire and salmon.

Analyze Visuals ▶
Describe the artwork on page 49. How is the use of color significant? Does the color treatment cause this coyote to reflect the **traits** of a trickster? Explain your answer.

No buffalo ever lived in the *Swah-netk'-qhu*[1] country. That was Coyote's fault. If he had not been so foolish and greedy, the people beside the *Swah-netk'-qhu* would not have had to cross the Rockies to hunt the *quas-peet-za*[2] (curled-hairs).

This is the way it happened:

Coyote was traveling over the plains beyond the big mountains. He came to a flat. There he found an old buffalo skull. It was the skull of Buffalo Bull. Coyote always had been afraid of Buffalo Bull. He remembered the many times Bull Buffalo had scared him, and he laughed upon seeing the old skull there on the flat.

"Now I will have some fun," Coyote remarked. "I will have revenge for the times Buffalo made me run."

He picked up the skull and threw it into the air; he kicked it and spat on it; he threw dust in the eye sockets. He did these things many times, until he grew tired. Then he went his way. Soon he heard a rumbling behind him. He thought it **A** was thunder, and he looked at the sky. The sky was clear. Thinking he must have imagined the sound, he walked on, singing. He heard the rumbling again, only

A TRICKSTER TALES
In the first paragraph, the Coyote is "foolish and greedy". The Joker, in Tim Burton's 1989 film *Batman,* also shares some of the traits of a trickster. Based on lines 5–13, what other **character traits** would you attribute to this trickster?

1. ***Swah-netk'-qhu*** (shwə-nĭt'kwə): the Salish name for the Columbia River and its waterfall.
2. ***quas-peet-za*** (kwəs-pēt'zä): a Salish word for buffalo.

Coyote Survivor, John Nieto. Serigraph, 29″ × 22″.

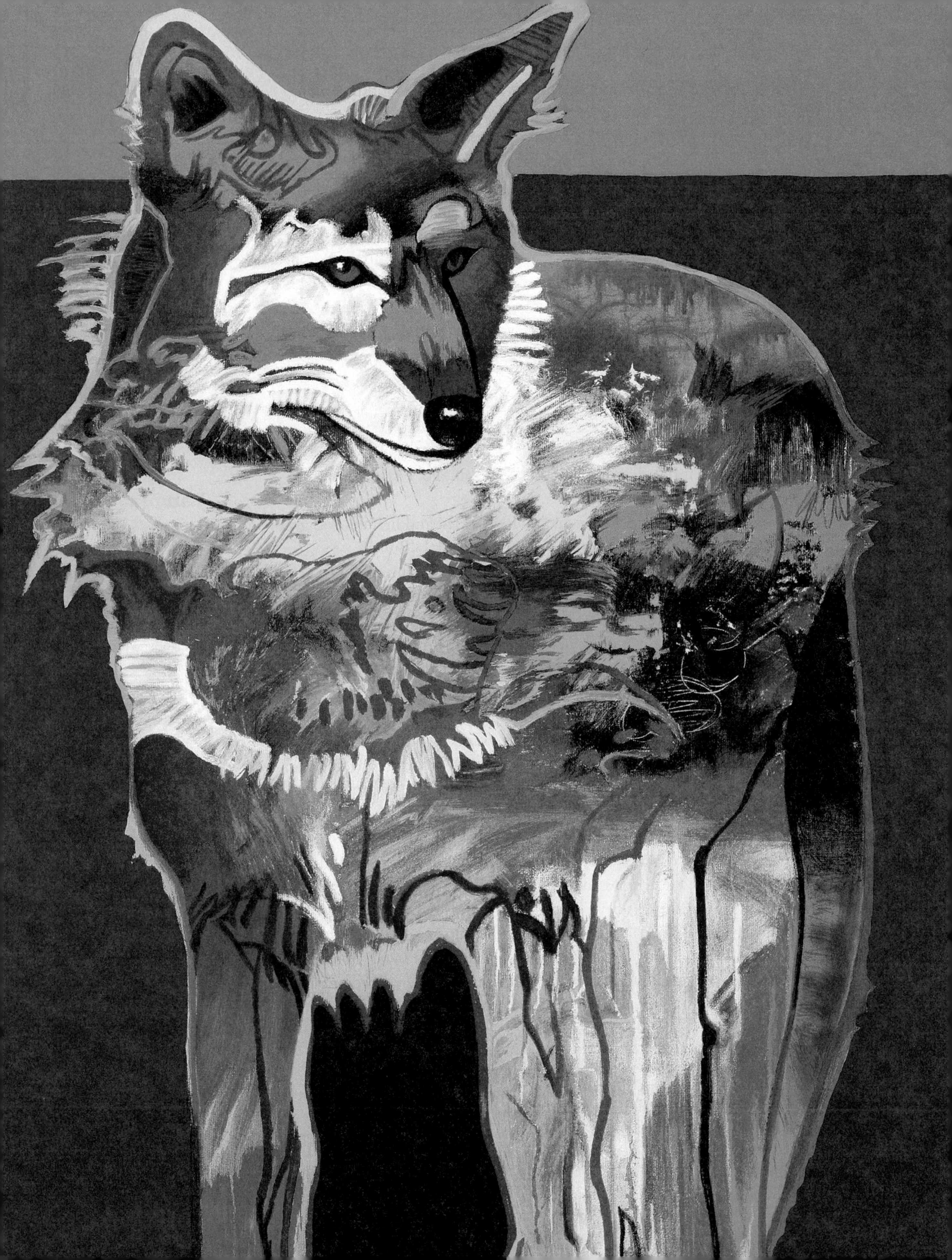

much closer and louder. Turning around, he saw Buffalo Bull pounding along after him, chasing him. His old enemy had come to life!

Coyote ran, faster than he thought he could run, but Buffalo gained steadily. Soon Buffalo was right at his heels. Coyote felt his hot breath.

"Oh, *Squas-tenk'*,[3] help me!" Coyote begged, and his power answered by putting three trees in front of him. They were there in the wink of an eye. Coyote jumped and caught a branch of the first tree and swung out of Buffalo's way. Buffalo rammed the tree hard, and it shook as if in a strong wind. Then Buffalo chopped at the trunk with his horns, first with one horn and then the other. He chopped fast, and in a little while over went the tree, and with it went Coyote. But he was up and into the second tree before Buffalo Bull could reach him. Buffalo soon laid that tree low, but he was not quick enough to catch Coyote, who scrambled into the third and last tree.

"Buffalo, my friend, let me talk with you," said Coyote, as his enemy hacked away at the tree's trunk. "Let me smoke my pipe. I like the *kinnikinnick*.[4] Let me smoke. Then I can die more content."

"You may have time for one smoke," grunted Bull Buffalo, resting from his chopping.

Coyote spoke to his medicine-power, and a pipe, loaded and lighted, was given to him. He puffed on it once and held out the pipe to Buffalo Bull.

"No, I will not smoke with you," said that one. "You made fun of my bones. I have enough enemies without you. Young Buffalo is one of them. He killed me and stole all my fine herd."

"My uncle,"[5] said Coyote, "you need new horns. Let me make new horns for you. Then you can kill Young Buffalo. Those old horns are dull and worn."

Bull Buffalo was pleased with that talk. He decided he did not want to kill Coyote. He told Coyote to get down out of the tree and make the new horns. Coyote jumped down and called to his power. It scolded him for getting into trouble, but it gave him a flint knife and a stump of pitchwood.[6] From this stump Coyote carved a pair of fine heavy horns with sharp points. He gave them to Buffalo Bull. All buffalo bulls have worn the same kind of horns since. **B**

Buffalo Bull was very proud of his new horns. He liked their sharpness and weight and their pitch-black color. He tried them out on what was left of the pitchwood stump. He made one toss and the stump flew high in the air, and he forgave Coyote for his mischief. They became good friends right there. Coyote said he would go along with Buffalo Bull to find Young Buffalo.

They soon came upon Young Buffalo and the big herd he had won from Buffalo Bull. Young Buffalo laughed when he saw his old enemy, and he walked out to meet him. He did not know, of course, about the new horns. It was not much of a fight,

Language Coach

Connotation The images or feelings connected to a word are its **connotation**. Why does Coyote refer to Buffalo Bull as "My uncle" in line 39 (see footnote 5)? How might the meaning differ if Coyote had used one of these terms to address Buffalo Bull: *Mister*, *Your Honor*, or *Worthy Opponent*?

B TRICKSTER TALES
This trickster tale is **mythic** in that it explains how something came to be—in this case, the lack of buffalo in a certain geographic area. What second mythic explanation is offered in lines 39–46?

---

3. ***Squas-tenk'*** (skwəs-tĭnk'): a Salish word referring to Coyote's spirit helper.
4. ***kinnikinnick*** (kĭn'ĭ-kĭ-nĭk'): the Salish word for the bearberry shrub. The Okanogan toasted bearberry leaves and then crumbled them and mixed them with tobacco for pipe smoking.
5. **my uncle:** Terms like *uncle, brother, sister,* and *cousin* were sometimes used as a sign of respect. Here, Coyote is using the term to flatter Buffalo Bull.
6. **pitchwood:** the sap-filled wood of a pine or fir tree.

that fight between Young Buffalo and Buffalo Bull. With the fine new horns, Buffalo Bull killed the other easily, and then he took back his herd, all his former wives and their children. He gave Coyote a young cow, the youngest cow, and he said:

"Never kill her, *Sin-ka-lip'!*[7] Take good care of her and she will supply you with meat forever. When you get hungry, just slice off some choice fat with a flint knife. Then rub ashes on the wound and the cut will heal at once." **C**

Coyote promised to remember that, and they parted. Coyote started back to his own country, and the cow followed. For a few suns he ate only the fat when he was hungry. But after awhile he became tired of eating fat, and he began to long for the sweet marrow-bones and the other good parts of the buffalo. He smacked his lips at the thought of having some warm liver.

C PREDICT
Consider what you know about the **archetypal** trickster character and think about Coyote's behavior thus far. How do you think Coyote will respond to Buffalo Bull's instructions? Give reasons for your prediction.

---

7. ***Sin-ka-lip'*** (sĭng'kə-lĭp'): the Salish name for Coyote; it means "imitator."

Buffalo, John Nieto. Acrylic, 30″× 40″.

"Buffalo Bull will never know," Coyote told himself, and he took his young cow down beside a creek and killed her.

As he peeled off the hide, crows and magpies came from all directions. They settled on the carcass and picked at the meat. Coyote tried to chase them away, but there were too many of them. While he was chasing some, others returned and ate the meat. It was not long until they had devoured every bit of the meat.

"Well, I can get some good from the bones and marrow-fat," Coyote remarked, and he built a fire to cook the bones. Then he saw an old woman walking toward him. She came up to the fire.

"Sin-ka-lip'," she said, "you are a brave warrior, a great chief. Why should you do woman's work? Let me cook the bones while you rest."

Vain Coyote! He was flattered. He believed she spoke her true mind. He stretched out to rest and he fell asleep. In his sleep he had a bad dream. It awoke him, and he saw the old woman running away with the marrow-fat and the boiled grease. He looked into the cooking-basket. There was not a drop of soup left in it. He chased the old woman. He would punish her! But she could run, too, and she easily kept ahead of him. Every once in awhile she stopped and held up the marrow-fat and shouted: *"Sin-ka-lip',* do you want this?" D

Finally Coyote gave up trying to catch her. He went back to get the bones. He thought he would boil them again. He found the bones scattered all around, so he gathered them up and put them into the cooking-basket. Needing some more water to boil them in, he went to the creek for it, and when he got back, there were no bones in the basket! In place of the bones was a little pile of tree limbs!

Coyote thought he might be able to get another cow from Buffalo Bull, so he set out to find him. When he came to the herd, he was astonished to see the cow he had killed. She was there with the others! She refused to go with Coyote again, and Buffalo Bull would not give him another cow. Coyote had to return to his own country without a buffalo.

That is why there never have been any buffalo along the *Swah-netk'-qhu.*

D TRICKSTER TALES
Coyote is not the only character who plays the role of trickster in this tale. Reread lines 77–83. Notice how the old woman turns the tables on Coyote, teasing him with some tricks of her own. An **archetype of mythic literature,** the trickster character appears frequently in American popular entertainment—from animated cartoons to superhero comic books and the hugely popular movies based on them. Tricks and counter-tricks have kept Wile E. Coyote in the American public eye since 1948. Where else have you seen a trickster such as Coyote in action?

Comprehension

1. **Recall** Why is Buffalo Bull so enraged at Coyote at the beginning of the story?
2. **Recall** How does Coyote convince Buffalo Bull to spare his life?
3. **Summarize** According to the story, why don't buffalo live in the *Swah-netk'-qhu* country?

Text Analysis

4. **Analyze Predictions** Review the chart you completed as you read. How accurate were your predictions? Did the fact that the trickster is a somewhat familiar **archetypal character** make it easier to predict Coyote's actions, or did his behavior surprise you? Explain your answer, referring to both your chart and the selection.
5. **Interpret Trickster Tales** Trickster tales endure, in part, simply because they are fun to read. But they also often serve to teach a lesson or moral. What does "Coyote and the Buffalo" teach or explain? Support your answer with specific lines from the story.
6. **Draw Conclusions** Trickster tales, like other forms of folk literature, offer readers insight into a society's way of life. What information about the following aspects of Okanogan culture did you glean from this tale?
   - traits or qualities the Okanogan admired as well as those they disapproved of
   - the traditional role of women in Okanogan society
   - Okanogan rituals and religious beliefs
7. **Make Judgments** Review the paragraph you wrote earlier about famous or compelling villains and tricksters. What character traits does Coyote share with these characters? In your opinion, is Coyote an admirable character? Explain, citing evidence from the text to support your opinion.

Text Criticism

8. **Critical Interpretations** Critic Paul Rodin has argued that a trickster "is at one and the same time creator and destroyer, giver and negator, he who dupes others and who is always duped himself. . . . He possesses no values, moral or social, is at the mercy of his passions and appetites." Identify the ways in which Coyote fits this definition of a trickster. Cite evidence from the selection to support your answer.

Why do we root for the "BAD GUY"?

What makes Coyote appealing, despite his character flaws? Can you think of a famous person who fits the "trickster" label?

COMMON CORE

RL 1 Cite textual evidence to support analysis of what the text says explicitly as well as inferences drawn from the text, including determining where the text leaves matters uncertain. **RL 3** Analyze the impact of the author's choices regarding how to develop and relate elements of a story. **RL 5** Analyze how an author's choices concerning how to structure specific parts of a text contribute to its overall structure and meaning as well as its aesthetic impact.

Themes Across Time

COMMON CORE

RI 5 Analyze and evaluate the effectiveness of the structure an author uses in his or her exposition, including whether the structure makes points clear, convincing, and engaging. **RI 6** Determine an author's point of view or purpose in a text in which the rhetoric is particularly effective, analyzing how style and content contribute to the power, persuasiveness, or beauty of the text. **L 5b** Analyze nuances in the meaning of words with similar denotations.

from The Way to Rainy Mountain

Memoir by N. Scott Momaday

Meet the Author

N. Scott Momaday born 1934

"The most important question one can ask is 'Who am I?'" N. Scott Momaday (mŏm'ə-dā') has asserted. "People tend to define you. As a child, you can't help that, but as you grow older, the goal is to garner enough strength to insist on your own definition of yourself." In his writing, Momaday focuses on the search for identity, and he locates the key to self-understanding in awareness of the past.

Native American Roots Momaday developed a deep sense of his own roots early on. His father, a successful artist and a member of the Kiowa (kī'ə-wô') tribe, routinely told him Kiowa folk tales. His mother, an accomplished writer of French, English, and Cherokee ancestry, instructed him in traditional ways. Momaday grew up on reservations in the Southwest and often spent his summers with his grandparents and other Kiowa relatives in Oklahoma.

The Making of a Writer Growing up on reservations, Momaday developed a reverence for the land and a strong Native American identity. "I saw people," he recalls, "who were deeply involved in their traditional life, in the memories of their blood. They had, as far as I could see, a certain strength and beauty that I find missing in the modern world at large." The lives of these people, together with the Southwestern landscape, inspired Momaday to begin writing at an early age. With the encouragement of his parents, Momaday began composing poetry. Years of hard work and determination paid off when he was awarded a poetry fellowship by Stanford University in 1959.

Voice of the Kiowa In both his poetry and prose, Momaday pays tribute to Native American storytelling traditions and culture. His first novel, *House Made of Dawn,* tells the story of one man's struggle to recover his identity after a stint in the U.S. Army. Original in both theme and structure, the novel was awarded the Pulitzer Prize in 1969. In one of his most popular works, *The Way to Rainy Mountain,* Momaday mixes Kiowa myths, legends, and history with autobiographical details. In addition to his poetry and fiction, Momaday has published essays and articles on preserving the environment. He says, "Writing is a way of expressing your spirit. So there's much more to it than the question of material success. You are out to save your soul after all, and be the best thing that you can be."

Author Online
THINK central
Go to thinkcentral.com. KEYWORD: HML11-54

DID YOU KNOW?

N. Scott Momaday . . .

- rode the bus 28 miles to and from school as a teenager.
- taught both middle school and high school on the Jicarilla reservation in New Mexico before becoming a professional writer.
- won the Pulitzer Prize, the most prestigious U.S. literary award, for his very first novel.

TEXT ANALYSIS: MEMOIR

A **memoir** is a form of autobiographical writing that shares personal experiences as well as observations of significant historical events or people. Memoirs often are written in a highly literary style that may include the use of rhetorical techniques such as understatement, overstatement, repetition, or parallel structure.

As you read N. Scott Momaday's memoir, note how he uses diction and tone to evoke emotion and to advance his purpose for writing. Also, try to distinguish between descriptions of personal experience and sections that comment on larger historical events.

READING SKILL: ANALYZE STRUCTURE

Writers usually arrange information using a **structure** that helps readers see how ideas are related. Momaday interweaves three distinct strands throughout his memoir: details about landscape, details about the Kiowa, and details about his grandmother. As you read, record details about each topic in a chart like the one below, and consider how the topics are related.

The Landscape	The Kiowa	Momaday's Grandmother

VOCABULARY IN CONTEXT

Momaday used the following words in this exploration of his heritage. To test your knowledge, substitute one vocabulary word for the boldfaced word or phrase in each sentence.

WORD LIST			
	enmity	opaque	solstice
	inherently	pillage	tenuous
	luxuriant	preeminently	
	nocturnal	profusion	

1. My mother's garden yields an **abundance** of flowers.
2. The feuding brothers eyed each other with **hostility**.
3. There is something **intrinsically** funny about seeing pictures of my father as a teenager.
4. The summer reunion is held on the **longest day of the year.**

Complete the activities in your **Reader/Writer Notebook**.

What is your HERITAGE?

What makes you who you are? Part of the answer lies in your heritage, or the beliefs, traditions, and culture passed down to you from preceding generations. Think of the things you have gained or learned from older relatives—the recipe for your favorite meal, perhaps, or a sense of humor, or an attitude toward hardship. How have the things you've learned helped shape who you are today? In the selection that follows, N. Scott Momaday offers his own perspective on the importance of heritage.

INTERVIEW Interview one of your classmates about his or her heritage. Ask your subject about a family tradition, an important belief or value, or a story about his or her family's roots. Find out if your classmate thinks heritage has affected his or her identity.

The Way to Rainy Mountain

N. Scott Momaday

BACKGROUND In the 1600s, after a bitter dispute between two chiefs, a band of Kiowa moved from what is now Montana to South Dakota's Black Hills. In around 1785, the Kiowa migrated farther south to escape attacks by neighboring tribes, settling in what is now western Kansas and Oklahoma. With their Comanche allies, the Kiowa ruled the southern Great Plains for a century. One of the last tribes to be defeated by the U.S. government, the Kiowa surrendered in 1875 and were forced onto a reservation in Oklahoma, where members of the tribe still live today.

A single knoll[1] rises out of the plain in Oklahoma, north and west of the Wichita Range. For my people, the Kiowas, it is an old landmark, and they gave it the name Rainy Mountain. The hardest weather in the world is there. Winter brings blizzards, hot tornadic winds arise in the spring, and in summer the prairie is an anvil's edge. The grass turns brittle and brown, and it cracks beneath your feet. There are green belts along the rivers and creeks, linear groves of hickory and pecan, willow and witch hazel. At a distance in July or August the steaming foliage seems almost to writhe in fire. Great green and yellow grasshoppers are everywhere in the tall grass, popping up like corn to sting the flesh, and tortoises crawl about on the red earth, going nowhere in the plenty of time. Loneliness is an aspect of the land. All things in the plain are isolate; there is no confusion of objects in the eye, but one hill or one tree or one man. To look upon that landscape in the early morning, with the sun at your back, is to lose the sense of proportion. Your imagination comes to life, and this, you think, is where Creation was begun. **A**

I returned to Rainy Mountain in July. My grandmother had died in the spring, and I wanted to be at her grave. She had lived to be very old and at last infirm.

Analyze Visuals ▸
Examine the portrait on page 57, and consider the photographer's use of high-contrast lighting. What **traits** are suggested by this emphasis of light and shadow? Do you think the subject might look stronger or more vulnerable in a different kind of light? Explain your answer.

A ANALYZE STRUCTURE
Reread lines 1–14, and notice how the highly descriptive opening paragraph functions as both a literal and figurative "beginning," leading to the phrase "where Creation was begun." What structural relationship do you see between the first paragraph and lines 15–16?

1. **knoll** (nōl): a small round hill.

Edward S. Curtis Collection. Library of Congress.

Her only living daughter was with her when she died, and I was told that in death her face was that of a child.

I like to think of her as a child. When she was born, the Kiowas were living the last great moment of their history. For more than a hundred years they had controlled the open range from the Smoky Hill River to the Red, from the headwaters of the Canadian to the fork of the Arkansas and Cimarron. In alliance with the Comanches, they had ruled the whole of the southern Plains. War was their sacred business, and they were among the finest horsemen the world has ever known. But warfare for the Kiowas was **preeminently** a matter of disposition rather than of survival, and they never understood the grim, unrelenting advance of the U.S. Cavalry. When at last, divided and ill-provisioned, they were driven onto the Staked Plains in the cold rains of autumn, they fell into panic. In Palo Duro Canyon they abandoned their crucial stores to **pillage** and had nothing then but their lives. In order to save themselves, they surrendered to the soldiers at Fort Sill[2] and were imprisoned in the old stone corral that now stands as a military museum. My grandmother was spared the humiliation of those high gray walls by eight or ten years, but she must have known from birth the affliction of defeat, the dark brooding of old warriors. **B**

Her name was Aho, and she belonged to the last culture to evolve in North America. Her forebears came down from the high country in western Montana nearly three centuries ago. They were a mountain people, a mysterious tribe of hunters whose language has never been positively classified in any major group. In the late seventeenth century they began a long migration to the south and east. It was a journey toward the dawn, and it led to a golden age. Along the way the Kiowas were befriended by the Crows,[3] who gave them the culture and religion of the Plains. They acquired horses, and their ancient nomadic spirit was suddenly free of the ground. They acquired Tai-me, the sacred Sun Dance doll, from that moment the object and symbol of their worship, and so shared in the divinity of the sun. Not least, they acquired the sense of destiny, therefore courage and pride. When they entered upon the southern Plains they had been transformed. No longer were they slaves to the simple necessity of survival; they were a lordly and dangerous society of fighters and thieves, hunters and priests of the sun. According to their origin myth, they entered the world through a hollow log. From one point of view, their migration was the fruit of an old prophecy, for indeed they emerged from a sunless world.

Although my grandmother lived out her long life in the shadow of Rainy Mountain, the immense landscape of the continental interior lay like memory in her blood. She could tell of the Crows, whom she had never seen, and of the Black Hills, where she had never been. I wanted to see in reality what she had seen more perfectly in the mind's eye, and traveled fifteen hundred miles to begin my pilgrimage.

preeminently (prē-ĕm′ə-nənt-lē) *adv.* above all; most importantly

pillage (pĭl′ĭj) *n.* the act of looting or plundering by force

COMMON CORE RI 6

B MEMOIR
An **author's purpose,** or reason for writing, usually fits into one of three categories: to entertain, to inform, or to persuade. The style, tone, and diction of a text are strong clues to an author's purpose. Reread lines 19–34, and note Momaday's use of words such as *driven, surrendered, imprisoned, humiliation, affliction,* and *defeat.* Think about the tone these words create, and then consider *why* Momaday may have chosen these specific words. Is his purpose only to entertain, only to inform, only to persuade, or some combination of the three?

2. **Fort Sill:** a U.S. army post established in 1869 in the Indian Territory (now Oklahoma).
3. **Crows:** a group of Native Americans who once inhabited the region between the Platte and Yellowstone rivers in the northern Great Plains. The Crows are now settled in Montana.

Yellowstone, it seemed to me, was the top of the world, a region of deep lakes and dark timber, canyons and waterfalls. But, beautiful as it is, one might have the sense of confinement there. The skyline in all directions is close at hand, the high wall of the woods and deep cleavages of shade. There is a perfect freedom in the mountains, but it belongs to the eagle and the elk, the badger and the bear. The Kiowas reckoned their stature by the distance they could see, and they were bent and blind in the wilderness.

Descending eastward, the highland meadows are a stairway to the plain. In July the inland slope of the Rockies is **luxuriant** with flax and buckwheat, stonecrop and larkspur. The earth unfolds and the limit of the land recedes. Clusters of trees, and animals grazing far in the distance, cause the vision to reach away and wonder to build upon the mind. The sun follows a longer course in the day, and the sky is immense beyond all comparison. The great billowing clouds that sail upon it are shadows that move upon the grain like water, dividing light. Farther down, in the land of the Crows and Blackfeet,[4] the plain is yellow. Sweet clover takes hold of the hills and bends upon itself to cover and seal the soil. There the Kiowas paused on their way; they had come to the place where they must change their lives. The sun is at home on the plains. Precisely there does it have the certain character of a god. When the Kiowas came to the land of the Crows, they could see the dark lees of the hills at dawn across the Bighorn River, the **profusion** of light on the grain shelves, the oldest deity ranging after the **solstices.** Not yet would they veer southward to the caldron of the land that lay below; they must wean their blood from the northern winter and hold the mountains a while longer in their view. They bore Tai-me in procession to the east.

A dark mist lay over the Black Hills, and the land was like iron. At the top of a ridge I caught sight of Devil's Tower upthrust against the gray sky as if in the birth of time the core of the earth had broken through its crust and the motion of the world was begun. There are things in nature that engender an awful quiet in the heart of man; Devil's Tower is one of them. Two centuries ago, because they could not do otherwise, the Kiowas made a legend at the base of the rock. My grandmother said:

Eight children were there at play, seven sisters and their brother. Suddenly the boy was struck dumb; he trembled and began to run upon his hands and feet. His fingers became claws, and his body was covered with fur. Directly there was a bear where the boy had been. The sisters were terrified; they ran, and the bear after them. They came to the stump of a great tree, and the tree spoke to them. It bade them climb upon it, and as they did so it began to rise into the air. The bear came to kill them, but they were just beyond its reach. It reared against the tree and scored the bark all around with its claws. The seven sisters were borne into the sky, and they became the stars of the Big Dipper.

luxuriant (lŭg-zhŏŏr'ē-ənt) *adj.* characterized by abundant growth

profusion (prə-fyōō'zhən) *n.* abundance; lavishness

solstice (sŏl'stĭs) *n.* either of two days of the year when the sun is farthest from the celestial equator; the summer solstice is the longest day of the year, and the winter solstice is the shortest.

COMMON CORE L 5b

Language Coach

Formal Language Note the formal tone of lines 89–97. For example, "It bade them climb upon it" could be expressed informally as "It asked them to climb it." Why is formal language appropriate for the telling of a legend?

---

4. **Blackfeet:** a group of Native Americans who once inhabited a region now occupied by parts of Montana and the Canadian provinces of Alberta and Saskatchewan.

From that moment, and so long as the legend lives, the Kiowas have kinsmen in the night sky. Whatever they were in the mountains, they could be no more. However **tenuous** their well-being, however much they had suffered and would suffer again, they had found a way out of the wilderness. **C**

tenuous (tĕn'yo͞o-əs) *adj.* having little substance or strength; flimsy

C ANALYZE STRUCTURE
Reread lines 98–101. What does Momaday mean when he says that "the Kiowas have kinsmen in the night sky"? How does the inclusion of this legend add depth to the personal elements of this memoir?

My grandmother had a reverence for the sun, a holy regard that now is all but gone out of mankind. There was a wariness in her, and an ancient awe. She was a Christian in her later years, but she had come a long way about, and she never forgot her birthright. As a child she had been to the Sun Dances; she had taken part in those annual rites, and by them she had learned the restoration of her people in the presence of Tai-me. She was about seven when the last Kiowa Sun Dance was held in 1887 on the Washita River above Rainy Mountain Creek. The buffalo were gone. In order to consummate the ancient sacrifice—to impale the head of a buffalo bull upon the medicine tree—a delegation of old men journeyed into Texas, there to beg and barter for an animal from the Goodnight herd.[5] She was ten when the Kiowas came together for the last time as a living Sun Dance culture. They could find no buffalo; they had to hang an old hide from the sacred tree. Before the dance could begin, a company of soldiers rode out from Fort Sill under orders to disperse the tribe. Forbidden without cause the essential act of their faith, having seen the wild herds slaughtered and left to rot upon the ground, the Kiowas backed away forever from the medicine tree. That was July 20, 1890, at the great bend of the Washita. My grandmother was there. Without bitterness, and for as long as she lived, she bore a vision of deicide.[6]

Now that I can have her only in memory, I see my grandmother in the several postures that were peculiar to her: standing at the wood stove on a winter morning and turning meat in a great iron skillet; sitting at the south window, bent above her beadwork, and afterwards, when her vision failed, looking down for a long time into the fold of her hands; going out upon a cane, very slowly as she did when the weight of age came upon her; praying. I remember her most often at prayer. She made long, rambling prayers out of suffering and hope, having seen many things. I was never sure that I had the right to hear, so exclusive were they of all mere custom and company. The last time I saw her she prayed standing by the side of her bed at night, naked to the waist, the light of a kerosene lamp moving upon her dark skin. Her long, black hair, always drawn and braided in the day, lay upon her shoulders and against her breasts like a shawl. I do not speak Kiowa, and I never understood her prayers, but there was something **inherently** sad in the sound, some merest hesitation upon the syllables of sorrow. She began in a high and descending pitch, exhausting her breath to silence; then again and again—and always the same intensity of effort, of something that is, and is not, like urgency in the human voice. Transported so in the dancing light among the shadows of her room, she seemed beyond the reach of time. But that was illusion; I think I knew then that I should not see her again.

Language Coach
Word Definitions
Postures in line 121 means "the positions of the body." Grandmother's postures are peculiar to her; they distinguish her from other people the speaker knows. What postures does Momaday list? How does each add to his description of his grandmother?

inherently (ĭn-hîr'ənt-lē') *adv.* related to part of something's inmost nature

5. **Goodnight herd:** a herd of Southern Plains bison established in the 1870s by Charles and Molly Goodnight for the purpose of preserving the animals from extinction.
6. **a vision of deicide** (dē'ə-sīd'): a picture in her mind of the killing of a god.

◀ Analyze Visuals
In your opinion, does this photograph convey the same **mood** that Momaday evokes in his autobiography? Explain your answer, citing details from both the photograph and the text.

Mandan Offering the Buffalo Skull, Edward S. Curtis, photographer. McCormick Library of Special Collections, Northwestern University Library.

Houses are like sentinels in the plain, old keepers of the weather watch. There, in a very little while, wood takes on the appearance of great age. All colors wear soon away in the wind and rain, and then the wood is burned gray and the grain appears and the nails turn red with rust. The windowpanes are black and **opaque;** you imagine there is nothing within, and indeed there are many ghosts, bones given up to the land. They stand here and there against the sky, and you approach them for a longer time than you expect. They belong in the distance; it is their domain. D

Once there was a lot of sound in my grandmother's house, a lot of coming and going, feasting and talk. The summers there were full of excitement and reunion. The Kiowas are a summer people; they abide the cold and keep to themselves, but when the season turns and the land becomes warm and vital they cannot hold still; an old love of going returns upon them. The aged visitors who came to my grandmother's house when I was a child were made of lean and leather, and they bore themselves upright. They wore great black hats and bright ample shirts

opaque (ō-pāk') *adj.* not allowing light to pass through

D MEMOIR
Reread lines 120–145. What words and phrases give you an indication of Momaday's **tone,** or attitude toward his subject matter?

that shook in the wind. They rubbed fat upon their hair and wound their braids with strips of colored cloth. Some of them painted their faces and carried the scars of old and cherished **enmities.** They were an old council of warlords, come to remind and be reminded of who they were. Their wives and daughters served them well. The women might indulge themselves; gossip was at once the mark and compensation of their servitude. They made loud and elaborate talk among themselves, full of jest and gesture, fright and false alarm. They went abroad in fringed and flowered shawls, bright beadwork and German silver. They were at home in the kitchen, and they prepared meals that were banquets.

enmity (ĕn′mĭ-tē) *n.* hostility; hatred

There were frequent prayer meetings, and great **nocturnal** feasts. When I was a child I played with my cousins outside, where the lamplight fell upon the ground and the singing of the old people rose up around us and carried away into the darkness. There were a lot of good things to eat, a lot of laughter and surprise. And afterwards, when the quiet returned, I lay down with my grandmother and could hear the frogs away by the river and feel the motion of the air.

nocturnal (nŏk-tûr′nəl) *adj.* occurring at night

Now there is a funeral silence in the rooms, the endless wake of some final word. The walls have closed in upon my grandmother's house. When I returned to it in mourning, I saw for the first time in my life how small it was. It was late at night, and there was a white moon, nearly full. I sat for a long time on the stone steps by the kitchen door. From there I could see out across the land; I could see the long row of trees by the creek, the low light upon the rolling plains, and the stars of the Big Dipper. Once I looked at the moon and caught sight of a strange thing. A cricket had perched upon the handrail, only a few inches away from me. My line of vision was such that the creature filled the moon like a fossil. It had gone there, I thought, to live and die, for there, of all places, was its small definition made whole and eternal. A warm wind rose up and purled like the longing within me. **E**

E MEMOIR
Think about how Momaday contrasts his grandmother's house as it was during his childhood visits with how it is now. What might this house **symbolize?**

The next morning I awoke at dawn and went out on the dirt road to Rainy Mountain. It was already hot, and the grasshoppers began to fill the air. Still, it was early in the morning, and the birds sang out of the shadows. The long yellow grass on the mountain shone in the bright light, and a scissortail hied[7] above the land. There, where it ought to be, at the end of a long and legendary way, was my grandmother's grave. Here and there on the dark stones were ancestral names. Looking back once, I saw the mountain and came away.

THEME AND GENRE
In mythic literature, the concept of the pilgrimage carries great significance. Momaday's pilgrimage to visit his mother's grave is emblematic of a spiritual journey to uncover his ancestral roots. A contemporary version of this journey is told in Jonathan Safran Foer's 2002 novel *Everything is Illuminated.* Which recent novels you've read include or allude to the mythic idea of the pilgrimage?

7. **a scissortail hied:** a fork-tailed bird of the Southwest hied, or hurried.

Comprehension

1. **Recall** Where is Rainy Mountain, and why does Momaday return there?
2. **Clarify** What two natural phenomena are explained by the Kiowa legend about the seven sisters and their brother?
3. **Summarize** What important events in Kiowa history does Momaday recount?

Text Analysis

4. **Draw Conclusions** In your opinion, what is the most important insight Momaday gains about his **heritage** during his pilgrimage from Yellowstone to his grandmother's grave at Rainy Mountain? Support your opinion with evidence from the text.
5. **Understand Memoirs** Reread lines 52–101. What does Momaday's account of the Kiowa's migration offer you that a description in a history book might not? Explain, citing specific lines of the selection that support your answer.
6. **Analyze Structure** Review the chart you created as you read, and summarize the geographical, historical, and personal details that Momaday includes in each of the three strands. How are they related? Describe the impact of Momaday's technique of weaving the three strands together.
7. **Examine Author's Style** Although best known as a novelist, Momaday is also an accomplished poet. In what way might this selection be described as poetic? In a chart like the one shown, record examples of the poetic elements Momaday uses in his memoir. Use your completed chart to explain what you think these stylistic choices add to the selection. (Refer to the **Glossary of Literary and Nonfiction Terms** on page R104 if needed.)

Poetic Elements		
Alliteration	*Consonance*	*Imagery*
"The grass turns brittle and brown . . ."		

Text Criticism

8. **Critical Interpretations** Teacher and scholar Kenneth M. Roemer has argued that "in *The Way to Rainy Mountain,* N. Scott Momaday links the survival of his people to their ability to remember, preserve and pass on stories." Do you agree that a culture's survival rests on this ability? Explain, using evidence from this selection to support your opinion.

What is your **HERITAGE?**

How is Momaday's identity shaped by his heritage? Can you think of ways your heritage has affected your life?

COMMON CORE

RI 5 Analyze and evaluate the effectiveness of the structure an author uses in his or her exposition, including whether the structure makes points clear, convincing, and engaging. **RI 6** Determine an author's point of view or purpose in a text in which the rhetoric is particularly effective, analyzing how style and content contribute to the power, persuasiveness, or beauty of the text.

Vocabulary in Context

▲ VOCABULARY PRACTICE

Choose the vocabulary word that answers each riddle.

1. I refer to things that do not happen in daylight.
2. I represent extremes of time, both shortest and longest.
3. I am the opposite of friendship.
4. I describe something uncertain or insubstantial.
5. I mean the same thing as *chiefly.*
6. I am the act of looting by force.
7. I am an adjective that could describe a field filled with wildflowers.
8. I am a noun indicating an abundance of wildflowers.
9. Air filled with dense fog is one example of what I am.
10. One of my meanings is "essentially."

WORD LIST

enmity
inherently
luxuriant
nocturnal
opaque
pillage
preeminently
profusion
solstice
tenuous

ACADEMIC VOCABULARY IN WRITING

• document • illustrate • interpret • promote • reveal

Write a paragraph explaining how Momaday uses this memoir to **document** not only the end of his grandmother's life but also the "end" of a specific way of life for the Kiowa people. Use at least one Academic Vocabulary word in your response.

VOCABULARY STRATEGY: SPECIALIZED VOCABULARY

The Kiowa recognize the importance of seasonal events such as the solstices. There are a number of terms that describe other natural phenomena relating Earth to the sun and the moon. Many of them have Latin and Greek roots. Some of these terms have only technical meanings, but others are also used in more general ways.

COMMON CORE

RI 4 Determine the meaning of words and phrases as they are used in a text including technical meanings. **L 4c** Consult general and specialized reference materials, both print and digital, to clarify a word's precise meaning.

PRACTICE Match each term with its definition. Consult a print or online dictionary if you need help. Then choose the term that also has a meaning not related to astronomy and write a definition for it.

1. apogee	**a.** two dates each year when day and night are of equal length
2. equinox	**b.** having a noncircular planetary orbits such as Earth's
3. diurnal	**c.** point when the moon is farthest from Earth
4. perigee	**d.** relating to the daily rotation of Earth
5. eccentric	**e.** point when the moon is closest to Earth

Native American Values

Native Americans have long been characterized by stereotypes in Western culture. Explorers, trappers, and settlers often had little prior knowledge of Native Americans, so early written accounts of encounters with Native Americans naturally reflect an ignorance and misunderstanding of their values. Although Europeans and Native Americans coexisted peacefully in many places for many years, hostile encounters—often prompted by government policies—encouraged later writers to indulge in blatant "cowboys and Indians" stereotyping. Reading historical and current literature by Native Americans can help you see beyond the stereotypes and gain a clearer understanding of the Native American experience.

Writing to Synthesize

When you synthesize information about a subject, you make connections between various sources, including your own prior knowledge. By combining ideas and facts from more than one source, you gain a deeper understanding of the subject and sometimes discover new insights into your own experience.

Look back through the selections in this section, and make a list of ideas and facts that connect all of the selections and your personal experience. Focus on the things that connect us all as people. Then, use your list to write one paragraph describing an early Native American value that many people still hold today. Write a second paragraph describing something normally condemned, or disapproved of, by both early Native Americans and most people today. You may want to use an outline like this one to develop your paragraphs.

Paragraph 1

Thesis statement (What value do people today hold in common with early Native Americans?)

Support for thesis (quotations or summaries from selections, areas of interest in the news, personal anecdotes)

Restatement of main idea

Paragraph 2

Thesis statement (What disagreeable actions or behaviors were similarly condemned by early Native Americans?)

Support for thesis (quotations or summaries from selections, areas of interest in the news, personal anecdotes)

Restatement of main idea

Extension Online

RESEARCH Historically, many university and professional sports teams have employed Native American mascots. In recent years, this practice has come under attack. With a partner, go online to **research** images of three such mascots and print them to share with the class. Also find out what routines or traditions each mascot has performed. Then, as a class, discuss why people might find such mascots offensive. As you discuss, be sure to consider what you learned from your reading.

The Buffalo Chase with Bow (1832), George Catlin. The Granger Collection, New York.

COMMON CORE

W 9 Draw evidence from literary texts to support analysis, reflection, and research. **SL 1** Initiate and participate effectively in a range of collaborative discussions. **SL 1a** Come to discussions prepared, having read and researched material under study.

Media Study

Changing Views of Native Americans

Film Clips on **Media Smart** DVD-ROM

COMMON CORE

RI 7 Integrate and evaluate multiple sources of information presented in different media or formats as well as in words in order to address a question or solve a problem.

How do media shape PERCEPTIONS?

In this unit, Native American voices from the past and present reveal their way of life and worldview. In contrast, many 20th-century films about the Old West lacked this Native American perspective, often reinforcing inaccurate **stereotypes** and creating new ones. In this lesson, you will watch three film clips that present images of Native Americans from three different time periods.

Background

How the Western Won America's fascination with the Old West began with late 19th-century dime-novel westerns. These low-priced, fast-paced stories were typically set in the frontier between the mid-1800s and the turn of the century. Alongside dime novels arose Wild West shows. These colorful, outdoor spectacles featured frontier figures, such as Buffalo Bill, Sitting Bull, and Annie Oakley, and staged reenactments of battles. Both dime novels and Wild West shows presented simplistic morality tales. To establish order and perhaps justify the taking of Native American lands and lives, the so-called good guys—cowboys and settlers—had to overcome the alleged bad guys—rampaging Indians or marauding outlaws. Thus was born a source for stereotyping that would endure in other forms.

At the start of the 20th century, as the motion picture industry evolved, the western film genre burst onto the screen. While Hollywood filmmakers glorified the frontier by shooting in spectacular locations, they recycled the simple formulas of the earlier western forms and perpetuated some of the inaccurate images.

By the mid-1900s, as TV became commonplace, westerns dominated both big and small screens. At the peak of the western's golden age, over 20 westerns were televised each week, exposing viewers to themes and images that went unquestioned. It didn't seem to matter if an Indian's costume wasn't historically accurate or if his or her language wasn't realistic. Little was said about the effects of western expansion on Native American life and culture. The Hollywood images took hold in the minds of viewers. Aware of this, filmmakers of more recent times have made deliberate efforts to bring more authentic portrayals to the screen.

Media Literacy: Images in Mass Media

The **western** is a film and TV genre that portrays the early days of the American frontier. In many TV shows and movies, particularly classic westerns, the film and TV industry depended on **stereotypes,** oversimplified or inaccurate representations of people. Stereotypes can create misconceptions, especially when there are no alternative portrayals to displace them. Use your knowledge of characterization and film techniques to help you spot these stereotypes.

STRATEGIES FOR ANALYZING FILM AND TELEVISION STEREOTYPES

A Character's Appearance	Look for how actors are costumed and how make-up is applied. Keep in mind that most often, little historical research was done to present Native Americans accurately. Costumes and language were often a mix of different tribes.	
A Character's Dialogue	Focus on how characters speak. Which characters speak dialogue in complete sentences? Which speak in simple words or phrases? Stereotypical characters are usually depicted as being somehow outside of the mainstream culture and as holding a different set of values.	
A Character's Actions	Ask yourself: Do characters behave according to a stereotype? Are the actions more negative than positive? Notice how **lighting** and **music** reinforce these impressions. How does the director film the actions? Be aware of camera placement. • **Low-angle shots** position the camera to look up at an object or a person. Such shots convey an imposing or powerful presence. • **High-angle shots** position the camera to look down, often conveying helplessness.	
Other Characters' Responses to the Character	Notice how other characters react to the individual. Do close-up shots reveal expressions of tolerance, condescension, or superiority? In what ways do the dialogue and the acting convey how the character is regarded?	

MediaSmart DVD-ROM

- **Film 1:** *Stagecoach*
- **Director:** John Ford
- **Genre:** Movie Western
- **Running Time:** 2 minutes

- **Film 2:** *The Lone Ranger*
- **Genre:** TV Western
- **Running Time:** 2 minutes

- **Film 3:** *Smoke Signals*
- **Director:** Chris Eyre
- **Rating:** PG-13
- **Genre:** Drama
- **Running Time:** 2.5 minutes

Viewing Guide for

Changing Views of Native Americans

Watch the first two clips to explore how Native Americans were portrayed during the glory days of the western. The scene from *Stagecoach* (1939) brings two groups into direct contact. In the clip from *The Lone Ranger* TV series (1949–1957), the two main characters prepare to take action. Watch the third clip to see a more recent Native American portrayal—one that challenges the old Hollywood images. In *Smoke Signals* (1998), friends Victor and Thomas engage in lively conversation during a road trip.

To critically analyze the clips, view them more than once. Examine the portrayals, and answer these questions.

NOW VIEW

FIRST VIEWING: Comprehension

1. **Recall** In *Stagecoach,* what do the travelers do as soon as they spot the Native Americans?
2. **Summarize** Think about Victor in *Smoke Signals.* Summarize his view of the acceptable look and behavior for "Indian" males.

CLOSE VIEWING: Media Literacy

3. **Identify Film Techniques** Consider how the use of music and the **high-** and **low-angle** shots contribute to characterization in the beginning of the *Stagecoach* clip. How might the effect reinforce **stereotypes?**
4. **Analyze Stereotypes** In *The Lone Ranger* clip, the character Tonto might be considered an improvement over past portrayals of Native Americans. However, what might still be **stereotypical** about this character?
5. **Analyze Characters** Recall how Victor in *Smoke Signals* describes "real Indian" behavior. Might their portrayal be perceived as a step forward? Why or why not?
6. **Evaluate Characterization** *Smoke Signals* director Chris Eyre has said, "I'm interested in telling stories about Indians who are normal, everyday people." How effectively do the character portrayals in the scene from his film counter the stereotypes in *Stagecoach* and *The Lone Ranger?* Base your opinion on the modern-day setting in *Smoke Signals* and on the characterizations of Thomas and Victor.

Produce Your Own Media

Compare Portrayals What impressions of Native Americans do you get from each clip? At the time each portrayal was first presented, how might it have affected perceptions of Native Americans? As you think about these clips, consider the following:

- the portrayals of individuals or groups
- the techniques of camera position, lighting, and music
- the fact that *Smoke Signals* was written and directed by Native Americans

Now that you have critiqued these clips, try creating a media award for a film or TV show. As a class, brainstorm about any films or TV shows that you think rise above the simplistic techniques of stereotyping. What character portrayals or story lines strike you as complex and true to life? How sensitively are different social groups portrayed? Create a name for the award, and devise criteria for judging the pieces.

Once your class has decided on the best nominees and chosen the winner, think about ways you can use multimedia to present the media award. You may want to use presentational software to display the title and attributes of each nominee. You also could use recorded music that is appropriate to each nominee, or a voice-over recording that details how one work succeeded where others failed.

COMMON CORE

RI 7 Integrate and evaluate multiple sources of information presented in different media or formats as well as in words in order to address a question or solve a problem. **SL 2** Integrate multiple sources of information presented in diverse formats and media in order to make informed decisions and solve problems, evaluating the credibility and accuracy of each source and noting any discrepancies among the data. **SL 3** Evaluate a speaker's point of view, assessing the tone used. **SL 5** Make strategic use of digital media in presentations to enhance understanding of findings, reasoning, and evidence and to add interest.

Further Exploration

Hold a Native American Film Festival According to Native American filmmaker Bird Runningwater, "Filmmaking provides a new way to merge a strong oral tradition of storytelling with technology and, in the process, revitalize ourselves." Research Native American films and reviews. If possible, rent movies to view as a group, and then critique them in a panel discussion.

Conduct a Native American Film Study Savage warrior. Noble savage. Sage protector of the earth. One hundred years of moviemaking hasn't begun to cover the complexity and diversity of Native American cultural groups. Research westerns ranging from the 1950s to the present. What historical inaccuracies are evident? In contemporary works, have attempts to present more positive depictions fully succeeded?

Text Analysis Workshop

Historical Narratives

If you wanted to know what life was like for someone 400 years ago, where could you get the information? History books could give you a general account, but what if you wanted to know the details of someone's daily life or what it was like to actually be at an important historical event? In American literature, there are many personal accounts that have been published and passed down through the centuries that give unique perspectives on the events of the past.

COMMON CORE

Included in this workshop:
RI 9 Analyze seventeenth- and eighteenth-century foundational U.S. documents of historical and literary significance for their themes, purposes, and rhetorical features. **RI 10** Read and comprehend literary nonfiction.

Recording the American Experience

Europeans began voyages by ship to the Americas in the late 15th century and reported news of their explorations and settlement. These historical narratives of the survivors told gripping adventure stories, written down in journals and letters, of the the first Europeans' experiences of coming to America. **Historical narratives** are accounts of real-life historical experiences, written by either a person who experienced those events or someone who studied or observed them. In many cases, the narratives became important historical documents that now exist as our principal record of events. Historical narratives can be divided into two categories:

Indian Summer, Regis François Gignoux. © Christie's Images/Corbis.

- **Primary sources** are materials written by people who were either participants in or observers of the events written about. Letters, diaries, journals, speeches, autobiographies, and interviews are all primary sources.
- **Secondary sources** are records of events written by people who were not directly involved in the events. Two typical examples of secondary sources are biographies and histories.

Bringing the Past to Life

Primary sources offer valuable insights into the thinking and culture of a given time period. Use these strategies to bring the information to life:

- Determine a document's origin.
- Try to understand the **perspective** and **motives** of the writer.
- Note **sensory details** that depict people, places, and events.
- Identify customs, values, or conditions of the **culture** or **time period.**

Álvar Núñez Cabeza de Vaca was one of many explorers who sailed to the New World after Christopher Columbus. The historical narrative *La Relación* (page 70) was Cabeza de Vaca's report to the king of Spain. Note the personal **perspective** he provides in this excerpt about one night in his crossing of the Atlantic Ocean.

> When night fell, only the navigator and I remained able to tend the barge. Two hours after dark he told me I must take over; he believed he was going to die that night.
>
> **—Álvar Núñez Cabeza de Vaca, *La Relación***

In 1620, the Puritans survived a journey across the Atlantic in the *Mayflower* and landed at Cape Cod. In 1630, William Bradford, Plymouth Colony's second governor, began writing *Of Plymouth Plantation* (page 104), a chronicle of his colony's experiences. Notice the use of **sensory details** in Bradford's description of the colony's first winter.

> The weather was very cold and it froze so hard as the spray of the sea lighting on their coats, they were as if they had been glazed.
>
> **—William Bradford, *Of Plymouth Plantation***

As the American colonies expanded from the 16th through the 18th centuries, the slave trade expanded as well. Olaudah Equiano was one of the millions of Africans captured and transported to the Americas. He survived this ordeal and published his autobiography in 1789. These lines from his autobiography describe the conditions below the decks of a slave ship and his first reaction to what he saw.

> When I looked round the ship too, and saw a large furnace of copper boiling, and a multitude of black people of every description chained together, every one of their countenances expressing dejection and sorrow, I no longer doubted of my fate.
>
> **—Olaudah Equiano, *The Interesting Narrative of the Life of Olaudah Equiano***

THE SLAVE NARRATIVE

The **slave narrative** is an American literary genre that portrays the daily life of slaves as written by the slaves themselves after gaining their freedom. Some 6,000 slave narratives are known to exist. The Reverend Ephraim Peabody wrote in 1849 about three recently published slave narratives:

> *We place these volumes without hesitation among the most remarkable productions of the age—remarkable as being pictures of slavery by the slave, remarkable as disclosing under a new light the mixed elements of American civilization, and not less remarkable as a vivid exhibition of the force and working of the native love of freedom in the individual mind.*
>
> **–The Reverend Ephraim Peabody**

Probably the most influential example of the genre is the autobiography of Frederick Douglass, *Narrative of the Life of Frederick Douglass, an American Slave*, published in 1845.

Close Read

Describe what you think were the writer's motives for recording the events in the first two **primary source** examples on this page.

Close Read

Point out details that are particularly vivid. Describe how you would visualize the scene.

from La Relación

Report by Álvar Núñez Cabeza de Vaca

COMMON CORE

RI 1 Cite textual evidence to support analysis of what the text says explicitly as well as inferences drawn from the text, including determining where the text leaves matters uncertain. **RI 6** Determine an author's point of view or purpose in a text. **RI 9** Analyze foundational U.S. documents of historical and literary significance for their themes, purposes, and rhetorical features.

DID YOU KNOW?

Cabeza de Vaca . . .

- recorded the only accounts of some now-extinct Native American groups.
- was the first European to cross North and South America.
- was accompanied by an enslaved African named Esteban.

Meet the Author

Álvar Núñez Cabeza de Vaca c. 1490–1557

In 1536, Spanish slave hunters raiding in northern Mexico were startled by a strange sight: a Spaniard "strangely dressed and in company with Indians." Long given up for dead, Álvar Núñez Cabeza de Vaca had survived one of the most disastrous expeditions in the history of the Spanish conquest to become the first European to cross North America.

Conquering Hero Cabeza de Vaca came from a family of Spanish *conquistadors,* or conquerors. He had been a soldier for nearly 20 years when, in 1527, he joined an expedition to Spanish North America. Appointed by the king of Spain, he became treasurer and second in command, assigned the task of colonizing the territory north and east of the Gulf of Mexico.

Disaster Strikes Led by Pánfilo de Narváez, the expedition sailed with five ships and 600 men. Two ships were lost in a hurricane; 200 men drowned or deserted. After landing in Tampa Bay, Narváez sent his ships north and ordered 300 men to march to New Spain (present-day Mexico), which he guessed to be a few weeks away. Months later, the ships were gone and the desperate landing party was eating its horses to survive. Using horsehide and nails made from melted armor, they built five barges and sailed along the Gulf Coast from Florida to Texas, hoping to reach Spanish settlements in northern Mexico. Two barges and 80 men washed up on or near Galveston Island. Ultimately, only Cabeza de Vaca and three other men survived.

Cabeza de Vaca survived by adapting to his new surroundings. For six years, he lived with dozens of Native American groups in various roles—as a captive, a trader, and a well-known healer. In 1534, the four survivors escaped, setting out across the desert in search of New Spain. In 1536, they finally reached their goal. A year later, Cabeza de Vaca returned to Spain, where he wrote his account of the expedition, *La Relación* (The Account), as a report to the king.

Conqueror No More The king rewarded Cabeza de Vaca by appointing him governor of a South American colony, where his humane treatment of Native Americans may have cost him his job. By 1545, he had been ousted from his position and convicted on a corruption charge in Spain. Exiled to Africa, Cabeza de Vaca was eventually pardoned. In 1552, he returned to Spain to end his days as a judge.

Author Online
Go to thinkcentral.com. KEYWORD: HML11-72

TEXT ANALYSIS: HISTORICAL CONTEXT

When you read historical works, you may notice statements that seem strange or even offensive. These remarks might be a reflection of the work's **historical context**—the ideas and details from the author's time that influence the written work.

It was amazing to see these wild, untaught savages howling like brutes in compassion for us.

The author's statement reflects views about Indians that most people of his time shared. While his **purpose** was to communicate the experience of a life-threatening adventure, his account was shaped by the culture that shaped him. To familiarize yourself with the historical context of *La Relación*, read the author biography on page 72 and the background information on page 74. Then, as you read the work, note details that reflect this context.

READING STRATEGY: READING A PRIMARY SOURCE

Unlike a history book, *La Relación* is an eyewitness report. Such **primary sources** give us special insight into history. When using these sources, consider the intended audience, the author's role in events, and where and when the document was written.

As you read, complete a chart like the one shown. Consult the author biography and background information as needed.

Questions	*Answers*
What do I know about the author and his times?	
What details tell me about life in 16th-century North America?	
What is the relationship between the author and his audience?	
What is the author's role in the events he describes?	

VOCABULARY IN CONTEXT

The following words help bring this explorer's account to life. Choose a synonym for each word from the numbered terms.

WORD LIST			
	cauterize	ingratiate	locomotion
	embody	inundate	tarry

1. movement **3.** burn **5.** flood

2. personify **4.** seek favor **6.** delay

Complete the activities in your **Reader/Writer Notebook.**

What's the STORY *behind the* GLORY?

Dreams of wealth, glory, and conquest lured adventurers to the Americas, but few were prepared for the harsh reality that awaited them. For every hero who claimed a fortune, there were hundreds of others who died trying. Often, the greatest prize of all was living to tell the tale. What enabled some to survive while others failed?

DISCUSS In a small group, share stories you've read or heard that describe a person's struggle to survive in desperate circumstances, such as a shipwreck, war, or a natural disaster. Then make a list of traits that those people or characters exhibit. Decide what qualities seem essential in a survivor.

La Relación

Álvar Núñez Cabeza de Vaca

BACKGROUND In the 1500s, Spanish conquistadors took to the seas to claim new land for Spain. Seeking gold and silver, they explored unfamiliar territory and encountered Native American cultures they did not understand. By the time Cabeza de Vaca sailed, Spaniards had conquered the Aztecs of Mexico and the Inca of Peru, two of the most advanced civilizations in the Americas. Millions of Native Americans would die in this often brutal cultural encounter. In *La Relación,* Cabeza de Vaca finds himself unexpectedly at the mercy of the people he came to conquer.

At this point in the account, Narváez's barge has abandoned the rest, and Cabeza de Vaca's barge has joined one commanded by two other officers. The next three chapters describe the shipwreck of Cabeza de Vaca's barge on Galveston Island and the crew's encounter with the Karankawa Indians who lived there.

A Sinking and a Landing

Our two barges continued in company for four days, each man eating a ration of half a handful of raw corn a day. Then the other barge was lost in a storm. Nothing but God's great mercy kept us from going down, too.

It was winter and bitterly cold, and we had suffered hunger and the heavy beating of the waves for many days. Next day, the men began to collapse. By sunset, all in my barge had fallen over on one another, close to death. Few were any longer conscious. Not five could stand. When night fell, only the navigator and I remained able to tend the barge. Two hours after dark he told me I must take over; he believed he was going to die that night. **A**

So I took the tiller. After midnight I moved over to see if he were dead. He said no, in fact was better, and would steer till daylight. In that hour I would have welcomed death rather than see so many around me in such a condition. When I had returned the helm to the navigator, I lay down to rest—but without much rest, for nothing was farther from my mind than sleep.

Near dawn I seemed to hear breakers resounding; the coast lying low, they roared louder. Surprised at this, I called to the navigator, who said he thought we

Analyze Visuals ▶
What **details** in the image convey the desperate situation of the shipwrecked men?

A PRIMARY SOURCE
Describe the **tone** of lines 4–9. In what ways might the author's choice of tone be influenced by his intended **audience?**

Illustration by Tom McNeely.

were coming close to land. We sounded and found ourselves in seven fathoms.[1] The navigator felt we should stay clear of the shore till daylight; so I took an oar and pulled it on the shore side, wheeling the stern to seaward about a league[2] out. As we drifted into shore, a wave caught us and heaved the barge a horseshoe-throw [about 42 feet] out of the water. The jolt when it hit brought the dead-looking men to. Seeing land at hand, they crawled through the surf to some rocks. Here we made a fire and parched some of our corn. We also found rain water. The men began to regain their senses, their **locomotion,** and their hope.

locomotion (lō'kə-mō'shən) *n.* the power to move from place to place

This day of our landing was November 6.

What Befell Oviedo with the Indians

After we ate, I ordered Lope de Oviedo, our strongest man, to climb one of the trees not far off and ascertain the lay of the land. He complied and found out from the treetop that we were on an island. [This was Galveston Island.] He also said that the ground looked as if cattle had trampled it and therefore that this must be a country of Christians. **B**

B HISTORICAL CONTEXT
In the 1500s, "Christians" was used as a synonym for Europeans. What does this suggest about how the Spaniards saw the world? How does such a belief shape the author's purpose?

I sent him back for a closer look, to see if he could find any worn trails, but warned him not to risk going too far. He went and came upon a path which he followed for half a league to some empty huts. The Indians were gone to shoal-flats[3] [to dig roots]. He took an earthen pot, a little dog, and a few mullets[4] and started back.

We had begun to worry what might have happened to him, so I detailed another two men to check. They met him shortly and saw three Indians with bows and arrows following him. The Indians were calling to him and he was gesturing them to keep coming. When he reached us, the Indians held back and sat down on the shore.

Half an hour later a hundred bowmen reinforced the first three individuals. Whatever their stature, they looked like giants to us in our fright. We could not hope to defend ourselves; not half a dozen of us could even stand up.

The Inspector [Solís] and I walked out and greeted them. They advanced, and we did our best to placate and **ingratiate.** We gave them beads and bells, and each one of them gave us an arrow in pledge of friendship. They told us by signs that they would return at sunrise and bring food, having none then.

ingratiate (ĭn-grā'shē-āt') *v.* to gain another's favor by deliberate effort

The Indians' Hospitality Before and After a New Calamity

As the sun rose next morning, the Indians appeared as they promised, bringing an abundance of fish and of certain roots which taste like nuts, some bigger than walnuts, some smaller, mostly grubbed from the water with great labor.

That evening they came again with more fish and roots and brought their women and children to look at us. They thought themselves rich with the little bells and beads we gave them, and they repeated their visits on other days.

---

1. **We sounded . . . fathoms:** We measured the depth of the water and found it to be about 42 feet. (A fathom is equal to 6 feet, or 1.83 meters.)
2. **league:** a unit of distance; Cabeza de Vaca probably used the Spanish league, equal to 3.1 miles (5 kilometers).
3. **shoal-flats:** stretches of level ground under shallow water.
4. **mullets:** certain edible fish.

Being provided with what we needed, we thought to embark again. It was a struggle to dig our barge out of the sand it had sunk in, and another struggle to launch her. For the work in the water while launching, we stripped and stowed our clothes in the craft.

Quickly clambering in and grabbing our oars, we had rowed two crossbow shots from shore when a wave **inundated** us. Being naked and the cold intense, we let our oars go. The next big wave capsized the barge. The Inspector and two others held fast, but that only carried them more certainly underneath, where they drowned.

inundate (ĭn'ŭn-dāt') *v.* to cover with water; to overwhelm

A single roll of the sea tossed the rest of the men into the rushing surf and back onto shore half-drowned.

We lost only those the barge took down; but the survivors escaped as naked as they were born, with the loss of everything we had. That was not much, but valuable to us in that bitter November cold, our bodies so emaciated we could easily count every bone and looked the very picture of death. I can say for myself that from the month of May I had eaten nothing but corn, and that sometimes raw. I never could bring myself to eat any of the horse-meat at the time our beasts were slaughtered; and fish I did not taste ten times. On top of everything else, a cruel north wind commenced to complete our killing. C

C PRIMARY SOURCE
Reread lines 68–71. What does the author's reponse to his current situation tell you about his usual diet?

The Lord willed that we should find embers while searching the remnants of our former fire. We found more wood and soon had big fires raging. Before them, with flowing tears, we prayed for mercy and pardon, each filled with pity not only for himself but for all his wretched fellows.

At sunset the Indians, not knowing we had gone, came again with food. When they saw us looking so strangely different, they turned back in alarm. I went after them calling, and they returned, though frightened. I explained to them by signs that our barge had sunk and three of our number drowned. They could see at their feet two of the dead men who had washed ashore. They could also see that the rest of us were not far from joining these two.

The Indians, understanding our full plight, sat down and lamented for half an hour so loudly they could have been heard a long way off. It was amazing to see these wild, untaught savages howling like brutes in compassion for us. It intensified my own grief at our calamity and had the same effect on the other victims.

When the cries died down, I conferred with the Christians about asking the Indians to take us to their homes. Some of our number who had been to New Spain warned that the Indians would sacrifice us to their idols.[5] But death being surer and nearer if we stayed where we were, I went ahead and beseeched the Indians. They were delighted. They told us to **tarry** a little while, then they would do as we wished.

tarry (tăr'ē) *v.* to delay

Presently thirty of them gathered loads of wood and disappeared to their huts, which were a long walk away; while we waited with the remainder until near nightfall. Then, supporting us under our arms, they hurried us from one

5. **New Spain . . . their idols:** New Spain included what is now the southwest United States, Mexico, Central America north of Panama, and some West Indian islands. In Mexico, conquistadors had encountered Aztecs who practiced human sacrifice.

to another of the four big fires they had built along the path. At each fire, when we regained a little warmth and strength, they took us on so swiftly our feet hardly touched ground. D

Thus we made their village, where we saw they had erected a hut for us with many fires inside. An hour later they began a dance celebration that lasted all night. For us there was no joy, feasting, or sleep, as we waited the hour they should make us victims.

In the morning, when they brought us fish and roots and acted in every way hospitably, we felt reassured and somewhat lost our anxiety of the sacrificial knife.

D **GRAMMAR AND STYLE**
Reread lines 93–98. Note how the author uses **prepositional phrases,** such as "until near nightfall" and "along the path," to add important details about where and when events are happening.

Cabeza de Vaca learned that men from one of the other barges had also landed on the island, bringing the number of Europeans there to about 90. In a matter of weeks, all but 16 of them died of disease, which spread to the Karankawas and killed half of them as well. Some of the Karankawas wanted to put the remaining Europeans to death but were dissuaded by Cabeza de Vaca's host. Cabeza de Vaca and his men were later forced to act as healers.

How We Became Medicine-Men

The islanders wanted to make physicians of us without examination or a review of diplomas. Their method of cure is to blow on the sick, the breath and the laying-on of hands supposedly casting out the infirmity. They insisted we should do this too and be of some use to them. We scoffed at their cures and at the idea we knew how to heal. But they withheld food from us until we complied. An Indian told me I knew not whereof I spoke in saying their methods had no effect. Stones and other things growing about in the fields, he said, had a virtue whereby passing a pebble along the stomach could take away pain and heal; surely extraordinary men like us **embodied** such powers over nature. Hunger forced us to obey, but disclaiming any responsibility for our failure or success.

embody (ĕm-bŏd'ē) *v.* to represent in human form

An Indian, falling sick, would send for a medicine-man, who would apply his cure. The patient would then give the medicine-man all he had and seek more from his relatives to give. The medicine-man makes incisions over the point of the pain, sucks the wound, and **cauterizes** it. This remedy enjoys high repute among the Indians. I have, as a matter of fact, tried it on myself with good results. The medicine-men blow on the spot they have treated, as a finishing touch, and the patient regards himself relieved.

cauterize (kô'tə-rīz') *v.* to burn or sear to destroy diseased tissue

Our method, however, was to bless the sick, breathe upon them, recite a *Pater noster* and *Ave Maria,*[6] and pray earnestly to God our Lord for their recovery. When we concluded with the sign of the cross, He willed that our patients should directly spread the news that they had been restored to health. E

In consequence, the Indians treated us kindly. They deprived themselves of food to give to us, and presented us skins and other tokens of gratitude.

Translated by Cyclone Covey

E **HISTORICAL CONTEXT**
In Cabeza de Vaca's time, no one had good knowledge of what caused disease. Reread lines 105–125. In what ways did the Spanish and the Karankawas have similiar ideas about healing?

---

6. ***Pater noster*** (pä'tər nŏs'tər) **and *Ave Maria*** (ä'vā mə-rē'ə): the Lord's Prayer ("Our Father") and the Hail Mary, named for the prayers' opening words in Latin.

Comprehension

1. **Summarize** What was life like for the Spaniards on the barges?
2. **Recall** What happened to Cabeza de Vaca's men when they tried to leave Galveston Island?
3. **Clarify** Why did the Karankawas enlist the Spaniards as healers?

Text Analysis

4. **Make Inferences** Based on the events and reactions Cabeza de Vaca describes, what appears to be the Karankawas' view of the Spaniards? Cite details to support your answer.
5. **Evaluate a Primary Source** Review the information you collected about *La Relación* as you read. In what ways would you consider this account a valuable and reliable source of information? What are its shortcomings? Explain your conclusions.
6. **Make Generalizations About Historical Context** To understand the historical context of a work, you need to consult sources outside of the work for information. Identify three passages from *La Relación* that reflect ideas, values, or events from the author's time. Then, using the footnotes to the text and the background information on page 74 as sources, explain the historical context of each example. Based on your results, what generalizations can you make about 16th-century Spanish perspectives? Create a chart to organize your notes.

Examples from Text	*Information from Other Sources*
• • •	• • •
Generalizations About Historical Context • • •	

Text Criticism

7. **Biographical Context** Later in life, Cabeza de Vaca spoke out against the enslavement of Native Americans. How might his experiences as a captive, trader, and healer among the Karankawas and other groups have influenced his position? Explain your answer, citing evidence from the text.

What's the STORY *behind the* GLORY?

What qualities of a hero and survivor does Cabeza de Vaca demonstrate in this selection? Support your answer with evidence from the landing on Galveston Island and from the narrator's encounters with the Karankawas.

COMMON CORE

RI 1 Cite textual evidence to support analysis of what the text says explicitly as well as inferences drawn from the text, including determining where the text leaves matters uncertain. **RI 6** Determine an author's point of view or purpose in a text. **RI 9** Analyze foundational U.S. documents of historical and literary significance for their themes, purposes, and rhetorical features.

Vocabulary in Context

▲ VOCABULARY PRACTICE

Choose the word that is not related in meaning to the other words.

1. (a) transit, (b) locomotion, (c) movement, (d) connection
2. (a) inane, (b) incompetent, (c) ingratiate, (d) inept
3. (a) deluge, (b) inundate, (c) wind, (d) overwhelm
4. (a) cauterize, (b) sear, (c) singe, (d) weep
5. (a) obtain, (b) dawdle, (c) tarry, (d) linger
6. (a) embody, (b) personify, (c) actualize, (d) construct

WORD LIST

cauterize
embody
ingratiate
inundate
locomotion
tarry

ACADEMIC VOCABULARY IN WRITING

• document • illustrate • interpret • promote • reveal

What cultural biases about Native Americans does Cabeza de Vaca **reveal** in this selection? **Document** your answer with evidence from the text. Try to use at least three of the Academic Vocabulary words as you write.

VOCABULARY STRATEGY: ETYMOLOGIES

Many English words have intriguing histories, or **etymologies.** The etymology of a word, or its origin and history, can provide insight into the word's meaning. Standard dictionaries, as well as etymological dictionaries, are excellent sources of word histories. Information about a word's etymology will often appear near the beginning or end of a dictionary entry, as in the following example:

> **cau•ter•ize** (kô′tə-rīz′) *tr.v.* **-ized, -iz•ing, -iz•es 1.** To burn or sear with a cautery. **2.** To deaden, as to feelings or moral scruples. [Middle English *cauterizen,* from Late Latin *cauterizare,* to cauterize, brand, from Latin *cauterium,* cautery.] **—cau•ter•i•za•tion** (-tər-ĭ-zā′shən) *n.*

COMMON CORE

L 4c Consult general and specialized reference materials, both print and digital, to determine or clarify a word's etymology. **L 6** Acquire and use accurately general and domain-specific words.

PRACTICE Consult a print or online dictionary to answer these questions.

1. From what language did *oratorio* enter English?
2. From which Greek word is *cynosure* derived? What is the word's current meaning?
3. What is the origin of the word *malaprop?*
4. Through which languages can the history of *querulous* be traced?

Language

◆ **GRAMMAR AND STYLE: Add Necessary Details**

Review the **Grammar and Style** note on page 78. Cabeza de Vaca uses numerous details throughout his account to help readers visualize his amazing journey. **Prepositional phrases** include details about what happens, as well as where, when, and how. Read this example from *La Relación:*

> *A single roll of the sea tossed the rest of the men into the rushing surf and back onto shore half-drowned.* (lines 63–64)

PRACTICE Rewrite each sentence, adding prepositional phrases that modify the boldfaced words. Follow the directions in parentheses. An example has been done for you.

> **EXAMPLE**
>
> The barges, filled with half-starved men, **drifted** for days. (Tell where they drifted.)
>
> *The barges, filled with half-starved men, drifted on the stormy seas for days.*

1. They told us they **would return** and bring us food. (Tell when they will return.)
2. We **traveled** through the woods to the **village.** (Add two phrases. Tell how long they traveled and where the village was located.)
3. We waited anxiously for **news.** (Tell what kind of news was expected.)

READING-WRITING CONNECTION

Expand your understanding of these excerpts from *La Relación* by responding to this prompt. Then use the **revising tips** to improve your journal entry.

WRITING PROMPT

EXPLORER'S ACCOUNT Explorers often keep journals of their experiences. These accounts—from the writings of Lewis and Clark to the reports of a modern astronaut—describe what the explorers see and how they are changed by their experiences.

Write a **two-to-four-paragraph journal entry** describing an interesting moment in an exploration. The journey can be real or fictional—a trip to a new town or galaxy, a trek across the desert, or the race to a new invention. Be sure to share your reactions to it.

REVISING TIPS

- Write in the first person, using the pronouns *I* and *me*.
- Clearly recount a specific event or moment in the narrator's exploration.
- Concentrate on action and momentum.
- Vividly describe surroundings, people, or events influencing the moment.
- Show the narrator's reactions to the events.

COMMON CORE

L 3 Apply knowledge of language to make effective choices for meaning or style. **L 3a** Vary syntax for effect. **W 3** Write narratives to develop real or imagined experiences or events using effective technique, well-chosen details, and well-structured event sequences. **W 3a, d** Engage and orient the reader by setting out a situation and its significance, establishing one point of view, and introducing a narrator and/or characters; use precise words and phrases, telling details, and sensory language to convey a vivid picture.

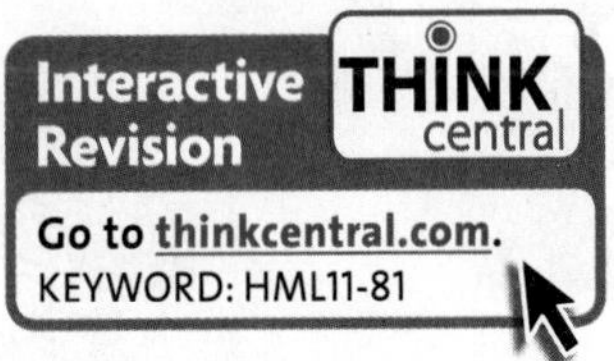

from The Interesting Narrative of the Life of Olaudah Equiano

Slave Narrative by Olaudah Equiano

HISTORY Video link at thinkcentral.com

COMMON CORE

RI 1 Cite textual evidence to support analysis of what the text says explicitly. **RI 3** Analyze a complex set of ideas or sequence of events and explain how specific individuals, ideas, or events interact and develop over the course of the text. **RI 5** Analyze and evaluate the effectiveness of the structure an author uses in his or her exposition or argument, including whether the structure makes points clear, convincing, and engaging. **L 2b** Spell correctly.

Meet the Author

Olaudah Equiano c. 1745–1797

Soldier, sailor, North Pole explorer—Olaudah Equiano led a remarkable life by the standards of any age. Writing as a former slave in the 1700s, Equiano left powerful testimony on the brutality of enslavement that became the model for a new genre, the slave narrative.

Ocean Crossings According to his autobiography, Equiano was born a chief's son in the Ibo (or Igbo) culture of present-day Nigeria. When he was 11, he was captured and sold as a slave to a series of African masters before making the miserable journey to the Americas known as the Middle Passage. Sold in the West Indies to British navy officer Michael Pascal, Equiano returned to sea with his new owner, who renamed him Gustavus Vassa.

Equiano spent years fighting for Britain, hoping to be freed for good service. Instead, in 1762 he was sold again, to Quaker merchant Robert King, who trained him in business. In 1766, after 21 years as a slave, Equiano bought back his freedom, moved to London, and promptly launched his business career. But by 1773, he was at sea again, first on an expedition to find a northwest passage, and later traveling to Central America and Turkey.

Turning Points In the late 1770s, Equiano returned to London where he got involved in antislavery efforts and converted to Christianity. In 1789, as public debate over abolishing the slave trade began in Britain, Equiano wrote, self-published, and promoted his narrative. Equiano's life story exposed the cruelty of the slave trade and made him an important public figure. He died in 1797, just ten years before Britain abolished the slave trade.

Historians Look More Closely Equiano's narrative includes a wealth of specific details, most of which check out against other sources. But, in 1999, English professor Vincent Carretta uncovered two documents that suggested Equiano was not born in Africa: his baptismal record from England and a ship's passenger list, both of which identify Equiano's birthplace as South Carolina. Historians continue to debate the evidence and how, if at all, it changes the value of *The Interesting Narrative.* Carretta himself points out that even if the narrative is based on the oral accounts of other slaves, its descriptions still provide a valuable portrait of early African life and the Middle Passage.

THINK central

Author Online

Go to thinkcentral.com. KEYWORD: HML11-82

DID YOU KNOW?

Olaudah Equiano . . .

- was a best-selling author in Britain.
- owned slaves in Central America.
- married an English woman and raised two daughters.
- died a wealthy man.

(background) Diagram of the cargo hold of a fully loaded slave ship

TEXT ANALYSIS: SLAVE NARRATIVE

Slave narratives, the life stories of people who survived slavery, help us understand the grim realities of this experience.

Olaudah Equiano wrote *The Interesting Narrative* at a time when many Africans remembered their lives before enslavement. Like other 18th-century slave narratives, his work

- portrays the culture shock of a newly captured African
- focuses criticism on slave traders, not slave owners
- includes religious and moral appeals against slavery

As you read, notice the author's purposeful use of language to both narrate and persuade .

READING SKILL: ANALYZE DETAILS

Equiano's readers had little contact with slavery. He chose powerful **descriptive details** to bring the experience to life.

The closeness of the place, and the heat of the climate, added to the number in the ship, which was so crowded that each had scarcely room to turn himself, almost suffocated us.

To reach his readers, Equiano uses

- **sensory details,** ones that appeal to the five senses
- descriptions of his own reactions
- **anecdotes,** brief stories that support his points

As you read, use a chart like the one shown to record effective examples of each kind of detail.

Sensory Details	Reactions	Anecdotes

VOCABULARY IN CONTEXT

Equiano used the following words in his argument against slavery. Restate each phrase, using a different word or words for the boldfaced term.

1. **copious** amounts of rain, causing a flood
2. the **nominal** boss, but with no real authority
3. her **countenance** betraying her fear
4. cruel rulers acting without worry or **scruple**
5. to our **consternation,** revealed all our plans
6. deadly effects of **pestilential** beetles

Complete the activities in your **Reader/Writer Notebook**.

What does it mean to be a SLAVE?

From the 1500s to the 1800s, millions of Africans were enslaved to work in the Americas. Their experiences have been documented in books and portrayed in films. What do you know about the realities of slavery?

TEST YOURSELF Decide whether each statement is true or false. Think about the facts or impressions that helped you choose your answer.

SLAVERY: *Fact or Fiction*

1. Slavery was a common practice in Africa.
   ☐ TRUE ○ FALSE
2. No Africans participated willingly in the slave trade.
   ☐ TRUE ○ FALSE
3. Most enslaved Africans were brought to North America.
   ☐ TRUE ○ FALSE
4. Captured Africans were packed like cargo into slave ships.
   ☐ TRUE ○ FALSE
5. Slave traders typically sold families as a single group.
   ☐ TRUE ○ FALSE

The Interesting Narrative of the Life of Olaudah Equiano

Olaudah Equiano

BACKGROUND As European colonies in the Americas expanded, so did the slave trade. Slaves were captured in Africa, then taken by ship to the West Indies—a journey called the Middle Passage. For two months, Africans lay tightly chained in storage compartments with hardly enough air to breathe. Millions died from bad food, harsh treatment, disease, and despair. Olaudah Equiano is one of the few to describe this horrific journey.

When Olaudah Equiano was 11 years old, he and his sister were kidnapped while the adults in his village were working in the fields. After being forced to travel for several days, Equiano and his sister were separated. For the next six or seven months, Equiano was sold several times to African masters in different countries. He was eventually taken to the west coast of Africa and carried aboard a slave ship bound for the West Indies.

The first object which saluted my eyes when I arrived on the coast, was the sea, and a slave ship, which was then riding at anchor, and waiting for its cargo. These filled me with astonishment, which was soon converted into terror, when I was carried on board. I was immediately handled, and tossed up to see if I were sound, by some of the crew; and I was now persuaded that I had gotten into a world of bad spirits, and that they were going to kill me. Their complexions, too, differing so much from ours, their long hair, and the language they spoke (which was very different from any I had ever heard), united to confirm me in this belief. (A) Indeed, such were the horrors of my views and fears at the moment, that, if ten thousand worlds had been my own, I would have freely parted with them all to

Analyze Visuals ▶
Describe the mood of this painting. What does the image reveal about the conditions on board a slave ship?

(A) SLAVE NARRATIVE
Note Equiano's use of **first-person point of view** in lines 1–8. In what ways might this description be startling to Equiano's mostly European audience?

Detail of *The Slave Ship* (1956), Robert Riggs. N.A. Courtesy of Les Mansfield, Cincinnati, Ohio.

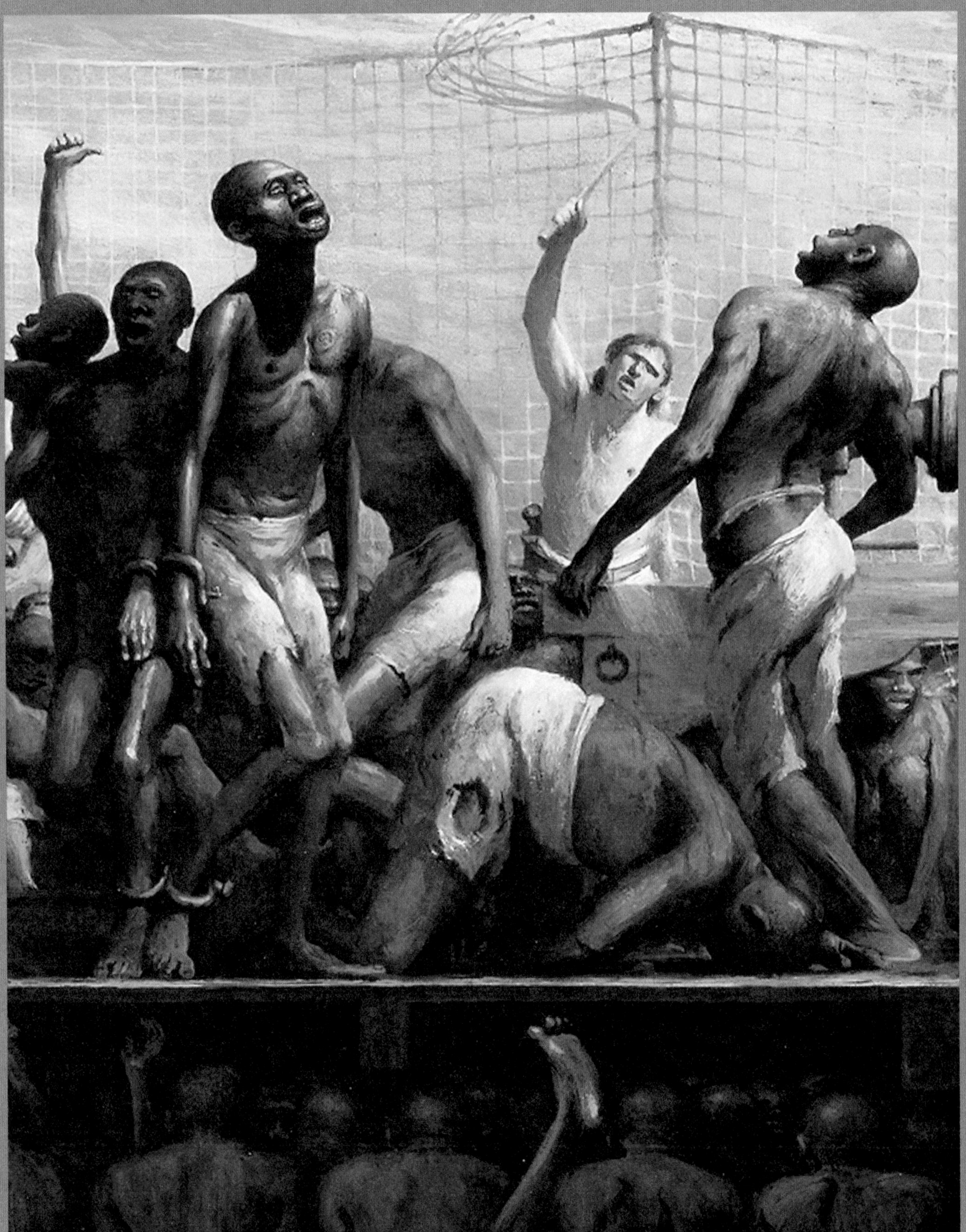

have exchanged my condition with that of the meanest slave[1] in my own country. When I looked round the ship too, and saw a large furnace of copper boiling, and a multitude of black people of every description chained together, every one of their **countenances** expressing dejection and sorrow, I no longer doubted of my fate; and, quite overpowered with horror and anguish, I fell motionless on the deck and fainted. When I recovered a little, I found some black people about me, who I believed were some of those who had brought me on board, and had been receiving their pay; they talked to me in order to cheer me, but all in vain. I asked them if we were not to be eaten by those white men with horrible looks, red faces, and long hair. They told me I was not, and one of the crew brought me a small portion of spirituous liquor in a wine glass; but, being afraid of him, I would not take it out of his hand. One of the blacks, therefore, took it from him and gave it to me, and I took a little down my palate, which, instead of reviving me, as they thought it would, threw me into the greatest **consternation** at the strange feeling it produced, having never tasted any such liquor before. Soon after this, the blacks who brought me on board went off, and left me abandoned to despair. **B**

I now saw myself deprived of all chance of returning to my native country, or even the least glimpse of hope of gaining the shore, which I now considered as friendly; and I even wished for my former slavery in preference to my present situation, which was filled with horrors of every kind, still heightened by my ignorance of what I was to undergo. I was not long suffered to indulge my grief; I was soon put down under the decks, and there I received such a salutation in my nostrils as I had never experienced in my life; so that, with the loathsomeness of the stench, and crying together, I became so sick and low that I was not able to eat, nor had I the least desire to taste anything. I now wished for the last friend, death, to relieve me; but soon, to my grief, two of the white men offered me eatables; and, on my refusing to eat, one of them held me fast by the hands, and laid me across, I think, the windlass,[2] and tied my feet, while the other flogged[3] me severely. I had never experienced anything of this kind before, and, although not being used to the water, I naturally feared that element the first time I saw it, yet, nevertheless, could I have got over the nettings,[4] I would have jumped over the side, but I could not; and besides, the crew used to watch us very closely who were not chained down to the decks, lest we should leap into the water; and I have seen some of these poor African prisoners most severely cut, for attempting to do so, and hourly whipped for not eating. This indeed was often the case with myself. In a little time after, amongst the poor chained men, I found some of my own nation, which in a small degree gave ease to my mind. I inquired of these what was to be done with us? They gave me to understand, we were to be carried to these white people's country to work for them. I then was a little revived, and thought, if it were no worse than working, my situation was not so desperate; but still I feared

countenance
(koun'tə-nəns) *n.*
appearance, especially the expression of the face

consternation
(kŏn'stər-nā'shən) *n.*
a state of paralyzing dismay; fear

B ANALYZE DETAILS
Reread lines 1–26. What details reinforce Equiano's impression that he has been captured by bad spirits?

THEME AND GENRE
A common theme in literature is the struggle to overcome adversity. Autobiographical narratives like Equiano's have influenced explorations of this theme in the context of race and slavery in films like *Amistad* (1997) and in *Roots* (1976), the groundbreaking novel and TV miniseries. Why do you think this theme of triumph over adversity is so universally appealing to modern audiences?

1. **the meanest slave:** the poorest or most wretched slave.
2. **windlass** (wĭnd'ləs): a device for raising and lowering a ship's anchor.
3. **flogged:** beat with a whip or rod.
4. **nettings:** networks of small ropes on the sides of a ship that were used for various purposes, such as stowing sails. On slave ships, the nettings helped keep the slaves from jumping overboard.

I should be put to death, the white people looked and acted, as I thought, in so savage a manner; for I had never seen among any people such instances of brutal cruelty; and this not only shown towards us blacks, but also to some of the whites themselves. One white man in particular I saw, when we were permitted to be on deck, flogged so unmercifully with a large rope near the foremast,[5] that he died in consequence of it; and they tossed him over the side as they would have done a brute. This made me fear these people the more; and I expected nothing less **C** than to be treated in the same manner. I could not help expressing my fears and apprehensions to some of my countrymen; I asked them if these people had no country, but lived in this hollow place (the ship)? They told me they did not, but came from a distant one. "Then," said I, "how comes it in all our country we never heard of them?" They told me because they lived so very far off. I then asked where were their women? had they any like themselves? I was told they had. "And why," said I, "do we not see them?" They answered, because they were left behind. I asked how the vessel could go? They told me they could not tell; but that there was cloth put upon the masts by the help of the ropes I saw, and then the vessel went on; and the white men had some spell or magic they put in the water when they liked, in order to stop the vessel. I was exceedingly amazed at this account, and really thought they were spirits. I therefore wished much to be from amongst them, for I expected they would sacrifice me; but my wishes were vain—for we were so quartered that it was impossible for any of us to make our escape. . . . **D**

At last, when the ship we were in, had got in all her cargo, they made ready with many fearful noises, and we were all put under deck, so that we could not see how they managed the vessel. But this disappointment was the least of my sorrow. The stench of the hold while we were on the coast was so intolerably loathsome, that it was dangerous to remain there for any time, and some of us had been permitted to stay on the deck for the fresh air; but now that the whole ship's cargo were confined together, it became absolutely **pestilential.** The closeness of the place, and the heat of the climate, added to the number in the ship, which was so crowded that each had scarcely room to turn himself, almost suffocated us. This produced **copious** perspirations, so that the air soon became unfit for respiration, from a variety of loathsome smells, and brought on a sickness among the slaves, of which many died. . . . This wretched situation was again aggravated by the galling[6] of the chains. . . . The shrieks of the women, and the groans of the dying, rendered the whole a scene of horror almost inconceivable. Happily perhaps, for myself, I was soon reduced so low here that it was thought necessary to keep me almost always on deck; and from my extreme youth I was not put in fetters. In this situation I expected every hour to share the fate of my companions, some of whom were almost daily brought upon deck at the point of death, which I began to hope would soon put an end to my miseries. . . . **E**

One day they had taken a number of fishes; and when they had killed and satisfied themselves with as many as they thought fit, to our astonishment who

C GRAMMAR AND STYLE
Reread lines 54–57. Note how Equiano uses **adverb clauses,** such as "when we were permitted to be on deck," to modify verbs and adverbs in the sentence.

D SLAVE NARRATIVE
Look back at lines 48–54. What does Equiano's reaction reveal about the way he regards slavery?

pestilential (pĕs'tə-lĕn'shəl) *adj.* deadly; poisonous

copious (kō'pē-əs) *adj.* in large amounts; abundant

E ANALYZE DETAILS
What details in lines 75–85 does Equiano use to describe conditions below deck? What kind of image do these details create? Support your answer with evidence from these lines.

5. **foremast** (fôr'məst): the mast (tall pole that supports sails and rigging) nearest the forward end of a sailing ship.
6. **galling:** rubbing or chafing, enough to produce sores.

were on deck, rather than give any of them to us to eat, as we expected, they tossed the remaining fish into the sea again, although we begged and prayed for some as well as we could, but in vain; and some of my countrymen, being pressed by hunger, took an opportunity, when they thought no one saw them, of trying to get a little privately; but they were discovered, and the attempt procured them some very severe floggings. One day, when we had a smooth sea and moderate wind, two of my wearied countrymen who were chained together (I was near them at the time), preferring death to such a life of misery, somehow made through the nettings and jumped into the sea; immediately, another quite dejected fellow, who, on account of his illness, was suffered to be out of irons, also followed their example; and I believe many more would very soon have done the same, if they had not been prevented by the ship's crew, who were instantly alarmed. . . .

COMMON CORE L 2b

Language Coach

English Spelling In *prayed* (line 94) and *wearied* (line 99), *-ed* is added to a word ending in *y* (*pray* and *weary*). *Prayed* keeps the *y*, because a vowel comes before *y*. For *weary*, the *y* is changed to an *i*. How would you spell *supply* + *-ed* or employ + *-ed*?

During the rest of his voyage to the West Indies, Equiano continued to endure hardships. After the ship anchored on the coast of Barbados, Equiano and the other slaves were brought ashore and herded together in a slave merchant's yard to be sold.

We were not many days in the merchant's custody, before we were sold after their usual manner, which is this: On a signal given (as the beat of a drum), the buyers rush at once into the yard where the slaves are confined, and make choice of that parcel[7] they like best. The noise and clamor with which this is attended, and the eagerness visible in the countenances of the buyers, serve not a little to increase the apprehension of terrified Africans, who may well be supposed to consider them as the ministers of that destruction to which they think themselves devoted. In this manner, without **scruple,** are relations and friends separated, most of them never to see each other again. I remember, in the vessel in which I was brought over, in the men's apartment, there were several brothers, who, in the sale, were sold in different lots; and it was very moving on this occasion, to see and hear their cries at parting. O, ye **nominal** Christians! might not an African ask you—Learned you this from your God, who says unto you, Do unto all men as you would men should do unto you? Is it not enough that we are torn from our country and friends, to toil for your luxury and lust of gain? Must every tender feeling be likewise sacrificed to your avarice? Are the dearest friends and relations now rendered more dear by their separation from their kindred, still to be parted from each other, and thus prevented from cheering the gloom of slavery, with the small comfort of being together, and mingling their sufferings and sorrows? Why are parents to lose their children, brothers their sisters, or husbands their wives? Surely, this is a new refinement in cruelty, which . . . thus aggravates distress, and adds fresh horrors even to the wretchedness of slavery. ~ F

scruple (skro͞o'pəl) *n.* feeling of uneasiness or guilt that keeps a person from doing something

nominal (nŏm'ə-nəl) *adj.* in name but not in reality

F SLAVE NARRATIVE
What point is Equiano making in lines 116–118? To what emotions is he appealing?

7. **parcel:** a group of slaves offered for sale as one "package."

Comprehension

1. **Recall** Who has brought Equiano to the slave ship?
2. **Recall** What does Equiano think will happen to him when he is brought on board ship?
3. **Clarify** What does Equiano mean when he refers to "nominal Christians"?

Text Analysis

4. **Analyze Descriptive Details** Review the chart you made while reading. Identify the details that had the strongest impact on you as a reader. Why were those details so effective?
5. **Compare and Contrast** Like Cabeza de Vaca, Equiano describes a journey to the Americas. In what ways does his narrative resemble *La Relación?* Identify at least two similarities and two differences.
6. **Synthesize Information** Review your answers to the quiz about **slavery** that you took before reading Equiano's narrative. What facts or details in his account most surprised you? Correct your quiz answers to reflect what you learned.
7. **Evaluate a Slave Narrative** Some historians have questioned whether Equiano's narrative is authentic. Read the information on this debate in the author's biography on page 82. Based on the issues raised, what you have learned about slave narratives, and your own reading, make an argument for or against the historical value of Equiano's account. Support your answer with details.

Text Criticism

8. **Biographical Context** In 1775, just 14 years before writing his life story, Equiano bought slaves to work on his Central American plantation. He explained his actions by saying he did what he could "to comfort the poor creatures, and render their condition easy." Do you find this explanation consistent with the views of slavery put forth in *The Interesting Narrative?* Cite evidence from the text to support your answer.

What does it mean to be a **SLAVE?**

How does this personal account add to your understanding of slavery? Cite details from the text to support your response.

COMMON CORE

RI 1 Cite textual evidence to support analysis of what the text says explicitly. **RI 3** Analyze a complex set of ideas or sequence of events and explain how specific individuals, ideas, or events interact and develop over the course of the text. **RI 5** Analyze and evaluate the effectiveness of the structure an author uses in his or her exposition or argument, including whether the structure makes points clear, convincing, and engaging.

Vocabulary in Context

▲ VOCABULARY PRACTICE

Choose the letter of the phrase that defines or is related to the boldfaced word.

1. **countenance:** (a) a sad expression, (b) a well-toned body, (c) a cash register
2. **consternation:** (a) a freight ship, (b) a serious accident, (c) a peace treaty
3. **copious:** (a) a nest of baby birds, (b) a xerographic machine, (c) a 20-inch snowfall
4. **pestilential:** (a) a contagious disease, (b) a cooking implement, (c) a vegetarian meal
5. **scruple:** (a) an attack of conscience, (b) a two-handed card game, (c) a ruffle on a skirt
6. **nominal:** (a) a stretch limousine, (b) a word derived from a foreign language, (c) a leader with no real power

WORD LIST

consternation
copious
countenance
nominal
pestilential
scruple

ACADEMIC VOCABULARY IN SPEAKING

• document • illustrate • interpret • promote • reveal

Olaudah Equiano's narrative serves as an eloquent **document** on the inhumanity of slavery. With a small group of your peers, discuss the details of this narrative that most forcefully **illustrate** what slavery was like. Use at least one of the Academic Vocabulary words in your contribution to the discussion.

VOCABULARY STRATEGY: SPANISH COGNATES

Many words in the English language are related to words in other languages by descent from a common language. When these words have identical or similar spellings and meanings, they are called **cognates.** For example, the English word "accident" has the same meaning as "accidente" in Spanish. You can use your knowledge of cognates to determine the meaning of unfamiliar words.

COMMON CORE

L 4d Verify the preliminary determination of the meaning of a word.

PRACTICE Choose the Spanish cognate that you think completes the meaning of each sentence. Then write the word as it is spelled in English. Verify your answers by consulting a print or online dictionary.

• categoria • eficiente • secreto • estudiante • opportunidad

1. I would like the _____ to attend college in another state.
2. The national hurricane center assigns a number to a hurricane to identify its_____ .
3. My parents want me to be a good ____.
4. It is important to be _____ in your work.

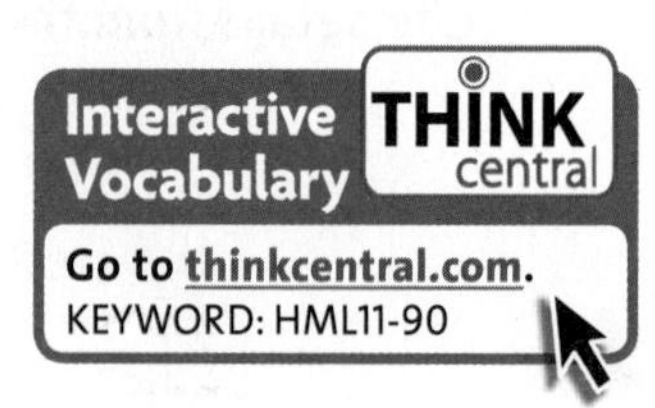

Interactive Vocabulary
THINK central
Go to thinkcentral.com.
KEYWORD: HML11-90

Language

COMMON CORE

L 3 Apply knowledge of language to make effective choices for meaning or style. **L 3a** Vary syntax for effect. **W 3** Write narratives to develop real or imagined experiences or events using effective technique, well-chosen details, and well-structured event sequences. **W 3a, d** Engage and orient the reader by setting out a situation and its significance, establishing one point of view; create a smooth progression of experiences or events; use precise words and phrases, telling details, and sensory language to convey a vivid picture.

GRAMMAR AND STYLE: Add Descriptive Details

Review the **Grammar and Style** note on page 87. Equiano uses elaborate and richly detailed sentences to describe his experiences. Some of the details are contained in **adverb clauses,** as in this example:

> *These filled me with astonishment, which was soon converted into terror, when I was carried on board.* (lines 2–4)

In this sentence, the adverb clause modifies *filled,* describing when the action occurred. Adverb clauses also help answer the questions *where, why, how,* or *to what degree.* Like other **subordinate clauses,** adverb clauses include a subject and a predicate, but they cannot stand alone as independent sentences. They are often introduced with words such as *as if, because, since, so that, until, while, when,* or *where.*

PRACTICE Add adverb clauses to the following sentences to modify the boldfaced words, as instructed in parentheses. A sample answer has been done for you.

EXAMPLE

He **saw** the ship for the first time. (Tell when he saw it.)

He saw the ship for the first time when he arrived at the harbor.

1. The men on the ship **had been captured.** (Tell why they were captured.)
2. The prisoners **were kept** in the ship's hold. (Tell how long they were kept there.)
3. Many slaves **became** ill. (Add two details. Tell why and when the slaves became ill.)

READING-WRITING CONNECTION

Expand your understanding of these excerpts from Equiano's narrative. Then use the **revising tips** to improve your journal entry.

WRITING PROMPT	REVISING TIPS
WRITE A PERSONAL ACCOUNT Equiano uses details to provide powerful first-person testimony. Choose an experience or a scene you want to describe. Write a **one-page account** to communicate the power of the experience. Include vivid details.	• Write in the first person, using the pronouns *I* or *me.* • Rely on vivid sensory details to capture the experience. • Describe the emotional impact of the experience. • Use adverbs to relate the sequence of events.

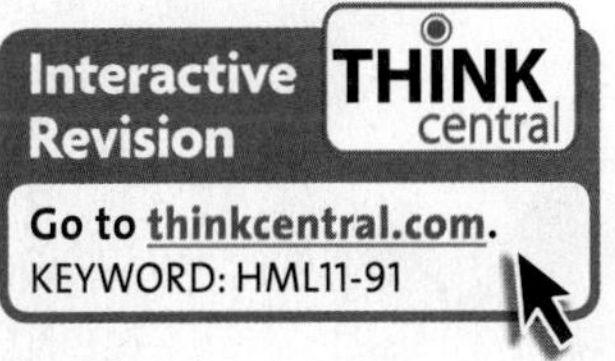

COMMON CORE

RI 4 Determine the meaning of words and phrases as they are used in a text, including technical meanings. **RI 5** Analyze and evaluate the effectiveness of the structure an author uses in his or her exposition, including whether the structure makes points clear, convincing, and engaging. **RI 6** Determine an author's point of view or purpose in a text in which the rhetoric is particularly effective. **RI 10** Read and comprehend literary nonfiction. **L 3a** Apply an understanding of syntax to the study of complex texts when reading.

from The General History of Virginia

Historical Narrative by John Smith

HISTORY Video link at thinkcentral.com

Meet the Author

John Smith c. 1580–1631

The author of one of the earliest works of American literature continues to inspire widely varied reactions among historians. Called a boastful bully by some and an early American hero by others, John Smith created a legend around himself that lasts to this day.

Great Adventures At age 16, Smith left England to become a soldier for hire and occasional pirate. In 1605, after traveling to Austria, Turkey, and North Africa, he returned to England. Smith's military experience made him a good leader in the eyes of the Virginia Company, the group of investors hoping for huge profits from their New World venture. They hired him to help run the Jamestown colony, where he arrived in 1607.

Struggles for Control Conflicts broke out in Jamestown almost immediately. The first president died and the next two were deposed; colonists mutinied and deserted the colony, living in the nearby woods. Smith took control of the colony in 1608. As he tells it, he focused on survival—safety, shelter, and food—and led forcefully, pushing settlers of all social levels to work as hard as he did. History tells us a slightly different story: Smith was nearly executed for the deaths of two colonists on an expedition he led. It also tells us, however, that Jamestown thrived under his command and fell into greed, chaos, and starvation after his departure in 1610.

Fact or Fiction? Shortly after arriving in Virginia, John Smith was captured by the Powhatan Indians. Smith writes several times of his 1607 capture and of being brought before the tribe's leader, Powhatan. Only in the final version, the 1624 *General History of Virginia,* does Smith mention his rescue by Powhatan's daughter Pocahontas, who would have been ten years old at the time. The story may have been an attempt by Smith to cash in on Pocahontas's later fame: she had visited England in 1616 and become a celebrity.

In the meantime, Smith had fallen on hard times. After one early success, his attempts to colonize New England were dismal failures. Smith wanted to prove that hard work was the smartest way to develop a colony, but he never got his chance. He made his living from tales of his adventurous life and died unemployed in London in 1631.

DID YOU KNOW?

John Smith . . .

- coined the name "New England."
- offered to accompany the Pilgrims—who chose Miles Standish instead.
- wrote a how-to manual on establishing colonies.
- left the Jamestown colony after two years and never went back.

THINK central
Author Online
Go to thinkcentral.com. KEYWORD: HML11-92

TEXT ANALYSIS: NARRATOR

A **narrator** is the voice that tells a story. The voice an author chooses shapes the way readers perceive the events described. Most nonfiction authors write about themselves in the **first person.** John Smith writes about himself mostly in the **third person,** using a voice that sounds like an objective observer.

As you read, notice how Smith uses the narrator to portray himself and his role in events. Consider how the third-person point of view affects your perceptions of the account.

READING STRATEGY: READING OLDER TEXTS

Reading centuries-old texts can be challenging. Use these strategies as you read this selection:

- Simplify difficult **syntax** (word order) by paraphrasing. For a difficult sentence, first establish who is doing what. Then sort out the meaning in the phrases and clauses.
- Use footnotes or side notes to translate **archaic expressions,** words, and phrases no longer in use.
- Note the many contrasts between the historical map on page 95 and the features of current maps. These differences can help you to appreciate the challenges of Smith's text.

In this case, your purpose for reading is to make sense of the conflicts among the Jamestown colonists. Use a chart like the one shown to take notes about these key individuals.

Individuals	*Connection to Smith*	*Actions*
President Wingfield		
Captain Kendall		
Robinson and Emry		
George Cassen		

VOCABULARY IN CONTEXT

Choose words from the list to complete the phrases below.

WORD LIST	depose	industry	mollify
	entreaty	interim	

1. a corrupt leader whom they voted to _______
2. a peacemaker trying to _____ the unruly crowd
3. a desperate _____ for our assistance
4. admired by coworkers for her _______

Complete the activities in your **Reader/Writer Notebook**.

What makes a LEADER?

In some societies, like 17th-century Britain, leaders were chosen on the basis of their social status. But men used to luxury and privilege didn't thrive in the Jamestown colony, where hard work and scarce supplies were facts of daily life. In this context, where leaders needed common sense and determination to succeed, a new standard of leadership emerged.

DISCUSS Working with a small group, brainstorm examples of strong leaders who demonstrate different leadership styles. Use your examples to debate the pros and cons of each style. Is any one style best in all situations?

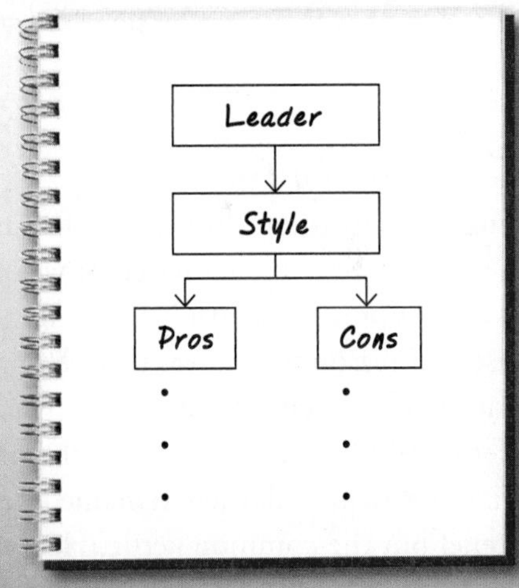

THE GENERAL HISTORY OF VIRGINIA

John Smith

BACKGROUND The Jamestown colony was modeled after a military expedition, transplanting about 100 hardy men into the Virginia wilderness in May 1607. Five members of Jamestown's ruling council—Edward Wingfield, Bartholomew Gosnold, John Ratcliffe, George Kendall, and John Smith—soon found themselves wrestling for control of the colony. As Smith's account opens, the colonists' ships have returned to England for supplies, leaving the men to survive on their own.

The Struggle for Jamestown

Being thus left to our fortunes, it fortuned that within ten days, scarce ten amongst us could either go or well stand, such extreme weakness and sickness oppressed us. And thereat none need marvel if they consider the cause and reason which was this: While the ships stayed, our allowance was somewhat bettered by a daily proportion of biscuit which the sailors would pilfer to sell, give, or exchange with us for money, sassafras, furs, or love. But when they departed, there remained neither tavern, beer-house, nor place of relief but the common kettle. Had we been as free from all sins as [we were free from] gluttony and drunkenness we might have been canonized for saints, but our President [Edward Wingfield] would never have been admitted for engrossing to his private, oatmeal, sack, oil, aqua vitae, beef, eggs, or what not but the kettle; that indeed he allowed equally to be distributed, and that was half a pint of wheat and as much barley boiled with water for a man a day, and this, having fried some twenty-six weeks in the ship's hold, contained as many worms as grains so that we might truly call it rather so much bran than corn; our drink was water, our lodgings castles in the air. **A**

Analyze Visuals ▶

You need no caption to know the **map** on the opposite page is very old. Notice two important ways it differs from current maps. First, it includes clearly **historical details** such as sailing ships and bows and arrows. Second, the map lacks proportion. The ships, for example, are **out of scale.** They are huge by comparison with the harbor and the islands. What additional non-standard, out-of-proportion map details can you identify?

8 common kettle: food that was available to everyone.

11 engrossing to his private: taking for his private use; **sack:** wine; **aqua vitae:** brandy.

A OLDER TEXTS
Using the side notes, restate lines 8–12 in modern English. What joke is Smith making?

Arrival of the English in Virginia (1585–1588), Theodore de Bry. Engraving © Giraudon/Art Resource, New York.

Pasquenoke
Dasamonquepeuc
Roanoac
Trinety harbor

With this lodging and diet, our extreme toil in bearing and planting palisades so strained and bruised us and our continual labor in the extremity of the heat had so weakened us, as were cause sufficient to have made us as miserable in our native country or any other place in the world.

From May to September, those that escaped lived upon sturgeon and sea crabs. Fifty in this time we buried; the rest seeing the President's projects to escape these miseries in our pinnace by flight (who all this time had neither felt want nor sickness) so moved our dead spirits as we **deposed** him and established Ratcliffe in his place (Gosnold being dead), Kendall deposed. Smith newly recovered, Martin and Ratcliffe were by his care preserved and relieved, and the most of the soldiers recovered with the skillful diligence of Master Thomas Wotton our surgeon general. **B**

But now was all our provision spent, the sturgeon gone, all helps abandoned, each hour expecting the fury of the savages, when God, the patron of all good endeavors, in that desperate extremity so changed the hearts of the savages that they brought such plenty of their fruits and provision as no man wanted.

The new President [Ratcliffe] and Martin, being little beloved, of weak judgment in dangers, and less **industry** in peace, committed the managing of all things abroad to Captain Smith, who, by his own example, good words, and fair promises, set some to mow, others to bind thatch, some to build houses, others to thatch them, himself always bearing the greatest task for his own share, so that in short time he provided most of them lodgings, neglecting any for himself. . . . **C**

A Surprise Attack

Smith, perceiving (notwithstanding their late misery) not any regarded but from hand to mouth, (the company being well recovered) caused the pinnace to be provided with things fitting to get provision for the year following, but in the **interim** he made three or four journeys and discovered the people of Chickahominy, yet what he carefully provided the rest carelessly spent.

Wingfield and Kendall, living in disgrace strengthened themselves with the sailors and other confederates to regain their former credit and authority, or at least such means aboard the pinnace (being fitted to sail as Smith had appointed for trade), to alter her course and to go for England.

Smith, unexpectedly returning, had the plot discovered to him, much trouble he had to prevent it, till with the store of saker and musket shot he forced them [to] stay or sink in the river: which action cost the life of Captain Kendall.

These brawls are so disgustful, as some will say they are better forgotten, yet all men of good judgment will conclude it were better their baseness should be manifest to the world, than the business bear the scorn and shame of their excused disorders.

19 palisades: walls made of tall, pointed wooden stakes.

24 pinnace: a small sailing ship.

depose (dĭ-pōz′) *v.* to remove from rule

B OLDER TEXTS
Reread lines 27–28. **Clarify** the pronoun referent for the word *his* in line 27. Who is responsible for healing Martin and Ratcliffe?

industry (ĭn′də-strē) *n.* hard work; diligence

37 abroad: outside the palisades.

C NARRATOR
Reread lines 35–41. Do Smith's claims sound more or less credible than they would if stated by a **first-person narrator**? Give reasons for your answer.

interim (ĭn′tər-ĭm) *n.* period in between; interval

46 Chickahominy (chĭ′kə-hä′mə-nē): a river in Virginia.

52 discovered: revealed.

53 saker: cannon shot.

55 Captain Kendall: Kendall was executed for mutiny in 1607.

57–59 it were . . . disorders: It is better to reveal the troublemakers than to have the "business" of the colony get a bad name.

Illustration of Jamestown Fort, Virginia, about 1608. Getty Images.

The President and Captain Archer not long after intended also to have abandoned the country, which project also was curbed and suppressed by Smith.

The Spaniard never more greedily desired gold than he [Smith] victual, nor his soldiers more to abandon the country than he to keep it. But [he found] plenty of corn in the river of Chickahominy, where hundreds of savages in divers places stood with baskets expecting his coming.

And now the winter approaching, the rivers became so covered with swans, geese, ducks, and cranes that we daily feasted with good bread, Virginia peas, pumpkins, and putchamins, fish, fowl, and divers sort of wild beasts as fast as we could eat them, so that none of our tuftaffety humorists desired to go for England.

But our comedies never endured long without a tragedy, some idle exceptions being muttered against Captain Smith for not discovering the head of Chickahominy river and [he being] taxed by the Council to be too slow in so worthy an attempt. The next voyage he proceeded so far that with much labor by cutting of trees asunder he made his passage, but when his barge could pass no farther, he left her in a broad bay of danger of shot, commanding none should go ashore till his return, himself with two English and two savages went up higher in a canoe, but he was not long absent but his men went ashore, whose want of government gave both occasion and opportunity to the savages to surprise one George Cassen whom they slew and much failed not to have cut off the boat and all the rest.

60 Captain Archer: Gabriel Archer had abandoned the colony and then returned. He did not support Smith.

63 victual: food.

69 putchamins: persimmons.

70 tuftaffety humorists: unreliable lace-wearers.

73 exceptions: objections.

80–82 whose want . . . the rest: the men's lack of discipline in going ashore led to the surprise attack on Cassen; only by some failure on the attackers' side did the others survive.

Smith little dreaming of that accident, being got to the marshes at the river's head twenty miles in the desert, had his two men [Robinson and Emry] slain (as is supposed) sleeping by the canoe, while himself by fowling sought them victual, who finding he was beset with 200 savages, two of them he slew, still defending himself with the aid of the savage his guide, whom he bound to his arms with his garters and used him as a buckler, yet he was shot in his thigh a little, and had many arrows that stuck in his clothes but no great hurt, till at last they took him prisoner. . . . **D**

84 desert: wilderness; **85–86 by fowling . . . victual:** hunted birds to find them food.

88 garters: shirtlaces; **buckler:** shield.

D NARRATOR
Reread lines 83–90. What details does the narrator include that suggest Smith is not responsible for the deaths of the two men?

At Powhatan's Court

At last they brought him to Werowocomoco, where was Powhatan, their Emperor. Here more than two hundred of those grim courtiers stood wondering at him, as [if] he had been a monster, till Powhatan and his train had put themselves in their greatest braveries. Before a fire upon a seat like a bedstead, he sat covered with a great robe made of raccoon skins and all the tails hanging by. On either hand did sit a young wench of sixteen or eighteen years and along on each side [of] the house, two rows of men and behind them as many women, with all their heads and shoulders painted red, many of their heads bedecked with the white down of birds, but every one with something, and a great chain of white beads around their necks.

94 greatest braveries: fanciest clothes.

At his entrance before the King, all the people gave a great shout. The Queen of Appomattoc was appointed to bring him water to wash his hands, and another brought him a bunch of feathers, instead of a towel, to dry them; having feasted him after their best barbarous manner they could, a long consultation was held, but the conclusion was, two great stones were brought before Powhatan; then as many as could, laid hands on him, dragged him to them, and thereon laid his head and being ready with their clubs to beat out his brains, Pocahontas, the King's dearest daughter, when no **entreaty** could prevail, got his head in her arms and laid her own upon his to save him from death, whereat the Emperor was contended he should live to make him hatchets, and her bells, beads, and copper, for they thought him as well of all occupations as themselves. For the King himself will make his own robes, shoes, bows, arrows, pots; plant, hunt, or do anything so well as the rest.

102 the Queen of Appomattoc (ăp'ə-măt'ək): the leader of the nearby village of Appomattoc.

entreaty (ĕn-trē'tē) *n.* plea

112 as well . . . themselves: The Indians thought Smith had varied skills as they did.

Two days after, Powhatan, having disguised himself in the most fearfulest manner he could, caused Captain Smith to be brought forth to a great house in the woods and there upon a mat by the fire to be left alone. Not long after, from behind a mat that divided the house, was made the most dolefulest noise he ever heard; then Powhatan more like a devil than a man, with some two hundred more as black as himself, came unto him and told him now that they were friends, and presently he should go to Jamestown to send him two great guns and a grindstone for which he would give him the country of Capahowasic and forever esteem him as his son Nantaquoud.

So to Jamestown with twelve guides Powhatan sent him. That night they quartered in the woods, he still expecting (as he had done all this long time of his imprisonment) every hour to be put to one death or other, for all

122–123 the country of Capahowasic (kăp'ə-hou'ə-sĭk') **. . . Nantaquoud** (nŏn'tə-kwo͞od'): Powhatan would give Smith control of a nearby village and also promised to think as highly of him as he did of his own son.

their feasting. But almighty God (by His divine providence) had **mollified** the hearts of those stern barbarians with compassion. The next morning betimes they came to the fort, where Smith having used the savages with what kindness he could, he showed Rawhunt, Powhatan's trusty servant, two demi-culverins and a millstone to carry [to] Powhatan; they found them somewhat too heavy, but when they did see him discharge them, being loaded with stones, among the boughs of a great tree loaded with icicles, the ice and branches came so tumbling down that the poor savages ran away half dead with fear. But at last we regained some conference with them and gave them such toys and sent to Powhatan, his women, and children such presents as gave them in general full content. **E**

Now in Jamestown they were all combustion, the strongest preparing once more to run away with the pinnace; which, with the hazard of his life, with saker falcon and musket shot, Smith forced now the third time to stay or sink.

Some, no better than they should be, had plotted with the President the next day to have him put to death by the Levitical law, for the lives of Robinson and Emry; pretending the fault was his that had led them to their ends; but he quickly took such order with such lawyers that he laid them by the heels till he sent some of them prisoners for England.

Now every once in four or five days, Pocahontas with her attendants brought him so much provision that saved many of their lives, that else for all this had starved with hunger.

His relation of the plenty he had seen, especially at Werowocomoco, and of the state and bounty of Powhatan (which till that time was unknown), so revived their dead spirits (especially the love of Pocahontas) as all men's fear was abandoned.

Thus you may see what difficulties still crossed any good endeavor; and the good success of the business being thus oft brought to the very period of destruction; yet you see by what strange means God hath still delivered it. ∾

mollify (mŏl′ə-fī′) *v.* to soothe; to reduce in intensity

131 demi-culverins (dĕm′ē-kŭl′vər-ĭnz): large cannons.

E OLDER TEXTS
Reread lines 128–137. What inferences can you make about how Europeans of the time viewed Native Americans? How does the map on page 95 reflect this view?

143 Levitical law: According to the Book of Leviticus in the Bible, "He that killeth any man shall surely be put to death."

Language Coach

Synonyms and Antonyms
Plenty and *bounty* (lines 150 and 151) are **synonyms,** words with similar meanings. What are their meanings? *Lack* is an **antonym** of *plenty* and *bounty:* It means the opposite of *plenty* and *bounty*. Define *lack*. What have the colonists experienced a lack of?

THEME AND GENRE
In his historical narrative of adventure and adversity in Jamestown, Smith creates an almost mythic self-portrait of a strong and successful leader. The 2005 film *The New World* offers a different portrayal and shows Smith arriving in America as a prisoner in chains. What other 21st-century films, novels, or plays about a historical subject reexamine the facts and give a new twist to an old story?

Comprehension

1. **Recall** Why does Ratcliffe become the leader of Jamestown?
2. **Recall** What leads to the killing of Captain Kendall?
3. **Clarify** How does Smith become Powhatan's captive?
4. **Summarize** What happens to Smith during his stay with Powhatan?

Text Analysis

5. **Interpret Older Texts** Review the character chart you made. Consider Smith's connection to each character. What motives might have influenced Smith's portrayal of his fellow colonists? Cite details to support your answer.
6. **Make Inferences About Historical Context** How does the map on page 95 lend to your understanding of John Smith and the events he narrates in this selection? Support your answer with features and details on the map that differ from features and details on current-day maps.
7. **Examine a Historical Narrative** Smith's account of his explorations along the Chickahominy River is filled with details that suggest he is a hero. But if you read closely, he reveals that he was severely criticized for the way he performed. Reread lines 72–90, and record the conflicting information in a chart like the one shown. What accusations is Smith defending himself against?

Smith's Version	*Accusations Against Him*

8. **Evaluate Narrator** Consider Smith's use of **third-person point of view** as well as the **motives** that influenced his writing. Given these factors, is Smith a credible narrator? Evaluate the reliability of Smith's narrative as a source on the following topics. Give reasons for your answers.
   - daily life in Jamestown
   - Native American culture
   - Smith's own actions
   - conflicts in Jamestown

Text Criticism

9. **Different Perspectives** If Wingfield had written a report, how might it have differed from Smith's description of these events? Cite details to support your answer.

What makes a LEADER?

What qualities of leadership does John Smith reveal in this selection? Cite evidence from the text to support your answer.

COMMON CORE

RI 4 Determine the meaning of words and phrases as they are used in a text, including technical meanings. **RI 5** Analyze and evaluate the effectiveness of the structure an author uses in his or her exposition, including whether the structure makes points clear, convincing, and engaging. **RI 6** Determine an author's point of view or purpose in a text in which the rhetoric is particularly effective. **RI 10** Read and comprehend literary nonfiction. **L 3a** Apply an understanding of syntax to the study of complex texts when reading.

Vocabulary in Context

▲ VOCABULARY PRACTICE

Decide whether the words in each pair are synonyms or antonyms.

1. depose/appoint
2. interim/gap
3. mollify/anger
4. industry/diligence
5. entreaty/plea

WORD LIST
depose
entreaty
industry
interim
mollify

ACADEMIC VOCABULARY IN WRITING

• document • illustrate • interpret • promote • reveal

Write a short paragraph to **illustrate** the conflict that sprang up among members of Smith's expedition. Use details to **document** your observations. Include at least two Academic Vocabulary words in your paragraph.

VOCABULARY STRATEGY: MULTIPLE MEANINGS

Many words have more than one meaning. To make sense of what you read, you need to make sure you understand which meaning a writer intends. This is particularly true with words that are used as more than one part of speech, or with words that occur in older texts. For example, the noun *industry* usually refers to a specific branch of manufacture or trade. Smith uses it to mean "dedication to a task." As you read authors such as Smith, be alert to the nuances of meaning in the words they use. If you encounter an unfamiliar word or a familiar word in an unfamiliar setting, examine the **context**—the surrounding words, phrases, and sentences—for clues to the writer's meaning.

COMMON CORE

L 4 Determine or clarify the meaning of unknown and multiple-meaning words and phrases. **L 4a, c–d** Use context as a clue to the meaning of a word or phrase; consult general and specialized reference materials, both print and digital, to clarify a word's precise meaning or its standard usage; verify the preliminary determination of the meaning of a word or phrase.

PRACTICE Determine the meaning of each boldfaced word as it is used in the sentence. Consult a print or online dictionary if you need to.

1. Was John Smith a **contemporary** of Olaudah Equiano?
2. The **gravity** of the situation required the presence of several police officers.
3. What **accommodations** have the two leaders managed to reach?
4. The governor intends to **commute** several prisoners' sentences.
5. At this point we cannot **countenance** any more delays.
6. The hotel employees **agitated** for better working conditions.

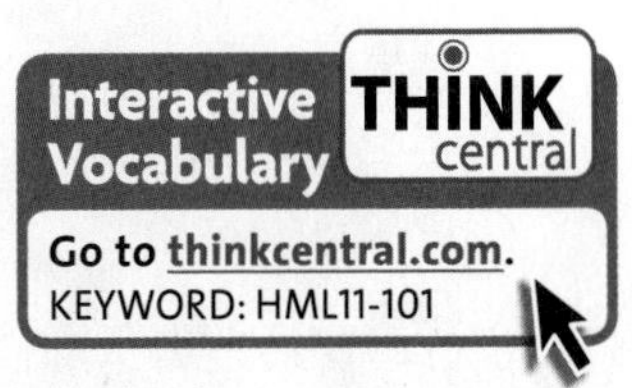

from Of Plymouth Plantation

Chronicle by William Bradford

COMMON CORE

RI 2 Determine two or more central ideas of a text and analyze their development over the course of the text, including how they interact and build on one another to provide a complex analysis; provide an objective summary of the text. **RI 9** Analyze seventeenth-century foundational U.S. documents of historical and literary significance for their themes, purposes, and rhetorical features.

Meet the Author

William Bradford c. 1590–1657

Long before there were holiday legends of Pilgrims and Indians, a group of English Puritans set off to create a new, pure society in the North American wilderness. Their leader was William Bradford.

Early Rebel Born into a time of religious upheaval in England, Bradford joined the crusade for religious reform at age 12. He was inspired by the ideals of the Puritans, a Protestant religious group that wanted to purify the Church of England and create simpler, more democratic ways to worship. By 17, Bradford had joined the radical Puritans known as Separatists, who called for a total break with the official church.

Not surprisingly, the Separatists clashed with the king of England, who also headed the church. Emigration to North America offered the hope of freedom, and Bradford helped plan and finance the voyage across the Atlantic. In 1620, Bradford and his wife, Dorothy, left behind their four-year-old son to join nearly 40 other Separatists on the ship *Mayflower*. Facing the journey with typical resolve, Bradford described the group as "pilgrims," or religious wanderers, the name we use for them today.

A Natural Leader Although the Pilgrims initiated the voyage, they made up fewer than half of the ship's 102 passengers. During the long, difficult journey, disagreements broke out among the group, and Bradford took decisive action. He helped craft the Mayflower Compact, often called the first U.S. Constitution. Signed by the 41 men on board, the compact was an agreement to work together for the good of the entire group. And they kept their promise. In April 1621, when the *Mayflower* returned to England, not one colonist left Plymouth Colony—a tribute to Bradford's sound leadership.

Bradford was also effective in forging alliances with local Native American tribes such as the Wampanoag (wäm′pə-nō′ăg), a union of tribes led by Massasoit (măs′ə-soit′). The Wampanoag, who had lost 80 percent of their people to smallpox shortly before the Pilgrims' arrival, faced their own struggle to survive. Out of mutual need, Bradford and Massasoit created a strong alliance that lasted throughout their lifetimes.

Historian in the Making With a historian's instinct, Bradford saved many documents from the trip's planning phase. During his 30 years as governor, he continued to document the challenges of the growing colony, which owed its survival to his energy, vision, and expert diplomacy. His chronicle, *Of Plymouth Plantation,* is our best history of these adventurous times.

Author Online

THINK central

Go to thinkcentral.com. KEYWORD: HML11-102

DID YOU KNOW?

William Bradford . . .

- lost his first wife to drowning shortly after the *Mayflower* landed.
- sold one of his farms to help pay Plymouth Colony's debts.
- was elected governor of Plymouth 30 times.

TEXT ANALYSIS: CULTURAL CHARACTERISTICS

Many texts, especially those about community life, reflect the **cultural characteristics** of the communities they describe, including their view of the human condition. *Of Plymouth Plantation* is a record of the Pilgrims' efforts to create a model Puritan society. In it, William Bradford describes the outcome of an Indian attack.

Thus it pleased God to vanquish their enemies and give them deliverance; and by His special providence so to dispose that not any one of them were either hurt or hit....

Bradford's description expresses the Puritan theme that victory is a gift from God. As you read, consider what else Bradford's descriptions and sometimes subtle word choice reveal about Puritan themes and the rhetorical appeal of shared beliefs. The appeal to common beliefs can influence not only what readers think but also how they feel about a subject.

READING STRATEGY: SUMMARIZE

When you **summarize,** you restate the **main ideas** and the most important **details** of what you read. This process will help you sift through Bradford's long, complex sentences for important clues to his beliefs and themes.

This excerpt from *Of Plymouth Plantation* has five sections. As you read each section, record the date or time of year events occur and a one- or two-sentence summary of the section.

Section: Their Safe Arrival at Cape Cod

Time of Year:
Summary:

VOCABULARY IN CONTEXT

The following boldfaced words help tell the story of the founding of Plymouth Colony. Use context clues to guess the meaning of each word; then, write a brief definition.

1. found **solace** in the peaceful woodland setting
2. her survival was an act of **providence**
3. will **tender** her resignation in a letter
4. chose a **rendezvous** convenient for everyone
5. tried to **procure** enough food for the family
6. an illness **feigned** in order to avoid work

Complete the activities in your **Reader/Writer Notebook**.

When does HARDSHIP *unite us?*

Hard times can bring people together or tear them apart. For example, in a blackout after a serious storm, people could respond by sharing supplies or by stealing what they need from unprotected homes. When does facing hardship become a source of strength and unity rather than one of distrust and division?

DISCUSS Working with a small group, list events you know from history or from the news that imposed great hardships on a community. Compare situations that had a unifying effect with those that divided the community. Identify factors that may account for the different responses.

Of Plymouth Plantation

William Bradford

BACKGROUND By the time the Pilgrims landed at Cape Cod, the local Native American tribes had had 100 years of contact and conflict with European explorers. Squanto, who became the Pilgrims' interpreter, had learned English when he was kidnapped by an English expedition in 1605. The Nauset Indians, who attacked the Pilgrims shortly after their arrival, had survived years of skirmishes with English explorers, including a 1609 battle with John Smith of Jamestown fame. Keep these events in mind as you read Bradford's account.

Their Safe Arrival at Cape Cod

But to omit other things (that I may be brief) after long beating at sea they[1] fell with that land which is called Cape Cod; the which being made and certainly known to be it, they were not a little joyful. . . .

Being thus arrived in a good harbor, and brought safe to land, they fell upon their knees and blessed the God of Heaven who had brought them over the vast and furious ocean, and delivered them from all the perils and miseries thereof, again to set their feet on the firm and stable earth, their proper element. . . . (A)

But here I cannot but stay and make a pause, and stand half amazed at this poor people's present condition; and so I think will the reader, too, when he well considers the same. Being thus passed the vast ocean, and a sea of troubles before in their preparation (as may be remembered by that which went before), they had now no friends to welcome them nor inns to entertain or refresh their weatherbeaten bodies; no houses or much less towns to repair to, to seek for

Analyze Visuals ▶
Describe the landscape that awaits the travellers. What emotional response might they have had to this sight?

(A) CULTURAL CHARACTERISTICS
Reread lines 4–7. What does this paragraph reveal about the way Puritans viewed God? How might this shared belief influence Bradford's readers?

1. **they:** Bradford refers to the Pilgrims in the third person, even though he is one of them.

The Landing of the Pilgrims (1803–1806), Michael Felice Corne. Tempera on canvas. Pilgrim Hall Museum. Plymouth, Massachusetts.

succor.[2] It is recorded in Scripture as a mercy to the Apostle and his shipwrecked company, that the barbarians showed them no small kindness in refreshing them,[3] but these savage barbarians, when they met with them (as after will appear) were readier to fill their sides full of arrows than otherwise. And for the season it was winter, and they that know the winters of that country know them to be sharp and violent, and subject to cruel and fierce storms, dangerous to travel to known places, much more to search an unknown coast. Besides, what could they see but a hideous and desolate wilderness, full of wild beasts and wild men—and what multitudes there might be of them they knew not. Neither could they, as it were, go up to the top of Pisgah[4] to view from this wilderness a more goodly country to feed their hopes; for which way soever they turned their eyes (save upward to the heavens) they could have little **solace** or content in respect of any outward objects. For summer being done, all things stand upon them with a weatherbeaten face, and the whole country, full of woods and thickets, represented a wild and savage hue. If they looked behind them, there was the mighty ocean which they had passed and was now as a main bar and gulf to separate them from all the civil parts of the world. . . . B

solace (sŏl′ĭs) *n.* comfort in sorrow or distress

B SUMMARIZE
Reread lines 16–30. What challenges confronted the colonists when they arrived at Cape Cod?

2. **to seek for succor:** to look for help or relief.
3. **It is . . . refreshing them:** a reference to the Biblical account of the courteous reception given to Paul ("the Apostle") and his companions by the inhabitants of Malta (Acts 27:41–28:2).
4. **Pisgah:** the mountain from whose peak Moses saw the Promised Land (Deuteronomy 34:1–4).

The First Winter of the Pilgrims in Massachusetts, 1620 (1800s). Colored engraving. The Granger Collection, New York.

The First Encounter

Being thus arrived at Cape Cod the 11th of November, and necessity calling them to look out a place for habitation (as well as the master's and mariners' importunity); they having brought a large shallop[5] with them out of England, stowed in quarters in the ship, they now got her out and set their carpenters to work to trim her up; but being much bruised and shattered in the ship with foul weather, they saw she would be long in mending. Whereupon a few of them **tendered** themselves to go by land and discover those nearest places, whilst the shallop was in mending; . . .

tender (tĕn′dər) *v.* to offer formally

After this, the shallop being got ready, they set out again for the better discovery of this place, and the master of the ship desired to go himself. So there went some thirty men but found it to be no harbor for ships but only for boats. There was also found two of their [the Indians'] houses covered with mats, and sundry of their implements in them, but the people were run away and could not be seen. Also there was found more of their corn and of their beans of various colors; the corn and beans they [the English] brought away, purposing to give them [the Indians] full satisfaction when they should meet with any of them as, about some six months afterward they did, to their good content.[6]

And here is to be noted a special **providence** of God, and a great mercy to this poor people, that here they got seed to plant them corn the next year, or else they might have starved, for they had none nor any likelihood to get any till the season had been past, as the sequel did manifest.[7] Neither is it likely they had had this, if the first voyage had not been made, for the ground was now all covered with snow and hard frozen; but the Lord is never wanting unto His in their greatest needs; let His holy name have all the praise. C

providence (prŏv′ĭ-dəns) *n.* an instance of divine care

COMMON CORE RI 9

C CULTURAL CHARACTERISTICS

As you have seen from your reading so far, William Bradford believes that God played a special role in the lives of the Puritan settlers. Reread lines 48–54. In the first sentence, notice the phrase "a special providence of God." The verb form of *providence* is *provide.* This word expresses Bradford's belief that God literally provides for the Puritan settlers by giving them seed corn to plant so that they will not starve. As you read the following paragraphs (lines 55–99), look for other places where the author expresses Puritan beliefs about the role of God in their lives.

The month of November being spent in these affairs, and much foul weather falling in, the 6th of December they sent out their shallop again with ten of their principal men and some seamen, upon further discovery, intending to circulate that deep bay of Cape Cod. The weather was very cold and it froze so hard as the spray of the sea lighting on their coats, they were as if they had been glazed. . . . [The next night they landed and] made them a barricado[8] as usually they did every night, with logs, stakes, and thick pine boughs, the height of a man, leaving it open to leeward,[9] partly to shelter them from the cold and wind (making their fire in the middle and lying round about it) and partly to defend them from any sudden assaults of the savages, if they should surround them; so being very weary, they betook them to rest. But about midnight they heard a hideous and great cry, and their sentinel called "Arm! arm!" So they bestirred them and stood to their arms and shot off a couple of muskets, and then the noise

5. **shallop** (shăl′əp): an open boat usually used in shallow waters.
6. **purposing . . . content:** intending to repay the Nauset Indians for the corn and beans they took, as they in fact did, to the Indians' satisfaction, six months later.
7. **as the sequel did manifest:** as the events that followed proved to be the case.
8. **barricado** (băr′ĭ-kä′dō): a barrier for defense.
9. **to leeward:** on the side sheltered from the wind.

ceased. They concluded it was a company of wolves or such like wild beasts, for one of the seamen told them he had often heard such a noise in Newfoundland.

So they rested till about five of the clock in the morning; for the tide, and their purpose to go from thence, made them be stirring betimes. So after prayer they prepared for breakfast, and it being day dawning it was thought best to be carrying things down to the boat. But some said it was not best to carry the arms down, others said they would be the readier, for they had lapped them up in their coats from the dew; but some three or four would not carry theirs till they went themselves. Yet as it fell out, the water being not high enough, they laid them down on the bank side and came up to breakfast.

But presently, all on the sudden, they heard a great and strange cry, which they knew to be the same voices they heard in the night, though they varied their notes; and one of their company being abroad came running in and cried, "Men, Indians! Indians!" And withal, their arrows came flying amongst them. Their men ran with all speed to recover their arms, as by the good providence of God they did. In the meantime, of those that were there ready, two muskets were discharged at them, and two more stood ready in the entrance of their **rendezvous** but were commanded not to shoot till they could take full aim at them. And the other two charged again with all speed, for there were only four had arms there, and defended the barricado, which was first assaulted. The cry of the Indians was dreadful, especially when they [the Indians] saw their men [the English] run out of the rendezvous toward the shallop to recover their arms, the Indians wheeling about upon them. But some running out with coats of mail on, and cutlasses in their hands, they [the English] soon got their arms and let fly amongst them [the Indians] and quickly stopped their violence. . . .

rendezvous (rän′dā-vo͞o) *n.* a gathering place

Thus it pleased God to vanquish their enemies and give them deliverance; and by His special providence so to dispose that not any one of them were either hurt or hit, though their arrows came close by them and on every side [of] them; and sundry of their coats, which hung up in the barricado, were shot through and through. Afterwards they gave God solemn thanks and praise for their deliverance, and gathered up a bundle of their arrows and sent them into England afterward by the master of the ship, and called that place the First Encounter. . . .

The Starving Time

But that which was most sad and lamentable was, that in two or three months' time half of their company died, especially in January and February, being the depth of winter, and wanting houses and other comforts; being infected with the scurvy[10] and other diseases which this long voyage and their inaccommodate condition had brought upon them. So as there died some times two or three of a day in the foresaid time, that of 100 and odd persons, scarce fifty remained. And of these, in the time of most distress, there was but six or seven sound persons who to their great commendations, be it spoken, spared no pains night nor day, but with abundance of toil and hazard of their own health fetched them wood, made them fires, dressed them meat, made their beds, washed their loathsome clothes,

Language Coach

Fixed Expressions
The phrase "depth of winter" in line 102 means "middle part of winter." Other phrases with *depth* are *in-depth* ("complete" or "thorough") and *depths of* ("the deepest point of"). Use *depths of despair* in a sentence about the colonists' situation.

10. **scurvy** (skûr′vē): a disease caused by lack of vitamin C.

The First Thanksgiving (1914), Jennie Augusta Brownscombe. © Burstein Collection/Corbis.

clothed and unclothed them. . . . In a word, did all the homely and necessary offices for them which dainty and queasy stomachs cannot endure to hear named; and all this willingly and cheerfully, without any grudging in the least, showing herein their true love unto their friends and brethren; a rare example and worthy to be remembered. Two of these seven were Mr. William Brewster, their reverend Elder, and Myles Standish, their Captain and military commander, unto whom myself and many others were much beholden in our low and sick condition. And yet the Lord so upheld these persons as in this general calamity they were not at all infected either with sickness or lameness. . . . D

Indian Relations

All this while the Indians came skulking about them, and would sometimes show themselves aloof off, but when any approached near them, they would run away; and once they [the Indians] stole away their [the colonists'] tools where they had been at work and were gone to dinner. But about the 16th of March, a certain Indian came boldly amongst them and spoke to them in broken English, which they could well understand but marveled at it. At length they understood by discourse with him, that he was not of these parts, but belonged to the eastern parts where some English ships came to fish, with whom he was acquainted and could name sundry of them by their names, amongst whom he had got his language. He became profitable to them in acquainting them with many things concerning the state of the country in the east parts where he lived, which was afterwards profitable unto them; as also of the people here, of their names, number and strength, of their situation and distance from this place, and who was chief amongst them. His name was Samoset. He told them also of another Indian whose name was Squanto, a native of this place, who had been in England and could speak better English than himself.

▲ Analyze Visuals

Contrast the scenery in this image with the landscape on page 105. How has the view of nature changed?

D CULTURAL CHARACTERISTICS

Reread lines 106–118. Notice how Bradford holds up seven colonists as examples. What values do these seven represent? What do they mean to Bradford, and how might their example influence Bradford's readers?

Being, after some time of entertainment and gifts dismissed, a while after he came again, and five more with him, and they brought again all the tools that were stolen away before, and made way for the coming of their great Sachem,[11] called Massasoit. Who, about four or five days after, came with the chief of his friends and other attendance, with the aforesaid Squanto. With whom, after friendly entertainment and some gifts given him, they made a peace with him (which hath now continued this 24 years) in these terms: **E**

1. That neither he nor any of his should injure or do hurt to any of their people.
2. That if any of his did hurt to any of theirs, he should send the offender, that they might punish him.
3. That if anything were taken away from any of theirs, he should cause it to be restored; and they should do the like to his.
4. If any did unjustly war against him, they would aid him; if any did war against them, he should aid them.
5. He should send to his neighbors confederates to certify them of this, that they might not wrong them, but might be likewise comprised in the conditions of peace.[12]
6. That when their men came to them, they should leave their bows and arrows behind them.

After these things he returned to his place called Sowams,[13] some 40 miles from this place, but Squanto continued with them and was their interpreter and was a special instrument sent of God for their good beyond their expectation. He directed them how to set their corn, where to take fish, and to **procure** other commodities, and was also their pilot to bring them to unknown places for their profit, and never left them till he died.

First Thanksgiving

They began now to gather in the small harvest they had, and to fit up their houses and dwellings against winter, being all well recovered in health and strength and had all things in good plenty. For as some were thus employed in affairs abroad, others were exercised in fishing, about cod and bass and other fish, of which they took good store, of which every family had their portion. All the summer there was no want; and now began to come in store of fowl, as winter approached, of which this place did abound when they came first (but afterward decreased by degrees). And besides waterfowl there was great store of wild turkeys, of which they took many, besides venison, etc. Besides they had about a peck a meal a week to a person, or now since harvest, Indian corn to that proportion. Which made many afterwards write so largely of their plenty here to their friends in England, which were not **feigned** but true reports.

E SUMMARIZE
Reread lines 122–141. What events led to the treaty with Massasoit?

procure (prō-kyŏŏr') *v.* to get by special effort; to obtain

Language Coach

Homophones Words that sound alike but have different meanings and spellings are called **homophones.** *Fowl* (line 166) means "birds." Look at "foul weather" in line 55 on page 107. What does *foul* mean? How is it pronounced?

feigned (fānd) *adj.* not real; pretended **feign** *v.*

---

11. **Sachem** (sā'chəm): chief.

12. **He should send . . . peace:** Massasoit was to send representatives to other tribes to let them know about the treaty with the Pilgrims.

13. **Sowams** (sō'əmz): near the site of present-day Barrington, Rhode Island.

Comprehension

1. **Recall** What happens to the colonists during "the starving time"?
2. **Recall** Who is Squanto?
3. **Clarify** In what ways did the Wampanoag help the colonists survive?

Text Analysis

4. **Make Inferences About Cultural Characteristics** Bradford's **word choice** and his choice of details provide subtle clues to Puritan beliefs. Reread Bradford's account of the arrival at Cape Cod (lines 4–30). What does his description reveal about Puritan attitudes toward nature? Use a chart like the one shown to gather evidence and make inferences.

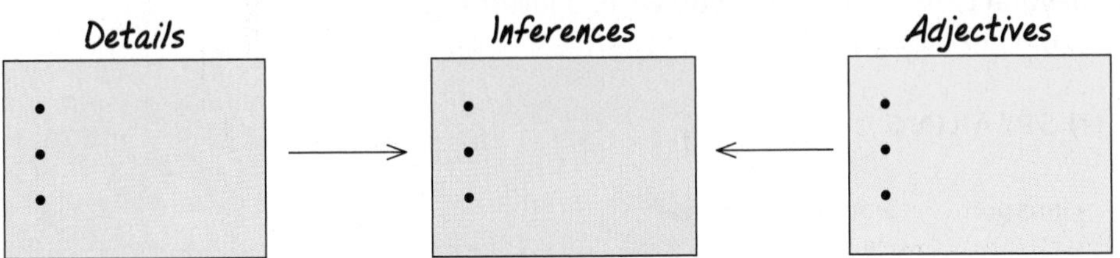

5. **Analyze Outcomes** Using the **summary** chart you created as you read, review the events of the first year at Plymouth. How did events change the colonists'
   - prospects for survival?
   - impressions of Native Americans?
   - attitude toward the region?
   - sense of providence?
6. **Analyze Form** A **chronicle** is a chronological, objective account of historical events. What features of Bradford's narrative might have changed had he written a personal account of his experiences?
7. **Make Judgments** Review the terms of the treaty between the Plymouth colonists and the Wampanoag (lines 142–154). Notice which terms apply to both parties equally and which do not. In your opinion, is the treaty fair? Explain your answer.

Text Criticism

8. **Different Perspectives** How might a Wampanoag historian's version of events differ from Bradford's? Choose an episode from *Of Plymouth Plantation* and cite specific details that might change to reflect this different perspective.

When does HARDSHIP *unite us?*

Which beliefs most contributed to the colonists' willingness to face hardships together? And how does Bradford's appeal to common beliefs influence readers—especially Bradford's Puritan contemporaries? Support your answer with details from Bradford's account.

COMMON CORE

RI 1 Cite textual evidence to support analysis of what the text says explicitly as well as inferences drawn from the text, including determining where the text leaves matters uncertain. **RI 2** Determine two or more central ideas of a text and analyze their development over the course of the text, including how they interact and build on one another to provide a complex analysis; provide an objective summary of the text. **RI 9** Analyze seventeenth-century foundational U.S. documents of historical and literary significance for their themes, purposes, and rhetorical features.

Vocabulary in Context

▲ VOCABULARY PRACTICE

Show you understand the vocabulary words by answering these questions.

1. If you wanted to **procure** something, would you go to a store or go swimming?
2. If someone's sorrow is **feigned,** is it genuine or bogus?
3. Is a **rendezvous** a good place to be alone?
4. What would be a sign of **providence**—an unexpected victory or a deadly accident?
5. Who would be in more need of **solace**—a person who has just won a race or someone whose grandmother has just died?
6. To **tender** yourself as a mayoral candidate, would you write a letter to the election board or tell a friend about your idea?

WORD LIST

feigned
procure
providence
rendezvous
solace
tender

ACADEMIC VOCABULARY IN SPEAKING

• document • illustrate • interpret • promote • reveal

With a small group of your peers, explain how William Bradford's narrative **promotes** Puritan beliefs. Include details from the selection to **document** your ideas. As you contribute, use at least one of the Academic Vocabulary words.

VOCABULARY STRATEGY: WORDS FROM FRENCH

Rendezvous is one of a number of words in English that comes directly from French. The meaning of some French words and terms may change slightly in English; *rendezvous,* for example, means "present yourself" in French. Other terms keep the same meaning. If you are not sure of the meaning of a French term when you hear or read it, consult a dictionary. Many unabridged dictionaries have short foreign-language dictionaries in the appendix where you can look up a word in a language such as French and see the English translation. Your school library may also have a French-English dictionary. Also, the Internet has many reliable resources on words and their origins. Use these kinds of references to increase your command of English words.

COMMON CORE

L 4c Consult general and specialized reference materials, both print and digital, to determine or clarify a word's precise meaning, its etymology, or its standard usage.

PRACTICE Create a three-column chart with these headings: *Term, Original Meaning,* and *Meaning in English.* Then, using a dictionary that contains etymologies, fill in the chart for each of the following terms.

1. laissez faire
2. vis-à-vis
3. hors d'oeuvre
4. noblesse oblige
5. faux pas
6. coup de grâce
7. esprit de corps
8. savoir-faire

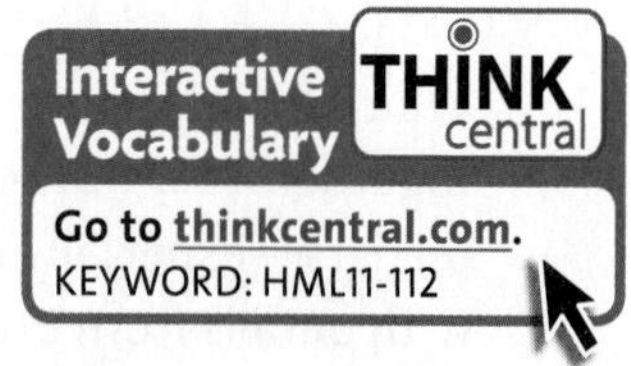

Personal Accounts of Exploration and Settlement

The selections in this section not only provide information about life in early America but are also sources of insight into the personal challenges and moral conflicts that shaped so much of our colonial culture. Because they are all firsthand accounts, the reader's understanding of the events, places, and people described is colored by the very personal feelings of each writer. Their fears, opinions, and doubts help bring this long-past world to life, as shown here.

"In that hour, I would have welcomed death rather than see so many around me in such a condition."

—Álvar Núñez Cabeza de Vaca

"I was soon put down under the decks, and there I received a salutation in my nostrils as I had never experienced in my life; so that, with the loathsomeness of the stench, and crying together, I became so sick and low that I was not able to eat.

—Olaudah Equiano

"That night they quartered in the woods, he still expecting (as he had done all this long time of his imprisonment) every hour to be put to one death or other, for all their feasting."

—Captain John Smith

"Besides, what could they see but a hideous and desolate wilderness, full of wild beasts and wild men—and what multitudes there might be of them they knew not."

—William Bradford

Pocahontas rescues John Smith.

Extension

SPEAKING & LISTENING In a group of four students **debate** the following statement:

The narrators of the selections in this section are unreliable because of their personal and emotional involvement in the events and experiences they relate.

Writing to Evaluate

Review the selections beginning on page 72 and choose two documents that give you the most complete picture of this historical period. In a brief essay, evaluate how various features of the texts bring the ideas and events of this period to life.

Consider

- the themes of each selection
- descriptive details, images, and dialogue that enhance meaning and advance the writer's purpose
- what the writer's personal feelings and ideas add to your understanding or interest in the work

COMMON CORE

RI 9 Analyze seventeenth- and eighteenth-century foundational U.S. documents of historical and literary significance for their themes, purposes, and rhetorical features. **W 2** Write explanatory texts to examine complex ideas. **SL 1** Initiate and participate effectively in a range of collaborative discussions.

To My Dear and Loving Husband *and* Upon the Burning of Our House, July 10th, 1666

Poetry by Anne Bradstreet

Huswifery

Poetry by Edward Taylor

VIDEO TRAILER THINK central KEYWORD: HML11-114A

COMMON CORE **RL 4** Determine the meaning of words and phrases as they are used in the text, including figurative meanings; analyze the impact of specific word choices on meaning and tone. **L 3a** Apply an understanding of syntax to the study of complex texts when reading. **L 4** Clarify the meaning of unknown words and phrases. **L 5a** Interpret figures of speech in context and analyze their role in the text.

Meet the Authors

Anne Bradstreet

c. 1612-1672

Anne Bradstreet was essentially the first notable American poet, man or woman. Considering that Puritan women were not encouraged to improve their minds—let alone express their ideas—this achievement is remarkable.

Coming to America Anne Dudley Bradstreet was born in England and raised on an estate, which her father managed for the Earl of Lincoln. With access to the earl's library, she received a good education. In 1628, 16-year-old Anne married Simon Bradstreet. Two years later, the young couple sailed for Massachusetts. After her privileged upbringing, Anne Bradstreet was not prepared for the harsh living conditions of colonial America. Her religious faith helped her endure these hardships—as did writing poetry.

Personal Poetry Bradstreet focused primarily on the realities of her life—her husband, her eight children, and her house. In 1650, without her knowledge, Bradstreet's brother-in-law had some of her verses published in London in a volume titled *The Tenth Muse Lately Sprung Up in America.* It was the first book of poetry ever published by an American colonist.

Edward Taylor 1642?–1729

For over 200 years, the work of Edward Taylor, one of colonial America's most inventive poets, remained unread. His poetry did not come to light until the 1930s when his long-forgotten manuscripts were discovered in the Yale University Library.

Frontier Parson and Poet Born in England, Taylor came to America in 1668 to escape religious persecution in his homeland. In 1671, after graduating from Harvard University, Taylor became the minister of a church in Westfield, Massachusetts. He held that position until his death 58 years later.

The wilderness town of Westfield presented many challenges to the highly intellectual Taylor. But he undertook his roles as farmer, physician, and minister with energy. He even called his flock to worship by beating a drum.

Like Anne Bradstreet—a volume of whose work he owned—Taylor wrote his poetry to glorify God. He found his subjects in human life, nature, and everyday activities. His poems on these topics served as a form of worship.

Author Online THINK central

Go to thinkcentral.com. KEYWORD: HML11-114B

TEXT ANALYSIS: FIGURATIVE LANGUAGE

Like all poets, Puritan poets used **figurative language** to create imagery and communicate ideas beyond the literal meaning of words. Figurative language helped the Puritan poets convey ideas about their religious faith and their personal lives. As you read the poems by Anne Bradstreet and Edward Taylor, look for the types of figures of speech listed below.

- A **metaphor** is a figure of speech that directly compares two unlike things without using *like* or *as*. (*Our house is our nest.*)
- An **extended metaphor** is one that draws the comparison out and compares the two things at length and in many ways. (*Our house is our nest; we fly away only to return to its snug protection.*)
- **Personification** is a figure of speech in which an object, animal, or idea is given human characteristics. (*Our house wraps our family in a warm embrace.*)
- **Hyperbole** is a figure of speech in which the truth is exaggerated for emphasis. (*Our house means more to us than all the money in the world.*)
- Also note the effect of any biblical **allusions,** or references, and how they enhance the meaning of the poem.

READING STRATEGY: CLARIFY MEANING IN OLDER POETRY

When reading works from the Puritan era, it is important to stop and **clarify meaning** by rereading and restating difficult passages as needed in order to fully appreciate the literature. Be aware of the following as you read the Puritan poets:

- **Archaic language—**words that were once in common use but that are now considered old-fashioned or out-of-date
- **Inverted syntax—**sentence structure in which the expected order of words is reversed

As you read each poem, use a chart like the one shown to record and restate examples of archaic language and inverted syntax.

"Upon the Burning of Our House"	
Archaic Language	*Inverted Syntax*
"blest" (blessed)	"when rest I took" (when I took rest)

 Complete the activities in your **Reader/Writer Notebook.**

What do you VALUE *most?*

The things that we value in life may be actual objects or they may be less tangible. For instance, a person might prize a favorite CD or jacket. On the other hand, the gift of family may outweigh more material possessions. The Puritan poets you are about to read valued family life and their religious faith above all things. What do you prize most in your life?

QUICKWRITE Imagine that a reality show has offered you the chance to win a million dollars. The catch is that you will have to give up an object, a person, or a belief that you truly value. Assume that you are not willing to make the sacrifice. Write a brief letter to explain why you must turn down the money.

To My Dear and Loving Husband

Anne Bradstreet

If ever two were one, then surely we.
If ever man were loved by wife, then thee;
If ever wife was happy in a man,
Compare with me, ye women, if you can.
I prize thy love more than whole mines of gold
Or all the riches that the East doth hold.
My love is such that rivers cannot quench, **A**
Nor ought but love from thee, give recompense.[1]
Thy love is such I can no way repay,
The heavens reward thee manifold, I pray.
Then while we live, in love let's so persevere[2]
That when we live no more, we may live ever. **B**

A FIGURATIVE LANGUAGE
Reread lines 5–7. How does the poet use **hyperbole** in these lines to emphasize her feelings for her husband?

B CLARIFY MEANING
Use conventional word order to restate the **inverted syntax** in lines 11–12. What relationship do the lines suggest between earthly love and eternal life?

Analyze Visuals ▸
Many Puritan women stitched samplers like the one shown here. The samplers often depicted nature scenes or stories from the Bible. What values are suggested by the subject matter of the sampler?

---

1. **recompense** (rĕk'əm-pĕns'): payment in return for something, such as a service.
2. **persevere:** In Bradstreet's time, *persevere* would have been pronounced pûr-səv'ər, which rhymes with *ever.*

Upon the Burning of Our House, July 10th, 1666

Anne Bradstreet

In silent night when rest I took
For sorrow near I did not look
I wakened was with thund'ring noise
And piteous shrieks of dreadful voice.
That fearful sound of "Fire!" and "Fire!"
Let no man know is my desire. **C**

I, starting up, the light did spy,
And to my God my heart did cry
To strengthen me in my distress
And not to leave me succorless.[1]
Then, coming out, beheld a space
The flame consume my dwelling place.

And when I could no longer look,
I blest His name that gave and took,[2]
That laid my goods now in the dust:
Yea, so it was, and so 'twas just.
It was His own, it was not mine,
Far be it that I should repine;[3]

C CLARIFY MEANING
Paraphrase lines 1–6 to clarify their meaning. How does the poet use contrast to convey a sense of fear?

Language Coach

Meanings of Idioms
The phrase "Far be it" in line 18 is an **idiom,** an expression whose overall meaning is different from that of the individual words. "Far be it" means "I wouldn't dare to. . . ." How does the speaker view herself in relation to God?

---

1. **succorless** (sŭk'ər-lĭs): without help or relief.
2. **I . . . took:** an allusion to Job 1:21 in the Bible—"The Lord gave, and the Lord hath taken away; blessed be the name of the Lord."
3. **repine:** to complain or fret; to long for something.

He might of all justly bereft,
But yet sufficient for us left.
When by the ruins oft I past,
My sorrowing eyes aside did cast,
And here and there the places spy
Where oft I sat and long did lie:

Here stood that trunk and there that chest,
There lay that store I counted best.
My pleasant things in ashes lie,
And them behold no more shall I.
Under thy roof no guest shall sit,
Nor at thy table eat a bit.

No pleasant tale shall e'er be told,
Nor things recounted done of old.
No candle e'er shall shine in thee,
Nor bridegroom's voice e'er heard shall be.
In silence ever shalt thou lie;
Adieu, Adieu, all's vanity.[4]

Then straight I 'gin my heart to chide,[5]
And did thy wealth on earth abide?
Didst fix thy hope on mold'ring dust? **D**
The arm of flesh didst make thy trust?
Raise up thy thoughts above the sky
That dunghill mists away may fly.

Thou hast an house on high erect,
Framed by that mighty Architect,
With glory richly furnishéd,
Stands permanent though this be fled.
It's purchaséd and paid for too
By Him who hath enough to do. **E**

A price so vast as is unknown
Yet by His gift is made thine own;
There's wealth enough, I need no more,
Farewell, my pelf,[6] farewell my store.
The world no longer let me love,
My hope and treasure lies above.

COMMON CORE RL 4

D ALLUSION
Bradstreet's Puritan readers were well acquainted with the language of the King James translation of the Bible, the authoritative English translation of their time. As daily readers of the Bible, they would have recognized numerous **biblical allusions** in the language of her poems. In the word *dust* (lines 15 and 39), they would have heard a reference to the Book of Genesis: "Dust thou art and unto dust shalt thou return." Reread lines 13–39. Then, check the footnote for the biblical allusion in line 36. How does this allusion work with the allusion in the word *dust* to express Bradstreet's theme in this poem? Explain your response.

E FIGURATIVE LANGUAGE
Reread lines 43–48. What two things does Bradstreet compare in the **metaphor** in these lines?

4. **all's vanity:** an allusion to Ecclesiastes 1:2 in the Bible—"All is vanity," meaning that all is temporary and meaningless.
5. **chide:** to scold mildly so as to correct or improve.
6. **pelf:** wealth or riches, especially when dishonestly acquired.

Huswifery

Edward Taylor

Make me, O Lord, Thy spinning wheel complete.
Thy holy word my distaff[1] make for me.
Make mine affections Thy swift flyers[2] neat,
And make my soul Thy holy spool to be.
My conversation make to be Thy reel,
And reel the yarn thereon spun of Thy wheel. **F**

Make me Thy loom then, knit therein this twine:
And make Thy holy spirit, Lord, wind quills:[3]
Then weave the web Thyself. The yarn is fine.
Thine ordinances make my fulling mills.[4]
Then dye the same in heavenly colors choice,
All pinked[5] with varnished flowers of paradise.

Then clothe therewith mine understanding, will,
Affections, judgment, conscience, memory;
My words and actions, that their shine may fill
My ways with glory and Thee glorify.
Then mine apparel shall display before Ye
That I am clothed in holy robes for glory. **G**

F CLARIFY MEANING
Huswifery means "housekeeping." What housekeeping activity is being described in lines 1–6?

G FIGURATIVE LANGUAGE
What **extended metaphor** does Taylor use throughout the poem to express his relationship to God?

---

1. **distaff:** staff on a spinning wheel for holding the wool or flax to be spun.
2. **flyers:** parts of spinning wheels that twist fibers into yarn.
3. **quills:** rods or spindles used to wind and hold yarn.
4. **fulling mills:** machines that beat and process woven cloth to make it denser and more compact.
5. **pinked:** decorated.

Comprehension

1. **Recall** In "To My Dear and Loving Husband," what does the speaker value more than gold?
2. **Recall** When the speaker in "Upon the Burning of Our House" wakes up to find her house on fire, what is her initial reaction?
3. **Clarify** The speaker in Taylor's "Huswifery" compares himself to a loom. Who or what is compared to the weaver?

Text Analysis

4. **Clarify Meaning** Review the examples of **archaic language** and **inverted syntax** you recorded as you read the poems. How would you restate lines 19–20 of "Upon the Burning of Our House": "He might of all justly bereft, / But yet sufficient for us left"?
5. **Draw Conclusions** Use details from the two poems by Anne Bradstreet to explain what she reveals about her
   - marriage
   - religious beliefs
   - daily life
6. **Make Inferences** What did Bradstreet **value** more than her house? How did this help her accept the loss of her house by fire?
7. **Analyze Figurative Language** How do the "holy robes for glory" mentioned in line 18 of "Huswifery" complete the poem's **extended metaphor**?
8. **Compare Literary Works** What do the poems by Bradstreet and Taylor have in common? What distinguishes one poet's work from the other's? In a chart like the one shown, compare and contrast the poets' work, noting the religious views expressed, the formality of each poet's **style,** and the personality revealed. Use specific details from the poems to complete the chart.

	Bradstreet	Taylor
Religious Views		
Style		
Personality		

Text Criticism

9. **Examine Social Context** The Puritans strongly disapproved of women writers. A Puritan minister even wrote a letter to his sister in England saying, "Your printing of a book, beyond the custom of your sex, doth rankly smell." In spite of this disapproval, do you think the Puritan community would have considered any aspects of Anne Bradstreet's poetry praiseworthy? Explain your answer.

What do you VALUE *most?*

Consider the various things that people value in modern society. What might the Puritans think of some modern values? What do you think of modern values?

COMMON CORE

RL 4 Determine the meaning of words and phrases as they are used in the text, including figurative meanings; analyze the impact of specific word choices on meaning and tone. **RL 9** Demonstrate knowledge of how two or more works from the same period treat similar themes or topics. **L 3a** Apply an understanding of syntax to the study of complex texts when reading. **L 5a** Interpret figures of speech in context and analyze their role in the text.

COMMON CORE

RI 3 Analyze a complex set of ideas and explain how specific ideas interact and develop over the course of the text. **RI 6** Determine an author's point of view or purpose in a text in which the rhetoric is particularly effective, analyzing how style and content contribute to the power, persuasiveness, or beauty of the text. **L 3** Apply knowledge of language to understand how language functions in different contexts and to comprehend more fully when reading.

from Sinners in the Hands of an Angry God

Sermon by Jonathan Edwards

VIDEO TRAILER THINK central KEYWORD: HML11-122A

DID YOU KNOW?

Jonathan Edwards . . .

- wrote a paper on spiders at age 11.
- died as a result of a smallpox inoculation.
- was the grandfather of Aaron Burr, vice-president under Thomas Jefferson.

Meet the Author

Jonathan Edwards 1703–1758

When Jonathan Edwards delivered a sermon, with its fiery descriptions of hell and eternal damnation, people listened. Edwards believed that religion should be rooted not only in reason but also in emotion. Although 19th-century editors tried to tone down his style, Edwards is recognized today as a masterful preacher. In fact, he is considered by many to be America's greatest religious thinker.

A Spiritual Calling Born in East Windsor, Connecticut, Edwards was a child prodigy and entered what is now Yale University at the age of 12. While a graduate student there, Edwards experienced a spiritual crisis that led to what he later described as "religious joy." He came to believe that such an intense religious experience was an important step toward salvation.

In 1722, after finishing his education, Edwards followed the path of his father and grandfather and became a Puritan minister. In 1726, Edwards began assisting his grandfather, who was the minister at the parish church in Northampton, Massachusetts. When his grandfather died three years later, Edwards became the church's pastor.

Religious Revivalist Edwards soon became an effective preacher. In 1734 and 1735, he delivered a series of sermons that resulted in a great number of conversions. The converts believed they had felt God's grace and were "born again" when they accepted Jesus Christ.

Edwards's sermons helped trigger the Great Awakening, a religious revival that swept through New England from 1734 to 1750. The movement grew out of a sense among some Puritan ministers that their congregations had grown too self-satisfied. Delivered at the height of the Great Awakening, "Sinners in the Hands of an Angry God" is the most famous of Edwards's nearly 1,200 sermons.

Last Years Although Edwards inspired thousands, his church dismissed him in 1750 because he wanted to limit membership to those who had undergone conversion. A year later, Edwards went to Stockbridge, Massachusetts, where he became a missionary in a Native American settlement. In 1757, he accepted an appointment as president of what is now Princeton University.

By the time of Edwards's death the following year, the extremism of the Great Awakening had been rejected. However, his vision of humanity suspended, like a spider, over the burning pit of hell still maintains its emotional impact.

Author Online THINK central

Go to thinkcentral.com. KEYWORD: HML11-122B

TEXT ANALYSIS: PERSUASION

Puritan theologian Jonathan Edwards delivered powerfully persuasive sermons. As in all persuasive writing, an Edwards sermon is shaped by the author's **purpose,** his **audience,** and his **context**—that is, his reason for preaching, his Puritan congregation, and the times in which the Puritans lived. One of Edwards's most prominent rhetorical or persuasive techniques is the use of biblical **allusions**—references to figures, events, or places in the Bible that he assumed his congregation would recognize.

As you read Edwards's sermon, look for passages that reveal how purpose and audience affect the tone of his sermon.

READING SKILL: ANALYZE EMOTIONAL APPEALS

Emotional appeals are messages designed to persuade an audience by creating strong feelings. They often include sensory language to create vivid imagery and loaded words to create these types of feelings:

- **fear,** which taps into a fear of losing one's safety or security
- **pity,** which draws on a sympathy or compassion for others
- **guilt,** which relies on one's sense of ethics or morality

As you read, use a chart like the one below to record examples of language that appeals to the emotions.

Examples	*Emotional Appeals*
"arrows of death fly unseen"	*appeals to fear by creating anxiety, unease*

VOCABULARY IN CONTEXT

Jonathan Edwards uses the listed words to help convey his spiritual message. Choose a word from the list that is a synonym for each of the numbered words.

WORD LIST			
	abhor	deliverance	mitigation
	abominable	discern	whet
	appease	incense	
	ascribe	induce	

1. detest **2.** easing **3.** sharpened **4.** anger greatly **5.** attribute

Complete the activities in your **Reader/Writer Notebook.**

What keeps you IN LINE?

A sense of morality probably keeps you from cheating on a test. In other words, you know cheating is wrong. But there are other reasons for behaving morally. Some people are anxious to please. Others fear the consequences of breaking the rules. Jonathan Edwards uses fear to get his point across in the sermon you're about to read.

ROLE-PLAY With a partner, take turns role-playing a conversation with a child who has been stealing. Your mission is to persuade him or her to stop. Before you begin, consider how best to keep the child in line. For example, you might frighten or shame the child or appeal to his or her pride.

Sinners in the Hands of an Angry God

Jonathan Edwards

BACKGROUND Jonathan Edwards delivered his sermon "Sinners in the Hands of an Angry God" in 1741 to a congregation in Enfield, Connecticut. Edwards read the sermon, as he always did, in a composed style, with few gestures or movements. However, the sermon had a dramatic effect on his parishioners, many of whom wept and moaned.

We find it easy to tread on and crush a worm that we see crawling on the earth; so it is easy for us to cut or singe a slender thread that any thing hangs by; thus easy is it for God when he pleases to cast his enemies down to hell. . . .

They[1] are now the objects of that very same *anger* and wrath of God, that is expressed in the torments of hell. And the reason why they do not go down to hell at each moment, is not because God, in whose power they are, is not then very angry with them; as angry as he is with many miserable creatures now tormented in hell, who there feel and bear the fierceness of his wrath. Yea, God is a great deal more angry with great numbers that are now on earth; yea, doubtless, with many that are now in this congregation, who it may be are at ease, than he is with many of those who are now in the flames of hell. (A)

Analyze Visuals ▶
This painting by Italian artist Giuseppe Arcimboldo presents an **allegory** of fire. What lesson or message does the painting seem to suggest about the meaning of fire?

(A) PERSUASION
Reread lines 8–11. Notice that Edwards directly addresses his **audience** in these lines. How do you imagine the audience responded to these words?

---

1. **they:** Earlier in the sermon, Edwards refers to all "unconverted men," whom he considers God's enemies. Unconverted men are people who have not been "born again," meaning that they have not accepted Jesus Christ.

Fire, allegory (1566), Giuseppe Arcimboldo. Painted for Emperor Maximillian II. Limewood, 66.5 cm × 51 cm. Inv. 1585. Kunsthistorisches Museum, Vienna. © Erich Lessing/Art Resource, New York.

So that it is not because God is unmindful of their wickedness, and does not resent it, that he does not let loose his hand and cut them off. God is not altogether such an one as themselves, though they may imagine him to be so. The wrath of God burns against them, their damnation does not slumber; the pit is prepared, the fire is made ready, the furnace is now hot, ready to receive them; the flames do now rage and glow. The glittering sword is **whet,** and held over them, and the pit hath opened its mouth under them. . . . B

Unconverted men walk over the pit of hell on a rotten covering, and there are innumerable places in this covering so weak that they will not bear their weight, and these places are not seen. The arrows of death fly unseen at noonday; the sharpest sight cannot **discern** them. God has so many different unsearchable ways of taking wicked men out of the world and sending them to hell, that there is nothing to make it appear, that God had need to be at the expense of a miracle, or go out of the ordinary course of his providence, to destroy any wicked man, at any moment. . . .

So that, thus it is that natural men[2] are held in the hand of God, over the pit of hell; they have deserved the fiery pit, and are already sentenced to it; and God is dreadfully provoked, his anger is as great towards them as to those that are actually suffering the executions of the fierceness of his wrath in hell; and they have done nothing in the least to **appease** or abate that anger, neither is God in the least bound by any promise to hold them up one moment; the devil is waiting for them, hell is gaping for them, the flames gather and flash about them, and would fain[3] lay hold on them, and swallow them up; the fire pent up in their own hearts is struggling to break out: and they have no interest in any Mediator,[4] there are no means within reach that can be any security to them. In short, they have no refuge, nothing to take hold of. . . . C

The bow of God's wrath is bent, and the arrow made ready on the string, and justice bends the arrow at your heart, and strains the bow, and it is nothing but the mere pleasure of God, and that of an angry God, without any promise or obligation at all, that keeps the arrow one moment from being made drunk with your blood. Thus all you that never passed under a great change of heart, by the mighty power of the Spirit of God upon your souls; all you that were never born again, and made new creatures, and raised from being dead in sin, to a state of new, and before altogether unexperienced light and life, are in the hands of an angry God. However you may have reformed your life in many things, and may have had religious affections, and may keep up a form of religion in your families and closets,[5] and in the house of God, it is nothing but his mere pleasure that keeps you from being this moment swallowed up in everlasting destruction. . . . D

The God that holds you over the pit of hell, much as one holds a spider, or some loathsome insect over the fire, **abhors** you, and is dreadfully provoked: his

whet (hwĕt) *adj.* sharpened

B **EMOTIONAL APPEALS** Reread lines 14–18. What **imagery** does Edwards use in these lines?

discern (dĭ-sûrn') *v.* to perceive or recognize something

appease (ə-pēz') *v.* to bring peace, quiet, or calm to; to soothe

C **EMOTIONAL APPEALS** **Loaded language,** or words with strong emotional associations, can be used to influence an audience's attitude. What examples of loaded language do you see in lines 27–30?

D **PERSUASION** The imagery in lines 38–42 is well suited to the serrmon's historical **context.** Why might the bow and arrow have held negative associations for Colonial Americans?

abhor (ăb-hôr') *v.* to regard with disgust

---

2. **natural men:** people who have not been born again.
3. **would fain:** would rather.
4. **Mediator:** Jesus Christ, who mediates, or is the means of bringing about, salvation.
5. **closets:** private rooms for meditation.

Babylon Burning. From the *Apocalypse of Saint John* (Revelations 18). Luther Bible, First Edition. 1530. Private collection. Photo © Art Resource, New York.

wrath towards you burns like fire; he looks upon you as worthy of nothing else, but to be cast into the fire; he is of purer eyes than to bear to have you in his sight; you are ten thousand times more **abominable** in his eyes, than the most hateful venomous serpent is in ours. You have offended him infinitely more than ever a stubborn rebel did his prince; and yet it is nothing but his hand that holds you from falling into the fire every moment. It is to be **ascribed** to nothing else, that you did not go to hell the last night; that you was suffered[6] to awake again in this world, after you closed your eyes to sleep. And there is no other reason to be given, why you have not dropped into hell since you arose in the morning, but that God's hand has held you up. There is no other reason to be given why you have not gone to hell, since you have sat here in the house of God, provoking his pure eyes by your sinful wicked manner of attending his solemn worship.

abominable (ə-bŏm′ə-nə-bəl) *adj.* thoroughly detestable

ascribe (ə-skrīb′) *v.* to attribute to a specified cause or source

6. **you was suffered:** you were permitted.

Yea, there is nothing else that is to be given as a reason why you do not this very moment drop down into hell. **E**

O sinner! Consider the fearful danger you are in: it is a great furnace of wrath, a wide and bottomless pit, full of the fire of wrath, that you are held over in the hand of that God, whose wrath is provoked and **incensed** as much against you, as against many of the damned in hell. You hang by a slender thread, with the flames of divine wrath flashing about it, and ready every moment to singe it, and burn it asunder;[7] and you have no interest in any Mediator, and nothing to lay hold of to save yourself, nothing to keep off the flames of wrath, nothing of your own, nothing that you ever have done, nothing that you can do, to **induce** God to spare you one moment. . . .

It is *everlasting* wrath. It would be dreadful to suffer this fierceness and wrath of Almighty God one moment; but you must suffer it to all eternity. There will be no end to this exquisite[8] horrible misery. When you look forward, you shall see a long forever, a boundless duration before you, which will swallow up your

E EMOTIONAL APPEALS
Notice the use of the **simile,** or comparison, in lines 50–65. In what way does comparing the audience to a spider appeal to fear?

incense (ĭn-sĕns′) *v.* to cause to be extremely angry

induce (ĭn-do͞os′) *v.* to succeed in persuading someone to do something

7. **burn it asunder** (ə-sŭn′dər): burn it into separate parts or pieces.
8. **exquisite** (ĕk′skwĭ-zĭt): intensely felt.

Detail of *Hell,* Hendrik met de Bles, Kunsthistorisches Museum, Vienna. © Erich Lessing/Art Resource, New York.

thoughts, and amaze your soul; and you will absolutely despair of ever having any **deliverance,** any end, any **mitigation,** any rest at all. You will know certainly that you must wear out long ages, millions of millions of ages, in wrestling and conflicting with this almighty merciless vengeance; and then when you have so done, when so many ages have actually been spent by you in this manner, you will know that all is but a point to what remains. So that your punishment will indeed be infinite. Oh, who can express what the state of a soul in such circumstances is! All that we can possibly say about it, gives but a very feeble, faint representation of it; it is inexpressible and inconceivable: For "who knows the power of God's anger?"[9]

How dreadful is the state of those that are daily and hourly in the danger of this great wrath and infinite misery! But this is the dismal case of every soul in this congregation that has not been born again, however moral and strict, sober and religious, they may otherwise be. . . .

And now you have an extraordinary opportunity, a day wherein Christ has thrown the door of mercy wide open, and stands in the door calling and crying with a loud voice to poor sinners; a day wherein many are flocking to him, and pressing into the kingdom of God. Many are daily coming[10] from the east, west, north, and south; many that were very lately in the same miserable condition that you are in, are now in a happy state, with their hearts filled with love to him who has loved them, and washed them from their sins in his own blood, and rejoicing in hope of the glory of God. How awful is it to be left behind at such a day! To see so many others feasting, while you are pining and perishing! To see so many rejoicing and singing for joy of heart, while you have cause to mourn for sorrow of heart, and howl for vexation of spirit! How can you rest one moment in such a condition? . . .

Therefore, let every one that is out of Christ, now awake and fly from the wrath to come. . . . (F)

deliverance (dĭ-lĭv'ər-əns) *n.* rescue from danger

mitigation (mĭt-ĭ-gā'shən) *n.* lessening of something that causes suffering

COMMON CORE **RI 3, RI 6**

(F) ALLUSION

Reread lines 75 to the end, and consider how purpose and audience influence Edwards's language in these lines. As habitual readers of the Bible, members of his congregation would be familiar with the biblical contrast between a God of wrath and a God of mercy. In lines 87–88, they would recognize a **biblical allusion** or reference in the quotation from Psalm 90. In line 99, they would hear echoes of biblical passages that identify Christ as the lamb of God and that associate Christ's blood with the cleansing of sin. How do allusions such as these increase the persuasive appeal of Edwards's sermon? Cite evidence from the selection to support your response.

---

9. **"who knows . . . anger?":** an allusion to Psalm 90:11 in the Bible—"Who knoweth the power of thine anger?"

10. **Many . . . coming:** a reference to the hundreds of people who were being converted during the Great Awakening.

Comprehension

1. **Recall** According to Jonathan Edwards's sermon, what is a constant threat to all human beings?
2. **Clarify** In Edwards's view, what must sinners do to be spared God's wrath?
3. **Summarize** What key image does Edwards use to persuade his audience?

Text Analysis

4. **Analyze Emotional Appeals** Review the examples of words, phrases, and images you recorded as you read. How does this language effectively appeal to the audience's emotions and get Edwards's message across?
5. **Analyze Persuasion** What role does the appeal to fear or terror play in Edwards's sermon? How do biblical allusions support the writer's appeal to fear? Cite evidence from the sermon to support your response.
6. **Draw Conclusions** How would you describe Jonathan Edwards's view of the following? Cite specific examples for each.
   - God
   - Christ
   - humanity
7. **Compare Literary Works** Use a chart like the one shown to compare some of Jonathan Edwards's and Anne Bradstreet's attitudes and beliefs. Cite specific details from their writings to support your ideas.

	Edwards	*Bradstreet*
Eternal Life		
God's Relation to People *Religious Beliefs*		
Human Frailty		

Text Criticism

8. **Historical Context** In the 18th century, many people died at a much younger age than they do today. How might awareness of the fragility of life have affected people's receptiveness to Edwards's sermon?

What keeps you IN LINE?

In this well-known sermon, Edwards acknowledges that his listeners may already be moral and religious. If he isn't trying to "scare" listeners into moral behavior, what is his true purpose?

COMMON CORE

RI 3 Analyze a complex set of ideas and explain how specific ideas interact and develop over the course of the text. **RI 6** Determine an author's point of view or purpose in a text in which the rhetoric is particularly effective, analyzing how style and content contribute to the power, persuasiveness, or beauty of the text. **L 3** Apply knowledge of language to understand how language functions in different contexts and to comprehend more fully when reading.

Vocabulary in Context

▲ VOCABULARY PRACTICE

Decide whether the boldface words make the statements true or false.

1. If a movie is said to be **abominable,** you should expect to hate it.
2. A good way to **appease** a friend is to criticize her.
3. Feeding the hungry would result in the **mitigation** of their suffering.
4. If you **discern** a difference between two documents, you notice that they are not alike.
5. A person who **abhors** you is probably a close friend.
6. When you **ascribe** a motive to a crime, you explain why someone did it.
7. One way to **incense** someone is to say something complimentary.
8. If you have trouble cutting a steak, it might help to **whet** your knife.
9. An example of **deliverance** is the rescue of passengers from a sinking ship.
10. If I **induce** you to help me do a hard job, I have managed to persuade you.

WORD LIST

abhor
abominable
appease
ascribe
deliverance
discern
incense
induce
mitigation
whet

ACADEMIC VOCABULARY IN WRITING

• document • illustrate • interpret • promote • reveal

What does Edwards's sermon **reveal** about Puritan thought on the human condition? Do you think the Puritans believed that they had full control over their own lives? Write a paragraph explaining how Puritans saw themselves in relation to God, and use at least one Academic Vocabulary word in your response.

VOCABULARY STRATEGY: CONNOTATION

Though some words may have the same definition, their **connotations,** or shades of meaning, can vary. In Edwards's sermon, for example, the word *incensed* suggests a stronger feeling than *angered*. As you read large sections of text, you can use context clues to determine a word's exact shade of meaning.

PRACTICE Based on context clues, select a more intense word from the following list to replace each boldface word in the paragraph.

• antipathy • disconsolate • contrive • momentous • negligible

Our debate team has placed second in state competition for the past three years. Next year, we have to **figure out** a way to take first place. The difference in our score and those of the teams that beat us has been **minor,** so we haven't been too **unhappy** about placing second. In fact, we have no **dislike** of the other teams. Nevertheless, bringing the trophy home next year will be a **very important** occasion.

COMMON CORE

RI 4 Determine the meaning of words as they are used in a text, including connotative meanings. **L 4a** Use context as a clue to the meaning of a word. **L 5** Demonstrate understanding of nuances in word meanings.

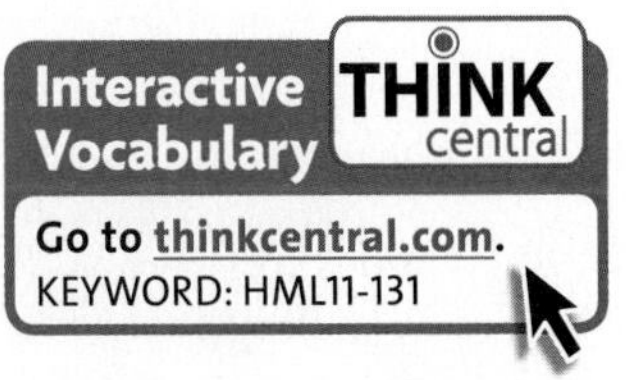

Text Analysis Workshop

American Drama

Have you ever gone to the theater or a movie and felt as if life were unfolding before you? Dramas that realistically portray events have a way of hitting a nerve. American playwrights, in particular, are known for writing dramas that reveal the truth of our everyday experience, and sometimes our not-so-everyday experience.

COMMON CORE

Included in this workshop: **RL 3** Analyze the impact of the author's choices regarding how to develop and relate elements of a drama. **RL 5** Analyze how an author's choices concerning how to structure specific parts of a text contribute to its overall structure and meaning as well as its aesthetic impact.

The Rise of American Drama

Though drama is one of the oldest forms of literature, it was one of the last of the literary genres to develop in the United States. The Puritans in New England regarded theatrical performances as frivolous, so few plays were staged in the 1600s. During the 18th and 19th centuries, drama gradually became an accepted form of entertainment. However, most of the plays performed in the United States were imported from Europe or were adapted from novels.

In 1920 the Broadway production of Eugene O'Neill's *Beyond the Horizon* marked a turning point in presenting true-to-life characters who were struggling to understand their lives. Building on O'Neill's achievement, American playwrights Thornton Wilder, Lillian Hellman, Tennessee Williams, and Arthur Miller created dramas in the 1930s and 1940s that met with critical and popular success. Following World War II, American dramatists Edward Albee and Lorraine Hansberry made significant contributions to the theater. Arthur Miller's 1953 *The Crucible* (page 134) is an example of a modern drama that portrays events from Puritan times.

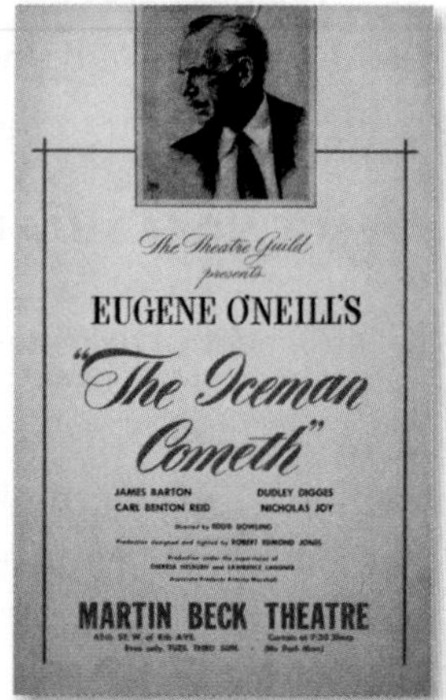

Eugene O'Neill's *The Iceman Cometh* became an American classic.

Conventions of Drama

The two main types of drama are tragedy and comedy. A **tragedy** recounts the downfall of a main character, and a **comedy** is light and humorous in tone, usually ending happily. Many dramas combine elements of both. In addition, most dramas follow similar conventions, or rules, in how they are presented. An understanding of basic dramatic conventions can help you imagine the performance as you read.

PLOT AND STRUCTURE

The **plot** in drama, as in fiction, introduces events and character interactions that produce a **conflict,** or struggle between opposing forces. The conflict builds as the action intensifies throughout the play's **acts** and **scenes,** finally reaching a peak and then resolution. Each scene serves as a building block in the stages of the plot: **exposition, rising action, climax, falling action,** and **resolution.**

TYPES OF CHARACTERS

Drama has many of the same types of characters that are found in fiction. The **protagonist** is the central character of the play. This character is at the center of the conflict and often undergoes radical changes during the course of the play. The **antagonist** often opposes the protagonist, giving rise to the central conflict of the play. Some plays also include a **foil,** a minor character who provides a striking contrast to another character. Interplay among these characters heightens the dramatic tension as the play develops. The names of all a play's characters are listed in the **cast of characters** at the beginning of the play.

SPEECH DEVICES

In drama, the playwright develops the story line through the characters' actions and dialogue. Virtually everything of consequence—from the plot details to the character revelations—flows from **dialogue,** or conversation between characters. Other **speech devices** used by playwrights include

- **monologue:** a long speech spoken by a single character to the audience or another character
- **soliloquy:** a reflective speech in which a character speaks his or her private thoughts aloud, unheard by other characters
- **aside:** a short speech or comment that is delivered by a character to the audience but is not heard by other characters who are present

STAGE AND SETTING

Stage directions are the italicized instructions in a play. The playwright includes the stage directions in order to describe the setting, props, lighting, scenery, sound effects, and costumes. Stage directions also describe the entrances and exits of characters and how the characters look, speak, and react to events or to others. These stage directions from *The Crucible* describe the stage set at the beginning of Act Four.

(*A cell in Salem jail, that fall.*)

(*At the back is a high barred window; near it, a great, heavy door. Along the walls are two benches.*)

(*The place is in darkness but for the moonlight seeping through the bars. It appears empty. Presently footsteps are heard coming down a corridor beyond the wall, keys rattle, and the door swings open.* Marshal Herrick *enters with a lantern.*)

—Arthur Miller, *The Crucible*

Close Read

Why is the description of the cell important to this scene? What effect does it have on the **mood** the scene evokes?

Themes Across Time

from The Crucible

Video link at thinkcentral.com

Drama by Arthur Miller

VIDEO TRAILER THINK central KEYWORD: HML11-134A

COMMON CORE

RL 1 Cite textual evidence to support analysis of what the text says explicitly as well as inferences drawn from the text, including determining where the text leaves matters uncertain. **RL 3** Analyze the impact of the author's choices regarding how to develop and relate elements of a drama. **RL 5** Analyze how an author's choices concerning how to structure specific parts of a text contribute to its overall structure and meaning as well as its aesthetic impact. **RL 7** Analyze multiple interpretations of a drama, evaluating how each version interprets the source text.

DID YOU KNOW?

Arthur Miller . . .

- was once rejected by the University of Michigan because of low grades.
- was once married to film star Marilyn Monroe.
- wrote *Death of a Salesman* in six weeks.

Meet the Author

Arthur Miller 1915–2005

Arthur Miller once paid playwright Edward Albee a compliment, saying that his plays were "necessary." Albee replied: "I will go one step further and say that Arthur's plays are 'essential.'" Miller's plays explore family relationships, morality, and personal responsibility. Many critics consider him the greatest American dramatist of the 20th century.

A Born Playwright Miller was born in New York City in 1915 into an upper-middle-class family. However, the family's comfortable life ended in the 1930s when Miller's businessman father was hit hard by the Great Depression. Unable to afford college, Miller worked in a warehouse to earn tuition money. He eventually attended the University of Michigan.

While in college, Miller won several awards for his plays. These successes inspired him to pursue a career in the theater. His first Broadway hit, *All My Sons* (1947), was produced when Miller was still in his early 30s. However, it was his masterpiece *Death of a Salesman* that made Miller a star. The play won a Pulitzer Prize in 1949 and earned rave reviews from both critics and the public.

Dramatic Years Miller's rise to fame occurred during a difficult period in American history. In the 1940s and 1950s, a congressional committee was conducting hearings to identify suspected Communists in American society. Miller himself was called before the congressional committee and questioned about his activities with the American Communist Party. Although Miller admitted that he had attended a few meetings years earlier, he refused to implicate others. For his refusal, he was cited for contempt of Congress—a conviction that was later overturned.

The hearings provided the inspiration for his 1953 play *The Crucible,* set during the Salem, Massachusetts, witch trials of 1692. Miller wrote the play to warn against mass hysteria and to plead for freedom and tolerance.

The Curtain Closes In the 1970s, Miller's career declined a bit. The plays he wrote did not earn the critical or popular success of his earlier work. In the 1980s and 1990s, however, he enjoyed a resurgence with revivals of *Death of a Salesman* on Broadway. He even directed a production of the play in Beijing.

To the end of his life, Miller continued to write. "It is what I do," he said in an interview. "I am better at it than I ever was. And I will do it as long as I can."

Author Online

Go to thinkcentral.com. KEYWORD: HML11-134B

TEXT ANALYSIS: CONVENTIONS OF DRAMA

Drama is literature in play form. It is meant to be performed and seen. However, an understanding of dramatic conventions can help you picture the performance when you read a script. As you read *The Crucible,* be aware of these drama conventions:

- **Stage directions,** which Miller uses not only to describe settings and characters but also to provide historical background in the form of expository mini-essays
- **Dialogue,** the lifeblood of drama, which moves the plot forward and reveals character traits
- **Types of characters**—heroes, villains, and foils—which Miller uses to heighten the tension of his drama
- **Plot,** which is driven by **conflict** that builds throughout each act

READING SKILL: DRAW CONCLUSIONS ABOUT CHARACTERS

Characters in drama reveal their personality traits through their words and actions. The descriptions in the stage directions can also provide insight into these characters. As you read *The Crucible,* **draw conclusions** about the play's main characters. Record their important traits and the evidence that reveals these traits in a chart like the one shown. Be sure to add characters to the chart as you encounter them.

	Abigail Williams	John Proctor	Reverend John Hale
Traits	proud	assertive	
Evidence			
Motivation	resentment	pride	

VOCABULARY IN CONTEXT

Arthur Miller uses the words shown here to help convey the atmosphere of the Salem witch trials. Place them in the following categories: words that describe character traits, words that describe actions, and words that are concepts.

WORD LIST			
	adamant	corroborate	imperceptible
	anarchy	deference	iniquity
	contentious	immaculate	subservient

Complete the activities in your **Reader/Writer Notebook**.

What fuels *a* MOB?

Visualize a mob of people rampaging through the streets, whipped into a frenzy by hysteria. The fear, anger, and panic produced by hysteria can make otherwise reasonable people do irrational things. In *The Crucible,* for example, the hysteria created by the Salem witch trials makes neighbor turn against neighbor.

DISCUSS What makes people act as a mob? What are some of the results of mob action? Think about news reports or historical accounts of mobs that you've come across. In a small group, discuss what caused these mobs to form and how they behaved.

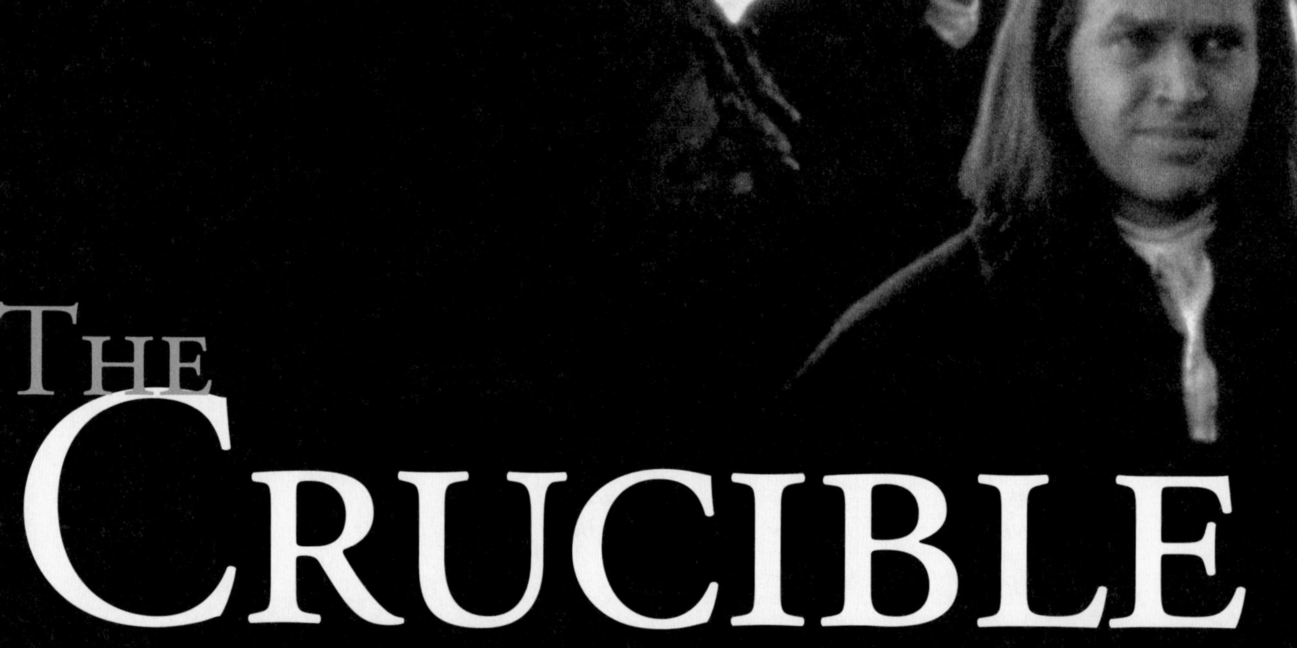

The Crucible

Arthur Miller

BACKGROUND *The Crucible* is based on the witch trials that took place in the Puritan community of Salem, Massachusetts, in 1692. At these trials, spectral evidence—the testimony of a church member who claimed to have seen a person's spirit performing witchcraft—was enough to sentence the accused to death. Miller studied the court records of the trials to gain insight into his characters—all of whom were real people—and get a feel for the Puritan way of speaking. Above all, he wanted to capture the mood of a time when no one was safe.

CAST OF CHARACTERS
(*in order of appearance*)

Reverend Samuel Parris
Betty Parris
Tituba
Abigail Williams
John Proctor
Elizabeth Proctor
Susanna Walcott
Mrs. Ann Putnam
Thomas Putnam
Mercy Lewis
Mary Warren
Rebecca Nurse
Giles Corey
Reverend John Hale
Francis Nurse
Ezekiel Cheever
Marshal Herrick
Judge Hathorne
Martha Corey
Deputy Governor Danforth
Girls of Salem
Sarah Good

Act *One*

An Overture

(*A small upper bedroom in the home of* Reverend Samuel Parris, *Salem, Massachusetts, in the spring of the year 1692.*

There is a narrow window at the left. Through its leaded panes the morning sunlight streams. A candle still burns near the bed, which is at the right. A chest, a chair, and a small table are the other furnishings. At the back a door opens on the landing of the stairway to the ground floor. The room gives off an air of clean spareness. The roof rafters are exposed, and the wood colors are raw and unmellowed.

As the curtain rises, Reverend Parris *is discovered kneeling beside the bed, evidently in prayer. His daughter,* Betty Parris, *aged ten, is lying on the bed, inert.*)

THEME AND GENRE
Imagine that you thought something terrible was happening but you weren't absolutely positive. Should you act? In *The Crucible,* characters do terrible things to stop what they think are crimes. In the Pulitzer-prize winning play *Doubt* (2005), characters confront the same question: What do we do if we think something is happening but we're not sure? Can you think of other characters in recent plays, films, or novels who had to make a difficult decision about whether to act or not act on their beliefs?

At the time of these events Parris was in his middle forties. In history he cut a villainous path, and there is very little good to be said for him. He believed he was being persecuted wherever he went, despite his best efforts to win people and God to his side. In meeting, he felt insulted if someone rose to shut the door without first asking his permission. He was a widower with no interest in children, or talent with them. He regarded them as young adults, and until this strange crisis he, like the rest of Salem, never conceived that the children were anything but thankful for being permitted to walk straight, eyes slightly lowered, arms at the sides, and mouths shut until bidden to speak.

His house stood in the "town"—but we today would hardly call it a village. The meeting house[1] was nearby, and from this point outward—toward the bay or inland—there were a few small-windowed, dark houses snuggling against the raw Massachusetts winter. Salem had been established hardly forty years before. To the European world the whole province was a barbaric frontier inhabited by a sect of fanatics who, nevertheless, were shipping out products of slowly increasing quantity and value.

No one can really know what their lives were like. They had no novelists—and would not have permitted anyone to read a novel if one were handy. Their creed forbade anything resembling a theater or "vain enjoyment." They did not celebrate Christmas, and a holiday from work meant only that they must concentrate even more upon prayer.

Which is not to say that nothing broke into this strict and somber way of life. When a new farmhouse was built, friends assembled to "raise the roof," and there would be special foods cooked and probably some potent cider passed around. There was a good supply of ne'er-do-wells in Salem, who dallied at the shovelboard[2] in Bridget Bishop's tavern. Probably more than the creed, hard work kept the morals of the place from spoiling, for the people were forced

1. **meeting house:** the most important building in the Puritan community, used both for worship and for meetings.
2. **shovelboard:** a game in which a coin or disc is shoved across a board by hand.

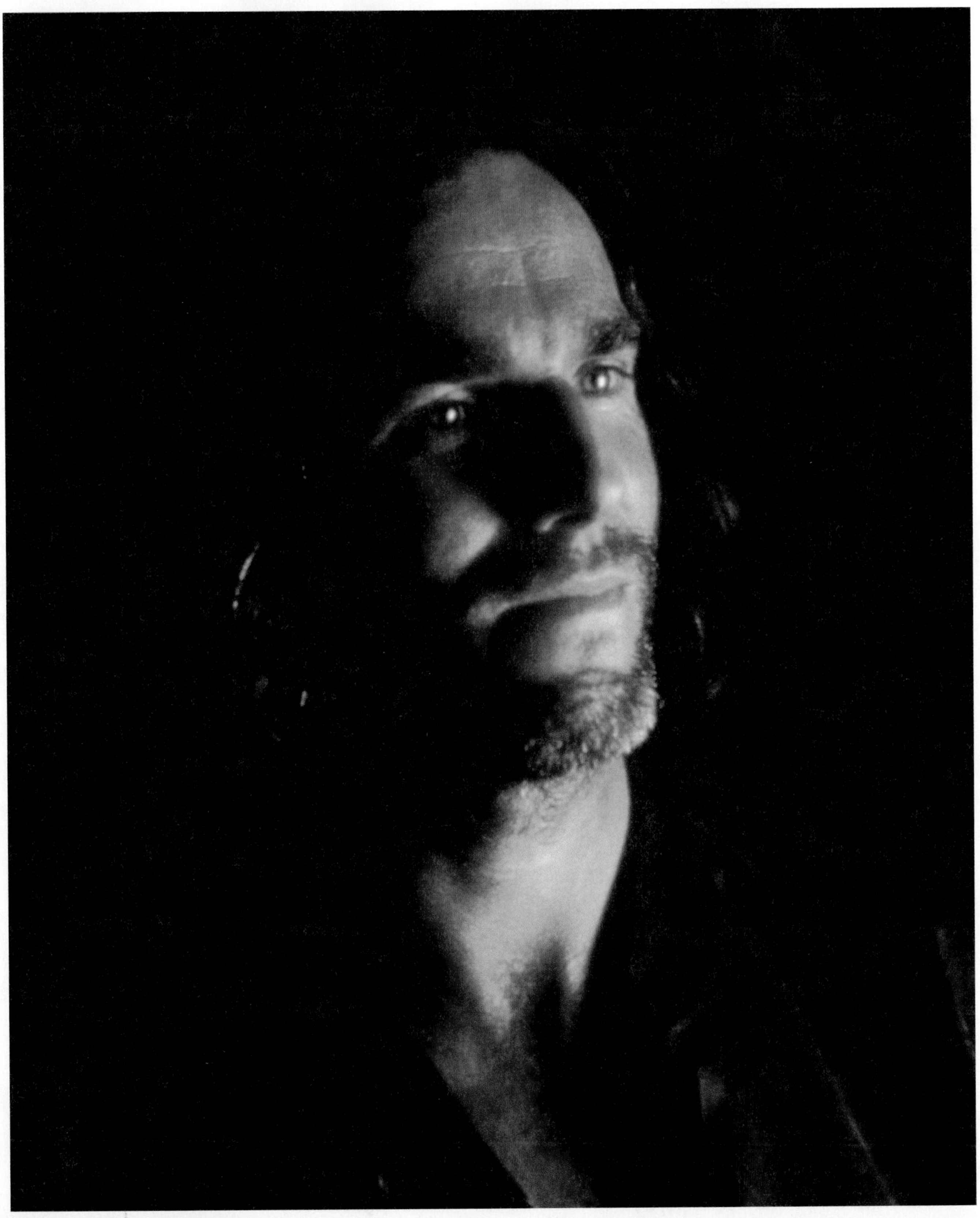

Daniel Day-Lewis as John Proctor

to fight the land like heroes for every grain of corn, and no man had very much time for fooling around.

That there were some jokers, however, is indicated by the practice of appointing a two-man patrol whose duty was to "walk forth in the time of God's worship to take notice of such as either lye about the meeting house, without attending to the word and ordinances, or that lye at home or in the fields without giving good account thereof, and to take the names of such persons, and to present them to the magistrates, whereby they may be accordingly proceeded against." This predilection for minding other people's business was time-honored among the people of Salem, and it undoubtedly created many of the suspicions which were to feed the coming madness. It was also, in my opinion, one of the things that a John Proctor would rebel against, for the time of the armed camp had almost passed, and since the country was reasonably—although not wholly—safe, the old disciplines were beginning to rankle. But, as in all such matters, the issue was not clear-cut, for danger was still a possibility, and in unity still lay the best promise of safety.

The edge of the wilderness was close by. The American continent stretched endlessly west, and it was full of mystery for them. It stood, dark and threatening, over their shoulders night and day, for out of it Indian tribes marauded from time to time, and Reverend Parris had parishioners who had lost relatives to these heathen.

The parochial snobbery of these people was partly responsible for their failure to convert the Indians. Probably they also preferred to take land from heathens rather than from fellow Christians. At any rate, very few Indians were converted, and the Salem folk believed that the virgin forest was the Devil's last preserve, his home base and the citadel of his final stand. To the best of their knowledge the American forest was the last place on earth that was not paying homage to God.

For these reasons, among others, they carried about an air of innate resistance, even of persecution. Their fathers had, of course, been persecuted in England. So now they and their church found it necessary to deny any other sect its freedom, lest their New Jerusalem[3] be defiled and corrupted by wrong ways and deceitful ideas.

They believed, in short, that they held in their steady hands the candle that would light the world. We have inherited this belief, and it has helped and hurt us. It helped them with the discipline it gave them. They were a dedicated folk, by and large, and they had to be to survive the life they had chosen or been born into in this country.

The proof of their belief's value to them may be taken from the opposite character of the first Jamestown settlement, farther south, in Virginia. The Englishmen who landed there were motivated mainly by a hunt for profit. They had thought to pick off the wealth of the new country and then return rich to England. They were a band of individualists, and a much more ingratiating group than the Massachusetts men. But Virginia destroyed them. Massachusetts tried to kill off the Puritans, but they combined; they set up a communal society which, in the beginning, was little more than an armed camp with an autocratic and very devoted leadership. It was, however, an autocracy by consent, for they were united from top to bottom by a commonly held ideology whose perpetuation was the reason and justification for all their sufferings. So their self-denial, their purposefulness, their suspicion of all vain pursuits, their hard-handed justice, were altogether perfect instruments for the conquest of this space so antagonistic to man.

But the people of Salem in 1692 were not quite the dedicated folk that arrived on the *Mayflower.* A vast differentiation had taken place, and in their own time a revolution had unseated the royal government and substituted a junta which was at this

3. **New Jerusalem:** in Christianity, a heavenly city and the last resting place of the souls saved by Jesus. It was considered the ideal city, and Puritans modeled their communities after it.

moment in power.[4] The times, to their eyes, must have been out of joint, and to the common folk must have seemed as insoluble and complicated as do ours today. It is not hard to see how easily many could have been led to believe that the time of confusion had been brought upon them by deep and darkling forces. No hint of such speculation appears on the court record, but social disorder in any age breeds such mystical suspicions, and when, as in Salem, wonders are brought forth from below the social surface, it is too much to expect people to hold back very long from laying on the victims with all the force of their frustrations.

The Salem tragedy, which is about to begin in these pages, developed from a paradox. It is a paradox in whose grip we still live, and there is no prospect yet that we will discover its resolution. Simply, it was this: for good purposes, even high purposes, the people of Salem developed a theocracy, a combine of state and religious power whose function was to keep the community together, and to prevent any kind of disunity that might open it to destruction by material or ideological enemies. It was forged for a necessary purpose and accomplished that purpose. But all organization is and must be grounded on the idea of exclusion and prohibition, just as two objects cannot occupy the same space. Evidently the time came in New England when the repressions of order were heavier than seemed warranted by the dangers against which the order was organized. The witch-hunt was a perverse manifestation of the panic which set in among all classes when the balance began to turn toward greater individual freedom.

When one rises above the individual villainy displayed, one can only pity them all, just as we shall be pitied someday. It is still impossible for man to organize his social life without repressions, and the balance has yet to be struck between order and freedom.

The witch-hunt was not, however, a mere repression. It was also, and as importantly, a long overdue opportunity for everyone so inclined to express publicly his guilt and sins, under the cover of accusations against the victims. It suddenly became possible—and patriotic and holy—for a man to say that Martha Corey had come into his bedroom at night, and that, while his wife was sleeping at his side, Martha laid herself down on his chest and "nearly suffocated him." Of course it was her spirit only, but his satisfaction at confessing himself was no lighter than if it had been Martha herself. One could not ordinarily speak such things in public.

Long-held hatreds of neighbors could now be openly expressed, and vengeance taken, despite the Bible's charitable injunctions. Land-lust which had been expressed before by constant bickering over boundaries and deeds, could now be elevated to the arena of morality; one could cry witch against one's neighbor and feel perfectly justified in the bargain. Old scores could be settled on a plane of heavenly combat between Lucifer and the Lord; suspicions and the envy of the miserable toward the happy could and did burst out in the general revenge.

(Reverend Parris *is praying now, and, though we cannot hear his words, a sense of his confusion hangs about him. He mumbles, then seems about to weep; then he weeps, then prays again; but his daughter does not stir on the bed.*

The door opens, and his Negro slave enters. Tituba *is in her forties.* Parris *brought her with him from Barbados, where he spent some years as a merchant before entering the ministry. She enters as one does who can no longer bear to be barred from the sight of her beloved, but she is also very frightened because her slave sense has warned her that, as always, trouble in this house eventually lands on her back.*)

Tituba (*already taking a step backward*). My Betty be hearty soon?

4. **a junta** (ho͝on′tə) **. . . power:** *Junta* is a Spanish term meaning "a small, elite ruling council." The reference here is to the group that led England's Glorious Revolution of 1688–1689.

Parris. Out of here!

Tituba (*backing to the door*). My Betty not goin' die . . .

Parris (*scrambling to his feet in a fury*). Out of my sight! (*She is gone.*) Out of my—(*He is overcome with sobs. He clamps his teeth against them and closes the door and leans against it, exhausted.*) Oh, my God! God help me! (*Quaking with fear, mumbling to himself through his sobs, he goes to the bed and gently takes* Betty*'s hand.*) Betty. Child. Dear child. Will you wake, will you open up your eyes! Betty, little one . . .

(*He is bending to kneel again when his niece,* Abigail Williams, *seventeen, enters—a strikingly beautiful girl, an orphan, with an endless capacity for dissembling. Now she is all worry and apprehension and propriety.*)

Abigail. Uncle? (*He looks to her.*) Susanna Walcott's here from Doctor Griggs.

Parris. Oh? Let her come, let her come.

Abigail (*leaning out the door to call to Susanna, who is down the hall a few steps*). Come in, Susanna.

(Susanna Walcott, *a little younger than* Abigail, *a nervous, hurried girl, enters.*)

Parris (*eagerly*). What does the doctor say, child?

Susanna (*craning around* Parris *to get a look at* Betty). He bid me come and tell you, reverend sir, that he cannot discover no medicine for it in his books.

Parris. Then he must search on.

Susanna. Aye, sir, he have been searchin' his books since he left you, sir. But he bid me tell you, that you might look to unnatural things for the cause of it.

Parris (*his eyes going wide*). No—no. There be no unnatural cause here. Tell him I have sent for Reverend Hale of Beverly, and Mr. Hale will surely confirm that. Let him look to medicine and put out all thought of unnatural causes here. There be none.

Susanna. Aye, sir. He bid me tell you. (*She turns to go.*)

Abigail. Speak nothin' of it in the village, Susanna.

Parris. Go directly home and speak nothing of unnatural causes.

Susanna. Aye, sir. I pray for her. (*She goes out.*)

Abigail. Uncle, the rumor of witchcraft is all about; I think you'd best go down and deny it yourself. The parlor's packed with people, sir. I'll sit with her.

Parris (*pressed, turns on her*). And what shall I say to them? That my daughter and my niece I discovered dancing like heathen in the forest?

Abigail. Uncle, we did dance; let you tell them I confessed it—and I'll be whipped if I must be. But they're speakin' of witchcraft. Betty's not witched.

Parris. Abigail, I cannot go before the congregation when I know you have not opened with me. What did you do with her in the forest?

Abigail. We did dance, uncle, and when you leaped out of the bush so suddenly, Betty was frightened and then she fainted. And there's the whole of it.

Parris. Child. Sit you down.

Abigail (*quavering, as she sits*). I would never hurt Betty. I love her dearly.

Parris. Now look you, child, your punishment will come in its time. But if you trafficked with[5] spirits in the forest I must know it now, for surely my enemies will, and they will ruin me with it.

Abigail. But we never conjured spirits.

Parris. Then why can she not move herself since midnight? This child is desperate! (Abigail *lowers her eyes.*) It must come out—my enemies will bring it out. Let me know what you done there. Abigail, do you understand that I have many enemies?

Abigail. I have heard of it, uncle.

Parris. There is a faction that is sworn to drive me from my pulpit. Do you understand that?

Abigail. I think so, sir.

Parris. Now then, in the midst of such disruption, my own household is discovered to be the very center of some obscene practice. Abominations are done in the forest—

---

5. **trafficked with:** met with.

Winona Ryder as Abigail Williams

Abigail. It were sport, uncle!

Parris (*pointing at* Betty). You call this sport? (*She lowers her eyes. He pleads.*) Abigail, if you know something that may help the doctor, for God's sake tell it to me. (*She is silent.*) I saw Tituba waving her arms over the fire when I came on you. Why was she doing that? And I heard a screeching and gibberish coming from her mouth. She were swaying like a dumb beast over that fire!

Abigail. She always sings her Barbados songs, and we dance.

Parris. I cannot blink what I saw, Abigail, for my enemies will not blink it. I saw a dress lying on the grass.

Abigail (*innocently*). A dress?

Parris (*It is very hard to say*). Aye, a dress. And I thought I saw—someone naked running through the trees!

Abigail (*in terror*). No one was naked! You mistake yourself, uncle!

Parris (*with anger*). I saw it! (*He moves from her. Then, resolved*) Now tell me true, Abigail. And I pray you feel the weight of truth upon you, for now my ministry's at stake, my ministry and perhaps your cousin's life. Whatever abomination you have done, give me all of it now, for I dare not be taken unaware when I go before them down there.

Abigail. There is nothin' more. I swear it, uncle.

Parris (*studies her, then nods, half convinced*). Abigail, I have fought here three long years to bend these stiff-necked people to me, and now, just now when some good respect is rising for me in the parish, you compromise my very character. I have given you a home, child, I have put clothes upon your back—now give me upright answer. Your name in the town—it is entirely white, is it not?

Abigail (*with an edge of resentment*). Why, I am sure it is, sir. There be no blush about my name.[6]

Parris (*to the point*). Abigail, is there any other cause than you have told me, for your being discharged from Goody[7] Proctor's service? I have heard it said, and I tell you as I heard it, that she comes so rarely to the church this year for she will not sit so close to something soiled. What signified that remark?

Abigail. She hates me, uncle, she must, for I would not be her slave. It's a bitter woman, a lying, cold, sniveling woman, and I will not work for such a woman!

Parris. She may be. And yet it has troubled me that you are now seven month out of their house, and in all this time no other family has ever called for your service.

Abigail. They want slaves, not such as I. Let them send to Barbados for that. I will not black my face for any of them! (*with ill-concealed resentment at him*) Do you begrudge my bed, uncle?

Parris. No—no.

Abigail (*in a temper*). My name is good in the village! I will not have it said my name is soiled! Goody Proctor is a gossiping liar!

(*Enter* Mrs. Ann Putnam. *She is a twisted soul of forty-five, a death-ridden woman, haunted by dreams.*)

Parris (*as soon as the door begins to open*). No—no, I cannot have anyone. (*He sees her, and a certain* ***deference*** *springs into him, although his worry remains.*) Why, Goody Putnam, come in.

Mrs. Putnam (*full of breath, shiny-eyed*). It is a marvel. It is surely a stroke of hell upon you.

Parris. No, Goody Putnam, it is—

Mrs. Putnam (*glancing at* Betty). How high did she fly, how high?

Parris. No, no, she never flew—

Mrs. Putnam (*very pleased with it*). Why, it's sure she did. Mr. Collins saw her goin' over Ingersoll's barn, and come down light as bird, he says!

Parris. Now, look you, Goody Putnam, she never—

---

6. **There be . . . my name:** There is nothing wrong with my reputation.

7. **Goody:** short for *Goodwife,* the Puritan equivalent of *Mrs.*

(*Enter* Thomas Putnam, *a well-to-do, hard-handed landowner, near fifty.*) Oh, good morning, Mr. Putnam.

Putnam. It is a providence the thing is out now! It is a providence. (*He goes directly to the bed.*)

Parris. What's out, sir, what's—?

(Mrs. Putnam *goes to the bed.*)

Putnam (*looking down at* Betty). Why, *her* eyes is closed! Look you, Ann.

Mrs. Putnam. Why, that's strange. (*to* Parris) Ours is open.

Parris (*shocked*). Your Ruth is sick?

Mrs. Putnam (*with vicious certainty*). I'd not call it sick; the Devil's touch is heavier than sick. It's death, y'know, it's death drivin' into them, forked and hoofed.

Parris. Oh, pray not! Why, how does Ruth ail?

Mrs. Putnam. She ails as she must—she never waked this morning, but her eyes open and she walks, and hears naught, sees naught, and cannot eat. Her soul is taken, surely.

(Parris *is struck.*)

Putnam (*as though for further details*). They say you've sent for Reverend Hale of Beverly?

Parris (*with dwindling conviction now*). A precaution only. He has much experience in all demonic arts, and I—

Mrs. Putnam. He has indeed; and found a witch in Beverly last year, and let you remember that.

Parris. Now, Goody Ann, they only thought that were a witch, and I am certain there be no element of witchcraft here.

Putnam. No witchcraft! Now look you, Mr. Parris—

Parris. Thomas, Thomas, I pray you, leap not to witchcraft. I know that you—you least of all, Thomas, would ever wish so disastrous a charge laid upon me. We cannot leap to witchcraft. They will howl me out of Salem for such corruption in my house.

A word about Thomas Putnam. He was a man with many grievances, at least one of which appears justified. Some time before, his wife's brother-in-law, James Bayley, had been turned down as minister of Salem. Bayley had all the qualifications, and a two-thirds vote into the bargain, but a faction stopped his acceptance, for reasons that are not clear.

Thomas Putnam was the eldest son of the richest man in the village. He had fought the Indians at Narragansett,[8] and was deeply interested in parish affairs. He undoubtedly felt it poor payment that the village should so blatantly disregard his candidate for one of its more important offices, especially since he regarded himself as the intellectual superior of most of the people around him.

His vindictive nature was demonstrated long before the witchcraft began. Another former Salem minister, George Burroughs, had had to borrow money to pay for his wife's funeral, and, since the parish was remiss in his salary, he was soon bankrupt. Thomas and his brother John had Burroughs jailed for debts the man did not owe. The incident is important only in that Burroughs succeeded in becoming minister where Bayley, Thomas Putnam's brother-in-law, had been rejected; the motif of resentment is clear here. Thomas Putnam felt that his own name and the honor of his family had been smirched by the village, and he meant to right matters however he could.

Another reason to believe him a deeply embittered man was his attempt to break his father's will, which left a disproportionate amount to a stepbrother. As with every other public cause in which he tried to force his way, he failed in this.

So it is not surprising to find that so many accusations against people are in the handwriting of Thomas Putnam, or that his name is so often found as a witness **corroborating** the supernatural testimony, or that his daughter led the crying-out at the most opportune junctures of the trials, especially when—But we'll speak of that when we come to it.

8. **fought the Indians at Narragansett:** The Puritans fought a series of battles against the Narragansett Indians over territory that both groups had settled on.

Putnam (*At the moment he is intent upon getting* Parris, *for whom he has only contempt, to move toward the abyss*). Mr. Parris, I have taken your part in all contention here, and I would continue; but I cannot if you hold back in this. There are hurtful, vengeful spirits layin' hands on these children.

Parris. But, Thomas, you cannot—

Putnam. Ann! Tell Mr. Parris what you have done.

Mrs. Putnam. Reverend Parris, I have laid seven babies unbaptized in the earth. Believe me, sir, you never saw more hearty babies born. And yet, each would wither in my arms the very night of their birth. I have spoke nothin', but my heart has clamored intimations.[9] And now, this year, my Ruth, my only—I see her turning strange. A secret child she has become this year, and shrivels like a sucking mouth were pullin' on her life too. And so I thought to send her to your Tituba—

Parris. To Tituba! What may Tituba—?

Mrs. Putnam. Tituba knows how to speak to the dead, Mr. Parris.

Parris. Goody Ann, it is a formidable sin to conjure up the dead!

Mrs. Putnam. I take it on my soul, but who else may surely tell us what person murdered my babies?

Parris (*horrified*). Woman!

Mrs. Putnam. They were murdered, Mr. Parris! And mark this proof! Mark it! Last night my Ruth were ever so close to their little spirits; I know it, sir. For how else is she struck dumb now except some power of darkness would stop her mouth? It is a marvelous sign, Mr. Parris!

Putnam. Don't you understand it, sir? There is a murdering witch among us, bound to keep herself in the dark. (Parris *turns to* Betty, *a frantic terror rising in him.*) Let your enemies make of it what they will, you cannot blink it more.

Parris (*to* Abigail). Then you were conjuring spirits last night.

Abigail (*whispering*). Not I, sir—Tituba and Ruth.

Parris (*turns now, with new fear, and goes to* Betty, *looks down at her, and then, gazing off*). Oh, Abigail, what proper payment for my charity! Now I am undone.

Putnam. You are not undone! Let you take hold here. Wait for no one to charge you—declare it yourself. You have discovered witchcraft—

Parris. In my house? In my house, Thomas? They will topple me with this! They will make of it a—

(*Enter* Mercy Lewis, *the Putnams' servant, a fat, sly, merciless girl of eighteen.*)

Mercy. Your pardons. I only thought to see how Betty is.

Putnam. Why aren't you home? Who's with Ruth?

Mercy. Her grandma come. She's improved a little, I think—she give a powerful sneeze before.

Mrs. Putnam. Ah, there's a sign of life!

Mercy. I'd fear no more, Goody Putnam. It were a grand sneeze; another like it will shake her wits together, I'm sure. (*She goes to the bed to look.*)

Parris. Will you leave me now, Thomas? I would pray a while alone.

Abigail. Uncle, you've prayed since midnight. Why do you not go down and—

Parris. No—no. (*to* Putnam) I have no answer for that crowd. I'll wait till Mr. Hale arrives. (*to get* Mrs. Putnam *to leave*) If you will, Goody Ann . . .

Putnam. Now look you, sir. Let you strike out against the Devil, and the village will bless you for it! Come down, speak to them—pray with them. They're thirsting for your word, Mister! Surely you'll pray with them.

Parris (*swayed*). I'll lead them in a psalm, but let you say nothing of witchcraft yet. I will not discuss it. The cause is yet unknown. I have had enough contention since I came; I want no more.

Mrs. Putnam. Mercy, you go home to Ruth, d'y'hear?

Mercy. Aye, mum.

(Mrs. Putnam *goes out.*)

---

9. **clamored intimations** (klăm′ərd ĭn′tə-mā′shənz): nagging suspicions.

Parris (*to* Abigail). If she starts for the window, cry for me at once.

Abigail. I will, uncle.

Parris (*to* Putnam). There is a terrible power in her arms today. (*He goes out with* Putnam.)

Abigail (*with hushed trepidation*). How is Ruth sick?

Mercy. It's weirdish, I know not—she seems to walk like a dead one since last night.

Abigail (*turns at once and goes to* Betty, *and now, with fear in her voice*). Betty? (Betty *doesn't move. She shakes her.*) Now stop this! Betty! Sit up now!

(Betty *doesn't stir.* Mercy *comes over.*)

Mercy. Have you tried beatin' her? I gave Ruth a good one and it waked her for a minute. Here, let me have her.

Abigail (*holding* Mercy *back*). No, he'll be comin' up. Listen, now; if they be questioning us, tell them we danced—I told him as much already.

Mercy. Aye. And what more?

Abigail. He knows Tituba conjured Ruth's sisters to come out of the grave.

Mercy. And what more?

Abigail. He saw you naked.

Mercy (*clapping her hands together with a frightened laugh*). Oh, Jesus!

(*Enter* Mary Warren, *breathless. She is seventeen, a* ***subservient,*** *naive, lonely girl.*)

Mary Warren. What'll we do? The village is out! I just come from the farm; the whole country's talkin' witchcraft! They'll be callin' us witches, Abby!

Mercy (*pointing and looking at* Mary Warren). She means to tell, I know it.

Mary Warren. Abby, we've got to tell. Witchery's a hangin' error, a hangin' like they done in Boston two year ago! We must tell the truth, Abby! You'll only be whipped for dancin', and the other things!

Abigail. Oh, *we'll* be whipped!

Mary Warren. I never done none of it, Abby. I only looked!

Villagers gathering to gossip

Mercy (*moving menacingly toward* Mary). Oh, you're a great one for lookin', aren't you, Mary Warren? What a grand peeping courage you have!

(Betty, *on the bed, whimpers.* Abigail *turns to her at once.*)

Abigail. Betty? (*She goes to* Betty.) Now, Betty, dear, wake up now. It's Abigail. (*She sits* Betty *up and furiously shakes her.*) I'll beat you, Betty! (Betty *whimpers.*) My, you seem improving. I talked to your papa and I told him everything. So there's nothing to—

Betty (*darts off the bed, frightened of* Abigail, *and flattens herself against the wall*). I want my mama!

Abigail (*with alarm, as she cautiously approaches* Betty). What ails you, Betty? Your mama's dead and buried.

Betty. I'll fly to Mama. Let me fly! (*She raises her arms as though to fly, and streaks for the window, gets one leg out.*)

Abigail (*pulling her away from the window*). I told him everything; he knows now, he knows everything we—

Betty. You drank blood, Abby! You didn't tell him that!

Abigail. Betty, you never say that again! You will never—

Betty. You did, you did! You drank a charm to kill John Proctor's wife! You drank a charm to kill Goody Proctor!

Abigail (*smashes her across the face*). Shut it! Now shut it!

Betty (*collapsing on the bed*). Mama, Mama! (*She dissolves into sobs.*)

Abigail. Now look you. All of you. We danced. And Tituba conjured Ruth Putnam's dead sisters. And that is all. And mark this. Let either of you breathe a word, or the edge of a word, about the other things, and I will come to you in the black of some terrible night and I will bring a pointy reckoning that will shudder you.[10] And you know I can do it; I saw Indians smash my dear parents' heads on the pillow next to mine, and I have seen some reddish work done at night, and I can make you wish you had never seen the sun go down! (*She goes to* Betty *and roughly sits her up.*) Now, you—sit up and stop this!

(*But* Betty *collapses in her hands and lies inert on the bed.*)

Mary Warren (*with hysterical fright*). What's got her? (Abigail *stares in fright at* Betty.) Abby, she's going to die! It's a sin to conjure, and we—

Abigail (*starting for* Mary). I say shut it, Mary Warren!

(*Enter* John Proctor. *On seeing him,* Mary Warren *leaps in fright.*)

Proctor was a farmer in his middle thirties. He need not have been a partisan of any faction in the town, but there is evidence to suggest that he had a sharp and biting way with hypocrites. He was the kind of man—powerful of body, even-tempered, and not easily led—who cannot refuse support to partisans without drawing their deepest resentment. In Proctor's presence a fool felt his foolishness instantly—and a Proctor is always marked for calumny[11] therefore.

But as we shall see, the steady manner he displays does not spring from an untroubled soul. He is a sinner, a sinner not only against the moral fashion of the time, but against his own vision of decent conduct. These people had no ritual for the washing away of sins. It is another trait we inherited from them, and it has helped to discipline us as well as to breed hypocrisy among us. Proctor, respected and even feared in Salem, has come to regard himself as a kind of fraud. But no hint of this has yet appeared on the surface, and as he enters from the crowded parlor below it is a man in his prime we see, with a quiet confidence and an unexpressed, hidden force. Mary Warren, his servant, can barely speak for embarrassment and fear.

10. **bring . . . shudder you:** inflict a terrifying punishment on you.

11. **marked for calumny** (kăl'əm-nē): singled out to have lies told about him.

Mary Warren. Oh! I'm just going home, Mr. Proctor.

Proctor. Be you foolish, Mary Warren? Be you deaf? I forbid you leave the house, did I not? Why shall I pay you? I am looking for you more often than my cows!

Mary Warren. I only come to see the great doings in the world.

Proctor. I'll show you a great doin' on your arse one of these days. Now get you home; my wife is waitin' with your work! (*Trying to retain a shred of dignity, she goes slowly out.*)

Mercy Lewis (*both afraid of him and strangely titillated*). I'd best be off. I have my Ruth to watch. Good morning, Mr. Proctor.

(Mercy *sidles out. Since* Proctor*'s entrance,* Abigail *has stood as though on tiptoe, absorbing his presence, wide-eyed. He glances at her, then goes to* Betty *on the bed.*)

Abigail. Gah! I'd almost forgot how strong you are, John Proctor!

Proctor (*looking at* Abigail *now, the faintest suggestion of a knowing smile on his face*). What's this mischief here?

Abigail (*with a nervous laugh*). Oh, she's only gone silly somehow.

Proctor. The road past my house is a pilgrimage to Salem all morning. The town's mumbling witchcraft.

Abigail. Oh, posh! (*Winningly she comes a little closer, with a confidential, wicked air.*) We were dancin' in the woods last night, and my uncle leaped in on us. She took fright, is all.

Proctor (*his smile widening*). Ah, you're wicked yet, aren't y'! (*A trill of expectant laughter escapes her, and she dares come closer, feverishly looking into his eyes.*) You'll be clapped in the stocks before you're twenty.

(*He takes a step to go, and she springs into his path.*)

Abigail. Give me a word, John. A soft word. (*Her concentrated desire destroys his smile.*)

Proctor. No, no, Abby. That's done with.

Abigail (*tauntingly*). You come five mile to see a silly girl fly? I know you better.

Proctor (*setting her firmly out of his path*). I come to see what mischief your uncle's brewin' now. (*with final emphasis*) Put it out of mind, Abby.

Abigail (*grasping his hand before he can release her*). John—I am waitin' for you every night.

Proctor. Abby, I never give you hope to wait for me.

Abigail (*now beginning to anger—she can't believe it*). I have something better than hope, I think!

Proctor. Abby, you'll put it out of mind. I'll not be comin' for you more.

Abigail. You're surely sportin' with me.

Proctor. You know me better.

Abigail. I know how you clutched my back behind your house and sweated like a stallion whenever I come near! Or did I dream that? It's she put me out, you cannot pretend it were you. I saw your face when she put me out, and you loved me then and you do now!

Proctor. Abby, that's a wild thing to say—

Abigail. A wild thing may say wild things. But not so wild, I think. I have seen you since she put me out; I have seen you nights.

Proctor. I have hardly stepped off my farm this sevenmonth.

Abigail. I have a sense for heat, John, and yours has drawn me to my window, and I have seen you looking up, burning in your loneliness. Do you tell me you've never looked up at my window?

Proctor. I may have looked up.

Abigail (*now softening*). And you must. You are no wintry man. I *know* you, John. I know you. (*She is weeping.*) I cannot sleep for dreamin'; I cannot dream but I wake and walk about the house as though I'd find you comin' through some door. (*She clutches him desperately*).

Proctor (*gently pressing her from him, with great sympathy but firmly*). Child—

Abigail (*with a flash of anger*). How do you call me child!

Proctor. Abby, I may think of you softly from time to time. But I will cut off my hand before I'll ever reach for you again. Wipe it out of mind. We never touched, Abby.

Abigail. Aye, but we did.

Proctor. Aye, but we did not.

Abigail (*with a bitter anger*). Oh, I marvel how such a strong man may let such a sickly wife be—

Proctor (*angered—at himself as well*). You'll speak nothin' of Elizabeth!

Abigail. She is blackening my name in the village! She is telling lies about me! She is a cold, sniveling woman, and you bend to her! Let her turn you like a—

Proctor (*shaking her*). Do you look for whippin'?

(*A psalm is heard being sung below.*)

Abigail (*in tears*). I look for John Proctor that took me from my sleep and put knowledge in my heart! I never knew what pretense Salem was, I never knew the lying lessons I was taught by all these Christian women and their covenanted[12] men! And now you bid me tear the light out of my eyes? I will not, I cannot! You loved me, John Proctor, and whatever sin it is, you love me yet! (*He turns abruptly to go out. She rushes to him.*) John, pity me, pity me!

(*The words "going up to Jesus" are heard in the psalm, and* Betty *claps her ears suddenly and whines loudly.*)

Abigail. Betty? (*She hurries to* Betty, *who is now sitting up and screaming.* Proctor *goes to* Betty *as* Abigail *is trying to pull her hands down, calling* "Betty!")

Proctor (*growing unnerved*). What's she doing? Girl, what ails you? Stop that wailing!

(*The singing has stopped in the midst of this, and now* Parris *rushes in.*)

Parris. What happened? What are you doing to her? Betty! (*He rushes to the bed, crying,* "Betty, Betty!" Mrs. Putnam *enters, feverish with curiosity, and with her* Thomas Putnam *and* Mercy Lewis. Parris, *at the bed, keeps lightly slapping* Betty*'s face, while she moans and tries to get up.*)

Abigail. She heard you singin' and suddenly she's up and screamin'.

Mrs. Putnam. The psalm! The psalm! She cannot bear to hear the Lord's name!

Parris. No. God forbid. Mercy, run to the doctor! Tell him what's happened here! (Mercy Lewis *rushes out.*)

Mrs. Putnam. Mark it for a sign, mark it!

(Rebecca Nurse, *seventy-two, enters. She is white-haired, leaning upon her walking-stick.*)

Putnam (*pointing at the whimpering* Betty). That is a notorious sign of witchcraft afoot, Goody Nurse, a prodigious sign!

Mrs. Putnam. My mother told me that! When they cannot bear to hear the name of—

Parris (*trembling*). Rebecca, Rebecca, go to her, we're lost. She suddenly cannot bear to hear the Lord's—

(Giles Corey, *eighty-three, enters. He is knotted with muscle, canny, inquisitive, and still powerful.*)

Rebecca. There is hard sickness here, Giles Corey, so please to keep the quiet.

Giles. I've not said a word. No one here can testify I've said a word. Is she going to fly again? I hear she flies.

Putnam. Man, be quiet now!

(*Everything is quiet.* Rebecca *walks across the room to the bed. Gentleness exudes from her.* Betty *is quietly whimpering, eyes shut.* Rebecca *simply stands over the child, who gradually quiets.*)

And while they are so absorbed, we may put a word in for Rebecca. Rebecca was the wife of Francis Nurse, who, from all accounts, was one of those men for whom both sides of the argument had to have respect. He was called upon to arbitrate disputes as though he were an unofficial judge, and

12. **covenanted** (kŭv'ə-nən-tĭd): In Puritan religious practice, the men of a congregation would make an agreement, or covenant, to govern the community and abide by its beliefs and practices.

Rebecca also enjoyed the high opinion most people had for him. By the time of the delusion,[13] they had three hundred acres, and their children were settled in separate homesteads within the same estate. However, Francis had originally rented the land, and one theory has it that, as he gradually paid for it and raised his social status, there were those who resented his rise.

Another suggestion to explain the systematic campaign against Rebecca, and inferentially against Francis, is the land war he fought with his neighbors, one of whom was a Putnam. This squabble grew to the proportions of a battle in the woods between partisans of both sides, and it is said to have lasted for two days. As for Rebecca herself, the general opinion of her character was so high that to explain how anyone dared cry her out for a witch—and more, how adults could bring themselves to lay hands on her—we must look to the fields and boundaries of that time.

As we have seen, Thomas Putnam's man for the Salem ministry was Bayley. The Nurse clan had been in the faction that prevented Bayley's taking office. In addition, certain families allied to the Nurses by blood or friendship, and whose farms were contiguous with the Nurse farm or close to it, combined to break away from the Salem town authority and set up Topsfield, a new and independent entity whose existence was resented by old Salemites.

That the guiding hand behind the outcry was Putnam's is indicated by the fact that, as soon as it began, this Topsfield-Nurse faction absented themselves from church in protest and disbelief. It was Edward and Jonathan Putnam who signed the first complaint against Rebecca; and Thomas Putnam's little daughter was the one who fell into a fit at the hearing and pointed to Rebecca as her attacker. To top it all, Mrs. Putnam—who is now staring at the bewitched child on the bed—soon accused Rebecca's spirit of "tempting her to **iniquity**," a charge that had more truth in it than Mrs. Putnam could know.

Mrs. Putnam (*astonished*). What have you done?

(Rebecca, *in thought, now leaves the bedside and sits.*)

Parris (*wondrous and relieved*). What do you make of it, Rebecca?

Putnam (*eagerly*). Goody Nurse, will you go to my Ruth and see if you can wake her?

Rebecca (*sitting*). I think she'll wake in time. Pray calm yourselves. I have eleven children, and I am twenty-six times a grandma, and I have seen them all through their silly seasons, and when it come on them they will run the Devil bowlegged keeping up with their mischief. I think she'll wake when she tires of it. A child's spirit is like a child, you can never catch it by running after it; you must stand still, and, for love, it will soon itself come back.

Proctor. Aye, that's the truth of it, Rebecca.

Mrs. Putnam. This is no silly season, Rebecca. My Ruth is bewildered, Rebecca; she cannot eat.

Rebecca. Perhaps she is not hungered yet. (*to* Parris) I hope you are not decided to go in search of loose spirits, Mr. Parris. I've heard promise of that outside.

Parris. A wide opinion's running in the parish that the Devil may be among us, and I would satisfy them that they are wrong.

Proctor. Then let you come out and call them wrong. Did you consult the wardens[14] before you called this minister to look for devils?

Parris. He is not coming to look for devils!

Proctor. Then what's he coming for?

Putnam. There be children dyin' in the village, Mister!

Proctor. I seen none dyin'. This society will not be a bag to swing around your head, Mr. Putnam. (*to* Parris) Did you call a meeting before you—?

Putnam. I am sick of meetings; cannot the man turn his head without he have a meeting?

Proctor. He may turn his head, but not to Hell!

Rebecca. Pray, John, be calm. (*Pause. He defers to her.*) Mr. Parris, I think you'd best send Reverend

13. **the time of the delusion:** the era of the witchcraft accusations and trials.

14. **wardens:** officers appointed to keep order.

Hale back as soon as he come. This will set us all to arguin' again in the society, and we thought to have peace this year. I think we ought rely on the doctor now, and good prayer.

Mrs. Putnam. Rebecca, the doctor's baffled!

Rebecca. If so he is, then let us go to God for the cause of it. There is prodigious danger in the seeking of loose spirits. I fear it, I fear it. Let us rather blame ourselves and—

Putnam. How may we blame ourselves? I am one of nine sons; the Putnam seed have peopled this province. And yet I have but one child left of eight—and now she shrivels!

Rebecca. I cannot fathom that.

Mrs. Putnam (*with a growing edge of sarcasm*). But I must! You think it God's work you should never lose a child, nor grandchild either, and I bury all but one? There are wheels within wheels in this village, and fires within fires!

Putnam (*to* Parris). When Reverend Hale comes, you will proceed to look for signs of witchcraft here.

Proctor (*to* Putnam). You cannot command Mr. Parris. We vote by name in this society, not by acreage.

Putnam. I never heard you worried so on this society, Mr. Proctor. I do not think I saw you at Sabbath meeting since snow flew.

Proctor. I have trouble enough without I come five mile to hear him preach only hellfire and bloody damnation. Take it to heart, Mr. Parris. There are many others who stay away from church these days because you hardly ever mention God any more.

Parris (*now aroused*). Why, that's a drastic charge!

Rebecca. It's somewhat true; there are many that quail to bring their children—

Parris. I do not preach for children, Rebecca. It is not the children who are unmindful of their obligations toward this ministry.

Rebecca. Are there really those unmindful?

Parris. I should say the better half of Salem village—

Putnam. And more than that!

Parris. Where is my wood? My contract provides I be supplied with all my firewood. I am waiting since November for a stick, and even in November I had to show my frostbitten hands like some London beggar!

Giles. You are allowed six pound a year to buy your wood, Mr. Parris.

Parris. I regard that six pound as part of my salary. I am paid little enough without I spend six pound on firewood.

Proctor. Sixty, plus six for firewood—

Parris. The salary is sixty-six pound, Mr. Proctor! I am not some preaching farmer with a book under my arm; I am a graduate of Harvard College.

Giles. Aye, and well instructed in arithmetic!

Parris. Mr. Corey, you will look far for a man of my kind at sixty pound a year! I am not used to this poverty; I left a thrifty business in the Barbados to serve the Lord. I do not fathom it, why am I persecuted here? I cannot offer one proposition but there be a howling riot of argument. I have often wondered if the Devil be in it somewhere; I cannot understand you people otherwise.

Proctor. Mr. Parris, you are the first minister ever did demand the deed to this house—

Parris. Man! Don't a minister deserve a house to live in?

Proctor. To live in, yes. But to ask ownership is like you shall own the meeting house itself; the last meeting I were at you spoke so long on deeds and mortgages I thought it were an auction.

Parris. I want a mark of confidence, is all! I am your third preacher in seven years. I do not wish to be put out like the cat whenever some majority feels the whim. You people seem not to comprehend that a minister is the Lord's man in the parish; a minister is not to be so lightly crossed and contradicted—

Putnam. Aye!

Parris. There is either obedience or the church will burn like Hell is burning!

Proctor. Can you speak one minute without we land in Hell again? I am sick of Hell!

Behind the Curtain

COMMON CORE RL 7

DRAMA AND FILM

These photographs show scenes from the 1996 film version of *The Crucible* that do not occur in Miller's play. One features a meeting between Proctor and Abigail; the other shows an incident that is mentioned in the play. As you study these photographs, keep in mind that on stage it is difficult and expensive to move the action from place to place by changing the set. As a result, Act I of Miller's play takes place in one bedroom. Films, however, make it possible to move a story's action rapidly from one setting to another.

- What are some advantages and disadvantages of adding these new scenes in the film version?
- What story elements is the film director trying to emphasize?

Parris. It is not for you to say what is good for you to hear!

Proctor. I may speak my heart, I think!

Parris (*in a fury*). What, are we Quakers?[15] We are not Quakers here yet, Mr. Proctor. And you may tell that to your followers!

Proctor. My followers!

Parris (*Now he's out with it*). There is a party in this church. I am not blind; there is a faction and a party.

Proctor. Against you?

Putnam. Against him and all authority!

Proctor. Why, then I must find it and join it.

(*There is shock among the others.*)

Rebecca. He does not mean that.

Putnam. He confessed it now!

Proctor. I mean it solemnly, Rebecca; I like not the smell of this "authority."

Rebecca. No, you cannot break charity[16] with your minister. You are another kind, John. Clasp his hand, make your peace.

Proctor. I have a crop to sow and lumber to drag home. (*He goes angrily to the door and turns to* Corey *with a smile.*) What say you, Giles, let's find the party. He says there's a party.

Giles. I've changed my opinion of this man, John. Mr. Parris, I beg your pardon. I never thought you had so much iron in you.

Parris (*surprised*). Why, thank you, Giles!

Giles. It suggests to the mind what the trouble be among us all these years. (*to all*) Think on it. Wherefore is everybody suing everybody else? Think on it now, it's a deep thing, and dark as a pit. I have been six time in court this year—

Proctor (*familiarly, with warmth, although he knows he is approaching the edge of* Giles' *tolerance with this*). Is it the Devil's fault that a man cannot say you good morning without you clap him for defamation?[17] You're old, Giles, and you're not hearin' so well as you did.

Giles (*He cannot be crossed*). John Proctor, I have only last month collected four pound damages for you publicly sayin' I burned the roof off your house, and I—

Proctor (*laughing*). I never said no such thing, but I've paid you for it, so I hope I can call you deaf without charge. Now come along, Giles, and help me drag my lumber home.

Putnam. A moment, Mr. Proctor. What lumber is that you're draggin', if I may ask you?

Proctor. My lumber. From out my forest by the riverside.

Putnam. Why, we are surely gone wild this year. What **anarchy** is this? That tract is in my bounds, it's in my bounds, Mr. Proctor.

Proctor. In your bounds! (*indicating* Rebecca) I bought that tract from Goody Nurse's husband five months ago.

Putnam. He had no right to sell it. It stands clear in my grandfather's will that all the land between the river and—

Proctor. Your grandfather had a habit of willing land that never belonged to him, if I may say it plain.

Giles. That's God's truth; he nearly willed away my north pasture but he knew I'd break his fingers before he'd set his name to it. Let's get your lumber home, John. I feel a sudden will to work coming on.

Putnam. You load one oak of mine and you'll fight to drag it home!

Giles. Aye, and we'll win too, Putnam—this fool and I. Come on! (*He turns to* Proctor *and starts out.*)

Putnam. I'll have my men on you, Corey! I'll clap a writ on you!

(*Enter* Reverend John Hale *of Beverly.*)

15. **Quakers:** a radical English religious sect—much hated by the Puritans—who often "spoke their heart" during their religious meetings.

16. **break charity:** break off; end the relationship.

17. **clap . . . defamation** (dĕf'ə-mā'shən): imprison him for slander.

Rob Campbell as Reverend Hale

Mr. Hale is nearing forty, a tight-skinned, eager-eyed intellectual. This is a beloved errand for him; on being called here to ascertain witchcraft he felt the pride of the specialist whose unique knowledge has at last been publicly called for. Like almost all men of learning, he spent a good deal of his time pondering the invisible world, especially since he had himself encountered a witch in his parish not long before. That woman, however, turned into a mere pest under his searching scrutiny, and the child she had allegedly been afflicting recovered her normal behavior after Hale had given her his kindness and a few days of rest in his own house. However, that experience never raised a doubt in his mind as to the reality of the underworld or the existence of Lucifer's many-faced lieutenants. And his belief is not to his discredit. Better minds than Hale's were—and still are—convinced that there is a society of spirits beyond our ken. One cannot help noting that one of his lines has never yet raised a laugh in any audience that has seen this play; it is his assurance that "We cannot look to superstition in this. The Devil is precise." Evidently we are not quite certain even now whether diabolism is holy and not to be scoffed at. And it is no accident that we should be so bemused.

Like Reverend Hale and the others on this stage, we conceive the Devil as a necessary part of a respectable view of cosmology.[18] Ours is a divided empire in which certain ideas and emotions and actions are of God, and their opposites are of Lucifer. It is as impossible for most men to conceive of a morality without sin as of an earth without "sky." Since 1692 a great but superficial change has wiped out God's beard and the Devil's horns, but the world is still gripped between two diametrically opposed

18. **cosmology** (kŏz-mŏl′ə-jē): a branch of philosophy dealing with the structure of the universe.

absolutes. The concept of unity, in which positive and negative are attributes of the same force, in which good and evil are relative, ever-changing, and always joined to the same phenomenon—such a concept is still reserved to the physical sciences and to the few who have grasped the history of ideas. When it is recalled that until the Christian era the underworld was never regarded as a hostile area, that all gods were useful and essentially friendly to man despite occasional lapses; when we see the steady and methodical inculcation into humanity of the idea of man's worthlessness—until redeemed—the necessity of the Devil may become evident as a weapon, a weapon designed and used time and time again in every age to whip men into a surrender to a particular church or church-state.

Our difficulty in believing the—for want of a better word—political inspiration of the Devil is due in great part to the fact that he is called up and damned not only by our social antagonists but by our own side, whatever it may be. The Catholic Church, through its Inquisition,[19] is famous for cultivating Lucifer as the arch-fiend, but the Church's enemies relied no less upon the Old Boy to keep the human mind enthralled. Luther[20] was himself accused of alliance with Hell, and he in turn accused his enemies. To complicate matters further, he believed that he had had contact with the Devil and had argued theology with him. I am not surprised at this, for at my own university a professor of history—a Lutheran, by the way—used to assemble his graduate students, draw the shades, and commune in the classroom with Erasmus.[21] He was never, to my knowledge, officially scoffed at for this, the reason being that the university officials, like most of us, are the children of a history which still sucks at the Devil's teats. At this writing, only England has held back before the temptations of contemporary diabolism. In the countries of the Communist ideology, all resistance of any import is linked to the totally malign capitalist succubi,[22] and in America any man who is not reactionary in his views is open to the charge of alliance with the Red hell. Political opposition, thereby, is given an inhumane overlay which then justifies the abrogation of all normally applied customs of civilized intercourse. A political policy is equated with moral right, and opposition to it with diabolical malevolence. Once such an equation is effectively made, society becomes a congerie of plots and counterplots, and the main role of government changes from that of the arbiter to that of the scourge of God.

The results of this process are no different now from what they ever were, except sometimes in the degree of cruelty inflicted, and not always even in that department. Normally the actions and deeds of a man were all that society felt comfortable in judging. The secret intent of an action was left to the ministers, priests, and rabbis to deal with. When diabolism rises, however, actions are the least important manifests of the true nature of a man. The Devil, as Reverend Hale said, is a wily one, and, until an hour before he fell, even God thought him beautiful in Heaven.[23]

The analogy, however, seems to falter when one considers that, while there were no witches then, there are Communists and capitalists now, and in each camp there is certain proof that spies of each side are at work undermining the other. But this is a snobbish objection and not at all warranted by the facts. I have no doubt that people *were* communing with, and even worshiping, the Devil in Salem,

19. **Inquisition:** a former tribunal in the Roman Catholic Church dedicated to the discovery and punishment of heresy.

20. **Luther:** Martin Luther (1483–1546), the German theologian who led the Protestant Reformation.

21. **Erasmus** (ĭ-răz′məs): Desiderius Erasmus (1466?–1536), a Dutch scholar who sought to restore Christian faith by a study of the Scriptures and classical texts.

22. **succubi** (sŭk′yə-bī): demons that assume female form. Demons that assume male form are called incubi (ĭn′kyə-bī).

23. **The Devil . . . beautiful in Heaven:** According to Christian belief, Lucifer was God's favorite angel until the angel rebelled and was cast out of Heaven.

and if the whole truth could be known in this case, as it is in others, we should discover a regular and conventionalized propitiation of the dark spirit. One certain evidence of this is the confession of Tituba, the slave of Reverend Parris, and another is the behavior of the children who were known to have indulged in sorceries with her.

There are accounts of similar *klatches* in Europe, where the daughters of the towns would assemble at night and, sometimes with fetishes, sometimes with a selected young man, give themselves to love, with some bastardly results. The Church, sharp-eyed as it must be when gods long dead are brought to life, condemned these orgies as witchcraft and interpreted them, rightly, as a resurgence of the Dionysiac forces[24] it had crushed long before. Sex, sin, and the Devil were early linked, and so they continued to be in Salem, and are today. From all accounts there are no more puritanical mores in the world than those enforced by the Communists in Russia, where women's fashions, for instance, are as prudent and all-covering as any American Baptist would desire. The divorce laws lay a tremendous responsibility on the father for the care of his children. Even the laxity of divorce regulations in the early years of the revolution was undoubtedly a revulsion from the nineteenth-century Victorian immobility of marriage and the consequent hypocrisy that developed from it. If for no other reasons, a state so powerful, so jealous of the uniformity of its citizens, cannot long tolerate the atomization of the family. And yet, in American eyes at least, there remains the conviction that the Russian attitude toward women is lascivious. It is the Devil working again, just as he is working within the Slav[25] who is shocked at the very idea of a woman's disrobing herself in a burlesque show. Our opposites are always robed in sexual sin, and it is from this unconscious conviction that demonology gains both its attractive sensuality and its capacity to infuriate and frighten.

Coming into Salem now, Reverend Hale conceives of himself much as a young doctor on his first call. His painfully acquired armory of symptoms, catchwords, and diagnostic procedures are now to be put to use at last. The road from Beverly is unusually busy this morning, and he has passed a hundred rumors that make him smile at the ignorance of the yeomanry in this most precise science. He feels himself allied with the best minds of Europe—kings, philosophers, scientists, and ecclesiasts of all churches. His goal is light, goodness and its preservation, and he knows the exaltation of the blessed whose intelligence, sharpened by minute examinations of enormous tracts, is finally called upon to face what may be a bloody fight with the Fiend himself.

(*He appears loaded down with half a dozen heavy books.*)

Hale. Pray you, someone take these!

Parris (*delighted*). Mr. Hale! Oh! it's good to see you again! (*taking some books*) My, they're heavy!

Hale (*setting down his books*). They must be; they are weighted with authority.

Parris (*a little scared*). Well, you do come prepared!

Hale. We shall need hard study if it comes to tracking down the Old Boy. (*noticing* Rebecca) You cannot be Rebecca Nurse?

Rebecca. I am, sir. Do you know me?

Hale. It's strange how I knew you, but I suppose you look as such a good soul should. We have all heard of your great charities in Beverly.

Parris. Do you know this gentleman? Mr. Thomas Putnam. And his good wife Ann.

Hale. Putnam! I had not expected such distinguished company, sir.

---

24. **Dionysiac** (dĭ′ə-nĭs′ē-ăk′) **forces:** forces associated with Dionysus, the Greek god of wine and ecstasy.
25. **Slav:** a generic reference to Russians and other Slavic-speaking peoples of Eastern Europe who were under the control of the Soviet Union.

Putnam (*pleased*). It does not seem to help us today, Mr. Hale. We look to you to come to our house and save our child.

Hale. Your child ails too?

Mrs. Putnam. Her soul, her soul seems flown away. She sleeps and yet she walks . . .

Putnam. She cannot eat.

Hale. Cannot eat! (*Thinks on it. Then, to* Proctor *and* Giles Corey.) Do you men have afflicted children?

Parris. No, no, these are farmers. John Proctor—

Giles Corey. He don't believe in witches.

Proctor (*to* Hale). I never spoke on witches one way or the other. Will you come, Giles?

Giles. No—no, John, I think not. I have some few queer questions of my own to ask this fellow.

Proctor. I've heard you to be a sensible man, Mr. Hale. I hope you'll leave some of it in Salem.

(Proctor *goes.* Hale *stands embarrassed for an instant.*)

Parris (*quickly*). Will you look at my daughter, sir? (*leads* Hale *to the bed*) She has tried to leap out the window; we discovered her this morning on the highroad, waving her arms as though she'd fly.

Hale (*narrowing his eyes*). Tries to fly.

Putnam. She cannot bear to hear the Lord's name, Mr. Hale; that's a sure sign of witchcraft afloat.

Hale (*holding up his hands*). No, no. Now let me instruct you. We cannot look to superstition in this. The Devil is precise; the marks of his presence are definite as stone, and I must tell you all that I shall not proceed unless you are prepared to believe me if I should find no bruise of hell upon her.

Parris. It is agreed, sir—it is agreed—we will abide by your judgment.

Hale. Good then. (*He goes to the bed, looks down at* Betty. *To* Parris.) Now, sir, what were your first warning of this strangeness?

Parris. Why, sir—I discovered her—(*indicating* Abigail) and my niece and ten or twelve of the other girls, dancing in the forest last night.

Hale (*surprised*). You permit dancing?

Parris. No, no, it were secret—

Mrs. Putnam (*unable to wait*). Mr. Parris's slave has knowledge of conjurin', sir.

Parris (*to* Mrs. Putnam). We cannot be sure of that, Goody Ann—

Mrs. Putnam (*frightened, very softly*). I know it, sir. I sent my child—she should learn from Tituba who murdered her sisters.

Rebecca (*horrified*). Goody Ann! You sent a child to conjure up the dead?

Mrs. Putnam. Let God blame me, not you, not you, Rebecca! I'll not have you judging me any more! (*to* Hale) Is it a natural work to lose seven children before they live a day?

Parris. Sssh!

(Rebecca, *with great pain, turns her face away. There is a pause.*)

Hale. Seven dead in childbirth.

Mrs. Putnam (*softly*). Aye. (*Her voice breaks; she looks up at him. Silence.* Hale *is impressed.* Parris *looks to him. He goes to his books, opens one, turns pages, then reads. All wait, avidly.*)

Parris (*hushed*). What book is that?

Mrs. Putnam. What's there, sir?

Hale (*with a tasty love of intellectual pursuit*). Here is all the invisible world, caught, defined, and calculated. In these books the Devil stands stripped of all his brute disguises. Here are all your familiar spirits—your incubi and succubi; your witches that go by land, by air, and by sea; your wizards of the night and of the day. Have no fear now—we shall find him out if he has come among us, and I mean to crush him utterly if he has shown his face! (*He starts for the bed.*)

Rebecca. Will it hurt the child, sir?

Hale. I cannot tell. If she is truly in the Devil's grip we may have to rip and tear to get her free.

Rebecca. I think I'll go, then. I am too old for this. (*She rises.*)

Parris (*striving for conviction*). Why, Rebecca, we may open up the boil of all our troubles today!

Rebecca. Let us hope for that. I go to God for you, sir.

Parris (*with trepidation—and resentment*). I hope you do not mean we go to Satan here! (*slight pause*)

Rebecca. I wish I knew. (*She goes out; they feel resentful of her note of moral superiority.*)

Putnam (*abruptly*). Come, Mr. Hale, let's get on. Sit you here.

Giles. Mr. Hale, I have always wanted to ask a learned man—what signifies the readin' of strange books?

Hale. What books?

Giles. I cannot tell; she hides them.

Hale. Who does this?

Giles. Martha, my wife. I have waked at night many a time and found her in a corner, readin' of a book. Now what do you make of that?

Hale. Why, that's not necessarily—

Giles. It discomfits me! Last night—mark this—I tried and tried and could not say my prayers. And then she close her book and walks out of the house, and suddenly—mark this—I could pray again!

Old Giles must be spoken for, if only because his fate was to be so remarkable and so different from that of all the others. He was in his early eighties at this time, and was the most comical hero in the history. No man has ever been blamed for so much. If a cow was missed, the first thought was to look for her around Corey's house; a fire blazing up at night brought suspicion of arson to his door. He didn't give a hoot for public opinion, and only in his last years—after he had married Martha—did he bother much with the church. That she stopped his prayer is very probable, but he forgot to say that he'd only recently learned any prayers and it didn't take much to make him stumble over them. He was a crank and a nuisance, but withal a deeply innocent and brave man. In court once, he was asked if it were true that he had been frightened by the strange behavior of a hog and had then said he knew it to be the Devil in an animal's shape. "What frighted you?" he was asked. He forgot everything but the word "frighted," and instantly replied, "I do not know that I ever spoke that word in my life."

Hale. Ah! The stoppage of prayer—that is strange. I'll speak further on that with you.

Giles. I'm not sayin' she's touched the Devil, now, but I'd admire to know what books she reads and why she hides them. She'll not answer me, y' see.

Hale. Aye, we'll discuss it. (*to all*) Now mark me, if the Devil is in her you will witness some frightful wonders in this room, so please to keep your wits about you. Mr. Putnam, stand close in case she flies. Now, Betty, dear, will you sit up? (Putnam *comes in closer, ready-handed.* Hale *sits* Betty *up, but she hangs limp in his hands.*) Hmmm. (*He observes her carefully. The others watch breathlessly.*) Can you hear me? I am John Hale, minister of Beverly. I have come to help you, dear. Do you remember my two little girls in Beverly? (*She does not stir in his hands.*)

Parris (*in fright*). How can it be the Devil? Why would he choose my house to strike? We have all manner of licentious people in the village!

Hale. What victory would the Devil have to win a soul already bad? It is the best the Devil wants, and who is better than the minister?

Giles. That's deep, Mr. Parris, deep, deep!

Parris (*with resolution now*). Betty! Answer Mr. Hale! Betty!

Hale. Does someone afflict you, child? It need not be a woman, mind you, or a man. Perhaps some bird invisible to others comes to you—perhaps a pig, a mouse, or any beast at all. Is there some figure bids you fly? (*The child remains limp in his hands. In silence he lays her back on the pillow. Now, holding out his hands toward her, he intones.*) In nomine Domini Sabaoth sui filiique ite ad infernos.[26] (*She does not stir. He turns to* Abigail, *his eyes narrowing.*) Abigail, what sort of dancing were you doing with her in the forest?

26. **In nomine . . . infernos** *Latin:* "In the name of the Father and Son, get thee back to Hell."

Abigail. Why—common dancing is all.

Parris. I think I ought to say that I—I saw a kettle in the grass where they were dancing.

Abigail. That were only soup.

Hale. What sort of soup were in this kettle, Abigail?

Abigail. Why, it were beans—and lentils, I think, and—

Hale. Mr. Parris, you did not notice, did you, any living thing in the kettle? A mouse, perhaps, a spider, a frog—?

Parris (*fearfully*). I—do believe there were some movement—in the soup.

Abigail. That jumped in, we never put it in!

Hale (*quickly*). What jumped in?

Abigail. Why, a very little frog jumped—

Parris. A frog, Abby!

Hale (*grasping Abigail*). Abigail, it may be your cousin is dying. Did you call the Devil last night?

Abigail. I never called him! Tituba, Tituba . . .

Parris (*blanched*). She called the Devil?

Hale. I should like to speak with Tituba.

Parris. Goody Ann, will you bring her up? (Mrs. Putnam *exits.*)

Hale. How did she call him?

Abigail. I know not—she spoke Barbados.

Hale. Did you feel any strangeness when she called him? A sudden cold wind, perhaps? A trembling below the ground?

Abigail. I didn't see no Devil! (*shaking* Betty) Betty, wake up. Betty! Betty!

Hale. You cannot evade me, Abigail. Did your cousin drink any of the brew in that kettle?

Abigail. She never drank it!

Hale. Did you drink it?

Abigail. No, sir!

Hale. Did Tituba ask you to drink it?

Abigail. She tried, but I refused.

Hale. Why are you concealing? Have you sold yourself to Lucifer?

Abigail. I never sold myself! I'm a good girl! I'm a proper girl!

(Mrs. Putnam *enters with* Tituba, *and instantly* Abigail *points at* Tituba.)

Abigail. She made me do it! She made Betty do it!

Tituba (*shocked and angry*). Abby!

Abigail. She makes me drink blood!

Parris. Blood!!

Mrs. Putnam. My baby's blood?

Tituba. No, no, chicken blood. I give she chicken blood!

Hale. Woman, have you enlisted these children for the Devil?

Tituba. No, no, sir, I don't truck with no Devil!

Hale. Why can she not wake? Are you silencing this child?

Tituba. I love me Betty!

Hale. You have sent your spirit out upon this child, have you not? Are you gathering souls for the Devil?

Abigail. She sends her spirit on me in church; she makes me laugh at prayer!

Parris. She have often laughed at prayer!

Abigail. She comes to me every night to go and drink blood!

Tituba. You beg *me* to conjure! She beg *me* make charm—

Abigail. Don't lie! (*to* Hale) She comes to me while I sleep; she's always making me dream corruptions!

Tituba. Why you say that, Abby?

Abigail. Sometimes I wake and find myself standing in the open doorway and not a stitch on my body! I always hear her laughing in my sleep. I hear her singing her Barbados songs and tempting me with—

Tituba. Mister Reverend, I never—

Hale (*resolved now*). Tituba, I want you to wake this child.

Tituba. I have no power on this child, sir.

Hale. You most certainly do, and you will free her from it now! When did you compact with the Devil?

Tituba. I don't compact with no Devil!

Parris. You will confess yourself or I will take you out and whip you to your death, Tituba!

Putnam. This woman must be hanged! She must be taken and hanged!

Tituba (*terrified, falls to her knees*). No, no, don't hang Tituba! I tell him I don't desire to work for him, sir.

Parris. The Devil?

Hale. Then you saw him! (Tituba *weeps.*) Now Tituba, I know that when we bind ourselves to Hell it is very hard to break with it. We are going to help you tear yourself free—

Tituba (*frightened by the coming process*). Mister Reverend, I do believe somebody else be witchin' these children.

Hale. Who?

Tituba. I don't know, sir, but the Devil got him numerous witches.

Hale. Does he! *It is a clue.* Tituba, look into my eyes. Come, look into me. (*She raises her eyes to his fearfully.*) You would be a good Christian woman, would you not, Tituba?

Tituba. Aye, sir, a good Christian woman.

Hale. And you love these little children?

Tituba. Oh, yes, sir, I don't desire to hurt little children.

Hale. And you love God, Tituba?

Tituba. I love God with all my bein'.

Hale. Now, in God's holy name—

Tituba. Bless Him. Bless Him. (*She is rocking on her knees, sobbing in terror.*)

Hale. And to His glory—

Tituba. Eternal glory. Bless Him—bless God . . .

Hale. Open yourself, Tituba—open yourself and let God's holy light shine on you.

Tituba. Oh, bless the Lord.

Hale. When the Devil comes to you does he ever come—with another person? (*She stares up into his face.*) Perhaps another person in the village? Someone you know.

Parris. Who came with him?

Putnam. Sarah Good? Did you ever see Sarah Good with him? Or Osburn?

Parris. Was it man or woman came with him?

Tituba. Man or woman. Was—was woman.

Parris. What woman? A woman, you said. What woman?

Tituba. It was black dark, and I—

Parris. You could see him, why could you not see her?

Tituba. Well, they was always talking; they was always runnin' round and carryin' on—

Parris. You mean out of Salem? Salem witches?

Tituba. I believe so, yes, sir.

(*Now* Hale *takes her hand. She is surprised.*)

Hale. Tituba. You must have no fear to tell us who they are, do you understand? We will protect you. The Devil can never overcome a minister. You know that, do you not?

Tituba (*kisses* Hale*'s hand*). Aye, sir, oh, I do.

Hale. You have confessed yourself to witchcraft, and that speaks a wish to come to Heaven's side. And we will bless you, Tituba.

Tituba (*deeply relieved*). Oh, God bless you, Mr. Hale!

Hale (*with rising exaltation*). You are God's instrument put in our hands to discover the Devil's agents among us. You are selected, Tituba, you are chosen to help us cleanse our village. So speak utterly, Tituba, turn your back on him and face God—face God, Tituba, and God will protect you.

Tituba (*joining with him*). Oh, God, protect Tituba!

Hale (*kindly*). Who came to you with the Devil? Two? Three? Four? How many?

(Tituba *pants, and begins rocking back and forth again, staring ahead.*)

Tituba. There was four. There was four.

Parris (*pressing in on her*). Who? Who? Their names, their names!

Tituba (*suddenly bursting out*). Oh, how many times he bid me kill you, Mr. Parris!

Parris. Kill me!

Tituba (*in a fury*). He say Mr. Parris must be kill! Mr. Parris no goodly man, Mr. Parris mean man and no gentle man, and he bid me rise out of my bed and cut your throat! (*They gasp.*) But I tell him "No! I don't hate that man. I don't want kill that man." But he say, "You work for me, Tituba, and I make you free! I give you pretty dress to wear, and put you way high up in the air, and you gone fly back to Barbados!" And I say, "You lie, Devil, you lie!" And then he come one stormy night to me, and he say, "Look! I have *white* people belong to me." And I look—and there was Goody Good.

Parris. Sarah Good!

Tituba (*rocking and weeping*). Aye, sir, and Goody Osburn.

Mrs. Putnam. I knew it! Goody Osburn were midwife to me three times. I begged you, Thomas, did I not? I begged him not to call Osburn because I feared her. My babies always shriveled in her hands!

Hale. Take courage, you must give us all their names. How can you bear to see this child suffering? Look at her, Tituba. (*He is indicating* Betty *on the bed.*) Look at her God-given innocence; her soul is so tender; we must protect her, Tituba; the Devil is out and preying on her like a beast upon the flesh of the pure lamb. God will bless you for your help.

(Abigail *rises, staring as though inspired, and cries out.*)

Abigail. I want to open myself! (*They turn to her, startled. She is enraptured, as though in a pearly light.*) I want the light of God, I want the sweet love of Jesus! I danced for the Devil; I saw him; I wrote in his book; I go back to Jesus; I kiss His hand. I saw Sarah Good with the Devil! I saw Goody Osburn with the Devil! I saw Bridget Bishop with the Devil!

(*As she is speaking,* Betty *is rising from the bed, a fever in her eyes, and picks up the chant.*)

Betty (*staring too*). I saw George Jacobs with the Devil! I saw Goody Howe with the Devil!

Parris. She speaks! (*He rushes to embrace* Betty.) She speaks!

Hale. Glory to God! It is broken, they are free!

Betty (*calling out hysterically and with great relief*). I saw Martha Bellows with the Devil!

Abigail. I saw Goody Sibber with the Devil! (*It is rising to a great glee.*)

Putnam. The marshal, I'll call the marshal!

(Parris *is shouting a prayer of thanksgiving.*)

Betty. I saw Alice Barrow with the Devil!

(*The curtain begins to fall.*)

Hale (*as* Putnam *goes out*). Let the marshal bring irons!

Abigail. I saw Goody Hawkins with the Devil!

Betty. I saw Goody Bibber with the Devil!

Abigail. I saw Goody Booth with the Devil!

(*On their ecstatic cries, the curtain falls.*)

Comprehension

1. **Recall** What is the cause for concern in the Parris household?
2. **Clarify** What has occurred between John Proctor and Abigail Williams before the time in which the play begins?
3. **Summarize** Why does Reverend Hale come to Salem?

Text Analysis

4. **Infer Character Motives** Reread lines 1017–1056 at the end of Act One. Why do you think Tituba and Abigail admit to having practiced witchcraft? Why do they name others?
5. **Draw Conclusions About Characters** Review the **traits** you recorded in your chart for the characters you have encountered so far. How would you describe the most important character traits of the following?
   - Abigail Williams
   - John Proctor
   - Reverend Hale
6. **Make Predictions** Based on what you have learned about Abigail in Act One, whom do you think she might accuse as the play goes on? Cite specific evidence to support your answer.
7. **Identify Beliefs** What do the characters in the play believe about witches? List their beliefs in a concept web like the one shown.

Witches

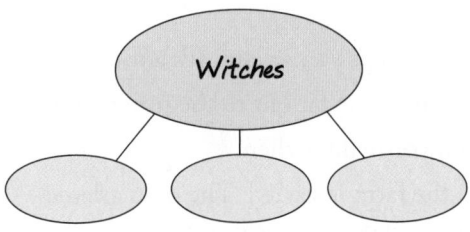

8. **Connect Setting and Mood** The setting of a literary work refers to the time and place in which the action occurs. How do you think Miller uses setting to help create mood in Act One?
9. **Analyze Conventions of Drama** Review the **stage directions** that take the form of mini-essays in Act One. What insights about America after the Second World War does Miller convey? Use details from the mini-essays in your answer.

Text Criticism

10. **Author's Style** The mini-essays in Act One are not usually included in a stage production of *The Crucible*. Why do you think this is so? Why do you think Miller included them in his drama?

What fuels a **MOB?**

What role does Abigail play in the group hysteria that develops as Act One draws to a close?

COMMON CORE

RL 1 Cite textual evidence to support analysis of what the text says explicitly as well as inferences drawn from the text, including determining where the text leaves matters uncertain. **RL 3** Analyze the impact of the author's choices regarding how to develop and relate elements of a drama. **RL 5** Analyze how an author's choices concerning how to structure specific parts of a text contribute to its overall structure and meaning as well as its aesthetic impact.

Act *Two*

(*The common room of* Proctor*'s house, eight days later.*

At the right is a door opening on the fields outside. A fireplace is at the left, and behind it a stairway leading upstairs. It is the low, dark, and rather long living room of the time. As the curtain rises, the room is empty. From above, Elizabeth *is heard softly singing to the children. Presently the door opens and* John Proctor *enters, carrying his gun. He glances about the room as he comes toward the fireplace, then halts for an instant as he hears her singing. He continues on to the fireplace, leans the gun against the wall as he swings a pot out of the fire and smells it. Then he lifts out the ladle and tastes. He is not quite pleased. He reaches to a cupboard, takes a pinch of salt, and drops it into the pot. As he is tasting again, her footsteps are heard on the stair. He swings the pot into the fireplace and goes to a basin and washes his hands and face.* Elizabeth *enters.*)

Elizabeth. What keeps you so late? It's almost dark.

Proctor. I were planting far out to the forest edge.

Elizabeth. Oh, you're done then.

Proctor. Aye, the farm is seeded. The boys asleep?

Elizabeth. They will be soon. (*And she goes to the fireplace, proceeds to ladle up stew in a dish.*)

Proctor. Pray now for a fair summer.

Elizabeth. Aye.

Proctor. Are you well today?

Elizabeth. I am. (*She brings the plate to the table, and, indicating the food.*) It is a rabbit.

Proctor (*going to the table*). Oh, is it! In Jonathan's trap?

Elizabeth. No, she walked into the house this afternoon; I found her sittin' in the corner like she come to visit.

Proctor. Oh, that's a good sign walkin' in.

Elizabeth. Pray God. It hurt my heart to strip her, poor rabbit. (*She sits and watches him taste it.*)

Proctor. It's well seasoned.

Elizabeth (*blushing with pleasure*). I took great care. She's tender?

Proctor. Aye. (*He eats. She watches him.*) I think we'll see green fields soon. It's warm as blood beneath the clods.

Elizabeth. That's well.

(Proctor *eats, then looks up.*)

Proctor. If the crop is good I'll buy George Jacob's heifer. How would that please you?

Elizabeth. Aye, it would.

Proctor (*with a grin*). I mean to please you, Elizabeth.

Elizabeth (*It is hard to say*). I know it, John.

(*He gets up, goes to her, kisses her. She receives it. With a certain disappointment, he returns to the table.*)

Proctor (*as gently as he can*). Cider?

Elizabeth (*with a sense of reprimanding herself for having forgot*). Aye! (*She gets up and goes and pours a glass for him. He now arches his back.*)

Joan Allen as Elizabeth Proctor

Proctor. This farm's a continent when you go foot by foot droppin' seeds in it.

Elizabeth (*coming with the cider*). It must be.

Proctor (*drinks a long draught, then, putting the glass down*). You ought to bring some flowers in the house.

Elizabeth. Oh! I forgot! I will tomorrow.

Proctor. It's winter in here yet. On Sunday let you come with me, and we'll walk the farm together; I never see such a load of flowers on the earth. (*With good feeling he goes and looks up at the sky through the open doorway.*) Lilacs have a purple smell. Lilac is the smell of nightfall, I think. Massachusetts is a beauty in the spring!

Elizabeth. Aye, it is.

(*There is a pause. She is watching him from the table as he stands there absorbing the night. It is as though she would speak but cannot. Instead, now, she takes up his plate and glass and fork and goes with them to the basin. Her back is turned to him. He turns to her and watches her. A sense of their separation rises.*)

Proctor. I think you're sad again. Are you?

Elizabeth (*She doesn't want friction, and yet she must*). You come so late I thought you'd gone to Salem this afternoon.

Proctor. Why? I have no business in Salem.

Elizabeth. You did speak of going, earlier this week.

Proctor (*He knows what she means*). I thought better of it since.

Elizabeth. Mary Warren's there today.

Proctor. Why'd you let her? You heard me forbid her go to Salem any more!

Elizabeth. I couldn't stop her.

Proctor (*holding back a full condemnation of her*). It is a fault, it is a fault, Elizabeth—you're the mistress here, not Mary Warren.

Elizabeth. She frightened all my strength away.

Proctor. How may that mouse frighten you, Elizabeth? You—

Elizabeth. It is a mouse no more. I forbid her go, and she raises up her chin like the daughter of a prince and says to me, "I must go to Salem, Goody Proctor; I am an official of the court!"

Proctor. Court! What court?

Elizabeth. Aye, it is a proper court they have now. They've sent four judges out of Boston, she says, weighty magistrates of the General Court, and at the head sits the Deputy Governor of the Province.

Proctor (*astonished*). Why, she's mad.

Elizabeth. I would to God she were. There be fourteen people in the jail now, she says. (Proctor *simply looks at her, unable to grasp it.*) And they'll be tried, and the court have power to hang them too, she says.

Proctor (*scoffing, but without conviction*). Ah, they'd never hang—

Elizabeth. The Deputy Governor promise hangin' if they'll not confess, John. The town's gone wild, I think. She speak of Abigail, and I thought she were a saint, to hear her. Abigail brings the other girls into the court, and where she walks the crowd will part like the sea for Israel. And folks are brought before them, and if they scream and howl and fall to the floor—the person's clapped in the jail for bewitchin' them.

Proctor (*wide-eyed*). Oh, it is a black mischief.

Elizabeth. I think you must go to Salem, John. (*He turns to her.*) I think so. You must tell them it is a fraud.

Proctor (*thinking beyond this*). Aye, it is, it is surely.

Elizabeth. Let you go to Ezekiel Cheever—he knows you well. And tell him what she said to you last week in her uncle's house. She said it had naught to do with witchcraft, did she not?

Proctor (*in thought*). Aye, she did, she did. (*now, a pause*)

Elizabeth (*quietly, fearing to anger him by prodding*). God forbid you keep that from the court, John. I think they must be told.

Proctor (*quietly, struggling with his thought*). Aye, they must, they must. It is a wonder they do believe her.

Elizabeth. I would go to Salem now, John—let you go tonight.

Proctor. I'll think on it.

Elizabeth (*with her courage now*). You cannot keep it, John.

Proctor (*angering*). I know I cannot keep it. I say I will think on it!

Elizabeth (*hurt, and very coldly*). Good, then, let you think on it. (*She stands and starts to walk out of the room.*)

Proctor. I am only wondering how I may prove what she told me, Elizabeth. If the girl's a saint now, I think it is not easy to prove she's fraud, and the town gone so silly. She told it to me in a room alone—I have no proof for it.

Elizabeth. You were alone with her?

Proctor (*stubbornly*). For a moment alone, aye.

Elizabeth. Why, then, it is not as you told me.

Proctor (*his anger rising*). For a moment, I say. The others come in soon after.

Elizabeth (*quietly—she has suddenly lost all faith in him*). Do as you wish, then. (*She starts to turn.*)

Proctor. Woman. (*She turns to him.*) I'll not have your suspicion any more.

Elizabeth (*a little loftily*). I have no—

Proctor. I'll not have it!

Elizabeth. Then let you not earn it.

Proctor (*with a violent undertone*). You doubt me yet?

Elizabeth (*with a smile, to keep her dignity*). John, if it were not Abigail that you must go to hurt, would you falter now? I think not.

Proctor. Now look you—

Elizabeth. I see what I see, John.

Proctor (*with solemn warning*). You will not judge me more, Elizabeth. I have good reason to think before I charge fraud on Abigail, and I will think on it. Let you look to your own improvement before you go to judge your husband any more. I have forgot Abigail, and—

Elizabeth. And I.

Proctor. Spare me! You forget nothin' and forgive nothin'. Learn charity, woman. I have gone tiptoe in this house all seven month since she is gone. I have not moved from there to there without I think to please you, and still an everlasting funeral marches round your heart. I cannot speak but I am doubted, every moment judged for lies, as though I come into a court when I come into this house!

Elizabeth. John, you are not open with me. You saw her with a crowd, you said. Now you—

Proctor. I'll plead my honesty no more, Elizabeth.

Elizabeth (*now she would justify herself*). John, I am only—

Proctor. No more! I should have roared you down when first you told me your suspicion. But I wilted, and, like a Christian, I confessed. Confessed! Some dream I had must have mistaken you for God that day. But you're not, you're not, and let you remember it! Let you look sometimes for the goodness in me, and judge me not.

Elizabeth. I do not judge you. The magistrate sits in your heart that judges you. I never thought you but a good man, John—(*with a smile*)—only somewhat bewildered.

Proctor (*laughing bitterly*). Oh, Elizabeth, your justice would freeze beer![1] (*He turns suddenly toward a sound outside. He starts for the door as* Mary Warren *enters. As soon as he sees her, he goes directly to her and grabs her by her cloak, furious.*) How do you go to Salem when I forbid it? Do you mock me? (*shaking her*) I'll whip you if you dare leave this house again!

(*Strangely, she doesn't resist him, but hangs limply by his grip.*)

Mary Warren. I am sick, I am sick, Mr. Proctor. Pray, pray, hurt me not. (*Her strangeness throws him off, and her evident pallor and weakness. He frees her.*) My insides are all shuddery; I am in the proceedings all day, sir.

1. **your justice . . . beer:** Alcoholic beverages freeze at very low temperatures, so Proctor is sarcastically calling his wife cold-hearted.

Proctor (*with draining anger—his curiosity is draining it*). And what of these proceedings here? When will you proceed to keep this house, as you are paid nine pound a year to do—and my wife not wholly well?

(*As though to compensate,* Mary Warren *goes to* Elizabeth *with a small rag doll.*)

Mary Warren. I made a gift for you today, Goody Proctor. I had to sit long hours in a chair, and passed the time with sewing.

Elizabeth (*perplexed, looking at the doll*). Why, thank you, it's a fair poppet.[2]

Mary Warren (*with a trembling, decayed voice*). We must all love each other now, Goody Proctor.

Elizabeth (*amazed at her strangeness*). Aye, indeed we must.

Mary Warren (*glancing at the room*). I'll get up early in the morning and clean the house. I must sleep now. (*She turns and starts off.*)

Proctor. Mary. (*She halts.*) Is it true? There be fourteen women arrested?

Mary Warren. No, sir. There be thirty-nine now—(*She suddenly breaks off and sobs and sits down, exhausted.*)

Elizabeth. Why, she's weepin'! What ails you, child?

Mary Warren. Goody Osburn—will hang!

(*There is a shocked pause, while she sobs.*)

Proctor. Hang! (*He calls into her face.*) Hang, y'say?

Mary Warren (*through her weeping*). Aye.

Proctor. The Deputy Governor will permit it?

Mary Warren. He sentenced her. He must. (*to* ***ameliorate*** *it*) But not Sarah Good. For Sarah Good confessed, y'see.

Proctor. Confessed! To what?

Mary Warren. That she—(*in horror at the memory*)—she sometimes made a compact with Lucifer, and wrote her name in his black book—with her blood—and bound herself to torment Christians till God's thrown down—and we all must worship Hell forevermore.

(*pause*)

Proctor. But—surely you know what a jabberer she is. Did you tell them that?

Mary Warren. Mr. Proctor, in open court she near to choked us all to death.

Proctor. How, choked you?

Mary Warren. She sent her spirit out.

Elizabeth. Oh, Mary, Mary, surely you—

Mary Warren (*with an indignant edge*). She tried to kill me many times, Goody Proctor!

Elizabeth. Why, I never heard you mention that before.

Mary Warren. I never knew it before. I never knew anything before. When she come into the court I say to myself, I must not accuse this woman, for she sleep in ditches, and so very old and poor. But then—then she sit there, denying and denying, and I feel a misty coldness climbin' up my back, and the skin on my skull begin to creep, and I feel a clamp around my neck and I cannot breathe air; and then (*entranced*) I hear a voice, a screamin' voice, and it were my voice—and all at once I remembered everything she done to me!

Proctor. Why? What did she do to you?

Mary Warren (*like one awakened to a marvelous secret insight*). So many time, Mr. Proctor, she come to this very door, beggin' bread and a cup of cider—and mark this: whenever I turned her away empty, she *mumbled.*

Elizabeth. Mumbled! She may mumble if she's hungry.

Mary Warren. But *what* does she mumble? You must remember, Goody Proctor. Last month—a Monday, I think—she walked away, and I thought my guts would burst for two days after. Do you remember it?

Elizabeth. Why—I do, I think, but—

Mary Warren. And so I told that to Judge Hathorne, and he asks her so. "Sarah Good," says he, "what curse do you mumble that this girl must fall sick after turning you away?" And then she replies

---

2. **fair poppet:** pretty doll.

(*mimicking an old crone*) "Why, your excellence, no curse at all. I only say my commandments;[3] I hope I may say my commandments," says she!

Elizabeth. And that's an upright answer.

Mary Warren. Aye, but then Judge Hathorne say, "Recite for us your commandments!" (*leaning avidly toward them*) and of all the ten she could not say a single one. She never knew no commandments, and they had her in a flat lie!

Proctor. And so condemned her?

Mary Warren (*now a little strained, seeing his stubborn doubt*). Why, they must when she condemned herself.

Proctor. But the proof, the proof!

Mary Warren (*with greater impatience with him*). I told you the proof. It's hard proof, hard as rock, the judges said.

Proctor (*pauses an instant, then*). You will not go to court again, Mary Warren.

Mary Warren. I must tell you, sir, I will be gone every day now. I am amazed you do not see what weighty work we do.

Proctor. What work you do! It's strange work for a Christian girl to hang old women!

Mary Warren. But, Mr. Proctor, they will not hang them if they confess. Sarah Good will only sit in jail some time (*recalling*) and here's a wonder for you; think on this. Goody Good is pregnant!

Elizabeth. Pregnant! Are they mad? The woman's near to sixty!

Mary Warren. They had Doctor Griggs examine her, and she's full to the brim. And smokin' a pipe all these years, and no husband either! But she's safe, thank God, for they'll not hurt the innocent child. But be that not a marvel? You must see it, sir, it's God's work we do. So I'll be gone every day for some time. I'm—I am an official of the court, they say, and I—(*She has been edging toward offstage.*)

Proctor. I'll official you! (*He strides to the mantel, takes down the whip hanging there.*)

Mary Warren (*terrified, but coming erect, striving for her authority*). I'll not stand whipping any more!

Elizabeth (*hurriedly, as Proctor approaches*). Mary, promise now you'll stay at home—

Mary Warren (*backing from him, but keeping her erect posture, striving, striving for her way*). The Devil's loose in Salem, Mr. Proctor; we must discover where he's hiding!

Proctor. I'll whip the Devil out of you! (*With whip raised he reaches out for her, and she streaks away and yells.*)

Mary Warren (*pointing at* Elizabeth). I saved her life today!

(*Silence. His whip comes down.*)

Elizabeth (*softly*). I am accused?

Mary Warren (*quaking*). Somewhat mentioned. But I said I never see no sign you ever sent your spirit out to hurt no one, and seeing I do live so closely with you, they dismissed it.

Elizabeth. Who accused me?

Mary Warren. I am bound by law, I cannot tell it. (*to* Proctor) I only hope you'll not be so sarcastical no more. Four judges and the King's deputy sat to dinner with us but an hour ago. I—I would have you speak civilly to me, from this out.

Proctor (*in horror, muttering in disgust at her*). Go to bed.

Mary Warren (*with a stamp of her foot*). I'll not be ordered to bed no more, Mr. Proctor! I am eighteen and a woman, however single!

Proctor. Do you wish to sit up? Then sit up.

Mary Warren. I wish to go to bed!

Proctor (*in anger*). Good night, then!

Mary Warren. Good night. (*Dissatisfied, uncertain of herself, she goes out. Wide-eyed, both,* Proctor *and* Elizabeth *stand staring.*)

Elizabeth (*quietly*). Oh, the noose, the noose is up!

Proctor. There'll be no noose.

3. **commandments:** the Ten Commandments in the Bible.

Elizabeth. She wants me dead. I knew all week it would come to this!

Proctor (*without conviction*). They dismissed it. You heard her say—

Elizabeth. And what of tomorrow? She will cry me out until they take me!

Proctor. Sit you down.

Elizabeth. She wants me dead, John, you know it!

Proctor. I say sit down! (*She sits, trembling. He speaks quietly, trying to keep his wits.*) Now we must be wise, Elizabeth.

Elizabeth (*with sarcasm, and a sense of being lost*). Oh, indeed, indeed!

Proctor. Fear nothing. I'll find Ezekiel Cheever. I'll tell him she said it were all sport.

Elizabeth. John, with so many in the jail, more than Cheever's help is needed now, I think. Would you favor me with this? Go to Abigail.

Proctor (*his soul hardening as he senses . . .*). What have I to say to Abigail?

Elizabeth (*delicately*). John—grant me this. You have a faulty understanding of young girls. There is a promise made in any bed—

Proctor (*striving against his anger*). What promise!

Elizabeth. Spoke or silent, a promise is surely made. And she may dote on it now—I am sure she does—and thinks to kill me, then to take my place.

(Proctor*'s anger is rising; he cannot speak.*)

Elizabeth. It is her dearest hope, John, I know it. There be a thousand names; why does she call mine? There be a certain danger in calling such a name—I am no Goody Good that sleeps in ditches, nor Osburn, drunk and half-witted. She'd dare not call out such a farmer's wife but there be monstrous profit in it. She thinks to take my place, John.

Proctor. She cannot think it! (*He knows it is true.*)

Elizabeth (*"reasonably"*). John, have you ever shown her somewhat of contempt? She cannot pass you in the church but you will blush—

Proctor. I may blush for my sin.

Elizabeth. I think she sees another meaning in that blush.

Proctor. And what see you? What see you, Elizabeth?

Elizabeth (*"conceding"*). I think you be somewhat ashamed, for I am there, and she so close.

Proctor. When will you know me, woman? Were I stone I would have cracked for shame this seven month!

Elizabeth. Then go and tell her she's a whore. Whatever promise she may sense—break it, John, break it.

Proctor (*between his teeth*). Good, then. I'll go. (*He starts for his rifle.*)

Elizabeth (*trembling, fearfully*). Oh, how unwillingly!

Proctor (*turning on her, rifle in hand*). I will curse her hotter than the oldest cinder in hell. But pray, begrudge me not my anger!

Elizabeth. Your anger! I only ask you—

Proctor. Woman, am I so base? Do you truly think me base?

Elizabeth. I never called you base.

Proctor. Then how do you charge me with such a promise? The promise that a stallion gives a mare I gave that girl!

Elizabeth. Then why do you anger with me when I bid you break it?

Proctor. Because it speaks deceit, and I am honest! But I'll plead no more! I see now your spirit twists around the single error of my life, and I will never tear it free!

Elizabeth (*crying out*). You'll tear it free—when you come to know that I will be your only wife, or no wife at all! She has an arrow in you yet, John Proctor, and you know it well!

(*Quite suddenly, as though from the air, a figure appears in the doorway. They start slightly. It is* Mr. Hale. *He is different now—drawn a little, and there is a quality of deference, even of guilt, about his manner now.*)

Hale. Good evening.

Proctor (*still in his shock*). Why, Mr. Hale! Good evening to you, sir. Come in, come in.

Hale (*to* Elizabeth). I hope I do not startle you.

Elizabeth. No, no, it's only that I heard no horse—

Hale. You are Goodwife Proctor.

Proctor. Aye; Elizabeth.

Hale (*nods, then*). I hope you're not off to bed yet.

Proctor (*setting down his gun*). No, no. (Hale *comes further into the room. And* Proctor, *to explain his nervousness.*) We are not used to visitors after dark, but you're welcome here. Will you sit you down, sir?

Hale. I will. (*He sits.*) Let you sit, Goodwife Proctor.

(*She does, never letting him out of her sight. There is a pause as* Hale *looks about the room.*)

Proctor (*to break the silence*). Will you drink cider, Mr. Hale?

Hale. No, it rebels[4] my stomach; I have some further traveling yet tonight. Sit you down, sir. (Proctor *sits.*) I will not keep you long, but I have some business with you.

Proctor. Business of the court?

Hale. No—no, I come of my own, without the court's authority. Hear me. (*He wets his lips.*) I know not if you are aware, but your wife's name is—mentioned in the court.

Proctor. We know it, sir. Our Mary Warren told us. We are entirely amazed.

Hale. I am a stranger here, as you know. And in my ignorance I find it hard to draw a clear opinion of them that come accused before the court. And so this afternoon, and now tonight, I go from house to house—I come now from Rebecca Nurse's house and—

Elizabeth (*shocked*). Rebecca's charged!

Hale. God forbid such a one be charged. She is, however—mentioned somewhat.

Elizabeth (*with an attempt at a laugh*). You will never believe, I hope, that Rebecca trafficked with the Devil.

Hale. Woman, it is possible.

Proctor (*taken aback*). Surely you cannot think so.

Hale. This is a strange time, Mister. No man may longer doubt the powers of the dark are gathered in monstrous attack upon this village. There is too much evidence now to deny it. You will agree, sir?

Proctor (*evading*). I—have no knowledge in that line. But it's hard to think so pious a woman be secretly a Devil's bitch after seventy year of such good prayer.

Hale. Aye. But the Devil is a wily one, you cannot deny it. However, she is far from accused, and I know she will not be. (*pause*) I thought, sir, to put some questions as to the Christian character of this house, if you'll permit me.

Proctor (*coldly, resentful*). Why, we—have no fear of questions, sir.

Hale. Good, then. (*He makes himself more comfortable.*) In the book of record that Mr. Parris keeps, I note that you are rarely in the church on Sabbath Day.

Proctor. No, sir, you are mistaken.

Hale. Twenty-six time in seventeen month, sir. I must call that rare. Will you tell me why you are so absent?

Proctor. Mr. Hale, I never knew I must account to that man for I come to church or stay at home. My wife were sick this winter.

Hale. So I am told. But you, Mister, why could you not come alone?

Proctor. I surely did come when I could, and when I could not I prayed in this house.

Hale. Mr. Proctor, your house is not a church; your theology must tell you that.

Proctor. It does, sir, it does; and it tells me that a minister may pray to God without he have golden candlesticks upon the altar.

Hale. What golden candlesticks?

4. **rebels:** upsets.

Proctor. Since we built the church there were pewter candlesticks upon the altar; Francis Nurse made them, y'know, and a sweeter hand never touched the metal. But Parris came, and for twenty week he preach nothin' but golden candlesticks until he had them. I labor the earth from dawn of day to blink of night, and I tell you true, when I look to heaven and see my money glaring at his elbows—it hurt my prayer, sir, it hurt my prayer. I think, sometimes, the man dreams cathedrals, not clapboard meetin' houses.

Hale (*thinks, then*). And yet, Mister, a Christian on Sabbath Day must be in church. (*pause*) Tell me—you have three children?

Proctor. Aye. Boys.

Hale. How comes it that only two are baptized?

Proctor (*starts to speak, then stops, then, as though unable to restrain this*). I like it not that Mr. Parris should lay his hand upon my baby. I see no light of God in that man. I'll not conceal it.

Hale. I must say it, Mr. Proctor; that is not for you to decide. The man's ordained, therefore the light of God is in him.

Proctor (*flushed with resentment but trying to smile*). What's your suspicion, Mr. Hale?

Hale. No, no, I have no—

Proctor. I nailed the roof upon the church, I hung the door—

Hale. Oh, did you! That's a good sign, then.

Proctor. It may be I have been too quick to bring the man to book,[5] but you cannot think we ever desired the destruction of religion. I think that's in your mind, is it not?

Hale (*not altogether giving way*). I—have—there is a softness in your record, sir, a softness.

Elizabeth. I think, maybe, we have been too hard with Mr. Parris. I think so. But sure we never loved the Devil here.

Hale (*nods, deliberating this. Then, with the voice of one administering a secret test*). Do you know your Commandments, Elizabeth?

Elizabeth (*without hesitation, even eagerly*). I surely do. There be no mark of blame upon my life, Mr. Hale. I am a convenanted Christian woman.

Hale. And you, Mister?

Proctor (*a trifle unsteadily*). I—am sure I do, sir.

5. **bring the man to book:** judge the man.

John Proctor and his sons

Hale (*glances at her open face, then at* John, *then*). Let you repeat them, if you will.

Proctor. The Commandments.

Hale. Aye.

Proctor (*looking off, beginning to sweat*). Thou shalt not kill.

Hale. Aye.

Proctor (*counting on his fingers*). Thou shalt not steal. Thou shalt not covet thy neighbor's goods, nor make unto thee any graven image. Thou shalt not take the name of the Lord in vain; thou shalt have no other gods before me. (*with some hesitation*) Thou shalt remember the Sabbath Day and keep it holy. (*Pause. Then.*) Thou shalt honor thy father and mother. Thou shalt not bear false witness. (*He is stuck. He counts back on his fingers, knowing one is missing.*) Thou shalt not make unto thee any graven image.

Hale. You have said that twice, sir.

Proctor (*lost*). Aye. (*He is flailing for it.*)

Elizabeth (*delicately*). Adultery, John.

Proctor (*as though a secret arrow had pained his heart*). Aye. (*trying to grin it away—to* Hale) You see, sir, between the two of us we do know them all. (Hale *only looks at* Proctor, *deep in his attempt to define this man.* Proctor *grows more uneasy.*) I think it be a small fault.

Hale. Theology, sir, is a fortress; no crack in a fortress may be accounted small. (*He rises; he seems worried now. He paces a little, in deep thought.*)

Proctor. There be no love for Satan in this house, Mister.

Hale. I pray it, I pray it dearly. (*He looks to both of them, an attempt at a smile on his face, but his misgivings are clear.*) Well, then—I'll bid you good night.

Elizabeth (*unable to restrain herself*). Mr. Hale. (*He turns.*) I do think you are suspecting me somewhat? Are you not?

Hale (*obviously disturbed—and evasive*). Goody Proctor, I do not judge you. My duty is to add what I may to the godly wisdom of the court. I pray you both good health and good fortune. (*to* John) Good night, sir. (*He starts out.*)

Elizabeth (*with a note of desperation*). I think you must tell him, John.

Hale. What's that?

Elizabeth (*restraining a call*). Will you tell him?

(*Slight pause.* Hale *looks questioningly at* John.)

Proctor (*with difficulty*). I—I have no witness and cannot prove it, except my word be taken. But I know the children's sickness had naught to do with witchcraft.

Hale (*stopped, struck*). Naught to do—?

Proctor. Mr. Parris discovered them sportin' in the woods. They were startled and took sick.

(*pause*)

Hale. Who told you this?

Proctor (*hesitates, then*). Abigail Williams.

Hale. Abigail!

Proctor. Aye.

Hale (*his eyes wide*). Abigail Williams told you it had naught to do with witchcraft!

Proctor. She told me the day you came, sir.

Hale (*suspiciously*). Why—why did you keep this?

Proctor. I never knew until tonight that the world is gone daft with this nonsense.

Hale. Nonsense! Mister, I have myself examined Tituba, Sarah Good, and numerous others that have confessed to dealing with the Devil. They have *confessed* it.

Proctor. And why not, if they must hang for denyin' it? There are them that will swear to anything before they'll hang; have you never thought of that?

Hale. I have. I—I have indeed. (*It is his own suspicion, but he resists it. He glances at* Elizabeth, *then at* John.) And you—would you testify to this in court?

Proctor. I—had not reckoned with goin' into court. But if I must I will.

Hale. Do you falter here?

Proctor. I falter nothing, but I may wonder if my story will be credited in such a court. I do wonder on it, when such a steady-minded minister as you will suspicion such a woman that never lied, and cannot, and the world knows she cannot! I may falter somewhat, Mister; I am no fool.

Hale (*quietly—it has impressed him*). Proctor, let you open with me now, for I have a rumor that troubles me. It's said you hold no belief that there may even be witches in the world. Is that true, sir?

Proctor (*He knows this is critical, and is striving against his disgust with* Hale *and with himself for even answering*). I know not what I have said, I may have said it. I have wondered if there be witches in the world—although I cannot believe they come among us now.

Hale. Then you do not believe—

Proctor. I have no knowledge of it; the Bible speaks of witches, and I will not deny them.

Hale. And you, woman?

Elizabeth. I—I cannot believe it.

Hale (*shocked*). You cannot!

Proctor. Elizabeth, you bewilder him!

Elizabeth (*to* Hale). I cannot think the Devil may own a woman's soul, Mr. Hale, when she keeps an upright way, as I have. I am a good woman, I know it; and if you believe I may do only good work in the world, and yet be secretly bound to Satan, then I must tell you, sir, I do not believe it.

Hale. But, woman, you do believe there are witches in—

Elizabeth. If you think that I am one, then I say there are none.

Hale. You surely do not fly against the Gospel, the Gospel—

Proctor. She believe in the Gospel, every word!

Elizabeth. Question Abigail Williams about the Gospel, not myself!

(Hale *stares at her.*)

Proctor. She do not mean to doubt the Gospel, sir, you cannot think it. This be a Christian house, sir, a Christian house.

Hale. God keep you both; let the third child be quickly baptized, and go you without fail each Sunday in to Sabbath prayer; and keep a solemn, quiet way among you. I think—

(Giles Corey *appears in doorway.*)

Giles. John!

Proctor. Giles! What's the matter?

Giles. They take my wife.

(Francis Nurse *enters.*)

Giles. And his Rebecca!

Proctor (*to* Francis). Rebecca's in the *jail!*

Francis. Aye, Cheever come and take her in his wagon. We've only now come from the jail, and they'll not even let us in to see them.

Elizabeth. They've surely gone wild now, Mr. Hale!

Francis (*going to* Hale). Reverend Hale! Can you not speak to the Deputy Governor? I'm sure he mistakes these people—

Hale. Pray calm yourself, Mr. Nurse.

Francis. My wife is the very brick and mortar of the church, Mr. Hale (*indicating* Giles) and Martha Corey, there cannot be a woman closer yet to God than Martha.

Hale. How is Rebecca charged, Mr. Nurse?

Francis (*with a mocking, half-hearted laugh*). For murder, she's charged! (*mockingly quoting the warrant*) "For the marvelous and supernatural murder of Goody Putnam's babies." What am I to do, Mr. Hale?

Hale (*turns from* Francis, *deeply troubled, then*). Believe me, Mr. Nurse, if Rebecca Nurse be tainted, then nothing's left to stop the whole green world from burning. Let you rest upon the justice of the court; the court will send her home, I know it.

Francis. You cannot mean she will be tried in court!

Hale (*pleading*). Nurse, though our hearts break, we cannot flinch; these are new times, sir. There is a misty plot afoot so subtle we should be criminal to cling to old respects and ancient friendships. I have seen too many frightful proofs in court—the Devil is alive in Salem, and we dare not quail to follow wherever the accusing finger points!

Proctor (*angered*). How may such a woman murder children?

Hale (*in great pain*). Man, remember, until an hour before the Devil fell, God thought him beautiful in Heaven.

Giles. I never said my wife were a witch, Mr. Hale; I only said she were reading books!

Hale. Mr. Corey, exactly what complaint were made on your wife?

Giles. That bloody mongrel Walcott charge her. Y'see, he buy a pig of my wife four or five year ago, and the pig died soon after. So he come dancin' in for his money back. So my Martha, she says to him, "Walcott, if you haven't the wit to feed a pig properly, you'll not live to own many," she says. Now he goes to court and claims that from that day to this he cannot keep a pig alive for more than four weeks because my Martha bewitch them with her books!

(*Enter* Ezekiel Cheever. *A shocked silence.*)

Cheever. Good evening to you, Proctor.

Proctor. Why, Mr. Cheever. Good evening.

Cheever. Good evening, all. Good evening, Mr. Hale.

Proctor. I hope you come not on business of the court.

Cheever. I do, Proctor, aye. I am clerk of the court now, y'know.

(*Enter* Marshal Herrick, *a man in his early thirties, who is somewhat shamefaced at the moment.*)

Giles. It's a pity, Ezekiel, that an honest tailor might have gone to Heaven must burn in Hell. You'll burn for this, do you know it?

Cheever. You know yourself I must do as I'm told. You surely know that, Giles. And I'd as lief[6] you'd not be sending me to Hell. I like not the sound of it, I tell you; I like not the sound of it. (*He fears* Proctor, *but starts to reach inside his coat.*) Now believe me, Proctor, how heavy be the law, all its tonnage I do carry on my back tonight. (*He takes out a warrant.*) I have a warrant for your wife.

Proctor (*to* Hale). You said she were not charged!

Hale. I know nothin' of it. (*to* Cheever) When were she charged?

Cheever. I am given sixteen warrant tonight, sir, and she is one.

Proctor. Who charged her?

Cheever. Why, Abigail Williams charge her.

Proctor. On what proof, what proof?

Cheever (*looking about the room*). Mr. Proctor, I have little time. The court bid me search your house, but I like not to search a house. So will you hand me any poppets that your wife may keep here?

Proctor. Poppets?

Elizabeth. I never kept no poppets, not since I were a girl.

Cheever (*embarrassed, glancing toward the mantel where sits* Mary Warren*'s poppet*). I spy a poppet, Goody Proctor.

Elizabeth. Oh! (*going for it*) Why, this is Mary's.

Cheever (*shyly*). Would you please to give it to me?

Elizabeth (*handing it to him, asks* Hale). Has the court discovered a text in poppets now?

Cheever (*carefully holding the poppet*). Do you keep any others in this house?

Proctor. No, nor this one either till tonight. What signifies a poppet?

Cheever. Why, a poppet—(*He gingerly turns the poppet over.*) a poppet may signify—Now, woman, will you please to come with me?

Proctor. She will not! (*to* Elizabeth) Fetch Mary here.

Cheever (*ineptly reaching toward* Elizabeth). No, no, I am forbid to leave her from my sight.

Proctor (*pushing his arm away*). You'll leave her out of sight and out of mind, Mister. Fetch Mary, Elizabeth. (Elizabeth *goes upstairs.*)

Hale. What signifies a poppet, Mr. Cheever?

---

6. **as lief** (lēf): rather.

Cheever (*turning the poppet over in his hands*). Why, they say it may signify that she—(*He has lifted the poppet's skirt, and his eyes widen in astonished fear.*) Why, this, this—

Proctor (*reaching for the poppet*). What's there?

Cheever. Why (*He draws out a long needle from the poppet.*) it is a needle! Herrick, Herrick, it is a needle!

(Herrick *comes toward him.*)

Proctor (*angrily, bewildered*). And what signifies a needle!

Cheever (*his hands shaking*). Why, this go hard with her, Proctor, this—I had my doubts, Proctor, I had my doubts, but here's calamity. (*to* Hale, *showing the needle*) You see it, sir, it is a needle!

Hale. Why? What meanin' has it?

Cheever (*wide-eyed, trembling*). The girl, the Williams girl, Abigail Williams, sir. She sat to dinner in Reverend Parris's house tonight, and without word nor warnin' she falls to the floor. Like a struck beast, he says, and screamed a scream that a bull would weep to hear. And he goes to save her, and, stuck two inches in the flesh of her belly, he draw a needle out. And demandin' of her how she come to be so stabbed, she (*to* Proctor *now*) testify it were your wife's familiar spirit[7] pushed it in.

Proctor. Why, she done it herself! (*to* Hale) I hope you're not takin' this for proof, Mister!

(Hale, *struck by the proof, is silent.*)

Cheever. 'Tis hard proof! (*to* Hale) I find here a poppet Goody Proctor keeps. I have found it, sir. And in the belly of the poppet a needle's stuck. I tell you true, Proctor, I never warranted to see such proof of Hell, and I bid you obstruct me not, for I—

(*Enter* Elizabeth *with* Mary Warren. Proctor, *seeing* Mary Warren, *draws her by the arm to* Hale.)

Proctor. Here now! Mary, how did this poppet come into my house?

Mary Warren (*frightened for herself, her voice very small*). What poppet's that, sir?

Proctor (*impatiently, pointing at the doll in* Cheever's *hand*). This poppet, this poppet.

Mary Warren (*evasively, looking at it*). Why, I—I think it is mine.

Proctor. It is your poppet, is it not?

Mary Warren (*not understanding the direction of this*). It—is, sir.

Proctor. And how did it come into this house?

Mary Warren (*glancing about at the avid faces*). Why—I made it in the court, sir, and—give it to Goody Proctor tonight.

Proctor (*to* Hale). Now, sir—do you have it?

Hale. Mary Warren, a needle have been found inside this poppet.

Mary Warren (*bewildered*). Why, I meant no harm by it, sir.

Proctor (*quickly*). You stuck that needle in yourself?

Mary Warren. I—I believe I did, sir, I—

Proctor (*to* Hale). What say you now?

Hale (*watching* Mary Warren *closely*). Child, you are certain this be your natural memory? May it be, perhaps, that someone conjures you even now to say this?

Mary Warren. Conjures me? Why, no, sir, I am entirely myself, I think. Let you ask Susanna Walcott—she saw me sewin' it in court. (*or better still*) Ask Abby, Abby sat beside me when I made it.

Proctor (*to* Hale, *of* Cheever). Bid him begone. Your mind is surely settled now. Bid him out, Mr. Hale.

Elizabeth. What signifies a needle?

Hale. Mary—you charge a cold and cruel murder on Abigail.

Mary Warren. Murder! I charge no—

Hale. Abigail were stabbed tonight; a needle were found stuck into her belly—

7. **familiar spirit:** the spirit or demon, most usually in the form of an animal such as a black cat, that was a companion and helper to a witch.

Elizabeth. And she charges me?

Hale. Aye.

Elizabeth (*her breath knocked out*). Why—! The girl is murder! She must be ripped out of the world!

Cheever (*pointing at* Elizabeth). You've heard that, sir! Ripped out of the world! Herrick, you heard it!

Proctor (*suddenly snatching the warrant out of* Cheever*'s hands*). Out with you.

Cheever. Proctor, you dare not touch the warrant.

Proctor (*ripping the warrant*). Out with you!

Cheever. You've ripped the Deputy Governor's warrant, man!

Proctor. Damn the Deputy Governor! Out of my house!

Hale. Now, Proctor, Proctor!

Proctor. Get y'gone with them! You are a broken minister.

Hale. Proctor, if she is innocent, the court—

Proctor. If *she* is innocent! Why do you never wonder if Parris be innocent, or Abigail? Is the accuser always holy now? Were they born this morning as clean as God's fingers? I'll tell you what's walking Salem—vengeance is walking Salem. We are what we always were in Salem, but now the little crazy children are jangling the keys of the kingdom, and common vengeance writes the law! This warrant's vengeance! I'll not give my wife to vengeance!

Elizabeth. I'll go, John—

Proctor. You will not go!

Herrick. I have nine men outside. You cannot keep her. The law binds me, John, I cannot budge.

Proctor (*to* Hale, *ready to break him*). Will you see her taken?

Hale. Proctor, the court is just—

Proctor. Pontius Pilate! God will not let you wash your hands of this![8]

Elizabeth. John—I think I must go with them. (*He cannot bear to look at her.*) Mary, there is bread enough for the morning; you will bake, in the afternoon. Help Mr. Proctor as you were his daughter—you owe me that, and much more. (*She is fighting her weeping. To* Proctor.) When the children wake, speak nothing of witchcraft—it will frighten them. (*She cannot go on.*)

Proctor. I will bring you home. I will bring you soon.

Elizabeth. Oh, John, bring me soon!

Proctor. I will fall like an ocean on that court! Fear nothing, Elizabeth.

Elizabeth (*with great fear*). I will fear nothing. (*She looks about the room, as though to fix it in her mind.*) Tell the children I have gone to visit someone sick.

(*She walks out the door,* Herrick *and* Cheever *behind her. For a moment,* Proctor *watches from the doorway. The clank of chain is heard.*)

Proctor. Herrick! Herrick, don't chain her! (*He rushes out the door. From outside.*) Damn you, man, you will not chain her! Off with them! I'll not have it! I will not have her chained!

(*There are other men's voices against his.* Hale, *in a fever of guilt and uncertainty, turns from the door to avoid the sight;* Mary Warren *bursts into tears and sits weeping.* Giles Corey *calls to* Hale.)

Giles. And yet silent, minister? It is fraud, you know it is fraud! What keeps you, man?

(Proctor *is half braced, half pushed into the room by two deputies and* Herrick.)

Proctor. I'll pay you, Herrick, I will surely pay you!

Herrick (*panting*). In God's name, John, I cannot help myself. I must chain them all. Now let you keep inside this house till I am gone! (*He goes out with his deputies.*)

(Proctor *stands there, gulping air. Horses and a wagon creaking are heard.*)

Hale (*in great uncertainty*). Mr. Proctor—

Proctor. Out of my sight!

Hale. Charity, Proctor, charity. What I have heard in

8. **Pontius** (pŏn′tē-əs) **Pilate . . . hands of this:** the Roman governor who presided over the trial and sentencing of Christ. Pilate publicly washed his hands to absolve himself of responsibility for Christ's death.

her favor, I will not fear to testify in court. God help me, I cannot judge her guilty or innocent—I know not. Only this consider: the world goes mad, and it profit nothing you should lay the cause to the vengeance of a little girl.

Proctor. You are a coward! Though you be ordained in God's own tears, you are a coward now!

Hale. Proctor, I cannot think God be provoked so grandly by such a petty cause. The jails are packed—our greatest judges sit in Salem now—and hangin's promised. Man, we must look to cause proportionate. Were there murder done, perhaps, and never brought to light? Abomination? Some secret blasphemy that stinks to Heaven? Think on cause, man, and let you help me to discover it. For there's your way, believe it, there is your only way, when such confusion strikes upon the world. (*He goes to* Giles *and* Francis.) Let you counsel among yourselves; think on your village and what may have drawn from heaven such thundering wrath upon you all. I shall pray God open up our eyes.

(Hale *goes out.*)

Francis (*struck by* Hale*'s mood*). I never heard no murder done in Salem.

Proctor (*He has been reached by* Hale*'s words*). Leave me, Francis, leave me.

Giles (*shaken*). John—tell me, are we lost?

Proctor. Go home now, Giles. We'll speak on it tomorrow.

Giles. Let you think on it. We'll come early, eh?

Proctor. Aye. Go now, Giles.

Giles. Good night, then.

(Giles Corey *goes out. After a moment.*)

Mary Warren (*in a fearful squeak of a voice*). Mr. Proctor, very likely they'll let her come home once they're given proper evidence.

Proctor. You're coming to the court with me, Mary. You will tell it in the court.

Mary Warren. I cannot charge murder on Abigail.

Proctor (*moving menacingly toward her*). You will tell the court how that poppet come here and who stuck the needle in.

Mary Warren. She'll kill me for sayin' that! (Proctor *continues toward her.*) Abby'll charge lechery on you, Mr. Proctor!

Proctor (*halting*). She's told you!

Mary Warren. I have known it, sir. She'll ruin you with it, I know she will.

Proctor (*hesitating, and with deep hatred of himself*). Good. Then her saintliness is done with. (Mary *backs from him.*) We will slide together into our pit; you will tell the court what you know.

Mary Warren (*in terror*). I cannot, they'll turn on me—

(Proctor *strides and catches her, and she is repeating, "I cannot, I cannot!"*)

Proctor. My wife will never die for me! I will bring your guts into your mouth but that goodness will not die for me!

Mary Warren (*struggling to escape him*). I cannot do it, I cannot!

Proctor (*grasping her by the throat as though he would strangle her*). Make your peace with it! Now Hell and Heaven grapple on our backs, and all our old pretense is ripped away—make your peace! (*He throws her to the floor, where she sobs, "I cannot, I cannot . . ." And now, half to himself, staring, and turning to the open door.*) Peace. It is a providence, and no great change; we are only what we always were, but naked now. (*He walks as though toward a great horror, facing the open sky.*) Aye, naked! And the wind, God's icy wind, will blow!

(*And she is over and over again sobbing, "I cannot, I cannot, I cannot," as the curtain falls.*)

Comprehension

1. **Recall** Why does Elizabeth want John to go to Salem?
2. **Clarify** Why does Hale come to the Proctors' home?
3. **Summarize** What proof leads to Elizabeth's arrest?

Text Analysis

4. **Form Opinions** Do you think Reverend Hale believes that Elizabeth Proctor is practicing witchcraft? Support your opinion with specific details.
5. **Draw Conclusions About Characters** Review the **traits** you recorded in your chart for Elizabeth Proctor. How would you describe her character?
6. **Analyze Conventions of Drama** What does **dialogue** reveal about the complicated relationship between John and Elizabeth in the following scenes?
   - Elizabeth learns that John was alone with Abigail (lines 132–138)
   - Elizabeth asks John to break his unspoken promise to Abigail (lines 398–422)
   - John threatens Mary Warren (lines 990–1005)
7. **Analyze Dramatic Irony** Dramatic irony occurs when the readers know more about a situation than a character does. Why is John struck by Hale's declaration that "some secret blasphemy" (lines 946–947) has caused all of the confusion?
8. **Make Judgments About a Character** How would you judge John's behavior so far? Cite evidence from the play to support your judgment.
9. **Compare Characters** Compare the following characters and determine which one has the greatest faith in the court proceedings. What accounts for their differing attitudes?
   - John Proctor • Hale • Cheever

Text Criticism

10. **Historical Context** Miller wrote that during the anti-Communist hearings, "I saw accepted the notion that conscience was no longer a private matter but one of state administration." How does this notion apply to the witch-hunts in Salem?

What fuels a MOB?

What role does Reverend Hale play in the mob mentality that develops in Salem during Act Two?

COMMON CORE

RL 1 Cite textual evidence to support analysis of what the text says explicitly as well as inferences drawn from the text, including determining where the text leaves matters uncertain. **RL 2** Provide an objective summary of the text. **RL 3** Analyze the impact of the author's choices regarding how to develop and relate elements of a drama. **RL 5** Analyze how an author's choices concerning how to structure specific parts of a text contribute to its overall structure and meaning as well as its aesthetic impact.

Act *Three*

(*The vestry room of the Salem meeting house, now serving as the anteroom*[1] *of the General Court.*

As the curtain rises, the room is empty, but for sunlight pouring through two high windows in the back wall. The room is solemn, even forbidding. Heavy beams jut out, boards of random widths make up the walls. At the right are two doors leading into the meeting house proper, where the court is being held. At the left another door leads outside.

There is a plain bench at the left, and another at the right. In the center a rather long meeting table, with stools and a considerable armchair snugged up to it.

Through the partitioning wall at the right we hear a prosecutor's voice, Judge Hathorne*'s, asking a question; then a woman's voice,* Martha Corey*'s, replying.*)

Hathorne's Voice. Now, Martha Corey, there is abundant evidence in our hands to show that you have given yourself to the reading of fortunes. Do you deny it?

Martha Corey's Voice. I am innocent to a witch. I know not what a witch is.

Hathorne's Voice. How do you know, then, that you are not a witch?

Martha Corey's Voice. If I were, I would know it.

Hathorne's Voice. Why do you hurt these children?

Martha Corey's Voice. I do not hurt them. I scorn it!

Giles' Voice (*roaring*). I have evidence for the court!

(*Voices of townspeople rise in excitement.*)

Danforth's Voice. You will keep your seat!

Giles' Voice. Thomas Putnam is reaching out for land!

Danforth's Voice. Remove that man, Marshal!

Giles' Voice. You're hearing lies, lies!

(*A roaring goes up from the people.*)

Hathorne's Voice. Arrest him, excellency!

Giles' Voice. I have evidence. Why will you not hear my evidence?

(*The door opens and* Giles *is half carried into the vestry room by* Herrick.)

Giles. Hands off, damn you, let me go!

Herrick. Giles, Giles!

Giles. Out of my way, Herrick! I bring evidence—

Herrick. You cannot go in there, Giles; it's a court!

(*Enter* Hale *from the court.*)

Hale. Pray be calm a moment.

Giles. You, Mr. Hale, go in there and demand I speak.

---

1. **vestry room . . . anteroom:** A vestry room is a room in a church used for nonreligious meetings or church business. An anteroom is a waiting room or a room that leads into another.

Paul Scofield as Deputy Governor Danforth

Hale. A moment, sir, a moment.

Giles. They'll be hangin' my wife!

(Judge Hathorne *enters. He is in his sixties, a bitter, remorseless Salem judge.*)

Hathorne. How do you dare come roarin' into this court! Are you gone daft, Corey?

Giles. You're not a Boston judge yet, Hathorne. You'll not call me daft!

(*Enter* Deputy Governor Danforth *and, behind him,* Ezekiel Cheever *and* Parris. *On his appearance, silence falls.* Danforth *is a grave man in his sixties, of some humor and sophistication that does not, however, interfere with an exact loyalty to his position and his cause. He comes down to* Giles, *who awaits his wrath.*)

Danforth (*looking directly at* Giles). Who is this man?

Parris. Giles Corey, sir, and a more **contentious**—

Giles (*to* Parris). I am asked the question, and I am old enough to answer it! (*to* Danforth, *who impresses him and to whom he smiles through his strain*) My name is Corey, sir, Giles Corey. I have six hundred acres, and timber in addition. It is my wife you be condemning now. (*He indicates the courtroom.*)

Danforth. And how do you imagine to help her cause with such contemptuous riot?[2] Now be gone. Your old age alone keeps you out of jail for this.

Giles (*beginning to plead*). They be tellin' lies about my wife, sir, I—

Danforth. Do you take it upon yourself to determine what this court shall believe and what it shall set aside?

Giles. Your Excellency, we mean no disrespect for—

Danforth. Disrespect indeed! It is disruption, Mister. This is the highest court of the supreme government of this province, do you know it?

Giles (*beginning to weep*). Your Excellency, I only said she were readin' books, sir, and they come and take her out of my house for—

Danforth (*mystified*). Books! What books?

Giles (*through helpless sobs*). It is my third wife, sir; I never had no wife that be so taken with books, and I thought to find the cause of it, d'y'see, but it were no witch I blamed her for. (*He is openly weeping.*) I have broke charity with the woman, I have broke charity with her. (*He covers his face, ashamed.* Danforth *is respectfully silent.*)

Hale. Excellency, he claims hard evidence for his wife's defense. I think that in all justice you must—

Danforth. Then let him submit his evidence in proper affidavit. You are certainly aware of our procedure here, Mr. Hale. (*to* Herrick) Clear this room.

Herrick. Come now, Giles. (*He gently pushes* Corey *out.*)

Francis. We are desperate, sir; we come here three days now and cannot be heard.

Danforth. Who is this man?

Francis. Francis Nurse, Your Excellency.

Hale. His wife's Rebecca that were condemned this morning.

Danforth. Indeed! I am amazed to find you in such uproar. I have only good report of your character, Mr. Nurse.

Hathorne. I think they must both be arrested in contempt, sir.

Danforth (*to* Francis). Let you write your plea, and in due time I will—

Francis. Excellency, we have proof for your eyes; God forbid you shut them to it. The girls, sir, the girls are frauds.

Danforth. What's that?

Francis. We have proof of it, sir. They are all deceiving you.

(Danforth *is shocked, but studying* Francis.)

Hathorne. This is contempt, sir, contempt!

Danforth. Peace, Judge Hathorne. Do you know who I am, Mr. Nurse?

---

2. **contemptuous** (kən-tĕmp'cho͞o-əs) **riot:** disrespectful, outrageous behavior.

Francis. I surely do, sir, and I think you must be a wise judge to be what you are.

Danforth. And do you know that near to four hundred are in the jails from Marblehead to Lynn,[3] and upon my signature?

Francis. I—

Danforth. And seventy-two condemned to hang by that signature?

Francis. Excellency, I never thought to say it to such a weighty judge, but you are deceived.

(*Enter* Giles Corey *from left. All turn to see as he beckons in* Mary Warren *with* Proctor. Mary *is keeping her eyes to the ground;* Proctor *has her elbow as though she were near collapse.*)

Parris (*on seeing her, in shock*). Mary Warren! (*He goes directly to bend close to her face.*) What are you about here?

Proctor (*pressing* Parris *away from her with a gentle but firm motion of protectiveness*). She would speak with the Deputy Governor.

Danforth (*shocked by this, turns to* Herrick). Did you not tell me Mary Warren were sick in bed?

Herrick. She were, Your Honor. When I go to fetch her to the court last week, she said she were sick.

Giles. She has been strivin' with her soul all week, Your Honor; she comes now to tell the truth of this to you.

Danforth. Who is this?

Proctor. John Proctor, sir. Elizabeth Proctor is my wife.

Parris. Beware this man, Your Excellency, this man is mischief.

Hale (*excitedly*). I think you must hear the girl, sir, she—

Danforth (*who has become very interested in* Mary Warren *and only raises a hand toward* Hale). Peace. What would you tell us, Mary Warren?

(Proctor *looks at her, but she cannot speak.*)

Proctor. She never saw no spirits, sir.

Danforth (*with great alarm and surprise, to* Mary). Never saw no spirits!

Giles (*eagerly*). Never.

Proctor (*reaching into his jacket*). She has signed a deposition, sir—

Danforth (*instantly*). No, no, I accept no depositions. (*He is rapidly calculating this; he turns from her to* Proctor.) Tell me, Mr. Proctor, have you given out this story in the village?

Proctor. We have not.

Parris. They've come to overthrow the court, sir! This man is—

Danforth. I pray you, Mr. Parris. Do you know, Mr. Proctor, that the entire contention of the state in these trials is that the voice of Heaven is speaking through the children?

Proctor. I know that, sir.

Danforth (*thinks, staring at* Proctor, *then turns to* Mary Warren). And you, Mary Warren, how came you to cry out people for sending their spirits against you?

Mary Warren. It were pretense, sir.

Danforth. I cannot hear you.

Proctor. It were pretense, she says.

Danforth. Ah? And the other girls? Susanna Walcott, and—the others? They are also pretending?

Mary Warren. Aye, sir.

Danforth (*wide-eyed*). Indeed. (*Pause. He is baffled by this. He turns to study* Proctor*'s face.*)

Parris (*in a sweat*). Excellency, you surely cannot think to let so vile a lie be spread in open court!

Danforth. Indeed not, but it strike hard upon me that she will dare come here with such a tale. Now, Mr. Proctor, before I decide whether I shall hear you or not, it is my duty to tell you this. We burn a hot fire here; it melts down all concealment.

Proctor. I know that, sir.

---

3. **Marblehead . . . Lynn:** two coastal towns in Massachusetts, near Salem.

Danforth. Let me continue. I understand well, a husband's tenderness may drive him to extravagance in defense of a wife. Are you certain in your conscience, Mister, that your evidence is the truth?

Proctor. It is. And you will surely know it.

Danforth. And you thought to declare this revelation in the open court before the public?

Proctor. I thought I would, aye—with your permission.

Danforth (*his eyes narrowing*). Now, sir, what is your purpose in so doing?

Proctor. Why, I—I would free my wife, sir.

Danforth. There lurks nowhere in your heart, nor hidden in your spirit, any desire to undermine this court?

Proctor (*with the faintest faltering*). Why, no, sir.

Cheever (*clears his throat, awakening*). I—Your Excellency.

Danforth. Mr. Cheever.

Cheever. I think it be my duty, sir—(*kindly, to* Proctor) You'll not deny it, John. (*to* Danforth) When we come to take his wife, he damned the court and ripped your warrant.

Parris. Now you have it!

Danforth. He did that, Mr. Hale?

Hale (*takes a breath*). Aye, he did.

Proctor. It were a temper, sir. I knew not what I did.

Danforth (*studying him*). Mr. Proctor.

Proctor. Aye, sir.

Danforth (*straight into his eyes*). Have you ever seen the Devil?

Proctor. No, sir.

Danforth. You are in all respects a Gospel Christian?

Proctor. I am, sir.

Parris. Such a Christian that will not come to church but once in a month!

Danforth (*restrained—he is curious*). Not come to church?

Proctor. I—I have no love for Mr. Parris. It is no secret. But God I surely love.

Cheever. He plow on Sunday, sir.

Danforth. Plow on Sunday!

Cheever (*apologetically*). I think it be evidence, John. I am an official of the court, I cannot keep it.

Proctor. I—I have once or twice plowed on Sunday. I have three children, sir, and until last year my land give little.

Giles. You'll find other Christians that do plow on Sunday if the truth be known.

Hale. Your Honor, I cannot think you may judge the man on such evidence.

Danforth. I judge nothing. (*Pause. He keeps watching* Proctor, *who tries to meet his gaze.*) I tell you straight, Mister—I have seen marvels in this court. I have seen people choked before my eyes by spirits; I have seen them stuck by pins and slashed by daggers. I have until this moment not the slightest reason to suspect that the children may be deceiving me. Do you understand my meaning?

Proctor. Excellency, does it not strike upon you that so many of these women have lived so long with such upright reputation, and—

Parris. Do you read the Gospel, Mr. Proctor?

Proctor. I read the Gospel.

Parris. I think not, or you should surely know that Cain were an upright man, and yet he did kill Abel.[4]

Proctor. Aye, God tells us that. (*to* Danforth) But who tells us Rebecca Nurse murdered seven babies by sending out her spirit on them? It is the children only, and this one will swear she lied to you.

(Danforth *considers, then beckons* Hathorne *to him.* Hathorne *leans in, and he speaks in his ear.* Hathorne *nods.*)

4. **Cain . . . Abel:** According to the Book of Genesis in the Bible, Cain and Abel were the sons of Adam and Eve, the first humans.

Hathorne. Aye, she's the one.

Danforth. Mr. Proctor, this morning, your wife send me a claim in which she states that she is pregnant now.

Proctor. My wife pregnant!

Danforth. There be no sign of it—we have examined her body.

Proctor. But if she say she is pregnant, then she must be! That woman will never lie, Mr. Danforth.

Danforth. She will not?

Proctor. Never, sir, never.

Danforth. We have thought it too convenient to be credited. However, if I should tell you now that I will let her be kept another month; and if she begin to show her natural signs, you shall have her living yet another year until she is delivered—what say you to that? (John Proctor *is struck silent.*) Come now. You say your only purpose is to save your wife. Good, then, she is saved at least this year, and a year is long. What say you, sir? It is done now. (*In conflict,* Proctor *glances at* Francis *and* Giles.) Will you drop this charge?

Proctor. I—I think I cannot.

Danforth (*now an almost imperceptible hardness in his voice*). Then your purpose is somewhat larger.

Parris. He's come to overthrow this court, Your Honor!

Proctor. These are my friends. Their wives are also accused—

Danforth (*with a sudden briskness of manner*). I judge you not, sir. I am ready to hear your evidence.

Proctor. I come not to hurt the court; I only—

Danforth (*cutting him off*). Marshal, go into the court and bid Judge Stoughton and Judge Sewall declare recess for one hour. And let them go to the tavern, if they will. All witnesses and prisoners are to be kept in the building.

Herrick. Aye, sir. (*very deferentially*) If I may say it, sir, I know this man all my life. It is a good man, sir.

Danforth (*It is the reflection on himself he resents*). I am sure of it, Marshal. (Herrick *nods, then goes out.*) Now, what deposition do you have for us, Mr. Proctor? And I beg you be clear, open as the sky, and honest.

Proctor (*as he takes out several papers*). I am no lawyer, so I'll—

Danforth. The pure in heart need no lawyers. Proceed as you will.

Proctor (*handing* Danforth *a paper*). Will you read this first, sir? It's a sort of testament. The people signing it declare their good opinion of Rebecca, and my wife, and Martha Corey. (Danforth *looks down at the paper.*)

Parris (*to enlist* Danforth*'s sarcasm*). Their good opinion! (*But* Danforth *goes on reading, and* Proctor *is heartened.*)

Proctor. These are all landholding farmers, members of the church. (*delicately, trying to point out a paragraph*) If you'll notice, sir—they've known the women many years and never saw no sign they had dealings with the Devil.

(Parris *nervously moves over and reads over* Danforth*'s shoulder.*)

Danforth (*glancing down a long list*). How many names are here?

Francis. Ninety-one, Your Excellency.

Parris (*sweating*). These people should be summoned. (Danforth *looks up at him questioningly.*) For questioning.

Francis (*trembling with anger*). Mr. Danforth, I gave them all my word no harm would come to them for signing this.

Parris. This is a clear attack upon the court!

Hale (*to* Parris, *trying to contain himself*). Is every defense an attack upon the court? Can no one—?

Parris. All innocent and Christian people are happy for the courts in Salem! These people are gloomy for it. (*to* Danforth *directly*) And I think you will want to know, from each and every one of them, what discontents them with you!

Hathorne. I think they ought to be examined, sir.

Danforth. It is not necessarily an attack, I think. Yet—

Francis. These are all covenanted Christians, sir.

Danforth. Then I am sure they may have nothing to fear. (*hands* Cheever *the paper*) Mr. Cheever, have warrants drawn for all of these—arrest for examination. (*to* Proctor) Now, Mister, what other information do you have for us? (Francis *is still standing, horrified.*) You may sit, Mr. Nurse.

Francis. I have brought trouble on these people; I have—

Danforth. No, old man, you have not hurt these people if they are of good conscience. But you must understand, sir, that a person is either with this court or he must be counted against it, there be no road between. This is a sharp time, now, a precise time—we live no longer in the dusky afternoon when evil mixed itself with good and befuddled the world. Now, by God's grace, the shining sun is up, and them that fear not light will surely praise it. I hope you will be one of those. (Mary Warren *suddenly sobs.*) She's not hearty,[5] I see.

Proctor. No, she's not, sir. (*to* Mary, *bending to her, holding her hand, quietly*) Now remember what the angel Raphael said to the boy Tobias.[6] Remember it.

Mary Warren (*hardly audible*). Aye.

Proctor. "Do that which is good, and no harm shall come to thee."

Mary Warren. Aye.

Danforth. Come, man, we wait you.

(Marshal Herrick *returns, and takes his post at the door.*)

Giles. John, my deposition, give him mine.

Proctor. Aye. (*He hands* Danforth *another paper.*) This is Mr. Corey's deposition.

Danforth. Oh? (*He looks down at it. Now* Hathorne *comes behind him and reads with him.*)

Hathorne (*suspiciously*). What lawyer drew this, Corey?

Giles. You know I never hired a lawyer in my life, Hathorne.

Danforth (*finishing the reading*). It is very well phrased. My compliments. Mr. Parris, if Mr. Putnam is in the court, will you bring him in? (Hathorne *takes the deposition, and walks to the window with it.* Parris *goes into the court.*) You have no legal training, Mr. Corey?

Giles (*very pleased*). I have the best, sir—I am thirty-three time in court in my life. And always plaintiff, too.

Danforth. Oh, then you're much put-upon.

Giles. I am never put-upon; I know my rights, sir, and I will have them. You know, your father tried a case of mine—might be thirty-five year ago, I think.

Danforth. Indeed.

Giles. He never spoke to you of it?

Danforth. No, I cannot recall it.

Giles. That's strange, he give me nine pound damages. He were a fair judge, your father. Y'see, I had a white mare that time, and this fellow come to borrow the mare—(*Enter* Parris *with* Thomas Putnam. *When he sees* Putnam, Giles' *ease goes; he is hard.*) Aye, there he is.

Danforth. Mr. Putnam, I have here an accusation by Mr. Corey against you. He states that you coldly prompted your daughter to cry witchery upon George Jacobs that is now in jail.

Putnam. It is a lie.

Danforth (*turning to* Giles). Mr. Putnam states your charge is a lie. What say you to that?

Giles (*furious, his fists clenched*). A fart on Thomas Putnam, that is what I say to that!

Danforth. What proof do you submit for your charge, sir?

Giles. My proof is there! (*pointing to the paper*) If Jacobs hangs for a witch he forfeit up his property—that's law! And there is none but Putnam with the

---

5. **hearty:** well.

6. **what the angel Raphael said . . . Tobias:** In the Book of Tobit in the Apocrypha, Tobit's son Tobias cured his father's blindness with the help of the angel Raphael.

coin to buy so great a piece. This man is killing his neighbors for their land!

Danforth. But proof, sir, proof.

Giles (*pointing at his deposition*). The proof is there! I have it from an honest man who heard Putnam say it! The day his daughter cried out on Jacobs, he said she'd given him a fair gift of land.

Hathorne. And the name of this man?

Giles (*taken aback*). What name?

Hathorne. The man that give you this information.

Giles (*hesitates, then*). Why, I—I cannot give you his name.

Hathorne. And why not?

Giles (*hesitates, then bursts out*). You know well why not! He'll lay in jail if I give his name!

Hathorne. This is contempt of the court, Mr. Danforth!

Danforth (*to avoid that*). You will surely tell us the name.

Giles. I will not give you no name. I mentioned my wife's name once and I'll burn in hell long enough for that. I stand mute.

Danforth. In that case, I have no choice but to arrest you for contempt of this court, do you know that?

Giles. This is a hearing; you cannot clap me for contempt of a hearing.

Danforth. Oh, it is a proper lawyer![7] Do you wish me to declare the court in full session here? Or will you give me good reply?

Giles (*faltering*). I cannot give you no name, sir, I cannot.

Danforth. You are a foolish old man. Mr. Cheever, begin the record. The court is now in session. I ask you, Mr. Corey—

Proctor (*breaking in*). Your Honor—he has the story in confidence, sir, and he—

Parris. The Devil lives on such confidences! (*to* Danforth) Without confidences there could be no conspiracy, Your Honor!

Hathorne. I think it must be broken, sir.

Danforth (*to* Giles). Old man, if your informant tells the truth let him come here openly like a decent man. But if he hide in anonymity I must know why. Now sir, the government and central church demand of you the name of him who reported Mr. Thomas Putnam a common murderer.

Hale. Excellency—

Danforth. Mr. Hale.

Hale. We cannot blink it more. There is a prodigious fear of this court in the country—

Danforth. Then there is a prodigious guilt in the country. Are *you* afraid to be questioned here?

Hale. I may only fear the Lord, sir, but there is fear in the country nevertheless.

Danforth (*angered now*). Reproach me not with the fear in the country; there is fear in the country because there is a moving[8] plot to topple Christ in the country!

Hale. But it does not follow that everyone accused is part of it.

Danforth. No uncorrupted man may fear this court, Mr. Hale! None! (*to* Giles) You are under arrest in contempt of this court. Now sit you down and take counsel with yourself, or you will be set in the jail until you decide to answer all questions.

(Giles Corey *makes a rush for* Putnam. Proctor *lunges and holds him.*)

Proctor. No, Giles!

Giles (*over* Proctor*'s shoulder at* Putnam). I'll cut your throat, Putnam, I'll kill you yet!

Proctor (*forcing him into a chair*). Peace, Giles, peace. (*releasing him*) We'll prove ourselves. Now we will. (*He starts to turn to* Danforth.)

---

7. **Oh . . . lawyer:** Oh, he thinks he is a real lawyer.

8. **moving:** active.

Giles. Say nothin' more, John. (*pointing at* Danforth) He's only playin' you! He means to hang us all!

(Mary Warren *bursts into sobs.*)

Danforth. This is a court of law, Mister. I'll have no **effrontery** here!

Proctor. Forgive him, sir, for his old age. Peace, Giles, we'll prove it all now. (*He lifts up* Mary*'s chin.*) You cannot weep, Mary. Remember the angel, what he say to the boy. Hold to it, now; there is your rock. (Mary *quiets. He takes out a paper, and turns to* Danforth.) This is Mary Warren's deposition. I—I would ask you remember, sir, while you read it, that until two week ago she were no different than the other children are today. (*He is speaking reasonably, restraining all his fears, his anger, his anxiety.*) You saw her scream, she howled, she swore familiar spirits choked her; she even testified that Satan, in the form of women now in jail, tried to win her soul away, and then when she refused—

Danforth. We know all this.

Proctor. Aye, sir. She swears now that she never saw Satan; nor any spirit, vague or clear, that Satan may have sent to hurt her. And she declares her friends are lying now.

(Proctor *starts to hand* Danforth *the deposition, and* Hale *comes up to* Danforth *in a trembling state.*)

Hale. Excellency, a moment. I think this goes to the heart of the matter.

Danforth (*with deep misgivings*). It surely does.

Hale. I cannot say he is an honest man; I know him little. But in all justice, sir, a claim so weighty cannot be argued by a farmer. In God's name, sir, stop here; send him home and let him come again with a lawyer—

Danforth (*patiently*). Now look you, Mr. Hale—

Hale. Excellency, I have signed seventy-two death warrants; I am a minister of the Lord, and I dare not take a life without there be a proof so **immaculate** no slightest qualm of conscience may doubt it.

Danforth. Mr. Hale, you surely do not doubt my justice.

Hale. I have this morning signed away the soul of Rebecca Nurse, Your Honor. I'll not conceal it, my hand shakes yet as with a wound! I pray you, sir, this argument let lawyers present to you.

Danforth. Mr. Hale, believe me; for a man of such terrible learning you are most bewildered—I hope you will forgive me. I have been thirty-two year at the bar, sir, and I should be confounded were I called upon to defend these people. Let you consider, now—(*to* Proctor *and the others*) And I bid you all do likewise. In an ordinary crime, how does one defend the accused? One calls up witnesses to prove his innocence. But witchcraft is *ipso facto,*[9] on its face and by its nature, an invisible crime, is it not? Therefore, who may possibly be witness to it? The witch and the victim. None other. Now we cannot hope the witch will accuse herself; granted? Therefore, we must rely upon her victims—and they do testify, the children certainly do testify. As for the witches, none will deny that we are most eager for all their confessions. Therefore, what is left for a lawyer to bring out? I think I have made my point. Have I not?

Hale. But this child claims the girls are not truthful, and if they are not—

Danforth. That is precisely what I am about to consider, sir. What more may you ask of me? Unless you doubt my probity?[10]

Hale (*defeated*). I surely do not, sir. Let you consider it, then.

Danforth. And let you put your heart to rest. Her deposition, Mr. Proctor.

(Proctor *hands it to him.* Hathorne *rises, goes beside* Danforth, *and starts reading.* Parris *comes to his other side.* Danforth *looks at* John Proctor, *then proceeds to read.* Hale *gets up, finds position near the judge, reads too.* Proctor *glances at* Giles. Francis *prays silently, hands pressed together.* Cheever *waits placidly, the*

9. ***ipso facto*** *Latin:* by that very fact.

10. **doubt my probity:** question my integrity.

sublime official, dutiful. Mary Warren *sobs once.* John Proctor *touches her head reassuringly. Presently* Danforth *lifts his eyes, stands up, takes out a kerchief and blows his nose. The others stand aside as he moves in thought toward the window.*)

Parris (*hardly able to contain his anger and fear*). I should like to question—

Danforth (*his first real outburst, in which his contempt for* Parris *is clear*). Mr. Parris, I bid you be silent! (*He stands in silence, looking out the window. Now, having established that he will set the gait.*) Mr. Cheever, will you go into the court and bring the children here? (Cheever *gets up and goes out upstage.* Danforth *now turns to* Mary.) Mary Warren, how came you to this turnabout? Has Mr. Proctor threatened you for this deposition?

Mary Warren. No, sir.

Danforth. Has he ever threatened you?

Mary Warren (*weaker*). No, sir.

Danforth (*sensing a weakening*). Has he threatened you?

Mary Warren. No, sir.

Danforth. Then you tell me that you sat in my court, callously lying, when you knew that people would hang by your evidence? (*She does not answer.*) Answer me!

Mary Warren (*almost inaudibly*). I did, sir.

Danforth. How were you instructed in your life? Do you not know that God damns all liars? (*She cannot speak.*) Or is it now that you lie?

Judge Danforth questioning Mary Warren

Mary Warren. No, sir—I am with God now.

Danforth. You are with God now.

Mary Warren. Aye, sir.

Danforth (*containing himself*). I will tell you this—you are either lying now, or you were lying in the court, and in either case you have committed perjury and you will go to jail for it. You cannot lightly say you lied, Mary. Do you know that?

Mary Warren. I cannot lie no more. I am with God, I am with God.

(*But she breaks into sobs at the thought of it, and the right door opens, and enter* Susanna Walcott, Mercy Lewis, Betty Parris, *and finally* Abigail. Cheever *comes to* Danforth.)

Cheever. Ruth Putnam's not in the court, sir, nor the other children.

Danforth. These will be sufficient. Sit you down, children. (*Silently they sit.*) Your friend, Mary Warren, has given us a deposition. In which she swears that she never saw familiar spirits, apparitions, nor any manifest of the Devil. She claims as well that none of you have seen these things either. (*slight pause*) Now, children, this is a court of law. The law, based upon the Bible, and the Bible, writ by Almighty God, forbid the practice of witchcraft, and describe death as the penalty thereof. But likewise, children, the law and Bible damn all bearers of false witness. (*slight pause*) Now then. It does not escape me that this deposition may be devised to blind us; it may well be that Mary Warren has been conquered by Satan, who sends her here to distract our sacred purpose. If so, her neck will break for it. But if she speak true, I bid you now drop your guile and confess your pretense, for a quick confession will go easier with you. (*pause*) Abigail Williams, rise. (Abigail *slowly rises.*) Is there any truth in this?

Abigail. No, sir.

Danforth (*thinks, glances at* Mary, *then back to* Abigail). Children, a very auger bit[11] will now be turned into your souls until your honesty is proved. Will either of you change your positions now, or do you force me to hard questioning?

Abigail. I have naught to change, sir. She lies.

Danforth (*to* Mary). You would still go on with this?

Mary Warren (*faintly*). Aye, sir.

Danforth (*turning to* Abigail). A poppet were discovered in Mr. Proctor's house, stabbed by a needle. Mary Warren claims that you sat beside her in the court when she made it, and that you saw her make it and witnessed how she herself stuck her needle into it for safe-keeping. What say you to that?

Abigail (*with a slight note of indignation*). It is a lie, sir.

Danforth (*after a slight pause*). While you worked for Mr. Proctor, did you see poppets in that house?

Abigail. Goody Proctor always kept poppets.

Proctor. Your Honor, my wife never kept no poppets. Mary Warren confesses it was her poppet.

Cheever. Your Excellency.

Danforth. Mr. Cheever.

Cheever. When I spoke with Goody Proctor in that house, she said she never kept no poppets. But she said she did keep poppets when she were a girl.

Proctor. She has not been a girl these fifteen years, Your Honor.

Hathorne. But a poppet will keep fifteen years, will it not?

Proctor. It will keep if it is kept, but Mary Warren swears she never saw no poppets in my house, nor anyone else.

Parris. Why could there not have been poppets hid where no one ever saw them?

Proctor (*furious*). There might also be a dragon with five legs in my house, but no one has ever seen it.

Parris. We are here, Your Honor, precisely to discover what no one has ever seen.

---

11. **auger** (ô′gər) **bit:** drill.

Proctor. Mr. Danforth, what profit this girl to turn herself about? What may Mary Warren gain but hard questioning and worse?

Danforth. You are charging Abigail Williams with a marvelous cool plot to murder, do you understand that?

Proctor. I do, sir. I believe she means to murder.

Danforth (*pointing at* Abigail, *incredulously*). This child would murder your wife?

Proctor. It is not a child. Now hear me, sir. In the sight of the congregation she were twice this year put out of this meetin' house for laughter during prayer.

Danforth (*shocked, turning to* Abigail). What's this? Laughter during—!

Parris. Excellency, she were under Tituba's power at that time, but she is solemn now.

Giles. Aye, now she is solemn and goes to hang people!

Danforth. Quiet, man.

Hathorne. Surely it have no bearing on the question, sir. He charges contemplation of murder.

Danforth. Aye. (*He studies* Abigail *for a moment, then.*) Continue, Mr. Proctor.

Proctor. Mary. Now tell the Governor how you danced in the woods.

Parris (*instantly*). Excellency, since I come to Salem this man is blackening my name. He—

Danforth. In a moment, sir. (*to* Mary Warren, *sternly, and surprised*) What is this dancing?

Mary Warren. I—(*She glances at* Abigail, *who is staring down at her remorselessly. Then, appealing to* Proctor.) Mr. Proctor—

Proctor (*taking it right up*). Abigail leads the girls to the woods, Your Honor, and they have danced there naked—

Parris. Your Honor, this—

Proctor (*at once*). Mr. Parris discovered them himself in the dead of night! There's the "child" she is!

Danforth (*It is growing into a nightmare, and he turns, astonished, to* Parris). Mr. Parris—

Parris. I can only say, sir, that I never found any of them naked, and this man is—

Danforth. But you discovered them dancing in the woods? (*Eyes on* Parris, *he points at* Abigail.) Abigail?

Hale. Excellency, when I first arrived from Beverly, Mr. Parris told me that.

Danforth. Do you deny it, Mr. Parris?

Parris. I do not, sir, but I never saw any of them naked.

Danforth. But she have *danced?*

Parris (*unwillingly*). Aye, sir.

(Danforth, *as though with new eyes, looks at* Abigail.)

Hathorne. Excellency, will you permit me? (*He points at* Mary Warren.)

Danforth (*with great worry*). Pray, proceed.

Hathorne. You say you never saw no spirits, Mary, were never threatened or afflicted by any manifest of the Devil or the Devil's agents.

Mary Warren (*very faintly*). No, sir.

Hathorne (*with a gleam of victory*). And yet, when people accused of witchery confronted you in court, you would faint, saying their spirits came out of their bodies and choked you—

Mary Warren. That were pretense, sir.

Danforth. I cannot hear you.

Mary Warren. Pretense, sir.

Parris. But you did turn cold, did you not? I myself picked you up many times, and your skin were icy. Mr. Danforth, you—

Danforth. I saw that many times.

Proctor. She only pretended to faint, Your Excellency. They're all marvelous pretenders.

Hathorne. Then can she pretend to faint now?

Proctor. Now?

Parris. Why not? Now there are no spirits attacking her, for none in this room is accused of witchcraft. So let her turn herself cold now, let her pretend she is attacked now, let her faint. (*He turns to* Mary Warren.) Faint!

Mary Warren. Faint?

Parris. Aye, faint. Prove to us how you pretended in the court so many times.

Mary Warren (*looking to* Proctor). I—cannot faint now, sir.

Proctor (*alarmed, quietly*). Can you not pretend it?

Mary Warren. I—(*She looks about as though searching for the passion to faint.*) I—have no *sense* of it now, I—

Danforth. Why? What is lacking now?

Mary Warren. I—cannot tell, sir, I—

Danforth. Might it be that here we have no afflicting spirit loose, but in the court there were some?

Mary Warren. I never saw no spirits.

Parris. Then see no spirits now, and prove to us that you can faint by your own will, as you claim.

Mary Warren (*stares, searching for the emotion of it, and then shakes her head*). I—cannot do it.

Parris. Then you will confess, will you not? It were attacking spirits made you faint!

Mary Warren. No, sir, I—

Parris. Your Excellency, this is a trick to blind the court!

Mary Warren. It's not a trick! (*She stands.*) I—I used to faint because I—I thought I saw spirits.

Danforth. *Thought* you saw them!

Mary Warren. But I did not, Your Honor.

Hathorne. How could you think you saw them unless you saw them?

Mary Warren. I—I cannot tell how, but I did. I—I heard the other girls screaming, and you, Your Honor, you seemed to believe them, and I—It were only sport in the beginning, sir, but then the whole world cried spirits, spirits, and I—I promise you, Mr. Danforth, I only thought I saw them but I did not.

(Danforth *peers at her.*)

Parris (*smiling, but nervous because* Danforth *seems to be struck by* Mary Warren*'s story*). Surely Your Excellency is not taken by this simple lie.

Danforth (*turning worriedly to* Abigail). Abigail. I bid you now search your heart and tell me this—and beware of it, child, to God every soul is precious and His vengeance is terrible on them that take life without cause. Is it possible, child, that the spirits you have seen are illusion only, some deception that may cross your mind when—

Abigail. Why, this—this—is a base question, sir.

Danforth. Child, I would have you consider it—

Abigail. I have been hurt, Mr. Danforth; I have seen my blood runnin' out! I have been near to murdered every day because I done my duty pointing out the Devil's people—and this is my reward? To be mistrusted, denied, questioned like a—

Danforth (*weakening*). Child, I do not mistrust you—

Abigail (*in an open threat*). Let *you* beware, Mr. Danforth. Think you to be so mighty that the power of Hell may not turn *your* wits? Beware of it! There is—(*Suddenly, from an accusatory attitude, her face turns, looking into the air above—it is truly frightened.*)

Danforth (*apprehensively*). What is it, child?

Abigail (*looking about in the air, clasping her arms about her as though cold*). I—I know not. A wind, a cold wind, has come. (*Her eyes fall on* Mary Warren.)

Mary Warren (*terrified, pleading*). Abby!

Mercy Lewis (*shivering*). Your Honor, I freeze!

Proctor. They're pretending!

Hathorne (*touching* Abigail*'s hand*). She is cold, Your Honor, touch her!

Mercy Lewis (*through chattering teeth*). Mary, do you send this shadow on me?

Mary Warren. Lord, save me!

Susanna Walcott. I freeze, I freeze!

Abigail (*shivering visibly*). It is a wind, a wind!

Mary Warren. Abby, don't do that!

Danforth (*himself engaged and entered by* Abigail). Mary Warren, do you witch her? I say to you, do you send your spirit out?

(*With a hysterical cry* Mary Warren *starts to run.* Proctor *catches her.*)

Mary Warren (*almost collapsing*). Let me go, Mr. Proctor, I cannot, I cannot—

Abigail (*crying to Heaven*). Oh, Heavenly Father, take away this shadow!

(*Without warning or hesitation,* Proctor *leaps at* Abigail *and, grabbing her by the hair, pulls her to her feet. She screams in pain.* Danforth, *astonished, cries, "What are you about?" and* Hathorne *and* Parris *call, "Take your hands off her!" and out of it all comes* Proctor*'s roaring voice.*)

Proctor. How do you call Heaven! Whore! Whore!

(Herrick *breaks* Proctor *from her.*)

Herrick. John!

Danforth. Man! Man, what do you—

Proctor (*breathless and in agony*). It is a whore!

Danforth (*dumbfounded*). You charge—?

Abigail. Mr. Danforth, he is lying!

Proctor. Mark her! Now she'll suck a scream to stab me with, but—

Danforth. You will prove this! This will not pass!

Proctor (*trembling, his life collapsing about him*). I have known her, sir. I have known her.

Danforth. You—you are a lecher?

Francis (*horrified*). John, you cannot say such a—

Proctor. Oh, Francis, I wish you had some evil in you that you might know me! (*to* Danforth) A man will not cast away his good name. You surely know that.

Danforth (*dumbfounded*). In—in what time? In what place?

Proctor (*his voice about to break, and his shame great*). In the proper place—where my beasts are bedded. On the last night of my joy, some eight months past. She used to serve me in my house, sir. (*He has to clamp his jaw to keep from weeping.*) A man may think God sleeps, but God sees everything, I know it now. I beg you, sir, I beg you—see her what she is. My wife, my dear good wife, took this girl soon after, sir, and put her out on the highroad. And being what she is, a lump of vanity, sir—(*He is being overcome.*) Excellency, forgive me, forgive me. (*Angrily against himself, he turns away from the* Governor *for a moment. Then, as though to cry out is his only means of speech left.*) She thinks to dance with me on my wife's grave! And well she might, for I thought of her softly. God help me, I lusted, and there *is* a promise in such sweat. But it is a whore's vengeance, and you must see it; I set myself entirely in your hands. I know you must see it now.

Danforth (*blanched, in horror, turning to* Abigail). You deny every scrap and tittle[12] of this?

Abigail. If I must answer that, I will leave and I will not come back again!

(Danforth *seems unsteady.*)

Proctor. I have made a bell of my honor! I have rung the doom of my good name—you will believe me, Mr. Danforth! My wife is innocent, except she knew a whore when she saw one!

Abigail (*stepping up to* Danforth). What look do you give me? (Danforth *cannot speak.*) I'll not have such looks! (*She turns and starts for the door.*)

Danforth. You will remain where you are! (Herrick *steps into her path. She comes up short, fire in her eyes.*) Mr. Parris, go into the court and bring Goodwife Proctor out.

Parris (*objecting*). Your Honor, this is all a—

12. **every scrap and tittle:** every tiny bit.

Danforth (*sharply to* Parris). Bring her out! And tell her not one word of what's been spoken here. And let you knock before you enter. (Parris *goes out.*) Now we shall touch the bottom of this swamp. (*to* Proctor) Your wife, you say, is an honest woman.

Proctor. In her life, sir, she have never lied. There are them that cannot sing, and them that cannot weep—my wife cannot lie. I have paid much to learn it, sir.

Danforth. And when she put this girl out of your house, she put her out for a harlot?[13]

Proctor. Aye, sir.

Danforth. And knew her for a harlot?

Proctor. Aye, sir, she knew her for a harlot.

Danforth. Good then. (*to* Abigail) And if she tell me, child, it were for harlotry, may God spread His mercy on you! (*There is a knock. He calls to the door.*) Hold! (*to* Abigail) Turn your back. Turn your back. (*to* Proctor) Do likewise. (*Both turn their backs*—Abigail *with indignant slowness.*) Now let neither of you turn to face Goody Proctor. No one in this room is to speak one word, or raise a gesture aye or nay. (*He turns toward the door, calls.*) Enter! (*The door opens.* Elizabeth *enters with* Parris. Parris *leaves her. She stands alone, her eyes looking for* Proctor.) Mr. Cheever, report this testimony in all exactness. Are you ready?

Cheever. Ready, sir.

Danforth. Come here, woman. (Elizabeth *comes to him, glancing at* Proctor*'s back.*) Look at me only, not at your husband. In my eyes only.

Elizabeth (*faintly*). Good, sir.

Danforth. We are given to understand that at one time you dismissed your servant, Abigail Williams.

Elizabeth. That is true, sir.

Danforth. For what cause did you dismiss her? (*Slight pause. Then* Elizabeth *tries to glance at* Proctor.) You will look in my eyes only and not at your husband. The answer is in your memory and you need no help to give it to me. Why did you dismiss Abigail Williams?

Elizabeth (*not knowing what to say, sensing a situation, wetting her lips to stall for time*). She—dissatisfied me. (*pause*) And my husband.

Danforth. In what way dissatisfied you?

Elizabeth. She were—(*She glances at* Proctor *for a cue.*)

Danforth. Woman, look at me! (Elizabeth *does.*) Were she slovenly? Lazy? What disturbance did she cause?

Elizabeth. Your Honor, I—in that time I were sick. And I—My husband is a good and righteous man. He is never drunk as some are, nor wastin' his time at the shovelboard, but always at his work. But in my sickness—you see, sir, I were a long time sick after my last baby, and I thought I saw my husband somewhat turning from me. And this girl—(*She turns to* Abigail.)

Danforth. Look at me.

Elizabeth. Aye, sir. Abigail Williams—(*She breaks off.*)

Danforth. What of Abigail Williams?

Elizabeth. I came to think he fancied her. And so one night I lost my wits, I think, and put her out on the highroad.

Danforth. Your husband—did he indeed turn from you?

Elizabeth (*in agony*). My husband—is a goodly man, sir.

Danforth. Then he did not turn from you.

Elizabeth (*starting to glance at* Proctor). He—

Danforth (*reaches out and holds her face, then*). Look at me! To your own knowledge, has John Proctor ever committed the crime of lechery? (*In a crisis of indecision she cannot speak.*) Answer my question! Is your husband a lecher!

Elizabeth (*faintly*). No, sir.

Danforth. Remove her, Marshal.

13. **for a harlot:** as a woman of low morals.

Proctor. Elizabeth, tell the truth!

Danforth. She has spoken. Remove her!

Proctor (*crying out*). Elizabeth, I have confessed it!

Elizabeth. Oh, God! (*The door closes behind her.*)

Proctor. She only thought to save my name!

Hale. Excellency, it is a natural lie to tell; I beg you, stop now before another is condemned! I may shut my conscience to it no more—private vengeance is working through this testimony! From the beginning this man has struck me true. By my oath to Heaven, I believe him now, and I pray you call back his wife before we—

Danforth. She spoke nothing of lechery, and this man has lied!

Hale. I believe him! (*pointing at* Abigail) This girl has always struck me false! She has—

(Abigail, *with a weird, wild, chilling cry, screams up to the ceiling.*)

Abigail. You will not! Begone! Begone, I say!

Danforth. What is it, child? (*But* Abigail, *pointing with fear, is now raising up her frightened eyes, her awed face, toward the ceiling—the girls are doing the same—and now* Hathorne, Hale, Putnam, Cheever, Herrick, *and* Danforth *do the same.*) What's there? (*He lowers his eyes from the ceiling, and now he is frightened; there is real tension in his voice.*) Child! (*She is transfixed—with all the girls, she is whimpering open-mouthed, agape at the ceiling.*) Girls! Why do you—?

Mercy Lewis (*pointing*). It's on the beam! Behind the rafter!

Danforth (*looking up*). Where!

Abigail. Why—? (*She gulps.*) Why do you come, yellow bird?

Proctor. Where's a bird? I see no bird!

Abigail (*to the ceiling*). My face? My face?

Proctor. Mr. Hale—

Danforth. Be quiet!

Proctor (*to* Hale). Do you see a bird?

Danforth. Be quiet!!

Abigail (*to the ceiling, in a genuine conversation with the "bird," as though trying to talk it out of attacking her*). But God made my face; you cannot want to tear my face. Envy is a deadly sin, Mary.

Mary Warren (*on her feet with a spring, and horrified, pleading*). Abby!

Abigail (*unperturbed, continuing to the "bird"*). Oh, Mary, this is a black art[14] to change your shape. No, I cannot, I cannot stop my mouth; it's God's work I do.

Mary Warren. Abby, I'm *here!*

Proctor (*frantically*). They're pretending, Mr. Danforth!

Abigail (*Now she takes a backward step, as though in fear the bird will swoop down momentarily*). Oh, please, Mary! Don't come down.

Susanna Walcott. Her claws, she's stretching her claws!

Proctor. Lies, lies.

Abigail (*backing further, eyes still fixed above*). Mary, please don't hurt me!

Mary Warren (*to* Danforth). I'm not hurting her!

Danforth (*to* Mary Warren). Why does she see this vision?

Mary Warren. She sees nothin'!

Abigail (*now staring full front as though hypnotized, and mimicking the exact tone of* Mary Warren*'s cry*). She sees nothin'!

Mary Warren (*pleading*). Abby, you mustn't!

Abigail and All the Girls (*all transfixed*). Abby, you mustn't!

Mary Warren (*to all the girls*). I'm here, I'm here!

Girls. I'm here, I'm here!

Danforth (*horrified*). Mary Warren! Draw back your spirit out of them!

Mary Warren. Mr. Danforth!

14. **a black art:** sorcery.

Girls (*cutting her off*). Mr. Danforth!

Danforth. Have you compacted with the Devil? Have you?

Mary Warren. Never, never!

Girls. Never, never!

Danforth (*growing hysterical*). Why can they only repeat you?

Proctor. Give me a whip—I'll stop it!

Mary Warren. They're sporting.[15] They—!

Girls. They're sporting!

Mary Warren (*turning on them all hysterically and stamping her feet*). Abby, stop it!

Girls (*stamping their feet*). Abby, stop it!

Mary Warren. Stop it!

Girls. Stop it!

Mary Warren (*screaming it out at the top of her lungs, and raising her fists*). Stop it!!

Girls (*raising their fists*). Stop it!!

(Mary Warren, *utterly confounded, and becoming overwhelmed by* Abigail*'s—and the girls'—utter conviction, starts to whimper, hands half raised, powerless, and all the girls begin whimpering exactly as she does.*)

Danforth. A little while ago you were afflicted. Now it seems you afflict others; where did you find this power?

Mary Warren (*staring at* Abigail). I—have no power.

Girls. I have no power.

Proctor. They're gulling you,[16] Mister!

Danforth. Why did you turn about this past two weeks? You have seen the Devil, have you not?

Hale (*indicating* Abigail *and the girls*). You cannot believe them!

Mary Warren. I—

Proctor (*sensing her weakening*). Mary, God damns all liars!

Danforth (*pounding it into her*). You have seen the Devil, you have made compact with Lucifer, have you not?

Proctor. God damns liars, Mary!

(Mary *utters something unintelligible, staring at* Abigail, *who keeps watching the "bird" above.*)

Danforth. I cannot hear you. What do you say? (Mary *utters again unintelligibly.*) You will confess yourself or you will hang! (*He turns her roughly to face him.*) Do you know who I am? I say you will hang if you do not open with me!

Proctor. Mary, remember the angel Raphael—do that which is good and—

Abigail (*pointing upward*). The wings! Her wings are spreading! Mary, please, don't, don't—!

Hale. I see nothing, Your Honor!

Danforth. Do you confess this power! (*He is an inch from her face.*) Speak!

Abigail. She's going to come down! She's walking the beam!

Danforth. Will you speak!

Mary Warren (*staring in horror*). I cannot!

Girls. I cannot!

Parris. Cast the Devil out! Look him in the face! Trample him! We'll save you, Mary, only stand fast against him and—

Abigail (*looking up*). Look out! She's coming down!

(*She and all the girls run to one wall, shielding their eyes. And now, as though cornered, they let out a gigantic scream, and* Mary, *as though infected, opens her mouth and screams with them. Gradually* Abigail *and the girls leave off, until only* Mary *is left there, staring up at the "bird," screaming madly. All watch her, horrified by this evident fit.* Proctor *strides to her.*)

Proctor. Mary, tell the Governor what they—(*He has hardly got a word out, when, seeing him coming for her, she rushes out of his reach, screaming in horror.*)

---

15. **sporting:** playing a game.

16. **gulling you:** deceiving you.

Behind the Curtain

COMMON CORE RL 7

DRAMA AND FILM

The photographs here depict the scene in which Abigail and the girls claim to see Mary Warren's spirit flying overhead. The upper photograph shows a staged version of the scene; the lower one shows the same moment from a film adaptation. As you examine the stage image, notice what is visible to the audience—the entire set and all the characters present in the scene. Theater directors rely on the actors and the lighting to draw the audience's attention to part of the set or to particular characters or groups of characters. By contrast, film directors can use the camera to focus on part of the action. In the lower photograph, the camera has zoomed in to let the actors' facial expressions register on the audience. As you read the last page of Act Three, imagine that you are directing a film version of *The Crucible*. Choose one moment in which you want the camera to zoom in on John Proctor, including a close-up with just his face onscreen.

Mary Warren. Don't touch me—don't touch me! (*At which the girls halt at the door.*)

Proctor (*astonished*). Mary!

Mary Warren (*pointing at* Proctor). You're the Devil's man! (*He is stopped in his tracks.*)

Parris. Praise God!

Girls. Praise God!

Proctor (*numbed*). Mary, how—?

Mary Warren. I'll not hang with you! I love God, I love God.

Danforth (*to* Mary). He bid you do the Devil's work?

Mary Warren (*hysterically, indicating* Proctor). He come at me by night and every day to sign, to sign, to—

Danforth. Sign what?

Parris. The Devil's book? He come with a book?

Mary Warren (*hysterically, pointing at* Proctor, *fearful of him*). My name, he want my name. "I'll murder you," he says, "if my wife hangs! We must go and overthrow the court," he says!

(Danforth*'s head jerks toward* Proctor, *shock and horror in his face.*)

Proctor (*turning, appealing to* Hale). Mr. Hale!

Mary Warren (*her sobs beginning*). He wake me every night, his eyes were like coals and his fingers claw my neck, and I sign, I sign . . .

Hale. Excellency, this child's gone wild!

Proctor (*as* Danforth*'s wide eyes pour on him*). Mary, Mary!

Mary Warren (*screaming at him*). No, I love God; I go your way no more. I love God, I bless God. (*Sobbing, she rushes to* Abigail.) Abby, Abby, I'll never hurt you more! (*They all watch, as* Abigail, *out of her infinite charity, reaches out and draws the sobbing* Mary *to her, and then looks up to* Danforth.)

Danforth (*to* Proctor). What are you? (Proctor *is beyond speech in his anger.*) You are combined with anti-Christ,[17] are you not? I have seen your power; you will not deny it! What say you, Mister?

Hale. Excellency—

Danforth. I will have nothing from you, Mr. Hale! (*to* Proctor) Will you confess yourself befouled with Hell, or do you keep that black allegiance yet? What say you?

Proctor (*his mind wild, breathless*). I say—I say—God is dead!

Parris. Hear it, hear it!

Proctor (*laughs insanely, then*). A fire, a fire is burning! I hear the boot of Lucifer, I see his filthy face! And it is my face, and yours, Danforth! For them that quail to bring men out of ignorance, as I have quailed, and as you quail now when you know in all your black hearts that this be fraud—God damns our kind especially, and we will burn, we will burn together!

Danforth. Marshal! Take him and Corey with him to the jail!

Hale (*starting across to the door*). I denounce these proceedings!

Proctor. You are pulling Heaven down and raising up a whore!

Hale. I denounce these proceedings, I quit this court! (*He slams the door to the outside behind him.*)

Danforth (*calling to him in a fury*). Mr. Hale! Mr. Hale!

(*The curtain falls.*)

---

17. **combined with anti-Christ:** working with the Devil.

Comprehension

1. **Recall** Why does Mary Warren come to the court?
2. **Recall** What does John Proctor admit to the court?
3. **Clarify** Why is Proctor arrested at the end of the act?

Text Analysis

4. **Recognize Verbal Irony** Verbal irony occurs when someone states one thing and means another. According to the stage directions, Abigail draws the sobbing, repentant Mary to her side "out of her infinite charity" (lines 1136–1137). Why is this comment ironic?
5. **Draw Conclusions About Characters** Review the character traits you recorded in your chart for Danforth. How do these traits influence his relationship with the following?
   - John Proctor
   - Reverend Hale
   - Abigail Williams
   - Reverend Parris
6. **Make Judgments** What is your opinion of the way Danforth is conducting the court? Use details from the play to support your opinion.
7. **Analyze Character Motives** Why does Elizabeth lie to Danforth about her husband's relationship with Abigail?
8. **Analyze Conventions of Drama** Review the information on **types of characters** in the **Text Analysis Workshop** on pages 132–133. Then determine the play's central character, or **protagonist,** its major **antagonists,** and **character foils.** List these characters in a chart like the one shown and take notes on their personalities and values. What effect does the interplay among these characters have on the play?

Character-Type	Personality	Values

Text Criticism

9. **Different Perspectives** The real Abigail Williams was 11 years old in 1692 and had not had an illicit relationship with John Proctor. How would the play differ if Arthur Miller had not embellished the truth? What would be lost?

What fuels a **MOB?**

How does Mary Warren contribute to the mob mentality that takes over the court room in Act Three?

COMMON CORE

RL 1 Cite textual evidence to support analysis of what the text says explicitly as well as inferences drawn from the text, including determining where the text leaves matters uncertain. **RL 3** Analyze the impact of the author's choices regarding how to develop and relate elements of a drama. **RL 5** Analyze how an author's choices concerning how to structure specific parts of a text contribute to its overall structure and meaning as well as its aesthetic impact. **RL 6** Analyze a case in which grasping point of view requires distinguishing what is directly stated in a text from what is really meant.

Act *Four*

(A cell in Salem jail, that fall.

At the back is a high barred window; near it, a great, heavy door. Along the walls are two benches.

The place is in darkness but for the moonlight seeping through the bars. It appears empty. Presently footsteps are heard coming down a corridor beyond the wall, keys rattle, and the door swings open. Marshal Herrick *enters with a lantern.*

He is nearly drunk, and heavy-footed. He goes to a bench and nudges a bundle of rags lying on it.)

Herrick. Sarah, wake up! Sarah Good! (*He then crosses to the other bench.*)

Sarah Good (*rising in her rags*). Oh, Majesty! Comin', comin'! Tituba, he's here, His Majesty's come!

Herrick. Go to the north cell; this place is wanted now. (*He hangs his lantern on the wall.* Tituba *sits up.*)

Tituba. That don't look to me like His Majesty; look to me like the marshal.

Herrick (*taking out a flask*). Get along with you now, clear this place. (*He drinks, and* Sarah Good *comes and peers up into his face.*)

Sarah Good. Oh, is it you, Marshal! I thought sure you be the devil comin' for us. Could I have a sip of cider for me goin'-away?

Herrick (*handing her the flask*). And where are you off to, Sarah?

Tituba (*as* Sarah *drinks*). We goin' to Barbados, soon the Devil gits here with the feathers and the wings.

Herrick. Oh? A happy voyage to you.

Sarah Good. A pair of bluebirds wingin' southerly, the two of us! Oh, it be a grand transformation, Marshal! (*She raises the flask to drink again.*)

Herrick (*taking the flask from her lips*). You'd best give me that or you'll never rise off the ground. Come along now.

Tituba. I'll speak to him for you, if you desires to come along, Marshal.

Herrick. I'd not refuse it, Tituba; it's the proper morning to fly into Hell.

Tituba. Oh, it be no Hell in Barbados. Devil, him be pleasure-man in Barbados, him be singin' and dancin' in Barbados. It's you folks—you riles him up 'round here; it be too cold 'round here for that Old Boy. He freeze his soul in Massachusetts, but in Barbados he just as sweet and—(*A bellowing cow is heard, and* Tituba *leaps up and calls to the window.*) Aye, sir! That's him, Sarah!

Sarah Good. I'm here, Majesty! (*They hurriedly pick up their rags as* Hopkins, *a guard, enters.*)

John Proctor going to the gallows

Hopkins. The Deputy Governor's arrived.

Herrick (*grabbing* Tituba). Come along, come along.

Tituba (*resisting him*). No, he comin' for me. I goin' home!

Herrick (*pulling her to the door*). That's not Satan, just a poor old cow with a hatful of milk. Come along now, out with you!

Tituba (*calling to the window*). Take me home, Devil! Take me home!

Sarah Good (*following the shouting* Tituba *out*). Tell him I'm goin', Tituba! Now you tell him Sarah Good is goin' too!

(*In the corridor outside* Tituba *calls on—"Take me home, Devil; Devil take me home!" and* Hopkins' *voice orders her to move on.* Herrick *returns and begins to push old rags and straw into a corner. Hearing footsteps, he turns, and enter* Danforth *and* Judge Hathorne. *They are in greatcoats and wear hats against the bitter cold. They are followed in by* Cheever, *who carries a dispatch case*[1] *and a flat wooden box containing his writing materials.*)

Herrick. Good morning, Excellency.

Danforth. Where is Mr. Parris?

Herrick. I'll fetch him. (*He starts for the door.*)

Danforth. Marshal. (Herrick *stops.*) When did Reverend Hale arrive?

Herrick. It were toward midnight, I think.

Danforth (*suspiciously*). What is he about here?

Herrick. He goes among them that will hang, sir. And he prays with them. He sits with Goody Nurse now. And Mr. Parris with him.

Danforth. Indeed. That man have no authority to enter here, Marshal. Why have you let him in?

Herrick. Why, Mr. Parris command me, sir. I cannot deny him.

Danforth. Are you drunk, Marshal?

Herrick. No, sir; it is a bitter night, and I have no fire here.

Danforth (*containing his anger*). Fetch Mr. Parris.

Herrick. Aye, sir.

Danforth. There is a prodigious stench in this place.

Herrick. I have only now cleared the people out for you.

Danforth. Beware hard drink, Marshal.

Herrick. Aye, sir. (*He waits an instant for further orders. But* Danforth, *in dissatisfaction, turns his back on him, and* Herrick *goes out. There is a pause.* Danforth *stands in thought.*)

Hathorne. Let you question Hale, Excellency; I should not be surprised he have been preaching in Andover[2] lately.

Danforth. We'll come to that; speak nothing of Andover. Parris prays with him. That's strange. (*He blows on his hands, moves toward the window, and looks out.*)

Hathorne. Excellency, I wonder if it be wise to let Mr. Parris so continuously with the prisoners. (Danforth *turns to him, interested.*) I think, sometimes, the man has a mad look these days.

Danforth. Mad?

Hathorne. I met him yesterday coming out of his house, and I bid him good morning—and he wept and went his way. I think it is not well the village sees him so unsteady.

Danforth. Perhaps he have some sorrow.

Cheever (*stamping his feet against the cold*). I think it be the cows, sir.

Danforth. Cows?

Cheever. There be so many cows wanderin' the highroads, now their masters are in the jails, and much disagreement who they will belong to now. I know Mr. Parris be arguin' with farmers all yesterday—

1. **dispatch case:** a case for carrying documents.

2. **Andover:** a town in Massachusetts northwest of Salem.

there is great contention, sir, about the cows. Contention make him weep, sir; it were always a man that weep for contention. (*He turns, as do* Hathorne *and* Danforth, *hearing someone coming up the corridor.* Danforth *raises his head as* Parris *enters. He is gaunt, frightened, and sweating in his greatcoat.*)

Parris (*to* Danforth, *instantly*). Oh, good morning, sir, thank you for coming, I beg your pardon wakin' you so early. Good morning, Judge Hathorne.

Danforth. Reverend Hale have no right to enter this—

Parris. Excellency, a moment. (*He hurries back and shuts the door.*)

Hathorne. Do you leave him alone with the prisoners?

Danforth. What's his business here?

Parris (*prayerfully holding up his hands*). Excellency, hear me. It is a providence. Reverend Hale has returned to bring Rebecca Nurse to God.

Danforth (*surprised*). He bids her confess?

Parris (*sitting*). Hear me. Rebecca have not given me a word this three month since she came. Now she sits with him, and her sister and Martha Corey and two or three others, and he pleads with them, confess their crimes and save their lives.

Danforth. Why—this is indeed a providence. And they soften, they soften?

Parris. Not yet, not yet. But I thought to summon you, sir, that we might think on whether it be not wise, to—(*He dares not say it.*) I had thought to put a question, sir, and I hope you will not—

Danforth. Mr. Parris, be plain, what troubles you?

Parris. There is news, sir, that the court—the court must reckon with. My niece, sir, my niece—I believe she has vanished.

Danforth. Vanished!

Parris. I had thought to advise you of it earlier in the week, but—

Danforth. Why? How long is she gone?

Parris. This be the third night. You see, sir, she told me she would stay a night with Mercy Lewis. And next day, when she does not return, I send to Mr. Lewis to inquire. Mercy told him she would sleep in *my* house for a night.

Danforth. They are both gone?!

Parris (*in fear of him*). They are, sir.

Danforth (*alarmed*). I will send a party for them. Where may they be?

Parris. Excellency, I think they be aboard a ship. (Danforth *stands agape.*) My daughter tells me how she heard them speaking of ships last week, and tonight I discover my—my strongbox is broke into. (*He presses his fingers against his eyes to keep back tears.*)

Hathorne (*astonished*). She have robbed you?

Parris. Thirty-one pound is gone. I am penniless. (*He covers his face and sobs.*)

Danforth. Mr. Parris, you are a brainless man! (*He walks in thought, deeply worried.*)

Parris. Excellency, it profit nothing you should blame me. I cannot think they would run off except they fear to keep in Salem any more. (*He is pleading.*) Mark it, sir, Abigail had close knowledge of the town, and since the news of Andover has broken here—

Danforth. Andover is remedied.[3] The court returns there on Friday, and will resume examinations.

Parris. I am sure of it, sir. But the rumor here speaks rebellion in Andover, and it—

Danforth. There is no rebellion in Andover!

Parris. I tell you what is said here, sir. Andover have thrown out the court, they say, and will have no part of witchcraft. There be a faction here, feeding on that news, and I tell you true, sir, I fear there will be riot here.

Hathorne. Riot! Why at every execution I have seen naught but high satisfaction in the town.

3. **remedied:** no longer a problem.

Parris. Judge Hathorne—it were another sort that hanged till now. Rebecca Nurse is no Bridget that lived three year with Bishop before she married him. John Proctor is not Isaac Ward that drank his family to ruin. (*to* Danforth) I would to God it were not so, Excellency, but these people have great weight yet in the town. Let Rebecca stand upon the gibbet[4] and send up some righteous prayer, and I fear she'll wake a vengeance on you.

Hathorne. Excellency, she is condemned a witch. The court have—

Danforth (*in deep concern, raising a hand to* Hathorne). Pray you. (*to* Parris) How do you propose, then?

Parris. Excellency, I would postpone these hangin's for a time.

Danforth. There will be no postponement.

Parris. Now Mr. Hale's returned, there is hope, I think—for if he bring even one of these to God, that confession surely damns the others in the public eye, and none may doubt more that they are all linked to Hell. This way, unconfessed and claiming innocence, doubts are multiplied, many honest people will weep for them, and our good purpose is lost in their tears.

Danforth (*after thinking a moment, then going to* Cheever). Give me the list.

(Cheever *opens the dispatch case, searches.*)

Parris. It cannot be forgot, sir, that when I summoned the congregation for John Proctor's excommunication[5] there were hardly thirty people come to hear it. That speak a discontent, I think, and—

Danforth (*studying the list*). There will be no postponement.

Parris. Excellency—

Danforth. Now, sir—which of these in your opinion may be brought to God? I will myself strive with him[6] till dawn. (*He hands the list to* Parris, *who merely glances at it.*)

Parris. There is not sufficient time till dawn.

Danforth. I shall do my utmost. Which of them do you have hope for?

Parris (*not even glancing at the list now, and in a quavering voice, quietly*). Excellency—a dagger—(*He chokes up.*)

Danforth. What do you say?

Parris. Tonight, when I open my door to leave my house—a dagger clattered to the ground. (*Silence.* Danforth *absorbs this. Now* Parris *cries out.*) You cannot hang this sort. There is danger for me. I dare not step outside at night!

(Reverend Hale *enters. They look at him for an instant in silence. He is steeped in sorrow, exhausted, and more direct than he ever was.*)

Danforth. Accept my congratulations, Reverend Hale; we are gladdened to see you returned to your good work.

Hale (*coming to* Danforth *now*). You must pardon them. They will not budge.

(Herrick *enters, waits.*)

Danforth (*conciliatory*). You misunderstand, sir; I cannot pardon these when twelve are already hanged for the same crime. It is not just.

Parris (*with failing heart*). Rebecca will not confess?

Hale. The sun will rise in a few minutes. Excellency, I must have more time.

Danforth. Now hear me, and beguile yourselves no more. I will not receive a single plea for pardon or postponement. Them that will not confess will hang. Twelve are already executed; the names of

4. **gibbet** (jĭb′ĭt): gallows.

5. **excommunication:** banishment from a church. For the Puritans in New England, this punishment resulted in the loss of church privileges.

6. **strive with him:** struggle with him through prayer.

these seven are given out, and the village expects to see them die this morning. Postponement now speaks a floundering on my part; reprieve or pardon must cast doubt upon the guilt of them that died till now. While I speak God's law, I will not crack its voice with whimpering. If retaliation is your fear, know this—I should hang ten thousand that dared to rise against the law, and an ocean of salt tears could not melt the resolution of the statutes. Now draw yourselves up like men and help me, as you are bound by Heaven to do. Have you spoken with them all, Mr. Hale?

Hale. All but Proctor. He is in the dungeon.

Danforth (*to* Herrick). What's Proctor's way now?

Herrick. He sits like some great bird; you'd not know he lived except he will take food from time to time.

Danforth (*after thinking a moment*). His wife—his wife must be well on with child now.

Herrick. She is, sir.

Danforth. What think you, Mr. Parris? You have closer knowledge of this man; might her presence soften him?

Parris. It is possible, sir. He have not laid eyes on her these three months. I should summon her.

Danforth (*to* Herrick). Is he yet **adamant?** Has he struck at you again?

Herrick. He cannot, sir, he is chained to the wall now.

Danforth (*after thinking on it*). Fetch Goody Proctor to me. Then let you bring him up.

Herrick. Aye, sir. (Herrick *goes. There is silence.*)

Hale. Excellency, if you postpone a week and publish to the town that you are striving for their confessions, that speak mercy on your part, not faltering.

Danforth. Mr. Hale, as God have not empowered me like Joshua to stop this sun from rising,[7] so I cannot withhold from them the perfection of their punishment.

Hale (*harder now*). If you think God wills you to raise rebellion, Mr. Danforth, you are mistaken!

Danforth (*instantly*). You have heard rebellion spoken in the town?

Hale. Excellency, there are orphans wandering from house to house; abandoned cattle bellow on the highroads, the stink of rotting crops hangs everywhere, and no man knows when the harlots' cry will end his life—and you wonder yet if rebellion's spoke? Better you should marvel how they do not burn your province!

Danforth. Mr. Hale, have you preached in Andover this month?

Hale. Thank God they have no need of me in Andover.

Danforth. You baffle me, sir. Why have you returned here?

Hale. Why, it is all simple. I come to do the Devil's work. I come to counsel Christians they should belie themselves. (*His sarcasm collapses.*) There is blood on my head! Can you not see the blood on my head!!

Parris. Hush! (*For he has heard footsteps. They all face the door.* Herrick *enters with* Elizabeth. *Her wrists are linked by heavy chain, which* Herrick *now removes. Her clothes are dirty; her face is pale and gaunt.* Herrick *goes out.*)

Danforth (*very politely*). Goody Proctor. (*She is silent.*) I hope you are hearty?

Elizabeth (*as a warning reminder*). I am yet six month before my time.

Danforth. Pray be at your ease, we come not for your life. We—(*uncertain how to plead, for he is not accustomed to it.*) Mr. Hale, will you speak with the woman?

Hale. Goody Proctor, your husband is marked to hang this morning.

(*pause*)

Elizabeth (*quietly*). I have heard it.

---

7. **like Joshua . . . rising:** According to the Bible, Joshua became leader of the Israelites after Moses died. He led the people to the Promised Land while the sun stood still.

Hale. You know, do you not, that I have no connection with the court? (*She seems to doubt it.*) I come of my own, Goody Proctor. I would save your husband's life, for if he is taken I count myself his murderer. Do you understand me?

Elizabeth. What do you want of me?

Hale. Goody Proctor, I have gone this three month like our Lord into the wilderness.[8] I have sought a Christian way, for damnation's doubled on a minister who counsels men to lie.

Hathorne. It is no lie, you cannot speak of lies.

Hale. It is a lie! They are innocent!

Danforth. I'll hear no more of that!

Hale (*continuing to* Elizabeth). Let you not mistake your duty as I mistook my own. I came into this village like a bridegroom to his beloved, bearing gifts of high religion; the very crowns of holy law I brought, and what I touched with my bright confidence, it died; and where I turned the eye of my great faith, blood flowed up. Beware, Goody Proctor—cleave to no faith when faith brings blood. It is mistaken law that leads you to sacrifice. Life, woman, life is God's most precious gift; no principle, however glorious, may justify the taking of it. I beg you, woman, prevail upon your husband to confess. Let him give his lie. Quail not before God's judgment in this, for it may well be God damns a liar less than he that throws his life away for pride. Will you plead with him? I cannot think he will listen to another.

Elizabeth (*quietly*). I think that be the Devil's argument.

Hale (*with a climactic desperation*). Woman, before the laws of God we are as swine! We cannot read His will!

Elizabeth. I cannot dispute with you, sir; I lack learning for it.

Danforth (*going to her*). Goody Proctor, you are not summoned here for disputation. Be there no wifely tenderness within you? He will die with the sunrise. Your husband. Do you understand it? (*She only looks at him.*) What say you? Will you contend with him? (*She is silent.*) Are you stone? I tell you true, woman, had I no other proof of your unnatural life, your dry eyes now would be sufficient evidence that you delivered up your soul to Hell! A very ape would weep at such calamity! Have the devil dried up any tear of pity in you? (*She is silent.*) Take her out. It profit nothing she should speak to him!

Elizabeth (*quietly*). Let me speak with him, Excellency.

Parris (*with hope*). You'll strive with him? (*She hesitates.*)

Danforth. Will you plead for his confession or will you not?

Elizabeth. I promise nothing. Let me speak with him.

(*A sound—the sibilance of dragging feet on stone. They turn. A pause.* Herrick *enters with* John Proctor. *His wrists are chained. He is another man, bearded, filthy, his eyes misty as though webs had overgrown them. He halts inside the doorway, his eye caught by the sight of* Elizabeth. *The emotion flowing between them prevents anyone from speaking for an instant. Now* Hale, *visibly affected, goes to* Danforth *and speaks quietly.*)

Hale. Pray, leave them, Excellency.

Danforth (*pressing* Hale *impatiently aside*). Mr. Proctor, you have been notified, have you not? (Proctor *is silent, staring at* Elizabeth.) I see light in the sky, Mister; let you counsel with your wife, and may God help you turn your back on Hell. (Proctor *is silent, staring at* Elizabeth.)

Hale (*quietly*). Excellency, let—

(Danforth *brushes past* Hale *and walks out.* Hale *follows.* Cheever *stands and follows,* Hathorne *behind.* Herrick *goes.* Parris, *from a safe distance, offers.*)

8. **like our Lord ... wilderness:** According to the New Testament, Jesus spent 40 days wandering in the desert.

Parris. If you desire a cup of cider, Mr. Proctor, I am sure I—(Proctor *turns an icy stare at him, and he breaks off.* Parris *raises his palms toward* Proctor.) God lead you now. (Parris *goes out.*)

(*Alone.* Proctor *walks to her, halts. It is as though they stood in a spinning world. It is beyond sorrow, above it. He reaches out his hand as though toward an embodiment not quite real, and as he touches her, a strange soft sound, half laughter, half amazement, comes from his throat. He pats her hand. She covers his hand with hers. And then, weak, he sits. Then she sits, facing him.*)

Proctor. The child?

Elizabeth. It grows.

Proctor. There is no word of the boys?

Elizabeth. They're well. Rebecca's Samuel keeps them.

Proctor. You have not seen them?

Elizabeth. I have not. (*She catches a weakening in herself and downs it.*)

Proctor. You are a—marvel, Elizabeth.

Elizabeth. You—have been tortured?

Proctor. Aye. (*Pause. She will not let herself be drowned in the sea that threatens her.*) They come for my life now.

Elizabeth. I know it.

(*pause*)

Proctor. None—have yet confessed?

Elizabeth. There be many confessed.

Proctor. Who are they?

Elizabeth. There be a hundred or more, they say. Goody Ballard is one; Isaiah Goodkind is one. There be many.

Proctor. Rebecca?

Elizabeth. Not Rebecca. She is one foot in Heaven now; naught may hurt her more.

Proctor. And Giles?

Elizabeth. You have not heard of it?

Proctor. I hear nothin', where I am kept.

Elizabeth. Giles is dead.

(*He looks at her incredulously.*)

Proctor. When were he hanged?

Elizabeth (*quietly, factually*). He were not hanged. He would not answer aye or nay to his indictment; for if he denied the charge they'd hang him surely, and auction out his property. So he stand mute, and died Christian under the law. And so his sons will have his farm. It is the law, for he could not be condemned a wizard without he answer the indictment, aye or nay.

Proctor. Then how does he die?

Elizabeth (*gently*). They press him, John.

Proctor. Press?

Elizabeth. Great stones they lay upon his chest until he plead aye or nay. (*with a tender smile for the old man*) They say he give them but two words. "More weight," he says. And died.

Proctor (*numbed—a thread to weave into his agony*). "More weight."

Elizabeth. Aye. It were a fearsome[9] man, Giles Corey.

(*pause*)

Proctor (*with great force of will, but not quite looking at her*). I have been thinking I would confess to them, Elizabeth. (*She shows nothing.*) What say you? If I give them that?

Elizabeth. I cannot judge you, John.

(*pause*)

Proctor (*simply—a pure question*). What would you have me do?

Elizabeth. As you will, I would have it. (*slight pause*) I want you living, John. That's sure.

Proctor (*pauses, then with a flailing of hope*). Giles' wife? Have she confessed?

Elizabeth. She will not.

---

9. **fearsome:** courageous.

(*pause*)

Proctor. It is a pretense, Elizabeth.

Elizabeth. What is?

Proctor. I cannot mount the gibbet like a saint. It is a fraud. I am not that man. (*She is silent.*) My honesty is broke, Elizabeth; I am no good man. Nothing's spoiled by giving them this lie that were not rotten long before.

Elizabeth. And yet you've not confessed till now. That speak goodness in you.

Proctor. Spite only keeps me silent. It is hard to give a lie to dogs. (*Pause. For the first time he turns directly to her.*) I would have your forgiveness, Elizabeth.

Elizabeth. It is not for me to give, John, I am—

Proctor. I'd have you see some honesty in it. Let them that never lied die now to keep their souls. It is pretense for me, a vanity that will not blind God nor keep my children out of the wind. (*pause*) What say you?

Elizabeth (*upon a heaving sob that always threatens*). John, it come to naught that I should forgive you, if you'll not forgive yourself. (*Now he turns away a little, in great agony.*) It is not my soul, John, it is yours. (*He stands, as though in physical pain, slowly rising to his feet with a great immortal longing to find his answer. It is difficult to say, and she is on the verge of tears.*) Only be sure of this, for I know it now: Whatever you will do, it is a good man does it. (*He turns his doubting, searching gaze upon her.*) I have read my heart this three month, John. (*pause*) I have sins of my own to count. It needs a cold wife to prompt lechery.

Proctor (*in great pain*). Enough, enough—

Elizabeth (*now pouring out her heart*). Better you should know me!

Proctor. I will not hear it! I know you!

Elizabeth. You take my sins upon you, John—

Proctor (*in agony*). No, I take my own, my own!

Elizabeth. John, I counted myself so plain, so poorly made, no honest love could come to me! Suspicion kissed you when I did; I never knew how I should say my love. It were a cold house I kept! (*In fright, she swerves, as* Hathorne *enters.*)

Hathorne. What say you, Proctor? The sun is soon up.

(Proctor, *his chest heaving, stares, turns to* Elizabeth. *She comes to him as though to plead, her voice quaking.*)

Elizabeth. Do what you will. But let none be your judge. There be no higher judge under Heaven than Proctor is! Forgive me, forgive me, John—I never knew such goodness in the world! (*She covers her face, weeping.*)

(Proctor *turns from her to* Hathorne; *he is off the earth, his voice hollow.*)

Proctor. I want my life.

Hathorne (*electrified, surprised*). You'll confess yourself?

Proctor. I will have my life.

Hathorne (*with a mystical tone*). God be praised! It is a providence! (*He rushes out the door, and his voice is heard calling down the corridor.*) He will confess! Proctor will confess!

Proctor (*with a cry, as he strides to the door*). Why do you cry it? (*In great pain he turns back to her.*) It is evil, is it not? It is evil.

Elizabeth (*in terror, weeping*). I cannot judge you, John, I cannot!

Proctor. Then who will judge me? (*suddenly clasping his hands*) God in Heaven, what is John Proctor, what is John Proctor? (*He moves as an animal, and a fury is riding in him, a tantalized search.*) I think it is honest, I think so; I am no saint. (*As though she had denied this he calls angrily at her.*) Let Rebecca go like a saint; for me it is fraud!

(*Voices are heard in the hall, speaking together in suppressed excitement.*)

Elizabeth. I am not your judge, I cannot be. (*as though giving him release*) Do as you will, do as you will!

Proctor. Would you give them such a lie? Say it. Would you ever give them this? (*She cannot answer.*) You would not; if tongs of fire were singeing you you would not! It is evil. Good, then—it is evil, and I do it!

(Hathorne *enters with* Danforth, *and, with them,* Cheever, Parris, *and* Hale. *It is a businesslike, rapid entrance, as though the ice had been broken.*)

Danforth (*with great relief and gratitude*). Praise to God, man, praise to God; you shall be blessed in Heaven for this. (Cheever *has hurried to the bench with pen, ink, and paper.* Proctor *watches him.*) Now then, let us have it. Are you ready, Mr. Cheever?

Proctor (*with a cold, cold horror at their efficiency*). Why must it be written?

Danforth. Why, for the good instruction of the village, Mister; this we shall post upon the church door! (*to* Parris, *urgently*) Where is the marshal?

Parris (*runs to the door and calls down the corridor*). Marshal! Hurry!

John and Elizabeth Proctor before the marshal

Danforth. Now, then, Mister, will you speak slowly, and directly to the point, for Mr. Cheever's sake. (*He is on record now, and is really dictating to* Cheever, *who writes.*) Mr. Proctor, have you seen the Devil in your life? (Proctor*'s jaws lock.*) Come, man, there is light in the sky; the town waits at the scaffold; I would give out this news. Did you see the Devil?

Proctor. I did.

Parris. Praise God!

Danforth. And when he come to you, what were his demand? (Proctor *is silent.* Danforth *helps.*) Did he bid you to do his work upon the earth?

Proctor. He did.

Danforth. And you bound yourself to his service? (Danforth *turns, as* Rebecca Nurse *enters, with* Herrick *helping to support her. She is barely able to walk.*) Come in, come in, woman!

Rebecca (*brightening as she sees* Proctor). Ah, John! You are well, then, eh?

(Proctor *turns his face to the wall.*)

Danforth. Courage, man, courage—let her witness your good example that she may come to God herself. Now hear it, Goody Nurse! Say on, Mr. Proctor. Did you bind yourself to the Devil's service?

Rebecca (*astonished*). Why, John!

Proctor (*through his teeth, his face turned from* Rebecca). I did.

Danforth. Now, woman, you surely see it profit nothin' to keep this conspiracy any further. Will you confess yourself with him?

Rebecca. Oh, John—God send his mercy on you!

Danforth. I say, will you confess yourself, Goody Nurse?

Rebecca. Why, it is a lie, it is a lie; how may I damn myself? I cannot, I cannot.

Danforth. Mr. Proctor. When the Devil came to you did you see Rebecca Nurse in his company? (Proctor *is silent.*) Come, man, take courage—did you ever see her with the Devil?

Proctor (*almost inaudibly*). No.

(Danforth, *now sensing trouble, glances at* John *and goes to the table, and picks up a sheet—the list of condemned.*)

Danforth. Did you ever see her sister, Mary Easty, with the Devil?

Proctor. No, I did not.

Danforth (*his eyes narrow on* Proctor). Did you ever see Martha Corey with the Devil?

Proctor. I did not.

Danforth (*realizing, slowly putting the sheet down*). Did you ever see anyone with the Devil?

Proctor. I did not.

Danforth. Proctor, you mistake me. I am not empowered to trade your life for a lie. You have most certainly seen some person with the Devil. (Proctor *is silent.*) Mr. Proctor, a score of people have already testified they saw this woman with the Devil.

Proctor. Then it is proved. Why must I say it?

Danforth. Why "must" you say it! Why, you should rejoice to say it if your soul is truly purged of any love for Hell!

Proctor. They think to go like saints. I like not to spoil their names.

Danforth (*inquiring, incredulous*). Mr. Proctor, do you think they go like saints?

Proctor (*evading*). This woman never thought she done the Devil's work.

Danforth. Look you, sir. I think you mistake your duty here. It matters nothing what she thought—she is convicted of the unnatural murder of children, and you for sending your spirit out upon Mary Warren. Your soul alone is the issue here, Mister, and you will prove its whiteness or you cannot live in a Christian country. Will you tell me now what persons conspired with you in the Devil's company? (Proctor *is silent.*) To your knowledge was Rebecca Nurse ever—

Proctor. I speak my own sins; I cannot judge another. (*crying out, with hatred*) I have no tongue for it.

Hale (*quickly to* Danforth). Excellency, it is enough he confess himself. Let him sign it, let him sign it.

Parris (*feverishly*). It is a great service, sir. It is a weighty name; it will strike the village that Proctor confess. I beg you, let him sign it. The sun is up, Excellency!

Danforth (*considers; then with dissatisfaction*). Come, then, sign your testimony. (*to* Cheever) Give it to him. (Cheever *goes to* Proctor, *the confession and a pen in hand.* Proctor *does not look at it.*) Come, man, sign it.

Proctor (*after glancing at the confession*). You have all witnessed it—it is enough.

Danforth. You will not sign it?

Proctor. You have all witnessed it; what more is needed?

Danforth. Do you sport with me? You will sign your name or it is no confession, Mister! (*His breast heaving with agonized breathing,* Proctor *now lays the paper down and signs his name.*)

Parris. Praise be to the Lord!

(Proctor *has just finished signing when* Danforth *reaches for the paper. But* Proctor *snatches it up, and now a wild terror is rising in him, and a boundless anger.*)

Danforth (*perplexed, but politely extending his hand*). If you please, sir.

Proctor. No.

Danforth (*as though* Proctor *did not understand*). Mr. Proctor, I must have—

Proctor. No, no. I have signed it. You have seen me. It is done! You have no need for this.

Parris. Proctor, the village must have proof that—

Proctor. Damn the village! I confess to God, and God has seen my name on this! It is enough!

Danforth. No, sir, it is—

Proctor. You came to save my soul, did you not? Here! I have confessed myself; it is enough!

Danforth. You have not con—

Proctor. I have confessed myself! Is there no good penitence but it be public? God does not need my name nailed upon the church! God sees my name; God knows how black my sins are! It is enough!

Danforth. Mr. Proctor—

Proctor. You will not use me! I am no Sarah Good or Tituba, I am John Proctor! You will not use me! It is no part of salvation that you should use me!

Danforth. I do not wish to—

Proctor. I have three children—how may I teach them to walk like men in the world, and I sold my friends?

Danforth. You have not sold your friends—

Proctor. Beguile me not! I blacken all of them when this is nailed to the church the very day they hang for silence!

Danforth. Mr. Proctor, I must have good and legal proof that you—

Proctor. You are the high court, your word is good enough! Tell them I confessed myself; say Proctor broke his knees and wept like a woman; say what you will, but my name cannot—

Danforth (*with suspicion*). It is the same, is it not? If I report it or you sign to it?

Proctor (*He knows it is insane*). No, it is not the same! What others say and what I sign to is not the same!

Danforth. Why? Do you mean to deny this confession when you are free?

Proctor. I mean to deny nothing!

Danforth. Then explain to me, Mr. Proctor, why you will not let—

Proctor (*with a cry of his whole soul*). Because it is my name! Because I cannot have another in my life! Because I lie and sign myself to lies! Because I am not worth the dust on the feet of them that hang! How may I live without my name? I have given you my soul; leave me my name!

Danforth (*pointing at the confession in* Proctor*'s hand*). Is that document a lie? If it is a lie I will not accept it! What say you? I will not deal in lies, Mister! (Proctor *is motionless.*) You will give me your honest confession in my hand, or I cannot keep you from the rope. (Proctor *does not reply.*) Which way do you go, Mister?

(*His breast heaving, his eyes staring,* Proctor *tears the paper and crumples it, and he is weeping in fury, but erect.*)

Danforth. Marshal!

Parris (*hysterically, as though the tearing paper were his life*). Proctor, Proctor!

Hale. Man, you will hang! You cannot!

Proctor (*his eyes full of tears*). I can. And there's your first marvel, that I can. You have made your magic now, for now I do think I see some shred of goodness in John Proctor. Not enough to weave a banner with, but white enough to keep it from such dogs. (Elizabeth, *in a burst of terror, rushes to him and weeps against his hand.*) Give them no tear! Tears pleasure them! Show honor now, show a stony heart and sink them with it! (*He has lifted her, and kisses her now with great passion.*)

Rebecca. Let you fear nothing! Another judgment waits us all!

Danforth. Hang them high over the town! Who weeps for these, weeps for corruption! (*He sweeps out past them.* Herrick *starts to lead* Rebecca, *who almost collapses, but* Proctor *catches her, and she glances up at him apologetically.*)

Rebecca. I've had no breakfast.

Herrick. Come, man.

(Herrick *escorts them out,* Hathorne *and* Cheever *behind them.* Elizabeth *stands staring at the empty doorway.*)

Parris (*in deadly fear, to* Elizabeth). Go to him, Goody Proctor! There is yet time!

(*From outside a drumroll strikes the air.* Parris *is startled.* Elizabeth *jerks about toward the window.*)

Parris. Go to him! (*He rushes out the door, as though to hold back his fate.*) Proctor! Proctor!

(*again, a short burst of drums*)

Hale. Woman, plead with him! (*He starts to rush out the door, and then goes back to her.*) Woman! It is pride, it is vanity. (*She avoids his eyes, and moves to the window. He drops to his knees.*) Be his helper!—What profit him to bleed? Shall the dust praise him? Shall the worms declare his truth? Go to him, take his shame away!

Elizabeth (*supporting herself against collapse, grips the bars of the window, and with a cry*). He have his goodness now. God forbid I take it from him!

(*The final drumroll crashes, then heightens violently.* Hale *weeps in frantic prayer, and the new sun is pouring in upon her face, and the drums rattle like bones in the morning air. The curtain falls.*)

Comprehension

1. **Recall** Why has Reverend Hale returned to Salem?
2. **Clarify** Why does Danforth summon Elizabeth Proctor?
3. **Summarize** What does John Proctor do when asked to sign a confession?

Text Analysis

4. **Infer Character Motives** Explain why each of the following characters wants John and the other prisoners to confess. Support your answer with evidence.
   - Danforth
   - Parris
   - Hale
5. **Examine Dialogue** Reread Elizabeth Proctor's dialogue at the end of Act Four (lines 782–783) when she says of her husband, "He have his goodness now." What do you think she means? Do you agree with her?
6. **Analyze Conventions of Drama** Much of the **plot** of *The Crucible* is built around the internal and external conflicts of John Proctor. An **internal conflict** is a struggle between opposing forces within a character. An **external conflict** pits a character against nature, society, or another character. Use a chart like the one shown to show the internal and external conflicts of John Proctor. How is each resolved?

Conflict	Internal or External?	How Resolved

7. **Draw Conclusions About Characters** Refer to the chart of character traits you have created. Which characters have changed over the course of the play? How have they changed? Cite specific details from the play.
8. **Interpret Symbol** A crucible is a severe test or trial. It is also a vessel in which materials are melted at high temperatures to produce a more refined substance. What do you think a crucible might symbolize in this drama?
9. **Synthesize Themes** A theme is a central idea the writer wishes to share with the reader. This idea may be a lesson about life or about people and their actions. What do you think are some of the themes of *The Crucible?*

Text Criticism

10. **Critical Interpretations** Many critics have observed that Miller's play goes beyond the historical events of 17th- and 20th-century America and explores universal conflicts. What universal conflicts does the play deal with?

What fuels a **MOB?**

In Act Four, what motivates several of the characters to resist the mob mentality that has swept through Salem?

COMMON CORE

RL 1 Cite textual evidence to support analysis of what the text says explicitly as well as inferences drawn from the text, including determining where the text leaves matters uncertain. **RL 2** Determine two or more themes or central ideas of a text and analyze their development over the course of the text, including how they interact and build on one another to produce a complex account; provide an objective summary of the text. **RL 3** Analyze the impact of the author's choices regarding how to develop and relate elements of a drama. **RL 5** Analyze how an author's choices concerning how to structure specific parts of a text contribute to its overall structure and meaning as well as its aesthetic impact.

Vocabulary in Context

▲ VOCABULARY PRACTICE

Decide whether the words in each pair are synonyms or antonyms.

1. iniquity/goodness
2. contentious/argumentative
3. adamant/unsure
4. immaculate/filthy
5. deference/impudence
6. anarchy/disorder
7. corroborate/substantiate
8. imperceptible/unnoticeable
9. subservient/subordinate

WORD LIST
adamant
anarchy
contentious
corroborate
deference
immaculate
imperceptible
iniquity
subservient

ACADEMIC VOCABULARY IN WRITING

• document • illustrate • interpret • promote • reveal

The plot of *The Crucible* **illustrates** how rapidly a situation can spiral out of control. Write about an experience in which you lost control of a situation. What could you have done to prevent it? In your response, try to use at least one additional Academic Vocabulary word.

VOCABULARY STRATEGY: CONTEXT CLUES

The words, sentences, paragraphs, and even punctuation marks that surround a word make up its **context.** Often context can help you figure out the meaning of an unfamiliar word or help you better understand the various shades of meaning that words can have.

COMMON CORE

L 4a Use context as a clue to the meaning of a word or phrase. **L 5b** Analyze nuances in the meaning of words with similar denotations.

PRACTICE Locate each word below in its context in the play. Then write the letter of the correct definition for each.

1. **subservient** (page 147): (a) forceful, (b) vengeful, (c) lower in importance
2. **iniquity** (page 151): (a) forgetfulness, (b) act of not caring, (c) wickedness
3. **ameliorate** (page 168): (a) improve, (b) aggravate, (c) move farther along
4. **contentious** (page 182): (a) angry, (b) generous, (c) misguided
5. **effrontery** (page 188): (a) patience, (b) presumptuousness, (c) desire to talk a lot

Language

◆ GRAMMAR AND STYLE: Use Realistic Dialogue

A play consists almost entirely of dialogue, so it is important that the characters' speech match the setting. In *The Crucible,* Arthur Miller's **word choice** and use of **inverted sentences** reflect the speech of the time, contributing to the author's realistic depiction of life in 17th-century Salem. Here are some examples:

> ***Parris.*** *. . . Let him look to medicine and put out all thought of unnatural causes here. There be none.* (Act One, lines 50–52)
>
> ***Susanna.*** *Aye, sir. . . .* (Act One, line 52)
>
> ***Abigail.*** *Now look you. All of you. We danced. . . .* (Act One, line 353)

Here, Miller uses *be* rather than *are,* the verb form we use in this context today. Instead of *yes,* he uses the word *aye,* a word that was commonplace in the 1600s but is rarely used today. Finally, he uses a type of inverted word order common to 17th-century speech, with the verb preceding the subject.

PRACTICE Rewrite the following sentences so that they better reflect the 17th-century speech patterns that Miller employs.

EXAMPLE

You go to the house!

Go you to the house!

1. Yes, it is true I saw the devil with Rebecca Nurse.
2. Are you sure of their guilt?
3. You confess to these sins!

COMMON CORE

L 3a Vary syntax for effect, consulting references for guidance as needed; apply an understanding of syntax to the study of complex texts when reading. **W 1** Write arguments to support claims in an analysis of substantive topics or texts, using valid reasoning and relevant and sufficient evidence. **W 1b** Develop claim(s) fairly and thoroughly, supplying the most relevant evidence.

READING-WRITING CONNECTION

Expand your understanding of Miller's play by responding to this prompt. Then, use the **revising tips** to improve your essay.

WRITING PROMPT	REVISING TIPS
ANALYZE MOTIVATIONS Why does John Proctor change his mind and tear up the confession? In **four or five paragraphs,** discuss Proctor's perception of a morally righteous person and how that perception affects his decision. Think about Rebecca Nurse's reaction to his confession and Elizabeth's assertion that "there be no higher judge under Heaven than Proctor is!"	• Explain the choices Proctor must make to arrive at his decision. • Clarify how Proctor's idea of morality differs from that of the judges. • Use quotations and examples from the play to support key points.

Reading for Information

The Crucible and McCarthyism

- Online Article, page 217
- Newspaper Article, page 218
- Memoir, page 220

Use with *The Crucible*, page 136.

While Arthur Miller was writing *The Crucible,* Senator Joseph McCarthy was conducting a campaign to root out communists in American public life. In his memoir, *Timebends,* Miller sees a connection between the Salem witch trials and McCarthy's campaign. The following selections will help you understand that connection by providing you with information about McCarthyism and its bearing on *The Crucible.* They will also provide you with the opportunity to evaluate the objectivity of writers who have a personal stake in the subject they address. As you read, look for connections between the main idea expressed by these writers and the themes you studied as you read *The Crucible.*

COMMON CORE

RI 1 Cite textual evidence to support analysis of what the text says explicitly. **RI 6** Determine an author's point of view or purpose in a text in which the rhetoric is particularly effective, analyzing how style and content contribute to the power, persuasiveness, or beauty of the text. **RI 7** Integrate and evaluate multiple sources of information presented in different media or formats as well as in words.

Standards Focus: Understand Historical Context

To varying degrees, every literary work reflects its **historical context**—the social and political conditions that shaped the culture of its time. *The Crucible,* produced in 1953, grew out of the controversy surrounding Senator McCarthy and his anti-communism campaign. Political speeches on both sides of the issue often contained **logical fallacies**—rhetorical flaws that were intended to inflame public emotions. The most common of these are still prominent in this country's political debates.

- The **either/or fallacy** insists that only two choices exist in a complex situation, as when a politician says, "You're either with us or against us."
- **Name-calling** occurs when politicians point the finger of blame, accusing their opponents of moral failings or lack of patriotism.
- When politicians lump all the members of an opposing group into a single negative **stereotype,** they have used **overgeneralization**.
- Finally, when a politician suggests that an opponent or an opponent's policies are to blame for what's wrong with the country, **false cause** is usually at work.

To better grasp the historical context of *The Crucible,* take notes on what you learn as you read the selections and evaluate the **objectivity** of each source. An objective source provides balanced information on a subject. The first selection is about McCarthyism. As you read it, try to determine whether the article takes a position on the subject. Each of the other selections was written by someone with a personal stake in the issue at hand. As you read, look for evidence of subjectivity—a personal stake in the subject that affects the writer's stance.

McCARTHYISM

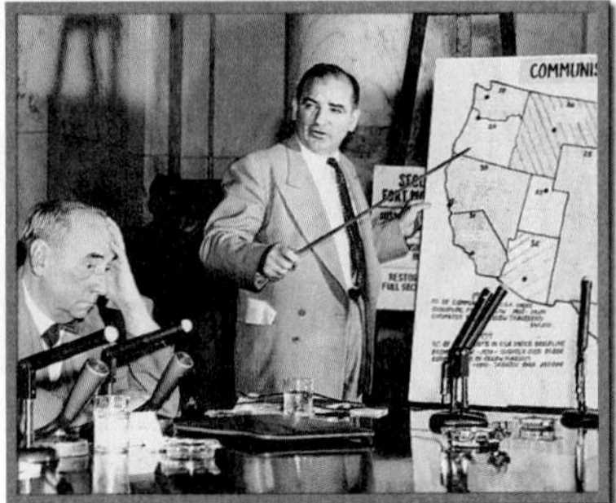
Army counsel Joseph N. Welch, left, and Senator Joseph McCarthy

Throughout the 1940s and 1950s America was overwhelmed with concerns about the threat of communism growing in Eastern Europe and China. Capitalizing on those concerns, a young Senator named Joseph McCarthy made a public accusation that more than two hundred "card-carrying" communists had infiltrated the United States government. Though eventually his accusations were proven to be untrue, and he was censured by the Senate for unbecoming conduct, his zealous campaigning ushered in one of the most repressive times in 20th-century American politics. **A**

While the House Un-American Activities Committee (HUAC) had been formed in 1938 as an anti-Communist organ, McCarthy's accusations heightened the political tensions of the times. Known as McCarthyism, the paranoid hunt for infiltrators was notoriously difficult on writers and entertainers, many of whom were labeled communist sympathizers and were unable to continue working. Some had their passports taken away, while others were jailed for refusing to give the names of other communists. The trials, which were well publicized, could often destroy a career with a single unsubstantiated accusation. Among those well-known artists accused of communist sympathies or called before the committee were Paul Robeson, Arthur Miller, Aaron Copland, Leonard Bernstein, Charlie Chaplin and Elia Kazan. In all, three hundred and twenty artists were blacklisted, and for many of them this meant the end of exceptional and promising careers. **B**

During this time there were few in the press willing to stand up against McCarthy and the anti-Communist machine. Among those few were comedian Mort Sahl, and journalist Edward R. Murrow, whose strong criticisms of McCarthy are often cited as playing an important role in his eventual removal from power. By 1954, the fervor had died down and many actors and writers were able to return to work. Though relatively short, these proceedings remain one of the most shameful moments in modern U.S. history.

Internet

A HISTORICAL CONTEXT
What preoccupied Americans during the 1940s and 1950s? Record your answer in your notes.

B HISTORICAL CONTEXT
Reread lines 15–29 and use the information presented to define McCarthyism. Does this paragraph explain McCarthyism objectively or does it take a position on the senator and his campaign? Support your answer with evidence from the selection.

Reprinted from
The New York Times

SUNDAY, SEPTEMBER 8, 1996 B16

Arthur Miller prepares to testify before the House Un-American Activities Commitee, 1956.

The Demons of Salem, With Us Still

by Victor Navasky

When Arthur Miller's drama *The Crucible* first opened on Broadway in 1953, the country was in a panic about the so-called Red Menace. Senator Joseph McCarthy, with his reckless charges of spies and "comsymps,"[1] occupied the front pages, while behind the scenes J. Edgar Hoover, the director of the F.B.I., presided over and manipulated a vast internal security bureaucracy, issuing periodic bulletins intended to fan the flames of the domestic cold war. **C**

C HISTORICAL CONTEXT
As you read this article, keep in mind that Victor Navasky is the author of *Naming Names,* a history of McCarthyism that depicts the subject in a dramatically negative light. His goal in this article is not simply to inform readers but to support his position on McCarthyism and *The Crucible.* As evidence Navasky cites **logical fallacies** in McCarthy's political language (lines 5–6). Which logical fallacy does a speaker commit by calling his opponents spies and "comsymps"?

In the center ring were the congressional inquisitor-investigators, asking "Are you now or have you ever been a member of the Communist Party?"

At the time, Mr. Miller and Tennessee Williams were regarded as the world's two foremost playwrights. But that lofty status was an invitation rather than an obstacle to the red-hunters who wanted to talk to Mr. Miller. In fact, when he was finally summoned to appear, the committee chairman, Representative Francis Walters, let Mr. Miller know that things might go easier for him if he persuaded his fiancee, Marilyn Monroe, to pose for a photograph with the chairman. Mr. Miller let that option lapse and was shortly indicted for contempt of Congress when he refused to answer the committee's questions about Communists he had known.

On the left, the hunt for subversives was routinely labeled a witch hunt, after the infamous Salem witch trials of the late 17th century. And so when *The Crucible,* set in Salem in 1692 but written in the overheated atmosphere of the domestic cold war, appeared, two questions were quickly asked: Was Mr. Miller's depiction of the inhabitants and events of 1692 Salem faithful to the original? And was the original an appropriate metaphor for McCarthyism?

1. **"comsymps":** Communist sympathizers.

On the historical front it was generally conceded when the play was written that Mr. Miller's research was accurate. His principal changes involved fusing some characters and raising the age of John Proctor's accuser, Abigail Williams, from 11 to 17 (to accommodate Mr. Miller's story of how a liaison between Abigail and John was intertwined with the accusations of witchcraft against Proctor's wife).

But even before the play was written, Mr. Miller was denounced for his metaphor. He had stopped off at the home of his friend and colleague Elia Kazan, who had directed Mr. Miller's two previous prize-winning hits, "All My Sons" and "Death of a Salesman," and who had been subpoenaed to appear before the House Committee on Un-American Activities (where he ultimately named names).

They went for a walk in the Connecticut woods and discussed Mr. Kazan's dilemma. On the one hand to be an informer was unpalatable, but on the other, as Mr. Kazan put it at the time, "Secrecy serves the Communists." **D**

In his memoir *Timebends,* Mr. Miller wrote that he was half inside his car when Molly, Kazan's wife, "came out and asked if I was staying at my house, half an hour away, and I said that I was on my way to Salem. She instantly understood what my destination meant, and her eyes widened in sudden apprehension and possible anger. 'You're not going to equate witches with this!'

Later, Mr. Kazan reported his wife's views in his own memoir, *A Life.*

"What's going on here and now is not to be compared with the witch trials of that time," she said. "Those witches did not exist. Communists do. Here and everywhere in the world. It's a false parallel. Witch hunt! The phrase would indicate that there are no Communists in government, none in the arts, none sending money from Hollywood to 12th Street." **E**

For me, the parallel worked. The term "Communist" had been so demonized that like the word "witch" it signified something that didn't really exist in its popular meaning. Certainly the entertainment community Communists like Mr. Kazan (and for a brief period, Mr. Miller himself, although he never fully joined the party) were not conscious agents of an international monolithic conspiracy to overthrow the Government by force and violence; they were, for the most part, do-gooders, who thought—misguidedly, most of them later concluded—that the Communist Party was the best agency to do something about the depression and racism at home and fascism abroad.

As it turned out, despite mixed notices for *The Crucible,* over the years it was to become Arthur Miller's most performed play, with productions in China, Poland, Britain, high schools and repertory theaters throughout the world. Now *The Crucible* is a $25 million motion picture, under the aegis of 20th Century Fox.

Although the playwright in Mr. Miller was originally drawn to think about the political and moral pressures of the domestic cold war years, when I asked him about the applicability of the play to the here and now he said:

"I have had immense confidence in the applicability of the play to almost any time, the reason being it's dealing with a paranoid situation. But that situation doesn't depend on any particular political or sociological development. I wrote it blind to the world. The enemy is within, and within stays within, and we can't get out of within. It's always on the edge of our minds that behind what we see is a nefarious plot." **F**

D HISTORICAL CONTEXT
Reread lines 61–78. In light of his comment, would you say that Elia Kazan took McCarthy's mission seriously? Explain.

E HISTORICAL CONTEXT
Given her husband's role in the McCarthy hearings, why do you think Molly Kazan might have objected to Miller's comparison between HUAC and Salem?

F HISTORICAL CONTEXT
Reread lines 79–145. Evaluate the **objectivity** of author Victor Navasky and of Molly Kazan and Arthur Miller, witnesses Navasky quotes in these paragraphs. An objective writer or witness is an observer who weighs all the evidence without being swayed by a personal stake in the subject. By contrast, a subjective writer or witness has a personal involvement and is swayed by personal beliefs on the subject. If you determine that Navasky or either of his witnesses is not objective, then carefully evaluate the evidence he or she presents. Weigh all the evidence before drawing conclusions of your own.

TIMEBENDS

by Arthur Miller

I had known about the Salem witchcraft phenomenon since my American history class at Michigan, but it had remained in mind as one of those inexplicable mystifications of the long-dead past when people commonly believed that the spirit could leave the body, palpably and visibly. My mother might believe it still, if only in one corner of her mind, and I suspected that there were a lot of other people who, like me, were secretly open to suggestion. As though it had been ordained, a copy of Marion Starkey's book *The Devil in Massachusetts* fell into my hands, and the bizarre story came back as I had recalled it, but this time in remarkably well-organized detail. **G**

Miller at his typewriter in 1959

G HISTORICAL CONTEXT
Reread lines 1–17. What details indicate the significance for Miller of finding Starkey's book?

At first I rejected the idea of a play on the subject. My own rationality was too strong, I thought, to really allow me to capture this wildly irrational outbreak. A drama cannot merely describe an emotion, it has to become that emotion. But gradually, over weeks, a living connection between myself and Salem, and between Salem and Washington, was made in my mind—for whatever else they might be, I saw that the hearings in Washington were profoundly and even avowedly ritualistic. After all, in almost every case the Committee knew in advance what they wanted the witness to give them; the names of his comrades in the Party. The FBI had long since infiltrated the Party, and informers had long ago identified the participants in various meetings. The main point of the hearings, precisely as in seventeenth-century Salem, was that the accused make public confession, damn his confederates as well as his Devil master, and guarantee his sterling new allegiance by breaking disgusting old vows—whereupon he was let loose to rejoin the society of extremely decent people. In other words, the same spiritual nugget lay folded within both procedures—an act of contrition done not in solemn privacy but out in the public air. The Salem prosecution was actually on more solid legal ground since the defendant, if guilty of familiarity with the Unclean One, had broken a law against the practice of witchcraft, a civil as well as a religious offense; whereas the offender against HUAC (House Un-American Activities Committee) could not be accused of any such violation but only of a spiritual crime, subservience to a political enemy's desires and ideology. He was summoned before the Committee to be called a bad name, but one that could destroy his career. **H**

H HISTORICAL CONTEXT
As you have seen by reading these selections, politics, journalism, and literature can share ideas from a particular historical context. One article provides information on the McCarthy hearings; another addresses both the hearings and the writing of *The Crucible*. The third provides personal testimony from Miller himself. To synthesize what you have read, identify a theme or idea that runs through all three selections.

Comprehension

1. **Recall** What was Senator McCarthy's mission?
2. **Recall** What kinds of professionals were targeted by McCarthy's accusations?
3. **Recall** What was the catalyst for Miller's interest in the Salem witch trials?

Text Analysis

4. **Evaluate Statements** Considering the historical context of *The Crucible* and Arthur Miller's own comments in *Timebends,* do you think Miller was really "blind to the world" when he wrote *The Crucible?* Support your opinion.
5. **Evaluate the Role of Historical Context** Is knowing *The Crucible*'s historical context necessary to understand the playwright's message? Explain.

COMMON CORE

RI 1 Cite textual evidence to support analysis of what the text says explicitly. **RI 6** Determine an author's point of view or purpose in a text in which the rhetoric is particularly effective, analyzing how style and content contribute to the power, persuasiveness, or beauty of the text. **RI 7** Integrate and evaluate multiple sources of information presented in different media or formats as well as in words. **W 2** Write informative/explanatory texts to examine and convey complex ideas, concepts, and information clearly and accurately through the effective selection, organization, and analysis of content. **W 2b** Develop the topic thoroughly by selecting the most significant and relevant facts, concrete details, or quotations.

Read for Information: Synthesize

WRITING PROMPT

Think about the social and political conditions of the time during which Arthur Miller was writing *The Crucible.* In what ways has looking through this historical lens colored your understanding of the play? In developing your new analysis, support your thesis with information from the articles you have just read and details from the play.

To answer this prompt, follow these steps:

1. In a sentence or two, summarize how reading these selections, evaluating their objectivity, and weighing the evidence they present has affected your understanding of the play and its historical context. Consider using this summary as your thesis statement.
2. In your notes, identify elements of the play that you now view differently. How has your sense of these elements changed? For example, are there things you now see more clearly? Does the play interest you more? Note the historical evidence that caused you to think differently.
3. Using your thesis statement and notes, write an essay in which you explain how the historical context of *The Crucible* affects your appreciation and understanding of the play.
4. Cite evidence from *The Crucible* and the selections in this Reading for Information feature.

Media Study

from The Crucible

Film Clips on MediaSmart DVD-ROM

COMMON CORE

RL 7 Analyze multiple interpretations of a drama, evaluating how each version interprets the source text.

From Page to Screen

From the classical tragedies of Ancient Greece to the Renaissance masterpieces of Shakespeare, playwrights have examined the impact of suspicion, hysteria, and revenge, building plays around the arc of destruction these impulses unleash. So effective was *The Crucible* in depicting these timeless themes that it was declared a classic when first staged. In this lesson, view a scene from the film version to explore how a different medium changes the structure of Arthur Miller's play.

The Filmmakers' Challenge

Translating a well-known play to the big screen poses a number of challenges. Writing the screenplay, perhaps the biggest hurdle, was made a little easier in the case of *The Crucible.* Arthur Miller adapted his own work and took an active role in the film's production. Consulting with the film's director, Miller took certain liberties with the play's structure. He changed where some scenes take place and added entirely new scenes. "I did some rewriting during production to take advantage of opportunities we had with this wonderful Hog Island [Massachusetts] location," Miller recalls.

On the set, Daniel Day-Lewis with Arthur Miller

Over the past five decades, *The Crucible*'s themes have reached far beyond its place and time. As Miller points out, the play's themes "find [their] relevance in every culture. I knew a woman imprisoned for six years under the [Chinese] Mao regime. . . . She told me that when she saw *The Crucible* in Shanghai she couldn't believe that a non-Chinese had written it, because the interrogations in *The Crucible* had been precisely the interrogations she had endured under the Cultural Revolution."

Comparing Texts: Dialogue

In taking his play from the page to the screen, Arthur Miller had to make certain decisions about how much of the original dialogue he would retain. During production, actors and directors will often make changes to the dialogue to fine-tune a scene.

Compare the dialogue from the play with the dialogue that appears in the film. Notice Miller's stage direction in the text and how actor Daniel Day-Lewis, in the role of John Proctor, interprets it.

Danforth (*with suspicion*). It is the same, is it not? If I report it or you sign it?

Proctor (*he knows it is insane*). No, it is not the same! What others say and what I sign is not the same!

Danforth. Why? Do you mean to deny this confession when you are free?

Proctor. I mean to deny nothing!

Danforth. Then explain to me, Mr. Proctor, why you will not let—

Proctor (*with a cry of his whole soul*). Because it is my name! Because I cannot have another in my life! Because I lie and sign myself to lies! Because I am not worth the dust on the feet of them that hang! How may I live without my name? I have given you my soul; leave me my name!

Viewing Guide

Media Smart DVD-ROM

- **Film:** *The Crucible*
- **Director:** Nicholas Hytner
- **Genre:** Drama
- **Running Time:** 5 minutes

In the clip from *The Crucible,* the character John Proctor has finally agreed to sign a false confession that will save him from death.

Plan on viewing the clip several times. To help you analyze the dialogue and performance, refer to the questions.

NOW VIEW

CLOSE VIEWING: Media Analysis

1. **Analyze Setting** In the play, this scene is set in jail. How does moving the setting affect (or not affect) the scene?
2. **Compare Dialogue** Compare the dialogue from the play with the dialogue in the movie. Why do you think Miller changed some of his original dialogue for the movie?
3. **Evaluate Actor's Performance** Read the stage direction the playwright included for Proctor's speech. Do you think the actor playing Proctor succeeded in portraying "a cry of his whole soul"? Cite evidence from the scene to support your opinion.

Reading for Information

MOVIE REVIEW *Rolling Stone* magazine reviewed Nicholas Hytner's film adaptation of *The Crucible* in 1996.

[REVIEW]

The Crucible

Peter Travers

Director Nicholas Hytner with cast

Arthur Miller is the first to admit that *The Crucible* must stand on its own. The playwright, now 81, sat near me at a screening of the film, unwittingly intimidating all around him. For the Pulitzer Prize–winning author of *Death of a Salesman,* attention must be paid. Miller asked for none of it. He talked with boyish zest of working with director Nicholas Hytner on re-crafting *The Crucible* as a $25 million film that would allow startling imagery to resonate with his language and burst the bounds of the stage.

Does it ever. *The Crucible,* despite some damaging cuts to the text, is a seductively exciting film that crackles with visual energy, passionate provocation and incendiary acting. . . .

The great Paul Scofield is triumphant, avoiding the easy caricature of Danforth as a fanatic. He brings the role something new: wit. We laugh with this judge, which heightens the horror later when he blinds himself to truth in the name of God and his own ambition. The scene in which he ignores Rev. Hale (Rob Campbell), who knows the girls are faking, and bullies the servant Mary Warren (Karron Graves) into delusion and madness chills the blood.

As the unforgiving wife whose "justice would freeze beer," in the words of her husband, Joan Allen is an absolute stunner in an award-caliber performance that is also a surprising source of warmth. By the seashore, where the pregnant Elizabeth has come to say goodbye to her condemned husband, she tells John, "I once counted myself so plain, so poorly made, that no honest love could come to me." Elizabeth's scene of tender reconciliation is the film's moral core. John need only sign a false confession of witchcraft to save himself from the gallows. Of course, he won't. "Because it is my name," he tells Danforth simply. "Because I cannot have another in my life."

In the film's most complex role, Daniel Day-Lewis performs with quiet power. Playing nobility can make actors insufferable, but Day-Lewis keeps John Proctor human even when saddled with smudgy makeup and fake brown teeth for his final scene. *The Crucible,* for all its timely denunciation of persecution masked as piety . . . comes down to individual resistance and how you search your heart to find it. The years haven't softened the rage against self-betrayal in *The Crucible.* This stirring film lets you feel the heat of Miller's argument and the urgent power of his kick.

The Puritan Legacy

In the minds of some, Puritanism is a thing of the past—an outmoded collection of beliefs from a dour and oddly-dressed group of people. Yet others insist that the spiritual, social, and cultural principles fostered by Puritanism are stubbornly present, in one way or another, in American society today. Somewhere in the middle of this debate are literary historians Richard Ruland and Malcolm Bradbury, who insist: "Puritans considered many of the literary questions we still ask today; they answered them differently."

Writing to Compare

We can all agree that the Puritan style of dress is out of fashion, but are Puritan ideas also outmoded? Consider these "literary questions" discussed in the selections you have just read:

What is true love?

Why do bad things happen to good people?

How can faith sustain us?

How can people best serve God?

Are people worthy?

Are people basically good or bad?

Choose one of the questions above, and in a brief essay explain how two of the Puritan authors in this section might have responded. (Although Arthur Miller's play was written in the twentieth century, you can include *The Crucible* since it accurately reflects the Puritan mind-set.) Give specific evidence from the texts to support your opinions and ideas.

Consider

- the themes, or central ideas, of the selections. Does the selection have a message related to one of the "literary questions" above?
- the topics, or subject that the work focuses on. The topic is what the writer describes, discusses, or talks about. A writer's choice of subject will often have an influence on the work's themes.

Extension

SPEAKING & LISTENING Imagine you are a Puritan villager in charge of welcoming new settlers. Using the selections you've just read as your resource, write and deliver an **informal speech** to your new neighbors, welcoming them and sharing a little about the values and beliefs of your community.

COMMON CORE

RL 9 Demonstrate knowledge of foundational works of American literature, including how two or more texts from the same period treat similar themes or topics. **W 9** Draw evidence from literary texts to support analysis, reflection, and research. **SL 6** Adapt speech to a variety of contexts and tasks.

The Puritan (1883–1886), Augustus Saint-Gaudens. Bronze figure. Private collection. © Art Resource, New York.

Text Analysis Workshop

Persuasive Rhetoric

Persuasion is built on the power of words—words that grab your attention, keep you riveted, and influence what you think. **Persuasive rhetoric** is the art of using language to argue and convince others to adopt a position or act in a certain way.

COMMON CORE

Included in this workshop: **RI 5** Analyze and evaluate the effectiveness of the structure an author uses in his or her exposition or argument, including whether the structure makes points clear, convincing, and engaging. **RI 6** Determine an author's point of view or purpose in a text in which the rhetoric is particularly effective, analyzing how style and content contribute to the power, persuasiveness, or beauty of the text. **RI 8** Delineate and evaluate the reasoning in seminal U.S. texts, including the application of constitutional principles and use of legal reasoning and the premises, purposes, and arguments in works of public advocacy. **RI 9** Analyze eighteenth-century foundational U.S. documents of historical and literary significance for their themes, purposes, and rhetorical features.

A Cause for Argument

America's history of persuasive rhetoric began with statesmen, writers, and orators who felt strongly about the future of the colonized states. These men vigorously debated freedom—from tyranny, taxes, and censorship. Writings, such as Thomas Jefferson's Declaration of Independence (page 238), were not only official state documents but well-crafted arguments.

The way ideas are organized in an **argument** can be key to the argument's persuasive power. A writer can develop an argument **deductively,** by beginning with a generalization, or premise, and proceeding to examples and supporting facts. Writers can also argue **inductively,** by beginning with examples or facts and proceeding to a conclusion.

A 1792 British caricature of Thomas Paine, who was ridiculed in England for his appeal to overthrow the monarchy

The Power of Language

To be effective, a persuasive work must engage both the minds and the emotions of its audience. Persuasive writers use words to develop sound reasoning, to arouse emotions, and to appeal to shared values. **Persuasive techniques** fall into three basic types.

- **Logical appeals** rely on reason and facts to support a claim. For example, the Declaration of Independence cites "injuries and usurpations" committed by King George III as evidence of the need for independence (page 242).
- **Emotional appeals** present ideas that elicit strong feelings. Jefferson, for example, uses the appeal of emotionally loaded words when he associates King George with "death, desolation, and tyranny" (page 244).
- **Ethical appeals** use values or moral standards to persuade an audience. The Declaration of Independence is loaded with the language of shared values—for example, the assertion that "all men are created equal" (page 240).

BASICS OF AN ARGUMENT

To be effective, an argument should include

- a **claim,** or clear statement of a position on an issue
- **support** for the claim in the form of reasons and evidence
- **counterarguments,** or statements that anticipate and refute opposing views
- sound **logic** and effective language
- a **conclusion** that sums up the reasons or the call for action

In addition to persuasive techniques, writers often use **rhetorical devices** to enhance their arguments:

- A **rhetorical question** does not require a reply because the answer is obvious. In a letter to her husband (page 262), Abigail Adams asks, "Shall we not be despised by foreign powers, for hesitating so long at a word?"
- **Antithesis** occurs when contrasting ideas are expressed in a grammatically balanced statement. Notice the juxtaposition of ideas in this phrase from Thomas Paine's "The Crisis" (page 252): "I call not upon a few, but upon all."
- **Repetition** is the use of the same word or phrase more than once for emphasis. **Parallelism,** a form of repetition in which a grammatical pattern is repeated, is used effectively in this famous passage from the Declaration of Independence (page 236): "We hold these truths to be self-evident:—That all men are created equal; that they are endowed by their Creator with certain unalienable rights; that among these are life, liberty and the pursuit of happiness."

Sometimes persuasive writing includes errors in logical thinking, called **logical fallacies**. Below are some common logical fallacies.

Type of Fallacy	Definition	Example
Circular reasoning	Supporting a statement by repeating the statement using different words.	Liberty is essential to humankind. Free people must have it.
Hasty generalization	A conclusion drawn from too little evidence or from evidence that is biased.	Candidate Smith voted against my bill. He is an enemy to freedom.
Non sequitur	A conclusion that does not follow logically from the "proof" offered to support it.	The incumbent candidate is hugely popular. He must be the best qualified for office.

Rhetorical devices and persuasive techniques can be used to create arguments that are valid and sincere or artificial and insincere. It is up to the reader or listener to evaluate whether the argument is based on sound reasoning, and therefore credible and convincing, or whether the words and appeals are the sole strength of the argument.

from Speech in the Virginia Convention

by Patrick Henry

COMMON CORE

RI 5 Analyze and evaluate the effectiveness of the structure an author uses in his or her argument, including whether the structure makes points clear, convincing, and engaging. **RI 6** Determine an author's point of view or purpose in a text in which the rhetoric is particularly effective, analyzing how style and content contribute to the power, persuasiveness, or beauty of the text. **L 3a** Apply an understanding of syntax to the study of complex texts. **L 4b** Identify and correctly use patterns of word changes that indicate different meanings or parts of speech.

DID YOU KNOW?

Patrick Henry . . .

- had 16 children—6 by his first wife, who died, and then 10 by his second wife.
- owned slaves.
- advocated the right to bear arms later guaranteed by the U.S. Constitution.
- strongly supported states' rights.

(background) Virginia House of Burgesses

Meet the Author

Patrick Henry 1736–1799

Known as "the Orator of Liberty," Patrick Henry made a name for himself with his speeches supporting American democracy. He was one of the earliest opponents of British rule in the American colonies. In 1765, after the British Parliament passed a tax bill called the Stamp Act, Henry was among the members of the Virginia legislature that challenged the legality of a British tax on the colonies. But he went farther than his colleagues by making a threat against the king. In his argument, so the story goes, he used a loaded analogy: "Caesar had his Brutus, Charles the First his Cromwell, and George III . . ."—at this point, shouts of "Treason!" erupted in the hall, but Henry continued—"may profit by their example." He ended his speech with the defiant words, "If this be treason, make the most of it." Henry did indeed make the most of his "treason," becoming a tireless and influential leader both before and after the Revolution.

Profitable Law Career Henry was born in Virginia to a prosperous landowner. His father, who had attended the University of Aberdeen in Scotland, gave him a classical education at home. His mother, Sarah Winston Syme, was from a wealthy family. Henry went out on his own at age 15. Although smart and industrious, he couldn't find success as a storekeeper or later as a tobacco planter. After marrying and starting a family, he decided to teach himself law, and in 1760, at the age of 24, he was admitted to the bar. Henry's eloquence, quick wit, and rhetorical gifts served him well, and his law practice grew increasingly profitable.

Popular Virginia Politician Henry is best known for his fervent "Speech in the Virginia Convention," which narrowly convinced the assembled leadership to prepare for war with Britain. In addition, he organized a Virginia militia that became part of the new Continental Army after independence was declared. He helped write the new state constitution and the Virginia Declaration of Rights, which was a major influence on the Bill of Rights added to the U.S. Constitution. He also served several terms as governor of Virginia and as a state legislator. Although President Washington offered him positions as secretary of state and Supreme Court justice, Henry declined and always remained suspicious of the federal government. In 1799, after being elected again to the state legislature, he died at his 700-acre plantation, Red Hill, before he could take office.

Author Online THINK central

Go to thinkcentral.com. KEYWORD: HML11-228

TEXT ANALYSIS: RHETORICAL DEVICES

Rhetorical devices are structures within language that appeal to readers or listeners and communicate ideas.

- A **rhetorical question** is a question to which no answer is expected. (*But when shall we be stronger?*)
- **Antithesis** expresses contrasting ideas in parallel grammatical structures. (*Give me liberty, or give me death!*)
- **Repetition** is the recurrence of words, phrases, or lines. (*Let it come! I repeat it, sir, let it come!*)
- **Parallelism** is a kind of repetition in which words or phrases in the same grammatical form connect ideas. (*Is life so dear, or peace so sweet . . .*)
- **Biblical allusions** are references to events, figures, or phrases from the Bible. In this selection, they have the rhetorical appeal of shared beliefs.

As you read Henry's speech, be on the lookout for rhetorical devices and how they might have affected his audience.

READING SKILL: READING A PERSUASIVE SPEECH

In this famous speech, Patrick Henry speaks to members of the Virginia convention, but clearly he is aware of a wider audience—even of future generations reading his words. As you read the speech, think about Henry's **audience** and how he uses language to appeal to his audience. What **tone** or attitude do you detect in his language, and how does his choice of words reveal his **purpose** as a speaker?

VOCABULARY IN CONTEXT

Use context clues to write a definition of each boldfaced word.

1. **Martial** Speech Sets Stage for War
2. Never **Supinely** Accept Tyranny, Henry Says
3. **Invincible** Patriot Army Will Repel Attacks
4. **Insidious** Spies Reveal Patriots' Plans
5. Nothing Can **Extenuate** Tory Traitors
6. Citizens Told to Be **Vigilant**
7. America Must Remain **Inviolate**

Complete the activities in your **Reader/Writer Notebook**.

When is it time *to* TAKE ACTION?

Whether it's the winning shot in the final seconds of the game, the right moment to ask someone out, or the decision to accept a job offer—timing is everything. In the spring of 1775, Patrick Henry had had enough of compromise with the British; it was time for armed resistance. His address to the Virginia Convention turned out to be a decisive moment not only in his own life but in the life of the United States as well.

DISCUSS With a partner, think of examples from sports, politics, or everyday life when the time was right for decisive action. Then, for one example, analyze why it was the right action at the right time.

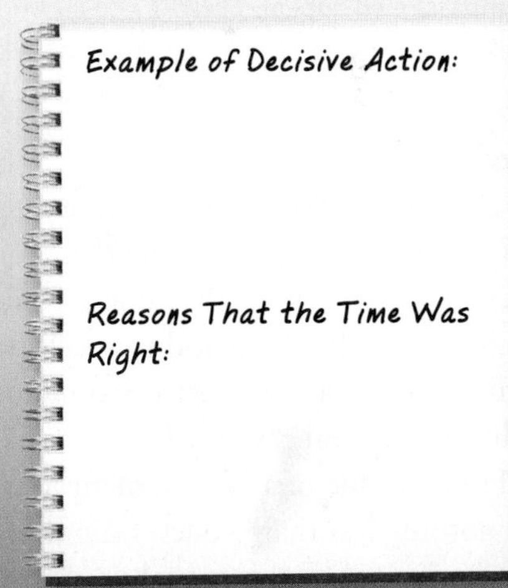

Example of Decisive Action:
Reasons That the Time Was Right:

SPEECH IN THE

Virginia Convention

Patrick Henry

BACKGROUND In the spring of 1775, delegates from the state of Virginia could not agree whether to press for a peaceful solution with Britain or to prepare for war. Patrick Henry introduced resolutions calling for military preparedness. After politely listening to his colleagues' objections to armed rebellion, he rose to deliver this impassioned appeal.

Analyze Visuals ▶
This painting shows Patrick Henry speaking to the Virginia House of Burgesses. What different attitudes are reflected in the faces and postures of his audience members?

March 23, 1775

Mr. President:[1] No man thinks more highly than I do of the patriotism, as well as abilities, of the very worthy gentlemen who have just addressed the House. But different men often see the same subject in different lights; and, therefore, I hope that it will not be thought disrespectful to those gentlemen, if, entertaining as I do opinions of a character very opposite to theirs, I shall speak forth my sentiments freely and without reserve. This is no time for ceremony. The question before the House is one of awful moment[2] to this country. For my own part I consider it as nothing less than a question of freedom or slavery; and in proportion to the magnitude of the subject ought to be the freedom of the debate. It is only in this way that we can hope to arrive at truth, and fulfill the great responsibility which we hold to God and our country. Should I keep back my opinions at such a Ⓐ

Ⓐ **RHETORICAL DEVICES**
Reread lines 1–11. What are some examples of **antithesis,** and what kind of emphasis does it create?

1. **Mr. President:** the president of the Virginia Convention, Peyton Randolph.
2. **of awful moment:** of very grave importance.

Patrick Henry Before the Virginia House of Burgesses (1851), Peter F. Rothermel. Red Hill, The Patrick Henry National Memorial, Brookneal, Virginia.

time, through fear of giving offense, I should consider myself as guilty of treason towards my country, and of an act of disloyalty towards the majesty of heaven, which I revere above all earthly kings. B

Mr. President, it is natural to man to indulge in the illusions of hope. We are apt to shut our eyes against a painful truth, and listen to the song of that siren, till she transforms us into beasts.[3] Is this the part of wise men, engaged in a great and arduous struggle for liberty? Are we disposed to be of the number of those who, having eyes, see not, and having ears, hear not,[4] the things which so nearly concern their temporal salvation? For my part, whatever anguish of spirit it may cost, I am willing to know the whole truth—to know the worst and to provide for it.

I have but one lamp by which my feet are guided; and that is the lamp of experience. I know of no way of judging of the future but by the past. And judging by the past, I wish to know what there has been in the conduct of the British ministry for the last ten years, to justify those hopes with which gentlemen have been pleased to solace themselves and the House? Is it that **insidious** smile with which our petition has been lately received? Trust it not, sir; it will prove a snare to your feet. Suffer not yourselves to be betrayed with a kiss.[5] C

Ask yourselves how this gracious reception of our petition comports[6] with these warlike preparations which cover our waters and darken our land. Are fleets and armies necessary to a work of love and reconciliation? Have we shown ourselves so unwilling to be reconciled that force must be called in to win back our love? Let us not deceive ourselves, sir. These are the implements of war and subjugation[7]—the last arguments to which kings resort. I ask gentlemen, sir, what means this **martial** array, if its purpose be not to force us to submission? Can gentlemen assign any other possible motives for it? Has Great Britain any enemy, in this quarter of the world, to call for all this accumulation of navies and armies? No, sir, she has none. They are meant for us; they can be meant for no other. They are sent over to bind and rivet upon us those chains which the British ministry have been so long forging. D

And what have we to oppose to them? Shall we try argument? Sir, we have been trying that for the last ten years. Have we anything new to offer on the subject? Nothing. We have held the subject up in every light of which it is capable; but it has been all in vain. Shall we resort to entreaty and humble supplication? What terms shall we find which have not been already exhausted? Let us not, I beseech you, sir, deceive ourselves longer. E

B PERSUASIVE SPEECH
In lines 1–14, notice how Henry uses the language of shared beliefs to appeal to his audience. What tone does he establish?

insidious (ĭn-sĭd′ē-əs) *adj.* treacherous

C RHETORICAL DEVICES
Reread lines 22–28 and read footnote 5. Why do you think Henry might have chosen this Biblical allusion, and what does the allusion reveal about Henry's awareness of his audience?

martial (mär′shəl) *adj.* warlike

D RHETORICAL DEVICES
Reread lines 29–40, answering each of the **rhetorical questions.** How is a listener likely to respond to Henry's final statements in lines 37–40?

E GRAMMAR AND STYLE
Reread lines 43–46. Notice the use of **declarative, interrogative,** and **imperative** sentences.

---

3. **the illusions of hope . . . into beasts:** In the *Odyssey* of Homer, the goddess Circe lures men to her island and then magically transforms them into pigs. Henry suggests that the "illusions of hope" may transform people in a similar way.
4. **having eyes . . . hear not:** an allusion to Ezekiel 12:2 in the Bible, which speaks of "who have eyes to see, but see not, who have ears to hear, but hear not."
5. **betrayed with a kiss:** an allusion to Luke 22:47–48 in the Bible, wherein Judas betrayed Jesus to the Roman soldiers by kissing him and thus identifying him.
6. **comports:** agrees or goes along with.
7. **subjugation:** control by conquering.

The Bloody Massacre perpetrated in. . . Boston on March 5th, 1770 (1770), Paul Revere. Colored engraving. Private collection. /Art Resource, New York.

Sir, we have done everything that could be done to avert the storm which is now coming on. We have petitioned; we have remonstrated[8]; we have supplicated; we have prostrated ourselves before the throne, and have implored its interposition[9] to arrest the tyrannical hands of the ministry and Parliament. Our petitions have been slighted; our remonstrances have produced additional violence and insult; our supplications have been disregarded; and we have been spurned, with contempt, from the foot of the throne. In vain, after these things, may we indulge the fond hope of peace and reconciliation. There is no longer any room for hope.

COMMON CORE L 4b

Language Coach

Suffixes Read the definition for *remonstrated* (line 48). Now, note the noun *remonstrances* in line 51. What **suffix** (word part at the end of a word that forms a new word) is added to make *remonstrate* a noun? Write a definition for *remonstrances.*

8. **remonstrated:** to object; to protest strongly.
9. **we have prostrated . . . interposition:** We have thrown ourselves at the feet of the king and have begged for intervention.

If we wish to be free—if we mean to preserve **inviolate** those inestimable privileges for which we have been so long contending—if we mean not basely to abandon the noble struggle in which we have been so long engaged, and which we have pledged ourselves never to abandon until the glorious object of our contest shall be obtained, we must fight! I repeat it, sir, we must fight! An appeal to arms and to the God of Hosts is all that is left us!

They tell us, sir, that we are weak—unable to cope with so formidable an adversary. But when shall we be stronger? Will it be the next week, or the next year? Will it be when we are totally disarmed, and when a British guard shall be stationed in every house? Shall we gather strength by irresolution and inaction? Shall we acquire the means of effectual resistance, by lying **supinely** on our backs, and hugging the delusive phantom of hope, until our enemies shall have bound us hand and foot?

Sir, we are not weak, if we make a proper use of those means which the God of nature hath placed in our power. Three millions of people, armed in the holy cause of liberty, and in such a country as that which we possess, are **invincible** by any force which our enemy can send against us. Besides, sir, we shall not fight our battles alone. There is a just God who presides over the destinies of nations, and who will raise up friends to fight our battles for us. The battle, sir, is not to the strong alone;[10] it is to the **vigilant,** the active, the brave. Besides, sir, we have no election.[11] If we were base enough to desire it, it is now too late to retire from the contest. There is no retreat but in submission and slavery! Our chains are forged! Their clanking may be heard on the plains of Boston! The war is inevitable—and let it come! I repeat it, sir, let it come! F

It is in vain, sir, to **extenuate** the matter. Gentlemen may cry, "Peace! peace!"—but there is no peace. The war is actually begun! The next gale that sweeps from the north[12] will bring to our ears the clash of resounding arms! Our brethren are already in the field! Why stand we here idle? What is it that gentlemen wish? What would they have? Is life so dear, or peace so sweet, as to be purchased at the price of chains and slavery? Forbid it, Almighty God! I know not what course others may take; but as for me, give me liberty, or give me death! G

inviolate (ĭn-vī′ə-lĭt) *adj.* not violated; intact

supinely (so͞o-pīn′lē) *adv.* in a manner with the face upward

invincible (ĭn-vĭn′sə-bəl) *adj.* unbeatable

vigilant (vĭj′ə-lənt) *adj.* alert; watchful

F RHETORICAL DEVICES
Why do you think Henry repeats the word *sir* so often in this paragraph? Explain the likely effect of this **repetition** as well as that of the phrase "let it come!"

extenuate (ĭk-stĕn′yo͞o-āt′) *v.* to lessen the seriousness of, especially by providing partial excuses

G PERSUASIVE SPEECH
Reread lines 80–86. Notice how the pace or momentum of the speech accelerates as Henry draws to a close. How does the change in pace affect the speaker's tone? What purpose do you detect in the pace and tone of Henry's closing lines? Cite evidence from the speech to support your answer.

10. **battle . . . strong alone:** an allusion to Ecclesiastes 9:11 in the Bible, "the race is not to the swift, nor the battle to the strong."

11. **election:** choice.

12. **the next gale . . . north:** Some colonists in Massachusetts had already shown open resistance to the British and were on the brink of war.

Comprehension

1. **Recall** What does Patrick Henry urge the colonists to do?
2. **Paraphrase** Reread lines 22–28. What methods had the colonists already used to express their complaints against the British?
3. **Clarify** How did the British respond to those complaints?

Text Analysis

4. **Analyze a Persuasive Speech** How do beliefs shared by speaker and audience advance Henry's purpose and affect his tone in this speech? Support your answer with evidence from the speech.
5. **Interpret Allusions** Review the following allusions to the Bible that Henry uses in his speech. Explain the rhetorical appeal of each allusion.
   - lines 18–19
   - lines 74–75
6. **Evaluate Appeals** How does Henry convince his audience that the **decisive moment** to fight is at hand? In a chart, summarize his reasons. Then, beside each, note whether he appeals mainly to logic or emotion. Which reasons are strongest? Explain.
7. **Make Judgments About Rhetorical Devices** Review the rhetorical devices discussed on page 229. Which devices occur most frequently in Henry's speech? Do you think that rhetorical devices are an effective way to communicate, or do you find them manipulative? Cite examples from the text to support your answer.

Reasons to Fight	Logical or Emotional
1. If we want to be free and keep the rights and privileges we have grown accustomed to, we have to fight. (lines 56–61)	logical
2.	

COMMON CORE

RI 5 Analyze and evaluate the effectiveness of the structure an author uses in his or her argument, including whether the structure makes points clear, convincing, and engaging. **RI 6** Determine an author's point of view or purpose in a text in which the rhetoric is particularly effective, analyzing how style and content contribute to the power, persuasiveness, or beauty of the text. **L 3a** Apply an understanding of syntax to the study of complex texts.

Text Criticism

8. **Different Perspectives** Imagine that the following people heard Henry's speech from the visitor's gallery. How might each have reacted, and why?
   - the wife of one of the delegates
   - a farmer whose parents live in England
   - a member of the Virginia militia
   - a clergyman
   - an African enslaved in the colony

When is it time to **TAKE ACTION?**

Patrick Henry's intense frustration compelled him to act. What circumstances in your life have triggered you to make a decision or to take action?

Vocabulary in Context

▲ VOCABULARY PRACTICE

Decide whether these statements about the vocabulary words are true or false.

1. An **invincible** chess champion is one who has not been beaten.
2. A statue that is lying **supinely** is lying face down.
3. A **vigilant** guard usually takes naps while on duty.
4. Circumstances that **extenuate** a bad decision are those that make it worse.
5. A country that is overrun by armies from another land is experiencing **subjugation.**
6. A vase that has broken into several pieces may be described as **inviolate.**
7. A **martial** gathering is one that is organized by peace demonstrators.

WORD LIST

extenuate
insidious
invincible
inviolate
martial
supinely
vigilant

ACADEMIC VOCABULARY IN SPEAKING

• document • illustrate • interpret • promote • reveal

Patrick Henry uses several persuasive techniques to **illustrate** his points. In a small group, discuss how he presents himself to the delegates and **promotes** his argument. Use at least three Academic Vocabulary words in your discussion.

VOCABULARY STRATEGY: ANALOGIES

One way to determine word meanings is through the use of **analogies,** or comparisons between pairs of words. Here are two examples of analogies that show different kinds of relationships.

vigilant : unobservant :: invincible : vulnerable
(Vigilant is to unobservant as invincible is to vulnerable.)
subjugation : prisoner :: election : governor
(Subjugation is to prisoner as election is to governor.)

In the first example, both pairs of words are near opposites. In the second example, the relationship is one of process. Just as a prisoner has experienced subjugation, a governor has experienced election.

PRACTICE Complete each analogy by choosing the word that creates the same relationship between both pairs of words. Use a dictionary if you are uncertain about a word's meaning.

1. animal : cat :: vehicle : (a) driving, (b) house, (c) bicycle, (d) theater
2. sad : depressed :: dry : (a) desiccated, (b) wet, (c) arid, (d) damp
3. roof : gable :: poem : (a) haiku, (b) prose, (c) rhyme, (d) stanza
4. vogue : anachronism :: obtuse : (a) dull, (b) cheerful, (c) acute, (d) angle

COMMON CORE

L 4d Verify the preliminary determination of the meaning of a word or phrase. **L 5** Demonstrate understanding of word relationships. **L 6** Acquire and use accurately general academic and domain-specific words and phrases, sufficient for reading, writing, and speaking.

Language

◆ **GRAMMAR AND STYLE:** Vary Sentence Types

Review the **Grammar and Style** note on page 232. Part of Henry's style is to vary his sentences among the four basic types:

- **Declarative,** which expresses a statement of fact, desire, intent, or feeling and ends with a period. *This is no time for ceremony.* (line 6)
- **Interrogative,** which asks a question and ends with a question mark. *Shall we try argument?* (line 41)
- **Imperative,** which gives a command and sometimes ends with an exclamation point. *Trust it not, sir.* (lines 27–28)
- **Exclamatory,** which expresses strong emotions and always ends with an exclamation point. *I repeat it, sir, we must fight!* (line 60)

Henry's skillful use of sentence variety creates an interesting melody. It also keeps the reader engaged by calling for frequent shifts in response.

PRACTICE For each sentence in this excerpt from Henry's speech, identify the type and compose your own sentence following his pattern.

EXAMPLE

The war is actually begun!

We won the game!

(1) The next gale that sweeps from the north will bring to our ears the clash of resounding arms! (2) Our brethren are already in the field! (3) Why stand we here idle? (4) What is it that gentlemen wish? (5) What would they have? (6) Is life so dear, or peace so sweet, as to be purchased at the price of chains and slavery? (7) Forbid it, Almighty God!

COMMON CORE

L 3a Vary syntax for effect, consulting references for guidance as needed; apply an understanding of syntax to the study of complex texts when reading. **W 1** Write arguments to support claims in an analysis of substantive topics or texts, using valid reasoning and relevant and sufficient evidence.

READING-WRITING CONNECTION

Expand your understanding of Henry's speech by responding to this prompt. Then, use the **revising tips** to improve your speech.

WRITING PROMPT

COMPOSE A PERSUASIVE SPEECH Patrick Henry's famous speech is a classic example of effective **oratory,** the art of public speaking. Using Henry's speech as a model, write a **three-to-five paragraph persuasive speech** on a topic you feel strongly about.

REVISING TIPS

- Present a clear argument.
- Cite reasons and evidence.
- Use rhetorical devices.
- Close with a strong statement.

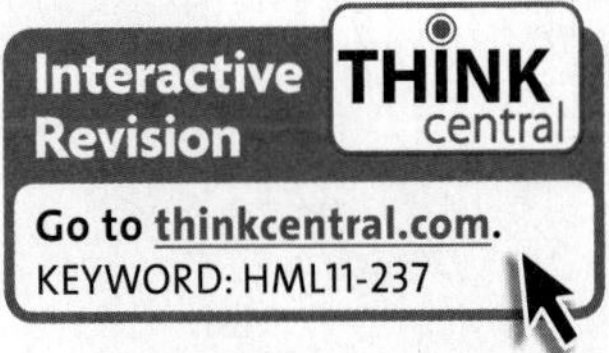

from The Declaration of Independence

Public Document by Thomas Jefferson

COMMON CORE

RI 4 Determine the meaning of words and phrases as they are used in a text, including technical meanings. **RI 5** Analyze and evaluate the effectiveness of the structure an author uses in his or her argument, including whether the structure makes points clear, convincing, and engaging. **RI 8** Delineate and evaluate the reasoning in seminal U.S. texts, including the application of constitutional principles and use of legal reasoning and the premises, purposes, and arguments in works of public advocacy. **L 3a** Apply an understanding of syntax to the study of complex texts when reading.

Meet the Author

Thomas Jefferson 1743–1826

Thomas Jefferson was one of the most accomplished founding fathers. Active in the cause for independence, he was governor of Virginia during the Revolutionary War and U.S. minister to France afterward. He also served the new country as the first secretary of state, the second vice-president, and the third president. As president, he acquired the vast Louisiana Territory west of the Mississippi River to the Rocky Mountains, essentially doubling the size of the country. But more important than any political office he held was the lasting impact of Jefferson's ideals of liberty and self-government so eloquently expressed in the Declaration of Independence.

Brilliant Legal Mind The son of a surveyor and gentleman farmer, Jefferson was born into a life of privilege in rural Virginia. Educated at the College of William and Mary, he was tutored in the law and practiced successfully before entering politics at age 26. As a member of the colonial Virginia legislature, he fell in with a group of radicals, among them Patrick Henry. Lacking Henry's oratorical gifts, Jefferson distinguished himself by his legal writing. Significantly, Jefferson's indelible mark on American life came largely from the many legal documents and laws he wrote promoting democracy.

Passion for Learning Jefferson had an insatiable curiosity about the world and often indulged in what he called his "canine appetite for reading." In addition to devouring works on the classics, history, law, science, and philosophy, he taught himself architecture from books. He designed his elaborate estate at Monticello and the buildings of the University of Virginia, which he also founded as the embodiment of his principles of education and individual freedom.

The Issue of Slavery Charges of hypocrisy on the issue of slavery have tarnished Jefferson's image as the "apostle of liberty." In his early writings, he denounced slavery and tried unsuccessfully to include the issue in the Declaration. Yet Jefferson always owned slaves—as many as 600 over the course of his lifetime—and in later years, he remained undecided on this issue. A defining conflict of this period in American history, the controversy over slavery is part of the historical context that shaped Jefferson's purpose as an individual and as the author of one of our most important historical documents.

DID YOU KNOW?

Thomas Jefferson . . .

- played the violin.
- was an amateur inventor.
- developed the policy of the separation of church and state.
- favored the rights of the states over the federal government.
- died on July 4, the same day as his friend and political rival, John Adams.

Jefferson's home at Monticello

Author Online THINK central

Go to thinkcentral.com. KEYWORD: HML11-238

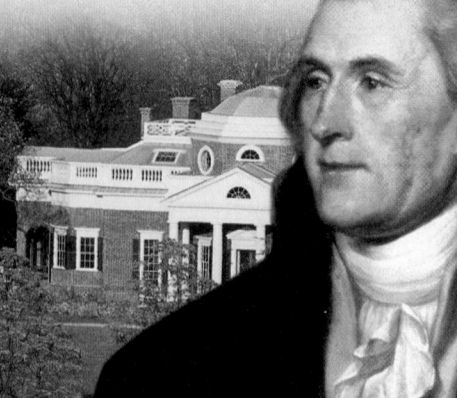

TEXT ANALYSIS: ARGUMENT

Jefferson's purpose in the Declaration of Independence was to make a logical argument for independence. An **argument** expresses an opinion on an issue and supports it with reasons and evidence. Beginning with a **claim,** the writer's position on the subject, an argument needs the **support** of reasons and evidence to prove its claim. A sound argument anticipates opposing views and provides **counterarguments** or **counterclaims** as evidence against them.

Jefferson's **purpose** with the Declaration was not simply to support a historically important argument. It was to inspire his **audience**—his fellow colonists, as well as future generations of Americans—to aspire to the ideals set forth in this document. As you read, look for these elements of an argument.

READING SKILL: ANALYZE TEXT STRUCTURE

The Declaration of Independence has four main sections:

1. a **preamble,** or **foreword,** that announces the reason for the document
2. a **declaration** of people's natural rights and relationship to government
3. a long **list** of complaints against George III, the British king
4. a **conclusion** that formally states America's independence

Each section expresses abstract and complex ideas. As you read, use a chart like the one shown to identify the most important point of each section and to record some of the complex ideas put forth by the author.

Section	Main Point	Complex Ideas
1 Preamble lines 1–6	Independence requires a public statement of reasons.	The laws of nature and God support justice.

VOCABULARY IN CONTEXT

Match each vocabulary word in the first column with the word or phrase in the second column that is closest in meaning.

1. abdicate	**a.** correction
2. redress	**b.** tyranny
3. despotism	**c.** treachery
4. impel	**d.** abandon
5. mercenary	**e.** drive
6. perfidy	**f.** hired soldier

When is REBELLION *justified?*

Many young people harbor a spirit of rebellion—against parents, teachers, bosses, rules, or any situation that "just isn't fair!" But how often do you attempt to explain your rebellion logically? In June of 1776, Thomas Jefferson and other colonial leaders had decided to rebel against British rule. But they needed to justify their dangerous action—to themselves, to the king, and to the world.

DISCUSS In a small group, think of several situations in which an individual or a group rebelled against a perceived injustice. The situations could be any of the following:

- local—an incident in your school or community, for example
- global—such as demonstrations against global trade policies
- historical—such as the American, French, or Russian revolutions

Then, as a group, evaluate the reasons for each rebellion and explain which ones you think are justified.

The Declaration of *Independence*

Thomas Jefferson

BACKGROUND In September 1774, 56 delegates met in Philadelphia at the First Continental Congress to draw up a declaration of colonial rights. They agreed to reconvene in May 1775 if their demands weren't met. At this Second Continental Congress, Thomas Jefferson joined Benjamin Franklin and John Adams on the committee to draft the Declaration of Independence. The task of writing it fell to Jefferson. Although Congress made many changes to the list of grievances, Jefferson's declaration of rights remained untouched—an abiding testament to "self-evident" truths for the nation and the world.

Analyze Visuals ▶
This is an original copy of the Declaration. What might be some of the advantages of having the whole document appear on one large sheet of paper?

In Congress, July 4, 1776

When, in the course of human events, it becomes necessary for one people to dissolve the political bands which have connected them with another, and to assume, among the powers of the earth, the separate and equal station to which the laws of nature and of nature's God entitle them, a decent respect to the opinions of mankind requires that they should declare the causes which **impel** them to the separation. Ⓐ

We hold these truths to be self-evident:—That all men are created equal; that they are endowed by their Creator with certain unalienable rights; that among these are life, liberty, and the pursuit of happiness. That, to secure these rights, governments are instituted among men, deriving their just powers from the consent of the governed; that, whenever any form of government becomes destructive of these ends, it is the right of the people to alter or to abolish it, and to institute a new government, laying its foundation on such principles, and organizing its powers in such form, as to them shall seem most likely to effect their safety and happiness. Prudence, indeed, will dictate that governments long established should not be changed for light and transient causes; and, accordingly,

impel (ĭm-pĕl′) *v.* to drive forward; force

Ⓐ **ARGUMENT**
What **claim** does Jefferson present in the preamble of the Declaration, and what **support** does he say he will provide?

IN CONGRESS. JULY 4, 1776.

The unanimous Declaration of the thirteen united States of America.

all experience hath shown that mankind are more disposed to suffer, while evils are sufferable, than to right themselves by abolishing the forms to which they are accustomed. But, when a long train of abuses and usurpations, pursuing invariably the same object, evinces a design to reduce them under absolute **despotism,** it is their right, it is their duty, to throw off such government, and to provide new guards for their future security. Such has been the patient sufferance of these colonies; and such is now the necessity that constrains them to alter their former systems of government. The history of the present King of Great Britain[1] is a history of repeated injuries and usurpations, all having, in direct object, the establishment of an absolute tyranny over these States. To prove this, let facts be submitted to a candid world. **B**

He has refused his assent to laws[2] the most wholesome and necessary for the public good. **C**

He has forbidden his Governors to pass laws of immediate and pressing importance, unless suspended in their operation till his assent should be obtained; and, when so suspended, he has utterly neglected to attend to them.

He has refused to pass other laws for the accommodation of large districts of people, unless these people would relinquish the right of representation in the legislature—a right inestimable to them, and formidable to tyrants only.

He has called together legislative bodies at places unusual, uncomfortable, and distant from the depository of their public records, for the sole purpose of fatiguing them into compliance with his measure.

He has dissolved representative houses repeatedly, for opposing, with manly firmness, his invasions on the rights of the people.

He has refused, for a long time after such dissolutions, to cause others to be elected; whereby the legislative powers, incapable of annihilation, have returned to the people at large for their exercise; the State remaining, in the meantime, exposed to all dangers of invasion from without, and convulsions within.

He has endeavored to prevent the population[3] of these States; for that purpose obstructing the laws for the naturalization of foreigners; refusing to pass others to encourage their migration hither, and raising the conditions of new appropriations of lands.

He has obstructed the administration of justice, by refusing his assent to laws for establishing judiciary powers.

He has made judges dependent on his will alone for the tenure of their offices,[4] and the amount and payment of their salaries.

He has erected a multitude of new offices, and sent hither swarms of officers to harass our people and eat out their substance.[5]

despotism (dĕs′pə-tĭz′əm) *n.* government by a ruler with unlimited power

B ARGUMENT
What opposing claim does Jefferson anticipate in lines 15–22? What **counterargument** does he make at the end of this paragraph, and what does he say he is about to do?

C TEXT STRUCTURE
Why might the list of complaints make up the largest part of the four-part structure?

Language Coach

Multiple-Meaning Words *Dissolved* can mean "caused to pass into solution" (such as sugar dissolved in tea). However, in line 39, *dissolved,* means "ended" or "terminated." Why would the king want to dissolve the representative houses?

1. **the present King of Great Britain:** George III, who reigned from 1760 to 1820.
2. **refused his assent to laws:** Laws passed in the colonies needed the king's approval; sometimes it took years for laws to be approved or rejected.
3. **to prevent the population:** to keep the population from growing.
4. **the tenure of their offices:** their job security.
5. **eat out their substance:** use up their resources.

Declaration of Independence in Congress, at the Independence Hall, Philadelphia, July 4, 1776 (1819), John Trumbull. Oil on canvas. The Granger Collection, New York.

He has kept among us, in times of peace, standing armies, without the consent of our legislatures.

He has affected to render the military independent of, and superior to, the civil power.

He has combined with others to subject us to a jurisdiction foreign to our constitutions,[6] and unacknowledged by our laws; giving his assent to their acts of pretended legislation:

For quartering large bodies of armed troops among us;

For protecting them, by a mock trial, from punishment for any murders which they should commit on the inhabitants of these States;

For cutting off our trade with all parts of the world;

For imposing taxes on us without our consent;

For depriving us, in many cases, of the benefits of trial by jury;

For transporting us beyond the seas, to be tried for pretended offenses;

For abolishing the free system of English laws in a neighboring province,[7] establishing there an arbitrary government, and enlarging its boundaries, so as to render it at once an example and fit instrument for introducing the same absolute rule into these colonies;

For taking away our charters, abolishing our most valuable laws, and altering, fundamentally, the forms of our governments;

For suspending our own legislatures, and declaring themselves invested with power to legislate for us in all cases whatsoever. **D**

COMMON CORE L 3a

D TEXT STRUCTURE
Reread lines 59–76 and study the arrangement of paragraphs. In lines 62-76, Jefferson lists violations the English king has committed against the colonies. Jefferson emphasizes these violations by devoting a separate paragraph to each one and by using **parallel structure.** Each paragraph begins with the preposition *for,* followed by a gerund such as *quartering* or *protecting.* Read lines 59–76 aloud. How does Jefferson's use of parallelism and paragraph structure contribute to the persuasive impact of these lines?

6. **subject us . . . our constitutions:** Parliament had passed the Declaratory Act in 1766, stating that the king and Parliament could make laws for the colonies.

7. **a neighboring province:** the province of Quebec, which at the time extended south to the Ohio River and west to the Mississippi.

He has **abdicated** government here, by declaring us out of his protection, and waging war against us.

He has plundered our seas, ravaged our coasts, burnt our towns,[8] and destroyed the lives of our people.

He is at this time transporting large armies of foreign **mercenaries** to complete the works of death, desolation, and tyranny, already begun with circumstances of cruelty and **perfidy** scarcely paralleled in the most barbarous ages, and totally unworthy the head of a civilized nation.

He has constrained our fellow citizens, taken captive on the high seas, to bear arms against their country, to become the executioners of their friends and brethren, or to fall themselves by their hands.

He has excited domestic insurrection amongst us,[9] and has endeavored to bring on the inhabitants of our frontiers the merciless Indian savages, whose known rule of warfare is an undistinguished destruction of all ages, sexes, and conditions.

In every stage of these oppressions we have petitioned for **redress,** in the most humble terms; our repeated petitions have been answered only by repeated injury. A prince whose character is thus marked by every act which may define a tyrant is unfit to be the ruler of a free people.

Nor have we been wanting in our attentions to our British brethren. We have warned them, from time to time, of attempts by their legislature to extend an unwarrantable jurisdiction over us. We have reminded them of the circumstances of our emigration and settlement here. We have appealed to their native justice and magnanimity; and we have conjured them, by the ties of our common kindred, to disavow these usurpations, which would inevitably interrupt our connections and correspondence. E

They, too, have been deaf to the voice of justice and of consanguinity.[10] We must, therefore, acquiesce in the necessity which denounces our separation; and hold them, as we hold the rest of mankind, enemies in war, in peace friends. F

We, Therefore, the Representatives of the United States of America, in General Congress assembled, appealing to the Supreme Judge of the world for the rectitude[11] of our intentions, do, in the name and by the authority of the good people of these colonies, solemnly publish and declare, that these United Colonies are, and of right ought to be, Free and Independent States; that they are absolved from all allegiance to the British crown, and that all political connection between them and the state of Great Britain is, and ought to be, totally dissolved; and that, as free and independent states, they have full power to levy war, conclude peace, contract alliances, establish commerce, and to do all other acts and things which independent states may of right do. And, for the support of this declaration, with a firm reliance on the protection of Divine Providence, we mutually pledge to each other our lives, our fortunes, and our sacred honor.

abdicate (ăb'dĭ-kāt') *v.* to give up responsibility for

mercenary (mûr'sə-nĕr'ē) *n.* a professional soldier hired to fight in a foreign army

perfidy (pûr'fĭ-dē) *n.* treachery

redress (rĭ-drĕs') *n.* the correction of a wrong; compensation

E **GRAMMAR AND STYLE**
Reread lines 98–101. Notice how Jefferson uses a **compound-complex sentence,** which has two or more independent clauses and one or more subordinate clauses, in order to show the complex relationships between ideas.

F **ARGUMENT**
Reread lines 95–104. Notice how Jefferson uses the first-person plural pronouns *we* and *our* to identify with his **audience** and to inspire unity of **purpose.** Examine Jefferson's **diction,** or choice of words. How does the language of these closing paragraphs support the writer's inspirational **tone** or attitude toward the idea of independence? Support your answer with evidence from the Declaration.

8. **plundered . . . our towns:** American seaports such as Norfolk, Virginia, had already been shelled.
9. **excited . . . amongst us:** George III had encouraged slaves to rise up and rebel against their masters.
10. **deaf to . . . consanguinity:** The British have ignored pleas based on their common ancestry with the colonists.
11. **rectitude:** morally correct behavior or thinking.

Comprehension

1. **Recall** Name three complaints that the colonists had against the king.
2. **Recall** What rights are specified in the Declaration?
3. **Clarify** What does Jefferson say is the purpose of government?
4. **Clarify** According to the Declaration, who gives people their rights?

Text Analysis

5. **Make Inferences** The Declaration clearly takes aim at the abuses of King George to justify the colonists' **rebellion.** But reread lines 102–104. To what extent does the document hold the British people responsible? What is the new relationship declared between Americans and their "British brethren," and how might it differ from the old?
6. **Analyze Elements of an Argument** How does Jefferson's awareness of his audience affect his diction—the words he chooses and the manner of their arrangement? Explain the persuasive appeal of the following words and phrases:
   - "We hold these truths to be self-evident" (line 7)
   - "endowed by their Creator" (line 8)
   - "unalienable rights" (line 8)
   - "secure these rights" (lines 9–10)
7. **Evaluate Text Structure** Review the chart you filled in. How effective is Jefferson's four-part structure in stating the colonists' case? Would reordering the parts make any difference? Explain your answer.
8. **Evaluate Elements of an Argument** Identify the major claim and the support given in the Declaration. In your opinion, is the support sufficient for the claim? Does it have to be? Explain your answer.

Text Criticism

9. **Historical Context** Jefferson's celebrated statement "All men are created equal" only applied to white men at the time. How has the meaning of Jefferson's statement changed over time? How has it stayed the same?

When is REBELLION *justified?*

Which set of reasons for breaking away from British rule strikes you as most important—the colonists' philosophical ideals, the hardships colonists suffered as a result of British policies, or the king's response to colonists' complaints? Explain your answer.

COMMON CORE

RI 1 Cite textual evidence to support inferences drawn from the text. **RI 4** Determine the meaning of words and phrases as they are used in a text, including technical meanings. **RI 5** Analyze and evaluate the effectiveness of the structure an author uses in his or her argument, including whether the structure makes points clear, convincing, and engaging. **RI 8** Delineate and evaluate the reasoning in seminal U.S. texts, including the application of constitutional principles and use of legal reasoning and the premises, purposes, and arguments in works of public advocacy.

Vocabulary in Context

▲ VOCABULARY PRACTICE

Choose the word that is not related in meaning to the other words.

1. (a) disloyalty, (b) perfidy, (c) honesty, (d) treachery
2. (a) despotism, (b) dictatorship, (c) tyranny, (d) righteousness
3. (a) monarch, (b) ruler, (c) mercenary, (d) king
4. (a) redress, (b) model, (c) remedy, (d) compensation
5. (a) abandon, (b) renounce, (c) confiscate, (d) abdicate
6. (a) mobilize, (b) impel, (c) propel, (d) restrain

WORD LIST
abdicate
despotism
impel
mercenary
perfidy
redress

ACADEMIC VOCABULARY IN WRITING

• document • illustrate • interpret • promote • reveal

The Declaration of Independence **reveals** many hardships the colonists suffered at the hands of King George. Write a short paragraph discussing how these trials affected the colonists and eventually led them to **promote** the cause for freedom. Use three Academic Vocabulary words in your paragraph.

VOCABULARY STRATEGY: POLITICAL WORDS

The content areas of social studies and political science use many terms to describe systems of government. Some terms identify specific types of government; others, like the vocabulary word *despotism,* describe the practices of a government. It is useful to understand the meanings of such terms.

PRACTICE Choose the political word described by each numbered item. Then use a dictionary to trace the etymology of each word.

oligarchy regency republic socialism totalitarianism

1. a few people have the ruling power
2. a person rules in place of the regular ruler, who may be ill or too young
3. production of goods and services is under the control of government
4. one political group rules and suppresses all opposition, often with force
5. citizens elect representatives to manage the government

COMMON CORE

RI 4 Determine the meaning of words and phrases as they are used in a text, including technical meanings. **L 4c** Consult general and specialized reference materials to determine or clarify a word's etymology. **L 6** Acquire and use accurately general academic and domain-specific words and phrases.

Language

◆ GRAMMAR AND STYLE: Vary Sentence Structure

Review the **Grammar and Style** note on page 244. Like most lawyers, who have to be precise as well as thorough, Jefferson uses **complex** and **compound-complex** sentences to pack in meaning.

- A **complex sentence** has one main clause (as in yellow), which can stand alone, and one or more subordinate clauses (as in green), which cannot.

  A prince whose character is thus marked by every act which may define a tyrant is unfit to be the ruler of a free people. (lines 93–94)

- A **compound-complex sentence** has two or more independent clauses (as in yellow) and one or more subordinate clauses (as in green).

  Such has been the patient sufferance of these colonies; and such is now the necessity that constrains them to alter their former systems of government. (lines 22–24)

PRACTICE Rewrite each pair of sentences as a complex or compound-complex sentence. Use the conjunction shown in parentheses.

> **EXAMPLE**
>
> The king exploits the people. The people move toward rebellion. (after)
>
> *After the king exploits the people, the people move toward rebellion.*

1. The people declare their grievances with British rule. The British king and parliament do not listen. (when)
2. The parliament learns of the dissatisfaction of the colonists. The parliament imposes even harsher laws. (as soon as)

COMMON CORE

L 3a Vary syntax for effect, consulting references for guidance as needed; apply an understanding of syntax to the study of complex texts when reading. **W 1** Write arguments to support claims in an analysis of substantive topics or texts, using valid reasoning and relevant and sufficient evidence.

READING-WRITING CONNECTION

Expand your understanding of Jefferson's Declaration of Independence by responding to this prompt. Then, use the **revising tips** to improve your declaration.

WRITING PROMPT	REVISING TIPS
TAKE A STAND The Declaration of Independence has served as a model in several historical instances. Write a **declaration** for a group or individual of your choosing. Your declaration should have at least **three paragraphs** and be modeled on the Declaration of Independence.	• Include a brief declaration of rights. • List at least ten complaints. • Conclude with a resolution.

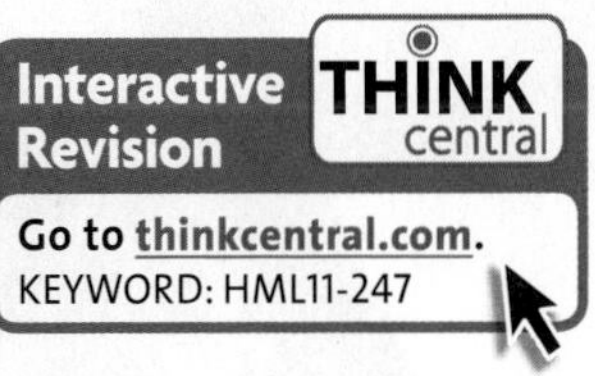

COMMON CORE

RI 2 Determine two or more central ideas of a text and analyze their development, including how they interact and build on one another to provide a complex analysis; provide an objective summary of the text. **RI 3** Analyze a complex set of ideas or sequence of events and explain how specific individuals, ideas, or events interact and develop. **RI 4** Analyze how an author uses and refines the meaning of a key term. **RI 5** Analyze and evaluate the effectiveness of the structure an author uses in his or her exposition or argument.

from The Crisis

Essay by Thomas Paine

Meet the Author

Thomas Paine 1737–1809

Brash, bold, and fearless—and at times angry and offensive—Thomas Paine was the firebrand of the American Revolution. In the fall of 1775, few American leaders dared to advocate openly for independence. Not only did they risk being accused of treason, they were uncertain how the common people would react to such a radical notion. They turned to Tom Paine to test the waters. Paine had arrived in Philadelphia from London only the year before but was already gaining a reputation as a revolutionary writer. He eagerly took up the task and in a few months wrote *Common Sense* (1776), a 50-page pamphlet that attacked the injustices of hereditary rule and urged the colonists to form their own independent country where "the law is king." Paine's pamphlet sold 120,000 copies in the first three months. Six months later, the colonies declared their independence.

New Voice for a New Political Audience Paine's political ideas in *Common Sense* were not particularly new or original. In the Age of Enlightenment, intellectual circles were buzzing with talk of natural rights and democracy. What was new was Paine's voice—raw, direct, full of energy. Unlike most political writers of the day, such as Thomas Jefferson, Paine addressed common men—farmers, craftsmen, and laborers—not the educated elite. His straightforward prose reinforced his democratic message that all men were capable of understanding and participating in government. People responded because Paine spoke their language. In his native England, he had worked as sailor, teacher, customs officer, grocer, and maker of ladies' corsets. He envisioned America as the place where working men like him could have political and economic power.

Limits of Success With American independence won, Paine left for Europe in 1787 to join the reform efforts brewing there. But his outspokenness got him into trouble in both conservative England and revolutionary France. His last major work, *The Age of Reason* (1794, 1795), attacked organized religion and alienated many of his supporters. By the time he returned to the United States in 1802, few politicians wanted to associate with him. He spent his last years in poverty and obscurity.

Legacy Despite Paine's later decline, his contribution to the intellectual and cultural life of Revolutionary America is indisputable. He was the radical the country needed, the spokesman for new American values and ideals.

DID YOU KNOW?

Thomas Paine . . .

- failed out of school by age 12.
- was fired twice from a job as tax collector.
- didn't come to America until he was 37 years old.
- became involved in the French Revolution.

Author Online THINK central

Go to thinkcentral.com. KEYWORD: HML11-248

TEXT ANALYSIS: PERSUASIVE TECHNIQUES

Thomas Paine used a number of **persuasive techniques** in *The Crisis* to persuade Americans to join the cause. He was a master of **rhetoric,** the use of language to persuade.

- **Emotional appeals** have powerful rhetorical impact. They persuade by eliciting strong feelings, such as pity or fear.
- **Ethical appeals** influence readers by appealing to their sense of right and wrong.
- **Appeals to association** suggest that readers will gain acceptance or prestige by taking the writer's position.
- **Appeals to authority** influence readers by citing experts or others who warrant respect.

As you read, notice Paine's patriotic **purpose** and his understanding of his fellow colonists—the readers who make up his **audience.** Examine how his purpose and his audience affects his **tone** or attitude in this important historical essay.

READING STRATEGY: SUMMARIZE MAIN IDEAS

Summarizing means identifying main ideas and combining them into a brief overview of a text. As you read Paine's essay, use a chart like the one shown to identify main ideas. Afterwards, combine the main ideas into a brief paragraph.

Main Ideas	Summary
I see no real cause for fear.	

VOCABULARY IN CONTEXT

Complete each phrase with the appropriate word from the list.

WORD LIST	ardor	prudent	tyranny
	celestial	relinquish	wrangling

1. _____ brothers who never seemed to get along
2. will fight _____ and other forms of oppression
3. a _____ decision in dangerous circumstances
4. would not _____ control of the property
5. music so sweet it seemed _____
6. expressed his _____ in mushy love poems

Complete the activities in your **Reader/Writer Notebook**.

Whose SIDE *are you on?*

Loyalty is a value easily expressed but often difficult to uphold. Situations change, doubts creep in, and conflicts arise that can test the strongest bonds of loyalty. Paine's essay addresses the crisis of loyalty threatening the ranks of American soldiers during the dark days of the Revolutionary War.

QUICKWRITE Think about a time when your loyalty was tested and you were tempted to switch sides or give up. In a short paragraph, briefly describe the situation and explain what you decided. What was the most crucial factor in your decision?

The CRISIS

Thomas Paine

BACKGROUND On the blustery Christmas Eve of 1776, the situation looked bleak for the Continental Army. General Washington's ragtag troops had retreated to the western banks of the Delaware River. Tom Paine was camped with them. The British were within striking distance of Philadelphia, and Washington knew he had to advance the next day or risk losing the war. To boost the morale of his ill-equipped and outnumbered soldiers, he ordered his officers to read aloud the following essay, which Paine had written the day before.

These are the times that try men's souls: The summer soldier and the sunshine patriot will, in this crisis, shrink from the service of his country; but he that stands it NOW, deserves the love and thanks of man and woman. **Tyranny,** like hell, is not easily conquered; yet we have this consolation with us, that the harder the conflict, the more glorious the triumph. What we obtain too cheap, we esteem too lightly:—' Tis dearness only that gives every thing its value. Heaven knows how to set a proper price upon its goods; and it would be strange indeed, if so **celestial** an article as FREEDOM should not be highly rated. Britain, with an army to enforce her tyranny, has declared, that she has a right (*not only to* TAX) but "to BIND us in ALL CASES WHATSOEVER,"[1] and if *being bound in that manner* is not slavery, then there is not such a thing as slavery upon earth. Even the expression is impious, for so unlimited a power can only belong to God. (A)

1. **"to BIND us in ALL CASES WHATSOEVER":** a reference to wording in the Declaratory Act of 1766, in which the British parliament asserted its "power and authority" to make and enforce laws over the American colonies.

Analyze Visuals ▶
A minuteman was pledged to be ready to fight on a minute's notice. What does this suggest about the preparedness of the colonists?

tyranny (tĭr′ə-nē) *n.* cruel and oppressive government or rule

celestial (sə-lĕs′chəl) *adj.* heavenly

(A) PERSUASIVE TECHNIQUES
Identify the **loaded language**—words with strong connotations—in lines 1–12. What kind of emotional appeal do these words have? What tone do they establish?

Minute Man: Liberty or Death. Private collection. © Scala/Art Resource, New York.

VINCE
AUT
MORIRE
LIBERTY
OR
DEATH
1774
-75
MINUTE MAN

Whether the Independence of the Continent was declared too soon, or delayed too long, I will not now enter into as an argument; my own simple opinion is, that had it been eight months earlier, it would have been much better. We did not make a proper use of last winter, neither could we, while we were in a dependant state. However, the fault, if it were one, was all our own; we have none to blame but ourselves. But no great deal is lost yet; all that Howe has been doing for this month past is rather a ravage than a conquest which the spirit of the Jersies a year ago would have quickly repulsed, and which time and a little resolution will soon recover. **B**

B MAIN IDEAS
Reread lines 13–21. What is Paine's main idea in this paragraph? Support your answer with evidence from the passage.

I have as little superstition in me as any man living, but my secret opinion has ever been, and still is, that God almighty will not give up a people to military destruction, or leave them unsupportedly to perish, who had so earnestly and so repeatedly sought to avoid the calamities of war, by every decent method which wisdom could invent. Neither have I so much of the infidel in me, as to suppose, that he has **relinquished** the government of the world, and given us up to the care of devils; and as I do not, I cannot see on what grounds the king of Britain can look up to heaven for help against us: A common murderer, a highwayman, or a housebreaker, has as good a pretense as he. . . .

relinquish (rĭ-lĭng'kwĭsh) *v.* to withdraw from; to give up

I once felt all that kind of anger, which a man ought to feel, against the mean principles that are held by the Tories:[2] A noted one, who kept a tavern at Amboy,[3] was standing at his door, with as pretty a child in his hand, about eight or nine years old, as most I ever saw, and after speaking his mind as freely as he thought was **prudent,** finished with this unfatherly expression, *"Well! give me peace in my day."* Not a man lives on the Continent but fully believes that a separation must some time or other finally take place, and a generous parent would have said, *"If there must be trouble, let it be in my day, that my child may have peace;"* and this single reflection, well applied, is sufficient to awaken every man to duty. Not a place upon earth might be so happy as America. Her situation is remote from all the **wrangling** world, and she has nothing to do but trade with them. A man may easily distinguish in himself between temper and principle, and I am as confident, as I am that God governs the world, that America will never be happy until she gets clear of foreign dominion. Wars, without ceasing, will break out until that period arrives, and the Continent must in the end be conqueror; for, though the flame of liberty may sometimes cease to shine, the coal never can expire. . . . **C**

prudent (pro͞od'nt) *adj.* showing caution or good judgment

wrangling (răng'glĭng) *adj.* arguing noisily **wrangle** *v.*

C PERSUASIVE TECHNIQUES
Notice that Paine makes an **ethical appeal** in lines 31–39. How does he say a parent should behave?

I turn with the warm **ardor** of a friend to those who have nobly stood, and are yet determined to stand the matter out: I call not upon a few, but upon all; not on this State or that State, but on every State; up and help us; lay your shoulders to the wheel; better have too much force than too little, when so great an object is at stake. Let it be told to the future world, that in the depth of winter, when nothing but hope and virtue could survive, that the city and the country, alarmed at one

ardor (är'dər) *n.* intense enthusiasm; passion

---

2. **the mean principles . . . Tories:** the small-minded beliefs of those colonists who remain loyal to Great Britain.

3. **Amboy:** probably Perth Amboy, a town in New Jersey.

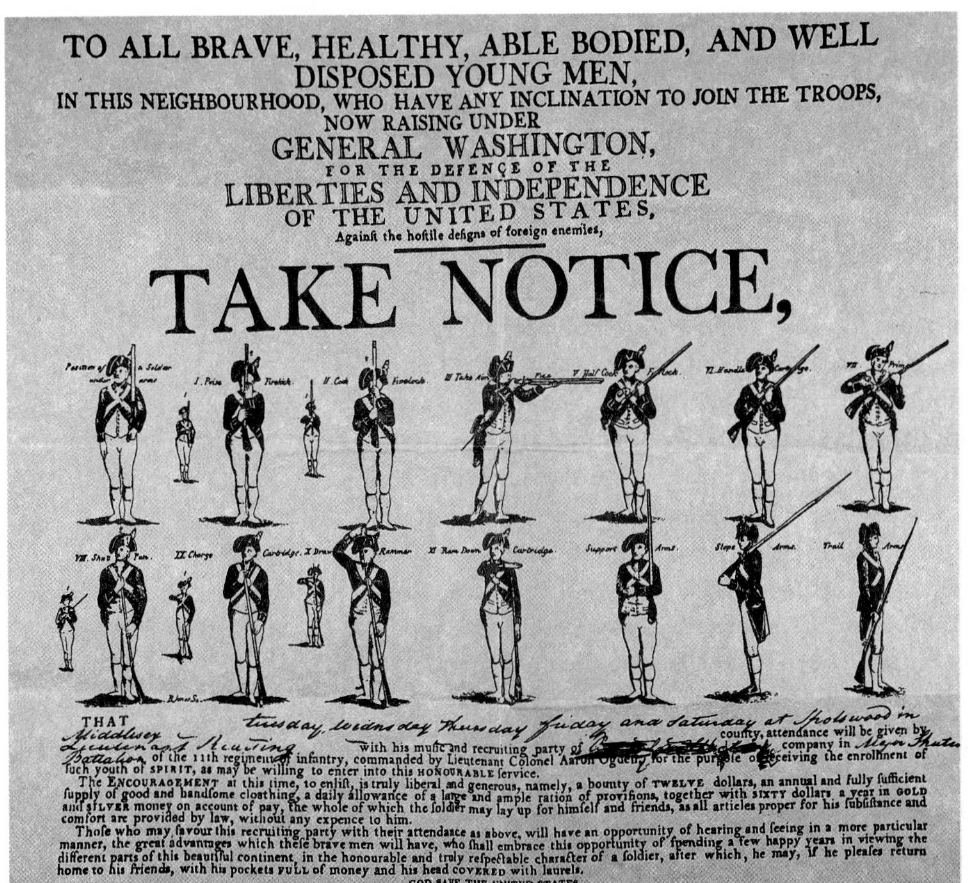

◀ Analyze Visuals

A broadside is a public notice printed on one side of a large sheet of paper. What feelings and emotions does this American Revolutionary War broadside appeal to?

common danger, came forth to meet and to repulse it. Say not, that thousands are gone, turn out your tens of thousands; throw not the burden of the day upon Providence, but *"shew your faith by your works,"* that God may bless you. It matters not where you live, or what rank of life you hold, the evil or the blessing will reach you all. The far and the near, the home counties and the back, the rich and the poor, shall suffer or rejoice alike. The heart that feels not now, is dead: The blood of his children shall curse his cowardice, who shrinks back at a time when a little might have saved the whole, and made *them* happy. I love the man that can smile in trouble, that can gather strength from distress, and grow brave by reflection. 'Tis the business of little minds to shrink; but he whose heart is firm, and whose conscience approves his conduct, will pursue his principles unto death. My own line of reasoning is to myself as strait and clear as a ray of light. **D** Not all the treasures of the world, so far as I believe, could have induced me to support an offensive war, for I think it murder; but if a thief break into my house, burn and destroy my property, and kill or threaten to kill me, or those that are in it, and to *"bind me in all cases whatsoever,"* to his absolute will, am I to suffer it?

D PERSUASIVE TECHNIQUES

Reread lines 47–64. Notice how Paine's persuasive **purpose** and his awareness of his **audience** contribute to his attitude or **tone** of passionate conviction. He identifies with his readers by calling himself a friend. He uses emotionally loaded words to appeal to beliefs shared by the colonists who read his essays. Choose an especially persuasive sentence from this passage. What is Paine's tone in this sentence? What purpose does the sentence reveal? Explain your response.

What signifies it to me, whether he who does it, is a king or a common man; my countryman or not my countryman? whether it is done by an individual villain, or an army of them? If we reason to the root of things we shall find no difference; neither can any just cause be assigned why we should punish in the one case, and pardon in the other. Let them call me rebel, and welcome, I feel no concern from it; but I should suffer the misery of devils, were I to make a whore of my soul by swearing allegiance to one, whose character is that of a sottish, stupid, stubborn, worthless, brutish man. I conceive likewise a horrid idea in receiving mercy from a being, who at the last day shall be shrieking to the rocks and mountains to cover him, and fleeing with terror from the orphan, the widow and the slain of America.

There are cases which cannot be overdone by language, and this is one. There are persons too who see not the full extent of the evil that threatens them; they solace themselves with hopes that the enemy, if they succeed, will be merciful. It is the madness of folly to expect mercy from those who have refused to do justice; and even mercy, where conquest is the object, is only a trick of war: The cunning of the fox is as murderous as the violence of the wolfe; and we ought to guard equally against both. Howe's first object is partly by threats and partly by promises, to terrify or seduce the people to deliver up their arms, and receive mercy. The ministry recommended the same plan to Gage, and this is what the Tories call making their peace; *"a peace which passeth all understanding" indeed!* A peace which would be the immediate forerunner of a worse ruin than any we have yet thought of. Ye men of Pennsylvania, do reason upon those things! Were the back counties to give up their arms, they would fall easy prey to the Indians, who are all armed: This perhaps is what some Tories would not be sorry for. Were the home counties to deliver up their arms, they would be exposed to the resentment of the back counties, who would then have it at their power to chastise their defection at pleasure. And were any one State to give up its arms, that State must be garrisoned by all Howe's army of Britons and Hessians to preserve it from the anger of the rest. Mutual fear is a principal link in the chain of mutual love, and woe be the State that breaks the compact. Howe is mercifully inviting you to barbarous destruction, and men must be either rogues or fools that will not see it. I dwell not upon the vapours of imagination; I bring reason to your ears; and in language, as plain as A, B, C, hold up truth to your eyes. **E**

I thank God that I fear not. I see no real cause for fear. I know our situation well, and can see the way out of it. While our army was collected, Howe dared not risk a battle, and it is no credit to him that he decamped from the White Plains, and waited a mean opportunity to ravage the defenceless Jersies; but it is great credit to us, that, with an handful of men, we sustained an orderly retreat for near an hundred miles, brought off our ammunition, all our field-pieces, the greatest part of our stores, and had four rivers to pass. None can say that our retreat was

COMMON CORE L 4c

Language Coach

Etymology *Horrid* (line 76) comes from the Latin *horrere*, meaning "to be afraid." *Horrid* means "very bad" or "terrible." Look up these related words in a dictionary: *horrendous* and *abhor*. Use each in a sentence about Paine's beliefs.

COMMON CORE RI 4

E MAIN IDEAS

Reread lines 79–101, and note Paine's repetition of the word *mercy* and its related forms *merciful* and *mercifully*. *Mercy* means receiving good treatment from someone who has power over you. How does the meaning of this key term develop and change in this paragraph? How does this development support Paine's comment in lines 97–98?

Washington Crossing the Delaware (1851), Eastman Johnson. Copy after the Emmanuel Leutze painting in the Metropolitan Museum, New York. Private collection. © Art Resource, New York.

▲ Analyze Visuals
What figures and objects are emphasized by the **composition,** or the arrangement of shapes? Consider what this emphasis adds to the painting's meaning.

precipitate, for we were near three weeks in performing it, and the country might have time to come in. Twice we marched back to meet the enemy and remained out till dark. The sign of fear was not seen in our camp, and had not some of the cowardly and disaffected inhabitants spread false alarms through the country, the Jersies had never been ravaged. Once more we are again collected and collecting; our new army at both ends of the Continent is recruiting fast, and we shall be able to open the next campaign with sixty thousand men, well armed and clothed. This is our situation, and who will may know it. By perseverance and fortitude we have the prospect of a glorious issue; by cowardice and submission, the sad choice of a variety of evils—a ravaged country—a depopulated city—habitations without safety, and slavery without hope—our homes turned into barracks and bawdy-houses for Hessians, and a future race to provide for whose fathers we shall doubt of. Look on this picture, and weep over it!—and if there yet remains one thoughtless wretch who believes it not, let him suffer it unlamented. ~ F

F MAIN IDEAS
Reread this paragraph, focusing on what Paine says about fear. What is the main point he makes about fear? Support your answer with evidence from the paragraph.

After Reading

Comprehension

1. **Recall** At the end of the essay, what two qualities does Paine say American troops need to win the war?
2. **Summarize** In the third paragraph, what reasons does Paine give for assuring the Americans that their cause is right?
3. **Clarify** What is implied by the terms "summer soldier" and "sunshine patriot" in the first paragraph?

Text Analysis

4. **Interpret Metaphor** A metaphor is a figure of speech that equates two unlike things. Explain what Paine means by the metaphor in lines 45–46. How might this metaphor serve to inspire the troops' loyalty?
5. **Summarize Main Ideas** Using the chart of main ideas you completed as you read, write a paragraph **summarizing** Paine's main ideas. Does a summary of this essay's main ideas lose the persuasive power of Paine's rhetoric? Explain your answer.
6. **Analyze Persuasive Techniques** Review the persuasive techniques on page 249. Then, find six examples of Paine's strong persuasive appeals. In a chart, record your examples and explain the types of appeals. How does Paine's use of persuasive language affect the tone of this essay? Cite evidence from your chart to support your answer.

Example from "The Crisis"	Kind of Appeal
Those soldiers who stand firm in the "service of [their] country" deserve the "love and thanks of man and woman." (lines 2–3)	ethical appeal of "service to country" plus emotional appeal of love and gratitude
"God almighty will not give up a people to military destruction. . . ." (lines 23–24)	appeal to authority—in this case, the ultimate authority

Text Criticism

7. **Critical Interpretations** John Adams, second U.S. president and no fan of Paine's, nonetheless acknowledged his crucial influence: "Without the pen of Paine the sword of Washington would have been wielded in vain." Use information from Paine's essay, as well as facts from his biography on page 248, to support Adams's assessment.

Whose **SIDE** *are you on?*

Political debates often compel people to decide which side they will be loyal to. Who or what deserves your loyalty? Why?

COMMON CORE

RI 2 Determine two or more central ideas of a text and analyze their development, including how they interact and build on one another to provide a complex analysis; provide an objective summary of the text. **RI 3** Analyze a complex set of ideas or sequence of events and explain how specific individuals, ideas, or events interact and develop. **RI 5** Analyze and evaluate the effectiveness of the structure an author uses in his or her exposition or argument.

Vocabulary in Context

▲ VOCABULARY PRACTICE

Choose the letter of the phrase that defines or is related to the boldfaced word.

1. **celestial:** (a) an instrument, (b) a star in the sky, (c) a slogan
2. **tyranny:** (a) a country with no freedoms, (b) an old bicycle, (c) a relay race
3. **ardor:** (a) a grove of trees, (b) a passion for justice, (c) an accounting mistake
4. **relinquish:** (a) a building site, (b) a surrender of territory, (c) a bad argument
5. **prudent:** (a) a cautious investor, (b) a distant relative, (c) car insurance
6. **wrangling:** (a) a favor, (b) a rowing machine, (c) towns with border disputes

WORD LIST

ardor
celestial
prudent
relinquish
tyranny
wrangling

ACADEMIC VOCABULARY IN SPEAKING

• document • illustrate • interpret • promote • reveal

Paine's essay was used to inspire Washington's army to victory. Today, people sometimes use speeches, blogs, and videos to inspire others. However, even these messages started out as words on a page. In a small group, discuss the importance of the written word in **promoting** a cause or in **illustrating** important points. Use two of the Academic Vocabulary words in your discussion.

VOCABULARY STRATEGY: WORDS FROM MIDDLE ENGLISH

Many modern words from Middle English originally derive from French. Others come from Old English, the earliest recognized form of the English language. To learn the derivation of a word, you need to understand how to read a dictionary entry. The entry below begins with the word in boldface, divided into syllables, followed by the pronunciation guide in parenthesis, and then the part of speech. Two numbered definitions are provided, as well as a highlighted summary of the word's etymology—its derivation from Middle English, Old French, and Latin.

> **ar•dor** (är der) *n.* **1.** Great intensity of feeling. **2.** Strong enthusiams or devotion: zeal. [Middle English *ardour,* from Old French, from Latin *ardor,* for *ardere,* to burn.]

PRACTICE The boldface words in these sentences derive from Middle English. Use context clues to write a definition for each word. Then, consult a print or online dictionary to learn the etymology and original meaning of each word.

1. He demonstrated his athletic **prowess** by participating in the triathlon.
2. She has been a **recluse** ever since the death of her husband.
3. Her **fulsome** praise of his decision greatly embarrassed him.
4. He had the perfect **rejoinder** for every accusation of the committee.
5. The garden held a **plenitude** of rare plants and flowers.

COMMON CORE

L 4c Consult general and specialized reference materials, both print and digital, to find the pronunciation of a word or determine or clarify its precise meaning, its part of speech, its etymology, or its standard usage. **L 6** Acquire and use accurately general academic and domain-specific words and phrases.

Interactive Vocabulary
THINK central
Go to thinkcentral.com.
KEYWORD: HML11-257

COMMON CORE

RI 6 Determine an author's point of view or purpose in a text in which the rhetoric is particularly effective, analyzing how style and content contribute to the power, persuasiveness, or beauty of the text. **RI 9** Analyze documents of historical and literary significance for their themes, purposes, and rhetorical features.

Letter to the Reverend Samson Occom

by Phillis Wheatley

Letter to John Adams

by Abigail Adams

Meet the Authors

Phillis Wheatley

c. 1753–1784

Phillis Wheatley was the first African-American poet to be published. Moreover, her unusual life is the stuff that movies are made of. Kidnapped at age seven in West Africa, she was sold to the prosperous Wheatley family at a Boston slave auction. Within 16 months, she had mastered English and could read the Bible. She went on to learn Latin and Greek well enough to read the classics.

Startling Success Story Encouraged by the Wheatley family, Phillis started writing poetry as a teenager; She earned fame in the colonies and England when newspapers began publishing her poems, most of them on moral and religious subjects. While in London in 1773 to publish her book of poetry, Wheatley was the toast of society, which included many nobles and dignitaries and the visiting American patriot Ben Franklin.

Life as a Free Black Woman By 1778, Wheatley had gained her freedom and married a free black man. Their life together was a losing struggle against poverty, however, for in many respects living as a free black in a colonial city was as hard as being a slave. In late 1779, Wheatley tried to get a second book of her poems published, but war-torn, financially strapped Boston had lost interest in her.

Abigail Adams

1744–1818

Abigail Adams was the wife of the second U.S. president, John Adams, and mother of the sixth, John Quincy Adams. But she is equally well-known for her outspoken opinions as expressed in thousands of personal letters.

Intelligent and Competent The daughter of a wealthy minister, young Abigail read extensively in her father's library. After marrying John Adams, she moved to a farm in Braintree, Massachusetts. As John became increasingly involved in colonial politics and the struggle for independence, Abigail managed the household and farm as well as John's business affairs.

An Early Feminist? Because of her support for women's education and her acute awareness of men's "absolute power," many have championed Abigail Adams as an early advocate of women's rights. However, although her thinking was clearly advanced for her time—she also favored the abolition of slavery—she held quite conventional views about a woman's subordinate role in society.

Author Online

Go to thinkcentral.com. KEYWORD: HML11-258

TEXT ANALYSIS: DICTION

Diction is a writer's choice of words. Diction includes both vocabulary (words) and syntax (arrangement of words). Diction can be formal or informal, common or technical, abstract or concrete. Note the formal diction in this excerpt from the letter written by Abigail Adams:

How many are the solitary hours I spend, ruminating upon the past, and anticipating the future, whilst you, overwhelmed with the cares of state, have but a few moments you can devote to any individual.

Writers often communicate **tone,** or attitude toward a subject, through their diction. As you read the letters, notice words and phrases that reveal each writer's attitude toward the issues of liberty and freedom.

READING STRATEGY: READING PRIMARY SOURCES

Primary sources are materials written or made by people who took part in or witnessed the events portrayed. These sources can provide unique insights on a subject. To get the most out of a primary source, consider the following:

- Who was the writer? The age, nationality, and social class of the writer can influence the point of view.
- What is the form of the document: letter, diary, speech? How might the form have affected the content?
- When and where was it written? The time and place of a primary source's writing can provide clues to the culture and history of the period.
- Who is the intended audience? In a private letter to a loved one, a writer might voice thoughts and feelings more freely than in an open letter to a public audience.

For help analyzing the letters of Wheatley and Adams, complete a chart such as the one shown here as you read each letter.

Writer:
Form:
When and Where Written:
Intended Purpose/Audience:

Complete the activities in your **Reader/Writer Notebook**.

Who gets to make the RULES?

Those in authority make the rules for others—whether it's in the halls of Congress or the classroom. The authors of these two letters, while agreeing wholeheartedly with the patriot cause, still felt left out of the process and the benefits of the American Revolution.

DISCUSS People today have not only more freedom than people did in colonial times but also more ways to change the laws. Think of at least three situations in which rules directly impact your life. Then for each situation, discuss ways that are available to change or modify those rules.

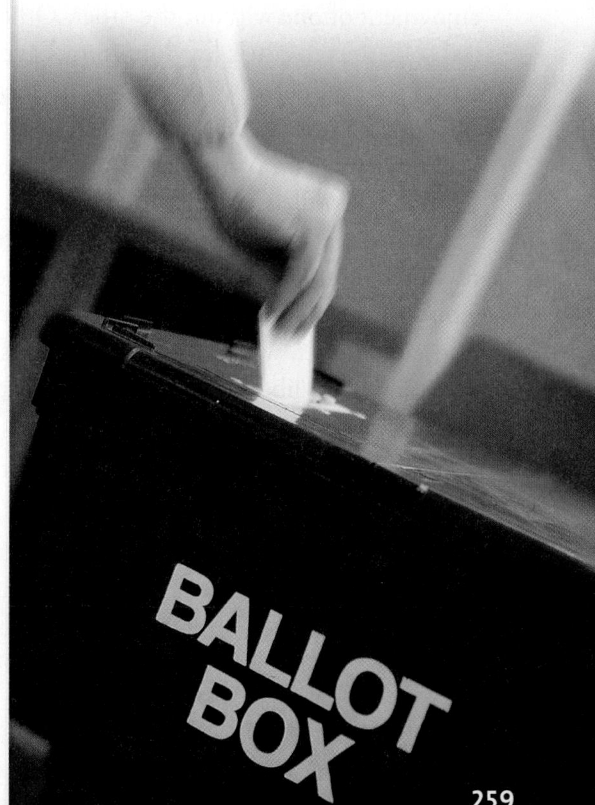

Letter to the Reverend Samson Occom

Phillis Wheatley

BACKGROUND The Reverend Samson Occom was a Mohegan Indian who became a minister after converting to Christianity. In a letter to Phillis Wheatley, he had criticized some of his fellow ministers for owning slaves. Wheatley's response to her friend, dated February 11, 1774, was later published in colonial newspapers.

Reverend and honored sir,

I have this day received your obliging kind epistle, and am greatly satisfied with your reasons respecting the negroes, and think highly reasonable what you offer in vindication of their natural rights: Those that invade them cannot be insensible that the divine light is chasing away the thick darkness which broods over the land of Africa;[1] and the chaos which has reigned so long, is converting into beautiful order, and reveals more and more clearly the glorious dispensation of civil and religious liberty, which are so inseparably united, that there is little or no enjoyment of one without the other: Otherwise, perhaps, the Israelites had been less solicitous for their freedom from Egyptian slavery;[2] I do not say they would have been contented without it, by no means; for in every human breast God has implanted a principle, which we call love of freedom; it is impatient (A) of oppression, and pants for deliverance; and by the leave of our modern Egyptians[3] I will assert, that the same principle lives in us. God grant deliverance in his own way and time, and get him honor upon all those whose avarice impels them to countenance and help forward the calamities of their fellow creatures. This I desire not for their hurt, but to convince them of the strange absurdity of their conduct, whose words and actions are so diametrically opposite. How well the cry for liberty, and the reverse disposition for the exercise of oppressive power over others agree—I humbly think it does not require the penetration[4] of a philosopher to determine.—

Phillis Wheatley

1. **insensible . . . the land of Africa:** unaware that Christianity is spreading throughout Africa.
2. **Israelites . . . Egyptian slavery:** a biblical allusion to the Israelites who were led out of Egypt by Moses.
3. **modern Egyptians:** the owners of African slaves.
4. **penetration:** understanding; insight.

Analyze Visuals ▶

This image shows a slave auction in New Amsterdam (New York). What does this tell you about slavery in colonial America?

(A) DICTION

Describe Wheatley's **diction** in lines 1–11. How might her way of writing have struck white readers at the time?

Language Coach

Word Definitions

Absurdity (line 16) means "unreasonableness," "illogicality," or "stupidity." Wheatley is saying that slave owners are saying one thing and doing another. How do their actions conflict with their words?

First Slave Auction in New Amsterdam, 1655.
The Granger Collection, New York.

Letter to John Adams

Abigail Adams

BACKGROUND In March of 1776, while John Adams was in Philadelphia with other delegates drafting a code of laws for the new independent country, Abigail wrote a letter asking him to "remember the ladies" in the new laws: "Be more generous and favorable to them than your ancestors. Do not put such unlimited power into the hands of husbands." John's response was to laugh and remark, "You are so saucy." The following is the next letter she sent to him.

Braintree, 7, May, 1776

How many are the solitary hours I spend, ruminating upon the past, and anticipating the future, whilst you, overwhelmed with the cares of state, have but a few moments you can devote to any individual. All domestic pleasures and enjoyments are absorbed in the great and important duty you owe your country, "for our country is, as it were, a secondary god, and the first and greatest parent. It is to be preferred to parents, wives, children, friends, and all things, the gods only excepted; for, if our country perishes, it is as impossible to save an individual, as to preserve one of the fingers of a mortified hand." Thus do I suppress every wish, and silence every murmur, acquiescing in a painful separation from the companion of my youth, and the friend of my heart. **B**

I believe 't is near ten days since I wrote you a line. I have not felt in a humor to entertain you if I had taken up my pen. Perhaps some unbecoming invective[1] might have fallen from it. The eyes of our rulers have been closed, and a lethargy has seized almost every member. I fear a fatal security has taken possession of them. Whilst the building is in flames, they tremble at the expense of water to quench it. In short, two months have elapsed since the evacuation of Boston,[2] and very little has been done in that time to secure it, or the harbor, from future

Analyze Visuals ▶
These pastel portraits of Abigail and John Adams were done in 1766, about two years after their marriage. How do these portraits compare with those that might be done today of a young couple?

B PRIMARY SOURCES
Does Adams's letter concern itself with private or public issues in lines 1–10? What does she say about the relationship between the private and the public?

1. **unbecoming invective:** inappropriate abusive language.
2. **two months . . . Boston:** British troops under General William Howe and more than a thousand Loyalists evacuated Boston on March 17, 1776.

invasion. The people are all in a flame, and no one among us, that I have heard of, even mentions expense. They think, universally, that there has been an amazing neglect somewhere. Many have turned out as volunteers to work upon Noddle's Island, and many more would go upon Nantasket,[3] if the business was once set on foot. "'T is a maxim of state, that power and liberty are like heat and moisture. Where they are well mixed, every thing prospers; where they are single, they are destructive."

A government of more stability is much wanted in this colony, and they are ready to receive it from the hands of the Congress. And since I have begun with maxims of state,[4] I will add another, namely, that a people may let a king fall, yet still remain a people; but, if a king let his people slip from him, he is no longer a king.[5] And as this is most certainly our case, why not proclaim to the world, in decisive terms, your own importance? **C**

Shall we not be despised by foreign powers, for hesitating so long at a word?

I cannot say that I think you are very generous to the ladies; for, whilst you are proclaiming peace and good-will to men, emancipating all nations, you insist upon retaining an absolute power over wives. But you must remember, that arbitrary power is like most other things which are very hard, very liable to be broken; and, notwithstanding all your wise laws and maxims, we have it in our power, not only to free ourselves, but to subdue our masters, and, without violence, throw both your natural and legal authority at our feet;—

"Charm by accepting, by submitting sway,
Yet have our humor most when we obey."[6] **D**

I thank you for several letters which I have received since I wrote last; they alleviate a tedious absence, and I long earnestly for a Saturday evening, and experience a similar pleasure to that which I used to find in the return of my friend upon that day after a week's absence. The idea of a year dissolves all my philosophy.

Our little ones, whom you so often recommend to my care and instruction, shall not be deficient in virtue or probity,[7] if the precepts of a mother have their desired effect; but they would be doubly enforced, could they be indulged with the example of a father alternately before them. I often point them to their sire,

"engaged in a corrupted state,
Wrestling with vice and faction."[8] **E**

A. Adams

COMMON CORE L 5

Language Coach

Similes A **simile** is a figure of speech that compares two similar things, using words such as *like* or *as*. What comparison does Adams mention in lines 22–24? How does the comparison express her ideas about the balance between power and liberty?

C DICTION
Reread lines 25–30. How does diction contribute to Adams's tone in these lines? And how does tone help the writer to express her purpose? Cite evidence to support your answer.

D PRIMARY SOURCES
What inconsistency in the attitudes of the times does Abigail Adams point out in lines 32–40?

E DICTION
Reread lines 46–51. What does the formal language used to discuss both public and private matters tell you about family relations at the time?

3. **Noddle's Island . . . Nantasket:** sites near the city of Boston. Noddle's Island is now called East Boston.
4. **maxims of state:** rules or short sayings related to government.
5. **king:** a reference to King George III, who ignored colonists' protests and put Massachusetts under military rule.
6. **"Charm . . . obey":** a couplet taken from Alexander Pope's poem *Moral Essays.*
7. **deficient . . . probity:** lacking in goodness or integrity.
8. **"engaged . . . faction":** lines taken from Joseph Addison's play *Cato.* Cato (234–149 B.C.) was a Roman politician who fought for high moral standards in the Roman Senate.

Comprehension

1. **Recall** What does Phillis Wheatley praise the Reverend Occom for doing?
2. **Clarify** In Wheatley's opinion, what is the cause of slavery?
3. **Recall** Why does Abigail Adams put her country before personal happiness?
4. **Clarify** What is the situation in Massachusetts that Adams complains to her husband about?

Text Analysis

5. **Compare and Contrast** In both letters, Wheatley and Adams reveal their powerlessness to change what they clearly see as wrong. How do they personally deal with this lack of **authority?** Discuss how they cope with the following situations:
   - slavery
   - lack of security due to inaction
   - absolute power of men
6. **Analyze Diction** For each letter, look for examples of diction that reveal the writer's **tone.** Then compare and contrast the tone of each, explaining possible reasons for any differences you find.
7. **Analyze Primary Sources** How are these personal letters letters useful or limited in their historical value? What insights do they provide that more formal documents, such as the Declaration of Independence, do not? How does the identity of the writer influence the content? Draw upon your chart to cite examples from the letters to prove your points.
8. **Evaluate Argument** Each woman makes an argument in her letter: Wheatley against slavery, and Adams against the "arbitrary power" of men. Who presents the stronger case? Cite evidence to support your opinion.

Text Criticism

9. **Historical Context** Personal letters, such as Wheatley's, offer a rare opportunity to hear women's voices from the past. What distinguishes Wheatley's and Adams's writing from the rhetoric of Patrick Henry, Thomas Jefferson, and Tom Paine? What do their letters reveal about how women were expected to behave in early America?

Who gets to make the RULES?

Rules are everywhere—from the laws in government down to the rules at your school or at home. Why are rules and people who are given **authority** to enforce rules important?

COMMON CORE

RI 5 Analyze and evaluate the effectiveness of the structure an author uses in his or her argument. **RI 6** Determine an author's point of view or purpose in a text in which the rhetoric is particularly effective, analyzing how style and content contribute to the power, persuasiveness, or beauty of the text. **RI 9** Analyze documents of historical and literary significance for their themes, purposes, and rhetorical features.

from The Autobiography

by Benjamin Franklin

Video link at thinkcentral.com

COMMON CORE

RI 1 Cite textual evidence to support inferences drawn from the text, including determining where the text leave matters uncertain. **RI 5** Analyze and evaluate the effectiveness of the structure an author uses in his or her exposition. **RI 6** Determine an author's point of view or purpose.

DID YOU KNOW?

Benjamin Franklin . . .

- started the first public library and fire department in America.
- founded what became the University of Pennsylvania.
- invented bifocal eyeglasses.

(background) Page from *Poor Richard's Almanack*

Meet the Author

Benjamin Franklin 1706–1790

Printer, publisher, writer, scientist, inventor, businessman, philosopher, statesman—Benjamin Franklin's numerous roles only hint at the man's tremendous versatility and talent. As the oldest founding father, Franklin had already lived a full life when at the age of 70 he joined 40-year-old John Adams and 33-year-old Thomas Jefferson to draft the Declaration of Independence. Soon afterward, he loaned Congress a large sum of his own money and sailed on a leaky ship to France to arrange for more loans and a crucial alliance to fight the British. His masterly efforts abroad on behalf of the American cause earned him a reputation as one of the most successful American diplomats of all time. Only a few years before he died, his presence at the Constitutional Convention helped unify the delegates. So great was his influence that he is credited with convincing them to approve the final document by a vote of 39 to 3. A man of great integrity, intelligence, and charm, Ben Franklin embodied the best of the new nation and became its first celebrity.

Pulling Himself Up Born in Boston as the youngest of 15 children, Franklin did not want to follow in his father's footsteps to become a candle and soap maker. Instead, he joined his brother in the printing business as an apprentice. With only two years of formal education, Franklin taught himself to write by imitating the great essayists of his day. At the age of 16, he was contributing satirical pieces to his brother's newspaper. By his own account "too saucy and provoking" as a youth, he soon quarreled with his brother and struck out on his own for Philadelphia. Franklin did very well in Philadelphia, prospering in his own printing business, running the successful *Pennsylvania Gazette* newspaper, writing his popular *Poor Richard's Almanack* for 26 years, and being active in colonial politics.

Citizen of the World Franklin's writing—from humorous satires and wise sayings to serious political essays and scientific observations on electricity—as well as his diplomacy and charismatic personality made him an international celebrity. Although respected by the great minds of his age, he never lost his connection to the common people. In the words of John Adams: "His reputation is greater than that of Newton, Frederick the Great or Voltaire, his character more revered than all of them. There's scarcely a coachman or a footman or scullery maid who does not consider him a friend of all mankind."

THINK central

Author Online

Go to thinkcentral.com. KEYWORD: HML11-266

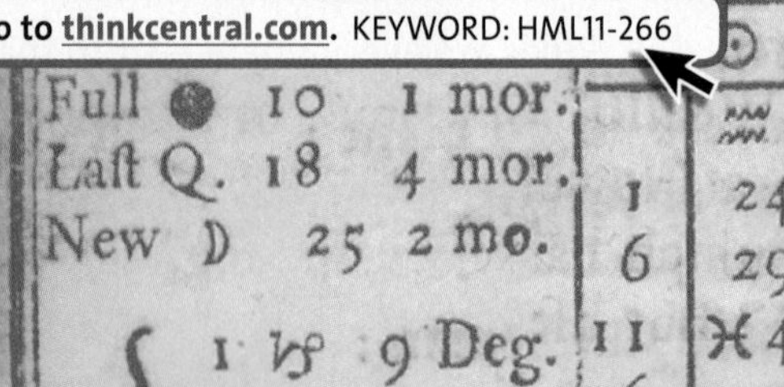

TEXT ANALYSIS: CHARACTERISTICS OF AUTOBIOGRAPHY

An **autobiography** is the story of a person's life, written by that person. As you read this excerpt from Franklin's autobiography, notice the following characteristics of autobiography:

- **First person:** The author of an autobiography usually writes from the first-person point of view.
- **Dual perspective:** Often the author of an autobiography writes as an older person looking back on him- or herself as a younger person, providing opportunities for reflection.
- **Significant moments:** Autobiographies may vary from straightforward chronological accounts to impressionistic narratives. In either case, especially important events and people in the author's life are highlighted.

READING SKILL: MAKE INFERENCES ABOUT THE AUTHOR

Making inferences means "reading between the lines"—making logical guesses based on evidence in the text to figure out what is not directly stated. As you read *The Autobiography,* make inferences about the values and motives that seem characteristic of Franklin's personality. Use a chart like the one shown to record details from the text about the 13 virtues he hopes to acquire and how he goes about doing so. What inferences can you make about him?

Details or Evidence from Text	*Inference*

Review: **Connect**

VOCABULARY IN CONTEXT

Franklin uses the following boldfaced words in describing his efforts to improve himself. Restate each phrase, using a different word or words for the boldfaced term.

1. **unremitting** storms that went on for weeks
2. **felicity** over her great good luck
3. a mansion as one symbol of **affluence**
4. dreamed up an **artifice** to avoid doing his job
5. **incorrigible** behavior that disgraced the family
6. a **trifling** problem, easily cleared up
7. would often **contrive** to secretly meet his friends

Complete the activities in your **Reader/Writer Notebook**.

Is PERFECTION *possible?*

As a young man, Benjamin Franklin believed that human beings could actually achieve perfection in a given area. All you needed was a reasonable plan and a lot of self-discipline. Many people today also aim for perfection, although their quest may take a different path. Bookstores have whole sections devoted to self-improvement in a variety of areas, including diet, exercise, careers, and dating.

QUICKWRITE Do you think perfection is possible or at least worth striving for? If you think so, outline a self-improvement plan that shows how you might achieve your goal. If you don't think perfection is possible, write a paragraph in which you explain why you think it is unattainable.

THE

Autobiography

Benjamin Franklin

BACKGROUND Franklin was a prolific writer, producing volumes of essays, travel journals, newspaper articles, satires, speeches, almanacs, letters, and even ballads. But his great masterpiece was his *Autobiography,* which is still very popular today. The following excerpt details Franklin's plan to achieve moral perfection. He was about 20 years old when he first conceived the idea on one of his long, trans-Atlantic voyages. The plan reveals his faith in reason, order, and human perfectibility, which was typical of 18th-century thought.

It was about this time I conceived the bold and arduous project of arriving at moral perfection. I wished to live without committing any fault at any time; I would conquer all that either natural inclination, custom, or company might lead me into. As I knew, or thought I knew, what was right and wrong, I did not see why I might not always do the one and avoid the other. But I soon found I had undertaken a task of more difficulty than I had imagined. While my care was employed in guarding against one fault, I was often surprised by another; habit took the advantage of inattention; inclination was sometimes too strong for reason. I concluded, at length, that the mere speculative conviction that it was our interest to be completely virtuous, was not sufficient to prevent our slipping; and that the contrary habits must be broken, and good ones acquired and established, before we can have any dependence on a steady, uniform rectitude of conduct. For this purpose I therefore contrived the following method. **A**

In the various enumerations of the moral virtues I had met with in my reading, I found the catalogue more or less numerous, as different writers included more or

Analyze Visuals ▶
What do the details of this famous painting suggest about Franklin?

A AUTOBIOGRAPHY
What characteristics of autobiography do you find in the first paragraph of this selection?

Benjamin Franklin (1767), David Martin. Oil on canvas.
© White House Historical Association, Washington, D.C.

fewer ideas under the same name. Temperance, for example, was by some confined to eating and drinking, while by others it was extended to mean the moderating every other pleasure, appetite, inclination, or passion, bodily or mental, even to our avarice and ambition. I proposed to myself, for the sake of clearness, to use rather more names, with fewer ideas annexed to each, than a few names with more ideas; and I included under thirteen names of virtues all that at that time occurred to me as necessary or desirable, and annexed to each a short precept, which fully expressed the extent I gave to its meaning.

These names of virtues, with their precepts were:

1. **Temperance.** Eat not to dullness; drink not to elevation.
2. **Silence.** Speak not but what may benefit others or yourself; avoid **trifling** conversation.
3. **Order.** Let all your things have their places; let each part of your business have its time.
4. **Resolution.** Resolve to perform what you ought; perform without fail what you resolve.
5. **Frugality.** Make no expense but to do good to others or yourself; *i.e.,* waste nothing.
6. **Industry.** Lose no time; be always employed in something useful; cut off all unnecessary actions.
7. **Sincerity.** Use no hurtful deceit; think innocently and justly; and, if you speak, speak accordingly.
8. **Justice.** Wrong none by doing injuries, or omitting the benefits that are your duty.
9. **Moderation.** Avoid extremes; forbear resenting injuries so much as you think they deserve.
10. **Cleanliness.** Tolerate no uncleanliness in body, clothes, or habitation.
11. **Tranquillity.** Be not disturbed at trifles, or at accidents common or unavoidable.
12. **Chastity.** Rarely use venery but for health or offspring, never to dulness, weakness, or the injury of your own or another's peace or reputation.
13. **Humility.** Imitate Jesus and Socrates.[1] B

My intention being to acquire the *habitude* of all these virtues, I judged it would be well not to distract my attention by attempting the whole at once, but to fix it on one of them at a time; and, when I should be master of that, then to proceed to another, and so on, till I should have gone through the thirteen; and, as the previous acquisition of some might facilitate the acquisition of certain others, I arranged them with that view, as they stand above. Temperance first, as it tends to

Language Coach

Conciseness in Writing Franklin's precepts (following line 24) are concise, or brief and clear. Reread lines 19–23, and explain Franklin's reasons for giving concise explanations of the virtues. Why are fewer words more effective?

trifling (trī′flĭng) *adj.* frivolous; inconsequential
trifle *v.*

B MAKE INFERENCES Based on Franklin's list of virtues, what inference can you make about his view of his own moral character? Explain.

---

1. **Socrates** (sŏk′rə-tēz′): Greek philosopher (470?–399 B.C.) who believed that true knowledge comes through dialogue and systematic questioning of ideas; he was executed for his beliefs.

procure that coolness and clearness of head, which is so necessary where constant vigilance was to be kept up, and guard maintained against the **unremitting** attraction of ancient habits, and the force of perpetual temptations. This being acquired and established, Silence would be more easy; and my desire being to gain knowledge at the same time that I improved in virtue, and considering that in conversation it was obtained rather by the use of the ears than of the tongue, and therefore wishing to break a habit I was getting into of prattling, punning, and joking, which only made me acceptable to trifling company, I gave *Silence* the second place. This and the next, *Order,* I expected would allow me more time for attending to my project and my studies. *Resolution,* once become habitual, would keep me firm in my endeavors to obtain all the subsequent virtues; *Frugality* and Industry freeing me from my remaining debt, and producing **affluence** and independence, would make more easy the practice of Sincerity and Justice, etc., etc. Conceiving then, that, agreeably to the advice of Pythagoras in his Golden Verses,[2] daily examination would be necessary, I **contrived** the following method for conducting that examination. **C**

unremitting (ŭn′rĭ-mĭt′ĭng) *adj.* constant; never stopping

affluence (ăf′lo͞o-əns) *n.* wealth

contrive (kən-trīv′) *v.* to plan skillfully; to design

C **MAKE INFERENCES**
What can you infer from lines 25–46 about Franklin's approach to problems?

I made a little book, in which I allotted a page for each of the virtues. I ruled each page with red ink, so as to have seven columns, one for each day of the week, marking each column with a letter for the day. I crossed these columns with thirteen red lines, marking the beginning of each line with the first letter of one of the virtues, on which line, and in its proper column, I might mark, by a little black spot, every fault I found upon examination to have been committed respecting that virtue upon that day.

Form of the pages.

TEMPERANCE							
eat not to dullness; drink not to elevation.							
	S.	M.	T.	W.	T.	F.	S.
T.							
S.	•	•		•		•	
O.	••	•	•		•	•	•
R.			•			•	
F.		•			•		
I.			•	•			
S.							
J.							
M.							
C.							
T.							
C.							
H.							

I determined to give a week's strict attention to each of the virtues successively. Thus, in the first week, my great guard was to avoid every[3] the least offense against *Temperance,* leaving the other virtues to their ordinary chance, only marking every evening the faults of the day. Thus, if in the first week I could keep my first line, marked T, clear of spots, I supposed the habit of that virtue so much strengthened, and its opposite weakened, that I might venture extending my attention to include the next, and for the following week keep both lines clear of spots. Proceeding

Language Coach

Easily Confused Words
Although *successively* (line 59) and *successfully* sound and look similar, their meanings are different. *Successively* means "following in order, one after another." *Successfully* means "with the result of achieving a goal." Use each word in a sentence to explain Franklin's plan for perfection.

2. **Pythagoras** (pĭ-thăg′ər-əs)**... Golden Verses:** Pythagoras was a Greek philosopher and mathematician (580?–500? B.C.).

3. **every:** even.

thus to the last, I could go through a course complete in thirteen weeks, and four courses in a year. And like him who, having a garden to weed, does not attempt to eradicate all the bad herbs at once, which would exceed his reach and his strength, but works on one of the beds at a time, and, having accomplished the first, proceeds to a second, so I should have, I hoped, the encouraging pleasure of seeing on my pages the progress I made in virtue, by clearing successively my lines of their spots, till in the end, by a number of courses, I should be happy in viewing a clean book, after thirteen weeks' daily examination. . . . **D**

D AUTOBIOGRAPHY
In what way do lines 47–80 provide an example of Franklin's **dual perspective?**

The precept of *Order* requiring that *every part of my business should have its allotted time,* one page in my little book contained the following scheme of employment for the twenty-four hours of a natural day.

	Hours	
The Morning. *Question.* What good shall I do this day?	5 6 7	Rise, wash, and address *Powerful Goodness!* Contrive day's business, and take the resolution of the day; prosecute the present study, and breakfast.
	8 9 10 11	Work.
Noon.	12 1	Read, or overlook my accounts, and dine.
	2 3 4 5	Work.
Evening. *Question.* What good have I done today?	6 7 8 9	Put things in their places. Supper. Music or diversion, or conversation. Conversation. Examination of the day.
Night.	10 11 12 1 2 3 4	Sleep.

I entered upon the execution of this plan for self-examination, and continued it with occasional intermissions for some time. I was surprised to find myself so much fuller of faults than I had imagined; but I had the satisfaction of seeing them diminish. To avoid the trouble of renewing now and then my little book, which, by scraping out the marks on the paper of old faults to make room for new ones in a new course, became full of holes, I transferred my tables and precepts to the ivory leaves of a memorandum book, on which the lines were drawn with red ink, that made a durable stain, and on those lines I marked my faults with a black-lead pencil, which marks I could easily wipe out with a wet sponge. After a while I went through one course only in a year, and afterward only one in several years, till at length I omitted them entirely, being employed in voyages and business abroad, with a multiplicity of affairs that interfered; but I always carried my little book with me. **E**

E MAKE INFERENCES
Reread lines 84–95. What can you infer about Franklin's persistence in pursuing his goals?

My scheme of *Order* gave me the most trouble; and I found that, though it might be practicable where a man's business was such as to leave him the disposition of his time, that of a journeyman printer, for instance, it was not possible to be exactly observed by a master, who must mix with the world, and often receive people of business at their own hours. *Order,* too, with regard to places for things, papers, etc., I found extremely difficult to acquire. I had not been early accustomed to it, and, having an exceeding good memory, I was not so sensible of the inconvenience attending want of method. This article, therefore, cost me so much painful attention, and my faults in it vexed me so much, and I made so little progress in amendment, and had such frequent relapses, that I was almost ready to give up the attempt, and content myself with a faulty character in that respect, like the man who, in buying an ax of a smith, my neighbor, desired to have the whole of its surface as bright as the edge. The smith consented to grind it bright for him if he would turn the wheel; he turned, while the smith pressed the broad face of the ax hard and heavily on the stone, which made the turning of it very fatiguing. The man came every now and then from the wheel to see how the work went on, and at length would take his ax as it was, without farther grinding. "No," said the smith, "turn on, turn on; we shall have it bright by-and-by; as yet, it is only speckled." "Yes," says the man, *"but I think I like a speckled ax best."* And I believe this may have been the case with many, who, having, for want of some such means as I employed, found the difficulty of obtaining good and breaking bad habits in other points of vice and virtue, have given up the struggle, and concluded that *"a speckled ax was best;"* for something, that pretended to be reason, was every now and then suggesting to me that such extreme nicety as I exacted of myself might be a kind of foppery in morals,[4] which, if it were known, would make me ridiculous; that a perfect character might be attended with the inconvenience of being envied and hated; and that a benevolent man should allow a few faults in himself, to keep his friends in countenance. **F**

F CONNECT
What insight does Franklin come to about his quest for perfection? Consider what you have learned in your own life about perfection. Does his insight seem reasonable?

In truth, I found myself **incorrigible** with respect to Order; and now I am grown old, and my memory bad, I feel very sensibly the want of it. But, on the whole, though I never arrived at the perfection I had been so ambitious of

incorrigible (ĭn-kôr′ĭ-jə-bəl) *adj.* incapable of being reformed or corrected

4. **foppery in morals:** excessive regard for and concern about one's moral appearance.

obtaining, but fell short of it, yet I was, by the endeavor, a better and a happier man than I otherwise should have been if I had not attempted it; as those who aim at perfect writing by imitating the engraved copies, though they never reach the wished-for excellence of those copies, their hand is mended by the endeavor, and is tolerable while it continues fair and legible. G

It may well be my posterity should be informed that to this little **artifice,** with the blessing of God, their ancestor owed the constant **felicity** of his life, down to his 79th year, in which this is written. What reverses may attend the reminder is in the hand of Providence; but, if they arrive, the reflection on past happiness enjoyed ought to help his bearing them with more resignation. To Temperance he ascribes his long-continued health, and what is still left to him of a good constitution; to Industry and Frugality, the early easiness of his circumstances and acquisition of his fortune, with all that knowledge that enabled him to be a useful citizen, and obtained for him some degree of reputation among the learned; to Sincerity and Justice, the confidence of his country, and the honorable employs it conferred upon him; and to the joint influence of the whole mass of the virtues, even in the the imperfect state he was able to acquire them, all that evenness of temper, and that cheerfulness in conversation, which makes his company still sought for, and agreeable even to his younger acquaintance. I hope, therefore, that some of my descendants may follow the example and reap the benefit.

G AUTOBIOGRAPHY
What **significant moment** or insight is described in this paragraph?

artifice (är'tə-fĭs) *n.* a clever means to an end

felicity (fĭ-lĭs'ĭ-tē) *n.* great happiness

from Poor Richard's Almanack

BENJAMIN FRANKLIN

He that cannot obey cannot command.

Don't count your chickens before they are hatched.

A mob's a monster; heads enough but no brains.

Well done is better than well said.

Lost time is never found again.

Early to bed, early to rise, makes a man healthy, wealthy and wise.

If you would know the worth of money, go and try to borrow some.

A friend in need is a friend indeed.

Fish and visitors smell in three days.

Love your neighbor; yet don't pull down your hedge.

God helps them that help themselves.

If you would keep your secret from an enemy, tell it not to a friend.

Be slow in choosing a friend, slower in changing.

Don't throw stones at your neighbors', if your own windows are glass.

Eat to live and not live to eat.

Love your enemies, for they tell you your faults.

Better slip with foot than tongue.

Three may keep a secret, if two of them are dead.

Never leave that till tomorrow, which you can do today.

A penny saved is a penny earned.

A rolling stone gathers no moss.

Make hay while the sun shines.

Beware of little expenses; a small leak will sink a great ship.

He that goes a borrowing goes a sorrowing.

Honesty is the best policy.

Little strokes fell big oaks.

He that lies down with dogs shall rise up with fleas.

Comprehension

1. **Recall** Who are Franklin's models for the virtue of humility?
2. **Clarify** Why does Franklin list the virtues in the order he does?
3. **Summarize** What is Franklin's method for acquiring the 13 virtues?

Text Analysis

4. **Make Inferences About the Author** Look at the details and inferences you recorded in your chart. Now assign each of Franklin's 13 virtues to one of the following categories. What can you infer about Franklin's beliefs and values in general from his list of virtues?
   - healthful living
   - succeeding in the world
   - getting along with others
5. **Analyze Autobiography** Like most autobiographies, Franklin's has a dual perspective in which he is both main character and narrator. Go back through the excerpt to find characterizations of Franklin as a young man and as an older man looking back on his life. Record your answers in two charts as shown. What differences do you find?

Young Franklin	
Character Trait	*Evidence in Text*
1. Ambitious	*1. "I conceived the bold and arduous project of arriving at moral perfection." (lines 1–2)*
2.	

Old Franklin	
Character Trait	*Evidence in Text*
1. Honest	*1. "In truth, I found myself incorrigible with respect to Order; and now I am grown old, . . . I feel very sensibly the want of it." (lines 124–125)*
2.	

6. **Analyze Aphorisms** Franklin wrote many **aphorisms**—brief, clever statements that make wise observations about life. How might Franklin's aphorisms have helped him and others come closer to perfection?

Text Criticism

7. **Critical Interpretations** Some critics consider Franklin self-righteous and materialistic; others have ridiculed his plan for moral perfection as regimented and superficial. Do you find any evidence for these charges in the excerpt? Explain.

Is PERFECTION *possible?*

Although Franklin worked diligently, he never reached perfection in all facets of his life. In what areas have you tried to reach perfection? How would you rate your efforts at **self-improvement**?

COMMON CORE

RI 1 Cite textual evidence to support inferences drawn from the text, including determining where the text leave matters uncertain. **RI 5** Analyze and evaluate the effectiveness of the structure an author uses in his or her exposition. **RI 6** Determine an author's point of view or purpose.

Vocabulary in Context

▲ VOCABULARY PRACTICE

Show your understanding of the vocabulary words by answering these questions.

1. Which would cause **felicity,** doing well on a test or having trouble sleeping?
2. If someone created an **artifice,** would that person be shrewd or naïve?
3. To **contrive,** would you act impulsively or by plan?
4. Who is more likely **incorrigible,** a person with five parking tickets or one with five burglary convictions?
5. Is a **trifling** problem one you should ignore or act on immediately?
6. If you wanted to hide your **affluence,** would you probably drive an inexpensive car or take a trip around the world?
7. Is a person with **unremitting** joy constantly happy or never happy?

WORD LIST

affluence
artifice
contrive
felicity
incorrigible
trifling
unremitting

ACADEMIC VOCABULARY IN WRITING

• document • illustrate • interpret • promote • reveal

Some people have **interpreted** Benjamin Franklin's autobiography in a negative light. Write a short paragraph discussing the kind of lifestyle Franklin **promoted.** In your paper, also discuss how close you think most people come to meeting his expectations. Use at least three Academic Vocabulary words in your writing.

VOCABULARY STRATEGY: COGNATES IN DIFFERENT LANGUAGES

The Romance languages—French, Italian, and Spanish—developed from Latin. Although English is not one of the Romance languages, many English words did originate in Latin. When words in different languages are descended from the same language and have similar or identical spellings and meanings, they are called cognates. For example, the spelling of "animal" is exactly the same in English and Spanish. The English word "rose" has a similar spelling, "rosa," in Spanish.

COMMON CORE

L 6 Demonstrate independence in gathering vocabulary knowledge when considering a word or phrase important to comprehension or expression.

PRACTICE Identify the English cognate of each of the following Spanish words. Then write an English sentence using the English word.

1. tecnología
2. novela
3. diccionario
4. arrogante
5. fotographia

Reading for Information

MAGAZINE ARTICLE Benjamin Franklin's drive for self-improvement may seem a little excessive, but it remains a great American ideal. This article looks at the continuing American urge to change oneself for the better.

50 Ways to Fix Your Life

by Carolyn Kleiner Butler

Americans have long been captivated by the notion of self-improvement—none more so than Benjamin Franklin. An accomplished printer, author, postmaster, scientist, inventor, and diplomat who taught himself to speak five languages, this Founding Father "conceiv'd the bold and arduous project of arriving at moral perfection."

Today, self-help is not just a way of life—it's practically a national obsession. There are 7,500 books on the topic on amazon.com alone, covering just about every imaginable bad habit or dilemma.

Such offerings "appeal to the deeply felt American idea of 'before and after,'" says Robert Thompson, professor of media and popular culture at Syracuse University in New York, who points out the underlying similarities between Franklin and, say, Dr. Phil. "If you were born a peasant in a medieval village, you knew who you were and it was very hard to change that, but here there is fluidity of class, and entire industries pop up that reflect the ultimate optimism that really anybody can be a 'swan' and completely turn [his or her] life around."

Time to change. The hard truth is that lasting change doesn't usually happen in a single TV season. In reality, of the 40 to 45 percent of people who will make New Year's resolutions come January, fewer than half will succeed within six months, according to John Norcross, professor of psychology at the University of Scranton in Pennsylvania and coauthor of *Changing for Good.* But the fact is that when someone makes a serious commitment to transform his or her life, it is possible.

How can you cross that far-off finish line? First and foremost, you really have to be ready to do it and understand that the pros outweigh the cons. Also, research shows that keeping track of your development in a visible way—charting your weight loss, for one, or graphing your heart rate and stamina—is associated with sustainable lifestyle change, as is social support, whether in the form of friends, online discussion groups, or reliable, proven, self-help books.

Lastly, and most important, don't give up if you tumble off the wagon now and then. Triumphant changers often see a setback as a reason to recommit to their goal, and they get back on the horse immediately.

In the end, simply making a concerted effort to improve your lifestyle can have lasting benefits, no matter what the final result. Indeed, Franklin recounts, "On the whole, tho' I never arrived at . . . perfection . . . I was, by the endeavour, a better and happier man than I otherwise should have been if I had not attempted it."

Revolutionary Ideas

For colonists living in the 1770s, there was one topic around which most conversation and writing revolved: the Revolution. The writing of this period was political, and it was persuasive. It had a life-and-death purpose: to win over the hearts and minds of American colonists—and the rest of the world—to the belief that rebellion was necessary.

Writing to Persuade

Reflect briefly on each of the pieces you have just read, and select two you find particularly persuasive. Then, imagine you are a colonist of the time and write a letter to your local paper in which you voice your support for the ideas of the writers chosen. Be sure to cite specific phrases or lines that you find convincing. Add your own thoughts and opinions to try to further persuade readers to support the rebellion.

Consider

- thought-provoking or incendiary sentences or passages
- your opinions on the issues discussed in the selections
- how to express your viewpoint clearly and convincingly

Extension

SPEAKING & LISTENING

Imagine yourself on the village green, part of an impassioned gathering of colonists arguing both sides of independence from England. Recast your letter as a **speech** and deliver it to your friends, neighbors, and political opponents.

COMMON CORE

RI 9 Analyze eighteenth-century foundational U.S. documents of historical and literary significance for their themes, purposes, and rhetorical features. **W 1** Write arguments to support claims in an analysis of substantive texts, using valid reasoning and relevant and sufficient evidence. **SL 4** Present information, findings, and supporting evidence, conveying a clear and distinct perspective.

Give Me Liberty or Give Me Death. Patrick Henry delivering his great speech on the *Rights of the Colonies* before the Virginia Assembly, Richmond, March 23, 1775. The Granger Collection, New York.

Persuasive Essay

You have seen how some of our country's founding fathers crafted arguments to support their **claims**, or positions, and to persuade readers to think a certain way. In this workshop, you will have the opportunity to assert a claim by writing a persuasive essay.

Complete the workshop activities in your **Reader/Writer Notebook.**

WRITE WITH A PURPOSE

WRITING TASK

Write a **persuasive essay** that argues a strong claim on an issue. Support your claim with reasons and evidence that will convince your audience to think or act in a certain way toward an issue that interests you.

Idea Starters

- an issue of interest to people in your school or community
- an issue involving the environment or social justice
- an issue about the freedoms and responsibilities of the media

THE ESSENTIALS

Here are some common purposes, audiences, and formats for persuasive writing.

PURPOSES	AUDIENCES	FORMATS
• to persuade people to agree with your claim • to motivate others to take action	• classmates and teacher • parents • community members • school board • customer service department • Web users	• essay for class • editorial • speech • commercial/PSA • message-board posting • business proposal • blog

COMMON CORE TRAITS

1. DEVELOPMENT OF IDEAS

- introduces a **precise, knowledgeable claim** and establishes its **significance**
- provides **valid reasons** and **relevant evidence** to support the claim
- acknowledges **opposing claims** and refutes them with **counterclaims**
- offers a **concluding section** that follows from and supports the claim

2. ORGANIZATION OF IDEAS

- **organizes** the claim, counterclaims, reasons, and evidence in a **logical sequence**
- uses varied **transitions**—words, phrases, and clauses—to create **cohesion** and **clarify relationships** among ideas

3. LANGUAGE FACILITY AND CONVENTIONS

- maintains a **formal style** and an **objective, authoritative tone**
- employs correct **grammar**, **mechanics**, and **spelling**

Planning/Prewriting

W 1a–e Write arguments to support claims with valid reasoning and relevant evidence. **W 5** Develop writing by planning. **W 7** Conduct short research projects; synthesize multiple sources. **W 8** Gather relevant information from authoritative sources.

Getting Started

CHOOSE A SUBSTANTIVE ISSUE

Make a list of issues that interest you and might interest others. Select a **substantive issue**—one that you feel strongly about and can make a convincing argument for or against. The issue should be something reasonable people can disagree about—there's no point in arguing, for example, that cars should stop at school crosswalks.

TIPS

To find out about important issues, you could try the following:

- Talk to friends, classmates, or parents.
- Read your local newspaper.
- Attend school council meetings, school board meetings, or city or town meetings.

THINK ABOUT AUDIENCE AND PURPOSE

Your **purpose** in writing a persuasive essay is to convince your **audience** to share your position on an issue and to take action. To convince your audience, you need to understand their background and perspective on the topic. Think about their concerns, values, and possible biases. Then you can choose the reasons and evidence that will be most convincing to them. To get your audience involved in your topic, be sure to establish the **significance** of viewpoint—why it should matter to them.

ASK YOURSELF:

- Who will read my essay?
- What interest do my readers have in the issue?
- How do my readers currently feel about the issue? How do I know?
- What reasons might readers have for opposing my claim?

STATE YOUR CLAIM

Every issue has at least two sides—for it and against it. As a writer, you need to adopt a viewpoint on the issue and confidently state your position in a **precise claim**. Make sure your claim is a statement that you can prove and support with valid reasons and evidence. If you discover that your claim can't be supported easily, then you should rework it. Using a graphic organizer may help you clearly state your claim.

WHAT DOES IT LOOK LIKE?

The Issue	Viewpoint	Claim
Cell phone use while driving	People should not be allowed to use cell phones while they drive.	Using cell phones—even hands-free models—to talk or send messages while driving must be banned now.

Planning/Prewriting *continued*

Getting Started

GATHER SUPPORT FOR YOUR CLAIM

Strong **reasons** tell why you believe what you do. They are **logical,** or clearly and directly in support of your claim. Each reason should be supported by **evidence** that is **relevant,** or strongly tied to your issue. Types of evidence include facts and statistics, examples, anecdotes (short personal stories), expert opinions, quotations, and commonly accepted beliefs.

To support your reasons, you will use evidence from both primary and secondary sources. Because a **primary source** is a document written by someone directly involved in an issue or event, it may be stronger and more authoritative than a **secondary source,** which is created later based on primary sources.

Be sure to evaluate your sources for:

- **accuracy**—Is the information correct?
- **credibility**—Can the source be trusted as authoritative?

As you gather support, synthesize the information you find. When you **synthesize,** you make connections between a variety of sources and your prior knowledge in order to draw original conclusions about your issue.

WHAT DOES IT LOOK LIKE?

Claim

"Using cell phones—even hands-free models—to talk or send messages while driving must be banned now."

Reason

When people talk or send messages on cell phones while driving, they endanger their own lives and the lives of others.

Evidence [expert opinion]

"It's absolutely clear from the research literature that talking or sending messages on a cell phone while driving does elevate the risk of a crash," said Dr. Donald Reinfurt.

ANTICIPATE READER CONCERNS

Some readers may have a claim that opposes your viewpoint. Anticipate their opposing claims and address them by providing a **counterclaim,** which is a statement that refutes their claim and explains why your viewpoint is more valid. Think of arguments you could develop to counter these claims.

WHAT DOES IT LOOK LIKE?

Opposing Claim: *People with limited time need to use their phones while they're driving.*

Counterclaim: *While their time may be limited, they would lose a lot more time if they were injured in an accident.*

PEER REVIEW Explain to a peer the claim you intend to assert and the evidence you are using to support your claim. Then ask: What other sources could I consult to provide accurate and credible information? What new approach could I take to strengthen my claim?

In your *Reader/Writer Notebook,* create graphic organizers like the ones on this page to plan your claim, reasons, evidence, and counterclaims.

W 4 Produce clear and coherent writing appropriate to task, purpose, and audience. **W 9b (RI 1)** Cite textual evidence. **L 3** Apply knowledge of language to make effective choices for meaning and style.

Drafting

The following chart shows a structure for organizing an effective persuasive essay.

Organizing Your Persuasive Essay

INTRODUCTION

- Grab the audience's attention with an engaging **fact, statistic,** or **anecdote.**
- Identify the issue and state your position in a **precise, knowledgeable claim.**
- Establish the **significance of the claim.**

BODY

- Present your reasons in a **logical sequence,** such as order of importance.
- Support each reason with **relevant** and **sufficient evidence.**
- Fairly address **opposing claims** and provide **well-supported counterclaims.** Acknowledge the strengths and limitations of your claim and counterclaims.
- Use transitions to create **cohesion,** or flow, and to **clarify relationships** among your ideas. **Vary your syntax** by using a mix of short and long, simple and complex sentences.
- Maintain a **formal style** by using an **objective,** or controlled, **tone.** Avoid being defensive or dismissive of other viewpoints.

CONCLUDING SECTION

- Restate your **claim.**
- End with a **call to action**—tell readers to do something if they agree with your position.

GRAMMAR IN CONTEXT: PARALLEL STRUCTURE

One technique you can use to emphasize your reasons and create cohesion is **parallel structure,** stating related ideas in similar grammatical ways. Use parallel structure when you coordinate ideas, compare or contrast ideas, or link ideas with correlative conjunctions such as these:

both . . . and *either . . . or* *neither . . . nor* *not only . . . but also*

In this example, notice how parallel structure links the variety of activities people can do while talking on a cell phone:

> People talk on the phone while watching a ballgame, while washing the dishes, and while driving to work.

Use the information in the chart to draft your persuasive essay. Include at least one instance of parallel structure to enhance your argument.

Revising

When you revise, you evaluate the content, development, and style of your persuasive essay. Your goal is to determine if you've achieved your purpose and effectively communicated your ideas to the intended audience. The questions, tips, and strategies in the following chart can help you revise or rewrite where necessary.

PERSUASIVE ESSAY

Ask Yourself	*Tips*	*Revision Strategies*
1. Do I capture the audience's attention in my opening lines and introduce a precise, knowledgeable claim?	**Bracket** interesting statements or thought-provoking questions. **Underline** the claim.	**Add** an attention-getting statement or quotation. **Add** your claim, or **replace** the claim with a stronger one.
2. Are there at least two valid reasons that support my claim? Is there relevant evidence to support each reason?	**Highlight** the reasons that support the claim. **Circle** the evidence that supports each reason. **Draw an arrow** from the evidence to the reason.	If necessary, **add** valid reasons to support the claim. **Add** examples, anecdotes, or quotations to bolster unsupported reasons. **Elaborate** on pieces of evidence by adding more details or explanation.
3. Do I acknowledge opposing claims and present counterclaims?	**Draw a wavy** line under the opposing claims and your responses to them.	If necessary, **add** counterclaims that acknowledge the merits of your opinion and the limitations of opposing claims.
4. Are the counterclaims, reasons, and evidence in a logical sequence?	**Number** your reasons to reflect your ranking of their strength (1 = strongest, etc.).	If your strongest reason isn't last or first, **reorder** your reasons and evidence for emphasis.
5. Do I use transitions to clarify the relationships among my claim, counterclaims, reasons, and evidence?	**Draw a star** next to each transitional word or phrase.	**Check** your starred transitions and **add** variety if necessary. **Reread** the parts that lack stars. **Add** appropriate transitions to link related ideas.
6. Does the concluding section restate my claim and give the reader something to think about?	**Put a check mark** next to the restatement. **Underline** the sentence that leaves the reader with an important insight or observation.	**Add** a restatement of the claim if it is missing. **Add** a thought-provoking question or statement about human nature.

PEER REVIEW Working with a peer, review your drafts together. Answer each question in the chart to decide how to improve your drafts and where to try a new approach. Use the strategies to help you strengthen your argument.

COMMON CORE

W 5 Develop and strengthen writing as needed by revising, editing, rewriting, or trying a new approach, focusing on how well purpose and audience have been addressed.

ANALYZE A STUDENT DRAFT

Read this student draft, and notice the comments on its strengths as well as the suggestions for improvement.

Cell Phone Use in Cars: Hang Up—Don't Bang Up!

by Bruce Lomibao, Plainview High School

A **memorable title** identifies the issue.

1 Something dangerous is happening around you. Every time a motorist talks on a cellular phone, that person is endangering his or her own life and the lives of others. Using cell phones—even hands-free models—to talk or send messages while driving must be banned now.

Bruce needs to revise the introduction to grab his audience's interest.

In the introduction, Bruce clearly states his **claim** on this issue.

2 A study by the Cellular Telecommunications & Internet Association found that more than 200 million Americans use cellular telephones. People talk on the phone while watching a ballgame, washing the dishes, or driving to work. Although talking on a cell phone distracts people in each case, this distraction can have serious consequences for drivers.

3 According to a study conducted by Dr. Donald Reinfurt of the University of North Carolina's Highway Safety Research Center, about one of every 600 driving accidents involved a cell phone. However, Reinfurt believes that "cell phones are involved in many more crashes" because most drivers won't admit they were on the phone. "Using a cell phone while driving is extremely dangerous," said Martha Kramer, whose son caused a car accident while talking on his cell phone. According to a study of drivers in Canada, "the risk of a collision when using a cellular telephone was four times higher than the risk when a cellular telephone was not being used."

Relevant and convincing **evidence,** including an expert opinion and a statistic, add **support** to Bruce's claim.

LEARN HOW **Grab the Audience's Attention** Bruce's first sentence may somewhat interest the audience, but it isn't descriptive enough to draw the reader fully into the essay. Bruce should add a startling fact, statistic, or anecdote to grab the audience's attention.

BRUCE'S REVISION TO PARAGRAPH 1

Picture this: a man gets into a car, puts on a blindfold, starts the engine, puts his foot on the gas, and takes his hands off the wheel. That would never happen, you say? Maybe not, but something just as dangerous is happening around you every day.

~~Something dangerous is happening around you.~~ Every time a motorist talks on a cellular phone, that person is endangering his or her own life and the lives of others.

ANALYZE A STUDENT DRAFT *continued*

4 Despite these statistics, some people may say their time is so valuable that they need to talk while driving. What they don't consider is how much time they'd lose if they were injured—or worse—in a car accident. Others might argue that if lawmakers ban cell-phone use, they will also have to ban distractions such as eating and listening to music. However, the Insurance Information Institute reports that "there is increasing evidence that the dangers associated with cell-phone use outweigh those of other distractions."

Bruce gives an accurate and honest representation of **opposing claims.** He then addresses each opposing claim with a **counterclaim.**

5 Obviously more people are noticing this problem, but what is being done about it? Nearly 50 countries have banned or restricted the use of cell phones while driving. Here in the U.S., several states prohibit all drivers from using handheld phones for talking or texting, and over half of the states restrict the use of cell phones by inexperienced drivers. Many other states and the federal government are considering legislation related to cell phones and driving.

6 You could be the next victim of a driver distracted by a cell-phone conversation. So before that happens, remember: "Hang up—don't bang up!"

Bruce restates his position in his concluding section, but he fails to include a **call to action.**

LEARN HOW **Include a Call to Action** The purposes of writing an argument are to persuade an audience to agree with a position and to motivate this audience to take action. An argument's body should persuade the audience to agree with the position, and the concluding section should include an obvious **call to action.**

BRUCE'S REVISION TO PARAGRAPH 6

You could be the next victim of a driver distracted by a cell-phone conversation. So before that happens, remember: "Hang up—don't bang up!" ^

Send letters or e-mails to your local, state, and federal legislators urging them to ban the use of cell phones in cars. Do it today.

Use the feedback from your peers and teacher, the revision strategies chart, and the two "Learn How" lessons to revise your persuasive essay. Evaluate how well your essay convinces readers to act on the issue through valid reasons, relevant and sufficient evidence, and a strong call to action.

Editing and Publishing

W 5 Develop and strengthen writing as needed by revising, editing, rewriting, or trying a new approach, focusing on how well purpose and audience have been addressed. **L 2b** Spell correctly.

In the editing stage, you proofread your essay to make sure that it is free of grammar, spelling, and punctuation errors. Careless spelling mistakes make you sound less authoritative to your audience. Read your essay slowly and carefully to correct any lingering misspelled words.

GRAMMAR IN CONTEXT: ESTABLISHING TONE

One of your goals in persuasive writing is to establish a **tone** of authority so that your readers take your arguments as seriously as you do. The strength of your argument can be compromised if you don't use accurate, credible sources. Whether you use a **primary source** or **secondary source,** you should always check that the information comes from a credible person or place. Use the following tips when examining primary and secondary sources to determine their suitability for citing in a convincing, authoritative essay:

- Online sources with addresses that end in *.edu* or *.gov* are generally more reliable than other sites. If you use sources with other endings, such as *.org* or *.com,* check to make sure the site was created by a trustworthy organization.
- When obtaining information from a book or magazine, be sure that the book, magazine, or newspaper was published recently.
- Always check the background of the source's author. The author should have the experience necessary to relay credible information or a valid opinion.

Notice how Bruce revised his essay to include a more credible source. This revision helps Bruce to strengthen the authoritative tone of his argument.

~~"Using a cell phone while driving is extremely dangerous," said Martha Kramer, whose son caused a car accident while talking on his cell phone.~~

"It's absolutely clear from the research literature that talking on a cell phone while driving does elevate the risk of a crash," said Dr. Reinfurt.

PUBLISH YOUR WRITING

Share your persuasive essay with an audience.

- Publish your argument as an editorial for your school or local newspaper.
- Post a blog for people interested in the subject matter of the essay.
- Develop your essay into a persuasive speech to present to your class.

Correct any errors in your essay by carefully proofreading it. Check that you have included accurate, credible sources and that you have assured your audience of their validity and reliability. Then, publish your final essay.

Scoring Rubric

Use the rubric below to evaluate your persuasive essay from the Writing Workshop or your response to the on-demand task on the next page.

PERSUASIVE ESSAY

SCORE	COMMON CORE TRAITS
6	• **Development** Asserts a precise, knowledgeable claim; supports the claim with valid reasons and relevant, sufficient evidence; fairly and thoroughly counters opposing claims with counterclaims; ends powerfully • **Organization** Has a logical, persuasive sequence; uses transitions to create cohesion and show the relationships among the claim, reasons, and evidence • **Language** Consistently maintains a formal style and objective, authoritative tone; shows a strong command of conventions
5	• **Development** States a precise, knowledgeable claim; offers valid reasons and relevant evidence; fairly counters opposing claims with counterclaims; ends with a strong concluding section • **Organization** Is logically sequenced; uses transitions to show the relationships among the claim, reasons, and evidence • **Language** Uses a formal style and objective tone; has a few errors in conventions
4	• **Development** States a precise claim; offers mostly valid support; needs to more fairly address opposing claims; has an adequate concluding section • **Organization** Reflects a logical sequence, with one or two exceptions; could use a few more transitions • **Language** Mostly uses a formal style, but sounds defensive at times; includes a few distracting errors in conventions
3	• **Development** States a vague claim; provides some relevant support but not enough; unfairly dismisses other viewpoints; concludes somewhat weakly • **Organization** Has some flaws in organization; needs more transitions to link ideas • **Language** Often lapses into an informal style or indecisive tone; has several errors in conventions
2	• **Development** Has an uninformed claim; offers irrelevant reasons and insufficient evidence; fails to acknowledge other viewpoints; has a weak concluding section • **Organization** Has major organizational flaws; lacks transitions throughout • **Language** Uses an informal style and indecisive tone; has many errors in conventions
1	• **Development** Lacks a claim; provides no support; ignores opposing claims; ends abruptly • **Organization** Has no organization and transitions • **Language** Uses an inappropriate style and tone; has major problems with grammar, mechanics, and spelling

Preparing for Timed Writing

W 10 Write routinely over shorter time frames for a range of tasks, purposes, and audiences.

1. ANALYZE THE TASK 5 MIN

Read the task carefully. Then, read it again, noting on your own paper the words that tell the audience, the topic, and the purpose.

WRITING TASK *Topic*

Your school is debating whether to adopt a school uniform policy or to continue allowing students to choose what they will wear to school. Consider how each option affects the student population, the teachers, and the school environment. What is your position on the issue? In a persuasive essay, convince the school board to agree with your position.

Purpose *Audience*

2. PLAN YOUR RESPONSE 10 MIN

- Use a chart to gather ideas. The pros are the reasons for the policy, and the cons are the reasons against the policy. Choose your viewpoint based on the number and strength of reasons. Write your claim.
- Support each reason with relevant evidence, such as facts, examples, and anecdotes. Also, address one possible opposing claim.
- Arrange your reasons and evidence in a logical sequence, such as order of importance.

School Uniforms	
Pros	
Cons	

3. RESPOND TO THE TASK 20 MIN

Begin drafting your essay. As you write, keep the following points in mind:

- In the introduction, grab your audience's interest and state a precise claim.
- In each paragraph, provide a valid reason and relevant evidence that supports it.
- Acknowledge and counter opposing claims.
- Conclude by restating your claim and proposing some action that your audience should take.

4. IMPROVE YOUR RESPONSE 5–10 MIN

Revising Review the key aspects of the essay. Do you state your claim clearly? Do you include valid reasons, relevant evidence, and a call to action?

Proofreading Proofread, or edit, your essay to correct errors in grammar, spelling, punctuation, and capitalization. Make sure edits are neat and the essay is legible.

Checking Your Final Copy Before you turn in your essay, read it one more time to catch any errors you may have missed and to make any finishing touches.

Speaking & Listening Workshop

Presenting and Evaluating a Persuasive Speech

If you have ever talked a friend into agreeing with your opinion, then you have spoken persuasively. Effective persuasive speeches incorporate the same techniques that are used in good persuasive essays. A speech, though, allows you to use your voice and body as well as words to make your point.

 Complete the workshop activities in your **Reader/Writer Notebook.**

SPEAK WITH A PURPOSE	COMMON CORE TRAITS
TASK	***A STRONG PERSUASIVE SPEECH . . .***
Adapt your **persuasive essay** into a **persuasive speech,** and present it to your class. Then, listen to and evaluate the persuasive speeches of others.	• asserts a claim that reflects the speaker's distinct perspective • organizes reasons and evidence in a logical order • addresses alternative or opposing perspectives • uses persuasive **rhetoric**, or language, effectively

COMMON CORE

SL 3 Evaluate a speaker's point of view, reasoning, and use of evidence and rhetoric. **SL 4** Present information, findings, and evidence, such that listeners can follow the line of reasoning. **SL 6** Adapt speech to a variety of contexts and tasks.

Adapt Your Essay

Since your audience will be listening to your argument rather than reading it, you will need to adapt your persuasive essay so that it works as a speech. To be convincing, you will need to state your claim, or **stance,** on the topic clearly and concisely so that your audience understands your distinct perspective. You must then support that claim with evidence that is compelling, logical, and supported by reliable research.

Introduction	Body	Concluding Section
• Start with a thought-provoking quotation or tell a vivid anecdote. • State your claim clearly. • Establish the significance of your claim.	• Organize your information in order of importance. • Present valid reasons and logical, sufficient evidence. • Consider alternative perspectives and offer reasons why your claim is more valid. • Use **rhetoric,** or persuasive language, to sway your audience.	• Sum up your points and restate your claim. • Summarize your strongest evidence and the significance of your claim. • End with a statement that gives your audience something to consider.

Considering your audience will help you decide on the style, organization, and substance of your speech. Will your audience be swayed by emotional or logical appeals? Will a reference to a common experience be convincing?

THINK central

Speaking & Listening Online

Go to thinkcentral.com.
KEYWORD: HML11-290

Deliver Your Speech

USE VERBAL AND NONVERBAL TECHNIQUES

Use these techniques to communicate your ideas effectively:

Verbal Techniques	Nonverbal Techniques
• Keep your **rate** of speech steady. Pause for effect when you reach key ideas. • **Enunciate** your words clearly.	• Engage your audience by making **eye contact** with individuals. • Use appropriate **gestures** to enforce key ideas.

EVALUATE PERSUASIVE SPEECHES

As you listen to your classmates' speeches, take careful notes. This will help you evaluate information and later ask pertinent questions that will stimulate a thoughtful, well-reasoned exchange of ideas. Use the following questions to focus your evaluation:

- Evaluate the speaker's **point of view.** What is the claim? On what **premises** or assumptions is the claim based? Do the premises seem logical and factual? Do they provide a strong foundation for the speaker's **stance,** or position on the issue?
- Examine the **reasoning.** Are the reasons valid and clearly linked? What reasons or ideas does the speaker emphasize? Are these **points of emphasis** effective for the audience?
- Assess the **evidence.** Is it reliable? Does it support the speaker's claim? Be on the lookout for flawed reasoning, such as overgeneralizations or exaggeration.
- Does the speaker fairly acknowledge alternate perspectives? Does he or she explain the strengths and limitations of other viewpoints?
- Analyze the speaker's language choices. Has the speaker used **rhetorical devices** such as understatement or hyperbole to influence you? Do the speaker's **tone** and **word choices** support or detract from the points made?

As a Speaker Deliver your speech to a classmate, incorporating verbal and nonverbal techniques. Speak persuasively, using formal English appropriate for the topic of your speech. Have your classmate offer suggestions for improvement.

As a Listener Listen to a classmate deliver his or her speech. Take notes on the organization, substance, and style of the speech, using the questions above to help you evaluate what you're hearing.

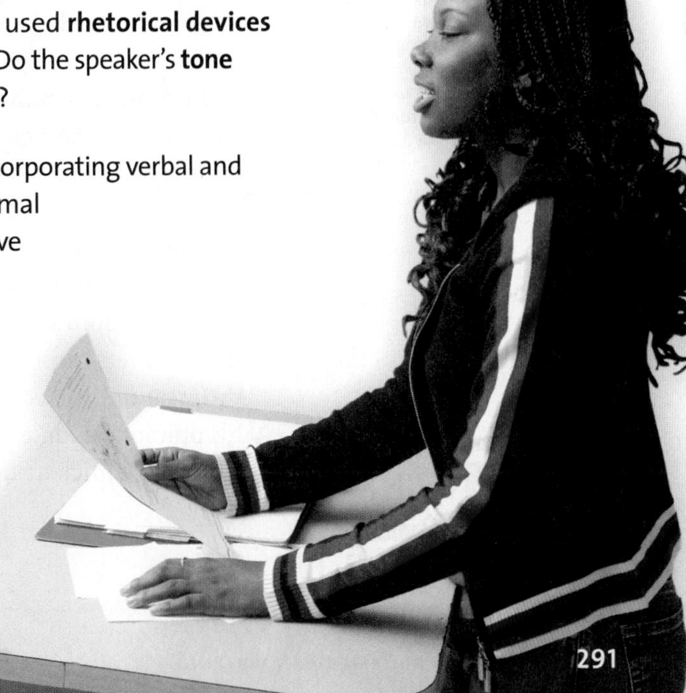

Assessment Practice

ASSESS
Taking this practice test will help you assess your knowledge of these skills and determine your readiness for the Unit Test.

REVIEW
After you take the practice test, your teacher can help you identify any standards you need to review.

COMMON CORE

RI 1 Cite strong and thorough textual evidence to support analysis of what the text says explicitly. **RI 6** Determine an author's point of view or purpose in a text in which the rhetoric is particularly effective, analyzing how style and content contribute to the power or persuasiveness of the text. **RI 8** Delineate and evaluate the reasoning in seminal U.S. texts, including the application of constitutional principles and use of legal reasoning and the premises, purposes, and arguments in works of public advocacy. **L 3a** Vary syntax for effect, consulting references for guidance as needed; apply an understanding of syntax to the study of complex texts when reading. **L 4a** Use context as a clue to the meaning of a word or phrase.

Practice Test THINK central
Take it at thinkcentral.com.
KEYWORD: HML11N-292

DIRECTIONS **Read these selections and answer the questions that follow.**

from Defense of the Constitutions of Government in Massachusetts During the Revolution

by John Adams

1 It is become a kind of fashion among writers, to admit, as a maxim, that if you could be always sure of a wise, active, and virtuous prince, monarchy would be the best of governments. But this is so far from being admissible, that it will forever remain true, that a free government has a great advantage over a simple monarchy. The best and wisest prince, by means of a freer communication with his people, and the greater opportunities to collect the best advice from the best of his subjects, would have an immense advantage in a free state over a monarchy. A senate consisting of all that is most noble, wealthy, and able in the nation, with a right to counsel the crown at all times, is a check to ministers, and a security against abuses, such as a body of nobles who never meet, and have no such right, can never supply. Another assembly, composed of representatives chosen by the people in all parts, gives free access to the whole nation, and communicates all its wants, knowledge, projects, and wishes to government; it excites emulation among all classes, removes complaints, redresses grievances, affords opportunities of exertion to genius, though in obscurity, and gives full scope to all the faculties of man; it opens a passage for every speculation to the legislature, to administration, and to the public; it gives a universal energy to the human character, in every part of the state, such as never can be obtained in a monarchy.

2 There is a third particular which deserves attention both from governments and people. In a simple monarchy, the ministers of state can never know their friends from their enemies; secret cabals undermine their influence, and blast their reputation. This occasions a jealousy ever anxious and irritated, which never thinks the government safe without an encouragement of informers and spies, throughout every part of the state, who interrupt the tranquillity of private life, destroy the confidence of families in their own domestics and in one another, and poison freedom in its sweetest retirements. In a free government, on the contrary, the ministers can have no enemies of consequence but among the members of the great or little council, where every man is obliged to take his side, and declare his opinion, upon every question. This circumstance alone, to every manly mind, would be sufficient to decide the preference in favor of a free government.

from Boston Tea Party *by George Hewes*

1 It was now evening, and I immediately dressed myself in the costume of an Indian, equipped with a small hatchet, which I and my associates denominated the tomahawk, with which, and a club, after having painted my face and hands with coal dust in the shop of a blacksmith, I repaired to Griffin's wharf, where the ships lay that contained the tea. When I first appeared in the street after being thus disguised, I fell in with many who were dressed, equipped and painted as I was, and who fell in with me and marched in order to the place of our destination. . . .

2 We then were ordered by our commander to open the hatches and take out all the chests of tea and throw them overboard, and we immediately proceeded to execute his orders, first cutting and splitting the chests with our tomahawks, so as thoroughly to expose them to the effects of the water.

3 In about three hours from the time we went on board, we had thus broken and thrown overboard every tea chest to be found in the ship, while those in the other ships were disposing of the tea in the same way, at the same time. We were surrounded by British armed ships, but no attempt was made to resist us.

4 We then quietly retired to our several places of residence, without having any conversation with each other, or taking any measures to discover who were our associates; nor do I recollect of our having had the knowledge of the name of a single individual concerned in that affair, except that of Leonard Pitt, the commander of my division, whom I have mentioned. There appeared to be an understanding that each individual should volunteer his services, keep his own secret, and risk the consequence for himself. No disorder took place during that transaction, and it was observed at that time that the stillest night ensued that Boston had enjoyed for many months. . . .

5 Another attempt was made to save a little tea from the ruins of the cargo by a tall, aged man who wore a large cocked hat and white wig, which was fashionable at that time. He had sleightly slipped a little into his pocket, but being detected, they seized him and, taking his hat and wig from his head, threw them, together with the tea, of which they had emptied his pockets, into the water. In consideration of his advanced age, he was permitted to escape, with now and then a slight kick.

6 The next morning, after we had cleared the ships of the tea, it was discovered that very considerable quantities of it were floating upon the surface of the water; and to prevent the possibility of any of its being saved for use, a number of small

GO ON

boats were manned by sailors and citizens, who rowed them into those parts of the harbor wherever the tea was visible, and by beating it with oars and paddles so thoroughly drenched it as to render its entire destruction inevitable.

Reading Comprehension

Use "Defense of the Constitutions of Government in Massachusetts During the Revolution" (p. 292) to answer questions 1–6.

1. Which position on government does Adams favor?

A. Monarchies are the best form of government because they have wise and virtuous rulers.

B. Writers should be consulted when a country forms its government because they are well informed.

C. A free state is the best form of government because its ideas and opinions come from the people.

D. Only the best and wisest prince who communicates with his subjects should rule a nation.

2. The words *enemies, informers,* and *spies* in paragraph 2 appeal to the emotion of—

A. anger **C.** fear

B. excitement **D.** guilt

3. Which claim does Adams make about a free government in paragraph 2?

A. The best way to run a free government is with a large assembly and a small one.

B. Members of a free government often take a tough-minded approach to governing.

C. People who serve in a free government have similar opinions.

D. The leaders in a free government usually have few hidden enemies.

4. "Every manly mind" in paragraph 2 is an example of which persuasive technique?

A. An appeal by association

B. An appeal to authority

C. An ethical appeal

D. Loaded language

5. Which quote is an example of loaded language?

A. *monarchy would be the best of governments*

B. *such as a body of nobles who never meet*

C. *gives free access to the whole nation*

D. *poison freedom in its sweetest retirements*

6. This excerpt reflects the view of colonists who —

A. believed that political rivalries would destroy the British monarchy

B. questioned British rule and tried to form a new government

C. upheld the ideals of a monarchy

D. had simple ideas about government

Use "Boston Tea Party" (pp. 293–294) to answer questions 7–12.

7. Which descriptive details most clearly place this account in its historical context?
   - **A.** Tomahawk, chests of tea, coal dust
   - **B.** Armed ships, hatches, small boats
   - **C.** Evening, three hours, next morning
   - **D.** Sailors, citizens, aged man

8. This narrative is a primary source because it is —
   - **A.** a political argument
   - **B.** a participant's report
   - **C.** an accurate history
   - **D.** a published document

9. This account by a colonial shoemaker calls attention to —
   - **A.** an alliance between Native Americans and tradespeople
   - **B.** a lack of leadership during the Revolutionary War
   - **C.** the tension between wealthy and poor people in the colonies
   - **D.** the role of the common people in the Revolution

10. The colonists most likely dressed as Native Americans to —
    - **A.** honor Native American traditions
    - **B.** forge an alliance against the British
    - **C.** protect themselves from the British
    - **D.** cause economic problems in the colonies

11. The descriptive anecdote in paragraph 5 suggests that —
    - **A.** tea was a prized commodity among the colonists in Boston
    - **B.** the elderly were treated with disrespect in colonial times
    - **C.** many participants thought the Boston Tea Party was amusing
    - **D.** violent attacks were characteristic of the Boston Tea Party

12. The descriptive details in this account emphasize that the Boston Tea Party was —
    - **A.** poorly planned
    - **B.** carried out in secret
    - **C.** led by Native Americans
    - **D.** authorized by the British

Use both selections to answer question 13.

13. Both primary sources give the reader insight into the —
    - **A.** origins of the United States
    - **B.** benefits of a constitution
    - **C.** advantages of a monarchy
    - **D.** fashions of the period

SHORT CONSTRUCTED RESPONSE

Write three or four sentences to answer this question.

14. Cite three details from George Hewes's account that identify it as a primary source.

Write two or three paragraphs to answer this question.

15. What argument does John Adams make in paragraph 1 in favor of an assembly of representatives? Cite three reasons he gives to support his argument.

Vocabulary

Use context clues and your knowledge of specialized vocabulary to answer the following questions based on "Defense of the Constitutions of Government in Massachusetts During the Revolution."

1. What is the most likely meaning of the word *monarchy* as it is used in paragraph 1?

A. A state headed by a leader who usually rules by hereditary right

B. A body of elected officials who hold the supreme power in a nation

C. A small group of persons who rule together

D. A government that shares power with the people

2. What is the most likely meaning of the word *cabals* as it is used in paragraph 2?

A. Social clubs

B. Religious denominations

C. Groups of conspirators

D. Military organizations

3. What is the most likely meaning of the word *ministers* as it is used in paragraph 2?

A. Church leaders

B. Public officials

C. Foreign diplomats

D. Business tycoons

Use context clues and your knowledge of multiple-meaning words to answer the following questions based on the excerpt from "Boston Tea Party."

4. Which meaning of the word *execute* is used in paragraph 2?

A. Carry out

B. Create

C. Kill

D. Validate

5. Which meaning of the word *several* is used in paragraph 4?

A. Distant

B. Separate

C. Humble

D. More than two or three

6. Which meaning of the word *measures* is used in paragraph 4?

A. Actions

B. Dimensions

C. Legislative bills

D. Quantities

Revising and Editing

DIRECTIONS Read this passage and answer the questions that follow.

(1) George Washington hired engineer Pierre L'Enfant to plan a new capitol city. (2) The new city would be called Federal City and would be located in Maryland. (3) L'Enfant was later fired. (4) Surveyor Andrew Ellicott redrew the plans but upheld much of L'Enfant's vision. (5) By 1800, President John Adams had moved into the White House. (6) It was far from finished. (7) It was damp. (8) The city was later renamed. (9) Today, Washington, D.C., reflects L'Enfants vision of a city of open space.

1. What change, if any, should be made in sentence 1?

A. Change ***engineer*** to **Engineer**

B. Insert a comma after ***L'Enfant***

C. Change ***capitol*** to **capital**

D. Make no change

2. What is the most effective way to combine sentences 3 and 4 to form a compound-complex sentence?

A. L'Enfant was later fired, but when surveyor Andrew Ellicott redrew the plans, he upheld much of L'Enfant's vision.

B. L'Enfant was later fired, and surveyor Andrew Ellicott redrew the plans but upheld much of L'Enfant's vision.

C. When redrawing the plans, surveyor Andrew Ellicott upheld much of L'Enfant's vision, even though L'Enfant was fired.

D. Much of L'Enfant's vision was upheld by surveyor Andrew Ellicott, who redrew the plans after L'Enfant was fired.

3. What is the most effective way to combine sentences 5 and 6 to form a complex sentence?

A. By 1800, President John Adams had moved into the White House, even though it was far from finished.

B. By 1800, President John Adams had moved into the White House, but it was far from finished.

C. By 1800, President John Adams had moved into the White House; however, it was far from finished.

D. By 1800, President John Adams had moved into the White House; it was far from finished.

4. Which prepositional phrase should be added to the end of sentence 8 to add descriptive detail?

A. Even as it grew

B. After Washington's death

C. To reflect Washington's involvement

D. Washington, D.C.

5. What change, if any, should be made in sentence 9?

A. Spell out ***D.C.***

B. Change ***L'Enfants*** to **L'Enfant's**

C. Change ***reflects*** to **reflected**

D. Make no change

Ideas for Independent Reading

Continue exploring the Questions of the Times on pages 20–21 with these additional works.

Who owns the LAND?

The Narrative of the Captivity and Restoration of Mrs. Mary Rowlandson
by Mary Rowlandson

In February 1676, during a land dispute called King Philip's War, a minister's wife named Mary Rowlandson was taken hostage by Wampanoag warriors. Packed with violence, cruelty, piety, and anger, Rowlandson's account of her three-month captivity became one of the first bestsellers in colonial America.

The Portable North American Indian Reader
edited by Fredrick W. Turner

As an introduction to the verbal art of Native Americans, this anthology has few equals. It includes myths, tales, poetry, and speeches from the many diverse Native American cultures who thrived before, during, and after contact with European explorers and settlers. Modern selections show how traditional Indian kinship with the land continues to the present day.

Finding the Center: The Art of the Zuni Storyteller
translated by Dennis Tedlock

Thought to have descended from the Anasazi, a cliff-dwelling people of 1,000 years ago, the Zuni of present-day New Mexico enjoy a rich oral heritage handed down from long before the first Europeans arrived. The folklorist Dennis Tedlock has collected, translated, and transcribed many key Zuni stories in this volume, placing the words on the page in a manner that mimics their oral performance.

What makes an EXPLORER?

The Four Voyages
by Christopher Columbus

In these journals and eyewitness accounts, Christopher Columbus comes across as a complex, driven, yet entirely understandable person. In place of the confident adventurer of story, we see a man of mixed motives, influenced equally by greed, religious passion, and scientific curiosity. These journals shed light on the impulses that pushed Columbus to make the most significant journeys of his time.

Love and Hate in Jamestown
by David Price

In 1607, 105 Englishmen arrived in what would become the Virginia settlement of Jamestown. They came seeking gold, a route to the Orient, and survivors from the lost Roanoke Colony. What they found instead were Native American people—some friendly, some brutally hostile—and day after day of challenges, hardship, and misery.

Voyages and Discoveries
by Richard Hakluyt

Early English explorers were a fascinating breed. These sailors were willing—even eager—to face unknown dangers for the sake of their country and the glory and adventure it would bring. Using ships' records, charts, and logs, Richard Hakluyt pulls together the stories of such adventurers as Sir Francis Drake, whose yen for exploration enabled the European settlement of America.

RL 10 Read and comprehend literature. **RI 10** Read and comprehend literary nonfiction.

Are people basically GOOD?

The Diary and Life of Samuel Sewall
edited by Mel Yazawa

Samuel Sewall served as one of the judges in the Salem witchcraft trials, voting to hang 19 people for wholly imaginary offenses. Yet in his diary, we see another side of this forbidding figure. He wrestles with lingering guilt over his role in that public hysteria, feels remorse over the unfair treatment of the Indians, recalls the pleasures of food and marriage, and grieves bitterly over the loss of friends and family.

A Short Account of the Destruction of the Indies
by Bartolomé de Las Casas

A Spanish priest and missionary, Las Casas was appalled by the abuse and enslavement of Native Americans. He dedicated himself to their emancipation, returning to Spain to plead their case before the king, then going back to the New World to serve as their official protector.

Letters from an American Farmer
by Michel Guillaume Jean de Crèvecœur

Crèvecœur's "letters," originally written as essays, paint a mesmerizing portrait of a fertile country populated with rough-mannered yet skilled and kindhearted people. Crèvecœur addresses such difficult topics as the hardships of the frontier, the plight of women, and the evils of slavery. Yet such problems fade before his faith in the righteousness of American individualism.

Who has the right to RULE?

1776
by David McCullough

How did a ragtag group of farmers manage to defeat the world's most powerful army? That is the question historian David McCullough explores in this fascinating look at one pivotal year in our nation's history. Persistence, optimism, ingenuity, leadership, luck, and weather are the elements to which McCullough attributes the colonists' success in the Revolutionary War.

The Puritan Dilemma: The Story of John Winthrop
by Edmund S. Morgan

As the leader of Massachusetts Bay Colony for nearly 20 years, John Winthrop spent his life combining religious devotion with power politics. This biography shines a spotlight upon issues that mattered most to Winthrop: the relationship between individual liberties and community harmony, and the legitimacy of political authority.

The Adams-Jefferson Letters
edited by Lester J. Cappon

Divided by political party and regional affiliation, Thomas Jefferson of Virginia and John Adams of Massachusetts were united in their love of country and their concern for the future of democracy. This collection of letters, including contributions by Abigail Adams (John Adams's gifted wife), touches upon virtually every major issue that faced the young republic.

Get Novel Wise THINK central

Go to thinkcentral.com.
KEYWORD: HML11-299

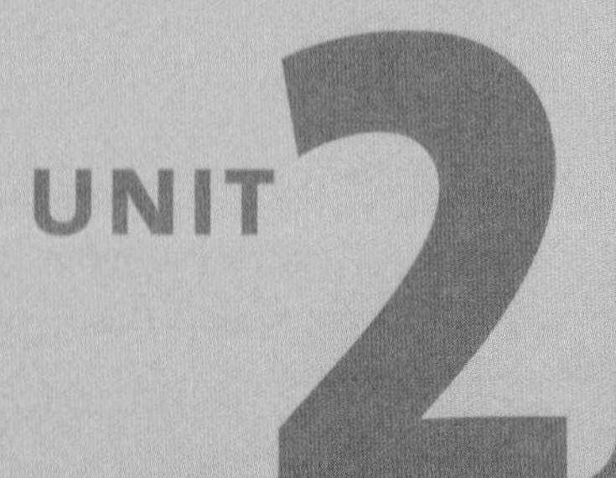

COMMON CORE

Preview Unit Goals

TEXT ANALYSIS	• Understand romanticism as a literary movement • Identify elements of transcendentalism • Identify and analyze blank verse • Identify and examine stanza, rhyme scheme, and meter • Analyze elements used to create mood; analyze theme • Identify and analyze sound devices and imagery • Interpret symbol and allegory • Identify and analyze satire and unity of effect • Analyze elements of an essay • Determine an author's point of view or purpose; analyze style and content
READING	• Paraphrase main ideas; summarize information; make inferences • Clarify meanings; examine complex sentences
WRITING AND LANGUAGE	• Write a short story • Use rhetorical questions • Identify and use parallelism and adjective clauses • Use imperative sentences and dashes
SPEAKING AND LISTENING	• Dramatize a script
VOCABULARY	• Use knowledge of word roots and affixes to determine word meaning • Research word origins
ACADEMIC VOCABULARY	• construct • expand • indicate • reinforce • role
MEDIA AND VIEWING	• Evaluate how meaning is conveyed in visual media

Find It Online!

Go to thinkcentral.com for the interactive version of this unit.

American Romanticism

1800–1855

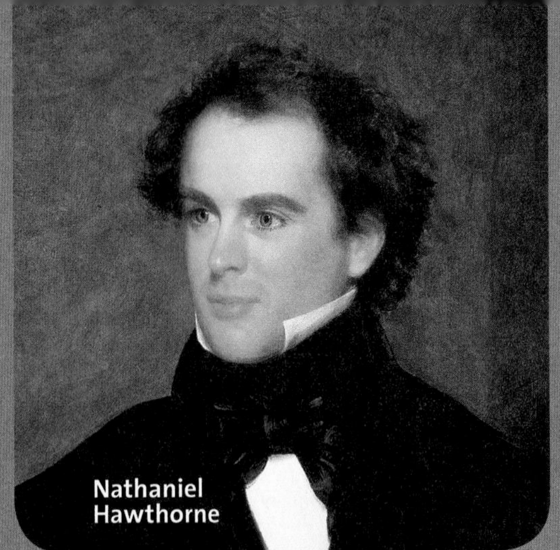

Nathaniel Hawthorne

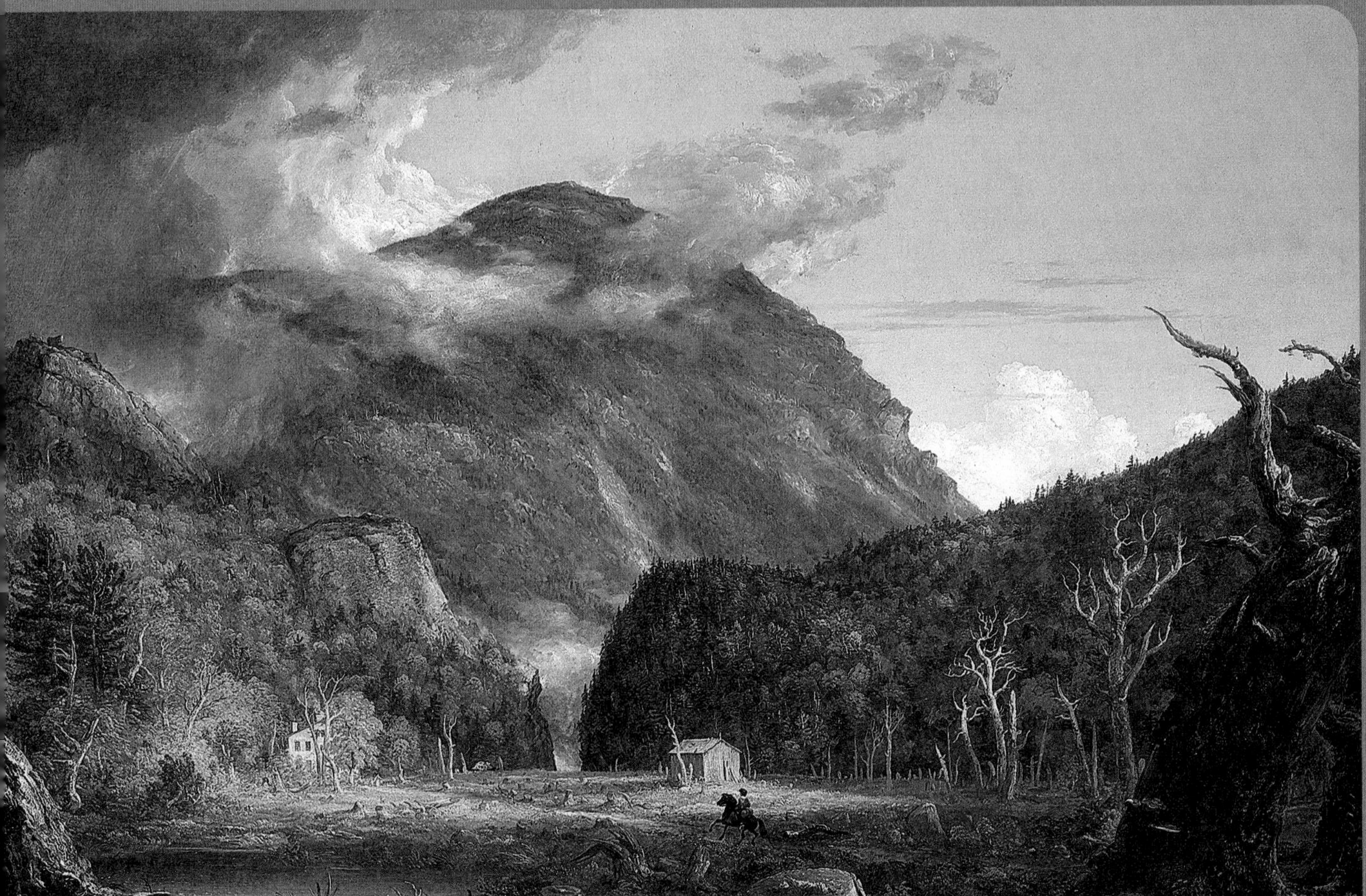

CELEBRATING THE INDIVIDUAL

- The Early Romantics
- The Fireside Poets
- The Transcendentalists
- American Gothic

MediaSmart DVD-ROM

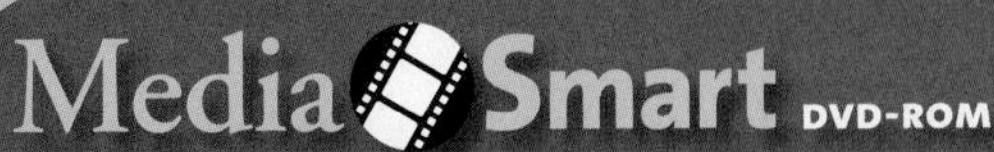

Illustrations Inspired by Poe

Examine evocative paintings and illustrations that take gothic into new dimensions. Page 460

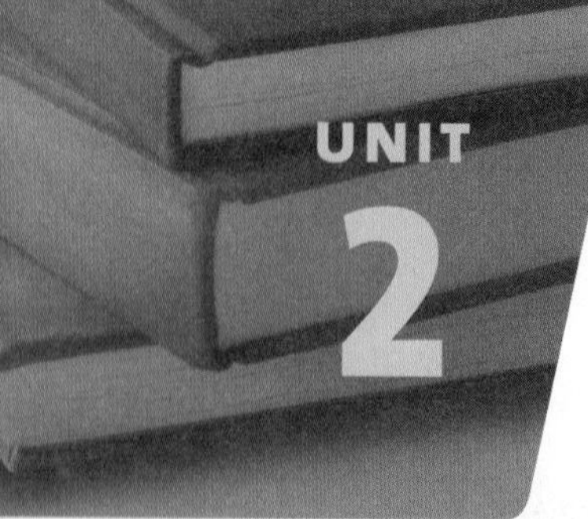

Questions of the Times

DISCUSS In small groups or as a class, discuss the following questions. Then read on to learn how writers—and other Americans—grappled with these issues during the American romantic period.

Is the price of progress ever TOO HIGH?

During the romantic period, America seemed limitless—new frontiers were being explored every day, and inventions advanced both farming and industry. Yet to many people, life felt frantic and soulless. Is progress always worth its price?

Is it patriotic to protest one's GOVERNMENT?

Democracy was flourishing in the early 19th century and citizens felt optimistic about their country. Yet the problems of the age—slavery, women's disenfranchisement, the mistreatment of workers—were severe, and protestors agitated for change. What role do you think activism plays in a democracy? Under what circumstances, if any, should citizens lose their right to protest?

COMMON CORE

RL 9 Demonstrate knowledge of nineteenth-century foundational works of American literature, including how two or more texts from the same period treat similar themes or topics. **RI 9** Analyze documents of historical and literary significance for their themes, purposes, and rhetorical features.

Does everyone have a "DARK SIDE"?

Although most romantic writers reflected the optimism of their times, some pondered the darker side of human nature. Edgar Allan Poe, for example, conjectured that in extreme situations people would reveal their true, evil natures. Do you think everyone has a dark side? What might make the dark side prevail?

Where do people look for TRUTH?

To escape the materialism and hectic pace of industrialization, many writers of the age turned to nature and to the self for simplicity, truth, and beauty. In earlier centuries, people had looked to reason or to God for answers. Where do you think people turn to make sense of their lives today?

American Romanticism 1800–1855

Celebrating the Individual

Patriotic and individualistic, urban and untamed, wealthy and enslaved—Americans in the first half of the 19th century embodied a host of contradictions. Struggling to make sense of their complex, inconsistent society, writers of the period turned inward for a sense of truth. Their movement, known as romanticism, explored the glories of the individual spirit, the beauty of nature, and the possibilities of the imagination.

Romanticism: Historical Context

Historical forces clearly shaped the literature of the American romantic period. Writers responded—positively and negatively—to the country's astonishing growth and to the booming Industrial Revolution.

COMMON CORE

RL 9 Demonstrate knowledge of nineteenth-century foundational works of American literature, including how two or more texts from the same period treat similar themes or topics. **RI 9** Analyze documents of historical and literary significance for their themes, purposes, and rhetorical features.

The Spirit of Exploration

WESTWARD EXPANSION Writers of the romantic period were witness to a period of great growth and opportunity for the young American nation. With that growth, however, came a price. In 1803, the Louisiana Purchase doubled the country's size. In the years that followed, explorers and settlers pushed farther and farther west. Settlers moved for largely practical reasons: to make money and to gain land. But each bit of land settled by white Americans was taken from Native American populations who had lived there for generations. The Indian Removal Act of 1830, for example, required Native Americans to relocate west. As whites invaded their homelands, many Native Americans saw no choice but to comply. And those who did not were simply—and often brutally—forced to leave.

Toward the middle of the century, Americans embraced the notion of **"manifest destiny"**—the idea that it was the destiny of the United States to expand to the Pacific Ocean and into Mexican territory. Mexicans disagreed, of course. When the Republic of Texas was annexed by the United States in 1845, it set off the Mexican-American War. Many Americans, including writer **Henry David Thoreau,** found the war to be immoral—a war fought mainly to expand slavery. "Can there not be a government," he wrote, "in which majorities do not virtually decide right and wrong, but conscience?" In the end, the United States defeated Mexico and, through treaties and subsequent land purchases from the Mexican government, established the current borders of the 48 contiguous United States.

▶ TAKING NOTES

Outlining As you read this introduction, use an outline to record the main ideas about the characteristics and the literature of the period. You can use article headings, boldfaced terms, and the information in these boxes as starting points. (See page R49 in the **Research Handbook** for more help with outlining.)

I. Historical Context
A. Spirit of Exploration
1. Westward Expansion
2. Manifest Destiny
B. Growth of Industry

Growth of Industry

The stories and essays of the romantic period reflect an enormous shift in the attitudes and working habits of many Americans. When the War of 1812 interrupted trade with the British, Americans were suddenly forced to produce many of the goods they had previously imported. The **Industrial Revolution** began, changing the country from a largely agrarian economy to an industrial powerhouse.

The factory system changed the way of life for many Americans, but not always for the better. People left their farms for the cities, working long hours for low wages in harsh conditions. In addition, Northeastern textile mills' demand for cotton played a role in the expansion of slavery in the South. Writers of this period reacted to the negative effects of industrialization—the commercialism, hectic pace, and lack of conscience—by turning to nature and to the self for simplicity, truth, and beauty.

Detail of *Summer Afternoon on the Hudson* (1852), Jasper Francis Crospey.

Cultural Influences

Many romantic writers were outspoken in their support for human rights. Their works created awareness of the injustice of slavery and called for reform in many other areas as well.

This antislavery medal was created to help grow support for the abolition movement.

The Tragedy of Slavery

From 1793 to 1860, cotton production rose greatly, due to the invention of the cotton gin and other farming machinery. So did the number of enslaved workers. Plantation owners were the wealthiest and most powerful people in the South, yet they were relatively few in number. Most Southern farmers held few or no slaves, but they aspired to. They felt that slavery had become necessary for increasing profits.

For slaves, life was brutal. Field workers—men, women, and children—rose before dawn and worked in the fields until bedtime. Many were beaten or otherwise abused. And worst of all, family members were sold away from one another. Often family members attempted to escape to be with one another again. Unfortunately, escapes were rarely successful.

Tension over slavery increased between the North and the South. Many in the North saw slavery as immoral and worked to have it abolished. Others worried as the balance of power between free and slave states shifted with each new state entering the Union. Romantic poets **James Russell Lowell** and **John Greenleaf Whittier** wrote abolitionist journalism and poetry, and even **Henry Wadsworth Longfellow** published a volume of antislavery poems. Perhaps the greatest social achievement of the romantics was to create awareness of slavery's cruelty.

A Voice from the Times

Men! Whose boast it is that ye
Come of fathers brave and free,
If there breathe on earth a slave,
Are ye truly free and brave?
If ye do not feel the chain,
When it works a brother's pain,
Are ye not base slaves indeed,
Slaves unworthy to be freed?

—James Russell Lowell
from "Stanzas on Freedom"

Call for Social Reform

By the mid-19th century, many Americans had joined together to fight slavery and the other social ills of the time. Many leading writers of the romantic movement were outspoken in their support for human rights. **William Cullen Bryant** and **James Russell Lowell,** for example, were prominent abolitionists who also supported workers' and women's rights.

The abolition movement began by advocating resettlement of blacks in Africa. But most enslaved African Americans had been born and raised in the United States and resented the idea of being forced to leave. Instead, white and black abolitionists (including women) began to join together to work for emancipation. They formed societies, spoke at conventions, published newspapers, and swamped Congress with petitions to end slavery.

In the 1830s and 1840s, workers began to agitate as well, protesting low wages and deteriorating working conditions. Many struck, but few were successful—a large pool of immigrants was always ready to take their places. Still, workers began forming unions, and slowly conditions improved.

Women in the early 19th century found much to protest. They could neither vote nor sit on juries. Their education rarely extended beyond elementary school. When they married, their property and money became their husband's. Many even lacked guardianship rights over their children. Throughout this period, women worked for change, gathering in 1848 at Seneca Falls, New York, to continue their long fight for women's rights.

Ideas of the Age

Reflecting the optimism of their growing country, American romantic writers forged a national literature for the very first time. Yet sectionalism threatened to tear the nation apart.

Nationalism vs. Sectionalism

In the early 1800s, many Supreme Court decisions strengthened the federal government's power over the states. At the same time, Secretary of State John Quincy Adams established a foreign policy guided by **nationalism**—the belief that national interests should be placed ahead of regional concerns or the interests of other countries. Reflecting the national pride and optimism of the American people, writers of this age forged a literature entirely the nation's own. For the first time, writers were not imitating their European counterparts, but were listening to their own voices and writing with a distinctly American accent.

However, this new spirit of nationalism was challenged by the question of slavery. Up until 1818, the United States had consisted of ten free and ten slave states. As new territories tried to enter the Union, the North and South wrangled over the balance of power between free and slave states. Economic interests also challenged nationalism. Tariffs on manufactured goods from Britain forced Southerners to buy more expensive, Northern-manufactured goods. From the South's point of view, the North was getting rich at the South's expense. Sectionalism, or the placing of the interests of one's own region ahead of the nation as a whole, began to take hold.

THE ARTISTS' GALLERY

The Hudson River School

The paintings on pages 301 and 304 are excellent examples of the works of the Hudson River School artists. This group of landscape painters flourished between 1825 and 1870. The artists knew one another and used similar techniques for portraying nature scenes.

American Style Thomas Cole painted *A View of the Mountain Pass Called the Notch of the White Mountains* (1839), shown here and on page 301. He and the other Hudson River artists created passionate wilderness scenes that appealed to the imagination and made earlier American landscapes seem weak and unobserved. Like the American romantic writers of the time, the Hudson River School artists made a conscious effort to create an American style—one based on nature and the emotions.

Real-Life Inspiration The painting shown in detail here has an interesting history. Author Nathaniel Hawthorne wrote a short story about a real-life landslide at Crawford Notch that took the lives of nine people. The story may have piqued Cole's interest in the scene. In the painting Cole highlights the insignificance and vulnerability of the human figures in the face of the coming storm. One barely notices the settlers' homes or the rider, who seems oblivious to the ominous clouds gathering at the upper left—hinting of disaster to come.

Romantic Literature

Themes of individualism and nature unified the writing of the American romantic movement, despite dramatic differences in the writers' focus and style.

The Early Romantics

The early American romantic writers may have been influenced more by the literature of another continent than by that of their own. **Romanticism** had first emerged in Europe in the late 18th century, in reaction to the neoclassicism of the period that had preceded it. Where neoclassical writers admired and imitated classical forms, the romantics looked to nature for inspiration. Where neoclassicists valued reason, the romantics celebrated emotions and the imagination. The first American romantic writers grew

▶ *For Your Outline*

THE EARLY ROMANTICS

- were inspired by the beauty of nature
- emphasized emotions and the imagination over reason
- celebrated the individual spirit

Kindred Spirits (1849), Asher B. Durand. © Francis G. Mayer/Corbis.

◀ **Analyze Visuals**

This painting is a memorial to painter Asher B. Durand's friend and fellow Hudson River School artist Thomas Cole (here shown with romantic poet William Cullen Bryant).

Although Durand was influenced by Cole, his works express stillness and a realistic imitation of nature, in contrast to Cole's more expressive rendering. Compare this painting with Cole's on the previous page. How are they similar? How are they different?

A collection of major works by early American romantics

out of this European tradition, shaping and molding it to fit their unique American identity. They too were reacting to what had come before—the rationality of the Age of Reason and the strict doctrines of Puritanism.

Indeed, much had changed since the Puritan era in America, and the writers of the early romantic period reflected the more modern sensibilities of their day. As the U.S. population exploded and the country's borders moved westward, American writers aimed to capture the energy and character of their growing country. They saw the limits of reason and instead celebrated the glories of the individual spirit, the emotions, and the imagination as basic elements of human nature. The splendors of nature inspired the romantics more than the fear of God, and some of them felt a fascination with the supernatural.

William Cullen Bryant's 1817 poem "Thanatopsis" went a long way toward establishing romanticism as the major force in the literature of mid-19th century America. Bryant followed the trend of the English romantics by celebrating nature in his work. Romanticism was not only a movement in poetry, however. **Washington Irving,** the first American writer esteemed abroad, pioneered the short story as a literary form. He put America on the literary map and also influenced other writers, particularly Nathaniel Hawthorne. **James Fenimore Cooper** is remembered for writing the first truly original American novel. He celebrated the American spirit in all his frontier novels, known as *The Leatherstocking Tales.* The early romantic writers were the pioneers of America's national literature, setting the course for those who would follow.

A Voice from the Times

To him who in the love of Nature holds
Communion with her visible forms, she speaks
A various language; for his gayer hours
She has a voice of gladness, and a smile
And eloquence of beauty, and she glides
Into his darker musings, with a mild
And healing sympathy, that steals away
Their sharpness, ere he is aware. . . .

—**William Cullen Bryant**
from "Thanatopsis"

The legendary Hiawatha, memorialized in Longfellow's poem "The Song of Hiawatha"

The Fireside Poets

Other writers influential in forging an American literature were the Fireside Poets, a group of New England poets whose work was morally uplifting and romantically engaging. The group's name came from the family custom of reading poetry aloud beside a fire, a common form of entertainment in the 19th century. With the Fireside Poets, the poetry of American writers was, for the first time, on equal footing with that of their British counterparts.

Henry Wadsworth Longfellow, the best-known member of the group, stressed individualism and an appreciation of nature in his work. His poems took for their subject matter the more colorful aspects of America's past. "Evangeline," for example, tells of lovers who are separated during the French and Indian War, while "The Song of Hiawatha" takes its themes from Native American folklore. Longfellow's fame was so great that after his death, he was honored with a plaque in Poets' Corner of Westminster Abbey in London—the only American poet ever to receive such an honor.

The other Fireside Poets, **James Russell Lowell, Oliver Wendell Holmes,** and **John Greenleaf Whittier,** were strongly committed to using poetry to bring about social reform. They were interested in such issues as abolition, women's rights, improvement of factory conditions, and temperance. They also championed the common person—perhaps as an outgrowth of the form of democracy that had been sweeping the land since President Jackson took office in 1829. Jackson had crusaded against control of the government by the wealthy and promised to look out for the interests of common people. One can see this regard for the common person in the work of Whittier, for example, who wrote of farmers, lumbermen, migrants, and the poor.

For Your Outline

THE FIRESIDE POETS

- emphasized moral themes in work
- were viewed as equals of British poets of the day
- stressed individualism and an appreciation of nature
- were committed to social reform

The Transcendentalists

By the mid-1800s, Americans were taking new pride in their emerging culture. **Ralph Waldo Emerson,** a New England writer, nurtured this pride. Emerson led a group practicing **transcendentalism**—a philosophical and literary movement that emphasized living a simple life and celebrating the truth found in nature and in personal emotion and imagination. Exalting the dignity of the individual, the transcendentalists stressed American ideas of optimism, freedom, and self-reliance.

The term *transcendentalism* came from Immanuel Kant, a German philosopher who wrote of "transcendent forms" of knowledge that exist beyond reason and experience. Emerson gave this philosophy a peculiarly American spin: he said that every individual is capable of discovering this higher truth on his or her own, through intuition. The transcendentalists believed that people are inherently good and should follow their own beliefs, however different these beliefs may be from the norm. Both Emerson's essay "Self-Reliance" and **Henry David Thoreau's** "Civil Disobedience" address this faith in the integrity of the individual.

Not surprisingly, a major target for the transcendentalists' criticism was their Puritan heritage, with its emphasis on material prosperity and rigid obedience to the laws of society. The transcendentalists disliked the commercial, financial side of American life and stressed instead spiritual well-being, achieved through intellectual activity and a close relationship to nature. Thoreau put his beliefs into practice by building a small cabin on Walden Pond and living there for two years, writing and studying nature.

Transcendental ideas lived on in American culture in the works of later poets such as Walt Whitman, Robert Frost, and Wallace Stevens and through the civil rights movement of the 20th century. In the short term, however, transcendentalists' optimism began to fade when confronted with the persistence of slavery and the difficulty in abolishing it.

For Your Outline

THE TRANSCENDENTALISTS

- emphasized living a simple life
- stressed a close relationship to nature
- celebrated emotions and the imagination
- stressed individualism and self-reliance
- believed intuition can lead to knowledge
- believed in the inherent goodness of people
- encouraged spiritual well-being over financial well-being

A replica of Thoreau's 10-by-15-foot cabin on the shore of Walden Pond

A Voice from the Times

Go confidently in the direction of your dreams! Live the life you've imagined. As you simplify your life, the laws of the universe will be simpler.

—Henry David Thoreau

American Gothic: The "Brooding" Romantics

Not all American romantics were optimistic or had faith in the innate goodness of humankind, however. Three other giants from this period, **Edgar Allan Poe, Nathaniel Hawthorne,** and **Herman Melville** are what have been called **"brooding" romantics** or **"anti-transcendentalists."** Theirs is a complex philosophy, filled with dark currents and a deep awareness of the human capacity for evil. While Irving had been satisfied if his work kept "mankind in good humor with one another," Hawthorne, Melville, and Poe were haunted by a darker vision of human existence. Their stories are characterized by a probing of the inner life of their characters, and examination of the complex and often mysterious forces that motivate human behavior. They are romantic, however, in their emphasis on emotion, nature, the individual, and the unusual.

> ***For Your Outline***
>
> **AMERICAN GOTHIC: THE "BROODING" ROMANTICS**
>
> - did not believe in the innate goodness of people
> - explored the human capacity for evil
> - probed the inner life of characters
> - explored characters' motivations
> - agreed with romantic emphasis on emotion, nature, and the individual
> - included elements of fantasy and the supernatural in works

EXPLORING THE DARKNESS Poe and Hawthorne, and to a lesser extent Melville, used **gothic** elements such as grotesque characters, bizarre situations, and violent events in their fiction. The gothic tradition had begun in Europe, perhaps inspired by the gothic architecture of the Middle Ages. European writers of the 19th century, such as Mary Shelley, author of *Frankenstein,* delighted readers with their deliciously creepy accounts of monsters, vampires, and humans with a large capacity for evil. The romantic movement itself also gave rise to gothic literature. Once the romantics freed the imagination from the restrictions of reason, they could follow it wherever it might go. For the dark romantics, the imagination led to the threshold of the unknown—that shadowy region where the fantastic, the demonic, and the insane reside.

Edgar Allan Poe, of course, was the master of the gothic form in the United States. He explored human psychology from the inside, using first-person narrators who were sometimes criminal or even insane. His plots involved extreme situations—not just murder, but live burials, physical and mental torture, and retribution from beyond the grave.

Nathaniel Hawthorne agreed with the romantic emphasis on emotion and the individual. However, he did not see these as completely positive forces. His works, such as *The Scarlet Letter* and "The Minister's Black Veil," examine the darker facets of the human soul—for example, the psychological effects sin and guilt may have on human life.

Herman Melville's early works were mostly adventure stories set in the South Pacific. *Moby Dick,* however, departed from that pattern. By concentrating on a ship's captain's obsessive quest for the whale that took his leg, Melville explores such issues as madness and the conflict of good and evil. Later, in "Bartleby the Scrivener," Melville

> **A Voice from the Times**
>
> *I looked upon the scene before me—upon the mere house, and the simple landscape features of the domain—upon the bleak walls—upon the vacant eye-like windows—upon a few rank sedges—and upon a few white trunks of decayed trees—with an utter depression of soul which I can compare to no earthly sensation more properly than to the after-dream of the reveller upon opium—the bitter lapse into every-day life—the hideous dropping off of the veil.*
>
> **—Edgar Allan Poe**
> *from* "The Fall of the House of Usher"

Like an Open-Doored Marble Tomb, George Klauba. Acrylic on panel, 18″ × 14.5″. Courtesy of Ann Nathan Gallery, Chicago, Illinois. © George Klamba.

reveals the dark side of material prosperity by exploring how the struggle for material gain affects the individual.

Perhaps the dark vision of Hawthorne, Melville, and Poe foreshadowed the tumult and tragedy that was soon to erupt in civil war in America. There is no question that these three writers profoundly affected the development of the American literary voice throughout the remainder of the 19th century.

Connecting Literature, History, and Culture

Use this timeline and the questions on the next page to gain insight about how developments during the American romantic period reflected what was happening in the world as a whole.

AMERICAN LITERARY MILESTONES

1800

1806 Noah Webster's first dictionary is published. It includes 5,000 words related to American customs that have never before been collected.

1809 Washington Irving publishes *A History of New York,* satirizing the young nation.

1810

1817 "Thanatopsis," composed by William Cullen Bryant at age 18, is published in *The North American Review.* ▼

1820

1824 Irving's "The Devil and Tom Walker" is published.

1826 James Fenimore Cooper writes *The Last of the Mohicans.*

1827 *Freedom's Journal,* the first African-American newspaper, is founded. ▼

FREEDOM'S JOURNAL.

HISTORICAL CONTEXT

1800

1803 Thomas Jefferson doubles ▲ the country's size by buying Louisiana Territory from France.

1807 Robert Fulton launches *Clermont*, the first steamboat.

1808 United States bans slave trade.

1810

1812 United States declares war ▲ on Great Britain. American industry booms.

1815 Quaker Levi Coffin establishes the Underground Railroad.

1820

1820 Missouri Compromise prohibits slavery in western territories but allows slavery in Arkansas Territory and Louisiana.

1823 The Monroe Doctrine bans European colonization in the Americas.

1825 The Erie Canal is opened, linking Lake Erie with the Hudson River.

1828 Construction begins on the first railroad in the United States.

WORLD CULTURE AND EVENTS

1800

1804 Napoleon is crowned emperor of France.

1806 The Holy Roman Empire reaches its last days.

1807 British slave trade is abolished.

1810

1813 Jane Austen publishes *Pride and Prejudice.*

1816 Rossini writes the comic opera *The Barber of Seville.*

1819 Factory work is outlawed in England for children under nine years old.

1820

1821 Venezuela and Mexico declare independence from Spain. ▶

1823 Beethoven completes his Ninth Symphony.

1829 Slavery is abolished in Mexico.

MAKING CONNECTIONS

- Which European authors were contemporaries of American romantic writers?
- What evidence do you see that slavery was not only an American problem?
- What nations were battling for independence or dealing with its challenges?
- What inventions were moving the world into a more technological age?

COMMON CORE

RI 7 Integrate and evaluate multiple sources of information presented in different media or formats as well as in words in order to address a question or solve a problem.

1830

1835 Emerson, Thoreau, Margaret Fuller, and others form the Transcendental Club.

1838 Henry Wadsworth Longfellow's "A Psalm of Life" is published.

1839 Edgar Allan Poe's "The Fall of the House of Usher" is published.

1840

1845 Henry David Thoreau moves to Walden Pond.

1846 Herman Melville's first novel, *Typee*, is published. ▼

1850

1850 Nathaniel Hawthorne's *The Scarlet Letter* is published.

1851 Sojourner Truth delivers her "Ain't I a Woman?" speech to the Women's Rights Convention in Akron, Ohio. ▶

1852 Harriet Beecher Stowe publishes *Uncle Tom's Cabin*.

1830

1830 Indian Removal Act authorizes relocation of southeastern Native American tribes to territories west of Mississippi River.

1832 Samuel B. Morse invents the telegraph. ▼

1840

1845 Florida and Texas become the 27th and 28th states.

1848 Gold discoveries in California lead to first gold rush. ▼

1850

1850 Congress passes the Fugitive Slave Act, forcing officials in Northern states to return escaped slaves to their owners.

1851 Isaac Singer devises the sewing machine. ▼

1830

1838 Slaves mutiny aboard the ▲ Spanish ship *Amistad*.

1840

1843 Charles Dickens writes *A Christmas Carol*.

1847 Emily Brontë publishes *Wuthering Heights*.

1848 Karl Marx and Friedrich Engels publish *The Communist Manifesto*.

1850

1852 David Livingstone is first European to explore Africa's Zambezi River.

1853 Verdi's opera *La Traviata* is first performed in Venice; Crimean War begins, involving Turkey, Russia, Britain, and France.

UNIT 2

The Legacy of the Era

Civil Rights

COMMON CORE

W 10 Write routinely over short time frames for a range of tasks, purposes, and audiences.
SL 1 Initiate and participate effectively in collaborative discussions, building on others' ideas and expressing their own clearly and persuasively.

When faced with unjust government actions, Henry David Thoreau called for Americans to practice civil disobedience in protest. This nonviolent form of protest attained full flower in the civil rights movement of the 1960s and remains an important tactic for activists today. In strikes, marches, and candlelight vigils, protestors across the United States use nonviolent means to make their voices heard.

DISCUSS As a class, think of recent examples of citizens using civil disobedience to protest government action. Were their protests successful? Was Thoreau right when he said, "If the alternative is to keep all just men in prison, or give up . . . , the State will not hesitate which to choose"?

Modern Gothic

The influence of Edgar Allan Poe is alive and well—make that undead and decaying—in the works of modern horror authors such as Stephen King and Anne Rice, and in many of the graphic novels lining today's bookstore shelves. Though their settings may be modern, these works share Poe's fascination with the dark side of humankind.

QUICKWRITE Why do you think people enjoy being frightened? Write a paragraph or two giving your reasons why so many people read gothic literature and enjoy films written in this same tradition.

The Romantic Hero

The romantic writers' focus on the individual led to the creation of a different kind of hero: unique, bold, sometimes brooding or eccentric. From the obsessed Captain Ahab, searching for his white whale in *Moby Dick,* to *The Last of the Mohicans'* noble Natty Bumppo, living on the fringes of society as both a white man and a Native American, romantic heroes were often larger than life, and always unforgettable. Their stories are still told today, and they have inspired a modern array of equally vivid characters.

CREATE With a small group, brainstorm a memorable hero for a new novel, TV show, or movie. Your hero should exemplify key aspects of the romantic spirit and must be utterly unique, a dynamic or mesmerizing individual who would capture people's imaginations.

Indiana Jones, from the movie *Raiders of the Lost Ark,* is a typical romantic hero.

The Devil and Tom Walker

Short Story by Washington Irving

COMMON CORE

RL 1 Cite textual evidence to support analysis of inferences drawn from the text. **RL 2** Determine two themes of a text and analyze their development. **RL 4** Analyze the impact of specific word choices on meaning and tone, including language that is fresh, engaging, or beautiful. **RL 6** Distinguish what is directly stated from what is really meant. **L 3** Apply knowledge of language to comprehend more fully when reading. **L 4a** Use context as a clue to the meaning of a word or phrase.

Meet the Author

Washington Irving 1783–1859

The Headless Horseman has thundered through readers' nightmares for nearly 200 years. Rip Van Winkle has been inspiring laughter for just as long. These characters, along with scores of others that populate his writing, helped make Washington Irving the first American writer to achieve an international reputation.

A Reluctant Lawyer Born when the nation was new and patriotism at its fiercest, Washington Irving was named for the country's first president. He began studying law at 16 but never showed much enthusiasm for it. He did, however, have a passion for writing, a playful mind, and keen powers of observation. "I was always fond of visiting new scenes and observing strange characters and manners," he once wrote. In 1807, he began publishing light satirical pieces about New York politics, culture, and theater.

Also Known As . . . In 1809, Irving penned *A History of New York from the Beginning of Time Through the End of the Dutch Dynasty,* a satire of both historical texts and the local politics they chronicled. It was considered a comic masterpiece, but for a time no one knew who had written it—the manuscript was said to have been left at an inn by an old lodger named Diedrich Knickerbocker. Knickerbocker was one of many eccentric narrators created by Irving, who didn't sign his own name to his works until he was over 40.

American Abroad In 1815, Irving began traveling through Europe, remaining there for 17 years. With the encouragement of Sir Walter Scott—the author of *Ivanhoe* and a fan of Irving's *History*—he began writing a series of stories that blended the legends of Europe with the tales he had heard while wandering as a young man through New York's Catskill Mountains and Hudson Valley. The stories, including both "The Legend of Sleepy Hollow"and "Rip Van Winkle," appeared in 1820 as *The Sketch-Book of Geoffrey Crayon, Gent.* The collection was wildly successful. However, in 1824, Irving published *Tales of a Traveller* (which contained "The Devil and Tom Walker"), and the book was not well received. In fact, the criticism was so harsh that Irving stopped writing fiction altogether.

Irving returned to America in 1832 to live with his brother on the Sunnyside estate. He died at the age of 76 and was buried near the haunting ground of his famous horseman—in New York's Sleepy Hollow Cemetery.

DID YOU KNOW?

Washington Irving . . .

- was a spectator at the trial of Aaron Burr.
- served as a colonel in the War of 1812.
- inspired the name of the New York Knicks basketball team.
- lost the love of his life when she died at 17.

Author Online THINK central

Go to thinkcentral.com. KEYWORD: HML11-318

TEXT ANALYSIS: SATIRE

Irving was a master of **satire,** a literary device in which people, customs, or institutions are ridiculed with the purpose of improving society. In this passage, Irving pokes fun at quarrelsome, complaining women:

. . . Though a female scold is generally considered to be a match for the devil, yet in this instance she appears to have had the worst of it.

Satire is often subtle, so as you read, watch for its indicators: humor, exaggeration, absurd situations, and irony.

READING SKILL: ANALYZE IMAGERY

Irving develops his characters and establishes mood through imagery—words and phrases that appeal to the five senses.

. . . There lived near this place a meager, miserly fellow, of the name of Tom Walker. He had a wife as miserly as himself. . . . They lived in a forlorn-looking house that stood alone and had an air of starvation.

As you read, use a chart like the one below to record images from the story. Also include your inferences about how the images support the story's characters and mood.

Images	Characterization	Mood
house with a look of starvation	Tom and his wife are miserly.	depressing

Review: **Make Inferences**

VOCABULARY IN CONTEXT

The following words are critical to the story of a miser who would trade his soul for money. Check your understanding of each one by rewording the sentence in which it appears.

1. The **melancholy** sight of the graveyard chilled him.
2. The **persecution** of the Puritans went unchallenged.
3. The mention of gold awakened his **avarice.**
4. The corrupt **usurer** charged 20 percent interest.
5. **Speculating** in land deals held the promise of quick profits.
6. Hard economic times are **propitious** for moneylenders.
7. People who flaunt their wealth are guilty of **ostentation.**
8. He was a strict **censurer** of other people's vices.

Complete the activities in your **Reader/Writer Notebook.**

Are you willing to PAY ANY PRICE?

People who'll stop at nothing to achieve wealth, success, or fame are often said to have "sold their soul." In other words, they have sacrificed something important—moral beliefs, privacy, family—in order to get what they want. Consider this kind of trade-off. Do you think it might ever be worth the consequences?

DISCUSS Working with a partner, list several people—real or fictional—who fit this profile. Then pick one such person and list his or her gains and their consequences. Assign a value to each item and decide whether, overall, the prize was worth the price. Share your conclusions with the rest of the class.

The DEVIL *and* Tom Walker

Washington Irving

BACKGROUND The story of Tom Walker is a variation on the legend of Faust, a 16th-century magician and astrologer who was said to have sold his soul to the devil for wisdom, money, and power. Washington Irving reinvented the tale, setting it in the 1720s in an area of New England settled by Quakers and Puritans. In Irving's comic retelling of the legend, the writer satirizes people who present a pious public image as they "sell their soul" for money.

A few miles from Boston in Massachusetts, there is a deep inlet, winding several miles into the interior of the country from Charles Bay, and terminating in a thickly wooded swamp or morass. On one side of this inlet is a beautiful dark grove; on the opposite side the land rises abruptly from the water's edge into a high ridge, on which grow a few scattered oaks of great age and immense size. Under one of these gigantic trees, according to old stories, there was a great amount of treasure buried by Kidd the pirate. The inlet allowed a facility to bring the money in a boat secretly and at night to the very foot of the hill; the elevation of the place permitted a good lookout to be kept that no one was at hand; while the remarkable trees formed good landmarks by which the place might easily be found again. The old stories add, moreover, that the devil presided at the hiding of the money and took it under his guardianship; but this, it is well-known, he always does with buried treasure, particularly when it has been ill-gotten. Be that as it may, Kidd never returned to recover his wealth; being shortly after seized at Boston, sent out to England, and there hanged for a pirate. **A**

Analyze Visuals ▶
Artist John Quidor is well-known for his series of fantastic paintings based on Irving's writings. In this detail, a man discovers a store of hidden gold. What clues from the painting's images, colors, and dark tones help you visualize and better understand the imagery in the story?

A IMAGERY
Reread lines 1–15. What details in the description suggest that this is an ill-fated place?

Detail of *The Money Diggers* (1832), John Quidor.

About the year 1727, just at the time that earthquakes were prevalent in New England, and shook many tall sinners down upon their knees, there lived near this place a meager, miserly fellow, of the name of Tom Walker. He had a wife as miserly as himself: they were so miserly that they even conspired to cheat each other. Whatever the woman could lay hands on, she hid away; a hen could not cackle but she was on the alert to secure the new-laid egg. Her husband was continually prying about to detect her secret hoards, and many and fierce were the conflicts that took place about what ought to have been common property. They lived in a forlorn-looking house that stood alone and had an air of starvation. A few straggling savin trees, emblems of sterility, grew near it; no smoke ever curled from its chimney; no traveler stopped at its door. A miserable horse, whose ribs were as articulate as the bars of a gridiron,[1] stalked about a field, where a thin carpet of moss, scarcely covering the ragged beds of puddingstone,[2] tantalized and balked his hunger; and sometimes he would lean his head over the fence, look piteously at the passerby and seem to petition deliverance from this land of famine. **B**

The house and its inmates had altogether a bad name. Tom's wife was a tall termagant,[3] fierce of temper, loud of tongue, and strong of arm. Her voice was often heard in wordy warfare with her husband; and his face sometimes showed signs that their conflicts were not confined to words. No one ventured, however, to interfere between them. The lonely wayfarer shrunk within himself at the horrid clamor and clapper-clawing;[4] eyed the den of discord askance;[5] and hurried on his way, rejoicing, if a bachelor, in his celibacy. **C**

One day that Tom Walker had been to a distant part of the neighborhood, he took what he considered a shortcut homeward, through the swamp. Like most shortcuts, it was an ill-chosen route. The swamp was thickly grown with great gloomy pines and hemlocks, some of them ninety feet high, which made it dark at noonday, and a retreat for all the owls of the neighborhood. It was full of pits and quagmires, partly covered with weeds and mosses, where the green surface often betrayed the traveler into a gulf of black, smothering mud; there were also dark and stagnant pools, the abodes of the tadpole, the bullfrog, and the water snake; where the trunks of pines and hemlocks lay half-drowned, half-rotting, looking like alligators sleeping in the mire. **D**

Tom had long been picking his way cautiously through this treacherous forest; stepping from tuft to tuft of rushes and roots, which afforded precarious footholds among deep sloughs; or pacing carefully, like a cat, along the prostrate trunks of trees; startled now and then by the sudden screaming of the bittern,[6] or the quacking of wild duck rising on the wind from some solitary pool. At length he arrived at a firm piece of ground, which ran out like a peninsula into the deep bosom of the swamp. It had been one of the strongholds of the Indians during their wars

COMMON CORE L 4a

Language Coach

Multiple-Meaning Words Find "common property" in line 23. *Common* here means "shared." What meaning does *common* have in the expression *common thief*?

B IMAGERY
Identify the images in lines 16–30 that help to characterize Tom and his wife. What **character traits** do these images reveal?

C SATIRE
In lines 31–37, Irving satirizes scolding women and the institution of marriage. What humorous details indicate this satire?

D IMAGERY
What kind of **mood** is established by the description of the swamp in lines 40–47?

---

1. **as articulate . . . gridiron:** as clearly separated as the bars of a grill.
2. **puddingstone:** a rock consisting of pebbles and gravel cemented together.
3. **termagant** (tûr′mə-gənt): a quarrelsome, scolding woman.
4. **clapper-clawing:** scratching or clawing with the fingernails.
5. **eyed . . . askance** (ə-skăns′): looked disapprovingly at the house filled with arguing.
6. **bittern:** a wading bird with mottled, brownish plumage and a deep, booming cry.

with the first colonists. Here they had thrown up a kind of fort, which they had looked upon as almost impregnable, and had used as a place of refuge for their squaws and children.

Nothing remained of the old Indian fort but a few embankments, gradually sinking to the level of the surrounding earth, and already overgrown in part by oaks and other forest trees, the foliage of which formed a contrast to the dark pines and hemlocks of the swamp.

It was late in the dusk of evening when Tom Walker reached the old fort, and he paused there awhile to rest himself. Anyone but he would have felt unwilling to linger in this lonely, **melancholy** place, for the common people had a bad opinion of it, from the stories handed down from the time of the Indian wars, when it was asserted that the savages held incantations[7] here, and made sacrifices to the evil spirit.

melancholy
(mĕl′ən-kŏl′ē) *adj.*
gloomy; sad

Tom Walker, however, was not a man to be troubled with any fears of the kind. He reposed himself for some time on the trunk of a fallen hemlock, listening to the boding cry of the tree toad, and delving with his walking staff into a mound of black mold at his feet. As he turned up the soil unconsciously, his staff struck against something hard. He raked it out of the vegetable mold, and lo! a cloven skull, with an Indian tomahawk buried deep in it, lay before him. The rust on the weapon showed the time that had elapsed since this death-blow had been given. It was a dreary memento of the fierce struggle that had taken place in this last foothold of the Indian warriors.

"Humph!" said Tom Walker, as he gave it a kick to shake the dirt from it. **E**

E MAKE INFERENCES
Look again at lines 68 and 77. What can you infer about Tom Walker from his reaction to the swamp and to his grisly discovery of the skull?

"Let that skull alone!" said a gruff voice. Tom lifted up his eyes, and beheld a great black man seated directly opposite him, on the stump of a tree. He was exceedingly surprised, having neither heard nor seen anyone approach; and he was still more perplexed on observing, as well as the gathering gloom would permit, that the stranger was neither Negro nor Indian. It is true he was dressed in a rude half-Indian garb, and had a red belt or sash swathed round his body; but his face was neither black nor copper-color, but swarthy and dingy, and begrimed with soot, as if he had been accustomed to toil among fires and forges. He had a shock of coarse black hair, that stood out from his head in all directions, and bore an ax on his shoulder.

He scowled for a moment at Tom with a pair of great red eyes.

"What are you doing on my grounds?" said the black man, with a hoarse, growling voice.

"Your grounds!" said Tom, with a sneer, "no more your grounds than mine; they belong to Deacon Peabody."

"Deacon Peabody be d—d," said the stranger, "as I flatter myself he will be, if he does not look more to his own sins and less to those of his neighbors. Look yonder, and see how Deacon Peabody is faring."

7. **incantations:** verbal charms or spells recited to produce a magic effect.

The Devil and Tom Walker (1856), John Quidor. Oil on canvas, 68.8 cm × 86.6 cm. © The Cleveland Museum of Art, Mr. and Mrs. William H. Marlatt Fund, 1967.18.

▲ Analyze Visuals
This Quidor painting illustrates the first meeting between Tom and the devil. In your opinion, how well do the artist's choices of color and shading and his depiction of Tom's **character** match the story? Explain.

Tom looked in the direction that the stranger pointed, and beheld one of the great trees, fair and flourishing without, but rotten at the core, and saw that it had been nearly hewn through, so that the first high wind was likely to blow it down. On the bark of the tree was scored the name of Deacon Peabody, an eminent man, who had waxed wealthy by driving shrewd bargains with the Indians. He now looked around, and found most of the tall trees marked with the name of some great man of the colony, and all more or less scored by the ax. The one on which he had been seated, and which had evidently just been hewn down, bore the name of Crowninshield; and he recollected a mighty rich man of that name, who made a vulgar display of wealth, which it was whispered he had acquired by buccaneering.[8] **F**

"He's just ready for burning!" said the black man, with a growl of triumph. "You see, I am likely to have a good stock of firewood for winter."

"But what right have you," said Tom, "to cut down Deacon Peabody's timber?"

"The right of a prior claim," said the other. "This woodland belonged to me long before one of your white-faced race put foot upon the soil."

"And pray, who are you, if I may be so bold?" said Tom.

"Oh, I go by various names. I am the wild huntsman in some countries; the black miner in others. In this neighborhood I am he to whom the red men consecrated this spot, and in honor of whom they now and then roasted a white man, by way of sweet-smelling sacrifice. Since the red men have been exterminated by you white savages, I amuse myself by presiding at the **persecutions** of Quakers and Anabaptists;[9] I am the great patron and prompter of slave dealers, and the grand master of the Salem witches." **G**

"The upshot of all which is that, if I mistake not," said Tom, sturdily, "you are he commonly called Old Scratch."[10]

"The same, at your service!" replied the black man, with a half-civil nod.

Such was the opening of this interview, according to the old story; though it has almost too familiar an air to be credited. One would think that to meet with such a singular personage, in this wild, lonely place, would have shaken any man's nerves; but Tom was a hard-minded fellow, not easily daunted, and he had lived so long with a termagant wife that he did not even fear the devil.

It is said that after this commencement they had a long and earnest conversation together, as Tom returned homeward. The black man told him of great sums of money buried by Kidd the pirate, under the oak trees on the high ridge, not far from the morass. All these were under his command, and protected by his power, so that none could find them but such as propitiated his favor. These he offered to place within Tom Walker's reach, having conceived an especial kindness for him; but they were to be had only on certain conditions. What these conditions were may be easily surmised, though Tom never disclosed them publicly. They must have been very hard, for he required time to think of them, and he was not a man

F MAKE INFERENCES
Reread lines 96–105. Why do you think the trees are marked with the men's names?

persecution
(pûr′sĭ-kyōō′shən) *n.* the act or practice of oppressing or harassing with ill-treatment, especially because of race, religion, gender, or beliefs

G SATIRE
Reread lines 115–118. What do they tell you about the author's attitude toward the activities of the early settlers? What led you to make that inference?

Language Coach

Word Definitions
Propitious means "helpful or advantageous; favorable." *Propitiated* in line 131 means "gained the good will of." On page 327, line 164, you'll see the phrase "propitiatory offering." What might *propitiatory* mean?

---

8. **buccaneering:** robbing ships at sea; piracy.
9. **presiding . . . Anabaptists:** exercising authority over the oppression of Christian groups that the Puritans considered heretical.
10. **Old Scratch:** a nickname for the devil.

Forest Landscape (1800s), Asher Brown Durand. Oil on canvas, 76.2 cm × 66 cm. © Brooklyn Museum of Art/ Bridgeman Art Library.

to stick at trifles when money was in view. When they had reached the edge of the swamp, the stranger paused. "What proof have I that all you have been telling me is true?" said Tom. "There's my signature," said the black man, pressing his finger on Tom's forehead. So saying, he turned off among the thickets of the swamp, and seemed, as Tom said, to go down, down, down, into the earth, until nothing but his head and shoulders could be seen, and so on, until he totally disappeared.

When Tom reached home, he found the black print of a finger burnt, as it were, into his forehead, which nothing could obliterate.

The first news his wife had to tell him was the sudden death of Absalom Crowninshield, the rich buccaneer. It was announced in the papers with the usual flourish that "a great man had fallen in Israel."[11]

COMMON CORE RL 2

THEME
The theme of the danger of greed goes back to ancient Greece. When the gods give greedy King Midas the ability to turn anything he touches into gold, Midas does not realize that his touch will accidentally kill his own daughter. Tom Walker also fails to understand that his greed for wealth will require a terrible personal sacrifice. This theme continues in 20th-century fiction. In John Steinbeck's novel, *The Pearl*, a humble pearl diver and his family become unexpectedly wealthy, until the greed of their neighbors and friends for a piece of that wealth leads to tragedy. Why do you think stories about the risks of greed continue to be written?

11. **a great man . . . Israel:** a biblical reference—"Know ye not that there is a prince and a great man fallen this day in Israel?" (2 Samuel 3:38)—used, with unconscious irony, by the papers to mean that an important member of God's people on earth had passed away.

Tom recollected the tree which his black friend had just hewn down and which was ready for burning. "Let the freebooter[12] roast," said Tom; "who cares!" He now felt convinced that all he had heard and seen was no illusion.

He was not prone to let his wife into his confidence; but as this was an uneasy secret, he willingly shared it with her. All her **avarice** was awakened at the mention of hidden gold, and she urged her husband to comply with the black man's terms, and secure what would make them wealthy for life. However Tom might have felt disposed to sell himself to the devil, he was determined not to do so to oblige his wife; so he flatly refused, out of the mere spirit of contradiction. Many and bitter were the quarrels they had on the subject; but the more she talked, the more resolute was Tom not to be damned to please her.

avarice (ăv′ə-rĭs) *n.* immoderate desire for wealth; greed

At length she determined to drive the bargain on her own account, and if she succeeded, to keep all the gain to herself. Being of the same fearless temper as her husband, she set off for the old Indian fort toward the close of a summer's day. She was many hours absent. When she came back, she was reserved and sullen in her replies. She spoke something of a black man, whom she met about twilight hewing at the root of a tall tree. He was sulky, however, and would not come to terms; she was to go again with a propitiatory offering, but what it was she forbore to say.

The next evening she set off again for the swamp, with her apron heavily laden. Tom waited and waited for her, but in vain; midnight came, but she did not make her appearance; morning, noon, night returned, but still she did not come. Tom now grew uneasy for her safety, especially as he found she had carried off in her apron the silver teapot and spoons, and every portable article of value. Another night elapsed, another morning came; but no wife. In a word, she was never heard of more.

What was her real fate nobody knows, in consequence of so many pretending to know. It is one of those facts which have become confounded by a variety of historians. Some asserted that she lost her way among the tangled mazes of the swamp, and sank into some pit or slough; others, more uncharitable, hinted that she had eloped with the household booty and made off to some other province; while others surmised that the tempter had decoyed her into a dismal quagmire, on the top of which her hat was found lying. In confirmation of this, it was said a great black man, with an ax on his shoulder, was seen late that very evening coming out of the swamp, carrying a bundle tied in a check apron, with an air of surly triumph. H

COMMON CORE L 3

Language Coach

Fixed Expressions Look at "confirmation of" in line 177. *Of* often follows *confirmation*, such as in the statement "I need *confirmation of* this information." Other phrases using *confirmation* include "[to] await confirmation" and "further confirmation." Use each phrase in a sentence of your own.

H GRAMMAR AND STYLE
Irving emphasizes ideas and creates lyricism through the use of **parallelism,** the repetition of grammatical structures. In lines 173–177, for example, the writer uses parallelism to present three possible fates of Tom's wife.

The most current and probable story, however, observes that Tom Walker grew so anxious about the fate of his wife and his property that he set out at length to seek them both at the Indian fort. During a long summer's afternoon he searched about the gloomy place, but no wife was to be seen. He called her name repeatedly, but she was nowhere to be heard. The bittern alone responded to his voice, as they flew screaming by; or the bullfrog croaked dolefully from a neighboring pool. At length, it is said, just in the brown hour of twilight, when the owls began to hoot, and the bats to flit about, his attention was attracted by the clamor of carrion crows[13] hovering about a cypress tree. He looked up, and beheld a bundle tied in a

12. **freebooter:** pirate.

13. **carrion crows:** crows that feed on dead or decaying flesh.

check apron, and hanging in the branches of the tree, with a great vulture perched hard by, as if keeping watch upon it. He leaped with joy; for he recognized his wife's apron and supposed it to contain the household valuables. **I**

"Let us get hold of the property," said he consolingly to himself, "and we will endeavor to do without the woman."

As he scrambled up the tree, the vulture spread its wide wings, and sailed off screaming into the deep shadows of the forest. Tom seized the checked apron, but, woeful sight! found nothing but a heart and liver tied up in it!

Such, according to this most authentic old story, was all that was to be found of Tom's wife. She had probably attempted to deal with the black man as she had been accustomed to deal with her husband; but though a female scold is generally considered a match for the devil, yet in this instance she appears to have had the worst of it. She must have died game, however; for it is said Tom noticed many prints of cloven feet stamped upon the tree, and found handfuls of hair that looked as if they had been plucked from the coarse black shock of the woodman. Tom knew his wife's prowess by experience. He shrugged his shoulders, as he looked at the signs of a fierce clapper-clawing. "Egad," said he to himself, "Old Scratch must have had a tough time of it!" **J**

Tom consoled himself for the loss of his property with the loss of his wife, for he was a man of fortitude. He even felt something like gratitude towards the black woodman, who, he considered, had done him a kindness. He sought, therefore, to cultivate a further acquaintance with him, but for some time without success; the old blacklegs played shy, for, whatever people may think, he is not always to be had for calling for: he knows how to play his cards when pretty sure of his game.

At length, it is said, when delay had whetted Tom's eagerness to the quick, and prepared him to agree to anything rather than not gain the promised treasure, he met the black man one evening in his usual woodsman's dress, with his ax on his shoulder, sauntering along the swamp, and humming a tune. He affected to receive Tom's advances with great indifference, made brief replies, and went on humming his tune.

By degrees, however, Tom brought him to business, and they began to haggle about the terms on which the former was to have the pirate's treasure. There was one condition which need not be mentioned, being generally understood in all cases where the devil grants favors; but there were others about which, though of less importance, he was inflexibly obstinate. He insisted that the money found through his means should be employed in his service. He proposed, therefore, that Tom should employ it in the black traffic; that is to say, that he should fit out a slave ship. This, however, Tom resolutely refused: he was bad enough in all conscience; but the devil himself could not tempt him to turn slave trader.

Finding Tom so squeamish on this point, he did not insist upon it, but proposed, instead, that he should turn **usurer;** the devil being extremely anxious for the increase of usurers, looking upon them as his peculiar people.

To this no objections were made, for it was just to Tom's taste.

"You shall open a broker's shop in Boston next month," said the black man.

"I'll do it tomorrow, if you wish," said Tom Walker.

"You shall lend money at two percent a month."

"Egad, I'll charge four!" replied Tom Walker.

I IMAGERY
Which images in lines 189–192 suggest that Tom's discovery won't be a pleasant one?

J SATIRE
How does Irving use **humor** and **exaggeration** to satirize a "female scold" in lines 199–207?

usurer (yo͞o'zhər-ər) *n.* one who lends money, at interest, especially at an unusually or unlawfully high rate of interest

"You shall extort bonds, foreclose mortgages, drive the merchants to bankruptcy—"

"I'll drive them to the d——l," cried Tom Walker.

"You are the usurer for my money!" said blacklegs with delight. "When will you want the rhino?"[14]

"This very night."

"Done!" said the devil.

"Done!" said Tom Walker. So they shook hands and struck a bargain. **K**

K SATIRE
Reread lines 232–243. How does Tom compare with the devil in terms of his greed and mercilessness? Decide what comment Irving is making about usurers in general.

A few days' time saw Tom Walker seated behind his desk in a countinghouse[15] in Boston.

His reputation for a ready-moneyed man, who would lend money out for a good consideration, soon spread abroad. Everybody remembers the time of Governor Belcher, when money was particularly scarce. It was a time of paper credit. The country had been deluged with government bills; the famous Land Bank[16] had been established; there had been a rage for **speculating;** the people had run mad with schemes for new settlements; for building cities in the wilderness; land-jobbers[17] went about with maps of grants, and townships, and Eldorados[18] lying nobody knew where, but which everybody was ready to purchase. In a word, the great speculating fever, which breaks out every now and then in the country, had raged to an alarming degree, and everybody was dreaming of making sudden fortunes from nothing. As usual the fever had subsided; the dream had gone off, and the imaginary fortunes with it; the patients were left in doleful plight, and the whole country resounded with the consequent cry of "hard times."

speculating
(spĕk'yə-lā'tĭng) *n.* engaging in risky business transactions on the chance of a quick or considerable profit

At this **propitious** time of public distress did Tom Walker set up as usurer in Boston. His door was soon thronged by customers. The needy and adventurous, the gambling speculator, the dreaming land-jobber, the thriftless tradesman, the merchant with cracked credit; in short, everyone driven to raise money by desperate means and desperate sacrifices hurried to Tom Walker.

propitious
(prə-pĭsh'əs) *adj.* helpful or advantageous; favorable

Thus Tom was the universal friend of the needy and acted like a "friend in need"; that is to say, he always exacted good pay and good security. In proportion to the distress of the applicant was the hardness of his terms. He accumulated bonds and mortgages; gradually squeezed his customers closer and closer; and sent them at length, dry as a sponge, from his door.

In this way he made money hand over hand, became a rich and mighty man, and exalted his cocked hat upon 'Change.[19] He built himself, as usual, a vast

14. **rhino:** a slang term for money.
15. **countinghouse:** an office in which a business firm conducts its bookkeeping, correspondence, and similar activities.
16. **Land Bank:** Boston merchants organized the Land Bank in 1739. Landowners could take out mortgages on their property and then repay the loans with cash or manufactured goods. When the Land Bank was outlawed in 1741, many colonists lost money.
17. **land-jobbers:** people who buy and sell land for profit.
18. **Eldorados:** places of fabulous wealth or great opportunity. Early Spanish explorers sought a legendary country named El Dorado, which was rumored to be rich with gold.
19. **exalted . . . 'Change:** proudly raised himself to a position of importance as a trader on the stock exchange.

house, out of **ostentation;** but left the greater part of it unfinished and unfurnished, out of parsimony. He even set up a carriage in the fullness of his vainglory,[20] though he nearly starved the horses which drew it; and as the ungreased wheels groaned and screeched on the axletrees, you would have thought you heard the souls of the poor debtors he was squeezing. L

As Tom waxed old, however, he grew thoughtful. Having secured the good things of this world, he began to feel anxious about those of the next. He thought with regret on the bargain he had made with his black friend, and set his wits to work to cheat him out of the conditions. He became, therefore, all of a sudden, a violent churchgoer. He prayed loudly and strenuously, as if heaven were to be taken by force of lungs. Indeed, one might always tell when he had sinned most during the week, by the clamor of his Sunday devotion. The quiet Christians who had been modestly and steadfastly traveling Zionward[21] were struck with self-reproach at seeing themselves so suddenly outstripped in their career by this new-made convert. Tom was as rigid in religious as in money matters; he was a stern supervisor and **censurer** of his neighbors, and seemed to think every sin entered up to their account became a credit on his own side of the page. He even talked of the expediency of reviving the persecution of Quakers and Anabaptists. In a word, Tom's zeal became as notorious as his riches. M

Still, in spite of all this strenuous attention to forms, Tom had a lurking dread that the devil, after all, would have his due.[22] That he might not be taken unawares, therefore, it is said he always carried a small Bible in his coat pocket. He had also a great folio Bible on his countinghouse desk, and would frequently be found reading it when people called on business; on such occasions he would lay his green spectacles in the book, to mark the place, while he turned round to drive some usurious bargain.

Some say that Tom grew a little crackbrained in his old days, and that fancying his end approaching, he had his horse new shod, saddled and bridled, and buried with his feet uppermost; because he supposed that at the last day the world would be turned upside down; in which case he should find his horse standing ready for mounting, and he was determined at the worst to give his old friend a run for it. This, however, is probably a mere old wives' fable. If he really did take such a precaution, it was totally superfluous; at least so says the authentic old legend, which closes his story in the following manner:

One hot summer afternoon in the dog days, just as a terrible black thundergust was coming up, Tom sat in his countinghouse, in his white linen cap and India silk morning gown. He was on the point of foreclosing a mortgage, by which he would complete the ruin of an unlucky land speculator for whom he had professed the greatest friendship. The poor land-jobber begged him to grant a few months' indulgence. Tom had grown testy and irritated, and refused another day.

ostentation
(ŏs´ tĕn-tā'shən) *n.* display meant to impress others; boastful showiness

L IMAGERY
Find the images in lines 264–275 that are used to describe both Tom and his clients. What do these images tell you about Tom and his methods?

censurer
(sĕn'shər-ər) *n.* one who expresses strong disapproval or harsh criticism

M SATIRE
What kind of churchgoer is represented by Tom in lines 276–289? Think about what Irving is suggesting about this kind of individual.

---

20. **vainglory:** boastful, undeserved pride in one's accomplishments or qualities.

21. **Zionward:** toward heaven.

22. **the devil . . . due:** a reference to the proverb "Give the devil his due," used to mean "Give even a disagreeable person the credit he or she deserves." Here, of course, the expression is used literally rather than figuratively.

"My family will be ruined and brought upon the parish," said the land-jobber. "Charity begins at home," replied Tom; "I must take care of myself in these hard times."

"You have made so much money out of me," said the speculator.

Tom lost his patience and his piety. "The devil take me," said he, "if I have made a farthing!"[23]

Just then there were three loud knocks at the street door. He stepped out to see who was there. A black man was holding a black horse, which neighed and stamped with impatience.

"Tom, you're come for," said the black fellow, gruffly. Tom shrank back, but too late. He had left his little Bible at the bottom of his coat pocket, and his big Bible on the desk buried under the mortgage he was about to foreclose; never was a sinner taken more unawares. The black man whisked him like a child into the saddle,

23. **farthing:** a coin worth one-fourth of a penny, formerly used throughout the British Empire.

▼ Analyze Visuals

What elements in this painting by Quidor emphasize the human fear of the supernatural and the consequences of greed? Explain.

Tom Walker's Flight (about 1856), John Quidor. Oil on canvas, 26 3/4" × 33 3/4". The Fine Arts Museums of San Francisco, Gift of Mr. and Mrs. John D. Rockefeller 3rd, 1979.7.84.

gave the horse the lash, and away he galloped, with Tom on his back, in the midst of the thunderstorm. The clerks stuck their pens behind their ears, and stared after him from the windows. Away went Tom Walker, dashing down the streets; his white cap bobbing up and down, his morning gown fluttering in the wind, and his steed striking fire out of the pavement at every bound. When the clerks turned to look for the black man, he had disappeared.

Tom Walker never returned to foreclose the mortgage. A countryman, who lived on the border of the swamp, reported that in the height of the thundergust he had heard a great clattering of hoofs and a howling along the road, and running to the window caught sight of a figure, such as I have described, on a horse that galloped like mad across the fields, over the hills, and down into the black hemlock swamp toward the old Indian fort; and that shortly after a thunderbolt falling in that direction seemed to set the whole forest in a blaze.

The good people of Boston shook their heads and shrugged their shoulders, but had been so much accustomed to witches and goblins, and tricks of the devil, in all kinds of shapes, from the first settlement of the colony, that they were not so much horror-struck as might have been expected. Trustees were appointed to take charge of Tom's effects. There was nothing, however, to administer upon. On searching his coffers[24] all his bonds and mortgages were found reduced to cinders. In place of gold and silver, his iron chest was filled with chips and shavings; two skeletons lay in his stable instead of his half-starved horses, and the very next day his great house took fire and burnt to the ground. **N**

N IMAGERY
Reread lines 341–345. What **message** do these images suggest about material possessions and those who seek them?

Such was the end of Tom Walker and his ill-gotten wealth. Let all griping money brokers lay this story to heart. The truth of it is not to be doubted. The very hole under the oak trees whence he dug Kidd's money is to be seen to this day; and the neighboring swamp and old Indian fort are often haunted in stormy nights by a figure on horseback, in morning gown and white cap, which is doubtless the troubled spirit of the usurer. In fact the story has resolved itself into a proverb so prevalent throughout New England, of "The Devil and Tom Walker."

COMMON CORE RL 2

THEME

Irving's story is a satirical version of the legend of Faust, who sold his soul to the devil. The Faust theme often appears in works of literature and film. One recent example is the best-selling 2003 novel, *The Devil Wears Prada,* and its 2006 film version. In this satire of the fashion industry, a young woman begins to lose herself as she tries to please her demanding boss in order to have a successful career. What other recent stories, novels, plays, or films can you think of that relate to the Faust theme?

---

24. **coffers:** safes or strongboxes designed to hold money or other valuable items.

Comprehension

1. **Recall** What character traits do Tom Walker and his wife share?
2. **Recall** What bargain does Tom make with the stranger in the forest?
3. **Summarize** How does Tom try to avoid fulfilling his end of the bargain?

Text Analysis

4. **Compare Character Traits** As Tom gets older, he begins to worry about his actions and becomes "a violent churchgoer." But does he really change? Support your opinion with examples from the text. Use a chart like the one shown to collect evidence.

	Before the Bargain	As He Ages
Attitude		
Statements		
Actions		

5. **Draw Conclusions** In your opinion, is there any way Tom could have escaped the consequences of his deal with the devil? Use evidence from the text and your own knowledge of human nature to support your answer.

6. **Analyze Imagery** What inferences can you make about how each of the following images supports characterization and mood?
   - the trees and the swamp (lines 40–47)
   - the hewn trees (lines 96-102)
   - Tom's new house (lines 270–272)
   - Tom as a churchgoer (lines 279–289)

7. **Analyze Satire** Through statements he makes about Tom Walker, his wife, and his community, what messages is Irving communicating about
   - women (lines 31–37)?
   - the slave trade (lines 224–227)?
   - the Puritan attitude (lines 115–118)?
   - moneylenders (lines 228–230)?

Text Criticism

8. **Critical Interpretations** The story of Tom Walker engaged readers both here and in Europe for many different, and sometimes conflicting, reasons. Look at the story again through the eyes of each of the following people. What reasons would you give for recommending the story to others?
   - revolutionary
   - Puritan
   - American politician
   - banker

Are you willing to **PAY ANY PRICE?**

Tom Walker goes to extreme lengths to acquire wealth. Are there things in life that are worth paying any price for? If so, what are they, and what are the consequences of seeking them?

COMMON CORE

RL 1 Cite evidence to support analysis of inferences drawn from the text. **RL 3** Analyze the impact of the author's choices regarding how to develop and relate elements of a story. **RL 4** Analyze the impact of specific word choices on meaning and tone, including language that is fresh, engaging, or beautiful. **RL 6** Distinguish what is directly stated from what is really meant.

Vocabulary in Context

▲ VOCABULARY PRACTICE

Choose the vocabulary word that best matches each description below.

1. someone who loves to nag, criticize, and sneer
2. your mood if you suddenly lost your job, your best friend, or your dog
3. what a hot day is to lemonade vendors
4. a pretentious display that is meant to impress others
5. what the Bill of Rights was written to prevent
6. what someone who buys stock in a struggling company is doing
7. a person you don't want to have help you out of financial difficulties
8. a feeling that can make someone drool in a department store

WORD LIST
avarice
censurer
melancholy
ostentation
persecution
propitious
speculating
usurer

ACADEMIC VOCABULARY IN WRITING

• construct • expand • indicate • reinforce • role

Irving uses several examples of wicked characters to **reinforce** the idea that greed is bad. In a short paragraph, **indicate** how Irving could have also included positive **role** models to illustrate moderation. Use three of the Academic Vocabulary words in your writing.

COMMON CORE

L 4b–c Identify and use patterns of word changes that indicate different parts of speech; consult reference materials to determine or clarify a word's part of speech. **L 6** Acquire and use academic words and phrases.

VOCABULARY STRATEGY: THE LATIN ROOT *spec*

When Tom Walker's neighbors speculated in land, they were hoping to spot opportunities for a quick profit. The Latin root *spec* in the word *speculating* actually means "to look at" or "to see or behold." Words containing this root, or the related forms *spect* and *spic*, usually have something to do with light, sight, or clarity.

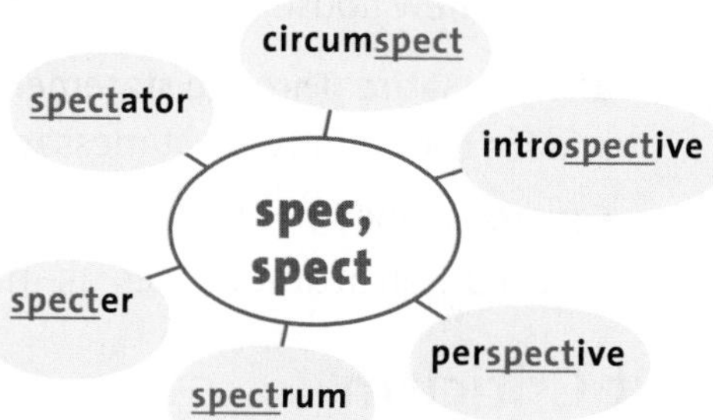

PRACTICE Match each definition below with the appropriate word from the word web, considering what you know about the origin of the Latin root *spec* and the other word parts shown. Then, say whether the words are nouns or adjectives, checking a dictionary if necessary.

1. tending to look within, at one's own thoughts or feelings
2. an observer of an event
3. a ghostly sight or apparition
4. showing unwillingness to act rashly; prudent
5. a point of view
6. a range of colored light

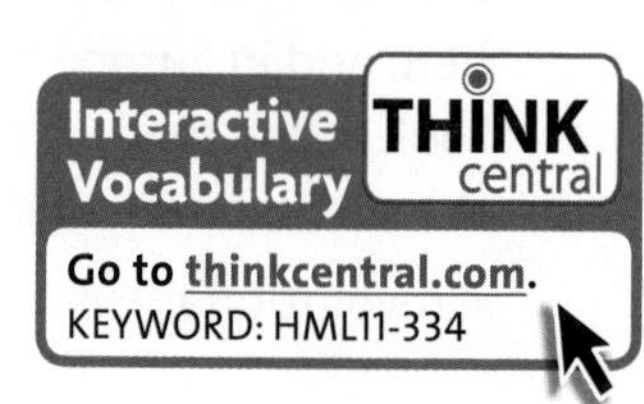

Interactive Vocabulary
THINK central
Go to thinkcentral.com.
KEYWORD: HML11-334

Language

COMMON CORE

L 3 Apply knowledge of language to to make effective choices for meaning or style. **L 3a** Vary syntax for effect. **W 3d** Write narratives using precise words and phrases.

GRAMMAR AND STYLE: Recognize Parallelism

Review the **Grammar and Style** note on page 327. Irving uses parallelism—the repetition of grammatical structures—to create emphasis or to add rhythm. Look at this example:

> *Tom's wife was a tall termagant, fierce of temper, loud of tongue, and strong of arm.* (lines 31–32)

Notice that each of the highlighted phrases contains an adjective (*fierce, loud,* and *strong*) followed by a prepositional phrase (*of temper, of tongue,* and *of arm*). How does the parallelism affect the description of Tom's wife?

PRACTICE Write down each of the following sentences from the selection. Then identify the parallel elements from each sentence as shown and write your own sentence with similar parallel elements.

EXAMPLE

. . . No smoke ever curled from its chimney; no traveler stopped at its door.

No frown ever crossed his face; no complaint crossed his lips.

1. "Oh, I go by various names. I am the wild huntsman in some countries; the black miner in others. . . . I am the great patron and prompter of slave dealers, and the grand master of the Salem witches."
2. . . . Midnight came, but she did not make her appearance; morning, noon, night returned, but still she did not come.
3. He built himself, as usual, a vast house, out of ostentation; but left the greater part of it unfinished and unfurnished, out of parsimony.

READING-WRITING CONNECTION

Expand your understanding of Irving's "The Devil and Tom Walker" by responding to this prompt. Then, use the **revising tips** to improve your story.

WRITING PROMPT

WRITE A STORY An archetypal plot is a basic story line that serves as a frame for stories across time and cultures. Write a **one- to three-page story** around a situation where a character makes a "deal with the devil" in a modern setting. Be sure to show the results of the main character's actions.

REVISING TIPS

- Use parallel verbs (such as *saw, went, bought*) to add rhythm and vary syntax.
- Use parallel phrases to enhance your style.
- Use parallel sentences to clarify meaning.

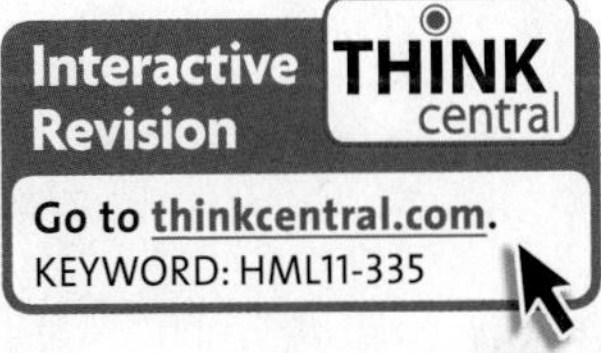

COMMON CORE

RL 4 Analyze the impact of specific word choice on meaning and tone. **RL 5** Analyze how an author's choices concerning how to structure a text contribute to its structure and meaning, as well as its aesthetic impact.

Thanatopsis

Poem by William Cullen Bryant

DID YOU KNOW?

William Cullen Bryant . . .

- could say the alphabet at 16 months of age.
- helped found the Republican Party.
- was an early abolitionist and staunch supporter of Abraham Lincoln.

Meet the Author

William Cullen Bryant 1794–1878

In his own day, William Cullen Bryant was a literary superstar. Schoolchildren recited his poetry. Adults pored over his newspaper editorials. And other writers praised his genius. James Fenimore Cooper even went so far as to call Bryant "the author of America" for helping to create a distinctive American literature.

All-American Poet Born in 1794 in Cummington, Massachusetts, Bryant began his writing career at an early age. At 10, he translated poems written in Latin; at 13, he published "The Embargo," a poem satirizing the policies of President Thomas Jefferson.

But the young Bryant was most inspired to write poetry about the natural world. As a boy, he spent hours exploring the forests and hills near his home. His earliest efforts reflected the influence of the English romantic poets.

In time, however, Bryant discovered his American voice. At the ripe old age of 18, he wrote "Thanatopsis," a poem inspired by his wanderings in the countryside. The American editor who published the poem was so struck by its brilliance that he asserted, "No one on this side of the Atlantic is capable of writing such a verse."

Career Moves At his father's urging, Bryant attended law school and spent ten years as a lawyer in Plainsfield, Massachusetts. But he was destined for a career in literature and writing. Leaving behind the "disagreeable drudgery" of his law practice, Bryant moved to New York City in 1825 to become a journalist.

Eventually, he became the editor-in-chief of the *New York Evening Post,* a position he held until his death. A committed political and social activist, Bryant used the newspaper to advocate for human rights and the protection of the environment.

Lifelong Naturalist Unfortunately, Bryant's journalistic work took a toll on his poetry. Nonetheless, Bryant left his mark on American literature as one of the first poets to overthrow what he called the "servile habit of copying" English poets.

Above all, Bryant is celebrated for his power to portray the wild American landscape. Walking up to 40 miles a day, he developed a deep knowledge of America's forests, streams, mountains, and valleys. "Even as an old man," noted one critic, "Bryant was never content unless he knew the name of every tree, bush, and weed in sight."

Author Online THINK central

Go to thinkcentral.com. KEYWORD: HML11-336

TEXT ANALYSIS: BLANK VERSE

William Cullen Bryant wrote "Thanatopsis" in a verse form known as blank verse. **Blank verse** is unrhymed poetry written in **iambic pentameter.** In this meter, each line has five iambic feet, a pattern consisting of an unstressed syllable (˘) followed by a stressed syllable (′). Poets who write in blank verse sometimes vary this rhythm, using loose iambic pentameter to add a conversational tone. Read the following lines from "Thanatopsis" aloud to hear the rhythm:

To him who in the love of Nature holds
Communion with her visible forms, she speaks

Notice that the first line above uses strict iambic pentameter, while the second is loose, adding a second unstressed syllable in the fourth foot. The effect of this variation is to make the poetry sound much like the way people talk. Bryant also achieves this effect through the use of **enjambment,** which means that one line ends without a pause and continues into the next line for its meaning. As you read "Thanatopsis," notice how the poem's rhythm imitates natural speech.

READING SKILL: UNDERSTAND STRUCTURE

In poetry, **structure** is the arrangement of words and lines to produce a desired effect. The structure of a poem usually emphasizes important aspects of content and can help a poet indicate shifts in mood. Use the following strategies to help you understand and make inferences about the structure and effects of Bryant's poem:

- Notice the indented line that indicates the beginning of each of the three verse sections in the poem.
- Summarize each section to understand the content and central ideas.
- Look for details and word choices that convey mood.

As you read "Thanatopsis," use a chart like the one shown to record the ideas and mood evoked in each section of the poem.

Section	Ideas	Mood
1st	Death comes to everyone.	bleak
2nd		
3rd		

Complete the activities in your **Reader/Writer Notebook**.

What can DEATH *teach us about life?*

Some people view death as the ultimate enemy. Others, however, consider it a natural part of life. Acceptance of that fact is a theme of William Cullen Bryant's "Thanatopsis." But death—and life—have other important lessons to teach us. One is recognizing that death, since it comes to us all, makes us all equal. What are some other important life lessons?

SURVEY With a partner, conduct a survey among your classmates, friends, and family and ask them to name the five greatest lessons that life—or death—has taught them. Compile the results and share them with the rest of the class.

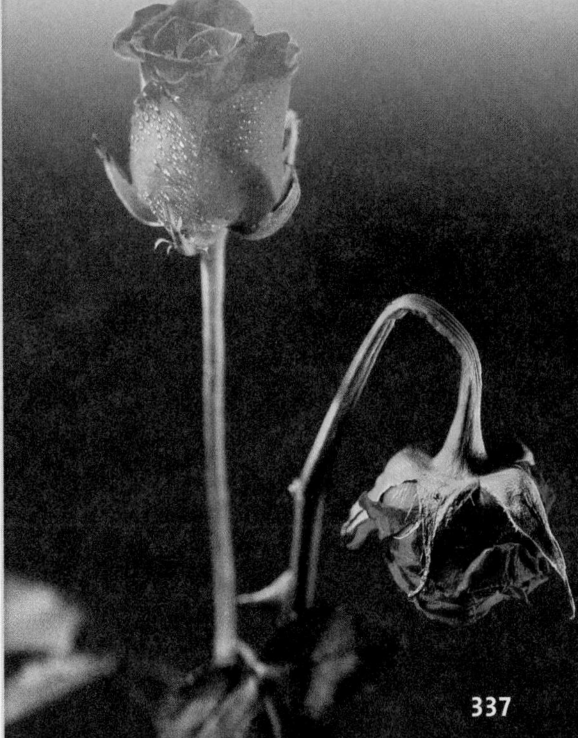

Thanatopsis

William Cullen Bryant

To him who in the love of Nature holds
Communion with her visible forms, she speaks
A various language; for his gayer hours
She has a voice of gladness, and a smile
And eloquence of beauty, and she glides
Into his darker musings, with a mild
And healing sympathy, that steals away
Their sharpness, ere he is aware. When thoughts **A**
Of the last bitter hour come like a blight
Over thy spirit, and sad images
Of the stern agony, and shroud, and pall,
And breathless darkness, and the narrow house,
Make thee to shudder, and grow sick at heart;—
Go forth, under the open sky, and list
To Nature's teachings, while from all around—
Earth and her waters, and the depths of air—
Comes a still voice—Yet a few days, and thee
The all-beholding sun shall see no more
In all his course; nor yet in the cold ground,
Where thy pale form was laid, with many tears,
Nor in the embrace of ocean, shall exist
Thy image. Earth, that nourished thee, shall claim
Thy growth, to be resolved to earth again,
And, lost each human trace, surrendering up
Thine individual being, shalt thou go
To mix forever with the elements,
To be a brother to the insensible rock
And to the sluggish clod, which the rude swain
Turns with his share, and treads upon. The oak
Shall send his roots abroad, and pierce thy mold. **B**

Yet not to thine eternal resting-place
Shalt thou retire alone—nor couldst thou wish
Couch more magnificent. Thou shalt lie down
With patriarchs of the infant world—with kings,
The powerful of the earth—the wise, the good,
Fair forms, and hoary seers of ages past,
All in one mighty sepulcher.—The hills
Rock-ribbed and ancient as the sun,—the vales

2 **communion:** a close relationship.

A BLANK VERSE
Reread lines 1–8 aloud. Identify the places where a phrase begins at the end of a line and continues on the next line. How does this **enjambment** affect the flow of the lines?

11–12 **shroud . . . the narrow house:** A shroud is a burial garment, while a pall is a heavy garment draped over a coffin. The narrow house is the grave or coffin.

28–29 **the sluggish clod . . . share:** the heavy mass of earth, which the farmer loosens with his plow.

B STRUCTURE
What is the central idea of the poem's first section, lines 1–30?

33 **couch:** bed.

36 **hoary seers:** ancient wise men.

37 **sepulcher:** grave.

Stretching in pensive quietness between;
The venerable woods—rivers that move
In majesty, and the complaining brooks
That make the meadows green; and, poured round all,
Old ocean's gray and melancholy waste,—
Are but the solemn decorations all
Of the great tomb of man. The golden sun, **C**
The planets, all the infinite host of heaven,
Are shining on the sad abodes of death,
Through the still lapse of ages. All that tread
The globe are but a handful to the tribes
That slumber in its bosom.—Take the wings
Of morning—and the Barcan desert pierce,
Or lose thyself in the continuous woods
Where rolls the Oregon, and hears no sound,
Save his own dashings—yet—the dead are there;
And millions in those solitudes, since first
The flight of years began, have laid them down
In their last sleep—the dead reign there alone.
So shalt thou rest—and what if thou withdraw
Unheeded by the living—and no friend
Take note of thy departure? All that breathe
Will share thy destiny. The gay will laugh
When thou art gone, the solemn brood of care
Plod on, and each one as before will chase
His favorite phantom; yet all these shall leave
Their mirth and their employments, and shall come
And make their bed with thee. As the long train **D**
Of ages glide away, the sons of men,
The youth in life's green spring, and he who goes
In the full strength of years, matron and maid,
The speechless babe, and the gray-headed man—
Shall one by one be gathered to thy side,
By those, who in their turn shall follow them.

So live, that when thy summons comes to join
The innumerable caravan, which moves
To that mysterious realm, where each shall take
His chamber in the silent halls of death,
Thou go not, like the quarry-slave at night,
Scourged to his dungeon, but, sustained and soothed
By unfaltering trust, approach thy grave,
Like one who wraps the drapery of his couch
About him, and lies down to pleasant dreams. **E**

40 venerable: impressive and worthy of respect because of age.

C STRUCTURE
Identify the **mood** in lines 31–45. How does it contrast with the mood in the first section?

51 Barcan desert: a desert region in northern Africa.

53 Oregon: old name for the Columbia River, which flows between the states of Washington and Oregon.

D BLANK VERSE
Tap your foot to the rhythm as you read lines 61–66. Note the motion described in these lines. How does the rhythm suggest this motion?

E STRUCTURE
Reread the last section of the poem, lines 73–81. How would you **summarize** these lines?

After Reading

Comprehension

COMMON CORE

RL 4 Analyze the impact of specific word choice on meaning and tone. **RL 5** Analyze how an author's choices concerning how to structure a text contribute to its structure and meaning, as well as its aesthetic impact.

1. **Recall** According to the speaker, how does nature help people cope during times of sadness?
2. **Recall** According to lines 22–30, what happens to people when they die?
3. **Clarify** Why, according to the speaker, should people greet death without fear?

Text Analysis

4. **Analyze Title** The title of the poem combines the Greek words *thanatos* ("death") and *opsis* ("a vision"). Cite specific details from the poem to explain the vision of death presented in "Thanatopsis."
5. **Understand Structure** Review the notes you recorded in your chart on the ideas and mood in each section of "Thanatopsis." Identify the central idea in each section, and draw conclusions about how the poem's structure helps develop an overall message.
6. **Draw Conclusions About Tone** A writer establishes his or her tone, or attitude toward a subject, through a variety of language choices. Use a chart to jot down important examples of Bryant's word choices, details, and direct statements. Then draw conclusions about the poem's tone.

Examples	Tone

7. **Evaluate Blank Verse** How would the impact of Bryant's message differ if he had used a strict meter and regular pattern of rhyme in his poem? Evaluate whether his use of blank verse is an effective or pleasing way to express his ideas. Give reasons for your opinion.
8. **Recognize Characteristics of Romanticism** How does "Thanatopsis" reflect Romantic notions of nature and democratic values?

Text Criticism

9. **Different Perspectives** Bryant wrote "Thanatopsis" when he was a very young man. He was also greatly influenced by the English romantic poets. Given what you have learned about the Puritans and the romantic poets, how do you think the following people might have reacted to the poem?
   - Bryant at age 70
   - a Puritan
   - an English romantic poet

What can **DEATH** *teach us about life?*

Death is a very popular topic in literature and music. Does death as a topic teach enough lessons to warrant a large number of poems and songs? Why or why not?

Wrap-Up: The Early Romantics

Elements of Style

On the surface, it seems as if William Cullen Bryant's "Thanatopsis" and Washington Irving's "The Devil and Tom Walker" could hardly be more different. One is an elegant nature poem written in formal language.

> *Go forth, under the open sky, and list / To Nature's teachings*
>
> *from* "Thanatopsis"

The other is a short story about strange, supernatural deeds and is written in a down-to-earth, casual style.

> *Tom's wife was a tall termagant, fierce of temper, loud of tongue, and strong of arm.*
>
> *from* "The Devil and Tom Walker"

But with a more careful reading, one can find elements of romanticism in each work.

Writing to Analyze

In general, America's romantic writers shared several characteristics. They looked to nature for inspiration, they celebrated individualism, they valued emotion and the imagination, and they sometimes explored the supernatural in their work. Which of these elements can you find in the two works you've just read? Create a chart like the one here, and use it to write a brief essay explaining why these two very different writers were each good examples of the romantic movement.

Element	***Selection(s)***	***Example(s)***
nature	*"Thanatopsis"*	*"To him who in the love of Nature holds / Communion with her visible forms, she speaks / A various language"*
	"The Devil and Tom Walker"	*"On one side of this inlet is a beautiful dark grove; on the opposite side the land rises abruptly from the water's edge into a high ridge, on which grow a few scattered oaks of great age and immense size."*
individualism		
emotion or passion		
imagination		
supernatural		

Extension

VIEWING & REPRESENTING

Romanticism was not only a literary movement; it was a movement of the other arts as well. Romantic artists shared many of the same concerns as writers of the day. Examine the painting shown here. (If you have trouble making out the painting's details, turn to page 326, where you can view it in a larger format.) With a partner, discuss what elements you think might indicate that the work is a good example of a romantic painting.

COMMON CORE

W 2 Write an explanatory text to examine complex ideas through organization and analysis of content. **SL 2** Integrate multiple sources of information presented in diverse formats and media in order to make informed decisions.

COMMON CORE

RL 4 Analyze the impact of specific word choices on meaning and tone, including language that is fresh, engaging or beautiful. **RL 5** Analyze how an author's choices concerning how to structure specific parts of a text contribute to overall structure and meaning, as well as aesthetic impact.

A Psalm of Life
The Tide Rises, the Tide Falls

Poetry by Henry Wadsworth Longfellow

VIDEO TRAILER THINK central KEYWORD: HML11-342A

DID YOU KNOW?

Henry Wadsworth Longfellow . . .

- was a child prodigy.
- spoke 11 languages.
- read 18 languages.
- grew a beard to hide the scars of a fire that killed his wife.

(background) Westminster Abbey

Meet the Author

Henry Wadsworth Longfellow 1807–1882

For nearly 150 years, Longfellow's "Paul Revere's Ride" has captivated readers. Its lines are as familiar as a nursery rhyme, and the image of Revere galloping into danger is imprinted on our minds. This poem, along with a number of others, made Henry Wadsworth Longfellow one of America's most popular poets.

Boy Genius Longfellow grew up in a literary household in Portland, Maine. His mother, Zilpah Wadsworth, often read aloud to him, while his father, Stephen, supplied him with numerous books. An exceptionally intelligent child, Longfellow entered school at the age of three and at six received this flattering report: "Master Henry Longfellow is one of the best boys we have in school. He spells and reads very well. He can also add and multiply numbers. His conduct is very correct and amiable."

Professor and Poet At age 13 Longfellow became a published poet, and at 15 he entered Bowdoin College in Maine where, like his classmate Nathaniel Hawthorne, he decided to devote his life to writing. While in college, he published poems in national magazines. Longfellow studied a number of foreign languages, including French, Spanish, and Italian. He was such a gifted translator that the college offered him upon graduation the first professorship in modern languages. Longfellow taught at Bowdoin until 1834, when he transferred to Harvard. He remained there until 1854.

Voice of America Although he worked hard to introduce European literature to an American audience, Longfellow wrote about American subjects. He sought inspiration in American history and lore, as well as in the country's landscape. A poet, argued Longfellow, should take his subjects from "nature and not from books" and should try to "fathom the recesses of his own mind, and bring up rich pearls from the secret depths of thought."

Literary Fame With the publication of his books *Evangeline, A Tale of Acadie* (1847) and *The Song of Hiawatha* (1855), Longfellow became a household name. Personal tragedy, however, cast a shadow over his achievement. His first wife died following a miscarriage and his second wife was fatally burned in a fire. Longfellow coped by immersing himself in his work. In his final years, Longfellow was showered with accolades. When he died, he became the first American writer to be honored with a bust in Poets' Corner of London's Westminster Abbey.

Author Online

Go to thinkcentral.com. KEYWORD: HML11-342B

TEXT ANALYSIS: STANZA AND RHYME SCHEME

Poets often organize their ideas and images in compact units known as **stanzas**—groups of lines sometimes characterized by a repeated pattern of rhyme and number of lines. Each stanza generally develops a separate idea, image, or example of figurative language; recognizing stanzas will help you trace this development.

A **rhyme scheme** is the pattern of end rhyme in a stanza or an entire poem. Rhyme helps to make the words of a poem memorable and is often used to emphasize important words in the poem.

Life is real! Life is earnest!
And the grave is not its goal;
Dust thou art, to dust returnest,
Was not spoken of the soul.

Here the rhyme scheme is *abab;* that is, the first and third lines (*a* and *a*) rhyme, as do the second and fourth lines (*b* and *b*).

As you read, note how Longfellow makes use of these conventions to organize his thoughts about life and express them in a form that the reader will remember.

READING STRATEGY: READING TRADITIONAL POETRY

To appreciate the musical qualities of these Longfellow poems, try the following strategies:

- Read each poem silently to interpret the basic meaning.
- Then, read them aloud, listening for the end rhyme. Notice which words are emphasized by rhyme.

In a web diagram like the one shown, note some important words that are emphasized through rhyme. You will need a separate diagram for each poem.

Complete the activities in your **Reader/Writer Notebook**.

What gives life PURPOSE?

People who live with purpose may be more likely to feel a sense of satisfaction or accomplishment. What is it that gives life value or meaning? Is it self-expression, creativity, following one's dream, or serving humanity? In the poems that follow, Longfellow offers his thoughts about how to lead a purposeful life.

QUICKWRITE Think of a person you know or have read about who has led a life you truly admire. How has this person made a difference in the world? Describe his or her impact on family, community, or country in a short paragraph.

A Psalm of Life

Henry Wadsworth Longfellow

What the Heart of the Young Man
Said to the Psalmist[1]

Tell me not, in mournful numbers,[2]
Life is but an empty dream!—
For the soul is dead that slumbers,
And things are not what they seem.

Life is real! Life is earnest!
And the grave is not its goal;
Dust thou art, to dust returnest,
Was not spoken of the soul. (A)

Not enjoyment, and not sorrow,
Is our destined end or way;
But to act, that each tomorrow
Find us farther than today.

Art is long, and Time is fleeting,
And our hearts, though stout[3] and brave,
Still, like muffled drums, are beating
Funeral marches to the grave.

In the world's broad field of battle,
In the bivouac[4] of Life,
Be not like dumb, driven cattle!
Be a hero in the strife!

(A) STANZA AND RHYME SCHEME
Review the rhyme scheme of the first two stanzas. How does the rhyme scheme contribute to the poem's **tone,** or attitude? Explain.

---

1. **Psalmist** (sä'mĭst): the author of the poems in the biblical Book of Psalms, many of which comment on the fleeting nature of life. King David of Israel is regarded as the author of most of the psalms.
2. **numbers:** metrical feet or lines; verses.
3. **stout:** strong.
4. **bivouac** (bĭv'o͞o-ak'): a temporary encampment of troops.

The Calm After the Storm (1866), Edward Moran. Oil on canvas. Private collection. © SuperStock, Inc./SuperStock.

Trust no Future, howe'er pleasant!
　Let the dead Past bury its dead!
Act,—act in the living Present!
　Heart within, and God o'erhead!

Lives of great men all remind us
　We can make our lives sublime,
And, departing, leave behind us
　Footprints on the sands of time; **B**

Footprints, that perhaps another,
　Sailing o'er life's solemn main,[5]
A forlorn and shipwrecked brother,
　Seeing, shall take heart again.

Let us, then, be up and doing,
　With a heart for any fate;
Still achieving, still pursuing,
　Learn to labor and to wait.

5. **main:** open ocean.

▲ Analyze Visuals

How might the title of this painting (*The Calm After the Storm*) connect to the **theme** of this poem?

B TRADITIONAL POETRY
Note the word emphasized by the end rhyme in lines 25 and 27. What might be the significance of this word?

THE TIDE RISES, *The Tide Falls*

Henry Wadsworth Longfellow

The tide rises, the tide falls,
The twilight darkens, the curlew[1] calls;
Along the sea sands damp and brown
The traveler hastens toward the town,
And the tide rises, the tide falls. **C**

Darkness settles on roofs and walls,
But the sea in the darkness calls and calls;
The little waves, with their soft white hands,
Efface[2] the footprints in the sands,
And the tide rises, the tide falls.

The morning breaks; the steeds in their stalls
Stamp and neigh, as the hostler[3] calls;
The day returns, but nevermore
Returns the traveler to the shore,
And the tide rises, the tide falls. **D**

C STANZA AND RHYME SCHEME
What rhyme occurs in three of the five lines of each stanza? What word is emphasized by this repeated rhyme? Consider the impact of this technique on the poem's meaning.

D TRADITIONAL POETRY
In terms of basic meaning, what is the difference between the day and the traveler in lines 13–14?

1. **curlew:** a type of large bird often found along the shoreline.
2. **efface:** to wear away; wipe out.
3. **hostler:** person who takes care of horses.

Singing Beach, Manchester (1863), Martin Johnson Heade. Oil on canvas, 50.8 cm × 91.4 cm. The Fine Arts Museums of San Francisco, Gift of Mr. and Mrs. John D. Rockefeller, 3rd, 1993.35.12.

Comprehension

COMMON CORE

RL 4 Analyze the impact of specific word choices on meaning and tone, including language that is fresh, engaging or beautiful. **RL 5** Analyze how an author's choices concerning how to structure specific parts of a text contribute to overall structure and meaning, as well as aesthetic impact.

1. **Recall** What record does the traveler leave behind in "The Tide Rises, the Tide Falls"? What happens to this record and to the traveler?
2. **Recall** What, according to the speaker of "A Psalm of Life," is "our destined end" or purpose?
3. **Paraphrase** What does the speaker say about the value of the lives of great people in "A Psalm of Life"?

Text Analysis

4. **Draw Conclusions About Traditional Poetry** Review the emphasized words you recorded in your web diagram for "A Psalm of Life." What can you conclude about the relationship between the poem's sound and its meaning?
5. **Analyze Metaphor** A metaphor compares two dissimilar things. Think about the metaphor in lines 17–18 of "A Psalm of Life." What is Longfellow saying about the world and life by comparing them to a battlefield and a bivouac?
6. **Examine Stanza and Rhyme Scheme** Identify the rhyme scheme used in "The Tide Rises, the Tide Falls." How does this rhyme scheme reflect the poem's central image?
7. **Interpret Repetition** Longfellow repeats the line "the tide rises, the tide falls" throughout his poem. What idea is he trying to emphasize about the difference between nature and human life through this repetition?
8. **Compare and Contrast** Reread lines 8–10 in "The Tide Rises . . ." and 25–32 in "A Psalm of Life." Consider what happens to the footprints in each poem. Based on this and other images, how would you say Longfellow's outlook on life and death in each poem is similar? In what way is it different? Use a Venn diagram like the one shown to organize your thoughts.

Text Criticism

9. **Critical Interpretations** "Longfellow," writes critic Alan Trachtenberg, "remains one of the nation's abidingly popular poets; more poems of his are probably still taken to heart and committed to memory than those of any of his more luminous 19th century peers. . . ." Why do you think Longfellow was, and still is, popular? Use evidence to support your conclusions.

What gives life **PURPOSE?**

What, according to the speaker of "A Psalm of Life," should people do to give their lives purpose? Do you agree or disagree?

COMMON CORE

RL 1 Cite evidence to support analysis of inferences drawn from the text. **RL 5** Analyze how an author's choices concerning how to structure a text contribute to its structure and meaning, as well as its aesthetic impact.

The Chambered Nautilus
Old Ironsides

Poetry by Oliver Wendell Holmes

Meet the Author

Oliver Wendell Holmes 1809–1894

Many people climb the ladder of success, but few make their mark in two very different fields. Oliver Wendell Holmes was both a prize-winning physician and a wildly popular poet. His discovery of the contagious nature of puerperal ("childbed") fever changed the practice of medicine. And his verse was so beloved that he was frequently called upon to write poems for public occasions.

A Cultural Elite Holmes grew up in a family steeped in history and tradition. He was descended from prominent Boston families and early Dutch settlers. His father, a Calvinist minister in Cambridge, Massachusetts, nurtured his interests in books, religion, and nature. "I am very thankful," wrote Holmes, "that the first part of my life was not passed shut in between high walls and treading the unimpressible and unsympathetic pavement."

Literary Triumph At 15, Holmes enrolled at Phillips Andover Academy, where he impressed his teachers by translating the Roman poet Virgil's *Aeneid.* After receiving a bachelor's degree and a medical degree from Harvard University, he entered private practice in Boston. Holmes achieved literary stardom at the age of 21 with the appearance of his poem "Old Ironsides." Written to protest the planned destruction of a ship that fought in the War of 1812, the poem won Holmes instant fame. Following its publication, the USS *Constitution* was returned to active duty.

Talent for Talk After his first book of poems was published in 1836, Holmes joined the lecture circuit, where he entranced audiences with his ready wit. He was equally charming in the classroom, causing his students at Harvard Medical School to greet his lectures with "a mighty shout and stamp of applause." Holmes's eloquence was also on display at the Saturday Club, a group including Ralph Waldo Emerson and Nathaniel Hawthorne. The writers met regularly to share their latest works.

Renaissance Man In addition to poetry, Holmes wrote three novels, a biography of Emerson, and numerous essays. Many of the essays appeared in *The Atlantic Monthly,* a magazine edited by Holmes's friend James Russell Lowell. Printed under the title "The Autocrat of the Breakfast Table," these essays combined prose and poetry and explored the themes of human destiny and freedom.

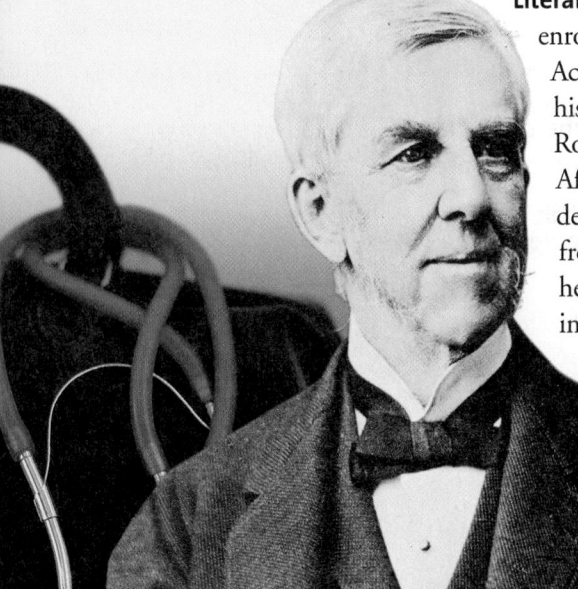

Author Online

Go to thinkcentral.com. KEYWORD: HML11-348

DID YOU KNOW?

Oliver Wendell Holmes . . .

- dropped out of law school because it bored him.
- became dean of the Harvard Medical School.
- called the subconscious mind "the underground workshop of thought" 20 years before Freud published his study of the unconscious.

TEXT ANALYSIS: METER

Meter is one of the tools used by poets to make language memorable and pleasing to the ear. It is defined as the repetition of a regular rhythmic unit in a line of poetry. Each unit, known as a **foot,** has one stressed syllable (indicated by a ´) and either one or two unstressed syllables (indicated by a ˘). The two basic types of metrical feet used by Holmes in these poems are the **iamb,** in which an unstressed syllable is followed by a stressed syllable (˘´), and the **trochee,** in which a stressed syllable is followed by an unstressed syllable (´˘). Two words are used to describe the meter of a line. The first word identifies the type of metrical foot—iambic, trochaic—and the second word indicates the number of feet in a line: **monometer** (one), **dimeter** (two), **trimeter** (three), **tetrameter** (four), **pentameter** (five), **hexameter** (six), and so forth. Here is a line from "Old Ironsides" with the meter marked:

Hĕr déck, ŏnce réd wĭth hérŏes' blóod

As you read these two poems by Holmes, note the meter in each and consider what it contributes to the poem's meaning and aesthetic appeal.

READING SKILL: MAKE INFERENCES

Making inferences involves "reading between the lines"—making logical guesses based on evidence in the text to figure out what is not directly stated. As you read these two poems by Holmes, you will need to make inferences to get at the author's meaning. For each poem, create a chart like the one shown.

"The Chambered Nautilus"		
Details or Evidence from Text	*What I Know from Experience*	*Ideas Inferred*
"Year after year beheld the silent toil / That spread his lustrous coil"	*It takes a lot of practice to become good at a sport.*	*Change requires effort.*

Complete the activities in your **Reader/Writer Notebook.**

When is it time to MOVE ON?

Sometimes people have to choose between cherishing the past and looking toward the future. For example, when you move out of your parents' house, will you expect them to keep your room exactly as it is or to convert it to a home office? Change can produce a renewed sense of well-being as well as a sense of loss.

DISCUSS Working with a partner, list situations or occasions in life when one must decide between holding on to the past and making a change. In each case, what are the benefits of either choice? After discussing this question with your partner, share your conclusions with others.

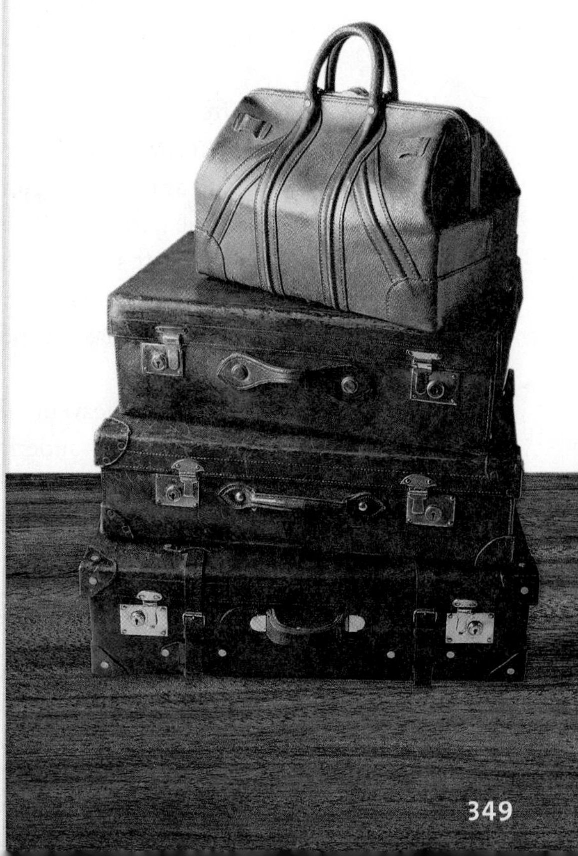

The Chambered Nautilus

Oliver Wendell Holmes

This is the ship of pearl, which, poets feign,[1]
Sails the unshadowed main,—
The venturous bark that flings
On the sweet summer wind its purpled wings
In gulfs enchanted, where the Siren[2] sings,
And coral reefs lie bare,
Where the cold sea-maids rise to sun their streaming hair.

Its webs of living gauze no more unfurl;
Wrecked is the ship of pearl!
And every chambered cell,
Where its dim dreaming life was wont to dwell,
As the frail tenant shaped his growing shell,
Before thee lies revealed,—
Its irised ceiling rent,[3] its sunless crypt unsealed! **A**

A METER
Although the basic meter of this poem is **iambic,** what kind of **foot** is substituted for the iamb at the beginning of many of the lines? How does this variation affect the feel of these lines?

Year after year beheld the silent toil
That spread his lustrous coil;
Still, as the spiral grew,
He left the past year's dwelling for the new,
Stole with soft step its shining archway through,
Built up its idle door,
Stretched in his last-found home, and knew the old no more.

Thanks for the heavenly message brought by thee,
Child of the wandering sea,
Cast from her lap, forlorn!
From thy dead lips a clearer note is born

---

1. **feign:** imagine.
2. **Siren:** a partly human female creature in Greek mythology that lured sailors to destruction with sweet, magical songs.
3. **its irised ceiling rent:** its rainbow-colored ceiling ripped apart.

Analyze Visuals
As the nautilus grows, it adds a new chamber to its spiral shell, abandoning the old chamber for the new one. What might this process of growth suggest about the role of change in life?

Than ever Triton blew from wreathèd horn![4]
While on mine ear it rings,
Through the deep caves of thought I hear a voice that sings:—

Build thee more stately mansions, O my soul,
As the swift seasons roll!
Leave thy low-vaulted past!
Let each new temple, nobler than the last,
Shut thee from heaven with a dome more vast,
Till thou at length art free,
Leaving thine outgrown shell by life's unresting sea! B

B MAKE INFERENCES
Reread lines 29–35. What inference can you make about what it might mean for the soul to escape its shell?

4. **Triton . . . wreathèd horn:** Triton, a sea god in Greek mythology, is usually pictured blowing a wreathed, or coiled, conch-shell horn.

OLD IRONSIDES

Oliver Wendell Holmes

Ay, tear her tattered ensign[1] down!
Long has it waved on high,
And many an eye has danced to see
That banner in the sky;
Beneath it rung the battle shout,
And burst the cannon's roar;—
The meteor of the ocean air
Shall sweep the clouds no more.

Her deck, once red with heroes' blood,
Where knelt the vanquished foe,
When winds were hurrying o'er the flood,
And waves were white below,
No more shall feel the victor's tread,
Or know the conquered knee;—
The harpies[2] of the shore shall pluck
The eagle of the sea! C

Oh, better that her shattered hulk
Should sink beneath the wave;
Her thunders shook the mighty deep,
And there should be her grave;
Nail to the mast her holy flag,
Set every threadbare sail,
And give her to the god of storms,
The lightning and the gale! D

C ALLUSION
Oliver Wendell Holmes assumed that his readers would be familiar with the basics of Greek mythology, so it is not surprising that his poems include classical **allusions**—references to characters, locations, or events in classical myths that enrich the reader's experience of Holmes's poems. Read foonote 2 on page 350 and footnote 2 at the bottom of this page. How do the allusions explained here contribute to your understanding of the poems? Explain your response.

D MAKE INFERENCES
Reread the third stanza. Based on what has been said in previous stanzas about the ship's gloried past, do you think the speaker is being sincere or **ironic** about the fate of Old Ironsides? Explain.

1. **ensign:** flag.
2. **harpies:** evil monsters from Greek mythology that are half woman and half bird.

After Reading

Comprehension

1. **Recall** What event involving Old Ironsides took place during the war?
2. **Recall** According to the speaker, what should be the ship's fate?
3. **Summarize** In lines 1–14 of "The Chambered Nautilus," what does the speaker imagine and notice about the nautilus?

Text Analysis

4. **Analyze Symbol** What do you think the chambered nautilus **symbolizes,** or represents, for the speaker of the poem? Use evidence to support your answer.
5. **Make Inferences** Look back at the inferences and evidence you recorded as you read. What ideas about change does Holmes convey in "The Chambered Nautilus"? How does Holmes use each of the following images to express his thoughts about change?
   - the shell's appearance in the speaker's hands (lines 8–14)
   - the growth of the shell (lines 15–21)
   - the message the shell conveys (lines 29–35)
6. **Identify Tone** The attitude that a writer takes toward a particular subject is called **tone.** How would you describe the tone of each poem? What words and figures of speech help establish this tone? Use a chart like the one shown to record your answers.

"Old Ironsides"
Tone: sardonic
Words: "Oh, better that her shattered hulk / Should sink beneath the wave" (lines 17–18)
"The Chambered Nautilus"
Tone:
Words:

7. **Interpret Meter** Review the metric pattern you identified in "Old Ironsides." Then read the poem aloud. How does this meter reflect the poem's subject matter? Explain.

Text Criticism

8. **Author's Style** Recall from Holmes's biography on page 348 that the poem "Old Ironsides" was instrumental in saving the USS *Constitution.* What techniques and details used in the poem might have motivated readers to act? Cite evidence to support your answer.

When is it time to MOVE ON?

Consider the "heavenly message" presented in "The Chambered Nautilus." In what ways might you leave your "low-vaulted past" and "build more stately mansions" throughout your life?

COMMON CORE

RL 1 Cite evidence to support analysis of inferences drawn from the text. **RL 2** Provide an objective summary of the text. **RL 4** Analyze the impact of specific words on meaning and tone. **RL 5** Analyze how an author's choices concerning how to structure a text contribute to its structure and meaning, as well as its aesthetic impact.

COMMON CORE

RL 1 Cite evidence to support analysis of inferences drawn from the text. **RL 4** Analyze the impact of specific word choices on meaning and tone, including language that is fresh, engaging, or beautiful. **RL 10** Read and comprehend literature.

from Snowbound

Poem by John Greenleaf Whittier

The First Snowfall

Poem by James Russell Lowell

Meet the Authors

John Greenleaf Whittier

1807–1892

John Greenleaf Whittier embodied the idealism of his age, which combined social activism and literary activity. He devoted most of his waking hours to the abolition of slavery, even risking his own life for the cause. Yet he also managed to write hundreds of poems. Many express an idyllic view of rural life and a profound moral aversion to slavery.

Rural Childhood Whittier's social consciousness derived from his modest background. Born to devout Quakers, Whittier was taught to believe in the equality of all people, the immorality of war, and the importance of thrift. Working long days on his family's farm in Haverhill, Massachusetts, Whittier also learned about nature.

Poet and Politician Unlike most of his literary contemporaries, Whittier received little formal schooling. He was, however, an avid reader, devouring the poetry of John Milton, Robert Burns, and other poets. When Whittier was 19, his poetry was discovered by the abolitionist and editor William Lloyd Garrison. In later years, Whittier contributed poems to various newspapers.

James Russell Lowell

1819–1891

To his contemporaries, James Russell Lowell was the quintessential New England man of letters. He wrote poetry that stirred the emotions, newspaper editorials that influenced public opinion, and literary criticism.

Rebel with a Cause Lowell was born into a prominent New England family. In 1834, he entered Harvard, where he exasperated his teachers with his spoiled, immature behavior. His flouting of school rules and his disregard for his studies eventually led to his suspension. In 1844, Lowell married Maria White, who set her husband on the path to more mature behavior. In later years, Lowell published several volumes of verse and numerous articles in support of the abolitionist movement. He opposed slavery, the Mexican War, and corruption in politics.

Poet and Diplomat Lowell's talents were not limited to writing. He served as editor of *The Atlantic Monthly,* as an American diplomat in Spain, and as ambassador to Great Britain. While he enjoyed much public success in these roles, Lowell is today best remembered for his poetry.

Author Online

Go to thinkcentral.com. KEYWORD: HML11-354

TEXT ANALYSIS: MOOD

Mood is the feeling or atmosphere that a writer creates for the reader. Although it may seem that mood is simply inherent in a piece, it is actually achieved through the use of various devices, such as the following:

- **figurative language:** language that communicates ideas beyond the literal meaning of words
- **imagery:** descriptive words and phrases a writer uses to re-create sensory experiences
- **meter:** repetition of a regular rhythmic unit in a line of poetry
- **rhyme:** similarity of sound between two words

Notice, for example, how Lowell uses all four devices in the following stanza from "The First Snowfall":

I stood and watched by the window
The noiseless work of the sky,
And the sudden flurries of snowbirds,
Like brown leaves whirling by.

As you read the poems by Lowell and Whittier, look for the devices that help to create a different mood in each poem.

READING STRATEGY: PARAPHRASE

Sometimes, the surest way to get through a difficult passage is to **paraphrase** it, or restate the ideas in simpler words. To paraphrase a line or stanza in a poem, determine its main idea and replace difficult words with easier ones. In some cases, footnotes will help you clarify meaning. Consider the following lines from Lowell's poem "The First Snowfall":

And the poorest twig on the elm-tree
Was ridged inch deep with pearl.

Here is a paraphrase of the lines above in simpler language:

An inch of snow covered the slender twig on the elm tree.

As you read, use a chart like the one shown to record difficult words or phrases and how you might paraphrase them.

Original Word(s)	*My Paraphrase*

Review: **Make Inferences**

Complete the activities in your **Reader/Writer Notebook**.

What can NATURE *teach us?*

What lessons about life have you learned from nature? Perhaps waiting out a thunderstorm taught you something about patience. Or maybe watching monkeys at the zoo helped you to understand group behavior. The selections that follow describe kernels of wisdom two poets gleaned from the natural world.

QUICKWRITE In your notebook, list some insights you have gained from nature. How could you apply these insights to your own life? Write down your thoughts and ideas in a short paragraph.

Scene or Event	*Insights*
thunderstorm	*Nature puts things in perspective.*

SNOWBOUND
A Winter Idyll

John Greenleaf Whittier

The sun that brief December day
Rose cheerless over hills of gray,
And, darkly circled, gave at noon
A sadder light than waning[1] moon.
Slow tracing down the thickening sky
Its mute and ominous prophecy,
A portent[2] seeming less than threat,
It sank from sight before it set. **A**
A chill no coat, however stout,
Of homespun stuff could quite shut out,
A hard, dull bitterness of cold,
That checked, mid-vein, the circling race
Of lifeblood in the sharpened face,
The coming of the snowstorm told.
The wind blew east; we heard the roar
Of Ocean on his wintry shore,
And felt the strong pulse throbbing there
Beat with low rhythm our inland air.

Meanwhile we did our nightly chores,—
Brought in the wood from out of doors,
Littered the stalls, and from the mows
Raked down the herd's grass for the cows:
Heard the horse whinnying for his corn;
And, sharply clashing horn on horn,
Impatient down the stanchion rows[3]

A MOOD
Poets often use structural elements, such as meter and rhyme scheme, to help create a particular **mood. Meter** is simply the repetition of a rhythmic unit, and **rhyme** is the use of words (most often at the end of lines) that share a similar sound. Reread the first eight lines of the poem, and write down the words that rhyme. How many pairs of rhyme words do you see? What mood do these words help create?

1. **waning:** lessening in intensity.
2. **portent:** omen.
3. **stanchion** (stăn′chən) **rows:** lines of devices that fit loosely around the necks of animals such as cows in order to limit their motion.

Analyze Visuals ▶
To what senses does this photograph appeal, in addition to sight?

The cattle shake their walnut bows;
While, peering from his early perch
Upon the scaffold's pole of birch,
The cock his crested helmet bent
And down his querulous[4] challenge sent.

Unwarmed by any sunset light
The gray day darkened into night,
A night made hoary with the swarm
And whirl-dance of the blinding storm,
As zigzag, wavering to and fro,
Crossed and recrossed the wingëd snow:
And ere the early bedtime came
The white drift piled the window frame,
And through the glass the clothesline posts
Looked in like tall and sheeted ghosts. **B**

So all night long the storm roared on:
The morning broke without a sun;
In tiny spherule[5] traced with lines
Of Nature's geometric signs,
In starry flake, and pellicle,[6]
All day the hoary meteor fell;
And, when the second morning shone,
We looked upon a world unknown,
On nothing we could call our own.
Around the glistening wonder bent
The blue walls of the firmament,
No cloud above, no earth below—
A universe of sky and snow! **C**
The old familiar sights of ours
Took marvelous shapes; strange domes and towers
Rose up where sty or corncrib stood,
Or garden wall, or belt of wood;
A smooth white mound the brush pile showed,
A fenceless drift what once was road;
The bridle post an old man sat
With loose-flung coat and high cocked hat;
The well curb[7] had a Chinese roof;

COMMON CORE L 3

Language Coach

Oral Fluency The two dots over the e in *wingëd* (line 36) indicate that the *e* should be pronounced. *Winged* is normally pronounced in one syllable as */weengd/*, but here it is pronounced in two syllables as */weeng ehd/*. Read lines 35–36, pronouncing *winged* in one syllable, then in two syllables. How does the sound of the lines change?

B MOOD
A **simile** is a figure of speech comparing two things using the words *like* or *as.* What mood does the poet create with the simile in lines 39–40?

C PARAPHRASE
How has the world been transformed by snow in lines 50–53?

4. **querulous** (kwĕr'ə-ləs): complaining.
5. **spherule** (sfîr'o͞ol): a little sphere.
6. **pellicle:** a thin film or skin.
7. **well curb:** framing around the neck of a well.

And even the long sweep,[8] high aloof,
In its slant splendor, seemed to tell
Of Pisa's leaning miracle.[9]

A prompt, decisive man, no breath
Our father wasted: "Boys, a path!"
Well pleased, (for when did farmer boy
Count such a summons less than joy?)
Our buskins[10] on our feet we drew;
With mittened hands, and caps drawn low,
To guard our necks and ears from snow,
We cut the solid whiteness through.
And, where the drift was deepest, made
A tunnel walled and overlaid
With dazzling crystal: we had read
Of rare Aladdin's wondrous cave,[11]
And to our own his name we gave,
With many a wish the luck were ours
To test his lamp's supernal[12] powers.
We reached the barn with merry din,
And roused the prisoned brutes within.
The old horse thrust his long head out,
And grave with wonder gazed about;
The cock his lusty greeting said,
And forth his speckled harem led;
The oxen lashed their tails, and hooked,
And mild reproach of hunger looked;
The hornëd patriarch of the sheep,
Like Egypt's Amun[13] roused from sleep,
Shook his sage head with gesture mute,
And emphasized with stamp of foot. **D**

All day the gusty north wind bore
The loosening drift its breath before;
Low circling round its southern zone,
The sun through dazzling snow-mist shone.
No church bell lent its Christian tone

COMMON CORE RL 5

TEXT STRUCTURE
Whittier's narrative poem "Snowbound" vividly describes the events and setting of one snowy evening. In a poem, each event is often set off in a separate stanza. In a novel, however, the events are usually separated into chapters. Can you think of other poems, novels, plays, or films that describe events that occur in a natural setting? How does the text structure of the work affect the way descriptions of setting are presented?

D MOOD
Identify examples of **figurative language** and **imagery** in lines 66–92. What is the mood created by this language?

---

8. **sweep:** a long pole connected to a bucket, used for raising water from a well.
9. **Pisa's leaning miracle:** the Leaning Tower of Pisa, Italy.
10. **buskins:** high leather boots.
11. **Aladdin's wondrous cave:** In *The Thousand and One Nights*, the boy Aladdin used a magic lamp to discover a treasure in a cave.
12. **supernal:** heavenly; supernatural.
13. **Amun** (ä'mən): the supreme god of the ancient Egyptians, often represented as having a ram's head.

To the savage air, no social smoke
Curled over woods of snow-hung oak.
A solitude made more intense
By dreary-voicëd elements,
The shrieking of the mindless wind,
The moaning tree boughs swaying blind,
And on the glass the unmeaning beat
Of ghostly fingertips of sleet.
Beyond the circle of our hearth
No welcome sound of toil or mirth
Unbound the spell, and testified
Of human life and thought outside. **E**
We minded that the sharpest ear
The buried brooklet could not hear,
The music of whose liquid lip
Had been to us companionship,
And, in our lonely life, had grown
To have an almost human tone.

E PARAPHRASE
Reread lines 106–109. What effect does the snowstorm have on the family's sense of itself and the world outside?

As night drew on, and, from the crest
Of wooded knolls that ridged the west,
The sun, a snow-blown traveler, sank
From sight beneath the smothering bank,
We piled, with care, our nightly stack
Of wood against the chimney back,—
The oaken log, green, huge, and thick,
And on its top the stout backstick;
The knotty forestick laid apart,
And filled between with curious art
The ragged brush; then, hovering near,
We watched the first red blaze appear,
Heard the sharp crackle, caught the gleam
On whitewashed wall and sagging beam,
Until the old, rude-furnished room
Burst, flowerlike, into rosy bloom;
While radiant with a mimic flame
Outside the sparkling drift became,
And through the bare-boughed lilac tree
Our own warm hearth seemed blazing free.
The crane and pendent trammels showed,
The Turks' heads on the andirons[14] glowed;

14. **The crane . . . the andirons:** The crane was the movable arm on which the trammels, or adjustable pothooks, hung. The andirons, or metal supports holding the fireplace wood, were topped with turbanlike knots.

While childish fancy, prompt to tell
The meaning of the miracle,
Whispered the old rhyme: *"Under the tree,*
When fire outdoors burns merrily,
There the witches are making tea." **F**

The moon above the eastern wood
Shone at its full; the hill range stood
Transfigured in the silver flood,
Its blown snows flashing cold and keen,
Dead white, save where some sharp ravine
Took shadow, or the somber green
Of hemlocks turned to pitchy black
Against the whiteness at their back.
For such a world and such a night
Most fitting that unwarming light,
Which only seemed where'er it fell
To make the coldness visible.

Shut in from all the world without,
We sat the clean-winged hearth[15] about,
Content to let the north wind roar
In baffled rage at pane and door,
While the red logs before us beat
The frost line back with tropic heat; **G**
And ever, when a louder blast
Shook beam and rafter as it passed,
The merrier up its roaring draught
The great throat of the chimney laughed;
The house dog on his paws outspread
Laid to the fire his drowsy head,
The cat's dark silhouette on the wall
A couchant[16] tiger's seemed to fall;
And, for the winter fireside meet,
Between the andirons' straddling feet,
The mug of cider simmered slow,
The apples sputtered in a row,
And, close at hand, the basket stood
With nuts from brown October's wood.

F MOOD
In lines 116–142, what techniques does the poet use to create a mood of security and warmth in the midst of nature's cold and snow?

COMMON CORE L 4a

Language Coach

Word Definitions At the end of line 155, you might read the word *without* and think "without what?" Here, *without* means "outside." In lines 155–160, how does the world *within* differ from the world *without*?

G MAKE INFERENCES
Reread lines 155–160. Why is the north wind baffled?

15. **clean-winged hearth:** Hearths were commonly swept with a turkey wing.
16. **couchant** (kou'chənt): lying down, but with head raised.

THE FIRST SNOWFALL

James Russell Lowell

The snow had begun in the gloaming,[1]
And busily all the night
Had been heaping field and highway
With a silence deep and white.

Every pine and fir and hemlock
Wore ermine[2] too dear for an earl,
And the poorest twig on the elm-tree
Was ridged inch deep with pearl.

From sheds new-roofed with Carrara[3]
Came Chanticleer's[4] muffled crow,
The stiff rails softened to swan's-down,
And still fluttered down the snow.

I stood and watched by the window
The noiseless work of the sky,
And the sudden flurries of snowbirds,
Like brown leaves whirling by. **H**

I thought of a mound in sweet Auburn[5]
Where a little headstone stood;
How the flakes were folding it gently,
As did robins the babes in the wood. **I**

Up spoke our own little Mabel,
Saying, "Father, who makes it snow?"
And I told of the good All-father
Who cares for us here below.

COMMON CORE L 5b

Language Coach

Synonyms Often the word *dear* (line 6) is used as a term of affection. However, *dear* can also mean "high-priced." Other words with similar meanings, or **synonyms,** of *dear* include *costly*, *valuable*, and *precious*. Read lines 5–8, and write down the words related to wealth or luxury. How are the descriptions in the poem enhanced by these words?

H MOOD
Reread lines 1–16. How would you describe the mood created by the poet's use of **rhyme** and **meter?** Explain your answer.

I PARAPHRASE
Paraphrase lines 17–20. How does the mood shift in these lines?

---

1. **gloaming:** twilight.
2. **ermine:** the expensive white fur of a type of weasel.
3. **Carrara:** Carrara marble, a white marble named after the Italian city where it is mined.
4. **Chanticleer's:** a rooster's.
5. **Auburn:** Mount Auburn Cemetery, located in Cambridge, Massachusetts.

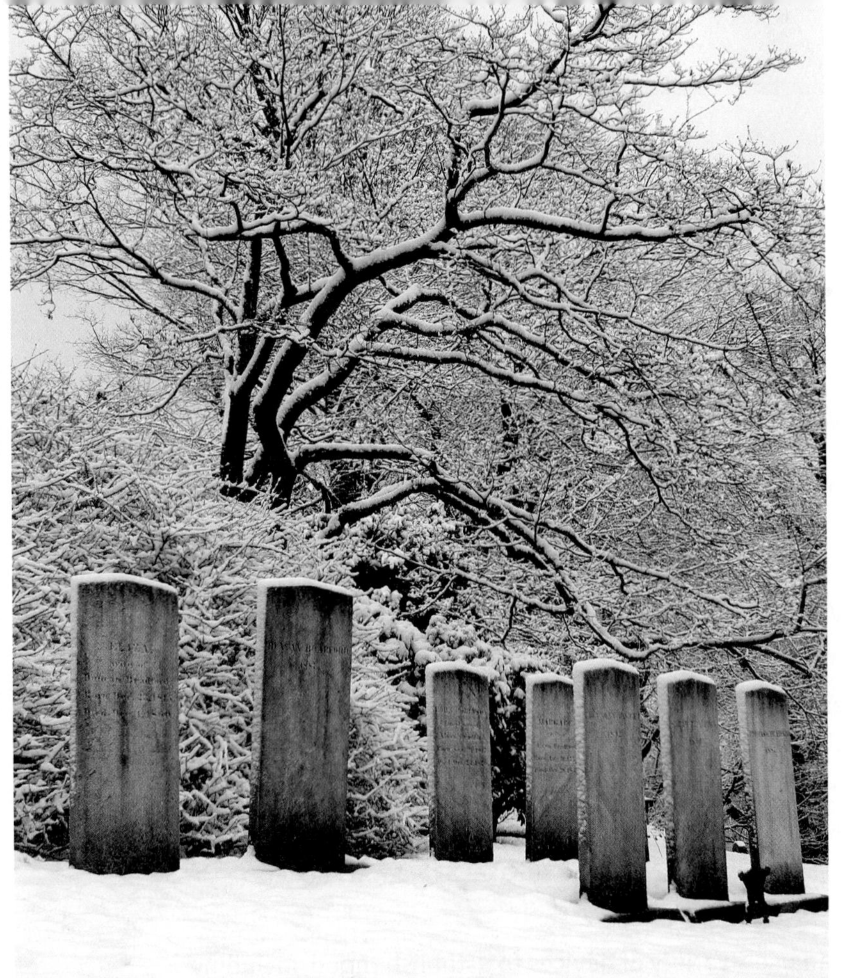

◀ Analyze Visuals
This photograph shows Mount Auburn Cemetery, which is mentioned in the poem. What **mood** is suggested by the photograph, what details support the mood, and how does the mood of the picture match that of the poem?

Again I looked at the snowfall,
    And thought of the leaden sky
That arched o'er our first great sorrow,
    When that mound was heaped so high. J

I remembered the gradual patience
    That fell from that cloud like snow,
Flake by flake, healing and hiding
    The scar that renewed our woe.

And again to the child I whispered,
    "The snow that husheth all,
Darling, the merciful Father
    Alone can make it fall!" K

Then, with eyes that saw not, I kissed her;
    And she, kissing back, could not know
That *my* kiss was given to her sister,
    Folded close under deepening snow.

J MAKE INFERENCES
In line 17, "mound" refers to the daughter's grave. What else does "mound" refer to in line 28?

K MOOD
What mood does the speaker create at the end of the poem by invoking the "merciful Father"?

Comprehension

1. **Recall** In what ways does the family in "Snowbound" prepare for and cope with the storm?
2. **Clarify** How does the family in "Snowbound" feel about being snowed in?
3. **Summarize** How does the snowfall transform the landscape in lines 1–14 of "The First Snowfall"?
4. **Clarify** In "The First Snowfall," what has happened to the family?

Text Analysis

5. **Make Inferences** How do the people in "Snowbound" react to the storm? What do their responses say about their relationship to one another?
6. **Interpret Figurative Language** Reread lines 29–32 of "The First Snowfall." What does the figurative language in this stanza suggest about the family's grief and the relation of their sorrow to the natural world?
7. **Paraphrase to Draw Conclusions** Review the paraphrases you made in your chart as you read Lowell's poem. Describe the speaker's religious beliefs. How do they help him cope with his pain?
8. **Analyze Mood** Poets can use a variety of devices to establish mood, including **figurative language, imagery, rhyme,** and **meter.** In each of the poems, identify two devices used to create mood, giving examples. For each poem, which device would you say is the more important? Explain.
9. **Associate Ideas** In these poems and elsewhere, snow is often referred to as having a quieting effect. What are some common metaphors or images used to express our associations with other kinds of weather, such as downpours, torrid heat, windstorms, and Indian summers?

Text Criticism

10. **Historical Context** Whittier and Lowell were two of a group known as the Fireside Poets. (See page 310.) This name refers to a popular family pastime of the period: reading poetry aloud in front of the fireplace after dinner. The poems of the group were very popular and read as entertainment not only in homes but also in schools. Why might the poetry of this group have played such an important role in people's lives? Support your opinion.

What can NATURE *teach us?*

In "The First Snowfall," the speaker draws a parallel between a natural weather event and the healing of a great grief. How does nature speak to you? Can you think of a natural object or event that has held special meaning for you?

COMMON CORE

RL 1 Cite evidence to support analysis of inferences drawn from the text. **RL 4** Analyze the impact of specific word choices on meaning and tone, including language that is fresh, engaging, or beautiful. **RL 9** Demonstrate knowledge of how two or more texts from the same period treat similar themes or topics. **RL 10** Read and comprehend poetry.

Fireside Poets in Perspective

The Fireside Poets were extremely popular in their day. Indeed, they were so beloved that many families read their works aloud by the fire as a form of nightly entertainment. They were respected as well, becoming the first poets to be considered on equal footing with their British counterparts. Over the years, however, the group's works fell out of favor with critics, who began to look upon them with more affection than respect. Only in recent years have critics again begun to appreciate the craft of the Fireside Poets.

Writing to Evaluate

With a group of classmates, come up with several criteria for evaluating the poems on pages 344–363. Then use your criteria to write a brief evaluation of the work of the Fireside Poets as a whole.

Consider

- what elements (vivid imagery, precise word choice, or thought-provoking themes) you think distinguish "good" poetry from "bad"
- whether the poems contain those elements
- whether your opinion of the poems changed upon rereading

Extension

SPEAKING & LISTENING Perform an **oral interpretation** of one poem from this group of Fireside Poets' work. Let your opinion of the Fireside Poets in general and of this work in particular inform your reading. For example, if you admire a particular poem, you may wish to read it in a lively and engaging voice. If, on the other hand, you found a poem too sentimental, let your reading reflect this judgment.

COMMON CORE

W 2 Write explanatory texts to examine complex ideas, concepts, and information through the analysis of content. **SL 6** Adapt speech to a variety of contexts and tasks.

Text Analysis Workshop

The Art of the Essay

When you write an essay for class, you are taking part in a literary tradition that goes back hundreds of years. In classroom writing, the essay may have many rules governing its structure and topic, but in the literary world, essays come in all shapes and sizes, accommodate any topic, and can be found in books, magazines, and daily newspapers.

COMMON CORE

Included in this workshop: **RI 6** Determine an author's point of view or purpose in a text in which the rhetoric is effective, analyzing how style and content contribute to the power, persuasiveness, or beauty of the text. **RI 9** Analyze documents of literary significance for their themes, purposes, and rhetorical features. **RI 10** Read and comprehend literary nonfiction.

First Attempts

An **essay** is a short work of nonfiction that offers a writer's opinion on a particular subject. The length can vary greatly. Some are personal, while others are coldly factual. The essay originated with the 16th-century French philosopher Michel de Montaigne, who first introduced the form when he published a collection of writings entitled *Essais,* a French word meaning "attempts." English writers began using the form, and eventually it became commonplace.

Two masters of the American essay in the 19th century were Ralph Waldo Emerson and Henry David Thoreau. These writers used the form to express their philosophies and personal views on a variety of topics, from the ideal lifestyle to the beauty of nature. Using notes he recorded in his journals, Emerson created essays that gave his ideas structure and refined his concepts. In turn they became the cornerstone of **transcendentalism,** a literary and philosophical movement that emphasized individualism and intuition as a means to understanding reality. Among Thoreau's works is a series of essays, entitled *Walden,* in which he describes his experience of living out the ideals of individualism at Walden Pond (see page 380).

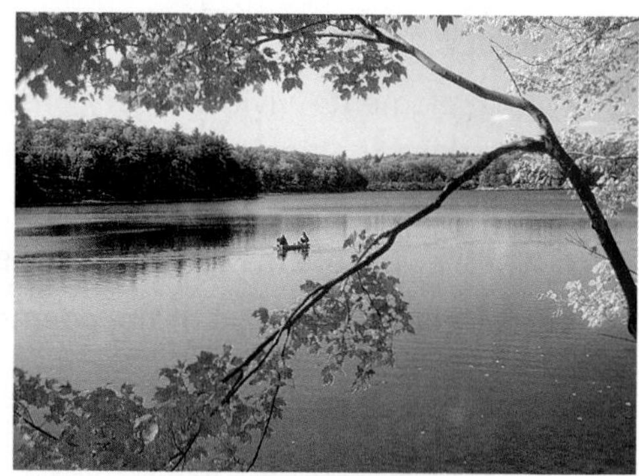

Thoreau's Walden Pond today, located just outside Concord, Massachusetts.

Emerson and Thoreau laid the groundwork for the American essay. Since then, numerous writers have gained reputations as respected authors of the form, including H. L. Mencken, Ernest Hemingway, E. B. White, Joan Didion, and Amy Tan.

The Craft of Expressing Ideas

Essays generally fall into one of two traditions. **Formal essays** explore topics in a serious and organized manner. **Informal essays** adopt a more casual tone and may include humor and unconventional topics. These essays are often more personal in nature. Emerson's "Self-Reliance" (see page 370) is a formal essay, whereas Thoreau's *Walden* essays are more informal.

Whether the essay's purpose is to be **persuasive, expository, descriptive,** or **narrative,** essayists typically rely on these elements to express their ideas:

- **Organization** is the arrangement of the main ideas and supporting details. Some essays may be narratives that read like a story, while others may follow a strict pattern of organization, such as **cause-and-effect** or **compare-and-contrast.**
- **Supporting details** include facts, opinions, reasons, sensory details, anecdotes, and examples that support the **main idea,** the most important idea about a topic.
- **Diction** is the way a writer uses and arranges language. Some writers use simple and casual words and sentences that may create a personal voice. Others are more formal, using elevated language and complex sentence structures.
- **Tone** is the expression of a writer's attitude toward a subject and may be described as serious, humorous, sarcastic, and so on. The writer's diction and details will provide clues to his or her tone.

"Self-Reliance" is a carefully constructed argument in the form of an essay. Emerson organizes his ideas step by step, leading the reader to the conclusion he wants them to reach—an understanding of his philosophy of individualism. Note Emerson's **opinions,** abstract **language,** and formal **tone** in this passage from "Self-Reliance":

> There is a time in every man's education when he arrives at the conviction that envy is ignorance; that imitation is suicide; that he must take himself for better for worse as his portion . . . .
>
> **—Ralph Waldo Emerson, "Self-Reliance"**

Close Read

What ideas does Emerson introduce in this sentence? Paraphrase his ideas in your own words.

Thoreau, on the other hand, takes a more personal and informal approach in *Walden*. Even though his **sentence structure** is complicated and lengthy, the **language** is simple, and the **details** are concrete.

> When first I took up my abode in the woods, that is, began to spend my nights as well as days there, which, by accident, was on Independence day, or the fourth of July 1845, my house was not finished for winter, but was merely a defense against the rain, without plastering or chimney, the walls being of rough weather-stained boards, with wide chinks, which made it cool at night.
>
> **—Henry David Thoreau, *Walden***

Close Read

Note the **diction** and **details** in this passage. What do they reveal about Thoreau's **tone?**

COMMON CORE

RI 2 Determine two or more central ideas of a text and analyze their development over the course of a text. **RI 3** Analyze a complex set of ideas and explain how specific ideas interact and develop over the course of the text. **RI 9** Analyze documents of literary significance for their themes, purposes, and rhetorical features. **L 5a** Interpret figures of speech in context and analyze their role in the text.

from Self-Reliance
from Nature

Essays by Ralph Waldo Emerson

VIDEO TRAILER THINK central KEYWORD: HML11-368A

DID YOU KNOW?

Ralph Waldo Emerson . . .

- entered Harvard when he was only 14.
- was named class poet at Harvard—but only after seven other students had refused the honor.
- published *Nature,* one of his most famous works, anonymously.

Old North Bridge, Concord, Massachusetts

Meet the Author

Ralph Waldo Emerson 1803–1882

As the acknowledged leader of the transcendentalists, Ralph Waldo Emerson, poet, essayist, and lecturer, was a towering figure in the 19th-century literary world. He helped shape a new, uniquely American body of literature and is often cited as one of the most significant writers in American history. "All life is an experiment," the radical thinker and writer once said. "The more experiments you make, the better."

An Average Student Emerson was born in Boston, Massachusetts. His father, a prominent Unitarian minister, died when Emerson was eight, plunging the family into financial trouble. Although money was tight, funds were found to enroll Emerson at Harvard. When he graduated in 1821, ranked 30th out of a class of 59, there was little indication that Emerson would soon become one of the most celebrated literary figures of all time.

Spiritual Crisis In 1825, Emerson returned to Harvard to study for the Unitarian ministry and was ordained in 1829. Just over a year later, his beloved wife, Ellen, died of tuberculosis. Ellen's death threw Emerson into a state of spiritual crisis, causing him to question many aspects of the Christian tradition and his duties as a minister. In 1832, after much consideration, Emerson resigned his post.

The Voice of Transcendentalism Following his wife's death, Emerson settled in Concord, Massachusetts, and devoted himself to the study of philosophy, religion, and literature. In 1836 Emerson published *Nature,* in which he eloquently articulated his transcendental philosophy, an outgrowth of European romanticism. That same year, Emerson formed the Transcendental Club with a group of like-minded friends, including Henry David Thoreau and Margaret Fuller. *Nature,* with its emphasis on self-reliance and individuality, became the group's unofficial manifesto.

The Sage of Concord Those who met Emerson in person often thought him a rather stiff and formal person, dressed always in black. He reserved his passion for the page and the podium, where he elaborated upon his ideas in essays and a series of popular lectures. By the 1840s the Sage of Concord, as he was known, had become a major literary force whose influence is still evident in American culture today.

Author Online THINK central

Go to thinkcentral.com. KEYWORD: HML11-368B

TEXT ANALYSIS: TRANSCENDENTALISM

Ralph Waldo Emerson's motto was "Trust thyself." This principle lies at the heart of **transcendentalism,** an intellectual movement that emphasized the dignity of the individual and advocated a simple, mindful life. The transcendentalists, led by Emerson himself, wanted to transcend—or go beyond—the limitations of the senses and everyday experience. Key tenets of transcendentalism include

- a theory that "transcendent forms" of truth exist beyond reason and experience; every individual is capable of discovering this truth on his or her own, through intuition
- a conviction that people are inherently good and should follow their own beliefs, however controversial they may be
- a belief that humankind, nature, and God are all interconnected

As you read, consider how Emerson's writing articulates his belief in the importance of the individual as well as his ideas about humankind's relationship to the natural world.

READING SKILL: IDENTIFY THEME

Theme is the underlying message or the central idea of a work, which can be stated in one sentence. Usually, writers do not state the theme directly; instead, readers must make inferences based on clues in the text. As you read "Self-Reliance" and *Nature,* record your inferences about each work's theme in a chart like the one below.

Theme of "Self-Reliance"	Theme of Nature

VOCABULARY IN CONTEXT

Emerson uses these words to state his convictions. Test your knowledge by deciding which word is suggested by each phrase.

WORD LIST			
	aversion	exhilaration	nonconformist
	decorum	importune	occult

1. a food you do not like
2. a race you have just won
3. a well-behaved crowd
4. a nagging younger sibling

Complete the activities in your **Reader/Writer Notebook.**

What is your MOTTO?

The ancient Roman poet Horace gravely advised, "Never despair." Modern comedian Woody Allen quipped that the secret to success in life is simple: "Eighty percent of success is showing up." Each of these mottos captures an individual's attitude toward life in one pithy phrase. Ralph Waldo Emerson's motto, "Trust thyself," distills the essence of the ideals he expressed in his essays and lectures.

QUICKWRITE Create your own personal motto. To get started, consider the traits or resources that helped you solve a difficult problem, or the best advice you have ever given a friend. Use your answers to develop a personal motto that is short and to the point.

Self-Reliance

RALPH WALDO EMERSON

There is a time in every man's education when he arrives at the conviction that envy is ignorance; that imitation is suicide; that he must take himself for better for worse as his portion; that though the wide universe is full of good, no kernel of nourishing corn can come to him but through his toil bestowed on that plot of ground which is given to him to till. . . .

Trust thyself: every heart vibrates to that iron string. Accept the place the divine providence has found for you, the society of your contemporaries, the connection of events. Great men have always done so, and confided themselves childlike to the genius of their age, betraying their perception that the absolutely trustworthy[1] was seated at their heart, working through their hands, predominating[2] in all their being. . . . **A**

Whoso would be a man, must be a **nonconformist.** He who would gather immortal palms[3] must not be hindered by the name of goodness, but must explore if it be goodness. Nothing is at last sacred but the integrity of your own mind. Absolve you to yourself, and you shall have the suffrage[4] of the world. I remember an answer which when quite young I was prompted to make to a valued adviser

Analyze Visuals ▶
What elements of **transcendentalism** are reflected in the painting on the opposite page?

A THEME
Re-read the ideas in lines 1–11. Based on these lines, what inferences can you make about the theme of this selection?

nonconformist
(nŏn′kən-fôr′mĭst) *n.* one who does not follow generally accepted beliefs, customs, or practices

---

1. **the absolutely trustworthy:** God.
2. **predominating:** being predominant, or having controlling influence.
3. **immortal palms:** everlasting triumph and honor. In ancient times, people carried palm leaves as a symbol of victory, success, or joy.
4. **suffrage:** approval; support.

Wanderer Above the Sea of Fog (1818), Caspar David Friedrich. Oil on canvas, 94.8 cm × 74.8 cm.

who was wont to **importune** me with the dear old doctrines of the church. On my saying, "What have I to do with the sacredness of traditions, if I live wholly from within?" my friend suggested—"But these impulses may be from below, not from above." I replied, "They do not seem to me to be such; but if I am the Devil's child, I will live then from the Devil." No law can be sacred to me but that of my nature. Good and bad are but names very readily transferable to that or this; the only right is what is after my constitution;[5] the only wrong what is against it. . . . B

What I must do is all that concerns me, not what the people think. This rule, equally arduous in actual and in intellectual life, may serve for the whole distinction between greatness and meanness.[6] It is the harder because you will always find those who think they know what is your duty better than you know it. It is easy in the world to live after the world's opinion; it is easy in solitude to live after our own; but the great man is he who in the midst of the crowd keeps with perfect sweetness the independence of solitude. . . . C

For nonconformity the world whips you with its displeasure. And therefore a man must know how to estimate a sour face. The by-standers look askance on him in the public street or in the friend's parlor. If this **aversion** had its origin in contempt and resistance like his own he might well go home with a sad countenance; but the sour faces of the multitude, like their sweet faces, have no deep cause, but are put on and off as the wind blows and a newspaper directs. . . .

The other terror that scares us from self-trust is our consistency; a reverence for our past act or word because the eyes of others have no other data for computing our orbit than our past acts, and we are loth to disappoint them. . . .

A foolish consistency is the hobgoblin[7] of little minds, adored by little statesmen and philosophers and divines.[8] With consistency a great soul has simply nothing to do. He may as well concern himself with his shadow on the wall. Speak what you think now in hard words and tomorrow speak what tomorrow thinks in hard words again, though it contradict everything you said today.—"Ah, so you shall be sure to be misunderstood."— Is it so bad then to be misunderstood? Pythagoras was misunderstood, and Socrates, and Jesus, and Luther, and Copernicus, and Galileo, and Newton,[9] and every pure and wise spirit that ever took flesh. To be great is to be misunderstood.

importune (ĭm'pôr-to͞on') *v.* to ask urgently or repeatedly; to annoy or trouble

B TRANSCENDENTALISM
Transcendentalists believed in disregarding external authority in favor of one's own experience and intuition. What is implied by the word *sacred* in line 21?

C GRAMMAR AND STYLE
Emerson adds detail and precision to his writing by using **adjective clauses,** which modify nouns and pronouns. In line 27 and lines 29–30, he uses adjective clauses beginning with *who* to describe specific types of people.

aversion (ə-vûr'zhən) *n.* a strong dislike

COMMON CORE L 5a

Language Coach

Figurative Language In lines 37–39, "computing our orbit" is an example of figurative language, language that communicates ideas beyond the literal meaning of words. "Computing our orbit" can be understood as "deciding what we'll do next." State lines 37–39 in your own words.

5. **after my constitution:** consistent with my nature.
6. **meanness:** the state of being inferior in quality, character, or value.
7. **hobgoblin:** a source of fear or dread.
8. **divines:** religious leaders.
9. **Pythagoras** (pĭ-thăg'ər-əs) **. . . Newton:** great thinkers whose radical theories and viewpoints caused controversy.

Nature

RALPH WALDO EMERSON

Nature is a setting that fits equally well a comic or a mourning piece. In good health, the air is a cordial of incredible virtue. Crossing a bare common, in snow puddles, at twilight, under a clouded sky, without having in my thoughts any occurrence of special good fortune, I have enjoyed a perfect **exhilaration.** I am glad to the brink of fear. In the woods too, a man casts off his years, as the snake his slough,[1] and at what period soever of life, is always a child. In the woods, is perpetual youth. Within these plantations of God, a **decorum** and sanctity reign, a perennial festival is dressed, and the guest sees not how he should tire of them in a thousand years. In the woods, we return to reason and faith. There I feel that nothing can befall me in life,—no disgrace, no calamity, (leaving me my eyes,) which nature cannot repair. Standing on the bare ground,—my head bathed by the blithe air, and uplifted into infinite space,—all mean egotism vanishes. I become a transparent eye-ball; I am nothing; I see all; the currents of the Universal Being circulate through me; I am part or particle of God. The name of the nearest friend sounds then foreign and accidental: to be brothers, to be acquaintances,—master or servant, is then a trifle and a disturbance. I am the lover of uncontained and immortal beauty. In the wilderness, I find something more dear and connate[2] than in streets or villages. In the tranquil landscape, and especially in the distant line of the horizon, man beholds somewhat as beautiful as his own nature. D

exhilaration (ĭg-zĭl′ə-rā′shən) *n.* a feeling of high spirits or lively joy

decorum (dĭ-kôr′əm) *n.* good taste in conduct or appearance

D TRANSCENDENTALISM
Review the elements of transcendentalism listed on page 369. Which aspect of transcendentalist thought is reflected in lines 12–19? Explain your answer.

1. **slough** (slŭf): the cast-off skin of a snake.
2. **connate:** agreeable; able to be related to.

The greatest delight which the fields and woods minister, is the suggestion of an **occult** relation between man and the vegetable. I am not alone and unacknowledged. They nod to me, and I to them. The waving of the boughs in the storm, is new to me and old. It takes me by surprise, and yet is not unknown. Its effect is like that of a higher thought or a better emotion coming over me, when I deemed I was thinking justly or doing right.

Yet it is certain that the power to produce this delight, does not reside in nature, but in man, or in a harmony of both. It is necessary to use these pleasures with great temperance. For, nature is not always tricked[3] in holiday attire, but the same scene which yesterday breathed perfume and glittered as for the frolic of the nymphs, is overspread with melancholy today. Nature always wears the colors of the spirit. To a man laboring under calamity, the heat of his own fire hath sadness in it. Then, there is a kind of contempt of the landscape felt by him who has just lost by death a dear friend. The sky is less grand as it shuts down over less worth in the population. ∾

occult (ə-kŭlt') *adj.* secret or hidden from view

Language Coach

Word Definitions In line 26, *reside* means "live" or "exist." (Think of related words: *residence* and *resident*.) Where does Emerson say the power to appreciate nature exists? Now, read lines 30–34. What is Emerson saying about our perception of the natural world?

3. **tricked:** dressed.

▼ Analyze Visuals

Emerson says that "nature always wears the colors of the spirit." What **mood** does this painting convey? Describe the elements of the painting that establish this mood.

Ben Lomond (1829–1830), Thomas Doughty. Oil on canvas. © Christie's Images/SuperStock.

Comprehension

1. **Recall** According to "Self-Reliance," what is the only law that Emerson can hold sacred?
2. **Summarize** What are three ways the woods can transform a man, according to Emerson in *Nature?*
3. **Clarify** In *Nature,* Emerson discusses the "delight" the natural world often inspires. What does Emerson think this power to delight comes from?

COMMON CORE

RI 2 Determine two or more central ideas of a text and analyze their development over the course of the text. **RI 3** Analyze a complex set of ideas and explain how specific ideas interact and develop over the course of the text. **RI 9** Analyze documents of literary significance for their themes, purposes, and rhetorical features.

Text Analysis

4. **Draw Conclusions** Reread lines 37–48 of "Self-Reliance." What is Emerson speaking of when he mentions consistency, and why does he berate it as "the hobgoblin of little minds"? Consider the following examples of Emerson's statements as you formulate your response:
   - "Good and bad are but names very readily transferable to that or this. . . ."
   - ". . . The sour faces of the multitude . . . have no deep cause, but are put on and off as the wind blows. . . ."
5. **Identify Elements of Transcendentalism** Review the elements of transcendentalism listed on page 369. Then reexamine "Self-Reliance" and *Nature,* identifying key ideas that reflect each tenet of transcendentalism. Record your answer in a chart like the one shown.

Element of Transcendentalism	Example from the Text
Every individual is capable of discovering higher truths on his or her own, through intuition.	"Nothing is at last sacred but the integrity of your own mind." ("Self-Reliance," line 14)

6. **Analyze Theme** Look at the themes you recorded for each of Emerson's writings. How does each theme relate to the ideals of transcendentalism?

Text Criticism

7. **Critical Interpretation** Writer Henry James argued that Emerson had no concept of the evil that exists in the world. In James's words, it was "a side of life as to which Emerson's eyes were thickly bandaged. . . . He had no great sense of wrong . . . no sense of the dark, the foul, the base." In your opinion, is this a valid criticism of Emerson? Citing evidence, explain why or why not.

What is your MOTTO?

What are some of the ideals, or beliefs, that you adhere to? How are your ideals different from those of the people you know best?

Vocabulary in Context

▲ VOCABULARY PRACTICE

Choose the vocabulary word that best completes each sentence.

1. An unexpected tragedy can quickly turn_____ into grief.
2. To constantly _____ a friend for favors can destroy the friendship.
3. One should act with _____ on serious or formal occasions.
4. It is not wise to pry into the _____ intrigues of others.
5. Certain values are held by every person, whether a traditionalist or a(n) _____.
6. It makes sense to avoid anything to which one has a(n) _____.

WORD LIST
aversion
decorum
exhilaration
importune
nonconformist
occult

ACADEMIC VOCABULARY IN SPEAKING

• construct • expand • indicate • reinforce • role

Although Emerson believed that nature played an important **role** in life, he also saw it as inferior to the power found in humans. In fact, Emerson believed that nature **reinforces** what is already present in humankind. In a small group, discuss how people view nature and self-sufficiency today. In your discussion, use at least three of the Academic Vocabulary words.

VOCABULARY STRATEGY: WORDS WITH MULTIPLE AFFIXES

You can decipher many long words if you are able to locate a recognizable base word within them. Removing the prefix and the suffix from the vocabulary word *nonconformist,* for example, reveals the base word *conform.* What meanings do the affixes add to the base word? Analyze similar words by separating them into a base word and affixes. Remember that many base words drop the final *e* before suffixes are added.

COMMON CORE

L 4b Identify and correctly use patterns of word changes that indicate different meanings or parts of speech. **L 6** Acquire and use accurately general academic words and phrases.

PRACTICE Write the base word and the affixes that make up each word listed. Then write a sentence that demonstrates the meaning of the longer word.

1. prefabricated
2. undiversified
3. disreputable
4. repagination
5. indefatigable
6. abnegation

Language

GRAMMAR AND STYLE: Use Descriptive Details

Review the **Grammar and Style** note on page 372. The precision of Emerson's prose owes much to his skillful use of **adjective clauses**—subordinate clauses that add important details about nouns and pronouns. An adjective clause usually follows the word it modifies and is introduced by words such as *when, who, whom, whose, that,* and *which.* Here is an example from "Self-Reliance":

> *There is a time in every man's education when he arrives at the conviction that envy is ignorance; that imitation is suicide; that he must take himself for better for worse as his portion. . . .* (lines 1–3)

Notice that each of the highlighted clauses offers information about the noun it modifies. The first clause tells you about the "time in every man's education" Emerson is discussing. The second, third, and fourth clauses explain what kind of conviction he embraces at this time.

PRACTICE Identify the adjective clause in each sentence from Emerson's work. Then write your own sentences, using adjective clauses as Emerson does.

EXAMPLE

He who would gather immortal palms must not be hindered by the name of goodness, but must explore if it be goodness.

Those who wish to make a true difference cannot worry what others might say behind their backs.

1. There is a kind of contempt of the landscape felt by him who has just lost by death a dear friend.
2. Nature is a setting that fits equally well a comic or a mourning piece.

READING-WRITING CONNECTION

Expand your understanding of Emerson's writing by responding to this prompt. Then, use the **revising tips** to improve your speech.

WRITING PROMPT	REVISING TIPS
UPDATE EMERSON'S MESSAGE Emerson's ideas about nonconformity are still relevant today. Write a **short speech** presenting an updated version of Emerson's message for an audience of contemporary high school students. Use at least one adjective clause in your speech.	• Direct your speech to your peers. • Check your examples to make sure they are current and that they support Emerson's ideas.

COMMON CORE

L 3 Apply knowledge of language to make effective choices for meaning and style. **W 2b** Develop the topic by selecting the most significant and relevant facts, extended definitions, concrete details, quotations, or other information and examples. **W 2d** Use precise language to manage the complexity of a topic.

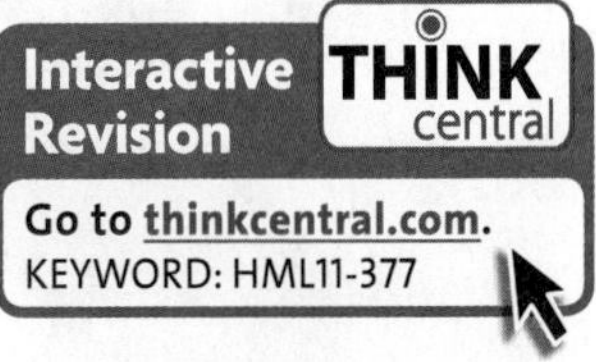

COMMON CORE

RI 2 Determine two or more central ideas of a text and analyze their development; provide an objective summary of the text. **RI 6** Determine an author's point of view or purpose in a text in which the rhetoric is effective, analyzing how style and content contribute to the power, persuasiveness, or beauty of the text. **RI 9** Analyze documents of literary significance for their themes, purposes, and rhetorical features.

from Walden
from Civil Disobedience

Video link at thinkcentral.com

Essays by Henry David Thoreau

VIDEO TRAILER THINK central KEYWORD: HML11-378A

Meet the Author

Henry David Thoreau 1817–1862

Henry David Thoreau (thə-rō') advocated simple, mindful living and rejected a lifestyle dedicated to the pursuit of wealth. Thoreau spent much of his life writing and observing nature, devoting only a minimum of time to earning a wage. He published just two books, both of which sold very poorly in his own lifetime. Few of his contemporaries would have judged him much of a success. In the years since his death, however, his reputation has grown tremendously. Today, he is regarded as a writer of uncommon vision and remembered as one of the first environmentalists.

Independent Spirit Thoreau was born and raised in Concord, Massachusetts, and attended Harvard University. After graduating, he returned to Concord to teach school. Though some of Thoreau's neighbors viewed him as eccentric, he was a careful observer and a deep thinker. Taking to heart the ideas of his friend Ralph Waldo Emerson, Thoreau tried to live by his own values, often doing odd jobs that would earn him just enough money to meet his own modest needs.

Defiant Nonconformist Thoreau's life was full of examples of his nonconformity to society's norms. As a Harvard student, he was required to wear a black coat but sported a green one instead. In his first year of teaching, he refused to punish his students physically, a harsh but common practice of the time, and resigned his post. In 1845, he conducted his famous experiment, living simply and frugally in a small cabin on the shores of Walden Pond. In 1846, he was arrested and spent a night in jail for refusing to pay a poll tax, an act of protest against the U.S. government's war with Mexico and its support of slavery. This exercise of conscience over law later became known as civil disobedience.

Influential Thinker At the time of Thoreau's death from tuberculosis at age 44, he was viewed as an unsuccessful nature writer. Today, however, he is known as the father of American nature writing and an important political thinker. His observations about the natural world and the value of the simple life, as well as his promotion of nonviolent protest, have helped bring about great societal change. He has provided inspiration to many, including conservationist John Muir and civil rights leader Martin Luther King Jr.

DID YOU KNOW?

Henry David Thoreau . . .

- worked off and on as a pencil maker in his family's pencil factory.
- kept a journal that when published filled 20 volumes.
- pared down his expenses to 27 cents a week, which he earned by working only six weeks a year.

Author Online THINK central

Go to thinkcentral.com. KEYWORD: HML11-378B

TEXT ANALYSIS: ESSAY

An **essay** is a work of nonfiction, often loosely structured, expressing the writer's personal views on a single subject. To analyze an essay, pay careful attention to the rhetorical or persuasive power of the following elements:

- the writer's **tone,** or attitude toward his or her subject
- **figurative language** that makes abstract ideas more appealing and easier to grasp
- **anecdotes,** or short accounts of personal incidents
- **imagery** that creates vivid impressions for the reader

As you read, consider how these rhetorical elements illuminate Thoreau's ideas and contribute to the power and persuasiveness of the text.

Review: Transcendentalism

READING SKILL: EVALUATE IDEAS

To **evaluate** a writer's ideas, you must examine them carefully and then make judgments about their value. **Summarizing** can help. As you read the selections from *Walden* and "Civil Disobedience," use a chart like the one shown to briefly restate Thoreau's main ideas. After you summarize each idea, note your reaction to it.

	Thoreau's Ideas and Beliefs	*My Reactions*
Walden		
"Civil Disobedience"		

VOCABULARY IN CONTEXT

Thoreau uses the following words to present his theories about simple, principled living. To see how many you know, choose the word that is closest in meaning to each numbered term.

WORD LIST

abject	impetuous	pervade
congenial	misgiving	transgress
deliberately	perturbation	

1. err	**4.** wretched	**7.** impulsive
2. disturbance	**5.** friendly	**8.** thoughtfully
3. doubt	**6.** permeate	

Complete the activities in your **Reader/Writer Notebook**.

Do you chart your own COURSE?

"Cranks," "crackpots," "oddballs"—society has been quick to apply a negative label to people outside the mainstream. Although Thoreau was probably never called an "oddball," he was certainly regarded as an eccentric. Nonconformity has never been an easy choice, as people often condemn nonconformists without bothering to find out why they embrace a different set of values. Nevertheless, history has shown that many nonconformists, like Thoreau, are often simply ahead of their time.

DISCUSS With a small group of classmates, create a list of famous nonconformists. How did the individuals you listed depart from the norms of their time? Were they punished for their actions? Were they able to win others to their point of view? Discuss these questions with your group.

WALDEN

Henry David Thoreau

BACKGROUND Like Ralph Waldo Emerson and other transcendentalists, Thoreau felt a need to affirm his unity with nature. On July 4, 1845, he began an experiment in what he thought of as "essential living"—living simply, studying the natural world, and seeking truth within himself. On land owned by Emerson near Concord, Massachusetts, Thoreau built a small cabin by Walden Pond and lived there for more than two years, writing and studying nature. *Walden* is the record of his experiences.

THEME
What is the right way to live? People have been asking this question for millennia. In *Walden,* Thoreau describes his attempt to live the "right way." In the recent movie *Into the Wild* (2007), a young man attempts to find his own way of living but meets with disastrous results. What characters in recent films, plays, or novels have tried to find a new or different way of living? How successful were they?

from Where I Lived, and What I Lived For

Analyze Visuals ▶
Consider the tranquil scene depicted in the photograph on the opposite page. What aspect of the photograph is most responsible for conveying this sense of tranquility, and why?

When first I took up my abode in the woods, that is, began to spend my nights as well as days there, which, by accident, was on Independence day, or the fourth of July, 1845, my house was not finished for winter, but was merely a defense against the rain, without plastering or chimney, the walls being of rough weather-stained boards, with wide chinks, which made it cool at night. The upright white hewn studs and freshly planed door and window casings gave it a clean and airy look, especially in the morning, when its timbers were saturated with dew, so that I fancied that by noon some sweet gum would exude from them. . . . Ⓐ

I was seated by the shore of a small pond, about a mile and a half south of the village of Concord and somewhat higher than it, in the midst of an extensive wood between that town and Lincoln, and about two miles south of that our only field known to fame, Concord Battle Ground; but I was so low in the woods that the opposite shore, half a mile off, like the rest, covered with wood, was my most distant horizon. For the first week, whenever I looked out on the pond it impressed me like a tarn high up

Ⓐ **ESSAY**
Think about Thoreau's **tone** as he describes his crude, unfinished house. What sense of the writer's views or personality do you get from these opening lines?

16 tarn: a small mountain lake or pool.

on the side of a mountain, its bottom far above the surface of other lakes, and, as the sun arose, I saw it throwing off its nightly clothing of mist, and here and there, by degrees, its soft ripples or its smooth reflecting surface was revealed, while the mists, like ghosts, were stealthily withdrawing in every direction into the woods, as at the breaking up of some nocturnal conventicle. The very dew seemed to hang upon the trees later into the day than usual, as on the sides of mountains. . . .

I went to the woods because I wished to live **deliberately,** to front only the essential facts of life, and see if I could not learn what it had to teach, and not, when I came to die, discover that I had not lived. I did not wish to live what was not life, living is so dear; nor did I wish to practice resignation, unless it was quite necessary. I wanted to live deep and suck out all the marrow of life, to live so sturdily and Spartan-like as to put to rout all that was not life, to cut a broad swath and shave close, to drive life into a corner, and reduce it to its lowest terms, and, if it proved to be mean, why then to get the whole and genuine meanness of it, and publish its meanness to the world; or if it were sublime, to know it by experience, and be able to give a true account of it in my next excursion. For most men, it appears to me, are in a strange uncertainty about it, whether it is of the devil or of God, and have *somewhat hastily* concluded that it is the chief end of man here to "glorify God and enjoy him forever." B

Still we live meanly, like ants; though the fable tells us that we were long ago changed into men; like pygmies we fight with cranes; it is error upon error, and clout upon clout, and our best virtue has for its occasion a superfluous and evitable wretchedness. Our life is frittered away by detail. An honest man has hardly need to count more than his ten fingers, or in extreme cases he may add his ten toes, and lump the rest. Simplicity, simplicity, simplicity! I say, let your affairs be as two or three, and not a hundred or a thousand; instead of a million count half a dozen, and keep your accounts on your thumbnail. In the midst of this chopping sea of civilized life, such are the clouds and storms and quicksands and thousand-and-one items to be allowed for, that a man has to live, if he would not founder and go to the bottom and not make his port at all, by dead reckoning, and he must be a great calculator indeed who succeeds. Simplify, simplify. Instead of three meals a day, if it be necessary eat but one; instead of a hundred dishes, five; and reduce other things in proportion. . . . C

Why should we live with such hurry and waste of life? We are determined to be starved before we are hungry. Men say that a stitch in time saves nine, and so they take a thousand stitches today to save nine to-morrow. As for *work,* we haven't any of any consequence. We have the Saint Vitus' dance, and cannot possibly keep our heads still. If I should only give a few pulls at the parish bell-rope, as for a fire, that is, without setting the bell, there is hardly a man on his farm in the outskirts of Concord, notwithstanding that press of engagements which was his excuse so many times this morning,

22 conventicle: a secret religious meeting.

deliberately (dĭ-lĭb'ər-ĭt-lē) *adv.* in an unhurried and thoughtful manner

29 Spartan-like: in a simple and disciplined way, like the inhabitants of the ancient city-state of Sparta.

B EVALUATE IDEAS

Reread lines 24–37. **Summarize** Thoreau's reasons for moving to the woods. What do you think of these reasons?

41 evitable: avoidable.

C ESSAY

In this essay, Thoreau often uses **figurative language** to present his observations. In lines 46–50, he likens civilized life to a rough sea. What might "the clouds and storms and quicksand" of life be? How might one "founder," or sink, in civilized life?

56 Saint Vitus' dance: a disorder of the nervous system, characterized by rapid, jerky, involuntary movements.

nor a boy, nor a woman, I might almost say, but would forsake all and follow that sound, not mainly to save property from the flames, but, if we will confess the truth, much more to see it burn, since burn it must, and we, be it known, did not set it on fire,—or to see it put out, and have a hand in it, if that is done as handsomely; yes, even if it were the parish church itself. Hardly a man takes a half hour's nap after dinner, but when he wakes he holds up his head and asks, "What's the news?" as if the rest of mankind had stood his sentinels. Some give directions to be waked every half hour, doubtless for no other purpose; and then, to pay for it, they tell what they have dreamed. After a night's sleep the news is as indispensable as the breakfast. "Pray tell me any thing new that has happened to a man any where on this globe,"—and he reads it over his coffee and rolls, that a man has had his eyes gouged out this morning on the Wachito River; never dreaming the while that he lives in the dark unfathomed mammoth cave of this world, and has but the rudiment of an eye himself. D

D ESSAY
What situation does Thoreau exaggerate in lines 66–75, and what is the rhetorical effect of his exaggeration? Would you respond differently to Thoreau's point if he stated his view here without exaggeration? Explain your answer.

For my part, I could easily do without the post-office. I think that there are very few important communications made through it. To speak critically, I never received more than one or two letters in my life—I wrote this some years ago—that were worth the postage. The penny-post is, commonly, an institution through which you seriously offer a man that penny for his thoughts which is so often safely offered in jest. And I am sure that I never read any memorable news in a newspaper. If we read of one man robbed, or murdered, or killed by accident, or one house burned, or one vessel wrecked, or one steamboat blown up, or one cow run over on the Western Railroad, or one mad dog killed, or one lot of grasshoppers in the winter,—we never need read of another. One is enough. . . .

79–81 penny-post . . . jest: Thoreau jokingly connects the postage rate at the time (a penny per letter) with the phrase "a penny for your thoughts."

Let us spend one day as deliberately as Nature, and not be thrown off the track by every nutshell and mosquito's wing that falls on the rails. Let us rise early and fast, or break fast, gently and without **perturbation;** let company come and let company go, let the bells ring and the children cry,—determined to make a day of it. . . .

perturbation (pûr′tər-bā′shən) *n.* disturbance of the emotions; agitation; uneasiness

Time is but the stream I go a-fishing in. I drink at it; but while I drink I see the sandy bottom and detect how shallow it is. Its thin current slides away, but eternity remains. I would drink deeper; fish in the sky, whose bottom is pebbly with stars. I cannot count one. I know not the first letter of the alphabet. I have always been regretting that I was not as wise as the day I was born. The intellect is a cleaver; it discerns and rifts its way into the secret of things. I do not wish to be any more busy with my hands than is necessary. My head is hands and feet. I feel all my best faculties concentrated in it. My instinct tells me that my head is an organ for burrowing, as some creatures use their snout and fore-paws, and with it I would mine and burrow my way through these hills. I think that the richest vein is somewhere hereabouts; so by the divining rod and thin rising vapors I judge; and here I will begin to mine. E

E EVALUATE IDEAS
Summarize lines 87–104. What does Thoreau want to spend his time trying to understand, and how does he plan to achieve this understanding? Decide what you think about this desire.

from Solitude

This is a delicious evening, when the whole body is one sense, and imbibes delight through every pore. I go and come with a strange liberty in Nature, a part of herself. As I walk along the stony shore of the pond in my shirt sleeves, though it is cool as well as cloudy and windy, and I see nothing special to attract me, all the elements are unusually **congenial** to me. The bullfrogs trump to usher in the night, and the note of the whippoorwill is borne on the rippling wind from over the water. Sympathy with the fluttering alder and poplar leaves almost takes away my breath; yet, like the lake, my serenity is rippled but not ruffled. These small waves raised by the evening wind are as remote from storm as the smooth reflecting surface. Though it is now dark, the wind still blows and roars in the wood, the waves still dash, and some creatures lull the rest with their notes. The repose is never complete. The wildest animals do not repose, but seek their prey now; the fox, and skunk, and rabbit, now roam the fields and woods without fear. They are Nature's watchmen,—links which connect the days of animated life. . . .

Men frequently say to me, "I should think you would feel lonesome down there, and want to be nearer to folks, rainy and snowy days and nights especially." I am tempted to reply to such,—This whole earth which we inhabit is but a point in space. How far apart, think you, dwell the two most distant inhabitants of yonder star, the breadth of whose disk cannot be appreciated by our instruments? Why should I feel lonely? Is not our planet in the Milky Way? This which you put seems to me not to be the most important question. What sort of space is that which separates a man from his fellows and makes him solitary? I have found that no exertion of the legs can bring two minds much nearer to one another. . . . F

congenial (kən-jēn′yəl) *adj.* suited to one's needs or nature; agreeable

COMMON CORE L 4c

Language Coach

Synonyms *Rippled* and *ruffled* (line 113) are synonyms, words with similar meanings. Thoreau contrasts their meanings, though. With a partner, look up each word in a dictionary; then, decide what difference in meaning Thoreau intended for them to have.

F EVALUATE IDEAS
Reread lines 121–130. **Summarize** Thoreau's ideas about loneliness. Do you agree with his assessment of this condition? Explain your answer.

from The Pond in Winter

Every winter the liquid and trembling surface of the pond, which was so sensitive to every breath, and reflected every light and shadow, becomes solid to the depth of a foot or a foot and a half, so that it will support the heaviest teams, and perchance the snow covers it to an equal depth, and it is not to be distinguished from any level field. Like the marmots in the surrounding hills, it closes its eye-lids and becomes dormant for three months or more. Standing on the snow-covered plain, as if in a pasture amid the hills, I cut my way first through a foot of snow, and then a foot of ice, and open a window under my feet, where, kneeling to drink, I look down into the quiet parlor of the fishes, **pervaded** by a softened light as through a window of

135 marmots: burrowing rodents that hibernate in winter; also known as groundhogs or woodchucks.

pervade (pər-vād′) *v.* to spread through every part of

ground glass, with its bright sanded floor the same as in summer; there a perennial waveless serenity reigns as in the amber twilight sky, corresponding to the cool and even temperament of the inhabitants. Heaven is under our feet as well as over our heads. . . . G

G TRANSCENDENTALISM
What transcendentalist ideal is reflected in lines 143–144?

from Spring

One attraction in coming to the woods to live was that I should have leisure and opportunity to see the spring come in. The ice in the pond at length begins to be honey-combed, and I can set my heel in it as I walk. Fogs and rains and warmer suns are gradually melting the snow; the days have grown sensibly longer; and I see how I shall get through the winter without adding to my woodpile, for large fires are no longer necessary. I am on the alert for the first signs of spring, to hear the chance note of some arriving bird, or the striped squirrel's chirp, for his stores must be now nearly exhausted, or see the woodchuck venture out of his winter quarters. . . .

The change from storm and winter to serene and mild weather, from dark and sluggish hours to bright and elastic ones, is a memorable crisis which all things proclaim. It is seemingly instantaneous at last. Suddenly an influx of light filled my house, though the evening was at hand, and the clouds of winter still overhung it, and the eaves were dripping with sleety rain. I looked out the window, and lo! where yesterday was cold gray ice there lay the transparent pond already calm and full of hope as in a summer evening, reflecting a summer evening sky in its bosom, though none was visible overhead, as if it had intelligence with some remote horizon. . . . H

149 sensibly: noticeably.

H ESSAY
Even when an essay does not argue a particular point, the writer uses **rhetorical techniques,** or methods that have persuasive appeal. For example, in lines 143–144, when Thoreau says "Heaven is under our feet," his use of figurative language has strong emotional appeal. Re-read lines 145–162. What effect does Thoreau's use of **imagery** have in this description?

from Conclusion

I left the woods for as good a reason as I went there. Perhaps it seemed to me that I had several more lives to live, and could not spare any more time for that one. It is remarkable how easily and insensibly we fall into a particular route, and make a beaten track for ourselves. I had not lived there a week before my feet wore a path from my door to the pond-side; and though it is five or six years since I trod it, it is still quite distinct. It is true, I fear that others may have fallen into it, and so helped to keep it open. The surface of the earth is soft and impressible by the feet of men; and so with the paths which the mind travels. How worn and dusty, then, must be the highways of the world, how deep the ruts of tradition and conformity! I did not wish to take a cabin passage, but rather to go before the mast and on the deck of

Language Coach

Figurative Language "Beaten track" (line 166) and "ruts" (line 172) can be used as figurative language, language that communicates ideas beyond the literal meaning of the words. How can "beaten track" and "ruts" be understood both literally and figuratively?

172–175 On a sailing ship, passengers stayed in private compartments, or cabins, near the middle of the ship, while the crew shared living quarters at the front, where more was visible.

the world, for there I could best see the moonlight amid the mountains. I do not wish to go below now. **I**

I learned this, at least, by my experiment; that if one advances confidently in the direction of his dreams, and endeavors to live the life which he has imagined, he will meet with a success unexpected in common hours. He will put some things behind, will pass an invisible boundary; new, universal, and more liberal laws will begin to establish themselves around and within him; or the old laws be expanded, and interpreted in his favor in a more liberal sense, and he will live with the license of a higher order of beings. In proportion as he simplifies his life, the laws of the universe will appear less complex, and solitude will not be solitude, nor poverty poverty, nor weakness weakness. If you have built castles in the air, your work need not be lost; that is where they should be. Now put the foundations under them. . . .

Why should we be in such desperate haste to succeed, and in such desperate enterprises? If a man does not keep pace with his companions, perhaps it is because he hears a different drummer. Let him step to the music which he hears, however measured or far away. It is not important that he should mature as soon as an appletree or an oak. Shall he turn his spring into summer? If the condition of things which we were made for is not yet, what were any reality which we can substitute? We will not be shipwrecked on a vain reality. Shall we with pains erect a heaven of blue glass over ourselves, though when it is done we shall be sure to gaze still at the true ethereal heaven far above, as if the former were not? . . . **J**

However mean your life is, meet it and live it; do not shun it and call it hard names. It is not so bad as you are. It looks poorest when you are richest. The fault-finder will find faults even in paradise. Love your life, poor as it is. You may perhaps have some pleasant, thrilling, glorious hours, even in a poorhouse. The setting sun is reflected from the windows of the almshouse as brightly as from the rich man's abode; the snow melts before its door as early in the spring. I do not see but a quiet mind may live as contentedly there, and have as cheering thoughts, as in a palace. The town's poor seem to me often to live the most independent lives of any. May be they are simply great enough to receive without **misgiving.** Most think that they are above being supported by the town; but it oftener happens that they are not above supporting themselves by dishonest means, which should be more disreputable. Cultivate poverty like a garden herb, like sage. Do not trouble yourself much to get new things, whether clothes or friends. Turn the old; return to them. Things do not change; we change. Sell your clothes and keep your thoughts. God will see that you do not want society. If I were confined to a corner of a garret all my days, like a spider, the world would be just as large to me while I had my thoughts about me. The philosopher said: "From an army of three divisions one can take away its general, and put it in disorder; from the man the most **abject** and vulgar one cannot take away his thought." Do not seek so anxiously to be developed, to subject

I ESSAY
To what does Thoreau compare life in lines 172–175? Explain how this **metaphor** conveys Thoreau's reasons for leaving Walden.

189–191 If a man . . . away: This is one of Thoreau's most famous passages. The "different drummer" evolved from a journal entry describing how he fell asleep to the sound of someone beating a drum "alone in the silence and the dark." The phrase "marching to the beat of a different drummer" became popular during the 1960s and 1970s.

J TRANSCENDENTALISM
What key feature of transcendentalism does Thoreau embrace in lines 189–191?

misgiving (mĭs-gĭv'ĭng) *n.* a feeling of doubt, mistrust, or uncertainty

215 the philosopher: Confucius (551–479 B.C.), Chinese teacher of moral living, who had an influence on Thoreau's ideas.

abject (ăb'jĕkt') *adj.* low; contemptible; wretched

yourself to many influences to be played on; it is all dissipation. Humility like darkness reveals the heavenly lights. The shadows of poverty and meanness gather around us, "and lo! creation widens to our view." We are often reminded that if there were bestowed on us the wealth of Croesus, our aims must still be the same, and our means essentially the same. Moreover, if you are restricted in your range by poverty, if you cannot buy books and newspapers, for instance, you are but confined to the most significant and vital experiences; you are compelled to deal with the material which yields the most sugar and the most starch. It is life near the bone where it is sweetest. You are defended from being a trifler. No man loses ever on a lower level by magnanimity on a higher. Superfluous wealth can buy superfluities only. Money is not required to buy one necessary of the soul. . . . K

The life in us is like the water in the river. It may rise this year higher than man has ever known it, and flood the parched uplands; even this may be the eventful year, which will drown out all our muskrats. It was not always dry land where we dwell. I see far inland the banks which the stream anciently washed, before science began to record its freshets. Every one has heard the story which has gone the rounds of New England, of a strong and beautiful bug which came out of the dry leaf of an old table of apple-tree wood, which had stood in a farmer's kitchen for sixty years, first in Connecticut, and afterward in Massachusetts,—from an egg deposited in the living tree many years earlier still, as appeared by counting the annual layers beyond it; which was heard gnawing out for several weeks, hatched perchance by the heat of an urn. Who does not feel his faith in a resurrection and immortality strengthened by hearing of this? Who knows what beautiful and winged life, whose egg has been buried for ages under many concentric layers of woodenness in the dead dry life of society, deposited at first in the alburnum of the green and living tree, which has been gradually converted into the semblance of its well-seasoned tomb,—heard perchance gnawing out now for years by the astonished family of man, as they sat round the festive board,—may unexpectedly come forth from amidst society's most trivial and handselled furniture, to enjoy its perfect summer life at last!

I do not say that John or Jonathan will realize all this; but such is the character of that morrow which mere lapse of time can never make to dawn. The light which puts out our eyes is darkness to us. Only that day dawns to which we are awake. There is more day to dawn. The sun is but a morning star.

222 Croesus (krē′səs): an ancient king legendary for his great wealth.

K EVALUATE IDEAS
Summarize Thoreau's ideas about poverty. Do you think his view of the poor and the lives they lead is realistic? Record your thoughts in your chart.

235 freshets: overflowings of a stream caused by heavy rain or melting snow.

245 alburnum (ăl-bûr′nəm): the part of a tree's trunk through which sap flows.

251 John or Jonathan: the common man (as in the more current expression "Tom, Dick, and Harry").

Comprehension

1. **Recall** What were Thoreau's reasons for moving to the woods?
2. **Recall** What does Thoreau advise people to do to ensure their lives are not "frittered away by detail"?
3. **Summarize** What are Thoreau's views on correspondence and the daily news?

Text Analysis

4. **Make Inferences** Thoreau rejects many things as inessential or unimportant. List at least three things that *were* important to him, citing specific lines from the text to support your answer.
5. **Analyze the Essay** Thoreau was a poet as well as an essayist, and in *Walden,* he uses **figurative language** to express abstract concepts. Complete the chart by finding examples of such language. Use your completed chart to describe what you think Thoreau's use of figurative language adds to this essay.

Type of Figurative Language	Examples from Walden
metaphor	"Time is but the stream I go a-fishing in."
simile	
personification	

6. **Evaluate Ideas** Review the philosophical ideas you summarized as you read. Choose two ideas—Thoreau's view of the poor, for example, or the way he feels about civilized life. Explain whether or not you think the ideas you chose have merit, citing reasons for your opinions.
7. **Compare Texts** In "Thoreau Still Beckons, *if* I Can Take My Laptop" on page 389, Cynthia G. La Ferle argues that "making choices is so much more difficult in a culture fueled by sheer busyness and commercialism. There are few places . . . where one can escape." Do you agree that it would be more challenging for a modern American to live as Thoreau did? Explain why or why not, using details from both texts to support your opinion.

Text Criticism

8. **Critical Interpretations** According to Frank Stewart, author of *A Natural History of Nature Writing,* nature writers are "moved by the joyous, wild, and dazzling beauty in the world." Do you think this comment applies to Thoreau? Cite examples from *Walden* to support your opinion.

Do you chart your own COURSE?

In his day, Thoreau's living habits were probably considered unusual and even eccentric. In what place and in what manner might a nonconformist today live?

COMMON CORE

RI 2 Determine two or more central ideas of a text and analyze their development; provide an objective summary of the text. **RI 6** Determine an author's point of view or purpose in a text in which the rhetoric is effective, analyzing how style and content contribute to the power, persuasiveness, or beauty of the text. **RI 9** Analyze documents of literary significance for their themes, purposes, and rhetorical features.

MAGAZINE ARTICLE Thoreau's call for a simpler life continues to resonate with Americans. Those struggling with a hectic lifestyle may recall his words with a particular sense of longing. Read on to hear one busy woman's reflection on the topic.

THOREAU STILL BECKONS, *if* I Can Take My Laptop

By Cynthia G. La Ferle

Thanks to the wonders of modern technology, I now have a mind-boggling array of options.

I can shop for birthday gifts on the Internet, watch a funeral in Britain on "live" television, and order a complete wardrobe from a computer catalog. . . .

Every day I have more choices than I can reasonably consider. And so, like other tired Americans, I carry the burden of complexity—a burden so overwhelming, in fact, that there are times when I imagine trading places with Henry David Thoreau.

It's only fitting that I rediscovered Thoreau the week I purged my home office with a dust rag and a vacuum cleaner. The autumn mornings felt ripe for pitching and sorting. "Walden," Thoreau's famous treatise on simple living, was jammed behind a pile of unread paperbacks. . . .

It occurred to me that things were vastly different for Thoreau. The "comforts of life" in the 1840s were not exactly cushy by today's standards. His concept of luxury might have been taking tea in his mother's bone china saucers. So what had he given up to commune with nature?

Even before he moved to Walden Pond, Thoreau hadn't accumulated three television sets or a closetful of designer clothes. He didn't own several pairs of expensive athletic shoes for all those philosophical walks he took. His cot in the cabin couldn't have been more lumpy than the straw-filled mattresses in most mid-19th-century homes. And Thoreau never had to trade a personal computer for a pencil.

With all due respect, I wonder, how tough was Thoreau's two-year sabbatical with simplicity? Is it true that he occasionally walked from Walden Pond back to Concord, where Emerson's wife had a home-cooked supper waiting for him? . . .

And yet, just as Thoreau did, I'd like to weed out, pare down, live deliberately, be a resident philosopher. . . .

Visiting the "real" Walden Pond this fall, I was amazed and disappointed to find the place overrun. Locals were strewn on its small beach. You couldn't walk the path around the pond without rubbing shoulders with other sightseers; there wasn't a spot left for solitary reflection.

If nothing else, my rendezvous with Thoreau got me thinking. What—and how much—do I really need? What price have I paid for modern technology and "convenience"? In which landfill will all my stuff end up? . . .

Could I survive in a one-room cabin with barely more than a chair, a wooden table, a bowlful of raw vegetables, and my laptop? Honestly, I wish I could.

Civil DISOBEDIENCE

Henry David Thoreau

Analyze Visuals ▶
The photographer who created the image on the opposite page chose to focus not on the people in the crowd, but on their shadows. Why might she have made this choice?

BACKGROUND Thoreau put into practice the ideas expressed in Ralph Waldo Emerson's "Self-Reliance." In 1846, he spent a night in jail for refusing to pay a poll tax—a tax one had to pay in order to vote—as an act of protest against the U.S. government. Thoreau was enraged by the government's support of slavery and its war against Mexico, which he viewed as a case of a stronger country overpowering a weaker one simply to expand its own borders. Inspired by his experience in jail, Thoreau wrote this essay to add his voice to the ongoing debate about a citizen's responsibility to pay for a war he did not support.

I heartily accept the motto, "That government is best which governs least;" and I should like to see it acted up to more rapidly and systematically. Carried out, it finally amounts to this, which also I believe,—"That government is best which governs not at all;" and when men are prepared for it, that will be the kind of government which they will have. Government is at best but an expedient; but most governments are usually, and all governments are sometimes, inexpedient. The objections which have **A** been brought against a standing army, and they are many and weighty, and deserve to prevail, may also at last be brought against a standing government. The standing army is only an arm of the standing government. The government itself, which is only the mode which the people have chosen to execute their will, is equally liable to be abused and perverted before the people can act through it. Witness the present Mexican war, the work of comparatively a few individuals using the standing government as their tool; for, in the outset, the people would not have consented to this measure. . . .

But, to speak practically and as a citizen, unlike those who call themselves no-government men, I ask for, not at once no government, but *at once* a

A EVALUATE IDEAS
Sometimes writers may make false or misleading statements, known as **logical fallacies,** to bolster their arguments. Examine Thoreau's progression of ideas in lines 1–10, when he says that if you accept the motto, "That government is best which governs least" then it naturally follows that "That government is best which governs not at all." Some might say that the second statement is a **non sequitur,** or a conclusion that does not follow from the evidence. What do you think? Explain why you think Thoreau's statement is or is not valid.

13 the present Mexican war: the 1846–1848 war between Mexico and the United States.

better government. Let every man make known what kind of government would command his respect, and that will be one step toward obtaining it.

After all, the practical reason why, when the power is once in the hands of the people, a majority are permitted, and for a long period continue, to rule is not because they are most likely to be in the right, nor because this seems fairest to the minority, but because they are physically the strongest. But a government in which the majority rule in all cases cannot be based on justice, even as far as men understand it. Can there not be a government in which majorities do not virtually decide right and wrong, but conscience?—in which majorities decide only those questions to which the rule of expediency is applicable? Must the citizen ever for a moment, or in the least degree, resign his conscience to the legislator? Why has every man a conscience, then? I think that we should be men first, and subjects afterward. It is not desirable to cultivate a respect for the law, so much as for the right. The only obligation which I have a right to assume is to do at any time what I think right. It is truly enough said, that a corporation has no conscience; but a corporation of conscientious men is a corporation *with* a conscience. Law never made men a whit more just; and, by means of their respect for it, even the well-disposed are daily made the agents of injustice. [B] A common and natural result of an undue respect for law is, that you may see a file of soldiers, colonel, captain, corporal, privates, powder-monkeys, and all, marching in admirable order over hill and dale to the wars, against their wills, ay, against their common sense and consciences, which makes it very steep marching indeed, and produces a palpitation of the heart. They have no doubt that it is a damnable business in which they are concerned; they are all peaceably inclined. Now, what are they? Men at all? or small movable forts and magazines, at the service of some unscrupulous man in power? Visit the Navy-Yard, and behold a marine, such a man as an American government can make, or such as it can make a man with its black arts—a mere shadow and reminiscence of humanity, a man laid out alive and standing, and already, as one may say, buried under arms with funeral accompaniments, though it may be,—

> "Not a drum was heard, not a funeral note,
> As his corse to the rampart we hurried;
> Not a soldier discharged his farewell shot
> O'er the grave where our hero we buried."

The mass of men serve the state thus, not as men mainly, but as machines, with their bodies. They are the standing army, and the militia, jailers, constables, *posse comitatus,* etc. In most cases there is no free exercise whatever of the judgment or of the moral sense; but they put themselves on a level with wood and earth and stones; and wooden men can perhaps be manufactured that will serve the purpose as well. Such command no more respect than men of straw or a lump of dirt. They have the same sort of worth only as horses and dogs. Yet such as these even are commonly

[B] EVALUATE IDEAS
Reread lines 21–37. What position does Thoreau take in the conflict between majority rule and individual conscience? On your chart, **summarize** and react to his position.

39 powder-monkeys: boys with the job of carrying gunpowder to artillery crews.

45 magazines: places where ammunition is stored.

47–48 black arts: witchcraft.

51–54 "Not a drum . . . we buried": opening lines of "The Burial of Sir John Moore After Corunna" by the Irish poet Charles Wolfe (1791–1823).

57 *posse comitatus* (pŏs'ē kŏm-ə-tā'-təs): group of people that can be called on by the sheriff to help enforce the law [*Latin,* literally, the power of the county].

esteemed good citizens. Others—as most legislators, politicians, lawyers, ministers, and office-holders—serve the state chiefly with their heads; and, as they rarely make any moral distinctions, they are as likely to serve the Devil, without *intending* it, as God. A very few—as heroes, patriots, martyrs, reformers in the great sense, and *men*—serve the state with their consciences also, and so necessarily resist it for the most part; and they are commonly treated as enemies by it. . . . **C**

C **EVALUATE IDEAS**
Reread lines 55–69. Which way of serving the state does Thoreau approve of? Which ways does he condemn? Decide whether you agree with his assessment of soldiers and others who serve.

Unjust laws exist: shall we be content to obey them, or shall we endeavor to amend them, and obey them until we have succeeded or shall we **transgress** them at once? Men generally, under such a government as this, think that they ought to wait until they have persuaded the majority to alter them. They think that, if they should resist, the remedy would be worse than the evil. But it is the fault of the government itself that the remedy *is* worse than the evil. *It* makes it worse. Why is it not more apt to anticipate and provide for reform? Why does it not cherish its wise minority? Why does it cry and resist before it is hurt? Why does it not encourage its citizens to be on the alert to point out its faults, and *do* better than it would have them? Why does it always crucify Christ, and excommunicate Copernicus and Luther, and pronounce Washington and Franklin rebels? . . . **D**

transgress (trăns-grĕs') *v.* to violate a command or law

80 Copernicus (kō-pûr'nə-kəs) **and Luther:** Radicals in their time, Polish astronomer Nicolaus Copernicus theorized that the sun rather than the earth was the center of our planetary system; German theologian Martin Luther was a leader in the Protestant Reformation.

If the injustice is part of the necessary friction of the machine of government, let it go, let it go: perchance it will wear smooth, certainly the machine will wear out. If the injustice has a spring, or a pulley, or a rope, or a crank, exclusively for itself, then perhaps you may consider whether the remedy will not be worse than the evil; but if it is of such a nature that it requires you to be the agent of injustice to another, then, I say, break the law. Let your life be a counter-friction to stop the machine. What I have to do is to see, at any rate, that I do not lend myself to the wrong which I condemn. . . .

D **GRAMMAR AND STYLE**
In lines 70–81, Thoreau adds emphasis and emotion to his writing by asking **rhetorical questions**—questions that do not require a reply because the writer assumes the answers are obvious.

I meet this American government, or its representative, the state government, directly, and face to face, once a year—no more—in the person of its tax-gatherer; this is the only mode in which a man situated as I am necessarily meets it; and it then says distinctly, Recognize me; and the simplest, most effectual, and, in the present posture of affairs, the indispensablest mode of treating with it on this head, of expressing your little satisfaction with and love for it, is to deny it then. My civil neighbor, the tax-gatherer, is the very man I have to deal with,—for it is, after all, with men and not with parchment that I quarrel,—and he has voluntarily chosen to be an agent of the government. How shall he ever know well what he is and does as an officer of the government, or as a man, until he is obliged to consider whether he shall treat me, his neighbor, for whom he has respect, as a neighbor and well-disposed man, or as a maniac and disturber of the peace, and see if he can get over this obstruction to his neighborliness without a ruder and more **impetuous** thought or speech corresponding with his action. I know this well, that if one thousand, if one hundred, if ten men

95 posture of affairs: situation.

impetuous (ĭm-pĕch'o͞o-əs) *adj.* acting with sudden or rash energy; hasty

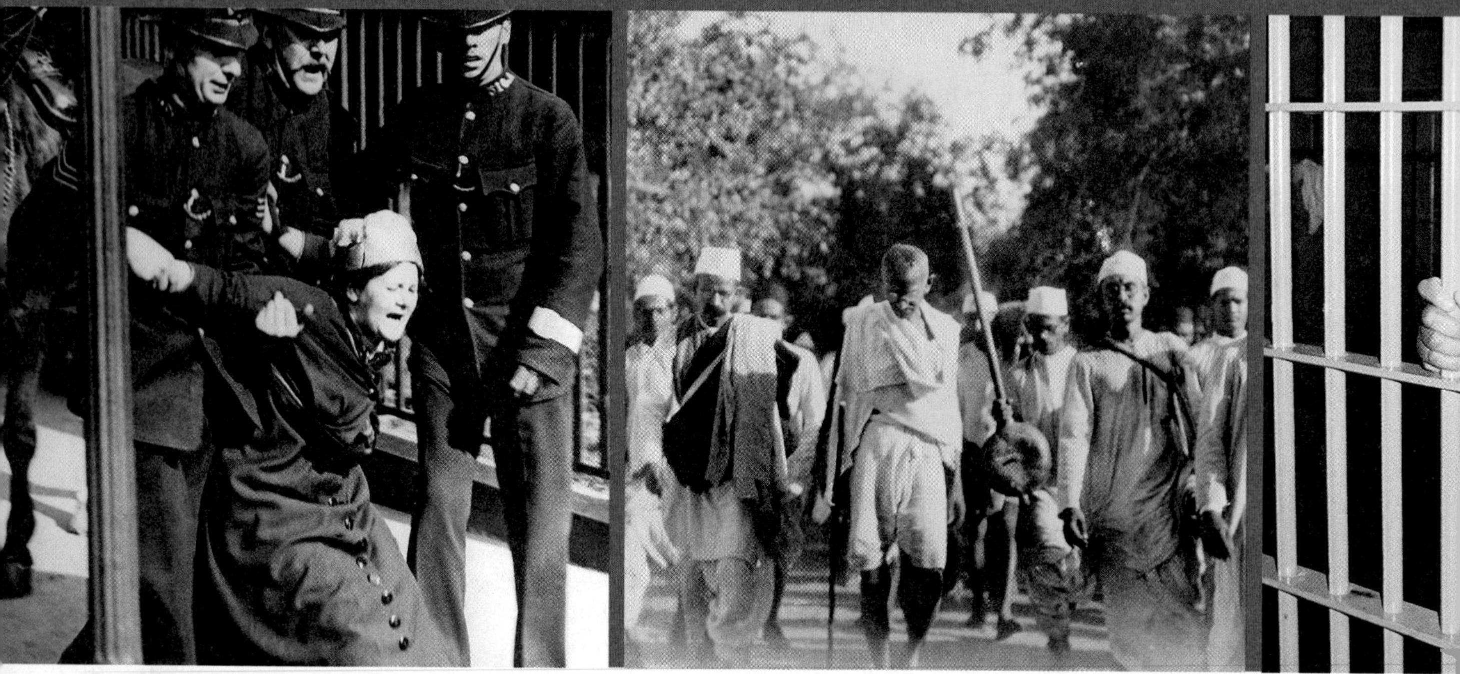

Left: London police arresting a suffragist, 1914; *center:* Gandhi marching to the sea, in defiance of the British salt monopoly

whom I could name,—if ten *honest* men only,—ay, if *one* honest man, in this State of Massachusetts, *ceasing to hold slaves,* were actually to withdraw from this copartnership, and be locked up in the county jail therefor, it would be the abolition of slavery in America. For it matters not how small the beginning may seem to be: what is once well done is done forever. But we love better to talk about it: that we say is our mission. Reform keeps many scores of newspapers in its service, but not one man. . . .

Under a government which imprisons any unjustly, the true place for a just man is also a prison. The proper place today, the only place which Massachusetts has provided for her freer and less desponding spirits, is in her prisons, to be put out and locked out of the State by her own act, as they have already put themselves out by their principles. It is there that the fugitive slave, and the Mexican prisoner on parole, and the Indian come to plead the wrongs of his race should find them; on that separate, but more free and honorable ground, where the State places those who are not *with* her, but *against* her,—the only house in a slave State in which a free man can abide with honor. If any think that their influence would be lost there, and their voices no longer afflict the ear of the State, that they would not be as an enemy within its walls, they do not know by how much truth is stronger than error, nor how much more eloquently and effectively he can combat injustice who has experienced a little in his own person. Cast your whole vote, not a strip of paper merely, but your whole influence. A minority is powerless while it conforms to the majority; it is not even a minority then; but it is irresistible when it clogs by its whole weight. If the alternative is to keep all just men in prison, or give up war and slavery, the State will not hesitate which to choose. If a thousand men were not to pay their tax bills

COMMON CORE RI 4

Language Coach

Connotation The images and feelings you connect to a word, adding a finer shade of meaning to it, are a word's **connotation.** *Abide* (line 123) can mean "withstand patiently" or simply "stay." How do *abide's* connotations of endurance and acceptance fit the phrase "abide with honor"?

Left: Dr. Martin Luther King Jr., jailed for civil disobedience; *center:* Vietnam war protester burns his military draft card; *right:* Beijing man stands in front of tanks during the 1989 Tiananmen Square uprising.

this year, that would not be a violent and bloody measure, as it would be to pay them, and enable the State to commit violence and shed innocent blood. This is, in fact, the definition of a peaceable revolution, if any such is possible. If the tax-gatherer, or any other public officer, asks me, as one has done, "But what shall I do?" my answer is, "If you really wish to do anything, resign your office." When the subject has refused allegiance, and the officer has resigned his office, then the revolution is accomplished. But even suppose blood should flow. Is there not a sort of blood shed when the conscience is wounded? Through this wound a man's real manhood and immortality flow out, and he bleeds to an everlasting death. I see this blood flowing now. . . . E

I have paid no poll-tax for six years. I was put into a jail once on this account, for one night; and, as I stood considering the walls of solid stone, two or three feet thick, the door of wood and iron, a foot thick, and the iron grating which strained the light, I could not help being struck with the foolishness of that institution which treated me as if I were mere flesh and blood and bones, to be locked up. I wondered that it should have concluded at length that this was the best use it could put me to, and had never thought to avail itself of my services in some way. I saw that, if there was a wall of stone between me and my townsmen, there was a still more difficult one to climb or break through before they could get to be as free as I was. I did not for a moment feel confined, and the walls seemed a great waste of stone and mortar. I felt as if I alone of all my townsmen had paid my tax. They plainly did not know how to treat me, but behaved like persons who are underbred. In every threat and in every compliment there was a blunder; for they thought that my chief desire was to stand the other side of

E EVALUATE IDEAS
Thoreau holds an **assumption**—an opinion or belief that is taken for granted—that civil disobedience is the only sensible and moral course to take. Reread lines 114–143. How convincing are the reasons Thoreau gives in support of his belief?

157 **underbred:** ill-mannered.

that stone wall. I could not but smile to see how industriously they locked the door on my meditations, which followed them out again without let or hindrance, and *they* were really all that was dangerous. As they could not reach me, they had resolved to punish my body; just as boys, if they cannot come at some person against whom they have a spite, will abuse his dog. I saw that the State was half-witted, that it was timid as a lone woman with her silver spoons, and that it did not know its friends from its foes, and I lost all my remaining respect for it, and pitied it. F

Thus the State never intentionally confronts a man's sense, intellectual or moral, but only his body, his senses. It is not armed with superior wit or honesty, but with superior physical strength. I was not born to be forced. I will breathe after my own fashion. Let us see who is the strongest. What force has a multitude? They only can force me who obey a higher law than I. They force me to become like themselves. I do not hear of *men* being *forced* to live this way or that by masses of men. What sort of life were that to live? When I meet a government which says to me, "Your money or your life," why should I be in haste to give it my money? It may be in a great strait, and not know what to do: I cannot help that. It must help itself; do as I do. It is not worth the while to snivel about it. I am not responsible for the successful working of the machinery of society. I am not the son of the engineer. I perceive that, when an acorn and a chestnut fall side by side, the one does not remain inert to make way for the other, but both obey their own laws, and spring and grow and flourish as best they can, till one, perchance, overshadows and destroys the other. If a plant cannot live according to its nature, it dies; and so a man. ❧ G

160–161 without let or hindrance: without encountering obstacles.

F **ESSAY**
Why do you think Thoreau includes this personal **anecdote** about his night in jail? Consider why he feels free as he stands in his cell, contemplating his own imprisonment.

G **ESSAY**
What **message** does Thoreau convey through his example of the acorn and the chestnut?

After Reading

Comprehension

1. **Recall** According to Thoreau, what should be respected more than the law?
2. **Summarize** What should a citizen do about an unjust law?
3. **Clarify** List the three ways Thoreau says a citizen may serve the state. With which did Thoreau agree?

COMMON CORE

RI 2 Determine two or more central ideas of a text and analyze their development; provide an objective summary of the text. **RI 5** Analyze and evaluate the effectiveness of the structure an author uses. **RI 6** Determine an author's point of view or purpose in a text in which the rhetoric is effective, analyzing how style and content contribute to the power, persuasiveness, or beauty of the text. **RI 9** Analyze documents of literary significance for their themes, purposes, and rhetorical features.

Text Analysis

4. **Make Judgments** Consider the **historical context** of Thoreau's essays. Would it be easier to practice nonconformity today? Consider the contemporary consequences of refusing to pay a tax ("Civil Disobedience," lines 144–166) or of celebrating or "cultivating" poverty (*Walden*, lines 198–230).
5. **Analyze Essays** Even when they discuss serious or even lofty ideas, essays are often loosely structured and highly personal. **Skim** *Walden* and "Civil Disobedience," noting passages in which Thoreau refers to himself. Identify his personal feelings and instances when he shares his own experiences, such as the night he spent in jail. How do these passages influence your acceptance of his arguments? Explain, citing specific lines from both essays.
6. **Interpret Paradox** A **paradox** seems to contradict itself but suggests an important truth. Reexamine both selections and record in a chart the examples of paradox you find. Then explain what truth or idea each paradox illustrates.

Paradox	Explanation
"I did not wish to live what was not life. . . ." (*Walden*, lines 26–27)	

7. **Evaluate Ideas** Ralph Waldo Emerson said of Thoreau, "No truer American ever lived." Review the political ideas you summarized as you read "Civil Disobedience." Do you consider Thoreau's arguments to be those of a patriot or those of a traitor? In your response, consider Thoreau's points on the necessity of government, how unjust laws may be changed, and majority rule.

Text Criticism

8. **Critical Interpretations** Critic Andrew Delbanco asserts that Thoreau is, "despite all the barricades he erected around himself, an irresistible writer; to read him is to feel wrenched away from the customary world and delivered into a place we fear as much as we need." What does it mean when we say we both need and fear the world Thoreau creates? Explain your response.

Do you chart your own **COURSE?**

The result of Thoreau's civil disobedience was a night spent in jail. In what ways do people today react to nonconformity? How do you act towards those who refuse to conform?

Vocabulary in Context

▲ VOCABULARY PRACTICE

Decide whether each statement is true or false.

1. If an odor were to **pervade** a room, it would be escaping through a chimney.
2. A person who is experiencing **perturbation** usually feels relaxed and confident.
3. An **impetuous** act is one that you do on the spur of the moment.
4. If you have some **misgiving** about attending a party, you should consider not going.
5. A **congenial** person usually gets along with others.
6. If you act **deliberately,** you act with haste and lack of concern.
7. **Abject** sorrow is sadness that will pass quickly.
8. If you **transgress** a law, you break it.

WORD LIST
abject
congenial
deliberately
impetuous
misgiving
perturbation
pervade
transgress

ACADEMIC VOCABULARY IN WRITING

• construct • expand • indicate • reinforce • role

Thoreau **expanded** on Emerson's ideas by living them out—even to the point of being jailed for civil disobedience. In a short paragraph, discuss how you have **reinforced** a belief in your life. Use at least three Academic Vocabulary words in your writing.

VOCABULARY STRATEGY: THE PREFIXES *ab-* AND *per-*

Though the prefixes *ab-* and *per-* are sometimes combined with recognizable base words, often they are attached to Latin roots, as in the vocabulary words *abject* and *pervade.* When you think you recognize the prefix *ab-* or *per-* in a word, look for context clues that support your guess. Then use the meaning of the prefix—and of the root, if you know it—to decipher the word's definition.

PRACTICE The prefix *ab-* or *per-* occurs in each boldfaced word below. Use context clues and root and prefix meanings—or a dictionary, if necessary—to define each word.

1. That man's **pernicious** lies have totally destroyed his son's reputation.
2. To get out of debt, I have decided to **abjure** going to the mall for three months.
3. The recruits immediately obeyed the officer's **peremptory** command.
4. **Abstemious** eating habits can help a person lose weight.
5. His **perfunctory** effort to learn who had **absconded** with the money was unsuccessful.

COMMON CORE

L 4b Identify and use patterns of word changes that indicate different meanings or parts of speech. **L 6** Acquire and use academic words and phrases.

Prefix	Meaning
ab-	"away"; "away from"
per-	"through"; "thoroughly, very"

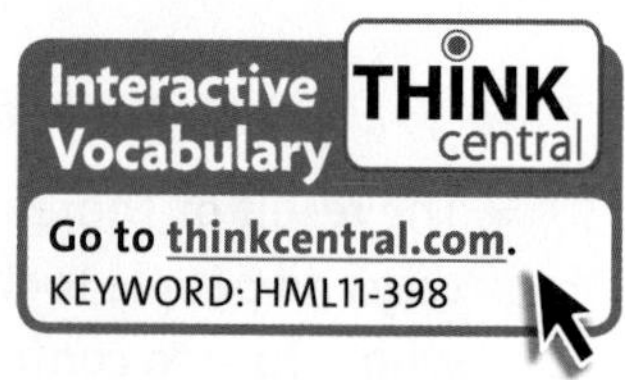

Language

COMMON CORE

L 3a Apply an understanding of syntax to the study of complex texts when reading. **W 1a–b** Introduce precise, knowledgeable claims; develop claims and counterclaims, supplying the most relevant evidence for each. **W 1d–e** Establish and maintain a formal style and objective tone; provide a concluding statement that follows from the argument presented.

GRAMMAR AND STYLE: Ask Rhetorical Questions

Review the **Grammar and Style** note on page 393. Thoreau asks a number of thought-provoking questions in "Civil Disobedience." But he's not expecting any answers. The questions he asks are **rhetorical questions;** they don't require a reply. Writers often use these types of **interrogative sentences** to drive home a point or evoke an emotional response. Here is an example from the text:

> *But even suppose blood should flow. Is there not a sort of blood shed when the conscience is wounded?* (lines 139–141)

Read this passage aloud. Consider how it would sound if it lacked a rhetorical question—if the second sentence read, "A sort of blood flows when the conscience is wounded." Do you think the rhetorical question makes Thoreau's argument more compelling?

PRACTICE Rewrite the following paragraph, changing some sentences to rhetorical questions.

> Thoreau suggests that if citizens disagree with their government's actions, they should stop paying taxes. However, if a large number of Americans refused to pay their taxes this year, the results would be disastrous. Public schools would collapse, salaries for police officers and firefighters would go unpaid, and services from public transportation to public hospitals would crumble. I do not see how a good citizen could allow this to happen. I do not see the honor in such an act.

READING-WRITING CONNECTION

Expand your understanding of Thoreau's writing by responding to this prompt. Then, use the **revising tips** to improve your letter.

WRITING PROMPT	REVISING TIPS
WRITE A LETTER TO THE EDITOR Thoreau proposed radical ideas in "Civil Disobedience." Some people found them thrilling; others found them threatening. Choose one of the ideas proposed in "Civil Disobedience." Write a **three-paragraph letter** to the editor of a local newspaper in which you explain the idea and argue for or against implementing it. Include at least two rhetorical questions in your letter.	• Check to make sure your letter includes a strong argument. • Include at least three reasons that support your argument. • Keep the tone of your letter polite. • End the letter with a request for action.

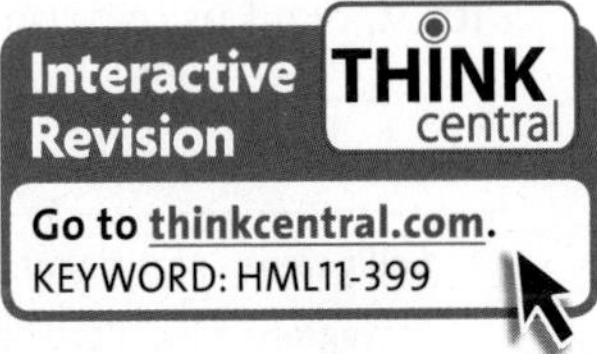

On *Civil Disobedience*

COMMON CORE

RI 2 Determine two or more central ideas of a text; provide an objective summary of the text.

Mohandas K. Gandhi

BACKGROUND Mohandas K. Gandhi (1869–1948), called Mahatma ("Great Soul"), helped free India of British rule. As a student, he greatly admired Thoreau's essay "Civil Disobedience." Thoreau's ideas helped shape Gandhi's key principle—*satyagraha* (sə-tyä'grə-hə), or "truth-force." In the following excerpt from a 1916 speech, Gandhi describes this powerful weapon for fighting oppression.

July 27, 1916

There are two ways of countering injustice. One way is to smash the head of the man who perpetrates injustice and to get your own head smashed in the process. All strong people in the world adopt this course. Everywhere wars are fought and millions of people are killed. The consequence is not the progress of a nation but its decline. . . . No country has ever become, or will ever become, happy through victory in war. A nation does not rise that way, it only falls further. In fact, what comes to it is defeat, not victory. And if, perchance, either our act or our purpose was ill-conceived, it brings disaster to both belligerents.[1]

But through the other method of combating injustice, we alone suffer the consequences of our mistakes, and the other side is wholly spared. This other method is *satyagraha.*[2] One who resorts to it does not have to break another's head; he may merely have his own head broken. He has to be prepared to die himself, suffering all the pain. In opposing the atrocious laws of the Government of South Africa,[3] it was this method that we adopted. We made it clear to the said Government that we would never bow to its outrageous laws. No clapping is possible without two hands to do it, and no quarrel without two persons to make it. Similarly, no State is possible without two entities, the rulers and the ruled. You are our sovereign, our Government, only so long as we consider ourselves your subjects. When we are not subjects, you are not the sovereign either. So long as it is your endeavour to control us with justice and love, we will let you to do so. But if you wish to strike at us from behind, we cannot permit it. Whatever you do in other matters, you will have to ask our opinion about the laws that concern us. If you make laws to keep us suppressed in a wrongful manner and without taking us into confidence, these laws will merely adorn the statute-books. We will never obey them. Award us for it what punishment you like, we will put up with it. Send us to prison and we will live there as in a paradise. Ask us to mount the

---

1. **belligerents:** participants in a war.
2. **satyagraha** (sə-tyä'grə-hə) *Sanskrit:* insistence on truth. Gandhi used this term to describe his policy of seeking reform by means of nonviolent resistance.
3. **atrocious laws . . . South Africa:** Gandhi led the Indian community in opposition to racial discrimination in South Africa, where he lived for several years.

Gandhi in 1948, after ending a six-day hunger strike for peace

scaffold[4] and we will do so laughing. Shower what sufferings you like upon us, we will calmly endure all and not hurt a hair of your body. We will gladly die and will not so much as touch you. But so long as there is yet life in these our bones, we will never comply with your arbitrary laws.

4. **mount the scaffold:** ascend the platform on which one is executed by hanging.

Text Analysis

1. **Summarize** What two ways of countering injustice does Gandhi describe? Explain which approach Gandhi adopted.
2. **Interpret** Reread lines 16–20. What point is Gandhi making about the relationship between a government and its citizens?
3. **Compare Texts** Henry David Thoreau's ideas influenced many 20th-century reformers, including Gandhi. What connections do you see between the views Thoreau presents in *Walden* and "Civil Disobedience" and Gandhi's beliefs? Cite evidence from both texts to support your answer.

from Woman in the Nineteenth Century

Nonfiction by Margaret Fuller

COMMON CORE

RI 2 Determine two or more central ideas of a text and analyze their development, including how they interact and build on one another. **RI 5** Analyze the effectiveness of the structure. **RI 6** Determine an author's point of view, analyzing how style and content contribute to the persuasiveness of the text. **RI 8** Evaluate purposes and arguments in works of public advocacy. **L 1a** Apply the understanding that usage can change over time.

DID YOU KNOW?

Margaret Fuller . . .

- learned to read when she was 3 years old.
- suffered from nightmares in which she dreamed horses were galloping across her head.
- inspired Edgar Allan Poe to quip, "There are three species: men, women, and Margaret Fuller."

Meet the Author

Margaret Fuller 1810–1850

Margaret Fuller spent much of her life fighting to make women equal members of society. At a time when a woman's only place was thought to be the small sphere of the home, Fuller became a respected author, a commanding public speaker, a popular journalist, and a key figure in the transcendentalist movement. One literary historian observed that Fuller "transcended virtually every stereotype American women had to endure in the first half of the 19th century."

A Demanding Childhood Sarah Margaret Fuller was born in Cambridgeport, Massachusetts. Her father, a stern and formidable man, had high expectations for her. When she was only 10 years old, he counseled that excelling "in all things should be your constant aim." As a teenager, Fuller typically started her studies at five in the morning and sometimes did not finish until eleven at night.

Coming into Her Own Fuller's father died suddenly when she was 25, and she became a teacher to help support her family. Through a mutual acquaintance, she met Ralph Waldo Emerson, who was much impressed by her intelligence and wit. She began attending meetings of the Transcendental Club. In 1840, Fuller became the editor of *The Dial,* a short-lived but highly influential literary magazine. Fuller solicited poems, essays, and fiction from leading transcendentalists and wrote much of the content herself.

An Influential Voice In 1844, Fuller started writing the literary column for the *New York Tribune,* perhaps the most widely read newspaper of its day. In addition to reviewing literary works, she addressed social issues such as poverty and slavery. In 1845, Fuller published *Woman in the Nineteenth Century,* a revolutionary feminist work that paid tribute to women's intellectual and creative abilities and declared that women must be accepted as equal to men. The first edition sold out in two weeks.

Romance and Tragedy In 1846, the *New York Tribune* sent Fuller to cover civil unrest in Europe. She settled in Rome, where she fell in love with and married Italian aristocrat Giovanni Angelo Ossoli. When revolution broke out in Rome in 1848, Fuller supported the cause by volunteering at a hospital while her husband fought for the republic. The revolution failed, and Fuller, Ossoli, and their young son sailed to the United States in 1850. With New York City almost in sight, their ship hit a sandbar and sank. Fuller, Ossoli, and their son drowned.

THINK central

Author Online

Go to thinkcentral.com. KEYWORD: HML11-402

TEXT ANALYSIS: AUTHOR'S PERSPECTIVE

Differences of opinion in politics, art, or any subject are often debated formally and informally in speech and writing. When people engage in a **debate,** they exchange their opinions on an issue, often approaching the discussion with a unique set of ideas and experiences. **Author's perspective** refers to the distinct combination of opinions, values, and beliefs that influence the way a writer looks at a topic. Margaret Fuller takes a unique approach to advocating her views in a debate with a fictional character. As you read, pay close attention to **rhetorical techniques**—the methods an author employs to influence readers and convey ideas. These techniques vary from writer to writer, but they always provide clues to a writer's view. To identify Margaret Fuller's perspective, examine the following rhetorical elements:

- the writer's **tone,** or attitude toward the subject
- **details** the writer chooses to include or emphasize
- rhetorical devices and logical fallacies
- how the writer portrays specific individuals

As you read this excerpt, use these elements to help you analyze the author's perspective.

READING STRATEGY: PARAPHRASE MAIN IDEAS

When you read challenging texts such as this one, it is important to pay careful attention to the author's **main ideas.** One way to make sure that you are understanding these key points is to **paraphrase** them, or restate the information in your own words. A good paraphrase is about the same length as the original text but is written in simpler language. As you read, paraphrase the annotated passages to achieve a better understanding of Fuller's main ideas. Record your work in a chart like the one shown.

Fuller's Main Ideas	My Paraphrases
"I was talking on this subject with Miranda, a woman, who, if any in the world could, might speak without heat or bitterness of the position of her sex."	I spoke about this with Miranda. If any woman can talk about gender issues calmly and rationally, Miranda can.

Complete the activities in your **Reader/Writer Notebook**.

What does society EXPECT *of us?*

In the 19th century, society expected women to be loving wives, adoring mothers, and expert housekeepers. Women were not expected to be great thinkers; they were to leave the thinking to men. Some women, including Margaret Fuller, rejected these limiting expectations.

SURVEY Does society still have different expectations for men and women? Complete the following survey, marking which jobs you think would most likely be held by men, which would mostly likely be held by women, and which would have roughly equal numbers of each. Then write a paragraph discussing what your results might indicate about how gender influences societal expectations.

Survey: *Gender and Jobs*

Occupation	Mostly Male	Mostly Female	Equal
1. Kindergarten teacher			
2. Carpenter			
3. Hairstylist			
4. Surgeon			
5. Firefighter			
6. College professor			
7. Personal shopper			
8. Architect			

Woman in the Nineteenth Century

Margaret Fuller

BACKGROUND From 1839 to 1844 in the context of the great debate about the equality of men and women, Fuller led a series of seminars for women called "Conversations." She lectured on topics ranging from ethics to art and then asked her listeners to discuss each topic, thus helping the women to recognize their own intellectual abilities. The sessions led Fuller to write *Woman in the Nineteenth Century,* in which she insists society accept women and men as equals. Here, Fuller presents her views as a debate between herself and the fictional "Miranda," a woman who, like Fuller, had from childhood been encouraged to exercise her mind.

I was talking on this subject with Miranda, a woman, who, if any in the world could, might speak without heat and bitterness of the position of her sex. Her father was a man who cherished no sentimental reverence for woman, but a firm belief in the equality of the sexes. She was his eldest child, and came to him at an age when he needed a companion. From the time she could speak and go alone, he addressed her not as a plaything, but as a living mind. Among the few verses he ever wrote was a copy addressed to this child, when the first locks were cut from her head, and the reverence expressed on this occasion for that cherished head, he never belied. It was to him the temple of immortal intellect. He respected his child, however, too much to be an indulgent parent. He called on her for clear judgment, for courage, for honor and fidelity; in short, for such virtues as he knew. In so far as he possessed the keys to the wonders of this universe, he allowed free use of them to her, and by the incentive of a high expectation, he forbade, as far as possible, that she should let the privilege lie idle. **A**

Thus this child was early led to feel herself a child of the spirit. She took her place easily, not only in the world of organized being, but in the world of mind. A dignified sense of self-dependence was given as all her portion,[1] and she found it a

Analyze Visuals ▶
In your opinion, what **traits** does the subject of this portrait project? After you've read the selection, revisit your answer. Tell whether you think the woman in the portrait might share any of Miranda's qualities.

A PARAPHRASE MAIN IDEAS
Paraphrase lines 2–4. What were Miranda's father's views on gender equality?

1. **all her portion:** something that she had a right to expect.

Portrait of Ann Cochrells (1848), David Parr. Oil on canvas, 9″ × 11″.

sure anchor. Herself securely anchored, her relations with others were established with equal security. She was fortunate in a total absence of those charms which might have drawn to her bewildering flatteries, and in a strong electric nature, which repelled those who did not belong to her; and attracted those who did. With men and women her relations were noble,—affectionate without passion, intellectual without coldness. The world was free to her, and she lived freely in it. Outward adversity came, and inward conflict, but that faith and self-respect had early been awakened which must always lead at last, to an outward serenity and an inward peace. **B**

Of Miranda I had always thought as an example, that the restraints upon the sex were insuperable[2] only to those who think them so, or who noisily strive to break them. She had taken a course of her own, and no man stood in her way. Many of her acts had been unusual, but excited no uproar. Few helped, but none checked her, and the many men, who knew her mind and her life, showed to her confidence, as to a brother, gentleness as to a sister. And not only refined, but very coarse men approved and aided one in whom they saw resolution and clearness of design. Her mind was often the leading one, always effective. **C**

When I talked with her upon these matters, and had said very much what I have written, she smilingly replied: "and yet we must admit that I have been fortunate, and this should not be. My good father's early trust gave the first bias, and the rest followed of course. It is true that I have had less outward aid, in after years, than most women, but that is of little consequence. Religion was early awakened in my soul, a sense that what the soul is capable to ask it must attain, and that, though I might be aided and instructed by others, I must depend on myself as the only constant friend. This self dependence, which was honored in me, is deprecated as a fault in most women. They are taught to learn their rule from without, not to unfold it from within.

"This is the fault of man, who is still vain, and wishes to be more important to woman than, by right, he should be." **D**

"Men have not shown this disposition toward you," I said.

"No! because the position I early was enabled to take was one of self-reliance. And were all women as sure of their wants as I was, the result would be the same. But they are so overloaded with precepts by guardians, who think that nothing is so much to be dreaded for a woman as originality of thought or character, that their minds are impeded by doubts till they lose their chance of fair free proportions. The difficulty is to get them to the point from which they shall naturally develop self-respect, and learn self-help. **E**

"Once I thought that men would help to forward this state of things more than I do now. I saw so many of them wretched in the connections they had formed in weakness and vanity. They seemed so glad to esteem women whenever they could.

"'The soft arms of affection,' said one of the most discerning spirits, 'will not suffice for me, unless on them I see the steel bracelets of strength.'"

2. **insuperable:** incapable of being overcome.

B AUTHOR'S PERSPECTIVE
Consider Fuller's **tone** in lines 15–26. What can you **infer** about the traits Fuller found admirable?

C PARAPHRASE MAIN IDEAS
Paraphrase the main idea Fuller states in lines 27–29. Of what does Fuller see Miranda as an "example"?

COMMON CORE RI 5

D ANALYZE STRUCTURE
Fuller begins her argument about women's equality with a portrayal of Miranda, a self-reliant and well-educated fictional friend. In a well-reasoned explanation, Miranda credits her father with raising her to be an intellectual equal of men. Reread Fuller's response in lines 45–46. Is this statement logical? Do you think Fuller has introduced a **logical fallacy** (an error in thinking), such as an **oversimplification** or a **hasty generalization?** Explain your answer.

E AUTHOR'S PERSPECTIVE
Consider the **details** Fuller chooses to focus on. By contrasting Miranda's upbringing with that of most 19th-century women, what type of upbringing is Fuller advocating?

But early I perceived that men never, in any extreme of despair, wished to be women. On the contrary they were ever ready to taunt one another at any sign of weakness, with,

Art thou not like the women, who—

The passage ends various ways, according to the occasion and rhetoric of the speaker. When they admired any woman they were inclined to speak of her as "above her sex." Silently I observed this, and feared it argued a rooted scepticism, which for ages had been fastening on the heart, and which only an age of miracles could eradicate. Ever I have been treated with great sincerity; and I look upon it as a signal instance of this, that an intimate friend of the other sex said, in a fervent moment, that I "deserved in some star to be a man." He was much surprised when I disclosed my view of my position and hopes, when I declared my faith that the feminine side, the side of love, of beauty, of holiness, was now to have its full chance, and that, if either were better, it was better now to be a woman, for even the slightest achievement of good was furthering an especial work of our time. He smiled incredulously. "She makes the best she can of it," thought he. "Let Jews believe the pride of Jewry, but I am of the better sort, and know better."[3] F

Another used as highest praise, in speaking of a character in literature, the words "a manly woman."

"So in the noble passage of Ben Jonson:

'I meant the day-star should not brighter ride,
Nor shed like influence from its lucent seat;
I meant she should be courteous, facile, sweet,
Free from that solemn vice of greatness, pride;
I meant each softest virtue there should meet,
Fit in that softer bosom to abide,
Only a learned and a manly *soul,*
I purposed her, that should with even powers,
The rock, the spindle, and the shears control
Of destiny, and spin her own free hours.'"[4]

"Methinks," said I, "you are too fastidious in objecting to this. Jonson in using the word 'manly' only meant to heighten the picture of this, the true, the intelligent fate, with one of the deeper colors."

"And yet," said she, "so invariable is the use of this word where a heroic quality is to be described, and I feel so sure that persistence and courage are the most womanly no less than the most manly qualities, that I would exchange these words for others of a larger sense at the risk of marring the fine tissue of the verse. Read 'A heavenward and instructed soul,' and I should be satisfied. Let it not be said, wherever there is energy or creative genius, 'She has a masculine mind.'"

F PARAPHRASE MAIN IDEAS
Paraphrase lines 65–68 in your chart. What way of thinking does Miranda describe, and how easy does she think it will be to reverse?

COMMON CORE L 1a

Language Coach

Archaic Expressions Words and phrases no longer in use are **archaic expressions.** *Methinks* is meaning "it seems to me" or "in my opinion." Write the sentence in lines 90–93 in your own—modern—words.

---

3. **'She makes . . . know better':** Miranda's male friend uses a religious slur to discount women.
4. **'I meant . . . free hours':** These lines are taken from the poem "On Lucy, Countess of Bedford." Their author, Ben Jonson (1573?–1637), was an English playwright and poet.

Comprehension

1. **Recall** What did Miranda's father believe in regard to the equality of the sexes?
2. **Clarify** What do the men Miranda describes mean when they comment that a woman they admire is "above her sex"?

Text Analysis

3. **Analyze Main Ideas** Examine the main ideas you **paraphrased** as you read. Then reread the selection's last two paragraphs. What is Fuller's main point about "heroic" qualities such as persistence, confidence, and creativity? Use your paraphrases and specific lines from the text to support your answer.
4. **Examine Author's Perspective** Recall that Fuller was in the Transcendental Club, and think about the ideals that this group embraced. Through her description of Miranda, what was Fuller saying about the traits a woman needed to transcend society's expectations? Restate Fuller's perspective in one or two sentences. Consider the following in your answer:
   - Miranda's statement that women "are taught to learn their rule from without, not to unfold it from within." (lines 43–44)
   - The contrast between Miranda's upbringing and that of women "so overloaded with precepts by guardians . . . that their minds are impeded by doubts." (lines 50–52)
5. **Draw Conclusions About Author's Perspective** Why might Fuller have chosen to present her views as a dialogue between herself and the fictional Miranda, instead of simply stating her beliefs and advocating her position outright? Explain the rhetorical impact of the dialogue—how it influences readers and conveys ideas. Cite at least one example from the text to support your analysis.
6. **Compare Texts** Compare Fuller's main ideas with the beliefs Ralph Waldo Emerson sets forth in "Self-Reliance" (page 370). What common elements do the two texts share? In what ways does their focus differ? Cite examples.

Text Criticism

7. **Historical Context** A friend of Fuller's once described her as possessing "what in woman is generally called a masculine mind; that is, its action was determined by ideas rather than sentiments." Do contemporary Americans still believe that men are governed by reason while women are driven by emotion? Explain your answer.

What does society **EXPECT** *of us?*

Margaret Fuller felt that society expected too little of women. What expectations do people, such as parents, teachers, mentors, and society, have of you?

COMMON CORE

RI 2 Determine two or more central ideas of a text and analyze their development, including how they interact and build on one another. **RI 5** Analyze the effectiveness of the structure. **RI 6** Determine an author's point of view, analyzing how style and content contribute to the persuasiveness of the text. **RI 8** Evaluate purposes and arguments in works of public advocacy.

The Transcendental Spirit

In the 19th century, transcendentalism emerged as a fresh intellectual framework for addressing social, economic, political, and cultural changes in America's increasingly complex society. Many of the issues writers of the day struggled with continue to be relevant today. Get into a "transcendental" frame of mind by taking the following quiz.

How TRANSCENDENTAL Are You?

- ∗ Do you ever take a walk with no destination in mind? ☐ yes ☐ no
- ∗ Do you express your opinions even when they aren't popular? ☐ yes ☐ no
- ∗ Would you accept very low pay for a job that you loved? ☐ yes ☐ no
- ∗ Do you think there are too many gadgets and gizmos in modern life and that we should all aim to simplify? ☐ yes ☐ no
- ∗ Would you go to jail rather than conform to a law that goes against your conscience? ☐ yes ☐ no

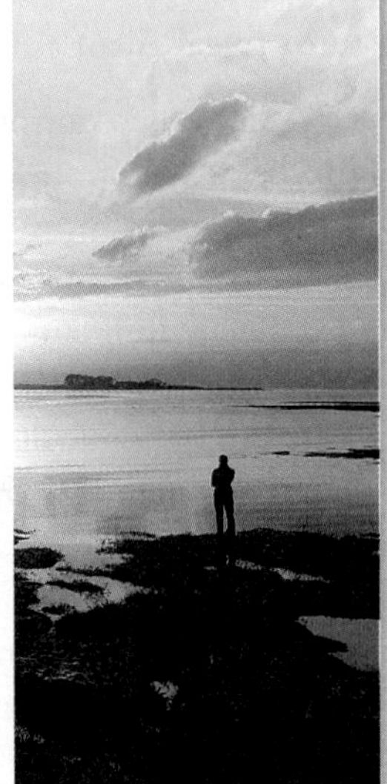

Writing to Analyze

Select one of the questions above and respond to it in a focused, well-developed paragraph. Give at least one example from your life to support your answer. Then write one more paragraph analyzing how one of the transcendental writers whose work you've just read might have responded to the same question.

Consider

- which question resonated with you the most
- what example(s) from your life might best reveal your beliefs to your audience
- how particular sentences or passages in the readings relate to the question you chose

Extension Online

INQUIRY & RESEARCH Search the Internet for evidence of Henry David Thoreau's legacy. Use the key words *Thoreau* and *Walden* to find several different types of memorials for one of transcendentalism's greatest thinkers. You will find many nonprofit organizations, projects, schools, and centers dedicated to promoting or remembering Thoreau's ideas. Of his various beliefs, which ones resonate most with modern day audiences? Report your findings to your class.

COMMON CORE

W 2 Write informative/explanatory texts to examine and convey complex ideas, concepts, and information clearly and accurately through the effective selection, organization, and analysis of content. **W 7** Conduct short research projects to answer a question or solve a problem.

The Fall of the House of Usher

Short Story by Edgar Allan Poe

HISTORY Video link at thinkcentral.com

COMMON CORE

RL 3 Analyze the impact of the author's choices regarding how to develop and relate elements of a story. **RL 4** Analyze the impact of specific word choices on meaning and tone. **L 1a** Apply the understanding that usage is a matter of convention and can change over time. **L 3a** Apply an understanding of syntax to the study of complex texts when reading. **L 4** Clarify the meaning of multiple-meaning words and phrases.

DID YOU KNOW?

Edgar Allan Poe . . .

- invented the modern detective story.
- inspired the name of the Baltimore Ravens football team.
- briefly wrote a literary gossip column.
- publicly denounced the work of Henry Wadsworth Longfellow.

(background) Baltimore, Maryland, scene of Poe's mysterious death

Meet the Author

Edgar Allan Poe c. 1809–1849

"The Raven" has been called the best-known poem in American literature; "The Fall of the House of Usher" is a masterpiece of Gothic horror. Both of these works were the creation of one feverish imagination, that of poet, critic, and fiction innovator Edgar Allan Poe.

Haunted by Death Once called one of literature's "most brilliant, but erratic, stars," Poe is as well-known for his unstable life as for his formidable talent. Abandoned by his father as an infant, Poe lost his mother to tuberculosis by the age of 3. He was taken in by John Allan, a wealthy Virginia businessman, but the two had a stormy relationship. At age 18, Poe got himself thrown out of college for gambling debts, beginning a lifelong pattern of self-sabotage. Estranged from Allan as a young man, Poe formed a new family with his aunt and his young cousin, Virginia Clemm. In 1836, he and Virginia married publicly, although they had probably married in secret the year before, when she was only 13. She died 11 years later, and the devastated Poe died 2 years after. Theories about the cause of his death range from alcohol poisoning to brain lesions to rabies.

Making Ends Meet For much of his adult life, Poe struggled to support his family. He landed promising positions at a series of literary magazines, spoiling one opportunity after another with his erratic behavior. At the same time, his scathing reviews made him a feared and respected critic, and his inventive short stories brought him acclaim. Although his life matched the Romantic ideal of the starving artist who suffered for the purity of his art, Poe's stories were designed to reach a wide audience. His successes with horror, science fiction, and detective stories proved his mastery of popular genres.

Tortured Soul Poe's distinctive themes included madness, untimely death, and obsession. Given his troubled life, many critics have interpreted Poe's deranged narrators as reflections of the author's own state of mind. But Poe was a brilliant and controlled stylist, whose theories of art championed rigorous structure, careful use of language, and the masterful creation of a single, calculated effect. His fascination with the macabre was equaled by his interest in logic; his supremely rational detective C. Auguste Dupin inspired Sir Arthur Conan Doyle's scientific sleuth Sherlock Holmes. Poe's life and work exemplify the deepest divisions of the self: the conflict of beautiful ideals and dark impulses.

Author Online THINK central

Go to thinkcentral.com. KEYWORD: HML11-410

TEXT ANALYSIS: UNITY OF EFFECT

Some writers insist that plot or character drives a story. Edgar Allan Poe wanted his stories to achieve a **unity of effect,** where every element—plot, character, setting, and imagery—helped create a single effect, or **mood,** as in this opening sentence from the selection:

During the whole of a dull, dark, and soundless day in the autumn of the year, when the clouds hung oppressively low . . .

The ominous details set a scene of instant gloom. As you read, note the choices Poe makes to achieve his intended effect.

READING SKILL: UNDERSTAND COMPLEX SENTENCES

Poe's sentences have a nervous, excited quality: they pile on details and jump from one subject to another. Use these strategies to help you understand Poe's complex sentences:

- Focus on the main idea. Finding the main subject and verb of a sentence can help you identify its main idea.
- Break long sentences into shorter ones that focus on one idea. Group modifiers with the words they describe.
- Keep reading. Poe often restates ideas, and a confusing sentence might be followed by one easier to understand.

Apply these strategies as you read. Using a chart like the one shown, paraphrase five especially complex sentences.

Line Numbers for Poe's Sentence	My Paraphrase

VOCABULARY IN CONTEXT

Poe was fascinated with unusual language. Review the vocabulary words, noting any familiar roots, prefixes, or suffixes that might help you unlock the meaning of the words.

WORD LIST			
	affinity	demeanor	insipid
	alleviation	equivocal	pertinacity
	anomaly	inordinate	vagary
	apathy		

Complete the activities in your **Reader/Writer Notebook**.

Where does TERROR *begin?*

Fear can be a reasonable response to an immediate danger, like the instant alarm you would feel upon seeing a car racing toward you. But some of the things we find most terrifying don't present any real threat. A strange noise in the night, a creepy phone call, a creaking door slowly opening—what makes us afraid of things that can't really hurt us?

QUICKWRITE Recall times when you were frightened for no good reason: a walk in a familiar place that seemed strangely spooky or a sudden paranoia about being home alone. Describe what triggered your fear and why. How much of your terror was the result of your own imagination?

THE FALL OF THE House of Usher

Edgar Allan Poe

Son coeur est un luth suspendu;
Sitôt qu'on le touche il résonne.
—De Béranger

"His heart is a hanging lute; / As soon as one touches it, it sounds" (lines from a poem by the 19th-century French poet Pierre Jean de Béranger).

During the whole of a dull, dark, and soundless day in the autumn of the year, when the clouds hung oppressively low in the heavens, I had been passing alone, on horseback, through a singularly dreary tract of country, and at length found myself, as the shades of the evening drew on, within view of the melancholy House of Usher. I know not how it was—but, with the first glimpse of the building, a sense of insufferable gloom pervaded my spirit. I say insufferable; for the feeling was unrelieved by any of that half-pleasurable, because poetic, sentiment with which the mind usually receives even the sternest natural images of the desolate or terrible. I looked upon the scene before me—upon the mere house, and the simple landscape features of the domain—upon the bleak walls—upon the vacant, eye-like windows—upon a few rank sedges—and upon a few white trunks of decayed trees—with an utter depression of soul which I can compare to no earthly sensation more properly than to the after-dream of the reveller

Analyze Visuals ▶
What mood does this image convey? Identify specific elements, such as color, texture, and composition, that contribute to this mood.

12 rank sedges: overgrown grassy plants.

Illustrations by Shane Rebenscheid.

upon opium—the bitter lapse into everyday life—the hideous dropping off of the veil. There was an iciness, a sinking, a sickening of the heart—an unredeemed dreariness of thought which no goading of the imagination could torture into *aught* of the sublime. What was it—I paused to think—what was it that so unnerved me in the contemplation of the House of Usher? It was a mystery all insoluble; nor could I grapple with the shadowy fancies that crowded upon me as I pondered. I was forced to fall back upon the unsatisfactory conclusion, that while, beyond doubt, there *are* combinations of very simple natural objects which have the power of thus affecting us, still the analysis of this power lies among considerations beyond our depth. It was possible, I reflected, that a mere different arrangement of the particulars of the scene, of the details of the picture, would be sufficient to modify, or perhaps to annihilate its capacity for sorrowful impression; and, acting upon this idea, I reined my horse to the precipitous brink of a black and lurid tarn that lay in unruffled lustre by the dwelling, and gazed down—but with a shudder even more thrilling than before—upon the remodelled and inverted images of the grey sedge, and the ghastly tree-stems, and the vacant and eye-like windows. Ⓐ

Language Coach

Homophones Words that sound alike but have different meanings and spellings are homophones. *Aught* (line 18) and *ought* are both pronounced /awt/. *Aught,* though, means "anything" or "all" and *ought* is similar to "should." What might "aught of the sublime" mean here?

28–29 precipitous . . . tarn: steep bank of a small black, repulsive-looking mountain lake.

Nevertheless, in this mansion of gloom I now proposed to myself a sojourn of some weeks. Its proprietor, Roderick Usher, had been one of my boon companions in boyhood; but many years had elapsed since our last meeting. A letter, however, had lately reached me in a distant part of the country—a letter from him—which, in its wildly importunate nature, had admitted of no other than a personal reply. The MS. gave evidence of nervous agitation. The writer spoke of acute bodily illness—of a mental disorder which oppressed him—and of an earnest desire to see me, as his best, and indeed his only personal friend, with a view of attempting, by the cheerfulness of my society, some **alleviation** of his malady. It was the manner in which all this, and much more, was said—it was the apparent *heart* that went with his request—which allowed me no room for hesitation; and I accordingly obeyed forthwith what I still considered a very singular summons.

Ⓐ **UNITY OF EFFECT**
Reread lines 16–32. Describe the **mood** of the scene. What details of the narrator's reactions contribute to this effect?

38 had admitted of no other than: had required; **MS.:** an abbreviation of *manuscript*.

alleviation (ə-lē'vē-ā'shən) *n.* relief

Although, as boys, we had been even intimate associates, yet I really knew little of my friend. His reserve had been always excessive and habitual. I was aware, however, that his very ancient family had been noted, time out of mind, for a peculiar sensibility of temperament, displaying itself, through long ages, in many works of exalted art, and manifested, of late, in repeated deeds of munificent yet unobtrusive charity, as well as in a passionate devotion to the intricacies, perhaps even more than to the orthodox and easily recognizable beauties, of musical science. I had learned, too, the very remarkable fact, that the stem of the Usher race, all time-honored as it was, had put forth, at no period, any enduring branch; in other words, that the entire family lay in the direct line of descent, and had always, with very trifling and very temporary variation, so lain. It was this

52 munificent yet unobtrusive: generous yet inconspicuous.

deficiency, I considered, while running over in thought the perfect keeping of the character of the premises with the accredited character of the people, and while speculating upon the possible influence which the one, in the long lapse of centuries, might have exercised upon the other—it was this deficiency, perhaps, of collateral issue, and the consequent undeviating transmission, from sire to son, of the patrimony with the name, which had, at length, so identified the two as to merge the original title of the estate in the quaint and **equivocal** appellation of the "House of Usher"—an appellation which seemed to include, in the minds of the peasantry who used it, both the family and the family mansion. **B**

I have said that the sole effect of my somewhat childish experiment—that of looking down within the tarn—had been to deepen the first singular impression. There can be no doubt that the consciousness of the rapid increase of my superstition—for why should I not so term it?—served mainly to accelerate the increase itself. Such, I have long known, is the paradoxical law of all sentiments having terror as a basis. And it might have been for this reason only, that, when I again uplifted my eyes to the house itself, from its image in the pool, there grew in my mind a strange fancy—a fancy so ridiculous, indeed, that I but mention it to show the vivid force of the sensations which oppressed me. I had so worked upon my imagination as really to believe that about the whole mansion and domain there hung an atmosphere peculiar to themselves and their immediate vicinity—an atmosphere which had no **affinity** with the air of heaven, but which had reeked up from the decayed trees, and the gray wall, and the silent tarn—a pestilent and mystic vapor, dull, sluggish, faintly discernible, and leaden-hued.

Shaking off from my spirit what *must* have been a dream, I scanned more narrowly the real aspect of the building. Its principal feature seemed to be that of an excessive antiquity. The discoloration of ages had been great. Minute fungi overspread the whole exterior, hanging in a fine tangled web-work from the eaves. Yet all this was apart from any extraordinary dilapidation. No portion of the masonry had fallen; and there appeared to be a wild inconsistency between its still perfect adaptation of parts, and the crumbling condition of the individual stones. In this there was much that reminded me of the specious totality of old wood-work which has rotted for long years in some neglected vault, with no disturbance from the breath of the external air. Beyond this indication of extensive decay, however, the fabric gave little token of instability. Perhaps the eye of a scrutinizing observer might have discovered a barely perceptible fissure, which, extending from the roof of the building in front, made its way down the wall in a zigzag direction, until it became lost in the sullen waters of the tarn. **C**

Noticing these things, I rode over a short causeway to the house. A servant in waiting took my horse, and I entered the Gothic archway of the hall. A valet, of stealthy step, thence conducted me, in silence, through many dark and intricate passages in my progress to the *studio* of his master.

62–63 this deficiency . . . issue: for some reason, the Ushers have few descendants.

equivocal (ĭ-kwĭv′ə-kəl) *adj.* ambiguous

B COMPLEX SENTENCES
Identify the main idea of lines 62–68. What are the two meanings of the phrase "the House of Usher"?

affinity (ə-fĭn′ĭ-tē) *n.* a kinship or likeness

92 specious totality: false appearance of soundness.

96 fissure: long narrow crack.

C GRAMMAR AND STYLE
Reread lines 95–98. Note how Poe uses the **participle** "scrutinizing" and the **participial phrase** "extending from the roof of the building in front" as modifiers.

Much that I encountered on the way contributed, I know not how, to heighten the vague sentiments of which I have already spoken. While the objects around me—while the carvings of the ceilings, the sombre tapestries of the walls, the ebon blackness of the floors, and the phantasmagoric armorial trophies which rattled as I strode, were but matters to which, or to such as which, I had been accustomed from my infancy—while I hesitated not to acknowledge how familiar was all this—I still wondered to find how unfamiliar were the fancies which ordinary images were stirring up. On one of the staircases, I met the physician of the family. His countenance, I thought, wore a mingled expression of low cunning and perplexity. He accosted me with trepidation and passed on. The valet now threw open a door and ushered me through into the presence of his master.

106–107 phantasmagoric (făn-tăz′mə-gôr′ĭk) **armorial trophies:** fantastic wall decorations bearing coats of arms.

The room in which I found myself was very large and lofty. The windows were long, narrow, and pointed, and at so vast a distance from the black oaken floor as to be altogether inaccessible from within. Feeble gleams of encrimsoned light made their way through the trellissed panes, and served to render sufficiently distinct the more prominent objects around; the eye, however, struggled in vain to reach the remoter angles of the chamber, or the recesses of the vaulted and fretted ceiling. Dark draperies hung upon the walls. The general furniture was profuse, comfortless, antique, and tattered. Many books and musical instruments lay scattered about, but failed to give any vitality to the scene. I felt that I breathed an atmosphere of sorrow. An air of stern, deep, and irredeemable gloom hung over and pervaded all.

121 vaulted and fretted: arched and decorated with interlaced designs.

Upon my entrance, Usher arose from a sofa on which he had been lying at full length, and greeted me with a vivacious warmth which had much in it, I at first thought, of an overdone cordiality—of the constrained effort of the *ennuyé* man of the world. A glance, however, at his countenance convinced me of his perfect sincerity. We sat down; and for some moments, while he spoke not, I gazed upon him with a feeling of half pity, half of awe. Surely, man had never before so terribly altered, in so brief a period, as had Roderick Usher! It was with difficulty that I could bring myself to admit the identity of the wan being before me with the companion of my early boyhood. Yet the character of his face had been at all times remarkable. A cadaverousness of complexion; an eye large, liquid, and luminous beyond comparison; lips somewhat thin and very pallid, but of a surpassingly beautiful curve; a nose of a delicate Hebrew model, but with a breadth of nostril unusual in similar formations; a finely moulded chin, speaking, in its want of prominence, of a want of moral energy; hair of a more than web-like softness and tenuity; these features, with an **inordinate** expansion above the regions of the temple, made up altogether a countenance not easily to be forgotten. And now in the mere exaggeration of the prevailing character of these features, and of the expression they were wont to convey, lay so much of change that I doubted to whom I spoke. The now ghastly pallor of the skin, and the now miraculous lustre of the eye, above all things startled and

129 *ennuyé* (än-nwē-yā′) *French:* bored.

136 cadaverousness of complexion: a corpselike appearance.

inordinate (ĭn-ôr′dn-ĭt) *adj.* exceeding reasonable limits; excessive even awed me. The silken hair, too, had been suffered to grow all unheeded, and as, in its wild gossamer texture, it floated rather than fell about the face, I could not, even with effort, connect its Arabesque expression with any idea of simple humanity. **D**

In the manner of my friend I was at once struck with an incoherence—an inconsistency; and I soon found this to arise from a series of feeble and futile struggles to overcome an habitual trepidancy—an excessive nervous agitation. For something of this nature I had indeed been prepared, no less by his letter, than by reminiscences of certain boyish traits, and by conclusions deduced from his peculiar physical conformation and temperament. His action was alternately vivacious and sullen. His voice varied rapidly from a tremulous indecision (when the animal spirits seemed utterly in abeyance) to that species of energetic concision—that abrupt, weighty, unhurried, and hollow-sounding enunciation—that leaden, self-balanced, and perfectly modulated guttural utterance, which may be observed in the lost drunkard, or the irreclaimable eater of opium, during the periods of his most intense excitement.

It was thus that he spoke of the object of my visit, of his earnest desire to see me, and of the solace he expected me to afford him. He entered, at some length, into what he conceived to be the nature of his malady. It was, he said, a constitutional and a family evil, and one for which he despaired to find a remedy—a mere nervous affection, he immediately added, which would undoubtedly soon pass off. It displayed itself in a host of unnatural sensations. Some of these, as he detailed them, interested and bewildered me; although, perhaps, the terms and the general manner of their narration had their weight. He suffered much from a morbid acuteness of the senses; the most **insipid** food was alone endurable; he could wear only garments of certain texture; the odors of all flowers were oppressive; his eyes were tortured by even a faint light; and there were but peculiar sounds, and these from stringed instruments, which did not inspire him with horror.

To an anomalous species of terror I found him a bounden slave. "I shall perish," said he, "I *must* perish in this deplorable folly. Thus, thus, and not otherwise, shall I be lost. I dread the events of the future, not in themselves, but in their results. I shudder at the thought of any, even the most trivial, incident, which may operate upon this intolerable agitation of soul. I have, indeed, no abhorrence of danger, except in its absolute effect—in terror. In this unnerved—in this pitiable, condition—I feel that the period will sooner or later arrive when I must abandon life and reason together, in some struggle with the grim phantasm, FEAR." **E**

I learned, moreover, at intervals, and through broken and equivocal hints, another singular feature of his mental condition. He was enchained by certain superstitious impressions in regard to the dwelling which he tenanted, and whence, for many years, he had never ventured forth—in regard to an influence whose suppositious force was conveyed in terms too

149 Arabesque (ăr′ə-bĕsk′): intricately interwoven, like the design of an Oriental rug.

D UNITY OF EFFECT
Reread lines 132–150. Poe often uses **exaggeration** to add drama to his descriptions. Which details of Roderick's appearance show this technique at work?

159 concision: terseness; brevity in use of words.

insipid (ĭn-sĭp′ĭd) *adj.* lacking in flavor; bland

175 but peculiar: only certain.

E COMPLEX SENTENCES
Reread the description of Roderick's state of mind in lines 177–185, and identify the idea that is repeatedly emphasized. What does Roderick seem to be afraid of?

190 suppositious: supposed.

shadowy here to be re-stated—an influence which some peculiarities in the mere form and substance of his family mansion had, by dint of long sufferance, he said, obtained over his spirit—an effect which the *physique* of the gray walls and turrets, and of the dim tarn into which they all looked down, had, at length, brought about upon the *morale* of his existence.

He admitted, however, although with hesitation, that much of the peculiar gloom which thus afflicted him could be traced to a more natural and far more palpable origin—to the severe and long-continued illness—indeed to the evidently approaching dissolution—of a tenderly beloved sister—his sole companion for long years—his last and only relative on earth. "Her decease," he said, with a bitterness which I can never forget, "would leave him (him, the hopeless and the frail) the last of the ancient race of the Ushers." While he spoke, the lady Madeline (for so she was called) passed through a remote portion of the apartment, and, without having noticed my presence, disappeared. I regarded her with an utter astonishment not unmingled with dread—and yet I found it impossible to account for such feelings. A sensation of stupor oppressed me as my eyes followed her retreating steps. When a door, at length, closed upon her, my glance sought instinctively and eagerly the countenance of the brother—but he had buried his face in his hands, and I could only perceive that a far more than ordinary wanness had overspread the emaciated fingers through which trickled many passionate tears.

The disease of the lady Madeline had long baffled the skill of her physicians. A settled **apathy,** a gradual wasting away of the person, and frequent although transient affections of a partially cataleptical character were the unusual diagnosis. Hitherto she had steadily borne up against the pressure of her malady, and had not betaken herself finally to bed; but on the closing in of the evening of my arrival at the house, she succumbed (as her brother told me at night with inexpressible agitation) to the prostrating power of the destroyer; and I learned that the glimpse I had obtained of her person would thus probably be the last I should obtain—that the lady, at least while living, would be seen by me no more.

For several days ensuing, her name was unmentioned by either Usher or myself; and during this period I was busied in earnest endeavors to alleviate the melancholy of my friend. We painted and read together, or I listened, as if in a dream, to the wild improvisations of his speaking guitar. And thus, as a closer and still closer intimacy admitted me more unreservedly into the recesses of his spirit, the more bitterly did I perceive the futility of all attempt at cheering a mind from which darkness, as if an inherent positive quality, poured forth upon all the objects of the moral and physical universe in one unceasing radiation of gloom. F

I shall ever bear about me a memory of the many solemn hours I thus spent alone with the master of the House of Usher. Yet I should fail in any attempt to convey an idea of the exact character of the studies, or of the

Analyze Visuals ▸
What techniques has the artist used to create contrast between Madeline and the two men?

apathy (ăp'ə-thē) *n.* lack of feeling or interest

215 transient . . . cataleptical (kăt'l-ĕp'tĭ-kəl) **character:** temporary episodes of a trancelike condition.

F COMPLEX SENTENCES
Reread lines 226–231. **Paraphrase** this sentence by breaking it into two shorter sentences, each beginning with the word *I.* What has changed in the narrator's relationship with Roderick?

occupations, in which he involved me, or led me the way. An excited and highly distempered ideality threw a sulphureous lustre over all. His long improvised dirges will ring forever in my ears. Among other things, I hold painfully in mind a certain singular perversion and amplification of the wild air of the last waltz of Von Weber. From the paintings over which his elaborate fancy brooded, and which grew, touch by touch, into vagueness at which I shuddered the more thrillingly, because I shuddered knowing not why,—from these paintings (vivid as their images now are before me) I would in vain endeavor to educe more than a small portion which should lie within the compass of merely written words. By the utter simplicity, by the nakedness of his designs, he arrested and over-awed attention. If ever mortal painted an ideal, that mortal was Roderick Usher. For me at least—in the circumstances then surrounding me—there arose out of the pure abstractions which the hypochondriac contrived to throw upon his canvas, an intensity of intolerable awe, no shadow of which felt I ever yet in the contemplation of the certainly glowing yet too concrete reveries of Fuseli.

One of the phantasmagoric conceptions of my friend, partaking not so rigidly of the spirit of abstraction, may be shadowed forth, although feebly, in words. A small picture presented the interior of an immensely long and rectangular vault or tunnel, with low walls, smooth, white, and without interruption or device. Certain accessory points of the design served well to convey the idea that this excavation lay at an exceeding depth below the surface of the earth. No outlet was observed in any portion of its vast extent, and no torch or other artificial source of light was discernable; yet a flood of intense rays rolled throughout, and bathed the whole in a ghastly and inappropriate splendor. G

I have just spoken of that morbid condition of the auditory nerve which rendered all music intolerable to the sufferer, with the exception of certain effects of stringed instruments. It was, perhaps, the narrow limits to which he thus confined himself upon the guitar which gave birth, in great measure, to the fantastic character of his performances. But the fervid *facility* of his *impromptus* could not be so accounted for. They must have been, and were, in the notes, as well as in the words of his wild fantasias (for he not unfrequently accompanied himself with rhymed verbal improvisations), the result of that intense mental collectedness and concentration to which I have previously alluded as observable only in particular moments of the highest artificial excitement. The words of one of these rhapsodies I have easily remembered. I was, perhaps, the more forcibly impressed with it as he gave it, because, in the under or mystic current of its meaning, I fancied that I perceived, and for the first time, a full consciousness on the part of Usher of the tottering of his lofty reason upon her throne. The verses, which were entitled "The Haunted Palace," ran very near, if not accurately, thus:—

236 distempered . . . sulphureous (sŭl-fər'ē-əs) **lustre:** diseased creativity gave a nightmarish quality.

239 Von Weber (vŏn vā'bər): the German romantic composer Karl Maria von Weber (1786–1826).

250 Fuseli (fyo͞o'zə-lē'): the Swiss-born British painter Henry Fuseli (1741–1825), many of whose works feature fantastic or gruesome elements.

COMMON CORE RL 3, RL 4

G UNITY OF EFFECT
Details of **setting** play a major role in this story's **mood**, or atmosphere, of unrelenting gloom. Reread lines 251–260, a description of one of Roderick Usher's paintings. Notice how **details** work together with **diction,** or choice of words, to create an imaginary setting every bit as disturbing as the story's actual setting. What do you see in Usher's painting? How does the painting reflect the artist's character?

266 *impromptus* (ăɴ-prôɴp-tü') *French:* musical pieces made up as they are played.

I

In the greenest of our valleys,
By good angels tenanted,
Once a fair and stately palace—
Radiant palace—reared its head.
In the monarch Thought's dominion—
It stood there!
Never seraph spread a pinion
Over fabric half so fair.

283–284 Never seraph (sĕr′əf) **. . . half so fair:** No angel ever spread its wing over half so beautiful a structure.

II

Banners yellow, glorious, golden,
On its roof did float and flow;
(This—all this—was in the olden
Time long ago)
And every gentle air that dallied,
In that sweet day,
Along the ramparts plumed and pallid,
A winged odor went away.

III

Wanderers in that happy valley
Through two luminous windows saw
Spirits moving musically
To a lute's well-tunèd law,
Round about a throne, where sitting
(Porphyrogene!)
In state his glory well befitting,
The ruler of the realm was seen.

298 Porphyrogene (pôr-fĭr′ə-jēn′): a son born to a ruling king.

IV

And all with pearl and ruby glowing
Was the fair palace door,
Through which came flowing, flowing, flowing
And sparkling evermore,
A troop of Echoes whose sweet duty
Was but to sing,
In voices of surpassing beauty,
The wit and wisdom of their king.

V

But evil things, in robes of sorrow,
Assailed the monarch's high estate;
(Ah, let us mourn, for never morrow
Shall dawn upon him, desolate!)
And, round about his home, the glory
That blushed and bloomed
Is but a dim-remembered story
Of the old time entombed.

VI

And travellers now within that valley,
Through the red-litten windows see
Vast forms that move fantastically
To a discordant melody;
While, like a rapid ghastly river,
Through the pale door,
A hideous throng rush out forever,
And laugh—but smile no more.

I well remember that suggestions arising from this ballad led us into a train of thought wherein there became manifest an opinion of Usher's which I mention not so much on account of its novelty (for other men have thought thus), as on account of the **pertinacity** with which he maintained it. This opinion, in its general form, was that of the sentience of all vegetable things. But, in his disordered fancy, the idea had assumed a more daring character, and trespassed, under certain conditions, upon the kingdom of inorganization. I lack words to express the full extent, of the earnest *abandon* of his persuasion. The belief, however, was connected (as I have previously hinted) with the gray stones of the home of his forefathers. The conditions of the sentience had been here, he imagined, fulfilled in the method of collocation of these stones—in the order of their arrangement, as well as in that of the many *fungi* which overspread them, and of the decayed trees which stood around—above all, in the long undisturbed endurance of this arrangement, and in its reduplication in the still waters of the tarn. Its evidence—the evidence of the sentience—was to be seen, he said (and I here started as he spoke), in the gradual yet certain condensation of an atmosphere of their own about the waters and the walls. The result was discoverable, he added, in that silent yet importunate and terrible influence which for centuries had moulded the destinies of his family, and which made *him* what I now saw him—what he was. Such opinions need no comment, and I will make none.

Our books—the books which, for years, had formed no small portion of the mental existence of the invalid—were, as might be supposed, in strict keeping with this character of phantasm. We pored together over such works

pertinacity (pûr′tn-ăs′ĭ-tē) ***n.*** **stubbornness; persistence**

329–330 sentience (sĕn′shəns) **of all vegetable things:** consciousness of all growing things.

as the Ververt et Chartreuse of Gresset; the Belphegor of Machiavelli; the Heaven and Hell of Swedenborg; the Subterranean Voyage of Nicholas Klimm by Holberg; the Chiromancy of Robert Flud, of Jean D'Indaginé, and of De la Chambre; the Journey into the Blue Distance of Tieck; and the City of the Sun of Campanella. Our favorite volume was a small octavo edition of the *Directorium Inquisitorium,* by the Dominican Eymeric de Gironne; and there were passages in Pomponius Mela, about the old African Satyrs and Aegipans, over which Usher would sit dreaming for hours. His chief delight, however, was found in the perusal of an exceedingly rare and curious book in quarto Gothic—the manual of a forgotten church—the *Vigiliae Mortuorum secundum Chorum Ecclesiae Maguntinae.*

350–356 Ververt et Chartreuse . . . Pomponius Mela: extravagantly imaginative works of fiction, theology, philosophy, and geography.

360 *Vigiliae Mortuorum secundum Chorum Ecclesiae Maguntinae* *Latin:* Wakes for the Dead, in the Manner of the Choir of the Church of Mainz.

I could not help thinking of the wild ritual of this work, and of its probable influence upon the hypochondriac, when, one evening, having informed me abruptly that the lady Madeline was no more, he stated his intention of preserving her corpse for a fortnight (previously to its final interment), in one of the numerous vaults within the main walls of the building. The worldly reason, however, assigned for this singular proceeding, was one which I did not feel at liberty to dispute. The brother had been led to his resolution (so he told me) by consideration of the unusual character of the malady of the deceased, of certain obtrusive and eager inquiries on the part of her medical men, and of the remote and exposed situation of the burial-ground of the family. I will not deny that when I called to mind the sinister countenance of the person whom I met upon the staircase, on the day of my arrival at the house, I had no desire to oppose what I regarded as at best but a harmless, and by no means an unnatural, precaution.

364–365 for a fortnight . . . interment: for two weeks prior to its final burial.

At the request of Usher, I personally aided him in the arrangements for the temporary entombment. The body having been encoffined, we two alone bore it to its rest. The vault in which we placed it (and which had been so long unopened that our torches, half smothered in its oppressive atmosphere, gave us little opportunity for investigation) was small, damp, and entirely without means of admission for light; lying, at great depth, immediately beneath that portion of the building in which was my own sleeping apartment. It had been used, apparently, in remote feudal times, for the worst purposes of a donjonkeep, and, in later days, as a place of deposit for powder, or some other highly combustible substance, as a portion of its floor, and the whole interior of a long archway through which we reached it, were carefully sheathed with copper. The door, of massive iron, had been, also, similarly protected. Its immense weight caused an unusually sharp, grating sound, as it moved upon its hinges. **H**

383 donjonkeep (dŏn′jən-kēp): dungeon.

H UNITY OF EFFECT
Reread lines 377–388. Why might Poe have provided so much **detail** about the structure of the vault?

Having deposited our mournful burden upon tressels within this region of horror, we partially turned aside the yet unscrewed lid of the coffin, and looked upon the face of the tenant. A striking similitude between the brother and sister now first arrested my attention; and Usher, divining, perhaps, my thoughts, murmured out some few words from which I learned

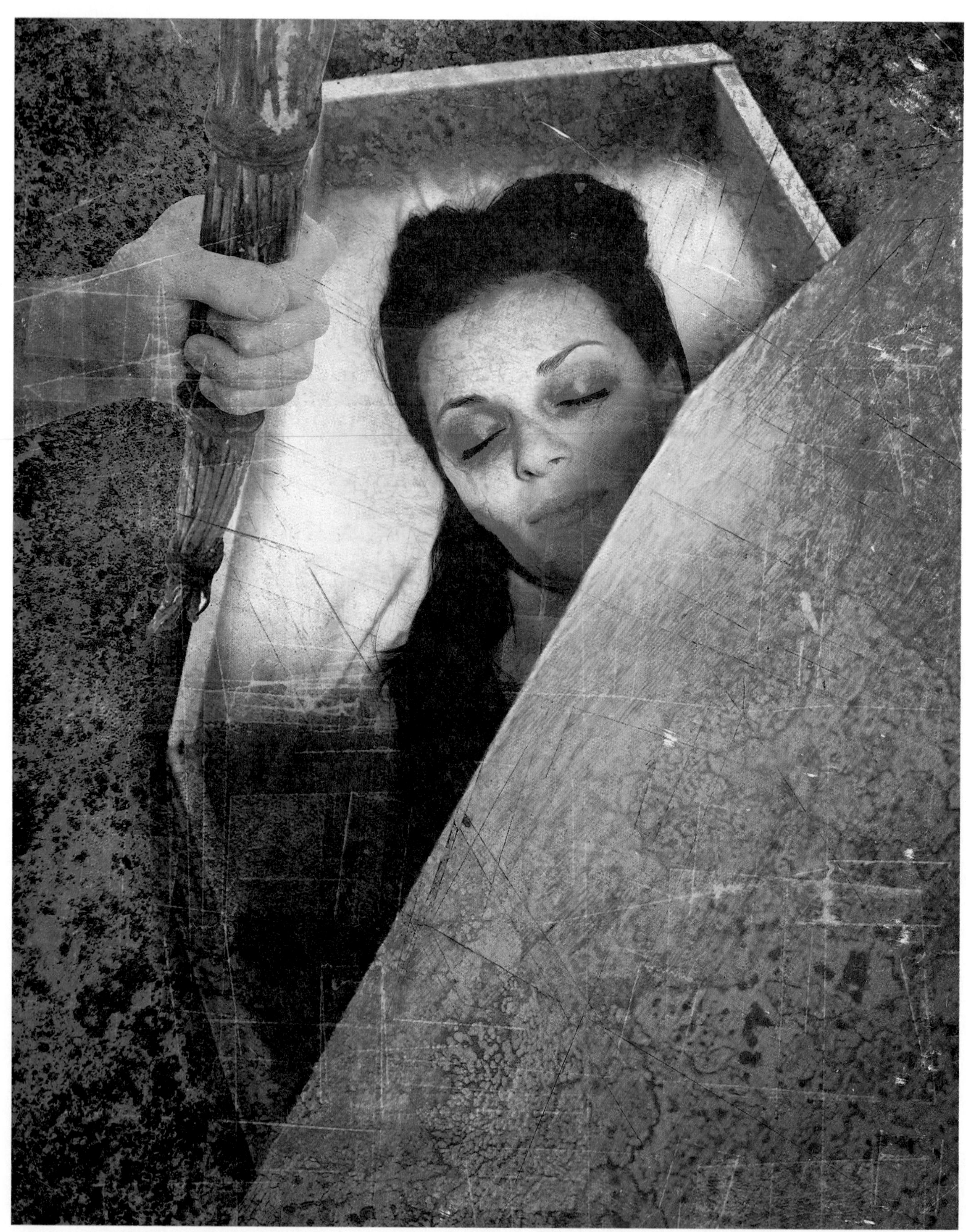

that the deceased and himself had been twins, and that sympathies of a scarcely intelligible nature had always existed between them. Our glances, however, rested not long upon the dead—for we could not regard her unawed. The disease which had thus entombed the lady in the maturity of her youth, had left, as usual in all maladies of a strictly cataleptical character, the mockery of a faint blush upon the bosom and the face, and that suspiciously lingering smile upon the lip which is so terrible in death. We replaced and screwed down the lid, and, having secured the door of iron, made our way, with toil, into the scarcely less gloomy apartments of the upper portion of the house.

And now, some days of bitter grief having elapsed, an observable change came over the features of the mental disorder of my friend. His ordinary manner had vanished. His ordinary occupations were neglected or forgotten. He roamed from chamber to chamber with hurried, unequal, and objectless step. The pallor of his countenance had assumed, if possible, a more ghastly hue—but the luminousness of his eye had utterly gone out. The once occasional huskiness of his tone was heard no more; and a tremulous quaver, as if of extreme terror, habitually characterized his utterance. There were times, indeed, when I thought his unceasingly agitated mind was laboring with some oppressive secret, to divulge which he struggled for the necessary courage. At times, again, I was obliged to resolve all into the mere inexplicable **vagaries** of madness, for I beheld him gazing upon vacancy for long hours, in an attitude of the profoundest attention, as if listening to some imaginary sound. It was no wonder that his condition terrified—that it infected me. I felt creeping upon me, by slow yet certain degrees, the wild influences of his own fantastic yet impressive superstitions.

vagary (vā′gə-rē) *n.* strange idea

It was, especially, upon retiring to bed late in the night of the seventh or eighth day after the placing of the lady Madeline within the donjon, that I experienced the full power of such feelings. Sleep came not near my couch—while the hours waned and waned away. I struggled to reason off the nervousness which had dominion over me. I endeavored to believe that much, if not all of what I felt, was due to the bewildering influence of the gloomy furniture of the room—of the dark and tattered draperies, which, tortured into motion by the breath of a rising tempest, swayed fitfully to and fro upon the walls, and rustled uneasily about the decorations of the bed. But my efforts were fruitless. An irrepressible tremor gradually pervaded my frame; and, at length, there sat upon my very heart an incubus of utterly causeless alarm. Shaking this off with a gasp and a struggle, I uplifted myself upon the pillows, and, peering earnestly within the intense darkness of the chamber, hearkened—I know not why, except that an instinctive spirit prompted me—to certain low and indefinite sounds which came, through the pauses of the storm, at long intervals, I knew not whence. Overpowered by an intense sentiment of horror, unaccountable yet unendurable, I threw on my clothes with haste (for I felt that I should sleep no more during the night), and endeavored to arouse myself from the pitiable condition into which I had fallen, by pacing rapidly to and fro through the apartment. [I]

423 couch: bed.

430 incubus: something that burdens like a nightmare.

[I] COMPLEX SENTENCES
Reread lines 431–435. Identify the main subject and verb of the sentence. Which participial phrases modify this subject?

I had taken but a few turns in this manner, when a light step on an adjoining staircase arrested my attention. I presently recognized it as that of Usher. In an instant afterward he rapped, with a gentle touch, at my door, and entered, bearing a lamp. His countenance was, as usual, cadaverously wan—but, moreover, there was a species of mad hilarity in his eyes—an evidently restrained *hysteria* in his whole **demeanor.** His air appalled me—but any thing was preferable to the solitude which I had so long endured, and I even welcomed his presence as a relief.

demeanor (dĭ-mē′nər) *n.* behavior

"And you have not seen it?" he said abruptly, after having stared about him for some moments in silence—"you have not then seen it?—but, stay! you shall." Thus speaking, and having carefully shaded his lamp, he hurried to one of the casements, and threw it freely open to the storm.

The impetuous fury of the entering gust nearly lifted us from our feet. It was, indeed, a tempestuous yet sternly beautiful night, and one wildly singular in its terror and its beauty. A whirlwind had apparently collected its force in our vicinity; for there were frequent and violent alterations in the direction of the wind; and the exceeding density of the clouds (which hung so low as to press upon the turrets of the house) did not prevent our perceiving the lifelike velocity with which they flew careering from all points against each other, without passing away into the distance. I say that even their exceeding density did not prevent our perceiving this—yet we had no glimpse of the moon or stars, nor was there any flashing forth of lightning. But the under surfaces of the huge masses of agitated vapor, as well as the terrestrial objects immediately around us, were glowing in the unnatural light of a faintly luminous and distinctly visible gaseous exhalation which hung about and enshrouded the mansion.

458 careering: going at top speed.

462–463 huge masses . . . terrestrial objects: the huge, fast-moving clouds, as well as the objects on the ground.

"You must not—you shall not behold this!" said I, shuddering, to Usher, as I led him, with a gentle violence, from the window to a seat. "These appearances, which bewilder you, are merely electrical phenomena not uncommon—or it may be that they have their ghastly origin in the rank miasma of the tarn. Let us close this casement;—the air is chilling and dangerous to your frame. Here is one of your favorite romances. I will read, and you shall listen;—and so we will pass away this terrible night together."

470 miasma (mī-ăz′mə): poisonous vapors.

The antique volume which I had taken up was the "Mad Trist" of Sir Launcelot Canning; but I had called it a favorite of Usher's more in sad jest than in earnest; for, in truth, there is little in its uncouth and unimaginative prolixity which could have had interest for the lofty and spiritual ideality of my friend. It was, however, the only book immediately at hand; and I indulged a vague hope that the excitement which now agitated the hypochondriac, might find relief (for the history of mental disorder is full of similar **anomalies**) even in the extremeness of the folly which I should read. Could I have judged, indeed, by the wild overstrained air of vivacity with which he hearkened, or apparently hearkened, to the words of the tale, I might well have congratulated myself upon the success of my design.

475–476 uncouth . . . prolixity (prō-lĭk′sĭ-tē): clumsy and unimaginative wordiness.

anomaly (ə-nŏm′ə-lē) *n.* departure from the normal rules

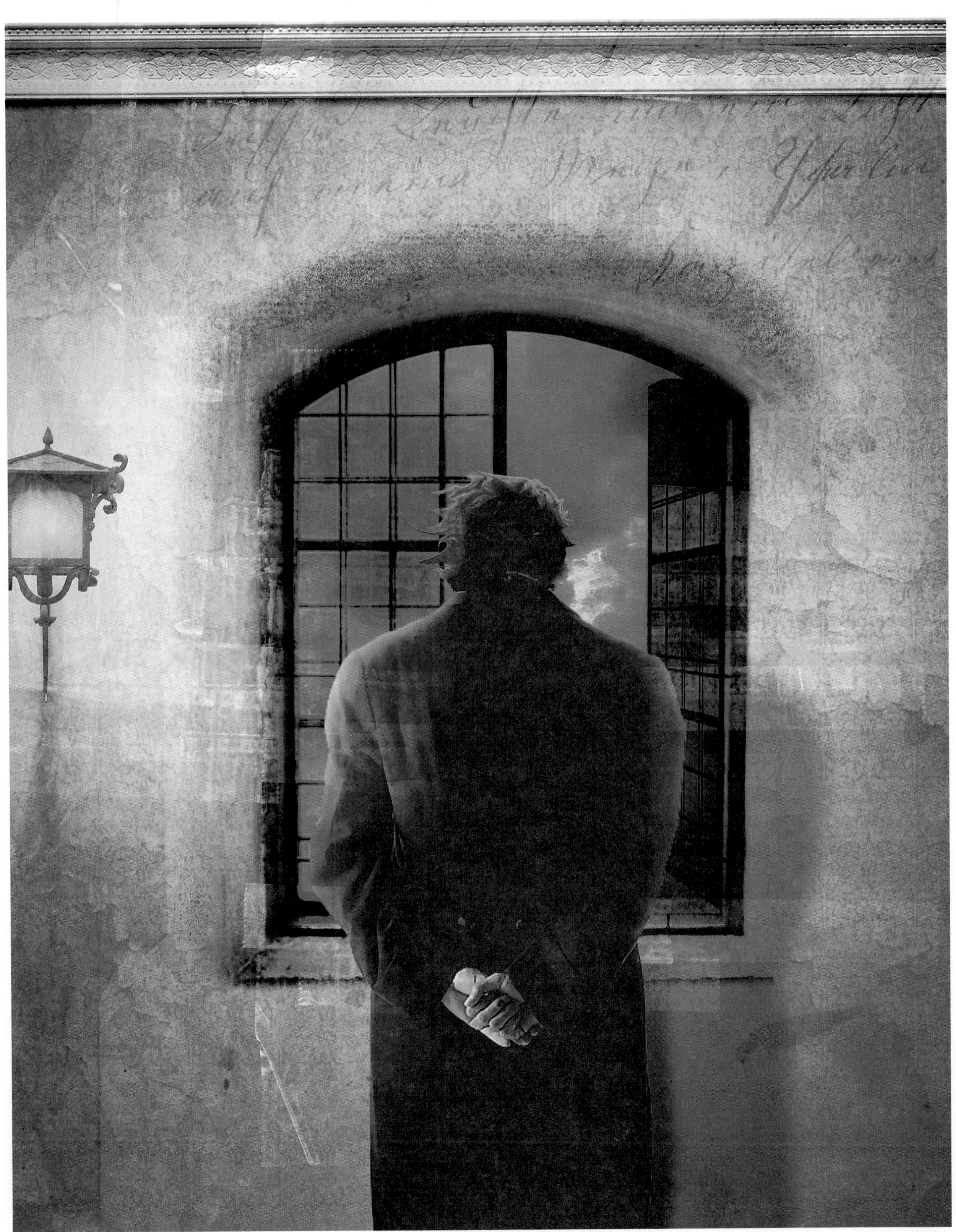

I had arrived at that well-known portion of the story where Ethelred, the hero of the Trist, having sought in vain for peaceable admission into the dwelling of the hermit, proceeds to make good an entrance by force. Here, it will be remembered, the words of the narrative run thus:

"And Ethelred, who was by nature of a doughty heart, and who was now mighty withal, on account of the powerfulness of the wine which he had drunken, waited no longer to hold parley with the hermit, who, in sooth, was of an obstinate and maliceful turn, but, feeling the rain upon his shoulders, and fearing the rising of the tempest, uplifted his mace outright, and, with blows, made quickly room in the plankings of the door for his gauntleted hand; and now pulling therewith sturdily, he so cracked, and ripped, and tore all asunder, that the noise of the dry and hollow-sounding wood alarumed and reverberated throughout the forest."

492–494 uplifted his mace . . . gauntleted hand: raised his spiked club and cut a space in the door for his armored, gloved hand.

COMMON CORE L 1a

Language Coach

Formal Language *Termination* (line 497) means "end" or "conclusion." *Termination* usually has a formal tone, and is often used these days in legal or official language. How is Poe using *termination* here, though?

At the termination of this sentence I started and, for a moment, paused; for it appeared to me (although I at once concluded that my excited fancy had deceived me)—it appeared to me that, from some very remote portion of the mansion, there came, indistinctly, to my ears, what might have been, in its exact similarity of character, the echo (but a stifled and dull one certainly) of the very cracking and ripping sound which Sir Launcelot had so particularly described. It was, beyond doubt, the coincidence alone which had arrested my attention; for, amid the rattling of the sashes of the casements, and the ordinary commingled noises of the still increasing storm, the sound, in itself, had nothing, surely, which should have interested or disturbed me. I continued the story:

"But the good champion Ethelred, now entering within the door, was sore enraged and amazed to perceive no signal of the maliceful hermit; but, in the stead thereof, a dragon of scaly and prodigious demeanor, and of a fiery tongue, which sate in guard before a palace of gold, with a floor of silver; and upon the wall there hung a shield of shining brass with this legend enwritten—

Who entereth herein, a conqueror hath bin;
Who slayeth the dragon, the shield he shall win;

And Ethelred uplifted his mace, and struck upon the head of the dragon, which fell before him, and gave up his pesty breath, with a shriek so horrid and harsh, and withal so piercing, that Ethelred had fain to close his ears with his hands against the dreadful noise of it, the like whereof was never before heard."

517 pesty: poisonous.

Here again I paused abruptly, and now with a feeling of wild amazement—for there could be no doubt whatever that, in this instance, I did actually hear (although from what direction it proceeded I found it impossible to say) a low and apparently distant, but harsh, protracted, and most unusual screaming or grating sound—the exact counterpart of what my fancy had conjured up for the dragon's unnatural shriek as described by the romancer. **J**

Oppressed, as I certainly was, upon the occurrence of this second and most extraordinary coincidence, by a thousand conflicting sensations, in which wonder and extreme terror were predominant, I still retained sufficient presence of mind to avoid exciting, by any observation, the sensitive nervousness of my companion. I was by no means certain that he had noticed the sounds in question; although, assuredly, a strange alteration had, during the last few minutes, taken place in his demeanor. From a position fronting my own, he had gradually brought round his chair, so as to sit with his face to the door of the chamber; and thus I could but partially perceive his features, although I saw that his lips trembled as if he were murmuring inaudibly. His head had dropped upon his breast—yet I knew that he was not asleep, from the wide and rigid opening of the eye as I caught a glance of it in profile. The motion of his body, too, was at variance with this idea—for he rocked from side to side with a gentle yet constant and uniform sway. Having rapidly taken notice of all this, I resumed the narrative of Sir Launcelot, which thus proceeded:

"And now, the champion, having escaped from the terrible fury of the dragon, bethinking himself of the brazen shield, and of the breaking up of the enchantment which was upon it, removed the carcass from out of the way before him, and approached valorously over the silver pavement of the castle to where the shield was upon the wall; which in sooth tarried not for his full coming, but fell down at his feet upon the silver floor, with a mighty great and terrible ringing sound."

No sooner had these syllables passed my lips, than—as if a shield of brass had indeed, at the moment, fallen heavily upon a floor of silver—I became aware of a distinct, hollow, metallic, and clangorous, yet apparently muffled, reverberation. Completely unnerved, I leaped to my feet; but the measured rocking movement of Usher was undisturbed. I rushed to the chair in which he sat. His eyes were bent fixedly before him, and throughout his whole countenance there reigned a stony rigidity. But, as I placed my hand upon his shoulder, there came a strong shudder over his whole person; a sickly smile quivered about his lips; and I saw that he spoke in a low, hurried, and gibbering murmur, as if unconscious of my presence. Bending closely over him, I at length drank in the hideous import of his words.

"Not hear it?—yes, I hear it, and *have* heard it. Long—long—long—many minutes, many hours, many days, have I heard it—yet I dared not—oh, pity me, miserable wretch that I am!—I dared not—I *dared* not speak! *We have put her living in the tomb!* Said I not that my senses were acute? I *now* tell you that I heard her first feeble movements in the hollow coffin. I heard them—many, many days ago—yet I dared not—*I dared not speak!* And now—to-night—Ethelred—ha ha!—the breaking of the hermit's door, and the death-cry of the dragon, and the clangor of the shield!—say, rather, the

J UNITY OF EFFECT
Reread lines 521–527. What coincidence is repeated?

COMMON CORE L4

Language Coach

Fixed Expressions The term ***fixed expression*** refers to the normal combination of words—the ways they are often used. Note "by no means certain" (line 532). *By no means* is often used before *certain*. Create a sentence with one of these fixed expressions: *almost certain, [to] grow certain.*

rending of her coffin, and the grating of the iron hinges of her prison, and her struggles within the coppered archway of the vault! Oh! whither shall I fly? Will she not be here anon? Is she not hurrying to upbraid me for my haste? Have I not heard her footstep on the stair? Do I not distinguish that heavy and horrible beating of her heart? MADMAN!"—here he sprang furiously to his feet, and shrieked out his syllables, as if in the effort he were giving up his soul—"MADMAN! I TELL YOU THAT SHE NOW STANDS WITHOUT THE DOOR!" (K)

As if in the superhuman energy of his utterance there had been found the potency of a spell, the huge antique panels to which the speaker pointed threw slowly back, upon the instant, their ponderous and ebony jaws. It was the work of the rushing gust—but then without those doors there did stand the lofty and enshrouded figure of the lady Madeline of Usher. There was blood upon her white robes, and the evidence of some bitter struggle upon every portion of her emaciated frame. For a moment she remained trembling and reeling to and fro upon the threshold—then, with a low moaning cry, fell heavily inward upon the person of her brother, and in her violent and now final death-agonies, bore him to the floor a corpse, and a victim to the terrors he had anticipated.

From the chamber, and from that mansion, I fled aghast. The storm was still abroad in all its wrath as I found myself crossing the old causeway. Suddenly there shot along the path a wild light, and I turned to see whence a gleam so unusual could have issued; for the vast house and its shadows were alone behind me. The radiance was that of the full, setting, and blood-red moon, which now shone vividly through that once barely discernible fissure, of which I have before spoken as extending from the roof of the building, in a zigzag direction, to the base. While I gazed, the fissure rapidly widened—there came a fierce breath of the whirlwind—the entire orb of the satellite burst at once upon my sight—my brain reeled as I saw the mighty walls rushing asunder—there was a long tumultuous shouting sound like the voice of a thousand waters—and the deep and dank tarn at my feet closed sullenly and silently over the fragments of the "HOUSE OF USHER."

(K) UNITY OF EFFECT
Reread lines 568–571. Recall the description of the vault you read earlier. In what way does that description help set up the situation of the story's **climax?**

Analyze Visuals ▶

Compare the image on the opposite page with the description in lines 581–587. Is the artist's interpretation of the scene effective? Support your answer with details from the selection.

THEME
Many works of literature touch on the theme of decay or decline. In "The Fall of the House of Usher," Poe explores this theme though his description of the Usher family and their decaying mansion. Stories that center on this theme tend to follow the same text structure: on the outside things seem to be stable or alive, but in fact they are decaying and rotting from the inside, leading to a dramatic collapse. For example, in the novels of William Faulkner, such as *The Sound and the Fury* (1929), Faulkner writes about the decline of a southern community. What other novels, plays, or films touch on the theme of decay and decline?

Comprehension

1. **Recall** Why does the narrator come to the House of Usher?
2. **Recall** What change in Madeline's condition occurs shortly after the narrator's arrival?
3. **Clarify** What are Roderick's reasons for placing Madeline in the vault below the house?

Text Analysis

4. **Examine Complex Sentences** Review the chart you created as you read. Compare your paraphrases with Poe's original sentences. Without Poe's elaborate language, does the story have the same **mood?** Explain.
5. **Interpret Title** Reread lines 58–68. Based on this passage, explain two possible meanings of the story's title. In what ways does the title help you anticipate the ending of the story?
6. **Analyze Unity of Effect** In what way does each of the following demonstrate Poe's principle of the single effect? Cite key details that show Poe's use of the specified story element to build **mood.**
   - setting (lines 115–125)
   - character traits (lines 172–176)
   - plot developments (lines 216–222)
   - imagery (lines 452–465)
7. **Evaluate Author's Technique** In your opinion, does Poe's technique of the unified effect accomplish its intended purpose? What, if any, are the disadvantages of his approach? Explain.

Text Criticism

8. **Critical Interpretations** The literary critic Cleanth Brooks dismissed "The Fall of the House of Usher" as an "essentially meaningless" exercise in horror for its own sake. Considering your own reading of the story, do you agree or disagree with this opinion? Cite details to support your answer.

Where does TERROR *begin?*

How does Poe's use of the first-person point of view help communicate the experience of terror?

COMMON CORE

RL 3 Analyze the impact of the author's choices regarding how to develop and relate elements of a story. **RL 4** Analyze the impact of specific word choices on meaning and tone. **L 3a** Apply an understanding of syntax to the study of complex texts when reading.

Vocabulary in Context

▲ VOCABULARY PRACTICE

Choose the word that is not related in meaning to the other words.

1. (a) dull, (b) uninteresting, (c) insipid, (d) insecure
2. (a) demeanor, (b) antique, (c) manner, (d) interaction
3. (a) conception, (b) delusion, (c) vagary, (d) tome
4. (a) connection, (b) disturbance, (c) affinity, (d) relationship
5. (a) deviation, (b) oddity, (c) representative, (d) anomaly
6. (a) bureaucratic, (b) extravagant, (c) extreme, (d) inordinate
7. (a) apathy, (b) ecstasy, (c) indifference, (d) unconcern
8. (a) agony, (b) torment, (c) alleviation, (d) anguish
9. (a) persistence, (b) perseverance, (c) pretense, (d) pertinacity
10. (a) hazy, (b) ambiguous, (c) contentious, (d) equivocal

WORD LIST

affinity
alleviation
anomaly
apathy
demeanor
equivocal
inordinate
insipid
pertinacity
vagary

ACADEMIC VOCABULARY IN WRITING

• construct • expand • indicate • reinforce • role

Poe uses a creepy setting, a disturbed character, and mounting suspense to **reinforce** horror in his story. Think about which of these elements had the most success in creating a sense of horror for you. Then, in a paragraph discuss why that particular element played such an important **role** in the story. Use at least three of the Academic Vocabulary words in your paragraph.

COMMON CORE

L 4b–c Identify and use patterns of word changes that indicate different meanings or parts of speech; consult general reference materials.

VOCABULARY STRATEGY: THE GREEK ROOT *path*

The vocabulary word *apathy* contains the Greek root *path*, which means "feel" or "suffer." This root is found in a number of English words. To understand words with *path*, use context clues as well as your knowledge of the root's meaning.

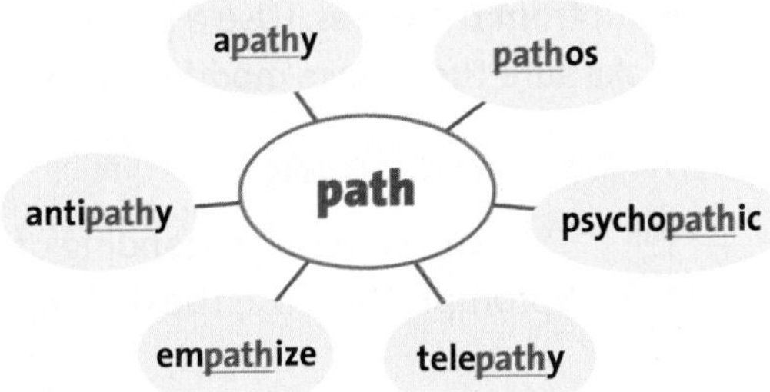

PRACTICE Choose the word from the word web that best completes each sentence. Consider what you know about the Greek root and the other word parts shown. If necessary, consult a dictionary.

1. Her brother's cruel actions caused her to feel a strong _____ for him.
2. The characters' tearful farewell evoked a sense of _____ in the audience.
3. Their thoughts were so aligned that it seemed they could communicate by _____.
4. Many criminals' behavior tends to be _____.
5. Parents are often able to _____ with their children's problems and frustrations.

Language

COMMON CORE

L 3 Apply knowledge of language to understand how language functions in different contexts, to make effective choices for meaning or style, and to comprehend more fully when reading. **W 3** Write narratives that use telling details and sensory language to convey a vivid picture of the experiences, events, setting and/or characters.

GRAMMAR AND STYLE: Add Descriptive Details

Review the **Grammar and Style** note on page 415. Poe is a master of elaborate, ornate descriptions that are packed with details. Some of his descriptive words are **participles,** verb forms that function as adjectives, as in this example:

His long improvised dirges will ring forever in my ears. (lines 236–237)

Participles usually end in *-ing* or *-ed* and can be combined with modifiers and complements to make **participial phrases.**

PRACTICE Read each of the following sentences from Poe's story, noting the boldfaced participle or participial phrase. Then, write your own sentence, using a participle as instructed in parentheses. An example has been done for you.

EXAMPLE

His countenance, I thought, wore a **mingled** expression of low cunning and perplexity. (Use a past participle, one that ends with *-ed.*)

The cat, I noticed, carried a mangled mouse in her jaws.

1. A sensation of stupor oppressed me as my eyes followed her **retreating** steps. (Use a present participle, one that ends with *-ing.*)
2. **Shaking off from my spirit what *must* have been a dream,** I scanned more narrowly the real aspect of the building. (Use a participial phrase to begin your sentence. Make sure your phrase modifies the subject.)
3. Minute fungi overspread the whole exterior, **hanging in a fine tangled web-work from the eaves.** (Use a participial phrase at the end of your sentence. Make sure the phrase modifies the subject.)

READING-WRITING CONNECTION

Expand your understanding of Poe's writing by responding to this prompt. Then, use the **revising tips** to improve your description.

WRITING PROMPT	REVISING TIPS
WRITE A DESCRIPTION You don't need far-off locales and crumbling castles to inspire **terror.** Using a few well-chosen details, you can turn a familiar scene into an unsettling backdrop for eerie events. Write a **two- to four-paragraph description** that makes an everyday location seem terrifying. Choose descriptive details that suggest something strange or unsettling is at work.	• Use descriptive details that appeal to the five senses. • Arrange your description in spatial order so readers can better understand what you are describing. • Include recognizable elements of terror that are subtle, yet alarming.

The Raven

Poem by Edgar Allan Poe

RL 1, RL 4, RL 5, L 4

TEXT ANALYSIS: SOUND DEVICES

First published in 1845, "The Raven" became an instant hit. Part of the poem's popularity was due to Poe's clever use of **sound devices**, patterns of word sounds used to create musical effects.

- **Rhyme,** the repetition of similar sounds, is one of the easiest sound devices to spot. Poe adds variety by using **internal rhyme,** rhyming words that fall inside a line.

  Ah, distinctly I remember it was in the bleak December;

- **Repetition,** of rhymes and of words and phrases, helps give "The Raven" its distinctive rhythm.

  As of someone gently rapping, rapping at my chamber door.

- **Alliteration,** the repetition of initial consonant sounds, is used to create rhythm or to stress key words.

  While I nodded, nearly napping . . .

- **Onomatopoeia** is the use of words that sound like their meaning, such as the word *rustling* in this example:

  And the silken, sad, uncertain rustling of each purple curtain

As you read, note how Poe combines these sound devices to form complex rhythmic patterns.

Review: **Stanza and Rhyme Scheme**

READING SKILL: MAKE INFERENCES

"The Raven" tells a story without directly stating all of the important details. You'll need to use clues in the poem to **make inferences** about the speaker's situation. As you read, use a chart like the one shown to record your inferences and the clues that helped you. By the end of the poem, you'll be able to **draw conclusions** about what the speaker experiences.

	Inferences About the Speaker	*Clues*
State of Mind		
Recent Experiences		

Complete the activities in your **Reader/Writer Notebook**.

How do people handle LOSS?

At some point in our lives, we all face loss—of someone we love, our favorite pet, or even a cherished dream. But even though the experience of loss is universal, people can choose many different ways to cope with the sadness and grief they feel. What do people need to do to face their grief and move on?

DISCUSS Working in small groups, think about some ways people respond to a serious loss. Discuss how they express their own feelings and what they do to adjust to the changes that the loss creates. What patterns can you identify?

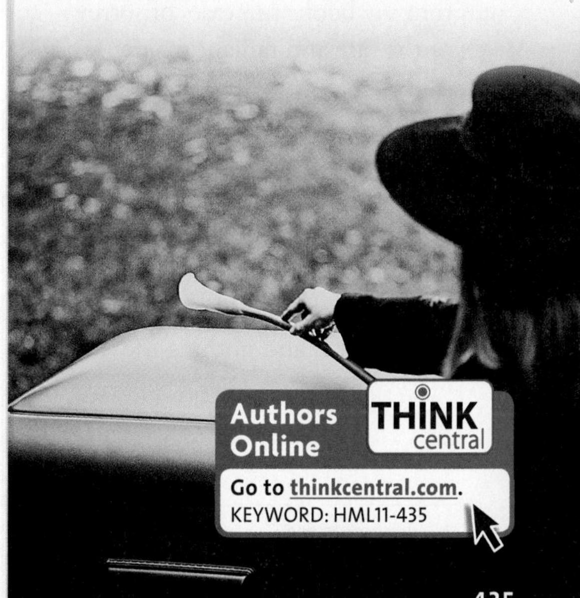

Authors Online THINK central

Go to thinkcentral.com. KEYWORD: HML11-435

The Raven

Edgar Allan Poe

Once upon a midnight dreary, while I pondered, weak and weary,
Over many a quaint and curious volume of forgotten lore—
While I nodded, nearly napping, suddenly there came a tapping,
As of someone gently rapping, rapping at my chamber door.
"'Tis some visitor," I muttered, "tapping at my chamber door—
Only this and nothing more." A

Ah, distinctly I remember it was in the bleak December;
And each separate dying ember wrought its ghost upon the floor.
Eagerly I wished the morrow;—vainly I had sought to borrow
From my books surcease[1] of sorrow—sorrow for the lost Lenore—
For the rare and radiant maiden whom the angels name Lenore—
Nameless *here* forevermore. B

And the silken, sad, uncertain rustling of each purple curtain
Thrilled me—filled me with fantastic terrors never felt before;
So that now, to still the beating of my heart, I stood repeating
"'Tis some visitor entreating entrance at my chamber door;—
Some late visitor entreating entrance at my chamber door;—
That it is and nothing more."

Analyze Visuals ▶
What techniques has the photographer used that make the raven on page 437 seem mysterious?

A SOUND DEVICES
Reread lines 1–6. What pattern of **internal rhyme** does Poe establish in the first stanza?

B MAKE INFERENCES
Reread lines 9–12. What does this passage imply about Lenore's connection to the speaker and the reason for her absence? Give details to support your answer.

1. **surcease:** an end.

Presently my soul grew stronger; hesitating then no longer,
"Sir," said I, "or Madam, truly your forgiveness I implore;
But the fact is I was napping, and so gently you came rapping,
And so faintly you came tapping, tapping at my chamber door,
That I scarce was sure I heard you"—here I opened wide the door;—
Darkness there and nothing more. **C**

C STANZA AND RHYME SCHEME
Recall that a poem's rhyme scheme is its pattern of **end rhyme.** Describe the rhyme scheme of this poem. How does Poe use **repetition** as part of the rhyme scheme?

Deep into that darkness peering, long I stood there wondering, fearing,
Doubting, dreaming dreams no mortal ever dared to dream before;
But the silence was unbroken, and the stillness gave no token,
And the only word there spoken was the whispered word, "Lenore!"
This I whispered, and an echo murmured back the word "Lenore!"
Merely this and nothing more.

Back into the chamber turning, all my soul within me burning,
Soon again I heard a tapping somewhat louder than before.
"Surely," said I, "surely that is something at my window lattice;
Let me see, then, what thereat is, and this mystery explore—
Let my heart be still a moment and this mystery explore;—
'Tis the wind and nothing more!"

Open here I flung the shutter, when, with many a flirt and flutter,
In there stepped a stately Raven of the saintly days of yore.[2]
Not the least obeisance[3] made he; not a minute stopped or stayed he;
But, with mien[4] of lord or lady, perched above my chamber door—
Perched upon a bust of Pallas[5] just above my chamber door—
Perched, and sat, and nothing more. **D**

D SOUND DEVICES
Reread lines 37–38. What example of **onomatopoeia** can you find?

Then this ebony bird beguiling my sad fancy into smiling,
By the grave and stern decorum of the countenance it wore,
"Though thy crest be shorn and shaven, thou," I said, "art sure no craven,[6]
Ghastly grim and ancient Raven wandering from the Nightly shore—
Tell me what thy lordly name is on the Night's Plutonian[7] shore!"
Quoth the Raven, "Nevermore." **E**

E SOUND DEVICES
Identify the **alliteration** in lines 45–46. What words are emphasized by using this technique?

Much I marveled this ungainly fowl to hear discourse so plainly,
Though its answer little meaning—little relevancy bore;
For we cannot help agreeing that no living human being

---

2. **days of yore:** days of long ago.
3. **obeisance** (ō-bā'səns): a gesture of respect.
4. **mien** (mēn): appearance.
5. **bust of Pallas:** statue of the head and shoulders of Pallas Athena, Greek goddess of wisdom.
6. **craven:** coward.
7. **Plutonian:** having to do with Pluto, Roman god of the dead and ruler of the underworld.

Ever yet was blessed with seeing bird above his chamber door—
Bird or beast upon the sculptured bust above his chamber door,
With such name as "Nevermore."

But the Raven, sitting lonely on the placid bust, spoke only
That one word, as if his soul in that one word he did outpour.
Nothing farther then he uttered—not a feather then he fluttered—
Till I scarcely more than muttered "Other friends have flown before—
On the morrow *he* will leave me, as my hopes have flown before."
Then the bird said, "Nevermore." **F**

Startled at the stillness broken by reply so aptly spoken,
"Doubtless," said I, "what it utters is its only stock and store
Caught from some unhappy master whom unmerciful Disaster
Followed fast and followed faster till his songs one burden[8] bore—
Till the dirges[9] of his Hope that melancholy burden bore
Of 'Never—nevermore.'"

But the Raven still beguiling all my fancy into smiling,
Straight I wheeled a cushioned seat in front of bird, and bust and door;
Then, upon the velvet sinking, I betook myself to linking
Fancy unto fancy, thinking what this ominous bird of yore—
What this grim, ungainly, ghastly, gaunt, and ominous bird of yore
Meant in croaking, "Nevermore." **G**

This I sat engaged in guessing, but no syllable expressing
To the fowl whose fiery eyes now burned into my bosom's core;
This and more I sat divining,[10] with my head at ease reclining
On the cushion's velvet lining that the lamp-light gloated o'er,
But whose velvet violet lining with the lamp-light gloating o'er,
She shall press, ah, nevermore!

Then, methought, the air grew denser, perfumed from an unseen censer
Swung by Seraphim[11] whose foot-falls tinkled on the tufted floor.
"Wretch," I cried, "thy God hath lent thee—by these angels he hath sent thee
Respite—respite and nepenthe[12] from thy memories of Lenore;
Quaff,[13] oh quaff this kind nepenthe and forget this lost Lenore!"
Quoth the Raven, "Nevermore."

F MAKE INFERENCES
Reread lines 58–59. What does this comment suggest about the speaker's past experiences and his current mood? Explain.

G SOUND DEVICES
Identify the sound device used in lines 71–72. What qualities of the raven are emphasized by the use of this device?

---

8. **burden:** the chorus or refrain of a song.
9. **dirges:** songs of mourning.
10. **divining:** guessing from incomplete evidence.
11. **censer / Swung by Seraphim** (sĕr'ə-fĭm): container of sweet burning incense swung by angels of the highest rank.
12. **respite . . . and nepenthe** (nĭ-pĕn'thē): temporary relief and a forgetfulness that eases grief.
13. **quaff:** drink deeply.

"Prophet!" said I, "thing of evil!—prophet still, if bird or devil!—
Whether Tempter[14] sent, or whether tempest tossed thee here ashore,
Desolate yet all undaunted, on this desert land enchanted—
On this home by Horror haunted—tell me truly, I implore—
Is there—*is* there balm in Gilead?[15]—tell me—tell me, I implore!"
    Quoth the Raven, "Nevermore."

"Prophet!" said I, "thing of evil!—prophet still, if bird or devil!
By that Heaven that bends above us—by that God we both adore—
Tell this soul with sorrow laden if, within the distant Aidenn,[16]
It shall clasp a sainted maiden whom the angels name Lenore—
Clasp a rare and radiant maiden whom the angels name Lenore."
    Quoth the Raven, "Nevermore." **H**

"Be that word our sign of parting, bird or fiend!" I shrieked, upstarting—
"Get thee back into the tempest and the Night's Plutonian shore!
Leave no black plume as a token of that lie thy soul hath spoken!
Leave my loneliness unbroken!—quit the bust above my door!
Take thy beak from out my heart, and take thy form from off my door!"
    Quoth the Raven, "Nevermore."

And the Raven, never flitting, still is sitting, *still* is sitting
On the pallid bust of Pallas just above my chamber door;
And his eyes have all the seeming of a demon's that is dreaming,
And the lamp-light o'er him streaming throws his shadow on the floor;
And my soul from out that shadow that lies floating on the floor
    Shall be lifted—nevermore!

COMMON CORE L 4

Language Coach

Words Easily Confused *Tempter* and *tempest* (both in line 86) are pronounced and spelled similarly, but have different meanings. *Tempter*, here, means "the Devil" and *tempest* means "violent storm." What effect does Poe's use of these similar sounding words have?

H MAKE INFERENCES Given the bird's repeated response, what does the speaker's persistent questioning of the raven suggest about his state of mind? Explain your answer.

14. **Tempter:** the devil.
15. **balm** (bäm) **in Gilead** (gĭl'ē-əd): relief from suffering.
16. **Aidenn** (ād'n): heaven (from the Arabic form of the word *Eden*).

Comprehension

1. **Recall** Where and when do the events of the poem take place?
2. **Recall** What is the raven's response to all of the speaker's questions?
3. **Clarify** What is the speaker's explanation of the raven's one response?

Text Analysis

4. **Make Inferences** Review the **inferences** you made as you read. What conclusions did you draw about the speaker and his emotional state?
5. **Examine Tone** For each of the following passages, describe the speaker's tone, or attitude, toward the raven. What explains the speaker's changing responses to his mysterious visitor?
   - the raven's first appearance (lines 43–44)
   - the thoughts the raven inspires (lines 71–74)
   - the purpose the speaker attributes to the raven (lines 81–84)
   - the speaker's command to the raven (lines 97–98)
6. **Compare and Contrast Imagery** Poe uses imagery to create a stark contrast between Lenore and the raven. Using a chart like the one shown, list images that describe each character. What do these images communicate about each character? Cite evidence.

Lenore	Raven

7. **Evaluate Sound Devices** Reread lines 79–84. Identify the rhymes and other sound devices used in this stanza, and give examples of each technique. Which of these devices do you find most compelling or effective? Explain your answer.

Text Criticism

8. **Author's Style** In an essay about "The Raven," Poe claimed that he started with the word *nevermore* (he liked its vowel sounds), then added the death of a beautiful woman ("the most poetical topic in the world"). Only later did he invent the story and characters that readers have found so moving and memorable. Poe seems to have been more interested in form than content. Which do you find more important in this poem? Cite details in your answer.

How do people handle **LOSS?**

Consider the speaker's changing responses to the raven throughout the poem. What does the speaker's conflict with the raven suggest about the behavior of people who are struggling with grief?

COMMON CORE

RL 1 Cite evidence to support analysis of inferences drawn from the text. **RL 4** Analyze the impact of specific word choices on meaning and tone. **RL 5** Analyze how an author's choices concerning how to structure a text contribute to its overall structure and meaning, as well as its aesthetic impact.

Language

COMMON CORE

L 2 Demonstrate command of the conventions of standard English capitalization and punctuation when writing. **W 3** Write narratives using effective technique, well-chosen details, and well-structured event sequences. **W 3b** Use narrative technique such as dialogue, to develop a character. **W 3d** Use precise words and phrases to convey a vivid picture of the character.

◆ GRAMMAR AND STYLE: Craft Effective Sentences

Poe uses **imperative sentences**—sentences that give orders or make requests—and **dashes** to convey his character's excitable state. The use of dashes and a tone of breathless urgency are distinctive features of Poe's style.

"Be that word our sign of parting, bird or fiend!" I shrieked, upstarting—
"Get thee back into the tempest and the Night's Plutonian shore!" (lines 97–98)

PRACTICE Using the following verse from "The Raven" as a model, compose your own stanza in the style of Poe, incorporating dashes and imperative sentences. Feel free to choose a different subject, but make sure to follow Poe's rhyme scheme and to echo his tone. A sample beginning is provided for you.

EXAMPLE

"Prophet!" said I, "thing of evil!—prophet still, if bird or devil!—
"You pest, begone!" I cried—near choking. "Take from me your wretched joking!"

"Prophet!" said I, "thing of evil!—prophet still, if bird or devil!—
Whether Tempter sent, or whether tempest tossed thee here ashore,
Desolate yet all undaunted, on this desert land enchanted—
On this home by Horror haunted—tell me truly, I implore—
Is there—*is* there balm in Gilead?—tell me—tell me, I implore!"
Quoth the Raven, "Nevermore."

READING-WRITING CONNECTION

Expand your understanding of Poe's "The Raven" by responding to this prompt. Then, use the **revising tips** to improve your monologue.

WRITING PROMPT

WRITE A MONOLOGUE A monologue is a lengthy passage or speech in which a single character expresses thoughts in an uninterrupted flow, with no other character's words intervening. Monologues in literature often explore a character's feelings. Write a **one-page prose monologue,** in your own voice or that of a fictional character, that explores an emotion, such as grief or joy. In your monologue reveal details about your speaker's personality and the reasons for his or her emotional response.

REVISING TIPS

- Include your speaker's thoughts, emotions, and spoken words.
- Use first-person pronouns, such as *I, me,* and *my.*
- Include at least one sentence that gives an order or makes a request.
- Use dashes to show pauses, urgency, or strong emotions.

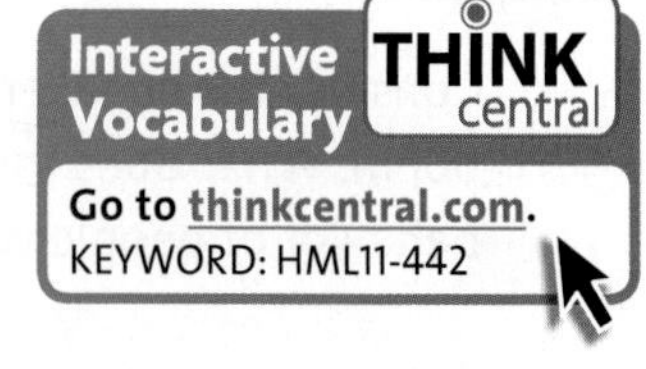

Connect: Poem

PARODY Like other well-known and well-loved works of literature, "The Raven" has inspired many a **parody**—a comic imitation of another work or type of literature. As you read the following parody, note the points of imitation in form or content. In what ways does the parodist turn Poe's ideas to comic effect?

What Troubled Poe's Raven

John Bennett

Could Poe walk again to-morrow, heavy with dyspeptic sorrow,
While the darkness seemed to borrow darkness from the night before,
From the hollow gloom abysmal, floating downward, grimly dismal,
Like a pagan curse baptismal from the bust above the door,
He would hear the Raven croaking from the dusk above the door,
"Never, never, nevermore!"

And, too angry to be civil, "Raven," Poe would cry "or devil,
Tell me why you will persist in haunting Death's Plutonian shore?"
Then would croak the Raven gladly, "I will tell you why so sadly,
I so mournfully and madly, haunt you, taunt you, o'er and o'er,
Why eternally I haunt you, daunt you, taunt you, o'er and o'er —
Only this, and nothing more.

"Forty-eight long years I've pondered, forty-eight long years I've wondered,
How a poet ever blundered into a mistake so sore.
How could lamp-light from your table ever in the world be able,
From *below*, to throw my sable shadow 'streaming on the floor,'
When I perched up here on Pallas, high above your chamber-door?
Tell me that — if nothing more!"

Then, like some wan, weeping willow, Poe would bend above his pillow,
Seeking surcease in the billow where mad recollections drown,
And in tearful tones replying, he would groan "There's no denying
Either I was blindly lying, or the world was upside down—
Say, by Joe!—it was just midnight—so the world *was* upside down—
Aye, the world was upside down!"

Comparing Texts

American Gothic

The Masque of the Red Death

Short Story by Edgar Allan Poe

from Danse Macabre

Essay by Stephen King

Wait Until Dark

Movie Poster

COMMON CORE **RL 3** Analyze the impact of the author's choices regarding how to develop and relate elements of a story. **RL 4** Determine the meanings of words and phrases as they are used in the text, including figurative and connotative meanings; analyze the impact of specific word choices on meaning and tone. **RI 4** Determine the meaning of words and phrases as they are used in a text, including figurative, connotative and technical meanings. **RI 7** Evaluate multiple sources of information presented in different media or formats as well as in words to address a question. **L 2b** Spell correctly. **L 4c** Consult reference materials to find the pronunciation of a word.

Meet the Authors

Edgar Allan Poe c. 1809–1849

Edgar Allan Poe was a master of the psychological thriller. His tales of the ghastly and the grotesque are peopled with distraught narrators, deranged heroes, and doomed heroines. They move beyond the sunlit, rational world to explore the dark, irrational depths of the human mind. (For more about Poe, see page 410.)

A Gothic Allegory "The Masque of the Red Death," first published in 1842, is timeless in its appeal. We can enjoy it for its thrills or as an **allegory**. In an allegory, characters and objects stand for abstract ideas such as good and evil. Often meant to teach moral lessons, allegories typically feature simple characters and unnamed settings, somewhat like fairy tales.

Poe's Enduring Legacy Generations of mystery and suspense writers have been influenced by the brooding atmosphere and eerie tension of Poe's stories. In fact, two of the most highly regarded American short stories written since Poe's death owe a debt to the Gothic master. "An Occurrence at Owl Creek Bridge" (page 604) has the ghostly mood of Poe's fiction. The creepy tension that pervades "A Rose for Emily" (page 1066) can be traced to Poe's haunted settings. In the twentieth century, with the advent of movies, Poe found a wider audience in films adapted from his stories. In 1964, for example, "The Masque of the Red Death" was made into a movie starring Vincent Price, a well-known horror-movie actor of the time.

Stephen King born 1947

Stephen King's phenomenal success began in 1974, with the publication of *Carrie*. Discouraged, King had thrown an unfinished manuscript of the novel in the trash. His wife retrieved it and urged him to finish it; the rest is history. King went on to become one of the bestselling writers of all time. His novels have contributed to a revival of horror fiction and horror movies. In fact, he's been called a "one-man entertainment industry."

Terror and Suspense No living American author has achieved the success we associate with King's Gothic page-turners and the movies that have been adapted from them. *Carrie* was a huge commercial success. Turned into a classic horror movie, also titled *Carrie*, it has inspired a movie sequel, a Broadway musical, a made-for-television movie, and a non-musical stage parody. His novels have sold in the millions, and the movies made from them have found a worldwide audience. They testify to the enduring appeal of the elements in fiction that both excite and frighten us.

THINK central

Author Online

Go to thinkcentral.com. KEYWORD: HMD11-444

TEXT ANALYSIS: SUSPENSE

One of the most important elements of a Gothic story is **suspense**—the combination of excitement and anxiety that readers feel about coming events in a plot. In "The Masque of the Red Death," readers feel excited about an extravagant masquerade party, but they begin to feel anxious when Poe describes a clock that makes the guests nervous each time it strikes the hour. As you read the story, notice the elements in the party that make you eager for more or that make you feel a sense of dread about the outcome. Then, when you read Stephen King's essay, notice how he explains the element of fear and terror in suspense. How does this nonfiction excerpt add to your appreciation of writers such as Poe?

READING STRATEGY: CLARIFY MEANING

Poe's unusual, archaic vocabulary reinforces this story's feeling of antiquity. To help you clarify the meaning of difficult words and phrases, consult the side notes for helpful information. In addition, use **context clues** in surrounding phrases to figure out unfamiliar words. Finally, **paraphrase** difficult passages, using simpler language. By contrast with the Poe story, Stephen King's nonfiction excerpt is written in contemporary, accessible language. As you read King, pay special attention to his comments about a closed door and the role it plays in suspense. Remember that the best way to understand any suspense story is to become engaged in the author's mixture of excitement and dread.

VOCABULARY IN CONTEXT

Poe used the following words in his eerie tale. Complete each phrase with an appropriate word from the list.

WORD LIST			
	blasphemous	disapprobation	propriety
	cessation	impede	reverie

1. wandered the halls lost in a ________
2. a peace treaty following the ________ of hostilities
3. her friends' ________ after her unwise decision
4. tried not to ________ the flow of traffic
5. deeply offended by his ________ arguments
6. acted with decorum and ________

Complete the activities in your **Reader/Writer Notebook**.

Is SAFETY *an illusion?*

We like to feel that there are steps we can take to keep ourselves safe. To protect ourselves from theft, we can install an alarm or add high-security locks. To protect our health, we can exercise and eat healthy food. But do our precautions really keep danger away, or do they just give us an illusion of safety?

What's the Connection?

As you study these texts, think about the elements that make a story, a movie, or even a movie poster suspenseful. With Edgar Allan Poe's story "The Masque of the Red Death," you will experience actual suspense in the hands of a master. Afterwards, as you read Stephen King's explanation of suspense, think about how it applies to your experience as a reader. Finally, when you examine the poster for *Wait Until Dark,* think about how images create suspense.

THE

Masque OF THE RED DEATH

Edgar Allan Poe

BACKGROUND Around 1350, Europe was struck by an epidemic of bubonic plague (Black Death) that killed more than a quarter of its population. The plague killed its victims quickly—within three to five days—and there was no cure. Artwork from that time is full of haunting symbols like the Dance of Death, where Death, personified as a skeleton, whirls anonymous figures to their graves. These grisly allegorical images spoke to the deepest fears of their audience, for whom death was a nearby presence. Note how Poe borrows from this history in his own tale of death.

The "Red Death" had long devastated the country. No pestilence had ever been so fatal, or so hideous. Blood was its Avatar and its seal—the redness and horror of blood. There were sharp pains, and sudden dizziness, and then profuse bleeding at the pores, with dissolution. The scarlet stains upon the body, and especially upon the face of the victim, were the pest ban which shut him out from the aid and from the sympathy of his fellow men. And the whole seizure, progress, and termination of the disease were the incidents of half an hour. A

But the Prince Prospero was happy and dauntless and sagacious. When his dominions were half depopulated, he summoned to his presence a thousand hale and lighthearted friends from among the knights and dames of his court,

2 **Avatar** (ăv′ə-tär′): the physical form of an unseen force.

5 **pest ban:** announcement of infection with the plague.

A **CLARIFY MEANING**
Use the **side notes** to help you restate lines 1–8. What can you **infer** about the mood of the country from this description?

and with these retired to the deep seclusion of one of his castellated abbeys. This was an extensive and magnificent structure, the creation of the prince's own eccentric yet august taste. A strong and lofty wall girdled it in. This wall had gates of iron. The courtiers, having entered, brought furnaces and massy hammers and welded the bolts. They resolved to leave means neither of ingress or egress to the sudden impulses of despair or of frenzy from within. The abbey was amply provisioned. With such precautions the courtiers might bid defiance to contagion. The external world could take care of itself. In the meantime it was folly to grieve, or to think. The prince had provided all the appliances of pleasure. There were buffoons, there were improvisatori, there were ballet-dancers, there were musicians, there was Beauty, there was wine. All these and security were within. Without was the "Red Death."

It was toward the close of the fifth or sixth month of his seclusion, and while the pestilence raged most furiously abroad, that the Prince Prospero entertained his thousand friends at a masked ball of the most unusual magnificence.

It was a voluptuous scene, that masquerade. But first let me tell of the rooms in which it was held. There were seven—an imperial suite. In many palaces, however, such suites form a long and straight vista, while the folding doors slide back nearly to the walls on either hand, so that the view of the whole extent is scarcely **impeded.** Here the case was very different; as might have been expected from the duke's love of the *bizarre.* The apartments were so irregularly disposed that the vision embraced but little more than one at a time. There was a sharp turn at every twenty or thirty yards, and at each turn a novel effect. To the right and left, in the middle of each wall, a tall and narrow Gothic window looked out upon a closed corridor which pursued the windings of the suite. These windows were of stained glass whose color varied in accordance with the prevailing hue of the decorations of the chamber into which it opened. That at the eastern extremity was hung, for example, in blue—and vividly blue were its windows. The second chamber was purple in its ornaments and tapestries, and here the panes were purple. The third was green throughout, and so were the casements. The fourth was furnished and lighted with orange—the fifth with white—the sixth with violet. The seventh apartment was closely shrouded in black velvet tapestries that hung all over the ceiling and down the walls, falling in heavy folds upon a carpet of the same material and hue. But in this chamber only, the color of the windows failed to correspond with the decorations. The panes here were scarlet—a deep blood color. Now in no one of the seven apartments were there any lamp or candelabrum amid the profusion of golden ornaments that lay scattered to and fro or depended from the roof. There was no light of any kind emanating from lamp or candle within the suite of chambers. But in the corridors that followed the suite, there stood, opposite to each window, a heavy tripod, bearing a brazier of fire that projected its rays through the tinted glass and so glaringly illumined the room. And thus were produced a multitude of gaudy and fantastic appearances. But in the western or black chamber the effect of the firelight that streamed upon the dark hangings through the blood-tinted panes, was

12 castellated abbeys (kăs′tə-lā′tĭd ăb′ēz): castle-like buildings once used as monasteries ("abbeys").

16–17 ingress (ĭn′grĕs′) **or egress** (ē′grĕs′): entry or exit.

18 provisioned: stocked with supplies.

21 improvisatori (ĭm-prŏv′ĭ-zə-tôr′ē): poets who compose verses aloud.

impede (ĭm-pēd′) *v.* to interfere with or slow the progress of

COMMON CORE **RL 3**

B SUSPENSE

Reread Poe's description of the seventh room used by guests of the masquerade party (lines 44–60). Notice that the details establish an eerie **mood**—an important part of Gothic **suspense.** Nothing frightening happens in these lines, but the **setting** itself gives the reader an unsettling sense that terror awaits. How does the narrator's description of the windows (lines 46-48) contribute to the story's suspenseful atmosphere? What effect does firelight in the room have on Prince Prospero's guests? Finally, how does their reaction add to the suspense?

53 brazier (brā′zhər): metal pan for holding a fire.

ghastly in the extreme, and produced so wild a look upon the countenances of those who entered, that there were few of the company bold enough to set foot within its precincts at all. (B)

It was in this apartment, also, that there stood against the western wall a gigantic clock of ebony. Its pendulum swung to and fro with a dull, heavy, monotonous clang; and when the minute hand made the circuit of the face, and the hour was to be stricken, there came from the brazen lungs of the clock a sound which was clear and loud and deep and exceedingly musical, but of so peculiar a note and emphasis that, at each lapse of an hour, the musicians of the orchestra were constrained to pause, momentarily, in their performance, to hearken to the sound; and thus the waltzers perforce ceased their evolutions; and there was a brief disconcert of the whole gay company; and, while the chimes of the clock yet rang, it was observed that the giddiest turned pale, and the more aged and sedate passed their hands over their

58 countenances (koun′tə-nəns-əz): faces.

62 ebony (ĕb′ə-nē): a hard, very dark wood.

64 brazen: brass.

69 evolutions: intricate patterns of movement; **disconcert:** state of confusion.

brows as if in confused **reverie** or meditation. But when the echoes had fully ceased, a light laughter at once pervaded the assembly; the musicians looked at each other and smiled as if at their own nervousness and folly, and made whispering vows, each to the other, that the next chiming of the clock should produce in them no similar emotion; and then, after the lapse of sixty minutes (which embrace three thousand and six hundred seconds of the Time that flies), there came yet another chiming of the clock, and then were the same disconcert and tremulousness and meditation as before. **C**

reverie (rĕv′ə-rē) *n.* daydream

C SUSPENSE
How does the clock described in lines 71-79 contribute to the story's developing suspense?

But, in spite of these things, it was a gay and magnificent revel. The tastes of the duke were peculiar. He had a fine eye for colors and effects. He disregarded the *decora* of mere fashion. His plans were bold and fiery, and his conceptions glowed with barbaric lustre. There are some who would have thought him mad. His followers felt that he was not. It was necessary to hear and see and touch him to be *sure* that he was not.

82 ***decora:*** fine things.

He had directed, in great part, the movable embellishments of the seven chambers, upon occasion of this great *fête;* and it was his own guiding taste which had given character to the masqueraders. Be sure they were grotesque. There were much glare and glitter and piquancy and phantasm—much of what has been seen since in *Hernani.* There were arabesque figures with unsuited limbs and appointments. There were delirious fancies such as the madman fashions. There was much of the beautiful, much of the wanton, much of the *bizarre,* something of the terrible, and not a little of that which might have excited disgust. To and fro in the seven chambers there stalked, in fact, a multitude of dreams. And these—the dreams—writhed in and about, taking hue from the rooms, and causing the wild music of the orchestra to seem as the echo of their steps. And, anon, there strikes the ebony clock which stands in the hall of velvet. And then, for a moment, all is still, and all is silent save the voice of the clock. The dreams are stiff-frozen as they stand. But the echoes of the chime die away—they have endured but an instant—and a light, half-subdued laughter floats after them as they depart. And now again the music swells, and the dreams live, and writhe to and fro more merrily than ever, taking hue from the many-tinted windows through which stream the rays of the tripods. But to the chamber which lies most westwardly of the seven, there are now none of the maskers who venture; for the night is waning away; and there flows a ruddier light through the blood-colored panes; and the blackness of the sable drapery appalls; and to him whose foot falls upon the sable carpet, there comes from the near clock of ebony a muffled peal more solemnly emphatic than any which reaches *their* ears who indulge in the more remote gaieties of the other apartments. **D**

90 ***Hernani*** (ĕr′nä-nē): a play by French writer Victor Hugo, first staged in 1830 and notable for its use of color and spectacle; **arabesque** (ăr′ə-bĕsk′): intricately designed.

D CLARIFY MEANING
Paraphrase lines 104–111. Why do none of the guests venture into the seventh room?

But these other apartments were densely crowded, and in them beat feverishly the heart of life. And the revel went whirlingly on, until at length there commenced the sounding of midnight upon the clock. And then the music ceased, as I have told; and the evolutions of the waltzes were quieted; and there was an uneasy **cessation** of all things as before. But now there were twelve strokes to be sounded by the bell of the clock; and thus

cessation (sĕ-sā′shən) *n.* a coming to an end; a stopping it happened, perhaps, that more of thought crept, with more of time, into the meditations of the thoughtful among those who reveled. And thus, too, it happened, perhaps, that before the last echoes of the last chime had utterly sunk into silence, there were many individuals in the crowd who had found leisure to become aware of the presence of a masked figure which had arrested the attention of no single individual before. And the rumor of this new presence having spread itself whisperingly around, there arose at length from the whole company a buzz, or murmur, expressive of **disapprobation** and surprise—then, finally of terror, of horror, and of disgust.

disapprobation (dĭs-ăp'rə-bā'shən) *n.* disapproval

In an assembly of phantasms such as I have painted, it may well be supposed that no ordinary appearance could have excited such sensation. In truth the masquerade license of the night was nearly unlimited; but the figure in question had out-Heroded Herod, and gone beyond the bounds of even the prince's indefinite decorum. There are chords in the hearts of the most reckless which cannot be touched without emotion. Even with the utterly lost, to whom life and death are equally jests, there are matters of which no jest can be made. The whole company, indeed, seemed now deeply to feel that in the costume and bearing of the stranger neither wit nor **propriety** existed. The figure was tall and gaunt, and shrouded from head to foot in the habiliments of the grave. The mask which concealed the visage was made so nearly to resemble the countenance of a stiffened corpse that the closest scrutiny must have had difficulty in detecting the cheat. And yet all this might have been endured, if not approved, by the mad revellers around. But the mummer had gone so far as to assume the type of the Red Death. His vesture was dabbled in *blood*—and his broad brow, with all the features of the face, was besprinkled with the scarlet horror. **E**

130 out-Heroded Herod: been more extreme than the biblical King Herod, who ordered the deaths of all male babies in order to kill the infant Jesus. This expression is also used in Shakespeare's *Hamlet.*

propriety (prə-prī'ĭ-tē) *n.* the quality of being proper; appropriateness

137 habiliments (hə-bĭl'ə-mənts): clothing.

E CLARIFY MEANING
Reread lines 127–143. Use **context clues** to determine the meaning of the words *decorum, visage,* and *vesture.* What details help explain why the figure's appearance is so shocking?

When the eyes of Prince Prospero fell upon this spectral image (which with a slow and solemn movement, as if more fully to sustain its *role,* stalked to and fro among the waltzers), he was seen to be convulsed, in the first moment with a strong shudder either of terror or distaste; but, in the next, his brow reddened with rage.

"Who dares?" he demanded hoarsely of the courtiers who stood near him—"who dares insult us with this **blasphemous** mockery? Seize him and unmask him—that we may know whom we have to hang at sunrise, from the battlements!"

blasphemous (blăs'fə-məs) *adj.* disrespectful or offensive

It was in the eastern or blue chamber in which stood the Prince Prospero as he uttered these words. They rang throughout the seven rooms loudly and clearly—for the prince was a bold and robust man, and the music had become hushed at the waving of his hand.

It was in the blue room where stood the prince, with a group of pale courtiers by his side. At first, as he spoke, there was a slight rushing movement of this group in the direction of the intruder, who at the moment was also near at hand, and now, with deliberate and stately step, made closer approach to the speaker. But from a certain nameless awe with which the mad assumptions of the mummer had inspired the whole party, there

162 mummer: a person dressed for a masquerade.

were found none who put forth hand to seize him; so that, unimpeded, he passed within a yard of the prince's person; and, while the vast assembly, as if with one impulse, shrank from the centers of the rooms to the walls, he made his way uninterruptedly, but with the same solemn and measured step which had distinguished him from the first, through the blue chamber to the purple—through the purple to the green—through the green to the orange—through this again to the white—and even thence to the violet, ere a decided movement had been made to arrest him. It was then, however, that the Prince Prospero, maddening with rage and the shame of his own momentary cowardice, rushed hurriedly through the six chambers while none followed him on account of a deadly terror that had seized upon all. He bore aloft a drawn dagger, and had approached, in rapid impetuosity, to within three or four feet of the retreating figure, when the latter, having attained the extremity of the velvet apartment, turned suddenly and confronted his pursuer. There was a sharp cry—and the dagger dropped gleaming upon the sable carpet, upon which, instantly afterwards, fell prostrate in death the Prince Prospero. Then, summoning the wild courage of despair, a throng of the revellers at once threw themselves into the black apartment, and seizing the mummer, whose tall figure stood erect and motionless within the shadow of the ebony clock, gasped in unutterable horror at finding the grave-cerements and corpselike mask, which they handled with so violent a rudeness, untenanted by any tangible form. **F**

And now was acknowledged the presence of the Red Death. He had come like a thief in the night. And one by one dropped the revellers in the blood-bedewed halls of their revel, and died each in the despairing posture of his fall. And the life of the ebony clock went out with that of the last of the gay. And the flames of the tripods expired. And Darkness and Decay and the Red Death held illimitable dominion over all.

COMMON CORE L 2b, L 4c

Language Coach

English Spelling Usually you write *ie* when the sound is long *e*, except after *c*. *Seize* (line 163), which has a long *e* sound, is an exception. Pronounce the following words aloud: *either, neighbor, protein, height*. Check your pronunciations in a dictionary.

183–184 finding the . . . form: ripping off the figure's burial garments and mask to find nothing underneath.

F SUSPENSE
How does the quickening pace of the plot's closing moments contribute to this story's suspense?

190 illimitable dominion (ĭ-lĭm′ĭ-tə-bəl də-mĭn′yən): unlimited power.

Comprehension

1. **Recall** Why does Prince Prospero seal himself and his guests in the abbey?
2. **Recall** What effect does the striking of the clock have on the revellers?
3. **Summarize** What happens after the mysterious figure is unmasked?

Text Analysis

4. **Make Inferences** What does each of the following reveal about Prince Prospero?
   - his response to the crisis in his country (lines 1–12)
   - his plans for the masquerade (lines 86–94)
   - his response to the masked figure (lines 144–152)
5. **Clarify Meaning** Explain how context clues and the author's use of suspense help you to understand the narrator's description of firelight (lines 51-60).
6. **Analyze Descriptive Details** For each of the following examples, identify the contrast drawn between the seventh room and the rest of Prince Prospero's suite. Based on these contrasts, what might the seventh room represent?
   - its decorations (lines 44–48)
   - its location (lines 104–105)
   - its atmosphere (lines 56–60)
   - what occurs there (lines 174–179)
7. **Evaluate Suspense** For you as a reader, what is the most suspenseful moment in Poe's story and how does the narrator create suspense at this point? Support your answer with evidence from the story.
8. **Analyze Mood** As you learned reading "The Fall of the House of Usher" (page 412), the mood or atmosphere of Poe's stories contributes to an overall unity of effect. What kind of mood does Poe establish in "The Masque of the Red Death"? How does the mood of the story contribute to the suspense? Support your response with evidence from the selection.

Text Criticism

9. **Critical Interpretations** Some critics have argued that "The Masque of the Red Death" takes place in Prospero's mind. Cite details from the story that support this interpretation. How does this view change the story's meaning?

Is SAFETY *an illusion?*

Consider the desperate measures the characters take to achieve safety. In what ways, if any, do their behaviors reflect real-world responses to a deadly threat?

COMMON CORE

RL 1 Cite evidence to support analysis of inferences drawn from the text. **RL 3** Analyze the impact of the author's choices regarding how to develop and relate elements of a story. **RL 4** Determine the meanings of words and phrases as they are used in the text, including figurative and connotative meanings; analyze the impact of specific word choices on meaning and tone. **L 4a** Use context as a clue to the meaning of a word or phrase.

Vocabulary in Context

▲ VOCABULARY PRACTICE

Show you understand the vocabulary words by answering these questions.

1. Will an attempt to **impede** the passage of a law speed up the process or slow it down?
2. Would a **blasphemous** comment be considered controversial or appeasing?
3. Which would more likely result in a parent's **disapprobation**—a detention or a school award?
4. Would someone's **reverie** make them attentive or distracted?
5. If I act with **propriety,** am I being polite or asking uncomfortable questions?
6. Which would cause the **cessation** of a conversation—one participant nodding in agreement or one participant walking away?

WORD LIST

blasphemous
cessation
disapprobation
impede
propriety
reverie

ACADEMIC VOCABULARY IN SPEAKING

• construct • expand • indicate • reinforce • role

Poe, who was a master of horror stories, sometimes **constructed** his stories around true accounts. In a small group, discuss what inspires you to write creatively. Then, **expand** this idea by brainstorming where professional writers get their inspiration. Use at least three of the Academic Vocabulary words in your discussion.

VOCABULARY STRATEGY: AFFIXES AND SPELLING CHANGES

Some base words are hard to recognize because they are spelled differently when affixes are added. For example, the vocabulary word *cessation* includes the base word *cease* and the suffix *-ation.* Note how the spelling of the base word changes in the new word. These spelling changes may reflect the word's etymology (its history and origins), or they may simply reflect new pronunciation that made the word easier to say. To decipher words of this type, look for related base words and use context clues to unlock meaning.

PRACTICE Identify the appropriate base word for each of the following numbered words. Then write a sentence that demonstrates the meaning of each numbered word. Finally, use a dictionary to research the word's origins. Did the spelling change as a result of the word's history?

1. derisive
2. contentious
3. impermeable
4. pomposity
5. acclamation
6. irrevocable
7. despicable
8. incessant
9. sobriety
10. commensurate

COMMON CORE

L 2b Spell correctly. **L 4b–c** Identify and use patterns of word changes that indicate different meanings or parts of speech; consult reference materials. **L 6** Acquire and use academic words and phrases.

Interactive Vocabulary THINK central

Go to thinkcentral.com.
KEYWORD: HML11-454

Essay

In "The Masque of the Red Death," you experienced suspense. Now, in an excerpt from Stephen King's *Danse Macabre*, you'll read about what creates suspense in a work of art.

from *Danse Macabre*

Essay by Stephen King

BACKGROUND Stephen King may well be the best-known writer of horror fiction since Edgar Allan Poe. In 1981, after writing a number of best-selling novels, King wrote *Stephen King's Danse Macabre*, a nonfiction work in which he discussed horror in literature and film and examined the psychology of terror. The book's title is a reference to the "Dance of Death," a symbolic representation of death, in the form of a skeleton, leading people to their graves. This dance was commonly depicted on cemetery walls and in the European art of the Middle Ages and the Renaissance.

I want to say something about imagination purely as a tool in the art and science of scaring people. The idea isn't original with me; I heard it expressed by William F. Nolan at the 1979 World Fantasy Convention. Nothing is so frightening as what's behind the closed door, Nolan said. You approach the door in the old, deserted house, and you hear something scratching at it. The audience holds its breath along with the protagonist as she or he (more often she) approaches that door. The protagonist throws it open, and there is a ten-foot-tall bug. The audience screams, but this particular scream has an oddly relieved sound to it. "A bug ten feet tall is pretty horrible," the audience thinks, "but I can deal with a ten-foot-tall bug. I was afraid it might be a *hundred* feet tall.". . . Ⓐ

Bill Nolan was speaking as a screenwriter when he offered the example of the big bug behind the door, but the point applies to all media. What's behind the door or lurking at the top of the stairs is never as frightening as the door or the staircase itself. And because of this, comes the paradox: the artistic work of horror is almost always a disappointment. It is the classic no-win situation. You can scare people with the unknown for a long, long time (the classic example, as Bill Nolan also pointed out, is the Jacques Tourneur film with Dana Andrews, *Curse of the Demon*), but sooner or later, as in poker, you have to turn your down cards up. You have to open the door and show the audience what's behind it. And if what happens to be behind it is a bug, not ten but a hundred feet tall, the audience heaves a sigh of relief (or utters a scream

Ⓐ **SUSPENSE**
In lines 4–10, how does the image of a door, with a giant bug behind it, contribute to your understanding of suspense? Explain.

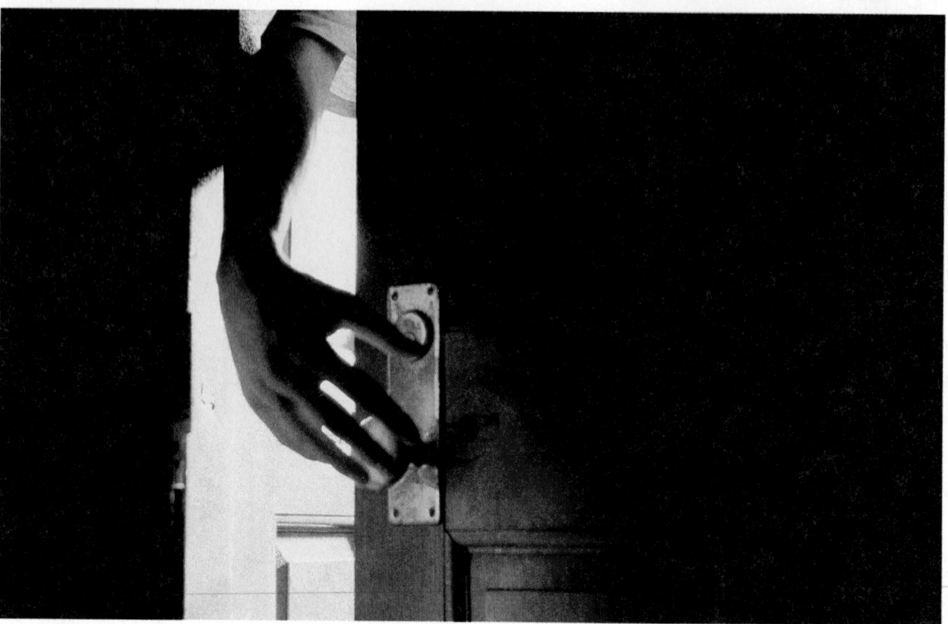

THEME
The most famous of all vampires, Dracula originated in Bram Stoker's novel of the same name. The mythic figure of the vampire inspired many literary, dramatic, and film versions. Some adaptations stay close to the spirit of Stoker's novel, in which Dracula was a disturbing, even repulsive character. But many portray vampires as desirable, mysterious, even romantic figures. Stephenie Meyer's series of vampire novels, beginning with *Twilight*, features a contemporary romance between two teenagers, one of whom is a vampire. Why do vampires continue to fascinate us?

of relief) and thinks, "A bug a hundred feet tall is pretty horrible, but I can deal with that. I was afraid it might be a *thousand* feet tall." . . . B

The danse macabre is a waltz with death. This is a truth we cannot afford to shy away from.

Like the rides in the amusement park which mimic violent death, the tale of horror is a chance to examine what's going on behind doors which we usually keep double-locked. Yet the human imagination is not content with locked doors. Somewhere there is another dancing partner, the imagination whispers in the night—a partner in a rotting ball gown, a partner with empty eyesockets, green mold growing on her elbow-length gloves, maggots squirming in the thin remains of her hair. To hold such a creature in our arms? Who, you ask me, would be so mad? Well . . . ?

"You will not want to open this door," Bluebeard tells his wife in that most horrible of all horror stories, "because your husband has forbidden it." But this, of course, only makes her all the more curious . . . and at last, her curiosity is satisfied. C

"You may go anywhere you wish in the castle," Count Dracula tells Jonathan Harker, "except where the doors are locked, where of course you will not wish to go." But Harker goes soon enough.

And so do we all. Perhaps we go to the forbidden door or window willingly because we understand that a time comes when we must go whether we want to or not . . . and not just to look, but to be pushed through. Forever.

B CLARIFY MEANING
Explain the meaning of *danse macabre,* and identify the context clues that help you understand what the phrase means.

C SUSPENSE
Reread lines 33–35. What does Bluebeard's wife reveal about the human response to suspense? Explain your answer, citing ideas from King's essay.

Movie Poster

The movie poster shown on this page advertised *Wait Until Dark*, a very successful movie from 1967. Based on a stage play, the film tells the story of a recently blind woman threatened by thugs in her basement apartment. The poster's split image shows a match flame in the dark and the dimly lit face of a woman opening her mouth to scream. Think about how the image works with the words in the poster to create suspense. Respond to the questions below, citing evidence from the poster to support your answers.

COMMON CORE

RI 7 Evaluate multiple sources of information presented in different media or formats as well as in words to address a question.

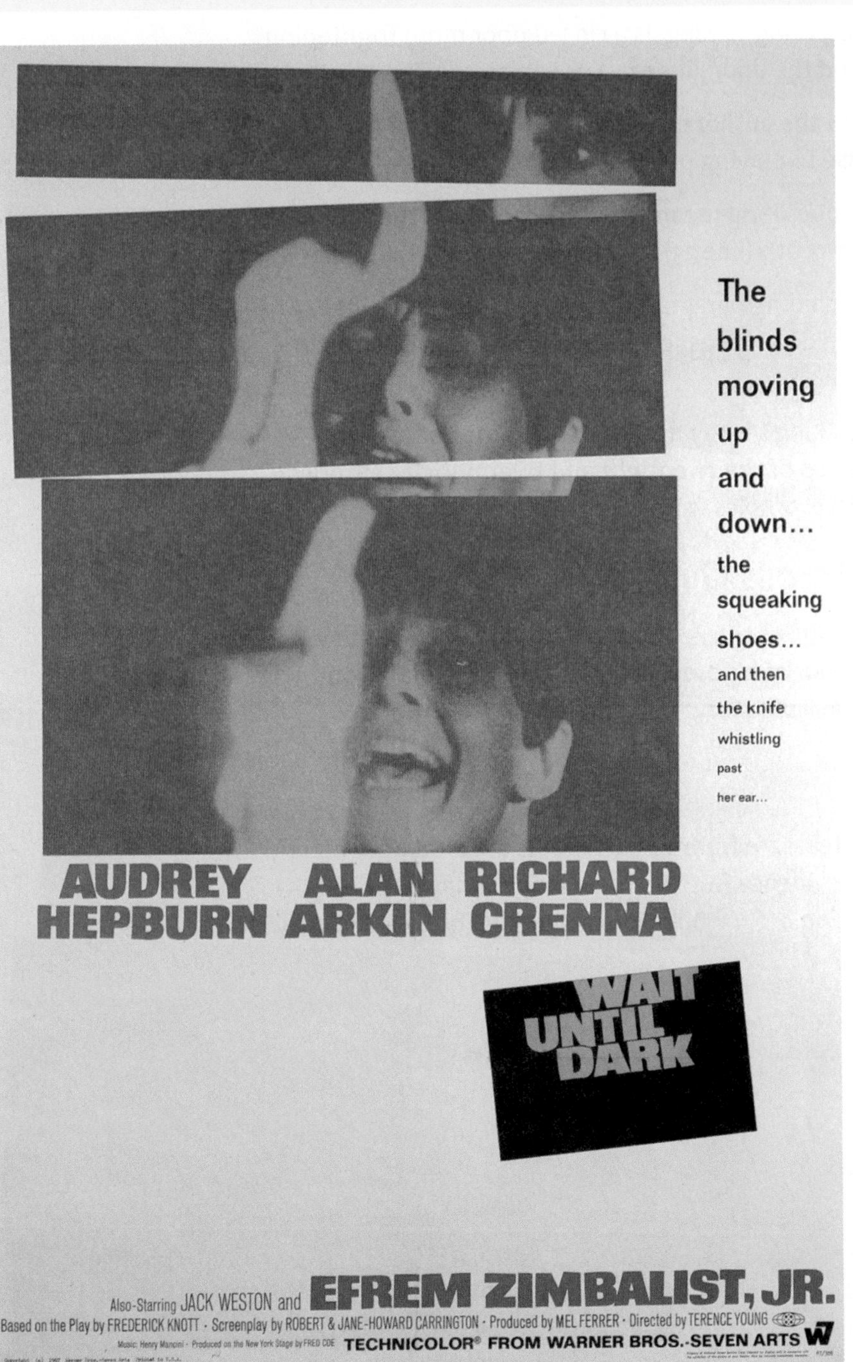

1. **ANALYZE**
   Study the split image in the poster. Examine the woman's facial expression and the contrast between darkness and the match flame. What kind of atmosphere do these elements create? If you had only the images to analyze, what kind of story would you expect them to represent?

2. **INTERPRET**
   Examine the language to the right of the split image. How do the words themselves and the diminishing type size contribute to the impact of the poster? What purpose do they help the poster to achieve?

Comprehension

1. **Summarize** According to Stephen King, what makes a closed door so frightening?
2. **Clarify** In this discussion of suspense, what do some amusement park rides have in common with tales of horror?

COMMON CORE

RI 1 Cite evidence to support analysis of inferences draw from the text. **RI 4** Determine the meaning of words and phrases as they are used in a text, including figurative, connotative and technical meanings.

Text Analysis

3. **Analyze Suspense** Why, according to King, is a closed door more frightening than what is actually behind the door (lines 12-13)? Explain.
4. **Clarify Meaning** What does the author mean, in lines 17-18, when he compares creating suspense to playing poker? Explain.
5. **Interpret Metaphor** What does King mean when he compares the experience of suspense to a waltz with death (line 23)?
6. **Clarify Meaning** In the concluding paragraph, why does King think we willingly open the forbidden door of suspense? Support your answer with evidence from the text.
7. **Make Inferences** How does King's essay help to explain the success of suspenseful books and movies of the twentieth and twenty-first centuries? Support your response with examples from your own reading or film viewing.

Comparing Themes Across Genres

8. What elements in "The Masque of the Red Death" (page 446) illustrate what King means with his metaphor of a closed, forbidden door? Explain your answer, citing evidence from Poe's story.

Is SAFETY *an illusion*?

A locked door can make us feel safe from threats. But is a locked door merely an illusion of safety? Using evidence from Stephen King's essay, explain how he would answer this question. How would you answer the question? Explain your answer.

Assessment Practice: Short Constructed Response

LITERARY TEXT: "THE MASQUE OF THE RED DEATH"

On assessments you are expected to read carefully and answer questions that focus on particular passages from a text. To strengthen your close-reading skills, read the **short constructed response question** at left below and practice the strategies suggested at right.

Examine Poe's description of the effect a masked figure has on guests at the masked ball. How does this description contribute to the story's developing suspense?

STRATEGIES IN ACTION

1. List words or phrases that have a foreboding tone.
2. Identify elements of the action that cause anxiety for the guests and the reader.
3. Use evidence you circled or underlined to support your answer.

NONFICTION TEXT: from DANSE MACABRE

On assessments you are expected to identify key ideas in a piece of text. Practice this skill as you respond to the **short constructed response question** below. Be sure to follow the steps outlined to the right of the question.

In the opening paragraph, King introduces a metaphor that expresses the central idea of the text. What is the metaphor and what idea does it express about suspense?

STRATEGIES IN ACTION

1. Reread the opening paragraph and identify a metaphor/idea that plays a key role in the rest of the essay.
2. Briefly explain the idea conveyed by the metaphor and identify why it is so important to King.

COMPARING LITERARY AND NONFICTION TEXTS

To succeed on assessments, you will need to identify thematic connections between literary and nonfiction texts. Practice this valuable skill by responding to the following **short constructed response question** about "The Masque of the Red Death" and the excerpt from *Danse Macabre*.

As a nonfiction text, *Danse Macabre* has an explicit main idea. Poe's short story, by contrast, has an implied theme. What is King's explicit main idea and how is it reflected in "The Masque of the Red Death"?

STRATEGIES IN ACTION

1. Reread King's opening paragraph and identify the essay's main idea.
2. From Poe's story, select two or three details or scenes that illustrate King's main idea.

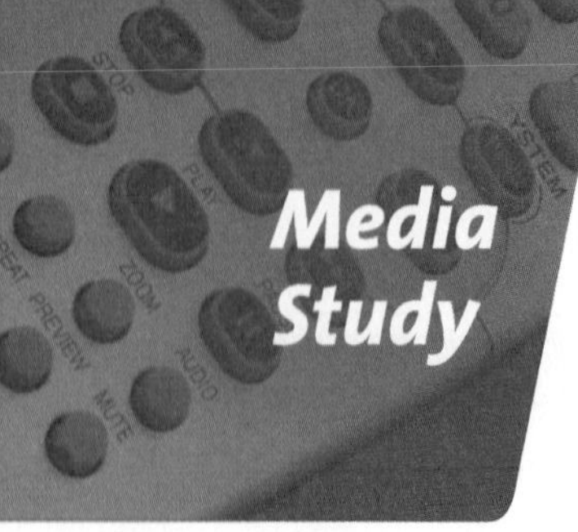

Media Study

Illustrations Inspired by Poe

Image Collection on MediaSmart DVD-ROM

COMMON CORE

RL 7 Analyze multiple interpretations of a story, evaluating how each version interprets the source text.

What does GOTHIC *look like?*

Shadows and gargoyles and pervading gloom all evoke the **gothic spirit** that Edgar Allan Poe depicted so well in his stories and poems. Countless artists have been inspired by Poe's works—writers, musicians, architects, and certainly visual artists. British illustrator Arthur Rackham had a particular affinity for Poe's writing. In examining Rackham's illustrations in this lesson, you'll see how an artist influenced by Poe's gothic style expresses his own personal interpretation.

Background

American Gothic It's not simply the plots and characters Poe created that have mesmerized readers and artists over time. It's what his writing revealed of our dark side, of our capacity for decadence and even insanity, that has given him such lasting influence. Though the term *gothic* has been applied to other art forms such as architecture and music, it is in Poe's writing that the psychological elements of gothic are most sharply defined.

At the time Poe's work was first published, illustrators were regularly hired to create images to accompany his text. As Poe's reputation grew and more people read his often disturbing stories, painters and artists found great imaginative fodder in Poe's phantasmagorical tales. You can see his influence in the work of countless illustrators over the past 150 years, including Poe contemporary Gustave Doré, Arthur Rackham, Edward Gorey, Charles Addams (creator of "The Addams Family" cartoon), and even popular children's book illustrator Stephen Gammell. Many of today's graphic novelists are heavily influenced by Poe's sense of gothic.

Media Literacy: Art Elements in Illustrations

In Edgar Allan Poe's writing, he often expresses his style through imagery that re-creates certain sensory experiences. In "The Fall of the House of Usher," Poe's description of the house is one of decay and desolation. In order to translate such descriptions into a visual image, an illustrator relies on the art elements of **color, line, shape,** and **texture** to evoke similar feelings. Another aspect of visual art is **dominance,** which is created when one or more parts of an image are given more importance than the others.

Consider these elements when analyzing this 1935 Arthur Rackham illustration for "The Fall of the House of Usher." Think about the deliberate stylistic choices made by the illustrator to match the mood and tone of Poe's writing.

STRATEGIES FOR ANALYZING ILLUSTRATIONS

1. **Color** is used to highlight important aspects and create mood in an image. To analyze an illustrator's use of color, think about the overall mood of the image. Are the colors warm (red and orange) or cool (blue and green)? Do the muted colors in this image seem to reflect Poe's descriptions?

2. **Line** is a stroke or a mark. Vertical, horizontal, jagged, curved—lines have expressive qualities. Look at the style of lines an artist uses. Here, for example, the vertical lines are strong and varied and suggest the dreary atmosphere of Poe's setting.

3. **Shape** is the outline of an object in an image. Notice the tension created by the strong yet warped lines of the dead trees against the severe lines of the house.

4. **Texture** is the surface quality of an image. Examine how this artist manipulates visual elements to create different textures. Ask yourself: If I could touch this image, how would it feel?

5. Be aware of the primary object that draws your eye. Here the house of Usher is the dominant image.

Media Smart DVD-ROM

- **Selection 1:** "The Fall of The House of Usher"
- **Selection 2:** "The Pit and the Pendulum"
- **Type:** Illustration
- **Illustrator:** Arthur Rackham

Viewing Guide for

Illustrations Inspired by Poe

Access the full-sized images on the DVD. Examine each image carefully, jotting down your initial impressions. Look for common elements, themes, and subjects in the images. To help you analyze each image in terms of color, shape, line, texture, and dominance, use the viewing strategies detailed on page 461. You can also refer to the Elements of Design section of the Media Handbook (pages R94–R95). Answer the questions to help you analyze the images.

NOW VIEW

FIRST VIEWING: Comprehension

1. **Describe** Where does the narrator of "The Fall of the House of Usher" appear in Rackham's illustration?
2. **Identify** Where is the man standing in "The Pit and the Pendulum" illustration?

CLOSE VIEWING: Media Literacy

3. **Analyze Color** What colors does Rackham use in the "House of Usher" illustration, and what mood do these create? Explain your answer.
4. **Compare Line** Look carefully at the way line is used in both illustrations. In which image is line used most effectively? Explain.
5. **Compare Dominance** Consider the images for "The Fall of the House of Usher" and "The Pit and the Pendulum." One part of each image is dominant. How does the illustrator achieve this effect? Think about
   - the use of shape in the images
   - how color is used to create dominance

Write or Discuss

Describe Unity of Effect Poe believed in writing to achieve "unity of effect," in which every detail of a work contributes to a single overall feeling. This idea guided his word choices, sentence structures, and subject matter. Look at the two Rackham illustrations in this Media Study. How do you think Rackham's decisions as an artist create unity of effect? Describe to your classmates what Rackham achieves with these gothic images. Consider these elements:

- Rackham's use of color, line, shape, and texture in the images
- the parts of Poe's stories that each work depicts
- the overall mood of each illustration

Produce Your Own Media

Create Gothic Artwork How would you visually represent something in the gothic style? Use your understanding of the term to create a gothic piece of **artwork.** It can be a photograph, a painting, a computer-generated image, a drawing, even a collage of magazine clippings.

HERE'S HOW Here are a few suggestions for creating gothic visual art:

- No matter what type of gothic piece you will create, make notes on your intentions and how you plan to achieve them.
- Decide on the psychological mood you want to express.
- Keep in mind the visual art elements.
- Consider what colors you'll need to use. If creating a gothic photograph, consider the lighting effects you might employ, or whether to use color or black-and-white film.
- Try to establish a dominant element in your piece, something that the viewer will quickly focus on.

Further Exploration

Contrasting Styles Revisit the variety of additional Poe-inspired images on the DVD, or look for other examples on your own. Explore how these works are all influenced by Poe's writing in some way. What Poe-inspired similarities can you find between the images? Cite specific elements from the images. Think about

- line, shape, color, and texture
- how the images reflect a gothic sensibility
- how the images express the psychological

Find the Gothic in Your Life Think about other art forms—movies, music, live theater—where you find gothic elements. Describe a movie, song, or play in which you can identify these elements.

COMMON CORE

RL 7 Analyze multiple interpretations of a story, evaluating how each version interprets the source text. **SL 1a** Research material under study and refer to evidence from the texts and other research to stimulate an exchange of ideas. **SL 2** Integrate information presented in diverse formats and media. **SL 4** Present findings, conveying a clear perspective, such that listeners can follow the line of reasoning, and the organization, development and style are appropriate to the purpose and audience.

Tech Tip

If available, use a design program to turn a photograph of a happy occasion into a gothic representation.

American Masterpiece

from Moby Dick

Novel by Herman Melville

Herman Melville

COMMON CORE

RL 3 Analyze the impact of the author's choices regarding how to develop and relate elements of a story.

BACKGROUND "Call me Ishmael," says the narrator of *Moby Dick* in the novel's famous opening words. Ishmael, the sole survivor of the lost whaling ship the *Pequod*, tells the story of Captain Ahab and his relentless pursuit of the great white whale, Moby Dick. A tale of harrowing adventure, *Moby Dick* is also a complex examination of obsession, of the conflict between fate and free will. A critical and financial failure during Herman Melville's lifetime (1819–1891), the novel is recognized today as one of the greatest works of American fiction.

TEXT ANALYSIS In the scene you are about to read, Captain Ahab speaks with several of his crewmen about Moby Dick. Melville uses **dialogue** to provide explicit information about the white whale, but in the way each of the characters speaks, the author also **characterizes** Captain Ahab and the crewmen present in this scene. As you read the scene, pay special attention to Captain Ahab as the main speaker. What do you learn from him about Moby Dick? What is his attitude toward the whale? What do you learn about Captain Ahab's personal history that can help you to understand his motivation for hunting the white whale?

UNDERSTAND DIALOGUE After you have read the scene, complete a chart like the one below, providing details for each category.

Dialogue	
News about Moby Dick:	Speaker's attitude:
News about Ahab:	Ahab's motivation:

Whenever you read dialogue, concentrate on two things—the information provided by speaking characters and the way their words convey what kind of characters they are.

"Whosoever of ye raises me a white-headed whale with a wrinkled brow and a crooked jaw; whosoever of ye raises me that white-headed whale, with three holes punctured in his starboard fluke—look ye, whosoever of ye raises me that same white whale, he shall have this gold ounce, my boys!"

"Huzza! huzza!" cried the seamen, as with swinging tarpaulins they hailed the act of nailing the gold to the mast.

"It's a white whale, I say," resumed Ahab, as he threw down the top-maul; "a white whale. Skin your eyes for him, men; look sharp for white water; if ye see but a bubble, sing out."

All this while Tashtego, Daggoo, and Queequeg had looked on with even more intense interest and surprise than the rest, and at the mention of the wrinkled brow and crooked jaw they had started as if each was separately touched by some specific recollection.

"Captain Ahab," said Tashtego, "that white whale must be the same that some call Moby Dick."

"Moby Dick?" shouted Ahab. "Do ye know the white whale then, Tash?"

"Does he fan-tail a little curious, sir, before he goes down?" said the Gay-Header deliberately.

"And has he a curious spout, too," said Daggoo, "very bushy, even for a parmacetty, and mighty quick, Captain Ahab?"

"And he have one, two, tree-oh! good many iron in him hide, too, Captain," cried Queequeg disjointedly, "all twisketee be-twisk, like him—him—" faltering hard for a word, and screwing his hand round and round as though uncorking a bottle—"like him—him—"

"Corkscrew!" cried Ahab, "aye, Queequeg, the harpoons lie all twisted and wrenched in him; aye, Daggoo, his spout is a big one, like a whole shock of wheat, and white as a pile of our Nantucket wool after the great annual sheep-shearing; aye, Tashtego, and he fan-tails like a split jib in a squall. Death and devils! men, it is Moby Dick ye have seen—Moby Dick—Moby Dick!"

"Captain Ahab," said Starbuck, who with Stubb and Flask, had thus far been eyeing his superior with increasing surprise, but at last seemed struck with a thought which somewhat explained all the wonder. "Captain Ahab, I have heard of Moby Dick—but it was not Moby Dick that took off thy leg?"

"Who told thee that?" cried Ahab; then pausing, "Aye, Starbuck, aye, my hearties all round; it was Moby Dick that dismasted me; Moby Dick that brought me to this dead stump I stand on now. Aye, aye," he shouted with a terrific, loud, animal sob, like that of a heart-stricken moose; "Aye, aye! it was that accursed white whale that razed me; made a poor pegging lubber of me forever and a day!" Then tossing both arms, with measureless imprecations he shouted out: "Aye, aye! and I'll chase him round Good Hope, and round the Horn, and round the Norway Maelstrom, and round perdition's flames before I give him up. And this is what ye have shipped for, men! to chase that white whale on both sides of land, and over all sides of earth, till he spouts black blood and rolls fin out. What say ye, men, will ye splice hands on it, now? I think ye do look brave."

"Aye, aye!" shouted the harpooneers and seamen, running closer to the excited old man: "A sharp eye for the White Whale; a sharp lance for Moby Dick!"

American Masterpiece

from The Scarlet Letter

Novel by Nathaniel Hawthorne

Nathaniel Hawthorne

COMMON CORE

RL 6 Analyze a case in which grasping a point of view requires distinguishing what is directly stated in a text from what is really meant. **W 4** Produce clear and coherent writing in which the development, organization, and style are appropriated to task, purpose, and audience.

BACKGROUND Published in 1850, *The Scarlet Letter* is a short historical novel set in Salem in the earliest days of the Massachusetts Bay colony. Vividly re-creating the world of Puritan New England, Nathaniel Hawthorne's novel explores universal themes of sin, retribution, and forgiveness. It traces the story of Hester Prynne, who commits the sin of adultery and is publicly punished for it, and the two men in her life—her one-time lover and her vengeful husband—who keep their own sins hidden from public view. Part of Hester's punishment is to wear, for all her life, a scarlet letter *A* sewn onto the bodice of her gown. "The publication of *The Scarlet Letter* was in the United States a literary event of the first importance," wrote author and critic Henry James. The carefully crafted novel, with its serious themes and complex symbolism, showed that writers in the young nation could produce literature equal to that of Britain and could draw on America's history and heritage in producing it.

TEXT ANALYSIS In the following scene from the novel's opening, Hester Prynne is about to appear in public for the first time with the scarlet letter on her gown. Waiting for her appearance outside the jail door, members of the community talk about her and her crime. As the focus shifts from one speaker to another, readers get slightly different perspectives on Hester. All of the women condemn her, but they each have their own point of view. Some are harsher than others, and some hint at Hester's strong and defiant personality, which will emerge as a major force in the novel. Read the passage carefully, and note how the shifts in point of view slowly reveal a subtle range of attitudes in the community.

WRITE We have all stood in a group of people and discussed (or heard discussed) another person's behavior or situation. In some cases, the tone might have been respectful and generous; in others, it may have been gossipy and judgmental. Imagine that you have just witnessed such a discussion about someone who is accused of committing a crime. Imagine what that crime was, what the speakers might say, and how their views and perspectives might be subtly or completely different. Then write the scene out, using the excerpt on the right as a model for formatting and punctuation.

Literature Connections
The Scarlet Letter
Nathaniel Hawthorne
And Related Readings
McDougal Littell

"Goodwives," said a hard-featured dame of fifty, "I'll tell ye a piece of my mind. It would be greatly for the public behoof, if we women, being of mature age and church-members in good repute, should have the handling of such malefactresses as this Hester Prynne. What think ye, gossips? If the hussy stood up for judgment before us five, that are now here in a knot together, would she come off with such a sentence as the worshipful magistrates have awarded? Marry, I trow not!"

"People say," said another, "that the Reverend Master Dimmesdale, her godly pastor, takes it very grievously to heart that such a scandal should have come upon his congregation."

"The magistrates are God-fearing gentlemen, but merciful overmuch, — that is a truth," added a third autumnal matron. "At the very least, they should have put the brand of a hot iron on Hester Prynne's forehead. Madam Hester would have winced at that, I warrant me. But she, — the naughty baggage, — little will she care what they put upon the bodice of her gown! Why, look you, she may cover it with a brooch, or such like heathenish adornment, and so walk the streets as brave as ever!"

"Ah, but," interposed, more softly, a young wife, holding a child by the hand, "let her cover the mark as she will, the pang of it will be always in her heart."

"What do we talk of marks and brands, whether on the bodice of her gown, or the flesh of her forehead?" cried another female, the ugliest as well as the most pitiless of these self-constituted judges. "This woman has brought shame upon us all, and ought to die. Is there not law for it? Truly there is, both in the Scripture and the statute-book. Then let the magistrates, who have made it of no effect, thank themselves if their own wives and daughters go astray!"

"Mercy on us, goodwife," exclaimed a man in the crowd, "is there no virtue in woman, save what springs from a wholesome fear of the gallows? That is the hardest word yet! Hush, now, gossips; for the lock is turning in the prison-door, and here comes Mistress Prynne herself."

American Gothic

The Minister's Black Veil

Short Story by Nathaniel Hawthorne

VIDEO TRAILER  KEYWORD: HML11-468A

COMMON CORE

RL 1 Cite evidence to support analysis of what the text says explicitly as well as inferences drawn from the text, including determining where the text leaves matters uncertain. **RL 3** Analyze the impact of the author's choices regarding how to develop and relate elements of a story. **L 4b–c** Identify and use patterns of word changes that indicate different meanings or parts of speech; consult reference materials.

DID YOU KNOW?

Nathaniel Hawthorne . . .

- achieved his first literary success writing stories for children.
- was a mentor to Herman Melville, who dedicated *Moby Dick* to him.
- wrote a campaign biography for his college friend Franklin Pierce, who became the 14th U.S. president.

Meet the Author

Nathaniel Hawthorne c. 1804–1864

An intensely private man who allowed few to know him well, Nathaniel Hawthorne was fascinated by the dark secrets of human nature. In his greatest novels and short stories, including his masterpieces *The Scarlet Letter* and *The House of the Seven Gables,* he explored such themes as sin, hypocrisy, and guilt. One of the first American writers to explore his characters' hidden motivations, Hawthorne broke new ground in American literature with his morally complex characters.

Legacy of Guilt Born in Salem, Hawthorne was a descendant of the Puritan settlers of Massachusetts. His great-great-grandfather was a judge at the infamous Salem witch trials—the only one who refused to apologize for his role in sentencing innocent people to death. Though he tried to distance himself from his family's dark legacy, Hawthorne shared the Puritan belief that people are basically sinful. But where Puritans believed that society could be purified by the actions of a righteous few, Hawthorne was more pessimistic: he believed that perfection was impossible and remained skeptical of all attempts to reform or improve society.

Difficult Compromises Throughout his life, Hawthorne was torn between his literary calling and his desire for a stable, respectable profession. By the time he left for Bowdoin College in 1821, Hawthorne knew he wanted to write. After graduation, he lived alone for 12 years, dedicated to building his literary career. By 1842, he had achieved some success and had married his great love, Sophia Peabody. Their otherwise happy marriage was constantly shadowed by financial woes. When times were tough, Hawthorne had well-connected friends set him up with government jobs, whose dull routines choked his imagination and limited his time to write. Although he never stopped writing, work, illness, and family duties dominated Hawthorne's later years. He died in 1864 of a sudden illness.

Challenging Questions One of Hawthorne's great talents was his mastery of symbolism. He often chose symbols whose meaning was ambiguous, forcing readers to think deeply about his characters and their conflicts. Despite his pessimism, he found hope in the redeeming power of love, a theme he developed in his mature works. Hawthorne's efforts to come to terms with his own past inspired profound reflections on American identity that still resonate today.

Author Online THINK central

Go to thinkcentral.com. KEYWORD: HML11-468B

TEXT ANALYSIS: SYMBOL

A **symbol** is something concrete—a person, a place, an object, or an action—used to stand for an abstract idea or feeling. In some works, symbols may be subtle and hard to identify. In this story, Hawthorne identifies his main symbol outright:

Know, then, this veil is a type and a symbol . . .

Stories of veiled or masked figures can be traced back to myth. Such stories continue to fascinate audiences today. The challenge for readers is to interpret the symbolism of the veil. A rich symbol has many possible meanings. To interpret the veil or mask story, pay close attention to the veil's context in the work, including ideas and feelings associated with it and how it affects the **plot,** or the structure of the story.

As you read, use a concept map to note details about the minister's black veil, the main symbol in this story.

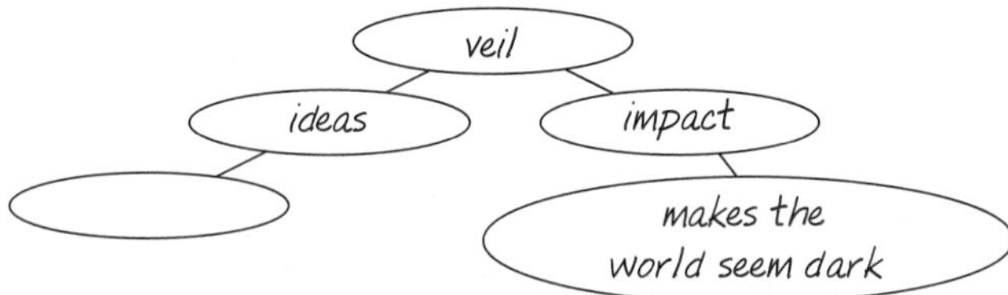

READING SKILL: IDENTIFY CULTURAL CHARACTERISTICS

As you read, keep in mind that the story is set in an 18th-century Puritan town. The parishioners' responses to their minister are meant to illustrate the traits that, in Hawthorne's eyes, define Puritan culture. As the story unfolds, think about the values, beliefs, and social constraints that are revealed by the parishioners' behavior.

VOCABULARY IN CONTEXT

The boldfaced words helped Hawthorne tell his tale of Puritan life. Use context clues to write a definition of each.

1. messages filled with confusion and **ambiguity**
2. a **zealous** speaker whose eyes blazed intensely
3. a tale of sin and **iniquity**
4. an event so unusual that it seemed **preternatural**
5. an **ostentatious** costume that made people stare
6. **imbued** with great hopes for the future
7. her **tremulous** voice that revealed her nervousness
8. a sign that might **portend** trouble ahead

Complete the activities in your **Reader/Writer Notebook**.

How does someone become a STRANGER?

Your best friend suddenly doesn't like the things she's always liked. Your brother comes home from college with a new haircut, listening to strange new music. What happens when someone you thought you knew changes? Can you still recognize the person you knew, or do his or her new behaviors lead to estrangement?

QUICKWRITE Recall a time when someone close to you changed in a way that made him or her seem like a different person. Write a paragraph to describe the change. Explain why it made you see the person so differently.

THE MINISTER'S BLACK VEIL

Nathaniel Hawthorne

BACKGROUND In the Puritan town of 18th-century Massachusetts, the meetinghouse was the center of the community life. Used for both religious and civil gatherings, meetinghouses were simple and plain, with no obviously religious decorations. Families did not sit together during religious services, which lasted most of the day on Sundays. Men and women sat on opposite sides, and worshipers were seated according to their age and social standing. The oldest and most distinguished citizens were rewarded with seats closest to the pulpit, the raised platform from which the pastor delivered his sermons. As services began, all eyes turned expectantly toward the pulpit, awaiting the pastor's entrance.

Analyze Visuals ▶
Simplicity was a central value of Puritan life. What elements of this painting help create its simple style? Consider the use of color, line, and texture, as well as the composition of the image, in your answer.

The sexton[1] stood in the porch of Milford meetinghouse, pulling lustily at the bell rope. The old people of the village came stooping along the street. Children, with bright faces, tripped merrily beside their parents, or mimicked a graver gait,[2] in the conscious dignity of their Sunday clothes. Spruce bachelors looked sidelong at the pretty maidens, and fancied that the Sabbath sunshine made them prettier than on weekdays. When the throng had mostly streamed into the porch, the sexton began to toll the bell, keeping his eye on the Reverend Mr. Hooper's door. The first glimpse of the clergyman's figure was the signal for the bell to cease its summons. **A**

A CULTURAL CHARACTERISTICS
Reread lines 1–9. What details reveal the importance of Sunday worship for the people of Milford?

1. **sexton:** church employee who takes care of church property and performs various other duties.
2. **mimicked a graver gait:** followed their parents' example and walked in a more dignified way.

Church at Head Tide #2 (1938–1940), Marsden Hartley. Oil on academy board, 37 1/4″ × 31 1/4″ × 2 1/4″. Gift of Mr. and Mrs. John Cowles. The Minneapolis Institute of Arts.

"But what has good Parson Hooper got upon his face?" cried the sexton in astonishment.

All within hearing immediately turned about, and beheld the semblance of Mr. Hooper, pacing slowly his meditative way towards the meetinghouse. With one accord they started, expressing more wonder than if some strange minister were coming to dust the cushions of Mr. Hooper's pulpit.

"Are you sure it is our parson?" inquired Goodman[3] Gray of the sexton.

"Of a certainty it is good Mr. Hooper," replied the sexton. "He was to have exchanged pulpits with Parson Shute of Westbury; but Parson Shute sent to excuse himself yesterday, being to preach a funeral sermon."

The cause of so much amazement may appear sufficiently slight. Mr. Hooper, a gentlemanly person about thirty, though still a bachelor, was dressed with due clerical neatness, as if a careful wife had starched his band, and brushed the weekly dust from his Sunday's garb. There was but one thing remarkable in his appearance. Swathed about his forehead, and hanging down over his face, so low as to be shaken by his breath, Mr. Hooper had on a black veil. On a nearer view, it seemed to consist of two folds of crape,[4] which entirely concealed his features, except the mouth and chin, but probably did not intercept his sight, farther than to give a darkened aspect to all living and inanimate things. With this gloomy shade before him, good Mr. Hooper walked onward, at a slow and quiet pace, stooping somewhat and looking on the ground, as is customary with abstracted[5] men, yet nodding kindly to those of his parishioners who still waited on the meetinghouse steps. But so wonder-struck were they that his greeting hardly met with a return.

"I can't really feel as if good Mr. Hooper's face was behind that piece of crape," said the sexton.

"I don't like it," muttered an old woman, as she hobbled into the meetinghouse. "He has changed himself into something awful, only by hiding his face."

"Our parson has gone mad!" cried Goodman Gray, following him across the threshold.

A rumor of some unaccountable phenomenon had preceded Mr. Hooper into the meetinghouse, and set all the congregation astir. Few could refrain from twisting their heads towards the door; many stood upright, and turned directly about; while several little boys clambered upon the seats, and came down again with a terrible racket. There was a general bustle, a rustling of the women's gowns and shuffling of the men's feet, greatly at variance with that hushed repose which should attend the entrance of the minister. But Mr. Hooper appeared not to notice the perturbation of his people. He entered with an almost noiseless step, bent his head mildly to the pews on each side, and bowed as he passed his oldest parishioner, a white-haired great-grandsire, who occupied an armchair in the centre of the aisle. It was strange to observe how slowly this venerable man became conscious of something singular in the appearance of his pastor. He seemed not

Language Coach

Word Definitions

Accord (line 14) means "agreement." *With one accord* means "all in agreement." What reaction are the churchgoers feeling with one accord?

3. **Goodman:** the Puritan equivalent of Mr.
4. **crape** (krāp): a piece of dark material worn as a sign of mourning. Also called *crepe.*
5. **abstracted:** preoccupied, or lost in thought.

fully to partake of the prevailing wonder till Mr. Hooper had ascended the stairs, and showed himself in the pulpit, face-to-face with his congregation, except for the black veil. That mysterious emblem was never once withdrawn. It shook with his measured breath as he gave out the psalm; it threw its obscurity between him and the holy page, as he read the Scriptures; and while he prayed, the veil lay heavily on his uplifted countenance. Did he seek to hide from the dread Being[6] whom he was addressing?

Such was the effect of this simple piece of crape, that more than one woman of delicate nerves was forced to leave the meetinghouse. Yet perhaps the pale-faced congregation was almost as fearful a sight to the minister as his black veil to them.

Mr. Hooper had the reputation of a good preacher, but not an energetic one: he strove to win his people heavenward by mild persuasive influences, rather than to drive them thither by the thunders of the Word. The sermon which he now delivered was marked by the same characteristics of style and manner as the general series of his pulpit oratory. But there was something, either in the sentiment of the discourse itself, or in the imagination of the auditors, which made it greatly the most powerful effort that they had ever heard from their pastor's lips. It was tinged, rather more darkly than usual, with the gentle gloom of Mr. Hooper's temperament. The subject had reference to secret sin, and those sad mysteries which we hide from our nearest and dearest, and would fain conceal from our own consciousness, even forgetting that the Omniscient[7] can detect them. A subtle power was breathed into his words. Each member of the congregation, the most innocent girl, and the man of hardened breast, felt as if the preacher had crept upon them, behind his awful veil, and discovered their hoarded **iniquity** of deed or thought. Many spread their clasped hands on their bosoms. There was nothing terrible in what Mr. Hooper said; at least, no violence; and yet, with every tremor of his melancholy voice, the hearers quaked. An unsought pathos came hand in hand with awe. So sensible were the audience of some unwonted attribute in their minister, that they longed for a breath of wind to blow aside the veil, almost believing that a stranger's visage would be discovered, though the form, gesture and voice were those of Mr. Hooper. **B**

At the close of the services, the people hurried out with indecorous confusion, eager to communicate their pent-up amazement, and conscious of lighter spirits the moment they lost sight of the black veil. Some gathered in little circles, huddled closely together, with their mouths all whispering in the centre; some went homeward alone, wrapped in silent meditation; some talked loudly, and profaned the Sabbath day with **ostentatious** laughter. A few shook their sagacious heads, intimating that they could penetrate the mystery; while one or two affirmed that there was no mystery at all, but only that Mr. Hooper's eyes were so weakened by the midnight lamp as to require a shade. After a brief interval, forth came good Mr. Hooper also, in the rear of his flock. Turning his veiled face from one group to another, he paid due reverence to the hoary heads, saluted the middle-aged with kind dignity, as their friend and spiritual guide, greeted the young with mingled

COMMON CORE L 4b

Language Coach

Suffixes A **suffix** is a word part that appears at the end of a root or base word to form a new word. The suffix *–ward* means "in the direction of." What do *heavenward* (line 63) and *homeward* (line 87) mean?

iniquity (ĭ-nĭk'wĭ-tē) *n.* wickedness

B SYMBOL

Reread lines 62–82. Describe the change that occurs in Mr. Hooper's preaching. What seems to cause the listeners' unusual response?

ostentatious (ŏs'tĕn-tā'shəs) *adj.* loud; overdone

---

6. **the dread Being:** the awe-inspiring God.
7. **the Omniscient:** a title for God, signifying that he is all-knowing.

authority and love, and laid his hands on the little children's heads to bless them. Such was always his custom on the Sabbath day. Strange and bewildered looks repaid him for his courtesy. None, as on former occasions, aspired to the honor of walking by their pastor's side. Old Squire Saunders, doubtless by an accidental lapse of memory, neglected to invite Mr. Hooper to his table, where the good clergyman had been wont to bless the food almost every Sunday since his settlement. He returned, therefore, to the parsonage, and at the moment of closing the door, was observed to look back upon the people, all of whom had their eyes fixed upon the minister. A sad smile gleamed faintly from beneath the black veil, and flickered about his mouth, glimmering as he disappeared. C

"How strange," said a lady, "that a simple black veil, such as any woman might wear on her bonnet, should become such a terrible thing on Mr. Hooper's face!"

"Something must surely be amiss with Mr. Hooper's intellects," observed her husband, the physician of the village. "But the strangest part of the affair is the effect of this vagary, even on a sober-minded man like myself. The black veil,

C CULTURAL CHARACTERISTICS
Reread lines 92–100. Identify details that convey Mr. Hooper's social status in Milford. What does the change in the villagers' behavior toward the minister suggest about their values?

The Last Halt: Stop of Hooker's Band in East Hartford before Crossing River (1939), Alton S. Tobey. Study for East Hartford, Connecticut Postal Office. Oil on fiberboard, 26" x 44 1/8". Transfer from General Services Administration. Smithsonian American Art Museum, Washington, D.C. Photo © Smithsonian American Art Museum, Washington, D.C./Art Resource, New York. © Alton Tobey Collection/www.altontobey.org

though it covers only our pastor's face, throws its influence over his whole person, and makes him ghost-like from head to foot. Do you not feel it so?"

"Truly do I," replied the lady; "and I would not be alone with him for the world. I wonder he is not afraid to be alone with himself!"

"Men sometimes are so," said her husband.

The afternoon service was attended with similar circumstances. At its conclusion, the bell tolled for the funeral of a young lady. The relatives and friends were assembled in the house, and the more distant acquaintances stood about the door, speaking of the good qualities of the deceased, when their talk was interrupted by the appearance of Mr. Hooper, still covered with his black veil. It was now an appropriate emblem. The clergyman stepped into the room where the corpse was laid, and bent over the coffin, to take a last farewell of his deceased parishioner. As he stooped, the veil hung straight down from his forehead so that, if her eyelids had not been closed forever, the dead maiden might have seen his face. Could Mr. Hooper be fearful of her glance, that he so hastily caught back the black veil? A person, who watched the interview between the dead and the living, scrupled not to affirm that, at the instant when the clergyman's features were disclosed, the corpse had slightly shuddered, rustling the shroud[8] and muslin cap, though the countenance retained the composure of death. A superstitious old woman was the only witness of this prodigy. From the coffin, Mr. Hooper passed into the chamber of the mourners, and thence to the head of the staircase, to make the funeral prayer. It was a tender and heart-dissolving prayer, full of sorrow, yet so **imbued** with celestial hopes, that the music of the heavenly harp, swept by the fingers of the dead, seemed faintly to be heard among the saddest accents of the minister. The people trembled, though they but darkly understood him, when he prayed that they, and himself, and all of mortal race might be ready, as he trusted this young maiden had been, for the dreadful hour that should snatch the veil from their faces. The bearers went heavily forth, and the mourners followed, saddening all the street, with the dead before them, and Mr. Hooper in his black veil behind. **D**

"Why do you look back?" said one in the procession to his partner.

"I had a fancy," replied she, "that the minister and the maiden's spirit were walking hand in hand."

"And so had I, at the same moment," said the other.

That night, the handsomest couple in Milford village were to be joined in wedlock. Though reckoned a melancholy man, Mr. Hooper had a placid cheerfulness for such occasions, which often excited a sympathetic smile, where livelier merriment would have been thrown away. There was no quality of his disposition which made him more beloved than this. The company at the wedding awaited his arrival with impatience, trusting that the strange awe, which had gathered over him throughout the day, would now be dispelled. But such was not the result. When Mr. Hooper came, the first thing that their eyes rested on was the same horrible black veil, which had added deeper gloom to the funeral, and could **portend** nothing but evil to the wedding. Such was its immediate effect on the guests, that a cloud seemed to have rolled duskily from beneath the

COMMON CORE L 4c

Language Coach

Topically Related Words
Lines 115–141 describe a scene from a funeral. Look up the following words in a dictionary: *deceased, corpse, coffin, farewell, shroud, mourner, bearer, procession*. Using the words listed, explain what is occurring at the funeral.

imbued (ĭm-byo͞od') *adj.* deeply influenced by **imbue** *v.*

D SYMBOL
Paraphrase lines 133–138. In this context, what could Mr. Hooper mean when he refers to "the dreadful hour that should snatch the veil from their faces"?

portend (pôr-tĕnd') *v.* to serve as an omen of; to signify

8. **shroud:** burial garment.

black crape, and dimmed the light of the candles. The bridal pair stood up before the minister. But the bride's cold fingers quivered in the **tremulous** hand of the bridegroom, and her death-like paleness caused a whisper that the maiden who had been buried a few hours before was come from her grave to be married. If ever another wedding were so dismal, it was that famous one where they tolled the wedding knell.[9] After performing the ceremony, Mr. Hooper raised a glass of wine to his lips, wishing happiness to the new-married couple, in a strain of mild pleasantry that ought to have brightened the features of the guests, like a cheerful gleam from the hearth. At that instant, catching a glimpse of his figure in the looking glass, the black veil involved his own spirit in the horror with which it overwhelmed all others. His frame shuddered—his lips grew white—he spilt the untasted wine upon the carpet—and rushed forth into the darkness. For the Earth, too, had on her Black Veil. (E)

tremulous (trĕm'yə-ləs) *adj.* trembling; quivering

The next day, the whole village of Milford talked of little else than Parson Hooper's black veil. That, and the mystery concealed behind it, supplied a topic for discussion between acquaintances meeting in the street, and good women gossiping at their open windows. It was the first item of news that the tavern keeper told to his guests. The children babbled of it on their way to school. One imitative little imp covered his face with an old black handkerchief, thereby so affrighting his playmates that the panic seized himself, and he well-nigh lost his wits by his own waggery.[10]

(E) SYMBOL
At this point in the story, note how the minister's veil has changed the way others react to him. Reactions to a veil or mask have been a part of mythic stories in every age and culture. The characters in ancient Greek plays were represented on stage by actors wearing different masks. This allowed male actors to also play female roles. Masks in African myths like the *Epic of Sundiata* were believed to be the place where spirits were created. What reaction or belief does the veil or mask generate here? Cite details from lines 159–166 to support your response.

It was remarkable that, of all the busybodies and impertinent people in the parish, not one ventured to put the plain question to Mr. Hooper, wherefore he did this thing. Hitherto, whenever there appeared the slightest call for such interference, he had never lacked advisers, nor shown himself averse to be guided by their judgment. If he erred at all, it was by so painful a degree of self-distrust that even the mildest censure would lead him to consider an indifferent action as a crime. Yet, though so well acquainted with this amiable weakness, no individual among his parishioners chose to make the black veil a subject of friendly remonstrance. There was a feeling of dread, neither plainly confessed nor carefully concealed, which caused each to shift the responsibility upon another, till at length it was found expedient to send a deputation to the church, in order to deal with Mr. Hooper about the mystery, before it should grow into a scandal. Never did an embassy so ill discharge its duties. The minister received them with friendly courtesy, but became silent, after they were seated, leaving to his visitors the whole burden of introducing their important business. The topic, it might be supposed, was obvious enough. There was the black veil, swathed round Mr. Hooper's forehead, and concealing every feature above his placid mouth, on which, at times, they could perceive the glimmering of a melancholy smile. But that piece of crape, to their imagination, seemed to hang down before his heart, the symbol of a fearful secret between him and them. Were the veil but cast aside, they might speak freely of it, but not till then. Thus they sat a considerable time, speechless,

9. **If . . . the wedding knell:** a reference to "The Wedding Knell," a story by Hawthorne in which a bell-tolling appropriate for a funeral is sounded at a wedding.
10. **waggery:** mischievous merriment.

confused, and shrinking uneasily from Mr. Hooper's eye, which they felt to be fixed upon them with an invisible glance. Finally, the deputies returned abashed to their constituents, pronouncing the matter too weighty to be handled, except by a council of the churches, if, indeed, it might not require a general synod.[11] **F**

But there was one person in the village unappalled by the awe with which the black veil had impressed all beside herself. When the deputies returned without an explanation, or even venturing to demand one, she, with the calm energy of her character, determined to chase away the strange cloud that appeared to be settling round Mr. Hooper, every moment more darkly than before. As his plighted wife,[12] it should be her privilege to know what the black veil concealed. At the minister's first visit, therefore, she entered upon the subject, with a direct simplicity, which made the task easier both for him and her. After he had seated himself, she fixed her eyes steadfastly upon the veil, but could discern nothing of the dreadful gloom that had so overawed the multitude: it was but a double fold of crape, hanging down from his forehead to his mouth, and slightly stirring with his breath. **G**

F CULTURAL CHARACTERISTICS
Paraphrase lines 175–199. Explain what motivates the parishioners to confront Mr. Hooper. What do their fears reveal about Puritan culture?

G SYMBOL
Reread lines 200–210. Contrast the response of the minister's fiancée to the veil with the responses of the other villagers. What might explain the difference in her response?

"No," said she aloud, and smiling, "there is nothing terrible in this piece of crape except that it hides a face which I am always glad to look upon. Come, good sir, let the sun shine from behind the cloud. First lay aside your black veil: then tell me why you put it on."

Mr. Hooper's smile glimmered faintly.

"There is an hour to come," said he, "when all of us shall cast aside our veils. Take it not amiss, beloved friend, if I wear this piece of crape till then."

"Your words are a mystery too," returned the young lady. "Take away the veil from them, at least."

"Elizabeth, I will," said he, "so far as my vow may suffer me. Know, then, this veil is a type and a symbol, and I am bound to wear it ever, both in light and darkness, in solitude and before the gaze of multitudes, and as with strangers, so with my familiar friends. No mortal eye will see it withdrawn. This dismal shade must separate me from the world: even you, Elizabeth, can never come behind it!"

"What grievous affliction hath befallen you," she earnestly inquired, "that you should thus darken your eyes forever?"

"If it be a sign of mourning," replied Mr. Hooper, "I, perhaps, like most other mortals, have sorrows dark enough to be typified by a black veil."

"But what if the world will not believe that it is the type of an innocent sorrow?" urged Elizabeth. "Beloved and respected as you are, there may be whispers that you hide your face under the consciousness of secret sin. For the sake of your holy office, do away this scandal!"

The color rose into her cheeks, as she intimated the nature of the rumors that were already abroad in the village. But Mr. Hooper's mildness did not forsake him. He even smiled again—that same sad smile, which always appeared like a faint glimmering of light proceeding from the obscurity beneath the veil.

"If I hide my face for sorrow, there is cause enough," he merely replied; "and if I cover it for secret sin, what mortal might not do the same?"

---

11. **a general synod:** a meeting of the governing body of the churches.
12. **plighted wife:** fiancée.

Portrait of Alice Irene Harvey (1912), Mark Gertler. Oil on canvas, 60.9 cm × 50.8 cm. © Leeds Museums and Galleries, Leeds, United Kingdom/Bridgeman Art Library.

And with this gentle but unconquerable obstinacy did he resist all her entreaties. At length Elizabeth sat silent. For a few moments she appeared lost in thought, considering, probably, what new methods might be tried to withdraw her lover from so dark a fantasy, which, if it had no other meaning, was perhaps a symptom of mental disease. Though of a firmer character than his own, the tears rolled down her cheeks. But, in an instant, as it were, a new feeling took the place of sorrow: her eyes were fixed insensibly on the black veil, when, like a sudden twilight in the air, its terrors fell around her. She arose, and stood trembling before him.

"And do you feel it then at last?" said he mournfully.

She made no reply, but covered her eyes with her hand, and turned to leave the room. He rushed forward and caught her arm.

"Have patience with me, Elizabeth!" cried he passionately. "Do not desert me, though this veil must be between us here on earth. Be mine, and hereafter there shall be no veil over my face, no darkness between our souls! It is but a mortal veil—it is not for eternity! Oh! you know not how lonely I am, and how frightened to be alone behind my black veil. Do not leave me in this miserable obscurity forever!"

"Lift the veil but once, and look me in the face," said she.

"Never! It cannot be!" replied Mr. Hooper.

"Then, farewell!" said Elizabeth.

She withdrew her arm from his grasp and slowly departed, pausing at the door to give one long, shuddering gaze that seemed almost to penetrate the mystery of the black veil. But even amid his grief, Mr. Hooper smiled to think that only a material emblem had separated him from happiness, though the horrors which it shadowed forth must be drawn darkly between the fondest of lovers.

From that time no attempts were made to remove Mr. Hooper's black veil or, by a direct appeal, to discover the secret which it was supposed to hide. By persons who claimed a superiority to popular prejudice, it was reckoned merely an eccentric whim, such as often mingles with the sober actions of men otherwise rational, and tinges them all with its own semblance of insanity. But with the multitude, good Mr. Hooper was irreparably a bugbear.[13] He could not walk the streets with any peace of mind, so conscious was he that the gentle and timid would turn aside to avoid him, and that others would make it a point of hardihood to throw themselves in his way. The impertinence of the latter class compelled him to give up his customary walk, at sunset, to the burial ground, for when he leaned pensively over the gate, there would always be faces behind the gravestones, peeping at his black veil. A fable went the rounds that the stare of the dead people drove him thence. It grieved him to the very depth of his kind heart to observe how the children fled from his approach, breaking up their merriest sports, while his melancholy figure was yet afar off. Their instinctive dread caused him to feel, more strongly than aught else, that a **preternatural** horror was interwoven with the threads of

◀ Analyze Visuals
In what ways does the woman depicted in the painting on the opposite page reflect the character of Elizabeth as described in lines 240–244? What could the woman's white dress **symbolize?**

preternatural
(prē′tər-năch′ər-əl) *adj.* supernatural

13. **bugbear:** a source of dread or fear.

the black crape. In truth, his own antipathy to the veil was known to be so great that he never willingly passed before a mirror, nor stooped to drink at a still fountain, lest, in its peaceful bosom, he should be affrighted by himself. This was what gave plausibility to the whispers that Mr. Hooper's conscience tortured him for some great crime too horrible to be entirely concealed, or otherwise than so obscurely intimated. Thus, from beneath the black veil there rolled a cloud into the sunshine, an **ambiguity** of sin or sorrow, which enveloped the poor minister, so that love or sympathy could never reach him. It was said that ghost and fiend consorted with him there. With self-shudderings and outward terrors, he walked continually in its shadow, groping darkly within his own soul, or gazing through a medium that saddened the whole world. Even the lawless wind, it was believed, respected his dreadful secret, and never blew aside the veil. But still good Mr. Hooper sadly smiled at the pale visages of the worldly throng as he passed by.

ambiguity (ăm′bĭ-gyo͞o′ĭ-tē) *n.* unclearness; uncertainty

Among all its bad influences, the black veil had the one desirable effect, of making its wearer a very efficient clergyman. By the aid of his mysterious emblem—for there was no other apparent cause—he became a man of awful power, over souls that were in agony for sin. His converts always regarded him with a dread peculiar to themselves, affirming, though but figuratively, that before he brought them to celestial light, they had been with him behind the black veil. Its gloom, indeed, enabled him to sympathize with all dark affections. Dying sinners cried aloud for Mr. Hooper, and would not yield their breath till he appeared; though ever, as he stooped to whisper consolation, they shuddered at the veiled face so near their own. Such were the terrors of the black veil, even when Death had bared his visage! Strangers came long distances to attend service at his church, with the mere idle purpose of gazing at his figure, because it was forbidden them to behold his face. But many were made to quake ere they departed! Once, during Governor Belcher's[14] administration, Mr. Hooper was appointed to preach the election sermon. Covered with his black veil, he stood before the chief magistrate, the council, and the representatives, and wrought so deep an impression that the legislative measures of that year were characterized by all the gloom and piety of our earliest ancestral sway.[15] **H**

H CULTURAL CHARACTERISTICS
Once Mr. Hooper is perceived to have intimate knowledge of sin, he becomes a famous and respected clergyman. Based on this fact, what would you conclude is the main concern of Puritan worshipers?

In this manner Mr. Hooper spent a long life, irreproachable in outward act, yet shrouded in dismal suspicions; kind and loving, though unloved, and dimly feared; a man apart from men, shunned in their health and joy, but ever summoned to their aid in mortal anguish. As years wore on, shedding their snows above his sable veil, he acquired a name throughout the New England churches, and they called him Father Hooper. Nearly all his parishioners, who were of a mature age when he was settled, had been borne away by many a funeral: he had one congregation in the church, and a more crowded one in the churchyard; and having wrought so late into the evening, and done his work so well, it was now good Father Hooper's turn to rest.

14. **Governor Belcher's:** referring to Governor Jonathan Belcher (1682–1757), colonial governor of the Massachusetts Bay Colony from 1730 to 1741, and later of New Jersey.

15. **earliest ancestral sway:** the Puritans who held power in 17th-century America.

Several persons were visible by the shaded candlelight in the death chamber of the old clergyman. Natural connections[16] he had none. But there was the decorously grave, though unmoved physician, seeking only to mitigate the last pangs of the patient whom he could not save. There were the deacons, and other eminently pious members of his church. There, also, was the Reverend Mr. Clark, of Westbury, a young and **zealous** divine, who had ridden in haste to pray by the bedside of the expiring minister. There was the nurse, no hired handmaiden of death, but one whose calm affection had endured thus long, in secrecy, in solitude, amid the chill of age, and would not perish, even at the dying hour. Who, but Elizabeth! And there lay the hoary head of good Father Hooper upon the death pillow, with the black veil still swathed about his brow and reaching down over his face, so that each more difficult gasp of his faint breath caused it to stir. All through life that piece of crape had hung between him and the world: it had separated him from cheerful brotherhood and woman's love, and kept him in that saddest of all prisons, his own heart; and still it lay upon his face, as if to deepen the gloom of his darksome chamber, and shade him from the sunshine of eternity.

zealous (zĕl'əs) *adj.* eager and enthusiastic

For some time previous, his mind had been confused, wavering doubtfully between the past and the present, and hovering forward, as it were, at intervals, into the indistinctness of the world to come. There had been feverish turns, which tossed him from side to side and wore away what little strength he had. But in the most convulsive struggles, and in the wildest vagaries of his intellect, when no other thought retained its sober influence, he still showed an awful solicitude lest the black veil should slip aside. Even if his bewildered soul could have forgotten, there was a faithful woman at his pillow, who, with averted eyes, would have covered that aged face, which she had last beheld in the comeliness of manhood. At length the death-stricken old man lay quietly in the torpor of mental and bodily exhaustion, with an imperceptible pulse, and breath that grew fainter and fainter, except when a long, deep, and irregular inspiration seemed to prelude the flight of his spirit.

The minister of Westbury approached the bedside.

"Venerable Father Hooper," said he, "the moment of your release is at hand. Are you ready for the lifting of the veil, that shuts in time from eternity?"

Father Hooper at first replied merely by a feeble motion of his head; then, apprehensive, perhaps, that his meaning might be doubtful, he exerted himself to speak.

"Yea," said he, in faint accents, "my soul hath a patient weariness until that veil be lifted."

"And is it fitting," resumed the Reverend Mr. Clark, "that a man so given to prayer, of such a blameless example, holy in deed and thought, so far as mortal judgment may pronounce; is it fitting that a father in the church should leave a shadow on his memory that may seem to blacken a life so pure? I pray you, my venerable brother, let not this thing be! Suffer us to be gladdened by your

16. **natural connections:** relatives.

triumphant aspect, as you go to your reward. Before the veil of eternity be lifted, let me cast aside this black veil from your face!"

And thus speaking, the Reverend Mr. Clark bent forward to reveal the mystery of so many years. But, exerting a sudden energy that made all the beholders stand aghast, Father Hooper snatched both his hands from beneath the bedclothes and pressed them strongly on the black veil, resolute to struggle, if the minister of Westbury would contend with a dying man.

"Never!" cried the veiled clergyman. "On earth, never!"

"Dark old man!" exclaimed the affrighted minister, "with what horrible crime upon your soul are you now passing to the judgment?"

Father Hooper's breath heaved; it rattled in his throat; but with a mighty effort, grasping forward with his hands, he caught hold of life, and held it back till he should speak. He even raised himself in bed; and there he sat shivering, with the arms of death around him, while the black veil hung down, awful, at that last moment, in the gathered terrors of a lifetime. And yet the faint, sad smile, so often there, now seemed to glimmer from its obscurity, and linger on Father Hooper's lips.

"Why do you tremble at me alone?" cried he, turning his veiled face round the circle of pale spectators. "Tremble also at each other! Have men avoided me, and women shown no pity, and children screamed and fled, only for my black veil? What, but the mystery which it obscurely typifies, has made this piece of crape so awful? When the friend shows his inmost heart to his friend; the lover to his best beloved; when man does not vainly shrink from the eye of his Creator, loathsomely treasuring up the secret of his sin; then deem me a monster, for the symbol beneath which I have lived, and die! I look around me, and, lo! On every visage a Black Veil!" ❶

❶ SYMBOL
Explain Father Hooper's reproach in lines 380–387. What do his comments suggest about the meaning of the veil?

While his auditors shrank from one another, in mutual affright, Father Hooper fell back upon his pillow, a veiled corpse, with a faint smile lingering on his lips. Still veiled, they laid him in his coffin, and a veiled corpse they bore him to the grave. The grass of many years has sprung up and withered on that grave, the burial stone is moss-grown, and good Mr. Hooper's face is dust; but awful is still the thought, that it mouldered beneath the Black Veil!

Comprehension

1. **Recall** What is the topic of the first sermon Mr. Hooper gives while wearing the veil?
2. **Recall** What reason does Mr. Hooper give Elizabeth for wearing the veil?
3. **Summarize** As time goes by, how do Mr. Hooper's relationships change?

Text Analysis

4. **Identify Cultural Characteristics** What does the story reveal about Puritan religious beliefs, rules of behavior, and values and ideals?
5. **Interpret Symbol** Review the concept map you created as you read. Based on this information, what does the black veil represent? Explain your answer.
6. **Examine Character Ambiguity** The minister is an ambiguous character: he can be seen as an innocent victim of others' fears or as a man driven to isolate himself, convinced of his own moral superiority. Identify at least two details that support each perspective. Which interpretation do you find more compelling? Give reasons for your answer.
7. **Make Judgments About Character Motivations** Mr. Hooper's wearing of the black veil leads to his isolation from his congregation. Based on the following passages, what argument would you make about the real causes of the villagers' discomfort in the minister's presence?
   - the first sighting of the minister (lines 34–39)
   - parishioners' comments after services (lines 105–113)
   - his arrival at the wedding (lines 147–152)
   - the attempt to confront him (lines 190–197)

Text Criticism

8. **Biographical Context** Reread the biography of Hawthorne on page 468. Explain the personal motives that inspired Hawthorne's critical portrayal of Puritan culture. In what ways might Mr. Hooper represent Hawthorne's struggle with his own guilt?

How does someone become a STRANGER?

In line 336, the narrator calls the human heart the "saddest of all prisons." What does this mean? What does it suggest about our relationships with others?

COMMON CORE

RL 1 Cite evidence to support analysis of what the text says explicitly as well as inferences drawn from the text, including determining where the text leaves matters uncertain.
RL 3 Analyze the impact of the author's choices regarding how to develop and relate elements of a story.

Vocabulary in Context

▲ VOCABULARY PRACTICE

Decide whether the words in each pair are synonyms or antonyms.

1. ostentatious/discreet
2. ambiguity/clarity
3. portend/predict
4. iniquity/vice
5. zealous/halfhearted
6. imbued/infused
7. preternatural/ordinary
8. tremulous/quaking

WORD LIST
ambiguity
imbued
iniquity
ostentatious
portend
preternatural
tremulous
zealous

ACADEMIC VOCABULARY IN SPEAKING

• construct • expand • indicate • reinforce • role

Appearance plays a powerful **role** in our society. With a partner, discuss whether you think someone's appearance reveals his or her identity or conceals it, or both. Support your opinion with specific examples and try to use at least one Academic Vocabulary word in your discussion.

VOCABULARY STRATEGY: THE LATIN ROOT *ambi*

The vocabulary word *ambiguity* contains the Latin root *ambi.* This root, which can mean either "both" or "around," can be found in many English words in all content areas, from science to philosophy. When you encounter the root *ambi* in a word, you can often use context clues to determine which meaning of the root is involved.

PRACTICE Choose the word from the word web that best completes each sentence. Consider what you know about the Latin root and the other word parts shown. If necessary, consult a dictionary.

1. Because Peter was _____, he could write with either hand.
2. Their home had a pleasant and gracious _____.
3. Beth was_____ about joining the group and could not make up her mind.
4. The ____ of their property extends to that line of trees.
5. The _____ temperature in the room was too warm to preserve the specimens.

COMMON CORE

L 4b Identify and use patterns of word changes that indicate different meanings or parts of speech. **L 6** Acquire and use academic words and phrases.

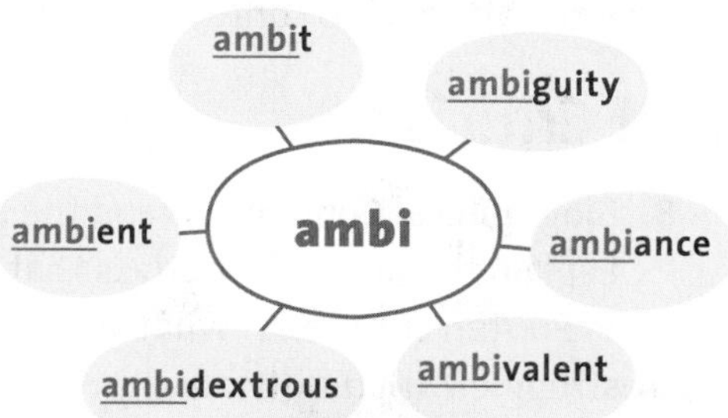

The Gothic Perspective

Although the romantic period was mostly characterized by a feeling of optimism, American gothic literature showed a fascination with the dark side of human nature. Sin, deception, hedonism, guilt, death—all are subjects upon which gothic writers based their dark tales, as illustrated beautifully in this excerpt from Edgar Allan Poe's "The Masque of the Red Death."

> *"The 'Red Death' had long devastated the country. No pestilence had ever been so fatal, or so hideous. Blood was its Avatar and its seal—the redness and horror of blood. There were sharp pains, and sudden dizziness, and then profuse bleeding at the pores, with dissolution. . . .*
>
> *But the Prince Prospero was happy and dauntless and sagacious. When his dominions were half depopulated, he summoned to his presence a thousand hale and lighthearted friends from among the knights and dames of his court, and with these retired to the deep seclusion of one of his castellated abbeys."*

Literary critic Paul Zweig has a few words to say about the importance of Poe's dark perspective.

> *"Poe's achievement . . . was to give literary expression to the dread that haunted America's dream of success in the 19th century. If anything was possible in this land of wealth and change, then personal failure, even simple unhappiness, was obscene, a skeleton in the cellar of democracy."*

Writing to Analyze

Nathaniel Hawthorne is also a master of the gothic genre. Do you think Zweig's comments about Poe can apply to Hawthorne's work as well? Write a brief analysis, citing evidence from "The Minister's Black Veil" to support your opinion.

Consider

- characters' personal failings
- characters' unhappiness or fears
- the message you take away from the story

Extension

SPEAKING & LISTENING

Although Poe and Hawthorne both wrote gothic literature, the nature of their work differs quite a bit. While Poe was the master of supernatural horror, Hawthorne focused on more everyday, realistic fears. With your classmates, **discuss** what frightens you more—the fantastic or the realistic?

COMMON CORE

W 2 Write informative/explanatory texts to examine and convey complex ideas, concepts and information through the selection, organization, and analysis of content.
SL 1 Participate in a range of collaborative discussions.

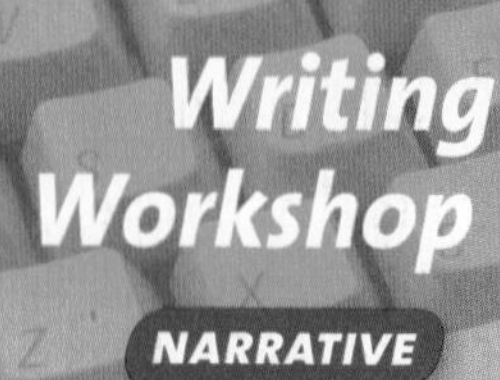

Short Story

You have seen how writers in past centuries wrote short stories to entertain readers and to provide insight into the way people think and feel. In this workshop, you will learn how to craft a short story that entertains and engages readers.

 Complete the workshop activities in your **Reader/Writer Notebook.**

WRITE WITH A PURPOSE

WRITING TASK

Write a **short story** that engages readers with a strong plot, complex characters, and a vivid setting. Build your story around a central conflict.

Idea Starters
- a real-life situation
- an interesting-looking person
- a news story
- a dream
- an inexplicable sound, smell, sight, or event

THE ESSENTIALS

Here are some common purposes, audiences, and formats for writing a short story.

PURPOSES	AUDIENCES	FORMATS
• to entertain your readers • to express yourself creatively	• classmates and teacher • other students in your school • Web users • contest judges	• story for class • school's literary magazine • school's Web site • short story contest

COMMON CORE TRAITS

1. DEVELOPMENT OF IDEAS
- focuses on a **central conflict**
- introduces and develops a **narrator** and **characters**
- uses techniques such as **dialogue, description, reflection,** and **multiple plot lines** to develop the plot and characters
- offers a **conclusion** that follows from the events in the story
- conveys the **significance** of the events in the story

2. ORGANIZATION OF IDEAS
- presents a smooth **progression of events** to create a coherent story
- uses effective **pacing** to advance the plot

3. LANGUAGE FACILITY AND CONVENTIONS
- maintains a consistent **point of view**
- uses **precise words, telling details,** and **sensory language**
- **formats** and **punctuates dialogue** correctly
- employs correct **grammar, mechanics,** and **spelling**

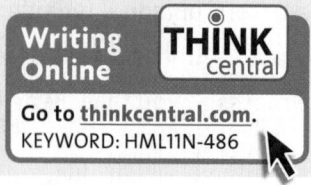

Writing Online THINK central
Go to thinkcentral.com.
KEYWORD: HML11N-486

Planning/Prewriting

W 3a–e Write narratives to develop real or imagined experiences or events using effective technique, well-chosen details, and well-structured event sequences. **W 5** Develop and strengthen writing as needed by planning.

Getting Started

EXPLORE STORY IDEAS

Using your imagination to explore "What if?" scenarios is a good way to brainstorm story ideas. Since your purpose is to entertain readers, try to think of "What if?" questions that have intriguing answers. The situation you decide on is the starting point for developing the rest of your story.

ASK YOURSELF:

- How would a person with a certain kind of temperament and background react to an unexpected, extraordinary event?
- What would happen if a historical or a current event had played out differently?
- How would life change if something that is now impossible became possible?

THINK ABOUT AUDIENCE AND PURPOSE

As you plan your short story, keep your audience and purpose in mind. Your **purpose** is to entertain readers and to express yourself creatively. Your **audience** will be your teacher and classmates but may also include a wider audience of teens and young adult readers.

ASK YOURSELF:

- What effect do I want my story to have on my audience?
- What do I want my audience to know about each scene?
- What do I want my audience to know that the characters in my story do not know?

IMAGINE CHARACTERS

Short stories usually focus on one or two **main characters** and sometimes include **minor characters** as well. Use these techniques to bring your characters to life:

- Reveal key character traits by providing **relevant, descriptive details** about the characters' appearance, behavior, and actions.
- Include **telling details,** or pieces of description or dialogue, that reveal important or interesting information about the characters.
- Use **dialogue** (the characters' actual words) and **interior monologue** (the characters' unspoken thoughts, feelings, and reflections) to reveal personality and **perspective,** or **point of view.**

ASK YOURSELF:

- How do the characters look and move?
- What do the characters' actions reveal?
- What distinctive gestures or expressions are typical of the characters?
- What causes conflicts for the characters?
- What personality traits come to light as the characters face their conflicts?
- How do the characters grow or change because of their conflicts?
- How do the characters speak and think?
- Is there any disconnect between what the characters say to others, what they think to themselves, and how they act?

IMAGINE SETTING

Imagine a **setting,** or time and place, for your story. **Sensory language** helps to paint a vivid picture of the setting.

ASK YOURSELF:

- What time period or place do I find interesting?
- If I were to visit an imaginary place, what would it look, sound, smell, and feel like?

Planning/Prewriting *continued*

Getting Started

PLOT YOUR STORY

To keep your readers interested in your story, something has to happen. The **sequence of events** in a short story is called the **plot.** Most plots begin with an **exposition,** which introduces the characters, their setting, and their **conflict**—a problem or situation to be solved. Next is the **rising action,** in which **complications** arise as the characters attempt to resolve their conflict. The conflict escalates until it reaches a turning point, or **climax.** During the **falling action** and the **resolution,** the conflict is resolved and the story ends.

As you plan your story, keep **pacing** in mind. You can create intensity or excitement by keeping the action moving from one event to the next and not focusing on unimportant details. You can build **suspense,** a feeling of uncertainty and curiosity about what will happen next, by lingering over details that describe characters or setting. You can create **tension** by speeding up the narrative.

If you plan to write a longer short story, experiment with **multiple plot lines,** or subplots, that relate to the main plot or central conflict.

WHAT DOES IT LOOK LIKE?

Plot Plan

Characters: David and Nadine

Setting: kitchen at David's house

Exposition: A college letter has arrived; David hesitates to open it. His conflict is internal. He fights his nervousness and uncertainty about his future.

Rising Action: Nadine comes in, gets a drink of water, and reads the letter silently.

Climax: Nadine tells David that he is accepted to college in Boston.

Falling Action: Nadine and David celebrate together and then catch their breath.

Resolution: Nadine and David watch a movie together, knowing everything has changed.

PEER REVIEW Describe your story's sequence of events to a peer. Then ask: Is the sequence clear and compelling? What kinds of details can I include to create suspense?

In your *Reader/Writer Notebook,* develop your plot plan. Ask yourself the following questions as you develop your plot:

- Do the main characters have a conflict with one another or with some other external or internal force?
- How do the main characters' actions or decisions further complicate the problem?
- What happens to make the conflict reach a climax, or turning point?
- How is the conflict resolved?
- How have the characters changed by the end of the story?
- What is the significance of what has happened?

W 3c Use a variety of techniques to sequence events. **W 4** Produce clear and coherent writing appropriate to task, purpose, and audience. **L 1** Demonstrate command of grammar and usage.

Drafting

The following chart shows a structure for organizing an effective short story.

Organizing Your Short Story

EXPOSITION

- Engage and orient your readers by introducing the **characters, setting,** and **central conflict.**
- Choose the point of view you will use throughout the story. The **point of view** is the **vantage point,** or **perspective,** from which a writer tells a story. If you are writing a longer short story, using **multiple points of view** gives readers more than one perspective on the characters, setting, and plot. Choose from the following points of view: first person, third-person limited, or third-person omniscient.
  - **First person:** The narrator is a character in the story. He or she tells only what he or she knows and experiences. The narrator uses first-person pronouns: *I, me, my, we, us.*
  - **Third-person limited:** The narrator is not a character. The narrator focuses on one character's knowledge and experiences. The narrator uses third-person pronouns: *he, she, they, his, her, their, them.*
  - **Third-person omniscient:** An all-knowing narrator tells the story, using third-person pronouns. The narrator knows what all characters are thinking and feeling.

▼

RISING ACTION AND CLIMAX

- Develop the characters with such techniques as **dialogue** and **reflection.**
- Introduce plot complications.
- Although you'll present most plot points in **chronological order,** you may sometimes skip forward **(flash-forward)** or backward in time **(flashback).**
- Include **precise words** and **phrases, telling details,** and **sensory language** to describe the characters and settings and to create a mood.
- Use **pacing** that helps keep the action moving and creates a smooth progression from one event to the next.
- Bring the plot to a **climax.**

▼

FALLING ACTION AND RESOLUTION

- **Resolve** the conflict and reveal the final outcome. Convey the **significance** of the events.

GRAMMAR IN CONTEXT: TRANSITIONAL EXPRESSIONS

Transitional expressions create **coherence,** or a strong connection between ideas. In short stories, they help the reader follow the progression of the plot. Transitional expressions may be prepositions or adverbs. Notice how an adverb is used as a transitional expression:

> *They laughed at the situation. **After** their laughter faded, Nadine congratulated David.*

Following the plot plan you created earlier and the chart on this page, write a draft of your short story. Be sure to use a consistent point of view, pacing that moves the story along, descriptive and sensory language, and transitional expressions.

Revising

When revising, consider your story's characters, setting, plot, pacing, and resolution. Your goal is to determine whether you've achieved your purpose and effectively expressed your story idea to your audience. The questions, tips, and strategies in the following chart can help you revise and improve your draft.

SHORT STORY

Ask Yourself	Tips	Revision Strategies
1. Does the story's exposition introduce the main characters and establish the setting? Does it initiate the central conflict? ▶	**Highlight** details about the main characters and setting. **Draw a wavy line** under the event or situation that initiates the central conflict. ▶	**Add** details about the main characters and setting. **Add** a sentence that initiates the central conflict.
2. Does the story have a clear point of view? Is the point of view developed consistently? ▶	**Underline** phrases that indicate the point of view. **Label** the point of view in the margin. ▶	**Delete** information that the narrator would not know. **Reword** sentences to make the point of view consistent.
3. Is the plot developed with actions and decisions that complicate the problem? Does the conflict build toward a climax? ▶	**Draw a star** by each plot complication. **Draw two stars** by the story's climax. Make sure that there is a smooth progression of events building toward the climax. ▶	**Add** actions or decisions that create complications. **Add** an event, an action, a decision, or a realization to bring about the climax.
4. Does the story use precise words and phrases, telling details, and sensory language to develop the plot and characters? ▶	**Draw a dotted line** under the characters' spoken words or unspoken thoughts and feelings. **Put parentheses** around descriptive details about characters. ▶	**Add** dialogue and interior monologue. **Elaborate** on characters with descriptions of physical appearance, behavior, and actions.
5. Is pacing used effectively to advance the plot? ▶	**Draw a box** around any details that are unrelated to the central conflict. ▶	**Delete** any unnecessary details to tighten the pace and move the action forward.
6. Does the story's conclusion resolve the conflict and show the significance of the events? ▶	**Circle** the sentences that resolve the conflict. **Bracket** the sentences that show the significance of events. ▶	**Add** sentences that resolve the conflict. **Add** a sentence or two to show the significance of events.

PEER REVIEW Working with a peer, review your draft. Answer each question in the chart to evaluate how to make improvements. Then, revise your draft, using the tips and revision techniques. If your story is not flowing smoothly, try a new approach to make it more cohesive.

W 3a–b Set out a problem and its significance; use dialogue to develop events and characters. **W 5** Develop and strengthen writing as needed by revising, editing, rewriting, or trying a new approach, focusing on addressing what is most significant for a specific purpose and audience.

ANALYZE A STUDENT DRAFT

Read this student draft; note the comments on its strengths as well as suggestions for improvement.

The Discovery

by Maile Cortese, Weddington High School

1 As David drove into the driveway, he became oddly calm. He turned down the radio so that he could hear his heart beating. Easing the door open, he stepped out of the car, walked down to the mailbox, and looked inside. "There it is." Hands shaking, he reached in for the letter.

2 David gently carried the envelope into the house as if it were made of glass. As he sat down at his kitchen table, he became numb. The envelope was addressed to him, but he didn't really feel like it was for him. He read the address line. "David Kalinger," he announced to no one in particular. "Yep, it's for me."

3 Fingers trembling, he slowly raised his hand to open it. He slid his thumb under the flap and tore the paper. The letter was sitting in the envelope so peacefully, waiting for someone to read its secret. Just as he was pulling the letter out of the envelope, his sister Nadine strolled in through the side door. David sighed.

4 Nadine explained that she rushed home to find out about the acceptance letter. Then, she reached into the cabinet to get a glass for water.

Maile presents the **main character** and uses telling details to characterize him as nervous.

Here, Maile introduces the **central conflict.**

This paragraph slows down the pacing to build **suspense**—Nadine's arrival postpones the opening of the letter.

Maile should use **dialogue** to show the reader what happens, rather than simply telling the reader what happens. An exchange of dialogue would help develop the characters and plot.

LEARN HOW **Develop Plot and Characters with Dialogue** Maile can develop the plot more effectively by inserting dialogue. Dialogue can be used to extend the moment and develop the characters and their relationship. It can also reveal information that is important to the plot. Maile decides to revise the fourth paragraph, replacing it with dialogue that creates suspense and provides information about the relationship between the two characters.

MAILE'S REVISION TO PARAGRAPH 4

~~Nadine explained that she rushed home to find out about the acceptance letter. Then, she reached into the cabinet to get a glass for water.~~

"Nadine! What are you doing here?" he asked.

"I heard you were getting your acceptance letter today, so I just ran over here. Man, I'm so out of breath! Can I get a glass of water?" she panted as she reached into the cabinet.

"Sure, go ahead," David muttered, knowing she already had. As Nadine sat down, David just stared at the envelope and held his breath.

ANALYZE A STUDENT DRAFT *continued*

5 "So have you even looked at it yet?" Nadine asked.

6 David shook his head miserably. "Would you do it for me?" he pleaded.

7 Nadine gave him an inquisitive look but then quickly snatched the envelope, opened the letter, and started to read it silently.

8 "What? What? Read it aloud! What are you doing?" he shouted in misery.

9 "Oh no, David. I was afraid of this," she said in a sorrowful voice, her face grim. David put his head in his hands, moaning softly.

10 "David, I'm not going to have you around here to keep me company any more. You've been accepted! You're going to Boston!" she shouted triumphantly.

11 David jumped to his feet, knocking over the chair, and gave Nadine a playful shove. "You'll be sorry!" he shouted as he reached for Nadine.

12 They fell to the floor, laughing hysterically.

Maile uses **dialogue** to heighten the **suspense.**

The story reaches its **climax** when Nadine tells David the contents of the letter.

This **conclusion** needs to be revised to show the **significance** of the event.

LEARN HOW **Show Significance in the Conclusion** Maile shows how David's central conflict has been resolved, but she does not show why the event is significant. Maile decides to add a few sentences to the resolution to reflect on why the event is significant to David and Nadine's relationship.

MAILE'S REVISION TO PARAGRAPH 12

They fell to the floor, laughing hysterically. *Soon, their howls ended and they stood up and hugged each other. After catching their breath, David set up the movie while Nadine made the popcorn, just like every other Friday night since they were young. However, they both knew that David's move to Boston would be a big change for them both.*

Use the feedback from your peers and teacher, the revision strategies chart, and the two "Learn How" lessons to revise or rework your story. Evaluate whether your audience will find your story entertaining and whether you have expressed your story idea in a creative, unique way.

W 5 Develop and strengthen writing as needed by revising, editing, rewriting, or trying a new approach. **L 1** Demonstrate a command of grammar and usage. **L 2** Demonstrate a command of capitalization, punctuation, and spelling.

Editing and Publishing

In the editing stage, you proofread your short story to make sure that it is free of grammar, usage, and punctuation errors. Pay close attention to your grammar and word usage, such as verb tenses and parts of speech. Make sure that you have chosen your words carefully. Also, read carefully to catch any spelling errors, even after doing a word-processing spell-check. These kinds of mistakes keep your audience from fully enjoying your story.

GRAMMAR IN CONTEXT: FORMATTING AND PUNCTUATING DIALOGUE

Since your short story will include a good amount of dialogue, you will need to make sure that it is formatted and punctuated correctly. Every time you have dialogue that comes from a new speaker, you should start a new paragraph.

When used with quotation marks, **commas** and **periods** are placed within the closing quotation marks.

"Oh no, David. I was afraid of this," she said in a sorrowful voice, her face grim.

Question marks and **exclamation points** are placed inside the closing quotation marks if the quotation itself is a question or an exclamation. Otherwise, they are placed outside the quotation marks.

"So have you even looked at it yet?" Nadine asked.

PUBLISH YOUR WRITING

Share your short story with an audience.

- Submit your story to your school's literary magazine or Web site.
- Submit your story to a short story contest. Ask your school librarian or media specialist to help you identify several contests.
- Adapt your short story into a script. Then, collaborate with classmates to perform your script for the class.

Proofread your final draft. As you proofread, check your dialogue to see that you have formatted and punctuated it correctly. Correct any errors you find in your story. Then, publish your completed work.

Scoring Rubric

Use the rubric below to evaluate your short story from the Writing Workshop or your response to the on-demand task on the next page.

SHORT STORY

SCORE	COMMON CORE TRAITS
6	• **Development** Skillfully introduces, develops, and resolves a conflict; develops compelling, believable characters; effectively uses dialogue, description, reflection, and one or more plot lines • **Organization** Has a smooth, coherent event sequence that builds to a strong conclusion; uses effective pacing • **Language** Consistently maintains one or more points of view; weaves in precise words, telling details, and sensory language; shows a strong command of conventions
5	• **Development** Effectively introduces, develops, and resolves a conflict; develops interesting, believable characters; ably uses dialogue, description, reflection, and one or more plot lines • **Organization** Has a coherent event sequence that builds to a conclusion; uses mostly effective pacing • **Language** Maintains one or more points of view; includes precise words, telling details, and sensory language; has a few errors in conventions
4	• **Development** Introduces, develops, and resolves a conflict; has interesting characters with some believable traits; could use some more dialogue, description, and reflection • **Organization** Includes some extraneous events, resulting in ineffective pacing • **Language** Mostly maintains a point of view; needs more precise words, telling details, and sensory language; has a few distracting errors in conventions
3	• **Development** Introduces and resolves a conflict, but it needs more development; has some underdeveloped characters; needs more dialogue, description, and reflection • **Organization** Has a confusing sequence caused by some extraneous events; has a lagging pace at times • **Language** Has a few lapses in point of view; lacks enough precise words, telling details, and sensory language; has some significant errors in conventions
2	• **Development** Introduces a conflict but does not develop or resolve it; inadequately develops characters; lacks sufficient dialogue, description, and reflection • **Organization** Includes too many events that distract from the plot; has choppy pacing • **Language** Uses an inconsistent point of view; mostly lacks precise words, telling details, and sensory language; has many distracting errors in conventions
1	• **Development** Has no identifiable conflict; includes underdeveloped characters; lacks any dialogue, description, and reflection • **Organization** Has no apparent organization • **Language** Never establishes a clear point of view; lacks precise words, telling details, and sensory language; has major problems with conventions

Preparing for Timed Writing

W 10 Write routinely over shorter time frames for a range of tasks, purposes, and audiences.

1. ANALYZE THE TASK — 5 MIN

Read the task carefully. Then, read it again, noting on your own paper the words that tell the topic, the purpose, and the audience.

WRITING TASK

Write a short story in which characters react to an unexpected event in their own neighborhood. In your story, try to entertain peers and adults by presenting a lively description of how the main character and others handle the unexpected event, and what happens as a result.

Topic → characters react to an unexpected event; *Purpose* → to entertain; *Audience* → peers and adults

2. PLAN YOUR RESPONSE — 10 MIN

Use a graphic organizer to brainstorm details for your story. Answer the questions below to fill in information for each part of the graphic organizer.

1. **Exposition:** What is the unexpected event? What does the main character say, think, feel, and do as a result of the event? What conflict does the event create?
2. **Rising Action:** What complications arise as the characters try to resolve the central conflict?
3. **Climax:** What is the most exciting or suspenseful part of the story? Who is involved?
4. **Falling Action:** What events or actions occur that indicate the conflict is close to being resolved?
5. **Resolution:** How is the conflict resolved? Do the neighborhood and characters change because of the unexpected event? If so, how?

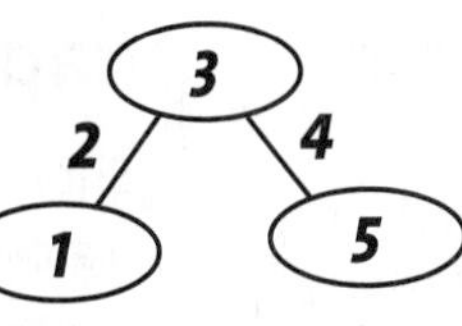

3. RESPOND TO THE TASK — 20 MIN

Begin drafting your short story. A quick way to begin is to write a short dialogue that introduces the characters and establishes the setting and central conflict. As you write the rest of your draft, be sure to maintain a consistent point of view.

4. IMPROVE YOUR RESPONSE — 5–10 MIN

Revising Go back to the key aspects of the task. Does your story have a vivid setting and an interesting main character? Have you developed a plot that begins with an unexpected event and then tells what happens? Is your point of view consistent? If not, add these elements.

Proofreading Correct errors in grammar, spelling, punctuation, and capitalization. Make sure that your edits are neat and that the paper is legible.

Checking Your Final Copy Before you turn in your paper, read it one more time to catch any errors you may have missed.

Speaking & Listening Workshop

Dramatizing a Script

You have probably seen actors perform in a play at school or in a local theater. Before these actors could perform, they needed a script to tell them what to say and how to act.

 Complete the workshop activities in your **Reader/Writer Notebook.**

SPEAK WITH A PURPOSE	COMMON CORE TRAITS
TASK Adapt your short story into a **script.** Play the main character, and select classmates to play the other roles. Practice your script, and then present it to your class.	***A STRONG SCRIPT . . .*** • develops and resolves a central conflict • uses dialogue to further the plot, reveal character traits and relationships, and develop and resolve conflicts • presents a smooth progression of events to create a coherent story • has stage directions that give guidance to the director, performers, and stage crew • conveys the significance of the events in the story

COMMON CORE

SL 1b, d Work with peers to promote civil discussions and decision-making, set clear goals and deadlines, and establish roles; respond thoughtfully to diverse perspectives. **SL 6** Adapt speech to a variety of contexts and tasks.

Adapt Your Short Story

Short stories and scripts are crafted differently, but they have the same goal—to tell a story. A script is the text of a play, film, or broadcast. It consists of dialogue and stage directions—the writer's instructions for the director, performers, and stage crew. Usually set in italics, they are located at the beginning of and throughout a script. Scripts are also divided into scenes. Each scene portrays a new setting.

Use the following tips and techniques to adapt your short story into a script:

- **Examine and Revise Dialogue** During a play, film, or broadcast, the only thing the audience hears is dialogue. Dialogue must further the plot, reveal character traits and relationships, develop and resolve conflicts, and convey the significance of the events. Make sure your dialogue accomplishes all of these things.
- **Add Stage Directions** Go through your short story and highlight precise words and phrases, telling details, and sensory language that convey the setting, plot details, character traits, and character relationships. Turn these details into stage directions that tell the actors how the characters should be portrayed and tell the director or stage crew how the scene should look.
- **Make the Significance of the Events Clear** Read your dialogue and stage directions. Does your script convey the significance of the events clearly? You can do this explicitly—in a direct manner—or implicitly—indirectly through clues. These clues could include characterization, mood, symbolism, foreshadowing, and irony. Be sure to include several kinds of clues to help your audience understand the significance of your story.

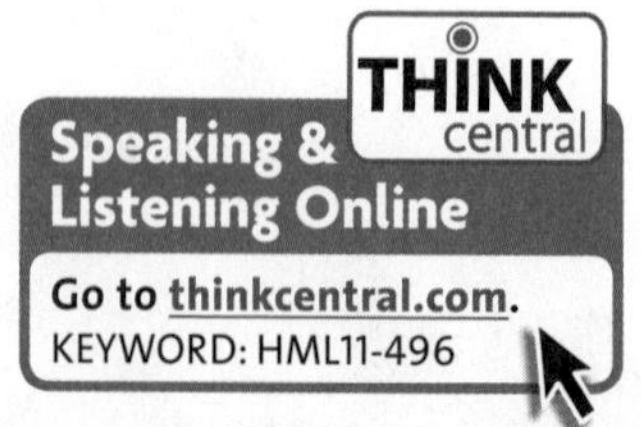

Present Your Script

CHOOSE TECHNIQUES FOR YOUR PERFORMANCE

As author of the story, you are the director of the performance. You should also portray the main character. Choose classmates to help you present your script and portray other characters. Read through the script with these classmates. As a group, discuss the different verbal and nonverbal techniques you should use to portray your characters. You and your classmates may disagree about the techniques. Respond respectfully to their viewpoints and try to resolve any differences. But if disagreement persists, you as the director may choose the techniques for the performance of your script.

Tips

VERBAL TECHNIQUES

- Decide what your **speaking rate** should be in various parts of the story. Base your speaking rate on the character's personality and situation. For instance, if your character is nervous, you might want to increase the rate of your speech.
- **Enunciate** your words clearly and speak loudly. Even if the script instructs a character to whisper, you should whisper loudly enough so the audience can hear you.

NONVERBAL TECHNIQUES

- Remember that your character's **body language** can convey important information. For instance, if a character is hunched over and always hovering in corners, the audience may conclude that this character is shy.
- Use **facial expressions** to convey your character's thoughts and emotions. For instance, an angry character may exhibit a prominent scowl.

PREPARE FOR YOUR PERFORMANCE

Review the criteria for adapting your short story into a script and the effective use of verbal and nonverbal techniques in the performance. Set clear goals for you and your classmates to work toward as you prepare for your performance. To do this, create a rubric or checklist using agreed upon criteria for evaluation. Set a deadline for when you will be ready for your performance. Rehearse your performance several times before presenting it to the class.

As a Speaker Use the rubric as you practice. Perform your script for the class. After your performance, promote discussion with your audience by asking for their feedback about the script and the performance. Use their feedback to revise your script and adjust your performance.

As a Listener Watch another group perform a script. Use the rubric that your group developed to evaluate the performance. After the performance, offer the writer feedback on the effectiveness of the script. Also, respond respectfully when you critique the actors' performances.

Assessment Practice

ASSESS

Taking this practice test will help you assess your knowledge of these skills and determine your readiness for the Unit Test.

REVIEW

After you take the practice test, your teacher can help you identify any standards you need to review.

COMMON CORE

RI 2 Determine two central ideas of a text and analyze their development over the course of the text. **RI 3** Analyze a sequence of events and explain how specific individuals interact and develop over the course of the text. **RI 4** Determine the meaning of words and phrases as they are used in the text, including figurative and connotative meanings. **RI 7** Evaluate information presented in different media or formats. **L 1** Demonstrate command of the conventions of standard English grammar and usage when writing. **L 2** Demonstrate command of the conventions of standard English capitalization, punctuation, and spelling. **L 3** Apply knowledge of language to make effective choices for meaning or style.

DIRECTIONS **Read the two selections and the viewing and representing piece. Then answer the questions that follow.**

The Daydreamer

by Magdalena Gómez

1 "I'm going to Spain," I announced to my Puerto Rican mother and Spanish gypsy father the night before my fourteenth birthday.

2 Looking over the top of the *Daily News*, my father, Virgilio Segarra-Fernandez, asked: "Huh?" Only one of his eardrums worked properly.

3 "To Spain. I'm going to Spain. I want to learn to dance like my grandmother. I want to see the castles in Valledolid. I want to go—"

4 "How? Your poor father doesn't even have a box to drop dead in," interrupted my mother, Lydia Segarra, as she pressed pleats into my birthday dress.

5 "I'm getting a job. Monday I can apply for working papers."

6 "No daughter of Virgilio Segarra-Fernandez is going to work. You go to school. You learn and go to college, then you can work anywhere you want," said my father, his attention going back to the *Daily News*.

7 "Your papí is right. And besides that, an educated woman doesn't have to get married if she doesn't want to."

8 Papí gave Mamí one of those serious looks of his when she said that. The air was getting thick and I thought maybe Papí's neck veins might start getting wiggly, so I just shut up.

9 That night, I hated my Castro Convertible bed in the living room more than ever. I would be fourteen years old in a matter of hours and didn't even have my own room. The radiator pipes played poor-people music all night long. Clink, clank, clunk, pssssst . . . clunk, clink, pssst, clank; Doña Rosa's French poodle tap-danced on the linoleum upstairs, and mice held their nightly festivals inside the walls. That was it! I'd had it! I was going to school *and* getting a job, and not just any job either. I was going to be a cashier in a supermarket. I would start by packing groceries and work my way up.

10 I took my notebook and a flashlight into bed and wrote down everything I had to do to get ready. The first thing was to talk my father into it; next, polish my dress shoes; next, practice my cursive for the job application; next, straighten my hair with big rollers so it wouldn't look frizzy—nobody who worked in the supermarket had frizzy hair, except the cleaning guy, Don Luis, and he was really old. He had fake teeth and would put them in his mouth weird to make us kids laugh. I secretly wished he was my grandfather, since I never had one. Anyway, I filled two pages in my notebook, no skipping lines, and fell asleep like I was dead.

11 In the morning, my mother sang "Happy Birthday" in Spanish and told me to take a good bath, brush my teeth, and braid my hair because all the family from

her side was coming for my birthday. My father didn't have a family in the Bronx. They all lived in Spain and didn't believe in taking airplanes. They were just scared of them, like my father was, but I pretended that I didn't know so that he wouldn't be embarrassed.

12 None of my friends from school were coming, except Amparo, because my mother thought they were all a bunch of good-for-nothings. Amparo lived with her strict grandmother and had to stay home all the time, just like me. I liked Amparo, but she was so pretty I always felt fat and ugly around her. All the boys liked her, but she had to act like she didn't care or her grandmother would have an attack of nerves. I *really* didn't care, because all I could think about was being a cashier in a pink uniform with my name embroidered on the pocket. I would do the embroidery myself. No plastic name tags for me. Sometimes you just have to be different or you feel boring.

13 I did all my birthday stuff, put on my dress, and waited in the kitchen for everybody to show up. The first one to arrive was Tía Consuelo. I saw the soft package under her flabby arm and I knew she had knitted me another hat with *lentejuelas* on it, those big tacky sequins. The kind of hat I wouldn't wear if my hair looked like Brillo and it was minus 100 degrees. God knows, I would never get a job wearing *that*. I thought to myself that when I did get that job, and I knew that I would, I would buy my own birthday presents, and a real fine hat made of velvet, the kind that is so soft it makes me want to cry.

14 A whole gang of cousins showed up, all of them too young or too old to play with. I got all kinds of presents: toys I had outgrown or clothes I'd have to grow into, but nothing that would help me get a job. One nice dress from my mother, a little too pink, good for a party, not for a job. I drank soda and ate cake, ice cream, candy—all the stuff my mom won't let me eat until I finish all my vegetables and what she calls "real food." No vegetables on my birthday; that was the best part. There was lots of real food, but with so many people to entertain, my mother didn't notice if I ate it or not.

15 Some neighbors showed up and told jokes that I didn't think were funny, but I laughed anyway. I didn't want to hurt their feelings. Grownups get hurt really easily and then they get mad. So everybody laughed, played music, and had a good time. Nobody seemed to really care if I was there or not, or if I was really happy. I was just the excuse for them to have a party.

16 It didn't matter. All I could think about was my new job that I didn't have yet.

17 When I got to school on Monday, I went to the guidance counselor, Mrs. Mason, to see about working papers. Mrs. Mason said my parents would have to sign them. I told her about my supermarket idea, and she said I should try babysitting

GO ON

first because she didn't think I was old enough to handle money. I told her I was an "A" student in math, and she just cleared her throat and adjusted her glasses. I said, "Thank you very much" and put my working papers in my sock, since I had left my book bag in class.

18 I went back to class and got in trouble during Social Studies. The teacher, Mr. Moss, said I was daydreaming and that I could do that on my own time. He said daydreamers don't get into college. I told him, "Yes, you're right. They become Albert Einstein." He turned beet red and sent me to the principal's office.

19 Outside Mr. No-Neck's office (his real name was Mr. Nobeck) the walls were the color of *café con leche* that's a little too strong, and there was one of those "Do Your Best" kind of posters on the wall with phony smiling kids on it.

20 I have to admit, I was sweating. If my parents ever found out I was kicked out of class, there's no way I'd get either of them to sign my working papers, not to mention the scolding I'd get. My mother would scream and my father would give me the silent treatment, then they'd scream at each other. "She's *your* daughter," my mother would yell. My father would sit there, his neck veins getting wiggly, thinking of something to say, and once he said it, World War Three would break out, and all the neighbors would know everything I'd done wrong since the day I was born.

21 Mr. No-Neck came out of his office and called me in. "Miss Segarra, I hear you have a very smart mouth. Mr. Moss is very upset. His note also says you were daydreaming in class," No-Neck said, trying hard to sound like he doesn't come from the Bronx.

22 "I didn't mean to be smart, and I was just thinking," I mumbled, my eyes looking down at my scuffed shoes.

23 "Thinking? And about exactly *what* were you thinking?" he asked, poking holes in the air with his finger.

24 "My job. The one I'm going to get, I mean, at the supermarket; I'm going to be a cashier and save money so I can go to Spain," I said, looking at his veiny nose.

25 "Spain? Why Spain?" He seemed really interested.

26 "Because that's where my father's from. I want to see the castles and learn to dance like my grandmother." I forgot I was nervous.

27 "You want to dance the flamingo?"

28 "No, I want to dance *flamenco*. No offense, Mr. Nobeck, but flamingo is a bird."

29 I couldn't help myself. I was tired of people getting away with that *flamingo* thing. It's like calling Puerto Rico Porto Reek-o. I bit my lip and waited for No-Neck to blow his top.

30 "Well, Miss Segarra, it seems you do indeed have a smart mouth, and I'm not so sure that's such a bad thing." He said it very softly. I got sweaty-suspicious. "How do you say it, fla-mink-ko?" he asked sincerely.

31 "No. *Fla-men-co,*" I said slowly. "Fla-maine-co. Fla-man-co. Flamenco." He kept trying until he got it. Then he got quiet for a really long time. I got nervous

again. "It's too bad you have your heart set on that supermarket job." As he spoke, his right pointer finger was bouncing off his lips.

32 "How come?" I asked.

33 "Well, some of the seniors could use a Spanish tutor after school."

34 "Seniors?" I gulped.

35 "Yes. They need a tutor so that *they* don't go around saying *flamingo* when they mean *flamenco*. But I don't suppose you'd be interested." Nobeck looked out his window.

36 "Maybe. What does the job pay?" I asked in my best business voice.

37 "Two dollars an hour," he said in a very flat voice, looking me dead in the eyes now.

38 My mind raced between Don Luis and his funny teeth and my name embroidered on the pink smock, and all the work I had done to prepare for my big interview.

39 "I would be happy to speak with your parents. We must have their permission," he said.

40 I figured he had a better chance talking my parents into it than I would, since grownups listen to each other more often than they listen to kids. "Okay, Mr. Nobeck, I'll try it." The thought of tutoring seniors made my stomach quake. "How many hours a week?" I asked, trying hard to act cool.

41 "An hour and a half, three times a week."

42 "That's only nine dollars a week." I felt limp.

43 "That's right."

44 "How many weeks?"

45 "Thirty. It's for the whole rest of the school year."

46 "That's two hundred seventy dollars." I was showing off how good my math was.

47 "Correct. Well?" He was standing up now.

48 "It's a deal."

49 I shook his hand. There was no turning back now. My parents had taught me that a handshake is your word of honor. They would have to sign the papers now, they would never, ever want me to go back on my word. I liked that about my parents. I didn't always like what they said, and I still hated vegetables and hats with lentejuelas, and my father's wiggly veins, and my mother's screaming, but they weren't so bad. They always kept their word. They just didn't remember how hard it was to be fourteen. Getting the rent paid was hard enough.

50 Nobeck said goodbye and added, "Einstein said that imagination is better than knowledge. I'm sure you'll get to Spain, Miss Segarra. And stay out of trouble. Don't stop daydreaming, just don't do it in class. And I expect you to apologize to Mr. Moss." His hands were in his pockets now.

51 "Yes, Mr. Nobeck. Thank you."

52 I left thinking about going to Puerto Rico next. Maybe I would invite Amparo. In my mind, I embroidered my name in the sky.

The Secret Latina

by Veronica Chambers
from *Essence*, July 2000

1 She's a platanos-frying, malta Dukesa-drinking, salsa-dancing Mamacita—my dark-skinned Panamanian mother. She came to this country when she was 21, her sense of culture intact, her Spanish flawless. Even today, more than 20 years since she left her home country to become an American citizen, my mother still considers herself Panamanian and checks 'Hispanic' on census forms.

2 As a Black woman in America, my Latin identity is murkier than my mother's, despite the fact that I, too, was born in Panama, and call that country 'home.' My father's parents came from Costa Rica and Jamaica, my mother's from Martinique. I left Panama when I was 2 years old. My family lived in England for three years then came to the States when I was 5. Having dark skin and growing up in Brooklyn in the 1970's meant I was Black, period. You could meet me and not know I was of Latin heritage. Without a Spanish last name or my mother's fluent Spanish at my disposal, I often felt isolated from the Latin community.

3 I found it almost impossible to explain to my elementary-school friends why my mother would speak Spanish at home. They would ask if I was Puerto Rican and look bewildered when I told them I was not. To them, Panama was a kind of nowhere. There weren't enough Panamanians in Brooklyn to be a force. Everybody knew where Jamaicans were from because of famous singers like Bob Marley. Panamanians had Ruben Blades, but most of my friends thought he was Puerto Rican, too.

4 In my neighborhood, where the smell of somebody's grandmother's cooking could transform a New York corner into Santo Domingo, Kingston or Port-au-Prince, a Panamanian was a sort of fish with feathers—assumed to be a Jamaican who spoke Spanish. The analogy was not without historical basis: A century ago, Panama's Black community was largely drawn to the country from all over the Caribbean as cheap labor to build the Panama Canal.

5 My father didn't mind that we considered ourselves Black rather than Latino. He named my brother Malcolm X, and if my mother hadn't put her foot down, I would have been called Angela Davis Chambers. It's not that my mother didn't admire Angela Davis, but you have only to hear how 'Veronica Victoria' flows off her Spanish lips to know that she was homesick for Panama and for those names that sang like timbales on carnival day. So between my father and my mother was a Black-Latin divide. Because of my father, we read and discussed books about Black history and civil rights. Because of my mother, we ate Panamanian food, listened to salsa and heard Spanish at home.

6 Still, it wasn't until my parents divorced when I was 10 that my mother tried to teach Malcolm and me Spanish. She was a terrible language teacher. She had no sense of how to explain structure, and her answer to every question was "That's just the way it is." A few short weeks after our Spanish lessons began, my mother gave up and we were all relieved. But I remained intent on learning my mother's language. When she spoke Spanish, her words were a fast current, a stream of language that was colorful, passionate, fiery. I wanted to speak Spanish because I wanted to swim in the river of her words, her history, my history, too.

7 At school I dove into the language, matching what little I knew from home with all that I learned. One day, when I was in the ninth grade, I finally felt confident enough to start speaking Spanish with my mother. I soon realized that by speaking Spanish with her, I was forging an important bond. When I'd spoken only English, I was the daughter, the little girl. But when I began speaking Spanish, I became something more—a hermanita, a sisterfriend, a Panamanian homegirl who could hang with the rest of them. Eventually this bond would lead me home.

8 Two years ago, at age 27, I decided it was finally time. I couldn't wait any longer to see Panama, the place my mother and my aunts had told me stories about. I enlisted my cousin Digna as a traveling companion and we made arrangements to stay with my godparents, whom I had never met. We planned our trip for the last week in February—carnival time.

9 Panama, in Central America, is a narrow sliver of a country: You can swim in the Caribbean Sea in the morning and backstroke across the Pacific in the afternoon. As our plane touched down, bringing me home for the first time since I was 2, I felt curiously comfortable and secure. In the days that followed, there was none of the culture shock that I'd expected—I had my mother and aunts to thank for that. My godmother Olga reminded me of them. The first thing she did was book appointments for Digna and me to get our eyebrows plucked and our nails and feet done with Panamanian-style manicures and pedicures. "It's carnival," Aunt Olga said, "and you girls have to look your best." We just laughed.

10 In Panama, I went from being a lone Black girl with a curious Latin heritage to being part of the Latinegro tribe or the Afro-Antillianos, as we were officially called. I was thrilled to learn there was actually a society for people like me. Everyone was Black, everyone spoke Spanish and everyone danced the way they danced at fiesta time back in Brooklyn, stopping only to chow down on a smorgasbord of souse, rice with black-eyed peas, beef patties, empanadas and codfish fritters. The carnival itself was an all-night bacchanal with elaborate floats, brilliantly colored costumes and live musicians. In the midst of all this, my godmother took my cousin and me to a photo studio to have our pictures taken in polleras, the traditional dress. After spending an hour on makeup and hair and donning a rented costume, I looked like Scarlett in Gone With the Wind.

11 Back in New York, I gave the photo to my mother. She almost cried. She says she was so moved to see me in a pollera because it was "such a patriotic thing to do." Her appreciation made me ridiculously happy; ever since I was a little girl, I'd wanted to be like my mother. In one of my most vivid memories, I am 7 or 8 and my parents are having a party. Salsa music is blaring and my mother is dancing and laughing. She sees me standing off in a corner, so she pulls me into the circle of grown-ups and tries to teach me how to dance to the music. Her hips are electric. She puts her hands on my sides and says, "Move these," and I start shaking my hip bones as if my life depends on it.

12 Now I am a grown woman, with hips to spare. I can salsa. My Spanish isn't shabby. You may look at me and not know that I am Panamanian, that I am an immigrant, that I am both Black and Latin. But I am my mother's daughter, a secret Latina, and that's enough for me.

Salsa, Tango, Rumba, Mambo,
Merengue, and more

Classes taught
by Salsa Champion
Victoria Marquez Salinas
at the Latin Dance Studio in
downtown Springville

Learn Latin Dance
for *FUN* and
EXERCISE

Sign up now!
Call 555-6759

¡El baile latino es muy caliente!

Reading Comprehension

Use "The Daydreamer" (pp. 498–501) to answer questions 1–11.

1. The main reason the narrator wants to get a job is —
   A. to help her family survive
   B. to travel and learn about her heritage
   C. to pay for college
   D. to buy herself a birthday present

2. Paragraphs 9 and 10 are mainly about —
   A. how excited the narrator is for her birthday
   B. the narrator's desire to change her circumstances
   C. how the narrator falls asleep
   D. the problems in the narrator's house

3. For the girl, the highlight of her birthday party is —
   A. her friends singing Happy Birthday in Spanish
   B. laughing at her neighbors' jokes
   C. receiving presents from her cousins
   D. eating only what she wants

4. An antonym for *flabby* in paragraph 13 is —
   A. firm
   B. healthy
   C. loose
   D. strong

5. The author inserts an extra space between paragraphs 16 and 17 to —
   A. introduce a new character
   B. write about a different theme
   C. indicate a passage of time
   D. tell a story about the father

6. In paragraph 17, the narrator tells the guidance counselor that she is an A student in math because —
   A. the counselor doesn't think she is smart enough to get a job
   B. the narrator is sharing part of her resume with the counselor
   C. the counselor is trying to convince the parents to let the narrator get a job
   D. the narrator is showing she can be responsible with money

7. In paragraph 19, *phony* means —
   A. authentic
   B. false
   C. distant
   D. loud

8. The narrator is sent out of class because —
   A. she will not answer the teacher's question
   B. she has embarrassed the teacher
   C. the principal wants to talk to her about a job
   D. she is not paying attention

9. Mr. Nobeck, the principal, doesn't get angry with the narrator when she corrects his pronunciation because —
   A. he was just testing her
   B. she said "No offense."
   C. he didn't hear her clearly
   D. she knew what she was talking about

10. Which of the following sentences from the selection best expresses a theme of the story?

A. You learn and go to college, then you can work anywhere you want.

B. It's too bad you have your heart set on that supermarket job.

C. Einstein said that imagination is better than knowledge.

D. My parents had taught me that a handshake is your word of honor.

11. The narrator ends the story talking about Puerto Rico because —

A. she has already made it to Spain in her mind

B. it is cheaper to go to Puerto Rico than to Spain

C. her friend Amparo is from Puerto Rico

D. she is bored in class

Use "The Secret Latina" (pp. 502–504) to answer questions 12–17.

12. Paragraph 1 is mainly about —

A. the eating and drinking habits of Panamanians

B. the mother's cultural identity

C. the requirements to be "Hispanic" on the census form

D. how long it takes to become an American citizen

13. In paragraph 2, the author says she considered herself Black because —

A. there weren't many Panamanians living in Brooklyn

B. she didn't have a Latin last name

C. other Latinos disliked Panamanians

D. she was a Latina with dark skin

14. The expression "a sort of fish with feathers" in paragraph 4 means —

A. a person new to a neighborhood

B. an unfamiliar combination of two familiar qualities

C. an everyday sight

D. a name for Jamaicans who speak Spanish

15. The father teaches his children about Black history and civil rights because —

A. he wants to teach them about his new identity

B. the mother wants the children to know about both cultures

C. he knows the mother can't teach them Spanish

D. the children consider themselves Black

16. In paragraph 9, the reader can conclude that the author didn't experience culture shock because —

A. she had been taught about the culture and language

B. she wasn't in Panama very long

C. her relatives planned everything for her

D. she went with her cousin

17. In paragraph 10, the word *smorgasbord* means —

A. one plate with lots of food

B. a buffet of hot and cold dishes

C. a party where food is served

D. a type of Panamanian food

GO ON

Use "The Daydreamer" and "The Secret Latina" to answer question 18.

18. The narrators of both selections would probably agree that —
    - **A.** Spanish is a difficult language to learn
    - **B.** parents don't understand their children
    - **C.** culture is an important part of identity
    - **D.** school is necessary for travel

Use the visual representation on page 505 to answer questions 19–20.

19. The purpose of the photograph on the poster is most likely to —
    - **A.** teach how to dance the tango
    - **B.** emphasize the importance of dramatic lighting
    - **C.** inspire viewers to take a dance class
    - **D.** model proper dance costuming

20. Which of these elements of the poster supports the dance studio's credibility?
    - **A.** *Come Learn All the Hottest Dances*
    - **B.** *Salsa, Tango, Rumba, Mambo, Merengue, and more*
    - **C.** *Learn to Dance for Fun, for Exercise*
    - **D.** *Classes taught by Salsa Champion Victoria Marquez Salinas*

SHORT CONSTRUCTED RESPONSE

Write a short constructed response to each question, using text evidence to support your response.

21. Who do you think has the greatest impact on the narrator of "The Daydreamer"? Support your response with evidence from the selection.

22. In what ways is "The Secret Latina" about discovering one's cultural heritage? In what ways is it about the changing relationship between a parent and child? Support your response with evidence from the selection.

Write a short constructed response to the following question, using text evidence from both selections to support your response.

23. What is one characteristic shared by both narrators? Support your response with evidence from **both** selections.

Revising and Editing

DIRECTIONS Read this passage and answer the questions that follow.

(1) The honeybee is well known for its production of honey and beeswax. (2) It is also renowned, however, for its exceptional memory and its language system, which is complex. (3) The honeybee has an excellent short-term memory. (4) It remembers where the best food sources are and knows when their quality is best. (5) The honeybee locates these food sources by remembering the color and scent of the flowers. (6) The honeybee forms a short-term memory of the flower's color. (7) It converts this initial memory to a long-term memory through a biological process. (8) Even after winter hibernation, these foragers go right to the flowers they visited the summer before. (9) One group of honeybees was even able to fly through a maze!

1. What change, if any, should be made in sentence 1?

A. Change ***its*** to **it's**

B. Change ***beeswax*** to **beezwax**

C. Insert a comma after ***honey***

D. Make no change

2. What is the most effective way to revise sentence 2?

A. It is also renowned, however, for its exceptional memory and complex language system.

B. It is also renowned, however, for its exceptional memory; also, its language system is complex.

C. It is also renowned, however, for its exceptional memory and has a language system that is complex.

D. It is also renowned, however, for its memory, which is exceptional, and it has a complex language system.

3. What is the most effective way to add details to sentence 5 using an adjective clause?

A. The honeybee dutifully locates these food sources by remembering the color and scent of the flowers.

B. The honeybee locates these food sources by remembering the rich color and aromatic scent of the flowers.

C. The honeybee locates these food sources by remembering the color and scent of the flowers that provide the best pollen and nectar.

D. The honeybee locates these food sources by remembering the best pollen and nectar food sources and the color and scent of the flowers.

4. What is the most effective way to improve the organization of the paragraph?

A. Move sentence 1 to the end of the paragraph

B. Switch sentences 8 and 9

C. Delete sentence 9

D. Switch sentences 6 and 7

Ideas for Independent Reading

Continue exploring the Questions of the Times on pages 302–303 with these additional works.

Is the price of progress ever TOO HIGH?

Rip Van Winkle and Other Stories
by Washington Irving

Behind the high jinks and folklore of the stories in this collection, there lurks a mingled sense of wonder and worry at the rapid changes taking place in America in the early 19th century. In the title tale, for example, Rip Van Winkle falls asleep in a British colony and wakes 20 years later in a new nation, his village's statue of King George replaced with one of George Washington. With insight and humor, Irving makes a profound social comment on the changes taking place in his time.

The Last of the Mohicans
by James Fenimore Cooper

The hero of this story, Natty Bumppo, lives on the borderline between two cultures—admired by both Indians and whites, but truly at home with neither. Here, Natty and his Indian friend Chingachgook escort two British maidens through hostile territory during the French and Indian War. Breathtaking chases and gun battles ensue. Yet through the course of the story a deeper theme emerges: that the United States, in its desire for wealth, may have forsaken the rewards of living in harmony with nature.

Is it patriotic to protest one's GOVERNMENT?

Uncle Tom's Cabin
by Harriet Beecher Stowe

Written toward the end of the romantic period, Stowe's novel changed history. Appalled by the institution of slavery, Stowe set out to make whites see slaves as human beings—mothers, fathers, children, *people* with hearts and souls like any other. Her work became immensely popular and did in fact influence opinions and garner support for the abolitionist movement. Indeed, the novel had so great an impact that it has often been cited as one of the causes of the Civil War.

The Night Thoreau Spent in Jail
by Jerome Lawrence and Robert E. Lee

Issues of moral and civic responsibility take center stage in this play dramatizing the risks Thoreau took to follow his conscience. As the curtain rises, Thoreau is behind bars—his punishment for committing an act of civil disobedience. When Ralph Waldo Emerson visits, Thoreau challenges him to defy a government that fosters injustice.

The Poetry of John Greenleaf Whittier: A Readers' Edition
by John Greenleaf Whittier

John Greenleaf Whittier was committed to using poetry to bring about social reform. This anthology includes several poems that explore the evils of slavery. One such poem, "Ichabod," savaged real-life senator Daniel Webster for his support of the Missouri Compromise and the Fugitive Slave Act.

RL 10 Read and comprehend literature. **RI 10** Read and comprehend literary nonfiction.

Does everyone have a "DARK SIDE"?

The Fall of the House of Usher and Other Writings
by Edgar Allan Poe

Does everyone have a "dark side"? Over and over again, Poe answered that question with a resounding yes. In so doing, he helped establish the modes of horror and fantasy, which to this day dominate much of American culture. For an overview of the best of Poe's writing, this edition is the book to read. Murderous delusions, decadent appetites, and unspeakable cruelty pepper the stories and poems found here.

The House of the Seven Gables
by Nathaniel Hawthorne

This gothic romance tells of the Pyncheon family (owners of "the house of the seven gables"), whose ancestor Colonel Pyncheon has cursed them with his wicked deeds. In the book's preface, Hawthorne conveys its theme: "The wrong-doing of one generation lives into the successive ones, and . . . becomes a pure and uncontrollable mischief."

American Gothic Tales
edited by Joyce Carol Oates

Oates's anthology of haunting tales shows the far reaches of the gothic imagination in American literature. The collection includes short stories from over 40 of the best American horror writers of the past 200 years, ranging from Washington Irving to Stephen King.

Where do people look for TRUTH?

The Portable Thoreau
by Henry David Thoreau

An icon of individualism, Henry David Thoreau looked for the truth in two main places: nature and himself. Generations of readers have concluded not only that those are good places to search for the truth, but also that Thoreau—for all his peculiarities—did a fine job of finding it. This edition contains the full text of *Walden,* as well as poems, notebooks, journal entries, and essays such as "Civil Disobedience." These works allow readers to see past the confident sage of Walden to the prickly, affectionate, politically motivated man beneath.

The Essential Transcendentalists
edited by Richard G. Geldard

America's best transcendentalist thinkers and writers grappled with many questions of their day: What is woman's role in society? When and how should a person protest the government? How can we live ethical lives? Where can one find the truth? The works in this collection explore these and many other ideas as relevant today as they were nearly 200 years ago.

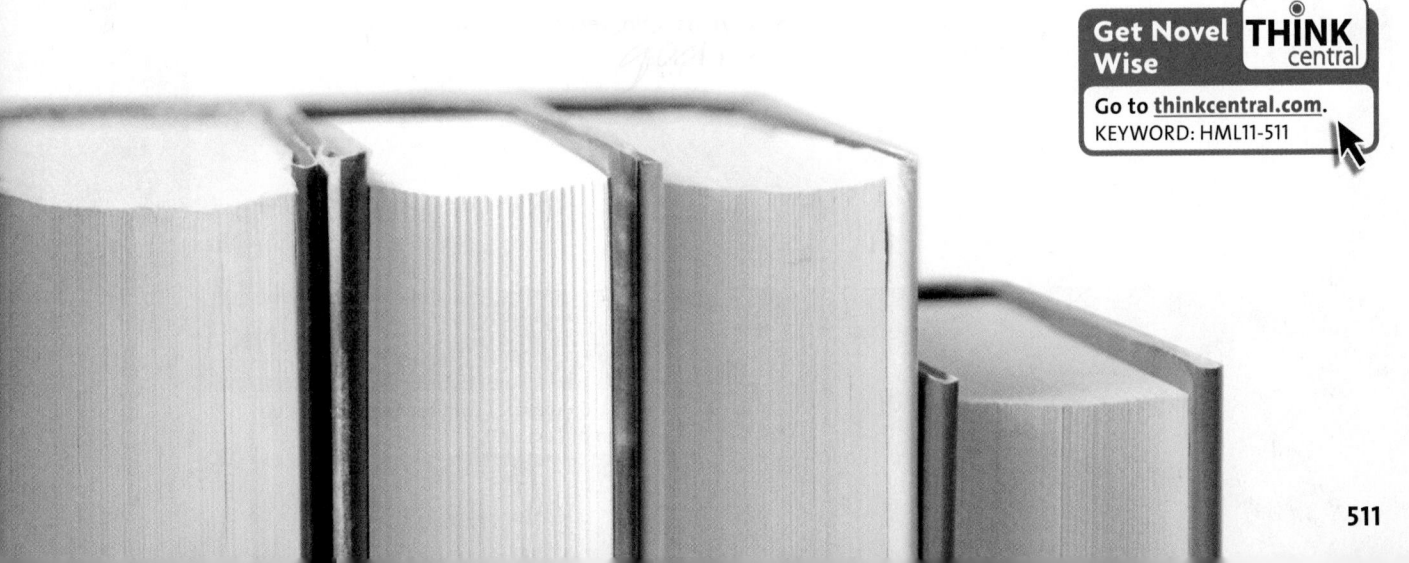

Get Novel Wise THINK central

Go to thinkcentral.com.
KEYWORD: HML11-511

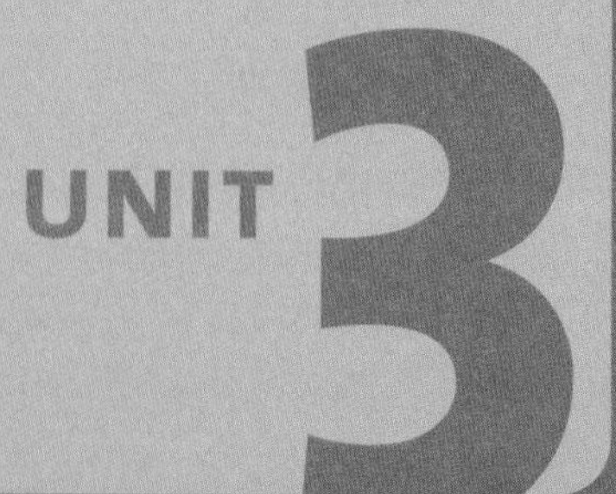

COMMON CORE

Preview Unit Goals

TEXT ANALYSIS	• Understand the historical and cultural contexts of romanticism and realism; understand realism as a literary movement • Analyze tone • Analyze and evaluate free verse • Analyze elements of style, including tone, sentence structure, figurative language, and dialogue • Analyze the styles of Whitman and Dickinson • Analyze narrative elements, including theme, structure, conflict, and characterization • Analyze primary sources • Analyze author's purpose • Evaluate the structure and reasoning used in a work
READING	• Take notes; synthesize information
WRITING AND LANGUAGE	• Make effective word choices; use vivid verbs • Use language that conveys tone • Write an informative article
VOCABULARY	• Use knowledge of Latin roots to understand word meaning
ACADEMIC VOCABULARY	• element • emphasis • conflict • create • perspective
MEDIA AND VIEWING	• Compare and contrast print and film versions of a work • Maintain an online feature article

Find It Online! THINK central

Go to thinkcentral.com for the interactive version of this unit.

From Romanticism to Realism 1855–1870

Frederick Douglass

AN AGE OF TRANSITION

- Brilliant Mavericks: Whitman and Dickinson
- Literature of the Civil War

Media Smart DVD-ROM

From Page to Screen

View a film version of "An Occurrence at Owl Creek Bridge" that evokes the dark-hued themes of Ambrose Bierce. Page 618

UNIT 3

Questions of the Times

DISCUSS After reading these questions and talking about them with a partner, share your views with the class as a whole. Then read on to explore the ways in which writers of the Civil War era dealt with the same issues.

What DIVIDES *a nation?*

In the years leading up to the Civil War, the agrarian South, whose economy depended upon slave labor, and the industrialized North, which became increasingly opposed to slavery, began to see each other as enemies. Slavery was one of many issues that divided Americans of the day. What issues or beliefs typically cause conflict between citizens? What divides Americans today?

Is anything worth DYING FOR?

During the Civil War, boys and young men on both sides of the conflict marched off to war with visions of becoming heroes in the service of a great cause. Hundreds of thousands never returned home. Was their sacrifice worthwhile? Would you ever be willing to risk your life for a flag, a group, or an idea?

COMMON CORE

RL 9 Demonstrate knowledge of nineteenth-century foundational works of American literature, including how two or more texts from the same period treat similar themes or topics. **RI 9** Analyze nineteenth-century foundational U.S. documents of historical and literary significance for their themes, purposes, and rhetorical features.

Why do people BREAK RULES?

Poets Walt Whitman and Emily Dickinson broke well-established conventions of poetic form and content, and today they are celebrated for their ingenuity. Yet, during their lives few readers recognized their genius because their work was radically different from the popular poetry of the day. Why do you think people break the rules if they will not be rewarded for it? Do artists, especially, tend to break the rules?

Is it important to FACE REALITY?

After the horrors of the Civil War, romantic attitudes no longer captured the spirit of America. Instead, artists and writers turned to a new movement known as realism, which reflected a different view of life—unsentimental, honest, and often harsh or even ugly. Do you think writers and artists should deal with life's realities or take us away from them?

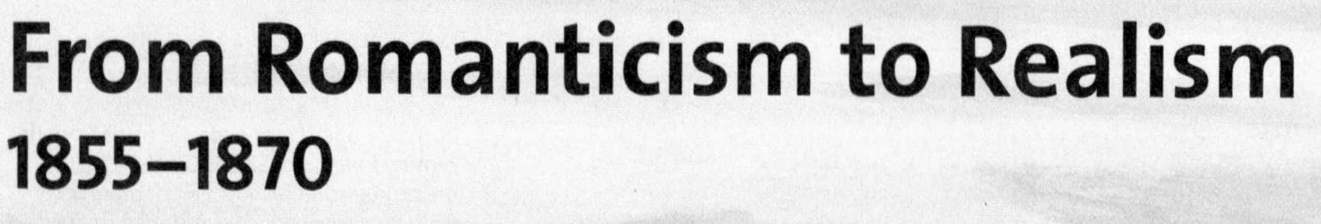

From Romanticism to Realism
1855–1870

An Age of Transition

The Civil War was a violent clash, not just of armies, but of ideas. Who was right, and who was wrong? What did it mean to be an American? Was any price too high to pay to keep the nation whole? There was nothing theoretical about the conflict—real people died, hundreds of thousands of them: fathers, sons, and brothers. But the war began before a single shot was ever fired. Writers served as its first soldiers, and the battle lines were drawn in ink.

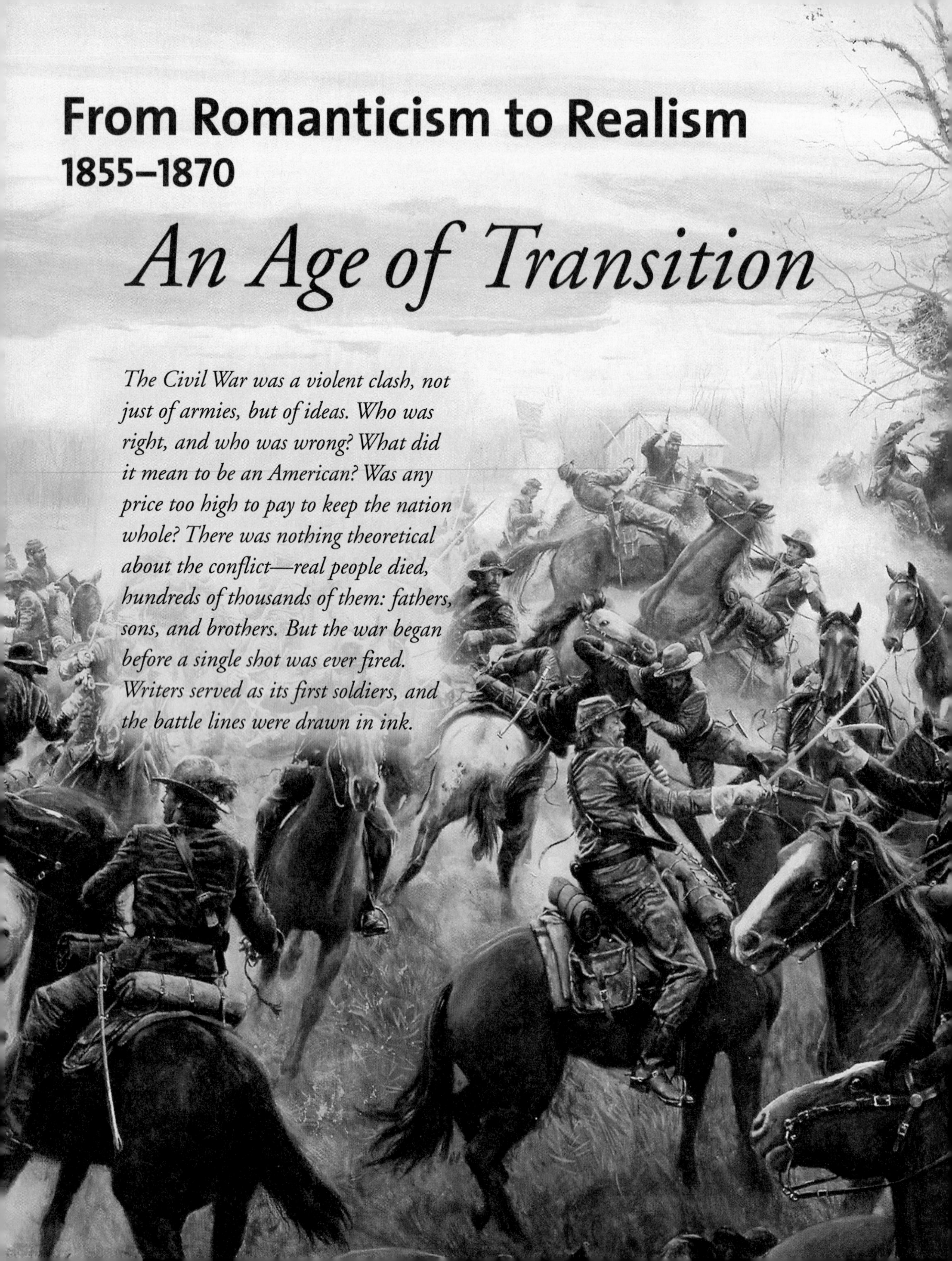

Emerging Realism: Historical Context

The central influence on literature of this period was the conflict between North and South that ended in the Civil War. Although romantic attitudes helped push the nation into war, four years of bitter fighting led to a new realism.

COMMON CORE

RL 9 Demonstrate knowledge of nineteenth-century foundational works of American literature, including how two or more texts from the same period treat similar themes or topics. **RI 9** Analyze nineteenth-century foundational U.S. documents of historical and literary significance for their themes, purposes, and rhetorical features.

A Cultural Divide

"A house divided against itself cannot stand," wrote **Abraham Lincoln** in 1858, referring to the bitterly divided United States. Since colonial times, the South and the North had shown strong regional differences. Most of the manufacturing and financial services of the nation were located in the North, whose economy was based primarily on trade and industry. In contrast, the South had developed an agricultural way of life—growing cotton, tobacco, and sugar cane for export to the North and Europe—that relied on the labor of nearly four million slaves. Most Southerners opposed any interference with slavery by the federal government because of the region's economic dependence on it, the widespread fear of slave unrest, and the belief that states should control their own affairs.

SLAVERY DIVIDES THE NATION Although national political leaders tried to sidestep the slavery issue, growing Northern opposition to slavery and its expansion into the West made confrontation inevitable. In the 1850s, several events moved the country to its breaking point. In Kansas, the vote over whether to join the Union as a free state or a slave state turned deadly when gun-toting mobs swarmed over the border from Missouri to cast illegal ballots in favor of slavery. Continuing violence between proslavery and antislavery settlers led people to begin calling the territory **Bleeding Kansas.** Abolitionist **John Brown** played a role in Bleeding Kansas in 1856, killing five proslavery men as revenge for the sacking of the antislavery town of Lawrence. Three years later, Brown again shocked the nation when he led a bloody raid on the federal arsenal at Harpers Ferry, hoping to spark a slave uprising. Writer **Henry David Thoreau** called Brown "an angel of light"; but fellow writer **Nathaniel Hawthorne** retorted, "No man was ever more justly hanged."

CONFLICT REACHES THE GOVERNMENT Even the floor of the U.S. Senate became a battleground. In 1856, Massachusetts senator Charles Sumner gave an impassioned speech against slavery, berating his colleagues for two days for their support of slavery. A few days later, Carolina congressman Preston S. Brooks retaliated by attacking Sumner with his cane, beating the Massachusetts senator unconscious. When writer **William Cullen Bryant** heard about the caning, he was outraged. "Has it come to this," he asked in the *New York Evening Post,* "that we must speak with bated breath in the presence of our Southern masters? . . . Are we, too, slaves, slaves for life, a

TAKING NOTES

Outlining As you read this introduction, use an outline to record main ideas about the historical characteristics and literature of this period. You can use headings, boldfaced terms, and the information in boxes like this one as starting points. (See page R49 in the **Research Handbook** for more help with outlining.)

I. Historical Context
  A. Cultural Divide
    1. Northern economy based on trade and industry; Southern based on agriculture and slavery
    2. slavery's expansion west provoked confrontation

Battle for the Shenandoah © Mort Künstler, Inc.

target for their brutal blows, when we do not comport ourselves to please them?" Meanwhile, newspapers across the South applauded the attack, describing abolitionists as unruly dogs to be collared and disciplined. Such angry name-calling and accusations reflected—and added to—the growing sense on both sides that Northerners and Southerners were no longer simply Americans from different regions, but foreigners and enemies.

In 1857, the Supreme Court entered the fray by hearing the case of **Dred Scott,** a slave whose owner had taken him to spend several years in a free state. Scott argued that living in a free state made him free; the Supreme Court ruled against him. Worse, it went on to say that even free blacks "had no rights which a white man was bound to respect." The *Dred Scott* decision sent shock waves through the already divided nation. Northerners were outraged and alarmed. Was the South's "peculiar institution" of slavery to become the law of the whole land?

SOUTHERN CHIVALRY — ARGUMENT VERSUS CLUB'S.
An 1856 cartoon of Congressman Preston S. Brooks attacking Senator Charles Sumner on the Senate floor.

The Civil War

Ironically, none of these acts led to the final break. Instead, the lawful election in 1860 of a politically moderate U.S. president, Abraham Lincoln, ignited war. Enraged at Lincoln's pledge to stop the western spread of slavery, the Southern states seceded to form the **Confederate States of America.**

For a generation that had grown up on the literary ideal of the brave, dashing **Romantic hero,** the booming of Confederate cannons firing on Fort Sumter in the spring of 1861 was a call to glory. Boys and young men rushed off to join the Union or Confederate army. Southerners boasted that a single one of them could lick ten Yankees; Northerners were sure that "Johnny Reb" would turn and run at the first shot. For many, the biggest fear was that the war would end too soon and they would miss their chance to become heroes.

The mood was nearly festive on the sunny July day when fresh Union forces marched south into Virginia to confront the rebels at Bull Run. Soldiers wandered from their lines to pick blackberries and drink cool water from the creek, and the cream of Washington society drove down in carriages with bottles of champagne and picnic baskets to enjoy the spectacle.

REALITY STRIKES By late afternoon, thousands of dead and wounded soldiers lay near the banks of Bull Run. On the losing side, panic-stricken Union soldiers stumbled away from the battlefield, their feet tangling in shawls and parasols that had been dropped by terrified civilians as they fled. The party was over.

A Voice from the Times

Future years will never know the seething hell and the black infernal background of countless minor scenes and interiors, (not the official surface courteousness of the Generals, not the few great battles) . . . the real war will never get in the books.

—Walt Whitman

The blood-soaked **Battle of Bull Run** gave everyone (especially the losing Union side) a taste of the reality of war, but it was only the beginning. Four long years of fighting followed. Names of battle sites became synonymous with death: Shiloh, Antietam, Fredericksburg, Gettysburg, Vicksburg. When the war ended at last, in April 1865, with **General Robert E. Lee's** surrender to **General Ulysses S. Grant** at Appomattox Courthouse, approximately 618,000 men had died—nearly as many Americans as have died in all other wars that the United States has ever fought. Much of the South lay in ruins, scarred by gutted plantation houses, burned bridges, and uprooted railroad lines.

Ideas of the Age

Americans in the postwar period embraced notions of freedom and unity. At the same time, they lost their taste for romanticism, having been confronted with the harsh realities of war.

A Voice from the Times

[W]e here highly resolve that these dead shall not have fought in vain—that this nation, under God, shall have a new birth of freedom—and that government of the people, by the people, for the people, shall not perish from the earth.

—Abraham Lincoln

Freedom and Unity

The United States was changed by the Civil War. It had suffered bitterly and was now a wiser, more somber nation. Yet the ideals of America's founders had survived the devastation of war. For the first time, the Declaration of Independence's notions of equality and liberty for all were brought closer to fruition. Slavery was dead—outlawed by Lincoln's bold **Emancipation Proclamation** and the **Thirteenth Amendment** to the Constitution. "We shout for joy that we live to record this righteous decree," said **Frederick Douglass.** "Free Forever!"

The Civil War had divided the country; its end brought the country back together. This time the country was united in a new way. Before the war, people were used to saying "The United States *are* . . . ," with the emphasis on the individual states more than on the united interests of all. After the war, people began saying "The United States *is* . . . ." A group of independent states had become one nation, indivisible, with the goal of liberty for all.

The Civil War changed not only American society but its literary culture as well. In the years following the war, American readers and writers found they had lost their taste for romanticism. Many had witnessed war's grim nature firsthand, and it shaped their view of life. Gallant heroism and adventure no longer suited America's tastes; nor did meditations on the beauty of nature or the worth of the individual. Writing became more honest, unsentimental, and ironic. A new style, **realism,** would predominate in the years to come.

Abraham Lincoln Reading the Emancipation Proclamation Before His Cabinet Members, undated color illustration after painting by Francis Bicknell Carpenter. © Bettmann/Corbis.

Literature of the Times

The Civil War was a transitional period for writers of the day. Groundbreaking poets, former slaves, famous public figures and everyday people all contributed their ideas as the country and its literature moved from romanticism to realism.

Brilliant Mavericks: Whitman and Dickinson

In 1842, when the conflicts leading to the Civil War were just beginning to brew and the romantic movement was going strong, writer **Ralph Waldo Emerson** issued a challenge to America. The nation needed a poet worthy of itself—a truly fresh voice with limitless passion and originality. "I look in vain," lamented Emerson, "for the poet whom I describe. We do not with sufficient plainness, or sufficient profoundness, address ourselves to life. . . ." In the coming decades, two poets would answer Emerson's bold call: **Walt Whitman** and **Emily Dickinson.**

Outwardly, Whitman and Dickinson had little in common. Whitman, big, bearded, and outspoken, was always in the thick of things and wrote many poems about current issues and events, from the sad plight of the slave to the shocking assassination of President Lincoln. Dickinson, on the other hand, was shy and reclusive, living her whole life in her native New England, and finding inspiration for her poetry in her own thoughts.

RULE-BREAKERS The two, however, were not entirely unalike. Both felt hemmed in by conventional ideas of how poems ought to look and what poems ought to say. Both wrote poetry so radical in form and content that it took many years for readers to appreciate it. (In Dickinson's case, appreciation didn't come until after her death.) Together, they broke poetry wide open, creating the most remarkable work of the Civil War era.

In 1855, Whitman published at his own expense a book of poetry called *Leaves of Grass.* The book was small, but it contained a huge ambition. Whitman saw America as a great poem, the greatest in the world, and his job was to capture it on paper. A sprawling, rowdy, vigorous young nation, he believed, could not be squeezed into traditional poetic forms. Instead, he wrote in **free verse,** unconfined by formal patterns of rhyme and meter. His lines were loose and rambling, his language colorful and vigorous, and he refused to limit himself to "poetic" subjects. If it was a part of American life, it was his to write about, even if it was a topic others might consider common or vulgar.

Emily Dickinson also found traditional poetic forms inadequate. Yet, where Whitman's poems were expansive, hers were terse and compressed—a few brief lines packed with complex, original images. Her subject matter was intensely personal, and her themes

▶ *For Your Outline*

BRILLIANT MAVERICKS

- Whitman and Dickinson answered Emerson's call for a national poet.
- Whitman was gregarious and outspoken; Dickinson, shy and reclusive.
- Both broke conventional rules of poetry.
- Whitman used free verse to write about everything American.
- Dickinson used compressed lines and complex imagery to explore personal themes.
- Both poets can be seen as transitional.

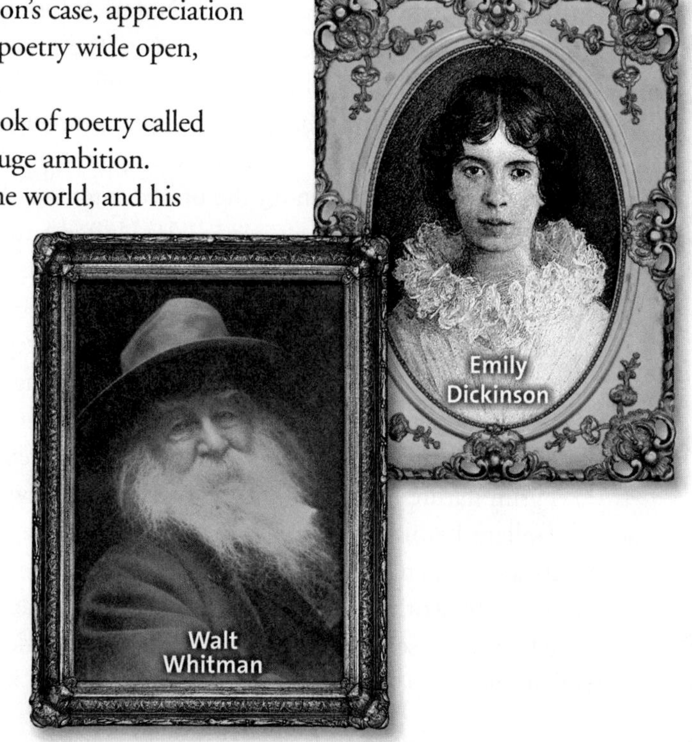
Emily Dickinson
Walt Whitman

© Tom Gauld/Heart USA Inc.

◀ Analyze Visuals

This cartoon is one artist's representation of Emily Dickinson's reclusive nature. What other personality traits does the artist suggest about Dickinson in these panels?

were the great themes of life: love, death, immortality, and nature. Although she wrote nearly 1,800 poems, only a handful appeared in print during her lifetime. In fact, she was virtually unknown in her time, living a reclusive life that belied the intense creative fervor of her inner world.

Neither Dickinson nor Whitman can be easily categorized. Although Whitman can be considered a romantic poet because of his emphasis on individualism, emotion, and nature, his exploration of topics others found vulgar was certainly not romantic. Dickinson, too, could be aggressively unromantic, with her images of ordinary household items and her abrupt, unemotional tone. Perhaps both poets can be seen as transitional, moving with Americans of the day from romanticism to realism.

Literature of the Civil War

Of all human actions, none speaks so dramatically nor so violently as war. Of all wars, civil war by its very nature divides a nation's voice into factions. Among the diverse literary voices heard during the Civil War, some of the most powerful were African American.

Often at the urging of abolitionists, former slaves who escaped to the North published **slave narratives** detailing their experiences. These tales of suffering were immensely important to the cause of antislavery. Not simply autobiography, they were testimony, giving lie to Southern claims that slaves were happy and well-treated, that slavery was a "positive good" for both master and slave, and that people of African descent were inferior to whites. More than that, the narratives made readers *care* by showing that slaves were real human beings who suffered and wept and longed for freedom.

For Your Outline

LITERATURE OF THE CIVIL WAR

- Slave narratives revealed the true nature of slavery and made readers care.
- Diaries and letters gave personal responses to historical events.
- Public documents influenced a large audience.
- Later fiction moved toward realism.

Fugitive slaves flee a Southern plantation at night in an attempt to reach the North.

Personal experience was central to the literature of the time, because everyday life now had great historical significance. Writers—male and female, white and black, from the highest-ranking general down to the common foot soldier—shared "their" Civil War in **diaries** and **letters**.

Voices from the Times

Many times I sat down in the mud determined to go no further, and willing to die to end my misery. But soon a friend would pass and urge me to make another effort, and I would stagger a mile further.

—Union soldier Elisha Rhodes

I daily part with my raiment for food. We find no one who will exchange eatables for Confederate money. So we are devouring our clothes.

—Southern diarist Mary Chesnut

While these writers addressed their words to friends and family (or even to themselves), others, such as President **Abraham Lincoln,** wrote for a larger audience. Still, Lincoln underestimated the reach of his words. "The world will little note, nor long remember, what we say here," he proclaimed in his **Gettysburg Address,** which in fact proved to be one of the most enduring works of the Civil War era.

Lincoln's speech, with its inspiring message and elevated language, represents the highest ideals of the period. The fiction created after the war by realistic writers such as **Ambrose Bierce** and **Stephen Crane,** however, shows the period in a harsher light. Their stories focus on the human tragedy of a war that destroyed hundreds of thousands of American lives, even as it freed many more.

In the years to come, **realism** would grow and refine itself to include the work of writers countrywide, from the frozen arctic north of Jack London to the plains of Willa Cather's frontier. It would develop to include the work of naturalist writers who viewed human beings as passive victims of their environment. Brought on by the brutalities of the Civil War, realism would become the form that to some extent still dominates American literature today.

THE ARTISTS' GALLERY

Prisoners from the Front (1866), Winslow Homer. Oil on canvas, 24″ × 38″. The Metropolitan Museum of Art, Gift of Mrs. Frank B. Porter, 1922 (22.207). Photo © 1995 The Metropolitan Museum of Art, New York.

Winslow Homer

Known for his bold technique and unsentimental style, **Winslow Homer** was one of the most admired artists of the 19th century. He first rose to acclaim during the Civil War.

Behind Union Lines When war broke out, *Harper's Weekly* sent Homer south, to draw illustrations for the magazine. The young artist camped out with the Union army and shared the soldiers' hardships, from meager rations to the deadly threat of typhoid fever.

Homer rarely drew a battle scene, spurning the romantic elements of high drama and heroism. Instead, he recorded the reality of everyday life in camp—the boredom and sadness of men far from home. In 1863, a critic praised him as "the first of our artists who has endeavored to tell us any truth about the war."

Civil War Masterpiece At first glance, the painting shown here might seem like nothing special, just soldiers standing in an empty field. Yet *Prisoners from the Front,* painted just after the war ended, won acclaim as the most powerful painting of the war. Why?

For Americans, this work had a deep symbolic meaning. In the soldiers, Homer conveys two opposing worldviews: the romantic, long-haired Southern officer confronts his Northern counterpart, who eyes him coolly. Behind them, the devastated landscape of the South tells the story of how the Civil War ends.

Connecting Literature, History, and Culture

As you read this timeline and answer the questions on the next page, think about the ways in which American literature was influenced by—and itself influenced—national and world events.

AMERICAN LITERARY MILESTONES

1855

1855 Frederick Douglass's autobiographical slave narrative, *My Bondage and My Freedom,* is published; Walt Whitman publishes the first edition of *Leaves of Grass* at his own expense.

1857 The *Atlantic Monthly,* a journal of literature and opinion, is founded. Over the years, Emerson, Longfellow, and other writers and editors will contribute to the magazine.

1859

1859 Henry David Thoreau writes "A Plea for Captain John Brown," in which he refers to the condemned abolitionist as "an angel of light."

1861 The first autobiography by a formerly enslaved woman, Harriet Jacobs's *Incidents in the Life of a Slave Girl,* is published. ▶

1862 Emily Dickinson writes 366 poems within the year.

HISTORICAL CONTEXT

1855

1856 Preston S. Brooks beats Massachusetts senator Charles Sumner with a cane on the floor of the Senate in retaliation for Sumner's antislavery speech.

1857 Supreme Court's *Dred Scott* decision declares that slaves and former slaves are not U.S. citizens and thus not entitled to basic rights. ▶

1859

1859 Abolitionist John Brown is hanged for treason after leading a raid on the federal arsenal at Harpers Ferry.

1860 Abraham Lincoln is elected president; in response, South Carolina secedes from the Union, followed eventually by ten other Southern states.

1861 Confederate guns fire on Fort Sumter, launching the Civil War. ▶

WORLD CULTURE AND EVENTS

1855

1855 British nurse Florence Nightingale introduces hygienic standards into military hospitals during the Crimean War. ▶

1856 Two states of Australia introduce the voting procedure known as the Australian, or secret, ballot.

1857 Indians rebel against British occupation of the subcontinent.

1859

1859 British naturalist Charles Darwin publishes *Origin of Species,* giving his theory of evolution.

1861 Czar Alexander II of Russia frees serfs; in England, Charles Dickens publishes *Great Expectations.*

1862 French physicist Jean Foucault calculates the speed of light; Victor Hugo publishes *Les Misérables.*

MAKING CONNECTIONS

- What examples do you see of American writers being influenced by political events?
- What evidence shows that the nation was sharply divided before the Civil War?
- How did African Americans contribute to the literary culture of America during this period?
- What important scientific theories and discoveries arose during this period?

COMMON CORE

RI 7 Integrate and evaluate multiple sources of information presented in different media or formats as well as in words in order to address a question or solve a problem.

1863

1863 Abraham Lincoln delivers Gettysburg Address. ▶

1864 The *New Orleans Tribune,* one of the first daily newspapers produced by African Americans, begins publication.

1865 Walt Whitman pens his classic ode to Abraham Lincoln, "When Lilacs Last in the Dooryard Bloom'd."

1867

1867 Mark Twain publishes *The Celebrated Jumping Frog of Calaveras County and Other Sketches.*

1868 Part 1 of *Little Women,* Louisa May Alcott's classic novel about four sisters, is published. ▶

1870 Bret Harte publishes story collection *The Luck of Roaring Camp and Other Sketches.*

1863

1863 Lincoln signs Emancipation Proclamation; the 54th Massachusetts Volunteer Infantry, one of the first African-American regiments, is founded. ▶

1864 Union general William Tecumseh Sherman marches from Atlanta to the Atlantic Ocean.

1865 Civil War ends; Lincoln is assassinated; 13th Amendment abolishes slavery.

1867

1867 United States buys Alaska from Russia.

1868 Congress passes 14th Amendment, prohibiting discrimination against African Americans.

1869 The hammering of a golden spike at Promontory Point, Utah, marks completion of the transcontinental railroad. ▼

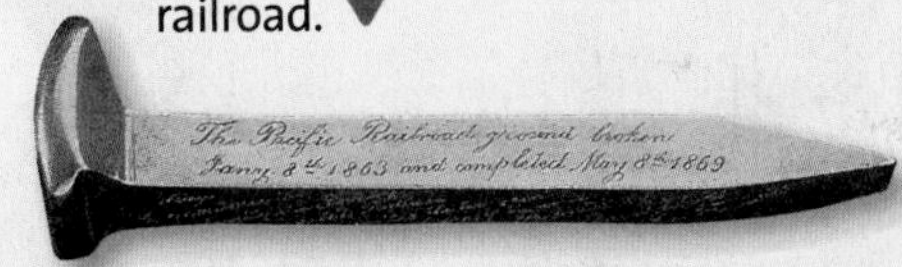

1870 The first African-American senator, Hiram R. Revels, takes his seat.

1863

1863 Leo Tolstoy publishes *War and Peace.*

1864 Louis Pasteur invents pasteurization.

1865 Telegraph cable is laid across the Atlantic Ocean. ▶

1866 Fyodor Dostoyevsky publishes *Crime and Punishment.*

1867

1868 Remains of Cro-Magnon man discovered in Europe; Meiji era in Japan begins period of modernization.

1869 Suez Canal is completed in Egypt.

1870 After a troubled reign, Queen Isabella II of Spain abdicates throne in favor of her son, Alfonso XII.

UNIT 3

The Legacy of the Era

War Stories

COMMON CORE

SL 1 Initiate and participate in a range of collaborative discussions, building on others' ideas and expressing their own clearly and persuasively.

Before the Civil War, most American writers depicted war romantically, focusing on the glory of a battle, the justness of a cause, or the heroism of a leader. Later, writers such as Stephen Crane began to depict war in all its grim reality, uncovering the daily discomforts of military life, the horrors of the battlefield, and the lasting and unexpected consequences of war. Americans today are still drawn to war stories of all kinds.

DISCUSS As a class, discuss which elements in current war stories (novels, movies, TV shows, news reports) are realistic and which are romantic in nature. Give specific examples.

Steven Spielberg's 1998 movie *Saving Private Ryan* was noted for its realistic portrayal of battle.

Artistic Innovators

Who are the blue men in this picture, and what do they have to do with Walt Whitman and Emily Dickinson? The Blue Man Group is just one example of many current artistic innovators who can tip their hats to the mavericks of an earlier era: Whitman and Dickinson. Since Whitman and Dickinson's bold experiments with poetic form and content in the 19th century, writers, musicians, and artists have increasingly pushed the limits of what is considered art, broadening Americans' tastes and imaginations in the process.

QUICKWRITE With your classmates, list as many artistic innovators as you can think of from the Civil War period to today. What do they have in common? What value do they bring to our society?

African-American Influence

One lasting legacy of the Civil War period has been the rise of African Americans to leadership positions and levels of prominence. Beginning with abolitionists such as Sojourner Truth and Frederick Douglass, African Americans have made their way into all spheres of American public life, from politics, education, and the sciences to the arts and entertainment.

CREATE With a partner, create a poster or collage highlighting the achievements of three African American leaders today. Include photographs of three leaders who are working in different fields, and list their accomplishments. Consult a dictionary of quotations or other sources for quotations by or about each person.

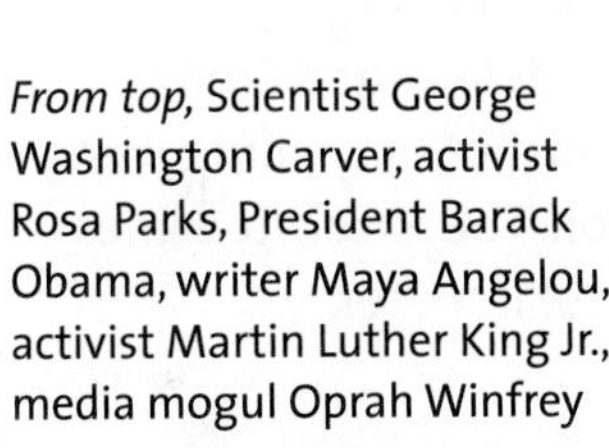

From top, Scientist George Washington Carver, activist Rosa Parks, President Barack Obama, writer Maya Angelou, activist Martin Luther King Jr., media mogul Oprah Winfrey

Text Analysis Workshop

Form and Content in Poetry

Do you think everything has already been said? Throughout American history, poets have prided themselves on finding new ways to say things, as well as inventing new poetic forms in which to say them.

COMMON CORE

Included in this workshop:
RL 1 Cite strong and thorough textual evidence to support analysis of what the text says explicity. **RL 5** Analyze how an author's choices concerning how to structure specific parts of a text contribute to its overall structure and meaning as well as its aesthetic impact. **RL 10** Read and comprehend literature, including poems.

Form and Function

All works of art have **form,** a particular organization of parts that makes a whole. In poetry, form is referred to as **poetic structure:** the way words are arranged in lines, lines are arranged in stanzas, and units of sound are organized to achieve rhythm and rhyme. In general, poetic forms fall into two categories, traditional and organic. Poems in **traditional form** follow certain fixed conventions. For example, they can have a limited number of lines, a specified meter and rhyme scheme, and a definite structure. Such poems are also called **fixed form** poems and include the **sonnet,** the **ballad,** the **epic,** the **elegy,** the **ode,** the **villanelle,** and **blank verse.** Often, poets choose a form that fits the subject matter. For example, a sonnet was originally intended only for the subject of love. The great English poets, such as William Shakespeare and John Milton, used traditional poetic forms, as did many early American poets.

Engraving of Walt Whitman by Max Beerbohm, 1904

The **organic form** of poetry, also known as **irregular form,** developed in the early 19th century. The English romantic poets wanted more flexible verse forms to fit the new content of their poetry. Unlike traditional forms, which provide an ideal pattern for poems to follow, organic form takes its shape and pattern from the content of the poem itself. That is, the form of a poem "grows" naturally out of what the poem says. A poem in organic form may have meter and rhyme, but the poet may vary the rhythm and rhyme scheme in irregular and unexpected ways. In searching for ways to find new expression, several American poets, such as Walt Whitman and Emily Dickinson, began experimenting with organic form.

Poetic Form in Action

One way to understand the difference between traditional and organic forms is to compare the poetry of Henry Wadsworth Longfellow and Emily Dickinson. Longfellow was somewhat conventional in most of his poems, using a predictable alternating rhyme scheme and punctuation. The excerpted lines shown here from Longfellow's "Psalm of Life" have a regular meter.

Tell me not, in mournful numbers, *a*

Life is but an empty dream!— *b*

For the soul is dead that slumbers, *a*

And things are not what they seem. *b*

—Henry Wadsworth Longfellow, "A Psalm of Life"

Close Read

Study the pattern of rhythm in the first two lines, and then sound out and note the stressed and unstressed syllables in lines 3 and 4.

Now look at the first stanza of a poem by Dickinson. She also used meter and rhyme, but she added rhythmical variations, which characterize it as organic. The first line has four accents, while the next three lines each have three accented syllables and are **enjambed,** or **run-on,** ending without a grammatical or normal speech pause.

My life closed twice before its close— *a*

It yet remains to see *b*

If Immortality unveil *c*

A third event to me *b*

—Emily Dickinson, "My life closed twice before its close"

Close Read

Notice the difference in rhythm between line 1 and lines 2–4. What effect does this shift have on the way the poem sounds? How might the change in rhythm emphasize the writer's meaning?

Free verse is an organic form that lacks regular meter and rhyme. Although free verse still has rhythm and may include an occasional rhyme within a line, it does not follow any strict rules. Like all forms of poetry, however, it may include a variety of sound devices, such as repetition and alliteration, to achieve a musical quality.

The great master of free verse in American poetry was Walt Whitman. At a time when American poetry followed traditional forms, Whitman went his own way and created a form that grew purely out of the ideas expressed. In this passage from "I Hear America Singing," notice the language and sound devices that create a poetic effect in sentences that are almost like those in prose.

I hear America singing, the varied carols I hear,
Those of mechanics, each one singing his as it should be blithe and strong,
The carpenter singing his as he measures his plank or beam,

—Walt Whitman, "I Hear America Singing"

Close Read

Examine and compare the three examples on this page. How do they vary in content?

COMMON CORE

RL 1 Cite textual evidence to support analysis of what the text says explicitly as well as inferences drawn from the text. **RL 4** Analyze the impact of specific word choices on meaning and tone, including words with multiple meanings or language that is particularly fresh, engaging, or beautiful. **RL 5** Analyze how an author's choices concerning how to structure specific parts of a text contribute to its overall structure and meaning as well as its aesthetic impact. **SL 1** Participate in collaborative discussions. **SL 2** Integrate multiple sources of information presented in diverse formats and media. **L 4** Determine or clarify the meaning of multiple-meaning words.

Selected Poetry

by Walt Whitman

VIDEO TRAILER THINK central KEYWORD: HML11-530A

Meet the Author

Walt Whitman 1819–1892

When Walt Whitman's book of poems *Leaves of Grass* first appeared, many people were shocked by its controversial content and revolutionary form. Of the 800 copies printed, most were eventually thrown away. However, a few readers recognized the poet's genius. In a letter to Whitman, Ralph Waldo Emerson called *Leaves of Grass* "the most extraordinary piece of wit and wisdom that America has yet contributed."

The Making of a Poet Nothing Whitman wrote before *Leaves of Grass* contained any hint of what was to come. He burst onto the literary scene full-bodied and brash, like one of his poems.

His early years offered little in the way of preparation. Born in 1819, Whitman grew up in rural Long Island and crowded Brooklyn. He held a series of jobs including office boy, typesetter, printer, newspaper editor, school teacher, carpenter, and journalist.

In the 1840s, Whitman published a number of poems and short stories—and even a fairly successful novel—but these were conventional efforts.

Apparently, however, Whitman was just waiting for the proper inspiration. Upon reading Emerson, he realized that he could celebrate all aspects of nature and humanity by using spiritual language. "I was simmering, simmering, simmering," he once declared. "Emerson brought me to a boil."

An American Bard In the early 1850s, Whitman quit his job as a journalist and worked on *Leaves of Grass.* Declaring a kind of literary Independence Day, he printed his 12-poem book on July 4, 1855, at his own expense; he even set some of the type himself. Throughout his lifetime, Whitman would continue to rewrite, revise, and expand *Leaves of Grass.* The ninth and final edition, published in 1892, contained nearly 400 poems.

Unfettered by traditional poetic conventions and grammatical structures, Whitman captured the vitality, optimism, and voice of his native land. He celebrated all aspects of American life—the unique and the commonplace, the beautiful and the ugly.

Whitman once claimed that "the proof of a poet is that his country absorbs him as affectionately as he has absorbed it." By that measure and any other, Whitman is one of the most successful poets in history. Today *Leaves of Grass* is widely regarded as the most influential book of poetry in American literature.

DID YOU KNOW?

Walt Whitman . . .

- dropped out of school at age 11.
- sent a copy of *Leaves of Grass* to poet John Greenleaf Whittier, who threw it into the fire.
- had Thomas Edison record him reading one of his poems.

Author Online THINK central

Go to thinkcentral.com. KEYWORD: HML11-530B

TEXT ANALYSIS: FREE VERSE

Walt Whitman is the great master of free verse in American poetry. **Free verse** is poetry that does not contain regular patterns of rhyme and meter. The lines in free verse often flow more naturally than do rhymed, metrical lines and so sound more like everyday speech. Note, however, that Whitman does use the following poetic devices to create rhythm:

- **cataloging:** frequent lists of people, things, and attributes

  The shoemaker singing as he sits on his bench, the hatter singing as he stands
- **repetition:** repeated words or phrases at the beginning of two or more lines

  Beat! beat! drums!—blow! bugles! blow!
- **parallelism:** related ideas phrased in similar ways

  Born here of parents born here from parents the same, and their parents the same

As you read the poems, notice how Whitman uses these devices to achieve rhythm, musical effects, and a style all his own.

READING SKILL: ANALYZE TONE

To help you understand Whitman's poems, pay attention to their tone. **Tone** is an expression of a writer's attitude toward his or her subject. For example, a writer's tone might be respectful, angry, or amused. Tone can be communicated through choice of words and details. Notice the triumphant tone in these lines from "Song of Myself":

I celebrate myself, and sing myself,
And what I assume you shall assume,
For every atom belonging to me as good belongs to you.

As you read Whitman's poems, jot down examples of words and details that communicate tone in a chart like the one shown.

	Examples	Tone
"I Hear America Singing"	"blithe and strong"	happy, confident
"Song of Myself"		
"A Noiseless Patient Spider"		
"Beat! Beat! Drums!"		

Complete the activities in your **Reader/Writer Notebook**.

What does AMERICA *look like?*

What images come to mind when you think about America? Maybe you see big cities or rolling farmland. Maybe you picture the mountains or the coasts. Or maybe you focus on the people rather than the land. Many of Walt Whitman's poems contain vivid images of America in the mid-1800s. What—and who—captures America's spirit and reality today?

DISCUSS Imagine that you have been asked to design a poster that will help introduce tourists and newcomers to America. Get together in a small group and discuss the images that represent the people and places of America. Be sure to include images that symbolize all aspects of the country.

I Hear America Singing

Walt Whitman

I hear America singing, the varied carols I hear,
Those of mechanics, each one singing his as it should be blithe and strong,
The carpenter singing his as he measures his plank or beam, **A**
The mason singing his as he makes ready for work, or leaves off work,
The boatman singing what belongs to him in his boat, the deckhand singing on the steamboat deck,
The shoemaker singing as he sits on his bench, the hatter singing as he stands,
The wood-cutter's song, the ploughboy's on his way in the morning, or at noon intermission or at sundown,
The delicious singing of the mother, or of the young wife at work, or of the girl sewing or washing,
Each singing what belongs to him or her and to none else,
The day what belongs to the day—at night the party of young fellows, robust, friendly,
Singing with open mouths their strong melodious songs. **B**

A FREE VERSE
Notice the use of **cataloging** throughout the poem. What rhythmic effect does the poet create with his list of the men and women at work in America?

B ANALYZE TONE
Reread lines 10–11. What attitude does the speaker express toward the young men? Note the words and details that help convey that attitude.

Text Analysis

1. **Summarize** What types of workers does Whitman celebrate in this poem?
2. **Clarify** What do you think singing represents in the poem?
3. **Make Inferences** Why do you think Whitman does not mention wealthy entrepreneurs, prominent leaders, or powerful politicians?

The Reaper (1878), Winslow Homer. Watercolor. Private collection. Photo © Art Resource, New York.

Song of Myself

Walt Whitman

1

I celebrate myself, and sing myself,
And what I assume you shall assume,
For every atom belonging to me as good belongs to you. **C**

I loaf and invite my soul,
I lean and loaf at my ease observing a spear of summer grass.

My tongue, every atom of my blood, form'd from this soil, this air,
Born here of parents born here from parents the same, and their parents the same,
I, now thirty-seven years old in perfect health begin,
Hoping to cease not till death.

Creeds and schools in abeyance,
Retiring back a while sufficed at[1] what they are, but never forgotten,
I harbor for good or bad, I permit to speak at every hazard,
Nature without check with original energy. **D**

C FREE VERSE
Read lines 1–3 aloud and listen to the rhythm created by **parallelism.** In what ways does the use of this technique reflect the relationship between the speaker and the reader?

D ANALYZE TONE
Compare the tone in lines 4–5 with that in lines 12–13. How does the tone change? How is the tone in both pairs of lines similar?

6

A child said *What is the grass?* fetching it to me with full hands,
How could I answer the child? I do not know what it is any more than he.
I guess it must be the flag of my disposition, out of hopeful green stuff woven.

Or I guess it is the handkerchief of the Lord,
A scented gift and remembrancer designedly dropt,[2]

---

1. **sufficed at:** satisfied with.
2. **remembrancer designedly dropt:** a purposely dropped token of affection.

Boys in Pasture, Winslow Homer. © Burstein Collection/Corbis.

Bearing the owner's name someway in the corners, that we may see
and remark, and say *Whose?*

Or I guess the grass is itself a child, the produced babe of the
vegetation.

Or I guess it is a uniform hieroglyphic,[3] E
And it means, Sprouting alike in broad zones and narrow zones,
Growing among black folks as among white,
Kanuck, Tuckahoe, Congressman, Cuff,[4] I give them the same, I
receive them the same.

And now it seems to me the beautiful uncut hair of graves.

Tenderly will I use you curling grass,
It may be you transpire[5] from the breasts of young men,
It may be if I had known them I would have loved them,
It may be you are from old people, or from offspring taken soon
out of their mothers' laps,
And here you are the mothers' laps. F

E **FREE VERSE**
Be aware of the **repetition** in lines 16–21. What is the relationship between the repeated elements?

F **ANALYZE TONE**
What attitude does the speaker express toward the dead in lines 25–30?

3. **hieroglyphic:** a system of symbols that represent meanings or speech sounds.
4. **Kanuck, Tuckahoe, . . . Cuff:** slang terms for various groups of people. A Kanuck (now spelled Canuck) is a Canadian, especially a French Canadian; a Tuckahoe is someone from the coast of Virginia; a Cuff is an African American.
5. **transpire:** emerge; ooze out.

This grass is very dark to be from the white heads of old mothers,
Darker than the colorless beards of old men,
Dark to come from under the faint red roofs of mouths.

O I perceive after all so many uttering tongues,
And I perceive they do not come from the roofs of mouths for nothing.

I wish I could translate the hints about the dead young men and women,
And the hints about old men and mothers, and the offspring taken soon out of their laps.

What do you think has become of the young and old men?
And what do you think has become of the women and children?

They are alive and well somewhere,
The smallest sprout shows there is really no death,
And if ever there was it led forward life, and does not wait at the end to arrest it,
And ceas'd the moment life appear'd.

All goes onward and outward, nothing collapses,
And to die is different from what any one supposed, and luckier. **G**

52

The spotted hawk swoops by and accuses me, he complains of my gab and my loitering.

I too am not a bit tamed, I too am untranslatable,
I sound my barbaric yawp[6] over the roofs of the world. **H**

The last scud[7] of day holds back for me,
It flings my likeness after the rest and true as any on the shadow'd wilds,
It coaxes me to the vapor and the dusk.

I depart as air, I shake my white locks at the runaway sun,
I effuse my flesh in eddies,[8] and drift it in lacy jags.

COMMON CORE RL 4, L 4

Language Coach

Multiple-Meaning Words You may be familiar with the meaning of *arrest* (line 42) in a law-enforcement context ("being taken into custody by law enforcement"). *Arrest* also means "to stop." Reread line 42–43. What does *arrest* mean here? What is Whitman saying about death?

G ANALYZE TONE
What words would you use to describe the tone in lines 38–45, where the speaker discusses life and death?

H FREE VERSE
Reread lines 47–48. What **poetic devices** in these lines emphasize the speaker's untamed nature?

6. **yawp:** loud, rough speech.
7. **scud:** wind-blown cloud.
8. **effuse . . . eddies:** scatter my flesh in swirling currents.

I bequeath[9] myself to the dirt to grow from the grass I love,
If you want me again look for me under your boot-soles. **I**

You will hardly know who I am or what I mean,
But I shall be good health to you nevertheless,
And filter and fibre your blood.

Failing to fetch me at first keep encouraged,
Missing me one place search another,
I stop somewhere waiting for you.

I **ANALYZE TONE**
What words and details does the poet use in lines 49–55 to create a defiant tone?

9. **bequeath:** hand over, as if in a will.

Text Analysis

1. **Clarify** According to the speaker, in lines 40–43, why is there "really no death"?
2. **Summarize** To what does the speaker compare himself in section 52?
3. **Analyze Symbols** What do you think grass symbolizes in this poem?

▼ **Analyze Visuals**
This painting by American artist Elliott Daingerfield shows a man returning home after working on his farm. What **images** in the painting are similar to those described in the poem?

Return from the Farm (1915–1920), Elliott Daingerfield. Smithsonian American Art Museum, Washington, D.C. Photo © Smithsonian American Art Museum/Art Resource, New York.

Crossing the Spider Web, Victor Hugo. Watercolor. Maison Victor Hugo. Musée de la Ville de Paris. Photo © Giraudon/Art Resource, New York.

A Noiseless **Patient Spider**

Walt Whitman

A noiseless patient spider,
I mark'd where on a little promontory[1] it stood isolated,
Mark'd how to explore the vacant vast surrounding,
It launch'd forth filament, filament, filament, out of itself,
Ever unreeling them, ever tirelessly speeding them.

And you O my soul where you stand,
Surrounded, detached, in measureless oceans of space,
Ceaselessly musing, venturing, throwing, seeking the spheres to connect them, J
Till the bridge you will need be form'd, till the ductile[2] anchor hold,
Till the gossamer[3] thread you fling catch somewhere, O my soul. K

1. **promontory:** a high ridge of land or rock jutting out over water or land.
2. **ductile:** capable of being drawn or stretched out.
3. **gossamer:** extremely light or fine.

J **FREE VERSE**
Compare the use of **parallelism** in lines 5 and 8. What do these parallel elements suggest about the relationship between the spider and speaker?

K **ANALYZE TONE**
What is the overall tone of the poem? What details communicate that tone?

Beat! Beat! Drums!

Walt Whitman

Beat! beat! drums!—blow! bugles! blow!
Through the windows—through doors—burst like a ruthless force,
Into the solemn church, and scatter the congregation,
Into the school where the scholar is studying;
Leave not the bridegroom quiet—no happiness must he have now with his bride,
Nor the peaceful farmer any peace, ploughing his field or gathering his grain,
So fierce you whirr and pound you drums—so shrill you bugles blow. **L**

Beat! beat! drums!—blow! bugles! blow!
Over the traffic of cities—over the rumble of wheels in the streets;
Are beds prepared for sleepers at night in the houses? no sleepers must sleep in those beds,
No bargainers' bargains by day—no brokers or speculators—would they continue?
Would the talkers be talking? would the singer attempt to sing?
Would the lawyer rise in the court to state his case before the judge?
Then rattle quicker, heavier drums—you bugles wilder blow.

Beat! beat! drums!—blow! bugles! blow!
Make no parley—stop for no expostulation,[1]
Mind not the timid—mind not the weeper or prayer,
Mind not the old man beseeching the young man,
Let not the child's voice be heard, nor the mother's entreaties,
Make even the trestles[2] to shake the dead where they lie awaiting the hearses,
So strong you thump O terrible drums—so loud you bugles blow. **M**

L ANALYZE TONE
Describe the tone in lines 1–7. Why is this tone appropriate for the subject matter?

M FREE VERSE
Notice the **parallel structure** in the last line of each stanza. What impact does this device have on the poem's message?

---

1. **parley:** a discussion or conference; **expostulation:** argument.
2. **trestles:** tables, in this case, upon which coffins sit until the undertaker comes to take them away.

Reading for Information

ESSAY Among the most important themes of Walt Whitman's poetry is the magnificence of America as seen in the nation's common people. In his preface to *Leaves of Grass,* his great life work, he introduces this idea quite emphatically.

from the Preface to *Leaves of* GRASS

Walt Whitman

The Americans of all nations at any time upon the earth have probably the fullest poetical nature. The United States themselves are essentially the greatest poem. In the history of the earth hitherto the largest and most stirring appear tame and orderly to their ampler largeness and stir. Here at last is something in the doings of man that corresponds with the broadcast doings of the day and night. Here is not merely a nation but a teeming nation of nations. Here is action untied from strings necessarily blind to particulars and details magnificently moving in vast masses. Here is the hospitality which forever indicates heroes. . . . Here are the roughs and beards and space and ruggedness and nonchalance that the soul loves. Here the performance disdaining the trivial unapproached in the tremendous audacity of its crowds and groupings and the push of its perspective spreads with crampless and flowing breadth and showers its prolific and splendid extravagance. One sees it must indeed own the riches of the summer and winter, and need never be bankrupt while corn grows from the ground or the orchards drop apples or the bays contain fish or men beget children upon women.

Other states indicate themselves in their deputies . . . but the genius of the United States is not best or most in its executives or legislatures, nor in its ambassadors or authors or colleges or churches or parlors, nor even in its newspapers or inventors . . . but always most in the common people. Their manners speech dress friendships—the freshness and candor of their physiognomy—the picturesque looseness of their carriage . . . their deathless attachment to freedom—their aversion to anything indecorous or soft or mean—the practical acknowledgment of the citizens of one state by the citizens of all other states—the fierceness of their roused resentment—their curiosity and welcome of novelty—their self-esteem and wonderful sympathy—their susceptibility to a slight—the air they have of persons who never knew how it felt to stand in the presence of superiors—the fluency of their speech—their delight in music, the sure symptom of manly tenderness and native elegance of soul . . . their good temper and openhandedness—the terrible significance of their elections—the President's taking off his hat to them not they to him—these too are unrhymed poetry. It awaits the gigantic and generous treatment worthy of it.

After Reading

Comprehension

1. **Recall** What two things does Whitman compare in "A Noiseless Patient Spider"?
2. **Summarize** In "Beat! Beat! Drums!" whom do the drums and bugles call to action?
3. **Paraphrase** How would you paraphrase lines 16–19 of "Beat! Beat! Drums!"?

Text Analysis

4. **Examine Imagery** Think about the images of mid-19th-century America that Whitman conveys in his poems. How do these images compare with what America looks like today? Cite specific details from the poems to support your comparisons.
5. **Analyze Tone** Review the examples of tone that you recorded as you read the poems. What can you conclude about Whitman's attitude toward the following?
   - manual labor
   - the soul
   - himself
   - war
6. **Analyze Metaphor** Reread lines 16–25 of "Song of Myself." What metaphors does the speaker use to describe what grass means to him? What ideas does each metaphor suggest?
7. **Compare Poems** Use a chart like the one shown to compare the **images** and **mood** of "A Noiseless Patient Spider" and "Beat! Beat! Drums!" Based on your notes, what is the overall impact of each poem?

	Images	*Mood*
"A Noiseless Patient Spider"		
"Beat! Beat! Drums!"		

8. **Compare Texts** In what ways are the pronouncements made in Whitman's preface (page 540) reflected in his poems? Consider the content of what he says as well as the manner in which he states it. Provide details to support your ideas.
9. **Evaluate Free Verse** Why is free verse an appropriate form for Whitman's poems? Support your opinion.

Text Criticism

10. **Author's Style** In another section of "Song of Myself," Whitman writes: "He most honors my style who learns under it to destroy the teacher." What does he mean? Do you think Whitman encourages this position in the poems you have read? Use evidence from the poems to support your opinion.

What does AMERICA *look like?*

In his poems, Walt Whitman explored many different aspects of Americans and their lives. Think about your classmates and the people in your community. Do you think they are a good representation of the many different kinds of people in America? Explain your answer.

COMMON CORE

RL 1 Cite textual evidence to support analysis of what the text says explicitly as well as inferences drawn from the text. **RL 2** Determine themes or central ideas of a text; provide an objective summary of the text. **RL 4** Analyze the impact of specific word choices on meaning and tone, including words with multiple meanings or language that is particularly fresh, engaging, or beautiful. **RL 5** Analyze how an author's choices concerning how to structure specific parts of a text contribute to its overall structure and meaning as well as its aesthetic impact. **RL 9** Demonstrate knowledge of how two or more texts from the same period treat similar themes or topics. **L 5** Demonstrate understanding of figurative language.

COMMON CORE

RL 4 Determine the meaning of words and phrases as they are used in the text, including figurative meanings; analyze the impact of specific word choices on meaning and tone, including words with multiple meanings or language that is particularly fresh, engaging, or beautiful.
L 5 Demonstrate understanding of figurative language.

Ode to Walt Whitman

Pablo Neruda

BACKGROUND Pablo Neruda (1904–1973), a Nobel Prize–winning poet from Chile, was greatly inspired by Walt Whitman's poetry. In a speech delivered in 1972, he said, "I was barely 15 when I discovered Walt Whitman, my primary creditor. I stand among you today still owing this marvelous debt that has helped me live." In the following poem, Neruda echoes Whitman's joyful exuberance and describes Whitman by using a variety of metaphors—a comparison of two things without using words such as *like* or *as*.

I do not remember
at what age
nor where:
in the great damp South
or on the fearsome
coast, beneath the brief
cry of the seagulls,
I touched a hand and it was
the hand of Walt Whitman.
I trod the ground
with bare feet,
I walked on the grass,
on the firm dew
of Walt Whitman.

During
my entire
youth
I had the company of that hand,
that dew,
its firmness of patriarchal pine, its
prairie-like expanse,
and its mission of circulatory peace.

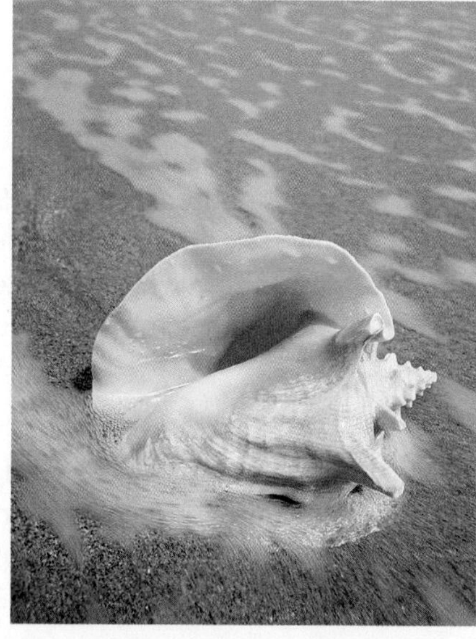

Not
disdaining
the gifts
of the earth,
nor the copious
curving of the column's capital,
nor the purple
initial
of wisdom,
you taught me
to be an American,
you raised
my eyes
to books,
towards
the treasure
of the grains:
broad,
in the clarity
of the plains,
you made me see
the high
tutelary
mountain. From subterranean
echoes,
you gathered
for me
everything;
everything that came forth
was harvested by you,
galloping in the alfalfa,
picking poppies for me,
visiting
the rivers,
coming into the kitchens
in the afternoon.

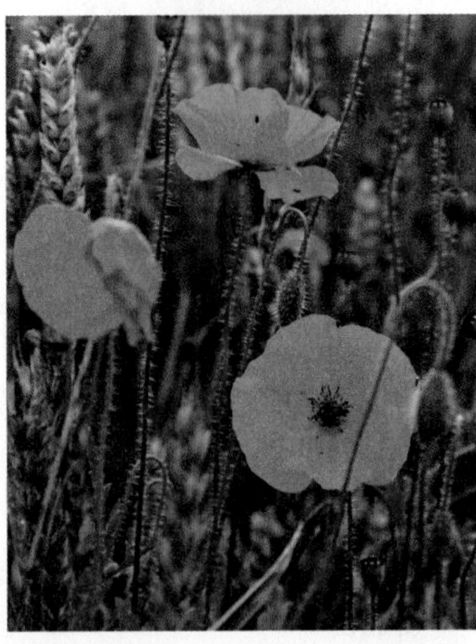

But not only
soil
was brought to light
by your spade:
you unearthed
man,
and the
slave
who was humiliated
with you, balancing
the black dignity of his stature,
walked on, conquering
happiness.

To the fireman
below,
in the stoke-hole,
you sent
a little basket
of strawberries.
To every corner of your town
a verse
of yours arrived for a visit,
and it was like a piece
of clean body,
the verse that arrived,
like
your own fisherman beard
or the solemn tread of your acacia
legs.

Your silhouette
passed among the soldiers:
the poet, the wound-dresser,
the night attendant
who knows
the sound
of breathing in mortal agony
and awaits with the dawn
the silent
return
of life.

Good baker!
Elder first cousin
of my roots,
araucaria's
cupola,
it is
now
a hundred
years
that over your grass
and its germinations,
the wind
passes
without wearing out your eyes

New
and cruel years in your Fatherland:
persecutions,
tears,
prisons,
poisoned weapons
and wrathful wars
have not crushed
the grass of your book;
the vital fountainhead
of its freshness.
And, alas!
those
who murdered
Lincoln
now
lie in his bed.
They felled
his seat of honor
made of fragrant wood,
and raised a throne
spattered
with misfortune and blood.

View from Neruda's house on Isla Negra, Chile, with antique sailboat figureheads hanging in the window

But
your voice
sings
in the suburban
stations,
in
the
vespertine
wharfs,
your word
splashes
like
dark water.
Your people,
white
and black,
poor
people,
simple people
like
all
people
do not forget
your bell:
They congregate singing
beneath
the magnitude
of your spacious life.
They walk among the peoples with your love
caressing
the pure development
of brotherhood on earth.

Text Analysis

1. **Analyze Metaphor** Neruda uses various metaphors to characterize Whitman's poems. What does each of these metaphors suggest about Whitman's verse?
   - Whitman's hand (lines 8–9)
   - Whitman as harvester (lines 47–70)
   - a basket of strawberries (lines 71–76)
   - a bell (lines 147–157)
2. **Compare Texts** Neruda has acknowledged Whitman's influence on his own verse. What elements of "Ode to Walt Whitman" reveal this influence? Be specific, citing evidence from this poem as well as from the Whitman poems you read on pages 532–539.

COMMON CORE

RL 1 Cite evidence to support analysis of what the text says explicitly as well as inferences drawn from the text. **RL 2** Determine two or more themes or central ideas of a text. **RL 4** Determine the meaning of words and phrases used in the text, including figurative meanings; analyze the impact of specific word choices on meaning and tone, including language that is particularly fresh, engaging, or beautiful. **RL 5** Analyze how an author's choices concerning how to structure specific parts of a text contribute to its overall structure and meaning as well as its aesthetic impact.

Selected Poetry

by Emily Dickinson

VIDEO TRAILER THINK central KEYWORD: HML11-546A

Meet the Author

Emily Dickinson 1830–1886

Emily Dickinson rarely ventured beyond the confines of her family home in Amherst, Massachusetts, but her restless mind and creativity knew no such boundaries. In her bedroom overlooking the village graveyard, Dickinson meditated on life and death and wrote about these subjects with startling originality. Today she and Walt Whitman are considered the greatest American poets of the 19th century.

Family Ties Dickinson was born in 1830 into a well-to-do family, which would become the center of her existence. She stood in awe of her father, a stern, imposing man committed to Puritan ideals, and felt estranged from her mother, who "did not," Dickinson once commented in a letter, "care for thought." However, she had a close relationship with her older brother, Austin, and her younger sister, Vinnie.

In 1847, Dickinson left home to attend Mount Holyoke Female Seminary in nearby South Hadley, but she left after just one year. She missed her family, but she also resented the intense pressure she felt there to join the church. All her life, Dickinson felt torn between her own convictions and the religious beliefs of those around her. This conflict is reflected in many of her poems.

A Writer's Life In the 1850s, Dickinson began to devote herself to poetry. Late at night, she wrote by candlelight. During the day, she jotted down her thoughts between household chores. Inspired by her own observations and experiences, Dickinson composed a remarkable number of profound, gemlike poems.

Perhaps because of this newfound focus on her writing, Dickinson gradually withdrew from the world. However, she did not become a total recluse. She entertained occasional visitors in her home and maintained contact with friends and family by means of a lively correspondence.

Poetic Legacy Early in 1886, Dickinson wrote a letter to her cousins that simply read "Called back." She seemed to have realized that she was dying. Following her death, her sister Vinnie discovered a box full of Dickinson's poems bound into neat booklets. As a result of Vinnie's perseverance, the first volume of Dickinson's poetry appeared four years after the poet's death. Her poems—1,775 in all—finally revealed to the world the passionate, witty woman who never flinched from the truth.

DID YOU KNOW?

Emily Dickinson . . .

- sometimes signed her letters "Uncle Emily."
- dressed only in white in the last 16 years of her life.
- had eye problems and feared that she might go blind.

Author Online THINK central

Go to thinkcentral.com. KEYWORD: HML11-546B

TEXT ANALYSIS: AUTHOR'S STYLE

Emily Dickinson's style is as unique and personal as her observations about the world. Here are some of the distinctive stylistic elements you will find in Dickinson's poetry:

- dense **quatrains,** or four-line stanzas, that echo the simple rhythms of church hymns
- **slant rhymes,** or words that do not exactly rhyme ("chill"/"Tulle")
- inventive punctuation and sentence structure, including the use of dashes to highlight important words and break up the rhythm of her poems
- irregular capitalization and inverted syntax to emphasize words
- surprisingly unconventional **figurative language,** including similes, metaphors, and personification

As you read, think about the effect of these style elements in Dickinson's poems.

READING STRATEGY: READING DICKINSON'S POETRY

To get the most out of Dickinson's poetry, try reading each poem three times.

- The first time, read for an overall impression. Pause when you encounter dashes, and be aware of the poem's **rhythm.**
- The second time, note the use of **imagery** and **figurative language.** Pay attention to the words capitalized for emphasis.
- The third time, read the poem aloud. Think about what the imagery and figurative language convey about meaning.

Use a chart like the one shown for each poem. Jot down your thoughts and ideas after each reading.

"Because I could not stop for Death"		
1st Reading	2nd Reading	3rd Reading
Poem has a calm, reflective mood.	Images of death are not frightening.	Poem suggests that death and dying are not frightening.

Complete the activities in your **Reader/Writer Notebook**.

What are life's ESSENTIAL TRUTHS?

Love, loss. Joy, death. When you focus on life's real meaning, you explore its essential truths. These truths, of course, are the natural focus of poets. For instance, in the poems that follow, Emily Dickinson has a great deal to say about death and dying. But does she—or any other poet—speak for you? What do you think about such weighty matters as death, success, and solitude? What is your truth?

QUICKWRITE Create your own top-five list of life's essential truths. Begin with number five and work your way up to number one. Feel free to express your truths in statements, phrases, questions, or any form you want.

Because I could not stop for Death—

Emily Dickinson

Because I could not stop for Death—
He kindly stopped for me—
The Carriage held but just Ourselves—
And Immortality. **A**

We slowly drove—He knew no haste
And I had put away
My labor and my leisure too,
For His Civility[1]—

We passed the School, where Children strove
At Recess—in the Ring—
We passed the Fields of Gazing Grain[2]—
We passed the Setting Sun—

Or rather—He passed Us—
The Dews drew quivering and chill—
For only Gossamer,[3] my Gown—
My Tippet—only Tulle[4]—

We paused before a House that seemed
A Swelling of the Ground—
The Roof was scarcely visible—
The Cornice[5]—in the Ground— **B**

Since then—'tis Centuries—and yet
Feels shorter than the Day
I first surmised the Horses' Heads
Were toward Eternity—

A AUTHOR'S STYLE
Reread lines 1–4 and notice the use of **personification,** a figure of speech in which an object, animal, or idea is given human characteristics. How is Death personified?

B DICKINSON'S POETRY
Note the **imagery** used to describe the house in lines 17–20. What do you think the house represents?

Analyze Visuals ▸
Why might the artist have chosen to keep this photograph out of focus?

---

1. **Civility:** politeness.
2. **Gazing Grain:** grain leaning toward the sun.
3. **Gossamer:** a thin, light cloth.
4. **My Tippet—only Tulle** (to͞ol): My shawl was only a fine net cloth.
5. **Cornice** (kôr′nĭs): the molding around the top of a building.

Success is counted sweetest

Emily Dickinson

Success is counted sweetest
By those who ne'er succeed.
To comprehend a nectar[1]
Requires sorest need.

Not one of all the purple Host[2]
Who took the Flag[3] today
Can tell the definition
So clear of Victory

As he defeated—dying—
On whose forbidden ear
The distant strains of triumph
Burst agonized and clear! **C**

C **DICKINSON'S POETRY** Read lines 9–12 aloud. What elements create the **rhythm** in these lines?

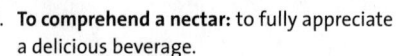

1. **To comprehend a nectar:** to fully appreciate a delicious beverage.
2. **Host:** army.
3. **took the Flag:** captured the enemy's flag as a token of victory.

Text Analysis

1. **Clarify** Who is the "purple Host" in line 5?
2. **Paraphrase** Reread lines 9–12. How would you paraphrase these lines?
3. **Form Opinions** Do you agree that those who fail are better able to appreciate success than those who win? Explain your answer.

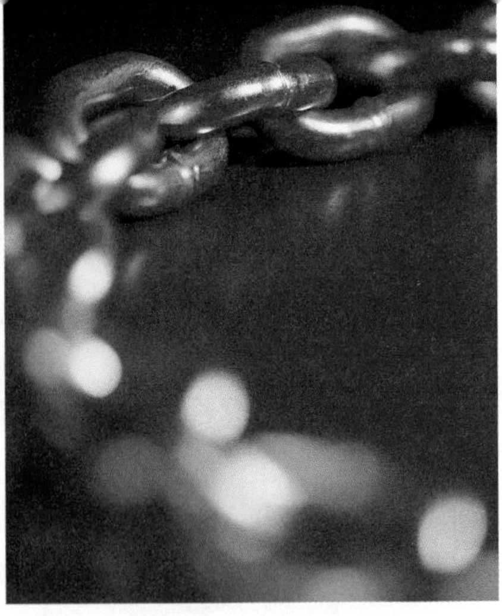

Much Madness is divinest Sense—

Emily Dickinson

Much Madness is divinest Sense—
To a discerning Eye—
Much Sense—the starkest Madness— D
'Tis the Majority
In this, as All, prevail—
Assent—and you are sane—
Demur[1]—you're straightway dangerous—
And handled with a Chain[2]—

D AUTHOR'S STYLE
Pay attention to the use of capitalization in lines 1–3. Which two words are twice capitalized? Why do you think Dickinson chose to capitalize those words?

1. **demur** (dĭ-mûr'): voice opposition; object.
2. **handled with a Chain:** In the 19th century, those who were considered insane were often kept chained in asylums.

My life closed twice before its close—

Emily Dickinson

My life closed twice before its close—
It yet remains to see
If Immortality unveil
A third event to me

So huge, so hopeless to conceive
As these that twice befell.
Parting is all we know of heaven,
And all we need of hell. E

E DICKINSON'S POETRY
After your first reading of the poem, what is your overall impression of its subject?

The Soul selects her own Society—

Emily Dickinson

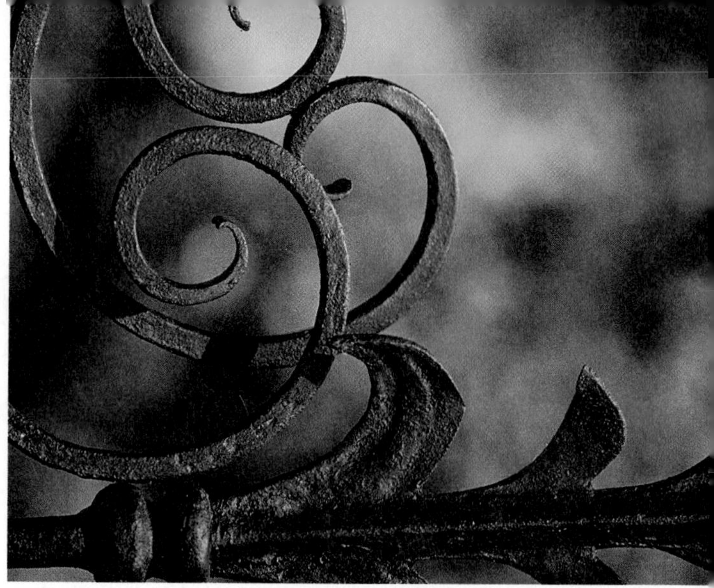

The Soul selects her own Society—
Then—shuts the Door—
To her divine Majority[1]—
Present no more—

Unmoved—she notes the Chariots[2]—pausing—
At her low Gate—
Unmoved—an Emperor be kneeling
Upon her Mat— **F**

I've known her—from an ample nation—
Choose One—
Then—close the Valves of her attention—
Like Stone— **G**

1. **divine Majority:** other souls.
2. **the Chariots:** the Emperor's chariots.

F DICKINSON'S POETRY
Reread lines 5–8. What are some of the effects of the dashes and the poet's abbreviated use of words?

COMMON CORE L 5

G AUTHOR'S STYLE
A poet's **style** can be recognized by the distinctive way he or she writes. In addition to Dickinson's unusual capitalization and use of dashes, she also uses creative similes. A **simile** is a figure of speech that compares two things that have something in common, using *like* or *as*. What image does the comparison in the last quatrain suggest?

Text Analysis

1. **Summarize** How would you summarize the second quatrain?
2. **Paraphrase** Reread lines 9–10. How would you paraphrase these lines?
3. **Draw Conclusions** What do you think the speaker means by "Society"?

I heard a Fly buzz—when I died—

Emily Dickinson

I heard a Fly buzz—when I died—
The Stillness in the Room
Was like the Stillness in the Air—
Between the Heaves[1] of Storm— **H**

The Eyes around—had wrung them dry—
And Breaths were gathering firm
For that last Onset—when the King[2]
Be witnessed—in the Room—

I willed my Keepsakes—Signed away
What portion of me be
Assignable—and then it was
There interposed[3] a Fly—

With Blue—uncertain stumbling Buzz—
Between the light—and me—
And then the Windows failed—and then
I could not see to see— **I**

H AUTHOR'S STYLE
Notice the **simile** in the first quatrain. What is being compared? Why is this comparison appropriate?

I DICKINSON'S POETRY
Reread lines 13–16. What final images does the speaker describe? What is ironic about this **imagery?**

---

1. **Heaves:** risings and fallings.
2. **the King:** God.
3. **interposed:** came between.

My Life had stood— a Loaded Gun—

Emily Dickinson

My Life had stood—a Loaded Gun—
In Corners—till a Day
The Owner passed—identified—
And carried Me away—

And now We roam in Sovereign Woods[1]—
And now We hunt the Doe—
And every time I speak for Him—
The Mountains straight reply—

And do I smile, such cordial light
Upon the Valley glow—
It is as a Vesuvian face
Had let its pleasure through— J

And when at Night—Our good Day done—
I guard My Master's Head—
'Tis better than the Eider-Duck's
Deep Pillow—to have shared—

To foe of His—I'm deadly foe—
None stir the second time—
On whom I lay a Yellow Eye—
Or an emphatic Thumb—

Though I than He—may longer live
He longer must—than I—
For I have but the power to kill,
Without—the power to die—

1. **Sovereign** (sŏv'ər-ĭn) **Woods:** God's woods.

COMMON CORE **RL 1, RL 2**

J ALLUSION
Reread lines 1–12. Notice that the narrator imagines herself to have the destructive power of a gun carried by its owner into the woods to hunt deer. In line 9, the narrator equates the firing of a gun with a smile—an image that she develops with a classical **allusion,** a reference to Mount Vesuvius that she assumes her readers will recognize. A volcanic mountain, Vesuvius erupted in A.D. 79 and buried the Roman city of Pompeii under hot ash. How does this allusion contribute to the poem's imagery and themes? Cite evidence from the poem to support your response.

Reading for Information

LETTER In April 1862, Thomas Wentworth Higginson wrote an essay offering advice to beginning writers, urging them, "Charge your style with life." Emily Dickinson, 32 years old at the time, responded to his essay, submitting four poems along with the following unsigned letter. In place of a signature, she enclosed a signed calling card.

Letter to Mr. T. W. Higginson

April 15, 1862

Mr Higginson,

Are you too deeply occupied to say if my Verse is alive?

The Mind is so near itself—it cannot see, distinctly—and I have none to ask—

Should you think it breathed—and had you the leisure to tell me, I should feel quick gratitude—

If I make the mistake—that you dared to tell me—would give me sincerer honor—toward you—

I enclose my name—asking you, if you please—Sir—to tell me what is true?

That you will not betray me—it is needless to ask—since Honor is it's own pawn—

Miss Emily E. Dickinson

Comprehension

1. **Recall** What has happened to the speaker in "Because I could not stop for Death—"?
2. **Clarify** What do you think is the speaker's attitude toward the Majority in "Much Madness is divinest Sense"?
3. **Summarize** How would you summarize lines 5–8 of "I heard a Fly buzz—when I died—"?

Text Analysis

4. **Make Inferences** What essential truths about death and dying does Dickinson convey in the following poems? Cite specific details.
   - "My life closed twice before its close—"
   - "I heard a Fly buzz—when I died—"
5. **Analyze Author's Style** What ideas are emphasized by the unusual use of capitalization in the following poems? Be specific.
   - "Much Madness is divinest Sense"
   - "The Soul selects her own Society—"
6. **Analyze Dickinson's Poetry** Review the thoughts and ideas you recorded as you read and reread the poems. Based on Dickinson's **imagery** and **figurative language,** how would you characterize the overall **tone** of her poems?
7. **Evaluate Paradox** A **paradox** is a statement that seems to contradict itself but may nevertheless suggest an important truth. Use a diagram like the one shown to identify the paradoxes in "Success is counted sweetest," "Much Madness is divinest Sense," and "My Life had stood—a Loaded Gun—." What truth does each paradox convey?

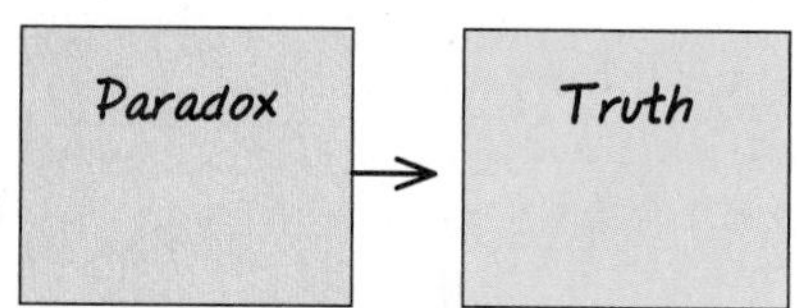

8. **Compare Texts** What style elements of the poet do you recognize in Emily Dickinson's letter to Thomas Wentworth Higginson (page 555)?

Text Criticism

9. **Different Perspectives** Until 1955, editors published "corrected" versions of Dickinson's poems with dashes removed, rhyme and meter made regular, and metaphors replaced with more conventional figures of speech. By eliminating these things, what was lost? Use details from the poems to support your ideas.

What are life's ESSENTIAL TRUTHS?

Dickinson, like many other poets, spent time focusing on important truths about life. Do you believe people today think often enough about the essential truths in life? Explain your answer.

COMMON CORE

RL 1 Cite evidence to support analysis of what the text says explicitly as well as inferences drawn from the text. **RL 4** Determine the meaning of words and phrases used in the text, including figurative meanings; analyze the impact of specific word choices on meaning and tone, including language that is particularly fresh, engaging, or beautiful. **RL 5** Analyze how an author's choices concerning how to structure specific parts of a text contribute to its overall structure and meaning as well as its aesthetic impact. **RL 9** Demonstrate knowledge of how two or more texts from the same period treat similar themes or topics. **L 5a** Interpret figures of speech in context and analyze their role in text.

The Innovations of Whitman and Dickinson

Although Emily Dickinson and Walt Whitman were both revolutionary in their approach to poetic form and content, their poems look quite different. Dickinson wrote short and concise lines; Whitman, long and sprawling ones.

Success is counted sweetest
By those who ne'er succeed.

—Emily Dickinson

I wish I could translate the hints about the dead young men
and women,
And the hints about old men and mothers, and the offspring taken
soon out of their laps.

—Walt Whitman

Dickinson concentrated on private and personal experiences; Whitman, on representative experiences of the American people.

I heard a Fly buzz—when I died—

—Emily Dickinson

I hear America singing, the varied carols I hear,

—Walt Whitman

Writing to Compare

Write an essay to further compare the work of Dickinson and Whitman. Cite specific lines from the poems on page 532 through 554 to support your comparison and thoroughly develop your ideas.

Consider

- each poet's style and form (that is, word choice, imagery, line length, stanzas, rhythm, rhyme), using precise terms to discuss poetic features
- the poems' subject matter and general themes
- which words, lines, or stanzas will provide you with effective evidence and details

Extension

SPEAKING & LISTENING

With a partner, create a dialogue between Whitman and Dickinson in which they discuss their topics, themes, and techniques. Then, **perform** your conversation for the class. Use speaking styles that you think are appropriate for the two poets, based on your understanding of their content and style.

COMMON CORE

W 2 Write explanatory texts to examine and convey complex ideas, concepts, and information. **W 9** Draw evidence from literary texts to support analysis. **SL 4** Present information such that substance and style are appropriate to purpose and task. **SL 6** Adapt speech to context and task. **L 3** Make effective choices for meaning or style.

COMMON CORE

RI 4 Determine the meaning of words and phrases as they are used in a text, including figurative and connotative meanings. **RI 6** Determine an author's point of view or purpose in a text in which the rhetoric is particularly effective, analyzing how style and content contribute to the power, persuasiveness, or beauty of a text. **L 3a** Apply an understanding of syntax to the study of complex texts when reading. **L 5** Demonstrate understanding of figurative language and nuances in word meanings.

from Narrative of the Life of Frederick Douglass, an American Slave

Video link at thinkcentral.com

Slave Narrative by Frederick Douglass

VIDEO TRAILER THINK central KEYWORD: HML11-558A

Meet the Author

Frederick Douglass c. 1817–1895

Frederick Douglass endured 21 years of slavery before he escaped to freedom in the North, where he became an outspoken and influential abolitionist. In the years leading up to the Civil War, his powerful speeches spurred the nation to move against slavery and to extend equal rights to all its citizens.

Forbidden Education As a boy, Douglass worked as a slave in the home of Hugh and Sophia Auld of Baltimore, Maryland. Although it was against the law, Mrs. Auld taught Douglass how to read. After Mr. Auld commanded his wife to stop her lessons, Douglass educated himself in secret, studying from a textbook on public speaking titled *The Columbian Orator.*

From Slave to Abolitionist Douglass escaped and in 1838 settled in New Bedford, Massachusetts. Three years later, he spoke so eloquently to the Massachusetts Anti-Slavery Society that they hired him to lecture about his experiences. Proslavery hecklers frequently attacked him, hurling insults and even rotten eggs and vegetables, but Douglass continued, undeterred.

In 1845, with the publication of his autobiography, *Narrative of the Life of Frederick Douglass, an American Slave,* Douglass rose to international fame—dangerous attention for a runaway slave. To avoid being recaptured, Douglass left for a two-year speaking tour of Great Britain. During the trip, two friends raised the money to purchase his freedom.

Tireless Reformer Returning to the United States as a free man, Douglass settled in Rochester, New York, and founded an antislavery newspaper, the *North Star.* During the Civil War, he advised President Abraham Lincoln and helped recruit the first African-American soldiers for the Union army. For Douglass, the end of slavery was only a first step to achieving a greater goal: full and equal civil rights for African Americans.

In the years after the Civil War, Douglass was appointed to several government posts, including U.S. marshal for the District of Columbia and minister to Haiti. To the end of his life, he continued his fight for full citizenship for African Americans and his support for other causes, including women's rights, land reform, and public education.

Author Online THINK central

Go to thinkcentral.com. KEYWORD: HML11-558B

DID YOU KNOW?

Frederick Douglass . . .

- escaped to the North by disguising himself as a sailor.
- made his home a stop on the Underground Railroad.
- was an early defender of women's rights.

TEXT ANALYSIS: STYLE

Style is a writer's distinctive way of expressing ideas—not what is said, but how it is said. Douglass uses a formal, elegant style that demonstrates his masterful command of language.

After running thus for a considerable distance, they finally upset the cart, dashing it with great force against a tree, and threw themselves into a dense thicket.

Elements that characterize style include

- **tone,** conveyed by choice of words and details
- **sentence patterns and structures**
- use of **figurative language**
- use of **dialogue**

Douglass combines crisp, factual narration with bursts of poetic language. As you read, note the choices Douglass makes that contribute to his sophisticated style. Examine how the author's style and tone contribute to his viewpoint or perspective on the institution of slavery.

READING SKILL: ANALYZE AUTHOR'S PURPOSE

An author creates a work to achieve a specific **purpose,** or goal. In general, an author writes to inform, to express thoughts or feelings, to persuade, or to entertain. However, a complex work will often have more than one purpose.

Frederick Douglass wrote his autobiography mainly to persuade readers that slavery should be abolished. To achieve his purpose, he described the physical realities that slaves endured and his responses to his life as a slave.

We were often in the field from the first approach of day till its last lingering ray had left us . . .

As you read, use a chart like the one shown to take notes on Douglass's experiences. Notice when he provides factual details about the general conditions of slave life and when he describes his personal responses to his situation.

Physical Realities	Responses to Situation

Complete the activities in your **Reader/Writer Notebook.**

Can you set yourself FREE?

Separated from his parents, denied the right to an education, and moved from place to place at the convenience of his owners, Frederick Douglass learned that nothing in his life was under his control. Rejecting the injustice of slavery, he risked his life to escape. With his decision to set himself free, he claimed the right to self-determination: he would be a man and not a slave.

QUICKWRITE Without mentioning any names, contrast two people you know of—one who has self-determination and one who does not. Would you attribute the differences beween them more to circumstances or to attitude?

A—	M—
stands up to defend the rights of others	afraid to disagree with her boyfriend

Narrative of the Life of Frederick Douglass

Frederick Douglass

BACKGROUND Douglass wrote his autobiography to convince skeptics that such an eloquent speaker had indeed once been a slave. His book became one of the most famous slave narratives ever published and played an enormous role in rallying support for the abolition of slavery. This excerpt recounts a period in Douglass's life during which his owner, Hugh Auld's brother, Thomas, had hired him out to a man with a reputation as a "slave breaker."

I left Master Thomas's house, and went to live with Mr. Covey, on the 1st of January, 1833. I was now, for the first time in my life, a field hand. In my new employment, I found myself even more awkward than a country boy appeared to be in a large city. I had been at my new home but one week before Mr. Covey gave me a very severe whipping, cutting my back, causing the blood to run, and raising ridges on my flesh as large as my little finger. The details of this affair are Ⓐ as follows: Mr. Covey sent me, very early in the morning of one of our coldest days in the month of January, to the woods, to get a load of wood. He gave me a team of unbroken oxen. He told me which was the in-hand ox, and which the off-hand[1] one. He then tied the end of a large rope around the horns of the in-hand ox, and gave me the other end of it, and told me, if the oxen started to run, that

Analyze Visuals ▶
Describe the **style** of this painting. What impression of its subject does the painting convey?

Ⓐ **STYLE**
Explain what Douglass means by "this affair" in line 6. What is surprising about his **word choice?**

1. **in-hand . . . off-hand:** In a team of animals trained to pull loads, the in-hand animal is the one on the left; the animal on the right is the off-hand one.

Panel 30 from *The Frederick Douglass Series* (1938–1939), Jacob Lawrence. Hampton University Museum.

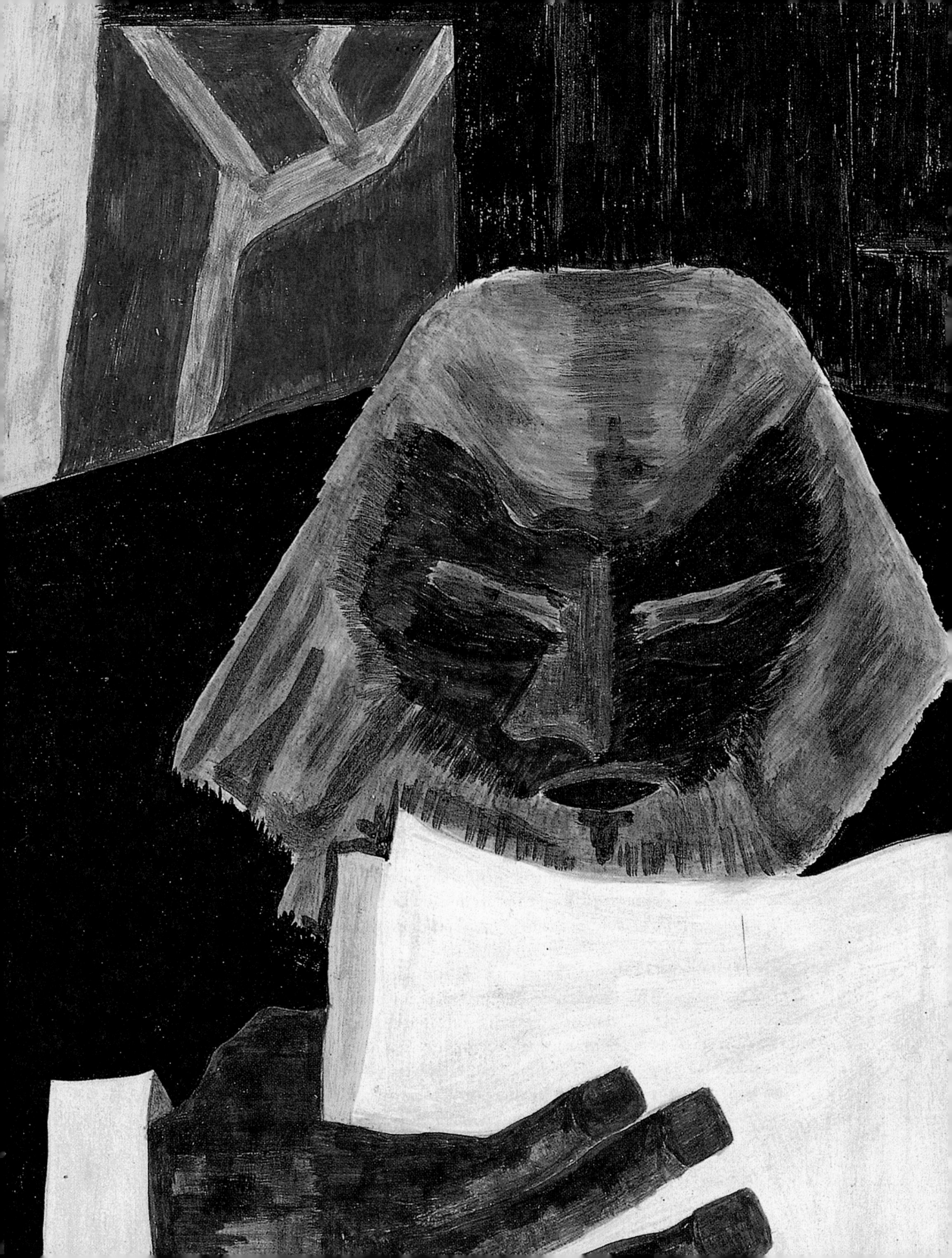

The Life of Harriet Tubman, #9 (1940), Jacob Lawrence. Casein tempera on hardboard, 12″ × 17 7/8″. Hampton University Museum. Photo courtesy of Gwendolyn Knight Lawrence/Art Resource, New York. © 2007 The Jacob and Gwendolyn Lawrence Foundation, Seattle/Artists Rights Society (ARS), New York.

I must hold on upon the rope. I had never driven oxen before, and of course I was very awkward. I, however, succeeded in getting to the edge of the woods with little difficulty; but I had got a very few rods[2] into the woods, when the oxen took fright, and started full tilt, carrying the cart against trees, and over stumps, in the most frightful manner. I expected every moment that my brains would be dashed out against the trees. After running thus for a considerable distance, they finally upset the cart, dashing it with great force against a tree, and threw themselves into a dense thicket.

How I escaped death, I do not know. There I was, entirely alone, in a thick wood, in a place new to me. My cart was upset and shattered, my oxen were entangled among the young trees, and there was none to help me. After a long spell of effort, I succeeded in getting my cart righted, my oxen disentangled, and again yoked to the cart. I now proceeded with my team to the place where I had, the day before, been chopping wood, and loaded my cart pretty heavily, thinking in this way to tame my oxen. I then proceeded on my way home. I had now

▲ Analyze Visuals
Identify details in this painting that are used to represent the experience of slavery. What effects are achieved by centering the image of the figures' feet?

2. **rods:** units of length equal to 5 1/2 yards.

consumed one half of the day. I got out of the woods safely, and now felt out of danger. I stopped my oxen to open the woods gate; and just as I did so, before I could get hold of my ox rope, the oxen again started, rushed through the gate, catching it between the wheel and the body of the cart, tearing it to pieces, and coming within a few inches of crushing me against the gate-post. Thus twice, in one short day, I escaped death by the merest chance. On my return, I told Mr. Covey what had happened, and how it happened. He ordered me to return to the woods again immediately. I did so, and he followed on after me. Just as I got into the woods, he came up and told me to stop my cart, and that he would teach me how to trifle away my time, and break gates. He then went to a large gum-tree, and with his axe cut three large switches, and, after trimming them up neatly with his pocket-knife, he ordered me to take off my clothes. I made him no answer, but stood with my clothes on. He repeated his order. I still made him no answer, nor did I move to strip myself. Upon this he rushed at me with the fierceness of a tiger, tore off my clothes, and lashed me till he had worn out his switches, cutting me so savagely as to leave the marks visible for a long time after. This whipping was the first of a number just like it, and for similar offenses. **B**

I lived with Mr. Covey one year. During the first six months, of that year, scarce a week passed without his whipping me. I was seldom free from a sore back. My awkwardness was almost always his excuse for whipping me. We were worked fully up to the point of endurance. Long before day we were up, our horses fed, and by the first approach of day we were off to the field with our hoes and ploughing teams. Mr. Covey gave us enough to eat, but scarce time to eat it. We were often less than five minutes taking our meals. We were often in the field from the first approach of day till its last lingering ray had left us; and at saving-fodder time, midnight often caught us in the field binding blades.[3] **C**

Covey would be out with us. The way he used to stand it, was this. He would spend the most of his afternoons in bed. He would then come out fresh in the evening, ready to urge us on with his words, example, and frequently with the whip. Mr. Covey was one of the few slaveholders who could and did work with his hands. He was a hard-working man. He knew by himself just what a man or a boy could do. There was no deceiving him. His work went on in his absence almost as well as in his presence; and he had the faculty of making us feel that he was ever present with us. This he did by surprising us. He seldom approached the spot where we were at work openly, if he could do it secretly. He always aimed at taking us by surprise. Such was his cunning, that we used to call him, among ourselves, "the snake." When we were at work in the cornfield, he would sometimes crawl on his hands and knees to avoid detection, and all at once he would rise nearly in our midst, and scream out, "Ha, ha! Come, come! Dash on, dash on!" This being **D** his mode of attack, it was never safe to stop a single minute. His comings were like a thief in the night. He appeared to us as being ever at hand. He was under every

Language Coach

Fixed Expressions The term ***fixed expression*** refers to the normal combination of words—the ways they are often used. "Merest chance" (line 32) means "only by chance." Other fixed expressions with *chance* are "strong chance" and "reasonable chance." Use each expression in a sentence.

B STYLE
Reread lines 31–43. What is the effect of Douglass's choice to use little imagery or figurative language in his narration?

C AUTHOR'S PURPOSE
Reread lines 46–52. What details does Douglass use to inform his readers about the working conditions of slaves?

D GRAMMAR AND STYLE
Reread lines 63–65. Note how Douglass uses the **vivid verbs** *crawl* and *scream* to characterize Covey's menacing behavior.

---

3. **saving- fodder . . . binding blades:** They are gathering and bundling ("binding") corn-plant leaves ("blades") to use for livestock ("fodder").

tree, behind every stump, in every bush, and at every window, on the plantation. He would sometimes mount his horse, as if bound to St. Michael's,[4] a distance of seven miles, and in half an hour afterwards you would see him coiled up in the corner of the wood-fence, watching every motion of the slaves. He would, for this purpose, leave his horse tied up in the woods. Again, he would sometimes walk up to us, and give us orders as though he was upon the point of starting on a long journey, turn his back upon us, and make as though he was going to the house to get ready; and, before he would get half way thither, he would turn short and crawl into a fence-corner, or behind some tree, and there watch us till the going down of the sun. . . .

If at any one time of my life more than another, I was made to drink the bitterest dregs of slavery, that time was during the first six months of my stay with Mr. Covey. We were worked in all weathers. It was never too hot or too cold; it could never rain, blow, hail, or snow, too hard for us to work in the field. Work, work, work, was scarcely more the order of the day than of the night. The longest days were too short for him, and the shortest nights too long for him. I was somewhat unmanageable when I first went there, but a few months of this discipline tamed me. Mr. Covey succeeded in breaking me. I was broken in body, soul, and spirit. My natural elasticity was crushed, my intellect languished, the disposition to read departed, the cheerful spark that lingered about my eye died; the dark night of slavery closed in upon me; and behold a man transformed into a brute! E

Sunday was my only leisure time. I spent this in a sort of beast-like stupor, between sleep and wake, under some large tree. At times I would rise up, a flash of energetic freedom would dart through my soul, accompanied with a faint beam of hope, that flickered for a moment, and then vanished. I sank down again, mourning over my wretched condition. I was sometimes prompted to take my life, and that of Covey, but was prevented by a combination of hope and fear. My sufferings on this plantation seem now like a dream rather than a stern reality. . . .

I have already intimated that my condition was much worse, during the first six months of my stay at Mr. Covey's, than in the last six. The circumstances leading to the change in Mr. Covey's course toward me form an epoch in my humble history. You have seen how a man was made a slave; you shall see how a slave was made a man. On one of the hottest days of the month of August, 1833, Bill Smith, William Hughes,[5] a slave named Eli, and myself, were engaged in fanning wheat.[6] Hughes was clearing the fanned wheat from before the fan. Eli was turning, Smith was feeding, and I was carrying wheat to the fan. The work was simple, requiring strength rather than intellect; yet, to one entirely unused to such work, it came very hard. About three o'clock of that day, I broke down; my strength failed me; I was seized with a violent aching of the head, attended with

COMMON CORE RI 4, L 5

Language Coach

Figurative Language "Bitterest dregs of slavery" is **figurative language,** language that communicates meaning beyond the literal meaning of the words. Read lines 78–80. (*Dregs* means "residue settled at the bottom of a liquid.") What does "bitterest dregs of slavery" mean?

E STYLE

Reread lines 78–88. Identify examples of metaphor, repetition, and parallelism. What **tone** is created by this use of language? What kind of perspective on slavery does it help the writer to achieve?

4. **St. Michael's:** a town southeast of Baltimore, on the east side of the Chesapeake Bay.
5. **Bill Smith, William Hughes:** Bill Smith was a hired man, and William Hughes was Mr. Covey's cousin.
6. **fanning wheat:** using a machine that blows air to separate grains of wheat from the unusable husks.

extreme dizziness; I trembled in every limb. Finding what was coming, I nerved myself up, feeling it would never do to stop work. I stood as long as I could stagger to the hopper[7] with grain. When I could stand no longer, I fell, and felt as if held down by an immense weight. The fan of course stopped; every one had his own work to do; and no one could do the work of the other, and have his own go on at the same time.

Mr. Covey was at the house, about one hundred yards from the treading-yard where we were fanning. On hearing the fan stop, he left immediately, and came to the spot where we were. He hastily inquired what the matter was. Bill answered that I was sick, and there was no one to bring wheat to the fan. I had by this time crawled away under the side of the post and rail-fence by which the yard was enclosed, hoping to find relief by getting out of the sun. He then asked where I was. He was told by one of the hands. He came to the spot, and, after looking at me awhile, asked me what was the matter. I told him as well as I could, for I scarce had strength to speak. He then gave me a savage kick in the side, and told me to get up. I tried to do so, but fell back in the attempt. He gave me another kick, and again told me to rise. I again tried, and succeeded in gaining my feet; but, stooping to get the tub with which I was feeding the fan, I again staggered and fell. While down in this situation, Mr. Covey took up the hickory slat with which Hughes had been striking off the half-bushel measure, and with it gave me a heavy blow upon the head, making a large wound, and the blood ran freely; and with this again told me to get up. I made no effort to comply, having now made up my **F** mind to let him do his worst. In a short time after receiving this blow, my head grew better. Mr. Covey had now left me to my fate. At this moment I resolved, for the first time, to go to my master, enter a complaint, and ask his protection. In order to do this, I must that afternoon walk seven miles; and this, under the circumstances, was truly a severe undertaking. I was exceedingly feeble; made so as much by the kicks and blows which I received, as by the severe fit of sickness to which I had been subjected. I, however, watched my chance, while Covey was looking in an opposite direction, and started for St. Michael's. I succeeded in getting a considerable distance on my way to the woods, when Covey discovered me, and called after me to come back, threatening what he would do if I did not come. I disregarded both his calls and his threats, and made my way to the woods as fast as my feeble state would allow; and thinking I might be overhauled by him if I kept the road,[8] I walked through the woods, keeping far enough from the road to avoid detection, and near enough to prevent losing my way. I had not gone far before my little strength again failed me. I could go no farther. I fell down, and lay for a considerable time. The blood was yet oozing from the wound on my head. For a time I thought I should bleed to death; and think now that I should have done so, but that the blood so matted my hair as to stop the wound. After lying there about three quarters of an hour, I nerved myself up again, and started on my

COMMON CORE RI 6

F AUTHOR'S PURPOSE
Reread lines 113–128. Notice the description of Mr. Covey's violence and the author's reaction to it. Without making judgments about Covey's behavior, Douglass advances a persuasive purpose—to expose slavery's unacceptable brutality. Now read lines 129–144, paying special attention to Douglass's tone and to what he reports about himself and Mr. Covey. How does Douglass advance his purpose in these lines?

7. **hopper:** a funnel-shaped container for storing grain.
8. **kept the road:** stayed on the road.

way, through bogs and briers, barefooted and bareheaded, tearing my feet sometimes at nearly every step; and after a journey of about seven miles, occupying some five hours to perform it, I arrived at master's store. I then presented an appearance enough to affect any but a heart of iron. From the crown of my head to my feet, I was covered with blood. My hair was all clotted with dust and blood; my shirt was stiff with blood. My legs and feet were torn in sundry places with briers and thorns, and were also covered with blood. I suppose I looked like a man who had escaped a den of wild beasts, and barely escaped them. In this state I appeared before my master, humbly entreating him to interpose his authority for my protection. I told him all the circumstances as well as I could, and it seemed, as I spoke, at times to affect him. He would then walk the floor, and seek to justify Covey by saying he expected I deserved it. He asked me what I wanted. I told him, to let me get a new home; that as sure as I lived with Mr. Covey again, I should live with but to die with him; that Covey would surely kill me; he was in a fair way for it. Master Thomas ridiculed the idea that there was any danger of Mr. Covey's killing me, and said that he knew Mr. Covey; that he was a good man, and that he could not think of taking me from him; that, should he do so, he would lose the whole year's wages; that I belonged to Mr. Covey for one year, and that I must go back to him, come what might; and that I must not trouble him with any more stories, or that he would himself *get hold of me.* After **G** threatening me thus, he gave me a very large dose of salts,[9] telling me that I might remain in St. Michael's that night, (it being quite late,) but that I must be off back to Mr. Covey's early in the morning; and that if I did not, he would get *hold of me,* which meant that he would whip me. I remained all night, and, according to his orders, I started off to Covey's in the morning, (Saturday morning,) wearied in body and broken in spirit. I got no supper that night, or breakfast that morning. I reached Covey's about nine o'clock; and just as I was getting over the fence that divided Mrs. Kemp's fields from ours, out ran Covey with his cowskin, to give me another whipping. Before he could reach me, I succeeded in getting to the cornfield; and as the corn was very high, it afforded me the means of hiding. He seemed very angry, and searched for me a long time. My behavior was altogether unaccountable. He finally gave up the chase, thinking, I suppose, that I must come home for something to eat; he would give himself no further trouble in looking for me. I spent that day mostly in the woods, having the alternative before me,—to go home and be whipped to death, or stay in the woods and be starved to death. That night, I fell in with Sandy Jenkins, a slave with whom I was somewhat acquainted. Sandy had a free wife who lived about four miles from Mr. Covey's; and it being Saturday, he was on his way to see her. I told him my circumstances, and he very kindly invited me to go home with him. I went home with him, and talked this whole matter over, and got his advice as to what course it was best for me to pursue. I found Sandy an old adviser. He told me, with great solemnity, I

G STYLE
Reread lines 159–167. Note that Douglass chooses to convey this dialogue without the use of quotations. What effect does he achieve instead by repeating the word *that?*

9. **salts:** mineral salts used to relieve faintness and headache or to reduce swelling.

Panel #10 from *The Frederick Douglass Series of 1938-1940,* Jacob Lawrence. © 2007 The Jacob and Gwendolyn Lawrence Foundation, Seattle/Artists Rights Society (ARS), New York.

must go back to Covey; but that before I went, I must go with him into another part of the woods, where there was a certain *root,* which, if I would take some of it with me, carrying it *always on my right side,* would render it impossible for Mr. Covey, or any other white man, to whip me. He said he had carried it for years; and since he had done so, he had never received a blow, and never expected to while he carried it. I at first rejected the idea, that the simple carrying of a root in my pocket would have any such effect as he had said, and was not disposed to take it; but Sandy impressed the necessity with much earnestness, telling me it could do no harm, if it did no good. To please him, I at length took the root, and, according to his direction, carried it upon my right side. This was Sunday morning. I immediately started for home; and upon entering the yard gate, out came Mr. Covey on his way to meeting.[10] He spoke to me very kindly, made me drive the pigs from a lot near by, and passed on towards the church. Now, this singular conduct of Mr. Covey really made me begin to think that there was something in the *root* which Sandy had given me; and had it been on any other day than Sunday, I could have attributed the conduct to no other cause than the influence of that root; and as it was, I was half inclined to think the *root* to be something more than I at first had taken it to be. All went well till Monday morning. On this morning, the virtue of the *root* was fully tested. Long before daylight, I was called to go and rub, curry, and feed, the horses. I obeyed, and was glad to obey. But whilst thus engaged, whilst in the act of throwing down some blades from the loft, Mr. Covey entered the stable with a long rope; and just as I was half out of the loft, he caught hold of my legs, and was about tying me. As soon as I found what he was up to, I gave a sudden spring, and as I did so, he holding to my legs, I was brought sprawling on the stable floor. Mr. Covey seemed now to think he had me, and could do what he pleased; but at this moment—from whence came the spirit I don't know—I resolved to fight; and, suiting my action to the resolution, I seized Covey hard by the throat; and as I did so, I rose. He held on to me, and I to him. My resistance was so entirely unexpected, that Covey seemed taken all aback. He trembled like a leaf. This gave me assurance, and I held him uneasy, causing the blood to run where I touched him with the ends of my fingers. Mr. Covey soon called out to Hughes for help. Hughes came, and, while Covey held me, attempted to tie my right hand. While he was in the act of doing so, I watched my chance, and gave him a heavy kick close under the ribs. This kick fairly sickened Hughes, so that he left me in the hands of Mr. Covey. This kick had the effect of not only weakening Hughes, but Covey also. When he saw Hughes bending over with pain, his courage quailed. He asked me if I meant to persist in my resistance. I told him I did, come what might; that he had used me like a brute for six months, and that I was determined to be used so no longer. With that, he strove to drag me to a stick that was lying just out of the stable door. He meant to knock me down. But just as he was leaning over to get

COMMON CORE RI 4, L 5b

Language Coach

Connotation A word's **connotations** are the images and feelings associated with the word. *Brute* (line 227) is very similar in meaning to *animal*, but its connotations are negative ("unable to reason," "cruel," "stupid"). Why is *brute* appropriate here?

10. **meeting:** church service.

the stick, I seized him with both hands by his collar, and brought him by a sudden snatch to the ground. By this time, Bill came. Covey called upon him for assistance. Bill wanted to know what he could do. Covey said, "Take hold of him, take hold of him!" Bill said his master hired him out to work, and not to help to whip me; so he left Covey and myself to fight our own battle out. We were at it for nearly two hours. Covey at length let me go, puffing and blowing at a great rate, saying that if I had not resisted, he would not have whipped me half so much. The truth was, that he had not whipped me at all. I considered him as getting entirely the worst end of the bargain; for he had drawn no blood from me, but I had from him. The whole six months afterwards, that I spent with Mr. Covey, he never laid the weight of his finger upon me in anger. He would occasionally say, he didn't want to get hold of me again. "No," thought I, "you need not; for you will come off worse than you did before."

This battle with Mr. Covey was the turning-point in my career as a slave. It rekindled the few expiring embers of freedom, and revived within me a sense of my own manhood. It recalled the departed self-confidence, and inspired me again with a determination to be free. The gratification afforded by the triumph was a full compensation[11] for whatever else might follow, even death itself. He only can understand the deep satisfaction which I experienced, who has himself repelled by force the bloody arm of slavery. I felt as I never felt before. It was a glorious resurrection, from the tomb of slavery, to the heaven of freedom. My long-crushed spirit rose, cowardice departed, bold defiance took its place; and I now resolved that, however long I might remain a slave in form, the day had passed forever when I could be a slave in fact. I did not hesitate to let it be known of me, that the white man who expected to succeed in whipping, must also succeed in killing me. **H**

From this time I was never again what might be called fairly whipped, though I remained a slave four years afterwards. I had several fights, but was never whipped.

COMMON CORE RI 4

Language Coach

Figurative Language "Getting . . . the worst end of the bargain" (line 238) means "having the loss while the other person has the gain"; it is **figurative language,** language that communicates meaning beyond the literal meaning of the words. Why does Douglass have the better position?

H AUTHOR'S PURPOSE Reread lines 243–253. How might this description have helped Douglass achieve his purpose?

11. **compensation:** payment; something of equivalent value.

Comprehension

1. **Recall** What was Covey's first reason for beating Douglass?
2. **Summarize** How did Master Thomas respond when Douglass asked for protection from Covey?
3. **Clarify** How was the battle with Covey a turning point in Douglass's life as a slave?

Text Analysis

4. **Analyze Author's Purpose** Review the chart you created as you read. Given his main purpose, why might Douglass have chosen to include both kinds of detail in his narrative? Explain your answer.
5. **Analyze Style** Describe the main elements of Douglass's style. Which elements, if any, help Douglass establish himself as a credible **narrator**? Support your answer with details.
6. **Examine Rhetorical Devices** Douglass was a great orator, and his style was influenced by his mastery of rhetorical devices. One of his signature techniques was his use of **inverted parallelism,** a reversal of ideas expressed in parallel phrases or clauses: "The longest days were too short for him, and the shortest nights too long for him." Identify the inverted parallelism in lines 99–100. In what ways does this reversal of ideas summarize Douglass's emotional experiences in this selection?
7. **Make Generalizations from Conflicts** What do the conflicts between Douglass and Covey reveal about slavery's effects on both slaves and masters? Use charts like the ones shown to make generalizations about slavery based on Douglass's experiences.

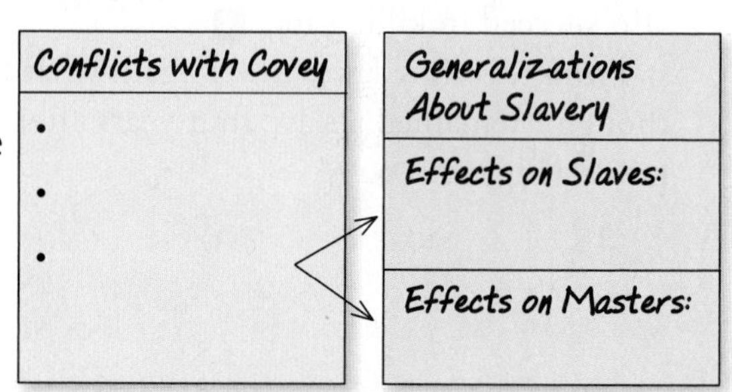

8. **Draw Conclusions** Consider how Douglass portrays his triumphant moment of self-determination. In what ways does his experience illustrate each of the following classic American ideas? Support your answers with details.
   - individual rights
   - self-reliance
   - resistance to tyranny

Text Criticism

9. **Different Perspectives** In what ways might a slave narrative written by an enslaved woman differ from Douglass's account? Explain your answer.

Can you set yourself **FREE?**

When Frederick Douglass eventually realized his dream of freedom, he declared his right to self-determination. In what areas do you think a free person is able to control his or her own life? What aspects of your life are you unable to control?

COMMON CORE

RI 2 Determine two or more central ideas of a text. **RI 4** Determine the meaning of words and phrases as they are used in a text, including figurative and connotative meanings. **RI 6** Determine an author's point of view or purpose in a text in which the rhetoric is particularly effective, analyzing how style and content contribute to the power, persuasiveness, or beauty of a text. **RI 9** Analyze nineteenth-century U.S. documents of literary significance for their themes, purposes, and rhetorical features. **L 3a** Apply an understanding of syntax to the study of complex texts when reading.

Language

GRAMMAR AND STYLE: Make Effective Word Choices

Review the **Grammar and Style** note on page 563. To convey the brutal conditions he endured as a slave, Douglass used **vivid verbs,** ones that convey precise actions or emotions and draw readers into the reality of his experiences.

> *I was seized with a violent aching of the head, attended with extreme dizziness; I trembled in every limb. Finding what was coming, I nerved myself up, feeling it would never do to stop work. I stood as long as I could stagger to the hopper with grain.* (lines 106–109)

The verbs *seized, trembled, nerved,* and *stagger* help communicate the urgency of Douglass's situation.

PRACTICE Rewrite each sentence, replacing the boldface words with vivid verbs. An example has been done for you.

EXAMPLE

I **walked** into the room where the baby was **crying** and **helped** her back to sleep.

I crept into the room where the baby was whimpering and coaxed her back to sleep.

1. The wind **blew** as he **walked** through the dark forest.
2. A sudden wave of illness made me **hold** my stomach.
3. The waves **moved** the ship back and forth as the storm **continued.**

READING-WRITING CONNECTION

Expand your understanding of Frederick Douglass by responding to this prompt. Then, use the **revising tips** to improve your description.

WRITING PROMPT

DESCRIBE A TURNING POINT Douglass viewed his fight with the cowardly overseer Covey as a turning point in his life. Think of an episode from your own life that you would describe as a turning point. Write a **three-paragraph description** of the episode. Make effective word choices to convey the significance of the event to your readers.

REVISING TIPS

- Include all the necessary background information to help readers understand the significance of the event.
- Tell your story using chrono-logical order.
- Use precise verbs and sensory details that vividly describe your experience.

COMMON CORE

L 3 Apply knowledge of language to make effective choices for meaning or style. **W 3** Write narratives to develop real or imagined experiences or events using effective technique, well-chosen details, and well-structured event sequences. **W 3d** Use precise words and phrases, telling details, and sensory language to convey a vivid picture of the experiences, events, setting, and/or characters.

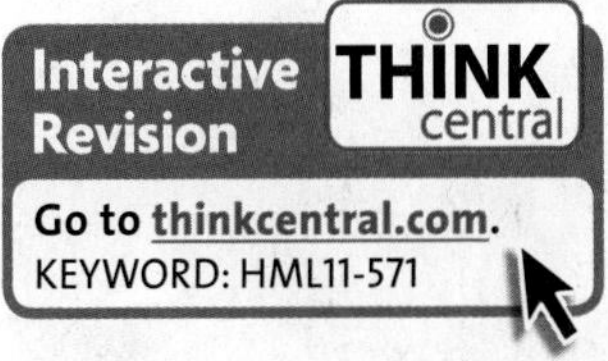

from Incidents in the Life of a Slave Girl

Slave Narrative by Harriet Jacobs

COMMON CORE

RI 3 Analyze a sequence of events and explain how specific individuals interact and develop over the course of the text. **L 4** Determine or clarify the meaning of multiple-meaning words. **L 4d** Verify the preliminary determination of the meaning of a word.

DID YOU KNOW?

Harriet Jacobs . . .

- was described in a runaway slave notice as having run away "without any known cause or provocation."
- used fictitious names in her autobiography because she "deemed it kind and considerate toward others."
- was asked by the son of her former owner for help in getting a job after the Civil War.

Meet the Author

Harriet Jacobs 1813–1897

Harriet Jacobs's *Incidents in the Life of a Slave Girl* is one of the few slave narratives to recount the anguish of slavery from a female point of view. The book ranks as one of the most powerful and important examples of the slave narrative genre.

Defying Her Owner Jacobs was born into slavery in Edenton, North Carolina. Her first owner was a relatively kind woman who taught her to read and sew. When Jacobs was 12, the woman died, and Jacobs was willed to the 3-year-old daughter of Dr. James Norcom—the man she calls "Dr. Flint" in her autobiography. Norcom began making sexual advances toward Jacobs when she was in her teens. Jacobs resisted him and instead started a relationship with Norcom's neighbor, a white lawyer named Samuel Sawyer ("Mr. Sands" in the narrative), hoping the relationship would put a stop to Norcom's unwanted attentions. Jacobs had two children with Sawyer, but Norcom continued harassing her. Infuriated by her refusals, he punished Jacobs by sending her and her young children to work for his son ("Mr. Flint"), who he hoped would be able to break her resistance.

Seven Years in Hiding Shortly after arriving at the son's plantation, Jacobs made the painful decision to run away and leave her children behind. She hoped that her leaving would make the Norcoms sell the children to their father, Sawyer. Unlike many runaways, Jacobs did not immediately flee north. She hid in a tiny attic space in her grandmother's house. She remained there for seven years, but was able to take comfort in the knowledge that her children had been bought by Sawyer and saved from plantation life. In 1842, friends arranged for Jacobs to escape to New York. Once there, she found work as a nanny for a white family. Even so, Jacobs was always in danger of losing her freedom. Fugitive slave laws allowed for slave catchers to capture slaves who had escaped to the North and return them to slavery in the South. Fortunately, in 1852, Jacobs's employer purchased Jacobs's freedom and that of her two children.

Abolitionist and Author In the North, Jacobs became involved in the abolitionist movement. Abolitionist friends encouraged her to write *Incidents in the Life of a Slave Girl,* which she published in 1861 under the pseudonym Linda Brent, the name she uses to refer to herself in the narrative.

Author Online THINK central

Go to thinkcentral.com. KEYWORD: HML11-572

TEXT ANALYSIS: NARRATIVE ELEMENTS

The events in Jacobs's autobiography are true, not fictional, yet Jacobs selects and arranges them to tell a compelling story. Critics have noted, not always admiringly, how much her book resembles a novel. As you read, notice the following narrative characteristics:

- Linda, the main character, experiences internal and external **conflicts** resulting from slavery. An **internal conflict** is a struggle within a character; an **external conflict** is a struggle between a character and an outside force.
- These conflicts result in **suspense,** or excitement and tension, as readers wonder about the outcome of the complex sequence of events.
- Direct comments and telling details develop the strong **characterizations** of Linda and the slave owners, making their personalities clear yet complex.

READING STRATEGY: READING A NARRATIVE

Numerous characters are mentioned in this selection, and because the excerpt is from the middle of the book, it is not always clear who they are. Some are never given names. Study Jacobs's biography on page 572, and then match characters in the narrative to the actual figures in Jacobs's life. Pay attention to the background paragraphs that precede each part of the selection. As you read, use a graphic organizer to keep track of the characters and their relation to the narrator. Note whether they support or oppose her.

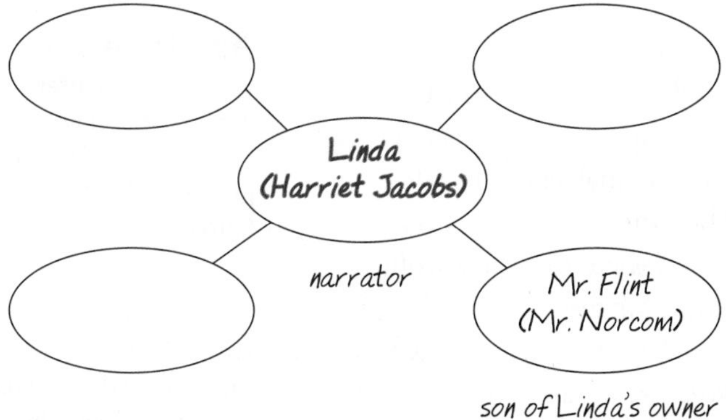

Complete the activities in your **Reader/Writer Notebook**.

What is the PRICE *of freedom?*

Parents often put their children's welfare before their own. In Harriet Jacobs's case, the sacrifice she made for her children was tremendous. Running away put her at risk of being caught and severely beaten, jailed, or sold. In addition, she deprived herself of the opportunity to play a role in the raising of her own children.

DISCUSS Think about sacrifices people have made for their own or their children's freedom. Discuss examples from the past or the present with a group of classmates. Can the price of freedom ever be too high?

The Ride for Freedom, The Fugitive Slaves (1862), Eastman Johnson. Oil. The Granger Collection, New York.

Incidents in the Life of a Slave Girl

Harriet Jacobs

BACKGROUND At this point in the narrative, Linda has spent six weeks at the plantation of old Dr. Flint's son, Mr. Flint, making the house ready for his new bride, who is now at the house. Mr. Flint has said openly that he plans to break Linda's willful spirit, as his father had not been able to do. In addition, Linda has learned that the next day, her children are to be brought from their grandmother's house, where they are loved, to the plantation, where they will be put to work and used to keep Linda in line. Be warned that this selection contains a racial slur.

The Flight

MR. FLINT was hard pushed for house servants, and rather than lose me he had restrained his malice. I did my work faithfully, though not, of course, with a willing mind. They were evidently afraid I should leave them. Mr. Flint wished that I should sleep in the great house instead of the servants' quarters. His wife agreed to the proposition, but said I mustn't bring my bed into the house, because it would scatter feathers on her carpet. I knew when I went there that they would never think of such a thing as furnishing a bed of any kind for me and my little one. I therefore carried my own bed, and now I was forbidden to use it. I did as I (A) was ordered. But now that I was certain my children were to be put in their power, in order to give them a stronger hold on me, I resolved to leave them that night. I remembered the grief this step would bring upon my dear old grandmother; and nothing less than the freedom of my children would have induced me to disregard her advice. I went about my evening work with trembling steps. Mr. Flint twice called from his chamber door to inquire why the house was not locked up. I replied that I had not done my work. "You have had time enough to do it," said he. "Take care how you answer me!"

Analyze Visuals ▶
What can you **infer** about the enslaved family pictured in this photograph from South Carolina?

(A) NARRATIVE ELEMENTS
Notice how the details in lines 1–8 build the **characterization** of the Flints. What kind of people are they?

I shut all the windows, locked all the doors, and went up to the third story, to wait till midnight. How long those hours seemed, and how fervently I prayed that God would not forsake me in this hour of utmost need! I was about to risk everything on the throw of a die; and if I failed, O what would become of me and my poor children? They would be made to suffer for my fault. **B**

At half past twelve I stole softly down stairs. I stopped on the second floor, thinking I heard a noise. I felt my way down into the parlor, and looked out of the window. The night was so intensely dark that I could see nothing. I raised the window very softly and jumped out. Large drops of rain were falling, and the darkness bewildered me. I dropped on my knees, and breathed a short prayer to God for guidance and protection. I groped my way to the road, and rushed towards the town with almost lightning speed. I arrived at my grandmother's house, but dared not see her. She would say, "Linda, you are killing me;" and I knew that would unnerve me. I tapped softly at the window of a room, occupied by a woman, who had lived in the house several years. I knew she was a faithful friend, and could be trusted with my secret. I tapped several times before she heard me. At last she raised the window, and I whispered, "Sally, I have run away. Let me in, quick." She opened the door softly, and said in low tones, "For God's sake, don't. Your grandmother is trying to buy you and de chillern. Mr. Sands was here last week. He tole her he was going away on business, but he wanted her to go ahead about buying you and de chillern, and he would help her all he could. Don't run away, Linda. Your grandmother is all bowed down wid trouble now." **C**

I replied, "Sally, they are going to carry my children to the plantation to-morrow; and they will never sell them to any body so long as they have me in their power. Now, would you advise me to go back?"

"No, chile, no," answered she. "When dey finds you is gone, dey won't want de plague[1] ob de chillern; but where is you going to hide? Dey knows ebery inch ob dis house."

I told her I had a hiding-place, and that was all it was best for her to know. I asked her to go into my room as soon as it was light, and take all my clothes out of my trunk, and pack them in hers; for I knew Mr. Flint and the constable would be there early to search my room. I feared the sight of my children would be too much for my full heart; but I could not go out into the uncertain future without one last look. I bent over the bed where lay my little Benny and baby Ellen. Poor little ones! fatherless and motherless! Memories of their father came over me. He wanted to be kind to them; but they were not all to him, as they were to my womanly heart. I knelt and prayed for the innocent little sleepers. I kissed them lightly, and turned away. **D**

As I was about to open the street door, Sally laid her hand on my shoulder, and said, "Linda, is you gwine all alone? Let me call your uncle."

"No, Sally," I replied, "I want no one to be brought into trouble on my account."

B NARRATIVE ELEMENTS
Describe the **conflicts** presented in lines 9–21. Which lines build **suspense?**

C READING A NARRATIVE
Reread lines 28–38. Who are Sally and Mr. Sands? How does Linda interact with them? Refer to Jacobs's biography on page 572 if necessary.

D GRAMMAR AND STYLE
Examine lines 50–54. Notice how the writer uses emotionally charged **adjectives** to express the depth of her despair.

---

1. **plague:** nuisance.

I went forth into the darkness and rain. I ran on till I came to the house of the friend who was to conceal me.

Early the next morning Mr. Flint was at my grandmother's inquiring for me. She told him she had not seen me, and supposed I was at the plantation. He watched her face narrowly, and said, "Don't you know any thing about her running off?" She assured him that she did not. He went on to say, "Last night she ran off without the least provocation. We had treated her very kindly. My wife liked her. She will soon be found and brought back. Are her children with you?" When told that they were, he said, "I am very glad to hear that. If they are here, she cannot be far off. If I find out that any of my niggers have had any thing to do with this damned business, I'll give 'em five hundred lashes." As he started to go to his father's, he turned round and added, persuasively, "Let her be brought back, and she shall have her children to live with her."

The tidings made the old doctor rave and storm at a furious rate. It was a busy day for them. My grandmother's house was searched from top to bottom. As my trunk was empty, they concluded I had taken my clothes with me. Before

COMMON CORE L 4, L 4d

Language Coach

Multiple-Meaning Words *Narrowly* (line 62) is a **multiple-meaning word,** a word with more than one meaning. Look up *narrow* in a dictionary, and select the meaning that fits the context of the sentence.

ten o'clock every vessel northward bound was thoroughly examined, and the law against harboring[2] fugitives was read to all on board. At night a watch was set over the town. Knowing how distressed my grandmother would be, I wanted to send her a message; but it could not be done. Every one who went in or out of her house was closely watched. The doctor said he would take my children, unless she became responsible for them; which of course she willingly did. The next day was spent in searching. Before night, the following advertisement was posted at every corner, and in every public place for miles round:—

> *$300 REWARD! Ran away from the subscriber,[3] an intelligent, bright, mulatto[4] girl, named Linda, 21 years of age. Five feet four inches high. Dark eyes, and black hair inclined to curl; but it can be made straight. Has a decayed spot on a front tooth. She can read and write, and in all probability will try to get to the Free States. All persons are forbidden, under penalty of the law, to harbor or employ said slave. $150 will be given to whoever takes her in the state, and $300 if taken out of the state and delivered to me, or lodged in jail. DR. FLINT.*

For a week, Linda hides in the house of an unnamed friend. Her pursuers come so close to finding her that she rushes from the house into the bushes, where she is bitten by a poisonous snake or lizard. She suffers greatly until an old woman treats her with a folk remedy. Vowing "give me liberty or death," she refuses to return to the Flints. Then a sympathetic white woman, an old friend of her grandmother's, offers to conceal Linda in a small storage room in her house. The woman makes them promise never to tell, as she is the wife of a prominent slaveholder. The woman sends her cook, Linda's friend Betty, to meet Linda and take her to the house.

Months of Peril

I went to sleep that night with the feeling that I was for the present the most fortunate slave in town. Morning came and filled my little cell with light. I thanked the heavenly Father for this safe retreat. Opposite my window was a pile of feather beds. On the top of these I could lie perfectly concealed, and command a view of the street through which Dr. Flint passed to his office. Anxious as I was, I felt a gleam of satisfaction when I saw him. Thus far I had outwitted him, and I triumphed over it. Who can blame slaves for being cunning? They are constantly compelled to resort to it. It is the only weapon of the weak and oppressed against the strength of their tyrants. (E)

(E) NARRATIVE ELEMENTS Consider how Jacobs develops the **characterization** of Linda in this paragraph. How are readers likely to feel toward her?

---

2. **harboring:** sheltering or protecting.
3. **the subscriber:** the person placing the notice, Dr. Flint.
4. **mulatto:** of mixed black and white ancestry.

I was daily hoping to hear that my master had sold my children; for I knew who was on the watch to buy them. But Dr. Flint cared even more for revenge than he did for money. My brother William, and the good aunt who had served in his family twenty years, and my little Benny, and Ellen, who was a little over two years old, were thrust into jail, as a means of compelling my relatives to give some information about me. He swore my grandmother should never see one of them again till I was brought back. They kept these facts from me for several days. When I heard that my little ones were in a loathsome jail, my first impulse was to go to them. I was encountering dangers for the sake of freeing them, and must I be the cause of their death? The thought was agonizing. My benefactress[5] tried to soothe me by telling me that my aunt would take good care of the children while they remained in jail. But it added to my pain to think that the good old aunt, who had always been so kind to her sister's orphan children, should be shut up in prison for no other crime than loving them. I suppose my friends feared a reckless movement on my part, knowing, as they did, that my life was bound up in my children. I received a note from my brother William. It was scarcely legible, and ran thus: "Wherever you are, dear sister, I beg of you not to come here. We are all much better off than you are. If you come, you will ruin us all. They would force you to tell where you had been, or they would kill you. Take the advice of your friends; if not for the sake of me and your children, at least for the sake of those you would ruin." **F**

Poor William! He also must suffer for being my brother. I took his advice and kept quiet. My aunt was taken out of jail at the end of a month, because Mrs. Flint could not spare her any longer. She was tired of being her own housekeeper. It was quite too fatiguing to order her dinner and eat it too. My children remained in jail, where brother William did all he could for their comfort. Betty went to see them sometimes, and brought me tidings. She was not permitted to enter the jail; but William would hold them up to the grated window while she chatted with them. When she repeated their prattle, and told me how they wanted to see their ma, my tears would flow. Old Betty would exclaim, "Lors, chile! what's you crying 'bout? Dem young uns vil kill you dead. Don't be so chick'n hearted! If you does, you vil nebber git thro' dis world." **G**

Language Coach

Antonyms An **antonym** is a word with a meaning opposite that of another word. *Reckless* (line 112) and *careful* are antonyms. Read lines 112–121. What reckless action might Linda take? What advice is Linda given?

F NARRATIVE ELEMENTS
What new **conflict** is presented in this paragraph?

G READING A NARRATIVE
Review the paragraph that begins "For a week . . ." on page 578. Who is Betty, mentioned in lines 124–130?

5. **benefactress:** a woman who gives aid.

Comprehension

1. **Recall** What prompts Linda to make the decision to escape?
2. **Summarize** What actions do the Flints take after they find out Linda has left?
3. **Clarify** Why does Linda want the Flints to sell her children?

COMMON CORE

RI 3 Analyze a complex sequence of events and explain how specific individuals or events interact and develop over the course of the text.

Text Analysis

4. **Reading a Narrative** Review the web you made as you read, considering how each person listed interacts with the narrator. Which characters support Linda and which oppose her? Share questions you have about them.
5. **Examine Narrative Elements** Describe different **conflicts**—internal and external—that develop through the events in this excerpt. What do these conflicts reveal about the institution of slavery and the sacrifices forced by it?
6. **Analyze Characterization** How does the writer present herself? Discuss what you learn about her character and values from
   - her attitude toward her work (lines 2–3)
   - her thoughts as she visits her children (lines 48–54)
   - her insistence upon escaping alone (line 57)
7. **Contrast Characterizations** Contrast the writer's portrayal of herself with her portrayal of the Flints. What does she reveal about the Flints' character and values?
8. **Draw Conclusions** How might the writer's political purpose and the knowledge that she was writing for an audience of Northern white women have influenced her characterizations?
9. **Compare Texts** Read "Free Labor" and "Go Down, Moses" on pages 582 and 583. How do they compare with Harriet Jacobs's narrative in their **tone** and their messages about slavery?

Text Criticism

10. **Author's Style** Jacobs's style was influenced by the literature popular in her time. Nineteenth-century women's novels were melodramatic, arousing readers' emotions with suspenseful plots that usually involved virtuous characters pitted against evil villains. *Uncle Tom's Cabin,* an immensely popular antislavery novel, included such elements as well. It also rendered the speech of slave characters in heavy dialect, a convention of the time. How do you, as a modern reader, respond to Jacobs's style? Evaluate the effects of her style on the power of her narrative.

What is the PRICE *of freedom?*

A person who makes a sacrifice always gives up something. What did Harriet Jacobs give up in order to be free? Do you think the end result (freedom) was worth what she had to give up? Why or why not?

Language

COMMON CORE

L 3 Apply knowledge of language to make effective choices for meaning or style. **W 3d** Use precise words to convey a vivid picture of the characters.

GRAMMAR AND STYLE: Establish Tone

Review the **Grammar and Style** note on page 576. **Tone** is a writer's attitude toward a subject. In Jacobs's compelling narrative, she uses emotionally charged language to establish a tone of melancholy and desperation. In the following example, the **adjectives** *loathsome* and *agonizing* succinctly convey the turmoil and conflict the narrator is experiencing and help elicit empathy from her readers.

> *When I heard my little ones were in a loathsome jail, my first impulse was to go to them. I was encountering dangers for the sake of freeing them, and must I be the cause of their death? The thought was agonizing.* (lines 106–108)

PRACTICE Copy the numbered sentences below. Then rewrite them, using adjectives, verbs, and additional phrases to effectively convey a tone of fear or sorrow. A sample answer has been done for you.

EXAMPLE

I fainted when I heard Linda had run off, leaving her children behind.

I collapsed to the floor when I heard poor Linda had run off, tearing herself away from the dear babies she cherished.

1. I'm an old woman, but I tried to be strong as Mr. Flint asked me questions about Linda.
2. The children cried when they heard their mother had left them behind.
3. It made me sad to see them feeling so bad. It is very hard for the little children.

READING-WRITING CONNECTION

Expand your understanding of Harriet Jacobs's writing by responding to this prompt. Then, use the **revising tips** to improve your response.

WRITING PROMPT	REVISING TIPS
EXPLORE POINT OF VIEW *Incidents in the Life of a Slave Girl* is told from the first-person point of view and thus focuses on the thoughts, words, and actions of the narrator, Linda (Harriet Jacobs). Choose one of the other people mentioned in the narrative—Sally, or Linda's grandmother, aunt, or brother. Write a **three-paragraph response,** told from that character's point of view, reacting to the news that Linda has run away. As a starting point, reread Linda's descriptions of how any of these characters did or would react.	• Use precise language to relate your character's thoughts, feelings, spoken words, and actions. • Use the first-person point of view in your response. • Choose a tone that you think is appropriate for your character.

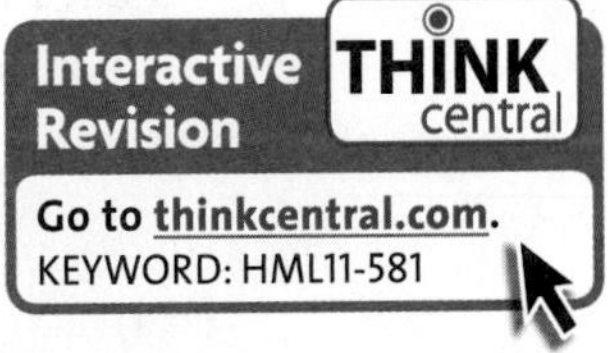

Interactive Revision
THINK central
Go to thinkcentral.com.
KEYWORD: HML11-581

Free Labor

Frances Ellen Watkins Harper

I wear an easy garment,
  O'er it no toiling slave
Wept tears of hopeless anguish,
  In his passage to the grave.

And from its ample folds
  Shall rise no cry to God,
Upon its warp and woof shall be
  No stain of tears and blood.

Oh, lightly shall it press my form,
  Unladened with a sigh,
I shall not 'mid its rustling hear,
  Some sad despairing cry.

This fabric is too light to bear
  The weight of bondsmen's tears,
I shall not in its texture trace
  The agony of years.

Too light to bear a smother'd sigh,
  From some lorn woman's heart,
Whose only wreath of household love
  Is rudely torn apart.

Then lightly shall it press my form,
  Unburden'd by a sigh;
And from its seams and folds shall rise,
  No voice to pierce the sky,

And witness at the throne of God,
  In language deep and strong,
That I have nerv'd Oppression's hand,
  For deeds of guilt and wrong.

Go Down, Moses

Traditional Spiritual

When Israel was in Egypt's land,
Let my people go!
Oppressed so hard they could not stand,
Let my people go!

Go down, Moses,
'Way down in Egypt's land,
Tell old Pharoah, "Let my people go!"

"Thus saith the Lord" bold Moses said,
Let my people go!
"If not I'll smite your first-born dead,"
Let my people go!

Go down, Moses,
'Way down in Egypt's land,
Tell old Pharoah, "Let my people go!"

No more in bondage shall they toil,
Let my people go!
Let them come out with Egypt's spoil,
Let my people go!

Go down, Moses,
'Way down in Egypt's land,
Tell old Pharoah, "Let my people go!"

COMMON CORE RL 7

COMPARE INTERPRETATIONS
As with any song, different singers of "Go Down, Moses" emphasize different phrases, affecting tone and meaning. Compare the recording of "Go Down, Moses" found on the *Literature* Audio Anthology with a version sung by civil-rights activist Paul Robeson (available online or at a library). Which interpretation do you find more powerful? Why?

COMMON CORE

RI 4 Analyze how an author uses and refines the meaning of a key term or terms over the course of a text. **RI 5** Analyze and evaluate the effectiveness of the structure an author uses in his or her exposition or argument, including whether the structure makes points clear, convincing, and engaging. **RI 8** Delineate and evaluate the reasoning in seminal U.S. texts, including the application of constitutional principles and use of legal reasoning. **RI 9** Analyze foundational U.S. documents of historical and literary significance for their themes, purposes, and rhetorical features. **L 3a** Apply an understanding of syntax to the study of complex texts when reading.

The Gettysburg Address

Speech by Abraham Lincoln

The Emancipation Proclamation

Proclamation by Abraham Lincoln

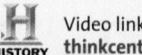

Video link at thinkcentral.com

DID YOU KNOW?

Abraham Lincoln . . .

- loved the works of Edgar Allan Poe.
- was a talented mimic who enjoyed playing practical jokes.
- made Thanksgiving Day a national holiday.
- suffered from bouts of depression.

Meet the Author

Abraham Lincoln 1809–1865

Abraham Lincoln led the United States during its greatest crisis—the Civil War. Dedicated to keeping the nation together, Lincoln guided the country toward a new national identity, that of a nation committed to the principle of union, in which slavery no longer had a place.

Humble Origins Born on the Kentucky frontier to illiterate parents, Lincoln rarely went to school and was largely self-educated. As a young man, he moved with his family to Illinois, where he worked as a shopkeeper, rail-splitter, and surveyor and studied law. He served in the state legislature from 1834 to 1841, becoming a lawyer in 1836.

Evolving Views Although Lincoln opposed slavery as "injustice and bad policy," he was not an abolitionist; he preferred to free slaves gradually. In 1854, he began a vigorous public campaign to block the expansion of slavery to the western territories. His eloquent speeches and famous debates with Senator Stephen A. Douglas raised his political profile and strengthened his opposition to slavery.

A House Divided In 1860, Lincoln was elected president on his antislavery platform, prompting seven Southern states to secede from the Union before he even took office. In 1861, two months after his inauguration, the Civil War began.

As the fighting wore on, Lincoln faced increasing pressure to move against slavery while he struggled to keep the loyalty of the Union states that permitted slavery within their borders. After nearly two years of fighting, Lincoln issued the Emancipation Proclamation, which freed slaves in the rebelling states.

Tragic Ending Throughout the war, Lincoln faced opposition and ridicule from the public, his generals, and his own cabinet. The prospect of a Union victory, however, earned him reelection, and the Confederate armies surrendered weeks into his second term. Just five days later, Lincoln was assassinated, the first such occurrence in American history. His shocking murder and the end of war made him an instant hero. Today, he is one of the country's most widely respected presidents.

THINK central

Author Online

Go to thinkcentral.com. KEYWORD: HML11-584

TEXT ANALYSIS: AUDIENCE AND FORM

Lincoln was a master orator and an expert lawyer. He was keenly aware that the **form** of a piece of writing affects what the writer can say to his or her **audience.**

- A **speech,** such as the Gettysburg Address, is often prepared for a specific audience. The speaker chooses rhetorical techniques that influence the audience and evoke emotion. Note Lincoln's effective use of parallel structure.

  The world will little note nor long remember what we say here, but it can never forget what they did here.

- A **proclamation,** such as the Emancipation Proclamation, is a legal document that announces official state business. As with any legal document, the writer is a person of authority and addresses the general public using clear reasoning and precise, technical language that can be clearly interpreted in a court of law.

  I, Abraham Lincoln, President of the United States, by virtue of the power in me vested as Commander-in-Chief . . .

As you read these texts, note how the structures conventional to each form shape the way Lincoln expresses his message or argument.

READING SKILL: ANALYZE AN AUTHOR'S BELIEFS

A thoughtful, principled man, Lincoln tried to act in accordance with his beliefs. To identify those beliefs in his writing, consider the ideals he invokes, the actions he takes, and the reasons he gives for his actions, as well as how he expresses the meaning of key terms such as *nation*, *consecrate*, and *freedom*. As you read, note details that reveal

- the reason he felt the war was necessary
- his views on the responsibilities of the president
- the reasons he opposed slavery

Use a chart like the one shown to record your notes.

Beliefs About . . .	Gettysburg Address	Emancipation Proclamation
the necessity of war		
the duties of the president		
slavery		

Complete the activities in your **Reader/Writer Notebook.**

What makes a great LEGACY?

Washington, Jefferson, Lincoln—these legendary figures top most lists of greatest American presidents. In each case, the legacy is more complicated than the heroic myths suggest. What are the real reasons some leaders hold such a prominent place in history?

TEST YOURSELF What ideas come to mind when you think of Abraham Lincoln and the times in which he lived? Decide whether each statement is fact or myth.

Myth or History?

1. Hard-working Abe Lincoln was a poor country boy who rose to become president.
   ☐ TRUE ○ FALSE
2. Lincoln led the fight to abolish slavery.
   ☐ TRUE ○ FALSE
3. The Civil War was fought to free the slaves.
   ☐ TRUE ○ FALSE
4. The Emancipation Proclamation ended slavery in the United States.
   ☐ TRUE ○ FALSE
5. All of the Union states opposed slavery.
   ☐ TRUE ○ FALSE

The Gettysburg Address

Abraham Lincoln

BACKGROUND The Battle of Gettysburg was fought July 1–3, 1863. The victory for Union forces marked a turning point in the Civil War, but the losses on both sides were staggering: 28,000 Confederate soldiers and 23,000 Union soldiers were killed or wounded. Lincoln delivered his Gettysburg Address on November 19, 1863, at a ceremony dedicating a national cemetery on the battle site.

Four score and seven years ago[1] our fathers brought forth on this continent a new nation, conceived in liberty, and dedicated to the proposition that all men are created equal.

Now we are engaged in a great civil war, testing whether that nation, or any nation so conceived and so dedicated, can long endure. We are met on a great battlefield of that war. We have come to dedicate a portion of that field as a final resting place for those who here gave their lives that that nation might live. It is altogether fitting and proper that we should do this. (A)

But, in a larger sense, we cannot dedicate—we cannot consecrate—we cannot hallow[2]—this ground. The brave men, living and dead, who struggled here have consecrated it far above our poor power to add or detract. The world will little note nor long remember what we say here, but it can never forget what they did (B) here. It is for us, the living, rather, to be dedicated here to the unfinished work which they who fought here have thus far so nobly advanced. It is rather for us to be here dedicated to the great task remaining before us—that from these honored dead we take increased devotion to that cause for which they gave the last full measure of devotion; that we here highly resolve that these dead shall not have died in vain; that this nation, under God, shall have a new birth of freedom; and that government of the people, by the people, for the people, shall not perish from the earth.

1. **four score . . . ago:** 87 years ago—that is, in 1776. (*Score* means "a group of 20.")
2. **hallow:** set apart as holy.

COMMON CORE L 3a

(A) AUDIENCE AND FORM
The Gettysburg Address is perhaps the most famous speech in the history of this country. In under 300 words, Lincoln crafted a masterpiece of oratory, using **parallel structure** and evocative language to inspire a nation. In the second paragraph, notice the rhythm Lincoln achieves with parallel clauses and phrases: *we are engaged, we are met, we have come; so conceived and so dedicated.* There is powerful emotional appeal here. After reading the speech silently, read it aloud. What effect does Lincoln's use of parallelism have on your delivery?

(B) GRAMMAR AND STYLE
Reread lines 9–13. Note how **repetition** emphasizes the verbs *dedicate* and *consecrate* and refines their meaning.

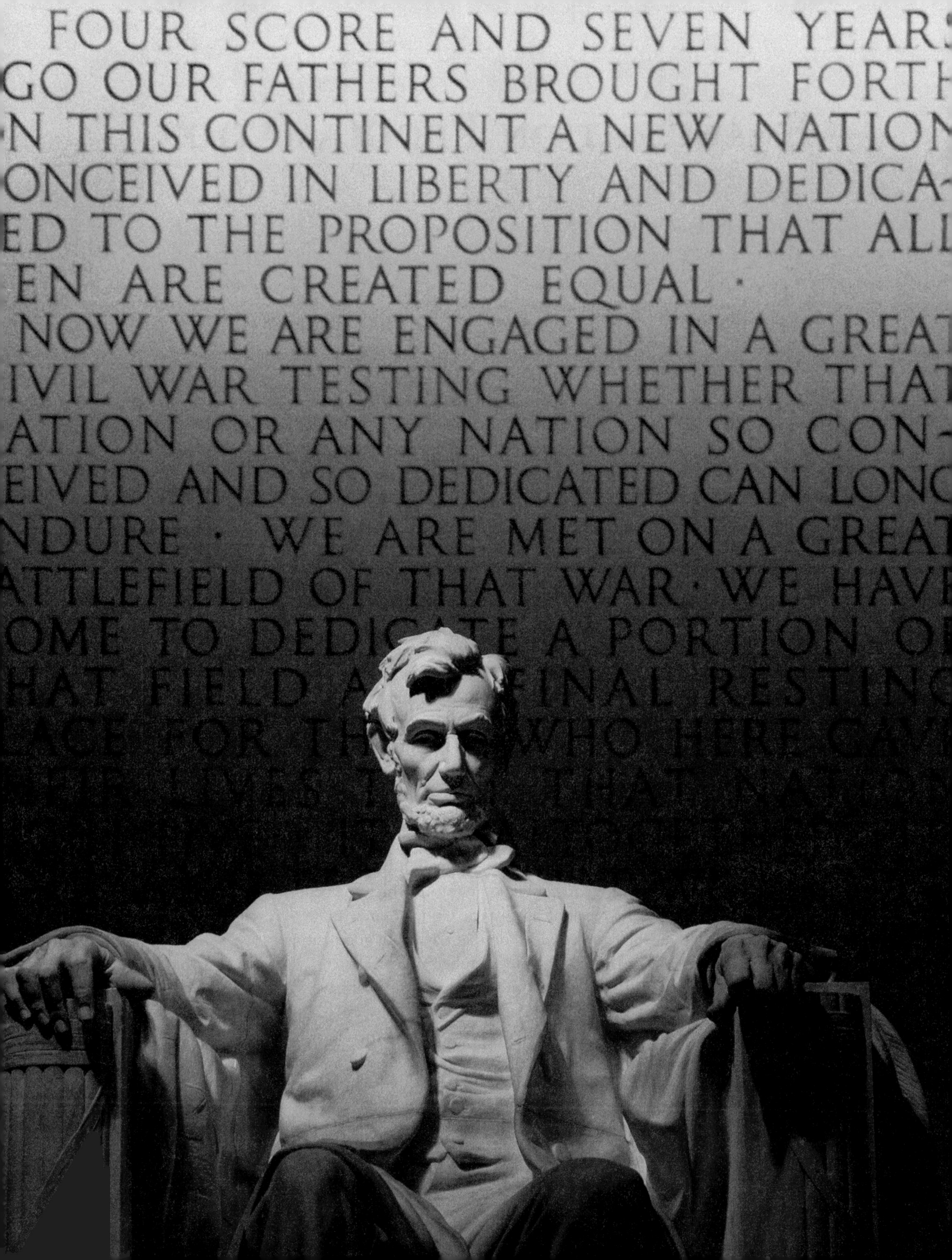

FOUR SCORE AND SEVEN YEARS
GO OUR FATHERS BROUGHT FORTH
N THIS CONTINENT A NEW NATION
ONCEIVED IN LIBERTY AND DEDICA-
ED TO THE PROPOSITION THAT ALL
EN ARE CREATED EQUAL ·
NOW WE ARE ENGAGED IN A GREAT
IVIL WAR TESTING WHETHER THAT
ATION OR ANY NATION SO CON-
EIVED AND SO DEDICATED CAN LONG
NDURE · WE ARE MET ON A GREAT
ATTLEFIELD OF THAT WAR · WE HAVE

The Emancipation Proclamation

January 1, 1863

Abraham Lincoln

BACKGROUND The Emancipation Proclamation was more of a symbolic gesture than an enforceable law. The document applied only to territory the Union did not control; it did not free slaves held by states that were loyal to the Union. Though the proclamation had little immediate legal impact, its promises inspired nearly 200,000 African Americans to join the Union army. Their efforts helped the North win the war.

A Transcription By the President of the United States of America: A Proclamation.

Whereas, on the twenty-second day of September, in the year of our Lord one thousand eight hundred and sixty-two, a proclamation was issued by the President of the United States, containing, among other things, the following, to wit: C

"That on the first day of January, in the year of our Lord one thousand eight hundred and sixty-three, all persons held as slaves within any State or designated part of a State, the people whereof shall then be in rebellion against the United States, shall be then, thenceforward, and forever free; and the Executive Government of the United States, including the military and naval authority thereof, will recognize and maintain the freedom of such persons, and will do no act or acts to repress such persons, or any of them, in any efforts they may make for their actual freedom.

"That the Executive will, on the first day of January aforesaid,[1] by proclamation, designate the States and parts of States, if any, in which the people thereof, respectively, shall then be in rebellion against the United States; and the fact that any State, or the people thereof, shall on that day be, in good faith, represented in the Congress of the United States by members chosen thereto at elections wherein a majority of the qualified voters of such State shall have participated, shall, in the absence of strong countervailing[2] testimony, be deemed conclusive evidence that such State, and the people thereof, are not then in rebellion against the United States." D

Now, therefore I, Abraham Lincoln, President of the United States, by virtue of the power in me vested as Commander-in-Chief, of the Army and Navy of

C AUDIENCE AND FORM
Describe the word choice and sentence structure of lines 1–3. In what ways does the form of the writing—namely, a presidential proclamation—affect Lincoln's **diction?** What technical terms does Lincoln use?

D AUDIENCE AND FORM
Paraphrase lines 12–20. What is Lincoln's legal reasoning for this proclamation? What is the **purpose** of the complicated and careful definitions in this paragraph?

1. **aforesaid:** mentioned earlier.
2. **countervailing:** contradicting.

the United States in time of actual armed rebellion against the authority and government of the United States, and as a fit and necessary war measure for suppressing said rebellion, do, on this first day of January, in the year of our Lord one thousand eight hundred and sixty-three, and in accordance with my purpose so to do publicly proclaimed for the full period of one hundred days, from the day first above mentioned, order and designate as the States and parts of States wherein the people thereof respectively, are this day in rebellion against the United States, the following, to wit:

Arkansas, Texas, Louisiana, (except the Parishes of St. Bernard, Plaquemines, Jefferson, St. John, St. Charles, St. James Ascension, Assumption, Terrebonne, Lafourche, St. Mary, St. Martin, and Orleans, including the City of New Orleans)[3] Mississippi, Alabama, Florida, Georgia, South Carolina, North Carolina, and Virginia, (except the forty-eight counties designated as West Virginia,[4] and also the counties of Berkley, Accomac, Northampton, Elizabeth City, York, Princess Ann, and Norfolk, including the cities of Norfolk and Portsmouth), and which excepted parts, are for the present, left precisely as if this proclamation were not issued.

And by virtue of the power, and for the purpose aforesaid, I do order and declare that all persons held as slaves within said designated States, and parts of States, are, and henceforward shall be free; and that the Executive government of the United States, including the military and naval authorities thereof, will recognize and maintain the freedom of said persons.

And I hereby enjoin upon[5] the people so declared to be free to abstain from all violence, unless in necessary self-defence; and I recommend to them that, in all cases when allowed, they labor faithfully for reasonable wages.

And I further declare and make known, that such persons of suitable condition, will be received into the armed service of the United States to garrison[6] forts, positions, stations, and other places, and to man vessels of all sorts in said service.

And upon this act, sincerely believed to be an act of justice, warranted by the Constitution, upon military necessity, I invoke the considerate judgment of mankind, and the gracious favor of Almighty God. **E**

In witness whereof, I have hereunto set my hand and caused the seal of the United States to be affixed.

Done at the City of Washington, this first day of January, in the year of our Lord one thousand eight hundred and sixty three, and of the Independence of the United States of America the eighty-seventh.

By the President: ABRAHAM LINCOLN
WILLIAM H. SEWARD, Secretary of State.

Language Coach

Word Definitions In line 41, *said* means "mentioned earlier." What purpose might the phrase "said designated States" serve here?

E AUTHOR'S BELIEFS
Reread lines 51–53. What constitutional principles does Lincoln cite for freeing the slaves?

---

3. **except the Parishes . . . New Orleans:** Parishes, or counties, occupied by Union forces.
4. **the forty-eight . . . Virginia:** the western counties of Virginia broke from the Confederacy to form a new state. West Virginia joined the Union as a slave state in 1863.
5. **enjoin upon:** to direct.
6. **garrison:** to occupy as troops.

Comprehension

1. **Recall** For what occasion did Lincoln deliver the Gettysburg Address?
2. **Clarify** According to Lincoln, for what cause or idea was the Battle of Gettysburg fought?
3. **Recall** What authority does Lincoln claim for issuing the Emancipation Proclamation?
4. **Summarize** What exceptions limit the effect of Lincoln's proclamation?

COMMON CORE

RI 1 Cite evidence to support inferences drawn from the text. **RI 4** Analyze how an author uses and refines the meaning of a key term or terms over the course of a text. **RI 5** Analyze and evaluate the effectiveness of the structure an author uses in his or her exposition or argument, including whether the structure makes points clear, convincing, and engaging. **RI 8** Delineate and evaluate the reasoning in seminal U.S. texts, including the application of constitutional principles and use of legal reasoning. **RI 9** Analyze foundational U.S. documents of historical and literary significance for their themes, purposes, and rhetorical features.

Text Analysis

5. **Examine Historical Context** Using details from the author's biography on page 584 and from the background paragraphs on pages 586 and 588, describe the historical context of each document. What political pressures influenced Lincoln's public statements? What legal reasoning did he use?
6. **Compare Audience and Form** Use a chart like the one shown to compare and contrast Lincoln's two works. In what ways does the form or structure used influence Lincoln's message or argument?

	Gettysburg Address	Emancipation Proclamation
Form		
Audience		
Diction		
Tone		

7. **Draw Conclusions About Author's Beliefs** Review the chart you created as you read. Based on your answers, what would you consider to be Lincoln's fundamental values? Cite evidence to support your answer.
8. **Evaluate Form** Which of the two works better conveys each of the following ideas? Support your answers with details.
   - a sense of presidential authority
   - the urgency of the national crisis
   - the value of freedom
   - Lincoln's personal voice

Text Criticism

9. **Critical Interpretations** Often critical of Lincoln's policies, Frederick Douglass also spoke warmly of his honesty and moral conviction. He stated, "The image of the man went out with his words, and those who read them knew him." Based on your own reading, what impressions do you have of Lincoln's character? Explain your answer.

What makes a great LEGACY?

Abraham Lincoln is remembered for his leadership during the Civil War and for helping to end slavery. What kind of legacy would you like to leave? Explain your answer.

Language

◆ GRAMMAR AND STYLE: Use Language Effectively

Review the **Grammar and Style** note on page 586. In the Gettysburg Address, Lincoln makes effective use of the rhetorical device of **repetition.** Here is an example:

> *It is for us, the living, rather, to be dedicated here to the unfinished work which they who fought here have thus far so nobly advanced. It is rather for us to be here dedicated to the great task remaining before us . . .* (lines 13–15)

To emphasize the purpose of the solemn occasion, Lincoln repeats the word *dedicate,* as well as other verbs and abstract nouns, throughout his address. As he repeats words, he sometimes introduces subtle shifts in their meaning, encouraging reflection among the mourners.

PRACTICE Rewrite the following paragraph, incorporating repetition to emphasize key points.

> I was among the mourners who heard your eloquent and inspiring speech at Gettysburg. It made me want to write to you, and it caused me to think about what we are fighting for. My son was 19 years old when he enlisted. He was 20 when he was killed. My family and I can hardly bear the loss, but we have no other choice. We can only hope that his death—and the loss of thousands of others—will not have been in vain. As a parent, it is my sincere hope this is true. Speaking as a citizen of the United States, I can only pray the soldiers have not died for nothing.

COMMON CORE

L 3 Apply knowledge of language to make effective choices for meaning or style. **W 1** Write arguments to support claims in an analysis of substantive topics or texts, using valid reasoning and relevant and sufficient evidence. **W 1b** Develop claim thoroughly in a manner that anticipates the audience's knowledge level, concerns, values, and possible biases. **W 9** Draw evidence from literary or informational texts to support reflection.

READING-WRITING CONNECTION

Expand your understanding of Abraham Lincoln's writing by responding to this prompt. Then, use the **revising tips** to improve your persuasive letter.

WRITING PROMPT

WRITE A PERSUASIVE LETTER Knowing he would be speaking to an audience of people mourning the tremendous losses of the Civil War, Lincoln chose his words carefully. To show his respect for their heavy sacrifices, he used elevated language that conveyed a sense of their importance in history.

Imagine that you had just heard Abraham Lincoln give his speech. Write a **three-paragraph persuasive letter** to your relatives supporting Lincoln's argument for the Civil War.

REVISING TIPS

- Include a strong statement expressing your opinion.
- Support your opinion by developing at least three examples that suit your audience.
- Use evidence such as facts, statistics, expert opinions, and personal examples in your letter.
- Conclude your letter by asking your relatives to take action in some way.

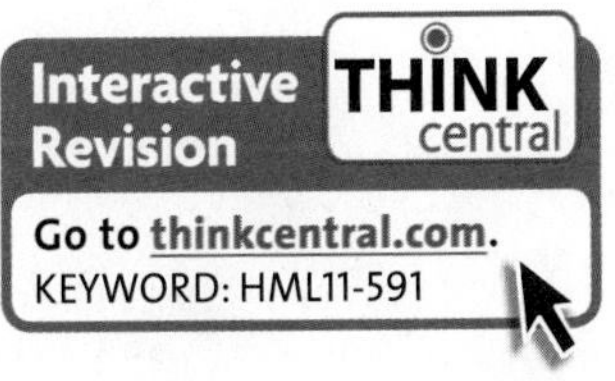

Reading for Information

Voices from the Civil War

- Letter, page 593
- Letter, page 594
- Diary Entry, page 595
- Speech, page 596

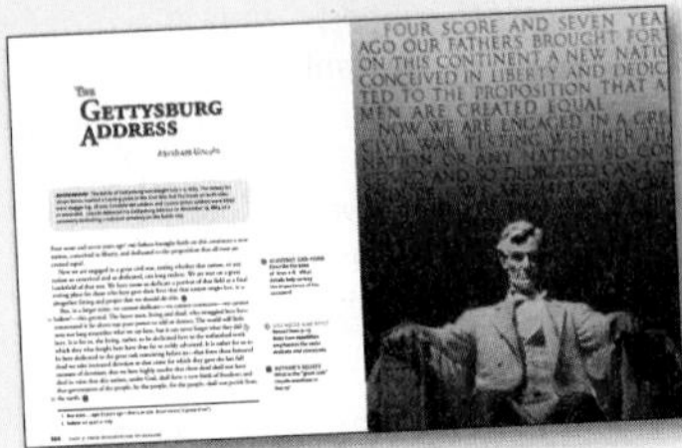

Use with the Gettysburg Address, page 586.

Abraham Lincoln delivered the Gettysburg Address to an audience gathered in honor of fallen Union soldiers. How do you think they reacted to it? Might the same speech have been received differently by a Southern audience? The following documents can give you some insight into differing perspectives on the Civil War. After reading each text, take a moment to imagine how each author might have responded to Lincoln's message; later, you'll be asked to write such a response.

COMMON CORE

RI 6 Determine an author's point of view or purpose in a text in which the rhetoric is particularly effective, analyzing how style and content contribute to the power, persuasiveness, or beauty of the text. **RI 8** Delineate and evaluate the reasoning in seminal U.S. texts, including the premises, purposes, and arguments in works of public advocacy. **L 4a** Use context as a clue to the meaning of a word. **L 5** Demonstrate understanding of figurative language.

Standards Focus: Analyze Primary Sources

Primary sources are documents written by people who participated in or witnessed the events described in the document. Consequently, primary sources can describe personal experiences that are usually lacking in a more removed account. Later in this unit, when reading "An Occurrence at Owl Creek Bridge" (page 604), you will have the opportunity to relate the main ideas in a literary work to these primary source documents.

The letters, diary entry, and speech you are about to read are all primary sources of information on the Civil War. Read the background paragraph before each document as well as its title and date, noting

- the form of the document (letter, diary entry, or speech)
- when and where it was written or delivered
- whether it was intended for a public or private audience
- some of the details that shaped the author's perspective

Record what you learn on a chart such as the one shown here. Then, as you read the texts, consider how these factors relate to the author's purpose for writing.

Author	Form of Writing	Time & Place Created	Intended Audience	Relevant Details About the Author
Robert E. Lee				
Sullivan Ballou				
Mary Chesnut				
Sojourner Truth				

Robert E. Lee had a distinguished career in the U.S. Army until his home state of Virginia seceded from the Union. At that point, his loyalty to Virginia compelled him to join the Confederate army, where he became a general and one of the Confederacy's greatest heroes.

Letter to His Son

January 23, 1861

. . . The South, in my opinion, has been aggrieved by the acts of the North, as you say. I feel the aggression, and am willing to take every proper step for redress. It is the principle I contend for, not individual or private gain. As an American citizen, I take pride in my country, her prosperity and institutions, and would defend any State if her rights were invaded. But I can anticipate no greater calamity for the country than a dissolution of the Union. It would be an accumulation of all the evils we complain of, and I am willing to sacrifice everything but honor for its preservation. **A** I hope, therefore, that all constitutional means will be exhausted before there is a recourse to force. Secession is nothing but revolution. The framers of our Constitution never exhausted so much labor, wisdom and forbearance in its formation, and surrounded it with so many guards and securities, if it was intended to be broken by every member of the Confederacy at will. It was intended for 'perpetual union' so expressed in the preamble, and for the establishment of a government, not a compact, which can only be dissolved by revolution, or the consent of all the people in convention assembled. It is idle to talk of secession. Anarchy would have been established, and not a government by Washington, Hamilton, Jefferson, Madison, and the other patriots of the Revolution. . . . Still, a Union that can only be maintained by swords and bayonets, and in which strife and civil war are to take the place of brotherly love and kindness, has no charm for me. I shall mourn for my country and for the welfare and progress of mankind. If the Union is dissolved, and the Government disrupted, I shall return to my native State and share the miseries of my people, and save in defence will draw my sword on none. **B**

COMMON CORE L 4a

Language Coach

Antonyms An **antonym** is a word with a meaning opposite that of another word. *Dissolution* (line 6) and *preservation* (line 8) are antonyms. Based on the context of the words, what does each word mean?

A PRIMARY SOURCES
Reread lines 5–8. What does Lee want to preserve at any cost but his honor? What is his point of view concerning secession?

B PRIMARY SOURCES
Based on lines 18–21, how does Lee feel about maintaining the Union "by swords and bayonets"? Why?

Major Sullivan Ballou of the Second Rhode Island Regiment wrote the following letter to his wife on July 14, 1861. He was killed about a week later, at the first battle of Bull Run.

Letter to Sarah Ballou

My very dear Sarah:

The indications are very strong that we shall move in a few days—perhaps tomorrow. Lest I should not be able to write again, I feel impelled to write a few lines that may fall under your eye when I shall be no more. . . .

I have no misgivings about, or lack of confidence in the cause in which I am engaged, and my courage does not halt or falter. I know how strongly American Civilization now leans on the triumph of the Government, and how great a debt we owe to those who went before us through the blood and sufferings of the Revolution. And I am willing—perfectly willing—to lay down all my joys in this life, to help maintain this Government, and to pay that debt. . . .

Sarah my love for you is deathless, it seems to bind me with mighty cables that nothing but Omnipotence could break; and yet my love of Country comes over me like a strong wind and bears me unresistibly on with all these chains to the battlefield.

The memories of the blissful moments I have spent with you come creeping over me, and I feel most gratified to God and to you that I have enjoyed them so long. And hard it is for me to give them up and burn to ashes the hopes of future years, when, God willing, we might still have lived and loved together, and seen our sons grown up to honorable manhood, around us. I have, I know, but few and small claims upon Divine Providence, but something whispers to me—perhaps it is the wafted prayer of my little Edgar, that I shall return to my loved ones unharmed. If I do not my dear Sarah, never forget how much I love you, and when my last breath escapes me on the battlefield, it will whisper your name. Forgive my many faults, and the many pains I have caused you. How thoughtless and foolish I have often times been! How gladly would I wash out with my tears every little spot upon your happiness. . . . C

But, O Sarah! If the dead can come back to this earth and flit unseen around those they loved, I shall always be near you; in the gladdest days and in the darkest nights . . . always, always, and if there be a soft breeze upon your cheek, it shall be my breath, as the cool air fans your throbbing temple, it shall be my spirit passing by. Sarah do not mourn me dead; think I am gone and wait for thee, for we shall meet again. . . .

C PRIMARY SOURCES
This letter from Sullivan Ballou is a **primary source** document of the Civil War. Because Major Ballou was a participant in the war, his reflections on its necessity and on his personal expectations provide valuable insight into the cultural and historical setting. Pay special attention to the sentiments expressed in lines 14–25. Then, as you read "An Occurrence at Owl Creek Bridge" later in this unit (page 604), consider how a main idea in that literary work relates to this primary source document.

Wife of a former South Carolina senator, James Chesnut, and a member of the Southern gentility, Mary Chesnut socialized with many prominent Confederates. In her extensive diaries, she kept notes on the social and political conditions in the wartime South.

A Diary from Dixie

1864

September 1st — The battle is raging at Atlanta, our fate hanging in the balance.

September 2nd — Atlanta is gone. Well that agony is over. Like David, when the child was dead, I will get up from my knees, will wash my face and comb my hair. There is no hope, but we will try to have no fear. . . .

September 21st — The President has gone West. He sent for Mr. Chesnut.

I went with Mrs. Rhett to hear Dr. Palmer. I did not know before how utterly hopeless was our situation. This man is so eloquent; it was hard to listen and not give way. Despair was his word, and martyrdom. He offered us nothing more in this world than the martyr's crown. He is not for slavery, he says; he is for freedom, the freedom to govern our own country as we see fit. He is against foreign interference in our state matters. That is what Mr. Palmer went to war for, it appears. Every day shows that slavery is doomed the world over. For that he thanked God. He spoke of this time of our agony; and then came the cry: "Help us, Oh God! Vain is the help of man." So we came away shaken to the depths. . . .

The end has come, no doubt of the fact. Our Army has so moved as to uncover Macon and Augusta. We are going to be wiped off the face of the earth. Now what is there to prevent Sherman taking General Lee in the rear. We have but two armies, and Sherman is between them now. **D**

September 29th — These stories of our defeats in the Valley fall like blows upon a dead body. Since Atlanta, I have felt as if all were dead within me, forever. Captain Ogden of General Chesnut's staff dined here today. Had ever a Brigadier with little or no brigade so magnificent a staff? The reserves, as somebody said, are gathered by robbing the cradle and the grave of men too old and boys too young. . . .

General Chesnut was away in Camden, but I could not wait. I gave the beautiful bride, Mrs. Darby, a dinner which was simply perfect. I was satisfied for once in my life with my own table, and I know pleasanter guests were never seated around any table whatsoever in the world. My house is always crowded. After all, what a number of pleasant people are thrown by war's catastrophes into Columbia. I call such society glorious. It is the wind-up, the Cassandra in me says; and the old life means to die royally.

COMMON CORE L 5

Language Coach

Similes A **simile** is a figure of speech that compares two things that have something in common, using a word such as *like* or *as*. Identify the simile in lines 2–4. To whom does Chesnut compare herself? What does she feel after the fall of Atlanta?

D PRIMARY SOURCES
According to Chesnut, why did Dr. Palmer go to war? What did he not fight for?

An advocate for the rights of blacks and women, and herself a former slave, Sojourner Truth delivered this candid address to a progressive audience not long after the Thirteenth Amendment abolished slavery in the United States.

Speech to the American Equal Rights Association

May 9, 1867

My friends, I am rejoiced that you are glad, but I don't know how you will feel when I get through. I come from another field—the country of the slave. They have got their liberty—so much good luck to have slavery partly destroyed; not entirely. I want it root and branch destroyed. Then we will all be free indeed. I feel that if I have to answer for the deeds done in my body just as much as a man, I have a right to have just as much as a man. There is a great stir about colored men getting their rights, but not a word about the colored women; and if colored men get their rights, and not colored women theirs, you see the colored men will be masters over the women, and it will be just as bad as it was before. So I am for keeping the thing going while things are stirring; because if we wait till it is still, it will take a great while to get it going again. . . . I want women to have their rights. In the courts women have no right, no voice; nobody speaks for them. I wish woman to have her voice there among the pettifoggers. If it is not a fit place for women, it is unfit for men to be there. **E**

E PRIMARY SOURCES
Is Sojourner Truth rejoicing over the outcome of the war? Why or why not?

I am above eighty years old; it is about time for me to be going. I have been forty years a slave and forty years free, and would be here forty years more to have equal rights for all. I suppose I am kept here because something remains for me to do; I suppose I am yet to help to break the chain. I have done a great deal of work; as much as a man, but did not get so much pay. I used to work in the field and bind grain, keeping up with the cradler; but men doing no more, got twice as much pay; so with the German women. They work in the field and do as much work, but do not get the pay. We do as much, we eat as much, we want as much. I suppose I am about the only colored woman that goes about to speak for the rights of the colored women. I want to keep the thing stirring, now that the ice is cracked. What we want is a little money. You men know that you get as much again as women when you write, or for what you do. When we get our rights we shall not have to come to you for money, for then we shall have money enough in our own pockets; and may be you will ask us for money. But help us now until we get it. It is a good consolation to know that when we have got this battle fought we shall not be coming to you any more. You have been having our rights so long, that you think, like a slaveholder, that you own us. I know that it is hard for one who has held the reins for so long to give up; it cuts like a knife. It will feel all the better when it closes up again. I have been in Washington about three years, seeing about these colored people. Now colored men have the right to vote. There ought to be equal rights now more than ever, since colored people have got their freedom. **F**

F PRIMARY SOURCES
What is Sojourner Truth advocating, or arguing for? What are two reasons she gives to support her claim?

Comprehension

1. **Recall** How did Robert E. Lee plan to respond if the Union was dissolved?
2. **Recall** What did Sullivan Ballou think would be his fate in battle?
3. **Recall** How did Mary Chesnut spend her time during the month of September 1864?
4. **Summarize** In the primary sources you just read, Union and Confederate soldiers and civilians reveal some of the motives they had for engaging in the Civil War. Summarize these motives.

Text Analysis

5. **Analyze Author's Purpose** Think about what Ballou shares with his wife, Sarah. For what purpose—or purposes—would you say he is writing to her? How do the style and content of the letter help him achieve this purpose?
6. **Evaluate Reasoning** Think about the context in which Sojourner Truth gave her speech. How effective do you think her audience would have found her reasoning in advocating for women's rights? Explain.
7. **Analyze Author's Perspective** An author's perspective is the combination of life experiences, culture, values, and beliefs that influences his or her view on a topic. Drawing upon the information you recorded on your chart, describe each author's perspective on the Civil War.

COMMON CORE

RI 2 Provide an objective summary of the text. **RI 6** Determine an author's point of view or purpose in a text in which the rhetoric is particularly effective, analyzing how style and content contribute to the power, persuasiveness, or beauty of the text. **RI 8** Delineate and evaluate the reasoning in seminal U.S. texts, including the premises, purposes, and arguments in works of public advocacy. **W 1** Write arguments to support claims in an analysis of texts.

Read for Information: Synthesize

WRITING PROMPT

Choose one of the four writers whose documents you just read, and imagine how this person might have responded to Lincoln's Gettysburg Address. Then summarize the imagined response, and support your ideas with evidence from the text.

To answer this prompt, choose a writer whose perspective on the war you think you understand well. Then follow these steps:

1. Reread the Gettysburg Address to remind yourself of Lincoln's message.
2. Bearing in mind the personal experiences and loyalties of your chosen writer and the thoughts and feelings he or she expresses about the war, imagine how he or she might have reacted to Lincoln's speech. Summarize this imaginary response.
3. Support your notion of that person's response with evidence from your chart and from the primary source written by that individual.

Text Analysis Workshop

Realism

Most modern readers expect stories to be like real life. In the mid-19th century, however, a "realistic" story was considered radical and was even criticized. Despite this outcry, several famous American writers persevered, and in doing so, they initiated one of the most enduring movements in literary history.

COMMON CORE

Included in this workshop:
RL 2 Determine two or more themes or central ideas of a text and analyze their development over the course of the text.
RL 3 Analyze the impact of the author's choices regarding how to develop and relate elements of a story. **L 1a** Apply the understanding that usage is a matter of convention and can change over time.

The Rise of Realism

Realism in literature refers to writing that offers an accurate and detailed portrayal of actual life. It also refers to a literary movement that first developed in France in the mid-19th century and then spread to England, Russia, and the United States. Realism was born as a reaction to **romanticism,** an artistic and literary movement that glorified the individual and celebrated the emotions and imagination; it dominated literature during the early 19th century. Unlike the romantics, realists did not want to glorify anything. They simply wanted to depict reality, no matter how ordinary the characters or their circumstances. In basing their literature on careful observations of commonplace events and people, the realists believed they could shed light on greater social issues and concerns.

New York City sweatshop, circa 1912

In the United States, realism was also the product of a rapidly changing society. By the end of the Civil War in 1865, America was changing from a predominantly rural society to an urban one and was experiencing the effects of the Industrial Revolution. Many writers were inspired to depict the effects of these dramatic social changes on the average citizen. The first American writers to experiment with realism—in the 1870s and 1880s—were Mark Twain, William Dean Howells, and Henry James. In the following decades, the realist movement spawned several related movements, such as **naturalism, regionalism,** and **local color** (see pages 656–657).

Characteristics of Realism

COMPLEX CHARACTERS IN ORDINARY PLACES

In realist fiction, character exploration and development became more important than plot. Often the characters were laborers, businessmen, or housewives from the lower and middle classes. Exploring details of a personality or a relationship could reveal important complexities, contradictions, and ironies, especially those related to social or economic issues.

The realist writer might write long, involved descriptions of a character's inner thoughts, usually focused on personal concerns or the mundane events of his or her everyday life. Realist fiction would typically

- focus on **complex characters** who are ordinary people, not heroes or villains
- portray ordinary **settings,** especially those that allow for accurate depictions of society and culture
- depict true-to-life **dialogue** that captures the dialects and idioms of conversation, reflecting the usage conventions of a particular time, place, and social group

DETACHED NARRATION

Realist writers adopted the scientific method of detached observation. This allows the narrator of a story to sound unbiased and distant, as if simply recording the complete facts of the story. The reader is then allowed to draw his or her own conclusions. Notice the detached perspective of the narrator and the detailed **description** in this passage.

> A man stood upon a railroad bridge in northern Alabama, looking down into the swift water twenty feet below. The man's hands were behind his back, the wrists bound with a cord. A rope closely encircled his neck.
>
> **—Ambrose Bierce, "An Occurrence at Owl Creek Bridge"**

SOCIAL THEMES

The literature of realism sought to explore the key issues of the time: What are the implications of modern technology? What are the effects of urbanization? Realist **themes** are typically concerned with class conflicts, urbanization, marriage, and family life. In his novel *The Rise of Silas Lapham,* author William Dean Howells tells the story of a family coming to terms with new wealth, acquisition, and corruption. In the following passage, Howells relates the family's initial responses to their newfound wealth.

> Their first years there were given to careful getting on Lapham's part, and careful saving on his wife's. Suddenly the money began to come so abundantly that she need not save; and then they did not know what to do with it. A certain amount could be spent on horses, and Lapham spent it; his wife spent on rich and rather ugly clothes and a luxury of household appointments. Lapham had not yet reached the picture-buying stage of the rich man's development, but they decorated their house with the costliest and most abominable frescoes. . . .
>
> **—William Dean Howells, *The Rise of Silas Lapham***

ROMANTICISM VS. REALISM

To understand the different perspectives and subject matter of romanticism and realism, consider these two prose examples:

Romanticism
In that moment of the afternoon, the sun fell upon the snow drifts in an ethereal light, and all the heavens seemed to shine down upon the frozen fields, as if promising, one day, the ascent of spring.

Realism
At 4:00 each afternoon, the sunlight cast long shadows along the frozen landscape. The whistle of the clothing factory would blow, and the workers would stream out from the opened doors and squint into the last light of the day.

Close Read

What effect does the detached perspective in Bierce's passage have on the reader? From these few lines, what is your reaction to this character?

Close Read

What do you think might happen to the Laphams, given what you know about the typical **themes** in realism?

American Masterpiece

from The Red Badge of Courage

Novel by Stephen Crane

Stephen Crane
1871–1900

COMMON CORE

RL 2 Determine two or more themes or central ideas of a text. **SL 1a** Refer to evidence from texts to stimulate a thoughtful, well-reasoned exchange of ideas. **SL 4** Present information, findings, and supporting evidence.

BACKGROUND Imagination, not experience, explains Stephen Crane's achievements in realism. His first novel, *Maggie: A Girl of the Streets*, exposed the brutal realities of New York slum life, but Crane wrote a first draft of the narrative while still in college, before moving to the slums himself in search of work as a journalist. Crane's talent for realism also explains *The Red Badge of Courage*, a Civil War novel acclaimed by soldiers and veterans for presenting combat realistically, despite the fact that the author had not served as a soldier or observed the battlefield firsthand. Crane's masterpiece focuses on a single, unnamed Civil War battle. The protagonist Henry Fleming, a young private in the Union army, is anything but heroic. Through Henry's eyes, readers experience the long and tedious waiting for battle, the utter chaos once the fighting begins, and the ironic twists of fate that determine who will survive and who will perish. Much of the action takes place in Henry's mind as he struggles to adapt to his environment, tries to comprehend his new experiences, and worries about whether he will prove courageous or cowardly.

TEXT ANALYSIS "There was no real literature of our Civil War," Ernest Hemingway once observed, "until Stephen Crane wrote *The Red Badge of Courage*." Crane's great novel is considered a pioneering work of **realism**, breaking with tradition in a number of ways. First, it focuses not on kings or generals but on a lowly private caught up in the action. Second, it ignores the great sweep of history and deals instead with one character's impressions. Finally, the novel is almost completely devoid of heroics. "The idea of falling like heroes on ceremonial battlefields," remarked novelist and critic Ford Madox Ford, "was gone forever."

DISCUSS After you read the excerpt, review the Text Analysis Workshop on Realism (pages 598–599). Then, with a small group of your peers, make a list of the characteristics of realism you see in the Crane excerpt. For each item on your list, include at least one quotation from the excerpt that illustrates the realist trait. When your group has finished, share your observations with the class as a whole. **Note:** Consider saving your notes from this activity so that you can refer to them when you read Stephen Crane's short story "The Open Boat" (page 736), a masterpiece of realist fiction.

"Here they come! Here they come!" Gun locks clicked.

Across the smoke-infested fields came a brown swarm of running men who were giving shrill yells. They came on, stooping and swinging their rifles at all angles. A flag, tilted forward, sped near the front.

As he caught sight of them the youth was momentarily startled by a thought that perhaps his gun was not loaded. He stood trying to rally his faltering intellect so that he might recollect the moment when he had loaded, but he could not.

A hatless general pulled his dripping horse to a stand near the colonel of the 304th. He shook his fist in the other's face. "You've got to hold 'em back!" he shouted, savagely; "you've got to hold 'em back!"

In his agitation the colonel began to stammer. "A-all r-right, General, all right, by Gawd! We-we'll do our—we-we'll d-d-do—do our best, General." The general made a passionate gesture and galloped away. The colonel, perchance to relieve his feelings, began to scold like a wet parrot. The youth, turning swiftly to make sure that the rear was unmolested, saw the commander regarding his men in a highly resentful manner, as if he regretted above everything his association with them.

The man at the youth's elbow was mumbling, as if to himself: "Oh, we're in for it now! oh, we're in for it now!"

The captain of the company had been pacing excitedly to and fro in the rear. He coaxed in schoolmistress fashion, as to a congregation of boys with primers. His talk was an endless repetition. "Reserve your fire, boys—don't shoot till I tell you—save your fire—wait till they get close up—don't be damned fools—"

Perspiration streamed down the youth's face, which was soiled like that of a weeping urchin. He frequently, with a nervous movement, wiped his eyes with his coat sleeve. His mouth was still a little way open.

He got the one glance at the foe-swarming field in front of him, and instantly ceased to debate the question of his piece being loaded. Before he was ready to begin—before he had announced to himself that he was about to fight—he threw the obedient, well-balanced rifle into position and fired a first wild shot. Directly he was working at his weapon like an automatic affair.

He suddenly lost concern for himself, and forgot to look at a menacing fate. He became not a man, but a member. He felt that something of which he was a part—a regiment, an army, a cause, or a country—was in a crisis. He was welded into a common personality which was dominated by a single desire. For some moments he could not flee, no more than a little finger can commit a revolution from a hand.

THEME

The narrative structure of Crane's novel reflects the themes of conflict, fear, and courage often found in stories of war. Recent films about World War II such as *Letters from Iwo Jima* and *Flags of Our Fathers* also develop a strong narrative to relate the horror and courage that shaped the war in the Pacific.

COMMON CORE

RL 2 Provide an objective summary of the text. **RL 3** Analyze the impact of the author's choices regarding how to develop and relate the elements of a story. **RL 4** Analyze the impact of specific word choices on meaning and tone, including words with multiple meanings. **RL 5** Analyze how an author's choices concerning how to structure specific parts of a text contribute to its overall structure and meaning as well as its aesthetic impact.

An Occurrence at Owl Creek Bridge

Short Story by Ambrose Bierce

VIDEO TRAILER THINK central KEYWORD: HML11-602A

Meet the Author

Ambrose Bierce 1842–c. 1914

As a Civil War soldier, Ambrose Bierce was an eyewitness to the harsh realities of war. The brutal contrast between soldiers' dreams of glory and the senselessness of warfare became a recurring theme in Bierce's postwar short stories, including his suspenseful tale "An Occurrence at Owl Creek Bridge."

In the Line of Fire Born into a poor, intensely religious family, Bierce spent his early years on an Indiana farm. At age 15, he left home for a job at a newspaper, where he set type. Three years later, the Civil War broke out, and the idealistic Bierce immediately volunteered for the Union army. Fighting in some of the war's bloodiest battles, Bierce watched many of his comrades die and nearly died himself from a head wound.

When the war was over, Bierce moved to San Francisco, which was then the literary center of the West. Determined to become a writer, Bierce took a job as a night watchman, which allowed him ample time for reading and for polishing his writing skills. He started writing a regular newspaper column and became famous for exposing bigotry, hypocrisy, and corruption with razor-sharp satire. His cutting wit earned him the title "the Wickedest Man in San Francisco." Such a reputation delighted Bierce, who kept on his desk a human skull that he claimed belonged to one of his critics.

A Morbid Imagination Bierce began publishing short stories in the 1870s, when realism was becoming the dominant literary style in American fiction. Although Bierce's true-to-life war stories inspired realist writers like Stephen Crane, his fiction often included surreal or ghostly events. Like Edgar Allan Poe, to whom he was often compared, Bierce was fascinated with strange and horrible deaths, and he described them with his characteristic dark humor and a sense of irony. Bierce also went beyond realism in his experiments with narration, pioneering the use of multiple points of view in a single story.

Vanished At 71, Bierce revisited Civil War battle sites where he had fought and then went to Mexico to report on the Mexican Revolution as an observer with Pancho Villa's rebel army. He never returned to the United States, and no trace of him was found. Before he left, he wrote to a niece, "If you hear of my being stood up against a Mexican stone wall and shot to rags, please know that I think that a pretty good way to depart this life. It beats old age, disease or falling down the cellar stairs."

Author Online THINK central
Go to thinkcentral.com. KEYWORD: HML11-602B

DID YOU KNOW?

Ambrose Bierce . . .

- was one of 13 children, whose names all began with the letter *A*.
- was awarded 15 commendations for bravery under fire.
- was nicknamed Bitter Bierce for his cynical humor and cruel wit.
- also wrote under the names Mrs. J. Milton Bowers and Dod Grile.

TEXT ANALYSIS: POINT OF VIEW

Because the narrator is the voice that tells a story, the reader knows only what the narrator is able to tell. Therefore, the narrator's point of view greatly affects the story's events as well as the internal and external development of characters. Types of **point of view** include

- **first person:** told by a character in the work whose knowledge is limited to his or her own experiences
- **third-person omniscient:** told by a voice outside the story who reveals the thoughts and feelings of all the characters
- **third-person limited:** told by a voice outside the story who focuses on one character's thoughts and feelings

As you read, look for clues in the narration that help identify the point of view in Ambrose Bierce's story, and consider the impact of that choice.

READING SKILL: ANALYZE STRUCTURE

To analyze the **structure** of a literary work, you examine the relationship between its parts and its content. This story is divided into three numbered sections, each of which occurs at a different point in time. After you read each section, summarize the events that occur and note when they take place. Use a chart like the one shown to record your notes.

	What Happens	When
Section 1		

VOCABULARY IN CONTEXT

Bierce used the words in Column A in his tale of a man facing death. Test your knowledge by matching each vocabulary word with its synonym in Column B.

Column A	Column B
1. interminable	a. swaying
2. poignant	b. painful
3. ineffable	c. predicting
4. summarily	d. unending
5. oscillation	e. indescribable
6. ludicrous	f. immediately
7. presaging	g. laughable

Complete the activities in your **Reader/Writer Notebook**.

Can we escape the INEVITABLE?

"An Occurrence at Owl Creek Bridge" opens with an execution about to take place. Standing on an isolated, heavily guarded bridge, with a noose around his neck, the protagonist is doomed. There is no escape. Or is there?

DISCUSS In a small group, list ways people respond when faced with a bad situation they cannot change. Classify each response as useful or destructive. When does it make sense to look for a way out, and when is it time to accept the inevitable?

An Occurrence at Owl Creek Bridge

Ambrose Bierce

I

A man stood upon a railroad bridge in northern Alabama, looking down into the swift water twenty feet below. The man's hands were behind his back, the wrists bound with a cord. A rope closely encircled his neck. It was attached to a stout cross-timber above his head and the slack fell to the level of his knees. Some loose boards laid upon the sleepers[1] supporting the metals of the railway supplied a footing for him and his executioners—two private soldiers of the Federal army, directed by a sergeant who in civil life may have been a deputy sheriff. At a short remove upon the same temporary platform was an officer in the uniform of his rank, armed. He was a captain. A sentinel at each end of the bridge stood with his rifle in the position known as "support," that is to say, vertical in front of the left shoulder, the hammer resting on the forearm thrown straight across the chest—a formal and unnatural position, enforcing an erect carriage of the body. It did not appear to be the duty of these two men to know what was occurring at the center of the bridge; they merely blockaded the two ends of the foot planking that traversed it. (A)

Beyond one of the sentinels nobody was in sight; the railroad ran straight away into a forest for a hundred yards, then, curving, was lost to view. Doubtless there was an outpost farther along. The other bank of the stream was open ground—a gentle acclivity[2] topped with a stockade of vertical tree trunks, loopholed for rifles, with a single embrasure[3] through which protruded the muzzle of a brass cannon commanding the bridge. Midway of the slope between bridge and fort were the spectators—a single company of infantry in line, at "parade rest," the butts of the rifles on the ground, the barrels inclining slightly backward against the right

Analyze Visuals ▶
Based on this image, what do you predict will happen in the story?

(A) POINT OF VIEW
Identify the point of view used in lines 1–15. What does the **tone** of the description tell you about the narrator's perspective?

1. **sleepers:** railroad ties.
2. **acclivity:** an upward slope.
3. **embrasure:** a flared opening in a wall for a gun, with sides angled so that the inside opening is larger than that on the outside.

shoulder, the hands crossed upon the stock.[4] A lieutenant stood at the right of the line, the point of his sword upon the ground, his left hand resting upon his right. Excepting the group of four at the center of the bridge, not a man moved. The company faced the bridge, staring stonily, motionless. The sentinels, facing the banks of the stream, might have been statues to adorn the bridge. The captain stood with folded arms, silent, observing the work of his subordinates, but making no sign. Death is a dignitary who when he comes announced is to be received with formal manifestations of respect, even by those most familiar with him. In the code of military etiquette silence and fixity are forms of deference.

The man who was engaged in being hanged was apparently about thirty-five years of age. He was a civilian, if one might judge from his habit, which was that of a planter. His features were good—a straight nose, firm mouth, broad forehead, from which his long, dark hair was combed straight back, falling behind his ears to the collar of his well-fitting frock-coat. He wore a mustache and pointed beard, but no whiskers; his eyes were large and dark gray, and had a kindly expression which one would hardly have expected in one whose neck was in the hemp. Evidently this was no vulgar assassin. The liberal military code makes provision for hanging many kinds of persons, and gentlemen are not excluded.

The preparations being complete, the two private soldiers stepped aside and each drew away the plank upon which he had been standing. The sergeant turned to the captain, saluted and placed himself immediately behind that officer, who in

Language Coach

Topically Related Words
Read lines 30–32. Look up *dignitary, etiquette,* and *deference* in a dictionary. How is each word related to the ideas of formality or respect?

4. **stock:** the wooden part of the rifle that serves as a handle.

turn moved apart one pace. These movements left the condemned man and the sergeant standing on the two ends of the same plank, which spanned three of the cross-ties of the bridge. The end upon which the civilian stood almost, but not quite, reached a fourth. This plank had been held in place by the weight of the captain; it was now held by that of the sergeant. At a signal from the former the latter would step aside, the plank would tilt and the condemned man go down between two ties. The arrangement commended itself to his judgment as simple and effective. His face had not been covered nor his eyes bandaged. He looked a moment at his "unsteadfast footing," then let his gaze wander to the swirling water of the stream racing madly beneath his feet. A piece of dancing driftwood caught his attention and his eyes followed it down the current. How slowly it appeared to move! What a sluggish stream! **B**

B POINT OF VIEW
Note that the third-person point of view narrows from omniscient to limited. What **sensory details** alert you to this change in perspective?

He closed his eyes in order to fix his last thoughts upon his wife and children. The water, touched to gold by the early sun, the brooding mists under the banks at some distance down the stream, the fort, the soldiers, the piece of drift—all had distracted him. And now he became conscious of a new disturbance. Striking through the thought of his dear ones was a sound which he could neither ignore nor understand, a sharp, distinct, metallic percussion like the stroke of a blacksmith's hammer upon the anvil; it had the same ringing quality. He wondered what it was, and whether immeasurably distant or near by—it seemed both. Its recurrence was regular, but as slow as the tolling of a death knell.[5] He awaited each stroke with impatience and—he knew not why—apprehension. The intervals of silence grew progressively longer; the delays became maddening. With their greater infrequency the sounds increased in strength and sharpness. They hurt his ear like the thrust of a knife; he feared he would shriek. What he heard was the ticking of his watch.

He unclosed his eyes and saw again the water below him. "If I could free my hands," he thought, "I might throw off the noose and spring into the stream. By diving I could evade the bullets and, swimming vigorously, reach the bank, take to the woods and get away home. My home, thank God, is as yet outside their lines; my wife and little ones are still beyond the invader's farthest advance."

As these thoughts, which have here to be set down in words, were flashed into the doomed man's brain rather than evolved from it the captain nodded to the sergeant. The sergeant stepped aside. **C**

C ANALYZE STRUCTURE
If the story were told in chronological order, what would you expect to happen next?

II

Peyton Farquhar was a well-to-do planter, of an old and highly respected Alabama family. Being a slave owner and like other slave owners a politician he was naturally an original secessionist and ardently devoted to the Southern cause. Circumstances of an imperious nature, which it is unnecessary to relate here, had prevented him from taking service with the gallant army that had fought the disastrous campaigns ending with the fall of Corinth,[6] and he chafed under the

5. **the tolling of a death knell:** the slow, steady ringing of a bell at a funeral or to indicate death.
6. **Corinth:** a town in Mississippi that was the site of a Civil War battle in 1862.

inglorious restraint, longing for the release of his energies, the larger life of the soldier, the opportunity for distinction. That opportunity, he felt, would come, as it comes to all in war time. Meanwhile he did what he could. No service was too humble for him to perform in aid of the South, no adventure too perilous for him to undertake if consistent with the character of a civilian who was at heart a soldier, and who in good faith and without too much qualification assented to at least a part of the frankly villainous dictum that all is fair in love and war.

One evening while Farquhar and his wife were sitting on a rustic bench near the entrance to his grounds, a gray-clad soldier rode up to the gate and asked for a drink of water. Mrs. Farquhar was only too happy to serve him with her own white hands. While she was fetching the water her husband approached the dusty horseman and inquired eagerly for news from the front.

"The Yanks are repairing the railroads," said the man, "and are getting ready for another advance. They have reached the Owl Creek bridge, put it in order and built a stockade on the north bank. The commandant has issued an order, which is posted everywhere, declaring that any civilian caught interfering with the railroad, its bridges, tunnels or trains will be **summarily** hanged. I saw the order." **D**

"How far is it to the Owl Creek bridge?" Farquhar asked.

"About thirty miles."

"Is there no force on this side the creek?"

"Only a picket post[7] half a mile out, on the railroad, and a single sentinel at this end of the bridge."

"Suppose a man—a civilian and student of hanging—should elude the picket post and perhaps get the better of the sentinel," said Farquhar, smiling, "what could he accomplish?"

The soldier reflected. "I was there a month ago," he replied. "I observed that the flood of last winter had lodged a great quantity of driftwood against the wooden pier at this end of the bridge. It is now dry and would burn like tow."[8]

The lady had now brought the water, which the soldier drank. He thanked her ceremoniously, bowed to her husband and rode away. An hour later, after nightfall, he repassed the plantation, going northward in the direction from which he had come. He was a Federal scout. **E**

summarily (sə-mĕr'ə-lē) *adv.* quickly and without ceremony

D ANALYZE STRUCTURE
Compare lines 97–101 with the description in lines 1–21. What details connect these two sections of the story?

E POINT OF VIEW
Reread lines 113–116. Explain what the reader knows that Peyton Farquhar does not. Which type of third-person point of view allows the author to give the reader details that are hidden from the characters?

III

As Peyton Farquhar fell straight downward through the bridge he lost consciousness and was as one already dead. From this state he was awakened—ages later, it seemed to him—by the pain of a sharp pressure upon his throat, followed by a sense of suffocation. Keen, **poignant** agonies seemed to shoot from his neck downward through every fiber of his body and limbs. These pains appeared to flash along well-defined lines of ramification[9] and to beat with an inconceivably rapid periodicity. They seemed like streams of pulsating fire heating

poignant (poin'yənt) *adj.* physically or mentally painful

7. **picket post:** the camp of soldiers who are assigned to guard against a surprise attack.
8. **tow** (tō): coarse, dry fiber.
9. **flash . . . ramification:** spread out rapidly along branches from a central point.

him to an intolerable temperature. As to his head, he was conscious of nothing but a feeling of fullness—of congestion. These sensations were unaccompanied by thought. The intellectual part of his nature was already effaced; he had power only to feel, and feeling was torment. He was conscious of motion. Encompassed in a luminous cloud, of which he was now merely the fiery heart, without material substance, he swung through unthinkable arcs of **oscillation,** like a vast pendulum. Then all at once, with terrible suddenness, the light about him shot upward with the noise of a loud plash; a frightful roaring was in his ears, and all was cold and dark. The power of thought was restored; he knew that the rope had broken and he had fallen into the stream. There was no additional strangulation; the noose about his neck was already suffocating him and kept the water from his lungs. To die of hanging at the bottom of a river!—the idea seemed to him **ludicrous.** He opened his eyes in the darkness and saw above him a gleam

oscillation (ŏs′ə-lā′shən) *n.* the action of swinging back and forth

ludicrous (lo͞o′dĭ-krəs) *adj.* laughably absurd; ridiculous

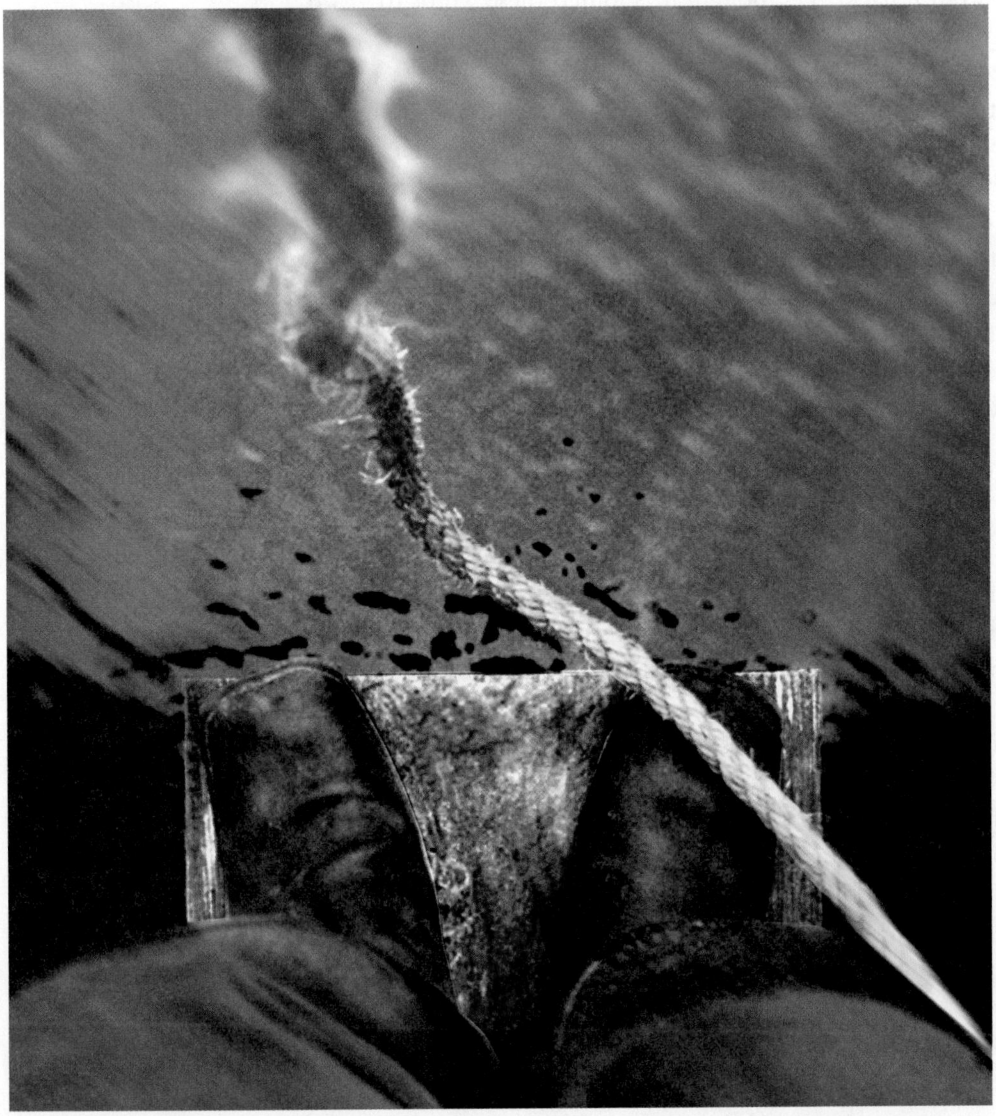

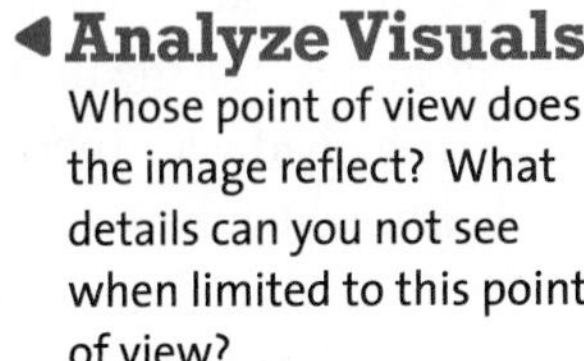

Analyze Visuals
Whose point of view does the image reflect? What details can you not see when limited to this point of view?

of light, but how distant, how inaccessible! He was still sinking, for the light became fainter and fainter until it was a mere glimmer. Then it began to grow and brighten, and he knew that he was rising toward the surface—knew it with reluctance, for he was now very comfortable. "To be hanged and drowned," he thought, "that is not so bad; but I do not wish to be shot. No; I will not be shot; that is not fair."

He was not conscious of an effort, but a sharp pain in his wrist apprised him that he was trying to free his hands. He gave the struggle his attention, as an idler might observe the feat of a juggler, without interest in the outcome. What splendid effort!—what magnificent, what superhuman strength! Ah, that was a fine endeavor! Bravo! The cord fell away; his arms parted and floated upward, the hands dimly seen on each side in the growing light. He watched them with a new interest as first one and then the other pounced upon the noose at his neck. They tore it away and thrust it fiercely aside, its undulations resembling those of a water-snake. "Put it back, put it back!" He thought he shouted these words to his hands, for the undoing of the noose had been succeeded by the direst pang that he had yet experienced. His neck ached horribly; his brain was on fire; his heart, which had been fluttering faintly, gave a great leap, trying to force itself out at his mouth. His whole body was racked and wrenched with an insupportable anguish![10] But his disobedient hands gave no heed to the command. They beat the water vigorously with quick, downward strokes, forcing him to the surface. He felt his head emerge; his eyes were blinded by the sunlight; his chest expanded convulsively, and with a supreme and crowning agony his lungs engulfed a great draught of air, which instantly he expelled in a shriek! F

He was now in full possession of his physical senses. They were, indeed, preternaturally keen and alert. Something in the awful disturbance of his organic system had so exalted and refined them that they made record of things never before perceived. He felt the ripples upon his face and heard their separate sounds as they struck. He looked at the forest on the bank of the stream, saw the individual trees, the leaves and the veining of each leaf—saw the very insects upon them: the locusts, the brilliant-bodied flies, the gray spiders stretching their webs from twig to twig. He noted the prismatic colors in all the dewdrops upon a million blades of grass. The humming of the gnats that danced above the eddies of the stream, the beating of the dragon-flies' wings, the strokes of the water-spiders' legs, like oars which had lifted their boat—all these made audible music. A fish slid along beneath his eyes and he heard the rush of its body parting the water.

He had come to the surface facing down the stream; in a moment the visible world seemed to wheel slowly round, himself the pivotal point, and he saw the bridge, the fort, the soldiers upon the bridge, the captain, the sergeant, the two privates, his executioners. They were in silhouette against the blue sky. They shouted and gesticulated, pointing at him. The captain had drawn his pistol, but did not fire; the others were unarmed. Their movements were grotesque and horrible, their forms gigantic.

COMMON CORE RL 3

F CHARACTERIZATION
Characterization refers to the techniques a writer uses to develop characters. With third-person limited point of view, Bierce can observe his main character from a distance, as he does in the first two parts of this story, conveying character externally through details of action and dialogue. In Part III, however, the point of view shifts to record the sensations and emotions of Peyton Farquhar's inner life. Reread lines 143–160. What details does the author use to capture the panic of a man in danger of drowning? How do these details contribute to character development? Cite evidence from the paragraph to support your response.

---

10. **racked . . . anguish:** stretched and twisted with unendurable physical pain.

Suddenly he heard a sharp report and something struck the water smartly within a few inches of his head, spattering his face with spray. He heard a second report, and saw one of the sentinels with his rifle at his shoulder, a light cloud of blue smoke rising from the muzzle. The man in the water saw the eye of the man on the bridge gazing into his own through the sights of the rifle. He observed that it was a gray eye and remembered having read that gray eyes were keenest, and that all famous marksmen had them. Nevertheless, this one had missed.

A counter-swirl had caught Farquhar and turned him half round; he was again looking into the forest on the bank opposite the fort. The sound of a clear, high voice in a monotonous singsong now rang out behind him and came across the water with a distinctness that pierced and subdued all other sounds, even the beating of the ripples in his ears. Although no soldier, he had frequented camps enough to know the dread significance of that deliberate, drawling, aspirated chant; the lieutenant on shore was taking a part in the morning's work. How coldly and pitilessly—with what an even, calm intonation, **presaging,** and enforcing tranquillity in the men—with what accurately measured intervals fell those cruel words:

"Attention, company! . . . Shoulder arms! . . . Ready! . . . Aim! . . . Fire!"

COMMON CORE RL 4

Language Coach

Multiple-Meaning Words
Report (line 180) is a **multiple-meaning word,** a word with more than one meaning. In this context, *report* means "loud, explosive noise." With a partner, identify the words in the paragraph that point to the appropriate meaning of this word.

presaging (prĕs′ĭj-ĭng) *adj.* predicting **presage** *v.*

Farquhar dived—dived as deeply as he could. The water roared in his ears like the voice of Niagara, yet he heard the dulled thunder of the volley and, rising again toward the surface, met shining bits of metal, singularly flattened, oscillating slowly downward. Some of them touched him on the face and hands, then fell away, continuing their descent. One lodged between his collar and neck; it was uncomfortably warm and he snatched it out.

As he rose to the surface, gasping for breath, he saw that he had been a long time under water; he was perceptibly farther down stream—nearer to safety. The soldiers had almost finished reloading; the metal ramrods flashed all at once in the sunshine as they were drawn from the barrels, turned in the air, and thrust into their sockets. The two sentinels fired again, independently and ineffectually.

The hunted man saw all this over his shoulder; he was now swimming vigorously with the current. His brain was as energetic as his arms and legs; he thought with the rapidity of lightning.

"The officer," he reasoned, "will not make that martinet's[11] error a second time. It is as easy to dodge a volley as a single shot. He has probably already given the command to fire at will. God help me, I cannot dodge them all!"

An appalling plash within two yards of him was followed by a loud, rushing sound, *diminuendo*,[12] which seemed to travel back through the air to the fort and died in an explosion which stirred the very river to its deeps! A rising sheet of water curved over him, fell down upon him, blinded him, strangled him! The cannon had taken a hand in the game. As he shook his head free from the commotion of the smitten water he heard the deflected shot humming through the air ahead, and in an instant it was cracking and smashing the branches in the forest beyond.

"They will not do that again," he thought; "the next time they will use a charge of grape.[13] I must keep my eye upon the gun; the smoke will apprise me—the report arrives too late; it lags behind the missile. That is a good gun."

Suddenly he felt himself whirled round and round—spinning like a top. The water, the banks, the forests, the now distant bridge, fort and men—all were commingled and blurred. Objects were represented by their colors only; circular horizontal streaks of color—that was all he saw. He had been caught in a vortex and was being whirled on with a velocity of advance and gyration that made him giddy and sick. In a few moments he was flung upon the gravel at the foot of the left bank of the stream—the southern bank—and behind a projecting point which concealed him from his enemies. The sudden arrest of his motion, the abrasion of one of his hands on the gravel, restored him, and he wept with delight. He dug his fingers into the sand, threw it over himself in handfuls and audibly blessed it. It looked like diamonds, rubies, emeralds; he could think of nothing beautiful which it did not resemble. The trees upon the bank were giant garden plants; he

Language Coach

Formal Language Read lines 210–211. Note the words "with the rapidity of lightning." Now, compare those words with these: "with lightning-fast speed." Which phrase do you find more formal? Consider both word order and word choice.

ANALYZE STRUCTURE

The structure of Bierce's story, in which events are not told in chronological order, is similar to the narrative technique employed by Charles Frazier in his 1997 Civil War novel, *Cold Mountain*, which was made into a film in 2003. The novel alternates between the stories of the two main characters, lovers who are separated by war. What are other examples of twentieth-century novels, plays, or films that use this non-sequential method of storytelling?

11. **martinet's:** alluding to a strict disciplinarian or person who demands that regulations be followed exactly.
12. ***diminuendo*** (dĭ-mĭn'yo͞o-ĕn'dō) *Italian*: gradually decreasing in loudness.
13. **grape:** short for grapeshot, a cluster of several small iron balls fired in one shot from a cannon.

noted a definite order in their arrangement, inhaled the fragrance of their blooms. A strange, roseate light shone through the spaces among their trunks and the wind made in their branches the music of æolian harps.[14] He had no wish to perfect his escape—was content to remain in that enchanting spot until retaken.

A whiz and rattle of grapeshot among the branches high above his head roused him from his dream. The baffled cannoneer had fired him a random farewell. He sprang to his feet, rushed up the sloping bank, and plunged into the forest.

All that day he traveled, laying his course by the rounding sun. The forest seemed **interminable;** nowhere did he discover a break in it, not even a woodman's road. He had not known that he lived in so wild a region. There was something uncanny in the revelation.

▲ Analyze Visuals
Compare this image with the description given in lines 237–240. What associations does each scene call to mind?

interminable
(ĭn-tûr'mə-nə-bəl)
adj. endless

14. **music of æolian** (ē-ō'lē-ən) **harps:** heavenly, or unearthly, music.

By night fall he was fatigued, footsore, famishing. The thought of his wife and children urged him on. At last he found a road which led him in what he knew to be the right direction. It was as wide and straight as a city street, yet it seemed untraveled. No fields bordered it, no dwelling anywhere. Not so much as the barking of a dog suggested human habitation. The black bodies of the trees formed a straight wall on both sides, terminating on the horizon in a point, like a diagram in a lesson in perspective. Overhead, as he looked up through this rift in the wood, shone great golden stars looking unfamiliar and grouped in strange constellations. He was sure they were arranged in some order which had a secret and malign significance. The wood on either side was full of singular noises, among which—once, twice, and again, he distinctly heard whispers in an unknown tongue.

His neck was in pain and lifting his hand to it he found it horribly swollen. He knew that it had a circle of black where the rope had bruised it. His eyes felt congested; he could no longer close them. His tongue was swollen with thirst; he relieved its fever by thrusting it forward from between his teeth into the cold air. How softly the turf had carpeted the untraveled avenue—he could no longer feel the roadway beneath his feet!

Doubtless, despite his suffering, he had fallen asleep while walking, for now he sees another scene—perhaps he has merely recovered from a delirium. He stands at the gate of his own home. All is as he left it, and all bright and beautiful in the morning sunshine. He must have traveled the entire night. As he pushes open the gate and passes up the wide white walk, he sees a flutter of female garments; his wife, looking fresh and cool and sweet, steps down from the veranda to meet him. At the bottom of the steps she stands waiting, with a smile of **ineffable** joy, an attitude of matchless grace and dignity. Ah, how beautiful she is! He springs forward with extended arms. As he is about to clasp her he feels a stunning blow upon the back of the neck; a blinding white light blazes all about him with a sound like the shock of a cannon—then all is darkness and silence! G

Peyton Farquhar was dead; his body, with a broken neck, swung gently from side to side beneath the timbers of the Owl Creek bridge. H

ineffable (ĭn-ĕf′ə-bəl) *adj.* beyond description; inexpressible

G PRIMARY SOURCE DOCUMENTS
Reread lines 270–279, and think about the main idea that is revealed by the changing point of view at the end. How do Peyton Farquhar's thoughts relate to those expressed in the **primary source** "Letter to Sarah Ballou," which you read earlier in this unit (page 594)? Remember that Sullivan Ballou was killed in battle about a week after writing the letter to his wife.

H ANALYZE STRUCTURE
"An Occurrence at Owl Creek Bridge" is a classic example of a story whose plot is structured to deliver a surprise ending. Such endings have the power to overturn all previous notions about the story. What surprise endings or intriguing plot twists can you cite from other works?

Comprehension

1. **Summarize** What is Peyton Farquhar's background?
2. **Recall** How does Farquhar die?
3. **Clarify** Why did the soldier who visited Farquhar give him such detailed information about the bridge?

Text Analysis

4. **Make Inferences** What is the Union soldiers' reason for hanging Farquhar? Cite evidence to support your inference.
5. **Analyze Structure** Review the chart you created as you read. How would the story be different if it were told in chronological order?
6. **Examine Point of View** Citing at least two examples from the story, explain how the shifts in point of view affect the level of **suspense.** What would be different about the story if it were told entirely from the **third-person omniscient** point of view?
7. **Make Inferences about Character Development** Bierce uses sensory details to suggest Farquhar's state of mind. In each of the following episodes, what sensory details suggest that Farquhar's perceptions may be unreliable?
   - on the bridge (lines 60–70)
   - in the river (lines 161–172)
   - reaching land (lines 231–240)
   - in the woods (lines 255–260)
8. **Interpret Themes** Reread lines 80–91. Based on Farquhar's dreams of glory and his ultimate fate, what point might Bierce be making about
   - heroism
   - the realities of war
   - the dangers of fantasy
9. **Evaluate Narrative Devices** In your opinion, did Bierce intend Farquhar's **escape** to seem believable? Cite textual evidence to support your view.

Text Criticism

10. **Author's Style** Compare Bierce's use of realistic and fantastic elements in this story. Which label—realistic or fantastic—best describes Bierce's style? Support your answer with details.

Can we escape the INEVITABLE?

As Peyton Farquhar awaited his fate on the bridge, his mind began to wander toward the possibility of escape. Was he giving rational consideration to escape, or was his mind merely "killing time"? Do you think his thoughts were useful or destructive? Why?

COMMON CORE

RL 2 Determine two or more themes or central ideas of a text and analyze their development over the course of the text. **RL 3** Analyze the impact of the author's choices regarding how to develop and relate the elements of a story. **RL 5** Analyze how an author's choices concerning how to structure specific parts of a text contribute to its overall structure and meaning as well as its aesthetic impact.

Vocabulary in Context

▲ VOCABULARY PRACTICE

Decide whether these statements using the vocabulary words are true or false.

1. A **ludicrous** TV show would probably make you cry.
2. A job that is performed **summarily** tends to take a long time.
3. An **ineffable** pleasure is likely to leave you speechless with joy.
4. Climbing a very steep ladder is an example of **oscillation.**
5. You would typically describe a standup comic's performance as **poignant.**
6. Messages **presaging** happiness tend to make a fortuneteller popular.
7. If a school day seems **interminable,** it feels like it will never be over.

WORD LIST
ineffable
interminable
ludicrous
oscillation
poignant
presaging
summarily

ACADEMIC VOCABULARY IN WRITING

• conflict • create • element • emphasis • perspective

An easily overlooked **element** of this story is the fact that Peyton Farquhar, a civilian, was "set up" by a Federal scout posing as a Confederate soldier. Write a paragraph from the **perspective** of the scout, justifying the deceit that resulted in Farquhar's death. Use at least one Academic Vocabulary word in your response.

VOCABULARY STRATEGY: THE LATIN ROOT *lud*

The vocabulary word *ludicrous* contains the root *lud,* meaning "play." This root, which may also be spelled *lus,* has its origin in Latin, the language of ancient Rome. *Lud* or *lus* is found in a number of English words from a variety of content areas. To understand words with *lud* or *lus,* use your knowledge of the root meaning and the meanings of affixes, as well as context clues.

COMMON CORE

L 4b Identify and correctly use patterns of word changes that indicate different meanings or parts of speech. **L 6** Acquire and use accurately general academic words.

PRACTICE Choose the word from the word web that best completes each sentence. Consider what you know about the Latin root and the context of each sentence. If necessary, consult a dictionary.

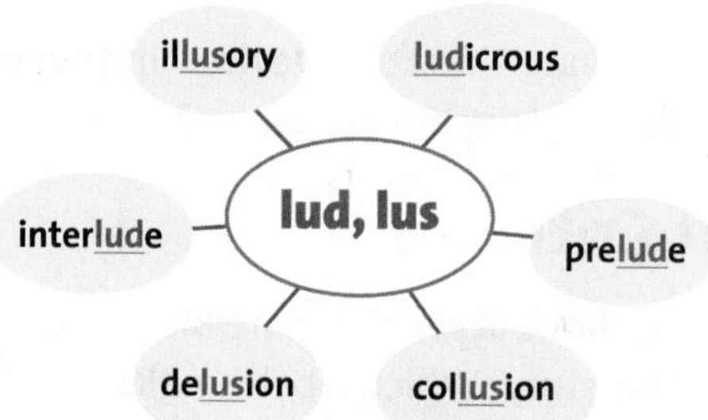

1. In the _____ between the scenes, a violinist performed for the audience.
2. He suffers from the _____ that he is a good golfer.
3. Though she dresses expensively, her wealth is more _____ than real.
4. As a ______ to the main act, a young, inexperienced band played.
5. As a result of the two guards' _____, a prisoner escaped.

Voices of the Civil War

Near the outbreak of the Civil War, writer Ralph Waldo Emerson remarked, "All arts disappear in the one art of war." In other words, the necessities of warfare—military, political, economic, and social—act somehow to discourage or diminish the creation of what might be termed "serious literature." Nevertheless, fine nonfiction writing about pressing national issues emerged in the years prior to, during, and immediately following the Civil War.

The selections beginning on page 558 include many forms of nonfiction: autobiographies, speeches, documents, letters, and diaries. Perhaps these forms served as better vehicles than poems or short stories might have for the people of the day who wanted to explore their personal responses to the war. In any case, the nonfiction here is valuable for several reasons:

- It gives readers a glimpse into the events and culture of the writers' troubled time.
- It provides each writer's personal response to what was happening all around.
- It presents a good overview of the many different factions that made up the country at the time.

Writing to Synthesize

Write an essay describing both the historical and personal insights you gained from reading the nonfiction in this unit.

Consider

- the historical facts you learned from the selections (important figures, dates, battles, and so forth)
- the personal concerns of the writers
- what you can infer about the country as a whole from the many voices of its writers

Conclude by making a comparison or analogy to our current events, concerns, and national mood.

Lincoln at Gettysburg II (1939–1942), William H. Johnson. Gouache and pen and ink on paper, 19 3/4″ × 17 1/16″.

Extension

SPEAKING & LISTENING

Examine the image of Lincoln shown here. Based on your reading and your prior knowledge of President Lincoln, give a brief **oral critique** of how he is portrayed in this painting. Discuss the style of the work as a whole, Lincoln's placement in relation to other figures in the painting, the colors used, and any other aspects you consider important. Be sure to use precise, formal language in your speech.

COMMON CORE

W 2 Write explanatory texts. **W 2d** Use techniques such as analogy to manage the complexity of the topic. **SL 4** Present information, findings, and supporting evidence, such that the development and substance are appropriate to purpose. **SL 6** Demonstrate a command of formal English when indicated.

Media Study

from An Occurrence at Owl Creek Bridge

Film Clips on MediaSmart DVD-ROM

COMMON CORE

RL 7 Analyze multiple interpretations of a story, evaluating how each version interprets the source text.

From Page to Screen

Since 1932, the short story "An Occurrence at Owl Creek Bridge" has been adapted for the screen at least four times. Its Civil War setting, heart-pounding suspense, and surprise ending make it an ideal story to adapt to film. One of the most famous versions appeared on the television series *The Twilight Zone*. In this lesson, you'll view three clips from the 2005 version to explore one of the ways Ambrose Bierce's tale has been adapted for the big screen.

The Filmmaker's Challenge

The fact that the main action of the story takes place in the mind of the character Peyton Farquhar creates a challenge for a filmmaker. To reveal a character's thoughts, a filmmaker must rely on such devices as **voice-over narration,** in which the character speaks his or her thoughts, and **flashbacks,** which present a scene from the character's memory.

In his film, director Brian James Egen provided only subtle clues that what the audience sees is not what is actually happening. "I had to create a feeling," Egen says, "from the time the rope breaks to the end, as if it was real. I wanted the audience to be taken completely by surprise, so we created the scenes as realistically as possible."

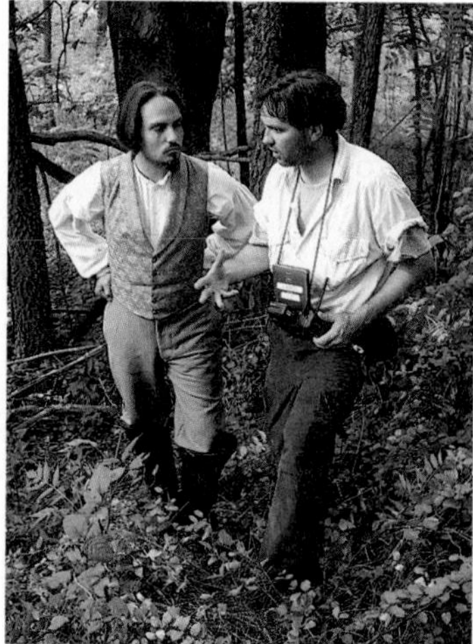

Brian James Egen directs an actor on location.

Comparing Texts: Point of View

Point of view in film can be either objective or subjective. In the **objective point of view,** the camera acts as a neutral recorder of action. It is used to show scenes as they would occur in reality. In the **subjective point of view,** the camera becomes a participant in the scene and seems to get inside a character's head by showing the viewer exactly what the character sees.

Read the following passage from the story and visualize the events. When you view the clips, pay special attention to this moment in the film. How close does the film come to the scene as you imagined it? Compare Bierce's use of the **third-person limited point of view** with the point of view used by the filmmaker. Notice the ways in which both the story and the film emphasize this moment.

Media Tools THINK central

Go to thinkcentral.com.
KEYWORD: HML11-619

He felt his head emerge; his eyes were blinded by the sunlight; his chest expanded convulsively, and with a supreme and crowning agony his lungs engulfed a great draught of air, which instantly he expelled in a shriek!

He was now in full possession of his physical senses. They were, indeed, preternaturally keen and alert. Something in the awful disturbance of his organic system had so exalted and refined them that they made record of things never before perceived. He felt the ripples upon his face and heard their separate sounds as they struck. He looked at the forest on the bank of the stream, saw the individual trees, the leaves and the veining of each leaf—saw the very insects upon them: the locusts, the brilliant-bodied flies, the gray spiders stretching their webs from twig to twig. He noted the prismatic colors in all the dewdrops upon a million blades of grass.

Viewing Guide

MediaSmart DVD-ROM

- **Film:** *An Occurrence at Owl Creek Bridge*
- **Director:** Brian James Egen
- **Genre:** Historical thriller
- **Running Time:** 14 minutes

The three clips you'll view from *An Occurrence at Owl Creek Bridge* include Farquhar's hanging and escape, his long walk through the night to reach his wife, and, of course, the sudden ending. You may want to watch the clips more than once in order to analyze them.

NOW VIEW

CLOSE VIEWING: **Media Analysis**

1. **Compare Point of View** Think about the scene in the film that corresponds to the passage shown from the story. Did the filmmaker use the **objective** or **subjective point of view?** What is the effect of this point of view in comparison with Bierce's use of the **third-person limited?**
2. **Analyze Montage** A **montage** is a succession of shots, often short and without dialogue, intended to create a particular effect or suggest meaning. What do you think the filmmaker wanted to convey with the montage of Farquhar's family and home in the third clip?
3. **Evaluate the Adaptation** How effective do you think the filmmaker was in adapting Bierce's story to the big screen? Think about the following:
   - the rising suspense in the hanging scene
   - the voice-over narration
   - moments in the film that do not appear in the story

Online Feature Article

In this unit, you discovered the events, figures, and literature of the Civil War. The World Wide Web is home to discussions about this era and about the significant issues of today. Now, you will write about one legacy of your era in an **online feature article**—an informative piece of writing on a topic or trend.

 Complete the workshop activities in your **Reader/Writer Notebook.**

WRITE WITH A PURPOSE

WRITING TASK

Inform your audience by writing an **online feature article** that answers this research question: What is one topic, trend, person, or phenomenon that has defined *your* time? Choose a topic that people will still read and talk about 100 years from now.

Idea Starters

- a ground-breaking technology
- an important figure, such as an inventor or human-rights crusader
- an event, such as a presidential election, a war, or a terrorist attack
- a social or environmental issue

THE ESSENTIALS

Here are some common purposes, audiences, and formats for online feature articles and other informative/explanatory writings.

PURPOSES	AUDIENCES	FORMATS
• to inform readers about a topic • to help readers gain a unique perspective on the topic • to develop and maintain an online readership	• classmates and teacher • friends and family on a social networking site • Web users with similar interests • community members	• magazine article • wiki article • news report • blog posting • podcast • video blog

COMMON CORE TRAITS

1. DEVELOPMENT OF IDEAS

- provides an engaging **introduction** with a clear **controlling idea**
- develops the topic and supports it with **evidence**, such as **facts, extended definitions, concrete details,** and **quotations**
- provides a **concluding section** that supports the information

2. ORGANIZATION OF IDEAS

- logically **organizes** complex ideas, concepts, and information to **create a unified whole**
- uses appropriate and varied **transitions** and **syntax** to create cohesion and connect ideas
- includes **formatting, links, graphics,** and **multimedia**

3. LANGUAGE FACILITY AND CONVENTIONS

- uses **precise language, domain-specific vocabulary,** and **literary techniques**
- establishes and maintains a **formal style** and **objective tone**
- employs correct **grammar, mechanics,** and **spelling**

Writing Online 

Go to thinkcentral.com.
KEYWORD: HML11N-620

W 2a–f Write informative/explanatory texts to examine and convey complex information. W 6 Use technology to produce and publish individual writing products. W 7 Conduct short research projects to answer a question.

Planning/Prewriting

Getting Started

CHOOSE A TOPIC

Use the Idea Starters on the previous page to brainstorm several topics that interest you and will likely interest your audience. Come up with at least three ideas for a topic, and then do a preliminary search online for each one. Choose a topic that has ample available information, but isn't so broad that you can't write a short article on it. Be sure to frame your topic in the form of a specific, tightly focused **research question** to help guide your research and writing.

TIPS FOR GENERATING TOPIC IDEAS:

- Review national and international news sources for interesting current events.
- Visit community Web sites for popular topics of conversation.
- Read blogs or wikis that your teachers or classmates recommend, especially ones that your peers contribute to.
- Consider major events that have affected your life.

THINK ABOUT AUDIENCE AND PURPOSE

As you prepare to write your article, consider your **audience** and **purpose.** Understanding your audience will help you know what information to include and what **voice** and **style** to use while writing. Knowing your audience and purpose will also help you decide where to publish your online article.

ASK YOURSELF:

- What **background information** do I need to include? For example, are there **domain-specific vocabulary terms** that I should explain or define?
- What aspects of this topic might my audience wish to learn more about?
- Where will I publish, or post, my article?

FIND MULTIPLE AUTHORITATIVE SOURCES

Look for reputable sources in your school and local libraries and on the Web. Determine the strengths and limitations of each source by considering whether it is appropriate for your **audience** and **purpose.**

Choose authoritative online sources by looking for sites that are developed by experts in their field and that include information that can be verified by other sources. Find articles from official news sources, such as magazines and newspapers, or educational publications. Make sure you don't rely too heavily on just one source.

Record the title, author, and page number or Web address for each source. Remember, it's your responsibility to avoid plagiarism.

See pages 1344–1351 for more information on locating and evaluating potential sources.

WHAT DOES IT LOOK LIKE?

Sources	Notes
www.cnn.com/ ELECTION/2008/ results/president/	results of 2008 election for U.S. president
Book: Narrative of the Life of Frederick Douglass	Frederick Douglass's autobiography
www.biography.com/ articles/Barack-Obama-12782369	comprehensive biography of Barack Obama

Planning/Prewriting *continued*

Getting Started

COLLECT AND SYNTHESIZE INFORMATION

While researching your topic, keep a record of **relevant quotations, facts, details, examples,** and **multimedia** that you come across. As you take notes, look for opportunities to **synthesize** information—to make connections and combine facts in a way that provides a broader understanding of the subject. Use a variety of reputable sources and your own previous knowledge to draw original conclusions about your topic.

WHAT DOES IT LOOK LIKE?

"From the first I saw no chance of bettering the condition of the freedman until he should . . . become a citizen." *–Frederick Douglass, 1892*	*"One hundred years later, the life of the Negro is still sadly crippled by the manacles of segregation and the chains of discrimination."* *–Martin Luther King Jr., 1963*

For over a century, influential African Americans fought for equality under the law in addition to freedom from slavery.

DRAFT A CONTROLLING IDEA

Craft a **controlling idea**, or thesis statement. Your research question can serve as the basis for your controlling idea, which should precisely identify what you want your audience to learn about your topic. Modify or refine your controlling idea as you draft.

WHAT DOES IT LOOK LIKE?

The years of struggle by past African-American leaders created the foundation for the historic election of the first African-American president of the United States.

GENERATE A STORYBOARD

Use a storyboard to outline how your information will appear on Web pages. Keep in mind that Web users are less likely to notice elements on the right side and bottom of the page, or on pages that appear cluttered. Use **text features,** such as headings and links, to organize your Web pages and to make them easy to read and navigate. Plan how you will use multimedia and where you will locate it on the page or via a link.

WHAT DOES IT LOOK LIKE?

The First African-American President

Sidebar
Contents
Links
Discussion

Introduction

Introduction text

Photo

Next

PEER REVIEW Show your **controlling idea** to another student and explain your **audience** and **purpose.** Discuss your evidence and how well it supports your controlling idea.

YOUR TURN

List possible topics in your *Reader/Writer Notebook*. Choose a specific topic that interests you and draft a research question. Gather your sources, synthesize the information, and draft a controlling idea. Generate a storyboard to plan your article.

W 4 Produce clear and coherent writing. **W 8** Gather information from multiple sources and follow a standard format for citation. **W 9b (RI 1)** Draw evidence from informational texts to support analysis. **L 2** Demonstrate command of conventions.

Drafting

The following chart shows a structure for outlining a **clear** and **coherent** online feature article.

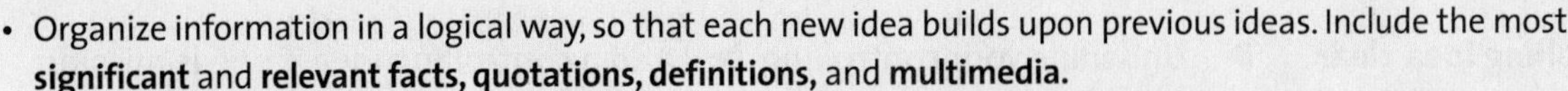

Organizing Your Online Feature Article

INTRODUCTION

- Grab your audience's attention with a **compelling quotation, question,** or **anecdote.**
- Supply your audience with the **background information** they need to grasp the topic.
- Use **precise language** to introduce a clear **controlling idea,** or thesis statement.
- Establish a **formal style** and an **objective tone,** or attitude.

BODY

- Organize information in a logical way, so that each new idea builds upon previous ideas. Include the most **significant** and **relevant facts, quotations, definitions,** and **multimedia.**
- Use appropriate **transitions** to link ideas, create cohesion, and clarify relationships.
- **Vary your syntax** instead of relying on the same words, phrases, and clauses.
- Use literary techniques, such as **metaphors, similes,** and **analogies,** to help your audience understand complex or abstract ideas and to add interest.
- Document the **source** of each idea. See pages 1344–1351 for information on citations.

CONCLUDING SECTION

- Restate your **controlling idea** and explain the significance of your topic.

GRAMMAR IN CONTEXT: INCORPORATING QUOTATIONS

Quoting primary sources and experts increases your credibility and gives readers a broader understanding of your topic. When quoting someone else's work, cite your source both in the running text of your article and in the Works Cited section. Follow these guidelines:

- Use quotation marks at both the beginning and the end of someone else's direct words.
- Integrate short quotations into your own sentences.
- Use ellipses to indicate where you've omitted any words from the quotation.
- Enclose the author's last name and the page number of the quote in parentheses at the end of the sentence. If you've already referenced the author, include only the page number.
- Hyperlink your in-text citation to your Works Cited section.

American historian Steven Lawson said of Obama's historic victory, "In becoming commander in chief, Obama has inherited the legacy of countless civil rights warriors who risked their lives . . . to gain the right to vote, not as an empty symbol, but as a genuine tool for freedom and equality" (2).

See pages 1376–1377 for Modern Language Association guidelines for creating a Works Cited list.

Develop a first draft of your online feature article. Make sure to integrate quotations. Add multimedia and links to aid understanding and navigation.

Revising

Best-selling author Michael Crichton once said, "Books aren't written—they're rewritten." Revising, rewriting, and, if necessary, trying a new approach are essential to the writing process. The following chart will help you revise and rewrite where necessary.

ONLINE FEATURE ARTICLE

Ask Yourself	*Tips*	*Revision Strategies*
1. Does my introduction grab the audience's attention?	**Highlight** attention-grabbing quotes, anecdotes, or facts.	**Add** a compelling question, quotation, or anecdote to engage your audience.
2. Is my controlling idea clear and appropriate for my task, purpose, and audience?	**Underline** your controlling idea, or thesis statement.	**Add** a controlling idea if one is missing. **Rework** your existing one if it is unclear or doesn't fit your task, purpose, or audience.
3. Is my organization logical, effective, and easy to navigate?	**Circle** headings, links, and menu options.	**Group** related paragraphs under boldfaced headings. **Add** more links to your menu to allow users to easily move to each section of your article.
4. Did I use significant and relevant evidence and multimedia to support my controlling idea?	**Place a check mark** next to relevant evidence and multimedia that supports your controlling idea.	**Delete** information that isn't relevant to your controlling idea. **Add** additional details for any ideas that are not sufficiently supported.
5. Does my concluding section restate my controlling idea and explain my topic's significance?	**Underline** your restated controlling idea and explanation of the topic's significance.	**Insert** sentences that restate your controlling idea and explain your topic's significance.
6. Are all of my sources correctly cited? Have I included a Works Cited section?	**Highlight** evidence. **Place a check mark** next to each citation and Works Cited entry.	**Add** in-text citations and/or Works Cited entries for any evidence that hasn't been properly cited.

PEER REVIEW Working with a partner, review your draft. Answer each question in the chart to decide how your draft can be improved. Ask: Is my use of multimedia distracting?

W 2a–b Include formatting, graphics, and multimedia; develop topic thoroughly by extended definitions or other information. **W 5** Develop and strengthen writing by revising, rewriting, or trying a new approach. **SL 5** Make strategic use of digital media.

ANALYZE A STUDENT DRAFT

Read this draft; notice the comments on its strengths as well as suggestions for improvement.

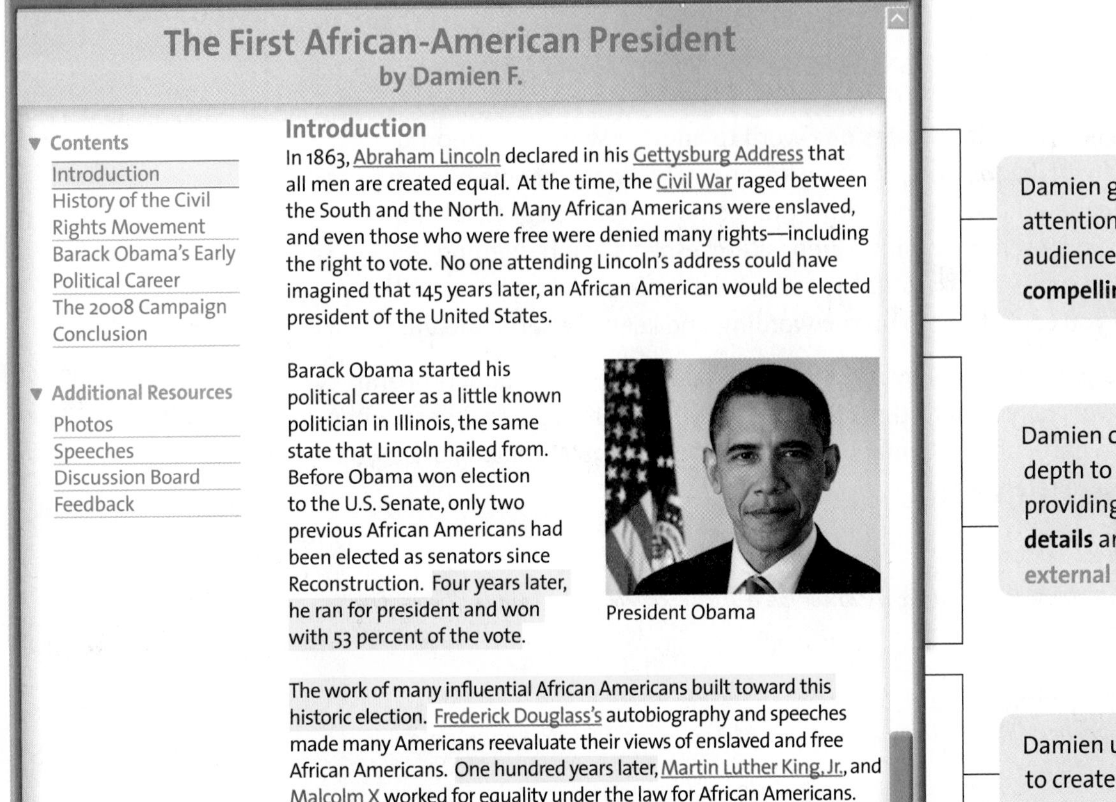

The First African-American President

by Damien F.

Contents

Additional Resources

Photos
Speeches
Discussion Board
Feedback

Introduction

In 1863, Abraham Lincoln declared in his Gettysburg Address that all men are created equal. At the time, the Civil War raged between the South and the North. Many African Americans were enslaved, and even those who were free were denied many rights—including the right to vote. No one attending Lincoln's address could have imagined that 145 years later, an African American would be elected president of the United States.

Barack Obama started his political career as a little known politician in Illinois, the same state that Lincoln hailed from. Before Obama won election to the U.S. Senate, only two previous African Americans had been elected as senators since Reconstruction. Four years later, he ran for president and won with 53 percent of the vote.

President Obama

The work of many influential African Americans built toward this historic election. Frederick Douglass's autobiography and speeches made many Americans reevaluate their views of enslaved and free African Americans. One hundred years later, Martin Luther King, Jr., and Malcolm X worked for equality under the law for African Americans. Though they all had different philosophies and methods, their efforts and those of many other Civil Rights leaders led to monumental changes in the law and throughout society.

Next: History of the Civil Rights Movement

Damien grabs the attention of his audience with a **compelling introduction.**

Damien could add more depth to his article by providing **additional details** and links to external sources.

Damien uses **transitions** to create cohesion and connect ideas.

LEARN HOW **Link to External Sources** Damien can provide his readers with links to **authoritative** Web sites for more background information, biographies, and extended definitions. He provides sufficient links in the bottom paragraph, but not in his second paragraph. He decided to add a link to the election results.

DAMIEN'S REVISION TO *INTRODUCTION*

Four years later, he ran for president and won with 53 percent of the vote.

Link to official 2008 presidential election results

YOUR TURN Use feedback from your peers and teacher as well as the "Learn How" lesson to revise or rewrite parts of your online feature article. Make sure that any links you provide are only to reliable Web sites.

Editing and Publishing

COMMON CORE

W 5 Strengthen writing by editing. **L 1a–b** Apply the understanding that usage is sometimes contested; resolve issues of contested usage. **L 2** Demonstrate command of the conventions of standard English capitalization, punctuation, and spelling.

In the editing stage, you proofread your article to eliminate errors. You also need to ensure that all of your links and multimedia elements are functioning properly. Lastly, do a final check to make sure that your pages are formatted consistently and are easy to read and navigate.

GRAMMAR IN CONTEXT: PREPOSITIONS AND USAGE

A **preposition** is a word that relates one word to another word. Common prepositions are *at, by, for, from, in, of, on, to,* and *with.* Many people believe that a sentence should never end with a preposition. In some cases, it is now acceptable to end a sentence with a preposition, especially if rewording the sentence would make it awkward. However, a sentence should not end with a preposition if you could tighten up the wording and keep the same meaning.

Discuss with a partner the following example from Damien's introduction and decide which version you both think is more appropriate. If your teacher requires you to follow a particular style manual, such as *The Chicago Manual of Style,* you may use that as a reference.

Damien's original sentence:

Barack Obama started his political career as a little known politician in Illinois, the same state that Lincoln hailed from.

Damien's revised sentence:

Like Lincoln, Barack Obama started his political career as a little known politician from Illinois.

PUBLISH YOUR WRITING

When you are finished proofreading your article, you are ready to post it online.

- Send an e-mail or text message to friends and family to notify them that your article is available for viewing.
- Post a link to your article in related forums or online communities.
- Update your status on any social media networks that you participate in to include a link to your article.
- Exchange links with classmates who have written articles on similar topics.

YOUR TURN Carefully proofread your article and correct any errors in conventions. Be sure to check that you have used prepositions effectively. After you've completed these final touches, publish your online feature article.

Scoring Rubric

Use the rubric below to evaluate your online feature article.

ONLINE FEATURE ARTICLE

SCORE	COMMON CORE TRAITS
6	• **Development** Effectively introduces a topic; states an insightful controlling idea; is well-developed with significant, relevant evidence; ends powerfully • **Organization** Organizes complex ideas to create a unified whole; uses appropriate transitions and varied syntax; effectively uses formatting and multimedia; correctly cites sources • **Language** Uses precise wording effectively; maintains formal style and objective tone; shows strong command of conventions
5	• **Development** Competently introduces a topic; states a clear controlling idea; is well-developed with relevant evidence; ends capably • **Organization** Logically organizes ideas; uses transitions and varied syntax; uses formatting and multimedia; correctly cites sources • **Language** Uses precise language; generally maintains formal style and objective tone; makes a few errors in conventions
4	• **Development** Adequately introduces a topic; states a controlling idea; includes some relevant evidence; ends adequately • **Organization** Is mostly well-organized; uses adequate transitions, syntax, formatting, and multimedia; cites most sources • **Language** Needs more precise words; mostly maintains formal style and objective tone; has some errors in conventions
3	• **Development** States a controlling idea, but lacks a compelling introduction and sufficient evidence; ends with a weak concluding section • **Organization** Has weaknesses in organization; uses some transitions and variety of syntax; has inconsistent formatting, multimedia, and source citations • **Language** Sometimes uses vague language; has inconsistent style and tone; has many errors in conventions
2	• **Development** Has a weak controlling idea and introduction; does not support most ideas; ends abruptly • **Organization** Has serious organizational flaws; often lacks transitions; lacks formatting and multimedia; rarely cites sources • **Language** Uses vague language; uses informal style and tone; has major errors in conventions
1	• **Development** Lacks a controlling idea, supporting evidence, and a concluding section • **Organization** Has no organization, formatting, multimedia, or citations • **Language** Often uses vague language; has an inappropriate style and tone; shows no command of conventions

Updating an Online Feature Article

Unlike an article published in a print periodical, an online feature article is always a work in progress. That's because the World Wide Web is never static; content is continually being added, updated, reorganized, or deleted to accommodate new information, new multimedia, and new ideas. As the author of an online feature article, you must regularly maintain your published work. If you want readers to consider your article a reliable source, you need to keep it updated. In this workshop, you will learn how to effectively update, improve, and enhance your online article.

Complete the workshop activities in your **Reader/Writer Notebook.**

PRODUCE WITH A PURPOSE	COMMON CORE TRAITS
TASK	***A SUCCESSFUL UPDATE . . .***
Update your online feature article to replace dead links, improve design and navigation, and provide updated information on your topic.	• replaces outdated information with new content from current and reliable sources • repairs broken links • responds promptly and respectfully to readers' questions, comments, and feedback • modifies design or navigation features for greater ease in viewing and navigation • promotes growth in readership by seeking new audiences and encouraging visitors to return

COMMON CORE

W 6 Use technology to update individual writing products in response to ongoing feedback. **SL 1c, d** Pose and respond to questions; synthesize comments; determine what additional information is required. **SL 5** Make strategic use of digital media.

Maintaining Your Article

Frequently visit your online feature article and spend a few minutes maintaining it. Use these guidelines to help you:

- **Keep Your Links Current** Web sites often move or remove pages. For this reason, it's essential that you regularly check all of your links and make sure that the Web address, or URL, is still functional and connects to the correct information. When you locate dead or incorrect links, update them to reflect the new URL, find suitable replacement links, or delete the links from your article.
- **Respond to Feedback** Promptly read all questions and comments posted to your article. Politely reply when appropriate; delete inappropriate comments right away. Replying thoughtfully to feedback can stimulate discussion, which encourages more reader participation and return visitors.
- **Include a *Last Updated* Date** Provide a line of text that states the date when you last updated your article. This note shows readers how current your information is and how committed you are to keeping it up-to-date.

Modifying and Improving Your Article

Part of updating an online article is modifying and improving it as you receive feedback and learn more about your topic. You might modify your article for a variety of reasons, including:

- **To Improve Content** As new information about your topic becomes available, delete out-of-date information and revise your article to include the updated content, such as new links and multimedia. Make sure that any information you consider adding comes from a reliable source. If you have chosen a topic about something that changes frequently, consider adding an Updates section. Subscribing to a Web feed is a good way to stay current on your topic.
- **To Address User Feedback** Readers may offer feedback on the accuracy of your facts, your site design, or your navigational features. Before making significant changes, synthesize feedback you've received and decide what additional information or research is required. Be willing to revise your work, or even try a new approach, to address valid reader feedback.
- **To Redesign Your Web Pages** Trying a new design can give your article a more contemporary look and keep it visually appealing. You could reorganize the navigational features, add new multimedia, or try a new font. Make sure that navigation remains simple and easy for your readers.
- **To Grow Your Readership** Anytime you update or redesign your article, consider posting a status update on social media networks. Send email updates to your readers and post a link to your article on forums that your audience frequents. This way you can encourage new readers to visit and old readers to return.

Bethany1 (reader) said . . .

Great article, but I think you need information on Rosa Parks. BTW, do you know any events planned for Black History Month?

January 15, 7:45 AM

Allan2 (reader) said . . .

I'm not sure information on Rosa Parks would fit well with Damien's topic. It might be distracting.

January 15, 1:18 PM

DamienF (Site Administrator) said . . .

Thanks for your feedback, Bethany and Allan! I'll do a little research and think about it. But can you tell me more about why you think Parks should/should not be included? Does anyone else have any thoughts?

January 15, 6:25 PM

NEWS FEED

DamienF Check out **my updated feature article!** I've added a new section on Civil Rights leaders and additional information on Obama's presidency. And look for a schedule of Black History Month events, coming soon!

Regularly visit your online feature article. Check if your links are still functional and update, replace, or delete dead links. Politely and thoughtfully respond to questions, comments, and feedback. Keep your content up-to-date to engage your current readers and attract new ones.

Assessment Practice

ASSESS
Taking this practice test will help you assess your knowledge of these skills and determine your readiness for the Unit Test.

REVIEW
After you take the practice test, your teacher can help you identify any standards you need to review.

COMMON CORE

RL 4 Determine the meaning of words and phrases as they are used in the text, including figurative and connotative meanings; analyze the impact of specific word choices on meaning and tone, including language that is particularly fresh, engaging, or beautiful. **RL 10** Read and comprehend literature, including poems. **L 2** Demonstrate command of the conventions of standard English capitalization, punctuation, and spelling. **L 3** Apply knowledge of language to make effective choices for meaning or style. **L 4a** Use context as a clue to the meaning of a word or phrase. **L 5a** Interpret figures of speech in context and analyze their role in text.

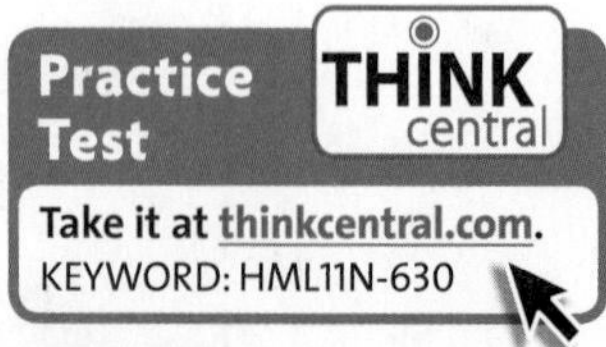

DIRECTIONS **Read these poems and answer the questions that follow.**

The Wind begun to knead the Grass—

by Emily Dickinson

The Wind begun to knead the Grass—
As Women do a Dough—
He flung a Hand full at the Plain—
A Hand full at the Sky—
The Leaves unhooked themselves from Trees—
And started all abroad—
The Dust did scoop itself like Hands—
And throw away the Road—

The Wagons quickened on the Street—
The Thunders gossiped low—
The Lightning showed a Yellow Head—
And then a livid Toe—
The Birds put up the Bars to Nests—
The Cattle flung to Barns—
Then came one drop of Giant Rain—
And then, as if the Hands
That held the Dams—had parted hold—
The Waters Wrecked the Sky—
But overlooked my Father's House—
Just Quartering a Tree—

Patroling Barnegat *by Walt Whitman*

Wild, wild the storm, and the sea high running,
Steady the roar of the gale, with incessant undertone muttering,
Shouts of demoniac laughter fitfully piercing and pealing,
Waves, air, midnight, their savagest trinity lashing,
Out in the shadows there milk-white combs careering,
On beachy slush and sand spirts of snow fierce slanting,
Where through the murk the easterly death-wind breasting,
Through cutting swirl and spray watchful and firm advancing,
(That in the distance! is that a wreck? is the red signal flaring?)
Slush and sand of the beach tireless till daylight wending,
Steadily, slowly, through hoarse roar never remitting,
Along the midnight edge by those milk-white combs careering,
A group of dim, weird forms, struggling, the night confronting,
That savage trinity warily watching.

Reading Comprehension

Use "The Wind begun to knead the Grass—" (p. 630) to answer questions 1–8.

1. What effect do the dashes have on your reading and understanding of the poem?
   A. They tell you to read some words without emphasis because they are less important to the poem's meaning.
   B. They show where similes and metaphors occur and help convey their meaning.
   C. They help establish the poem's rhythm and indicate a pause after each description.
   D. They call attention to rhyming words and mark the end of sentences within the poem.

2. What does the simile in lines 1–2 suggest about the wind?
   A. The wind is gently ruffling the grass.
   B. A windy day is a good day for baking.
   C. The direction of the wind is inconsistent.
   D. The wind is strong as it pushes against the grass.

3. Dickinson uses similes and personification to describe different aspects of —
   A. someone's personality
   B. a thunderstorm
   C. a dam breaking
   D. small-town life

4. The personification of the wind, the leaves, and the dust conveys a sense of —
   A. natural order
   B. gentle guidance
   C. unpredictable power
   D. domestic happiness

5. The slant rhyme of *abroad* and *road* in lines 6 and 8 draws attention to the —
   A. wagons hurrying on the road
   B. chaotic unruliness of the wind
   C. travelers caught by the weather
   D. contrast of the leaves against the dust

6. The speaker's tone in lines 1–18 is best described as —
   A. fearful and serious
   B. gloomy and somber
   C. exhilarated and playful
   D. optimistic and confident

7. Dickinson most likely uses irregularly capitalized words in this poem to emphasize —
   A. key words that tell the story
   B. the rhythm of the rain
   C. her opinion of the events
   D. emotions conveyed in the poem

8. Dickinson personifies the "Thunders" in line 10 as people who gossip to call attention to thunder's —
   A. dramatic display
   B. sinister rumbling
   C. meaningless noise
   D. frightening power

Use "Patroling Barnegat" (p. 631) to answer questions 9–14.

9. Which poetic devices does Whitman use in line 1 to make a dramatic exclamation?
   A. Cataloging and parallelism
   B. Simile and personification
   C. Repetition and inverted word order
   D. Slant rhymes and inventive punctuation

10. By ending each line with a participle, Whitman is using —
   A. imagery to convey an idea
   B. parallelism to create rhythm
   C. details to communicate tone
   D. personification to describe an object

11. Whitman uses the irregular meter of free verse to —
   A. convey the wildness of the storm
   B. present a contrast with the subject
   C. suggest daily life near the sea
   D. establish movement in the poem

12. The effect of Whitman's catalog of sights and sounds on the beach is to —
   A. build tension
   B. emphasize ideas
   C. honor people
   D. celebrate everyday diction

13. What effect does Whitman achieve by repeating the word *through* in lines 7–11?
   A. He interrupts the chronological order of events.
   B. He mimics the sound of the wind blowing across the beach.
   C. He emphasizes the relentlessness of the darkness, the waves, and the wind.
   D. He focuses attention on how a storm damages the surrounding area.

14. Whitman's tone in lines 1–8 is —
   A. hysterical
   B. suspenseful
   C. tragic
   D. triumphant

Use both poems to answer question 15.

15. Which statement best contrasts the tone at the end of the two poems?
   A. The Dickinson poem is factual; the Whitman poem is reflective.
   B. The Dickinson poem is sad; the Whitman poem is exuberant.
   C. The Dickinson poem is peaceful; the Whitman poem is frantic.
   D. The Dickinson poem is menacing; the Whitman is distant.

SHORT CONSTRUCTED RESPONSE

Write three or four sentences to answer this question.

16. Whitman often repeats words and phrases in his poetry. What effect does he achieve in "Patroling Barnegat" by writing the phrases "savagest trinity" in line 4, "savage trinity" in line 14, and "milk-white combs careering" in lines 5 and 12?

Write two or three paragraphs to answer this question.

17. Compare Whitman's and Dickinson's writing styles. Which poetic devices does Dickinson use to describe a storm? Which poetic devices does Whitman use?

Vocabulary

Use context clues and the Latin word and root definitions to answer the following questions.

1. The Latin word *livere* means "to be bluish." The most likely meaning of the word *livid* as it is used in line 12 of "The Wind begun to knead the Grass—" is —
   - **A.** extremely calm
   - **B.** very pale
   - **C.** in a state of shock
   - **D.** leaden colored

2. The Latin prefix *in-* means "not" and the Latin word *cessare* means "to stop." The most likely meaning of the word *incessant* as it is used in line 2 of "Patroling Barnegat" is —
   - **A.** continuing without interruption
   - **B.** concluding a recent action
   - **C.** pausing periodically
   - **D.** resuming activity

3. The word *remit* comes from the Latin prefix *re-*, which means "backward," and the Latin word *mittere*, which means "to send." The most likely meaning of the word *remitting* as it is used in line 11 of "Patroling Barnegat" is —
   - **A.** letting up
   - **B.** waiting
   - **C.** forgiving
   - **D.** restoring

Use context clues to answer the following questions.

4. What is the most likely meaning of the word *quartering* as it is used in line 20 of "The Wind begun to knead the Grass—"?
   - **A.** Locating
   - **B.** Making visible
   - **C.** Measuring
   - **D.** Splitting into parts

5. The most likely meaning of *demoniac* as it is used in line 3 of "Patroling Barnegat" is —
   - **A.** comical
   - **B.** fiendish
   - **C.** sincere
   - **D.** thunderous

6. The most likely meaning of the word *careering* as it is used in lines 5 and 12 of "Patroling Barnegat" is —
   - **A.** falling
   - **B.** growing
   - **C.** pounding
   - **D.** rushing

Revising and Editing

DIRECTIONS Read this passage and answer the questions that follow.

(1) With a weight of 13,632 tons and a length of 729 feet, the *Edmund Fitzgerald* was the largest carrier on the Great Lakes when it first sailed in 1958. (2) Seventeen years later, the ship would sink in Lake Superior. (3) At 2:20 p.m. on November 9th, 1975, the *Fitzgerald* departed, Superior, Wisconsin, destined for Detroit. (4) The National Weather Service issued gale warnings for the area. (5) The next day, winds gusting up to 70 knots and waves cresting as high as 30 feet shook the ship. (6) Water came onto the deck. (7) At approximately 7:15 that evening, the ship vanished from radar observation, and all 29 crew members were lost. (8) That fateful day of November 10, 1975, will always be remembered. (9) It was later discovered that the ship had dropped about 530 feet to the bottom of Lake Superior.

1. What change, if any, should be made in sentence 1?

A. Change ***tons*** to **ton's**
B. Insert a comma after ***Lakes***
C. Change ***sailed*** to **sailing**
D. Make no change

2. What is the most effective way to revise sentence 2 to convey a more somber tone?

A. Seventeen years later, the hefty ship would sink in Lake Superior.
B. Seventeen short years later, the ship would sink in Lake Superior.
C. Seventeen productive years later, the ship would sink in Lake Superior.
D. Seventeen years later, the doomed ship would sink in Lake Superior.

3. What change, if any, should be made in sentence 3?

A. Delete the comma after ***departed***
B. Change ***9th*** to **Ninth**
C. Delete the comma after ***Wisconsin***
D. Make no change

4. Which transition word or phrase should be added to the beginning of sentence 4?

A. As a result,
B. In short,
C. Shortly afterwards,
D. Therefore,

5. Which vivid verb should replace the verb in sentence 6?

A. Crashed
B. Seeped
C. Squirted
D. Washed

6. What is the most effective way to revise the underlined portion of sentence 7 to convey a more somber tone?

A. all 29 crew members were tragically lost
B. all 29 crew members were unfortunately lost
C. all 29 crew members were suddenly lost
D. all 29 crew members were definitely lost

7. What is the most effective way to improve the organization of the paragraph?

A. Delete sentence 5
B. Switch sentences 5 and 6
C. Delete sentence 7
D. Move sentence 8 to the end of the paragraph

Ideas for Independent Reading

Continue exploring the Questions of the Times on pages 514–515 with these additional works.

What DIVIDES *a nation?*

Classic Slave Narratives
edited by Henry Louis Gates Jr.

This collection of classic slave narratives provides testimony to the horrors of bondage and sheds light on the American slave experience. The volume contains two of the best-known examples of "literature of escape"—the stories of Frederick Douglass and Olaudah Equiano—as well as two narratives by women—Harriet Jacobs and Mary Prince.

Battle Cry of Freedom
by James M. McPherson

This history of the Civil War brings all aspects of the conflict to vivid life, from the momentous episodes that preceded the war, to the battles, politics, and personalities of the war itself. James McPherson provides readers with the framework they need to understand the complex economic, political, and social forces that divided the nation and led the country to war.

Journal of a Residence on a Georgian Plantation in 1838–1839
by Frances Anne Kemble

After her marriage, Fanny Kemble discovered the source of her wealthy husband's income: rice plantations that depended upon the labor of more than 600 slaves. This journal, published after her divorce, describes the appalling conditions Fanny found on one of the plantations and her attempts to improve life for the slaves there.

Is anything worth DYING FOR?

The Personal Memoirs of Ulysses S. Grant
by Ulysses S. Grant

Dying of throat cancer, Ulysses S. Grant spent his last days looking back upon the most important years of his life—the years he spent as the commander of the Union army in the Civil War. Here, in what Mark Twain called "the best [memoirs] of any general's since Caesar," Grant recalls how he managed to defeat Robert E. Lee and the Confederate army.

Co. Aytch: A Confederate Memoir of the Civil War
by Sam R. Watkins

Sam Watkins was 21 years old when the Civil War broke out. A native of Columbia, Tennessee, he didn't want to miss out on the "big show." Volunteering as a private, he served in Company H of the Maury Grays, First Tennessee Regiment. From that lowly position, Watkins fought in almost every major clash, from the battle of Shiloh to the battle of Nashville.

Lincoln
by David Herbert Donald

Pulitzer Prize–winning author David Donald tells the story of Abraham Lincoln, the man who managed to hold together a nation of vastly differing regional interests during the turmoil and tragedy of the Civil War. Donald's Lincoln emerges as ambitious yet fallible, with a remarkable capacity for growth—a man who spent his whole life learning and growing to eventually become one of our nation's greatest presidents.

COMMON CORE

RL 10 Read and comprehend literature. **RI 10** Read and comprehend literary nonfiction.

Why do people BREAK RULES?

Leaves of Grass
by Walt Whitman

Walt Whitman created a daring new kind of poetry that would become a major force in the world of literature. Whitman first published this volume himself, in 1855, with only 12 poems. He expanded and revised the book over the course of his life as his experiences and the nation's history changed and grew.

Letters of Emily Dickinson
by Emily Dickinson

Emily Dickinson's ingenuity, sensitivity, and wit course through her letters as well as her poetry. Compiled by a close friend, Dickinson's letters were first published in 1894, eight years after her death. Although she became increasingly reclusive and rarely saw her friends in her later years, this volume of letters shows that she thought of them often and affectionately.

Daisy Miller
by Henry James

In this short novel, a wealthy young woman named Daisy Miller takes the grand tour of Europe. In the 19th century, such a long trip was a rite of passage for well-to-do young Americans. In Rome, Daisy's friendship with an Italian man, though innocent, causes her to be shunned by her peers. Yet she refuses to change her carefree ways. By disregarding the social rules of her community, Daisy sets herself up for tragedy.

Is it important to FACE REALITY?

Shiloh: A Novel
by Shelby Foote

This modern novel gives readers an up-close impression of the battle of Shiloh from the perspectives of many different soldiers who fought in it. Each chapter consists of the first-person accounts of various narrators, Union and Confederate, telling of what transpires in their own little corner of the battle.

Ambrose Bierce's Civil War
by Ambrose Bierce, edited by William McCann

Ambrose Bierce is one of the few writers of his day who actually fought in the Civil War. As a result, his gritty depictions of battle and close observation of soldiers' daily lives have the ring of authenticity. This collection includes both personal memoirs and fictional accounts of the war.

Life in the Iron Mills
by Rebecca Harding Davis

Decades before most Americans took notice, Rebecca Harding Davis unveiled the human costs of industrialism in *Life in the Iron Mills*. She concentrated on the stunted lives of factory workers, showing the dirty hovels where they lived, their unwholesome food, their constant labor, and their lack of education. Her story was one of the first works of American fiction to acknowledge such realities. Yet Davis also looked beyond social conditions to explore her characters' hidden yearnings for artistic expression and lasting love.

Get Novel Wise THINK central

Go to thinkcentral.com.
KEYWORD: HML11-637

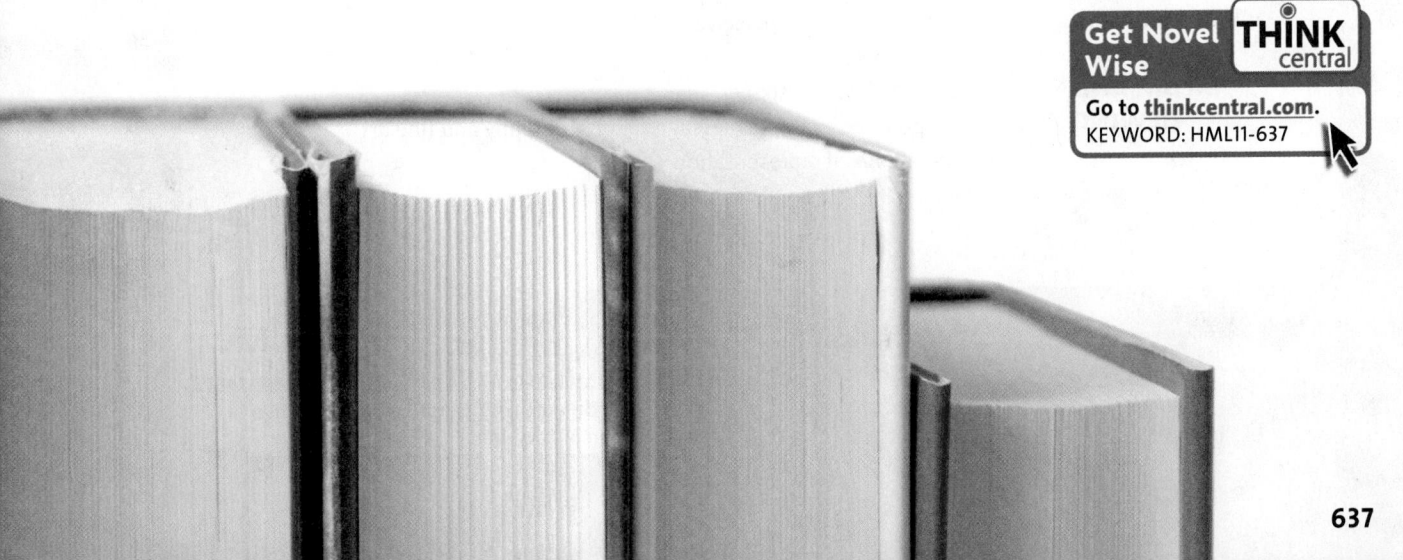

UNIT 4

COMMON CORE

Preview Unit Goals

TEXT ANALYSIS	• Analyze descriptive language, including imagery, figurative language, repetition, and diction • Analyze regionalism and naturalism as literary movements • Analyze rhetorical techniques in literature • Identify and analyze literary elements, including setting, plot, conflict, theme, tone, and character development • Analyze irony, hyperbole, and understatement • Analyze author's perspective • Analyze primary sources • Analyze how an author's choice of genre or text structure affects the expression of a theme or topic
READING	• Make inferences and draw conclusions about characters
WRITING AND LANGUAGE	• Write an analytical essay • Use gerunds and gerund phrases • Use passive and active voice effectively
VOCABULARY	• Use knowledge of Latin and Greek roots to understand word meanings • Discriminate between connotative and denotative meanings of words • Use context clues to detemine shades of meanings • Read and understand analogies
ACADEMIC VOCABULARY	• apparent • confine • expose • focus • perceive
MEDIA AND VIEWING	• Create a class newspaper • Interpret and evaluate messages in photography and fine art • Create a visual representation

Find It Online!

Go to thinkcentral.com for the interactive version of this unit.

Regionalism and Naturalism

1870–1910

Willa Cather

CAPTURING THE AMERICAN LANDSCAPE

- Regionalism and Local Color Writing
- The Rise of Naturalism
- A New Role for Women

MediaSmart DVD-ROM

American Landscapes

Discover the techniques used to create stirring images of America. Page 730

Questions of the Times

DISCUSS Consider the following questions with your classmates. Then read on to learn how these issues affected people living during this period and how the questions were reflected in the writing of the time.

What makes a place UNIQUE?

In the post–Civil War years, the United States was growing and changing at such a rapid pace that many Americans felt they were losing their regional identities. People were proud of the things they felt made them unique, and writers responded to this impulse by attempting to record the character of the country's distinct regions. What is it exactly that makes a place unique?

Does the universe CARE?

Life was quite difficult for many Americans during this period. Native Americans, African Americans, immigrants, factory workers, laborers, and farmers struggled daily against poverty and oppression. To many, it seemed that life was unfair—that despite their efforts, they could not escape their fate. Do you think people can control their destiny, or are they simply victims of circumstance?

COMMON CORE

RL 9 Demonstrate knowledge of nineteenth- and early-twentieth-century foundational works of American literature, including how two or more texts from the same period treat similar themes or topics. **RI 9** Analyze documents of historical and literary significance for their themes, purposes, and rhetorical features.

How are women's ROLES CHANGING?

Women of this era were becoming more educated, politically aware, and ambitious. Yet they were not allowed to vote, and those who stepped outside their homes to become artists, writers, and reformers faced strong disapproval and warnings that such activities were "unnatural" for women. How have women's roles evolved over the years?

Why are there "haves" and "HAVE-NOTS"?

This period was a time of harsh extremes. Industry was controlled by a handful of businesses owned by a few people who became very wealthy. These businesses were supported by countless laborers who worked long hours for low wages in dangerous conditions. Why do some people reap huge benefits while others are locked into hardship? Should the government ensure opportunity for all?

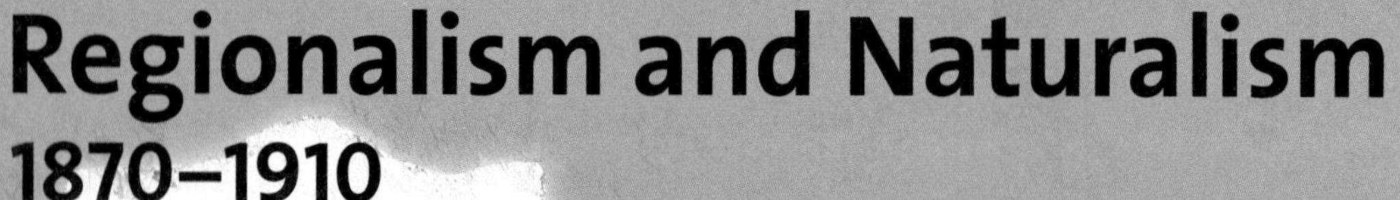

Regionalism and Naturalism

1870–1910

Capturing the American Landscape

Vast, varied, filled with seemingly limitless possibility—that was the United States in the years following the Civil War. Yet, all around them in this land of hope and opportunity, writers saw fellow Americans living lives of hardship and even despair. Regionalism tried to capture the reality of ordinary people's lives; naturalism searched for explanations.

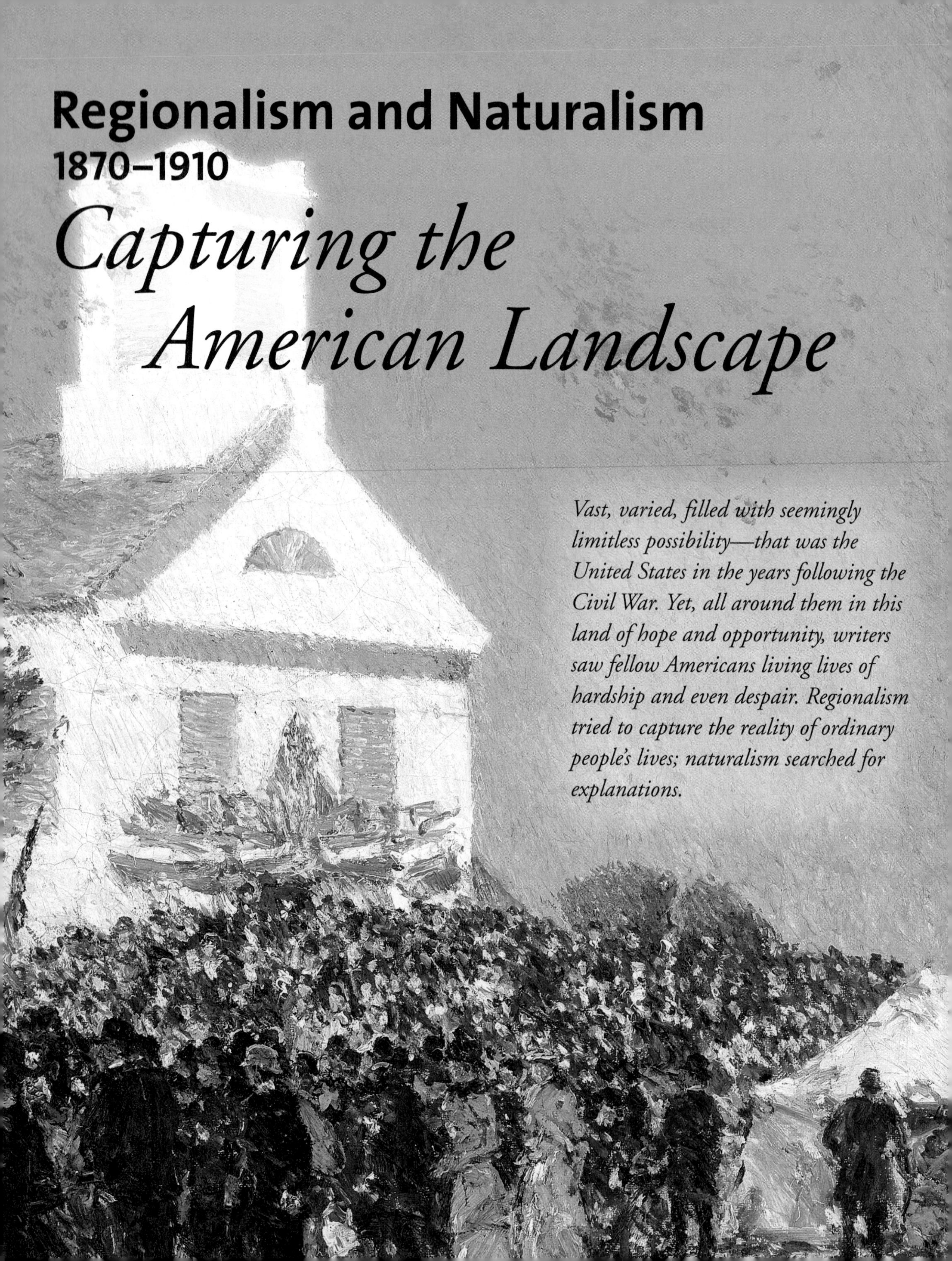

Regionalism and Naturalism: Historical Context

The post–Civil War period saw the nation reunited and transformed. Writers responded by attempting to preserve in their writing the distinct character of America's regions and to come to terms with some of its harsh new realities.

COMMON CORE

RL 9 Demonstrate knowledge of nineteenth- and early-twentieth-century foundational works of American literature, including how two or more texts from the same period treat similar themes. **RI 9** Analyze documents of historical and literary significance for their themes, purposes, and rhetorical features.

Reconstruction's Failures and Successes

The Civil War left the South in ruins. Its primary labor system, slavery, had been abolished. Freed African Americans lacked money, property, education, and opportunity. Farms, factories, and plantations had been destroyed, and rail lines were unusable. The federal government had to come up with a plan to solve these problems and to readmit the Southern states to the union. That plan was **Reconstruction.**

Reconstruction did not go smoothly. The president and Congress clashed over how to best carry it out. Southern states resisted many of the protections granted to newly freed blacks, while blacks felt that too little was being done to ensure their civil rights and economic independence. However, Reconstruction did succeed in a few significant ways. African Americans gained citizenship and equal protection under the law as well as the right to vote, and all of the Confederate states returned to the Union.

Although Americans were glad to move past the divisiveness of the war years, they regretted losing their regional identities and were unsettled by the many changes taking place in the country. These circumstances influenced writers of the time to begin trying to capture the customs, character, and landscapes of the nation's distinct regions—a type of writing that would come to be called **regionalism.**

TAKING NOTES

Outlining As you read this introduction, use an outline to record the main ideas about the characteristics and literature of the period. You can use headings, boldfaced terms, and the information in these boxes as starting points. (See page R49 in the **Research Handbook** for more help with outlining.)

I. *Historical Context*
- A. *Reconstruction*
  - 1. *Failures*
  - 2. *Successes*
  - 3. *Effect on writers*
- B. *Transformed Nation*

A Nation Transformed

In the decades following the Civil War, the country as a whole changed radically. In 1869, the first **transcontinental railroad** was completed. It was an event of huge importance. The railroad brought a flood of new settlers west—so many, in fact, that in 1890 the government announced the closing of the frontier. This westward expansion was yet another influence on writers of the time. It created an appreciation for America's diversity, which was celebrated by **local color writers** such as **Mark Twain** and **Bret Harte.**

The railroad also expanded industry. By 1885, four transcontinental lines had been completed, creating manufacturing hubs in Pittsburgh, Cleveland, Detroit, and Chicago. In turn, cities grew exponentially as more and more people came looking for work. In 1850, Chicago was a small town of 20,000; by 1910, the population was more than 2 million. Yet although new technologies and industrial modernization ensured the nation's prosperity, much of its wealth lay in the hands of only a few.

Country Fair, New England (1890), Childe Hassam. 24 ¼" × 20 ⅛".

The Hatch Family (1871), Eastman Johnson. Oil on canvas, 48″ × 73 3/8″. The Metropolitan Museum of Art, Gift of Frederic H. Hatch, 1926 (26.97). Photo © 1999 The Metropolitan Museum of Art.

◀ **Analyze Visuals**
What might have been the artist's purpose in rendering the scene in this painting? What conclusions can you draw about these people based on their clothing and surroundings?

Cultural Influences

Industry's success created a better life for many Americans. For a few, it brought great wealth, but others suffered poverty and hardship. Both regional and naturalist writers were influenced by these developments.

The Gilded Age

As the 1800s drew to an end, a very small group of men controlled the vast majority of industry, including the enormously profitable steel, railroad, oil, and meatpacking sectors. Captains of industry such as John D. Rockefeller, the oil tycoon, and Cornelius Vanderbilt, the railroad magnate, enjoyed showing off the vast fortunes they had made. They built palatial mansions, draped their wives and daughters in diamonds, and threw extravagant parties (at one, guests were handed silver shovels and invited to dig in a sandbox filled with jewels)—in short, they did everything but actually coat themselves in gold. When writers **Mark Twain** and **Charles Dudley Warner** dubbed this period "the Gilded Age," they did not exaggerate. It was a time of sparkle and glitter, luxury and excess.

A Voice from the Times

The only way not to think about money is to have a great deal of it.

—Edith Wharton

Many ordinary people had more money too and all sorts of new things to spend it on. They could take the train to an amusement park and ride the Ferris wheel, then snack on soda and a candy bar. City dwellers could shop in the new department stores, while country folks pored over the mail-order catalog from Sears, Roebuck (known as "the wish book," it offered everything from skin lotion to bicycles, and even an entire house—assembly required).

There were telephones now, thanks to Alexander Graham Bell. In 1908 Henry Ford brought out the first Model T, a "horseless carriage" cheap enough for his own factory workers to buy. Thomas Edison alone patented more than 1,000 inventions, from the phonograph to the electric light bulb.

The Have-Nots

Unfortunately, the Gilded Age was not so shiny for many other Americans. The settling of the West forced Native Americans off their land and onto reservations. Although Native Americans fought back—among them **Chief Joseph** of the Nez Perce and the legendary Sioux warriors Crazy Horse and Sitting Bull—there was no stopping the tide.

Life was hard for freed African Americans as well. The failures of Reconstruction in the South left many poor and powerless, held down by segregationist Jim Crow laws and forced to work as sharecroppers under conditions much like slavery.

Others who found themselves facing hard times during this period were many immigrants who had come to America in search of freedom and opportunity. Russian, Italian, Scandinavian, German, Dutch, and Japanese immigrants—all were seeking a better life. Some joined the settlers heading west; others stayed in the cities, where they lived in crowded tenements and found work in factories. Unfortunately, many of these new city-dwelling Americans found themselves working 16-hour days in airless sweatshops for subsistence wages.

A Voice from the Times

I Will Fight No More Forever

Tell General Howard I know his heart. What he told me before, I have in my heart. I am tired of fighting. Our chiefs are killed. Looking Glass is dead. Toohoolhoolzote is dead. The old men are all dead. It is the young men who say yes or no. He who led on the young men is dead. It is cold and we have no blankets. The little children are freezing to death. My people, some of them, have run away to the hills, and have no blankets, no food; no one knows where they are—perhaps freezing to death. I want to have time to look for my children and see how many of them I can find. Maybe I shall find them among the dead. Hear me, my chiefs! I am tired; my heart is sick and sad. From where the sun now stands I will fight no more forever.

—Chief Joseph of the Nez Perce,
from his 1877 surrender speech

Even independent farmers faced hard times. They borrowed money from the banks for new machinery that made them more productive than ever before; but high yields meant low prices, and when they couldn't pay back their loans they lost their farms.

People knew that they were missing out on the prosperity that others were enjoying, and it made them angry. Workers began to form **labor unions;** many farmers, white and black, joined the **Populist Party,** hoping to make the government more responsive to workers' needs. However, the opposition had money and power, and these early efforts often ended in bitter defeat.

More and more, the individual seemed helpless, at the mercy of forces beyond his or her understanding or control. Life became a constant struggle, and the world appeared to be a harsh, uncaring place. These feelings found their voice in a literary movement called **naturalism.** Naturalist writers, such as **Stephen Crane,** were concerned with the impact of social and natural forces on the individual. These writers tended to portray characters victimized by brutal forces and unable to control their lives.

Industrialist John D. Rockefeller is portrayed as a wealthy king, with the oil and railroad industries as the "jewels" in his crown.

Ideas of the Age

During this period, some Americans believed in "survival of the fittest," while others worked for social justice.

Laissez Faire vs. Progressivism

Many of the naturalists' ideas corresponded to new scientific, political, and economic theories emerging at the time. Various thinkers of the day felt that Charles Darwin's theory of natural selection could be applied to human society. An English philosopher named Herbert Spencer called this idea **survival of the fittest,** claiming that those who rose to the top of society were "fit," while those who suffered at the bottom were best left to die out. **Social Darwinists** used these ideas to justify the huge gap between rich and poor and to push a governmental policy of **laissez faire** (French for "allow to do"), meaning that business should not be regulated, because the law of nature would ensure success for the "fittest" and inevitable failure for everyone else.

This self-serving philosophy infuriated many Americans. A **progressive movement** emerged, which aimed to restore economic opportunities and correct injustices in American life. The progressives did not see inequality as the way of the world. They believed that social change was possible and necessary and that it was the job of the government to make laws to protect people.

A Voice from the Times

Let no one underestimate the need of pity. We live in a stony universe whose hard, brilliant forces rage fiercely.

—Theodore Dreiser

Regional and Naturalist Literature

The country's rapid growth and change was reflected in new literary movements and voices, including regionalism, naturalism, and women's writing.

Regionalism and Local Color Writing

The end of the Civil War, the country's rapid expansion, and the growth of industry all led to the birth of local color writing, a form of regionalism. Aware of the speed with which the nation was changing, regional writers sought to record for the future the unique character of their areas.

Prominent among the early local colorists were **Bret Harte** and **Mark Twain.** Their versions of life on the frontier captured the imagination of readers in the more settled communities of the East, Midwest, and South. For those who could not hop aboard the new transcontinental train and see the country for themselves, reading all about it was the next best thing. Americans were endlessly fascinated by tales of life in the mining camps, on the cattle ranches, and in the frontier towns. The new regionalist literature satisfied this curiosity with its honest portrayals of the people and their way of life in different areas of the country, especially the West. Writers carefully recorded how ordinary people spoke, dressed, acted, thought, and looked, from the knobby, roughened hands of a Nebraska farm woman to the dust-covered boots of a California gambler.

AN OUTGROWTH OF REALISM Regionalism, with its emphasis on everyday experience and accuracy, grew out of **realism.** Many regionalist writers, such as **Willa Cather,** shared the realist goal of showing ordinary lives as they

▶ *For Your Outline*

REGIONALISM AND LOCAL COLOR

- Writing was influenced by end of Civil War, country's expansion, and industry's growth.
- Regionalists sought to record for the future the unique character of a region.
- Regionalists captured life on the frontier and in other regions.
- Regionalism was an outgrowth of realism.
- Native American oral literature was a form of regionalism.
- *Huckleberry Finn* is a masterpiece of regionalism.

were, without romance or sentimentality. Cather's story, "A Wagner Matinee," for example, gives a very unromantic view of life on the plains. Other writers tended to exaggerate a bit, either for comic effect—as in Twain's "The Notorious Jumping Frog of Calaveras County"—or to make their stories livelier. Our national legend of the Wild West, with its gunslingers, saloons, and sheriffs, had its origins in the picturesque settings and characters of writers like **Bret Harte.**

> **A Voice from the Times**
>
> *Authorship is not a trade, it is an inspiration; authorship does not keep an office, its habitation is all out under the sky, and everywhere the winds are blowing and the sun is shining and the creatures of God are free.*
>
> —Mark Twain

NATIVE AMERICAN LITERATURE While this kind of regional literature thrived, another was under siege. For generations, Native American tribes had passed down from one generation to the next folk tales, legends, and other **oral literature,** relying on the memories of traditional storytellers and their audiences. Now, the tribes found themselves scattered. Children were forcibly taken from their elders and sent away to "Indian schools," where teachers demanded they forget their language and heritage and assimilate into American society. Entire cultures were rapidly disappearing. However, through the efforts of Native Americans and sympathetic outsiders who helped them write their stories down, some of the literature was saved, thus giving another view of life in the West.

AN "AMERICAN" NOVEL With the publication in 1884 of Mark Twain's ***The Adventures of Huckleberry Finn,*** regionalism and local color writing reached a zenith. *Huckleberry Finn* was the first novel written entirely in "American"—that is, it was told in the colorful, colloquial, and often ungrammatical voice of its young narrator, Huck. Twain was known for using his gift of humor to make a serious point, and in this novel he used biting satire to tackle the issue of racism in America. Despite Twain's immense popularity with readers worldwide, critics of the time dismissed *Huckleberry Finn,* calling it vulgar and immoral, and libraries banned the book from their shelves as "the veriest trash." Today, many consider it not only Twain's finest work but possibly the best book ever written by an American author. The novel had a huge influence on later writers, among them Ernest Hemingway, who said, "All modern American literature comes from one book by Mark Twain called *Huckleberry Finn.* There was nothing before. There has been nothing as good since."

The Rise of Naturalism

As the 19th century came to a close, several factors led to the rise of a literary movement called **naturalism.** The final decades of the century were a time of rapid change and sharp contrasts—a time when "captains of industry" amassed vast fortunes by exploiting the cheap labor of immigrants and other workers who flooded the cities in search of work. By 1916, the majority of American workers were industrial laborers in factories.

WRITING REFLECTS REALITY The work of naturalist writers, such as Theodore Dreiser, reflected this harsh new reality. In the first pages of his novel *The Financier,* for example, a boy named Frank stares through the window of a fish shop at a lobster and a squid that have been placed together in a tank. Day after day, the two creatures battle it out, the sharp-clawed lobster attacking, the squid fighting for its life. At last, the lobster devours the squid. That's the way of the world, Frank thinks—one creature lives off another. When Frank grows up and becomes a banker, he applies this lesson to the ruthless world of business.

Why do people do the things they do? Are humans capable of choice, or do they act on instinct, like other animals? Is life a losing battle? Looking to the theories of Darwin and other scientists, naturalists such as **Dreiser, Frank Norris, Jack London,** and **Stephen Crane** saw human beings as helpless creatures moved by forces beyond their understanding or control.

Despite this grim attitude, many naturalist writers were quite popular. Some, like Frank Norris, gave a voice to ordinary people and portrayed the rich and influential in an unflattering light, as in his famous 1901 novel *The Octopus,* which attacked the railroad interests in his home state of California. Jack London, on the other hand, captured readers with his tales of an arctic world entirely outside their everyday experience. Riveted by the exotic setting and thrilling action of novels such as *White Fang* and *The Call of the Wild,* readers were willing to accept less-than-happy endings.

A Voice from the Times

A man said to the universe:
"Sir, I exist!"
"However," replied the universe,
"The fact has not created in me
A sense of obligation."

—Stephen Crane

▶ ***For Your Outline***

THE RISE OF NATURALISM

- Naturalism reflected time of rapid changes and sharp contrasts, when wealth was concentrated in few hands.
- Naturalists saw humans as helpless from forces beyond their control.

A New Role for Women

Women writing in this period in the United States tended to be realists. Some were regionalists and others embraced naturalist themes, but all were breaking barriers as women's roles slowly shifted. "The power of a woman is in her refinement, gentleness, and elegance; it is she who makes etiquette, and it is she who preserves the order and decency of society." So said a popular book of etiquette in 1880, voicing a widely held notion about women's place in society.

At the same time, however, the movement to give women the **right to vote** was reemerging after a period of inactivity in the years immediately following the Civil War, when male reformers argued that black and white women should wait until black men gained their rights. Women were growing impatient, not just for the vote, but to have a larger voice in every aspect of public life, from politics to literature.

▶ *For Your Outline*

A NEW ROLE FOR WOMEN

- Women writers tended to be realists, whether working as regionalists or naturalists.
- They broke barriers as women's roles shifted.
- The women's suffrage movement reemerged.
- University education became more available to women.
- Women's writing reflected society's limitations.

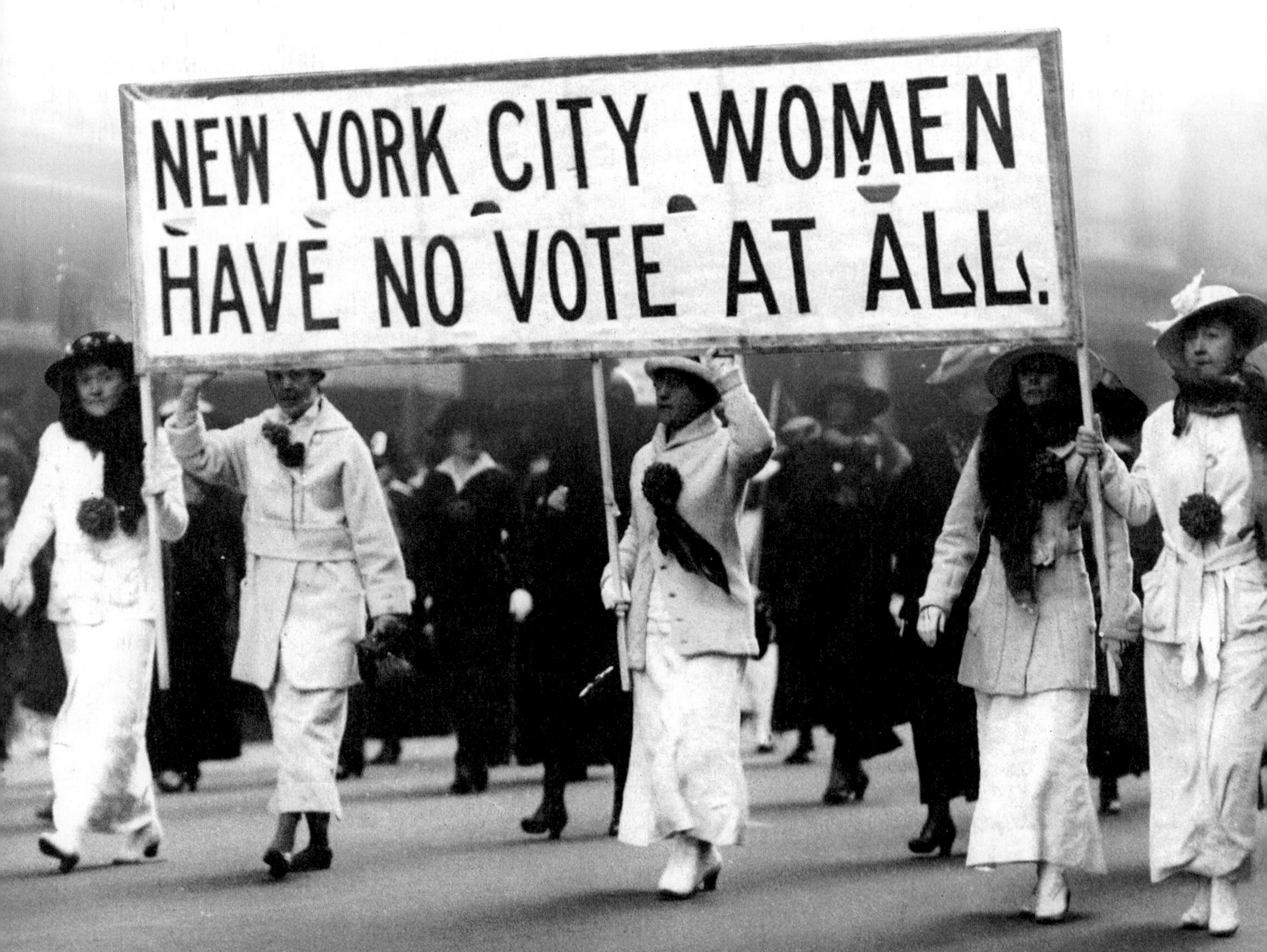

One important factor in the growth of the women's movement was the spread of **university education** among women of the era. Newspapers of the day trumpeted the dangers of this development. An 1896 *New York Journal* headline proclaimed: "Are We Destroying Woman's Beauty? The Startling Warning of a Great English Physician Against Higher Education of Women. How Intellectual Work Destroys Beauty." Despite such dire warnings, women continued to seek education. Then they found that the limited roles assigned them did not make full use of their abilities and knowledge.

BREAKTHROUGH WRITERS Charlotte Perkins Gilman—related on her father's side to a noted family of writers and social reformers that included Harriet Beecher Stowe, the author of *Uncle Tom's Cabin*—became one of the most well-known advocates for women. Fleeing a repressive marriage, **Gilman** moved from the East Coast to California, where she wrote and spoke out on behalf of women's rights and against male domination. One of her most famous stories is "The Yellow Wallpaper," about a woman writer who, as treatment for her "nervous condition," is forbidden to write.

Kate Chopin wrote fiction that articulates the frustrations of generations of women confined to a sort of extended childhood by the men in their lives. Her gentle stories depicting some of the most obvious of women's troubles were extremely popular in the 1890s. Her 1899 novel *The Awakening,* however, stepped over the line in its portrayal of a woman's hidden passion, arousing a public protest so vigorous that Chopin ceased writing completely.

Works by women of this period often end tragically, in madness, ruin, scandal, and death. In part, this was a reflection of their **naturalist** leanings; at the same time, though, it grew out of their own experiences in a culture that did not encourage women's artistic goals. **Edith Wharton,** who in novels such as *The Age of Innocence* and *The House of Mirth* decried the stifling small-mindedness of upper-class society, made her own escape by running off to Paris, only to have her marriage fall apart. Facing overwhelming obstacles, women writers fought with, in the words of New England's local color writer **Mary Wilkins Freeman**, "little female weapons." When the weapon was a pen, the impact could be revolutionary.

As the country moved farther into the 20th century, writers would begin to turn from regionalism and naturalism to the more experimental works that characterize modernism. Thankfully Twain, London, Chopin, and the other writers of their time captured for future generations the unique spirit of late 19th- and early 20th-century America.

THE ARTISTS' GALLERY

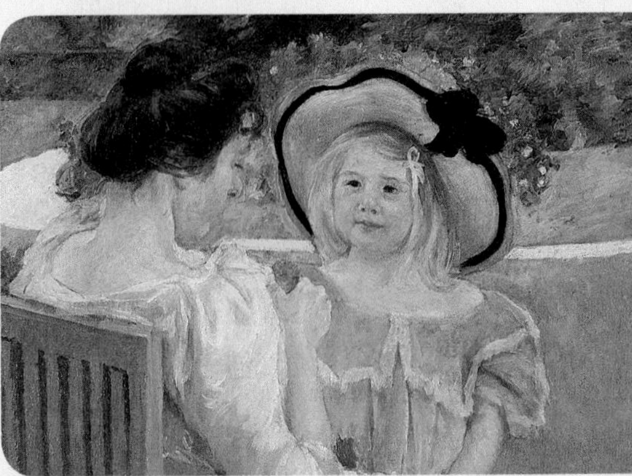

American Impressionism

During this period, the revolutionary style pioneered by French painters such as Claude Monet and Auguste Renoir made its mark in the United States. American artists took the basic goal of **impressionism**—to capture reality as we actually see it in the moment, not as formal rules of art say we should see it—and adapted it to their own situation.

Style and Subject Like their European counterparts, American impressionists focused on the effects of light and color and liked to paint outdoors. Often they painted what a new American leisure class wanted to buy: idyllic landscapes that let them "get away" and portraits of themselves relaxing in their homes or picnicking at the seaside. Paintings like these were not only a pleasure to look at but a status symbol too—proof that the owner (perhaps the son or grandson of a penniless immigrant) had acquired taste and culture.

Progressive Woman One of the few women who exhibited with the impressionists in Paris was an American artist named **Mary Cassatt,** whose work *In the Garden* (1904) is shown here. At a time when no respectable woman traveled alone, lived alone, or pursued a career in art, Cassatt did all three. Known as "a painter of mothers and children," her works reflect a surprisingly modern sensibility. Though her paintings show women in conventional settings, she gives them a new sense of purpose. Cassatt's women do not exist just to be looked at; they are the heroes of their own lives.

Connecting Literature, History, and Culture

Use the timeline and the questions on the next page to gain insight about how developments in the United States during this period reflected those in the world as a whole.

AMERICAN LITERARY MILESTONES

1870

1870 Bret Harte publishes his story collection *The Luck of Roaring Camp and Other Sketches.* ▶

1876 Mark Twain completes *The Adventures of Tom Sawyer* and begins writing *The Adventures of Huckleberry Finn.*

1880

1881 Henry James publishes *The Portrait of a Lady.*

1883 Mark Twain's *Life on the Mississippi* is published. ▶

1885 Libraries across America ban Mark Twain's *The Adventures of Huckleberry Finn,* published the previous year; William Dean Howells publishes *The Rise of Silas Lapham.*

1887 Diary of Chief Seattle is published.

HISTORICAL CONTEXT

1870

1872 Susan B. Anthony is arrested and fined for leading a group of women to test their right to vote. ▶

1876 Alexander Graham Bell patents first telephone; at Battle of Little Bighorn, 1,500 Sioux and Cheyenne warriors defeat and kill about 200 U.S. Army troops, commanded by George A. Custer.

1877 Chief Joseph of the Nez Perce tribe surrenders to U.S. Army; Thomas Edison invents the phonograph.

1880

1880 John D. Rockefeller's Standard Oil Company of Ohio controls U.S. refining; George Eastman patents his rolled camera film.

1883 The first metal-framed skyscraper, ten stories high, is built in Chicago.

1886 The Statue of Liberty, a gift from France to the United States, is dedicated in New York Harbor. ▶

WORLD CULTURE AND EVENTS

1870

1871 Franco-Prussian War ends and Germany is unified; French naturalist writer Émile Zola publishes the first book in his 20-novel series *Les Rougon-Macquart.*

1872 Critics coin the term *impressionism* after viewing Claude Monet's painting *Impression: Sunrise.*

1879 The British defeat the Zulus in South Africa.

1880

1883 The Orient Express makes its first rail run from Paris to Istanbul.

1887 Fictional detective Sherlock Holmes makes his first appearance in *A Study in Scarlet,* by Sir Arthur Conan Doyle. ▶

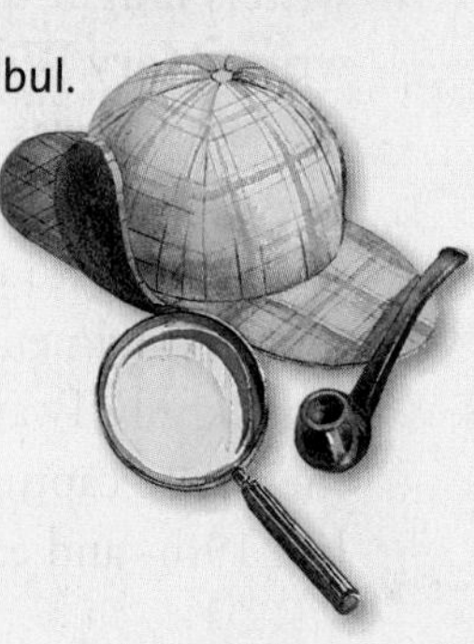

1889 The Eiffel Tower is completed in Paris.

MAKING CONNECTIONS

- Who were some inventors at work in Europe and the United States?
- How did American women fare in gaining the right to vote as compared with New Zealand women?
- What evidence do you see that the United States was becoming an imperial power?
- Name two works of American literature from this period that describe real people or events.

COMMON CORE

RI 7 Integrate and evaluate multiple sources of information presented in different formats as well as in words in order to address a question or solve a problem.

1890

1890 Charlotte Perkins Gilman describes the emotional and intellectual decline of a young wife and mother in "The Yellow Wallpaper."

1893 Stephen Crane publishes *Maggie: A Girl of the Streets;* Paul Laurence Dunbar publishes his first volume of poetry, *Oak and Ivy,* while working as an elevator operator.

1899 Kate Chopin publishes her novel *The Awakening*.

1900

1900 Theodore Dreiser publishes *Sister Carrie*.

1901 Booker T. Washington publishes *Up From Slavery: An Autobiography.*

1903 Jack London publishes *The Call of the Wild;* W. E. B. Du Bois publishes *The Souls of Black Folk.*

1905 Edith Wharton publishes *The House of Mirth.*

1906 Upton Sinclair's *The Jungle* ▶ exposes dangerous conditions in meatpacking factories.

1890

1892 New York's Ellis Island becomes entry point for European immigrants.

1896 Supreme Court upholds "separate but equal" doctrine of Jim Crow laws, widely used to discriminate against African Americans; the Klondike gold rush begins in Alaska and Canada.

1898 The Spanish-American War results in United States gaining control of Guam, Puerto Rico, and the Philippines; U.S. also annexes Hawaii.

1900

1901 William McKinley is assassinated; Theodore Roosevelt becomes president of the United States.

1903 Near Kitty Hawk, North Carolina, Orville and Wilbur Wright make first flight in engine-powered airplane.

1906 Earthquake and fire destroy much of San Francisco.

1908 Ford Motor Company brings out the first Model T automobile.

1890

1893 New Zealand becomes first country to grant women suffrage.

1894 Rudyard Kipling publishes *The Jungle Book.*

1896 Italian physicist Guglielmo Marconi invents first radio; first modern Olympic games are held in Athens.

1897 Edmond Rostand publishes *Cyrano de Bergerac.*

1900

1900 The Boxer Rebellion protests foreign influence in China.

1901 After 64 years as ruler of Great Britain, Queen Victoria dies. ▶

1902 Joseph Conrad publishes *Heart of Darkness.*

1904 James Joyce begins *Dubliners.*

1905 Albert Einstein formulates his theory of relativity.

The Legacy of the Era

The Wild, Wild West

COMMON CORE

W 7 Conduct short research projects to answer a question. **W 10** Write over shorter time frames for a range of tasks and purposes. **SL 2** Integrate multiple sources of information. **SL 4** Present information, findings, and supporting evidence.

It's high noon and two cowboys face off on a deserted street, spurs jingling, fingers twitching. Sound familiar? Although the real Wild West lasted just a few decades, it lives on today in Westerns—a genre of novels, television shows, and movies inspired originally by the stories of Bret Harte and other regionalist writers such as Zane Grey and Owen Wister.

QUICKWRITE What is it about the Wild West that makes it so appealing to Americans? Write a paragraph or two explaining why, in your opinion, the legend lives on.

The Labor Movement

In the post–Civil War period, many laborers, unhappy with the appalling working conditions of their day, began to join unions and strike for better wages and conditions. Business leaders feared the growth of unions and tried to break their power with lockouts, firings, and even violence. Slowly, however, unions increased their membership and their power, eventually changing the way many Americans worked.

ONLINE RESEARCH Today, workers consider 8 hours a full day. Contrast that with the 10 to 12 hours typically worked in the 19th century, and you will see one benefit won by early unions. What issues are today's unions focusing on? Visit the Web site of a modern labor union, and report to the class on its top concerns.

Regionalism Today

Local color writing is still very popular in America. Writers such as Garrison Keillor, Larry McMurtry, and Fannie Flagg capture regions as we know them today, from small-town Minnesota to the great spaces of Texas to sleepy towns of the South.

REPORT Do some research to find out if there are any writers working today who are capturing the flavor of the region in which you live. Report to the class on the writer or writers you discover. What have they written? Is their work well-known? Do they write in dialect, describe landscapes or towns, work in fiction or nonfiction? Explore these and any other questions that arise as you research.

Garrison Keillor

Text Analysis Workshop

Setting in Regional Literature

Many places in the world are fascinating, but some of the most ordinary places can be interesting, too, if you notice what is unique about them. In the last half of the 19th century, regional writers in the United States strove to depict in their stories the unique aspects of a specific place and of its people. These enduring tales give readers a glimpse into the past and inspire a tradition that continues to this day.

COMMON CORE

Included in this workshop: **RL 3** Analyze the impact of the author's choices regarding how to develop and relate elements of a story. **L 1a** Apply the understanding that usage is a matter of convention. **L 3** Apply knowledge of language to make effective choices for meaning or style.

The Growth of Regional Literature

Regional literature arose from an effort to accurately represent the speech, manners, habits, history, folklore, and beliefs of people in specific geographical areas. Although regionalism is considered an offshoot of realism, it has been part of American literature from the beginning. Washington Irving's tales of Dutch New York and Nathaniel Hawthorne's stories of Puritan New England are just two examples. After the Civil War, however, when realism became the dominant literary movement, writers began to focus on the lives of ordinary people and to avoid the supernaturalism and sentimentality found in much of the work of Irving, Hawthorne, and Edgar Allan Poe.

Mark Twain relaxes on a ship's deck.

A factor that contributed to the growth of regional writing was the boom in publishing in the late 1800s. Popular magazines sprang up all over the United States to meet the demand for information about the rest of the country. Mark Twain's "The Notorious Jumping Frog of Calaveras County," for example, was first published in a New York magazine and became an immediate sensation.

The Importance of Setting

The effectiveness of regional writing depends to a large extent on the depiction of **setting,** the time and place in which a story's events occur. Key elements of setting in regional literature include the following:

- geographical location and physical features, such as a river, a camp, a house, or a mode of transportation
- the time in which the events take place—a season of the year or a historical period
- the jobs and daily activities of the characters
- the culture of the characters, including their religious and moral beliefs and the social and economic conditions in which they live

Two means of conveying setting that are commonly found in regional literature are the use of **dialects**—distinctive forms of language spoken in particular areas or by particular groups of people—and **detailed descriptions** of location. Read this example from Twain's "The Notorious Jumping Frog of Calaveras County" (page 684).

"Rev. Leonidas W. H'm, Reverend Le— Well, there was a feller here once by the name of Jim Smiley, in the winter of '49—or maybe it was the spring of '50—I don't recollect exactly, somehow, though what makes me think it was one or the other is because I remember the big flume warn't finished when he first come to the camp. . . ."

—Mark Twain, "The Notorious Jumping Frog of Calaveras County"

The pronunciations indicated by the spellings *feller* and *warn't*, the expression "I don't recollect," and the use of *come* rather than *came* all contribute to the regional flavor of the piece. Although this dialect is not standard English, its conventions are established by its speakers.

Now look at this description from Willa Cather's "A Wagner Matinee" (page 718), in which the narrator recalls the Nebraska farm where he grew up. Notice the harshness and the lack of color in the setting described; both the landscape and the evidence of human habitation are black, pitted, and bare.

I saw again the tall, naked house on the prairie, black and grim as a wooden fortress; the black pond where I had learned to swim, its margin pitted with sun-dried cattle tracks; the rain gullied clay banks about the naked house, the four dwarf ash seedlings where the dish-cloths were always hung to dry before the kitchen door.

—Willa Cather, "A Wagner Matinee"

In regional literature, setting, characters, and plot are usually inseparable. As you read regional writing, notice the relationship between the characters and the setting. Ask yourself how the characters react to the setting. Then decide how this relationship is significant to the story's plot.

LOCAL COLOR REALISM

Prospectors pan for gold during the gold rush, 1889.

In 1868, a popular story about the California gold rush—Bret Harte's "The Luck of Roaring Camp"—launched a specific form of regional writing called **local color writing.** Mark Twain, with his memorable characters, was a master of this form. Other local color realists of the time include Joel Chandler Harris in the South and Sarah Orne Jewett and Mary Wilkins Freeman in New England. Later regional writers, such as Willa Cather, William Faulkner, and Flannery O'Connor, developed sophisticated ways of making universal statements about the human condition while focusing on the local and the particular.

Close Read

What feeling about life on the frontier do you get from the description? How could you rewrite the passage to change that feeling?

COMMON CORE

RI 1 Cite evidence to support inferences drawn from the text. **RI 6** Determine an author's point of view or purpose in a text in which the rhetoric is effective. **SL 1** Participate effectively in collaborative discussions, building on others' ideas and expressing their own. **L 5a** Interpret figures of speech in context and analyze their role in the text.

from The Autobiography of Mark Twain

by Mark Twain

HISTORY Video link at thinkcentral.com

VIDEO TRAILER THINK central KEYWORD: HML11-658A

Meet the Author

Mark Twain 1835–1910

Readers of all ages have followed the youthful adventures of Huck Finn and Tom Sawyer for more than 100 years. Many have also enjoyed the witty and sharp social commentary in Mark Twain's lectures and journalism. A man who found humor in a life filled with tragedy, Mark Twain remains one of America's greatest literary voices.

Life on the River Samuel Langhorne Clemens—as Twain was named at birth—grew up in the Mississippi River town of Hannibal, Missouri. The river and the town shaped young Clemens's early years. After his father's death, he began working at an early age to help support his family. Work for a printer and a newspaper began a lifelong connection to journalism and led to his first published writing—a humorous sketch. Planning to write travel sketches, Clemens signed on with a river pilot. He spent four years on the river, where he met many different kinds of people. After the Civil War, river travel was largely replaced by railroad travel, but Clemens remembered the river's lessons as he took the pen name by which his readers came to know him.

On the Move Twain kept traveling, first to the American West, where he panned for gold. He gained literary recognition with his tall tale "The Notorious Jumping Frog of Calaveras County," set in California. Twain also traveled the world, sharing his experiences in sketches, letters, and lectures. Travel writings such as *The Innocents Abroad* artfully combined wit and serious information and were vastly popular.

Twain's Great Legacy After his 1870 marriage, Twain based his growing family in Hartford, Connecticut, where he produced his most lasting works, *The Adventures of Tom Sawyer* and *The Adventures of Huckleberry Finn.* These books secured Twain's place as a great American novelist.

Tragedy Haunts the Later Years Despite literary success, Twain found himself in debt from unsuccessful business ventures. Facing bankruptcy in 1893, he traveled once again, delivering humorous lectures amidst the great personal sorrow of two daughters' deaths and his wife's fading health. Twain's last works reflect the sorrow and anger of this period, which lasted until his death.

Author Online THINK central

Go to thinkcentral.com. KEYWORD: HML11-658B

DID YOU KNOW?

Mark Twain . . .

- used multiple pen names, including S. L. C., Josh, and Thomas Jefferson Snodgrass.
- served briefly in the Confederate Army.
- took his name from a nautical term for water depth meaning "two fathoms deep."

TEXT ANALYSIS: IRONY AND OVERSTATEMENT

In Mark Twain's true-life adventure stories, Twain often used life's absurdities to evoke emotions and influence readers. To help create meaning and generate humor, Twain used the following literary techniques:

- **situational irony**—a contrast between what is expected and what actually happens
- **dramatic irony**—when readers know more about a situation or character than the characters do
- **verbal irony**—a contrast between what is stated and what is meant
- **overstatement**—an exaggeration for emphasis or for humorous effect (also called *hyperbole*)

Watch for examples of irony and overstatement as you read.

READING STRATEGY: PREDICT

When you **predict,** you use text clues to make a reasonable guess about what will happen in a story. Sometimes a story will surprise you with a plot twist; sometimes your predictions will hit the mark. Either way, watching for text clues can help you find the situational irony in Twain's story. As you read, use a chart like the one shown to record your predictions and the clues from the text that led you to make your educated guess.

Predictions	*Text Clues*
I predict he'll find a way to get involved.	*Narrator says he can't resist the temptation to be a subject.*

VOCABULARY IN CONTEXT

Match each vocabulary word in the first column with the word in the second column that is closest in meaning.

1. unassailable	**a.** trust
2. multifariously	**b.** peeved
3. minutest	**c.** spellbound
4. implacable	**d.** overtrusting
5. credulity	**e.** tiniest
6. rapt	**f.** unquestionable
7. nettled	**g.** unyielding
8. gullible	**h.** variously

Complete the activities in your **Reader/Writer Notebook**.

Have you ever put on an ACT?

Occasionally we are tempted to try to fool others into thinking we are smarter, cooler, richer, or more popular than we really are. Sometimes it's as simple as putting on a new pair of sunglasses or pretending to know more about something than we really do. In his autobiography, Mark Twain recalls from his youth a more extreme version of this kind of deception.

DISCUSS With your classmates, come up with a list of ways in which people pretend to be something they're not. Examples can range from simple social posing to more outrageous, even criminal, forms of falsified identity. Then review these examples, considering people's motives for such deception.

The Autobiography of Mark Twain

Mark Twain

BACKGROUND This excerpt from Mark Twain's autobiography focuses on a traveling show that visited Twain's small town around 1850. These entertainment shows were popular in a time before radio, television, or computers. They featured magic acts, ventriloquists, and mesmerizers (or hypnotists). Hypnotists placed people in suggestible, trancelike states and then ordered them to perform various antics.

An exciting event in our village was the arrival of the mesmerizer.[1] I think the year was 1850. As to that I am not sure but I know the month—it was May; that detail has survived the wear of fifty years. A pair of connected little incidents of that month have served to keep the memory of it green for me all this time; incidents of no consequence and not worth embalming,[2] yet my memory has preserved them carefully and flung away things of real value to give them space and make them comfortable. The truth is, a person's memory has no more sense than his conscience and no appreciation whatever of values and proportions. However, never mind those trifling incidents; my subject is the mesmerizer now. **A**

He advertised his show and promised marvels. Admission as usual: 25 cents, children half price. The village had heard of mesmerism in a general way but had not encountered it yet. Not many people attended the first night but next day they had so many wonders to tell that everybody's curiosity was fired and after

Analyze Visuals ▶
Look at the poster on page 661, especially at the image in the top circle. What can you **infer** about the mesmerizer depicted?

A PREDICT
Based on the clues presented in this first paragraph, what can you predict about what might happen in the story?

1. **mesmerizer:** hypnotist; from the name of an Austrian physician, Franz Anton Mesmer, who popularized hypnotism in the 1770s.
2. **embalming:** preserving.

THE MESMERIZER

that for a fortnight[3] the magician had prosperous times. I was fourteen or fifteen years old, the age at which a boy is willing to endure all things, suffer all things short of death by fire, if thereby he may be conspicuous and show off before the public; and so, when I saw the "subjects" perform their foolish antics on the platform and make the people laugh and shout and admire I had a burning desire to be a subject myself. (B)

Every night for three nights I sat in the row of candidates on the platform and held the magic disk[4] in the palm of my hand and gazed at it and tried to get sleepy, but it was a failure; I remained wide awake and had to retire defeated, like the majority. Also, I had to sit there and be gnawed with envy of Hicks, our journeyman;[5] I had to sit there and see him scamper and jump when Simmons the enchanter exclaimed, "See the snake! See the snake!" and hear him say, "My, how beautiful!" in response to the suggestion that he was observing a splendid sunset; and so on—the whole insane business. I couldn't laugh, I couldn't applaud; it filled me with bitterness to have others do it and to have people make a hero of Hicks and crowd around him when the show was over and ask him for more and more particulars of the wonders he had seen in his visions and manifest in many ways that they were proud to be acquainted with him. Hicks—the idea! I couldn't stand it; I was getting boiled to death in my own bile.

On the fourth night temptation came and I was not strong enough to resist. When I had gazed at the disk a while I pretended to be sleepy and began to nod. Straightway came the professor and made passes over my head and down my body and legs and arms, finishing each pass with a snap of his fingers in the air to discharge the surplus electricity;[6] then he began to "draw" me with the disk, holding it in his fingers and telling me I could not take my eyes off it, try as I might; so I rose slowly, bent and gazing, and followed that disk all over the place, just as I had seen the others do. Then I was put through the other paces. Upon suggestion I fled from snakes, passed buckets at a fire, became excited over hot steamboat-races, made love to imaginary girls and kissed them, fished from the platform and landed mud cats that outweighed me—and so on, all the customary marvels. But not in the customary way. I was cautious at first and watchful, being afraid the professor would discover that I was an impostor and drive me from the platform in disgrace; but as soon as I realized that I was not in danger, I set myself the task of terminating Hicks's usefulness as a subject and of usurping his place.

It was a sufficiently easy task. Hicks was born honest, I without that incumbrance[7]—so some people said. Hicks saw what he saw and reported accordingly, I saw more than was visible and added to it such details as could help. Hicks had no imagination; I had a double supply. He was born calm, I was

COMMON CORE L 5a

(B) OVERSTATEMENT
Remember that **overstatement**, or hyperbole, is an exaggeration used to emphasize a point or create humor. Reread lines 14–19, looking for instances of Twain's use of this rhetorical technique. Why do you think Twain uses overstatement here? How might his use of overstatement in a work of nonfiction affect readers?

Language Coach

Etymology *Usurping* (line 47) means "taking control by force." *Usurp* comes from the Latin word *usurpare*, meaning "to seize for use." Read lines 44–47. Why does Twain want to usurp Hicks's place? Explain your answer, using the word *usurp*.

---

3. **fortnight:** 14 days.
4. **magic disk:** the object used by the mesmerizer to focus a subject's attention, helping him or her to achieve a hypnotic state.
5. **journeyman:** a competent and experienced, but not brilliant, craftsman.
6. **discharge . . . electricity:** It was once erroneously believed that hypnosis was linked to electricity and magnetism.
7. **incumbrance:** earlier spelling of *encumbrance*, here meaning "burden; obligation."

born excited. No vision could start a rapture in him and he was constipated as to language, anyway; but if I saw a vision I emptied the dictionary onto it and lost the remnant of my mind into the bargain.

At the end of my first half-hour Hicks was a thing of the past, a fallen hero, a broken idol, and I knew it and was glad and said in my heart, "Success to crime!" Hicks could never have been mesmerized to the point where he could kiss an imaginary girl in public or a real one either, but I was competent. Whatever Hicks had failed in, I made it a point to succeed in, let the cost be what it might, physically or morally. He had shown several bad defects and I had made a note of them. For instance, if the magician asked, "What do you see?" and left him to invent a vision for himself, Hicks was dumb and blind, he couldn't see a thing nor say a word, whereas the magician soon found out that when it came to seeing visions of a stunning and marketable sort I could get along better without his help than with it.

COMMON CORE L 5a

Language Coach

Metaphors A **metaphor** is a figure of speech that compares two things that have something in common. In lines 55–56, Twain directly compares Hicks to a fallen hero and a broken idol. What does Twain mean by this comparison?

Then there was another thing: Hicks wasn't worth a tallow dip[8] on mute mental suggestion. Whenever Simmons stood behind him and gazed at the back of his skull and tried to drive a mental suggestion into it, Hicks sat with vacant face and never suspected. If he had been noticing he could have seen by the **rapt** faces of the audience that something was going on behind his back that required a response. Inasmuch as I was an impostor I dreaded to have this test put upon me, for I knew the professor would be "willing" me to do something, and as

rapt (răpt) *adj.* deeply moved, delighted, or absorbed

8. **wasn't worth a tallow dip:** wasn't any good. A tallow dip was an inexpensive candle.

I couldn't know what it was, I should be exposed and denounced. However, when my time came, I took my chance. I perceived by the tense and expectant faces of the people that Simmons was behind me willing me with all his might. I tried my best to imagine what he wanted but nothing suggested itself. I felt ashamed and miserable then. I believed that the hour of my disgrace was come and that in another moment I should go out of that place disgraced. I ought to be ashamed to confess it but my next thought was not how I could win the compassion of kindly hearts by going out humbly and in sorrow for my misdoings, but how I could go out most sensationally and spectacularly. **C**

C PREDICT
Reread lines 66–81. How do you predict Twain will respond to the challenge of "mute mental suggestion" from Simmons?

There was a rusty and empty old revolver lying on the table among the "properties" employed in the performances. On May Day two or three weeks before there had been a celebration by the schools and I had had a quarrel with a big boy who was the school bully and I had not come out of it with credit.[9] That boy was now seated in the middle of the house, halfway down the main aisle. I crept stealthily and impressively toward the table, with a dark and murderous scowl on my face, copied from a popular romance, seized the revolver suddenly, flourished it, shouted the bully's name, jumped off the platform and made a rush for him and chased him out of the house before the paralyzed people could interfere to save him. There was a storm of applause, and the magician, addressing the house, said, most impressively—

"That you may know how really remarkable this is and how wonderfully developed a subject we have in this boy, I assure you that without a single spoken word to guide him he has carried out what I mentally commanded him to do, to the **minutest** detail. I could have stopped him at a moment in his vengeful career by a mere exertion of my will, therefore the poor fellow who has escaped was at no time in danger."

minutest (mī-no͞o′tĭst) *adj.* smallest; most precise

So I was not in disgrace. I returned to the platform a hero and happier than I have ever been in this world since. As regards mental suggestion, my fears of it were gone. I judged that in case I failed to guess what the professor might be willing me to do, I could count on putting up something that would answer just as well. I was right, and exhibitions of unspoken suggestion became a favorite with the public. Whenever I perceived that I was being willed to do something I got up and did something—anything that occurred to me—and the magician, not being a fool, always ratified it. When people asked me, "How *can* you tell what he is willing you to do?" I said, "It's just as easy," and they always said admiringly, "Well, it beats *me* how you can do it."

Hicks was weak in another detail. When the professor made passes over him and said "his whole body is without sensation now—come forward and test him, ladies and gentlemen," the ladies and gentlemen always complied eagerly and stuck pins into Hicks, and if they went deep Hicks was sure to wince, then that poor professor would have to explain that Hicks "wasn't sufficiently under the influence." But I didn't wince; I only suffered and shed tears on the inside. The miseries that a conceited boy will endure to keep up his "reputation"! And so

9. **credit:** honor or distinction.

will a conceited man; I know it in my own person and have seen it in a hundred thousand others. That professor ought to have protected me and I often hoped he would, when the tests were unusually severe, but he didn't. It may be that he was deceived as well as the others, though I did not believe it nor think it possible. Those were dear good people but they must have carried simplicity and **credulity** to the limit. They would stick a pin in my arm and bear on it until they drove it a third of its length in, and then be lost in wonder that by a mere exercise of will power the professor could turn my arm to iron and make it insensible to pain. Whereas it was not insensible at all; I was suffering agonies of pain.

credulity (krĭ-do͞o'lĭ-tē) *n.* an inclination to believe too readily

After that fourth night, that proud night, that triumphant night, I was the only subject. Simmons invited no more candidates to the platform. I performed alone every night the rest of the fortnight. Up to that time a dozen wise old heads, the intellectual aristocracy of the town, had held out as **implacable** unbelievers. I was as hurt by this as if I were engaged in some honest occupation. There is nothing surprising about this. Human beings feel dishonor the most, sometimes, when they most deserve it. That handful of overwise old gentlemen kept on shaking their heads all the first week and saying they had seen no marvels there that could not have been produced by collusion; and they were pretty vain of their unbelief too and liked to show it and air it and be superior to the ignorant and the **gullible.** Particularly old Dr. Peake, who was the ringleader of the irreconcilables and very formidable; for he was an F.F.V.,[10] he was learned, white-haired and venerable, nobly and richly clad in the fashions of an earlier and a courtlier day, he was large and stately, and he not only seemed wise but was what he seemed in that regard. He had great influence and his opinion upon any matter was worth much more than that of any other person in the community. When I conquered him at last, I knew I was undisputed master of the field; and now after more than fifty years I acknowledge with a few dry old tears that I rejoiced without shame. **D**

implacable (ĭm-plăk'ə-bəl) *adj.* impossible to satisfy

gullible (gŭl'ə-bəl) *adj.* easily deceived or tricked

D IRONY
Reread lines 125–142. Identify the **situational irony** in Twain's reaction to the skeptical wise old men in the crowd. What does this suggest about him?

In 1847 we were living in a large white house on the corner of Hill and Main Streets—a house that still stands but isn't large now although it hasn't lost a plank; I saw it a year ago and noticed that shrinkage. My father died in it in March of the year mentioned but our family did not move out of it until some months afterward. Ours was not the only family in the house; there was another, Dr. Grant's. One day Dr. Grant and Dr. Reyburn argued a matter on the street with sword canes and Grant was brought home **multifariously** punctured. Old Dr. Peake caulked the leaks and came every day for a while to look after him.

multifariously (mŭl'tə-fâr'ē-əs-lē) *adv.* in many and various ways

The Grants were Virginians, like Peake, and one day when Grant was getting well enough to be on his feet and sit around in the parlor and talk, the conversation fell upon Virginia and old times. I was present but the group were probably unconscious of me, I being only a lad and a negligible quantity. Two of

10. **F.F.V.:** First Family of Virginia. Dr. Peake has high social status because his ancestors were among the first settlers of Virginia.

the group—Dr. Peake and Mrs. Crawford, Mrs. Grant's mother—had been of the audience when the Richmond theater burned down thirty-six years before, and they talked over the frightful details of that memorable tragedy. These were eyewitnesses, and with their eyes I saw it all with an intolerable vividness: I saw the black smoke rolling and tumbling toward the sky, I saw the flames burst through it and turn red, I heard the shrieks of the despairing, I glimpsed their faces at the windows, caught fitfully through the veiling smoke, I saw them jump to their death or to mutilation worse than death. The picture is before me yet and can never fade.

In due course they talked of the colonial mansion of the Peakes, with its stately columns and its spacious grounds, and by odds and ends I picked up a clearly defined idea of the place. I was strongly interested, for I had not before heard of such palatial things from the lips of people who had seen them with their own eyes. One detail, casually dropped, hit my imagination hard. In the wall by the great front door there was a round hole as big as a saucer—a British cannon ball had made it in the war of the Revolution. It was breathtaking; it made history real; history had never been real to me before.

Very well, three or four years later, as already mentioned, I was king bee and sole "subject" in the mesmeric show; it was the beginning of the second week; the performance was half over; just then the majestic Dr. Peake with his ruffled bosom and wrist-bands and his gold-headed cane entered, and a deferential citizen vacated his seat beside the Grants and made the great chief take it. This happened while I was trying to invent something fresh in the way of vision, in response to the professor's remark—

"Concentrate your powers. Look—look attentively. There—don't you see something? Concentrate—concentrate! Now then—describe it." **E**

Without suspecting it, Dr. Peake, by entering the place, had reminded me of the talk of three years before. He had also furnished me capital and was become my confederate, an accomplice in my frauds. I began on a vision, a vague and dim one (that was part of the game at the beginning of a vision; it isn't best to see it too clearly at first, it might look as if you had come loaded with it). The vision developed by degrees and gathered swing, momentum, energy. It was the Richmond fire. Dr. Peake was cold at first and his fine face had a trace of polite scorn in it; but when he began to recognize that fire, that expression changed and his eyes began to light up. As soon as I saw that, I threw the valves wide open and turned on all the steam and gave those people a supper of fire and horrors that was calculated to last them one while! They couldn't gasp when I got through—they were petrified. Dr. Peake had risen and was standing—and breathing hard. He said, in a great voice:

"My doubts are ended. No collusion could produce that miracle. It was totally impossible for him to know those details, yet he has described them with the clarity of an eyewitness —and with what **unassailable** truthfulness God knows I know!" **F**

I saved the colonial mansion for the last night and solidified and perpetuated

Language Coach

Word Definitions *Eyewitnesses* (line 158) means "people who have seen something personally and can report on it." What had Dr. Peake and Mrs. Crawford personally seen? Answer the question using the phrases *give eyewitness accounts of* or *eyewitnesses to.*

E PREDICT
Predict how Twain will win over the wise old men of the town.

unassailable (ŭn′ə-sā′lə-bəl) *adj.* impossible to dispute or disprove

F IRONY
What do you know that Dr. Peake doesn't? Explain how this **dramatic irony** affects your impression of the characters involved, including young Twain.

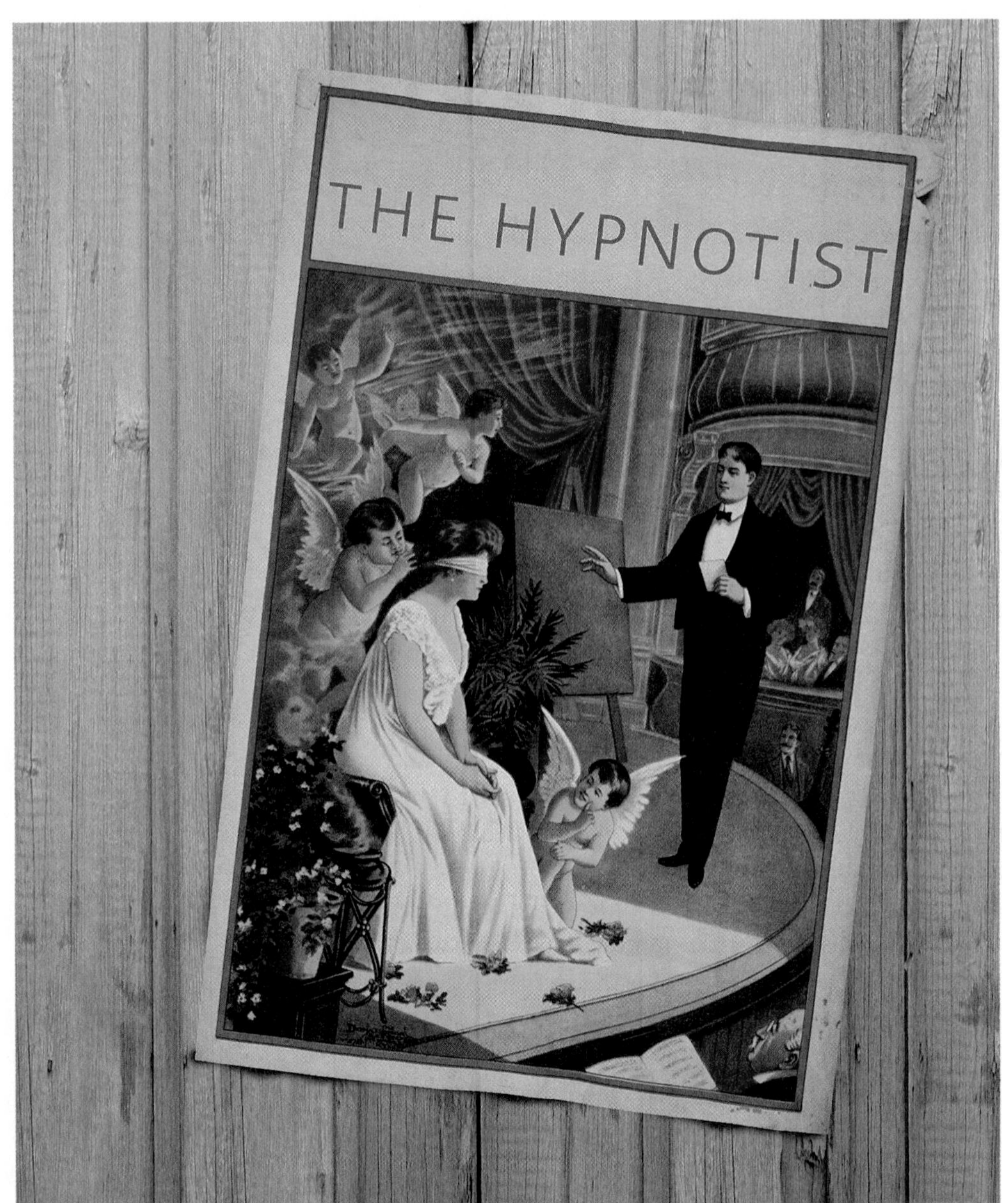

Dr. Peake's conversion with the cannon-ball hole. He explained to the house that I could never have heard of that small detail, which differentiated this mansion from all other Virginian mansions and perfectly identified it, therefore the fact stood proven that I had *seen* it in my vision. Lawks![11]

It is curious. When the magician's engagement closed there was but one person in the village who did not believe in mesmerism and I was the one. All the others were converted but I was to remain an implacable and unpersuadable disbeliever in mesmerism and hypnotism for close upon fifty years. This was because I never would examine them, in after life. I couldn't. The subject revolted me. Perhaps it brought back to me a passage in my life which for pride's sake I wished to forget;

11. **Lawks!:** an expression of wonder or amusement, shortened from "Lord, have mercy!"

though I thought, or persuaded myself I thought, I should never come across a "proof" which wasn't thin and cheap and probably had a fraud like me behind it.

The truth is I did not have to wait long to get tired of my triumphs. Not thirty days, I think. The glory which is built upon a lie soon becomes a most unpleasant incumbrance. No doubt for a while I enjoyed having my exploits told and retold and told again in my presence and wondered over and exclaimed about, but I quite distinctly remember that there presently came a time when the subject was wearisome and odious to me and I could not endure the disgusting discomfort of it. I am well aware that the world-glorified doer of a deed of great and real splendor has just my experience; I know that he deliciously enjoys hearing about it for three or four weeks and that pretty soon after that he begins to dread the mention of it and by and by wishes he had been with the damned before he ever thought of doing that deed. I remember how General Sherman[12] used to rage and swear over "While we were marching through Georgia," which was played at him and sung at him everywhere he went; still, I think I suffered a shade more than the legitimate hero does, he being privileged to soften his misery with the reflection that his glory was at any rate golden and reproachless in its origin, whereas I had no such privilege, there being no possible way to make mine respectable.

How easy it is to make people believe a lie and how hard it is to undo that work again! Thirty-five years after those evil exploits of mine I visited my old mother, whom I had not seen for ten years; and being moved by what seemed to me a rather noble and perhaps heroic impulse, I thought I would humble myself and confess my ancient fault. It cost me a great effort to make up my mind; I dreaded the sorrow that would rise in her face and the shame that would look out of her eyes; but after long and troubled reflection, the sacrifice seemed due and right and I gathered my resolution together and made the confession. **G**

G PREDICT
Reread lines 227–234. How do you think Twain's mother will respond to his confession? Explain why you think this.

To my astonishment there were no sentimentalities, no dramatics, no George Washington effects; she was not moved in the least degree; she simply did not believe me and said so! I was not merely disappointed, I was **nettled** to have my costly truthfulness flung out of the market in this placid and confident way when I was expecting to get a profit out of it. I asserted and reasserted, with rising heat, my statement that every single thing I had done on those long-vanished nights was a lie and a swindle; and when she shook her head tranquilly and said she knew better, I put up my hand and *swore* to it—adding a triumphant, "*Now* what do you say?"

nettled (nĕt'əld) *adj.* irritated; annoyed **nettle** *v.*

It did not affect her at all; it did not budge her the fraction of an inch from her position. If this was hard for me to endure, it did not begin with the blister she put upon the raw[13] when she began to put my sworn oath out of court with *arguments* to prove that I was under a delusion and did not know what I was talking about. Arguments! Arguments to show that a person on a man's outside can know better what is on his inside than he does himself. I had cherished some

12. **General Sherman:** William Tecumseh Sherman, Union commander who led a destructive march in 1864 from Atlanta, Georgia, to the Atlantic, cutting the Confederacy in two.

13. **the blister . . . raw:** a bad thing made even worse.

contempt for arguments before, I have not enlarged my respect for them since. She refused to believe that I had invented my visions myself; she said it was folly: that I was only a child at the time and could not have done it. She cited the Richmond fire and the colonial mansion and said they were quite beyond my capacities. Then I saw my chance! I said she was right—I didn't invent those, I got them from Dr. Peake. Even this great shot did not damage. She said Dr. Peake's evidence was better than mine, and he had said in plain words that it was impossible for me to have heard about those things. Dear, dear, what a grotesque and unthinkable situation: a confessed swindler convicted of honesty and condemned to acquittal by circumstantial evidence furnished by the swindled! (H)

I realized with shame and with impotent vexation that I was defeated all along the line. I had but one card left but it was a formidable one. I played it and stood from under. It seemed ignoble to demolish her fortress after she had defended it so valiantly but the defeated know not mercy. I played that master card. It was the pin-sticking. I said solemnly—

"I give you my honor, a pin was never stuck into me without causing me cruel pain."

She only said—

"It is thirty-five years. I believe you do think that now but I was there and I know better. You never winced."

She was so calm! and I was so far from it, so nearly frantic.

"Oh, my goodness!" I said, "let me *show* you that I am speaking the truth. Here is my arm; drive a pin into it—drive it to the head—I shall not wince."

She only shook her gray head and said with simplicity and conviction—

"You are a man now and could dissemble the hurt; but you were only a child then and could not have done it."

And so the lie which I played upon her in my youth remained with her as an unchallengeable truth to the day of her death. Carlyle[14] said "a lie cannot live." It shows that he did not know how to tell them. If I had taken out a life policy on this one the premiums would have bankrupted me ages ago. ∾

(H) **IRONY**
Reread lines 244–259. Identify the **situational irony** that underlies Twain's confession to his mother. What statement is Twain making about honesty and deception?

14. **Carlyle:** Thomas Carlyle, a British historian and essayist.

Connect: Epigrams

A popular writer and a sought-after public speaker, Mark Twain was full of witty remarks. What do these **epigrams—**short, clever, and sometimes paradoxical statements—reveal about Twain's view of human nature?

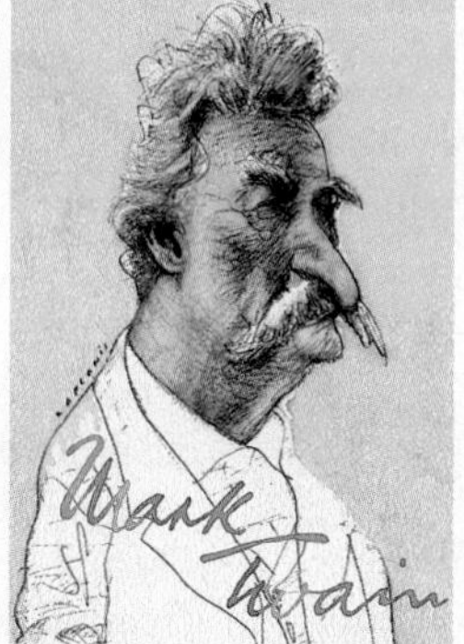

Epigrams

Mark Twain

Don't, like the cat, try to get more out of an experience than there is in it. The cat, having sat upon a hot stove lid, will not sit upon a hot stove lid again. Nor upon a cold stove lid.

....

It is by the goodness of God that in our country we have those three unspeakably precious things: freedom of speech, freedom of conscience, and the prudence never to practice either of them.

....

Man is the only animal that blushes. Or needs to.

....

I am an old man and have known a great many troubles, but most of them have never happened.

....

Nothing so needs reforming as other people's habits.

....

When I was a boy of fourteen, my father was so ignorant I could hardly stand to have the old man around. But when I got to be twenty-one, I was astonished at how much the old man had learned in seven years.

....

Put all your eggs in one basket, and—watch the basket.

There are several good protections against temptations, but the surest is cowardice.

....

If you pick up a starving dog and make him prosperous, he will not bite you. This is the principal difference between a dog and a man.

....

Good breeding consists in concealing how much we think of ourselves and how little we think of the other person.

....

To promise not to do a thing is the surest way in the world to make a body want to go and do that very thing.

....

Habit is habit, and not to be flung out of the window by any man, but coaxed downstairs a step at a time.

....

One of the most striking differences between a cat and a lie is that a cat only has nine lives.

....

Each person is born to one possession which outvalues all the others—his last breath.

....

Everyone is a moon, and has a dark side which he never shows to anybody.

Comprehension

1. **Recall** What position or role does young Twain want to have? Why?
2. **Summarize** What weaknesses made Hicks a bad subject?
3. **Clarify** What does Twain do to get the mesmerizer to choose him?

COMMON CORE

RI 1 Cite evidence to support inferences drawn from the text. **RI 6** Determine an author's point of view or purpose in a text in which the rhetoric is effective.

Text Analysis

4. **Examine Predictions** Review your list of predictions and clues. Were you able to correctly predict everything that happened? Or were you surprised by how some aspects of the story developed? Cite details from the story in your answer.
5. **Contrast Characters** To become the mesmerizer's subject, Twain must displace Hicks. Twain presents himself as very different from Hicks. Based on this contrast, what does Twain seem to value and admire in a person? Use a chart like the one shown to collect evidence.

Hicks	Twain

6. **Analyze Irony** By its very nature, irony presents a degree of tension wherever it appears—the tension between expectations and reality. In many cases, it also adds humor. Review Twain's use of irony in the following passages. What's funny about them?
   - "Hicks was born honest, I without that incumbrance [burden]—so some people said." (lines 48–49)
   - Young Twain is genuinely hurt by those who do not believe his performances. (lines 127–129)
   - Twain identifies with great heroes who tire of hearing their praises sung. (lines 213–223)
7. **Draw Conclusions About Changing Perspective** In writing this piece, the adult Twain had a different view of himself, his boyhood deception, and the people of his hometown than he had as a young boy. What does this dual perspective show you about his growth from boyhood to adulthood?

Text Criticism

8. **Author's Perspective** Reread Twain's epigrams on page 670. What view of human nature do they reflect? Explain how this view is played out in the *Autobiography,* giving evidence from both texts to support your answer.

Have you ever put on an **ACT?**

Mark Twain indicates in his autobiography that as a young person, he was not very honest. Based on Twain's views later in life and those expressed in his epigrams, what effect do you think deception had on Twain?

Vocabulary in Context

▲ VOCABULARY PRACTICE

Decide whether these statements about the vocabulary words are true or false.

1. Someone with many career changes can be said to have worked **multifariously.**
2. Believing everything a fortuneteller tells you is an example of **credulity.**
3. A person who pays **rapt** attention to a performance is probably bored with it.
4. You might feel **nettled** if it rains on your picnic.
5. If you are **gullible,** you have an enormous appetite for sweet foods.
6. A defendant with an **unassailable** alibi should feel confident testifying in court.
7. If you record the **minutest** facts about an event, you are noting only how long it took.
8. A person with **implacable** demands is not likely to be easily satisfied.

WORD LIST

credulity
gullible
implacable
minutest
multifariously
nettled
rapt
unassailable

ACADEMIC VOCABULARY IN SPEAKING

• apparent • confine • expose • focus • perceive

Mark Twain used his autobiography to **expose** some of the humorous and interesting things that happened in his life. In a small group, discuss some of the pros and cons of using an autobiographical format to tell a story. Use at least two of the Academic Vocabulary words in your discussion.

VOCABULARY STRATEGY: DIFFERENCES IN WORD MEANINGS

Homographs are words that are spelled the same but differ in meaning, derivation, or pronunciation. Sometimes these words have totally different meanings, and sometimes the shifts in meaning are more nuanced, or subtle. An example of a word with totally different meanings is *minute* (mī-no͞ot'), meaning "small," and *minute* (mĭn'ĭt), meaning "60 seconds." An example of a word with a slight, or subtle, shift in meaning is *relative*, which may mean "kinship or relationship by blood" or may mean "relevant or pertinent." To determine the meaning of such a word, analyze the context of the sentence or paragraph and check the meanings in a dictionary.

COMMON CORE

L 4d Verify the preliminary determination of the meaning of a word or phrase. **L 6** Acquire and use accurately general academic words.

PRACTICE Write the definition of each boldfaced word in the sentence below. After each definition, write a new sentence using a different meaning of the word. If the pronunciation is different, write P.

a. Take the household **refuse** to the dump.
b. The band has a new upright **bass** player.
c. They found the tusk of a **mammoth** in our state.
d. The wind from the storm began to **buffet** the boat.
e. The scientist proposed a theoretical **construct.**

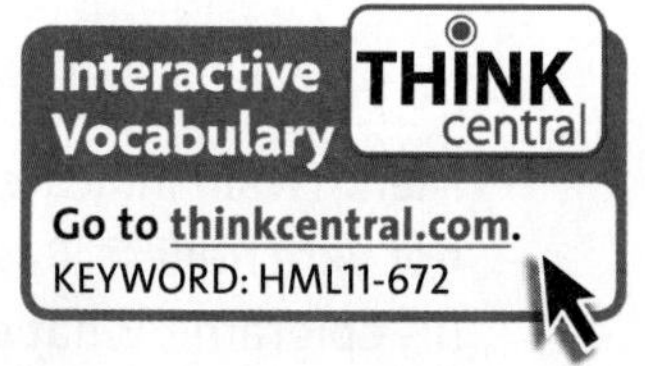

from Life on the Mississippi

Memoir by Mark Twain

COMMON CORE

RI 6, L 1b, L 3, L 5a–b

TEXT ANALYSIS: VOICE

Voice is a writer's unique use of language. It allows a reader to "hear" the writer's personality in his or her writing. Mark Twain's distinctive voice is full of dry wit.

Here was something fresh—this thing of getting up in the middle of the night. . . . It was a detail . . . that had never occurred to me at all. I knew that boats ran all night, but somehow I had never happened to reflect that somebody had to get up out of a warm bed to run them.

A writer's voice is established through **diction**, or word choice and order, and **tone**, or attitude toward the subject. As you read, look for Twain's ironic or humorous tone.

READING STRATEGY: PARAPHRASE

Twain often uses deadpan humor. However, it can take some digging to figure out just what he's saying. **Paraphrasing** can help; if you slow down and restate hard sentences in simpler language, you'll find it easier to follow them. By recognizing his use of **understatement** (downplaying the importance of things) or his use of **overstatement** (exaggeration, or hyperbole) and other figures of speech, you can paraphrase better.

Within ten seconds more I was set aside in disgrace, and Mr. Bixby was . . . flaying me alive with abuse of my cowardice.

With a dictionary, you can paraphrase this sentence.

1. **Paraphrase it literally:** "I was promptly disgraced, and Mr. Bixby was skinning me alive and calling me a coward."
2. **Notice where Twain is stretching the truth:** Bixby is not really skinning him alive, but abusing him verbally.

Your final paraphrase can read, "Soon I had gotten into trouble and Mr. Bixby was shouting at me, calling me a coward." Record your paraphrases in a chart like the one shown.

Difficult Passage	*Literal Paraphrase*	*Final Paraphrase (when appropriate)*

Complete the activities in your **Reader/Writer Notebook.**

Is IGNORANCE *really bliss?*

People who don't pay attention to the news or world affairs are sometimes described as burying their heads in the sand. This is not a compliment. However, it's also acknowledged that these people are sometimes happier or less worried than those who experience more. Mark Twain discovers that his experiences on the Mississippi River come at a price.

PRESENT Consider people you know who seek varied experiences and others who prefer to remain sheltered. Then list the advantages and disadvantages of each approach. Decide which approach makes the most sense to you, and identify two reasons for your choice. Share your conclusions with the class.

Life on the Mississippi

Mark Twain

BACKGROUND In this excerpt from his memoir, Mark Twain describes his first days as an apprentice riverboat pilot. Piloting a paddle steamboat was dangerous and tricky, because the Mississippi was constantly changing. The powerful current moved from one side to the other, especially in the windy parts of the river. Along this twisting course lurked hidden sandbars and submerged wrecks. Riverboat pilots gathered—and exchanged—precious information about the river's changing current.

A Cub-Pilot's Experience

What with lying on the rocks four days at Louisville, and some other delays, the poor old *Paul Jones* fooled away about two weeks in making the voyage from Cincinnati to New Orleans. This gave me a chance to get acquainted with one of the pilots, and he taught me how to steer the boat, and thus made the fascination of river life more potent than ever for me. . . .

I soon discovered two things. One was that a vessel would not be likely to sail for the mouth of the Amazon under ten or twelve years; and the other was that the nine or ten dollars still left in my pocket would not suffice for so impossible an exploration[1] as I had planned, even if I could afford to wait for a ship. Therefore it followed that I must contrive a new career. The *Paul Jones* was now bound for

Analyze Visuals ▶

What does this illustrated map tell you about the size of the Mississippi River compared with the town on its banks? What other impressions of the river do you glean?

1. **mouth of the Amazon . . . exploration:** Twain, having read that an American expedition had been unable to finish its exploration of the Amazon River, went to New Orleans with the idea that he would be able to travel to South America and complete the job.

SEVENTH ST
SIXTH ST
BIRD ST
FIFTH ST
HILL ST
FOURTH ST
NORTH ST
ROCK ST
PALMYRA
HANNIBAL & MOBERLY R.R.
T. JASPER

St. Louis. I planned a siege against my pilot, and at the end of three hard days he surrendered. He agreed to teach me the Mississippi River from New Orleans to St. Louis for five hundred dollars, payable out of the first wages I should receive after graduating. I entered upon the small enterprise of "learning" twelve or thirteen hundred miles of the great Mississippi River with the easy confidence of my time of life. If I had really known what I was about to require of my faculties, I should not have had the courage to begin. I supposed that all a pilot had to do was to keep his boat in the river, and I did not consider that that could be much of a trick, since it was so wide. **A**

The boat backed out from New Orleans at four in the afternoon, and it was "our watch" until eight. Mr. Bixby, my chief, "straightened her up," plowed her along past the sterns of the other boats that lay at the Levee,[2] and then said, "Here, take her; shave those steamships as close as you'd peel an apple." I took the wheel, and my heartbeat fluttered up into the hundreds; for it seemed to me that we were about to scrape the side off every ship in the line, we were so close. I held my breath and began to claw the boat away from the danger; and I had my own opinion of the pilot who had known no better than to get us into such peril, but I was too wise to express it. In half a minute I had a wide margin of safety intervening between the *Paul Jones* and the ships; and within ten seconds more I was set aside in disgrace, and Mr. Bixby was going into danger again and flaying me alive with abuse of my cowardice. I was stung, but I was obliged to admire the easy confidence with which my chief loafed from side to side of his wheel, and trimmed the ships so closely that disaster seemed ceaselessly imminent. When he had cooled a little he told me that the easy water was close ashore and the current outside, and therefore we must hug the bank, upstream, to get the benefit of the former, and stay well out, downstream, to take advantage of the latter. In my own mind I resolved to be a downstream pilot and leave the upstreaming to people dead to prudence.[3] **B**

Now and then Mr. Bixby called my attention to certain things. Said he, "This is Six-Mile Point." I assented. It was pleasant enough information, but I could not see the bearing of it. I was not conscious that it was a matter of any interest to me. Another time he said, "This is Nine-Mile Point." Later he said, "This is Twelve-Mile Point." They were all about level with the water's edge; they all looked about alike to me; they were monotonously unpicturesque. I hoped Mr. Bixby would change the subject. But no; he would crowd up around a point, hugging the shore with affection, and then say: "The slack water ends here, abreast this bunch of China trees; now we cross over." So he crossed over. He gave me the wheel once or twice, but I had no luck. I either came near chipping off the edge of a sugar plantation, or I yawed[4] too far from shore, and so dropped back into disgrace again and got abused.

The watch was ended at last, and we took supper and went to bed. At midnight the glare of a lantern shone in my eyes, and the night watchman said, "Come!

A VOICE
Reread lines 6–19. What does Twain's **tone** suggest about his youthful confidence?

B PARAPHRASE
Reread and paraphrase lines 33–38. What does Twain learn about the upstream and downstream currents? What decision does he make about the future?

---

2. **Levee** (lĕv'ē): a landing place for boats on a river.
3. **dead to prudence:** lacking good judgment.
4. **yawed:** swerved.

Turn out!" And then he left. I could not understand this extraordinary procedure; so I presently gave up trying to, and dozed off to sleep. Pretty soon the watchman was back again, and this time he was gruff. I was annoyed. I said,

"What do you want to come bothering around here in the middle of the night for? Now, as like as not, I'll not get to sleep again to-night."

The watchman said, "Well, if this ain't good, I'm blessed."

The "offwatch"[5] was just turning in, and I heard some brutal laughter from them, and such remarks as "Hello, watchman! ain't the new cub turned out yet? He's delicate, likely. Give him some sugar in a rag, and send for the chambermaid to sing 'Rock-a-by Baby' to him." **C**

About this time Mr. Bixby appeared on the scene. Something like a minute later I was climbing the pilothouse steps with some of my clothes on and the rest in my arms. Mr. Bixby was close behind, commenting. Here was something fresh—this thing of getting up in the middle of the night to go to work. It was a detail in piloting that had never occurred to me at all. I knew that boats ran all night, but somehow I had never happened to reflect that somebody had to get up out of a warm bed to run them. I began to fear that piloting was not quite so romantic as I had imagined it was; there was something very real and worklike about this new phase of it. . . .

Mr. Bixby made for the shore and soon was scraping it, just the same as if it had been daylight. And not only that, but singing:

Father in heaven, the day is declining, etc.

It seemed to me that I had put my life in the keeping of a peculiarly reckless outcast. Presently he turned on me and said, "What's the name of the first point above New Orleans?"

I was gratified to be able to answer promptly, and I did. I said I didn't know.

"Don't *know?*"

This manner jolted me. I was down at the foot[6] again, in a moment. But I had to say just what I had said before.

"Well, you're a smart one!" said Mr. Bixby. "What's the name of the *next* point?" Once more I didn't know.

"Well, this beats anything. Tell me the name of *any* point or place I told you."

I studied awhile and decided that I couldn't.

"Look here! What do you start out from, above Twelve-Mile Point, to cross over?"

"I—I—don't know."

"You—you—don't know?" mimicking my drawling manner of speech. "What *do* you know?"

"I—I—nothing, for certain."

"By the great Caesar's ghost, I believe you! You're the stupidest dunderhead I ever saw or ever heard of, so help me Moses! The idea of *you* being a pilot—*you!* Why, you don't know enough to pilot a cow down a lane."

C PARAPHRASE
Twain's frequent use of **dialogue** and **dialect,** or regional speech, is one of the challenging qualities about his writing. Paraphrase the dialogue in lines 51–62. What are the other crew members saying about him?

COMMON CORE L 1b

Language Coach
Word Definitions *Made for* in line 72 means "went toward." Look up *make* in a dictionary, and note the different prepositions that can be combined with *made* to create new meanings. What do *make up, make off with,* and *make over* mean?

---

5. **"offwatch":** those sailors who had just completed their watch.
6. **down at the foot:** at the bottom of the class.

Oh, but his wrath was up! He was a nervous man, and he shuffled from one side of his wheel to the other as if the floor was hot. He would boil awhile to himself, and then overflow and scald me again.

"Look here! What do you suppose I told you the names of those points for?"

I tremblingly considered a moment, and then the devil of temptation provoked me to say, "Well to—to—be entertaining, I thought."

This was a red rag to the bull.[7] He raged and stormed so (he was crossing the river at the time) that I judged it made him blind, because he ran over the steering oar of a trading scow.[8] Of course the traders sent up a volley of red-hot profanity. Never was a man so grateful as Mr. Bixby was, because he was brimful, and here were subjects who could *talk back.* He threw open a window, thrust his head out, and such an irruption followed as I never had heard before. The fainter and farther away the scowmen's curses drifted, the higher Mr. Bixby lifted his voice and the weightier his adjectives grew. When he closed the window he was empty. You could have drawn a seine[9] through his system and not caught curses enough to disturb your mother with. Presently he said to me in the gentlest way, "My boy, you must get a little memorandum book; and every time I tell you a thing, put it down right away. There's only one way to be a pilot, and that is to get this entire river by heart. You have to know it just like A B C." **D**

That was a dismal revelation to me, for my memory was never loaded with anything but blank cartridges. However, I did not feel discouraged long. I judged that it was best to make some allowances, for doubtless Mr. Bixby was "stretching." . . .[10]

By the time we had gone seven or eight hundred miles up the river, I had learned to be a tolerably plucky upstream steersman, in daylight; and before we reached St. Louis I had made a trifle of progress in night work, but only a trifle. I had a notebook that fairly bristled with the names of towns, "points," bars, islands, bends, reaches, etc.; but the information was to be found only in the notebook—none of it was in my head. It made my heart ache to think I had only got half of the river set down; for as our watch was four hours off and four hours on, day and night, there was a long four-hour gap in my book for every time I had slept since the voyage began. . . . **E**

The face of the water, in time, became a wonderful book—a book that was a dead language to the uneducated passenger, but which told its mind to me without reserve, delivering its most cherished secrets as clearly as if it uttered them with a voice. And it was not a book to be read once and thrown aside, for it had a new story to tell every day. Throughout the long twelve hundred miles there was never a page that was void of interest, never one that you could leave unread without loss, never one that you would want to skip, thinking you could find higher enjoyment in some other thing. There never was so wonderful a book

COMMON CORE L 5a

Language Coach

Figurative Language "He would boil . . . and scald me again" (lines 95–96) is an example of **figurative language,** language that communicates meaning beyond the literal meaning of the words. How do words about boiling water express Mr. Bixby's anger?

D VOICE
Reread this paragraph, focusing on lines 104–112. Notice the elaborate **diction** Twain uses to describe Mr. Bixby's behavior, especially as Mr. Bixby finally quiets down. How does this choice of language affect the pacing and humor of this paragraph?

E VOICE
Reread lines 117–125. What **tone** does Twain take here in describing his own progress? Give details from the text to support your answer.

7. **a red rag to the bull:** Bullfighters wave capes to both provoke and distract the bull.
8. **scow:** a flat-bottomed boat used chiefly to transport freight.
9. **seine** (sān): large fishing net.
10. **"stretching":** exaggerating.

written by man; never one whose interest was so absorbing, so unflagging, so sparklingly renewed with every reperusal.[11] The passenger who could not read it was charmed with a peculiar sort of faint dimple on its surface (on the rare occasions when he did not overlook it altogether); but to the pilot that was an *italicized* passage; indeed, it was more than that, it was a legend of the largest capitals,[12] with a string of shouting exclamation points at the end of it, for it meant that a wreck or a rock was buried there that could tear the life out of the strongest vessel that ever floated. It is the faintest and simplest expression the water ever makes, and the most hideous to a pilot's eye. In truth, the passenger who could not read this book saw nothing but all manner of pretty pictures in it,

---

11. **reperusal** (rē′pə-ro͞o′zəl): rereading.
12. **a legend of the largest capitals:** an inscription in large capital letters.

painted by the sun and shaded by the clouds, whereas to the trained eye these were not pictures at all, but the grimmest and most dead earnest of reading matter.

Now when I had mastered the language of this water, and had come to know every trifling feature that bordered the great river as familiarly as I knew the letters of the alphabet, I had made a valuable acquisition. But I had lost something, too. I had lost something which could never be restored to me while I lived. All the grace, the beauty, the poetry, had gone out of the majestic river! I still keep in mind a certain wonderful sunset which I witnessed when steamboating was new to me. A broad expanse of the river was turned to blood; in the middle distance the red hue brightened into gold, through which a solitary log came floating, black and conspicuous; in one place a long, slanting mark lay sparkling upon the water; in another the surface was broken by boiling, tumbling rings, that were as many-tinted as an opal; where the ruddy flush was faintest, was a smooth spot that was covered with graceful circles and radiating lines, ever so delicately traced; the shore on our left was densely wooded, and the somber shadow that fell from this forest was broken in one place by a long, ruffled trail that shone like silver; and high above the forest wall a clean-stemmed dead tree waved a single leafy bough that glowed like a flame in the unobstructed splendor that was flowing from the sun. There were graceful curves, reflected images, woody heights, soft distances; and over the whole scene, far and near, the dissolving lights drifted steadily, enriching it every passing moment with new marvels of coloring. (F)

(F) VOICE
Consider Twain's **tone** and **diction** earlier in the selection, as he was first learning his way around the ship. Then reread lines 126–164. How does Twain's voice change as he explains his increased knowledge of the river? Give details.

Champions of the Mississippi, Currier and Ives. Lithograph. Museum of the City of New York, New York. © Scala/Art Resource, New York.

I stood like one bewitched. I drank it in, in a speechless rapture. The world was new to me, and I had never seen anything like this at home. But as I have said, a day came when I began to cease from noting the glories and the charms which the moon and the sun and the twilight wrought upon the river's face; another day came when I ceased altogether to note them. Then, if that sunset scene had been repeated, I should have looked upon it without rapture, and should have commented upon it, inwardly, after this fashion: "This sun means that we are going to have wind tomorrow; that floating log means that the river is rising, small thanks to it; that slanting mark on the water refers to a bluff reef[13] which is going to kill somebody's steamboat one of these nights, if it keeps on stretching out like that; those tumbling 'boils' show a dissolving bar and a changing channel there; the lines and circles in the slick water over yonder are a warning that that troublesome place is shoaling up[14] dangerously; that silver streak in the shadow of the forest is the 'break' from a new snag, and he has located himself in the very best place he could have found to fish for steamboats; that tall dead tree, with a single living branch, is not going to last long, and then how is a body ever going to get through this blind place at night without the friendly old landmark?"

No, the romance and beauty were all gone from the river. All the value any feature of it had for me now was the amount of usefulness it could furnish toward compassing the safe piloting of a steamboat. Since those days, I have pitied doctors from my heart. What does the lovely flush in a beauty's cheek mean to a doctor but a "break" that ripples above some deadly disease? Are not all her visible charms sown thick with what are to him the signs and symbols of hidden decay? Does he ever see her beauty at all, or doesn't he simply view her professionally, and comment upon her unwholesome condition all to himself? And doesn't he sometimes wonder whether he has gained most or lost most by learning his trade? G

COMMON CORE L 5b

Language Coach

Synonyms A **synonym** is a word with a meaning similar to that of another word. *Bewitched* (line 165) means "placed under a spell" or "enthralled." Synonyms of *bewitched* are *charmed* and *enchanted*. What common theme do these words have?

G PARAPHRASE

Reread lines 184–190 and paraphrase the comments about what a doctor sees. What parallel is Twain drawing between the doctor's plight and his own?

13. **bluff reef:** an underwater ridge of rock.
14. **shoaling up:** becoming too shallow for safe navigation because of a buildup of sand or silt in the riverbed.

After Reading

Comprehension

1. **Recall** What new job does Mark Twain begin?
2. **Recall** How does Twain react to Mr. Bixby's initial instruction?
3. **Summarize** As Twain's training continues, what does he learn?

COMMON CORE

RI 6 Determine an author's point of view or purpose in a text in which the rhetoric is particularly effective. **L 3** Apply knowledge of language to comprehend more fully when reading. **L 5a** Interpret figures of speech in context and analyze their role in the text.

Text Analysis

4. **Examine Paraphrases** Review the paraphrases you recorded as you read. In the end, what were the most difficult aspects of Twain's writing? Explain.
5. **Analyze Humor** In any piece of humorous writing, the humor usually springs from a general underlying attitude toward the subject. Review the following humorous passages from the selection and in each case identify the attitude expressed. What do the passages have in common?
   - Twain tries to steer the boat for the first time (lines 23–38)
   - Twain fails to show up for his first night watch (lines 51–71)
   - Twain learns that he has to learn the entire river by heart (lines 75–112)
6. **Analyze Voice** Twain's voice undergoes a distinct change at line 126. Describe his voice both up to and after this point in terms of its **diction** and **tone.** What change in attitude is reflected by this change in voice?
7. **Draw Conclusions** In this selection, Twain develops an **extended metaphor** comparing the river with a book. In a chart like this one, identify the points of this comparison. Through this metaphor, what is he saying about the river and his experience as a student pilot?

Line Numbers	Passage	What It Says About the River
126–127	"The face of the water . . . became a wonderful book—a book that was a dead language to the uneducated passenger"	It's "wonderful" but cannot be understood by the uneducated.

Text Criticism

8. **Author's Style** *Life on the Mississippi* first appeared serially in the *Atlantic Monthly* magazine in 1875. In 1874, Twain wrote the magazine's editor that he liked writing for the audience of the *Atlantic* "for the simple reason that it don't require a 'humorist' to paint himself stripèd and stand on his head every fifteen minutes." In other words, he liked an audience that appreciated subtle humor. Do you find this sensibility reflected in the selection you have just read? Explain.

Is IGNORANCE *really bliss?*

Twain states that after he learned his trade, he was never able to see the Mississippi the same way again. What has experience caused you to see differently? What kinds of revelations can be negative? Explain.

The Notorious Jumping Frog of Calaveras County

Short Story by Mark Twain

COMMON CORE

RL 3, RL 4, L 1a, L 5a

TEXT ANALYSIS: TALL TALE

The **tall tale** is a distinctively American form of storytelling featuring outlandish characters and events, often with a comic effect. Based on oral tradition, the tall tale generally aims to fool or impress the listener or reader, using various devices. Look for these techniques and consider their impact:

- **Hyperbole**—a figure of speech exaggerating or overstating a claim or point
- **Understatement**—the technique of downplaying the significance of the outlandish, often to ironic or humorous effect
- **Local color**—writing that brings a region alive by portraying its dress, mannerisms, customs, character types, and speech

READING SKILL: UNDERSTAND DIALECT

Dialect is the distinct form of a language spoken in one geographic area or by a particular group. Writers use dialect to establish setting, provide local color, and develop characters. In this story, Twain uses a frontier dialect. Because of its unfamiliar usage, idioms, and strange spellings, dialect can be challenging to read. These strategies will help:

- **Read slowly**—Try reading aloud to help you recognize words you may have heard but don't normally see in print.
- **Use context clues**—When Twain writes, "You'd see that frog whirling in the air like a doughnut—see him turn one summerset," context tells you that *summerset* must mean the same as *somersault*.

As you read, jot down unfamiliar words and what you think they mean.

VOCABULARY IN CONTEXT

Which of the following words do you know? Write definitions for the words and then check the definitions as you read.

WORD LIST			
	cavorting	enterprising	infamous
	conjecture	garrulous	tranquil
	dilapidated	indifferent	

Complete the activities in your **Reader/Writer Notebook**.

Can you spot a TALL TALE?

You listen to a friend recount the events of the weekend and you're pretty sure the story is way too wild to be true. You hear a politician describe great accomplishments and you just know it's a stretch. These situations inspire the skepticism you need to read about a frog that turns somersaults.

DISCUSS Work with a small group to play the game "Two Truths and a Lie." Take a few minutes for each of you to come up with two truths and one lie. The statements can be about anything from personal experience to oddball facts. Take turns sharing statements. Can you guess which are the lies and which are the truths? Compare your answers and explain what made you believe or disbelieve each statement.

The Notorious JUMPING FROG of Calaveras County

Mark Twain

BACKGROUND Twain got the idea for this story during his days panning for gold in California. Local storytellers told this tale without cracking a smile, teaching Twain two important lessons about humor: one, that the manner in which a person tells a story is what makes it funny, and two, that a humorist should always pretend to be dead serious.

Analyze Visuals ▶
What techniques in this illustration can be compared with the storytelling techniques of a tall tale? Explain.

In compliance with the request of a friend of mine who wrote me from the East, I called on good-natured, **garrulous** old Simon Wheeler and inquired after my friend's friend, Leonidas W. Smiley, as requested to do, and I hereunto append[1] the result. I have a lurking suspicion that *Leonidas W.* Smiley is a myth, that my friend never knew such a personage, and that he only **conjectured** that if I asked old Wheeler about him, it would remind him of his **infamous** *Jim* Smiley and he would go to work and bore me to death with some exasperating reminiscence of him as long and as tedious as it should be useless to me. If that was the design, it succeeded.

garrulous (găr′ə-ləs) *adj.* extremely talkative

conjecture (kən-jĕk′chər) *v.* to guess

infamous (ĭn′fə-məs) *adj.* having a very bad reputation; disgraceful

1. **hereunto append:** add to this document.

W.J.WELCH.Sc

I found Simon Wheeler dozing comfortably by the barroom stove of the **dilapidated** tavern in the decayed mining camp of Angel's, and I noticed that he was fat and baldheaded and had an expression of winning gentleness and simplicity upon his **tranquil** countenance. He roused up and gave me good day. I told him that a friend of mine had commissioned me to make some inquiries about a cherished companion of his boyhood named *Leonidas W.* Smiley—*Rev. Leonidas W.* Smiley, a young minister of the Gospel, who he had heard was at one time a resident of Angel's Camp. I added that if Mr. Wheeler could tell me anything about this Rev. Leonidas W. Smiley, I would feel under many obligations to him.

Simon Wheeler backed me into a corner and blockaded me there with his chair, and then sat down and reeled off the monotonous narrative which follows this paragraph. He never smiled, he never frowned, he never changed his voice from the gentle-flowing key to which he tuned his initial sentence, he never betrayed the slightest suspicion of enthusiasm, but all through the interminable narrative there ran a vein of impressive earnestness and sincerity which showed me plainly that, so far from his imagining that there was anything ridiculous or funny about his story, he regarded it as a really important matter and admired its two heroes as men of transcendent genius in *finesse.*[2] I let him go on in his own way and never interrupted him once.

"Rev. Leonidas W. H'm, Reverend Le—Well, there was a feller here once by the name of *Jim* Smiley, in the winter of '49—or maybe it was the spring of '50—I don't recollect exactly, somehow, though what makes me think it was one or the other is because I remember the big flume[3] warn't finished when he first come to the camp; but anyway, he was the curiousest man about always betting on anything that turned up you ever see, if he could get anybody to bet on the other side, and if he couldn't he'd change sides. Any way that suited the other man would suit *him*—any way just so's he got a bet, *he* was satisfied. But still he was lucky, uncommon lucky; he most always come out winner. He was always ready and laying for a chance; there couldn't be no solit'ry thing mentioned but that feller'd offer to bet on it and take ary side you please, as I was just telling you. If there was a horse race, you'd find him flush or you'd find him busted at the end of it; if there was a dogfight, he'd bet on it; if there was a cat fight, he'd bet on it; if there was a chicken fight, he'd bet on it; why, if there was two birds setting on a fence, he would bet you which one would fly first; or if there was a camp meeting, he would be there reg'lar to bet on Parson Walker, which he judged to be the best exhorter about here, and so he was too, and a good man. If he even see a straddlebug[4] start to go anywheres, he would bet you how long it would take him to get to—to wherever he was going to, and if you took him up, he would foller that straddlebug to Mexico but what he would find out where he was bound for and how long he was on the road. Lots of the boys here has seen that Smiley and can tell you about him. Why, it never made no difference to *him*—he'd bet on

dilapidated
(dĭ-lăp'ĭ-dā'tĭd) *adj.*
in a state of disrepair; rundown **dilapidate** *v.*

tranquil (trăng'kwəl) *adj.*
undisturbed; peaceful

Language Coach

Word Definitions
Monotonous (line 20) means "having little variety in tone or pitch." Reread lines 21–23. What surrounding words and phrases hint at the meaning of *monotonous*?

COMMON CORE L 5a

TALL TALE
In his tall tales, Twain perfected a mixture of humor and exaggeration that calls on readers to go along with wildly unbelievable events. The characteristics of the tall tale that we see in Twain's story can also be found in comic-book superhero films. What are some examples of tall tales that you have enjoyed recently in novels, plays, or movies?

2. **men of . . . *finesse*:** exceptionally brilliant men.
3. **flume:** a wooden trough built as a channel for running water—used in gold mining for separating particles of gold.
4. **straddlebug:** a long-legged beetle.

any thing—the dangdest feller. Parson Walker's wife laid very sick once for a good while, and it seemed as if they warn't going to save her; but one morning he come in and Smiley up and asked him how she was, and he said she was considerable better—thank the Lord for his inf'nite mercy—and coming on so smart that with the blessing of Prov'dence she'd get well yet; and Smiley, before he thought, says, 'Well, I'll resk two-and-a-half she don't anyway.' **B**

"Thish-yer Smiley had a mare—the boys called her the fifteen-minute nag but that was only in fun, you know, because of course she was faster than that—and he used to win money on that horse, for all she was so slow and always had the asthma, or the distemper, or the consumption,[5] or something of that kind. They used to give her two or three hundred yards' start and then pass her under way, but always at the fag end[6] of the race she'd get excited and desperatelike, and come **cavorting** and straddling up and scattering her legs around limber, sometimes in the air and sometimes out to one side among the fences, and kicking up m-o-r-e dust and raising m-o-r-e racket with her coughing and sneezing and blowing her nose—and always fetch up at the stand just about a neck ahead, as near as you could cipher it down.[7]

"And he had a little small bull-pup, that to look at him you'd think he warn't worth a cent but to set around and look ornery and lay for a chance to steal something. But as soon as money was up on him he was a different dog; his underjaw'd begin to stick out like the fo'castle[8] of a steamboat and his teeth would uncover and shine like the furnaces. And a dog might tackle him and bullyrag[9] him, and bite him and throw him over his shoulder two or three times, and Andrew Jackson—which was the name of the pup—Andrew Jackson would never let on but what *he* was satisfied and hadn't expected nothing else—and the bets being doubled and doubled on the other side all the time, till the money was all up; and then all of a sudden he would grab that other dog jest by the j'int of his hind leg and freeze to it—not chaw, you understand, but only just grip and hang on till they throwed up the sponge,[10] if it was a year. Smiley always come out winner on that pup till he harnessed a dog once that didn't have no hind legs, because they'd been sawed off in a circular saw, and when the thing had gone along far enough and the money was all up and he come to make a snatch for his pet holt,[11] he see in a minute how he'd been imposed on and how the other dog had him in the door, so to speak, and he 'peared surprised, and then he looked sorter discouragedlike and didn't try no more to win the fight, and so he got shucked out bad. He give Smiley a look, as much as to say his heart was broke, and it was *his* fault for putting up a dog that hadn't no hind legs for him to take holt of, which was his main dependence in a fight, and

B DIALECT
Paraphrase the passage written in dialect in lines 29–56. What point is Simon Wheeler making about Smiley?

cavorting (kə-vôr'tĭng) *adj.* prancing about in a playful manner **cavort** *v.*

COMMON CORE L 1a

Language Coach

Regional Dialects Reread lines 57–67, paying special attention to the dialect. As noted on page 683, Twain uses frontier dialect in this story to reflect the usage and pronunciations conventional to a certain group of people. Using the Internet or a history of the English language—a historical reference book that discusses the origins and uses of English—make a list of regional dialects in the United States.

5. **distemper . . . consumption:** Distemper is a viral disease caught by dogs and other four-legged mammals. Consumption is an old-fashioned name for tuberculosis.
6. **fag end:** final part.
7. **cipher** (sī'fər) **it down:** calculate it; figure it.
8. **fo'castle** (fōk'səl): forecastle—here, the protruding front deck of a steamboat.
9. **bullyrag:** harass.
10. **throwed up the sponge:** gave up.
11. **pet holt:** favorite grip.

then he limped off a piece and laid down and died. It was a good pup, was that Andrew Jackson, and would have made a name for hisself if he'd lived, for the stuff was in him and he had genius—I know it, because he hadn't no opportunities to speak of, and it don't stand to reason that a dog could make such a fight as he could under them circumstances if he hadn't no talent. It always makes me feel sorry when I think of that last fight of his'n and the way it turned out. C

C TALL TALE
Reread lines 68–93. What device characteristic of the tall tale is on display in this paragraph?

"Well, thish-yer Smiley had rat terriers, and chicken cocks, and tomcats and all them kind of things till you couldn't rest, and you couldn't fetch nothing for him to bet on but he'd match you. He ketched a frog one day and took him home, and said he cal'lated[12] to educate him; and so he never done nothing for three months but set in his back yard and learn that frog to jump. And you bet you he *did* learn him, too. He'd give him a little punch behind, and the next minute you'd see that frog whirling in the air like a doughnut—see him turn one summerset, or maybe a couple if he got a good start, and come down flatfooted and all right, like a cat. He got him up so in the matter of ketching flies, and kep' him in practice so constant, that he'd nail a fly every time as fur as he could see him. Smiley said all a frog wanted was education and he could do 'most anything—and I believe him. Why, I've seen him set Dan'l Webster down here on this floor—Dan'l Webster was the name of the frog—and sing out, 'Flies, Dan'l, flies!' and quicker'n you could wink he'd spring straight up and snake a fly off'n the counter there, and flop down on the floor ag'in as solid as a gob of mud, and fall to scratching the side of his head with his hind foot as **indifferent** as if he hadn't no idea he'd been doin' any more'n any frog might do. You never see a frog so modest and straight-for'ard as he was, for all he was so gifted. And when it come to fair and square jumping on a dead level, he could get over more ground at one straddle than any animal of his breed you ever see. Jumping on a dead level was his strong suit, you understand; and when it come to that, Smiley would ante up money on him as long as he had a red.[13] Smiley was monstrous proud of his frog, and well he might be for fellers that had traveled and been everywheres all said he laid over any frog that ever *they* see. D

indifferent (ĭn-dĭf'ər-ənt) *adj.* having no particular interest

D DIALECT
Reread lines 110–111. How does the dialect in this sentence, and throughout the paragraph, help to characterize the frog?

"Well, Smiley kep' the beast in a little lattice box, and he used to fetch him downtown sometimes and lay for a bet. One day a feller—a stranger in the camp, he was—come acrost him with his box and says:

"'What might it be that you've got in the box?'

"And Smiley says, sorter indifferent-like, 'It might be a parrot, or it might be a canary, maybe, but it ain't—it's only just a frog.'

"And the feller took it and looked at it careful, and turned it round this way and that, and says, 'H'm—so 'tis. Well, what's *he* good for?'

"'Well,' Smiley says, easy and careless, 'he's good enough for *one* thing, I should judge—he can outjump any frog in Calaveras County.'

"The feller took the box again and took another long, particular look, and give it back to Smiley and says, very deliberate, 'Well,' he says, 'I don't see no p'ints[14] about that frog that's any better'n any other frog.'

---

12. **cal'lated:** calculated; intended.
13. **a red:** a red cent (slang for a penny).
14. **p'ints:** points.

Frog of Calaveras County. The Granger Collection, New York.

"'Maybe you don't,' Smiley says. 'Maybe you understand frogs and maybe you don't understand 'em; maybe you've had experience and maybe you ain't only a amature, as it were. Anyways, I've got *my* opinion, and I'll resk forty dollars that he can outjump any frog in Calaveras County.'

"And the feller studied a minute and then says, kinder sad-like, 'Well, I'm only a stranger here and I ain't got no frog; but if I had a frog, I'd bet you.'

"And then Smiley says, 'That's all right—that's all right—if you'll hold my box a minute, I'll go and get you a frog.' And so the feller took the box and put up his forty dollars along with Smiley's, and set down to wait. **E**

"So he set there a good while thinking and thinking to himself, and then he got the frog out and prized his mouth open and took a teaspoon and filled him full of quail shot[15]—filled him pretty near up to his chin—and set him on the floor. Smiley he went to the swamp and slopped around in the mud for a long time, and finally he ketched a frog and fetched him in and give him to this feller, and says:

"'Now, if you're ready, set him alongside of Dan'l, with his forepaws just even with Dan'l's, and I'll give the word.' Then he says, 'One—two—three—*git!*' and him and the feller touched up the frogs from behind, and the new frog hopped off

E TALL TALE
Reread the dialogue in lines 120–138. What does the straightfaced understatement reveal about the two characters?

15. **quail shot:** small lead pellets for firing from a shotgun.

lively, but Dan'l give a heave and hysted up his shoulders—so—like a Frenchman, but it warn't no use—he couldn't budge; he was planted as solid as a church, and he couldn't no more stir than if he was anchored out. Smiley was a good deal surprised, and he was disgusted too, but he didn't have no idea what the matter was, of course. F

"The feller took the money and started away, and when he was going out at the door, he sorter jerked his thumb over his shoulder—so—at Dan'l and says again, very deliberate, 'Well,' he says, *'I* don't see no p'ints about that frog that's any better'n any other frog.'

"Smiley he stood scratching his head and looking down at Dan'l a long time, and at last he says, 'I do wonder what in the nation that frog throw'd off for—I wonder if there ain't something the matter with him—he 'pears to look mighty baggy, somehow.' And he ketched Dan'l by the nap of the neck and hefted him, and says, 'Why, blame my cats if he don't weigh five pound!' and turned him upside down and he belched out a double handful of shot. And then he see how it was, and he was the maddest man—he set the frog down and took out after that feller, but he never ketched him. And—"

[Here Simon Wheeler heard his name called from the front yard and got up to see what was wanted.] And turning to me as he moved away, he said: "Just set where you are, stranger, and rest easy—I ain't going to be gone a second."

But, by your leave, I did not think that a continuation of the history of the **enterprising** vagabond *Jim* Smiley would be likely to afford me much information concerning the Rev. *Leonidas W.* Smiley and so I started away.

At the door I met the sociable Wheeler returning, and he buttonholed me and recommenced:[16]

"Well, thish-yer Smiley had a yaller one-eyed cow that didn't have no tail, only just a short stump like a bannanner, and—"

However, lacking both time and inclination, I did not wait to hear about the afflicted cow but took my leave. ∾

F **GRAMMAR AND STYLE**
Reread lines 144–151. Notice how Twain uses **coordinating conjunctions** and **dashes** to convey Simon's breathless retelling of the story.

enterprising
(ĕn'tər-prī'zĭng) *adj.* possessing imagination and initiative

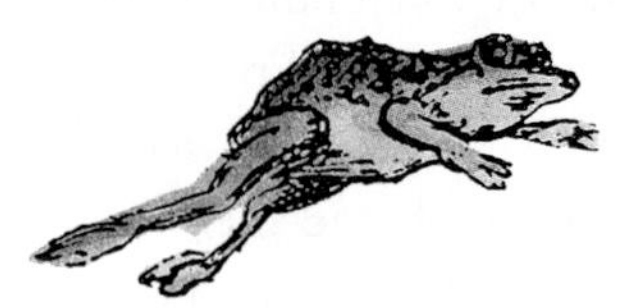

16. **buttonholed . . . recommenced:** detained me for conversation and began talking again.

After Reading

Comprehension

1. **Recall** How does the narrator hear the story of the jumping frog?
2. **Recall** What is Smiley always willing to do?
3. **Summarize** What happens to Smiley's frog?

Text Analysis

4. **Make Inferences About Characters** What can you infer about Jim Smiley based on each of the following examples?
    - Smiley betting on the health of the parson's wife
    - Smiley spending three months teaching a frog to jump
    - Smiley studying why the frog couldn't jump
5. **Understand Dialect** Review the dialect and translations you recorded as you read. In general, what does the use of dialect contribute to **characterization** and **setting** in this story? Cite specific examples.
6. **Analyze Overstatement** Simon Wheeler makes liberal use of overstatement, or hyperbole, in describing Jim Smiley; some of what he says is totally improbable, and some is simply a bit of a stretch. List several examples of overstatement and rate each on a scale of one to five, with five being the most outrageous. At any point, did your doubts prevent you from enjoying the story? Explain.
7. **Make Judgments About the Tall Tale** Twain sets this story in a **frame**—a story within a story—in which the first-person narrator asks about a man named Leonidas Smiley but gets a story about Jim Smiley instead. In the end, the narrator makes a show of going away disappointed. How does this device contribute to the impact of the tall tale? Explain how the story would have been different if the original first-person narrator had simply told the story in his own voice, or if Wheeler himself had been the first-person narrator. Do you think this frame is an effective technique? Why or why not?

Text Criticism

8. **Critical Interpretations** According to one critic, Twain's organization of this tale "seems wholly directionless," yet "actually it is carefully molded for climax." Do you agree? Look back at the story and explain how the elaborate setup affects the impact of the story's punchline. Use examples from the story to support your ideas.

Can you spot a TALL TALE?

A tall tale, like this one by Twain, usually makes people laugh because they know it's not true. What stories and ideas in real life cause people to be skeptical? Do you think any of those stories have a basis in fact? Why or why not?

COMMON CORE

RL 3 Analyze the impact of the author's choices regarding how to develop and relate elements of a story. **RL 4** Analyze the impact of specific word choices on meaning and tone. **RL 5** Analyze how an author's choices concerning how to structure specific parts of a text contribute to its overall structure and meaning as well as its aesthetic impact. **L 1a** Apply the understanding that usage is a matter of convention. **L 5a** Interpret figures of speech in context and analyze their role in the text.

Vocabulary in Context

▲ VOCABULARY PRACTICE

Choose the word that is not related in meaning to the other words.

1. (a) dilapidated, (b) decaying, (c) neglected, (d) lonesome
2. (a) chatty, (b) argumentative, (c) garrulous, (d) verbose
3. (a) serene, (b) tranquil, (c) unhappy, (d) placid
4. (a) unusual, (b) infamous, (c) disreputable, (d) notorious
5. (a) comfort, (b) condolence, (c) consolation, (d) conjecture
6. (a) imaginative, (b) expensive, (c) enterprising, (d) resourceful
7. (a) unconcerned, (b) detached, (c) indifferent, (d) unnoticeable
8. (a) cavorting, (b) trembling, (c) shaking, (d) jarring

WORD LIST

cavorting
conjecture
dilapidated
enterprising
garrulous
indifferent
infamous
tranquil

ACADEMIC VOCABULARY IN WRITING

• apparent • confine • expose • focus • perceive

Tall tales often **focus** on larger-than-life heroes and amazing exploits. In a short paragraph, discuss some modern-day people and events that could be made into tall tales. Be sure to include why you think the people and events are worthy of a tall tale. Use at least one Academic Vocabulary word in your paragraph.

VOCABULARY STRATEGY: THESAURI AND WORD KNOWLEDGE

A thesaurus is a reference book that helps you find specific, or precise, words for more general terms. In a thesaurus, words are arranged by their meanings and by their parts of speech rather than by alphabetical order, as in a dictionary. You can use a thesaurus to choose a specific word to show a subtle difference in meaning or to avoid monotony in your writing. For example, to replace the vocabulary word *infamous*, you could find *wrong*, *disreputable*, and *dishonorable*.

COMMON CORE

L 4c Consult general and specialized reference materials to determine or clarify a word's precise meaning. **L 5b** Analyze nuances in the meaning of words with similar denotations. **L 6** Acquire and use accurately general academic words and phrases.

PRACTICE Use a thesaurus to identify the following words.

1. Three nouns you might use when talking about "wealth"
2. Two or three verbs related to the noun "flattery"
3. Words that could replace "middle" in referring to distance or space
4. Three adjectives to describe the feeling of being "cold"
5. Words to suggest what you might do rather than "advise"

Language

GRAMMAR AND STYLE: Create Realistic Characters

Review the **Grammar and Style** note on page 690. Mark Twain creates convincing dialogue to help establish the character of Simon Wheeler. Look at this example from the story:

> *And a dog might tackle him and bullyrag him, and bite him and throw him over his shoulder two or three times, and Andrew Jackson—which was the name of the pup—Andrew Jackson would never let on but what* he *was satisfied and hadn't expected nothing else. . . .* (lines 72–75)

Notice how Twain uses the highlighted **coordinating conjunctions** to reflect Simon's long, rambling sentences. He also uses **dashes** to show how Simon interrupts himself. Finally, the underlined word is **dialect**, showing that Simon is rooted in his local culture.

PRACTICE After you respond to the prompt below, rewrite the conversation in dialect. You may use either the same Western dialect that Twain uses or a dialect from a different place and time that is familiar to you. Make use of coordinating conjunctions, dashes, and regional vocabulary, as well as any special spellings or contractions that will help your reader "hear" the dialect as it would be spoken.

EXAMPLE

"My goodness! If I had known you felt that way about it, I never would have said anything in the first place."

"Well, shut my mouth! If I'da known you felt that way 'bout it, I never woulda said nothin' in th' first place."

COMMON CORE

L 1a Apply the understanding that usage is a matter of convention and can change over time. **L 2** Demonstrate command of the conventions of standard English punctuation and spelling when writing. **W 3b** Use narrative techniques, such as dialogue and pacing, to develop characters.

READING-WRITING CONNECTION

Expand your understanding of Twain's writing by responding to this prompt. Then use the **revising tips** to improve your dialogue.

WRITING PROMPT

WRITE A DIALOGUE A **conversation** can reveal a great deal about its participants. Characters' words and gestures as well as the pace and flow of their speech all make a story's characters believable.

Write a **one-page conversation** between two real people or fictional characters. Like Twain, have them share amazing—and possibly exaggerated—experiences.

REVISING TIPS

- Start a new paragraph to indicate a change in speakers and to reflect the pacing of the conversation.
- Be sure to set punctuation, such as commas and periods, inside closing quotation marks.
- Use exaggeration and irony to make your experiences humorous.

American Masterpiece

from The Adventures of Huckleberry Finn

Novel by Mark Twain

COMMON CORE

RL 6 Analyze a case in which grasping point of view requires distinguishing what is directly stated in a text from what is really meant. **L 1** Demonstrate command of the conventions of English grammar and usage when writing. **L 1a** Apply the understanding that usage is a matter of convention and can change over time.

BACKGROUND Although Mark Twain first won fame as a Western humorist writing about life in the California gold-mining camps, he drew on his Missouri childhood for many of his best-known works, including *The Adventures of Huckleberry Finn*, widely regarded as one of the greatest American novels. Set in the years before the Civil War, when slavery was still legal in Missouri, the novel follows its protagonist Huck and a runaway slave named Jim on an adventure by raft down the Mississippi River. With the novel's hero, Twain depicts the conflict between what society expects and what conscience demands of individuals. In the excerpt on the following page, for example, Huck has just done what his society has taught him is the right thing to do: he has written a note to Miss Watson, reporting the whereabouts of her runaway slave, Jim. However, Huck has deep misgivings about this action.

TEXT ANALYSIS Twain narrates Huck's tale in first person point of view, taking the voice of Huck himself—an uneducated Missouri boy of the mid-nineteenth century. Huck's story is sprinkled with **colloquial language**—words and phrases taken from informal English. The result is a book that sounds not like Mark Twain writing but like Huck Finn speaking. His language includes slang, as well as incorrect grammar conventional to the place and time of the story.

Twain achieves much more, however, in writing *Huck Finn* from the point of view of an uneducated, somewhat naïve, young man. The author uses **irony** to comment on the values of Huck's society. **Dramatic irony** occurs when readers know more than a character knows. Early in the story, for example, Huck tells about his chance to join a gang led by his friend Tom Sawyer: "... he hunted me up and said he was going to start a band of robbers, and I might join if I would go back to the widow and be respectable." Readers know that joining a group of thieves is the opposite of "respectable," but Huck does not. This is also an example of **verbal irony.** Twain is clearly being ironic when he has Huck use the word "respectable." The author is saying one thing but meaning its opposite.

DISCUSS Read the passage with a small group of your peers. Make a list of colloquial words and phrases that make the writing sound as if Huck is speaking to you. Then, read the passage a second time and identify at least one instance of irony—a place in the writing where both readers and author know more than Huck knows. Afterward, share your findings with your class as a whole.

I felt good and all washed clean of sin for the first time I had ever felt so in my life, and I knowed I could pray now. But I didn't do it straight off, but laid the paper down and set there thinking—thinking how good it was all this happened so, and how near I come to being lost and going to hell. And went on thinking. And got to thinking over our trip down the river; and I see Jim before me, all the time, in the day, and in the nighttime, sometimes moonlight, sometimes storms, and we a floating along, talking, and singing, and laughing. But somehow I couldn't seem to strike no places to harden me against him, but only the other kind. I'd see him standing my watch on top of his'n, stead of calling me, so I could go on sleeping; and see him how glad he was when I come back out of the fog; and when I come to him again in the swamp, up there where the feud was; and such-like times; and would always call me honey, and pet me, and do everything he could think of for me, and how good he always was; and at last I struck the time I saved him by telling the men we had small-pox aboard, and he was so grateful, and said I was the best friend old Jim ever had in the world, and the only one he's got now; and then I happened to look around, and see that paper.

It was a close place. I took it up, and held it in my hand. I was a trembling, because I'd got to decide, forever, betwixt two things, and I knowed it. I studied a minute, sort of holding my breath, and then says to myself:

"All right, then, I'll *go* to hell"—and tore it up.

It was awful thoughts, and awful words, but they was said. And I let them stay said; and never thought no more about reforming. I shoved the whole thing out of my head; and said I would take up wickedness again, which was in my line, being brung up to it, and the other warn't. And for a starter, I would go to work and steal Jim out of slavery again; and if I could think up anything worse, I would do that, too; because as long as I was in, and in for good, I might as well go the whole hog.

Then I set to thinking over how to get at it, and turned over considerable many ways in my mind; and at last fixed up a plan that suited me. So then I took the bearings of a woody island that was down the river a piece, and as soon as it was fairly dark I crept out with my raft and went for it, and hid it there, and then turned in. I slept the night through, and got up before it was light, and had my breakfast, and put on my store clothes, and tied up some others and one thing or another in a bundle, and took the canoe and cleared for shore. I landed below where I judged was Phelps's place, and hid my bundle in the woods, and then filled up the canoe with water, and loaded rocks into her and sunk her where I could find her again when I wanted her, about a quarter mile below a little steam sawmill that was on the bank.

The Outcasts of Poker Flat

Video link at thinkcentral.com

Short Story by Bret Harte

COMMON CORE

RL 1 Cite evidence to support analysis of what the text says explicitly. **RL 3** Analyze the impact of the author's choices regarding how to develop and relate elements of a story. **SL 1a–d** Draw on preparation to stimulate a thoughtful, well-reasoned exchange of ideas; work with peers to promote civil, democratic discussions; pose and respond to questions that probe reasoning and evidence; ensure a hearing for a full range of positions on a topic or issue; clarify, verify, or challenge ideas and conclusions; promote divergent and creative perspectives; respond thoughtfully to diverse perspectives; synthesize comments, claims, and evidence on an issue.

DID YOU KNOW?

Bret Harte . . .

- was called "Dickens among the pines" for the vivid and recognizable characters he created.
- worked as a shotgun rider on a California stagecoach.
- worked as an abolitionist during the Civil War, often speaking out against the harsh treatment of minorities.

Meet the Author

Bret Harte 1836–1902

Many of the familiar characters in Western stories and films—saloon keepers, fallen ladies, hard-bitten gamblers, mining prospectors, and dewy-eyed youngsters—can be found in the stories of Bret Harte. Harte's colorful writing helped shape the Western genre. It also inspired emigration to the developing region of the American west. Harte's writing made him—for a short while—one of America's most popular and highly paid literary figures.

A Man of Many Hats Born into an educated but financially struggling family, Bret Harte moved often during his childhood. Although the frequent moves and his poor health kept him from formal schooling, he read widely on his own and published his first writing at age 11. After his father died, Harte began working—first for a pharmacist, then a lawyer, and later as a tutor, a miner, and finally a journalist for a newspaper in California, where the family had moved after his mother's remarriage. It was at this newspaper that Harte began to publish his stories and articles.

Good Times In the early 1860s, Harte moved to San Francisco and began to hone his literary craft. He wrote and edited stories, articles, humor, and literary criticism for two newspapers, the *Golden Era* and then the *Californian.* At the *Californian,* Harte helped along the career of a young, unknown Mark Twain. Becoming founding editor of the *Overland Monthly,* Harte soon wrote and published "The Luck of Roaring Camp" and "The Outcasts of Poker Flat," stories of outcasts with hearts of gold. These stories put him on the literary map. Suddenly, he was the talk of the town with his work much discussed, often imitated, and highly sought after. When the *Atlantic Monthly* in Boston offered Harte an annual contract with a big salary, he moved his family back east.

. . . And Bad Times Harte was careless about fulfilling his *Atlantic Monthly* contract, and it was not renewed. He tried lecturing, novel writing (*Gabriel Conroy*), and playwriting with Mark Twain (*Ah Sin*), but was left with a failing literary career. His marriage had also deteriorated. Finally, in 1877, friends helped Harte get an appointment as U.S. consul in Germany. By 1885 he had landed in London. Bret Harte, who played a key role in creating the popular portrait of the Old West, lived in London for the rest of his life, dying there in 1902.

Author Online THINK central

Go to thinkcentral.com. KEYWORD: HML11-696

TEXT ANALYSIS: REGIONALISM

A natural outgrowth of realism, **regionalism** was a literary movement of the 19th century that focused on the speech, habits, history, and beliefs of people in a specific geographic area. In "The Outcasts of Poker Flat," the **setting**—the physical features of a particular landscape and its time period—plays a prominent role in the plot. Harte has assembled a representative group of characters from the rapidly-expanding American West. Readers meet a gambler, two women with bad reputations, and a town drunk. Regionalist writers like Harte were so successful with these **character types,** or characters with a similar set of traits, that their creations continue to show up in literature, in movies, and in television shows today. As you read, pay careful attention to how Harte creates and develops these traditional characters in this specific time and place.

READING SKILL: CLARIFY MEANING

As you read this story, make sure to **clarify** any portions of the story that seem unclear on first reading. Stop and ask yourself questions such as these:

- What just happened?
- What do the characters' words and actions reveal about them?
- What meaning can be extracted from the narrator's comments and expressions?

VOCABULARY IN CONTEXT

Harte uses a rich and challenging vocabulary in this story of the Old West. Choose the word from the list that you would associate with or use to describe an individual who

1. can see into the future
2. is constantly joking
3. criticizes others
4. complains all the time
5. utters a curse
6. is friendly to everyone
7. is an exile
8. has a steady outlook
9. weeps in sad movies
10. is avoided by others

WORD LIST			
	amicable	jocular	prescience
	anathema	maudlin	querulous
	equanimity	pariah	vituperative
	expatriated		

Complete the activities in your **Reader/Writer Notebook**.

What does it mean to be an OUTCAST?

In ancient times, people were sent into exile as a form of punishment. They were cast out of society and set adrift, often in harsh and dangerous wilderness. In this story, the characters are exiled into the California mountains, where they face both psychological and physical challenges.

DEBATE In a small group, prepare arguments for or against the statement "We need society to live." In developing your argument, consider the consequences of living outside of society. Conduct a debate, providing evidence for your position and asking questions that probe the reasoning of the opposing position. Respond thoughtfully to a range of ideas different from your own. After the debate, discuss whether you would support exile as a form of modern punishment.

The Outcasts of Poker Flat

Bret Harte

BACKGROUND Many of Bret Harte's stories highlighted both the lure of gold in California and the challenge of battling a harsh landscape of huge spaces and towering mountains. During the California Gold Rush, which began in 1848, thousands of people poured into the state, creating towns such as the one in this story. These towns, which developed from miners' camps, were often rough and featured the homemade style of justice that sets this story's events in motion.

As Mr. John Oakhurst, gambler, stepped into the main street of Poker Flat on the morning of the twenty-third of November, 1850, he was conscious of a change in its moral atmosphere since the preceding night. Two or three men, conversing earnestly together, ceased as he approached, and exchanged significant glances. There was a Sabbath lull in the air, which, in a settlement unused to Sabbath influences, looked ominous. **A**

Mr. Oakhurst's calm, handsome face betrayed small concern in these indications. Whether he was conscious of any predisposing cause, was another question. "I reckon they're after somebody," he reflected; "likely it's me." He returned to his pocket the handkerchief with which he had been whipping away the red dust of Poker Flat from his neat boots, and quietly discharged his mind of any further conjecture.

In point of fact, Poker Flat was "after somebody." It had lately suffered the loss of several thousand dollars, two valuable horses, and a prominent citizen. It was experiencing a spasm of virtuous reaction, quite as lawless and ungovernable as any of the acts that had provoked it. A secret committee had determined to rid the town of all improper persons. This was done permanently in regard of two

Analyze Visuals ▶
Describe the sense of time and place conveyed in this image. What details give you this sense?

A CLARIFY MEANING
Reread the first paragraph. What has happened thus far?

Deadwood, South Dakota, 1877. The Granger Collection, New York.

BLOOM'S
FURNISHING GOODS
HAT
BOOT & SHOE
HOUSE
WELCH'S HOTEL
CORNFORTH'S
FRUITS & PRODUCE
H.J. BRENDLINGER
OCCIDENTAL
CHOP HOUSE & SAMPLE ROOM
LODGING
LAW OFFICE
nt Shop

men who were then hanging from the boughs of a sycamore in the gulch, and temporarily in the banishment of certain other objectionable characters. I regret to say that some of these were ladies. It is but due to the sex, however, to state that their impropriety was professional, and it was only in such easily established standards of evil that Poker Flat ventured to sit in judgment. **B**

B CLARIFY MEANING
Reread lines 13–22. What is the narrator's attitude toward the "virtuous reaction" of Poker Flat?

Mr. Oakhurst was right in supposing that he was included in this category. A few of the committee had urged hanging him as a possible example, and a sure method of reimbursing themselves from his pockets of the sums he had won from them. "It's agin justice," said Jim Wheeler, "to let this yer young man from Roaring Camp[1]—an entire stranger—carry away our money." But a crude sentiment of equity residing in the breasts of those who had been fortunate enough to win from Mr. Oakhurst overruled this narrower local prejudice. **C**

C REGIONALISM
What can you **infer** about life in Poker Flat?

Mr. Oakhurst received his sentence with philosophic calmness, none the less coolly that he was aware of the hesitation of his judges. He was too much of a gambler not to accept Fate. With him life was at best an uncertain game, and he recognized the usual percentage in favor of the dealer.

A body of armed men accompanied the deported wickedness of Poker Flat to the outskirts of the settlement. Besides Mr. Oakhurst, who was known to be a coolly desperate man, and for whose intimidation the armed escort was intended, the **expatriated** party consisted of a young woman familiarly known as "The Duchess," another who had won the title of "Mother Shipton,"[2] and "Uncle Billy," a suspected sluice-robber[3] and confirmed drunkard. The cavalcade provoked no comments from the spectators, nor was any word uttered by the escort. Only, when the gulch which marked the uttermost limit of Poker Flat was reached, the leader spoke briefly and to the point. The exiles were forbidden to return at the peril of their lives.

expatriated (ĕk-spā′trē-ā′tĭd) *adj.* sent out of a country or area; banished **expatriate** *v.*

As the escort disappeared, their pent-up feelings found vent in a few hysterical tears from the Duchess, some bad language from Mother Shipton, and a Parthian volley of expletives[4] from Uncle Billy. The philosophic Oakhurst alone remained silent. He listened calmly to Mother Shipton's desire to cut somebody's heart out, to the repeated statements of the Duchess that she would die in the road, and to the alarming oaths that seemed to be bumped out of Uncle Billy as he rode forward. With the easy good-humor characteristic of his class, he insisted upon exchanging his own riding-horse, "Five Spot," for the sorry mule which the Duchess rode. But even this act did not draw the party into any closer sympathy. The young woman readjusted her somewhat draggled plumes with a feeble, faded coquetry; Mother Shipton eyed the possessor of "Five Spot" with malevolence, and Uncle Billy included the whole party in one sweeping **anathema**. **D**

anathema (ə-năth′ə-mə) *n.* a strong denunciation; a curse

D CLARIFY MEANING
Reread lines 44–55. What is your impression of Oakhurst at this point in the story? Compare him with the other outcasts.

---

1. **Roaring Camp:** name applied to a wild California settlement that was established in the 1830s by Isaac Graham. Harte used the name in his story "The Luck of Roaring Camp."
2. **"Mother Shipton":** originally, a 16th-century English woman who was accused of being a witch.
3. **sluice-robber** (slo͞os′rŏb-ər): a person who steals gold from sluices, or the water troughs used by miners to sift gold.
4. **Parthian volley of expletives:** crude or hostile remarks made when leaving. Soldiers from the ancient Asian land of Parthia typically shot at their enemies while pretending to retreat on horseback.

The road to Sandy Bar—a camp that, not having as yet experienced the regenerating influences of Poker Flat, consequently seemed to offer some invitation to the emigrants—lay over a steep mountain range. It was distant a day's severe travel. In that advanced season, the party soon passed out of the moist, temperate regions of the foot-hills into the dry, cold, bracing air of the Sierras.[5] The trail was narrow and difficult. At noon the Duchess, rolling out of her saddle upon the ground, declared her intention of going no farther, and the party halted.

The spot was singularly wild and impressive. A wooded amphitheatre, surrounded on three sides by precipitous cliffs of naked granite, sloped gently toward the crest of another precipice that overlooked the valley. It was, (E) undoubtedly, the most suitable spot for a camp, had camping been advisable. But Mr. Oakhurst knew that scarcely half the journey to Sandy Bar was accomplished, and the party were not equipped or provisioned for delay. This fact he pointed out to his companions curtly, with a philosophic commentary on the folly of "throwing up their hand before the game was played out." But they were furnished with liquor, which in this emergency stood them in place of food, fuel, rest, and **prescience.** In spite of his remonstrances, it was not long before they were more or less under its influence. Uncle Billy passed rapidly from a bellicose state into one of stupor, the Duchess became **maudlin,** and Mother Shipton snored. Mr. Oakhurst alone remained erect, leaning against a rock, calmly surveying them.

Mr. Oakhurst did not drink. It interfered with a profession which required coolness, impassiveness, and presence of mind, and, in his own language, he "couldn't afford it." As he gazed at his recumbent fellow-exiles, the loneliness begotten of his **pariah**-trade, his habits of life, his very vices, for the first time seriously oppressed him. He bestirred himself in dusting his black clothes, washing his hands and face, and other acts characteristic of his studiously neat habits, and for a moment forgot his annoyance. The thought of deserting his weaker and more pitiable companions never perhaps occurred to him. Yet he could not help feeling the want of that excitement which, singularly enough, was most conducive to that calm **equanimity** for which he was notorious. He looked at the gloomy walls that rose a thousand feet sheer above the circling pines around him; at the sky, ominously clouded; at the valley below, already deepening into shadow. And, doing so, suddenly he heard his own name called.

A horseman slowly ascended the trail. In the fresh, open face of the new-comer Mr. Oakhurst recognized Tom Simson, otherwise known as "The Innocent" of Sandy Bar. He had met him some months before over a "little game," and had, with perfect equanimity, won the entire fortune—amounting to some forty dollars—of that guileless youth. After the game was finished, Mr. Oakhurst drew the youthful speculator behind the door and thus addressed him: "Tommy, you're a good little man, but you can't gamble worth a cent. Don't try it over again." He then handed him his money back, pushed him gently from the room, and so made a devoted slave of Tom Simson.

(E) **REGIONALISM**
Setting, the place and time in which a story is set, is an essential element of Regionalism. Reread lines 56–65, and note Harte's **diction,** or word choice, as he describes the characters' physical surrounding: "steep mountain range"; "bracing air"; "singularly wild"; "precipitous cliffs"; "naked granite." Do you see words in the passage that indicate the time in history or time of season in which the story is set?

prescience (prĕsh'əns) *n.* knowledge of events before they occur

maudlin (môd'lĭn) *adj.* excessively sentimental

pariah (pə-rī'ə) *n.* an outcast, someone or something looked down on by others

equanimity (ē'kwə-nĭm'ĭ-tē) *n.* evenness of temper, especially under stress

5. **Sierras:** the Sierra Nevada range of mountains, in eastern California.

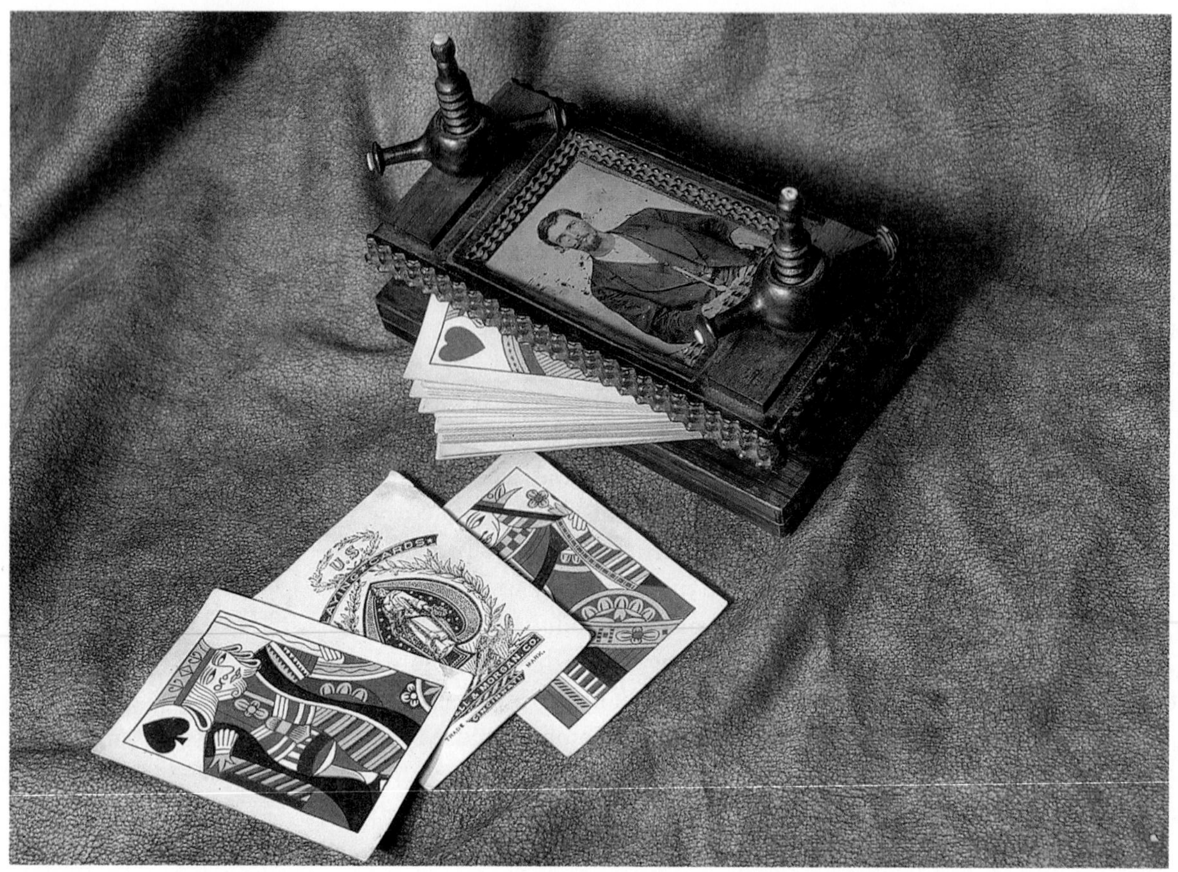

There was a remembrance of this in his boyish and enthusiastic greeting of Mr. Oakhurst. He had started, he said, to go to Poker Flat to seek his fortune. "Alone?" No, not exactly alone; in fact (a giggle), he had run away with Piney Woods. Didn't Mr. Oakhurst remember Piney? She that used to wait on the table at the Temperance House?[6] They had been engaged a long time, but old Jake Woods had objected, and so they had run away, and were going to Poker Flat to be married, and here they were. And they were tired out, and how lucky it was they had found a place to camp and company. All this the Innocent delivered rapidly, while Piney, a stout, comely damsel of fifteen, emerged from behind the pine tree, where she had been blushing unseen, and rode to the side of her lover.

Mr. Oakhurst seldom troubled himself with sentiment, still less with propriety; but he had a vague idea that the situation was not fortunate. He retained, however, his presence of mind sufficiently to kick Uncle Billy, who was about to say something, and Uncle Billy was sober enough to recognize in Mr. Oakhurst's kick a superior power that would not bear trifling. He then endeavored to dissuade Tom Simson from delaying further, but in vain. He even pointed out the fact that there was no provision, nor means of making a camp. But, unluckily, the Innocent met this objection by assuring the party that he was provided with an extra mule loaded with provisions, and by the discovery of a rude attempt at a log house near the trail. "Piney can stay with Mrs. Oakhurst," said the Innocent, pointing to the Duchess, "and I can shift for myself."

6. **Temperance House:** a place where customers could not drink.

Nothing but Mr. Oakhurst's admonishing foot saved Uncle Billy from bursting into a roar of laughter. As it was, he felt compelled to retire up the canyon until he could recover his gravity. There he confided the joke to the tall pine trees, with many slaps of his leg, contortions of his face, and the usual profanity. But when he returned to the party, he found them seated by a fire—for the air had grown strangely chill and the sky overcast—in apparently **amicable** conversation. Piney was actually talking in an impulsive, girlish fashion to the Duchess, who was listening with an interest and animation she had not shown for many days. The Innocent was holding forth, apparently with equal effect, to Mr. Oakhurst and Mother Shipton, who was actually relaxing into amiability. "Is this yer a d—d picnic?" said Uncle Billy, with inward scorn, as he surveyed the sylvan group, the glancing firelight, and the tethered animals in the foreground. Suddenly an idea mingled with the alcoholic fumes that disturbed his brain. It was apparently of a **jocular** nature, for he felt impelled to slap his leg again and cram his fist into his mouth. F

As the shadows crept slowly up the mountain, a slight breeze rocked the tops of the pine trees, and moaned through their long and gloomy aisles. The ruined cabin, patched and covered with pine boughs, was set apart for the ladies. As the lovers parted, they unaffectedly exchanged a kiss, so honest and sincere that it might have been heard above the swaying pines. The frail Duchess and the malevolent Mother Shipton were probably too stunned to remark upon this last evidence of simplicity, and so turned without a word to the hut. The fire was replenished, the men lay down before the door, and in a few minutes were asleep. G

Mr. Oakhurst was a light sleeper. Toward morning he awoke benumbed and cold. As he stirred the dying fire, the wind, which was now blowing strongly, brought to his cheek that which caused the blood to leave it—snow!

He started to his feet with the intention of awakening the sleepers, for there was no time to lose. But turning to where Uncle Billy had been lying, he found him gone. A suspicion leaped to his brain and a curse to his lips. He ran to the spot where the mules had been tethered; they were no longer there. The tracks were already rapidly disappearing in the snow.

The momentary excitement brought Mr. Oakhurst back to the fire with his usual calm. He did not waken the sleepers. The Innocent slumbered peacefully, with a smile on his good-humored, freckled face; the virgin Piney slept beside her frailer sisters as sweetly as though attended by celestial guardians, and Mr. Oakhurst, drawing his blanket over his shoulders, stroked his mustaches and waited for the dawn. It came slowly in a whirling mist of snowflakes, that dazzled and confused the eye. What could be seen of the landscape appeared magically changed. He looked over the valley, and summed up the present and future in two words—"snowed in!"

A careful inventory of the provisions, which, fortunately for the party, had been stored within the hut, and so escaped the felonious fingers of Uncle Billy, disclosed the fact that with care and prudence they might last ten days longer.

amicable (ăm'ĭ-kə-bəl) *adj.* characterized by friendly goodwill

jocular (jŏk'yə-lər) *adj.* humorous

F CLARIFY MEANING
Reread lines 117–133. What effect has the arrival of Tom and Piney had on the outcasts?

G GRAMMAR AND STYLE
Reread lines 134–135. Note that the **verbs** *crept* and *moaned* are used to **personify** the shadows and the breeze.

COMMON CORE RL 4, L 5b

Language Coach

Word Choice *Felonious* (line 159) means "criminal" and is related to the word *felony* (a term for a serious crime). Read lines 158 –160. Why do you think Harte might have chosen to use the word *felonious* instead of *criminal*?

"That is," said Mr. Oakhurst, *sotto voce*[7] to the Innocent, "if you're willing to board us." If you ain't—and perhaps you'd better not—you can wait till Uncle Billy gets back with provisions." For some occult reason, Mr. Oakhurst could not bring himself to disclose Uncle Billy's rascality, and so offered the hypothesis that he had wandered from the camp and had accidentally stampeded the animals. He dropped a warning to the Duchess and Mother Shipton, who of course knew the facts of their associate's defection. "They'll find out the truth about us *all* when they find out anything," he added, significantly, "and there's no good frightening them now."

Tom Simson not only put all his worldly store at the disposal of Mr. Oakhurst, but seemed to enjoy the prospect of their enforced seclusion. "We'll have a good camp for a week, and then the snow'll melt, and we'll all go back together." The cheerful gaiety of the young man and Mr. Oakhurst's calm infected the others. The Innocent, with the aid of pine boughs, extemporized a thatch for the roofless cabin, and the Duchess directed Piney in the rearrangement of the interior with a taste and tact that opened the blue eyes of that provincial maiden to their fullest extent. "I reckon now you're used to fine things at Poker Flat," said Piney. The Duchess turned away sharply to conceal something that reddened her cheeks through its professional tint, and Mother Shipton requested Piney not to "chatter." But when Mr. Oakhurst returned from a weary search for the trail, he heard the sound of happy laughter echoed from the rocks. He stopped in some alarm, and his thoughts first naturally reverted to the whiskey, which he had prudently cached.[8] "And yet it don't somehow sound like whiskey," said the gambler. It was not until he caught sight of the blazing fire through the still-blinding storm and the group around it that he settled to the conviction that it was "square fun." **H**

Whether Mr. Oakhurst had cached his cards with the whiskey as something debarred the free access of the community, I cannot say. It was certain that, in Mother Shipton's words, he "didn't say cards once" during the evening. Haply the time was beguiled by an accordion, produced somewhat ostentatiously by Tom Simson from his pack. Notwithstanding some difficulties attending the manipulation of this instrument, Piney Woods managed to pluck several reluctant melodies from its keys, to an accompaniment by the Innocent on a pair of bone castanets. But the crowning festivity of the evening was reached in a rude camp-meeting hymn, which the lovers, joining hands, sang with great earnestness and vociferation. I fear that a certain defiant tone and Covenanter's swing[9] to its chorus, rather than any devotional quality, caused it speedily to infect the others, who at last joined the refrain:

> "I'm proud to live in the service of the Lord,
> And I'm bound to die in His army."[10] **I**

COMMON CORE L4

Language Coach

Word Definitions
Often when people think of the word *occult*, they think of the supernatural. *Occult* (line 163) as an adjective can mean "related to the supernatural," or it can mean "secret" or "unknown." Which definition fits in this context?

H CLARIFY MEANING
Reread lines 170–185. What is Piney's impression of the Duchess? of Poker Flat?

I REGIONALISM
Reread lines 186–199. From the information given, what can you **infer** about the characters and the culture to which they belong?

---

7. ***sotto voce*** (sŏt'ō vō'chē) *Italian*: in a low voice.
8. **prudently cached** (kăshd): wisely hidden away.
9. **Covenanter's swing:** the strong rhythms of songs sung by Scottish Presbyterians, who made covenants or agreements to oppose the Church of England.
10. **"I'm proud . . . army":** lines from the early American spiritual "Service of the Lord."

The pines rocked, the storm eddied and whirled above the miserable group, and the flames of their altar leaped heavenward, as if in token of the vow.

At midnight the storm abated, the rolling clouds parted, and the stars glittered keenly above the sleeping camp. Mr. Oakhurst, whose professional habits had enabled him to live on the smallest possible amount of sleep, in dividing the watch with Tom Simson, somehow managed to take upon himself the greater part of that duty. He excused himself to the Innocent, by saying that he had "often been a week without sleep." "Doing what?" asked Tom. "Poker!" replied Oakhurst, sententiously; "when a man gets a streak of luck, he don't get tired. The luck gives in first. Luck," continued the gambler, reflectively, "is a mighty queer thing. All you know about it for certain is that it's bound to change. And it's finding out when it's going to change that makes you. We've had a streak of bad luck since we left Poker Flat—you come along, and slap you get into it, too. If you can hold your cards right along you're all right. For," added the gambler, with cheerful irrelevance,

> "I'm proud to live in the service of the Lord,
> And I'm bound to die in His army."

The third day came, and the sun, looking through the white-curtained valley, saw the outcasts divide their slowly decreasing store of provisions for the morning meal. It was one of the peculiarities of that mountain climate that its rays diffused a kindly warmth over the wintry landscape, as if in regretful commiseration of the past. But it revealed drift on drift of snow piled high around the hut—a hopeless, uncharted, trackless sea of white lying below the rocky shores to which the castaways still clung. Through the marvelously clear air the smoke of the pastoral village of Poker Flat rose miles away. Mother Shipton saw it, and from a remote pinnacle of her rocky fastness, hurled in that direction a final malediction.[11] It was her last **vituperative** attempt, and perhaps for that reason was invested with a certain degree of sublimity. It did her good, she privately informed the Duchess. "Just you go out there and cuss, and see." She then set herself to the task of amusing "the child," as she and the Duchess were pleased to call Piney. Piney was no chicken, but it was a soothing and original theory of the pair thus to account for the fact that she didn't swear and wasn't improper.

When night crept up again through the gorges, the reedy notes of the accordion rose and fell in fitful spasms and long-drawn gasps by the flickering campfire. But music failed to fill entirely the aching void left by insufficient food, and a new diversion was proposed by Piney—storytelling. Neither Mr. Oakhurst nor his female companions caring to relate their personal experiences, this plan would have failed, too, but for the Innocent. Some months before he had chanced upon a stray copy of Mr. Pope's ingenious translation of the *Iliad*.[12] He now proposed

vituperative
(vī-to͞o′pər-ə-tĭv) *adj.*
abusively critical

COMMON CORE RL 4, L 5a

Language Coach

Figurative Language
Read lines 232–233. Knowing that *spasms* are involuntary muscle movements and *gasps* are labored or difficult breaths, can you tell what Harte is saying through his description of Piney's accordion playing?

11. **malediction:** curse.
12. **Mr. Pope's . . . *Iliad*:** British poet Alexander Pope published his translation of Homer's *Iliad* in 1720.

to narrate the principal incidents of that poem—having thoroughly mastered the argument and fairly forgotten the words—in the current vernacular of Sandy Bar. And so for the rest of that night the Homeric demigods again walked the earth. Trojan bully and wily Greek wrestled in the winds, and the great pines in the canyon seemed to bow to the wrath of the son of Peleus.[13] Mr. Oakhurst listened with quiet satisfaction. Most especially was he interested in the fate of "Ash-heels," as the Innocent persisted in denominating the "swift-footed Achilles." **J**

So with small food and much of Homer and the accordion, a week passed over the heads of the outcasts. The sun again forsook them, and again from leaden skies the snowflakes were sifted over the land. Day by day closer around them drew the snowy circle, until at last they looked from their prison over drifted walls of dazzling white, that towered twenty feet above their heads. It became more and more difficult to replenish their fires, even from the fallen trees beside them, now half hidden in the drifts. And yet no one complained. The lovers turned from the dreary prospect and looked into each other's eyes, and were happy. Mr. Oakhurst settled himself coolly to the losing game before him. The Duchess, more cheerful than she had been, assumed the care of Piney. Only Mother Shipton—once the strongest of the party—seemed to sicken and fade. At midnight on the tenth day she called Oakhurst to her side. "I'm going," she said, in a voice of **querulous** weakness, "but don't say anything about it. Don't waken the kids. Take the bundle from under my head and open it." Mr. Oakhurst did so. It contained Mother Shipton's rations for the last week, untouched. "Give 'em to the child," she said, pointing to the sleeping Piney. "You've starved yourself," said the gambler. "That's

J CHARACTER TYPES
Reread lines 232–245. Notice how the fireside storytelling adds to the **characterization** of Tom Simson. His humorous retelling of the *Iliad* adds to his reputation as the Innocent. He is just one of several **character types** in a story of characters in exile. Characters who become outcasts appear repeatedly in American novels such as *The Great Gatsby* and *To Kill a Mockingbird*. What are some characters who are outcasts in recent films you have seen?

querulous (kwĕr′ə-ləs) *adj.* complaining

13. **son of Peleus** (pē′lē-əs): Achilles (ə-kĭl′ēz), the Greek hero in the *Iliad.* Tom Simson mispronounces his name as "Ash-heels."

what they call it," said the woman, querulously, as she lay down again, and, turning her face to the wall, passed quietly away. **K**

The accordion and the bones were put aside that day, and Homer was forgotten. When the body of Mother Shipton had been committed to the snow, Mr. Oakhurst took the Innocent aside, and showed him a pair of snowshoes, which he had fashioned from the old pack saddle. "There's one chance in a hundred to save her yet," he said, pointing to Piney; "but it's there," he added, pointing toward Poker Flat. "If you can reach there in two days she's safe." "And you?" asked Tom Simson. "I'll stay here," was the curt reply.

The lovers parted with a long embrace. "You are not going, too?" said the Duchess, as she saw Mr. Oakhurst apparently waiting to accompany him. "As far as the canyon," he replied. He turned suddenly, and kissed the Duchess, leaving her pallid face aflame, and her trembling limbs rigid with amazement.

Night came, but not Mr. Oakhurst. It brought the storm again and the whirling snow. Then the Duchess, feeding the fire, found that someone had quietly piled beside the hut enough fuel to last a few days longer. The tears rose to her eyes, but she hid them from Piney.

The women slept but little. In the morning, looking into each other's faces, they read their fate. Neither spoke; but Piney, accepting the position of the stronger, drew near and placed her arm around the Duchess's waist. They kept this attitude for the rest of the day. That night the storm reached its greatest fury, and, rendering asunder[14] the protecting pines, invaded the very hut.

Toward morning they found themselves unable to feed the fire, which gradually died away. As the embers slowly blackened, the Duchess crept closer to Piney, and broke the silence of many hours: "Piney, can you pray?" "No, dear," said Piney,

K CLARIFY MEANING
What happens to Mother Shipton? Explain whether or not you were surprised by this development, and why or why not.

COMMON CORE L 4

Language Coach

Multiple-Meaning Words
Attitude (line 282) is most often associated with a mental or emotional state. *Attitude* can also mean "posture" or "position." Why are Piney and the Duchess keeping this attitude?

14. **rending asunder:** forcefully ripping apart.

simply. The Duchess, without knowing exactly why, felt relieved, and, putting her head upon Piney's shoulder, spoke no more. And so reclining, the younger and purer pillowing the head of her soiled sister upon her virgin breast, they fell asleep.

The wind lulled as if it feared to waken them. Feathery drifts of snow, shaken from the long pine boughs, flew like white-winged birds, and settled about them as they slept. The moon through the rifted clouds looked down upon what had been the camp. But all human stain, all trace of earthly travail, was hidden beneath the spotless mantle mercifully flung from above.

They slept all that day and the next, nor did they waken when voices and footsteps broke the silence of the camp. And when pitying fingers brushed the snow from their wan faces, you could scarcely have told from the equal peace that dwelt upon them, which was she that had sinned. Even the law of Poker Flat recognized this, and turned away, leaving them still locked in each other's arms. **L**

L CLARIFY MEANING
Summarize what has happened to the Duchess and Piney. What point does the narrator seem to be making in lines 279–299?

But at the head of the gulch, on one of the largest pine trees, they found the deuce of clubs[15] pinned to the bark with a bowie-knife. It bore the following, written in pencil, in a firm hand:

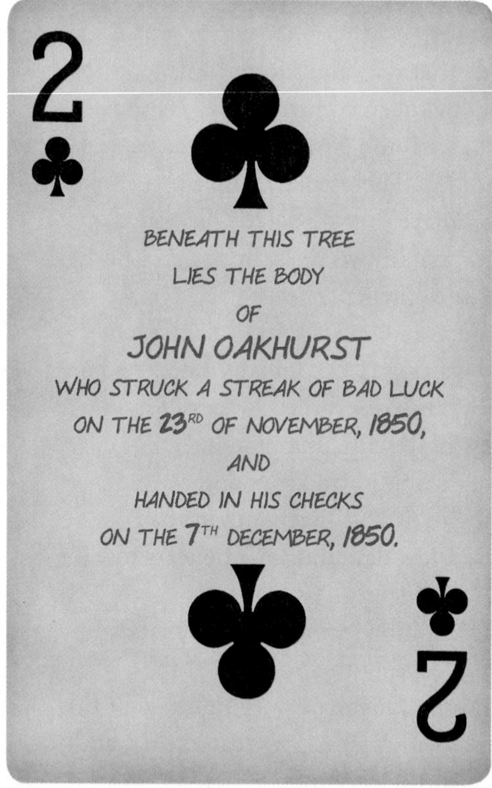

2
BENEATH THIS TREE
LIES THE BODY
OF
JOHN OAKHURST
WHO STRUCK A STREAK OF BAD LUCK
ON THE 23RD OF NOVEMBER, 1850,
AND
HANDED IN HIS CHECKS
ON THE 7TH DECEMBER, 1850.
2

And pulseless and cold, with a Derringer[16] by his side and a bullet in his heart, though still calm as in life, beneath the snow lay he who was at once the strongest and yet the weakest of the outcasts of Poker Flat. **M**

M CLARIFY MEANING
Why has Oakhurst committed this final act?

---

15. **deuce of clubs:** the lowest card in a deck of playing cards—thus a loser's card.

16. **Derringer:** a short-barreled pistol invented by American gunsmith Henry Derringer.

After Reading

Comprehension

1. **Recall** Why do Mr. Oakhurst and the others leave Poker Flat?
2. **Recall** Who joins the traveling group at their camp?
3. **Summarize** What happens to the travelers at the camp?

COMMON CORE

RL 1 Cite evidence to support analysis of what the text says explicitly. **RL 2** Determine two or more themes or central ideas of a text. **RL 3** Analyze the impact of the author's choices regarding how to develop and relate elements of a story.

Text Analysis

4. **Clarify Meaning** Review the following quotations within the context of the story and paraphrase what they mean:
   - "There was a Sabbath lull in the air, which, in a settlement unused to Sabbath influences, looked ominous." (lines 5–6)
   - "Mr. Oakhurst seldom troubled himself with sentiment, still less with propriety; but he had a vague idea that the situation was not fortunate." (lines 108–109)
5. **Examine the Main Character** Bret Harte was known for portraying the character type of an outcast with a heart of gold. How does John Oakhurst fit this formula of the character with contradictory traits? Use a chart to explore this question.

Outcast Traits	Virtuous Traits

6. **Interpret Author's Perspective** Personal experience and historical context influence the characters and conflicts that a writer chooses to depict. Based on events in this story and their outcome, how would you describe Harte's opinion of the following?
   - John Oakhurst
   - society in the Old West
   - human nature
7. **Evaluate Use of Regionalism** The goal of regionalists was to capture life at a particular time in history. In your opinion, how well did Harte convey the region, the people, and the times in "The Outcasts of Poker Flat"? Cite evidence to support your view.

Text Criticism

8. **Critical Interpretations** Mark Twain said that it was Bret Harte who "trimmed and schooled me patiently until he changed me from an awkward utterer of coarse grotesqueness to a writer of paragraphs and chapters." Harte also influenced Ambrose Bierce and Rudyard Kipling. Why do you think Harte might have had a strong impact on so many writers?

What does it mean to be an **OUTCAST?**

Besides being literally "cast out" of Poker Flat, in what way are Oakhurst, the Duchess, Mother Shipton, and Uncle Billy exiles from society? What moral statement does the author make about their fellow townspeople?

Vocabulary in Context

▲ VOCABULARY PRACTICE

Show you understand the vocabulary words by answering these questions.

1. If I handled a situation with **equanimity,** would I be upset about it or calm?
2. Which could be considered **maudlin,** a stern lecture or a mushy love story?
3. Would a **querulous** person be more likely to enjoy a party or find fault with it?
4. If I am **expatriated,** am I living in exile or returning to my own country?
5. Is a party host or a prosecuting lawyer more likely to be **amicable?**
6. Is a **pariah** shunned or welcomed into gatherings?
7. If a person utters an **anathema,** is he or she expressing anger or compassion?
8. Who is more likely to be **jocular,** a runner or a comedian?
9. Does someone with **prescience** predict future events or excel in chemistry?
10. Would a **vituperative** tutor encourage her students or scold them?

WORD LIST
amicable
anathema
equanimity
expatriated
jocular
maudlin
pariah
prescience
querulous
vituperative

ACADEMIC VOCABULARY IN WRITING

• apparent • confine • expose • focus • perceive

Which character, in your opinion, proves to be the most admirable? After you select a character, write a paragraph describing when it becomes **apparent** that the character is admirable. **Focus** your description on some specific action of the character, and use at least one Academic Vocabulary word in your response.

COMMON CORE

L 4b Identify and correctly use patterns of word changes that indicate different meanings or parts of speech. **L 6** Acquire and use accurately general academic words and phrases.

VOCABULARY STRATEGY: THE LATIN ROOT *equ*

The origin of the root *equ,* which means "even," "just," or "equal," is the Latin language. The vocabulary word *equanimity* contains this root. Occasionally spelled *iqu,* this root is found in a number of English words. In its prefix form *equi,* it is sometimes combined with existing words to form new words, as in *equiprobable.* To understand words with *equ,* use context clues and your knowledge of root and affix meanings.

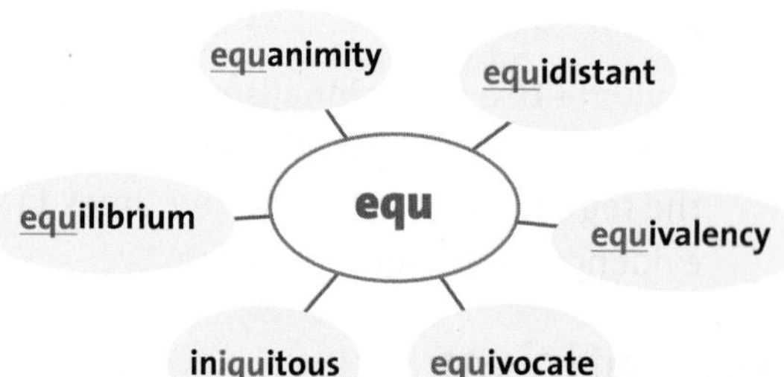

PRACTICE Apply what you know about *equ, equi,* and other word parts to help you understand the words in the web. Then choose the word that best completes each sentence. If necessary, consult a dictionary.

1. If you _____, it may be said that you are talking out of both sides of your mouth.
2. What town is _____ between Chicago and Milwaukee?
3. The accident affected her _____, and she often felt dizzy.
4. Passing a high school ____ test can take the place of actually graduating.

Language

GRAMMAR AND STYLE: Add Descriptive Details

Review the **Grammar and Style** note on page 703. Harte uses **personification**—the attribution of human qualities to objects or ideas—to enliven his descriptions of inanimate objects. Here is an example from the story:

> *The third day came, and the sun, looking through the white-curtained valley, saw the outcasts divide their slowly decreasing store of provisions for the morning meal.* (lines 217–219)

Harte's use of the highlighted **participial phrase** and **verb** creates an ethereal image of the sun "watching" the outcasts.

PRACTICE Rewrite each of the following sentences to include personification.

EXAMPLE

We could see the town at the top of the mountain but couldn't see most of its buildings.

The town seemed to turn its back on us, hiding its buildings from our view down in the valley.

1. The mountain was solid rock, very steep, and very tall.
2. Lights were shining in some of the windows.
3. Snow began to fall, making it harder to see the town way above us.

COMMON CORE

L 3 Apply knowledge of language to make effective choices for style. **W 3b, e** Use narrative techniques, such as description; provide a conclusion that follows from and reflects on what is observed.

READING-WRITING CONNECTION

Expand your understanding of "The Outcasts of Poker Flat" by responding to this prompt. Then, use the **revising tips** to improve your description.

WRITING PROMPT	REVISING TIPS
WRITE A DESCRIPTION Think of a real or fictional society that you might like to write about in a short story. Then, write a three- or four-paragraph description of that society from the perspective of a person who has been sent into exile and must live just on the outskirts of the city or town. Your character should conclude by reflecting on the good and bad points about the place.	• Add precise words and sensory details to make your description vivid and realistic. • Write from a first-person point of view, using the personal pronoun I. • Include a description of setting, the time and place in which your society exists.

COMMON CORE

RL 3 Analyze the impact of the author's choices regarding how to develop and relate elements of a story. **RL 6** Analyze a case in which grasping point of view requires distinguishing what is directly stated in a text from what is really meant. **L 1a** Apply the understanding that usage is a matter of convention.

from Lake Wobegon Days

Garrison Keillor

BACKGROUND Garrison Keillor follows in the tradition of such great regional storytellers as Mark Twain and Will Rogers. Like his predecessors, Keillor draws on childhood experiences to paint whimsical pictures of the characters and local color of small-town life. *Lake Wobegon Days* is a novel set in Wobegon, Minnesota, a fictionalized version of his hometown. Keillor, a Minnesota native, originally wrote many of the Wobegon stories for a weekly variety show on public radio called *A Prarie Home Companion*. The show first aired in 1974 and, with one six-year hiatus, continued into the 21st century. Keillor's stories of life in rural Minnesota share an especially close kinship with Twain's stories of life along the Mississippi River in Missouri.

People who visit Lake Wobegon come to see somebody, otherwise they missed the turn on the highway and are lost. *Ausländers,* the Germans call them. They don't come for Toast 'n Jelly Days, or the Germans' quadrennial Gesuffa Days, or Krazy Daze, or the Feast Day of St. Francis, or the three-day Mist County Fair with its exciting Death Leap from the top of the grandstand to the arms of the haystack for only ten cents. What's special about here isn't special enough to draw a major crowd, though Flag Day—you could drive a long way on June 14 to find another like it.

Flag Day, as we know it, was the idea of Herman Hochstetter, Rollie's dad, who ran the dry goods store and ran Armistice Day, the Fourth of July, and Flag Day. For the Fourth, he organized a double-loop parade around the block which allowed people to take turns marching and watching. On Armistice Day, everyone stepped outside at 11 A.M and stood in silence for two minutes as Our Lady's bell tolled eleven times.

Flag Day was his favorite. For a modest price, he would install a bracket on your house to hold a pole to hang your flag on, or he would drill a hole in the sidewalk in the front of your store with his drill gun powered by a .22 shell. *Bam!* And in went the flag. On patriotic days, flags flew all over; there were flags on the tall poles, flags on the short, flags in the brackets on the pillars and the porches, and if you were flagless you could expect to hear from Herman. His hairy arm around your shoulder, his poochlike face close to yours, he would say how proud he was that so many people were proud of their country, leaving you to see the obvious, that you were a gap in the ranks.

In June 1944, the day after D-Day, a salesman from Fisher Hat called on Herman and offered a good deal on red and blue baseball caps. "Do you have white also?" Herman asked. The salesman thought that white caps could be had for the same wonderful price. Herman ordered two hundred red, two hundred white, and one hundred blue. By the end of the year, he still had four hundred and eighty-six caps. The inspiration of the Living Flag was born from that overstock.

On June 14, 1945, a month after V-E Day, a good crowd assembled in front of the Central Building in response to Herman's ad in the paper:

> Honor "AMERICA" June 14 AT 4 P.M. Be proud of "Our Land & People". Be part of the "LIVING FLAG". Don't let it be said that Lake Wobegon was "Too Busy". Be on time. 4 P.M. "Sharp".

His wife Louise handed out the caps, and Herman stood on a stepladder and told people where to stand. He lined up the reds and whites into stripes, then got the blues into their square. Mr. Hanson climbed up on the roof of the Central Building and took a photograph, they sang the national anthem, and then the Living Flag dispersed. The photograph appeared in the paper the next week. Herman kept the caps.

In the flush of victory, people were happy to do as told and stand in place, but in 1946 and 1947, dissension cropped up in the ranks: people complained about the heat and about Herman—what gave *him* the idea he could order *them* around? "People! Please! I need your attention! You blue people, keep your hats on! Please! Stripe No. 4, you're sagging! You reds, you're up here! We got too many white people, we need more red ones! Let's do this without talking, people! I can't get you straight if you keep moving around! Some of you are not paying attention! Everybody shut up! Please!"

One cause of resentment was the fact that none of them got to see the Flag they were in; the picture in the paper was black and white. Only Herman and Mr. Hanson got to see the real Flag, and some boys too short to be needed down below. People wanted a chance to go up to the roof and witness the spectacle for themselves. **A**

"How can you go up there if you're supposed to be down here?" Herman said. "You go up there to look, you got nothing to look at. Isn't it enough that you're doing your part?"

On Flag Day, 1949, just as Herman said, "That's it! Hold it now!" one of the reds made a break for it—dashed up four flights of stairs to the roof and leaned over and had a long look. Even with the hole he left behind, it was a magnificent sight. The

COMMON CORE RL 6

A CHARACTER TYPES
As an offshoot of Realism, **Regionalism** sought to accurately portray the speech, manners, and habits of people from a particular geographic region. Like Mark Twain a century before him, Keillor favors common characters whose sincerity and humility are often in stark contrast to the absurdity of their words and actions. Twain was exceptionally skilled at creating humor through irony. Reread lines 40–51, and look for ways in which Keillor uses irony to reveal the humor of his characters' words and actions.

Living Flag filled the street below. A perfect Flag! The reds so brilliant! He couldn't take his eyes off it. "Get down here! We need a picture!" Herman yelled up to him. "How does it look?" people yelled up to him. "Unbelievable! I can't describe it!" he said.

So then everyone had to have a look. "No!" Herman said, but they took a vote and it was unanimous. One by one, members of the Living Flag went up to the roof and admired it. It *was* marvelous! It brought tears to the eyes, it made one reflect on this great country and on Lake Wobegon's place in it. One wanted to stand up there all afternoon and just drink it in. So, as the first hour passed, and only forty of the five hundred had been to the top, the others got more and more restless. "Hurry up! Quit dawdling! *You've* seen it! Get down here and give someone else a chance!" Herman sent people up in groups of four, and then ten, but after two hours, the Living Flag became the Sitting Flag and then began to erode, as the members who had had a look thought about heading home to supper, which infuriated the ones who hadn't. "Ten more minutes!" Herman cried, but ten minutes became twenty and thirty, and people snuck off and the Flag that remained for the last viewer was a Flag shot through by cannon fire.

In 1950, the Sons of Knute took over Flag Day. Herman gave them the boxes of caps. Since then, the Knutes have achieved several good Flags, though most years the attendance was poor. You need at least four hundred to make a good one. Some years the Knutes made a "no-look" rule, other years they held a lottery. One year they experimented with a large mirror held by two men over the edge of the roof, but when people leaned back and looked up, the Flag disappeared, of course.

Text Analysis

1. **Analyze Local Color** One of the primary characteristics of regional writing is **local color,** or writing that portrays the customs, character types, mannerisms, and speech of a region. What elements of local color do you find in this excerpt? Citing evidence from the text, characterize the residents of small-town Minnesota as portrayed by Keillor.

2. **Compare Texts** As Twain does in the excerpt from his *Autobiography* and in "The Notorious Jumping Frog of Calaveras County," Keillor depicts a community event in a small town. Which author uses dialect or local conventions of language usage more effectively to portray setting? Explain, citing evidence from the texts.

COMMON CORE

RL 1 Cite evidence to support inferences drawn from the text. **RL 3** Analyze the impact of the author's choices regarding how to develop and relate elements of a story. **L 2a** Observe hyphenation conventions.

A Wagner Matinee

Short Story by Willa Cather

Meet the Author

Willa Cather 1873–1947

Willa Cather believed that "the most basic material a writer works with is acquired before the age of 15." Indeed, it was the American West of Cather's early years that inspired the majority of her literary successes.

The Power of Place At age nine, Virginia-born Willa Cather moved to Nebraska with her family. The prairie challenged Cather—and almost all other settlers—with its "erasure of personality" and made her feel that she "would go under." But after a difficult transition, Cather grew to love the harsh prairie and to admire the immigrants—especially women—who struggled daily against an unforgiving climate. Though they lived by hard physical labor, many of these immigrants were educated people. They introduced Cather to French and German literature, also teaching her Latin and Greek. Nebraska and Cather's childhood neighbors —whose stories "went round and round in [her] head"— dramatically influenced her writing.

Seeing the World After college, where she did some writing, Cather went back east and worked as a journalist, teacher, and magazine editor. During this time, she met her best friend, Isabelle McClung, who sparked in her a lifelong interest in music, which can be seen in "A Wagner Matinee." She also formed lifelong relationships with her companion Edith Lewis and writer Sarah Orne Jewett. Cather also saw something of the world on several trips to France and then to the American Southwest.

Developing a Voice Around 1906, Cather moved to New York City and began a full-time writing career. Though she never lived in Nebraska again, the prairie was never far from her work. Many of her 12 novels and 58 stories had prairie settings or immigrant characters, showing Cather's respect for the grit needed to endure everyday life. Some of these characters were directly drawn from real people Cather had known, such as childhood friend Annie (Anna) who formed the basis of the main character in her novel *My Ántonia.*

Choices Willa Cather chose an artist's life rather than the everyday family life she so closely observed in her Nebraska neighbors. She once said to a friend that "nothing mattered to her but writing books, and living the kind of life that makes it possible to write them." Willa Cather lived that life until her death in 1947.

DID YOU KNOW?

Willa Cather . . .

- had such a sharp memory for mannerisms and turns of speech that she never took notes.
- wrote six novels about her home town of Red Cloud, Nebraska, while living in New York's Greenwich Village.
- received the Pulitzer Prize in 1923.

Author Online THINK central

Go to thinkcentral.com. KEYWORD: HML11-716

TEXT ANALYSIS: SETTING

In Willa Cather's fiction, the development of the plot and characters is heavily influenced by the **setting,** or the time and place in which the story occurs. In "A Wagner Matinee," the narrator's aunt has moved from Boston to the Nebraska frontier; these places determine the kind of person she becomes. Setting can also serve as a **symbol.** As you read, note the details of each location and what they seem to represent.

READING SKILL: DRAW CONCLUSIONS ABOUT CHARACTER

Understanding a character in a story is like getting to know a real person. You **draw conclusions,** or make reasonable judgments, about the person by combining the impressions you have already formed with new facts you discover. To become better acquainted with Aunt Georgiana, the main character in "A Wagner Matinee," look closely at the details as you read the story. Create a chart like the one shown, using it to record details and **make inferences** about Aunt Georgiana. At the end of the story, you will use these specific inferences to draw larger conclusions about her character.

Observations About ...	What They Reveal
physical appearance: • •	
major decision: • •	
actions and reactions: • •	

VOCABULARY IN CONTEXT

Cather uses the listed words to develop setting and character. Choose a word from the list to complete each phrase.

WORD LIST	callow	overture	tentatively
	excruciatingly	somnambulant	veritable
	myriad	sordid	

1. _____ employees with more bravado than experience
2. _____ tasks to complete—almost too many to count
3. living in _____, disgusting conditions
4. agreed _____ to take on the additional work

Complete the activities in your **Reader/Writer Notebook.**

Does it matter where we LIVE?

Imagine life on an island with only a few dozen other people. How would it shape your social life? your work habits? your relationship to nature? Now think about life in a big city. How would these things be different? The places we live really shape our personality and values.

DISCUSS As a class, choose two very different places and discuss the lifestyles of the people who live there. Then consider how life in each place would shape the personalities of its inhabitants.

A Wagner Matinee

Willa Cather

BACKGROUND "A Wagner Matinee" takes place in Nebraska and Boston around 1900. At the time, Bostonians could attend concerts of works by European composers such as Richard Wagner (väg′nər). Americans who moved west, such as Willa Cather's family and Aunt Georgiana in this story, left such worldly pleasures behind. Instead, the settlers endured long hours of strenuous labor, and natural disasters such as drought, flood, and prairie fires.

Analyze Visuals ▶
Look at the painting on page 719. What might souvenirs like these signify to a settler who left the city for life on the prairie? Explain.

THEME
When you grow old, will you be satisfied with the life you've lived? That's a question people have been asking for ages. Several modern writers and filmmakers have created characters who have regrets about their lives. Can you think of any 21st-century works that share this focus?

I received one morning a letter, written in pale ink on glassy, blue-lined note-paper, and bearing the postmark of a little Nebraska village. This communication, worn and rubbed, looking as though it had been carried for some days in a coat pocket that was none too clean, was from my Uncle Howard and informed me that his wife had been left a small legacy by a bachelor relative who had recently died, and that it would be necessary for her to go to Boston to attend to the settling of the estate. He requested me to meet her at the station and render her whatever services might be necessary. On examining the date indicated as that of her arrival, I found it no later than tomorrow. He had characteristically delayed writing until, had I been away from home for a day, I must have missed the good woman altogether. **A**

A SETTING
What does the **description** of the letter tell you about the place the letter was sent from? What does the description suggest about the place the letter was sent to? Give details to support your answer.

The name of my Aunt Georgiana called up not alone her own figure, at once pathetic and grotesque, but opened before my feet a gulf of recollection so wide and deep, that, as the letter dropped from my hand, I felt suddenly a stranger to all the present conditions of my existence, wholly ill at ease and out of place amid the familiar surroundings of my study. I became, in short, the gangling farmer-boy

Old Souvenirs (about 1881–1901), John F. Peto. Bequest of Oliver Burr Jennings, 1968 (68.205.3). Metropolitan Museum of Art, New York.

Bulletin.
PRICE THREE CENTS
ADELPHIA
FIRE
INSURANCE
RO
POSTAL CARD
NEW YORK
PHILADELPHIA
13
IMPORTANT INFORMATION INSID

my aunt had known, scourged with chilblains[1] and bashfulness, my hands cracked and sore from the corn husking. I felt the knuckles of my thumb **tentatively,** as though they were raw again. I sat again before her parlor organ, fumbling the scales with my stiff, red hands, while she, beside me, made canvas mittens for the huskers.[2]

tentatively (tĕn′tə-tĭv-lē) *adv.* in a hesitant or uncertain manner

The next morning, after preparing my landlady somewhat, I set out for the station. When the train arrived I had some difficulty in finding my aunt. She was the last of the passengers to alight, and it was not until I got her into the carriage that she seemed really to recognize me. She had come all the way in a day coach; her linen duster[3] had become black with soot and her black bonnet grey with dust during the journey. When we arrived at my boarding-house the landlady put her to bed at once and I did not see her again until the next morning.

Whatever shock Mrs. Springer experienced at my aunt's appearance, she considerately concealed. As for myself, I saw my aunt's misshapen figure with that feeling of awe and respect with which we behold explorers who have left their ears and fingers north of Franz-Josef-Land, or their health somewhere along the Upper Congo.[4] My Aunt Georgiana had been a music teacher at the Boston Conservatory, somewhere back in the latter sixties. One summer, while visiting in the little village among the Green Mountains[5] where her ancestors had dwelt

Language Coach

Prefixes *Misshapen* (line 30) means "badly shaped" or "deformed." The prefix *mis-* means "wrong," "badly," or "not." Using this information, give the meanings of the following words: *misadvise, misdeed, misunderstood.*

1. **scourged with chilblains:** tormented with painful swelling or sores on the hands or feet caused by exposure to the cold.
2. **huskers:** farm workers who remove cornhusks by hand.
3. **duster:** a long, lightweight overgarment to protect clothing from dust.
4. **Franz-Josef-Land . . . Upper Congo:** Franz-Josef-Land is a group of small, mostly ice-covered islands in the Arctic Ocean, north of Russia. The Upper Congo is part of a major river in central Africa.
5. **Green Mountains:** a mountain range in Vermont.

Family and Their Dugout (1870s), Anonymous. Photo 11″ × 14″. Near McCook, Nebraska. © Nebraska State Historical Society, Lincoln, Nebraska.

for generations, she had kindled the **callow** fancy of the most idle and shiftless of all the village lads, and had conceived for this Howard Carpenter one of those extravagant passions which a handsome country boy of twenty-one sometimes inspires in an angular, spectacled woman of thirty. When she returned to her duties in Boston, Howard followed her, and the upshot of this inexplicable infatuation was that she eloped with him, eluding the reproaches of her family and the criticisms of her friends by going with him to the Nebraska frontier. Carpenter, who, of course, had no money, had taken a homestead in Red Willow County,[6] fifty miles from the railroad. There they had measured off their quarter section themselves by driving across the prairie in a wagon, to the wheel of which they had tied a red cotton handkerchief, and counting off its revolutions. They built a dugout in the red hillside, one of those cave dwellings whose inmates so often reverted to primitive conditions. Their water they got from the lagoons where the buffalo drank, and their slender stock of provisions was always at the mercy of bands of roving Indians. For thirty years my aunt had not been further than fifty miles from the homestead. **B**

But Mrs. Springer knew nothing of all this, and must have been considerably shocked at what was left of my kinswoman. Beneath the soiled linen duster which, on her arrival, was the most conspicuous feature of her costume, she wore a black stuff[7] dress, whose ornamentation showed that she had surrendered herself unquestioningly into the hands of a country dressmaker. My poor aunt's figure, however, would have presented astonishing difficulties to any dressmaker. Originally stooped, her shoulders were now almost bent together over her sunken chest. She wore no stays, and her gown, which trailed unevenly behind, rose in a sort of peak over her abdomen. She wore ill-fitting false teeth, and her skin was as yellow as a Mongolian's from constant exposure to a pitiless wind and to the alkaline water which hardens the most transparent cuticle into a sort of flexible leather. **C**

I owed to this woman most of the good that ever came my way in my boyhood, and had a reverential affection for her. During the years when I was riding herd for my uncle, my aunt, after cooking the three meals—the first of which was ready at six o'clock in the morning—and putting the six children to bed, would often stand until midnight at her ironing-board, with me at the kitchen table beside her, hearing me recite Latin declensions and conjugations,[8] gently shaking me when my drowsy head sank down over a page of irregular verbs. It was to her, at her ironing or mending, that I read my first Shakespeare, and her old text-book on mythology was the first that ever came into my empty hands. She taught me my scales and exercises, too—on the little parlor organ, which her husband had bought her after fifteen years, during which she had not so much as seen any instrument, but an accordion that belonged to one of the Norwegian farmhands. She would sit beside me by the hour, darning and counting while I struggled with the "Joyous Farmer,"[9] but she seldom talked to me about music, and I understood why. She was a pious

callow (kăl'ō) *adj.* lacking adult experience; immature

B SETTING
Consider the **description** of the homestead in lines 43–51. How do you think life in such a place might affect a woman with Aunt Georgiana's background?

C DRAW CONCLUSIONS
Reread lines 52–62. What can you **infer** about Aunt Georgiana based on Cather's vivid description of her physical appearance?

6. **Red Willow County:** county in southwestern Nebraska, bordering on Kansas.
7. **stuff:** a woolen material.
8. **Latin declensions and conjugations:** forms of Latin nouns and verbs representing different cases and tenses.
9. **"Joyous Farmer":** one of a series of musical pieces for children by German composer Robert Schumann.

woman; she had the consolations of religion and, to her at least, her martyrdom was not wholly **sordid.** Once when I had been doggedly beating out some easy passages from an old score of *Euryanthe*[10] I had found among her music books, she came up to me and, putting her hands over my eyes, gently drew my head back upon her shoulder, saying tremulously, "Don't love it so well, Clark, or it may be taken from you. Oh! dear boy, pray that whatever your sacrifice may be, it be not that." **D**

When my aunt appeared on the morning after her arrival, she was still in a semi-**somnambulant** state. She seemed not to realize that she was in the city where she had spent her youth, the place longed for hungrily half a lifetime. She had been so wretchedly train-sick throughout the journey that she had no recollection of anything but her discomfort, and, to all intents and purposes, there were but a few hours of nightmare between the farm in Red Willow County and my study on Newbury Street. I had planned a little pleasure for her that afternoon, to repay her for some of the glorious moments she had given me when we used to milk together in the straw-thatched cowshed and she, because I was more than usually tired, or because her husband had spoken sharply to me, would tell me of the splendid performance of the *Huguenots*[11] she had seen in Paris, in her youth. At two o'clock the Symphony Orchestra was to give a Wagner program, and I intended to take my aunt; though, as I conversed with her, I grew doubtful about her enjoyment of it. Indeed, for her own sake, I could only wish her taste for such things quite dead, and the long struggle mercifully ended at last. I suggested our visiting the Conservatory and the Common[12] before lunch, but she seemed altogether too timid to wish to venture out. She questioned me absently about various changes in the city, but she was chiefly concerned that she had forgotten to leave instructions about feeding half-skimmed milk to a certain weakling calf, "old Maggie's calf, you know, Clark," she explained, evidently having forgotten how long I had been away. She was further troubled because she had neglected to tell her daughter about the freshly-opened kit of mackerel in the cellar, which would spoil if it were not used directly.

I asked her whether she had ever heard any of the Wagnerian operas,[13] and found that she had not, though she was perfectly familiar with their respective situations, and had once possessed the piano score of *The Flying Dutchman.* I began to think it would have been best to get her back to Red Willow County without waking her, and regretted having suggested the concert.

From the time we entered the concert hall, however, she was a trifle less passive and inert, and for the first time seemed to perceive her surroundings. I had felt some trepidation lest she might become aware of the absurdities of her attire, or might experience some painful embarrassment at stepping suddenly into the world to which she had been dead for a quarter of a century. But, again, I found how superficially I

sordid (sôr′dĭd) *adj.* wretched; dirty; morally degraded

D DRAW CONCLUSIONS
Reread lines 63–82. What does Aunt Georgiana's treatment of her nephew reveal about her?

somnambulant (sŏm-năm′byə-lənt′) *adj.* sleepwalking

COMMON CORE L 2a

Language Coach

Compound Adjectives *Freshly-opened* (line 104) is an example of a **compound adjective.** This phrase modifies the noun *kit.* To avoid confusion, the words in a compound adjective are normally separated by a hyphen (-) when they appear immediately before the word they modify. If they follow the word they modify, no hyphen is needed: *The kit of mackerel was freshly opened.* What are some other common compound adjectives?

10. ***Euryanthe*** (yo͝or′ē-ăn′thē): an opera by German composer Carl Maria von Weber.
11. ***Huguenots*** (hyo͞o′gə-nŏts′): an opera by German composer Giacomo Meyerbeer.
12. **the Common:** Boston Common, a public park.
13. **Wagnerian operas:** The orchestra will play selections from several operas composed by Wagner, including *The Flying Dutchman, Tannhäuser, Tristan and Isolde,* and a cycle of four operas called *The Ring of the Nibelung.*

had judged her. She sat looking about her with eyes as impersonal, almost as stony, as those with which the granite Rameses[14] in a museum watches the froth and fret that ebbs and flows[15] about his pedestal—separated from it by the lonely stretch of centuries. I have seen this same aloofness in old miners who drift into the Brown hotel at Denver, their pockets full of bullion,[16] their linen soiled, their haggard faces unshaven; standing in the thronged corridors as solitary as though they were still in a frozen camp on the Yukon, conscious that certain experiences have isolated them from their fellows by a gulf no haberdasher[17] could bridge.

We sat at the extreme left of the first balcony, facing the arc of our own and the balcony above us, **veritable** hanging gardens, brilliant as tulip beds. The matinée audience was made up chiefly of women. One lost the contour of faces and figures, indeed any effect of line whatever, and there was only the color of bodices past counting, the shimmer of fabrics soft and firm, silky and sheer; red, mauve, pink, blue, lilac, purple, ecru, rose, yellow, cream, and white, all the colors that an impressionist[18] finds in a sunlit landscape, with here and there the dead shadow of a frock coat. My Aunt Georgiana regarded them as though they had been so many daubs of tube-paint on a palette.

veritable (vĕr′ĭ-tə-bəl) *adj.* true; not unreal or imaginary

When the musicians came out and took their places, she gave a little stir of anticipation and looked with quickening interest down over the rail at that invariable grouping, perhaps the first wholly familiar thing that had greeted her eye since she had left old Maggie and her weakling calf. I could feel how all those details sank into her soul, for I had not forgotten how they had sunk into mine when I came fresh from ploughing forever and forever between green aisles of corn, where, as in a treadmill, one might walk from daybreak to dusk without perceiving a shadow of change. The clean profiles of the musicians, the gloss of their linen, the dull black of their coats, the beloved shapes of the instruments, the patches of yellow light thrown by the green shaded lamps on the smooth, varnished bellies of the 'cellos and the bass viols in the rear, the restless, wind-tossed forest of fiddle necks and bows—I recalled how, in the first orchestra I had ever heard, those long bow strokes seemed to draw the heart out of me, as a conjurer's stick reels out yards of paper ribbon from a hat. **E**

E SETTING
Reread lines 133–146. How does Aunt Georgiana respond to the setting of the Boston concert hall?

The first number was the *Tannhauser* **overture.** When the horns drew out the first strain of the Pilgrim's chorus, my Aunt Georgiana clutched my coat sleeve. Then it was I first realized that for her this broke a silence of thirty years; the inconceivable silence of the plains. With the battle between the two motives, with the frenzy of the Venusberg theme and its ripping of strings, there came to me an overwhelming sense of the waste and wear we are so powerless to combat;

overture (ō′vər-cho͞or′) *n.* the orchestral introduction to a musical dramatic work

14. **Rameses** (răm′ĭ-sēz′): one of the ancient kings of Egypt of that name.
15. **froth . . . flows:** happiness and sadness that come and go.
16. **bullion:** gold.
17. **haberdasher:** a dealer in men's clothing and accessories.
18. **impressionist:** a follower of a movement in French painting that emphasized the play of light and color.

and I saw again the tall, naked house on the prairie, black and grim as a wooden fortress; the black pond where I had learned to swim, its margin pitted with sun-dried cattle tracks; the rain-gullied clay banks about the naked house, the four dwarf ash seedlings where the dish-cloths were always hung to dry before the kitchen door. The world there was the flat world of the ancients; to the east, a cornfield that stretched to daybreak; to the west, a corral that reached to sunset; between, the conquests of peace, dearer bought than those of war.

The overture closed, my aunt released my coat sleeve, but she said nothing. She sat staring at the orchestra through a dullness of thirty years, through the films made little by little by each of the three hundred and sixty-five days in every one of them. What, I wondered, did she get from it? She had been a good pianist in her day I knew, and her musical education had been broader than that of most music teachers of a quarter of a century ago. She had often told me of Mozart's operas and Meyerbeer's, and I could remember hearing her sing, years ago, certain melodies of Verdi's. When I had fallen ill with a fever in her house she used to sit by my cot in the evening—when the cool, night wind blew in through the faded mosquito netting tacked over the window and I lay watching a certain bright star that burned red above the cornfield—and sing "Home to our mountains, O, let us return!" in a way fit to break the heart of a Vermont boy near dead of homesickness already.

I watched her closely through the prelude to *Tristan and Isolde,* trying vainly to conjecture what that seething turmoil of strings and winds might mean to her, but she sat mutely staring at the violin bows that drove obliquely downward, like the pelting streaks of rain in a summer shower. Had this music any message for her? Had she enough left to at all comprehend this power which had kindled the world since she had left it? I was in a fever of curiosity, but Aunt Georgiana sat silent upon her peak in Darien.[19] She preserved this utter immobility throughout the number from *The Flying Dutchman,* though her fingers worked mechanically upon her black dress, as though, of themselves, they were recalling the piano score they had once played. Poor old hands! They had been stretched and twisted into mere tentacles to hold and lift and knead with; the palms unduly swollen, the fingers bent and knotted—on one of them a thin, worn band that had once been a wedding ring. As I pressed and gently quieted one of those groping hands, I remembered with quivering eyelids their services for me in other days.

Soon after the tenor began the "Prize Song," I heard a quick drawn breath and turned to my aunt. Her eyes were closed, but the tears were glistening on her cheeks, and I think, in a moment more, they were in my eyes as well. It never really died, then—the soul that can suffer so **excruciatingly** and so interminably; it withers to the outward eye only; like that strange moss which can lie on a dusty shelf half a century and yet, if placed in water, grows green again. She wept so throughout the development and elaboration of the melody. **F**

Language Coach

Fixed Expressions A **fixed expression** is a group of words that are usually combined in the same way to express a specific meaning. The fixed expression "fallen ill" (line 167) has to do with illness. Explain these fixed expressions about illness: *come down with, [have] a bout of.*

excruciatingly (ĭk-skro͞o′shē-ā′tĭng-lē) *adv.* in a way that causes great pain or distress

F DRAW CONCLUSIONS Reread lines 187–193. What **inferences** can you make about Aunt Georgiana's feeling for music, based upon her reaction to it?

19. **peak in Darien:** a mountain in what is now Panama, referred to in English poet John Keats's "On First Looking into Chapman's Homer" as a place where the Pacific was contemplated with silence and awe by Spanish explorers.

During the intermission before the second half of the concert, I questioned my aunt and found that the "Prize Song" was not new to her. Some years before there had drifted to the farm in Red Willow County a young German, a tramp cow puncher, who had sung the chorus at Bayreuth,[20] when he was a boy, along with the other peasant boys and girls. Of a Sunday morning he used to sit on his gingham-sheeted bed in the hands' bedroom which opened off the kitchen, cleaning the leather of his boots and saddle, singing the "Prize Song," while my aunt went about her work in the kitchen. She had hovered about him until she had prevailed upon him to join the country church, though his sole fitness for this step, in so far as I could gather, lay in his boyish face and his possession of this divine melody. Shortly afterward he had gone to town on the Fourth of July, been drunk for several days, lost his money at a faro table, ridden a saddled Texas steer on a bet, and disappeared with a fractured collar-bone. All this my aunt told me huskily, wanderingly, as though she were talking in the weak lapses of illness. **G**

G DRAW CONCLUSIONS
Reread lines 194–207. How does Cather use a plot event to further the internal development of the narrator and the external development of Aunt Georgiana?

20. **Bayreuth** (bī-roit′): a town in the Bavarian region of Germany where annual Wagner music festivals are held.

Two on the Aisle (1927), Edward Hopper © Francis G. Mayer/Corbis. © Heirs of Josephine N. Hopper, licensed by the Whitney Museum of American Art.

"Well, we have come to better things than the old *Trovatore*[21] at any rate, Aunt Georgie?" I queried, with a well meant effort at jocularity.

Her lip quivered and she hastily put her handkerchief up to her mouth. From behind it she murmured, "And you have been hearing this ever since you left me, Clark?" Her question was the gentlest and saddest of reproaches.

The second half of the program consisted of four numbers from the *Ring*, and closed with Siegfried's funeral march. My aunt wept quietly, but almost continuously, as a shallow vessel overflows in a rainstorm. From time to time her dim eyes looked up at the lights which studded the ceiling, burning softly under their dull glass globes; doubtless they were stars in truth to her. I was still perplexed as to what measure of musical comprehension was left to her, she who had heard nothing but the singing of Gospel Hymns at Methodist services in the square frame school-house on Section Thirteen for so many years. I was wholly unable to gauge how much of it had been dissolved in soapsuds, or worked into bread, or milked into the bottom of a pail. **H**

H SETTING
Reread lines 220–222. What does this **metaphor** suggest about how a place might affect one's appreciation of music?

The deluge of sound poured on and on; I never knew what she found in the shining current of it; I never knew how far it bore her, or past what happy islands. From the trembling of her face I could well believe that before the last numbers she had been carried out where the **myriad** graves are, into the grey, nameless burying grounds of the sea; or into some world of death vaster yet, where, from the beginning of the world, hope has lain down with hope and dream with dream and, renouncing, slept.

myriad (mîr'ē-əd) *adj.* exceedingly numerous

The concert was over; the people filed out of the hall chattering and laughing, glad to relax and find the living level again, but my kinswoman made no effort to rise. The harpist slipped its green felt cover over his instrument; the flute-players shook the water from their mouthpieces; the men of the orchestra went out one by one, leaving the stage to the chairs and music stands, empty as a winter cornfield.

I spoke to my aunt. She burst into tears and sobbed pleadingly. "I don't want to go, Clark, I don't want to go!"

I understood. For her, just outside the door of the concert hall, lay the black pond with the cattle-tracked bluffs; the tall, unpainted house, with weather-curled boards; naked as a tower, the crook-backed ash seedlings where the dish-cloths hung to dry; the gaunt, molting turkeys picking up refuse about the kitchen door.

---

21. ***Trovatore*** (trō'vä-tôr'ĕ): *Il Trovatore* is an opera by the Italian composer Giuseppe Verdi.

Comprehension

1. **Recall** Why does Aunt Georgiana travel to Boston?
2. **Recall** Why does Clark take his aunt to the concert?
3. **Summarize** How do Clark and his aunt respond to the concert?

COMMON CORE

RL 1 Cite evidence to support inferences drawn from the text.
RL 3 Analyze the impact of the author's choices regarding how to develop and relate elements of a story.

Text Analysis

4. **Predict Events** In your opinion, will Aunt Georgiana return to Nebraska, or will she stay in Boston? Give evidence to support your answer.
5. **Make Inferences** Aunt Georgiana warns Clark, "Don't love it so well, Clark, or it may be taken from you." What does this suggest about the role of music in her own life?
6. **Draw Conclusions About Character** Look back at the **inferences** you recorded in your chart as you read. Judging from the choices that Aunt Georgiana has made in her life, what conclusions can you draw about her character? What emotions does she seem to experience, and how does she handle them?
7. **Contrast Settings** The two settings in this story—the Nebraska prairie and the Boston concert hall—are both significant for Aunt Georgiana. What do they **symbolize?** Support your answer with details from the story.
8. **Make Judgments** How might Aunt Georgiana be different if she had stayed in Boston? Use examples from the story and your views about the importance of place to support your answer.

Text Criticism

9. **Biographical Context** "A Wagner Matinee" created a stir when it appeared in 1904. Cather's family objected to the fictional portrait of her real-life aunt Franc. One of her friends remarked: "The stranger to this state will associate Nebraska with the aunt's wretched figure, her ill-fitting false teeth, her skin yellowed by the weather." Do you agree? Examine the **imagery** and **figurative language** used to describe the people and scenes of Nebraska. Do you think Cather's Nebraska relatives were justified in taking offense? Cite evidence from the story to support your answer.

Does it matter where we **LIVE?**

What effect has frontier life in Nebraska had on Aunt Georgiana? In what way has place had no effect at all on Aunt Georgiana? In your opinion, how does the place we live affect our true character, if at all?

Vocabulary in Context

▲ VOCABULARY PRACTICE

Choose the word from the list that best completes each sentence.

WORD LIST
callow
excruciatingly
myriad
overture
somnambulant
sordid
tentatively
veritable

1. Though uncertain whether Aunt Georgiana would enjoy the concert, Clark ____ made plans to go.
2. Earlier, his aunt had seemed dazed, walking around in an almost _____ state.
3. Her life on the farm, while not _____, was certainly harsh and difficult.
4. She was worn down from the _____ jobs she performed from dawn to dusk.
5. But Aunt Georgiana was not a(n) _____ young girl with no experience or culture.
6. She was a(n) _____ treasure chest of musical knowledge.
7. When the _____ was played, she became a new woman.
8. Yet she found it _____ difficult to listen to the beautiful music.

ACADEMIC VOCABULARY IN WRITING

• apparent • confine • expose • focus • perceive

Assume the role of Aunt Georgiana, and write several paragraphs describing your return to Boston. **Expose** Aunt Georgiana's innermost feelings during the concert, when she **perceives** what she has missed by living on the frontier. Use at least one Academic Vocabulary word in your response.

VOCABULARY STRATEGY: MUSIC TERMINOLOGY

Knowledge of the academic vocabulary used in specific content areas is important to your success in school. Many academic vocabulary words have their origins in other languages. For example, *sociology* comes from the French *sociologie*, *history* from the Latin word *historia*. Many of the academic words associated with music come from Italian or French. For example, the vocabulary word *overture*, which refers to the introductory piece in an opera or other musical drama, is derived from a French word.

COMMON CORE

L 6 Acquire and use accurately general academic and domain-specific words and phrases.

PRACTICE Match each term in the lefthand column with its definition in the righthand column. Research the origin of each word to determine whether it is Italian, French, or some other language.

1. concerto	**a.** an elaborate melody in an opera, sung by one person
2. contralto	**b.** a moderately slow tempo, or pace
3. aria	**c.** a man who sings with a higher voice
4. diva	**d.** a woman who sings with a lower voice
5. andante	**e.** a leading woman soloist in an opera company
6. tenor	**f.** a piece in which a soloist performs with an orchestra

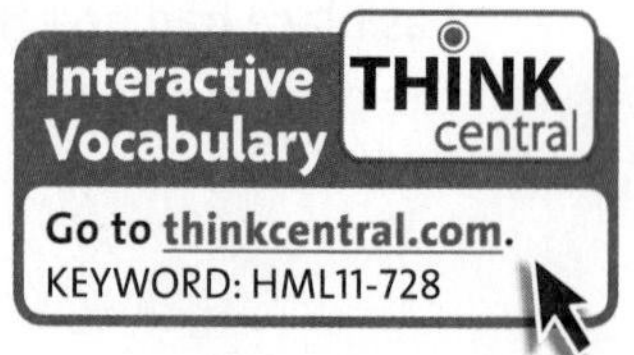

America's Literary Regions

Indiana author Edward Eggleston made this claim in 1892.

> *"It used to be a matter of no little jealousy to us, I remember, that the manners, customs, thoughts and feelings of New England country people filled so large a place in books, while our life, not less interesting, not less romantic, and certainly not less filled with humorous and grotesque material, had no place in literature. It was as though we were shut out of good society."*

By the end of the 19th century, however, virtually every region of the country—from the cities of the Northeast, to the mining camps of California, to the Southern bayou, to the northern plains—had its own local colorist capturing the region's distinctive features in writing. These local color writers portrayed the dialects, dress, mannerisms, customs, character types, and landscapes of their regions with an eye for accurate detail.

Writing to Synthesize

Make a chart like the one shown, listing each of the selections you've read in this section (pages 658–728). On your chart, note what you've learned about the way the people in each region speak, the way they dress, their customs, and their landscapes. Then use your chart to write a one-paragraph description of each region you've encountered in your reading. Based on all of your descriptions, write a concluding sentence or two in which you sum up what the regions have in common.

	How People Speak	How People Dress	Local Customs	Local Landscape
The Autobiography of Mark Twain				

Extension

VIEWING & REPRESENTING

Create a **single-frame cartoon** to represent the region you live in. You may want to focus on the way people speak and dress, or you may prefer to characterize the landscape.

COMMON CORE

W 2 Write informative/explanatory texts to examine and convey complex ideas, concepts, and information clearly and accurately.
W 2b Develop the topic thoroughly by selecting the most significant and relevant facts, concrete details, or other information and examples.

A homesteader's dugout house in Pie Town, New Mexico

Media Study

American Landscapes

Image Collection on  DVD-ROM

COMMON CORE

RI 7 Integrate and evaluate multiple sources of information presented in different media or formats.

Can pictures
DEVELOP
new frontiers?

Paintings and photographs can have a profound effect on us. They can enlighten us, frighten us, elicit our sympathies, even inspire us. In this lesson, you'll examine the landscape work of two 19th-century artists and discover how paintings and photographs helped to spur **Western expansion.**

Background

Framing New Views In the late 1800s, at a time when writer Mark Twain portrayed a romanticized view of the West, the new medium of photography gained popularity for revealing American life as it really was. For many painters of the day, photography posed a new challenge. While some saw it as displacing traditional forms of representation, others embraced it as a liberating artistic force.

Photography was also having an impact on the mass media. Because people were increasingly interested in facts and in realistic portrayals of events, they turned to the burgeoning newspaper industry and the day's more "realistic" writers. With the portability of cameras, photographers could supply newspapers, magazines, and advertisers with images in a short period of time, exposing viewers to faraway locations.

At the same time, Western expansion was being promoted by the federal government and by land developers from the East and Midwest. Photographic images of the new frontier were frequently used by advertisers and marketers to entice Americans to go West and settle the sparsely populated territory. In 1871, painter Thomas Moran joined forces with photographer William Henry Jackson and embarked on a geological expedition to document Western lands. These two artists found inspiration in surroundings of astounding natural beauty. Examples of their work appear in this lesson.

Media Literacy: Photographs and Paintings

The paintings of Thomas Moran and the photographs of William Henry Jackson were instrumental in convincing Congress to declare Yellowstone, in 1872, the country's first national park. Shown here are a painting by Moran and a photograph by Jackson of a canyon scene. Analyze these images by considering how each artist used certain elements to achieve compelling landscape art.

STRATEGIES FOR ANALYZING PHOTOGRAPHS AND PAINTINGS

Composition is the arrangement of subject elements within an image. Scan each image from top to bottom, side to side, and corner to corner, noting how each artist has arranged the elements in the frame. Ask yourself: Where is the **focal point,** or main focus, of the painting and of the photograph? What section of the image first catches my eye? In both of these images, the focal point is the waterfall.

For painters, **perspective** is a technique that creates the illusion of depth, making objects look three-dimensional. To determine the perspective of an image, try to identify the **horizon line,** the horizontal section that appears to your eye to be at the farthest distance in a landscape. In both of these images, the horizon line appears near the top, where the sky meets the uppermost part of the valley.

Depth of field is the area in front of and behind a focused subject in which the image appears sharp. Photographers achieved this effect by adjusting camera lenses. Notice in the photograph how depth of field creates an impression of distance.

Texture is the surface quality of an image—what the image would feel like if we could touch it. Ask yourself:

- What materials or techniques did the photographer use to create a sense of texture?
- With paintings, where does the paint seem to rise slightly from the canvas?

In these canyon images, your own knowledge of what is being depicted adds to your interpretation and appreciation of the textures conveyed.

Media Smart DVD-ROM

Paintings by Thomas Moran
- **Selection 2:** "Grand Canyon of the Yellowstone"
- **Selection 4:** "Castle Geyser"

Photographs by William Henry Jackson
- **Selection 1:** "Grand Canyon of the Yellowstone"
- **Selection 3:** "Castle Geyser"

Viewing Guide for

American Landscape Artists

Look at the full-sized images on the DVD. Examine each image carefully, jotting down your initial impressions. To help you analyze the paintings of Thomas Moran and the photographs of William Henry Jackson in terms of certain design elements, refer to the details on page 731. You can also refer to the Elements of Design section of the Media Handbook (pages R94–R95) to review the visual art elements of color, shape, line, and texture. Then consider these questions to help you analyze the images.

NOW VIEW

FIRST VIEWING: Comprehension

1. **Identify** In both Grand Canyon images, what elements of nature do you see?
2. **Clarify** Which Grand Canyon image has people in it?

CLOSE VIEWING: Media Literacy

3. **Analyze Composition** In each of the Grand Canyon images, the artist chose to depict the widest possible view. Through this composition, what effect do you think each artist was trying to achieve?
4. **Compare Texture** Consider both Moran paintings. Which appears to have more texture? Explain your choice.
5. **Analyze Perspective** In the color painting "Castle Geyser" by Thomas Moran, find the horizon line. Name whatever objects you can that rise up from this line.
6. **Compare Images** Both the painting and the photograph of the geyser on this page have an otherworldly look and feel. Which image looks more alien to you? Support your response in terms of your view of
   - in the painting, the stark color contrast between the deep blue of the pool and the lighter tone of the sky
   - in the photograph, the placement of the camera and the lens to make the pool seem as large as possible

Write or Discuss

Judge an Image The landscape paintings and photographs of this lesson not only inspired thousands to journey to the West but also inspired the protection of one of America's most striking natural regions. Among these four images, pick one that you think is the most interesting. In a short oral or written evaluation, describe what elements it has that make it a fine example of landscape art. If possible, include the image in your presentation. Base your criteria on these considerations:

- the **composition** and **perspective** in the paintings or the effect of the **depth of field** in the photographs
- the aim of Thomas Moran and William Henry Jackson to capture stunning scenes of natural beauty
- the aspects of the painting or photograph that especially appeal to you (for example, the specific subject matter, use or absence of color, overall mood or feeling)

RI 7 Integrate and evaluate multiple sources of information presented in different media or formats. **SL 5** Make strategic use of digital media in presentations to enhance understanding of findings, reasoning, and evidence and to add interest.

Produce Your Own Media

Create Your Personal Landscape Think of a favorite place. How would you represent it visually? Create a landscape image of your choice. It can be a photograph, a painting, a computer-generated image, or a drawing.

HERE'S HOW Decide what landscape you want to capture and which medium you want to use. Here are some things to keep in mind:

- Be aware of composition. What you show and don't show in an image defines your vision of the landscape. Is there a dominant element you want to focus on?
- Try to provide some texture to your image regardless of the medium you've chosen.
- Give your work a horizontal landscape orientation. Experiment with giving your image an illusion of depth. For a drawing or painting, determine where to position the lines that will establish the perspective. For a photograph, determine the depth of field by adjusting lenses or camera position.
- No matter what type of image you create, make notes on what your intentions were and how you planned to create it.

Tech Tip

Use a software program to experiment with various effects.

Further Exploration

View More Photographs The equipment the early photographers used was quite unwieldy. Photographers had to carry their big box cameras and heavy film plates to their subjects, so you can imagine the rigors of filming a vast and remote landscape like the Grand Canyon.

Look at the early photographs on the DVD or research your own examples of early photography, and choose an image that most interests you.

The Open Boat

Short Story by Stephen Crane

COMMON CORE

RL 2 Determine two or more themes or central ideas of a text and analyze how they interact to produce a complex account. **RL 3** Analyze the impact of the author's choices regarding how to develop and relate elements of a story. **RL 4** Determine the meaning of words and phrases as they are used in the text, including figurative meanings; analyze the impact of specific word choices on meaning and tone, including words with multiple meanings.

DID YOU KNOW?

Stephen Crane . . .

- spent most of his two semesters in college playing baseball.
- claimed that his understanding of combat in *The Red Badge of Courage* came from watching football games.
- wrote powerful poetry, including "Do Not Weep, Maiden, for War Is Kind."

Meet the Author

Stephen Crane 1871–1900

When Crane's novel *The Red Badge of Courage* was published in 1895, it caused a literary sensation. Critics hailed its unromanticized portrayal of a young soldier's struggles during one battle of the Civil War. As one reviewer exclaimed, "The style is as rough as it is direct. . . . But the original power of the book is great enough to set a new fashion in literature." War veterans, unimpressed by literary fashion, were struck by the graphic depiction of combat. So vivid was the battlefield experience in the novel that they assumed the story was a factual eyewitness account. But the author was only 23 years old at the time and had not yet seen war. Such was the power of Crane's imagination that he was able in his short life to create works of great integrity as well as artistic force.

Living on the Edge Born in Newark, New Jersey, the youngest of 14 children, Stephen Crane came from a family of writers. His father, a Methodist minister, and his mother both wrote religious articles, and two of his brothers were journalists. A stint in military school nourished the teenage Crane's interest in the Civil War, but college life bored him. "Not that I disliked books," he insisted, but that "humanity was a much more interesting study." And study it he did—first as a freelance journalist living in the slums of New York City's Bowery, then as a reporter traveling in Mexico and the American Wild West, and finally as a war correspondent shipping out to hot spots in Cuba and Greece. Twelve years of living on the edge gave Crane material not only for numerous news articles but also for three novels, several volumes of poetry, and some of the best-known short stories in American literature, including "The Open Boat," "The Blue Hotel," and "The Bride Comes to Yellow Sky."

The Cost of Adventure Adventure often comes at a price. Biographers cite the deprivations of Crane's years in the New York slums, the dangers of traveling to far-off places, and his own neglect of his health as contributing to his death from tuberculosis at age 28. But Crane had matured far beyond his years. True to his early intentions, he was a great student of humanity, and he developed a philosophy described by one critic as a "bold and robust humanism." As a naturalist writer, Crane believed that nature was a powerful force that shaped our lives. But as a humanist, he also had faith in his fellow humans' ability to act responsibly and honestly.

Author Online THINK central

Go to thinkcentral.com. KEYWORD: HML11-734

TEXT ANALYSIS: NATURALISM

Naturalism is an offshoot of **realism,** the 19th-century literary movement that examines the effect of natural and social forces on the individual. While naturalism aims to depict people accurately, it tends toward pessimism by showing human beings at the mercy of the environment and their own instincts. With an emphasis on setting, theme, conflict, and irony, naturalism paints human destiny as beyond individual control.

Naturalist writers often chose **mythic situations,** retelling ancient stories from a naturalist perspective. For example, stories about individuals at the mercy of the ocean are included in the myths of many ancient cultures. "The Open Boat" is a naturalistic version of such a story. As you read, look for characteristics of naturalism in the story, and compare Crane's story with other tales about individuals lost at sea.

READING SKILL: ANALYZE DESCRIPTIVE LANGUAGE

Naturalist writers use vivid and detailed **descriptive language** in their study of human behavior. Effective description relies on various literary elements.

- **imagery**—descriptive words that create sensory experiences
- **figurative language**—language that goes beyond the literal to make a vivid comparison
- **tone**—a writer's attitude toward the subject
- **mood**—the feeling the writer creates for the reader

As you read, record examples of Crane's use of these elements.

VOCABULARY IN CONTEXT

Match each vocabulary word in the first column with the word or phrase in the second column that is closest in meaning.

1. dearth	**a.** comply
2. ingenuously	**b.** abnormality
3. aberration	**c.** raucous
4. acquiesce	**d.** compel
5. motley	**e.** shortage
6. epithet	**f.** relief
7. respite	**g.** insulting name
8. obstreperous	**h.** naively
9. coerce	**i.** assorted

Complete the activities in your **Reader/Writer Notebook**.

Does NATURE *play fair?*

A lioness kills an antelope. An earthquake destroys one small town and leaves other nearby towns untouched. Diseases kill millions worldwide. Does this seem fair? Does nature stack the deck against certain creatures? As one of the leading writers in the naturalist movement, Stephen Crane addresses this issue in "The Open Boat."

DISCUSS With a small group, discuss how you explain the inequities found in nature. First, list some specific natural disasters or dangers that you know of. Then, discuss the reasons why each one may have happened the way it did.

THE OPEN BOAT

STEPHEN CRANE

BACKGROUND On New Year's Eve, 1896, Stephen Crane was traveling on the ship *Commodore* to Cuba to report on an impending revolution. Loaded with ammunition and Cuban rebels, the ship was damaged by a sandbar outside of Jacksonville, Florida, and two days later sank in the open sea. Most survivors filled the lifeboats, but Crane and four others ended up in a much smaller boat. This is the story he wrote about his harrowing ordeal. It has been called one of the world's great short stories.

A tale intended to be after the fact. Being the experience of four men from the sunk steamer *Commodore.*

I

None of them knew the color of the sky. Their eyes glanced level, and were fastened upon the waves that swept toward them. These waves were the hue of slate, save for the tops, which were of foaming white, and all of the men knew the colors of the sea. The horizon narrowed and widened, and dipped and rose, and at all times its edge was jagged with waves that seemed thrust up in points like rocks. **A**

Many a man ought to have a bathtub larger than the boat which here rode upon the sea. These waves were most wrongfully and barbarously abrupt and tall, and each froth top was a problem in small boat navigation.

Analyze Visuals ▸
Look at the art on page 737. Apart from the men's appearance, what do the colors of the water and the sky suggest about their situation? Explain.

A DESCRIPTIVE LANGUAGE
The first paragraph is not really about the color of the sky. What does Crane emphasize by beginning the story this way?

German Shipwreck Survivors (image manipulated), Achille Beltrame. Engraving in Italian newspaper *La Domenica del Corriere,* February 1941. © Dagli Orti/The Art Archive.

The cook squatted in the bottom and looked with both eyes at the six inches of gunwale[1] which separated him from the ocean. His sleeves were rolled over his fat forearms, and the two flaps of his unbuttoned vest dangled as he bent to bail out the boat. Often he said: "Gawd! That was a narrow clip." As he remarked it he invariably gazed eastward over the broken sea.

The oiler,[2] steering with one of the two oars in the boat, sometimes raised himself suddenly to keep clear of water that swirled in over the stern. It was a thin little oar and it seemed often ready to snap.

The correspondent, pulling at the other oar, watched the waves and wondered why he was there.

The injured captain, lying in the bow, was at this time buried in that profound dejection and indifference which comes, temporarily at least, to even the bravest and most enduring when, willy nilly, the firm fails, the army loses, the ship goes down. The mind of the master of a vessel is rooted deep in the timbers of her, though he command for a day or a decade, and this captain had on him the stern impression of a scene in the grays of dawn of seven turned faces, and later a stump of a topmast with a white ball on it that slashed to and fro at the waves, went low and lower, and down. Thereafter there was something strange in his voice. Although steady, it was deep with mourning, and of a quality beyond oration or tears. **B**

"Keep'er a little more south, Billie," said he.

"'A little more south,' sir," said the oiler in the stern.

A seat in this boat was not unlike a seat upon a bucking bronco, and, by the same token, a bronco is not much smaller. The craft pranced and reared, and plunged like an animal. As each wave came, and she rose for it, she seemed like a horse making at a fence outrageously high. The manner of her scramble over these walls of water is a mystic thing, and, moreover, at the top of them were ordinarily these problems in white water, the foam racing down from the summit of each wave, requiring a new leap, and a leap from the air. Then, after scornfully bumping a crest, she would slide, and race, and splash down a long incline and arrive bobbing and nodding in front of the next menace. **C**

A singular disadvantage of the sea lies in the fact that after successfully surmounting one wave you discover that there is another behind it just as important and just as nervously anxious to do something effective in the way of swamping boats. In a ten-foot dinghy[3] one can get an idea of the resources of the sea in the line of waves that is not probable to the average experience, which is never at sea in a dinghy. As each slaty wall of water approached, it shut all else from the view of the men in the boat, and it was not difficult to imagine that this particular wave was the final outburst of the ocean, the last effort of the grim water. There was a terrible grace in the move of the waves, and they came in silence, save for the snarling of the crests.

Language Coach

Word Definitions *Willy nilly* (line 24) means "spontaneously" or "without regard to choice." How do you think the captain, the person ultimately responsible for the ship, would feel when his ship goes down?

B NATURALISM

Reread lines 22–31. What can you **infer** about the "seven turned faces" and the "stump of a topmast"? Consider what these things tell you about the captain's recent experience.

C DESCRIPTIVE LANGUAGE

Notice the descriptive language in lines 34–42. What quality of the boat does the bronco **metaphor** emphasize? Explain your answer.

---

1. **gunwale** (gŭn′əl): the upper edge of a boat.
2. **oiler:** a worker who cares for the machinery in the engine room of a ship.
3. **dinghy** (dĭng′ē): a small open boat.

In the wan light, the faces of the men must have been gray. Their eyes must have glinted in strange ways as they gazed steadily astern. Viewed from a balcony, the whole thing would doubtlessly have been weirdly picturesque. But the men in the boat had no time to see it, and if they had had leisure there were other things to occupy their minds. The sun swung steadily up the sky, and they knew it was broad day because the color of the sea changed from slate to emerald green, streaked with amber lights, and the foam was like tumbling snow. The process of the breaking day was unknown to them. They were aware only of this effect upon the color of the waves that rolled toward them.

In disjointed sentences the cook and the correspondent argued as to the difference between a lifesaving station and a house of refuge. The cook had said: "There's a house of refuge just north of the Mosquito Inlet Light, and as soon as they see us, they'll come off in their boat and pick us up."

"As soon as who see us?" said the correspondent.

"The crew," said the cook.

"Houses of refuge don't have crews," said the correspondent. "As I understand them, they are only places where clothes and grub are stored for the benefit of shipwrecked people. They don't carry crews."

"Oh, yes, they do," said the cook.

"No, they don't," said the correspondent.

"Well, we're not there yet, anyhow," said the oiler, in the stern.

"Well," said the cook, "perhaps it's not a house of refuge that I'm thinking of as being near Mosquito Inlet Light. Perhaps it's a lifesaving station."

"We're not there yet," said the oiler, in the stern. **D**

II

As the boat bounced from the top of each wave, the wind tore through the hair of the hatless men, and as the craft plopped her stern down again the spray slashed past them. The crest of each of these waves was a hill, from the top of which the men surveyed, for a moment, a broad tumultuous expanse, shining and wind-riven. It was probably splendid. It was probably glorious, this play of the free sea, wild with lights of emerald and white and amber.

"Bully good thing it's an on-shore wind,"[4] said the cook. "If not, where would we be? Wouldn't have a show."

"That's right," said the correspondent.

The busy oiler nodded his assent.

Then the captain, in the bow, chuckled in a way that expressed humor, contempt, tragedy, all in one. "Do you think we've got much of a show, now, boys?" said he.

Whereupon the three were silent, save for a trifle of hemming and hawing. To express any particular optimism at this time they felt to be childish and stupid, but they all doubtless possessed this sense of the situation in their mind. A young man thinks doggedly at such times. On the other hand, the ethics of their condition was decidedly against any open suggestion of hopelessness. So they were silent.

4. **on-shore wind:** wind that blows toward the shore.

D PRIMARY SOURCES
Following this short story, you will find several newspaper accounts of the 1897 sinking of the *Commodore*. The article written by Stephen Crane, "Stephen Crane's Own Story" (page 765), is an excellent example of a **primary source**—an account of the disaster written by a participant in the event. Reread lines 62–76. Then, read Crane's newspaper article, and note the similarities you find between this literary work and the primary source document.

Language Coach

Formal Language
Whereupon is a formal word meaning "following afterward and as a result of." Read lines 87–94. Why are the men silent, and what are they responding to?

"Oh, well," said the captain, soothing his children, "we'll get ashore all right."

But there was that in his tone which made them think, so the oiler quoth: "Yes! If this wind holds!"

The cook was bailing. "Yes! If we don't catch hell in the surf."

Canton flannel gulls[5] flew near and far. Sometimes they sat down on the sea, near patches of brown seaweed that rolled over the waves with a movement like carpets on a line in a gale. The birds sat comfortably in groups, and they were envied by some in the dinghy, for the wrath of the sea was no more to them than it was to a covey of prairie chickens a thousand miles inland. Often they came very close and stared at the men with black bead-like eyes. At these times they were uncanny and sinister in their unblinking scrutiny, and the men hooted angrily at them, telling them to be gone. One came, and evidently decided to alight on the top of the captain's head. The bird flew parallel to the boat and did not circle, but made short sidelong jumps in the air in chicken fashion. His black eyes were wistfully fixed upon the captain's head. "Ugly brute," said the oiler to the bird. "You look as if you were made with a jackknife." The cook and the correspondent swore darkly at the creature. The captain naturally wished to knock it away with the end of the heavy painter,[6] but he did not dare do it, because anything resembling an emphatic gesture would have capsized this freighted boat, and so with his open hand, the captain gently and carefully waved the gull away. After it had been discouraged from the pursuit the captain breathed easier on account of his hair, and others breathed easier because the bird struck their minds at this time as being somehow gruesome and ominous. **E**

E NATURALISM
Reread lines 99–117. How does the author suggest the indifference or even hostility of nature in these lines?

In the meantime the oiler and the correspondent rowed. And also they rowed.

They sat together in the same seat, and each rowed an oar. Then the oiler took both oars; then the correspondent took both oars; then the oiler; then the correspondent. They rowed and they rowed. The very ticklish part of the business was when the time came for the reclining one in the stern to take his turn at the oars. By the very last star of truth, it is easier to steal eggs from under a hen than it was to change seats in the dinghy. First the man in the stern slid his hand along the thwart[7] and moved with care, as if he were of Sèvres.[8] Then the man in the rowing seat slid his hand along the other thwart. It was all done with the most extraordinary care. As the two sidled past each other, the whole party kept watchful eyes on the coming wave, and the captain cried: "Look out now! Steady there!"

The brown mats of seaweed that appeared from time to time were like islands, bits of earth. They were traveling, apparently, neither one way nor the other. They were, to all intents, stationary. They informed the men in the boat that it was making progress slowly toward the land.

The captain, rearing cautiously in the bow, after the dinghy soared on a great swell, said that he had seen the lighthouse at Mosquito Inlet. Presently the cook

---

5. **canton flannel gulls:** gulls looking as if they were made of canton flannel, a heavy type of cotton that is soft on one side and ribbed on the other.
6. **painter:** a line used for towing or securing a boat.
7. **thwart:** a seat that extends across a boat.
8. **Sèvres:** a type of fine china made in Sèvres, France.

remarked that he had seen it. The correspondent was at the oars, then, and for some reason he too wished to look at the lighthouse, but his back was toward the far shore and the waves were important, and for some time he could not seize an opportunity to turn his head. But at last there came a wave more gentle than the others, and when at the crest of it he swiftly scoured the western horizon.

"See it?" said the captain.

"No," said the correspondent, slowly, "I didn't see anything."

"Look again," said the captain. He pointed. "It's exactly in that direction."

At the top of another wave, the correspondent did as he was bid, and this time his eyes chanced on a small still thing on the edge of the swaying horizon. It was precisely like the point of a pin. It took an anxious eye to find a lighthouse so tiny.

"Think we'll make it, Captain?"

"If this wind holds and the boat don't swamp, we can't do much else," said the captain.

The little boat, lifted by each towering sea, and splashed viciously by the crests, made progress that in the absence of seaweed was not apparent to those in her. She seemed just a wee thing wallowing, miraculously, top up, at the mercy of five oceans. Occasionally, a great spread of water, like white flames, swarmed into her. F

"Bail her, cook," said the captain, serenely.

"All right, Captain," said the cheerful cook.

F **NATURALISM**
In lines 149–152, what images, words, and phrases suggest the overwhelming power of nature and the smallness of humanity?

III

It would be difficult to describe the subtle brotherhood of men that was here established on the seas. No one said that it was so. No one mentioned it. But it dwelt in the boat, and each man felt it warm him. They were a captain, an oiler, a cook, and a correspondent, and they were friends, friends in a more curiously ironbound degree than may be common. The hurt captain, lying against the water jar in the bow, spoke always in a low voice and calmly, but he could never command a more ready and swiftly obedient crew than the **motley** three of the dinghy. It was more than a mere recognition of what was best for the common safety. There was surely in it a quality that was personal and heartfelt. And after this devotion to the commander of the boat there was this comradeship that the correspondent, for instance, who had been taught to be cynical of men, knew even at the time was the best experience of his life. But no one said that it was so. No one mentioned it.

motley (mŏt'lē) *adj.* composed of diverse, often mismatched elements

"I wish we had a sail," remarked the captain. "We might try my overcoat on the end of an oar and give you two boys a chance to rest." So the cook and the correspondent held the mast and spread wide the overcoat. The oiler steered, and the little boat made good way with her new rig. Sometimes the oiler had to scull[9] sharply to keep a sea from breaking into the boat, but otherwise sailing was a success.

Meanwhile the lighthouse had been growing slowly larger. It had now almost assumed color, and appeared like a little gray shadow on the sky. The man at the

9. **scull:** to propel a boat by rowing from side to side, reversing the oar at each turn.

The Much Resounding Sea (1884), Thomas Moran. 25″ × 62″.

oars could not be prevented from turning his head rather often to try for a glimpse of this little gray shadow.

At last, from the top of each wave the men in the tossing boat could see land. Even as the lighthouse was an upright shadow on the sky, this land seemed but a long black shadow on the sea. It certainly was thinner than paper. "We must be about opposite New Smyrna,"[10] said the cook, who had coasted this shore often in schooners. "Captain, by the way, I believe they abandoned that lifesaving station there about a year ago."

"Did they?" said the captain.

The wind slowly died away. The cook and the correspondent were not now obliged to slave in order to hold high the oar. But the waves continued their old

10. **New Smyrna:** New Smyrna Beach, a city on the eastern coast of Florida, about 15 miles south of Daytona Beach.

impetuous swooping at the dinghy, and the little craft, no longer under way, struggled woundily over them. The oiler or the correspondent took the oars again.

Shipwrecks are *apropos* of nothing. If men could only train for them and have them occur when the men had reached pink condition, there would be less drowning at sea. Of the four in the dinghy none had slept any time worth mentioning for two days and two nights previous to embarking in the dinghy, and in the excitement of clambering about the deck of a foundering[11] ship they had also forgotten to eat heartily. G

For these reasons, and for others, neither the oiler nor the correspondent was fond of rowing at this time. The correspondent wondered **ingenuously** how in the name of all that was sane could there be people who thought it amusing to row a boat. It was not an amusement; it was a diabolical punishment, and even

G **NATURALISM**
In lines 189–194, the author uses **verbal irony,** suggesting something different from what is literally meant. In this paragraph, what is Crane suggesting about the timing of shipwrecks? Explain.

ingenuously
(ĭn-jĕn′yo͞o-əs-lē) *adv.* in a manner showing childlike innocence or simplicity

11. **foundering:** sinking.

a genius of mental **aberrations** could never conclude that it was anything but a horror to the muscles and a crime against the back. He mentioned to the boat in general how the amusement of rowing struck him, and the weary-faced oiler smiled in full sympathy. Previously to the foundering, by the way, the oiler had worked double watch in the engine room of the ship.

aberration (ăb'ə-rā'shən) *n.* a disorder of the mind

"Take her easy, now, boys," said the captain. "Don't spend yourselves. If we have to run a surf[12] you'll need all your strength, because we'll sure have to swim for it. Take your time."

Slowly the land arose from the sea. From a black line it became a line of black and a line of white—trees and sand. Finally, the captain said that he could make out a house on the shore. "That's the house of refuge, sure," said the cook. "They'll see us before long, and come out after us."

The distant lighthouse reared high. "The keeper ought to be able to make us out now, if he's looking through a glass," said the captain. "He'll notify the lifesaving people."

"None of those other boats could have got ashore to give word of the wreck," said the oiler, in a low voice. "Else the lifeboat would be out hunting us."

Slowly and beautifully the land loomed out of the sea. The wind came again. It had veered from the northeast to the southeast. Finally, a new sound struck the ears of the men in the boat. It was the low thunder of the surf on the shore. "We'll never be able to make the lighthouse now," said the captain. "Swing her head a little more north, Billie."

"'A little more north' sir," said the oiler.

Whereupon the little boat turned her nose once more down the wind, and all but the oarsman watched the shore grow. Under the influence of this expansion doubt and direful apprehension was leaving the minds of the men. The management of the boat was still most absorbing, but it could not prevent a quiet cheerfulness. In an hour, perhaps, they would be ashore.

Their backbones had become thoroughly used to balancing in the boat and they now rode this wild colt of a dinghy like circus men. The correspondent thought that he had been drenched to the skin, but happening to feel in the top pocket of his coat, he found therein eight cigars. Four of them were soaked with seawater; four were perfectly scatheless. After a search, somebody produced three dry matches, and thereupon the four waifs rode impudently in their little boat, and with an assurance of an impending rescue shining in their eyes, puffed at the big cigars and judged well and ill of all men. Everybody took a drink of water. **H**

H DESCRIPTIVE LANGUAGE
Reread lines 227–234. Cite examples of the author's language that suggests the assurance of the men might be premature.

IV

"Cook," remarked the captain, "there don't seem to be any signs of life about your house of refuge."

"No," replied the cook. "Funny they don't see us!"

A broad stretch of lowly coast lay before the eyes of the men. It was of dunes topped with dark vegetation. The roar of the surf was plain, and sometimes they

12. **run a surf:** row through the surf to get to shore.

could see the white lip of a wave as it spun up the beach. A tiny house was blocked out black upon the sky. Southward, the slim lighthouse lifted its little gray length.

Tide, wind, and waves were swinging the dinghy northward. "Funny they don't see us," said the men.

The surf's roar here dulled, but its tone was, nevertheless, thunderous and mighty. As the boat swam over the great rollers, the men sat listening to this roar. "We'll swamp sure," said everybody.

It is fair to say here that there was not a lifesaving station within twenty miles in either direction, but the men did not know this fact and in consequence they made dark and **opprobrious** remarks concerning the eyesight of the nation's lifesavers. Four scowling men sat in the dinghy and surpassed records in the invention of **epithets.**

opprobrious (ə-prō'brē-əs) *adj.* scornful; derogatory

epithet (ĕp'ə-thĕt') *n.* an abusive word or phrase

"Funny they don't see us."

The lightheartedness of a former time had completely faded. To their sharpened minds it was easy to conjure pictures of all kinds of incompetency and blindness and, indeed, cowardice. There was the shore of the populous land, and it was bitter and bitter to them that from it came no sign. **I**

I NATURALISM
Dramatic irony is the technique of allowing the reader to know more than the characters do about their own situation. What does the author emphasize with his use of dramatic irony in lines 247–256?

"Well," said the captain, ultimately, "I suppose we'll have to make a try for ourselves. If we stay out here too long, we'll none of us have strength left to swim after the boat swamps."

And so the oiler, who was at the oars, turned the boat straight for the shore. There was a sudden tightening of muscles. There was some thinking.

"If we don't all get ashore—" said the captain. "If we don't all get ashore, I suppose you fellows know where to send news of my finish?"

They then briefly exchanged some addresses and admonitions. As for the reflections of the men, there was a great deal of rage in them. Perchance they might be formulated thus: "If I am going to be drowned—if I am going to be drowned—if I am going to be drowned, why, in the name of the seven mad gods who rule the sea,[13] was I allowed to come thus far and contemplate sand and trees? Was I brought here merely to have my nose dragged away as I was about to nibble the sacred cheese of life? It is preposterous. If this old ninny-woman, Fate, cannot do better than this, she should be deprived of the management of men's fortunes. She is an old hen who knows not her intention. If she has decided to drown me, why did she not do it in the beginning and save me all this trouble. The whole affair is absurd. . . . But, no, she cannot mean to drown me. She dare not drown me. She cannot drown me. Not after all this work." Afterward the man might have had an impulse to shake his fist at the clouds. "Just you drown me, now, and then hear what I call you!" **J**

J NATURALISM
Reread lines 264–277. What techniques does the author use here to suggest the indifference or hostility of nature?

The billows that came at this time were more formidable. They seemed always just about to break and roll over the little boat in a turmoil of foam. There was a preparatory and long growl in the speech of them. No mind unused to the sea would have concluded that the dinghy could ascend these sheer heights in time.

13. **seven mad . . . the sea:** possibly a reference to the gods of the seven major seas of the world.

The shore was still afar. The oiler was a wily surfman. "Boys," he said, swiftly, "she won't live there minutes more and we're too far out to swim. Shall I take her to sea again, Captain?"

"Yes! Go ahead!" said the captain.

This oiler, by a series of quick miracles, and fast and steady oarsmanship, turned the boat in the middle of the surf and took her safely to sea again.

There was a considerable silence as the boat bumped over the furrowed sea to deeper water. Then somebody in gloom spoke. "Well, anyhow, they must have seen us from the shore by now."

The gulls went in slanting flight up the wind toward the gray desolate east. A squall, marked by dingy clouds, and clouds brick-red, like smoke from a burning building, appeared from the southeast.

"What do you think of those lifesaving people? Ain't they peaches?"

"Funny they haven't seen us."

"Maybe they think we're out here for sport! Maybe they think we're fishin'. Maybe they think we're damned fools."

It was a long afternoon. A changed tide tried to force them southward, but wind and wave said northward. Far ahead, where coastline, sea, and sky formed their mighty angle, there were little dots which seemed to indicate a city on the shore.

"St. Augustine?"[14]

The captain shook his head. "Too near Mosquito Inlet."

And the oiler rowed, and then the correspondent rowed. Then the oiler rowed. It was a weary business. The human back can become the seat of more aches and pains than are registered in books for the composite anatomy of a regiment. It is a limited area, but it can become the theatre of innumerable muscular conflicts, tangles, wrenches, knots, and other comforts.

"Did you ever like to row, Billie?" asked the correspondent.

"No," said the oiler. "Hang it."

When one exchanged the rowing seat for a place in the bottom of the boat, he suffered a bodily depression that caused him to be careless of everything save an obligation to wiggle one finger. There was cold seawater swashing to and fro in the boat, and he lay in it. His head, pillowed on a thwart, was within an inch of the swirl of a wave crest, and sometimes a particularly **obstreperous** sea came inboard and drenched him once more. But these matters did not annoy him. It is almost certain that if the boat had capsized he would have tumbled comfortably out upon the ocean as if he felt sure that it was a great soft mattress.

"Look! There's a man on the shore!"

"Where?"

"There! See 'im? See 'im?"

"Yes, sure! He's walking along."

"Now he's stopped. Look! He's facing us!"

"He's waving at us!"

COMMON CORE RL 4

Language Coach

Figurative Language
Peaches (line 294) is an example of figurative language, language that communicates meaning beyond the literal meaning of the words. Here, *peaches* means "people who have peachlike qualities—sweet, wonderful." Read lines 294–297. What do the men think of the people?

obstreperous
(ŏb-strĕp'ər-əs) *adj.* very noisy and unruly

14. **St. Augustine:** a city about 65 miles north of New Smyrna Beach, along the northeastern coast of Florida.

"So he is! By thunder!"

"Ah, now, we're all right! Now we're all right! There'll be a boat out here for us in half an hour."

"He's going on. He's running. He's going up to that house there."

The remote beach seemed lower than the sea, and it required a searching glance to discern the little black figure. The captain saw a floating stick and they rowed to it. A bath towel was by some weird chance in the boat, and, tying this on the stick, the captain waved it. The oarsman did not dare turn his head, so he was obliged to ask questions.

"What's he doing now?"

"He's standing still again. He's looking, I think. . . . There he goes again. Toward the house. . . . Now he's stopped again."

"Is he waving at us?"

"No, not now! He was, though."

"Look! There comes another man!"

"He's running."

"Look at him go, would you."

"Why, he's on a bicycle. Now he's met the other man. They're both waving at us. Look!"

"There comes something up the beach."

"What the devil is that thing?"

"Why, it looks like a boat."

"Why, certainly it's a boat."

"No, it's on wheels."

"Yes, so it is. Well, that must be the lifeboat. They drag them along shore on a wagon."

"That's the lifeboat, sure."

"No, by——it's—it's an omnibus."[15]

"I tell you it's a lifeboat."

"It is not! It's an omnibus. I can see it plain. See? One of those big hotel omnibuses."

"By thunder, you're right. It's an omnibus, sure as fate. What do you suppose they are doing with an omnibus? Maybe they are going around collecting the lifecrew, hey?"

"That's it, likely. Look! There's a fellow waving a little black flag. He's standing on the steps of the omnibus. There come those two other fellows. Now they're all talking together. Look at the fellow with the flag. Maybe he ain't waving it!"

"That ain't a flag, is it? That's his coat. Why, certainly, that's his coat."

"So it is. It's his coat. He's taken it off and is waving it around his head. But would you look at him swing it!"

"Oh, say, there isn't any lifesaving station there. That's just a winter resort hotel omnibus that has brought over some of the boarders to see us drown."

"What's that idiot with the coat mean? What's he signaling, anyhow?"

"It looks as if he were trying to tell us to go north. There must be a lifesaving

15. **omnibus:** bus. At this time, a bus would have been pulled by horses.

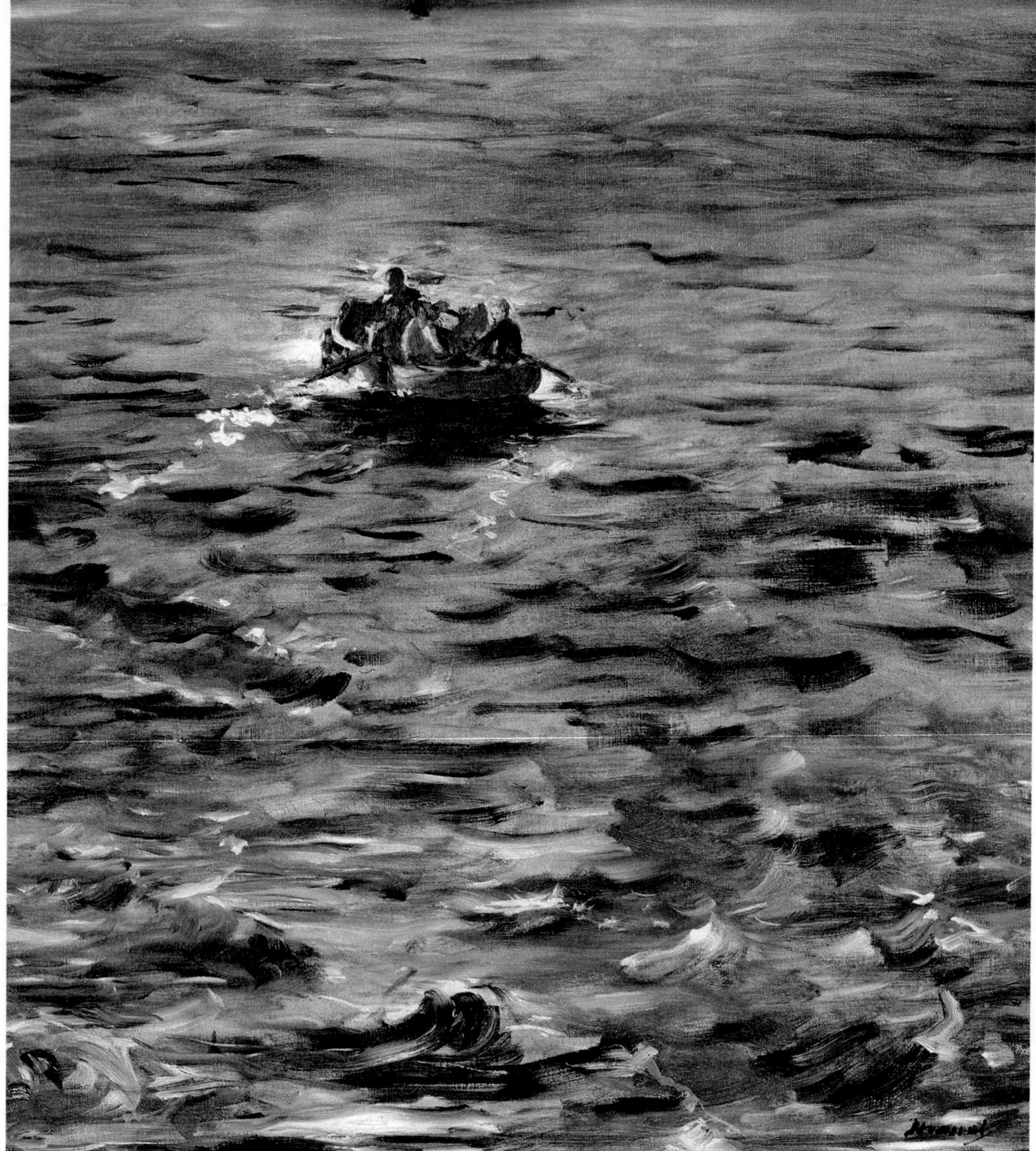

The Escape of Henri de Rochefort, March 20, 1874 (1880–1881), Edouard Manet. Oil on canvas, 80 cm × 73 cm. Musée d'Orsay, Paris.

station up there."

"No! He thinks we're fishing. Just giving us a merry hand. See? Ah, there, Willie."

"Well, I wish I could make something out of those signals. What do you suppose he means?"

"He don't mean anything. He's just playing."

"Well, if he'd just signal us to try the surf again, or to go to sea and wait, or go north, or go south, or go to hell—there would be some reason in it. But look at him. He just stands there and keeps his coat revolving like a wheel. The ass!"

"There come more people."

"Now there's quite a mob. Look! Isn't that a boat?"

"Where? Oh, I see where you mean. No, that's no boat."

"That fellow is still waving his coat."

"He must think we like to see him do that. Why don't he quit it. It don't mean anything."

"I don't know. I think he is trying to make us go north. It must be that there's a lifesaving station there somewhere."

"Say, he ain't tired yet. Look at 'im wave."

"Wonder how long he can keep that up. He's been revolving his coat ever since he caught sight of us. He's an idiot. Why aren't they getting men to bring a boat out. A fishing boat—one of those big yawls[16]—could come out here all right. Why don't he do something?"

"Oh, it's all right, now."

"They'll have a boat out here for us in less than no time, now that they've seen us."

A faint yellow tone came into the sky over the low land. The shadows on the sea slowly deepened. The wind bore coldness with it, and the men began to shiver.

"Holy smoke!" said one, allowing his voice to express his impious mood, "if we keep on monkeying out here! If we've got to flounder out here all night!"

"Oh, we'll never have to stay here all night! Don't you worry. They've seen us now, and it won't be long before they'll come chasing out after us."

The shore grew dusky. The man waving a coat blended gradually into this gloom, and it swallowed in the same manner the omnibus and the group of people. The spray, when it dashed uproariously over the side, made the voyagers shrink and swear like men who were being branded. **K**

"I'd like to catch the chump who waved the coat. I feel like soaking him one, just for luck."

"Why? What did he do?"

"Oh, nothing, but then he seemed so damn cheerful."

In the meantime the oiler rowed, and then the correspondent rowed, and then the oiler rowed. Gray-faced and bowed forward, they mechanically, turn by turn, plied the leaden oars. The form of the lighthouse had vanished from the southern horizon, but finally a pale star appeared, just lifting from the sea. The streaked saffron in the west passed before the all-merging darkness, and the sea to the east was black. The land had vanished, and was expressed only by the low and drear thunder of the surf.

"If I am going to be drowned—if I am going to be drowned—if I am going to be drowned, why, in the name of the seven mad gods who rule the sea, was I allowed to come thus far and contemplate sand and trees? Was I brought here merely to have my nose dragged away as I was about to nibble the sacred cheese of life?" **L**

The patient captain, drooped over the water jar, was sometimes obliged to speak to the oarsman.

K DESCRIPTIVE LANGUAGE
What mood is established by the **description** in lines 394–403?

L NATURALISM
Reread lines 415–419. There is something almost comical about the repeated image of a man "about to nibble the sacred cheese of life." Why do you think Crane might have chosen to strike such a **tone** in reference to such a serious topic? Explain.

16. **yawls:** sailboats with two masts.

"Keep her head up! Keep her head up!"

"'Keep her head up,' sir." The voices were weary and low.

This was surely a quiet evening. All save the oarsman lay heavily and listlessly in the boat's bottom. As for him, his eyes were just capable of noting the tall black waves that swept forward in a most sinister silence, save for an occasional subdued growl of a crest.

The cook's head was on a thwart, and he looked without interest at the water under his nose. He was deep in other scenes. Finally he spoke. "Billie," he murmured, dreamfully, "what kind of pie do you like best?"

V

"Pie," said the oiler and the correspondent, agitatedly. "Don't talk about those things, blast you!"

"Well," said the cook, "I was just thinking about ham sandwiches, and—"

A night on the sea in an open boat is a long night. As darkness settled finally, the shine of the light, lifting from the sea in the south, changed to full gold. On the northern horizon a new light appeared, a small bluish gleam on the edge of the waters. These two lights were the furniture of the world. Otherwise there was nothing but waves.

Two men huddled in the stern, and distances were so magnificent in the dinghy that the rower was enabled to keep his feet partly warmed by thrusting them under his companions. Their legs indeed extended far under the rowing seat until they touched the feet of the captain forward. Sometimes, despite the efforts of the tired oarsman, a wave came piling into the boat, an icy wave of the night, and the chilling water waked them anew. They would twist their bodies for a moment and groan, and sleep the dead sleep once more, while the water in the boat gurgled about them as the craft rocked.

The plan of the oiler and the correspondent was for one to row until he lost the ability, and then arouse the other from his seawater couch in the bottom of the boat.

The oiler plied the oars until his head drooped forward, and the overpowering sleep blinded him. And he rowed yet afterward. Then he touched a man in the bottom of the boat, and called his name. "Will you spell me for a little while?" he said, meekly.

"Sure, Billie," said the correspondent, awakening and dragging himself to a sitting position. They exchanged places carefully, and the oiler, cuddling down in the seawater at the cook's side, seemed to go to sleep instantly.

The particular violence of the sea had ceased. The waves came without snarling. The obligation of the man at the oars was to keep the boat headed so that the tilt of the rollers would not capsize her, and to preserve her from filling when the crests rushed past. The black waves were silent and hard to be seen in the darkness. Often one was almost upon the boat before the oarsman was aware.

In a low voice the correspondent addressed the captain. He was not sure that the captain was awake, although this iron man seemed to be always awake. "Captain, shall I keep her making for that light north, sir?"

The same steady voice answered him. "Yes. Keep it about two points off the port bow."[17]

The cook had tied a life belt around himself in order to get even the warmth which this clumsy cork contrivance could donate, and he seemed almost stovelike when a rower, whose teeth invariably chattered wildly as soon as he ceased his labor, dropped down to sleep.

The correspondent, as he rowed, looked down at the two men sleeping under foot. The cook's arm was around the oiler's shoulders, and, with their fragmentary clothing and haggard faces, they were the babes of the sea, a grotesque rendering of the old babes in the wood.[18]

Later he must have grown stupid at his work, for suddenly there was a growling of water, and a crest came with a roar and a swash into the boat, and it was a wonder that it did not set the cook afloat in his life belt. The cook continued to sleep, but the oiler sat up, blinking his eyes and shaking with the new cold. (M)

"Oh, I'm awfully sorry, Billie," said the correspondent, contritely.

"That's all right, old boy," said the oiler, and lay down again and was asleep.

Presently it seemed that even the captain dozed, and the correspondent thought that he was the one man afloat on all the oceans. The wind had a voice as it came over the waves, and it was sadder than the end.

There was a long, loud swishing astern of the boat, and a gleaming trail of phosphorescence, like blue flame, was furrowed on the black waters. It might have been made by a monstrous knife.

Then there came a stillness, while the correspondent breathed with the open mouth and looked at the sea.

Suddenly there was another swish and another long flash of bluish light, and this time it was alongside the boat, and might almost have been reached with an oar. The correspondent saw an enormous fin speed like a shadow through the water, hurling the crystalline spray and leaving the long glowing trail.

The correspondent looked over his shoulder at the captain. His face was hidden, and he seemed to be asleep. He looked at the babes of the sea. They certainly were asleep. So, being bereft of sympathy, he leaned a little way to one side and swore softly into the sea.

But the thing did not then leave the vicinity of the boat. Ahead or astern, on one side or the other, at intervals long or short, fled the long sparkling streak, and there was to be heard the whiroo of the dark fin. The speed and power of the thing was greatly to be admired. It cut the water like a gigantic and keen projectile. (N)

The presence of this biding thing did not affect the man with the same horror that it would if he had been a picnicker. He simply looked at the sea dully and swore in an undertone.

(M) GRAMMAR AND STYLE
Reread lines 475–478. With his unusual use of the **gerund phrase** "a growling of water," Crane characterizes the sea as a wild or angry animal, emphasizing its danger.

(N) NATURALISM
Reread lines 484–501. What might the shark symbolize? Consider what this symbol contributes to the development of the **theme.**

17. **two points off the port bow:** two compass points, or a total of 45 degrees, to the left.
18. **babes in the wood:** a reference to an old nursery rhyme in which two children are abandoned in the woods and die there in the night.

Nevertheless, it is true that he did not wish to be alone with the thing. He wished one of his companions to awaken by chance and keep him company with it. But the captain hung motionless over the water jar and the oiler and the cook in the bottom of the boat were plunged in slumber.

VI

"If I am going to be drowned—if I am going to be drowned—if I am going to be drowned, why, in the name of the seven mad gods who rule the sea, was I allowed to come thus far and contemplate sand and trees?" **O**

O NATURALISM
What is the tone of this third repetition of the men's outcry against fate?

During this dismal night, it may be remarked that a man would conclude that it was really the intention of the seven mad gods to drown him, despite the abominable injustice of it. For it was certainly an abominable injustice to drown a man who had worked so hard, so hard. The man felt it would be a crime most unnatural. Other people had drowned at sea since galleys[19] swarmed with painted sails, but still—

When it occurs to a man that nature does not regard him as important, and that she feels she would not maim the universe by disposing of him, he at first wishes to throw bricks at the temple, and he hates deeply the fact that there are no bricks and no temples. Any visible expression of nature would surely be pelleted with his jeers. **P**

P NATURALISM
What does the author say about nature's regard for the individual in lines 518–522?

Then, if there be no tangible thing to hoot he feels, perhaps, the desire to confront a personification and indulge in pleas, bowed to one knee, and with hands supplicant, saying: "Yes, but I love myself."

A high cold star on a winter's night is the word he feels that she says to him. Thereafter he knows the pathos of his situation.

The men in the dinghy had not discussed these matters, but each had, no doubt, reflected upon them in silence and according to his mind. There was seldom any expression upon their faces save the general one of complete weariness. Speech was devoted to the business of the boat.

To chime the notes of his emotion, a verse mysteriously entered the correspondent's head. He had even forgotten that he had forgotten this verse, but it suddenly was in his mind.

> *A soldier of the Legion lay dying in Algiers,*
> *There was lack of woman's nursing, there was* ***dearth*** *of woman's tears;*
> *But a comrade stood beside him, and he took that comrade's hand,*
> *And he said: "I never more shall see my own, my native land."*[20]

dearth (dûrth) *n.* lack

In his childhood, the correspondent had been made acquainted with the fact that a soldier of the Legion lay dying in Algiers, but he had never regarded it as important. Myriads of his schoolfellows had informed him of the soldier's plight, but the dinning had naturally ended by making him perfectly indifferent. He had never considered it his affair that a soldier of the Legion lay dying in Algiers, nor

19. **galleys:** large medieval ships propelled by sails and oars.

20. ***A soldier . . . native land:*** condensed first stanza of Caroline E. S. Norton's poem "Bingen on the Rhine." The Legion is the French Foreign Legion; Algiers is the capital city of the African nation Algeria.

had it appeared to him as a matter for sorrow. It was less to him than the breaking of a pencil's point.

Now, however, it quaintly came to him as a human, living thing. It was no longer merely a picture of a few throes in the breast of a poet, meanwhile drinking tea and warming his feet at the grate; it was actuality—stern, mournful, and fine.

The correspondent plainly saw the soldier. He lay on the sand with his feet out straight and still. While his pale left hand was upon his chest in an attempt to thwart the going of his life, the blood came between his fingers. In the far Algerian distance, a city of low square forms was set against a sky that was faint with the last sunset hues. The correspondent, plying the oars and dreaming of the slow and slower movements of the lips of the soldier, was moved by a profound and perfectly impersonal comprehension. He was sorry for the soldier of the Legion who lay dying in Algiers. **Q**

Q DESCRIPTIVE LANGUAGE
The description in lines 549–556 paints the correspondent's mental picture of the soldier in the poem. What does this **imagery** suggest about the correspondent's own plight?

The thing which had followed the boat and waited had evidently grown bored at the delay. There was no longer to be heard the slash of the cutwater,[21] and there was no longer the flame of the long trail. The light in the north still glimmered, but it was apparently no nearer to the boat. Sometimes the boom of the surf rang in the correspondent's ears, and he turned the craft seaward then and rowed harder. Southward, some one had evidently built a watch fire on the beach. It was too low and too far to be seen, but it made a shimmering, roseate reflection upon the bluff back of it, and this could be discerned from the boat. The wind came stronger, and sometimes a wave suddenly raged out like a mountain-cat and there was to be seen the sheen and sparkle of a broken crest.

The captain, in the bow, moved on his water jar and sat erect. "Pretty long night," he observed to the correspondent. He looked at the shore. "Those lifesaving people take their time."

"Did you see that shark playing around?"

"Yes, I saw him. He was a big fellow, all right."

"Wish I had known you were awake."

Later the correspondent spoke into the bottom of the boat.

"Billie!" There was a slow and gradual disentanglement. "Billie, will you spell me?"

"Sure," said the oiler.

As soon as the correspondent touched the cold comfortable seawater in the bottom of the boat, and had huddled close to the cook's life belt he was deep in sleep, despite the fact that his teeth played all the popular airs. This sleep was so good to him that it was but a moment before he heard a voice call his name in a tone that demonstrated the last stages of exhaustion. "Will you spell me?"

"Sure, Billie."

The light in the north had mysteriously vanished, but the correspondent took his course from the wide-awake captain.

Later in the night they took the boat farther out to sea, and the captain directed the cook to take one oar at the stern and keep the boat facing the seas. He was to

COMMON CORE RL 4

Language Coach

Multiple-Meaning Words *Airs* (line 579) is a multiple-meaning word, a word with more than one meaning. Here, *airs* means "melodies." What does Crane mean by teeth playing melodies?

21. **cutwater:** the front part of a ship.

call out if he should hear the thunder of the surf. This plan enabled the oiler and the correspondent to get **respite** together. "We'll give those boys a chance to get into shape again," said the captain. They curled down and, after a few preliminary chatterings and trembles, slept once more the dead sleep. Neither knew they had bequeathed to the cook the company of another shark, or perhaps the same shark.

respite (rĕs′pĭt) *n.* a period of rest or relief

As the boat caroused on the waves, spray occasionally bumped over the side and gave them a fresh soaking, but this had no power to break their repose. The ominous slash of the wind and the water affected them as it would have affected mummies.

"Boys," said the cook, with the notes of every reluctance in his voice, "she's drifted in pretty close. I guess one of you had better take her to sea again." The correspondent, aroused, heard the crash of the toppled crests.

As he was rowing, the captain gave him some whiskey and water, and this steadied the chills out of him. "If I ever get ashore and anybody shows me even a photograph of an oar—"

At last there was a short conversation.

"Billie. . . . Billie, will you spell me?"

"Sure," said the oiler.

VII

When the correspondent again opened his eyes, the sea and the sky were each of the gray hue of the dawning. Later, carmine and gold was painted upon the waters. The morning appeared finally, in its splendor, with a sky of pure blue, and the sunlight flamed on the tips of the waves. R

R DESCRIPTIVE LANGUAGE
Note the change in mood. What descriptive language has been used to achieve this?

On the distant dunes were set many little black cottages, and a tall white windmill reared above them. No man, nor dog, nor bicycle appeared on the beach. The cottages might have formed a deserted village.

The voyagers scanned the shore. A conference was held in the boat. "Well," said the captain, "if no help is coming, we might better try a run through the surf right away. If we stay out here much longer we will be too weak to do anything for ourselves at all." The others silently **acquiesced** in this reasoning. The boat was headed for the beach. The correspondent wondered if none ever ascended the tall wind tower, and if then they never looked seaward. This tower was a giant, standing with its back to the plight of the ants. It represented in a degree, to the correspondent, the serenity of nature amid the struggles of the individual—nature in the wind, and nature in the vision of men. She did not seem cruel to him then, nor beneficent, nor treacherous, nor wise. But she was indifferent, flatly indifferent. It is, perhaps, plausible that a man in this situation, impressed with the unconcern of the universe, should see the innumerable flaws of his life and have them taste wickedly in his mind and wish for another chance. A distinction between right and wrong seems absurdly clear to him, then, in this new ignorance of the grave edge, and he understands that if he were given another opportunity he would mend his conduct and his words, and be better and brighter during an introduction, or at a tea. S

acquiesce (ăk′wē-ĕs′) *v.* to comply or give in

S NATURALISM
Reread lines 612–628. Which sentence in this paragraph do you think most effectively expresses the indifference of nature to the struggles of the individual? Explain.

Moonlit Shipwreck at Sea (1901), Thomas Moran. 30″ × 40 ¼″. © Christie's Images Limited.

"Now, boys," said the captain, "she is going to swamp sure. All we can do is to work her in as far as possible, and then when she swamps, pile out and scramble for the beach. Keep cool now, and don't jump until she swamps sure."

The oiler took the oars. Over his shoulders he scanned the surf. "Captain," he said, "I think I'd better bring her about, and keep her head-on to the seas and back her in."

"All right, Billie," said the captain. "Back her in." The oiler swung the boat then and, seated in the stern, the cook and the correspondent were obliged to look over their shoulders to contemplate the lonely and indifferent shore.

The monstrous inshore rollers[22] heaved the boat high until the men were again enabled to see the white sheets of water scudding up the slanted beach. "We won't get in very close," said the captain. Each time a man could wrest his

▲ Analyze Visuals
In your opinion, how well does this painting reflect the men's situation? Reread the description of the waves on this page and compare them to the waves as portrayed by the artist.

22. **inshore rollers:** long waves swelling close to the shore.

attention from the rollers, he turned his glance toward the shore, and in the expression of the eyes during this contemplation there was a singular quality. The correspondent, observing the others, knew that they were not afraid, but the full meaning of their glances was shrouded.

As for himself, he was too tired to grapple fundamentally with the fact. He tried to **coerce** his mind into thinking of it, but the mind was dominated at this time by the muscles, and the muscles said they did not care. It merely occurred to him that if he should drown it would be a shame.

coerce (kō-ûrs') *v.* to force

There were no hurried words, no pallor, no plain agitation. The men simply looked at the shore. "Now, remember to get well clear of the boat when you jump," said the captain.

Seaward the crest of a roller suddenly fell with a thunderous crash, and the long white comber[23] came roaring down upon the boat.

"Steady now," said the captain. The men were silent. They turned their eyes from the shore to the comber and waited. The boat slid up the incline, leaped at the furious top, bounced over it, and swung down the long back of the wave. Some water had been shipped and the cook bailed it out.

But the next crest crashed also. The tumbling boiling flood of white water caught the boat and whirled it almost perpendicular. Water swarmed in from all sides. The correspondent had his hands on the gunwale at this time, and when the water entered at that place he swiftly withdrew his fingers, as if he objected to wetting them.

The little boat, drunken with this weight of water, reeled and snuggled deeper into the sea. T

"Bail her out, cook! Bail her out," said the captain.

"All right, Captain," said the cook.

"Now, boys, the next one will do for us, sure," said the oiler. "Mind to jump clear of the boat."

The third wave moved forward, huge, furious, implacable. It fairly swallowed the dinghy, and almost simultaneously the men tumbled into the sea. A piece of life belt had lain in the bottom of the boat, and as the correspondent went overboard he held this to his chest with his left hand.

The January water was icy, and he reflected immediately that it was colder than he had expected to find it off the coast of Florida. This appeared to his dazed mind as a fact important enough to be noted at the time. The coldness of the water was sad; it was tragic. This fact was somehow so mixed and confused with his opinion of his own situation that it seemed almost a proper reason for tears. The water was cold.

When he came to the surface he was conscious of little but the noisy water. Afterward he saw his companions in the sea. The oiler was ahead in the race. He was swimming strongly and rapidly. Off to the correspondent's left, the cook's great white and corked back bulged out of the water, and in the rear the captain was hanging with his one good hand to the keel of the overturned dinghy.

T NATURALISM

Ancient literature in every culture includes stories of people at the mercy of natural forces. From the epic flood in the Babylonian story *Gilgamesh* to Odysseus' dangerous sea voyage, there are many stories about humans cast loose on unstill waters. These stories are as old as human history and as recent as the hugely successful television series *Lost*. They include Ernest Hemingway's powerful novel *The Old Man and the Sea* as well as the 2000 film *The Perfect Storm*. Reread lines 645–664. How does this passage compare with stories you've read or seen in which humans struggle against storms or other violent natural forces?

23. **comber:** a large wave that breaks on a beach.

There is a certain immovable quality to a shore, and the correspondent wondered at it amid the confusion of the sea.

It seemed also very attractive, but the correspondent knew that it was a long journey, and he paddled leisurely. The piece of life preserver lay under him, and sometimes he whirled down the incline of a wave as if he were on a hand sled.

But finally he arrived at a place in the sea where travel was beset with difficulty. He did not pause swimming to inquire what manner of current had caught him, but there his progress ceased. The shore was set before him like a bit of scenery on a stage, and he looked at it and understood with his eyes each detail of it.

As the cook passed, much farther to the left, the captain was calling to him, "Turn over on your back, cook! Turn over on your back and use the oar."

"All right, sir." The cook turned on his back, and, paddling with an oar, went ahead as if he were a canoe.

Presently the boat also passed to the left of the correspondent with the captain clinging with one hand to the keel. He would have appeared like a man raising himself to look over a board fence, if it were not for the extraordinary gymnastics of the boat. The correspondent marveled that the captain could still hold to it.

They passed on, nearer to shore—the oiler, the cook, the captain—and following them went the water jar, bouncing gaily over the seas.

The correspondent remained in the grip of this strange new enemy—a current. The shore, with its white slope of sand and its green bluff, topped with little silent cottages, was spread like a picture before him. It was very near to him then, but he was impressed as one who in a gallery looks at a scene from Brittany[24] or Holland.

He thought: "I am going to drown? Can it be possible? Can it be possible? Can it be possible?" Perhaps an individual must consider his own death to be the final phenomenon of nature. **U**

U NATURALISM
Reread lines 707–709. How does the correspondent come to view death as he is faced with the prospect of drowning?

But later a wave perhaps whirled him out of this small deadly current, for he found suddenly that he could again make progress toward the shore. Later still, he was aware that the captain, clinging with one hand to the keel of the dinghy, had his face turned away from the shore and toward him, and was calling his name. "Come to the boat! Come to the boat!"

In his struggle to reach the captain and the boat, he reflected that when one gets properly wearied, drowning must really be a comfortable arrangement, a cessation of hostilities accompanied by a large degree of relief, and he was glad of it, for the main thing in his mind for some moments had been horror of the temporary agony. He did not wish to be hurt.

Presently he saw a man running along the shore. He was undressing with most remarkable speed. Coat, trousers, shirt, everything flew magically off him.

"Come to the boat," called the captain.

"All right, Captain." As the correspondent paddled, he saw the captain let himself down to bottom and leave the boat. Then the correspondent performed his one little marvel of the voyage. A large wave caught him and flung him with

---

24. **Brittany:** a region in northwestern France.

ease and supreme speed completely over the boat and far beyond it. It struck him even then as an event in gymnastics, and a true miracle of the sea. An overturned boat in the surf is not a plaything to a swimming man.

The correspondent arrived in water that reached only to his waist, but his condition did not enable him to stand for more than a moment. Each wave knocked him into a heap, and the undertow pulled at him.

Then he saw the man who had been running and undressing, and undressing and running, come bounding into the water. He dragged ashore the cook, and then waded toward the captain, but the captain waved him away, and sent him to the correspondent. He was naked, naked as a tree in winter, but a halo was about his head, and he shone like a saint. He gave a strong pull, and a long drag, and a bully heave at the correspondent's hand. The correspondent, schooled in the minor formulæ, said: "Thanks, old man." But suddenly the man cried: "What's that?" He pointed a swift finger. The correspondent said: "Go."

In the shallows, face downward, lay the oiler. His forehead touched sand that was periodically, between each wave, clear of the sea.

The correspondent did not know all that transpired afterward. When he achieved safe ground he fell, striking the sand with each particular part of his body. It was as if he had dropped from a roof, but the thud was grateful to him.

It seems that instantly the beach was populated with men with blankets, clothes, and flasks, and women with coffeepots and all the remedies sacred to their minds. The welcome of the land to the men from the sea was warm and generous, but a still and dripping shape was carried slowly up the beach, and the land's welcome for it could only be the different and sinister hospitality of the grave.

When it came night, the white waves paced to and fro in the moonlight, and the wind brought the sound of the great sea's voice to the men on shore, and they felt that they could then be interpreters.

Comprehension

1. **Recall** Which character in the story doesn't survive?
2. **Clarify** Why don't the men row the boat directly onto the beach?
3. **Clarify** Why don't the people on shore rescue the men?

Text Analysis

4. **Make Inferences About Conflict** The sea is the great **antagonist** in Crane's story. Are the men saved primarily by their own efforts or by chance? How does their struggle compare to stories you've read or movies you've seen in which water plays the role of antagonist?
5. **Examine Naturalism** Reread lines 509–522 at the beginning of section VI, where the correspondent rails against the "abominable injustice" of **nature.** Is nature really unjust in the story? What characteristics of nature are suggested in these lines and in other places in the story?
6. **Examine Dramatic Irony** Naturalistic writers often use irony to express their worldview. Find two instances in "The Open Boat" in which the characters' perceptions don't match the reality of the situation. Then, explain how the two examples of irony interact to build toward Crane's naturalistic theme.
7. **Analyze Tone** The narrative voice of this story is quite detached, relating highly dramatic events with a mild and even slightly humorous tone. Find examples of this detachment. How does this tone affect the story's message or overall impact? Explain.
8. **Evaluate Descriptive Language** Identify the section of the story (a page or more) that you find most compelling. Now review the examples of descriptive elements that you recorded as you read. What role does descriptive writing play in this passage? How do you think the description affects your feelings about it? Cite details from the text to support your answer.

Text Criticism

9. **Author's Style** One writer described Stephen Crane's stories as "intensely realistic." He attributed this realism to Crane's training as a reporter, saying "his English flow[s] simple and pure." Do you agree? Explain why or why not, citing evidence from the story to support your answer.

Does NATURE *play fair?*

In "The Open Boat," do you think Crane portrays "nature" as evil, kind, or indifferent to humans? Why might he have chosen "nature," "Fate," and "the seven mad gods who rule the sea" as the ambiguous objects of his questions?

COMMON CORE

RL 2 Determine two or more themes or central ideas of a text and analyze how they interact to produce a complex account. **RL 3** Analyze the impact of the author's choices regarding how to develop and relate elements of a story. **RL 4** Analyze the impact of specific word choices on meaning and tone, including language that is particularly fresh, engaging, or beautiful. **RL 6** Analyze a case in which grasping point of view requires distinguishing what is directly stated in a text from what is really meant.

Vocabulary in Context

▲ VOCABULARY PRACTICE

Choose the letter of the phrase that defines or is related to the boldfaced word.

1. **coerce:** (a) someone being robbed, (b) someone singing, (c) someone writing
2. **epithet:** (a) a sincere apology, (b) a two-handed card game, (c) a show of anger
3. **motley:** (a) polka dots with plaid, (b) a portrait of twins, (c) a thunderstorm
4. **obstreperous:** (a) a severe cold, (b) a noisy argument, (c) a lazy summer day
5. **dearth:** (a) a large fireplace, (b) a song played at funerals, (c) a shortage of good ideas
6. **respite:** (a) halftime at a game, (b) jealous anger, (c) paying back a debt
7. **aberration:** (a) a pilot in training, (b) a small city park, (c) the habits of an eccentric
8. **ingenuously:** (a) a sudden change in weather, (b) a believer in fairy tales, (c) a clever invention
9. **opprobrious:** (a) a clever comedian, (b) a scornful laugh, (c) a wildlife refuge
10. **acquiesce:** (a) an army's surrender, (b) a child's naptime, (c) a bird's piercing call

WORD LIST

aberration
acquiesce
coerce
dearth
epithet
ingenuously
motley
obstreperous
opprobrious
respite

ACADEMIC VOCABULARY IN WRITING

• apparent • confine • expose • focus • perceive

How does the correspondent initially **perceive** his situation in "The Open Boat"? Write a paragraph explaining how his attitude changes by the end of the story, and use at least one Academic Vocabulary word in your response.

VOCABULARY STRATEGY: THE GREEK PREFIX *epi-*

The prefix *epi-*, which has its origin in the Greek language, means "upon," "among," or "in addition." *Epi-* is found in a number of English words, including the vocabulary word *epithet*. You can use your knowledge of the origin of this prefix, in addition to the context of a word, to help determine the word's meaning.

PRACTICE Choose the word from the word web that best completes each sentence. Consider what you know about the Greek prefix and the other word parts shown. If necessary, consult a dictionary.

1. The _____ of the earthquake was 200 miles from the city.
2. The top layer of skin in humans is called the _____.
3. The _____ spread illness and disease throughout the region.

COMMON CORE

L 4d Verify the preliminary determination of the meaning of a word. **L 6** Acquire and use accurately general academic words and phrases.

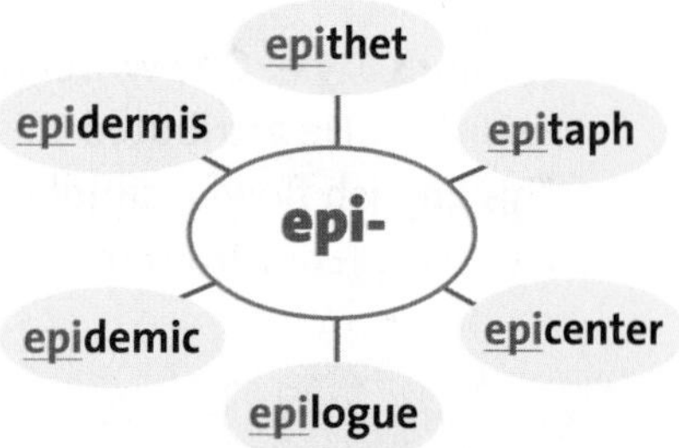

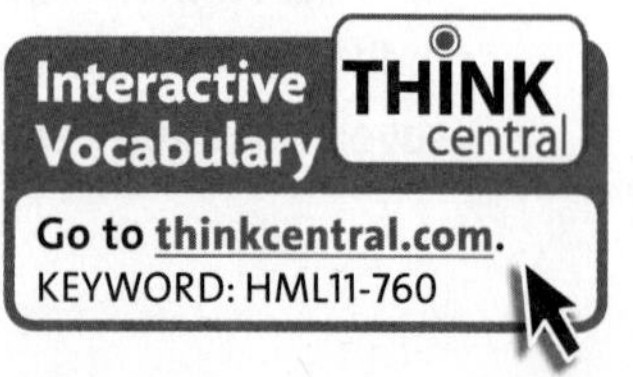

Interactive Vocabulary
THINK central
Go to thinkcentral.com.
KEYWORD: HML11-760

Language

◆ GRAMMAR AND STYLE: Use Effective Description

Review the **Grammar and Style** note on page 751. Crane uses gerunds and gerund phrases in some unusual ways, creating energetic phrases and sentences. A **gerund** is a verb form that ends in *-ing* and functions as a noun. A **gerund phrase** includes a gerund and its modifiers and complements. In this example from "The Open Boat," notice how "snarling of the crests" functions as a noun in the sentence:

> *There was a terrible grace in the move of the waves, and they came in silence, save for the snarling of the crests.* (lines 51–52)

The gerund emphasizes the action of the waves more than the simple noun *snarl* would. It's a subtle difference that, when used strategically in your writing, can have a cumulative impact.

PRACTICE Rewrite each of the following sentences so that it contains a gerund phrase. You may want to change an existing verb into a gerund or add an entirely new idea. (Remember that a participial phrase, which also uses the *-ing* form of a verb, is used as an adjective, whereas a gerund phrase is used as a noun.)

EXAMPLE

The sun sank gradually, and their hearts sank soon after.

The gradual sinking of the sun was followed by the sinking of their hearts.

1. The surf roared, announcing the nearness of the shore.
2. The gulls cried and gave voice to their own despair.
3. The men looked warily at the shark fin as it coolly sliced the water.

COMMON CORE

L 1 Demonstrate command of the conventions of standard English grammar when writing. **L 3** Apply knowledge of language to make effective choices for meaning or style. **W 3b** Use narrative techniques, such as description and reflection, to develop characters.

READING-WRITING CONNECTION

Expand your understanding of "The Open Boat" by responding to this prompt. Then, use the **revising tips** to improve your character sketch.

WRITING PROMPT

WRITE A CHARACTER SKETCH The most compelling character in "The Open Boat" is the sea. To describe the sea, Crane frequently uses **personification,** a figure of speech in which an object is given human features.

Write a **short character sketch** about a non-human character such as the sea in "The Open Boat." Use Crane's story as a model for your character sketch.

REVISING TIPS

- Use personification to make your non-human character come to life.
- Include descriptive details as well as a reflection on the importance or effect of the subject.
- Use precise words and phrases that will convey a vivid mood.

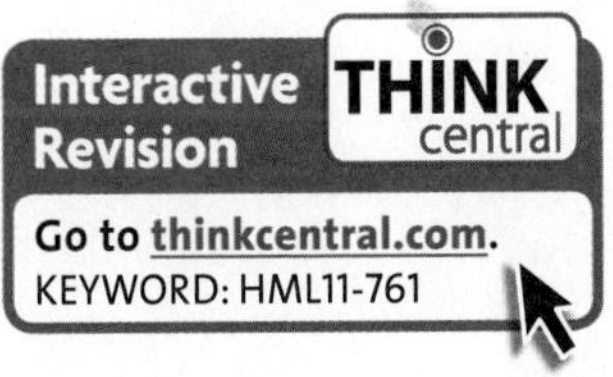

Reading for Information

The Wreck of the *Commodore*

Newspaper Articles

Use with "The Open Boat," page 736.

COMMON CORE

RI 1 Cite textual evidence to support inferences drawn from the text, including determining where the text leaves matters uncertain. **RI 5** Analyze and evaluate the effectiveness of the structure an author uses in his or her exposition, including whether the structure makes points clear and engaging. **RI 9** Analyze nineteenth-century documents of historical significance.

"The Open Boat" was based on Stephen Crane's experience with the wreck of the *Commodore,* a ship on a private mission to arm rebels fighting in the Cuban civil war. Crane had joined these filibusters, as these men were known, in search of adventure and a good story. When the ship went down, however, he acted as far more than a journalist. You'll now read news stories about this sensational event, including an account by Crane himself.

Standards Focus: Analyze Primary Sources

The 1897 articles about the wreck of the *Commodore* are **primary sources** of information on that event. You can also look to them as evidence of the kind of writing that appeared in newspapers of the day. As you read the articles, make connections between the three texts and synthesize, or bring together, your ideas about the event. Keep the following questions in mind:

- Who is the intended **audience**?
- What techniques are used to capture the readers' interest?
- What is the **tone** of the piece?
- What is its **scope** and **focus**? In other words, how much is covered, and what in the piece is most important?
- What **structure** is used to organize the information in the piece?
- How much **imagery** or other colorful language does it contain?
- How does the piece differ from something you might find in a newspaper today?

Note your observations and textual evidence in a chart such as this one.

"The Commodore Sinks at Sea"	"More of the Filibusters Safe"	"Stephen Crane and His Work"	"Stephen Crane's Own Story"
lots of stacked headlines			

THE FLORIDA TIMES-UNION

SUNDAY, JANUARY 3, 1897 PRICE 5 CENTS.

THE COMMODORE SINKS AT SEA

The Little Vessel Lost with Her Cargo of Arms and Ammunition

HER NUMEROUS COMPANY REACH LAND IN SAFETY

They are Compelled to Take to the Boats and Abandon the Sinking Vessel

An Overload of Coal the Probable Cause A

THE STEAMER COMMODORE, which left here Thursday night with an expedition for the Cuban insurgents, is now resting on the bottom of the sea, twenty fathoms below the surface, about eighteen miles northeast of Mosquito Inlet.

All of the men on the vessel, twenty-eight in number, reached the shore in safety, and twelve of them arrived in Jacksonville last night over the Florida East Coast railway. The other sixteen are still down the coast, but are expected to arrive here on a special train this morning. . . .

DETAILS OF THE ACCIDENT

About 12 o'clock Friday night it was discovered that the boat was leaking badly. The swash of the water in the hold as the vessel rolled from side to side soon alarmed everyone on board. A panic ensued, but Captain Murphy, Stephen Crane, R. A. Delgado and one or two others soon quieted the excitement and put everybody to work on the pumps and with buckets. The steam pump was started and for two hours the water was poured over the sides in streams.

At 2:30 A.M., it was seen that the water was steadily gaining, and it was decided to abandon the vessel.

IN THE BOATS

Paul Rojo, R. A. Delgado, Franco Blanco, the old Cuban pilot, and nine other men took one of the boats and left the steamer. Captain Murphy, the first and second mate, the engineer and assistant, Stephen Crane and ten men took the large yawl boat, and at 3 o'clock they left the Commodore to her fate. The night was dark and they could not see what became of her, but as she was rapidly filling with water, they are all confident that she is now resting on the bottom, and old Neptune has been supplied with enough arms and ammunition to blow up the island of Cuba. . . . B

A PRIMARY SOURCES
Compare these headlines with those in papers today. Why do you think there are so many?

Language Coach

Fixed Expressions "Panic ensued" in line 21 means "panic followed." Other **fixed expressions**—normal combinations of words—are *panic broke out* and *panic spread through*. Explain the cause of the panic, using one of these fixed expressions.

B PRIMARY SOURCES
Reread lines 43–47. What does the writer mean by this comment?

The New York Press

MONDAY, JANUARY 4, 1897 SECTION 1

MORE OF THE FILIBUSTERS SAFE

STEPHEN CRANE, NOVELIST, SWIMS ASHORE

DAYTONA, Fla., Jan. 3.—"That newspaper feller was a nervy man," said the cook of the ill-fated Commodore tonight in reference to Stephen Crane, the novelist, who is after material for stories. "He didn't seem to know what fear was. When we started out he insisted upon doing a seaman's work, and he did it well, too.

"When the boats were launched he was the last one, except Captain Murphy, to get in, and his nerve greatly encouraged all hands. In the small dingy he rowed as well as the others, notwithstanding he was so worn out that he could hardly hold his oar straight in the terrific seas.

SAVES A DROWNING MAN

"Both he and Captain Murphy were thrown out on the same side. Crane was partially thrown under the overturned boat and but for Captain Murphy's readiness in catching him by the collar he would have gone under. We all battled there in the water for hours, it seemed to us. Crane was a good swimmer, and he really saved one of the sailors, as the man could not swim a stroke, and Crane had to keep him up by the aid of an oar. These newspaper fellers have got spunk, if they do tell such awful woppers at times," concluded the cook, as he took another big swig of the "life preservative" provided by the good people here. . . . **C**

Language Coach

Word Definitions *Nervy* (line 2) means "bold" or "strong." Reread the first paragraph. What details does the cook give to back up his assessment of Crane?

C PRIMARY SOURCES Note that this article consists entirely of a quotation by the cook. Why do you think the writer of this article chose to quote him at such length?

STEPHEN CRANE AND HIS WORK

How He Came to Be on the Unlucky Commodore

TO WRITE FOR THE PRESS

Brilliant Author Not of the Sort to Give Up His Cuban Letters Because of Shipwreck

STEPHEN CRANE, the writer, is safe and readers of The Press may expect in a short time a treat from his versatile pen. . . .

Mr. Crane was on the way to Cuba to write about the war there. He will get to Cuba as soon as he can. He is not of the sort who are frightened by an experience in a lifeboat. His letters will appear in The Press as soon as they arrive.

Mr. Crane has not intimated just what he is going to write; probably he does not know himself. But that his letters will be intensely interesting and true to life readers of his stories, "The Red Badge of Courage," "The Third Violet," "George's Mother" and "Maggie, a Girl of the Streets," feel assured. **D**

D PRIMARY SOURCES This paper portrays Crane as quite a hero, citing his bravery and pluck. In this article, why do you think the editors have chosen to make so much of his "Cuban letters," or his work as a foreign correspondent?

The New York Press

THURSDAY, JANUARY 7, 1897 SECTION 1

STEPHEN CRANE'S OWN STORY

JACKSONVILLE, FLA., Jan. 6.—It was the afternoon of New Year's. The Commodore lay at her dock in Jacksonville and negro stevedores processioned steadily toward her with box after box of ammunition and bundle after bundle of rifles. Her hatch, like the mouth of a monster, engulfed them. It might have been the feeding time of some legendary creature of the sea. It was in broad daylight and the crowd of gleeful Cubans on the pier did not forbear to sing the strange patriotic ballads of their island. . . . The revenue cutter Boutwell, the old isosceles triangle that protects United States interests in the St. John's, lay at anchor, with no sign of excitement aboard her.

SLEEP IMPOSSIBLE

As darkness came upon the waters, the Commodore was a broad, flaming path of blue and silver phosphorescence, and as her stout bow lunged at the great black waves she threw flashing, roaring cascades to either side. And all that was to be heard was the rhythmical and mighty pounding of the engines.

THE COOK IS HOPEFUL

The cook was asleep on a bench in the galley. He woke as I entered the galley and delivered himself of some dolorous sentiments: "I don't feel right about this ship, somehow. It strikes me that something is going to happen to us. I don't know what it is, but the old ship is going to get it in the neck, I think."

Author Stephen Crane

"Well, how about the men on board of her?" said I. "Are any of us going to get out, prophet?"

"Yes," said the cook. "Sometimes I have these damned feelings come over me, and they are always right, and it seems to me, somehow, that you and I will both get [out] and meet again somewhere, down at Coney Island, perhaps, or some place like that."

Here I first came to know a certain young oiler named Billy Higgins. He was sloshing around this inferno filling buckets with water and passing them to a chain of men that extended up the ship's side. **E**

A WHISTLE OF DESPAIR

Now the whistle of the Commodore had been turned loose, and if there ever was a voice of despair and death, it was in the voice of this whistle. It had gained a new tone. It was as if its throat was already choked by the water, and this cry on the sea at night, with a wind blowing

continued

COMMON CORE RI 1

E PRIMARY SOURCES
The very title "Stephen Crane's Own Story" tells you that the article is a primary-source document. It is Crane's first-person narrative of his experience during the *Commodore* disaster. Reread lines 45–50. Then compare the datelines of the three articles, and consider why Crane provides so little information about why the men are passing buckets of water. What other connections can you make between the articles? Based on these accounts, what conclusion can you draw about Stephen Crane himself?

F PRIMARY SOURCES
Reread lines 51–63. Identify the **imagery** used to describe the *Commodore*. What **mood** does Crane achieve with this language?

G PRIMARY SOURCES
Reread lines 81–102. What happened to the men still aboard the ship?

H PRIMARY SOURCES
What **tone** does Crane adopt in the last paragraph? Explain how this tone affects your perception of these events.

JANUARY 7, 1897 THE NEW YORK PRESS SECTION 1

the spray over the ship, and the waves roaring over the bow, and swirling white along the decks, was to each of us probably a song of man's end. The boat moved at last and swung down toward the water. F

IN THE TEN-FOOT DINGY

The captain was just about to swing over the rail when a dark form came forward and a voice said: "Captain, I go with you."

The captain answered: "Yes, Billy; get in."

HIGGINS LAST TO LEAVE SHIP

It was Billy Higgins, the oiler. Billy dropped into the boat and a moment later the captain followed, bringing with him an end of about forty yards of lead line. The other end was attached to the rail of the ship.

As we swung back to leeward the captain said: "Boys, we will stay right near the ship till she goes down."

This cheerful information, of course, filled us all with glee.

When came the gray shade of dawn, the form of the Commodore grew slowly clear to us as our little ten-foot boat rose over each swell. She was floating with such an air of buoyancy that we laughed when we had time, and said "What a gag it would be on those other fellows if she didn't sink at all."

But later we saw men aboard of her, and later still they began to hail us.

We rowed back to the ship, but did not approach too near, because we were four men in a ten-foot boat, and we knew that the touch of a hand on our gunwale would assuredly swamp us. . . .

THE COMMODORE SINKS

The cook let go of the line. We rowed around to see if we could not get a line from the chief engineer, and all this time, mind, there were no shrieks, no groans, but silence, silence and silence, and then the Commodore sank. G

She lurched to windward, then swung afar back, righted and dove into the sea, and rafts were suddenly swallowed by this frightful maw of the ocean. And then by the men of the ten-foot dingy were words said that were still not words—something far beyond words.

The lighthouse of Mosquito Inlet stuck up above the horizon like the point of a pin. We turned our dingy toward the shore.

The history of life in an open boat for thirty hours would no doubt be instructive for the young, but none is to be told here and now. For my part I would prefer to tell the story at once, because from it would shine the splendid manhood of Captain Edward Murphy and of William Higgins, the oiler, but let it suffice at this time to say that when we were swamped in the surf and making the best of our way toward the shore the captain gave orders amid the wildness of the breakers as clearly as if he had been on the quarter deck of a battleship.

John Kitchell of Daytona came running down the beach, and as he ran the air was filled with clothes. If he had pulled a single lever and undressed, even as the fire horses harness, he could not seem to me to have stripped with more speed. He dashed into the water and dragged the cook. Then he went after the captain, but the captain sent him to me, and then it was that he saw Billy Higgins lying with his forehead on sand that was clear of the water, and he was dead. H

STEPHEN CRANE

Comprehension

1. **Summarize** What happened to the *Commodore* and her crew?

Text Analysis

2. **Examine Text Features** Review the headlines of these articles. Consider their content and number. What logical connections can you make between them, in terms of **tone?** Explain. How do they support the structure of the articles?
3. **Analyze Primary Sources** Consider the headlines, contents, and tone of the articles. Based on these examples, how would you synthesize your ideas into a general statement about 19th-century journalism? Cite evidence to support your generalization.

COMMON CORE

RI 1 Cite textual evidence to support inferences drawn from the text. **RI 2** Provide an objective summary of the text. **RI 5** Analyze and evaluate the effectiveness of the structure an author uses in his or her exposition. **RI 9** Analyze nineteenth-century documents of historical significance. **W 2** Write explanatory texts to examine and convey complex ideas clearly and accurately through the effective selection, organization, and analysis of content. **W 2c** Use appropriate transitions to clarify the relationships among complex ideas and concepts. **W 7** Synthesize multiple sources on a subject.

Read for Information: Compare Forms

WRITING PROMPT

In Stephen Crane's article about the wreck of the *Commodore*, he wrote:

The history of life in an open boat for thirty hours would no doubt be instructive for the young, but none is to be told here and now. . . . I would prefer to tell the story at once, because from it would shine the splendid manhood of Captain Edward Murphy and of William Higgins, the oiler.

Based on your reading of "The Open Boat" and "Stephen Crane's Own Story," why might Crane have reserved the tale of the open boat for a short story? What does he do with the short story that he can't or doesn't do in the article?

The following steps will help you answer the prompt:

1. Compare the short story and the article, considering the following elements:

	Article	Short Story
Audience and Purpose	to describe shipwreck for newspaper readers	
Character Development		
Coverage of Events		
Imagery and Figurative Language		
Theme and Main Idea		

2. Based on this comparison, consider why Crane may have made the choices he did in writing each piece.
3. Finally, try to explain Crane's decision to write "The Open Boat" by evaluating the strengths of the short story over the article. Support your ideas with details from each text, and use appropriate transitions to show the connections between your ideas.

The Law of Life

Short Story by Jack London

COMMON CORE

RL 2 Determine two or more themes or central ideas of a text and analyze their development over the course of the text. **RL 3** Analyze the impact of the author's choices regarding how to develop and relate elements of a story. **RL 4** Analyze the impact of specific word choices on meaning and tone, including words with multiple meanings. **RL 9** Demonstrate knowledge of early-twentieth-century works of American literature. **L 4b** Identify and correctly use patterns of word changes that indicate different meanings or parts of speech.

DID YOU KNOW?

Jack London . . .

- was the first American author to become a millionaire from his writing.
- pioneered the field of sports writing.
- covered the Russo-Japanese War and the Mexican Revolution as a correspondent.

Meet the Author

Jack London 1876–1916

According to critic Alfred Kazin, "The greatest story Jack London ever wrote was the story he lived." Before London had turned 21 he had had more adventures than a Hollywood action hero. Once he began publishing stories about his experiences, he became an international celebrity. His works, many set in the wilds of Alaska and the American West, brought before the reading public a fresh style and subject matter that proved popular and profitable.

The Call of Adventure Born in San Francisco, Jack London grew up in Oakland, California. Disowned by his biological father, he took the name of his stepfather, John London. Although a decent man, the stepfather couldn't make much of a living, so London spent much of his youth working. Periods of backbreaking manual labor—in factories, canneries, a power plant, and a laundry—alternated with high adventure. The 16-year-old Jack became an oyster pirate in San Francisco Bay before switching sides to join the shore police. At age 17, he boarded a ship for a seal-hunting expedition to the Bering Sea. At 18, he quit work altogether to travel the country as a hobo. These escapades came to an abrupt halt when he was arrested for vagrancy in New York State and jailed for 30 days. Moved by the hard-luck stories of the men he had met on the road and in prison, London could see where his life was heading and decided to turn it around. I ran back to California and opened the books," he explained. By the time he was 20, he had enrolled at the University of California at Berkeley and become a writer.

From Rags to Riches Although writing steadily, London could get nothing published. News of the Klondike Gold Rush in 1897 inspired him to head to Alaska in hopes of striking it rich. Instead of finding gold, however, he got a bad case of scurvy and returned home after less than a year. Still, London admitted, "It was in the Klondike that I found myself." Equally important, he found a wealth of material and formulated the naturalistic philosophy that would make him a blockbuster writer. He shot to international fame with *The Call of the Wild* (1903), and within six years had produced most of his greatest works—*The Sea Wolf* (1904), *White Fang* (1906), *The Road* (1907), the autobiographical *Martin Eden* (1909), and several collections of short stories. London inspired many in the next generation of writers, including Ernest Hemingway, Jack Kerouac, and Norman Mailer.

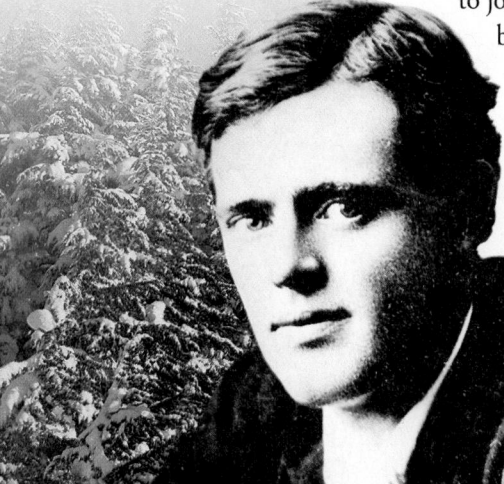

Author Online THINK central

Go to thinkcentral.com. KEYWORD: HML11-768

TEXT ANALYSIS: THEME

Theme is the central message communicated by a literary work. It may be stated directly, but it usually emerges through literary elements as a comment on the human condition. The answers to certain questions can help you identify a story's theme or themes.

- What is the resolution of the primary **conflict?**
- What traits do the main **characters** display?
- What about the physical or cultural **setting** is significant?
- What **point of view** is used to describe the experiences of the main character?
- What meaning does the **title** convey?

Ask yourself these questions as you read "The Law of Life," recording the answers and other details in a chart.

Details Revealing Theme					
Conflict	Character	Setting	Point of View	Symbol	Title

Review: Naturalism

READING SKILL: ANALYZE AUTHOR'S PERSPECTIVE

An **author's perspective** is the unique combination of background, experiences, beliefs, and values that influences the way a writer looks at a topic and the choices he or she makes in writing about it. This story reflects London's experiences in Alaska and the Klondike, where he had gone in hopes of striking it rich in the goldfields. Reread London's biography on page 768. As you read the story, draw on what you know of London's life to help you understand his perspective on such subjects as youth and old age, strength and weakness, survival and death.

VOCABULARY IN CONTEXT

Restate each phrase, using a different word or words for the boldfaced term.

1. need to **replenish** the water supply
2. a **slovenly** fellow, with dirty hair and unshined shoes
3. the **inexorable** passage of time
4. willing to **attest** to his honesty
5. a cat attempting to **harry** the mouse it caught

 Complete the activities in your **Reader/Writer Notebook**.

How do people face DEATH?

Death comes to all of us, but different cultures approach the inevitable end in various ways. The death described in London's story may seem cruel to you, but consider the cultural context of the community described in the story.

QUICKWRITE Think about how your own culture treats people who are dying. Are they treated with indifference or respect? In a more hostile environment, such as a natural disaster, do you think society could maintain the same customs? In your notebook, jot down your thoughts about these issues.

THE LAW OF LIFE

JACK LONDON

BACKGROUND Written when London was about 25 years old, this story was included in his second collection of short stories about Alaska, *Children of the Frost* (1902). The characters are members of a nomadic native tribe whose customs are shaped by the harsh conditions of the Arctic. The law they live by expresses London's naturalistic vision at its most brutal.

Analyze Visuals ▶
Look at the image on page 771. What elements of the man's clothing and facial expression give clues to the photo's **setting?** Explain.

Old Koskoosh listened greedily. Though his sight had long since faded, his hearing was still acute, and the slightest sound penetrated to the glimmering intelligence which yet abode behind his withered forehead, but which no longer gazed forth upon the things of the world. Ah! that was Sit-cum-to-ha, shrilly anathematizing the dogs as she cuffed and beat them into the harness. Sit-cum-to-ha was his daughter's daughter, but she was too busy to waste a thought upon her broken grandfather, sitting alone there in the snow, forlorn and helpless. Camp must be broken. The long trail waited while the short day refused to linger. Life called her, and the duties of life, not death. And he was very close to death now. Ⓐ

The thought made the old man panicky for the moment, and he stretched forth a palsied hand which wandered tremblingly over the small heap of dry wood beside him. Reassured that it was indeed there, his hand returned to the shelter of his mangy furs, and he again fell to listening. The sulky crackling of half-frozen hides told him that the chief's moose-skin lodge had been struck, and

Ⓐ **THEME**
What is significant about the **setting** described in the first paragraph, and what **mood** does it create?

even then was being rammed and jammed into portable compass. The chief was his son, stalwart and strong, head man of the tribesmen, and a mighty hunter. As the women toiled with the camp luggage, his voice rose, chiding them for their slowness. Old Koskoosh strained his ears. It was the last time he would hear that voice. There went Geehow's lodge! And Tusken's! Seven, eight, nine; only the shaman's[1] could be still standing. There! They were at work upon it now. He could hear the shaman grunt as he piled it on the sled. A child whimpered, and a woman soothed it with soft, crooning gutturals.[2] Little Koo-tee, the old man thought, a fretful child, and not overstrong. It would die soon, perhaps, and they would burn a hole through the frozen tundra and pile rocks above to keep the wolverines away. Well, what did it matter? A few years at best, and as many an empty belly as a full one. And in the end, Death waited, ever-hungry and hungriest of them all. **B**

What was that? Oh, the men lashing the sleds and drawing tight the thongs. He listened, who would listen no more. The whip-lashes snarled and bit among the dogs. Hear them whine! How they hated the work and the trail! They were off! Sled after sled churned slowly away into the silence. They were gone. They had passed out of his life, and he faced the last bitter hour alone. No. The snow crunched beneath a moccasin; a man stood beside him; upon his head a hand rested gently. His son was good to do this thing. He remembered other old men whose sons had not waited after the tribe. But his son had. He wandered away into the past, till the young man's voice brought him back.

"Is it well with you?" he asked.

And the old man answered, "It is well."

"There be wood beside you," the younger man continued, "and the fire burns bright. The morning is gray, and the cold has broken. It will snow presently. Even now it is snowing."

"Ay, even now it is snowing."

"The tribesmen hurry. Their bales are heavy, and their bellies flat with lack of feasting. The trail is long and they travel fast. I go now. It is well?"

"It is well. I am as a last year's leaf, clinging lightly to the stem. The first breath that blows, and I fall. My voice is become like an old woman's. My eyes no longer show me the way of my feet, and my feet are heavy, and I am tired. It is well."

He bowed his head in content till the last noise of the complaining snow had died away, and he knew his son was beyond recall. Then his hand crept out in haste to the wood. It alone stood between him and the eternity that yawned in upon him. At last the measure of his life was a handful of fagots.[3] One by one they would go to feed the fire, and just so, step by step, death would creep upon him. When the last stick had surrendered up its heat, the frost would begin to gather strength. First his feet would yield, then his hands; and the numbness would travel, slowly, from the extremities to the body. His head would fall forward upon his knees, and he would rest. It was easy. All men must die. **C**

COMMON CORE RL 4

Language Coach

Multiple-Meaning Words *Compass* (line 15) is a **multiple-meaning word,** a word with more than one meaning. *Compass* can mean "device for determining direction," but here it means "a limited space." What activity is the old man listening to?

B THEME
Reread lines 10–27. From whose **point of view** are we experiencing the events described? What are some of the contrasting ideas running through this character's mind?

C AUTHOR'S PERSPECTIVE
Reread the biography on page 768 and consider the experience that forced London to leave Alaska. How might this experience be reflected in lines 48–56? Explain.

1. **shaman's:** belonging to a priest who uses magic to cure the sick or predict events.
2. **gutturals:** sounds that are made in the throat.
3. **fagots:** sticks of wood.

He did not complain. It was the way of life, and it was just. He had been born close to the earth, close to the earth had he lived, and the law thereof was not new to him. It was the law of all flesh. Nature was not kindly to the flesh. She had no concern for that concrete thing called the individual. Her interest lay in the species, the race. This was the deepest abstraction old Koskoosh's barbaric mind was capable of, but he grasped it firmly. He saw it exemplified in all life. The rise of the sap, the bursting greenness of the willow bud, the fall of the yellow leaf—in this alone was told the whole history. But one task did Nature set the individual. Did he not perform it, he died. Did he perform it, it was all the same, he died. Nature did not care; there were plenty who were obedient, and it was only the obedience in this matter, not the obedient, which lived and lived always. The tribe of Koskoosh was very old. The old men he had known when a boy, had known old men before them. Therefore it was true that the tribe lived, that it stood for the obedience of all its members, way down into the forgotten past, whose very resting-places were unremembered. They did not count; they were episodes. They had passed away like clouds from a summer sky. He also was an episode, and would pass away. Nature did not care. To life she set one task, gave one law. To perpetuate was the task of life, its law was death. A maiden was a good creature to look upon, full-breasted and strong, with spring to her step and light in her eyes. But her task was yet before her. The light in her eyes brightened, her step quickened, she was now bold with the young men, now timid, and she gave them of her own unrest. And ever she grew fairer and yet fairer to look upon, till some hunter, able no longer to withhold himself, took her to his lodge to cook and toil for him and to become the mother of his children. And with the coming of her offspring her looks left her. Her limbs dragged and shuffled, her eyes dimmed and bleared, and only the little children found joy against the withered cheek of the old squaw by the fire. Her task was done. But a little while, on the first pinch of famine or the first long trail, and she would be left, even as he had been left, in the snow, with a little pile of wood. Such was the law. **D**

He placed a stick carefully upon the fire and resumed his meditations. It was the same everywhere, with all things. The mosquitoes vanished with the first frost. The little tree-squirrel crawled away to die. When age settled upon the rabbit it became slow and heavy, and could no longer outfoot its enemies. Even the big bald-face grew clumsy and blind and quarrelsome, in the end to be dragged down by a handful of yelping huskies. He remembered how he had abandoned his own father on an upper reach of the Klondike one winter, the winter before the missionary came with his talk-books and his box of medicines. Many a time had Koskoosh smacked his lips over the recollection of that box, though now his mouth refused to moisten. The "painkiller" had been especially good. But the missionary was a bother after all, for he brought no meat into the camp, and he ate heartily, and the hunters grumbled. But he chilled his lungs on the divide by the Mayo,[4] and the dogs afterwards nosed the stones away and fought over his bones.

COMMON CORE L 4b

Language Coach

Related Words
Exemplified (line 62) means "shown by example." How can you tell that the words *example* and *exemplified* are related? When might you use *example*, and when might you use *exemplify*?

D THEME
Reread lines 57–85. In one or two sentences, summarize the theme expressed here about the relationship between nature and the individual. What kind of comment on the human condition does this naturalist theme express? Explain your response.

4. **the Mayo:** a small river in the Yukon Territory in northwestern Canada.

Koskoosh placed another stick on the fire and harked back deeper into the past. There was the time of the Great Famine, when the old men crouched empty-bellied to the fire, and let fall from their lips dim traditions of the ancient day when the Yukon ran wide open for three winters, and then lay frozen for three summers. He had lost his mother in that famine. In the summer the salmon run had failed, and the tribe looked forward to the winter and the coming of the caribou. Then the winter came, but with it there were no caribou. Never had the like been known, not even in the lives of the old men. But the caribou did not come, and it was the seventh year, and the rabbits had not **replenished,** and the dogs were naught but bundles of bones. And through the long darkness the children wailed and died, and the women, and the old men; and not one in ten of the tribe lived to meet the sun when it came back in the spring. That *was* a famine!

replenish (rĭ-plĕn′ĭsh) *v.* to fill up again

But he had seen times of plenty, too, when the meat spoiled on their hands, and the dogs were fat and worthless with overeating—times when they let the game go unkilled, and the women were fertile, and the lodges were cluttered with sprawling men-children and women-children. Then it was the men became high-stomached, and revived ancient quarrels, and crossed the divides to the south to kill the Pellys, and to the west that they might sit by the dead fires of the Tananas.[5] He remembered, when a boy, during a time of plenty, when he saw a moose pulled down by the wolves. Zing-ha lay with him in the snow and watched—Zing-ha, who later became the craftiest of hunters, and who, in the end, fell through an air-hole on the Yukon. They found him, a month afterward, just as he had crawled halfway out and frozen stiff to the ice.

But the moose. Zing-ha and he had gone out that day to play at hunting after the manner of their fathers. On the bed of the creek they struck the fresh track of a moose, and with it the tracks of many wolves. "An old one," Zing-ha, who was quicker at reading the sign, said—"an old one who cannot keep up with the herd. The wolves have cut him out from his brothers, and they will never leave him." And it was so. It was their way. By day and by night, never resting, snarling on his heels, snapping at his nose, they would stay by him to the end. How Zing-ha and he felt the blood-lust quicken! The finish would be a sight to see! E

E THEME
In lines 124–131, the third-person-limited point of view reveals Koskoosh's memory of the old moose and his own reaction at the time. What is **ironic** about this recollection?

Eager-footed, they took the trail, and even he, Koskoosh, slow of sight and an unversed tracker, could have followed it blind, it was so wide. Hot were they on the heels of the chase, reading the grim tragedy, fresh-written, at every step. Now they came to where the moose had made a stand. Thrice the length of a grown man's body, in every direction, had the snow been stamped about and uptossed. In the midst were the deep impressions of the splay-hoofed game, and all about, everywhere, were the lighter footmarks of the wolves. Some, while their brothers **harried** the kill, had lain to one side and rested. The full-stretched impress of their bodies in the snow was as perfect as though made the moment before. One wolf had been caught in a wild lunge of the maddened victim and trampled to death. A few bones, well picked, bore witness.

harry (hăr′ē) *v.* to torment, often by constant attack

5. **Pellys . . . Tananas:** *Pellys* probably refers to native peoples who lived near the Pelly River. The Tananas are native people who traditionally lived in areas of Alaska and the Yukon.

Again, they ceased the uplift of their snowshoes at a second stand. Here the great animal had fought desperately. Twice had he been dragged down, as the snow **attested,** and twice had he shaken his assailants clear and gained footing once more. He had done his task long since, but none the less was life dear to him. Zing-ha said it was a strange thing, a moose once down to get free again; but this one certainly had. The shaman would see signs and wonders in this when they told him. F

And yet again, they came to where the moose had made to mount the bank and gain the timber. But his foes had laid on from behind, till he reared and fell back upon them, crushing two deep into the snow. It was plain the kill was at hand, for their brothers had left them untouched. Two more stands were hurried past, brief in time-length and very close together. The trail was red now, and the clean stride of the great beast had grown short and **slovenly.** Then they heard the first sounds of the battle—not the full-throated chorus of the chase, but the short, snappy bark which spoke of close quarters and teeth to flesh. Crawling up the wind, Zing-ha bellied it through the snow, and with him crept he, Koskoosh, who was to be chief of the tribesmen in the years to come. Together they shoved aside the under branches of a young spruce and peered forth. It was the end they saw.

The picture, like all of youth's impressions, was still strong with him, and his dim eyes watched the end played out as vividly as in that far-off time. Koskoosh

attest (ə-tĕst') *v.* to affirm to be true; to be proof of

F THEME
Reread lines 143–149. What is surprising about the moose's struggle with the wolves? Consider the significance of this **conflict.**

slovenly (slŭv'ən-lē) *adj.* untidy in personal appearance marvelled at this, for in the days which followed, when he was a leader of men and a head of councillors, he had done great deeds and made his name a curse in the mouths of the Pellys, to say naught of the strange white man he had killed, knife to knife, in open fight. **G**

For long he pondered on the days of his youth, till the fire died down and the frost bit deeper. He replenished it with two sticks this time, and gauged his grip on life by what remained. If Sit-cum-to-ha had only remembered her grandfather, and gathered a larger armful, his hours would have been longer. It would have been easy. But she was ever a careless child, and honored not her ancestors from the time the Beaver, son of the son of Zing-ha, first cast eyes upon her. Well, what mattered it? Had he not done likewise in his own quick youth? For a while he listened to the silence. Perhaps the heart of his son might soften, and he would come back with the dogs to take his old father on with the tribe to where the caribou ran thick and the fat hung heavy upon them.

He strained his ears, his restless brain for the moment stilled. Not a stir, nothing. He alone took breath in the midst of the great silence. It was very lonely. Hark! What was that? A chill passed over his body. The familiar, long-drawn howl broke the void, and it was close at hand. Then on his darkened eyes was projected the vision of the moose—the old bull moose—the torn flanks and bloody sides, the riddled mane, and the great branching horns, down low and tossing to the last. He saw the flashing forms of gray, the gleaming eyes, the lolling tongues, the slavered fangs. And he saw the **inexorable** circle close in till it became a dark point in the midst of the stamped snow. **H**

A cold muzzle thrust against his cheek, and at its touch his soul leaped back to the present. His hand shot into the fire and dragged out a burning fagot. Overcome for the nonce[6] by his hereditary fear of man, the brute retreated, raising a prolonged call to his brothers; and greedily they answered, till a ring of crouching, jaw-slobbered gray was stretched round about. The old man listened to the drawing in of this circle. He waved his brand wildly, and sniffs turned to snarls; but the panting brutes refused to scatter. Now one wormed his chest forward, dragging his haunches after, now a second, now a third; but never a one drew back. Why should he cling to life? he asked, and dropped the blazing stick into the snow. It sizzled and went out. The circle grunted uneasily, but held its own. Again he saw the last stand of the old bull moose, and Koskoosh dropped his head wearily upon his knees. What did it matter after all? Was it not the law of life? ~

G AUTHOR'S PERSPECTIVE
Reread lines 162–166. What sensibility about human relationships is revealed in the struggle described here? Consider how this sensibility might be rooted in London's life experiences.

inexorable
(ĭn-ĕk'sər-ə-bəl) *adj.* relentless

H THEME
Reread lines 177–185. What does the old bull moose represent? Consider the thematic message suggested by this **symbol.**

---

6. **for the nonce:** for the time being.

Comprehension

1. **Recall** How does Koskoosh die?
2. **Clarify** How has he expected to die?
3. **Summarize** Describe the conditions of life for the tribe.

COMMON CORE

RL 2 Determine two or more themes or central ideas of a text and analyze their development over the course of the text. **RL 3** Analyze the impact of the author's choices regarding how to develop and relate elements of a story. **RL 9** Demonstrate knowledge of nineteenth- and early-twentieth-century works of American literature, including how two or more texts from the same period treat similar themes or topics.

Text Analysis

4. **Interpret Theme** Look back at the details about narrative elements you recorded in your chart as you read. Taken together, what do these details suggest about the fate of Koskoosh and all humans?
5. **Analyze Cultural Context** Explain how each of the following factors might contribute to the tribe's attitude about death:
   - the tribe's connection "to the earth" (lines 57–67)
   - what the tribe sees as "the task of life" (lines 73–85)
   - the Arctic environment (lines 101–123)
6. **Analyze Point of View** Imagine that this story had been written without any insight into Koskoosh's thoughts. What information or ideas would be missing? With this in mind, explain whether or not you think the point of view plays a crucial role in expressing the story's **theme.** Cite evidence from the story to support your view.
7. **Examine Author's Perspective** In your opinion, has London created a credible portrayal of the Native Americans and their values? How do you think this portrayal reflects London's own life experiences? In developing your answer, give details from the story as well as from the biography on page 768.
8. **Compare Expressions of Naturalism** Compare and contrast London's portrayal of nature in this story with Crane's in "The Open Boat." Consider in particular the characters' fates and any differences in tone. Record your answers with evidence from the stories in a Venn diagram. In which version of nature would you prefer to live? Explain.

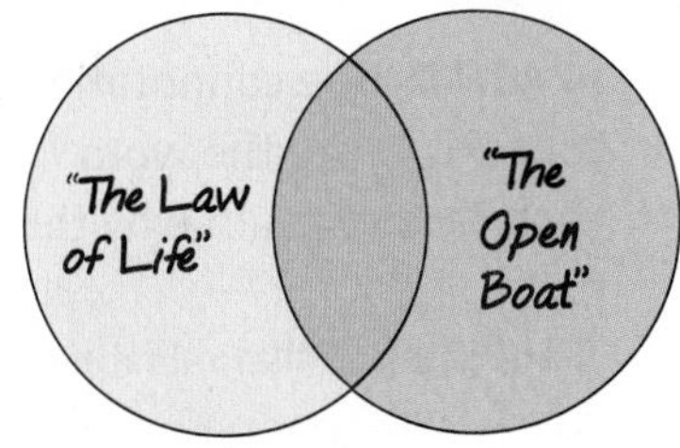

Text Criticism

9. **Critical Interpretation** The writer E. L. Doctorow said, "It was Jack London's capacity for really living in the world, for taking it on in self-conscious and often reckless acts of courage, that made him our first writer-hero." Given what you have read in London's biography and your reading of "The Law of Life," do you agree with the notion of London as a hero? Explain.

How do people face **DEATH?**

What comment on the human condition does London make through Koskoosh's last thoughts? Do you think this attitude toward death is ultimately hopeful or hopeless? Explain.

Vocabulary in Context

▲ VOCABULARY PRACTICE

Determine the relationship between the first pair of words in each analogy. Then choose the vocabulary word that best completes the second pair.

1. *Nurse* is to *care* as *pest* is to _____.
2. *Impressive* is to *splendid* as _____ is to *unyielding.*
3. *Agree* is to *contradict* as _____ is to *deplete.*
4. *Well-groomed* is to *dandy* as _____ is to *slob.*
5. *Refuse* is to *decline* as _____ is to *declare.*

WORD LIST

attest
harry
inexorable
replenish
slovenly

ACADEMIC VOCABULARY IN WRITING

• apparent • confine • expose • focus • perceive

In a few paragraphs, make a case for or against leaving elderly people to die in a society such as the one in this story. You may **confine** your argument to practical aspects of the practice, or you may choose to **focus** on the relative value of life that it implies. Use at least one Academic Vocabulary word in your response.

VOCABULARY STRATEGY: DENOTATION AND CONNOTATION

Every word has a **denotation,** or basic dictionary meaning. Some words have additional nuances, or shades of meaning. We call such a subtle distinction of meaning a **connotation.** For example, the word *slovenly* means "untidy," but it has a more strongly negative connotation. When you encounter a new word, analyze its context to draw a conclusion about any connotation it might have.

COMMON CORE

L 5b Analyze nuances in the meaning of words with similar denotations. **L 6** Acquire and use accurately general academic words and phrases.

PRACTICE The connotation of each boldfaced word makes it inappropriate in the context. Write the word from the list provided that would be more suitable in each case. Explain why the word you chose is a better match for the context.

charlatan discriminating ostentatious resolute subservient traditional

1. His **picky** taste was evident in his beautiful suits and well-chosen ties.
2. That **beguiler!** She convinced the children that she was their long-lost aunt.
3. I admire **inflexible** leaders who make hard decisions and then stick with them.
4. Her **humble** attitude impressed her employers, but behind their backs she belittled them constantly.
5. The **elegant** ballroom had more than its share of gold chandeliers, gaudy silk couches, and overly elaborate draperies.
6. The mayor espouses **reactionary** values such as hard work and love of family.

Naturalistic Perspectives

As illustrated in the short stories by Stephen Crane and Jack London you have just read, the central assumption of naturalism is that human beings have very little control over their own lives, but instead are at the mercy of the natural world and the impersonal force of fate. The following quotations all explore a similarly naturalistic attitude.

"Nature, to be commanded, must be obeyed."

—Sir Francis Bacon

"It clearly matters very little to nature whether man has a mind or not."

—Eugène Delacroix

"At no time and in no place, will nature ever ask your permission."

—Fyodor Dostoyevsky

"Man and nature have such different views about the good of the world."

—George Gissing

"In nature there are neither rewards nor punishments—there are consequences."

—R. G. Ingersoll

Writing to Evaluate

Choose the quotation on this page that you think best represents a key theme of "The Open Boat" or "The Law of Life." Write an essay defending your choice, using details from the story as support.

Consider

- the main message of each story
- the subtle and sometimes not-so-subtle differences between the quotations
- which details from the story support your choice of quotation

Extension Online

INQUIRY & RESEARCH A tornado demolishes a house yet skips its neighbor; a marathon runner dies of a heart attack; a woman loses her retirement fund after working loyally for a company for 25 years. Every day it seems there is another story in the newspaper about the randomness of nature or the inability of humans to control their own lives. **Search** three online newspapers for stories that seem to support the naturalistic viewpoint. Print out one story to share with your classmates.

COMMON CORE

W 4 Produce clear and coherent writing in which the development, organization, and style are appropriate to task, purpose, and audience. **W 8** Gather relevant information from multiple authoritative digital sources. **W 9a (RL 2)** Determine themes or central ideas of a text and analyze their development.

Text Analysis Workshop

Social Themes in Fiction

People often talk about social issues—such as poverty, racism, or crime—in a general sense, but how do these issues affect individuals' lives in reality? In 19th-century America, writers began to explore these issues in fiction.

COMMON CORE

Included in this workshop:
RL 9 Demonstrate knowledge of early-twentieth-century foundational works of American literature, including how two or more texts from the same period treat similar themes or topics.

Dramatizing Social Issues

Typical themes in literature deal with issues that are common to most people, such as the loss of innocence, difficult family relationships, or a new love. **Social themes,** however, deal with issues that concern a particular group of people, such as those in a certain neighborhood, geographical region, or religious community. These issues are usually specific to a time and place, but they may echo in other cultures and times as well. For example, the dynamics of Puritan society inspired a number of great literary works with social themes, from Nathaniel Hawthorne's *The Scarlet Letter* (1850) to Arthur Miller's *The Crucible* (1953). While Hawthorne explored the effects of Puritan morality on individual lives, Miller chose to expose the wrongs committed in the name of righteousness during the Salem witch trials as a way to explore parallel events of his own time.

Two suffragettes, circa 1905, stand on an American city street, promoting women's rights.

In the late 19th and early 20th centuries, novels and short stories with a contemporary social theme typically dealt with issues that generated strong public reaction and debate for that era. These issues included industrialism, urbanization, and the displacement of Native Americans. In this way, literature became a powerful tool for social change.

Identifying Social Themes

Novels and short stories of the period often portray characters struggling against poverty, prejudice, and other social obstacles. One social issue in particular that emerged in the second half of the 19th century was the role of women in society. This issue preoccupied writers of many nationalities during this time and inspired feminist writers in the 20th century. All of the stories in this part of Unit 4 address this issue in one way or another. To help you identify the social themes in these and other stories, consider the following:

- Look for **characters** who have little control over their fate, and ask yourself what **social factors** contribute to their situation.

- Clarify the **conflicts** in the story and determine to what extent they are caused by forces beyond a character's control.
- Examine direct statements of a **character's or narrator's opinions** to see whether these provide clues to a theme.
- Think about the **author's reason** for writing the story. What was he or she trying to achieve?

Works that address social issues often focus on people who have few, if any, rights and privileges in society. The first-person narrator of "The Yellow Wallpaper" (page 798), although comfortably middle-class, has no control over her life. Early in the story, she explains her complete submission to her doctor and her husband.

> So I take phosphates . . . and tonics, and journeys, and air, and exercise, and am absolutely forbidden to "work" until I am well again.
>
> Personally, I disagree with their ideas.
>
> Personally, I believe that congenial work, with excitement and change, would do me good.
>
> But what is one to do?
>
> **—Charlotte Perkins Gilman, "The Yellow Wallpaper"**

Close Read

Based on the narrator's statements in this passage, how would you describe her relationship with the doctor and her husband?

In "The Story of an Hour" (page 784), the main character, after hearing that her husband is dead, reflects on the control he has exercised over her. Notice how her thoughts are a statement on the relationships between men and women in general.

> There would be no one to live for her during those coming years; she would live for herself. There would be no powerful will bending hers in that blind persistence with which men and women believe they have a right to impose a private will upon a fellow creature.
>
> **—Kate Chopin, "The Story of an Hour"**

Close Read

How is this character's attitude different from that expressed in "The Yellow Wallpaper"?

A New Role for Women

The Story of an Hour

Short Story by Kate Chopin

VIDEO TRAILER THINK central KEYWORD: HML11-782A

COMMON CORE

RL 2 Determine themes or central ideas of a text. **RL 5** Analyze how an author's choices concerning how to structure specific parts of a text contribute to its overall structure and meaning as well as its aesthetic impact.
RI 2 Determine two or more central ideas of a text and analyze their development over the course of the text. **RI 5** Analyze and evaluate the effectiveness of the structure an author uses in his or her exposition or argument, including whether the structure makes points clear, convincing, and engaging. **RI 7** Integrate and evaluate multiple sources of information presented in different media or formats as well as in words in order to address a question.

Joyas Voladoras

Essay by Brian Doyle

Calvin and Hobbes

Cartoon Strip by Bill Watterson

Meet the Author

Kate Chopin 1850–1904

When her second volume of short stories was published in 1897, Kate Chopin's literary career was already thriving. Critics had praised her first collection, *Bayou Folk,* for its local-color realism, calling her tales "charming" and "quaint." Two years later came the bombshell: Chopin published *The Awakening,* a novel about a housewife's sexual and artistic awakening, complete with an adulterous affair and suicide as a last, desperate act of freedom. A chorus of outraged reviewers reviled the novel as immoral, drowning out the few brave enough to praise it. No publisher would touch her next collection, *A Vocation and a Voice,* which included "The Story of an Hour." Chopin died soon after, and *The Awakening* languished out of print for 50 years.

Faithful Wife and Mother Born into a socially prominent family, and esteemed for her beauty, intelligence, and wit, Kate Chopin married when she was 19. She and her husband settled in New Orleans, where their six children were born. Chopin had no difficulty reconciling the demands of her family with her strong independent streak. With the support of her husband, she smoked cigarettes and explored the city unescorted—scandalous behavior for an upper-class woman at the time.

A Budding Writer Chopin started writing at the age of 32. After her husband died, she returned to St. Louis, where her doctor suggested she write stories to work through her grief. Encouraged that her very first story was published, Chopin studied the work of French short story master Guy de Maupassant and honed her craft. She gradually developed an interest in complex issues such as the longing for freedom and self-fulfillment among women.

A Late-Blooming Classic Though *The Awakening* ended its author's career, it went on, after her death, to become a classic. Critics in the 1950s rediscovered the novel and, proclaiming Chopin "ahead of her time," sparked renewed interest in her modern sensibilities. Of *The Awakening*'s heroine, Edna Pontellier, Chopin once said, "I never dreamed of Mrs. Pontellier making such a mess of things. . . . If I had the slightest intimation of such a thing I would have excluded her from the company." The controversial heroine made Chopin a legend. Today, *The Awakening* is among the five most-read American novels in colleges and universities.

Author Online THINK central

Go to thinkcentral.com. KEYWORD: HML11-782B

TEXT ANALYSIS: THEME

At the heart of every effective piece of writing is a **theme**—a message the writer wants readers to understand or a perception about life the writer wants to share. A good short story writer doesn't express his or her theme explicitly but rather expects readers to draw their own conclusions about the story's central meaning. A rich story may have more than one theme. In "The Story of an Hour," Kate Chopin focuses on the internal life of a woman in the immediate aftermath of traumatic news. As you read the story, pay attention to Mrs. Mallard's reactions to the story's opening event. Use a chart like the one below to record clues to the story's theme or themes.

Mrs. Mallard's feelings	Mrs. Mallard's thoughts	Mrs. Mallard's actions
"wept with sudden wild abandonment"		

By contrast with a short story, an essay usually has an explicit theme—often expressed in an easily identified **thesis statement.** "Joyas Voladoras," however, is an essay without an explicit message. Instead of supporting a thesis statement, Brian Doyle reflects on the hummingbird, its heart, and the hearts of other animals. As you read the essay, pay special attention to the writer's attitude. Doyle's clearly emotional response to his subject provides clues to his themes.

READING SKILL: ANALYZE PATTERNS OF ORGANIZATION

Short story and essay writers organize their material in very different ways. Short stories follow a **plot**—from exposition and rising action to **climax**, falling action, and **resolution**. Kate Chopin organizes "The Story of an Hour" by tracing the rising action to a climax. She starts with a shocking event and follows its aftermath chronologically. As you read, trace the rising action by noting Mrs. Mallard's emotional state. In Brian Doyle's essay, look for a pattern that takes the place of plot. Notice that Doyle begins with the hummingbird and its heart. Then, each paragraph takes up a related subject. Following this essay is like following a writer's train of thought.

Complete the activities in your **Reader/Writer Notebook**.

Do all CAGES *have bars?*

Prisons and detention centers, animal cages, even children's playpens—all have bars to keep their inhabitants from escaping. But are these the only kinds of constraints that restrict freedom? In "The Story of an Hour," Kate Chopin explores just how restrictive invisible bars can be.

What's the Connection?

As you study the texts in this section, look for thematic connections among them. In "The Story of an Hour," a woman with a heart condition reacts to two shocking events in a short period of time. In "Joyas Voladoras," Brian Doyle reflects with awe on the hummingbird heart and on related subjects. In the *Calvin and Hobbes* cartoon strip, a young boy muses on how short life is. What kind of attitude toward life do you find in each of these selections?

The Story of an Hour

KATE CHOPIN

BACKGROUND This story takes place around 1900, when the status of women was radically different than it is today. Because women could not vote, they had almost no political or legal power; because they could not own property and had few chances to gain education or employment, they had little or no financial independence. Few careers were open to middle- and upper-class women, who were expected to be supported by their husbands. In most American marriages of the time, the husband was the undisputed head of the household.

Analyze Visuals ▸
In the era in which this story is set, women were deemed fragile, sensitive, and submissive. What artistic elements help to convey these attributes in the painting on page 785?

Knowing that Mrs. Mallard was afflicted with a heart trouble, great care was taken to break to her as gently as possible the news of her husband's death.

It was her sister Josephine who told her, in broken sentences; veiled hints that revealed in half concealing. Her husband's friend Richards was there, too, near her. It was he who had been in the newspaper office when intelligence of the railroad disaster was received, with Brently Mallard's name leading the list of "killed." He had only taken the time to assure himself of its truth by a second telegram, and had hastened to forestall any less careful, less tender friend in bearing the sad message.

A Sketch of a Faraway Look, Herman Jean Joseph Richir. Bonhams, London.

She did not hear the story as many women have heard the same, with a paralyzed inability to accept its significance. She wept at once, with sudden, wild abandonment, in her sister's arms. When the storm of grief had spent itself she went away to her room alone. She would have no one follow her.

There stood, facing the open window, a comfortable, roomy armchair. Into this she sank, pressed down by a physical exhaustion that haunted her body and seemed to reach into her soul.

She could see in the open square before her house the tops of trees that were all aquiver with the new spring life. The delicious breath of rain was in the air. In the street below a peddler was crying his wares. The notes of a distant song which someone was singing reached her faintly, and countless sparrows were twittering in the eaves.

There were patches of blue sky showing here and there through the clouds that had met and piled one above the other in the west facing her window.

She sat with her head thrown back upon the cushion of the chair, quite motionless, except when a sob came up into her throat and shook her, as a child who has cried itself to sleep continues to sob in its dreams.

She was young, with a fair, calm face, whose lines bespoke repression and even a certain strength. But now there was a dull stare in her eyes, whose gaze was fixed away off yonder on one of those patches of blue sky. It was not a glance of reflection, but rather indicated a suspension of intelligent thought.

There was something coming to her and she was waiting for it, fearfully. What was it? She did not know; it was too subtle and elusive to name. But she felt it, creeping out of the sky, reaching toward her through the sounds, the scents, the color that filled the air. A

Now her bosom rose and fell tumultuously. She was beginning to recognize this thing that was approaching to possess her, and she was striving to beat it back with her will—as powerless as her two white slender hands would have been. B

When she abandoned herself a little whispered word escaped her slightly parted lips. She said it over and over under her breath: "free, free, free!" The vacant stare and the look of terror that had followed it went from her eyes. They stayed keen and bright. Her pulses beat fast, and the coursing blood warmed and relaxed every inch of her body. C

She did not stop to ask if it were or were not a monstrous joy that held her. A clear and exalted perception enabled her to dismiss the suggestion as trivial.

She knew that she would weep again when she saw the kind, tender hands folded in death; the face that had never looked save with love upon her, fixed and gray and dead. But she saw beyond that bitter moment a long procession of years to come that would belong to her absolutely. And she opened and spread her arms out to them in welcome.

A GRAMMAR AND STYLE
Reread lines 30–33. Notice how Chopin uses the **active voice,** with the subjects performing the action in the sentences. Contrast this with her use of the **passive voice** in the first sentence of the story.

B PATTERNS OF ORGANIZATION
Reread lines 13–36. What kind of pattern do you see in Mrs. Mallard's emotions and how does this pattern lend organization to the story?

C THEME
What does Mrs. Mallard mean when she says, "free, free, free"? What kind of idea or message do you think these words convey? Explain.

There would be no one to live for her during those coming years; she would live for herself. There would be no powerful will bending hers in that blind persistence with which men and women believe they have a right to impose a private will upon a fellow creature. A kind intention or a cruel intention made the act seem no less a crime as she looked upon it in that brief moment of illumination.

And yet she had loved him—sometimes. Often she had not. What did it matter! What could love, the unsolved mystery, count for in face of this possession of self-assertion which she suddenly recognized as the strongest impulse of her being!

"Free! Body and soul free!" she kept whispering.

Josephine was kneeling before the closed door with her lips to the keyhole, imploring for admission. "Louise, open the door! I beg; open the door—you will make yourself ill. What are you doing, Louise? For heaven's sake open the door."

"Go away. I am not making myself ill." No; she was drinking in a very elixir of life[1] through that open window.

Her fancy was running riot along those days ahead of her. Spring days, and summer days, and all sorts of days that would be her own. She breathed a quick prayer that life might be long. It was only yesterday she had thought with a shudder that life might be long. **D**

She arose at length and opened the door to her sister's importunities. There was a feverish triumph in her eyes, and she carried herself unwittingly like a goddess of Victory. She clasped her sister's waist, and together they descended the stairs. Richards stood waiting for them at the bottom.

Someone was opening the front door with a latchkey. It was Brently Mallard who entered, a little travel-stained, composedly carrying his grip-sack[2] and umbrella. He had been far from the scene of accident, and did not even know there had been one. He stood amazed at Josephine's piercing cry; at Richards' quick motion to screen him from the view of his wife.

But Richards was too late.

When the doctors came they said she had died of heart disease—of joy that kills. **E**

D PATTERS OF ORGANIZATION
Reread lines 49–67, with close attention to Mrs. Mallard and her emotional state. What kind of order do you detect in this part of the story? Explain.

E THEME
In the story's closing line, are the doctors correct in saying that Mrs. Mallard died "of joy that kills"? And how does the closing line add to the message or idea you have found in Mrs. Mallard's thoughts and feelings as the story developed? Explain your answer, citing evidence from the story.

1. **elixir of life:** a medicine that restores vigor or the essence of life.
2. **grip-sack:** a small traveling bag or satchel.

After Reading

Comprehension

1. **Summarize** Describe the news Mrs. Mallard receives at the beginning of the story and explain how she reacts.
2. **Clarify** What happens at the end of the story?

Text Analysis

3. **Analyze Theme** Examine your chart on Mrs. Mallard's feelings, her thoughts, and her actions. What messages or key ideas can you infer from the interactions of the items on your chart? Explain.
4. **Analyze Patterns of Organization** Chopin uses a traditional plot to structure this story. What starts the rising action and where does the story reach its climax? Support your answer with evidence from the story.
5. **Interpret Imagery** Reread lines 16–22. How does Chopin's use of imagery contribute to your understanding of Mrs. Mallard's character and situation? Did the imagery make you more or less sympathetic toward her? Explain, citing specific lines from the story that influenced your response.
6. **Compare Characters** Both Mrs. Mallard and Aunt Georgiana in "A Wagner Matinee" by Willa Cather (page 718) face **constraints** that confine them to a specific way of life. In a Venn diagram like the one shown, compare and contrast these two characters' situations. Use your completed diagram to explain what message each author might be trying to convey through her main character.

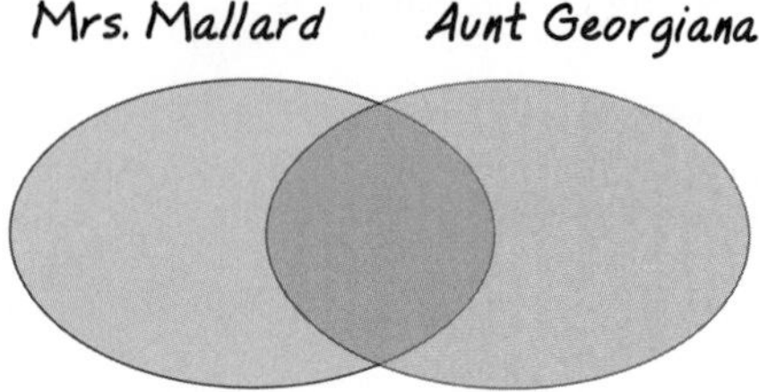

Text Criticism

7. **Social Context** Women's roles have certainly changed since Chopin wrote this story, but has the institution of marriage? Reread lines 49–54 of "The Story of an Hour." Is the imposition of will by both men and women that Chopin describes still an issue in contemporary marriages? Explain your opinion.

Do all **CAGES** *have bars?*

Before the beginning of "The Story of an Hour," what made Mrs. Mallard feel confined? Why, during the story, does she feel as if she has been released from a cage? Cite evidence from the story to support your answer.

COMMON CORE

RL 1 Cite evidence to support inferences drawn from the text. **RL 2** Determine two or more themes or central ideas of a text, including how they interact and build on one another to produce a complex account; provide an objective summary of the text. **RL 5** Analyze how an author's choices concerning how to structure specific parts of a text contribute to its overall structure and meaning as well as its aesthetic impact. **RL 9** Demonstrate knowledge of how two or more texts from the same period treat similar themes or topics.

Language

◆ GRAMMAR AND STYLE: Use Effective Voice

Review the **Grammar and Style** note on page 786. The **active voice** indicates that the subject of a sentence is *performing* the action. The **passive voice** indicates that the subject of a sentence is *receiving* the action. A writer may use the passive voice to create a particular effect or to indicate that the performer of an action is indefinite or unknown. Here are examples of each type of voice:

Active: *Someone was opening the front door with a latchkey.* (line 72)

Passive: *It was he who had been in the newspaper office when intelligence of the railroad disaster was received....* (lines 5–6)

Kate Chopin effectively uses the active and passive voices to mirror her character's emotional transition from repression to liberation. She begins the story in the passive voice, when Mrs. Mallard is still under constraint, but later switches to the active voice as Mrs. Mallard begins to acknowledge her own identity.

PRACTICE Change the voice of the following sentences as indicated in parentheses.

> **EXAMPLE**
>
> He gave me my freedom. (Change to the passive voice.)
>
> *Freedom was given to me.*

1. A life of adventure is desired by everyone. (Change to the active voice.)
2. I will spend my days as I wish. (Change to the passive voice.)
3. No one will be consulted about my plans. (Change to the active voice.)

COMMON CORE

L 3 Apply knowledge of language to make effective choices for meaning or style. **W 9** Draw evidence from literary texts to support reflection. **W 10** Write over shorter time frames for a range of tasks.

READING-WRITING CONNECTION

Expand your understanding of "The Story of an Hour" by responding to this prompt. Then, use the **revising tips** to improve your journal entry.

WRITING PROMPT	REVISING TIPS
COMPOSE A JOURNAL ENTRY "The Story of an Hour" focuses on Mrs. Mallard's feelings about her husband's reported death. Think about the moment her feelings suddenly shift from sorrow to joy. Imagine you are Mrs. Mallard. Write a **three-paragraph journal entry** in which you detail some of the thoughts that might have gone through her mind as she pondered her future.	• Make sure your entry reflects Mrs. Mallard's struggle with her feelings, showing a clear progression from grief to joy. • Give concrete examples of how she believes her life might change. • Use language and sentence types that capture her emotions.

Essay

In Kate Chopin's short story, you saw how a lifetime can fit into the space of an hour. In "Joyas Voladoras," you'll read about the short life of the hummingbird and the remarkable heart that keeps the bird alive.

Joyas Voladoras

Brian Doyle

BACKGROUND We are often fascinated with extremes in nature: minute, complex organisms that function at a high level of efficiency, as well as enormous animals that make us feel insignificant by comparison. In the following essay, Brian Doyle reflects on the tiny hummingbird and its incredibly fast heart. From the hummingbird, Doyle moves on to consider the blue whale and its absurdly large heart. Finally, he expands his subject to the properties of the heart that cannot be weighed or counted. Brian Doyle is the author of several books of essays, including *The Wet Engine*, a meditation on the heart.

Consider the hummingbird for a long moment. A hummingbird's heart beats ten times a second. A hummingbird's heart is the size of a pencil eraser. A hummingbird's heart is a lot of the hummingbird. *Joyas voladoras,* flying jewels, the first white explorers in the Americas called them, and the white men had never seen such creatures, for hummingbirds came into the world only in the Americas, nowhere else in the universe, more than three hundred species of them whirring and zooming and nectaring in hummer time zones nine times removed from ours, their hearts hammering faster than we could clearly hear if we pressed our elephantine ears to their infinitesimal chests.

Each one visits a thousand flowers a day. They can dive at sixty miles an hour. They can fly backward. They can fly more than five hundred miles without pausing to rest. But when they rest they come close to death: on frigid nights, or when they are starving, they retreat into torpor, their metabolic rate slowing to a fifteenth of their normal sleep rate, their hearts sludging nearly to a halt, barely beating, and if they are not soon warmed, if they do not soon find that which is sweet, their hearts grow cold, and they cease to be. Consider for a moment those hummingbirds who did not open their eyes again today, this very day, in the Americas: bearded helmetcrests and booted racket-tails, violet-tailed sylphs and violet-capped woodnymphs, crimson topazes and purple-crowned fairies, red-tailed comets and amethyst woodstars, rainbow-bearded thornbills and glittering-bellied emeralds, velvet-purple coronets and golden-bellied star-frontlets, fiery-tailed awlbills and Andean hillstars, spatuletails and pufflegs, each the most amazing thing you have never seen, each thunderous wild heart the size of an infant's fingernail, each mad heart silent, a brilliant music stilled. (A)

(A) THEME
In lines 9–22, the writer's **tone**—his attitude toward hummingbirds—provides clues to the theme of this message. How would you describe the writer's tone in these lines? What message do you infer from this tone? Explain.

Hummingbirds, like all flying birds but more so, have incredible enormous immense ferocious metabolisms. To drive those metabolisms they have race car hearts that eat oxygen at an eye-popping rate. Their hearts are built of thinner, leaner fibers than ours. Their arteries are stiffer and more taut. They have more mitochondria in their heart muscles—anything to gulp more oxygen. Their hearts are stripped to the skin for the war against gravity and inertia, the mad search for food, the insane idea of flight. The price of their ambition is a life closer to death; they suffer more heart attacks and aneurysms and ruptures than any other living creature. It's expensive to fly. You burn out. You fry the machine. You melt the engine. Every creature on earth has approximately two billion heartbeats to spend in a lifetime. You can spend them slowly, like a tortoise, and live to be two hundred years old, or you can spend them fast, like a hummingbird, and live to be two years old. B

The biggest heart in the world is inside the blue whale. It weighs more than seven tons. It's as big as a room. It *is* a room, with four chambers. A child could walk around in it, head high, bending only to step through the valves. The valves are as big

B PATTERNS OF ORGANIZATION
In the first three paragraphs, this essay addresses a wide range of subjects related to the hummingbird—all of them organized around the writer's repetition of the word *heart*. Why do you think the author chose this word as the organizing focus for his essay? Explain.

as the swinging doors in a saloon. This house of a heart drives a creature a hundred feet long. When this creature is born it is twenty feet long and weighs four tons. It is waaaaay bigger than your car. It drinks a hundred gallons of milk from its mama every day and gains two hundred pounds a day, and when it is seven or eight years old it endures an unimaginable puberty and then it essentially disappears from human ken, for next to nothing is known of the mating habits, travel patterns, diet, social life, language, social structure, diseases, spirituality, wars, stories, despairs, and arts of the blue whale. There are perhaps ten thousand blue whales in the world, living in every ocean on earth, and of the largest mammal who ever lived we know nearly nothing. But we know this: the animals with the largest hearts in the world generally travel in pairs, and their penetrating moaning cries, their piercing yearning tongue, can be heard underwater for miles and miles. C

Mammals and birds have hearts with four chambers. Reptiles and turtles have hearts with three chambers. Fish have hearts with two chambers. Insects and mollusks have hearts with one chamber. Worms have hearts with one chamber, although they may have as many as eleven single-chambered hearts. Unicellular bacteria have no hearts at all; but even they have fluid eternally in motion, washing from one side of the cell to the other, swirling and whirling. No living being is without interior liquid motion. We all churn inside.

So much held in a heart in a lifetime. So much held in a heart in a day, an hour, a moment. We are utterly open with no one, in the end—not mother and father, not wife or husband, not lover, not child, not friend. We open windows to each but we live alone in the house of the heart. Perhaps we must. Perhaps we could not bear to be so naked for fear of a constantly harrowed heart. When young we think there will come one person who will savor and sustain us always; when we are older we know this is the dream of a child, that all hearts finally are bruised and scarred, scored and torn, repaired by time and will, patched by force of character, yet fragile and rickety forevermore, no matter how ferocious the defense and how many bricks you bring to the wall. You can brick up your heart as stout and tight and hard and cold and impregnable as you possibly can and down it comes in an instant, felled by a woman's second glance, a child's apple breath, the shatter of glass in the road, the words "I have something to tell you", a cat with a broken spine dragging itself into the forest to die, the brush of your mother's papery ancient hand in the thicket of your hair, the memory of your father's voice early in the morning echoing from the kitchen where he is making pancakes for his children. D

C PATTERNS OF ORGANIZATION
After three paragraphs about the hummingbird, in line 35 Brian Doyle changes the subject and writes about the blue whale. Reread lines 35–49. Then explain why you think Doyle included this paragraph in the essay.

D THEME
The first two sentences of Doyle's last paragraph have the same beginning: "So much held in a heart." What message do you think the author wants to convey to you in this statement? Explain.

Cartoon

COMMON CORE

RI 7 Integrate and evaluate multiple sources of information presented in different media or formats as well as in words in order to address a question.

You have studied a short story about sudden news and sudden death, as well as an essay about the hearts of hummingbirds and other creatures. Now you will examine *Calvin and Hobbes,* a popular cartoon strip by Bill Watterson. As you study each frame and read the dialogue, think about how the images and words work together to convey meaning. Then, respond to the questions alongside the cartoon, citing evidence to support your answers.

1. **ANALYZE** Examine the first two frames of the cartoon. How do the words and the cartoonist's drawings work together to convey a theme?

2. **INTERPRET** Examine the last frame in this cartoon strip, paying special attention to facial expressions and the night sky behind Calvin and Hobbes. What purpose does the cartoonist achieve with this image? Why do you think he closes the strip without words?

Comprehension

1. **Recall** What happens to hummingbirds when they are cold or starving?
2. **Explain** Why do hummingbirds have such a short life cycle?

Text Analysis

3. **Analyze Theme** Describe the writer's tone in the last paragraph of the essay and explain how the tone conveys a theme. Support your answer with evidence from the essay.
4. **Analyze Patterns of Organization** How does the writer keep this essay focused and organized, even when he changes the subject? Explain your answer.
5. **Analyze Metaphor** What do you think Doyle means by the line, "we live alone in the house of the heart" (lines 59–60)? Cite evidence from the essay to support your answer.
6. **Analyze Diction** What effect does the writer achieve by using ornate, elaborate language?
7. **Evaluate Imagery** How does Doyle's use of **imagery,** or language that appeals to the senses, enhance the effectiveness of this essay? Cite examples in your response.

Comparing Themes Across Genres

8. **Analyze Theme** What messages about life does Brian Doyle's essay share with Kate Chopin's "The Story of an Hour"? Cite evidence from both the essay and the story to support your answer.

Do all **CAGES** *have bars?*

In "Joyas Voladoras," Brian Doyle celebrates the heart as an organ and the heart as a metaphor for much, much more. How are human beings both restricted and made free by the heart? Support your response with evidence from Doyle's essay.

COMMON CORE

RI 2 Determine two or more central ideas of a text. **RI 5** Analyze and evaluate the effectiveness of the structure an author uses in his or her exposition or argument, including whether the structure makes the points clear, convincing, and engaging. **RI 6** Analyze how style and content contribute to the power, persuasiveness, or beauty of the text.

Assessment Practice: Short Constructed Response

LITERARY TEXT: "THE STORY OF AN HOUR"

On assessments you are expected to make inferences as you read. Practice this skill as you answer the **short constructed response question** below. Be sure to follow the steps outlined to the right of the question.

This story closes with an instance of dramatic irony. Irony always involves a contrast between appearance and reality. Dramatic irony occurs when readers know more about something in a story than the characters know. What is the dramatic irony that closes this story and how does it express the author's theme?

STRATEGIES IN ACTION

1. *Make a list of words that describe Mrs. Mallard's state of mind during the time she spends alone after hearing that her husband has died in a train accident.*
2. *In light of your list, why do you think Mrs. Mallard cries out when she discovers that her husband is alive?*
3. *Identify the mistake the doctors make when they explain why Mrs. Mallard dies. The dramatic irony that lies in their misunderstanding is a clue to the theme.*

NONFICTION TEXT: "JOYAS VOLADORAS"

On assessments you are expected to read carefully and answer questions that focus on particular passages from a text. To strengthen your close-reading skills, read the **short constructed response question** at left below and practice the strategies suggested at right.

In the second-to-last paragraph of this essay, what purpose does the writer achieve by describing the hearts of numerous kinds of animals?

STRATEGIES IN ACTION

1. *Closely reread the paragraph, looking for clues to Doyle's purpose in the descriptions themselves.*
2. *Look for a message from the writer in the paragraph's opening or closing sentence.*

COMPARING LITERARY AND NONFICTION TEXTS

On assessments you will need to identify thematic connections between literary and nonfiction texts. Practice this valuable skill by responding to the **short constructed response question** at left below and using the strategies provided at right.

How do the authors of both "The Story of an Hour" and "Joyas Voladoras" use the heart as a metaphor?

STRATEGIES IN ACTION

1. *Doyle explicitly discusses the heart throughout. Briefly write what "heart" means to him.*
2. *Identify something in Mrs. Mallard's heart and life that resembles your answer to number 1.*

The Yellow Wallpaper

Short Story by Charlotte Perkins Gilman

COMMON CORE

RL 1 Cite evidence to support analysis of what the text says explicitly as well as inferences drawn from the text, including determining where the text leaves matters uncertain. **RL 3** Analyze the impact of the author's choices regarding how to develop and relate elements of a story. **RL 9** Demonstrate knowledge of nineteenth-century foundational works of American literature. **L 3** Apply knowledge of language to comprehend more fully when reading.

DID YOU KNOW?

Charlotte Perkins Gilman . . .

- moved 19 times in her first 18 years.
- produced eight novels, six nonfiction books, almost 200 short stories, hundreds of poems, and thousands of essays.
- founded and ran her own feminist magazine, the *Forerunner.*

Meet the Author

Charlotte Perkins Gilman 1860–1935

As a feminist writer, social activist, public lecturer, editor, and publisher, Charlotte Perkins Gilman rode the wave of reform that washed over the United States in the late 19th and early 20th centuries. Her 1898 landmark study, *Women and Economics*—called "the Bible of the woman's movement" at the time—argued persuasively that women's economic dependence on men made them veritable slaves in U.S. society. To rectify the inequities, she advocated child-care centers and communal kitchens so that women could earn money outside the home. In addition, her startlingly original story "The Yellow Wallpaper," published in 1892, discredited a popular treatment for women's so-called "nervous disorders." Looking beyond suffrage, Gilman sought to free women from domestic servitude and foster their intellectual and emotional growth.

Formative Early Years Gilman got a rather shaky start in life. Her father abandoned the family shortly after her birth in Hartford, Connecticut. Her mother, possibly in reaction to her dire circumstances, adopted the odd child-rearing habits of withholding affection and forbidding her daughter to read fiction or form close friendships. Fortunately, financial hardship forced the family to live with relatives, the most prominent among them being Harriet Beecher Stowe, the abolitionist author of *Uncle Tom's Cabin,* and the feminists Catherine Beecher and Isabella Beecher Hooker. Guided by her strong, successful aunts, young Charlotte grew into a well-adjusted, independent woman.

Sweetening Reform with Humor Gilman's first published work was a volume of poetry, *In This Our World,* which attracted attention for the humorous way she ridiculed social injustice and inequality. *Women and Economics* garnered similar praise despite its frontal assault on conventional marriage. One reviewer praised the "wit and sarcasm" that made Gilman's "profound social philosophy" such an entertaining read. After publishing several more sociological studies, Gilman returned to writing fiction. *Herland* (1915) is a science-fiction satire about the comic misadventures of three men who stumble upon an all-female society. Still, Gilman's most popular work continues to be "The Yellow Wallpaper," the grim but fascinating portrait of a woman's descent into madness. The one-of-a-kind story has never gone out of print.

Author Online
THINK central
Go to thinkcentral.com. KEYWORD: HML11-796

TEXT ANALYSIS: FIRST-PERSON NARRATOR

A story's **narrator**—the character or voice that relates events to the reader—can have a marked effect on how you perceive the events of the story. A **first-person narrator** is a character in the story. This story is narrated by a woman diagnosed with a "nervous condition." From reading her journal entries, you learn what she is experiencing mentally and emotionally. As you read, ask yourself how she changes and what causes her to change. Consider whether she is a reliable source of information and what might be left out of her narration.

READING SKILL: UNDERSTAND SOCIAL CONTEXT

Social context, or the social conditions that inspired or influenced the author, is key to this story's **setting**. In 1892, when the story was written, women held a very different place in society than they do today. Use your own knowledge, as well as the background on page 796, to analyze the social context of this story. Note what the annotated passages reveal about how women were treated and how they were expected to behave. Consider what Gilman may have thought about these conditions and how they influence the way she chooses to present her narrator in "The Yellow Wallpaper."

Story Passages	*Notes on Social Context*
"John laughs at me, of course, but one expects that in marriage."	*The narrator does not expect that a husband would take his wife's ideas seriously. At this time, men wielded the power in most American households.*

VOCABULARY IN CONTEXT

Gilman uses these words in her harrowing story of stress and power. Determine the meaning of each word from its context.

1. doctor's orders **misconstrued** because of their complexity
2. a **recurrent** ailment, returning every few months
3. a delicate **temperament,** prone to worrying
4. disturbed by intense, **lurid** dreams
5. flashy, **flamboyant** drawings representing her state of mind
6. **undulating** patterns that made her feel seasick
7. a twisted **convolution** of nightmarish thoughts
8. ignorant remarks that demonstrated her **fatuity**

Complete the activities in your **Reader/Writer Notebook**.

What if no one took you SERIOUSLY?

A friend rolls his or her eyes in disbelief as you tell a story. Your parents don't believe that you really are sick, not just feigning illness to get out of a test. A teacher or coach refuses to listen to your perspective before launching into a lecture. On at least one occasion, you've probably felt the sting of someone dismissing your feelings or refusing to listen to you. An isolated instance is bad enough, but if everyone around you refused to take you seriously, you might feel utterly powerless.

QUICKWRITE Try to imagine a whole day during which, no matter what happened, no one took you seriously. Envision yourself in the middle of such a day; then write a journal entry describing your reaction.

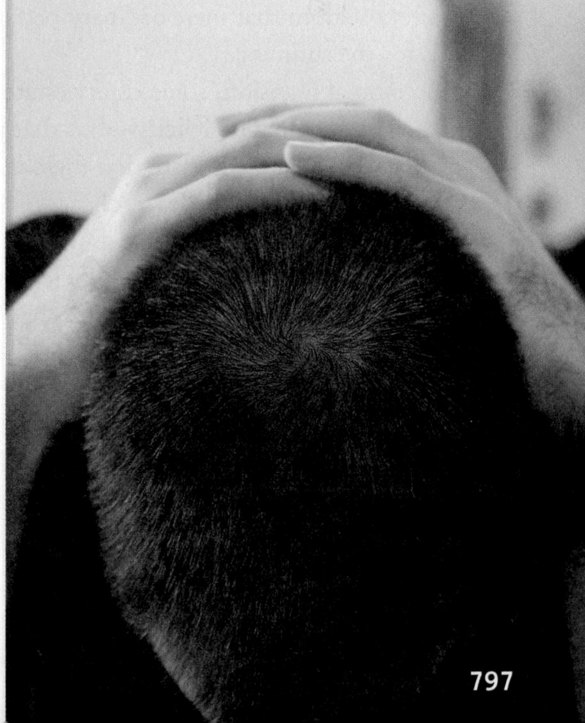

The Yellow WALLPAPER

CHARLOTTE PERKINS GILMAN

BACKGROUND If a woman sought medical treatment for a disorder such as depression or anxiety in 1892, her ills were often diagnosed as trivial "nervous conditions," curable through isolation and prolonged rest. Today it is believed that some of these disorders were caused in part by the stress of living within the rigid social roles to which women were confined. Doctors of the time, however, typically felt that their patients' gender lay at the root of the problem. Many saw women as weak and emotionally unstable, and thus predisposed to illness.

Analyze Visuals ▶
Examine this painting. Describe the woman's size, position, and coloring relative to the flowers in the foreground. How does she look next to the flowers? Explain.

It is very seldom that mere ordinary people like John and myself secure ancestral halls for the summer.

A colonial mansion, a hereditary estate, I would say a haunted house, and reach the height of romantic felicity—but that would be asking too much of fate!

Still I will proudly declare that there is something queer about it.

Else, why should it be let so cheaply? And why have stood so long untenanted?

John laughs at me, of course, but one expects that in marriage.

John is practical in the extreme. He has no patience with faith, an intense horror of superstition, and he scoffs openly at any talk of things not to be felt and seen and put down in figures.

John is a physician, and *perhaps*—(I would not say it to a living soul, of course, but this is dead paper and a great relief to my mind)—*perhaps* that is one reason I do not get well faster.

You see he does not believe I am sick!

And what can one do? **A**

A SOCIAL CONTEXT
Consider what you learned from the background paragraph at the top of this page. How does Gilman convey the belief prevalent in her time that women were emotionally unstable and prone to illness?

Geraniums (1888), Childe Hassam. 18 1/4″ × 12 7/8″. The Hyde Collection, Glens Falls, New York. Photo © Michael Fredericks.

If a physician of high standing, and one's own husband, assures friends and relatives that there is really nothing the matter with one but temporary nervous depression—a slight hysterical[1] tendency—what is one to do?

My brother is also a physician, and also of high standing, and he says the same thing.

So I take phosphates or phosphites—whichever it is, and tonics, and journeys, and air, and exercise, and am absolutely forbidden to "work" until I am well again.

Personally, I disagree with their ideas.

Personally, I believe that congenial work, with excitement and change, would do me good.

But what is one to do?

I did write for a while in spite of them; but it *does* exhaust me a good deal—having to be so sly about it, or else meet with heavy opposition.

I sometimes fancy that in my condition if I had less opposition and more society and stimulus—but John says the very worst thing I can do is to think about my condition, and I confess it always makes me feel bad.

So I will let it alone and talk about the house.

The most beautiful place! It is quite alone, standing well back from the road, quite three miles from the village. It makes me think of English places that you read about, for there are hedges and walls and gates that lock, and lots of separate little houses for the gardeners and people.

There is a *delicious* garden! I never saw such a garden—large and shady, full of box-bordered paths, and lined with long grape-covered arbors with seats under them.

There were greenhouses, too, but they are all broken now.

There was some legal trouble, I believe, something about the heirs and coheirs; anyhow, the place has been empty for years.

That spoils my ghostliness, I am afraid, but I don't care—there is something strange about the house—I can feel it.

I even said so to John one moonlight evening, but he said what I felt was a *draft,* and shut the window.

I get unreasonably angry with John sometimes. I'm sure I never used to be so sensitive. I think it is due to this nervous condition.

But John says if I feel so, I shall neglect proper self-control; so I take pains to control myself—before him, at least, and that makes me very tired. **B**

I don't like our room a bit. I wanted one downstairs that opened on the piazza and had roses all over the window, and such pretty old-fashioned chintz hangings![2] but John would not hear of it.

He said there was only one window and not room for two beds, and no near room for him if he took another.

He is very careful and loving, and hardly lets me stir without special direction.

Language Coach

Antonyms An **antonym** is a word with a meaning opposite that of another word. Gilman is contrasting the words *opposition* and *society* in lines 29–31. Knowing that *opposition* means "action working against something or someone," what must *society* mean here?

B FIRST-PERSON NARRATOR

Reread lines 32–50. Notice how the narrator combines details of the house with her personal feelings about it. How does the author's use of first-person point of view lend to the internal development of the narrator? Support your answer with evidence from the selection.

1. **hysterical:** Hysteria is the presence of a physical ailment with no underlying physical cause.
2. **chintz hangings:** curtains made out of chintz, a printed cotton fabric.

I have a schedule prescription for each hour in the day; he takes all care from me, and so I feel basely ungrateful not to value it more.

He said we came here solely on my account, that I was to have perfect rest and all the air I could get. "Your exercise depends on your strength, my dear," said he, "and your food somewhat on your appetite; but air you can absorb all the time." So we took the nursery at the top of the house.

It is a big, airy room, the whole floor nearly, with windows that look all ways, and air and sunshine galore. It was nursery first and then playroom and gymnasium, I should judge; for the windows are barred for little children, and there are rings and things in the walls.

The paint and paper look as if a boys' school had used it. It is stripped off—the paper—in great patches all around the head of my bed, about as far as I can reach, and in a great place on the other side of the room low down. I never saw a worse paper in my life.

One of those sprawling **flamboyant** patterns committing every artistic sin.

flamboyant (flăm-boi′ənt) *adj.* marked by strikingly elaborate or colorful display

It is dull enough to confuse the eye in following, pronounced enough to constantly irritate and provoke study, and when you follow the lame uncertain curves for a little distance they suddenly commit suicide—plunge off at outrageous angles, destroy themselves in unheard of contradictions.

The color is repellent, almost revolting; a smouldering unclean yellow, strangely faded by the slow-turning sunlight.

It is a dull yet **lurid** orange in some places, a sickly sulphur tint in others.

lurid (lo͝or′ĭd) *adj.* shocking; gruesome

No wonder the children hated it! I should hate it myself if I had to live in this room long.

There comes John, and I must put this away, —he hates to have me write a word.

We have been here two weeks, and I haven't felt like writing before, since that first day.

I am sitting by the window now, up in this atrocious nursery, and there is nothing to hinder my writing as much as I please, save lack of strength. C

C GRAMMAR AND STYLE Notice that Gilman chose to tell this story in the **present tense.** This lends the narrative a sense of immediacy and allows readers to feel as though they're witnessing new developments in the narrator's condition as they unfold.

John is away all day, and even some nights when his cases are serious.

I am glad my case is not serious!

But these nervous troubles are dreadfully depressing.

John does not know how much I really suffer. He knows there is no *reason* to suffer, and that satisfies him.

Of course it is only nervousness. It does weigh on me so not to do my duty in any way!

I meant to be such a help to John, such a real rest and comfort, and here I am a comparative burden already!

Nobody would believe what an effort it is to do what little I am able,—to dress and entertain, and order things.

It is fortunate Mary is so good with the baby. Such a dear baby!

And yet I *cannot* be with him, it makes me so nervous.

I suppose John never was nervous in his life. He laughs at me so about this wallpaper!

At first he meant to repaper the room, but afterwards he said that I was letting it get the better of me, and that nothing was worse for a nervous patient than to give way to such fancies.

He said that after the wallpaper was changed it would be the heavy bedstead, and then the barred windows, and then that gate at the head of the stairs, and so on.

"You know the place is doing you good," he said, "and really, dear, I don't care to renovate the house just for a three months' rental."

"Then do let us go downstairs," I said, "there are such pretty rooms there."

Then he took me in his arms and called me a blessed little goose, and said he

A Woman Seated at a Table by a Window, Carl Holsoe. Oil on canvas. © SuperStock.

◀ Analyze Visuals

How would you describe the **mood** of this painting? In your opinion, is it similar to or different from the mood of the story? Explain, citing specific details from each that influenced your answer.

would go down to the cellar, if I wished, and have it whitewashed into the bargain. **D**

But he is right enough about the beds and windows and things.

It is an airy and comfortable room as anyone need wish, and, of course, I would not be so silly as to make him uncomfortable just for a whim.

I'm really getting quite fond of the big room, all but that horrid paper.

Out of one window I can see the garden, those mysterious deepshaded arbors, the riotous old-fashioned flowers, and bushes and gnarly trees.

Out of another I get a lovely view of the bay and a little private wharf belonging to the estate. There is a beautiful shaded lane that runs down there from the house. I always fancy I see people walking in these numerous paths and arbors, but John has cautioned me not to give way to fancy in the least. He says that with my imaginative power and habit of story-making, a nervous weakness like mine is sure to lead to all manner of excited fancies, and that I ought to use my will and good sense to check the tendency. So I try.

I think sometimes that if I were only well enough to write a little it would relieve the press of ideas and rest me.

But I find I get pretty tired when I try.

It is so discouraging not to have any advice and companionship about my work. When I get really well, John says we will ask Cousin Henry and Julia down for a long visit; but he says he would as soon put fireworks in my pillowcase as to let me have those stimulating people about now.

I wish I could get well faster.

But I must not think about that. This paper looks to me as if it *knew* what a vicious influence it had!

There is a **recurrent** spot where the pattern lolls like a broken neck and two bulbous eyes stare at you upside down.

I get positively angry with the impertinence of it and the everlastingness. **E** Up and down and sideways they crawl, and those absurd, unblinking eyes are everywhere. There is one place where two breadths didn't match, and the eyes go all up and down the line, one a little higher than the other.

I never saw so much expression in an inanimate thing before, and we all know how much expression they have! I used to lie awake as a child and get more entertainment and terror out of blank walls and plain furniture than most children could find in a toy store.

I remember what a kindly wink the knobs of our big, old bureau used to have, and there was one chair that always seemed like a strong friend.

I used to feel that if any of the other things looked too fierce I could always hop into that chair and be safe.

The furniture in this room is no worse than inharmonious, however, for we had to bring it all from downstairs. I suppose when this was used as a playroom they had to take the nursery things out, and no wonder! I never saw such ravages as the children have made here.

D SOCIAL CONTEXT
Reread lines 99–110 and describe the relationship between the narrator and her husband. What might Gilman be saying about how women were viewed in the late 1800s?

recurrent (rĭ-kûr′ənt) *adj.* occurring time after time

E FIRST-PERSON NARRATOR
How are the narrator's feelings about the wallpaper changing? Explain whether or not her response to the room's décor seems rational to you.

The wallpaper, as I said before, is torn off in spots, and it sticketh closer than a brother—they must have had perseverance as well as hatred.

Then the floor is scratched and gouged and splintered, the plaster itself is dug out here and there, and this great heavy bed which is all we found in the room, looks as if it had been through the wars.

But I don't mind it a bit—only the paper.

There comes John's sister. Such a dear girl as she is, and so careful of me! I must not let her find me writing.

She is a perfect and enthusiastic housekeeper, and hopes for no better profession. I verily believe she thinks it is the writing which made me sick!

But I can write when she is out, and see her a long way off from these windows. **F**

There is one that commands the road, a lovely shaded winding road, and one that just looks off over the country. A lovely country, too, full of great elms and velvet meadows.

This wallpaper has a kind of sub-pattern in a different shade, a particularly irritating one, for you can only see it in certain lights, and not clearly then.

But in the places where it isn't faded and where the sun is just so—I can see a strange, provoking, formless sort of figure, that seems to skulk about behind that silly and conspicuous front design.

There's sister on the stairs!

F SOCIAL CONTEXT
Examine the narrator's description of John's sister in lines 158–162. How do these lines add to your understanding of the story's setting and how it affects the narrator?

Well, the Fourth of July is over! The people are all gone and I am tired out. John thought it might do me good to see a little company, so we just had mother and Nellie and the children down for a week.

Of course I didn't do a thing. Jennie sees to everything now.

But it tired me all the same.

John says if I don't pick up faster he shall send me to Weir Mitchell[3] in the fall.

But I don't want to go there at all. I had a friend who was in his hands once, and she says he is just like John and my brother, only more so! **G**

Besides, it is such an undertaking to go so far.

I don't feel as if it was worth while to turn my hand over for anything, and I'm getting dreadfully fretful and querulous.

I cry at nothing, and cry most of the time.

Of course I don't when John is here, or anybody else, but when I am alone.

And I am alone a good deal just now. John is kept in town very often by serious cases, and Jennie is good and lets me alone when I want her to.

So I walk a little in the garden or down that lovely lane, sit on the porch under the roses, and lie down up here a good deal.

I'm getting really fond of the room in spite of the wallpaper. Perhaps *because* of the wallpaper.

It dwells in my mind so!

I lie here on this great immovable bed—it is nailed down, I believe—and

G SOCIAL CONTEXT
Reread lines 177–179. What is suggested or highlighted by the fact that all the male characters in the story share common **traits?** What role does the social context play in shaping the story's setting? Cite evidence to support your answer.

3. **Weir Mitchell:** Dr. Silas Weir Mitchell, a physician famous for his "rest cure" for nervous diseases, which is no longer considered effective.

follow that pattern about by the hour. It is as good as gymnastics, I assure you. I start, we'll say, at the bottom, down in the corner over there where it has not been touched, and I determine for the thousandth time that I *will* follow that pointless pattern to some sort of a conclusion.

I know a little of the principle of design, and I know this thing was not arranged on any laws of radiation, or alternation, or repetition, or symmetry, or anything else that I ever heard of.

It is repeated, of course, by the breadths, but not otherwise.

Looked at in one way each breadth stands alone, the bloated curves and flourishes—a kind of "debased Romanesque" with *delirium tremens*[4]—go waddling up and down in isolated columns of **fatuity.**

fatuity (fə-to͞o'ĭ-tē) *n.* something foolish or stupid

But, on the other hand, they connect diagonally, and the sprawling outlines run off in great slanting waves of optic horror, like a lot of wallowing seaweeds in full chase.

The whole thing goes horizontally, too, at least it seems so, and I exhaust myself in trying to distinguish the order of its going in that direction.

They have used a horizontal breadth for a frieze, and that adds wonderfully to the confusion.

There is one end of the room where it is almost intact, and there, when the crosslights fade and the low sun shines directly upon it, I can almost fancy radiation after all,—the interminable grotesques seem to form around a common center and rush off in headlong plunges of equal distraction.

It makes me tired to follow it. I will take a nap I guess.

I don't know why I should write this.

I don't want to.

I don't feel able.

And I know John would think it absurd. But I *must* say what I feel and think in some way—it is such a relief!

But the effort is getting to be greater than the relief.

Half the time now I am awfully lazy, and lie down ever so much.

John says I mustn't lose my strength, and has me take cod liver oil and lots of tonics and things, to say nothing of ale and wine and rare meat.

Dear John! He loves me very dearly, and hates to have me sick. I tried to have a real earnest reasonable talk with him the other day, and tell him how I wish he would let me go and make a visit to Cousin Henry and Julia.

But he said I wasn't able to go, nor able to stand it after I got there; and I did not make out a very good case for myself, for I was crying before I had finished. H

It is getting to be a great effort for me to think straight. Just this nervous weakness I suppose.

And dear John gathered me up in his arms, and just carried me upstairs and laid me on the bed, and sat by me and read to me till it tired my head.

H FIRST-PERSON NARRATOR
Reread lines 223–229. Imagine the "real earnest reasonable talk" the narrator describes. How might the account of this scene be different if John were the narrator? How do you think the change in point of view would affect your perception of the main character? Explain your answer.

---

4. **"debased Romanesque" with *delirium tremens*:** Romanesque is an artistic style characterized by simple ornamentation. *Delirium tremens* refers to violent trembling and hallucinations caused by excessive drinking.

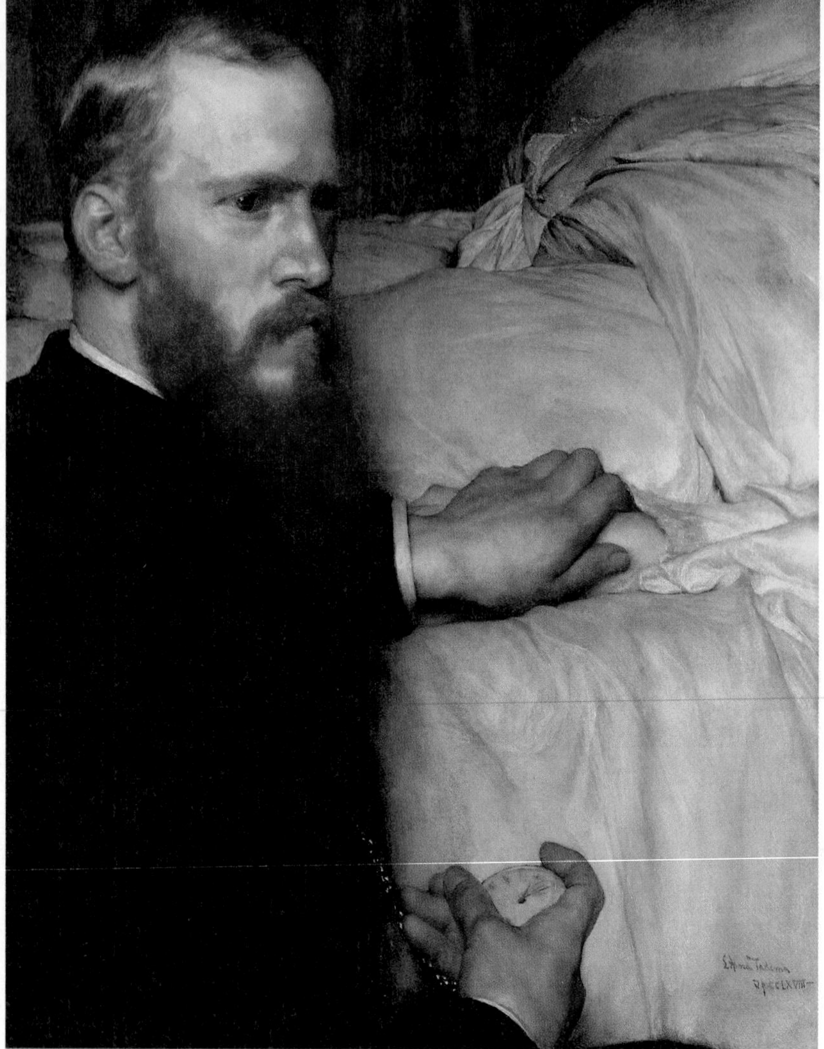

Portrait of Dr. Washington Epps, My Doctor (1885), Sir Lawrence Alma-Tadema. Oil on canvas, 64.2 cm × 51 cm. Private collection. © Bridgeman Art Library.

◂ Analyze Visuals
Study this painting, then describe the emotion conveyed by the subject's facial expression. Does this image make you feel more or less sympathetic toward John, the narrator's husband? Explain your answer.

He said I was his darling and his comfort and all he had, and that I must take care of myself for his sake, and keep well.

He says no one but myself can help me out of it, that I must use my will and self-control and not let any silly fancies run away with me.

There's one comfort, the baby is well and happy, and does not have to occupy this nursery with the horrid wallpaper.

If we had not used it, that blessed child would have! What a fortunate escape! Why, I wouldn't have a child of mine, an impressionable little thing, live in such a room for worlds.

I never thought of it before, but it is lucky that John kept me here after all, I can stand it so much easier than a baby, you see.

Of course I never mention it to them any more—I am too wise,—but I keep watch of it all the same.

There are things in that paper that nobody knows but me, or ever will.

Behind that outside pattern the dim shapes get clearer every day.

It is always the same shape, only very numerous.

And it is like a woman stooping down and creeping about behind that pattern. I don't like it a bit. I wonder—I begin to think—I wish John would take me away from here!

It is so hard to talk with John about my case, because he is so wise, and because he loves me so.

But I tried it last night.

It was moonlight. The moon shines in all around just as the sun does.

I hate to see it sometimes, it creeps so slowly, and always comes in by one window or another.

John was asleep and I hated to waken him, so I kept still and watched the moonlight on that **undulating** wallpaper till I felt creepy.

undulating (ŭn'jə-lā'tĭng) *adj.* appearing to move in waves **undulate** *v.*

The faint figure behind seemed to shake the pattern, just as if she wanted to get out.

I got up softly and went to feel and see if the paper *did* move, and when I came back John was awake.

"What is it, little girl?" he said. "Don't go walking about like that—you'll get cold."

I thought it was a good time to talk, so I told him that I really was not gaining here, and that I wished he would take me away.

"Why darling!" said he, "our lease will be up in three weeks, and I can't see how to leave before.

"The repairs are not done at home, and I cannot possibly leave town just now. Of course if you were in any danger, I could and would, but you really are better, dear, whether you can see it or not. I am a doctor, dear, and I know. You are gaining flesh and color, your appetite is better, I feel really much easier about you."

"I don't weigh a bit more," said I, "nor as much; and my appetite may be better in the evening when you are here, but it is worse in the morning when you are away!"

"Bless her little heart!" said he with a big hug, "she shall be as sick as she pleases! But now let's improve the shining hours[5] by going to sleep, and talk about it in the morning!"

"And you won't go away?" I asked gloomily.

"Why, how can I, dear? It is only three weeks more and then we will take a nice little trip of a few days while Jennie is getting the house ready. Really dear you are better!"

"Better in body perhaps—" I began, and stopped short, for he sat up straight and looked at me with such a stern, reproachful look that I could not say another word.

"My darling," said he, "I beg of you, for my sake and for our child's sake, as well as for your own, that you will never for one instant let that idea enter your mind! There is nothing so dangerous, so fascinating, to a **temperament** like yours. It is a false and foolish fancy. Can you not trust me as a physician when I tell you so?"

temperament (tĕm'prə-mənt) *n.* a person's characteristic mode of emotional response

5. **improve the shining hours:** make good use of time—an allusion to the poem "Against Idleness and Mischief" by Isaac Watts.

So of course I said no more on that score, and we went to sleep before long. He thought I was asleep first, but I wasn't, and lay there for hours trying to decide whether that front pattern and the back pattern really did move together or separately.

On a pattern like this, by daylight, there is a lack of sequence, a defiance of law, that is a constant irritant to a normal mind.

The color is hideous enough, and unreliable enough, and infuriating enough, but the pattern is torturing.

You think you have mastered it, but just as you get well underway in following, it turns a back-somersault and there you are. It slaps you in the face, knocks you down, and tramples upon you. It is like a bad dream.

The outside pattern is a florid arabesque,[6] reminding one of a fungus. If you can imagine a toadstool in joints, an interminable string of toadstools, budding and sprouting in endless **convolutions**—why, that is something like it.

That is, sometimes!

There is one marked peculiarity about this paper, a thing nobody seems to notice but myself, and that is that it changes as the light changes.

When the sun shoots in through the east window—I always watch for that first long, straight ray—it changes so quickly that I never can quite believe it.

That is why I watch it always.

By moonlight—the moon shines in all night when there is a moon—I wouldn't know it was the same paper.

At night in any kind of light, in twilight, candle light, lamplight, and worst of all by moonlight, it becomes bars! The outside pattern I mean, and the woman behind it is as plain as can be.

I didn't realize for a long time what the thing was that showed behind, that dim sub-pattern, but now I am quite sure it is a woman.

By daylight she is subdued, quiet. I fancy it is the pattern that keeps her so still. It is so puzzling. It keeps me quiet by the hour.

I lie down ever so much now. John says it is good for me, and to sleep all I can.

Indeed he started the habit by making me lie down for an hour after each meal.

It is a very bad habit I am convinced, for you see I don't sleep.

And that cultivates deceit, for I don't tell them I'm awake—O no!

The fact is I am getting a little afraid of John.

He seems very queer sometimes, and even Jennie has an inexplicable look.

It strikes me occasionally, just as a scientific hypothesis,—that perhaps it is the paper!

I have watched John when he did not know I was looking, and come into the room suddenly on the most innocent excuses, and I've caught him several times *looking at the paper!* And Jennie too. I caught Jennie with her hand on it once.

She didn't know I was in the room, and when I asked her in a quiet, a very quiet voice, with the most restrained manner possible, what she was doing with

FIRST-PERSON NARRATOR
Consider the narrator's statement in lines 294–295. Based on her description of the wallpaper, would you say she has "a normal mind"? Explain your answer.

convolution (kŏn'və-lo͞o'shən) *n.* a form or shape that is folded into curved, complicated windings

Language Coach

Prefixes A **prefix** is a word part attached to the beginning of a word root. The prefix *sub-* means "under" or "beneath." What does *sub-pattern* (line 316) mean, and what clues to its meaning can you find in lines 315–316?

6. **florid arabesque:** an elaborate interwoven pattern.

the paper—she turned around as if she had been caught stealing, and looked quite angry—asked me why I should frighten her so!

Then she said that the paper stained everything it touched, that she had found yellow smooches[7] on all my clothes and John's, and she wished we would be more careful!

Did not that sound innocent? But I know she was studying that pattern, and I am determined that nobody shall find it out but myself! J

Life is very much more exciting now than it used to be. You see I have something more to expect, to look forward to, to watch. I really do eat better, and am more quiet than I was.

John is so pleased to see me improve! He laughed a little the other day, and said I seemed to be flourishing in spite of my wallpaper.

I turned it off with a laugh. I had no intention of telling him it was *because* of the wallpaper—he would make fun of me. He might even want to take me away.

I don't want to leave now until I have found it out. There is a week more, and I think that will be enough.

I'm feeling ever so much better! I don't sleep much at night, for it is so interesting to watch developments; but I sleep a good deal in the daytime.

In the daytime it is tiresome and perplexing.

There are always new shoots on the fungus, and new shades of yellow all over it. I cannot keep count of them, though I have tried conscientiously.

It is the strangest yellow, that wallpaper! It makes me think of all the yellow things I ever saw—not beautiful ones like buttercups, but old foul, bad yellow things.

But there is something else about that paper—the smell! I noticed it the moment we came into the room, but with so much air and sun it was not bad. Now we have had a week of fog and rain, and whether the windows are open or not, the smell is here.

It creeps all over the house.

I find it hovering in the dining room, skulking in the parlor, hiding in the hall, lying in wait for me on the stairs.

It gets into my hair.

Even when I go to ride, if I turn my head suddenly and surprise it—there is that smell!

Such a peculiar odor, too! I have spent hours in trying to analyze it, to find what it smelled like.

It is not bad—at first, and very gentle, but quite the subtlest, most enduring odor I ever met.

In this damp weather it is awful, I wake up in the night and find it hanging over me.

It used to disturb me at first. I thought seriously of burning the house—to reach the smell.

J FIRST-PERSON NARRATOR

Reread lines 323–338. How has the narrator's attitude toward John and Jennie changed? What do you think they might say about her feelings if they were aware of them?

Language Coach

Word Definitions

Skulking (line 360) means "moving in a secretive manner" or "hiding with a bad intent." What human qualities is the narrator giving to the smell?

---

7. **smooches:** smudges.

In Bed (1878), Federico Zandomeneghi. Oil on canvas, 60.5 cm × 73.5 cm. Galleria d'Arte Moderna, Florence. © Alinari/Art Resource, New York.

But now I am used to it. The only thing I can think of that it is like is the *color* of the paper! A yellow smell. **K**

There is a very funny mark on this wall, low down, near the mopboard. A streak that runs round the room. It goes behind every piece of furniture, except the bed, a long, straight, even *smooch*, as if it had been rubbed over and over.

I wonder how it was done and who did it, and what they did it for. Round and round and round—round and round and round—it makes me dizzy!

I really have discovered something at last.

Through watching so much at night, when it changes so, I have finally found out.

The front pattern *does* move—and no wonder! The woman behind shakes it!

Sometimes I think there are a great many women behind, and sometimes only one, and she crawls around fast, and her crawling shakes it all over.

K FIRST-PERSON NARRATOR

How would an impartial, omniscient narrator describe the woman's mind at this point? How would this change in the story's point of view affect Gilman's depiction of her main character? Explain your answer.

Then in the very bright spots she keeps still, and in the very shady spots she just takes hold of the bars and shakes them hard.

And she is all the time trying to climb through. But nobody could climb through that pattern—it strangles so; I think that is why it has so many heads.

They get through, and then the pattern strangles them off and turns them upside down, and makes their eyes white!

If those heads were covered or taken off it would not be half so bad.

I think that woman gets out in the daytime!

And I'll tell you why—privately—I've seen her!

I can see her out of every one of my windows!

It is the same woman, I know, for she is always creeping, and most women do not creep by daylight.

I see her on that long road under the trees, creeping along, and when a carriage comes she hides under the blackberry vines.

I don't blame her a bit. It must be very humiliating to be caught creeping by daylight!

I always lock the door when I creep by daylight. I can't do it at night, for I know John would suspect something at once.

And John is so queer now, that I don't want to irritate him. I wish he would take another room! Besides, I don't want anybody to get that woman out at night but myself.

I often wonder if I could see her out of all the windows at once.

But, turn as fast as I can, I can only see out of one at one time.

And though I always see her, she *may* be able to creep faster than I can turn!

I have watched her sometimes away off in the open country, creeping as fast as a cloud shadow in a high wind.

If only that top pattern could be gotten off from the under one! I mean to try it, little by little.

I have found out another funny thing, but I shan't tell it this time! It does not do to trust people too much.

There are only two more days to get this paper off, and I believe John is beginning to notice. I don't like the look in his eyes.

And I heard him ask Jennie a lot of professional questions about me. She had a very good report to give.

She said I slept a good deal in the daytime.

John knows I don't sleep very well at night, for all I'm so quiet!

He asked me all sorts of questions, too, and pretended to be very loving and kind.

As if I couldn't see through him! L

L FIRST-PERSON NARRATOR
Consider the narrator's statements in lines 403–404 and line 423. Why is she turning against her husband? Explain what John's real concerns might be.

Still, I don't wonder he acts so, sleeping under this paper for three months.

It only interests me, but I feel sure John and Jennie are secretly affected by it.

Hurrah! This is the last day, but it is enough. John to stay in town overnight, and won't be out until this evening.

Jennie wanted to sleep with me—the sly thing! but I told her I should undoubtedly rest better for a night all alone.

That was clever, for really I wasn't alone a bit! As soon as it was moonlight and that poor thing began to crawl and shake the pattern, I got up and ran to help her.

I pulled and she shook, I shook and she pulled, and before morning we had peeled off yards of that paper.

A strip about as high as my head and half around the room.

And then when the sun came and that awful pattern began to laugh at me, I declared I would finish it today!

We go away tomorrow, and they are moving all my furniture down again to leave things as they were before.

Jennie looked at the wall in amazement, but I told her merrily that I did it out of pure spite at the vicious thing.

She laughed and said she wouldn't mind doing it herself, but I must not get tired.

How she betrayed herself that time! Ⓜ

But I am here, and no person touches this paper but me,—not *alive!*

She tried to get me out of the room—it was too patent! But I said it was so quiet and empty and clean now that I believed I would lie down again and sleep all I could; and not to wake me even for dinner—I would call when I woke.

So now she is gone, and the servants are gone, and the things are gone, and there is nothing left but that great bedstead nailed down, with the canvas mattress we found on it.

We shall sleep downstairs tonight, and take the boat home tomorrow.

I quite enjoy the room, now it is bare again.

How those children did tear about here!

This bedstead is fairly gnawed!

But I must get to work.

I have locked the door and thrown the key down into the front path.

I don't want to go out, and I don't want to have anybody come in, till John comes.

I want to astonish him.

I've got a rope up here that even Jennie did not find. If that woman does get out, and tries to get away, I can tie her!

But I forgot I could not reach far without anything to stand on!

This bed will *not* move!

I tried to lift and push it until I was lame, and then I got so angry I bit off a little piece at one corner—but it hurt my teeth.

Then I peeled off all the paper I could reach standing on the floor. It sticks horribly and the pattern just enjoys it! All those strangled heads and bulbous eyes and waddling fungus growths just shriek with derision!

Ⓜ FIRST-PERSON NARRATOR

The anonymous narrator of this story influenced the development of a character type in American literature and film—the emotionally disturbed wife. Sue Kaufman's 1967 novel *Diary of a Mad Housewife*, which was later made into a film, owes much to Gilman's disturbing experiment in first-person narration. Laura Brown, a character in the novel and film *The Hours*, is a more recent example of the "mad housewife." Reread lines 426–442. Which details in this section of the narrative do you find compelling? Explain your answer.

I am getting angry enough to do something desperate. To jump out of the window would be admirable exercise, but the bars are too strong even to try.

Besides I wouldn't do it. Of course not. I know well enough that a step like that is improper and might be **misconstrued.**

I don't like to *look* out of the windows even—there are so many of those creeping women, and they creep so fast.

I wonder if they all come out of that wallpaper as I did? Ⓝ

But I am securely fastened now by my well-hidden rope—you don't get *me* out in the road there!

I suppose I shall have to get back behind the pattern when it comes night, and that is hard!

It is so pleasant to be out in this great room and creep around as I please!

I don't want to go outside. I won't, even if Jennie asks me to.

For outside you have to creep on the ground, and everything is green instead of yellow.

But here I can creep smoothly on the floor, and my shoulder just fits in that long smooch around the wall, so I cannot lose my way.

Why there's John at the door!

It is no use, young man, you can't open it!

How he does call and pound!

Now he's crying for an axe.

It would be a shame to break down that beautiful door!

"John dear!" said I in the gentlest voice, "the key is down by the front steps, under a plantain leaf!"

That silenced him for a few moments.

Then he said—very quietly indeed, "Open the door, my darling!"

"I can't," said I. "The key is down by the front door under a plantain leaf!"

And then I said it again, several times, very gently and slowly, and said it so often that he had to go and see, and he got it of course, and came in. He stopped short by the door.

"What is the matter?" he cried. "What are you doing!"

I kept on creeping just the same, but I looked at him over my shoulder.

"I've got out at last," said I, "in spite of you and Jane.[8] And I've pulled off most of the paper, so you can't put me back!"

Now why should that man have fainted? But he did, and right across my path by the wall, so that I had to creep over him every time!

misconstrued (mĭs′kən-stro͞od′) *adj.* misunderstood; misinterpreted **misconstrue** *v.*

Ⓝ **FIRST-PERSON NARRATOR**
What does the narrator now believe about the wallpaper?

8. **in spite of you and Jane:** As Jane is previously unmentioned, the name may be a typographical error by the original printer of the story in place of the name of the housekeeper, Jennie, or Cousin Julia; or it may denote the narrator herself, freed from her commonplace, wifely, "Jane" persona.

Reading for Information

JOURNAL ARTICLE Charlotte Perkins Gilman herself suffered a profound depression and was prescribed a "rest cure" by a noted neurologist of the day. In this 1913 article from her feminist journal *Forerunner,* she says she wrote "The Yellow Wallpaper" to bear witness to the horrors of this "cure" and to attest to her recovery.

THE
FORERUNNER
A MONTHLY MAGAZINE
CHARLOTTE PERKINS GILMAN

WHY I WROTE "THE YELLOW WALLPAPER"

Many and many a reader has asked that. When the story first came out, in the *New England Magazine* about 1891, a Boston physician made protest in *The Transcript.* Such a story ought not to be written, he said; it was enough to drive anyone mad to read it.

Another physician, in Kansas I think, wrote to say that it was the best description of incipient insanity he had ever seen, and—begging my pardon—had I been there?

Now the story of the story is this:

For many years I suffered from a severe and continuous nervous breakdown tending to melancholia—and beyond. During about the third year of this trouble I went, in devout faith and some faint stir of hope, to a noted specialist in nervous diseases, the best known in the country. This wise man put me to bed and applied the rest cure, to which a still good physique responded so promptly that he concluded there was nothing much the matter with me, and sent me home with solemn advice to "live as domestic a life as far as possible," to "have but two hours' intellectual life a day," and "never to touch pen, brush or pencil again as long as I lived." This was in 1887.

I went home and obeyed those directions for some three months, and came so near the border line of utter mental ruin that I could see over.

Then, using the remnants of intelligence that remained, and helped by a wise friend, I cast the noted specialist's advice to the winds and went to work again—work, the normal life of every human being; work, in which is joy and growth and service, without which one is a pauper and a parasite; ultimately recovering some measure of power.

Being naturally moved to rejoicing by this narrow escape, I wrote *The Yellow Wallpaper,* with its embellishments and additions to carry out the ideal (I never had hallucinations or objections to my mural decorations) and sent a copy to the physician who so nearly drove me mad. He never acknowledged it.

The little book is valued by alienists and as a good specimen of one kind of literature. It has to my knowledge saved one woman from a similar fate—so terrifying her family that they let her out into normal activity and she recovered.

But the best result is this. Many years later I was told that the great specialist had admitted to friends of his that he had altered his treatment of neurasthenia since reading *The Yellow Wallpaper.*

It was not intended to drive people crazy, but to save people from being driven crazy, and it worked.

Comprehension

1. **Summarize** Describe the "rest cure" treatment and explain why it is prescribed for the narrator.
2. **Recall** Why does the narrator hate the wallpaper at first?
3. **Clarify** Who does the narrator think she is at the end of the story?

Text Analysis

4. **Analyze First-Person Narrator** The narrator of this story is **unreliable**—you can't always trust that what she says is accurate or complete. How does her highly subjective account contribute to your perception of her character's internal development? Cite evidence from the story to support your answer.
5. **Interpret Symbolism** Reread lines 380–391 and consider the narrator's **powerlessness.** What might the yellow wallpaper symbolize in the story? Consider the following as you formulate your answer:
   - the narrator's attitude toward both her "condition" and her marriage
   - what she sees in the "strangling" pattern of the paper
   - her exhilaration when she rips the wallpaper off the wall
6. **Understand Social Context** Examine the chart you filled in as you read. What conclusions can you draw about the social context of this story? Citing evidence from both the short story and the article on page 814, explain
   - how wives were expected to behave in the 1890s
   - how women seem to have been treated by the men—husbands, brothers, doctors—who cared for them
   - what Gilman thought about women's being denied meaningful work and personal power, and how she addresses these issues in this story

Text Criticism

7. **Different Perspectives** At the time "The Yellow Wallpaper" was published, most critics read it as a horror tale about madness or, after Gilman's explanation appeared in 1913, as an exposé of women's medical treatment. Only a few saw what feminists in the 1970s would interpret as Gilman's **political assumptions.** Feminists read the story as a criticism of marriage and the oppression of women. Explain which of these interpretations you favor, citing evidence from the text.

What if no one took you SERIOUSLY?

In "The Yellow Wallpaper," the narrator is doubted by the doctor and her own husband, with devastating consequences. Is it possible to believe in yourself if no one else seems to? Explain your answer.

COMMON CORE

RL 1 Cite evidence to support inferences drawn from the text, including determining where the text leaves matters uncertain. **RL 3** Analyze the impact of the author's choices regarding how to develop and relate elements of a story. **RL 9** Demonstrate knowledge of nineteenth-century foundational works of American literature. **RI 1** Cite evidence to support analysis of what the text says explicitly as well as inferences drawn from the text.

Vocabulary in Context

▲ VOCABULARY PRACTICE

Choose the word that is not related in meaning to the other words.

1. (a) extravagant, (b) showy, (c) flamboyant, (d) lowly
2. (a) undulating, (b) flying, (c) soaring, (d) gliding
3. (a) consideration, (b) convolution, (c) intricacy, (d) complexity
4. (a) periodic, (b) repeated, (c) refused, (d) recurrent
5. (a) fatuity, (b) favor, (c) silliness, (d) folly
6. (a) miscellaneous, (b) misconstrued, (c) various, (d) diversified
7. (a) vivid, (b) lurid, (c) sensational, (d) vapid
8. (a) humidity, (b) personality, (c) disposition, (d) temperament

WORD LIST
convolution
fatuity
flamboyant
lurid
misconstrued
recurrent
temperament
undulating

ACADEMIC VOCABULARY IN WRITING

• apparent • confine • focus • expose • perceive

"The Yellow Wallpaper" **exposes** social issues from the late 1800s. If you were writing a short story, which issues would you **focus** on? Explain your answer in a short paragraph, using at least two of the Academic Vocabulary words.

VOCABULARY STRATEGY: WORD ANALOGIES

A **word analogy** is a statement that compares, or shows the relationships, between pairs of words. Relationships frequently expressed include synonyms, antonyms, cause and effect, part and whole, and location. Analogies are normally written like the following example.

FLAMBOYANT : PLAIN :: textured : smooth

Studying the word relationships in analogies can increase your vocabulary.

PRACTICE For each item, choose the word pair that expresses a relationship most similar to that of the capitalized words. Then identify the relationship type.

1. HURRICANE : FLOOD ::
   a. plumber : pipes **b.** calm : agitated **c.** drought : famine **d.** lawyer : court
2. SAGACIOUS : SHREWD ::
   a. messy : tidy **b.** shy : careless **c.** joy : gloom **d.** retribution : punishment
3. EXTRAVAGANT : FRUGAL ::
   a. accept : forbid **b.** crime : robbery **c.** merry : cheerful
   d. courage : bravery
4. CHOIR : TENOR ::
   a. key : lock **b.** rider : horse **c.** shallow : deep **d.** garden : tomato

COMMON CORE

L 5 Demonstrate understanding of word relationships. **L 6** Acquire and use accurately general academic words and phrases.

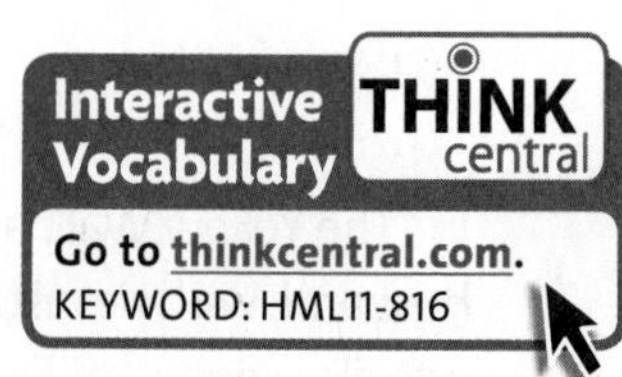

Language

◆ GRAMMAR AND STYLE: Choose Effective Verb Tense

Review the **Grammar and Style** note on page 801. The immediacy and power of "The Yellow Wallpaper" come in part from Gilman's choice to have the narrator tell the story mostly in the **present tense** as though writing in a diary. In this way, the reader plunges directly into the narrator's mind and follows its dark descent. Notice the use of **present-tense verbs** in this chilling example from the end of the story:

> *But I am securely fastened now by my well-hidden rope—you don't get* me *out in the road there!* (lines 475–476)

PRACTICE The following paragraph is a sample from another short story. Notice how the past-tense verbs create a certain distance between the reader and the events. Revise the paragraph, writing it in the present tense to achieve a different effect.

> I threw another log on the fire, waiting for Ahmer to come home. Dinner sat on the table, growing cold. Ahmer had been gone for hours and I was sure he had left with hurt feelings. Why did we always argue this way on special occasions? It was as though we didn't really want to celebrate, or didn't know how.

COMMON CORE

L 1 Demonstrate command of the conventions of standard English grammar and usage when writing. **W 1** Write arguments to support claims in an analysis of texts, using valid reasoning and relevant and sufficient evidence. **W 1a–b** Introduce a precise claim; develop claim and counterclaims fairly and thoroughly, supplying the most relevant evidence for each in a manner that anticipates the audience's possible biases.

READING-WRITING CONNECTION

Expand your understanding of "The Yellow Wallpaper" by responding to this prompt. Then, use the **revising tips** to improve your analysis.

WRITING PROMPT

WRITE AN ANALYSIS Although most contemporary readers respond positively to "The Yellow Wallpaper," the editor of the *Atlantic Monthly* in 1892 rejected it for publication. By way of explanation, he offered this candid reaction: "I could not forgive myself if I made others as miserable as I have made myself." How did the story affect you? Write a **three-to-five-paragraph analysis** explaining your own thoughts and feelings about the story. In your analysis, discuss the effect Gilman's present-tense narration had on you.

REVISING TIPS

- In your first paragraph, include a thesis statement that brings out the controlling idea of your analysis.
- Cite examples and quotations from the story to support your conclusions.
- Include your personal thoughts and comments about the examples you used from the story.
- Respond to any opposing claims that you expect readers might make.

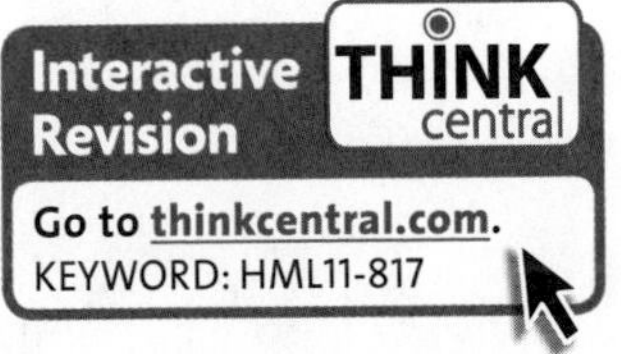

American Masterpiece

from Ethan Frome

Novel by Edith Wharton

Edith Wharton
1862-1937

COMMON CORE

RL 3 Analyze the impact of the author's choices regarding how to develop and relate elements of a story. **SL 1a** Come to discussions prepared, having read and researched material under study; draw on that preparation by referring to evidence from texts to stimulate a thoughtful, well-reasoned exchange of ideas.

BACKGROUND Edith Wharton grew up in the rarefied atmosphere of New York wealth and wrote about it in most of her novels. Yet *Ethan Frome*, one of her best-known works, was set not in upper-crust New York society, but rather in a poor New England village. A novella, *Ethan Frome* takes place in a Massachusetts village called Starkfield, the name clearly evoking the bleak lifestyle that Wharton wished to portray. The story is told by an engineer who visits Starkfield and grows interested in a "ruin of a man" he sees there named Ethan Frome. Frome himself, we learn, had always wanted to be an engineer and to live in cities, "where there were lectures and big libraries." Instead, poverty and tradition have restricted him to a barren farm and an equally barren marriage. A visit from his sickly wife Zeena's young cousin, Mattie Silver, brings a spark of joy into Frome's grim life. His tragic attempt to grasp that joy forms the central conflict of the tale.

TEXT ANALYSIS Told in prose as spare and lean as the New England farm on which it is set, *Ethan Frome* contrasts sharply with Wharton's urban novels—lushly detailed portraits of Gilded Age Manhattan. *Ethan Frome* is similar to Wharton's other books, however, in that its characters seem to have very little influence over their own lives. In this respect, Wharton was a **naturalist** writer, exploring how human beings are shaped by forces beyond their control.

The excerpt on the opposite page describes Ethan Frome's changing relationship with Mattie Silver and the strong emotions that she has awakened in him. As you read the text, notice Wharton's subtle **characterization** of both her protagonist and the young woman who has come to spend time on his farm. The novelist gives readers access to the entire range of Frome's character—**internal** and **external.** We observe the lonely farmer's thoughts and feelings, as well as how his environment and his visitor shape his character. By contrast, readers see Mattie Silver exclusively from the outside. The author shares with us only what her protagonist sees of this new influence in Frome's life.

DISCUSS After you have read the excerpt from *Ethan Frome*, join a small group of your peers and review the characteristics of naturalism, which are described on pages 648–649. Then, discuss Wharton's characterization of Ethan Frome and Mattie Silver. How does her characterization, especially of Frome, reflect the way naturalist writers viewed the world? Finally, discuss your predictions for Ethan Frome. What kind of impact will Mattie's presence have on him in the end? If time allows, share your group's perceptions with the rest of the class.

Frome was in the habit of walking into Starkfield to fetch home his wife's cousin, Mattie Silver, on the rare evenings when some chance of amusement drew her to the village. It was his wife who had suggested, when the girl came to live with them, that such opportunities should be put in her way. Mattie Silver came from Stamford, and when she entered the Fromes' household to act as her cousin Zeena's aid it was thought best, as she came without pay, not to let her feel too sharp a contrast between the life she had left and the isolation of a Starkfield farm. But for this—as Frome sardonically reflected—it would hardly have occurred to Zeena to take any thought for the girl's amusement.

When his wife first proposed that they should give Mattie an occasional evening out he had inwardly demurred at having to do the extra two miles to the village and back after his hard day on the farm; but not long afterward he had reached the point of wishing that Starkfield might give all its nights to revelry.

Mattie Silver had lived under his roof for a year, and from early morning till they met at supper he had frequent chances of seeing her; but no moments in her company were comparable to those when, her arm in his, and her light step flying to keep time with his long stride, they walked back through the night to the farm. He had taken to the girl from the first day, when he had driven over to the Flats to meet her, and she had smiled and waved to him from the train, crying out, "You must be Ethan!" as she jumped down with her bundles, while he reflected, looking over her slight person: "She don't look much on housework, but she ain't a fretter, anyhow." But it was not only that the coming to his house of a bit of hopeful young life was like the lighting of a fire on a cold hearth. The girl was more than the bright serviceable creature he had thought her. She had an eye to see and an ear to hear: he could show her things and tell her things, and taste the bliss of feeling that all he imparted left long reverberations and echoes he could wake at will.

It was during their night walks back to the farm that he felt most intensely the sweetness of this communion. He had always been more sensitive than the people about him to the appeal of natural beauty. His unfinished studies had given form to this sensibility and even in his unhappiest moments field and sky spoke to him with a deep and powerful persuasion. But hitherto the emotion had remained in him as a silent ache, veiling with sadness the beauty that evoked it. He did not even know whether any one else in the world felt as he did, or whether he was the sole victim of this mournful privilege. Then he learned that one other spirit had trembled with the same touch of wonder: that at his side, living under his roof and eating his bread, was a creature to whom he could say: "That's Orion down yonder; the big fellow to the right is Aldebaran, and the bunch of little ones—like bees swarming—they're the Pleiades . . . ."

April Showers

Short Story by Edith Wharton

COMMON CORE

RL 1 Cite evidence to support inferences drawn from the text. **RL 3** Analyze the impact of the author's choices regarding how to develop and relate elements of a story. **RL 4** Determine the meaning of words and phrases as they are used in the text, including connotative meanings. **L 5b** Analyze nuances in the meaning of words with similar denotations.

DID YOU KNOW?

Edith Wharton . . .

- privately published her first book of poetry at age 16.
- published a book each year from 1902 until her death in 1937.
- entertained President Theodore Roosevelt at her home in France.
- had such a forceful personality that her friends pretended to cower in fear when they saw her coming.

Meet the Author

Edith Wharton 1862–1937

To understand Edith Wharton is to know something about the insular upper-class society that produced her. Rich and fashionable "old New York" consisted of established families, like Wharton's own, descended from English and Dutch colonists and having inherited "old money" made in banking, shipping, and real estate. For Wharton, it was a restrictive world of narrow minds and rigid, arbitrary rules, where "'bad manners' were the supreme offense." It was a world already starting to disintegrate in the late 19th and early 20th century as new immigrants poured into New York and "new money" was being made in industry and manufacturing. But it was the world Wharton struggled with and wrote about with the satiric wit of an insider who had found a way to be free.

The Compensations of Wealth Wharton was educated at home by governesses and spent her youth as expected, traveling with her parents to Europe and dutifully attending the lavish balls and dinners during New York's social season. Her happiest times, however, were spent in her father's large library, reading and writing. Her cold, domineering mother thwarted the young Edith's literary ambitions by limiting her supply of paper and forcing her to marry a rich banker 12 years her senior. Depressed by her empty marriage and frivolous social life, Wharton used her characteristic moral strength and imaginative powers to break out. She had her own country estate built in Lenox, Massachusetts, where she could associate with people who shared her interests in art and literature. She also escaped to Europe each winter, where she cultivated friendships with famous artists and writers, such as her mentor, rival, and long-time friend, Henry James. Ultimately, she divorced her husband and moved permanently to France, living alternately outside Paris and on the Riviera.

Fame and Fulfillment? The novel that brought Wharton her first great success was *The House of Mirth* (1905), the story of a young woman crushed by the ranks of old New York when she tries to live by her own moral standards. Many of Wharton's other novels and stories sympathetically portray individuals who try but fail to find happiness in unconventional ways. *Ethan Frome* (1911), perhaps her best-known novel, depicts a doomed pair of lovers in a poor farming community. Wharton was the most celebrated American woman writer of her time but had a rather skeptical view of personal fulfillment. "If only we'd stop trying to be happy," she once said, "we could have a pretty good time."

Author Online THINK central

Go to thinkcentral.com. KEYWORD: HML11-820

TEXT ANALYSIS: CHARACTER DEVELOPMENT

Sometimes writers develop characters by revealing directly what characters think or feel. At other times, writers tell you indirectly about the character's thoughts and feelings by describing how the character acts, speaks, and reacts. Often, though, writers use both methods to develop their characters.

In "April Showers," the writer describes some of Theodora's thoughts and feelings, but much of her character is revealed through her actions. As you read, analyze Theodora's actions and ask yourself what they say about her.

READING SKILL: MAKE INFERENCES ABOUT CHARACTERS

Writers don't reveal everything about their characters directly. Instead, they expect readers to **make inferences,** or logical assumptions, about characters based on how those characters think and behave. Inferences must be supported by evidence from the text. As you read, jot down revealing actions and dialogue, as well as the inferences you draw from them.

Evidence from the Text	*My Inferences*
"Lingeringly, tenderly she gathered up the pages of her novel . . . and tied them with the blue satin ribbon. . . . She had meant to wear the ribbon with her new dotted muslin on Sundays, but this was putting it to a nobler use. She bound it round her manuscript, tying the ends in a pretty bow."	*Theodora cares more abut her novel than she does about her clothes. But she's also dressing up the novel like a doll, not just sending it out, as a serious, more experienced writer would do.*

VOCABULARY IN CONTEXT

Wharton uses these words in her story about a writer waiting for a lucky break. Choose the word that completes each phrase.

WORD LIST			
	admonitory	harassing	predecessor
	commiseration	impending	retrospective
	dastardly	interrogation	

1. wrote stories of evil villains and their _____ deeds
2. ignored _____ advice that success doesn't come overnight
3. modeled herself after her famous _____
4. sent impatient letters _____ those reviewing her work
5. feared _____ failure when no one responded

Complete the activities in your **Reader/Writer Notebook.**

What is your DREAM JOB?

You've probably answered the question "What do you want to be when you grow up?" more than a few times. But take a minute to think about your ultimate ambition. What is it about your dream job that's so appealing? Money? Fame? The thrill of doing something you love? The main character in this story dreams of becoming a writer, but does she have what it takes?

QUICKWRITE Imagine that you're filling out an application for your dream job (even if your chosen job—be it rock star or international soccer sensation—isn't one you'd typically fill out an application to get). What skills or traits make you the perfect candidate for the job? Why do you want it? What are you willing to do to get it?

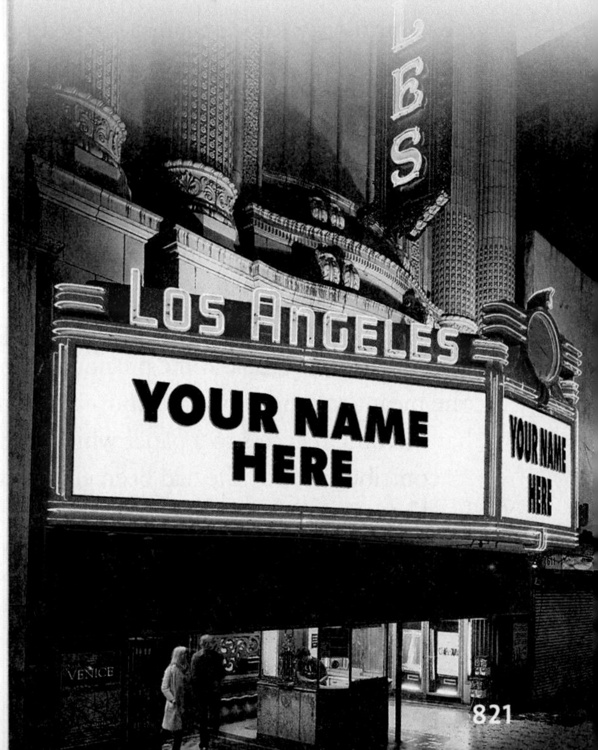

April Showers

EDITH WHARTON

BACKGROUND By the turn of the 20th century, popular magazines—*Scribner's, Harper's, Century,* the *Atlantic Monthly,* and *Ladies' Home Journal*—paid good money to publish short stories, essays, and also longer works in serial form as, say, several chapters per issue. Edith Wharton first published her stories in magazines and serialized her Pulitzer Prize–winning novel, *The Age of Innocence,* as well as her autobiography. Such a publishing bonanza was great encouragement for writers of varying degrees of talent.

Analyze Visuals ▶ Describe the **mood** suggested in this painting. Which is more responsible for conveying the mood, the subject's pose and expression or the artist's use of light and shadow? Explain your choice.

"But Guy's heart slept under the violets on Muriel's grave."

It was a beautiful ending; Theodora had seen girls cry over last chapters that weren't half as pathetic. She laid her pen aside and read the words over, letting her voice linger on the fall of the sentence; then, drawing a deep breath, she wrote across the foot of the page the name by which she had decided to become known in literature—Gladys Glyn. **A**

Downstairs the library clock struck two. Its muffled thump sounded like an **admonitory** knock against her bedroom floor. Two o' clock! and she had promised her mother to be up early enough to see that the buttons were sewn on Johnny's reefer, and that Kate had her cod-liver oil[1] before starting for school!

Lingeringly, tenderly she gathered up the pages of her novel—there were five hundred of them—and tied them with the blue satin ribbon that her Aunt Julia had given her. She had meant to wear the ribbon with her new dotted muslin on Sundays, but this was putting it to a nobler use. She bound it round her manuscript, tying the ends in a pretty bow. Theodora was clever at making bows, and could have trimmed hats beautifully, had not all her spare moments been given to literature. Then, with a last look at the precious pages, she sealed and addressed the package. She meant to send it off next morning to the *Home Circle*.[2] She knew it would be hard to obtain access to a paper which numbered so many popular authors among its contributors, but she had been encouraged to make the venture by something her Uncle James had said the last time he had come down from Boston.

A CHARACTER DEVELOPMENT
Wharton uses **third-person limited point of view** for this story, focusing on Theodora and her thoughts and feelings. In lines 1–6, what does Theodora think of the novel she has finished, and what do her thoughts reveal about her character?

admonitory
(ăd-mŏn′ĭ-tôr′ē) *adj.* warning

1. **cod-liver oil:** a foul-tasting liquid once commonly taken as a source of vitamins A and D.
2. ***Home Circle:*** a magazine popular in the late 19th and early 20th centuries.

Girl Reading (1909), Edmund Charles Tarbell. Oil on canvas, 32 1/4″ × 28 1/2″. The Hayden Collection, Charles Henry Hayden Fund 09.209. © Museum of Fine Arts, Boston.

He had been telling his brother, Doctor Dace, about his new house out at Brookline.[3] Uncle James was prosperous, and was always moving into new houses with more "modern improvements." Hygiene was his passion, and he migrated in the wake of sanitary plumbing.

"The bathrooms alone are worth the money," he was saying, cheerfully, "although it *is* a big rent. But then, when a man's got no children to save up for—" he glanced compassionately round Doctor Dace's crowded table "—and it *is* something to be in a neighborhood where the drainage is A-one. That's what I was telling our neighbor. Who do you suppose she is, by the way?" He smiled at Theodora. "I rather think that young lady knows all about her. Ever heard of Kathleen Kyd?"

Kathleen Kyd! The famous "society novelist," the creator of more "favorite heroines" than all her **predecessors** put together had ever turned out, the author of *Fashion and Passion, An American Duchess, Rhona's Revolt*. Was there any intelligent girl from Maine to California whose heart would not have beat faster at the mention of that name? **B**

predecessor (prĕd'ĭ-sĕs'ər) *n.* a person who precedes or comes before

B CHARACTER DEVELOPMENT
Reread lines 22–37. What does the dialogue reveal about Dr. Dace and Uncle James? What does third-person limited point of view reveal about Theodora? How does she differ from her father and uncle? Support your answer with evidence from these lines.

"Why, yes," Uncle James was saying, "Kathleen Kyd lives next door. Frances G. Wollop is her real name, and her husband's a dentist. She's a very pleasant, sociable kind of woman; you'd never think she was a writer. Ever hear how she began to write? She told me the whole story. It seems she was a saleswoman in a store, working on starvation wages, with a mother and a consumptive[4] sister to support. Well, she wrote a story one day, just for fun, and sent it to the *Home Circle*. They'd never heard of her, of course, and she never expected to hear from them. She did, though. They took the story and passed their plate for more. She became a regular contributor and eventually was known all over the country. Now she tells me her books bring her in about ten thousand a year. Rather more than you and I can boast of, eh, John? Well, I hope *this* household doesn't contribute to her support." He glanced sharply at Theodora. "I don't believe in feeding youngsters on sentimental trash; it's like sewer gas—doesn't smell bad, and infects the system without your knowing it." **C**

C MAKE INFERENCES
Why does Uncle James distinguish between "pleasant, sociable" women and female writers? Explain what you can infer about his character from these lines.

Theodora listened breathlessly. Kathleen Kyd's first story had been accepted by the *Home Circle,* and they had asked for more! Why should Gladys Glyn be less fortunate? Theodora had done a great deal of novel reading—far more than her parents were aware of—and felt herself competent to pronounce upon the quality of her own work. She was almost sure that "April Showers" was a remarkable book. If it lacked Kathleen Kyd's lightness of touch, it had an emotional intensity never achieved by that brilliant writer. Theodora did not care to amuse her readers; she left that to more frivolous talents. Her aim was to stir the depths of human nature, and she felt she had succeeded. It was a great thing for a girl to be able to feel that about her first novel. Theodora was only seventeen; and she remembered, with a touch of **retrospective** compassion, that George Eliot[5] had not become famous till she was nearly forty.

retrospective (rĕt'rə-spĕk'tĭv) *adj.* looking back into the past

3. **Brookline:** a town in Massachusetts, just west of Boston.
4. **consumptive:** having consumption, or tuberculosis.
5. **George Eliot:** the pseudonym of the great 19th-century English novelist Mary Ann Evans.

No, there was no doubt about the merit of "April Showers." But would not an inferior work have had a better chance of success? Theodora recalled the early struggles of famous authors, the notorious antagonism of publishers and editors to any new writer of exceptional promise. Would it not be wiser to write the book down to the average reader's level, reserving for some later work the great "effects" into which she had thrown all the fever of her imagination? The thought was sacrilege! Never would she lay hands on the sacred structure she had reared; never would she resort to the inartistic expedient of modifying her work to suit the popular taste. Better obscure failure than a vulgar triumph. The great authors never stooped to such concessions, and Theodora felt herself included in their ranks by the firmness with which she rejected all thought of conciliating an unappreciative public. The manuscript should be sent as it was. **D**

She woke with a start and a heavy sense of apprehension. The *Home Circle* had refused "April Showers"! No, that couldn't be it; there lay the precious manuscript, waiting to be posted. What was it, then? Ah, that ominous thump below stairs—nine o'clock striking! It was Johnny's buttons!

She sprang out of bed in dismay. She had been so determined not to disappoint her mother about Johnny's buttons! Mrs. Dace, helpless from chronic rheumatism, had to entrust the care of the household to her eldest daughter; and Theodora honestly meant to see that Johnny had his full complement of buttons, and that Kate and Bertha went to school tidy. Unfortunately, the writing of a great novel leaves little time or memory for the lesser obligations of life, and Theodora usually found that her good intentions matured too late for practical results.

Her contrition was softened by the thought that literary success would enable her to make up for all the little negligences of which she was guilty. She meant to spend all her money on her family; and already she had visions of a wheeled chair for her mother, a fresh wallpaper for the doctor's shabby office, bicycles for the girls, and Johnny's establishment at a boarding school where sewing on his buttons would be included in the curriculum. If her parents could have guessed her intentions, they would not have found fault with her as they did; and Doctor Dace, on this particular morning, would not have looked up to say, with his fagged, ironical air:

"I suppose you didn't get home from the ball till morning?"

Theodora's sense of being in the right enabled her to take the thrust with a dignity that would have awed the unfeeling parent of fiction.

"I'm sorry to be late, father," she said.

Doctor Dace, who could never be counted on to behave like a father in a book, shrugged his shoulders impatiently.

"Your sentiments do you credit, but they haven't kept your mother's breakfast warm." **E**

"Hasn't mother's tray gone up yet?"

"Who was to take it, I should like to know? The girls came down so late that

D MAKE INFERENCES
Consider Theodora's sympathy for George Eliot in lines 61–63 and her opinion of the "average reader." What inferences can you make about Theodora's character based on her thoughts about her own work?

E MAKE INFERENCES
Theodora muses repeatedly that Dr. Dace does not act as a father in a work of fiction would. What does she mean by this?

I had to hustle them off before they'd finished breakfast, and Johnny's hands were so dirty that I sent him back to his room to make himself decent. It's a pretty thing for the doctor's children to be the dirtiest little savages in Norton!"

Theodora had hastily prepared her mother's tray, leaving her own breakfast untouched. As she entered the room upstairs, Mrs. Dace's patient face turned to her with a smile much harder to bear than her father's reproaches.

"Mother, I'm *so* sorry—"

"No matter, dear. I suppose Johnny's buttons kept you. I can't think what that boy does to his clothes!"

Theodora sat the tray down without speaking. It was impossible to own to having forgotten Johnny's buttons without revealing the cause of her forgetfulness. For a few weeks longer she must bear to be misunderstood; then—ah, then if her novel were accepted, how gladly would she forget and forgive! But what if it were refused? She turned aside to hide the dismay that flushed her face. Well, then she would admit the truth—she would ask her parents' pardon, and settle down without a murmur to an obscure existence of mending and combing.

She had said to herself that after the manuscript had been sent, she would have time to look after the children and catch up with the mending; but she had reckoned without the postman. He came three times a day; for an hour before each ring she was too excited to do anything but wonder if he would bring an answer this time, and for an hour afterward she moved about in a leaden stupor of disappointment. The children had never been so trying. They seemed to be always coming to pieces, like cheap furniture; one would have supposed they had been put together with bad glue. Mrs. Dace worried herself ill over Johnny's tatters, Bertha's bad marks at school, and Kate's open abstention from cod-liver oil; and Doctor Dace, coming back late from a long round of visits to a fireless office with a smoky lamp, called out furiously to know if Theodora would kindly come down and remove the "East, West, home's best" that hung above the empty grate.

In the midst of it all, Miss Sophy Brill called. It was very kind of her to come, for she was the busiest woman in Norton. She made it her duty to look after other people's affairs, and there was not a house in town but had the benefit of her personal supervision. She generally came when things were going wrong, and the sight of her bonnet on the doorstep was a surer sign of calamity than a crepe bow on the bell.[6] After she left, Mrs. Dace looked very sad, and the doctor punished Johnny for warbling down the entry:

"Miss Sophy Brill
Is a bitter pill!"

while Theodora, locking herself in her room, resolved with tears that she would never write another novel. F

The week was a long nightmare. Theodora could neither eat nor sleep. She was up early enough, but instead of looking after the children and seeing that breakfast

Language Coach

Word Definitions
"Reckoned without" (line 124) means "hadn't taken into consideration." Read lines 122–127. How has Theodora's plan for the day been disrupted by the postman?

F **CHARACTER DEVELOPMENT**
What kind of person is Miss Brill? Why does her visit have such a dramatic effect on Theodora? Cite evidence from the story to support your response.

6. **crepe bow on the bell:** a signal that someone had died. Clothing made from black crepe (a silk material) used to be worn by those in mourning.

was ready, she wandered down the road to meet the postman, and came back wan and empty-handed, oblivious of her morning duties. She had no idea how long the suspense would last; but she didn't see how authors could live if they were kept waiting more than a week.

Then suddenly, one afternoon—she never quite knew how or when it happened—she found herself with a *Home Circle* envelope in her hands, and her dazzled eyes flashing over a wild dance of words that wouldn't settle down and make sense.

"Dear Madam:" (They called her *Madam!* And then; yes, the words were beginning to fall into line now.) "Your novel, 'April Showers,' has been received, and we are glad to accept it on the usual terms. A serial on which we were counting for immediate publication has been delayed by the author's illness, and the first chapters of 'April Showers' will therefore appear in our midsummer number. Thanking you for favoring us with your manuscript, we remain," and so forth.

Theodora found herself in the wood beyond the schoolhouse. She was kneeling on the ground, brushing aside the dead leaves and pressing her lips to the little bursting green things that pushed up eager tips through last year's decay. It was spring—spring! Everything was crowding toward the light and in her own heart hundreds of germinating hopes had burst into sudden leaf. She wondered if the thrust of those little green fingers hurt the surface of the earth as her springing raptures hurt—yes, actually hurt!—her hot, constricted breast! She looked up through interlacing boughs at a tender, opaque blue sky full of the coming of a milky moon. She seemed enveloped in an atmosphere of loving comprehension. The brown earth throbbed with her joy, the treetops trembled with it, and a sudden star broke through the branches like an audible "I know!"

COMMON CORE RL 4, L 5b

Language Coach

Connotation The images or feelings you connect to a word add a finer shade of meaning, called **connotation.** Read lines 161–171. What connotations do the words *bursting, springing,* and *enveloped* have in your mind? How do they reflect Theodora's feelings?

Theodora, on the whole, behaved very well. Her mother cried, her father whistled and said he supposed he must put up with grounds in his coffee now, and be thankful if he ever got a hot meal again; while the children took the most deafening and **harassing** advantage of what seemed a sudden suspension of the laws of nature.

harassing (hə-răs′ĭng) *adj.* persistently annoying **harass** *v.*

Within a week everybody in Norton knew that Theodora had written a novel, and that it was coming out in the *Home Circle.* On Sundays, when she walked up the aisle, her friends dropped their prayer books and the soprano sang false in her excitement. Girls with more pin money than Theodora had ever dreamed of copied her hats and imitated her way of speaking. The local paper asked her for a poem; her old school teachers stopped to shake hands and grew shy over their congratulations; and Miss Sophy Brill came to call. She had put on her Sunday bonnet and her manner was almost abject. She ventured, very timidly, to ask her young friend how she wrote, whether it "just came to her," and if she had found that the kind of pen she used made any difference; and wound up by begging Theodora to write a sentiment in her album.

Even Uncle James came down from Boston to talk the wonder over. He called Theodora a "sly baggage," and proposed that she should give him her earnings to invest in a new patent grease-trap company. From what Kathleen Kyd had told him, he thought Theodora would probably get a thousand dollars for her story. He concluded by suggesting that she should base her next romance on the subject of sanitation, making the heroine nearly die of sewer gas poisoning because her parents won't listen to the handsome young doctor next door, when he warns them that their plumbing is out of order. That was a subject that would interest everybody, and do a lot more good than the sentimental trash most women wrote.

At last the great day came. Theodora had left an order with the bookseller for the midsummer number of the *Home Circle* and before the shop was open she was waiting on the sidewalk. She clutched the precious paper and ran home without opening it. Her excitement was almost more than she could bear. Not heeding her father's call to breakfast, she rushed upstairs and locked herself in her room. Her hands trembled so that she could hardly turn the pages. At last—yes, there it was: "April Showers."

The paper dropped from her hands. What name had she read beneath the title? Had her emotion blinded her?

"April Showers, by *Kathleen Kyd.*"

Kathleen Kyd! Oh, cruel misprint! Oh, **dastardly** typographer! Through tears of rage and disappointment Theodora looked again; yes, there was no mistaking the hateful name. Her glance ran on. She found herself reading a first paragraph

dastardly (dăs'tərd-lē) *adj.* characterized by underhandedness or treachery

In the Station Waiting Room, Boston (1915), Edmund Charles Tarbell. Oil on canvas, 24 3/8" × 32". Gift of Dr. Joseph R. Fazzano. © Crocker Art Museum, Sacramento, California.

that she had never seen before. She read farther. All was strange. The horrible truth burst upon her: *It was not her story!*

She never knew how she got back to the station. She struggled through the crowd on the platform, and a gold-banded arm pushed her into the train just starting for Norton. It would be dark when she reached home; but that didn't matter—nothing mattered now. She sank into her seat, closing her eyes in the vain attempt to shut out the vision of the last few hours; but minute by minute memory forced her to relive it; she felt like a rebellious school child dragged forth to repeat the same detested "piece."

Although she did not know Boston well, she had made her way easily enough to the *Home Circle* building; at least, she supposed she had, since she remembered nothing till she found herself ascending the editorial stairs as easily as one does incredible things in dreams. She must have walked very fast, for her heart was beating furiously, and she had barely breath to whisper the editor's name to a young man who looked out at her from a glass case, like a zoological specimen. The young man led her past other glass cases containing similar specimens to an inner enclosure which seemed filled by an enormous presence. Theodora felt herself enveloped in the presence, submerged by it, gasping for air as she sank under its rising surges.

Gradually fragments of speech floated to the surface. "'April Showers?' Mrs. Kyd's new serial? *Your* manuscript, you say? You have a letter from me? The name, please? Evidently some unfortunate misunderstanding. One moment." And then a bell ringing, a zoological specimen ordered to unlock a safe, her name asked for again, the manuscript, her own precious manuscript, tied with Aunt Julia's ribbon, laid on the table before her, and her outcries, her protests, her **interrogations,** drowned in a flood of bland apology: "An unfortunate accident—Mrs. Kyd's manuscript received the same day—extraordinary coincidence in the choice of a title—duplicate answers sent by mistake—Miss Dace's novel hardly suited to their purpose—should of course have been returned—regrettable oversight—accidents would happen—sure she understood."

The voice went on, like the steady pressure of a surgeon's hand on a shrieking nerve. When it stopped she was in the street. A cab nearly ran her down, and a car bell jangled furiously in her ears. She clutched her manuscript, carrying it tenderly through the crowd, like a live thing that had been hurt. She could not bear to look at its soiled edges and the ink stain on Aunt Julia's ribbon.

The train stopped with a jerk and she opened her eyes. It was dark, and by the windy flare of gas on the platform she saw the Norton passengers getting out. She stood up stiffly and followed them. A warm wind blew into her face the fragrance of the summer woods, and she remembered how, two months earlier, she had knelt among the dead leaves, pressing her lips to the first shoots of green. Then for the first time she thought of home. She had fled away in the morning without a word, and her heart sank at the thought of her mother's fears. And her father—how angry he would be! She bent her head under the coming storm of his derision.

Language Coach

Fixed Expressions The term ***fixed expression*** refers to the normal combination of words—the ways they are often used. "Vain attempt" (line 215) means an "unsuccessful effort." ("Futile attempt" and "botched attempt" are similar expressions.) Use one of these expressions in a sentence.

interrogation (ĭn-tĕr′ə-gā′shən) *n.* a questioning

The night was cloudy, and as she stepped into the darkness beyond the station a hand was slipped in hers. She stood still, too weary to feel frightened, and a voice said, quietly:

"Don't walk so fast, child. You look tired."

"Father!" Her hand dropped from his, but he recaptured it and drew it through his arm. When she found voice, it was to whisper, "You were at the station?"

"It's such a good night I thought I'd stroll down and meet you."

Her arm trembled against his. She could not see his face in the dimness, but the light of his cigar looked down on her like a friendly eye, and she took courage to falter out: "Then you knew—"

"That you'd gone to Boston? Well, I rather thought you had."

They walked on slowly, and presently he added, "You see, you left the *Home Circle* lying in your room."

How she blessed the darkness and the muffled sky! She could not have borne the scrutiny of the tiniest star.

"Then mother wasn't very much frightened?"

"Why, no, she didn't appear to be. She's been busy all day over some toggery of Bertha's."

Theodora choked. "Father, I'll—" She groped for words, but they eluded her. "I'll do things—differently; I haven't meant—" Suddenly she heard herself bursting out: "It was all a mistake, you know—about my story. They didn't want it; they won't have it!" and she shrank back involuntarily from his **impending** mirth.

She felt the pressure of his arm, but he didn't speak, and she figured his mute hilarity. They moved on in silence. Presently he said:

"It hurts a bit just at first, doesn't it?"

"O father!"

He stood still, and the gleam of his cigar showed a face of unexpected participation.

"You see I've been through it myself."

"You, father? You?"

"Why, yes. Didn't I ever tell you? I wrote a novel once. I was just out of college, and didn't want to be a doctor. No; I wanted to be a genius, so I wrote a novel."

The doctor paused, and Theodora clung to him in a mute passion of **commiseration.** It was as if a drowning creature caught a live hand through the murderous fury of the waves.

"Father—O father!"

"It took me a year—a whole year's hard work; and when I'd finished it the public wouldn't have it, either; not at any price and that's why I came down to meet you, because I remembered my walk home." G

impending (ĭm-pĕn'dĭng) *adj.* to be about to occur **impend** *v.*

commiseration (kə-mĭz'ə-rā'shən) *n.* a feeling of sympathy or pity

G CHARACTER DEVELOPMENT
Reread lines 281–291. What does the dialogue reveal about Theodora's father? What kind of lesson does Theodora learn here? Explain your answer.

Comprehension

1. **Summarize** Describe Theodora's family situation and responsibilities.
2. **Recall** What does Theodora plan to do with the money she expects to earn?
3. **Clarify** How does the *Home Circle* editor explain the mix-up?
4. **Clarify** What does Theodora's father reveal to her at the end of the story?

COMMON CORE

RL 1 Cite evidence to support inferences drawn from the text. **RL 3** Analyze the impact of the author's choices regarding how to develop and relate elements of a story. **RL 6** Analyze a case in which grasping point of view requires distinguishing what is directly stated in a text from what is really meant.

Text Analysis

5. **Analyze Character Development** Reread lines 52–75. What clues does Wharton provide in these lines to indicate that Theodora might not be the "great author" she thinks herself to be? Cite specific evidence from these lines to support your answer.
6. **Make Inferences About Characters** Review the inferences you recorded as you read, and recall Theodora's disappointment that her father does not act the way she thinks the parent in a novel would. How might their relationship change as a result of the disastrous "April Showers" incident?
7. **Interpret Satire** A **satire** ridicules ideas and behavior to expose human faults or weakness. Satire is sometimes hard to detect, but a writer's tone is often an indication—reading a satire can feel as though the author were winking at you while telling the story. Explain what characters and behavior Wharton satirizes in this story by filling out a chart like the one shown.

Character	*Satirized for . . .*	*Evidence in Story*
Uncle James	*being crude and materialistic*	• *talks obsessively about indoor plumbing and "sewer gas" at the dinner table (lines 24–51)* • *brags about his money and even asks Theodora to invest the money from her novel in one of his schemes (lines 26–29, 188–196)*

Text Criticism

8. **Historical Context** A contemporary critic commented, "When we look beneath the high surface gloss of Wharton's world, we see a marketplace, pure and simple. Hers is an almost purely economic conception of life." What insights does this story give you into the economic position of women at the turn of the 20th century? What kinds of work were available to them, and at what kinds of wages? Is it surprising that an educated young woman would try to make money by writing? Support your answer with evidence.

What is your DREAM JOB?

In "April Showers," Theodora's ambition is to write a novel. Do you think there are positive as well as negative motivations for choosing a career? Explain your answer.

Vocabulary in Context

▲ VOCABULARY PRACTICE

Show that you understand the vocabulary words by answering these questions.

1. Which is a **dastardly** deed, betraying a friend or voting in an election?
2. If an investigation is **impending,** is it over or about to happen?
3. Would an artist have a **retrospective** exhibit early or late in his or her career?
4. What is the intent of a **harassing** letter, to schedule an appointment or to irritate the recipient into action?
5. If I make an **admonitory** statement, do I expect you to laugh or take it seriously?
6. Is an **interrogation** intended to get information or rehearse a performance?
7. Which would be a gesture of **commiseration,** sending flowers or watching a lengthy movie?
8. Who would be your mother's **predecessor** in life, you or your grandmother?

WORD LIST
admonitory
commiseration
dastardly
harassing
impending
interrogation
predecessor
retrospective

ACADEMIC VOCABULARY IN SPEAKING

• apparent • confine • expose • focus • perceive

The reason for Theodora's lack of interest in daily affairs becomes **apparent** when her family realizes that she has written a novel and sent it off to be published. In a small group, discuss your thoughts about Theodora's actions and whether you agree or disagree with her excuses. Use at least three Academic Vocabulary words in your discussion.

VOCABULARY STRATEGY: THE LATIN ROOT *rog*

The word root *rog,* which has its origin in Latin, means "ask," "ask for," or "propose." *Rog* is found in a number of English words, including the vocabulary word *interrogation.* To understand words built around *rog,* use your knowledge of the Latin origin and meaning of the root and affixes as well as context clues.

COMMON CORE

L 4b Identify and correctly use patterns of word changes that indicate different meanings or parts of speech. **L 6** Acquire and use accurately general academic words and phrases.

PRACTICE Apply what you know about the Latin root *rog* and the other word parts to help you understand the words in the web. Then choose the word that best completes each sentence. If necessary, consult a dictionary.

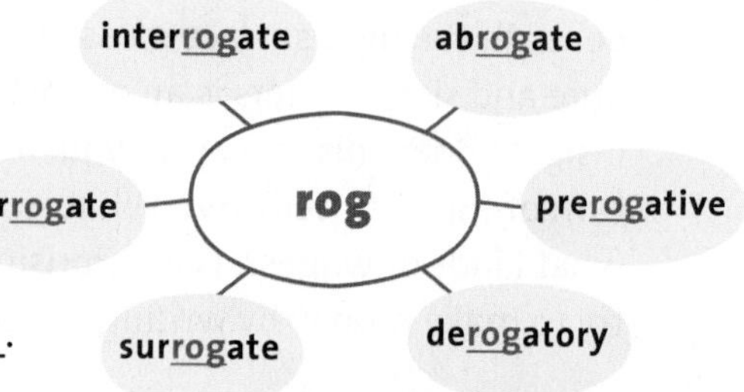

1. It is the race winner's _____ to wear the yellow jersey.
2. The official could not attend the ceremony, so he sent a(n) _____.
3. They feared that the new judge would _____ to herself powers that belonged to the legislature.
4. Jake tends to make _____ remarks about people he does not like.
5. People _____ their responsibility when they do not care for their pets.

Women's Changing Roles

A woman's role in American society was rigidly defined in the late 19th and early 20th centuries. Women of this period could not vote, few owned businesses, and few gained a higher education. Yet women were increasingly agitating for change in both big and small ways. The writers in this section (pages 782–832) gave voice to the struggles of women attempting to fashion a new role for themselves and break free from restricting social expectations. As critic Richard Gray noted, "Humanity, if it is repressed, will always have its revenge."

Writing to Compare

Think about how women's roles have changed since the times of Kate Chopin and Edith Wharton. Using the stories you have just read and your knowledge of American society today, write a comparison of women's roles then and now.

Consider

- what each text tells you about society's expectations for women at that time
- how things have or have not changed since the days these writers were working
- what details from the texts best illustrate women's roles in the past
- what examples from today best illustrate women's roles now

Extension

SPEAKING & LISTENING

With a partner, **role-play** a conversation between two of the main characters from this section of the book. You will need to prepare by working together to select characters, review the stories, and draft your character's words before your first rehearsal. Discuss your family life, your work, your frustrations, and so on. Alternatively, role-play two of the main characters' husbands or fathers discussing the women in their lives. Adapt your speech to suit the characters' language conventions.

COMMON CORE

W 2 Write informative/explanatory texts to examine and convey complex ideas, concepts, and information clearly and accurately through the effective selection and analysis of content. **SL 1a–b** Draw on preparation by referring to evidence from texts; work with peers to set clear goals and deadlines and establish individual roles as needed. **SL 6** Adapt speech to a variety of contexts and tasks.

Writing Workshop

INFORMATIVE TEXT

Analytical Essay

As you have seen in this unit, literature often reveals more than just a series of events. It can mirror the beliefs and ideas of a specific region, convey thoughts about cultural or societal change, or explore philosophical questions. In this workshop, you will write an analytical essay to examine how an author's works reflect broader ideas and movements.

Complete the workshop activities in your **Reader/Writer Notebook.**

WRITE WITH A PURPOSE

WRITING TASK

Write an **analytical essay** that examines a literary movement or the broader ideas reflected in an author's various works. Keep your audience in mind as you gather evidence and details to support your controlling idea.

Idea Starters

- a literary movement associated with a specific author
- beliefs of a specific culture or historical period
- social change as presented in an author's works

THE ESSENTIALS

Here are some common purposes, audiences, and formats for writing an analytical essay.

PURPOSES	AUDIENCES	FORMATS
• to analyze how an author's works reflect literary movements or cultural ideas • to convey your understanding of an author's works	• classmates and teacher • other students • Web users	• essay for class • Web site • classroom bulletin board display • class newspaper

COMMON CORE TRAITS

1. DEVELOPMENT OF IDEAS

- includes an **introduction** that clearly identifies the **topic** and **controlling idea**
- uses **significant and relevant evidence**—facts, extended definitions, concrete details, and quotations—to develop the topic
- offers a **concluding section** that supports the information

2. ORGANIZATION OF IDEAS

- **organizes** ideas and evidence in a **logical way**
- uses **transitions** to create **cohesion** and **clarify relationships** among ideas

3. LANGUAGE FACILITY AND CONVENTIONS

- maintains a **formal style** and **objective tone**
- uses **precise language, domain-specific vocabulary,** and **literary techniques**
- aligns **subject-verb agreement**
- employs correct **grammar, mechanics,** and **spelling**

Go to thinkcentral.com.
KEYWORD: HML11N-834

W 2a–f Write informative texts to convey complex ideas clearly and accurately. **W 5** Develop writing by planning. **W 7** Conduct short research projects; synthesize multiple sources. **W 8** Gather information from multiple sources.

Planning/Prewriting

Getting Started

CHOOSE A TOPIC

Choose an author whose works reflect an important idea. You might want to explore an author whose work you already know. Conduct a short research project to determine whether the author's writing reflects a particular literary movement or broader idea and to get general information about the author's historical and geographical background. You will need to read several of the author's texts, so choose an author who wrote shorter texts, such as short stories or poems.

Once you have a sense of the author's overall work and impact, narrow your **topic** to a specific idea or movement. Make sure that your focus is broad enough for a full-length essay.

WHAT DOES IT LOOK LIKE?

Questions and answers

What short story or poem from this book or elsewhere left a lasting impression on me? **Jack London's "The Law of Life"**

Is it possible that the author's works might reflect a literary movement or a cultural idea? **Yes, it is possible. "The Law of Life" reflects the literary movement called naturalism, so maybe London's other works reflect this movement as well.**

Has the author written other short stories or poems that I can read and analyze for my essay? **Yes, Jack London has written other short stories that I can read and analyze for my essay.**

Will I be able to find a variety of sources about this author? **Yes, Jack London is a famous writer.**

THINK ABOUT AUDIENCE AND PURPOSE

When planning an analytical essay, consider your **purpose** for writing—to analyze a topic and convey your insights. Also, consider your **audience,** in this case your teacher and classmates. When referring to literary texts in your essay, assume that your audience has not read them. Be sure to provide readers with adequate **context** and background information about literary texts and historical time periods.

Consider **domain-specific vocabulary,** such as literary terms, that may not be understood by your audience. You might explain unfamiliar topics by using a comparison. For example, you could use a **metaphor, simile,** or **analogy** to compare the ideas of a literary movement to a subject that is more familiar to the audience.

ASK YOURSELF:

- What background information will my audience need in order to understand my analysis?
- What story or poem details would a reader need in order to understand my reference to a particular literary text?
- Have I equipped an uninformed reader with everything he or she needs to understand my analysis?

Planning/Prewriting *continued*

Getting Started

GATHER AND REVIEW SOURCES

As you gather information from multiple sources, evaluate their reliability, relevance, and authority. Sources should contain accurate information and credible ideas and should come from reputable publishers. Evaluate Internet sources carefully to see who created the site and where the author found the information. Use sources that convey a variety of perspectives on the topic.

For this essay, begin by collecting sources about the author's historical time period and the literary movements that were prevalent during that time period. Then, collect several of the author's literary texts. As you read, take notes about relevant facts or concrete details that reflect a literary movement or broader idea. You will use the notes to **synthesize**, or make connections between, the information you gather from these authoritative sources.

TIPS

- For online sources offering authoritative literary scholarship, start with addresses that end in *.edu*, which indicates that the site is affiliated with a college or university. If you use sources with other endings, such as *.org* or *.com*, confirm that the site was created by a reliable organization.
- When using information from the Web sites of educational institutions (*.edu* Web addresses), be sure that the information comes from a source that is an authority on the author or literary movement, rather than from a student paper.
- When researching information about current issues, look for the most current sources. For some topics, such as those involving historical time periods, older sources—especially primary sources—may be more relevant.

DRAFT AND SUPPORT YOUR CONTROLLING IDEA

Review your notes, and write a sentence or two summarizing the topic of your essay. This is your **controlling idea,** or thesis statement. Next, use your notes to develop main points that support your controlling idea. Use the **evidence** that you have drawn from the literary and informative texts to support your main points.

WHAT DOES IT LOOK LIKE?

Controlling Idea: *London's works promote the naturalistic view in two distinct ways, showing how both harsh natural forces and human society can defeat human will.*

First Main Point: *In "The Law of Life," he expresses a naturalistic view by showing how a man who resigns himself to death by brutal cold is defeated by nature's unexpected cruelty.*

PEER REVIEW Share your controlling idea, main points, and evidence with a partner. Ask whether the evidence sufficiently supports the main points and controlling idea. If the evidence is not sufficient, revise or rework your plan to provide more support for your main points.

After you have gathered and reviewed sources, draft a controlling idea in your *Reader/Writer Notebook.* Then, develop main points and decide which evidence you should use to support your main points and controlling idea.

W 4 Produce clear and coherent writing appropriate to task, purpose, and audience. **W 9** Draw evidence from texts to support analysis. **L 3** Apply knowledge of language to make effective choices for meaning.

Drafting

The following chart shows how to organize your draft to create an effective analytical essay.

Organizing Your Analytical Essay

INTRODUCTION

- Draw the reader into your analysis by including a **memorable quotation** or **interesting detail.**
- Introduce your **topic**, state your **controlling idea**, and identify the author(s) on whom you will focus.

BODY

- Organize the information in your essay so that each idea builds on the one that precedes it. You may choose **comparison-contrast** (similarities and differences between two ideas), **logical order** (related ideas grouped together), **order of importance** (most to least important ideas or vice versa), or a combination of these.
- Include your main points and **relevant textual evidence** that supports your main points and controlling idea. If necessary, include **parenthetical citations**—sources enclosed in parentheses.
- Establish and maintain a **formal style** and **objective tone.**
- Provide **context** so that your audience can fully understand your points.
- Use **precise language**, define any **domain-specific vocabulary,** and weave in **metaphors, similes,** or **analogies** to help your audience understand complex ideas.
- Use **varied transitions** to create cohesion and clarify relationships among the main points and textual evidence.

CONCLUDING SECTION

- Restate your controlling idea and main points, noting the **implications,** or significance, of the topic.
- Include a Works Cited list. (See example on page 840.)

GRAMMAR IN CONTEXT: TEXTUAL EVIDENCE

You must include **sufficient textual evidence**, such as relevant facts, concrete details, extended definitions, quotations, paraphrases, and summaries, from your sources to support your main points. A quotation is the actual text from the source. A paraphrase is a restatement of information in one's own words. A summary is a brief retelling of the main ideas of a piece of writing.

Include a citation if you are paraphrasing, stating the author's original ideas, or if you are providing specific, little-known facts. Keep in mind that you do not need to include a citation for general, well-known information. The example below shows one way of directly quoting text.

> *Naturalism blends realism's practical focus with an emerging philosophy known as determinism, which can be described as the belief "that humans have little ability to impose will upon their own destinies" ("The American Novel").*

Using your notes and the information in the chart, write a draft of your essay. Be sure to support your main points with textual evidence.

Revising

When you revise, your goal is to determine whether you have effectively presented your topic to your audience and supported it with relevant evidence. The questions, tips, and strategies in the following chart can help you revise or rewrite where necessary.

ANALYTICAL ESSAY

Ask Yourself	*Tips*	*Revision Strategies*
1. Does the introduction draw the audience into the analysis? Does it introduce the topic and the author and state a clear controlling idea?	▶ **Circle** text that draws the audience into the analysis. **Underline** the topic and the name of the author. **Double underline** the controlling idea.	▶ **Add** a memorable quotation or interesting detail. **Add** a sentence introducing the topic. **Add** the author's name. **Add** a clearer controlling idea.
2. Do main points support the controlling idea and build on one another? Does evidence support each main point?	▶ **Bracket** each main point. **Highlight** evidence that supports each main point.	▶ **Replace** paragraphs or sentences that don't support the controlling idea. **Add** relevant textual evidence to support the main points.
3. Is the essay's organization logical and effective? Are transitions used to clarify relationships among the main points and textual evidence?	▶ **Put a plus sign** next to sentences that help the organization. **Put a minus sign** next to sentences that stray from the organization. **Circle** transitional words and phrases.	▶ **Rearrange** the order of ideas to reflect the desired organization. **Add** appropriate transitions to link related ideas.
4. Do context, precise language, and definitions help the audience understand information?	▶ **Place a box** around context, language, and definitions that help the reader understand information from sources.	▶ **Add** relevant facts, details, precise language, and definitions of domain-specific vocabulary.
5. Do I maintain a formal style and objective tone throughout the analysis?	▶ **Draw a wavy line** under any contractions, casual slang, or informal language.	▶ **Reword** text to avoid slang. **Replace** instances of informal language with precise, formal words.
6. Does the concluding section restate the controlling idea and explain its significance?	▶ **Underline** the sentence or sentences that restate the controlling idea.	▶ **Restate** the controlling idea. **Elaborate** on why it is significant.

PEER REVIEW Working with a classmate, review each other's drafts. Ask about confusing sections and give each other specific, constructive suggestions about how to revise or try a new approach with the essays.

W 2f Provide a concluding section that follows from and supports the information. **W 5** Develop and strengthen writing as needed by revising, editing, rewriting, or trying a new approach, addressing a specific purpose.

ANALYZE A STUDENT DRAFT

Read these excerpts from a student draft, and note the comments on its strengths as well as suggestions for improvement.

London's Naturalistic Expressions

by Omar Bradford, Randall High School

1 Throughout American history, societal beliefs and philosophies have had a strong influence on literary movements. The naturalistic literary movement of the late 19th century and early 20th century was no exception. Commonly recognized as an offshoot of realism, naturalism blends realism's practical focus with an emerging philosophy known as determinism, which can be described as the belief "that humans have little ability to impose will upon their own destinies" ("The American Novel"). One author whose name is synonymous with this naturalistic movement is Jack London. London's works promote the naturalistic view in two distinct ways, showing how both harsh natural forces and human society can defeat human will.

2 The power of nature is a theme that runs rampant through London's writing. London's short story "The Law of Life" displays the naturalistic belief in the inability of human will to triumph over natural forces. The main character contemplates his life and death, eventually relinquishing his will to live with the knowledge that the harsh severity of death is the natural way of things and that he should simply succumb to it.

Omar defines **domain-specific vocabulary** to help his audience understand this concept.

The **controlling idea** summarizes Omar's analysis.

Although Omar explains how the story relates to the controlling idea, he does not provide enough context for the reader.

LEARN HOW **Provide Context** In his second paragraph, Omar discusses how the short story "The Law of Life" expresses naturalism. Omar successfully explains the story's connection with naturalism, but he does not provide enough context for the audience to understand the events of the story. Omar revised the paragraph to provide more context.

OMAR'S REVISION TO PARAGRAPH 2

The story details an older tribesman's last hours. After his people leave him alone in the snow, he ~~The main character~~ contemplates his life and death, eventually relinquishing his will to live with the knowledge that the harsh severity of death is the natural way of things and that he should simply succumb to it.

ANALYZE A STUDENT DRAFT *continued*

3 In contrast, London uses manmade, societal forces to express naturalism in the short story "Li-Wan the Fair." The main character, Li-Wan, is a tribeswoman whose will has been smothered by the people around her. As a child, she dreams of her past. Her tribe discount her dreams, insisting that they are crazy imaginings. Eventually, Li-Wan's beliefs fall in line with the beliefs of the societal forces that surround her. She concurs that the dreams were " 'ill dreams of childhood, shadows of things not real' " (London 461). Then, after she has been taken from her tribe and forced to marry a brutal renegade named Canim, she finally realizes the truth about her dreams. She gains the will to escape her situation, but once again the force of the people around her thwarts her will. Canim, along with two unsympathetic women and a language barrier, force her to remain in her desperate situation. Despite her strong will to escape, societal forces mar Li-Wan's efforts—revealing the story's naturalistic framework.

Omar uses the **transitional phrase** "In contrast" to link ideas between main points and to show that he is using comparison-contrast organization.

4 Whether London expresses naturalism through the power of natural or societal forces, he successfully explores one of the philosophies that was on the minds of many during that time in history.

Omar restates his controlling idea in his concluding section, but he does not discuss the implications, or significance, of the information.

Works Cited

"The American Novel." pbs.org. March 2007. 10 March 2009. <http://www.pbs.org/wnet/americannovel/timeline/naturalism.html>

London, Jack. Jack London: The Call of the Wild, White Fang, The Sea-Wolf, 40 Short Stories. Ed. Paul Horowitz. New York: Chatham River Press, 1983.

LEARN HOW Strengthen Your Concluding Section In his last paragraph, Omar restates his controlling idea effectively, but he does not leave the audience with something to think about. Omar revised the paragraph to explain the significance of his analysis.

OMAR'S REVISION TO PARAGRAPH 4

. . . he successfully explores one of the philosophies that was on the minds of many during that time in history.^ *Through his work and the work of his contemporaries, we can better understand the ideas of those who lived before us and the ways they helped shape modern thought.*

Use the feedback from your peers and teacher, the revision strategies chart, and the two "Learn How" lessons to revise or rework your essay. Evaluate how well you have presented your analysis and supported your controlling idea.

COMMON CORE

W 5 Develop and strengthen writing by editing. L 1 Demonstrate command of standard English grammar and usage. L 2b Spell correctly.

Editing and Publishing

In the editing stage, you proofread your analytical essay to make sure that it is free of grammar, spelling, and punctuation errors. Read your essay slowly and carefully to correct any remaining misspelled words. Careless spelling mistakes make you sound less authoritative to your audience.

GRAMMAR IN CONTEXT: SUBJECT-VERB AGREEMENT

When you edit, check for errors in **subject-verb agreement** throughout your writing. Keep the following guidelines in mind:

- If a compound subject is combined with *and,* it usually requires a plural verb. If a compound subject is combined with *or, nor, neither . . . nor,* or *either . . . or,* the verb agrees with the subject that is closest to it.

Incorrect	Correct
Societal beliefs and philosophies **has** had a strong influence on literary movements.	Societal beliefs and philosophies **have** had a strong influence on literary movements.

- If a prepositional phrase comes between the subject and the verb, be careful not to mistake the object of the preposition for the subject.

Incorrect	Correct
The naturalistic literary movement of the late 19th century and early 20th century **were** no exception.	The naturalistic literary movement of the late 19th century and early 20th century **was** no exception.

As Omar edited his essay, he realized he had used a plural verb with a collective noun that refers to a single group. He changed the verb to give the collective noun a singular sense.

Incorrect	Correct
Her tribe **discount** her dreams . . .	Her tribe **discounts** her dreams . . .

PUBLISH YOUR WRITING

Share your analytical essay with an audience.

- Create a display of your essay and a photo of the author you wrote about.
- Include your essay in a class newspaper that you create with classmates.
- Publish your essay on your school Web site.
- Find a Web site about the author you focused on in your essay. Send an e-mail to the creators of the site, asking if they will publish your analytical essay online.

Proofread your essay to correct any errors. Make sure that you have achieved subject-verb agreement. Then, publish your completed essay for your audience.

Scoring Rubric

Use the rubric below to evaluate your analytical essay from the Writing Workshop or your response to the on-demand task on the next page.

ANALYTICAL ESSAY

SCORE	COMMON CORE TRAITS
6	• **Development** Has an engaging introduction that clearly identifies the controlling idea; is developed thoroughly with significant and relevant evidence; ends powerfully • **Organization** Arranges ideas in an effective, logical order, creating a unified whole; uses varied transitions to create cohesion and link ideas • **Language** Consistently maintains a formal style and objective tone; uses precise language; shows a strong command of conventions
5	• **Development** States a clear controlling idea; develops ideas with relevant evidence; has a strong concluding section • **Organization** Arranges ideas logically; uses transitions to create cohesion and link ideas • **Language** Uses a formal style and objective tone; has few errors in conventions
4	• **Development** States a controlling idea; develops ideas with adequate evidence; provides a satisfactory concluding section • **Organization** Arranges ideas logically, with a few exceptions; needs more transitions to strengthen cohesion • **Language** Mostly uses a formal style; includes some vague language and a few distracting errors in conventions
3	• **Development** States a controlling idea that could be more precise; provides some evidence; has a weak concluding section • **Organization** Has flaws in organization; needs more transitions to link ideas • **Language** Often lapses into an informal style or subjective tone; has several errors
2	• **Development** Has a vague controlling idea; offers mostly irrelevant and insufficient evidence; has a weak concluding section • **Organization** Has major organizational flaws; lacks transitions throughout, with little cohesion • **Language** Uses an inappropriate style and subjective tone; has many errors
1	• **Development** Lacks a controlling idea; fails to use evidence; ends abruptly • **Organization** Has no organization, no transitions, and no sense of cohesion • **Language** Uses an inappropriate style and tone; has major problems with grammar, mechanics, and spelling

Preparing for Timed Writing

W 10 Write routinely over shorter time frames for a range of tasks, purposes, and audiences.

1. ANALYZE THE TASK — 5 MIN

Read the task carefully. Then, read it again, underlining words that tell the topic, the audience, and the purpose.

WRITING TASK

Write a comparison-contrast essay about two of your favorite literary texts. *(Topic)* Your essay should concentrate on key aspects of the texts, such as characters, theme, setting, plot, and conflict. Your essay should give your audience, such as your teacher and classmates, *(Audience)* new insights into the literary texts. *(Purpose)*

2. PLAN YOUR RESPONSE — 10 MIN

Begin by choosing two literary texts that you know well. Then, use a Venn diagram to compare and contrast several aspects of the two texts. Be sure to include aspects that are listed in the task.

3. RESPOND TO THE TASK — 20 MIN

Begin drafting your essay. Write a controlling idea that summarizes your essay's main points. Keep the following guidelines in mind as you write:

- In the introduction, catch your audience's attention with a question, quotation, or interesting detail.
- Choose either a point-by-point (compares and contrasts both texts, one point at a time), or subject-by-subject (discusses the first literary text, then moves on to the second) organization. Support each point with relevant textual evidence.
- Use transitions such as *both, like, similarly,* and *also* to show similarities, and *in contrast, instead, on the other hand,* and *however* to show differences.
- Give your audience something to think about in your concluding section. Consider adding a summary of your comparison or a new but related idea.

4. IMPROVE YOUR RESPONSE — 5–10 MIN

Revising Check your draft against the task. Have you focused on key aspects of the texts? Have you offered additional insights into the texts?

Proofreading Correct errors in grammar, usage, spelling, punctuation, and capitalization. Make sure that your paper and any edits are neatly written and legible.

Checking Your Final Copy Before you turn in your paper, read it one more time to catch any errors you may have missed.

Creating a Class Newspaper

Think of a newspaper that you have read before. What types of articles did you like reading? What types of articles did you dislike? In this workshop, you and your classmates will create a newspaper using publishing technology such as layout and design software.

 Complete the workshop activities in your **Reader/Writer Notebook.**

PRODUCE WITH A PURPOSE	COMMON CORE TRAITS
TASK	***A STRONG CLASS NEWSPAPER . . .***
Work with classmates to gather and develop content for a **class newspaper.** Then, use computer software to create your newspaper.	• contains clearly written, thoroughly researched, and informative articles • contains relevant graphics and images

COMMON CORE

W 6 Use technology to produce and publish writing products. **SL 1b** Work with peers to promote decision-making, set clear goals and deadlines, and establish individual roles. **SL 2** Integrate multiple sources of information. **SL 5** Make strategic use of digital media in presentations.

Plan Your Newspaper

PLAN THE NEWSPAPER'S SECTIONS

With classmates, decide on the newspaper's name and sections. You may want to include sections that cover issues and events in your school, your community, and the world beyond. As you discuss options, recognize that in order to be productive, you will need to listen to a range of ideas. Here are some additional ideas:

- a section that highlights upcoming school or community events
- a section that details students' recent achievements in academics, sports, or music
- a section that shares students' opinions about current issues

PLAN THE STAFF AND CONTENTS

Work with your classmates to establish an editorial team for each section. Teams should meet to brainstorm ideas for articles, graphics, and images and decide who will write each article and who will create or obtain each graphic and image. After teams have established their roles and plans, have the entire staff regroup. Create a chart like the one below to summarize your plan for the newspaper. As a group, set a deadline for the publication of your newspaper. Discuss and set any intermediate deadlines that each team should meet.

Section	Articles/Writers	Graphics and Images/Artists and Researchers

Create the Newspaper

Before your editorial team begins to create content using publishing software, take time to plan the layout of your section. Consider how pages will be formatted, including how many columns of text will appear on a page and where headlines and graphics will go. While planning articles, each member of your team should keep in mind any space limitations needed to fit your planned format.

GATHER INFORMATION AND CREATE CONTENT

When creating and gathering content for the newspaper, keep the following guidelines in mind:

- When gathering information for an article, interview knowledgeable people. Take notes or use an audio recorder during the interview. Refer to your notes or recording to find interesting quotations to put into your article.
- When researching information for an article, look at multiple sources of information. Be sure to evaluate the credibility and accuracy of each source before using the information in your article. If you find any discrepancies in the information, do additional research to determine which source is correct.
- When writing articles, answer the 5 W's *(Who? What? Where? When?* and *Why?).* Think of a title that tells your reader the basic focus of your article. Begin your article with a **lead,** an interest-grabbing sentence that states the main idea of the article.
- Edit one another's articles to be sure they are free of grammar, usage, and spelling errors.
- When gathering graphics or images, respect copyright laws by using only materials that don't require permission.

CREATE AND DISTRIBUTE THE FINAL PRODUCT

- Work with your classmates to insert the articles, graphics, and images into the publishing program your team is using. If necessary, cut, add, or revise material to meet space requirements.
- Print several copies of your newspaper and distribute them throughout your school. If your newspaper covers community issues, distribute it to members of the community as well.

As a class, discuss and make decisions on criteria for evaluating your class newspaper. Distribute your newspaper and ask for volunteers to use the rubric to provide feedback.

Assessment Practice

ASSESS

Taking this practice test will help you assess your knowledge of these skills and determine your readiness for the Unit Test.

REVIEW

After you take the practice test, your teacher can help you identify any standards you need to review.

COMMON CORE

RL 1 Cite evidence to support analysis of what the text says explicitly as well as inferences drawn from the text. **RL 2** Determine themes or central ideas of a text. **RL 3** Analyze the impact of the author's choices regarding how to develop and relate elements of a story. **RL 4** Determine the meaning of words and phrases as they are used in the text, including figurative meanings. **RL 6** Distinguish what is directly stated in a text from what is really meant. **RI 1** Cite evidence to support analysis of what the text says explicitly. **RI 7** Evaluate sources of information presented in different media or formats as well as in words. **L 1** Demonstrate command of the conventions of standard English grammar. **L 4** Determine the meaning of multiple-meaning words. **L 4a** Use context as a clue to the meaning of a word.

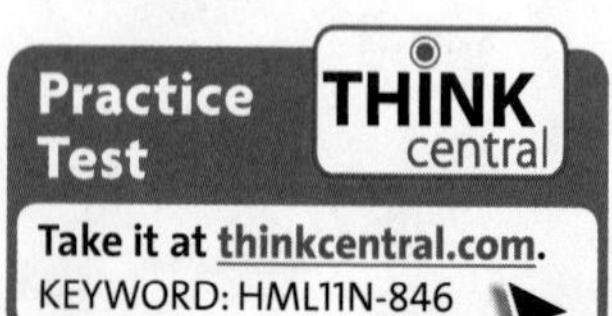

DIRECTIONS **Read the two selections and the viewing and representing piece. Then answer the questions that follow.**

A Call Loan *by O. Henry*

1 In those days the cattlemen were the anointed. They were the grandees of the grass, kings of the kine, lords of the lea, barons of beef and bone. They might have ridden in golden chariots had their tastes so inclined. The cattleman was caught in a stampede of dollars. It seemed to him that he had more money than was decent. But when he had bought a watch with precious stones set in the case so large that they hurt his ribs, and a California saddle with silver nails and Angora skin *suaderos*, and ordered everybody up to the bar for whisky—what else was there for him to spend money for?

2 Not so circumscribed in expedient for the reduction of surplus wealth were those lairds of the lariat who had womenfolk to their name. In the breast of the rib-sprung sex the genius of purse lightening may slumber through years of inopportunity, but never, my brothers, does it become extinct.

3 So, out of the chaparral came Long Bill Longley from the Bar Circle Branch on the Frio—a wife-driven man—to taste the urban joys of success. Something like half a million dollars he had, with an income steadily increasing.

4 Long Bill was a graduate of the camp and trail. Luck and thrift, a cool head, and a telescopic eye for mavericks had raised him from cowboy to be a cowman. Then came the boom in cattle, and Fortune, stepping gingerly among the cactus thorns, came and emptied her cornucopia at the doorstep of the ranch.

5 In the little frontier city of Chaparosa, Longley built a costly residence. Here he became a captive, bound to the chariot of social existence. He was doomed to become a leading citizen. He struggled for a time like a mustang in his first corral, and then he hung up his quirt and spurs. Time hung heavily on his hands. He organised the First National Bank of Chaparosa, and was elected its president.

6 One day a dyspeptic man, wearing double-magnifying glasses, inserted an official-looking card between the bars of the cashier's window of the First National Bank. Five minutes later the bank force was dancing at the beck and call of a national bank examiner.

7 This examiner, Mr. J. Edgar Todd, proved to be a thorough one.

8 At the end of it all the examiner put on his hat, and called the president, Mr. William R. Longley, into the private office.

9 "Well, how do you find things?" asked Longley, in his slow, deep tones. "Any brands in the round-up you didn't like the looks of?"

10 "The bank checks up all right, Mr. Longley," said Todd; "and I find your loans in very good shape—with one exception. You are carrying one very bad

bit of paper—one that is so bad that I have been thinking that you surely do not realise the serious position it places you in. I refer to a call loan of $10,000 made to Thomas Merwin. Not only is the amount in excess of the maximum sum the bank can loan any individual legally, but it is absolutely without endorsement or security. Thus you have doubly violated the national banking laws, and have laid yourself open to criminal prosecution by the Government. A report of the matter to the Comptroller of the Currency—which I am bound to make—would, I am sure, result in the matter being turned over to the Department of Justice for action. You see what a serious thing it is."

11 Bill Longley was leaning his lengthy, slowly moving frame back in his swivel chair. His hands were clasped behind his head, and he turned a little to look the examiner in the face. The examiner was surprised to see a smile creep about the rugged mouth of the banker, and a kindly twinkle in his light-blue eyes. If he saw the seriousness of the affair, it did not show in his countenance.

12 "Of course, you don't know Tom Merwin," said Longley, almost genially. "Yes, I know about that loan. It hasn't any security except Tom Merwin's word. Somehow, I've always found that when a man's word is good it's the best security there is. Oh, yes, I know the Government doesn't think so. I guess I'll see Tom about that note."

13 Mr. Todd's dyspepsia seemed to grow suddenly worse. He looked at the chaparral banker through his double-magnifying glasses in amazement.

14 "You see," said Longley, easily explaining the thing away, "Tom heard of 2000 head of two-year-olds down near Rocky Ford on the Rio Grande that could be had for $8 a head. I reckon 'twas one of old Leandro Garcia's outfits that he had smuggled over, and he wanted to make a quick turn on 'em. Those cattle are worth $15 on the hoof in Kansas City. Tom knew it and I knew it. He had $6,000, and I let him have the $10,000 to make the deal with. His brother Ed took 'em on to market three weeks ago. He ought to be back 'most any day now with the money. When he comes Tom'll pay that note."

15 The bank examiner was shocked. It was, perhaps, his duty to step out to the telegraph office and wire the situation to the Comptroller. But he did not. He talked pointedly and effectively to Longley for three minutes. He succeeded in making the banker understand that he stood upon the border of a catastrophe. And then he offered a tiny loophole of escape.

16 "I am going to Hilldale's to-night," he told Longley, "to examine a bank there. I will pass through Chaparosa on my way back. At twelve o'clock to-morrow I shall call at this bank. If this loan has been cleared out of the way by that time it will not be mentioned in my report. If not—I will have to do my duty."

17 With that the examiner bowed and departed.

GO ON

18 The President of the First National lounged in his chair half an hour longer, and then he lit a mild cigar, and went over to Tom Merwin's house. Merwin, a ranchman in brown duck, with a contemplative eye, sat with his feet upon a table, plaiting a rawhide quirt.

19 "Tom," said Longley, leaning against the table, "you heard anything from Ed yet?"

20 "Not yet," said Merwin, continuing his plaiting. "I guess Ed'll be along back now in a few days."

21 "There was a bank examiner," said Longley, "nosing around our place to-day, and he bucked a sight about that note of yours. You know I know it's all right, but the thing *is* against the banking laws. I was pretty sure you'd have paid it off before the bank was examined again, but the son-of-a-gun slipped in on us, Tom. Now, I'm short of cash myself just now, or I'd let you have the money to take it up with. I've got till twelve o'clock to-morrow, and then I've got to show the cash in place of that note or—"

22 "Or what, Bill?" asked Merwin, as Longley hesitated.

23 "Well, I suppose it means be jumped on with both of Uncle Sam's feet."

24 "I'll try to raise the money for you on time," said Merwin, interested in his plaiting.

25 "All right, Tom," concluded Longley, as he turned toward the door; "I knew you would if you could."

26 Merwin threw down his whip and went to the only other bank in town, a private one, run by Cooper & Craig.

27 "Cooper," he said, to the partner by that name, "I've got to have $10,000 to-day or to-morrow. I've got a house and lot there that's worth about $6,000 and that's all the actual collateral. But I've got a cattle deal on that's sure to bring me in more than that much profit within a few days."

28 Cooper began to cough.

29 "Now, for God's sake don't say no," said Merwin. "I owe that much money on a call loan. It's been called, and the man that called it is a man I've laid on the same blanket with in cow-camps and ranger-camps for ten years. He can call anything I've got. He can call the blood out of my veins and it'll come. He's got to have the money. He's in a devil of a—Well, he needs the money, and I've got to get it for him. You know my word's good, Cooper."

30 "No doubt of it," assented Cooper, urbanely, "but I've a partner, you know. I'm not free in making loans. And even if you had the best security in your hands, Merwin, we couldn't accommodate you in less than a week. We're just making a shipment of $15,000 to Myer Brothers in Rockdell, to buy cotton with. It goes down on the narrow-gauge to-night. That leaves our cash quite short at present. Sorry we can't arrange it for you."

31 Merwin went back to his little bare office and plaited at his quirt again. About four o'clock in the afternoon he went to the First National Bank and leaned over the railing of Longley's desk.

32 "I'll try to get that money for you to-night—I mean to-morrow, Bill."

33 "All right, Tom," said Longley quietly.

34 At nine o'clock that night Tom Merwin stepped cautiously out of the small frame house in which he lived. It was near the edge of the little town, and few citizens were in the neighbourhood at that hour. Merwin wore two six-shooters in a belt, and a slouch hat. He moved swiftly down a lonely street, and then followed the sandy road that ran parallel to the narrow-gauge track until he reached the water-tank, two miles below the town. There Tom Merwin stopped, tied a black silk handkerchief about the lower part of his face, and pulled his hat down low.

35 In ten minutes the night train for Rockdell pulled up at the tank, having come from Chaparosa.

36 With a gun in each hand Merwin raised himself from behind a clump of chaparral and started for the engine. But before he had taken three steps, two long, strong arms clasped him from behind, and he was lifted from his feet and thrown, face downward upon the grass. There was a heavy knee pressing against his back, and an iron hand grasping each of his wrists. He was held thus, like a child, until the engine had taken water, and until the train had moved, with accelerating speed, out of sight. Then he was released, and rose to his feet to face Bill Longley.

37 "The case never needed to be fixed up this way, Tom," said Longley. "I saw Cooper this evening, and he told me what you and him talked about. Then I went down to your house to-night and saw you come out with your guns on, and I followed you. Let's go back, Tom."

38 They walked away together, side by side.

39 " 'Twas the only chance I saw," said Merwin presently. "You called your loan, and I tried to answer you. Now, what'll you do, Bill, if they sock it to you?"

40 "What would you have done if they'd socked it to you?" was the answer Longley made.

41 "I never thought I'd lay in a bush to stick up a train," remarked Merwin; "but a call loan's different. A call's a call with me. We've got twelve hours yet, Bill, before this spy jumps onto you. We've got to raise them spondulicks somehow. Maybe we can—Great Sam Houston! do you hear that?"

42 Merwin broke into a run, and Longley kept with him, hearing only a rather pleasing whistle somewhere in the night rendering the lugubrious air of "The Cowboy's Lament."

43 "It's the only tune he knows," shouted Merwin, as he ran. "I'll bet—"

44 They were at the door of Merwin's house. He kicked it open and fell over an old valise lying in the middle of the floor. A sunburned, firm-jawed youth, stained by travel, lay upon the bed puffing at a brown cigarette.

GO ON

45 "What's the word, Ed?" gasped Merwin.

46 "So, so," drawled that capable youngster. "Just got in on the 9:30. Sold the bunch for fifteen, straight. Now, buddy, you want to quit kickin' a valise around that's got $29,000 in greenbacks in its in'ards."

The Next Frontier

by S. C. Gwynne
***from* Texas Monthly**

1 It is a fine, sunny, mid-April morning in South Texas. The weather has been unusually cool and rainy, and the spacious, pool-table-flat wedge of land between the Nueces River and the Mexican border—which the Spanish once called El Desierto de los Muertos[1]—today looks as green as Ireland. I am in a pickup, bouncing through a pasture on the 237,348-acre Norias division of the King Ranch, one of four massive chunks of land that make up the 825,000-acre (1,300-square-mile) spread. The truck belongs to Dave DeLaney, a rangy 51-year-old who runs the ranch's cattle operation. With roughly 43,500 head, it is the nation's largest. DeLaney is giving me the grand tour, which will ultimately take the better part of two days. . . .

2 What is most striking about the place, not surprisingly, is its tremendous scale—nearly unimaginable for those of us who live in places where real estate is calibrated in fractions of city blocks. The pasture we are in, for example, encompasses 30,000 acres—or 47 square miles. The live oak grove (or motte, as they call it here) we just drove through comprises 60,000 acres. And the land is not only vast. It is also beautiful. Though beauty is not a quality generally associated with South Texas, Norias is one of the loveliest pieces of coastal real estate I've ever seen, a place of swaying bluestem grasses; lush, wide-open coastal plain; rolling bone-white sand dunes; and rain-detonated explosions of daisies, coreopsis, and dayflowers. Animals are everywhere we look: scores of wild turkeys, some of them in mating dances; white-tailed deer and bobwhite quail in almost every meadow; ducks; javelinas; feral hogs; brilliantly colored scissor-tailed flycatchers; and red-winged blackbirds.

1. **El Desierto de los Muertos:** Spanish for The Desert of the Dead.

3 Beyond the size and beauty of the physical environment, there is the weight of history. The King Ranch was the first ranch in Texas, the cornerstone of the cattle business in the West, one of the originators of the great cattle drives to the Kansas railheads and later of the fenced pastures that killed the drives off. At the time of his death, in 1885, founder Richard King owned half a million acres and was the wealthiest man in Texas. His grandson Robert J. Kleberg Jr. built the business into a 15-million-acre global empire, with ranches spread from Argentina to Australia. Kleberg invented the Santa Gertrudis, the first American cattle breed and the first new breed anywhere in one hundred years; he bred the first registered American quarter horse and the Thoroughbred stallion Assault, which won the Triple Crown in 1946. If that wasn't enough, Kleberg also invented the root plow and the cattle prod, eradicated Texas tick fever, and arranged the largest oil lease ever on private land.

4 All this history lives on, pervasive as the mesquite and huisache trees. I can feel it in the vast muscular land and see it in the glorious Main House, with its battlements, multichromatic terra-cotta tiles, Tiffany-designed furniture and art glass, Italian marble stairs, and teak floors. Drifting along the ranch's two thousand miles of asphalt, caliche, and dirt roads, I can't help feeling a certain sense of timelessness, as though nothing on this splendid Rhode Island–size ranch has really changed since the days when Captain King's *vaqueros* rounded up tens of thousands of cattle for the northern trail drives.

5 But those are appearances only, mirages of the South Texas heat. The truth is that the King Ranch is not at all what it once was. As a business, it is profoundly and irreversibly changed from the time when Kleberg would receive potentates[2] and movie stars on the Main House porch and sit like a Middle Eastern pasha[3] in his reviewing stand, gazing at million-dollar horses. Fifty-six years of enlightened despotism had left the ranch singularly dependent on him, and when he died, in 1974, the machinery of empire immediately began to creak and then to fail. Battles of succession led to wars of secession. Family members forced the ranch to buy them out, causing it to incur massive debt; lawsuits followed, then the remaining heirs grabbed most of the oil royalties that had been floating the operation for forty years. Drained of most of its oil money, the business staggered forward under the burden of its archaic, nearly feudal cradle-to-grave welfare system for the hundreds of workers and their families who resided on the King Ranch. Had things gone only slightly differently, these forces might have easily led to the breakup of the King Ranch, as they have for thousands of other family-owned outfits.

2. **potentates** (pō-tən-tāts): people who have great power or sway.

3. **pasha** (pə-ˈshä): a man of high rank or office.

GO ON

6 But this did not happen. Instead came sweeping change, driven by an entirely new concept of the ranch. What Captain King founded was a simple cattle operation. Then it became a cattle and oil business. As the King Ranch struggled to survive, it came to be seen as a business, to be sure, but also as a *legacy*, something to be shielded, protected, and preserved. The result is that over the past quarter century its owners have, laboriously and at considerable risk, built an elaborate financial carapace[4] around the 825,000 acres of the home ranches in South Texas. Ironically, in order to protect the four divisions of this acreage (Santa Gertrudis, Laureles, Norias, and Encino), the King Ranch has been forced to branch out into new enterprises that are antithetical to everything the ranch once held holy. The business is now built around commercial hunting leases, which let thousands of outsiders into the private kingdom, and farming, long considered by ranch folk as a pedestrian, second-class business and pointedly banned by Kleberg. With 36,000 acres of Florida citrus groves, the King Ranch is the leading citrus grower in America. It is also one of the nation's ten-biggest sugarcane producers. It owns huge sod, cotton, and milo farms in Texas and Florida. Buffered from the cruel volatility of the markets, the ranch lives on, working cattle and sustaining its old romance. But today the King Ranch exists in the form of a large and diversified agribusiness conglomerate, carefully designed to prevent the sacred acres from ever being sold.

7 Along the way it has become something the previous generations could never have foreseen or imagined. "If Captain King sat down with us today, he'd say, 'Well, how are things going?'" said Helen Kleberg Groves, known as Helenita, Kleberg's only child and one of the matriarchs of the family. "And we'd say, 'They are going fine. We don't have that many cattle or horses anymore. It is hard to make any money at ranching. We've got hunting leases and citrus groves and sod and cane farms.' He would think we had lost our minds."

4. **carapace** (ker-ə-pās): a protective shell.

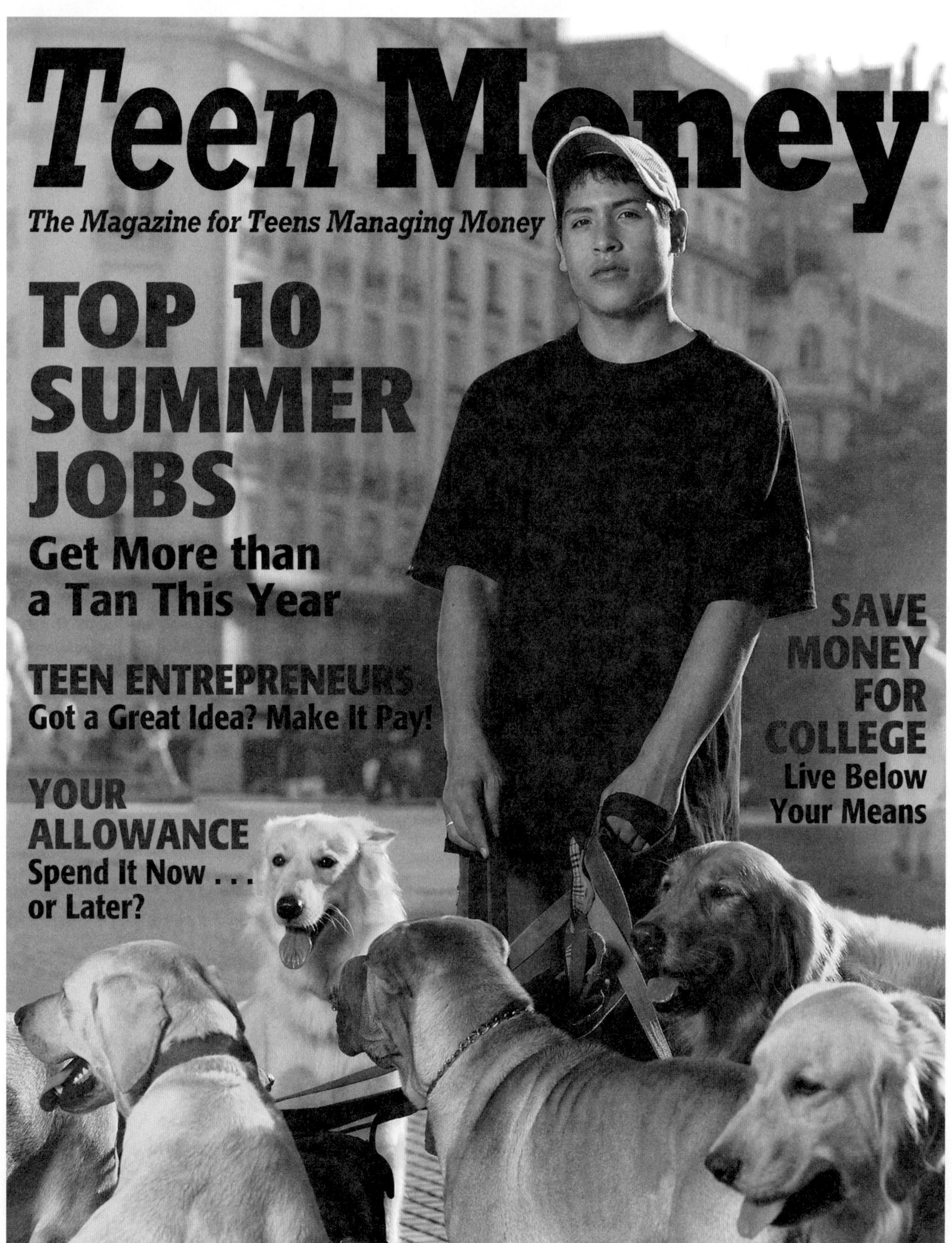
Teen Money
The Magazine for Teens Managing Money
TOP 10 SUMMER JOBS
Get More than a Tan This Year
TEEN ENTREPRENEURS
Got a Great Idea? Make It Pay!
YOUR ALLOWANCE
Spend It Now . . . or Later?
SAVE MONEY FOR COLLEGE
Live Below Your Means

Reading Comprehension

Use "A Call Loan" (pp. 846–850) to answer questions 1–12.

1. The author chooses to begin the story by relating —
   - **A.** how expensive cattle ranching is
   - **B.** how hard it is to make a living raising cattle
   - **C.** how much money could be made in cattle ranching
   - **D.** how cattlemen spend their money

2. In paragraph 6, the word *dyspeptic* means —
   - **A.** content
   - **B.** disgruntled
   - **C.** lean
   - **D.** satisfied

3. One of the reasons the bank president doesn't want to call Tom Merwin's loan is that —
   - **A.** he doesn't like government interference
   - **B.** the bank examiner is corrupt
   - **C.** Cooper & Craig will get more business
   - **D.** he knows Tom keeps his word

4. Based on the description and behavior of the national bank examiner, the reader can conclude that —
   - **A.** the author probably didn't like bank examiners
   - **B.** the examiner is the main character in the story
   - **C.** the bank president enjoyed his visits
   - **D.** the examiner didn't like the bank president

5. Which word from paragraphs 18–27 help the reader understand the meaning of the word *quirt*?
   - **A.** Collateral
   - **B.** Note
   - **C.** Table
   - **D.** Whip

6. In paragraph 29, Tom Merwin says that Bill Longley "can call the blood out of my veins." The author uses this statement to —
   - **A.** show how much respect Tom has for Bill
   - **B.** foreshadow that Tom will die trying to repay the loan
   - **C.** imply that Tom doesn't want to repay the loan
   - **D.** establish security for Tom to repay the loan

7. A source of internal conflict for Tom Merwin is —
   - **A.** his rivalry with Bill Longley
   - **B.** his disagreement with Cooper
   - **C.** his desire to make things right
   - **D.** his disgust for the bank examiner

8. The tone of paragraph 41 changes from —
   - **A.** serious to humorous
   - **B.** despair to hope
   - **C.** tolerable to bitter
   - **D.** sympathetic to thoughtless

9. In paragraph 41, the word *spondulicks* means —
   - **A.** beef
   - **B.** cash
   - **C.** cows
   - **D.** trains

10. When Ed says things are "So, so" in response to Tom's breathless question, it is an example of —
   A. connotation
   B. sarcasm
   C. satire
   D. understatement

11. Based on paragraph 46, the reader can infer that —
   A. the bank examiner reports First National Bank of Chaparosa to the Department of Justice
   B. Long Bill Longley leaves town
   C. Tom Merwin pays the call loan
   D. Ed, Tom's brother, keeps all the money

12. Which of the following best expresses a theme of the selection?
   A. A friend should do whatever it takes to pay back a friend.
   B. Keeping one's word is important, especially to a friend.
   C. Banks should not be trusted to loan money.
   D. Mixing business and friendship is never good.

Use "The Next Frontier" (pp. 850–852) to answer questions 13–18.

13. In paragraph 1, the fact that the land was called *El Desierto de los Muertos* ("The Desert of the Dead") is ironic now because the land —
   A. receives plenty of rain
   B. is filled with graves
   C. is green and lush
   D. is empty and unusable

14. Read the following dictionary entry.

   scale \'skāl\ *n* **1.** a series of musical notes **2.** a series of marks or points at known intervals used to measure distances **3.** a distinctive relative size, extent, or degree **4.** a graded series of tests to rate individual achievement or intelligence

   Which definition best matches the meaning of the word *scale* as it is used in paragraph 2?
   A. Definition 1
   B. Definition 2
   C. Definition 3
   D. Definition 4

15. The author includes background information on the ranch to —
   A. show how the King Ranch is like other places in South Texas
   B. reveal how the King Ranch failed
   C. highlight the importance and the achievements of the King Ranch
   D. explain the author's connection to the King Ranch

16. Problems for the King Ranch began when —
   A. members of the family wanted to get out of the business
   B. Robert J. Kleberg Jr. didn't have any children
   C. the farm equipment began to fail
   D. Richard King died in 1885

17. In paragraph 6, the word *antithetical* means —
   A. analogous
   B. contradictory
   C. hypothetical
   D. similar

18. According to the article, the King Ranch operates largely through —

A. tourism

B. cattle and horses

C. oil

D. farming and hunting leases

Use "A Call Loan" and "The Next Frontier" to answer question 19.

19. The authors of both selections would agree that —

A. cattle ranching used to be a lucrative business

B. money trouble follows a family for many generations

C. it is important to stay with one career

D. bankers do not trust farmers

Use the visual representation on page 853 to answer questions 20–21.

20. A reader turning to the article "Teen Entrepreneurs: Got a Great Idea? Make it Pay!" will find tips on —

A. affording the latest electronics

B. saving for college

C. creating a successful business

D. finding a summer job

21. The designer most likely chose the photograph to —

A. illustrate a teen entrepreneur at work

B. persuade teens to buy more dogs

C. convince teens to take their jobs seriously

D. show that urban teens have unique job opportunities

SHORT CONSTRUCTED RESPONSE

Write a short constructed response to each question, using text evidence to support your response.

22. Why does O. Henry use dialogue? Support your response with evidence from the selection.

23. How does the King Ranch change from the beginning of the article to the end? Support your response with evidence from the selection.

Write a short constructed response to the following question, using text evidence from both selections to support your response.

24. Which rancher from "A Call Loan" and "The Next Frontier" would you like to have as a friend? Support your response with evidence from **both** selections.

Revising and Editing

DIRECTIONS Read this passage and answer the questions that follow.

(1) In the 1770s, the first permanent settlement in Chicago was established by a Haitian trader named Jean Baptiste Point du Sable. (2) The community developed slowly at first. (3) The growth of Chicago was spur by the construction of railroads in the mid-1800s. (4) Its progress came to a halt when the city was destroyed by a fire in 1871. (5) Organizations immediately offered aid, however. (6) Triumphantly, the city bounced back. (7) In 1893, Chicago hosted the World's Fair.

1. What is the most effective way to revise sentence 1?

A. In the 1770s, a Haitian trader named Jean Baptiste du Sable established the first permanent settlement in Chicago.

B. The first permanent settlement in Chicago was established in the 1770s by a Haitian trader named Jean Baptiste Point du Sable.

C. In Chicago in the 1770s, the first permanent settlement was established by a Haitian trader named Jean Baptiste Point du Sable.

D. The first permanent settlement in Chicago was established by a Haitian trader named Jean Baptiste Point du Sable in the 1770s.

2. What change, if any, should be made in sentence 3?

A. Change ***growth*** to **grow**

B. Insert a comma after ***spur***

C. Change ***spur*** to **spurred**

D. Make no change

3. Which transition could best be added to the beginning of sentence 4?

A. In addition,

B. Finally,

C. Therefore,

D. Unfortunately,

4. What is the most effective way to revise sentence 5?

A. Organizations immediately started to arrange clean-up crews to assist the city, however.

B. Organizations immediately started forming relief and clean-up crews, however.

C. Organizations immediately helped, however.

D. Assisting organizations immediately helped, however.

5. What is the most effective way to combine sentences 6 and 7?

A. Triumphantly, the city bounced back; however, in 1893, Chicago hosted the World's Fair.

B. Triumphantly, the city bounced back and hosted the World's Fair in 1893.

C. In 1893, Chicago hosted the World's Fair, but triumphantly, the city bounced back.

D. In 1893, Chicago hosted the World's Fair; otherwise, the city triumphantly bounced back.

Ideas for Independent Reading

Continue exploring the Questions of the Times on pages 640–641 with these additional works.

What makes a place UNIQUE?

My Ántonia
by Willa Cather

This novel, recognized as Willa Cather's finest, depicts through the voice of the immigrant Ántonia Shimerda the hardships and rewards of pioneer life and the strength of America's frontier women. As Ántonia grows into womanhood, she overcomes poverty, disappointment, and family tragedy to become a mother and a successful farmer—a woman who "had not lost the fire of life."

American Indian Stories, Legends, and Other Writings
by Zitkala-Sa

This collection of works by Sioux writer and activist Zitkala-Sa (1876–1938) contains retellings of traditional Native American legends as well as stories, poems, essays, and speeches focused on the Native American experience.

The Virginian: A Horseman of the Plains
by Owen Wister

The strong-but-silent cowboy, the saintly schoolmarm, the climactic shootout—all have become standards of American Westerns but were brand-new ideas when Owen Wister penned *The Virginian* in 1902. His story of "the Virginian," a man torn between his love for a woman and his quest for justice, was the first true American Western.

Does the universe CARE?

Sister Carrie
by Theodore Dreiser

Carrie Meeber arrives in Chicago filled with vague hopes of fun and comfort. Meanwhile, across town, George Hurstwood, a well-to-do restaurant manager, is living the life of his dreams, respected by his peers and hobnobbing with famous actors. In *Sister Carrie,* Dreiser brings these two people together and lets us watch, amazed and appalled, as Carrie is taken to heights of glory while Hurstwood falls to the depths of despair.

The Best Short Stories of Jack London
by Jack London

No issue engaged writer Jack London more consistently than the clash between a seemingly uncaring natural world and the striving creatures who inhabit it. Intense, thrilling, and thought-provoking, the ten short stories in this collection show why London was so popular in his day and remains one of the most widely read of all American authors.

McTeague: A Story of San Francisco
by Frank Norris

Frank Norris set the literary establishment on its ear when he published *McTeague,* a naturalistic story of a San Francisco dentist. The title character, spurred by a strange force of self-destruction, makes one bad decision after another. Finally, he commits a murder and winds up fighting for his life in the harsh alkali deserts of California.

RL 10 Read and comprehend literature. **RI 10** Read and comprehend literary nonfiction.

How are women's ROLES CHANGING?

The Awakening
by Kate Chopin

Causing a storm of controversy when published in 1899, *The Awakening* follows the daily life of an attractive, well-to-do New Orleans matron named Edna Pontellier. Married into a prominent family, Edna leads a very comfortable existence, with good friends, a fine house, and nothing very pressing to do. Yet Edna is assailed by a nameless discontent. Although she cannot articulate exactly what she wants, she knows that the options open to women in her society are slowly making her die inside.

The House of Mirth
by Edith Wharton

The daughter of a failed New York businessman, Lily Bart is pretty, independent-minded, and cultivated. She is also penniless. Living with her rich yet miserly aunt, she spends her time socializing with New York's aristocrats. In such a situation, Lily's course of action is obvious to everyone. If she wants to maintain her lifestyle, she must find a rich man and marry him. Yet selling her beauty to the highest bidder strikes Lily as savage. Unable to find a path that would bring her both self-respect and material comfort, Lily drifts from party to party, trying not to think about what is going to happen to her. Lily's ultimately tragic fate is clearly the blame of a society that values wealth and convention above all.

Why are there "haves" and "HAVE-NOTS"?

The Jungle
by Upton Sinclair

No other novel in American literature has had a more direct impact upon daily life than *The Jungle*. Based upon extensive research conducted in Chicago's slaughterhouses, Sinclair's novel was intended to turn a blinding light on unfair labor practices and rally readers to the cause of socialism. Instead, its descriptions of unclean meatpacking practices caused a steep decline in the sales of beef and pork and brought about federal laws to keep food healthy. "I aimed at the public's heart, and by accident hit it in the stomach," Sinclair ruefully remarked. Nevertheless, *The Jungle* remains jarring in its description of the appalling conditions laborers were forced to endure.

A Hazard of New Fortunes
by William Dean Howells

In this novel of class conflict, a mild-mannered editor moves to New York from Boston, looking to enhance his career. He takes charge of a magazine sponsored by a ruthless financier and comes into contact with his old German tutor, who has become a political radical. Torn between his sympathy for the working poor and his need to stay on good terms with his rich patron, the editor does not know what to do. When a violent streetcar strike breaks out, he can no longer remain a bystander. He has to decide whether to support what he knows is right or to play it safe and keep his job.

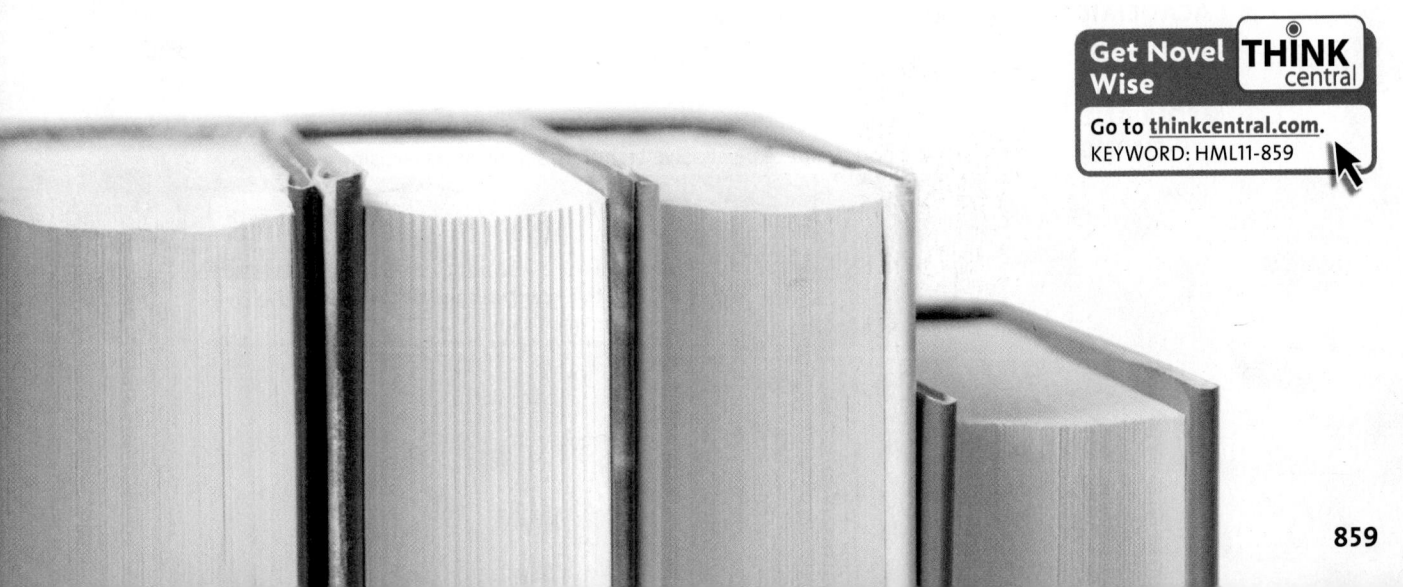

Get Novel Wise THINK central

Go to thinkcentral.com. KEYWORD: HML11-859

UNIT 5

COMMON CORE

Preview Unit Goals

TEXT ANALYSIS	• Understand Harlem Renaissance and modernism as literary movements • Identify and analyze literary elements, including tone, theme, diction, voice, mood, irony, imagery, setting, and character development • Identify and analyze rhyme scheme in poetry • Identify and analyze individual styles, including Frost's and Hemingway's • Analyze and interpret modern, narrative, and imagist poetry • Identify and analyze author's purpose and viewpoint • Distinguish literal from figurative meaning
READING	• Make inferences and draw conclusions • Identify explicit and implicit main ideas
WRITING AND LANGUAGE	• Write a persuasive essay • Craft effective sentences by using vivid language, phrases, and coordinating conjunctions
SPEAKING AND LISTENING	• Participate in a debate
VOCABULARY	• Use knowledge of Latin and Greek word roots to understand word meaning • Use a thesaurus to find precise words and understand nuances of words
ACADEMIC VOCABULARY	• conclude • criteria • despite • justify • maintain
MEDIA AND VIEWING	• Interpret and evaluate information presented in media and illustrations • Analyze and evaluate persuasive techniques in print advertising

Find It Online!

Go to thinkcentral.com for the interactive version of this unit.

The Harlem Renaissance & Modernism

1910–1940

Langston Hughes

A CHANGING AWARENESS

- The Harlem Renaissance
- The New Poetry
- The Modern Short Story
- Journalism as Literature

MediaSmart DVD-ROM

Zora Neale Hurston's Biography

Explore how documentary filmmakers bring a writer and her world to vivid life. Page 916

Questions of the Times

DISCUSS Share your views about the following questions with a small group or in a whole-class discussion. As you read the selections in this unit, reflect on how the writing of the Harlem Renaissance and the modernist period was shaped by these questions.

What is MODERN?

Americans in the first half of the 20th century consciously moved away from the traditions of their past and embraced all things modern. From the shiny new automobiles rolling off Henry Ford's assembly line to the esoteric poetry of T. S. Eliot—Americans' love affair with modernism was in full swing. What does *modern* mean to you? Why do you think people like to be on the "cutting edge"?

Can ideals survive CATASTROPHE?

The years between 1910 and 1940 were scarred by two historical events: World War I and the Great Depression. Faced with a world at war followed by deep economic instability at home, many American writers began to see the world with a new cynicism. How can people hold on to their idealism in light of dire events? Is it even possible?

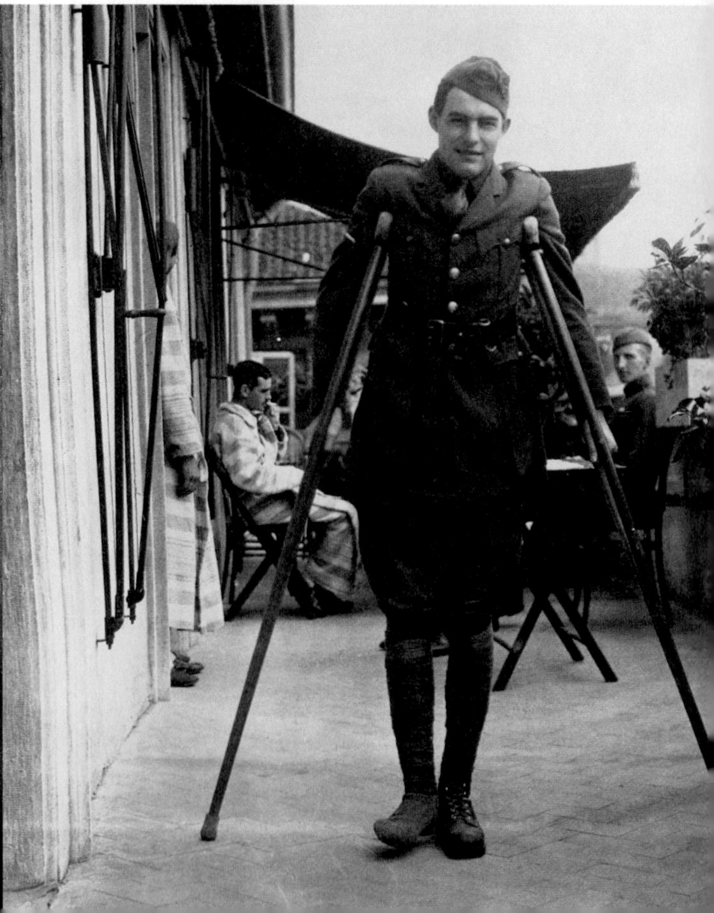

COMMON CORE

RL 9 Demonstrate knowledge of early-twentieth-century foundational works of American literature, including how two or more texts from the same period treat similar themes or topics. **RI 9** Analyze documents of historical and literary significance for their themes, purposes, and rhetorical features.

How can people honor their HERITAGE?

The writers of the Harlem Renaissance were quite diverse stylistically, yet they shared a pride in their heritage that shines through their work. Why do you think writing might be a good vehicle for honoring one's past? How else do people honor their heritage?

What drives HUMAN BEHAVIOR?

Newly familiar with Sigmund Freud's groundbreaking work in human psychology, American writers of this period began to examine the unconsious motivations that affect human behavior. Do you think people regulate their behavior through reason and understanding, or are they driven by unconscious desires?

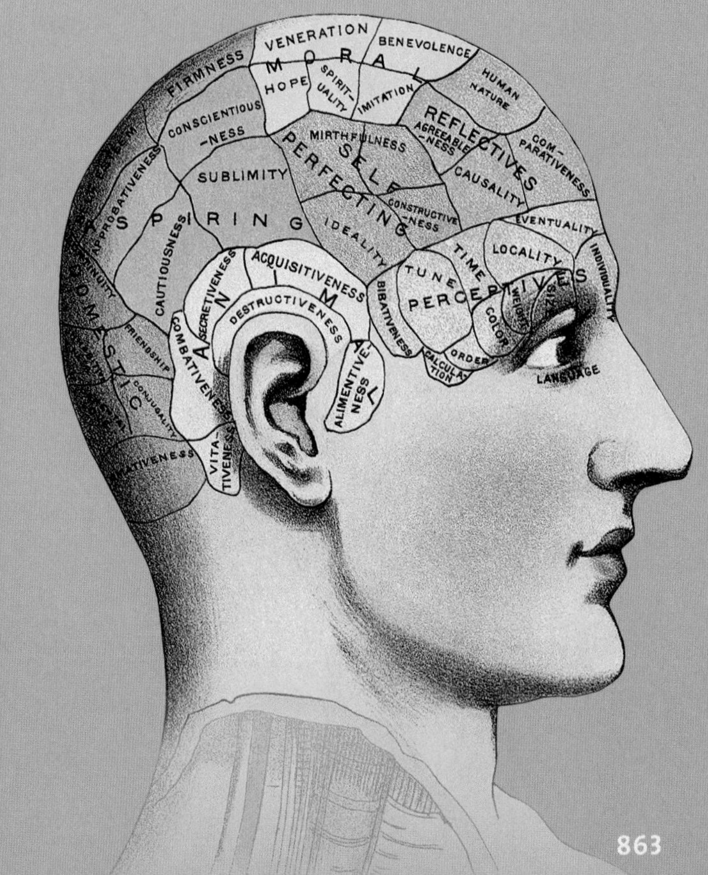

The Harlem Renaissance and Modernism

1910–1940

A Changing Awareness

Change was the only constant for Americans in the early 20th century. In 30 short years, they faced a world war, an economic boom followed by the Great Depression, shifting attitudes toward women's place in society, and a mass culture that isolated and alienated the individual. In this swirl of uncertainty, traditional values seemed to slip out of reach or were actively discarded as Americans—writers and nonwriters alike—searched for truths in what felt like a whole new world.

The Harlem Renaissance and Modernism: Historical Context

Catastrophic historical events—including a devastating war and a deep economic depression—as well as rapid societal change profoundly affected the writing of this period.

COMMON CORE

RL 9 Demonstrate knowledge of early-twentieth-century foundational works of American literature, including how two or more texts from the same period treat similar themes or topics. **RI 9** Analyze documents of historical and literary significance for their themes, purposes, and rhetorical features.

A World at War

World War I—the **Great War**—was perhaps the most influential force on American writers of the early 20th century. The war broke out in Europe in 1914; before it ended in 1918, it involved 32 nations, including the United States, and took the lives of over 20 million people. It was a new kind of war, waged on a massive scale with terrible new weapons that reflected the technological advances of the time—machine guns, poison gases, airplane bombers, and submarines. Old ideals about the purposes and meaning of war were destroyed in the carnage. As Lieutenant Frederic Henry, a character in **Ernest Hemingway's** 1929 novel ***A Farewell to Arms,*** observed: "Words such as glory, honor, courage, or hallow were obscene." For many Americans, the war signaled an end to idealism and ushered in an era marked by hedonism, political corruption, and ruthless business practices.

TAKING NOTES

Outlining As you read each section of this introduction, add the information you learn to an outline like the one started for you here. You can use headings, boldfaced terms, and the information in these boxes as starting points. (See page R49 in the **Research Handbook** for more help with outlining.)

I. Historical Context
- A. A World at War
  1. influence on writers
  2. affected millions
  3. new kind of war
  4. destroyed ideals
- B. The Jazz Age

The Jazz Age

Some Americans, disillusioned with the traditional values that had led to war, sought escape in the pleasures of entertainment and good times. The 1920s, with its booming economy, became known as the **Roaring Twenties.** Writer **F. Scott Fitzgerald** called this decade "the greatest, gaudiest spree in history." As incomes rose, people were able to spend more money on goods and leisure activities. In addition, many young people began, for the first time, to rebel as a group against the values of the past and the authority of their elders. They experimented with new fashions and new attitudes, actively seeking out fun and freedom.

A NEW ERA FOR WOMEN Women of the period saw their lives change in fundamental ways. In 1920, the passage of the **19th Amendment** finally gave women the right to vote. But the vote was just one facet of the changing nature of womanhood. The 1920s saw the emergence of the **flapper,** an emancipated young woman who embraced new fashions and the urban attitudes of the day. By 1930, ten million American women were earning wages in the workplace—another new frontier. In addition, family life was made increasingly easier by technological innovations, from ready-made clothes to sliced bread. Many women writers, such as **Edna St. Vincent Millay** and **Dorothy Parker,** were celebrated as much for their modern lifestyles as for their writing. In turn, they often wrote about the clash between traditional and modern values, celebrating youth, independence, and freedom from social constraints.

The City from Greenwich Village (1922), John Sloan. Gift of Helen Farr Sloan.

JAZZ CULTURE This period also saw the passage of **Prohibition** (1920–1933), in which alcohol was made illegal. In defiance of this restriction, many people drank in illegal nightclubs called speakeasies, as gangsters made fortunes running and supplying the clubs. At the fancy Cotton Club in New York's Harlem neighborhood, the guests—nearly all whites—rubbed shoulders with celebrities and gangsters as they listened to the great jazz performers—nearly all blacks—who helped give the era its name: the **Jazz Age.**

The Great Depression

The good times came to a dramatic end when the stock market crashed in October 1929, plunging the nation into economic depression. During the **Great Depression**, so called for its length and severity, many banks failed, businesses floundered, and workers lost their jobs. By 1933, the unemployment rate had grown to 25 percent. Unable to pay their bills, thousands of people lost their homes, and millions went hungry.

THE DUST BOWL A severe drought that began in the early 1930s added to the nation's pain. When the drought began, winds picked up dirt from the dry, exhausted fields of the Great Plains. Huge dust storms arose, damaging farms across a 150,000-square-mile region called the **Dust Bowl.**

Ruined farmers set off with their families to find work, many traveling west to California. Unfortunately, little work was to be found in California, for it, like the rest of the nation, was suffering through the Great Depression. Writers such as **John Steinbeck** captured the uncertainty and despair of the times: "Carloads, caravans, homeless and hungry; twenty thousand and fifty thousand and a hundred thousand and two hundred thousand. They streamed over the mountains, hungry and restless—restless as ants, scurrying to find work to do."

Migrant Mother by Dorothea Lange, 1936. This photograph of Florence Owens Thompson with her children came to symbolize the Great Depression for many Americans.

THE NEW DEAL The country was desperate for help. During his presidential campaign in 1932, Franklin Delano Roosevelt pledged to give the country a "new deal." When elected, he fulfilled his promise by enacting various **New Deal** programs—relief for the homeless and hungry, recovery for agriculture and business, and various economic reforms to prevent such a severe depression from occurring again. Yet in truth, it was the massive spending and production spurred by World War II that finally brought the economic crisis to an end.

Cultural Influences

A developing mass culture and ideas that challenged traditional thought provided fodder for writers of the time.

New Directions

MASS CULTURE The 1920s was the first decade to be significantly shaped by **mass media.** New goods—from cars to toasters to beauty products—were flooding the market, and businesses relied on advertising to sell them. Thanks to advertising, items people had formerly considered luxuries were now deemed necessities. Mass media quickly became the ultimate source for this manufacturing of desire.

Mass production quickly and efficiently produced Americans' newfound necessities, but efficiency came with a price. Henry Ford perfected the assembly-line system, but its repetitiveness and monotony reduced workers to nameless, faceless cogs in the production process. And its products, efficiently mass-produced, led to the homogenization of American culture. **Sinclair Lewis** and many other significant writers of the day were alienated by the new values and lifestyles of their peers and soon began to criticize what they saw as Americans' conformity and materialism.

Print advertisements from the 1920s and 1930s

NEW IDEAS The writers of this period were also influenced by exciting new ideas that were challenging Americans' traditional views. A literary technique called **stream of consciousness** developed from the psychoanalytic theories of **Sigmund Freud,** who proposed that unconscious forces drive human beings and that the key to understanding behavior lay in this deeper realm of the mind. **Karl Marx's** socioeconomic theories—that history is a constant struggle between classes, for example—found their way into some of the literature of the day, mainly that of Depression-era writers. And **Albert Einstein's** theory of relativity, which overturned long-held beliefs about the nature of the universe, offered writers a fresh new way of looking at the world.

A Voice from the Times

It's the fellow with four to ten thousand a year . . . and an automobile and a nice little family in a bungalow . . . that makes the wheels of progress go round! That's the type of fellow that's ruling America today[!]

—Sinclair Lewis
from *Babbitt*

Modern Literature and the Harlem Renaissance

The writers of this period, working in a variety of genres and focusing on discrete themes, were markedly influenced by the events and culture of the day. Many responded by embracing all things new, while others celebrated their heritage.

The New Poetry

At the beginnning of the century, rapid industrialization and urbanization caused many Americans to feel that the social order governing their lives was crumbling. Poets of the day began to explore in their work the impact of rapid change and uncertainty on the individual.

Edgar Lee Masters, in his famous collection *Spoon River Anthology,* used free verse to probe the discontent beneath the apparent stability of small-town life in the United States. *Spoon River Anthology* found a wide audience, in part because it voiced concerns shared by many Americans about the transformation from a rural to an industrialized society. Like Masters, **Edwin Arlington Robinson** also exposed the tensions underlying small-town life. His poems draw psychological portraits of characters isolated in the midst of American society. In portraying their isolation, Robinson was a forerunner of the modernist movement. These poets charted new territory by challenging conventional attitudes.

Others, such as **Carl Sandburg, Robert Frost,** and **Edna St. Vincent Millay,** seemed to be more connected to earlier traditions that focused on nature and common people. Yet they, too, revealed an awareness of the changes sweeping the American landscape. For this reason, Millay, Sandburg, and Frost can be called transitional poets, those who connect past traditions with modern thought.

Works by transitional poets Millay, Frost, and Sandburg

MODERNISM Other poets of this period belong to the literary movement called **modernism** (see page 934). Modernism arose as a direct response to the social and intellectual forces shaping the 20th century. Modernist writers, many of whom were expatriates living in Europe, responded to the loss of idealism they felt in the wake of World War I. Living abroad, they experienced both the immediate and the long-term effects of World War I more acutely than did Americans at home. Most modernists also saw mass society as a threat to the individual, especially the artist. They felt that the standardization of culture resulted in alienation—a theme they captured in their work.

Experimentation was a distinguishing characteristic of these writers. "Make it new," extolled **Ezra Pound** as he urged fellow poets to abandon the artifice of past forms and search for their individual voices. **Harriet Monroe,** editor of *Poetry* magazine, wrote that the new poetry "has set before itself an ideal of absolute simplicity and sincerity—an ideal which implies an individual, unstereotyped diction; and an individual, unstereotyped rhythm." The lack of

▶ *For Your Outline*

THE NEW POETRY

- Poets began to challenge conventional thought.
- Modernists responded to historical forces such as WWI and an increasing mass society.
- Experimentation characterized modernism.
- Imagists believed that poetry should be expressed through the "rendering of concrete objects."
- Imagists favored free verse.
- In objectivist poetry, objects speak for themselves.

"stereotypes," however, made any recognizable movement hard to sustain: as soon as a style became accepted, it also became a new standard against which to rebel. The result was that modernist poetry as a body of work is as fragmented as many of its individual poems.

IMAGISM Many of the so-called new poets did, however, share the belief that poetry is most profoundly expressed through the "rendering of concrete objects." Ezra Pound called this kind of poetry **imagism** because it sought to re-create an image—not comment on it, not interpret it, but just present it. Pound became the center of a circle of poets, including **H. D.** (Hilda Doolittle) and **Amy Lowell**, who cast off the sentimentality, formal structures, and rhyme schemes of their predecessors and exploded into **free verse** (poetry without a predictable rhyme or metric scheme). Ezra Pound was especially taken with the poetry of **T. S. Eliot,** whose *The Waste Land* is considered one of the most representative and influential of modernist poems.

A Voice from the Times

so much depends
upon

a red wheel
barrow

glazed with rain
water

beside the white
chickens.

—**William Carlos Williams**
"The Red Wheelbarrow"

OBJECTIVISM One modernist poet, **William Carlos Williams,** however, vehemently disliked *The Waste Land* for its intellectualism and its references to classical literature. In response to Eliot's complex ideas and academic references, Williams famously stated that there are "no ideas but in things." Williams became the center of a new movement in modernist poetry called **objectivism,** in which poets let the objects they rendered speak for themselves. These poets invited readers to experience the homely simplicity of an object for no other reason than to understand its "this-ness."

The modernist movement had an enormous impact on later poets. Many poets today prefer to communicate through images rather than direct statements. They believe in economy of words and continue to experiment with free verse. Poetry had been altered irrevocably.

Sculpture inspired by William Carlos Williams's poem
The Red Wheelbarrow (1992), Frank Jensen. © Frank Jensen.

The Modern Short Story

Poetry was not the only form popular during this period. In fact, the period from 1890 to 1930 has been called "the Age of the Short Story" in American literature. The great popularity of the short story has often been attributed to the American temperament. Americans living in the first half of the 20th century were too impatient and too much in a hurry to read longer works. They wanted "fast" literature, just as Americans today want fast food.

Other factors contributed to the popularity of the short story as well. New methods of advertising had brought about a boom in magazine publication. As the number of magazines grew, so did the demand for short stories. In turn, magazines paid their writers handsome fees. At one point, **F. Scott Fitzgerald** was receiving as much as $4,000 for a single story. **William Faulkner,** who complained that writing short stories interfered with his more serious, longer works, earned more from the sale of four short stories to the *Saturday Evening Post* than he did from his first four novels.

THEMES PULLED FROM LIFE The upheavals of this period in American history provided rich fodder for short story writers. World War I turned many Americans' idealism into uncertainty. Civilization as people had known it was being destroyed, and writers sought to capture in their work the resulting alienation and confusion. Indeed, World War I shook the ideological foundations of some young American writers so profoundly that **Gertrude Stein,** an American writer living in Paris, called them **"the lost generation."**

These alienated writers broke with the traditions of the past, turning to new methods and stylistic devices to carry their themes. **Ernest Hemingway** and other writers composed short, fragmentary stories without traditional beginnings or endings. They left out a narrrative voice, leaving readers alone to figure out what might be going on or what a character might be feeling."I always try to write on the principle of the iceberg," Hemingway said. "There is seven-eighths of it under water for every part that shows."

The boom years of the Roaring Twenties inspired its own literature. Writers such as **F. Scott Fitzgerald** revealed the negative side of the period's gaiety and freedom by portraying wealthy and attractive people leading empty lives in their gilded surroundings. Writer **John Steinbeck** is most closely identified with the bust years of the Great Depression. Declaring that a writer's duty is to "set down his time as nearly as he can understand it," Steinbeck managed to tell, perhaps better than anyone else, the stories of ordinary people caught up

▶ *For Your Outline*

MODERN SHORT STORY

- 1890–1930 called "the Age of the Short Story"
- stories' popularity due to American temperament and growth of magazines
- "lost generation" alienated by WWI
- wrote fragmentary stories without traditional beginning or ending

THE HARLEM RENAISSANCE

- a flowering of African-American arts
- expressions of what it meant to be black in a white-dominated world
- came to an end with the Great Depression

An illustration of the Roaring Twenties high life, which served as inspiration for writers such as F. Scott Fitzgerald

in the Great Depression and lost from the devastation of the Dust Bowl.

Steinbeck, **Eudora Welty,** and many other writers of the time were beneficiaries of one of President Roosevelt's New Deal programs, the Works Progress Administration (WPA). The WPA was set up to create as many jobs as possible, as quickly as possible, including work for the nation's artists and writers. As the head of the WPA put it, "They've got to eat just like other people." Eudora Welty traveled around Mississippi for the WPA, writing articles about various projects under way in the state. She later said that these travels introduced her to the very different ways in which people lived, inspiring her later writing.

The Harlem Renaissance

Beginning in 1916 and continuing throughout the 1920s, in what came to be known as the **Great Migration,** millions of black farmers and sharecroppers moved to the urban North in search of opportunity and freedom from oppression and racial hostility. Thousands of these migrants settled in Harlem, a New York City neighborhood that quickly became the cultural center of African-American life.

Soon, the very air in Harlem seemed charged with creativity as black men and women drew on their own cultural resources—their folk traditions as well as a new urban awareness—to produce unique forms of expression. Harlem attracted worldly and race-conscious African Americans who nurtured each other's artistic, musical, and literary talents and created a flowering of African-American arts known as the **Harlem Renaissance.**

A LITERARY MOVEMENT The event that unofficially kicked off the Harlem Renaissance as a literary movement was a dinner given on March 21, 1924. Some of the nation's most celebrated writers and thinkers, black and white, gathered at New York City's Civic Club. The sponsors of the dinner—an older generation of African-American intellectuals that included **W. E. B. Du Bois, James Weldon Johnson,** and **Charles S. Johnson**—had begun organizations such as the National Urban League and the National Association for the Advancement of Colored People to promote equality for African Americans. These organizations published journals in which the writings of a younger generation were first published. **Countee Cullen, Zora Neale Hurston,** and **Langston Hughes** were among the young writers who received recognition and sometimes cash awards for

THE ARTISTS' GALLERY

The Migration of the Negro Panel no. 1 (1940–1941), Jacob Lawrence. Casein tempera on hardboard, 12″ x 18″. Acquired 1942. The Phillips Collection, Washington, D.C. © The Estate of Gwendolyn Knight Lawrence/Artist Rights Society (ARS), New York.

Jacob Lawrence

The Harlem Renaissance was not only a literary movement but a flourishing movement of the visual arts as well. Since it was difficult for black Americans of the day to attend art academies as their white counterparts did, the art schools and workshops of Harlem provided vital training for many of America's finest black artists. Jacob Lawrence was one of the first to be educated by the African-American community in Harlem.

Harlem as Muse Lawrence found inspiration in the streets of Harlem. His early work depicted the community—its people, sidewalks, streets, and storefronts—in bold colors and elemental shapes. He once said that 1930s "was actually a wonderful period in Harlem. . . . There was real vitality in the community." Lawrence rubbed elbows there with writers and artists such as Langston Hughes, Claude McKay, Romare Bearden, and Augusta Savage, all of whom emphasized their cultural identity in their work.

The Migration Series The painting shown here was the first in a 60-panel series on the Great Migration. It shows a crowd of Southern migrants about to embark on a journey to three Northern cities. Lawrence's decision to show no faces but only the shapes of hats and coats and luggage enhances the viewer's sense of a crowd surging as one entity toward the station. Lawrence based the paintings in this series on the experiences of his family and other members of his community who took part in the Great Migration.

their work in these journals, and many were present at this "coming-out party" for the writers of the Harlem Renaissance.

These young writers considered themselves the founders of a new era in literature. They looked inward and expressed what it meant to be black in a white-dominated world. They represented what came to be called "the New Negro," a sophisticated and well-educated African American with strong racial pride and self-awareness. In fact, connections made at that dinner led to a popular and enduring anthology of writing, published in 1925, titled *The New Negro.*

Zora Neale Hurston, Harlem Renaissance writer

MANY VOICES Yet this new generation of writers did not speak with only one voice. Harvard-educated **Countee Cullen,** for example, used a classical style to explore the black struggle. Others cast off more formal language and styles and wrote with the pulse of jazz rhythms. "Jazz is a heartbeat," wrote Langston Hughes, "and its heartbeat is yours." Some, like Jamaican-born **Claude McKay,** were militant. McKay's poem "If We Must Die," written after race riots in 1919, ends with an image of African Americans "pressed to the wall, dying, but fighting back!" Others, such as **Jean Toomer,** were more interested in exploring their own identities than the concerns of a whole race. "I was inescapably myself," he wrote. Despite their varied perspectives, however, these writers shared a deep pride in their heritage and asserted their cultural identity through their work.

The Harlem Renaissance was brought to a premature end by the economic collapse of the Great Depression. Many of the writers who had gathered in Harlem were forced to scatter and take other jobs to support themselves. Nevertheless, their work planted seeds that continue to generate important writing from the African-American perspective.

Journalism as Literature

In the early decades of the 20th century, journalism came into its own as an influential part of the literary scene (see page 1092). The sensationalism and reckless misinterpretation of facts that had characterized journalism in the last decades of the 19th century were being replaced by an interest in stylistic quality and the recognition that there was more to news than scandal. Many of the writers who were to become major figures in American literature learned their craft—and developed some of their most compelling subjects—writing for newspapers or magazines.

REPORTING THE ERA Fresh out of high school in 1917, **Ernest Hemingway** worked as a reporter for the *Kansas City Star.* The newspaper's strict rules of

> ***For Your Outline***
>
> **JOURNALISM AS LITERATURE**
>
> - Journalism turned from sensationalism.
> - Writers honed their craft at newspapers and magazines.
> - Hemingway, Porter, and Steinbeck reported on the day's big news.
> - White, Thurber, and Parker built their reputations at *New Yorker.*

style helped him develop the clear, provocative prose that characterizes his work: "Use short sentences. Use short first paragraphs. Use vigorous English. Be positive, not negative." Hemingway was also a war correspondent who reported on the Spanish Civil War, and he was the first Allied journalist to enter Paris on August 25, 1944—the day it was liberated from Nazi control.

Some other writers who became well-known for their fiction produced fine journalism as well. **Katherine Anne Porter,** for example, worked for several newspapers and magazines. On assignment in 1920, she traveled to Mexico and arrived in the middle of a revolution. Her observations of this conflict later became the subject of several short stories in a collection called *Flowering Judas* (1930), which launched her literary career. **John Steinbeck** turned his hand to journalism as well, reporting in 1936 for the *San Francisco News* about the plight of California's migrant farm workers and working in 1943 as a war correspondent for the *New York Herald Tribune.*

A Voice from the Times

This is not a novel to be tossed aside lightly. It should be thrown with great force.

—Dorothy Parker
from a literary review

MAGAZINES ON THE RISE In the first decades of the 20th century, the popular magazine came into its own as new magazines were created to satisfy every taste and interest. The *New Yorker,* which first appeared in 1925, was founded by one-time newspaperman **Harold Ross.** To staff his new magazine, Ross sought writers with newspaper experience, writers who could grind out "the gleams and sparkles of humor and satire from the grist of human nature and the news of the world." Among them were **E. B. White, James Thurber,** and **Dorothy Parker,** who went on to write poetry, short stories, and novels. Yet these writers' reputations as witty, satiric observers of contemporary society were built on the essays, commentary, and book and theater reviews (and in the case of Thurber, cartoons too) that they contributed to the *New Yorker.*

Like poetry and short stories, literary journalism continues to be popular. Today's writers can thank the innovators of the modernist movement, America's giants of the short story form, the groundbreaking writers of the Harlem Renaissance, and the literary journalists of this earlier era for many of the themes, styles, and forms currently in use.

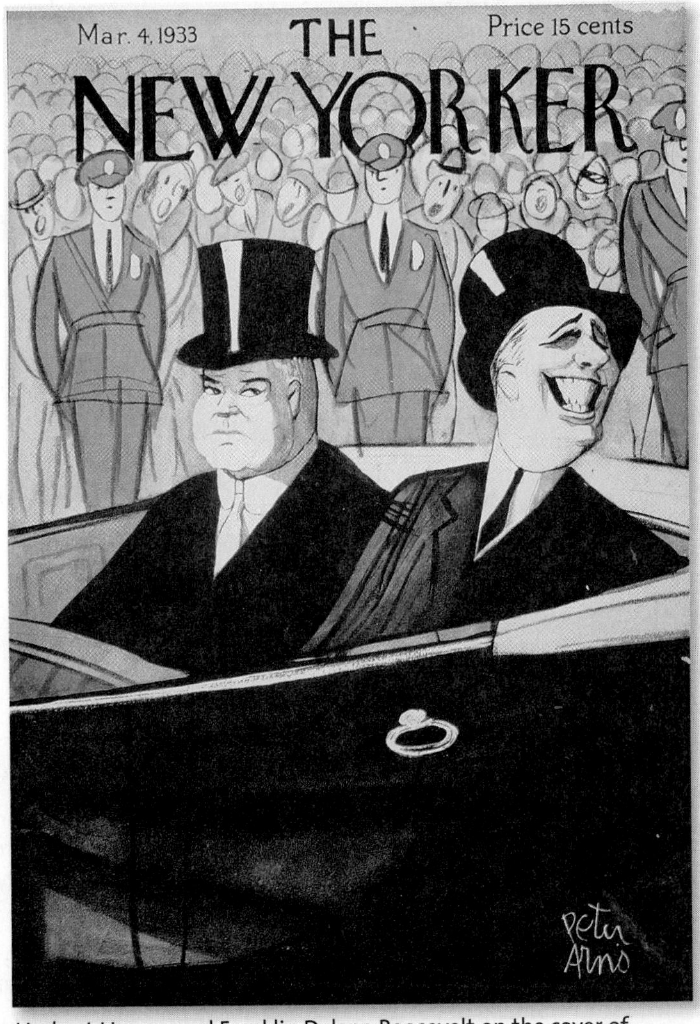

Herbert Hoover and Franklin Delano Roosevelt on the cover of the *New Yorker,* 1933

Connecting Literature, History, and Culture

The literature and culture of the United States during this period reflect developments occurring elsewhere in the world. Use the timeline and the questions on the next page to find connections.

AMERICAN LITERARY MILESTONES

1910

1912 Harriet Monroe ▶ founds *Poetry: A Magazine of Verse;* Edna St. Vincent Millay publishes "Renascence."

1913 Ezra Pound forms a group of imagist poets in London.

1915

1915 Edgar Lee Masters examines small-town life in *Spoon River Anthology.*

1916 Carl Sandburg publishes *Chicago Poems.*

1919 Claude McKay publishes his militant "If We Must Die."

1920

1920 Edith Wharton's *The Age of Innocence* is published.

1921 Langston Hughes's poem "The Negro Speaks of Rivers" appears in *The Crisis* magazine.

1922 T. S. Eliot's *The Waste Land* captures modern sensibilities.

1924 Robert Frost wins the first of his four Pulitzer Prizes.

HISTORICAL CONTEXT

1910

1911 The National Urban League is founded.

1912 The *Titanic* sinks, killing more than 1,500 people.

1913 The Armory Show in New York City introduces European modernist paintings and sculpture to shocked Americans.

1915

1916 Jeannette Rankin of Montana becomes the first woman elected to the U.S. House of Representatives.

1917 The United States enters World War I. ▶

1919 Race riots break out in 25 U.S. cities.

1920

1920 The 18th Amendment ushers in the era of Prohibition, and the 19th Amendment assures women of the right to vote.

1921 Albert Einstein presents a lecture in New York City about his theory of relativity. ▶

1924 Native Americans win full citizenship.

WORLD CULTURE AND EVENTS

1910

1911 Marie Curie wins the Nobel Prize in chemistry. ▶

1914 World War I begins with the assassination of Archduke Francis Ferdinand of Austria.

1915

1915 The short story "Rashomon" by Japanese modernist writer Akutagawa Ryunosuke is published.

1918 A flu pandemic kills more than 20 million people worldwide.

1919 The Treaty of Versailles spells out the peace terms for the end of World War I.

1920

1922 James Joyce publishes his masterpiece, *Ulysses.*

1923 Sigmund Freud publishes *The Ego and the Id,* examining the causes of human behavior. ▶

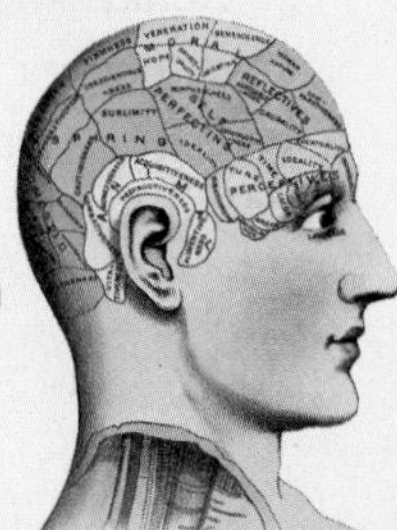

MAKING CONNECTIONS

- Why was the year 1913 an important one for poetry and art?
- Violence stirred in the years between 1910 and 1940. Give an example from each of the three main sections of the timeline that support this observation.
- Name three women of this period who were gaining recognition or breaking barriers in literature, politics, and science.

COMMON CORE

RI 7 Integrate and evaluate multiple sources of information presented in different media or formats as well as in words in order to address a question or solve a problem.

1925

1925 F. Scott Fitzgerald's *The Great Gatsby* explores the American dream.

1926 Ernest Hemingway's novel *The Sun Also Rises* chronicles expatriates after WWI.

1929 William Faulkner's *The Sound and the Fury* experiments with stream of consciousness and multiple viewpoints.

1930

1930 *Flowering Judas* by Katherine Anne Porter is published. ▶

1932 Pearl S. Buck wins a Pulitzer Prize for *The Good Earth.*

1933 William Faulkner's *A Green Bough* is published.

1935

1936 Margaret Mitchell publishes *Gone with the Wind.*

1937 Zora Neale Hurston's *Their Eyes Were Watching God* is published.

1940 Richard Wright's *Native Son* is published.

1925

1927 Charles Lindbergh makes his historic solo nonstop flight from New York to Paris; the first talking movie, *The Jazz Singer,* stars Al Jolson.

1929 The Wall Street stock market crashes and the Great Depression begins. ▼

STAGE BROADWAY SCREEN

VARIETY

PRICE 25¢

NEW YORK, WEDNESDAY, OCTOBER 30, 1929

WALL ST. LAYS AN EGG

1930

1931 The Empire State building is completed. ▶

1932 Franklin Delano Roosevelt is elected president for the first of his four terms.

1933 Roosevelt's New Deal tries to put Americans back to work.

1935

1938 The Fair Labor Standards Act sets a minimum wage and limits the workweek to 40 hours.

1939 Judy Garland stars in *The Wizard of Oz.* ▼

1925

1925 Virginia Woolf's innovative novel *Mrs. Dalloway* is published in England.

1928 Joseph Stalin becomes dictator of Communist Russia. Chiang Kai-shek becomes head of the Nationalist government in China.

1930

1930 Mahatma Gandhi leads a nonviolent march to protest British taxes.

1932 Japan takes control of Manchuria.

1933 Adolf Hitler takes control of Germany.

1935

1936 The Spanish Civil War breaks out.

1937 Japan invades China.

1939 World War II begins with the German invasion of Poland.

UNIT 5

The Legacy of the Era

Mass Culture

COMMON CORE

SL 1 Initiate and participate effectively in a range of collaborative discussions.
W 7 Conduct short research projects to answer a question.
W 10 Write routinely over shorter time frames for a range of tasks and purposes.

Many American writers of the early 20th century were reacting against a rising mass culture and the conformity and materialism they saw as its inevitable effects. These writers would likely be astounded to see the extent to which mass culture has overtaken the United States today. From the restaurant business, with nationwide chains replacing family-owned places, to a fashion scene in which only a very few styles (and sizes) are considered desirable—mass culture is everywhere you look.

DISCUSS In small groups, brainstorm ten examples of our current mass culture. Then discuss what you see as the effects—positive and negative—of mass culture on our society as a whole.

Trends in Journalism

Many of the best writers of the early 20th century, such as Ernest Hemingway, E. B. White, and William Faulkner, sharpened their skills writing for newspapers and magazines. Today there is no shortage of talented journalists, yet the nature of the business has changed. Thousands of newspapers and magazines—one for nearly every conceivable interest—are printed every day. Twenty-four-hour news stations and Web sites give minute-by-minute accounts of current events, and blogs allow people to respond personally to the news.

QUICKWRITE With all of the venues available for today's writers to publish their ideas, how much of it is worthwhile literature? Is some simply a lot of hot air? Write several paragraphs sharing your opinions about today's journalists and the everyday people who, thanks to the Internet, can reach the masses with their words.

The New Deal Today

Several of President Roosevelt's New Deal programs remain in place today: Social Security (to pay out retirement pensions), the FDIC (to insure bank deposits), agricultural price supports (to protect farmers from price devaluation), and the SEC (to regulate the stock market). Yet some of these long-running programs have become politically controversial in today's world.

RESEARCH With a partner, research one of these programs. Summarize for your class why the program is politically controversial, what suggestions have been made to reform or eliminate it, and your opinion of its merit.

COMMON CORE

RL 4 Determine the meaning of words and phrases as they are used in the text, including figurative and connotative meanings. **RL 5** Analyze how an author's choices concerning how to structure specific parts of a text contribute to its overall structure and meaning as well as its aesthetic impact.

Selected Poetry

by Langston Hughes

VIDEO TRAILER THINK central KEYWORD: HML11-878A

DID YOU KNOW?

Langston Hughes . . .

- was one of the first African Americans to earn a living solely from writing.
- was dubbed the "poet low-rate" of Harlem by some African-American intellectuals.
- wrote radio jingles during World War II to promote the purchase of war bonds.

Meet the Author

Langston Hughes 1902–1967

Langston Hughes was one of the leading poets of the Harlem Renaissance as well as an accomplished novelist, playwright, and essayist. His writings center on poor and working-class African Americans, a group whom literature had generally ignored.

Early Inspirations James Mercer Langston Hughes started writing poetry in seventh grade, when his classmates elected him class poet. He admired the work of Paul Laurence Dunbar and Carl Sandburg, two poets known for their efforts to capture the voices of everyday Americans. After graduating from high school, Hughes went to live with his father in Mexico, where he became fluent in Spanish. On the train journey south, he composed what would become one of his most famous poems, "The Negro Speaks of Rivers."

Busboy Poet In 1921, Hughes enrolled at Columbia University in New York City. He left after one year to travel the world as a cook's assistant aboard a ship. In 1925, Hughes settled in Washington, D.C., and took a job busing tables at a hotel restaurant. One day Vachel Lindsay, a well-known poet, came to the hotel. Hughes mustered the courage to slip three of his poems, including "The Weary Blues," beside Lindsay's plate. Lindsay liked the poems, and the next morning's newspapers reported Lindsay's discovery of the "busboy poet."

A year later, Hughes published his first poetry collection, *The Weary Blues.* His gritty depiction of "workers, roustabouts, and singers and job hunters" angered some African-American critics who felt that members of the race should always be portrayed in the best possible light. Hughes responded to these criticisms, saying, "I knew only the people I had grown up with, and they weren't people whose shoes were always shined. . . . But they seemed to me good people, too."

Poet Laureate of Harlem As a poet, Hughes kept his language direct; he made no attempt to be obscure or pretentious. He celebrated the lively nightlife and the everyday experiences of working-class African Americans, often re-creating the structures and rhythms of blues and jazz music in works such as *Montage of a Dream Deferred* (1951), a book-length suite of related poems. Hughes became informally known as the Poet Laureate of Harlem and today is universally recognized as the most influential voice of the Harlem Renaissance.

Author Online THINK central
Go to thinkcentral.com. KEYWORD: HML11-878B

TEXT ANALYSIS: SPEAKER

You know that the **speaker** of a poem, like the narrator of a story, is the voice that talks to the reader. In his poems, Langston Hughes created speakers who represented important aspects of African-American culture. Sometimes his speaker is the voice of the culture itself.

I've known rivers ancient as the world and older than the
flow of human blood in human veins.

Hughes also uses his speakers to portray the joys and struggles of working-class African Americans.

In a deep song voice with a melancholy tone
I heard that Negro sing, that old piano moan—

As you read each poem, try to identify the speaker of the poem and what aspects of African-American life the speaker describes.

READING SKILL: ANALYZE RHYTHM AND REPETITION

When Hughes began writing, most African-American poets tried to sound like the white poets they read in school. Instead, Hughes drew his inspiration from jazz and blues music, using the rhythm and repetition of these musical forms to structure his poetry. Musical elements found in Hughes's poetry include

- jazz-influenced **rhythm** (the pattern of stressed and unstressed syllables) that features strong accents, quick changes in rhythm, and irregular beats
- rhythmic **repetition** of words and phrases, like that used in blues lyrics
- the **refrain,** one or more repeated lines of poetry that function like the chorus of a song

As you read each poem, use a chart like the one shown to record examples of these musical patterns.

Rhythm	Repetition	Refrain

Complete the activities in your **Reader/Writer Notebook**.

What shapes your IDENTITY?

Hughes wrote poetry to honor his African-American heritage, but he didn't limit himself to great heroes and historical events. For Hughes, it was the vibrant culture of everyday people—their music, their slang, and their experiences of life in the city—that shaped his sense of identity.

DISCUSS What everyday experiences help shape your identity? List images and activities that characterize the way you live: the sounds and smells of your neighborhood, the places you go, the foods you eat, and so on. In a small group, compare your answers. Which experiences, if any, do group members have in common?

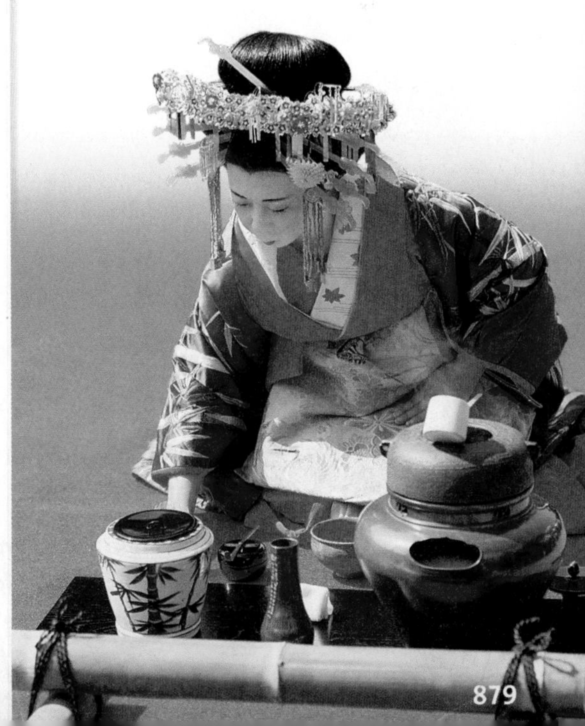

Harlem

Langston Hughes

What happens to a dream deferred?

Does it dry up
like a raisin in the sun?
Or fester like a sore—
And then run?
Does it stink like rotten meat?
Or crust and sugar over—
like a syrupy sweet? A

Maybe it just sags
like a heavy load.

Or does it explode?

Analyze Visuals ▶
What elements of this painting help capture the thriving street life in Harlem?

A RHYTHM AND REPETITION
Identify the pattern of stresses in lines 2–8. Which words are emphasized by this rhythm?

Text Analysis

1. **Clarify** What does the speaker mean by "a dream deferred"?
2. **Make Inferences** What social or political consequences are hinted at in the poem's last line?
3. **Interpret Figurative Language** List the **similes** the speaker uses to describe the effect of a deferred dream. What do these comparisons reveal about the speaker's attitude?

Street Shadows (1959), Jacob Lawrence. Egg tempera on hardboard, 24″ × 30″. Private collection, New York. Photograph courtesy of Gwendolyn Knight Lawrence/Art Resource, New York. © 2008 The Jacob and Gwendolyn Lawrence Foundation, Seattle/ Artists Rights Society (ARS), New York.

The Negro Speaks of Rivers (1998), Phoebe Beasley. Silkscreen. © Phoebe Beasley.

The Negro Speaks *of* Rivers

Langston Hughes

I've known rivers:
I've known rivers ancient as the world and older than the
flow of human blood in human veins. **B**

My soul has grown deep like the rivers.

I bathed in the Euphrates[1] when dawns were young.
I built my hut near the Congo and it lulled me to sleep.
I looked upon the Nile and raised the pyramids above it.
I heard the singing of the Mississippi when Abe Lincoln
went down to New Orleans,[2] and I've seen its muddy
bosom turn all golden in the sunset.

I've known rivers:
Ancient, dusky[3] rivers.

My soul has grown deep like the rivers. **C**

B SPEAKER
Reread lines 1–2. What traits of the speakers are emphasized by Hughes's word choice?

C RHYTHM AND REPETITION
Reread the poem. Which line serves as the poem's **refrain?**

1. **Euphrates** (yo͞o-frā′tēz): a river flowing through present-day Turkey, Syria, and Iraq. The valley between the Tigris and Euphrates rivers was the site of one of the world's earliest civilizations.
2. **when Abe Lincoln went down to New Orleans:** Lincoln's first glimpse of the horrors of slavery reportedly came on his trip to New Orleans as a young man.
3. **dusky:** dark; shadowy.

I, Too

Langston Hughes

I, too, sing America.

I am the darker brother.
They send me to eat in the kitchen
When company comes,
But I laugh,
And eat well,
And grow strong. **D**

Tomorrow,
I'll be at the table
When company comes.
Nobody'll dare
Say to me,
"Eat in the kitchen,"
Then.

Besides,
They'll see how beautiful I am
And be ashamed—

I, too, am America.

D SPEAKER
Reread lines 1–7. Identify the speaker of the poem. What aspects of the African-American experience does the speaker describe?

Text Analysis

1. **Summarize** In "I, Too," what is the speaker's attitude toward America?
2. **Interpret Imagery** What is the significance of the four rivers mentioned in "The Negro Speaks of Rivers"?
3. **Compare and Contrast Speakers** What qualities do the speakers of both poems share? In what ways are they different?

The *Weary* Blues

Langston Hughes

Droning a drowsy syncopated[1] tune,
Rocking back and forth to a mellow croon,
I heard a Negro play.
Down on Lenox Avenue[2] the other night
By the pale dull pallor[3] of an old gas light
He did a lazy sway. . . .
He did a lazy sway. . . .
To the tune o' those Weary Blues.
With his ebony hands on each ivory key
He made that poor piano moan with melody.
O Blues!
Swaying to and fro on his rickety stool
He played that sad raggy tune like a musical fool.
Sweet Blues!
Coming from a black man's soul.
O Blues!
In a deep song voice with a melancholy tone
I heard that Negro sing, that old piano moan—
"Ain't got nobody in all this world,
Ain't got nobody but ma self.
I's gwine to quit ma frownin'
And put ma troubles on the shelf."
Thump, thump, thump, went his foot on the floor.
He played a few chords then he sang some more— **E**
"I got the Weary Blues
And I can't be satisfied.
Got the Weary Blues
And can't be satisfied—
I ain't happy no mo'
And I wish that I had died."
And far into the night he crooned that tune.
The stars went out and so did the moon.
The singer stopped playing and went to bed
While the Weary Blues echoed through his head.
He slept like a rock or a man that's dead.

COMMON CORE RL 4

Language Coach

Connotation The images or feelings you connect to a word add a finer shade of meaning, called **connotation.** *Croon* (line 2) means "soft, sentimental song." What other words in lines 1–2 share croon's calm connotations?

E RHYTHM AND REPETITION
Identify three examples of repetition in the poem thus far. Which line or phrase might be considered the poem's refrain?

1. **syncopated** (sĭng′kə-pā′tĭd): characterized by a shifting of stresses from normally strong to normally weak beats.
2. **Lenox Avenue:** a main north-south street in Harlem.
3. **pallor** (păl′ər): lack of color.

Comprehension

1. **Clarify** What hope does the speaker of "I, Too" express?
2. **Recall** Who are the individuals described in "The Weary Blues"?
3. **Summarize** What happens to the speaker of "The Weary Blues"?

COMMON CORE

RL 4 Determine the meaning of words and phrases as they are used in the text, including figurative and connotative meanings. **RL 5** Analyze how an author's choices concerning how to structure specific parts of a text contribute to its overall structure and meaning as well as its aesthetic impact.

Text Analysis

4. **Identify Sensory Details** Many of Hughes's poems are rich in details that appeal to the five senses. Reread "Harlem" and "The Weary Blues." For each poem, use a chart like the one shown to record examples of each kind of sensory detail. Which example did you find especially vivid? Explain your answer.

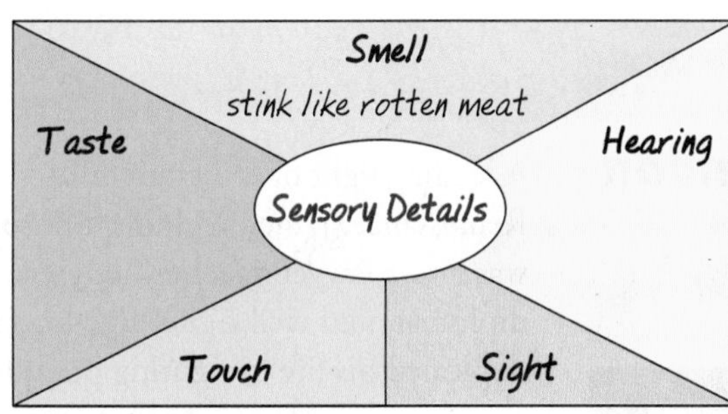

5. **Analyze Rhythm and Repetition** Review the chart you created while reading. Which poem is most influenced by jazz music? Cite examples from the poem.
6. **Draw Conclusions About Author's Perspective** Use the events, situations, and ideas presented in each of Hughes's poems to draw conclusions about his views on African-American identity. In Hughes's eyes, what characteristics define African-American culture?
7. **Evaluate Speakers** Consider the four poems you read. In your opinion, which speaker best achieves each of the following goals? Cite details from the poems in your answers.
   - captures Hughes's pride in African-American culture
   - reflects the everyday life of African Americans
   - conveys the sounds of African-American speech

Text Criticism

8. **Critical Interpretations** In a review of Hughes's poetry collection *The Weary Blues,* poet Countee Cullen criticized Hughes for "too much emphasis on strictly Negro themes" and questioned whether jazz poems belong to "that select and austere circle of high literary expression which we call poetry." Do you agree with Cullen's concerns? Why or why not?

What shapes your IDENTITY?

Much of Langston Hughes's **identity** was shaped by his environment. How did he feel about the people and places he wrote about in his poetry? Explain your answer using examples from Hughes's poems.

COMMON CORE

RL 5 Analyze how an author's choices concerning how to structure specific parts of a text contribute to its overall structure and meaning as well as its aesthetic impact. **RL 9** Demonstrate knowledge of early-twentieth-century works of American literature, including how two or more texts from the same period treat similar themes or topics.

My City

Poem by James Weldon Johnson

If We Must Die

Poem by Claude McKay

Meet the Authors

James Weldon Johnson

1871–1938

A leading light of the Harlem Renaissance, James Weldon Johnson was also a lawyer, teacher, songwriter, diplomat, and civil rights activist. He dedicated his life to fighting prejudice and inspiring African Americans to new heights of social and literary achievement.

Unstoppable Talent After graduating from Atlanta University in 1894, Johnson worked as a school principal, founded a daily newspaper, and became the first African-American lawyer since Reconstruction to be admitted to the Florida bar. In 1901, the restless Johnson traveled to New York, where he and his younger brother became successful Broadway songwriters. One of their early songs, "Lift Every Voice and Sing," eventually became known as the African-American national anthem.

Renaissance Man Johnson also published works in many genres of literature. Among his best-known works are his novel *The Autobiography of an Ex-Colored Man,* his poetry collection *God's Trombones,* and a cultural history, *Black Manhattan.* He also edited several groundbreaking collections of African-American poetry and spirituals.

Claude McKay

c. 1890–1948

Hailed by James Weldon Johnson as "the poet of rebellion," Jamaican-born Festus Claudius McKay made his name as a fierce critic of racism in the United States. His poetry collection *Harlem Shadows,* published in 1922, is considered one of the founding works of the Harlem Renaissance.

Poet of Rebellion Already established as a poet, 23-year-old McKay arrived in the United States in 1912. In 1919, the country was torn apart by a wave of violent attacks against African Americans. Racial tensions erupted into 26 riots across the country during a period known as the Red Summer. "If We Must Die" was McKay's anguished response, which became instantly popular among African Americans.

Enduring Message During World War II, the poem took on new meaning when British Prime Minister Sir Winston Churchill quoted from it during a speech. The poem went on to become a battle cry for the Allies in their fight against the Nazis. McKay often complained that the fame of this one poem had overshadowed his other work, which included the novels *Home to Harlem* and *Banana Bottom.*

Author Online THINK central

Go to thinkcentral.com. KEYWORD: HML11-886

TEXT ANALYSIS: SONNET

New ideas help keep poetic traditions alive. The centuries-old **sonnet,** a 14-line lyric poem with specific patterns of rhythm and rhyme, has been reimagined by many poets. The poems in this lesson are based on two classic types of sonnets.

- The **Italian,** or **Petrarchan, sonnet** is divided into two metrics: an **octave,** or eight-line grouping, and a **sestet,** or six-line grouping. The usual rhyme scheme for the octave is *abbaabba.* The rhyme scheme for the sestet varies but is often *cdccde* or *cdccdc.*
- The **English,** or **Shakespearean, sonnet** has a rhyme scheme of *abab cdcd efef gg.* This divides the poem into four distinct line groups: three **quatrains,** or four-line units, followed by a **couplet,** a pair of rhymed lines.

Sonnets are often written in **iambic pentameter.** In this meter, each line includes five pairs of syllables, the first unstressed, the second stressed. However, modern poets often break the rules when writing sonnets. As you read, note how each poet adapts the sonnet's structure to fit a modern message.

READING SKILL: UNDERSTAND FORM AND MEANING

Understanding a sonnet's structure can help you interpret its meaning. Keep in mind the following:

- In many sonnets, quatrains, octaves, and other line groupings are not set apart by stanza breaks. Use the rhyme scheme to determine the poem's line groupings.
- Each line grouping usually expresses one main idea.
- The first line grouping of the sonnet describes the speaker's situation or problem. The last line grouping resolves, concludes, or reacts to that situation.

As you begin to read each sonnet, identify the line groupings, listing them in a chart like the one shown. Also record in your chart the main idea expressed in each line grouping.

Title:	
Line Grouping	Main Idea
1st quatrain	

Complete the activities in your **Reader/Writer Notebook.**

When does old become NEW *again?*

When CDs came on the market, vinyl records seemed doomed. Then, hip-hop artists made the scratching of a needle on vinyl the signature sound of a new style of music. Artists often bring back old ideas to give them new meaning. Poets James Weldon Johnson and Claude McKay did just that with their revival of the sonnet, breathing new life into a 700-year-old poetic form.

PRESENT Think of an artist, a musician, or a writer from the past whose work you admire. Create a plan to adapt this person's work to make a creation of your own, and present your plan to the class.

My City

James Weldon Johnson

When I come down to sleep death's endless night,
The threshold of the unknown dark to cross,
What to me then will be the keenest loss,
When this bright world blurs on my fading sight?
Will it be that no more I shall see the trees
Or smell the flowers or hear the singing birds
Or watch the flashing streams or patient herds?
No, I am sure it will be none of these. **A**

But, ah! Manhattan's sights and sounds, her smells,
Her crowds, her throbbing force, the thrill that comes
From being of her a part, her subtle spells,
Her shining towers, her avenues, her slums—
O God! the stark, unutterable pity,
To be dead, and never again behold my city! **B**

Analyze Visuals ▶
What details in this photo correspond to the poet's vision of his city?

A FORM AND MEANING
Use the **stanza break** to identify the line groupings of this poem. What is the main idea of lines 1–8?

B SONNET
Judging from its line groupings, what type of sonnet is this?

View of Broadway near Times Square in Manhattan, 1920s

CAPITOL
Maxwell House Coffee
REGINALD DENNY
MICHAEL STROGOFF
CHEVROLET
General Outdoor Adv Co
FOLLOW THE ARROW AND YOU FOLLOW THE STYLE
ARROW COLLARS
COLUMBIA
COLUMBIA BURLESQUE
PALACE

If We Must Die

Claude McKay

If we must die, let it not be like hogs
Hunted and penned in an inglorious[1] spot,
While round us bark the mad and hungry dogs,
Making their mock at our accursed lot.
If we must die, O let us nobly die,
So that our precious blood may not be shed
In vain; then even the monsters we defy
Shall be constrained[2] to honor us though dead! **C**
O kinsmen! we must meet the common foe!
Though far outnumbered let us show us brave,
And for their thousand blows deal one deathblow!
What though before us lies the open grave?
Like men we'll face the murderous, cowardly pack,
Pressed to the wall, dying, but fighting back! **D**

C SONNET
State the **rhyme scheme** of lines 1–8. Considering the rhyme scheme, what type of sonnet is this?

D FORM AND MEANING
By the end of the poem, what resolution has the speaker reached?

1. **inglorious:** shameful; disgraceful.
2. **constrained:** forced.

Comprehension

1. **Recall** In "My City," what will the speaker most regret about death?
2. **Clarify** In "If We Must Die," what type of death does the speaker argue for?
3. **Paraphrase** In "If We Must Die," what is the meaning of the phrase "making their mock at our accursed lot"?

Text Analysis

4. **Identify Form** McKay's poem closely follows the conventions of a traditional sonnet. Which kind of sonnet is it? Explain your answer.
5. **Make Inferences About Audience** Recall the events that inspired McKay to write "If We Must Die." What audience can you infer the speaker is addressing? Describe the speaker's relationship to this audience.
6. **Classify Sonnet** Johnson's poem includes features of both Shakespearean and Petrarchan sonnets. Using a chart like the one shown, decide whether each listed feature of the poem's structure is characteristic of Shakespearean sonnets, Petrarchan sonnets, or both. Based on your answers, which label is the better description of Johnson's sonnet?

	Shakespearean	*Petrarchan*
Structure		
Rhyme Scheme		
Meter		
Final Couplet		

7. **Analyze Form and Meaning** Review the chart you completed as you read. Notice Johnson's use of a stanza break, whereas McKay uses none. In your opinion, how does this choice contribute to each poem's meaning? Explain.
8. **Examine Author's Purpose** Consider the motives that might have inspired African-American poets to express themselves in European poetic forms. What artistic and social messages are suggested by the Harlem Renaissance revival of the sonnet?

Text Criticism

9. **Critical Interpretations** Claude McKay once stated that he hoped his poems could convey universal meaning. Reread the background on "If We Must Die" included in the author biography. Does the poem's history suggest McKay was successful in his goal? Explain your answer.

When does old become **NEW** *again?*

In the last decade or so, recycling has become a main focus of American society. What value do you see in reusing old or outdated things? Explain your answer.

COMMON CORE

RL 5 Analyze how an author's choices concerning how to structure specific parts of a text contribute to its overall structure and meaning as well as its aesthetic impact. **RL 9** Demonstrate knowledge of early-twentieth-century works of American literature, including how two or more texts from the same period treat similar themes or topics.

Any Human to Another

Poem by Countee Cullen

Storm Ending

Poem by Jean Toomer

A Black Man Talks of Reaping

Poem by Arna Bontemps

COMMON CORE

RL 4 Determine the meaning of words and phrases as they are used in the text, including figurative and connotative meanings; analyze the impact of specific word choices on meaning and tone. **RL 9** Demonstrate knowledge of how two or more texts from the same period treat similar themes or topics.

Meet the Authors

Countee Cullen
1903–1946

In 1925, while still an undergraduate at New York University, Countee Cullen (kŭl'ən) published his first poetry collection, *Color,* which won immediate critical acclaim.

Cullen's greatest poetic influences were the English Romantic poets, especially John Keats. Although some of Cullen's poetry deals directly with experiences specific to African Americans, much of his work addresses universal concerns such as love and faith. Cullen adamantly believed that poetry could break down racial barriers and disliked being pigeonholed, once stating, "If I am going to be a poet at all, I am going to be a Poet and not a Negro Poet."

Jean Toomer
1894–1967

Born in Washington, D.C., Nathan Eugene Toomer grew up in a prominent, racially mixed family. Toomer could pass for white, and as a young man, often changed his racial identification from white to black and back again. As an adult, he rejected the concept of race altogether and embraced an idealistic vision of himself as a founder of a "united human race."

Toomer was drawn to Eastern philosophy and Imagist poetry—poetry that conveys meaning through the use of precise, striking images. His reputation rests mainly on his novel *Cane* (1923), an experimental work exploring the African-American experience through fragments of poetry and prose.

Arna Bontemps
1902–1973

After graduating from college in 1923, Arna Bontemps (bôn-täN') discovered a thriving literary scene in Harlem that he called a "foretaste of paradise." Despite his love for the bustle of the Northern cities, Bontemps was most deeply inspired by the Southern roots of African-American culture. Nearly all of his stories, novels, and plays are set in the South and provide vivid portrayals of rural life.

Bontemps, who earned his living as an educator, left Harlem in 1931 and spent most of his career in the South. His major works include the short story collection *The Old South* and the novel *God Sends Sunday,* which is often cited as the final work of the Harlem Renaissance.

Author Online

TEXT ANALYSIS: THEME

In poetry, the speaker's descriptions of the world will often help you identify a poem's **theme,** its underlying message about life or human nature. In most works, the theme is implied, rather than directly stated. Consider these lines:

Your grief and mine
Must intertwine

The speaker might be talking to a loved one or making a general point about sorrow. To uncover the message of a poem, use these strategies:

- Consider the title. What information does it reveal?
- Identify the speaker. Is the speaker the voice of an individual or of a group?
- Notice key images and think about their meaning.
- Consider the mood, or feeling, the speaker conveys.

Readers notice different details and often find different themes in the same work. As you read, try to draw your own conclusions about each poet's message.

READING SKILL: DISTINGUISH FIGURATIVE FROM LITERAL MEANING

You've learned that poets use **figurative language,** such as similes, metaphors, and personification, to go beyond the literal meaning of words. Use these steps to uncover this extra level of meaning:

- Read each poem once to grasp its overall meaning.
- Reread the poem, noting important words and phrases.
- Ask questions about comparisons you notice. What is being compared, and how are these things alike?
- Uncover hidden metaphors by noting descriptive details. What do these details remind you of?

As you read each poem, record examples of figurative language in a chart like the one shown. Then, jot down some of the impressions created by the words the poet chooses.

Example	Impressions
like an arrow	

Complete the activities in your **Reader/Writer Notebook**.

How do you VIEW *the world?*

You can see a glass as half empty or half full. You can see a pile of old newspapers as trash to be thrown away or as the makings of papier-mâché. The way you see things—your outlook—says a lot about who you are.

QUICKWRITE Many factors shape your outlook—your personality, your life experiences, your state of mind. Write one or two sentences describing your outlook. Then, explain the factors you think have most influenced the way you look at the world.

Any Human to Another

Countee Cullen

The ills I sorrow at
Not me alone
Like an arrow,
Pierce to the marrow,
Through the fat
And past the bone.

Your grief and mine
Must intertwine
Like sea and river,
Be fused and mingle,
Diverse yet single,
Forever and forever. **A**

Let no man be so proud
And confident,
To think he is allowed
A little tent
Pitched in a meadow
Of sun and shadow
All his little own.

Joy may be shy, unique,
Friendly to a few,
Sorrow never scorned to speak
To any who
Were false or true. **B**

Your every grief
Like a blade
Shining and unsheathed[1]
Must strike me down.
Of bitter aloes[2] wreathed,
My sorrow must be laid
On your head like a crown.

COMMON CORE RL 9

A THEME
Remember that **theme** is a work's underlying message about life or human nature. Reread lines 1–12, and then consider the title of the poem. In your own words, state the theme of the poem in one sentence. Then, discuss whether you think this theme is relevant to life.

B FIGURATIVE MEANING
Identify two examples of **personification** in lines 20–24. What qualities are indicated by these lines?

---

1. **unsheathed:** removed from its protective case.
2. **bitter aloes:** spiny-leafed plants whose juice is used to make a bad-tasting medicine.

Storm Ending

Jean Toomer

Thunder blossoms gorgeously above our heads,
Great, hollow, bell-like flowers,
Rumbling in the wind,
Stretching clappers to strike our ears . . **C**
Full-lipped flowers
Bitten by the sun
Bleeding rain
Dripping rain like golden honey—
And the sweet earth flying from the thunder.

C FIGURATIVE MEANING
What is thunder compared to in lines 1–4? Explain what qualities are emphasized by this comparison.

Field and Storm (2003), April Gornik. Oil on linen, 74″ × 95″. Courtesy of the artist and Danese Gallery, New York.

A Black Man Talks of Reaping

Arna Bontemps

Sunflowers, Charly Palmer. Mixed media collage on canvas, 48″ × 24″. © Charly Palmer.

I have sown beside all waters in my day.
I planted deep, within my heart the fear
That wind or fowl would take the grain away.
I planted safe against this stark, lean year. **D**

I scattered seed enough to plant the land
In rows from Canada to Mexico,
But for my reaping[1] only what the hand
Can hold at once is all that I can show.

Yet what I sowed and what the orchard yields
My brother's sons are gathering stalk and root,
Small wonder then my children glean[2] in fields
They have not sown, and feed on bitter fruit. **E**

▲ Analyze Visuals
What elements of this painting reflect the theme of the poem?

D FIGURATIVE MEANING
Reread lines 1–4. What idea do the words *sown, planted,* and *grain* have in common?

E THEME
In lines 11–12, why are the children's gleanings described as "bitter fruit"?

1. **reaping:** harvesting grain.
2. **glean:** gather grain left behind by reapers.

Comprehension

1. **Summarize** In "Any Human to Another," what comparisons does the speaker use to describe grief?
2. **Clarify** In "Storm Ending," what event is described in the last line of the poem?
3. **Clarify** In "A Black Man Talks of Reaping," how much has the speaker reaped from all the seed he has scattered?

Text Analysis

4. **Distinguish Figurative from Literal Meaning** Review the notes you took on Bontemps's poem. Bontemps uses an **extended metaphor,** a lengthy comparison of two things that have many points in common. Identify the extended metaphor Bontemps uses. What is this metaphor meant to suggest?
5. **Examine Imagery** "Storm Ending" includes several examples of **synesthesia,** imagery that uses one type of sensory experience to describe a different one—for example, a sound decribed as a smell. Identify two examples of synesthesia in the poem. Which two senses are combined in each image?
6. **Compare and Contrast Tone** Describe the tone, or attitude toward the subject, of Cullen's and Bontemps's poems. What **outlook** on the prospects for social equality does each poem suggest?
7. **Analyze Theme** Complete a chart like the one shown for each poem. What do you conclude is the theme of each poem?

Title Reveals:	Speaker's Identity:
Key Images:	Mood:

Text Criticism

8. **Biographical Context** Reread the author biographies on page 892. In each case, what connections can you make between the poet's life story and the worldview expressed in his work? Be specific.

How do you **VIEW** *the world?*

People's views in life often change as they get older. Viewpoints change from generation to generation, too. Why do you think this happens? How is your outlook different from that of your parents?

COMMON CORE

RL 4 Determine the meaning of words and phrases as they are used in the text, including figurative and connotative meanings; analyze the impact of specific word choices on meaning and tone. **RL 9** Demonstrate knowledge of how two or more texts from the same period treat similar themes or topics. **L 5a** Interpret figures of speech in context and analyze their role in the text.

How It Feels to Be Colored Me

Essay by Zora Neale Hurston

COMMON CORE

RI 1 Cite textual evidence to support analysis of what the text says explicitly as well as inferences drawn from the text. **RI 2** Determine two or more central ideas of a text and analyze their development over the course of the text. **RI 5** Analyze and evaluate the effectiveness of the structure an author uses in his or her exposition or argument, including whether the structure makes points clear, convincing, and engaging. **RI 10** Read and comprehend literary nonfiction. **L 3a** Apply an understanding of syntax to the study of complex texts when reading.

DID YOU KNOW?

Zora Neale Hurston . . .

- dressed so flamboyantly that one acquaintance referred to her as a "macaw of brilliant plumage."
- shocked some people by wearing pants in public.
- became a fan of British poet John Milton after rescuing one of his books from the trash.

Meet the Author

Zora Neale Hurston c. 1891–1960

Raised in the all-black town of Eatonville, Florida, Zora Neale Hurston followed her mother's advice to "jump at de sun"—to follow her dreams, no matter how impossible they seemed. In 1925, she arrived in New York with "$1.50, no job, no friends, and a lot of hope." Hurston's flair, talent, and sheer nerve soon made her one of the leading African-American novelists of the 1930s.

Early Days When Hurston was 13 years old, her family life fell apart. Her mother died, her father remarried, and by the age of 14, Hurston was on her own. Working an endless series of menial jobs, Hurston tried for years to earn enough money to send herself back to school. After 12 years of trials and adventures, she finally completed high school and scraped together a year's tuition for Howard University, "the Negro Harvard," where in 1921 she published her first story.

Collector of Stories By 1925, Hurston's efforts began to pay off. She won a scholarship to Barnard College, where she studied with the renowned anthropologists Franz Boas and Ruth Benedict. After graduating from Barnard in 1928—the first known African American to do so—Hurston returned to the South to collect African-American folklore. "I had to go back, dress as they did, talk as they did, live their life," she said, "so I could get into my stories the world I knew as a child." The lively, hilarious stories she collected soon became material for her own fiction. In the 1930s and '40s, she published a series of major works, including the folklore collection *Mules and Men* (1935), the novel *Their Eyes Were Watching God* (1937), and her autobiography, *Dust Tracks on a Road* (1942).

Down But Not Out Hurston often came under fire by African-American writers who felt she minimized the seriousness of racial prejudice. By the late 1940s, her books had fallen out of favor and out of print. During the last 20 years of her life, Hurston struggled to earn a living, once again working as a maid to pay her bills. In 1960, Hurston died in a welfare home, poor and nearly forgotten, and was buried in an unmarked grave in Fort Pierce, Florida. Thanks to the efforts of author Alice Walker, Hurston's work was rediscovered in the 1970s. Hurston is now acknowledged as an influential figure in the history of African-American literature.

Author Online THINK central

Go to thinkcentral.com. KEYWORD: HML11-898

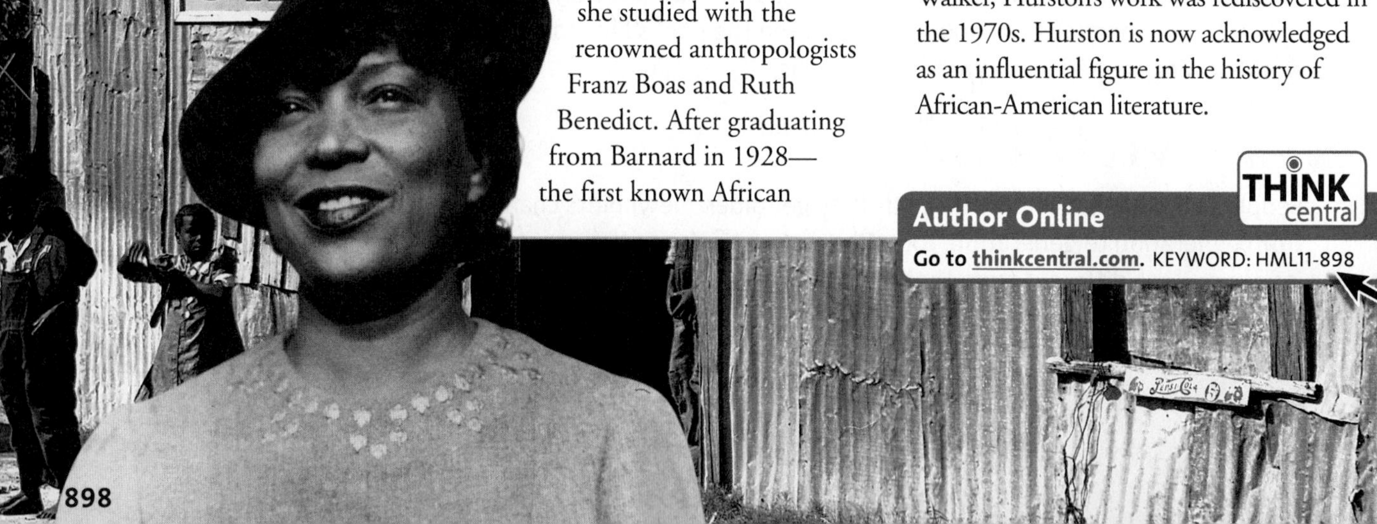

TEXT ANALYSIS: RHETORICAL TECHNIQUES

Famously outspoken, Zora Neale Hurston wasn't afraid to stand out from the crowd in a unique way. In this essay, Hurston uses the following **rhetorical techniques** to discuss her views about race.

- **repetition**—when a sound, word, phrase, or line is repeated for emphasis or unity.
- **parallel structure**—the use of similar grammatical constructions to express ideas that are related or equal in importance.

As you read, notice how Hurston uses these rhetorical techniques to make her ideas come alive.

READING SKILL: IDENTIFY MAIN IDEAS

You know that the **main idea** of a paragraph is the basic point it makes. Sometimes, the main idea is **explicit,** or directly stated in the text. However, main ideas may also be **implicit**—suggested or hinted at by the details in the text. In such cases, you'll need to analyze the details the author presents to discover the main idea.

As you read, use a chart like the one shown to record the main idea of each paragraph. If the main idea is implicit, note key details that helped you identify the main idea.

Paragraph	Main Idea	Key Details
1	I'm not ashamed to be colored.	offers no "extenuating circumstances"

VOCABULARY IN CONTEXT

Hurston uses the following words to make her points about African-American identity. Restate each phrase, using a different word or words for the boldfaced term.

1. collected a **miscellany** of objects on her travels
2. did not use **pigmentation** to judge character
3. excused from penalties because of **extenuating** factors
4. dressed in colorful **raiment**
5. spoke **exultingly** of her triumphs
6. saw herself as **cosmic** rather than small and narrow

Complete the activities in your **Reader/Writer Notebook**.

What makes you YOU?

Think of the things that make you unique: your style, your sense of humor, the way you keep your head (or don't) when things get tense. Of all the qualities and behaviors that make you who you are, which ones do you think best define your personality?

The Insider's Guide to Me

1. To find me in a crowd, look/listen for ___________.
2. The story my friends/family all tell about me is ___________.
3. Most people in school know me as ___________.
4. The thing I do that is most "me" is ___________.

How It Feels to Be Colored Me

Zora Neale Hurston

BACKGROUND Between 1865 and 1900, more than 100 independent towns were founded by African Americans trying to escape racial prejudice. Eatonville, Florida, a small town just north of Orlando, was the oldest of these self-governing black communities. Growing up in Eatonville, Zora Neale Hurston was sheltered from the experiences of exclusion and contempt that shaped the lives of many African Americans. As you read this essay, think about how these early experiences influenced Hurston's opinions on race.

Analyze Visuals ▶
What words would you use to describe the girl in the painting? Identify the techniques or elements that lend her these qualities.

I am colored but I offer nothing in the way of **extenuating** circumstances except the fact that I am the only Negro in the United States whose grandfather on the mother's side was *not* an Indian chief.

extenuating
(ĭk-stĕn′yo͞o-a′tĭng) *adj.* lessening the severity of **extenuate** *v.*

I remember the very day that I became colored. Up to my thirteenth year I lived in the little Negro town of Eatonville, Florida. It is exclusively a colored town. The only white people I knew passed through the town going to or coming from Orlando. The native whites rode dusty horses, the Northern tourists chugged down the sandy village road in automobiles. The town knew the Southerners and never stopped cane chewing when they passed. But the Northerners were something else again. They were peered at cautiously from behind curtains by the timid. The more venturesome would come out on the porch to watch them go past and got just as much pleasure out of the tourists as the tourists got out of the village. **A**

A RHETORICAL TECHNIQUES
Reread lines 4–12. Which lines have parallel structures? How do these comparisons help you understand more about Hurston and her hometown?

The front porch might seem a daring place for the rest of the town, but it was a gallery seat to me. My favorite place was atop the gate-post. Proscenium box for a born first-nighter.[1] Not only did I enjoy the show, but I didn't mind the actors knowing that I liked it. I actually spoke to them in passing. I'd wave at them and when they returned my salute, I would say something like this: "Howdy-do-well-

1. **proscenium . . . first-nighter:** A proscenium box is a box seat near the stage. A first-nighter is a person who attends the opening night of a performance.

Girl in a Red Dress (1934), Charles Alston. Oil on canvas, 71″ × 55.9″. © The Harmon and Harriet Kelley Collection of African American Art. © Estate of Charles Alston. Courtesy of Michael Rosenfeld Gallery, LLC, New York.

I-thank-you-where-you-goin'?" Usually automobile or the horse paused at this, and after a queer exchange of compliments, I would probably "go a piece of the way" with them, as we say in farthest Florida. If one of my family happened to come to the front in time to see me, of course negotiations would be rudely broken off. But even so, it is clear that I was the first "welcome-to-our-state" Floridian, and I hope the Miami Chamber of Commerce will please take notice.

During this period, white people differed from colored to me only in that they rode through town and never lived there. They liked to hear me "speak pieces" and sing and wanted to see me dance the parse-me-la,[2] and gave me generously of their small silver for doing these things, which seemed strange to me for I wanted to do them so much that I needed bribing to stop. Only they didn't know it. The colored people gave no dimes. They deplored any joyful tendencies in me, but I was their Zora nevertheless. I belonged to them, to the nearby hotels, to the county—everybody's Zora.

But changes came in the family when I was thirteen, and I was sent to school in Jacksonville. I left Eatonville, the town of the oleanders,[3] as Zora. When I disembarked from the riverboat at Jacksonville, she was no more. It seemed that I had suffered a sea change.[4] I was not Zora of Orange County any more, I was now a little colored girl. I found it out in certain ways. In my heart as well as in the mirror, I became a fast brown—warranted not to rub nor run.

But I am not tragically colored. There is no great sorrow dammed up in my soul, nor lurking behind my eyes. I do not mind at all. I do not belong to the sobbing school of Negrohood who hold that nature somehow has given them a low-down dirty deal and whose feelings are all hurt about it. Even in the helter-skelter skirmish that is my life, I have seen that the world is to the strong regardless of a little **pigmentation** more or less. No, I do not weep at the world—I am too busy sharpening my oyster knife.[5] B

Someone is always at my elbow reminding me that I am the grand-daughter of slaves. It fails to register depression with me. Slavery is sixty years in the past. The operation was successful and the patient is doing well, thank you. The terrible struggle that made me an American out of a potential slave said "On the line!" The Reconstruction said "Get set!"; and the generation before said "Go!" I am off to a flying start and I must not halt in the stretch to look behind and weep. Slavery is the price I paid for civilization, and the choice was not with me. It is a bully adventure and worth all that I have paid through my ancestors for it. No one on earth ever had a greater chance for glory. The world to be won and nothing to be lost. It is thrilling to think—to know that for any act of mine, I shall get twice as much praise or twice as much blame. It is quite exciting to hold the center of the national stage, with the spectators not knowing whether to laugh or to weep. C

Language Coach

Fixed Expressions Note "negotiations would be . . . broken off" (lines 21–22). A **fixed expression**, or standard combination of words, *break off negotiations* means "stop negotiations." What must the fixed expressions *enter into negotiations* and *resume negotiations* mean?

pigmentation (pĭg'mən-tā'shən) *n.* coloring

B MAIN IDEAS
State the main idea of lines 38–44. What criticism is implied by the author's statement?

C RHETORICAL TECHNIQUES
Reread lines 45–48. What important word does Hurston repeat in these sentences? What effect does this repetition have on Hurston's message?

2. **parse-me-la:** a dance movement popular with Southern African Americans of the period.
3. **oleanders** (ō'lē-ăn'dərz): evergreen shrubs with fragrant flowers.
4. **sea change:** complete transformation.
5. **oyster knife:** a reference to the saying "The world is my oyster," implying that the world contains treasure waiting to be taken, like the pearl in an oyster.

Empress of the Blues (1974), Romare Bearden. Collage, 36″ × 48″. Photo © Smithsonian American Art Museum/Art Resource, New York. © The Romare Bearden Foundation/Licensed by VAGA, New York.

The position of my white neighbor is much more difficult. No brown specter pulls up a chair beside me when I sit down to eat. No dark ghost thrusts its leg against mine in bed. The game of keeping what one has is never so exciting as the game of getting.

I do not always feel colored. Even now I often achieve the unconscious Zora of Eatonville before the Hegira.[6] I feel most colored when I am thrown against a sharp white background.

For instance at Barnard. "Beside the waters of the Hudson"[7] I feel my race. Among the thousand white persons, I am a dark rock surged upon, overswept by a creamy sea. I am surged upon and overswept, but through it all, I remain myself. When covered by the waters, I am; and the ebb but reveals me again.

Sometimes it is the other way around. A white person is set down in our midst, but the contrast is just as sharp for me. For instance, when I sit in the drafty basement that is The New World Cabaret with a white person, my color comes. We enter chatting about any little nothing that we have in common and are seated by the jazz waiters. In the abrupt way that jazz orchestras have, this one plunges into a number. It loses no time in circumlocutions, but gets right down to business. It constricts the thorax and splits the heart with its tempo and narcotic harmonies. This orchestra grows rambunctious, rears on its hind legs and attacks

Language Coach

Context Clues The words, sentences, paragraphs, and even punctuation marks that surround a word make up its **context.** *Specter* (line 57) means "visible spirit." In lines 57–59, what context clues can you find for the word *specter*?

6. **Hegira** (hĭ-jī′rə): journey (from the name given to Muhammad's journey from Mecca to Medina in 622).
7. **Barnard . . . Hudson":** Barnard is the college in New York City from which Hurston graduated in 1928. "Beside the waters . . ." is a reference to the first line of the college song.

the tonal veil with primitive fury, rending it, clawing it until it breaks through to the jungle beyond. I follow those heathen—follow them **exultingly.** I dance wildly inside myself; I yell within, I whoop; I shake my assegai[8] above my head, I hurl it true to the mark *yeeeeooww!* I am in the jungle and living in the jungle way. My face is painted red and yellow, and my body is painted blue. My pulse is throbbing like a war drum. I want to slaughter something—give pain, give death to what, I do not know. But the piece ends. The men of the orchestra wipe their lips and rest their fingers. I creep back slowly to the veneer we call civilization with the last tone and find the white friend sitting motionless in his seat, smoking calmly.

exultingly (ĭg-zŭlt′ĭng-lē) *adv.* joyfully

"Good music they have here," he remarks, drumming the table with his fingertips.

Music! The great blobs of purple and red emotion have not touched him. He has only heard what I felt. He is far away and I see him but dimly across the ocean and the continent that have fallen between us. He is so pale with his whiteness then and I am *so* colored. D

D MAIN IDEAS
Describe the two responses that are contrasted in lines 88–91. What does this contrast imply about the differences between whites and blacks?

At certain times I have no race, I am *me.* When I set my hat at a certain angle and saunter down Seventh Avenue, Harlem City, feeling as snooty as the lions in front of the Forty-Second Street Library, for instance. So far as my feelings are concerned, Peggy Hopkins Joyce on the Boule Mich[9] with her gorgeous **raiment,** stately carriage, knees knocking together in a most aristocratic manner, has nothing on me. The **cosmic** Zora emerges. I belong to no race nor time, I am the eternal feminine with its string of beads.

raiment (rā′mənt) *n.* clothing; garments

cosmic (kŏz′mĭk) *adj.* of or relating to the universe

I have no separate feeling about being an American citizen and colored. I am merely a fragment of the Great Soul that surges within the boundaries. My country, right or wrong.

Sometimes, I feel discriminated against, but it does not make me angry. It merely astonishes me. How *can* any deny themselves the pleasure of my company! It's beyond me.

But in the main, I feel like a brown bag of **miscellany** propped against a wall. Against a wall in company with other bags, white, red, and yellow. Pour out the contents, and there is discovered a jumble of small things priceless and worthless. A first-water[10] diamond, an empty spool, bits of broken glass, lengths of string, a key to a door long since crumbled away, a rusty knife-blade, old shoes saved for a road that never was and never will be, a nail bent under the weight of things too heavy for any nail, a dried flower or two, still a little fragrant. In your hand is the E brown bag. On the ground before you is the jumble it held—so much like the jumble in the bags, could they be emptied, that all might be dumped in a single heap and the bags refilled without altering the content of any greatly. A bit of colored glass more or less would not matter. Perhaps that is how the Great Stuffer of Bags filled them in the first place—who knows?

miscellany (mĭs′ə-lā′nē) *n.* a mixture of various things

E GRAMMAR AND STYLE
Reread lines 105–111. Note how Hurston uses **sentence fragments** to highlight specific details in her description.

---

8. **assegai** (ăs′ə-gī′): a type of light spear used in southern Africa.
9. **Peggy . . . Boule Mich:** a wealthy woman of Hurston's day, walking along the Boulevard Saint-Michel in Paris.
10. **first-water:** of the highest quality or purity.

Comprehension

1. **Recall** In Hurston's description, what kind of community was Eatonville?
2. **Recall** What was the big change Hurston experienced at age 13?
3. **Paraphrase** What is Hurston's view on slavery?

Text Analysis

4. **Identify Main Ideas** Review the chart you created as you read. What is the main idea of the essay? In what ways does race shape Hurston's sense of identity?
5. **Analyze Rhetorical Techniques** What effect is created by Hurston's use of rhetorical techniques to show how she belonged in Eatonville (lines 30–31), to reveal her thoughts at Barnard (lines 64–67), and to emphasize her connection with jazz (lines 68–85).
6. **Make Inferences** Judging from the anecdotes Hurston includes in her essay, what experiences and traits does she consider distinctively African-American? Support your answer with details.
7. **Interpret Analogy** An **analogy** is a comparison using one thing or idea to make sense of another. Look at the analogy in lines 105–116. What is being compared? Be sure to explain each part of the analogy, including the colored bags, the "Great Stuffer of Bags," and the bags' contents.
8. **Compare and Contrast Author's Perspectives** Hurston's views set her apart from most of her Harlem Renaissance contemporaries. Choose one of the poets you have read in this unit, and use a chart like the one shown to contrast his perspectives with Hurston's. What similarities and differences do you find?

	Hurston's Views	*_______'s Views*
What Defines Black Identity		
Goals of Black Writers		
Opinions of Whites		

Text Criticism

9. **Critical Interpretations** The author Alice Walker, one of Hurston's greatest admirers, finds Hurston's views sometimes "exasperating." She notes that this essay "presents two stereotypes: the 'happy darky' who sings and dances for white folks, for money and for joy; and the educated black person who is, underneath the thin veneer of civilization, still a 'heathen.'" Do you agree with Walker's views? Why or why not? Be specific in your response.

What makes you YOU?

Those who study people often debate whether nature or nurture most defines someone's personality. In other words, is the person born that way or is he or she shaped more by the environment. What do you think? Do you believe your personality is shaped more by nature or nurture? Explain your answer.

COMMON CORE

RI 1 Cite textual evidence to support analysis of what the text says explicitly as well as inferences drawn from the text. **RI 2** Determine two or more central ideas of a text and analyze their development over the course of the text. **RI 5** Analyze and evaluate the effectiveness of the structure an author uses in his or her exposition or argument, including whether the structure makes points clear, convincing, and engaging. **RI 10** Read and comprehend literary nonfiction. **L 3a** Apply an understanding of syntax to the study of complex texts when reading.

Vocabulary in Context

▲ VOCABULARY PRACTICE

Choose the word that is not related in meaning to the other words.

1. (a) collection, (b) miscellany, (c) regulation, (d) assortment
2. (a) apparel, (b) clothing, (c) weathering, (d) raiment
3. (a) vast, (b) cosmic, (c) universal, (d) fictional
4. (a) shading, (b) pigmentation, (c) zoology, (d) coloration
5. (a) determinedly, (b) exultingly, (c) delightedly, (d) ecstatically
6. (a) extenuating, (b) moderating, (c) mitigating, (d) exaggerating

WORD LIST
cosmic
extenuating
exultingly
miscellany
pigmentation
raiment

ACADEMIC VOCABULARY IN SPEAKING

• conclude • criteria • despite • justify • maintain

Zora Neale Hurston was upbeat and positive **despite** being the grand-daughter of slaves. In a group, discuss how the past influences the future. Do difficulties in the past **justify** someone being angry and resentful today? Use at least three Academic Vocabulary words in your discussion.

COMMON CORE

L 4b Identify and correctly use patterns of word changes that indicate different meanings or parts of speech. **L 6** Acquire and use accurately general academic and domain-specific words and phrases.

VOCABULARY STRATEGY: THE GREEK ROOT *cosm* OR *cosmo*

The origin of the root word *cosm*, which may also be spelled *cosmo*, is the Greek language. *Cosm* is derived from the Greek word *kosmos*, meaning "world" or "universe." This Greek root is found in the vocabulary word *cosmic* as well as a number of other English words. You can use your knowledge of the origin and meaning of this root word, in addition to the context of a word, to help determine the word's meaning.

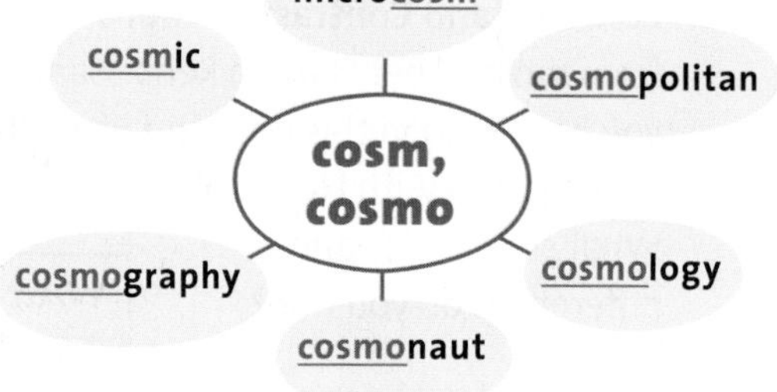

PRACTICE Apply what you know about the Greek root *cosm* or *cosmo* to the words in the web. Then, choose the word from the web that best completes each sentence. If you need to, consult a dictionary.

1. Many myths of creation also include a _________, or a theory of the universe.
2. A _________ is an explorer of outer space.
3. The science called _________ includes astronomy, geography, and geology.
4. A _________ can be any type of miniature community or world.
5. A _________ person tends to have a sophisticated view of the world.

Interactive Vocabulary
THINK central
Go to thinkcentral.com.
KEYWORD: HML11-906

Language

◆ GRAMMAR AND STYLE: Vary Sentence Structure

Review the **Grammar and Style** note on page 904. Zora Neale Hurston's independent and unconventional personality shines through in her writing style. She wasn't afraid to bend the rules of formal writing, adding punch and emphasis through the use of **sentence fragments.** Here are two examples from the essay:

> *I feel most colored when I am thrown against a sharp white background. For instance at Barnard.* (lines 62–64)
>
> *I am merely a fragment of the Great Soul that surges within the boundaries. My country, right or wrong.* (lines 99–101)

The fragment "My country, right or wrong" brings the reader to an abrupt halt, creating a dramatic and strong statement. The change in sentence rhythm helps emphasize the finality of Hurston's belief about her place in the world.

PRACTICE Rewrite the following paragraph in Zora Neale Hurston's style, incorporating one or two intentional sentence fragments. Add or delete any words as necessary.

> My parents were always finding opportunities to point out how much the world owed to China. We learned that our Chinese ancestors had invented paper, books, kites, gunpowder, compasses, fishing reels, and umbrellas. Was there anything that hadn't been invented by the Chinese? One day we went to eat at an Italian restaurant. As I dug into my plate of pasta, I told my mom, "Well, here's one thing the Chinese didn't invent." I was wrong! The Chinese invented pasta, she explained, and they invented restaurants, too!

COMMON CORE

L 1a Apply the understanding that usage is a matter of convention, can change over time, and is sometimes contested. **L 3a** Vary syntax for effect, consulting references for guidance as needed. **W 3** Write narratives to develop imagined experiences or events using effective technique, well-chosen details, and well-structured event sequences.

READING-WRITING CONNECTION

Expand your understanding of Hurston's essay by responding to this prompt. Then, use the **revising tips** to improve your essay.

WRITING PROMPT	REVISING TIPS
WRITE AN AUTOBIOGRAPHICAL ESSAY Imagine that you have entered a writing contest sponsored by a heritage society. Draft a **three-to-five-paragraph autobiographical essay**, modeled after Hurston's essay, in which you share your feelings about your own heritage. In your essay, include at least two sentence fragments that help emphasize important points.	• Focus on one or two important details about your heritage. • Use personal examples, explanations, and anecdotes to show why your heritage is important. • End with a conclusion that wraps up the thoughts in your essay.

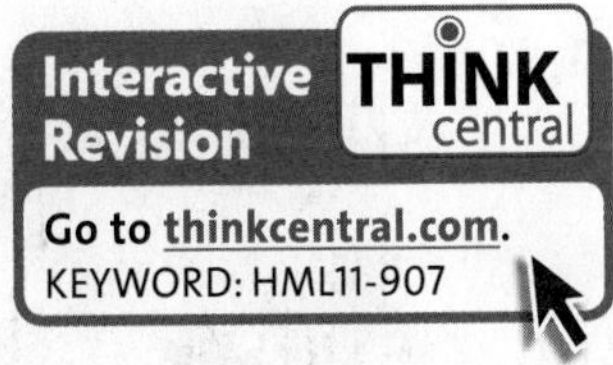

Themes Across Time

Thoughts on the African-American Novel

Literary Criticism by Toni Morrison

COMMON CORE

RI 2 Determine two or more central ideas of a text and analyze their development over the course of the text. **RI 4** Analyze how an author uses and refines the meaning of a key term or terms over the course of a text. **RI 6** Determine an author's point of view or purpose in a text in which the rhetoric is particularly effective, analyzing how content contributes to the power, persuasiveness, or beauty of the text.

Meet the Author

Toni Morrison born 1931

Toni Morrison was born Chloe Anthony Wofford in Lorain, Ohio. This working-class town had a small, close-knit African-American community with a vibrant oral culture. In stories, songs, and everyday speech, Morrison heard an imaginative blend of biblical phrases, rhetorical devices, slang, and conventional English. This early awareness of the power of language and storytelling was a powerful influence on Morrison's work.

Accidental Novelist After earning a bachelor's degree from Howard University (1953) and a master's in English from Cornell University (1955), Morrison embarked on a teaching career. While teaching at Howard, she joined a writers' group for fun, showing up at meetings with what she called "old junk" that she'd written in high school. When she ran out of "junk" before one meeting, she quickly scribbled down a story—a story that later inspired her first novel, *The Bluest Eye.* Published in 1969, the book recounts the story of a troubled African-American girl who, conditioned by white society's ideals of beauty, longs to have blue eyes. The novel's themes, such as the trauma of racism and the importance of community, set the stage for Morrison's later work.

A Major Literary Force The novels *Sula* (1973), *Song of Solomon* (1977), and *Tar Baby* (1981) established Morrison as a major author with a unique voice. Her novels typically have richly symbolic plots that include supernatural or fantastic elements. Within this imaginative context, Morrison provides a realistic treatment of social issues. Her characters, who often have allegorical or biblical names, confront the central struggles of African-American life: the impact of violence and injustice on their lives and the search for cultural identity.

Morrison has been nominated for every major literary honor; she has received, among others, the National Book Critics Circle Award, the Pulitzer Prize, and the Nobel Prize in Literature. She has written several novels and numerous works of commentary and cultural analysis. More recent novels include *Paradise* (1998) and *Love* (2003). Morrison lectures and teaches at various universities across the country. She is widely considered one of the most innovative stylists in contemporary American literature.

DID YOU KNOW?

Toni Morrison . . .

- was once a textbook editor.
- raised two sons as a single mother after her first marriage ended.
- changed her first name in college because "Chloe" was hard to pronounce.
- was the first African American to win the Nobel Prize in literature.

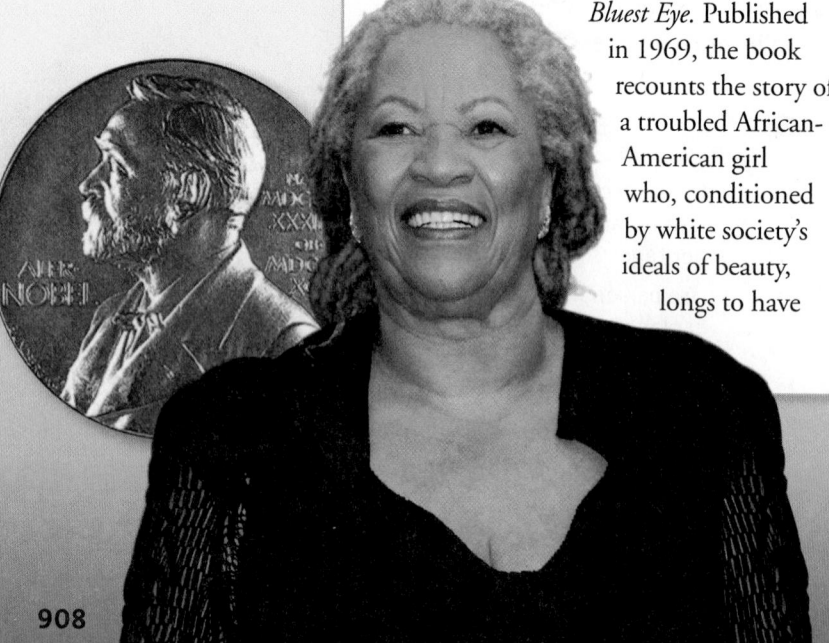

Author Online THINK central

Go to thinkcentral.com. KEYWORD: HML11-908

TEXT ANALYSIS: RHETORICAL TECHNIQUES

Literary criticism, including this essay by Toni Morrison, aims to make readers more knowledgeable about, and appreciative of the literature they read. In this critical essay Morrison uses the following rhetorical devices to make her words more effective:

- **personal accounts:** anecdotes or stories of personal experience that support the writer's message
- **repetition:** the recurrence of particular words, sounds, or ideas

As you read, think about how Morrison uses each rhetorical technique to clarify her meaning and to evoke a response from her readers.

READING SKILL: IDENTIFY AUTHOR'S VIEWPOINT

Works of literary criticism are written to communicate a position, or an opinion, on a topic. To identify an author's **position,** look for direct statements that express the author's viewpoint, such as the following:

I don't regard Black literature as simply books written by *Black people, or simply as literature written* about *Black people . . .*

You'll also want to look for the specific reasons and evidence the writer presents to support his or her opinion. As you read, identify Morrison's position on the importance of the novel to society and on the characteristics that define the African-American novel. In a chart like the one shown, record the reasons and evidence she uses to support her positions. Consider whether you find these positions persuasive.

	Position	*Reasons and Evidence*
Importance of the Novel		
What Defines the African-American Novel		

Complete the activities in your **Reader/Writer Notebook**.

Can CULTURE *be captured in words?*

You can think of culture as the things people make, such as food, books, music, and crafts. But culture is also the things people do: the way they talk, the relationships they build, the values they hold dear. In this essay, Toni Morrison talks about her struggle to capture the essence of African-American culture on the printed page.

QUICKWRITE Think about the cultures you belong to—your ethnicity, your religion, even your region or town. If you were writing about one of these cultures, what would you need to include? List three or more features you would use to capture the experience of that culture.

Thoughts on the African-American Novel

Toni Morrison

The label "novel" is useful in technical terms because I write prose that is longer than a short story. My sense of the novel is that it has always functioned for the class or the group that wrote it. The history of the novel as a form began when there was a new class, a middle class, to read it, it was an art form that they needed. The lower classes didn't need novels at that time because they had an art form already: they had songs, and dances, and ceremony, and gossip, and celebrations. The aristocracy didn't need it because they had the art that they had patronized, they had their own pictures painted, their own houses built, and they made sure their art separated them from the rest of the world. But when the industrial revolution began, there emerged a new class of people who were neither peasants nor aristocrats. In large measure they had no art form to tell them how to behave in this new situation. So they produced an art form: we call it the novel of manners, an art form designed to tell people something they didn't know. That is, how to behave in this new world, how to distinguish between the good guys and the bad guys. How to get married. What a good living was. What would happen

Analyze Visuals ▶
Read lines 1–15. How might the painting on page 911 be compared with the "novel of manners" referred to in lines 12–13? Explain.

Family (1955), Charles H. Alston. Oil on canvas, 48¼″ × 35¾″. Whitney Museum of American Art, New York. Purchase, with funds from the Artists and Students Assistance Fund 55.47.

Alston

if you strayed from the fold. So that early works such as *Pamela,* by Samuel Richardson, and the Jane Austen material[1] provided social rules and explained behavior, identified outlaws, identified the people, habits, and customs that one should approve of. They were didactic[2] in that sense. That, I think, is probably why the novel was not missed among the so-called peasant cultures. They didn't need it, because they were clear about what their responsibilities were and who and where was evil, and where was good.

But when the peasant class, or lower class, or what have you, confronts the middle class, the city, or the upper classes, they are thrown a little bit into disarray. For a long time, the art form that was healing for Black people was music. That music is no longer *exclusively* ours, we don't have exclusive rights to it. Other people sing it and play it; it is the mode of contemporary music everywhere. So another form has to take that place, and it seems to me that the novel is needed by African-Americans now in a way that it was not needed before—and it is following along the lines of the function of novels everywhere. We don't live in places where we can hear those stories anymore; parents don't sit around and tell their children those classical, mythological archetypal[3] stories that we heard years ago. But new information has got to get out, and there are several ways to do it. One is in the novel. I regard it as a way to accomplish certain very strong functions—one being the one I just described. **A**

It should be beautiful, and powerful, but it should also *work.* It should have something in it that enlightens; something in it that opens the door and points the way. Something in it that suggests what the conflicts are, what the problems are. But it need not solve those problems because it is not a case study,[4] it is not a recipe. There are things that I try to incorporate into my fiction that are directly and deliberately related to what I regard as the major characteristics of Black art, wherever it is. One of which is the ability to be both print and oral literature: to combine those two aspects so that the stories can be read in silence, of course, but one should be able to hear them as well. It should try deliberately to make you stand up and make you feel something profoundly in the same way that a Black preacher requires his congregation to speak, to join him in the sermon, to behave in a certain way, to stand up and to weep and to cry and to accede or to change and to modify—to expand on the sermon that is being delivered. In the same way that a musician's music is enhanced when there is a response from the audience. Now in a book, which closes, after all—it's of some importance to me to try to make that connection—to try to make that happen also. And, having at my disposal only the letters of the alphabet and some punctuation, I have to provide the places and spaces so that the reader can participate. Because it is the affective

COMMON CORE RI 2

A ANALYZE

In order to summarize a text effectively, it is necessary to identify and understand the author's main ideas. To learn this important skill, pause periodically as you read. Examine what you've read since the last pause and jot down the main ideas in your own words. Reread lines 23–35. How would you summarize Morrison's opinion about the importance of the novel?

Language Coach

Word Definitions

Disposal (line 52) means "power to use as one wants." Read lines 51–53. What does Morrison have at her disposal? What task does she wish to accomplish with it?

1. **the Jane Austen material:** Jane Austen (1775–1817) wrote several novels focused on middle-class life in her era.
2. **didactic** (dī-dăk'tĭk): intended to instruct.
3. **archetypal** (är'kĭ-tī'pəl): serving as a pattern for later examples.
4. **case study:** an intensive analysis of a group, individual or unit and its development.

and participatory relationship between the artist or the speaker and the audience that is of primary importance, as it is in these other art forms that I have described. B

To make the story appear oral, meandering, effortless, spoken—to have the reader *feel* the narrator without *identifying* that narrator, or hearing him or her knock about, and to have the reader work *with* the author in the construction of the book—is what's important. What is left out is as important as what is there. To describe sexual scenes in such a way that they are not clinical, not even explicit[5]—so that the reader brings his own sexuality to the scene and thereby participates in it in a very personal way. And owns it. To construct the dialogue so that it is heard. So that there are no adverbs attached to them: "loudly," "softly," "he said menacingly." The menace should be in the sentence. To use, even formally, a chorus. The real presence of a chorus. Meaning the community or the reader at large, commenting on the action as it goes ahead.

In the books that I have written, the chorus has changed but there has always been a choral note, whether it is the "I" narrator of *Bluest Eye,* or the town functioning as a character in *Sula,* or the neighborhood and the community that responds in the two parts of town in *Solomon.*[6] Or, as extreme as I've gotten, all of nature thinking and feeling and watching and responding to the action going on in *Tar Baby,* so that they are in the story: the trees hurt, fish are afraid, clouds report, and the bees are alarmed. Those are the ways in which I try to incorporate, into that traditional genre the novel, unorthodox novelistic characteristics—so that it is, in my view, Black, because it uses the characteristics of Black art. I am not suggesting that some of these devices have not been used before and elsewhere—only the reason why I do. I employ them as well as I can. And those are just some; I wish there were ways in which such things could be talked about in the criticism. My general disappointment in some of the criticism that my work has received has nothing to do with approval. It has something to do with the vocabulary used in order to describe these things. I don't like to find my books condemned as bad or praised as good, when that condemnation or that praise is based on criteria from other paradigms.[7] I would much prefer that they were dismissed or embraced based on the success of their accomplishment within the culture out of which I write. C

I don't regard Black literature as simply books written *by* Black people, or simply as literature written *about* Black people, or simply as literature that uses a certain mode of language in which you just sort of drop *g*'s. There is something very special and very identifiable about it and it is my struggle to *find* that elusive but identifiable style in the books. My joy is when I think that I have approached it; my misery is when I think I can't get there. D

B RHETORICAL TECHNIQUES
Reread lines 36–56. What personal account does Morrison use in this passage to help readers understand what she is saying?

C AUTHOR'S POSITION
Reread lines 68–86. What examples from her own work does Morrison cite as **evidence** for her position?

D RHETORICAL TECHNIQUES
Reread lines 87–92. What important key terms does Morrison repeat in this paragraph? Why does she use repetition here?

---

5. **not clinical, not even explicit:** not coldly impersonal or even clearly detailed.
6. ***Solomon:*** Morrison's novel *Song of Solomon.*
7. **paradigms** (păr′ə-dīmz′): theoretical frameworks or patterns.

Comprehension

1. **Recall** With what social class does Morrison associate the novel?
2. **Clarify** According to Morrison, why is the novel especially important for African Americans?
3. **Clarify** Why is it important to Morrison to include a chorus in her fiction?

Text Analysis

4. **Examine Author's Position** Review the chart you created as you read. In your opinion, does Morrison provide compelling support for her views on the nature of the African-American novel? Explain your answer.
5. **Analyze Rhetorical Techniques** Morrison uses rhetorical techniques, such as personal accounts and repetition, to make important points about African-American novels. Do you think her use of these devices is effective? Why or why not?
6. **Analyze Details** Explain the comparison Morrison makes in lines 44–48. What does this comparison reveal about the way Morrison views her work?
7. **Compare and Contrast Authors' Perspectives** Consider the aspects of African-American culture Morrison tries to capture in her novels. What artistic goals does Morrison share with the writers of the Harlem Renaissance? How does her vision of black culture compare with theirs? Explain your answer.
8. **Evaluate Author's Purpose** Literary criticism has three main purposes: to inform readers, to express the writer's opinions, and to persuade readers to accept those opinions. Based on your reading, which of these purposes was Morrison trying to achieve with her essay? Which, if any, did she achieve? Support your answer with details.

Text Criticism

9. **Critical Interpretations** Consider the qualities Morrison identifies as characteristic of African-American art forms. Which of the Harlem Renaissance works you read would meet Morrison's criteria for African-American art? Cite details in your answer.

Can **CULTURE** *be captured in words?*

Think about different cultures you have either read about or experienced first-hand. What cultures other than your own do you find interesting? Why?

COMMON CORE

RI 4 Analyze how an author uses and refines the meaning of a key term or terms over the course of a text. **RI 6** Determine an author's point of view or purpose in a text in which the rhetoric is particularly effective, analyzing how content contributes to the power, persuasiveness, or beauty of the text.

Perspectives on the Harlem Renaissance

Literary historian Richard Gray states the following about the writers of the Harlem Renaissance.

> *"[W]hat is notable about them is how they explored different literary forms to express the condition of African Americans in their times. Facing a racial experience the determining feature of which was that it was mixed and conflicted, they were prepared individually to confront and collectively to debate the question of just how their experience should be turned into literature."*

Because the experiences of the Harlem Renaissance writers were "mixed and conflicted," their works naturally examined different aspects of African-American life.

Writing to Analyze

Imagine that you are a publisher who is planning to print the works beginning on page 878 in a slim anthology called *The Harlem Renaissance.* You'd like to organize the works into thematic groupings to help your readers gain a sense of some of the issues and concerns that these writers, despite their varied experiences, collectively held in common. With a partner, work together to create a table of contents for your book, with the works grouped under thematic headings, such as "Social Protest" or "Reflections on Heritage." Then write a brief explanation of why you grouped the works as you did.

Consider

- which selections deal with similar topics or themes (some selections may explore several themes, giving you the option to group them in more than one way)
- what overarching phrases might best express those topics or themes
- what, specifically, from each selection led you to place it in its particular grouping

Writers Jessie Fauset, Langston Hughes, and Zora Neale Hurston

Extension Online

RESEARCH Go online to find two additional works by Harlem Renaissance writers to add to your anthology. You may choose works by writers already represented in your anthology, or works by other Harlem Renaissance writers, such as Paul Laurence Dunbar or Helene Johnson. Give an **oral reading** for the class, and explain where you would place the works in your anthology.

COMMON CORE

RL 9 Demonstrate knowledge of early-twentieth-century foundational works of American literature, including how two or more texts from the same period treat similar themes or topics. **RI 9** Analyze documents of historical and literary significance for their themes, purposes, and rhetorical features. **W 7** Conduct short research projects. **W 9a (RL 2)** Determine two or more themes or central ideas of a text and analyze their development. **SL 4** Present information, findings, and supporting evidence, conveying a clear and distinct perspective.

Media Study

Jump at the Sun

Documentary on MediaSmart DVD-ROM

COMMON CORE

RI 7 Integrate and evaluate multiple sources of information presented in different media or formats as well as in words in order to address a question or solve a problem.

How do you DOCUMENT *a life?*

KEY IDEA Think about how you would tell the story of your life. What events would you include to help someone understand the essential you? What would you leave out? Filmmakers face similar questions when they make a biographical **documentary.** The many details of a person's life must be boiled down to the key events that influenced and shaped that person. As you view *Jump at the Sun,* notice the details chosen to tell Zora Neale Hurston's life story.

Background

A Vibrant Life Zora Neale Hurston lived her life fully by following her mother's advice. "Mama exhorted her children at every opportunity to 'jump at de sun,'" Hurston explained. "We might not land on the sun, but at least we would get off the ground."

Hurston was a passionate woman who celebrated her role as a black female writer at a time when that was not an easy role to play. She was confident and proud of her heritage, making no apologies for who she was or what she did.

Hurston's dazzling personality and the dynamic times she lived through made her an ideal subject for a documentary film. Thus, the idea for *Jump at the Sun* was born. The filmmakers faced a challenge, though—Hurston died nearly a half-century ago, and film footage of her was not available. The filmmakers, therefore, had to find a way to bring her strong personality to life for the viewer, relying primarily on photographs, paintings, music, and readings from Hurston's own work. The filmmakers' challenge was to shape this material into a coherent and interesting film that tells the story of her life and work.

Jump at the Sun imparts to the viewer both the facts—the actual events that made up Hurston's life—and the exuberance of her personality. As you study the film, you'll explore the techniques used to bring life to the Harlem Renaissance and one of its most spirited writers.

Zora Neale Hurston

Media Literacy: Documentary

A **documentary** is a nonfiction film that often presents social, political, or historical subject matter. Prominent people make good subjects, as they allow the filmmaker to explore both an interesting life and its greater social context.

Feature filmmakers and other storytellers often repeat an old adage: "Show, don't tell." Many documentary filmmakers follow the same principle, presenting their material as a story that unfolds before the viewer's eyes. The use of **primary sources,** which include photographs, film clips, letters, and eyewitness accounts, helps to immerse the viewer in the subject's world.

DOCUMENTARY TOOLS AND TECHNIQUES

Visual

- Footage is recorded material used to reveal information about a subject. It includes film clips, news reports, photographs, interviews, and text. Footage can be used to create a visual and emotional impression of the times.
- Camera movement—such as zooming in from a long shot to a close-up, and tracking shots, which move the camera parallel to the object being filmed—can give a dynamic feel to a still picture.

Sound

- Voice-over narration is the voice of an unseen speaker that can be heard in a documentary.
- The style and tempo of the music will generally match the mood of the story and signal transitions to different settings or time periods.
- Sound effects are often used to help re-create a scene. For example, filmmakers may add crowd and traffic noise over a picture of a city.

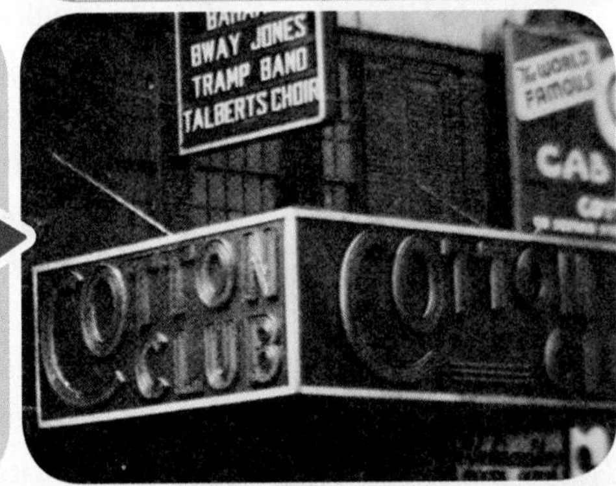

STRATEGIES FOR VIEWING

As you view a documentary, consider the filmmakers' purpose in creating the film. Realize that documentaries reflect the point of view of the filmmaker. They do not always represent objective truth.

- Notice the different types of **footage** used in a documentary. Pay special attention to the use of **primary sources.** Note how they help to bring the story to life by using the "show, don't tell" principle.
- Listen to the different types of **voice-over narration.** In this documentary, the main narrator provides the facts of the subject's life story. The second narrator evokes Hurston's personality with a lively reading of her work.
- Consider how the **visual** and **sound techniques** work together. Think about why the particular footage was chosen to accompany each type of voice-over narration. Notice how the music changes with each major shift in the story.

Media Smart DVD-ROM

- **Film:** *Jump at the Sun*
- **Genre:** Documentary
- **Voice-Over Narrator:** Veronica Chambers
- **Running Time:** 9 minutes

Viewing Guide for

Jump at the Sun

Filmmakers face a difficult challenge when they set out to tell a true story. They must carefully choose which details are necessary to bring the tale to life. Consider the documentary techniques you examined as you view the Zora Neale Hurston biography. Think about how each element contributes to the story being told. You may need to watch the documentary more than once in order to analyze it properly.

NOW VIEW

FIRST VIEWING: Comprehension

1. **Recall** What poet's work so influenced Hurston that she was moved to devote herself to literature?
2. **Clarify** What were Hurston's feelings about whether African-American writers have a duty to write about race relations?

CLOSE VIEWING: Media Literacy

3. **Identify Filmmakers' Purpose** Documentaries are made for a variety of purposes. For example, they can educate, inform, or influence opinion. What do you think the makers of *Jump at the Sun* wanted to achieve? Explain.
4. **Analyze the Voice-Over** The documentary is narrated by the writer Veronica Chambers. Why do you think the filmmakers chose a young writer to narrate the story of Hurston's life?
5. **Analyze Visuals** What types of images are shown to depict Hurston's hometown? Why do you think this type of footage was chosen?
6. **Evaluate Technique** In your opinion, which of the techniques in *Jump at the Sun* is the most effective in conveying Hurston's personality? Cite evidence from the film to support your opinion. Think about
   - the use of such **primary sources** as photographs, film clips, and the actual text read from Hurston's *Dust Tracks on a Road*
   - **music** that suggests the 1920s
   - the two types of **voice-over narration**

Write or Discuss

Compare the Texts Zora Neale Hurston was known for her unique personality. Think about the most memorable parts of Hurston's essay "How It Feels to Be Colored Me." Now consider the ways Hurston is depicted in the documentary. Write a paragraph that compares the Zora portrayed in the film with the Zora you know from the text. Think about

- the tone evident in the essay and in the documentary
- the quotes from Hurston's work that are included in the film, and the style in which they're read
- the selection of images and music in the film

Produce and Present Your Own Media

Plan a Documentary Make a documentary about someone you know well. Gather the materials you'll need to film your documentary. They should include **primary source material** from your subject's life, **interviews** with friends or family members, and a script for the **voice-over narration.**

HERE'S HOW Write interview questions about your subject for two or three friends or family members to answer. Write a script for the voice-over narration that gives a brief overview of the life you're describing. Collect your primary source material. Consider these suggestions:

- Find out about the people or events that have had the greatest impact on your subject's life. Find ways to represent them visually.
- Decide what music might be appropriate. Match it to the events you'll cover.
- Decide how you will portray your subject—through photographs, original video footage, or both.

Further Exploration

Create Your Documentary Now that you've gathered the materials for your documentary, plan how you will shoot it. Decide on the best image to start your film. Plan where you'll use the interviews you conducted, and over what images the voice-over narration will play. Decide at what point you will play the music. Remember that your film should both inform your audience and keep them interested throughout. Next, film your documentary using the notes you've created as a guide. Show your completed documentary to your classmates and ask them for constructive, or helpful, criticism.

COMMON CORE

RI 7 Integrate and evaluate multiple sources of information presented in different media or formats as well as in words in order to address a question or solve a problem. **W 2** Write informative/explanatory texts to examine and convey complex ideas, concepts, and information clearly and accurately through the effective selection, organization, and analysis of content. **SL 1** Initiate and participate effectively in a range of collaborative discussions. **SL 5** Make strategic use of digital media in presentations.

Tech Tip

If a video camera is available, film your documentary. If you do not have a video camera, try using photographs to create a digital story.

COMMON CORE

RL 3 Analyze the impact of the author's choices regarding how to develop and relate elements of a story. **RL 6** Analyze a case in which grasping point of view requires distinguishing what is directly stated in a text from what is really meant. **RL 9** Demonstrate knowledge of how two or more texts from the same period treat similar themes or topics.

Richard Cory
Miniver Cheevy

Poetry by Edwin Arlington Robinson

Lucinda Matlock

Poetry by Edgar Lee Masters

Meet the Authors

Edwin Arlington Robinson
1869–1935

Failure is a familiar subject in the poetry of Edwin Arlington Robinson, and one the artist knew well. Robinson wrote poetry for years before achieving recognition, and he witnessed family members suffer one personal defeat after another.

A Difficult Youth His father's financial struggles forced Robinson to curtail his studies at Harvard University. The family's fortunes continued to decline and Robinson's mother died of diphtheria in 1896. In addition, he lost both of his brothers to fatal addictions.

Devotion to His Craft Despite his tragic past and his own struggles with alcoholism, Robinson devoted his life to his craft. Over time he gained a reputation as one of the country's most accomplished narrative poets.

Reflections of the Past Robinson's best known poems explore the inner lives of the citizens of Tilbury Town, a fictional community modeled on Robinson's hometown of Gardiner, Maine. Many poems grew out of the tragic experiences of his family and childhood acquaintances. Often, the poems focus on individuals who are brought low because of their own personal failings and the town's repressive, materialistic culture.

Edgar Lee Masters
1868–1950

When his brilliant portrait of rural life, *Spoon River Anthology,* first appeared in 1915, Edgar Lee Masters became a literary sensation. Both the general public and renowned critics embraced the book, making it an American classic.

The Making of a Poet The book grew out of Masters's memories of growing up in the central Illinois towns of Lewiston and Petersburg. Living on his grandparents' farm in Petersburg and in the semi-industrialized Lewiston, Masters acquired both an appreciation and a distaste for rural culture. While he admired the hard work and resilience of rural folk, he despised their small-mindedness and bigotry. Eventually Masters left rural Illinois for the big city, residing in Chicago and New York City.

Literary Masterpiece Masters remains most famous for his *Spoon River Anthology.* In this book, 244 deceased inhabitants of the fictional town of Spoon River deliver monologues in which they bare their souls. The cast of characters is varied, ranging from prostitutes and thieves to librarians and Masters's own grandmother Lucinda, the model for "Lucinda Matlock."

Authors Online THINK central
Go to thinkcentral.com.
KEYWORD: HML11-920

TEXT ANALYSIS: CHARACTERIZATION IN NARRATIVE POETRY

While most modernist poets turned their efforts to lyric poetry, Edward Arlington Robinson and Edgar Lee Masters continued to develop the tradition of narrative poetry, often telling stories of interesting characters in the context of their communities. Like fiction, **narrative poetry** tells a story using elements of plot, character, and setting. To develop character, poets may adapt methods of **characterization** typically used in fiction.

- physical description of the character, including vivid **imagery**
- the character's own actions, words, thoughts, and feelings
- comments, thoughts, or actions of other characters
- direct comments about the character by the poem's speaker

As you read these poems, pay attention to the methods used by the poet to develop the characters.

Review: **Meter**

READING SKILL: ANALYZE SPEAKER'S ATTITUDE

In many poems, the **speaker** has a persona that is distinct from the poet. It is the speaker's **attitude** that shapes our view of the poem's subject. In each of the following poems, a speaker delivers a character sketch; in one case, the speaker is describing herself. By noticing the details and phrases the speaker uses to describe the character, we can learn about his or her attitude not only toward the character but toward life.

To analyze the speaker's attitude toward the character in each poem, use a chart like the one shown. As you read, jot down the details and phrases from each poem that reflect that attitude. One example has been filled in for you.

Details and Phrases Reflecting Speaker's Attitude		
"Richard Cory"	"Miniver Cheevy"	"Lucinda Matlock"
"He was a gentleman from sole to crown"		

Complete the activities in your **Reader/Writer Notebook**.

What makes for a FULL LIFE?

Everyone wants to be happy, but happiness comes more easily to some people than to others. What is the secret? Some seek happiness in close, loving relationships. Others pursue their dreams and try to remain true to their inner voice. Still others strive for the comforts of material success and prosperity. The following poems portray characters who have met with varying degrees of success in their search for contentment.

DISCUSS With a partner, make a list of some different ways in which people seek happiness. Which are the most likely to succeed? Which are the least likely? After discussing these questions, present your conclusions to the class.

Richard Cory

Edwin Arlington Robinson

Whenever Richard Cory went down town,
We people on the pavement looked at him:
He was a gentleman from sole to crown,
Clean favored,[1] and imperially slim.

And he was always quietly arrayed,
And he was always human when he talked;
But still he fluttered pulses when he said,
"Good-morning," and he glittered when he walked. **A**

And he was rich—yes, richer than a king—
And admirably schooled in every grace:[2]
In fine,[3] we thought that he was everything
To make us wish that we were in his place.

So on we worked, and waited for the light,
And went without the meat, and cursed the bread;
And Richard Cory, one calm summer night,
Went home and put a bullet through his head. **B**

A CHARACTERIZATION
Reread lines 1–8. Describe Richard Cory's appearance and manners. What do you think the speaker means by "he fluttered pulses" and "he glittered when he walked"?

B SPEAKER'S ATTITUDE
Reread lines 11–16. What contrast does the speaker draw between Richard Cory and the townspeople? How do they seem to regard him?

1. **clean favored:** having a tidy appearance.
2. **schooled in every grace:** extremely well-mannered and cultured.
3. **in fine:** in short.

Sir Philip Sassoon (1923), John Singer Sargent. Oil on canvas, 95.2 cm x 57.8 cm. Tate Gallery, London.

Miniver Cheevy

Edwin Arlington Robinson

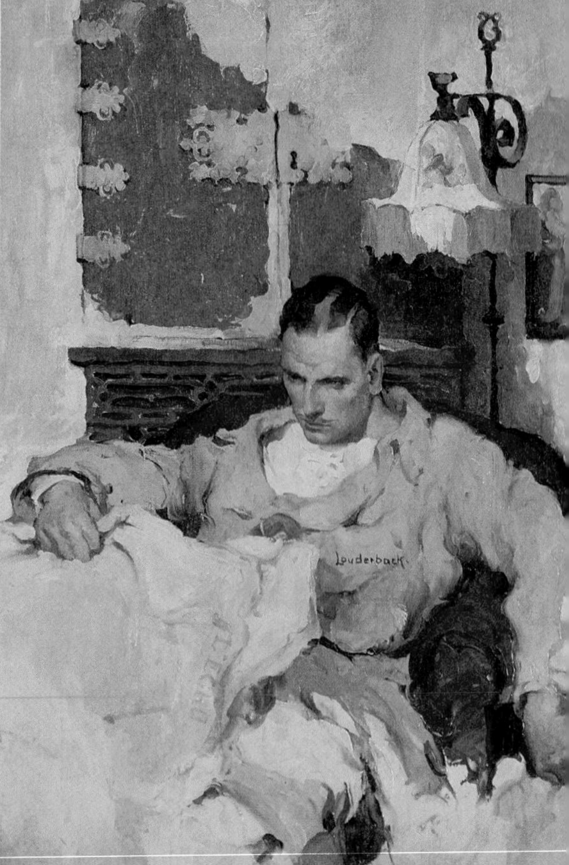

Reading in a Study, Walt Louderback. Oil on plywood, 76.2 cm × 59.7 c
collection. Photo © Bridgeman Art Library.

Miniver Cheevy, child of scorn,
    Grew lean while he assailed[1] the seasons;
He wept that he was ever born,
    And he had reasons.

Miniver loved the days of old
    When swords were bright and steeds
        were prancing;
The vision of a warrior bold
    Would set him dancing. (C)

Miniver sighed for what was not,
    And dreamed, and rested from his labors;
He dreamed of Thebes and Camelot,
    And Priam's neighbors.[2]

Miniver mourned the ripe renown
    That made so many a name so fragrant;
He mourned Romance, now on the town,
    And Art, a vagrant.

Miniver loved the Medici,[3]
    Albeit[4] he had never seen one;
He would have sinned incessantly
    Could he have been one. (D)

(C) METER
Reread lines 1–8. In each stanza, which line has a meter that stands out from the others? What emphasis is achieved by this change in **rhythm?**

(D) CHARACTERIZATION
Reread lines 9–20. Identify the primary means of characterization in these lines. What is the main **trait** conveyed here?

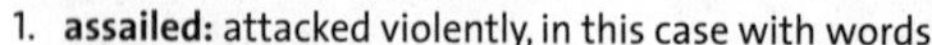

1. **assailed:** attacked violently, in this case with words.
2. **Thebes** (thēbz) **... Camelot ... Priam's** (prī'əmz) **neighbors:** Thebes was an ancient Greek city, the setting of many famous legends; Camelot was the site of King Arthur's legendary court; Priam's neighbors were participants in the Trojan War, during which Priam was king of Troy.
3. **Medici** (mĕd'ə-chē): a powerful Italian family that funded the arts and ruled Florence, sometimes with cruel and immoral leaders, during the Renaissance.
4. **albeit** (ôl-bē'ĭt): even though.

Miniver cursed the commonplace
And eyed a khaki suit with loathing;
He missed the medieval grace
Of iron clothing. **E**

Miniver scorned the gold he sought,
But sore annoyed was he without it;
Miniver thought, and thought, and thought,
And thought about it.

Miniver Cheevy, born too late,
Scratched his head and kept on thinking;
Miniver coughed, and called it fate,
And kept on drinking. **F**

Language Coach

Word Definitions *To eye something* means "to look at something closely." In line 22, why is Miniver eyeing the khaki suit with loathing?

E SPEAKER'S ATTITUDE
Identify the **irony** in lines 23–24. What does this irony suggest about the speaker's attitude toward Miniver's love of the medieval?

F METER
How does the last line of the poem change your understanding of Miniver? Recall your earlier analysis of the poem's meter, and explain its effect in this stanza.

Text Analysis

1. **Recall** What is the townspeople's initial impression of Richard Cory?
2. **Recall** Why does Miniver Cheevy claim to be unhappy?
3. **Compare Texts** What is similar about the ways the two poems end? In each case, how do the last two lines change your view of the character?

LUCINDA MATLOCK

Edgar Lee Masters

Detail of *Cowboy Dance* (mural study, Anson, Texas, post office) (1941), Jenne Magafan. Oil on fiberboard. Photo © Smithsonian American Art Museum, Washington, D.C./Art Resource, New York.

I went to the dances at Chandlerville,
And played snap-out[1] at Winchester.
One time we changed partners,
Driving home in the moonlight of middle June,
And then I found Davis.
We were married and lived together for seventy years,
Enjoying, working, raising the twelve children,
Eight of whom we lost
Ere I had reached the age of sixty.
I spun, I wove, I kept the house, I nursed the sick,
I made the garden, and for holiday
Rambled over the fields where sang the larks,
And by Spoon River gathering many a shell,
And many a flower and medicinal weed—
Shouting to the wooded hills, singing to the green valleys. G
At ninety-six I had lived enough, that is all,
And passed to a sweet repose.[2]
What is this I hear of sorrow and weariness,
Anger, discontent and drooping hopes?
Degenerate[3] sons and daughters,
Life is too strong for you—
It takes life to love Life. H

▲ Analyze Visuals
What qualities do you sense in the dancers portrayed in this painting? Do you find them to have anything in common with Lucinda Matlock? Explain.

G CHARACTERIZATION
Reread lines 1–15. What does the speaker's behavior reveal about her?

H SPEAKER'S ATTITUDE
Whom do you think the speaker is addressing in lines 18–22? How does she seem to feel about them? Explain.

---

1. **snap-out:** a game in which players join hands in a line, then run about trying to shake off those at the end of the line.
2. **repose:** here, the peaceful sleep of death.
3. **degenerate** (dĭ-jĕn′ər-ĭt): showing a decline in vigor or moral strength.

Comprehension

1. **Recall** What pleasures and sorrows did Lucinda Matlock experience in her life?
2. **Clarify** Overall, was Lucinda content with the life she lived?

COMMON CORE

RL 3 Analyze the impact of the author's choices regarding how to develop and relate elements of a story. **RL 6** Analyze a case in which grasping point of view requires distinguishing what is directly stated in a text from what is really meant. **RL 9** Demonstrate knowledge of how two or more texts from the same period treat similar themes or topics.

Text Analysis

3. **Compare Characters** Richard Cory, Miniver Cheevy, and Lucinda Matlock have found widely varying degrees of **contentment.** In your view, what is the primary reason for each character's happiness or unhappiness? Give details to support your answer.
4. **Examine Characterization in Narrative Poetry** What details does Robinson use to reveal each of the following character traits of Richard Cory and Miniver Cheevy? What impact does this characterization have on your sympathy or distaste for the characters? Explain.
   - Richard's perfectionism
   - Richard's self-restraint
   - Miniver's laziness
   - Miniver's romanticism
5. **Analyze Speaker's Attitude** Review the chart you created as you read. What attitude does the speaker of each poem express toward the main character? Would you say that the speaker is sympathetic to or critical of the character described? In each case, what does this attitude tell you about the speaker's own personality and values? Give evidence to support your answer.
6. **Evaluate Author's Style** Robinson's poems use **rhyme, meter,** and **humor** in a playful way that is somewhat at odds with the grim revelations made in the last lines. How does this playfulness shape the impact of these final lines? Explain whether or not you find this an effective technique, and why.

Text Criticism

7. **Critical Interpretations** Critic Bill Peschel has said that in Robinson's Tilbury Town poems, "the town's Puritan ethic, portrayed as repressive and critical, combined with the materialistic aspects of society, conspires to bring down its citizens." Do you find evidence of this repressive Puritan ethic in the attitudes of the speakers in the Robinson poems? Explain why or why not.

What makes for a FULL LIFE?

The speaker in "Lucinda Matlock" appears to have the most reasons to be happy. What, then, is her source of contentment? What do you think makes for a contented life?

Chicago
Grass

Poetry by Carl Sandburg

COMMON CORE

RL 4 Determine the meaning of words and phrases as they are used in the text, including figurative and connotative meanings; analyze the impact of specific word choices on meaning and tone, including words with multiple meanings or language that is particularly fresh, engaging, or beautiful. **RL 5** Analyze how an author's choices concerning how to structure specific parts of a text contribute to its overall structure and meaning as well as its aesthetic impact.

Meet the Author

Carl Sandburg 1878–1967

When Carl Sandburg died in 1967, President Lyndon Johnson was among the first to sing his praises. "Carl Sandburg," the president declared, "was more than the voice of America, more than the poet of its strength and genius. He was America." Johnson's feelings were not unique. Americans everywhere cherished Sandburg, believing his verse celebrated their spirit and speech as well as championed their cause.

A Hobo at Heart Sandburg grew up in America's heartland in Galesburg, Illinois. From his Swedish immigrant parents, August and Clara Sandburg, he learned to value hard work and education. His family's poverty, however, forced Sandburg to curtail his schooling at 13 in order to go to work. He labored at various jobs, ranging from shining shoes to delivering milk. When he turned 19, he left home to explore the American West, becoming one of the many hoboes who hopped freight trains in order to travel free.

Social Activist When the Spanish-American War erupted in 1898, Sandburg served for eight months in Puerto Rico. After his return, he studied at Lombard College but left without receiving a diploma. Overtaken once again by wanderlust, he rambled about the country, soaking up America's sights and songs. When he ran out of money, he returned to the Midwest, writing for journals in Chicago and joining the lecture circuit. His skill as an orator eventually earned him a job in Milwaukee as an organizer for the Wisconsin Social-Democratic Party. While living there, he married Lillian Steichen, who, like Sandburg, was committed to fighting social injustice.

Literary Celebrity In 1912, the couple moved to Chicago, where Sandburg became a reporter, editorial writer, and columnist for the *Chicago Daily News.* Two years later, his verse began to appear in *Poetry,* a prominent literary magazine. With the publication of his poetry collections *Chicago Poems, Cornhuskers,* and *Smoke and Steel,* Sandburg gained a reputation as the poet of the common people. The poetry readings he gave further heightened his popularity. Interspersing poetry with commentary and folk songs sung in his melodious baritone, Sandburg enthralled audiences wherever he went.

Sandburg won a number of awards and honors, including the 1951 Pulitzer Prize for poetry for *Complete Poems* and the 1939 Pulitzer Prize for history for *Abraham Lincoln: The War Years,* the last volume in a six-volume biography.

DID YOU KNOW?

Carl Sandburg . . .

- considered running for president of the United States.
- worked as a war correspondent during World War I.
- wrote books for children.
- spoke before Congress about Abraham Lincoln.

Author Online THINK central

Go to thinkcentral.com. KEYWORD: HML11-928

TEXT ANALYSIS: TONE AND DICTION

Some poems exhibit a subtle tone that is difficult to perceive and nearly impossible to describe. Others practically break forth with trumpets in the first stanza. Whether gently or boldly, poets generally convey tone, or attitude toward the subject, through **diction** (word choice and syntax) and choice of details. In the first lines of "Chicago," Carl Sandburg's diction creates a tone of admiration for a hard-working city:

Hog Butcher for the World,
Tool Maker, Stacker of Wheat,
Player with Railroads and the Nation's Freight Handler;
Stormy, husky, brawling,
City of the Big Shoulders. . . .

Read these two poems by Sandburg aloud to help you identify the tone of each. If you read with emotion, your tone of voice may provide you with clues to the poem's tone.

Review: **Personification**

READING SKILL: SYNTHESIZE DETAILS

In "Chicago," Sandburg presents a long list, or catalog, of qualities, images, and statements about the city. Collectively, this **sensory language** helps create vivid **imagery** of the city. As you read, pay close attention to the sensory language that Sandburg employs, and note how he uses it to create imagery. After you read the poem, you'll be asked to **synthesize** numerous **details** into a single, coherent impression.

Complete the activities in your **Reader/Writer Notebook**.

Would you rather live in the CITY *or the* COUNTRY?

"If you would be known, and not know, vegetate in a village; if you would know, and not be known, live in a city," wrote the poet Reverend Charles Caleb Colton. What benefits and drawbacks do you associate with city living? with country living? What kind of place inspires you the most? In the poems that follow, Carl Sandburg explores different settings that have affected him.

QUICKWRITE Think about a city or a place in the country where you would like to live. What aspects of this setting particularly appeal to you? How might living there enrich your life? Spend a few minutes writing in response to these questions.

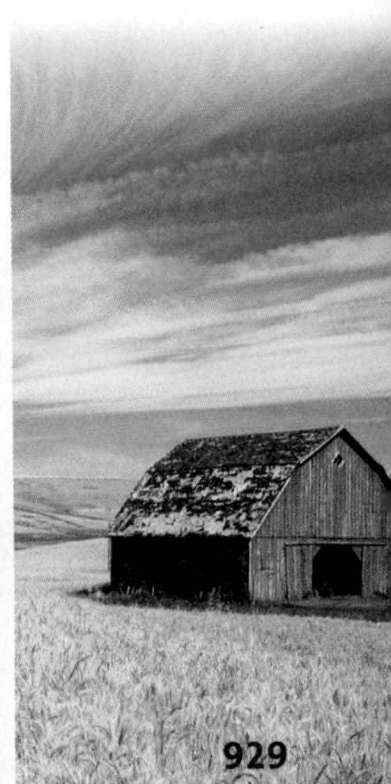

Chicago

Carl Sandburg

Hog Butcher for the World,
Tool Maker, Stacker of Wheat,
Player with Railroads and the Nation's Freight Handler;
Stormy, husky, brawling,
City of the Big Shoulders: **A**

They tell me you are wicked and I believe them, for I have seen your painted women under the gas lamps luring the farm boys.
And they tell me you are crooked and I answer: Yes, it is true I have seen the gunman kill and go free to kill again.
And they tell me you are brutal and my reply is: On the faces of women and children I have seen the marks of wanton[1] hunger.
And having answered so I turn once more to those who sneer at this my city, and I give them back the sneer and say to them:
Come and show me another city with lifted head singing so proud to be alive and coarse and strong and cunning. **B**
Flinging magnetic curses amid the toil of piling job on job, here is a tall bold slugger set vivid against the little soft cities;
Fierce as a dog with tongue lapping for action, cunning as a savage pitted against the wilderness,
Bareheaded,
Shoveling,

A SYNTHESIZE DETAILS
The brief descriptive phrases in lines 1–5, also known as **epithets,** are almost like nicknames; in fact, some of them have come into common use. What do they tell you about the city's economy and industry?

B TONE AND DICTION
Lines 6–8 contain harsh words such as *wicked* and *brutal.* Identify the language in lines 9–10 that counters this harshness. What does it reveal about Sandburg's feelings toward the city as well as its critics?

1. **wanton:** without limitation.

South of the Loop (1936), Charles Turzak. Color woodcut, Image $10\frac{2}{3}''$ × $11\frac{3}{4}''$, sheet $11\frac{1}{4}''$ × $15''$. Mary and Leigh Block Museum of Art, Northwestern University, 1992.73 © Joan Turzak Van Hees.

Wrecking,
Planning,
Building, breaking, rebuilding,

Under the smoke, dust all over his mouth, laughing with white teeth,
Under the terrible burden of destiny laughing as a young man laughs,
Laughing even as an ignorant fighter laughs who has never lost a battle,
Bragging and laughing that under his wrist is the pulse, and under his ribs the heart of the people,
Laughing!
Laughing the stormy, husky, brawling laughter of Youth, half-naked, sweating, proud to be Hog
Butcher, Tool Maker, Stacker of Wheat, Player with Railroads and Freight Handler to the Nation.

▲ Analyze Visuals

What qualities of the city are emphasized by both the horizontal and the vertical lines in this woodcut? Refer to specific areas of the print when giving your answer.

Grass

Carl Sandburg

Pile the bodies high at Austerlitz and Waterloo.[1]
Shovel them under and let me work—
I am the grass; I cover all. **C**

And pile them high at Gettysburg
And pile them high at Ypres and Verdun.[2]
Shovel them under and let me work.
Two years, ten years, and passengers ask the conductor:
What place is this?
Where are we now?

I am the grass.
Let me work. **D**

C PERSONIFICATION
Reread lines 1–3. Sandburg uses personification in establishing the speaker for this poem. Who is the speaker and what is its role in these scenes?

D TONE AND DICTION
Identify several examples of **repetition** in this poem. What **tone** is established by the repetition of these words and/or phrases?

1. **Austerlitz** (ô′stər-lĭts′) **and Waterloo:** sites of significant battles during the Napoleonic Wars (1800–1815).
2. **Ypres** (ē′prə) **and Verdun** (vər-dŭn′): sites of significant battles during World War I.

Le Plateau de Bolante (1917), Félix Vallotton. Oil on canvas. Musée d'Histoire Contemporaine, Paris. © Musée d'Histoire Contemporaine-BDIC.

Comprehension

1. **Recall** What negative aspects of Chicago are presented in lines 6–8?
2. **Clarify** What scenes are referred to in "Grass"?

Text Analysis

3. **Synthesize Details** Think about the **litany,** or list, of images and ideas in "Chicago." Based on the accumulation of detail in this poem, what general statement can you make about the people who live and work in the city?
4. **Compare Tone and Diction** Identify the tone of each poem. Are the tones similar or different? Cite at least three examples of diction that reveal tone in each poem.
5. **Evaluate Personification** Sandburg uses personification in "Chicago" as well as in "Grass," giving human characteristics to objects, animals, or ideas. Describe the figure who personifies Chicago. What words and phrases capture his most important traits?
6. **Analyze Style** What poetic or other stylistic devices underscore Sandburg's characterization of Chicago as a brash, brawling, vibrant city? Consider such elements as line and stanza shape, rhythm, and other formal conventions. Be specific, citing examples from the text.
7. **Interpret Setting and Theme** Both "Chicago" and "Grass" depict a strong sense of place, each containing some contradiction. For each poem, identify this contradiction and use it to help you formulate a theme statement. Give evidence to support your answers.
8. **Compare and Contrast Writers** Carl Sandburg was greatly influenced by the poetry of Walt Whitman (see page 530). Compare and contrast the two poets in terms of the following points, citing specific lines from their work. Can you see Whitman's influence in Sandburg's poems? Explain why or why not.
   - use of **catalog** or **litany**
   - use of **repetition** and **parallelism**
   - **tone** and **diction**
   - ideas about America

Text Criticism

9. **Critical Interpretations** Imagist poet William Carlos Williams once criticized Sandburg's poetry as "formless." Even some of Sandburg's supporters conceded that this was true. Do you agree or disagree? Cite evidence to support your response, also explaining whether you would count yourself among his supporters or his critics, and why.

Would you rather live in the **CITY** *or the* **COUNTRY?**

In his poems "Chicago" and "Grass," Carl Sandburg uses vivid imagery to make surprising statements about the city and the country. If you were going to write a poem about the city or the country, what imagery would you use? Explain.

COMMON CORE

RL 4 Determine the meaning of words and phrases as they are used in the text, including figurative and connotative meanings; analyze the impact of specific word choices on meaning and tone, including words with multiple meanings or language that is particularly fresh, engaging, or beautiful. **RL 5** Analyze how an author's choices concerning how to structure specific parts of a text contribute to its overall structure and meaning as well as its aesthetic impact.

Text Analysis Workshop

Modernism

Although **modernism** has its roots in the nineteenth century, it was not until World War I that this movement in art, architecture, music, and literature transformed American poetry and fiction. Prior to the war, traditional Victorian ideas dominated Western culture, including the belief that human beings are rational and that progress always moves us forward. Grand language—words about courage and sacrifice in "the war to end all wars"—played a role in drawing the world into war. However, the horrors of modern warfare changed everything, undermining the old traditions with skepticism and accelerating the pace of change and experimentation.

COMMON CORE

Included in this workshop: **RL 3** Analyze the impact of the author's choices regarding how to develop and relate elements of a story or drama. **RL 5** Analyze how an author's choices concerning how to structure specific parts of a text contribute to its overall structure and meaning as well as its aesthetic impact. **RL 9** Demonstrate knowledge of early-twentieth-century foundational works of American literature, including how two or more texts from the same period treat similar themes or topics.

Achievements in Language

Modernism inspired writers to consider language as language more deliberately than had ever been done before. Experiments with language and its limits changed the face of American fiction. Consider the modernism of Ernest Hemingway. The simple, spare, direct sentences of his early work represent a radical departure from the prose of his predecessors.

Experimental photograph of Ezra Pound, 1916

While Hemingway cut from his sentences the flowery language he associated with Victorian rhetoric, others pursued the subjectivity of human experience and the fragmented nature of human consciousness. Painters and photographers used visual distortions to express a fractured point of view, as in the photograph of Ezra Pound shown here. Some modernist poets and novelists experimented with **stream of consciousness,** a narrative in first-person point of view that presents the jumbled flow of a character's thoughts and sensations. Others, most notably William Faulkner, explored the subjectivity of experience by following the highly emotional perspectives of **multiple narrators** in a single story.

Shifting Perspectives

In 1929, with the publication of *The Sound and the Fury*, William Faulkner achieved a high point in fiction's depiction of human consciousness. The novel has three first-person narrators, and none of them is a reliable witness to the events that form the plot. Benjy Compson narrates the first section of the novel, but his mental ability is so severely restricted that he can't tell the difference between what happens to him in the present and what he remembers from the past. The second section of the novel jumps back in time almost two decades and relates a single day from the point of view of Benjy's intellectual brother, Quentin, who is so absorbed in abstraction and obsession that he too is incapable of distinguishing between what is "real" and what is not. After Quentin's day reaches an end, a third brother, Jason, takes over as narrator. Jason is so consumed with rage that, like the two brothers before him, he cannot be trusted with his own story.

Faulkner concludes *The Sound and the Fury* with a section narrated from limited third-person point of view. But it is his implementation of multiple first-person narrators that makes this novel a crowning achievement of psychological modernism. It is not possible to find in *The Sound and the Fury* a single coherent, traditional plot of the kind seen in nineteenth-century writers such as Nathaniel Hawthorne and Stephen Crane. But for readers who surrender to the magic of Faulkner's multiple voices, the novel provides a breathtaking glimpse into the subjective nature of experience.

T. S. Eliot and Katherine Anne Porter can help you to see how modernist American writers revolutionized point of view. Eliot's "The Love Song of J. Alfred Prufrock" is stream of consciousness at its best, tracing the musings of a man paralyzed by indecision. Note how the narrative jumps from trivial questions to an idle fantasy, much as the mind jumps while daydreaming.

> Shall I part my hair behind? Do I dare to eat a peach?
> I shall wear white flannel trousers, and walk upon the beach.
> I have heard the mermaids singing, each to each.
>
> **—T. S. Eliot, "The Love Song of J. Alfred Prufrock"**

Katherine Anne Porter writes "The Jilting of Granny Weatherall" in limited third-person point of view, closely following the perspective of an elderly woman as her mind wonders. As you examine Granny Weatherall's subjective sensations, notice how her consciousness moves into the past when an anonymous "he" appears in the narrative.

> The pillow rose about her shoulders and pressed against her heart and the memory was being squeezed out of it: oh, push down the pillow, somebody: it would smother her if she tried to hold it. Such a fresh breeze blowing and such a green day with no threats in it. But he had not come, just the same. What does a woman do when she has put on the white veil and set out the white cake for a man and he doesn't come?
>
> **—Katherine Anne Porter, "The Jilting of Granny Weatherall"**

AMERICANS IN PARIS

French painter Henri Matisse was an inspiration to American writers in Paris.

At loose ends after World War I, many disillusioned Americans remained in Europe, often settling in the Left Bank district of Paris, where they were joined by numerous writers and artists. Ezra Pound, Ernest Hemingway, Gertrude Stein, F. Scott Fitzgerald, James Joyce, and George Orwell were just some of the many writers who lived for a time in Paris during the 1920s. Many of the expatriate community saw it as a place where they could be more open to life—in a way that was impossible in the United States. For others, it served for inspiration: The simplicity of both Ernest Hemingway's and Gertrude Stein's styles is said to have been inspired by the art of French painters Paul Cezanne and Henri Matisse. Ironically, Paris became known as the place where American literary style was cultivated and crafted.

Close Read

Point out details in the Porter excerpt that capture her character's subjective sensations. In the last sentence of this excerpt, locate clues that tell you what the character is remembering. What aspect of modernism does this passage illustrate?

Selected Poetry

by Robert Frost

COMMON CORE

RL 1 Cite strong and thorough textual evidence to support analysis of what the text says explicitly as well as inferences drawn from the text, including determining where the text leaves matters uncertain. **RL 4** Analyze the impact of specific word choices on meaning and tone, including words with multiple meanings or language that is particularly fresh, engaging, or beautiful. **RL 6** Analyze a case in which grasping point of view requires distinguishing what is directly stated in a text from what is really meant (e.g., irony or understatement).

DID YOU KNOW?

Robert Frost . . .

- was unable to read a poem at John F. Kennedy's inauguration because of bright sunlight and so recited one from memory.
- won 44 honorary degrees from prestigious universities but never earned a college degree himself.

Meet the Author

Robert Frost 1874–1963

Robert Frost once remarked that his life's goal was to write "a few poems it will be hard to get rid of." Undoubtedly, he succeeded. Frost's best poems lodge themselves in the reader's imagination and refuse to go away. As a result, Frost is one of the most beloved American poets.

Awakening to Poetry Although Frost is associated with rural New England, he spent his first 11 years in San Francisco. Following his father's death in 1885, Frost's mother brought her two children east, eventually settling in the industrial city of Lawrence, Massachusetts. As a boy, Frost developed a passion for baseball and poetry. By the time he graduated from high school, he knew he would be a poet.

Aimless Years Frost's early manhood was nonetheless filled with change. He enrolled at both Dartmouth College and Harvard University but did not remain at either place, tiring of the routine of college life. For several years he drifted working as a mill hand, a school teacher, and a reporter. One stabilizing event in his life was his marriage in 1895 to Elinor White, his high school sweetheart.

Voice of New England In 1900, Frost abandoned the indoor life of teaching for the outdoor life of farming. During the day Frost worked his poultry farm, and at night he wrote. The 11 years Frost spent farming were some of his most creative. Inspired by the rugged New Hampshire countryside and its plain-spoken inhabitants, Frost wrote poems that probed the mysteries of nature and the human heart.

Literary Acclaim At the age of 38, Frost moved his family to England, where he could "write and be poor." Less than two months later, a London publisher accepted the manuscript of *A Boy's Will* (1913) for publication. By the time Frost returned to the United States in 1915, he was hailed as a leading American poet.

In 1924, Frost's collection *New Hampshire* won a Pulitzer Prize, the first of four that he would receive. His public success, however, was overshadowed by personal tragedy. Between 1934 and 1940, Frost lost a daughter, his wife, and a son; another daughter was institutionalized for mental illness. As a result, his later poems often convey a bleak outlook on life.

Author Online

THINK central

Go to thinkcentral.com. KEYWORD: HML11-936

TEXT ANALYSIS: FROST'S STYLE

Some of Robert Frost's poems seem so simple, yet they move people deeply. Why? It certainly has something to do with his powerful choice of theme and subject matter, but it's also a matter of his unique **style**—the distinctive way in which he uses words and poetic devices. For one thing, he makes skillful use of traditional rhyme, meter, and stanza form. He also uses other elements in a distinctive way.

- **Diction**—word choice and syntax, or word order
- **Imagery**—the descriptive phrases that appeal to the senses
- **Mood**—the overall feeling or atmosphere that a writer creates for the reader (often created with imagery)

Notice these elements in the opening lines of "'Out, Out—'":

The buzz saw snarled and rattled in the yard
And made dust and dropped stove-length sticks of wood,
Sweet-scented stuff when the breeze drew across it.

As you read these poems by Frost, pay close attention to his diction and his use of imagery and mood.

READING SKILL: RECOGNIZE AMBIGUITY

Many people approach poems like riddles; they are certain that the true meaning must lie in a single interpretation. This approach fails to take into account the **ambiguity** that lends richness and beauty to so many poems. Literature of the **modernist** movement often lends itself to more than one meaning; it is open to various, even opposing, interpretations, as in the opening lines of "Nothing Gold Can Stay."

Nature's first green is gold,
Her hardest hue to hold.

Are these lines referring to a golden hue of green, or are they making the point that nature's first green is precious, like gold? You don't have to choose between these meanings; skilled readers of poetry recognize ambiguity and live with it, even enjoy it, as they read and consider a poem. As you read, record different interpretations of lines from each poem.

"Acquainted with the Night"	"Nothing Gold Can Stay"	"'Out, Out—'"
	lines 1–2: • golden shade of green • green is precious, like gold	

Complete the activities in your **Reader/Writer Notebook**.

What does it mean to be ALONE?

Does solitude make you lonely? Or is it precious to you? It's a powerful idea, being alone. Some people can't get enough of it, and others have it in painful abundance. In any event, it offers opportunity for reflection. In "Acquainted with the Night," Robert Frost explores one person's emotional reaction to being alone.

QUICKWRITE What images and feelings does the word *solitude* evoke in you? Write a short poem describing a moment alone.

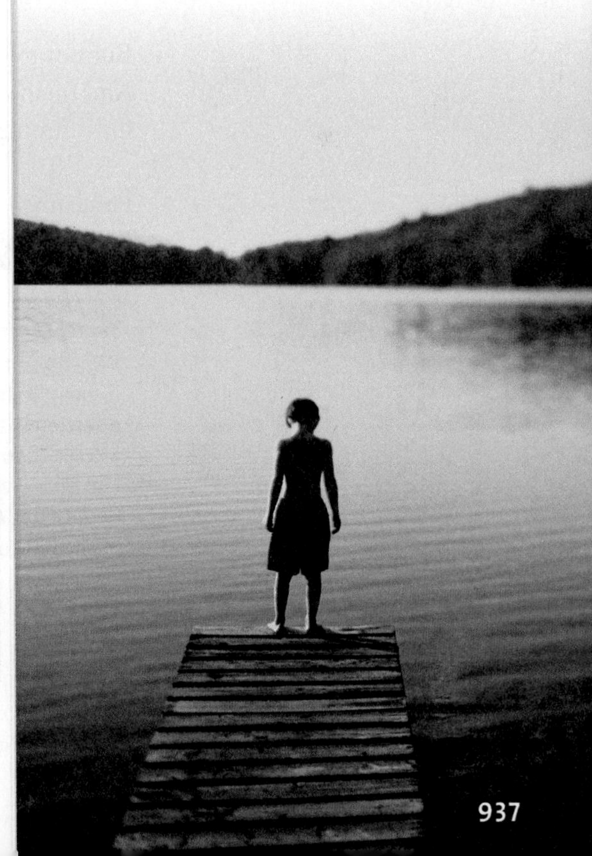

Acquainted *with the* Night

Robert Frost

I have been one acquainted with the night.
I have walked out in rain—and back in rain.
I have outwalked the furthest city light.

I have looked down the saddest city lane.
I have passed by the watchman on his beat
And dropped my eyes, unwilling to explain.

I have stood still and stopped the sound of feet
When far away an interrupted cry
Came over houses from another street,

But not to call me back or say good-by; **A**
And further still at an unearthly height
One luminary[1] clock against the sky

Proclaimed the time was neither wrong nor right.
I have been one acquainted with the night. **B**

THEME
Why do some people become depressed? What does it mean to feel depressed about one's life? This is a question that poets, novelists, and playwrights have always thought about. For example, the recent movie *The Hours* (2002) explores Virginia Woolf's battle with depression. Can you think of any other films, novels, or plays that touch on this same theme?

Analyze Visuals ▶
Notice the shadowy human figures in relation to other objects in the photograph. What mood is established by the **composition,** or arrangement of shapes? How do the figures appear in relation to each other? Explain.

A FROST'S STYLE
Reread lines 1–10. How does the poet's use of parallel structure and rhyme contribute to the poem's developing mood? Explain your answer.

B RECOGNIZE AMBIGUITY
Reread lines 11–14. Identify at least two possible meanings of "the time was neither wrong nor right." What does this proclamation suggest about the "luminary clock"? Explain.

1. **luminary:** giving off light.

Nothing Gold Can Stay

Robert Frost

Haystacks and Barn (1909), George Wesley Bellows. Oil on canvas, 56.5 cm × 71.4 cm. © Museum of Fine Arts, Houston, Texas/Bridgeman Art Library.

Nature's first green is gold,
Her hardest hue to hold.
Her early leaf's a flower;
But only so an hour.
Then leaf subsides to leaf.
So Eden[1] sank to grief,
So dawn goes down to day.
Nothing gold can stay. C

C **FROST'S STYLE**
What is the **mood** of this poem? Identify the **diction** or **imagery** that most strongly establishes this mood for you.

1. **Eden:** the biblical Garden of Eden, from which Adam and Eve were expelled for disobeying God.

Text Analysis

1. **Clarify** What does the speaker of the first poem mean when he says he's been "acquainted with the night"?
2. **Summarize** What does the speaker of "Acquainted with the Night" see and hear on his walk?
3. **Interpret Analogies** In "Nothing Gold Can Stay," how is the fate of a leaf similar to that of the Garden of Eden?

"Out, Out—"

Robert Frost

The buzz saw snarled and rattled in the yard
And made dust and dropped stove-length sticks of wood,
Sweet-scented stuff when the breeze drew across it.
And from there those that lifted eyes could count
Five mountain ranges one behind the other
Under the sunset far into Vermont.
And the saw snarled and rattled, snarled and rattled,
As it ran light, or had to bear a load. **D**
And nothing happened: day was all but done.
Call it a day, I wish they might have said
To please the boy by giving him the half hour
That a boy counts so much when saved from work.
His sister stood beside them in her apron
To tell them "Supper." At the word, the saw,
As if to prove saws knew what supper meant,
Leaped out at the boy's hand, or seemed to leap—
He must have given the hand. However it was,
Neither refused the meeting. But the hand! **E**
The boy's first outcry was a rueful[1] laugh,
As he swung toward them holding up the hand
Half in appeal, but half as if to keep
The life from spilling. Then the boy saw all—
Since he was old enough to know, big boy
Doing a man's work, though a child at heart—
He saw all spoiled. "Don't let him cut my hand off—
The doctor, when he comes. Don't let him, sister!"
So. But the hand was gone already.
The doctor put him in the dark of ether.[2]
He lay and puffed his lips out with his breath.
And then—the watcher at his pulse took fright.
No one believed. They listened at his heart.
Little—less—nothing!—and that ended it.
No more to build on there. And they, since they
Were not the one dead, turned to their affairs. **F**

D FROST'S STYLE
Frost's title is taken from a famous passage in Shakespeare—the words spoken by Macbeth upon news of his wife's death. Vivid **images** in the original passage convey a **mood** of heavy gloom that can be traced from the classical dramas of ancient Greece to present-day horror and action movies. Reread lines 1–8. What kind of mood do Frost's images convey? Why might he have chosen Macbeth's grief-stricken words as his title?

E FROST'S STYLE
Reread lines 13–18. What does the **diction** in these lines suggest about the accidental meeting of the saw and the hand? Explain the **irony** in these lines.

F RECOGNIZE AMBIGUITY
Identify the ambiguity in the last two lines of the poem. What does their **understatement** and lack of sentiment suggest about the survivors and their attitude toward the boy's death?

1. **rueful:** expressing sorrow or regret.
2. **ether:** a liquid used as an anesthetic. Its fumes cause unconsciousness when deeply inhaled.

Comprehension

1. **Clarify** What is the setting, including the time of day, of "'Out, Out—'"?
2. **Summarize** What happens to the boy?

Text Analysis

3. **Identify Rhymes** Examine the pairs of rhyming words in "Nothing Gold Can Stay." What ideas do the rhymes help Frost convey about the nature of beauty?
4. **Examine Theme** "'Out, Out—'" provides a portrait of **solitude** even among family. Identify words and phrases in which Frost suggests the solitude of these characters in the face of tragedy. What theme emerges about human relationships?
5. **Interpret Allusion** The title of "'Out, Out—'" is an **allusion,** or indirect reference to a well-known person, place, or literary work—in this case, a famous speech in Shakespeare's *Macbeth* (Act Five, Scene 5). How does the following quotation from *Macbeth* color your sense of Frost's poem?

   . . . Out, out brief candle!
   Life's but a walking shadow, a poor player
   That struts and frets his hour upon the stage
   And then is heard no more.

6. **Analyze Frost's Style** Identify several lines in any one of the three poems where Frost's **diction,** his use of **imagery,** and/or **mood** is particularly striking. Explain why you find it noteworthy and how Frost's style helps deliver the poem's message.
7. **Evaluate Ambiguity** Consult the chart in which you recorded different interpretations as you read. Identify the ambiguity that you found the most puzzling, contradictory, or profound. In your opinion, what does the ambiguity add to each poem? Explain.

Text Criticism

8. **Critical Interpretation** The critic and scholar Lionel Trilling hailed Frost for his "representation of the terrible actualities of life in a new way." Apply this comment to the three Frost poems you have just read. What are the "terrible actualities of life" in each poem? What might be considered "new" or unusual about Frost's portrayal of these realities? Explain.

What does it mean to be **ALONE?**

In "Acquainted with the Night," does the speaker seem to enjoy his solitude or long for companionship? Do you enjoy being alone? Explain.

COMMON CORE

RL 1 Cite strong and thorough textual evidence to support analysis of what the text says explicitly as well as inferences drawn from the text, including determining where the text leaves matters uncertain. **RL 4** Analyze the impact of specific word choices on meaning and tone, including words with multiple meanings or language that is particularly fresh, engaging, or beautiful. **RL 6** Analyze a case in which grasping point of view requires distinguishing what is directly stated in a text from what is really meant (e.g., irony or understatement).

The New Poetry

The Death of the Hired Man

Poem by Robert Frost

COMMON CORE

RL 1, RL 3, RL 5

KEYWORD: HML11-943

TEXT ANALYSIS: NARRATIVE POETRY

"The Death of the Hired Man" is **narrative poetry**, but unlike the poems by Robinson and Masters on pages 922–926, this poem has a more fully developed plot, setting, and characters.

- **Dialogue**—This poem consists almost entirely of a conversation between two people, so the dialogue plays a greater role than usual in developing the narrative elements.
- **Plot**—Although the "now-time" of the poem consists almost entirely of a single conversation, the dialogue itself indirectly relates events that have unfolded over years.
- **Characterization**—Frost conveys the characters' traits through their own words and what others say about them.
- **Setting**—Again, Frost conveys time and place primarily through what the characters say about their work and their relationships.

Review: **Blank Verse**

READING SKILL: UNDERSTAND FORM IN POETRY

In poetry, **form** generally refers to the shape of text on the page. In a larger sense, however, it can refer to any technique used to convey meaning. The dialogue in this poem can be hard to follow; you won't find many *he said*'s or *she said*'s. However, Frost uses other devices to show who's speaking.

- **Quotation marks**—Double quotation marks indicate the beginning and end of each speech. Single quotation marks indicate dialogue within a speech.
- **Line breaks**—Frost leaves a blank line when the speaker changes; he never changes speaker in the middle of a line.
- **Point of view**—The poem's speaker uses only the third person; in dialogue, the characters speak in the first person.

Use a chart to keep track of who is speaking in the poem.

Elements of Form Used to Show Speakers		
Line Numbers	*Who Is Speaking*	*How I Know*

Complete the activities in your **Reader/Writer Notebook**.

How do you know you're HOME?

It's the moment when you close the door behind you, drop your bag on the floor, take off your coat, and kick off your shoes. Or maybe it's the greeting you get from a family member or even a pet. Walking up the driveway, seeing a familiar face, smelling a familiar food: we recognize home in various ways.

QUICKWRITE Identify the place where you feel the most at home. Then write a brief description of some moment or event that captures the features that make home different from other places.

The DEATH of the HIRED MAN

Robert Frost

Mary sat musing on the lamp-flame[1] at the table,
Waiting for Warren. When she heard his step,
She ran on tiptoe down the darkened passage
To meet him in the doorway with the news
And put him on his guard. "Silas is back."
She pushed him outward with her through the door
And shut it after her. "Be kind," she said.
She took the market things from Warren's arms
And set them on the porch, then drew him down
To sit beside her on the wooden steps. **A**

"When was I ever anything but kind to him?
But I'll not have the fellow back," he said.
"I told him so last haying,[2] didn't I?
If he left then, I said, that ended it.
What good is he? Who else will harbor him
At his age for the little he can do?
What help he is there's no depending on.
Off he goes always when I need him most.
He thinks he ought to earn a little pay,
Enough at least to buy tobacco with,
So he won't have to beg and be beholden.
'All right,' I say, 'I can't afford to pay
Any fixed wages, though I wish I could.'
'Someone else can.' 'Then someone else will have to.' **B**
I shouldn't mind his bettering himself
If that was what it was. You can be certain,
When he begins like that, there's someone at him
Trying to coax him off with pocket money—
In haying time, when any help is scarce.
In winter he comes back to us. I'm done."

"Sh! not so loud: he'll hear you," Mary said.

Analyze Visuals ▸ Notice the shapes of the landscape in this image. How do these shapes compare with the outlines of the human figures? What might this suggest about the relationship between humans and nature? Explain.

A NARRATIVE POETRY Reread lines 1–10. What clues do they contain about the poem's **setting?** Explain.

B FORM IN POETRY Reread lines 11–24. Summarize these lines. Who is speaking? What is happening in lines 22–24?

---

1. **musing on the lamp-flame:** looking thoughtfully at the flame of an oil lamp.
2. **last haying:** the last time the hay was cut.

Detail of *Island Hay* (1945), Thomas Hart Benton.

"I want him to: he'll have to soon or late."

"He's worn out. He's asleep beside the stove.
When I came up from Rowe's I found him here,
Huddled against the barn door fast asleep,
A miserable sight, and frightening, too—
You needn't smile—I didn't recognize him—
I wasn't looking for him—and he's changed.
Wait till you see." C

"Where did you say he'd been?"

"He didn't say. I dragged him to the house,
And gave him tea and tried to make him smoke.
I tried to make him talk about his travels.
Nothing would do: he just kept nodding off."

"What did he say? Did he say anything?"

"But little."

"Anything? Mary, confess
He said he'd come to ditch[3] the meadow for me."

"Warren!"

"But did he? I just want to know."

"Of course he did. What would you have him say? D
Surely you wouldn't grudge the poor old man
Some humble way to save his self-respect.
He added, if you really care to know,
He meant to clear the upper pasture, too.
That sounds like something you have heard before?
Warren, I wish you could have heard the way
He jumbled everything. I stopped to look
Two or three times—he made me feel so queer—
To see if he was talking in his sleep.
He ran on[4] Harold Wilson—you remember—
The boy you had in haying four years since.
He's finished school, and teaching in his college.
Silas declares you'll have to get him back.
He says they two will make a team for work:
Between them they will lay this farm as smooth! E

C **NARRATIVE POETRY**
Reread Mary's description of Silas in lines 31–39. What **character traits** are revealed about Silas in these lines? about Mary?

D **FORM IN POETRY**
Reread lines 38–48. Identify the speaker of each speech. What devices indicate this? Explain what the rapid change of speakers emphasizes about the tone of this discussion.

E **BLANK VERSE**
Poetry written in unrhymed **iambic pentameter,** or blank verse, is said to be the poetic form that most resembles English speech. Read aloud lines 58–63. Would you agree? Explain.

3. **ditch:** plow.
4. **ran on:** talked about without stopping.

The way he mixed that in with other things.
He thinks young Wilson a likely lad, though daft
On[5] education—you know how they fought
All through July under the blazing sun,
Silas up on the cart to build the load,
Harold along beside to pitch it on."

"Yes, I took care to keep well out of earshot."

"Well, those days trouble Silas like a dream.
You wouldn't think they would. How some things linger!
Harold's young college-boy's assurance piqued[6] him.
After so many years he still keeps finding
Good arguments he sees he might have used.
I sympathize. I know just how it feels
To think of the right thing to say too late.
Harold's associated in his mind with Latin.
He asked me what I thought of Harold's saying
He studied Latin, like the violin,
Because he liked it—that an argument!
He said he couldn't make the boy believe
He could find water with a hazel prong[7]—
Which showed how much good school had ever done him.
He wanted to go over that. But most of all
He thinks if he could have another chance
To teach him how to build a load of hay—" **F**

"I know, that's Silas' one accomplishment.
He bundles every forkful in its place,
And tags and numbers it for future reference,
So he can find and easily dislodge it
In the unloading. Silas does that well.
He takes it out in bunches like big birds' nests.
You never see him standing on the hay
He's trying to lift, straining to lift himself."

"He thinks if he could teach him that, he'd be
Some good perhaps to someone in the world.
He hates to see a boy the fool of books.
Poor Silas, so concerned for other folk,
And nothing to look backward to with pride,

Language Coach

Word Definitions *Shot* can mean "range" or "reach." Read lines 65–70. What must *earshot* (line 70) mean?

F NARRATIVE POETRY
Reread lines 79–87. How are Silas and Harold characterized in these lines?

---

5. **daft on:** crazy about; obsessed with.
6. **piqued** (pēkt): aroused resentment in.
7. **find . . . prong:** a reference to the practice of dowsing, in which a person uses a forked stick made of hazel wood to try to find underground water.

And nothing to look forward to with hope,
So now and never any different."

Part of a moon was falling down the west,
Dragging the whole sky with it to the hills.
Its light poured softly in her lap. She saw it
And spread her apron to it. She put out her hand
Among the harplike morning-glory strings,
Taut[8] with the dew from garden bed to eaves,
As if she played unheard some tenderness
That wrought on[9] him beside her in the night. G
"Warren," she said, "he has come home to die:
You needn't be afraid he'll leave you this time."

"Home," he mocked gently.
"Yes, what else but home?
It all depends on what you mean by home.
Of course he's nothing to us, any more
Than was the hound that came a stranger to us
Out of the woods, worn out upon the trail."

"Home is the place where, when you have to go there,
They have to take you in."
"I should have called it
Something you somehow haven't to deserve."

Warren leaned out and took a step or two,
Picked up a little stick, and brought it back
And broke it in his hand and tossed it by.
"Silas has better claim on us you think
Than on his brother? Thirteen little miles
As the road winds would bring him to his door.
Silas has walked that far no doubt today.
Why doesn't he go there? His brother's rich,
A somebody—director in the bank."

"He never told us that."
"We know it, though." H

"I think his brother ought to help, of course.
I'll see to that if there is need. He ought of right
To take him in, and might be willing to—

G FORM IN POETRY
Reread lines 103–110. The poem's speaker has interrupted the dialogue between Mary and Warren. How does this shift in **point of view** affect the poem's **mood?**

Language Coach
Multiple-Meaning Words *Somebody* (line 129) is a multiple-meaning word, a word with more than one meaning. *Somebody* often means "an unspecified person." Here it means "an important person." How can you tell which definition is meant?

H NARRATIVE POETRY
Reread lines 124–130. What do these lines add to your understanding of Silas?

---

8. **taut:** pulled tight; straight.
9. **wrought** (rôt) **on:** worked on.

He may be better than appearances.[10]
But have some pity on Silas. Do you think
If he had any pride in claiming kin
Or anything he looked for from his brother,
He'd keep so still about him all this time?"

"I wonder what's between them."

"I can tell you.
Silas is what he is—we wouldn't mind him—
But just the kind that kinsfolk can't abide.[11]
He never did a thing so very bad.
He don't know why he isn't quite as good
As anybody. Worthless though he is,
He won't be made ashamed to please his brother."

"*I* can't think Si ever hurt anyone."

"No, but he hurt my heart the way he lay
And rolled his old head on that sharp-edged chair-back.
He wouldn't let me put him on the lounge.[12]
You must go in and see what you can do.
I made the bed up for him there tonight.
You'll be surprised at him—how much he's broken.
His working days are done; I'm sure of it."

"I'd not be in a hurry to say that."

"I haven't been. Go, look, see for yourself.
But, Warren, please remember how it is:
He's come to help you ditch the meadow.
He has a plan. You mustn't laugh at him.
He may not speak of it, and then he may.
I'll sit and see if that small sailing cloud
Will hit or miss the moon." (1)

It hit the moon.
Then there were three there, making a dim row,
The moon, the little silver cloud, and she.

Warren returned—too soon, it seemed to her—
Slipped to her side, caught up her hand and waited.

"Warren?" she questioned.

"Dead," was all he answered.

(1) **NARRATIVE POETRY**
In lines 150–161, the dialogue between Mary and Warren is coming to a head. What turn in the **plot** do you foresee?

---

10. **better than appearances:** better than he looks.
11. **abide:** put up with.
12. **lounge:** couch.

Comprehension

1. **Recall** Who is Silas, and what is his relationship to Mary and Warren?
2. **Recall** How does Silas look and act when Mary finds him?
3. **Clarify** Why is Warren angry with Silas?
4. **Clarify** In Mary's mind, why has Silas returned to the farm?

Text Analysis

5. **Analyze Characterization** What does the **dialogue** between Mary and Warren reveal about their differing attitudes toward the following subjects?
   - Silas's return (lines 5–30)
   - Silas's appearance and plans (lines 42–61)
   - Silas's skills (lines 88–102)
   - Silas's relationship to his brother (lines 124–145)

   Based on these attitudes, identify Mary's and Warren's chief personality traits.
6. **Draw Conclusions** Silas has a long history with Mary and Warren. Based on what they say about him and their past interactions with them, why do you think he has come to regard their farm as home?
7. **Examine Narrative Poetry** Compare the events that occur during the conversation between Mary and Warren with those events—revealed through **dialogue**—that have taken place over the entire time they have known Silas. How would the poem's **plot** be different if Mary and Warren had not talked at such length about these earlier events? Explain.
8. **Evaluate Form in Poetry** Review the chart in which you kept track of the changing speakers. In your opinion, what is gained or lost by Frost's style of writing dialogue in terms of the following elements? Overall, do you think his technique was effective? Explain.
   - clarity
   - rhythm
   - sense of drama

Text Criticism

9. **Biographical Context** Robert Frost spent 11 years farming and drew tremendous inspiration from farm life. The poet Ezra Pound, reviewing Frost's second book of poetry, wrote, "I know more of farm life than I did before I had read his poems. That means I know more of 'Life.'" Think of the Frost poems you've read. In what ways can the themes of farm life as depicted by Frost be said to reflect life in general?

How do you know you're **HOME?**

Who or what is home to Silas in "The Death of the Hired Man"? Do you agree with Silas's view, or does home mean something different to you? Explain.

COMMON CORE

RL 1 Cite textual evidence to support analysis of what the text says explicitly as well as inferences drawn from the text, including determining where the text leaves matters uncertain. **RL 3** Analyze the impact of the author's choices regarding how to develop and relate elements of a story. **RL 5** Analyze how an author's choices concerning how to structure specific parts of a text contribute to its overall structure and meaning.

Language

◆ **GRAMMAR AND STYLE:** Use Language Effectively

Poets strive to use words and phrases that will give their poems a musical quality and convey emphasis. One kind of phrase Frost uses frequently is the **infinitive phrase,** consisting of an infinitive—a verb form that begins with *to*—plus its modifiers and complements. Infinitive phrases can function as nouns, adjectives, or adverbs. For instance, in the examples below, Frost uses parallel infinitive phrases, highlighted in yellow, as adverbs modifying the verbs highlighted in green.

She ran on tiptoe down the darkened passage
To meet him in the doorway with the news (lines 3–4)

She took the market things from Warren's arms
And set them on the porch, then drew him down
To sit beside her on the wooden steps. (lines 8–10)

Notice that the infinitive phrases help to give the poem a predictable rhythm and to call attention to Mary's actions.

PRACTICE Fill in the blank lines in the following poem with infinitive phrases that modify the boldfaced words.

He **ran** out to the garage

____

A pair of bargain-hunters
Were fighting over a toaster.
He **tried** his best

____

Offering a waffle iron,
But neither was satisfied.

COMMON CORE

L 3a Vary syntax for effect, consulting references for guidance as needed; apply an understanding of syntax to the study of complex texts when reading. **W 2** Write informative/explanatory texts to examine and convey complex ideas, concepts, and information clearly and accurately through the effective selection, organization, and analysis of content. **W 4** Produce clear and coherent writing in which the development, organization, and style are appropriate to task, purpose, and audience.

READING-WRITING CONNECTION

Expand your understanding of "The Death of the Hired Man" by responding to this prompt. Then, use the **revising tips** to improve your essay.

WRITING PROMPT	REVISING TIPS
ANALYZE THEME Write an **essay** in which you identify the central message or theme of "The Death of the Hired Man." First make a list of all the perceptions about life or people conveyed in the poem. Then, determine which one is the most fully developed. Finally, describe the theme of the poem in **three or four paragraphs.** To support your analysis, include details and quotations.	• Include a clear statement of the poem's theme. • Discuss how details support the theme. • Organize your essay in a clear and logical order.

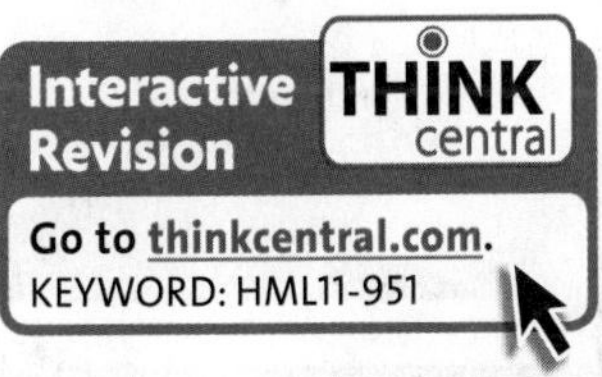

The New Poetry

In a Station of the Metro

Poetry by Ezra Pound

Helen

Poetry by H. D.

Spring and All / This Is Just to Say

Poetry by William Carlos Williams

COMMON CORE

RL 1 Cite strong and thorough textual evidence to support analysis of what the text says explicitly as well as inferences drawn from the text, including determining where the text leaves matters uncertain. **RL 4** Analyze the impact of specific word choices on meaning and tone, including words with multiple meanings or language that is particularly fresh, engaging, or beautiful.

Meet the Authors

Ezra Pound
1885–1972

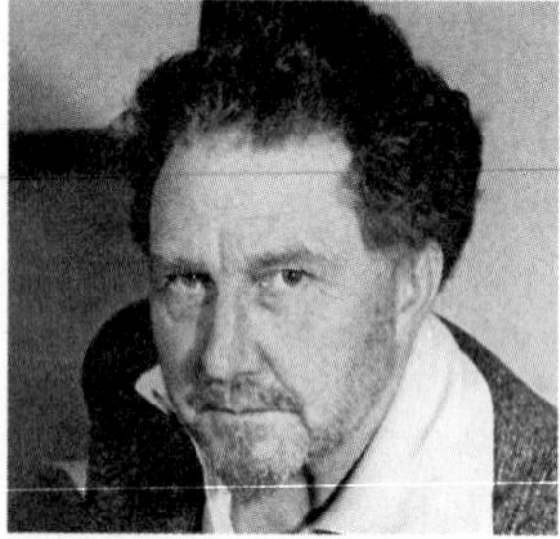

Ezra Pound may have been the most influential poet of the 20th century, promoting the careers of experimental writers and founding the literary movement known as imagism. Pound encouraged poets to use everyday language and to express emotions and ideas through precise, concrete images. In his own work, Pound drew upon the poetic traditions of numerous countries; his masterwork, *The Cantos,* features heroic figures from world history. In life, he was an inflammatory figure. During World War II, he made anti-American radio broadcasts from Rome. He was eventually arrested and confined to a mental hospital. Following his release, he lived a quiet, secluded life in Italy.

H. D. (Hilda Doolittle)
1886–1961

As a young woman, Hilda Doolittle coped with the pain of alienation by befriending other artists. At 15, she met the poet Ezra Pound, who became her close friend and, briefly, her fiancé. A few years later she met the poets Marianne Moore and William Carlos Williams, beginning lifelong nurturing friendships.

Although no longer romantically involved with Pound, Doolittle joined his circle of friends when she moved to London in 1911. Her first published poems appeared in *Poetry* magazine (1913) under the signature "H. D., *Imagiste,*" as suggested by Pound. That year she married Richard Aldington, another imagist, who shared her fascination with the classical world. H. D.'s best poems retell Greek myths from the perspective of women who have suffered injustice.

William Carlos Williams
1883–1963

William Carlos Williams crammed two lives into one. He worked full time as a doctor in Rutherford, New Jersey, yet managed to publish more than 40 books of poetry, fiction, plays, and essays. Often, he found inspiration while caring for his patients.

Born to an English father and a Puerto Rican mother, Williams grew up in Rutherford and considered America his home. While his contemporaries fled to Europe, he decided to write poems about the world around him. Williams felt strongly that a poem should be rooted in everyday life and not abstract ideas.

Author Online THINK central

Go to thinkcentral.com. KEYWORD: HML11-952

TEXT ANALYSIS: IMAGISM

Early in the 20th century, a number of American and British poets undertook a collective effort to rejuvenate poetry in English, freeing it from standard conventions of form and subject matter. The **imagists,** influenced by Japanese haiku as well as ancient Greek lyric and French symbolist poetry, wrote according to strict principles.

- to use the language of **common speech;** yet also to choose words with extreme precision and economy
- to create new **rhythms** as a way of expressing new moods; this generally meant writing in **free verse**
- to have complete freedom in choice of **subject matter**
- to present a clear and highly concentrated **image**

The images in these poems do not generally carry a specific meaning; rather, they suggest a certain feeling or idea.

Ezra Pound and H. D. were among the most important founding members of imagism; William Carlos Williams emerged a few years later, making his own distinctive mark on the style. As you read their work, consider the principles outlined above. Be attuned to the images in these poems and think about what ideas or feelings they might suggest.

READING SKILL: MAKE INFERENCES

Imagist poems are tightly compressed, leaving out details and explanations in favor of sharp, spare images. They can be seen as highly efficient, saying a lot with very few words. This economic use of language can occasionally leave room for confusion, often requiring you to **make inferences,** or logical guesses based on the text (or prior knowledge), about what is not directly stated. This is often referred to as "reading between the lines." As you read each poem, use a chart like the one shown to record your inferences and the evidence on which you base them.

"Helen"	
Inferences	*Details from Text or Prior Knowledge*
Helen is beautiful.	*First stanza focuses on her white skin and its "lustre."*

 Complete the activities in your **Reader/Writer Notebook**.

How do you capture a MOMENT?

"I'll never forget the sight of that wet scarf hanging out the car door." Many experiences leave us with a lingering mental image, which then becomes our means of remembering the experience. The gleaming surface of an empty swimming pool, a towering pile of unwashed dishes—something about such an image communicates the meaning or feeling of a moment. What is that meaning or feeling? How might you capture it?

QUICKWRITE Choose an image that stands out in your mind, whether it's from an important experience (your first day of school) or an ordinary moment (a walk to the store on a hot day). Then write a brief list of the sensory details that make the image so compelling for you.

In a Station of the Metro[1]

Ezra Pound

The apparition of these faces in the crowd;
Petals on a wet, black bough. **A**

A MAKE INFERENCES
Note the use of the word *apparition* to describe the faces in the crowd. What does this suggest about the people?

Helen

H. D.

All Greece hates
the still eyes in the white face,
the lustre as of olives
where she stands,
and the white hands. **B**

All Greece reviles[2]
the wan face when she smiles,
hating it deeper still
when it grows wan and white,
remembering past enchantments
and past ills.

Greece sees unmoved,
God's daughter[3], born of love,
the beauty of cool feet
and slenderest knees,
could love indeed the maid,
only if she were laid,
white ash amid funereal cypresses.[4] **C**

B IMAGISM
Helen of Troy, "the face that launched a thousand ships," is one of the best known characters of classical literature. She has been featured in numerous films, including epic retellings of the Trojan War. What is it about this figure from classical literature that fascinates audiences today? Reread the first stanza of this poem about Helen. Identify the **images** that account for Helen's grip on the imagination.

C MAKE INFERENCES
Based on information you find in the text, why do you think the Greeks hate Helen?

1. **the Metro:** the subway in Paris.
2. **reviles:** to attack with hateful language.
3. **God's daughter:** Helen was a daughter of Zeus, the king of the gods; and Leda, a mortal.
4. **funereal cypresses:** The cypress, a type of evergreen tree, has been associated with death and funeral services since ancient times.

Spring and All

William Carlos Williams

By the road to the contagious hospital[1]
under the surge of the blue
mottled clouds driven from the
northeast—a cold wind. Beyond, the
waste of broad, muddy fields
brown with dried weeds, standing and fallen

patches of standing water
the scattering of tall trees

All along the road the reddish
purplish, forked, upstanding, twiggy
stuff of bushes and small trees
with dead, brown leaves under them
leafless vines— D

Lifeless in appearance, sluggish[2]
dazed spring approaches—

They enter the new world naked,
cold, uncertain of all
save that they enter. All about them
the cold, familiar wind— E

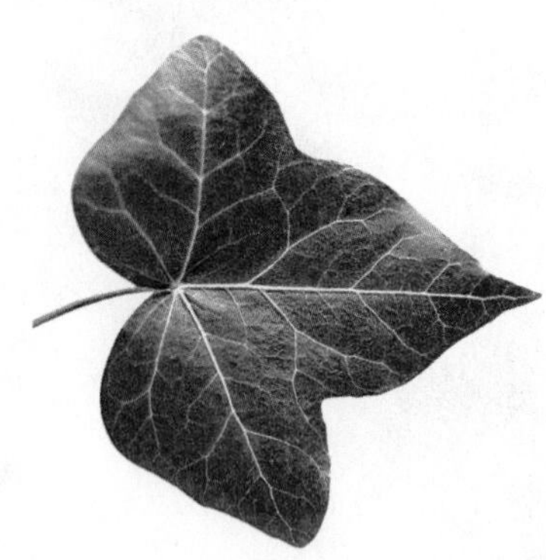

Now the grass, tomorrow
the stiff curl of wildcarrot leaf

One by one objects are defined—
It quickens:[3] clarity, outline of leaf

But now the stark dignity of
entrance—Still, the profound change
has come upon them: rooted, they
grip down and begin to awaken

D IMAGISM
Identify the colors named in lines 1–13. What aspect of spring is emphasized by these colors?

E IMAGISM
Reread lines 16–19. What words and phrases does Williams use to characterize the newly growing plants in these lines? Then identify the language in lines 20–27 that describes the change that comes upon them.

---

1. **contagious hospital:** place where people with contagious diseases are hospitalized.
2. **sluggish:** slow to respond.
3. **quickens:** comes alive; revives.

This Is Just to Say

William Carlos Williams

I have eaten
the plums
that were in
the icebox

and which
you were probably
saving
for breakfast

Forgive me
they were delicious
so sweet
and so cold (F)

(F) IMAGISM
Williams has chosen to invoke only two senses in this poem. What are they? Explain how this choice affects your perception of those sensory details.

Comprehension

1. **Clarify** In "Helen," what would it take for the Greeks to love Helen?
2. **Summarize** What signs of new life does the speaker of "Spring and All" notice by the road?

Text Analysis

3. **Make Inferences** Based on the chart you created for "Helen," what can you say about Helen's past and present relationship with the Greeks?
4. **Analyze Allusion** The title "Helen" is an allusion to Helen of Troy, a great beauty whose abduction by Paris, a Trojan prince, prompted the Greeks to take up arms against Troy in a war that lasted for ten years. How does this information help you understand the poem? Explain, citing evidence from the text.
5. **Examine Metaphor** The juxtaposition of the two images in "In a Station of the Metro" has the effect of a metaphor. What does the image in line 2 suggest about the faces in line 1?
6. **Interpret Imagist Poetry** Choose one of the poems in this lesson and identify its most prominent image or images. What feeling or idea are you left with at the end of the poem? Citing evidence from the text, explain what it is about the imagery that suggests this feeling.
7. **Compare Diction** William Carlos Williams favored the use of everyday language over highly formal poetic diction. Identify several examples of his ordinary diction in "Spring and All" and "This Is Just to Say." Compare Williams's language with the language H. D. uses in "Helen." Which, in your opinion, is more approachable? Which is more interesting? Cite details from the texts to support your opinion.

Text Criticism

8. **Author's Style** Like other modernist poets, the Imagists eschewed the use of traditional rhyme schemes, meters, and other formal elements. Yet form was important to them; you may recall from page 933 that Williams once criticized Carl Sandburg's poetry as "formless." Choose one of the three poets featured in this lesson and examine his or her use of the following poetic devices, when relevant:

   - rhythm
   - rhyme
   - line breaks
   - stanza breaks

   In your opinion, does the use of these elements seem deliberate or random? Cite evidence from the poem or poems to support your answer.

How do you capture a **MOMENT?**

Ezra Pound draws a similarity between two very dissimilar images in his two-line poem "In a Station of the Metro." What comparison can you make between two familiar, dissimilar images?

COMMON CORE

RL 1 Cite strong and thorough textual evidence to support analysis of what the text says explicitly as well as inferences drawn from the text, including determining where the text leaves matters uncertain. **RL 4** Analyze the impact of specific word choices on meaning and tone, including words with multiple meanings or language that is particularly fresh, engaging, or beautiful.

Language

◆ GRAMMAR AND STYLE: Create Imagery

Writers use fresh, **vivid adjectives** to create images that bring scenes to life. In the poem "Spring and All," for instance, Williams uses adjectives that lead readers to picture the way a landscape looks in the change from late winter to early spring. Carefully examine the adjectives Williams uses in the following lines. Notice how keenly they evoke the sight of a landscape in transition.

All along the road the reddish
purplish, forked, upstanding, twiggy
stuff of bushes and small trees (lines 9–11)

Lifeless in appearance, sluggish
dazed spring approaches— (lines 14–15)

COMMON CORE

L 3 Apply knowledge of language to make effective choices for meaning or style. **W 3d** Use telling details to convey a vivid picture of the experiences, events, setting, and/or characters.

PRACTICE Write down each of the following sentences. Then, try to enliven these sentences by inserting vivid adjectives. An example has been done for you.

EXAMPLE

The crowd stared at Helen's hands and face.

The angry crowd stared at Helen's delicate hands and ash-colored face.

1. She noticed fields and weeds by the side of the road.
2. I saw faces looking out from the windows of the train.
3. Slowly, the girl ate the peaches that we had plucked from the tree.

READING-WRITING CONNECTION

Expand your understanding of imagist poetry by responding to this prompt. Then, use the revising tips to improve your poem.

WRITING PROMPT	REVISING TIPS
WRITE AN IMAGIST POEM Think of a place that has inspired powerful emotions in you. What images come to mind when you think about that place? What feelings do your memories evoke in you? Use your responses to these questions as the starting point for an **eight-to-ten-line poem.** As you write, try to include concrete images that convey both emotions and meaning.	• Use sensory language to create vivid imagery. • Use precise descriptive language with vivid adjectives. • Write in free verse, but try to achieve a sense of rhythm.

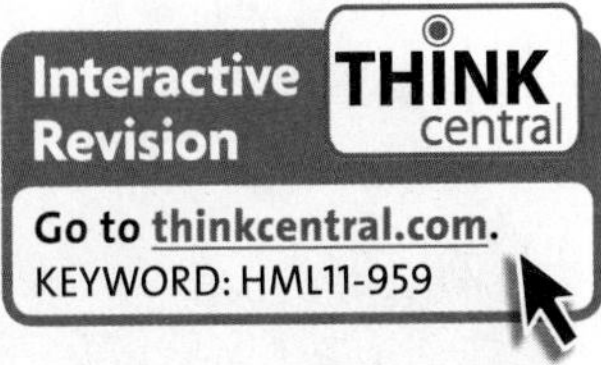

COMMON CORE

RL 5 Analyze how an author's choices concerning how to structure specific parts of a text contribute to its overall structure and meaning as well as its aesthetic impact. **RL 10** Read and comprehend literature, including poems.

anyone lived in a pretty how town

Poetry by E. E. Cummings

Poetry

Poetry by Marianne Moore

Recuerdo

Poetry by Edna St. Vincent Millay

Meet the Authors

E. E. Cummings
1894–1962

E. E. Cummings believed deeply in two things: love and human individuality. He felt that both being an individual and being in a loving relationship led to joy and personal growth. His poems honor love in all its variety and pay tribute to people who resist group conformity and conventional thought.

Cummings's faith in love grew out of his tender relationship with his parents. His father encouraged Cummings's literary ambitions and secured his release when he was imprisoned in France during World War I. After the war, Cummings lived in New York's Greenwich Village, a community of free-thinking artists and intellectuals, where he spent his days painting and writing. By the 1950s, Cummings's playful, innovative style had made him enormously popular.

Marianne Moore
1887–1972

Marianne Moore was a true original. Her interests ranged from baseball to Muhammad Ali to exotic animals, which she scrutinized during her frequent trips to the zoo. Gifted with an eye for detail, she wrote precise, witty descriptions of these and other subjects. Moore also affected an eccentric public appearance, often sporting a three-cornered hat and a black cape.

When she was 31, Moore moved to New York City, where she hobnobbed with other writers, served as editor of the prestigious literary journal *The Dial,* and wrote poetry. A highly innovative poet, she mixed direct observation with quoted material and experimented with stanza forms and line lengths. Her complex, meticulously crafted poems earned her the esteem of other poets, as well as a Pulitzer Prize.

Edna St. Vincent Millay
1892–1950

In both her life and her art, Edna St. Vincent Millay expressed emotional extremes. This intensity, coupled with Millay's revolt against cultural expectations for women, made her a symbol of the "new woman" of the 1920s.

Although Millay endured childhood poverty and deprivation, she nevertheless managed to excel in school and to win poetry awards. After graduating from Vassar College, she became a central figure among the avant-garde set in New York's Greenwich Village. There, she led a bohemian lifestyle, juggling relationships and living in poverty so that she had ample time to write.

Author Online THINK central

Go to thinkcentral.com. KEYWORD: HML11-960

TEXT ANALYSIS: FORM IN MODERN POETRY

Like other modernists, modern poets are known for challenging and experimenting with literary **form.** The term *form* refers primarily to the arrangement of words on the page and to the use of rhyme and meter, but also to the standard conventions of written language (spelling, punctuation, etc.). E. E. Cummings is widely noted for his playful sense of experimentation. In "anyone lived in a pretty how town," he abandons many rules of punctuation, spelling, grammar, and capitalization, creating striking (and sometimes puzzling) effects. Millay's "Recuerdo" is more traditional, with regular rhyme, stanzas, and meter.

Moore's poem "Poetry" is somewhere between these two. It observes the standard conventions of written language, yet it lacks regular rhyme, meter, and line length, giving it a more prose like feel than the other two poems. As you read, note how each poet responds to traditional form, whether by letting go of convention or adapting it. Remember that all good poets use form to help deliver or emphasize meaning.

READING STRATEGY: READING MODERN POETRY

Many readers enjoy the playful, unpredictable quality of modern poetry; others find it confusing or meaningless. There are a number of strategies that can help any reader enjoy these poems.

- **Paraphrase**—If a word, phrase, or sentence seems difficult, try restating it in your own words.
- **Read aloud**—Reading a poem aloud can sometimes help you hear the flow of a line or stanza and clarify its meaning, as well as emphasizing its musical qualities.
- **Observe mechanics**—Note the punctuation, spelling, capitalization, and grammar. How does this affect the sound or sense of the poem?

Using a chart like the one below, monitor your comprehension of each poem by paraphrasing difficult lines.

"anyone lived in a pretty how town"	"Poetry"	"Recuerdo"
Paraphrase: A character named "anyone" lived in some kind of town, year round, singing and dancing.		

Complete the activities in your **Reader/Writer Notebook**.

Do poems have to follow the RULES?

If it doesn't rhyme, is it still a poem? What if it's only two lines long? Do the lines have to break in a regular place? What if some of the words are upside-down on the page? The modernist poets asked questions like this, breaking rules right and left. Their work changed the accepted ideas about what poetry is.

DISCUSS With a small group, brainstorm a list of all the qualities you might find in a poem. From that list, come up with a set of rules that all poems follow.

Poetry Rules
• has to sound rhythmic
• must contain images

anyone lived in a pretty how town

E. E. Cummings

anyone lived in a pretty how town
(with up so floating many bells down)
spring summer autumn winter
he sang his didn't he danced his did.

Women and men(both little and small)
cared for anyone not at all
they sowed their isn't they reaped their same
sun moon stars rain **A**

children guessed(but only a few
and down they forgot as up they grew
autumn winter spring summer)
that noone loved him more by more

when by now and tree by leaf
she laughed his joy she cried his grief
bird by snow and stir by still
anyone's any was all to her **B**

someones married their everyones
laughed their cryings and did their dance
(sleep wake hope and then)they
said their nevers they slept their dream

stars rain sun moon
(and only the snow can begin to explain
how children are apt to forget to remember
with up so floating many bells down)

one day anyone died i guess
(and noone stooped to kiss his face)
busy folk buried them side by side
little by little and was by was

all by all and deep by deep
and more by more they dream their sleep
noone and anyone earth by april
wish by spirit and if by yes. **C**

Women and men(both dong and ding)
summer autumn winter spring
reaped their sowing and went their came
sun moon stars rain

Analyze Visuals ▶
Painter Marc Chagall is known for his whimsical and dream like images. Identify some unrealistic elements in the painting on page 963. What do they suggest about the couple depicted? Explain.

A FORM IN MODERN POETRY
Many words in these stanzas are used in strange ways, but the verbs are still pretty straight forward. In lines 1–8, which actions are attributed to "anyone" and which to the women and men? What does this suggest about the differences between them?

B READING MODERN POETRY
Paraphrase lines 13–16. How does "noone" feel about "anyone"?

C FORM IN MODERN POETRY
Reread lines 25–32. Identify some ways in which Cummings breaks with the conventions of **mechanics.** How does this affect your sense of the poem? Explain.

Couple Above St. Paul, Marc Chagall. Private collection.

Poetry

Marianne Moore

I, too, dislike it: there are things that are important beyond all this fiddle.
Reading it, however, with a perfect contempt for it, one discovers in
it, after all, a place for the genuine.
Hands that can grasp, eyes
that can dilate,[1] hair that can rise
if it must, these things are important not because a

high-sounding interpretation can be put upon them but because they are
useful. When they become so derivative[2] as to become unintelligible,
the same thing may be said for all of us, that we
do not admire what
we cannot understand: the bat **D**
holding on upside down or in quest of something to

eat, elephants pushing, a wild horse taking a roll, a tireless wolf under
a tree, the immovable critic twitching his skin like a horse that feels a flea,
the base-
ball fan, the statistician—
nor is it valid
to discriminate against "business documents and

school-books"; all these phenomena are important. One must make a
distinction
however: when dragged into prominence by half poets, the result is not
poetry, **E**
nor till the poets among us can be
"literalists[3] of
the imagination"—above
insolence and triviality and can present

D READING MODERN POETRY
Reread and **paraphrase** lines 1–11. What is important about "Hands that can grasp, eyes / that can dilate, hair that can rise"?

Analyze Visuals ▸
Consider what the speaker of this poem has to say about poetry. How do you think she might respond to this abstract painting?

E FORM IN MODERN POETRY
Note the extremely indented lines at lines 15, 20, and 22. What do these oddities of form contribute to the poem's meaning? Explain.

1. **dilate** (dī-lāt'): enlarge; open wide.
2. **derivative:** lacking originality.
3. **literalists:** people who interpret words in their usual or most basic sense.

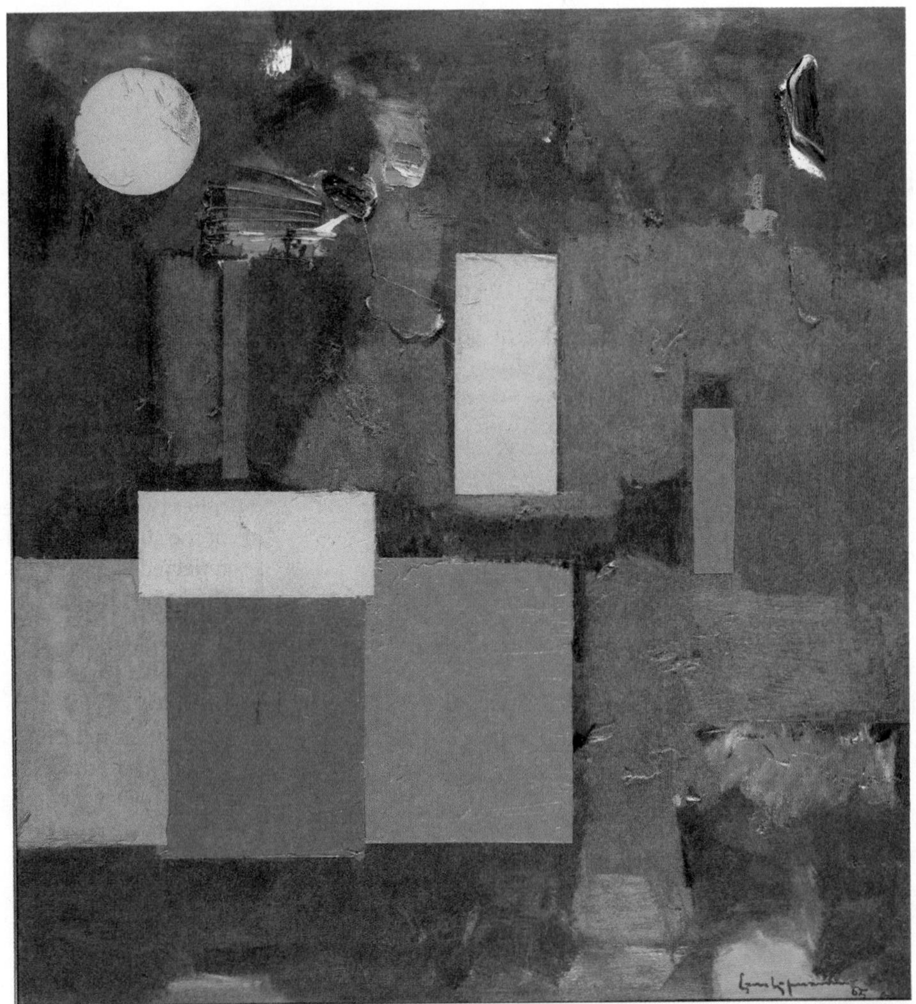

Rising Moon (1965), Hans Hofmann. Private collection. © 2008 Estate of Hans Hofmann/Artists Rights Society (ARS), New York/Art Resource, New York.

for inspection, "imaginary gardens with real toads in them," shall we have
 it. In the meantime, if you demand on the one hand,
 the raw material of poetry in
  all its rawness and
  that which is on the other hand
   genuine, you are interested in poetry. F

F READING MODERN POETRY
Reread lines 28–32 aloud. How, if at all, does this change your sense of the line breaks?

Recuerdo

Edna St. Vincent Millay

We were very tired, we were very merry—
We had gone back and forth all night on the ferry.
It was bare and bright, and smelled like a stable—
But we looked into a fire, we leaned across a table,
We lay on a hill-top underneath the moon;
And the whistles kept blowing, and the dawn came soon.

We were very tired, we were very merry—
We had gone back and forth all night on the ferry;
And you ate an apple, and I ate a pear,
From a dozen of each we had bought somewhere;
And the sky went wan,[1] and the wind came cold,
And the sun rose dripping, a bucketful of gold. G

We were very tired, we were very merry,
We had gone back and forth all night on the ferry.
We hailed, "Good morrow, mother!" to a shawl-covered head,
And bought a morning paper, which neither of us read;
And she wept, "God bless you!" for the apples and pears,
And we gave her all our money but our subway fares. H

G READING MODERN POETRY
Read aloud lines 1–12. How does this poem sound different from the other two? What aspect of the subject matter is reflected by the poem's **rhyme** and **meter?**

H FORM IN MODERN POETRY
Identify the **repetition** that helps to shape each stanza. What meaning is emphasized by this device?

1. **wan:** pale.

Port Scene, Paul Klee. Atheneum Museum, Helsinki, Finland. © Giraudon/Art Resource, New York. © 2007 Artists Rights Society (ARS), New York/VG Bild-Kunst, Bonn.

Comprehension

1. **Clarify** Who are the lovers described in "anyone lived in a pretty how town"?
2. **Clarify** What does the speaker of "Poetry" dislike about poetry? What does she value in it?
3. **Clarify** Where and when does "Recuerdo" take place?

COMMON CORE

RL 5 Analyze how an author's choices concerning how to structure specific parts of a text contribute to its overall structure and meaning as well as its aesthetic impact. **RL 10** Read and comprehend literature, including poems.

Text Analysis

4. **Analyze Modern Poetry** Review the chart you filled in as you read. In the Cummings poem, it is important not to try to read every line literally, but rather aim for the gist of these nonsense phrases. Choose one stanza from this poem and explain the general impression you get from the language in each line. Then paraphrase the entire stanza, making use of these impressions.
5. **Interpret Ideas** In "Poetry," what idea about poetry is represented by each of the following items? Explain.
   - "hands that can grasp" (line 4)
   - "elephants pushing" (line 13)
   - "business documents and school-books" (lines 18–19)
   - "'imaginary gardens with real toads in them'" (line 27)
6. **Evaluate Form in Modern Poetry** Each of these poems has a playful, irreverent quality, sometimes achieved by breaking rules of traditional poetry and sometimes by following them. Examine the poems in this lesson, identifying the most playful elements of each. In your opinion, which poem is the most radical? Cite evidence to support your answer.

Text Criticism

7. **Critical Interpretations** In a review, the critic Edmund Wilson argued that "Behind [the] formidable barrier of punctuations for which Mr. Cummings seems unfortunately to have achieved most celebrity, his emotions are conventional and simple in the extreme." Do you agree or disagree with Wilson's argument? Whether or not you agree, do you view Wilson's statement as a positive or negative comment? Cite evidence to support your opinion.

Do poems have to follow the RULES?

You probably found "Recuerdo" the easiest of the three poems to read because it employs a familiar sense of rhyme and meter. What "rules," then, do you think are broken in "Recuerdo"? Do you think poetry—or any form of art, for that matter—should adhere to particular "rules"? Explain.

The Love Song of J. Alfred Prufrock

Poem by T. S. Eliot

VIDEO TRAILER THINK central KEYWORD: HML11-968A

COMMON CORE

RL 2 Determine two or more themes or central ideas of a text and analyze their development over the course of the text, including how they interact and build on one another to produce a complex account; provide an objective summary of the text. **RL 5** Analyze how an author's choices concerning how to structure specific parts of a text contribute to its overall structure and meaning as well as its aesthetic impact.

Meet the Author

T. S. Eliot 1888–1965

When he was alive, T. S. Eliot was one of the most influential poets in the English-speaking world. His invention of new poetic rhythms, forms, and themes had an enormous impact on other writers and helped usher in a new era in poetry. Eliot, remarked the composer Igor Stravinsky, was "not only a great sorcerer of words, but the very key keeper of the language."

A Lover of Philosophy Eliot grew up in St. Louis, Missouri, in a household steeped in culture and tradition. His mother, Charlotte Champe Stearns, was an amateur poet, and his father, Henry Ware Eliot, was a successful businessman with New England roots. Eliot received a broad education, studying at Milton Academy and Harvard University. After earning both bachelor's and master's degrees from Harvard, Eliot continued his studies in philosophy at the Sorbonne in Paris and then back at Harvard. However, he never completed those studies. While on a traveling fellowship in Europe, he met the poet Ezra Pound, who encouraged Eliot's poetic ambitions.

Literary Success Pound helped Eliot gain entry into London's avant-garde circle of writers, and he introduced Eliot's poetry to Harriet Monroe of *Poetry* magazine. In 1915, Eliot's masterpiece "The Love Song of J. Alfred Prufrock" appeared in *Poetry.* That same year, Eliot married Vivien Haigh-Wood, an Englishwoman. Struggling to make a living as a writer, Eliot worked as a teacher, a bank clerk, and finally as an editor.

Breakthroughs in Poetry The 1917 publication of Eliot's first book, *Prufrock and Other Observations,* signaled a distinct break with the past. Using colloquial speech laced with slang, Eliot created a new, highly original poetic diction. He also explored new poetic themes, such as the splendors and horrors of modern life and the effects of alienation. With the appearance of *The Waste Land* in 1922, Eliot's reputation was solidified. In this poem, Eliot articulated the disgust and disillusionment felt by his generation in the wake of World War I, as well as its longing for meaning in a chaotic, sometimes frightening, world.

Inspired by Religion Though a pioneer in poetry, Eliot became increasingly conservative in his personal views. Struggling with anxiety over his domestic troubles, he joined the Church of England in 1927 and embraced its traditional pieties. In his later collections, *Ash Wednesday* (1930) and *Four Quartets* (1943), he used poetry to stress the significance of accepting religious discipline.

Author Online THINK central

Go to thinkcentral.com. KEYWORD: HML11-968B

DID YOU KNOW?

T. S. Eliot . . .

- was also an acclaimed playwright.
- wrote the book that inspired the musical *Cats.*
- won the Nobel Prize in literature in 1948.

TEXT ANALYSIS: STREAM OF CONSCIOUSNESS

Modern poets explored many ways of breaking free from the standard conventions of poetic form and even content, changing the nature of both narrative and lyric poetry. One of the most dramatic breaks from convention in the modern era was the development of **stream of consciousness.** Used by both poets and fiction writers, this technique presents a sometimes chaotic flow of images and ideas, meant to represent the unfiltered thoughts of the speaker or protagonist. "The Love Song of J. Alfred Prufrock" is a **dramatic monologue** in which Prufrock, the speaker, addresses a silent listener with a tumble of associative thoughts, allusions, and daydreams.

And indeed there will be time
For the yellow smoke that slides along the street
Rubbing its back upon the window-panes

As you read the poem, try not to be distracted by the seemingly nonsensical nature of some verses, but be alert to any feelings or ideas that the images seem to suggest.

READING STRATEGY: SUMMARIZE STANZAS

The difficult thing about reading stream of consciousness is figuring out how to connect seemingly unrelated ideas. A writer will often jump from one thought to the next without any clear transition. Fortunately, Eliot has done us the favor of grouping his thoughts in **stanzas.** If you read the stanzas closely, you will notice that each one expresses a fairly coherent idea. Once you **summarize** and identify the central idea or image of each stanza, you will have an easier time tracing the arc, and the sense, of the entire poem.

As you read, record your summary of each stanza in a chart like the one shown. Some stanzas have only two or three lines; in these cases, don't worry about providing a summary as much as a brief description of the central idea or image.

Stanza	*Summary/Central Idea*
1	*Speaker suggests that listener join him on an evening trip through the lonely city streets.*

Complete the activities in your **Reader/Writer Notebook**.

What is ALIENATION?

So many of us know the feeling of standing at the edge of a party, wanting to join but having no idea what to say or do. Everyone else is having more fun, making better jokes, or wearing nicer clothes. And it's all the worse if you are hoping to approach the object of your affections; do you even stand a chance? In this poem, J. Alfred Prufrock approaches a party with a similar sense of alienation. Full of dread and self-doubt and fearful of female rejection, he wonders whether he dares to step in and draw attention to himself.

QUICKWRITE Create a list of images that suggest alienation or isolation to you. They could be explicit, such as that of a person hesitating at the edge of a group, or implicit, such as the image of a lonely window lit in the darkness.

THE LOVE SONG OF J. Alfred Prufrock

T. S. Eliot

S'io credessi che mia risposta fosse
a persona che mai tornasse al mondo,
questa fiamma staria senza più scosse.
Ma per ciò che giammai di questo fondo
non tornò vivo alcun, s'i'odo il vero,
senza tema d'infamia ti rispondo.

S'io credessi . . . ti rispondo: These lines are from the *Inferno,* written in the early 14th century by Italian poet Dante Alighieri. As Dante visits hell, one of the damned agrees to speak of his torment only because he believes that Dante cannot return to the living world to repeat the tale.

Let us go then, you and I,
When the evening is spread out against the sky
Like a patient etherised upon a table;
Let us go, through certain half-deserted streets,
The muttering retreats
Of restless nights in one-night cheap hotels
And sawdust restaurants with oyster-shells:
Streets that follow like a tedious argument
Of insidious intent
To lead you to an overwhelming question . . .
Oh, do not ask, "What is it?"
Let us go and make our visit.

In the room the women come and go
Talking of Michelangelo.

The yellow fog that rubs its back upon the window-panes,
The yellow smoke that rubs its muzzle on the window-panes,
Licked its tongue into the corners of the evening,
Lingered upon the pools that stand in drains,
Let fall upon its back the soot that falls from chimneys,

3 etherised: given ether, a liquid used as an anesthetic.

9 insidious (ĭn-sĭd'ē-əs)**:** more dangerous than it seems.

Slipped by the terrace, made a sudden leap,
And seeing that it was a soft October night,
Curled once about the house, and fell asleep. **A**

And indeed there will be time
For the yellow smoke that slides along the street
Rubbing its back upon the window-panes;
There will be time, there will be time
To prepare a face to meet the faces that you meet;
There will be time to murder and create,
And time for all the works and days of hands
That lift and drop a question on your plate;
Time for you and time for me,
And time yet for a hundred indecisions,
And for a hundred visions and revisions,
Before the taking of a toast and tea.

In the room the women come and go
Talking of Michelangelo.

And indeed there will be time
To wonder, "Do I dare?" and, "Do I dare?"
Time to turn back and descend the stair,
With a bald spot in the middle of my hair—
(They will say: "How his hair is growing thin!")
My morning coat, my collar mounting firmly to the chin,
My necktie rich and modest, but asserted by a simple pin—
(They will say: "But how his arms and legs are thin!")
Do I dare
Disturb the universe?
In a minute there is time
For decisions and revisions which a minute will reverse. **B**

For I have known them all already, known them all—
Have known the evenings, mornings, afternoons,
I have measured out my life with coffee spoons;
I know the voices dying with a dying fall
Beneath the music from a farther room.
So how should I presume?

And I have known the eyes already, known them all—
The eyes that fix you in a formulated phrase,
And when I am formulated, sprawling on a pin,
When I am pinned and wriggling on the wall,
Then how should I begin

A STREAM OF CONSCIOUSNESS
Stream of consciousness is a writing technique that presents a narrator's flow of thoughts as they might in reality occur, enabling the reader to see "inside" the narrator's head. Reread lines 1–22, and consider the dreamlike quality of the narrator's wandering thoughts. What mood is created by the narrator's puzzling comparisons? As you reread the first 22 lines, write down any details that indicate the stream of consciousness technique.

Language Coach

Prefixes A prefix is a word part attached to the beginning of a word. *Re-* means "again." Read lines 31–34. How do *visions* and *revisions* differ in meaning? How does the word *indecisions* relate to line 33?

B SUMMARIZE STANZAS
Summarize lines 37–48. What do Prufrock's repeated questioning and his preoccupation with his appearance indicate about his state of mind?

54 presume: act overconfidently; dare.

56 formulated: reduced to a formula.

55–58 And I have . . . on the wall: Prufrock recalls being scrutinized by women at other parties. He portrays himself as a live insect that has been classified, labeled, and mounted for display.

To spit out all the butt-ends of my days and ways?
And how should I presume?

And I have known the arms already, known them all—
Arms that are braceleted and white and bare
(But in the lamplight, downed with light brown hair!)
Is it perfume from a dress
That makes me so digress?
Arms that lie along a table, or wrap about a shawl.
And should I then presume?
And how should I begin?

• • • • •

Shall I say, I have gone at dusk through narrow streets
And watched the smoke that rises from the pipes
Of lonely men in shirt-sleeves, leaning out of windows? . . .

I should have been a pair of ragged claws
Scuttling across the floors of silent seas.

• • • • •

And the afternoon, the evening, sleeps so peacefully!
Smoothed by long fingers,
Asleep . . . tired . . . or it malingers,
Stretched on the floor, here beside you and me.
Should I, after tea and cakes and ices,
Have the strength to force the moment to its crisis?
But though I have wept and fasted, wept and prayed,
Though I have seen my head (grown slightly bald) brought in
upon a platter,
I am no prophet—and here's no great matter;
I have seen the moment of my greatness flicker,
And I have seen the eternal Footman hold my coat, and snicker,
And in short, I was afraid.

And would it have been worth it, after all,
After the cups, the marmalade, the tea,
Among the porcelain, among some talk of you and me,
Would it have been worth while,
To have bitten off the matter with a smile,
To have squeezed the universe into a ball
To roll it towards some overwhelming question,
To say: "I am Lazarus, come from the dead,
Come back to tell you all, I shall tell you all"—
If one, settling a pillow by her head,
Should say: "That is not what I meant at all.
That is not it, at all." C

Language Coach

Word Definitions *Digress* (line 66) means "wander away from the main topic; ramble." What causes the speaker to digress?

73–74 I should . . . silent seas: Here Prufrock presents an image of himself as a crayfish.

77 malingers (mə-lĭng′ərz)**:** pretends illness in order to avoid duty or work.

81–83 But though . . . prophet: an allusion to the biblical story of John the Baptist, who is imprisoned by King Herod (Matthew 14; Mark 6). At the request of his wife, Herod had the Baptist's head cut off and brought to him on a platter.

94 Lazarus: In the biblical story (John 11:17–44) Lazarus lay dead in his tomb for four days before Jesus brought him back to life.

C STREAM OF CONSCIOUSNESS

Reread lines 75–98. Prufrock casts himself in three different **images** in this stanza, two of which are biblical allusions. Identify these images and explain what they have in common.

And would it have been worth it, after all,
Would it have been worth while,
After the sunsets and the dooryards and the sprinkled streets,
After the novels, after the teacups, after the skirts that trail along
the floor—
And this, and so much more?—
It is impossible to say just what I mean!
But as if a magic lantern threw the nerves in patterns on a
screen:
Would it have been worth while
If one, settling a pillow or throwing off a shawl,
And turning toward the window, should say:
"That is not it at all,
That is not what I meant, at all."

• • • • •

No! I am not Prince Hamlet, nor was meant to be;
Am an attendant lord, one that will do
To swell a progress, start a scene or two,
Advise the prince; no doubt, an easy tool,
Deferential, glad to be of use,
Politic, cautious, and meticulous;
Full of high sentence, but a bit obtuse;
At times, indeed, almost ridiculous—
Almost, at times, the Fool.

I grow old . . . I grow old . . .
I shall wear the bottoms of my trousers rolled. **D**

Shall I part my hair behind? Do I dare to eat a peach?
I shall wear white flannel trousers, and walk upon the beach.
I have heard the mermaids singing, each to each.

I do not think that they will sing to me.

I have seen them riding seaward on the waves
Combing the white hair of the waves blown back
When the wind blows the water white and black.

We have lingered in the chambers of the sea
By sea-girls wreathed with seaweed red and brown
Till human voices wake us, and we drown.

105 magic lantern: a forerunner of the slide projector.

115 deferential: yielding to someone else's opinion.

116 meticulous: extremely careful and precise about details.

117 obtuse: slow to understand; dull.

D STREAM OF CONSCIOUSNESS
What similarities can you detect between the "attendant lord" described in lines 112–119 and Prufrock's image of himself in lines 120–121? Explain.

124–125 mermaids . . . to me: In mythology, mermaids attract mortal men by their beauty and their singing, sometimes allowing men to live with them in the sea.

Comprehension

1. **Recall** What social situation does Prufrock reflect upon in this poem?
2. **Recall** How does he feel about this situation?
3. **Clarify** What is Prufrock's primary feeling about himself?

Text Analysis

4. **Synthesize Summaries** Review the summaries and central ideas you recorded as you read. Now, viewing this series of ideas as a **narrative** with a conflict, a climax, and a resolution, write a summary of Prufrock's internal journey.
5. **Examine Poetic Devices** Review Eliot's use of **repetition** and **rhyme** in lines 23–34. Explain how these devices are used to convey Prufrock's sense of anxiety.
6. **Analyze Stream of Consciousness** In the final lines of the poem (lines 122–131), Prufrock offers his final reflection. For each of the following passages, offer an explication, or careful analysis. What does each group of lines suggest about Prufrock's sense of himself and his place in the world? What resonating idea are we left with at the poem's end?
   - lines 120–121 ("I grow old . . . trousers rolled.")
   - lines 122–123 ("Shall I part . . . walk upon the beach.")
   - lines 124–125 ("I have heard the mermaids . . . sing to me.")
   - lines 126–131 ("I have seen them riding seaward . . . and we drown.")
7. **Evaluate Form and Content** Consider the feelings and ideas that Eliot was trying to express; in what way can the stream of consciousness technique be said to reflect these ideas? Explain whether or not you think this technique is effective, citing evidence.

Text Criticism

8. **Critical Interpretations** Critic Donald R. Fryxell wrote, "Prufrock is a trimmer . . . trimmers were those souls in Dante's *Inferno* who were condemned to the vestibule of hell because they had never really lived, although they were supposedly alive. . . . The Trimmers were lifeless, spiritless, mindless people." Do you agree or disagree with this statement? Give evidence from the text to support your answer.

What is ALIENATION?

The narrator in "The Love Song of J. Alfred Prufrock" sees himself as set apart from the crowd. His self-conscious ruminations reflect a profound fear of rejection. Whom or what might he fear? Have you ever had similar feelings of alienation? Explain.

COMMON CORE

RL 1 Cite textual evidence to support analysis of what the text says explicitly as well as inferences drawn from the text, including determining where the text leaves matters uncertain. **RL 5** Analyze how an author's choices concerning how to structure specific parts of a text contribute to its overall structure and meaning as well as its aesthetic impact.

Modernist Style

While there is no one thing that makes a poem "modern," most modernist literature does share some defining features.

Features of Modernism:

- nontraditional subject matter and themes
- a focus on alienated individuals rather than heroes
- use of understatement and irony to reveal emotions and ideas
- use of symbols and images to suggest meaning
- experimentation with style and language

Writing to Synthesize

Review the poems beginning on page 922 to get a feel for how they incorporate the features of modernism. Then write your own poem in the modernist style.

Consider

- what your poem will be about (remember that traditional themes and topics, such as love, were rejected or reinterpreted by the modernists)
- whether your poem will feature a speaker, and what he or she will be like
- how to use understatement or irony to bring out emotions
- what symbols or images might best convey your meaning
- whether you wish to experiment with language or style

Extension

SPEAKING & LISTENING

Choose a more traditional poem from Units 1–4, such as Poe's "The Raven," and modernize it. **Rewrite** two stanzas of the poem as a modernist poet might, using the features of modernism as a guideline. Then **recite** your stanzas for your classmates, and discuss the techniques you used to "update" the poem. You may need to write out your stanzas on poster board to show how you manipulated line length, stanza form, capitalization and punctuation, or other elements of style.

COMMON CORE

RL 9 Demonstrate knowledge of early-twentieth-century foundational works of American literature, including how two or more texts from the same period treat similar themes or topics. **SL 4** Present information, findings, and supporting evidence, conveying a clear and distinct perspective.

COMMON CORE

RL 2 Analyze the development of two or more themes or central ideas over the course of the text, including how they interact and build on one another to produce a complex account. **RL 3** Analyze the impact of the author's choices regarding how to develop and relate elements of a story. **RL 4** Determine the meaning of words and phrases as they are used in the text, including figurative and connotative meanings. **L 2a** Observe hyphenation conventions.

Winter Dreams

Short Story by F. Scott Fitzgerald

Meet the Author

F. Scott Fitzgerald 1896–1940

F. Scott Fitzgerald experienced, and depicted in his fiction, both the material success and the crushing disillusionment that characterized the 1920s—a decade he dubbed the Jazz Age. He died young, famous for his flashy lifestyle, not his writing. But today, thanks to his dazzling prose style and piercing insight, Fitzgerald is heralded as the spokesperson of his era and as an American literary giant.

Midwest Boy Makes Good Born in St. Paul, Minnesota, Fitzgerald grew up in comfortable circumstances. His parents could afford to send him to prep school and then Princeton University, where he spent his time writing for the literary magazine and creating musical comedies. Low grades and the intervention of World War I kept him from graduating, but he left with a big dream. "I want to be one of the greatest writers who ever lived," he told a friend.

Jazz Age Romance In 1918, Fitzgerald fell madly in love with a flirtatious 18-year-old named Zelda Sayre. Zelda was as rich as she was beautiful and refused to marry him until he could support her financially. Two years later, Fitzgerald's first novel, *This Side of Paradise,* was finally published. Hailed as a daringly original story of the postwar generation's revolt against tradition, it more than doubled Fitzgerald's income, earned him widespread exposure as "the philosopher of the flapper," and won Zelda over. The two married and soon became the golden couple of the 1920s, partying at glamorous locations in the United States and Europe and living beyond the income Fitzgerald made from his writing.

Fall and Redemption Like the decade the Fitzgeralds epitomized, their high life came crashing down. In 1930, Zelda began the first of many hospital stays for mental illness, while Scott fell deeply into debt and alcoholism. *The Beautiful and Damned* (1922), a novel about the unraveling lives of a once-glamorous couple, was deemed "depressing" by reviewers, and Fitzgerald's masterpiece, *The Great Gatsby* (1925), was not the popular success he had hoped for. He died of a heart attack in 1940, at age 44, and it was years before he came to be regarded as anything more than a writer of showy period pieces. The reexamination of Fitzgerald's work was spurred not by critics, many of whom had always appreciated his talent, but by a new generation of readers who discovered the brilliance of his writing and told their friends. The year he died, his book sales—just 40 copies total—earned him $13.13 in royalties. Today, however, *The Great Gatsby* is a beloved American classic, and Fitzgerald's books sell about 500,000 copies annually.

DID YOU KNOW?

F. Scott Fitzgerald . . .

- was named after his distant relative Francis Scott Key, who wrote the words to "The Star-Spangled Banner."
- wrote his first novel while in the army, working on it solely on the weekends for just three months.

Author Online THINK central

Go to thinkcentral.com. KEYWORD: HML11-976

TEXT ANALYSIS: CHARACTER MOTIVATION AND TRAITS

Some characters are so vividly portrayed, they seem like real people. The characters' traits and motivations are often familiar to us; we see them in ourselves or in others we know. **Character traits** are those qualities shown by a character, as implied by his or her physical appearance and expressions of personality, such as boldness or gentleness. By recognizing a character's traits, you are able to better understand the **character's motivation**—the stated or implied reason(s) behind the character's actions. As you read, note the words, actions, thoughts, and appearance of the **protagonist,** or main character, as well as of the **antagonist,** the person against which the protagonist struggles. What do these descriptions indicate about the characters' traits and motivations?

Review: **Theme**

READING STRATEGY: PREDICT STORY DEVELOPMENT

Predicting is the process of using text clues to make a reasonable guess about what will happen in a story. Sometimes your predictions will hit the mark, and other times the characters' actions and the story's events may surprise you. As you come to know the characters in "Winter Dreams," see if you can predict what will happen to them next, or how they will react or feel toward other characters and events. Record your predictions and the text clues that led you to make them.

Predictions	*Text Clues*

VOCABULARY IN CONTEXT

Fitzgerald uses the boldfaced words in his story of love and status. Determine the definition of each word from its context.

1. a girl whose mere presence could **precipitate** a sudden crush
2. due to her **patrimony,** would inherit a **surfeit** of money
3. attended parties surrounded by her **retinue**
4. flirted **blatantly,** without a trace of self-consciousness
5. pouting and **petulance** that seemed to attract men
6. unfriendly to women—no **camaraderie** with them
7. turned her nose up at **mundane,** ordinary things
8. enjoyed the **flux** of life, its **precarious** nature

Complete the activities in your **Reader/Writer Notebook.**

Will STATUS *make you happy?*

It's easy to get caught up in the pursuit of wealth and status—and to imagine that obtaining them would guarantee a perfect life. But would it? Can money buy love, and does high status guarantee happiness?

QUICKWRITE Envision the life you hope to lead ten years from now. Wealth and status top the list of many people's "must-haves," but what else holds a prominent place in your dreams? Jot down some of your aspirations on a graph like the one shown. Then fill in the graph, rating on a scale of 1 to 10 the importance you attach to each goal. Use your completed graph to write a short paragraph explaining which goal holds the top spot on your list, and why.

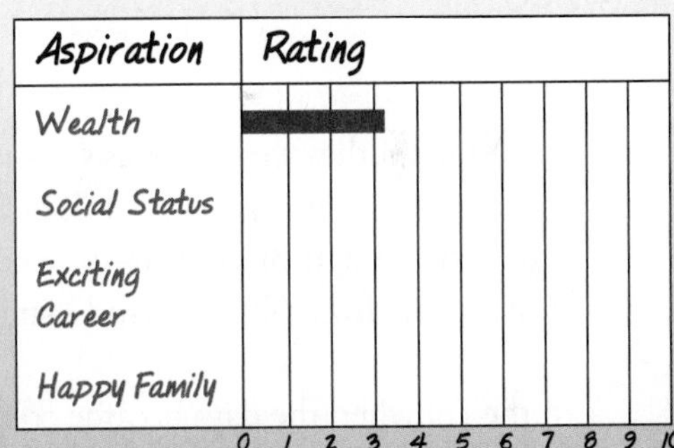

Winter *Dreams*

F. Scott Fitzgerald

BACKGROUND Behind the glitz and glamour of the 1920s lay a profound loss of idealism. Though World War I gave rise to new opportunities and freedoms, especially for women, the shift to the modern age left a gap in values that the new generation struggled to fill. "Winter Dreams" mostly takes place before 1920, when a restless uncertainty was first being felt. The story appeared in the collection *All the Sad Young Men* (1926), a title that expresses Fitzgerald's deeper understanding of the decade.

Analyze Visuals ▶
How would you describe the subject of this portrait? Describe the **traits** you think he projects, citing details from the painting to support your answer.

I

Some of the caddies were poor as sin and lived in one-room houses with a neurasthenic[1] cow in the front yard, but Dexter Green's father owned the second best grocery-store in Black Bear—the best one was "The Hub," patronized by the wealthy people from Sherry Island—and Dexter caddied only for pocket-money. **A**

A MOTIVATION AND TRAITS
Consider the kind of information you receive in the story's very first paragraph. What do you learn about Dexter's family and social position?

In the fall when the days became crisp and gray, and the long Minnesota winter shut down like the white lid of a box, Dexter's skis moved over the snow that hid the fairways of the golf course. At these times the country gave him a feeling of profound melancholy—it offended him that the links should lie in enforced fallowness, haunted by ragged sparrows for the long season. It was dreary, too, that on the tees where the gay colors fluttered in summer there were now only the desolate sand-boxes knee-deep in crusted ice. When he crossed the hills the wind blew cold as misery, and if the sun was out he tramped with his eyes squinted up against the hard dimensionless glare.

1. **neurasthenic** (nŏŏr′əs-thĕn′ĭk): weak and lacking in vigor.

Homme au Chapeau (1900s), Jean Berque. Waterhouse and Dodd, London. © Bridgeman Art Library.

In April the winter ceased abruptly. The snow ran down into Black Bear Lake scarcely tarrying for the early golfers to brave the season with red and black balls. Without elation, without an interval of moist glory, the cold was gone.

Dexter knew that there was something dismal about this Northern spring, just as he knew there was something gorgeous about the fall. Fall made him clinch his hands and tremble and repeat idiotic sentences to himself, and make brisk abrupt gestures of command to imaginary audiences and armies. October filled him with hope which November raised to a sort of ecstatic triumph, and in this mood the fleeting brilliant impressions of the summer at Sherry Island were ready grist to his mill.[2] He became a golf champion and defeated Mr. T. A. Hedrick in a marvelous match played a hundred times over the fairways of his imagination, a match each detail of which he changed about untiringly—sometimes he won with almost laughable ease, sometimes he came up magnificently from behind. Again, stepping from a Pierce-Arrow automobile,[3] like Mr. Mortimer Jones, he strolled frigidly into the lounge of the Sherry Island Golf Club—or perhaps, surrounded by an admiring crowd, he gave an exhibition of fancy diving from the spring-board of the club raft. . . . Among those who watched him in open-mouthed wonder was Mr. Mortimer Jones. B

And one day it came to pass that Mr. Jones—himself and not his ghost—came up to Dexter with tears in his eyes and said that Dexter was the —— best caddy in the club, and wouldn't he decide not to quit if Mr. Jones made it worth his while, because every other —— caddy in the club lost one ball a hole for him—regularly—

"No, sir," said Dexter decisively, "I don't want to caddy any more." Then, after a pause: "I'm too old."

"You're not more than fourteen. Why the devil did you decide just this morning that you wanted to quit? You promised that next week you'd go over to the State tournament with me."

"I decided I was too old."

Dexter handed in his "A Class" badge, collected what money was due him from the caddy-master, and walked home to Black Bear Village.

"The best —— caddy I ever saw," shouted Mr. Mortimer Jones over a drink that afternoon. "Never lost a ball! Willing! Intelligent! Quiet! Honest! Grateful!"

The little girl who had done this was eleven—beautifully ugly as little girls are apt to be who are destined after a few years to be inexpressibly lovely and bring no end of misery to a great number of men. The spark, however, was perceptible. There was a general ungodliness in the way her lips twisted down at the corners when she smiled, and in the—Heaven help us!—in the almost passionate quality of her eyes. Vitality is born early in such women. It was utterly in evidence now, shining through her thin frame in a sort of glow. C

COMMON CORE RL 3

B SETTING
Reread lines 17–31. Notice how vividly Fitzgerald renders the **setting** here—the golf course that plays an important role in the development of this story. Notice also how the author transforms the actual setting into a fantasy setting. What is it about this setting that motivates Dexter to fantasize about his future? What does his fantasy reveal about his character? Support your response with evidence from the story.

C PREDICT
Consider what you've learned about both Dexter and the "beautifully ugly" girl. How might she cause him to quit his job? Give reasons for your prediction.

---

2. **grist to his mill:** something that he could make good use of.
3. **Pierce-Arrow automobile:** a luxury car of the day.

She had come eagerly out onto the course at nine o'clock with a white linen nurse and five small new golf-clubs in a white canvas bag which the nurse was carrying. When Dexter first saw her she was standing by the caddy house, rather ill at ease and trying to conceal the fact by engaging her nurse in an obviously unnatural conversation graced by startling and irrelevant grimaces from herself.

"Well, it's certainly a nice day, Hilda," Dexter heard her say. She drew down the corners of her mouth, smiled, and glanced furtively around, her eyes in transit falling for an instant on Dexter.

Then to the nurse:

"Well, I guess there aren't very many people out here this morning, are there?"

The smile again—radiant, **blatantly** artificial—convincing.

blatantly (blāt'n-tlē) *adv.* in an extremely obvious way; conspicuously

"I don't know what we're supposed to do now," said the nurse, looking nowhere in particular.

"Oh, that's all right. I'll fix it up."

Dexter stood perfectly still, his mouth slightly ajar. He knew that if he moved forward a step his stare would be in her line of vision—if he moved backward he would lose his full view of her face. For a moment he had not realized how young she was. Now he remembered having seen her several times the year before—in bloomers.[4]

Suddenly, involuntarily, he laughed, a short abrupt laugh—then, startled by himself, he turned and began to walk quickly away.

"Boy!"

Dexter stopped.

"Boy—"

Beyond question he was addressed. Not only that, but he was treated to that absurd smile, that preposterous smile—the memory of which at least a dozen men were to carry into middle age.

COMMON CORE RL 4

Language Coach

Synonyms The words *absurd* and *preposterous* (line 79) are **synonyms,** words with meanings similar to each other. Both words mean "unreasonable" or "ridiculous." What is Dexter saying about the girl's smile?

"Boy, do you know where the golf teacher is?"

"He's giving a lesson."

"Well, do you know where the caddy-master is?"

"He isn't here yet this morning."

"Oh." For a moment this baffled her. She stood alternately on her right and left foot.

"We'd like to get a caddy," said the nurse. "Mrs. Mortimer Jones sent us out to play golf, and we don't know how without we get a caddy."

Here she was stopped by an ominous glance from Miss Jones, followed immediately by the smile.

"There aren't any caddies here except me," said Dexter to the nurse, "and I got to stay here in charge until the caddy-master gets here."

"Oh."

Miss Jones and her **retinue** now withdrew, and at a proper distance from Dexter became involved in a heated conversation, which was concluded by Miss Jones taking one of the clubs and hitting it on the ground with violence. For

retinue (rĕt'n-o͞o') *n.* a group of attendants or followers

---

4. **bloomers:** baggy pants that end just below the knee, formerly worn by girls.

further emphasis she raised it again and was about to bring it down smartly upon the nurse's bosom, when the nurse seized the club and twisted it from her hands.

"You little mean old *thing!*" cried Miss Jones wildly.

Another argument ensued. Realizing that the elements of comedy were implied in the scene, Dexter several times began to laugh, but each time restrained the laugh before it reached audibility. He could not resist the monstrous conviction that the little girl was justified in beating the nurse.

The situation was resolved by the fortuitous appearance of the caddy-master, who was appealed to immediately by the nurse.

"Miss Jones is to have a little caddy, and this one says he can't go."

"Mr. McKenna said I was to wait here till you came," said Dexter quickly.

"Well, he's here now." Miss Jones smiled cheerfully at the caddy-master. Then she dropped her bag and set off at a haughty mince[5] toward the first tee.

"Well?" The caddy-master turned to Dexter. "What you standing there like a dummy for? Go pick up the young lady's clubs."

"I don't think I'll go out today," said Dexter.

"You don't—"

"I think I'll quit."

The enormity of his decision frightened him. He was a favorite caddy, and the thirty dollars a month he earned through the summer were not to be made elsewhere around the lake. But he had received a strong emotional shock, and his perturbation required a violent and immediate outlet.

It is not so simple as that, either. As so frequently would be the case in the future, Dexter was unconsciously dictated to by his winter dreams. **D**

Analyze Visuals ▶
How does this painting differ—in both content and style—from the portrait on page 979? How might these differences be said to echo the changes in Dexter Green?

D MOTIVATION AND TRAITS
Why does Dexter quit caddying? Explain what his decision adds to your understanding of him.

II

Now, of course, the quality and the seasonability of these winter dreams varied, but the stuff of them remained. They persuaded Dexter several years later to pass up a business course at the State university—his father, prospering now, would have paid his way—for the **precarious** advantage of attending an older and more famous university in the East, where he was bothered by his scanty funds. But do not get the impression, because his winter dreams happened to be concerned at first with musings on the rich, that there was anything merely snobbish in the boy. He wanted not association with glittering things and glittering people—he wanted the glittering things themselves. Often he reached out for the best without knowing why he wanted it—and sometimes he ran up against the mysterious denials and prohibitions in which life indulges. It is with one of those denials and not with his career as a whole that this story deals.

He made money. It was rather amazing. After college he went to the city from which Black Bear Lake draws its wealthy patrons. When he was only twenty-three and had been there not quite two years, there were already people who liked to say: "Now *there's* a boy—" All about him rich men's sons were peddling bonds precariously, or investing **patrimonies** precariously, or plodding through the two dozen volumes of the "George Washington Commercial Course," but Dexter

precarious (prĭ-kâr′ē-əs) *adj.* risky; uncertain

patrimony (păt′rə-mō′nē) *n.* estate or money inherited from ancestors

5. **at a haughty mince:** taking short, dainty steps in an arrogant, snobbish way.

Portrait of Marquess Sommi (1925), Tamara De Lempicka. Oil on canvas, 100 cm × 73 cm. Albert and Victoria Benalloul. © 2007 Artists Rights Society (ARS), New York/ADAGP, Paris.

borrowed a thousand dollars on his college degree and his confident mouth, and bought a partnership in a laundry.

It was a small laundry when he went into it but Dexter made a specialty of learning how the English washed fine woolen golf-stockings without shrinking them, and within a year he was catering to the trade that wore knickerbockers.[6] Men were insisting that their Shetland hose and sweaters go to his laundry just as they had insisted on a caddy who could find golf-balls. A little later he was doing their wives' lingerie as well—and running five branches in different parts of the city. Before he was twenty-seven he owned the largest string of laundries in his section of the country. It was then that he sold out and went to New York. But the part of his story that concerns us goes back to the days when he was making his first big success.

When he was twenty-three Mr. Hart—one of the gray-haired men who liked to say "Now there's a boy"—gave him a guest card to the Sherry Island Golf Club for a weekend. So he signed his name one day on the register, and that afternoon played golf in a foursome with Mr. Hart and Mr. Sandwood and Mr. T. A. Hedrick. He did not consider it necessary to remark that he had once carried Mr. Hart's bag over this same links, and that he knew every trap and gully with his eyes shut—but he found himself glancing at the four caddies who trailed them, trying to catch a gleam or gesture that would remind him of himself, that would lessen the gap which lay between his present and his past.

It was a curious day, slashed abruptly with fleeting, familiar impressions. One minute he had the sense of being a trespasser—in the next he was impressed by the tremendous superiority he felt toward Mr. T. A. Hedrick, who was a bore and not even a good golfer any more.

Then, because of a ball Mr. Hart lost near the fifteenth green, an enormous thing happened. While they were searching the stiff grasses of the rough there was a clear call of "Fore!" from behind a hill in their rear. And as they all turned abruptly from their search a bright new ball sliced abruptly over the hill and caught Mr. T. A. Hedrick in the abdomen.

"By Gad!" cried Mr. T. A. Hedrick, "they ought to put some of these crazy women off the course. It's getting to be outrageous."

A head and a voice came up together over the hill:

"Do you mind if we go through?"

"You hit me in the stomach!" declared Mr. Hedrick wildly.

"Did I?" The girl approached the group of men. "I'm sorry. I yelled 'Fore!'"

Her glance fell casually on each of the men—then scanned the fairway for her ball.

"Did I bounce into the rough?"

It was impossible to determine whether this question was ingenuous or malicious. In a moment, however, she left no doubt, for as her partner came up over the hill she called cheerfully:

"Here I am! I'd have gone on the green except that I hit something."

COMMON CORE L 2a

Language Coach

Compound Numbers and Fractions Notice that the word *twenty-seven* in line 147 has a **hyphen** (-) in the middle that joins the two numbers. This is the normal convention for writing out the numbers twenty-one to ninety-nine as words. Hyphens are also used to connect the parts of a fraction when it's expressed in words: *One-half of the students went on a field trip that took up two-thirds of the school day.* With a partner, compose a sentence that includes a written out number and fraction that both require hyphens.

6. **knickerbockers:** loose pants that end in a gathering just below the knee and are worn with long socks. Formerly popular as golf wear.

As she took her stance for a short mashie[7] shot, Dexter looked at her closely. She wore a blue gingham dress, rimmed at throat and shoulders with a white edging that accentuated her tan. The quality of exaggeration, of thinness, which had made her passionate eyes and down-turning mouth absurd at eleven, was gone now. She was arrestingly beautiful. The color in her cheeks was centered like the color in a picture—it was not a "high" color, but a sort of fluctuating and feverish warmth, so shaded that it seemed at any moment it would recede and disappear. This color and the mobility of her mouth gave a continual impression of **flux,** of intense life, of passionate vitality—balanced only partially by the sad luxury of her eyes.

flux (flŭks): *n.* change

She swung her mashie impatiently and without interest, pitching the ball into a sand-pit on the other side of the green. With a quick, insincere smile and a careless "Thank you!" she went on after it. **E**

E MOTIVATION AND TRAITS
Reread lines 171–193. What **character** traits are revealed by the description of Judy and her actions? Support your response with evidence from the story.

"That Judy Jones!" remarked Mr. Hedrick on the next tee, as they waited—some moments—for her to play on ahead. "All she needs is to be turned up and spanked for six months and then to be married off to an old-fashioned cavalry captain."

"My God, she's good-looking!" said Mr. Sandwood, who was just over thirty.

"Good-looking!" cried Mr. Hedrick contemptuously, "she always looks as if she wanted to be kissed! Turning those big cow-eyes on every calf in town!"

It was doubtful if Mr. Hedrick intended a reference to the maternal instinct.

"She'd play pretty good golf if she'd try," said Mr. Sandwood.

"She has no form," said Mr. Hedrick solemnly.

"She has a nice figure," said Mr. Sandwood.

"Better thank the Lord she doesn't drive a swifter ball," said Mr. Hart, winking at Dexter.

Later in the afternoon the sun went down with a riotous swirl of gold and varying blues and scarlets, and left the dry, rustling night of Western summer. Dexter watched from the veranda of the Golf Club, watched the even overlap of the waters in the little wind, silver molasses under the harvest-moon. Then the moon held a finger to her lips and the lake became a clear pool, pale and quiet. Dexter put on his bathing-suit and swam out to the farthest raft, where he stretched dripping on the wet canvas of the springboard.

There was a fish jumping and a star shining and the lights around the lake were gleaming. Over on a dark peninsula a piano was playing the songs of last summer and of summers before that—songs from "Chin-Chin" and "The Count of Luxemburg" and "The Chocolate Soldier"[8]—and because the sound of a piano over a stretch of water had always seemed beautiful to Dexter he lay perfectly quiet and listened.

The tune the piano was playing at that moment had been gay and new five years before when Dexter was a sophomore at college. They had played it at a prom once when he could not afford the luxury of proms, and he had stood

7. **mashie:** an old name for the golf club now known as a five iron.

8. **"Chin-Chin" . . . "The Chocolate Soldier":** three popular Broadway musicals, first performed in 1914, 1912, and 1909, respectively.

outside the gymnasium and listened. The sound of the tune **precipitated** in him a sort of ecstasy and it was with that ecstasy he viewed what happened to him now. It was a mood of intense appreciation, a sense that, for once, he was magnificently attuned to life and that everything about him was radiating a brightness and a glamour he might never know again.

precipitate (prĭ-sĭp'ĭ-tāt') *v.* to bring about, especially abruptly

A low, pale oblong detached itself suddenly from the darkness of the Island, spitting forth the reverberated sound of a racing motor-boat. Two white streamers of cleft water rolled themselves out behind it and almost immediately the boat was beside him, drowning out the hot tinkle of the piano in the drone of its spray. Dexter raising himself on his arms was aware of a figure standing at the wheel, of two dark eyes regarding him over the lengthening space of water—then the boat had gone by and was sweeping in an immense and purposeless circle of spray round and round in the middle of the lake. With equal eccentricity one of the circles flattened out and headed back toward the raft.

"Who's that?" she called, shutting off her motor. She was so near now that Dexter could see her bathing-suit, which consisted apparently of pink rompers.[9]

The nose of the boat bumped the raft, and as the latter tilted rakishly he was precipitated toward her. With different degrees of interest they recognized each other.

"Aren't you one of those men we played through this afternoon?" she demanded.

He was.

"Well, do you know how to drive a motor-boat? Because if you do I wish you'd drive this one so I can ride on the surf-board behind. My name is Judy Jones"—she favored him with an absurd smirk—rather, what tried to be a smirk, for, twist her mouth as she might, it was not grotesque, it was merely beautiful—"and I live in a house over there on the Island, and in that house there is a man waiting for me. When he drove up at the door I drove out of the dock because he says I'm his ideal." (F)

(F) MOTIVATION AND TRAITS
Do you think Judy has changed since Dexter first encountered her on the golf course years before? Cite **details** and **dialogue** to support your conclusion.

There was a fish jumping and a star shining and the lights around the lake were gleaming. Dexter sat beside Judy Jones and she explained how her boat was driven. Then she was in the water, swimming to the floating surf-board with a sinuous crawl. Watching her was without effort to the eye, watching a branch waving or a sea-gull flying. Her arms, burned to butternut, moved sinuously among the dull platinum ripples, elbow appearing first, casting the forearm back with a cadence of falling water, then reaching out and down, stabbing a path ahead.

They moved out into the lake; turning, Dexter saw that she was kneeling on the low rear of the now uptilted surf-board.

"Go faster," she called, "fast as it'll go."

Obediently he jammed the level forward and the white spray mounted at the bow. When he looked around again the girl was standing up on the rushing board, her arms spread wide, her eyes lifted toward the moon.

"It's awful cold," she shouted. "What's your name?"

---

9. **rompers:** a loose-fitting one-piece garment with bloomer like pants.

He told her.

"Well, why don't you come to dinner tomorrow night?"

His heart turned over like the fly-wheel of the boat, and, for the second time, her casual whim gave a new direction to his life.

III

Next evening while he waited for her to come downstairs, Dexter peopled the soft deep summer room and the sun-porch that opened from it with the men who had already loved Judy Jones. He knew the sort of men they were—the men who when he first went to college had entered from the great prep schools with graceful clothes and the deep tan of healthy summers. He had seen that, in one sense, he was better than these men. He was newer and stronger. Yet in acknowledging to himself that he wished his children to be like them he was admitting that he was but the rough, strong stuff from which they eternally sprang.

When the time had come for him to wear good clothes, he had known who were the best tailors in America, and the best tailors in America had made him the suit he wore this evening. He had acquired that particular reserve peculiar to his university, that set it off from other universities. He recognized the value to him of such a mannerism and he had adopted it; he knew that to be careless in dress and manner required more confidence than to be careful. But carelessness was for his children. His mother's name had been Krimslich. She was a Bohemian of the peasant class and she had talked broken English to the end of her days. Her son must keep to the set patterns.

At a little after seven Judy Jones came downstairs. She wore a blue silk afternoon dress, and he was disappointed at first that she had not put on something more elaborate. This feeling was accentuated when, after a brief greeting, she went to the door of a butler's pantry and pushing it open called: "You can serve dinner, Martha." He had rather expected that a butler would announce dinner, that there would be a cocktail. Then he put these thoughts behind him as they sat down side by side on a lounge and looked at each other.

"Father and mother won't be here," she said thoughtfully.

He remembered the last time he had seen her father, and he was glad the parents were not to be here tonight—they might wonder who he was. He had been born in Keeble, a Minnesota village fifty miles farther north, and he always gave Keeble as his home instead of Black Bear Village. Country towns were well enough to come from if they weren't inconveniently in sight and used as footstools by fashionable lakes. G

They talked of his university, which she had visited frequently during the past two years, and of the near-by city which supplied Sherry Island with its patrons, and whither Dexter would return next day to his prospering laundries.

During dinner she slipped into a moody depression which gave Dexter a feeling of uneasiness. Whatever **petulance** she uttered in her throaty voice worried him. Whatever she smiled at—at him, at a chicken liver, at nothing—it disturbed him

Language Coach

Word Analysis Read lines 274–277. What contrast is Dexter making in his mind? What words show you that ideas are being contrasted?

G MOTIVATION AND TRAITS
Reread lines 270–300. **Summarize** Dexter's ideas about social class and the status it confers. How does Dexter see himself? To what does he aspire?

petulance (pĕch'ə-ləns) *n.* ill temper; annoyance

that her smile could have no root in mirth, or even in amusement. When the scarlet corners of her lips curved down, it was less a smile than an invitation to a kiss.

Then, after dinner, she led him out on the dark sun-porch and deliberately changed the atmosphere.

"Do you mind if I weep a little?" she said.

"I'm afraid I'm boring you," he responded quickly.

"You're not. I like you. But I've just had a terrible afternoon. There was a man I cared about, and this afternoon he told me out of a clear sky that he was poor as a church-mouse. He'd never even hinted it before. Does this sound horribly **mundane**?"

mundane (mŭn-dān′) *adj.* characteristic of or concerned with the ordinary

"Perhaps he was afraid to tell you."

"Suppose he was," she answered. "He didn't start right. You see, if I'd thought of him as poor—well, I've been mad about loads of poor men, and fully intended to marry them all. But in this case, I hadn't thought of him that way, and my interest in him wasn't strong enough to survive the shock. As if a girl calmly informed her fiancé that she was a widow. He might not object to widows, but—

"Let's start right," she interrupted herself suddenly. "Who are you, anyhow?"

For a moment Dexter hesitated. Then:

"I'm nobody," he announced. "My career is largely a matter of futures."

"Are you poor?"

"No," he said frankly, "I'm probably making more money than any man my age in the Northwest. I know that's an obnoxious remark, but you advised me to start right."

There was a pause. Then she smiled and the corners of her mouth drooped and an almost imperceptible sway brought her closer to him, looking up into his eyes. A lump rose in Dexter's throat, and he waited breathless for the experiment, facing the unpredictable compound that would form mysteriously from the elements of their lips. Then he saw—she communicated her excitement to him, lavishly, deeply, with kisses that were not a promise but a fulfillment. They aroused in him not hunger demanding renewal but **surfeit** that would demand more surfeit . . . kisses that were like charity, creating want by holding back nothing at all.

surfeit (sûr′fĭt) *n.* a fullness beyond the point of satisfaction

It did not take him many hours to decide that he had wanted Judy Jones ever since he was a proud, desirous little boy.

IV

It began like that—and continued, with varying shades of intensity, on such a note right up to the dénouement. Dexter surrendered a part of himself to the most direct and unprincipled personality with which he had ever come in contact. Whatever Judy wanted, she went after with the full pressure of her charm. There was no divergence of method, no jockeying for position or premeditation of effects—there was a very little mental side to any of her affairs. She simply made men conscious to the highest degree of her physical loveliness. Dexter had no desire to change her. Her deficiencies were knit up with a passionate energy that transcended and justified them.

When, as Judy's head lay against his shoulder that first night, she whispered, "I don't know what's the matter with me. Last night I thought I was in love with a man and tonight I think I'm in love with you—"—it seemed to him a beautiful and romantic thing to say. It was the exquisite excitability that for the moment he controlled and owned. But a week later he was compelled to view this same quality in a different light. She took him in her roadster[10] to a picnic supper, and after supper she disappeared, likewise in her roadster, with another man. Dexter became enormously upset and was scarcely able to be decently civil to the other people present. When she assured him that she had not kissed the other man, he knew she was lying—yet he was glad that she had taken the trouble to lie to him. **H**

He was, as he found before the summer ended, one of a varying dozen who circulated about her. Each of them had at one time been favored above all others—about half of them still basked in the solace of occasional sentimental

H **MOTIVATION AND TRAITS**
Reread lines 340–358. Dexter's thoughts convey information about Judy, but they also reveal much about Dexter himself. Explain what you learn about him from these lines.

10. **roadster:** a sporty, two-seat, open automobile.

Young Woman in Green (1927), Tamara de Lempicka. Musée National d'Art Moderne, Centre Georges Pompidou, Paris. © CNAC/MNAM/Dist. Réunion des Musées Nationaux/Art Resource, New York. © 2007 Artists Rights Society (ARS), New York/ADAGP, Paris.

revivals. Whenever one showed signs of dropping out through long neglect, she granted him a brief honeyed hour, which encouraged him to tag along for a year or so longer. Judy made these forays upon the helpless and defeated without malice, indeed half unconscious that there was anything mischievous in what she did.

When a new man came to town every one dropped out—dates were automatically canceled.

The helpless part of trying to do anything about it was that she did it all herself. She was not a girl who could be "won" in the kinetic sense—she was proof against cleverness, she was proof against charm; if any of these assailed her too strongly she would immediately resolve the affair to a physical basis, and under the magic of her physical splendor the strong as well as the brilliant played her game and not their own. She was entertained only by the gratification of her desires and by the direct exercise of her own charm. Perhaps from so much youthful love, so many youthful lovers, she had come, in self-defense, to nourish herself wholly from within. **1**

1 MOTIVATION AND TRAITS
Consider characters or people you've encountered who are similar to Judy Jones. What might **motivate** Judy to act as she does? Cite details you used to draw this **conclusion.**

Succeeding Dexter's first exhilaration came restlessness and dissatisfaction. The helpless ecstasy of losing himself in her was opiate rather than tonic.[11] It was fortunate for his work during the winter that those moments of ecstasy came infrequently. Early in their acquaintance it had seemed for a while that there was a deep and spontaneous mutual attraction—that first August, for example—three days of long evenings on her dusky veranda, of strange wan kisses through the late afternoon, in shadowy alcoves or behind the protecting trellises of the garden arbors, of mornings when she was fresh as a dream and almost shy at meeting him in the clarity of the rising day. There was all the ecstasy of an engagement about it, sharpened by his realization that there was no engagement. It was during those three days that, for the first time, he had asked her to marry him. She said "maybe some day," she said "kiss me," she said "I'd like to marry you," she said "I love you"—she said—nothing.

The three days were interrupted by the arrival of a New York man who visited at her house for half September. To Dexter's agony, rumor engaged them. The man was the son of the president of a great trust company. But at the end of a month it was reported that Judy was yawning. At a dance one night she sat all evening in a motor-boat with a local beau, while the New Yorker searched the club for her frantically. She told the local beau that she was bored with her visitor, and two days later he left. She was seen with him at the station, and it was reported that he looked very mournful indeed.

On this note the summer ended. Dexter was twenty-four, and he found himself increasingly in a position to do as he wished. He joined two clubs in the city and lived at one of them. Though he was by no means an integral part of the stag-lines at these clubs, he managed to be on hand at dances where Judy Jones was likely to appear. He could have gone out socially as much as he liked—he was an eligible young man, now, and popular with downtown fathers. His confessed devotion to Judy Jones had rather solidified his position. But he had no social aspirations and rather despised the dancing men who were always on tap for the Thursday

11. **opiate . . . tonic:** deadening rather than stimulating.

or Saturday parties and who filled in at dinners with the younger married set. Already he was playing with the idea of going East to New York. He wanted to take Judy Jones with him. No disillusion as to the world in which she had grown up could cure his illusion as to her desirability.

Remember that—for only in the light of it can what he did for her be understood.

Eighteen months after he first met Judy Jones he became engaged to another girl. Her name was Irene Scheerer, and her father was one of the men who had always believed in Dexter. Irene was light-haired and sweet and honorable, and a little stout, and she had two suitors whom she pleasantly relinquished when Dexter formally asked her to marry him.

Summer, fall, winter, spring, another summer, another fall—so much he had given of his active life to the incorrigible lips of Judy Jones. She had treated him with interest, with encouragement, with malice, with indifference, with contempt. She had inflicted on him the innumerable little slights and indignities possible in such a case—as if in revenge for having ever cared for him at all. She had beckoned him and yawned at him and beckoned him again and he had responded often with bitterness and narrowed eyes. She had brought him ecstatic happiness and intolerable agony of spirit. She had caused him untold inconvenience and not a little trouble. She had insulted him, and she had ridden over him, and she had played his interest in her against his interest in his work—for fun. She had done everything to him except to criticize him—this she had not done—it seemed to him only because it might have sullied the utter indifference she manifested and sincerely felt toward him. [J]

When autumn had come and gone again it occurred to him that he could not have Judy Jones. He had to beat this into his mind but he convinced himself at last. He lay awake at night for a while and argued it over. He told himself the trouble and the pain she had caused him, he enumerated her glaring deficiencies as a wife. Then he said to himself that he loved her, and after a while he fell asleep. For a week, lest he imagine her husky voice over the telephone or her eyes opposite him at lunch, he worked hard and late, and at night he went to his office and plotted out his years.

At the end of a week he went to a dance and cut in on her once. For almost the first time since they had met he did not ask her to sit out with him or tell her that she was lovely. It hurt him that she did not miss these things—that was all. He was not jealous when he saw that there was a new man tonight. He had been hardened against jealousy long before. [K]

He stayed late at the dance. He sat for an hour with Irene Scheerer and talked about books and about music. He knew very little about either. But he was beginning to be master of his own time now, and he had a rather priggish notion that he—the young and already fabulously successful Dexter Green—should know more about such things.

That was in October, when he was twenty-five. In January, Dexter and Irene became engaged. It was to be announced in June, and they were to be married three months later.

[J] GRAMMAR AND STYLE
Reread lines 416–428. Fitzgerald's long sentences, held together by the **coordinating conjunction** *and* and broken up by **dashes,** convey Dexter's perplexed thoughts about Judy's behavior.

[K] THEME
How does Dexter's response to this autumn compare with his reactions to the season at the beginning of the story? What theme in the story is suggested by the change in Dexter?

The Minnesota winter prolonged itself interminably, and it was almost May when the winds came soft and the snow ran down into Black Bear Lake at last. For the first time in over a year Dexter was enjoying a certain tranquillity of spirit. Judy Jones had been in Florida, and afterward in Hot Springs,[12] and somewhere she had been engaged, and somewhere she had broken it off. At first, when Dexter had definitely given her up, it had made him sad that people still linked them together and asked for news of her, but when he began to be placed at dinner next to Irene Scheerer people didn't ask him about her any more—they told him about her. He ceased to be an authority on her.

May at last. Dexter walked the streets at night when the darkness was damp as rain, wondering that so soon, with so little done, so much of ecstasy had gone from him. May one year back had been marked by Judy's poignant, unforgivable, yet forgiven turbulence—it had been one of those rare times when he fancied she had grown to care for him. That old penny's worth of happiness he had spent for this bushel of content. He knew that Irene would be no more than a curtain spread behind him, a hand moving among gleaming tea-cups, a voice calling to children . . . fire and loveliness were gone, the magic of nights and the wonder of the varying hours and seasons . . . slender lips, downturning, dropping to his lips and bearing him up into a heaven of eyes. . . . The thing was deep in him. He was too strong and alive for it to die lightly. **L**

L PREDICT
Identify the **metaphors** that come to Dexter's mind with regard to Irene. What do they suggest about his feelings toward her? Predict how Dexter will treat Irene in the future. Cite text clues that helped you make this guess.

In the middle of May when the weather balanced for a few days on the thin bridge that led to deep summer he turned in one night at Irene's house. Their engagement was to be announced in a week now—no one would be surprised at it. And tonight they would sit together on the lounge at the University Club and look on for an hour at the dancers. It gave him a sense of solidity to go with her—she was so sturdily popular, so intensely "great."

He mounted the steps of the brownstone house and stepped inside.

"Irene," he called.

Mrs. Scheerer came out of the living-room to meet him.

"Dexter," she said, "Irene's gone upstairs with a splitting headache. She wanted to go with you but I made her go to bed."

"Nothing serious, I—"

"Oh, no. She's going to play golf with you in the morning. You can spare her for just one night, can't you, Dexter?"

Her smile was kind. She and Dexter liked each other. In the living-room he talked for a moment before he said good night.

Returning to the University Club, where he had rooms, he stood in the doorway for a moment and watched the dancers. He leaned against the door-post, nodded at a man or two—yawned.

"Hello, darling."

The familiar voice at his elbow startled him. Judy Jones had left a man and crossed the room to him—Judy Jones, a slender enameled doll in cloth of gold: gold in a band at her head, gold in two slipper points at her dress's hem. The fragile glow of her face seemed to blossom as she smiled at him. A breeze of

12. **Hot Springs:** a spa city in west-central Arkansas.

warmth and light blew through the room. His hands in the pockets of his dinner-jacket tightened spasmodically. He was filled with a sudden excitement.

"When did you get back?" he asked casually.

"Come here and I'll tell you about it."

She turned and he followed her. She had been away—he could have wept at the wonder of her return. She had passed through enchanted streets, doing things that were like provocative music. All mysterious happenings, all fresh and quickening hopes, had gone away with her, come back with her now.

She turned in the doorway.

"Have you a car here? If you haven't, I have."

"I have a coupé."

In then, with a rustle of golden cloth. He slammed the door. Into so many cars she had stepped—like this—like that—her back against the leather, so—her elbow resting on the door—waiting. She would have been soiled long since had there been anything to soil her—except herself—but this was her own self-outpouring.

Autoportrait (1925), Tamara De Lempicka. Oil on wood, 35 cm × 26 cm. Private collection. © 2007 Artists Rights Society (ARS), New York/ADAGP, Paris.

◀ Analyze Visuals
Tamara De Lempicka's posterlike oil paintings are often described as dramatic and aggressive. How does this description fit this particular painting? Explain, citing details.

With an effort he forced himself to start the car and back into the street. This was nothing, he must remember. She had done this before, and he had put her behind him, as he would have crossed a bad account from his books.

He drove slowly downtown and, affecting abstraction,[13] traversed the deserted streets of the business section, peopled here and there where a movie was giving out its crowd or where consumptive or pugilistic[14] youth lounged in front of pool halls. The clink of glasses and the slap of hands on the bars issued from saloons, cloisters[15] of glazed glass and dirty yellow light.

Language Coach

Antonyms An antonym is a word with a meaning opposite that of another word. In lines 512–515, which word is an antonym of *deserted* (line 512)? Refer to a dictionary if necessary.

She was watching him closely and the silence was embarrassing, yet in this crisis he could find no casual word with which to profane the hour. At a convenient turning he began to zigzag back toward the University Club.

"Have you missed me?" she asked suddenly.

"Everybody missed you."

He wondered if she knew of Irene Scheerer. She had been back only a day—her absence had been almost contemporaneous with his engagement.

"What a remark!" Judy laughed sadly—without sadness. She looked at him searchingly. He became absorbed in the dashboard.

"You're handsomer than you used to be," she said thoughtfully. "Dexter, you have the most rememberable eyes."

He could have laughed at this, but he did not laugh. It was the sort of thing that was said to sophomores. Yet it stabbed at him.

"I'm awfully tired of everything, darling." She called every one darling, endowing the endearment with careless, individual **camaraderie.** "I wish you'd marry me."

camaraderie (kä'mə-rä'də-rē) *n.* a spirit of friendly good-fellowship

The directness of this confused him. He should have told her now that he was going to marry another girl, but he could not tell her. He could as easily have sworn that he had never loved her.

"I think we'd get along," she continued, on the same note, "unless probably you've forgotten me and fallen in love with another girl."

Her confidence was obviously enormous. She had said, in effect, that she found such a thing impossible to believe, that if it were true he had merely committed a childish indiscretion—and probably to show off. She would forgive him, because it was not a matter of any moment but rather something to be brushed aside lightly.

"Of course you could never love anybody but me," she continued, "I like the way you love me. Oh, Dexter, have you forgotten last year?"

"No, I haven't forgotten."

"Neither have I!"

Was she sincerely moved—or was she carried along by the wave of her own acting?

"I wish we could be like that again," she said, and he forced himself to answer: "I don't think we can."

---

13. **affecting abstraction:** pretending to be lost in thought.
14. **consumptive or pugilistic** (pyo͞o'jə-lĭs'-tĭc): sickly or aggressive.
15. **cloisters:** here, places to escape from life's problems.

"I suppose not. . . . I hear you're giving Irene Scheerer a violent rush."

There was not the faintest emphasis on the name, yet Dexter was suddenly ashamed.

"Oh, take me home," cried Judy suddenly; "I don't want to go back to that idiotic dance—with those children."

Then, as he turned up the street that led to the residence district, Judy began to cry quietly to herself. He had never seen her cry before.

The dark street lightened, the dwellings of the rich loomed up around them, he stopped his coupé in front of the great white bulk of the Mortimer Joneses' house, somnolent, gorgeous, drenched with the splendor of the damp moonlight. Its solidity startled him. The strong walls, the steel of the girders, the breadth and beam and pomp of it were there only to bring out the contrast with the young beauty beside him. It was sturdy to accentuate her slightness—as if to show what a breeze could be generated by a butterfly's wing.

He sat perfectly quiet, his nerves in wild clamor, afraid that if he moved he would find her irresistibly in his arms. Two tears had rolled down her wet face and trembled on her upper lip.

"I'm more beautiful than anybody else," she said brokenly, "why can't I be happy?" Her moist eyes tore at his stability—her mouth turned slowly downward with an exquisite sadness: "I'd like to marry you if you'll have me, Dexter. I suppose you think I'm not worth having, but I'll be so beautiful for you, Dexter."

A million phrases of anger, pride, passion, hatred, tenderness fought on his lips. Then a perfect wave of emotion washed over him, carrying off with it a sediment of wisdom, of convention, of doubt, of honor. This was his girl who was speaking, his own, his beautiful, his pride.

"Won't you come in?" He heard her draw in her breath sharply.

Waiting. M

"All right," his voice was trembling, "I'll come in."

M **PREDICT**
Do you think Judy has really changed? Will she really marry Dexter? Give reasons for your predictions.

V

It was strange that neither when it was over nor a long time afterward did he regret that night. Looking at it from the perspective of ten years, the fact that Judy's flare for him endured just one month seemed of little importance. Nor did it matter that by his yielding he subjected himself to a deeper agony in the end and gave serious hurt to Irene Scheerer and to Irene's parents, who had befriended him. There was nothing sufficiently pictorial about Irene's grief to stamp itself on his mind.

Dexter was at bottom hard-minded. The attitude of the city on his action was of no importance to him, not because he was going to leave the city, but because any outside attitude on the situation seemed superficial. He was completely indifferent to popular opinion. Nor, when he had seen that it was no use, that he did not possess in himself the power to move fundamentally or to hold Judy Jones, did he bear any malice toward her. He loved her, and he would love her until the day he was too old for loving—but he could not have her. So he tasted the deep pain that is reserved only for the strong, just as he had tasted for a little while the deep happiness.

Even the ultimate falsity of the grounds upon which Judy terminated the engagement—that she did not want to "take him away" from Irene—Judy, who had wanted nothing else—did not revolt him. He was beyond any revulsion or any amusement.

He went East in February with the intention of selling out his laundries and settling in New York—but the war came to America in March and changed his plans. He returned to the West, handed over the management of the business to his partner, and went into the first officers' training-camp in late April. He was one of those young thousands who greeted the war with a certain amount of relief, welcoming the liberation from webs of tangled emotion.

Language Coach

Related Words *Falsity* (line 595) is related to the word *falsehood* and means essentially the same thing ("something false, incorrect, or dishonest"). What falsity or falsehood does Judy use to explain her reasons for breaking up?

VI

This story is not his biography, remember, although things creep into it which have nothing to do with those dreams he had when he was young. We are almost done with them and with him now. There is only one more incident to be related here, and it happens seven years farther on.

It took place in New York, where he had done well—so well that there were no barriers too high for him. He was thirty-two years old, and, except for one flying trip immediately after the war, he had not been West in seven years. A man named Devlin from Detroit came into his office to see him in a business way, and then and there this incident occurred, and closed out, so to speak, this particular side of his life.

"So you're from the Middle West," said the man Devlin with careless curiosity. "That's funny—I thought men like you were probably born and raised on Wall Street. You know—wife of one of my best friends in Detroit came from your city. I was an usher at the wedding."

Dexter waited with no apprehension of what was coming.

"Judy Simms," said Devlin with no particular interest; "Judy Jones she was once."

"Yes, I knew her." A dull impatience spread over him. He had heard, of course, that she was married—perhaps deliberately he had heard no more.

"Awfully nice girl," brooded Devlin meaninglessly, "I'm sort of sorry for her."

"Why?" Something in Dexter was alert, receptive, at once.

"Oh, Lud Simms has gone to pieces in a way. I don't mean he ill-uses her, but he drinks and runs around—"

"Doesn't she run around?"

"No. Stays at home with her kids."

"Oh."

"She's a little too old for him," said Devlin.

"Too old!" cried Dexter. "Why, man, she's only twenty-seven."

He was possessed with a wild notion of rushing out into the streets and taking a train to Detroit. He rose to his feet spasmodically.

"I guess you're busy," Devlin apologized quickly. "I didn't realize—"

"No, I'm not busy," said Dexter, steadying his voice. "I'm not busy at all. Not busy at all. Did you say she was—twenty-seven? No, I said she was twenty-seven."

"Yes, you did," agreed Devlin dryly.

"Go on, then. Go on."

"What do you mean?"

"About Judy Jones."

Devlin looked at him helplessly.

"Well, that's—I told you all there is to it. He treats her like the devil. Oh, they're not going to get divorced or anything. When he's particularly outrageous she forgives him. In fact, I'm inclined to think she loves him. She was a pretty girl when she first came to Detroit."

A pretty girl! The phrase struck Dexter as ludicrous.

"Isn't she—a pretty girl, any more?"

"Oh, she's all right."

"Look here," said Dexter, sitting down suddenly. "I don't understand. You say she was a 'pretty girl' and now you say she's 'all right.' I don't understand what you mean—Judy Jones wasn't a pretty girl, at all. She was a great beauty. Why, I knew her, I knew her. She was—"

Devlin laughed pleasantly.

"I'm not trying to start a row,"[16] he said. "I think Judy's a nice girl and I like her. I can't understand how a man like Lud Simms could fall madly in love with her, but he did." Then he added: "Most of the women like her." N

N MOTIVATION AND TRAITS
Based on Devlin's description of Judy, how would you say she has changed since Dexter knew her? What might have caused these changes?

Dexter looked closely at Devlin, thinking wildly that there must be a reason for this, some insensitivity in the man or some private malice.

"Lots of women fade just like *that,*" Devlin snapped his fingers. "You must have seen it happen. Perhaps I've forgotten how pretty she was at her wedding. I've seen her so much since then, you see. She has nice eyes."

A sort of dullness settled down upon Dexter. For the first time in his life he felt like getting very drunk. He knew that he was laughing loudly at something Devlin had said, but he did not know what it was or why it was funny. When, in a few minutes, Devlin went he lay down on his lounge and looked out the window at the New York sky-line into which the sun was sinking in dull lovely shades of pink and gold.

He had thought that having nothing else to lose he was invulnerable at last—but he knew that he had just lost something more, as surely as if he had married Judy Jones and seen her fade away before his eyes.

The dream was gone. Something had been taken from him. In a sort of panic he pushed the palms of his hands into his eyes and tried to bring up a picture of the waters lapping on Sherry Island and the moonlit veranda, and gingham on

16. **row** (rou): a noisy argument or dispute.

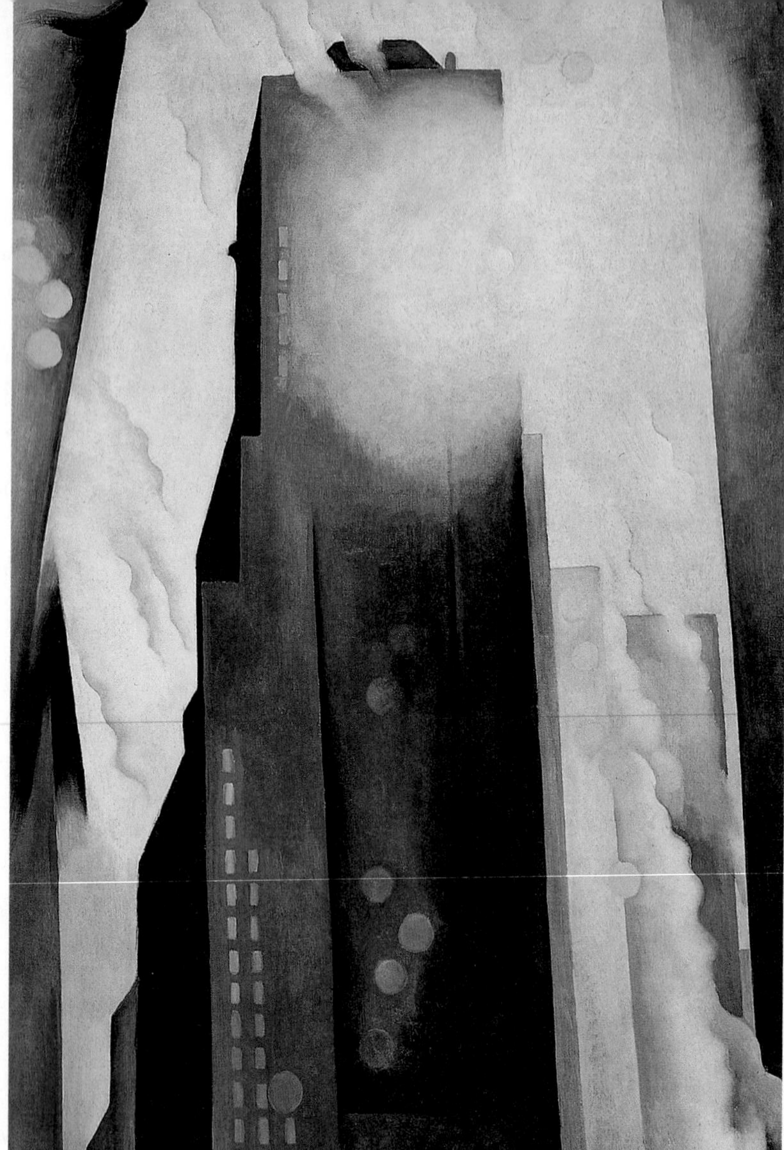

Detail of *The Shelton with Sunspots* (1926), Georgia O'Keeffe. Oil on canvas, 123.1 cm × 76.8 cm. The Art Institute of Chicago, gift of Leigh B. Block (1985.206) © 2007 The Georgia O'Keeffe Museum/Artists Rights Society (ARS), New York. Photo © 1994 The Art Institute of Chicago, all rights reserved.

the golf-links and the dry sun and the gold color of her neck's soft down. And her mouth damp to his kisses and her eyes plaintive with melancholy and her freshness like new fine linen in the morning. Why, these things were no longer in the world! They had existed and they existed no longer.

For the first time in years the tears were streaming down his face. But they were for himself now. He did not care about mouth and eyes and moving hands. He wanted to care, and he could not care. For he had gone away and he could never go back any more. The gates were closed, the sun was gone down, and there was no beauty but the gray beauty of steel that withstands all time. Even the grief he could have borne was left behind in the country of illusion, of youth, of the richness of life, where his winter dreams had flourished.

"Long ago," he said, "long ago, there was something in me, but now that thing is gone. Now that thing is gone, that thing is gone. I cannot cry. I cannot care. That thing will come back no more." ~

Comprehension

1. **Recall** How does Dexter's social **status** change in the story, and why?
2. **Clarify** Why doesn't Dexter marry either Judy Jones or Irene Scheerer?
3. **Summarize** What has happened to Judy Jones by the end of the story?

Text Analysis

4. **Predict Story Development** Review your list of predictions and clues. Were you able to predict everything that happened? Or were you surprised by how some aspects of the story developed? Support your answer with evidence from the story.
5. **Analyze Character Motivation and Traits** What kind of man is Dexter Green? Consider his values and beliefs. Does he deserve sympathy, criticism, or both? Using examples from the text, describe Dexter's traits and the motivations for his actions and feelings.
6. **Examine Symbol** Reread lines 490–494. Consider how Dexter pursues and responds to Judy throughout "Winter Dreams," and think about the young man's feelings regarding **status.** What might Judy **symbolize** in this story? Explain, citing evidence to support your answer.
7. **Analyze Imagery** Fitzgerald is celebrated for his use of imagery, which infuses his fiction with the flush of highly tuned emotions. Locate four or five examples of imagery in "Winter Dreams" that successfully convey the emotional intensity of Dexter and Judy's entanglement. Then explain how each example achieves this purpose.
8. **Interpret Theme** Reread lines 669–688 and consider what exactly Dexter has lost. What theme, or message about the human condition, does Fitzgerald convey through this loss?

Text Criticism

9. **Critical Interpretations** Critic Marius Bewley has argued that Fitzgerald's main subject is always "the American Dream, in which . . . his principal heroes are all trapped." How well does this statement apply to "Winter Dreams"? Use examples from the story to support your opinion.

Will STATUS *make you happy?*

In lines 128–129, Fitzgerald says of Dexter, "He wanted not association with glittering things and glittering people—he wanted the glittering things themselves." What does this tell you about Dexter's reasons for seeking **status**?

COMMON CORE

RL 2 Analyze the development of two or more themes or central ideas over the course of the text, including how they interact and build on one another to produce a complex account; provide an objective summary of the text. **RL 3** Analyze the impact of the author's choices regarding how to develop and relate elements of a story. **RL 4** Determine the meaning of words and phrases as they are used in the text, including figurative and connotative meanings.

Vocabulary in Context

▲ VOCABULARY PRACTICE

Decide whether the words in each pair are synonyms or antonyms.

1. precipitate/prevent
2. flux/change
3. retinue/troupe
4. petulance/pleasure
5. mundane/extraordinary
6. patrimony/inheritance
7. surfeit/shortage
8. blatantly/secretly
9. camaraderie/friendship
10. precarious/secure

WORD LIST
blatantly
camaraderie
flux
mundane
patrimony
petulance
precarious
precipitate
retinue
surfeit

ACADEMIC VOCABULARY IN WRITING

• conclude • criteria • despite • justify • maintain

In "Winter Dreams," Fitzgerald provides clues to Judy's disposition during two golf games. Reread lines 78-99 and lines 164-181. In a paragraph discuss what you **conclude** about Judy based on these two scenes. Use at least three Academic Vocabulary words in your paragraph.

VOCABULARY STRATEGY: WORDS FROM THE JAZZ AGE

The Jazz Age is a good example of a time when many new words were coined and old words took on new meanings. These words and phrases were clever and colorful, often providing subtle, **nuanced shifts in meaning** from existing words. For example, a "pushover," a Jazz Age term, is more than just a "victim." A "pushover" is someone who is incapable of offering any resistance. Whether "pushover" or "victim" would be the better word choice is dependent on **context.**

COMMON CORE

L 1a Apply the understanding that usage can change over time. **L 5b** Analyze nuances in the meaning of words with similar denotations.

PRACTICE For each pair in the following paragraph, choose the best word or words to fit the context and explain your choice. Refer to a dictionary if needed.

During the 1930's a young man would have been very happy to have had an old *(1. jalopy, car)* to drive. He would have *(2. strutted, swaggered)* as he walked toward the street where it was parked. Young people today would feel differently about having to drive such a vehicle. They would find it a *(3. hassle, struggle)* as well as *(4. depressing, a bummer).*

Language

COMMON CORE

L 2 Demonstrate command of the conventions of standard English punctuation when writing. **L 3a** Vary syntax for effect, consulting references for guidance as needed; apply an understanding of syntax to the study of complex texts when reading. **W 1** Write arguments to support claims in an analysis of substantive topics or texts, using valid reasoning and relevant and sufficient evidence.

GRAMMAR AND STYLE: Craft Effective Sentences

Review the **Grammar and Style** note on page 991. Fitzgerald's rich, evocative style in "Winter Dreams" comes in part from long sentences held together by the **coordinating conjunction** *and*. He often breaks up those long descriptions with **dashes** and **phrases** in a series.

> *Early in their acquaintance it had seemed for a while that there was a deep and spontaneous mutual attraction—that first August, for example—three days of long evenings on her dusky veranda, of strange wan kisses through the late afternoon, in shadowy alcoves or behind the protecting trellises of the garden arbors, of mornings when she was fresh as a dream and almost shy at meeting him in the clarity of the rising day. There was all the ecstasy of an engagement about it, sharpened by his realization that there was no engagement.* (lines 379–385)

Notice that this description has no action verbs and consists almost entirely of prepositional phrases. In this way, Fitzgerald perfectly expresses Dexter's emotional surrender in both style and content.

PRACTICE Study the following paragraph from the story, noting

- coordinating conjunctions in the first sentence that connect multiple images
- participial phrases that add a sense of motion and emotional significance

Continue these stylistic elements by writing two or three additional sentences.

> *There was a fish jumping and a star shining and the lights around the lake were gleaming. Dexter sat beside Judy Jones and she explained how her boat was driven. Then she was in the water, swimming to the floating surf-board with a sinuous crawl. Watching her was without effort to the eye, watching a branch waving or a seagull flying. Her arms, burned to butternut, moved sinuously among the dull platinum ripples, elbow appearing first, casting the forearm back with a cadence of falling water, then reaching out and down, stabbing a path ahead.* (lines 252–258)

READING-WRITING CONNECTION

Expand your understanding of "Winter Dreams" by responding to this prompt. Then, use the **revising tips** to improve your letter.

WRITING PROMPT	REVISING TIPS
COMPOSE A LETTER OF ADVICE If Dexter were your close friend, what advice would you give to him? In a **three-paragraph letter** (or email) to Dexter, explain what you think he should do to improve the quality of his life. Be sure to recommend something to fill the great void left by the loss of his youthful illusions.	• State your advice in clear, persuasive language. • Provide evidence for why you believe your advice is trustworthy. • Use appeals to logic, emotions, and eithical beliefs.

American Masterpiece

from The Great Gatsby

Novel by F. Scott Fitzgerald

F. Scott Fitzgerald
1896–1940

COMMON CORE

RL 3 Analyze the impact of the author's choices regarding how to develop and relate elements of a story.

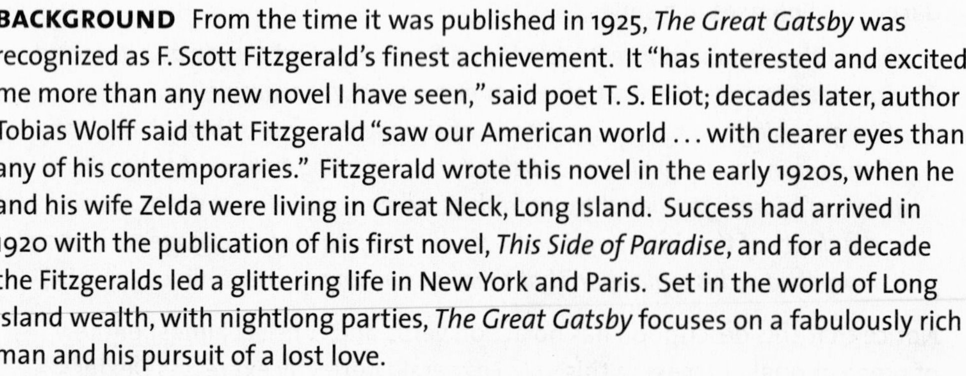

BACKGROUND From the time it was published in 1925, *The Great Gatsby* was recognized as F. Scott Fitzgerald's finest achievement. It "has interested and excited me more than any new novel I have seen," said poet T. S. Eliot; decades later, author Tobias Wolff said that Fitzgerald "saw our American world . . . with clearer eyes than any of his contemporaries." Fitzgerald wrote this novel in the early 1920s, when he and his wife Zelda were living in Great Neck, Long Island. Success had arrived in 1920 with the publication of his first novel, *This Side of Paradise*, and for a decade the Fitzgeralds led a glittering life in New York and Paris. Set in the world of Long Island wealth, with nightlong parties, *The Great Gatsby* focuses on a fabulously rich man and his pursuit of a lost love.

TEXT ANALYSIS Fitzgerald's challenge in *The Great Gatsby* was how to **characterize** his protagonist, a glamorous and perhaps dangerous man about whom little is known except hearsay and gossip. Through **dialogue,** the novel conveys various glimpses and conflicting stories about Gatsby, creating the impression of a complex—and perhaps unknowable—figure. The genius of this approach is that it brings us into the story as readers, leaving us with the task of sorting through what we hear about Jay Gatsby and trying to form a complete image of him. Always, Gatsby hovers just out of reach. Always, there seems more to him than the dialogue provides. In the end, he remains a mystery, one of the most engaging mysteries in American fiction.

WRITE Read the passage twice, paying close attention in the dialogue to how competing bits of gossip and hearsay create an impression of Gatsby. Then choose a subject about whom there are competing stories, conflicting versions of the truth. You might choose a controversial public figure such as a singer, a movie star, or a politician. If you prefer, you can create a character of your own, as Fitzgerald did in *The Great Gatsby*. Next, imagine a conversation in which several people share bits and pieces of what they've heard about your subject. Write this scene, concentrating on the dialogue. Your goal is to convey an air of mystery or misunderstanding about your character.

"This is an unusual party for me. I haven't even seen the host. I live over there—" I waved my hand at the invisible hedge in the distance, "and this man Gatsby sent over his chauffeur with an invitation."

For a moment he looked at me as if he failed to understand.

"I'm Gatsby," he said suddenly.

"What!" I exclaimed. "Oh, I beg your pardon."

"I thought you knew, old sport. I'm afraid I'm not a very good host."

He smiled understandingly—much more than understandingly. It was one of those rare smiles with a quality of eternal reassurance in it, that you may come across four or five times in life. It faced—or seemed to face—the whole external world for an instant, and then concentrated on *you* with an irresistible prejudice in your favor. It understood you just as far as you wanted to be understood, believed in you as you would like to believe in yourself, and assured you that it had precisely the impression of you that, at your best, you hoped to convey. Precisely at that point it vanished—and I was looking at an elegant young roughneck, a year or two over thirty, whose elaborate formality of speech just missed being absurd. Some time before he introduced himself I'd got a strong impression that he was picking his words with care.

Almost at the moment when Mr. Gatsby identified himself, a butler hurried toward him with the information that Chicago was calling him on the wire. He excused himself with a small bow that included each of us in turn.

"If you want anything just ask for it, old sport," he urged me. "Excuse me. I will rejoin you later."

When he was gone I turned immediately to Jordan—constrained to assure her of my surprise. I had expected that Mr. Gatsby would be a florid and corpulent person in his middle years.

"Who is he?" I demanded. "Do you know?"

"He's just a man named Gatsby."

"Where is he from, I mean? And what does he do?"

"Now *you're* started on the subject," she answered with a wan smile. "Well, he told me once he was an Oxford man."

A dim background started to take shape behind him, but at her next remark it faded away.

"However, I don't believe it."

"Why not?"

"I don't know," she insisted, "I just don't think he went there."

Something in her tone reminded me of the other girl's "I think he killed a man," and had the effect of stimulating my curiosity. I would have accepted without question the information that Gatsby sprang from the swamps of Louisiana or from the lower East Side of New York. That was comprehensible. But young men didn't—at least in my provincial inexperience I believed they didn't—drift coolly out of nowhere and buy a palace on Long Island Sound.

"Anyhow, he gives large parties," said Jordan, changing the subject with an urban distaste for the concrete. "And I like large parties. They're so intimate. At small parties there isn't any privacy."

Media Study

Advertising in the Jazz Age

Print Advertisements on MediaSmart DVD-ROM

COMMON CORE

RI 7 Integrate and evaluate multiple sources of information presented in different media or formats as well as in words in order to address a question or solve a problem.

Whose DREAM *are you buying?*

KEY IDEA As a struggling writer, F. Scott Fitzgerald worked briefly for an advertising firm and became leery of the industry's emerging practices. In his writing, Fitzgerald expressed his views about materialism and the impact of advertising on the contemporary culture of his day. For him, advertising was part of the glittering surface of the **American dream,** a dream of success, whose cost was often underestimated. In this lesson, you'll study magazine ads of the 1920s to uncover persuasive techniques that took root during the Jazz Age and flourish to this day.

Background

Spending Spree The first years of the 1920s were a time of "more." Because of mass production, such innovations as the automobile and the radio were more available and affordable. Electrical power spread beyond big cities, enabling more Americans to use new, time-saving appliances. As modern-day conveniences took hold and salaries steadily rose, ordinary people reaped the benefits of more leisure time and more money to spend. "Buy now, pay later" installment plans made expensive items appear more obtainable by allowing consumers to pay bills over an extended period of time.

Because merchandise was now flooding the marketplace, a fundamental shift had to occur in how Americans spent money. Before, thriftiness had been the rule. To fuel consumer spending, advertising agencies enlisted the expertise of psychologists to find ways to motivate buyers. The result was advertising designed to appeal to the public's desire for convenience, youth, beauty, and, particularly, wealth and luxury.

With an emphasis on the visual, Jazz Age ads protrayed the lavish lifestyles of the rich. Over time, print ads in newspapers, magazines, and billboards changed. Rather than just providing product details, ad writers of the 1920s changed the tone of the ads. Their purpose changed from informing the public to persuading ordinary Americans that they could live a lifestyle similar to that of the "beautiful people." Due in part to the persuasive power of such ads, the United States became a nation of shoppers and thus a consumer society.

Media Literacy: Persuasion in 1920s Ads

The Jazz Age marks the period when the advertising industry developed. Numerous agencies were established on Madison Avenue in New York City, and ads began to appear in the new medium of mass-circulation magazines. As *Time*, the *New Yorker*, and the *Saturday Evening Post* became popular, the ads within them exposed a nationwide audience to a vast array of products and services.

Advertisers also devised more deliberate ways to persuade. In earlier decades, ads contained straightforward details about product features and prices. Magazine ads of the 1920s shifted away from the product, using a light and informal tone to appeal more directly to the potential buyer. To explore some persuasive techniques commonly used in the 1920s, examine this automobile ad.

STRATEGIES FOR RECOGNIZING PERSUASIVE TECHNIQUES

- Understand the overall message. Behind the 1920s ads was the implication that purchases could bring higher social status and self-fulfillment.
- Look for the **tone**, or the writer's attitude toward the subject. Notice the words *steady*, *flow*, *power*, *smoothly*, and *swiftly*. Think about the attitude these words suggest about the car.
- Try to spot the **slogan,** the short phrase that, used in most ads, expresses something about the quality of the product or the company that makes it. Beginning in the 1920s, a slogan helped to make a product's name and purpose memorable to potential buyers.
- Recognize the technique of **transfer,** which refers to an advertiser's attempt to connect a product with someone or something that's pleasing or admired. Ask yourself: What might images of the rich at leisure have conveyed to working-class Americans of the 1920s?

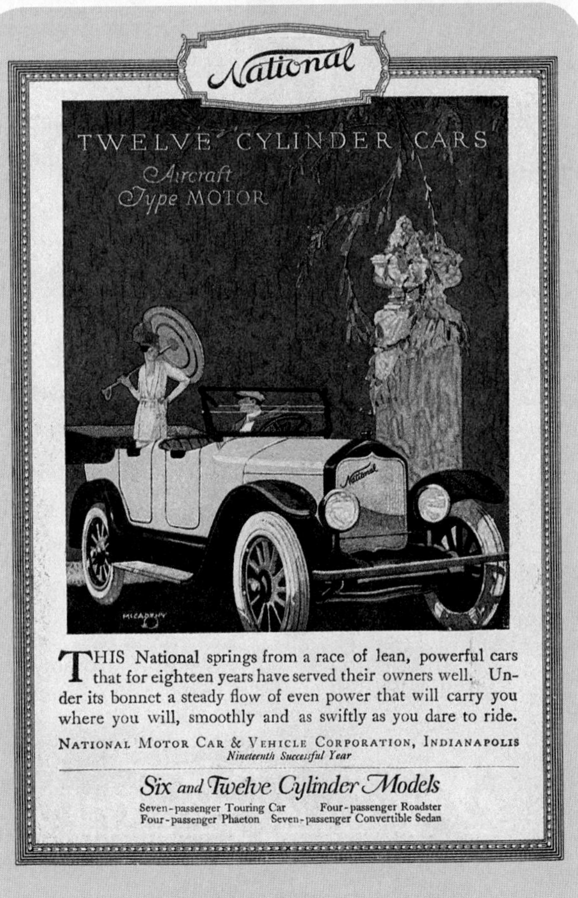

National
TWELVE CYLINDER CARS
Aircraft
Type MOTOR
THIS National springs from a race of lean, powerful cars that for eighteen years have served their owners well. Under its bonnet a steady flow of even power that will carry you where you will, smoothly and as swiftly as you dare to ride.
NATIONAL MOTOR CAR & VEHICLE CORPORATION, INDIANAPOLIS
Nineteenth Successful Year
Six and Twelve Cylinder Models
Seven-passenger Touring Car Four-passenger Roadster
Four-passenger Phaeton Seven-passenger Convertible Sedan

Media Smart DVD-ROM

- **Selection 1:** National Motor Car and Vehicle
- **Selection 2:** Eastman Kodak Company
- **Genre:** Print advertisements of the 1920s

For the out-of-doors days

KODAK

And not merely the alluring picture story, but on every negative at least a date; and a title, too, if you like. Titling is the work of but an instant with an Autographic Kodak; is as simple as making the picture itself—and there is no extra charge for Autographic film.

If it isn't an Eastman, it isn't a Kodak.

Viewing Guide for

Jazz Age Advertisements

To carefully examine the two advertisements, use the DVD. As you study them, keep in mind the high spirits and optimism of the Roaring Twenties. Use these questions as you examine the image and words of each ad.

NOW VIEW

FIRST VIEWING: Comprehension

1. **Recall** What product is advertised by a woman holding a bright orange parasol?
2. **Clarify** What leisure activity is depicted in the Kodak camera ad?

CLOSE VIEWING: Media Literacy

3. **Interpret Visuals** *Glamorous* and *elegant* are two words that would describe the images in these ads. What other words would you use to describe them?
4. **Analyze the Message** Note that in the National car ad, an expensive sports car is the dominant part of the visual presentation. What message do you think the 1920s advertisers specifically wanted to convey to their audience? Why do you think they promoted this message?
5. **Compare Advertisements** In what ways is the Kodak camera ad shown here similar to the ad for National cars?
6. **Evaluate an Advertisement** Choose the ad that appeals to you more. Evaluate it in terms of the effectiveness of its persuasive techniques. Think about
   - the ad's appeal to status, luxury, and style
   - the design of the visual and the choice and placement of text
   - how favorably you think 1920s Americans might have viewed the ad

Write or Discuss

Evaluate the Print Ads F. Scott Fitzgerald once wrote about the advertising profession: "Advertising is a racket. . . . You cannot be honest without admitting that its constructive contribution to humanity is exactly minus zero." In Fitzgerald's day, the advertising industry was taking root. Today, advertising is an integral part of everyday life. Think about the print ads in this lesson and how similar they might be to ads for similar products today. What persuasive techniques are still effective? Write a short evaluation of each ad. Keep the following points in mind:

- the deliberate appeals you saw that were embedded within the advertisements' visuals and text
- how potential buyers of the 1920s ads compare to today's buyers
- your own views about today's consumer society

COMMON CORE

RI 7 Integrate and evaluate multiple sources of information presented in different media or formats as well as in words in order to address a question or solve a problem. **SL 1** Initiate and participate effectively in a range of collaborative discussions. **SL 5** Make strategic use of digital media in presentations. **W 2** Write informative/explanatory texts to examine and convey complex ideas, concepts, and information clearly and accurately through the effective selection, organization, and analysis of content.

Produce and Present Your Own Media

Create a Contemporary Ad Poster Using one of the 1920s ads in this lesson as a model, create an advertisement as a modern-day counterpart. Individually or with a partner, decide on the product, target an audience of working-class buyers for the product, and determine the persuasive techniques you'll apply. Represent the ad in the form of a billboard poster. When you're done, present your ad to the whole class, and discuss the effectiveness of the ad.

HERE'S HOW As you design the ad, consider these suggestions:

- Put as much thought into the ad's visual design as into its wording. You might want to concentrate on designing the image of the ad while a partner focuses on devising the copy.
- Be sure to include appeals to status, wealth, and luxury through both the visual design and the text. Think about the leisure activities of today's wealthy people and what working people might find desirable about them.

Tech Tip

If you create the ad on a computer, choose font styles and sizes with care.

Further Exploration

Explore Ads Across the 20th Century On the DVD, access examples of ads that exhibit the persuasive techniques of the 1920s in product advertisements from ensuing decades. What cleverly designed image or turn of phrase turns objects into necessities? What evidence do you see of such techniques as appeals to youth, beauty, wealth, and luxury? Examining these ads can offer insights into the evolving consumer culture of the United States.

Comparing Texts

The Modern Short Story

In Another Country

Video link at thinkcentral.com

Short Story by Ernest Hemingway

Healing War's Wounds

Magazine Article by Karen Breslau

Moving a Nation to Care

Book Cover

COMMON CORE

RL 1 Cite textual evidence to support analysis of what the text says explicitly as well as inferences drawn from the text, including determining where the text leaves matters uncertain. **RL 4** Analyze the impact of specific word choices on meaning and tone, including words with multiple meanings or language that is particularly fresh, engaging, or beautiful. **RI 1** Cite textual evidence to support analysis of what the text says explicitly as well as inferences drawn from the text, including determining where the text leaves matters uncertain. **RI 4** Determine the meaning of words and phrases as they are used in a text, including figurative, connotative, and technical meanings. **RI 7** Integrate and evaluate multiple sources of information presented in different media or formats as well as in words in order to address a question.

Meet the Author

Ernest Hemingway 1899–1961

Whether trout fishing in Michigan, skiing in Switzerland, cheering for bullfighters in Spain, big-game hunting in Africa, marlin fishing off the coast of Key West, or drinking wine in a Paris café, Ernest Hemingway was the embodiment of rugged individualism. He experienced first hand the major events of his time—the Italian front in World War I, Paris in the 1920s, the Spanish Civil War, and D-day and the Battle of the Bulge during World War II. Behind the legendary persona, however, Hemingway was first and foremost a writer. His experiences provided the raw material for a body of work that captured the essence of modernity and left his indelible stamp on the century.

Irrepressible Energy and Drive Hemingway grew up in Oak Park, Illinois, a suburb of Chicago. After high school he got a job as a reporter for the *Kansas City Star,* where he developed both his deceptively simple writing style and a devotion to the truth. During World War I he volunteered as an ambulance driver for the American Red Cross and was severely wounded. After the war he made his way to Paris as a correspondent for the *Toronto Star.* Paris in the 1920s was a magnet for young artists and writers of the new modernist movement, and the vibrant, sociable Hemingway soon became a star. By the end of the decade, he had made his own contribution by publishing two collections of short stories, *In Our Time* (1925) and *Men Without Women* (1927), as well as two highly acclaimed novels, *The Sun Also Rises* (1926) and *A Farewell to Arms* (1929).

End of an Epic Life Hemingway was living in Cuba when he wrote what many consider his finest novel, *For Whom the Bell Tolls* (1940), based on his reporting of the Spanish Civil War. When World War II broke out, he served as a journalist, often putting himself in dangerous combat situations. His last major work published in his lifetime was the highly popular *The Old Man and the Sea* (1952). In his final years he suffered a variety of ills—including diabetes, liver problems, hypertension, and depression—that led to his suicide at age 62. He left behind five unpublished manuscripts and a towering literary legacy.

For more on Hemingway's days as a war correspondent, see the biography on page 1094.

Author Online THINK central

Go to thinkcentral.com. KEYWORD: HML11-1008

TEXT ANALYSIS: TONE

Hemingway began his literary career as a newspaper reporter. The spare, direct prose of his short stories reflects his journalistic roots. Reporters adopt a detached, objective tone or attitude toward their subject. This kind of detachment characterizes "In Another Country," but examine the narrator's surface detachment for evidence of the loss he feels. You will find clues to Hemingway's view of the human condition.

When you read Karen Breslau's magazine article, look for clues to her attitude toward the wounded soldiers she chose as her subject. Is her attitude detached and objective? Or has she made another choice with this piece of journalism? Finally, what does her tone tell you about her view of human potential?

READING SKILL: MAKE INFERENCES

One aspect of Hemingway's style is that he is not explicit about the effect of important events on his characters. He relates events and leaves it up to his readers to look for clues and **make inferences,** or logical assumptions, about the impact of events. As you read, look for revealing details, statements in the dialogue, and other clues to help you infer how the characters feel about their situation.

Likewise, when you read "Healing War's Wounds," examine the language Karen Breslau uses to describe recovering soldiers. The events, details, and dialogue she includes provide clues to her purpose in writing this article and to the message she wants readers to take from her story.

VOCABULARY IN CONTEXT

Hemingway uses these words to write about soldiers in a wartime hospital. Choose the word that you associate with each type of patient.

WORD LIST	citation	detached	lurch
	resign		

1. a patient who remains aloof and uninterested
2. a decorated soldier
3. one who stoically tries to make the best of his situation
4. a soldier who has trouble walking due to injury

Complete the activities in your **Reader/Writer Notebook**.

What are the COSTS *of war?*

Some costs of war can be counted. World War I, the setting of Hemingway's story, claimed the lives of about 9 million soldiers and 13 million civilians. But what about the millions who survived the trauma of the bloodiest and most destructive war in history up to that time? What price did they pay?

What's the Connection?

In a famous short story about World War I, Ernest Hemingway examines a group of soldiers undergoing new and ineffective physical therapy. In a magazine article, Karen Breslau focuses on an innovative approach to therapy for severely wounded soldiers from the war in Iraq. Finally, a book cover combines text with the image of a soldier's bowed head. Before you study these texts, think about what you already know about the psychological effects of war on combat soldiers. What is post-traumatic stress disorder? In what ways might it connect these texts?

In ANOTHER *Country*

Ernest Hemingway

BACKGROUND World War I was called the Great War and the War to End All Wars. It was the first large-scale modern war with the killing power of new technological weapons. Among the 21 million wounded was 18-year-old Ernest Hemingway, who later wrote this story about soldiers recuperating in Milan, Italy. "In the first war I was hurt very badly," he explained, "in the body, mind, and spirit, and also morally."

In the fall the war was always there, but we did not go to it any more. It was cold in the fall in Milan[1] and the dark came very early. Then the electric lights came on, and it was pleasant along the streets looking in the windows. There was much game hanging outside the shops, and the snow powdered in the fur of the foxes and the wind blew their tails. The deer hung stiff and heavy and empty, and small birds blew in the wind and the wind turned their feathers. It was a cold fall and the wind came down from the mountains. (A)

We were all at the hospital every afternoon, and there were different ways of walking across the town through the dusk to the hospital. Two of the ways were alongside canals, but they were long. Always, though, you crossed a bridge across a canal to enter the hospital. There was a choice of three bridges. On one of them a woman sold roasted chestnuts. It was warm, standing in front of her charcoal fire, and the chestnuts were warm afterward in your pocket. The hospital was very old and very beautiful, and you entered through a gate and walked across a courtyard and out a gate on the other side. There were usually funerals starting from the courtyard. Beyond the old hospital were the new brick pavilions, and there we met every afternoon and were all very polite and interested in what was the matter, and sat in the machines that were to make so much difference.

The doctor came up to the machine where I was sitting and said: "What did you like best to do before the war? Did you practise a sport?"

I said: "Yes, football."

"Good," he said. "You will be able to play football again better than ever."

My knee did not bend and the leg dropped straight from the knee to the ankle without a calf, and the machine was to bend the knee and make it move as in riding a tricycle. But it did not bend yet, and instead the machine **lurched** when it came to the bending part. The doctor said: "That will all pass. You are a fortunate young man. You will play football again like a champion."

In the next machine was a major who had a little hand like a baby's. He winked at me when the doctor examined his hand, which was between two leather straps that bounced up and down and flapped the stiff fingers, and said: "And will I too

1. **Milan:** a city in northern Italy.

(A) TONE
In the first paragraph of this story, Hemingway reveals his mastery at establishing tone. What kinds of details does he use and what kind of feeling is conveyed by these details? What kind of rhythm does the narrator achieve by repeating the coordinating conjunction *and*? How does this rhythm contribute to the tone of the paragraph?

Analyze Visuals ▶
The photo on the opposite page shows a young Ernest Hemingway at a Red Cross hospital in Milan in 1918. How does this photo, depicting real people in a real place, affect the way you read this work of fiction? Explain.

lurch (lûrch) *v.* to lean or roll suddenly to one side; stagger

play football, captain-doctor?" He had been a very great fencer,[2] and before the war the greatest fencer in Italy.

The doctor went to his office in a back room and brought a photograph which showed a hand that had been withered almost as small as the major's, before it had taken a machine course, and after was a little larger. The major held the photograph with his good hand and looked at it very carefully. "A wound?" he asked.

"An industrial accident," the doctor said.

"Very interesting, very interesting," the major said, and handed it back to the doctor.

"You have confidence?"

"No," said the major. **B**

B MAKE INFERENCES
In lines 16–41, Hemingway doesn't directly state how the soldiers feel about the machines. What can you infer about their emotions from their statements and reactions? Explain, citing evidence.

There were three boys who came each day who were about the same age I was. They were all three from Milan, and one of them was to be a lawyer, and one was to be a painter, and one had intended to be a soldier, and after we were finished with the machines, sometimes we walked back together to the Café Cova, which was next door to the Scala.[3] We walked the short way through the communist quarter because we were four together. The people hated us because we were officers, and from a wine-shop some one would call out, "A basso gli ufficiali!"[4] as we passed. Another boy who walked with us sometimes and made us five wore a black silk handkerchief across his face because he had no nose then and his face was to be rebuilt. He had gone out to the front from the military academy and been wounded within an hour after he had gone into the front line for the first time. They rebuilt his face, but he came from a very old family and they could never get the nose exactly right. He went to South America and worked in a bank. But this was a long time ago, and then we did not any of us know how it was going to be afterward. We only knew then that there was always the war, but that we were not going to it any more.

We all had the same medals, except the boy with the black silk bandage across his face, and he had not been at the front long enough to get any medals. The tall boy with a very pale face who was to be a lawyer had been a lieutenant of Arditi[5] and had three medals of the sort we each had only one of. He had lived a very long time with death and was a little **detached.** We were all a little detached, and there was nothing that held us together except that we met every afternoon at the hospital. Although, as we walked to the Cova through the tough part of town, walking in the dark, with light and singing coming out of the wine-shops, and sometimes having to walk into the street when the men and women would crowd together on the sidewalk so that we would have had to jostle them to get by, we felt held together by there being something that had happened that they, the people who disliked us, did not understand.

detached (dĭ-tăcht′) *adj.* reserved; aloof **detach** *v.*

We ourselves all understood the Cova, where it was rich and warm and not too brightly lighted, and noisy and smoky at certain hours, and there were always girls

2. **fencer:** one who fences—that is, practices the art of attack and defense using blunted swords or sabers.
3. **the Scala:** La Scala, a famous opera house in Milan.
4. **"A basso gli ufficiali!"** (ä bä′sō lē o͞o′fē-chä′lē) *Italian:* "Down with officers!"
5. **Arditi:** a carefully chosen group of volunteers who specialized in dangerous campaigns.

at the tables and the illustrated papers on a rack on the wall. The girls at the Cova were very patriotic, and I found that the most patriotic people in Italy were the café girls—and I believe they are still patriotic.

The boys at first were very polite about my medals and asked me what I had done to get them. I showed them the papers, which were written in very beautiful language and full of *fratellanza* and *abnegazione*,[6] but which really said, with the adjectives removed, that I had been given the medals because I was an American. After that their manner changed a little toward me, although I was their friend against outsiders. I was a friend, but I was never really one of them after they had read the **citations,** because it had been different with them and they had done very different things to get their medals. I had been wounded, it was true; but we all knew that being wounded, after all, was really an accident. I was never ashamed of the ribbons, though, and sometimes, after the cocktail hour, I would imagine myself having done all the things they had done to get their medals; but walking home at night through the empty streets with the cold wind and all the shops closed, trying to keep near the street lights, I knew that I would never have done such things, and I was very much afraid to die, and often lay in bed at night by myself, afraid to die and wondering how I would be when I went back to the front again. **C**

citation (sī-tā'shən) *n.* a formal statement praising a soldier's achievements

C MAKE INFERENCES
Consider how the narrator describes his relationship with his fellow soldiers. How might such interactions affect him?

The three with the medals were like hunting-hawks; and I was not a hawk, although I might seem a hawk to those who had never hunted; they, the three, knew better and so we drifted apart. But I stayed good friends with the boy who had been wounded his first day at the front, because he would never know now how he would have turned out; so he could never be accepted either, and I liked him because I thought perhaps he would not have turned out to be a hawk either. **D**

D MAKE INFERENCES
Reread lines 90–95. How does the **metaphor** about hawks further describe the difference between the narrator and the young Italian soldiers? What sense do you get of how the narrator feels about this difference?

The major, who had been the great fencer, did not believe in bravery, and spent much time while we sat in the machines correcting my grammar. He had complimented me on how I spoke Italian, and we talked together very easily. One day I had said that Italian seemed such an easy language to me that I could not take a great interest in it; everything was so easy to say. "Ah, yes," the major said. "Why, then, do you not take up the use of grammar?" So we took up the use of grammar, and soon Italian was such a difficult language that I was afraid to talk to him until I had the grammar straight in my mind.

The major came very regularly to the hospital. I do not think he ever missed a day, although I am sure he did not believe in the machines. There was a time when none of us believed in the machines, and one day the major said it was all nonsense. The machines were new then and it was we who were to prove them. It was an idiotic idea, he said, "a theory, like another." I had not learned my grammar, and he said I was a stupid impossible disgrace, and he was a fool to have bothered with me. He was a small man and he sat straight up in his chair with his right hand thrust into the machine and looked straight ahead at the wall while the straps thumped up and down with his fingers in them.

"What will you do when the war is over if it is over?" he asked me. "Speak grammatically!"

---

6. ***fratellanza* and *abnegazione*** (frä'tĕ-län'zä; äb-nĕ-gä-zē-o'nĕ) *Italian*: brotherhood and self-denial.

"I will go to the States."

"Are you married?"

"No, but I hope to be."

"The more of a fool you are," he said. He seemed very angry. "A man must not marry."

"Why, Signor Maggiore?"[7]

"Don't call me 'Signor Maggiore.'"

"Why must not a man marry?"

"He cannot marry. He cannot marry," he said angrily. "If he is to lose everything, he should not place himself in a position to lose that. He should not place himself in a position to lose. He should find things he cannot lose."

He spoke very angrily and bitterly, and looked straight ahead while he talked.

"But why should he necessarily lose it?"

"He'll lose it," the major said. He was looking at the wall. Then he looked down at the machine and jerked his little hand out from between the straps and slapped it hard against his thigh. "He'll lose it," he almost shouted. "Don't argue with me!" Then he called to the attendant who ran the machines. "Come and turn this thing off."

He went back into the other room for the light treatment and the massage. Then I heard him ask the doctor if he might use his telephone and he shut the door. When he came back into the room, I was sitting in another machine. He was wearing his cape and had his cap on, and he came directly toward my machine and put his arm on my shoulder.

"I am so sorry," he said, and patted me on the shoulder with his good hand. "I would not be rude. My wife has just died. You must forgive me."

"Oh—" I said, feeling sick for him. "I am *so* sorry."

He stood there biting his lower lip. "It is very difficult," he said. "I cannot **resign** myself."

He looked straight past me and out through the window. Then he began to cry. "I am utterly unable to resign myself," he said and choked. And then crying, his head up looking at nothing, carrying himself straight and soldierly, with tears on both his cheeks and biting his lips, he walked past the machines and out the door. E

The doctor told me that the major's wife, who was very young and whom he had not married until he was definitely invalided[8] out of the war, had died of pneumonia. She had been sick only a few days. No one expected her to die. The major did not come to the hospital for three days. Then he came at the usual hour, wearing a black band on the sleeve of his uniform. When he came back, there were large framed photographs around the wall, of all sorts of wounds before and after they had been cured by the machines. In front of the machine the major used were three photographs of hands like his that were completely restored. I do not know where the doctor got them. I always understood we were the first to use the machines. The photographs did not make much difference to the major because he only looked out of the window. F

resign (rĭ-zīn') *v.* to submit or yield without complaint

E TONE

Reread lines 133–146. What news does the major receive here? How does this news affect the major and the narrator's tone? Then, as you read the last paragraph, focus on the narrator's attitude. Hemingway closes the story with an image of the major at the window. What do you think is on his mind as he looks out the window? How does his mental state contribute to the story's tone?

F GRAMMAR AND STYLE

Reread lines 149–157. Note that though Hemingway describes a highly emotional situation, his short, **declarative sentences** and **plain diction** keep his **tone** detached and objective.

7. **Signor Maggiore** (sēn-yôr' mäd-jō'rĕ) *Italian:* Mr. Major—a respectful way of addressing an officer.

8. **invalided:** removed from active service because of sickness or injury.

Comprehension

1. **Recall** Why is the narrator in Milan?
2. **Recall** What did the major do before the war?
3. **Summarize** How is the narrator different from the other young soldiers?

Text Analysis

4. **Make Inferences** Review the inferences you made as you read. The narrator of this story is literally "in another country"—he is far from home, in a foreign, war-torn nation. What other aspects of his situation serve to further isolate or alienate him? Describe the text clues and prior knowledge that allowed you to infer how the narrator's situation affects him. Be sure to address each of the following:
   - how the narrator differs from the young Italian officers
   - the Italian civilians' response to the soldiers
   - how the narrator's circumstances differ from the major's at the story's end
5. **Analyze Tone** Reread the dialogue between the narrator and the major (lines 113–146). What kind of loss has the major experienced here, and how does he respond to his loss? What is the narrator's attitude toward the major? Cite evidence from the text to support your answer.
6. **Analyze Style** Reexamine the text, looking for examples of the following elements of Hemingway's prose **style**: short sentences; few adverbs or adjectives; and sharp, concrete images. Explain how Hemingway's style causes this story to be so emotionally charged despite the lack of direct commentary on the characters' emotions.

Text Criticism

7. **Historical Context** Influential author and patron Gertrude Stein formed a community with Fitzgerald, Hemingway, and other modernist writers living as expatriates in Paris in the 1920s. Their particular disillusionment prompted her to characterize them as a "lost generation." In what way do the characters in both "Winter Dreams" on page 978 and "In Another Country" remain "lost" at the end of each story? What might this say about the era in which these stories were written? Explain, citing evidence from both stories.

What are the **COSTS** *of war?*

Wounds suffered by soldiers on the battlefield are among the costs of war on display in this story. What other costs of war are endured by the soldiers here? Support your answer with evidence from the story.

COMMON CORE

RL 1 Cite textual evidence to support analysis of what the text says explicitly as well as inferences drawn from the text, including determining where the text leaves matters uncertain. **RL 4** Analyze the impact of specific word choices on meaning and tone, including words with multiple meanings or language that is particularly fresh, engaging, or beautiful.

Vocabulary in Context

▲ VOCABULARY PRACTICE

Choose the word from the word list that best completes each sentence.

1. Though only a few soldiers had received a(n) _____ for bravery, many of the others had also performed commendably.
2. Some of the soldiers sought companionship, while others remained aloof and _____.
3. It was painful to see young men _____ around on unsteady legs.
4. Was it better to struggle or to _____ oneself to one's fate?

WORD LIST

citation

detached

lurch

resign

ACADEMIC VOCABULARY IN WRITING

• conclude • criteria • despite • justify • maintain

The protagonist and other soldiers of "In Another Country" **maintain** a particular attitude toward life in the aftermath of combat. What kind of attitude do you recommend during times of stress? In a paragraph, identify this attitude and **justify** it to your readers. Use at least three of the Academic Vocabulary words in your writing.

VOCABULARY STRATEGY: THE ORIGIN OF ACADEMIC WORDS

As the narrator of this story would have noticed in his study of Italian, many English words are derived from that language, especially in the content areas of music and the arts. Academic vocabulary words, which include the words that apply to a specific content area, are important to your success in school. Many of those words are derived from other languages. You can use your knowledge of the word origins to improve your knowledge of academic vocabulary.

COMMON CORE

L 6 Acquire and use accurately general academic and domain-specific words and phrases, sufficient for reading, writing, speaking, and listening at the college and career readiness level.

PRACTICE Match each boldfaced academic term with its meaning. Then identify the language of origin.

1. **rotunda**	a. the art of painting on fresh moist plaster
2. **fjord**	b. a colorless and transparent mineral
3. **economy**	c. the efficient use of material resources
4. **parliament**	d. a narrow section of sea set between rocky cliffs
5. **fresco**	e. a slow movement in a piece of music
6. **adagio**	f. a circular part of a building, usually with a dome
7. **archaeology**	g. the science that studies the remains of past human life
8. **quartz**	h. a major legislative body

Language

COMMON CORE

L 3a Vary syntax for effect.
W 2e Establish and maintain an objective tone while attending to discipline-specific norms and conventions.

GRAMMAR AND STYLE: Establish Tone

Review the **Grammar and Style** note on page 1014. **Tone** is the expression of a writer's attitude toward a subject. Hemingway's early training as a newspaper reporter heavily influenced the tone of his fiction, giving it the emotional detachment and objectivity of a news report. Such a tone is achieved partly through his use of short, **declarative sentences** and **plain diction,** a style he also picked up from newspapers. Notice the simple language and understated quality of the following sentences:

It was cold in the fall in Milan and the dark came very early. Then the electric lights came on, and it was pleasant along the streets looking in the windows. There was much game hanging outside the shops, and the snow powdered in the fur of the foxes and the wind blew their tails. The deer hung stiff and heavy and empty, and small birds blew in the wind and the wind turned their feathers. It was a cold fall and the wind came down from the mountains. (lines 1–7)

PRACTICE Rewrite the following paragraph, adapting the language and sentence types to mimic Hemingway's objectivity.

The horrible, fiery inferno had completely annihilated everything, like an angry, vengeful God. Only the charred foundation of the Harlington Hotel remained, with its lone chimney of chipped and blackened stone standing forlornly amid the devastation like a victim of survivor guilt. Never again would we see the thick forest in its green majestic splendor! Ugly black stumps studded the land like tombstones. It was the landscape of damnation! Gone were the songs of birds, the chirps of chipmunks, and the laughter of children! A deafening silence enveloped the area for miles around. Only black grasshoppers flitted about the soot, sending up tiny clouds of ash.

READING-WRITING CONNECTION

Expand your understanding of "In Another Country" by responding to this prompt. Then, use the **revising tips** to improve your profile.

WRITING PROMPT	REVISING TIPS
WRITE A CHARACTER PROFILE Most of Hemingway's male protagonists share such strikingly similar traits that critics have named this type of character the "Hemingway hero." Using the examples of the narrator and the major in this story, create a **three-to-five-paragraph profile** of the Hemingway hero.	• Check your thesis statement to be sure you have defined the Hemingway hero. • Since tone is an essential feature of the Hemingway narrator, be sure that your essay focuses on a particular kind of attitude. • Examine the story's conclusion and be sure that you use it as supporting evidence.

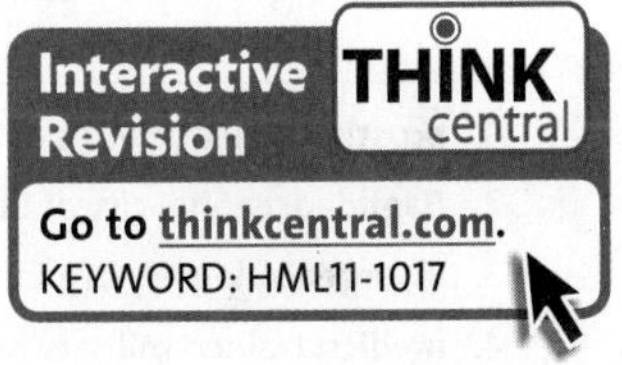

Magazine Article

In Hemingway's short story, you read about soldiers undergoing physical therapy for wounds suffered on the Italian front in World War I. In Karen Breslau's article, you'll discover how soldiers injured in the Iraq war use extreme sports to regain their physical and mental health.

HEALING WAR'S WOUNDS

Karen Breslau

BACKGROUND The conflict in Iraq started in March 2003, when a coalition led by the United States entered the country and toppled the government of Saddam Hussein. U.S. troops in Iraq have been threatened by violent opposition to the American presence there. Because of medical advances, severely wounded soldiers often survive to face difficult and lengthy recoveries. Karen Breslau, who writes about these soldiers in "Healing War's Wounds," is *Newsweek*'s San Francisco bureau chief.

"Hey, have any of y'all seen the crocodile that got my arm?" U.S. Army Maj. Anthony Smith hoists his prosthetic[1] hook, tied to a paddle, as he floats down Idaho's Salmon River in a large blue raft, manned by a cackling crew of fellow amputees. Momentarily rattled, a group of rafters resting onshore stare as Smith's boat glides by, before someone on the beach points down the rapids and yells, "He went that-a-way." Smith, digging his paddle back into the water, growls with mock pirate glee. "You should see what happens when I'm in a restaurant and I say to the waitress 'Can you give me a hand?'" **A**

He can laugh now. It's the surest sign yet of the progress he's made since April 24, 2004, when Smith, then a captain with an Arkansas National Guard unit stationed near Baghdad[2], was struck by a rocket-propelled grenade. . . . As Smith staggered to his feet, insurgents[3] opened fire, shooting him four times. By the time medics[4] reached him minutes later, Smith had "flat-lined." Finding no pulse or respiration, they loaded him into a body bag and put his name on the list of those KIA, killed in action. Only as a soldier was preparing to zip shut the bag did she notice an air bubble in the blood oozing from Smith's neck wound. "They said, 'Hey, this guy's still alive,'" Smith says.

A MAKING INFERENCES Examine the dialogue in the opening paragraph. What can you infer about the soldiers from the way they speak? Explain, citing evidence.

---

1. **prosthetic:** artificial, as of a replacement for a missing body part.
2. **Baghdad:** capital city of Iraq.
3. **insurgents:** loosely organized fighters who oppose the presence of the U.S. military in Iraq.
4. **medics:** trained military personnel who rescue wounded soldiers and administer life-saving first aid.

Analyze Visuals
What mood does the photographer capture with this image? How does the photograph support the tone of the article it accompanies? Cite details from the photograph and the selection to support your response.

Two and a half years later, Smith recounts his own resurrection in vivid detail—not because he remembers (he was in a coma for six weeks), but because he has pieced the story together from conversations with his wife, Jackie, and the dozens of doctors who labored to save him. Smith has endured more than 30 surgical procedures to reconstruct his abdomen, the remains of his right arm, his burned face and the gaping wound in his hip, now painfully infected. He must be constantly monitored for signs of traumatic brain injury that may have resulted from the force of his skull's slamming against the inside of his helmet. B

B TONE
Reread lines 18–25, with special attention to the information the writer provides about Major Smith. What do you learn from this passage about Major Smith and the writer's attitude toward him? Support your answer with details from the paragraph.

Though Smith's tale of survival is extreme, it is no longer unheard of. . . . But it also presents a huge challenge for the military as this sizable population of wounded veterans returns to society, bearing complex disabilities that will require lifelong care.

To address the problem, the military has adopted a holistic[5] mind-body approach, deploying a fleet of experts ranging from orthopedic[6] surgeons to therapists to work on the wounded. Doctors insist on group therapy to help cope with the guilt that often dogs survivors who have lost—or left—comrades on the battlefield. Of special concern are the service members, like Smith, classified by the Pentagon as "severely injured"—having lost limbs or eyesight, or suffering burns, paralysis or debilitating brain injuries that will not emerge fully in some cases for years. "Technology has advanced to the point where we can salvage patients who would not have survived before," says Lt. Col. John McManus of the Army's Institute for Surgical Research in San Antonio, Texas. "The bigger test is psychological. Can we restore a life worth living?"

The Pentagon has recently begun testing more experimental methods, rehabilitating wounded service members with extreme sports designed to build muscle—and self-confidence. . . . Patients who work out regularly, lifting weights and yanking pulleys from their wheelchairs, often with burned and mangled limbs, are rewarded with all-expenses-paid outdoor expeditions. It was just such an invitation that brought Smith, two other wounded service members and their wives to the

5. **holistic:** relating to the whole of something instead of its parts.
6. **orthopedic:** medically related to the bones, joints, or muscles.

◂ Analyze Visuals
What emotions do you think the veteran in the paragliding harness was feeling at the moment the photograph was taken? What details of the scene help you identify his emotions?

Salmon River last month. They were the guests of Sun Valley Adaptive Sports—one of several private nonprofits consulting with the Pentagon. On the week's agenda: white-water rafting, paragliding, rock climbing and horseback riding. With the group is Erik Schultz, a backcountry sports enthusiast who was paralyzed in a skiing accident eight years ago. During his darkest depression, says Schultz, friends "literally dragged me" on a camping trip. After a week in the wilderness, "I was bursting with self-confidence. Things didn't seem that hard anymore." He hopes that his presence in a wheelchair, fly-fishing from a rocky beach and whooping his way down the river, will help "demystify" disabled life for the wounded service members. **C**

Free from their hospital routines, and the weight of their wounds, Smith and the others spend their days splashing like kids. U.S. Marine S/Sgt. Damion Jacobs, who lost his right leg below the knee to an IED[7] near Fallujah six months ago, removes his prosthetic and props it in the sand like a coffee table; he leans against it while watching the show. Jacobs plans to take his Marine Corps physical and return to active duty. Army Spc. Andrew Soule, an intense, dignified 25-year-old who has emerged as the star of BAMC's rehab program, says that before his injury, he wasn't "much of an athlete." A year ago Soule lost both legs and suffered a severe arm injury in a bomb blast in Afghanistan. Now he kayaks, hand-cycles and surfs. On the first day of the river trip, one of Soule's carbon-fiber prosthetics is fractured. He tosses the limb aside and, for the next five days, kayaks legless, dragging his body over rocky beaches, even climbing stairs, with his arms. "People have this tendency to overreact," says Soule, who left Texas A&M after 9/11 to join the Army. "They don't know how much you can do for yourself." **D**

Even Soule is amazed by how far he has come. As he lay tourniqueted[8] on the ground last year next to the wreckage of his Humvee near the Pakistani border, waiting for a helicopter to rescue him, Soule's squad leader leaned over him and instructed the young soldier to repeat over and over, "I'm going to live. I'm going to live." It's a lesson he carried with him, down the Salmon River and beyond.

C TONE
The author clearly admires the soldiers for participating in extreme adventure sports. What details in this paragraph convey her admiring tone?

D MAKING INFERENCES
Reread lines 54–67. What kind of message about the soldiers and about life can you infer from the details the writer includes here? Cite evidence to support your answer.

7. **IED:** improvised explosive device; the military term for a homemade bomb.
8. **tourniqueted:** fitted with a device to prevent blood loss from a major wound.

Book Cover

This book cover features the bowed head of a combat soldier. The subtitle identifies the book's subject: "returning troops." Breslau's magazine article focuses also on returning troops, while Hemingway's short story features wounded soldiers in treatment near the front. As you study the book cover, think about how the words come together with the image to engage potential readers. Respond to the questions below, citing evidence from the book cover to support your answers.

RI 7 Integrate and evaluate multiple sources of information presented in different media or formats as well as in words in order to address a question.

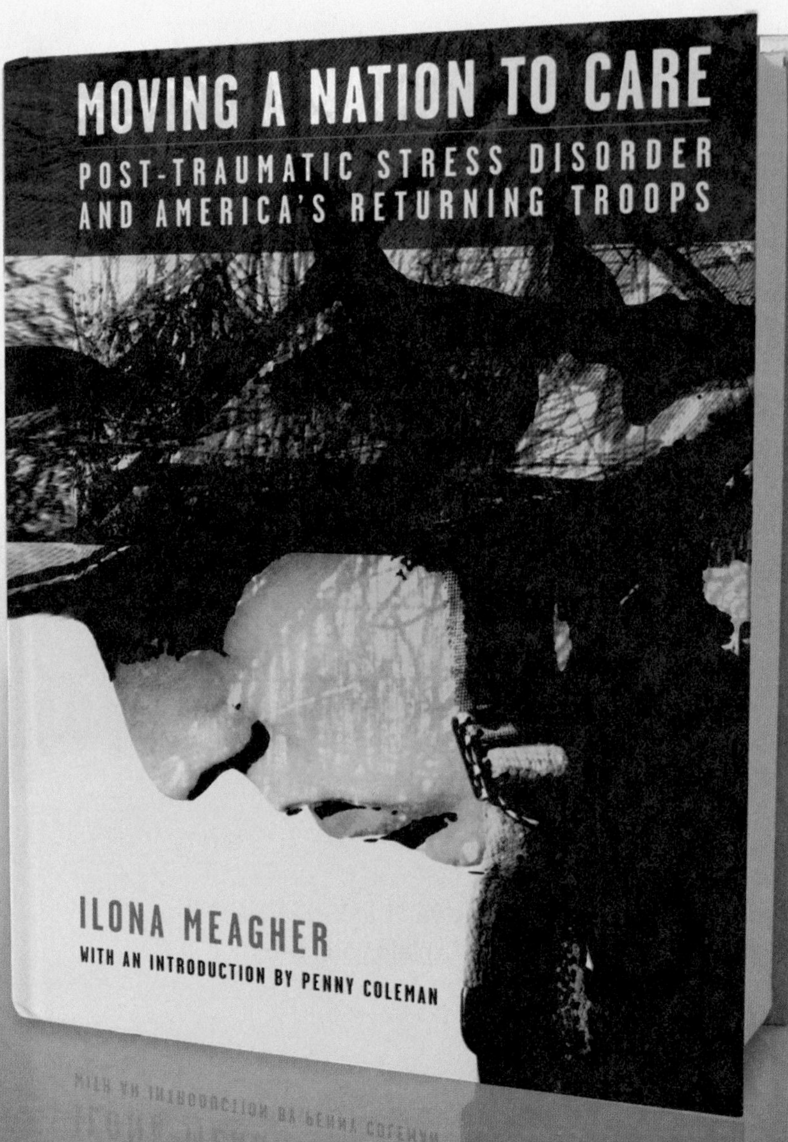

1. **INTERPRET** Examine the image of the soldier. Notice the camouflaged helmet, which indicates that he is on active duty. Notice also that his head is bowed and that his eyes are in shadow. What kind of mood does the image convey? Why do you think the publisher chose this image for a book about post-traumatic stress disorder in returning soldiers?

2. **MAKE INFERENCES** What persuasive message does the book title convey? What purpose does the publisher achieve by running the title in large block letters across the top of the cover? Explain your responses.

Comprehension

1. **Recall** Describe the military's "holistic mind-body approach" to treating injured soldiers.
2. **Clarify** How did spending a week in the wilderness boost Erik Schultz's self-confidence?
3. **Summarize** How does participating in extreme sports benefit injured soldiers mentally and physically?

COMMON CORE

RI 1 Cite textual evidence to support analysis of what the text says explicitly as well as inferences drawn from the text, including determining where the text leaves matters uncertain. **RI 4** Determine the meaning of words and phrases as they are used in a text, including figurative, connotative, and technical meanings.

Text Analysis

4. **Make Inferences** Breslau begins her article with a humorous anecdote, followed by a horrific description of Major Smith's near-fatal injuries. Why do you think she chose to begin the article this way? Explain your answer.
5. **Evaluate Tone** How successful is the writer in conveying her attitude toward the soldiers she writes about here? Cite evidence from the article to support your answer.
6. **Evaluate Diction** Breslau refers to Major Smith's recovery as a "resurrection." Considering the facts surrounding his injury, is this word appropriate here? Explain your answer.
7. **Make Inferences** Reread the article's closing sentence. What lesson do you think Soule carried with him? What lesson do you think Breslau wants readers to carry with them after reading her article? Explain your answer.

Comparing Themes Across Genres

8. **Analyze Theme** Both Hemingway's short story and Breslau's magazine article focus on wounded soldiers in therapy, but the two writers convey strikingly different attitudes toward the possibility of recovery. Describe the contrast in attitude between the two selections, citing evidence from both to support your answer.

What are the **COSTS** *of war?*

After reading "Healing War's Wounds," what responsibility do you think a society has to soldiers who have suffered the costs of war? Explain your answer.

Assessment Practice: Short Constructed Response

LITERARY TEXT: "IN ANOTHER COUNTRY"

On assessments you are often expected to make inferences as you read. Practice this skill as you answer the **short constructed response question** below. Be sure to follow the steps outlined to the right of the question.

When the narrator first mentions physical therapy machines, he says "the machines were to make so much difference." What kind of difference do these machines make for the soldiers in the story? Support your response with evidence from the text.

STRATEGIES IN ACTION

1. *Make a quick list of muscular damage the machines are supposed to repair.*
2. *List any improvements the machines produce.*
3. *Describe the attitude of the soldiers toward the machines.*
4. *Use steps 1–3 to help you answer the question.*

NONFICTION TEXT: "HEALING WAR'S WOUNDS"

On assessments you are often expected to read carefully and answer questions that focus on particular passages from a text. To strengthen your close-reading skills, read the **short constructed response question** at left below and practice the strategies suggested at right.

What kind of attitude toward life does Andrew Soule display after he fractures one of his prosthetic legs? Support your response with evidence from the text.

STRATEGIES IN ACTION

1. *Examine the details of Soule's behavior in the sentences following his prosthetic fracture.*
2. *What kind of attitude goes with his behavior here?*

COMPARING LITERARY AND NONFICTION TEXTS

On assessments you will need to identify thematic connections between literary and nonfiction texts. Practice this valuable skill by answering the **short constructed response question** at left below and using the strategies provided at right.

Describe the contrast in tone between the closing paragraphs of the short story "In Another Country" and the article "Healing War's Wounds." Support your response with evidence from both texts.

STRATEGIES IN ACTION

1. *Examine Hemingway's closing paragraph and write down a single word that describes his tone.*
2. *Complete step 1 for Breslau's article.*
3. *Use the two words you chose to describe tone to answer the question.*

American Masterpiece

from The Grapes of Wrath

Novel by John Steinbeck

John Steinbeck
1902–1968

COMMON CORE

RL 5 Analyze how an author's choices concerning how to structure specific parts of a text contribute to its overall structure and meaning as well as its aesthetic impact.

BACKGROUND The blockbuster novel of 1939, *The Grapes of Wrath* is the story of the Joads, a family of Oklahoma farmers who leave their Dustbowl farm and make their way to California to find work. John Steinbeck depicts the grueling conditions of Depression life with vivid details about the Joads, as well as short chapters on migrant farmers as a whole. Torn from the headlines of the times, the novel gave eloquent voice to photographic images of displaced farmers published in newspapers and other publications during the Depression. Two years later, James Agee and Walker Evans published *Let Us Now Praise Famous Men*, which combined Evans's powerful photographs of Southern sharecroppers with Agee's eloquent testimony to their bleak lives.

TEXT ANALYSIS Steinbeck's **tone** in the following passage can be summed up in a single phrase: *reverence toward the endurance of hardship*. In this excerpt from one of his short chapters on migrant farmers as a group, the author achieves an almost Biblical tone through **repetition** and **parallel structure.** As you read, notice the many repetitions of the conjunction *and*, as well as the connector *so that*. Notice also series of parallel phrases or clauses that give the prose a poetic rhythm. The second sentence includes an effective example: "made them with their tents and their hearts and their brains."

WRITE Read the excerpt twice, concentrating on tone. What idea about migrant farmers does the author convey through tone? Support your answer with details from the text. Then, after you have studied the photo essay that begins on page 1027, write a short paragraph explaining how these documents from the Depression relate to Steinbeck's view of migrant workers.

And the worlds were built in the evening. The people, moving in from the highways, made them with their tents and their hearts and their brains.

In the morning the tents came down, the canvas was folded, the tent poles tied along the running board, the beds put in place on the cars, the pots in their places. And as the families moved westward, the technique of building up a home in the evening and tearing it down with the morning light became fixed; so that the folded tent was packed in one place, the cooking pots counted in their box. And as the cars moved westward, each member of the family grew into his proper place, grew into his duties; so that each member, old and young, had his place in the car; so that in the weary, hot evenings, when the cars pulled into the camping places, each member had his duty and went to it without instruction: children to gather wood, to carry water; men to pitch the tents and bring down the beds; women to cook the supper and to watch while the family fed. And this was done without command. The families, which had been units of which the boundaries were a house at night, a farm by day, changed their boundaries. In the long hot light, they were silent in the cars moving slowly westward; but at night they integrated with any group they found.

Thus they changed their social life—changed as in the whole universe only man can change. They were not farm men any more, but migrant men. And the thought, the planning, the long staring silence that had gone out to the fields, went now to the roads, to the distance, to the West. That man whose mind had been bound with acres lived with narrow concrete miles. And his thought and his worry were not any more with rainfall, with wind and dust, with the thrust of the crops. Eyes watched the tires, ears listened to the clattering motors, and minds struggled with oil, with gasoline, with the thinning rubber between air and road. Then a broken gear was tragedy. Then water in the evening was the yearning, and food over the fire. Then health to go on was the need and strength to go on, and spirit to go on. The wills thrust westward ahead of them, and fears that had once apprehended drought or flood now lingered with anything that might stop the westward crawling.

The camps became fixed—each a short day's journey from the last.

And on the road the panic overcame some of the families, so that they drove night and day, stopped to sleep in the cars, and drove on to the West, flying from the road, flying from movement. And these lusted so greatly to be settled that they set their faces into the West and drove toward it, forcing the clashing engines over the roads.

But most of the families changed and grew quickly into the new life. And when the sun went down—

Time to look out for a place to stop.

And—there's some tents ahead.

The car pulled off the road and stopped, and because others were there first, certain courtesies were necessary. And the man, the leader of the family, leaned from the car.

Can we pull up here an' sleep?

Why, sure, be proud to have you.

Reading for Information

Photo Essay: The Grapes of Wrath

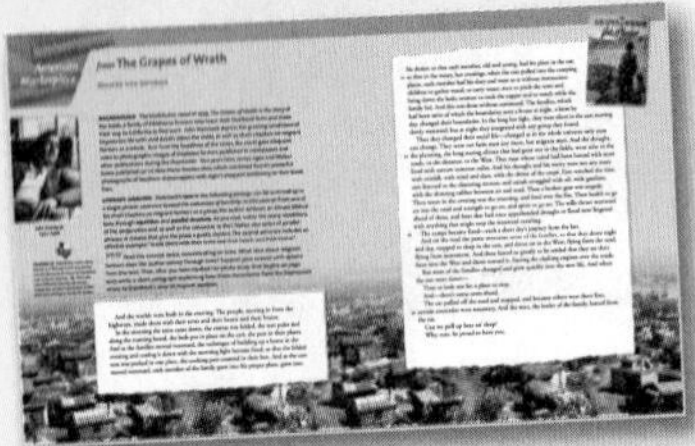

Use with *The Grapes of Wrath*, page 1024.

COMMON CORE

RI 7 Integrate and evaluate multiple sources of information presented in different media or formats as well as in words in order to address a question or solve a problem.

Before John Steinbeck wrote *The Grapes of Wrath,* he traveled through California's migrant labor camps with *Life* magazine photographer Horace Bristol. The following pictures were taken by Bristol at that time. The captions are Steinbeck's and the accompanying essay appeared along with the photos and captions. As you view "the worlds [that] were built in the evening" and the people who built and inhabited them, bear in mind that you will later be asked to decide which is more compelling, the photo essay or the excerpt from the novel.

Standards Focus: Analyze Photographs and Text

Reading a photo essay is a very different experience from reading a page of prose or looking at photographs on their own. The task requires an **interactive approach**, a willingness to reread text after examining a related photograph and to look at photographs in the light shed by a piece of writing.

As you examine a photograph, look for a **focal point**, the place that draws your attention. Study the **lighting** and how it affects you. What do **facial expressions** and **posture** convey about the people in a photo? What kind of **details** do you see, and how do they contribute to the **mood** of the image?

Captions make up some of the text in this photo essay. By quoting the words of people in the photographs, they add a personal voice to the images. A standard essay also accompanies the photographs on these pages. More impersonal than the captions, the essay supplies information and ideas that can help you understand the lives of the people in the photographs.

After you have examined the photographs and read the captions and the essay, choose three images that you find especially powerful. For each one, complete a chart like the one below.

Photograph		Caption	Interaction of all elements
Focal point:			
Lighting:			
Faces/posture:		Essay Text	
Details:			
Mood:			

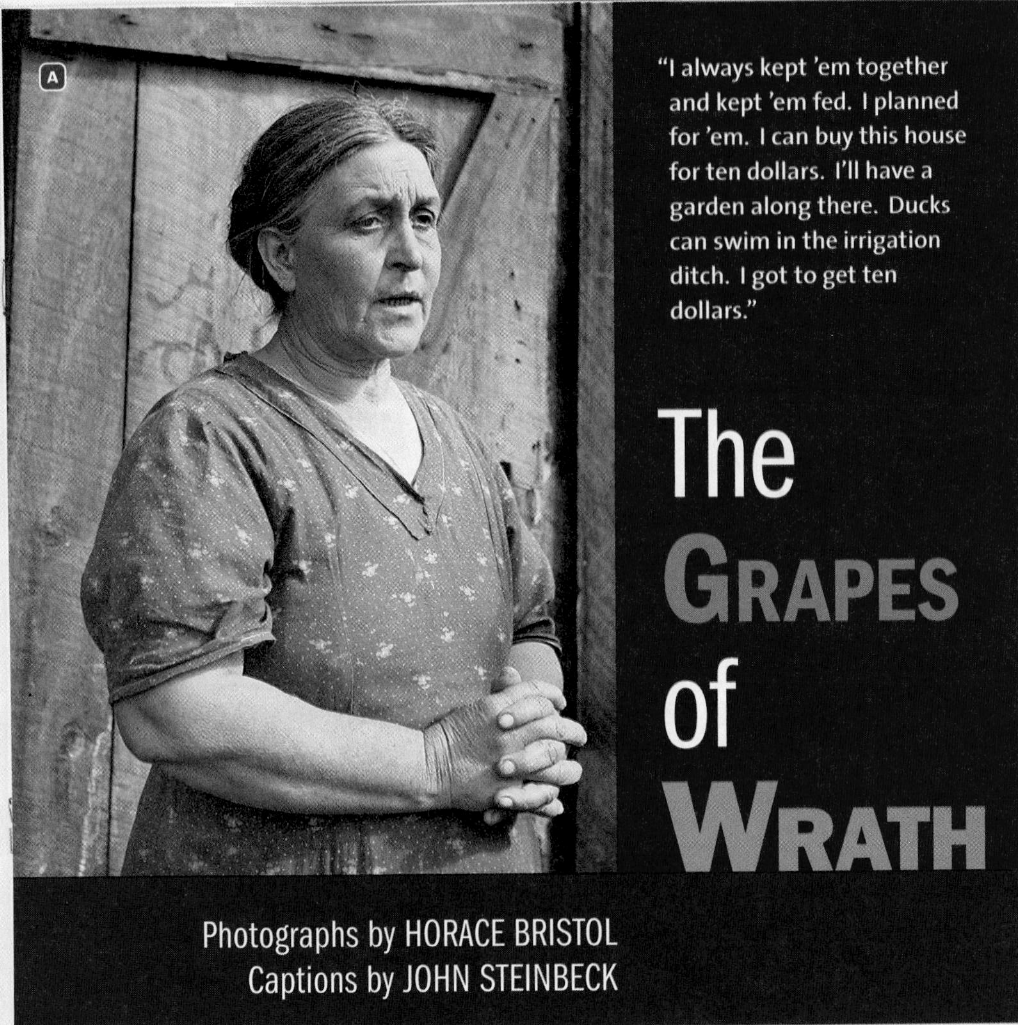

"I always kept 'em together and kept 'em fed. I planned for 'em. I can buy this house for ten dollars. I'll have a garden along there. Ducks can swim in the irrigation ditch. I got to get ten dollars."

The Grapes of Wrath

Photographs by HORACE BRISTOL
Captions by JOHN STEINBECK

In 1934, when the rest of the U.S. began to rise out of Depression, dust began to blow in Oklahoma and Montana, Arkansas and the Dakotas. Thousands of bewildered farmers and farm hands lost their holdings or their jobs and began to drift West. By the time the dust stopped blowing, the banks and the land companies found that mechanized farming over huge areas could make the land pay when individual farmers could not. The drift Westward continued and grew. Lured by assurances of green land and good money, the farmers sold their old tools and older houses, their livestock and furniture for anything they would bring. They used the money to buy shaky old cars, sawing off the bodies to make sedans into flimsy trucks. Along Route 66, through the Texas Panhandle, New Mexico and Arizona, they squeaked and rattled by tens of thousands, a bedraggled leaderless horde, camping beside the creeks and prairie villages, headed for California as a promised land.

A ANALYZE PHOTOGRAPHS AND TEXT
Image and text work together on this page in several important ways. The placement of the photograph emphasizes its importance here: the eye starts at the upper left of any page of text or photos. What kind of woman is depicted in the photograph? What can you tell about her from her **facial expression,** her **posture,** and her hands? When you read the **caption** beside her, how do the words add to the impression conveyed by the photo? The actual spoken words of a migrant make up the caption. The text beneath, by contrast, uses the language of journalism and is an **essay**—a factual account of Dustbowl conditions in 1934. How does the photograph lend to your understanding of the text—both caption and essay? How does the text contribute to your perception of the woman in the photograph?

B ANALYZE PHOTOGRAPHS AND TEXT
Study the photograph and reread the **caption.** How does the text affect the impact of the photograph? Explain.

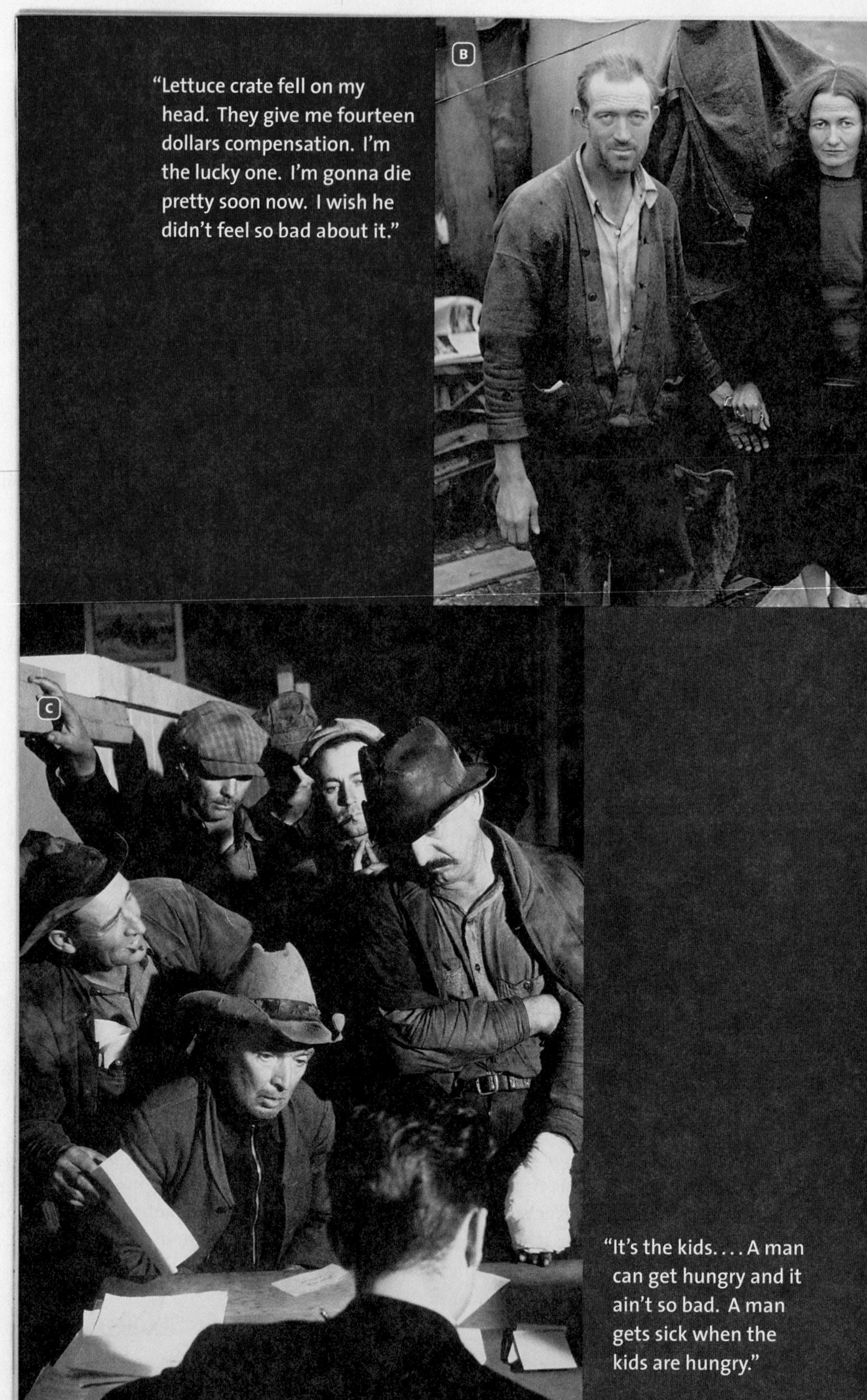

"Lettuce crate fell on my head. They give me fourteen dollars compensation. I'm the lucky one. I'm gonna die pretty soon now. I wish he didn't feel so bad about it."

"It's the kids. . . . A man can get hungry and it ain't so bad. A man gets sick when the kids are hungry."

C ANALYZE PHOTOGRAPHS AND TEXT
What is the **focal point** of this photograph and how does **lighting** draw your eye to the focal point? How do **facial expressions** and the **caption** contribute to the impact of the image?

In California the migrants found no promised land. Instead, they found that thousands of their own kind had already glutted the market for cheap itinerant labor. Furthermore, scrabbling about the State to look for work, fighting each other for jobs, they learned that California hated them because they were hungry and desperate. Because most of them came from Oklahoma, they were scornfully called "Okies," harried along between scarce jobs. Migrants are still in California, squatting in hideous poverty and squalor on the thin margins of the world's richest land. Of the one-third of a nation which is ill-housed, ill-clad, ill-nourished these are the bitterest dregs.

The problem of the Okies, though grim, is not insoluble. Some hope of a solution is suggested by the fact that an American writer can not only write about the Okies but that the result can be hailed by U.S. critics as the book of the decade. In *The Grapes of Wrath* (The Viking Press, $2.75), John Steinbeck (*Of Mice and Men*) presents the Okies in all their stink and misery, their courage and confusion. His 600-page novel, which may become a 20th Century *Uncle Tom's Cabin,* is now a nationwide best-seller. Last week, Producer Darryl Zanuck paid $75,000 for the right to make it into a movie.

"We just got in. Gonna work in the peas. Got a han'bill that says they's good wages pickin' peas."

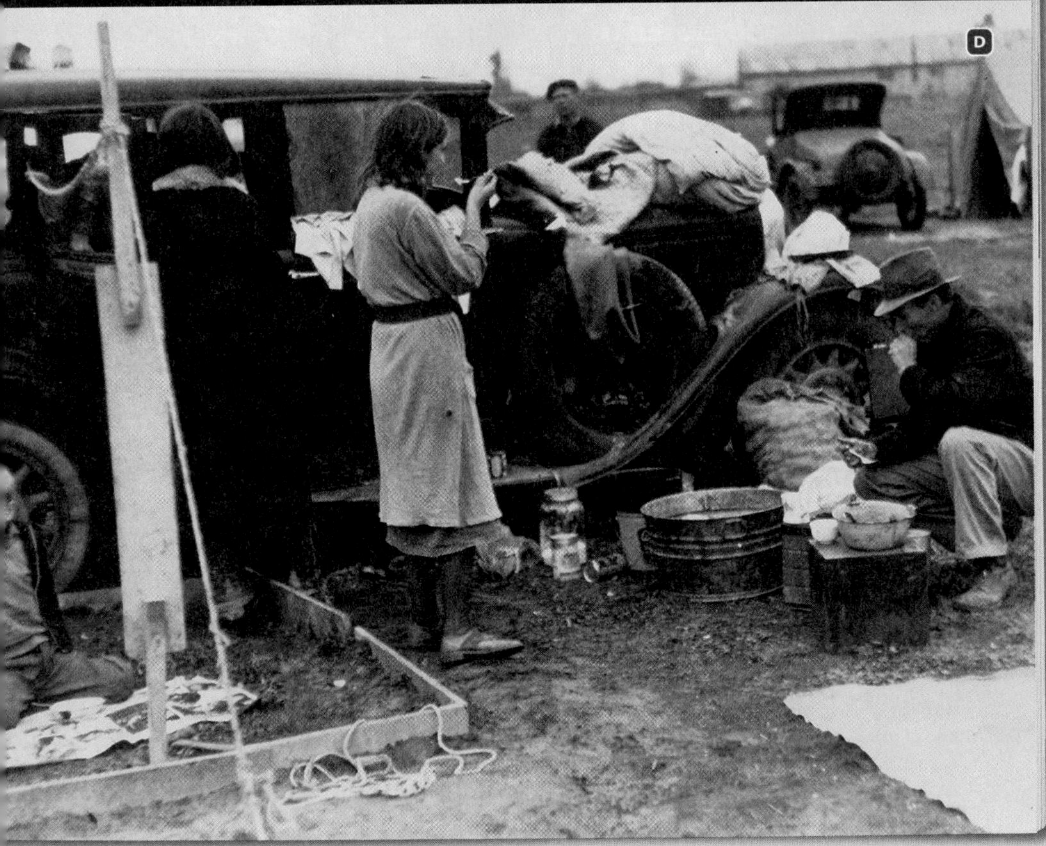

D ANALYZE PHOTOGRAPHS AND TEXT
What details of Depression-era migrant worker life does this photograph record, and what **mood** do the details establish? How does the **essay text** in the top half of this column contribute to the photograph's impression of migrant life?

E ANALYZE PHOTOGRAPHS AND TEXT
Reread the caption. What information does it convey about the company? Based on the information, what can you infer about the company? Finally, how does the photograph contribute to the impression of the company you inferred from the caption?

"The company lets us live in 'em when we're pickin' cotton. When we ain't workin', we pay rent. Water's comin' up in 'em now." E

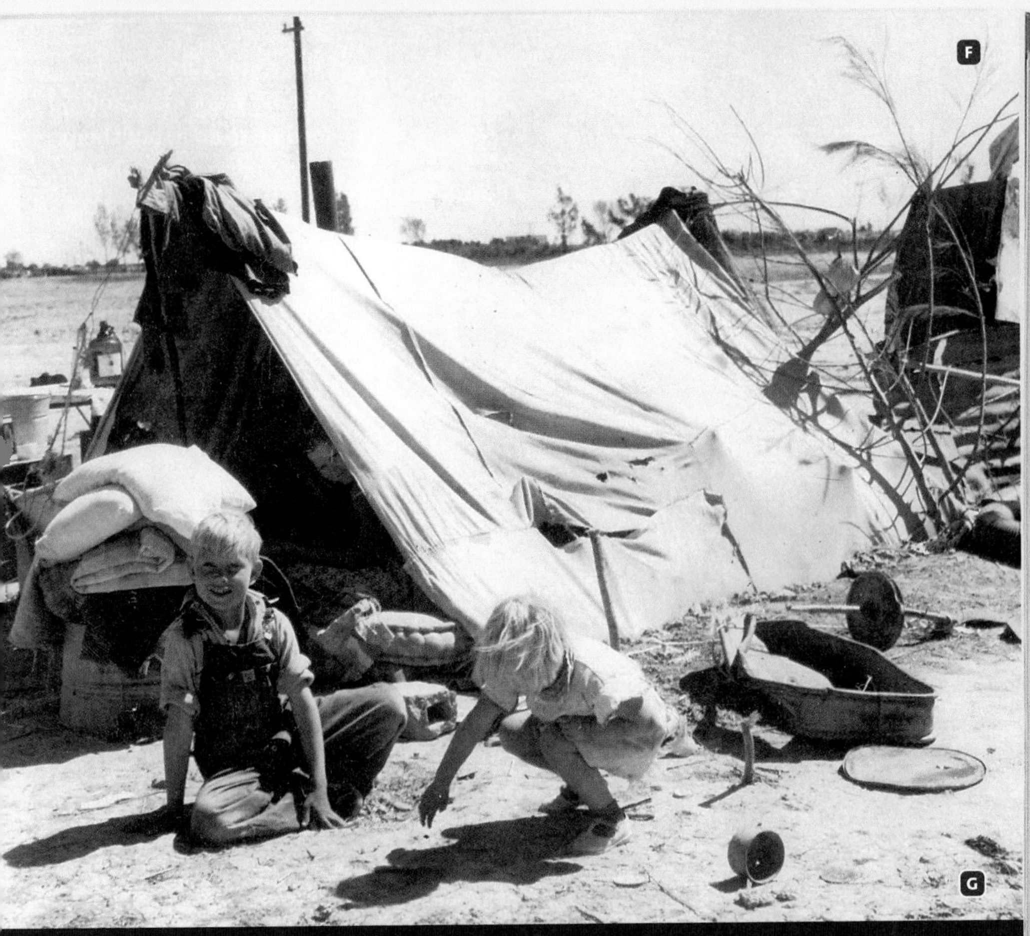

"We got to have a house when the rains come . . . jus' so's it's got a roof and a floor. Just to keep the little fellas off'n the groun'."

F ANALYZE PHOTOGRAPHS AND TEXT
How would you contrast the **mood** of the photographs on pages 1030 and 1031? What elements in the photographs account for this contrast?

G ANALYZE PHOTOGRAPHS AND TEXT
What role does the presence of children play in the impact of this photograph? How does the caption affect this impact? Explain your answer.

The pictures on [these pages] are not simply types which resemble those described in *The Grapes of Wrath*. They are the people of whom Author Steinbeck wrote. Before starting his book, he lived in California's migratory labor camps. LIFE Photographer Horace Bristol accompanied him. The woman on [page 981] might well be Ma Joad, Author Steinbeck's heroine. The man with the double-edged ax [page 986] is a counterpart of his hero, Tom Joad. Captions for their pictures and all others on these pages were written by Steinbeck. Some are excerpts from his book. Others were written especially for LIFE's photographs.

H ANALYZE PHOTOGRAPHS AND TEXT
Horace Bristol could have **cropped,** or cut, the background figure out of this image without losing any part of the man and ax in the foreground. Reread the caption. What is the impact of having the second man in the background?

"The whole thing's nuts. There's work to do and people to do it, but them two can't get together. There's food to eat and people to eat it, and them two can't get together neither."

"She's awful pretty. An' she been to high school. She could help a man with figuring and stuff like that."

I ANALYZE PHOTOGRAPHS AND TEXT
From this last photograph and caption, what might you gather about people's attitudes toward their circumstances? How might the photographer's **vantage point** be said to contribute to this idea?

Comprehension

1. **Recall** In the late 1930s, what combination of events and promises prompted many farmers in the plains states to travel westward?
2. **Recall** Who wrote the captions for the photographs in this photo essay? Are they fiction, nonfiction, or a mixture of both?
3. **Summarize** What typically happened to the Midwestern farmers who migrated to California? How were they regarded by Californians?

Text Analysis

4. **Analyze Tone** How would you describe the attitude of the speaker in the caption for the image on page 1030? How does the information conveyed by the photograph and caption on page 1031 help you understand this attitude?
5. **Analyze Photographs and Text** What have you learned from this photo essay about the living conditions and attitudes of Depression-era migrant workers?
6. **Evaluate** Reread lines 23–30 of the essay text. Do you agree or disagree with the writer's assertion? Explain.

COMMON CORE

RI 7 Integrate and evaluate multiple sources of information presented in different media or formats as well as in words in order to address a question or solve a problem. **W 4** Produce clear and coherent writing in which the development, organization, and style are appropriate to task, purpose, and audience. **W 9** Draw evidence from literary or informational texts to support analysis, reflection, and research.

Read for Information: Compare and Evaluate

WRITING PROMPT

Reflect on the excerpt you read from *The Grapes of Wrath* and on the photo essay you just studied. In your opinion, which paints a more powerful portrait of the migrant farmworkers? Why?

The following steps will help you answer the prompt:

1. Review the selections and decide, based on your first reaction, which piece you find more powerful.
2. Now go back and analyze each piece, taking notes on the following elements:
   - the amount of information provided
   - the kinds of **details** and information conveyed
   - the ideas or **themes** emphasized
   - the **author's perspective** and the photographer's vantage point
   - the literary elements and the artistic techniques
   - the **mood** and thoughts evoked
3. Review your analysis. As you look at the relative strengths of each piece, do you still have the same opinion about which is more compelling? Why or why not?
4. Now state your opinion about which selection is more compelling, and give the reasons for your opinion, comparing the strengths and weaknesses of each piece.

COMMON CORE

RL 1 Cite textual evidence to support analysis of what the text says explicitly as well as inferences drawn from the text. **RL 3** Analyze the impact of the author's choices regarding how to develop and relate elements of a story. **RL 5** Analyze how an author's choices concerning how to structure specific parts of a text contribute to its overall structure and meaning as well as its aesthetic impact.

The Jilting of Granny Weatherall

Short Story by Katherine Anne Porter

DID YOU KNOW?

Katherine Anne Porter . . .

- was a distant relative of the frontiersman Daniel Boone.
- taught singing and dancing as a teenager to help support her family.

Meet the Author

Katherine Anne Porter 1890–1980

Katherine Anne Porter has been called a "writer's writer"; in her lifetime she was more popular with critics and her fellow writers than with the public. She wrote mostly short fiction, a form with which it was difficult to build a popular reputation. What's more, all of her 27 short stories, including those technically classified as novellas (short novels), could fit into a single book. Still, Porter's work is celebrated for its nearly flawless consistency and style. Each one of her stories is a polished gem reflecting a hard truth about human experience.

Survival and Resiliency She was born Callie Russell Porter on a scrappy dirt farm in central Texas, where she dreamed of becoming an actress. She had the good looks, the drive, and the talent for performing but lacked the stamina. A two-year bout with tuberculosis permanently dashed her dreams of acting. However, while recuperating at a sanitorium, Porter befriended a journalist who helped her start writing for newspapers.

Living in Denver in 1918, Porter was again stricken by illness, this time by the deadly flu epidemic that swept the globe after World War I, killing 550,000 people in the United States and at least 25 million worldwide. This second brush with death inspired an idea that was later to become part of her novella *Pale Horse, Pale Rider* (1939). After her recovery, convinced of her true calling, Porter left Denver for the New York literary scene and the wider world.

Deep in the Heart of Texas Like many writers of her generation, Porter traveled widely, living in Mexico, Bermuda, Germany, Switzerland, and France, as well as New York for much of the 1920s and 1930s. Some of these places inspired her fiction: her time in Mexico enriched her first published story, "Maria Concepción" (1922), and several others, while pre–World War II Berlin informed "The Leaning Tower" (1944). But for the most part, foreign travel provided what Porter called a "constant exercise of memory" and brought her closer to her native land. Some of her best fiction—notably, "Noon Wine" (1937), "Old Mortality" (1939), and a series called "The Old Order" (1955)—takes place in Texas. Many of these stories, and "The Jilting of Granny Weatherall" (1929) in particular, include a dynamic grandmother based on Porter's own who raised her until age 11 and exerted a strong influence. Porter even took her grandmother's name after she divorced her first husband and began life on her own.

Author Online THINK central

Go to thinkcentral.com. KEYWORD: HML11-1034

TEXT ANALYSIS: STREAM OF CONSCIOUSNESS

The very first paragraph of this story plunges readers directly into the thoughts of its protagonist. This literary technique, **stream of consciousness,** presents the main events of a story, or the **plot,** using a character's seemingly unconnected thoughts, responses, and sensations. Rather than offering a logical account of events, it presents a series of associative connections, with one impression giving rise to another. Use these strategies to help you keep track of the plot:

- Remember that you are seeing the "inside" or internal development of the main character. The depictions of people and events you find there may not be completely reliable.
- Look for quotation marks to determine when Granny is speaking aloud and when she is not.
- Keep track of the twists and turns of Granny's thoughts to understand what she is reacting to.
- Keep in mind that the plot of this story moves back and forth between the present and the past.

READING SKILL: CLARIFY SEQUENCE

In this narrative, Porter shuffles together the past and the present to depict the distorted way Granny perceives the **sequence** of events. Porter achieves this effect in part through the use of **flashback,** in which she relates events that happened before the beginning of the story's "now" time. As you travel through Granny's memory, use a timeline to untangle the sequence of the main events in her life.

VOCABULARY IN CONTEXT

Porter uses these words to take readers into the mind of a woman on her deathbed. Complete each phrase with a word from the list.

WORD LIST	amethyst	dwindle	plague
	assign	embroidered	

1. kept an elaborately _____ blanket on the sickbed
2. had a valuable _____ ring to pass on to her daughter
3. felt her time _____ as she got weaker and weaker

Complete the activities in your **Reader/Writer Notebook**.

What makes a MEMORY *linger?*

That perfect first date. The humiliating moment you realized you had failed your driving test. The elated, screaming crowd jumping to its feet as the last seconds of the big game ticked away. Whether pleasant or painful, there are some memories you just can't shake. In this story, as Granny Weatherall lies on her deathbed, she's haunted by an event that still affects her almost as powerfully as it did when she experienced it as a young woman.

QUICKWRITE Write a paragraph about a memory of your own that you can still recall in crisp detail. What images, feelings, sounds, or smells come to mind? Why do you think this moment lingers in your memory?

The *Jilting* of Granny Weatherall

Katherine Anne Porter

She flicked her wrist neatly out of Doctor Harry's pudgy careful fingers and pulled the sheet up to her chin. The brat ought to be in knee breeches.[1] Doctoring around the country with spectacles on his nose! "Get along now, take your schoolbooks and go. There's nothing wrong with me." **A**

Doctor Harry spread a warm paw like a cushion on her forehead where the forked green vein danced and made her eyelids twitch. "Now, now, be a good girl, and we'll have you up in no time."

"That's no way to speak to a woman nearly eighty years old just because she's down. I'd have you respect your elders, young man."

"Well, Missy, excuse me." Doctor Harry patted her cheek. "But I've got to warn you, haven't I? You're a marvel, but you must be careful or you're going to be good and sorry."

"Don't tell me what I'm going to be. I'm on my feet now, morally speaking. It's Cornelia. I had to go to bed to get rid of her."

Her bones felt loose, and floated around in her skin, and Doctor Harry floated like a balloon around the foot of the bed. He floated and pulled down his waistcoat and swung his glasses on a cord. "Well, stay where you are, it certainly can't hurt you."

A STREAM OF CONSCIOUSNESS
In lines 1–4, how does Porter create the effect that you, the reader, are "inside" Granny's mind? Explain how your intimacy with this character affects your impression of her.

Analyze Visuals ▶
What does this unusual portrait suggest about its subject's thoughts or state of mind? Explain, citing details.

1. **knee breeches:** short pants formerly worn by young boys.

HAYES

"Get along and doctor your sick," said Granny Weatherall. "Leave a well woman alone. I'll call for you when I want you. . . . Where were you forty years ago when I pulled through milk-leg[2] and double pneumonia? You weren't even born. Don't let Cornelia lead you on," she shouted, because Doctor Harry appeared to float up to the ceiling and out. "I pay my own bills, and I don't throw my money away on nonsense!"

She meant to wave good-by, but it was too much trouble. Her eyes closed of themselves, it was like a dark curtain drawn around the bed. The pillow rose and floated under her, pleasant as a hammock in a light wind. She listened to the leaves rustling outside the window. No, somebody was swishing newspapers: no, Cornelia and Doctor Harry were whispering together. She leaped broad awake, thinking they whispered in her ear. **B**

B STREAM OF CONSCIOUSNESS
What insight do lines 25–30 give you into Granny Weatherall's character? What do they tell you about her physical condition?

"She was never like this, *never* like this!" "Well, what can we expect?" "Yes, eighty years old. . . ."

Well, and what if she was? She still had ears. It was like Cornelia to whisper around doors. She always kept things secret in such a public way. She was always being tactful and kind. Cornelia was dutiful; that was the trouble with her. Dutiful and good: "So good and dutiful," said Granny, "that I'd like to spank her." She saw herself spanking Cornelia and making a fine job of it.

"What'd you say, Mother?"

Granny felt her face tying up in hard knots.

"Can't a body think, I'd like to know?"

"I thought you might want something."

"I do. I want a lot of things. First off, go away and don't whisper."

She lay and drowsed, hoping in her sleep that the children would keep out and let her rest a minute. It had been a long day. Not that she was tired. It was always pleasant to snatch a minute now and then. There was always so much to be done, let me see: tomorrow.

Language Coach

Word Definitions
Drowsed (line 43) means "slept lightly." Why is *drowsed* more effective than *slept* would be?

Tomorrow was far away and there was nothing to trouble about. Things were finished somehow when the time came; thank God there was always a little margin over for peace: then a person could spread out the plan of life and tuck in the edges orderly. It was good to have everything clean and folded away, with the hair brushes and tonic bottles sitting straight on the white **embroidered** linen: the day started without fuss and the pantry shelves laid out with rows of jelly glasses and brown jugs and white stone-china jars with blue whirligigs[3] and words painted on them: coffee, tea, sugar, ginger, cinnamon, allspice: and the bronze clock with the lion on top nicely dusted off. The dust that lion could collect in twenty-four hours! The box in the attic with all those letters tied up, well, she'd have to go through that tomorrow. All those letters—George's letters and John's letters and her letters to them both—lying around for the children to find afterwards made her uneasy. Yes, that would be tomorrow's business. No use to let them know how silly she had been once.

embroidered
(ĕm'broi'dərd) *adj.* decorated with stitched designs **embroider** *v.*

2. **milk-leg:** a painful swelling of the leg experienced by some women after giving birth.
3. **stone-china . . . whirligigs** (hwûr'lĭ-gĭgz'): jars made of thick pottery with blue spiral designs.

While she was rummaging around she found death in her mind and it felt clammy and unfamiliar. She had spent so much time preparing for death there was no need for bringing it up again. Let it take care of itself now. When she was sixty she had felt very old, finished, and went around making farewell trips to see her children and grandchildren, with a secret in her mind: This is the very last of your mother, children! Then she made her will and came down with a long fever. That was all just a notion like a lot of other things, but it was lucky too, for she had once for all got over the idea of dying for a long time. Now she couldn't be worried. She hoped she had better sense now. Her father had lived to be one hundred and two years old and had drunk a noggin of strong hot toddy[4] on his last birthday. He told the reporters it was his daily habit, and he owed his long life to that. He had made quite a scandal and was very pleased about it. She believed she'd just **plague** Cornelia a little. **C**

"Cornelia! Cornelia!" No footsteps, but a sudden hand on her cheek. "Bless you, where have you been?"

"Here, Mother."

"Well, Cornelia, I want a noggin of hot toddy." **D**

"Are you cold, darling?"

"I'm chilly, Cornelia. Lying in bed stops the circulation. I must have told you that a thousand times."

Well, she could just hear Cornelia telling her husband that Mother was getting a little childish and they'd have to humor her. The thing that most annoyed her was that Cornelia thought she was deaf, dumb, and blind. Little hasty glances and tiny gestures tossed around her and over her head saying, "Don't cross her, let her have her way, she's eighty years old," and she sitting there as if she lived in a thin glass cage. Sometimes Granny almost made up her mind to pack up and move back to her own house where nobody could remind her every minute that she was old. Wait, wait, Cornelia, till your own children whisper behind your back!

In her day she had kept a better house and had got more work done. She wasn't too old yet for Lydia to be driving eighty miles for advice when one of the children jumped the track, and Jimmy still dropped in and talked things over: "Now, Mammy, you've a good business head, I want to know what you think of this? . . ." Old. Cornelia couldn't change the furniture around without asking. Little things, little things! They had been so sweet when they were little. Granny wished the old days were back again with the children young and everything to be done over. It had been a hard pull, but not too much for her. When she thought of all the food she had cooked, and all the clothes she had cut and sewed, and all the gardens she had made—well, the children showed it. There they were, made out of her, and they couldn't get away from that. Sometimes she wanted to see John again and point to them and say, Well, I didn't do so badly, did I? But that would have to wait. That was for tomorrow. She used to think of him as a man, but now all the children were older than their father, and he would be a child beside her if she saw him now. It seemed strange and there was something wrong in the idea. Why, he couldn't possibly recognize her. She had fenced in a hundred

plague (plāg) *v.* to annoy; harass

C STREAM OF CONSCIOUSNESS
Reread lines 47–73 and consider how Porter conveys the flow of Granny's thoughts. What idea triggers Granny's thoughts of death?

D CLARIFY SEQUENCE
Reread lines 61–77. Identify clues about the timing of Granny's father's "scandal" and subsequent death. What connection do you see between this memory and Granny's desire to "plague" Cornelia?

Language Coach

Word Definitions *Hard pull* (line 96) means "lengthy effort or struggle." Read lines 94–98. What caused the hard pull?

4. **noggin . . . toddy:** mug of a strong alcoholic drink.

acres once, digging the post holes herself and clamping the wires with just a negro boy to help. That changed a woman. John would be looking for a young woman with the peaked Spanish comb in her hair and the painted fan. Digging post holes changed a woman. Riding country roads in the winter when women had their babies was another thing: sitting up nights with sick horses and sick negroes and sick children and hardly ever losing one. John, I hardly ever lost one of them! John would see that in a minute, that would be something he could understand, she wouldn't have to explain anything! **E**

It made her feel like rolling up her sleeves and putting the whole place to rights again. No matter if Cornelia was determined to be everywhere at once, there were a great many things left undone on this place. She would start tomorrow and do them. It was good to be strong enough for everything, even if all you made melted and changed and slipped under your hands, so that by the time you finished you almost forgot what you were working for. What was it I set out to do? she asked herself intently, but she could not remember. A fog rose over the valley, she saw it marching across the creek swallowing the trees and moving up the hill like an army of ghosts. Soon it would be at the near edge of the orchard, and then it was time to go in and light the lamps. Come in, children, don't stay out in the night air.

Lighting the lamps had been beautiful. The children huddled up to her and breathed like little calves waiting at the bars in the twilight. Their eyes followed the match and watched the flame rise and settle in a blue curve, then they moved away from her. The lamp was lit, they didn't have to be scared and hang on to mother any more. Never, never, never more. God, for all my life I thank Thee. Without Thee, my God, I could never have done it. Hail, Mary, full of grace.[5]

I want you to pick all the fruit this year and see that nothing is wasted. There's always someone who can use it. Don't let good things rot for want of using. You waste life when you waste good food. Don't let things get lost. It's bitter to lose things. Now, don't let me get to thinking, not when I am tired and taking a little nap before supper. . . .

The pillow rose about her shoulders and pressed against her heart and the memory was being squeezed out of it: oh, push down the pillow, somebody: it would smother her if she tried to hold it. Such a fresh breeze blowing and such a green day with no threats in it. But he had not come, just the same. What does a woman do when she has put on the white veil and set out the white cake for a man and he doesn't come? She tried to remember. No, I swear he never harmed me but in that. He never harmed me but in that . . . and what if he did? There was the day, the day, but a whirl of dark smoke rose and covered it, crept up and over into the bright field where everything was planted so carefully in orderly rows. That was hell, she knew hell when she saw it. For sixty years she had prayed against remembering him and against losing her soul in the deep pit of hell, and now the two things were mingled in one and the thought of him was a smoky cloud from hell that moved and crept in her head when she had just got rid of Doctor Harry and was trying to rest a minute. Wounded vanity, Ellen, said a **F** sharp voice in the top of her mind. Don't let your wounded vanity get the upper

E **CLARIFY SEQUENCE**
Why does Granny say that today, John would be a child compared to her? Record on your timeline the information you learn in this paragraph.

F **GRAMMAR AND STYLE**
Reread lines 143–147. Porter uses **repetition** as well as short clauses joined by the **coordinating conjunction** *and* to present the circular nature of Granny's thoughts.

5. **Hail . . . grace:** the beginning of a Roman Catholic prayer to the Virgin Mary.

hand of you. Plenty of girls get jilted. You were jilted, weren't you? Then stand up to it. Her eyelids wavered and let in streamers of blue-gray light like tissue paper over her eyes. She must get up and pull the shades down or she'd never sleep. She was in bed again and the shades were not down. How could that happen? Better turn over, hide from the light, sleeping in the light gave you nightmares. "Mother, how do you feel now?" and a stinging wetness on her forehead. But I don't like having my face washed in cold water! G

Hapsy? George? Lydia? Jimmy? No, Cornelia, and her features were swollen and full of little puddles. "They're coming, darling, they'll all be here soon." Go wash your face, child, you look funny.

Instead of obeying, Cornelia knelt down and put her head on the pillow. She seemed to be talking but there was no sound. "Well, are you tongue-tied? Whose birthday is it? Are you going to give a party?"

Cornelia's mouth moved urgently in strange shapes. "Don't do that, you bother me, daughter."

"Oh, no, Mother. Oh, no. . . ."

Nonsense. It was strange about children. They disputed your every word. "No what, Cornelia?"

"Here's Doctor Harry."

"I won't see that boy again. He just left five minutes ago."

"That was this morning, Mother. It's night now. Here's the nurse." H

"This is Doctor Harry, Mrs. Weatherall. I never saw you look so young and happy!"

"Ah, I'll never be young again—but I'd be happy if they'd let me lie in peace and get rested."

She thought she spoke up loudly, but no one answered. A warm weight on her forehead, a warm bracelet on her wrist, and a breeze went on whispering, trying to tell her something. A shuffle of leaves in the everlasting hand of God, He blew on them and they danced and rattled. "Mother, don't mind, we're going to give you a little hypodermic."[6] "Look here, daughter, how do ants get in this bed? I saw sugar ants yesterday." Did you send for Hapsy too?

It was Hapsy she really wanted. She had to go a long way back through a great many rooms to find Hapsy standing with a baby on her arm. She seemed to herself to be Hapsy also, and the baby on Hapsy's arm was Hapsy and himself and herself, all at once, and there was no surprise in the meeting. Then Hapsy melted from within and turned flimsy as gray gauze and the baby was a gauzy shadow, and Hapsy came up close and said, "I thought you'd never come," and looked at her very searchingly and said, "You haven't changed a bit!" They leaned forward to kiss, when Cornelia began whispering from a long way off, "Oh, is there anything you want to tell me? Is there anything I can do for you?"

Yes, she had changed her mind after sixty years and she would like to see George. I want you to find George. Find him and be sure to tell him I forgot him. I want him to know I had my husband just the same and my children and my house like any other woman. A good house too and a good husband that I

6. **hypodermic:** injection.

G **STREAM OF CONSCIOUSNESS**
Describe the major event revealed by Granny's thoughts in lines 134–155. Based on the title of the story, what significance do these details reveal about the plot?

H **STREAM OF CONSCIOUSNESS**
What clues in lines 156–169 reveal to readers how much Granny's condition is deteriorating?

Language Coach

Idioms An **idiom** is an expression whose overall meaning is different from the meaning of the individual words. The idiom *just the same* (line 191) means "in spite of what happened before." What is Granny saying in lines 190–192?

loved and fine children out of him. Better than I hoped for even. Tell him I was given back everything he took away and more. Oh, no, oh, God, no, there was something else besides the house and the man and the children. Oh, surely they were not all? What was it? Something not given back. . . . Her breath crowded down under her ribs and grew into a monstrous frightening shape with cutting edges; it bored up into her head, and the agony was unbelievable: Yes, John, get the Doctor now, no more talk, my time has come.

When this one was born it should be the last. The last. It should have been born first, for it was the one she had truly wanted. Everything came in good time. Nothing left out, left over. She was strong, in three days she would be as well as ever. Better. A woman needed milk in her to have her full health. **I**

I STREAM OF CONSCIOUSNESS
Reread lines 189–203. What has Granny decided about George? Trace the path of her thoughts from this decision to the memory of the birth of her child.

"Mother, do you hear me?"

"I've been telling you—"

"Mother, Father Connolly's here."

"I went to Holy Communion only last week. Tell him I'm not so sinful as all that."

"Father just wants to speak to you."

He could speak as much as he pleased. It was like him to drop in and inquire about her soul as if it were a teething baby, and then stay on for a cup of tea and a round of cards and gossip. He always had a funny story of some sort, usually about an Irishman who made his little mistakes and confessed them, and the point lay in some absurd thing he would blurt out in the confessional showing his struggles between native piety and original sin. Granny felt easy about her soul. Cornelia, where are your manners? Give Father Connolly a chair. She had her secret comfortable understanding with a few favorite saints who cleared a straight road to God for her. All as surely signed and sealed as the papers for the new Forty Acres. Forever . . . heirs and **assigns** forever. Since the day the wedding cake was not cut, but thrown out and wasted. The whole bottom dropped out of the world, and there she was blind and sweating with nothing under her feet and the walls falling away. His hand had caught her under the breast, she had not fallen, there was the freshly polished floor with the green rug on it, just as before. He had cursed like a sailor's parrot and said, "I'll kill him for you." Don't lay a hand on him, for my sake leave something to God. "Now, Ellen, you must believe what I tell you. . . ."

assign (ə-sīn') *n.* a person to whom property is transferred in a will or other legal document

So there was nothing, nothing to worry about any more, except sometimes in the night one of the children screamed in a nightmare, and they both hustled out shaking and hunting for the matches and calling, "There, wait a minute, here we are!" John, get the doctor now, Hapsy's time has come. But there was Hapsy standing by the bed in a white cap. "Cornelia, tell Hapsy to take off her cap. I can't see her plain."

Her eyes opened very wide and the room stood out like a picture she had seen somewhere. Dark colors with the shadows rising towards the ceiling in long angles. The tall black dresser gleamed with nothing on it but John's picture, enlarged from a little one, with John's eyes very black when they should have been blue. You never saw him, so how do you know how he looked? But the man insisted the copy was perfect, it was very rich and handsome. For a picture, yes, but it's not my husband. The table by the bed had a linen cover and a candle and a crucifix.[7] The light was blue from Cornelia's silk lampshades. No sort of light at all, just frippery. You had to live forty years with kerosene lamps to appreciate honest electricity. She felt very strong and she saw Doctor Harry with a rosy nimbus[8] around him.

"You look like a saint, Doctor Harry, and I vow that's as near as you'll ever come to it."

"She's saying something."

"I heard you, Cornelia. What's all this carrying-on?"

"Father Connolly's saying—"

Cornelia's voice staggered and bumped like a cart in a bad road. It rounded corners and turned back again and arrived nowhere. Granny stepped up in the cart very lightly and reached for the reins, but a man sat beside her and she knew him by his hands, driving the cart. She did not look in his face, for she knew without seeing, but looked instead down the road where the trees leaned over and bowed to each other and a thousand birds were singing a Mass. She felt like singing too, but she put her hand in the bosom of her dress and pulled out a rosary,[9] and Father Connolly murmured Latin in a very solemn voice and tickled her feet. My God, will you stop that nonsense? I'm a married woman. What if he did run away and leave me to face the priest by myself? I found another a whole world better. I wouldn't have exchanged my husband for anybody except St. Michael himself, and you may tell him that for me with a thank you in the bargain.

Light flashed on her closed eyelids, and a deep roaring shook her. Cornelia, is that lightning? I hear thunder. There's going to be a storm. Close all the windows. Call the children in. . . . "Mother, here we are, all of us." "Is that you, Hapsy?" "Oh, no, I'm Lydia. We drove as fast as we could." Their faces drifted above her, drifted away. The rosary fell out of her hands and Lydia put it back. Jimmy tried to help, their hands fumbled together, and Granny closed two fingers around Jimmy's thumb. Beads wouldn't do, it must be something alive. She was so amazed her thoughts ran round and round. So, my dear Lord, this is my death and I wasn't even thinking about it. My children have come to see me die. But I can't, it's not time. Oh, I always hated surprises. I wanted to give Cornelia the **amethyst** set—Cornelia, you're to have the amethyst set, but Hapsy's to wear it when she wants, and, Doctor Harry, do shut up. Nobody sent for you. Oh, my dear Lord, do wait a minute. I meant to do something about the Forty Acres, Jimmy doesn't need it and Lydia will later on, with that worthless husband of hers. I meant to finish the altar cloth and send six bottles of wine to Sister Borgia for her dyspepsia.[10] I want to send six bottles of wine to Sister Borgia, Father Connolly, now don't let me forget.

amethyst (ăm'ə-thĭst) *n.* a purple-colored quartz used as a gemstone

Cornelia's voice made short turns and tilted over and crashed. "Oh, Mother, oh, Mother, oh, Mother. . . ."

---

7. **crucifix** (kro͞o'sə-fĭks'): a cross bearing a sculptured representation of the crucified Christ.
8. **nimbus** (nĭm'bəs): halo of light.
9. **rosary** (rō'zə-rē): a string of beads used by Roman Catholics to count their prayers.
10. **dyspepsia** (dĭs-pĕp'shə): indigestion.

Blue House (2004), Philip Hershberger. Encaustic on panel, 78″ × 48″. © Philip Hershberger.

"I'm not going, Cornelia. I'm taken by surprise. I can't go." J

You'll see Hapsy again. What about her? "I thought you'd never come." Granny made a long journey outward, looking for Hapsy. What if I don't find her? What then? Her heart sank down and down, there was no bottom to death, she couldn't come to the end of it. The blue light from Cornelia's lampshade drew into a tiny point in the center of her brain, it flickered and winked like an eye, quietly it fluttered and **dwindled.** Granny lay curled down within herself, amazed and watchful, staring at the point of light that was herself; her body was now only a deeper mass of shadow in an endless darkness and this darkness would curl around the light and swallow it up. God, give a sign!

For the second time there was no sign. Again no bridegroom and the priest in the house. She could not remember any other sorrow because this grief wiped them all away. Oh, no, there's nothing more cruel than this—I'll never forgive it. She stretched herself with a deep breath and blew out the light.

J STREAM OF CONSCIOUSNESS
Reread lines 266–279. What is **ironic** about Granny's response to the imminence of her death?

dwindle (dwĭn′dl) *v.* to become steadily less; to shrink

Comprehension

1. **Recall** Which characters mentioned in the story belong exclusively to Granny Weatherall's past?
2. **Recall** Who is with Granny when she dies?
3. **Clarify** Who is Hapsy?

Text Analysis

4. **Clarify Sequence** Using your timeline, retell the key events of Granny's life in chronological order. Which events mark the best and worst of Granny's life? Explain, citing Granny's own thoughts and feelings about each event.
5. **Make Inferences About Character** Go back through the story, noting thoughts and **memories** that linger in Granny's mind. What do they reveal about the kind of person she is? Record your answers in a chart like this one.

Granny's Thoughts	Character Traits Revealed
"It was good to have everything clean and folded away . . . nicely dusted off." (lines 50–55)	She likes putting things in order and having control in life.

6. **Analyze Stream of Consciousness** Porter uses stream of consciousness to dramatize Granny's interior life. What effect does this approach have on her readers? For example, how might your reaction to the story have been different if Porter had presented the same events with a more traditional plot? Cite specific examples from the story in your response.
7. **Analyze Theme** Which of the following statements best expresses the themes Porter conveys in this story? Support your choice with evidence from the text.
   - There is no deed so wrong it can't be forgiven.
   - In youth we are all foolish; with age comes true wisdom.
   - Life does not provide the answers or reassurances that people want, even at the moment of death.

Text Criticism

8. **Critical Interpretations** Novelist Reynolds Price asserts that Porter's stories are "lethal to the most widely cherished illusions of the species"—in other words, they destroy our sentimental notions about things like romance, self-regard, and parenthood. What "cherished illusions" does Porter destroy here? What truths does she portray instead? Support your answer.

COMMON CORE

RL 1 Cite textual evidence to support analysis of what the text says explicitly as well as inferences drawn from the text. **RL 3** Analyze the impact of the author's choices regarding how to develop and relate elements of a story. **RL 5** Analyze how an author's choices concerning how to structure specific parts of a text contribute to its overall structure and meaning as well as its aesthetic impact.

What makes a MEMORY *linger?*

Much like Granny in this story, we often remember things differently from how they actually happened . After all, memories are what people remember—not necessarily the truth. Why do you think this discrepancy between reality and memories happens?

Vocabulary in Context

▲ VOCABULARY PRACTICE

Decide whether each statement is true or false.

1. If your supplies have begun to **dwindle,** you probably need to find a way to get more.
2. An **amethyst** is a special shawl worn for good luck.
3. A tablecloth that is **embroidered** has beautiful designs painted on it.
4. If I am an **assign** in your will, I should expect to inherit at least a portion of what you have.
5. People who **plague** others are transmitting symptoms of a serious disease.

WORD LIST
amethyst
assign
dwindle
embroidered
plague

ACADEMIC VOCABULARY IN SPEAKING

• conclude • criteria • despite • justify • maintain

Granny Weatherall tries unsuccessfully to **maintain** some kind of control, but readers easily **conclude** that she has lost her grip on reality. In a small group, discuss the **criteria** by which you judge this character's sanity. Use at least one Academic Vocabulary word in your contribution to the discussion.

VOCABULARY STRATEGY: THESAURI AND WORD CHOICE

When you need to choose the most appropriate word from two or more words with similar meanings, you can turn to a thesaurus. A **thesaurus** is a reference book that helps you find specific, or precise, words for more general ideas. In a thesaurus, words are arranged by their meanings and by their parts of speech rather than by alphabetical order, as in a dictionary. For example, if the vocabulary word *dwindle* doesn't have the exact meaning you are looking for, a thesaurus can help you choose among such verbs as *recede, diminish,* or *shrink.*

COMMON CORE

L 4c Consult general and specialized reference materials, both print and digital, to determine or clarify a word's precise meaning and its part of speech. **L 5b** Analyze nuances in the meaning of words with similar denotations.

PRACTICE Use a thesaurus to choose an alternative word to replace each of the words in boldface. Explain how each new word changes the meaning of the sentence.

1. Ben **peppered** his explanation with "unbelievable!" and other expressions of surprise.
2. Despite their **refusal** to help her, Pauline harbored no ill will toward her brothers.
3. Through hard work and clever planning, they **engineered** an election victory for the underdog candidate.
4. These **conclusions** are anchored in several months of experimentation and solid research.

Language

COMMON CORE

L 3a Vary syntax for effect, consulting references for guidance as needed; apply an understanding of syntax to the study of complex texts when reading. **W 3** Write narratives to develop real or imagined experiences or events using effective technique, well-chosen details, and well-structured event sequences.

GRAMMAR AND STYLE: Craft Effective Sentences

Review the **Grammar and Style** note on page 1040. Porter skillfully crafts her prose in "The Jilting of Granny Weatherall" to depict Granny's interior life—her secret longings, wishes, and memories. Through her use of **repetition** and the **coordinating conjunction** *and,* Porter reveals Granny's circular thoughts and hazy memories.

> *Then Hapsy melted from within and turned flimsy as gray gauze and the baby was a gauzy shadow, and Hapsy came up close and said, "I thought you'd never come," and looked at her very searchingly and said, "You haven't changed a bit!"* (lines 183–186)

Notice the dreamlike quality of the sentence, with its many *and*'s linking the images as well as its repetition of *gauze* and *gauzy* and related terms *flimsy* and *shadow.*

PRACTICE The following passage presents a character's thoughts as they might appear in a traditional third-person narrative. Rewrite the paragraph as a third-person stream of consciousness.

Ron walked down the street whistling, his hands shoved deep into his pockets. He squinted up at the weak rays fighting to break through the winter cloud cover. When his gaze returned to street level, he almost tripped over his own feet. Abby was walking toward him.

"I wonder if she'll even recognize me," Ron thought to himself, quickening his pace and trying to clear his face of emotion.

READING-WRITING CONNECTION

YOUR TURN

Expand your understanding of "The Jilting of Granny Weatherall" by responding to this prompt. Then, use the **revising tips** to improve your narrative.

WRITING PROMPT	REVISING TIPS
USE STREAM OF CONSCIOUSNESS Katherine Anne Porter wasn't the only modernist to experiment with stream of consciousness; T. S. Eliot, James Joyce, and William Faulkner all used it to explore the intricacies of the human mind. Some writers use it today. Now you'll get a chance to try it for yourself. Write a **three- or four-paragraph narrative** in stream of consciousness, depicting the thoughts and impressions of a character having a particular experience. You can either write about yourself or create a fictional character.	• Include details of time and place as part of your character's consciousness. • Focus on your character's thoughts but include spoken words in quotation marks, too. • Use images from both the past and the present to show how your character sees what is happening now and what has happened in the past.

A Worn Path

Short Story by Eudora Welty

COMMON CORE

RL 2 Determine two or more themes or central ideas of a text and analyze their development over the course of the text, including how they interact and build on one another to produce a complex account; provide an objective summary of the text. **RL 10** Read and comprehend literature, including stories. **L 4b** Identify and correctly use patterns of word changes that indicate different meanings.

DID YOU KNOW?

Eudora Welty . . .

- was voted "Best All-Round Girl" in high school.
- was awarded the Presidential Medal of Freedom in 1980.
- inspired the name of an e-mail program, "Eudora," so named by a Web designer who loved her stories.

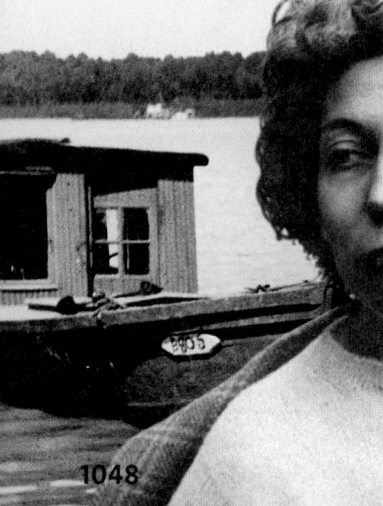

Meet the Author

Eudora Welty 1909–2001

Mississippi born and bred, Eudora Welty wrote about her fellow Southerners at a crucial time in U.S. history. When she first began publishing her stories in the late 1930s, vestiges of the Old South still colored daily life. But Welty lived long enough to see the changes wrought by the civil rights movement in the 1960s and the rise of the New South on the eve of the new millennium. All the while, she recorded the lives of ordinary people, depicting the family life that sustained them and the small acts of heroism that dignified them. She was a modernist who believed in love, a Southerner who had faith in tolerance and change, and a successful, unmarried woman at a time when single women in Mississippi were not allowed to buy a house. At first dismissed as a regionalist and even a "feminine" writer, Welty lived long enough to see her fiction recognized for its artistic vision and universal appeal. Through it all, she accepted the changes with her characteristic sense of humor, modesty, and grace.

A Photographer's Eye Nourished by books and a close-knit community of family and friends, Welty lived most of her life in the house her father built in Jackson, Mississippi. Although she wrote stories even in childhood and attended college, her education as a writer didn't seriously begin until 1933, when she landed a job as a publicity agent with the federal government's Works Progress Administration (WPA). Interviewing and photographing all kinds of people throughout Mississippi during the Great Depression—one of the most impoverished regions during the poorest time in the nation's history—was an eye opener for Welty and gave her the first "real germ" of her writing. Her early stories, such as "Why I Live at the P.O." and "A Worn Path," are like photographs, capturing a specific moment that reveals something significant about a person and at the same time a greater truth about the human condition.

A Long, Productive Life Welty received numerous awards and honors for her works, including a Pulitzer Prize for her novel *The Optimist's Daughter* (1972) and an O. Henry Award for "A Worn Path." Her award-winning memoir, *One Writer's Beginnings* (1984), was a runaway bestseller. Despite being very articulate about her writing, sitting graciously through countless interviews, and receiving large numbers of young fans at her home, Welty remained a very private person who always maintained that "a fiction writer should let writing speak for itself."

Author Online THINK central

Go to thinkcentral.com. KEYWORD: HML11-1048

TEXT ANALYSIS: UNIVERSAL THEME

You know that theme is the underlying message a writer wants readers to understand. A **universal theme** is a message that can be found throughout literature of all times and places. Works that convey a universal theme often contain **archetypes**—basic patterns found in a variety of works from different cultures throughout history. The perilous journey is one such archetype; the main character in this story travels a long and uncertain path in search of something.

As you read, consider what this journey might symbolize. Think about the main character's traits and how she deals with obstacles on the path, as well as the story's title and its setting. Taken together, what universal theme do these elements suggest?

READING STRATEGY: MONITOR COMPREHENSION

This story has a dreamlike quality that can make it challenging to follow. **Monitoring** is the strategy of checking your comprehension as you are reading and using techniques such as **questioning** and **clarifying** to aid your understanding. As you read, stop every once in a while to consider how well you are comprehending the story. Jot down any questions that come to mind. Review what you do understand and use context clues and analysis of key words and details to clarify the meaning of anything you don't.

Question:
If Phoenix is alone on her journey, why does she keep speaking aloud?
Clarification:

VOCABULARY IN CONTEXT

Welty uses the boldfaced words in her story of one woman's pilgrimage. Replace each boldfaced word with a new word or phrase.

1. **Limber** branches swayed back and forth in the breeze.
2. She gazed at the **radiation** of ripples each raindrop created on the pond's surface.
3. He could not shake his **obstinate** cough.
4. The **meditative** hiker gazed at the sky.

Complete the activities in your **Reader/Writer Notebook**.

What keeps us GOING?

Endurance is crucial in any long-distance sport, and it's a necessity for surviving harsh conditions or extreme adventures. But what kind of endurance is required for daily life? And where does this type of endurance come from?

DISCUSS With a small group of classmates, discuss the preceding questions. Begin by talking about what you think motivates champion athletes or people facing extreme conditions. Then consider what motivates ordinary people to endure—to keep attending night school while working two day jobs, for example, or to sacrifice a favorite after school activity in order to drive younger siblings to theirs. In your opinion, is the motivation the same in both the extreme and the ordinary cases? If not, what's the difference?

A Worn Path

Eudora Welty

BACKGROUND This story takes place in rural Mississippi in the 1930s, an era in which segregation laws and racism, combined with the economic devastation of the Great Depression, restricted most Southern blacks to lives of rural poverty and hardship. Eudora Welty saw the need and inequality surrounding her. She based this story on an old woman she observed crossing a field: "I thought, she is bent on an errand. And I know it isn't for herself. It was just the look of her figure. . . . She was a black woman. But then I suppose it would be more likely to be a black woman who would be in such desperate need and live so remotely away from help and who would have so far to go."

Analyze Visuals ▶
What thematic ideas might you ascribe to this painting? Identify the elements of the painting that suggest these ideas.

It was December—a bright frozen day in the early morning. Far out in the country there was an old Negro woman with her head tied in a red rag, coming along a path through the pinewoods. Her name was Phoenix Jackson. She was very old and small and she walked slowly in the dark pine shadows, moving a little from side to side in her steps, with the balanced heaviness and lightness of a pendulum in a grandfather clock. She carried a thin, small cane made from an umbrella, and with this she kept tapping the frozen earth in front of her. This made a grave and persistent noise in the still air, that seemed **meditative** like the chirping of a solitary little bird. Ⓐ

meditative (mĕd'ĭ-tā'tĭv) *adj.* engaged in serious thought or reflection

Ⓐ **UNIVERSAL THEME**
What details in lines 1–9 suggest that Phoenix is in for a long journey? As you read, keep in mind other **archetypal** journeys you know of.

Brooding Silence (date unknown), John Fabian Carlson. Smithsonian American Art Museum, Washington, D.C. © Smithsonian American Art Museum, Washington, D.C./Art Resource, New York.

She wore a dark striped dress reaching down to her shoe tops, and an equally long apron of bleached sugar sacks, with a full pocket: all neat and tidy, but every time she took a step she might have fallen over her shoelaces, which dragged from her unlaced shoes. She looked straight ahead. Her eyes were blue with age. Her skin had a pattern all its own of numberless branching wrinkles and as though a whole little tree stood in the middle of her forehead, but a golden color ran underneath, and the two knobs of her cheeks were illumined by a yellow burning under the dark. Under the red rag her hair came down on her neck in the frailest of ringlets, still black, and with an odor like copper.

Now and then there was a quivering in the thicket. Old Phoenix said, "Out of my way, all you foxes, owls, beetles, jack rabbits, coons and wild animals! . . . Keep out from under these feet, little bob-whites.[1] . . . Keep the big wild hogs out of my path. Don't let none of those come running my direction. I got a long way." Under her small black-freckled hand her cane, **limber** as a buggy whip, would switch at the brush as if to rouse up any hiding things.

On she went. The woods were deep and still. The sun made the pine needles almost too bright to look at, up where the wind rocked. The cones dropped as light as feathers. Down in the hollow was the mourning dove—it was not too late for him.

The path ran up a hill. "Seem like there is chains about my feet, time I get this far," she said, in the voice of argument old people keep to use with themselves. "Something always take a hold of me on this hill—pleads I should stay."

After she got to the top she turned and gave a full, severe look behind her where she had come. "Up through pines," she said at length. "Now down through oaks."

Her eyes opened their widest, and she started down gently. But before she got to the bottom of the hill a bush caught her dress.

Her fingers were busy and intent, but her skirts were full and long, so that before she could pull them free in one place they were caught in another. It was not possible to allow the dress to tear. "I in the thorny bush," she said. "Thorns, you doing your appointed work. Never want to let folks pass, no sir. Old eyes thought you was a pretty little *green* bush."

Finally, trembling all over, she stood free, and after a moment dared to stoop for her cane.

"Sun so high!" she cried, leaning back and looking, while the thick tears went over her eyes. "The time getting all gone here." **B**

At the foot of this hill was a place where a log was laid across the creek.

"Now comes the trial," said Phoenix.

Putting her right foot out, she mounted the log and shut her eyes. Lifting her skirt, leveling her cane fiercely before her, like a festival figure in some parade, she began to march across. Then she opened her eyes and she was safe on the other side.

"I wasn't as old as I thought," she said.

COMMON CORE L 4b

Language Coach

Suffixes A suffix is a word part that appears at the end of a root or base word to form a new word. The suffix *–let* means "small." Words with *–let* include *booklet, droplet,* and *owlet.* What does *ringlet* (line 18) mean?

limber (lĭm′bər) *adj.* bending or moving easily; supple

B UNIVERSAL THEME
Reread lines 34–44 and explain what you think the thorny bush might **symbolize.** What does Phoenix's way of dealing with this obstacle suggest about her character?

1. **bob-whites:** game birds that are a type of quail.

But she sat down to rest. She spread her skirts on the bank around her and folded her hands over her knees. Up above her was a tree in a pearly cloud of mistletoe. She did not dare to close her eyes, and when a little boy brought her a plate with a slice of marble-cake on it she spoke to him. "That would be acceptable," she said. But when she went to take it there was just her own hand in the air. **C**

So she left that tree, and had to go through a barbed-wire fence. There she had to creep and crawl, spreading her knees and stretching her fingers like a baby trying to climb the steps. But she talked loudly to herself: she could not let her dress be torn now, so late in the day, and she could not pay for having her arm or her leg sawed off if she got caught fast where she was.

At last she was safe through the fence and risen up out in the clearing. Big dead trees, like black men with one arm, were standing in the purple stalks of the withered cotton field. There sat a buzzard. **D**

"Who you watching?"

In the furrow she made her way along.

"Glad this not the season for bulls," she said, looking sideways, "and the good Lord made his snakes to curl up and sleep in the winter. A pleasure I don't see no two-headed snake coming around that tree, where it come once. It took a while to get by him, back in the summer."

She passed through the old cotton and went into a field of dead corn. It whispered and shook and was taller than her head. "Through the maze now," she said, for there was no path. **E**

Then there was something tall, black, and skinny there, moving before her.

At first she took it for a man. It could have been a man dancing in the field. But she stood still and listened, and it did not make a sound. It was as silent as a ghost.

"Ghost," she said sharply, "who be you the ghost of? For I have heard of nary[2] death close by."

But there was no answer—only the ragged dancing in the wind.

She shut her eyes, reached out her hand, and touched a sleeve. She found a coat and inside that an emptiness, cold as ice.

"You scarecrow," she said. Her face lighted. "I ought to be shut up for good," she said with laughter. "My senses is gone. I too old. I the oldest people I ever know. Dance, old scarecrow," she said, "while I dancing with you."

She kicked her foot over the furrow, and with mouth drawn down, shook her head once or twice in a little strutting way. Some husks blew down and whirled in streamers about her skirts.

Then she went on, parting her way from side to side with the cane, through the whispering field. At last she came to the end, to a wagon track where the silver grass blew between the red ruts. The quail were walking around like pullets,[3] seeming all dainty and unseen.

C MONITOR
Reread lines 51–56. What is happening in these lines? **Clarify** the meaning by considering the trials Phoenix has faced thus far, as well as how she feels at this point in her journey.

D UNIVERSAL THEME
Examine the images in lines 62–64. What **mood** do they help create? Explain.

E GRAMMAR AND STYLE
Welty uses a variety of sensory **details** to make Phoenix's journey riveting for readers. Reread lines 71–73, noting how the **verbs** *whispered* and *shook* conjure sights and sounds in your mind.

---

2. **nary:** not any.
3. **pullets:** young hens.

Snowy Woods at Dusk (date unknown), Dennis Sheehan. Oil, 20″ × 16″. Courtesy of Susan Powell Fine Art, Madison, Connecticut.

"Walk pretty," she said. "This the easy place. This the easy going." F

She followed the track, swaying through the quiet bare fields, through the little strings of trees silver in their dead leaves, past cabins silver from weather, with the doors and windows boarded shut, all like old women under a spell sitting there. "I walking in their sleep," she said, nodding her head vigorously.

In a ravine she went where a spring was silently flowing through a hollow log. Old Phoenix bent and drank. "Sweet-gum[4] makes the water sweet," she said, and drank more. "Nobody know who made this well, for it was here when I was born."

The track crossed a swampy part where the moss hung as white as lace from every limb. "Sleep on, alligators, and blow your bubbles." Then the track went into the road.

Deep, deep the road went down between the high green-colored banks. Overhead the live-oaks[5] met, and it was as dark as a cave.

A black dog with a lolling tongue came up out of the weeds by the ditch. She was meditating, and not ready, and when he came at her she only hit him a little with her cane. Over she went in the ditch, like a little puff of milkweed.

F UNIVERSAL THEME
Consider Phoenix's statement in line 93. What does her familiarity with each leg of this trek, in addition to the story's **title,** suggest about her journey?

4. **sweet-gum:** a tree of the witch hazel family.
5. **live-oaks:** oak trees of a type that has evergreen foliage.

Down there, her senses drifted away. A dream visited her, and she reached her hand up, but nothing reached down and gave her a pull. So she lay there and presently went to talking. "Old woman," she said to herself, "that black dog come up out of the weeds to stall you off, and now there he sitting on his fine tail, smiling at you."

A white man finally came along and found her—a hunter, a young man, with his dog on a chain. **G**

"Well, Granny!" he laughed. "What are you doing there?"

"Lying on my back like a June-bug waiting to be turned over, mister," she said, reaching up her hand.

He lifted her up, gave her a swing in the air, and set her down. "Anything broken, Granny?"

"No sir, them old dead weeds is springy enough," said Phoenix, when she had got her breath. "I thank you for your trouble."

"Where do you live, Granny?" he asked, while the two dogs were growling at each other.

"Away back yonder, sir, behind the ridge. You can't even see it from here."

"On your way home?"

"No sir, I going to town."

"Why, that's too far! That's as far as I walk when I come out myself, and I get something for my trouble." He patted the stuffed bag he carried, and there hung down a little closed claw. It was one of the bob-whites, with its beak hooked bitterly to show it was dead. "Now you go on home, Granny!"

"I bound to go to town, mister," said Phoenix. "The time come around."

He gave another laugh, filling the whole landscape. "I know you old colored people! Wouldn't miss going to town to see Santa Claus!"

But something held old Phoenix very still. The deep lines in her face went into a fierce and different **radiation.** Without warning, she had seen with her own eyes a flashing nickel fall out of the man's pocket onto the ground.

"How old are you, Granny?" he was saying.

"There is no telling, mister," she said, "no telling."

Then she gave a little cry and clapped her hands and said, "Git on away from here, dog! Look! Look at that dog!" She laughed as if in admiration. "He ain't scared of nobody. He a big black dog." She whispered, "Sic him!"

"Watch me get rid of that cur," said the man. "Sic him, Pete! Sic him!"

Phoenix heard the dogs fighting, and heard the man running and throwing sticks. She even heard a gunshot. But she was slowly bending forward by that time, further and further forward, the lids stretched down over her eyes, as if she were doing this in her sleep. Her chin was lowered almost to her knees. The yellow palm of her hand came out from the fold of her apron. Her fingers slid down and along the ground under the piece of money with the grace and care they would have in lifting an egg from under a setting hen. Then she slowly straightened up,

G MONITOR

Reread lines 106–115. How can you tell when Phoenix is experiencing actual events or interacting with real people and when she has "drifted away" into her own imagination? Write two **questions** that help you understand what is real and what is not.

radiation (rā′dē-ā′shən) *n.* the movement of lines or rays from a center point she stood erect, and the nickel was in her apron pocket. A bird flew by. Her lips moved. "God watching me the whole time. I come to stealing."

The man came back, and his own dog panted about them. "Well, I scared him off that time," he said, and then he laughed and lifted his gun and pointed it at Phoenix.

She stood straight and faced him.

"Doesn't the gun scare you?" he said, still pointing it.

"No, sir, I seen plenty go off closer by, in my day, and for less than what I done," she said, holding utterly still.

He smiled, and shouldered the gun. "Well, Granny," he said, "you must be a hundred years old, and scared of nothing. I'd give you a dime if I had any money with me. But you take my advice and stay home, and nothing will happen to you." **H**

H MONITOR
Keep the story's **setting** in mind as you contemplate the way the hunter treats Phoenix. What does their interaction tell you about this time and place in history?

"I bound to go on my way, mister," said Phoenix. She inclined her head in the red rag. Then they went in different directions, but she could hear the gun shooting again and again over the hill. **I**

I UNIVERSAL THEME
Reread lines 114–166, and describe the **character traits** Phoenix exhibits during this episode with the hunter. How do her traits help her overcome this particular obstacle in her journey?

She walked on. The shadows hung from the oak trees to the road like curtains. Then she smelled wood-smoke, and smelled the river, and she saw a steeple and the cabins on their steep steps. Dozens of little black children whirled around her. There ahead was Natchez shining. Bells were ringing. She walked on.

In the paved city it was Christmas time. There were red and green electric lights strung and criss-crossed everywhere, and all turned on in the daytime. Old Phoenix would have been lost if she had not distrusted her eyesight and depended on her feet to know where to take her.

She paused quietly on the sidewalk where people were passing by. A lady came along in the crowd, carrying an armful of red-, green- and silver-wrapped presents; she gave off perfume like the red roses in hot summer, and Phoenix stopped her.

"Please, missy, will you lace up my shoe?" She held up her foot.

"What do you want, Grandma?"

"See my shoe," said Phoenix. "Do all right for out in the country, but wouldn't look right to go in a big building."

"Stand still then, Grandma," said the lady. She put her packages down on the sidewalk beside her and laced and tied both shoes tightly.

"Can't lace 'em with a cane," said Phoenix. "Thank you, missy. I doesn't mind asking a nice lady to tie up my shoe, when I gets out on the street."

Moving slowly and from side to side, she went into the big building, and into a tower of steps, where she walked up and around and around until her feet knew to stop.

She entered a door, and there she saw nailed up on the wall the document that had been stamped with the gold seal and framed in the gold frame, which matched the dream that was hung up in her head.

Analyze Visuals ▶
What elements of this portrait give the woman a look of inner strength and determination? Be specific.

Woman Peeling Apples (1924), Archibald J. Motley, Jr. Oil on canvas, 32¼″ × 28″. Art and Artifacts Division, Schomberg Center for Research in Black Culture, The New York Public Library, Astor, Lenox and Tilden Foundations.

"Here I be," she said. There was a fixed and ceremonial stiffness over her body.

"A charity case, I suppose," said an attendant who sat at the desk before her.

But Phoenix only looked above her head. There was sweat on her face, the wrinkles in her skin shone like a bright net.

"Speak up, Grandma," the woman said. "What's your name? We must have your history, you know. Have you been here before? What seems to be the trouble with you?"

Old Phoenix only gave a twitch to her face as if a fly were bothering her.

"Are you deaf?" cried the attendant.

But then the nurse came in.

"Oh, that's just old Aunt Phoenix," she said. "She doesn't come for herself—she has a little grandson. She makes these trips just as regular as clockwork. She lives away back off the Old Natchez Trace."[6] She bent down. "Well, Aunt Phoenix, why don't you just take a seat? We won't keep you standing after your long trip." She pointed.

The old woman sat down, bolt upright in the chair.

"Now, how is the boy?" asked the nurse.

Old Phoenix did not speak.

"I said, how is the boy?"

But Phoenix only waited and stared straight ahead, her face very solemn and withdrawn into rigidity.

"Is his throat any better?" asked the nurse. "Aunt Phoenix, don't you hear me? Is your grandson's throat any better since the last time you came for the medicine?"

With her hands on her knees, the old woman waited, silent, erect and motionless, just as if she were in armor.

"You mustn't take up our time this way, Aunt Phoenix," the nurse said. "Tell us quickly about your grandson, and get it over. He isn't dead, is he?"

At last there came a flicker and then a flame of comprehension across her face, and she spoke.

"My grandson. It was my memory had left me. There I sat and forgot why I made my long trip."

"Forgot?" The nurse frowned. "After you came so far?"

Then Phoenix was like an old woman begging a dignified forgiveness for waking up frightened in the night. "I never did go to school, I was too old at the Surrender,"[7] she said in a soft voice. "I'm an old woman without an education. It was my memory fail me. My little grandson, he is just the same, and I forgot it in the coming."

"Throat never heals, does it?" said the nurse, speaking in a loud, sure voice to old Phoenix. By now she had a card with something written on it, a little list. "Yes. Swallowed lye.[8] When was it?—January—two-three years ago—"

Language Coach

Phrasal Verbs A phrasal verb contains a verb and a preposition or adverb. *Speak up* ("speak loud enough to be heard") in line 196 has a different meaning than *speak* does. Referring to a dictionary if necessary, define *speak down to, speak out,* and *speak to.*

---

6. **Old Natchez Trace:** The Natchez Trace was an important wilderness road during the 18th and early 19th centuries, extending from Natchez, Mississippi, to Nashville, Tennessee.
7. **the Surrender:** the end of the Civil War, after which time slaves were free.
8. **lye:** a strong alkaline liquid used especially in making soap.

Phoenix spoke unasked now. "No, missy, he not dead, he just the same. Every little while his throat begin to close up again, and he not able to swallow. He not get his breath. He not able to help himself. So the time come around, and I go on another trip for the soothing medicine." J

"All right. The doctor said as long as you came to get it, you could have it," said the nurse. "But it's an **obstinate** case."

"My little grandson, he sit up there in the house all wrapped up, waiting by himself," Phoenix went on. "We is the only two left in the world. He suffer and it don't seem to put him back at all. He got a sweet look. He going to last. He wear a little patch quilt and peep out holding his mouth open like a little bird. I remembers so plain now. I not going to forget him again, no, the whole enduring time. I could tell him from all the others in creation."

"All right." The nurse was trying to hush her now. She brought her a bottle of medicine. "Charity," she said, making a check mark in a book.

Old Phoenix held the bottle close to her eyes, and then carefully put it into her pocket.

"I thank you," she said.

"It's Christmas time, Grandma," said the attendant. "Could I give you a few pennies out of my purse?"

"Five pennies is a nickel," said Phoenix stiffly.

"Here's a nickel," said the attendant.

Phoenix rose carefully and held out her hand. She received the nickel and then fished the other nickel out of her pocket and laid it beside the new one. She stared at her palm closely, with her head on one side.

Then she gave a tap with her cane on the floor.

"This is what come to me to do," she said. "I going to the store and buy my child a little windmill they sells, made out of paper. He going to find it hard to believe there such a thing in the world. I'll march myself back where he waiting, holding it straight up in this hand."

She lifted her free hand, gave a little nod, turned around, and walked out of the doctor's office. Then her slow step began on the stairs, going down.

J **UNIVERSAL THEME**
What have you learned about Phoenix's **motivation** for making her perilous journey, and what can you **infer** about how often she makes it? Explain why Welty might have delayed revealing this information until the story's end.

obstinate (ŏb′stə-nĭt) *adj.* hard to control or treat

Language Coach
Word Definitions *Stiffly* (line 251) here means "awkwardly formal" or "not in a graceful manner." How must Phoenix feel in lines 249–252?

THEME AND GENRE
Phoenix Jackson continues the tradition of the mythic hero who must go on a long journey and face difficult obstacles in order to reach a goal. This archetype is also the basis for many popular films today. The heroes of *The Lord of the Rings* and Harry Potter films, *WALL-E*, and *Spider-Man* all face serious challenges that test their strength, courage, and self-knowledge. Can you think of other works that share this same theme?

Reading for Information

MEMOIR Always shy of biographers, Eudora Welty published her own memoir at the age of 74. This account of growing up in the South pays special attention to her development as a writer.

One Writer's Beginnings

Eudora Welty

Eudora Welty, early in her career

The characters who go to make up my stories and novels are not portraits. Characters I invent along with the story that carries them. Attached to them are what I've borrowed, perhaps unconsciously, bit by bit, of persons I have seen or noticed or remembered in the flesh—a cast of countenance here, a manner of walking there, that jump to the visualizing mind when a story is underway. (Elizabeth Bowen said, "Physical detail cannot be invented." It can only be chosen.) I don't write by invasion into the life of a real person: my own sense of privacy is too strong for that; and I also know instinctively that living people to whom you are close—those known to you in ways too deep, too overflowing, ever to be plumbed outside love—do not yield to, could never fit into, the demands of a story. On the other hand, what I do make my stories out of is the *whole* fund of my feelings, my responses to the real experiences of my own life, to the relationships that formed and changed it, that I have given most of myself to, and so learned my way toward a dramatic counterpart. Characters take on life sometimes by luck, but I suspect it is when you can write most entirely out of yourself, inside the skin, heart, mind, and soul of a person who is not yourself, that a character becomes in his own right another human being on the page.

Comprehension

1. **Recall** Why does Phoenix Jackson travel to the city of Natchez?
2. **Recall** What does she intend to do with the ten cents she collects?
3. **Summarize** What physical problems does Phoenix seem to have, and how do they affect her on her journey?

Text Analysis

4. **Monitor Comprehension** Look over the chart you filled in as you read. Identify a passage in the story that was challenging to understand. What clues in the text helped you **clarify** its meaning? Explain how they helped.
5. **Analyze Figurative Language** "A Worn Path" is rich with figurative language, especially **similes.** Skim the story, identifying examples of figurative language used to accomplish the following purposes. For each purpose, cite at least two examples.
   - give readers a clear mental picture of Phoenix's appearance
   - highlight Phoenix's main character traits
   - convey Phoenix's feelings about her grandson
6. **Understand Symbolism** In mythology, a phoenix is an immortal bird that represents renewal. It sets its nest on fire every 500 years; from the ashes, the phoenix is reborn. Why might Welty have bestowed this name upon her main character? In what way does the name fit the person who bears it?
7. **Interpret Universal Theme** Consider the trials and triumphs Phoenix faces on her journey, and think about what motivates her to **endure** her arduous trek. In what way does this **archetypal** journey mirror life itself? Use your answer to this question to formulate a sentence that states the theme of the story. Then explain what makes this theme universal.

Text Criticism

8. **Critical Interpretations** This story's ambiguity has fascinated readers for years. Many students have written Welty to ask if Phoenix's grandson is really alive at the story's end, or if Phoenix keeps making this journey though the boy is already gone. The author has replied, "It is the journey, the going of the errand, that is the story. . . . *Phoenix* is alive." In your opinion, does Welty bring this story to a satisfying conclusion? Explain why or why not, citing details from the text as well as your reaction to Welty's explanation.

What keeps us GOING?

Motivated by love for her grandson, Phoenix makes the difficult journey to town in spite of many obstacles. What motivates you to finish a difficult task?

COMMON CORE

RL 2 Determine two or more themes or central ideas of a text and analyze their development over the course of the text, including how they interact and build on one another to produce a complex account; provide an objective summary of the text. **RL 10** Read and comprehend literature, including stories.

Vocabulary in Context

▲ VOCABULARY PRACTICE

Demonstrate your understanding of the vocabulary words by answering these questions.

1. Would an **obstinate** cold go away in a few days or drag on for weeks?
2. If your leg muscles are **limber,** would you be more likely to excel at stretching exercises or to cramp up while swimming?
3. Would you expect someone to be **meditative** in a pep rally, or in a quiet garden?
4. Does **radiation** from the sun provide or absorb heat and light?

WORD LIST
limber
meditative
obstinate
radiation

ACADEMIC VOCABULARY IN SPEAKING

• conclude • criteria • despite • justify • maintain

Phoenix Jackson faces many obstacles as she walks to town—things that a younger person might not see as obstacles at all. In a small group, discuss three of the obstacles she faces. What can you **conclude** about Phoenix's age and her walk to town? Use at least three Academic Vocabulary words in your discussion.

VOCABULARY STRATEGY: SPANISH COGNATES

The English language has picked up thousands of words and word parts from other languages. When the words picked up from other languages have identical or similar spellings and meanings to those in the original languages, they are called cognates. The Spanish language and the English language have many cognates. For example, the English word *monitor* has the same meaning and same spelling in Spanish. The English word *position* is spelled *posicion* in Spanish. You can use your knowledge of a cognate in one language to determine its meaning in a different language.

COMMON CORE

L 2b Spell correctly. **L 6** Acquire and use accurately general academic and domain-specific words and phrases.

PRACTICE Write the letter of the Spanish cognate that you think completes the meaning of each sentence. Then write the word as it is spelled in English.

1. Because that actress is so _____, almost no one wants to spend time with her.
2. Some of the best films in recent years have been produced by _____ filmmakers.
3. The _____ has made a huge difference in the development of special effects in movies.
4. The students in the film class obviously think that films are ______.

a. realista
b. interesante
c. arrogante
d. computadora
e. independiente

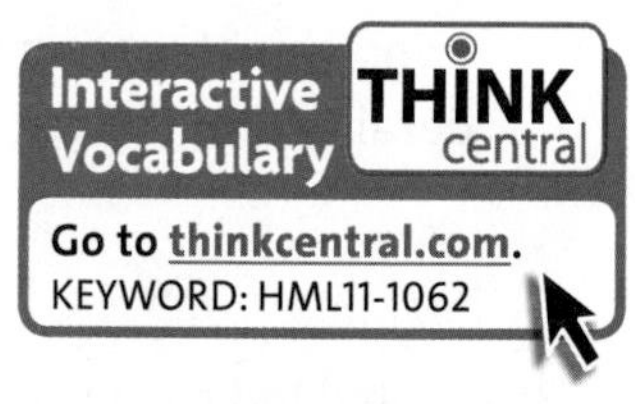

Language

GRAMMAR AND STYLE: Add Descriptive Details

Review the **Grammar and Style** note on page 1053. Welty's descriptions in the story give a wealth of sensory details that help readers get a clear picture of Phoenix and her actions. Welty makes particularly good use of **action verbs** (in yellow) and **participial phrases** (in green), as in this description of Phoenix crossing the precarious log bridge:

> *Putting her right foot out, she mounted the log and shut her eyes. Lifting her skirt, leveling her cane fiercely before her, like a festival figure in some parade, she began to march across.* (lines 47–49)

The highlighted participial phrases add key details to help readers visualize Phoenix. The first highlighted action verb, *mounted,* shows the physical exertion required for her to get on top of the log, while the third verb, *march,* works with the simile to suggest her regal bearing and sense of purpose.

PRACTICE The following sentences were written in response to the writing prompt below. Rewrite each sentence, adding more action verbs and participial phrases that help describe how things look, sound, smell, touch, or taste.

EXAMPLE

The sun was low on the horizon and made shadows between the bushes.

The sun crouched low on the horizon, casting long shadows between the scrubby bushes.

1. Tashi, a refugee fleeing her war-torn village, was on the high bank above the river.
2. She knew she had to cross in the shallows where the sand bar was.
3. The baby was still asleep in her arms but would wake soon and be hungry.

READING-WRITING CONNECTION

Expand your understanding of "A Worn Path" by responding to this prompt. Then, use the **revising tips** to improve your story.

WRITING PROMPT	REVISING TIPS
WRITE A STORY Think of an extreme situation today in which a contemporary Phoenix makes a perilous journey. What hazards does she or he face? What values and strengths does she or he need in order to endure? Write a **one-to-three-page story** updating Welty's tale.	• Give clear details about the setting for your story. • Show how your character confronts conflicts. • Use action verbs and participial phrases to show rather than tell.

COMMON CORE

L 3 Apply knowledge of language to understand how language functions in different contexts, to make effective choices for meaning or style, and to comprehend more fully when reading or listening. **W 3** Write narratives to develop imagined experiences or events using effective technique, well-chosen details, and well-structured event sequences. **W 3a** Engage and orient the reader by setting out a problem or situation and its significance, establishing one or multiple point(s) of view, and introducing a narrator and/or characters.

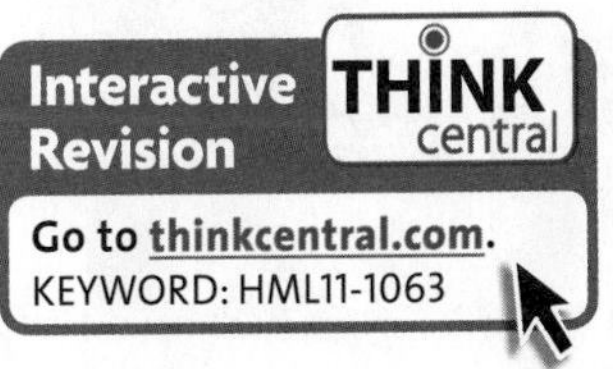

COMMON CORE

RL 3 Analyze the impact of the author's choices regarding how to develop and relate elements of a story (e.g., where a story is set, how the action is ordered, how the characters are introduced and developed). **RL 4** Analyze the impact of specific word choices on meaning and tone, including words with multiple meanings or language that is particularly fresh, engaging, or beautiful. **RL 5** Analyze how an author's choices concerning how to structure specific parts of a text contribute to its overall structure and meaning as well as its aesthetic impact.

A Rose for Emily

Short Story by William Faulkner

VIDEO TRAILER THINK central KEYWORD: HML11-1064A

Meet the Author

William Faulkner 1897–1962

Today, William Faulkner is considered one of the literary giants of the 20th century. This distinction didn't come easily, however. Faulkner took a while to find himself and his subject. Only after he decided to focus on his home state of Mississippi and his colorful family history was the full force of his creativity unleashed. Over an astonishing 13-year span, Faulkner churned out one masterpiece after another—among them, *The Sound and the Fury* (1929), *As I Lay Dying* (1930), *Sanctuary* (1931), *Absalom, Absalom!* (1936), and *Go Down, Moses* (1942). Of these artistic achievements, only *Sanctuary* was a bestseller—partly due to its scandalous subject matter—and none of the books earned Faulkner enough money to support his growing family. Although some critics raved about him, many others agreed with the *New York Times* that his South was "too often vicious, depraved, decadent, corrupt." By 1945, most of his books were out of print.

Narrative Challenges A glance at Faulkner's work would explain why readers and critics resisted his fiction. He wrote narratives on the cutting edge of the new modernism, and for the most part, he refused to compromise with the typical reader's desire for a coherent, chronological story. His novels weave numerous flashbacks into multiple story lines. They push sentence length to new limits, and two of his best-known modernist works increase the reader's challenge by using several highly unreliable narrators to tell the story. *The Sound and the Fury* has three first-person narrators (see pages 934-935). *As I Lay Dying* has fifteen. The story of a mother's dying wish, Faulkner's fifth novel switches narrators with each chapter, supplying readers with the perspective of various family members and others involved in the story. It is anything but an easy read.

Resurgence In 1946, an enterprising editor named Malcolm Cowley published *The Portable Faulkner,* a collection of stories and novel excerpts that untangled Faulkner's elaborate saga. Cowley's blueprint plus a helpful introduction sparked new interest in Faulkner. With the anxieties of the Great Depression and World War II behind them, more readers were ready to accept Faulkner's challenge to revisit the crimes and passions of the South—and America itself—through a modern consciousness.

DID YOU KNOW?

William Faulkner . . .

- dropped out of high school and took only a few college classes as a special student.
- worked almost three years at the post office, where he was considered lazy and inattentive, before he resigned.

Author Online THINK central

Go to thinkcentral.com. KEYWORD: HML11-1064B

TEXT ANALYSIS: POINT OF VIEW

As you've already learned, Faulkner is a pioneer of modernist fiction (see pages 934-935 and page 1064). He uses **stream of consciousness,** mimicking the flow of a character's thoughts and sensations to convey the subjective nature of experience. He uses **multiple narrators,** taking the point of view of several characters in a single novel. With each work of fiction, he crafts a point of view uniquely suited to the story being told. "A Rose for Emily," is the story of a small town's struggle to understand one of its residents. Using multiple narrators would be difficult in a short story. Using stream of consciousness would not convey what is most important here—the public perception of Miss Emily. Faulkner's choice for point of view, then, is **first-person-plural**—an unnamed *we*, the voice of the townspeople themselves.

As you read, notice the narrator's use of first-person pronouns such as *we* and *our*. What role does this point of view play in your understanding of Miss Emily and her story? How might other points of view change the narrative?

Review: **Mood**

READING SKILL: ANALYZE SEQUENCE

Faulkner often rearranges the **sequence** of events in his fiction, using **flashbacks** to offer a window into a character's past or dropping hints that **foreshadow** what is yet to come. As you read, keep a chart like the one shown. In the left column, record the story's events as you read about them. When you finish the story, number the events in chronological order.

Order in Which Narrator Reveals Events	Order in Which Events Occur
1. Miss Emily dies.	8
2. The aldermen visit about taxes.	7

VOCABULARY IN CONTEXT

Faulkner uses these words to create a story rich with atmosphere. Try to define each, based on its context.

1. The **cabal** executed their shady plans in secret.
2. The swaggering boy approached him with **temerity.**
3. Moonlight made the rickety house into a terrifying **tableau.**
4. Her **imperviousness** made her impossible to frighten.

Complete the activities in your **Reader/Writer Notebook**.

What makes *your* SKIN CRAWL?

As the girl steps outside into the alley, the overpowering smell of rotting garbage assaults her nostrils. Her stomach turns as she tries not to stare at a mass of maggots eating a discarded hamburger, and she shies away from the dumpster, with its squeaking and squirming inhabitants. Certain scenes from books or movies are so evocative that they leave you shaky and nauseated. Part of what you're responding to is the creepy atmosphere the writers or directors have created to mesmerize and repulse you.

DISCUSS In a small group, talk about the one thing that really gives you the creeps. Spiders, rats, the sight of blood—do any of these make your skin crawl? What movies or books have used these things to create an atmosphere that makes you shudder? Which works top your "creepiness scale"? Record the responses of your group to share with others.

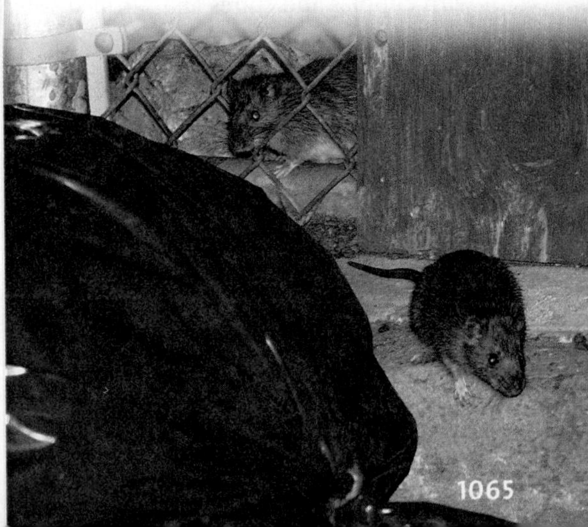

A Rose for Emily

William Faulkner

BACKGROUND "A Rose for Emily," like the majority of Faulkner's stories, takes place in the fictional Yoknapatawpha County, Mississippi. Published in 1930, the story portrays social customs of the small-town South at the turn of the 20th century. Be warned that the narrator refers to African Americans with a term that is offensive to contemporary readers.

I

When Miss Emily Grierson died, our whole town went to her funeral: the men through a sort of respectful affection for a fallen monument, the women mostly out of curiosity to see the inside of her house, which no one save an old manservant—a combined gardener and cook—had seen in at least ten years. (A)

It was a big, squarish frame house that had once been white, decorated with cupolas and spires and scrolled balconies in the heavily lightsome style of the seventies,[1] set on what had once been our most select street. But garages and cotton gins had encroached and obliterated even the august names of that neighborhood; only Miss Emily's house was left, lifting its stubborn and coquettish decay above the cotton wagons and the gasoline pumps—an eyesore among eyesores. And now Miss Emily had gone to join the representatives of those august names where they lay in the cedar-bemused[2] cemetery among the ranked and anonymous graves of Union and Confederate soldiers who fell at the battle of Jefferson.

(A) **POINT OF VIEW**
Identify the first-person-plural pronoun that establishes Faulkner's point of view in the opening paragraph. For whom does the narrator speak?

1. **the seventies:** the 1870s.
2. **cedar-bemused:** almost lost in cedar trees.

Alive, Miss Emily had been a tradition, a duty, and a care; a sort of hereditary obligation upon the town, dating from that day in 1894 when Colonel Sartoris, the mayor—he who fathered the edict that no Negro woman should appear on the streets without an apron—remitted her taxes, the dispensation dating from the death of her father on into perpetuity.[3] Not that Miss Emily would have accepted charity. Colonel Sartoris invented an involved tale to the effect that Miss Emily's father had loaned money to the town, which the town, as a matter of business, preferred this way of repaying. Only a man of Colonel Sartoris' generation and thought could have invented it, and only a woman could have believed it.

When the next generation, with its more modern ideas, became mayors and aldermen, this arrangement created some little dissatisfaction. On the first of the year they mailed her a tax notice. February came, and there was no reply. They wrote her a formal letter, asking her to call at the sheriff's office at her convenience. A week later the mayor wrote her himself, offering to call or to send his car for her, and received in reply a note on paper of an archaic shape, in a thin, flowing calligraphy in faded ink, to the effect that she no longer went out at all. The tax notice was also enclosed, without comment. **B**

They called a special meeting of the Board of Aldermen. A deputation waited upon her, knocked at the door through which no visitor had passed since she ceased giving china-painting lessons eight or ten years earlier. They were admitted by the old Negro into a dim hall from which a stairway mounted into still more shadow. It smelled of dust and disuse—a close, dank smell. The Negro led them into the parlor. It was furnished in heavy, leather-covered furniture. When the Negro opened the blinds of one window, they could see that the leather was cracked; and when they sat down, a faint dust rose sluggishly about their thighs, spinning with slow motes in the single sun-ray. On a tarnished gilt easel before the fireplace stood a crayon portrait of Miss Emily's father.

They rose when she entered—a small, fat woman in black, with a thin gold chain descending to her waist and vanishing into her belt, leaning on an ebony cane with a tarnished gold head. Her skeleton was small and spare; perhaps that was why what would have been merely plumpness in another was obesity in her. She looked bloated, like a body long submerged in motionless water, and of that pallid hue. Her eyes, lost in the fatty ridges of her face, looked like two small pieces of coal pressed into a lump of dough as they moved from one face to another while the visitors stated their errand. **C**

She did not ask them to sit. She just stood in the door and listened quietly until the spokesman came to a stumbling halt. Then they could hear the invisible watch ticking at the end of the gold chain.

Her voice was dry and cold. "I have no taxes in Jefferson. Colonel Sartoris explained it to me. Perhaps one of you can gain access to the city records and satisfy yourselves."

"But we have. We are the city authorities, Miss Emily. Didn't you get a notice from the sheriff, signed by him?"

B ANALYZE SEQUENCE
Explain when the events of the story's first paragraph happen in relation to those described in lines 15–31. Why might Faulkner have chosen to immediately announce Emily's death before revealing more about her life? Explain.

C MOOD
What is your initial reaction to Emily? Cite two examples of **figurative language** in lines 42–49 and explain what feeling they create.

3. **remitted . . . perpetuity:** released her from paying taxes forever from the time of her father's death.

"I received a paper, yes," Miss Emily said. "Perhaps he considers himself the sheriff . . . I have no taxes in Jefferson."

"But there is nothing on the books to show that, you see. We must go by the—"

"See Colonel Sartoris. I have no taxes in Jefferson."

"But, Miss Emily—"

"See Colonel Sartoris." (Colonel Sartoris had been dead almost ten years.) "I have no taxes in Jefferson. Tobe!" The Negro appeared. "Show these gentlemen out."

II

So she vanquished them, horse and foot, just as she had vanquished their fathers thirty years before about the smell. That was two years after her father's death and a short time after her sweetheart—the one we believed would marry her—had deserted her. After her father's death she went out very little; after her sweetheart went away, people hardly saw her at all. A few of the ladies had the **temerity** to call, but were not received, and the only sign of life about the place was the Negro man—a young man then—going in and out with a market basket.

temerity (tə-mĕr′ĭ-tē) *n.* foolish boldness

"Just as if a man—any man—could keep a kitchen properly," the ladies said; so they were not surprised when the smell developed. It was another link between the gross, teeming world and the high and mighty Griersons.

A neighbor, a woman, complained to the mayor, Judge Stevens, eighty years old.

"But what will you have me do about it, madam?" he said.

"Why, send her word to stop it," the woman said. "Isn't there a law?"

"I'm sure that won't be necessary," Judge Stevens said. "It's probably just a snake or a rat that nigger of hers killed in the yard. I'll speak to him about it."

The next day he received two more complaints, one from a man who came in diffident deprecation.[4] "We really must do something about it, Judge. I'd be the last one in the world to bother Miss Emily, but we've got to do something." That night the Board of Aldermen met—three graybeards and one younger man, a member of the rising generation.

"It's simple enough," he said. "Send her word to have her place cleaned up. Give her a certain time to do it in, and if she don't . . ."

"Dammit, sir," Judge Stevens said, "will you accuse a lady to her face of smelling bad?" **D**

So the next night, after midnight, four men crossed Miss Emily's lawn and slunk about the house like burglars, sniffing along the base of the brickwork and at the cellar openings while one of them performed a regular sowing motion with his hand out of a sack slung from his shoulder. They broke open the cellar door and sprinkled lime there, and in all the outbuildings. As they recrossed the lawn, a window that had been dark was lighted and Miss Emily sat in it, the light behind her, and her upright torso motionless as that of an idol. They crept quietly across the lawn and into the shadow of the locusts that lined the street. After a week or two the smell went away.

COMMON CORE RL 3, RL 5

D POINT OF VIEW

Reread lines 65–88. Notice that the opening paragraph summarizes events in Miss Emily's life. Faulkner's unique **point of view** here—first person plural—makes it possible for this narrative summary to include the townspeople's perceptions of his main character. Then, in the dialogue, Faulkner captures both gossip and the conflict among small-town perspectives. Think about how the point of view might change if Faulkner had the length of a novel to tell Miss Emily's story. He could, for example, write entire passages from the points of view of a neighbor woman, one of the complaining citizens, and the judge. How would the use of **multiple narrators** affect this story?

4. **diffident deprecation:** timid disapproval.

That was when people had begun to feel really sorry for her. People in our town, remembering how old lady Wyatt, her great-aunt, had gone completely crazy at last, believed that the Griersons held themselves a little too high for what they really were. None of the young men were quite good enough for Miss Emily and such. We had long thought of them as a **tableau,** Miss Emily a slender figure in white in the background, her father a spraddled silhouette in the foreground, his back to her and clutching a horsewhip, the two of them framed by the back-flung front door. So when she got to be thirty and was still single, we were not pleased exactly, but vindicated; even with insanity in the family she wouldn't have turned down all of her chances if they had really materialized. E

tableau (tăb'lō') *n.* a dramatic scene or picture

When her father died, it got about that the house was all that was left to her; and in a way, people were glad. At last they could pity Miss Emily. Being left alone, and a pauper, she had become humanized. Now she too would know the old thrill and the old despair of a penny more or less.

E GRAMMAR AND STYLE
Reread lines 98–107. The **pronouns** *we* and *our* indicate that this story is told from the **first-person-plural point of view.** The narrator is not a single character, but the collective voice of the townspeople.

The day after his death all the ladies prepared to call at the house and offer condolence and aid, as is our custom. Miss Emily met them at the door, dressed as usual and with no trace of grief on her face. She told them that her father was not dead. She did that for three days, with the ministers calling on her, and the doctors, trying to persuade her to let them dispose of the body. Just as they were about to resort to law and force, she broke down, and they buried her father quickly.

We did not say she was crazy then. We believed she had to do that. We remembered all the young men her father had driven away, and we knew that with nothing left, she would have to cling to that which had robbed her, as people will.

III

She was sick for a long time. When we saw her again, her hair was cut short, making her look like a girl, with a vague resemblance to those angels in colored church windows—sort of tragic and serene. F

F POINT OF VIEW
Reread lines 119–124. What is Faulkner's point of view in these paragraphs, and which personal pronoun signals the point of view? Explain what makes this point of view unique in fiction. Cite evidence from the story to support your answer.

The town had just let the contracts for paving the sidewalks, and in the summer after her father's death they began the work. The construction company came with niggers and mules and machinery, and a foreman named Homer Barron, a Yankee—a big, dark, ready man, with a big voice and eyes lighter than his face. The little boys would follow in groups to hear him cuss the niggers, and the niggers singing in time to the rise and fall of picks. Pretty soon he knew everybody in town. Whenever you heard a lot of laughing anywhere about the square, Homer Barron would be in the center of the group. Presently we began to see him and Miss Emily on Sunday afternoons driving in the yellow-wheeled buggy and the matched team of bays from the livery stable.

At first we were glad that Miss Emily would have an interest, because the ladies all said, "Of course a Grierson would not think seriously of a Northerner, a day laborer." But there were still others, older people, who said that even grief could not cause a real lady to forget *noblesse oblige*[5]—without calling it *noblesse oblige.*

---

5. ***noblesse oblige*** (nō-blĕs' ō-blēzh'): the responsibility of people in a high social position to behave in a noble fashion.

They just said, "Poor Emily. Her kinsfolk should come to her." She had some kin in Alabama; but years ago her father had fallen out with them over the estate of old lady Wyatt, the crazy woman, and there was no communication between the two families. They had not even been represented at the funeral.

And as soon as the old people said, "Poor Emily," the whispering began. "Do you suppose it's really so?" they said to one another. "Of course it is. What else could . . ." This behind their hands; rustling of craned silk and satin behind jalousies[6] closed upon the sun of Sunday afternoon as the thin, swift clop-clop-clop of the matched team passed: "Poor Emily."

She carried her head high enough—even when we believed that she was fallen. It was as if she demanded more than ever the recognition of her dignity as the last Grierson; as if it had wanted that touch of earthiness to reaffirm her **imperviousness.** Like when she bought the rat poison, the arsenic. That was over a year after they had begun to say "Poor Emily," and while the two female cousins were visiting her.

imperviousness (ĭm-pûr′vē-əs-nəs) *n.* an inability to be affected or disturbed

"I want some poison," she said to the druggist. She was over thirty then, still a slight woman, though thinner than usual, with cold, haughty black eyes in a face the flesh of which was strained across the temples and about the eye-sockets as you imagine a lighthouse-keeper's face ought to look. "I want some poison," she said.

6. **jalousies** (jăl′ə-sēz): blinds or shutters containing overlapping slats that can be opened or closed.

"Yes, Miss Emily. What kind? For rats and such? I'd recom—"

"I want the best you have. I don't care what kind."

The druggist named several. "They'll kill anything up to an elephant. But what you want is—"

"Arsenic," Miss Emily said. "Is that a good one?"

"Is . . . arsenic? Yes, ma'am. But what you want—"

"I want arsenic."

The druggist looked down at her. She looked back at him, erect, her face like a strained flag. "Why, of course," the druggist said. "If that's what you want. But the law requires you to tell what you are going to use it for."

Miss Emily just stared at him, her head tilted back in order to look him eye for eye, until he looked away and went and got the arsenic and wrapped it up. The Negro delivery boy brought her the package; the druggist didn't come back. When she opened the package at home there was written on the box, under the skull and bones: "For rats." **G**

G ANALYZE SEQUENCE
Reread lines 154–172. What does this exchange indicate about Emily's character? What **foreshadowing** do you sense in her refusal to comply with the law?

IV

So the next day we all said, "She will kill herself"; and we said it would be the best thing. When she had first begun to be seen with Homer Barron, we had said, "She will marry him." Then we said, "She will persuade him yet," because Homer himself had remarked—he liked men, and it was known that he drank with the younger men in the Elks' Club—that he was not a marrying man. Later we said, "Poor Emily" behind the jalousies as they passed on Sunday afternoon in the glittering buggy, Miss Emily with her head high and Homer Barron with his hat cocked and a cigar in his teeth, reins and whip in a yellow glove.

Then some of the ladies began to say that it was a disgrace to the town and a bad example to the young people. The men did not want to interfere, but at last the ladies forced the Baptist minister—Miss Emily's people were Episcopal—to call upon her. He would never divulge what happened during that interview, but he refused to go back again. The next Sunday they again drove about the streets, and the following day the minister's wife wrote to Miss Emily's relations in Alabama.

So she had blood-kin under her roof again and we sat back to watch developments. At first nothing happened. Then we were sure that they were to be married. We learned that Miss Emily had been to the jeweler's and ordered a man's toilet set in silver, with the letters H. B. on each piece. Two days later we learned that she had bought a complete outfit of men's clothing, including a nightshirt, and we said, "They are married." We were really glad. We were glad because the two female cousins were even more Grierson than Miss Emily had ever been.

So we were not surprised when Homer Barron—the streets had been finished some time since—was gone. We were a little disappointed that there was not a public blowing-off,[7] but we believed that he had gone on to prepare for Miss Emily's coming, or to give her a chance to get rid of the cousins. (By that time it was a **cabal,** and we were all Miss Emily's allies to help circumvent the cousins.)

cabal (kə-băl') *n.* a group united in a secret plot

7. **blowing-off:** here, a celebration.

Sure enough, after another week they departed. And, as we had expected all along, within three days Homer Barron was back in town. A neighbor saw the Negro man admit him at the kitchen door at dusk one evening.

And that was the last we saw of Homer Barron. And of Miss Emily for some time. The Negro man went in and out with the market basket, but the front door remained closed. Now and then we would see her at a window for a moment, as the men did that night when they sprinkled the lime, but for almost six months she did not appear on the streets. Then we knew that this was to be expected too; as if that quality of her father which had thwarted her woman's life so many times had been too virulent and too furious to die.

When we next saw Miss Emily, she had grown fat and her hair was turning gray. During the next few years it grew grayer and grayer until it attained an even pepper-and-salt iron-gray, when it ceased turning. Up to the day of her death at seventy-four it was still that vigorous iron-gray, like the hair of an active man.

From that time on her front door remained closed, save for a period of six or seven years, when she was about forty, during which she gave lessons in china-painting. She fitted up a studio in one of the downstairs rooms, where the daughters and granddaughters of Colonel Sartoris' contemporaries were sent to her with the same regularity and in the same spirit that they were sent to church on Sundays with a twenty-five-cent piece for the collection plate. Meanwhile her taxes had been remitted.

Then the newer generation became the backbone and the spirit of the town, and the painting pupils grew up and fell away and did not send their children to her with boxes of color and tedious brushes and pictures cut from the ladies' magazines. The front door closed upon the last one and remained closed for good. When the town got free postal delivery, Miss Emily alone refused to let them fasten the metal numbers above her door and attach a mailbox to it. She would not listen to them.

Daily, monthly, yearly we watched the Negro grow grayer and more stooped, going in and out with the market basket. Each December we sent her a tax notice, which would be returned by the post office a week later, unclaimed. Now and then we would see her in one of the downstairs windows—she had evidently shut up the top floor of the house—like the carven torso of an idol in a niche, looking or not looking at us, we could never tell which. Thus she passed from generation to generation—dear, inescapable, impervious, tranquil, and perverse. **H**

And so she died. Fell ill in the house filled with dust and shadows, with only a doddering Negro man to wait on her. We did not even know she was sick; we had long since given up trying to get any information from the Negro. He talked to no one, probably not even to her, for his voice had grown harsh and rusty, as if from disuse.

She died in one of the downstairs rooms, in a heavy walnut bed with a curtain, her gray head propped on a pillow yellow and moldy with age and lack of sunlight.

H POINT OF VIEW
Reread lines 227–233. When the narrator says that "we sent her a tax notice" and "we would see her in one of the downstairs windows," whom does "we" indicate? And how does this pronoun help to convey the story's point of view? Support your answer with evidence from the story.

V

The Negro met the first of the ladies at the front door and let them in, with their hushed, sibilant voices and their quick, curious glances, and then he disappeared. He walked right through the house and out the back and was not seen again.

The two female cousins came at once. They held the funeral on the second day, with the town coming to look at Miss Emily beneath a mass of bought flowers, with the crayon face of her father musing profoundly above the bier[8] and the ladies sibilant and macabre; and the very old men—some in their brushed Confederate uniforms—on the porch and the lawn, talking of Miss Emily as if she had been a contemporary of theirs, believing that they had danced with her and courted her perhaps, confusing time with its mathematical progression, as the old do, to whom all the past is not a diminishing road but, instead, a huge meadow which no winter ever quite touches, divided from them now by the narrow bottle-neck of the most recent decade of years.

Already we knew that there was one room in that region above stairs which no one had seen in forty years, and which would have to be forced. They waited until Miss Emily was decently in the ground before they opened it.

The violence of breaking down the door seemed to fill this room with pervading dust. A thin, acrid pall[9] as of the tomb seemed to lie everywhere upon this room decked and furnished as for a bridal: upon the valance curtains of faded rose color, upon the rose-shaded lights, upon the dressing table, upon the delicate array of crystal and the man's toilet things backed with tarnished silver, silver so tarnished that the monogram was obscured. Among them lay a collar and tie, as if they had just been removed, which, lifted, left upon the surface a pale crescent in the dust. Upon a chair hung the suit, carefully folded; beneath it the two mute shoes and the discarded socks.

The man himself lay in the bed.

For a long while we just stood there, looking down at the profound and fleshless grin. The body had apparently once lain in the attitude of an embrace, but now the long sleep that outlasts love, that conquers even the grimace of love, had cuckolded him.[10] What was left of him, rotted beneath what was left of the nightshirt, had become inextricable from the bed in which he lay; and upon him and upon the pillow beside him lay that even coating of the patient and biding dust.

Then we noticed that in the second pillow was the indentation of a head. One of us lifted something from it, and leaning forward, that faint and invisible dust dry and acrid in the nostrils, we saw a long strand of iron-gray hair. ❧ 1

COMMON CORE RL 4

1 MOOD

This story ends with a grotesque discovery, but from page one the author's dark, gothic **mood** has prepared us for a creepy revelation in the end. With "A Rose for Emily" and other stories and novels, Faulkner invented a unique vision of the South—a **mythic narrative** weighed down by gloom and peopled by deeply flawed characters. Faulkner's mythic South has influenced Southern fiction ever since—from the short stories of Flannery O'Connor to more recent fiction by writers such as Alan Gurganus and Edward P. Jones. What makes a story like "A Rose for Emily" so compelling? Explain your answer.

---

8. **bier:** coffin along with its stand.
9. **acrid pall:** bitter-smelling gloom.
10. **cuckolded him:** made his wife or lover unfaithful to him.

Comprehension

1. **Recall** Why was it difficult for Emily to meet suitable men in her youth?
2. **Clarify** What happened to Homer Barron?
3. **Clarify** What does the condition of the upstairs room in the Grierson house and the iron-gray hair on the pillow indicate?

Text Analysis

4. **Make Inferences** Use clues in the story to infer Emily's **motivation** for murdering Homer. Why was the relationship considered a "disgrace" and a "bad example to the young people"? What were Homer's intentions?
5. **Examine Methods of Characterization** Explain how Faulkner uses physical descriptions of Miss Emily, stories of her conflicts with the townspeople, and the revelation of the story's final paragraph to characterize his protagonist. Support your answer with evidence from the story.
6. **Analyze Mood** How would you describe the overall mood of "A Rose for Emily"? Skim the story, identifying at least three passages that create an especially strong **atmosphere** for the reader. Explain which literary elements contribute to each passage's mood.
7. **Analyze Point of View** What point of view does Faulkner use to narrate "A Rose for Emily"? Explain how this point of view contributes to the characterization of Miss Emily's town and how it compares to Faulkner's modernist experiments with point of view.
8. **Evaluate Sequence** Examine the chart you filled in as you read. How does the order in which the story's major events occur differ from the order in which the narrator presents them? Consider the effect created by Faulkner's manipulation of the story's sequence. What would the story lose if it were told in strict chronological order?

Text Criticism

9. **Historical Context** Faulkner lived, as one critic put it, "with one foot deep in the traditions of the Old South and the other poised for the possibilities of a modern era." What are some of the indications that this story was written in another time? Citing evidence, describe how Faulkner's story reflects an American society different from our own.

What makes your SKIN CRAWL?

How does the last sentence of "A Rose for Emily" confirm the story's creepy atmosphere? Explain your answer.

COMMON CORE

RL 3 Analyze the impact of the author's choices regarding how to develop and relate elements of a story (e.g., where a story is set, how the action is ordered, how the characters are introduced and developed). **RL 4** Analyze the impact of specific word choices on meaning and tone, including words with multiple meanings or language that is particularly fresh, engaging, or beautiful. **RL 5** Analyze how an author's choices concerning how to structure specific parts of a text contribute to its overall structure and meaning as well as its aesthetic impact.

Vocabulary in Context

▲ VOCABULARY PRACTICE

Chose the word that is not related in meaning to the other words.

1. (a) overconfidence, (b) temerity, (c) dismay, (d) brashness
2. (a) contempt, (b) cabal, (c) disdain, (d) scorn
3. (a) endurance, (b) imperviousness, (c) decency, (d) resistance
4. (a) tableau, (b) mesa, (c) plateau, (d) upland

WORD LIST
cabal
imperviousness
tableau
temerity

ACADEMIC VOCABULARY IN WRITING

• conclude • criteria • despite • justify • maintain

Faulkner **concludes** "A Rose for Emily" by solving the mystery of his main character. What are your **criteria** for a successful ending? Develop your answer in a short paragraph. Use at least three Academic Vocabulary words in your response.

VOCABULARY STRATEGY: ETYMOLOGIES

Many English words have intriguing histories, or **etymologies.** The vocabulary word *cabal*, for instance, can be traced back to *kabbala*, the name of an ancient Jewish mystical belief system. We can often develop a better understanding of the current meaning of a word by learning about its history. Standard dictionaries, we all as etymological dictionaries, are excellent sources of word histories. A typical word history may show the history of the word in the English language (its form in Middle English, for example) as well as its relationship to words from other Germanic languages or to the Romance languages.

COMMON CORE

L 4c Consult general and specialized reference materials, both print and digital, to determine or clarify a word's etymology.

PRACTICE Using a standard dictionary, an etymological dictionary, or the Internet, research the histories of the following words. Look for the history of the word in the English language as well as its relationship to words in other contemporary languages (German, Dutch, Italian, French, etc.) and in Latin.

1. trivial
2. decimate
3. abacus
4. aardvark
5. quarantine
6. malaria
7. ketchup
8. dexterity

Language

GRAMMAR AND STYLE: Choose Effective Point of View

Review the **Grammar and Style** note on page 1070. Part of what makes "A Rose for Emily" so interesting is the first-person-plural point of view—using *we* and related **pronouns** to tell the story. Usually, the first-person point of view is singular, an *I* who acts as both narrator and character. Faulkner's use of the plural creates a curious mixture of intimacy and anonymity. That is, the voice behind the *we* sounds personal, but readers don't know exactly who the voice is:

> *We learned that Miss Emily had been to the jeweler's and ordered a man's toilet set in silver, with the letters H. B. on each piece. Two days later we learned that she had bought a complete outfit of men's clothing, including a nightshirt, and we said, "They are married." We were really glad.* (lines 189–192)

This kind of narrator has the effect of making the town appear as a complete entity with a personality and opinions all its own.

PRACTICE Try using the first-person-plural point of view to create a narrative of your own. Choose a group—a family, for example, or a sports team—and describe, in a paragraph, an event or experience from their point of view. Be sure to use the correct pronouns—*we, us, our, ours*—in your narrative.

COMMON CORE

L 3 Apply knowledge of language to understand how language functions in different contexts, to make effective choices for meaning or style. **W 1** Write arguments to support claims in an analysis of substantive topics or texts, using valid reasoning and relevant and sufficient evidence.

READING-WRITING CONNECTION

Expand your understanding of "A Rose for Emily" by responding to the prompt below. Then, use the **revising tips** to improve your essay.

WRITING PROMPT	REVISING TIPS
WRITE AN ARGUMENT Do you think the townspeople in "A Rose for Emily" bear any responsibility for what becomes of Emily? Why did they initially think she would use the arsenic to kill herself—and what did they seemingly think of this decision? What if they had stopped the minister's wife from writing to her cousins? Why didn't they think to investigate Homer Barron's disappearance? Review the story, especially sections III and IV, to clarify your opinion and gather evidence. Then write a **three-to-five-paragraph argument** to try to convince someone else.	• Share your essay with a peer who has supported an opposing claim. • Ask your peer to identify unconvincing ideas and passages in your essay. • Strengthen your reasoning and find additional evidence to support your position.

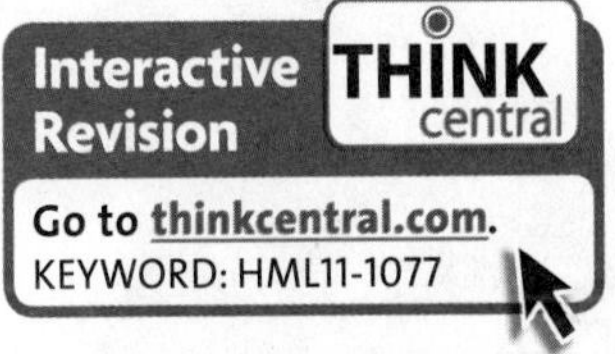

The Life You Save May Be Your Own

Short Story by Flannery O'Connor

COMMON CORE

RL 1 Cite textual evidence to support analysis of what the text says explicitly as well as inferences drawn from the text, including determining where the text leaves matters uncertain. **RL 6** Analyze a case in which grasping point of view requires distinguishing what is directly stated in a text from what is really meant.

DID YOU KNOW?

Flannery O'Connor . . .

- began writing and illustrating stories at the age of 6.
- enrolled in college at age 16, graduating three years later.
- created cartoons for her high school newspaper.
- raised peacocks on her farm in Georgia.

Meet the Author

Flannery O'Connor 1925–1964

As a child, Flannery O'Connor had a pet chicken that could walk backwards as well as forwards. News reporters—including a photographer all the way from New York City—were dispatched to her home in Savannah, Georgia, to take pictures of the unusual chicken. This experience, O'Connor later said, marked her for life. It began her preoccupation with the grotesque, a fascination she shares with other writers belonging to the literary tradition known as Southern Gothic. "Whenever I am asked why Southern writers particularly have a penchant for writing about freaks," O'Connor once commented, "I say it is because we are still able to recognize one."

Born to Write Always a bit shy but self-confident and spirited, O'Connor seemed born to be a writer. She wrote stories from an early age and described herself as a "pigeon-toed only child with a receding chin and a you-leave-me-alone-or-I'll-bite-you complex." In high school, she listed her hobby as "collecting rejection slips," as she was already sending out her stories to major literary journals. After graduating from college, she received a scholarship to attend the famed Writers' Workshop at the University of Iowa. In the late 1940s, she was twice invited to Yaddo, an exclusive artists' colony in upstate New York. In both places, she made lasting friends and developed the contacts she needed to succeed in the literary world.

A Life Cut Short At the age of 25, while writing her first novel, *Wise Blood* (1952), O'Connor was stricken with lupus, an autoimmune disease that had killed her father 9 years earlier. She moved with her mother to a farm outside of Milledgeville, Georgia, where she used her remaining 14 years to produce two highly acclaimed volumes of stories and another novel, *The Violent Bear It Away* (1960).

Defined by Region and Religion Being a Catholic in largely Protestant Georgia gave O'Connor a unique perspective. The South offered rich subject matter—sometimes violent, often humorous—and her Catholicism provided a unifying vision of the divine in everyday life. Her works, often difficult to categorize and to fully understand, weren't bestsellers and took some time to gain a following. Today, critics consider O'Connor one of the greatest short story writers of her time. Her novels and stories are more popular now than they've ever been.

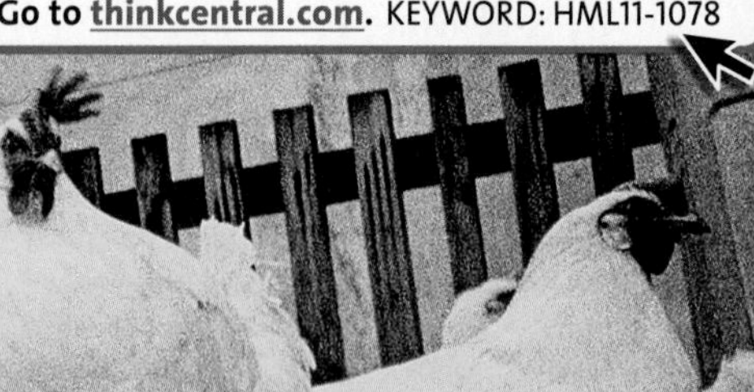

Author Online THINK central

Go to thinkcentral.com. KEYWORD: HML11-1078

TEXT ANALYSIS: IRONY

Irony is a contrast between appearance and actuality. You'll notice two kinds of irony at work in the story you're about to read.

- **Dramatic irony** occurs when readers know more about a situation than the characters themselves know—as though the writer is letting you in on a secret the characters aren't privy to.
- **Situational irony** is a contrast between what a character or reader expects to happen and what actually does happen. This kind of irony often takes the reader by surprise.

Irony is often indirect and subtle, making it difficult to detect. Recognizing it, however, can make a work infinitely more striking and memorable. As you read "The Life You Save May Be Your Own," look for examples of both situational and dramatic irony.

READING SKILL: ANALYZE DESCRIPTIVE DETAILS

O'Connor asserted that "distortion is the only way to make people see." To that end, she employed a wealth of **descriptive details** to flesh out her grotesque characters and their often perverse situations. As you read, use a chart like the one shown to note examples of these details. Record your personal reactions as well as your analysis of what these details reveal or highlight about the characters and their bizarre behavior.

Striking Details from the Story	*My Reactions*	*Analysis*
"He offered the old woman a piece [of gum] but she only raised her upper lip to indicate she had no teeth."	*This old woman gives me the creeps. I can picture her hostile stance and her toothless gums.*	*The woman lives in a poor, isolated area and probably doesn't have access to dental or medical care. But she's not ashamed of her circumstances, and she doesn't waste words explaining herself.*

 Complete the activities in your **Reader/Writer Notebook**.

Could you spot a CON ARTIST?

We've all seen—or heard of or read about—an instance in which someone was duped by a con artist. If you've ever watched a schemer in action, you may have thought to yourself, "I never would have fallen for that one." But literature, movies, and even newspapers are full of stories of people being conned. Why? What makes a con artist's deception so hard to spot?

QUICKWRITE Write a quick description of a con you've seen—on the big screen or in real life—or read about. Why do you think the victim fell for the con artist's antics? What traits did the con artist possess? If you'd been in the victim's shoes, do you honestly think you could have seen through the con artist's scheme, or would you too have been duped?

The Life You Save May Be Your Own

Flannery O'Connor

The old woman and her daughter were sitting on their porch when Mr. Shiftlet came up their road for the first time. The old woman slid to the edge of her chair and leaned forward, shading her eyes from the piercing sunset with her hand. The daughter could not see far in front of her and continued to play with her fingers. Although the old woman lived in this desolate spot with only her daughter and she had never seen Mr. Shiftlet before, she could tell, even from a distance, that he was a tramp and no one to be afraid of. His left coat sleeve was folded up to show there was only half an arm in it, and his gaunt figure listed slightly to the side as if the breeze were pushing him. He had on a black town suit and a brown felt hat that was turned up in the front and down in the back and he carried a tin tool box by a handle. He came on, at an amble, up her road, his face turned toward the sun which appeared to be balancing itself on the peak of a small mountain.

The old woman didn't change her position until he was almost into her yard; then she rose with one hand fisted on her hip. The daughter, a large girl in a short blue organdy dress, saw him all at once and jumped up and began to stamp and point and make excited speechless sounds. **A**

Mr. Shiftlet stopped just inside the yard and set his box on the ground and tipped his hat at her as if she were not in the least afflicted; then he turned toward the old woman and swung the hat all the way off. He had long black slick hair that hung flat from a part in the middle to beyond the tips of his ears on either side. His face descended in forehead for more than half its length and ended suddenly with his features just balanced over a jutting steel-trap jaw. He seemed to be a young man but he had a look of composed[1] dissatisfaction as if he understood life thoroughly.

"Good evening," the old woman said. She was about the size of a cedar fence post and she had a man's gray hat pulled down low over her head.

Analyze Visuals ▶
What compositional elements lend this scene a sense of isolation? Cite specific examples in your answer.

A ANALYZE DETAILS
Reread lines 1–16, recording in your chart the descriptive details O'Connor includes about each character. What does the old woman's body language suggest about her character? What does the girl's behavior indicate?

---

1. **composed:** calm; cool and collected.

Light of Lagrange (1997), Billy Morrow Jackson. Watercolor, 22″ × 29″. © Billy Morrow Jackson.

The tramp stood looking at her and didn't answer. He turned his back and faced the sunset. He swung both his whole and his short arm up slowly so that they indicated an expanse of sky and his figure formed a crooked cross. The old woman watched him with her arms folded across her chest as if she were the owner of the sun, and the daughter watched, her head thrust forward and her fat helpless hands hanging at the wrists. She had long pink-gold hair and eyes as blue as a peacock's neck.

He held the pose for almost fifty seconds and then he picked up his box and came on to the porch and dropped down on the bottom step. "Lady," he said in a firm nasal voice, "I'd give a fortune to live where I could see me a sun do that every evening."

"Does it every evening," the old woman said and sat back down. The daughter sat down too and watched him with a cautious sly look as if he were a bird that had come up very close. He leaned to one side, rooting in his pants pocket, and in a second he brought out a package of chewing gum and offered her a piece. She took it and unpeeled it and began to chew without taking her eyes off him. He offered the old woman a piece but she only raised her upper lip to indicate she had no teeth.

Mr. Shiftlet's pale, sharp glance had already passed over everything in the yard—the pump near the corner of the house and the big fig tree that three or four chickens were preparing to roost in—and had moved to a shed where he saw the square rusted back of an automobile. "You ladies drive?" he asked.

"That car ain't run in fifteen year," the old woman said. "The day my husband died, it quit running."

"Nothing is like it used to be, lady," he said. "The world is almost rotten."

"That's right," the old woman said. "You from around here?"

"Name Tom T. Shiftlet," he murmured, looking at the tires.

"I'm pleased to meet you," the old woman said. "Name Lucynell Crater and daughter Lucynell Crater. What you doing around here, Mr. Shiftlet?"

He judged the car to be about a 1928 or '29 Ford. "Lady," he said, and turned and gave her his full attention, "lemme tell you something. There's one of these doctors in Atlanta that's taken a knife and cut the human heart—the human heart," he repeated, leaning forward, "out of a man's chest and held it in his hand," and he held his hand out, palm up, as if it were slightly weighted with the human heart, "and studied it like it was a day-old chicken, and lady," he said, allowing a long significant pause in which his head slid forward and his clay-colored eyes brightened, "he don't know no more about it than you or me."

"That's right," the old woman said.

"Why, if he was to take that knife and cut into every corner of it, he still wouldn't know no more than you or me. What you want to bet?"

"Nothing," the old woman said wisely. "Where you come from, Mr. Shiftlet?"

He didn't answer. He reached into his pocket and brought out a sack of tobacco and a package of cigarette papers and rolled himself a cigarette, expertly with one hand, and attached it in a hanging position to his upper lip. Then he took a box of wooden matches from his pocket and struck one on his shoe. He held the burning match as if he were studying the mystery of flame while it traveled dangerously

Language Coach

Informal Pronunciation
Lemme (line 57) is an example of informal pronunciation. Instead of saying "Let me" distinctly, Mr. Shiftlet runs the two words together. Similar words are *dunno* ("don't know") and *gimme* ("give me"). How does informal speech suit this character?

toward his skin. The daughter began to make loud noises and to point to his hand and shake her finger at him, but when the flame was just before touching him, he leaned down with his hand cupped over it as if he were going to set fire to his nose and lit the cigarette. B

He flipped away the dead match and blew a stream of gray into the evening. A sly look came over his face. "Lady," he said, "nowadays, people'll do anything anyways. I can tell you my name is Tom T. Shiftlet and I come from Tarwater, Tennessee, but you never have seen me before: how you know I ain't lying? How you know my name ain't Aaron Sparks, lady, and I come from Singleberry, Georgia, or how you know it's not George Speeds and I come from Lucy, Alabama, or how you know I ain't Thompson Bright from Toolafalls, Mississippi?"

"I don't know nothing about you," the old woman muttered, irked.

"Lady," he said, "people don't care how they lie. Maybe the best I can tell you is, I'm a man; but listen lady," he said and paused and made his tone more ominous still, "what is a man?"

The old woman began to gum a seed. "What you carry in that tin box, Mr. Shiftlet?" she asked.

"Tools," he said, put back. "I'm a carpenter."

"Well, if you come out here to work, I'll be able to feed you and give you a place to sleep but I can't pay. I'll tell you that before you begin," she said.

There was no answer at once and no particular expression on his face. He leaned back against the two-by-four that helped support the porch roof. "Lady," he said slowly, "there's some men that some things mean more to them than money." The old woman rocked without comment and the daughter watched the trigger that moved up and down in his neck. He told the old woman then that all most people were interested in was money, but he asked what a man was made for. He asked her if a man was made for money, or what. He asked her what she thought she was made for but she didn't answer, she only sat rocking and wondered if a one-armed man could put a new roof on her garden house. He asked a lot of questions that she didn't answer. He told her that he was twenty-eight years old and had lived a varied life. He had been a gospel singer, a foreman on the railroad, an assistant in an undertaking parlor, and he come over the radio for three months with Uncle Roy and his Red Creek Wranglers. He said he had fought and bled in the Arm Service of his country and visited every foreign land and that everywhere he had seen people that didn't care if they did a thing one way or another. He said he hadn't been raised thataway. C

A fat yellow moon appeared in the branches of the fig tree as if it were going to roost there with the chickens. He said that a man had to escape to the country to see the world whole and that he wished he lived in a desolate place like this where he could see the sun go down every evening like God made it to do.

"Are you married or are you single?" the old woman asked.

There was a long silence. "Lady," he asked finally, "where would you find you an innocent woman today? I wouldn't have any of this trash I could just pick up."

The daughter was leaning very far down, hanging her head almost between her knees watching him through a triangular door she had made in her overturned

B ANALYZE DETAILS
Consider the wealth of details O'Connor offers about Tom Shiftlet in lines 45–76. Which details serve to reveal his important **traits?**

C IRONY
Reread lines 105–108. Explain the irony of Shiftlet's statement that he served in the "Arm Service."

hair; and she suddenly fell in a heap on the floor and began to whimper. Mr. Shiftlet straightened her out and helped her get back in the chair.

"Is she your baby girl?" he asked.

"My only," the old woman said, "and she's the sweetest girl in the world. I would give her up for nothing on earth. She's smart too. She can sweep the floor, cook, wash, feed the chickens, and hoe. I wouldn't give her up for a casket of jewels." D

"No," he said kindly, "don't ever let any man take her away from you."

"Any man come after her," the old woman said, " 'll have to stay around the place."

Mr. Shiftlet's eye in the darkness was focused on a part of the automobile bumper that glittered in the distance. "Lady," he said, jerking his short arm up as if he could point with it to her house and yard and pump, "there ain't a broken thing on this plantation that I couldn't fix for you, one-arm jackleg[2] or not. I'm a man," he said with a sullen dignity, "even if I ain't a whole one. I got," he said, tapping his knuckles on the floor to emphasize the immensity of what he was going to say, "a moral intelligence!" and his face pierced out of the darkness into a shaft of doorlight and he stared at her as if he were astonished himself at this impossible truth.

The old woman was not impressed with the phrase. "I told you you could hang around and work for food," she said, "if you don't mind sleeping in that car yonder."

"Why listen, Lady," he said with a grin of delight, "the monks of old slept in their coffins!"

"They wasn't as advanced as we are," the old woman said.

The next morning he began on the roof of the garden house while Lucynell, the daughter, sat on a rock and watched him work. He had not been around a week before the change he had made in the place was apparent. He had patched the front and back steps, built a new hog pen, restored a fence, and taught Lucynell, who was completely deaf and had never said a word in her life, to say the word "bird." The big rosy-faced girl followed him everywhere, saying "Burrttddt ddbirrrttdt," and clapping her hands. The old woman watched from a distance, secretly pleased. She was ravenous for a son-in-law.

Mr. Shiftlet slept on the hard narrow back seat of the car with his feet out the side window. He had his razor and a can of water on a crate that served him as a bedside table and he put up a piece of mirror against the back glass and kept his coat neatly on a hanger that he hung over one of the windows.

In the evenings he sat on the steps and talked while the old woman and Lucynell rocked violently in their chairs on either side of him. The old woman's three mountains were black against the dark blue sky and were visited off and on by various planets and by the moon after it had left the chickens. Mr. Shiftlet pointed out that the reason he had improved this plantation was because he had taken a personal interest in it. He said he was even going to make the automobile run.

D IRONY
O'Connor employs irony not just in her descriptions of her characters, but in their dialogue, as well. Reread lines 120–124. What double meaning might be suggested by the phrase "I would give her up for nothing on earth"?

Analyze Visuals ▶
Note that the painting on the opposite page is titled *The Interloper*. An interloper is an intruder. What does this title suggest about the man and the farmhouse depicted? How does the title work with the elements of the painting to establish a mood?

2. **jackleg:** someone who does work he or she has not been trained to do.

The Interloper (1958), Billy Morrow Jackson. Collection of Mrs. Virginia Penofsky.

He had raised the hood and studied the mechanism and he said he could tell that the car had been built in the days when cars were really built. You take now, he said, one man puts in one bolt and another man puts in another bolt and another man puts in another bolt so that it's a man for a bolt. That's why you have to pay so much for a car: you're paying all those men. Now if you didn't have to pay but one man, you could get you a cheaper car and one that had had a personal interest taken in it, and it would be a better car. The old woman agreed with him that this was so.

Mr. Shiftlet said that the trouble with the world was that nobody cared, or stopped and took any trouble. He said he never would have been able to teach Lucynell to say a word if he hadn't cared and stopped long enough. E

"Teach her to say something else," the old woman said.

"What you want her to say next?" Mr. Shiftlet asked.

The old woman's smile was broad and toothless and suggestive. "Teach her to say 'sugarpie,'" she said.

Mr. Shiftlet already knew what was on her mind. F

The next day he began to tinker with the automobile, and that evening he told her that if she would buy a fan belt, he would be able to make the car run.

The old woman said she would give him the money. "You see that girl yonder?" she asked, pointing to Lucynell who was sitting on the floor a foot away, watching

E IRONY
A "1928 or '29 Ford" like this one would, in fact, have been made on an assembly line, a feature that greatly reduced the cost of automobiles. What does this knowledge, combined with Shiftlet's statements in lines 160–170, tell you about his character? Explain which type of irony O'Connor is using here.

F ANALYZE DETAILS
What are Mrs. Crater's **motives** for wanting Lucynell to learn to say "sugarpie"? What details in line 173 suggest this?

him, her eyes blue even in the dark. "If it was ever a man wanted to take her away, I would say, 'No man on earth is going to take that sweet girl of mine away from me!' but if he was to say, 'Lady, I don't want to take her away, I want her right here,' I would say, 'Mister, I don't blame you none. I wouldn't pass up a chance to live in a permanent place and get the sweetest girl in the world myself. You ain't no fool,' I would say."

"How old is she?" Mr. Shiftlet asked casually.

"Fifteen, sixteen," the old woman said. The girl was nearly thirty but because of her innocence it was impossible to guess.

"It would be a good idea to paint it too," Mr. Shiftlet remarked. "You don't want it to rust out."

"We'll see about that later," the old woman said.

The next day he walked into town and returned with the parts he needed and a can of gasoline. Late in the afternoon, terrible noises issued from the shed and the old woman rushed out of the house, thinking Lucynell was somewhere having a fit. Lucynell was sitting on a chicken crate, stamping her feet and screaming, "Burrddttt! bddurrddtttt!" but her fuss was drowned out by the car. With a volley of blasts it emerged from the shed, moving in a fierce and stately way. Mr. Shiftlet was in the driver's seat, sitting very erect. He had an expression of serious modesty on his face as if he had just raised the dead.

That night, rocking on the porch, the old woman began her business at once. "You want you an innocent woman, don't you?" she asked sympathetically. "You don't want none of this trash."

"No'm, I don't," Mr. Shiftlet said.

"One that can't talk," she continued, "can't sass you back or use foul language. That's the kind for you to have. Right there," and she pointed to Lucynell sitting cross-legged in her chair, holding both feet in her hands.

"That's right," he admitted. "She wouldn't give me any trouble."

"Saturday," the old woman said, "you and her and me can drive into town and get married."

Mr. Shiftlet eased his position on the steps.

"I can't get married right now," he said. "Everything you want to do takes money and I ain't got any."

"What you need with money?" she asked.

"It takes money," he said. "Some people'll do anything anyhow these days, but the way I think, I wouldn't marry no woman that I couldn't take on a trip like she was somebody. I mean take her to a hotel and treat her. I wouldn't marry the Duchesser Windsor,"[3] he said firmly, "unless I could take her to a hotel and give her something good to eat.

"I was raised thataway and there ain't a thing I can do about it. My old mother taught me how to do."

"Lucynell don't even know what a hotel is," the old woman muttered. "Listen here, Mr. Shiftlet," she said, sliding forward in her chair, "you'd be getting a

---

3. **Duchesser Windsor:** Duchess of Windsor. The title was given to the American divorcée Wallace Simpson upon her marriage to the former Edward VIII of England in 1937.

permanent house and a deep well and the most innocent girl in the world. You don't need no money. Lemme tell you something: there ain't any place in the world for a poor disabled friendless drifting man."

The ugly words settled in Mr. Shiftlet's head like a group of buzzards in the top of a tree. He didn't answer at once. He rolled himself a cigarette and lit it and then he said in an even voice, "Lady, a man is divided into two parts, body and spirit."

The old woman clamped her gums together.

"A body and a spirit," he repeated. "The body, lady, is like a house: it don't go anywhere; but the spirit, lady, is like a automobile: always on the move, always . . ."

"Listen, Mr. Shiftlet," she said, "my well never goes dry and my house is always warm in the winter and there's no mortgage on a thing about this place. You can go to the courthouse and see for yourself. And yonder under that shed is a fine automobile." She laid the bait carefully. "You can have it painted by Saturday. I'll pay for the paint."

In the darkness, Mr. Shiftlet's smile stretched like a weary snake waking up by a fire. After a second he recalled himself and said, "I'm only saying a man's spirit means more to him than anything else. I would have to take my wife off for the week end without no regards at all for cost. I got to follow where my spirit says to go."

"I'll give you fifteen dollars for a week end trip," the old woman said in a crabbed voice. "That's the best I can do."

"That wouldn't hardly pay for more than the gas and the hotel," he said. "It wouldn't feed her."

"Seventeen-fifty," the old woman said. "That's all I got so it isn't any use you trying to milk me. You can take a lunch."

Mr. Shiftlet was deeply hurt by the word "milk." He didn't doubt that she had more money sewed up in her mattress but he had already told her he was not interested in her money. "I'll make that do," he said and rose and walked off without treating[4] with her further. **G**

G ANALYZE DETAILS
At this point in the story, what **conclusions** can you draw about each character? Cite details in lines 178–250 that influenced your judgments.

On Saturday the three of them drove into town in the car that the paint had barely dried on and Mr. Shiftlet and Lucynell were married in the Ordinary's[5] office while the old woman witnessed. As they came out of the courthouse, Mr. Shiftlet began twisting his neck in his collar. He looked morose and bitter as if he had been insulted while someone held him. "That didn't satisfy me none," he said. "That was just something a woman in an office did, nothing but paper work and blood tests. What do they know about my blood? If they was to take my heart and cut it out," he said, "they wouldn't know a thing about me. It didn't satisfy me at all."

"It satisfied the law," the old woman said sharply.

"The law," Mr. Shiftlet said and spit. "It's the law that don't satisfy me."

He had painted the car dark green with a yellow band around it just under the windows. The three of them climbed in the front seat and the old woman said, "Don't Lucynell look pretty? Looks like a baby doll." Lucynell was dressed up in a white dress that her mother had uprooted from a trunk and there was a Panama

4. **treating:** discussing terms; negotiating.
5. **Ordinary's:** judge's.

hat on her head with a bunch of red wooden cherries on the brim. Every now and then her placid expression was changed by a sly isolated little thought like a shoot of green in the desert. "You got a prize!" the old woman said.

Mr. Shiftlet didn't even look at her.

They drove back to the house to let the old woman off and pick up the lunch. When they were ready to leave, she stood staring in the window of the car, with her fingers clenched around the glass. Tears began to seep sideways out of her eyes and run along the dirty creases in her face. "I ain't ever been parted with her for two days before," she said.

Mr. Shiftlet started the motor.

"And I wouldn't let no man have her but you because I seen you would do right. Good bye, Sugarbaby," she said, clutching at the sleeve of the white dress. Lucynell looked straight at her and didn't seem to see her there at all. Mr. Shiftlet eased the car forward so that she had to move her hands.

The early afternoon was clear and open and surrounded by pale blue sky. Although the car would go only thirty miles an hour, Mr. Shiftlet imagined a terrific climb and dip and swerve that went entirely to his head so that he forgot his morning bitterness. He had always wanted an automobile but he had never been able to afford one before. He drove very fast because he wanted to make Mobile[6] by nightfall.

Occasionally he stopped his thoughts long enough to look at Lucynell in the seat beside him. She had eaten the lunch as soon as they were out of the yard and now she was pulling the cherries off the hat one by one and throwing them out the window. He became depressed in spite of the car. He had driven about a hundred miles when he decided that she must be hungry again and at the next small town they came to, he stopped in front of an aluminum-painted eating place called The Hot Spot and took her in and ordered her a plate of ham and grits. The ride had made her sleepy and as soon as she got up on the stool, she rested her head on the counter and shut her eyes. There was no one in The Hot Spot but Mr. Shiftlet and the boy behind the counter, a pale youth with a greasy rag hung over his shoulder. Before he could dish up the food, she was snoring gently. **H**

"Give it to her when she wakes up," Mr. Shiftlet said. "I'll pay for it now."

The boy bent over her and stared at the long pink-gold hair and the half-shut sleeping eyes. Then he looked up and stared at Mr. Shiftlet. "She looks like an angel of Gawd," he murmured.

"Hitch-hiker," Mr. Shiftlet explained. "I can't wait. I got to make Tuscaloosa."[7]

The boy bent over again and very carefully touched his finger to a strand of the golden hair, and Mr. Shiftlet left.

He was more depressed than ever as he drove on by himself. The late afternoon had grown hot and sultry and the country had flattened out. Deep in the sky a storm was preparing very slowly and without thunder as if it meant to drain every drop of air from the earth before it broke. There were times when Mr. Shiftlet

H IRONY
Consider what most people would expect from an establishment called The Hot Spot. What is ironic about this restaurant's name?

6. **Mobile:** a city in southwestern Alabama, along the Gulf Coast.

7. **Tuscaloosa:** a city in west-central Alabama.

preferred not to be alone. He felt too that a man with a car had a responsibility to others, and he kept his eye out for a hitch-hiker. Occasionally he saw a sign that warned: "Drive carefully. The life you save may be your own." ❶

The narrow road dropped off on either side into dry fields and here and there a shack or a filling station stood in a clearing. The sun began to set directly in front of the automobile. It was a reddening ball that through his windshield was slightly flat on the bottom and top. He saw a boy in overalls and a gray hat standing on the edge of the road and he slowed the car down and stopped in front of him. The boy didn't have his hand raised to thumb the ride, he was only standing there, but he had a small cardboard suitcase and his hat was set on his head in a way to indicate that he had left somewhere for good. "Son," Mr. Shiftlet said, "I see you want a ride."

The boy didn't say he did or he didn't but he opened the door of the car and got in, and Mr. Shiftlet started driving again. The child held the suitcase on his lap and folded his arms on top of it. He turned his head and looked out the window away from Mr. Shiftlet. Mr. Shiftlet felt oppressed. "Son," he said after a minute, "I got the best old mother in the world so I reckon you only got the second best."

The boy gave him a quick dark glance and then turned his face back out the window.

"It's nothing so sweet," Mr. Shiftlet continued, "as a boy's mother. She taught him his first prayers at her knee, she give him love when no other would, she told him what was right and what wasn't, and she seen that he done the right thing. Son," he said, "I never rued a day in my life like the one I rued when I left that old mother of mine."

The boy shifted in his seat but he didn't look at Mr. Shiftlet. He unfolded his arms and put one hand on the door handle.

"My mother was a angel of Gawd," Mr. Shiftlet said in a very strained voice. "He took her from heaven and giver to me and I left her." His eyes were instantly clouded over with a mist of tears. The car was barely moving.

The boy turned angrily in the seat. "You go to the devil!" he cried. "My old woman is a flea bag and yours is a stinking pole cat!" and with that he flung the door open and jumped out with his suitcase into the ditch.

Mr. Shiftlet was so shocked that for about a hundred feet he drove along slowly with the door still open. A cloud, the exact color of the boy's hat and shaped like a turnip, had descended over the sun, and another, worse looking, crouched behind the car. Mr. Shiftlet felt that the rottenness of the world was about to engulf him. He raised his arm and let it fall again to his breast. "Oh Lord!" he prayed. "Break forth and wash the slime from this earth!"

The turnip continued slowly to descend. After a few minutes there was a guffawing peal of thunder from behind and fantastic raindrops, like tin-can tops, crashed over the rear of Mr. Shiftlet's car. Very quickly he stepped on the gas, and with his stump sticking out the window he raced the galloping shower into Mobile.

❶ **IRONY**
What is the irony in Shiftlet's reasons for looking for a hitchhiker?

Language Coach

Word Definitions *Rued* (line 329) means "regretted" or "felt the consequences of." *Rue* is often used with *day*, as in lines 329–330. What does Mr. Shiftlet say he regrets?

Comprehension

1. **Recall** What are Lucynell's disabilities?
2. **Summarize** What is the bargain struck between Mr. Shiftlet and Mrs. Crater over her daughter, Lucynell?
3. **Clarify** What does Mr. Shiftlet's treatment of Lucynell at the end reveal about his intentions all along?

Text Analysis

4. **Analyze Descriptive Details** Review the chart you created as you read. Because Mr. Shiftlet and Mrs. Crater are both hiding something during much of the story, readers must mine the details given about each character for clues to their true selves. Since Mr. Shiftlet's words and thoughts can't be trusted, what can you learn about him from the descriptions of his physical appearance? What details reveal the flaws in Mrs. Crater's character and give her motives away? Support your analysis with evidence from the text.
5. **Interpret Irony** In this story, much of O'Connor's wry humor comes from **situational** and **dramatic irony.** Review the story to find at least two examples of each kind of irony. Also, see whether you can find one example that reveals both kinds at once. What do these multiple ironies suggest about O'Connor's view of her fellow human beings?
6. **Make Judgments** What is the significance of the story's title, taken from a road sign? Explain how you think O'Connor judges Tom T. Shiftlet, as well as how you yourself do. Be sure to address the following:
   - the way in which Mr. Shiftlet is a potential savior of his own life and the lives of others
   - how and why he fails in this role
   - whether you think he has any redeeming features or whether you see him as hopelessly lost

Text Criticism

7. **Author's Style** For Flannery O'Connor, a devout Catholic, evidence of divine grace was everywhere, and her stories are full of religious **imagery.** Find at least two examples of religious imagery in this story and explain what they contribute to its meaning and its message.

Could you spot a **CON ARTIST?**

Mr. Shiftlet's motivation for swindling is Mrs. Crater's car. What are some other reasons con artists deceive people? Do you have any sympathy for their motivations? Why or why not?

COMMON CORE

RL 1 Cite textual evidence to support analysis of what the text says explicitly as well as inferences drawn from the text, including determining where the text leaves matters uncertain. **RL 6** Analyze a case in which grasping point of view requires distinguishing what is directly stated in a text from what is really meant.

The Essence of a Short Story

Stories by modernist writers, such as Fitzgerald, Hemingway, and Faulkner, are often complex or ambiguous. These works demand much of readers, who must pay attention to details of character, setting, plot, dialogue, and language in order to decipher meaning.

Writing to Evaluate

After reflecting on each of the short stories you have just read, choose two stories and evaluate them in order to distill their essence—that which is utterly indispensable—in no more than 300 of the author's own words. You may use portions of sentences and combine them, if appropriate and necessary. In addition, you may create your own paragraphing structure in order to give your distillations a desirable "flow."

Consider

- introductions or important descriptions of characters
- plot events essential to the stories, especially the climax
- details that introduce the stories' topic, or subject
- dialogue that reveals character, motivation, or theme
- particularly meaningful language

Extension

VIEWING & REPRESENTING
Working with a partner, **choose or create an image** that you feel captures the essence of the story you evaluated. You may look for an image from a magazine, Web site, book of art, or other source, or you may create your own. Share your image with the class, and explain why you feel it represents or illustrates the story's essence.

COMMON CORE

RL 9 Demonstrate knowledge of early-twentieth-century foundational works of American literature, including how two or more texts from the same period treat similar themes or topics.

Ernest Hemingway, working as a war correspondent, 1944

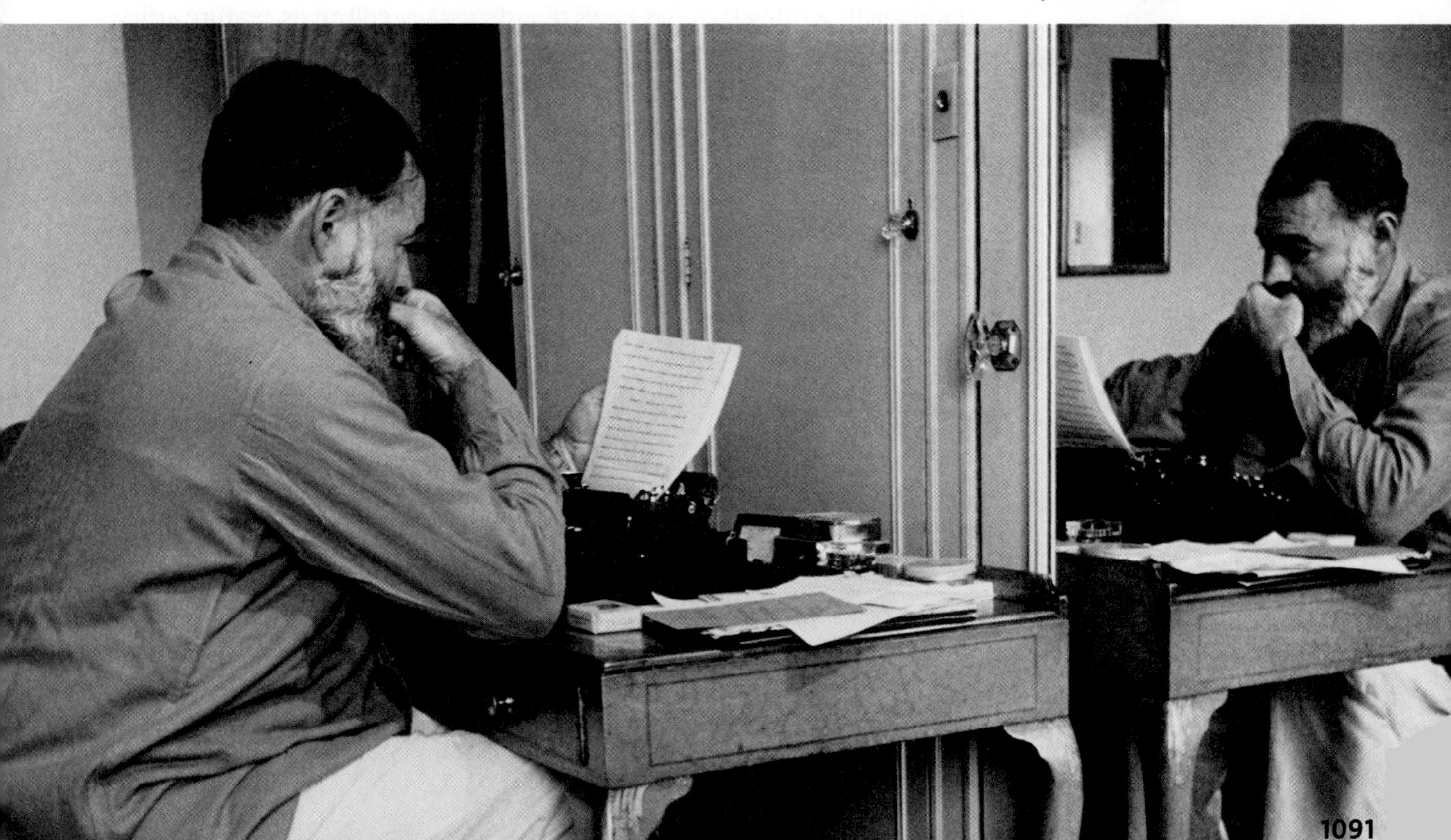

Text Analysis Workshop

Journalism

Some journalists put together a news story or an opinion piece that is so well written and riveting that the article is elevated to the realm of literature. Have you ever read a news report or editorial that seemed to stand out from anything else you'd read in the newspaper? If so, you may have read an emerging literary classic.

COMMON CORE

Included in this workshop:
RI 5 Analyze and evaluate the effectiveness of the structure an author uses in his or her exposition or argument, including whether the structure makes points clear, convincing, and engaging. **RI 6** Determine an author's point of view or purpose in a text in which the rhetoric is particularly effective, analyzing how style and content contribute to the power, persuasiveness, or beauty of the text.

The Fine Art of Journalism

Traditionally, journalism and literature are considered to be very different forms. **Journalism** is known for being factual, informative, and written for the moment. **Literature,** on the other hand, is built from the imagination and meant to last. Its language is often figurative, its images are symbolic, and the setting and characters are representative of deeper meaning. When journalism becomes literature, it's not the imaginative use of facts that makes it so; rather, it's the imaginative use of language that transforms it from a standard news story into a piece of art.

Journalistic writing includes news reports, essays, editorials, feature articles, and critical reviews and has a long history in the United States. Many of the big issues of the day, since pre-Revolutionary times, have been debated in newspapers, magazines, and pamphlets. In the early 20th century, a number of serious literary writers began their writing careers as journalists, including Ernest Hemingway, E. B. White, and Dorothy Parker. The tradition of journalism as literature continued with writers such as Truman Capote, Tom Wolfe, and Joan Didion. In the 1960s, Wolfe coined the term "New Journalism" to describe the work of a journalist who sets out to create journalistic writing that uses literary techniques.

Tools of the Trade

Journalism that transcends the mundane and becomes literature is usually characterized by the use of certain literary techniques.

- **Imagery**—Traditionally, news writing contains only essential details, without any embellishment of description. In literary writing, the writer includes words and phrases that express sensory experiences in order to create a vivid picture or strong impression for the reader.

- **Narrative elements**—In the world of journalism, an article is figuratively called "a story." At times, this might be literally true, especially when a journalist relates an incident with all the elements of a good tale, including a suspenseful plot, detailed characterization and setting, and a well-defined point of view.
- **Style and voice**—Style is a writer's unique way of communicating ideas, and voice is the expression of his or her personality. Most news writing is made up of spare, plain prose, written for a mass audience. In literary writing, the writer may use figurative language, coin new words, or interject descriptive phrases. Each of these elements can add up to an original style and voice.
- **Writer's tone**—News reporters historically have tried to maintain an objective, unbiased tone in their writing. However, writers such as Hemingway and Jack London often used the tone of their writing to advance a particular cause and to convey a very personal perspective. They wrote personal narratives of news events, including war experiences and unusual adventures, in which they interjected their own observations and opinions.

In the following passage from "A New Kind of War" (page 1096), notice how Hemingway included his observations instead of merely reporting the facts.

> In the war that I had known, men often lied about the manner of their wounding. Not at first; but later. I'd lied a little myself in my time. Especially late in the evening.
>
> **—Ernest Hemingway, "A New Kind of War"**

Close Read

What does Hemingway reveal about himself in this passage? Why wouldn't this be typical of journalism, which is known for being factual?

Dorothy Parker was always known for her acerbic wit. In the following excerpt from a literary review, notice the imagery and figurative language she uses in exaggerating the critics' reactions to Hemingway's first novel.

> Promptly upon its publication, Ernest Hemingway was discovered, the Stars and Stripes were reverentially raised over him, eight hundred and forty-seven book reviewers formed themselves into the word "welcome," and the band played "Hail to the Chief" in three concurrent keys.
>
> **—Dorothy Parker, "A Book of Great Short Stories"**

Close Read

In each of these examples, the writer's voice is well developed. How would you describe the personality of the writer in each?

A New Kind of War

Video link at thinkcentral.com

News Dispatch by Ernest Hemingway

COMMON CORE

RI 1 Cite textual evidence to support analysis of what the text says explicitly as well as inferences drawn from the text, including determining where the text leaves matters uncertain. **RI 6** Determine an author's point of view or purpose in a text in which the rhetoric is particularly effective, analyzing how style and content contribute to the power, persuasiveness, or beauty of the text. **RI 10** Read and comprehend literary nonfiction. **L 5b** Analyze nuances in the meaning of words with similar denotations.

Meet the Author

Ernest Hemingway 1899–1961

Ernest Hemingway never considered his journalism as important as his fiction, but his journalism was admired anyway, particularly his war correspondence. Before he published his first stories and novels in the 1920s, he reported on European affairs for the *Toronto Star.* He covered the Greco-Turkish War of 1922, describing 20 miles of Greek refugees trudging through the rain. He also interviewed the fascist Italian dictator Benito Mussolini, calling him the "biggest bluff in Europe."

Taking Sides in Spain By the 1930s, Hemingway had become a famous literary figure. He returned to war reporting in 1937 after civil war broke out in Spain, the country that he loved. Hemingway is perhaps most identified with this conflict, in which the right-wing army of General Francisco Franco (the Nationalists) fought against supporters of the left-wing elected government of Spain (the Loyalists or Republicans). This war was widely seen as a struggle against fascism, or dictatorial government. Many world writers, including Hemingway, were sympathetic to the Loyalist side. These writers were greatly disheartened by Franco's eventual victory in 1939.

Celebrity Journalist Hemingway covered the war for the North American Newspaper Alliance (NANA), receiving the highest fee ever paid a war correspondent. His NANA dispatches have been called "a new style of reporting that told the public about every facet of the war, especially . . . its effects on the common man, woman, and child." One of these dispatches, "A New Kind of War," is considered classic.

Writer or Fighter? After World War II broke out, Hemingway once again became a war reporter, this time for *Collier's* magazine. He memorably described the D-day landing at Normandy, the liberation of Paris, and the Allied movement into Germany in 1944. His command of a French guerrilla band and his storage of weapons in his hotel room led him to be investigated for violating the Geneva Convention, which forbids journalists to take up arms. He was cleared of misconduct and later awarded a Bronze Star for his service as a war correspondent.

See also the biography on page 1008, which covers Hemingway's entire career.

Author Online

Go to thinkcentral.com. KEYWORD: HML11-1094

DID YOU KNOW?

Ernest Hemingway . . .

- began a romance in Spain with fellow war reporter Martha Gellhorn, who became his third wife.
- hunted Nazi submarines off the coast of Cuba in his private fishing boat.

(background) Hemingway, center, among other correspondents covering the Spanish Civil War

TEXT ANALYSIS: SUBJECTIVITY IN REPORTING

News reporters are trained to be **objective,** presenting facts without the intrusion of their own personal feelings or opinions. You will notice, however, that Hemingway does not strive for this ideal in his reporting on the Spanish Civil War. His writing is quite **subjective,** expressing his personal reactions to what he sees. He wants his readers to be in Madrid with him, experiencing exactly what he does. Toward this end he uses both the **second-person point of view** ("as you lie in bed, you hear the firing in the front line") and the **first-person point of view** ("I did not believe a word of it").

As you read, notice ways in which Hemingway reveals his purpose through personal feelings and opinions. Consider what his subjectivity offers that an objective news report could not.

Review: **Dialogue**

READING SKILL: ANALYZE DESCRIPTIVE DETAILS

Hemingway makes powerful use of descriptive details. Many of these are **sensory details,** which appeal to the senses of sight, hearing, touch, smell, and taste. Notice the visual details in the following passage. What can you conclude from them?

On the corner, twenty yards away, is a heap of rubble, smashed cement and thrown up dirt, a single dead man, his torn clothes dusty, and a great hole in the sidewalk from which the gas from a broken main is rising. . . .

Other descriptive details are not sensory, but they still convey important ideas. What might it mean, for example, that the large rooms at the front of Hemingway's hotel only cost a dollar a day? As you read, jot down descriptive details about

- Madrid and the hotel
- Raven, the wounded soldier Hemingway meets
- Raven's commander, Jock Cunningham

React to these details and make inferences from them.

 Complete the activities in your **Reader/Writer Notebook**.

What can we learn from WAR?

The Spanish Civil War did not have immediate consequences for most Americans, yet American newspapers thought it was important enough to cover. Consider our own times. Why do newspapers and broadcast networks send reporters to cover fighting in foreign countries? What do these reports usually show or tell an audience about war?

DISCUSS Think about war coverage you have read, seen on television, or heard on the radio. Working in a small group, list types of information you would expect to be included in such reporting—the number of people killed in an attack, for example. After completing your list, discuss insights about war that you have gained from journalists.

A New Kind of War

Ernest Hemingway

BACKGROUND Hemingway and other journalists covering the Spanish Civil War stayed at the Hotel Florida in Madrid, the Spanish capital, which was under siege by General Franco's Nationalist forces. Franco was aided by the fascist governments of Italy and Nazi Germany, which sent troops and weapons. The Loyalist forces of the Spanish government were aided by the Soviet Union and volunteer International Brigades from across Europe and the United States. The soldiers that Hemingway profiles in this article were part of the International Brigades.

NANA Dispatch · APRIL 14, 1937

MADRID—The window of the hotel is open and, as you lie in bed, you hear the firing in the front line seventeen blocks away. There is a rifle fire all night long. The rifles go tacrong, capong, craang, tacrong, and then a machine gun opens up. It has a bigger calibre and is much louder, rong, cararong, rong, rong. Then there is the incoming boom of a trench mortar shell and a burst of machine gun fire. You lie and listen to it and it is a great thing to be in bed with your feet stretched out gradually warming the cold foot of the bed and not out there in University City or Carabanchel.[1] A man is singing hard-voiced in the street below and three drunks are arguing when you fall asleep. (A)

In the morning, before your call comes from the desk, the roaring burst of a high explosive shell wakes you and you go to the window and look out to see a man, his head down, his coat collar up, sprinting desperately across the paved

Analyze Visuals ▶
Examine the composition, or arrangement, of shapes in the photograph on the opposite page. What does the angle of the photo contribute to its impact? Explain.

(A) SUBJECTIVITY IN REPORTING
What are Hemingway's thoughts and sensations in the first paragraph? In a report on war, why might he include details of his hotel room and the sound of a voice singing in the street?

1. **University City or Carabanchel** (kär'-ə-bän-chel'): scenes of bloody battles in or on the outskirts of Madrid.

square. There is the acrid smell of high explosive you hoped you'd never smell again, and, in a bathrobe and bedroom slippers, you hurry down the marble stairs and almost into a middle-aged woman, wounded in the abdomen, who is being helped into the hotel entrance by two men in blue workmen's smocks. She has her two hands crossed below her big, old-style Spanish bosom and from between her fingers the blood is spurting in a thin stream. On the corner, twenty yards away, is a heap of rubble, smashed cement and thrown up dirt, a single dead man, his torn clothes dusty, and a great hole in the sidewalk from which the gas from a broken main is rising, looking like a heat mirage in the cold morning air. B

"How many dead?" you ask a policeman.

"Only one," he says. "It went through the sidewalk and burst below. If it would have burst on the solid stone of the road there might have been fifty."

A policeman covers the top of the trunk, from which the head is missing; they send for someone to repair the gas main and you go in to breakfast. A charwoman,[2] her eyes red, is scrubbing the blood off the marble floor of the corridor. The dead man wasn't you nor anyone you know and everyone is very hungry in the morning after a cold night and a long day the day before up at the Guadalajara[3] front. C

"Did you see him?" asked someone else at breakfast.

"Sure," you say.

"That's where we pass a dozen times a day. Right on that corner." Someone makes a joke about missing teeth and someone else says not to make that joke. And everyone has the feeling that characterizes war. It wasn't me, see? It wasn't me. D

The Italian dead up on the Guadalajara front weren't you, although Italian dead, because of where you had spent your boyhood, always seemed, still, like our dead.[4] No. You went to the front early in the morning in a miserable little car with a more miserable little chauffeur who suffered visibly the closer he came to the fighting. But at night, sometimes late, without lights, with the big trucks roaring past, you came on back to sleep in a bed with sheets in a good hotel, paying a dollar a day for the best rooms on the front. The smaller rooms in the back, on the side away from the shelling, were considerably more expensive. After the shell that lit on the sidewalk in front of the hotel you got a beautiful double corner room on that side, twice the size of the one you had had, for less than a dollar. It wasn't me they killed. See? No. Not me. It wasn't me anymore. E

Then, in a hospital given by the American Friends of Spanish Democracy, located out behind the Morata front along the road to Valencia,[5] they said, "Raven wants to see you."

"Do I know him?"

"I don't think so," they said, "but he wants to see you."

---

2. **charwoman:** a woman employed to clean houses or offices.
3. **Guadalajara:** a city in Spain to the northeast of Madrid, strategically important because of its nearness to the capital. Battle had raged there through most of March 1937, with the Loyalists finally winning.
4. **Italian dead . . . our dead:** Italian forces fought on the side of the Nationalists; however, Hemingway had spent a long time in an Italian hospital as a young man during World War I.
5. **Morata . . . Valencia:** Morata de Tejuña, a small town southeast of Madrid, was heavily damaged at this time. Valencia is on the eastern coast of Spain, about 240 miles southeast of Madrid.

B DESCRIPTIVE DETAILS
Notice the accumulation of **sensory details** in lines 10–21. What effect do they have on you as a reader? What purpose might they serve for the writer?

C GRAMMAR AND STYLE
Reread lines 28–30. Notice how the use of the **second-person pronoun** *you* places the reader in Hemingway's shoes.

D SUBJECTIVITY IN REPORTING
In the aftermath of a civilian casualty, Hemingway includes a joke made by survivors and his own highly personal conclusion about what the survivors are thinking. What purpose do you think it serves to include this material? Explain your answer.

E SUBJECTIVITY IN REPORTING
Reread lines 36–46. What is Hemingway's **tone** here—his attitude toward the Italian dead? his chauffeur? his hotel room? Cite evidence from this paragraph to support your response.

"Where is he?"

"Upstairs."

In the room upstairs they are giving a blood transfusion to a man with a very gray face who lay on a cot with his arm out, looking away from the gurgling bottle and moaning in a very impersonal way. He moaned mechanically and at regular intervals and it did not seem to be him that made the sound. His lips did not move.

"Where's Raven?" I asked.

"I'm here," said Raven.

The voice came from a high mound covered by a shoddy gray blanket. There were two arms crossed on the top of the mound and at one end there was something that had been a face, but now was a yellow scabby area with a wide bandage cross where the eyes had been.

"Who is it?" asked Raven. He didn't have lips, but he talked pretty well without them and with a pleasant voice. **F**

"Hemingway," I said. "I came up to see how you were doing."

"My face was pretty bad," he said. "It got sort of burned from the grenade, but it's peeled a couple of times and it's doing better."

"It looks swell," I said. "It's doing fine."

I wasn't looking at it when I spoke.

"How are things in America?" he asked. "What do they think of us over there?"

"Sentiment's changed a lot," I said. "They're beginning to realize the government is going to win this war."

COMMON CORE L 5b

Language Coach

Synonyms A **synonym** is a word with a meaning similar to that of another word. *Impersonal* and *mechanical* are synonyms meaning "not influenced by emotion or personality." What picture do "moaning in a very impersonal way" and "moaned mechanically" in line 56 create?

F DESCRIPTIVE DETAILS
Reread lines 54–66. Describe the emotional impact of the details in these lines. What purpose do you think it serves for Hemingway to include this description? Explain your response.

Members of the International Brigades near Madrid in late 1936

"Do you think so?"

"Sure," I said.

"I'm awfully glad," he said. "You know, I wouldn't mind any of this if I could just watch what was going on. I don't mind the pain, you know. It never seemed important really. But I was always awfully interested in things and I really wouldn't mind the pain at all if I could just sort of follow things intelligently. I could even be some use. You know, I didn't mind the war at all. I did all right in the war. I got hit once before and I was back and rejoined the battalion in two weeks. I couldn't stand to be away. Then I got this." G

G DIALOGUE
Reread lines 67–83. What does the dialogue reveal about the speakers? How does it add to the impression of war the writer has created in this article? Explain your response.

He had put his hand in mine. It was not a worker's hand. There were no callouses and the nails on the long, spatulate[6] fingers were smooth and rounded.

"How did you get it?" I asked.

"Well, there were some troops that were routed and we went over to sort of reform them and we did and then we had quite a fight with the fascists and we beat them. It was quite a bad fight, you know, but we beat them and then someone threw this grenade at me."

Holding his hand and hearing him tell it, I did not believe a word of it. What was left of him did not sound like the wreckage of a soldier somehow. I did not know how he had been wounded, but the story did not sound right. It was the sort of way everyone would like to have been wounded. But I wanted him to think I believed it.

"Where did you come from?" I asked.

"From Pittsburgh. I went to the University there."

"What did you do before you joined up here?"

"I was a social worker," he said. Then I knew it couldn't be true and I wondered how he had really been so frightfully wounded and I didn't care. In the war that I had known, men often lied about the manner of their wounding. Not at first; but later. I'd lied a little myself in my time. Especially late in the evening. But I was glad he thought I believed it, and we talked about books, he wanted to be a writer, and I told him about what happened north of Guadalajara and promised to bring some things from Madrid next time we got out that way. I hoped maybe I could get a radio. H

H SUBJECTIVITY IN REPORTING
Why doesn't Hemingway believe Raven? Do you believe Raven? Explain why or why not.

"They tell me Dos Passos and Sinclair Lewis[7] are coming over, too," he said.

"Yes," I said. "And when they come I'll bring them up to see you."

"Gee, that will be great," he said. "You don't know what that will mean to me."

"I'll bring them," I said.

"Will they be here pretty soon?"

"Just as soon as they come I'll bring them."

"Good boy, Ernest," he said. "You don't mind if I call you Ernest, do you?"

The voice came very clear and gentle from that face that looked like some hill that had been fought over in muddy weather and then baked in the sun.

"Hell, no," I said. "Please. Listen, old-timer, you're going to be fine. You'll be a lot of good, you know. You can talk on the radio."

---

6. **spatulate** (spăch'ə-lĭt): having a broad, rounded end.

7. **Dos Passos and Sinclair Lewis:** well-known American writers.

"Maybe," he said. "You'll be back?"

"Sure," I said. "Absolutely."

"Goodbye, Ernest," he said.

"Goodbye," I told him.

Downstairs they told me he'd lost both eyes as well as his face and was also badly wounded all through the legs and in the feet.

"He's lost some toes, too," the doctor said, "but he doesn't know that."

"I wonder if he'll ever know it."

"Oh, sure he will," the doctor said. "He's going to get well."

And it still isn't you that gets hit but it is your countryman now. Your countryman from Pennsylvania, where once we fought at Gettysburg.

Then, walking along the road, with his left arm in an airplane splint, walking with the gamecock walk of the professional British soldier that neither ten years of militant party work nor the projecting metal wings of the splint could destroy, I met Raven's commanding officer, Jock Cunningham, who had three fresh rifle wounds through his upper left arm (I looked at them, one was septic[8]) and another rifle bullet under his shoulder blade that had entered his left chest, passed through, and lodged there. He told me, in military terms, the history of the attempt to rally retiring troops on his battalion's right flank, of his bombing raid down a trench which was held at one end by the fascists and at the other end by the government troops, of the taking of this trench and, with six men and a Lewis gun,[9] cutting off a group of some eighty fascists from their own lines, and of the final desperate defense of their impossible position his six men put up until the government troops came up and, attacking, straightened out the line again. He told it clearly, completely convincingly, and with a strong Glasgow[10] accent. He had deep, piercing eyes sheltered like an eagle's, and, hearing him talk, you could tell the sort of soldier he was. For what he had done he would have had a V.C.[11] in the last war. In this war there are no decorations. Wounds are the only decorations and they do not award wound stripes. ❶

"Raven was in the same show," he said. "I didn't know he'd been hit. Ay, he's a good mon. He got his after I got mine. The fascists we'd cut off were very good troops. They never fired a useless shot when we were in that bad spot. They waited in the dark there until they had us located and then opened with volley fire. That's how I got four in the same place."

We talked for a while and he told me many things. They were all important, but nothing was as important as what Jay Raven, the social worker from Pittsburgh with no military training, had told me was true. This is a strange new kind of war where you learn just as much as you are able to believe.

COMMON CORE RI 6

❶ SUBJECTIVITY IN REPORTING

Reread lines 129–146. Notice the writer's **tone,** the hard and cynical attitude revealed by this powerful description of one soldier and his career in the Spanish Civil War. The writing here follows a pattern established earlier in the article. The writer focuses on the details of a particular scene or event and then surprises readers with a blunt message about the nature of war. As you read the article's concluding paragraphs look for final clues to Hemingway's tone. What **purpose** does his tone reveal?

---

8. **septic:** infected with bacteria.
9. **Lewis gun:** a lightweight machine gun.
10. **Glasgow:** a city in Scotland.
11. **V.C.:** the Victoria Cross, an award for valor "in the face of the enemy," given by Great Britain.

After Reading

Comprehension

1. **Recall** What happens in front of Hemingway's hotel before breakfast?
2. **Recall** Who is Raven, and what are his injuries?
3. **Clarify** What is the truth about how Raven was wounded?

Text Analysis

4. **Analyze Descriptive Details** Look back at the descriptive details you noted and circle the ones you found most vivid or affecting. What do you infer from any of these details that Hemingway doesn't tell you outright?
5. **Analyze Subjectivity in Reporting** Hemingway's article differs greatly from an objective news report. How does each of the following highly personal passages contribute to the writer's tone and purpose?
   - his recurrent thought "It wasn't me" (lines 35 and 46)
   - his reaction to the sight of Raven and to the story Raven tells (lines 61–106)
   - his description of Jock Cunningham (lines 129–146)
   - his belief about the most important thing he was told (lines 152–155)
6. **Examine Dialogue** A written news report often contains quotations from sources, but rarely does it contain dialogue between two people. Why might Hemingway have chosen to include dialogue in his dispatch?
7. **Interpret Title** What makes this conflict "a new kind of war"? Note what seems to surprise Hemingway about it.
8. **Synthesize Themes** The Spanish Civil War ended more than 65 years ago. What value is there in reading Hemingway's article today? What insights about war does it provide?
9. **Compare Texts** What similarities in **style** and **theme** do you see in "A New Kind of War" and "In Another Country," the Hemingway short story on page 1010?

Text Criticism

10. **Critical Interpretations** When the New York University journalism department compiled its list of the 100 best works of 20th-century American journalism, Hemingway's Spanish Civil War reporting was ranked 33rd. Do you agree that it should be esteemed so highly? Support your answer.

What can we learn from WAR?

Hemingway was skeptical of Raven's story when he first heard it. Do you think he changed his mind after hearing the story told by Jock Cunningham? How do you determine the truth when you watch a news report about war? Explain.

COMMON CORE

RI 1 Cite textual evidence to support analysis of what the text says explicitly as well as inferences drawn from the text, including determining where the text leaves matters uncertain. **RI 2** Determine two or more central ideas of a text. **RI 6** Determine an author's point of view or purpose in a text in which the rhetoric is particularly effective, analyzing how style and content contribute to the power, persuasiveness, or beauty of the text. **RI 10** Read and comprehend literary nonfiction.

Language

◆ GRAMMAR AND STYLE: Choose Effective Point of View

Review the **Grammar and Style** note on page 1098. At the beginning of his dispatch, Hemingway uses the **second-person pronoun** *you* to report his own experiences, where you would normally expect him to write in the first person. This has the effect of placing the reader ("you") at the point of the action. It also temporarily removes the narrator himself, creating a sense of detachment.

> *After the shell that lit on the sidewalk in front of the hotel you got a beautiful double corner room on that side, twice the size of the one you had had, for less than a dollar.* (lines 43–45)

Hemingway does periodically revert to the first person, as in the continuation of the preceding passage:

> *It wasn't me they killed. See? No. Not me. It wasn't me anymore.* (lines 45–46)

With this shifting point of view, Hemingway seems to step in and out of the narrative. The resulting detachment allows the reader to encounter the experience of war without added comment or sentiment.

PRACTICE Rewrite the following passage, inserting either first- or second-person pronouns to change the sense of immediacy or detachment.

> Hundreds of runners and spectators gather in Jonquil Park at dawn on Mother's Day. The air is crisp and the grass damp. The predominant color in the crowd is pink: pink ribbons, pink caps, pink shirts. Many people wear signs reading "In memory of . . ." There is an electric air of expectancy until the horn blasts. The runners are off!

COMMON CORE

L 3 Apply knowledge of language to understand how language functions in different contexts. **W 3a, e** Engage and orient the reader by setting out a situation and establishing one or multiple point(s) of view; create a smooth progression of experiences or events; provide a conclusion that follows from and reflects on what is experienced, observed, or resolved over the course of the narrative.

READING-WRITING CONNECTION

Expand your understanding of "A New Kind of War" by responding to this prompt. Then, use the **revising tips** to improve your report.

WRITING PROMPT	REVISING TIPS
WRITE A SUBJECTIVE REPORT In his Spanish Civil War dispatches, Hemingway was able to report events in such a way that readers felt they were right there with him. Go to a newsworthy event or recall one that you attended—a concert, a charity race, or a memorial service, for example. Write a **one-page report** that makes your readers seem to experience your thoughts and sensations during the event. Include dialogue, as Hemingway does, if it seems appropriate.	• Clearly identify the event and its participants. • Include sensory details to describe the setting. • Include personal reactions, and use an effective point of view.

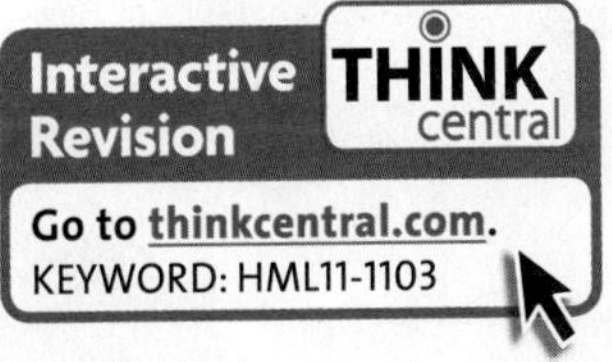

A Book of Great Short Stories

Book Review by Dorothy Parker

COMMON CORE

RI 3 Analyze a complex set of ideas or sequence of events and explain how ideas or events interact and develop over the course of the text. **RI 6** Determine an author's point of view or purpose in a text in which the rhetoric is particularly effective, analyzing how style and content contribute to the power, persuasiveness, or beauty of the text.

Meet the Author

Dorothy Parker 1893–1967

Dorothy Parker's sophisticated and witty voice made her one of the most quoted women of the 20th century. She belonged to the Algonquin Round Table, an informal group of writers who met daily at New York's Algonquin Hotel for lunch and clever conversation. Nicknamed the "Vicious Circle," they helped shape the literary tastes of the country.

Caustic Critic A well-read but smart-mouthed student, Parker left school at 14. When she was 19, her father died, and she was forced to find a job. After selling a poem to *Vanity Fair,* she was hired to write captions for its sister magazine, *Vogue.* She rose to become drama critic at *Vanity Fair* but was fired in 1920 for panning a play that starred the wife of one of the magazine's advertisers. She landed on her feet, becoming drama critic for another magazine, *Ainslee's.* She was also one of the founding editors of the *New Yorker* and served as its book reviewer for six years. Signing her reviews "Constant Reader," she championed writers she admired and demolished those she didn't. About one book she pronounced, "This is not a novel to be tossed aside lightly. It should be thrown with great force."

Popular Poet Parker's own books of poetry, *Enough Rope* and *Sunset Gun,* were bestsellers. They contained rueful verses, usually about failed love. One of her most quoted poems is "Résumé," which ends, "Guns aren't lawful; / Nooses give; / Gas smells awful; / You might as well live." Though often humorous, her poems grew out of great personal pain. She had an unhappy marriage to Edwin Parker, who returned from World War I with a drug addiction. Before divorcing him, she had disastrous love affairs that led her to several suicide attempts.

Screenwriter and Activist In 1933, Parker married Alan Campbell and moved with him to Hollywood, where they collaborated on screenplays. She also became more politically active, protesting racism, organizing the Screenwriters Guild, founding an anti-Nazi group, and going to Madrid to report on the Spanish Civil War. Her socialist sympathies caused her to be brought before the House Un-American Activities Committee in the 1950s. After she died of a heart attack in 1967, it was discovered that she had left her literary estate to Dr. Martin Luther King Jr. and the NAACP.

Author Online THINK central

Go to thinkcentral.com. KEYWORD: HML11-1104

DID YOU KNOW?

Dorothy Parker . . .

- was expelled from convent school for making smart remarks.
- originated the saying "Men seldom make passes / At girls who wear glasses".
- proposed "Excuse my dust" as her epitaph.

TEXT ANALYSIS: STYLE

Style is determined not by what is written, but by *how* it is written. Imagery, figurative language, exaggeration, dialogue, and diction are some of the rhetorical techniques that contribute to a particular writer's style. Dorothy Parker's style is characterized by witty diction and ironic exaggeration. Her book reviews are not merely informative. They are playful and persuasive, clearly aimed to influence readers. Consider Parker's style in this passage:

After all the high screaming about The Sun Also Rises, *I feared for Mr. Hemingway's next book. You know how it is—as soon as they all start acclaiming a writer, that writer is just about to slip downward.*

What kind of person do you imagine is speaking? Male or female? Friendly or distant? Serious or playful? As you read, notice what makes Dorothy Parker's style so effective and persuasive. Use her comments to form an impression of her personality and attitude toward the literary world.

READING STRATEGY: READING A BOOK REVIEW

Most book reviews are published in newspapers and magazines. They usually

- describe a new or newly republished book
- give an evaluation of its literary worth
- offer reasons for this evaluation

As you read Dorothy Parker's review, look for the lines that fulfill these functions. She discusses three of Ernest Hemingway's books, not just one, and she mentions others' opinions as well as her own, so it may help to take notes on a chart like the one shown.

	Description	Parker's Evaluation	Reasons
The Sun Also Rises			
In Our Time			
Men Without Women			

Complete the activities in your **Reader/Writer Notebook**.

What makes a GREAT *short story?*

During your school years, you've read many classic stories described as "great," such as "The Necklace" by Guy de Maupassant and "The Tell-Tale Heart" by Edgar Allan Poe. But how can you learn about new stories that might be just as great? Would you trust a book reviewer's evaluation?

QUICKWRITE Think about the best short story you ever read, in school or on your own. With its qualities in mind, jot down the recipe for a great short story. What must one contain, in your opinion? In a small group, share your recipes. Do you all have similar tastes, or are your standards unique?

A Book of Great Short Stories

Dorothy Parker

October 29, 1927

Ernest Hemingway wrote a novel called *The Sun Also Rises*. Promptly upon its publication, Ernest Hemingway was discovered, the Stars and Stripes were reverentially raised over him, eight hundred and forty-seven book reviewers formed themselves into the word "welcome," and the band played "Hail to the Chief" in three concurrent keys. All of which, I should think, might have made Ernest Hemingway pretty reasonably sick. **A**

For, a year or so before *The Sun Also Rises,* he had published *In Our Time,* a collection of short pieces. The book caused about as much stir in literary circles as an incompleted dogfight on upper Riverside Drive. True, there were a few that went about quick and stirred with admiration for this clean, exciting prose, but most of the reviewers dismissed the volume with a tolerant smile and the word "stark." It was Mr. Mencken[1] who slapped it down with "sketches in the bold, bad manner of the Café du Dôme," and the smaller boys, in their manner, took similar pokes at it. Well, you see, Ernest Hemingway was a young American living on the left bank of the Seine in Paris, France; he had been seen at the Dôme and the Rotonde and the Select and the Closerie des Lilas.[2] He knew Pound, Joyce, and Gertrude Stein. There is something a little—well, a little *you*-know—in all of those things. You wouldn't catch Bruce Barton or Mary Roberts Rinehart[3] doing them. No, sir.

Analyze Visuals ▶
What ideas are suggested by the cover designs of these books by Ernest Hemingway?

A RHETORICAL TECHNIQUES
A writer's style is determined by his or her use of **rhetorical techniques,** such as wit, exaggeration, and irony. Dorothy Parker uses these techniques to make readers laugh while conveying information about another writer's work and persuading readers to accept her view of that writer's work. Reread lines 1–6. How does Parker's use of ironic exaggeration contribute to the persuasive appeal of her wit?

1. **Mr. Mencken:** H. L. Mencken, an American journalist and literary critic.
2. **Dôme . . . des Lilas:** cafés in Paris that were frequented by young American writers.
3. **Pound . . . Rinehart:** Ezra Pound and Gertrude Stein were experimental American writers living in Paris; James Joyce was an experimental Irish writer. Bruce Barton and Mary Roberts Rinehart were more conventional American writers who lived in the United States.

in our time

by

ernest hemingway

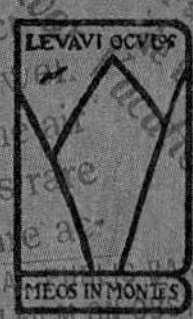

paris

three mountains press

1924

THE SUN ALSO RISES

ERNEST HEMINGWAY

Author of

"IN OUR TIMES" and "THE TORRENTS OF SPRING"

MEN WITHOU
WOMEN

BY

ERNEST HEMINGWAY

AUTHOR OF

THE SUN ALSO RISES

CHARLES SCRIBNER'S SONS

Dorothy Parker and Ernest Hemingway

And besides, *In Our Time* was a book of short stories. That's no way to start off. People don't like that; they feel cheated. Any bookseller will be glad to tell you, in his interesting *argot,*[4] that "short stories don't go." People take up a book of short stories and say, "Oh, what's this? Just a lot of those short things?" and put it right down again. Only yesterday afternoon at four o'clock sharp, I saw and heard a woman do that to Ernest Hemingway's new book, *Men Without Women*. She had been one of those most excited about his new novel. **B**

Literature, it appears, is here measured by a yard-stick. As soon as *The Sun Also Rises* came out, Ernest Hemingway was the white-haired boy. He was praised, adored, analyzed, best-sold, argued about, and banned in Boston; all the trimmings were accorded him. People got into feuds about whether or not his story was worth the telling. (You see this silver scar left by a bullet, right up here under my hair? I got that the night I said that any well-told story was worth the telling. An eighth of an inch nearer the temple, and I wouldn't be sitting here doing this sort of tripe.) They affirmed, and passionately, that the dissolute expatriates[5] in this novel of "a lost generation" were not worth bothering about; and then they devoted most of their time to discussing them. There was a time, and it went on for weeks, when you could go nowhere without hearing of *The Sun Also Rises*. Some thought it without excuse; and some, they of the cool, tall foreheads, called it the greatest American novel, tossing *Huckleberry Finn* and *The Scarlet Letter*[6] lightly out the window. They hated it or they revered it. I may say, with due respect to Mr. Hemingway, that I was never so sick of a book in my life.

B STYLE
Reread lines 20–26, and notice the informal diction and use of dialogue. What is your reaction to this style?

Language Coach
Synonyms A synonym is a word with a meaning similar to that of another word. Read lines 34–36. Which word is a synonym of *asserted* or *declared*? What point were people asserting?

4. ***argot*** (är'gō) *French:* expressions and vocabulary that are used by a particular group.
5. **dissolute expatriates:** loose-living people—in this case, Americans—residing in a foreign land.
6. ***Huckleberry Finn*** **and** ***The Scarlet Letter:*** novels by Mark Twain and Nathaniel Hawthorne, respectively.

Now *The Sun Also Rises* was as "starkly" written as Mr. Hemingway's short stories; it dealt with subjects as "unpleasant." Why it should have been taken to the slightly damp bosom of the public while the (as it seems to me) superb *In Our Time* should have been disregarded will always be a puzzle to me. As I see it—I knew this conversation would get back to me sooner or later, preferably sooner—Mr. Hemingway's style, this prose stripped to its firm young bones, is far more effective, far more moving, in the short story than in the novel. He is, to me, the greatest living writer of short stories; he is, also to me, not the greatest living novelist. C

C BOOK REVIEW
Reread lines 42–50. Restate Parker's opinion of *In Our Time.* What does she say about Hemingway's **style?**

After all the high screaming about *The Sun Also Rises,* I feared for Mr. Hemingway's next book. You know how it is—as soon as they all start acclaiming a writer, that writer is just about to slip downward. The littler critics circle like literary buzzards above only the sick lions. D

D GRAMMAR AND STYLE
In lines 51–54, notice how Parker uses the **first-person pronoun** *I* to refer to herself and addresses the reader with the **second-person pronoun** *you.* She also sets off her side remark with a **dash.** These choices establish an intimate conversational **voice.** Also notice her use of simile, comparing the critics to circling buzzards.

So it is a warm gratification to find the new Hemingway book, *Men Without Women,* a truly magnificent work. It is composed of thirteen short stories, most of which have been published before. They are sad and terrible stories; the author's enormous appetite for life seems to have been somehow appeased. You find here little of that peaceful ecstasy that marked the camping trip in *The Sun Also Rises* and the lone fisherman's days in "Big Two-Hearted River" in *In Our Time.* The stories include "The Killers," which seems to me one of the four great American short stories. (All you have to do is drop the nearest hat, and I'll tell you what I think the others are. They are Wilbur Daniel Steele's "Blue Murder," Sherwood Anderson's "I'm a Fool," and Ring Lardner's "Some Like Them Cold," that story which seems to me as shrewd a picture of every woman at some time as is Chekhov's[7] "The Darling." Now what do *you* like best?) The book also includes "Fifty Grand," "In Another Country," and the delicate and tragic "Hills like White Elephants." I do not know where a greater collection of stories can be found.

Ford Madox Ford[8] has said of this author, "Hemingway writes like an angel." I take issue (there is nothing better for that morning headache than taking a little issue.) Hemingway writes like a human being. I think it is impossible for him to write of any event at which he has not been present; his is, then, a reportorial talent, just as Sinclair Lewis's[9] is. But, or so I think, Lewis remains a reporter and Hemingway stands a genius because Hemingway has an unerring sense of selection. He discards details with a magnificent lavishness; he keeps his words to their short path. His is, as any reader knows, a dangerous influence. The simple thing he does looks so easy to do. But look at the boys who try to do it. E

E BOOK REVIEW
Reread lines 70–78. How highly does Parker rate Hemingway, and why?

7. **Wilbur . . . Chekhov's:** Steele, Anderson, and Lardner were popular American writers of the era; Anton Chekhov was a 19th-century Russian short story writer and playwright.
8. **Ford Madox Ford:** an English writer, editor, and critic who lived for a time in Paris.
9. **Sinclair Lewis's:** Lewis was an American novelist and social critic who published articles in several popular magazines.

Comprehension

COMMON CORE

RI 3 Analyze a complex set of ideas or sequence of events and explain how ideas or events interact and develop over the course of the text. **RI 6** Determine an author's point of view or purpose in a text in which the rhetoric is particularly effective, analyzing how style and content contribute to the power, persuasiveness, or beauty of the text.

1. **Recall** What was Hemingway's latest book at the time Parker's review was written?
2. **Clarify** How did the reception of *In Our Time* compare to the reception of *The Sun Also Rises?*
3. **Paraphrase** What does Parker say is the difference between Hemingway and Sinclair Lewis?

Text Analysis

4. **Reading a Book Review** Look back at the notes you took while reading, then summarize Parker's opinions of the three Hemingway books she discusses. With what evidence does she support her opinions?
5. **Analyze Style** How would you describe Parker's style in this book review? Explain the rhetorical appeal of each of the following:
   - use of the first-person *I*
   - exaggeration
   - similes and metaphors
   - informal diction
6. **Interpret Tone** What is Parker's attitude toward book reviewers and the reading public? Support your answer with details.
7. **Evaluate Author's Work** Review Parker's statements about Hemingway's short stories (lines 42–50, 55–78). Then skim "In Another Country" (page 1010). Do you agree with Parker's **evaluation** of Hemingway's short stories? Use a chart like the one shown to organize your thoughts.

"In Another Country"		
	Yes	No
Clean, Stripped-Down Prose		
Unpleasant Subject		
Sadness		
Reportorial Talent		
Effectiveness in Moving Readers		

Text Criticism

8. **Critical Interpretations** One scholar wrote, "It is through Parker's refusal to claim authority . . . that her book reviews achieve it. She presents readers with an unpretentious, sometimes self-mocking voice that, while it expresses strong opinions, pretends no Olympian knowledge or status." Do you agree with this critic about the source of Parker's authority or trustworthiness? Explain your view.

What makes a GREAT *short story?*

Dorothy Parker is at once critical and complimentary of Hemingway's writing. She thinks his novel is overrated and his short stories are underrated. Why might some readers tend to take novels more seriously than short stories? What do *you* think makes a great short story?

Language

◆ GRAMMAR AND STYLE: Establish Voice

Review the **Grammar and Style** note on page 1109. Dorothy Parker's voice is intimate, enthusiastic, and wittily self-involved. Here is an example from her review:

> *As I see it—I knew this conversation would get back to me sooner or later, preferably sooner—Mr. Hemingway's style, this prose stripped to its firm young bones, is far more effective, far more moving, in the short story than in the novel.* (lines 45–48)

Notice Parker's use of the **first-person pronoun** *I* and her use of **dashes** to enclose a parenthetical comment about herself. It's as if Parker is having a conversation with the reader. Additionally, her use of **figurative language**—comparing Hemingway's prose to a fleshless body—creates a far more striking image than had she merely described it as "lean." You can use these and other elements to establish your own voice.

PRACTICE Rewrite each of the following sentences, using pronouns, figurative language, and punctuation, to achieve a voice that sounds like Dorothy Parker's. A sample answer has been done for you.

EXAMPLE

This book is not good.

This volume—in my view—is appallingly, criminally bad.

1. Other reviewers have disliked this book.
2. Sales have been high.
3. Reviewing books can seem useless.

READING-WRITING CONNECTION

Expand your understanding of "A Book of Great Short Stories" by responding to this prompt. Then, use the **revising tips** to improve your review.

WRITING PROMPT

WRITE A BOOK REVIEW Dorothy Parker wrote book reviews for many years, and to one critic, they are the best expression of her literary sensibility. Choose a great book, or an "ungreat book," and write a **three-to-five-paragraph** review in your own personal voice. You might be as funny as Dorothy Parker, but in a different way. Or you might inspire readers to discover a book that could transform their lives. Think about what your own voice sounds like—perhaps tape-record yourself talking about the book. Then try to reproduce that voice in writing.

REVISING TIPS

- Provide a thorough description of the book.
- Offer a positive or negative evaluation.
- Provide evidence to support your evaluation.
- Write in a distinctive voice.

COMMON CORE

L 2 Demonstrate command of the conventions of standard English punctuation when writing.
W 1 Write arguments to support claims in an analysis of texts, using valid reasoning and relevant and sufficient evidence.

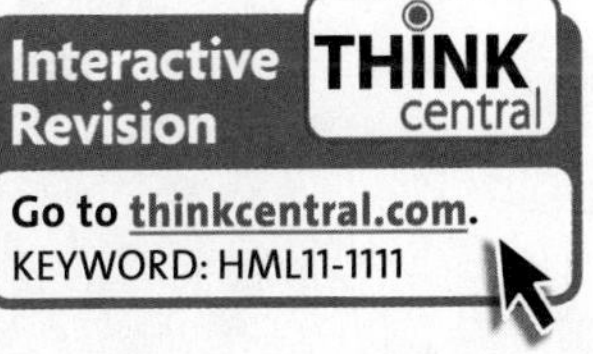

COMMON CORE

RI 6 Determine an author's point of view or purpose in a text in which the rhetoric is particularly effective, analyzing how style and content contribute to the power, persuasiveness, or beauty of the text.

The Duty of Writers

Essay by E. B. White

Meet the Author

E. B. White 1899–1985

Admired for his graceful style and gentle humor, E. B. White has been called the best essayist of the 20th century. For years readers looked forward to his columns in the *New Yorker* and *Harper's* magazines. Midcareer, he became a beloved children's author, writing the classics *Stuart Little* and *Charlotte's Web.* Later, he gained more fame with his update of *The Elements of Style,* a handbook used by millions of student writers.

New York Wit White enjoyed writing even as a child and won his first award when he was nine, for a poem about a mouse. In 1925, following unsuccessful stints in reporting and advertising, he was hired by a new magazine, the *New Yorker*. Its editor wanted it to be light, witty, and satirical. White did much to give it that voice. He wrote its opening "Notes and Comment" page and composed newsbreaks, fillers between articles with such headings as "Letters We Never Finished Reading" and "Neatest Trick of the Week." He did captions for cartoons and even once illustrated the magazine's cover. The *New Yorker* provided White with an outlet for his talent—and a wife: he married the fiction editor, Katharine, living happily with her for 48 years.

Up on the Farm Eventually White felt constrained by the brief length and sheer number of the pieces he had to write for the *New Yorker.* He took a leave from the magazine and moved to a farmhouse in Maine in 1938. There he raised chickens, geese, sheep, and a milk cow. He also began a monthly column for *Harper's* called "One Man's Meat" (an allusion to the saying "One man's meat is another man's poison.") Some of his most memorable essays were published in this column, including "Once More to the Lake," about revisiting the place where he vacationed as a child.

"Unfit for Children" In Maine, White wrote his first children's book, *Stuart Little,* about a family that has a mouse for a son. The head children's librarian at the New York Public Library called his manuscript "unfit for children," but he published it anyway in 1945. Young people loved it, and in 1952 he followed it up with *Charlotte's Web,* about a literate spider who saves a pig from slaughter.

White lived quietly until his death at 86 from Alzheimer's disease. Among his many awards were the Presidential Medal of Freedom and a special Pulitzer Prize for his entire body of work.

Author Online THINK central

Go to thinkcentral.com. KEYWORD: HML11-1112

DID YOU KNOW?

E. B. White . . .

- hated his given name, Elwyn Brooks, and answered to his college nickname, Andy.
- preferred sailing to reading.
- was so afraid of public speaking that he made others deliver his acceptance speeches.

TEXT ANALYSIS: STYLE AND DICTION

Style is the particular way in which a piece of literature is written. It is not what is said, but how it is said. An essential element of style is **diction,** an author's choice of words and syntax. E. B. White's style is both casual and elegant. In the following passage, which particular words or phrases create casualness? elegance?

I was sorry to hear the other day that a certain writer, appalled by the cruel events of the world, had pledged himself never to write anything that wasn't constructive and significant and liberty-loving. I have an idea that this, in its own way, is bad news.

As you read this essay, notice what White's diction contributes to his style. Also, if an expression strikes you as humorous, think about what makes it so.

READING SKILL: INTERPRET AUTHOR'S MESSAGE

An **author's message** is the main idea of a particular work, or the point it makes. White's essay presents his personal opinions on a topic, the duty of writers. These opinions are signaled by such words and phrases as

- "I have an idea that"
- "I don't think"
- "should"
- "shouldn't"
- "This seems to me"

As you read, use such clues to identify what kind of writing White favors and what he opposes. Make notes on a chart like the one shown.

Favors	*Opposes*
	writing only what is constructive, significant, and liberty-loving

Complete the activities in your **Reader/Writer Notebook.**

What do writers OWE *us?*

People often debate what writers should write. Should writers uplift the community or constantly denounce wrongs? Should they report every detail about a war or protect national security? Can they be blasphemous? frivolous? Decide what you believe is the duty of writers. Do they have a special responsibility in troubled times?

EVALUATE AND DISCUSS Explore your own ideas about a writer's obligations by completing this sentence: "I hate it when a writer . . ." In a small group discuss your completed sentences. Is there any agreement about what writers should or should not do?

"Write about dogs!"

The Duty of Writers

E. B. White

BACKGROUND This essay appeared in White's column for *Harper's* magazine in January 1939. It was a disturbing time, when it was clear that world war loomed. England and France had just appeased Hitler by allowing him to take over part of Czechoslovakia. The Nazis had looted and burned Jewish homes and businesses on a night that became known as Kristallnacht. Fascist forces were winning in the Spanish Civil War, and Japan had invaded China. In his State of the Union address, President Franklin D. Roosevelt warned that the freedoms Americans enjoyed were in danger.

I was sorry to hear the other day that a certain writer, appalled by the cruel events of the world, had pledged himself never to write anything that wasn't constructive and significant and liberty-loving. I have an idea that this, in its own way, is bad news.

All word-mongers,[1] at one time or another, have felt the divine necessity of using their talents, if any, on the side of right—but I didn't realize that they

1. **word-mongers:** those who deal in words for a living.

were making any resolutions to that effect, and I don't think they should. When liberty's position is challenged, artists and writers are the ones who first take up the sword. They do so without persuasion, for the battle is peculiarly their own. In the nature of things, a person engaged in the flimsy business of expressing himself on paper is dependent on the large general privilege of being heard. Any intimation that this privilege may be revoked throws a writer into a panic. His is a double allegiance to freedom—an intellectual one springing from the conviction that pure thought has a right to function unimpeded, and a selfish one springing from his need, as a bread-winner, to be allowed to speak his piece. America is now liberty-conscious. In a single generation it has progressed from being toothbrush-conscious, to being air-minded, to being liberty-conscious. The transition has been disturbing, but it has been effected, and the last part has been accomplished largely by the good work of writers and artists, to whom liberty is a blessed condition that must be preserved on earth at all costs. A

But to return to my man who has foresworn everything but what is good and significant. He worries me. I hope he isn't serious, but I'm afraid he is. Having resolved to be nothing but significant, he is in a fair way to lose his effectiveness. A writer must believe in something, obviously, but he shouldn't join a club. Letters flourish not when writers amalgamate,[2] but when they are contemptuous of one another. (Poets are the most contemptuous of all the writing breeds, and in the long run the most exalted and influential.) Even in evil times, a writer should cultivate only what naturally absorbs his fancy, whether it be freedom or cinch bugs, and should write in the way that comes easy. B

The movement is spreading. I know of one gifted crackpot who used to be employed gainfully in the fields of humor and satire, who has taken a solemn pledge not to write anything funny or light-hearted or "insignificant" again till things get straightened around in the world. This seems to me distinctly deleterious[3] and a little silly. A literature composed of nothing but liberty-loving thoughts is little better than the propaganda which it seeks to defeat. C

In a free country it is the duty of writers to pay no attention to duty. Only under a dictatorship is literature expected to exhibit an harmonious design or an inspirational tone. A despot doesn't fear eloquent writers preaching freedom—he fears a drunken poet who may crack a joke that will take hold. His gravest concern is lest gaiety, or truth in sheep's clothing, somewhere gain a foothold, lest joy in some unguarded moment be unconfined. I honestly don't believe that a humorist should take the veil[4] today; he should wear his bells night and day, and squeeze the uttermost jape,[5] even though he may feel more like writing a strong letter to the *Herald Tribune*. D

COMMON CORE **RI 6**

A DICTION
Reread lines 1–19, with special attention to White's **diction,** or choice of words. Notice the **irony** he achieves by using grand words and phrases for ordinary situations and events. In the first sentence, for example, White uses the phrase "appalled by the cruel events of the world" to describe a single moment in the life of an anonymous writer. By using overly serious words such as *appalled*, White lightly mocks writers who take themselves too seriously. What other words and phrases in these lines contribute to White's lightly ironic tone? Explain your response.

B AUTHOR'S MESSAGE
In lines 26–28, what does White state that a writer should do?

C STYLE AND DICTION
What phrasings add humor to this paragraph?

D AUTHOR'S MESSAGE
Reread lines 37–43. What value does White see in humor?

2. **Letters . . . amalgamate:** Writing and literature do not do well when writers form groups.
3. **deleterious:** harmful.
4. **take the veil:** become a nun or, here, a serious, religious person.
5. **wear his bells . . . jape:** consistently act like a jester (who wears a cap with bells) and see the humor in everything.

Comprehension

1. **Recall** At the beginning of the essay, what is White "sorry to hear"?
2. **Clarify** How has America changed in a generation, according to White?
3. **Paraphrase** What does White mean when he says, "Having resolved to be nothing but significant, he is in a fair way to lose his effectiveness"?

Text Analysis

4. **Interpret Author's Message** Look back at the chart you created as you read. What kind of writing does White favor, and what does he oppose? Summarize his main message.
5. **Evaluate Opinions** Do you agree with White's opinions about the **responsibility** of writers? React to each of the following statements:
   - "A literature composed of nothing but liberty-loving thoughts is little better than the propaganda which it seeks to defeat." (lines 33–34)
   - "Even in evil times, a writer should cultivate only what naturally absorbs his fancy. . . ." (lines 26–27)
   - "In a free country it is the duty of writers to pay no attention to duty." (line 35)
   - "A despot doesn't fear eloquent writers preaching freedom—he fears a drunken poet who may crack a joke that will take hold." (lines 37–38)
6. **Analyze Style and Diction** Choose a sentence from the essay that you find particularly thought provoking. Does it contain expressions that are casual, elegant, humorous, or a combination? Explain your answer.
7. **Compare Texts** Both White and Dorothy Parker (page 1104) wrote for the *New Yorker* magazine. How is White's **voice** different from Parker's? What do both essays suggest about the magazine's **tone?**

Text Criticism

8. **Historical Context** White was writing at a time when fascism was on the rise overseas but America had not yet become involved in World War II. Do you think his message would have been the same if he were writing later, say, after the horrors of the Holocaust had become known? Would it have been the same if America had been turning toward fascism?

What do writers **OWE** *us?*

E.B. White expresses the view that "the duty of writers" is to write about whatever interests them, regardless of the prevailing social, cultural, or political climate. Do you think writers should be free to write whatever they want whenever they want? Explain.

COMMON CORE

RI 6 Determine an author's point of view or purpose in a text in which the rhetoric is particularly effective, analyzing how style and content contribute to the power, persuasiveness, or beauty of the text.

Journalism Beyond the Facts

Journalism is typically regarded as writing whose purpose is to convey to readers the facts as they are known—to answer the questions *who? what? when? where?* and *how?* Depending on their assignment and its purpose, journalists may strive for detached objectivity or may more subjectively shape the stories they report, the ideas they explore, and the claims they make.

Writing to Evaluate

Each of the selections beginning on page 1096 goes beyond "just the facts" and conveys the writer's perspective on a particular topic. This perspective largely determines the structure and flow of each piece. Skim each selection and look for words, phrases, or sentences that help you discern the writer's perspective. Then try your own hand at writing a news story that conveys more than just the facts. Choose an event, such as a school play, a varsity track meet, or even a typical lunch break in the cafeteria, and report it from your own perspective. Use the selections in this section as your inspiration.

Consider

- how the authors in this section revealed their personal perspectives and how their perspectives shaped their writing
- what basic facts you need to convey about your topic
- how best to reveal your thoughts about the event you witness

Extension

SPEAKING & LISTENING Much of journalism is distinguished by its tone. From factual, unemotional reporting to lurid mudslinging—today's journalism encompasses it all. Find three examples of current news stories that range widely in tone. You might search for stories in traditional newspapers, entertainment magazines, home decorating magazines, supermarket tabloids, or online news sources. Create a **poster** with copies of the stories and their headlines and **present** it to the class, explaining why you think—or do not think—the tone of each story is appropriate for its content.

COMMON CORE

RI 9 Analyze U.S. documents of literary significance for their themes, purposes, and rhetorical features. **W 4** Produce clear and coherent writing in which the style is appropriate to task, purpose, and audience. **W 9b (RI 6)** Determine an author's point of view or purpose in a text. **L 1** Demonstrate command of the conventions of standard English usage when speaking.

Persuasive Essay

The writers and artists you have read about in this unit were not afraid to state their opinions. Through their work, they argued about what it meant to be modern. They also asserted claims about how best to preserve their heritage and ideals. In this workshop, you will learn how to build an effective argument by writing a persuasive essay about an issue relevant to today's world.

 Complete the workshop activities in your **Reader/Writer Notebook.**

WRITE WITH A PURPOSE

WRITING TASK

Write a **persuasive essay** that asserts a claim about a substantive issue of our time. Support your claim with reasons and evidence that will convince your audience to accept your position or take a specific action.

Idea Starters

- What should be the government's role in responding to a national crisis?
- What, if any, responsibilities do advertisers have—and to whom?
- In times of challenge, is escapism necessary or irresponsible?
- Has the field of journalism changed for the better or for the worse?

THE ESSENTIALS

Here are some common purposes, audiences, and formats for persuasive writing.

PURPOSES	AUDIENCES	FORMATS
• to persuade people to agree with your claim • to motivate others to take action	• classmates and teacher • parents • community members • government representatives • Web users	• essay for class • editorial • speech • video or multimedia presentation • commercial/PSA • blog

COMMON CORE TRAITS

1. DEVELOPMENT OF IDEAS

- includes an **introduction** that identifies an issue and states a **precise knowledgeable claim**
- fairly and thoroughly develops the claim with **valid reasons** and **relevant evidence**
- anticipates **opposing claims** and provides **counterclaims**
- has a **concluding section** that supports the argument

2. ORGANIZATION OF IDEAS

- **sequences** claims, counterclaims, and evidence in a **logical way**
- uses **transitions** to create **cohesion** and link ideas

3. LANGUAGE FACILITY AND CONVENTIONS

- maintains a **formal style** and an **objective tone**
- uses **parallelism** for effect
- employs correct **grammar**, **mechanics**, and **spelling**

Planning/Prewriting

W 1a–e Write arguments to support claims in an analysis of substantive topics or texts, using valid reasoning and relevant and sufficient evidence. **W 5** Develop and strengthen writing as needed by planning.

Getting Started

CHOOSE A SUBSTANTIVE ISSUE

For your argument, consider meaningful, **substantive issues** that matter to many people and that are open to disagreement. Be sure to focus on issues that you care about. List a few of these issues, noting the most commonly held opinions about each. Then choose an issue about which you can make a strong, persuasive argument.

WHAT DOES IT LOOK LIKE?

Responsibility of advertisers

* *Advertisers should not market violent video games to kids.*
* *An advertiser's job is to sell products. Parents must guide their children to avoid buying or playing such games.*

How journalism has changed

* *News programs no longer offer well-researched news stories, only sensationalized information.*
* *News programs today are more interesting because they appeal to viewers' interests.*

THINK ABOUT AUDIENCE AND PURPOSE

As you explore your issue in greater depth, keep in mind your **purpose** for writing: to persuade your **audience** to agree with your claim. Consider your audience's knowledge of the topic and their potential concerns.

ASK YOURSELF:

- Who is my audience, and how does this issue affect them? How much do they already know about the issue? What opinions do they hold?
- What position do I want my audience to take? What do I want them to do?
- How receptive might my audience be to my position? What objections might they have?

STATE YOUR CLAIM

State your position in a strong, knowledgeable **claim.** This statement will be the focus of your argument, so make sure it is **significant** and **precise.** You must be able to support your claim with reasons and evidence. If you find that you cannot support your claim, rework it or choose a different issue. Once you are satisfied with your claim, think about your **call to action,** or what you want your audience to do once they are persuaded by your argument.

WHAT DOES IT LOOK LIKE?

Issue	*Claim*	*Call to action*
How journalism has changed	*The standards of journalism have declined sharply in recent years.*	*Contact your local newspaper or TV station when you read or see a story that is misleading or inaccurate.*

Planning/Prewriting *continued*

Getting Started

GATHER SUPPORT FOR YOUR CLAIM

Reasons explain why you believe your claim is true. A reason is valid only if it is supported by **relevant** and **sufficient** evidence. In other words, each piece of evidence must strongly relate to the reason it supports. Also, you must provide enough evidence to convince your audience. Most evidence falls into one of the following categories:

- **anecdote**— specific example, incident, or personal experience
- **analogy**— an illustration of an unfamiliar concept by comparing it to something familiar
- **expert opinion**— informed opinion attributed to a credible source
- **fact** or **statistic**— indisputable information and numerical data

WHAT DOES IT LOOK LIKE?

Evidence

Anecdote: *Yesterday I read a newspaper article about our mayor that I knew could not be true.*	***Analogy:*** *If I write a term paper full of unsupported claims, I get a failing grade; when newspapers print unsubstantiated stories, they don't even apologize.*
Expert Opinion: *One prominent reporter and university lecturer agrees that journalism standards are in serious decline.*	***Statistic:*** *A recent study of local TV stations found that 65 percent of "news" stories contained factual inaccuracies.*

ANTICIPATE OPPOSING CLAIMS

Remember that members of your audience may hold different opinions about the issue than you do. Anticipate these **alternate** or **opposing claims** and be prepared to respond. Think carefully about each opposing claim so that you can acknowledge both its strengths and its limitations. Then develop your **counterclaim** with solid reasons and evidence.

WHAT DOES IT LOOK LIKE?

Opposing Claim: *News programs today are more interesting because they appeal to viewers' interests.*

Counterclaim and Evidence: *Entertainment is not the main goal of journalism. The American Society of News Editors states that the responsibility of news media is to inform people so they can make decisions about important issues.*

PEER REVIEW Share your claim, reasons, and evidence with a peer. Ask: Is my evidence sufficient to persuade my audience? Discuss the kinds of reasons and evidence that would provide better support for your claim.

In your *Reader/Writer Notebook*, use a chart like the one on page 1119 to develop your claim. List reasons for the claim, and then gather strong, credible evidence from a variety of sources to support each reason. Jot down anecdotal evidence from your experience that relates to your topic.

COMMON CORE

W 1c Use words, phrases, and clauses to clarify the relationships between claims and reasons, reasons and evidence, claims and counterclaims. **W 4** Produce clear and coherent writing appropriate to task, purpose, and audience.

Drafting

The following chart shows how to organize your draft to create a coherent and effective persuasive essay.

Organizing Your Persuasive Essay

INTRODUCTION

- Grab your audience's attention with an interesting **fact**, **quotation**, or **anecdote**.
- Identify the issue and state a precise, knowledgeable **claim**.

BODY

- Present your **reasons** in a **logical order**, such as order of importance.
- Explain each reason with **relevant**, **varied**, and **sufficient evidence**.
- Distinguish your claim from **opposing claims**. Fairly and thoroughly describe each opposing claim and present **counterclaims**.
- Maintain a **formal style** and an **objective tone**. Avoid being defensive or dismissive of other viewpoints.

CONCLUDING SECTION

- Restate your **claim** and its **significance**.
- End with a **call to action** that urges your audience to respond in a specific way.

GRAMMAR IN CONTEXT: USE VARIED TRANSITIONS

To craft a **coherent** argument, you need to connect all the related ideas. **Transitions** are the words, phrases, and clauses that show how the parts of your argument are related. This chart shows a variety of transitions that you might use in your essay.

Type of Transition	*Examples*	*Usage*
Support or opposition	*furthermore, but, conversely, in reality*	***Recently***, *technology has sped up the pace of news delivery.* ***As a result***, *we have witnessed the birth of the "24/7 News Monster." This beast—a hungry conglomeration of Web sites, bloggers, and cable channels—must be fed hourly. But,* ***in reality***, *reporters cannot produce quality journalism at this frenzied pace.*
Cause or effect	*because of, as a result*	
Examples	*frequently, for example*	
Sequence	*before, after, next, recently, over time*	

Develop a first draft of your essay, following the structure outlined in the chart above. Use at least five transitions to connect your ideas.

Revising

Revising means evaluating the development, organization, and style of your argument. Your goal is to determine if you have achieved your purpose and effectively communicated your ideas to a specific audience. The questions, tips, and strategies in the following chart can help you revise and rewrite as needed.

PERSUASIVE ESSAY

Ask Yourself	*Tips*	*Revision Strategies*
1. Does the introduction grab the audience's attention and include a precise claim?	**Bracket** the attention-grabbing text. **Draw a wavy line** under the claim.	**Add** an attention-grabbing fact, quotation, or anecdote. **Rework** the existing claim to make it more precise.
2. Are there at least three valid reasons to support the claim? Is each reason supported by relevant and sufficient evidence?	**Underline** each reason. **Circle** each piece of evidence and **draw an arrow** to the reason it supports.	**Add** reasons or **revise** existing ones to strengthen their validity. **Add** relevant evidence, such as facts and statistics, to support the argument.
3. Do I use varied transitions to link my claim, reasons, and evidence?	**Circle** each transitional word, phrase, or clause. **Note** any transitions used more than once or twice.	**Add** words, phrases, or clauses to link ideas and create a smooth flow. **Replace** repeated transitions with ones that haven't been used.
4. Are the reasons presented in the most persuasive order?	**Number** the reasons in the margin, ranking them according to strength.	**Rearrange** the reasons into a more logical order, such as strength of evidence.
5. Are opposing claims fairly acknowledged and refuted with counterclaims?	**Put a plus sign** by each sentence that addresses an opposing claim.	**Add** sentences that address opposing claims, refuting each with a counterclaim.
6. Does the concluding section restate the claim and include a call to action?	**Put a box** around the restatement of the claim. **Highlight** the call to action.	**Add** a sentence that restates the claim. **Add** a call to action.

PEER REVIEW Exchange your argument with a classmate or read it aloud to a partner. Use the chart above to help each other identify parts of your essays that need strengthening, reworking, or a new approach.

COMMON CORE

W 1a Introduce a precise claim.
W 5 Strengthen writing by revising, editing, rewriting, or trying a new approach.

ANALYZE A STUDENT DRAFT

Read this student's draft, noting the comments about its strengths as well as suggestions for improvement.

What's Happened to the News?

by Mia Bloom, Brookfield High School

1 "Election fraud? Join us after the break to hear why Mayor David Silva may not be a city resident." This story aired last night on Channel 7 news. Were it true, this fact would invalidate Silva's election—but it's not. Channel 7 based its story on a single source: Sarah Franklin, who is running for mayor against Silva. Is this acceptable journalism? On the contrary. It's just one more example of bad journalism.

Mia grabs her audience's attention with an **anecdote** that introduces her **topic**.

Mia needs to strengthen her claim to make it more precise.

2 What Channel 7 did is not an isolated incident. So-called "news stories" like these are part of a growing national trend. According to Dan Rather, one-time anchor of the CBS Evening News, "traditional journalism is under siege." For one thing, newspapers are cutting staff or closing up shop. One study reveals that since 2000, employment in print newsrooms has dropped by more than 15,000. This dramatic cut in staff means less fact-checking and more inaccurate stories being rushed to production.

3 Additionally, TV stations now consider news an entertainment division that must turn a profit. In order to gain viewers, news programs rush to be the first to report a story, sometimes without all the facts or with deliberately misleading information designed for shock value. Either way, the results are the same. Citizens are not equipped to make informed decisions. Rather believes the situation is so dire that media reform should be "an immediate national priority."

A quotation provides **relevant evidence** for Mia's argument.

LEARN HOW **Strengthen Your Claim** Mia states a claim in her first paragraph, but it's not as precise as it could be. She reworked this section, crafting a new claim that better explains her opinion and describes the troubling effects of the problem.

MIA'S REVISION TO PARAGRAPH 1

Is this acceptable journalism? On the contrary. ~~It's just one more example of bad journalism.~~

It's just one more example of journalism's declining standards. Television news reporters are not upholding their responsibility to inform the general public, which prevents citizens from making informed decisions.

ANALYZE A STUDENT DRAFT *continued*

4 According to the standards of the American Society of News Editors (ASNE), "Good faith with the reader is the foundation of good journalism. Every effort must be made to assure that the news content is accurate . . . and that all sides are presented fairly." By failing to present both sides of the story about Mayor Silva, Channel 7 violated this principle. Now, there may be some of you who believe that Channel 7 did nothing wrong. After all, the station did not state that Silva was ineligible to be mayor—it simply allowed his opponent to do so. Information that is deliberately misleading for ratings' sake is just as bad as inaccurate information.

5 We citizens must act. In running this one-sided story, Channel 7 abandoned its role and violated the public trust. Actions such as this can have huge ramifications on our ability to elect effective leaders. When you see instances of unbalanced reporting in any form of public media, take it upon yourself to contact the newspaper or TV station and encourage your community to do the same. As citizens, it is our responsibility to let the media know that they must be more vigilant in upholding their responsibility to the public they serve.

Mia addresses an **opposing claim** and responds with a **counterclaim.** However, her ideas are not arranged in a **logical sequence.**

In her concluding section, Mia **restates her claim** and provides a **call to action.**

LEARN HOW **Use a Logical Sequence** The information in Mia's fourth paragraph is confusing because the sequence is out of order. To strengthen her reasoning, she shifted the opposing claim and added a transition.

MIA'S REVISION TO PARAGRAPH 4

According to the standards of the American Society of News Editors (ASNE), "Good faith with the reader is the foundation of good journalism. Every effort must be made to assure that the news content is accurate . . . and that all sides are presented fairly." By failing to present both sides of the story about Mayor Silva, Channel 7 violated this principle. Now, there may be some of you who believe that Channel 7 did nothing wrong. After all, the station did not state that Silva was ineligible to be mayor—it simply allowed his opponent to do so. However, Information that is deliberately misleading for ratings' sake is just as bad as inaccurate information.

Use feedback from your peers and your teacher as well as the two "Learn How" lessons to revise your argument. Evaluate how well your essay uses compelling reasons, strong evidence, and a clear call to action.

COMMON CORE — **W 1a** Create an organization that logically sequences claims, counterclaims, reasons, and evidence. **W 5** Strengthen writing by editing. **L 2b** Spell correctly. **L 3a** Vary syntax for effect.

Editing and Publishing

When you write a persuasive essay, you want to show your knowledge and authority on the topic. Mistakes in grammar, usage, and punctuation can distract your audience from focusing on your argument. In the editing stage, you proofread your essay to make sure it is free of such errors. Also, check for spelling errors that your word-processing spell-check function may not have caught.

GRAMMAR IN CONTEXT: PARALLELISM AND SYNTAX

Good writers vary their **syntax**—the order of words and phrases in sentences—to make their writing more engaging. However, when used as a stylistic device, repetition can be effective. **Parallelism**, or the use of repeated grammatical structures, can heighten the persuasive effect of an argument. For example, read this famous line from President John F. Kennedy's 1961 inauguration speech. Through the use of parallelism, Kennedy makes what could have been a simple message much more memorable.

Ask not what your country can do for you—ask what you can do for your country.

—President John F. Kennedy

As she reviewed her essay, Mia found a good place to add two questions with parallel structures. Notice how her revision helps emphasize why people should care about the problem.

Why should we be worried about one little story on the local news? Why should we care about one small station's journalistic "standards"?
^ What Channel 7 did is not an isolated incident.

PUBLISH YOUR WRITING

Share your persuasive essay with your intended audience. Consider these options:

- Send your argument to an organization or a publication that has an interest in your issue or has the power to implement your proposed change.
- Upload your essay to the school Web site or a personal blog.
- Adapt your essay into a speech and deliver it to your audience.
- Turn your claim into a question and debate the topic with a small group of students.

Review some examples of effective writing in this unit to see how writers use repetition and parallelism. Add interest to your essay by experimenting with these stylistic elements. Then correct any errors and publish your final essay where it is most likely to reach your audience.

Scoring Rubric

Use the rubric below to evaluate your persuasive essay from the Writing Workshop or your response to the on-demand writing task on the next page.

PERSUASIVE ESSAY

SCORE	COMMON CORE TRAITS
6	• **Development** Asserts a precise, knowledgeable claim on a substantive topic; supports the claim with valid reasons and relevant, sufficient evidence; ably counters opposing claims with counterclaims; ends powerfully with a call to action • **Organization** Logically organizes claims, reasons, and evidence to persuasive effect; uses transitions to create cohesion and show relationships among ideas • **Language** Consistently maintains a formal style and an objective tone; shows a strong command of conventions
5	• **Development** States a precise claim on an interesting topic; offers valid reasons and evidence; counters opposing claims with counterclaims; ends with a strong concluding section • **Organization** Is logically organized; uses transitions to show relationships among the claim, reasons, and evidence • **Language** Uses a formal style and an objective tone; has a few errors in conventions
4	• **Development** States a clear claim; offers mostly valid support; needs to more fairly address opposing claims; has an adequate concluding section • **Organization** Reflects a logical organization, with one or two exceptions; could use a few more transitions • **Language** Mostly uses a formal style, but sounds defensive at times; includes a few distracting errors in conventions
3	• **Development** States a claim that could be more precise; provides some relevant support but not enough to be sufficient; unfairly dismisses other viewpoints; has a somewhat weak concluding section • **Organization** Has some flaws in organization; needs more transitions to show relationships among ideas • **Language** Often lapses into an informal style or a defensive tone; has several errors in conventions
2	• **Development** Has a weak claim; offers irrelevant reasons and insufficient evidence; fails to acknowledge other viewpoints; has a weak concluding section • **Organization** Has major organizational flaws; lacks transitions throughout • **Language** Uses an informal style and a defensive tone; has many errors in conventions
1	• **Development** Lacks a clear claim; provides no support for reasons; ignores opposing claims; ends abruptly • **Organization** Lacks organization; has no transitions • **Language** Uses an inappropriate style and tone; has major problems with grammar, mechanics, and spelling

Preparing for Timed Writing

COMMON CORE

W 9 Draw evidence from texts to support analysis. **W 10** Write routinely over shorter time frames for a range of tasks, purposes, and audiences.

1. ANALYZE THE TASK

5 MIN 

Read the task carefully. Then reread it, underlining the topic, the audience, and the purpose. Circle the type of writing you are being asked to do.

WRITING TASK

Read the following quotation from Daniel Singal's *American Quarterly* article entitled "Towards a Definition of American Modernism":

> Modernism "represents an attempt to restore a sense of order to human experience under the often chaotic conditions of twentieth-century existence."

Audience ↘ Purpose ↘ Topic ↘

Write a persuasive essay that tells your classmates why you agree or disagree with Singal's definition. Support your claim with valid reasons and relevant evidence.

2. PLAN YOUR RESPONSE

10 MIN 

Which side can you defend more effectively? Jot down names of modernist writers, their views, and their effect on society at the time. Then, decide on your claim and note your support in a chart. Identify a possible opposing claim and a counterclaim to refute it.

Reasons	Evidence
Opposing Claim: Counterclaim:	

3. RESPOND TO THE TASK

20 MIN 

Begin drafting your essay. Keep these guidelines in mind as you write:

- In the introduction, grab your audience's attention and state a precise claim.
- Present your reasons in a logical order. In each body paragraph, give one reason for your claim, supporting it with relevant evidence. Acknowledge and counter an opposing claim.
- Conclude by restating your claim and wrapping up your essay with a memorable phrase.

4. IMPROVE YOUR RESPONSE

5–10 MIN 

Revising Review key elements of your essay. Do you state a precise claim? Do you include enough support to be persuasive?

Proofreading Neatly correct any errors in grammar, spelling, and usage.

Checking Your Final Copy Before you turn in your essay, examine it once more to catch any errors you may have missed.

Speaking & Listening Workshop

Participating in a Debate

If you've ever tried to settle a disagreement with friends or siblings, you've used persuasive techniques to engage in a **debate**—a discussion in which individuals or teams argue opposing sides of an issue.

Complete the workshop activities in your **Reader/Writer Notebook.**

SPEAK WITH A PURPOSE	COMMON CORE TRAITS
TASK Participate in a **debate** about a substantive issue involving your school, community, or society. Be sure to allow adequate time to research supporting evidence for your argument.	***PARTICIPANTS IN AN EFFECTIVE DEBATE . . .*** • work productively with others in teams • present precise claims supported by valid reasons and sufficient evidence • evaluate other speakers' viewpoints, reasoning, evidence, and **rhetoric,** or language • respond thoughtfully to diverse perspectives and resolve contradictions when possible • speak clearly and persuasively using standard formal English

COMMON CORE

SL 1a–d Participate effectively in collaborative group discussions. **SL 3** Evaluate a speaker's point of view, reasoning, and use of evidence and rhetoric. **SL 4** Present information, findings, and supporting evidence, conveying a clear perspective, such that listeners can follow the line of reasoning.

Planning the Debate

A debate allows participants and audience members to consider and evaluate both sides of an issue. Follow these planning suggestions:

- **Identify Debate Teams** Form groups of six to debate the opposing sides of your chosen issue. Divide the group into two teams, with three members arguing for the affirmative side and three arguing for the negative side.

  Affirmative: *Yes, journalism standards have declined dramatically.*

  Negative: *No, journalism standards have not declined.*
- **Appoint a Moderator** The moderator plays a neutral role in the debate, promoting a civil discussion and keeping everyone on task. The moderator begins by introducing the topic of the debate and then recognizes speakers, alternating between affirmative and negative.
- **Research and Prepare Notes** Search print and online sources for information that will support your claim and stimulate a thoughtful exchange of ideas. Note the most common opposing claims and gather evidence to refute them. Meet with your team to share research and compile notes that you can use during the debate.
- **Assign Debate Roles** One member introduces the team's claim with supporting reasons and evidence. Another team member exchanges questions with a member of the opposing team to clarify and challenge reasoning. The last member presents a strong closing argument.

Holding the Debate

A well-run debate can be a vehicle for expressing your opinions in an assertive but respectful manner. Participating in a debate challenges you to synthesize comments made on both sides of an issue, pose probing questions, clarify ideas, and appreciate divergent perspectives.

GETTING STARTED

The moderator begins the debate by stating the topic and introducing the participants. Participants follow the moderator's instructions about whose turn it is to speak and how much time remains for each speaker.

Use the following debate format:

Speaker	*Role*	*Time*
Affirmative Speaker 1	Present the claim and supporting evidence for the affirmative ("pro") side of the argument.	5 minutes
Negative Speaker 1	Ask probing questions that will prompt the other team to address flaws in their argument.	3 minutes
Affirmative Speaker 2	Respond to the questions posed by the opposing team and counter any concerns.	3 minutes
Negative Speaker 2	Present the claim and supporting evidence for the negative ("con") side of the argument.	5 minutes
Affirmative Speaker 3	Summarize the claim and evidence for the affirmative side and explain why your reasoning is more valid.	3 minutes
Negative Speaker 3	Summarize the claim and evidence for the negative side and explain why your reasoning is more valid.	3 minutes

As a Speaker Follow the moderator's instructions. Speak clearly and persuasively, using formal English appropriate for a structured debate. Maintain a respectful tone regardless of your perspective.

As a Listener When the other team is presenting its side, evaluate the speaker's point of view, reasoning, and evidence. Take notes, identifying points of disagreement and noting any **fallacious,** or flawed, reasoning. Listen for persuasive rhetoric that serves to disguise exaggerated or distorted evidence. Be prepared to address these flaws during your team's response time.

Assessment Practice

ASSESS
Taking this practice test will help you assess your knowledge of these skills and determine your readiness for the Unit Test.

REVIEW
After you take the practice test, your teacher can help you identify any standards you need to review.

COMMON CORE

RL 1 Cite textual evidence to support analysis of what the text says. **RL 3** Analyze the impact of the author's choices regarding how to develop and relate elements of a story. **RL 4** Determine the meaning of words and phrases as they are used in the text; analyze the impact of specific word choices. **RL 6** Analyze a case in which grasping point of view requires distinguishing what is directly stated in a text from what is really meant. **RI 1** Cite textual evidence to support analysis of what the text says. **RI 6** Determine an author's point of view or purpose. **RI 7** Integrate and evaluate multiple sources of information presented in different media or formats. **W 5** Develop and strengthen writing by revising or editing. **W 9** Draw evidence from literary or informational texts to support analysis or reflection. **L 4a** Use context as a clue to the meaning of a word or phrase.

DIRECTIONS **Read the two selections and the viewing and representing piece. Then answer the questions that follow.**

The Sky Blue Ball

by Joyce Carol Oates

1 In a long-ago time when I didn't know *Yes I was happy, I was myself and I was happy*. In a long-ago time when I wasn't a child any longer yet I wasn't entirely not-a-child. In a long-ago time when I seemed often to be alone, and imagined myself lonely. *Yet this is your truest self: alone, lonely.*

2 One day I found myself walking beside a high brick wall the color of dried blood, the aged bricks loose and moldering, and over the wall came flying a spherical[1] object so brightly blue I thought it was a bird!-until it dropped a few yards in front of me, bouncing at a crooked angle off the broken sidewalk, and I saw that it was a rubber ball. A child had thrown a rubber ball over the wall, and I was expected to throw it back.

3 Hurriedly I let my things fall into the weeds, ran to snatch up the ball, which looked new, smelled new, spongy and resilient[2] in my hand like a rubber ball I'd played with years before as a little girl; a ball I'd loved and had long ago misplaced; a ball I'd loved and had forgotten. "Here it comes!" I called, and tossed the ball back over the wall; I would have walked on except, a few seconds later, there came the ball again, flying back.

4 *A game*, I thought. *You can't quit a game.*

5 So I ran after the ball as it rolled in the road, in the gravelly dirt, and again snatched it up, squeezing it with pleasure, how spongy how resilient a rubber ball, and again I tossed it over the wall; feeling happiness in swinging my arm as I hadn't done for years since I'd lost interest in such childish games. And this time I waited expectantly, and again it came!—the most beautiful sky blue rubber ball

1. **spherical** (sfîr′ ĭ-kəl) *adj.*: having the form of a sphere; globular.
2. **resilient** (rĭ-zĭl′yənt) *adj.*: able to return to original form after being bent, compressed, or stretched.

rising high, high into the air above my head and pausing for a heartbeat before it began to fall, to sink, like an object possessed of its own willful volition; so there was plenty of time for me to position myself beneath it and catch it firmly with both hands.

6 "Got it!"

7 I was fourteen years old and did not live in this neighborhood, nor anywhere in the town of Strykersville, New York (population 5,600). I lived on a small farm eleven miles to the north and I was brought to Strykersville by school bus, and consequently I was often alone; for this year, ninth grade, was my first at the school and I hadn't made many friends. And though I had relatives in Strykersville these were not relatives close to my family; they were not relatives eager to acknowledge me; for we who still lived in the country, hadn't yet made the inevitable move into town, were perceived inferior to those who lived in town. And in fact, my family was poorer than our relatives who lived in Strykersville.

8 At our school teachers referred to the nine farm children bussed there as "North Country children." We were allowed to understand that "North Country children" differed significantly from Strykersville children.

9 I was not thinking of such things now, I was smiling thinking it must be a particularly playful child on the other side of the wall, a little girl like me; like the little girl I'd been; though the wall was ugly and forbidding with rusted signs EMPIRE MACHINE PARTS and PRIVATE PROPERTY NO TRESPASSING. On the other side of the Chautauqua & Buffalo railroad yard was a street of

small wood-frame houses; it must have been in one of these that the little girl, my invisible, playmate, lived. She must be much younger than I was; for fourteen-year-old girls didn't play such heedless games with strangers, we grew up swiftly if our families were not well-to-do.

10 I threw the ball back over the wall, calling, "Hi! Hi, there!" But there was no reply. I waited; I was standing in broken concrete, amid a scrubby patch of weeds. Insects buzzed and droned around me as if in curiosity, yellow butterflies no larger than my smallest fingernail fluttered and caught in my hair, tickling me. The sun was bright as a nova in a pebbled-white soiled sky that was like a thin chamois cloth about to be lifted away and I thought, *This is the surprise I've been waiting for.* For somehow I had acquired the belief that a surprise, a nice surprise, was waiting for me. I had only to merit it, and it would happen. (And if I did not merit it, it would not happen.) Such a surprise could not come from God but only from strangers, by chance.

11 Another time the sky blue ball sailed over the wall, after a longer interval of perhaps thirty seconds; and at an unexpected angle, as if it had been thrown away from me, from my voice, purposefully. Yet there it came, as if it could not not come: my invisible playmate was obliged to continue the game. I had no hope of catching it but ran blindly into the road (which was partly asphalt and partly gravel and not much traveled except by trucks) and there came a dump truck headed at me, I heard the ugly shriek of brakes and a deafening angry horn and I'd fallen onto my knees, I'd cut my knees that were bare, probably I'd torn my skirt, scrambling quickly to my feet, my cheeks smarting with shame, for wasn't I too grown a girl for such behavior? "Get the hell out of the road!" a man's voice was furious in rectitude, the voice of so many adult men of my acquaintance, you did not question such voices, you did not doubt them, you ran quickly to get out of their way, already I'd snatched up the ball, panting like a dog, trying to hide the ball in my skirt as I turned, shrinking and ducking so the truck driver couldn't see my face, for what if he was someone who knew my father, what if he recognized me, knew my name. But already the truck was thundering past, already I'd been forgotten.

12 Back then I ran to the wall, though both my knees throbbed with pain, and I was shaking as if shivering, the air had grown cold, a shaft of cloud had pierced

the sun. I threw the ball back over the wall again, underhand, so that it rose high, high—so that my invisible playmate would have plenty of time to run and catch it. And it disappeared behind the wall and I waited, I was breathing hard and did not investigate my bleeding knees, my torn skirt. More clouds pierced the sun and shadows moved swift and certain across the earth like predator fish. After a while I called out hesitantly, "Hi? Hello?" It was like a ringing telephone you answer but no one is there. You wait, you inquire again, shyly, "Hello?" A vein throbbed in my forehead, a tinge of pain glimmered behind my eyes, that warning of pain, of punishment, following excitement. The child had drifted away, I supposed; she'd lost interest in our game, if it was a game. And suddenly it seemed silly and contemptible to me, and sad: there I stood, fourteen years old, a long-limbed weed of a girl, no longer a child yet panting and bleeding from the knees, the palms of my hands, too, chafed and scraped and dirty; there I stood alone in front of a moldering brick wall waiting for—what?

13 It was my school notebook, my several textbooks I'd let fall into the grass and I would afterward discover that my math textbook was muddy, many pages damp and torn; my spiral notebook in which I kept careful notes of the intransigent[3] rules of English grammar and sample sentences diagrammed was soaked in a virulent-smelling chemical and my teacher's laudatory comments in red and my grades of A (for all my grades at Strykersville Junior High were A, of that I was obsessively proud) had become illegible as if they were grades of C, D, F. I should have taken up my books and walked hurriedly away and put the sky blue ball out of my mind entirely but I was not so free, through my life I've been made to realize that I am not free, as others appear to be free, at all. For the "nice" surprise carries with it the "bad" surprise and the two are intricately entwined and they cannot be separated, nor even defined as separate. So though my head pounded I felt obliged to look for a way over the wall. Though my knees were scraped and bleeding I located a filthy oil drum and shoved it against the wall and climbed shakily up on it, dirtying my hands and arms, my legs, my clothes, even more. And I hauled myself over the wall, and jumped down, a drop of about ten feet, the breath knocked out of me as I landed, the shock of impact reverberating through me, along my spine, as if I'd been struck a sledge-hammer blow to the soles of my feet. At once I saw that there could be no little girl here, the factory

GO ON

3. **intransigent** (ĭn-trăn′sə-jənt) *adj.:* uncompromising.

yard was surely deserted, about the size of a baseball diamond totally walled in and overgrown with weeds pushing through cracked asphalt, thistles, stunted trees, and clouds of tiny yellow butterflies clustered here in such profusion I was made to see that they were not beautiful creatures, but mere insects, horrible. And rushing at me as if my very breath sucked them at me, sticking against my sweaty face, and in my snarled hair.

14 Yet stubbornly I searched for the ball. I would not leave without the ball. I seemed to know that the ball must be there, somewhere on the other side of the wall, though the wall would have been insurmountable[4] for a little girl. And at last, after long minutes of searching, in a heat of indignation I discovered the ball in a patch of chicory. It was no longer sky blue but faded and cracked; its dun-colored rubber showed through the venous-cracked surface, like my own ball, years ago. Yet I snatched it up in triumph, and squeezed it, and smelled it—it smelled of nothing: of the earth: of the sweating palm of my own hand.

4. **insurmountable** (ĭn′sər-moun′tə-bəl) *adj.:* not capable of being overcome.

Change of Heart

My neighbors and I just couldn't get along.

By Mary A. Fischer
from *Reader's Digest*

Being in the Minority

1 In 1992, like many people in Los Angeles, I watched TV news reports of Rodney King speaking to the press after four officers accused of beating him in 1991 were acquitted, leading to riots in the city. As King spoke to reporters, he plaintively asked, "Can we all get along?"

2 "No! We can't," I shouted back at the TV, though no one else was in the room to hear me. Mine was not an idle, uninformed response. I knew what I was talking about. In late 1989, I had bought a house in an affordable eastside neighborhood of Los Angeles called Highland Park, which was being transformed by waves of new immigrants, and I was convinced racial harmony was impossible. Statistics said that each year, tens of thousands of new immigrants, mostly from Latin America and Asia, were pouring into Southern California, yet for most whites, these trends remained in the abstract realm of statistics.

3 When I moved to Highland Park, however, the statistics became my daily reality and brought my prejudices to the surface. Many of my neighbors were from Mexico, El Salvador, the Philippines and Vietnam, and for the first time, I was in the minority and didn't like it.

4 Convinced that we had nothing in common, I fortressed myself in my lovely pink Spanish house on the hill. I rarely spoke to my neighbors, waving occasionally when we took out our trash cans or passed by in our cars. I fit their stereotype—the unfriendly white "gringa" who owned the nicest house on the block—just as they fit my preconceived notions of immigrants who stubbornly refused to assimilate.

5 I was annoyed when Hispanic salespeople in Radio Shack didn't understand when I asked for lithium batteries or extension cords. It irritated me that the local supermarkets didn't carry things like blue cheese or soy milk, and that some billboard ads for movies and cars were written in Spanish.

6 For years, I complained to various officials when my neighbors behaved in ways I didn't agree with. One woman from El Salvador kept a rooster in her backyard that woke me up at 5:00 every morning. When I reported her to the Animal Regulation Department, she responded to the complaint by cutting off the bird's head. I felt guilty about being the impetus for the rooster's brutal demise, but rationalized it as being necessary to restore peace and quiet to the neighborhood.

7 When my neighbors from Mexico played their music too loud, I called the police, who put a stop to it. Surmising that I had reported them, my neighbors

GO ON

stopped speaking to me. It was a punishment I could live with, since I reasoned that I was bringing the neighborhood into compliance with my values.

8 Then, two years ago, something happened that changed me and how I live in my neighborhood. In a matter of two days, I lost the things that mattered most to me. My six-figure job as a senior writer for a national magazine came to an end, and a relationship with a man I loved ended badly. Suddenly, all my anchors were gone and, sunk deep in grief, I wondered how—or if—I would be able to pull myself out.

9 The losses I experienced humbled me and made me vulnerable, but as a consequence I began to connect more fully with my neighbors and the world around me. I discovered how extraordinary they were. They were nothing like my biases had made them out to be. They were hard-working, honorable people who, like me, were just looking to live well and experience some measure of happiness.

10 I learned that the woman from El Salvador had fled her country with two young daughters after death squads murdered her husband. She cleaned houses to make ends meet and send her daughters to college. I learned that when my neighbors from Mexico came to Los Angeles 15 years ago, they did not speak English and the father cleaned offices for $8 an hour. Later, he drove delivery trucks. Today he owns three apartment buildings and has made more money than I probably ever will in my lifetime.

11 Now, many of my neighbors are my friends. At Christmas, I give them red wine and cakes and they give me potted flowers and platters of burritos. When my car wouldn't start a few months ago, and it looked like it would have to be towed, another neighbor from Guatemala, a sweet man named Angel who's a gardener, quickly brought out his jumper cables and got the car started.

12 Today, I would answer Rodney King's question differently. I'd say that it is possible for us to get along if people from different cultures don't make the mistake I did. When I first moved to my neighborhood, I neglected to view my neighbors as individuals and I saw them as different and apart from me. I see now how their lives and mine include experiences universal to us all: loss, disappointment, hope and love.

13 Last month, I heard a rooster crow early in the morning. It seems my neighbor from El Salvador got another one, but I no longer mind. I like watching the rooster as it wanders the neighborhood. Somehow, he makes me feel like I'm home.

King Street Community Garden
Farmer's Market

Come Taste What Your Neighbors Have Been Growing

9:00-12:00
First & Third Saturdays of the Month, June - October
Corner of King Street & Park Avenue

Vegetables from Around the World ... in Your Own Community

Reading Comprehension

Use "The Sky Blue Ball" (pp. 1130–1134) to answer questions 1–11.

1. The narrator believes her truest self is lonely because —

A. she doesn't understand who she is
B. she has made only a few friends
C. her parents just don't understand her
D. her family is poor

2. The brick wall symbolizes —

A. challenges in adult life
B. cooperation
C. childhood that cannot be regained
D. boundaries

3. In paragraph 2, *moldering* means —

A. forming a shape
B. crumbling into pieces
C. blending together
D. grinding thoroughly

4. Strykersville children —

A. are inferior to North Country children
B. have to ride the bus long distances to school
C. have to work on farms
D. are wealthier than North Country children

5. In paragraph 9, *heedless* means —

A. attentive
B. fun
C. thoughtless
D. unselfish

6. Why does the narrator try to hide her face from the truck driver in paragraph 11?

A. The truck driver recognizes her.
B. She wants to stay anonymous.
C. She recognizes the truck driver.
D. The truck driver's voice is loud.

7. For the narrator, the game of catch represents —

A. a sense of hope to make friends
B. a chore that needs to be completed
C. an unexpected return to childhood
D. a barrier to growing up

8. In paragraph 12, *contemptible* means —

A. admirable
B. important
C. serious
D. disdainful

9. The author chose to use a rubber ball as a meaningful symbol because —

A. it is an ordinary object associated with children
B. it looks like the earth
C. few people have played catch with rubber balls
D. many people have kept a rubber ball as a souvenir of childhood

10. How does the girl feel about finding the ball?

A. Angry
B. Disappointed
C. Excited
D. Sad

11. At the end of the story, the ball represents —

A. the negative experiences of childhood

B. the innocence of childhood

C. the triumph over childhood helplessness

D. a new friendship

Use "Change of Heart" (pp. 1135–1136) to answer questions 12–18.

12. The article is mostly about —

A. immigrants adjusting to life in the United States

B. learning to live in a multicultural neighborhood

C. living up to someone's prejudices

D. the Rodney King riots in Los Angeles

13. Read the following dictionary entry.

idle \'ī-dəl\ *adj* **1.** lacking worth or basis, vain **2a.** not occupied or employed **b.** not turned to normal or appropriate use **c.** not scheduled to compete **3a.** shiftless, lazy **b.** having no evident lawful means of support

Which definition best matches the meaning of the word *idle* as it is used in paragraph 2 of the selection?

A. Definition 1

B. Definition 2a

C. Definition 2b

D. Definition 3a

14. What does the following sentence mean?

Statistics said that each year, tens of thousands of new immigrants, mostly from Latin America and Asia, were pouring into Southern California, yet for most whites, these trends remained in the abstract realm of statistics.

A. Latin Americans and Asians were the only immigrants coming to Southern California.

B. Whites and new immigrants, mostly from Latin America and Asia, cooperate.

C. Latin Americans and Asians help whites understand statistics.

D. Whites rarely interacted with new immigrants.

15. What can the reader conclude about the author from her reaction in paragraph 6?

A. She cooperates with city officials and departments to stop illegal behavior in her neighborhood.

B. She likes getting up early in the morning.

C. She wants her neighbors to behave as she would.

D. She is in charge of the neighborhood watch program.

16. In paragraph 7, *surmising* means —

A. inferring from little evidence

B. knowing for a fact

C. learning after the fact

D. informing

17. According to paragraph 8, a great part of the author's identity was in her —

A. biases

B. boat

C. job

D. neighborhood

GO ON

18. In what way is this selection ironic?

A. The author's neighbors finally assimilate to living in the United States.

B. The author decides that she doesn't like her neighborhood.

C. The author is the one whose behavior changes.

D. The author realizes that people who are different cannot get along.

Use "The Sky Blue Ball" and "Change of Heart" to answer question 19.

19. The reader can conclude that the narrators in both selections —

A. respect tradition

B. adapt with their circumstances

C. stay the same

D. like to get into trouble

Use the visual representation on page 1137 to answer questions 20–21.

20. The organizers of the King Street Community Garden hope to improve the neighborhood by —

A. providing healthier food for the community

B. allowing neighbors to become friends through working together

C. providing soil, straw, and community tools to all who participate

D. charging tuition for gardening classes that benefit the organization

21. The designer of the poster chose the photograph to emphasize —

A. that gardening involves working in the dirt

B. that specialized tools are necessary to garden productively

C. the communal aspect of the garden

D. that soil, straw, and tools are provided

SHORT CONSTRUCTED RESPONSE

Write a short constructed response to each question, using text evidence to support your response.

22. How does the author of "The Sky Blue Ball" use imagery to bring the setting and her narrator's experiences to life? Support your response with evidence from the selection.

23. Why is "Change of Heart" a good title for this selection? Support your response with evidence from the selection.

Write a short constructed response to the following question, using text evidence from both selections to support your response.

24. What impact does the point of view have in "The Sky Blue Ball" and "Change of Heart"? Support your response with evidence from **both** selections.

Revising and Editing

DIRECTIONS Read this passage and answer the questions that follow.

(1) My twin sister, Natasha and I used to engage in unceasing hostilities. (2) We would fight over everything: clothes, bathroom space, chores, *everything*. (3) The week after we turned fifteen, we got news that changed our lives. (4) Natasha had been feeling sick for a while, and medical tests determined that she had leukemia. (5) The type of leukemia she had held a strong chance of survival, but it would require chemotherapy and some sacrifice and determination from our family. (6) I reevaluated my relationship with my sister, since I thought I might lose her.

1. What change, if any, should be made in sentence 1?
   - **A.** Change ***sister,*** to **sister:**
   - **B.** Insert a comma after ***Natasha***
   - **C.** Change ***unceasing*** to **ceasing**
   - **D.** Make no change

2. Which transition should be added to the beginning of sentence 3?
   - **A.** In fact,
   - **B.** Likewise,
   - **C.** Otherwise,
   - **D.** Then,

3. What change, if any, should be made in sentence 4?
   - **A.** Change ***that*** to **than**
   - **B.** Change ***for*** to **since**
   - **C.** Insert a comma after ***determined***
   - **D.** Make no change

4. What is the most effective way to revise sentence 6?
   - **A.** The thought of losing my sister made me to reevaluate our relationship.
   - **B.** To reevaluate our relationship happened at the thought of losing my sister.
   - **C.** While thinking about losing my sister, I began to reevaluate our relationship.
   - **D.** When thinking about losing my sister, I admitted to reevaluate our relationship.

5. To make a connection between the experience and life in general, which sentence could the writer add?
   - **A.** I learned that life is too precious to waste time fighting over trivial things.
   - **B.** I learned to love and appreciate my life.
   - **C.** I learned how the doctors planned to treat my sister's cancer.
   - **D.** I learned to value different people's points of view.

6. What would the next paragraph of this essay most likely contain?
   - **A.** Details about the sisters' fights
   - **B.** Details about other family members
   - **C.** Statistics about leukemia from a credible source
   - **D.** Examples of how the relationship changed

Ideas for Independent Reading

Continue exploring the Questions of the Times on pages 862–863 by reading these additional works.

What is MODERN?

Prufrock and Other Observations
by T. S. Eliot

This volume contains 12 early poems by T.S. Eliot, including "The Love Song of J. Alfred Prufrock," regarded by some as the first modernist poem. The collection also includes "Portrait of a Lady," "Preludes," and "Rhapsody on a Windy Night," three other great poems about loneliness and alienation. Ezra Pound praised the book for "its fine tone, its humanity, and its realism."

Spoon River Anthology
by Edgar Lee Masters

This is Edgar Lee Masters's best-known work, a collection of free-verse monologues written in the voices of inhabitants of a small-town cemetery. The interconnected poems reveal the hidden loves, thwarted longings, and bitterness of people who lived and died in the confines of a small town.

The Autobiography of Alice B. Toklas
by Gertrude Stein

Gertrude Stein was at the center of a sparkling community of American writers who lived in Europe following World War I. She knew Picasso, Matisse, Joyce, Hemingway, and other important modernist figures. This book is her memoir of those heady days in Paris, playfully written in the voice of her lifelong companion, Alice B. Toklas.

Can ideals survive CATASTROPHE?

The Sun Also Rises
by Ernest Hemingway

After the end of World War I, a group of American expatriates in Europe try to wrest pleasure from a life that has lost meaning. They meet in Paris bistros, fish in the trout streams of Spain, and watch bullfights in Pamplona. Can such pleasures compensate them for their lost illusions? *The Sun Also Rises* leaves this question unanswered.

Blood on the Forge
by William Attaway

Following World War I, three African-American brothers—Big Mat, Chinatown, and Melody—flee the rural South for jobs in the steel mills of Pittsburgh. In search of a better life, they instead find dangerous work, terrible living conditions, and ethnic conflict. Each of the three brothers copes with his new life in a different way.

Waiting for Lefty
by Clifford Odets

During the time of reexamination that followed the Great Depression, the plays of Clifford Odets were a jolt of working-class lightning. Their affirmation of hope energized theatergoers from coast to coast. *Waiting for Lefty* dramatizes the courage and doubts of a group of cabdrivers who are debating whether to strike for a living wage.

RL 10 Read and comprehend literature. **RI 10** Read and comprehend literary nonfiction

How can people honor their HERITAGE?

The Souls of Black Folk
by W. E. B. Du Bois

This collection of essays, published in 1903, is unified by the idea of African-Americans' "double consciousness." As Americans, they are heirs to the nation's ideals of liberty and equality. But as a despised minority, they are barred from full participation in these ideals. W.E.B. Du Bois describes the struggles African Americans face and the gifts they offer the nation.

Their Eyes Were Watching God
by Zora Neale Hurston

Zora Neale Hurston brings an all-black Florida town to life in this moving love story. Janie Crawford has been taught by a fearful grandmother to value economic security over love. She marries an ambitious businessman who views her as a trophy rather than as a partner. When he dies, Janie finds fulfillment with the younger, free-spirited Tea Cake.

Cane
by Jean Toomer

Cane is a groundbreaking work of the Harlem Renaissance by a writer of mixed ancestry. It is composed of stories, poems, vignettes, and a short play. Part I, set in rural Georgia, presents the beauty of the land and the violence residents inflict on one another. Part II, set in the urban North, portrays a world of spiritual deadness. In Part III, a figure resembling Jean Toomer returns to the South to seek his identity.

What drives HUMAN BEHAVIOR?

As I Lay Dying
by William Faulkner

The dying wish of Addie Bundren, the wife of a Mississippi farmer, is to be buried in the county seat with the rest of her family. Her husband and children place her coffin in a wagon and undertake a dangerous odyssey. In a series of interior monologues, the characters—even the dead Addie—reveal the complex motivations that spur them forward.

Babbitt
by Sinclair Lewis

This satirical novel added a new word to American speech—*babbitt,* meaning "a smugly conventional person." When George Babbitt, a successful Midwestern businessman of the 1920s, rebels against his empty, conformist life, his friends reject him. Eventually he realizes that he is too old to rebel but that he can support his son's unconventional dreams.

Native Son
by Richard Wright

In this classic American novel, Wright questions whether people who are born poor, without any real opportunities, can ever be "free." Bigger Thomas is an impoverished African-American youth who resents the world of white power around him. Hired as a chauffeur by a white millionaire, he commits a shocking crime that seems oddly predestined. Who is responsible for Bigger's tragic life?

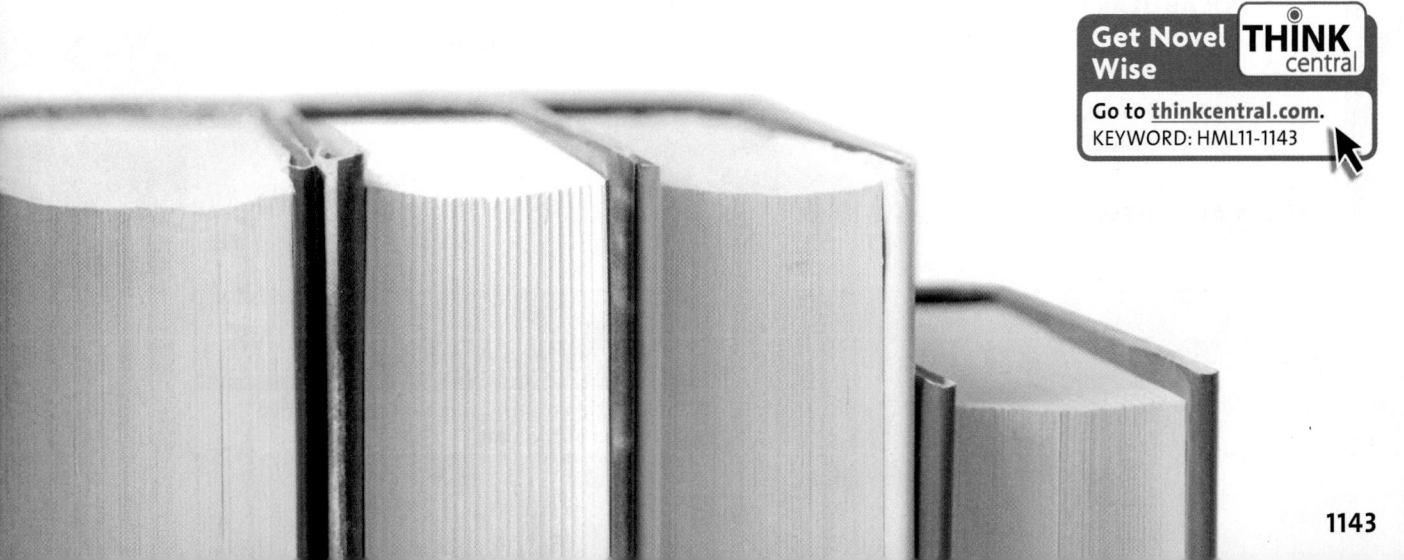

Get Novel Wise THINK central

Go to thinkcentral.com.
KEYWORD: HML11-1143

UNIT 6

COMMON CORE

Preview Unit Goals

TEXT ANALYSIS	• Understand and analyze historical and cultural context of contemporary literature • Identify and interpret allusions • Identify and interpret rhetorical devices, including paradox and repetition • Identify and analyze tone, imagery, voice, personification, and sound devices • Analyze primary and secondary source documents • Analyze and trace elements of an argument, including claim, reasons, evidence, and counterargument • Identify faulty reasoning, including circular logic and non-sequiturs • Make inferences about theme, genre, structure, and elements of drama in different cultural and historical contexts
READING	• Identify and evaluate main ideas and supporting details • Analyze inductive and deductive reasoning
WRITING AND LANGUAGE	• Write a resumé • Use word choice, sentence structure, and tone to establish voice • Use word choice, imagery, and tone to create mood
SPEAKING AND LISTENING	• Analyze an argument in a newspaper article • Compare and contrast perspectives in news reports
VOCABULARY	• Understand and use Greek prefixes to determine word meaning • Use context clues to determine the meaning of idioms
ACADEMIC VOCABULARY	• complex • economic • establish • ethnic • evolve
MEDIA AND VIEWING	• Create a Web site

Find It Online!

Go to thinkcentral.com for the interactive version of this unit.

Contemporary Literature

1940–PRESENT

Sandra Cisneros

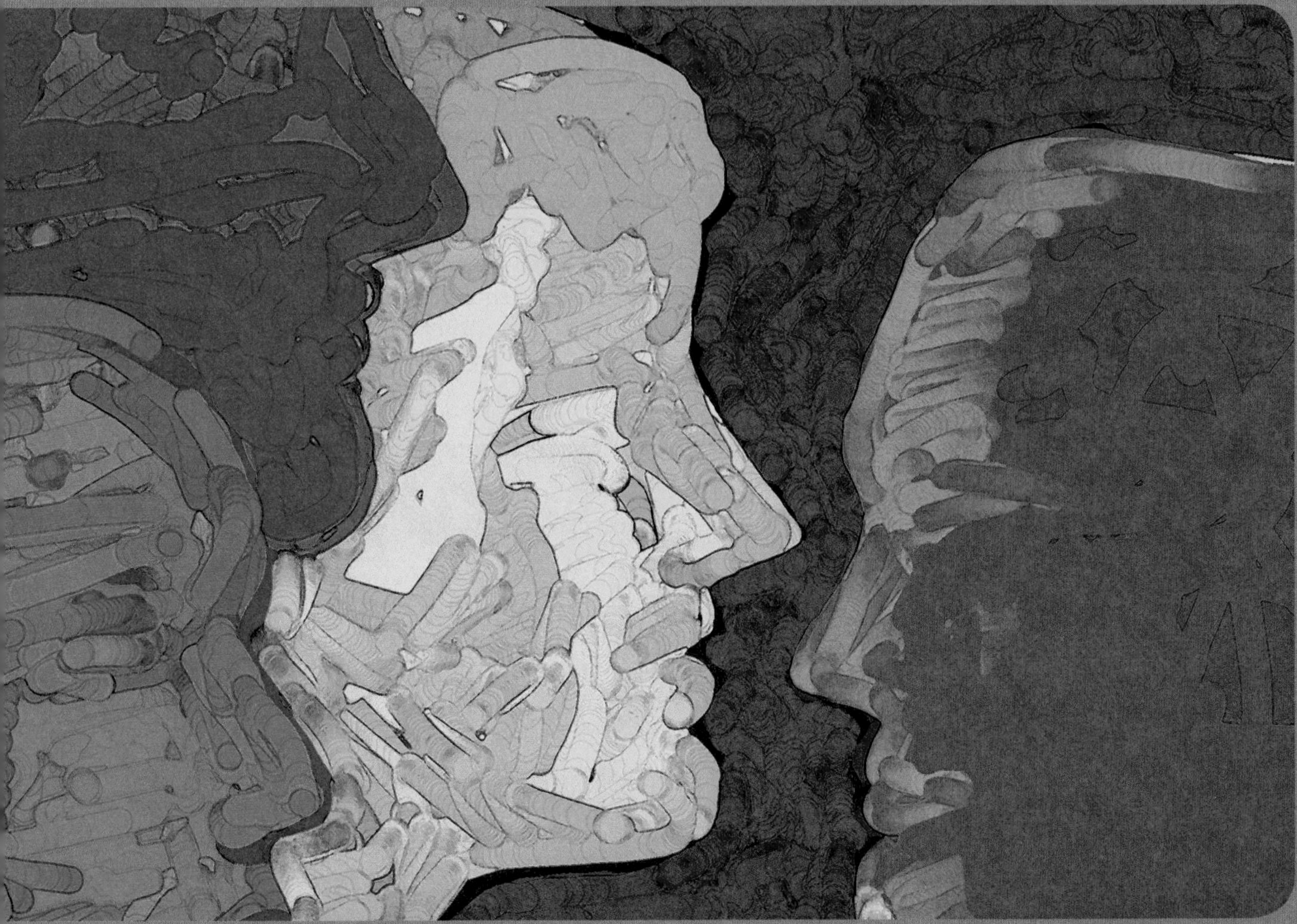

NEW PERSPECTIVES

- Modern American Drama
- Responses to War
- Civil Rights and Protest Literature
- A Mosaic of American Voices

MediaSmart DVD-ROM

Perspectives in the News

Deconstruct news reports to see how they can shape audience perceptions of historical events and figures. Page 1234

Questions of the Times

DISCUSS After reading these questions and talking about them with a partner, share with the class as a whole. Then read on to explore the ways in which writers of the contemporary era have dealt with the same issues.

Are we responsible for the WHOLE WORLD?

World War II brought the United States into a new role of increased power and involvement in the world, a role that expanded even further with the Cold War, Vietnam, and the "War on Terror." Do you believe America has a responsibility to intervene in other nations' conflicts? Does it have the right?

Can America achieve EQUAL RIGHTS?

In 1963, one hundred years after emancipation, African Americans still found themselves treated as second-class citizens, denied equal education, jobs, even the right to vote. The civil rights movement secured the legal right to equality, but in reality racism and injustice linger on. Do you believe America will ever achieve true equality?

ARE YOU
DOING ALL YOU CAN?

COMMON CORE

RL 9 Demonstrate knowledge of twentieth-century foundational works of American literature, including how two or more texts from the same period treat similar themes and topics. **RI 9** Analyze documents of historical and literary significance for their themes, purposes, and rhetorical features.

What makes an AMERICAN?

American writers of the 21st century reflect the diversity of the country itself. The United States has become a multicultural society whose citizens' experiences are endlessly varied. With no single "American experience" to bond citizens together, it seems logical to ask: What makes an American? Patriotism? Independence? Mere citizenship? Or something else?

What is the AMERICAN DREAM?

The Pilgrims and the Puritans dreamed of a new world where they would be free to practice their religion. Later immigrants dreamed of a country where any child could grow up to be the president. In the postwar era of the 1950s, the dream focused on consumer goods—"a car in every garage." How do you define the American dream?

Contemporary Literature
1940–PRESENT
New Perspectives

In the 1950s, America entered the Space Age—a beginning foray into our modern technological times. Looking down from space, the country's first astronauts marveled at the blue marble that was Earth floating in the blackness. From space, Earth looked peaceful and whole, with no divisions between nations, no conflict between races. It was a new way of looking at the world—just one of many new perspectives on modern life.

Contemporary Literature: Historical Context

Literature of the modern age reflects the uncertainty and anxiety brought on by the realities of war.

COMMON CORE

RL 9 Demonstrate knowledge of twentieth-century foundational works of American literature, including how two or more texts from the same period treat similar themes and topics. **RI 9** Analyze documents of historical and literary significance for their themes and purposes.

Modern Warfare

WORLD WAR II "Not a place on earth might be so happy as America," wrote Thomas Paine in the winter of 1776. "Her situation is remote from all the wrangling world." More than a century and a half later, as the Nazi army surged across Europe and Japan's expansionist government seized territories in Asia, many Americans still clung to the dream of isolationism—until **Pearl Harbor** woke them from their illusions.

On December 7, 1941, Japanese bombers struck the American naval base at Pearl Harbor, Hawaii, sinking ships, destroying planes, and killing over two thousand people. Though it lasted less than two hours, this surprise attack changed the course of history, bringing a reluctant United States into World War II.

The U.S. entry into the war turned the tide in favor of the Allies—England, France, and the Soviet Union—but it was a long, hard fight. By the time Germany and Japan surrendered to the Allied forces in 1945, more than 78 million people had been killed or wounded, including around six million Jews systematically murdered by the Nazis in what became known as the **Holocaust.** World War II was a catastrophe of epic dimensions, the first war in history in which more civilians than soldiers died. Never before had so many soldiers fought. Never before had such wholesale slaughter occurred. Writers such as **Randall Jarrell,** who had personal experience with the war, struggled to both document and examine the meaning of war on such a grand scale. Others, such as **Kurt Vonnegut** and **Bernard Malamud,** examined the rampant anti-Semitism that fueled the Holocaust. Malamud once remarked, "People say I write so much about misery, but you write about what you write best. As you are grooved, so you are grieved."

THE COLD WAR America came out of World War II a world power, wielding a new weapon of unparalleled destructive force: the atomic bomb. But along with strength and influence came deep uneasiness. The Soviet Union, once an ally, emerged as a rival superpower with equally large ambitions and a political system—communism—which many saw as a threat to the American way of life. Knowing any direct confrontation could end in nuclear annihilation, the two nations fought a "Cold War," each side racing to develop more and more devastating weapons while they jostled for strategic influence around the globe. As the arms race spiraled upward, ordinary citizens felt less and less secure. In literature, this pervasive fear of known and unknown dangers prompted a boom in **science fiction** writing, as writers pondered what might arise if the current trends continued.

TAKING NOTES

Outlining As you read this introduction, use an outline to record the main ideas about the characteristics and literature of the period. You can use article headings, boldfaced terms, and the information in these boxes as starting points. (See page R49 in the **Research Handbook** for more help with outlining.)

I. Historical Context
A. World War II
1. isolationism
2. Pearl Harbor
3. Holocaust
B. Cold War

MODERN CONFLICTS Meanwhile, in an effort to contain the spread of communism, the U.S. military became deeply involved in civil wars first in Korea, then in Vietnam. The major American involvement in the **Vietnam War** lasted about nine years and bred a degree of domestic conflict unseen since the Civil War. As the death toll among U.S. soldiers rose—reaching about 58,000 in all—many Americans questioned the wisdom of our intervention and took to the streets in protest. The literature of the time reflects the conflicts within the country. Writer **Tim O'Brien** once remarked that "It's not really Vietnam that I was concerned about . . . ; rather, it was to have readers care about what's right and wrong and about the difficulty of doing right, the difficulty of saying no to a war."

The Cold War finally came to an end with the breakup of the Soviet Union in 1991, but America was not finished with warfare. That same year, U.S. troops were sent to counter the Iraqi invasion of Kuwait in the first Persian Gulf War. A longer struggle began on September 11, 2001, when hijackers flew commercial airplanes into the Pentagon and the World Trade Center, killing thousands and leading to U.S. invasions of Afghanistan and Iraq. At the same time, violence raged around the globe, and with nuclear weapons no longer limited to two superpowers, possibilities for worldwide disaster loomed. Writers of the last several generations have been profoundly affected by the sense of instability that has been brought on by near-constant war. "At all times," wrote novelist **John Updike,** "an old world is collapsing and a new world arising."

A Voice from the Times

Mankind must put an end to war, or war will put an end to mankind.

—John F. Kennedy

U. S. Marines training for Operation Desert Shield, 1990

Segregated drinking fountains, North Carolina

Cultural Influences

Writers have both recorded and reflected upon the civil rights movement of the 1950s and 1960s—perhaps the most important social change in modern time.

The Civil Rights Movement

The civil rights movement had its roots in protests and legal actions of the 1950s. In 1954, the Supreme Court's ***Brown v. Board of Education*** ruling struck down school segregation as unconstitutional. Other civil rights advances followed, pushed along by black and white activists who organized protest marches, boycotts, voter registration drives, and sit-ins. **Dr. Martin Luther King Jr.** emerged as a leader during these times. King advocated nonviolent civil disobedience based on the philosophies of Henry David Thoreau and Indian social reformer Mohandas Gandhi.

Sadly, many of the peaceful demonstations of the civil rights movement were met with mob violence and police brutality. While the nation watched on television, protestors were beaten, attacked by police dogs, and sprayed with fire hoses. King himself endured repeated imprisonment for his efforts. But the violence did not stop the movement.

During the famous March on Washington in 1963, which drew 200,000 participants, demonstrators demanded civil rights legislation at the national level, backed strongly by federal enforcement. Largely as a result of King's efforts, Congress passed the 1964 **Civil Rights Act** outlawing segregation in public places and guaranteeing legal equality to black citizens. In the years since, America has still not achieved true equality and opportunity for all, yet the civil rights movement has brought it much closer to King's dream of a land where people would "not be judged by the color of their skin, but by the content of their character."

A Voice from the Times

I have a dream that one day this nation will rise up and live out the true meaning of its creed: "We hold these truths to be self-evident, that all men are created equal."

—Martin Luther King Jr.

Seattle-area neighborhood, 1955

Ideas of the Age

Modern writers have responded in a variety of ways to a peculiarly American philosophy: that of the American dream.

The American Dream

For earlier generations, the **American dream** had meant many things—political and religious freedom, economic opportunity, the chance to achieve a better life through talent, education, and hard work. After living through the Great Depression and two World Wars, however, many Americans in the 1950s whittled that dream down to something much simpler: the chance to own a home in a stable neighborhood.

For millions of mainly white Americans, life in the suburbs became the American dream. Families sought out communities with affordable single-family homes, good schools, shopping malls, and parking that was free and easy to find. People didn't care if their houses looked alike; they just wanted a safe place to raise their children.

As the years passed and the economy boomed, however, Americans began to add to their once-simple dream. *Things* became more important: a new television, car, or washing machine came to be seen as symbols of success. Soon the dream seemed to narrow to a vision of a consumer society in which conformity and "keeping up with the Joneses" was valued above all.

Writers from the mid-century to today have wrangled with the idea of the American dream. In the mid-'50s, **"beatniks"** such as **Jack Kerouac** and **Allen Ginsberg** protested the shallowness and conformity of American society. Dramatists such as **Arthur Miller** examined the strivings of ordinary Americans reaching for that American dream. Poets, novelists, short story writers—all have explored the many facets of the American dream.

Literature of the Times

The years between World War II and the present brought dramatic changes in the subjects and forms of literature, as well as a wider variety of authors represented.

> ***For Your Outline***
>
> **MODERN AMERICAN DRAMA**
> - postwar revival in theater
> - common theme was American dream
> - characterized by disillusionment and experimental style
> - broke boundaries and opened doors

Modern American Drama

In the years following World War II, some of the best and most influential writing was occurring within the community of American theater. Dramatists in the post-war years began to experiment stylistically and create works of social relevance that would prompt a revival in theater not only in America, but in Europe as well. Dramatists such as Arthur Miller and **Tennessee Williams** served as models of the liberated playwright—experimenting with stagecraft as well as modern themes often deemed provocative.

One of the most common themes explored by these playwrights was that of the American dream. "The American dream is the largely unacknowledged screen in front of which all American writing plays itself out," Arthur Miller once said. Indeed, Miller's Willy Loman, the main character in his *Death of a Salesman,* became the trademark figure of postwar American theater. A lowly salesman who has been discarded by the system to which he has mistakenly devoted his life, Willy Loman proved how the American dream could become twisted and broken.

A general disillusionment paired with an experimental style characterized many of the works of this period. While a play such as **Thornton Wilder's** *Our Town,* first produced in 1938, experimented with stagecraft by showing life literally "behind the scenes" on a stage bare of scenery, it still took a gentle view of small-town America. Works written in the 1940s and 1950s, however, were far less sympathetic. In *The Glass Menagerie* and *A Streetcar Named Desire,* for example, Southerner Tennessee Williams portrayed characters who, unsuited to modern life, retreat into the fantasy world of an earlier era. And Miller's critique of modern values in *Death of a Salesman* was found to be so threatening that Hollywood executives wanted to release the movie version along with a short film depicting the life of a salesman as blissful and carefree. Miller, however, protested.

Vivien Leigh and Marlon Brando in *A Streetcar Named Desire*

Lorraine Hansberry's *A Raisin in the Sun,* written in 1957, looked at the American dream from the perspective of those who had been excluded. The first major Broadway play by an African-American writer, *A Raisin in the Sun* was hailed by critics as "universal," while also capturing unique aspects of the African-

American experience. Writer **James Baldwin** said of the play, "[I]n order for a person to bear his life, he needs a valid re-creation of that life, which is why, as Ray Charles might put it, blacks chose to sing the blues. This is why *Raisin in the Sun* meant so much to black people . . . . In the theater, a current flowed back and forth between the audience and the actors, flesh and blood corroborating flesh and blood—as we say, testifying. . . ." In addition, the play opened the door to writers from outside the mainstream, who would revitalize American theater in the decades to follow.

A Voice from the Times

One of the most sound ideas in dramatic writing is that, in order to create the universal, you must pay very great attention to the specific.

—Lorraine Hansberry

Responses to War

War, with all its moral complexities and attendant brutality, has had a strong influence on writers throughout the 20th and 21st centuries. World War II brought with it previously unimaginable horrors: millions of casualties, the genocide of the Holocaust, the use of nuclear weapons. Struggling to come to terms with such destruction, some writers worked in the **modernist** style—giving detailed, realistic, and somewhat detached accounts of the war, as if told by an outside observer such as a journalist.

In fact, much of the most powerful literature of World War II was straight nonfiction, such as war correspondent **John Hersey's** *Hiroshima,* an unforgettable account of the first hours and days after the United States dropped atomic bombs on two Japanese cities, bringing massive destruction and an end to the war. **John Steinbeck,** better known for his Depression-era literature, worked as a war correspondent as well, spending time with troops in North Africa and England. His essay "Why Soldiers Won't Talk" explores how soldiers cope with the things they have witnessed.

Many writers of this period wrote of their own experiences—including the horrors of the Holocaust. **Elie Wiesel,** who was born in Europe and became an American citizen much later in life, was taken as a 15-year-old boy to a Nazi concentration camp in Poland. His memoir, *Night,* describes his nightmarish experiences in the camp, where he was beaten, starved, and nearly worked to death. Most members of his family did not survive.

In the 1960s, **Joseph Heller's** *Catch-22* and **Kurt Vonnegut's** *Slaughterhouse-Five* introduced a new style of war literature. Both writers had seen combat in World War II, and their novels shared a dark, ironic humor that focused on the absurdity of war. One such absurdity is the "catch" in Catch-22. It refers to a mysterious Air Force regulation which asserts that any person willing to go into battle should be considered insane, yet the very act of asking to be excused would prove one's sanity—and send a pilot back into battle. With their cynicism toward authority and sense of helplessness in the face of huge, inhuman forces, Heller and Vonnegut spoke to a younger generation caught up in a very different war: Vietnam.

Where World War II had united Americans in moral certainty against a common enemy, Vietnam drove them apart. Protesters—among them

For Your Outline

RESPONSES TO WAR

- war influenced 20th- and 21st- century writers
- some worked in modernist style
- others wrote powerful nonfiction
- later focus is on absurdity of war
- postmodern style questioned conventions
- some blurred line between fiction and nonfiction

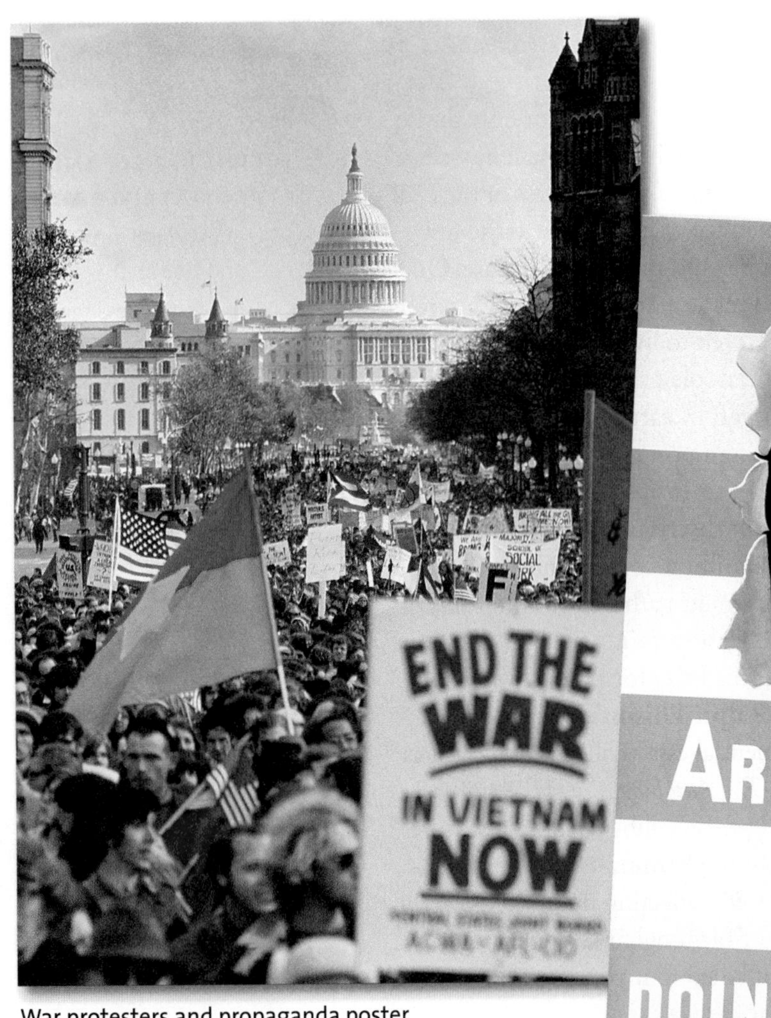

War protesters and propaganda poster

students, pacifists, and some returning veterans—marched in the streets, calling for an end to the war.

Writers of this time questioned authority, conventional values, and even the nature of reality. Some experimented with a "postmodern" style of fiction that drew attention to its own artificiality, pointing out the presence of the author by displaying its inner workings like a clock without a face. Others, like Vietnam veteran Tim O'Brien, wrote stories that blurred the lines between fiction and nonfiction. In *The Things They Carried*, O'Brien writes about telling his daughter how he killed a man in Vietnam—but this Tim O'Brien is a character, and the real O'Brien neither killed a man nor has a daughter. Can something that "didn't really happen" still be true? Postmodernism asks, What is fiction? What is truth?

▲ Analyze Visuals

The World War II propaganda poster shown here was meant to inspire support for the war. In your opinion, is it persuasive? How might the Vietnam War protesters shown in the other image have answered the question posed? How might they have responded to the intent of the poster?

Civil Rights and Protest Literature

The questioning of authority and conventional values applied not only to the writers of the Vietnam era but to those of the civil rights movement as well. To change laws, first it was necessary to change minds. The success of the civil rights movement depended on getting the message of justice out to the rest of America—telling people what was happening and making them care. One hundred years before, abolitionist writers had made a deep impact with novels and slave narratives that showed readers how it felt to live in bondage. In the 20th century, the written word still had a crucial role to play.

Even before the civil rights movement began in earnest, writers were examining issues of race and equality. Building upon the work of earlier Harlem Renaissance writers, black writers of the 1940s explored the dynamics of race relations and the injustice of discrimination in novels such as **Ann Petry's** *The Street,* which sold over a million copies, and **Richard Wright's** *Native Son.* As the civil rights movement gathered momentum in the early 1950s, African-American writers began to gain wider recognition, winning prestigious awards such as the Pulitzer Prize for poet **Gwendolyn Brooks** and the National Book Award for **Ralph Ellison's** *Invisible Man.*

The 1960s brought **James Baldwin's** influential essay collections as well as many important autobiographies, including *The Autobiography of Malcolm X* and **Anne Moody's** *Coming of Age in Mississippi.* By telling their own stories, these writers made a powerful statement about the harmful effects of racism and the need for change. Poets chimed in as well, reflecting upon the powerful events of the day. **Dudley Randall's** "Ballad of Birmingham," for example, was in response to the 1963 church bombing that killed four young girls.

For Your Outline

CIVIL RIGHTS AND PROTEST LITERATURE

- questioned authority and tradition
- delivered message of justice
- examined race and equality
- reflected African-American experience
- showed varying viewpoints

A MOSAIC OF AMERICAN VOICES

- current outpouring from writers of various ethnicities
- new appreciation for diversity
- universal themes, yet rooted in culture

Martin Luther King Jr. and Malcolm X

A Voice from the Times

We are not fighting for integration, nor are we fighting for separation. We are fighting for recognition as human beings.

—Malcolm X

Malcolm X and **Martin Luther King Jr.,** two leaders of the civil rights movement, held opposing viewpoints on the use of violence as a means for change. Inspired by Thoreau and Gandhi, as well as the Bible, King's speeches and writings combined a steadfast belief in nonviolent resistance with a bold determination to bring an end to injustice. In his 1963 "I Have a Dream" speech, King argued, "Let us not seek to satisfy our thirst for freedom by drinking from the cup of bitterness and hatred. We must forever conduct our struggle on the high plane of dignity and discipline. We must not allow our creative protest to degenerate into physical violence." Malcolm X, on the other hand, advocated the use of militant armed resistance as a response to discrimination. "I *am* for violence," he said, "if nonviolence means we continue postponing a solution to the black man's problem—just to *avoid* violence." Their writings give readers insight into the various, and sometimes opposing, factions that made up the civil rights movement.

A Mosaic of American Voices

The last 30 years have seen an outpouring of talent from American writers of many different ethnic backgrounds, along with an increasingly widespread appreciation of diversity. Just a few decades ago, the literary scene was still dominated almost exclusively by men of European descent. Now, they have been joined by Native American writers such as **N. Scott Momaday** and **Louise Erdrich,** Asian-American writers such as **Maxine Hong Kingston** and **Amy Tan,** Hispanic writers such as **Rudolfo Anaya** and **Sandra Cisneros,** and African-American writers such as **Alice Walker, Rita Dove, Toni Morrison,** and **Maya Angelou,** to name just a few. Many of the most exciting contemporary writers are women; many, too, such as **Bharati Mukherjee** and **Edwidge Danticat,** were born outside the United States and bring a global perspective to American literature.

While earlier writers of color often focused on the experience of discrimination, writers today draw on different aspects of life in America, positive and negative, from family memories and relationships to contemporary politics. With such a broad array of published voices, no longer is any one author assumed to speak for all people of a given group. Instead, the most compelling work of today's literary marketplace is both expressive of the individual and rooted in culture and place, while still managing to speak to universal human concerns. American literature has changed, again, and will continue to evolve as long as writers continue to write.

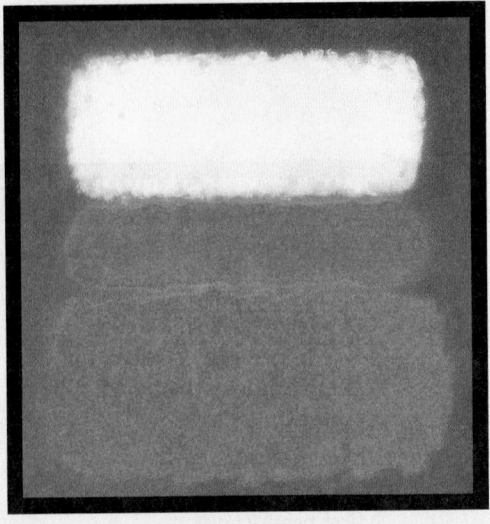

THE ARTISTS' GALLERY

Modern American Art

The power shift from Europe to the United States in the years after World War II had a parallel in the world of art. For the first time, international attention focused not on Paris's salon or London's Royal Academy but on the studios and galleries of New York City.

Abstract Expressionism During the 1940s and 1950s, a group of artists including **Mark Rothko** and **Jackson Pollock** dominated the New York art scene. Their style was abstract, intensely emotional, and focused as much on the process of painting as on the work itself. Jackson Pollock, who was famous for laying a giant canvas on the floor and throwing paint on it, described his art as "energy and motion made visible." Mark Rothko's signature style—floating rectangles of color aligned vertically against a colored background—is illustrated beautifully in his work *White Cloud Over Purple* (1957), shown here.

Pop Art In the early 1960s, a very different kind of art burst into public view. Pop art used familiar images from consumer culture to ask the question *What is art?* From **Andy Warhol,** with his silkscreened movie stars and soup cans, to **Roy Lichtenstein's** enormous blow-ups of comic strip panels, pop art celebrated modern methods of production while it subtly undermined the barrage of messages shaping Americans' attitudes and everyday lives.

Connecting Literature, History, and Culture

Use this timeline and the questions on the next page to gain insight about how American developments during this period reflected those in the world as a whole.

AMERICAN LITERARY MILESTONES

1940

1945 Richard Wright details coming of age in *Black Boy;* Randall Jarrell publishes World War II poem "The Death of the Ball Turret Gunner."

1947 Tennessee Williams's *A Streetcar Named Desire* is first produced.

1950

1951 J. D. Salinger's novel *The Catcher in the Rye* is published.

1952 Bernard Malamud publishes his baseball novel, *The Natural.*

1953 Arthur Miller's *The Crucible* reflects contemporary "witch hunt" of McCarthyism.

1960

1961 Joseph Heller's satirical war novel, *Catch-22,* is published.

1969 Kurt Vonnegut publishes *Slaughterhouse-Five;* N. Scott Momaday's *House Made of Dawn* wins Pulitzer Prize. ▶

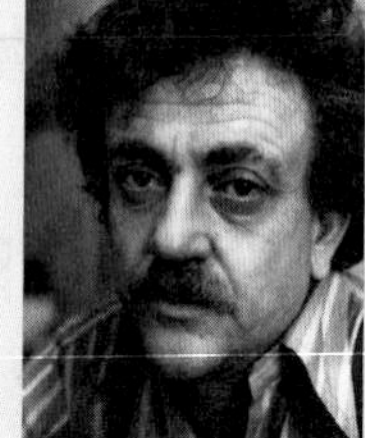

HISTORICAL CONTEXT

1940

1941 Japanese bomb Pearl Harbor, ▲ bringing United States into World War II.

1945 United States drops two atomic bombs on Japan, ending the war in the Pacific.

1950

1954 In *Brown v. Board of Education,* the Supreme Court declares segregated schools unconstitutional. ▼

1959 Alaska and Hawaii join the Union as the 49th and 50th states.

1960

1963 Martin Luther King gives "I Have a Dream" speech in Washington, D.C.; President John F. Kennedy is assassinated in Dallas.

1965 Malcolm X is assassinated.

1967 Thurgood Marshall becomes the first African-American justice on the Supreme Court.

1968 Assassinations of Martin Luther King Jr., and Robert F. Kennedy shock the nation.

WORLD CULTURE AND EVENTS

1940

1940 German forces conquer much of Europe.

1945 Germany surrenders to Allies.

1948 State of Israel is founded; South African policy of apartheid begins.

1950

1953 Korean War ends.

1957 Soviet Union launches first space satellite, *Sputnik.*

1959 Fidel Castro takes control of Cuba after ouster of dictator.

1960

1965 First U.S. combat forces land in Vietnam.

1966 Mao Zedong launches Cultural Revolution in China (to 1976). ▶

1969 U.S. astronauts land on moon.

MAKING CONNECTIONS

- What important roles have new technologies played in this era?
- What evidence do you see that "American" and "world" events have become harder to separate?
- Which political and cultural trends have influenced American literature?

COMMON CORE

RI 7 Integrate and evaluate multiple sources of information presented in different formats, as well as in words, to address a question or solve a problem.

1970

1970 Maya Angelou publishes autobiographical *I Know Why the Caged Bird Sings.*

1983 Sandra Cisneros publishes *The House on Mango Street.* ▶

1985

1985 Anne Tyler publishes *The Accidental Tourist.*

1989 Amy Tan's *The Joy Luck Club* is published.

1993 Rita Dove becomes first African- American poet laureate; Toni Morrison wins Nobel Prize for literature. ▶

2000

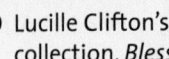

2000 Lucille Clifton's poetry collection, *Blessing the Boats,* wins National Book Award.

2002 Diane McWhorter's history of Birmingham during the Civil Rights Movement, *Carry Me Home,* wins the Pulitzer Prize for Nonfiction.

2007 Cormac McCarthy's *The Road* wins Pulitzer Prize.

1970

1974 President Richard M. Nixon resigns to avoid impeachment over Watergate scandal.

1977 First practical home computer, Apple II, hits market.

1981 The space shuttle *Columbia* launches; Sandra Day O'Connor becomes the first woman to be appointed to the U.S. Supreme Court.

1985

1989 The oil tanker *Exxon Valdez* ▲ runs aground, creating a huge oil spill along Alaskan coast.

1991 The Persian Gulf War begins; the United States leads allied coalition against Iraq.

2000

2001 Hijackers fly commercial planes into World Trade Center and Pentagon, killing thousands.

2005 Hurricane Katrina hits New Orleans and surrounding area, causing massive destruction. ▼

2009 Barack Obama becomes first African American president in U. S. history.

1970

1975 South Vietnam surrenders as North Vietnamese troops occupy Saigon.

1979 Egypt's Anwar Sadat and Israel's Menachem Begin sign treaty ending war between Egypt and Israel.

1985

1989 The Berlin Wall comes down; ▶ student protesters in China are killed in Tiananmen Square.

1991 Soviet Union breaks up into 15 republics.

2000

2003 U.S. troops invade Iraq, deposing leader Saddam Hussein.

2004 Poland joins European Union.

2008 China hosts the Summer Olympic Games.

UNIT 6

The Legacy of the Era

A New American Dream?

COMMON CORE

W 10 Write routinely over shorter time frames for a range of tasks, purposes, and audiences. **SL 1** Initiate and participate in discussions, building on others' ideas and expressing their own clearly and persuasively. **SL 4** Present findings such that the organization, development, substance, and style are appropriate to purpose, audience, and a range of formal and informal tasks.

As rapid changes in society have given rise to fresh concerns about education, social mobility, family and community, the environment, and the hectic pace of modern life, it may be time to redefine the American dream for a new generation.

CREATE What might be the American dream for students and young adults today? For new immigrants? Working-class people? Others? As a class, share your thoughts. Then break into groups of four and create posters or collages that depict different aspects of today's American dream. Consult a book of quotations to find varying interpretations of the American dream. Be sure to cite the speaker of each quotation.

What the Future Holds

Technology has affected both the form and content of literary and nonfiction texts, offering new possibilities from hypertext to hand-held e-books to online publishing—though the predicted death of the printed book (and of narrative as we know it) has not come to pass. What do you think literature and nonfiction will be like in 20 years?

QUICKWRITE Taking the role of a future critic, write a "book review" discussing one new form of literature or nonfiction. Include your opinions about the limitations and possibilities this form presents.

Living in the Global Village

America's isolationism ended abruptly with the attack on Pearl Harbor in World War II. In the postwar years, international trade and travel greatly expanded. Today, huge improvements in communications and transportation have made globalism possible on many levels: political, economic, and cultural. Day by day, Americans are becoming more aware of their ties with the rest of the world.

DISCUSS How does globalization affect your everyday life? Brainstorm ideas with a small group, then report back to the class. If you're stuck, try thinking about what you wear, what you eat, and how you earn and spend money.

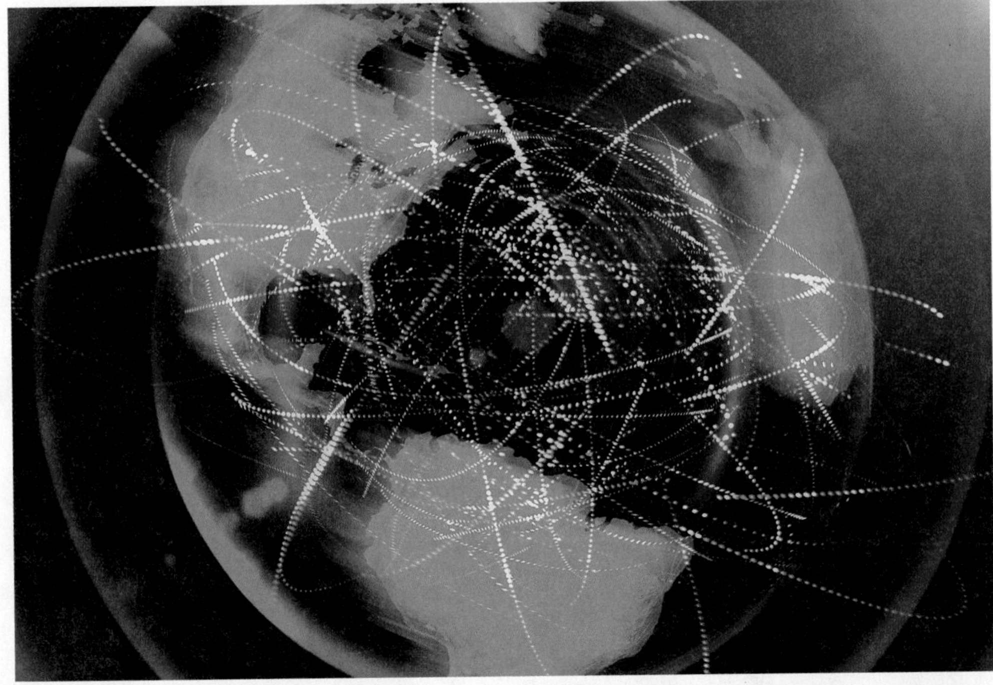

American Masterpiece

from Our Town

Drama by Thornton Wilder

Thornton Wilder

COMMON CORE

RL 3 Analyze the impact of the author's choices regarding how to develop and relate elements of a drama. **SL 1** Initiate and participate in a range of collaborative discussions.

BACKGROUND Since *Our Town* first appeared on Broadway in 1938, not a day has gone by when it has not been staged somewhere in the world. Set in the small town of Grover's Corners, New Hampshire, the play traces the everyday experiences of two neighboring families, the Gibbses and the Webbs. Spanning a dozen years at the beginning of the twentieth century, *Our Town* has several unusual touches: it is performed on a stage bare of all scenery; it depicts some characters from beyond the grave; and it employs a folksy but omniscient narrator called the Stage Manager, who reveals past and future events and comments on the geology of the region, as well as the history and sociology of the town.

TEXT ANALYSIS Both the title and the characters in *Our Town* are **allegorical.** As a typical small town of its time, inhabited by typical American families, Grover's Corners represents the life of every small-town American family—yours, mine, ours. The scene on the opposite page depicts George Gibbs and Emily Webb at the beginning of their courtship. They aren't sure of one another yet, and they have differing opinions about men and women. As readers, we face two tasks when we study **dialogue** or **characters in conflict.** One is to make inferences about the characters themselves. The other is to look for clues to how they view the world and to watch as differing views develop so that we can identify the play's **theme**—the message it expresses for the author.

DISCUSS Working in a small group, have two group members read the dialogue in this excerpt aloud. Then, look for clues that George and Emily are fond of one another. Does one character criticize the other as a way of hiding affection? If so, what clues show you the underlying fondness? What differing statements do Emily and George make about being male or female? Do they settle their difference by the end of the scene? After you have discussed these questions with your group, share your insights with the class as a whole.

George. Emily, why are you mad at me?

Emily. I'm not mad at you.

George. You've been treating me so funny lately.

Emily. Well, since you ask me, I might as well say it right out, George,— (*She catches sight of a teacher passing.*) Good-by, Miss Corcoran.

George. Good-by, Miss Corcoran. —Wha—what is it?

Emily (*not scoldingly; finding it difficult to say*). I don't like the whole change that's come over you in the last year. I'm sorry if that hurts your feelings, but I've got to—tell the truth and shame the devil.

George. A *change?* —Wha—what do you mean?

Emily. Well, up to a year ago, I used to like you a lot. And I used to watch you as you did everything . . . because we'd been friends so long . . . and then you began spending all your time at *baseball* . . . and you never stopped to speak to anybody any more. Not even to your own family you didn't . . . and, George, it's a fact, you've got awful conceited and stuck-up, and all the girls say so. They may not say so to your face, but that's what they say about you behind your back, and it hurts me to hear them say it, but I've got to agree with them a little. I'm sorry if it hurts your feelings . . . but I can't be sorry I said it.

George. I . . . I'm glad you said it, Emily. I never thought that such a thing was happening to me. I guess it's hard for a fella not to have faults creep into his character.

(*They take a step or two in silence, then stand still in misery.*)

Emily. I always expect a man to be perfect and I think he should be.

George. Oh . . . I don't think it's possible to be perfect, Emily.

Emily. Well, my *father* is, and as far as I can see *your* father is. There's no reason on earth why you shouldn't be, too.

George. Well, I feel it's the other way round. That men aren't naturally good; but girls are.

Emily. Well, you might as well know right now that I'm not perfect. It's not as easy for a girl to be perfect as a man, because we girls are more—more—nervous.—Now I'm sorry I said all that about you. I don't know what made me say it.

George. Emily,—.

Emily. Now I can see it's not the truth at all. And I suddenly feel that it isn't important, anyway.

George. Emily . . . would you like an ice-cream soda, or something, before you go home?

Emily. Well, thank you. . . . I would.

American Masterpiece

from The Glass Menagerie

Drama by Tennessee Williams

Tennessee Williams

BACKGROUND For *The Glass Menagerie*, Tennessee Williams (1911–1983) drew on his own youth. Williams had an abusive, frequently absent father; a much-loved sister who suffered from mental illness; and a strong-willed mother who tried to hold the family together while longing for the days of her Southern girlhood. *The Glass Menagerie* features Amanda, a mother much like Williams's; her son Tom, who supports his mother and sister at a job he hates; and her frail, painfully shy daughter Laura, who collects tiny glass animals—the menagerie of the play's title.

TEXT ANALYSIS Before you read the scene excerpted here, review what you learned about **dialogue, conflict,** and **theme** on page 1162. In the scene you read from *Our Town*, Wilder depicts two characters in gentle conflict. In *The Glass Menagerie*, the three major characters are frequently on stage at the same time, leaving the audience with the complex task of following *multiple conflicts* as the **dialogue** among the three unfolds. Williams increases the challenge by using **dramatic irony** in this scene, a moment when a character reveals something about himself or herself to the audience but is clearly not aware of it.

WRITE As you read this scene, pay special attention to Tom. What kind of conflict does he have with his mother Amanda? How does he view his sister Laura? When he informs his mother that he is "going to the movies," what makes his statement ironic? (Hint: Examine what he says about Laura before announcing that he will go to the movies and what his mother says about him afterwards.) Use your answers to these questions to write a paragraph on Tom and his conflicts in the play at this moment.

COMMON CORE

RL 3 Analyze the impact of the author's choices regarding how to develop and relate elements of a drama. **RL 6** Distinguish what is directly stated in a text from what is really meant. **W 9** Draw evidence from literary texts to support analysis and reflection.

Tom. Mother, you mustn't expect too much of Laura.

Amanda. What do you mean?

Tom. Laura seems all those things to you and me because she's ours and we love her. We don't even notice she's crippled any more.

Amanda. Don't say crippled! You know that I never allow that word to be used!

Tom. But face facts, Mother. She is and—that's not all—

Amanda. What do you mean "not all"?

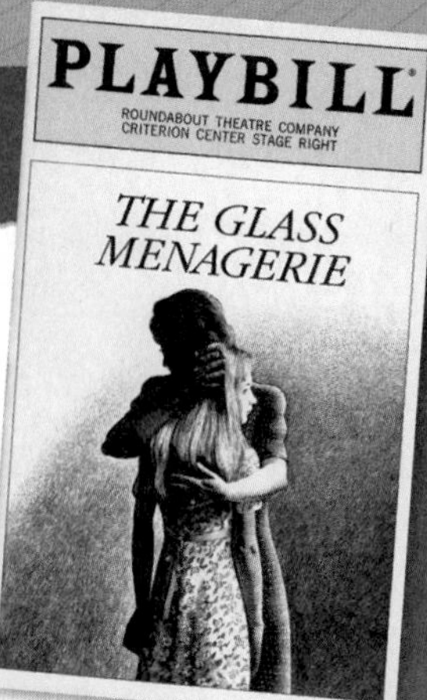

Tom. Laura is very different from other girls.

Amanda. I think the difference is all to her advantage.

Tom. Not quite all—in the eyes of others—strangers—she's terribly shy and lives in a world of her own and those things make her seem a little peculiar to people outside the house.

Amanda. Don't say peculiar.

Tom. Face the facts. She is.

(*The dance-hall music changes to a tango that has a minor and somewhat ominous tone.*)

Amanda. In what way is she peculiar—may I ask?

Tom (*gently*). She lives in a world of her own—a world of little glass ornaments, Mother. . . . (*He gets up.* Amanda *remains holding the brush, looking at him, troubled.*) She plays old phonograph records and—that's about all—

(*He glances at himself in the mirror and crosses to the door.*)

Amanda (*sharply*). Where are you going?

Tom. I'm going to the movies. (*He goes out the screen door.*)

Amanda. Not to the movies, every night to the movies! (*She follows quickly to the screen door.*) I don't believe you always go to the movies! (*He is gone.* Amanda *looks worriedly after him for a moment. Then vitality and optimism return and she turns from the door, crossing to portieres.*) Laura! Laura! (Laura *answers from kitchenette.*)

Laura. Yes, Mother.

Amanda. Let those dishes go and come in front! (Laura *appears with a dish towel. Amanda speaks to her gaily.*) Laura, come here and make a wish on the moon!

(*screen image: the moon*)

Laura (*entering*). Moon—moon?

Amanda. A little silver slipper of a moon. Look over your left shoulder, Laura, and make a wish! (Laura *looks faintly puzzled as if called out of sleep.* Amanda *seizes her shoulders and turns her at an angle by the door.*) Now! Now, darling, *wish!*

Laura. What shall I wish for, Mother?

Amanda (*her voice trembling and her eyes suddenly filling with tears*). Happiness! Good fortune!

(*The sound of the violin rises and the stage dims out.*)

American Masterpiece

from Death of a Salesman

Drama by Arthur Miller

Arthur Miller

BACKGROUND Arthur Miller (1915–2005) won the Pulitzer Prize in 1949 for *Death of a Salesman.* It is widely regarded as his finest work and one of the greatest American plays of the twentieth century. Some critics see it as a brilliant dissection of the American dream; others commend its perceptive portrayal of family tensions and personal failings. Willy Loman, the protagonist, acts the successful businessman, husband, and father, but he is a deeply troubled man. A career-long traveling salesman, he no longer earns a salary but only his commission on sales. His position is further threatened by his declining performance on the road. At home, a long-buried conflict with his elder son Biff threatens Willy's increasingly fragmented sense of self.

TEXT ANALYSIS So far, in two dramatic scenes from American Masterpieces (pages 1162–1163 and 1164–1165), you have observed a gentle **conflict** between two young people at the start of a courtship and a more difficult conflict among three family members over how they perceive each other. Now, in the scene on the opposite page, you will see how **dialogue** can express the conflict between two ways of viewing the world. Here, Willy Loman, an aging and increasingly unreliable salesman, faces Howard Wagner, a much younger man, now in charge of the company that employs Willy. By listening to the opposing voices in this scene and by considering the validity of their claims, you can make inferences about the author's **theme**—the message about the world he wishes to express in the play.

COMMON CORE

RL 1 Cite evidence to support analysis of what the text says explicitly, was well as inferences drawn from the text. **RL 3** Analyze the impact of the author's choices regarding how to develop and relate elements of a drama.

DISCUSS Read the scene once to get an impression of Willy and Howard. Then, read it a second time and concentrate on the stories Willy tells Howard. Search for clues to Willy's definition of success and his view of the business world. Howard says much less than Willy in this excerpt. Examine his short lines for clues to a different view of business and success.

After you have made inferences about Willy and Howard, discuss the two characters in a small group of your peers. Summarize Willy's view of success and the business world, and contrast his views with Howard's. Then, discuss what the group thinks Willy and Howard would say next. Finally, write a page of dialogue that develops this scene and the conflict between two ways of seeing the world.

Willy (*angrily*). Business is definitely business, but just listen for a minute. You don't understand this. When I was a boy—eighteen, nineteen—I was already on the road. And there was a question in my mind as to whether selling had a future for me. Because in those days I had a yearning to go to Alaska. See, there were three gold strikes in one month in Alaska, and I felt like going out. Just for the ride, you might say.

Howard (*barely interested*). Don't say.

Willy. Oh, yeah, my father lived many years in Alaska. He was an adventurous man. We've got quite a little streak of self-reliance in our family. I thought I'd go out with my older brother and try to locate him, and maybe settle in the North with the old man. And I was almost decided to go, when I met a salesman in the Parker House. His name was Dave Singleman. And he was eighty-four years old, and he'd drummed merchandise in thirty-one states. And old Dave, he'd go up to his room, y'understand, put on his green velvet slippers—I'll never forget—and pick up his phone and call the buyers, and without ever leaving his room, at the age of eighty-four, he made his living. And when I saw that, I realized that selling was the greatest career a man could want. 'Cause what could be more satisfying than to be able to go, at the age of eighty-four, into twenty or thirty different cities, and pick up a phone, and be remembered and loved and helped by so many different people? Do you know? when he died—and by the way he died the death of a salesman, in his green velvet slippers in the smoker of the New York, New Haven and Hartford, going into Boston—when he died, hundreds of salesmen and buyers were at his funeral. Things were sad on a lotta trains for months after that. (*He stands up.* Howard *has not looked at him.*) In those days there was personality in it, Howard. There was respect, and comradeship, and gratitude in it. Today, it's all cut and dried, and there's no chance for bringing friendship to bear—or personality. You see what I mean? They don't know me any more.

Howard (*moving away, to the right*). That's just the thing, Willy.

Willy. If I had forty dollars a week—that's all I'd need. Forty dollars, Howard.

Howard. Kid, I can't take blood from a stone, I—

Willy (*desperation is on him now*). Howard, the year Al Smith was nominated, your father came to me and—

Howard (*starting to go off*). I've got to see some people, kid.

Willy (*stopping him*). I'm talking about your father! There were promises made across this desk! You mustn't tell me you've got people to see—I put thirty-four years into this firm, Howard, and now I can't pay my insurance! You can't eat the orange and throw the peel away—a man is not a piece of fruit!

American Masterpiece

from A Raisin in the Sun

Drama by Lorraine Hansberry

Lorraine Hansberry

BACKGROUND "What happens to a dream deferred? / Does it dry up / like a raisin in the sun?" These lines from Langston Hughes's poem "Harlem" provided Lorraine Hansberry (1930–1965) with her title for *A Raisin in the Sun*, the story of the Youngers, an African-American family whose long-cherished dreams are almost realized when Mama, the family's matriarch, comes into some money. But Mama's plans to buy a house in a white neighborhood nearly destroy the family. Hansberry had difficulty finding backers to fund her play. With its all-black cast and racial themes, *A Raisin in the Sun* was very daring for its time. But once it finally opened, it received the New York Drama Critics' Circle Award for the best American play of 1959. Hansberry was the youngest person and the first African American to win the award.

The New York Times called *A Raisin in the Sun* the play that "changed American theater forever." It inspired a generation of young black writers and actors and brought a whole new audience to the theater. A glimpse into the private lives of African Americans was also a revelation for Broadway's white audiences. As Hansberry once observed, "The intimacy of knowledge which the Negro may culturally have of white Americans does not exist in the reverse."

COMMON CORE

RL 1 Cite evidence to support analysis of inferences drawn from the text. **RL 2** Determine two or more themes or central ideas of a text, and analyze their development over the course of the text. **W 10** Write routinely over shorter time frames.

TEXT ANALYSIS With the excerpt from *Death of a Salesman* (pages 1166–1167), you studied **dialogue** for conflicting views of the world. With the scene from *A Raisin in the Sun*, you will encounter a single character who voices one of Hansberry's **themes.** While writers of fiction can use the narrator to convey a message, playwrights rely exclusively on action and dialogue to express themes about humanity. Readers of drama—or members of a staged performance—will discover complex and fascinating ideas if they listen attentively and make subtle inferences about the characters, their actions, and their voices.

WRITE As you read this dialogue, in which a mother discusses her son with her daughter, look for conflicting ideas about love for and duty to family members. Which character has a stronger voice here, Mama or Beneatha? Write a paragraph on the dominant character and the theme she expresses.

Beneatha. That is not a man. That is nothing but a toothless rat.

Mama. Yes—death done come in this here house. (*She is nodding, slowly, reflectively.*) Done come walking in my house on the lips of my children. You what supposed to be my beginning again. You—what supposed to be my harvest. (*to* Beneatha) You—you mourning your brother?

Beneatha. He's no brother of mine.

Mama. What you say?

Beneatha. I said that that individual in that room is no brother of mine.

Mama. That's what I thought you said. You feeling like you better than he is today? (Beneatha *does not answer.*) Yes? What you tell him a minute ago? That he wasn't a man? Yes? You give him up for me? You done wrote his epitaph too—like the rest of the world? Well, who give you the privilege?

Beneatha. Be on my side for once! You saw what he just did, Mama! You saw him—down on his knees. Wasn't it you who taught me to despise any man who would do that? Do what he's going to do?

Mama. Yes—I taught you that. Me and your daddy. But I thought I taught you something else too . . . I thought I taught you to love him.

Beneatha. Love him? There is nothing left to love.

Mama. There is *always* something left to love. And if you ain't learned that, you ain't learned nothing. (*looking at her*) Have you cried for that boy today? I don't mean for yourself and for the family 'cause we lost the money. I mean for him: what he been through and what it done to him. Child, when do you think is the time to love somebody the most? When they done good and made things easy for everybody? Well then, you ain't through learning—because that ain't the time at all. It's when he's at his lowest and can't believe in hisself 'cause the world done whipped him so! When you starts measuring somebody, measure him right, child, measure him right. Make sure you done taken into account what hills and valleys he come through before he got to wherever he is.

Responses to War

COMMON CORE

RL 4 Analyze the impact of specific word choices on meaning and tone. **RI 2** Determine two or more central ideas of a text and analyze their development over the course of a text. **RI 4** Determine the meaning of words and phrases as they are used in a text.

Why Soldiers Won't Talk

Essay by John Steinbeck

The Death of the Ball Turret Gunner

Poem by Randall Jarrell

VIDEO TRAILER THINK central KEYWORD: HML11-1170A

Meet the Authors

John Steinbeck
1902–1968

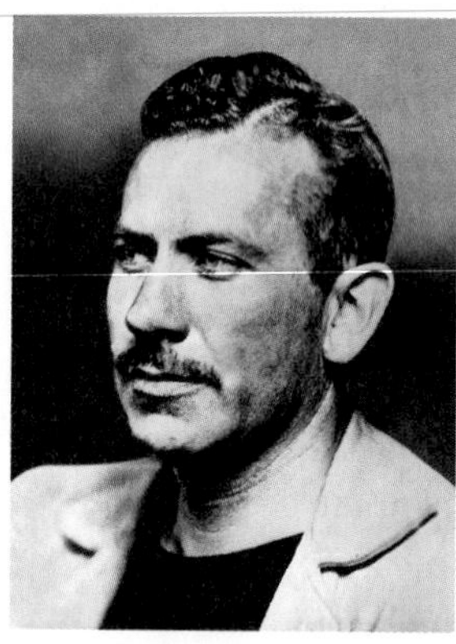

John Steinbeck created many memorable characters, from the downtrodden but dogged Joads in *The Grapes of Wrath* to George and Lennie in *Of Mice and Men.* Many of Steinbeck's characters convey his belief that people must fit into their surroundings—especially their natural surroundings—in order to find peace.

Childhood on the Land John Steinbeck grew up in the agricultural community of Salinas, California. The land profoundly influenced Steinbeck, who set many of his best works in these childhood scenes. He began to write early, encouraged by a high school teacher's praise.

Blending Life and Art While studying at Stanford University, Steinbeck worked in a factory and on road crews. Portraying people who lived by their hands became another key focus of Steinbeck's life and work. *The Grapes of Wrath* (1939) received a Pulitzer Prize for portraying down-and-out Oklahoma farmers during the Great Depression. Exhausted from writing the novel, Steinbeck moved in new directions. In 1943 he spent six months as a World War II correspondent, producing such writings as the following essay about the response of soldiers to combat. In 1962, he received the Nobel Prize in Literature "for his realistic as well as his imaginative writings."

Randall Jarrell
1914–1965

Respected as a literary critic, Randall Jarrell is nonetheless best known for his searing poetry about World War II, notably a "stark five-line lyric . . . the ultimate poem of war." That poem is "The Death of the Ball Turret Gunner."

On the Road Again Born in Nashville, Tennessee, Jarrell moved often during his childhood. One important move took the family to a ranch in California. Later, Jarrell returned to California to live with his grandparents during his parents' divorce. Memories of this time filtered into one of Jarrell's best poems, "The Lost World," and childhood is a frequent, haunting topic throughout his work.

Making a Name With the help of a wealthy uncle, Jarrell went to college and began a lifelong career teaching literature in universities. At the same time, he worked at his own poetry. In 1942, he enlisted in the service, where he trained pilots and wrote poems capturing the horror and dreariness of military life.

Authors Online THINK central

Go to thinkcentral.com. KEYWORD: HML11-1170B

TEXT ANALYSIS: TONE AND IMAGERY

A writer sometimes conveys **tone,** his or her attitude toward a subject, through imagery. **Imagery** consists of the descriptive words and phrases used to re-create sensory experiences. One of the interesting aspects of John Steinbeck's essay is the contrast between his clinical, detached, almost scientific tone and his use of sensory-rich imagery to support his conclusions on war. Jarrell's poem also uses vivid imagery to convey an attitude about that same subject. As you read each text, think about the relationship between tone and imagery. Decide what each of these elements adds to the experience of reading.

READING STRATEGY: ADJUST READING STRATEGIES

As you read "Why Soldiers Won't Talk," you need to apply reading strategies appropriate to an essay. First, identify the author's **main ideas**. Then, examine the pattern of reasoning the author uses to express these ideas.

In this essay, look for **deductive reasoning.** Deductive reasoning is arriving at a conclusion by applying a general principle to a specific situation. An example of a general principle is that people want to help themselves. Given a specific situation in which individuals face a choice between working for an income and relying on someone else for support, deductive reasoning would lead you to conclude that these individuals would choose work.

A poem such as "The Death of the Ball Turret Gunner" requires dramatically different reading strategies from those used when reading essays. The poem you will read is short and full of **images**; however, it does not explain itself. Use the illustration on page 1175 to help you picture the ball turret of a warplane. Then, read the poem several times—aloud, if possible. Picture the images and pay attention to language that expresses tone.

As you read these two texts, make use of these strategies and any others that work for you. Take notes about the essay's main ideas and its pattern of reasoning. Then, note the poem's imagery and tone.

Complete the activities in your **Reader/Writer Notebook**.

When is SILENCE *louder than words?*

People who have suffered greatly—fighting in a war, losing a loved one, witnessing tragedy—sometimes find it hard to communicate with others. Perhaps they cannot put their experiences and emotions into words. Perhaps they believe no one will understand. Others find silence and watchfulness more comfortable than talk and social engagement. Consider what silence can signify in a person's behavior, especially a soldier's in wartime.

QUICKWRITE Think of friends, family, peers, or even a character in a film or book. Identify someone you think of as more silent than talkative. Write a brief character description of this person. Read your description aloud, then share your ideas about why your subject is silent.

Why Soldiers Won't Talk

John Steinbeck

BACKGROUND Randall Jarrell's experience training pilots for the U.S. Army Air Force gained him firsthand knowledge of planes and gunners, including the view from the ball turret of a bomber. From this plexiglas bubble on the underside of the plane, gunners—totally exposed from below—fired at the enemy. During Steinbeck's time as a war correspondent, he too learned about bomber crews, as well as soldiers in the infantry.

During the years between the last war and this one, I was always puzzled by the reticence of ex-soldiers about their experiences in battle. If they had been reticent men it would have been different, but some of them were talkers and some were even boasters. They would discuss their experiences right up to the time of battle and then suddenly they wouldn't talk any more. This was considered heroic in them. It was thought that what they had seen or done was so horrible that they didn't want to bring it back to haunt them or their listeners. But many of these men had no such consideration in any other field.

Only recently have I found what seems to be a reasonable explanation, and the answer is simple. They did not and do not remember—and the worse the battle was, the less they remember. **A**

In all kinds of combat the whole body is battered by emotion. The ductless glands[1] pour their fluids into the system to make it able to stand up to the great demand on it. Fear and ferocity are products of the same fluid. Fatigue toxins[2] poison the system. Hunger followed by wolfed food distorts the metabolic pattern already distorted by the adrenaline[3] and fatigue. The body and the mind so disturbed are really ill and fevered. But in addition to these ills, which come from the inside of a man and are given him so that he can temporarily withstand pressures beyond his ordinary ability, there is the further stress of explosion.

Under extended bombardment or bombing the nerve ends are literally beaten. The eardrums are tortured by blast and the eyes ache from the constant hammering.

This is how you feel after a few days of constant firing. Your skin feels thick and insensitive. There is a salty taste in your mouth. A hard, painful knot is in your stomach where the food is undigested. Your eyes do not pick up much detail and the sharp outlines of objects are slightly blurred. Everything looks a little unreal. When

A ADJUST READING STRATEGIES
Reread lines 1–11. What puzzles Steinbeck about soldiers, and what **main idea** provides the solution to his puzzlement? Write down the main idea and label it as the **conclusion** to a pattern of deductive reasoning you will examine on the essay's second page.

Analyze Visuals ▶
How would you describe the look on this soldier's face? Explain what features convey this look.

1. **ductless glands:** glands, such as the thyroid or the pituitary gland, that secrete directly into the bloodstream.
2. **toxins:** poisons produced by the body that are capable of causing disease.
3. **adrenaline** (ə-drĕn′ə-lĭn): a substance secreted by the adrenal gland in response to stress.

you walk, your feet hardly seem to touch the ground and there is a floaty feeling all over your body. Even the time sense seems to be changed. Men who are really moving at a normal pace seem to take forever to pass a given point. And when you move it seems to you that you are very much slowed down, although actually you are probably moving more quickly than you normally do. **B**

Under the blast your eyeballs are so beaten that the earth and the air seem to shudder. At first your ears hurt, but then they become dull and all your other senses become dull, too. There are exceptions, of course. Some men cannot protect themselves this way and they break, and they are probably the ones we call shell-shock cases.[4]

In the dullness all kinds of emphases change. Even the instinct for self-preservation is dulled so that a man may do things which are called heroic when actually his whole fabric of reaction is changed. The whole world becomes unreal. You laugh at things which are not ordinarily funny and you become enraged at trifles. During this time a kind man is capable of great cruelties and a timid man of great bravery, and nearly all men have resistance to stresses beyond their ordinary ability.

Then sleep can come without warning and like a drug. Gradually your whole body seems to be packed in cotton. All the main nerve trunks are deadened, and out of the battered cortex[5] curious dreamlike thoughts emerge. It is at this time that many men see visions. The eyes fasten on a cloud and the tired brain makes a face of it, or an angel or a demon. And out of the hammered brain strange memories are jolted loose, scenes and words and people forgotten, but stored in the back of the brain. These may not be important things, but they come back with startling clarity into the awareness that is turning away from reality. And these memories are almost visions. **C**

And then it is over. You can't hear, but there is a rushing sound in your ears. And you want sleep more than anything, but when you do sleep you are dream-ridden, your mind is uneasy and crowded with figures. The anesthesia your body has given you to protect you is beginning to wear off, and, as with most anesthesia, it is a little painful.

And when you wake up and think back to the things that happened they are already becoming dreamlike. Then it is not unusual that you are frightened and ill. You try to remember what it was like, and you can't quite manage it. The outlines in your memory are vague. The next day the memory slips farther, until very little is left at all. A woman is said to feel the same way when she tries to remember what childbirth was like. And fever leaves this same kind of vagueness on the mind. Perhaps all experience which is beyond bearing is that way. The system provides the shield and then removes the memory, so that a woman can have another child and a man can go into combat again. **D**

It slips away so fast. Unless you made notes on the spot you could not remember how you felt or the way things looked. Men in prolonged battle are not normal men. And when afterward they seem to be reticent—perhaps they don't remember very well.

B TONE AND IMAGERY Reread lines 22–30, and note Steinbeck's use of **sensory detail.** What does this scene reveal about the soldier's mental state?

C GRAMMAR AND STYLE Reread lines 42–47. Notice how Steinbeck establishes his voice partly by using descriptions that contain realistic sensory **adjectives** and **verbs,** such as *battered, hammered,* and *jolted.*

D ADJUST READING STRATEGIES
Reread lines 55–63. This paragraph suggests the **premise** in a pattern of **deductive reasoning.** The premise is that acute stress induces a shock that causes the person under stress to forget the painful details of the experience. From this premise, Steinbeck uses an **analogy,** or a comparison, to suggest that both childbirth and combat are acutely stressful. In your own words, explain the **conclusion** to this line of reasoning for combat soldiers and women who have given birth.

4. **shell-shock cases:** soldiers with a psychological disturbance as a result of prolonged exposure to active warfare.
5. **cortex:** part of the brain that plays an active role in consciousness.

The Death of the Ball Turret Gunner

RANDALL JARRELL

From my mother's sleep I fell into the State,
And I hunched in its belly till my wet fur froze.
Six miles from earth, loosed from its dream of life,
I woke to black flak[1] and the nightmare fighters.
When I died they washed me out of the turret with a hose. (E)

(E) **TONE AND IMAGERY** What does the imagery of the last line suggest about the speaker's attitude toward death?

1. **flak:** the fire of anti-aircraft guns.

Comprehension

1. **Recall** According to Steinbeck, why don't soldiers talk about combat?
2. **Summarize** What physical changes does Steinbeck say happen during combat?
3. **Summarize** In Jarrell's poem, what happens to the speaker?

Text Analysis

4. **Examine Author's Purpose** Steinbeck uses the second-person *you* in his recounting of the physical effects of combat. Why do you think he chose this **stylistic device?**
5. **Interpret the Poem** In reference to his poem, Jarrell wrote that the gunner, who sat hunched up and revolved with the turret, looked like a fetus in the womb. Based on this information, how would you interpret the first four lines of the poem?
6. **Analyze Tone and Imagery** Skim the two texts, and make a list of notable images found in each work. Based on these images, what would you say is Jarrell's attitude toward the ball turret gunner and his predicament? What is Steinbeck's attitude toward combat and its effect on soldiers? Describe the overall tone of each work.
7. **Compare Texts** Jarrell and Steinbeck address the topic of war from different angles and through different genres. Do you think the two authors offer consistent or conflicting accounts of what combat feels like? Support your opinion with details from each text.
8. **Evaluate Reading Strategies** Look back at the notes you took as you read the essay and poem. For each work, which strategy was most useful in helping you understand the ideas and images presented? What helped you understand how Steinbeck structured both his claims and his evidence? What strategy helped you make sense of Jarrell's use of imagery or his tone? How did these strategies differ? How were they similar?

Text Criticism

9. **Critical Interpretations** In discussing "The Death of the Ball Turret Gunner," one critic stated, "In the combination of death and consciousness is the awakening and final recognition on the part of the gunner that he exists only to be a victim." Do you agree with this interpretation? Explain.

When is **SILENCE** *louder than words?*

Explain how this question applies to the silence of combat soldiers in "Why Soldiers Won't Talk." Cite evidence from the essay to support your answer.

COMMON CORE

RL 4 Analyze the impact of specific word choices on meaning and tone. **RI 2** Determine two or more central ideas of a text and analyze their development over the course of a text. **RI 4** Determine the meaning of words and phrases as they are used in a text. **RI 5** Analyze and evaluate the effectiveness of the structure an author uses, including whether the structure makes points clear, convincing, and engaging.

Language

◆ GRAMMAR AND STYLE: Establish Voice

Review the **Grammar and Style** note on page 1174. Voice is the unique way a writer uses **word choice, sentence structure,** and **tone** to express his or her personality or vision. Steinbeck's voice reflects his personal experience with war. It flows from his short sentences, straightforward tone, and sensory language.

> *The eardrums are tortured by blast and the eyes ache from the constant hammering.* (line 21)

> *This is how you feel after a few days of constant firing. Your skin feels thick and insensitive. There is a salty taste in your mouth. A hard, painful knot is in your stomach where the food is undigested.* (lines 22–24)

These examples include percussive-sounding words that reflect the pain of combat. The sentences imply that all information is essential and honest.

PRACTICE In the following sentences, revise the sentence structure and word choice to match Steinbeck's voice. Note how the revisions made to the example help to capture Steinbeck's voice.

EXAMPLE

Like a jackhammer pounding at solid concrete, the TV announcer gabs on and on, creating perpetual background noise that pollutes our homes.

The TV announcer talks on, creating a persistent, polluting noise.

1. The announcer chooses a topic, pushing it and pushing it as if it were bread dough, then kneading it into yet a new shape.
2. Must we sit there like zombies and put up with this endless chatter as though there were no alternative?

READING-WRITING CONNECTION

Expand your understanding of the effects of war by responding to this prompt. Then, use the **revising tips** to improve your essay.

WRITING PROMPT

PERSUASIVE ESSAY Think about the adjustments veterans must make when they return from combat. What does society do to help ease their transition back into civilian life? Write a **three- to five-paragraph essay** on the importance of supporting veterans during this time of transition. Include specific suggestions of ways this might be effectively achieved.

REVISING TIPS

- Contact a local veterans organization, and ask what can be done for veterans.
- Use the Internet to research for innovative treatment and support programs for veterans.
- Integrate information you find to help strengthen your essay.

COMMON CORE

L 3 Apply knowledge of language to understand how language functions to make effective choices for meaning or style, and to comprehend more fully when reading. **W 1** Write arguments to support claims in an analysis of substantive topics or texts, using valid reasoning and relevant and sufficient evidence. **W 8** Gather relevant information from multiple authoritative print and digital sources, using advanced searches effectively; integrate information into the text selectively to maintain the flow of ideas.

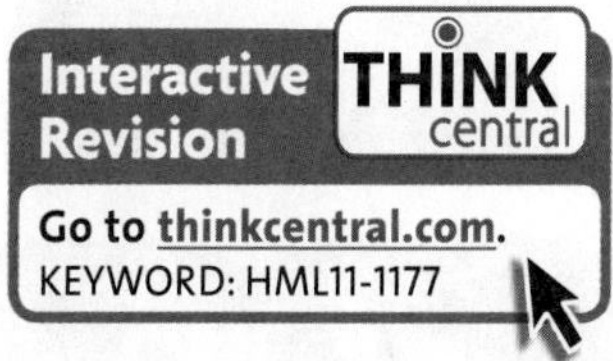

Comparing Texts

Responses to War

Adam
Short Story by Kurt Vonnegut, Jr.

from Survival in Auschwitz
Memoir by Primo Levi

Auschwitz-Birkenau Concentration Camp
Photograph

COMMON CORE

RL 3 Analyze the impact of the author's choices regarding how to develop and relate elements of a story. **RL 4** Analyze the impact of specific word choices on meaning and tone. **RI 3** Analyze a complex set of ideas or sequence of events and explain how specific individuals, ideas, or events interact and develop over the course of the text. **RI 6** Determine an author's point of view or purpose in a text in which the rhetoric is particularly effective, analyzing how style and content contribute to the power of the text. **RI 7** Integrate and evaluate multiple sources of information presented in multiple media or formats as well as words in order to address a question or solve a problem.

Meet the Authors

Kurt Vonnegut, Jr. 1922–2007

Kurt Vonnegut, Jr., blended black humor, science fiction, and fantasy to create a unique body of work. From the cult classic of *Cat's Cradle* to the international success of *Slaughterhouse-Five* to the semi-autobiographical *Timequake* that capped his career as a novelist, Vonnegut pushed at the boundaries of fiction, helping to re-define and revitalize the novel.

Art from Life As an infantry combat scout serving in Germany during World War II, Vonnegut was captured and held as a prisoner of war in Dresden. He survived the 1945 Allied bombing of the city because the American prisoners took shelter in a meat locker three stories below the ground. Protected from the firestorm that destroyed much of the city, the prisoners emerged to discover that thousands had been killed. Years later, Vonnegut transformed this experience into the fictional world of *Slaughterhouse-Five*.

A Study in Contrasts Despite the somewhat pessimistic outlook of works in which human beings are victims of circumstance in an indifferent universe, Vonnegut's fiction is preoccupied with moral issues.

Primo Levi 1919–1987

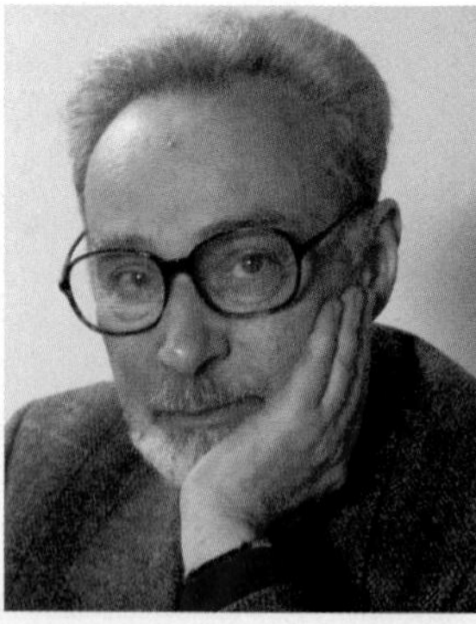

Known internationally as a writer of Holocaust literature, Primo Levi was born in Turin, Italy, and educated as a chemist. A survivor of Auschwitz, the notorious Nazi concentration camp near Krakow, Poland, he achieved international recognition for writings that recorded his experience of the war years.

Survivor In the chaos that engulfed Italy as World War II progressed, Levi joined the Italian resistance movement. Captured by the Fascist militia, he was held for several months at an Italian internment camp for Jews. After the camp fell to German control, early in 1944, the Jewish inmates were sent to Auschwitz. Of the 650 Italian Jews who entered Auschwitz with him, Levi was one of only twenty still alive eleven months later, when the advancing Russian army liberated Auschwitz.

Witness Levi recorded his Holocaust experience in *Survival in Auschwitz*.

Author Online

Go to thinkcentral.com. KEYWORD: HML11-1178

TEXT ANALYSIS: CHARACTERIZATION AND TONE

In fiction, writers bring characters to life by describing their physical appearance, by letting readers know what characters think and feel, by letting readers hear characters in dialogue, and sometimes by having the narrator comment on the characters. In a story such as "Adam," these methods of **characterization** also provide important clues to the tone of the story. **Tone** is the narrator's attitude toward his or her subject—sometimes even the narrator's attitude toward life. As you read "Adam," write notes about the four major methods of characterization. What tone—or attitude toward life—does Vonnegut convey through his characters?

Physical Appearance	Thoughts and Feelings	Dialogue	Narrator's Comments

By contrast with Vonnegut's story, the excerpt from Primo Levi's memoir *Survival in Auschwitz* doesn't spend much time on traditional characterization, but it does strongly convey the author's attitude toward his subject and toward life using diction and other stylistic techniques. As you read the excerpt, ask yourself how Levi's techniques account for the tone of the memoir.

READING SKILL: ANALYZE HISTORICAL CONTEXT

When you read a literary work with a particular historical setting, it is important to focus on the **historical context**—the conditions and events that shape the characters and their story. Vonnegut's short story, for example, is set in the aftermath of the Holocaust. During World War II, millions of people died from executions, beatings, disease, and malnutrition in Nazi concentration camps. As you read "Adam," use this information and the background information on page 1181, in addition to what you already know about World War II and the concentration camps, to help you understand the story's main character and the author's tone. Keep the same goal in mind as you read the excerpt by Levi. How does the episode he narrates affect your perception of Vonnegut's main character, Heinz Knechtmann?

Complete the activities in your **Reader/Writer Notebook**.

How do you AFFIRM LIFE?

In the aftermath of tragedy or heartbreak, people are often counseled that "time heals all wounds." Some are able to bounce back, whether from grave illness, a traumatic car accident, or even the horrors of war and genocide. Others cannot find this resilience and instead struggle to carry on.

What's the Connection?

As you study the texts in this section, think about what you already know about the tragic experiences of European Jews during World War II. Vonnegut's story "Adam," presents characters who survived this horrible experience and found the strength and will to start again. After you read "Adam," you'll study Levi's memoir "from *Survival in Auschwitz*," and a visual representation that convey the realities faced by Holocaust victims as they struggled to survive.

Adam

Kurt Vonnegut Jr.

BACKGROUND In the short story "Adam," set during the early 1950s, the main character, Heinz Knechtmann (knĕKHt'män), has survived the atrocities of the Holocaust and, like many Jewish survivors, has come to the United States seeking a better life. As the story begins, he and another expectant father, Mr. Sousa, are in the waiting room of a maternity hospital.

It was midnight in a Chicago lying-in hospital.

"Mr. Sousa," said the nurse, "your wife had a girl. You can see the baby in about twenty minutes."

"I know, I know, I know," said Mr. Sousa, a sullen gorilla, plainly impatient with having a tiresome and familiar routine explained to him. He snapped his fingers. "Girl! Seven, now. Seven girls I got now. A houseful of women. I can beat the stuffings out of ten men my own size. But, what do I get? Girls."

"Mr. Knechtmann," said the nurse to the other man in the room. She pronounced the name, as almost all Americans did, a colorless Netman. "I'm sorry. Still no word on your wife. She is keeping us waiting, isn't she?" She grinned glassily and left.

Sousa turned on Knechtmann. "Some little son of a gun like you, Netman, you want a boy, bing! You got one. Want a football team, bing, bing, bing, eleven, you got it." He stomped out of the room.

The man he left behind, all alone now, was Heinz Knechtmann, a presser in a dry-cleaning plant, a small man with thin wrists and a bad spine that kept him slightly hunched, as though forever weary. His face was long and big-nosed and thin-lipped, but was so overcast with good-humored humility as to be beautiful. **A** His eyes were large and brown, and deep-set and longlashed. He was only twenty-two, but seemed and felt much older. He had died a little as each member of his family had been led away and killed by the Nazis, until only in him, at the age of ten, had life and the name of Knechtmann shared a soul. He and his wife, Avchen, had grown up behind barbed wire.

Analyze Visuals ▶
What ideas are suggested by the images in the collage on page 1181? What is the cumulative impact of these images taken together? Explain.

A CHARACTERIZATION
Reread lines 15–18. Here Vonnegut combines his physical description of Heinz Knechtmann with a reflection on his personality. What might it look like to see a person "so overcast with good-humored humility as to be beautiful"?

Fatherhood (1990s). Ed Roskowski.

He had been staring at the walls of the waiting room for twelve hours now, since noon, when his wife's labor pains had become regular, the surges of slow rollers coming in from the sea a mile apart, from far, far away. This would be his second child. The last time he had waited, he had waited on a straw tick in a displaced-persons camp in Germany. The child, Karl Knechtmann, named after Heinz's father, had died, and with it, once more, had died the name of one of the finest cellists ever to have lived. **B**

When the numbness of weary wishing lifted momentarily during this second vigil, Heinz's mind was a medley of proud family names, gone, all gone, that could be brought to life again in this new being—if it lived. Peter Knechtmann, the surgeon; Kroll Knechtmann, the botanist; Friederich Knechtmann, the playwright. Dimly recalled uncles. Or if it was a girl, and if it lived, it would be Helga Knechtmann, Heinz's mother, and she would learn to play the harp as Heinz's mother had, and for all Heinz's ugliness, she would be beautiful. The Knechtmann men were all ugly, the Knechtmann women were all lovely as angels, though not all angels. It had always been so—for hundreds and hundreds of years.

"Mr. Netman," said the nurse, "it's a boy, and your wife is fine. She's resting now. You can see her in the morning. You can see the baby in twenty minutes."

Heinz looked up dumbly.

"It weighs five pounds nine ounces." She was gone again, with the same prim smile and officious, squeaking footsteps.

"Knechtmann," murmured Heinz, standing and bowing slightly to the wall. "The name is Knechtmann." He bowed again and gave a smile that was courtly and triumphant. He spoke the name with an exaggerated Old World pronunciation, like a foppish footman announcing the arrival of nobility, a guttural drum roll, unsoftened for American ears. "KhhhhhhhhhhhhhhNECHT! mannnnnnnnnnnnn." **C**

"Mr. Netman?" A very young doctor with a pink face and close cropped red hair stood in the waiting-room door. There were circles under his eyes, and he spoke through a yawn.

"Dr. Powers!" cried Heinz, clasping the man's right hand between both of his. "Thank God, thank God, thank God, and thank you."

"Um," said Dr. Powers, and he managed to smile wanly.

"There isn't anything wrong, is there?"

"Wrong?" said Powers. "No, no. Everything's fine. If I look down in the mouth, it's because I've been up for thirty-six hours straight." He closed his eyes, and leaned against the doorframe. "No, no trouble with your wife," he said in a faraway voice. "She's made for having babies. Regular pop-up toaster. Like rolling off a log. Schnip-schnap."

"She is?" said Heinz incredulously.

Dr. Powers shook his head, bringing himself back to consciousness. "My mind—conked out completely. Sousa—I got your wife confused with Mrs. Sousa. They finished in a dead heat. Netman, you're Netman. Sorry. Your wife's the one with pelvis trouble."

B HISTORICAL CONTEXT
Reread lines 19–30. With the help of the historical information on pages 1178–1179 and the Background on page 1180, explain the various events that happened to Heinz and his family.

C CHARACTERIZATION
Reread lines 45–50. How does Heinz's pride in the birth of his son express itself in his words and actions?

"Malnutrition as a child," said Heinz. **D**

"Yeah. Well, the baby came normally, but, if you're going to have another one, it'd better be a Caesarean. Just to be on the safe side."

"I can't thank you enough," said Heinz passionately.

Dr. Powers licked his lips, and fought to keep his eyes open. "Uh huh. 'S O.K.," he said thickly. "'Night. Luck." He shambled out into the corridor.

The nurse stuck her head into the waiting room. "You can see your baby, Mr. Netman."

"Doctor—" said Heinz, hurrying out into the corridor, wanting to shake Powers' hand again so that Powers would know what a magnificent thing he'd done. "It's the most wonderful thing that ever happened." The elevator doors slithered shut between them before Dr. Powers could show a glimmer of response.

"This way," said the nurse. "Turn left at the end of the hall, and you'll find the nursery window there. Write your name on a piece of paper and hold it against the glass."

Heinz made the trip by himself, without seeing another human being until he reached the end. There, on the other side of a large glass panel, he saw a hundred of them cupped in shallow canvas buckets and arranged in a square block of straight ranks and files.

Heinz wrote his name on the back of a laundry slip and pressed it to the window. A fat and placid nurse looked at the paper, not at Heinz's face, and missed seeing his wide smile, missed an urgent invitation to share for a moment his ecstasy.

She grasped one of the buckets and wheeled it before the window. She turned away again, once more missing the smile.

"Hello, hello, hello, little Knechtmann," said Heinz to the red prune on the other side of the glass. His voice echoed down the hard, bare corridor, and came back to him with embarrassing loudness. He blushed and lowered his voice. "Little Peter, little Kroll," he said softly, "little Friederich—and there's Helga in you, too. Little spark of Knechtmann, you little treasure house. Everything is saved in you."

"I'm afraid you'll have to be more quiet," said a nurse, sticking her head out from one of the rooms.

"Sorry," said Heinz. "I'm very sorry." He fell silent, and contented himself with tapping lightly on the window with a fingernail, trying to get the child to look at him. Young Knechtmann would not look, wouldn't share the moment, and after a few minutes the nurse took him away again.

Heinz beamed as he rode on the elevator and as he crossed the hospital lobby, but no one gave him more than a cursory glance. He passed a row of telephone booths and there, in one of the booths with the door open, he saw a soldier with whom he'd shared the waiting room an hour before.

"Yeah, Ma—seven pounds six ounces. Got hair like Buffalo Bill. No, we haven't had time to make up a name for her yet . . . That you, Pa? Yup, mother and daughter doin' fine, just fine. Seven pounds six ounces. Nope, no name. . . .

D HISTORICAL CONTEXT
Consider why Heinz's wife might have suffered malnutrition as a child. What does this suggest about the impact of history on the present?

That you, Sis? Pretty late for you to be up, ain't it? Doesn't look like anybody yet. Let me talk to Ma again. . . . That you, Ma? Well, I guess that's all the news from Chicago. Now, Mom, Mom, take it easy—don't worry. It's a swell-looking baby, Mom. Just the hair looks like Buffalo Bill, and I said it as a joke, Mom. That's right, seven pounds six ounces. . . ."

There were five other booths, all empty, all open for calls to anyplace on earth. Heinz longed to hurry into one of them breathlessly, and tell the marveolus news. But there was no one to call, no one waiting for the news. **E**

E TONE
Reread lines 117–119. How would you describe the tone of the story at this point?

But Heinz still beamed, and he strode across the street and into a quiet tavern there. In the dank twilight there were only two men, têtê-à-têtê, the bartender and Mr. Sousa.

"Yes sir, what'll it be?"

"I'd like to buy you and Mr. Sousa a drink," said Heinz with a heartiness strange to him. "I'd like the best brandy you've got. My wife just had a baby!"

"That so?" said the bartender with polite interest.

"Five pounds nine ounces," said Heinz.

"Huh," said the bartender. "What do you know."

"Netman," said Sousa, "Wha'dja get?"

"Boy," said Heinz proudly.

"Never knew it to fail," said Sousa bitterly. "It's the little guys, all the time the little guys."

"Boy, girl," said Heinz, "it's all the same, just as long as it lives. Over there in the hospital, they're too close to it to see the wonder of it. A miracle over and over again—the world made new."

"Wait'll you've racked up seven, Netman," said Sousa. "Then you come back and tell me about the miracle."

"You got seven?" said the bartender. "I'm one up on you. I got eight." He poured three drinks.

"Far as I'm concerned," said Sousa, "you can have the championship."

Heinz lifted his glass. "Here's long life and great skill and much happiness to—to Peter Karl Knechtmann." He breathed quickly, excited by the decision.

"There's a handle to take ahold of," said Sousa. "You'd think the kid weighed two hundred pounds."

"Peter is the name of a famous surgeon," said Heinz, "the boy's great-uncle, dead now. Karl was my father's name." **F**

F HISTORICAL CONTEXT
Reread lines 141–146. Why do you think Vonnegut focuses so much attention on the naming of the baby?

"Here's to Pete K. Netman," said Sousa, with a cursory salute.

"Pete," said the bartender, drinking.

"And here's to your little girl—the new one," said Heinz.

Sousa sighed and smiled wearily. "Here's to her. God bless her."

"And now, I'll propose a toast," said the bartender, hammering on the bar with his fist. "On your feet, gentlemen. Up, up, everybody up."

Heinz stood, and held his glass high, ready for the next step in camaraderie, a toast to the whole human race, of which the Knechtmanns were still a part.

"Here's to the White Sox!" roared the bartender.

"Minoso, Fox, Mele," said Sousa.

"Fain, Lollar, Rivera!" said the bartender. He turned to Heinz. "Drink up, boy! The White Sox! Don't tell me you're a Cub fan."

"No," said Heinz, disappointed. "No—I don't follow baseball, I'm afraid." The other two men seemed to be sinking away from him. "I haven't been able to think about much but the baby."

The bartender at once turned his full attention to Sousa. "Look," he said intensely, "they take Fain off of first, and put him at third, and give Pierce first. Then move Minoso in from left field to shortstop. See what I'm doing?"

"Yep, yep," said Sousa eagerly.

"And then we take that no-good Carrasquel and . . ."

Heinz was all alone again, with twenty feet of bar between him and the other two men. It might as well have been a continent.

He finished his drink without pleasure, and left quietly.

At the railroad station, where he waited for a local train to take him home to the South Side, Heinz's glow returned again as he saw a co-worker at the dry-cleaning plant walk in with a girl. They were laughing and had their arms around each other's waist.

"Harry," said Heinz, hurrying toward them. "Guess what, Harry. Guess what just happened." He grinned broadly.

Harry, a tall, dapper, snub-nosed young man, looked down at Heinz with mild surprise. "Oh—hello, Heinz. What's up, boy?"

The girl looked on in perplexity, as though asking why they should be accosted at such an odd hour by such an odd person. Heinz avoided her slightly derisive eyes. **G**

"A baby, Harry. My wife just had a boy."

"Oh," said Harry. He extended his hand. "Well, congratulations." The hand was limp. "I think that's swell, Heinz, perfectly swell." He withdrew his hand and waited for Heinz to say something else.

"Yes, yes—just about an hour ago," said Heinz. "Five pounds nine ounces. I've never been happier in my life."

"Well, I think it's perfectly swell, Heinz. You should be happy."

"Yes, indeed," said the girl.

There was a long silence, with all three shifting from one foot to the other.

"Really good news," said Harry at last.

"Yes, well," said Heinz quickly, "Well, that's all I had to tell you."

"Thanks," said Harry. "Glad to hear about it."

There was another uneasy silence.

"See you at work," said Heinz, and strode jauntily back to his bench, but with his reddened neck betraying how foolish he felt.

The girl giggled.

Back home in his small apartment, at two in the morning, Heinz talked to himself, to the empty bassinet, and to the bed. He talked in German, a language he had sworn never to use again. **H**

"They don't care," said Heinz. "They're all too busy, busy, busy to notice life, to feel anything about it. A baby is born." He shrugged. "What could be duller?

G CHARACTERIZATION
What character trait of Heinz's does Vonnegut reveal through the sentence "Heinz avoided her slightly derisive eyes"?

H HISTORICAL CONTEXT
Reread lines 197–199. What is Vonnegut's purpose in including this description of Heinz's use of and feelings about speaking German? Explain.

Who would be so stupid as to talk about it, to think there was anything important or interesting about it?"

He opened a window on the summer night, and looked out at the moonlit canyon of gray wooden porches and garbage cans. "There are too many of us, and we are all too far apart," said Heinz. "Another Knechtmann is born, another O'Leary, another Sousa. Who cares? Why should anyone care? What difference does it make? None."

He lay down in his clothes on the unmade bed, and, with a rattling sigh, went to sleep.

I CHARACTERIZATION AND TONE
Reread lines 226–243. How does the story's final section of dialogue contribute to your understanding of the main character and his wife? What tone does Vonnegut convey by closing the story with this particular conversation?

He awoke at six, as always. He drank a cup of coffee, and with a wry sense of anonymity, he jostled and was jostled aboard the downtown train. His face showed no emotion. It was like all the other faces, seemingly incapable of surprise or wonder, joy or anger.

He walked across town to the hospital with the same detachment, a gray, uninteresting man, a part of the city.

In the hospital, he was as purposeful and calm as the doctors and nurses bustling about him. When he was led into the ward where Avchen slept behind white screens, he felt only what he had always felt in her presence—love and aching awe and gratitude for her.

"You go ahead and wake her gently, Mr. Netman," said the nurse.

"Avchen—" He touched her on her white-gowned shoulder. "Avchen. Are you all right, Avchen?"

"Mmmmmmmmmm?" murmured Avchen. Her eyes opened to narrow slits. "Heinz. Hello, Heinz."

"Sweetheart, are you all right?"

"Yes, yes," she whispered. "I'm fine. How is the baby, Heinz?"

"Perfect. Perfect, Avchen."

"They couldn't kill us, could they, Heinz?"

"No."

"And here we are, alive as we can be."

"Yes."

"The baby, Heinz—" She opened her dark eyes wide. "It's the most wonderful thing that ever happened, isn't it?"

"Yes," said Heinz. ∾ I

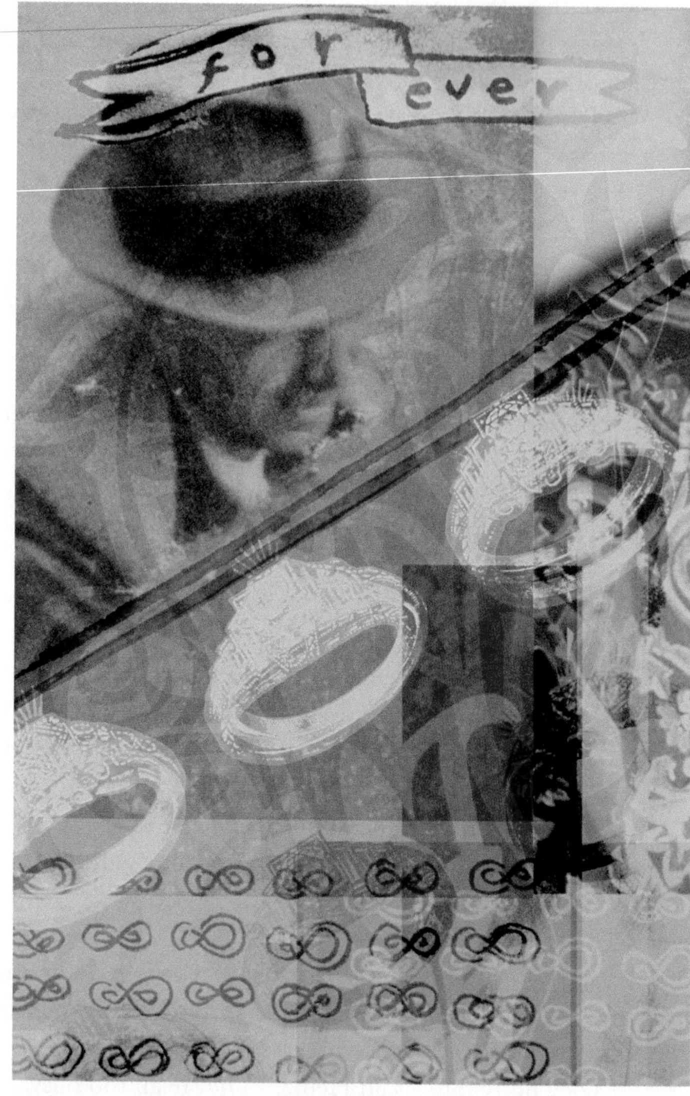

Life Decisions (1995), Ed Roskowski. © Ed Roskowski/Corbis.

Comprehension

1. **Recall** From what country and historical events is Heinz Knechtmann a refugee?
2. **Recall** Why is he at the hospital?
3. **Summarize** Why is he so amazed that he and his wife have had a child?

Text Analysis

4. **Analyze Characterization** In lines 4–7, how does Vonnegut use dialogue and details of physical appearance to characterize Mr. Sousa? Cite evidence from these lines to support your answer.
5. **Interpret Symbolism** In lines 78–79, what does the image of the closing elevator doors symbolize?
6. **Analyze Tone** Examine the short paragraph in lines 204–208. Describe the tone of this paragraph and explain how it differs from Vonnegut's tone in the dialogue that concludes "Adam" (lines 238–243).
7. **Analyze Historical Context** In the story's closing scene, the main character's wife says, "They couldn't kill us, could they, Heinz?" (line 236). Whom does she mean by "they"? To which historical events does she refer when she says, "They couldn't kill us"? Explain.
8. **Analyze Historical Context** In the barroom scene (lines 120–169), contrast Mr. Sousa and the bartender's life with Heinz Knechtmann's experience before immigrating to the United States. How does this contrast affect communication between the Americans and the Jewish immigrant in this scene?
9. **Analyze Allusion** The title of the story is an **allusion**—a reference to someone or something outside the story. To whom does the title refer? How does the title contribute to the meaning of the story?

Text Criticism

10. **Social Context** Explain whether you agree with Heinz's conclusion that people in this country are "too busy," "too many," and "too far apart" to care about one another. Give reasons for your response.

How do you AFFIRM LIFE?

In your opinion, what accounts for the resilience of the main character and his wife in "Adam"? Cite evidence from the story and your own experience to support your answer.

COMMON CORE

RL 3 Analyze the impact of the author's choices regarding how to develop and relate elements of a story. **RL 4** Analyze the impact of specific word choices on meaning and tone.

Memoir

In "Adam," you read about Holocaust survivors who came to America to begin a new life. In Primo Levi's memoir, you'll discover firsthand some of the horrors Holocaust victims endured in Nazi death camps.

from Survival in Auschwitz

Primo Levi

BACKGROUND Primo Levi spent the last year of World War II as an inmate at Auschwitz, a Nazi concentration camp in Poland. Levi wrote about his nightmarish experiences in objective, scientific detail, believing that subjective commentary was unnecessary and that the events would speak for themselves. The following excerpt from his memoir describes the ritual in which prisoners were selected for execution.

Today is working Sunday, *Arbeitssonntag:* we work until 1 P.M., then we return to camp for the shower, shave and general control for skin diseases and lice. And in the yards, everyone knew mysteriously that the selection would be today. **A**

The news arrived, as always, surrounded by a halo of contradictory or suspect details: the selection in the infirmary took place this morning; the percentage was seven per cent of the whole camp, thirty, fifty per cent of the patients. At Birkenau,[1] the crematorium chimney has been smoking for ten days. Room has to be made for an enormous convoy arriving from the Poznan ghetto.[2] The young tell the young that all the old ones will be chosen. The healthy tell the healthy that only the ill will be chosen. Specialists will be excluded. German Jews will be excluded. Low Numbers[3] will be excluded. You will be chosen. I will be excluded. **B**

At 1 P.M. exactly the yard empties in orderly fashion, and for two hours the gray unending army files past the two control stations where, as on every day, we are counted and recounted, and past the military band which for two hours without interruption plays, as on every day, those marches to which we must synchronize our steps at our entrance and our exit.

A HISTORICAL CONTEXT
Reread the opening paragraph (lines 1–3). How do the facts related here contribute to your understanding of life for Jewish prisoners in Auschwitz?

B CHARACTERIZATION
Reread lines 8–11 (from "The young tell the young" to the end of the paragraph). What human trait does the behavior of the Jewish prisoners reveal? Explain.

1. **Birkenau** (bûr'kən-ou): Also known as Auschwitz II, this camp stood about two miles from an older camp, called Auschwitz I. Between 1 million and 4 million people were murdered at Auschwitz-Birkenau during the years 1942–1945.
2. **Poznan** (pōz'năn') **ghetto:** the area of the Polish city of Poznan in which Jews were forced to live.
3. **Low Numbers:** prisoners with low identification numbers.

The shoes of victims, on display at the Auschwitz Museum

It seems like every day, the kitchen chimney smokes as usual, the distribution of the soup is already beginning. But then the bell is heard, and at that moment we realize that we have arrived.

Because this bell always sounds at dawn, when it means the reveille;[4] but if it sounds during the day, it means "*Blocksperre,*" enclosure in huts, and this happens when there is a selection to prevent anyone avoiding it, or when those selected leave for the gas, to prevent anyone seeing them leave. C

Our *Blockältester*[5] knows his business. He has made sure that we have all entered, he has the door locked, he has given everyone his card with his number, name, profession, age and nationality and he has ordered everyone to undress completely, except for shoes. We wait like this, naked, with the card in our hands, for the commission to

▲ Analyze Visuals

How does this photograph add to your understanding of Vonnegut's short story and Levi's testimony about life in Auschwitz? Explain your response.

C TONE

Describe the tone of lines 20–23. Explain how Levi's tone contrasts with the situation he describes here.

4. **reveille** (rĕv′ə-lē): a signal used to awaken people.
5. ***Blockältester*** (blŏ′käl-tĕs′tər) German: block elder—a prisoner cooperating with the German guards by serving as the head of a block, or barracks.

reach our hut. We are hut 48, but one can never tell if they are going to begin at hut 1 or hut 60. At any rate, we can rest quietly at least for an hour, and there is no reason why we should not get under the blankets on the bunk and keep warm.

Many are already drowsing when a barrage of orders, oaths and blows proclaims the imminent arrival of the commission. The *Blockältester* and his helpers, starting at the end of the dormitory, drive the crowd of frightened, naked people in front of them and cram them in the *Tagesraum* which is the Quartermaster's office.[6] The *Tagesraum* is a room seven yards by four: when the drive is over, a warm and compact human mass is jammed into the *Tagesraum,* perfectly filling all the corners, exercising such a pressure on the wooden walls as to make them creak. . . .

The *Blockältester* has closed the connecting-door and has opened the other two which lead from the dormitory and the *Tagesraum* outside. Here, in front of the two doors, stands the arbiter[7] of our fate, an SS subaltern.[8] On his right is the *Blockältester,* on his left, the quartermaster of the hut. Each one of us, as he comes naked out of the *Tagesraum* into the cold October air, has to run the few steps between the two doors, give the card to the SS man and enter the dormitory door. The SS man, in the fraction of a second between two successive crossings, with a glance at one's back and front, judges everyone's fate, and in turn gives the card to the man on his right or his left, and this is the life or death of each of us. In three or four minutes a hut of two hundred men is "done," as is the whole camp of twelve thousand men in the course of the afternoon.

Jammed in the charnel-house[9] of the *Tagesraum,* I gradually felt the human pressure around me slacken, and in a short time it was my turn. Like everyone, I passed by with a brisk and elastic step, trying to hold my head high, my chest forward and my muscles contracted and conspicuous. With the corner of my eye I tried to look behind my shoulders, and my card seemed to end on the right.

As we gradually come back into the dormitory we are allowed to dress ourselves. Nobody yet knows with certainty his own fate, it has first of all to be established whether the condemned cards were those on the right or the left. By now there is no longer any point in sparing each other's feelings with superstitious scruples. Everybody crowds around the oldest, the most wasted-away, and most "muselmann";[10] if their cards went to the left, the left is certainly the side of the condemned.

Even before the selection is over, everybody knows that the left was effectively the "*schlechte Seite,*" the bad side. There have naturally been some irregularities: René, for example, so young and robust, ended on the left; perhaps it was because he has glasses, perhaps because he walks a little stooped like a myope,[11] but more probably because of a simple mistake. . . .

There is nothing surprising about these mistakes: the examination is too quick and summary, and in any case, the important thing for the Lager[12] is not that the most useless prisoners be eliminated, but that free posts be quickly created, according to a certain percentage previously fixed. ∾ **D**

D HISTORICAL CONTEXT
Reread the last two paragraphs of the selection (lines 60–68). How does Levi explain the mistake that has been made? How does his explanation contribute to your understanding of the Holocaust? Explain.

---

6. **Quartermaster's office:** the office of the person who distributes food and clothing to the prisoners.
7. **arbiter** (är'bĭ-tər): judge; decider.
8. **SS subaltern:** a low-ranking officer in the Nazi special security force.
9. **charnel-house:** vault for the bones of the dead (used here figuratively).
10. **"muselmann"** (mo͞o'zəl-män): concentration-camp slang for a person near death from starvation.
11. **myope** (mī'ōp'): nearsighted person.
12. **Lager** (lä'gər) *German:* camp.

Photograph

This photograph shows the German slogan *Arbeit macht frei* ("Work will make you free") that Jews saw posted above the gate as they entered the Auschwitz-Birkenau Concentration Camp that Levi writes about in the memoir you just read. Analyze how the image and the words in this visual work together to convey meaning. Respond to the questions below, citing evidence from the visual to support your answers.

COMMON CORE

RI 7 Integrate and evaluate multiple sources of information presented in multiple media or formats as well as words in order to address a question or solve a problem.

1. **INTERPRET**
   Examine the colors in this photograph—pavement, grounds, building, trees, and sky. What kind of mood do these colors convey? What purpose do they help the photographer to achieve?

2. **ANALYZE**
   What purpose does the photographer achieve by prominently featuring the infamous slogan that was posted above the gate to Auschwitz?

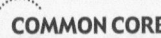

Comprehension

1. **Clarify** What is the purpose of the "selection" Levi tells about in this excerpt? What evidence can you cite to support your answer?
2. **Explain** In lines 65–68, why is it unimportant to those running the camp that mistakes were made during the "selection"?

Text Analysis

3. **Analyze Tone** Levi writes about the selection as if he were reciting ordinary events from an ordinary day, using ordinary diction and descriptions. Why might he use an almost matter-of-fact tone to describe horrific events? Explain.
4. **Analyze Characterization** Reread lines 31–37. What traits does this passage convey about the *Blockältester* and the Jewish prisoners, and how does their behavior here contribute to your understanding of conditions at Auschwitz? Support your answer by citing evidence from the passage.
5. **Examine Irony** Reread lines 60–64. What is ironic about Levi's reference to the "simple mistake" of Rene's selection?
6. **Analyze Historical Context** Briefly explain how the short excerpt from Levi's memoir contributes to your knowledge of the Holocaust. Cite evidence from the text to support your answer.

Comparing Themes Across Genres

7. **Analyze Theme** What do "Adam" and the excerpt from *Survival in Auschwitz* have to say about the theme of man's inhumanity to man? Support your answer with evidence from both texts.

How do you AFFIRM LIFE?

Like many Holocaust survivors, Levi felt the need to serve as a "witness" and tell his story so that such events would never be repeated. Do you think memoirs such as Levi's can prevent something similar from happening again, or are such events inevitable? Explain your response.

COMMON CORE

RI 2 Determine two or more central ideas of a text and analyze their development across the course of a text. **RI 3** Analyze a complex set of ideas or sequence of events and explain how specific individuals, ideas, or events interact and develop over the course of the text. **RI 6** Determine an author's point of view or purpose in a text in which the rhetoric is particularly effective, analyzing how style and content contribute to the power of the text.

Assessment Practice: Short Constructed Response

LITERARY TEXT: "ADAM"

On assessments you are expected to make inferences as you read. Practice this skill as you respond to the **short constructed response** below. Be sure to follow the steps outlined to the right of the question.

Examine Vonnegut's description of the young doctor. What do the details in these lines convey to you about the doctor? Explain.

STRATEGIES IN ACTION

1. Identify words and phrases that describe the young doctor.
2. List two character traits revealed by the words and phrases you identified.
3. Use the character traits from step 2 to write a thesis statement for your answer.
4. Use evidence you identified in step 1 to support your thesis.

NONFICTION TEXT: FROM "SURVIVAL IN AUSCHWITZ"

On assessments you are expected to read carefully and answer questions that focus on particular passages from a text selection. To strengthen your close-reading skills, read the **short constructed response** at left below and practice the strategies suggested at right.

Levi identifies only one Nazi in this excerpt, describing an SS soldier briefly. What traits does this passage convey about the soldier and the Nazi regime he represents? Explain.

STRATEGIES IN ACTION

1. List phrases that describe the SS soldier.
2. Identify a character trait to go with each phrase on your list. What does it tell you about the soldier, for example, that he makes each decision "in the fraction of a second"?

COMPARING LITERARY AND NONFICTION TEXTS

On assessments you will need to identify thematic connections between literary and nonfiction texts. Practice this valuable skill by responding to the **short constructed response** at left below and using the strategies provided at right.

One way to identify an author's theme or message is to ask yourself, "What's the moral of the story?" or "What did this text teach me about life or about people?" For each text, write a short sentence to answer these questions. What themes or ideas do the story and the memoir share? Cite evidence from both texts to support your response.

STRATEGIES IN ACTION

1. Remember that evidence from the text can take the form of a direct quotation, a paraphrase, or a specific synopsis.
2. Notice that the second part of the question is asking you to compare the texts. Be sure to include evidence to support each similarity you identify.

Ambush

Short Story by Tim O'Brien

COMMON CORE

RL 3 Analyze the impact of the author's choices regarding how to develop and relate elements of a story. **RL 5** Analyze how an author's choices concerning how to structure specific parts of a text contribute to its overall structure and meaning, as well as its aesthetic impact.

Meet the Author

Tim O'Brien born 1946

Over and over again, Tim O'Brien has presented characters who are marked by the Vietnam War. From an infantryman on his first tour of duty, to a veteran struggling to readjust to his hometown, to an antiwar radical obsessed with death, his protagonists bring to life the complex issues raised by the war.

Opening New Doors O'Brien's writing career began at an early age. One day he fled from humiliation in the Little League to the Worthington, Minnesota, library. There he found the book *Larry of the Little League,* and soothed himself by writing an imitation of it. The library's other books became an escape from"loneliness and frustration" and an outlet for O'Brien's fertile imagination. O'Brien realized that fiction would let him experience "what could have been or should have been."

A Critical Choice As a young man, O'Brien faced another new door. He returned from four years at Macalaster College, where the Vietnam War was on students' minds, to find a draft notice waiting for him. O'Brien, who opposed the war, struggled mightily with his conscience and even considered fleeing the country to avoid service. In the end, he could not bring himself to run, and he reported for duty.

What Can You Teach? O'Brien was an army infantryman from 1968 to 1970, seeing combat in Vietnam's Quang Nai province and receiving a Purple Heart. After the war, he studied at Harvard University, worked as a reporter for the *Washington Post,* and began writing novels. He asked himself, "What can you teach people, just for having been in a war?" He concluded that he could offer insight into the "complexity and ambiguity of a set of moral issues—but without preaching a moral lesson." O'Brien's nine books have all been connected to Vietnam and have vividly explored "its aftermath and effect on the human heart and mind."

Higher Ambitions Even after great success—a National Book Award and a Pulitzer Prize nomination—O'Brien still hopes to achieve more. He'd like to write a bestseller, and he works at it every day, no matter what. "You shape your own universe," he has said. "You practice all the time, then practice some more."

Author Online THINK central

Go to thinkcentral.com. KEYWORD: HML11-1194

DID YOU KNOW?

Tim O'Brien . . .

- described his own experiences fighting in Vietnam in the memoir *If I Die in a Combat Zone.*
- wrote stories about a fictional character, also named Tim O'Brien, in *The Things They Carried.*
- does not actually have a daughter, as the fictional Tim O'Brien does.

TEXT ANALYSIS: CONFLICT

A story's **conflict** is the struggle between opposing forces that is the basis of the story's plot. **External conflict**—a struggle between a character and some outside force—is usually easy to identify in a work of fiction. **Internal conflict**—a struggle within a character—may be more subtle and complex. For example, an internal conflict may revolve around a decision a character has to make, or it may be reflected in behavior that is contradictory. As you read this story, watch for the development of internal conflicts in the main character.

READING SKILL: ANALYZE STRUCTURE

The **structure** of a literary work is the way in which it is put together—the arrangement of its parts. Tim O'Brien's story "Ambush" includes a **frame story,** or a story within a story. The first paragraph provides a frame—the narrator recalls answering a question his daughter once asked him. In the second paragraph, he begins to recount in a **flashback** an experience he had earlier, during the war. As you read, use a chart like the one below to summarize what happens within the outer story and the inner story.

Beginning of Story 1:

Beginning of Story 2:

Middle of Story 2:

End of Story 2:

End of Story 1:

 Complete the activities in your **Reader/Writer Notebook.**

How does the PAST *affect the present?*

Perhaps more than any group in society, war veterans carry a difficult past. Some remember combat experiences vividly, some block them out entirely. The lucky ones find a way to reconcile their past with the present, to use the lessons of battle to inform their present perceptions and choices.

QUICKWRITE Think about war veterans you know or have heard about. They might have served in Vietnam, in the Persian Gulf, or in an international peacekeeping mission. Imagine one specific way in which a veteran's past experiences might affect his or her present life. How might they affect a father's relationship with his children, for example? Write down your thoughts and discuss them in a group.

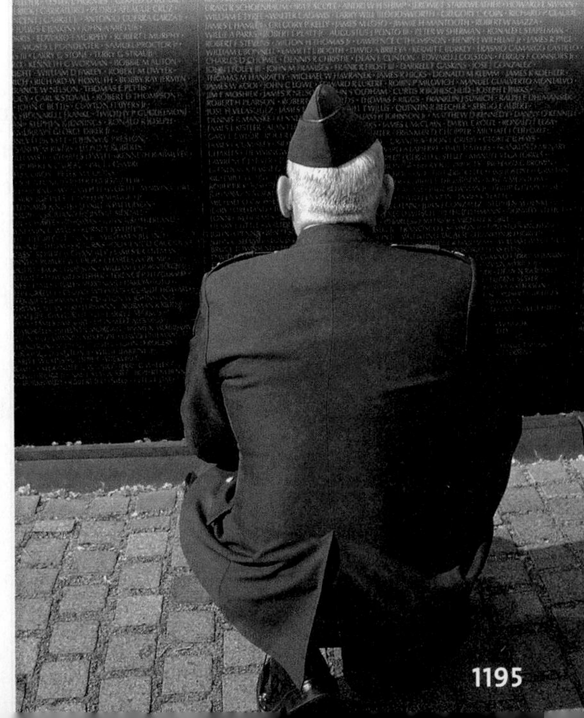

Ambush

Tim O'Brien

BACKGROUND "Ambush" is a short story based upon the writer's combat experiences in Vietnam. The Vietnam War lasted nine years, left 58,000 Americans dead, and left another 365,000 Americans wounded. Although they were better equipped and trained than the enemy, American troops fought in an unfamiliar landscape for a cause that many of them did not support or understand. Vietnamese Communists were skilled guerilla fighters whose tactics created a climate of frustration, confusion, and fear. American soldiers never knew when an attack might come and were haunted by their memories long after the war.

Analyze Visuals ▶
What **tone** is conveyed by this image?

When she was nine, my daughter Kathleen asked if I had ever killed anyone. She knew about the war; she knew I'd been a soldier. "You keep writing these war stories," she said, "so I guess you must've killed somebody." It was a difficult moment, but I did what seemed right, which was to say, "Of course not," and then to take her onto my lap and hold her for a while. Someday, I hope, she'll ask again. But here I want to pretend she's a grown-up. I want to tell her exactly what happened, or what I remember happening, and then I want to say to her that as a little girl she was absolutely right. This is why I keep writing war stories: (A)

He was a short, slender young man of about twenty. I was afraid of him—afraid of something—and as he passed me on the trail I threw a grenade that exploded at his feet and killed him. (B)

(A) **CONFLICT**
Reread lines 1–8. What **internal conflict** does the narrator face in the first paragraph?

(B) **ANALYZE STRUCTURE**
Reread lines 9–11. How does the **setting** of the story shift in the second paragraph?

The Green Machine (1977), Frank Dahmer. Screenprint on paper, $13\frac{1}{2}$″ × $17\frac{1}{4}$″. © National Vietnam Veterans Art Museum.

Or to go back: **C**

Shortly after midnight we moved into the ambush site outside My Khe. The whole platoon was there, spread out in the dense brush along the trail, and for five hours nothing at all happened. We were working in two-man teams—one man on guard while the other slept, switching off every two hours—and I remember it was still dark when Kiowa shook me awake for the final watch. The night was foggy and hot. For the first few moments I felt lost, not sure about directions, groping for my helmet and weapon. I reached out and found three grenades and lined them up in front of me; the pins had already been straightened for quick throwing. And then for maybe half an hour I kneeled there and waited. Very gradually, in tiny slivers, dawn began to break through the fog, and from my position in the brush I could see ten or fifteen meters up the trail. The mosquitoes were fierce. I remember slapping at them, wondering if I should wake up Kiowa and ask for some repellent, then thinking it was a bad idea, then looking up and seeing the young man come out of the fog. He wore black clothing and rubber sandals and a gray ammunition belt. His shoulders were slightly stooped, his head cocked to the side as if listening for something. He seemed at ease. He carried his weapon in one hand, muzzle down, moving without any hurry up the center of the trail. There was no sound at all—none that I can remember. In a way, it seemed, he was part of the morning fog, or my own imagination, but there was also the reality of what was happening in my stomach. I had already pulled the pin on a grenade. I had come up to a crouch. It was entirely automatic. I did not hate the young man; I did not see him as the enemy; I did not ponder issues of morality or politics or military duty. I crouched and kept my head low. I tried to swallow whatever was rising from my stomach, which tasted like lemonade, something fruity and sour. I was terrified. There were no thoughts about killing. The grenade was to make him go away—just evaporate—and I leaned back and felt my mind go empty and then felt it fill up again. I had already thrown the grenade before telling myself to throw it. The brush was thick and I had to lob it high, not aiming, and I remember the grenade seeming to freeze above me for an instant, as if a camera had clicked, and I remember ducking down and holding my breath and seeing little wisps of fog rise from the earth. The grenade bounced once and rolled across the trail. I did not hear it, but there must've been a sound, because the young man dropped his weapon and began to run, just two or three quick steps, then he hesitated, swiveling to his right, and he glanced down at the grenade and tried to cover his head but never did. It occurred to me then that he was about to die. I wanted to warn him. The grenade made a popping noise—not soft but not loud either—not what I'd expected—and there was a puff of dust and smoke—a small white puff—and the young man seemed to jerk upward as if pulled by invisible wires. He fell on his back. His rubber sandals had been blown off. There was no wind. He lay at the center of the trail, his right leg bent beneath him, his one eye shut, his other eye a huge star-shaped hole. **D**

C ANALYZE STRUCTURE
In terms of the structure of this story, what does this line signal?

D ANALYZE STRUCTURE
Summarize what happens in lines 13–53. How do these lines relate to the first paragraph of the story?

Come a Little Closer (1997), Michael Brostowitz. Oil on board, 15¼″ × 19¾″. © National Vietnam Veterans Art Museum.

It was not a matter of live or die. There was no real peril. Almost certainly the young man would have passed by. And it will always be that way.

Later, I remember, Kiowa tried to tell me that the man would've died anyway. He told me that it was a good kill, that I was a soldier and this was a war, that I should shape up and stop staring and ask myself what the dead man would've done if things were reversed.

None of it mattered. The words seemed far too complicated. All I could do was gape at the fact of the young man's body. (E)

Even now I haven't finished sorting it out. Sometimes I forgive myself, other times I don't. In the ordinary hours of life I try not to dwell on it, but now and then, when I'm reading a newspaper or just sitting alone in a room, I'll look up and see the young man coming out of the morning fog. I'll watch him walk toward me, his shoulders slightly stooped, his head cocked to the side, and he'll pass within a few yards of me and suddenly smile at some secret thought and then continue up the trail to where it bends back into the fog. ~ (F)

(E) **CONFLICT**
Reread lines 54–61. What **internal conflict** does the narrator express?

(F) **CONFLICT**
How does the vision the narrator imagines in lines 63–68 help resolve his conflict?

Comprehension

1. **Recall** What does the narrator tell his daughter when she asks if he ever killed someone?
2. **Summarize** What happened to the narrator outside My Khe?
3. **Clarify** What vision does the narrator sometimes see in his mind?

Text Analysis

4. **Examine Conflicts** Identify the **internal conflicts** the narrator experiences in this story. How would you describe the way he resolves or tries to resolve them? Explain your answer.
5. **Analyze Structure** What does the **frame** contribute to the impact of this story? Consider what would be lost without the first and last paragraphs.
6. **Interpret Title** In what ways does the title "Ambush" relate to the events of the story? Think about the frame as well as the inner story.
7. **Evaluate a Character's Actions** Kiowa tells the narrator that this "was a good kill." Do you agree? In your opinion, can there be a "good kill"?
8. **Apply Theme** What does this story suggest about the effects of the **past** on the present?
9. **Compare Texts** Compare "Ambush" and "Why Soldiers Won't Talk" (page 1172) as portrayals of a soldier's experience. On a chart, note what each presents as the physical sensations and emotional aftereffects of war. Which piece—the story or the essay—had more impact on you? Why?

	Physical Sensations	*Emotional Aftereffects*
"Ambush"		
"Why Soldiers Won't Talk"		

Text Criticism

10. **Author's Style** "Ambush" is a work of fiction, but the story reads like a nonfiction account of a true event. To readers who wonder how much of his work is actually true, O'Brien responds, "The literal truth is . . . irrelevant." Do you agree? Does it matter that O'Brien the writer does not have a daughter and does not know whether he ever killed anyone?

How does the **PAST** *affect the present?*

How does O'Brien's story convey the effects of the past on the present? Cite evidence from the story to support your answer.

COMMON CORE

RL 3 Analyze the impact of the author's choices regarding how to develop and relate elements of a story. **RL 5** Analyze how an author's choices concerning how to structure specific parts of a text contribute to its overall structure and meaning, as well as its aesthetic impact.

Wrap-Up: Responses to War

The Literary Legacy of War

Modernist writer Gertrude Stein once said, "War is never fatal but always lost. Always lost." One after another, the wars of the 20th century forced Americans to reconcile their sense of patriotism with the disillusionment that naturally comes from facing the realities of modern warfare. If it is an artist's job to find meaning, what meaning can be discerned from the act of war?

Writing to Synthesize

Each of the texts you have just read presents a variety of ideas and images in response to World War II and the Vietnam War. What do these pieces have in common? Reread the selections, pulling words or phrases from each that you find especially compelling—whether beautiful, ugly, moving, or surprising. When you have gathered 15–30 phrases, combine them artfully to create a poem that delivers a coherent impression about war. Your poem might tell a story, describe an image, or deliver a set of thoughts or pronouncements. It can take place on the battlefield or on the home front.

Consider

- what primary thought or feeling you were left with after reading all of the texts
- which parts of each selection had the strongest impact on you
- how to arrange the phrases in a way that communicates your own response to the texts

Extension

SPEAKING AND LISTENING Give an **oral reading** of your poem, using your voice, posture, and gestures to emphasize its meaning. If you think it would be effective, consider performing a choral reading with some of your classmates or setting your poem to music.

COMMON CORE

W 9 Draw evidence from literary or informational texts to support analysis, reflection, and research. **SL 6** Adapt speech to a variety of contexts and tasks.

American soldiers in Vietnam

from Letter from Birmingham Jail

Video link at thinkcentral.com

Letter by Martin Luther King Jr.

VIDEO TRAILER THINK central KEYWORD: HML11-1202A

COMMON CORE

RI 1 Cite textual evidence to support analysis of what the text says explicitly as well as inferences drawn from the text. **RI 4** Determine the meaning of words and phrases as they are used in a text, including figurative and connotative meanings; analyze how an author uses and refines the meaning of a key term or terms over the course of a text. **RI 6** Determine an author's point of view or purpose in a text in which the rhetoric is particularly effective, analyzing how style and content contribute to the power, persuasiveness, or beauty of the text. **RI 8** Delineate and evaluate the reasoning in seminal U.S. texts, including the premises, purposes, and arguments in works of public advocacy.

Meet the Author

Martin Luther King Jr. 1929–1968

An eloquent orator, a shrewd tactician, and a visionary leader, Martin Luther King Jr. became the catalyst for some of the most far-reaching social changes in U.S. history. Under his skillful leadership, the civil rights movement spurred passage of the Civil Rights Act of 1964 and the Voting Rights Act of 1965, laws that legally abolished racial segregation and voting discrimination. A tireless advocate for justice, King wrote five books, delivered about 2,500 speeches, and traveled more than 6 million miles in an effort to make his dream of equality a reality.

Boycott in Montgomery It was in Alabama that King first emerged as a civil rights leader to be reckoned with. In 1955, when Rosa Parks was arrested for breaking Montgomery's bus segregation laws, local civil rights advocates banded together to form a protest organization. They chose King, then pastor of the Dexter Avenue Baptist Church, to lead the new group. King mobilized African Americans to boycott city buses. The 381-day boycott tested the endurance of the entire black community, especially King, who was subjected to threats and bomb attacks. The steadfast boycotters ultimately triumphed, and the U.S. Supreme Court struck down the city's bus segregation laws. The success of the boycott launched the charismatic young leader onto the national stage, where he promoted his bold strategy: using nonviolent, direct action to achieve social change.

Expanding Influence King cautiously expanded the civil rights struggle throughout the South. He was particularly effective at organizing interracial coalitions to put pressure on lawmakers. One shining moment came at the 1963 March on Washington, a gathering of about 250,000 peaceful demonstrators supporting civil rights legislation. King's impassioned "I Have a Dream" speech, delivered on the steps of the Lincoln Memorial, is considered one of the greatest speeches in U.S. history.

Warrior for Peace King never wavered in his commitment to nonviolence and tried to extend his campaign to fight poverty and end the Vietnam War. Ultimately, he was unable to stem the surge of violence that overtook the country in the mid-1960s. In 1968, King was assassinated in Memphis, where he had gone to support a sanitation workers' strike. In the 12 years between the Montgomery boycott and his death, he had helped achieve the greatest advance in racial justice since the abolition of slavery.

DID YOU KNOW?

Martin Luther King Jr. . . .

- enrolled in college when he was 15 years old.
- was the first African American to be named *Time* magazine's "Man of the Year."
- won the Nobel Peace Prize in 1964.
- was arrested 30 times for his activism.

Author Online

THINK central

Go to thinkcentral.com. KEYWORD: HML11-1202B

TEXT ANALYSIS: ALLUSION

An **allusion** is a reference within a work to historical, literary, or cultural details from outside the work. Writers choose allusions that are familiar to their target audience. In this case, because King is writing to fellow clergymen, he uses references to the Bible and to religious scholars to make his points.

I would agree with St. Augustine that "an unjust law is no law at all."

King's allusions help connect current events with respected historical and religious figures. As you read, use the footnotes to help you understand King's allusions.

READING SKILL: ELEMENTS OF AN ARGUMENT

King's letter is a beautifully written **argument** defending his activism. In it, King uses **deductive reasoning** to respond to public criticism. Deductive reasoning occurs when a writer arrives at a conclusion by applying a general principal to a specific situation. As you read, use King's restatements to infer what the opposing positions are and record them in a chart like the one below. Then, record the general principle King gives as a counterargument and the reasons and evidence he uses to support them.

Position of Opponents	*General Principles*	*Reasons and Evidence*
King doesn't belong in Birmingham.	*"I am here because I have organizational ties here."*	• *leads the SCLC* • *invited by affiliated organization*

VOCABULARY IN CONTEXT

King uses the following words to argue his views. Test yourself by replacing each boldfaced term with one vocabulary word.

WORD LIST			
	affiliated	moratorium	scintillating
	cognizant	paradoxical	substantive
	estrangement	rabid	
	latent	retaliating	

1. **aware** of the difficulties involved
2. **hidden** emotions called up by the encounter
3. **contradictory** views seemed to say two things at once
4. **temporary stoppage** on further discussions

Complete the activities in your **Reader/Writer Notebook**.

When does ACTION *speak louder than words?*

When you're trying to confront a difficult issue, words are your first option. But once you've explained your position, presented your demands, and tried unsuccessfully to convince others to make a change, you're at the point when words give way to action. Martin Luther King Jr. explains how civil rights activists in Birmingham, Alabama, faced their own decisive moment in 1963.

DISCUSS When do you respond with words and when do you turn to action? Working with a small group, brainstorm situations that call for each type of response. What guidelines did you use to classify your examples?

Letter from Birmingham Jail

Martin Luther King Jr.

BACKGROUND In the spring of 1963, Martin Luther King Jr. and his organization, the Southern Christian Leadership Conference (SCLC), targeted Birmingham, Alabama, with a series of peaceful demonstrations aimed at ending segregation. The police reacted violently with attack dogs and high-pressure fire hoses. Hundreds of protesters, including King, were jailed. At first, King was criticized for taking on Birmingham; eight white clergymen published a letter calling his actions "unwise and untimely." But he responded with his own letter citing philosophers, religious scholars, and biblical figures to justify his actions.

April 16, 1963
My Dear Fellow Clergymen:

While confined here in the Birmingham city jail, I came across your recent statement calling my present activities "unwise and untimely." Seldom do I pause to answer criticism of my work and ideas. If I sought to answer all the criticisms that cross my desk, my secretaries would have little time for anything other than such correspondence in the course of the day, and I would have no time for constructive work. But since I feel that you are men of genuine good will and that your criticisms are sincerely set forth, I want to try to answer your statement in what I hope will be patient and reasonable terms.

I think I should indicate why I am here in Birmingham, since you have been influenced by the view which argues against "outsiders coming in." I have the honor of serving as president of the Southern Christian Leadership Conference, an organization operating in every Southern state, with headquarters in Atlanta, Georgia. We have some eighty-five **affiliated** organizations across the South, and one of them is the Alabama Christian Movement for Human Rights. Frequently we share staff, educational, and financial resources with our affiliates. Several months ago the affiliate here in Birmingham asked us to be on call to engage in a nonviolent direct-action program if such were deemed necessary. We readily consented, and when the hour came, we lived up to our promise. So I, along with several members of my staff, am here because I was invited here. I am here because I have organizational ties here. **A**

But more basically, I am in Birmingham because injustice is here. Just as the prophets of the eighth century B.C. left their villages and carried their "thus saith the Lord" far beyond the boundaries of their home towns, and just as the Apostle Paul left his village of Tarsus and carried the gospel of Jesus Christ to the

Analyze Visuals ▶
Look at this photograph of King in his jail cell in Birmingham. Based on the photo, what impressions do you have of his state of mind while in jail?

affiliated (ə-fĭl'ē-ā'tĭd) *adj.* joined in close association **affiliate** *v.*

A **ELEMENTS OF AN ARGUMENT**
Reread lines 10–21. Which sentence refers to the position that King is arguing against?

King in his jail cell in Birmingham

far corners of the Greco-Roman world, so am I compelled to carry the gospel of freedom beyond my own hometown. Like Paul, I must constantly respond to the Macedonian call for aid.[1] B

Moreover, I am **cognizant** of the interrelatedness of all communities and states. I cannot sit idly by in Atlanta and not be concerned about what happens in Birmingham. Injustice anywhere is a threat to justice everywhere. We are caught in an inescapable network of mutuality, tied in a single garment of destiny. Whatever affects one directly, affects all indirectly. Never again can we afford to live with the narrow, provincial "outside agitator" idea. Anyone who lives inside the United States can never be considered an outsider anywhere within its bounds.

You deplore the demonstrations taking place in Birmingham. But your statement, I am sorry to say, fails to express a similar concern for the conditions that brought about the demonstrations. I am sure that none of you would want to rest content with the superficial kind of social analysis that deals merely with effects and does not grapple with underlying causes. It is unfortunate that demonstrations are taking place in Birmingham, but it is even more unfortunate that the city's white power structure left the Negro community with no alternative.

In any nonviolent campaign there are four basic steps: collection of the facts to determine whether injustices exist; negotiation; self-purification; and direct action. We have gone through all these steps in Birmingham. There can be no gainsaying the fact that racial injustice engulfs this community. Birmingham is probably the most thoroughly segregated city in the United States. Its ugly record of brutality is widely known. Negroes have experienced grossly unjust treatment in the courts. There have been more unsolved bombings of Negro homes and churches in Birmingham than in any other city in the nation. These are the hard, brutal facts of the case. On the basis of these conditions, Negro leaders sought to negotiate with the city fathers. But the latter consistently refused to engage in good-faith negotiations. C

Then, last September, came the opportunity to talk with leaders of Birmingham's economic community. In the course of the negotiations, certain promises were made by the merchants— for example, to remove the stores' humiliating racial signs.[2] On the basis of these promises, the Reverend Fred Shuttlesworth and the leaders of the Alabama Christian Movement for Human Rights agreed to a **moratorium** on all demonstrations. As the weeks and months went by, we realized that we were the victims of a broken promise. A few signs, briefly removed, returned; the others remained.

As in so many past experiences, our hopes had been blasted, and the shadow of deep disappointment settled upon us. We had no alternative except to prepare for direct action, whereby we would present our very bodies as a means of laying our case before the conscience of the local and the national community. Mindful of the difficulties involved, we decided to undertake a process of self-purification.

B ALLUSION
Explain why King's allusions in lines 22–28 are appropriate for his audience. What shared beliefs does King appeal to?

cognizant (kŏg′nĭ-zənt) *adj.* aware

C ELEMENTS OF AN ARGUMENT
Reread lines 46–54. What **reasons** and **evidence** does King use to support his **claim** that there is racial injustice in Birmingham?

moratorium (môr′ə-tôr′ē-əm) *n.* a temporary stoppage or waiting period

1. **Macedonian** (măs′ĭ-dō′nē-ən) **call for aid:** According to the Bible (Acts 16), the apostle Paul received a vision calling him to preach in Macedonia, an area north of Greece.
2. **racial signs:** signs marking segregated buildings and other facilities.

We began a series of workshops on nonviolence, and we repeatedly asked ourselves: "Are you able to accept blows without **retaliating?**" "Are you able to endure the ordeal of jail?" We decided to schedule our direct-action program for the Easter season, realizing that except for Christmas, this is the main shopping period of the year. Knowing that a strong economic-withdrawal program[3] would be the by-product of direct action, we felt that this would be the best time to bring pressure to bear on the merchants for the needed change.

retaliating (rĭ-tăl'ē-ā'tĭng) *n.* taking revenge **retaliate** *v.*

Then it occurred to us that Birmingham's mayoral election was coming up in March, and we speedily decided to postpone action until after election day. When we discovered that the Commissioner of Public Safety, Eugene "Bull" Connor, had piled up enough votes to be in the runoff, we decided again to postpone action until the day after the runoff so that the demonstrations could not be used to cloud the issues. Like many others, we waited to see Mr. Connor defeated, and to this end we endured postponement after postponement. Having aided in this community need, we felt that our direct-action program could be delayed no longer.

COMMON CORE RI 4

Language Coach

Figurative Language
Cloud in line 80 means "confuse or make unclear" and is an example of figurative language, language that communicates meaning beyond the literal meaning of the words. How might a boycott or economic-withdrawal program cloud the issues during an election?

You may well ask: "Why direct action? Why sit-ins, marches, and so forth? Isn't negotiation a better path?" You are quite right in calling for negotiation. Indeed, this is the very purpose of direct action. Nonviolent direct action seeks to create such a crisis and foster such a tension that a community which has constantly refused to negotiate is forced to confront the issue. It seeks so to dramatize the issue that it can no longer be ignored. My citing the creation of tension as part of the work of the nonviolent-resister may sound rather shocking. But I must confess that I am not afraid of the word "tension." I have earnestly opposed violent tension, but there is a type of constructive, nonviolent tension which is necessary for growth. Just as Socrates[4] felt that it was necessary to create a tension in the mind so that individuals could rise from the bondage of myths and half-truths to the unfettered realm of creative analysis and objective appraisal, so must we see the need for nonviolent gadflies to create the kind of tension in society that will help men rise from the dark depths of prejudice and racism to the majestic heights of understanding and brotherhood.

The purpose of our direct-action program is to create a situation so crisis-packed that it will inevitably open the door to negotiation. I therefore concur with you in your call for negotiation. Too long has our beloved Southland been bogged down in a tragic effort to live in monologue rather than dialogue.

One of the basic points in your statement is that the action that I and my associates have taken in Birmingham is untimely. Some have asked: "Why didn't you give the new city administration time to act?" The only answer that I can give to this query is that the new Birmingham administration must be prodded about as much as the outgoing one, before it will act. . . . My friends, I must say to you that we have not made a single gain in civil rights without determined legal and nonviolent pressure. Lamentably, it is a historical fact that privileged groups

3. **economic-withdrawal program:** boycott.
4. **Socrates** (sŏk'rə-tēz'): Greek philosopher (470–399 B.C.) who was a major influence in the development of Western thought.

seldom give up their privileges voluntarily. Individuals may see the moral light and voluntarily give up their unjust posture; but, as Reinhold Niebuhr[5] has reminded us, groups tend to be more immoral than individuals.

We know through painful experience that freedom is never voluntarily given by the oppressor; it must be demanded by the oppressed. Frankly, I have yet to engage in a direct-action campaign that was "well-timed" in the view of those who have not suffered unduly from the disease of segregation. For years now I have heard the word "Wait!" It rings in the ear of every Negro with piercing familiarity. This "Wait" has almost always meant "Never." We must come to see, with one of our distinguished jurists, that "justice too long delayed is justice denied."

We have waited for more than 340 years for our constitutional and God-given rights. The nations of Asia and Africa are moving with jetlike speed toward gaining political independence, but we still creep at horse-and-buggy pace toward gaining a cup of coffee at a lunch counter. Perhaps it is easy for those who have never felt the stinging darts of segregation to say, "Wait." But when you have seen vicious mobs lynch your mothers and fathers at will and drown your sisters and brothers at whim; when you have seen hate-filled policemen curse, kick, and even kill your black brothers and sisters; when you see the vast majority of your twenty million Negro brothers smothering in an airtight cage of poverty in the midst of an affluent society; when you suddenly find your tongue twisted and your speech stammering as you seek to explain to your six-year-old daughter why she can't go to the public amusement park that has just been advertised on television, and see tears welling up in her eyes when she is told that Funtown is closed to colored children, and see ominous clouds of inferiority beginning to form in her little mental sky, and see her beginning to distort her personality by developing an unconscious bitterness toward white people; when you have to concoct an answer for a five-year-old son who is asking: "Daddy, why do white people treat colored people so mean?"; when you take a cross-country drive and find it necessary to sleep night after night in the uncomfortable corners of your automobile because no motel will accept you; when you are humiliated day in and day out by nagging signs reading "white" and "colored"; when your first name becomes "nigger," your middle name becomes "boy" (however old you are) and your last name becomes "John," and your wife and mother are never given the respected title "Mrs."; when you are harried by day and haunted by night by the fact that you are a Negro, living constantly at tiptoe stance, never quite knowing what to expect next, and are plagued with inner fears and outer resentments; when you are forever fighting a degenerating sense of "nobodiness"—then you will understand why we find it difficult to wait. There comes a time when the cup of endurance runs over, and men are no longer willing to be plunged into the abyss of despair. I hope, sirs, you can understand our legitimate and unavoidable impatience. D

D GRAMMAR AND STYLE
Reread lines 124–147. Note how King establishes **parallelism** by starting each subordinate clause with the words *when you.*

You express a great deal of anxiety over our willingness to break laws. This is certainly a legitimate concern. Since we so diligently urge people to obey the

5. **Reinhold Niebuhr** (nē'bŏŏr'): American theologian (1892–1971) whose writings deal mainly with moral and social problems.

Supreme Court's decision of 1954 outlawing segregation in the public schools,[6] at first glance it may seem rather **paradoxical** for us consciously to break laws. One may well ask: "How can you advocate breaking some laws and obeying others?" The answer lies in the fact that there are two types of laws: just and unjust. I would be the first to advocate obeying just laws. One has not only a legal but a moral responsibility to obey just laws. Conversely, one has a moral responsibility to disobey unjust laws. I would agree with St. Augustine[7] that "an unjust law is no law at all."

Now, what is the difference between the two? How does one determine whether a law is just or unjust? A just law is a man-made code that squares with the moral law or the law of God. An unjust law is a code that is out of harmony with the moral law. To put it in the terms of St. Thomas Aquinas:[8] An unjust law is a human law that is not rooted in eternal law and natural law. Any law that uplifts human personality is just. Any law that degrades human personality is unjust. All segregation statutes are unjust because segregation distorts the soul and damages the personality. It gives the segregator a false sense of superiority and the segregated a false sense of inferiority. Segregation, to use the terminology of the Jewish philosopher Martin Buber,[9] substitutes an "I-it" relationship for an "I-thou" relationship and ends up relegating persons to the status of things. Hence segregation is not only politically, economically, and sociologically unsound, it is morally wrong and sinful. Paul Tillich[10] has said that sin is separation. Is not segregation an existential expression of man's tragic separation, his awful **estrangement,** his terrible sinfulness? Thus it is that I can urge men to obey the 1954 decision of the Supreme Court, for it is morally right; and I can urge them to disobey segregation ordinances, for they are morally wrong. **E**

Let us consider a more concrete example of just and unjust laws. An unjust law is a code that a numerical or power majority group compels a minority group to obey but does not make binding on itself. This is *difference* made legal. By the same token, a just law is a code that a majority compels a minority to follow and that it is willing to follow itself. This is *sameness* made legal.

Let me give another explanation. A law is unjust if it is inflicted on a minority that, as a result of being denied the right to vote, had no part in enacting or devising the law. Who can say that the legislature of Alabama which set up that state's segregation laws was democratically elected? Throughout Alabama all sorts of devious methods are used to prevent Negroes from becoming registered voters, and there are some counties in which, even though Negroes constitute a majority of the population, not a single Negro is registered. Can any law enacted under such circumstances be considered democratically structured?

paradoxical (păr'ə-dŏk'sĭ-kəl) *adj.* self-contradictory

estrangement (ĭ-strānj'mənt) *n.* separation; alienation

E ELEMENTS OF AN ARGUMENT
Reread lines 160–176. How does King use deductive reasoning to support his conclusion that people should disobey segregation laws?

---

6. **Supreme Court decision . . . public schools:** the United States Supreme Court's decision in the case *Brown v. Board of Education of Topeka, Kansas.*
7. **St. Augustine** (ô'gə-stēn'): North African bishop (A.D. 354–430) regarded as a founding father of Christianity.
8. **St. Thomas Aquinas** (ə-kwī'nəs): noted philosopher and theologian (1225–1274).
9. **Martin Buber** (bo͞o'bər): influential philosopher (1878–1965) with great impact on Jewish and Christian theology.
10. **Paul Tillich** (tĭl'ĭk): German-born American theologian (1886–1965).

High school students jailed in Birmingham protests of 1963

Sometimes a law is just on its face and unjust in its application. For instance, I have been arrested on a charge of parading without a permit. Now, there is nothing wrong in having an ordinance which requires a permit for a parade. But such an ordinance becomes unjust when it is used to maintain segregation and to deny citizens the First Amendment privilege of peaceful assembly and protest.

I hope you are able to see the distinction I am trying to point out. In no sense do I advocate evading or defying the law, as would the **rabid** segregationist. That would lead to anarchy. One who breaks an unjust law must do so openly, lovingly, and with a willingness to accept the penalty. I submit that an individual who breaks a law that conscience tells him is unjust, and who willingly accepts the penalty of imprisonment in order to arouse the conscience of the community over its injustice, is in reality expressing the highest respect for law.

rabid (răb'ĭd) *adj.* unreasonably extreme; fanatical

Of course, there is nothing new about this kind of civil disobedience. It was evidenced sublimely in the refusal of Shadrach, Meshach, and Abednego to obey the laws of Nebuchadnezzar,[11] on the ground that a higher moral law was at stake. It was practiced superbly by the early Christians, who were willing to face hungry lions and the excruciating pain of chopping blocks rather than submit to certain unjust laws of the Roman Empire. To a degree, academic freedom is a reality today because Socrates practiced civil disobedience. In our own nation, the Boston Tea Party[12] represented a massive act of civil disobedience. (F)

(F) ALLUSION
Reread lines 202–209. What message about civil disobedience does King send with his choice of allusions?

11. **the refusal . . . Nebuchadnezzar** (nĕb'ə-kəd-nĕz'ər): In the Bible (Daniel 3), Shadrach (shăd'răk), Meshach (mē'shăch), and Abednego (ə-bĕd'nĭ-gō') are three Hebrews condemned to death for refusing to worship an idol set up by Nebuchadnezzar, king of Babylon. However, they were miraculously protected from the flames in the furnace into which they were thrown.

12. **Boston Tea Party:** In 1773, American rebels dumped 15,000 pounds of tea into Boston Harbor to protest the British Tea Act.

We should never forget that everything Adolf Hitler did in Germany was "legal" and everything the Hungarian freedom fighters[13] did in Hungary was "illegal." It was "illegal" to aid and comfort a Jew in Hitler's Germany. Even so, I am sure that, had I lived in Germany at the time, I would have aided and comforted my Jewish brothers. If today I lived in a Communist country where certain principles dear to the Christian faith are suppressed, I would openly advocate disobeying that country's antireligious laws.

I must make two honest confessions to you, my Christian and Jewish brothers. First, I must confess that over the past few years I have been gravely disappointed with the white moderate. I have almost reached the regrettable conclusion that the Negro's great stumbling block in his stride toward freedom is not the White Citizen's Counciler or the Ku Klux Klanner,[14] but the white moderate, who is more devoted to "order" than to justice; who prefers a negative peace which is the absence of tension to a positive peace which is the presence of justice; who constantly says: "I agree with you in the goal you seek, but I cannot agree with your methods of direct action"; who paternalistically believes he can set the timetable for another man's freedom; who lives by a mythical concept of time and who constantly advises the Negro to wait for a "more convenient season." Shallow understanding from people of goodwill is more frustrating than absolute misunderstanding from people of ill will. Lukewarm acceptance is much more bewildering than outright rejection.

Language Coach

Word Definitions
Stumbling block (line 220) means "obstacle to advancement; something that gets in the way." (Picture a person tripping over a large piece of wood while walking.) Who or what does King say the stumbling block is?

I had hoped that the white moderate would understand that law and order exist for the purpose of establishing justice and that when they fail in this purpose, they become the dangerously structured dams that block the flow of social progress. I had hoped that the white moderate would understand that the present tension in the South is a necessary phase of the transition from an obnoxious negative peace, in which the Negro passively accepted his unjust plight, to a **substantive** and positive peace, in which all men will respect the dignity and worth of human personality. Actually, we who engage in nonviolent direct action are not the creators of tension. We merely bring to the surface the hidden tension that is already alive. We bring it out in the open, where it can be seen and dealt with. Like a boil that can never be cured so long as it is covered up but must be opened with all its ugliness to the natural medicines of air and light, injustice must be exposed, with all the tension its exposure creates, to the light of human conscience and the air of national opinion before it can be cured.

substantive (sŭb'stən-tĭv) *adj.* significant; with a strong basis

In your statement you assert that our actions, even though peaceful, must be condemned because they precipitate violence. But is this a logical assertion? Isn't this like condemning a robbed man because his possession of money precipitated the evil act of robbery? Isn't this like condemning Socrates because his unswerving commitment to truth and his philosophical inquiries precipitated the act by the misguided populace in which they made him drink hemlock? Isn't this like

13. **Hungarian freedom fighters:** Hungarians who participated in an unsuccessful 1956 rebellion against the Communist government of their homeland. The rebellion was crushed by Soviet troops.

14. **the White . . . Klanner:** members of white supremacist groups.

condemning Jesus because his unique God-consciousness and never-ceasing devotion to God's will precipitated the evil act of crucifixion? We must come to see that, as the federal courts have consistently affirmed, it is wrong to urge an individual to cease his efforts to gain his basic constitutional rights because the quest may precipitate violence. Society must protect the robbed and punish the robber. . . .

Oppressed people cannot remain oppressed forever. The yearning for freedom eventually manifests itself, and that is what has happened to the American Negro. Something within has reminded him of his birthright of freedom, and something without has reminded him that it can be gained. Consciously or unconsciously, he has been caught up by the *Zeitgeist,*[15] and with his black brothers of Africa and his brown and yellow brothers of Asia, South America, and the Caribbean, the United States Negro is moving with a sense of great urgency toward the promised land of racial justice. If one recognizes this vital urge that has engulfed the Negro community, one should readily understand why public demonstrations are taking place. The Negro has many pent-up resentments and **latent** frustrations, and he must release them. So let him march; let him make prayer pilgrimages to the city hall; let him go on freedom rides—and try to understand why he must do so. If his repressed emotions are not released in nonviolent ways, they will seek expression through violence; this is not a threat but a fact of history. So I have not said to my people: "Get rid of your discontent." Rather, I have tried to say that this normal and healthy discontent can be channeled into the creative outlet of nonviolent direct action. And now this approach is being termed extremist.

latent (lāt'nt) *adj.* existing in a hidden form

But though I was initially disappointed at being categorized as an extremist, as I continued to think about the matter, I gradually gained a measure of satisfaction from the label. Was not Jesus an extremist for love: "Love your enemies, bless them that curse you, do good to them that hate you, and pray for them which despitefully use you, and persecute you." Was not Amos[16] an extremist for justice: "Let justice roll down like waters and righteousness like an ever-flowing stream." Was not Paul an extremist for the Christian gospel: "I bear in my body the marks of the Lord Jesus." Was not Martin Luther[17] an extremist: "Here I stand; I cannot do otherwise, so help me God." And John Bunyan:[18] "I will stay in jail to the end of my days before I make a butchery of my conscience." And Abraham Lincoln: "This nation cannot survive half slave and half free." And Thomas Jefferson: "We hold these truths to be self-evident, that all men are created equal. . . ." So the question is not whether we will be extremists, but what kind of extremists we will be. Will we be extremists for hate or for love? Will we be extremists for the preservation of injustice or for the extension of justice? In that dramatic scene on Calvary's hill[19] three men were crucified. We must never forget that all

COMMON CORE RI 4

Language Coach

Connotation A word's **connotations** are the connected images or feelings that add a finer shade of meaning to the word. What connotations do you think *extremist* has? Contrast those connotations with *activist.* How do the connotations differ?

15. ***Zeitgeist*** (tsīt'gīst') *German*: the spirit of the time; that is, the beliefs and attitudes shared by most people living in a particular period.
16. **Amos:** Hebrew prophet whose words are recorded in the Old Testament book bearing his name.
17. **Martin Luther:** German monk (1483–1546) who launched the Protestant Reformation.
18. **John Bunyan:** English preacher and author (1628–1688) who was twice imprisoned for unlicensed preaching.
19. **Calvary's hill:** the site of Jesus' crucifixion.

three were crucified for the same crime—the crime of extremism. Two were extremists for immorality, and thus fell below their environment. The other, Jesus Christ, was an extremist for love, truth, and goodness, and thereby rose above his environment. Perhaps the South, the nation and the world are in dire need of creative extremists. . . . **G**

I wish you had commended the Negro sit-inners and demonstrators of Birmingham for their sublime courage, their willingness to suffer, and their amazing discipline in the midst of great provocation. One day the South will recognize its real heroes. They will be the James Merediths,[20] with the noble sense of purpose that enables them to face jeering and hostile mobs, and with the agonizing loneliness that characterizes the life of the pioneer. They will be old, oppressed, battered Negro women, symbolized in a seventy-two-year-old woman in Montgomery, Alabama, who rose up with a sense of dignity and with her people decided not to ride segregated buses, and who responded with ungrammatical profundity to one who inquired about her weariness: "My feets is tired, but my soul is at rest." They will be the young high school and college students, the young ministers of the gospel and a host of their elders, courageously and nonviolently sitting in at lunch counters and willingly going to jail for conscience' sake. One day the South will know that when these disinherited children of God sat down at lunch counters, they were in reality standing up for what is best in the American dream and for the most sacred values in our Judaeo-Christian heritage, thereby bringing our nation back to those great wells of democracy which were dug deep by the founding fathers in their formulation of the Constitution and the Declaration of Independence.

Never before have I written so long a letter. I'm afraid it is much too long to take your precious time. I can assure you that it would have been much shorter if I had been writing from a comfortable desk, but what else can one do when he is alone in a narrow jail cell, other than write long letters, think long thoughts, and pray long prayers?

If I have said anything in this letter that overstates the truth and indicates an unreasonable impatience, I beg you to forgive me. If I have said anything that understates the truth and indicates my having a patience that allows me to settle for anything less than brotherhood, I beg God to forgive me.

I hope this letter finds you strong in the faith. I also hope that circumstances will soon make it possible for me to meet each of you, not as an integrationist or a civil-rights leader but as a fellow clergyman and a Christian brother. Let us all hope that the dark clouds of racial prejudice will soon pass away and the deep fog of misunderstanding will be lifted from our fear-drenched communities, and in some not too distant tomorrow the radiant stars of love and brotherhood will shine over our great nation with all their **scintillating** beauty.

Yours for the cause of Peace and Brotherhood,

Martin Luther King Jr.

COMMON CORE RI 4

G ALLUSION
Reread lines 275–293. Think about the usual connotations of the word *extremist*. At first, King says that he was "disappointed" at being called an extremist, but then he embraces the label. Why? How does King use biblical and historical allusions to support his reevaluation of this term?

scintillating (sĭn'tl-ā'tĭng) *adj.* sparkling **scintillate** *v.*

---

20. **James Merediths:** people like James Meredith, who endured violent opposition from whites to become the first African American to attend the University of Mississippi.

Ballad of Birmingham

Dudley Randall

"Mother dear, may I go downtown
instead of out to play,
and march the streets of Birmingham
in a freedom march today?"

"No, baby, no, you may not go,
for the dogs are fierce and wild,
and clubs and hoses, guns and jails
ain't good for a little child."

"But, mother, I won't be alone.
Other children will go with me,
and march the streets of Birmingham
to make our country free."

"No, baby, no, you may not go,
for I fear those guns will fire.
But you may go to church instead,
and sing in the children's choir."

She has combed and brushed her nightdark hair,
and bathed rose petal sweet,
and drawn white gloves on her small brown hands,
and white shoes on her feet.

The mother smiled to know her child
was in the sacred place,
but that smile was the last smile
to come upon her face.

For when she heard the explosion,
her eyes grew wet and wild.
She raced through the streets of Birmingham
calling for her child.

She clawed through bits of glass and brick,
then lifted out a shoe.
"O, here's the shoe my baby wore,
but, baby, where are you?"

Comprehension

1. **Summarize** What led to the decision to start the protests in Birmingham?
2. **Recall** What are the four steps involved in King's nonviolent campaigns?
3. **Clarify** What exactly does King mean by "nonviolent direct action"?
4. **Summarize** In King's view, what is the difference between defying the law and breaking an "unjust" law?

Text Analysis

5. **Examine Elements of an Argument** Review the chart you created as you read. Which of King's **arguments** did you find most persuasive? Consider both his position, or claim, and his reasons and evidence in your answer.
6. **Understand Analogy** An analogy is an extended, point-by-point comparison of two different things, often using a familiar example to explain a complex or abstract idea. Analyze King's analogy in lines 241–244 and discuss the persuasive appeal the analogy lends to King's argument in this letter.
7. **Interpret Allusions** Allusions can refer to people, places, events, or literary works. Choose four of King's allusions. Using the footnotes, interpret each allusion, and tell why you think King included them. Record your answers in a chart like the one shown.

Allusion	*Possible Meaning*	*Why Included*

8. **Analyze Persuasive Techniques** King's writings and speeches are filled with allusions that reveal his rhetorical mastery and breadth of knowledge. In what ways, if any, do his allusions also help him achieve the following possible purposes? Cite specific allusions that support your answers.
   - appealing to his readers' sense of right and wrong
   - establishing his credibility
   - making his ideas accessible to a wider audience
9. **Compare Texts** Compare the "Ballad of Birmingham" (page 1214) with King's letter. How is Randall's poem also an argument for acting against injustice?

Text Criticism

10. **Author's Style** King is a master of the **aphorism,** a short statement of principle or truth. Here's a memorable one: "Injustice anywhere is a threat to justice everywhere" (line 31). Find two more aphorisms and explain their effects.

When does ACTION *speak louder than words?*

Taking a stand requires action as well as words. On what issues have you been outspoken? What actions have you taken to back up your words?

COMMON CORE

RI 1 Cite textual evidence to support analysis of what the text says explicitly as well as inferences drawn from the text. **RI 4** Determine the meaning of words and phrases as they are used in a text, including figurative and connotative meanings; analyze how an author uses and refines the meaning of a key term or terms over the course of a text. **RI 6** Determine an author's point of view or purpose in a text in which the rhetoric is particularly effective, analyzing how style and content contribute to the power, persuasiveness, or beauty of the text.

Vocabulary in Context

▲ VOCABULARY PRACTICE

Show your understanding of the vocabulary words by answering these questions.

1. If I am **cognizant** of your plans, do I know about them or have I forgotten them?
2. Would a **paradoxical** statement be easy or difficult to make sense of?
3. Would a **substantive** contribution be minimal or significant?
4. Would a **rabid** response involve shouting furiously or agreeing silently?
5. If my company is **affiliated** with yours, are they competitors or partners?
6. Which might cause a **moratorium** in road building, a bad storm or potholes?
7. Is a diamond or gold more accurately described as **scintillating?**
8. Which is a **latent** ailment, a toothache or a broken arm?
9. Would an argument cause **estrangement** or a meeting with a stranger?
10. Which might be a cause for **retaliating,** losing a game or taking a taxi?

WORD LIST
affiliated
cognizant
estrangement
latent
moratorium
paradoxical
rabid
retaliating
scintillating
substantive

ACADEMIC VOCABULARY IN SPEAKING

• complex • economic • establish • ethnic • evolve

Reread King's letter, looking for specific examples of his tone. Then, in a small group discuss what kind of tone King **establishes** in his letter and what his tone says about nonviolent protest and King as a leader. Use at least two Academic Vocabulary words in your discussion.

VOCABULARY STRATEGY: WORDS AND ANALOGIES

An **analogy** compares two items or word meanings that are alike in one or more ways. Analyzing an analogy is one way of determining the meaning of unfamiliar words in context. Word analogy statements show the relationship by comparing one set of words to another set of words. For example, the following pairs are opposites, or antonyms.

rabid : calm and *affiliated : unrelated*

Word analogies can include relationships such as *synonyms, antonyms, part and whole, cause and effect,* and *location.*

PRACTICE For each word pair, create another word pair to express the same relationship. Then, identify the type of relationship.

1. architect : building ::
2. systematic : chaotic ::
3. book : page ::
4. obligatory : necessary ::
5. war : death ::

COMMON CORE

L 5 Demonstrate understanding of word relationships.

Language

COMMON CORE

L 3a Vary syntax for effect; apply an understanding of syntax to the study of complex texts when reading. **W 1** Write arguments to support claims in an analysis of substantive topics.

GRAMMAR AND STYLE: Use Rhetorical Devices

Review the Grammar and Style note on page 1208. In his letter, King uses **parallelism**—the repetition of grammatical structures—to create emphasis and to show comparisons, as in the following example:

> *Just as the prophets of the eighth century* B.C. *left their villages and carried their "thus saith the Lord" far beyond the boundaries of their home towns, and just as the Apostle Paul left his village of Tarsus and carried the gospel of Jesus Christ to the far corners of the Greco-Roman world, so am I compelled to carry the gospel of freedom beyond my own hometown.* (lines 22–27)

Notice how King uses parallel adverb clauses beginning with "just as" to set up a comparison between himself and the biblical figures he cites. What is the impact of this comparison?

PRACTICE Identify the parallel adjective clauses in the following passage from King. Then, write a paragraph of your own using similar parallel elements.

> [T]he Negro's great stumbling block in his stride toward freedom is not the White Citizen's Counciler or the Ku Klux Klanner, but the white moderate, who is more devoted to "order" than to justice; who prefers a negative peace which is the absence of tension to a positive peace which is the presence of justice; who constantly says: "I agree with you in the goal you seek, but I cannot agree with your methods of direct action"; who paternalistically believes he can set the timetable for another man's freedom; who lives by a mythical concept of time and who constantly advises the Negro to wait for a "more convenient season."

READING-WRITING CONNECTION

Expand your understanding of Martin Luther King Jr.'s letter by responding to this prompt. Then, use the **revising tips** to improve your argument.

WRITING PROMPT

WRITE A PERSUASIVE ARGUMENT Civil disobedience has been controversial ever since Henry David Thoreau first advocated it in 1847. Opposition to Martin Luther King, Jr.'s brand of nonviolent resistance came from some black activists as well as white segregationists. People still argue over the issue today.

Write a **four- to six-paragraph persuasive argument** explaining your position on the issue of nonviolent civil disobedience. Model your argument on King's, using counterarguments to anticipate objections to your view.

REVISING TIPS

- Present a clear thesis statement that states your main point.
- Use logical reasoning based on facts, expert opinions, and quotation from valid sources.
- Honestly and accurately present opposing views.
- Use persuasive language and rhetorical devices such as appeals to logic.

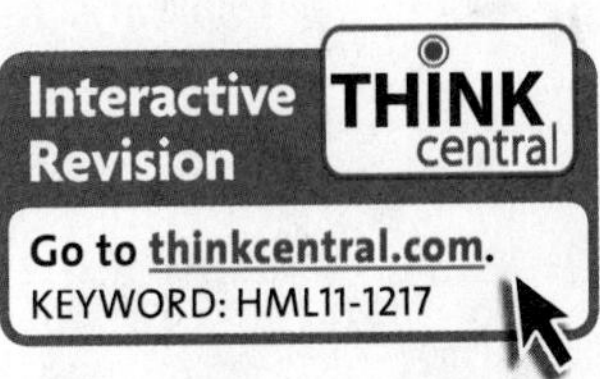

COMMON CORE

RI 2 Determine two or more central ideas of a text and analyze their development over the course of the text, including how they interact and build on one another to provide a complex analysis. **RI 5** Analyze and evaluate the effectiveness of the structure an author uses in his or her argument, including whether the structure makes points clear, convincing, and engaging. **RI 6** Determine an author's point of view or purpose in a text in which the rhetoric is particularly effective, analyzing how style and content contribute to the power, persuasiveness, or beauty of the text.

from Stride Toward Freedom

Nonfiction by Martin Luther King Jr.

For a biography of Martin Luther King Jr., see page 1202.

Necessary to Protect Ourselves

Interview with Malcolm X by Les Crane

Meet the Author

Malcolm X 1925–1965

In 1944, while Martin Luther King Jr. was attending college classes in Atlanta, 19-year-old Malcolm Little was hustling on the streets of Harlem. By 1952, a jailhouse conversion transformed Little into the political firebrand we know as Malcolm X, whose separatist views posed a serious challenge to King's integrationist vision.

Bitter Legacy Where King grew up comfortably middle-class, Little's childhood was scarred by poverty and racial violence. His outspoken father, Earl Little, was an early advocate of black separatism who was murdered by white supremacists. His mother, left alone to raise eight children in dire poverty, suffered a mental breakdown. Her children, including Malcolm, were sent to separate foster homes.

By the time he was sent to prison in 1946, Little had been brutally disillusioned about his prospects in white-dominated society. While reading in the prison library, he discovered the teachings of a small religious sect called the Nation of Islam, or the Black Muslims, who called white people "a race of devils" and promoted a vision of black pride. They advocated a radical solution to the race problem: the establishment of a separate, self-reliant black nation.

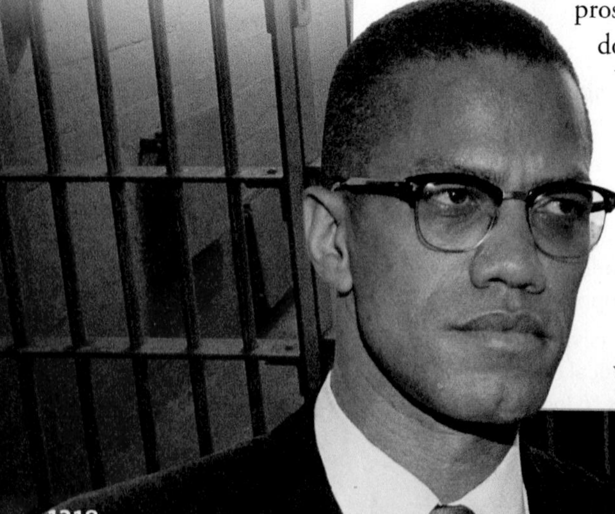

Change of Heart Inspired by the Black Muslim vision, Malcolm Little converted to Islam and changed his last name to X, symbolizing his lost African name. Once released from prison, he became an influential spokesman for the Nation of Islam and was named their first national minister. Over time, however, he became critical of the organization. In 1964, Malcolm X experienced a second spiritual conversion while making a pilgrimage to Mecca. The sight of Muslims of many races worshipping together caused him to renounce all forms of racial hatred. On his return home, Malcolm X broke with the Nation of Islam and formed the Organization of Afro-American Unity, dedicated to promoting unity among black people all over the world.

Marked Man This new direction angered many Black Muslims, including the young Louis Farrakhan, who labeled Malcolm X a traitor. In February 1965, as Malcolm X was speaking to a crowd of 400 in Harlem, he was gunned down by three assassins, two of whom were Black Muslims.

THINK central

Author Online

Go to thinkcentral.com. KEYWORD: HML11-1218

TEXT ANALYSIS: ANALYZE GENRES

The works you are about to read are two different types of writing, or **genres.** You will read part of an autobiography by Martin Luther King Jr., and an interview with Malcolm X. An **autobiography** is the story of a person's life written by that person. Autobiographies include important events from the person's life, as well as reflections on personal beliefs. An **interview** is a conversation conducted by a reporter in which responses are elicited from another person, recorded, then broadcast or published. In written format, interviews include questions by the reporter and answers by the person being interviewed. As you read, look for the distinguishing characteristics of each genre.

READING SKILL: SYNTHESIZING SOURCES

When you compare two or more sources, it is important to **synthesize,** or to bring together, the main ideas and supporting details from each text. Follow these steps for synthesizing:

- Find the main idea in each work.
- Look for details that support the main ideas.
- Compare and contrast the information in the sources to find similarities and differences.
- Put it all together by recording your findings.

As you read, fill out a chart like the one below. Then, using your chart, synthesize the information and compare the two texts.

	Main Ideas	*Supporting Details*
King		
Malcolm X		

VOCABULARY IN CONTEXT

King and Malcolm X use the boldfaced words to express their opposing views. Restate each phrase, using a different word or words for the boldfaced term.

1. need to **repudiate** those who oppress us
2. by not speaking out, **tacitly** accepting bad situations
3. cannot **succumb** to defeatist attitudes
4. realize that prejudice is applied **indiscriminately**
5. success through a **synthesis** of ideas and approaches
6. rioting and **anarchy** in the streets

 Complete the activities in your **Reader/Writer Notebook**.

How do we fight INJUSTICE?

Most people would agree that it's important to stand up for your rights if you're being treated unfairly. However, there are many different opinions about the best way to fight back against injustice. In this lesson, Martin Luther King Jr. and Malcolm X argue two very different perspectives on this issue. Traditionally they were on opposite sides of the debate about using violence as an appropriate political tool.

PRESENT What considerations do you think are important when choosing how to respond to injustice? Working in a small group, make a list of relevant concerns, such as obeying the law or achieving quick results. Then, rank them in order of importance. Share your opinions with the class.

STRIDE TOWARD FREEDOM

Martin Luther King Jr.

BACKGROUND In the 1950s, the civil rights movement focused its efforts on overturning the so-called Jim Crow laws, the segregation laws that kept African Americans from equal participation in public life. In 1954, the Supreme Court issued its decision in the landmark case *Brown v. Board of Education.* In this decision, the court declared that "separate but equal" education, a central provision of segregationist policy, was inherently discriminatory. Buoyed by this win, civil rights activists began to challenge Jim Crow through other forms of peaceful protest, such as the year-long mass boycott of segregated buses in Montgomery, Alabama, beginning in 1955. In *Stride Toward Freedom,* published in 1958, a confident and optimistic King describes the philosophy behind the successful boycott.

Analyze Visuals ▶
What does this photo reveal about the risks of nonviolent protest?

Oppressed people deal with their oppression in three characteristic ways. One way is acquiescence: the oppressed resign themselves to their doom. They **tacitly** adjust themselves to oppression, and thereby become conditioned to it. In every movement toward freedom some of the oppressed prefer to remain oppressed. Almost 2,800 years ago Moses set out to lead the children of Israel from the slavery of Egypt to the freedom of the promised land.[1] He soon discovered that slaves do not always welcome their deliverers. They become accustomed to being slaves. They would rather bear those ills they have, as Shakespeare pointed out, than flee to others that they know not of.[2] They prefer the "fleshpots of Egypt"[3] to the ordeals of emancipation. **A**

tacitly (tăs'ĭt-lē) *adj.* silently

A SYNTHESIZE RESOURCES
Reread lines 1–10. What does this paragraph tell you about the main idea?

1. **promised land:** the land of Canaan, promised by God in the Bible (Genesis 12:1–3, 7) to Abraham's descendants.
2. **bear those ills . . . know not of:** an allusion to a line in Act 3, Scene 1, of *Hamlet* by William Shakespeare.
3. **prefer the "fleshpots of Egypt":** an allusion to a line in the book of Exodus in the Bible. As Moses was leading the Israelites out of Egypt, some of them grumbled and wished they had stayed there.

Civil rights protestors being sprayed with high-pressure hoses

There is such a thing as the freedom of exhaustion. Some people are so worn down by the yoke of oppression that they give up. A few years ago in the slum areas of Atlanta, a Negro guitarist used to sing almost daily: "Been down so long that down don't bother me." This is the type of negative freedom and resignation that often engulfs the life of the oppressed.

But this is not the way out. To accept passively an unjust system is to cooperate with that system; thereby the oppressed become as evil as the oppressor. Noncooperation with evil is as much a moral obligation as is cooperation with good. The oppressed must never allow the conscience of the oppressor to slumber. Religion reminds every man that he is his brother's keeper.[4] To accept injustice or segregation passively is to say to the oppressor that his actions are morally right. It is a way of allowing his conscience to fall asleep. At this moment the oppressed fails to be his brother's keeper. So acquiescence—while often the easier way—is not the moral way. It is the way of the coward. The Negro cannot win the respect of his oppressor by acquiescing; he merely increases the oppressor's arrogance and contempt. Acquiescence is interpreted as proof of the Negro's inferiority. The Negro cannot win the respect of the white people of the South or the peoples of the world if he is willing to sell the future of his children for his personal and immediate comfort and safety. **B**

A second way that oppressed people sometimes deal with oppression is to resort to physical violence and corroding hatred. Violence often brings about momentary results. Nations have frequently won their independence in battle. But in spite of temporary victories, violence never brings permanent peace. It solves no social problem; it merely creates new and more complicated ones.

Violence as a way of achieving racial justice is both impractical and immoral. It is impractical because it is a descending spiral ending in destruction for all. The old law of an eye for an eye[5] leaves everybody blind. It is immoral because it seeks to humiliate the opponent rather than win his understanding; it seeks to annihilate rather than to convert. Violence is immoral because it thrives on hatred rather than love. It destroys community and makes brotherhood impossible. It leaves society in monologue rather than dialogue. Violence ends by defeating itself. It creates bitterness in the survivors and brutality in the destroyers. A voice echoes through time saying to every potential Peter, "Put up your sword."[6] History is cluttered with the wreckage of nations that failed to follow this command. **C**

If the American Negro and other victims of oppression **succumb** to the temptation of using violence in the struggle for freedom, future generations will be the recipients of a desolate night of bitterness, and our chief legacy to them will be an endless reign of meaningless chaos. Violence is not the way.

Language Coach

Word Definitions
Engulfs (line 15) means "flow over and swallow up" or "overwhelm." (Imagine water overflowing an island.) What does King say can overwhelm a person who is exhausted from oppression?

B SYNTHESIZE SOURCES
In lines 19–28, King states his position on how the oppressed should respond to oppression. What words and phrases reveal the specific historical example that has shaped King's thinking?

C SYNTHESIZE SOURCES
What support does King provide for his statement that violent resistance is unprofitable?

---

4. **his brother's keeper:** In the book of Genesis, after Cain killed his brother Abel, he denied knowing Abel's whereabouts by asking, "Am I my brother's keeper?" In general, the saying refers to a reluctance to accept responsibility for others.
5. **an eye for an eye:** an allusion to Exodus 21:23–25: "You shall give life for life, eye for eye. . . ."
6. **Peter . . . sword":** When Jesus' disciple Peter drew his sword to try to protect Jesus, Jesus condemned his use of violence.

succumb (sə-kŭm') *v.* to give in, especially to overpowering force or strength

The third way open to oppressed people in their quest for freedom is the way of nonviolent resistance. Like the **synthesis** in Hegelian philosophy,[7] the principle of nonviolent resistance seeks to reconcile the truths of two opposites—acquiescence and violence—while avoiding the extremes and immoralities of both. The nonviolent resister agrees with the person who acquiesces that one should not be physically aggressive toward his opponent but he balances the equation by agreeing with the person of violence that evil must be resisted. He avoids the nonresistance of the former and the violent resistance of the latter. With nonviolent resistance, no individual or group need submit to any wrong, nor need anyone resort to violence in order to right a wrong.

synthesis (sĭn'thĭ-sĭs) *n.* the union of parts or elements into a whole

It seems to me that this is the method that must guide the actions of the Negro in the present crisis in race relations. Through nonviolent resistance the Negro will be able to rise to the noble height of opposing the unjust system while loving the perpetrators of the system. The Negro must work passionately and unrelentingly for full stature as a citizen, but he must not use inferior methods to gain it. He must never come to terms with falsehood, malice, hate, or destruction. **D**

D ANALYZE GENRES
Reread lines 58–63. What characteristics help you understand that this is an autobiography?

Nonviolent resistance makes it possible for the Negro to remain in the South and struggle for his rights. The Negro's problem will not be solved by running away. He cannot listen to the glib suggestion of those who would urge him to migrate en masse to other sections of the country. By grasping his great opportunity in the South he can make a lasting contribution to the moral strength of the nation and set a sublime example of courage for generations yet unborn.

By nonviolent resistance, the Negro can also enlist all men of good will in his struggle for equality. The problem is not a purely racial one, with Negroes set against whites. In the end, it is not a struggle between people at all, but a tension between justice and injustice. Nonviolent resistance is not aimed against oppressors but against oppression. Under its banner consciences, not racial groups, are enlisted.

If the Negro is to achieve the goal of integration, he must organize himself into a militant and nonviolent mass movement. All three elements are indispensable. The movement for equality and justice can only be a success if it has both a mass and militant character; the barriers to be overcome require both. Nonviolence is an imperative in order to bring about ultimate community. **E**

E SYNTHESIZE SOURCES
In lines 70–80, what does King say is the best way to confront racism? How does he support this view?

A mass movement of a militant quality that is not at the same time committed to nonviolence tends to generate conflict, which in turn breeds anarchy. The support of the participants and the sympathy of the uncommitted are both inhibited by the threat that bloodshed will engulf the community. This reaction in turn encourages the opposition to threaten and resort to force. When, however, the mass movement **repudiates** violence while moving resolutely toward its goal, its opponents are revealed as the instigators and practitioners of violence if it occurs. Then public support is magnetically attracted to the advocates of nonviolence, while those who employ violence are literally disarmed by overwhelming sentiment against their stand.

repudiate (rĭ-pyo͞o'dē-āt') *v.* to reject or renounce

7. **Hegelian** (hā-gā'lē-ən) **philosophy:** the philosophy of Georg Hegel (1770–1831), which proposed that each situation has an opposite and that both extremes will eventually be reconciled.

NECESSARY *to* PROTECT OURSELVES

Interview with Malcolm X by Les Crane

BACKGROUND Malcolm X gave the following TV interview in 1964, at a time when violence against civil rights workers had escalated. Shocking images of protestors being beaten, clubbed, and tear-gassed had become staples of daily news coverage. Across the South, white supremacists tried to squelch the growing movement with murder, rifle attacks, bombings, and arson, crimes that frequently went unpunished. As attacks increased, many African Americans grew impatient with King's nonviolent tactics, expressing anger that chilled white listeners.

Events came to a head in 1964, with the Freedom Summer in Mississippi. Thousands of idealistic college students joined local civil rights activists in a massive voter registration drive, and violence exploded. Three young civil rights workers were murdered by local Klansmen with the help of the police. Despite increased FBI presence in the state, by summer's end 4 workers were dead, 80 had been beaten, and scores of black churches and businesses had been torched or bombed.

Analyze Visuals ▶
Based on this photo, what impressions do you have of Malcolm X as a leader?

Crane: You've been a critic of some of the Negro leadership in this country—Martin Luther King, Roy Wilkins, Abernathy,[1] and others—have you changed in your feelings toward them of late? F

Malcolm X: I think all of us should be critics of each other. Whenever you can't stand criticism you can never grow. I don't think that it serves any purpose for the leaders of our people to waste their time fighting each other needlessly. I think that we accomplish more when we sit down in private and iron out

F ANALYZE GENRES
What details tell you that this is an interview?

1. **Roy Wilkins, Abernathy:** Roy Wilkins (1901–1981) was executive secretary of the National Association for the Advancement of Colored People (NAACP) from 1955 to 1977. Ralph Abernathy (1926–1990) helped Martin Luther King Jr. found the Southern Christian Leadership Conference to combat racism.

Malcolm X at a Black Muslim rally

Nation of Islam members at a community event in Harlem

whatever differences that may exist and try and then do something constructive for the benefit of our people. But on the other hand, I don't think that we should be above criticism. I don't think that anyone should be above criticism.

Crane: Violence or the threat of violence has always surrounded you. Speeches that you've made have been interpreted as being threats. You have made statements reported in the press about how the Negroes should go out and arm themselves, form militias of their own. I read a thing once, a statement I believe you made that every Negro should belong to the National Rifle Association— **G**

Malcolm X: No, I said this: That in areas of this country where the government has proven its—either its inability or its unwillingness to protect the lives and property of our people, then it's only fair to expect us to do whatever is necessary to protect ourselves. And in situations like Mississippi, places like Mississippi where the government actually has proven its inability to protect us—and it has been proven that ofttimes the police officers and sheriffs themselves are involved in the murder that takes place against our people—then I feel, and I say that anywhere, that our people should start doing what is necessary to protect ourselves. This doesn't mean

Language Coach

Word Definitions Read lines 16–19. What is the difference between *inability* and *unwillingness* (line 17)? Refer to a dictionary if necessary. What would you think about a government that was unable to protect you? What about a government that was unwilling to do so?

G SYNTHESIZE SOURCES Usually in an interview, the reporter sets the agenda for the questions, and thus, determines the main ideas. Based on this comment from Crane, what is one of the main points in this interview?

that we should buy rifles and go out and initiate attacks **indiscriminately** against whites. But it does mean that we should get whatever is necessary to protect ourselves in a country or in an area where the governmental ability to protect us has broken down—

indiscriminately (ĭn'dĭ-skrĭm'ə-nĭt-lē) *adv.* randomly

Crane: Therefore you do not agree with Dr. King's Gandhian philosophy[2]—

Malcolm X: My belief in brotherhood would never restrain me in any way from protecting myself in a society from a people whose disrespect for brotherhood makes them feel inclined to put my neck on a tree at the end of a rope.[3] [*Applause*]

Crane: Well, it sounds as though you could be preaching a sort of an **anarchy**—

anarchy (ăn'ər-kē) *n.* an absence of political authority

Malcolm X: No, no. I respect government and respect law. But does the government and the law respect us? If the FBI, which is what people depend upon on a national scale to protect the morale and the property and the lives of the people, can't do so when the property and lives of Negroes and whites who try and help Negroes are concerned, then I think that it's only fair to expect elements to do whatever is necessary to protect themselves.

And this is no departure from normal procedure. Because right here in New York City you have vigilante committees[4] that have been set up by groups who see where their neighborhood community is endangered and the law can't do anything about it. So—and even their lives aren't at stake. So—but the fear, Les, seems to come into existence only when someone says Negroes should form vigilante committees to protect their lives and their property. **H**

I'm not advocating the breaking of any laws. But I say that our people will never be respected as human beings until we react as other normal, intelligent human beings do. And this country came into existence by people who were tired of tyranny and oppression and exploitation and the brutality that was being inflicted upon them by powers higher than they, and I think that it is only fair to expect us, sooner or later, to do likewise.

COMMON CORE RI 5, RI 7

H SYNTHESIZE SOURCES
Synthesizing sources from two different genres requires you to see past obvious differences—differences in format, intended audience, or layout—and to focus closely on the ideas and arguments in the two texts. In lines 39–44, Malcolm X talks about the role of violence in the civil rights movement. Where does King discuss violence in the previous text? Find specific passages on violence that show how the two men disagree or agree. How does each author support his arguments?

---

2. **Gandhian** (gän'dē-ən) **philosophy:** Mohandas Gandhi (1869–1948) was an Indian nationalist and spiritual leader. His use of nonviolent civil disobedience forced the British to grant India its independence in 1947.
3. **put my neck . . . rope:** an allusion to lynching, the practice of putting someone to death without due process of law. Many African Americans were lynched, usually by hanging.
4. **vigilante** (vĭj'ə-lăn'tē) **committees:** volunteer citizen groups that unlawfully assume powers such as pursuing and punishing suspected criminals or offenders.

After Reading

Comprehension

1. **Recall** What three ways of dealing with oppression does Martin Luther King Jr. identify?
2. **Clarify** In King's view, what three qualities must a movement have in order to achieve the goal of integration?
3. **Summarize** How does Malcolm X justify his criticisms of other civil rights leaders?

COMMON CORE

RI 2 Determine two or more central ideas of a text and analyze their development over the course of the text, including how they interact and build on one another to provide a complex analysis; provide an objective summary of the text. **RI 5** Analyze and evaluate the effectiveness of the structure an author uses in his or her argument, including whether the structure makes points clear, convincing, and engaging. **RI 6** Determine an author's point of view or purpose in a text in which the rhetoric is particularly effective, analyzing how style and content contribute to the power, persuasiveness, or beauty of the text.

Text Analysis

4. **Identify Allusion** Reread lines 47–50 of "Necessary to Protect Ourselves." Identify the historical event that Malcolm X is alluding to. What point does he make by invoking this event?
5. **Synthesize Sources** Review the chart you created as you read both texts. What are the main differences between the two leaders? What beliefs, if any, do they have in common? Be specific in your answers.
6. **Analyze Genres** Think about the two works you just read. How do these two genres allow people to express their opinions in similar and different ways?
7. **Analyze Structure** The structure of King's argument follows the formal logic of Hegelian philosophy, in which two opposing ideas are merged into a unified concept, or synthesis. To analyze this structure, complete a diagram like the one shown. In what way does the third response resolve the problems of the first two?

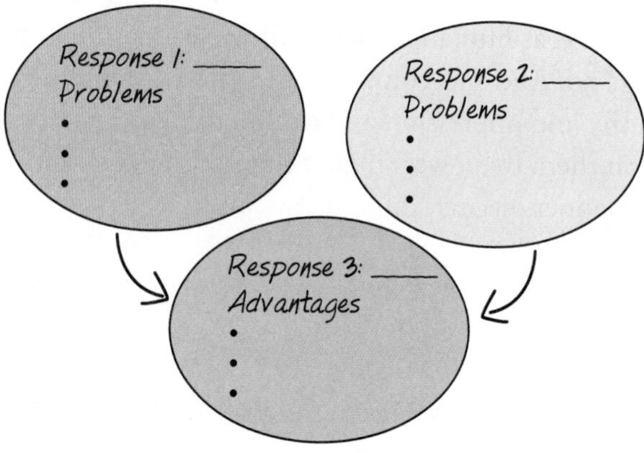

8. **Make Judgments** Many commentators criticized Martin Luther King Jr., for using radical and provocative tactics. In what ways might perceptions of King's philosophy have changed after Malcolm X gained public prominence?

Text Criticism

9. **Biographical Context** Reread the author biographies of King (page 1202) and Malcolm X (page 1218). What aspects of their personal histories may have influenced their different approaches to fighting racial injustice?

How do we fight INJUSTICE?

Today, many people around the world are persecuted. If you could talk to one such person, what would you tell him or her? How would you advise this person to fight injustice?

Vocabulary in Context

▲ VOCABULARY PRACTICE

Choose the letter of the phrase that defines or is related to the boldfaced word.

1. **succumb:** (a) a golfer practicing, (b) an army surrendering, (c) a teenager voting
2. **synthesis:** (a) a proposal combining several views, (b) a detailed analysis of a plan, (c) a group of protestors
3. **anarchy:** (a) an art auction, (b) an angry mob, (c) hereditary rule
4. **indiscriminately:** (a) a decision based on evidence, (b) a choice made without thought, (c) unfair hiring practices
5. **repudiate:** (a) retype a report, (b) vote someone out of office, (c) renew a promise
6. **tacitly:** (a) agree by nodding, (b) disagree by shouting, (c) celebrate by singing

WORD LIST
anarchy
indiscriminately
repudiate
succumb
synthesis
tacitly

ACADEMIC VOCABULARY IN SPEAKING

• complex • economic • establish • ethnic • evolve

Imagine that Martin Luther King Jr. and Malcolm X were discussing their respective beliefs about confronting racism. What do you think they would say to each other? In a small group, debate this **complex** issue by representing these two men's beliefs. Remember to keep the debate polite, focused, and in line with the beliefs of Malcolm X and King. Use at least three Academic Vocabulary words in your debate.

COMMON CORE

L 4b Identify and correctly use patterns of word changes that indicate different meanings or parts of speech. **SL 1b** Work with peers to promote civil, democratic discussions. **SL 1c** Ensure a hearing for a full range of positions on an issue.

VOCABULARY STRATEGY: THE GREEK PREFIX *syn-*

The **origin** of the prefix *syn-*, which appears at the beginning of the vocabulary word *synthesis*, is the Greek language. *Syn-* means "together" or "at the same time." This prefix, which may also be spelled *sym-* or *syl-*, is found in a number of English words, both scientific and nonscientific. To understand words with *syn-*, use your knowledge of the origin of the prefix, look for context clues, or consult a dictionary.

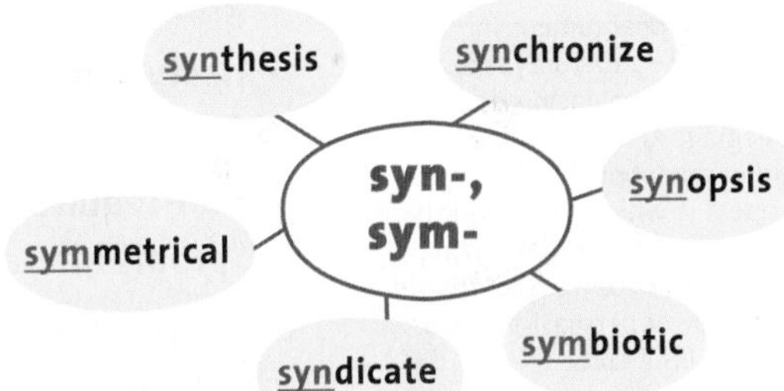

PRACTICE Choose the word from the word web that best completes each sentence. Use context clues to help you or, if necessary, check a dictionary.

1. They were able to _____ their watches and meet promptly at noon.
2. Though the halves of people's faces aren't exactly _____, they are fairly close.
3. Some animals have a _____ relationship and depend on each other for survival.
4. Groups or individuals in a _____ work together for some common interest.
5. A _____ can provide a quick overview of a story, play, or report.

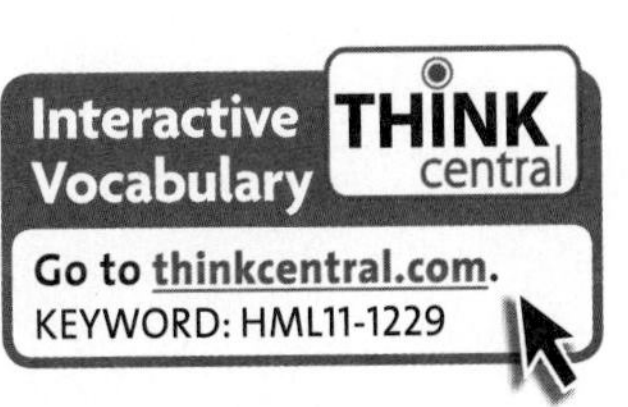

Interactive Vocabulary
THINK central
Go to thinkcentral.com.
KEYWORD: HML11-1229

Reading for Information

Martin Luther King Jr.: He Showed Us the Way

Essay

Use with "Stride Toward Freedom" and "Necessary to Protect Ourselves," beginning on pages 1220 and 1224.

COMMON CORE

RI 5 Analyze and evaluate the effectiveness of the structure an author uses in his or her exposition or argument, including whether the structure makes points clear, convincing, and engaging. **RI 6** Determine an author's point of view or purpose in a text in which the rhetoric is particularly effective, analyzing how style and content contribute to the power, persuasiveness, or beauty of the text.

You have just read two civil rights leaders' positions on the use of force in political resistance. Now you will learn why César Chávez, a leader in the crusade for the fair treatment of migrant farm workers, advocated nonviolence to achieve his goals. As you read his argument, bear in mind that later you will be asked to support your own opinion on this weapon for social change.

Standards Focus: Analyze an Argument

A well-formed argument typically contains a **claim,** the writer or speaker's position on a problem or issue; **support,** which consists of logical reasons and valid evidence that help to justify the claim; and a **counterargument,** brief arguments that refute or answer objections to any opposing claims. A strong argument is based on a **general principle** that clearly links the verifiable support to the claim. If you can't accept the general principle as a truth, then the entire argument falls apart.

Sometimes, though, writers and speakers use faulty reasoning, or **logical fallacies,** to support their claims. Some common logical fallacies include

- **circular logic:** supporting a statement by stating it in different words;
- **stereotyping:** broad statements about people on the basis of their gender, ethnicity, race, or political, social, professional, or religious group;
- **hasty generalization:** a conclusion drawn from too little evidence or from evidence that is biased;
- **non-sequitur:** a conclusion that does not follow logically from the "proof" offered to support it.

As you read, analyze the argument made by Chávez, completing a chart similar to the one below.

	Notes
Claim	Nonviolence is the "only weapon that Christians who struggle for social change can claim as their own."
General Principle	
Support	
Counterargument(s)	

MARTIN LUTHER KING JR.: He Showed Us the Way

César Chávez

In honoring Martin Luther King Jr.'s memory we also acknowledge nonviolence as a truly powerful weapon to achieve equality and liberation—in fact, the only weapon that Christians who struggle for social change can claim as their own.

Dr. King's entire life was an example of power that nonviolence brings to bear in the real world. It is an example that inspired much of the philosophy and strategy of the farm workers' movement. This observance of Dr. King's death gives us the best possible opportunity to recall the principles with which our struggle has grown and matured. **A**

Our conviction is that human life is a very special possession given by God to man and that no one has the right to take it for any reason or for any cause, however just it may be.

We are also convinced that nonviolence is more powerful than violence. Nonviolence supports you if you have a just and moral cause. Nonviolence provides the opportunity to stay on the offensive, and that is of crucial importance to win any contest.

If we resort to violence then one of two things will happen: either the violence will be escalated and there will be many injuries and perhaps deaths on both sides, or there will be total demoralization of the workers. **B**

Nonviolence has exactly the opposite effect. If, for every violent act committed against us, we respond with nonviolence, we attract people's support. We can gather the support of millions who have a conscience and would rather see a nonviolent resolution to problems. We are convinced that when people are faced with a direct appeal from the poor struggling nonviolently against great odds, they will react positively. The American people and people everywhere still yearn for justice. It is to that yearning that we appeal.

A ANALYZE AN ARGUMENT
Notice that Chávez states his **claim** in his opening sentence. Now reread lines 4–7 to identify his first piece of **support** for this claim. Note this on your chart.

B ANALYZE AN ARGUMENT
Reread lines 11–16. What reasons does Chávez give to support his conviction that "nonviolence is more powerful than violence"? Note these reasons as "support" in your chart.

Language Coach

Fixed Expressions "Work on the theory" is a **fixed expression**—a normal, often used combination of words—meaning "function under a certain belief." Another verb used with *theory* is *advance.* Use a fixed expression with *advance* in a sentence of your own.

C ANALYZE AN ARGUMENT
In this paragraph, Chávez anticipates objection to his claim about the advantages of nonviolence. Identify these objections.

D ANALYZE AN ARGUMENT
What counterarguments does Chávez provide to refute the objections he just anticipated? Note these in your chart.

E ANALYZE AN ARGUMENT
What does Chávez say about those who espouse violence?

But if we are committed to nonviolence only as a strategy or tactic, then if it fails our only alternative is to turn to violence. So we must balance the strategy with a clear understanding of what we are doing. However important the struggle is and however much misery, poverty and exploitation exist, we know that it cannot be more important than one human life. We work on the theory that men and women who are truly concerned about people are nonviolent by nature. These people become violent when the deep concern they have for people is frustrated and when they are faced with seemingly insurmountable odds.

We advocate militant nonviolence as our means of achieving justice for our people, but we are not blind to the feelings of frustration, impatience and anger which see the inside every farm worker. The burdens of generations of poverty and powerlessness lie heavy in the fields of America. If we fail, there are those who will see violence as the shortcut to change. **C**

It is precisely to overcome these frustrations that we have involved masses of people in their own struggle throughout the movement. Freedom is best experienced through participation and self-determination, and free men and women instinctively prefer democratic change to any other means. Thus, demonstrations and marches, strikes and boycotts are not only weapons against the growers, but our way of avoiding the senseless violence that brings no honor to any class or community. The boycott, as Gandhi taught, is the most nearly perfect instrument of nonviolent change, allowing masses of people to participate actively in a cause.

When victory comes through violence, it is a victory with strings attached. If we beat the growers at the expense of violence, victory would come at the expense of injury and perhaps death. Such a thing would have a tremendous impact on us. We would lose regard for human beings. Then the struggle would become a mechanical thing. When you lose your sense of life and justice, you lose your strength. **D**

The greater the oppression, the more leverage nonviolence holds. Violence does not work in the long run and if it is temporarily successful, it replaces one violent form of power with another just as violent. People suffer from violence. Examine history. Who gets killed in the case of violent revolution? The poor, the workers. The people of the land are the ones who give their bodies and don't really gain that much for it. We believe it is too big a price to pay for not getting anything. Those who espouse violence exploit people. To call men to arms with many promises, to ask them to give up their lives for a cause and then not produce for them afterwards, is the most vicious type of oppression. **E**

We know that most likely we are not going to do anything else the rest of our lives except build our union. For us there is nowhere else to go. Although we would like to see victory come soon, we are willing to wait. In this sense time is our ally. We learned many years ago that the rich may have money, but the poor have time.

It has been our experience that few men or women ever have the opportunity to know the true satisfaction that comes with giving one's life totally in the nonviolent struggle for justice. Martin Luther King Jr., was one of these unique servants and from him we learned many of the lessons that have guided us. For these lessons and for his sacrifice for the poor and oppressed, Dr. King's memory will be cherished in the hearts of the farm workers forever.

Comprehension

1. **Clarify** In addition to serving as weapons against growers, how do boycotts benefit the masses of people who participate in them?

Text Analysis

2. **Examine General Principle** What is Chávez's basic assumption about social change and just people? Might someone disagree with him? Explain.
3. **Analyze an Argument** Chávez acknowledges that nonviolent resistance has certain limitations. How does he answer each of the following objections?
   - People who have been oppressed may feel legitimately frustrated or impatient and turn to violence as a shortcut to change.
   - Violence does sometimes bring about victory.

COMMON CORE

RI 5 Analyze and evaluate the effectiveness of the structure an author uses in his or her argument, including whether the structure makes points clear, convincing, and engaging. **RI 6** Determine an author's point of view or purpose in a text in which the rhetoric is particularly effective, analyzing how style and content contribute to the power, persuasiveness, or beauty of the text. **W 2** Write informative/explanatory texts to examine and convey complex ideas, concepts, and information through the effective selection and analysis of content. **W 9** Draw evidence from informational texts to support analysis, reflection, and research.

Read for Information: Analyze an Argument

WRITING PROMPT

Find an article in a newspaper that argues a position. Analyze the argument to determine if the writer clearly states his or her claim, includes strong supporting evidence, and addresses possible opposing claims with counterarguments.

Use these questions to help you with the writing prompt:

1. What claim is the writer making? What general principle is the claim based on? Do you agree or disagree with the general principle?
2. What support does the writer give to uphold his or her claim? Does the writer cite specific facts, statistics, expert opinions, and true-life examples as evidence? Or does the writer include unfounded opinions as evidence?
3. Does the writer use any logical fallacies, such as hasty generalizations or stereotypes?
4. What counterarguments does the writer include? Are they valid arguments to objections that someone might raise?
5. Overall, how well do you think the writer argues his or her point?

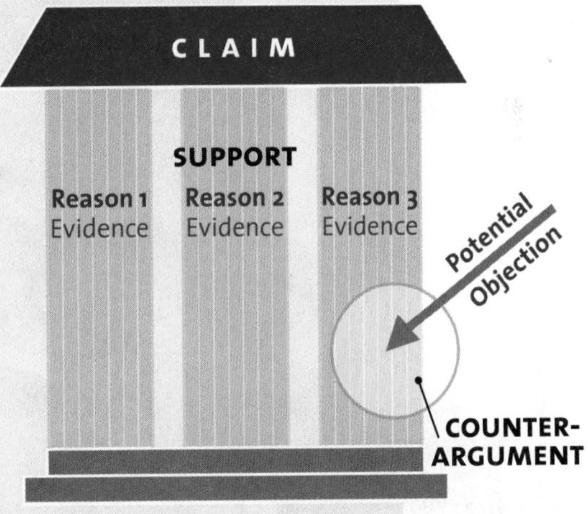

Media Study

Perspectives in the News

TV Newscast Clip / Magazine Article on Media Smart DVD-ROM

COMMON CORE

RI 7 Integrate and evaluate multiple sources of information presented in different media or formats as well as in words in order to address a question or solve a problem.

Does the news SHAPE *history?*

Recall the last time the news reported the death of someone who had played a pivotal role in history. Did the report provide new insights or change your opinion of the individual? Or did it reinforce your prior perceptions? In this lesson, you'll examine the way two different news forms covered a national figure and analyze the ways news reports can shape your **impressions** of that figure.

Background

Cultivating Activism As a teenager, César Chávez worked the fields of California with his family. After serving in the U.S. Navy in World War II, he returned to the fields but grew more politically active.

Inspired by the life and nonviolent teachings of Mohandas Gandhi and the activism of Martin Luther King Jr., Chávez helped found the National Farm Workers Association (NFWA) in 1962. "Nonviolence in action is a very potent force and it can't be stopped," said Chávez of the NFWA's founding principle. By staging peaceful strikes, marches, and boycotts, as well as fasting (as Gandhi had) in protest, Chávez garnered a wide swath of support for *La Causa* (the cause). Followers rallied to the call "*¡Sí Se Puede!*" which, translated to English, means "Yes, we can!"

Another force contributing to Chávez's cause, as well as to the larger American civil rights movement of the 1950s and 60s, was mass media. Print and network TV news coverage of marches, boycotts, and other acts of protest helped to fuel a spirit of activism nationwide. Millions were stirred by coverage that spotlighted both extraordinary leaders like Chávez and ordinary people.

César Chávez died in 1993. In following the peaceful legacy of Gandhi and King, Chávez created one of his own.

Media Literacy: Historical Perspectives in the News

The news media uses images and words to depict the work of political figures who, in time, become history makers. Just as writers of literature present their perspectives through the use of tone and diction, journalists convey certain ideas, values, and beliefs through those elements and others that are unique to news reports. In addition, journalists can shape an audience's perceptions by reporting on the individual from a particular perspective.

News reports can appear in both electronic and print forms. To help you analyze the perspective of a news report, examine the images and statements to determine the overall purpose of the report. Then think about how the report affects your perceptions of the person depicted.

STRATEGIES FOR ANALYZING NEWS REPORTS

TV News Reports

A typical TV news report is quite brief. To convey a strong impression of the report's subject, journalists choose the visual and verbal elements carefully.

- Focus on the **footage**—the film, videotape, and photographs that are edited into a report. The footage compiled on a historical figure can be edited to portray the individual in different ways.
- Notice what the **anchor** says in the **lead-in,** the introduction. The emphasis journalists put on certain words can suggest a figure's historical significance.
- Pay attention to descriptive words used in a reporter's **voice-over,** the narration that plays as images are shown. Also, listen for **sound bites,** statements excerpted from interviews or speeches that are edited into the report. Sound bites can be selected to create a certain impression of subject.

Magazine Article

The typical magazine feature article might cover a subject in more than one page, providing in-depth coverage.

- Consider how the **headline** and **subhead** frame the content of the article for a reader.
- Preview the **opening paragraph,** which often sets the tone for the article and is intended to draw in the reader.
- Make inferences about the **images.** Think about why certain photographs were chosen for an article.
- Scrutinize **quotes,** which might be made by the subject of the article or by others. Determine what the quotes reveal about the subject.

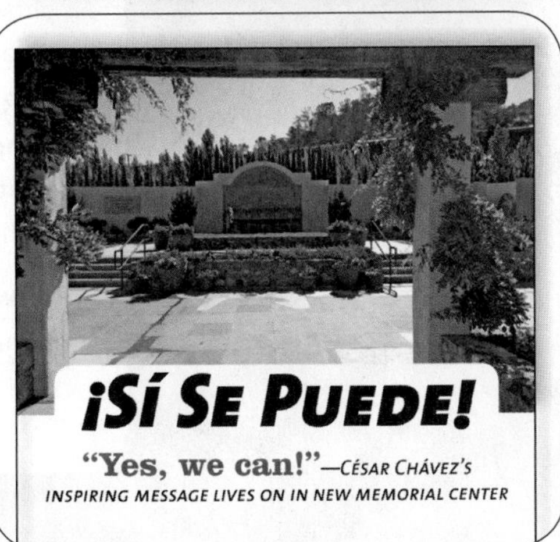

¡SÍ SE PUEDE!
"Yes, we can!"—CÉSAR CHÁVEZ'S
INSPIRING MESSAGE LIVES ON IN NEW MEMORIAL CENTER

Media Smart DVD-ROM

- **Selection 1:** "Chávez" from the CBS Nightly News
- **Type:** Newscast clip
- **Anchor:** Dan Rather
- **Reporter:** John Blackstone
- **Running time:** 2.5 minutes
- **Selection 2:** "¡Sí Se Puede!"
- **Type:** Magazine article

Viewing Guide for

News Perspectives

View the news clip and access the full text of the magazine article on the DVD. As you watch the TV news report, focus on the images that are used to tell César Chávez's story and listen for any descriptive words about Chávez's life and work. As you read the magazine article, look for the ways in which the writer describes Chávez and his legacy. To help you analyze these pieces, refer to these questions.

NOW VIEW

FIRST VIEWING: Comprehension

1. **Recall** In the TV news report, what does Chávez say he regards as his "biggest single accomplishment"?
2. **Summarize** Based on your review of the headline, subhead, and opening paragraph of the magazine article, summarize the ways Chávez has been honored since his death.

CLOSE VIEWING: Media Literacy

3. **Analyze Statements** What **descriptions** did you notice in the news anchor's **lead-in,** or introduction to the Chávez piece, or in the reporter's **voice-over** that reveal respect for the historical figure's accomplishments?
4. **Analyze Sound Bites** The clip includes a **sound bite** in which an individual states about Chávez, "His biggest legacy was to give his life for other people." Why do you think the news report includes this sound bite?
5. **Make Judgments** Briefly review the magazine article to choose a word or phrase that you think was carefully chosen to comment on the legacy of César Chávez. Describe what meaning this choice would have for viewers who had not been old enough to be aware of the leader in his lifetime.
6. **Compare Purposes** When and why do you think the TV news report was created? When and why was the magazine article published? Examine each news format and use a comparison chart to compare the purposes.

News Report	When First Reported	Purpose for Report
"Chávez"		
"¡Sí Se Puede!"		

Write or Discuss

Determine Perspectives In two brief statements, describe the perspective of both the newscast clip and the magazine article. Review the reports closely, jotting down any descriptive words or phrases about César Chávez that give you a sense of him as a person and as a leader. In addition, refer to the chart you devised to compare the purposes of the news forms. Think about

- the overall tone each news report conveys
- the details each piece presents about Chávez's life and times
- the visual elements
- the use of sources who provide sound bites and quotes

COMMON CORE

RI 7 Integrate and evaluate multiple sources of information presented in different media or formats as well as in words in order to address a question or solve a problem. **W 2** Write informative/explanatory texts to examine and convey complex ideas, concepts, and information clearly and accurately through the effective selection, organization, and analysis of content. **SL 2** Integrate multiple sources of information presented in diverse formats and media in order to make informed decisions and solve problems.

Produce Your Own Media

Create a News Feature Celebrate the life of someone who has made a positive impact on your community by creating a news feature. The subject could be a friend, a family member, or anyone else you admire. The feature can be a visual piece, in the form of video, or a written piece with photographs that illustrate it in the style of a magazine.

HERE'S HOW Here are some suggestions for creating your news feature:

- Decide on your perspective for the feature. The basis for your perspective might be the subject's achievements or personal qualities.
- Research your subject: do interviews, gather facts and any visual images you may want to use. If possible, interview the people who know the subject.
- For a TV news story, write a script that plots out which visuals you will use with your voice-over narration. Allow plenty of time for actually putting your scrapbook, video, or presentation piece together.
- For a magazine article based on your research, write a first draft that covers as much of the material as you see fit. Then, edit your article with an eye on where you might be able to use an image or two of the person in the layout.

Tech Tip

You can use digital pictures with a presentation software program and provide the voice-over in real time.

Further Exploration

Analyze Words With a partner or in a small group, find two different types of media that cover the same subject or event. For example, the report could be a TV newscast and a weekly newsmagazine about a development in the U.S. space program, or a hometown newspaper and a national sports magazine reporting on steroid use in baseball, and so on. Look closely at each news source and jot down the adjectives and adverbs used to describe the event or people involved. What perspective do you think these words convey? Consider

- who created the news piece and what their opinion of the subject might be
- what audience the news piece is written for

Cite specific examples from the media sources to support your impressions.

COMMON CORE

RI 3 Analyze a complex set of ideas or sequence of events and explain how specific individuals, ideas, or events interact and develop over the course of the text. **RI 6** Determine an author's point of view or purpose in a text in which the rhetoric is particularly effective, analyzing how content contributes to the power, persuasiveness, or beauty of the text.

from Coming of Age in Mississippi

Autobiography by Anne Moody

Meet the Author

Anne Moody born 1940

Anne Moody was one of many dedicated college students who were on the frontlines in the battle for civil rights. In her award-winning autobiography, she details the dangers she and other young activists faced as they challenged segregation laws across the South. Her unflinching descriptions of taunts, beatings, and intimidation reveal the violent realities of nonviolent protest. They also call to mind the words of Martin Luther King Jr., who commended these brave young men and women for "their sublime courage, their willingness to suffer, and their amazing discipline in the midst of great provocation."

Climate of Fear Moody was the oldest of nine children born to desperately poor African-American farmers in rural Mississippi. When she was just nine years old, Moody began working after school as a maid to help her family pay for food and clothing. Periodic acts of racist violence effectively intimidated the black community in Moody's hometown. When local white supremacists set fire to her neighbor's shack, killing the family inside, her mother advised her, "Just act like you don't know nothing." But Moody was part of a new generation that would no longer be silenced.

Dedicated Activist Moody first attended Natchez Junior College and later transferred to Tougaloo College, graduating in 1964. As a college student, she worked with major civil rights organizations such as the Congress for Racial Equality (CORE) and the National Association for the Advancement of Colored People (NAACP). Later, she became civil rights coordinator at Cornell University. Throughout her time in the movement, Moody faced constant threats to her life and worked to the point of exhaustion to integrate public facilities, extend voting rights, and promote literacy. Commenting on King's famous speech "I Have a Dream," she once quipped, "We never have time to sleep, much less dream." Often frustrated and discouraged at the slow pace of social change, Moody came to see the civil rights struggle as part of a larger fight for universal human rights. As she explained, "It's the fight of every ethnic and racial minority, every suppressed and exploited person, every one of the millions who daily suffer one or another of the indignities of the powerless and voiceless masses." Her autobiography is a moving testament to the dedication and courage that inspired hundreds of thousands of people to take action for social justice.

DID YOU KNOW?

Anne Moody . . .

- went to college on a basketball scholarship.
- left the civil rights movement over concerns about black nationalism.
- rarely gives interviews or makes public appearances.

Author Online THINK central

Go to thinkcentral.com. KEYWORD: HML11-1238

Negro Sitdowns Stir Fear Of Wider Unrest in South

TEXT ANALYSIS: EYEWITNESS ACCOUNT

Anne Moody wrote this **eyewitness account** to document the violence she faced as a civil rights worker in Mississippi. Like a camera, Moody records events from her vantage point on the scene. She uses precise, factual **diction** to capture what she sees.

At exactly 11 A.M., Pearlena, Memphis, and I entered Woolworth's from the rear entrance.

Moody is not a journalist; rather, she is recording events as part of her personal story. Moody's **tone**, or attitude toward her subject, is for the most part objective as she describes what happens to her. However, she includes some subjective details about her thoughts and feelings, too.

But something happened to me as I got more and more involved in the Movement. It no longer seemed important to prove anything.

As you read Moody's account, think about how her perspective influences the way she describes events.

READING STRATEGY: READING A PRIMARY SOURCE

Because Anne Moody had firsthand knowledge of the events she describes, her account is considered a **primary source.** From her recollections, you can learn about an important turning point in America's history and culture. Moody's **purpose** is to provide accurate background information to show the difficulties she and other African Americans faced.

In her account, Moody gives precise details about times and places:

Seconds before 11:15 we were occupying three seats at the previously segregated Woolworth's lunch counter.

Moody's careful attention to details helps validate her writing as a trustworthy primary source.

As you read, record in a chart like the one below specific details Moody includes in her account.

Details	Time	Place

Complete the activities in your **Reader/Writer Notebook**.

Who makes HISTORY?

Most people assume that history is made by great leaders, the ones who get their pictures in textbooks. But those leaders don't make history by themselves. Their achievements depend on the combined efforts of people like your parents, your teachers, and you.

DISCUSS Working in a small group, think of three or four historical events. In what ways did these events depend on the efforts of ordinary people? Make a list for each event.

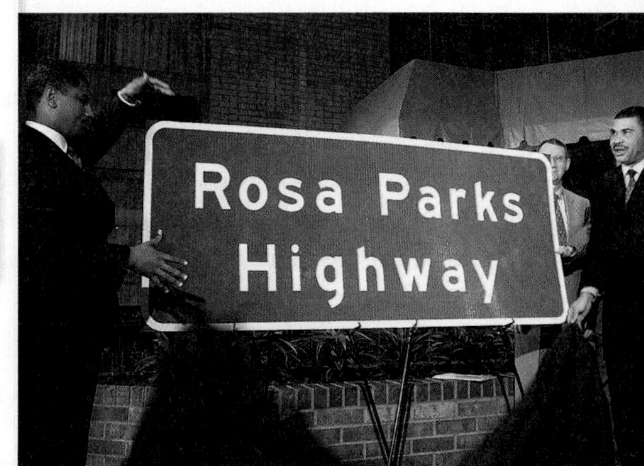

Coming of Age in Mississippi

Anne Moody

BACKGROUND On February 1, 1960, four African-American college freshmen seated themselves at a whites-only lunch counter in Greensboro, North Carolina, refusing to leave until they were served. Within a week, 300 people had joined the sit-in; within two months, sit-ins were being held in 54 cities across the South, most of them organized by college and high school students. By August 1961, more than 70,000 protesters, black and white, had participated in sit-ins. Students, impatient with the slow pace of change, had decided to confront segregation head-on. As you'll read in Anne Moody's account, those confrontations made the ugliness of racism impossible to ignore. Be warned that in relating the confrontations, Moody repeats certain offensive racial epithets.

I had counted on graduating in the spring of 1963, but as it turned out, I couldn't because some of my credits still had to be cleared with Natchez College. A year before, this would have seemed like a terrible disaster, but now I hardly even felt disappointed. I had a good excuse to stay on campus for the summer and work with the Movement, and this was what I really wanted to do. I couldn't go home again anyway, and I couldn't go to New Orleans—I didn't have money enough for bus fare.

During my senior year at Tougaloo,[1] my family hadn't sent me one penny. I had only the small amount of money I had earned at Maple Hill.[2] I couldn't afford to eat at school or live in the dorms, so I had gotten permission to move off campus. I had to prove that I could finish school, even if I had to go hungry every

Analyze Visuals ▶
What details in the photo help convey the tension of the scene at the protest?

Left to right: John Salter, Joan Trumpauer, and Anne Moody, seated at the Woolworth's lunch counter

1. **Tougaloo:** Tougaloo College, a traditionally African-American college on the northern edge of Jackson, Mississippi.
2. **Maple Hill:** a restaurant in New Orleans where Moody had worked in the summer.

day. I knew Raymond and Miss Pearl[3] were just waiting to see me drop out. But something happened to me as I got more and more involved in the Movement. It no longer seemed important to prove anything. I had found something outside myself that gave meaning to my life. **A**

I had become very friendly with my social science professor, John Salter, who was in charge of NAACP[4] activities on campus. All during the year, while the NAACP conducted a boycott of the downtown stores in Jackson, I had been one of Salter's most faithful canvassers[5] and church speakers. During the last week of school, he told me that sit-in demonstrations were about to start in Jackson and that he wanted me to be the spokesman for a team that would sit-in at Woolworth's lunch counter. The two other demonstrators would be classmates of mine, Memphis and Pearlena. Pearlena was a dedicated NAACP worker, but Memphis had not been very involved in the Movement on campus. It seemed that the organization had had a rough time finding students who were in a position to go to jail. I had nothing to lose one way or the other. Around ten o'clock the morning of the demonstrations, NAACP headquarters alerted the news services. As a result, the police department was also informed, but neither the policemen nor the newsmen knew exactly where or when the demonstrations would start. They stationed themselves along Capitol Street and waited.

To divert attention from the sit-in at Woolworth's, the picketing started at J. C. Penney's a good fifteen minutes before. The pickets were allowed to walk up and down in front of the store three or four times before they were arrested. At exactly 11 A.M., Pearlena, Memphis, and I entered Woolworth's from the rear entrance. We separated as soon as we stepped into the store, and made small purchases from various counters. Pearlena had given Memphis her watch. He was to let us know when it was 11:14. At 11:14 we were to join him near the lunch counter and at exactly 11:15 we were to take seats at it.

Seconds before 11:15 we were occupying three seats at the previously segregated Woolworth's lunch counter. In the beginning the waitresses seemed to ignore us, as if they really didn't know what was going on. Our waitress walked past us a couple of times before she noticed we had started to write our own orders down and realized we wanted service. She asked us what we wanted. We began to read to her from our order slips. She told us that we would be served at the back counter, which was for Negroes. **B**

"We would like to be served here," I said.

The waitress started to repeat what she had said, then stopped in the middle of the sentence. She turned the lights out behind the counter, and she and the other waitresses almost ran to the back of the store, deserting all their white customers. I guess they thought that violence would start immediately after the whites at the counter realized what was going on. There were five or six other people at the counter. A couple of them just got up and walked away. A girl sitting next to me

A EYEWITNESS ACCOUNT
Reread lines 1–15. In what ways do Moody's personal challenges motivate her to get involved in the civil rights movement?

COMMON CORE RI 6

B AUTHOR'S PURPOSE
Remember that one of Moody's overall purposes is to give detailed background information about an event during the civil rights movement. Reread lines 26-38. Then, summarize the timeline of the sit-in. Why does Moody give such specific details about the planning of the protest? What effect does her **diction,** or choice of words, have on her tone? How does her tone in this passage reinforce her central argument?

3. **Raymond and Miss Pearl:** Moody's stepfather and step-grandmother.
4. **NAACP:** National Association for the Advancement of Colored People, an organization that works to end discrimination against African Americans and other minorities.
5. **canvassers:** people who go from door to door to get support for a cause or gather opinions on an issue.

finished her banana split before leaving. A middle-aged white woman who had not yet been served rose from her seat and came over to us. "I'd like to stay here with you," she said, "but my husband is waiting."

The newsmen came in just as she was leaving. They must have discovered what was going on shortly after some of the people began to leave the store. One of the newsmen ran behind the woman who spoke to us and asked her to identify herself. She refused to give her name, but said she was a native of Vicksburg[6] and a former resident of California. When asked why she had said what she had said to us, she replied, "I am in sympathy with the Negro movement." By this time a crowd of cameramen and reporters had gathered around us taking pictures and asking questions, such as Where were we from? Why did we sit-in? What organization sponsored it? Were we students? From what school? How were we classified?

I told them that we were all students at Tougaloo College, that we were represented by no particular organization, and that we planned to stay there even after the store closed. "All we want is service," was my reply to one of them. After they had finished probing for about twenty minutes, they were almost ready to leave.

At noon, students from a nearby white high school started pouring in to Woolworth's. When they first saw us they were sort of surprised. They didn't know how to react. A few started to heckle and the newsmen became interested again. Then the white students started chanting all kinds of anti-Negro slogans. We were called a little bit of everything. The rest of the seats except the three we were occupying had been roped off to prevent others from sitting down. A couple of the boys took one end of the rope and made it into a hangman's noose. Several attempts were made to put it around our necks. The crowds grew as more students and adults came in for lunch.

We kept our eyes straight forward and did not look at the crowd except for occasional glances to see what was going on. All of a sudden I saw a face I remembered—the drunkard from the bus station sit-in. My eyes lingered on him just long enough for us to recognize each other. Today he was drunk too, so I don't think he remembered where he had seen me before. He took out a knife, opened it, put it in his pocket, and then began to pace the floor. At this point, I told Memphis and Pearlena what was going on. Memphis suggested that we pray. We bowed our heads, and all hell broke loose. A man rushed forward, threw Memphis from his seat, and slapped my face. Then another man who worked in the store threw me against an adjoining counter.

Down on my knees on the floor, I saw Memphis lying near the lunch counter with blood running out of the corners of his mouth. As he tried to protect his face, the man who'd thrown him down kept kicking him against the head. If he had worn hard-soled shoes instead of sneakers, the first kick probably would have

Language Coach

Synonyms A synonym is a word with a meaning similar to that of another word. Synonyms of *sympathy* (line 61) include *accord* and *agreement*. Use one of these synonyms to restate the woman's statement in line 61.

Language Coach

Idioms An **idiom** is an expression whose overall meaning is different from the meaning of the individual words. "All hell broke loose" (line 87) means "everything was suddenly chaotic and confusing." In what way did things get out of control?

---

6. **Vicksburg:** a city in Mississippi, west of Jackson.

killed Memphis. Finally a man dressed in plain clothes identified himself as a police officer and arrested Memphis and his attacker. **C**

Pearlena had been thrown to the floor. She and I got back on our stools after Memphis was arrested. There were some white Tougaloo teachers in the crowd. They asked Pearlena and me if we wanted to leave. They said that things were getting too rough. We didn't know what to do. While we were trying to make up our minds, we were joined by Joan Trumpauer.[7] Now there were three of us and we were integrated. The crowd began to chant, "Communists, Communists, Communists." Some old man in the crowd ordered the students to take us off the stools.

"Which one should I get first?" a big husky boy said.

"That white nigger," the old man said.

The boy lifted Joan from the counter by her waist and carried her out of the store. Simultaneously, I was snatched from my stool by two high school students. I was dragged about thirty feet toward the door by my hair when someone made them turn me loose. As I was getting up off the floor, I saw Joan coming back inside. We started back to the center of the counter to join Pearlena. Lois Chaffee, a white Tougaloo faculty member, was now sitting next to her. So Joan and I just climbed across the rope at the front end of the counter and sat down. There were now four of us, two whites and two Negroes, all women. The mob started smearing us with ketchup, mustard, sugar, pies, and everything on the counter. Soon Joan and I were joined by John Salter, but the moment he sat down he was hit on the jaw with what appeared to be brass knuckles. Blood gushed from his face and someone threw salt into the open wound. Ed King, Tougaloo's chaplain, rushed to him. **D**

At the other end of the counter, Lois and Pearlena were joined by George Raymond, a CORE[8] field worker and a student from Jackson State College. Then a Negro high school boy sat down next to me. The mob took spray paint from the counter and sprayed it on the new demonstrators. The high school student had on a white shirt; the word "nigger" was written on his back with red spray paint.

We sat there for three hours taking a beating when the manager decided to close the store because the mob had begun to go wild with stuff from other counters. He begged and begged everyone to leave. But even after fifteen minutes of begging, no one budged. They would not leave until we did. Then Dr. Beittel, the president of Tougaloo College, came running in. He said he had just heard what was happening.

About ninety policemen were standing outside the store; they had been watching the whole thing through the windows, but had not come in to stop the mob or do anything. President Beittel went outside and asked Captain Ray to come and escort us out. The captain refused, stating the manager had to invite him in before he could enter the premises, so Dr. Beittel himself brought us out.

C EYEWITNESS ACCOUNT
Reread lines 90–95. Identify details that convey the danger of the protesters' situation. What is surprising about Moody's **tone** in this passage?

D GRAMMAR AND STYLE
Reread lines 113–118. Note how Moody uses a serious tone and strong **verbs** and **verbals** like *smearing* and *gushed* to recreate the mood of the violent scene.

---

7. **Joan Trumpauer:** a white classmate of Moody's from Tougaloo College, who had been active in voter registration.

8. **CORE:** Congress of Racial Equality, a civil rights organization that coordinated marches and demonstrations in the 1960s.

Anne Moody and other protesters leaving the sit-in

He had told the police that they had better protect us after we were outside the store. When we got outside, the policemen formed a single line that blocked the mob from us. However, they were allowed to throw at us everything they had collected. Within ten minutes, we were picked up by Reverend King in his station wagon and taken to the NAACP headquarters on Lynch Street.

After the sit-in, all I could think of was how sick Mississippi whites were. They believed so much in the segregated Southern way of life, they would kill to preserve it. I sat there in the NAACP office and thought of how many times they had killed when this way of life was threatened. I knew that the killing had just begun. "Many more will die before it is over with," I thought. Before the sit-in, I had always hated the whites in Mississippi. Now I knew it was impossible for me to hate sickness. The whites had a disease, an incurable disease in its final stage. What were our chances against such a disease? I thought of the students, the young Negroes who had just begun to protest, as young interns. When these young interns got older, I thought, they would be the best doctors in the world for social problems. E

E EYEWITNESS ACCOUNT
Reread lines 140–150. In what ways have Moody's attitudes and beliefs changed due to her experience at the sit-in?

Before we were taken back to campus, I wanted to get my hair washed. It was stiff with dried mustard, ketchup and sugar. I stopped in at a beauty shop across the street from the NAACP office. I didn't have on any shoes because I had lost them when I was dragged across the floor at Woolworth's. My stockings were sticking to my legs from the mustard that had dried on them. The hairdresser took one look at me and said, "My land, you were in the sit-in, huh?"

"Yes," I answered. "Do you have time to wash my hair and style it?"

"Right away," she said, and she meant right away. There were three other ladies already waiting, but they seemed glad to let me go ahead of them. The hairdresser was real nice. She even took my stockings off and washed my legs while my hair was drying.

There was a mass rally that night at the Pearl Street Church in Jackson, and the place was packed. People were standing two abreast in the aisles. Before the speakers began, all the sit-inners walked out on the stage and were introduced by Medgar Evers.[9] People stood and applauded for what seemed like thirty minutes or more. Medgar told the audience that this was just the beginning of such demonstrations. He asked them to pledge themselves to unite in a massive offensive against segregation in Jackson, and throughout the state. The rally ended with "We Shall Overcome" and sent home hundreds of determined people. It seemed as though Mississippi Negroes were about to get together at last. **F**

Before I demonstrated, I had written Mama. She wrote me back a letter, begging me not to take part in the sit-in. She even sent ten dollars for bus fare to New Orleans. I didn't have one penny, so I kept the money. Mama's letter made me mad. I had to live my life as I saw fit. I had made that decision when I left home. But it hurt to have my family prove to me how scared they were. It hurt me more than anything else—I knew the whites had already started the threats and intimidations. I was the first Negro from my hometown who had openly demonstrated, worked with the NAACP, or anything. When Negroes threatened to do anything in Centreville, they were either shot like Samuel O'Quinn or run out of town, like Reverend Dupree.[10]

I didn't answer Mama's letter. Even if I had written one, she wouldn't have received it before she saw the news on TV or heard it on the radio. I waited to hear from her again. And I waited to hear in the news that someone in Centreville had been murdered. If so, I knew it would be a member of my family. ~

Language Coach

Interjections An interjection is a word used to show emotion, such as "my land" in line 156. Similar interjections include "my goodness" and "oh, my." What emotion is the hairdresser showing? Why does she feel that emotion?

F PRIMARY SOURCE
Reread lines 162–170. What does this paragraph tell you about the rally? Why would rallies like the one described be important to the success of the movement?

---

9. **Medgar Evers:** civil rights leader and organizer for the NAACP in Mississippi from 1954 until 1963, when he was killed by a sniper.

10. **Centreville . . . Samuel O'Quinn . . . Reverend Dupree:** In Centreville, the Mississippi town where Moody grew up, Samuel O'Quinn had been suspected of being associated with the NAACP. The Reverend Dupree had mentioned the NAACP in a sermon he preached.

Revolutionary Dreams

Nikki Giovanni

Love Letter I (1971), Charles Wilbert White. Color lithograph, 30" x 22 1/2". Gift of June Wayne. Image © 2007 Board of Trustees, National Gallery of Art, Washington, D.C. 1974.99.158.(B-27792)/PR. © 1971 The Charles White Archives.

i used to dream militant
dreams of taking
over america to show
these white folks how it should be
done
i used to dream radical dreams
of blowing everyone away with my perceptive powers
of correct analysis
i even used to think i'd be the one
to stop the riot and negotiate the peace
then i awoke and dug
that if i dreamed natural
dreams of being a natural
woman doing what a woman
does when she's natural
i would have a revolution

Comprehension

1. **Recall** What kinds of abuses were directed at the protesters during the sit-in?
2. **Recall** What role did the police play in the sit-in?
3. **Clarify** Why didn't the protesters fight back?

Text Analysis

4. **Make Inferences** After the sit-in, why was Anne Moody worried that a member of her family would be killed?
5. **Draw Conclusions from a Primary Source** Review the chart you created as you read. How does Moody's record of these events add to the validity of the account as a trustworthy primary source document?
6. **Synthesize Details** In what ways were students critical to the success of the movement? Use details from the background and the selection in your answer.
7. **Analyze Author's Perspective** Consider what you learn about Moody's character and private life from the account. What factors contributed to her decision to take action and become part of history? Be specific in your answers.
8. **Evaluate an Eyewitness Account** In your opinion, is Moody a credible reporter of events? In your answer, consider each of the following aspects of her account:
   - presentation of facts (lines 31–38)
   - diction and tone (lines 106–118)
   - opinions expressed (lines 140–147)
   - character traits (lines 171–180)
9. **Compare Texts** Reread the poem on page 1247. In what ways are Nikki Giovanni's thoughts about social change similar to Moody's? Cite details in your answer.

Text Criticism

10. **Different Perspectives** Anne Moody and Martin Luther King Jr., provide different views of the struggle for civil rights: that of a rank-and-file activist and that of a movement leader. In what ways do their accounts reflect their different roles within the movement? Support your answer with details.

Who makes HISTORY?

When you consider great people from history, do you also think about everyone who helped make them great? Anne Moody mentions several people who helped her and her friends during and after the sit-in. In your opinion, how important was the contribution of these people? Explain your answer.

COMMON CORE

RI 3 Analyze a complex set of ideas or sequence of events and explain how specific individuals, ideas, or events interact and develop over the course of the text. **RI 6** Determine an author's point of view or purpose in a text in which the rhetoric is particularly effective, analyzing how content contributes to the power, persuasiveness, or beauty of the text.

Language

GRAMMAR AND STYLE: Create Mood

Review the **Grammar and Style** note on page 1244. **Mood** is the feeling that a writer creates for the reader through such elements as **word choice, imagery,** and **tone.** Moody's account has a tense, serious mood. She uses plain, powerful language, avoiding sensationalism to let the mob's actions speak for themselves.

> *Simultaneously, I was snatched from my stool by two high school students. I was dragged about thirty feet toward the door by my hair when someone made them turn me loose.* (lines 107–109)

The author's choice of strong **verbs** like *snatched* and *dragged* allows her to convey the violence of the scene while maintaining a calm, controlled tone. Note that Moody uses straightforward **declarative sentences** to describe her experiences, without adding details about her own responses to what occurs.

PRACTICE The following paragraph is written to create a tense, dramatic mood. Rewrite the paragraph, adjusting word choice, imagery, and tone to create a lighter, more comic mood. A sample beginning is provided for you.

> We all sat quietly, waiting for news. My palms began to sweat and I had trouble swallowing. I looked over at my friend, seated two rows away, but I couldn't catch her eye. She looked like she was about to cry. I was hoping the news wouldn't be as bad as we feared. Then, the door opened and he walked in. I couldn't believe it. All the rumors were true: we'd been assigned the toughest teacher in the entire school for homeroom. It was going to be a long, long year.

EXAMPLE

"Hi, everybody!" our new teacher said, holding a bunch of balloons. "Welcome to homeroom!"

READING-WRITING CONNECTION

Expand your understanding of Moody's account by responding to this prompt. Then, use the **revising tips** to improve your report.

WRITING PROMPT

WRITE AN EYEWITNESS REPORT An effective eyewitness report puts the reader in the midst of the action while providing the context needed to understand the events described. Write a **three- to five-paragraph eyewitness report** on an event of your choosing, such as a sporting event or a community gathering. Use precise details and a clear, logical structure to make the event accessible to your audience.

REVISING TIPS

- Use descriptive language to describe the event.
- Use action verbs to show rather than tell.
- Choose an appropriate tone for your subject matter.
- Include an explanation of why the event was meaningful to you.

COMMON CORE

L 5b Analyze nuances in the meaning of words with similar denotations. **W 3** Write narratives to develop real or imagined experiences or events using effective technique, well-chosen details, and well-structured event sequences. **W 3d–e** Use precise words and phrases, telling details, and sensory language to convey a vivid picture of the experiences, events, setting, and/or characters; provide a conclusion that follows from and reflects on what is experienced, observed, or resolved over the course of the narrative.

My Dungeon Shook: Letter to My Nephew

Open Letter by James Baldwin

COMMON CORE

RI 1 Cite strong and thorough textual evidence to support analysis of what the text says explicitly as well as inferences drawn from the text, including determining where the text leaves matters uncertain. **RI 6** Determine an author's point of view or purpose in a text in which the rhetoric is particularly effective, analyzing how style and content contribute to the power, persuasiveness, or beauty of the text. **L 5a** Interpret figures of speech (e.g., paradox) in context and analyze their role in the text.

Meet the Author

James Baldwin 1924–1987

In the turbulent 1960s, James Baldwin became one of the country's most sought-after commentators on racial politics. But Baldwin never considered himself a spokesperson. Rather, he saw his role as bearing witness "to whence I came, where I am . . . to what I've seen and the possibilities that I think I see." This autobiographical vantage point is the hallmark of Baldwin's greatest works, from his moving first novel, *Go Tell It on the Mountain* (1953), to the provocative essays collected in *Notes of a Native Son* (1955), *Nobody Knows My Name* (1961), and *The Fire Next Time* (1963).

Early Struggles Born and raised in Harlem, Baldwin never knew his biological father and had a strained relationship with his stepfather, a domineering, bitter man who preached at a storefront evangelical church on weekends. A star pupil and voracious reader, the young James also helped his overworked mother raise his eight brothers and sisters. After a dramatic religious conversion at age 14, he gained local acclaim as a "boy-preacher." Then, at 18, a crisis of faith drove Baldwin to break with the church and leave home.

Emerging Artist Working to establish his literary career, Baldwin supported himself by writing book reviews and waiting tables. Baldwin achieved some success but felt increasingly stifled by the racist climate of the United States. In a life-changing decision in 1948, he bought a one-way plane ticket to Paris. "Once I found myself on the other side of the ocean," he later explained, "I could see where I came from very clearly, and I could see that I carried myself, which is my home, with me. You can never escape that."

Long-Distance Outrage With their penetrating insight and apocalyptic tone, Baldwin's essay collections were bestsellers. By the mid-1960s, he was an international celebrity, popular on the lecture circuit and in public debates, interviews, and panel discussions in the United States and Europe. In writing about his perceptions and personal torments, Baldwin made white Americans deeply, painfully aware of the realities of African-American life. As black leaders in the 1950s and 1960s looked outward to break down barriers, Baldwin looked inward to examine the psychological damage of racism and the search for black identity and self-realization. In the words of playwright Amiri Baraka, "Jimmy's voice, as much as Dr. King's or Malcolm X's, helped shepherd and guide us toward black liberation."

Author Online THINK central

Go to thinkcentral.com. KEYWORD: HML11-1250

DID YOU KNOW?

James Baldwin . . .

- was mentored by poet Countee Cullen in high school.
- moved to Paris at age 24 and only returned to the United States for visits.
- was working on a biography of Martin Luther King Jr., when he died.

(background) Harlem in 1937

TEXT ANALYSIS: RHETORICAL DEVICES

Baldwin is known for his passionate and poetic **style,** which is based on his skillful use of **rhetorical devices.** Baldwin uses these techniques to drive home his points and to create rhythmic effects that echo spoken language:

- A **paradox** is a statement that seems contradictory but really points to an important truth. Baldwin uses this device to push his readers to think more deeply about familiar ideas.

  It is the innocence which constitutes the crime.

- **Repetition** is the use of the same word, phrase, or sentence more than once for emphasis. Baldwin uses repetition expressively, to convey deep emotions.

  You must accept them and accept them with love. . . .

As you read, note the rhetorical devices Baldwin uses, and consider their effects.

READING STRATEGY: IDENTIFY PURPOSE

Baldwin's sentences do more than simply explain his points; they stir powerful emotional responses in the reader. Often, the meaning of his statements becomes apparent only after careful thought and reflection. As you read this letter, study Baldwin's **purpose** for writing. In a chart like the one below, note key sentences that convey Baldwin's purpose. Then, after you have finished the letter, summarize the reasons why Baldwin wrote this letter.

Baldwin's Sentence	Purpose

VOCABULARY IN CONTEXT

Baldwin uses the following words in his eloquent appeal. Complete each sentence with one of the words.

WORD LIST			
	constitute	mediocrity	unassailable
	impertinent	truculent	

1. You conceal your fears with a(n) _____ attitude.
2. Don't settle for _____; strive for excellence.
3. It is never _____ to speak honestly.
4. Know exactly what tasks and obligations _____ your duty.
5. Let your convictions be strong and your truth _______.

Complete the activities in your **Reader/Writer Notebook**.

What protects your sense of SELF?

Part of growing up is deciding who you want to be and how to make your vision a reality. But how do you keep your sense of self strong when others tell you who you can and cannot be? James Baldwin offers his nephew some advice on protecting his self-worth from the crushing forces of racism.

QUICKWRITE Think about the messages you get about yourself from family, friends, media, and other sources. Which ones support you and which ones seem to hold you back? List at least two examples in each category. Based on your list, what in your life most helps you protect your self-worth?

Support	Hold Back
1. With hard work you can achieve your dreams (my mom). 2.	1. College is too expensive and not worth it (my friend George). 2.

My Dungeon Shook

Letter to My Nephew on the One Hundredth Anniversary of the Emancipation

James Baldwin

BACKGROUND In 1963, as the nation's perspective on the race problem grew more pessimistic, James Baldwin published his essay collection *The Fire Next Time.* Expressing the pain and anger that African Americans had concealed for so long, Baldwin addressed his provocative essays to a sympathetic white audience that had failed to grasp the full magnitude of racial injustice. His searing attack fit the national mood, and the collection soared up the bestseller lists. Its success made Baldwin an icon of black rage and a widely televised commentator on racial issues throughout the 1960s. The following letter, taken from *The Fire Next Time,* captures the extremes of Baldwin's style: the righteous anger that made him famous and his fervent belief in the redeeming power of love.

Analyze Visuals ▶
Describe the story that this painting seems to tell. Which elements help the artist connect the two figures in the foreground with the main story of the painting?

Dear James:

I have begun this letter five times and torn it up five times. I keep seeing your face, which is also the face of your father and my brother. Like him, you are tough, dark, vulnerable, moody—with a very definite tendency to sound **truculent** because you want no one to think you are soft. You may be like your grandfather in this, I don't know, but certainly both you and your father resemble him very much physically. Well, he is dead, he never saw you, and he had a terrible life; he was defeated long before he died because, at the bottom of his heart, he really believed what white people said about him. This is one of the reasons that he became so holy.[1] I am sure that your father has told you something about all that. Neither you nor your father exhibit any tendency towards holiness: you really *are*

truculent (trŭk'yə-lənt) *adj.* eager for a fight; fierce

1. **so holy:** Baldwin's stepfather was a minister who raised his children in a strict, conservative, religious environment.

Father, Charly Palmer. Mixed media collage on wood. 18″ × 12″. © Charly Palmer.

I AM A MAN
I AM A MAN
I AM A MAN
I AM A MAN
I AM A MAN
I AM A MAN

of another era, part of what happened when the Negro left the land and came into what the late E. Franklin Frazier[2] called "the cities of destruction." You can only be destroyed by believing that you really are what the white world calls a *nigger*. I tell you this because I love you, and please don't you ever forget it.

I have known both of you all your lives, have carried your Daddy in my arms and on my shoulders, kissed and spanked him and watched him learn to walk. I don't know if you've known anybody from that far back; if you've loved anybody that long, first as an infant, then as a child, then as a man, you gain a strange perspective on time and human pain and effort. Other people cannot see what I see whenever I look into your father's face, for behind your father's face as it is today are all those other faces which were his. Let him laugh and I see a cellar your father does not remember and a house he does not remember and I hear in his present laughter his laughter as a child. Let him curse and I remember him falling down the cellar steps, and howling, and I remember, with pain, his tears, which my hand or your grandmother's so easily wiped away. But no one's hand can wipe away those tears he sheds invisibly today, which one hears in his laughter and in his speech and in his songs. I know what the world has done to my brother and how narrowly he has survived it. And I know, which is much worse, and this is the crime of which I accuse my country and my countrymen, and for which neither I nor time nor history will ever forgive them, that they have destroyed and are destroying hundreds of thousands of lives and do not know it and do not want to know it. One can be, indeed one must strive to become, tough and philosophical concerning destruction and death, for this is what most of mankind has been best at since we have heard of man. (But remember: *most* of mankind is not all of mankind.) But it is not permissible that the authors of devastation should also be innocent. It is the innocence which **constitutes** the crime. (A)

Now, my dear namesake, these innocent and well-meaning people, your countrymen, have caused you to be born under conditions not very far removed from those described for us by Charles Dickens[3] in the London of more than a hundred years ago. (I hear the chorus of the innocents screaming, "No! This is not true! How *bitter* you are!"—but I am writing this letter to *you,* to try to tell you something about how to handle *them,* for most of them do not yet really know that you exist. I *know* the conditions under which you were born, for I was there. Your countrymen were *not* there, and haven't made it yet. Your grandmother was also there, and no one has ever accused her of being bitter. I suggest that the innocents check with her. She isn't hard to find. Your countrymen don't know that *she* exists, either, though she has been working for them all their lives.)

Well, you were born, here you came, something like fifteen years ago; and though your father and mother and grandmother, looking about the streets through which they were carrying you, staring at the walls into which they brought you, had every reason to be heavyhearted, yet they were not. For here

Language Coach

Word Definitions
Shed tears means "lose tears" or "cry." What does Baldwin mean by "tears he sheds invisibly" (line 27)? What are invisible tears?

constitute (kŏn′stĭ-to͞ot′) *v.* to amount to; equal

(A) **RHETORICAL DEVICES**
Consider the **paradox** in lines 36–37. What point is Baldwin making?

---

2. **E. Franklin Frazier:** African-American sociologist (1894–1962) who studied the structure of black communities.

3. **described . . . by Charles Dickens:** Dickens (1812–1870) was a British novelist whose works frequently described the hardships suffered by the poor in London.

you were, Big James, named for me—you were a big baby, I was not—here you were: to be loved. To be loved, baby, hard, at once, and forever, to strengthen you against the loveless world. Remember that: I know how black it looks today, for you. It looked bad that day, too, yes, we were trembling. We have not stopped trembling yet, but if we had not loved each other none of us would have survived. And now you must survive because we love you, and for the sake of your children and your children's children. **B**

This innocent country set you down in a ghetto in which, in fact, it intended that you should perish. Let me spell out precisely what I mean by that, for the heart of the matter is here, and the root of my dispute with my country. You were born where you were born and faced the future that you faced because you were black and *for no other reason.* The limits of your ambition were, thus, expected to be set forever. You were born into a society which spelled out with brutal clarity, and in as many ways as possible, that you were a worthless human being. You were not expected to aspire to excellence: you were expected to make peace with **mediocrity**. Wherever you have turned, James, in your short time on this earth, you have been told where you could go and what you could do (and *how* you could do it) and where you could live and whom you could marry. I know your countrymen do not agree with me about this, and I hear them saying, "You exaggerate." They do not know Harlem, and I do. So do you. Take no one's word for anything, including mine—but trust your experience.

Know whence you came. If you know whence you came, there is really no limit **C** to where you can go. The details and symbols of your life have been deliberately constructed to make you believe what white people say about you. Please try to remember that what they believe, as well as what they do and cause you to endure, does not testify to your inferiority but to their inhumanity and fear. Please try to be clear, dear James, through the storm which rages about your youthful head today, about the reality which lies behind the words *acceptance* and *integration.* There is no reason for you to try to become like white people and there is no basis whatever for their **impertinent** assumption that *they* must accept *you.* The really terrible thing, old buddy, is that *you* must accept *them.* And I mean that very seriously. You must accept them and accept them with love. For these innocent people have no other hope. They are, in effect, still trapped in a history which they do not understand; and until they understand it, they cannot be released from it. They have had to believe for many years, and for innumerable reasons, that black men are inferior to white men. Many of them, indeed, know better, but, as you will discover, people find it very difficult to act on what they know. To act is to be committed, and to be committed is to be in danger. In this case, the danger, in the minds of most white Americans, is the loss of their identity. Try to imagine how you would feel if you woke up one morning to find the sun shining and all the stars aflame. You would be frightened because it is out of the order of nature. Any upheaval in the universe is terrifying because it so profoundly attacks one's sense of one's own reality. Well, the black man has functioned in the white man's world as a fixed star, as an immovable pillar: and as he moves out of his place, heaven and earth are shaken to their foundations. You, don't be afraid. I said that it was intended that you should perish in the ghetto, perish by never

B RHETORICAL DEVICES
Identify words and phrases that are repeated in lines 52–59. What does this **repetition** contribute to the paragraph's impact?

mediocrity
(mē'dē-ŏk'-rĭ-tē) *n.* lack of quality or excellence

C IDENTIFY PURPOSE
Reread lines 60–74. What is Baldwin's main point? How do these ideas add to your understanding of his purpose for writing?

impertinent
(ĭm-pûr'tn-ənt) *adj.* rude; ill-mannered

Language Coach

Synonyms A **synonym** is a word with a meaning similar to that of another word. As they are used in line 96, *fixed* and *immovable* are synonyms. How do these synonyms emphasize the non-changing "role" the black man had played?

Thinking (1990), Carlton Murrell. Oil on board. Private collection. © Bridgeman Art Library.

being allowed to go behind the white man's definitions, by never being allowed to spell your proper name. You have, and many of us have, defeated this intention; and, by a terrible law, a terrible paradox, those innocents who believed that your imprisonment made them safe are losing their grasp of reality. But these men are your brothers —your lost, younger brothers. And if the word *integration* means anything, this is what it means: that we, with love, shall force our brothers to see themselves as they are, to cease fleeing from reality and begin to change it. For this is your home, my friend, do not be driven from it; great men have done great things here, and will again, and we can make America what America must become. It will be hard, James, but you come from sturdy, peasant stock, men who picked cotton and dammed rivers and built railroads, and, in the teeth of[4] the most terrifying odds, achieved an **unassailable** and monumental dignity. You come from a long line of great poets, some of the greatest poets since Homer. One of them said, *The very time I thought I was lost, My dungeon shook and my chains fell off.*[5] **D**

You know, and I know, that the country is celebrating one hundred years of freedom one hundred years too soon. We cannot be free until they are free. God bless you, James, and Godspeed.

Your uncle,
James

unassailable (ŭn′ə-sā′lə-bəl) *adj.* undeniable

D IDENTIFY PURPOSE
Reread lines 100–113. Which sentence best states Baldwin's purpose in these lines?

---

4. **in the teeth of:** in spite of.
5. ***The very time . . . fell off:*** a quotation from the traditional spiritual "My Dungeon Shook." It alludes to the Biblical story of Paul and Silas (Acts 16), who were freed from an unjust imprisonment by the action of an earthquake.

Comprehension

1. **Recall** In Baldwin's view, why was the boy's grandfather defeated?
2. **Recall** What does Baldwin say *acceptance* means?
3. **Clarify** What crime does Baldwin accuse his country of committing?

Text Analysis

4. **Identify Purpose** Review the sentences you recorded in your chart. Which one best conveys the purpose of this letter? Explain your answer.
5. **Examine Rhetorical Devices** Baldwin sums up the themes of his letter with two concluding **paradoxes.** Reread lines 114–115. What perspective on the problem of race in America do these two statements convey?
6. **Analyze Audience** Baldwin addressed this **open letter** to his 15-year-old nephew but published it in *The Fire Next Time.* In each of the following passages, which details are directed to the nephew and which seem directed to a wider audience? Support your answer with details.
   - Baldwin's memories of his brother (lines 20–33)
   - criticisms of his readers (lines 38–44)
   - his advice to his nephew (lines 78–84)
   - his description of whites' fears (lines 90–97)
7. **Compare Style** Baldwin shared many of Martin Luther King Jr.'s values, goals, and religious influences. What is similar and different about the authors' styles? In your answer, consider each author's tone as well as his use of logical arguments, allusions, and rhetorical devices.
8. **Make Judgments** Consider Baldwin's solution to the problem of racism. In your opinion, does Baldwin's letter contain useful advice for protecting his nephew's self-worth? Explain your opinions.

Text Criticism

9. **Critical Interpretations** In *Soul on Ice* (1968), black activist Eldridge Cleaver criticized James Baldwin for his "grueling, agonizing, total hatred of the blacks, particularly of himself" and his "shameful, fanatical, fawning, sycophantic love of the whites." Do you see any evidence to support these accusations? Explain your answer, citing details from Baldwin's letter.

What protects your sense of **SELF?**

Sometimes people's view of themselves is too high. At other times, they suffer from low self-esteem. In your opinion, what is a good balance between these two extremes? How do you keep a proper perspective on yourself?

COMMON CORE

RI 1 Cite strong and thorough textual evidence to support analysis of what the text says explicitly as well as inferences drawn from the text, including determining where the text leaves matters uncertain. **RI 6** Determine an author's point of view or purpose in a text in which the rhetoric is particularly effective, analyzing how style and content contribute to the power, persuasiveness, or beauty of the text. **L 5a** Interpret figures of speech (e.g., paradox) in context and analyze their role in the text.

Vocabulary in Context

▲ VOCABULARY PRACTICE

Choose the word that is closest in meaning to the boldfaced vocabulary word.

1. **impertinent:** (a) insolent, (b) impossible, (c) unfriendly
2. **mediocrity:** (a) ordinariness, (b) indifference, (c) complexity
3. **unassailable:** (a) landlocked, (b) unknown, (c) indisputable
4. **truculent:** (a) uncivilized, (b) ferocious, (c) boorish
5. **constitute:** (a) connect, (b) compose, (c) conclude

WORD LIST
constitute
impertinent
mediocrity
truculent
unassailable

ACADEMIC VOCABULARY IN WRITING

• complex • economic • establish • ethnic • evolve

James Baldwin wrote a letter to his nephew offering advice about how to live in a **complex** society. In a short paragraph, discuss where you seek advice. Use at least two Academic Vocabulary words in your writing.

VOCABULARY STRATEGY: CONTEXT AND THE MEANING OF IDIOMS

An **idiom** is an expression whose overall meaning is different from the meaning of the individual words that it includes. For example, in "My Dungeon Shook" Baldwin uses the expression *in the teeth of* to describe overcoming difficult odds. Some idioms are very common and you will automatically know their meaning. However, if an idiom is unfamiliar to you, you may at first try to determine the meaning of the sentence or paragraph by focusing on the meanings of the individual words. Only by looking at the surrounding **context** will you be able to draw the conclusion that the words are working together as a part of an idiom with a special meaning.

COMMON CORE

L 4a Use context as a clue to the meaning of a word or phrase. **L 5a** Interpret figures of speech in context and analyze their role in the text.

PRACTICE Use context clues to identify the five idioms in the following paragraph and determine their meaning. Then, write the meaning, or a definition, of each idiom.

No matter what trouble she's in, she always gets herself off the hook. Even when she creates a disaster for everyone else, she gets away without any egg on her face. Sometimes her mistakes are just a matter of putting her foot in her mouth. At other times she actually thumbs her nose at other people's needs and concerns. We can only hope that someone will take her under his wing and teach her how to behave.

The March Toward Equality

In 1963, psychology professor Dr. Kenneth Clark conducted a series of interviews with Dr. Martin Luther King Jr., Malcolm X, and James Baldwin. Aired during a time of intense racial conflict, these interviews explored the differences in the ideals and world views of these three leading activists and thinkers. In his introduction to the interviews, Dr. Clark made this statement.

> "We have now come to the point where there are only two ways that America can avoid continued racial explosions. One would be total oppression. The other, total equality. There is no compromise. I believe, I hope, that we are on the threshold of a truly democratic America. It is not going to be easy to cross that threshold. But the achievement of the goals of justice, equality, and democracy for all American citizens involves the very destiny of our nation."

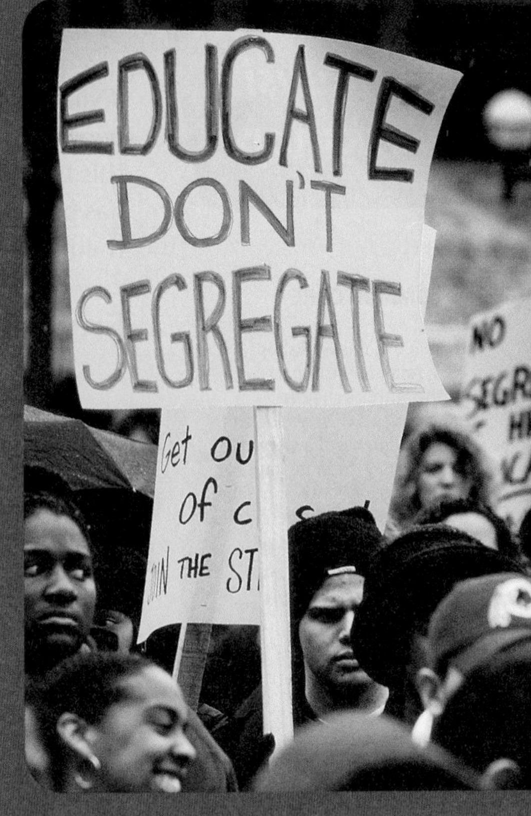

Writing to Persuade

Consider the state of civil rights in America today, in light of the goals and visions of the writers you have just read. In your opinion, have we reached total equality? Or would you say that we have arrived somewhere in between total equality and total oppression? Review the literature in this section and write a retrospective editorial in which you support a claim about whether or not the goals and visions of these writers have been realized.

Consider

- which ideas and details from the selections will help you articulate the vision of the civil rights leaders
- what stories, examples, or other details will help you support your view of civil rights in America today
- who your audience will be and what you want them to think or do
- how to express your argument clearly and respectfully

Extension Online

INQUIRY & RESEARCH Use the Internet to **research** contemporary topics in civil rights. Look for news and commentary in mainstream and lesser-known publications, including private blogs. Also look for Web sites of organizations devoted to advancing civil rights. Choose three issues that seem important or surprising to you and share them with your class.

COMMON CORE

RI 9 Analyze documents of historical and literary significance for their themes and purposes. **W 1** Write arguments to support claims in an analysis of substantive topics or texts. **W 9a–b** Apply grade 11 Reading standards to literature and to literary nonfiction.

Text Analysis Workshop

Voice in Contemporary Literature

If you go into a bookstore and browse the "New Fiction" section, what types of books do you find? How are they different from literature of the past? Throughout this textbook, you have witnessed the evolution of American literature. Each period has been characterized by literary movements that determined the styles and themes in writing. What do you think the trends have been in your generation?

COMMON CORE

Included in this workshop: **RL 3** Analyze the impact of the author's choices regarding how to develop and relate elements of a story or drama. **RL 9** Demonstrate knowledge of how two or more texts from the same period treat similar themes or topics.

From Modern to Contemporary

The era of contemporary literature began around 1946, immediately after World War II. War has a way of changing a nation's literature because of its effects on an entire generation. Realism had risen from the ashes of the Civil War, while modernism had defined its vision through the ruins of World War I. After World War II, the development of the Cold War, the Vietnam War, and the civil violence of the 1960s, American literature changed again. Literature began to focus on personal experience as seen in the context of society. Writers began to address the emotional effects of wars, for example, as well as other issues of social, political, and cultural relevance.

Amy Tan

One of the most significant changes in American literature has been its increasing diversity—not only in forms and techniques, but in voices. With its history as the great "melting pot," the United States has been in a unique position to cultivate a literary community of authors from a wide variety of races, ethnicities, and religions. Increased publishing opportunities have given a public voice to more and more writers of African, Asian, Latino, and Native American descent, who often provide a new perspective on living in two cultures at once. Authors who have addressed such issues include Amy Tan, Sandra Cisneros, Rita Dove, Gwendolyn Brooks, Alice Walker, and N. Scott Momaday.

Rita Dove

N. Scott Momaday

Diverse Works, Common Ground

Several defining features set contemporary literature apart from the previous era of modernist literature.

Voice in literature is the expression of the writer's or narrator's personality. With its emphasis on personal experience, contemporary literature is often told from the first-person point of view, through a persona that represents the writer or main character. This persona has a distinctive personality that shapes a reader's experience with the text.

Tone is the attitude that a writer takes toward a subject. For the modernists, the numbing effects of the early 20th century led to a detached, unemotional tone. For example, Prufrock's failure at the end of T. S. Eliot's poem (page 970) is conveyed in a matter-of-fact tone that is sympathetic but distant. Compare this modernist aloofness to Tim O'Brien's Vietnam story "Ambush" (page 1196). The tone of this contemporary story is one of engagement rather than detachment.

> I did not hate the young man; I did not see him as the enemy; I did not ponder issues of morality or politics or military duty. I crouched and kept my head low. I tried to swallow whatever was rising from my stomach, which tasted like lemonade, something fruity and sour. I was terrified.
>
> **—Tim O'Brien, "Ambush"**

Close Read

How would you characterize the narrator of this passage? Do you think he would be personable? distant? intimidating?

As a rule, modernist writers did not view the irony of life as humorous; instead, they often expressed defeat in the face of life's irony. Contemporary writers, however, look at the absurdity of such situations as a cause for humor, which may then be expressed through an **ironic** presentation of characters and events.

Modernist writers typically viewed the individual in isolation, whereas contemporary writers present the individual in relation to the larger social context. Often contemporary writers hint at **social criticism.** They present a situation with only a suggestion of the social obstacles, and the reader must infer the writer's opinion. In her poem "Primer for Blacks" (page 1297), Gwendolyn Brooks encourages African Americans to appreciate their heritage. Note the unspoken message about social barriers for African Americans that Brooks conveys in this passage.

> Blackness
> is a title,
> is a preoccupation,
> is a commitment Blacks
> are to comprehend—
> and in which you are
> to perceive your Glory.
>
> **—Gwendolyn Brooks, "Primer for Blacks"**

Close Read

What is the social barrier for African Americans that Brooks wants her reader to infer?

Brooks is making an argument for self-respect and self-esteem among African Americans. However, she does not state what she is arguing against; she leaves it up to the reader to infer the social barriers she is addressing.

COMMON CORE

RI 2 Determine two or more central ideas of a text and analyze their development over the course of the text. **RI 3** Analyze a complex set of ideas or sequence of events and explain how specific individuals, ideas, or events interact and develop over the course of the text. **RI 6** Determine an author's point of view, analyzing how style and content contribute to the power, persuasiveness, or beauty of the text. **L 2a** Observe hyphenation conventions.

Mother Tongue

HISTORY Video link at thinkcentral.com

Essay by Amy Tan

Meet the Author

Amy Tan born 1952

In 1989, Amy Tan's first book, *The Joy Luck Club,* spent 40 weeks on the *New York Times* bestseller list. Praised for its authentic dialogue and its rich portrayal of Chinese history, the book established Tan as an insightful chronicler of the Chinese-American experience and of the fierce and conflicted love between mothers and daughters.

Troubled Times Born in Oakland, California in 1952, Tan spent her early childhood in the San Francisco Bay area. She enjoyed her first literary success at the age of eight, winning first prize in an elementary school contest for her essay "What My Library Means to Me." Six years later, Tan's life took a tragic turn when both her father and her brother died from brain tumors. Her grief-stricken mother moved teenaged Amy and her surviving brother to Europe, settling in Montreux, Switzerland, where Tan graduated from high school in 1969.

Although her mother had pushed her to become a neurosurgeon, the rebellious Tan defied her mother's wishes and studied literature and linguistics in college. In 1974, she enrolled in a doctoral program in linguistics, but she abandoned her studies after a close friend was murdered. Tan then put her expertise to work as a language development consultant for programs serving children with disabilities. Five years later, she adopted a new career as a freelance technical writer.

Confronting the Past Tan took up writing fiction as a form of therapy, hoping to curb her workaholic tendencies. Her first short story, "End Game," appeared in *Seventeen* magazine, bringing her to the attention of prominent literary agent Sandra Dijkstra. With Dijkstra's encouragement, Tan began writing a series of stories that evolved into *The Joy Luck Club.* For this tightly woven collection of short stories, Tan drew upon her personal story, exploring the generational and cultural gap between Chinese mothers and their American-born daughters.

Two years later, Tan published her second book, *The Kitchen God's Wife,* a novel inspired by her mother's life in China. Though she switched her focus from mother-daughter love to sisterhood in her third novel, *The Hundred Secret Senses,* she once again drew on her mother's life story in her fourth, *The Bonesetter's Daughter.* As Tan explains, "My books have amounted to taking her stories—a gift to me—and giving them back to her. To me, it was the ultimate thing I ever could have done for myself and my mother."

Author Online

THINK central

Go to thinkcentral.com. KEYWORD: HML11-1262

DID YOU KNOW?

Amy Tan . . .

- plays in a band called the Rock Bottom Remainders with Stephen King and other literary celebrities.
- has visited the White House five times.
- has had her works translated into more than 20 languages.

TEXT ANALYSIS: PERSONAL ESSAY

Amy Tan could have written a research paper to get across her points about language and cultural identity. Instead, she chose to write a **personal essay,** in which she combines her insights on the topic with details from her own life.

Just last week, as I was walking down the street with [my mother], I again found myself conscious of the English I was using, the English I do use with her.

Unlike a scholarly paper or a newspaper article, a personal essay gives the reader a snapshot of the writer's life or personality as well as his or her thoughts on a specific topic. As evidenced by the excerpt above, personal essays are written as first-person narratives. The author appeals to the reader's emotions through the rhetorical or persuasive power of personal experiences. Tan uses anecdotes, or autobiographical incidents, to create meaning and to persuade the reader to understand her point of view. As you read this essay, note how Tan connects her ideas about the power of language with her own experiences.

READING SKILL: IDENTIFY MAIN IDEAS

Amy Tan's essay is organized into a series of paragraphs, most of which develop one **main idea,** or central point. Facts, descriptions, or examples that are related to the main idea are called **supporting details.** When a main idea is not directly stated, you can figure it out by asking yourself how these supporting details fit together.

Amy Tan uses vivid supporting details, drawn from deeply felt personal experiences, to make her points. As you read, use a diagram like the one shown to record the main idea of each paragraph and list the details that support that main idea.

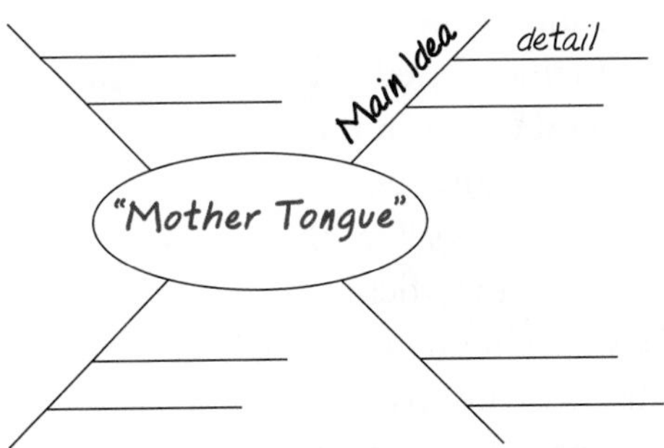

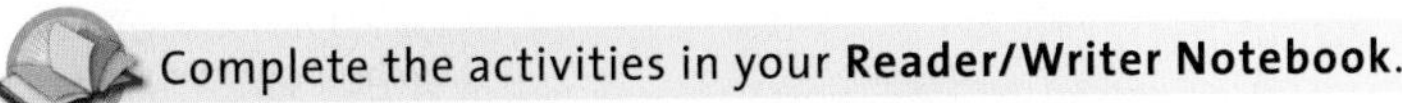
Complete the activities in your **Reader/Writer Notebook**.

What LANGUAGES *do you speak?*

Think about how you change the way you speak based on where you are and whom you're with. You might use slang when talking with friends but polite, formal language with adults. You might speak English at school and another language at home. In "Mother Tongue," you will read one writer's thoughts on her own different languages.

QUICKWRITE Make a list of places and situations where you use a different language or way of speaking. Then, for each situation, write a brief quotation that captures the sound of the language you use in that context.

Mother Tongue

Amy Tan

I am not a scholar of English or literature. I cannot give you much more than personal opinions on the English language and its variations in this country or others.

I am a writer. And by that definition, I am someone who has always loved language. I am fascinated by language in daily life. I spend a great deal of my time thinking about the power of language—the way it can evoke an emotion, a visual image, a complex idea, or a simple truth. Language is the tool of my trade. And I use them all—all the Englishes I grew up with. Ⓐ

Recently, I was made keenly aware of the different Englishes I do use. I was giving a talk to a large group of people, the same talk I had already given to half a dozen other groups. The talk was about my writing, my life, and my book, *The Joy Luck Club,* and it was going along well enough, until I remembered one major difference that made the whole talk sound wrong. My mother was in the room. And it was perhaps the first time she had heard me give a lengthy speech, using the kind of English I have never used with her. I was saying things like "the intersection of memory and imagination" and "There is an aspect of my fiction that relates to thus-and-thus"—a speech filled with carefully wrought grammatical phrases, burdened, it suddenly seemed to me, with nominalized[1] forms, past perfect tenses, conditional phrases, forms of standard English that I had learned in school and through books, the forms of English I did not use at home with my mother.

1. **nominalized** (nŏm′ə-nəl-īz′d) **forms:** nouns formed from other parts of speech.

Analyze Visuals ▶
In this painting, the artist represents an apple in three different ways. What point about language might the artist be making?

Ⓐ **PERSONAL ESSAY**
Reread lines 1–8. How do you respond to the author's use of first-person testimony? Explain your response.

Apple (1983), Andy Warhol. Synthetic polymer paint and silkscreen ink on canvas, 14″ × 11″. © The Andy Warhol Foundation for the Visual Arts/Artists Rights Society (ARS), New York. © The Andy Warhol Foundation, Inc./Art Resource, New York.

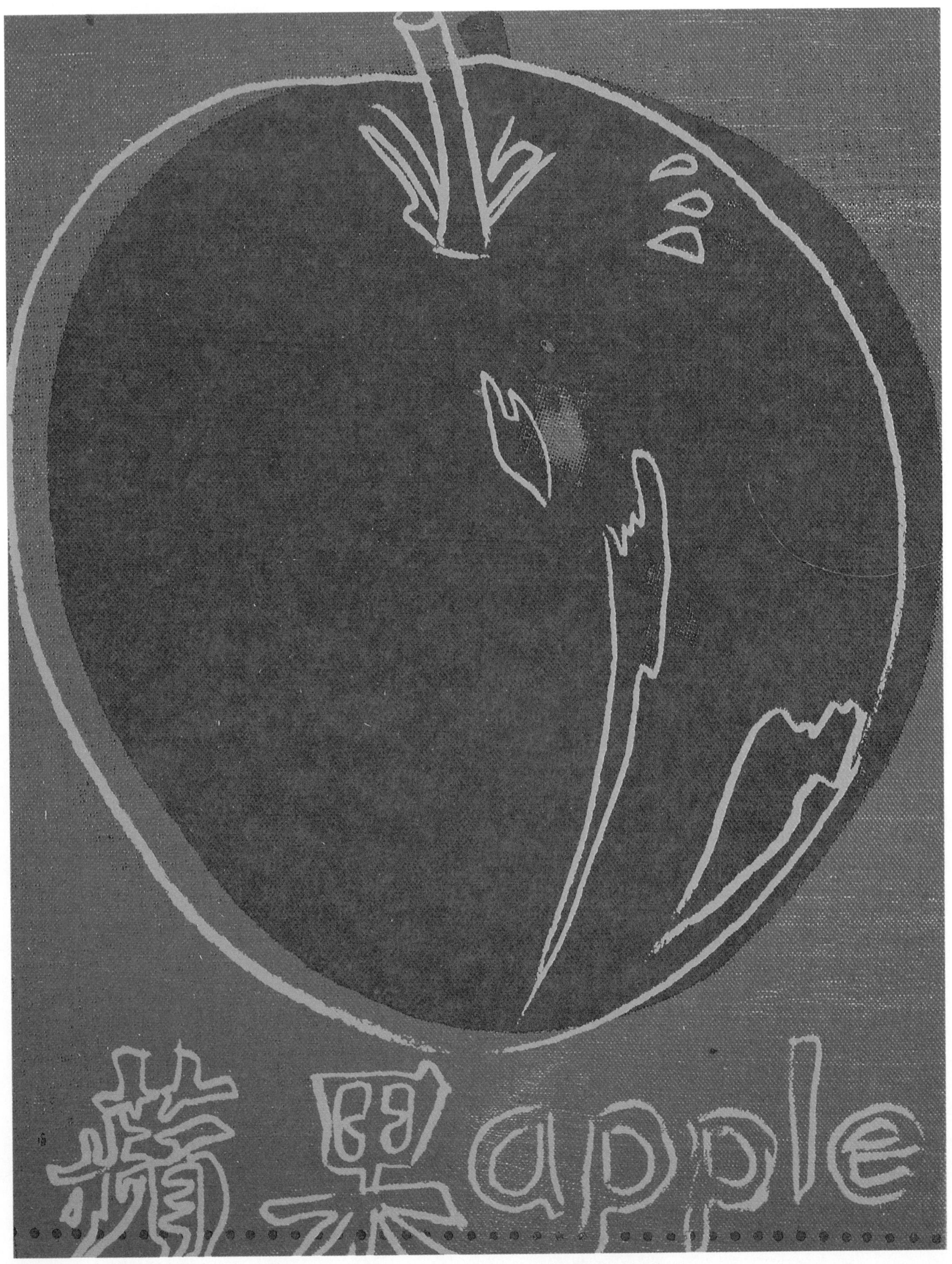
蘋果 apple

Just last week, as I was walking down the street with her, I again found myself conscious of the English I was using, the English I do use with her. We were talking about the price of new and used furniture, and I heard myself saying this: "Not waste money that way." My husband was with us as well, and he didn't notice any switch in my English. And then I realized why. It's because over the twenty years we've been together I've often used that same kind of English with him, and sometimes he even uses it with me. It has become our language of intimacy, a different sort of English that relates to family talk, the language I grew up with.

So that you'll have some idea of what this family talk sounds like, I'll quote what my mother said during a conversation that I videotaped and then transcribed. During this conversation, she was talking about a political gangster in Shanghai who had the same last name as her family's, Du, and how in his early years the gangster wanted to be adopted by her family, who were rich by comparison. Later, the gangster became more powerful, far richer than my mother's family, and he showed up at my mother's wedding to pay his respects. Here's what she said in part: B

"Du Yusong having business like fruit stand. Like off-the-street kind. He is Du like Du Zong—but not Tsung-ming Island[2] people. The local people call *putong*. The river east side, he belong to that side local people. That man want to ask Du Zong father take him in like become own family. Du Zong father wasn't look down on him, but didn't take seriously, until that man big like become a mafia. Now important person, very hard to inviting him. Chinese way, came only to show respect, don't stay for dinner. Respect for making big celebration, he shows up. Mean gives lots of respect. Chinese custom. Chinese social life that way. If too important won't have to stay too long. He come to my wedding. I didn't see, I heard it. I gone to boy's side, they have YMCA dinner. Chinese age I was nineteen."

You should know that my mother's expressive command of English belies how much she actually understands. She reads the *Forbes*[3] report, listens to *Wall Street Week*, converses daily with her stockbroker, reads Shirley MacLaine's books[4] with ease—all kinds of things I can't begin to understand. Yet some of my friends tell me they understand fifty percent of what my mother says. Some say they understand eighty to ninety percent. Some say they understand none of it, as if she were speaking pure Chinese. But to me, my mother's English is perfectly clear, perfectly natural. It's my mother tongue. Her language, as I hear it, is vivid, direct, full of observation and imagery. That was the language that helped shape the way I saw things, expressed things, made sense of the world. C

Lately I've been giving more thought to the kind of English my mother speaks. Like others, I have described it to people as "broken" or "fractured" English. But I wince when I say that. It has always bothered me that I can think of no way to describe it other than "broken," as if it were damaged and needed to be fixed, as if

B GRAMMAR AND STYLE
Reread lines 31–33. Note how Tan addresses her readers as *you*, as though in conversation. This use of **informal language** helps her create a warm, personal voice.

Language Coach
Pronunciation *Belies* (line 49) is pronounced with the stress on the second syllable (bih LYZ). (A word with a similar pronunciation is *replies*.) *Belies* means "misrepresents" or "gives an inaccurate idea of." What does her mother's command of English belie?

C MAIN IDEAS
Reread lines 49–58. What **supporting details** does Tan include to describe the way her mother uses English?

2. **Tsung-ming** (tsŏŏng-mĭng) **Island:** an island near the mouth of the Yangtze River, near Shanghai, in eastern China.
3. ***Forbes:*** a financial magazine.
4. **Shirley MacLaine's books:** works by the American actress Shirley MacLaine (born 1934), many of which deal with reincarnation.

it lacked a certain wholeness and soundness. I've heard other terms used, "limited English," for example. But they seem just as bad, as if everything is limited, including people's perceptions of the limited-English speaker.

I know this for a fact, because when I was growing up, my mother's "limited" English limited my perception of her. I was ashamed of her English. I believed that her English reflected the quality of what she had to say. That is, because she expressed them imperfectly, her thoughts were imperfect. And I had plenty of empirical evidence[5] to support me: the fact that people in department stores, at banks, and in restaurants did not take her seriously, did not give her good service, pretended not to understand her, or even acted as if they did not hear her.

My mother has long realized the limitations of her English as well. When I was a teenager, she used to have me call people on the phone and pretend I was she. In this guise, I was forced to ask for information or even to complain and yell at people who had been rude to her. One time it was a call to her stockbroker in New York. She had cashed out her small portfolio, and it just so happened we were going to New York the next week, our first trip outside California. I had to get on the phone and say in an adolescent voice that was not very convincing, "This is Mrs. Tan."

My mother was standing in the back whispering loudly, "Why he don't send me check, already two weeks late. So mad he lie to me, losing me money."

And then I said in perfect English on the phone, "Yes, I'm getting rather concerned. You had agreed to send the check two weeks ago, but it hasn't arrived."

Then she began to talk more loudly. "What he want, I come to New York tell him front of his boss, you cheating me?" And I was trying to calm her down, make her be quiet, while telling the stockbroker, "I can't tolerate any more excuses. If I don't receive the check immediately, I am going to have to speak to your manager when I'm in New York next week." And sure enough, the following week, there we were in front of this astonished stockbroker, and I was sitting there red-faced and quiet, and my mother, the real Mrs. Tan, was shouting at his boss in her impeccable broken English. **D**

We used a similar routine more recently, for a situation that was far less humorous. My mother had gone to the hospital for an appointment to find out about a CAT scan[6] she had had a month earlier. She said she had spoken very good English, her best English, no mistakes. Still, she said, the hospital did not apologize when they informed her they had lost the CAT scan and she had come for nothing. She said they did not seem to have any sympathy when she told them she was anxious to know the exact diagnosis, since her husband and her son had died of brain tumors. She said they would not give her any more information until the next time and she would have to make another appointment for that. So she said she would not leave until the doctor called her daughter. She wouldn't budge. And when the doctor finally called her daughter, me, who spoke in perfect English—lo and behold—we had assurances the CAT scan would be found, promises that a conference call on Monday would be held, and apologies for any suffering my mother had gone through for a most regrettable mistake.

5. **empirical evidence:** evidence derived from observation.

6. **CAT scan:** a three-dimensional image of structures inside the human body.

COMMON CORE RI 6

D PERSONAL ESSAY

Writing in the **first-person point of view** is a **rhetorical technique** with considerable persuasive appeal. A gifted writer such as Amy Tan can cite the facts of her personal experiences and present them so vividly that readers feel as if they are sharing moments from her life. Reread lines 66–91. Notice that the author makes her point here by relating a **personal anecdote**—a vivid experience drawn from her own life. How does the dialogue in this anecdote appeal to your emotions and create meaning for you? Cite evidence from the essay to support your response.

I think my mother's English almost had an effect on limiting my possibilities in life as well. Sociologists and linguists probably will tell you that a person's developing language skills are more influenced by peers than by family. But I do think that the language spoken in the family, especially in immigrant families which are more insular,[7] plays a large role in shaping the language of the child. And I believe that it affected my results on achievement tests, IQ tests, and the SAT. While my English skills were never judged poor, compared with math, English could not be considered my strong suit. In grade school I did moderately well, getting perhaps B's, sometimes B-pluses, in English and scoring perhaps in the sixtieth or seventieth percentile on achievement tests. But those scores were not good enough to override the opinion that my true abilities lay in math and science, because in those areas I achieved A's and scored in the ninetieth percentile or higher.

This was understandable. Math is precise; there is only one correct answer. Whereas, for me at least, the answers on English tests were always a judgment call, a matter of opinion and personal experience. Those tests were constructed around items like fill-in-the-blank sentence completion, such as, "Even though Tom was ________, Mary thought he was________." And the correct answer always seemed to be the most bland combinations, for example, "Even though Tom was shy, Mary thought he was charming," with the grammatical structure "even though" limiting the correct answer to some sort of semantic opposites,[8] so you wouldn't get answers like, "Even though Tom was foolish, Mary thought he was ridiculous." Well, according to my mother, there were very few limitations as to what Tom could have been and what Mary might have thought of him. So I never did well on tests like that.

The same was true with word analogies, pairs of words for which you were supposed to find some sort of logical semantic relationship, for instance, "Sunset is to nightfall as ________ is to________." And here you would be presented with a list of four possible pairs, one of which showed the same kind of relationship: *red* is to *stoplight, bus* is to *arrival, chills* is to *fever, yawn* is to *boring.* Well, I could never think that way. I knew what the tests were asking, but I could not block out of my mind the images already created by the first pair, *sunset* is to *nightfall*—and I would see a burst of colors against a darkening sky, the moon rising, the lowering of a curtain of stars. And all the other pairs of words—*red, bus, stoplight, boring*—just threw up a mass of confusing images, making it impossible for me to see that saying "A sunset precedes nightfall" was as logical as saying "A chill precedes a fever." The only way I would have gotten that answer right was to imagine an associative situation,[9] such as my being disobedient and staying out past sunset, catching a chill at night, which turned into feverish pneumonia as punishment—which indeed did happen to me.

I have been thinking about all this lately, about my mother's English, about achievement tests. Because lately I've been asked, as a writer, why there are not more Asian-Americans represented in American literature. Why are

COMMON CORE L 2a

Language Coach

Hyphens In line 121, the phrase *fill-in-the-blank* modifies, or gives information about, the noun phrase *sentence completion.* Notice that hyphens are used to connect all of the words in this phrase. Some other examples of long hyphenated phrases are: *hard-to-remember name, behind-the-back pass,* and *not-too-friendly look.* Work with a partner to come up with more examples of hyphenated phrases.

PERSONAL ESSAY
Reread lines 107–129. How does this anecdote appeal to you as a reader and contribute to your understanding of the author's ideas? Explain.

7. **insular:** isolated.
8. **semantic opposites:** words opposite in meaning.
9. **associative situation:** a circumstance or story based on mental connections.

there few Asian-Americans enrolled in creative writing programs? Why do so many Chinese students go into engineering? Well, these are broad sociological questions I can't begin to answer. But I have noticed in surveys—in fact, just last week—that Asian-American students, as a whole, do significantly better on math achievement tests than on English tests. And this makes me think that there are other Asian-American students whose English spoken in the home might also be described as "broken" or "limited." And perhaps they also have teachers who are steering them away from writing and into math and science, which is what happened to me.

Fortunately, I happen to be rebellious and enjoy the challenge of disproving assumptions made about me. I became an English major my first year in college, after being enrolled as pre-med. I started writing nonfiction as a freelancer the week after I was told by my boss at the time that writing was my worst skill and I should hone my talents toward account management. **F**

F MAIN IDEAS
Identify the main idea of lines 157–161. What details support this main idea?

But it wasn't until 1985 that I began to write fiction. At first I wrote using what I thought to be wittily crafted sentences, sentences that would finally prove I had mastery over the English language. Here's an example from the first draft of a story that later made its way into *The Joy Luck Club,* but without this line: "That was my mental quandary in its nascent state."[10] A terrible line, which I can barely pronounce.

Fortunately, for reasons I won't get into here, I later decided I should envision a reader for the stories I would write. And the reader I decided on was my mother, because these were stories about mothers. So with this reader in mind—and in fact she did read my early drafts—I began to write stories using all the Englishes I grew up with: the English I spoke to my mother, which for lack of a better term might be described as "simple"; the English she used with me, which for lack of a better term might be described as "broken"; my translation of her Chinese, which could certainly be described as "watered down"; and what I imagined to be her translation of her Chinese if she could speak in perfect English, her internal language, and for that I sought to preserve the essence, but neither an English nor a Chinese structure. I wanted to capture what language ability tests can never reveal: her intent, her passion, her imagery, the rhythms of her speech and the nature of her thoughts.

Apart from what any critic had to say about my writing, I knew I had succeeded where it counted when my mother finished reading my book and gave me her verdict: "So easy to read." ~

10. **my mental quandary . . . state:** my mental predicament in its earliest form.

Comprehension

1. **Recall** What words does Tan typically use to describe her mother's English?
2. **Summarize** In general, how did people react to Mrs. Tan's use of English?
3. **Recall** According to Tan, what aspects of language do achievement tests fail to reveal?

Text Analysis

4. **Identify the Main Idea** Review the diagram you created as you read. Based on your notes, what is the main idea of the entire essay? Explain your answer.
5. **Compare Roles** Tan describes situations in which she was forced to act as a go-between for her mother. In what ways do these interactions differ from the typical mother-daughter relationship? Explain your response.
6. **Make Judgments** Tan describes her mother's English as "vivid, direct, full of observation and imagery." Reread the story Tan's mother tells in lines 39–48. Do you agree with Tan's opinion of her mother's speech? Why or why not?
7. **Analyze a Personal Essay** Describe Tan's changing perceptions of her mother's use of English. In what way did her changing views toward her mother influence Tan's observations about the power of language? How does Tan's personal testimony influence your own views about language? Cite evidence from the essay to support your response.
8. **Interpret Title** Tan uses the expression "mother tongue" as the title of her essay. State the usual meaning of this expression. Then, use each of the following examples to develop a different or expanded meaning for this term:
   - the idea of family talk (lines 28–30)
   - Tan's description of her mother's speech (lines 55–58)
   - Tan's thoughts on language development (lines 107–110)

Text Criticism

9. **Different Perspectives** Look at the essay again through the eyes of the following individuals. What important lessons about life and the uses of language might each draw from this essay?
   - an immigrant
   - the child of an immigrant
   - a doctor
   - a teacher

COMMON CORE

RI 2 Determine two or more central ideas of a text and analyze their development over the course of the text, including how they interact and build on one another to provide a complex analysis. **RI 3** Analyze a complex set of ideas or sequence of events and explain how specific individuals, ideas, or events interact and develop over the course of the text. **RI 6** Determine an author's point of view, analyzing how style and content contribute to the power, persuasiveness, or beauty of the text.

What LANGUAGES *do you speak?*

Tan claims that the language spoken within the family does more to shape the way a child speaks than the language spoken by his or her peers. Do you agree with Tan's opinion? Explain.

Language

◆ **GRAMMAR AND STYLE:** Use Appropriate Language

Review the **Grammar and Style** note on page 1266. For this essay, Tan chooses a casual, conversational style that lets her establish a strong connection with her readers. One strategy that helps Tan create this distinctive style is her use of **informal language** that contains **contractions** and idiosyncratic terms like *Englishes*. She also addresses her readers in a personal voice, using the **pronoun** *you*, as in the following excerpt:

> *You should know that my mother's expressive command of English belies how much she actually understands. She reads the* Forbes *report, listens to* Wall Street Week, *converses daily with her stockbroker, reads Shirley MacLaine's books with ease—all kinds of things I can't begin to understand.* (lines 49–52)

Whenever you write, consider the audience you are addressing and choose the appropriate level of formality.

PRACTICE Rewrite the following sentences using informal language.

EXAMPLE

It is often difficult to make sense of the rules of effective language.

Sometimes it's hard to understand what makes language work well.

1. A lack of education caused my mother to speak a damaged, limited kind of English.
2. To demonstrate my use of these techniques, I have included some excerpts from my recent work.
3. A substantial portion of my fiction relates to my personal experiences.

COMMON CORE

L 3 Apply knowledge of language to understand how language functions in different contexts, to make effective choices for meaning or style, and to comprehend more fully when reading. **W 2a–b** Introduce a topic; organize information so that each new element builds on that which precedes it; develop the topic thoroughly by selecting the most significant and relevant examples appropriate to the audience's knowledge of the topic. **W 4** Produce clear and coherent writing in which the development, organization, and style are appropriate to task, purpose, and audience.

READING-WRITING CONNECTION

Expand your understanding of "Mother Tongue" by responding to the prompt. Then, use the **revising tips** to improve your essay.

WRITING PROMPT	REVISING TIPS
WRITE AN ESSAY Choose a topic that lets you draw on your personal experiences—a longtime hobby, a trip you took, your family history. Write an **one-page essay** that communicates your unique perspective on this subject. Be sure to include relevant details from your own experiences in the essay.	• Use an attention-grabbing opening. • Include appropriate and effective personal details. • Create a compelling voice that conveys your personality.

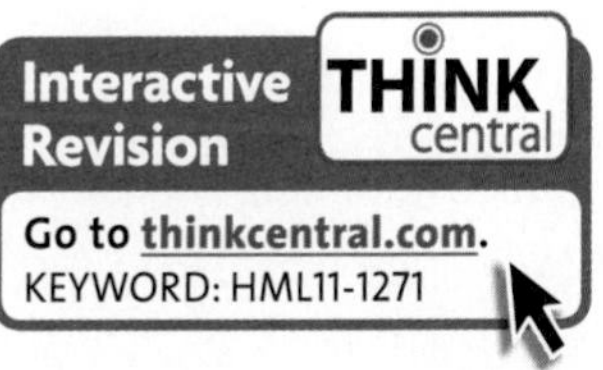

Interactive Revision
THINK central
Go to thinkcentral.com.
KEYWORD: HML11-1271

Reading for Information

Census Data: The U.S. Population

Government Documents

Use with "Mother Tongue," page 1264.

COMMON CORE

RI 5 Analyze and evaluate the effectiveness of the structure an author uses in his or her exposition or argument, including whether the structure makes points clear, convincing, and engaging. **RI 7** Integrate and evaluate multiple sources of information presented in different media or formats as well as in words in order to address a question or solve a problem.

The writers in this section, A Mosaic of American Voices, include Alice Walker, Sandra Cisneros, and Gwendolyn Brooks, who represent the diversity in the American population today. Their stories, poems, and essays, such as Amy Tan's essay "Mother Tongue," reflect the experiences of people living in a diverse culture. As you read the following government report, which presents the data the government has collected about America's diversity, consider how the data does or does not reflect the experiences of these writers.

Standards Focus: Analyze Text and Graphics

The U.S. Census Bureau conducts a national census every ten years and then compiles a report for the nation. The following portion of the 2000 census report focuses on the distribution and composition of the nation at that time. As you read the report, keep the following questions in mind:

- What is the report's tone, and who is the intended audience?
- What is the purpose of the report?
- What is the sequence of the information, and what are the major topics, or categories of information, in the report?
- How does this report's information on diversity reflect, or differ from, Amy Tan's experience as the daughter of an immigrant?
- How are maps and charts used to provide data and information?

To analyze the text and graphics in this report, note your observations and conclusions in a chart such as the one shown.

	Notes
Audience and tone	
Purpose	
Sequence of information/topics	

ALL ACROSS THE U.S.A.:
Population Distribution and Composition, 2000

During the 1990s, the population center of the United States shifted 12 miles south and 33 miles west, from a location near Steelville, Missouri, to a spot near Edgar Springs, Missouri.

Counting every person living in the United States is always a colossal undertaking. Census 2000 was the largest census in the history of the United States, counting 281 million people. In fact, the 33 million people added to the U.S. population between 1990 and 2000 is the largest census-to-census increase ever. New questions and procedures in Census 2000 provide unprecedented geographic[1] and racial detail. And new innovations in products and access modes will provide more data to more people faster than ever. **A**

Figure 2-1.
Percentage Change in Metropolitan and Nonmetropolitan Populations by Region: 1990 to 2000 **B**

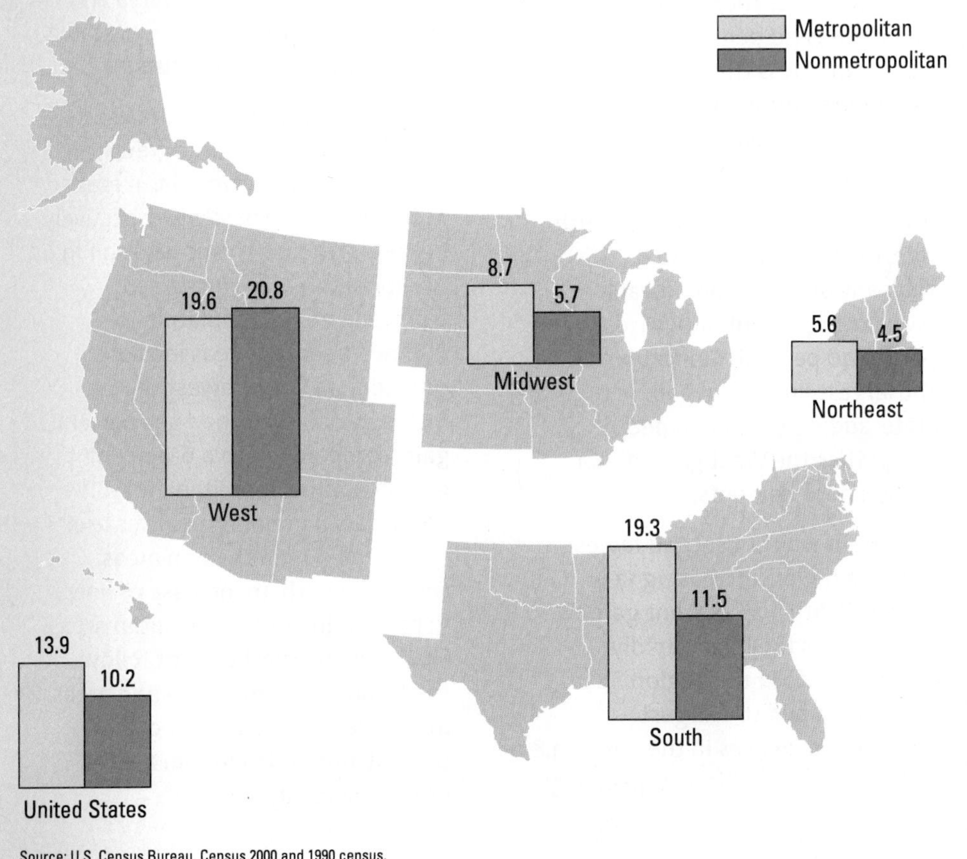

Source: U.S. Census Bureau, Census 2000 and 1990 census.

COMMON CORE RI 7

A ANALYZE TEXT AND GRAPHICS
Before reading further, examine the first two pages of this report from the U.S. Census Bureau. Notice that each section of the report begins with a one-sentence headline in green letters. Notice also that the paragraphs are presented as un-indented blocks of text, with space between paragraphs. The purpose of these features is to help readers grasp major points of the report and quickly identify pieces of information in separate paragraphs. Before you continue, glance at the next page of the report. What do you learn from the small headlines that will help you as you read the block paragraphs?

B ANALYZE TEXT AND GRAPHICS
Examine Figure 2-1. Which area of the country experienced the greatest growth in metropolitan population? the least growth of metropolitan population? What do you think might explain those changes?

1. The minimum population for Census Designated Places was dropped, generating more information on small areas than ever before.

Words That Count

- **Resident population** includes all people living in the United States.
- **The four statistical regions of the United States** are groups of states for which data are presented. They include the Northeast, the Midwest, the South, and the West.
- **Median age** is the age at which half the population is older and half is younger.

The decade of the 1990s was the only decade of the 20th century when every state gained population.

The growth rate during the 1990s (13 percent) was more than the rate in the 1980s (10 percent), but significantly less than the rate experienced during the 1950s — when a baby boom contributed appreciably to the 18-percent gain.

With an overall 20 percent growth rate, the West grew more rapidly than any other region. Nevada swelled 66 percent and Arizona gained 40 percent. California had the largest numerical gain of any state, adding 4.1 million people. Altogether, the West gained 10.4 million new residents.

The South was the second fastest growing region, increasing 17 percent. With a 26 percent gain, Georgia was the most rapidly growing state in this region. Texas and Florida had the largest numerical increases in the South, 3.8 million and 3.0 million, respectively. The total gain for the South (nearly 14.8 million) was the most of any region.

The population in the Midwest grew almost 8 percent, adding 4.7 million people. Minnesota was the Midwest's fastest growing state, increasing by more than 12 percent. A band of counties stretching across the Great Plains from the Canadian border to the Mexican border lost population.

The increase in the Northeast was 6 percent or 2.8 million people. Within the region, New Hampshire was the fastest growing state, increasing 11 percent. A band of slow growth counties included much of the interior Northeast and Appalachia, extending from Maine through western Pennsylvania and spilling over into the southern states of West Virginia and Kentucky.

In general, metropolitan areas across the United States grew faster than nonmetropolitan areas, 14 percent and 10 percent, respectively. In the Northeast, the population in metropolitan areas increased 6 percent, while population in nonmetropolitan areas increased 5 percent. In the Midwest the metropolitan areas had a 9-percent gain, compared with a 6-percent gain in nonmetropolitan areas. The South saw a population increase of 19 percent in metropolitan areas, compared with an increase of only 12 percent in nonmetropolitan areas. However, the West did not follow the trend. While metropolitan areas in the West increased almost 20 percent, nonmetropolitan areas grew 21 percent.

Table 2-1.
Population by Race and Hispanic Origin for the United States: 2000 **C**

Race and Hispanic or Latino	Number (in thousands)	Percent of total population
RACE		
Total Population....	281,421	100.0
One race..............	274,595	97.6
White............	211,460	75.1
Black or African American....	34,658	12.3
American Indian and Alaska Native.........	2,475	0.9
Asian..............	10,242	3.6
Native Hawaiian and Other Pacific Islander.......	399	0.1
Some other race...	15,359	5.5
Two or more races.................	6,826	2.4
HISPANIC OR LATINO		
Total Population....	281,421	100.0
Hispanic or Latino................	35,305	12.5
Not Hispanic or Latino................	246,116	87.5

Source: U.S. Census Bureau, Census 2000.

For the first time ever, respondents to the census were allowed to indicate more than one race.

The overwhelming majority of respondents to Census 2000 (98 percent) reported only one race. The largest group (75 percent) reported White alone. Another 12 percent reported Black or African American alone. Just under 1 percent of the population indicated only American Indian and Alaska Native, and 4 percent indicated Asian only. Among those indicating only one race, the smallest race group was the population of Native Hawaiians and Other Pacific Islanders, accounting for only 0.1 percent of the total U.S. population. The remainder of the single-race respondents (5 percent) indicated that they were Some other race alone.

Just over 2 percent of the population indicated more than one race. The most common combination was "White ***and*** Some other race," accounting for 32 percent of all respondents in this category. This group was followed by "White ***and*** American Indian and Alaska Native" (16 percent), "White ***and*** Asian" (13 percent), and "White ***and*** Black or African American" (11 percent). Of all respondents reporting more than one race, 7 percent indicated three or more races.

The federal government considers race and Hispanic origin to be two separate and distinct concepts. For Census 2000, about 13 percent of the total U.S. population indicated that they were Hispanic or Latino. The racial distribution of this group contrasted sharply with the racial distribution of the population as a whole. Nearly half (48 percent) of Hispanics indicated that they were White alone. Another 42 percent indicated that they were Some other race alone. Less than 4 percent reported Black or African American alone, American Indian and Alaska Native alone, or Native Hawaiian and Other Pacific Islander alone. Approximately 6 percent of all

COMMON CORE RI 7

C ANALYZE TEXT AND GRAPHICS
Review the information presented here in table form. Which racial group forms the greatest percentage of the population? What group is identified by a category other than race? In your notes, write a two-sentence summary of the information in this table.

Figure 2-2.
U.S. Age Distribution in Percent: 1990 and 2000 **D**

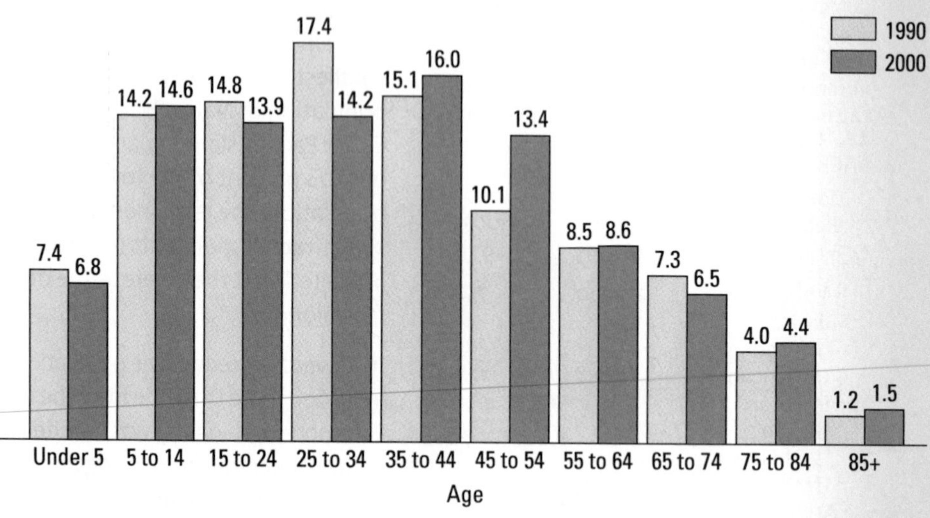

Source: U.S. Census Bureau, Census 2000 and 1990 census.

COMMON CORE RI 7

D ANALYZE TEXT AND GRAPHICS
Review the chart in which information on age distribution is presented in graphic form. What do the yellow columns represent? What do the green columns represent? How does the information presented here add to what you have learned by reading the Census Bureau report? Support your response with evidence from the chart and the report.

Hispanics reported two or more races. In fact nearly one-third of all respondents reporting more than one race were also Hispanic.

The U.S. population is growing older. **E**

The median age of the U.S. population in 2000 was 35.3 — the highest it has ever been. In 1990, the median was 32.9. The rise reflects a 4-percent decline in the number of people aged 18 to 34 and a 28-percent increase in the number aged 35 to 64. As the large generation of baby boomers[2] began passing their 45th birthday, the population aged 45 to 54 swelled 49 percent during the decade.

For the first time in the history of the census, the population aged 65 and older increased at a slower rate than the population as a whole. The percentage of people in this age group fell from 12.6 percent in 1990 to 12.4 percent in 2000. Relatively low birth rates during the late 1920s and early 1930s meant a relatively small number of people celebrated their 65th birthday in time for Census 2000. **F**

The Census Bureau Can Tell You More

- For more detailed information, see the following Census 2000 Briefs, *Population Change and Distribution* by Marc J. Perry and Paul J. Mackun and *Overview of Race and Hispanic Origin* by Elizabeth M. Grieco and Rachel C. Cassidy.
- Look for detailed tables on the Census Bureau's World Wide Web site (*www.census.gov*) and select "Census 2000."
- Contact the Statistical Information Staff of the U.S. Census Bureau at 301-457-2422 or e-mail *pop@census.gov*.

E ANALYZE TEXT AND GRAPHICS
This is one of four subheads in this report. What are those subheads? What is their purpose?

F ANALYZE TEXT AND GRAPHICS
Reread this last paragraph. How would you describe the tone? Has this tone remained consistent throughout the report? Is the audience of the report average Americans, government employees, or both?

2. Baby boomers are generally defined as people born from 1946 to 1964.

Comprehension

1. **Recall** In 2000 what percentage of the population was Hispanic or Latino? White? Black? Other?
2. **Summarize** What did the report conclude about the age distribution of the United States?

Text Analysis

3. **Analyze Sequence of Information** How is the information on race organized? What other sequence might be used to present this information? Explain.
4. **Analyze Graphic Presentations** Examine Figure 2-1. How did metropolitan and nonmetropolitan populations change between 1990 and 2000?
5. **Draw Conclusions** Which gives you a better sense of race in America, the Amy Tan essay or the census report? Why?

COMMON CORE

RI 5 Analyze and evaluate the effectiveness of the structure an author uses in his or her exposition or argument, including whether the structure makes points clear, convincing, and engaging. **RI 7** Integrate and evaluate multiple sources of information presented in different media or formats as well as in words in order to address a question or solve a problem. **W 1** Write arguments to support claims in an analysis of substantive texts, using valid reasoning and relevant and sufficient evidence. **W 8** Gather relevant information from multiple authoritative print and digital sources.

Read for Information: Synthesize

WRITING PROMPT

The 2000 census report identifies four categories of change in the American population—geographical center, population size, race and origin, and age. Which category of change do you think will have the greatest effect on America in the 21st century? State your opinion and support it with reasons and evidence from the census report you have just read, the Census Bureau Web site, at least one other Internet or print resource, and, if you wish, examples from your own experience.

The following steps will help you answer the prompt:

1. To determine which category of population change will have the greatest impact on the 21st century, study all of your sources, analyzing the information about the various categories of change. Write a clear statement of your opinion, or claim.
2. Take notes from your sources, identifying facts, statistics, and other evidence to support your claim.

Source 1	Source 2	Source 3
Evidence	Evidence	Evidence

3. Identify at least three reasons to support your claim and organize the evidence for the body of your essay under those reasons.
4. Take your thesis statement from step 1. Use step 4 to develop the body of your essay.

from In Search of Our Mothers' Gardens

Essay by Alice Walker

COMMON CORE

RI 5 Analyze and evaluate the effectiveness of the structure an author uses in his or her exposition or argument, including whether the structure makes points clear, convincing, and engaging. **RI 6** Determine an author's point of view or purpose in a text in which the rhetoric is particularly effective, analyzing how style and content contribute to the power, persuasiveness, or beauty of the text. **L 4c** Consult reference materials, both print and digital. **L 5** Demonstrate understanding of nuances in word meanings.

Meet the Author

Alice Walker born 1944

Best known for her novels, author and activist Alice Walker also writes poems, short stories, and essays. Often inspired by her personal experiences, Walker portrays the struggles of African-American women to transcend the limits imposed on their lives by racism and sexism. Though her characters typically face violence and great hardships, Walker emphasizes the power of hope and the strength of the human will to survive.

Early Influences The daughter of a sharecropper, Walker grew up poor in Eatonton, Georgia. When she was eight, an accident left her permanently blind in her right eye. A shy and self-conscious Walker withdrew from the world and turned to poetry to soothe her feelings of isolation.

Although uneducated herself, Walker's mother supported her daughter's creative ambitions. Walker was an exceptional student who became class valedictorian and won a scholarship to Spelman College, a historically black women's college in Atlanta, Georgia. When Walker left for college, her mother gave her three gifts: a typewriter, a sewing machine, and a suitcase. For Walker, these gifts represented creativity, domesticity, and freedom—a legacy of hopes, dreams, and unfulfilled longings passed from mother to daughter.

Fighting for Equality In 1965, after graduating from college, Walker received a travel fellowship to Senegal. Instead, she went to Mississippi to help fight for racial justice. "That summer," explains Walker, "marked the beginning of a realization that I could never live happily in Africa—or anywhere else—until I could live freely in Mississippi." In 1967, she defied state law to marry white civil rights lawyer Melvyn Leventhal. In retaliation for their interracial marriage, the couple was subjected to constant harassment and even death threats.

Speaking for the Oppressed During the 1970s, Walker published two novels and volumes of poetry and short stories. Her breakthrough came with the publication of her third novel, *The Color Purple* (1982), which was later made into a successful film. Many critics attacked this novel for its unflattering portrayals of African-American men. In response, Walker insisted her work reflected the painful realities of many black women's lives: "The black woman," she explained, "is one of America's greatest heroes. . . . Not enough credit has been given to the black woman who has been oppressed beyond recognition."

Author Online THINK central

Go to thinkcentral.com. KEYWORD: HML11-1278

DID YOU KNOW?

Alice Walker . . .

- became the first black woman to win the Pulitzer Prize for fiction.
- helped readers rediscover the writer Zora Neale Hurston.
- is an active environmentalist.

TEXT ANALYSIS: AUTHOR'S MESSAGE

Authors write for a reason: they have a point to get across. In most nonfiction, you can find direct statements that reveal the **author's message,** as in this example:

And so our mothers and grandmothers have, more often than not anonymously, handed on the creative spark, the seed of the flower they themselves never hoped to see. . . .

Walker reaches this conclusion by a pattern of **inductive reasoning.** Her essay proceeds from specific examples or pieces of evidence to a generalization such as the one quoted above. As you read, pay special attention to Walker's anecdotes, the brief stories she tells about her mother and women like her. See if you can anticipate the generalization Walker will infer from these anecdotes.

Walker also includes one of her poems in the essay. In the poem, her message is expressed indirectly, through elements such as **mood, imagery,** and **figurative language.** As you read the essay, notice the different techniques Walker uses to reveal her message.

READING SKILL: UNDERSTAND CULTURAL CONTEXT

When you analyze the **cultural context** of a text, you consider the social and cultural conditions that influenced how and why the text was written. Alice Walker's work reflects two key influences: her childhood experiences as a poor African-American girl in the South and her adult commitment to feminist ideals. To fully appreciate Walker's points, use the following strategies:

- Before reading, study the details about cultural context provided in the background information on page 1280.
- As you read, consult the footnotes to clarify Walker's references to cultural details.
- Apply what you know about the social conditions that shaped the lives of African Americans in the South.

As you read, note details that reveal how Walker's social and cultural influences have shaped her views.

Complete the activities in your **Reader/Writer Notebook**.

When does LIFE *become art?*

Some people have an irresistible urge to create. Maybe they express it by sewing stylish clothes or cooking elaborate meals, by singing as they work, or by telling hilarious stories. For these people, even everyday chores can provide the creative outlet they need to release their artistic impulses.

DISCUSS In a small group, think of several ways that people express their creativity in everyday life. What do you think drives people to be creative? Record your responses and compare them with those of other groups.

In Search of Our Mothers' Gardens

Alice Walker

BACKGROUND Alice Walker wrote this essay in 1974, after decades of civil rights activism had broken down many barriers for African Americans. At the same time, the women's movement had begun to raise awareness of the social constraints imposed on women's lives. Women of Walker's generation were poised to claim personal and social freedoms that earlier generations of women could never have dreamed of. As these women looked back into history to find role models for their own lives, they began to appreciate the extraordinary sacrifices these earlier generations had made. In this essay, Walker examines her mother's life to uncover a hidden legacy of resilience, strength, and overlooked talent passed on to the women of her own time.

In the late 1920s my mother ran away from home to marry my father. Marriage, if not running away, was expected of seventeen-year-old girls. By the time she was twenty, she had two children and was pregnant with a third. Five children later, I was born. And this is how I came to know my mother: she seemed a large, soft, loving-eyed woman who was rarely impatient in our home. Her quick, violent temper was on view only a few times a year, when she battled with the white landlord who had the misfortune to suggest to her that her children did not need to go to school.

She made all the clothes we wore, even my brothers' overalls. She made all the towels and sheets we used. She spent the summers canning vegetables and fruits. She spent the winter evenings making quilts enough to cover all our beds. **A**

During the "working" day, she labored beside—not behind—my father in the fields. Her day began before sunup, and did not end until late at night. There was never a moment for her to sit down, undisturbed, to unravel her own private thoughts; never a time free from interruption—by work or the noisy inquiries of her many children. And yet, it is to my mother—and all our mothers who were not famous—that I went in search of the secret of what has fed that muzzled and often mutilated,[1] but vibrant, creative spirit that the black woman has inherited, and that pops out in wild and unlikely places to this day.

Analyze Visuals ▶
Describe the style of this painting. In what ways does the artist's use of color, line, and texture contrast with the activity depicted?

Language Coach
Prefixes A **prefix** is a word part attached to the beginning of a word. *Mis-* means "bad." *Fortune,* here, means "luck." What happened to the landlord as a result of his remark? Why is Walker's use of *misfortune* (line 7) humorous?

A CULTURAL CONTEXT
What details in lines 1–11 convey the social conditions of African-American women in the early 20th century?

1. **mutilated** (myo͞ot'l-ā'tĭd): irreparably damaged.

Washerwoman, James Amos Porter. Oil on canvas, 18″ × 13″. Private collection. Reproduction rights given by the Dorothy Porter Wesley Research Center, Fort Lauderdale, Florida.

But when, you will ask, did my overworked mother have time to know or care about feeding the creative spirit?

The answer is so simple that many of us have spent years discovering it. We have constantly looked high, when we should have looked high—and low.

For example: in the Smithsonian Institution in Washington, D.C., there hangs a quilt unlike any other in the world. In fanciful, inspired, and yet simple and identifiable figures, it portrays the story of the Crucifixion.[2] It is considered rare, beyond price. Though it follows no known pattern of quilt-making, and though it is made of bits and pieces of worthless rags, it is obviously the work of a person of powerful imagination and deep spiritual feeling. Below this quilt I saw a note that says it was made by "an anonymous Black woman in Alabama, a hundred years ago."

If we could locate this "anonymous" black woman from Alabama, she would turn out to be one of our grandmothers—an artist who left her mark in the only materials she could afford, and in the only medium her position in society allowed her to use. **B**

As Virginia Woolf[3] wrote further, in *A Room of One's Own:*

Yet genius of a sort must have existed among women as it must have existed among the working class. [Change this to "slaves" and "the wives and daughters of sharecroppers."] Now and again an Emily Brontë or a Robert Burns [change this to "a Zora Hurston or a Richard Wright"[4]] blazes out and proves its presence. But certainly it never got itself on to paper. When, however, one reads of a witch being ducked, of a woman possessed by devils [or "Sainthood"[5]], of a wise woman selling herbs [our root workers], or even a very remarkable man who had a mother, then I think we are on the track of a lost novelist, a suppressed poet, of some mute and inglorious Jane Austen[6]. . . . Indeed, I would venture to guess that Anon, who wrote so many poems without signing them, was often a woman. . . . **C**

And so our mothers and grandmothers have, more often than not anonymously, handed on the creative spark, the seed of the flower they themselves never hoped to see: or like a sealed letter they could not plainly read.

And so it is, certainly, with my own mother. Unlike "Ma" Rainey's songs, which retained their creator's name even while blasting forth from Bessie Smith's[7] mouth, no song or poem will bear my mother's name. Yet so many of the stories that I write, that we all write, are my mother's stories. Only recently did I fully

COMMON CORE L 4c

Language Coach

History of English Many common English words, such as *years* (line 22), *high* (line 23), *work* (line 28), and *deep* (line 29) come from Old English. Use an electronic or print version of a history of the English language to find two interesting facts about Old English.

B AUTHOR'S MESSAGE
Reread Walker's description of the quilt in lines 24–34. Which sentence best states the message behind Walker's observations?

C CULTURAL CONTEXT
Reread lines 36–45. Consulting the footnotes as needed, explain how Walker adapts the Virginia Woolf quotation to her own cultural context. Why might Walker have chosen to quote this particular author?

---

2. **Crucifixion:** the death of Jesus Christ, who was nailed to a cross.
3. **Virginia Woolf:** English novelist, critic, and pioneering feminist (1882–1941). Her works frequently explore the inner lives of women living under severe social constraints.
4. **Emily Brontë . . . Richard Wright:** Brontë (1818–1848) was an English novelist and poet, and Burns (1759–1796) was a Scottish poet. Hurston (1891–1960) and Wright (1908–1960) were African-American writers.
5. **"Sainthood":** a reference to certain black women in the South called Saints. They were intensely spiritual women who were driven to madness by their unfulfilled creativity.
6. **Jane Austen:** British novelist (1775–1817), best known for *Pride and Prejudice.*
7. **"Ma" Rainey's . . . Bessie Smith's:** Ma Rainey was the nickname of Gertrude Malissa Nix Pridgett Rainey (1886–1939), a blues singer considered to be the mother of the blues. Bessie Smith (1894–1937), another blues singer, was mentored by Ma Rainey.

realize this: that through years of listening to my mother's stories of her life, I have absorbed not only the stories themselves, but something of the manner in which she spoke, something of the urgency that involves the knowledge that her stories—like her life—must be recorded. It is probably for this reason that so much of what I have written is about characters whose counterparts in real life are so much older than I am.

But the telling of these stories, which came from my mother's lips as naturally as breathing, was not the only way my mother showed herself as an artist. For stories, too, were subject to being distracted, to dying without conclusion. Dinners must be started, and cotton must be gathered before the big rains. The artist that was and is my mother showed itself to me only after many years. This is what I finally noticed:

Like Mem, a character in *The Third Life of Grange Copeland,*[8] my mother adorned with flowers whatever shabby house we were forced to live in. And not just your typical straggly country stand of zinnias, either. She planted ambitious gardens—and still does—with over fifty different varieties of plants that bloom profusely from early March until late November. Before she left home for the fields, she watered her flowers, chopped up the grass, and laid out new beds. When she returned from the fields she might divide clumps of bulbs, dig a cold pit,[9] uproot and replant roses, or prune branches from her taller bushes or trees—until night came and it was too dark to see.

Whatever she planted grew as if by magic, and her fame as a grower of flowers spread over three counties. Because of her creativity with her flowers, even my memories of poverty are seen through a screen of blooms—sunflowers, petunias, roses, dahlias, forsythia, spirea, delphiniums, verbena . . . and on and on.

And I remember people coming to my mother's yard to be given cuttings from her flowers; I hear again the praise showered on her because whatever rocky soil she landed on, she turned into a garden. A garden so brilliant with colors, so original in its design, so magnificent with life and creativity, that to this day people drive by our house in Georgia—perfect strangers and imperfect strangers—and ask to stand or walk among my mother's art.

I notice that it is only when my mother is working in her flowers that she is radiant, almost to the point of being invisible—except as Creator: hand and eye. She is involved in work her soul must have. Ordering the universe in the image of her personal conception of Beauty.

Her face, as she prepares the Art that is her gift, is a legacy of respect she leaves to me, for all that illuminates and cherishes life. She has handed down respect for the possibilities—and the will to grasp them.

For her, so hindered and intruded upon in so many ways, being an artist has still been a daily part of her life. This ability to hold on, even in very simple ways, is work black women have done for a very long time. D

COMMON CORE L5

Language Coach

Connotation The images or feelings you connect to a word add a finer shade of meaning, called **connotation.** Read lines 49–56. What did Walker absorb? Why are the connotations of *absorbed* (line 54) more appropriate than *heard* or *noted*?

COMMON CORE RI 5, RI 6

D AUTHOR'S MESSAGE
Before you read further, review the opening paragraph of this essay. Notice that Walker does not begin with a thesis statement—an idea about her mother that she intends to support in the body of the essay. Instead, she follows a pattern of **inductive reasoning.** She begins with specific anecdotes about her mother and leads from these specifics to generalizations like the one quoted on page 1282. Reread lines 59–93. Notice Walker's focus on the details of her mother's life. What inductive generalization about women does she draw from the evidence on this page?

8. ***The Third Life of Grange Copeland:*** Alice Walker's first novel, published in 1970.
9. **cold pit:** shallow pit, usually covered with glass, used for rooting or sheltering young plants from temperature variations in the spring.

This poem is not enough, but it is something, for the woman who literally covered the holes in our walls with sunflowers:

They were women then
My mama's generation
Husky of voice—Stout of
Step
With fists as well as
Hands
How they battered down
Doors
And ironed
Starched white
Shirts
How they led
Armies
Headragged Generals
Across mined
Fields
Booby-trapped
Kitchens
To discover books
Desks
A place for us
How they knew what we
Must know
Without knowing a page
Of it
Themselves. E

E AUTHOR'S MESSAGE
Reread the poem in lines 96–121. Identify images Walker uses to describe these women. What qualities are emphasized by these images?

Guided by my heritage of a love of beauty and a respect for strength—in search of my mother's garden, I found my own.

And perhaps in Africa over two hundred years ago, there was just such a mother; perhaps she painted vivid and daring decorations in oranges and yellows and greens on the walls of her hut; perhaps she sang—in a voice like Roberta Flack's[10]—*sweetly* over the compounds of her village; perhaps she wove the most stunning mats or told the most ingenious stories of all the village storytellers. Perhaps she was herself a poet—though only her daughter's name is signed to the poems that we know.

Perhaps Phillis Wheatley's mother was also an artist.

Perhaps in more than Phillis Wheatley's[11] biological life is her mother's signature made clear.

---

10. **Roberta Flack's:** Flack is a popular African-American singer-songwriter.
11. **Phillis Wheatley's:** American poet Phillis Wheatley (1753?–1783), was born in Africa and brought to America in slavery. She is often referred to as the first African-American poet.

After Reading

Comprehension

1. **Recall** On what occasions did Walker's mother lose her temper?
2. **Summarize** What did Walker's mother do in a typical day?
3. **Recall** According to Walker, what change occurred in her mother as she worked in her garden?

Text Analysis

4. **Make Inferences** Recall that a **paradox** is a statement that may appear contradictory but in fact communicates an important truth. Identify the paradox in Walker's poem in lines 117–121. What point is Walker making?
5. **Analyze Author's Message** Reread the conclusion of Walker's essay in lines 124–133. Explain what Walker means by her reference to Phillis Wheatley's mother. In what way does this passage express the message of Walker's essay?
6. **Examine Cultural Context** Consider the conditions that constrained Walker's mother's life. Within this context, what is so remarkable about what her mother achieved? Support your answer with details.
7. **Make Generalizations** Consider Walker's descriptions of the following works of art by African-American women. What does each example tell you about this artistic tradition?
   - the description of the quilt (lines 24–34)
   - Walker's comments on her mother's stories (lines 49–56)
   - the garden Walker's mother plants (lines 65–77)
8. **Draw Conclusions** Think back to your discussion about the creative outlets people use to express their artistic impulses. Consider the creative outlets described in question 7. In your opinion, what inspires these women to make art despite the obstacles they face?

Text Criticism

9. **Critical Interpretations** "Walker's optimism," writes critic Donna Haisty Winchell, "is ultimately born of her belief that something of the divine exists in every human and nonhuman participant in the universe. The inhabitants of her fictional world search . . . for that divine spark that makes them uniquely who they are." How might this quote apply to the women in this essay? Cite evidence from the text to support your conclusions.

When does LIFE *become art?*

Alice Walker views her mother's passion for creating beautiful flower gardens as an artistic expression. Can you think of other ways people express artistry in nontraditional ways? Explain.

COMMON CORE

RI 1 Cite evidence to support analysis of inferences drawn from the text. **RI 5** Analyze and evaluate the effectiveness of the structure an author uses in his or her exposition or argument, including whether the structure makes points clear, convincing, and engaging. **RI 6** Determine an author's point of view or purpose in a text in which the rhetoric is particularly effective, analyzing how style and content contribute to the power, persuasiveness, or beauty of the text.

Straw into Gold: The Metamorphosis of the Everyday

VIDEO TRAILER THINK central KEYWORD: HML11-1286A

COMMON CORE

RI 4 Determine the meaning of words and phrases as they are used in the text, including figurative and connotative meanings. **RI 5** Analyze and evaluate the effectiveness of the structure an author uses in his or her exposition or argument, including whether the structure makes points clear, convincing, and engaging.

Meet the Author

Sandra Cisneros born 1954

"I'm trying to write the stories that haven't been written," Sandra Cisneros has proclaimed. With her rich, intimate portraits of Mexican and Mexican-American characters, Cisneros hopes to make readers of all races aware of the complexities of straddling two cultures. She sees herself as a voice for the voiceless. "I'm determined," she explains, "to fill a literary void."

Fighting Tradition Born to a Mexican father and a Mexican-American mother, Cisneros grew up on Chicago's South Side. The only girl among seven children, she felt as if she had "seven fathers" because her brothers tried to control her behavior. Like their father, they thought Sandra should adopt a quiet, traditional lifestyle. Fortunately, she was blessed with a mother "brave enough to raise her daughter in a nontraditional way." "My mother didn't force me to learn how to cook," says Cisneros. "And she always told me, 'Make sure you can take care of yourself.'"

Growing Up Lonely Cisneros formed few lasting friendships in early childhood, because her family moved frequently between Chicago and Mexico. "The moving back and forth, the new school, were very upsetting to me as a child," she once said. Retreating into herself, Cisneros became a keen observer of others and a secret writer of poetry. After years of clandestine composition, she encountered a teacher in high school who appreciated her experiences and her writing. With the teacher's encouragement, Cisneros began to share her work with her classmates.

The Value of Heritage In 1976, Cisneros entered the University of Iowa's prestigious Writers' Workshop. Surrounded by people from more privileged backgrounds, Cisneros felt intimidated. Soon, however, she came to realize that she could write about something her classmates could not. "It was not until this moment," Cisneros recalls, "when I separated myself, when I considered myself truly distinct, that my writing acquired a voice." Cisneros's realization gave rise to her acclaimed *The House on Mango Street* (1984), a series of interlocking prose poems about a poor Mexican-American family. Her reputation was cemented with the publication in 1991 of *Woman Hollering Creek,* a collection of stories. "In everything I've done in my life," she maintains, "including all the choices I've made as a writer, I've followed my gut and my heart. It's taken me where I've needed to go so far."

DID YOU KNOW?

Sandra Cisneros . . .

- wrote in secret as a child because she knew her family would disapprove.
- won a MacArthur "genius grant," a large monetary award given to honor "exceptional creativity and originality."
- has had poems on display on Chicago subways and buses.

Author Online THINK central

Go to thinkcentral.com. KEYWORD: HML11-1286B

TEXT ANALYSIS: VOICE

A writer's **voice** is his or her unique style of expression. This unique use of language is what allows you to "hear" a human personality behind the words you read. In "Straw into Gold," Sandra Cisneros writes:

I'd never seen anybody make corn tortillas. Ever.

The informal tone, the use of a contraction, the everyday words, the short sentence followed by a fragment, and the pauses before and after the word *ever*—all help create Cisneros's voice in this essay—one that is personal, relaxed, and conversational. The voice is consistently natural, even with this essay's central **allusion**—an indirect reference the author assumes her readers will recognize. The mythological story to which Cisneros alludes is familiar to most children. As you read, look for instances when you "hear" Cisneros behind her words. Note the stylistic elements that help create this unique effect.

READING SKILL: ANALYZE STRUCTURE

The **structure** of a text, or how its different parts are organized, is directly tied to the author's purpose. Cisneros reveals two purposes in this essay, and she uses two methods of reasoning—two kinds of structures—to achieve them. Her primary structure is anecdotal. Using **inductive reasoning,** she shares with readers some of her formative experiences—moments that helped shape her life as a writer. Then she draws general conclusions from those specific experiences.

At the heart of this essay, you will also find an example of **deductive reasoning.** The writer arrives at a conclusion by applying a general principle to a specific situation. The general principle is that weaving straw into gold reveals magical power. The specific situation is that Cisneros, in her own way, can weave straw into gold. Finally, the specific conclusion is that as a writer, Cisneros also has magical power.

Personal essays are often loosely structured, and "Straw into Gold" is no exception. Cisneros begins the essay with an **anecdote**—a brief story that makes a point. As you read, use a chart like the one shown to list these anecdotes and the author's inductive generalizations about them.

Anecdote or Recollection	*Inductive Generalization*
learning to make tortillas	

Complete the activities in your **Reader/Writer Notebook**.

Where do writers get their MATERIAL?

Writers harvest ideas for their work in a variety of places. Some writers find inspiration in controversies ripped from the headlines. Others are intrigued by a particular moment in history. Literature can be inspired by a writer's travels around the world, but just as often, powerful stories start closer to home. In "Straw into Gold," you will meet a writer who has unearthed a wealth of ideas in her own experiences and heritage.

QUICKWRITE Think of a work of literature you're familiar with. Where do you think the writer came by his or her ideas? Whether it's a lyric poem about lost love or a novel about a historical event, try to imagine the writer's source of material. Explain your thoughts in a short paragraph.

Straw into Gold:

The Metamorphosis of the Everyday

Sandra Cisneros

BACKGROUND Cisneros originally delivered the text of "Straw into Gold" as a speech. The essay still retains some characteristics of an oral work—for example, the voice has a distinctly conversational character. The phrase "Straw into Gold" refers to the challenge faced by the heroine in "Rumplestiltskin." In this fairy tale, as you may recall, a miller's daughter will be put to death unless she can do the seemingly impossible—namely, spin gold out of mere straw. The word *metamorphosis* in the subtitle means "transformation."

Analyze Visuals ▸
What does the image on the opposite page suggest about women's roles in traditional Mexican culture? Read the essay and then revisit your answer, citing details from the text.

When I was living in an artists' colony in the south of France, some fellow Latin-Americans who taught at the university in Aix-en-Provence[1] invited me to share a homecooked meal with them. I had been living abroad almost a year then on an NEA[2] grant, subsisting mainly on French bread and lentils so that my money could last longer. So when the invitation to dinner arrived, I accepted without hesitation. Especially since they had promised Mexican food.

What I didn't realize when they made this invitation was that I was supposed to be involved in preparing the meal. I guess they assumed I knew how to cook Mexican food because I am Mexican. They wanted specifically tortillas, though I'd never made a tortilla in my life. **A**

A VOICE
Reread lines 1–10. What stylistic elements allow Cisneros's informal, conversational voice to emerge? Cite specific examples.

1. **Aix-en-Provence** (äk'sän-prō-väns'): French city about ten miles north of the Mediterranean Sea.
2. **NEA:** the National Endowment for the Arts, a federal agency that funds artistic projects of organizations and individuals.

It's true I had witnessed my mother rolling the little armies of dough into perfect circles, but my mother's family is from Guanajuato;[3] they are *provincianos*, country folk. They only know how to make flour tortillas. My father's family, on the other hand, is *chilango*[4] from Mexico City. We ate corn tortillas but we didn't make them. Someone was sent to the corner tortilleria to buy some. I'd never seen anybody make corn tortillas. Ever.

Somehow my Latino hosts had gotten a hold of a packet of corn flour, and this is what they tossed my way with orders to produce tortillas. *Así como sea.* Any ol' way, they said and went back to their cooking.

Why did I feel like the woman in the fairy tale who was locked in a room and ordered to spin straw into gold? I had the same sick feeling when I was required to **B** write my critical essay for the MFA[5] exam—the only piece of noncreative writing necessary in order to get my graduate degree. How was I to start? There were rules involved here, unlike writing a poem or story, which I did intuitively. There was a step by step process needed and I had better know it. I felt as if making tortillas—or writing a critical paper, for that matter—were tasks so impossible I wanted to break down into tears.

Somehow though, I managed to make tortillas—crooked and burnt, but edible nonetheless. My hosts were absolutely ignorant when it came to Mexican food; they thought my tortillas were delicious. (I'm glad my mama wasn't there.) Thinking back and looking at an old photograph documenting the three of us consuming those lopsided circles I am amazed. Just as I am amazed I could finish my MFA exam. I've managed to do a lot of things in my life I didn't think I was capable of and which many others didn't think I was capable of either. Especially because I am a woman, a Latina, an only daughter in a family of six men. My father would've liked to have seen me married long ago. In our culture men and women don't leave their father's house except by way of marriage. I crossed my father's threshold with nothing carrying me but my own two feet. A woman whom no one came for and no one chased away. **C**

To make matters worse, I left before any of my six brothers had ventured away from home. I broke a terrible taboo. Somehow, looking back at photos of myself as a child, I wonder if I was aware of having begun already my own quiet war.

I like to think that somehow my family, my Mexicanness, my poverty, all had something to do with shaping me into a writer. I like to think my parents were preparing me all along for my life as an artist even though they didn't know it. From my father I inherited a love of wandering. He was born in Mexico City but as a young man he traveled into the U.S. vagabonding. He eventually was drafted and thus became a citizen. Some of the stories he has told about his first months in the U.S. with little or no English surface in my stories in *The House on Mango Street*[6] as well as others I have in mind to write in the future. From him I inherited

B ALLUSION
An **allusion** is an indirect reference to a person, a place, an event, or a literary work that the writer believes readers will recognize. Cisneros uses a literary allusion in lines 20–21 to compare her challenge (making tortillas) with that of a character in "Rumplestiltskin." As you read, consider the essay's title. How does Cisneros carry the allusion through the essay, and what is its greater meaning?

Language Coach
Word Definitions
Intuitively (line 24) means "done in a manner requiring no active thought or knowledge." What does Cisneros do intuitively? How does she contrast intuitive tasks and non-intuitive tasks?

C ANALYZE STRUCTURE
What does Cisneros's completion of her MFA exam have in common with the experience recounted in the tortilla anecdote? Explain how these experiences make Cisneros feel like "the woman in the fairy tale" she alludes to in lines 20–21.

3. **Guanajuato** (gwä'nä-hwä'tō): state in central Mexico.
4. ***chilango*** (chē-läng'gō) *Mexican slang*: native to Mexico City.
5. **MFA:** Master of Fine Arts, an academic degree.
6. ***The House on Mango Street:*** Cisneros's first book of fiction, published in 1983.

a sappy heart. (He still cries when he watches Mexican soaps—especially if they deal with children who have forsaken their parents.)

My mother was born like me—in Chicago but of Mexican descent. It would be her tough streetwise voice that would haunt all my stories and poems. An amazing woman who loves to draw and read books and can sing an opera. A smart cookie. **D**

When I was a little girl we traveled to Mexico City so much I thought my grandparents' house on La Fortuna, number 12, was home. It was the only constant in our nomadic ramblings from one Chicago flat to another. The house on Destiny Street, number 12, in the colonia Tepeyac would be perhaps the only home I knew, and that nostalgia for a home would be a theme that would obsess me.

My brothers also figured greatly in my art. Especially the older two; I grew up in their shadows. Henry, the second oldest and my favorite, appears often in poems I have written and in stories which at times only borrow his nickname, Kiki. He played a major role in my childhood. We were bunk-bed mates. We were co-conspirators. We were pals. Until my oldest brother came back from studying in Mexico and left me odd woman out for always.

What would my teachers say if they knew I was a writer now? Who would've guessed it? I wasn't a very bright student. I didn't much like school because we moved so much and I was always new and funny looking. In my fifth-grade report card I have nothing but an avalanche of C's and D's, but I don't remember being that stupid. I was good at art and I read plenty of library books and Kiki laughed at all my jokes. At home I was fine, but at school I never opened my mouth except when the teacher called on me.

When I think of how I see myself it would have to be at age eleven. I know I'm thirty-two on the outside, but inside I'm eleven. I'm the girl in the picture with skinny arms and a crumpled skirt and crooked hair. I didn't like school because all they saw was the outside me. School was lots of rules and sitting with your hands folded and being very afraid all the time. I liked looking out the window and thinking. I liked staring at the girl across the way writing her name over and over again in red ink. I wondered why the boy with the dirty collar in front of me didn't have a mama who took better care of him.

I think my mama and papa did the best they could to keep us warm and clean and never hungry. We had birthday and graduation parties and things like that, but there was another hunger that had to be fed. There was a hunger I didn't even have a name for. Was this when I began writing? **E**

In 1966 we moved into a house, a real one, our first real home. This meant we didn't have to change schools and be the new kids on the block every couple of years. We could make friends and not be afraid we'd have to say goodbye to them and start all over. My brothers and the flock of boys they brought home would become important characters eventually for my stories—Louie and his cousins, Meme Ortiz and his dog with two names, one in English and one in Spanish.

My mother flourished in her own home. She took books out of the library and taught herself to garden—to grow flowers so envied we had to put a lock

D VOICE
Reread Cisneros's description of her parents in lines 43–55. Identify the informal words, as well as the short sentences and fragments, that establish Cisneros's voice here.

E ANALYZE STRUCTURE
Identify the six recollections Cisneros presents in lines 43–86. What do they have in common? What is the inductive conclusion Cisneros draws from them?

on the gate to keep out the midnight flower thieves. My mother has never quit gardening.

This was the period in my life, that slippery age when you are both child and woman and neither, I was to record in *The House on Mango Street.* I was still shy. I was a girl who couldn't come out of her shell.

How was I to know I would be recording and documenting the women who sat their sadness on an elbow and stared out a window? It would be the city streets of Chicago I would later record, as seen through a child's eyes.

I've done all kinds of things I didn't think I could do since then. I've gone to a prestigious university, studied with famous writers, and taken an MFA degree. I've taught poetry in schools in Illinois and Texas. I've gotten an NEA grant and run away with it as far as my courage would take me. I've seen the bleached and bitter mountains of the Peloponnesus.[7] I've lived on an island. I've been to Venice twice. I've lived in Yugoslavia. I've been to the famous Nice[8] flower market behind the opera house. I've lived in a village in the pre-Alps and witnessed the daily parade of promenaders.

I've moved since Europe to the strange and wonderful country of Texas, land of polaroid-blue skies and big bugs. I met a mayor with my last name. I met famous Chicana and Chicano artists and writers and *políticos.*[9]

Texas is another chapter in my life. It brought with it the Dobie-Paisano Fellowship,[10] a six-month residency on a 265-acre ranch. But most important, Texas brought Mexico back to me.

In the days when I would sit at my favorite people-watching spot, the snakey Woolworth's counter across the street from the Alamo[11] (the Woolworth's which has since been torn down to make way for progress), I couldn't think of anything else I'd rather be than a writer. I've traveled and lectured from Cape Cod to San Francisco, to Spain, Yugoslavia, Greece, Mexico, France, Italy, and now today to Texas. Along the way there has been straw for the taking. With a little imagination, it can be spun into gold. **F**

COMMON CORE RI 5

F ANALYZE STRUCTURE
The author concludes this essay with a pattern of **inductive reasoning** that she has used throughout—moving from specific experiences to a generalization about these experiences. However, as you learned before reading this selection, Cisneros weaves **deductive reasoning** into her reflections here. Review the information about deductive reasoning on page 1287. Then, identify the three parts of the author's deductive argument: the general principle, the specific situation, and the conclusion. What part does the essay's closing sentence play in this deductive structure?

7. **Peloponnesus** (pĕl′ə-pə-nē′-səs): peninsula forming the southern part of mainland Greece.
8. **Nice** (nēs): port city in southern France.
9. ***políticos*** (pō-lē′tē-kōs) *Spanish*: politicians.
10. **Dobie-Paisano** (dō′bē pī-zä′nō) **Fellowship:** a prestigious award offered to authors who are from or write about Texas. It includes cash as well as the use of living quarters.
11. **Alamo:** a mission chapel in San Antonio, Texas, site of a famous battle in Texas's war of independence from Mexico.

Comprehension

1. **Recall** What misunderstanding does Cisneros recount at the beginning of the essay?
2. **Recall** What traits do Cisneros and her father have in common?
3. **Summarize** As a child, how did Cisneros feel at school?

Text Analysis

4. **Make Inferences** What childhood events and circumstances inspired Cisneros to become a writer? Cite evidence from the selection to support your inferences.
5. **Interpret Allusion** An allusion is an indirect reference to a person, a place, an event, or a literary work with which the writer believes the reader will be familiar. Reread lines 120–123 and consider the essay's title. By incorporating allusions to the fairy tale "Rumplestiltskin," what point is Cisneros making about ordinary experiences? What is she saying about the imagination? Cite evidence from the essay to support your response.
6. **Analyze Structure** Review the chart you created. What idea does Cisneros return to throughout the essay? What is the function of this recurring idea in developing her message? Support your answer with evidence from the text.
7. **Compare Voice** In a chart, record examples of the stylistic elements that create Cisneros's unique voice. Then choose another prose selection from this unit, and analyze the voice of its author as well. Use your completed chart to explain how Cisneros's voice differs from that of the other writer's.

	Sentence Type/Length	Word Choice	Tone
Cisneros			
Other Writer			

Text Criticism

8. **Critical Interpretations** Cisneros's candid recollections prompted one critic to say, "The memories that Cisneros offers . . . sometimes wrinkle the nose and scorch the palate." He went on to praise her talent for "evoking the sensations of the past in their full complexity." Why do you think Cisneros shares her insecurities and painful experiences as well as her triumphs? How might failing to do this have altered the essay's message? Explain, citing evidence.

Where do writers get their **MATERIAL?**

Like many writers, Cisneros uses personal experiences and real people as material for her literary creations. How "creative" do you think it is to use personal experiences as the raw material for writing? Explain.

COMMON CORE

RI 1 Cite evidence to support analysis of what the text says explicitly as well as inferences drawn from the text. **RI 4** Determine the meaning of words and phrases as they are used in the text, including figurative and connotative meanings. **RI 5** Analyze and evaluate the effectiveness of the structure an author uses in his or her exposition or argument, including whether the structure makes points clear, convincing, and engaging.

COMMON CORE

RL 2 Determine two or more themes or central ideas of a text and analyze their development over the course of the text. **RL 4** Analyze the impact of specific word choices on meaning and tone. **RL 5** Analyze how an author's choices regarding how to structure specific parts of a text contribute to its overall structure and meaning, as well as its aesthetic impact.

Life for My Child Is Simple
Primer for Blacks

Poetry by Gwendolyn Brooks

Meet the Author

Gwendolyn Brooks 1917–2000

Decades before urban musicians introduced Americans to rap and hip hop, Gwendolyn Brooks captured some of these same rhythms in her writing. In verse celebrated for its lyrical beauty, Brooks portrays the thoughts, feelings, and, often, extraordinary heroism of African Americans living amidst poverty and segregation.

An Early Start Though born in Topeka, Kansas, Brooks spent almost her entire life in Chicago. Even as a young girl, she loved to write. When she was 7, Brooks began filling composition books with "careful rhymes," prompting her mother to exclaim, "You are going to be the lady Paul Laurence Dunbar." By the age of 16, Brooks was a frequent contributor to *The Defender,* a prominent black newspaper in Chicago. During her teenage years, leading African-American poets James Weldon Johnson and Langston Hughes also recognized her immense talent.

Literary Triumph At 28, Brooks published *A Street in Bronzeville,* named for the bustling black enclave on Chicago's South Side. Written in a range of traditional forms, the poems explored the difficult lives of those around her. "I wrote about what I saw and heard in the street," Brooks said. "I lived in a small second-floor apartment at the corner, and I could look first on one side and then the other. There was my material." In 1949, Brooks published *Annie Allen,* a series of poems that trace the life of a Bronzeville girl. The book achieved literary acclaim and propelled its author into the spotlight. In 1950, Brooks became the first African-American writer to receive the Pulitzer Prize. The award brought her worldwide fame. "Sometimes," she quipped, "I feel that my name is Gwendolyn Pulitzer Brooks."

A Fateful Encounter Brooks experienced another turning point in 1967, when she attended a conference of black writers, meeting young African-American poets. Impressed by their commitment to a black aesthetic and issues of racial justice, Brooks became interested in writing a new kind of poetry. "If it hadn't been for these young people," she later remarked, "I wouldn't know what I know about this society. By associating with them I know who I am." Brooks began to experiment with free verse and to focus on the problems of color and justice. She started a poetry workshop for members of a Chicago street gang and became a lifelong advocate for the next generation. "My greatest interest," Brooks once said, "is being involved with young people."

DID YOU KNOW?

Gwendolyn Brooks . . .

- published her first poem at age 13.
- was the first African American to win a Pulitzer Prize.
- paid for prizes for student literary contests out of her own pocket.

Brooks at home on Chicago's South Side, 1960

THINK central
Author Online
Go to thinkcentral.com. KEYWORD: HML11-1294

TEXT ANALYSIS: REPETITION

What keeps a song or a poem stuck in your mind long after you've heard it on the radio or read it in the classroom? Often, the answer lies in the writer's use of **repetition,** a technique in which a sound, word, phrase, or line is repeated for emphasis or to create rhythm. A related technique is **anaphora,** in which the same word or phrase is repeated at the beginning of two or more lines. Consider this example from "Primer for Blacks":

Blackness
is a title,
is a preoccupation,
is a commitment . . .

As you read, pay close attention to Brooks's use of repetition and especially of anaphora. Consider what these techniques emphasize in each poem, and note the rhythm they help build.

READING SKILL: COMPARE AND CONTRAST POEMS

Brooks's poetry career spanned six decades. She wrote "Life for My Child Is Simple" early in her career; it comes from *Annie Allen,* which traces the life of a fictional character but draws much of its inspiration from Brooks's own experiences. "Primer for Blacks" was written many years later, when Brooks was developing a deeper commitment to political and social issues. As you read, **compare and contrast** these two poems in a chart as shown. The following tips can help you:

- Ask yourself about the **subject** of each poem. Is it personal or political? Does it focus on a group or an individual?
- Describe the **tone.**
- Consider **stylistic elements** such as diction, punctuation, and capitalization.
- Identify the **theme** of each poem. What message does each suggest about life?

	"Life for My Child Is Simple"	"Primer for Blacks"
Subject		
Tone		
Speaker		
Style		
Theme		

Complete the activities in your **Reader/Writer Notebook**.

What should we REACH *for?*

Gwendolyn Brooks advised her readers to "exhaust the little moment"—to live richly and strive higher in each moment of their lives. What, in your opinion, is worth striving for?

QUICKWRITE Brainstorm a list of things that are worth reaching for. Start by listing personal goals. Then move on to more global issues: if you had unlimited resources, what would you fix or change? Come up with a top-ten list of the things most worth striving for.

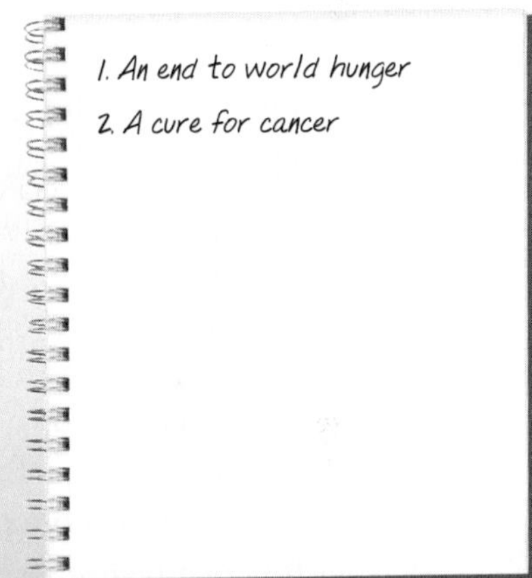

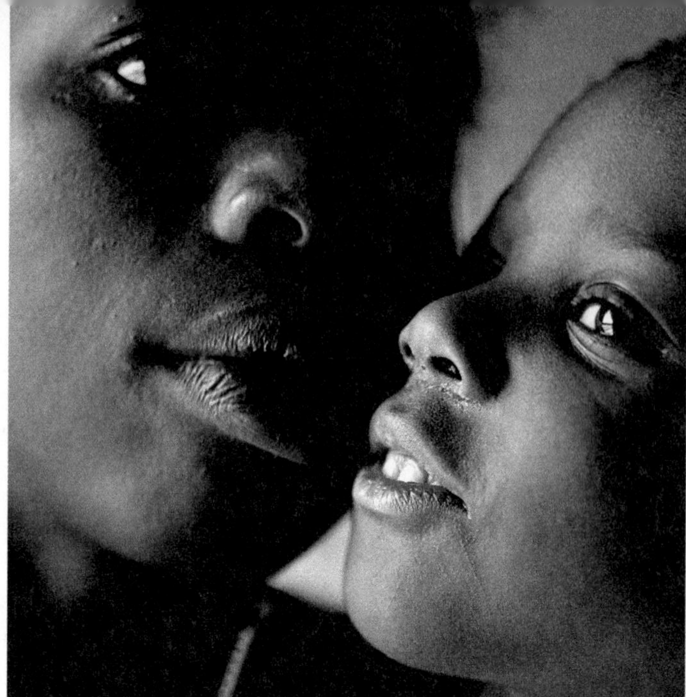

Life for My Child Is Simple

Gwendolyn Brooks

Life for my child is simple, and is good.
He knows his wish. Yes, but that is not all.
Because I know mine too.
And we both want joy of undeep and unabiding[1] things,
Like kicking over a chair or throwing blocks out of a window
Or tipping over an ice box pan[2]
Or snatching down curtains or fingering an electric outlet
Or a journey or a friend or an illegal kiss.
No. There is more to it than that. **A**
It is that he has never been afraid.
Rather, he reaches out and lo the chair falls with a beautiful crash,
And the blocks fall, down on the people's heads,
And the water comes slooshing sloppily out across the floor.
And so forth.
Not that success, for him, is sure, infallible.[3]
But never has he been afraid to reach.
His lesions are legion.[4]
But reaching is his rule.

A REPETITION
Reread lines 4–9 aloud. What happens to the poem's pace as the repetition builds? Describe the feeling created by the **rhythm** in these lines.

1. **unabiding:** not lasting; continually changing.
2. **ice box pan:** a pan for collecting melted ice in an old-fashioned refrigerator.
3. **infallible:** foolproof.
4. **His lesions are legion:** His injuries are many.

Primer for Blacks

Gwendolyn Brooks

Everyman, Brenda Joysmith. 345″ × 58 1/4″. © Brenda Joysmith. Courtesy of Joysmith Gallery.

Blackness
is a title,
is a preoccupation,[1]
is a commitment Blacks
are to comprehend—
and in which you are
to perceive your Glory.

The conscious shout
of all that is white is
"It's Great to be white."
The conscious shout
of the slack[2] in Black is
"It's Great to be white."
Thus all that is white
has white strength and yours. **B**

The word Black
has geographic power,
pulls everybody in:
Blacks here—
Blacks there—
Blacks wherever they may be.
And remember, you Blacks, what they told you—
remember your Education:
"one Drop—one Drop[3]
maketh a brand new Black."

Oh mighty Drop.
And because they have given us kindly
so many more of our people

B COMPARE AND CONTRAST POEMS
So far, how does this poem differ from "Life for My Child Is Simple" in both **content** and **style?** Cite examples from both poems to support your answer.

Language Coach
Word Definitions *Drop* means "a very small amount of liquid." Read lines 22–26, including the footnote. How could something so small, a mere drop, be considered mighty?

---

1. **preoccupation:** something requiring full attention.
2. **slack:** lack of force.
3. **"one Drop":** At times in U.S. history, a person with only "one drop" of African blood has been considered black.

Blackness
stretches over the land.
Blackness—
the Black of it,
the rust-red of it,
the milk and cream of it,
the tan and yellow-tan of it,
the deep-brown middle-brown high-brown of it,
the "olive" and ochre[4] of it—
Blackness
marches on. **C**

The huge, the pungent[5] object of our prime out-ride
is to Comprehend,
to salute and to Love the fact that we are Black,
which *is* our "ultimate Reality,"[6]
which is the lone ground
from which our meaningful metamorphosis,
from which our prosperous staccato,[7]
group or individual, can rise.

Self-shriveled Blacks.
Begin with gaunt and marvelous concession:
YOU are our costume and our fundamental bone.

All of you—
you COLORED ones,
you NEGRO ones,
those of you who proudly cry
"I'm half INDian"—
those of you who proudly screech
"I'VE got the blood of George WASHington in MY veins"—
ALL of you—
you proper Blacks,
you half-Blacks,
you wish-I-weren't Blacks,
Niggeroes and Niggerenes.

You.

C REPETITION
Reread lines 31–39. What does Brooks's use of **anaphora** emphasize about the many shades of blackness she lists? What point is she making here?

4. **ochre** (ō'kər): brownish orange-yellow.
5. **pungent** (pŭn'jənt): sharp and intense, like a powerful odor.
6. **the fact . . . "ultimate Reality":** a rewording of a quotation from black activist Ron Karenga.
7. **staccato** (stə-kä'tō): the playing of musical notes in a crisp, disconnected way.

After Reading

Comprehension

1. **Recall** In "Life for My Child Is Simple," what things does the child enjoy doing?
2. **Clarify** How do the child's feelings differ from his mother's?
3. **Clarify** Reread lines 16–30 of "Primer for Blacks." Why does "the word Black" have "geographic power"?
4. **Clarify** What, according to Brooks, is the object of blacks' "prime out-ride," or most important undertaking?

Text Analysis

5. **Interpret** Reread lines 10–18 of "Life for My Child Is Simple." Why has the speaker's son never been afraid of striving for what he wants? Why, in contrast, might the speaker have felt fearful?
6. **Examine Author's Purpose** Determine Brooks's intended audience for "Primer for Blacks." What do you think she wants her audience to feel? What action does she want her audience to take? Cite specific lines from the poem to support your answers.
7. **Analyze Style** Review "Primer for Blacks," noting Brooks's use of nonstandard capitalization. Why do you think she does this? How does this unorthodox capitalization affect the poem's meaning and contribute to the voice of the speaker?
8. **Analyze Repetition** Reconsider the annotated examples of repetition in Brooks's poems. Then find at least one other example in each work. Do your examples qualify as **anaphora?** In each case, what is the impact of repetition on the meaning?
9. **Compare and Contrast Poems** Using the chart you filled in as you read, summarize the similarities and the differences you found in the two poems. In your opinion, do the poems suggest similar or different ways of approaching life? Explain, citing evidence.

Text Criticism

10. **Author's Style** In the late 1960s, Brooks began experimenting with **free verse,** believing she was no longer living in "a sonnet kind of time." Why do you think Brooks chose free verse for these two poems? In your opinion, is free verse an appropriate poetic form for these works? Explain your opinions.

What should we REACH *for?*

In "Life for My Child Is Simple," Brooks implies that unlike her child, she has at times been "afraid to reach." What are some of the reasons why people might be afraid to reach? Explain.

COMMON CORE

RL 2 Determine two or more themes or central ideas of a text and analyze their development over the course of the text. **RL 4** Analyze the impact of specific word choices on meaning and tone. **RL 5** Analyze how an author's choices regarding how to structure specific parts of a text contribute to its overall structure and meaning, as well as its aesthetic impact.

Adolescence—III
Testimonial

Poetry by Rita Dove

COMMON CORE

RL 1 Cite evidence to support analysis of what the text says explicitly as well as inferences drawn from the text, including where the text leaves matters uncertain. **RL 4** Analyze the impact of specific word choices on meaning and tone, including words with multiple meanings or language that is fresh, engaging, or beautiful.

The Pulitzer Prize, which Dove won in 1987

Meet the Author

Rita Dove born 1952

For Rita Dove, the personal and the historical are equally important. "I've been fascinated," she says, "by what I've called before 'the underside of history,' the dramas of ordinary people." In her poetry, Dove often interweaves historical events with personal narratives, producing lyric images of everyday life.

High Achiever The daughter of a research chemist who broke the color barrier in the tire industry, Dove was always encouraged, she says, "to go as far as [she] could." Her parents drove Dove to excel in school and counseled her to never give up. Their guidance served her well. As a teenager, she was one of only 100 high school seniors named Presidential Scholar. She also distinguished herself in college, graduating Phi Beta Kappa from Miami University in 1973.

A Passion for Words Dove first became aware of the power of storytelling as a young girl. Listening to local storytellers in her hometown of Akron, Ohio, Dove discovered "the delight of shaping life with words." She also began a lifelong love affair with poetry, sparked by her discovery of an anthology in the local library. Though Dove began writing as a child, she did not fully embrace literary pursuits until college. Determining then that she wanted to be a writer, she applied and was accepted to the prestigious Iowa Writers' Workshop.

National Acclaim Publication in magazines had already earned Dove widespread praise when her first poetry collection, *The Yellow House on the Corner,* came out in 1980. Over the next few years, she published several more books, including *Thomas and Beulah,* hailed as her masterpiece. The book, which drew its inspiration from the quiet heroism of Dove's grandparents' lives, won a Pulitzer Prize in 1987. Since then, Dove has gone on to collect numerous literary honors.

Illuminating the Everyday Though she touches on issues of race, her poems, Dove asserts, "are about humanity." They attempt to convey something about the gamut of human experiences, not just the positive moments. "All the moments that make up a human being," Dove says, "have to be written about, talked about, painted, danced, in order to really talk about life."

DID YOU KNOW?

Rita Dove . . .

- was the youngest person and first African American named poet laureate.
- produced her own TV show.
- is a classically trained singer and musician, as well as a ballroom dancer.

Author Online THINK central

Go to thinkcentral.com. KEYWORD: HML11-1300

TEXT ANALYSIS: SOUND DEVICES

A musician as well as a poet, Rita Dove believes a poem's sound is paramount. "If a poem doesn't have a sense of music," she explains, "then that poem probably won't move me very much." To infuse her poems with this quality, Dove employs **sound devices**—patterns of word sounds that create musical or rhythmic effects. As you read Dove's poems, listen for the following sound devices:

- **alliteration**—the repetition of initial consonant sounds
- **assonance**—the repetition of vowel sounds within words
- **consonance**—the repetition of consonant sounds within and at the ends of words

Think about how these sound devices impart a musical quality to the poems. Also consider what words, images, and feelings these devices serve to highlight.

READING SKILL: MAKE INFERENCES ABOUT SPEAKERS

The language in Dove's poems is often restrained and concise. She characterizes the **speaker** in each poem with a few well-chosen details but does not offer much explicit description or commentary. It is up to you to read between the lines, or **make inferences,** about each speaker's situation and state of mind. As you read, collect clues that tell you about each speaker's age, situation, and mindset. After you read, you'll use this information to **draw conclusions** about each speaker's experiences.

Clues from the Text	My Inferences and Reactions
"... Mom and I worked/ The dusky rows of tomatoes." (lines 1–2)	The speaker and her mother probably live in a rural area, not the city. They work hard in the fields.

Complete the activities in your **Reader/Writer Notebook**.

How does your PERSPECTIVE *change?*

As you get older, the way you think and feel about important events in your life changes. And your perspective on something that looms in your future—graduation, for instance—will probably change once that event has actually happened.

QUICKWRITE Think of a big event or an important moment from your recent past; write a paragraph describing your feelings about it. Then imagine how you will feel about this same event ten years from now. How might your perspective have changed? Pretending to be your future self, write a second paragraph describing the event from this later perspective.

Adolescence—III

Rita Dove

BACKGROUND Dove wrote "Adolescence—III" early in her career, for her first published collection of poems. She composed "Testimonial" many years later and read it in the spring of 2001 at Howard University's commencement. "Whenever you think back," Dove told the graduating seniors, "and wonder where the future is going to lead you, remember that others have stood at this position and wondered, too. What you should do is take a step, one step at a time."

With Dad gone, Mom and I worked
The dusky rows of tomatoes.
As they glowed orange in sunlight
And rotted in shadow, I too
Grew orange and softer, swelling out
Starched cotton slips. **A**

The texture of twilight made me think of
Lengths of Dotted Swiss.[1] In my room
I wrapped scarred knees in dresses
That once went to big-band dances;
I baptized my earlobes with rosewater.
Along the window-sill, the lipstick stubs
Glittered in their steel shells. **B**

Looking out at the rows of clay
And chicken manure, I dreamed how it would happen:
He would meet me by the blue spruce,
A carnation over his heart, saying,
"I have come for you, Madam;
I have loved you in my dreams."
At his touch, the scabs would fall away.
Over his shoulder, I see my father coming toward us:
He carries his tears in a bowl,
And blood hangs in the pine-soaked air.

1. **Dotted Swiss:** crisp, sheer cotton fabric decorated with raised dots.

Analyze Visuals ▶
What words would you use to describe the girl in the painting? What details support your impressions?

A MAKE INFERENCES
What inferences can you make about the **speaker's** age from lines 1–6 and the poem's title? Do you get a sense of her family's situation in life? Explain.

B SOUND DEVICES
Reread lines 7–13. Find one example of **alliteration** and one of **assonance** in these lines. What words or images are emphasized by these devices?

Evening Thoughts, Ernest Crichlow. Lithograph, 25″ × 18″. Arisca Fine Art.

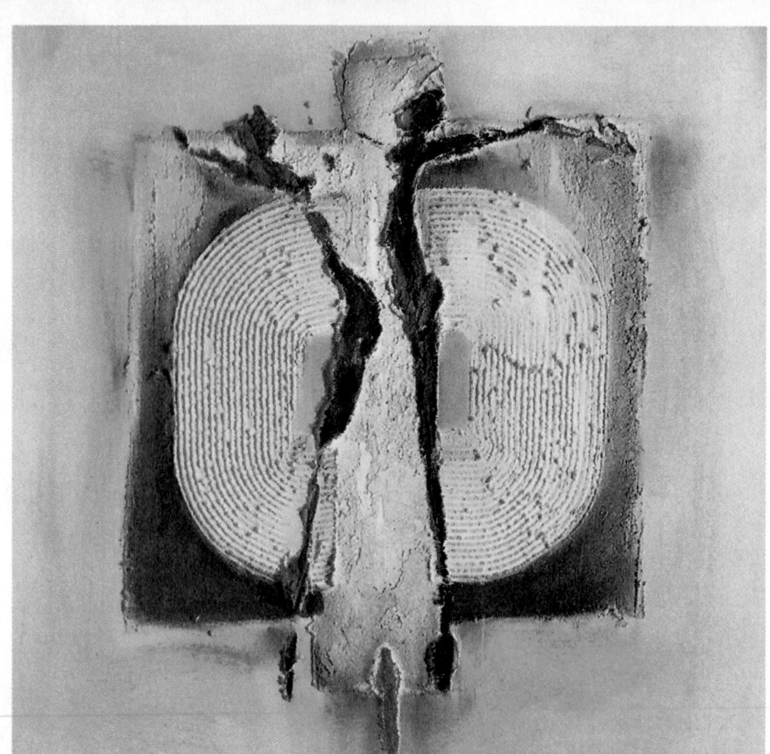

Discovery I, Alfred Gockel. 39 1/4″ × 39 1/4″. © Alfred Gockel.

Testimonial

Rita Dove

Back when the earth was new
and heaven just a whisper,
back when the names of things
hadn't had time to stick;

back when the smallest breezes
melted summer into autumn,
when all the poplars quivered
sweetly in rank and file . . .

the world called, and I answered.
Each glance ignited to a gaze.
I caught my breath and called that life,
swooned between spoonfuls of lemon sorbet. **C**

I was pirouette[1] and flourish,
I was filigree[2] and flame.
How could I count my blessings
when I didn't know their names?

Back when everything was still to come,
luck leaked out everywhere.
I gave my promise to the world,
and the world followed me here.

C MAKING INFERENCES
Who is the speaker in the poem? Rita Dove presents "Testimonial" in the voice of a goddess archetype, a powerful female figure from Greek myths and dramas. What words or phrases suggest the mythic character of the speaker? How does the language of this poem strengthen the power of the speaker's voice? Cite evidence to support your response.

1. **pirouette** (pĭr′o͞o-ĕt′): in ballet, a full turn of the body on one foot.
2. **filigree:** delicate ornamentation, often made of wire.

Comprehension

1. **Recall** In "Adolescence—III," what task occupies the speaker and her mother?
2. **Summarize** What does the adolescent speaker dream will happen to her?
3. **Summarize** In "Testimonial," how did the speaker respond to the world as a young person?

Text Analysis

4. **Draw Conclusions About Speakers** Review the **inferences** you made as you read. Using this information, explain the conclusions you can draw about each speaker's situation and state of mind. How do the two speakers' **perspectives** differ? Explain, citing evidence from both poems.
5. **Interpret Imagery** Many critics admire Dove's use of imagery. Look back over the images listed below. What does each one tell you about Dove's thoughts on the nature of youth?
   - the description of the world in "Testimonial" (lines 1–9)
   - the kind of life the speaker of "Testimonial" leads (lines 11–14)
   - the changes the speaker of "Adolescence—III" undergoes (lines 4–11)
6. **Analyze Sound Devices** Reexamine the two poems, looking for examples of each sound device listed in the chart. Use your completed chart to explain what tone and sensibility is established by the sound devices in each poem.

Sound Device	*"Adolescence—III"*	*"Testimonial"*
alliteration		
assonance		
consonance		

Text Criticism

7. **Cultural Context** Commenting on **themes** in her poetry, Dove has stated, "Obviously, as a black woman, I am concerned with race. . . . But certainly not every poem of mine mentions the fact of being black. They are poems about humanity, and sometimes humanity happens to be black." How does this view differ from the sensibility expressed by Gwendolyn Brooks in "Primer for Blacks" on page 1297? Explain your answer, citing evidence from each poet's work.

COMMON CORE

RL 1 Cite evidence to support analysis of what the text says explicitly as well as inferences drawn from the text, including where the text leaves matters uncertain. **RL 4** Analyze the impact of specific word choices on meaning and tone, including words with multiple meanings or language that is fresh, engaging, or beautiful.

How does your PERSPECTIVE *change?*

In "Testimonial," Dove writes "How could I count my blessings/when I didn't know their names?" What statement is she making about how her perspective has changed? How might *your* perspective change as you grow older? Explain.

COMMON CORE

RL 2 Determine two or more themes or central ideas of a text and analyze their development over the course of the text. **RL 4** Analyze the impact of specific word choices on meaning and tone, including words with multiple meanings or language that is fresh, engaging, or beautiful.

The Man in the Moon
Forgetfulness

Poetry by Billy Collins

Meet the Author

Billy Collins born 1941

Billy Collins is that rare thing—a celebrity poet. His books break poetry sales records, his readings pack concert halls, and his poems elicit rave reviews from writers and critics alike. Indeed, no American poet since Robert Frost has managed to acquire such a broad and devoted following.

New York Roots Born in a New York City hospital where poet William Carlos Williams once worked, Collins is a nearly lifelong New Yorker. Growing up in Queens, he displayed an early flair for writing and a deep passion for literature. After college, he earned a doctoral degree in Romantic poetry from the University of California. Today, however, Collins feels a certain aversion to this poetry. "The Romantics killed off humor," he once explained.

Grammar Teacher Makes It Big In 1971, Collins began teaching English at the City University of New York and writing poetry in his spare time. Absorbed by his teaching, Collins did not publish his first collection, *Pokerface* (1977), until he was 36. In the next 11 years, he published two additional collections. However, Collins did not achieve a widespread following until his fourth collection, *Questions About Angels* (1991), won the National Poetry Series competition. Since then his popularity has grown explosively, thanks in part to his charismatic poetry readings.

America's Poet In recognition of his poetic achievements, Collins was named U.S. poet laureate in 2001. During his two-year tenure, he encouraged the enjoyment of poetry in America's high schools, since "that's really where for most people poetry dies off and gets buried under other adolescent pursuits."

The Enigma of the Ordinary Though Collins has publicly expressed his political views, he is not a political poet. His poems are primarily concerned with the mystery of ordinary things and of everyday experiences. "Poetry is a home for ambiguity," he once noted. "It is one of the few places where ambiguity is honored." Often, a Collins poem begins with a humorous observation and then takes an unexpected turn, inviting readers to look afresh at the world around them.

DID YOU KNOW?

Billy Collins . . .

- broke the record for a bestselling poetry book—and then broke his own record twice.
- launched a Web site, Poetry 180, specifically designed to appeal to high school students.
- read a poem before Congress to honor the victims of the 9/11 attacks.

Author Online THINK central

Go to thinkcentral.com. KEYWORD: HML11-1306

TEXT ANALYSIS: IMAGERY

When you read a poem, you enter a world filled with sights, sounds, smells, and textures all its own. Poets draw you into this world by using **imagery,** words that re-create sensory experiences for the reader. Billy Collins owes some of his enormous popularity to the world he creates for his readers—a world that is often intensely familiar. In these lines from "The Man in the Moon," note the words that appeal to your senses of sight and touch:

He used to frighten me in the nights of childhood,
the wide adult face, enormous, stern, aloft.
I could not imagine such loneliness, such coldness.

As you read, look for language that appeals to your senses. Notice how Collins supports his images with **allusions** to classical mythology—indirect references to characters and places in Greek myths that the author assumes readers will recognize. Think about how images and allusions work together to create a vivid experience for you as the reader.

READING SKILL: TRACE THE DEVELOPMENT OF AN IDEA

Appreciating the sensory experience that a poem creates is one crucial aspect of analyzing poetry. Also important, however, is examining the **ideas** the poet presents. As you read, use the following strategies to trace the ideas Collins puts forth in "The Man in the Moon" and "Forgetfulness." Use a chart like the one shown to organize your notes.

- Consider each poem's **title.** What idea does each suggest?
- Note the concept introduced or elaborated upon in each **stanza.** Consider how each stanza builds upon the one preceding it.
- Analyze Collins's **tone.** What attitude is expressed in each group of lines? Does the tone remain consistent throughout the poem, or does it change?

"The Man in the Moon"		
	Ideas Suggested	Tone
Title	The title makes me think of a children's story.	playful
Stanza 1		
Stanza 2		

Complete the activities in your **Reader/Writer Notebook**.

What do the YEARS *take with them?*

As we age, we gain some things, such as maturity and wisdom. Other things—energy, for example, or idealism—seem to slip from us. In your opinion, do the years take more than they give?

ROLE-PLAY With a partner, improvise a scene in which two characters talk about growing older. First, discuss what the characters might say to each other about the joys and ordeals of aging—maybe they miss letting their imaginations run wild, or perhaps they appreciate the wisdom they've developed over the years. Decide whether your scene will be a comic or a serious one. Then write a dialogue between the characters and act it out for the class.

The Man in the **Moon**

Billy Collins

He used to frighten me in the nights of childhood,
the wide adult face, enormous, stern, aloft.
I could not imagine such loneliness, such coldness.

But tonight as I drive home over these hilly roads
I see him sinking behind stands of winter trees
and rising again to show his familiar face. A

And when he comes into full view over open fields
he looks like a young man who has fallen in love
with the dark earth,

a pale bachelor, well-groomed and full of melancholy,
his round mouth open
as if he had just broken into song. B

A TRACE IDEAS
Reread lines 1–6. How do you know what Collins is referring to when he says *He*? Explain how Collins's description of his subject changes from one stanza to the next. Record your answer in your chart.

B IMAGERY
Identify details that allow you to **visualize** the sight Collins describes. How does this description underscore the changing attitude of the speaker?

Forgetfulness

Billy Collins

The name of the author is the first to go
followed obediently by the title, the plot,
the heartbreaking conclusion, the entire novel
which suddenly becomes one you have never read, never
even heard of,

as if, one by one, the memories you used to harbor
decided to retire to the southern hemisphere of the brain,
to a little fishing village where there are no phones. **C**

Long ago you kissed the names of the nine Muses[1] goodbye
and watched the quadratic equation[2] pack its bag,
and even now as you memorize the order of the planets,

something else is slipping away, a state flower perhaps,
the address of an uncle, the capital of Paraguay.

Whatever it is you are struggling to remember
it is not poised on the tip of your tongue,
not even lurking in some obscure corner of your spleen.

It has floated away down a dark mythological river
whose name begins with an *L* as far as you can recall,
well on your own way to oblivion where you will join those
who have even forgotten how to swim and how to ride a
bicycle. **D**

No wonder you rise in the middle of the night
to look up the date of a famous battle in a book on war.
No wonder the moon in the window seems to have drifted
out of a love poem that you used to know by heart.

C TRACE IDEAS
Reread lines 1–8. Describe Collins's **tone** as he introduces the idea of forgetfulness. What words and phrases help him achieve this tone? Note any changes in tone as you continue to read.

COMMON CORE RL 4

D IMAGERY
In lines 17–18, Collins creates the image of a river. He expands on the image by inserting an **allusion,** an indirect reference that the author assumes readers will recognize. This allusion—"a dark mythological river / whose name begins with an *L*"—refers to Lethe, a river in classical mythology that causes one to forget the past. Explain how this allusion contributes to the imagery in lines 17-21 and to the theme of the poem.

1. **nine Muses:** in Greek mythology, goddesses of various fine arts and sciences.
2. **quadratic equation:** equation involving squaring of an unknown quantity or quantities, such as x^2.

Comprehension

1. **Summarize** In "The Man in the Moon," how does the speaker's attitude toward the moon change as he gets older?
2. **Recall** List three things that the speaker of "Forgetfulness" has forgotten.
3. **Clarify** In "Forgetfulness," what troubles the speaker in the middle of the night?

Text Analysis

4. **Examine Allusion** In "Forgetfulness," what ideas are developed or underscored by the allusion to the Muses, the Greek goddesses who preside over the arts and sciences (line 9)?
5. **Analyze Personification** The giving of human qualities to an object, animal, or idea is called personification. Find at least two examples of personification in "Forgetfulness." What does Collins's use of this technique contribute to the poem's **tone?**
6. **Analyze Imagery** Reread lines 22–25 of "Forgetfulness." Compare the concrete image of the moon—the only real image that appears in the poem—with the fleeting, intangible nature of the things the speaker has forgotten. What does this contrast emphasize about the poem's meaning? Explain, citing lines that support your answer.
7. **Trace the Development of an Idea** Collins is known for writing poems that begin with humor and end in mystery and seriousness. Review the graphic organizer you filled in as you read. How, if at all, does the **tone** change over the course of each poem? Do the two poems present similar or different ideas about aging? Explain your answers, citing evidence from both poems.

Text Criticism

8. **Critical Interpretations** Collins is beloved by readers for his fresh and often funny poems; he even won the Mark Twain Poetry Award, given for the "contribution of humor" to American verse. However, some critics argue that Collins's humor is hollow, weakened by clichés and lacking in originality and insight. On the basis of your reading of these poems, do you agree or disagree with this criticism? Explain your answer.

What do the YEARS *take with them?*

In his poem "Forgetfulness," Collins playfully laments the loss of memory that sometimes comes with age. However, memory loss is also the hallmark of Alzheimer's disease, a tragic and debilitating disease that can leave its victims unable to recognize their own family members. How would you feel if you began to lose your memories? Explain.

COMMON CORE

RL 2 Determine two or more themes or central ideas of a text and analyze their development over the course of the text.
RL 4 Analyze the impact of specific word choices on meaning and tone, including words with multiple meanings or language that is fresh, engaging, or beautiful.

A New Diversity

Late in the 20th century, it grew increasingly apparent that there was no single "American experience" and therefore no typical American voice. Once primarily the province of white men, the American literary canon—the body of works considered representative—exploded into a diverse chorus of ethnic voices. The number and range of voices continues to grow today.

Writing to Reflect

Every writer of any significance brings something new to a literary tradition, whether in subject matter, style, or way of looking at the world. As you reflect on the selections you have just read, consider what unique contributions might be attributed to each writer. Choose one author and write an essay about how his or her writing, as shown in this unit, can be said to do something different from writers of previous generations.

Consider

- the author's choice of subject matter
- his or her use of language, including style and tone
- any cultural or philosophical lens through which the author views the subject matter

Extension

VIEWING & REPRESENTING

Gather clippings of articles and literary texts from print media, photographs and other images of writers, and quotations from the selections in this section. Use these items to create a **collage**—your own "Mosaic of American Voices" representing the vibrancy and diversity of contemporary American literature.

COMMON CORE

W 9 Draw evidence from literary texts to support analysis, reflection, and research. **W 9a–b** Apply grade 11 Reading standards to literature and to literary nonfiction.

Increíbles Las Cosas Q'se Ven, 2001. Mural at Ashland Avenue and 19th Street in Chicago. © Jeffrey Zimmermann.

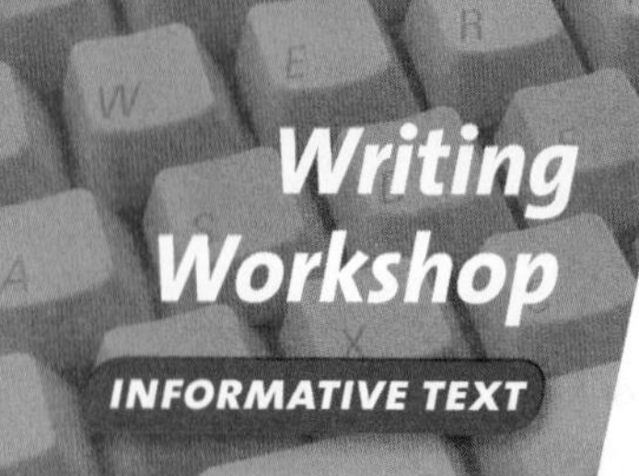

Résumé

As you have seen in this unit, literature often has lofty aspirations, such as to expose prejudice or push for change. However, capable writers also need the skills necessary to write effective work-related documents. When written effectively, these types of documents can open doors to opportunity. In this workshop, you will learn how to write a résumé for a potential employer.

Complete the workshop activities in your **Reader/Writer Notebook.**

WRITE WITH A PURPOSE

WRITING TASK

Write a **résumé** for a potential employer. Be sure to highlight the work, educational, and personal experiences and skills that qualify you for the position.

Idea Starters

- internships listed on Internet job sites or in a newspaper's classified section
- a hypothetical job position or internship that would interest you
- a local company or organization for whom you would like to work

THE ESSENTIALS

Here are some common purposes, audiences, and formats for writing a résumé.

PURPOSES	AUDIENCES	FORMATS
• to provide accurate information clearly and concisely • to make information and ideas accessible to a specific audience	• future employers • college admissions staff • co-workers	• résumé • job or college application • online employment site • Web site

COMMON CORE TRAITS

1. DEVELOPMENT OF IDEAS

- selects the most **significant** and **relevant facts** and **concrete details**
- focuses on information, details, and examples that are appropriate for a **specific purpose** and **audience**

2. ORGANIZATION OF IDEAS

- **organizes** information in a logical way
- employs **formatting** to aid comprehension and follow standard conventions

3. LANGUAGE FACILITY AND CONVENTIONS

- establishes and maintains a **formal style** and **objective tone**
- includes **precise language**
- uses **active verbs**
- employs correct **grammar, punctuation, capitalization,** and **spelling**

Planning/Prewriting

W 2a Format to aid comprehension. **W 2b** Develop a topic by selecting significant and relevant facts and concrete details. **W 5** Develop writing by planning and focusing on what is most significant for a specific purpose and audience.

Getting Started

THINK ABOUT AUDIENCE AND PURPOSE

A résumé is a description of the skills and experiences that qualify you for a job. When you create this type of document, you must think about what an employer needs to know about you in order to feel confident about your ability to perform the job. The employer is your **audience,** and the **purpose** is to clearly and accurately describe the qualifications that show you are the right person for the position.

WHAT DOES IT LOOK LIKE?

Résumé

* ***Audience:*** *potential employer*
* ***Purpose:*** *to convince the employer that I would be an asset to the company or organization*
* ***Audience's needs:*** *The employer needs to hire a competent person who has had experience creating sets for play productions.*

COLLECT INFORMATION

Résumés require you to effectively select **relevant facts and details** and organize them in a clear and logical way. When planning, it is important to consider information that is significant to an employer and specifically related to the requirements of the job. Before you begin to create a résumé, you should familiarize yourself with a variety of samples. You can find examples of professional résumés in books or on many reputable Web sites. Here are some tips for planning your résumé:

- Make a list of the work, educational, volunteer, and extracurricular experiences and accomplishments that qualify you for the desired position.
- Describe what you were required to do for each experience and the skills you gained through the experience. Use accessible language to describe any technical skills or tasks that you used or learned.
- Verify the names of the organizations you worked for and the dates you worked there.

WHAT DOES IT LOOK LIKE?

Information for résumé:

* ***School experience:*** *in charge of set design for the school's production of Macbeth;* ***Requirements and skills:*** *supervising team members; working within a budget; completing work within a tight timeframe; fixing set problems during performances*
* ***School experience:*** *staff writer for school newsletter;* ***Requirements and skills:*** *cover theater and art news; conduct interviews; write accurate and grammatically correct articles*
* ***Work experience:*** *hostess at Salina's Bistro;* ***Requirements and skills:*** *planning seating arrangements for reservations; juggling tasks; making adjustments to accommodate unexpected situations; appeasing dissatisfied customers; working efficiently in a fast-paced environment; effectively communicating with managers, busboys, and waiters to seat customers in a timely manner;* ***Dates:*** *February 2009 to January 2010*
* ***Volunteer experience:*** *collect donated items from local stores; deliver items to various homeless shelters;* ***Dates:*** *May 2009 to present*

Planning/Prewriting *continued*

Getting Started

CHOOSE A FORMAT

Résumés must present information in a format that is easy for employers to read and understand. A properly formatted résumé looks professional and helps you look professional when you apply for a position.

After looking through samples of résumés, create a formatting plan for your document. Use one of the common formatting layouts, but feel free to adjust the format to accommodate the information you will include. For example, you may use standard headings for parts of your document but tailor other headings to meet the specific needs of your information.

As you choose a format for your résumé, keep in mind the two most common types of résumés:

- **Functional résumés** focus on skills, rather than work history.
- **Chronological résumés** focus on work history, detailing job responsibilities and accomplishments.

You may also use ideas from both types of résumés. The most important thing is to create a format that allows you to highlight your strengths.

TIPS

- Maintain a consistent format throughout the document, including fonts, headings, margins, and other elements.
- To make your organization clearer, you might need to add subheadings below your main headings.
- Avoid inserting a section that states or mentions references. Instead, bring a list of references with you to interviews.
- As you create your résumé, you may change your mind about the format that is best for the amount of information or the way you decide to present it. If necessary, revise, rewrite, or try a new approach to your résumé to develop and strengthen it.

PEER REVIEW With a peer, share the information and format you plan to use in your résumé. Ask whether you have used **relevant, sufficient facts and concrete details** that successfully highlight your strengths relative to the job requirements. Discuss whether your formatting plan is an effective way to present your information.

After establishing your audience and purpose, collect and review sample documents. Then, brainstorm and collect information for your résumé in your *Reader/Writer Notebook*. Finally, choose a formatting plan.

W 4 Produce clear and coherent writing.
L 2 Demonstrate command of standard English capitalization, punctuation, and spelling.

Drafting

The following chart shows a structure for organizing an effective résumé.

Organizing Your Résumé

BEGINNING

- Choose a **font** and **style** for your résumé. Avoid unusual or ornate fonts that may distract the employer from the content of your résumé.
- Begin your résumé with your name, address, phone number, and e-mail address.
- After your contact information, state your **objective,** which is a statement of the job you are seeking or a statement of your goals in relation to the job you are seeking.
- Include **uniform spacing** between the various sections of your résumé.

▼

MIDDLE

- **Follow your formatting plan** consistently. Make adjustments to format when necessary.
- Arrange each detail about skills, experiences, or accomplishments underneath the **proper heading.** Format headings in **boldface.** Use **bullet points** to separate information beneath headings.
- Provide **dates** and **time spans** for each of your experiences and achievements.
- Use appropriately **formal style** and language. Maintain an **objective tone** by avoiding first-person pronouns (*I, me, my*). Avoid slang.
- Be as **concise** as possible in your wording. Use strong action verbs throughout, maintaining consistent verb tense and parallel structure.

▼

END

- Place the least relevant information at the end.
- Restrict your résumé to **no more than two pages** in length.

GRAMMAR IN CONTEXT: CAPITALIZING AND PUNCTUATING ADDRESSES

If a potential employer sees a capitalization or punctuation mistake in your mailing address, he or she will be immediately skeptical. When writing an address, capitalize the street name, city, and state. Abbreviate state names with the common two-letter postal abbreviation. Do not place a period after the abbreviation. Place a comma between the city and the state abbreviation. If a street name contains an abbreviated compass point with one letter *(N, S, E,* or *W),* follow the letter with a period. However, if it has two letters *(NE),* do not follow it with a period. Here is an example of a properly capitalized and punctuated address:

834 N. Clarington Road
Columbus, OH 54312

Using your prewriting notes and the information in the chart on this page, write a draft of your résumé. Be sure that you have capitalized and punctuated addresses correctly.

Revising

When you revise, you should focus on whether you have addressed the most significant information, experiences, and accomplishments in your résumé. Your goal is to determine whether you've presented your qualifications for the position clearly, accurately, and coherently to your potential employer. The questions, tips, and strategies in the following chart can help you revise and improve your draft.

RÉSUMÉ

Ask Yourself	*Tips*	*Revision Strategies*
1. Are my name, address, phone number, and e-mail address correctly stated?	**Bracket** your name, address, phone number, and e-mail address.	**Add** your contact information. Make sure the information, spelling, capitalization, and punctuation are correct.
2. Is an objective included? Does the objective state the job I am seeking or a related professional goal?	**Circle** your objective.	**Add** an objective if one is missing. **Revise** an existing objective to clearly address the job you are seeking or a professional goal.
3. Are work, educational, volunteer, and extracurricular experiences and accomplishments listed? Are dates and time spans included?	**Place stars** next to work, educational, volunteer, and extracurricular experiences. **Draw boxes** around dates and time spans.	**Add** work, educational, volunteer, or extracurricular experiences. **Add** dates and time spans for each experience.
4. Have the relevant skills associated with each of my work experiences been stated?	**Double underline** relevant skills.	**Add** the relevant skills and concrete descriptive details associated with each experience.
5. Does the résumé include action verbs and concise language? Have I avoided first-person pronouns?	**Highlight** action verbs. **Place an X** through wordy language and first-person pronouns.	**Add** action verbs. **Revise** wordy language. **Replace** first-person pronouns.
6. Is the least relevant information placed at the end of the résumé?	**Underline** the least relevant piece of information on your résumé.	**Rearrange** information so that the least relevant information is stated at the end of the résumé.

PEER REVIEW Before you revise, exchange papers with a peer and ask for suggestions about how you might improve your résumé. Use the chart to review your peer's draft, and write a short critique, pointing out its strengths and weaknesses.

COMMON CORE

W 5 Develop and strengthen writing by revising, editing, rewriting, or trying a new approach, focusing on what is most significant for a specific purpose or audience.

ANALYZE A STUDENT DRAFT

Read these excerpts from a student draft, and note the comments on its strengths as well as suggestions for improvement.

1

Monique Sanchez
834 N. Clarington Road
Columbus, OH 54312
msanchez3748@evernet.com
(361) 555-8671

2 **OBJECTIVE**
Obtain an internship

Monique's objective needs to be more specific.

3 **EDUCATIONAL AND EXTRACURRICULAR ACTIVITIES**

Monique lists her educational and extracurricular **experiences** first because these are the most significant for the internship she is trying to obtain.

Lead set designer, Allentown High School's production of *Macbeth*
February 2010–April 2010

- designed and created the production's set
- supervised and closely worked with a team of five fellow students
- completed work within a given timeframe and budget
- addressed and repaired set problems during performances

Staff Writer, *Allentown High Weekly News*
September 2010–present

- cover the school's theater and art programs for the school paper
- write accurate and grammatically correct articles
- conduct student, teacher, and administrator interviews

Monique provides the **time span** in which she has worked as a staff writer for the school newspaper.

LEARN HOW **State an Objective** A potential employer should immediately understand what you are trying to accomplish by submitting your résumé. Therefore, you should state your specific goal in your objective. Avoid vague statements that do not relate to the job position. Monique added relevant details to her objective to make it more specific.

MONIQUE'S REVISION TO THE OBJECTIVE 2

a summer internship as a set production assistant
Obtain ~~an internship~~

4 WORK EXPERIENCE

Hostess, Salina's Bistro
February 2009–January 2010

- figured out where people should sit and helped them find their tables
- worked efficiently, juggling multiple tasks in a fast-paced environment
- communicated effectively with managers, busboys, and waiters to keep customers' wait to a minimum
- made adjustments to accommodate unexpected situations
- appeased dissatisfied customers

Monique uses parallel verb structure and clearly states the **responsibilities** of her job as well as the **skills** she learned while working in the position.

5 VOLUNTEER EXPERIENCE

Hopeful Ones Delivery Service
May 2009–present

- get donated food and clothing from local stores
- make sure various homeless shelters have items

Monique fails to use strong action verbs to describe details about her volunteer work.

LEARN HOW Add Strong Action Verbs Although Monique includes details about her volunteer work, her writing would be more effective and specific if she used strong actions verbs. Monique revised these bullet points to add strong action verbs.

MONIQUE'S REVISION TO SECTION 5

- ~~get~~ *collect* donated food and clothing from local stores
- ~~make sure various homeless shelters have items~~ *monitor needs of homeless shelters and distribute items as needed*

Revise your résumé using feedback from your peers and teacher, the revision strategies chart, and the two "Learn How" lessons. Evaluate whether you've effectively shown your potential employer that you are a desirable choice for the job position. Try a new approach to formatting or organization if your résumé is less successful.

W 2e Maintain a formal style and objective tone. **W 5** Develop and strengthen your writing by revising, editing, rewriting, or trying a new approach. **L 3** Apply knowledge of language to make effective choices for meaning or style.

Editing and Publishing

In the editing stage, you proofread your résumé to make sure that it is free of grammar, spelling, and punctuation errors. These types of mistakes can cause employers to question the abilities of even the most qualified job applicant.

GRAMMAR IN CONTEXT: FORMAL VERSUS INFORMAL LANGUAGE

Informal, or casual, language is appropriate in some instances, such as when you are writing a letter to a friend or when you are writing dialogue for a story. However, when you are creating a résumé, you should always use formal, or traditional, language. As Monique edited her résumé, she noticed a bullet point that included informal language.

planned seating arrangements for reservations and seated customers in a timely manner
~~figured out where people should sit and helped them find their tables~~

PUBLISH YOUR WRITING

Share your résumé with an audience, such as classmates, your teacher, or someone you know who is responsible for hiring employees.

- Make several copies of your résumé and hand them out to your teacher and classmates. Ask for feedback.
- Submit your résumé to a potential employer. If necessary, write a cover letter to accompany your résumé.
- Bring your résumé to a community career fair.
- Publish your résumé on your school Web site. Before posting to the Internet be sure to remove your home address. Have employers contact you by e-mail.
- Share your résumé with a prominent business owner or manager in your community. Ask for specific suggestions for improvement.

Proofread your résumé to correct any errors. Make sure that you have used formal language throughout your résumé. Then, submit your completed résumé to your desired audience.

Scoring Rubric

Use the rubric below to evaluate your procedural document from the Writing Workshop or your response to the on-demand prompt on the next page.

RÉSUMÉ

SCORE	COMMON CORE TRAITS
6	• **Development** Has a specific, focused objective; lists experiences relevant to the purpose; is well-supported with significant facts and concrete details • **Organization** Uses a clear, consistent format throughout to organize information appropriately; uses headings and other style elements • **Language** Consistently maintains a formal style and objective tone; uses active verbs consistently; shows a strong command of conventions
5	• **Development** Includes a specific objective; lists relevant experiences; includes significant facts and concrete details • **Organization** Uses a consistent format with headings; organizes information appropriately • **Language** Maintains a formal style; uses active verbs; has a few errors in conventions
4	• **Development** Includes a specific objective; lists experiences; includes adequate facts and details • **Organization** Uses inconsistent styles for format; includes irrelevant information with relevant experience • **Language** Mostly maintains a formal style; uses some active verbs; has a few distracting errors in conventions
3	• **Development** Has a general objective; includes a few relevant experiences; lists some extraneous or unrelated facts and details • **Organization** Uses inconsistent format, which is difficult to read; lists experiences with no thought to relevance • **Language** Frequently lapses into an informal style; uses active verbs inconsistently; has some significant errors in conventions
2	• **Development** Has a brief general objective; lists experiences with few or no relevant facts and details; missing dates • **Organization** Provides little more than a list, with no seeming order of relevance • **Language** Uses an informal style and vague language; has many distracting errors in conventions
1	• **Development** Has no objective; lists unrelated experiences; lacks relevant details • **Organization** Provides a short list with no overall organization • **Language** Uses an inappropriate style and language; has major problems with grammar, usage, and spelling

Preparing for Timed Writing

W 10 Write routinely over shorter time frames for a range of tasks, purposes, and audiences.

1. ANALYZE THE TASK

5 MIN 

Read the writing task carefully. Then, read it again, noting the words that indicate the topic, the audience, and the purpose.

WRITING TASK

You want to apply for a job as a coach or tutor in an after-school program. Create a one-page résumé for the hiring committee, listing your experience and qualifications for the job. Begin by choosing the type of activities you would like to coach or tutor. Then think of the jobs and experiences you have had that are relevant to that position. Provide concrete facts and details that clearly convey your qualifications.

2. PLAN YOUR RESPONSE

10 MIN 

Think about the specific job that you would like and the requirements that it would entail. Use that to write an objective and your relevant experience in the chart. Note whether the experience is related to work, education, volunteering, or extracurricular activities. Be sure to include the requirements for each experience and the skills you used.

Objective	
Experience 1	
Experience 2	
Experience 3	

3. RESPOND TO THE TASK

20 MIN 

Use the information you listed in your chart to begin drafting a résumé. If you cannot use word-processing software to format the résumé, try to use a neat and consistent format in a handwritten draft. As you write, keep the following points in mind.

- In your objective, make it clear to your audience what job you are applying for.
- Remember to add dates and job requirements to each experience you list. Make sure the skills and experiences you selected contain concrete details that relate to the job you want.

4. IMPROVE YOUR RESPONSE

5–10 MIN 

Revising Review the language you used. Do you establish a formal style and maintain an objective tone by avoiding personal pronouns? Do you use active verbs and parallel structure? Did you select the most significant and relevant experiences?

Proofreading Correct errors in grammar, spelling, punctuation, and capitalization. Make sure your edits are neat and the résumé is legible.

Checking Your Final Copy Before you turn in your paper, read it one more time to catch any errors you may have missed.

Creating a Web Site

Many job-seekers create electronic résumés that they publish on Web sites. By providing multiple formats for your résumé, you can add visual interest and enhanced access to information for employers. A Web site also makes it easy to respond to ongoing feedback so you can quickly update your résumé whenever necessary.

Complete the workshop activities in your **Reader/Writer Notebook.**

PRODUCE WITH A PURPOSE	COMMON CORE TRAITS
TASK Create a **Web site** for your school that shares student résumés with potential employers. Focus on ways to use technology to enhance the information in the résumés.	***A STRONG WEB SITE . . .*** • targets a specific audience • contains accurate information • contains relevant and appropriate graphics, images, and/or sound

COMMON CORE

W 6 Use technology to publish writing products. **SL 2** Integrate information presented in diverse formats and media in order to solve problems. **SL 5** Make strategic use of digital media.

Plan the Web Site

Before you begin, think about your audience. Are you trying to reach business owners, volunteer coordinators, people who arrange internships, or all three? Once you choose an audience, follow the steps below to plan your Web site.

1. **Brainstorm elements to include on your Web site.** Begin by planning information and navigational features. Consider the following ideas:
   - The home page might list areas of interest and link to résumés within each category.
   - Hyperlinks in the résumés can lead to examples of the student's work and accomplishments.
   - Each résumé can provide a "Contact Me" link that opens an outgoing e-mail message to a general mailbox. (Do not provide your personal e-mail address online.)
2. **Consider graphics and sound.** Résumé pages can include images and be designed individually. Keep your audience and purpose in mind when choosing images and colors, fonts, and graphics. Use digital media strategically to make sure it complements the information you present. Remember that you can be creative, but you also want to look professional. If you use graphics that you did not create, check copyright restrictions and include a source line. Also consider adding sound to your Web site such as background music, interviews, or speeches that support or add to the information.
3. **Make a storyboard showing the design of each page.** Draw rough sketches showing the placement of titles, text, graphics, and navigation buttons.

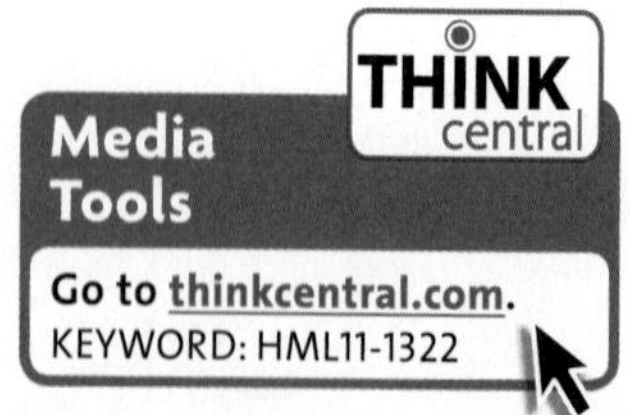

THINK
central
Media
Tools
Go to thinkcentral.com.
KEYWORD: HML11-1322

Produce the Web Site

Use your storyboard and notes as references as you produce your Web site. If you encounter problems while creating the site, ask your teacher or the school's computer specialist for guidance.

1. **Create or collect the content.** Ask classmates to contribute résumés to the site. Encourage your classmates to design their own pages to add interest. Use the following guidelines:
    - Because pages will be posted online, do not include your address, phone number, or photo.
    - Try to integrate different sources of information and diverse media, such as photos, graphics, and audio elements.
    - Follow standard formatting for résumés and include details that allow employers to make informed decisions.
2. **Build your site.** Ask your school's computer specialist for advice on which authoring program to use. An authoring program allows you to combine media elements into a Web document. Think of a domain name, or Web address, that reflects the content of your Web site. If you are unfamiliar with building a Web site, allow yourself plenty of time to accomplish the task. Consider the following tips as you build your site:
    - Place important hyperlinks across the top of your home page and/or in a running side column.
    - Emphasize headings by placing them in boldface and/or in color.
    - Make your Web site as easy to navigate as possible. Avoid inserting too many hyperlinks and confusing, overly busy design elements.
3. **Test the site and make necessary revisions.** Proofread the text, check graphics for correct positioning, and test all links and navigation buttons. Create a short survey or questionnaire, and ask teachers or classmates to review your site and provide feedback. Make revisions as needed.
4. **Upload your site.** Ask the computer specialist for permission to make your site available on your school's internal server or on the Web.

Using the steps and guidelines listed, create your Web site. After you have finished development, ask school officials if you can advertise your Web site in the school or local newspaper or add a hyperlink on the school's Web site. By integrating all of these résumés on one Web site, you make it possible for classmates and employers to easily share and update information.

Assessment Practice

ASSESS
Taking this practice test will help you assess your knowledge of these skills and determine your readiness for the Unit Test.

REVIEW
After you take the practice test, your teacher can help you identify any standards you need to review.

COMMON CORE

RL 2 Determine two or more themes or central ideas of a text and analyze their development over the course of a text. **RL 4** Determine the meaning of words and phrases as they are used in the text, including figurative and connotative meanings. **RL 10** Read and comprehend literature. **RI 4** Determine the meaning of words and phrases as they are used in the text, including figurative, connotative, and technical meanings. **RI 7** Evaluate information presented in different media or formats. **RI 10** Read and comprehend literary nonfiction. **L 1** Demonstrate command of the conventions of standard English grammar and usage when writing. **L 2** Demonstrate command of the conventions of standard English capitalization, punctuation, and spelling. **L 3** Apply knowledge of language to make effective choices for meaning or style. **L 4a** Use context as a clue to the meaning of a word or phrase.

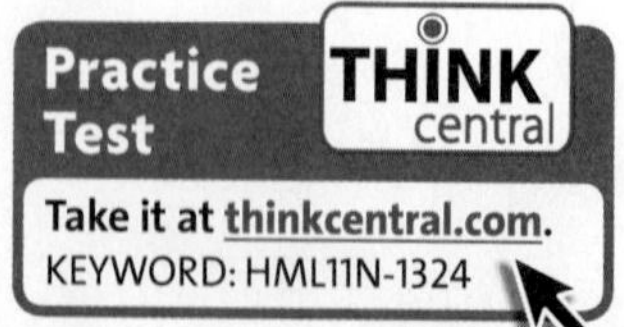

DIRECTIONS Read the two selections and the viewing and representing piece. Then answer the questions that follow.

from The Secret Life of Walter Mitty

by James Thurber

1 "WE'RE going through!" The Commander's voice was like thin ice breaking. He wore his full-dress uniform, with the heavily braided white cap pulled down rakishly over one cold gray eye. "We can't make it, sir. It's spoiling for a hurricane, if you ask me." "I'm not asking you, Lieutenant Berg," said the Commander. "Throw on the power lights! Rev her up to 8500! We're going through!" The pounding of the cylinders increased: ta-pocketa-pocketa-pocketa-*pocketa-pocketa.* The Commander stared at the ice forming on the pilot window. He walked over and twisted a row of complicated dials. "Switch on No. 8 auxiliary!" he shouted. "Switch on No. 8 auxiliary!" repeated Lieutenant Berg. "Full strength in No. 3 turret!" shouted the Commander. "Full strength in No. 3 turret!" The crew, bending to their various tasks in the huge, hurtling eight-engined Navy hydroplane, looked at each other and grinned. "The Old Man'll get us through," they said to one another. "The Old Man ain't afraid of Hell!" . . .

2 "Not so fast! You're driving too fast!" said Mrs. Mitty. "What are you driving so fast for?"

3 "Hmm?" said Walter Mitty. He looked at his wife, in the seat beside him, with shocked astonishment. She seemed grossly unfamiliar, like a strange woman who had yelled at him in a crowd. "You were up to fifty-five," she said. "You know I don't like to go more than forty. You were up to fifty-five." Walter Mitty drove on toward Waterbury in silence, the roaring of the SN202 through the worst storm in twenty years of Navy flying fading in the remote, intimate airways of his mind. "You're tensed up again," said Mrs. Mitty. "It's one of your days. I wish you'd let Dr. Renshaw look you over."

4 Walter Mitty stopped the car in front of the building where his wife went to have her hair done. "Remember to get those overshoes while I'm having my hair done," she said. "I don't need overshoes," said Mitty. She put her mirror back into her bag. "We've been all through that," she said, getting out of the car. "You're not a young man any longer." He raced the engine a little. "Why don't you wear your gloves? Have you lost your gloves?" Walter Mitty reached in a pocket and brought out the gloves. He put them on, but after she had turned and gone into the building and he had driven on to a red light, he took them off again. "Pick it

up, brother!" snapped a cop as the light changed, and Mitty hastily pulled on his gloves and lurched ahead. He drove around the streets aimlessly for a time, and then he drove past the hospital on his way to the parking lot.

5 . . . "It's the millionaire banker, Wellington McMillan," said the pretty nurse. "Yes?" said Walter Mitty, removing his gloves slowly. "Who has the case?" "Dr. Renshaw and Dr. Benbow, but there are two specialists here, Dr. Remington from New York and Dr. Pritchard-Mitford from London. He flew over." A door opened down a long, cool corridor and Dr. Renshaw came out. He looked distraught and haggard. "Hello, Mitty," he said. "We're having the devil's own time with McMillan, the millionaire banker and close personal friend of Roosevelt. Obstreosis of the ductal tract. Tertiary. Wish you'd take a look at him." "Glad to," said Mitty.

6 In the operating room there were whispered introductions: "Dr. Remington, Dr. Mitty. Dr. Pritchard-Mitford, Dr. Mitty." "I've read your book on streptothricosis," said Pritchard-Mitford, shaking hands. "A brilliant performance, sir." "Thank you," said Walter Mitty. "Didn't know you were in the States, Mitty," grumbled Remington. "Coals to Newcastle, bringing Mitford and me up here for a tertiary." "You are very kind," said Mitty. A huge, complicated machine, connected to the operating table, with many tubes and wires, began at this moment to go pocketa-pocketa-pocketa. "The new anesthetizer is giving away!" shouted an intern. "There is no one in the East who knows how to fix it!" "Quiet, man!" said Mitty, in a low, cool voice. He sprang to the machine, which was now going pocketa-pocketa-queep-pocketa-queep. He began fingering delicately a row of glistening dials. "Give me a fountain pen!" he snapped. Someone handed him a fountain pen. He pulled a faulty piston out of the machine and inserted the pen in its place. "That will hold for ten minutes," he said. "Get on with the operation." A nurse hurried over and whispered to Renshaw, and Mitty saw the man turn pale. "Coreopsis has set in," said Renshaw nervously. "If you would take over, Mitty?" Mitty looked at him and at the craven figure of Benbow, who drank, and at the grave, uncertain faces of the two great specialists. "If you wish," he said. They slipped a white gown on him, he adjusted a mask and drew on thin gloves; nurses handed him shining . . .

7 "Back it up, Mac! Look out for that Buick!" Walter Mitty jammed on the brakes. "Wrong lane, Mac," said the parking-lot attendant, looking at Mitty closely. "Gee. Yeh," muttered Mitty. He began cautiously to back out of the lane marked "Exit Only." "Leave her sit there," said the attendant. "I'll put her away." Mitty got out of the car. "Hey, better leave the key." "Oh," said Mitty, handing

GO ON

the man the ignition key. The attendant vaulted into the car, backed it up with insolent skill, and put it where it belonged.

8 They're so damn cocky, thought Walter Mitty, walking along Main Street; they think they know everything. Once he had tried to take his chains off, outside New Milford, and he had got them wound around the axles. A man had had to come out in a wrecking car and unwind them, a young, grinning garageman. Since then Mrs. Mitty always made him drive to a garage to have the chains taken off. The next time, he thought, I'll wear my right arm in a sling; they won't grin at me then. I'll have my right arm in a sling and they'll see I couldn't possibly take the chains off myself. He kicked at the slush on the sidewalk. "Overshoes," he said to himself, and he began looking for a shoe store.

9 When he came out into the street again, with the overshoes in a box under his arm, Walter Mitty began to wonder what the other thing was his wife had told him to get. She had told him, twice before they set out from their house for Waterbury. In a way he hated these weekly trips to town—he was always getting something wrong. Kleenex, he thought, Squibb's, razor blades? No. Tooth paste, toothbrush, bicarbonate, carborundum, initiative and referendum? He gave it up. But she would remember it. "Where's the what's-its-name?" she would ask. "Don't tell me you forgot the what's-its-name." A newsboy went by shouting something about the Waterbury trial.

10 . . . "Perhaps this will refresh your memory." The District Attorney suddenly thrust a heavy automatic at the quiet figure on the witness stand. "Have you ever seen this before?" Walter Mitty took the gun and examined it expertly. "This is my Webley-Vickers 50.80," he said calmly. An excited buzz ran around the courtroom. The Judge rapped for order. "You are a crack shot with any sort of firearms, I believe?" said the District Attorney, insinuatingly. "Objection!" shouted Mitty's attorney. "We have shown that the defendant could not have fired the shot. We have shown that he wore his right arm in a sling on the night of the fourteenth of July." Walter Mitty raised his hand briefly and the bickering attorneys were stilled. "With any known make of gun," he said evenly, "I could have killed Gregory Fitzhurst at three hundred feet with my left hand." Pandemonium broke loose in the courtroom. A woman's scream rose above the bedlam and suddenly a lovely, dark-haired girl was in Walter Mitty's arms. The District Attorney struck at her savagely. Without rising from his chair, Mitty let the man have it on the point of the chin. "You miserable cur!" . . .

11 "Puppy biscuit," said Walter Mitty. He stopped walking and the buildings of Waterbury rose up out of the misty courtroom and surrounded him again. A woman who was passing laughed. "He said 'Puppy biscuit,'" she said to her companion. "That man said 'Puppy biscuit' to himself." Walter Mitty hurried on. He went into an A. & P., not the first one he came to but a smaller one farther up

the street. "I want some biscuit for small, young dogs," he said to the clerk. "Any special brand, sir?" The greatest pistol shot in the world thought a moment. "It says 'Puppies Bark for It' on the box," said Walter Mitty.

12 His wife would be through at the hairdresser's in fifteen minutes Mitty saw in looking at his watch, unless they had trouble drying it; sometimes they had trouble drying it. She didn't like to get to the hotel first, she would want him to be there waiting for her as usual. He found a big leather chair in the lobby, facing a window, and he put the overshoes and the puppy biscuit on the floor beside it. He picked up an old copy of *Liberty* and sank down into the chair. "Can Germany Conquer the World Through the Air?" Walter Mitty looked at the pictures of bombing planes and of ruined streets.

13 . . . "The cannonading has got the wind up in young Raleigh, sir," said the sergeant. Captain Mitty looked up at him through tousled hair. "Get him to bed," he said wearily, "with the others. I'll fly alone." "But you can't, sir," said the sergeant anxiously. "It takes two men to handle that bomber and the Archies are pounding hell out of the air. Von Richtman's circus is between here and Saulier." "Somebody's got to get that ammunition dump," said Mitty. "I'm going over. Spot of brandy?" He poured a drink for the sergeant and one for himself. War thundered and whined around the dugout and battered at the door. There was a rending of wood and splinters flew through the room. "A bit of a near thing," said Captain Mitty carelessly. 'The box barrage is closing in," said the sergeant. "We only live once, Sergeant," said Mitty, with his faint, fleeting smile. "Or do we?" He poured another brandy and tossed it off. "I never see a man could hold his brandy like you, sir," said the sergeant. "Begging your pardon, sir." Captain Mitty stood up and strapped on his huge Webley-Vickers automatic. "It's forty kilometers through hell, sir," said the sergeant. Mitty finished one last brandy. "After all," he said softly, "what isn't?" The pounding of the cannon increased; there was the rat-tat-tatting of machine guns, and from somewhere came the menacing pocketa-pocketa-pocketa of the new flame-throwers. Walter Mitty walked to the door of the dugout humming "Aupres de Ma Blonde." He turned and waved to the sergeant. "Cheerio!" he said. . . .

14 Something struck his shoulder. "I've been looking all over this hotel for you," said Mrs. Mitty. "Why do you have to hide in this old chair? How did you expect me to find you?" "Things close in," said Walter Mitty vaguely. "What?" Mrs. Mitty said. "Did you get the what's-its-name? The puppy biscuit? What's in that box?" "Overshoes," said Mitty. "Couldn't you have put them on in the store?" "I was thinking," said Walter Mitty. "Does it ever occur to you that I am sometimes thinking?" She looked at him. "I'm going to take your temperature when I get you home," she said.

GO ON

15 They went out through the revolving doors that made a faintly derisive whistling sound when you pushed them. It was two blocks to the parking lot. At the drugstore on the corner she said, "Wait here for me. I forgot something. I won't be a minute." She was more than a minute. Walter Mitty lighted a cigarette. It began to rain, rain with sleet in it. He stood up against the wall of the drugstore, smoking. . . He put his shoulders back and his heels together. "To hell with the handkerchief," said Walter Mitty scornfully. He took one last drag on his cigarette and snapped it away. Then, with that faint, fleeting smile playing about his lips, he faced the firing squad; erect and motionless, proud and disdainful, Walter Mitty the Undefeated, inscrutable to the last.

Virtual Worlds

August 8, 2007
LONDON, England (CNN)

1 It's 2020. You get home from work, kick off your shoes and relax—on your very own tropical island. That night, your friends teleport over with other glamorous guests for a party at your five-star beach house, decked out in expensively understated chrome, crystal and fine Italian furniture.

2 But this is no billionaire way of life. If virtual worlds become the next Facebook phenomenon, experts predict that logging on to a luxury lifestyle could be attainable for all of us—and we might even spend more money on our online homes than on our real-life surroundings.

3 By 2020, virtual worlds may have surpassed social networking sites as the place to spend time online. Experts believe that the draw of 3-D spaces where our avatars can hang out with our friends—and meet new ones—may tempt away even the most ardent Facebook addict.

4 David Knighton is one of many netizens exploring virtual worlds. He's been visiting a site for over a year and told CNN that he enjoys its social dimension. "I've met several good friends who are still friends to this day in the 'real world' " he said.

5 But what is the draw of a virtual world? Are they only attractive to tech-heads? David doesn't think so. He says, "Experience plays a role in acceptance to be sure, but a virtual world takes hold more on a social and creative level. Someone who signs in and recognizes those aspects will immediately be hooked."

6 This is backed up by blogger and writer Caleb Booker, who has tracked virtual worlds from phone "party lines" through the first one-player text-based computer

adventures to the two- and three-dimensional Internet worlds that are burgeoning today.

7 Booker believes that, in a society that's increasingly mobile, virtual worlds help us hold our far-flung social networks together. He cites the example of his mother-in-law, who recently moved to a new city and uses a social networking site to stay in touch with her three daughters. "They're all busy, so virtual world technologies and Web 2.0 apps are the best and most convenient ways to keep up," he told CNN.

8 Booker says that virtual worlds take this interaction to a more sophisticated level. "I don't even have to worry about cab fare if I want to have a little get-together with my friends from the UK and the US tonight," he said.

9 And he thinks that it's only a matter of time before virtual worlds explode in popularity. "Bottom line: if people are using email for social interaction, they'll probably be interested in other ways to be social online."

Life-like avatars

10 Interaction on social networking sites is mainly limited to text, with the ability for users to add photos and video. But in a virtual world, people are represented by avatars: computer-generated figures which can look uncannily like ourselves—if we choose. They can walk like us, they'll soon talk like us and they can interact with each other.

11 As 3-D technology becomes increasingly sophisticated, Booker says that photo-realistic avatars are just around the corner, and will become increasingly convincing.

12 "Eye movement, breathing, and realistic expressions will be the easy part," he revealed. "The hard part will come with things like synching mouth movements with voice recognition. That's something we might not quite have nailed by 2020, but there will definitely be some kind of engine that attempts it by then."

13 Holographic projections of 3-D objects are in development, but it will be some time before virtual reality offers us experiences akin to Star Trek's holodecks: touching and tasting virtual matter is still some way off.

14 "We're a long, long way away from having a completely immersive Matrix-like world," he told CNN. "But then again, technology can surprise you. I remember joking with a friend about a guy who bought a brand-new VGA monitor. It could display 256 colors at once—who could honestly need something like that?"

Spartan life offline, exotic life online

15 The authors of the "Metaverse Roadmap," a briefing document that explores the possible development of virtual worlds over the next 20 years, agree that a boom within a decade is likely. Their research has indicated that by 2016, half of us will have interactive avatars, with those aged between 13 and 30 spending around 10 hours a week socializing in 3-D visual environments.

16 And the draw of virtual worlds may encourage some of us to forsake our mundane real-life surroundings for a luxury life online.

17 The Metaverse Roadmap points to the millions of youths who already use worlds and suggests that "Youth raised in such conditions might live increasingly Spartan lives in the physical world, and rich, exotic lives in virtual space." It makes a certain kind of sense: why cripple yourself with huge mortgage payments on "real" real-estate when in a virtual world you can buy an entire island for $1,600 and $300/month maintenance?

18 The uses for virtual worlds don't stop at socializing. Virtual environments are already being built for education, like Edward Castronova's "Arden" project at Indiana University, which will transport users into a Shakespearean world. The applications for interior designers are clear, while a team at the U.S. National Institute of Mental Health (NIMH) in Bethesda, Maryland have used the virtual shoot-em-up "Duke Nukem" to diagnose depression in players.

Business collaboration

19 Booker believes that virtual worlds will be used increasingly as business tools. "They're very well suited to collaborative work," he explained. "We're not sure why yet, but there's something about seeing everybody's avatar in the room with yours that makes the whole experience far more effective than if you were to simply have a conference call. It creates a real shared experience."

20 "The common feeling is that by 2020 virtual worlds will be as widespread as the World Wide Web is now," states Booker.

21 With that popularity comes opportunity—and not only for Internet land barons but also virtual builders, landscapers and interior decorators, designers of avatar clothing and accessories, and even community moderators and governors. "A significant percentage of the world's population will be able to make a living working in virtual worlds," says Booker.

22 And he thinks that this potential is just around the corner. "The truth is that, as far as virtual worlds go, we're living in the flash point at the beginning of the explosion."

You Deserve the Vacation of Your Dreams

Sail Away

to New Adventures in an Ocean Paradise
Discover Fun, Relaxation, and Freedom

Enjoy the Time of Your Life!

Paradise

Adventure

Fun

Discovery

Freedom

Call 800-555-1234 • BOOK YOUR GETAWAY TODAY!

Reading Comprehension

Use "The Secret Life of Walter Mitty" (pp. 1324–1328) to answer questions 1–10.

1. Read the following dictionary entry.

   remote \rĭ-mōt'\ *adj* **1.** separated by an interval or space greater than usual **2.** far removed in space, time, or relation **3.** small in degree **4.** secluded, out-of-the-way

   Which definition best matches the use of the word *remote* in paragraph 3?

   A. Definition 1

   B. Definition 2

   C. Definition 3

   D. Definition 4

2. Which of the following lines from the selection supports the idea that Walter Mitty daydreams often?

   A. *He looked at his wife, in the seat beside him, with shocked astonishment.*

   B. *"It's one of your days."*

   C. *She seemed grossly unfamiliar, like a strange woman who had yelled at him in a crowd.*

   D. *When he came out into the street again, . . . Walter Mitty began to wonder what the other thing was his wife had told him to get.*

3. In paragraphs 4 and 5, Walter Mitty's daydream is caused by —

   A. Mitty's dislike for overshoes

   B. the cop's snapping at Mitty

   C. the sight of the hospital

   D. Mitty's illness

4. Paragraphs 5 and 6 are mainly about —

   A. Walter Mitty's visit to his doctor's office

   B. Walter Mitty's meeting a millionaire

   C. Walter Mitty's fantasy of being a surgeon

   D. Walter Mitty's day at work

5. In paragraph 7, *insolent* means —

   A. careful

   B. cowardly

   C. disrespectful

   D. fair

6. Mrs. Mitty, the cop, and the parking attendant are similar because they —

   A. criticize Walter when he makes a mistake

   B. laugh at Walter's mistakes

   C. are characters in Walter's daydreams

   D. teach Walter the best way to do things

7. Which words from paragraph 10 help the reader understand the meaning of the word *bedlam*?

   A. Buzz

   B. Cur

   C. Pandemonium

   D. Webley-Vickers

8. What pattern do the events in the story follow?

   A. The same thing causes each daydream.

   B. Someone interrupts Walter Mitty's daydreams.

   C. Walter Mitty daydreams about the same thing.

   D. People around Walter Mitty become characters in his daydreams.

9. The best way to describe Walter Mitty's secret life is —

   A. dramatic and adventurous

   B. romantic and unsatisfying

   C. satisfying and lonely

   D. tragic and flawed

10. Walter Mitty's daydreams indicate that he is —

A. calm in a crisis

B. in love with his wife

C. unhappy in his everyday life

D. just like everybody else

Use "Virtual Worlds" (pp. 1328–1330) to answer questions 11–16.

11. Read the following dictionary entry.

deck /dĕk/ *v* **1.** clothe in a striking or elegant manner **2.** decorate **3.** furnish with a deck **4.** knock down with force

Which definition best matches the use of the word *decked* in paragraph 1?

A. Definition 1

B. Definition 2

C. Definition 3

D. Definition 4

12. Paragraph 9 is mainly about —

A. how virtual worlds are really popular

B. how similar email and virtual worlds are

C. how easy it will be for people to try virtual worlds

D. how virtual worlds are only a passing fad

13. In paragraph 10, *uncannily* means —

A. eerily

B. basically

C. exactly

D. usually

14. Paragraphs 12 and 13 mainly discuss —

A. improvements made in avatars so far

B. the best way to synch mouth movements of avatars with voice recognition

C. how difficult it is to make an avatar

D. what avatars will eventually be able to do

15. Which of the following can the reader conclude from the information in paragraphs 19–21?

A. Avatars will eliminate the need for people to work.

B. Virtual worlds will create new jobs.

C. Virtual worlds will make business more like a game.

D. Businesses will not use virtual worlds because they are for entertainment only.

16. Which of the following is the best summary of the article?

A. Virtual worlds currently use 3-D technology and holograms to offer people a better lifestyle.

B. Virtual worlds will continue to grow and provide social, educational, and business opportunities.

C. Facebook is the fastest growing Web site worldwide.

D. Although avatars are available now, most people prefer to use sites like Facebook and MySpace.

Use "The Secret Life of Walter Mitty" and "Virtual Worlds" to answer question 17.

17. Virtual worlds and Walter Mitty's secret life are both —

A. ways to escape boring routines of normal life

B. works of fiction

C. lifestyles of wealthy people

D. symptoms of mental illness

GO ON

Use the visual representation on page 1331 to answer questions 18–19.

18. One underlying message of the advertisement is that —
    - **A.** a cruise is an expensive vacation
    - **B.** a cruise offers fun adventures
    - **C.** the food is fantastic on a cruise
    - **D.** the ship will not go too far out to sea

19. In this advertisement, the designer is attempting to —
    - **A.** compare a cruise to a car trip
    - **B.** outline activities available on board a cruise ship
    - **C.** inform viewers of cruise ship dangers
    - **D.** persuade viewers to go on a cruise

SHORT CONSTRUCTED RESPONSE

Write a short constructed response to each question, using text evidence to support your response.

20. What might the author of "The Secret Life of Walter Mitty" be saying about male gender roles? Support your response with evidence from the selection.

21. Why does the author start "Virtual Worlds" with a story set in the future? Support your response with evidence from the selection.

Write a short constructed response to the following question, using text evidence from both selections to support your response.

22. What similar concern do the authors of "The Secret Life of Walter Mitty" and "Virtual Worlds" share? Support your response with evidence from **both** selections.

Revising and Editing

DIRECTIONS Read this passage and answer the questions that follow.

(1) The storm was over, but it had been bad. (2) We had seen the TV footage and read the newspapers, but no one was prepared for the mud-caked debris we find when we returned. (3) Where had our pristine home gone? (4) Louise covered her face—as if by blocking this sight, she could erase the devastation before us. (5) Despondently, we joined our neighbors. (6) They had found an heirloom that had somehow survived the ferocious winds, endless rains, and raging floods. (7) It reminded us that we had once lived happily in this now beleaguered city. (8) As I held the heirloom in my hand, I asked my mother, "Where do we go from here."

1. What is the most effective way to revise sentence 1?

A. The unpleasant storm was over.
B. What a storm it had been!
C. Although the fury of the storm had subsided, it left misery in its wake.
D. The storm caused a lot of damage.

2. What change, if any, should be made in sentence 2?

A. Change ***was prepared*** to **prepared**
B. Change ***find*** to **found**
C. Insert a comma after ***find***
D. Make no change

3. Which transition could best be added to the beginning of sentence 4?

A. Besides,
B. First,
C. Thus,
D. Unless,

4. What is the most effective way to combine sentences 5 and 6?

A. Despondently, we joined our neighbors; they had found an heirloom that had somehow survived the ferocious winds, endless rains, and raging floods.
B. Despondently, we joined our neighbors, yet they had found an heirloom that had somehow survived the ferocious winds, endless rains, and raging floods.
C. Because our neighbors had found an heirloom that had somehow survived the ferocious winds, endless rains, and raging floods, despondently, we joined our neighbors.
D. Despondently, we joined our neighbors, who had found an heirloom that had somehow survived the ferocious winds, endless rains, and raging floods.

5. What change, if any, should be made in sentence 8?

A. Change the **.** to a **?** at the end of the sentence
B. Delete the comma after ***hand***
C. Change ***asked*** to **ask**
D. Make no change

Ideas for Independent Reading

Continue exploring the Questions of the Times on pages 1146–1147 with these additional works.

Are we responsible for the WHOLE WORLD?

Catch-22
by Joseph Heller

This hilarious, heartbreaking novel brilliantly satirizes the "logic" of warfare. In the words of WWII airman Yossarian: "The enemy . . . is anybody who's going to get you killed, no matter which side he's on." Unfortunately for Yossarian, each time he completes the number of missions required for his discharge, that number is raised by his commanders.

Hiroshima
by John Hersey

In 1945, faced with a war that seemed as if it might never end, President Truman made the decision to drop an atomic bomb on the Japanese city of Hiroshima, killing between 70,000 and 80,000 people. John Hersey recorded the stories of Hiroshima survivors shortly after the explosion, bringing home for Americans the magnitude of the devastation and loss.

The Things They Carried
by Tim O'Brien

This collection of short stories focuses on a platoon of American soldiers in Vietnam. The things they carry—letters, photographs, Bibles, hand grenades—hint at the confused inner landscape of each young man. In this masterpiece of war literature, O'Brien makes clear that the burdens of war continue to weigh on the troops long after they lay down their arms.

Can America achieve EQUAL RIGHTS?

At Canaan's Edge: America in the King Years, 1965–68
by Taylor Branch

Third in a series on civil rights leader Martin Luther King Jr., *At Canaan's Edge* discusses the final years of King's life. The book begins with King's last great success: the marches in Selma, Alabama, that led to the passage of the Voting Rights Act. It then moves through the Vietnam years to the national tragedy of King's untimely death.

Vintage Baldwin
by James Baldwin

Author James Baldwin was extremely influential in exposing America's racial divide. Much of his writing focuses on the civil rights movement and the experience of African Americans living in white-controlled America. This collection includes short stories, essays, an excerpt from a novel, and a play.

A Gathering of Old Men
by Ernest Gaines

This quiet novel of race relations begins with the killing of a white bully by the only African-American man who has the courage to stand up for his rights. Eighteen elderly African-American men arrive at the scene of the crime, each carrying a shotgun with discharged shells. When the sheriff arrives, all 18 claim to be the murderer, forcing the community to reconsider how they treat one another.

COMMON CORE

RL 10 Read and comprehend literature. **RI 10** Read and comprehend literary nonfiction.

What makes an AMERICAN?

The Woman Warrior
by Maxine Hong Kingston

In this classic memoir, Maxine Hong Kingston encapsulates the confusion, anger, pleasure, and wonder of growing up Chinese American in California, the daughter of immigrants. Haunted by her mother's tales of the magical if sometimes brutal world she left behind, the young narrator is equally unsure about where she fits in among the "ghosts," her parents' term for the non-Chinese people they live among.

Arranged Marriage
by Chitra Banerjee Divakaruni

In this collection of short stories, Chitra Divakaruni focuses on the experiences of women living in India and of Indian women who have moved to America. The contrast between their two worlds, coupled with their inherent roles and expectations, is a common theme running throughout the stories.

Unsettling America
Edited by Maria Mazziotti Gillian and Jennifer Gillian

A diverse chorus of voices comment on ethnic pride and heritage, personal identity, and cultural stereotypes in this anthology of contemporary multicultural poetry. Pat Mora, Lucille Clifton, Li-Young Lee, Louise Erdrich, and Lawrence Ferlinghetti are among the notable poets included in this collection.

What is the AMERICAN DREAM?

The Portable Arthur Miller
by Arthur Miller, edited by Christopher Bigsby

Playwright Arthur Miller once said, "Whoever is writing in the United States is using the American Dream as an ironical pole of his story. People elsewhere tend to accept, to a far greater degree anyway, that the conditions of life are hostile to man's pretensions." Miller's best work examines the average American's pursuit of the American dream and how that dream can become twisted or unattainable. This collection includes complete texts of his masterpieces *The Death of a Salesman* and *The Crucible,* as well as several later plays and excerpts from his memoir *Timebends.*

The Stories of John Cheever
by John Cheever

These stories describe a world that could be considered the epitome of the American dream—a place of leafy suburbs, summer homes, and cocktail parties. But beneath the surface lurks a darkness. Cheever's characters face a myriad of problems—aging, financial blunders, embarrassment, death. Cheever's graceful prose illuminates this world and makes readers care about the imperfect people who inhabit it.

Get Novel Wise THINK central

Go to thinkcentral.com.
KEYWORD: HML11-1337

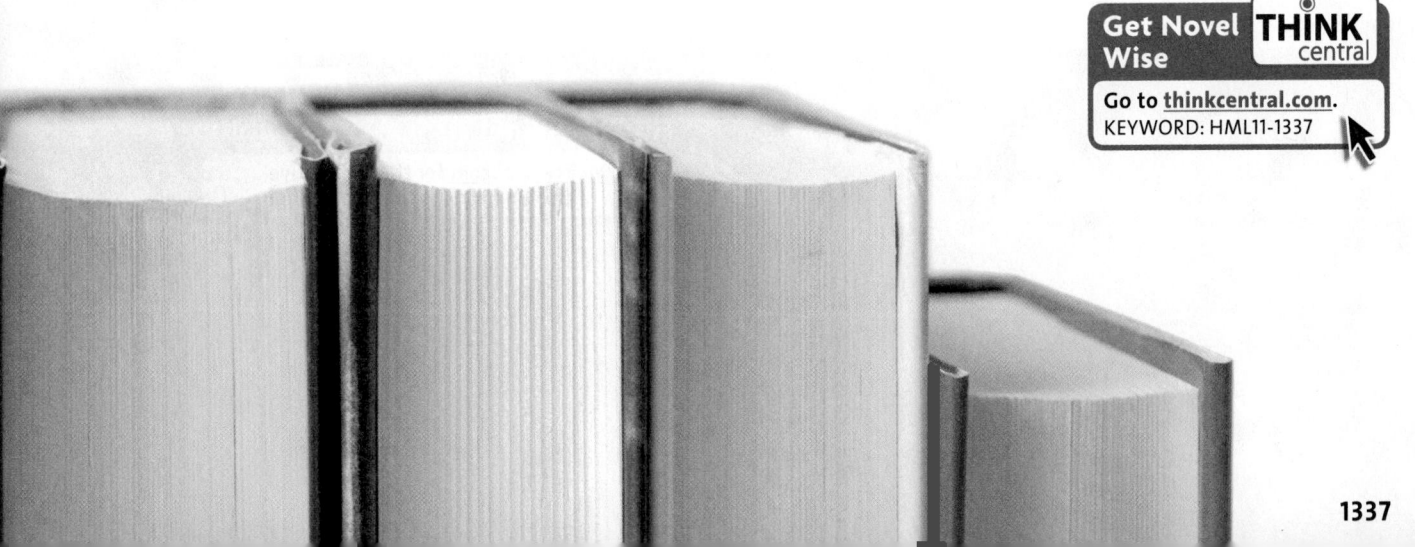

UNIT 7

COMMON CORE

Preview Unit Goals

DEVELOPING RESEARCH SKILLS

- Select and shape a topic
- Plan research
- Find relevant information from multiple print and digital sources, including primary and secondary sources and online resources; use advanced searches effectively
- Assess the credibility, as well as the strengths and limitations, of each source, including nonfiction books, newspapers, periodicals, and Web sites
- Make source cards and take notes
- Paraphrase and summarize information
- Avoid plagiarism by quoting directly and crediting sources
- Verify information, detect bias, and develop own perspective

WRITING AND LANGUAGE

- Write a research paper
- Document sources
- Prepare Works Cited list
- Format your paper
- Use punctuation with parenthetical citations
- Use correct style for direct quotations

ACADEMIC VOCABULARY

- adequate
- consult
- investigate
- objective
- qualitative

MEDIA AND VIEWING

- Produce a documentary

Find It Online!

Go to thinkcentral.com for the interactive version of this unit.

The Power of Research

INVESTIGATION AND DISCOVERY

- Research Strategies
- Writing Research Papers

Writing and Research in a Digital Age

From online news feeds and electronic archives to podcasts and digital notebooks, technology tools can help you tackle any research project. Find out how.

KEYWORD: HML11-1339

UNIT 7

What Is the Power of Research?

Throughout this book, you have explored the "big questions" of literature, history, and life. You can take these questions to a new, more challenging level through formal research.

What is it like to be AT WAR?

You might investigate this question by writing a **historical research paper** that explores why some 18- and 19-year-olds enlisted to fight in Vietnam. Or you might create a **personal research paper** that describes how a particular war or conflict affected you or someone you know. How did that personal experience relate to the conflict as a whole?

How does SCIENCE *affect you?*

Is acid rain present in your community? Do high school students improve their academic performance if they eat breakfast each day? When and where was the last earthquake in your state? When you write a **scientific research paper,** you present data that you have collected yourself as well as the findings of others.

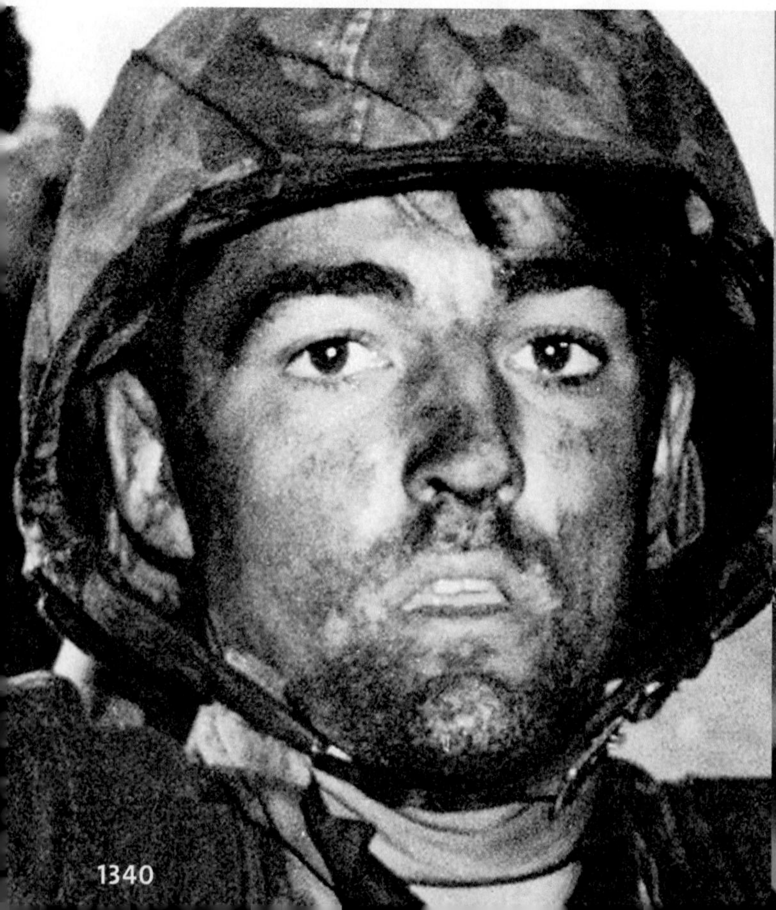

COMMON CORE

W 9 Draw evidence from literary or informational texts to support analysis, reflection and research. **W 10** Write over extended time frames (research, reflection, revision) for a range of tasks, purposes, and audiences.

How does LIFE *influence literature?*

Novels, stories, and poems reflect how authors see the world. They can also shape our view of places and events. One way to explore a work of literature is to write a **literary research paper** that traces how history influenced a particular literary work or vice versa. For instance, you could learn more about the real people who inspired John Steinbeck to write *The Grapes of Wrath*.

Are we ready for the next natural DISASTER?

The question that captivates you may touch on several fields of study. A **multidisciplinary research paper** allows you to ask questions related to science, government, history, and many other subject areas and to investigate how those subjects relate to each other.

UNIT 7

Research Strategies Workshop

Beginning Your Investigation

When you create a top-quality research paper, you go beyond merely gathering information. Instead, you investigate, analyze, develop new perspectives, and synthesize collected information to reach your own conclusions.

Deciding on a Topic

COMMON CORE

RI 7 Evaluate multiple sources of information presented in different media or formats. **W 6** Use technology, including the Internet, to produce writing products in response to ongoing feedback. **W 7** Conduct research projects to answer a question or solve a problem; synthesize multiple sources on the subject, demonstrating understanding of the subject under investigation. **W 8** Gather relevant information from multiple authoritative print and digital sources, using advanced searches effectively; assess strengths and limitations of each source in terms of task, purpose, and audience; integrate information selectively, avoiding plagiarism and overreliance on any one source. **W 9** Draw evidence from literary or informational texts to support analysis, reflection, and research. **L 6** Acquire and use academic and domain-specific words and phrases.

When writing a research paper, you may be asked to generate your own topic or put your own spin on an assigned topic. For instance, perhaps you need to write a paper for your American literature or American history class. Reading *The Grapes of Wrath* has heightened your interest in the historical events of that period, but you know that a topic like "the Dust Bowl" is too broad. Because you will spend hours researching and writing, you want to decide upon a topic that will hold your interest over time. How can you shape a general idea into the right research topic for you?

TRY OUT DIFFERENT "LENSES"

To discover a unique approach to a particular topic, view it through different "lenses," or perspectives. A historian, an economist, a scientist, and an artist would look at the topic of the Dust Bowl in different ways. This cluster diagram illustrates types of questions you might ask when brainstorming different aspects of a topic.

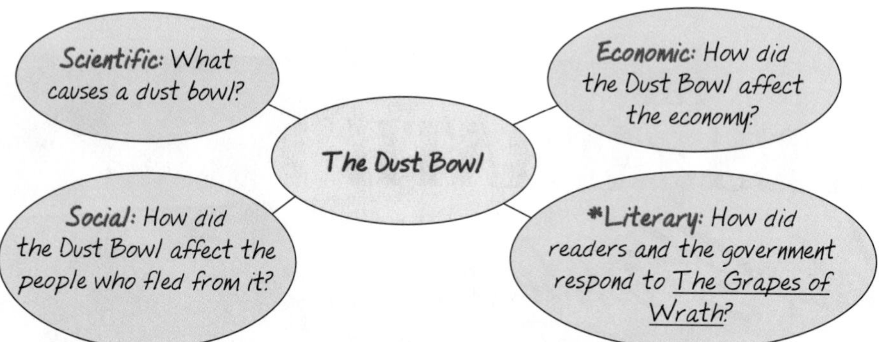

Choose the question that intrigues you the most and develop a plan for answering it. You might consult with other students in your class to get feedback on your question. You will want to end up with an open-ended question, one that cannot be answered with a "yes" or "no."

> **QUESTION:** *Did The Grapes of Wrath affect the government response to the Dust Bowl?*
>
> **OPEN-ENDED QUESTION:** *How did The Grapes of Wrath affect government response to the Dust Bowl?*

Your research question will develop into your thesis after you have read, evaluated, and synthesized information from a variety of sources.

Planning Your Research

To make your search efficient and effective, develop open-ended research questions and then formulate a plan for engaging in in-depth research on your topic.

FORMULATE RESEARCH QUESTIONS

You may want to write several open-ended research questions to help you begin and then refocus as you search for sources. Think about different perspectives on the topic of investigation. Remember, you may have to revise your research question depending on the results of your research.

- *How did the Dust Bowl affect the United States?*
- *Why did Steinbeck write The Grapes of Wrath? How did he do the research?*
- *What did the government do to help migrant workers like the Joad family?*

IDENTIFY THE MOST RELEVANT SOURCES

You will want to locate a range of relevant and credible sources to answer your research question. Take a few minutes to consider which sources make the most sense for the early stages of your research.

- **Encyclopedia articles** can provide a helpful overview of your topic as you begin researching.
- For the specific details you need, try **specialized reference works.** Almanacs provide facts and statistics, biographical references provide information on famous people, and atlases provide maps, charts, and graphics. See page R44 to learn more about reference works.
- **Documentaries** often include valuable interviews, speeches, and "you are there" footage that help you understand historical, literary, and scientific topics.
- **Magazines and newspapers** can give insights into a topic's perceived importance. Has your topic ever been front-page news, or is it rarely covered? How has coverage of your topic changed over time? For topics related to economics, popular culture, or history, take a look at related **advertisements.**
- **Interviews and oral histories** are firsthand testimony about history and culture. Look for them on audio, on video, in books, or on Web sites.
- **Original research** is information you discover yourself. For example, you might interview an expert, listen to a speech or lecture, create a questionnaire, perform an experiment, or conduct field research. To learn more about original research, see page R47.
- Be creative as you search. You might find valuable information in illustrations, maps, photographs, obituaries, statistical data, government publications, or museum exhibits.

Share your research questions with a librarian. He or she can suggest print and electronic resources that you may not have considered.

Find It Online!
THINK central
Go to thinkcentral.com for the interactive version of this unit.

Finding Relevant Sources

As you delve into your research, you will learn more about what sources are available and where you can find them, as well as how to assess their strengths and limitations.

Primary and Secondary Sources

Most research papers include both primary and secondary sources. As this chart shows, the two types have distinct differences, advantages, and disadvantages.

PRIMARY SOURCE	SECONDARY SOURCE
Definition: materials written or created by people who took part in events or observed them	**Definition:** records created after events occurred by people who were not directly involved
Examples: letters, diaries, speeches, photographs, autobiographies, e-mails, some Weblogs, first-person newspaper and magazine articles, public documents such as birth certificates	**Examples:** biographies, textbooks, encyclopedias, some Weblogs, third-person newspaper and magazine articles, most documentaries
Advantages: provide firsthand information; can give insight into attitudes and beliefs of the times; may contain very specific details	**Advantages:** sometimes include excerpts from many primary sources; often include a broad perspective and many viewpoints; can be useful for getting an overview of a topic
Disadvantages: offer limited perspective; may need interpretation; may be biased	**Disadvantages:** are only as credible as the sources on which they are based; may be biased

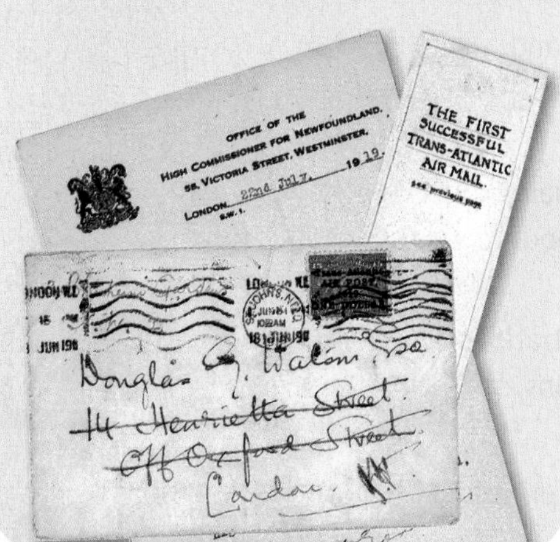

TERMS FOR THE LIBRARY

You will use these terms when doing research in a library or media center:

- primary source
- secondary source
- database
- catalog
- abstract
- bibliography
- index
- appendix
- preface

Using Library Resources

Today many print resources can also be found in electronic form. Most of your searches, however, will be conducted electronically on the Internet or through a library catalog. The following pages will show you where to look for sources and how to improve your search skills.

USING SEARCH ENGINES

When using a search engine (such as Google or Yahoo!) to find information on the Web, you will need to come up with **keywords** that will help you locate the most relevant sources. For best results, use your search engine's "advanced search" or "search tips" link. Follow these general tips for effective Internet searches.

- **Be specific.** Try combining two or three keywords. If you want to find out about labor camps in California, be sure *California* is one of your search terms.
- **Use search limiters.** Enclose phrases in quotation marks—for example, a search for *"The Grapes of Wrath"* will result in pages that have those words in that order. Some search engines allow you to add AND or a plus sign to be sure that certain results are included: *Depression AND California;* or *+Depression +California.* To exclude certain terms, use the word NOT or a minus sign: *evacuees NOT Katrina;* or *+evacuees -Katrina.* To learn more, see page R46.
- **Choose the most relevant pages.** Scan the first 10 to 15 descriptions the search engine provides. Which sites could help you answer your research questions? Consider adding, deleting, or changing keywords to improve your results.

Examine Search Engine Results

Which of these results do you think would yield the most useful information?

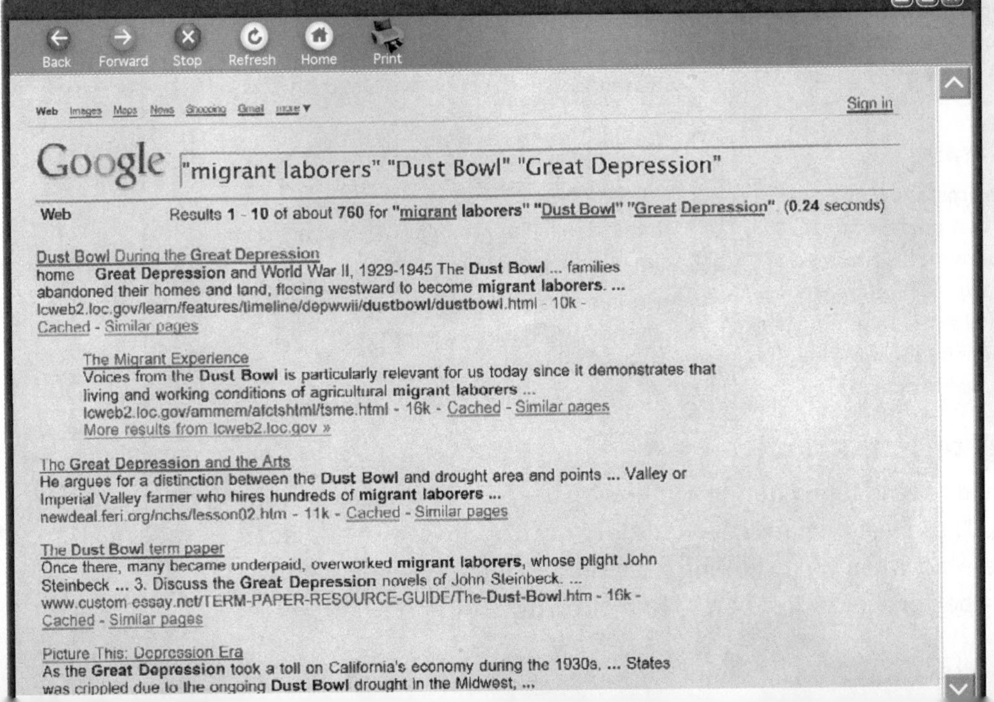

TERMS FOR THE INTERNET

Here are terms you will use when discussing the Internet:

- Web page
- Web site
- URL (uniform resource locator, also called Web address)
- search engine
- keyword search
- hyperlink
- menu

Close Read

1. This researcher did a search that combined three terms: "migrant laborers," "Dust Bowl," and "Great Depression." What are the advantages and disadvantages of doing such a specific search?
2. How might the search results change if the search was for "migrant laborers," "Dust Bowl," and "Oklahoma"?
3. What other search terms can you think of that might yield answers to the research questions on pages 1342–1343?

EXPLORE DATABASES

A **database** is any organized collection of data, whether print or electronic. Some of the databases in this chart are free to all; others may be available for free through your library's or media center's Web site.

TYPES OF SOURCES	EXAMPLES
LIBRARY CATALOGS Most library catalogs are available online, allowing you to search the catalog electronically and create a customized database of sources. Results will provide you with bibliographic data and a call number to locate the material in the library.	http://www.nypl.org/ http://www.lib.unc.edu/ http://bpl.org/catalogs/ http://www.lib.uchicago.edu/e/cat/
BOOKS Use your library's catalog to search for books by title, author, subject, or keyword. Once you find a book, use the book's index to locate specific information. In addition, some Web sites include full text of reference books and other older publications.	Bartleby.com offers free access to reference books, poetry, and classic literature online. books.google.com offers full text, previews, and reference information for books on a variety of subjects. Amazon.com offers previews of books, including tables of contents, excerpts, and front and back covers.
NEWSPAPERS AND PERIODICALS Most libraries have print indexes and electronic databases of newspapers and periodicals. You can search databases to find bibliographic citations or access to full-text articles. Full-text articles are often available at the Web sites of specific publications.	*Readers' Guide to Periodical Literature* is available in print and online, offering both full-text articles and indexing of over 400 periodicals. TIME magazine provides free access to archived articles online. *The New York Times Index* is available in print and online.
GENERAL DATABASES Libraries have access to many types of databases that provide full-text articles or bibliographic citations on a range of topics. A reference librarian can help you determine which databases might be the most helpful for the topic you are researching.	Academic Search Premier indexes articles from all major fields of study. MiddleSearch Plus provides full-text articles from middle school magazines. African American Experience indexes articles and primary source documents on African American history.

ADVANTAGES OF DATABASES

"Why should I spend time figuring out how to use these databases?" you might ask. "I can just type my keywords into my favorite search engine." That's true—but when you're writing a research paper, specialized databases are often a better choice. Read on to find out why.

- **Specificity**—Some databases, such as the Internet Movie Database, cover only certain topics. Others cover only one type of material, such as articles from medical journals. Because these databases are targeted, you don't have to sift through pages of search results that have little or no relation to your topic.
- **No advertisements**—Unlike many search engines, most specialized databases do not have distracting pop-up windows or sidebar advertisements. No advertiser has paid to have a page show up first or in the top ten.
- **Access to the "invisible Web"**—Librarians call pages that are accessible through the Internet, but not through search engines, the "invisible Web." Many millions of Web pages are available through subscription-only databases—but if your library or media center subscribes to such databases, all you may need to access them is the bar code number on your library card.
- **Abstracts**—Many databases include an abstract—a short summary of an article's content—for each article. By reading abstracts, you can quickly decide whether the entire article is worth reading.

To find the most relevant results on a targeted database, read the article titles and notice the names of the publications the articles come from. Click on the most promising titles and read the abstracts, or skim the first few paragraphs of each.

Examine Database Results

These results are from a database called InfoTrac. Examine them and think about whether this search is effective.

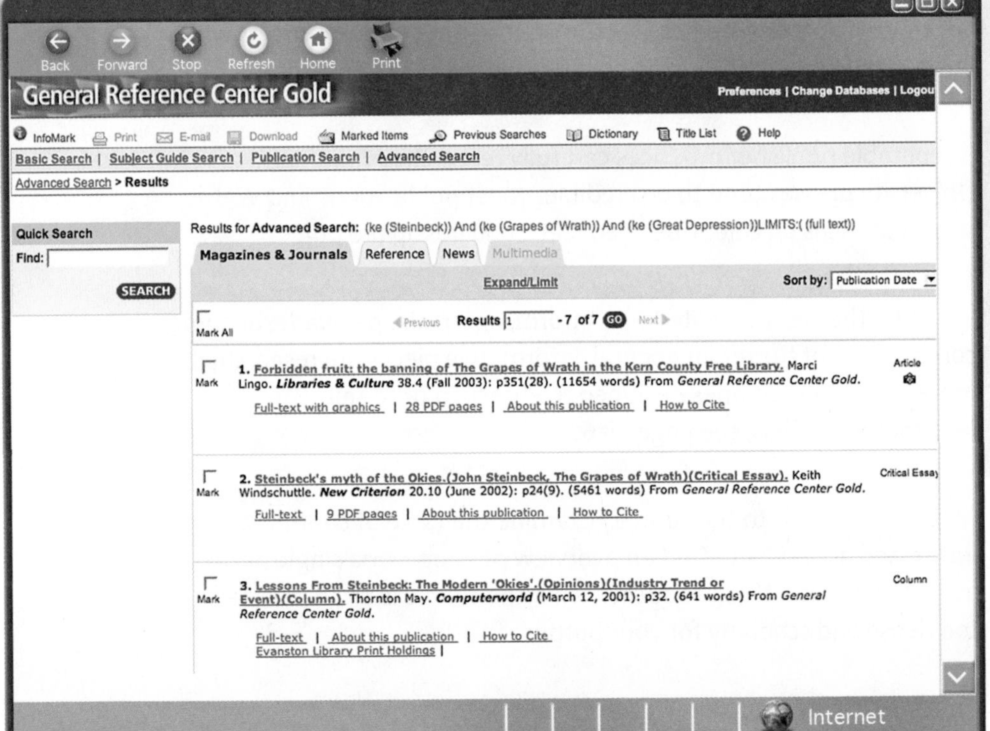

Close Read

1. Which three keyword phrases did this researcher use? On this database, the abbreviation *ke* stands for "keyword."
2. Which result includes graphics? How do you know?
3. Of the three results shown here, which one is not likely to be useful? How do you know?
4. What other information does this database provide that the search engine on page 1345 does not? Give three examples.

Evaluating Sources

In this section, you will learn how to select the most credible and accurate sources, whether print or online, and assess each source's strengths and limitations.

GUIDELINES FOR EVALUATING SOURCES

Relevance	Is the source related to the open-ended question and research questions you wrote on pages 1342–1343? Your goals and questions may change as you write; however, don't allow interesting but irrelevant sources to distract you.
Timeliness	Topics in science, medicine, and sports often require recently updated information. Older sources can be valuable for historical or literary topics. For a print source, check the copyright page. For a documentary, look for a copyright notice on the label. For online materials, look for a "last updated" notice.
Accuracy	Most encyclopedias, dictionaries, and almanacs are accurate because they are updated regularly and go through a rigorous review process. Online sources can have information that is even more accurate because of frequent updates. Some online sources, however, may not go through the same rigorous review process. Whenever possible, verify and clarify facts using more than one source.
Author's Credentials	Look for an author who has written on the same topic before or who has a position or job title that qualifies him or her as an expert.
Publisher's Credentials	A reputable publisher produces carefully researched materials. University presses tend to be credible. Most publications and Web sites that focus on celebrities, fad diets, and gossip are not.
Author's Purpose	Why was the source created—to inform, entertain, persuade, or some combination of these? In general, informative pieces are researched more carefully than ones designed to entertain or to sell. For information on bias, see page 1356.
Breadth and Depth of Information	Match your needs to the source. Examine the table of contents, index, and appendix to find an overview of a topic or a single detailed aspect of it. Also, think about whether the source is either too basic or too dense and scholarly for your purposes.

Finding Credible Web Sites

Anyone can create a Web site, so it is important to evaluate sites thoroughly.

QUESTIONS TO ASK ABOUT A WEB SITE

- **What does the address tell me?** Most sites with *.com* or *.net* in the address are personal or commercial sites. A personal site might be the work of one person, so its information may not have been carefully checked. Commercial sites exist to make a profit, so negative information about a product or service may be left out. Sites with the abbreviations *.edu* (educational institution), *.org* (nonprofit organization), or *.gov* (U.S. government) are more likely to be credible because they are the work of groups of people.
- **Who created this site?** Look for sections labeled "About Us" or "Contact Us." How can you tell if an individual rather than an organization created a site? The lack of an institution name or logo is one clue. Other clues are the lack of author biographies, the absence of documentation for sources, and hyperlinks that lead nowhere or only to the author's own sites. You can also consult a domain lookup site, such as *easywhois.com*.

TIP Some *.org* and *.edu* sites are personal sites that are not reviewed by the sponsoring institution. A personal *.edu* address includes a forward slash and a tilde (/~) followed by a name or initials, as in *okies.utc.edu/~haylee.*

Evaluate a Web Site

Would this site be useful for researching the open-ended question on page 1342?

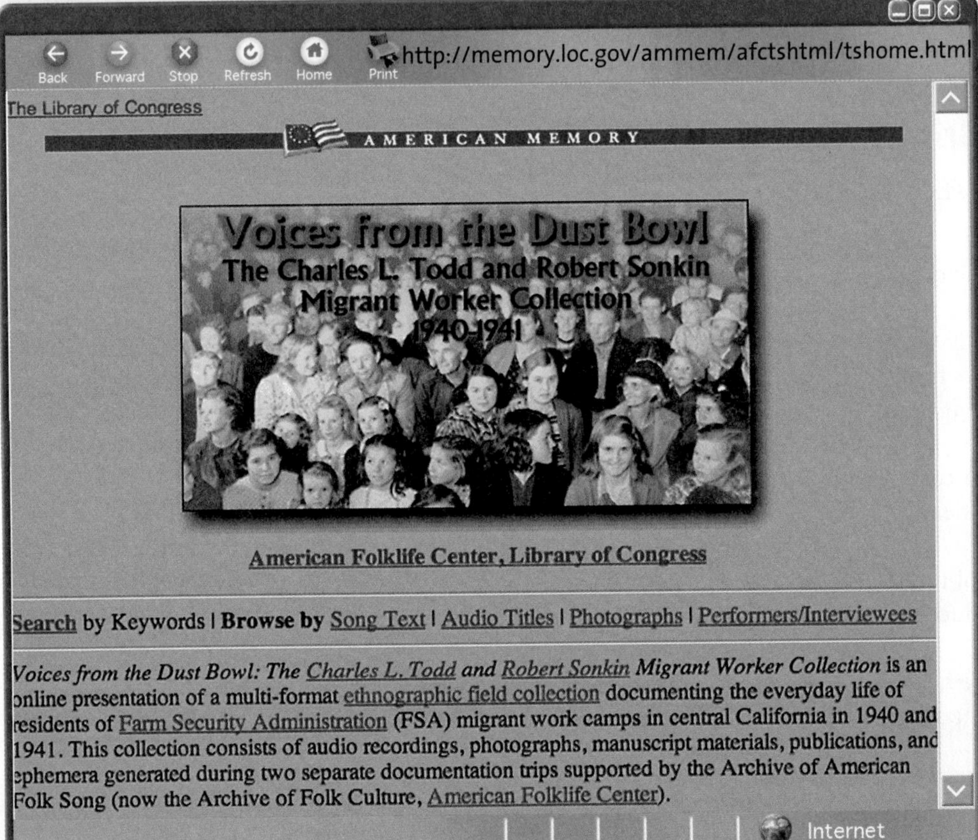

Close Read

1. What organization maintains this site? How do you know?
2. Why was the site created?
3. What clues do you have about the accuracy of the information on this site?

Evaluating Newspapers and Periodicals

When you assess magazines, newspapers, and scholarly journals, you need to assess the publication itself, the author of the article, and the article's content.

QUESTIONS TO ASK ABOUT NEWSPAPERS AND PERIODICALS

- **Is the publication well known and well respected?** Most large-circulation newspapers and national magazines are credible sources. Beware of supermarket tabloids and other sensationalist publications.
- **Who is the author?** Look for the writer's credentials. Generally, staff writers are as credible as the publication in which they appear.
- **How old is the information?** Depending on your topic, you may need up-to-the-minute information, or you might need information from a specific era.
- **Did the article originally appear in another source?** If so, make sure the original source is credible. News services such as AP (Associated Press) and the *New York Times* News Service are the original sources of many reprinted articles.
- **Can the information be verified?** The best way to tell if a particular piece of information is accurate is to check it against other sources.

Evaluate a Newspaper Article

Read and evaluate this newspaper article.

from the Los Angeles Times, July 9, 1939

Dust Bowl Book Brings Trouble

BY TOM CAMERON, TIMES STAFF REPRESENTATIVE

LOS GATOS, July 8. (Exclusive)—John Steinbeck, author of the best-selling novel, *Grapes of Wrath*, has betaken himself to Moody Gulch, a secluded canyon three miles from here, and padlocked himself against the world.

For the first time in his career, Steinbeck is inaccessible to friend and enemy alike. . . .

There have been reports of threats against the author which induced him to retreat to an almost inaccessible citadel—a refuge from the very economic refugees he sought to befriend. . . .

"It isn't the refugees who have taken exception to what I wrote," he asserted. "It's the moneyed people back there in Oklahoma—the big oil men and outfits like the Oklahoma City Chamber of Commerce. If anybody's sore at me for the book it's that kind of people." . . .

Regarding the report that Ruth Comfort Mitchell planned to write a refutation of some of the statements in his book, Steinbeck laughed in scorn.

"I know what I was talking about. I lived, off and on, with those Okies for the last three years. Anyone who tries to refute me will just become ridiculous."

Close Read

1. Briefly summarize this article.
2. The *Los Angeles Times* is California's most widely read newspaper, so would you expect this article to be credible? Give reasons for your answer.
3. Is this article useful even though it is dated? Explain.

Choosing Credible Books

Just as you write for different purposes and audiences, publishers put books on the market for different reasons. Some books are rushed to market and aimed at making money fast. Others are the result of years of work and have undergone multiple reviews, edits, and rewrites.

QUESTIONS TO ASK ABOUT NONFICTION BOOKS

- **Is the author an expert on this subject?** Check for information about the author on the book jacket, at the beginning of the book, and at the end.
- **Is the book research-based?** Check the back of the book for a bibliography. Look for footnotes in which the author credits his or her sources and provides additional insights or information. Check for an appendix, which might add other information, such as maps, statistical tables, or family trees.
- **What is the author's or publisher's purpose?** This may be stated in a **preface,** a short introductory essay. The preface may also tell you more about the writer's background and research.
- **What is the copyright date?** A series of updates and printings is often a sign that the source has been highly regarded for years and is probably credible.

Evaluate a Nonfiction Book

Decide whether this book, *Dust Bowl Migration,* would be useful to someone focusing on governmental response to the needs of Dust Bowl evacuees.

Index (continued)

Library of Congress Cataloging-in-Publication Data
Mulligan, Judith.
Dust Bowl Migration–1st ed.
1. Dust Bowl Era–1931-1939.
2. Droughts–Great Plains–History.

Contents

Close Read

1. Does this book contain information on federal policies that were related to the Dust Bowl? How do you know?
2. How useful might this book be to someone researching governmental response to the needs of Dust Bowl evacuees? Use page numbers and/or chapter numbers to support your answer.

Note Taking and Plagiarism

As you read and take notes from many sources, do not use the ideas of others without giving them credit. Plagiarism is dishonest and may result in your failing a class or being expelled.

TIP Cutting and pasting phrases, sentences, or paragraphs from a Web page or other electronic file into your research paper is plagiarism—unless you credit the source.

Recording Information

By taking careful notes, you will gather information and guard against plagiarism. You can record your information on an electronic document, use special "note-taking" software, or simply use index cards.

SOURCE LIST

Begin by listing each of your sources. If you are using index cards, make one source card for every source. Assign each source a number, and then record the author and/or editor (if given), the title of the publication or Web page, and the date and medium of publication. Also record the following for these sources:

- **Web source**—date created or posted, date accessed
- **Book**—publisher and publisher's location, library call number, relevant page numbers
- **Encyclopedia**—name and year of encyclopedia, publisher, publisher's location
- **Periodical article**—name of periodical, page numbers of article

Encyclopedia Article

Source 2

Kite, Steven. "Dust Bowl." *Encyclopedia of the Great Depression and New Deal*. Ed. James Ciment. 2 vols. Armonk, NY: Sharpe, 2001. Print.

NOTES

Before you take your first note, identify its source by noting its number from your source list. For example, if you are taking notes from an encyclopedia article that you numbered 6 on your source list, begin your notes with that number. Using this system will ensure that you will be able to identify the source of the note.

In addition to listing the source number, also include a specific heading or subtopic for your notes. This will help you group similar ideas as you take more notes. For example, someone writing about how *The Grapes of Wrath* influenced governmental response to the Dust Bowl might create note headings such as *Dust Bowl—living conditions, bank failures;* or *Steinbeck—early writings about Dust Bowl.* Then quote, paraphrase, or summarize your source. End each card with a page number, if one is available.

See page R48 for examples of source cards and notes.

PARAPHRASES AND SUMMARIES

A **paraphrase** is a restatement of an author's ideas in your own words. It includes all the ideas in the original statement and is about the same length as the original text. A **summary** is also a restatement, but it includes only key ideas and is therefore shorter than the original text. As these examples show, paraphrasing and summarizing carefully will help you avoid plagiarism.

Original Source

> With the introduction of the Soil Conservation Service (SCS) in 1935, the federal government began educating farmers in environmentally friendly farming techniques, such as shelterbelts, crop rotation, and introduction of soil-stabilizing grasses, terracing, and contour plowing.
>
> Kite, Steven. "Dust Bowl." *Encyclopedia of the Great Depression and New Deal*

Responsible Paraphrase

> Government response to dust storms Source 2
>
> The government also established the Soil Conservation Service in 1935. This program taught farmers to terrace their crops, plow along naturally occuring contours in the land, rotate crops, and practice other farming techniques that would protect the topsoil (110).

Carefully restates information; provides source number and page number

Responsible Summary

> Government response to dust storms Source 2
>
> The government also established the Soil Conservation Service in 1935, which taught farmers techniques to protect the topsoil (110).

Skillfully condenses original passage; includes source number and page number

The following examples show how sloppy paraphrasing and careless summarizing can lead to plagiarism.

Plagiarized Paraphrase

> Government response to dust storms
>
> The government introduced the Soil Conservation Service in 1935 to educate farmers in environmentally friendly farming techniques, including crop rotation, terracing, and contour plowing.

Reproduces several phrases from the original without explaining where words and ideas came from

Plagiarized Summary

> Government response to dust storms
>
> In 1935 the federal government introduced the Soil Conservation Service to teach farmers environmentally friendly farming techniques.

Takes a key phrase—"environmentally friendly farming techniques"—from the source without credit

Avoiding Plagiarism

By quoting and crediting information properly, you can include important ideas in your paper without plagiarizing them.

QUOTE INFORMATION ACCURATELY

Sometimes an idea is so significant or original that you want to reproduce it exactly as it was originally expressed. Place quotation marks around every word or phrase you take verbatim, or word for word, from a source. If you change the whole sentence except for one key phrase, that phrase still belongs to its author.

Original Source

Life in what the newspapers call the Dust Bowl is becoming a gritty nightmare.

Low, Ann Marie. *Dust Bowl Diary*. Qtd. in McElvaine, Robert S. *The Depression and New Deal: A History in Documents*

Plagiarized

Dust Bowl—Impact on farm families Source 7

In human terms, the Dust Bowl was a time of terrible suffering. Day by day, it was a gritty nightmare.

Does a good job of creating a new context, but the words "gritty nightmare" are not enclosed in quotation marks.

Correctly Quoted

Dust Bowl—Impact on farm families Source 7

In human terms, the Dust Bowl was a time of terrible suffering. Day by day, it was "a gritty nightmare," a young North Dakotan named Ann Marie Low wrote in her diary (135).

Quotation marks and attribution show that the phrase "gritty nightmare" comes from a source.

CREDIT INFORMATION AND IDEAS FROM OTHERS

Sometimes it is difficult to know what needs to be credited and what does not. These tips can help you decide:

- **You must credit others' ideas.** Authors don't just compile facts and quotations; they give opinions and draw conclusions as well. If your paper includes a theory, explanation, or suggestion that you did not develop yourself, be sure to cite its source. For example, if one of your sources states that the Dust Bowl was more devastating than the stock-market crash, you must tell your reader where you found that assertion.
- **You do not need to credit facts that are considered common knowledge.** For instance, well-known historical information such as "Abraham Lincoln was president of the United States" does not need documentation. Neither do well-known sayings such as "Beauty is only skin deep" or general information such as "The sun rises in the east" and "Governments collect taxes from citizens and businesses." However, when in doubt, cite your source or sources.

Becoming a Critical Researcher

A critical researcher is one who carefully considers information from different sources and synthesizes that information to develop his or her own view of a topic.

Verifying Information

As you examine multiple sources, you may find information that appears to be incorrect. Here's how to review and evaluate sources that contradict each other.

RECONCILE DIFFERENCES

Even credible experts can disagree. For example, historians disagree on exactly when the Dust Bowl era started and on how many people abandoned their homes because of it. When you encounter varying sources, use the criteria listed on page 1348 to determine which sources are credible. If they all appear to be credible, you could state in your paper that opinions vary and then describe the range that the different sources present.

Where can you check facts? Consult reputable print and online sources, such as encyclopedias, almanacs, and library databases. Here are some examples of reputable online sources.

FOR MORE INFORMATION . . .	TRY THIS ONLINE SOURCE
U.S. population statistics	www.census.gov (U.S. Bureau of the Census)
Primary sources, maps, audio, and video related to American history	www.loc.gov (Library of Congress)
Facts about the U.S. government	www.firstgov.gov (official U.S. government Web portal)
Facts about your state's history	your state's official Web site (visit www.firstgov.gov and click on "State Government")
International data	www.un.org (United Nations)
Information on technology	www.computerhistory.org (Computer History Museum) www.cnn.com/tech (CNN Technology News)
Data and resources on the environment	www.epa.gov (Environmental Protection Agency) www.webdirectory.com (The Environment Directory)
Information on space science	www.nasa.gov (NASA)

Detecting Bias

Bias is a preference or an attitude that can prevent a person from presenting information clearly and truthfully. Personal preferences and beliefs can sometimes be presented as facts. Sometimes bias is obvious; at other times it is very subtle.

QUESTIONS TO HELP YOU DETECT BIAS

- Who is the author, and what is his or her **background?** Does this person have ethical beliefs or personal experiences that might influence the writing?
- Why did the author write this piece? Did the **intent** influence his or her point of view? A person wishing to persuade readers may not fully present opposing viewpoints. For example, someone who contends that John Steinbeck single-handedly changed the government's response to migrant workers might leave out information about early government programs, private charities' efforts, and other artists' and writers' coverage of the problem.
- Are the writer's statements based on **verifiable evidence,** or are they speculation?
- Are **enough facts** presented to give a solid basis for the conclusions?
- Is the evidence **balanced,** or does one side get more support?
- How has the **time period** influenced the author's view of events or issues being discussed? For instance, a person writing during the Depression might be affected by the anxiety and despair of the time.
- Does the writer use **loaded language** that has extremely positive or extremely negative connotations, such as "Greedy bankers grew rich while despairing farmers starved"?

Developing Your Own Perspective

Each time you take notes, make connections by mentally attaching that note to something else you have read or discovered. As you synthesize more information, you will begin to develop your own viewpoint on your topic.

MAKE INFERENCES AND DRAW CONCLUSIONS

As you research, read between the lines of the author's words to find implied meanings and attitudes. An **inference** is a logical assumption that is based on observations or information in a text and one's own knowledge and experience. This chart shows the inference that one student made.

What the Source Says	What I Already Know	My Inference
Between 1929 and 1932, farm prices fell 55 percent.	The Great Depression started in 1929. The Dust Bowl started in the early 1930s.	Farmers were in serious trouble even before the Dust Bowl started.

If making an inference is "reading between the lines," then drawing a conclusion is "reading beyond the lines." A **conclusion** is a judgment or statement of belief based on evidence, experience, and reasoning. Making inferences is one of the necessary steps in drawing a conclusion, as you can see in this example.

What Sources Say	My Inferences	My Conclusion
John Steinbeck lived with migrant workers for about three years before he published The Grapes of Wrath. →	Steinbeck's portrayal of the migrants was probably accurate. →	The Grapes of Wrath was accurate, but not everyone wanted to believe its message.
Some growers in California got The Grapes of Wrath banned from several public libraries. →	The book was controversial. →	

DRAFT YOUR THESIS

As you read and take notes, think about what you are learning. Your thesis should be taking shape in your mind. That is, you will synthesize all that you have learned and thought about during your research. You will draw a larger conclusion about the topic you named in your goal statement.

This chart demonstrates the process of drafting a thesis based on your research.

Facts from My Research	My Conclusions	My Thesis
The Grapes of Wrath was published in 1939 and immediately became a best seller. →	The Grapes of Wrath was one of the most important and influential novels of its era. →	The Grapes of Wrath did not significantly affect the government's response to those who suffered from the effects of the Dust Bowl.
The President and the First Lady publicly discussed the book. →		
As early as 1935, there were government programs to help Dust Bowl victims. →	John Steinbeck was just one of many politicians, artists, and activists who were deeply concerned about the migrants. →	
Many other writers and photographers chronicled the problems of the migrant laborers. →		

Now it's time to put all your research and thinking to good use. In the next section, you will learn how to draft, revise, and perfect a research paper.

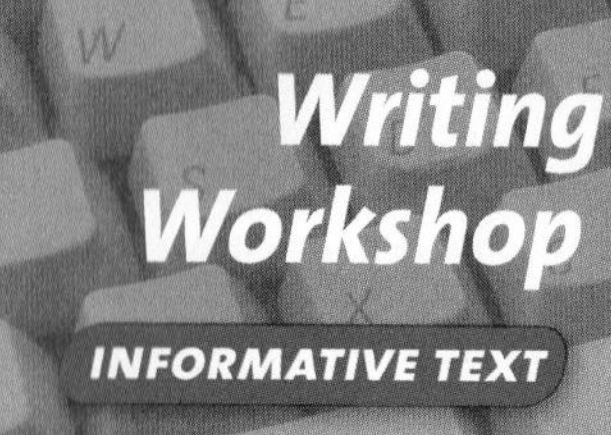

Research Paper

As you have seen in this unit, the purpose of conducting research isn't simply to repeat information that you have read elsewhere. Rather, the goal is to draw your own conclusions about a research question based on a variety of sources. In this workshop, you will select, organize, synthesize, and analyze information in a carefully documented research paper.

Complete the workshop activities in your **Reader/Writer Notebook.**

WRITE WITH A PURPOSE

WRITING TASK

Think of a research question that interests you, and write a **research paper** that fully investigates the question and answers it with ample evidence. Keep your audience in mind as you gather evidence and details to support your controlling idea.

Idea Starters

- how cable news channels affect political campaigns
- the effect of *The Grapes of Wrath* on perceptions of Dust Bowl migrants
- how big-box chain stores have changed small towns in the United States

THE ESSENTIALS

Here are some common purposes, audiences, and formats for research papers.

PURPOSES	AUDIENCES	FORMATS
• to share your research with others who are interested in the subject • for personal education • to fulfill a requirement at work or school	• classmates and teacher • friends with a shared interest in the topic • academic journal readers • co-workers	• research paper for class • school's literary magazine • school's Web site • an academic journal • Web log

COMMON CORE TRAITS

1. DEVELOPMENT OF IDEAS

- introduces a clearly defined **topic** and states a **controlling idea** that answers a research question
- supports the topic with **evidence** from multiple authoritative sources
- provides a **concluding section** that supports the information

2. ORGANIZATION OF IDEAS

- organizes ideas, information, and evidence in a **logical way**
- uses **appropriate transitions** to create **cohesion** and **clarify relationships** among ideas

3. LANGUAGE FACILITY AND CONVENTIONS

- maintains a **formal style** and **objective tone**
- uses **precise language** and **domain-specific vocabulary**
- uses **standard formatting** for quoting or citing sources
- employs correct **grammar, mechanics,** and **spelling**

W 2a–f Write informative/explanatory texts to examine complex ideas clearly and accurately. **W 5** Develop and strengthen writing as needed. **W 7** Conduct research projects to answer a question or solve a problem.

Planning/Prewriting

Getting Started

ANALYZE THE TASK

As you review the writing task, circle words and phrases that tell you what you have to produce. Underline important details about the assignment. Take a few minutes to think about what you have to do and how you will do it. If you have questions about acceptable topics, format, paper length, or anything else, now is the time to ask your teacher.

WHAT DOES IT LOOK LIKE?

Analyzing the task:

Think of a research question that interests you

This is my starting point for exploring a topic.

...and write a research paper

This is the genre for my writing.

...that fully investigates the question and answers it with ample evidence.

This is what will make my research paper successful.

SELECT A TOPIC

Explore a subject that interests you by brainstorming, asking questions, freewriting, or conferring with others. Try to settle on a topic for which you will be able to find a variety of sources. You must go beyond other people's ideas and find an original approach. Your topic should be narrow enough to be fully developed, yet not too narrow to support a full-length research paper.

WHAT DOES IT LOOK LIKE?

Freewrite

The Grapes of Wrath is such a vivid picture of what one family went through in Oklahoma, on the road, and in California. Maybe Steinbeck was just writing a good story, or maybe he was trying to be a political activist and cause change. I wonder whether this book caused people to make changes to help others who were going through these difficult times. Did Steinbeck's novel really make a difference?

THINK ABOUT AUDIENCE AND PURPOSE

Consider your **purpose** for writing: to answer a research question, support your findings with evidence, and share your findings with your **audience** (a wide range of teens and adults). Keep in mind that when you share the information, you should avoid merely repeating facts. Instead, produce a paper that **synthesizes,** or combines, information from multiple authoritative sources, analyzes it, and draws conclusions. You will need to be able to articulate the **significance** of your topic.

ASK YOURSELF:

- What might my audience already know about this topic? What information might be new to them?
- How can I help my audience better understand complex information?
- What background information do I need to present to enable my audience to grasp concepts and ideas?
- What **domain-specific vocabulary,** or specialized terminology, will my audience already be familiar with?

Planning/Prewriting *continued*

Getting Started

WRITE A RESEARCH QUESTION

Look for encyclopedia articles, Web sites, or videos about your topic. Don't take notes yet; just read or view to develop background knowledge. Then, use this background knowledge to write a research question.

▶ WHAT DOES IT LOOK LIKE?

Research Question

Did Steinbeck's novel cause the government to respond to the plight of migrant workers?

IDENTIFY RELATED QUESTIONS

After you have written a research question, generate additional, **related focused questions** for further research and investigation. This will help you to identify if you need to broaden or narrow your research.

TIP As you identify related questions, you may decide to revise or adopt one of the related questions as your research question.

▶ WHAT DOES IT LOOK LIKE?

Was Steinbeck the only writer or artist to shed light on the plight of migrant workers?

Did government programs address the plight of migrant workers before Steinbeck's book was published?

MAKE A RESEARCH PLAN

Develop a research plan that outlines your purpose, audience, research question, potential sources, and schedule. Before embarking on your research, you may want to have your teacher review your research plan and offer suggestions for improvement.

▶ WHAT DOES IT LOOK LIKE?

Name: ....
Purpose: ....
Audience: ....
Research Question: ....
....
Potential Sources: ....
....

SCHEDULE

Research Due: ....
First Draft Due: ....
Final Draft Due: ....

Teacher Approval/Suggestions: ....
....

PEER REVIEW Describe your research topic and research plan to a peer. Then, ask: Is my research topic narrow enough? Is it too narrow? Will my research plan allow me to explore a variety of perspectives? Do you have any suggestions for other types of sources I could explore?

Decide on a topic for your research paper. Then, after developing background knowledge, create a research question, related questions, and a research plan in your *Reader/Writer Notebook*.

W 8 Gather relevant information from multiple sources; assess the strength and limitations of each source; avoid plagiarism and overreliance on one source; follow a standard format for citation. **W 9** Draw evidence from texts to support research.

Researching

Following Your Research Plan

INVESTIGATE POSSIBLE SOURCES

Make sure you investigate multiple sources for your research. This will help you build a broader understanding of your topic and encounter the perspectives of a variety of authorities. Also, try to locate both primary and secondary sources. **Primary sources** are firsthand, original accounts, and **secondary sources** include information derived from, or about, primary or other secondary sources.

Make use of both print and digital resources. In addition to what you might find at the library or on the Internet, consider other sources, such as museums, historical sites, or personal interviews.

ASK YOURSELF:

- Where can I find texts that have been written for informed audiences?
- Where can I find an expert on my topic whom I can interview?
- Where can I write a letter or an e-mail requesting additional information from someone?
- How can I locate a museum or historical site that I can visit to find applicable information?
- What databases could provide me with relevant information?
- Which librarian or teacher who could help me access appropriate databases and search engines?

ASSESS EACH SOURCE

Before taking the time to read or further explore sources, assess the strengths and limitations of each source by evaluating its relevance, reliability, and accuracy. A source is **relevant** if it relates to the topic you are researching and **credible** when the information it presents is reliable and well-documented. For **accuracy,** seek up-to-date information published by major universities or established, credible publishing companies.

Evaluate Internet sources to see who created the site and where the person or institution found the information. Avoid Web sites with *.com* or *.net* in their addresses. Usually, Web sites with *.org*, *.gov*, or *.edu* in their addresses are more reliable.

TIP When conducting research using digital sources or the Internet, make the most effective use of the advanced searches by filling in as many of the search parameters as you can. This will help filter out any unwanted sources or Web sites, narrowing down the number of sources you need to look through.

WHAT DOES IT LOOK LIKE?

Reasons for Rejecting or Accepting Sources

"Dust Bowl Days": *This Web site doesn't name the author's credentials. It has no footnotes or bibliography. Therefore, I should reject this source.*

"Best Sellers of the Week": *I acquired this newspaper article from an established, credible newspaper (New York Times). The article was published in 1939; however, it is a primary source, so its date of publication is acceptable. Therefore, I can accept this source.*

"On the Cause of the 1930s Dust Bowl": *This is an article about the weather patterns that created the Dust Bowl. Although it is a well-documented article, it doesn't relate to my specific topic. Therefore, I should reject this source.*

Researching *continued*

Following Your Research Plan

PREPARE A SOURCE LIST

When you have decided which sources to keep, create an electronic source list or a series of source cards. Assign each source a number. Record full publishing information for each source and write short notes about the content and value of the source. Also note library call numbers. This information will help you later as you take notes. It will also help you follow a standard format when you compile a Works Cited list.

WHAT DOES IT LOOK LIKE?

Sources	Comments
"Timeline." *American Experience: Surviving the Dust Bowl.* Pub. Broadcasting Svc. n.d. Web. 17 Apr. 2010.	• lists several government responses to Dust Bowl • Dust Bowl events and responses are shown in an easy-to-read timeline format

TAKE NOTES

Read each source carefully as you look for answers to your research question and related questions. If necessary, modify the research question to accommodate the information you encounter. Use these guidelines for taking notes:

1. **Use an electronic file or note-taking software to record notes.** Make your notes easy to sort and group by entering notes on individual pages, or make separate databases or worksheet entries for each note. If you would rather write notes, use a notebook or index cards.
2. **Write a label or heading.** In the upper left-hand corner of the file, identify the main idea of your note.
3. **Record each piece of information.**
   Quote directly: Use the writer's exact words, enclosed in quotation marks.
   Paraphrase: Rewrite a passage in your own words and style.
   Summarize: Present only the main points of a passage.
4. **Record the source number and page number(s).** In the upper right-hand corner of each note, write the number of your source. Write page numbers at the bottom of your notes.

WHAT DOES IT LOOK LIKE?

Separate electronic worksheet entries for sources

Federal programs before *The Grapes of Wrath* 1

The Shelterbelt program started in 1937. The government paid farmers to plant trees so that less topsoil would blow away. By 1938, the tree planting and other methods had reduced blowing soil by 65 percent (4).

Firsthand account of Dust Bowl conditions 5

Ann Marie Low, a young North Dakotan, wrote in her diary that each day was "a gritty nightmare." She stated that sometimes dirt "lay inches deep on everything. Every towel and curtain was just black" (134, 135).

President Franklin Roosevelt's response to the book 5

In a January 1940 radio address, President Franklin Roosevelt said, "I have read a book recently; it is called *Grapes of Wrath.* There are 500,000 Americans that live in the covers of that book" (148).

Researching *continued*

Following Your Research Plan

DRAFT A CONTROLLING IDEA

Review your notes, and then develop your research question into a **controlling idea,** or thesis statement. Your controlling idea should have an original focus and should clearly present an interesting question that will be explored in the body of your research report. You can use the following equation to draft a controlling idea to guide you in your writing, but you'll want to polish it up for your final draft.

TOPIC: ______________________
+ RESEARCH QUESTION: ______________
= CONTROLLING IDEA: _______________

ASK YOURSELF:

- What recurring ideas appear in the different sources?
- How does all the information I have collected fit together?
- What larger point, or general conclusion, does the information support?
- Are my original ideas about the topic supported or contradicted by the information I have collected?
- Does my controlling idea accurately reflect the information I have collected? If it does not accurately reflect the information, how should I rework it ?

CREATE AN OUTLINE

A basic outline can help you organize your ideas, ensuring that each new idea builds on the one preceding it and creates a cohesive research report. Sort your notes into groups with similar headings or labels. Keep rearranging them until you find an order that makes sense. Most writers use one of these types of organization:

- **chronological order:** the order in which events occur
- **logical order:** related ideas grouped together
- **order of importance:** most important ideas to least important or vice versa

You will probably use a combination of these organizational patterns to arrange your main ideas and your supporting examples and details.

WHAT DOES IT LOOK LIKE?

Partial example of an outline

***The Grapes of Wrath* and the Dust Bowl**

I. Background information: The Dust Bowl
  A. What and where it was
  B. When it took place
  C. What people's lives were like
    1. "A gritty nightmare" (Low's diary)
    2. Dust killed children, animals
II. Background information: *The Grapes of Wrath*
  A. Based on Steinbeck's own research
  B. Reaction to the book

Follow your research plan to begin investigating possible sources. Assess each source to determine which ones you plan on using, and compile these sources in a list. Take notes about your sources, and use the notes to write a controlling idea and an outline in your *Reader/Writer Notebook.* If necessary, narrow or broaden your research question so that you can answer it thoroughly in your research paper.

Drafting

The following chart shows how to organize your draft to create an effective research paper.

Organizing Your Research Paper

INTRODUCTION

- Begin your paper by drawing the reader into the research. You might include a memorable **quotation** or an interesting **fact** or **detail.**
- Provide background information, an overview of your topic, and a **controlling idea** that includes a clear research question. The controlling idea is often the last sentence of the introductory paragraph.
- Establish and maintain a **formal style** and **objective tone.**
- Use a style manual, such as one produced by the MLA (Modern Language Association).

▼

BODY

- Using your outline as a guide, develop and support each **main point** in a separate paragraph. Incorporate **relevant facts, extended definitions, concrete details, quotations,** and **examples** from your notes to support your main points.
- **Synthesize,** or combine, the ideas and information from multiple sources. If appropriate, compare and contrast ideas from different sources, or show how one source complements, enlarges, or expands on another.
- Analyze a variety of ideas, and provide your own interpretations of them.
- Maintain the **organizational pattern** or combination of organizational patterns that you chose in your outline.
- Include **varied and appropriate transitions** and **syntax** (arrangement of words and phrases) to clarify relationships among ideas and to create cohesion.
- Use **precise language** and define any **domain-specific,** or specialized, **vocabulary** to help clarify concepts for your audience.
- Each time you quote, paraphrase, or summarize information from a source, **document** the source by including a **parenthetical reference** at the end of the sentence or sentences. Do not document information that can be found in several sources or standard reference books.

▼

CONCLUDING SECTION

- Restate the research question and controlling idea that follows from the research you gathered. Summarize the paper's main points.
- Leave your reader with something compelling to think about. For example, you could reflect on the overall **significance** of your topic, or include a compelling quotation.

▼

WORKS CITED LIST

- List all of the sources, print and nonprint, that you credit in your paper. Do not credit sources that you consulted but did not cite in your paper.
- Refer to the MLA guidelines on pages 1376–1377 to list your sources properly.

W 4 Produce clear and coherent writing. **W 8** Integrate information into the text selectively to avoid plagiarism; follow a standard format for citation. **L 2** Demonstrate a command of the conventions of standard English punctuation.

Drafting *continued*

LEARN HOW **Document Your Sources** To avoid plagiarism, or copying someone else's work, you must correctly document your sources. Within your paper, use **parenthetical citations,** source references enclosed in parentheses. In general, a parenthetical citation includes the **author's last name** and the **page number** (Himmelberg 9). There are, however, many variations on the use of parenthetical citations.

- **Author already mentioned in sentence:** Give only the page number (110).
- **Author not known:** Use a shortened form of the title of the work ("First Lady").
- **More than one author:** Include last names for up to three authors (Lange and Taylor 409). For more than three authors, use the first author's last name and *et al.* (Zielonka et al. 138–145).
- **More than one source:** Separate the information for each source with a semicolon (Kite 107; "Timeline").
- **More than one work by the same author:** Include a shortened form of the work's title (Steinbeck, *Dubious* 61).

GRAMMAR IN CONTEXT: PUNCTUATING PARENTHETICAL CITATIONS

A **parenthetical citation** should provide enough information to lead the reader to the full source entry in your Works Cited list. Place the citation as close as possible to the material being cited, as in the following MLA guidelines:

Always place the citation before the punctuation mark within a sentence that contains the information from the source.	When Steinbeck wrote "the dawn came, but no day," he was referring to the black clouds that swirled over the Great Plains during these desperate years (Steinbeck 5).
If a quotation ends a sentence, put the citation after the quotation mark, but before the end punctuation.	"I know what I was talking about," he told a reporter in July 1939. "I lived, on and off, with those Okies for the last three years" (Cameron A2).
For a block quotation, insert the final punctuation mark at the end of the quotation. Then, place the citation two spaces after the final punctuation mark.	. . . during the Dust Bowl of the 1930s. Some 2.5 million people fled the Plains states, many bound for California, where the promise of sunshine and a better life often collided with the reality of scarce, poorly paid work as migrant farm laborers. ("Great Depression")

Using the information in the chart on the previous page, write a draft of your research paper. Maintain a formal style and objective tone, and make sure your draft is of sufficient length and complexity to address the topic. Also, be sure to include correctly formatted parenthetical citations and a Works Cited list.

Revising

When you revise, your goal is to determine whether you've effectively explored and answered a research question based on a variety of evidence. The questions, tips, and strategies in the chart can help you revise or rewrite where necessary.

RESEARCH PAPER

Ask Yourself	*Tips*	*Revision Strategies*
1. Does my introduction draw readers in, give an overview of the topic, and clearly state the research question in the controlling idea?	**Underline** the sentence that draws readers in; **bracket** the overview of the topic; **circle** the research question.	**Add** a quotation or interesting detail or fact. **Add** or **elaborate** on background information. **Add** a sentence that clarifies the controlling idea and research question, if necessary.
2. Is the research question explored through several main points? Do facts, details, definitions, quotations, and examples support the main points?	In the margin, **check** each main point that develops the research question. In the text, **double-check** at least one piece of evidence for each main point.	**Add** main points to develop your research. **Delete** points that do not support or relate to the research question. **Elaborate** on each point with relevant textual evidence.
3. Are sources cited when necessary? Do the citations follow a consistent format?	**Place stars** by direct quotations and facts that are not common knowledge.	**Add** documentation for quoted, paraphrased, or summarized material. **Revise** incorrect citations.
4. Are main points organized in a logical way?	**Number** your main points. **Revise** if the organization makes no sense or is unclear.	**Rearrange** the order of ideas for clarity. Try logical or chronological order.
5. Do I maintain a formal style and objective tone throughout the research report?	**Draw a wavy line** under any contractions, slang, or informal or biased language.	**Reword** text to avoid contractions. **Replace** instances of informal language with precise, formal words.
6. Does the concluding section restate the research question, clearly present my concluding statement, and summarize the main points?	**Bracket** the restatement of the research question and your concluding statement. **Highlight** the summary of main ideas.	**Add** a sentence that reminds the reader of the research question. **Clarify** your concluding statement. **Add** a summary of main points.

PEER REVIEW Working with a peer, use this chart to review your draft. Then, revise your paper by making the changes suggested in the right-hand column. Ask your partner if he or she has any suggestions for improvement. If necessary, rework or try a new approach to further improve your paper.

COMMON CORE **W 5** Strengthen writing by revising, editing, rewriting, or trying a new approach.

ANALYZE A STUDENT DRAFT

Read these excerpts from a student draft; notice the comments on its strengths as well as suggestions for improvement.

Barron 1

Chris Barron
Mrs. Machado
English III
29 April 2010

The Grapes of Wrath: A Reflection of Real Life

1 John Steinbeck's *The Grapes of Wrath,* now considered an American masterpiece, tells the gripping story of a family that abandons its Oklahoma farm during the Dust Bowl of the 1930s. Many people believe that the controversial novel raised public awareness about the suffering of "Okies" who moved to California in search of a better life but found only poverty. Some experts also contend that Steinbeck's novel was the key factor in motivating the government to help these migrant workers.

In order to present a more effective controlling idea, Chris needs to clarify his major research question.

The Dust Bowl and Worsening Hard Times

2 To determine how much of an impact Steinbeck's novel had, it is important to have a clear understanding of what the Dust Bowl was and how it affected people. The Dust Bowl was a severe drought combined with high heat and high winds. It occurred mainly in Oklahoma, Nebraska, Kansas, Texas, New Mexico, and Colorado, and it had its center at the Oklahoma panhandle.

Chris provides **background information** to help his audience understand the topic.

LEARN HOW **Craft an Effective Controlling Idea** In his controlling idea, Chris mentions the possibility that the novel influenced government policy, but he does not present a clear research question. Note how Chris revised his controlling idea to include his research question.

CHRIS'S REVISION TO PARAGRAPH 1

~~Some experts also contend that Steinbeck's novel was the key factor in motivating the government to help these migrant workers.~~

To what degree, then, might Steinbeck's novel have motivated the federal government to implement policies to aid these migrant workers?

These conditions lasted about eight years, long enough to carry off tons of topsoil from the over-plowed fields in the region (Egan xi, 5). When Steinbeck wrote "the dawn came, but no day," he was referring to the black clouds that swirled over the Great Plains during these desperate years (Steinbeck 5).

3 Not all sources agree on when the Dust Bowl started, but some say that the first devastating storms hit in 1931 and suggest that the full-blown condition now called the Dust Bowl actually developed between 1933 and 1935 (Kite 107; "Timeline"). However, hard times were widespread in the area before the drought occurred. The Great Depression began in 1929 when the stock market crashed. The following year, people all across the country lost their jobs, and many banks could not pay their depositors (Egan 95). Farm prices fell sharply, too: between 1929 and 1932, they dove 55 percent (Himmelberg 9). By the time the Dust Bowl started, Midwestern farm families had endured years of low prices and bank failures, and high unemployment rates meant that family members could not find work in nearby cities.

Chris uses **appropriate and varied transitions** to clarify for the reader the relationships among the ideas.

4 In human terms, the Dust Bowl was a time of terrible suffering. Each day was "a gritty nightmare," a young North Dakotan named Ann Marie Low wrote in her diary. Sometimes dirt "lay inches deep on everything. Every towel and curtain was just black" (McElvaine 134, 135). Homes had to be shoveled out; nothing could be used before it was washed. The dust also choked and killed cattle—and even some children (Egan 5–6). Unable to grow anything on the land, many farm families had to leave the Dust Bowl or die there. The estimate of just how many left varies widely. Depending on how one defines the Dust Bowl area and its dates, the number ranges from 16,000 to 315,000 (Windschuttle). Many families traveled to California in search of work, as Steinbeck describes in his novel.

Chris includes **direct quotations** and uses **parenthetical citations** correctly.

Barron 3

Reactions to *The Grapes of Wrath*

5 Before Steinbeck began *The Grapes of Wrath,* he wrote newspaper articles about living conditions in the California labor camps (Windschuttle). He used this knowledge in his novel. "I know what I was talking about," he told a reporter in July 1939. "I lived, on and off, with those Okies for the last three years" (Cameron A2). The way the migrants were treated angered and disturbed Steinbeck. In one of the most haunting passages in *The Grapes of Wrath,* he wrote, "[I]n the eyes of the hungry there is a growing wrath. In the souls of the people the grapes of wrath are filling and growing heavy, growing heavy for the vintage" (Steinbeck 477). Because Steinbeck knew his topic so well and presented it with such emotional power, the novel was a huge success. Just two weeks after its publication, it topped bestseller lists in New York, Philadelphia, Washington, Atlanta, San Francisco, and Los Angeles ("Best Sellers").

Chris synthesizes **facts and details** from **multiple sources, quoting** the most memorable and **paraphrasing** or **summarizing** the others.

6 However, the book was not without controversy. When the *Los Angeles Times* reported that some of the migrant workers had sent Steinbeck threatening letters, he responded that it is not: "the refugees who have taken exception to what I wrote. It's the moneyed people back there in Oklahoma . . . If anybody's sore at me for the book it's that kind of people" (Cameron A1–2). Steinbeck's shocking novel brought him some influential enemies.

Chris needs to revise the way that he has incorporated the textual evidence into this sentence.

LEARN HOW **Incorporate Textual Evidence** Sentence-length quotations should be incorporated into text with either an introductory phrase followed by a comma or a full sentence followed by a colon. However, if you are using a shorter quote, make the quoted words part of your own sentence. Notice how Chris used more of the direct quote and revised its introduction.

CHRIS'S REVISION TO PARAGRAPH 6

When the *Los Angeles Times* reported that some of the migrant workers had sent Steinbeck threatening letters, he ~~responded that it is not: "the~~ responded, "It isn't the refugees who have taken exception to what I wrote. It's the moneyed people back there in Oklahoma. . . . If anybody's sore at me for the book it's that kind of people" (Cameron A1–2).

7 However, not every response to Steinbeck's work was negative. In December 1939, First Lady Eleanor Roosevelt responded publicly to the book. She said that although she had read and heard others' criticisms about the novel, she knew from her own travels and investigations that the living conditions depicted in the book were at least "partly true" ("First Lady"). Then, in a January 1940 radio address, President Franklin Roosevelt said, "I have read a book recently; it is called *Grapes of Wrath.* There are 500,000 Americans that live in the covers of that book" (McElvaine 148).

In this paragraph, Chris states his point at the beginning and uses the rest of the paragraph to **support this point with relevant facts and details.**

Assessing the Novel's Impact

8 It is clear that Steinbeck's novel made a tremendous impression on some of the most powerful and influential people in the country. Yet it is not easy to establish any cause-and-effect relationship between *The Grapes of Wrath* and improvements in the lives of Dust Bowl evacuees. The government had begun to respond to the problems of the Dust Bowl long before the book's publication. In 1935, four years before anyone read *The Grapes of Wrath,* the Emergency Relief Appropriation Act created jobs for unemployed farmers, set aside money for ranchers to feed their livestock and farmers to buy seeds, and funded the construction of work camps for youths. In 1935, the Resettlement Administration began relocating farmers to better farming areas (Kite 107; "FSA Camp").

Chris includes **his own ideas and interpretations** throughout the paper.

9 The government also established the Soil Conservation Service in 1935. This program taught farmers techniques to protect the topsoil (Kite 110). One of the most important soil-saving programs was the Shelterbelt Project. This anti-erosion measure called for planting trees across the entire Great Plains. The program was already reducing blowing dirt by 1938, a year before *The Grapes of Wrath* appeared ("Timeline").

Chris uses **detailed evidence** to support a main point. He also **credits sources** properly using **correct formats and style.**

Barron 5

10 It is also a mistake to assume that Steinbeck's novel was the sole reason that Americans focused their attention on victims of the Dust Bowl. For one thing, there were loads of people talking about injustice. Woody Guthrie had long been writing social protest songs about the Okies. Bibliographies and library catalogs show several other books that could also be read as protests. For example, in 1939, Carey McWilliams published *Factories in the Field,* an account of exploited migrants. It is also clear to anyone looking at Dorothea Lange's "Migrant Mother" and her other photographs that she was deeply concerned with the problems of poor people in California (McElvaine 105, 126, 175).

Chris needs to revise this sentence to **maintain his formal style and objective tone.**

LEARN HOW **Maintain a Formal Style and Objective Tone** The tone is the writer's attitude toward his or her subject. A writer's tone should be appropriate to the subject matter, purpose, and audience. For some subjects, a lighthearted, humorous, or informal tone is appropriate. For instance, if you were writing a lighthearted short story or a letter to a friend, a humorous tone would be appropriate.

However, when writing a research paper about a serious subject—such as a tragic event in American history—you should always use a formal style, avoiding casual language, comedic references, and subjective wording with bias or exaggeration. This formal style and objective tone will convey a serious sense of purpose, which is essential in a research paper, to your audience. Notice how Chris revised the highlighted sentence to maintain his formal style and objective tone:

CHRIS'S REVISION TO PARAGRAPH 10

~~For one thing, there were loads of people talking about injustice.~~ ^

For one thing, Steinbeck's was not the only voice crying out for justice.

11 Steinbeck's novel and many other works raised awareness of the grim lives of the Okies. However, history makes it clear that what really changed Americans' lives in the years after the publication of *The Grapes of Wrath* was the buildup to World War II. By 1940, many new jobs had become available in factories—and in the military. The Great Depression ended; coincidentally, the drought in the Midwest also ended in 1939 ("Timeline"). These large forces are what truly put American workers back on the road to prosperity.

This paragraph reflects Chris's interest in and **enthusiasm for the subject matter.**

A Great Novel, but Only One Factor Among Many

12 *The Grapes of Wrath* is one of the most important novels of the 20th century. At the time of its publication it captivated thousands of readers, including the president of the United States, and it helped to make the suffering of California migrant workers an issue of national importance. However, it is overstating the case to claim that the book motivated the government to help these workers. Many government programs were already in place at the time of the book's publication, and many other writers and activists helped bring the problem to public attention. Other, larger factors—the end of the drought, an improved economy, and the looming possibility of another world war—also had important effects on the migrant workers' situation. Although Steinbeck's novel was factually accurate and artistically important, a thorough evaluation of the evidence shows that it did not change the course of history.

Chris concludes by **summarizing** his main points and **answering his research question** with original ideas. Also, he gives his audience **something compelling to think about** by reflecting on the overall significance of the topic.

Barron 7

Works Cited

"Best Sellers of the Week." *New York Times* 1 May 1939:19. Print.

Cameron, Tom. "Dust Bowl Book Brings Trouble." *Los Angeles Times* 9 July 1939: A1+. Print.

Egan, Timothy. *The Worst Hard Time.* Boston: Houghton, 2006. Print.

"First Lady Stresses Community Interests." *New York Times* 8 Dec. 1939: 16. Print.

"FSA Migratory Labor Camp." *Documenting America* Chapter 6. Lib. Of Congress. 2001. Web. 9 Apr. 2010.

Himmelberg, Robert F. *The Great Depression and the New Deal.* Westport: Greenwood, 2001. Print.

Kite, Steven. "Dust Bowl." *Encyclopedia of the Great Depression and the New Deal.* Ed. James Ciment. 2 vols. Armonk, NY: Sharpe, 2001. Print.

McElvaine, Robert S. *The Depression and New Deal: A History in Documents.* New York: Oxford UP, 2000. 132–7. Print.

Steinbeck, John. *The Grapes of Wrath.* 1939. New York: Viking, 1964. Print.

~~"Steinbeck's Myth of the Okies." Windschuttle, Keith. *New Criterion* June 2002: 24+. Print.~~

"Timeline." *American Experience: Surviving the Dust Bowl.* Pub. Broadcasting Svc. n.d. Web. 17 Apr. 2010.

Windschuttle, Keith. "Steinbeck's Myth of the Okies." New Criterion June 2002: 24+. Print.

LEARN HOW Format a Works Cited List Correctly

When creating a Works Cited list, follow these formatting guidelines:

- Begin the list on a separate page, after the essay.
- Begin each entry on a separate line, aligned with the left margin.
- When an entry has more than one line, give additional lines a hanging indent of one-half inch.
- List sources alphabetically by authors' last names. If no author is listed, sort by title. Ignore *A, An,* and *The.*
- When two or more sources are written by one author, list the author's name only in the first entry. Begin additional entries with three hyphens (---), followed by a period.

Notice Chris's revision in blue.

Use the feedback from your peers and teacher, the revision strategies chart, and the "Learn How" lessons to revise or rework your essay. Evaluate whether you've provided adequate evidence to support your concluding statement.

Editing and Publishing

W 5 Strengthen writing by editing. **L 2** Demonstrate command of the conventions of standard English capitalization, punctuation, and spelling.

In the editing stage, you proofread your research paper to make sure that it is free of grammar, usage, spelling, and punctuation errors. Also, be sure that you format your paper according to the following guidelines:

- Double-space everything.
- Leave a one-inch margin at the left, right, top, and bottom of each page (except for page numbers).
- At the top left of the first page, type your name, your teacher's name, the class, and the date. On the rest of the pages, type your last name and the page number in the upper right corner.
- Indent all paragraphs one-half inch (or five spaces) and indent quotations of four or more lines one inch (or ten spaces) from the left margin.

See the *MLA Handbook for Writers of Research Papers* for additional guidelines.

GRAMMAR IN CONTEXT: OMITTING OR ADDING WORDS IN QUOTATIONS

Whenever you provide a direct quotation from a source, be sure to integrate it smoothly and correctly into your text. Use three spaced periods (. . .), called **ellipsis points,** to mark omissions from the original quotation. If the omission falls at the end of a quotation fragment that could stand as a complete sentence, insert the ellipses *after* an ending period, question mark, or exclamation point. Use **brackets** to mark additions to a quotation. As Chris edited his paper, he noticed a quotation fragment that should have an ending period before the ellipses. The fragment can stand as a complete sentence.

> When the *Los Angeles Times* reported that some of the migrant workers had sent Steinbeck threatening letters, he responded, "It isn't the refugees who have taken exception to what I wrote. It's the moneyed people back there in Oklahoma. . . . If anybody's sore at me for the book it's that kind of people" (Cameron A1–2).

PUBLISH YOUR WRITING

Here are some suggestions for sharing your research paper with an audience:

- Save your research paper as a writing sample to submit with a college or job application.
- Turn your paper into a documentary.
- Ask your school librarian or media specialist to help you locate academic journals to which you might submit your paper.

Correct any errors in your research paper, and make sure you have used correct style for adding or omitting text in quotations. Then, publish your completed work.

Scoring Rubric

Use the rubric below to evaluate your research paper from the Writing Workshop.

RESEARCH PAPER

SCORE	COMMON CORE TRAITS
6	• **Development** Effectively introduces a topic; states an insightful, well-researched controlling idea; thoroughly supports the controlling idea with main points and relevant evidence; ends powerfully • **Organization** Logically organizes information; effectively uses varied, appropriate transitions; includes formatting and graphics to enhance the information • **Language** Ably uses precise words; consistently maintains a formal style and objective tone; shows a strong command of conventions; correctly cites all sources
5	• **Development** Competently introduces a topic; states a well-researched controlling idea; offers main points and relevant evidence; has a strong concluding section • **Organization** Is logically organized; effectively uses transitions; includes formatting and graphics • **Language** Uses a formal style and objective tone; has a few errors in conventions; correctly cites sources
4 	• **Development** Sufficiently introduces a topic; states a clear controlling idea; offers mostly valid support; has an adequate concluding section • **Organization** Is mostly logically organized; needs more transitions; could use some formatting or graphics • **Language** Needs more precise words; has frequent lapses in style and tone; includes a few distracting errors in conventions; incorrectly formats a few source citations
3	• **Development** States a controlling idea, but the introduction could be more engaging; provides insufficient support; has a weak concluding section • **Organization** Has some flaws in organization; needs more transitions; doesn't include enough formatting or graphics • **Language** Lacks precise words; uses an informal style and subjective tone; has several errors in conventions; incorrectly formats some source citations
2	• **Development** Has an unclear controlling idea; does not support most ideas; ends abruptly • **Organization** Has organizational flaws; lacks transitions throughout; lacks formatting and graphics throughout • **Language** Lacks precise words; uses an informal style and subjective tone; has many errors in conventions; does not cite all sources and cites many incorrectly
1 	• **Development** Lacks a controlling idea; fails to develop the topic; ends abruptly • **Organization** Has no organization, transitions, or formatting • **Language** Uses vague words; has an inappropriate style and tone; has major problems in conventions; plagiarizes or does not credit sources

REVIEW MLA GUIDELINES

MLA Citation Guidelines

Today, you can find free Web sites that help you create citations for research papers using information you provide. Such sites have some time-saving advantages when you're developing a Works Cited list. However, you should always check your citations carefully before you turn in your final paper. If you are following MLA style, use these guidelines to evaluate and finalize your work.

BOOKS

One author

Steinbeck, John. *The Grapes of Wrath.* 1939. New York: Viking, 1964. Print.

Two authors or editors

Lange, Dorothea, and Paul Schuster Taylor. *An American Exodus: A Record of Human Erosion.* New York: Reynal & Hitchcock, 1939. Print.

Three authors or editors

Scheibel, Jeremy, Anne Chatsworth, and Ridley Davis, eds. *Stories from the Great Depression.* Princeton: Princeton UP, 2008. Print.

Four or more authors or editors

List the first author only. Then use the abbreviation* et al.*, which means "and others."

Rutkowski, J., et al. *American Immigration and Migration in the 1930s.* Topeka: Sanders-Ellis, 2007. Print.

No author given

American Literature: 1865 to the Present. Chicago: Omni, 2007. Print.

PARTS OF BOOKS

An introduction, a preface, a foreword, or an afterword written by someone other than the author(s) of a work

Gorton, Terry. Foreword. *John Steinbeck: A Centennial Tribute.* Ed. Stephen K. George. Westport: Praeger, 2002. xvii–xviii. Print.

A poem, a short story, an essay, or a chapter in a collection of works

Steinbeck, John. "The Leader of the People." *The Portable Steinbeck.* Ed. Pascal Covici, Jr. New York: Penguin, 1978. 397–415. Print.

A poem, a short story, an essay, or a chapter in an anthology of works by several authors

Steinbeck, John. "The Red Pony." *The American Short Story: A Collection of the Best Known and Most Memorable Short Stories by the Great American Authors.* Ed. Thomas K. Parkes. New York: Galahad, 1994. 886–948. Print.

A novel or play in a collection

Steinbeck, John. *The Grapes of Wrath. The Grapes of Wrath and Other Writings, 1936–1941.* New York: Library of America, 1996. Print.

W 8 Gather relevant information from multiple print and digital sources; follow a standard format for citation.

MAGAZINES, NEWSPAPERS, AND ENCYCLOPEDIAS

An article in a newspaper

Patel, Vikram. "Recalling the Days of Wrath." *Los Angeles Times* 8 Jan. 2008: 9. Print.

An article in a magazine

Schubert, Siegfried D., et al. "On the Cause of the 1930s Dust Bowl." *Science* 19 Mar. 2004: 1855–60. Print.

An article in an encyclopedia

Kite, Steven. "Dust Bowl." *Encyclopedia of the Great Depression and New Deal.* Ed. James Ciment. 2 vols. Armonk, NY: Sharpe, 2001. Print.

MISCELLANEOUS NONPRINT SOURCES

An interview

Sorenson, Elvina. Personal interview. 3 Feb. 2010.

A video recording or film

Our Daily Bread. Dir. King Vidor. Perf. Karen Morley, Tom Keene, Barbara Pepper, John Qualen. 1934. Film Preservation Assoc., 1999. DVD.

A sound recording

Guthrie, Woody. *Library of Congress Recordings/Woody Guthrie.* Rounder, 1988. CD.

ELECTRONIC PUBLICATIONS

A document from an Internet site

Include as much of the following information as available in the order given.

Author or compiler	Title or description of document	Title of Internet site	Site sponsor
Neary, Walter.	"Steinbeck & Salinas."	*About John Steinbeck.*	National Steinbeck Center.

Date of document	Medium of Publication	Date of access
June 1995.	Web.	2 Apr. 2010.

AN ONLINE BOOK OR E-BOOK

Wunder, John R., Frances Kaye, and Vernon Carstensen, eds. *Americans View Their Dust Bowl Experience.* Niwot: UP Colorado, 1999. Questia Media America. Web. 10 Apr. 2010.

A CD-ROM

"Dust Bowl." *Britannica Student Encyclopedia.* 2004 ed. Chicago: Encyclopaedia Britannica, 2004. CD-ROM.

Producing a Documentary

You have probably seen documentaries on historical figures or events, such as those commonly shown on public television. A documentary is a creative, engaging, and memorable way to present research.

Complete the workshop activities in your **Reader/Writer Notebook.**

PRODUCE WITH A PURPOSE	COMMON CORE TRAITS
TASK Produce a **documentary** that uses graphics, images, and sound to present research you conducted for the topic of your research report.	***A STRONG DOCUMENTARY . . .*** • focuses on a compelling subject • integrates information from multiple sources • makes strategic use of text, graphic, audio, and visual elements to enhance understanding and add interest

COMMON CORE

W 6 Use technology to produce, publish, and update individual or shared writing products. **SL 2** Integrate multiple sources of information presented in diverse formats and media. **SL 5** Make strategic use of digital media in presentations to enhance understanding and to add interest.

Plan Your Documentary

Be creative and selective as you choose what to include in your documentary. Keep your audience in mind as you decide how to arrange the various materials to enhance their interest in and understanding of your topic.

The following tips and techniques can help you plan your documentary:

- **Identify sources of information.** Review the notes you compiled while developing your research paper. Identify if any of those sources would lend themselves to being used in a documentary. Be sure to integrate information from multiple sources on the topic, such as photographs and illustrations, or an interview with an expert. As you identify sources, make sure you evaluate their credibility and accuracy. Ask yourself, is the source **credible**, or reliable and trustworthy? Is the information **accurate**, or up-to-date, well-documented, and written or furnished by an expert on the topic?
- **Look for audio and visual materials.** When choosing materials, include a variety of elements, such as text, graphics, and audio. Select the element that will best enhance the audience's understanding of the information that is being addressed. Also, select elements that will add to the visual and audio interest of the documentary. Be sure to respect copyright laws and use only materials for which you have permission.
- **Create a script.** Using your collected materials for guidance, create a **script** for your documentary. Include voice-over narration, interview footage, and music. Voice-over narration should provide necessary background information and relevant details about the visuals you present. Choose music that reflects the tone of the accompanying images.
- **Develop a storyboard.** Plan what your audience will see and hear. Include several types of camera positions, such as **establishing shots** (wide-angle shots that set the scene), **medium shots,** and **close-ups,** as well as a variety of camera angles. You can find examples at the library or on the Internet.

Produce Your Documentary

When producing your documentary, allow yourself plenty of time to gather equipment, record the material, and revise or rework your documentary. If technological problems occur and you're not sure how to proceed, ask a teacher, a parent, or an informed classmate for help.

Follow these steps as you produce your documentary:

- **Find out what equipment is available.** Your school may have a camcorder that you can borrow. If you have video editing software, you can record scenes in any order; if not, you will have to film each scene sequentially.
- **Record the video and the voice-overs.** Follow your script and storyboard carefully. When recording your voice-overs, follow the verbal techniques in the following chart:

Verbal Techniques

- Enunciate your words clearly.
- Maintain a formal style to help your audience focus on the information.
- Emphasize important words or points by speaking slightly louder and with more force.
- Pause for a moment after an important point to encourage the audience to reflect on it.
- Speak slowly enough to allow your audience to follow you, but not so slowly that they become bored.

- **Pull it together.** Review your footage, reshooting as necessary. Be sure that your documentary flows smoothly from one shot to the next. If necessary, add transitional words and phrases to your voice-overs to ensure that your documentary flows smoothly.

After you have followed all of the instructions for planning and producing your documentary, screen your documentary for family members or classmates. Ask for specific feedback, and then use the feedback to improve your documentary. After you have made improvements, think about sharing your documentary with a larger audience. Use one or more of the following techniques to find your larger audience:

- Work with other classmates to organize and hold a school film festival in which you can premiere all of your documentaries.
- Find an organization or reputable Web site that is devoted to your subject. Contact this organization or the Web site's creator about using your documentary.
- Enter your documentary in a documentary contest. Be sure to research each contest to determine the types of entries accepted and the rules.

Student Resource Bank

Reading any text—short story, poem, magazine article, newspaper, Web page—requires the use of special strategies. For example, you might plot events in a short story on a diagram, while you might use text features to spot main ideas in a magazine article. You also need to identify patterns of organization in the text. Using such strategies can help you read different texts with ease and also help you understand what you're reading.

COMMON CORE

Included in this handbook:
RL 3, RL 5, RI 2–7, SL 2, SL 5

1 Reading Literary and Nonfiction Texts

Literary and nonfiction texts include short stories, novels, poems, dramas, biographies, autobiographies, and essays. To appreciate and analyze literary and nonfiction texts, you will need to understand the characteristics of each type of text.

1.1 READING A SHORT STORY

Strategies for Reading

- Read the title. As you read the story, you may notice that the title has a special meaning.
- Keep track of events as they happen. Plot the events on a diagram like this one.

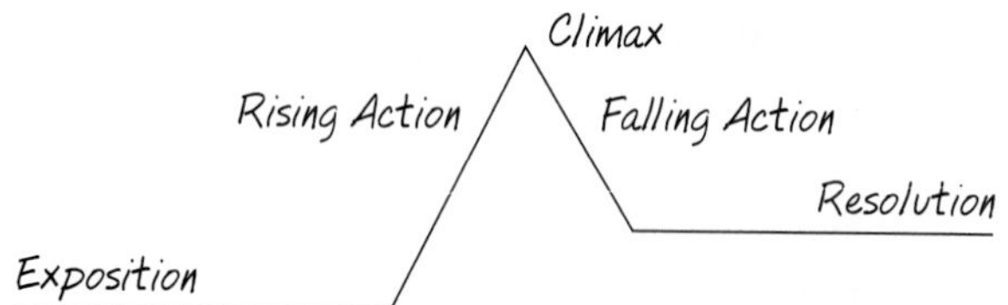

- Using the details the writer provides, **visualize** the characters. **Predict** what they might do next.
- Look for specific adjectives that help you visualize the **setting**—the time and place in which events occur.
- Note **cause-and-effect relationships** and how these affect the **conflict.**

1.2 READING A POEM

Strategies for Reading

- Notice the **form** of the poem, or the arrangement of its lines and stanzas on the page.
- Read the poem aloud a few times. Listen for and note the **rhymes** and **rhythms.**
- **Visualize** the images and comparisons.
- **Connect** with the poem by asking yourself what message the poet is trying to send.
- Create a word web or another **graphic organizer** to record your reactions and questions.

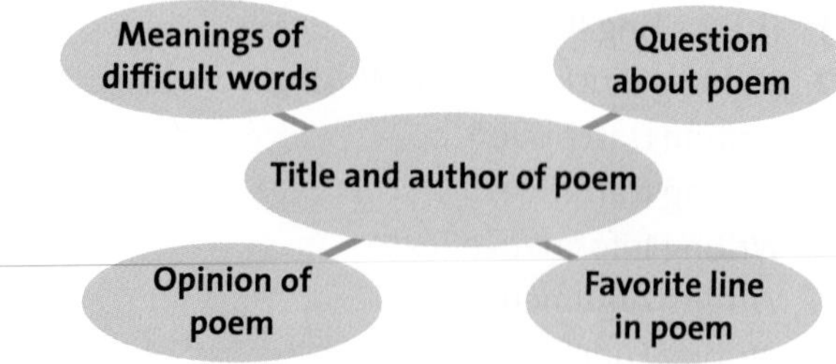

1.3 READING A PLAY

Strategies for Reading

- Read the stage directions to help you **visualize** the setting and characters.
- **Question** what the title means and why the playwright chose it.
- Identify the main conflict (struggle or problem) in the play. To **clarify** the conflict, make a chart that shows what the conflict is and how it is resolved.
- **Evaluate** the characters. What do they want? How do they change during the play? You may want to make a chart that lists each character's name, appearance, and traits.

1.4 READING NONFICTION

Strategies for Reading

- If you are reading a biography, an autobiography, or another type of biographical writing, such as a diary or memoir, use a family tree to keep track of the people mentioned.
- When reading an essay, **analyze** and **evaluate** the writer's ideas and reasoning. Does the writer present a thesis statement? use sound logic? adequately support opinions with facts and other evidence?
- For all types of nonfiction, be aware of the **author's purpose,** and note any personal **bias** of the writer's that might influence the presentation of information.

2 Reading Informational Texts: Text Features

An informational text is nonfiction writing that provides factual information. Informational materials, such as chapters in textbooks and articles in magazines, encyclopedias, and newspapers, usually contain elements that help the reader recognize their purposes, organization, and key ideas. These elements are known as **text features.**

2.1 UNDERSTANDING TEXT FEATURES

Text features are design elements of a text that indicate its organizational structure or otherwise make its key ideas and information understandable. Text features include titles, headings, subheadings, boldface type, bulleted and numbered lists, and graphic aids, such as charts, graphs, illustrations, and photographs. Notice how the text features help you find key information on the textbook page shown.

A The **title** identifies the topic.

B A **subheading** indicates the start of a new topic or section and identifies the focus of that section.

C **Boldface type** is used to make key terms obvious.

D A **bulleted list** shows items of equal importance.

E **Graphic aids,** such as illustrations, photographs, charts, graphs, diagrams, maps, and timelines, often clarify ideas in the text.

PRACTICE AND APPLY

1. What are the subheadings on the textbook page shown?
2. What are the key terms on the page? How do you know?
3. How do the bulleted list and the photograph help you understand the information on this page?

A **New Deal Programs: Helping the American People**

While working on banking and financial matters, the Roosevelt administration also implemented programs to provide relief to farmers, perhaps the hardest hit by the depression. It also aided other workers and attempted to stimulate economic recovery.

B RURAL ASSISTANCE The **Agricultural Adjustment Act (AAA)** C sought to raise crop prices by lowering production, which the government achieved by paying farmers to leave a certain amount of every acre of land unseeded. The theory was that reduced supply would boost prices. In some cases, crops were too far advanced for the acreage reduction to take effect. As a result, the government paid cotton growers $200 million to plow under 10 million acres of their crop. It also paid hog farmers to slaughter 6 million pigs. This policy upset many Americans, who protested the destruction of food when many people were going hungry. It did, however, help raise farm prices and put more money in farmers' pockets.

Background See *supply and demand* on page R46 in the Economics Handbook.

An especially ambitious program of regional development was the Tennessee Valley Authority (TVA), established on May 18, 1933. (See Geography Spotlight on page 520.) Focusing on the badly depressed Tennessee River Valley, the TVA renovated five existing dams and constructed 20 new ones, created thousands of jobs, and provided flood control, hydroelectric power, and other benefits to an impoverished region.

PROVIDING WORK PROJECTS The administration also established programs to provide relief through work projects and cash payments. One important program, the **Civilian Conservation Corps (CCC),** put young men aged 18 to 25 to work building roads, developing parks, planting trees, and helping in soil-erosion and flood-control projects. By the time the program ended in 1942, almost 3 million young men had passed through the CCC. The CCC paid a small wage, $30 a month, of which $25 was automatically sent home to the worker's family. It also supplied free food and uniforms and lodging in work camps. Many of the camps were located on the Great Plains, where, within a period of eight years, the men of the CCC planted more than 200 million trees. This tremendous reforestation program was aimed at preventing another Dust Bowl.

Civilian Conservation Corps

D
- The CCC provided almost 3 million men aged 18–25 with work and wages between 1933 and 1942.
- The men lived in work camps under a strict regime. The majority of the camps were racially segregated.
- By 1938, the CCC had an 11 percent African-American enrollment.
- Accomplishments of the CCC include planting over 3 billion trees, developing over 800 state parks, and building more than 46,000 bridges.

The Public Works Administration (PWA), created in June 1933 as part of the **National Industrial Recovery Act (NIRA),** provided money to states to create jobs chiefly in the construction of schools and other community buildings. When these programs failed to make a sufficient dent in unemployment, President Roosevelt established the Civil Works Administration in November 1933. It provided 4 million immediate jobs during the winter of 1933–1934. Although some critics of the CWA claimed that the programs were "make-work" projects and a waste of money, the CWA built 40,000 schools and paid the salaries of more than 50,000 schoolteachers in America's rural areas. It also built more than half a million miles of roads. C

MAIN IDEA **Analyzing Effects** C How did New Deal programs affect various regions of the United States?

E

The New Deal **491**

2.2 USING TEXT FEATURES

You can use text features to locate information, to help you understand it, and to categorize it. Just use the following strategies when you encounter informational text.

Strategies for Reading

- Scan the title, headings, and subheadings to get an idea of the main concepts and the way the text is organized.
- Before you begin reading the text more thoroughly, read any questions that appear at the end of a lesson or chapter. Doing this will help you set a purpose for your reading.
- Turn subheadings into questions. Then use the text below the subheadings to answer the questions. Your answers will be a summary of the text.
- Take notes by turning headings and subheadings into main ideas. You might enter them in a chart like the following.

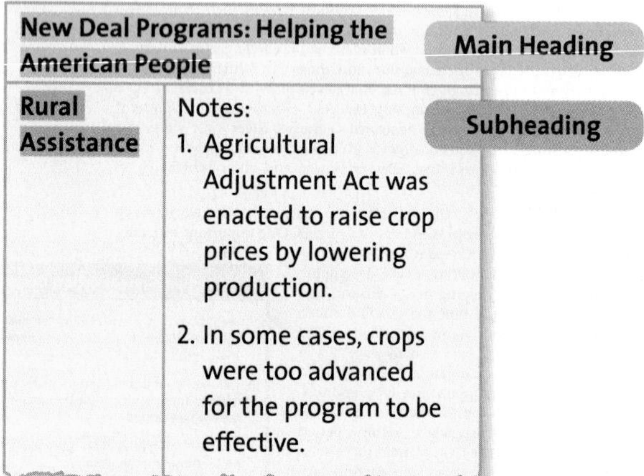

New Deal Programs: Helping the American People	
Rural Assistance	Notes: 1. Agricultural Adjustment Act was enacted to raise crop prices by lowering production. 2. In some cases, crops were too advanced for the program to be effective.

2.3 TURNING TEXT HEADINGS INTO OUTLINE ENTRIES

You can also use text features to take notes in outline form. The following outline shows how one student used text headings from the sample page on page R3. Study the outline and use the strategies that follow to create an outline based on text features.

I. New Deal Programs: Helping the American People
   A. Rural Assistance
      1. Agricultural Adjustment Act was enacted to raise crop prices by lowering production.
      2. In some cases, crops were too advanced for the program to be effective.

Main Heading Roman numeral entry

Subheading capital letter entry

Detail number entry

Strategies for Using Text Headings

- Preview the headings and subheadings in the text to get an idea of what different kinds there are and what their positions might be in an outline.
- Be consistent. Note that subheadings that are the same size and color should be used consistently in Roman-numeral or capital-letter entries in the outline. If you decide that a chapter heading should appear with a Roman numeral, then that's the level at which all other chapter headings should appear.
- Write the headings and subheadings that you will use as your Roman-numeral and capital-letter entries first. As you read, fill in numbered details from the text under the headings and subheadings in your outline.

PRACTICE AND APPLY

Find a suitable chapter in one of your textbooks and, using its text features, take notes on the chapter in outline form.

Preview the subheadings in the text to get an idea of the different kinds. Write the headings and subheadings you are using as your Roman-numeral and capital-letter entries first. Then fill in the details.

2.4 GRAPHIC AIDS

Information is communicated not only with words but also with graphic aids. **Graphic aids** are visual representations of verbal statements. They can be charts, webs, diagrams, graphs, photographs, or other visual representations of information. Graphic aids usually make complex information easier to understand. For that reason, graphic aids are often used to organize, simplify, and summarize information for easy reference.

Graphs

Graphs are used to illustrate statistical information. A **graph** is a drawing that shows the relative values of numerical quantities. Different kinds of graphs are used to show different numerical relationships.

Strategies for Reading

- **A** Read the title.
- **B** Find out what is being represented or measured.
- **C** In a circle graph, compare the sizes of the parts.
- **D** In a line graph, study the slant of the line. The steeper the line, the faster the rate of change.
- **E** In a bar graph, compare the lengths of the bars.

A **circle graph,** or **pie graph,** shows the relationships of parts to a whole. The entire circle equals 100 percent. The parts of the circle represent percentages of the whole.

MODEL: CIRCLE GRAPH

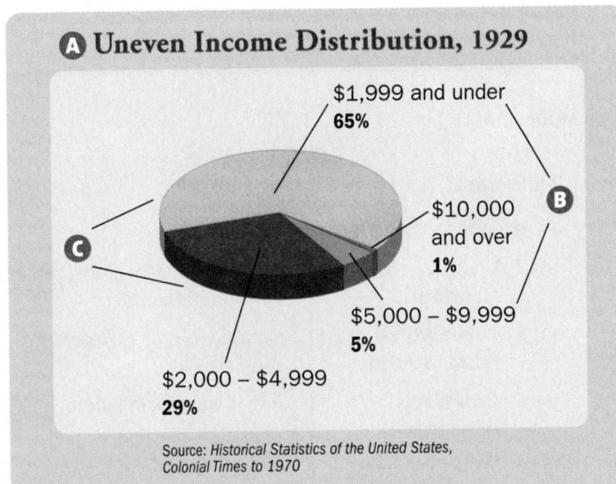

Line graphs show changes in numerical quantities over time and are effective in presenting trends, such as unemployment rates. A line graph is made on a grid. Here, the vertical axis indicates the percentage of the work force that is unemployed, and the horizontal axis shows years. Points on the graph indicate data. The lines that connect the points indicate the trends or patterns.

MODEL: LINE GRAPH

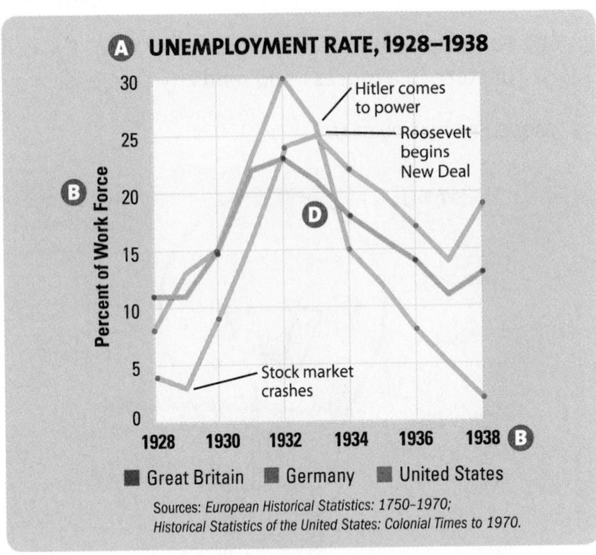

In a **bar graph,** vertical or horizontal bars are used to show or compare categories of information, such as average annual income during wartime. The lengths of the bars typically indicate quantities.

MODEL: BAR GRAPH

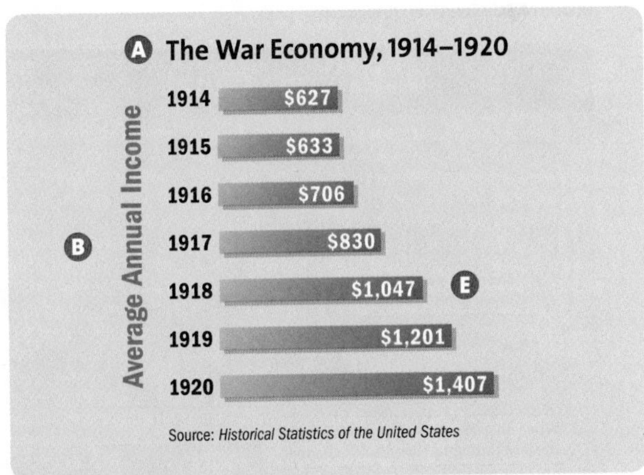

WATCH OUT! Evaluate carefully the information presented in graphs. For example, circle graphs show major factors and differences well but tend to minimize smaller factors and differences.

Diagrams

A **diagram** is a drawing that shows how something works or how its parts relate to one another.

A **picture diagram** is a picture or drawing of the subject being discussed.

Strategies for Reading

A Read the title.

B Read each label and look at the part it identifies.

C Follow any arrows or numbers that show the order of steps in a process, and read any captions.

MODEL: PICTURE DIAGRAM

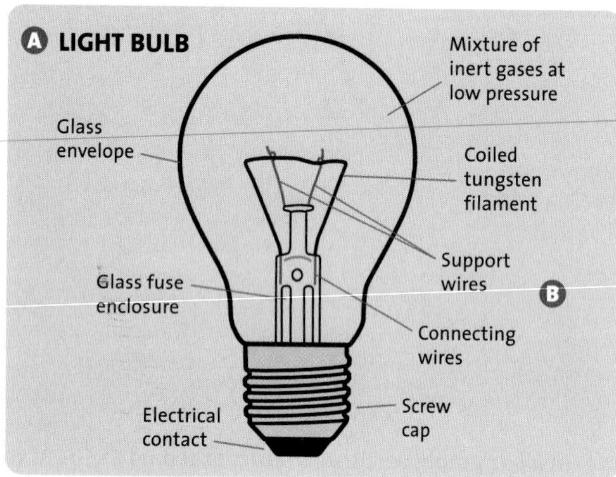

In a **schematic diagram,** lines, symbols, and words are used to help readers visualize processes or objects they wouldn't normally be able to see.

MODEL: SCHEMATIC DIAGRAM

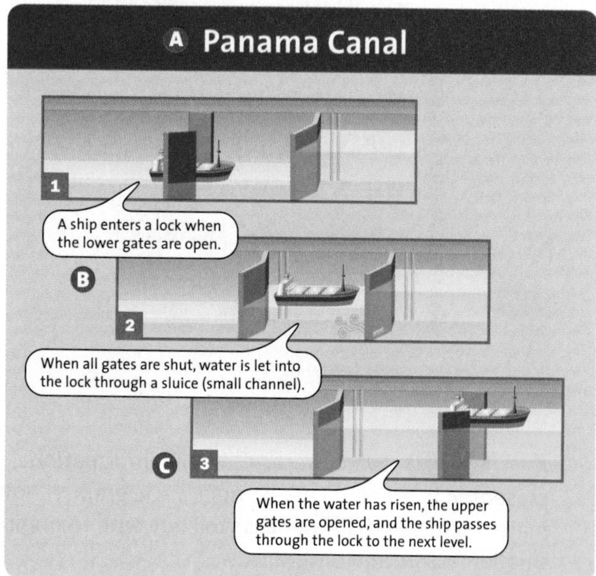

A Panama Canal
1
A ship enters a lock when the lower gates are open.
B
2
When all gates are shut, water is let into the lock through a sluice (small channel).
C
3
When the water has risen, the upper gates are opened, and the ship passes through the lock to the next level.

Charts and Tables

A **chart** presents information, shows a process, or makes comparisons, usually in rows or columns. A **table** is a specific type of chart that presents a collection of facts in rows and columns and shows how the facts relate to one another.

Strategies for Reading

A Read the title to learn what information the chart or table covers.

B Study column headings and row labels to determine the categories of information presented.

C Look down columns and across rows to find specific information.

MODEL: CHART

Geographic Distribution of U.S. Population, 1930–1970 A

Year	Central Cities	Suburbs	B Rural Areas and Small Towns
1930	31.8%	18.0%	50.2%
1940	31.6%	19.5%	48.9%
1950	32.3%	23.8%	43.9%
1960	32.6%	30.7%	36.7%
1970	31.4%	37.6%	31.0%

C

Source: Adapted from U.S. Bureau of the Census, *Decennial Censuses, 1930–1970*

MODEL: TABLE

New Deal A

EMPLOYMENT PROJECTS		PURPOSE B
1933	Civilian Conservation Corps	Provided jobs for single males on conservation projects
1933	Public Works Administration	Created jobs on government projects
1933	Civil Works Administration	Provided work in federal jobs
1935	Works Progress Administration	Quickly created as many jobs as possible—from construction jobs to positions in symphony orchestras
1935	National Youth Administration	Provided job training for unemployed young people and part-time jobs for needy students

C

Maps

A **map** visually represents a geographic region, such as a state or country. It provides information about areas through lines, colors, shapes, and symbols. There are different kinds of maps.

- **Political maps** show political features, such as national borders, states and capitols, and population demographics.
- **Physical maps** show the landforms in areas.
- **Road or travel maps** show streets, roads, and highways.
- **Thematic maps** show information on a specific topic, such as climate, weather, or natural resources.

Strategies for Reading

Ⓐ Read the title to find out what kind of map it is.

Ⓑ Read the labels to get an overall sense of what the map shows.

Ⓒ Look at the **key** or **legend** to find out what the symbols and colors on the map stand for.

MODEL: THEMATIC MAP

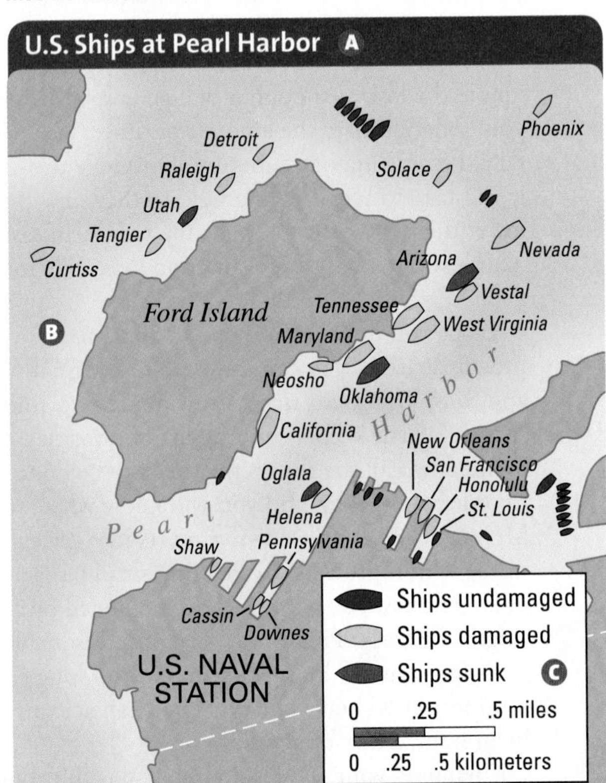

MODEL: ROAD MAP

PRACTICE AND APPLY

Use the graphic aids on pages R5–R7 to answer the following questions.

1. According to the circle graph, what percentage of the population in the 1920s earned $10,000 or over?
2. According to the line graph, which country had the highest unemployment rate in 1936?
3. According to the bar graph, by how much did the average annual income increase between 1914 and 1920?
4. What is used to contain the inert gases in a light bulb, according to the picture diagram?
5. Using the schematic diagram of the Panama Canal, describe the function of a sluice in the lock system.
6. According to the chart, in which type of area did the population steadily decrease between 1930 and 1970?
7. Use the table to determine the types of jobs found through the Public Works Administration.
8. On the thematic map, identify three ships that were sunk.
9. Use the 1920s map of Harlem to give directions from the Apollo Theatre to the Savoy Theatre.

3 Reading Informational Texts: Patterns of Organization

Reading any type of writing is easier once you recognize how it is organized. Writers usually arrange ideas and information in ways that best reveal how they are related. Here are the most common organizational patterns:

- order of importance
- chronological order
- cause-effect organization
- compare-and-contrast organization

3.1 ORDER OF IMPORTANCE

Order of importance is a pattern of organization in which information is arranged by its degree of importance. The information is often arranged in one of two ways: from **most important to least important** or from **least important to most important.** In the first way, the most important quality, characteristic, or fact is presented at the beginning of the text, and the remaining details are presented in an order ending with the least significant. The second pattern is the reverse: the text builds from the less important elements to the most important one. Order of importance is frequently used in persuasive writing.

Strategies for Reading

- To identify order of importance in a piece of writing, skim the text to see if it moves from items of greater importance to items of lesser importance, or the reverse.
- Next, read the text carefully. Look for words and phrases such as *first, second, mainly, more important, less important, least important* and *most important* to indicate the relative importance of the ideas and information.
- Identify the topic of the text and what aspect of the topic is being discussed—its complexity, size, effectiveness, varieties, or some other aspect. Note what the most important fact or idea seems to be.
- If you are having difficulty understanding the topic, try asking *who, what, when, where, why,* and *how* about the ideas or events.

Notice the degrees of importance of the ideas in the following model.

Subject | Words showing order of importance

MODEL

Why are some of us tempted to put off tasks when they could easily be done right away? In a word: procrastination. It affects all areas of life and can have some hefty consequences. By putting off tasks, we can cause unnecessary stress for ourselves and those around us. Many procrastinators say, "I work well under pressure," and this might be true. But better planning would lead to better grades, a more impressive report, and even career advancement. What can you do to curb your tendencies to delay the inevitable?

First, determine the cause of your procrastination. If you're honest with yourself, you might find that you set unrealistic goals, that you have a fear of failure or criticism, or that you feel guilty for delaying. Any of these reasons can paralyze your efforts to move forward.

The next important thing is to identify *the way in which* you procrastinate. Maybe you ignore the task as though it will go away. Maybe you underestimate the amount of time a task will take. Procrastinators sometimes misjudge the time it will take to prepare for a task, or they may even lower their standards to make the task seem easier. Think about what procrastination looks like for you.

Once you understand the *why* and *how* of procrastination, you can move on to the final and most important stage—turning "being" into "doing." First, keep a running list of priorities. Write down all the things that need to be done in order of urgency, and you will know where to begin. Second, break down projects into several tasks, or miniprojects. By creating small tasks out of larger ones, you won't feel overwhelmed by a single large task. Finally, set clear and reasonable goals for yourself. Be specific about how long each miniproject will take and what you can accomplish in an hour, a day, or a week.

Changing your ways is definitely possible, but it will take some honest evaluation. Hopefully, after the process of examining the *why* and *how* of procrastination, you will be ready to change your ways. Why not start right now?

PRACTICE AND APPLY

Read each paragraph, and then do the following:

1. Identify whether the order is from most important to least important or from least important to most important.
2. Identify key words and phrases that helped you figure out the order.
3. What is the order of importance indicated in the paragraph beginning, "Once you understand . . . "? What are the key words?

3.2 CHRONOLOGICAL ORDER

Chronological order is the arrangement of events in their order of occurrence. This type of organization is used in fictional narratives, historical writing, biographies, and autobiographies. To indicate the order of events, writers use words such as *before, after, next,* and *later* and words and phrases that identify specific times of day, days of the week, and dates, such as *the next morning, Tuesday,* and *on July 4, 1776.*

Strategies for Reading

- Look in the text for headings and subheadings that may indicate a chronological pattern of organization.
- Look for words and phrases that identify times, such as *in a year, three hours earlier, in 1871,* and *the next day.*
- Look for words that signal order, such as *first, afterward, then, during,* and *finally,* to see how events or steps are related.
- Note that a paragraph or passage in which ideas and information are arranged chronologically will have several words or phrases that indicate time order, not just one.
- Ask yourself: Are the events in the paragraph or passage presented in time order?

Notice the words and phrases that signal time order in the first three paragraphs of the following model.

MODEL

History of the National Weather Service

Today, the U.S. National Weather Service is one of the best-known federal agencies. It was not always so popular, especially in its early years.

The first incarnation of the National Weather Service was founded in the wake of the Civil War, as an agency in the Army Signal Service Corps. Its mission was to "take observations at military stations and to warn of storms on the Great Lakes and on the Atlantic and Gulf Coasts." Very early in its existence the agency earned a reputation for the corruption of its personnel and the unreliability of its forecasting. In 1881, William Howgate, the chief financial manager of the agency, was arrested for embezzling a quarter million dollars. . . . During this time the U.S. military budget was about 40 million dollars. Howgate was tried and convicted, only to escape a year later. Other servicemen in stations around the country were investigated throughout the 1880s and fired in large numbers for reckless neglect. . . . Moreover, the agency's weather predictions were frequently and dangerously wrong. On March 12, 1888, the New York station's forecast called for "fair weather"; instead of fair weather, New York got the Blizzard of '88, which dumped 21 inches of snow on the city and killed 400 people throughout the Northeast. . . .

In 1891, the Army Signal Service Corps's weather service was honorably discharged from the Department of War and given a new home in the civilian Department of Agriculture. It was named the Weather Bureau: it would not be called the National Weather Service until 1970. During the years leading up to 1900, the Weather Bureau's servicemen took regular measurement of such atmospheric conditions as temperature, wind speed, air pressure, rainfall, and cloud conditions. They transmitted their findings to one another via wireless telegraphy.

Time words and phrases

Order words and phrases

Events

PRACTICE AND APPLY

Refer to the preceding model to do the following:

1. List at least five words or phrases from the model that indicate time order. Do not use words that are already highlighted.
2. Draw a timeline beginning in 1881 and ending with "today." On the timeline chart major events in the formation of the National Weather Service as described in the model.
3. Sometimes more than one pattern of organization is used to help organize a text. Reread paragraph two, and find at least three causes for the Army Signal Service Corps's reputation as a corrupt and unreliable agency. Use the "multiple causes with a single effect" form shown on this page to chart this information.

3.3 CAUSE-EFFECT ORGANIZATION

Cause-effect organization is a pattern of organization that establishes causal relationships between events, ideas, and trends. Cause-effect relationships may be directly stated or merely implied by the order in which the information is presented. Writers often use the cause-effect pattern in historical and scientific writing. Cause-effect relationships may take several forms.

One cause with one effect

One cause with multiple effects

Multiple causes with a single effect

A chain of causes and effects

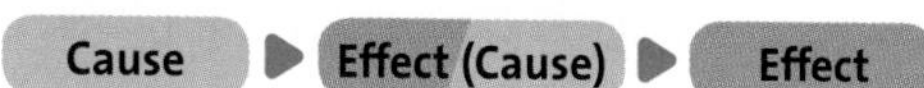

Strategies for Reading

- Look for headings and subheadings that indicate a cause-effect pattern of organization, such as "The Effects of Improved Weather Forecasting."
- To find the effect or effects, read to answer the question, What happened?
- To find the cause or causes, read to answer the question, Why did it happen?
- Look for words and phrases that help you identify specific relationships between events, such as *because, since, so, had the effect of, led to, as a result, resulted in, for that reason, due to, therefore, if . . . then,* and *consequently.*
- Evaluate each cause-effect relationship. Do not assume that because one event happened before another, the first event caused the second event.
- Use graphic organizers like the diagrams shown to record cause-effect relationships as you read.

Notice the words that signal causes and effects in the following model.

MODEL

The Formation of a Hurricane: What Does It Take?

Hurricanes have waged war on U.S. cities like no other enemy. Each year, up to ten tropical storms may form in the Atlantic Ocean and make their way west. Typically, three to five have the potential to become a full-blown hurricane. These high-speed monsters are fueled by the simplest of natural elements: water, wind, and air. Given the right conditions, these essential elements for life can become lethal.

The first condition for the formation of a hurricane involves warming ocean water in a relatively tranquil and tropical region of the Atlantic. By late summer, the surface water becomes thoroughly heated and begins to evaporate, or rise into the air. This process creates warm, moist air, which then rises and eventually condenses to form clouds and rain. During this process, energy is released, warming the air further.

Causes

Effect that in turn becomes a cause

The second condition, ironically, is the lack of wind. In the tropical regions of the Atlantic, the air may be relatively stagnant in places, which causes the warm, moist air to remain in one spot. Because the air is continuing to warm and gain energy, it needs to move, and so it does: upward. This column of upward-moving warm air creates an area of low pressure over the water, which in turn draws even more air from the surrounding area toward the center of the column. In addition, the inward-moving air causes the warm air to rise even faster, which then draws even more air and increases its wind speed. Thus, the transfer of energy from ocean to air begins to fuel itself with ever-increasing speed.

Signal words and phrases

As the air moves toward the column's center, it does not move in a straight line, but moves in a circular motion as a result of the earth's rotation. As the air moves up the column, it continues swirling.

A storm that continues in this cycle may grow up to 500 miles in diameter. Its westward movement ensures that it will eventually hit land if it doesn't dissipate, and what began as a simple combination of water, wind, and air could turn into a catastrophic storm.

PRACTICE AND APPLY

Refer to the preceding model to do the following:

1. Use the pattern of multiple causes with a single effect illustrated on page R10 to make a graphic organizer showing the causes described in the text and the effect of those causes.
2. List any words and phrases the writer uses to signal cause and effect in the third paragraph.

3.4 COMPARE-AND-CONTRAST ORGANIZATION

Compare-and-contrast organization is a pattern of organization that serves as a framework for examining similarities and differences in two or more subjects. A writer may use this pattern of organization to analyze two or more subjects, such as characters or movies, in terms of their important points or characteristics. These points or characteristics are called points of comparison. The compare-and-contrast pattern of organization may be developed in either of two ways.

Point-by-point organization—The writer discusses one point of comparison for both subjects, then goes on to the next point.

Subject-by-subject organization—The writer covers all points of comparison for one subject and then all points of comparison for the next subject.

Strategies for Reading

- Look in the text for headings, subheadings, and sentences that may suggest a compare-and-contrast pattern of organization, such as "East Coast and West Coast Living: More than a Continent Apart." These will help you identify where similarities and differences are addressed.
- To find similarities, look for words and phrases such as *like, similarly, both, also,* and *in the same way.*
- To find differences, look for words and phrases such as *unlike, but, on the other hand, in contrast,* and *however.*
- Use a graphic organizer, such as a Venn diagram or a compare-and-contrast chart, to record points of comparison and similarities and differences.

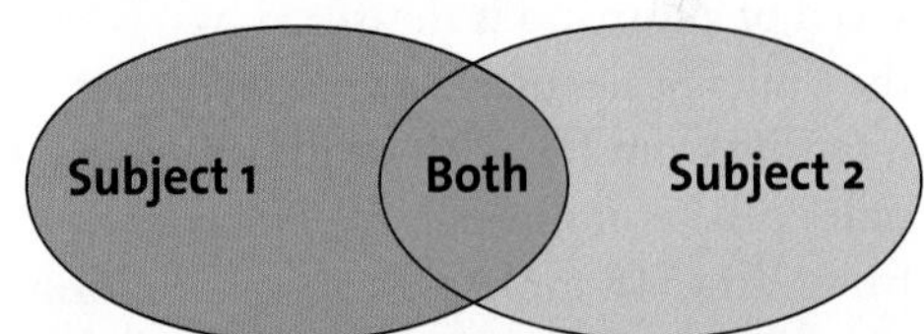

	Subject 1	Subject 2
Point 1		
Point 2		
Point 3		

Read the following models. As you read, use the signal words and phrases to identify the similarities and differences between the subjects and how the details are organized in each text.

MODEL 1

A Tale of Two Furies: Hurricane vs. Tornado

Two of the deadliest types of storms are hurricanes and tornadoes. While both are ferocious wind storms and require similar elements to form, each varies in speed and duration.

Subjects

Hurricanes, like tornadoes, require the meeting of cool and warm air and begin as rain or thunderstorms. However, one major difference between the two is that a hurricane forms at sea and moves toward land, while a tornado forms over, and remains on, land. Hurricanes require large amounts of warmth and moisture from ocean water to form, while tornadoes rely on the moisture already in the air. The duration of a hurricane is one week, on average. A few rare hurricanes have been known to last between 17 and 27 days. The average tornado, however, lasts 10 to 30 minutes, and may "touch down" on land for up to a minute.

Contrast words and phrases

Both tornadoes and hurricanes can be measured. The difference is in *how* and *when.* The wind speed of a tornado is measured by the Fujita Scale, or F-Scale, which rates intensity from F0, with winds less than 73 miles per hour, through F5, with winds from 261–318 mph. Since tornados form very quickly and cannot be accurately predicted, the F-Scale can only measure the strength of a tornado *after* it has occurred. In contrast, the intensity of hurricanes can be measured *while* they are forming. This is because unlike tornados, hurricanes form slowly and can be photographed using satellite imagery. The satellite pictures are then studied, and the results applied to a scale of measure called the Saffir-Simpson Hurricane Scale. This scale rates intensity from Category One through the most intense Category 5 storm.

Comparison words

MODEL 2

Same Goal, Different Methods

Booker T. Washington and W. E. B. Du Bois were alike in many ways. Both were devoted to helping their fellow African Americans attain equal rights. Both were educated black men with university teaching positions. Both also worked passionately toward their goal at the beginning of the 20th century. Nevertheless, they were not allies. Why? They had very different ideas about how blacks should go about attaining equal rights.

Subjects

Comparison words

Contrast words and phrases

Washington believed that for black people to achieve equal status and power as citizens they needed to focus on learning crafts, farming, and industrial skills. He argued that by gaining vocational skills and economic security, black people would naturally earn the respect and acceptance of the white community. To achieve these goals, however, Washington believed black people would need to let go temporarily of the fight for civil rights and political power.

In contrast to Washington, W. E. B. Du Bois believed that black people could not afford to stop fighting for civil rights and political power. In his opinion, only agitation and protest would achieve social change. According to Du Bois, in the climate of extreme racism that existed in America at the time, Washington's approach would merely cause blacks to suffer even more oppression.

So although these two African-American contemporaries had the same goal, their different approaches to achieving this goal made them adversaries rather than allies.

PRACTICE AND APPLY

Refer to the preceding models to do the following:

For each model, create a compare-and-contrast chart. In your chart, list the points of comparison in each model, and identify the similarities and differences between each model's subjects.

4 Reading Informational Texts: Forms

Magazines, newspapers, Web pages, and procedural, public, and workplace documents are all examples of informational materials. To understand and analyze informational texts, pay attention to text features and patterns of organization.

4.1 READING A MAGAZINE ARTICLE

Because people often skim magazines for topics of interest, magazine publishers use devices to attract attention to articles and to highlight key information.

Strategies for Reading

- **A** Read the **title** and other **headings** to find out more about the article's topic and organization.
- **B** Notice whether or not the article has a **byline,** a line naming the author, and make note of the date and source.
- **C** Examine **illustrations, photos,** or other **graphic aids** that visually convey or illustrate additional information, or information from the text.
- **D** Notice **pull quotes,** or quotations that a publisher has pulled out of the text and displayed to get your attention.

PRACTICE AND APPLY

Refer to the article to answer the following questions:

1. What does the title indicate the topic will be?
2. Why is this particular pull quote significant? What information does it convey?
3. Considering the information in the text and the visual image in the photo, what can you conclude about the severity of the hurricane mentioned in the article?

Katrina's South American Sister

A **Was Catarina an omen of things to come?**

C 

For people along the Gulf Coast, Hurricane Katrina was an unimaginable disaster. In meteorological terms, however, she was not unusual—a major storm for sure, but not atypical of what comes across the North Atlantic at that time of year. The one thing experts did note was that ocean temperatures in the Gulf of Mexico are especially warm these days.

For hurricane watchers, however, the real shocker had come 18 months earlier. And her name was Catarina.

Catarina came ashore in Brazil on March 28, 2004—a category-one hurricane that damaged 30,000 homes. Scientists were baffled. Brazilian meteorologists didn't even use the term "hurricane" at first—not until they looked closely at the satellite images. Why? Very simply, no hurricanes had ever been recorded before in the South Atlantic. Conventional wisdom was that cool ocean temperatures and atmospheric differences made it impossible for hurricanes to form there.

But here was Hurricane Catarina, and, indeed, a couple of months earlier, on January 19th, a smaller tropical storm had also developed off the coast of Brazil.

D **"The real shocker had come 18 months earlier . . . And her name was Catarina."**

The entire phenomenon was unprecedented. . . . Is it another indicator of global warming? Researchers say that any such analysis is, at this stage, speculative. Regardless, it might make sense to plan for the worst, rather than continually hoping for the best.

4.2 READING A TEXTBOOK

Each textbook that you use has its own system of organization, based on the content in the book. Often an introductory unit will explain the book's organization and special features. If your textbook has such a unit, read it first.

Strategies for Reading

A Before you begin reading the lesson or chapter, read any **questions** that appear at the end of it. Then use the questions to set your purpose for reading.

B **Read slowly and carefully** to better understand and remember the ideas presented in the text. When you come to an unfamiliar word, first try to figure out its meaning from **context clues.** If necessary, find the meaning of the word in a **sidenote** on the page, in a **glossary** at the back of the book, or in a dictionary. Avoid interrupting your reading by constantly looking up words in a dictionary.

C Use the book's **graphic aids,** such as illustrations, diagrams, and photos, to clarify your understanding of the text.

D Take notes as you read. Use text features such as **subheadings** and **boldfaced terms** to help you organize your notes. Use graphic organizers, such as cause-effect charts, to help you clarify relationships among ideas.

The New Deal Comes Under Attack

D THREE FIERY CRITICS In 1934, some of the strongest conservative opponents of the New Deal banded together to form an organization called the American Liberty League. The American Liberty League opposed New Deal measures that it believed violated respect for the rights of individuals and property. Three of the toughest critics the president faced, however, were three men who expressed views that appealed to poor Americans: Charles Coughlin, Dr. Francis Townsend, and Huey Long.

Every Sunday, Father Charles Coughlin, a Roman Catholic priest from a suburb of Detroit, broadcast radio sermons that combined economic, political, and religious ideas. Initially a supporter of the New Deal, Coughlin soon turned against Roosevelt. He favored a guaranteed annual income and the **nationalization** of banks. At the height of his popularity, Father Coughlin claimed a radio audience of as many as 40–45 million people, but his increasingly anti-Semitic (anti-Jewish) views eventually cost him support.

B **Vocabulary**
nationalization: conversion from private to governmental ownership

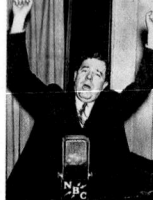

Another critic of New Deal policies was Dr. Francis Townsend, a physician and health officer in Long Beach, California. He believed that Roosevelt wasn't doing enough to help the poor and elderly, so he devised a pension plan that would provide monthly benefits to the aged. The plan found strong backing among the elderly, thus undermining their support for Roosevelt.

D Perhaps the most serious challenge to the New Deal came from Senator **Huey Long** of Louisiana. Like Coughlin, Long was an early supporter of the New Deal, but he, too, turned against Roosevelt. Eager to win the presidency for himself, Long proposed a nationwide social program called Share-Our-Wealth. Under the banner "Every Man a King," he promised something for everyone.

C

Huey Long

A PERSONAL VOICE HUEY LONG

"**We owe debts in America today, public and private, amounting to $252 billion. That means that every child is born with a $2,000 debt tied around his neck. . . . We propose that children shall be born in a land of opportunity, guaranteed a home, food, clothes, and the other things that make for living, including the right to education.**"

—*Record*, 74 Congress, Session 1

Long's program was so popular that by 1935 he boasted of having perhaps as many as 27,000 Share-Our-Wealth clubs and 7.5 million members. That same year, however, at the height of his popularity, Long was assassinated by a lone gunman.

As the initial impetus of the New Deal began to wane, President Roosevelt started to look ahead. He knew that much more needed to be done to help the people and to solve the nation's economic problems.

A SECTION 1 ASSESSMENT

SECTION REVIEW

- Name the three outspoken critics of Roosevelt's New Deal.
- Describe one New Deal program, and explain one opponent's view of the New Deal.
- **Critical Thinking** Of the New Deal programs discussed, which do you consider the most important? Consider scope, impact, and type of assistance offered by each.

The New Deal **493**

PRACTICE AND APPLY

1. What is the definition of *nationalization?*
2. Where on the page do you find the combined private and public debt owed during this time? What was the total amount?
3. Use the text on this page and on R3 to answer the second question in the Section Review of the textbook page.

4.3 READING PROCEDURAL DOCUMENTS

Procedural documents are functional documents that accompany products and services. They usually provide information about the use, care, operation, or assembly of the products they accompany. Some common procedural documents are contracts, warranties, manuals, instructions, schedules, and Web pages.

Strategies for Reading

A Read the **title** to identify the purpose of the document.

B Read the **general directions** to get started.

C Look for **numbers** or **letters** that indicate the steps to be followed. Note whether the steps must be done in order and whether there are signal words such as *first, next, then,* and *finally* that indicate the order in which the steps should be followed. Follow the steps in order.

D Refer to any **illustrations, diagrams,** or other **graphic aids** that accompany the numbered instructions. Use the graphic aids to help you understand each step.

E Look for **verbs that describe actions you should take,** such as *press, use,* and *hold.*

PRACTICE AND APPLY

1. Explain the function of key number 10.
2. Identify the number of the key that allows you to engage the phone's locking function.

INSTRUCTIONS FOR USING A CELL PHONE

A ## PHONE OVERVIEW

B **Use this guide to get a quick overview of your phone's functions.**

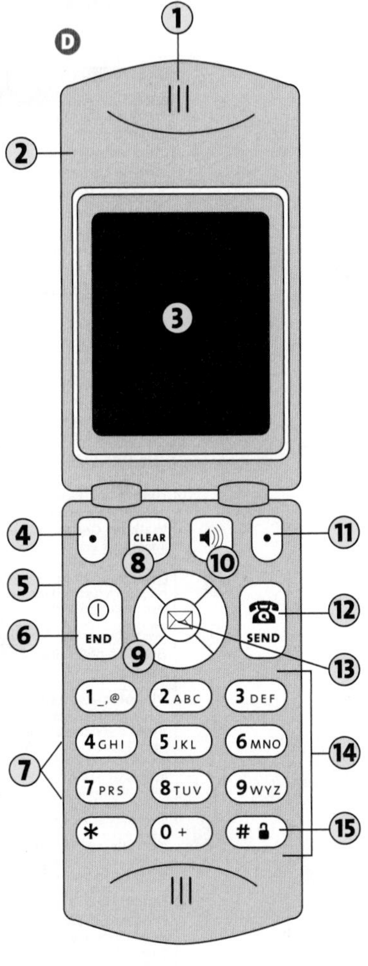

C 1. **Earpiece** **E**
2. **Flip** Flip open the case to answer incoming calls and close to end calls.
3. **LCD Screen** Displays messages and icons.
4. **Left Soft Key** Use to display the function-setting menu.
5. **Headset Jack**
6. **END/POWER Key** Use to turn the power on or off and to end a call.
7. **Side Keys** Use to adjust the ringer volume in standby mode and the earpiece volume during a call.
8. **CLEAR Key** Press to delete a single space or character. Press and hold to delete entire words. Press this key once in a menu to go back one level.
9. **Navigation Key** Use for quick access to messages or Web.
10. **Speaker Key** Use to set Speaker on or off.
11. **Right Soft Key** Use to select an action in a menu.
12. **SEND Key** Use to place or answer calls.
13. **Message Key** Use to retrieve or send voice and text messages.
14. **Alphanumeric Keypad** Use the keys to enter numbers and characters and to select menu items.
15. **Lock Mode Key** Use in standby mode to set the lock function by pressing and holding the key for about 3 seconds.

4.4 READING A PUBLIC DOCUMENT

Public documents are functional documents that are written for the public to provide information that is of public interest or concern. These documents are often free. They can be federal, state, or local government documents. They can be speeches or historical documents. They may even be laws, posted warnings, signs, or rules and regulations. The following is a public document that has been posted on a U.S. government Web site and can be printed as a document.

Strategies for Reading

- **A** Look at the **title** on the page to discover what the text is about.
- **B** Note the **source** of the document.
- **C** Carefully read **column headings** in the table. Items in a table are usually essential pieces of information.
- **D** Be sure to read **parenthetical text** if there is any. This information may help clarify meaning, provide examples, or further explain an entry.
- **E** Pay attention to **notes** and **asterisks** (*) and their accompanying footnotes. These will help clarify exceptions or exemptions to the rules, or add additional detail.

PRACTICE AND APPLY

Reread the TSA page and then answer the following questions:

1. Are knives allowed as a carry-on item? as a checked item?
2. Name the three types of scissors that are allowed as carry-on items.
3. Walking canes are allowed as a carry-on and as a checked item. Why do they need to be inspected?
4. Guidelines for acceptable carry-on and checked items on flights are revised periodically. Verify that the items listed here are up-to-date by checking the Transportation Security Administration Web site: www.tsa.gov. Search the site for a list of permitted and prohibited items. Key words to look for are *Travelers* and *Prohibited Items.*

RULES AND REGULATIONS FOR CARRY-ON ITEMS IN AIR TRAVEL

U.S. Department of Homeland Security
Transportation Security Administration
Arlington, VA 22202

A **Permitted and Prohibited Items**

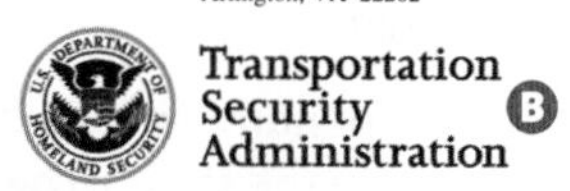

B

C

Can I take it?	Carry-on	Checked
Personal Items		
Cigar Cutters	Yes	Yes
Corkscrews	Yes	Yes
Cuticle Cutters	Yes	Yes
Eyeglass Repair Tools (including screwdrivers) **D**	Yes	Yes
Eyelash Curlers	Yes	Yes
Knitting and Crochet Needles	Yes	Yes
Knives - prohibited as carry-on except for plastic or round bladed butter knives.	**No**	Yes
Nail Clippers	Yes	Yes
Nail Files	Yes	Yes
Personal care or toiletries with aerosols, in limited quantities (such as hairsprays, deodorants)	Yes	Yes
Safety Razors (including disposable razors)	Yes	Yes
Scissors - plastic or metal with blunt tips	**Yes**	**Yes**
Scissors - metal with pointed tips and blades longer than four inches in length	**No**	**Yes**
Toy Transformer Robots	Yes	Yes
Toy Weapons (if not realistic replicas)	Yes	Yes
Tweezers	Yes	Yes
Umbrellas (allowed in carry-on baggage once they have been inspected to ensure that prohibited items are not concealed)	Yes	Yes
Walking Canes (allowed in carry-on baggage once they have been inspected to ensure that prohibited items are not concealed)	Yes	Yes
E Note Some personal care items containing aerosol are regulated as hazardous materials. The FAA regulates hazardous materials. This information is summarized at www.faa.gov, click on *Passengers*, then *Preparing to Fly*.		
Medication and Special Needs Devices		
Braille Note-Taker, Slate and Stylus, Augmentation Devices	Yes	Yes
Diabetes-Related Supplies/Equipment, (once inspected to ensure prohibited items are not concealed) including: insulin and insulin loaded dispensing products; vials or box of individual vials; jet injectors; pens; infusers; and preloaded syringes; and an unlimited number of unused syringes, when accompanied by insulin; lancets; blood glucose meters; blood glucose meter test strips; insulin pumps; and insulin pump supplies. Insulin in any form or dispenser must be properly marked with a professionally printed label identifying the medication or manufacturer's name or pharmaceutical label.	Yes	Yes
Nitroglycerine pills or spray for medical use (if properly marked with a professionally printed label identifying the medication or manufacturer's name or pharmaceutical label)	Yes	Yes
Ostomy Scissors All scissors with blades four inches or less	Yes	Yes
Prosthetic Device Tools and Appliances, including drill, allen wrenches, pullsleeves used to put on or remove prosthetic devices, if carried by the individual with the prosthetic device or his or her companion	Yes	Yes

U.S. Department of Homeland Security
TSA- Rev. 12-1-2005

Page 3 of 5

4.5 READING A WORKPLACE DOCUMENT

Workplace documents are materials that are produced or used within a workplace, usually to aid in the functioning of a business. These documents include meeting minutes, sales reports, statements of company policy or organizational structure, and explanations of operating procedures. Workplace documents also include memos, business letters, job applications, and résumés.

Strategies for Reading

Ⓐ Use **headings** and **subheadings** to help you locate information that is relevant or important to you.

Ⓑ Read a workplace document slowly and carefully, as it may contain **details** that should not be overlooked.

Ⓒ Notice how to contact the creator of the document. You will need this information to clear up anything that you don't understand.

PRACTICE AND APPLY

Refer to the company policy statement to answer the following questions:

1. How long does an employee need to work at HBA before he or she is eligible for three weeks of paid vacation?
2. Under which section(s) would you look if you traveled extensively for work and were interested in insurance that specifically covered accidents while traveling?
3. Does the company offer supplemental life insurance? Does the company or the employee pay for it?
4. How much short-term disability coverage does the company provide free of charge to an employee?

COMPANY POLICY STATEMENT

HBA Company
Employee Benefits Policy

Ⓐ Ⓑ

Medical Benefits

HBA offers four medical choices, which include two options that are at no cost to our employees. We also offer dental, vision, and an Employee Assistance Program at no cost to employees.

Retirement and Savings Plan Ⓐ

HBA's contributions to your retirement plan are guaranteed at 5% of your annual earnings, plus up to an additional 10% variable contribution (based on company performance).

Life Insurance

At no cost to the employee, life insurance is provided for three times his or her annual base salary, not to exceed $500,000. Employees may also elect to purchase supplemental life insurance for themselves, their spouse, and eligible dependent children.

Disability Programs

Accidental Death and Dismemberment Insurance—Eligible employees are covered for up to three times their annual base salary, not to exceed $500,000, depending on the extent of injury.

Short-Term Disability—Eligible employees receive a short-term disability benefit of 60% of their salary and may elect to "buy-up" additional coverage to a maximum 70% benefit.

Long-Term Disability—Eligible employees are provided coverage at a benefit amount of 50% of their salary and may elect to "buy-up" additional coverage to a total benefit level of 67%.

Travel Accident Insurance—Eligible employees are covered for $35,000 to $500,000, depending on their annual base salary.

Time Off Benefits

Vacation—Employees earn time off at the rate of two weeks per year for the first five years of employment, three weeks per year after five years of employment, and four weeks per year after ten years of employment.

Sick Leave—Employees earn at a rate of one week per year.

Holidays—Employees are paid for eight calendar holidays. Employees also receive three floating holidays per calendar year after six months of employment.

Ⓒ If you have any questions, contact the HBA Human Resources Department.

4.6 READING ELECTRONIC TEXT

Electronic text is any text that is in a form that a computer can store and display on a screen. Electronic text can be part of Web pages, CD-ROMs, search engines, and documents that you create with your computer software. Like books, Web pages often provide aids to finding information. However, each Web page is designed differently, and information is not in the same location on each page. It is important to know the functions of different parts of a Web page so that you can easily find the information you want.

Strategies for Reading

- **A** Look at the **title** of a page to determine what topics it covers.
- **B** For an online source, such as a Web page or a search engine, note the **Web address,** known as a **URL** (uniform resource locator), in case you need to return to the page later or cite it as a source.
- **C** Look for the **menu options,** or navigation options that allow you to navigate through the site's main categories and pages. These options are **links** to other pages providing more in-depth information on the topic listed.
- **D** Read **introductory text** to get a sense of the site's subject matter and purpose.
- **E** Use **hyperlinks** to get to other pages on the site. Hyperlinks may lead to pages listed in the menu options or to other Web sites related in subject matter.
- **F** Look for **graphic aids,** such as photos, illustrations, or animation, that will provide you with more information about the site's topic(s).

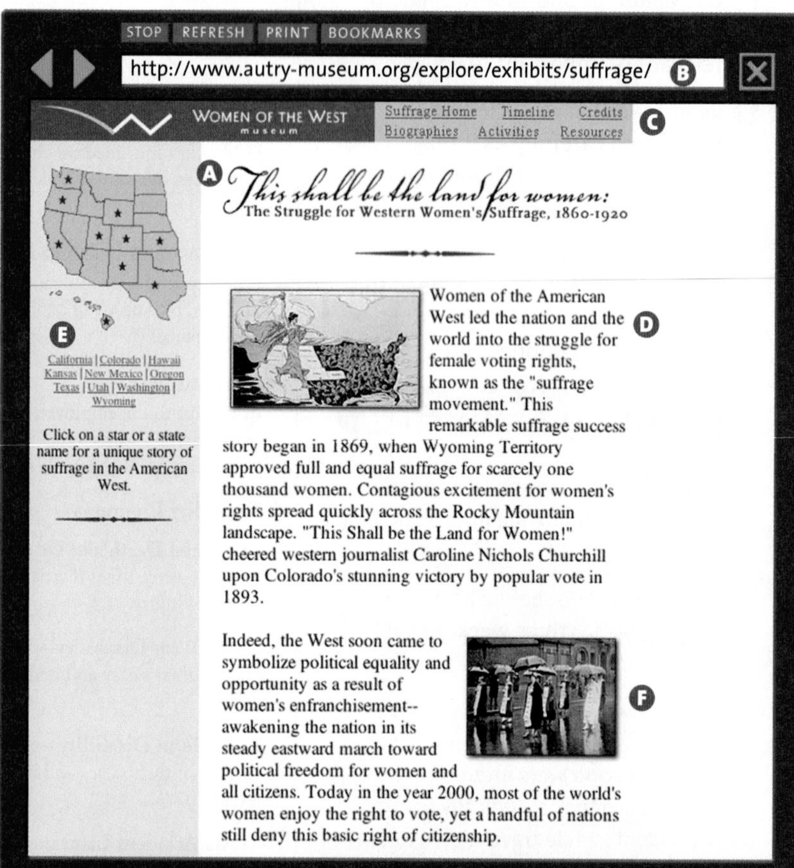

PRACTICE AND APPLY

1. What is the topic of this site?
2. If you were searching for information on suffrage in New Mexico, which links or hyperlinks would you use?
3. Who has produced this Web site?
4. Verify the information on women's suffrage in the Wyoming Territory presented on this Web page by consulting a reference source, such as an encyclopedia, or a government document.

5 Reading Persuasive Texts

5.1 ANALYZING AN ARGUMENT

An **argument** expresses a position on an issue or problem and supports it with reasons and evidence. Being able to analyze and evaluate arguments will help you distinguish between claims you should accept and those you should not. A sound argument should appeal strictly to reason. However, arguments are often used in texts that also contain other types of persuasive devices. An argument includes the following elements:

- A **claim** is the writer's position on an issue or problem.
- **Support** is any material that serves to prove a claim. In an argument, support usually consists of reasons and evidence.
- **Reasons** are declarations made to justify an action, a decision, or a belief—for example, "You should sleep on a good mattress *in order to avoid spinal problems.*"
- **Evidence** consists of the specific references, quotations, facts, examples, and opinions that support a claim. Evidence may also consist of statistics, reports of personal experience, or the views of experts.
- A **counterargument** is an argument made to oppose another argument. A good argument anticipates the opposition's objections and provides counterarguments to disprove or answer them.

Claim	Walt Whitman is one of the most important figures in American poetry.
Reason	He experimented with poetic form and content and created a quintessentially American voice in literature.
Evidence	His poetry influenced generations of poets. His poems celebrated the diversity and spirit of American culture.
Counterargument	No American poet before Whitman broke with tradition in the ways he did.

PRACTICE AND APPLY

In the early 1900s, Elinore Pruitt Stewart (formerly Rupert), was living in Burnt Fork, Wyoming, as a homesteader, a person who received public land free of charge under the Homestead Act of 1862. In the following letter to a friend, she makes an argument for homestead living over an impoverished city existence. Use a chart like the one shown to identify the claim, reason, evidence, and counterargument in her letter.

January 23, 1913

Dear Mrs. Coney,—

. . . When I read of the hard times among the Denver poor, I feel like urging them every one to get out and file on land. I am very enthusiastic about women homesteading. It really requires less strength and labor to raise plenty to satisfy a large family than it does to go out to wash, with the added satisfaction of knowing that their job will not be lost to them if they care to keep it. Even if improving the place does go slowly, it is that much done to stay done. Whatever is raised is the homesteader's own, and there is no house-rent to pay. This year Jerrine cut and dropped enough potatoes to raise a ton of fine potatoes. She wanted to try, so we let her, and you will remember that she is but six years old. We had a man to break the ground and cover the potatoes for her and the man irrigated them once. That was all that was done until digging time, when they were ploughed out and Jerrine picked them up. Any woman strong enough to go out by the day could have done every bit of the work and put in two or three times that much, and it would have been so much more pleasant than to work so hard in the city and then be on starvation rations in the winter.

To me, homesteading is the solution of all poverty's problems, but I realize that temperament has much to do with success in any undertaking, and persons afraid of coyotes and work and loneliness had better let ranching alone. At the same time, any woman who can stand her own company, can see the beauty of the sunset, loves growing things, and is willing to put in as much time at careful labor as she does over the washtub, will certainly succeed; will have independence, plenty to eat all the time, and a home of her own in the end.

5.2 RECOGNIZING PERSUASIVE TECHNIQUES

Persuasive texts typically rely on more than just the logical appeal of an argument to be convincing. They also rely on ethical and emotional appeals, as well as other **persuasive techniques**—devices that can sway you to adopt a position or take an action.

The chart shown here explains several of these techniques. Learn to recognize them, and you will be less likely to be influenced by them.

Persuasive Technique	Example
Appeals by Association	
Bandwagon appeal Suggests that a person should believe or do something because "everyone else" does	Join the millions who've contributed to The Cause: buy your 'Be Well' bracelet today.
Testimonial Relies on endorsements from well-known people or satisfied customers	DJ Super Dawg keeps songs spinning all day long with his new CompactM3 disc player. Give it a whirl!
Snob appeal Taps into people's desire to be special or part of an elite group	In Smart and Sassy cosmetics, you'll look and feel like the princess you are.
Transfer Connnects a product, candidate, or cause with a positive emotion or idea	Rediscover peace and tranquility with Back in Balance aromatherapy candles.
Appeal to loyalty Relies on people's affiliation with a particular group	Only Substantial Bank offers long-term customers better rates.
Emotional Appeals	
Appeals to pity, fear, or vanity Use strong feelings, rather than facts, to persuade	The cost of one candy bar can help buy a whole meal for a starving family.
Word Choice	
Glittering generality Makes a generalization that includes a word or phrase with positive connotations, such as *freedom* and *honor*, to promote a product or idea.	Improve your children's future: plant a tree on World Tree Day.

PRACTICE AND APPLY

Identify the persuasive techniques used in the model.

The Real Scoop

On my last trip to the Splendid Dan's Ice Cream Shoppe to get a Swirling Fantasia Double Dip Delight, I was thrilled to find yet another reason that makes buying dessert at Dan's feel so splendid. During the next 30 days at the downtown location, a whopping 40 percent of Dan's proceeds will go toward helping the homeless in our city. Forty percent! No wonder so many local celebrities, like news anchor Tandy Marquez and Mayor Donald Townsend, have been spotted at Dan's. They know that with each purchase, they are also providing food, clothing, and shelter for those in need. If you join them, you'll have not only the most amazing ice cream on the planet, but also the added joy of providing life's basic necessities to the less fortunate. It's the least we can do to better our city, so stop by Splendid Dan's—he's got the "real scoop."

5.3 ANALYZING LOGIC AND REASONING

When you evaluate an argument, you need to look closely at the writer's logic and reasoning. In doing this, it is helpful to identify the type of reasoning the writer is using.

The Inductive Mode of Reasoning

When a writer leads from specific evidence to a general principle or generalization, that writer is using **inductive reasoning.** Here is an example of inductive reasoning.

SPECIFIC FACTS

Fact 1 Harriet Beecher Stowe's *Uncle Tom's Cabin* helped alert Americans to the horrors of slavery.

Fact 2 Rachel Carson's *Silent Spring* helped make the public aware of the dangers of overuse of pesticides.

Fact 3 Betty Friedan's *The Feminine Mystique* prompted women to seek equal rights.

GENERALIZATION

Literature can sometimes help to shape public opinion.

Strategies for Determining the Soundness of Inductive Arguments

Ask yourself the following questions to evaluate an inductive argument:

- **Is the evidence valid and sufficient support for the conclusion?** Inaccurate facts lead to inaccurate conclusions. Make sure all facts are accurate.
- **Does the conclusion follow logically from the evidence?** Make sure the writer has used sound reasons—those that can be proved—as the basis for the conclusion and has avoided logical fallacies, such as circular logic and oversimplification.
- **Is the evidence drawn from a large enough sample?** The three facts listed in the example are enough to support the claim. By qualifying the generalization with words such as *sometimes, some,* or *many,* the writer indicates the generalization is limited to a specific group.

The Deductive Mode of Reasoning

When a writer arrives at a conclusion by applying a general principle to a specific situation, the writer is using **deductive reasoning.** Here's an example.

People have the right to revolt when oppressed. — General principle or premise

The American colonies are oppressed by British rule. — Specific situation

The American colonies are justified in fighting for freedom from British rule. — Specific conclusion

Strategies for Determining the Soundness of Deductive Arguments

Ask yourself the following questions to evaluate a deductive argument:

- **Is the general principle stated, or is it implied?** Note that writers often use deductive reasoning in an argument without stating the general principle. They assume readers will understand the principle. You may want to identify the general principle for yourself.
- **Is the general principle sound?** Don't assume the general principle is sound. Determine whether it is proven.
- **Is the conclusion valid?** To be valid, a conclusion in a deductive argument must follow logically from the general principle and the specific situation.

The following chart shows two conclusions drawn from the same general principle.

General Principle: All government offices were closed last Monday.	
Accurate Deduction	**Inaccurate Deduction**
West Post Office is a government office; therefore, West Post Office was closed last Monday.	Soon-Lin's Spa was closed last Monday; therefore, Soon-Lin's Spa is a government office.

The conclusion that Soon-Lin's Spa is a government office does not make logical sense because other factors determine whether or not it is a government office.

PRACTICE AND APPLY

Identify the mode of reasoning used in the following:

> Detailed research shows that using a cell phone while driving is a key cause of traffic accidents. Many states have already passed laws making "hands free" devices mandatory for cell phone users while driving. However, ear pieces or speaker phones provide very few true safety benefits. The problem is not the way in which a driver is distracted, but the distraction itself. Looking up a phone number, dialing, and concentrating on the conversation can all take a driver's focus, and eyes, off the road.
>
> Betsie Edens, a 19-year-old college student, says she uses her cell phone to get in touch with family, old friends, and fellow college students while making the three-hour drive from her parent's house to Denton State University. "I talk on the phone or send text messages at least two and a half of the three hours it takes to get there," she says.
>
> Betsie is one of millions of teenagers worldwide who do more talking on a cell phone than safe driving. It is time these unsafe drivers focus more on the road and less on their friends' gossip. For the sake of everybody's safety, cell phones must be turned off while on the road.

Identifying Faulty Reasoning

Sometimes an argument at first appears to make sense but isn't valid because it is based on a fallacy. A **logical fallacy** is an error in logic. Learn to recognize these common fallacies.

TYPE OF FALLACY	DEFINITION	EXAMPLE
Circular logic	Supporting a statement by simply repeating it in different words	Sport utility vehicles are popular **because more people buy them than any other category of new cars.**
Either/or fallacy	A statement that suggests that there are only two choices available in a situation that really offers more than two options	**Either** we raise the legal driving age **or** accidents caused by teenage drivers will continue to happen.
Oversimplification	An explanation of a complex situation or problem as if it were much more simple than it is	If we would only be more tolerant of people's differences, there would be **no more wars.**
Overgeneralization	A generalization that is too broad. You can often recognize overgeneralizations by the use of words such as *all, everyone, every time, anything, no one,* and *none.*	**Every time** I want to do something my way, my parents say no.
Stereotyping	A dangerous type of overgeneralization. Stereotypes are broad statements about people on the basis of their gender, ethnicity, race, or political, social, professional, or religious group.	**People who work for large corporations** are followers, not leaders.
Attacking the person or name-calling	An attempt to discredit an idea by attacking the person or group associated with it. Candidates often engage in name-calling during political campaigns.	The governor wants to eliminate candy machines in school cafeterias, but **he doesn't know what he's talking about.**
Evading the issue	Refuting an objection with arguments and evidence that do not address its central point	I know I wasn't supposed to use the car last night, **but I did fill up the tank and check the tire pressure.**
Non sequitur	A conclusion that does not follow logically from the "proof" offered to support it. A non sequitur is sometimes used to win an argument by diverting the reader's attention to proof that can't be challenged.	Mr. Crandall is my guidance counselor. **I will definitely get accepted to a private college.**
False cause	The mistake of assuming that because one event occurred after another event in time, the first event caused the second one to occur	The cheerleading squad did the Super Slam Dance, **and because of that, Donny slam-dunked the basketball, and we won the game.**
False analogy	A comparison that doesn't hold up because of a critical difference between the two subjects	Jenny didn't do well in Spanish, **so she'll probably fail German as well.**
Hasty generalization	A conclusion drawn from too little evidence or from evidence that is biased	Two jet planes crashed this year. **Air travel is extremely unsafe.**

PRACTICE AND APPLY

Look for examples of logical fallacies in the following argument. Identify each one and explain why you identified it as such.

Elephants should be banned from circuses. Leaders of circus companies claim that healthy living environments are provided for the animals, but they, like most business owners, are liars. Sharp bullhooks are used for training, and the elephants are beaten severely everyday. Abuse makes animals more aggressive, everyone knows that. In the last 15 years, captive elephants have killed 65 people and injured 130, so it is clear the elephants are abused by their trainers. Legislation to stop this cruelty should be passed immediately!

5.4 EVALUATING PERSUASIVE TEXTS

Learning how to evaluate persuasive texts and identify bias will help you become more selective when doing research and also help you improve your own reasoning and arguing skills. **Bias** is an inclination for or against a particular opinion or viewpoint. A writer may reveal a strongly positive or negative opinion on an issue by presenting only one way of looking at it or by heavily weighting the evidence on one side of the argument. Additionally, the presence of either of the following is often a sign of bias:

Loaded language consists of words with strongly positive or negative connotations that are intended to influence a reader's attitude.

EXAMPLE: *The superior All-Star Road Warrior offers unparalleled excellence in all-wheel-drive capability and can outperform any car on the road.* (*Superior, unparalleled, excellence,* and *outperform* have positive connotations.)

Propaganda is any form of communication that is so distorted that it conveys false or misleading information. Many logical fallacies—such as name-calling, the either/or fallacy, and false causes—are often used in propaganda. The following example shows an oversimplification. The writer uses one fact to support a particular point of view but does not reveal another fact that does not support that viewpoint.

EXAMPLE: *Since the new administration took office, unemployment rates have been cut in half.* (The writer does not include information about legislation, passed by the previous administration, that created thousands of jobs.)

*For more information, see **Identifying Faulty Reasoning,** page R22.*

Strategies for Evaluating Evidence

It is important to have a set of standards by which you can evaluate persuasive texts. Use the questions below to help you critically assess facts and opinions that are presented as evidence.

- **Are the facts presented verifiable?** Facts can be proved by eyewitness accounts, authoritative sources such as encyclopedias and almanacs, experts, or research.
- **Are the opinions presented credible?** Any opinions offered should be supported by facts, research, eyewitness accounts, or the opinions of experts on the topic.
- **Is the evidence thorough?** Thorough evidence leaves no reasonable questions unanswered. If a choice is offered, background for making the choice should be provided. If taking a side is called for, all sides of the issue should be presented.
- **Is the evidence biased?** Be alert to evidence that contains loaded language or other signs of bias.
- **Is the evidence authoritative?** The people, groups, or organizations that provided the evidence should have credentials that verify their credibility.
- **Is it important that the evidence be current?** Where timeliness is crucial, as in the areas of medicine and technology, the evidence should reflect the latest developments in the areas.

PRACTICE AND APPLY

Read the argument below. Identify the facts, opinions, and elements of bias.

> In our city neighborhood, unnecessary speed bumps are being built on residential streets. Cars park bumper to bumper along both sides of the street, day and night. There is no place to pull over, causing cars to stop in the middle of the street to pick up and drop off passengers. My point is that it is impossible to drive fast on these streets anyway! Why do no-good politicians spend a lot of taxpayer money on a ridiculous irritation for drivers? They must figure wrongly that either they build speed bumps, or some little kid will get killed. That's never happened and it never will.

Strategies for Evaluating an Argument

Make sure that all or most of the following statements are true:

- The argument presents a claim or thesis.
- The claim is connected to its support by a general principle that most readers would readily agree with. Valid general principle: *It is the job of a corporation to provide adequate health benefits to full-time employees.* Invalid general principle: *It is the job of a corporation to ensure its employees are healthy and physically fit.*
- The reasons make sense.
- The reasons are presented in a logical and effective order.
- The claim and all reasons are adequately supported by sound evidence.
- The evidence is adequate, accurate, and appropriate.
- The logic is sound. There are no instances of logical fallacies.
- The argument adequately anticipates reader concerns and addresses them with counterarguments.

PRACTICE AND APPLY

Use the preceding criteria to evaluate the strength of the following editorial:

> This town needs an ice skating rink. Everybody knows that ice skating is the only real way to learn balance and coordination, while also exercising. It is, after all, an Olympic event. That is why I believe it is the responsibility of the town council to put aside funding for a year-round ice skating rink.
>
> Our town has always believed that our children's future relies on good development. For intellectual stimulation, the council has provided the public library and the Nature Museum. For creativity, the council has funded the Community Art Center, where kids can learn to make pottery, paint, dance, and sing. But when it comes to a place where youth can go to develop physical skills of balance, rhythm, and strength, we have absolutely nothing.
>
> We also need a rink because ice skating is fun! The town council members are themselves boring individuals and don't think kids should have fun. As one member put it, "There are many places in this town built especially with youth in mind. Ice skating is not a top priority on our list of community needs this year." They obviously feel this way because our football team came in fifth in the conference last year.
>
> But the biggest reason we need an ice skating rink is so that kids can have a place to ice skate. And let's not forget, adults like ice skating, too. Most of the people who make it to the Olympics are over 18.
>
> Either the town council will help our children develop by putting up the rink, or they prove themselves stingy politicians who do not have the town's best interest at heart.

6 Adjusting Reading Rate to Purpose

You may need to change the way you read certain texts in order to understand what you read. To properly adjust the way you read, you need to be aware of what you want to get out of the text you are reading. Once you know your purpose for reading, you can adjust the speed at which you read in response to your purpose and the difficulty of the material.

Determine Your Purpose for Reading

You read different types of materials for different purposes. You may read a novel for enjoyment. You may read a textbook unit to learn a new concept or to master the content for a test. When you read for enjoyment, you naturally read at a pace that is comfortable for you. When you read for information, you need to read material more slowly and thoroughly. When you are being tested on material, you may think you have to read fast, especially if the test is being timed. However, you can actually increase your understanding of the material if you slow down.

Determine Your Reading Rate

The rate at which you read most comfortably is called your **independent reading level.** It is the rate that you use to read materials that you enjoy. To learn to adjust your reading rate to read materials for other purposes, you need to be aware of your independent reading level. You can figure out your reading level by following these steps:

1. Select a passage from a book or story you enjoy.
2. Have a friend or classmate time you as you begin reading the passage silently.
3. Read at the rate that is most comfortable for you.
4. Stop when your friend or classmate tells you one minute has passed.
5. Determine the number of words you read in that minute and write down the number.
6. Repeat the process at least two more times, using different passages.
7. Add the numbers and divide the sum by the number of times your friend timed you. The number you end up with is the average number of words you read per minute—your independent reading rate.

Reading Techniques for Informational Material

Use the following techniques to adapt your reading for informational texts, to prepare for tests, and to better understand what you read:

- **Skimming** is reading quickly to get the general idea of a text. To skim, read only the title, headings, graphic aids, and highlighted words of the text, as well as the first sentence of each paragraph. In addition, read any introduction, conclusion, or summary. Skimming can be especially useful when taking a test. Before reading a passage, you can skim questions that follow it in order to find out what is expected and to better focus on the important ideas in the text.

  When researching a topic, skimming can help you determine whether a source has information that is pertinent to your topic.
- **Scanning** is reading quickly to find a specific piece of information, such as a fact or a definition. When you scan, your eyes sweep across a page, looking for key words that may lead you to the information you want. Use scanning to review for tests and to find answers to questions.
- **Changing pace** is speeding up or slowing down the rate at which you read parts of a particular text. When you come across familiar concepts, you might be able to speed up without misunderstanding them. When you encounter unfamiliar concepts or material presented in an unpredictable way, however, you may need to slow down to process and absorb the information better.

WATCH OUT! Reading too slowly can diminish your ability to comprehend what you read. Make sure you aren't just reading one word at a time.

PRACTICE AND APPLY

Find an article in a magazine or textbook. Skim the article. Then answer the following questions:

1. What did you notice about the organization of the article?
2. What is the main idea of the article?

Writing is a process, a journey of discovery in which you can explore your thoughts, experiment with ideas, and search for connections. Through writing, you can explore and record your thoughts, feelings, and ideas for yourself alone, or you can communicate them to an audience.

Included in this handbook:
W 1a–e, W 2a–e, W 3a–e, W 4–6

1 The Writing Process

The writing process consists of the following stages: prewriting, drafting, revising and editing, proofreading, and publishing. These are not stages that you must complete in a set order. Rather, you may return to an earlier stage at any time to improve your writing.

1.1 PREWRITING

In the prewriting stage, you explore what you want to write about, what your purpose for writing is, whom you are writing for, and what form you will use to express your ideas. Ask yourself the following questions to get started.

Topic	• Is my topic assigned, or can I choose it? • What am I interested in writing about?
Purpose	• Am I writing to entertain, to inform, or to persuade—or some combination of these? • What effect do I want to have on my readers?
Audience	• Who is the audience? • What might the audience members already know about my topic? • What about the topic might interest them?
Format	• Which format will work best: essay, poem, speech, short story, article, or research paper?

Find Ideas for Writing

Here are some methods for generating topics:

- Browse through magazines, newspapers, and Web sites.
- Start a file of articles to save for future reference.
- With a group, brainstorm as many ideas as you can. Compile your ideas into a list.
- Interview an expert on a particular topic.
- Write down anything that comes into your head.
- Use a cluster map to explore subordinate ideas that relate to a general topic.

Organize Ideas

Once you've chosen a topic, you will need to compile and organize your ideas. If you are writing a description, you may need to gather sensory details. Or you may need to record information from different sources for an essay or a research paper. To record notes from sources you read or view, use any or all of these methods:

- **Summarize:** Briefly retell the main ideas of a piece of writing in your own words.
- **Paraphrase:** Restate all or almost all of the information in your own words.
- **Quote:** Record the author's exact words.

Depending on what form your writing takes, you may also need to arrange your ideas in a certain pattern.

*For more information, see the **Writing Handbook**, pages R32–R39.*

1.2 DRAFTING

In the drafting stage, you put your ideas on paper and allow them to develop and change as you write. You don't need to worry about correct grammar and spelling at this stage. There are two ways that you can write a draft:

Discovery drafting is a good approach when you are not quite sure what you think about your subject. You just start writing and let your feelings and ideas lead you in developing the topic.

Planned drafting may work better if you know that your ideas have to be arranged in a certain way, as in a research paper. Try making a writing plan or an informal outline before you begin drafting.

1.3 REVISING AND EDITING

The revising and editing stage allows you to polish your draft and make changes in its content, organization, and style. Use the questions that follow to assess problems and determine what changes would improve your work.

- Does my writing have a **main idea** or central focus? Is my controlling idea clear?
- Have I used **precise** nouns, verbs, and modifiers?

- Have I incorporated **adequate detail** and **evidence?** Where might I include a telling detail, a revealing statistic, or a vivid example?
- Is my writing **unified?** Do all ideas and supporting details pertain to my main idea or advance my thesis?
- Is my writing clear and **coherent?** Is the flow of sentences and paragraphs smooth and logical?
- Have I used a consistent **point of view?**
- Do I need to add **transitional words, phrases,** or **sentences** to clarify relationships among ideas?
- Have I used a **variety of sentence types?** Are they well constructed? What sentences might I combine to improve the rhythm of my writing?
- Have I used a **tone** appropriate for my audience and purpose?

1.4 PROOFREADING

When you are satisfied with your revision, proofread your paper for mistakes in grammar, usage, and mechanics. You may want to do this several times, looking for a different type of mistake each time. Use the following questions to help you correct errors:

- Have I corrected any errors in **subject-verb agreement** and **pronoun-antecedent agreement?**
- Have I double-checked for errors in **confusing word pairs,** such as *it's/its, than/then,* and *too/to?*
- Have I corrected any **run-on sentences** and **sentence fragments?**
- Have I followed rules for **correct capitalization?**
- Have I used **punctuation marks** correctly?
- Have I checked the **spellings of all unfamiliar words** in the dictionary?

TIP If possible, don't begin proofreading just after you've finished writing. Put your work away for at least a few hours. When you return to it, it will be easier for you to identify and correct mistakes.

*For more information, see the **Grammar Handbook** and the **Vocabulary and Spelling Handbook,** pages R50–R79.*

Use the proofreading symbols in the chart to mark changes on your draft.

Proofreading Symbols	
∧ Add letters or words.	/ Make a capital letter lowercase.
⊙ Add a period.	¶ Begin a new paragraph.
≡ Capitalize a letter.	Delete letters or words.
⊂ Close up space.	∿ Switch the positions of letters or words.
∧ Add a comma.	

1.5 PUBLISHING AND REFLECTING

Always consider sharing your finished writing with a wider audience. Reflecting on your writing is another good way to finish a project.

Publishing Ideas

- Post your writing on a Weblog.
- Create a multimedia presentation and share it with classmates.
- Publish your writing in a school newspaper, local newspaper, or literary magazine.
- Present your work orally in a report, speech, reading, or dramatic performance.

Reflecting on Your Writing

Think about your writing process and whether you would like to add what you have written to your writing portfolio. You might attach a note in which you answer questions like these:

- Which parts of the process did I find easiest? Which parts were more difficult?
- What was the biggest problem I faced during the writing process? How did I solve the problem?
- What changes have occurred in my writing style?
- Have I noticed any features in the writing of published authors or my peers that I can apply to my own work?

Writing Online
THINK central
Go to thinkcentral.com.
KEYWORD: HML11N-R27

1.6 PEER RESPONSE

Peer response consists of the suggestions and comments you make about the writing of your peers and also the comments and suggestions they make about your writing. You can ask a peer reader for help at any time in the writing process.

Using Peer Response as a Writer

- Indicate whether you are more interested in feedback about your ideas or about your presentation of them.
- Ask open-ended questions that will help you get specific information about your writing. Avoid questions that require yes-or-no answers.
- Encourage your readers to be honest.

Being a Peer Reader

- Respect the writer's feelings.
- Offer positive reactions first.
- Make sure you understand what kind of feedback the writer is looking for, and then respond accordingly.

For more information on the writing process, see the ***Introductory Unit,*** *pages 14–17.*

2 Building Blocks of Good Writing

Whatever your purpose in writing, you need to capture your reader's interest and organize your thoughts clearly.

2.1 INTRODUCTIONS

An introduction should capture your reader's attention and present a controlling idea.

Kinds of Introductions

There are a number of ways to begin an introduction. The one you choose depends on who the audience is and on your purpose for writing.

Make a Surprising Statement Beginning with a startling statement or an interesting fact can arouse your reader's curiosity about a subject, as in the following model.

MODEL

Although she wrote nearly 1,800 poems, Emily Dickinson probably did not want to publish any of them. Most of her poems were first published almost 100 years after they were written.

Provide a Description A vivid description sets a mood and brings a scene to life for your reader. In the following model, details about a horse's actions set the tone for an essay about horse training.

MODEL

Dust flew as the horse stomped the ground. The puffs of moisture blowing from his nostrils and the laid-back ears let the spectators know the stomping was not some clever performance. As the trainer approached cautiously, she could see the wild look in the horse's eyes.

Pose a Question Beginning with a question can make your reader want to find the answer. The model below asks questions about a respected writer.

MODEL

Zora Neale Hurston was one of the most successful writers of the Harlem Renaissance period. She wrote plays, novels, and essays that were enthusiastically received. How did it happen that such a talented and popular author died in poverty?

Relate an Anecdote Beginning with an anecdote, or brief story, can hook your reader and help you make a point in a dramatic way. The following anecdote introduces an interview with a retired school teacher.

MODEL

"Down in the valley
Where the green grass grows. . . ."

The words of the chanting children on the playground brought tears to Clara Jones's eyes. Though she could barely see them, she knew exactly how the old jump-rope game went.

I began softly to ask her about her 45 years of teaching at Pleasant Hills Elementary School.

Use a Quotation A witty quotation can hook your reader's attention and help you make an important point. You can find quotes in printed books of quotations or online.

MODEL

"Genius without education is like silver in the mine" is a quote by Benjamin Franklin, who probably would have advocated higher education for everyone. However, should everyone go to college?

Address the Reader Speaking directly to your reader establishes a friendly, informal tone and involves the reader in your topic.

MODEL

Do you know how many trees will be cut down for the new shopping mall to be built? Do you know how many families will have to give up their homes so that some shoppers can have yet another department store that sells the same things as five others in our area?

Begin with a Controlling Idea A controlling idea, or thesis statement, expressing a main idea may be woven into both the beginning and the end of a piece of nonfiction writing. The following is a controlling idea that introduces a literary analysis.

MODEL

In "The Death of the Hired Man," Robert Frost uses the hushed conversation of a husband and wife to explore the meaning of a lonely person's life. The whole poem seems to take place in whispers, though the message is strong.

TIP To write a strong introduction, you may want to try more than one of the methods and then decide which is the most effective for your purpose and audience.

2.2 PARAGRAPHS

A paragraph is made up of sentences that work together to develop an idea or accomplish a purpose. Whether or not it contains a topic sentence stating the main idea, a good paragraph must have unity and coherence.

Unity

A paragraph has unity when all the sentences support and develop one stated or implied idea. Use the following techniques to create unity in your paragraphs:

Write a Topic Sentence A topic sentence states the main idea of the paragraph; all other sentences in the paragraph provide supporting details. A topic sentence is often the first sentence in a paragraph. However, it may also appear later in a paragraph or at the end, to summarize or reinforce the main idea, as shown in the model that follows.

MODEL

Cats purr when they are being stroked by humans. Cats purr when they cuddle up with other cats. Many cats purr when they are in the veterinarian's office. Some cats purr when they are frightened. Since cats seem to purr in situations of both joy and stress, the cause of purring is still a mystery to humans.

Relate All Sentences to an Implied Main Idea A paragraph can be unified without a topic sentence as long as every sentence supports an implied, or unstated, main idea. In the example, all the sentences work together to create a unified impression of a frustrated writer trying to begin writing.

MODEL

He picked up his pencil at 9:27 and set it down purposefully on the writing pad. A minute or so passed. Well, maybe he should sharpen the pencil. That took 30 seconds—now 9:29. He set his pencil down again. He readjusted his chair. He raked his left hand through his thick hair. Was there a spot of thinning hair? He got up to go look in the mirror. No, not yet. At 9:31 he sat down again and took up the pencil. This time he moved the pad a little to the right.

Coherence

A paragraph is coherent when all its sentences are related to one another and each flows logically to the next. The following techniques will help you achieve coherence in paragraphs:

- Present your ideas in the most logical order.
- Use pronouns, synonyms, and repeated words to connect ideas.
- Use transitional devices to show relationships among ideas.

In the model shown here, the writer used some of these techniques to create a unified paragraph.

MODEL

After you figure out how big to make the model ship for your film of a shipwreck, you will need to take some other factors into account as well. You will have to figure out how much to stir the water and what speed to set the film. Perhaps even more important is to be sure no real objects at full size can be seen by the camera. In other words, don't let your towels and soap dish sneak into the picture and be sure the cat is locked out of the bathroom.

2.3 TRANSITIONS

Transitions are words and phrases that show connections among details. Clear transitions help show how your ideas relate to one another.

Kinds of Transitions

The types of transitions you choose depend on the ideas you want to convey.

Time or Sequence Some transitions help to clarify the sequence of events over time. When you are telling a story or describing a process, you can connect ideas with such transitional words as *first, second, always, then, next, later, soon, before, finally, after, earlier, afterward,* and *tomorrow.*

MODEL

Before a blood donation can be used, it must be processed carefully. First, a sample is tested for infectious diseases and identified by blood type. Next, preservatives are added. Finally, a blood cell separator breaks up the blood into its parts, such as red blood cells, platelets, and plasma.

Spatial Relationships Transitional words and phrases such as *in front, behind, next to, along, nearest, lowest, above, below, underneath, on the left,* and *in the middle* can help your reader visualize a scene.

MODEL

Two rows of corn grew along the south side of the garden. In front of them stood the tomatoes climbing on wire enclosures and a couple of okra plants. In the middle rows were medium-height plants—bush beans, peas, potatoes, and a few peppers. Low-growing plants filled the front of the garden—radishes on the right, then rows of lettuce, spinach, and onions. On the left, squash and cucumber vines spread over the ground.

Degree of Importance Transitional words and phrases such as *mainly, strongest, weakest, first, second, most important, least important, worst,* and *best* may be used to rank ideas or to show degrees of importance.

MODEL

There are several reasons to eat plenty of fresh fruits and vegetables. The most important reason is that they help to fortify your immune system!

Compare and Contrast Words and phrases such as *similarly, likewise, also, like, as, neither . . . nor,* and *either . . . or* show similarity between details. *However, by contrast, yet, but, unlike, instead, whereas,* and *while* show difference. Note the use of both types of transitions in the model.

MODEL

Although I like to shop in the big stores in the mall, when I'm really serious about buying something I go to a small store. Like big stores, many small stores carry a good selection of merchandise. Whereas the big stores may have lower prices, the small stores have more personal service and clerks who know about the products they sell.

TIP Both *but* and *however* can be used to join two independent clauses. When *but* is used as a coordinating conjunction, it is preceded by a comma. When *however* is used as a conjunctive adverb, it is preceded by a semicolon and followed by a comma.

Cause and Effect When you are writing about a cause-effect relationship, use transitional words and phrases such as *since, because, thus, therefore, so, due to, for this reason,* and *as a result* to help clarify that relationship and make your writing coherent.

MODEL

Due to the unusual amount of rain this summer, the grass is still lush and green in August.

2.4 CONCLUSIONS

A conclusion should leave readers with a strong final impression.

Kinds of Conclusions

Good conclusions sum up ideas in a variety of ways. Here are some techniques you might try:

Restate Your Controlling Idea A good way to conclude an essay is by restating your controlling idea, or thesis, in different words. The following conclusion restates the controlling idea introduced on page R29.

MODEL

In Robert Frost's "The Death of the Hired Man," a sad human life unfolds in the whispered conversations between Mary and Warren. Quiet compassion is also evident and is the point of the poem.

Ask a Question Try asking a question that sums up what you have said and gives your reader something new to think about. The following question concludes an appeal for preventing unwanted cats and dogs.

MODEL

Considering how many kittens, puppies, cats, and dogs are put to sleep or die on the streets, don't you think it makes sense that all household pets be spayed or neutered?

Make a Recommendation When you are persuading your audience to take a position on an issue, you can conclude by recommending a specific course of action.

MODEL

Help protect animals from careless humans. Volunteer at an animal shelter. Distribute literature around your neighborhood.

Make a Prediction Readers are concerned about matters that may affect them and therefore are moved by a conclusion that predicts the future.

MODEL

If the city council approves the new shopping mall, we will lose the woodlands that help make our neighborhood quiet and attractive. In their place, we will have traffic congestion, exhaust fumes, bright lights long into the night, and a source of danger to our children.

Summarize Your Information Summarizing reinforces your main idea, leaving a strong, lasting impression. The model concludes with a statement that summarizes a book review.

MODEL

Patricia McKissack's biography gives a strong picture of W. E. B. Du Bois, who was a link between Frederick Douglass, whom he knew early in life, and Martin Luther King Jr., whom he knew late in life.

2.5 ELABORATION

Elaboration is the process of developing an idea by providing specific supporting details that are relevant and appropriate to the purpose and form of your writing. In some cases, you may want to present support with a visual aid.

Facts and Statistics A fact is a statement that can be verified, and a statistic is a fact expressed as a number. Make sure the facts and statistics you supply are from reliable, up-to-date sources, and support your statements, as in the following model.

MODEL

A student who has an eye for beautiful gardens might consider a career in landscape architecture. The American Society of Landscape Architects has over 12,000 members, up 20 percent in the last five years. The average income of landscape architects is $74,644, which is higher than that of building architects.

Sensory Details Details that show how something looks, sounds, tastes, smells, or feels can enliven a description, making readers feel they are actually experiencing what you are describing.

MODEL

Sliding along on her cross-country skis, Sasha felt she was truly on top of the world. The action of the snow, skis, and sturdy boots massaged her feet. She opened her mouth to taste the sprinkles of snow. The view was a rainbow of color as snowflakes made tiny speckled prisms on her goggles.

Incidents From our earliest years, we are interested in "stories." One way to illustrate a point is to relate an incident or tell a story, as shown in the example.

MODEL

The East India Company had a monopoly on supplying tea to the American Colonies. Tea shipments took on the symbolism of the increasing tyranny of the English government. On December 16, 1773, a group of about 150 colonists put burnt cork on their faces, dressed as Mohawk warriors, boarded the tea-carrying ships, and proceeded to dump the entire tea cargoes into Boston Harbor.

Examples An example can help make an abstract idea concrete or can serve to clarify a complex point.

MODEL

Many of the stars and galaxies we see at night are showing us light from ancient times. Who knows where they really are today? For example, the light from the galaxy Andromeda has taken over 2 million years to get here.

Quotations Choose quotations that clearly support your points, and be sure that you copy each quotation word for word. Remember always to credit the source.

MODEL

Do you know anyone who says "you all" to mean "the group of you"? "Have you all seen this movie?" McCrum, Cran, and MacNeil explain in *The Story of English* that this famous Southern expression comes from a Scots-Irish translation of the plural for *you.* They say the expression "is typical both of Ulster and of the (largely southern) states of America." Did you all know that?

3 Writing Description

Descriptive writing allows you to paint word pictures about anything, from events of global importance to the most personal feelings. It is an essential part of almost every piece of writing.

RUBRIC: Standards for Writing

Successful descriptive writing should

- have a clear focus and sense of purpose
- use sensory details and precise words to create a vivid image, establish a mood, or express emotion
- present details in a logical order

3.1 KEY TECHNIQUES

Consider Your Goals What do you want to accomplish with your description? Do you want to show why something is important to you? Do you want to make a person or scene more memorable? Do you want to explain an event?

Identify Your Audience Who will read your description? How familiar are they with your subject? What background information will they need? Which details will they find most interesting?

Think Figuratively What figures of speech might help make your description vivid and interesting? What simile or metaphor comes to mind? What imaginative comparisons can you make? What living thing does an inanimate object remind you of?

Gather Sensory Details Which sights, smells, tastes, sounds, and textures make your subject come alive? Which details stick in your mind when you observe or recall your subject? Which senses does it most strongly affect?

You might want to use a chart like the one shown here to collect sensory details about your subject.

Sights	Sounds	Textures	Smells	Tastes

Create a Mood What feelings do you want to evoke in your readers? Do you want to soothe them with comforting images? Do you want to build tension with ominous details? Do you want to evoke sadness or joy?

3.2 OPTIONS FOR ORGANIZATION

Option 1: Spatial Order Choose one of these options to show the spatial order of elements in a scene you are describing.

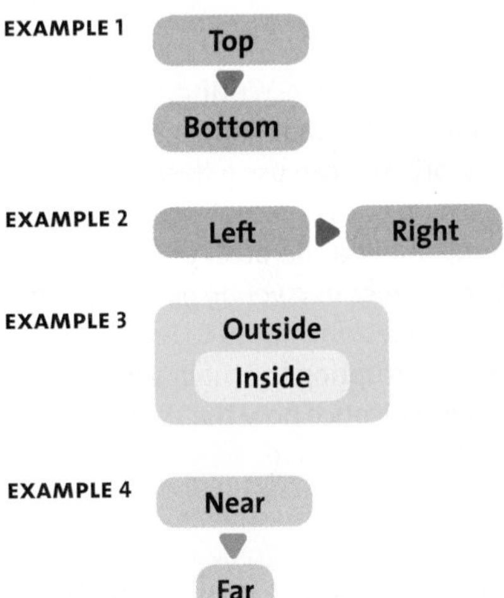

MODEL

Peering through the goggles, the diver surveyed the reef. To the left, a school of silvery fish swam near the surface. Below them, the reef was a rainbow of color. In the middle of the scene, bright, tiny fish nosed along the reef. Below them on the sand, a crab looked for food. Further right, a cluster of fan coral waved its purple fronds in the gentle current. Beyond it lay the barnacle-encrusted shape of a ship's propeller.

Option 2: Order of Impression Order of impression is the order in which you notice details.

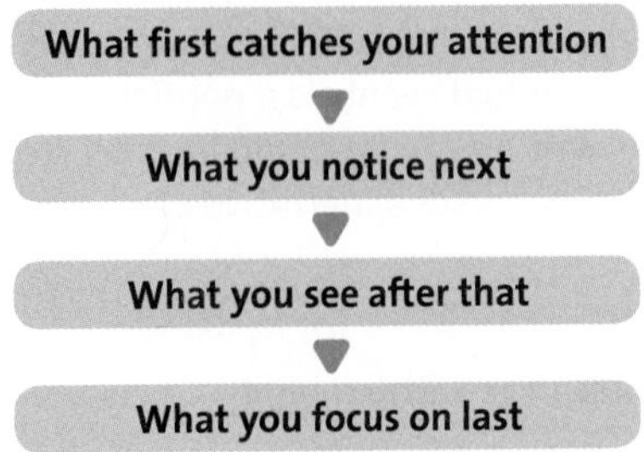

MODEL

Rain pelted against the windshield. Robbie narrowed his eyes to try to see the road in the brief clearing spasms between swipes of wiper blades. He could barely see that there was a little clearing far off in the horizon. Dark clouds made distinct shapes. Suddenly he noticed that against a small patch of lighter color was a swirling black cloud beginning to take the shape of a funnel.

TIP Use transitions that help readers understand the order of the impressions you are describing. Some useful transitions are *after, next, during, first, before, finally,* and *then.*

Option 3: Order of Importance You can use order of importance as the organizing structure for a description.

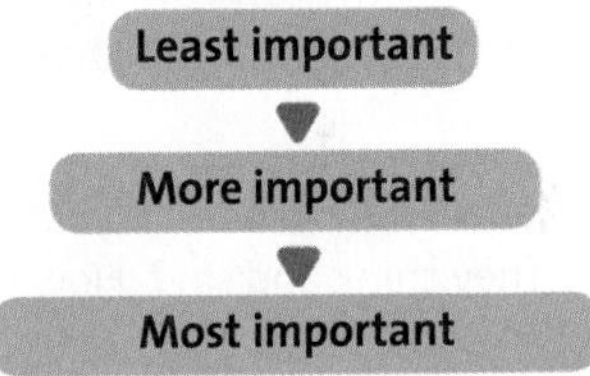

MODEL

I checked my backpack for the comforting essentials. Book? Yes. Journal and pencil? Yes. Water bottle? Yes. Tissues? Yes. Then I checked for the required essentials. Passport? Yes. Airline ticket? Yes. Map? Yes. Last of all, I checked the most important possession for this trip—a light heart and a sense of adventure. I was beginning my first real vacation in two years!

For more information, see ***Transitions**, page R30.*

4 Writing Narratives

Narrative writing tells a story. If you write a story from your imagination, it is a fictional narrative. A true story about actual events is a nonfictional narrative. Narrative writing can be found in short stories, novels, news articles, personal narratives, and biographies.

RUBRIC: Standards for Writing

A successful narrative should

- hook the reader's attention with a strong introduction
- include descriptive details and dialogue to develop the characters, setting, and plot
- have a clear beginning, middle, and end
- have a logical organization, with clues and transitions that help the reader understand the order of events
- maintain a consistent tone and point of view
- use language that is appropriate to the audience
- demonstrate the significance of events or ideas

4.1 KEY TECHNIQUES

Identify the Main Events What are the most important events in your narrative? Is each event needed to tell the story?

Describe the Setting When do the events occur? Where do they take place? How can you use setting to create mood and to set the stage for the characters and their actions?

Depict Characters Vividly What do your characters look like? What do they think and say? How do they act? What details can show what they are like?

TIP Dialogue is an effective means of developing characters in a narrative. As you write dialogue, choose words that express your characters' personalities and that show how the characters feel about one another and about the events in the plot.

4.2 OPTIONS FOR ORGANIZATION

Option 1: Chronological Order One way to organize a piece of narrative writing is to arrange the events in chronological order, as shown in the following example.

EXAMPLE

A contemporary Navajo boy in New Mexico is nearing adulthood. His father wants him to learn the lore of his ancestors. His mother wants him to prepare for school instead.

Introduction *Characters and setting*

The boy wants to please both his parents. He goes into the mountains to seek wisdom.

Event 1

Animals visit the boy, representing both the old ways and the new.

Event 2

The boy finds that he does not have to disappoint either parent. He finds that he must work hardest on learning what he himself is best suited for.

End *Perhaps showing the significance of the events*

Option 2: Flashback In narrative writing, it is also possible to introduce events that happened before the beginning of the story. You can use a flashback to show how past events led up to the present situation or to provide background about a character or event. Use clue words such as *last summer, as a young girl, the previous school year,* and *his earliest memories* to let your reader know that you are interrupting the main action to describe earlier events. Notice how the flashback interrupts the action in the model.

MODEL

Mr. Robbins picked up the small, white ball that had just smashed his kitchen window and felt angry that the boys playing across the street could be so careless. Then he remembered a summer day over 50 years ago, when he himself had hit a home run – right into the Nelsons' living room. How frightened he had been when Mrs. Nelson walked out of her front door, holding the baseball! But she had simply laughed as she gave it back to him and said, "Boys will be boys." Mr. Robbins shook his head at the memory and looked back at his broken pane of glass.

Option 3: Focus on Conflict When a fictional narrative focuses on a central conflict, the story's plot may be organized as shown in the following example.

EXAMPLE

The day after their high school graduation, Angela and her twin brother, Alex, decided to take their canoe out on the river that ran past their family home. They had done it many times since childhood, and the river was familiar to both of them.

Describe main characters and setting.

For two hours they traversed the river under a calm, clear sky, but by noon, rather ominous clouds had rolled in. Meanwhile, they had floated far downstream, and had taken a winding inlet off the river. Soon, they heard thunder in the distance, and Angela looked off to the southwest where she had noticed lightning. She alerted Alex and insisted they turn back immediately. Alex did not seem concerned, however, and refused to go back.

Present conflict.

As the storm began to get nearer, Angela again insisted they turn around, but Alex, who was steering the boat, said the storm was too far away to hurt them. As the rain began to fall on them, Angela began to plead with her brother that they either pull over to the shore or turn back immediately. To prove her point, she stopped paddling.

Relate events that make conflict complex and cause characters to change.

Alex ignored his sister and continued to paddle himself and steer them further downstream. Finally a bolt of lightning hit close by, and the rain started to pour. "Now do you believe me?!" shouted Angela through the driving rain. Alex turned the boat toward shore and didn't say a word.

Present resolution or outcome of conflict.

5 Writing Informative Texts

Expository writing informs and explains. You can use it to evaluate the effects of a new law, to compare two movies, to analyze a piece of literature, or to examine the problem of greenhouse gases in the atmosphere. There are many types of expository writing. Think about your topic and select the type that presents the information most clearly.

5.1 COMPARISON AND CONTRAST

Compare-and-contrast writing examines the similarities and differences between two or more subjects. You might, for example, compare and contrast two short stories, the main characters in a novel, or two movies.

RUBRIC: Standards for Writing

Successful compare-and-contrast writing should

- hook the reader's attention with a strong introduction
- clearly identify the subjects that are being compared and contrasted
- include specific, relevant details
- follow a clear plan of organization
- use language and details appropriate to the audience
- use transitional words and phrases to clarify similarities and differences

Options for Organization

Compare-and-contrast writing can be organized in different ways. The examples that follow demonstrate point-by-point organization and subject-by-subject organization.

Option 1: Point-by-Point Organization

EXAMPLE

I. Different beliefs about burial practices. **Point 1**

Subject A. Leon: traditional Laguna way.

Subject B. Father Paul: last rites and a funeral mass.

II. Both want a proper burial. **Point 2**

Subject A. Leon: painted face, feather in hair, body to graveyard, cornmeal and pollen.

Subject B. Father Paul: decide whether to sprinkle holy water without full Catholic rites.

Option 2: Subject-by-Subject Organization

EXAMPLE

I. Leon: — Subject A

Point 1. Believes in traditional Laguna burial.

Point 2. Proper burial: painted face, feather in hair, body to graveyard, corn meal and pollen.

II. Father Paul: — Subject B

Point 1. Believes burial requires last rites and a funeral mass.

Point 2. Must decide whether to sprinkle holy water without full Catholic rites.

For more information, see ***Writing Workshop: Online Feature Article*** *pages 620–627;* ***Writing Workshop: Analytical Essay,*** *pages 834–843;* ***Writing Workshop: Research Paper,*** *pages 1358–1377.*

5.2 CAUSE AND EFFECT

Cause-effect writing explains why something happened, why certain conditions exist, or what resulted from an action or a condition. You might use cause-effect writing to explain a character's actions, the progress of a disease, or the outcome of a war.

RUBRIC: Standards for Writing

Successful cause-effect writing should

- hook the reader's attention with a strong introduction
- clearly state the cause-and-effect relationship
- show clear connections between causes and effects
- present causes and effects in a logical order and use transitions effectively
- use facts, examples, and other details to illustrate each cause and effect
- use language and details appropriate to the audience

Options for Organization

Your organization will depend on your topic and your purpose for writing.

Option 1: Effect-to-Cause Organization If you want to explain the causes of an event, such as the closing of a factory, you might first state the effect and then examine its causes.

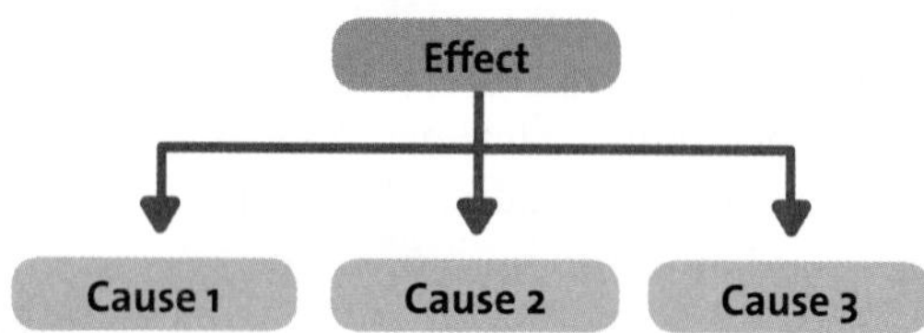

Option 2: Cause-to-Effect Organization If your focus is on explaining the effects of an event, such as the passage of a law, you might first state the cause and then explain the effects.

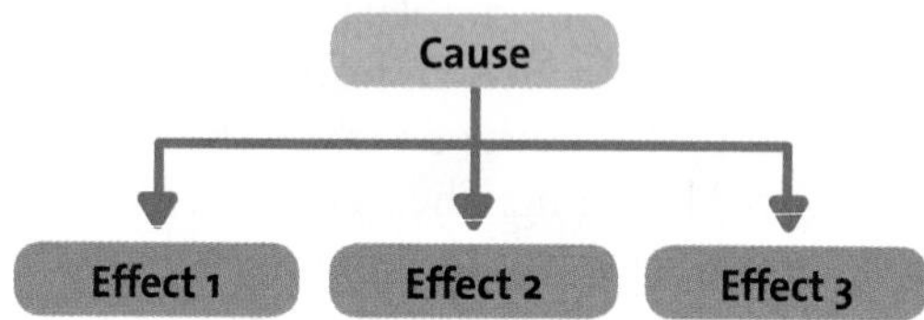

Option 3: Cause-Effect Chain Organization Sometimes you'll want to describe a chain of cause-effect relationships to explore a topic, such as the disappearance of tropical rain forests or the development of the Internet.

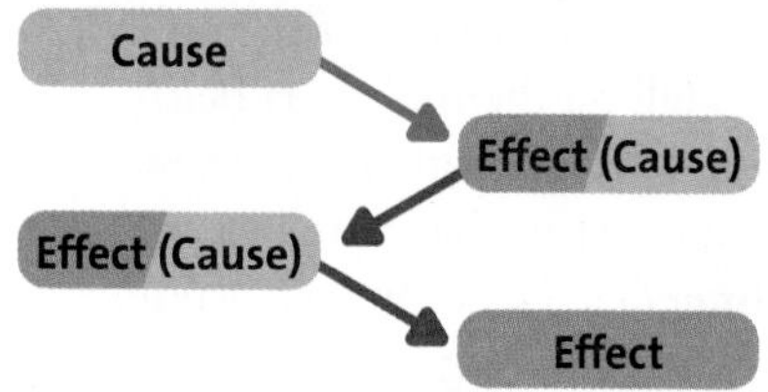

TIP Don't assume that a cause-effect relationship exists just because one event follows another. Look for evidence that the later event could not have happened if the first event had not caused it.

5.3 PROBLEM-SOLUTION

Problem-solution writing clearly states a problem, analyzes the problem, and proposes a solution to the problem. It can be used to identify and solve a conflict between characters, investigate global warming, or tell why the home team keeps losing.

RUBRIC: Standards for Writing

Successful problem-solution writing should

- hook the reader's attention with a strong introduction
- identify the problem and help the reader understand the issues involved
- analyze the causes and effects of the problem
- include quotations, facts, and statistics
- explore possible solutions to the problem and recommend the best one(s)
- use language, details, and a tone appropriate to the audience

Options for Organization

Your organization will depend on the goal of your problem-solution piece, your intended audience, and the specific problem you have chosen to address. The organizational methods that follow are effective for different kinds of problem-solution writing.

Option 1: Simple Problem-Solution

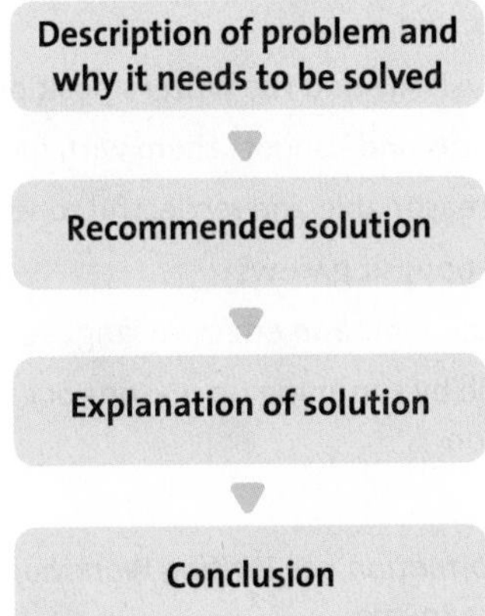

Option 2: Deciding Between Solutions

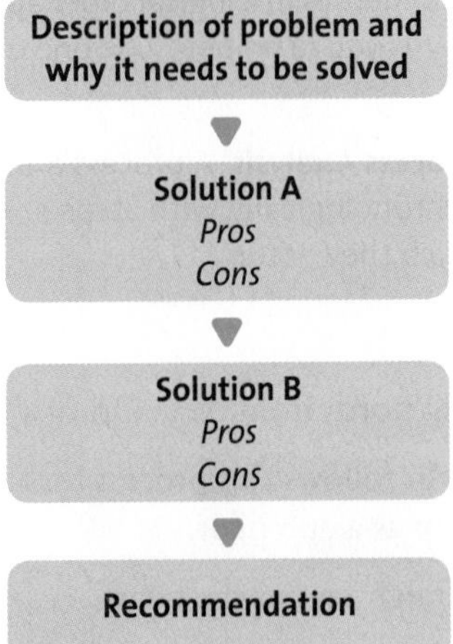

5.4 ANALYSIS

In writing an analysis, you explain how something works, how it is defined, or what its parts are.

RUBRIC: Standards for Writing

A successful analysis should

- hook the reader's attention with a strong introduction
- clearly define the subject and its parts
- use a specific organizing structure to provide a logical flow of information
- show connections among facts and ideas through transitional words and phrases
- use language and details appropriate for the audience

Options for Organization

Organize your details in a logical order appropriate to the kind of analysis you're writing. Use one of the following options:

Option 1: Process Analysis A process analysis is usually organized chronologically, with steps or stages in the order in which they occur.

EXAMPLE

Navigating north from New Orleans — **Introduce process.**

Mark Twain follows this process for his first trip as a cub pilot. — **Give background.**

Step 1: Straighten out the boat. — **Explain steps.**

Step 2: Stay close to the moored boats.

Step 3: Pass Six-Mile, Nine-Mile, and Twelve-Mile points.

Step 4: Cross the river when the calm water ends.

Option 2: Definition Analysis You can organize the details of a definition analysis in order of importance or impression.

EXAMPLE

A successful riverboat pilot must be a keen observer. — **Introduce term.**

The riverboat pilot must observe the surface of the river, the landmarks along the shore, and signs of nature. — **General definition.**

Quality 1: The surface can tell of rising water or hidden hazards. — **Explain features or qualities.**

Quality 2: Landmarks tell where the boat is; pilot must recall what dangers to avoid at that point.

Quality 3: The sky can give hints about what weather may be coming.

Option 3: Parts Analysis A parts analysis is organized as a listing of the subject's parts, with each explained.

EXAMPLE

Piloting a riverboat requires several skills. — **Introduce subject.**

Part 1: recognize how weather might threaten the boat — **Explain parts.**

Part 2: observe floating objects that could show a rising river; see ripples in the water surface that could indicate a hazard

Part 3: use landmarks to know where boat is and where dangers lie

*For more information, see **Writing Workshop: Analytical Essay,** pages 834–843.*

6 Writing Arguments

Persuasive writing allows you to use the power of language to inform and influence others. It includes speeches, persuasive essays, newspaper editorials, advertisements, and critical reviews.

RUBRIC: Standards for Writing

Successful persuasive writing should

- hook the reader's attention with a strong introduction
- state the issue and the writer's position
- give claims and support them with facts or reasons
- have a reasonable and respectful tone
- answer opposing views
- use sound logic and effective language
- conclude by summing up reasons or calling for action

*For more information, see **Writing Workshop: Persuasive Essay,** pages 280–289.*

6.1 KEY TECHNIQUES

Clarify Your Claim What do you believe about the issue? Determine how you can express your opinion most clearly.

Know Your Audience Who will read your writing? Think about what your audience already knows and believes about the issue. Imagine any objections to your position that your audience might have. Determine what additional information they will need. Decide on the tone and approach that would be most effective.

Support Your Opinion Why do you feel the way you do about the issue? Use facts, statistics, examples, quotations, anecdotes, or expert opinions to support your view. Think of reasons that will convince your readers and evidence that can answer their objections.

Ways to Support Your Argument	
Statistics	facts that are stated in numbers
Expert Opinions	information from a professional
Observations	events or situations you yourself have seen
Anecdotes	brief stories that illustrate points
Quotations	direct statements from authorities

*For more information, see **Identifying Faulty Reasoning**, page R22.*

Begin and End with a Bang How can you hook your readers and make a lasting impression? Think of a quotation, an anecdote, or a statistic that will catch your reader's attention and remain memorable. Create a strong summary or call to action with which you can conclude.

MODEL

Beginning

Stop before you call your doctor for medicine to cure that cold or ease that sore throat. You might be doing your body more harm than good by taking an antibiotic.

Conclusion

Listen to doctors when they suggest that antibiotics should be reserved for serious illness. Take the doctor's advice to drink lots of liquids and get bed rest instead of taking drugs for a less serious illness. Maybe humanity can win the battle with microbes by slowing their evolution into supermicrobes that resist antibiotics.

6.2 OPTIONS FOR ORGANIZATION

In a two-sided persuasive essay, you want to show the weaknesses of other opinions as you explain the strengths of your own.

Option 1: Reasons for Your Opinion

- Introduction states issue and your position on it.
- Reason 1 with evidence and support
- Reason 2 with evidence and support
- Reason 3 with evidence and support
- Objections to whole argument
- Response to objections
- Conclusion includes restatement of your position and recommended action.

Option 2: Point-by-Point Basis

- Introduction states issue and your position on it.
- Reason 1 with evidence and support
- Objections and responses for reason 1
- Reason 2 with evidence and support
- Objections and responses for reason 2
- Reason 3 with evidence and support
- Objections and responses for reason 3
- Conclusion includes restatement of your position and recommended action.

7 Writing Functional Texts

Business writing is writing done in a workplace to support the work of a company or business. Several types of formats, such as memos, letters, e-mails, applications, and bylaws, have been developed to make communication easier.

RUBRIC: Standards for Writing

Successful business writing should

- be courteous
- use language that is geared to its audience
- state the purpose clearly in the opening sentences or paragraph
- have a formal tone and not contain slang, contractions, or sentence fragments
- use precise words
- present only essential information
- present details in a logical order
- conclude with a summary of important points

7.1 KEY TECHNIQUES

Think About Your Purpose Ask yourself why you are doing this writing. Do you want to promote yourself to a college admissions committee or a job interviewer? Do you want to order or complain about a product? Do you want to set up a meeting or respond to someone's ideas? Are you writing bylaws for an organization?

Identify Your Audience Determine who will read your writing. What background information will they need? What tone or language is appropriate?

Use a Pattern of Organization That Is Appropriate to the Content If you have to compare and contrast two products in a memo, for example, you can use the same compare-and-contrast organization that you would use in an essay.

Support Your Points What specific details might clarify your ideas? What reasons do you have for your statements?

Finish Strongly Determine the best way to sum up your statements. What is your main point? What action do you want the recipients to take?

Revise and Proofread Your Writing Just as you are graded on the quality of an essay you write for a class, you will be judged on the quality of your writing in the workplace.

7.2 MATCHING THE FORMAT TO THE OCCASION

E-mail messages, memos, and letters have similar purposes but are used in different situations. The chart shows how each format can be used.

Format	Occasion
Memo	Use to send correspondence **inside** the workplace only.
E-mail message	Use to send correspondence **inside or outside** the company.
Letter	Use to send correspondence **outside** the company.

TIP Memos are often sent as e-mail messages in the workplace. Remember that both require formal language and standard spelling, capitalization, and punctuation.

PRACTICE AND APPLY

Refer to the documents on page R41 to complete the following:

1. Draft a response to the letter. Then revise your letter as necessary according to the rubric at the beginning of this section. Make sure you have included the necessary information and have written in an appropriate tone. Proofread your letter for grammatical errors and spelling mistakes. Follow the format of the model and use appropriate spacing between elements.
2. Write a memo in response to the memo. Tell the recipient what actions you have taken. Follow the format of the model.

For more information, see ***Writing Workshop: Procedural Documents,*** *pages 1312–1321.*

7.3 FORMATS

Business letters usually have a formal tone and a specific format as shown below. The key to writing a business letter is to get to the point as quickly as possible and to present your information clearly.

MODEL: BUSINESS LETTER

84 Mariposa Lane
El Paso, TX 79935
April 16, 2011

Heading *Where the letter comes from and when*

Dr. Larry Raines, Chair
English Department
Lincoln University
1127 University Drive
Tempe, AZ 85282

Inside address *To whom the letter is being sent*

Dear Dr. Raines:

Salutation *Greeting*

As a high school junior, I am investigating colleges to visit during this summer. My special interest is in English literature, and I know that Lincoln University has a fine department in this field.

Please send me information about applying to Lincoln and also requirements for entering your department.

Thank you.

Body *Text of the message*

Sincerely,
Lianna Chavez
Lianna Chavez

Closing

Memos are often used in workplaces as a way of conveying information in a direct and concise manner. They can be used to announce or summarize meetings and to request actions or specific information.

MODEL: MEMO

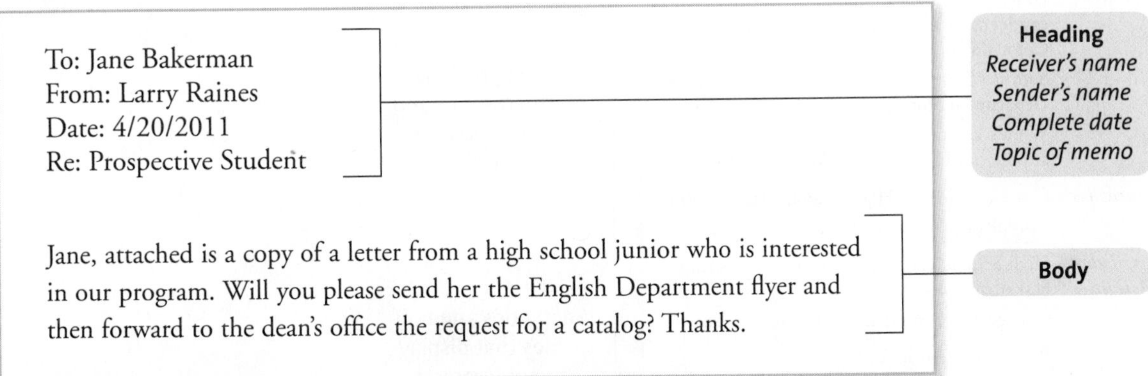

To: Jane Bakerman
From: Larry Raines
Date: 4/20/2011
Re: Prospective Student

Jane, attached is a copy of a letter from a high school junior who is interested in our program. Will you please send her the English Department flyer and then forward to the dean's office the request for a catalog? Thanks.

TIP Don't forget to write the topic of your memo in the subject line. This will help the receiver determine the importance of your memo.

When you apply for a job, you may be asked to fill out an application form. Application forms vary, but most of them ask for similar kinds of information. If you are mailing your application, you may want to include a brief letter.

MODEL: JOB APPLICATION

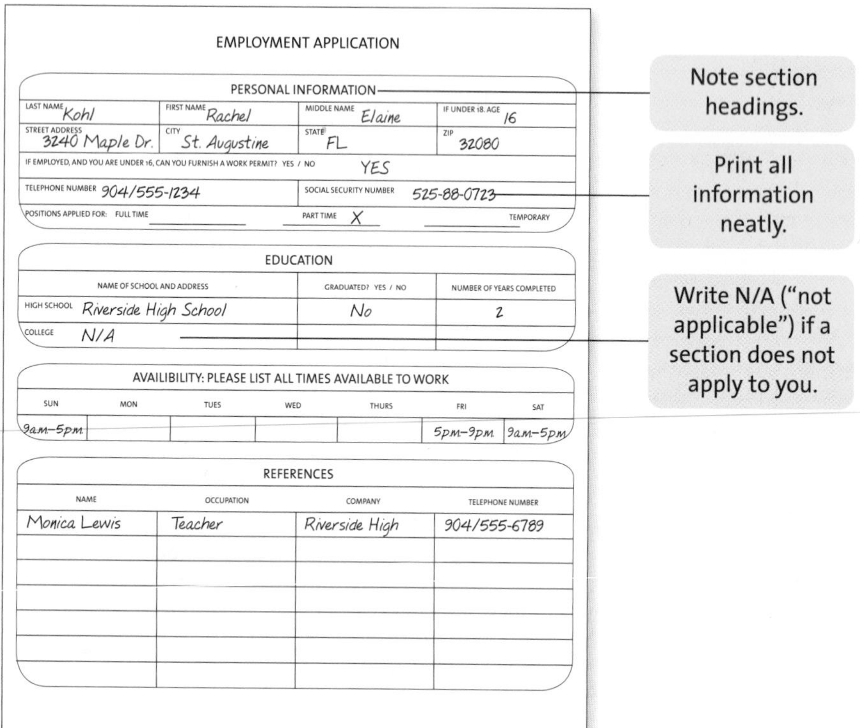

EMPLOYMENT APPLICATION

PERSONAL INFORMATION

LAST NAME Kohl	FIRST NAME Rachel	MIDDLE NAME Elaine	IF UNDER 18, AGE 16
STREET ADDRESS 3240 Maple Dr.	CITY St. Augustine	STATE FL	ZIP 32080
IF EMPLOYED, AND YOU ARE UNDER 16, CAN YOU FURNISH A WORK PERMIT? YES / NO YES			
TELEPHONE NUMBER 904/555-1234		SOCIAL SECURITY NUMBER 525-88-0723	
POSITIONS APPLIED FOR: FULL TIME ____		PART TIME X	TEMPORARY ____

EDUCATION

	NAME OF SCHOOL AND ADDRESS	GRADUATED? YES / NO	NUMBER OF YEARS COMPLETED
HIGH SCHOOL	Riverside High School	No	2
COLLEGE	N/A		

AVAILIBILITY: PLEASE LIST ALL TIMES AVAILABLE TO WORK

SUN	MON	TUES	WED	THURS	FRI	SAT
9am–5pm					5pm–9pm	9am–5pm

REFERENCES

NAME	OCCUPATION	COMPANY	TELEPHONE NUMBER
Monica Lewis	Teacher	Riverside High	904/555-6789

Note section headings.
Print all information neatly.
Write N/A ("not applicable") if a section does not apply to you.

MODEL: RÉSUMÉ

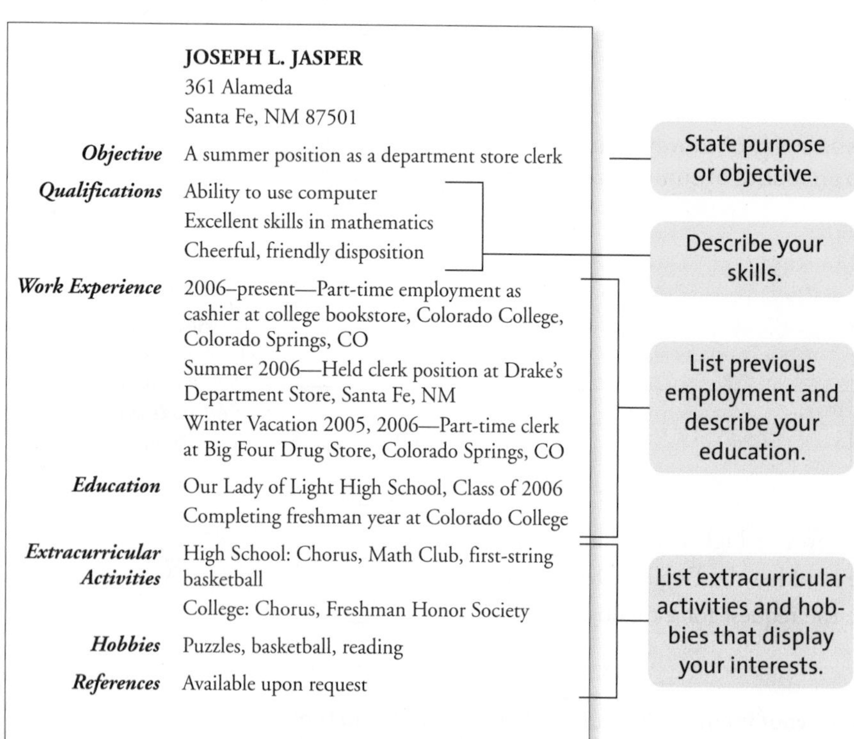

JOSEPH L. JASPER
361 Alameda
Santa Fe, NM 87501

Objective A summer position as a department store clerk

Qualifications Ability to use computer
Excellent skills in mathematics
Cheerful, friendly disposition

Work Experience 2006–present—Part-time employment as cashier at college bookstore, Colorado College, Colorado Springs, CO
Summer 2006—Held clerk position at Drake's Department Store, Santa Fe, NM
Winter Vacation 2005, 2006—Part-time clerk at Big Four Drug Store, Colorado Springs, CO

Education Our Lady of Light High School, Class of 2006
Completing freshman year at Colorado College

Extracurricular Activities High School: Chorus, Math Club, first-string basketball
College: Chorus, Freshman Honor Society

Hobbies Puzzles, basketball, reading

References Available upon request

State purpose or objective.
Describe your skills.
List previous employment and describe your education.
List extracurricular activities and hobbies that display your interests.

Sometimes you may have to write technical documents, such as a list of procedures for conducting a meeting, a manual on rules of behavior, or the minutes of a meeting. These documents contain written descriptions of rules, regulations, and meetings and enable organizations and businesses to run smoothly. These bylaws for a poetry club include a description of the organization and information about how the club operates.

MODEL: BYLAWS DOCUMENT

Article I Name

SECTION 1. The name of this organization is the Free Verse Poets Society of North Shore High School.

Article II Purpose

SECTION 1. The purpose of this organization is to stimulate young developing poets, to create enthusiasm for poetry, to promote the scholarly study of poetry, and to inform the school and community about poetry.

Article III Membership Requirements

SECTION 1. To qualify for membership, a candidate must be a student at North Shore High School.

SECTION 2. Membership in Free Verse Poets Society is voluntary. However, all members are required to attend semimonthly meetings, participate in any club fundraisers, and assist in the quarterly publication of the club newsletter, *Plutonian Shore.*

Article IV Meetings

SECTION 1. Meetings will be held twice a month on a day designated by voting members. Meetings will be held in a classroom designated by the faculty advisor.

SECTION 2. A quorum shall consist of eight (8) members; at least two (2) student officers and the faculty advisor are required to be present at each meeting.

SECTION 3. All student officers are voting members of the Free Verse Poets Society; however, the faculty advisor may be called upon in the event of an evenly split vote.

Article V Officers

SECTION 1. This organization shall be governed by a faculty advisor and a panel of four (4) student officers: the president, vice-president, scribe, and treasurer. Each student officer will be elected at the start of the school year.

SECTION 2. For members to be eligible for election, they must have served one (1) year as a member in the Free Verse Poets Society. Freshmen are not eligible for election. Only seniors are eligible for the office of society president.

SECTION 3. The president will preside over regular and special meetings.

SECTION 4. The vice-president will guide activities of appointed committees.

SECTION 5. The scribe will record and distribute meeting minutes.

SECTION 6. The treasurer will be responsible for all money collected by the society.

PRACTICE AND APPLY

Refer to the documents on pages R42 and R43 to complete the following:

1. Visit a business and request an employment application for a job you would like to have. Make sure you understand what each question is asking before you begin to write. Fill out the application as neatly and completely as possible.
2. Write a set of bylaws for an organization that you already belong to or one that you would like to form. Follow the format of the document on page R43.

Included in this handbook:
W 7–9

Good research involves using a variety of sources and materials. With an abundance of information at your fingertips, knowing where to go, how to access information, and how to record your findings are important skills and strategies.

1 Finding Sources

The **library** or **media center** and the **Internet** are the first places you will begin your research. Both the library and the Internet offer a wealth of resources, which include reference works, books, newspapers and periodicals, film, databases, catalogs, and other miscellaneous sources, such as music scores and maps.

1.1 REFERENCE WORKS

Reference works provide quick information that can help you refine or narrow your search. Reference works are roughly divided into two categories: general reference and specialized reference. Specialized reference works are focused on a particular field or area of study.

Reference Works	Examples
Encyclopedias—detailed information on nearly every subject, arranged alphabetically	*Encyclopaedia Britannica* Encyclopedia.com *Encyclopedia of Economics*
Dictionaries—word definitions, spellings, usage, pronunciations, and origins	*The American Heritage Dictionary* *Bartlett's Familiar Quotations*
Almanacs and Yearbooks—current facts and statistics	*World Almanac and Book of Facts*
Thesauri—lists of synonyms and antonyms	*Roget's International Thesaurus*
Biographical References—information on the lives of noteworthy people	*The Riverside Dictionary of Biography* *The International Who's Who*
Atlases—geographical and historical maps, charts, and graphics	*Rand McNally Atlas of the World*
Directories—names, addresses, and phone numbers of people and organizations	telephone books lists of business organizations, agencies, and publications
Indexes—alphabetical lists of newspaper and magazine articles	*Readers' Guide to Periodical Literature*

1.2 BOOKS

Nonfiction books provide in-depth information on specific topics. Your research may also require that you access fiction, poetry, or dramatic works. The following parts of a book will help you find information quickly and easily:

- **Title page**—a page that gives the book's name and the name of its author and publisher; usually the first full page of a book
- **Copyright page**—a page that gives the copyright date, or the date the book was published; usually located on the reverse side of the title page
- **Table of contents**—a list at the front of the book that gives the title of each chapter or section of the text and the page number on which it begins
- **Preface**—a short, preliminary section of a book in which the writer of the book briefly provides background information and, possibly, acknowledgments
- **Bibliography**—a list of related books and other materials used to write a text; usually placed at the end of the book
- **Glossary**—an alphabetized list of important and/or specialized words and their definitions; usually placed at the end of the book
- **Appendix**—a collection of additional materials that supply background or other related information on subject matter discussed in the main portion of the text; usually located at the end of the book
- **Index**—an alphabetized list of important topics, terms, and details covered in the book and the page numbers on which they can be found; located at the end of the book; useful for quickly finding specific information on a topic

*For more information, see **Choosing Reliable Books,** page 1351.*

Two basic systems are used to classify nonfiction books. Most high school and public libraries use the Dewey decimal system. University and research libraries generally use the Library of Congress system.

DEWEY DECIMAL SYSTEM

000–099	General works
100–199	Philosophy and psychology
200–299	Religion
300–399	Social science
400–499	Language
500–599	Natural sciences and mathematics
600–699	Technology (applied sciences)
700–799	Arts and recreation
800–899	Literature and rhetoric
900–999	Geography and history

LIBRARY OF CONGRESS SYSTEM

A	General works
B	Philosophy, psychology, religion
C	History
D	General history and history of Europe
E–F	American history
G	Geography, anthropology, recreation
H	Social sciences
J	Political science
K	Law
L	Education
M	Music
N	Fine arts
P	Language and literature
Q	Science
R	Medicine
S	Agriculture
T	Technology
U	Military science
V	Naval science
Z	Bibliography and library science

1.3 NEWSPAPERS AND PERIODICALS

Newspapers, magazines, and scholarly journals provide concise and current information on specific topics and the news of the day. Microforms are newspapers, periodicals, and reports stored on film (microfilm) or cards (microfiche) and viewable on special machines found at the library.

Types of Publications	Examples
Newspapers—published daily, weekly, or monthly; provide news reports, specialized features, and commentary; may be general or specialized	*New York Times* *Chicago Tribune* *Sacramento Bee*
Magazines—published monthly, quarterly, or at other intervals; provide news, articles on specific topics, and commentary; more in-depth than newspapers	*Newsweek* *Time* *Musician*
Journals—usually academic in scope; related to a specific field of study; highly specialized information	*Journal of Music Theory* *New England Journal of Medicine*

For more information, see ***Evaluating Newspapers and Periodicals,*** *page 1350.*

1.4 ELECTRONIC RESOURCES

Electronic resources include DVDs, videos, e-books, CD-ROMs, and audio resources. These resources may contain reference materials, movies, documentaries, television programs, books, music, speeches, textbooks, and various other content. While most documentaries, movies, and interviews are available on DVDs or CDs, you may want to directly access a film version. To quickly determine whether the piece is useful for your research, check the following:

- **Description or summary** of the piece—Does it contain the information you need, or is it otherwise relevant to your topic? Is it nonfiction or fiction?
- **Copyright date**—How current is the documentary or interview?
- **Producer** of the piece and its **participants**—Is the producer or creator reputable? Who is interviewed or featured?

1.5 DATABASES AND ONLINE CATALOGS

The library and Internet also offer large databases that allow you to search for articles on any number of topics. Often the library will subscribe to a database service, such as InfoTrac, Newsbank, or SIRS Researcher. The information on these databases is updated regularly.

Electronic catalogs have mostly replaced the card catalog system of book listings. Formerly filed in labeled drawers in libraries, listings can now be accessed from a library's Web site on the Internet.

1.6 OTHER RESOURCES

In addition to reference works found in the library or media center and on the Internet, you can get information from the following sources: corporate and nonprofit publications, lectures, correspondence, career guides, recordings, and television programming.

PRACTICE AND APPLY

1. If you were looking through a nonfiction book on penguins, which part of the book would you search in order to find information on emperor penguins, a specific type of penguin?
2. If you wanted the most current information on a given topic, which source(s) would you search first?
3. Describe a situation in which you might find it useful to search microfiche.

1.7 WEB SOURCES

Whole libraries are on the Internet, as are thousands of other reliable and comprehensive sources for research. To conduct a search efficiently and find the best information for your topic, familiarize yourself with the following terms and procedures.

The main search tools for finding information on the Web are search engines, metasearch tools, and directories. In addition, there are virtual libraries and a host of other sites, such as newspaper archives, news associations, encyclopedias, the Library of Congress, and specialized databases.

Search engines—A search engine is a Web site that allows you to look for information on the World Wide Web. Examples include Google, Yahoo!, and Bing.

Metasearch tools—A metasearch tool is similar to a search engine, except that it simultaneously searches multiple search engines for the keywords you request. Examples include Dogpile, SurfWax, and Metacrawler.

Directories—Directories arrange Internet resources into subject categories and are useful when you are researching a general topic. Examples include Lycos, Galaxy, Yahoo!, Web Directory, and About.com.

Keyword searches—In a keyword search, you access a search engine and type in a phrase or term related to your subject. This allows you to retrieve Web sites and documents that have those keywords in them. Here are some tips for doing a keyword search:

- In the search box, type in a specific word or two that clearly identify your subject.
- When you want to find an exact phrase, or words in a certain order, such as *recording studio* (and not just *recording* or just *studio*), use quotation marks around the entire phrase. For instance, "recording studio" will provide results using those words in that order.
- If necessary, replace the end of a word with an asterisk. For example, the keyword *music** leads to sites that contain *music, musician,* and *musicianship.*

Boolean searches—A Boolean search lets you specify how the keywords in your search are related. This type of search allows you to refine, narrow, or expand your search so that your results are more focused on your topic needs. Use the following tips to conduct a Boolean search:

- For a search containing two or more words that do not need to be in a specific order, use the word AND between the words to indicate that the site or document should contain all the words specified. For example, *internship* AND *radio* will produce results containing both those words, but not in any particular order. For some search engines, you can use a plus sign instead of AND.
- The word OR broadens the search to include all documents that contain either word (*job* OR *career*).
- The word NOT—or, for some search engines, a minus sign—excludes unwanted terms from the search (*songwriting* NOT *commercials*).

Each Web site you encounter in your search will have a **URL** (uniform resource locator), which is its Web address. The abbreviation usually located at the end of the URL indicates the type and purpose of the Web site.

URL ABBREVIATIONS AND MEANINGS

.COM	commercial—product information and sales; personal sites; some combinations of products and information, such as World Book Online
.EDU	education—information about schools, courses, campus life, and research projects; students' and teachers' personal sites
.GOV	United States government—official sites of the White House and of NASA, the FBI, and other government agencies and offices
.MIL	United States military—official sites of the army, navy, air force, and marines, as well as of the Department of Defense and related agencies
.NET	network—product information and sales
.ORG	organization—charities, libraries, and other nonprofits; political parties

*For more information, see **Using Library Resources,** pages 1345–1347.*

1.8 YOUR OWN ORIGINAL DATA

Sometimes you will need information that you just can't find in books or online. A good way to get in-depth, firsthand information is by interviewing experts, conducting surveys, and recording data from your own observations, fieldwork, or experiments.

Interviews with experts—Whatever the subject of your research, look for people who have knowledge or experience in that field. For example, if you were researching shipwrecks on the Great Lakes, you might interview someone from the Great Lakes Maritime Society or a captain of a ship on the Great Lakes. Use the following tips when conducting an interview:

1. Plan your questions and rehearse what you will say.
2. During the interview, listen carefully and take notes. Ask permission if you want to record the interview.
3. Request clarification and ask follow-up questions when necessary.
4. After the interview, review your notes and summarize the conversation. If you recorded the conversation, you might want to transcribe it.
5. Identify strong statements you might want to quote directly.
6. Send a thank-you note to the interviewee.

Oral histories—For some kinds of presentations and papers, you may want to include an **oral history,** or a story of a person's experiences told in his or her own words. For example, if you were writing a paper on Native Americans and reservation life, you might want to include an oral history of someone who is experiencing that life and who knows how his or her tribe came to live on the reservation. To conduct an oral history, follow all the tips for conducting an interview.

Surveys—Surveys allow you to gather information from a broad range of people through the use of a **questionnaire.** For example, you may want to gather and compare people's opinions, preferences, or beliefs about a current news topic. Use the following tips to conduct a survey or to distribute a questionnaire:

1. Plan the survey. Choose whether you want to ask multiple-choice questions, yes/no questions, open-ended questions, true/false questions, or questions that refer to a rating scale. Prepare your questionnaire.
2. Determine the sample population, or group of people, you want to survey.
3. Administer the survey the same way to each person. You may ask people to respond in person, on the phone, or by e-mail, but your method should be the same for each, with the questions asked in the same manner and order.
4. Once the questionnaires have been completed, compile and interpret the responses. Was there a clear preference or opinion from the entire group? Do certain groups of people think one way while others think another? What conclusions can you draw from the results?
5. Summarize your results in writing; use charts or other graphic aids to provide a visual representation of the data.

Independent observation and field research—Field research and independent observation include any purposeful observations you make at a site or an event related to your topic. For example, you might visit a movie set to learn more about how movies are made and then record the activity you observed. For some research projects you may want to set up a **field study,** which is a systematic series of observations or a planned course of data collection. For some topics you might conduct experiments, as for a report in a science class.

2 Collecting Information

Once you have located your sources, you will need to sort through the information. To make it useful and manageable, you will want to take detailed notes, arrange your information in a logical and organized manner, and make sure your sources are reliable and credible.

2.1 TAKING NOTES

As you go through your sources, record information that is relevant to your search.

Source cards—You will need to document the sources where you find your information or evidence so that you can credit the sources in your work. To create source cards, record all the information needed to identify each source you use in your research. Organize your notes so that you can easily refer to them when adding documentation to your research.

> Ackerman, Diane. *A Natural History of the Senses.* New York: Vintage, 1990. Print.

HERE'S HOW

MAKING SOURCE CARDS

Follow these guidelines when you make source cards:

- **Book** Record the author's or editor's complete name, the title, the location and name of the publisher, and the copyright date.
- **Magazine or Newspaper Article** Include the author's complete name (unless the article is unsigned), the title of the article, the name and date of the publication, and the page number(s) of the article.
- **Encyclopedia Article** Include the author's complete name (unless the article is unsigned), the title of the article, and the name and copyright date of the encyclopedia.
- **World Wide Web Site** Record the author's or editor's complete name (if available), the title of the document, publication information for any print version of it, the date of its electronic publication, the name of any institution or organization responsible for the site, and the date when you accessed the site.

Notes—As you read your sources, record all relevant facts, quotations, statistics, anecdotes, and examples electronically, or on **note cards.** When you're ready to draft your paper, you can arrange and organize your notes in different ways to present the information and then choose the best method of organization. Here is an example of a note with an exact quotation from the Diane Ackerman book.

> **Insects and photoreception**
> "Bees can judge the angle at which light hits their photoreceptors, and therefore locate the position of the sun in the sky, even on a partly cloudy day" (265).

HERE'S HOW

TAKING NOTES

Follow these guidelines as you take your notes:

- Organize information in separate pieces that can be easily arranged and sifted through.
- **Include a heading** indicating the subject of the note.
- **Record the number of the corresponding source card** on each note.
- **Put direct quotations in quotation marks.**
- **Record the number of the page** where you found the material.

When recording information for your notes, you can use the following forms of **restatement** to avoid **plagiarism,** or presenting someone else's work as your own:

Paraphrase—When you paraphrase, you restate the writer's idea in your own words. Be sure to enclose in quotation marks any of the author's exact words that you include in a paraphrase.

Summary—When you summarize, you restate the main idea of the original, including key facts and statistics, but in a shorter version, usually about one-third the length of the original. A summary omits unnecessary details.

Quotation—When you use a writer's exact statement, you will need to place quotation marks around it. Be sure to copy the words exactly as the writer wrote them, including all punctuation. Use quotations for

- extremely important ideas that might be misrepresented by paraphrases
- clear and concise explanations
- ideas presented in unusually lively or vivid language

2.2 OUTLINING

Once you've arranged your notes in a pattern of organization that is suitable for your topic, you can create a formal **outline** of how the information will be arranged in your report. An outline can be written in one of two ways: as a sentence outline or as a topic outline. The **sentence outline** contains entries written in sentence form; the **topic outline** contains only phrases or words that represent the ideas. With either choice, each main idea in the outline is designated by a Roman numeral. The subtopics that support the main ideas are designated with indented capital letters. The details that explain the subtopics are designated with numerals and lowercase letters.

MODEL: SENTENCE OUTLINE

Introduction: The human senses are varied and differ from those in animals.

I. Humans are believed to have five senses: sight, hearing, touch, taste, and smell.
   A. Aristotle, a Greek philosopher, first categorized the senses.
   B. Modern physics and physiology reclassified the senses.

II. Photoreceptors are those sense organs in living organisms that react to light.
   A. The human eye is a photoreceptor.
   B. Animal photoreception can be superior to that of humans.
      1. Insects have specialized eyes.
      2. Nocturnal animals can see in the dark.
      3. Some animals see the world in colors that are different from those perceived by humans.

MODEL: TOPIC OUTLINE

Introduction: The human senses are varied and differ from those in animals.

I. Five senses in humans
   A. First categorization of senses
   B. Modern reclassification of senses

II. Photoreception
   A. Human sight and photoreception
   B. Animal sight and photoreception
      1. Insects
      2. Nocturnal animals
      3. Animals vs. humans in perceiving colors

2.3 CHECKLIST FOR EVALUATING SOURCES

The information . . .

- ☑ is relevant to the topic you are researching
- ☑ is up-to-date (This point is especially important when researching time-sensitive topics in areas such as science, medicine, and sports.)
- ☑ is from an author who is qualified to write about the topic
- ☑ is from a trusted source that is updated or reviewed regularly
- ☑ makes the author's or institution's purpose for writing clear
- ☑ is written at the right level for your needs (For example, a children's book is probably too simplistic, while a scientific paper may be too complex.)
- ☑ has the level of detail you need—neither too general nor too specific
- ☑ can be verified in more than one source

3 Sharing Your Research

At last you have established your research goals, located sources of information, evaluated the materials, and taken notes on what you learned. Now you have a chance to share the results with people in your world—and even beyond. Here are some options you may choose to present your work:

- Give a speech to your classmates or to people in your community.
- Create a power presentation using desktop publishing software and share it with classmates, friends, or family members.
- Describe your research findings on your own Web site.
- Summarize the information in a newsletter or brochure.
- Share the results of your research in a formal research paper.

Writing that has a lot of mistakes can confuse or even annoy a reader. A business letter with a punctuation error might lead to a miscommunication and delay a reply. A sentence fragment might lower your grade on an essay. Paying attention to grammar, punctuation, and capitalization rules can make your writing clearer and easier to read.

COMMON CORE

Included in this handbook:
L 1, L 2a, L 3a, L 4a–d

Quick Reference: Parts of Speech

PART OF SPEECH	FUNCTION	EXAMPLES
Noun	names a person, a place, a thing, an idea, a quality, or an action	
Common	serves as a general name, or a name common to an entire group	coyote, hunter, spear, bonfire
Proper	names a specific, one-of-a-kind person, place, or thing	Rainy Mountain, Virginia, Puritans
Singular	refers to a single person, place, thing, or idea	field, pony, child, man
Plural	refers to more than one person, place, thing, or idea	fields, ponies, children, men
Concrete	names something that can be perceived by the senses	lemon, shores, wind, canoe
Abstract	names something that cannot be perceived by the senses	fear, intelligence, honesty
Compound	expresses a single idea through a combination of two or more words	birthright, folk tale, Sky-World
Collective	refers to a group of people or things	species, army, flock
Possessive	shows who or what owns something	America's, Douglass's, men's, slaves'
Pronoun	takes the place of a noun or another pronoun	
Personal	refers to the person(s) making a statement, the person(s) being addressed, or the person(s) or thing(s) the statement is about	I, me, my, mine, we, us, our, ours, you, your, yours, she, he, it, her, him, hers, his, its, they, them, their, theirs
Reflexive	follows a verb or preposition and refers to a preceding noun or pronoun	myself, yourself, herself, himself, itself, ourselves, yourselves, themselves
Intensive	emphasizes a noun or another pronoun	(same as reflexives)
Demonstrative	points to one or more specific persons or things	this, that, these, those
Interrogative	signals a question	who, whom, whose, which, what
Indefinite	refers to one or more persons or things not specifically mentioned	both, all, most, many, anyone, everybody, several, none, some
Relative	introduces an adjective clause by relating it to a word in the clause	who, whom, whose, which, that

PART OF SPEECH	FUNCTION	EXAMPLES
Verb	expresses an action, a condition, or a state of being	
Action	tells what the subject does or did, physically or mentally	run, reaches, listened, consider, decides, dreamed
Linking	connects the subject to something that identifies or describes it	am, is, are, was, were, sound, taste, appear, feel, become, remain, seem
Auxiliary	precedes the main verb in a verb phrase	be, have, do, can, could, will, would, may, might
Transitive	directs the action toward someone or something; always has an object	The wind **snapped** the young tree in half.
Intransitive	does not direct the action toward someone or something; does not have an object	The young tree **snapped.**
Adjective	modifies a noun or pronoun	**frightened** man, **two** epics, **enough** time
Adverb	modifies a verb, an adjective, or another adverb	walked **out, really** funny, **far** away
Preposition	relates one word to another word	at, by, for, from, in, of, on, to, with
Conjunction	joins words or word groups	
Coordinating	joins words or word groups used the same way	and, but, or, for, so, yet, nor
Correlative	used as a pair to join words or word groups used the same way	both . . . and, either . . . or, neither . . . nor
Subordinating	introduces a clause that cannot stand by itself as a complete sentence	although, after, as, before, because, when, if, unless
Interjection	expresses emotion	whew, yikes, uh-oh

Quick Reference: The Sentence and Its Parts

The diagrams that follow will give you a brief review of the essentials of a sentence and some of its parts.

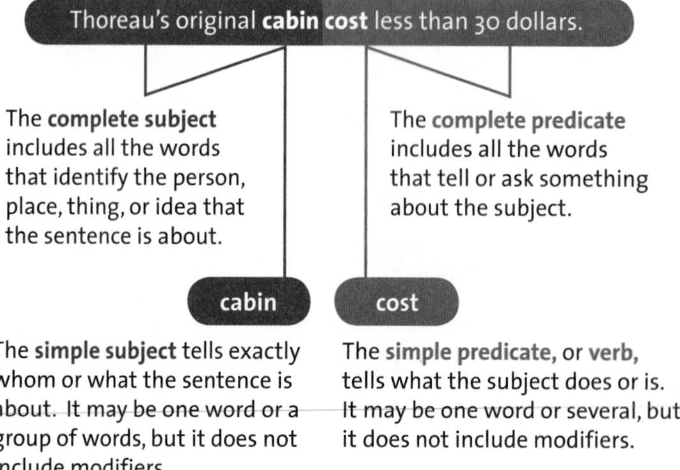

Thoreau's original **cabin cost** less than 30 dollars.
The **complete subject** includes all the words that identify the person, place, thing, or idea that the sentence is about.
The **complete predicate** includes all the words that tell or ask something about the subject.
cabin
cost
The **simple subject** tells exactly whom or what the sentence is about. It may be one word or a group of words, but it does not include modifiers.
The **simple predicate, or verb,** tells what the subject does or is. It may be one word or several, but it does not include modifiers.

Every word in a sentence is part of a complete subject or a complete predicate.

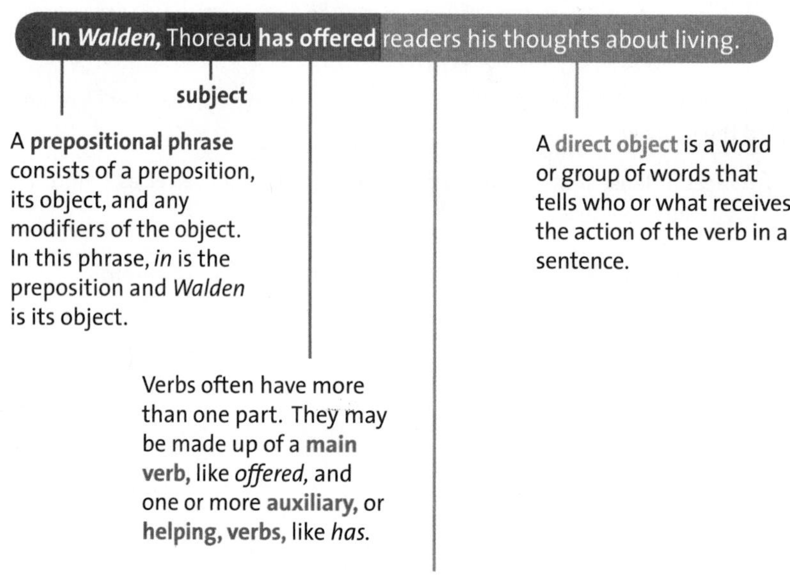

In *Walden,* Thoreau **has offered** readers his thoughts about living.
subject
A **prepositional phrase** consists of a preposition, its object, and any modifiers of the object. In this phrase, *in* is the preposition and *Walden* is its object.
A **direct object** is a word or group of words that tells who or what receives the action of the verb in a sentence.
Verbs often have more than one part. They may be made up of a **main verb,** like *offered,* and one or more **auxiliary,** or **helping, verbs,** like *has.*
An **indirect object** is a word or group of words that tells *to whom* or *for whom* or *to what* or *for what* about the verb. A sentence can have an indirect object only if it has a direct object. The indirect object always comes before the direct object in a sentence.

Quick Reference: Punctuation

MARK	FUNCTION	EXAMPLES
End Marks period, question mark, exclamation point	end a sentence	The games begin today. Who is your favorite contestant? What a play Jamie made!
period	follows an initial or abbreviation **Exception:** postal abbreviations of states	Prof. Ted Bakerman, D. H. Lawrence, Houghton Mifflin Co., P.M., A.D., oz., ft., Blvd., St. NE (Nebraska), NV (Nevada)
period	follows a number or letter in an outline	I. Volcanoes A. Central-vent 1. Shield
Comma	separates parts of a compound sentence	I had never disliked poetry, but now I really love it.
	separates items in a series	She is brave, loyal, and kind.
	separates adjectives of equal rank that modify the same noun	The slow, easy route is best.
	sets off a term of address	America, I love you. Come to the front, children.
	sets off a parenthetical expression	Hard workers, as you know, don't quit. I'm not a quitter, believe me.
	sets off an introductory word, phrase, or dependent clause	Yes, I forgot my key. At the beginning of the day, I feel fresh. While she was out, I was here. Having finished my chores, I went out.
	sets off a nonessential phrase or clause	Ed Pawn, the captain of the chess team, won. Ed Pawn, who is the captain, won. The two leading runners, sprinting toward the finish line, finished in a tie.
	sets off parts of dates and addresses	Send it by August 18, 2010, to Cherry Jubilee, Inc., 21 Vernona St., Oakland, Minnesota.
	follows the salutation and closing of a letter	Dear Jim, Sincerely yours,
	separates words to avoid confusion	By noon, time had run out. What the minister does, does matter. While cooking, Jim burned his hand.
Semicolon	separates items in a series if one or more items contain commas	We invited my sister, Jan; her friend, Don; my uncle Jack; and Mary Dodd.
	separates parts of a compound sentence that are not joined by a coordinating conjunction	The small books are on the top shelves; the large books are below. I dusted the books; however, I didn't wipe the shelves.
	separates parts of a compound sentence when the parts contain commas	After I ran out of money, I called my parents; but only my sister was home, unfortunately.

MARK	FUNCTION	EXAMPLES
Colon	introduces a list	Those we wrote were the following: Dana, John, and Will.
	introduces a long quotation	Thomas Jefferson wrote: "We the people of the United States, in order to form a more perfect union. . . ."
	follows the salutation of a business letter	Dear Ms. Williams: Dear Senator Wiley:
	separates certain numbers	1:28 P.M., Genesis 2:5
Dash	indicates an abrupt break in thought	I was thinking of my mother—who is arriving tomorrow—just as you walked in.
Parentheses	enclose less important material	Throughout her life (though some might think otherwise), she worked hard. The temperature on this July day (would you believe it?) is 65 degrees!
Hyphen	joins parts of a compound adjective before a noun	She lives in a first-floor apartment.
	joins parts of a compound with *all-*, *ex-*, *self-*, or *-elect*	The president-elect is a well-respected woman.
	joins parts of a compound number (to ninety-nine)	Today, I turn twenty-one.
	joins parts of a fraction	My cup is one-third full.
	joins a prefix to a word beginning with a capital letter	Life may have seemed simpler in pre-Civil War days. It's very chilly for mid-June.
	indicates that a word is divided at the end of a line	Did you know that school segrega- tion has been illegal since 1954?
Apostrophe	used with *s* to form the possessive of a noun or an indefinite pronoun	my friend's book, my friends' books, anyone's guess, somebody else's problem
	replaces one or more omitted letters in a contraction or numbers in a date	don't (omitted *o*), he'd (omitted *woul*), the class of '99 (omitted *19*)
	used with *s* to form the plural of a letter	I had two A's on my report card.
Quotation Marks	set off a speaker's exact words	Sara said, "I'm finally ready." "I'm ready," Sara said, "finally." Did Sara say, "I'm ready"? Sara said, "I'm ready!"
	set off the title of a story, an article, a short poem, an essay, a song, or a chapter	I liked Oates's "Hostage," Steinem's "Sisterhood," and Plath's "Mirror." Chapter II is titled "Our Gang's Dark Oath."
Ellipses	replace material omitted from a quotation	"We the people . . . in order to form a more perfect union . . . ."
Italics	indicate the title of a book, a play, a magazine, a long poem, an opera, a film, or a TV series, or the names of ships, trains, and spacecraft	***The Scarlet Letter, The Crucible, Time, The Death of the Hired Man, West Side Story, Citizen Kane, The Spirit of St. Louis, The Best of Frank Sinatra, Lusitania***

Quick Reference: Capitalization

CATEGORY	EXAMPLES
People and Titles	
Names and initials of people	Emily Dickinson, T. S. Eliot
Titles used before or in place of names	Professor Holmes, Senator Long
Deities and members of religious groups	Jesus, Allah, Buddha, Zeus, Baptists, Roman Catholics
Names of ethnic and national groups	Hispanics, Jews, African Americans
Geographical Names	
Cities, states, countries, continents	New York, Maine, Haiti, Africa
Regions, bodies of water, mountains	the South, Lake Erie, Mount Katahdin
Geographic features, parks	Continental Divide, Everglades, Yellowstone
Streets and roads, planets	55 East Ninety-fifth Street, Maple Lane, Venus, Jupiter
Organizations, Events, Etc.	
Companies, organizations, teams	General Motors, Lions Club, Utah Jazz
Buildings, bridges, monuments	the Alamo, Golden Gate Bridge, Lincoln Memorial
Documents, awards	the Constitution, World Cup
Special named events	Super Bowl, World Series
Government bodies, historical periods and events	the Supreme Court, U.S. Senate, Harlem Renaissance, World War II
Days and months, holidays	Friday, May, Easter, Memorial Day
Specific cars, boats, trains, planes	Mustang, *Titanic*, *California Zephyr*
Proper Adjectives	
Adjectives formed from proper nouns	American League, French cooking, Emersonian period, Arctic waters
First Words and the Pronoun I	
First word in a sentence or quotation	This is it. He said, "Let's go."
First word of sentence in parentheses that is not within another sentence	The spelling rules are covered in another section. (Consult that section for more information.)
First words in the salutation and closing of a letter	Dear Madam, Very truly yours,
First word in each line of most poetry Personal pronoun *I*	Then am I A happy fly If I live Or if I die.
First word, last word, and all important words in a title	"The Fall of the House of Usher," *Incidents in the Life of a Slave Girl*

1 Nouns

A **noun** is a word used to name a person, a place, a thing, an idea, a quality, or an action. Nouns can be classified in several ways.

*For more information on different types of nouns, see **Quick Reference: Parts of Speech,** page R50.*

1.1 COMMON NOUNS

Common nouns are general names, common to entire groups.

EXAMPLES: *writer, song, bravery*

1.2 PROPER NOUNS

Proper nouns name specific, one-of-a-kind things.

Common	Proper
writer, song, bravery, hunter	Mourning Dove, Mississippi, Granny

*For more information, see **Quick Reference: Capitalization,** page R55.*

1.3 SINGULAR AND PLURAL NOUNS

A noun may take a singular or a plural form, depending on whether it names a single person, place, thing, or idea or more than one. Make sure you use appropriate spellings when forming plurals.

Singular	Plural
church, lily, wife	churches, lilies, wives

*For more information, see **Forming Plural Nouns,** page R78.*

1.4 COMPOUND AND COLLECTIVE NOUNS

Compound nouns are formed from two or more words but express a single idea. They are written as single words, as separate words, or with hyphens. Use a dictionary to check the correct spelling of a compound noun.

EXAMPLES: *birthright, folk tale, Sky-World*

Collective nouns are singular nouns that refer to groups of people or things.

EXAMPLES: *army, flock, class, species*

1.5 POSSESSIVE NOUNS

A **possessive noun** shows who or what owns something.

EXAMPLES: *Welty's, jury's, children's*

*For more information, see **Forming Possessives,** page R78.*

2 Pronouns

A **pronoun** is a word that is used in place of a noun or another pronoun. The word or word group to which the pronoun refers is called its **antecedent.**

2.1 PERSONAL PRONOUNS

Personal pronouns change their form to express person, number, gender, and case. The forms of these pronouns are shown in the following chart.

	Nominative	Objective	Possessive
Singular			
First person	I	me	my, mine
Second person	you	you	your, yours
Third person	she, he, it	her, him, it	her, hers, his, its
Plural			
First person	we	us	our, ours
Second person	you	you	your, yours
Third person	they	them	their, theirs

2.2 AGREEMENT WITH ANTECEDENT

Pronouns should agree with their antecedents in number, gender, and person.

If an antecedent is singular, use a singular pronoun.

EXAMPLE: ***Sarah** laughed as her dog splashed in the lake.*

If an antecedent is plural, use a plural pronoun.

EXAMPLES:

***Sarah** and **Barbara** took turns holding the leash as they walked the dog home.*

***Andrew** and **Ryan** finished the race before the rest of their teammates.*

The gender of a pronoun must be the same as the gender of its antecedent.

EXAMPLES:

*The little **girl** ran outside without tying her shoelaces.*

***Daniel** waved to his friends before boarding the plane.*

The person of the pronoun must be the same as the person of its antecedent. As the chart in Section 2.1 shows, a pronoun can be in first-, second-, or third-person form.

EXAMPLE:

*Those of **you** who like animals should consider getting your degree in veterinary science.*

GRAMMAR PRACTICE

Rewrite each sentence so that the underlined pronoun agrees with its antecedent.

1. *The World on the Turtle's Back* is a myth that tells about a pregnant woman and how it helped create the earth.
2. Many of the sea creatures and birds tried to retrieve the dirt at the bottom of the ocean, but they could not reach him.
3. The woman circles the earth with their daughter, helping the plants to grow.
4. Both of the twins molded clay animals and gave it life.

2.3 PRONOUN CASE

Personal pronouns change form to show how they function in sentences. Different functions are shown by different **cases.** The three cases are **nominative, objective,** and **possessive.** For examples of these pronouns, see the chart in Section 2.1.

A **nominative pronoun** is used as a subject or a predicate nominative in a sentence.

An **objective pronoun** is used as a direct object, an indirect object, or the object of a preposition.

SUBJECT — OBJECT — OBJECT OF PREPOSITION

He explained it to me.

A **possessive pronoun** shows ownership. The pronouns *mine, yours, hers, his, its, ours,* and *theirs* can be used in place of nouns.

EXAMPLE: *These letters are yours.*

The pronouns *my, your, her, his, its, our,* and *their* are used before nouns.

EXAMPLE: *These are your letters.*

WATCH OUT! Many spelling errors can be avoided if you watch out for *its* and *their.* Don't confuse the possessive pronoun *its* with the contraction *it's,* meaning "it is" or "it has." The homonyms *they're* (a contraction of *they are*) and *there* ("in that place") are often mistakenly used for *their.*

TIP To decide which pronoun to use in a comparison, such as "He tells better tales than (I *or* me)," fill in the missing word(s): *He tells better tales than I* ***tell.***

GRAMMAR PRACTICE

Replace the underlined words in each sentence with an appropriate pronoun and identify the pronoun as a nominative, objective, or possessive pronoun.

1. Arthur Miller was a playwright from New York.
2. *The Crucible* is one of Arthur Miller's most well-known plays.
3. John Proctor and Reverend Parris are two of the main characters.
4. Reverend Hale tries to convince Rebecca Nurse and John Proctor to falsely confess to practicing witchcraft.
5. The Salem witch hunt illustrates how the town's strict Christian principles indirectly caused the deaths of innocent villagers.

2.4 REFLEXIVE AND INTENSIVE PRONOUNS

These pronouns are formed by adding *-self* or *-selves* to certain personal pronouns. Their forms are the same, and they differ only in how they are used.

A **reflexive pronoun** follows a verb or preposition and reflects back on an earlier noun or pronoun.

EXAMPLES:

He threw himself forward.

Danielle mailed herself the package.

Intensive pronouns intensify or emphasize the nouns or pronouns to which they refer.

EXAMPLES:

The queen herself would have been amused.

I saw it myself.

WATCH OUT! Avoid using *hisself* or *theirselves.* Standard English does not include these forms.

NONSTANDARD: *He had painted hisself into a corner.*

STANDARD: *He had painted himself into a corner.*

2.5 DEMONSTRATIVE PRONOUNS

Demonstrative pronouns point out things and persons near and far.

	Singular	Plural
Near	this	these
Far	that	those

2.6 INDEFINITE PRONOUNS

Indefinite pronouns do not refer to specific persons or things and usually have no antecedents. The chart shows some commonly used indefinite pronouns.

Singular	Plural	Singular or Plural	
another	both	all	none
anybody	few	any	some
no one	many	more	most
neither	several		

TIP Indefinite pronouns that end in *one, body,* or *thing* are always singular.

INCORRECT: *Does anybody think their hamburger is overcooked?*

CORRECT: *Does anybody think his or her hamburger is overcooked?*

If the indefinite pronoun might refer to either a male or a female, *his or her* may be used to refer to it, or the sentence may be rewritten.

EXAMPLES: *Everyone received his or her script.*

All the actors received their scripts.

2.7 INTERROGATIVE PRONOUNS

An **interrogative pronoun** is used to ask a question. The interrogative pronouns are *who, whom, whose, which,* and *what.*

EXAMPLES: *Whose backpack is on the kitchen table?*

Which dress do you prefer?

TIP *Who* is used as a subject, *whom* as an object. To find out which pronoun you need to use in a question, change the question to a statement.

QUESTION: *(Who/Whom) did you meet there?*

STATEMENT: *You met (?) there.*

Since the verb has a subject (*you*), the needed word must be the object form, *whom.*

EXAMPLE: *Whom did you meet there?*

WATCH OUT! A special problem arises when you use an interrupter, such as *do you think,* within a question.

EXAMPLE: *(Who/Whom) do you believe is the more influential musician?*

If you eliminate the interrupter, it is clear that the word you need is *who.*

2.8 RELATIVE PRONOUNS

Relative pronouns relate, or connect, dependent (or subordinate) clauses to the words they modify in sentences. The relative pronouns are *that, what, whatever, which, whichever, who, whoever, whom, whomever,* and *whose.*

Sometimes short sentences with related ideas can be combined by using a relative pronoun.

SHORT SENTENCE: *Mark Twain may be America's greatest humorist.*

RELATED SENTENCE: *Mark Twain wrote* Huckleberry Finn.

COMBINED SENTENCE: *Mark Twain, who wrote* Huckleberry Finn, *may be America's greatest humorist.*

GRAMMAR PRACTICE

Choose the appropriate interrogative or relative pronoun from the words in parentheses.

1. "The Notorious Jumping Frog" was written by Samuel Clemens, (who/whom) wrote under the pseudonym Mark Twain.
2. The story gained national fame for Mark Twain, (who/that) first published it in 1865.
3. (Who/Whom) do you think is funnier, Jim Smiley or the storyteller Simon Wheeler?
4. Smiley spent months educating his frog, (which/whose) fame as a jumper spread throughout the gold camps.

2.9 PRONOUN REFERENCE PROBLEMS

The referent of a pronoun should always be clear.

An **indefinite reference** occurs when the pronoun *it, you,* or *they* does not clearly refer to a specific antecedent.

UNCLEAR: *In the review, it claimed the movie is well done.*

CLEAR: *The review claimed the movie is well done.*

A **general reference** occurs when the pronoun *it, this, that, which,* or *such* is used to refer to a general idea rather than a specific antecedent.

UNCLEAR: *Stella tutors students every day after school. This lets her help kids who are struggling with their schoolwork.*

CLEAR: *Stella tutors students every day after school. Tutoring lets her help kids who are struggling with their schoolwork.*

Ambiguous means "having more than one possible meaning." An **ambiguous reference** occurs when a pronoun could refer to two or more antecedents.

UNCLEAR: *Stacey made Miranda a sandwich while she talked on the phone.*

CLEAR: *While Stacey talked on the phone, she made Miranda a sandwich.*

GRAMMAR PRACTICE

Rewrite the following sentences to correct indefinite, ambiguous, and general pronoun references.

1. In the poem "The Raven," it tells about a man who is grieving for his lover.
2. The raven refused to abandon its perch above the door. This frustrated the narrator.
3. The narrator told the raven that he thought he was a messenger from Lenore.
4. The raven always responded, "Nevermore." This frightened and confused the speaker.

3 Verbs

A **verb** is a word that expresses an action, a condition, or a state of being.

For more information, see ***Quick Reference: Parts of Speech,*** *page R50.*

3.1 ACTION VERBS

Action verbs express mental or physical activity.

EXAMPLE: *I walked to the store.*

3.2 LINKING VERBS

Linking verbs join subjects with words or phrases that rename or describe them.

EXAMPLE: *You are my friend.*

3.3 PRINCIPAL PARTS

Action and linking verbs typically have four principal parts, which are used to form verb tenses. The principal parts are the **present,** the **present participle,** the **past,** and the **past participle.**

Action verbs and some linking verbs also fall into two categories: regular and irregular. A **regular verb** is a verb that forms its past and past participle by adding *-ed* or *-d* to the present form.

Present	Present Participle	Past	Past Participle
perform	(is) performing	performed	(has) performed
hope	(is) hoping	hoped	(has) hoped
stop	(is) stopping	stopped	(has) stopped
marry	(is) marrying	married	(has) married

An **irregular verb** is a verb that forms its past and past participle in some other way than by adding *-ed* or *-d* to the present form.

Present	Present Participle	Past	Past Participle
bring	(is) bringing	brought	(has) brought
swim	(is) swimming	swam	(has) swum
steal	(is) stealing	stole	(has) stolen
grow	(is) growing	grew	(has) grown

3.4 VERB TENSE

The **tense** of a verb indicates the time of the action or state of being. An action or state of being can occur in the present, the past, or the future. There are six tenses, each expressing a different range of time.

The **present tense** expresses an action or state that is happening at the present time, occurs regularly, or is constant or generally true. Use the present part.

NOW: *That poet reads well.*

REGULAR: *I swim every day.*

GENERAL: *Time flies.*

The **past tense** expresses an action that began and ended in the past. Use the past part.

EXAMPLE: *The storyteller finished his tale.*

The **future tense** expresses an action or state that will occur. Use *shall* or *will* with the present part.

EXAMPLE: *They will attend the next festival.*

The **present perfect tense** expresses an action or state that (1) was completed at an indefinite time in the past or (2) began in the past and continues into the present. Use *have* or *has* with the past participle.

EXAMPLE: *Poetry has inspired readers throughout the ages.*

The **past perfect tense** expresses an action in the past that came before another action in the past. Use *had* with the past participle.

EXAMPLE: *The witness had testified before the defendant confessed.*

The future perfect tense expresses an action in the future that will be completed before another action in the future. Use *shall have* or *will have* with the past participle.

EXAMPLE: *They will have finished the novel before seeing the movie version of the tale.*

TIP The past-tense form of an irregular verb is not paired with an auxiliary verb, but the past-perfect-tense form of an irregular verb is always paired with an auxiliary verb.

INCORRECT: *I have went to that restaurant before.*

INCORRECT: *I gone to that restaurant before.*

CORRECT: *I have gone to that restaurant before.*

3.5 PROGRESSIVE FORMS

The progressive forms of the six tenses show ongoing actions. Use forms of *be* with the present participles of verbs.

PRESENT PROGRESSIVE: *She is rehearsing her lines.*

PAST PROGRESSIVE: *She was rehearsing her lines.*

FUTURE PROGRESSIVE: *She will be rehearsing her lines.*

PRESENT PERFECT PROGRESSIVE: *She has been rehearsing her lines.*

PAST PERFECT PROGRESSIVE: *She had been rehearsing her lines.*

FUTURE PERFECT PROGRESSIVE: *She will have been rehearsing her lines.*

WATCH OUT! Do not shift from tense to tense needlessly. Watch out for these special cases:

- In most compound sentences and in sentences with compound predicates, keep the tenses the same.

  INCORRECT: *Every morning they get up and went to work.*

  CORRECT: *Every morning they get up and go to work.*

- If one past action happened before another, indicate this with a shift in tense.

  INCORRECT: *She thought she forgot her toothbrush.*

  CORRECT: *She thought she had forgotten her toothbrush.*

GRAMMAR PRACTICE

Identify the tense of the verb(s) in each of the following sentences. If you find an unnecessary tense shift, correct it.

1. The setting of *The Crucible* is the late 17th century in Salem, Massachusetts.
2. Before the witch trials ended, people had lost their ability to make objective judgments.
3. Playwright Arthur Miller knew that the play pertains to his own time.
4. People will read it far into the future, and many will apply its message to their own time.
5. In the play some accuse others of being witches, even though they knew the accusation was false.

3.6 ACTIVE AND PASSIVE VOICE

The voice of a verb tells whether its subject performs or receives the action expressed by the verb. When the subject performs the action, the verb is in the **active voice.** When the subject is the receiver of the action, the verb is in the **passive voice.**

Compare these two sentences:

ACTIVE: *The Puritans did not celebrate Christmas.*

PASSIVE: *Christmas was not celebrated by the Puritans.*

To form the passive voice, use a form of *be* with the past participle of the verb.

WATCH OUT! Use the passive voice sparingly. It can make writing awkward and less direct.

AWKWARD: *The stories of hysterical witnesses were believed by gullible and fearful jurors.*

BETTER: *Gullible and fearful jurors believed the stories of hysterical witnesses.*

There are occasions when you will choose to use the passive voice because

- you want to emphasize the receiver: *The king was shot.*
- the doer is unknown: *My books were stolen.*
- the doer is unimportant: *French is spoken here.*

GRAMMAR PRACTICE

For the five items below, identify the boldfaced verb phrase as active or passive.

1. *The Crucible* **has played** in theaters throughout the world.
2. It **was written** by Arthur Miller, one of America's greatest dramatists.
3. Miller **did** not **approve** of Reverend Parris's greed for gold.
4. **Has** the reputation of the minister **been maligned?**

4 Modifiers

Modifiers are words or groups of words that change or limit the meanings of other words. Adjectives and adverbs are common modifiers.

4.1 ADJECTIVES

Adjectives modify nouns and pronouns by telling which one, what kind, how many, or how much.

WHICH ONE: *this, that, these, those*

EXAMPLE: *That couch needs to be reupholstered.*

WHAT KIND: *large, unique, anxious, moldy*

EXAMPLE: *The anxious speaker shuffled through her notes.*

HOW MANY: *ten, many, several, every, each*

EXAMPLE: *Each child grabbed several candies from the bowl.*

HOW MUCH: *more, less, little*

EXAMPLE: *There was more snow on the ground in the morning.*

4.2 PREDICATE ADJECTIVES

Most adjectives come before the nouns they modify, as in the previous examples. A **predicate adjective,** however, follows a linking verb and describes the subject.

EXAMPLE: *My friends are very intelligent.*

Be especially careful to use adjectives (not adverbs) after such linking verbs as *look, feel, grow, taste,* and *smell.*

EXAMPLE: *The weather grows cold.*

4.3 ADVERBS

Adverbs modify verbs, adjectives, and other adverbs by telling where, when, how, or to what extent.

WHERE: *The children played outside.*

WHEN: *The author spoke yesterday.*

HOW: *We walked slowly behind the leader.*

TO WHAT EXTENT: *He worked very hard.*

Adverbs may occur in many places in sentences, both before and after the words they modify.

EXAMPLES: *Suddenly the wind shifted.*

The wind suddenly shifted.

The wind shifted suddenly.

4.4 ADJECTIVE OR ADVERB?

Many adverbs are formed by adding *-ly* to adjectives.

EXAMPLES: *sweet, sweetly; gentle, gently*

However, *-ly* added to a noun will usually yield an adjective.

EXAMPLES: *friend, friendly; woman, womanly*

4.5 COMPARISON OF MODIFIERS

Modifiers can be used to compare two or more things. The form of a modifier shows the degree of comparison. Both adjectives and adverbs have three forms: the **positive,** the **comparative,** and the **superlative**.

The **positive form** is used to describe individual things, groups, or actions.

EXAMPLES:

Stephen Crane was a great writer.

His descriptions are vivid.

The **comparative form** is used to compare two things, groups, or actions.

EXAMPLES:

I think that Stephen Crane was a greater writer than Jack London.

Crane's descriptions are more vivid.

The **superlative form** is used to compare more than two things, groups, or actions.

EXAMPLES:

I think that Crane was the greatest writer of his era.

Crane's descriptions are the most vivid I have ever read.

4.6 REGULAR COMPARISONS

Most one-syllable and some two-syllable adjectives and adverbs have comparatives and superlatives formed by adding *-er* and *-est.* All three-syllable and most two-syllable modifiers have comparatives and superlatives formed with *more* and *most.*

Modifier	Comparative	Superlative
tall	taller	tallest
kind	kinder	kindest
droopy	droopier	droopiest
expensive	more expensive	most expensive
wasteful	more wasteful	most wasteful

WATCH OUT! Note that spelling changes must sometimes be made to form the comparatives and superlatives of modifiers.

EXAMPLES:

friendly, friendlier (Change *y* to *i* and add the ending.)

sad, sadder (Double the final consonant and add the ending.)

4.7 IRREGULAR COMPARISONS

Some commonly used modifiers have irregular comparative and superlative forms. They are listed in the following chart.

Modifier	Comparative	Superlative
good	better	best
bad	worse	worst
far	farther *or* further	farthest *or* furthest
little	less *or* lesser	least
many	more	most
well	better	best
much	more	most

4.8 PROBLEMS WITH MODIFIERS

Study the tips that follow to avoid common mistakes:

Farther* and *Further Use *farther* for distances; use *further* for everything else.

Double Comparisons Make a comparison by using *-er/-est* or by using *more/most.* Using *-er* with *more* or using *-est* with *most* is incorrect.

INCORRECT: *I like her more better than she likes me.*

CORRECT: *I like her better than she likes me.*

Illogical Comparisons An illogical or confusing comparison results when two unrelated things are compared or when something is compared with itself. The word *other* or the word *else* should be used in a comparison of an individual member to the rest of a group.

ILLOGICAL: *The narrator was more curious about the war than any student in his class.* (implies that the narrator isn't a student in the class)

LOGICAL: *The narrator was more curious about the war than any other student in his class.* (identifies that the narrator is a student)

Bad* vs. *Badly *Bad,* always an adjective, is used before a noun or after a linking verb. *Badly,* always an adverb, never modifies a noun. Be sure to use the right form after a linking verb.

INCORRECT: *Ed felt badly after his team lost.*

CORRECT: *Ed felt bad after his team lost.*

Good* vs. *Well *Good* is always an adjective. It is used before a noun or after a linking verb. *Well* is often an adverb meaning "expertly" or "properly." *Well* can also be used as an adjective after a linking verb when it means "in good health."

INCORRECT: *Helen writes very good.*

CORRECT: *Helen writes very well.*

CORRECT: *Yesterday I felt bad; today I feel well.*

Double Negatives If you add a negative word to a sentence that is already negative, the result will be an error known as a double negative. When using *not* or *-n't* with a verb, use *any-* words, such as *anybody* or *anything,* rather than *no-* words, such as *nobody* or *nothing,* later in the sentence.

INCORRECT: *I don't have no money.*

CORRECT: *I don't have any money.*

Using *hardly, barely,* or *scarcely* after a negative word is also incorrect.

INCORRECT: *They couldn't barely see two feet ahead.*

CORRECT: *They could barely see two feet ahead.*

Misplaced Modifiers Sometimes a modifier is placed so far away from the word it modifies that the intended meaning of the sentence is unclear. Prepositional phrases and participial phrases are often misplaced. Place modifiers as close as possible to the words they modify.

MISPLACED: *The ranger explained how to find ducks in her office.* (The ducks were not in the ranger's office.)

CLEARER: *In her office, the ranger explained how to find ducks.*

Dangling Modifiers Sometimes a modifier doesn't appear to modify any word in a sentence. Most dangling modifiers are participial phrases or infinitive phrases.

DANGLING: *Coming home with groceries, our parrot said, "Hello!"*

CLEARER: *Coming home with groceries, we heard our parrot say, "Hello!"*

GRAMMAR PRACTICE

Choose the correct word or words from each pair in parentheses.

1. Flannery O'Connor's story is (better/more better) than other stories I have read recently.
2. Mr. Shiftlet and Mrs. Crater (could/couldn't) hardly be less honest with each other.
3. Mr. Shiftlet says there isn't (any/no) broken thing on the farm that he can't fix.
4. He feels (good/well) about fixing the car.
5. Who do you think is the (stranger/strangest) person—Mr. Shiftlet or Mrs. Crater?
6. Mr. Shiftlet feels (bad/badly) about the rottenness of the world.
7. As Mr. Shiftlet drove on alone he felt (depresseder/more depressed) than ever.
8. Mr. Shiftlet didn't feel very (well/good) about being alone, so he picked up a hitchhiker.
9. One wonders how many other great stories Flannery O'Connor would have written had she lived (longer/more longer).

5 Prepositions, Conjunctions, and Interjections

5.1 PREPOSITIONS

A preposition is a word used to show the relationship between a noun or a pronoun and another word in the sentence.

Commonly Used Prepositions			
above	down	near	through
at	for	of	to
before	from	on	up
below	in	out	with
by	into	over	without

A preposition is always followed by a word or group of words that serves as its object. The preposition, its object, and modifiers of the object are called the **prepositional phrase.** In each example below, the prepositional phrase is highlighted and the object of the preposition is in boldface type.

EXAMPLES:

The future of the entire ***kingdom*** *is uncertain.*

We searched through the deepest ***woods.***

Prepositional phrases may be used as adjectives or as adverbs. The phrase in the first example is used as an adjective modifying the noun *future.* In the second example, the phrase is used as an adverb modifying the verb *searched.*

WATCH OUT! Prepositional phrases must be as close as possible to the word they modify.

MISPLACED: *We have clothes for leisurewear of many colors.*

CLEARER: *We have clothes of many colors for leisurewear.*

5.2 CONJUNCTIONS

A conjunction is a word used to connect words, phrases, or sentences. There are three kinds of conjunctions: **coordinating conjunctions, correlative conjunctions,** and **subordinating conjunctions.**

Coordinating conjunctions connect words or word groups that have the same function in a sentence. They include *and, but, or, for, so, yet,* and *nor.*

Coordinating conjunctions can join nouns, pronouns, verbs, adjectives, adverbs, prepositional phrases, and clauses in a sentence.

These examples show coordinating conjunctions joining words of the same function:

EXAMPLES:

I have many friends but few enemies. (two noun objects)

We ran out the door and into the street. (two prepositional phrases)

They are pleasant yet seem aloof. (two predicates)

We have to go now, or we will be late. (two clauses)

Correlative conjunctions are similar to coordinating conjunctions. However, correlative conjunctions are always used in pairs.

Correlative Conjunctions		
both . . . and	neither . . . nor	whether . . . or
either . . . or	not only . . . but also	

Subordinating conjunctions introduce subordinate clauses—clauses that cannot stand by themselves as complete sentences. The subordinating conjunction shows how the subordinate clause relates to the rest of the sentence. The relationships include time, manner, place, cause, comparison, condition, and purpose.

Subordinating Conjunctions	
Time	*after, as, as long as, as soon as, before, since, until, when, whenever, while*
Manner	*as, as if*
Place	*where, wherever*
Cause	*because, since*
Comparison	*as, as much as, than*
Condition	*although, as long as, even if, even though, if, provided that, though, unless, while*
Purpose	*in order that, so that, that*

In the example below, the boldface word is the conjunction, and the highlighted words form a subordinate clause:

EXAMPLE: *Walt Whitman was a man of the people,* ***although*** *many did not appreciate his poems.*

Walt Whitman was a man of the people is an independent clause, because it can stand alone as a complete sentence. *Although many did not appreciate his poems* cannot stand alone as a complete sentence; it is thus a subordinate clause.

Conjunctive adverbs are used to connect clauses that can stand by themselves as sentences. Conjunctive adverbs include *also, besides, finally, however, moreover, nevertheless, otherwise,* and *then.*

EXAMPLE: *She loved the fall; however, she also enjoyed winter.*

5.3 INTERJECTIONS

Interjections are words used to show emotion, such as *wow* and *cool.* Interjections are usually set off from the rest of a sentence by a comma or by an exclamation mark.

EXAMPLE: *Thoreau lived in the woods by himself. Amazing!*

6 The Sentence and Its Parts

A **sentence** is a group of words used to express a complete thought. A complete sentence has a subject and a predicate.

For more information, see ***Quick Reference: The Sentence and Its Parts,*** *page R52.*

6.1 KINDS OF SENTENCES

There are four basic types of sentences.

Type	Definition	Example
Declarative	states a fact, a wish, an intent, or a feeling	I wrote an essay on "The Weary Blues" for class.
Interrogative	asks a question	Are you familiar with Langston Hughes?
Imperative	gives a command or direction	Read "The Weary Blues" aloud.
Exclamatory	expresses strong feeling or excitement	It sounds like a song!

6.2 COMPOUND SUBJECTS AND PREDICATES

A compound subject consists of two or more subjects that share the same verb. They are typically joined by the coordinating conjunction *and* or *or.*

EXAMPLE: *Courtney and Eric enjoy the theater.*

A compound predicate consists of two or more predicates that share the same subject. They too are typically joined by a coordinating conjunction, usually *and, but,* or *or.*

EXAMPLE: *The main character in "Winter Dreams" attended a prestigious university and became a successful businessman.*

6.3 COMPLEMENTS

A **complement** is a word or group of words that completes the meaning of the sentence. Some sentences contain only a subject and a verb. Most sentences, however, require additional words placed after the verb to complete the meaning of the sentence. There are three kinds of complements: direct objects, indirect objects, and subject complements.

Direct objects are words or word groups that receive the action of action verbs. A direct object answers the question *what* or *whom.*

EXAMPLES:

The students asked many questions. (Asked what?)

The teacher quickly answered the students. (Answered whom?)

Indirect objects tell to whom or what or for whom or what the actions of verbs are performed. Indirect objects come before direct objects. In the examples that follow, the indirect objects are highlighted.

EXAMPLES:

My sister usually gave her *friends* good advice. (Gave to whom?)

Her brother sent the store a heavy package. (Sent to what?)

Subject complements come after linking verbs and identify or describe the subjects. A subject complement that names or identifies a subject is called a **predicate nominative.** Predicate nominatives include **predicate nouns** and **predicate pronouns.**

EXAMPLES:

My friends are very hard workers.

The best writer in the class is she.

A subject complement that describes a subject is called a **predicate adjective.**

EXAMPLE: *The pianist appeared very energetic.*

7 Phrases

A **phrase** is a group of related words that does not contain a subject and a predicate but functions in a sentence as a single part of speech.

7.1 PREPOSITIONAL PHRASES

A **prepositional phrase** is a phrase that consists of a preposition, its object, and any modifiers of the object. Prepositional phrases that modify nouns or pronouns are called **adjective phrases.** Prepositional phrases that modify verbs, adjectives, or adverbs are **adverb phrases.**

ADJECTIVE PHRASE: *The central character of the story is a villain.*

ADVERB PHRASE: *He reveals his nature in the first scene.*

7.2 APPOSITIVES AND APPOSITIVE PHRASES

An **appositive** is a noun or pronoun that identifies or renames another noun or pronoun. An **appositive phrase** includes an appositive and modifiers of it.

An appositive can be either **essential** or **nonessential.** An **essential appositive** provides information that is needed to identify what is referred to by the preceding noun or pronoun.

EXAMPLE: The Glass Menagerie *was written by playwright Tennessee Williams.*

A **nonessential appositive** adds extra information about a noun or pronoun whose meaning is already clear. Nonessential appositives and appositive phrases are set off with commas.

EXAMPLE: *Williams uses Laura's glass menagerie, a collection of fragile animal figurines, to represent her relationship to reality.*

8 Verbals and Verbal Phrases

A **verbal** is a verb form that is used as a noun, an adjective, or an adverb. A **verbal phrase** consists of a verbal along with its modifiers and complements. There are three kinds of verbals: **infinitives, participles,** and **gerunds.**

8.1 INFINITIVES AND INFINITIVE PHRASES

An **infinitive** is a verb form that usually begins with *to* and functions as a noun, an adjective, or an adverb. An **infinitive phrase** consists of an infinitive plus its modifiers and complements. The examples that follow show several uses of infinitive phrases.

NOUN: *To know her is my only desire.* (subject)

I'm planning to walk with you. (direct object)

Her goal was to promote women's rights. (predicate nominative)

ADJECTIVE: *We saw his need to be loved.* (adjective modifying *need*)

ADVERB: *She wrote to voice her opinions.* (adverb modifying *wrote*)

Because infinitives usually begin with *to,* it is usually easy to recognize them. However, sometimes *to* may be omitted.

EXAMPLE: *Let no one dare [to] enter this shrine.*

8.2 PARTICIPLES AND PARTICIPIAL PHRASES

A **participle** is a verb form that functions as an adjective. Like adjectives, participles modify nouns and pronouns. Most participles are present-participle forms, ending in *-ing,* or past-participle forms ending in *-ed* or *-en.* In the examples that follow, the participles are highlighted:

MODIFYING A NOUN: *The jogging woman completed another lap on the track.*

MODIFYING A PRONOUN: *Bored, he began to doodle in the margins of his notebook.*

Participial phrases are participles with all their modifiers and complements.

MODIFYING A NOUN: *Changing tactics, the attorney questioned the witness.*

MODIFYING A PRONOUN: *Dismissed for the day, they filed out of the courtroom.*

8.3 DANGLING AND MISPLACED PARTICIPLES

A participle or participial phrase should be placed as close as possible to the word that it modifies. Otherwise the meaning of the sentence may not be clear.

MISPLACED: *The boys were looking for squirrels searching the trees.*

CLEARER: *The boys searching the trees were looking for squirrels.*

A participle or participial phrase that does not clearly modify anything in a sentence is called a **dangling participle.** A dangling participle causes confusion because it appears to modify a word that it cannot sensibly modify. Correct a dangling participle by providing a word for the participle to modify.

DANGLING: *Running like the wind, my hat fell off.* (The hat wasn't running.)

CLEARER: *Running like the wind, I lost my hat.*

8.4 GERUNDS AND GERUND PHRASES

A **gerund** is a verb form ending in *-ing* that functions as a noun. Gerunds may perform any function nouns perform.

SUBJECT: *Running is my favorite pastime.*

DIRECT OBJECT: *I truly love running.*

INDIRECT OBJECT: *You should give running a try.*

SUBJECT COMPLEMENT: *My deepest passion is running.*

OBJECT OF PREPOSITION: *Her love of running keeps her strong.*

Gerund phrases are gerunds with all their modifiers and complements.

SUBJECT: *Wishing on a star never got me far.*

OBJECT OF PREPOSITION: *I will finish before leaving the office.*

APPOSITIVE: *Her avocation, flying airplanes, finally led to full-time employment.*

GRAMMAR PRACTICE

Identify the underlined phrases as appositive phrases, infinitive phrases, participial phrases, or gerund phrases.

1. In "The Masque of the Red Death," Poe uses allegory, <u>a device representing abstract qualities.</u>
2. <u>To escape the plague,</u> Prince Prospero seals himself and his courtiers in a walled abbey.
3. <u>Feeling protected from the Red Death,</u> Prospero holds a lavish masquerade ball.
4. There suddenly appears in the last room a masked figure, <u>the Red Death in a ghastly shroud.</u>
5. <u>Killing the apparition</u> is impossible.

9 Clauses

A **clause** is a group of words that contains a subject and a verb. There are two kinds of clauses: independent clauses and subordinate clauses.

9.1 INDEPENDENT AND SUBORDINATE CLAUSES

An **independent clause** can stand alone as a sentence, as the word *independent* suggests.

INDEPENDENT CLAUSE: *Frederick Douglass was an eloquent speaker.*

A sentence may contain more than one independent clause.

EXAMPLE: *Frederick Douglass was an eloquent speaker, but he encountered a lot of opposition.*

In the preceding example, the coordinating conjunction *but* joins two independent clauses.

For more information, see ***Conjunctions,*** *page R63.*

A **subordinate clause** cannot stand alone as a sentence. It is subordinate to, or dependent on, an independent clause.

EXAMPLE: *Although Frederick Douglass was a runaway slave, he frequently appeared in public to raise support for the abolitionist movement.*

The highlighted clause cannot stand by itself; it must be joined with an independent clause to form a complete sentence.

9.2 ADJECTIVE CLAUSES

An **adjective clause** is a subordinate clause used as an adjective. It usually follows the noun or pronoun it modifies. Adjective clauses are typically introduced by the relative pronoun *who, whom, whose, which,* or *that.*

EXAMPLES: *Frederick Douglass wrote objectively about the whippings that Corey frequently gave him.*

The autobiographer whom I liked best was Frederick Douglass.

He was a man who was determined to find freedom.

For more information, see ***Relative Pronouns,*** *page R58.*

An adjective clause can be either essential or nonessential. An **essential adjective clause** provides information that is necessary to identify the preceding noun or pronoun.

EXAMPLE: *The couch that we picked out will not be delivered for three weeks.*

A **nonessential adjective clause** adds additional information about a noun or pronoun whose meaning is already clear. Nonessential clauses are set off with commas.

EXAMPLE: *Joel's grandmother, who was born in Italy, makes the best lasagna.*

TIP The relative pronouns *whom, which,* and *that* may sometimes be omitted when they are objects in adjective clauses.

EXAMPLE: *The autobiographer [whom] I liked best was Frederick Douglass.*

9.3 ADVERB CLAUSES

An **adverb clause** is a subordinate clause that is used to modify a verb, an adjective, or an adverb. It is introduced by a subordinating conjunction.

For more information, see ***Conjunctions,*** *page R63.*

Adverb clauses typically occur at the beginning or end of sentences.

MODIFYING A VERB: *When we need you, we will call.*

MODIFYING AN ADVERB: *I'll stay here where there is shelter from the rain.*

MODIFYING AN ADJECTIVE: *Roman felt as good as he had ever felt.*

9.4 NOUN CLAUSES

A **noun clause** is a subordinate clause that is used as a noun. A noun clause may be used as a subject, a direct object, an indirect object, a predicate nominative, or the object of a preposition. Noun clauses are introduced either by pronouns, such as *that, what, who, whoever, which,* and *whose,* or by subordinating conjunctions, such as *how, when, where, why,* and *whether.*

For more information, see ***Conjunctions,*** *page R63.*

TIP Because the same words may introduce adjective and noun clauses, you need to consider how a clause functions within its sentence. To determine if a clause is a noun clause, try substituting *something* or *someone* for the clause. If you can do it, it is probably a noun clause.

EXAMPLES: *I know whose woods these are.*

("I know *something.*" The clause is a noun clause, direct object of the verb *know.*)

Give a copy to whoever wants one. ("Give a copy to *someone.*" The clause is a noun clause, object of the preposition *to.*)

10 The Structure of Sentences

When classified by their structure, there are four kinds of sentences: simple, compound, complex, and compound-complex.

10.1 SIMPLE SENTENCES

A **simple sentence** is a sentence that has one independent clause and no subordinate clauses. Various parts of simple sentences may be compound, and simple sentences may contain grammatical structures such as appositive and verbal phrases.

EXAMPLES:

Ambrose Bierce and Stephen Crane, two great American writers, both wrote during the latter half of the 19th century. (compound subject and an appositive)

Crane, best known for writing fiction, also wrote great poetry. (participial phrase containing a gerund phrase)

10.2 COMPOUND SENTENCES

A **compound sentence** consists of two or more independent clauses. The clauses in compound sentences are joined with commas and coordinating conjunctions (*and, but, or, nor, yet, for, so*) or with semicolons. Like simple sentences, compound sentences do not contain any subordinate clauses.

EXAMPLES:

I enjoyed the free pottery class, and I would like to go again.

Carl Sandburg's "Chicago" seems to celebrate the youthful energy of a booming industrial city; however, the poem dwells on the negative impacts of growth.

WATCH OUT! Do not confuse compound sentences with simple sentences that have compound parts.

EXAMPLE: *The center fielder caught the ball and immediately threw it toward second base.* (Here *and* joins parts of a compound predicate, not a compound sentence.)

10.3 COMPLEX SENTENCES

A **complex sentence** consists of one independent clause and one or more subordinate clauses. Each subordinate clause can be used as a noun or as a modifier. If it is used as a modifier, a subordinate clause usually modifies a word in the independent clause, and the independent clause can stand alone. However, when a subordinate clause is a noun clause, it is a part of the independent clause; the two cannot be separated.

MODIFIER: *One should not complain unless one has a better solution.*

NOUN CLAUSE: *We sketched pictures of whoever we wished.* (The noun clause is the object of the preposition *of* and cannot be separated from the rest of the sentence.)

10.4 COMPOUND-COMPLEX SENTENCES

A **compound-complex sentence** contains two or more independent clauses and one or more subordinate clauses. Compound-complex sentences are, simply, both compound and complex. If you start with a compound sentence, all you need to do to form a compound-complex sentence is add a subordinate clause.

COMPOUND: *All the students knew the answer, yet they were too shy to volunteer.*

COMPOUND-COMPLEX: *All the students knew the answer that their teacher expected, yet they were too shy to volunteer.*

10.5 PARALLEL STRUCTURE

When you write sentences, make sure that coordinate parts are equivalent, or **parallel,** in structure.

NOT PARALLEL: *Erin loved basketball and to play hockey.* (*Basketball* is a noun; *to play hockey* is a phrase.)

PARALLEL: *Erin loved basketball and hockey.* (*Basketball* and *hockey* are both nouns.)

NOT PARALLEL: *He wanted to rent an apartment, a new car, and traveling around the country.* (*To rent* is an infinitive, *car* is a noun, and *traveling* is a gerund.)

PARALLEL: *He wanted to rent an apartment, to drive a new car, and to travel around the country.* (*To rent, to drive,* and *to travel* are all infinitives.)

11 Writing Complete Sentences

Remember, a sentence is a group of words that expresses a complete thought. In formal writing, try to avoid both sentence fragments and run-on sentences.

11.1 CORRECTING FRAGMENTS

A **sentence fragment** is a group of words that is only part of a sentence. It does not express a complete thought and may be confusing to a reader or listener. A sentence fragment may be lacking a subject, a predicate, or both.

FRAGMENT: *Waited for the boat to arrive.* (no subject)

CORRECTED: *We waited for the boat to arrive.*

FRAGMENT: *People of various races, ages, and creeds.* (no predicate)

CORRECTED: *People of various races, ages, and creeds gathered together.*

FRAGMENT: *Near the old cottage.* (neither subject nor predicate)

CORRECTED: *The burial ground is near the old cottage.*

In your writing, fragments may be a result of haste or incorrect punctuation. Sometimes fixing a fragment will be a matter of attaching it to a preceding or following sentence.

FRAGMENT: *We saw the two girls. Waiting for the bus to arrive.*

CORRECTED: *We saw the two girls waiting for the bus to arrive.*

11.2 CORRECTING RUN-ON SENTENCES

A **run-on sentence** is made up of two or more sentences written as though they were one. Some run-ons have no punctuation within them. Others may have only commas where conjunctions or stronger punctuation marks are necessary. Use your judgment in correcting run-on sentences, as you have choices. You can make a run-on two sentences if the thoughts are not closely connected. If the thoughts are closely related, you can keep the run-on as one sentence by adding a semicolon or a conjunction.

RUN-ON: *We found a place for the picnic by a small pond it was three miles from the village.*

MAKE TWO SENTENCES: *We found a place for the picnic by a small pond. It was three miles from the village.*

RUN-ON: *We found a place for the picnic by a small pond it was perfect.*

USE A SEMICOLON: *We found a place for the picnic by a small pond; it was perfect.*

ADD A CONJUNCTION: *We found a place for the picnic by a small pond, and it was perfect.*

WATCH OUT! When you form compound sentences, make sure you use appropriate punctuation: a comma before a coordinating conjunction, a semicolon when there is no coordinating conjunction. A very common mistake is to use a comma alone instead of a comma and a conjunction. This error is called a **comma splice.**

INCORRECT: *He finished the apprenticeship, he left the village.*

CORRECT: *He finished the apprenticeship, and he left the village.*

GRAMMAR PRACTICE

Rewrite the following paragraph, correcting all fragments and run-ons.

The narrator in Charlotte Perkins Gilman's story "The Yellow Wallpaper" expects that her husband will laugh at her, that's an odd response, in my opinion. She could have lived more happily. If the relationship between her and her husband were an equal partnership. We can acknowledge that men and women may be different in some ways. Without believing that they are as different as this story suggests. The male character acts practical and "strong," the female character acts nervous and weak.

12 Subject-Verb Agreement

The subject and verb in a clause must agree in number. Agreement means that if the subject is singular, the verb is also singular, and if the subject is plural, the verb is also plural.

12.1 BASIC AGREEMENT

Fortunately, agreement between subjects and verbs in English is simple. Most verbs show the difference between singular and plural only in the third person of the present tense. In the present tense, the third-person singular form ends in *-s.*

Present-Tense Verb Forms

Singular	Plural
I eat	we eat
you eat	you eat
she, he, it eats	they eat

12.2 AGREEMENT WITH *BE*

The verb *be* presents special problems in agreement, because this verb does not follow the usual verb patterns.

Forms of *Be*

Present Tense		Past Tense	
Singular	Plural	Singular	Plural
I am	we are	I was	we were
you are	you are	you were	you were
she, he, it is	they are	she, he, it was	they were

12.3 WORDS BETWEEN SUBJECT AND VERB

A verb agrees only with its subject. When words come between a subject and a verb, ignore them when considering proper agreement. Identify the subject, and make sure the verb agrees with it.

EXAMPLES:

A story in the newspapers tells about the 1890s.

Dad as well as Mom reads the paper daily.

12.4 AGREEMENT WITH COMPOUND SUBJECTS

Use plural verbs with most compound subjects joined by the word *and.*

EXAMPLE: *My mother and her sisters call each other every Sunday.*

To confirm that you need a plural verb, you could substitute the plural pronoun *they* for *my mother and her sisters.*

If a compound subject is thought of as a unit, use a singular verb. Test this by substituting the singular pronoun *it.*

EXAMPLE: *Liver and onions [it] is Robert's least favorite dish.*

Use a singular verb with a compound subject that is preceded by *each, every,* or *many a.*

EXAMPLE: *Not every dog and cat at the shelter makes a good pet.*

When the parts of a compound subject are joined by *or, nor,* or the correlative conjunctions *either . . . or* or *neither . . . nor,* make the verb agree with the noun or pronoun nearest the verb.

EXAMPLES:

Baseball or football is my favorite sport.

Either my rabbits or my turtle was loose in my room.

Neither Mrs. Howard nor her two sons were home at the time of the accident.

12.5 PERSONAL PRONOUNS AS SUBJECTS

When using a personal pronoun as a subject, make sure to match it with the correct form of the verb *be.* (See the chart in Section 12.2.) Note especially that the pronoun *you* takes the forms *are* and *were,* regardless of whether it is singular or plural.

WATCH OUT! *You is* and *you was* are nonstandard forms and should be avoided in writing and speaking. *We was* and *they was* are also forms to be avoided.

INCORRECT: *You is facing the wrong direction.*

CORRECT: *You are facing the wrong direction.*

INCORRECT: *We was telling ghost stories.*

CORRECT: *We were telling ghost stories.*

12.6 INDEFINITE PRONOUNS AS SUBJECTS

Some indefinite pronouns are always singular; some are always plural.

Singular Indefinite Pronouns			
another	either	neither	one
anybody	everybody	nobody	somebody
anyone	everyone	no one	someone
anything	everything	nothing	something
each	much		

EXAMPLES:

Each of the writers was given an award.

Somebody in the room upstairs is sleeping.

Plural Indefinite Pronouns			
both	few	many	several

EXAMPLES:

Many of the books in our library are not in circulation.

Few have been returned recently.

Still other indefinite pronouns may be either singular or plural.

Singular or Plural Indefinite Pronouns		
all	more	none
any	most	some

The number of the indefinite pronoun *any* or *none* often depends on the intended meaning.

EXAMPLES:

Any of these topics has potential for a good article. (any one topic)

Any of these topics have potential for good articles. (all of the many topics)

The indefinite pronouns *all, some, more, most,* and *none* are singular when they refer to quantities or parts of things. They are plural when they refer to numbers of individual things. Context will usually give a clue.

EXAMPLES:

All of the flour is gone. (referring to a quantity)

All of the flowers are gone. (referring to individual items)

12.7 INVERTED SENTENCES

Problems in agreement often occur in inverted sentences beginning with *here* or *there;* in questions beginning with *how, when, why, where,* or *what;* and in inverted sentences beginning with phrases. Identify the subject—wherever it is—before deciding on the verb.

EXAMPLES:

There clearly are far too many cooks in this kitchen.

What is the correct ingredient for this stew?

Far from the embroiled cooks stands the master chef.

GRAMMAR PRACTICE

Locate the subject of each clause in the sentences below. Then choose the correct verb.

1. Many poets have written great poetry, but few (is/are) as talented as Emily Dickinson.
2. There (is/are) many lines in her work that her readers (treasures/treasure).
3. Some of her readers (appreciates/appreciate) her use of dashes, while others (finds/find) it confusing.
4. Each of her poems (presents/present) an idea to think about.
5. What (is/are) the dominant vowel sound in the last four lines of "Much Madness is divinest Sense"?
6. The consonant that prevails in the same poem (seems/seem) to be *s*.
7. I can't decide whether the poem's sound or its ideas (is/are) more striking.

12.8 SENTENCES WITH PREDICATE NOMINATIVES

When a predicate nominative serves as a complement in a sentence, use a verb that agrees with the subject, not the complement.

EXAMPLES:

The hunting habits of the North American wolf are an example of how change in the environment affects animals. (The subject is the plural noun *habits*—not *wolf*—and it takes the plural verb *are.*)

An example of how change in the environment affects animals is seen in the hunting habits of the North American wolf. (The subject is the singular noun *example*, and it takes the singular verb *is seen.*)

12.9 *DON'T* AND *DOESN'T* AS AUXILIARY VERBS

The auxiliary verb *doesn't* is used with singular subjects and with the personal pronouns *she, he,* and *it*. The auxiliary verb *don't* is used with plural subjects and with the personal pronouns *I, we, you,* and *they.*

SINGULAR: *She doesn't have a costume for the rehearsal.*

Doesn't the doctor have an appointment Wednesday morning?

PLURAL: *They don't think they did very well on that math test.*

The cats don't need to be fed more than twice a day.

12.10 COLLECTIVE NOUNS AS SUBJECTS

Collective nouns are singular nouns that name groups of persons or things. *Team,* for example, is the collective name of a group of individuals. A collective noun takes a singular verb when the group acts as a single unit. It takes a plural verb when the members of the group act separately.

EXAMPLES:

Our team usually wins. (The team as a whole wins.)

Our team vote differently on most issues. (The individual members vote.)

12.11 RELATIVE PRONOUNS AS SUBJECTS

When the relative pronoun *who, which,* or *that* is used as a subject in an adjective clause, the verb in the clause must agree in number with the antecedent of the pronoun.

SINGULAR: *Have you selected one of the poems that is meaningful to you?*

The antecedent of the relative pronoun *that* is the singular *one;* therefore, *that* is singular and must take the singular verb *is.*

PLURAL: *The fairy tales, which have been collected from many different sources, are annotated.*

The antecedent of the relative pronoun *which* is the plural *fairy tales. Which* is plural, and it takes the plural verb *have been collected.*

The key to becoming an independent reader is to develop a toolkit of vocabulary strategies. By learning and practicing the strategies, you'll know what to do when you encounter unfamiliar words while reading. You'll also know how to refine the words you use for different situations—personal, school, and work.

Being a good speller is important when communicating your ideas in writing. Learning basic spelling rules and checking your spelling in a dictionary will help you spell words that you may not use frequently.

COMMON CORE

Included in this handbook:
L 2b, L 4a–c, L 6

1 Using Context Clues

The context of a word is made up of the punctuation marks, words, sentences, and paragraphs that surround the word. A word's context can give you important clues about its meaning.

1.1 GENERAL CONTEXT

Sometimes you need to infer the meaning of an unfamiliar word by reading all the information in a passage.

> *I told my parents I wanted to quit playing the piano, but they told me to persevere anyway.*

You can figure out from the context that *persevere* means "continue."

1.2 SPECIFIC CONTEXT CLUES

Sometimes writers help you understand the meanings of words by providing specific clues such as those shown in the chart.

1.3 IDIOMS, SLANG, AND FIGURATIVE LANGUAGE

Use context clues to figure out the meanings of idioms, figurative language, and slang.

An **idiom** is an expression whose overall meaning is different from the meaning of the individual words.

> *If you're going to buy a house with a garden, you'd better have a green thumb. (Green thumb* means "ability to grow plants.")

Figurative language is language that communicates meaning beyond the literal meaning of the words. Note this example from "A Chip of Glass Ruby" by Nadine Gordimer:

> *There was the feeling, in the house, that he had wept and raged at her, that boulders of reproach had thundered down upon her absence, and yet he had said not one word. (Boulders of reproach had thundered down upon her absence* means he was very angry that she was gone.)

Slang is informal language composed of made-up words and ordinary words that are used to mean something different from their meanings in formal English.

> *My parents freaked out when I told them that I went to the concert without their permission. (Freaked out* means "became greatly distressed.")

Specific Context Clues

Type of Clue	Key Words/ Phrases	Example
Definition or restatement of the meaning of the word	or, which is, that is, in other words, also known as, also called	*Perennials*—**plants that live for more than two years**—make up only one-third of the garden's exhibit.
Example following an unfamiliar word	such as, like, as if, for example, especially, including	Their new apartment was *arrayed* with many beautiful things, **such as a crystal lamp and a porcelain vase.**
Comparison with a more familiar word or concept	as, like, also, similar to, in the same way, likewise	The prairie grasses *undulated* in the wind **like the waves in the ocean.**
Contrast with a familiar word or experience	unlike, but, however, although, on the other hand, on the contrary	My dog is usually very **calm, unlike** our neighbor's dog, which is very *rowdy.*

For more information, see ***Vocabulary Strategy: Context Clues,*** *pages 101, 131, 214, 672, 1000, and 1258.*

2 Analyzing Word Structure

Many words can be broken into smaller parts, such as base words, roots, prefixes, and suffixes.

2.1 BASE WORDS

A **base word** is a word part that by itself is also a word. Other words or word parts can be added to base words to form new words.

2.2 ROOTS

A **root** is a word part that contains the core meaning of the word. Many English words contain roots that come from older languages such as Greek, Latin, Old English (Anglo-Saxon), and Norse. Knowing the meaning of a word's root can help you determine the word's meaning.

Root	Meaning	Example
aster, astr (Greek)	star	asterisk
fic/ fac/ fec (Latin)	make, do	factory
spec/ spect/ spic (Latin)	look at, see, behold	spectator
ten (Latin)	stretch	tendon
derm/ derma (Greek)	skin	epidermis

For more information, see ***Vocabulary Strategy: Word Roots,*** *pages 90, 277, 334, 433, 484, 616, 710, 832, and 906.*

2.3 PREFIXES

A **prefix** is a word part attached to the beginning of a word. Most prefixes come from Greek, Latin, or Old English.

Prefix	Meaning	Example
un- (Old English)	not	unafraid
epi- (Greek)	upon, on, over	epicenter
syn- (Greek)	together, at the same time	synthesis
hexa- (Greek)	six	hexagram
geo- (Greek)	earth	geography
trans- (Latin)	across, beyond	transatlantic
dis- (Latin)	lack of, not	distrust
circum- (Latin)	around	circumvent
hemi- (Latin)	half	hemisphere

For more information, see ***Vocabulary Strategy: Prefixes,*** *pages 376, 398, 760, and 1229.*

2.4 SUFFIXES

A **suffix** is a word part that appears at the end of a root or base word to form a new word. Some suffixes do not change word meaning. These suffixes are

- added to nouns to change the number of persons or objects
- added to verbs to change the tense
- added to modifiers to change the degree of comparison

Suffix	Meaning	Example
-s, -es	to change the number of a noun	trunk + s = trunks
-d, -ed, -ing	to change verb tense	sprinkle + d = sprinkled
-er, -est	to change the degree of comparison in modifiers	cold + er = colder icy + est = iciest

Other suffixes can be added to a root or base to change the word's meaning. These suffixes can also determine a word's part of speech.

Suffix	Meaning	Example
-ence	state or condition of	independence
-ous	full of	furious
-ate	to make	activate
-ly, -ily	manner	quickly

For more information, see ***Vocabulary Strategy: Suffixes,*** *pages 376 and 454.*

Strategies for Understanding Unfamiliar Words

- Look for any prefixes or suffixes. Remove them to isolate the base word or the root.
- See if you recognize any elements—prefix, suffix, root, or base—of the word. You may be able to guess its meaning by analyzing one or two elements.
- Consider the way the word is used in the sentence. Use the context and the word parts to make a logical guess about the word's meaning.
- Consult a dictionary to see whether you are correct.

PRACTICE AND APPLY

Make inferences about the meanings of the following words from the fields of science and math. Consider what you have learned in this section about Greek, Latin, and Anglo-Saxon (Old English) word parts.

astronomy	efficacy	hexagonal
circumference	epidermis	spectrum
distend	geosciences	uncertainty

3 Understanding Word Origins

3.1 ETYMOLOGIES

Etymologies show the origin and historical development of a word. When you study a word's history and origin, you can find out when, where, and how the word came to be.

am•bas•sa•dor (ăm-băs′ə-dər, -dôr′) *n.* A diplomatic official of the highest rank appointed and accredited as representative in residence by one government or sovereign to another, usually for a specific length of time. [Middle English *ambassadour,* from Old French *ambassadeur,* from Medieval Latin *ambactia,* mission, from Latin *ambactus,* servant, ultimately of Celtic origin.]

com•mu•ni•ty (kə-myo͞o′nĭ-tē) *n., pl.* **-ties** A group of people living in the same locality and under the same government. [Middle English *communite,* citizenry, from Old French, from Latin *commūnitās,* fellowship, from *commūnis,* common.]

*For more information, see **Vocabulary Strategy: Etymologies,** pages 80, 257, and 1076.*

PRACTICE AND APPLY

Trace the etymology of the words below, often used in the fields of history and political science.

diplomat	independence	legislature
government	justice	revolution
immigrant	laissez-faire	treaty

3.2 WORD FAMILIES

Words that have the same root make up a word family and have related meanings. The chart shows a common Greek and a common Latin root. Notice how the meanings of the example words are related to the meanings of their roots.

Latin Root	*med:* "middle"
English Words	**mediate** resolve or settle **mediocre** ordinary **media**[2] middle wall of a blood vessel **medial** toward the middle **medium** action midway between two extremes
Greek Root	***chron:* "time"**
English Words	**chronicle** detailed narrative report **chronic** of long duration **synchronize** occur at same time **anachronism** out of proper order in time

*For more information, see **Vocabulary Strategy: Word Family,** pages 334, 433, 616, 710, and 906.*

3.3 WORDS FROM CLASSICAL MYTHOLOGY

The English language includes many words from classical mythology. You can use your knowledge of these myths to understand the origins and meanings of these words. For example, *herculean task* refers to the strongman Hercules. Thus, *herculean task* probably means "a job that is large or difficult." The chart shows a few common words from mythology.

Greek	Roman	Norse
panic	cereal	Wednesday
atlas	mercurial	gun
adonis	Saturday	berserk
mentor	January	valkyrie

PRACTICE AND APPLY

Look up the etymology of each word in the chart and locate the myth associated with it. Use the information from the myth to explain the origin and meaning of each word.

3.4 FOREIGN WORDS

The English language includes words from diverse languages, such as French, Dutch, Spanish, Italian, and Chinese. Many words stayed the way they were in their original language.

French	Dutch	Spanish	Italian
entree	maelstrom	rodeo	pasta
nouveau riche	trek	salsa	opera
potpourri	cookie	bronco	vendetta
tête-à-tête	snoop	tornado	grotto

For more information, see ***Vocabulary Strategy: Foreign Words,*** *page 1016.*

4 Synonyms and Antonyms

4.1 SYNONYMS

A **synonym** is a word with a meaning similar to that of another word. You can find synonyms in a thesaurus or a dictionary. In a dictionary, synonyms are often given as part of the definition of a word. The following word pairs are synonyms:

dry/arid   enthralled/fascinated   gaunt/thin

4.2 ANTONYMS

An **antonym** is a word with a meaning opposite that of another word. The following word pairs are antonyms:

friend/enemy   absurd/logical

courteous/rude   languid/energetic

5 Denotation and Connotation

5.1 DENOTATION

A word's dictionary meaning is called its **denotation.** For example, the denotation of the word *rascal* is "an unethical, dishonest person."

5.2 CONNOTATION

The images or feelings you connect to a word add a finer shade of meaning, called **connotation.** The connation of a word goes beyond its basic dictionary definition. Writers use connotations of words to communicate positive or negative feelings.

Positive	Neutral	Negative
save	store	hoard
fragrance	smell	stench
display	show	flaunt

Make sure you understand the denotation and connotation of a word when you read it or use it in your writing.

For more information, see ***Vocabulary Strategy: Denotation and Connotation,*** *pages 101, 131, 214, and 778.*

6 Analogies

An **analogy** is a comparison between two things that are similar in some way but are otherwise dissimilar. Analogies are sometimes used in writing when unfamiliar subjects or ideas are explained in terms of familiar ones. Analogies often appear on tests as well, usually in a format like this:

TERRIER : DOG ::
A) rat : fish
B) kitten : cat
C) trout : fish
D) fish : trout
E) poodle : collie

Follow these steps to determine the correct answer:

- Read the part in capital letters as "*bird* is to *fly* as . . ."
- Read the answer choices as "*rat* is to *fish,*" "*kitten* is to *cat,*" and so on.
- Ask yourself how the words *terrier* and *dog* are related. (A terrier is a type of dog.)
- Ask yourself which of the choices shows the same relationship. (A kitten is a kind of cat, but not in the same way that a terrier is a kind of dog. A kitten is a baby cat. A trout however, is a type of fish in the sense that a terrier is a type of dog. Therefore, the answer is C.)

For more information, see ***Vocabulary Strategy: Analogies,*** *pages 236, 816, and 1216.*

7 Homonyms and Homophones

7.1 HOMONYMS

Homonyms are words that have the same spelling and sound but have different origins and meanings.

I don't want to bore you with a story about how I had to bore through the living room wall.

Bore can mean "cause a person to lose interest," but an identically spelled word means "to drill a hole."

My dog likes to bark while it scratches the bark on the tree in the backyard.

Bark can mean "the sound made by a dog." However, another identically spelled word means "the outer covering of a tree." Each word has a different meaning and its own dictionary entry.

Sometimes only one of the meanings of two homonyms may be familiar to you. Use context clues to help you figure out the meaning of an unfamiliar word.

7.2 HOMOPHONES

Homophones are words that sound alike but have different meanings and spellings. The following homophones are frequently misused:

it's/its	they're/their/there
to/too/two	stationary/stationery

Many misused homophones are pronouns and contractions. Whenever you are unsure whether to write *your* or *you're* and *who's* or *whose,* ask yourself if you mean *you are* or *who is/has.* If you do, write the contraction. For other homophones, such as *scent* and *sent,* use the meaning of the word to help you decide which one to use.

8 Words with Multiple Meanings

Some words have acquired additional meanings over time that are based on the original meaning.

EXAMPLES: *I was in a hurry so I jammed my clothes into the suitcase. Unfortunately, I jammed my finger in the process.*

These two uses of *jam* have different meanings, but both of them have the same origin. You will find all the meanings of *jam* listed in one entry in the dictionary.

9 Specialized Vocabulary

Specialized vocabulary is special terms suited to a particular field of study or work. For example, science, mathematics, and history all have their own technical or specialized vocabularies. To figure out specialized terms, you can use context clues and reference sources, such as dictionaries on specific subjects, atlases, or manuals.

For more information, see ***Vocabulary Strategy: Specialized Vocabulary,*** *pages 64, 246, 454, and 728.*

10 Using Reference Sources

10.1 DICTIONARIES

A **general dictionary** will tell you not only a word's definitions but also its pronunciation, its parts of speech, and its history and origin. A **specialized dictionary** focuses on terms related to a particular field of study or work. Use a dictionary to check the spelling of any word you are unsure of in your English class and other subjects as well.

10.2 THESAURI

A **thesaurus** (plural, thesauri) is a dictionary of synonyms. A thesaurus can be helpful when you find yourself using the same modifiers over and over again.

10.3 SYNONYM FINDERS

A **synonym finder** is often included in word-processing software. It enables you to highlight a word and be shown a display of its synonyms.

10.4 GLOSSARIES

A **glossary** is a list of specialized terms and their definitions. It is often found in the back of textbooks and sometimes includes pronunciations. In fact, this textbook has four glossaries: the **Glossary of Literary and Nonfiction Terms,** the **Glossary of Reading & Informational Terms,** the **Glossary of Academic Vocabulary in English & Spanish,** and the **Glossary of Vocabulary in English & Spanish.** Use these glossaries to help you understand how terms are used in this textbook.

For more information, see ***Vocabulary Strategy: Reference Sources,*** *pages 112, 257, 692, 1046, and 1076.*

11 Spelling Rules

11.1 WORDS ENDING IN A SILENT *E*

Before adding a suffix beginning with a vowel or ***y*** to a word ending in a silent ***e,*** drop the ***e*** (with some exceptions).

amaze + -ing = amazing
love + -able = lovable
create + -ed = created
nerve + -ous = nervous

Exceptions: *change + -able = changeable; courage + -ous = courageous.*

When adding a suffix beginning with a consonant to a word ending in a silent ***e***, keep the ***e*** (with some exceptions).

late + -ly = lately
spite + -ful = spiteful
noise + -less = noiseless
state + -ment = statement

Exceptions: *truly, argument, ninth, wholly, awful,* and others.

When a suffix beginning with ***a*** or ***o*** is added to a word with a final silent ***e***, the final ***e*** is usually retained if it is preceded by a soft ***c*** or a soft ***g***.

bridge + -able = bridgeable
peace + -able = peaceable
outrage + -ous = outrageous
advantage + -ous = advantageous

When a suffix beginning with a vowel is added to words ending in ***ee*** or ***oe***, the final silent ***e*** is retained.

agree + -ing = agreeing **free + -ing = freeing**
hoe + -ing = hoeing **see + -ing = seeing**

11.2 WORDS ENDING IN *Y*

Before adding most suffixes to a word that ends in ***y*** preceded by a consonant, change the ***y*** to ***i***.

easy + -est = easiest
crazy + -est = craziest
silly + -ness = silliness
marry + -age = marriage

Exceptions: *dryness, shyness,* and *slyness.*

However, when you add ***-ing***, the ***y*** does not change.

empty + -ed = emptied but
empty + -ing = emptying

When adding a suffix to a word that ends in ***y*** preceded by a vowel, the ***y*** usually does not change.

play + -er = player
employ + -ed = employed
coy + -ness = coyness
pay + -able = payable

11.3 WORDS ENDING IN A CONSONANT

In one-syllable words that end in one consonant preceded by one short vowel, double the final consonant before adding a suffix beginning with a vowel, such as ***-ed*** or ***-ing***.

dip + -ed = dipped **set + -ing = setting**
slim + -est = slimmest **fit + -er = fitter**

The rule does not apply to words of one syllable that end in a consonant preceded by two vowels.

feel + -ing = feeling **peel + -ed = peeled**
reap + -ed = reaped **loot + -ed = looted**

In words of more than one syllable, double the final consonant when (**1**) the word ends with one consonant preceded by one vowel and (**2**) the word is accented on the last syllable.

be•gin´ **per•mit´** **re•fer´**

In the following examples, note that in the new words formed with suffixes, the accent remains on the same syllable:

be•gin´ + -ing = be•gin´ ning = beginning
per•mit´ + -ed = per•mit´ ted = permitted

In some words with more than one syllable, though the accent remains on the same syllable when a suffix is added, the final consonant is nevertheless not doubled, as in the following examples:

tra´vel + -er = tra´vel•er = traveler
mar´ket + -er = mar´ket•er = marketer

In the following examples, the accent does not remain on the same syllable; thus, the final consonant is not doubled:

re•fer´ + -ence = ref´er•ence = reference
con•fer´ + -ence = con´fer•ence = conference

11.4 PREFIXES AND SUFFIXES

When adding a prefix to a word, do not change the spelling of the base word. When a prefix creates a double letter, keep both letters.

dis- + approve = disapprove
re- + build = rebuild
ir- + regular = irregular
mis- + spell = misspell
anti- + trust = antitrust
il- + logical = illogical

When adding ***-ly*** to a word ending in ***l***, keep both ***l***'s, and when adding ***-ness*** to a word ending in ***n***, keep both ***n***'s.

careful + -ly = carefully
sudden + -ness = suddenness
final + -ly = finally
thin + -ness = thinness

11.5 FORMING PLURAL NOUNS

To form the plural of most nouns, just add *-s.*

prizes dreams circles stations

For most singular nouns ending in ***o,*** add *-s.*

solos halos studios photos pianos

For a few nouns ending in ***o,*** add *-es.*

heroes tomatoes potatoes echoes

When the singular noun ends in ***s, sh, ch, x,*** or ***z,*** add *-es.*

waitresses brushes ditches
axes buzzes

When a singular noun ends in ***y*** with a consonant before it, change the ***y*** to ***i*** and add *-es.*

army—armies candy—candies
baby—babies diary—diaries
ferry—ferries conspiracy—conspiracies

When a vowel (***a, e, i, o, u***) comes before the ***y,*** just add *-s.*

boy—boys way—ways
array—arrays alloy—alloys
weekday—weekdays jockey—jockeys

For most nouns ending in ***f*** or ***fe,*** change the ***f*** to ***v*** and add *-es* or *-s.*

life—lives calf—calves knife—knives
thief—thieves shelf—shelves loaf—loaves

For some nouns ending in ***f,*** add *-s* to make the plural.

roofs chiefs reefs beliefs

Some nouns have the same form for both singular and plural.

deer sheep moose salmon trout

For some nouns, the plural is formed in a special way.

man—men goose—geese
ox—oxen woman—women
mouse—mice child—children

For a compound noun written as one word, form the plural by changing the last word in the compound to its plural form.

stepchild—stepchildren firefly—fireflies

If a compound noun is written as a hyphenated word or as two separate words, change the most important word to the plural form.

brother-in-law—brothers-in-law
life jacket—life jackets

11.6 FORMING POSSESSIVES

If a noun is singular, add ***'s.***

mother—my mother's car Ross—Ross's desk

Exception: The ***s*** after the apostrophe is dropped after *Jesus', Moses',* and certain names in classical mythology (*Zeus'*). These possessive forms can be pronounced easily.

If a noun is plural and ends with ***s,*** just add an apostrophe.

parents—my parents' car
the Santinis—the Santinis' house

If a noun is plural but does not end in ***s,*** add ***'s.***

people—the people's choice
women—the women's coats

11.7 SPECIAL SPELLING PROBLEMS

Only one English word ends in ***-sede:*** *supersede.* Three words end in ***-ceed:*** *exceed, proceed,* and *succeed.* All other verbs ending in the sound "seed" are spelled with ***-cede.***

concede precede recede secede

In words with ***ie*** or ***ei,*** when the sound is long ***e*** (as in *she*), the word is spelled ***ie*** except after ***c*** (with some exceptions).

i* before *e **thief relieve field**
piece grieve pier

except after *c* **conceit perceive ceiling**
receive receipt

Exceptions: *either, neither, weird, leisure, seize.*

12 Commonly Confused Words

WORDS	DEFINITIONS	EXAMPLES
accept/except	The verb ***accept*** means "to receive or believe"; ***except*** is usually a preposition meaning "excluding."	**Except** for some of the more extraordinary events, I can **accept** that the *Odyssey* recounts a real journey.
advice/advise	***Advise*** is a verb; ***advice*** is a noun naming that which an ***adviser*** gives.	I **advise** you to take that job. Whom should I ask for **advice?**
affect/effect	As a verb, ***affect*** means "to influence." ***Effect*** as a verb means "to cause." If you want a noun, you will almost always want ***effect***.	Did Circe's wine **affect** Odysseus' mind? It did **effect** a change in Odysseus' men. In fact, it had an **effect** on everyone else who drank it.
all ready/already	***All ready*** is an adjective meaning "fully ready." ***Already*** is an adverb meaning "before or by this time."	He was **all ready** to go at noon. I have **already** seen that movie.
allusion/illusion	An ***allusion*** is an indirect reference to something. An ***illusion*** is a false picture or idea.	There are many **allusions** to the works of Homer in English literature. The world's apparent flatness is an **illusion.**
among/between	***Between*** is used when you are speaking of only two things. ***Among*** is used for three or more.	**Between** *Hamlet* and *King Lear,* I prefer the latter. Emily Dickinson is **among** my favorite poets.
bring/take	***Bring*** is used to denote motion toward a speaker or place. ***Take*** is used to denote motion away from such a person or place.	**Bring** the books over here, and I will **take** them to the library.
fewer/less	***Fewer*** refers to the number of separate, countable units. ***Less*** refers to bulk quantity.	We have **less** literature and **fewer** selections in this year's curriculum.
leave/let	***Leave*** means "to allow something to remain behind." ***Let*** means "to permit."	The librarian will **leave** some books on display but will not **let** us borrow any.
lie/lay	***Lie*** means "to rest or recline." It does not take an object. ***Lay*** always takes an object.	Rover loves to **lie** in the sun. We always **lay** some bones next to him.
loose/lose	***Loose*** (lo͞os) means "free, not restrained"; ***lose*** (lo͞oz) means "to misplace or fail to find."	Who turned the horses **loose?** I hope we won't **lose** any of them.
precede/proceed	***Precede*** means "to go or come before." Use ***proceed*** for other meanings.	Emily Dickinson's poetry **precedes** that of Alice Walker. You may **proceed** to the next section of the test.
than/then	Use ***than*** in making comparisons; use ***then*** on all other occasions.	Who can say whether Amy Lowell is a better poet **than** Denise Levertov? I will read Lowell first, and **then** I will read Levertov.
their/there/they're	***Their*** means "belonging to them." ***There*** means "in that place." ***They're*** is the contraction for "they are."	**There** is a movie playing at 9 P.M. **They're** going to see it with me. Sakara and Jessica drove away in **their** car after the movie.
two/too/to	***Two*** is the number. ***Too*** is an adverb meaning "also" or "very." Use ***to*** before a verb or as a preposition.	Meg had **to** go **to** town, **too.** We had **too** much reading **to** do. **Two** chapters is **too** many.

Effective oral communication occurs when the audience understands a message the way the speaker intends it. Good speakers and listeners do more than just talk and hear. They use specific techniques to present their ideas effectively, and they are attentive and critical listeners.

Included in this handbook:
SL 1a–d, SL 2–6

1 Speech

In school, in business, and in community life, a speech is one of the most effective means of communicating.

1.1 AUDIENCE, PURPOSE, AND OCCASION

When developing and delivering a speech, your goal is to deliver a focused, coherent presentation that conveys your ideas clearly and relates to the background of your audience. By understanding your audience, you can tailor your speech to them appropriately and effectively.

- **Know Your Audience** What kind of group are you presenting to? Fellow classmates? A group of teachers? What are their interests and backgrounds? Understanding their different points of view can help you organize the information so that they understand and are interested in it.
- **Understand Your Purpose** Keep in mind your purpose for speaking. Are you trying to persuade the audience to do something? Perhaps you simply want to entertain them by sharing a story or experience. Your reason for giving the speech will guide you in organizing your thoughts and deciding on how to deliver it.
- **Know the Occasion** Are you speaking at a special event? Is it formal? Will others be giving speeches besides you? Knowing the type of occasion will help you tailor the language and length of your speech for the event.

1.2 PREPARING YOUR SPEECH

There are several approaches to preparing a speech. Your teacher may tell you which one to use.

- **Manuscript** Prepare a complete script of the speech in advance and use it to deliver the speech. Use for formal occasions, such as graduation speeches and political addresses, and to present technical or complicated information.
- **Memory** Prepare a written text in advance and then memorize it in order to deliver the speech word for word. Use for short speeches, as when introducing another speaker or accepting an award.
- **Extemporaneous** Prepare the speech and deliver it using an outline or notes. Use for informal situations, for persuasive messages, and to make a more personal connection with the audience.

1.3 DRAFTING YOUR SPEECH

If you are writing your speech beforehand, rather than working from notes, use the following guidelines to help you:

- **Create a Unified Speech** Do this first by organizing your speech into paragraphs, each of which develops a single main idea. All the sentences in a paragraph should support the main idea of the paragraph, and all the paragraphs should support the main idea of the speech. Be sure that your speech has an introduction and a conclusion. Just as in a written product, use a pattern of organization that is appropriate to your subject and purpose.
- **Use Appropriate Language** The subject of your speech—and the way you choose to present it—should match your audience, your purpose, and the occasion. You can use informal language, such as slang, to share a story with your classmates. For a persuasive speech in front of a school assembly, use formal, standard American English. If you are giving an informative presentation, be sure to explain any terms that the audience may not be familiar with.
- **Provide Evidence** Include relevant facts, statistics, and incidents; quote experts to support your ideas and opinions. Elaborate—provide specific details, perhaps with visual or media displays—to clarify what you are saying.
- **Emphasize Important Points** To help your audience follow the main ideas and concepts of your speech, be sure to draw attention to important points. You can use rhyme, repetition, parallelism, and other rhetorical devices. You can also use figurative language for effect.
- **Use Precise Language** Use precise language to convey your ideas, and vary the structure and length of your sentences. You can keep the audience's attention with a word that elicits strong emotion. You can use a question or an interjection to make a personal connection with the audience.

- **Start Strong, Finish Strong** As you begin your speech, consider using a "hook"—an interesting question or statement meant to capture your audience's attention. At the end of the speech, restate your main ideas simply and clearly. Perhaps conclude with a powerful example or anecdote to reinforce your message.
- **Revise Your Speech** After you write your speech, revise, edit, and proofread it as you would a written report. Use a variety of sentence structures to achieve a natural rhythm. Check for correct subject-verb agreement and consistent verb tense. Correct run-on sentences and sentence fragments. Use parallel structure to emphasize ideas. Make sure you use complete sentences and correct punctuation and capitalization, even if no one else will see it. Your written speech should be clear and error-free.

1.4 DELIVERING YOUR SPEECH

Confidence is the key to a successful presentation. Use these techniques to help you prepare and present your speech:

Prepare

- **Review Your Information** Reread your notes and review any background research. You'll feel more confident during your speech.
- **Organize Your Notes** Some people prefer to include only key points. Others prefer the entire script. Write each main point, or each paragraph, of your speech on a separate numbered index card. Be sure to include your most important evidence and examples.
- **Plan Your Visual Aids and Sound Effects** If you are planning on using visual aids, such as slides, posters, charts, graphs, video clips, transparencies, or computer projections, now is the time to design your visual and sound elements and work them into your speech.

Practice

- **Rehearse** Rehearse your speech several times, possibly in front of a practice audience. Maintain good posture by standing with your shoulders back and your head up. If you are using visual aids, practice handling them. Adapt your rate of speaking, pitch, and tone of voice to your audience and setting. Glance at your notes to refresh your memory, but avoid reading them word for word. Your style of performance should express the purpose of your speech. Use the following chart to help you.

Purpose	Pace	Pitch	Tone
to persuade	fast but clear	even	urgent
to inform	using plenty of pauses	even	authoritative
to entertain	usually building to a "punch"	varied to create characters or drama	funny or dramatic

- **Use Audience Feedback** If you had a practice audience, ask them specific questions about your delivery: Did I use enough eye contact? Was my voice at the right volume? Did I stand straight, or did I slouch? Use the audience's comments to evaluate the effectiveness of your delivery and to set goals for future rehearsals.
- **Evaluate Your Performance** When you have finished each rehearsal, evaluate your performance. Did you pause to let an important point sink in, or use gestures for emphasis? Make a list of the aspects of your presentation that you will try to improve for your next rehearsal.

Present

- **Begin Your Speech** Try to look relaxed and smile.
- **Make Eye Contact** Try to make eye contact with as many audience members as possible. This will establish personal contact and help you determine if the audience understands your speech.
- **Remember to Pause** A slight pause after important points will provide emphasis and give your audience time to think about what you're saying.
- **Speak Clearly** Speak loud enough to be heard clearly, but not so loud that your voice is overwhelming. Use a conversational tone.
- **Maintain Good Posture** Stand up straight and avoid nervous movements that may distract the audience's attention from what you are saying.
- **Use Expressive Body Language** Use facial expressions to show your feelings toward your topic. Lean forward when you make an important point; move your hands and arms for emphasis. Use your body language to show your own style and reflect your personality.

- **Watch the Audience for Responses** If they start fidgeting or yawning, speak a little louder or get to your conclusion a little sooner. Use what you learn to decide what areas need improvement for future presentations.
- **Close your speech** As part of your closing remarks, be sure to thank your audience.

Respond to Questions

Depending on the content of your speech, your audience may have questions. Follow these steps to make sure that you answer questions in an appropriate manner:

- Think about what your audience may ask and prepare answers before your speech.
- Tell your audience at the beginning of your speech that you will take questions at the end. This helps avoid audience interruptions that may make your speech hard to follow.
- Call on audience members in the order in which they raise their hands.
- Repeat each question before you answer it to ensure that everyone has heard it. This step also gives you time to prepare your answer.

2 Different Types of Oral Presentations

2.1 INFORMATIVE SPEECH

When you deliver an informative speech, you give the audience new information, provide a better understanding of information, or enable the audience to use the information in a new way.

Use the following questions to evaluate your own presentation or that of a peer or a public figure.

Evaluate an Informative Speech

- Did the speaker have a specific, clearly focused topic?
- Did the speaker take the audience's previous knowledge into consideration?
- Did the speaker cite sources for the information?
- Did the speaker communicate the information objectively?
- Did the speaker explain technical terms?
- Did the speaker use visual aids effectively?
- Did the speaker anticipate and address any audience concerns or misunderstandings?
- Is the speech informative and accurate?

2.2 PERSUASIVE SPEECH

When you deliver a persuasive speech, you offer a thesis or clear statement on a subject, you provide relevant evidence to support your position, and you attempt to convince the audience to accept your point of view.

Use the following questions to evaluate the presentation of a peer or a public figure, or your own presentation.

For more information, see ***Speaking and Listening: Persuasive Speech,*** *page 290.*

Evaluate a Persuasive Speech

- Did the speaker present a clear thesis or argument?
- Did the speaker anticipate and address audience concerns, biases, and counterclaims?
- Did the speaker use sound logic and reasoning in developing the argument?
- Did the speaker support the argument with valid evidence, examples, facts, expert opinions, and quotations?
- Did the speaker use rhetorical devices, such as emotional appeals, to support assertions?
- Were the speaker's voice, facial expressions, and gestures effective?
- Is your reaction to the speech similar to that of other audience members?
- Did you believe the speaker to be truthful and ethical?

2.3 DEBATE

A debate is a balanced argument covering both sides of an issue. In a debate, two teams compete to win the support of the audience. In a formal debate, two teams, each with two members, present their arguments on a given proposition or policy statement. One team argues for the proposition or statement, and the other argues against it. Each debater must consider the proposition closely and must research both sides of it.

Preparing for the Debate

In preparing for a debate, the debaters prepare a **brief,** an outline of the debate, accounting for the evidence and arguments of both sides of the **proposition** (topic). Debaters also prepare a **rebuttal,** a follow-up speech to support their arguments and counter the opposition's. Propositions are usually one of four types:

- **Proposition of fact**—determines whether a statement is true or false. An example is "Deforestation is ruining the rain forest."
- **Proposition of value**—determines the value of a person, place, or thing. An example is "Free trade will help small countries develop."
- **Proposition of problem**—determines whether a problem exists and whether it requires action.
- **Proposition of policy**—determines the action that will be taken. An example is "Students will provide tutoring services."

The two groups of debaters who argue a topic are called the **affirmative side** and the **negative side.** The affirmative side tries to convince the audience that the proposition should be accepted. The negative side argues against the proposition.

Use the following steps to prepare a brief:

- **Gather Information** Consult a variety of primary and secondary sources to gather the most reliable, up-to-date information about the proposition.
- **Identify Key Ideas** Sort out the important points and arrange them in order of importance.
- **List Arguments for and Against Each Key Idea** Look for strong arguments that support your side of the proposition and also note those that support your opponents' side.
- **Support Your Arguments** Find facts, quotations, expert opinions, and examples that support your arguments and counter your opponents'.
- **Write the Brief** Begin your brief with a statement of the proposition. Then list the arguments and evidence that support both sides of the proposition.

Planning the Rebuttal

The rebuttal is the opportunity to rebuild your case. Use the following steps to build a strong rebuttal:

- Listen to your opponents respectfully. Note the points you wish to overturn.
- Defend what the opposition has challenged.
- Cite weaknesses in their arguments, such as points they overlooked.
- Present counterclaims and supporting evidence.
- Offer your summary arguments. Restate and solidify your stance.

Use the following questions to evaluate a debate.

Evaluate a Team in a Debate

- Did the team prove that a significant problem does or does not exist? How thorough was the team's analysis of the problem?
- How did the team convince you that the proposition is or is not the best solution to the problem?
- How effectively did the team present reasons and evidence supporting the case?
- How effectively did the team refute and rebut arguments made by the opposing team?
- Did the speakers maintain eye contact and speak at an appropriate rate and volume?
- Did the speakers observe proper debate etiquette?

PRACTICE AND APPLY

View a political debate for a local, state, or national election. Use the preceding criteria to evaluate it.

2.4 NARRATIVE SPEECH

When you deliver a narrative speech, you tell a story or present a subject using a story-type format. A good narrative keeps an audience informed and entertained. It also allows you to deliver a message in a creative way.

Use the following questions to evaluate a speaker or your own presentation.

Evaluate a Narrative Speech

- Did the speaker choose a context that makes sense and contributes to a believable narrative?
- Did the speaker locate scenes and incidents in specific places?
- Does the plot flow well?
- Did the speaker use words that convey the appropriate mood and tone?
- Did the speaker use sensory details that allow the audience to experience the sights, sounds, and smells of a scene and the specific actions, gestures, and thoughts of the characters?
- Did the speaker use a range of narrative devices to keep the audience interested?
- Is your reaction to the presentation similar to that of other audience members?

2.5 REFLECTIVE SPEECH

In a reflective speech, you describe a personal experience and explore its significance. Use vivid description, visuals, and sound effects to re-create the experience for your audience and convey meaning.

Use the following questions to evaluate a speaker or your own presentation.

Evaluate a Reflective Speech

- Did the speaker describe an important experience in his or her life?
- Did the speaker use figurative language, sensory details, or other techniques to re-create the event for the audience?
- Did the speaker explain the significance of the event to the audience?
- Does the experience relate to a broader theme or a more general abstract idea about life?
- Did the speaker convey the message through one specific event or several related incidents?
- Did the speaker encourage the audience to think about the significance of the experience and apply it to their own lives?
- Was your reaction to the presentation similar to that of other audience members?

2.6 DESCRIPTIVE SPEECH

In a descriptive speech, you describe a subject with which you are personally familiar. A good description will enable your listeners to tell how you feel toward your subject.

Use the following questions to evaluate a speaker or your own presentation.

Evaluate a Descriptive Speech

- Did the speaker make clear his or her point of view toward the subject being described?
- Did the speaker use sensory details, figurative language, and factual details?
- Did the speaker use tone and pitch to emphasize important details?
- Did the speaker use facial expressions to emphasize his or her feelings toward the subject?
- Did the speaker change vantage points to help the audience see the subject from another position?
- Did the speaker change perspectives to show how someone else might feel toward the subject?

2.7 ORAL INTERPRETATION

When you perform an oral interpretation, you use appropriate vocal intonations, facial expressions, and gestures to bring a literature selection to life.

In an **oral reading,** you will present or read a poem, monologue, or passage from a literary selection, in which you assume the voice of a character, the narrator, or the speaker. An oral reading can also be a presentation of a dialogue between two or more characters, in which you, as the sole performer, take on all the roles.

Use the following techniques when giving an oral reading:

- **Speak Clearly** As you speak, pronounce your words clearly.
- **Control Your Volume** Make sure that you are loud enough to be heard, but do not shout.
- **Pace Yourself** Read at a moderate rate, but vary your pace if it seems appropriate to the emotions of the character or to the action you perform.
- **Vary Your Voice** Use a different voice for each character. Stress important words and phrases. Use your voice to express different emotions.

In a **dramatic reading,** several speakers participate in the reading of a play or some other work. Use the following techniques in your dramatic reading:

- **Prepare** Rehearse your material several times. Become familiar with the humorous and serious parts of the script. Develop a special voice that fits the personality of the character you portray.
- **Project** As you read your lines, aim your voice toward the back of the room to allow everyone to hear you.
- **Perform** React to the other characters as if you were hearing their lines for the first time. Deliver your own lines with the appropriate emotion. Use not only hand gestures and facial expressions but also other body movements to express your emotions.

*For more information, see **Speaking and Listening: Presenting a Script,** page 496.*

Use the following questions to evaluate an artistic performance by a peer or a public presenter, a media presentation, or your own performance.

Evaluate an Oral Interpretation

- Did the speaker speak clearly, enunciating each word carefully?
- Did the speaker maintain eye contact with the audience?
- Did the speaker control his or her volume, projecting without shouting?
- Did the speaker vary the rate of speech appropriately to express emotion, mood, and action?
- Did the speaker use a different voice for each character?
- Did the speaker stress important words or phrases?
- Did the speaker's presentation allow you to identify and appreciate elements of the text such as character development, rhyme, imagery, and language?

PRACTICE AND APPLY

Develop an oral reading and present it to your class; evaluate the oral readings of your classmates, using the preceding criteria.

2.8 ORAL RESPONSE TO LITERATURE

An oral response to literature is a personal, analytical interpretation of a writer's story, novel, poem, or drama.

Use the following questions to evaluate a speaker or your own presentation.

Evaluate an Oral Response to Literature

- Did the speaker choose an interesting piece that he or she understands and feels strongly about?
- Did the speaker make a judgment that shows an understanding of significant ideas from the text?
- Did the speaker direct the audience to specific parts of the piece that support his or her ideas?
- Did the speaker identify and analyze the use of artistic elements such as imagery, figurative language, and character development?
- Did the speaker demonstrate an appreciation of the author's style?
- Did the speaker discuss any ambiguous or difficult passages and the impact of those passages on the audience?

PRACTICE AND APPLY

Listen as a classmate delivers an oral response to a selection you have read. Use the preceding criteria to evaluate the presentation.

3 Other Types of Communication

3.1 GROUP DISCUSSION

Successful groups assign a role to each member. These roles distribute responsibility among the members and help keep discussions focused.

Role	Responsibilities
Chairperson	• introduces topic • explains goal or purpose • participates in discussion and keeps it on track • helps resolve conflicts • helps group reach goal
Recorder	• takes notes on discussion • reports on suggestions and decisions • organizes and writes up notes • participates in discussion
Participants	• contribute relevant facts or ideas to discussion • respond constructively to one another's ideas • reach agreement or vote on final decision • evaluate the effectiveness of the discussion using agreed-upon criteria

3.2 INTERVIEWS

An **interview** is a formal type of conversation with a definite purpose and goal. To conduct a successful interview, use the following guidelines:

Prepare for the Interview

- Select your interviewee carefully. Identify who has the kind of knowledge and experience you are looking for.
- Set a time, a date, and a place. Ask permission to tape-record the interview.

- Learn all you can about the person you will interview or the topic you want information on.
- Prepare a list of questions. Create questions that encourage detailed responses instead of yes-or-no answers. Arrange your questions in order from most important to least important.
- Arrive on time with everything you need.

Conduct the Interview

- Ask your questions clearly and listen to the responses carefully. Give the person whom you are interviewing plenty of time to answer.
- Be flexible; follow up on any responses you find interesting.
- Avoid arguments; be tactful and polite.
- Even if you tape an interview, take notes on important points.
- Thank the person for the interview, and ask if you can call with any follow-up questions.

Follow Up on the Interview

- Summarize your notes or make a written copy of the tape recording as soon as possible.
- If any points are unclear or if information is missing, call and ask more questions while the person is still available.
- Select the most appropriate quotations to support your ideas.
- If possible, have the person you interviewed review your work to make sure you haven't misrepresented what he or she said.
- Send a thank-you note to the person in appreciation of his or her time and effort.

Evaluate an Interview

You can determine how effective your interview was by asking yourself these questions:

- Did you get the type of information you were looking for?
- Were your most important questions answered to your satisfaction?
- Were you able to keep the interviewee focused on the subject?

Responding to a Job Interview

In a job interview, you will be the person being interviewed. The person asking you questions will have several objectives in mind, and you will need to be prepared to respond in a professional manner. Keep these strategies in mind when you are being interviewed for employment:

- Prior to the interview, prepare a short list of questions relevant to the position.
- Respond honestly and effectively to each question, and use language that conveys sensitivity, maturity, and respect.
- Give responses that demonstrate knowledge of the subject or organization.
- Use active listening skills, as outlined in the next section.

4 Active Listening

Active listening is the process of receiving, interpreting, evaluating, and responding to a message. Whether you listen to a class discussion or a formal speech, use the following strategies to get as much as you can from the message.

Before Listening

- Learn what the topic is beforehand. You may need to read background information about the topic or learn technical terms in order to understand the speaker's message.
- Think about what you know or want to know about the topic.
- Have a pen and paper or a laptop computer to take notes.
- Establish a purpose for listening.

While Listening

- Focus your attention on the speaker.
- Listen for the speaker's purpose (usually stated at the beginning), which alerts you to main ideas.
- Listen for words or phrases that signal important points, such as *to begin with, in addition, most important, finally,* and *in conclusion.*
- Listen for varied sentences: simple, compound, and complex. Think about how the choice of syntax emphasizes the speaker's ideas.

- Take notes. Write down only the most important points. Use an outline or list format to organize main ideas and supporting points.
- Note comparisons and contrasts, causes and effects, or problems and solutions.
- Note how the speaker uses word choice, voice pitch, posture, and gestures to convey meaning.

After Listening

- Ask relevant questions to clarify anything that was unclear or confusing.
- Review your notes to make sure you understand what was said.
- Summarize and paraphrase the speaker's ideas.
- You may also wish to compare your interpretation of the speech with the interpretations of others who listened to it.

4.1 CRITICAL LISTENING

Critical listening involves interpreting and analyzing a spoken message to judge its accuracy and reliability. Use these strategies as you listen to messages from advertisers, politicians, lecturers, and others:

- **Determine the Speaker's Purpose** Think about the background, viewpoint, and possible motives of the speaker. Separate facts from opinions. Listen carefully to details and evidence that a speaker uses to support the message.
- **Listen for the Main Idea** Figure out the speaker's main message before allowing yourself to be distracted by seemingly convincing facts and details.
- **Recognize the Use of Persuasive Techniques** Pay attention to a speaker's choice of words. Speakers may slant information to persuade you to buy a product or accept an idea. Persuasive devices such as inaccurate generalizations, either/or reasoning, and bandwagon or snob appeal may represent faulty reasoning and provide misleading information.

  *For more information, see **Persuasive Techniques**, page R20.*
- **Observe Verbal and Nonverbal Messages** A speaker's gestures, facial expressions, and tone of voice should reinforce the message. If they don't, you should question the speaker's sincerity and the reliability of his or her message.
- **Give Appropriate Feedback** An effective speaker looks for verbal and nonverbal cues from you, the listener, to gauge how the message is being received. For example, if you understand or agree with the message, you might nod your head. If possible, during or after a presentation, ask questions to clarify understanding.

4.2 VERBAL FEEDBACK

At times you will be asked to give direct feedback to a speaker. You may be asked to evaluate the way the speaker delivers the presentation as well as the content of the presentation.

Use the following questions to evaluate a speaker's delivery.

Evaluate Delivery

- Did the speaker articulate words clearly and distinctly?
- Did the speaker pronounce words correctly?
- Did the speaker vary his or her rate?
- Did the speaker's voice sound natural and not strained?
- Was the speaker's voice loud enough?

Use the following guidelines to give constructive suggestions for improvement on content.

Evaluate Content

Be Specific Don't make statements like "Your charts need work." Offer concrete suggestions, such as "Please make the type bigger so we can read the poster from the back of the room."

Discuss Only the Most Important Points Don't overload the speaker with too much feedback about too many details. Focus on important points, such as:

- Is the topic too advanced for the audience?
- Are the supporting details well organized?
- Is the conclusion weak?

Give Balanced Feedback Tell the speaker not only what didn't work but also what did work: "Consider dropping the last two slides, since you covered those points earlier. The first two slides got my attention."

Every day you are exposed to hundreds of images and messages from television, radio, movies, newspapers, and the Internet. What is the effect of all this media? What do you need to know to be a smart media consumer? Being media literate means that you have the ability to think critically about media messages. It means that you are able to analyze and evaluate media messages and how they influence you and your world. To become media literate, you'll need the tools to study media messages.

COMMON CORE

Included in this handbook:
RI 7, SL 2, SL 5

1 Five Core Concepts in Media Literacy

from The Center for Media Literacy

The five core concepts of media literacy provide you with the basic ideas you can consider when examining media messages.

All media messages are "constructed." All media messages are made by someone. In fact, they are carefully thought out and researched and have attitudes and values built into them. Much of the information that you use to make sense of the world comes from the media. Therefore, it is important to know how media are put together so you can better understand the message it conveys.

Media messages are constructed using a creative language with its own rules. Each means of communication—whether it is film, television, newspapers, magazines, radio, or the Internet—has its own language and design. Therefore, the content of a message must use the language and design of the medium that conveys the message. Thus, the medium actually shapes the message. For example, a horror film may use music to heighten suspense, or a newspaper may use a big headline to signal the significance of a story. Understanding the language of each medium can increase your enjoyment of it as well as alert you to obvious and subtle influences.

Different people experience the same media messages differently. Personal factors such as age, education, and experience will affect the way a person responds to a media message. How many times has your interpretation of a film or book differed from that of a friend? Everyone interprets media messages through their own personal lens.

Media have embedded values and points of view. Media messages carry underlying values, which are purposely built into them by the creators of the message. For example, a commercial's main purpose may be to persuade you to buy something, but it also conveys the value of a particular lifestyle. Understanding not only the core message but also the embedded points of view will help you decide whether to accept or reject the message.

Most media messages are organized to gain profit and/or power. The creators of media messages often provide a commodity, such as information or entertainment, in order to make money. The bigger the audience, the higher the cost of advertising. Consequently, media outlets want to build large audiences in order to bring in more revenue from advertising. For example, a television network creates programming that appeals to the largest audience possible, and then uses the viewer ratings to attract more advertising dollars.

2 Media Basics

2.1 MESSAGE

When a film or TV show is created, it becomes a media product. Each media product is created to send a **message,** or an expression of belief or opinion, that serves a specific purpose. In order to understand the message, you will need to deconstruct it.

Deconstruction is the process of analyzing a media presentation. To analyze a media presentation you will need to look at its content, its purpose, the audience it's aimed at, and the techniques and elements that are used to create certain effects.

2.2 AUDIENCE

A **target audience** is a specific group of people that a product or presentation is aimed at. The members of a target audience usually share certain characteristics, such as age, gender, ethnic background, values, or lifestyle. For example, a target audience may be adults ages 40 to 60 who want to exercise and eat healthful foods.

Demographics are the characteristics of a population, including age, gender, profession, income, education, ethnicity, and geographic location. Media decision makers use demographics to shape their content to suit the needs and tastes of a target audience.

Nielsen ratings are the system used to track TV audiences and their viewing preferences. Nielsen Media Research, the company that provides this system, monitors TV viewing in a random sample of 5,000 U.S. households selected to represent the population as a whole.

2.3 PURPOSE

The **purpose,** or intent, of a media presentation is the reason it was made. Most media messages have more than one purpose, but each has a **core purpose.** To discover that purpose, think about why its creator paid for and produced the message. For example, an ad might entertain you with humor, but its core purpose is to persuade you to buy something.

2.4 TYPES AND GENRES OF MEDIA

The term ***media*** refers to television, newspapers, magazines, radio, movies, and the Internet. Each is a **medium,** or means for carrying information, entertainment, and advertisements to a large audience.

Each type of media has different characteristics, strengths, and weaknesses. Understanding how different types of media work and the role they play will help you become more informed about the choices you make in response to the media.

2.5 PRODUCERS AND CREATORS

People who control the media are known as **gatekeepers.** Gatekeepers decide what information to share with the public and the ways it will be presented. The following diagram gives some examples.

Who Controls the Media?

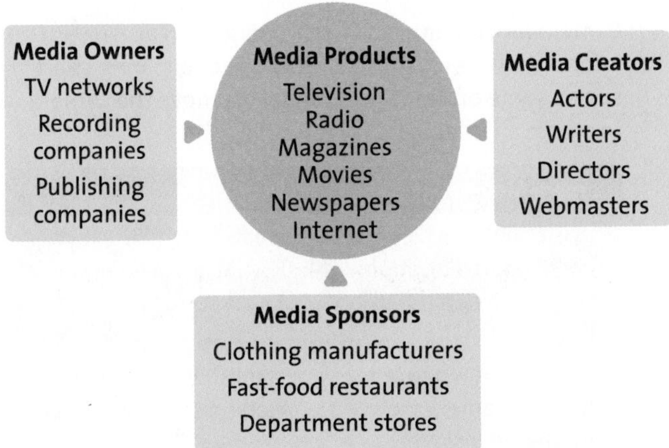

Some forms of media are independently owned, while others are part of a corporate family. Some corporate families might own several different kinds of media. For example, a company may own three radio stations, five newspapers, a publishing company, and a small television station. Often a corporate "parent" decides the content for all of its holdings.

2.6 LAWS GOVERNING MEDIA

Four main laws and policies affect the content, delivery, and use of mass media.

The First Amendment to the Constitution forbids Congress to limit speech or the press.

Copyright law protects the rights of authors and other media creators against the unauthorized publishing, reproduction, and selling of their works.

Laws prohibit **censorship,** any attempt to suppress or control people's access to media messages.

Laws prohibit **libel,** the publication of false statements that damage a person's reputation.

2.7 INFLUENCE OF MEDIA

By sheer volume alone, media influences our very existence, values, opinions, and beliefs. Our environment is saturated with media messages from television, billboards, radio, newspapers, magazines, video games, and so on. Each of these media products is selling one message and conveying another—a message about values—in the subtext. For example, a car ad is meant to sell a car, but if you look closer, you will see that it is using a set of values, such as a luxurious lifestyle, to make the car attractive to the target audience. One message of the ad is that if you buy the car, you'll have the luxurious lifestyle. The other message is that the luxurious lifestyle is good and desirable. TV shows, movies, and news programs also convey subtexts of values and beliefs.

Media can also shape your opinions about the world. For example, news about crime shapes our understanding about how much and what type of crime is prevalent in the world around us. TV news items, talk show interviews, and commercials may shape our perception of a political candidate, a celebrity, an ethnic group, a country, or a region. As a consequence, our knowledge of someone or someplace may be completely based on the information we receive from the television or other media.

3 Film and TV

Films and television programs come in a variety of types. Films include comedies, dramas, documentaries, and animated features. Televison programs cover an even wider array, including dramas, sitcoms, talk shows, reality shows, newscasts, and so on. Producers of films and producers of television programs rely on many of the same elements to convey their messages. Among these elements are scripts, visual and sound elements, special effects, and editing.

3.1 SCRIPT AND WRITTEN ELEMENTS

The writer and editor craft a story for television or film using a script and storyboard. A **script** is the text or words of a film or television show. A **storyboard** is a device often used to plan the shooting of a film and to help the director envision and convey what the finished product will look like. It consists of a sequence of sketches showing what will appear in the film's shots, often with explanatory notes and dialogue written beside or underneath them as shown in the example.

For more information, see ***Speaking and Listening: Producing a Documentary,*** *page 1378.*

Where is the cat?

I don't know. I haven't seen her.

Neither have I.

3.2 VISUAL ELEMENTS

Visual elements in film and television include camera shots, angles, and movements, as well as film components such as mise en scène, set design, props, and visual special effects.

A **camera shot** is a single, continuous view taken by a camera. **Camera angle** is the angle at which the camera is positioned during the recording of a shot or image. Each angle is carefully planned to create an effect. The following chart explains the different shots and angles.

Camera Shot/Angle	Effect
Establishing shot introduces viewers to the location of a scene, usually by presenting a wide view of an area	establishes the setting of a film
Close-up shot shows a detailed view of a person or an object	helps to create emotion and make viewers feel as if they know the character
Medium shot shows a view wider than a close-up but narrower than an establishing or long shot	shows part of an object or a character from the knees or waist up
Long shot is a wide view of a scene, showing the full figure(s) of a person or group and their surroundings	allows the viewer to see the "big picture" and shows the relationship between characters and the environment
Reaction shot shows someone reacting to something that occurred in a previous shot	allows the viewer to see how the subject feels in order to create empathy in the viewer
Low-angle shot looks up at an object or a person	makes a character, object, or scene appear more important or threatening
High-angle shot looks down on an object or a person	makes a character, object, or scene seem vulnerable or insignificant
Point-of-view (POV) shot shows a part of the story through a character's eyes	helps viewers identify with that character

Camera movement can create energy, reveal information, or establish a mood. The following chart shows some of the ways filmmakers move the camera to create an effect.

Camera Movement	Effect
Pan is a shot in which the camera scans a location from right to left or left to right	reveals information by showing a sweeping view of an area
Tracking shot is a shot in which the camera moves with the subject	establishes tension or creates a sense of drama
Zoom is the movement of the camera as it closes in on or moves farther away from the subject	captures action or draws the viewer's attention to detail

Mise en scène is a French term that refers to the arrangement of actors, props, and action on a film set. It is used to describe everything that can be seen in a frame, including the setting, lighting, visual composition, costumes, and action.

Framing is capturing people and objects within the "frame" of a screen or image. Framing is what the camera sees.

Composition is the arrangement of objects, characters, shapes, and colors within a frame and the relationship of the objects to one another.

3.3 SOUND ELEMENTS

Sound elements in film and television include music, voice-over, and sound effects.

Music may be used to set the mood and atmosphere in a scene. Music can have a powerful effect on the way viewers feel about a story. For example, fast-paced music helps viewers feel excited during an action scene.

Voice-over is the voice of the unseen commentator or narrator of a film, TV program, or commercial.

Sound effects are the sounds added to films, TV programs, and commercials during the editing process. Sound effects, such as laugh tracks or the sounds of punches in a fight scene, can create humor, emphasize a point, or contribute to the mood.

3.4 SPECIAL EFFECTS

Special effects include computer-generated animation, manipulated video images, and fast- or slow-motion sequences in films, TV programs, and commercials.

Animation on film involves the frame-by-frame photography of a series of drawings or objects. When these frames are projected—at a rate of 24 per second—the illusion of movement is achieved.

A **split screen** is a special-effects shot in which two or more separate images are shown in the same frame. One example is when two people, actually a distance apart, are shown talking to each other.

3.5 EDITING

Editing is the process of selecting and arranging shots in a sequence. The editor decides which scenes or shots to use, as well as the length of each shot, the number of shots, and their sequence. Editing establishes pace, mood, and a coherent story.

Cut is the transition from one shot to another. To create excitement, editors often use quick cuts, which are a series of short shots strung together.

Dissolve is a transitional device in which one scene fades into another.

Fade-in is a transitional device in which a white or black shot fades in to reveal the beginning of a new scene.

Fade-out is a transitional device in which a shot fades to darkness to end a scene.

Jump cut is an abrupt and jarring change from one shot to another. A jump cut shows a break in time or continuity.

Pace is the length of time each shot stays on the screen and the rhythm that is created by the transitions between shots. Short, quick cuts create a fast pace in a story. Long cuts slow down a story.

Parallel editing is a technique that cuts from one shot to another so as to suggest simultaneous action—often in different locations.

4 News

The **news** is information on events, people, and places in your community, your region, the nation, and the world. The news can be categorized by type, as shown in the chart.

Type	Description	Examples
Hard news	fact-based accounts of current events	local newspapers, newscasts, online wire services
Soft news	human-interest stories and other accounts that are less current or urgent than hard news	magazines and tabloid TV shows such as *Sports Illustrated, Access Hollywood*
News features	stories that elaborate on news reports	documentaries such as history reports on PBS
Commentary and opinion	essays and perspectives by experts, professionals, and media personalities	editorial pages, personal Web pages

4.1 CHOOSING THE NEWS

Newsworthiness is the significance of an event or action that makes it worthy of media reporting. Journalists and their editors usually weigh the following criteria in determining which stories should make the news:

Timeliness is the quality of being very current. Timely events usually take priority over previously reported events. For example, a car accident with fatalities will be timely on the day it occurs. Because of its timeliness it may be on the front page of a newspaper or the lead story on a newscast.

Widespread impact refers to the importance of an event and the number of people it could affect. The more widespread the impact of an event, the more likely it is to be newsworthy.

Proximity gauges the nearness of an event to a particular city, region, or country. People tend to be more interested in stories that take place locally and affect them directly.

Human interest is a quality of stories that cause readers or listeners to feel emotions such as happiness, anger, or sadness. People are interested in reading stories about other people.

Uniqueness refers to uncommon events or circumstances that are likely to be interesting to an audience.

Compelling video and **photographs** grab people's attention and stay in their minds.

4.2 REPORTING THE NEWS

While developing a news story, a journalist makes a variety of decisions about how to construct the story, such as what information to include and how to organize it. The following elements are commonly used in news stories:

5 *W*'s and *H* are the six questions reporters answer when writing news stories—*who, what, when, where, why,* and *how.* It is a journalist's job to answer these questions in any type of news report. These questions also serve as a structure for writing and editing a story.

Inverted pyramid is the means of organizing information according to importance. In the inverted pyramid diagram below, the most important information (the answers to the 5 *W*'s and *H*) appears at the top of the pyramid. The less important details appear at the bottom. Not all stories are reported using the inverted pyramid form. The style remains popular, however, because it enables a reader to get the essential information without reading the entire story. Notice the following example.

About 2,000 people gathered at the Vietnam Veterans Memorial Wall on Friday in an antiwar demonstration.

Demonstrators carried signs and sat peacefully as speakers from peace organizations around the world spoke on issues of ending the war.

Speakers called for an immediate end to the war and urged citizens to voice their opinions to state officials and legislators.

Angle or slant is the point of view from which a story is written. Even an objective report must have an angle.

Consider these two headlines that describe a war demonstration.

The first headline suggests that the article following it will be focused on the sentiment or mood of the crowd gathered to demonstrate against a war. The second headline suggests the article will be focused on the event.

Standards for News Reporting

The ideal of journalism is to present news in a way that is objective, accurate, and thorough. The best news stories contain the following elements:

- **Objectivity** The story takes a balanced point of view toward the issues; it is not biased, nor does it reflect a specific attitude or opinion.
- **Accuracy** The story presents factual information that can be verified.
- **Thoroughness** The story presents all sides of an issue; it includes background information, telling *who, what, when, where, why,* and *how.*

Balanced Versus Biased Reporting

Objectivity in news reporting can be measured by how balanced or biased the story is.

Balanced reporting represents all sides of an issue equally and fairly.

A balanced news story

- represents people and subjects in a neutral light
- treats all sides of an issue equally
- does not include inappropriate questions
- does not show stereotypes or prejudice toward people of a particular race, gender, age, religion, or other group
- does not leave out important background information that is needed to establish a context or perspective

Biased reporting is reporting in which one side is favored over another or in which the subject is unfairly represented. Biased reporting may show an overly negative view of a subject, or it may encourage racial, gender, or other stereotypes and prejudices. Sometimes biased reporting is apparent in the journalist's choice of sources.

Sources are the people interviewed for the news report, and also any written materials and documents the journalist used for background information. From each source, the journalist gets a different point of view. To decide whether news reporting is balanced or biased, you will need to pay attention to the sources. For a news story on a new medicinal drug, for instance, if the journalist's only source is a representative from the company that made the drug, the report may be biased. But if the journalist also includes the perspective of someone neutral, such as a scientist who is objectively studying the effects of drugs, the report may be more balanced. It is important to evaluate the **credibility,** or believability and trustworthiness, of both a source and the report itself. The following chart shows which sources are credible.

Sources for News Stories

Credible Sources	Weak Sources
• experts in a field • people directly affected by the reported event (eyewitnesses) • published reports that are specifically mentioned or shown	• unnamed or anonymous sources • people who are not involved in the reported event (for example, people who heard about a story from a friend) • research, data, or reports that are not specifically named or are referred to only in vague terms (for example, "Research shows that . . .")

5 Advertising

Advertising is a sponsor's paid use of various media to promote products, services, or ideas. Some common forms of advertising are shown in the chart.

Type of Ad	Characteristics
Billboard	large outdoor advertising sign
Print ad	typically appears in magazines and newspapers; uses eye-catching graphics and persuasive copy
Flyer	print ad that is circulated by hand or mail
Infomercial	an extended ad on TV that usually includes detailed product information, demonstrations, and testimonials
Public service announcement	a message aired on radio or TV to promote ideas that are considered to be in the public interest
Political ad	broadcast on radio or TV to promote political candidates
Trailer	a short film promoting an upcoming movie, TV show, or video game

Marketing is the process of transferring products and services from producer to consumer. It involves determining the packaging and pricing of a product, how it will be promoted and advertised, and where it will be sold. One way companies market their products is by becoming media sponsors.

Sponsors pay for their products to be advertised. These companies hire advertising agencies to create and produce specific campaigns for their products. They then buy television or radio airtime or magazine, newspaper, or billboard space to feature ads where the target audience is sure to see them. Because selling time and space to advertisers generates much of the income the media need to function, the media need advertisers just as much as advertisers need the media.

Product placement is the intentional and identifiable featuring of brand-name products in movies, television shows, video games, and other media. The intention is to have viewers feel positive about a product because they see a favorite character using it. Another purpose may be to promote product recognition.

5.1 PERSUASIVE TECHNIQUES

Persuasive techniques are the methods used to convince an audience to buy a product or adopt an idea. Advertisers use a combination of visuals, sound, special effects, and words to persuade their target audience. Recognizing the following techniques can help you evaluate persuasive media messages and identify misleading information:

Emotional appeals use strong feelings rather than factual evidence to persuade consumers. An example of an emotional appeal that targets people's fear is a statement such as this: "Is your identity safe? Protect yourself with ProTech software."

Bandwagon appeal uses the argument that a person should believe or do something because "everyone else" does. These appeals take advantage of people's desire to be socially accepted. Purchasing a popular product seems less risky when many others also find it worthy to buy. An example of a bandwagon appeal is "More and more people are switching to Bright 'n' Fresh laundry detergent."

Slogans are memorable phrases used in advertising campaigns. Slogans substitute catchy phrases for factual information.

Logical appeals rely on logic and facts, appealing to a consumer's reason and his or her respect for authority. Two examples of logical appeals are expert opinions and product comparison.

Celebrity ads use one of the following two categories of spokesperson:

- **Celebrity authorities** are experts in a particular field. Advertisers hope that audiences will transfer the respect or admiration they have for the person to the product. For example, a famous chef may endorse a particular brand of cookware. The manufacturers of the cookware want you to think that it is a good product because a cooking expert wouldn't endorse poor-quality pots and pans.
- **Celebrity spokespeople** are famous people who endorse a product. Advertisers hope that audiences will associate the product with the celebrity.

Product comparison involves comparing a product with its competition. The competing product is portrayed as inferior. The intended effect is for people to question the quality of the competing product and to believe the featured product is superior.

6 Elements of Design

The design of a media message is just as important as the words are in conveying the message. Like words, visuals are used to persuade, inform, and entertain.

Graphics and images, such as charts, diagrams, maps, timelines, photographs, illustrations, cartoons, book covers, and symbols, present information that can be quickly and easily understood. The following basic elements are used to give meaning to visuals:

Color can be used to highlight important elements such as headlines and subheads. It can also create mood, because many colors have a strong emotional or psychological impact on the reader or viewer. For example, warm colors more readily draw the eye and are often associated with happiness and comfort. Cool colors are often associated with feelings of peace and contentment or sometimes sadness.

Lines—strokes or marks—can be thick or thin, long or short, and smooth or jagged. They can focus attention and create a feeling of depth. They can frame an object. They can also direct a viewer's eye or create a sense of motion.

Texture is the surface quality or appearance of an object. For example, an object's texture can be glossy, rough, wet, or shiny. Texture can be used to create contrast. It can also be used to make an image look "real." For example, a pattern on wrapping paper can create a feeling of depth even though the texture is only visual and cannot be felt.

Shape is the external outline of an object. Shapes can be used to symbolize living things or geometric objects. They can emphasize visual elements and add interest. Shapes can also symbolize ideas.

Notice how this photograph uses these design elements to convey a message.

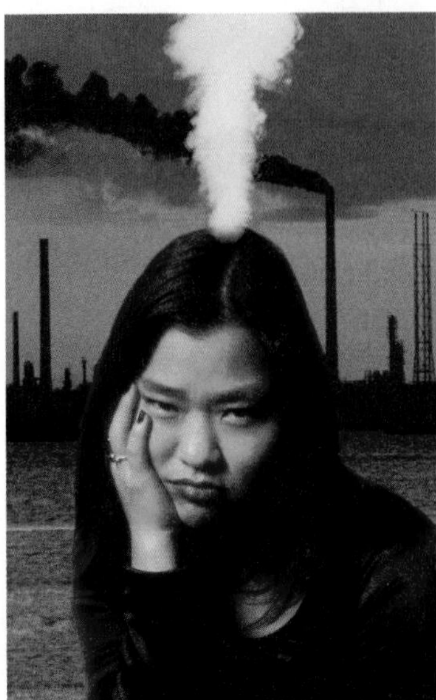

In "reading" this visual image for its message, take note of the following:

- The **foreground image** in this photo is of an unhappy young woman with a plume of smoke rising from her head, indicating she is angry or unhappy—presumably with the situation depicted behind her. The **background images** include smokestacks spewing smoke into the environment. This would suggest that the message concerns her feelings about the environment.
- The **colors** orange and black suggest danger, the need to be alert, or a threatening situation. The colors in this scene indicate that the situation is threatening or dangerous.
- The smokestacks in the background are in silhouette and can only be defined by their **shape.** This suggestion of the image lends an air of mystery and foreboding to the message.
- The **lines** in this picture are primarily vertical (the smokestacks, the young woman, and the white smoke plume). The vertical lines draw your focus toward the top of the photo, where it centers on the crossed smoke plumes.

Considering all the design elements in this photograph, what is its message?

7 Evaluating Media Messages

Being able to respond critically to media images and messages will help you evaluate the reliability of the content and make informed decisions. Here are six questions to ask about any media message:

Who made—and who sponsored—this message, and for what purpose? The source of the message is a clue to its purpose. If the source of the message is a private company, that company may be trying to sell you a product. If the source is a government agency, that agency may be trying to promote a program or philosophy. To discover the purpose, think about why its creator paid for and produced the message.

Who is the target audience and how is the message specifically tailored to it? Think about the age group, ethnic group, gender, and/or profession the message is targeting. Decide how it relates to you. Consider the tone and formality of the message. How do these two elements relate to similar messages you have heard in other media?

What are the different techniques used to inform, persuade, entertain, and attract attention? Analyze the elements, such as humor, music, special effects, and graphics, that have been used to create the message. Think about how visual and sound effects, such as symbols, color, photographs, words, and music, support the purpose behind the message.

What messages are communicated (and/or implied) about certain people, places, events, behaviors, lifestyles, and so forth? The media try to influence who we are, what we believe in, how we view things, and what values we hold. Look or listen closely to determine whether certain types of behavior are being depicted and if judgments or values are communicated through those behaviors. What are the biases in the message?

How current, accurate, and credible is the information in this message? Think about the reputation of the source. Note the broadcast or publication date of the message and whether the message might change quickly. If a report or account is not supported by facts, authoritative sources, or eyewitness accounts, you should question the credibility of the message.

What is left out of this message that might be important to know? Think about what the message is asking you to believe. Also think about what questions come to mind as you watch, read, or listen to the message.

Applying Strategies to the SAT* and ACT

The test items in this section are modeled after test formats that are used on the SAT and ACT. The strategies presented here will help you prepare for these tests and others. This section offers general test-taking strategies and tips for answering multiple-choice items in critical reading and writing, as well as samples for impromptu writing and essay writing. For each test, read the tips in the margin. Then apply the tips to the practice items. You can also apply the tips to Assessment Practice tests in this book.

1 General Test-Taking Strategies

- Arrive on time and be prepared. Be sure to bring either sharpened pencils with erasers or pens—whichever you are told to bring.
- If you have any questions, ask them before the test begins. Make sure you understand the test procedures, the timing, and the rules.
- Read the test directions carefully. Look at the passages and questions to get an overview of what is expected.
- Tackle the questions one at a time rather than thinking about the whole test.
- Refer back to the reading selections as needed. For example, if a question asks about an author's attitude, you might have to reread a passage for clues.
- If you are not sure of your answer, make a logical guess. You can often arrive at the correct answer by reasoning and eliminating wrong answers.
- As you fill in answers on your answer sheet, make sure you match the number of each test item to the numbered space on the answer sheet.
- Don't look for patterns in the positions of correct choices.
- Only change an answer if you are sure your original choice is incorrect. If you do change an answer, erase your original choice neatly and thoroughly.
- Look for main ideas as you read passages. They are often stated at the beginning or the end of a paragraph. Sometimes the main idea is implied.
- Check your answers and reread your essay.

2 Critical Reading

Most tests contain a critical reading section that measures your ability to read, understand, and interpret passages. The passages may be either fiction or nonfiction, and they can be 100 words or 500 to 850 words. They are drawn from literature, the humanities, social studies, and the natural sciences.

Directions: Read the following passage. Base your answers to questions 1 and 2 on what is stated or implied in the passage.

PASSAGE

The chemical composition of diamond is extremely simple; like graphite it is composed of only one element: carbon. But the similarity ends there, for no two minerals could be more diverse. Diamond is hard, lustrous, and transparent; graphite is soft, dull, and opaque. Diamond has a specific gravity of 3.5, high for a nonmetallic mineral. Graphite's specific gravity is 2.2, extremely low for a metallic mineral. These strikingly different properties of the same element result from the way in which the carbon atoms are packed together. In diamond they are close together and held by strong electrical bonds, whereas in graphite they are far apart and have weak bonds.

Diamond is valued for its remarkable physical properties. It is harder and more resistant to abrasion than any other natural mineral; nothing can scratch it except another diamond. It is also insoluble in all acids and alkalis. Because of these resistant properties, the Greeks called the mineral *adamas,* meaning "invincible," and its present name derives from that.

—Cornelius Hurlbut, from *Minerals and Man*

1. The (main) idea of the first paragraph is that ❷
   - (A) diamond and graphite consist of the same element but have different properties
   - (B) the atoms in diamond and graphite are held together by electrical bonds
   - (C) diamond is hard, lustrous, and transparent, while graphite is soft, dull, and opaque
   - (D) diamond and graphite have a simple chemical composition consisting of one element
   - (E) the specific gravity of diamond is high; graphite's specific gravity is low

❸ choices

2. The Greek word *adamas* is a fitting description of diamond's ❹
   - (A) international reputation
   - (B) great value
   - (C) jewelry applications ❺
   - (D) resistant properties
   - (E) ancient lineage

Tips: Multiple Choice

A multiple-choice question consists of a stem and a set of choices. On some tests, there are four choices. On the SAT, there are five. The stem is usually in the form of a question or an incomplete sentence. One of the choices correctly answers the question or completes the sentence.

❶ Read the stem carefully and try to answer the question without looking at the choices.

❷ Pay attention to key words in the stem. They may direct you to the correct answer. Question 1 is looking for the *main* idea. Choices (B) through (E) focus on minor details.

❸ Read all the choices before deciding on the correct answer.

❹ Some questions ask you to interpret a word or a figure of speech. Question 2, for example, asks you to describe the character of a diamond based on the etymology of its name.

❺ After reading all of the choices, eliminate any that you know are incorrect. In question 2, you can safely eliminate choice (C) because this passage focuses on the scientific properties of diamond, not its uses.

Answers: 1. (A), **2.** (D)

Directions: Base your answers to questions 1 and 2 on the two passages below.

PASSAGE 1

❷

The president helps people make sense of politics. Congress is a tangle of committees, the bureaucracy is a maze of agencies. The president is one man trying to do a job—a picture much more understandable to the mass of people who find themselves in the same boat. Furthermore, he is the top man. He ought to know what is going on and set it right. So when the economy goes sour, or war drags on, or domestic violence erupts, the president is available to take the blame. Then when things go right, it seems the president must have had a hand in it. ❸

—James David Barber, "The Presidential Character"

PASSAGE 2

No man or group at either end of Pennsylvania Avenue shares his peculiar status in our government and politics. ❷ That is why his services are in demand. By the same token, though, the obligations of all other men are different from his own. His Cabinet officers have departmental duties and constituents. His legislative leaders head Congressional parties, one in either House. His national party organization stands apart from his official family. His political allies in the states need not face Washington, or one another. The private groups that seek him out are not compelled to govern. And friends abroad are not compelled to run in our elections. ❹ Lacking his position and prerogatives, these men cannot regard his obligations as his own. They have their jobs to do; none is the same as his.

—Richard E. Neustadt, "Presidential Power"

❶ 1. In Passage 1, what does the author mean when he says, "The president helps people make sense of politics"?

(A) The government is sponsoring political education classes for voters.

(B) People see the president in personal terms, as someone with a job to do.

(C) The White House has valuable information about the legislative process.

(D) Congress is an impenetrable maze of agencies and committees.

(E) Citizens have to think about international issues before they vote.

2. The authors of both passages would probably agree with which one of these statements about government? ❺

(A) It is difficult to penetrate the maze of government bureaucracies.

(B) Many elected officials are only concerned with local issues.

(C) Each president leaves an indelible imprint on the nation.

(D) Not everyone supports the president or his policies.

(E) The president holds a unique position in our political system.

Tips: Two Passages

Questions are sometimes based on a pair of related passages, which may have completely different views or may simply describe different aspects of the same subject. The two passages here discuss the role of the U.S. president.

❶ Before reading the passages, skim all the questions to see what information you will need.

❷ Find topic sentences and ask yourself whether the passages support or refute their topic sentences. In this case, both passages support their claims with examples and discussion.

❸ You can determine an author's attitude toward a subject by his or her choice of words. In passage 1, the words *tangle* and *maze* convey a subtle disapproval of government bureaucracies.

❹ Analyze supporting details. The author of passage 2 supports his claim that the president has unique responsibilities by contrasting his position with those of others.

❺ When working with two passages, look for related or contrasting ideas. To answer question 2, you have to find a common thread in the discussions of the presidency. Eliminate any answers that pertain to only one of the passages.

Answers: 1. (B), **2.** (E)

Directions: Read the following passage, taken from a novel published in 1900. Based on what is stated or implied in the passage, answer questions 1 through 5, which appear on the next page.

PASSAGE

When Caroline Meeber boarded the afternoon train for Chicago, her total outfit consisted of a small trunk, a cheap imitation alligator-skin satchel, a small lunch in a paper box, and a yellow leather snap purse containing her ticket, a scrap of paper with her sister's address in Van Buren Street, and four dollars in money. It was in August, 1889. She was eighteen years of age, bright, timid, and full of the illusions of ignorance and youth. Whatever touch of regret at parting characterized her thoughts, it was certainly not for advantages now being given up. A gush of tears at her mother's farewell kiss, a touch in her throat when the cars clacked by the flour mill where her father worked by the day, a pathetic sign as the familiar green environs of the village passed in review, and the threads which bound her so lightly to girlhood and home were irretrievably broken.

To be sure, there was always the next station, where one might descend and return. There was the great city, bound more closely by these very trains which came up daily. Columbia City was not so very far away, even once she was in Chicago. What, pray, is a few hours—a few hundred miles? She looked at the little slip bearing her sister's address and wondered. She gazed at the green landscape, now passing in swift review, until her swifter thoughts replaced its impression with vague conjectures of what Chicago might be.

When a girl leaves her home at eighteen, she does one of two things. Either she falls into saving hands and becomes better, or she rapidly assumes the cosmopolitan standard of virtue and becomes worse. Of an intermediate balance, under the circumstances, there is no possibility. The city has its cunning wiles, no less than the infinitely smaller and more human tempter. There are large forces which allure with all the soulfulness of expression possible in the most cultured human. The gleam of a thousand lights is often as effective as the persuasive light in a wooing and fascinating eye. Half of the undoing of the unsophisticated and natural mind is accomplished by forces wholly superhuman. A blare of sound, a roar of life, a vast array of human hives, appeal to the astonished senses in equivocal terms. Without a counselor at hand to whisper cautious interpretations, what falsehoods may not these things breathe into the unguarded ear! Unrecognized for what they are, their beauty, like music, too often relaxes, then weakens, then perverts the simpler human perceptions.

—Theodore Dreiser, *Sister Carrie*

Tips: Reading Text

1. Notice the characters who are presented in a passage. Be alert to details about their appearance, personality, or behavior.
2. Identify the point of view from which the story is being told. In a first-person narrative, the narrator is a character in the story and uses the pronouns *I* and *me.* In a third-person narrative, the narrator is outside the story and uses the pronouns *he, she,* and *they.*
3. Try to visualize the setting as you read, filling in details as they are presented. In this passage we see a young woman on a train headed for Chicago in 1889. She has left behind the "familiar green environs" of her home in the small town of Columbia City.
4. Remember that a word can have several different meanings or subtle shades of meaning.
5. Some test questions will ask you to interpret a figure of speech or an image. Try to understand why the author chose that particular image and what effect it achieves.

Answers: 1. (D), **2.** (B), **3.** (A), **4.** (C), **5.** (E)

1. The catalog of Caroline's belongings in lines 2–5 helps to

(A) foreshadow her destiny

(B) mock her appearance

(C) create sympathy for her

(D) convey her social status

(E) portray her personality

2. What is implied about Caroline's life in the statement "Whatever touch of regret at parting characterized her thoughts, it was certainly not for advantages now being given up"?

(A) It was hard for Caroline to leave behind the comforts of home.

(B) Caroline's life at home offered few material benefits.

(C) Caroline hated the life of poverty she led at home.

(D) Moving to the city required a sacrifice on Caroline's part.

(E) Once she left home, Caroline never looked back.

3. The description in lines 21–24 suggests that the city is a place that should be viewed with

(A) distrust

(B) respect

(C) enthusiasm

(D) contempt

(E) nostalgia

4. The image of a tempter in lines 24–30 suggests the

(A) evils of human nature

(B) simple beauty of music

(C) corrupting influence of the city

(D) vulnerable innocence of youth

(E) pleasures of materialism

5. In line 29, "natural" most nearly means

(A) normal

(B) inborn

(C) logical

(D) real

(E) naive

The critical reading section may feature sentence completion questions that test your knowledge of vocabulary. They may also measure your ability to figure out how different parts of a sentence logically fit together.

Directions: Choose the word or set of words that, when inserted, best fits the meaning of the complete sentence.

1. The investigator constructed a _______ of events to _______ the cause of the accident. ❶
   (A) chronology . . ascertain
   (B) timeline . . predict ❷
   (C) typology . . determine
   (D) collation . . understand
   (E) history . . prosecute

2. Russian author Alexander Solzhenitsyn tried to _______ government censorship by _______ some of his writings out of the country.
   (A) encircle . . translating
   (B) disrupt . . carrying
   (C) circumvent . . smuggling ❸
   (D) evade . . banishing
   (E) prevent . . propelling

3. Automakers can _______ the effects of global warming by ❹ reducing carbon-dioxide and other _______ emissions from cars and trucks.
   (A) minimize . . natural
   (B) misuse . . harmful
   (C) correct . . excessive
   (D) mitigate . . toxic
   (E) relieve . . acute

4. Because ❺ they have a _______ appetite, bears will raid cabins, backpacks, and picnic areas in search of anything that smells of food. ❻
   (A) vicious
   (B) voracious
   (C) refined
   (D) notorious
   (E) selective

Tips: Sentence Completion

❶ When you are completing sentences with two words missing, think about which pair of suggested words fits both blanks.

❷ If one word in the answer choice is wrong, eliminate that choice from consideration. In sentence 1, *timeline* makes sense, but *predict* does not, because the accident occurred in the past.

❸ A prefix can help to unlock the meaning of a word. The Latin prefix *circum-* means "around." The writer was trying to circumvent, or go around, government censorship.

❹ Look for key words or phrases that link the ideas in a sentence. The word *by* introduces a phrase that explains how to do something—in this case, how to reduce global warming.

❺ Look for words that link the ideas in a sentence. The word *because* in sentence 4 signals a cause-and-effect relationship between appetite and behavior.

❻ If you don't know a word's meaning, look for clues within the sentence. For sentence 4, ask yourself: What sort of appetite would lead a bear to eat almost anything? An animal with a *refined* (C) or *selective* (E) appetite, for example, would choose only certain foods.

Answers: 1. (A), **2.** (C), **3.** (D), **4.** (B)

B Writing

The writing section of standardized tests measures your ability to express ideas clearly and correctly. You will be asked to identify errors in grammar and usage and to improve sentences and paragraphs.

Directions: The following sentence contains either a single error or no error. If it does contains an error, select the underlined part that must be changed to make the sentence correct. If the sentence is correct as written, select answer choice (E).

1. Neither (A) the Supreme Court nor (B) the president have (C) ❷ the power to create laws, because the Constitution entrusts (D) ❸ that responsibility to Congresss alone. No error (E) ❶

Directions: Determine if the underlined part of the following sentence needs improvement. If it does, select the best change presented. If the original phrasing is best, select answer (A).

2. Ancient Greeks believed in mythical creatures, they combined human and animal traits.

(A) creatures, they combined ❹

(B) creatures, and they combined

(C) creatures that combined ❺

(D) creatures, and which combined

(E) creatures such as could combine

Directions: Following is an early draft of an essay. Read it and answer the question.

Controlling E-Waste

(1) It is estimated that Americans generate about 2 million tons of technology-related trash each year. (2) Computer circuit boards, monitors, and printers are piling up in landfills. (3) They decay. (4) They can leak mercury and other toxic substances as a result of the decay. (5) Some public health officials think the U.S. should develop a federal law that requires technology companies to take back their used products and reduce the amount of hazardous material they use in manufacturing.

3. Which one of the following sentences combines sentences 3 and 4? ❻

(A) They can decay, also leaking mercury and other toxic substances.

(B) When they decay, they can leak mercury and other toxic substances.

(C) They decay; then they can leak mercury and other toxic substances.

(D) They decay, and thus leak mercury and other toxic substances.

(E) They can leak toxic substances such as mercury.

Tips: Grammar and Style

❶ Read the entire sentence or passage to grasp its overall meaning. Pay particular attention to any underlined portions.

❷ Watch for subject-verb agreement when using *neither . . . nor.* If both subjects are singular, the verb must be singular.

❸ Use prefixes to help you understand the meaning of words. The prefix *en-* in the word *entrust* means "in" or "within."

❹ Read through all of the choices before you decide which revision is best. In this case, answer (A) is *not* correct, because joining two independent clauses with only a comma creates a run-on sentence.

❺ Understand how to use *that* and *which. That* introduces an essential defining clause. *Which* introduces a nonessential clause. Use *which* if the clause can be omitted without changing the meaning of the sentence. Nonessential clauses are set off with commas.

❻ When combining sentences, think about how the ideas are related. Subordinating conjunctions such as *while, when, before, after,* and *until* express a relationship of time. *Because* and *since* indicate cause and effect.

Answers: 1. (C), **2.** (C), **3.** (B)

4 Essay

To determine how well you can develop and express ideas, many tests ask you to write an essay in response to an assignment, or prompt. The essay will represent a first draft and be scored based on the following criteria:

- **Focus** Establish a point of view in the opening paragraph.
- **Organization** Maintain a logical progression of ideas.
- **Support for Ideas** Use details and examples to develop an argument.
- **Style/Word Choice** Use words accurately and vary your sentences.
- **Grammar** Use Standard English and proofread for errors.

Think carefully about the issue presented in this quotation and the assignment below.

> Arts education and physical education both enjoy public support and help students grow and develop in many ways. In recent years, these programs have sometimes been marginalized or discontinued due to budget cuts or redirection of school resources. Sometimes schools have had to choose between these programs.

> **Assignment:** If a school had to choose between funding its arts program and funding its physical education program, which option would you support? Plan and write an essay in which you develop your opinion on this issue. Support your position with specific reasons and examples taken from your studies and experience.

SAMPLE ESSAY

If I had to decide whether to cut arts or physical education programs from the curriculum, I would choose to save the arts. 1

It's hard to cut physical education programs when our nation is struggling with an obesity epidemic. We all know that Americans don't get enough exercise. We drive everywhere, and we spend hours in front of the TV. 2 But physical fitness is a medical and lifestyle issue, not an academic pursuit. Exercise and good nutrition require a personal, lifelong commitment, and that goes beyond what can be taught in a gym class.

The arts, on the other hand, are as much an academic pursuit as science, history, or literature. Acting in a play requires reading and interpreting a work of literature. Composing even a simple tune requires knowledge of harmony, rhythm, and timing. Painting and drawing require some understanding of the principles of light, color, and perspective. 3 Whereas high school athletes often struggle with academics because of the demands of their sport, students in music and performing arts don't seem to experience those conflicting demands in the same way.

Arts education encourages students to be creative and to take risks. There are no right or wrong answers in art, so students who might not excel in other areas of academic life can gain respect through their music or dancing.

Music, painting, literature, dance, and theater not only enrich our lives but also stimulate us and teach us life lessons that a gym class never could. 4

Tips: Writing an Essay

The SAT allows only 25 minutes for you to write an essay. Before you begin writing, take a few minutes to jot down the main points you want to make. Allow time to reread and proofread your essay before you hand it in.

1. When you're writing a persuasive essay, state your point of view in the introduction. Be sure to keep your purpose in mind as you write.
2. Take the opposing point of view into consideration and respond to it.
3. Include concrete examples in the body of your essay to clarify your points and strengthen your arguments.
4. Make sure your essay has a conclusion, even if it is just a single sentence. A conclusion pulls your ideas together and lets the reader know that you have finished.
5. There will not be time to recopy your essay, so if you have to make a correction, do so neatly and legibly.
6. You don't have to write a long essay. Length is less important than clarity of thought and correctness of expression. Your essay could range from 200 to 400 words.

Glossary of Literary and Nonfiction Terms

Act An act is a major unit of action in a play, similar to a chapter in a book. Depending on their lengths, plays can have as many as five acts. Arthur Miller's play *The Crucible* has four acts.

See also **Drama; Scene.**

Allegory An allegory is a work with two levels of meaning, a literal one and a symbolic one. In such a work, most of the characters, objects, settings, and events represent abstract qualities. Personification is often used in traditional allegories. As in a fable or parable, the purpose of an allegory may be to convey truths about life, to teach religious or moral lessons, or to criticize social institutions.

Example: In Edgar Allan Poe's "The Masque of the Red Death," the main character Prospero, the sequence and the decorations of the rooms in the castle, and objects such as the ebony clock all have allegorical meaning.

See page 444.

Alliteration Alliteration is the repetition of consonant sounds at the beginnings of words. Poets use alliteration to impart a musical quality to their poems, to create mood, to reinforce meaning, to emphasize particular words, and to unify lines or stanzas. Note the examples of alliteration in the following line:

> **Doubting, dreaming dreams no mortal ever dared to dream before.**
>
> **—Edgar Allan Poe, "The Raven"**

See pages 435, 1301.

Allusion An allusion is an indirect reference to a person, place, event, or literary work with which the author believes the reader will be familiar.

Example: In "Speech in the Virginia Convention," Patrick Henry warns colonists not to be "betrayed with a kiss"—an allusion to the Apostle Judas, who betrayed Jesus by kissing him.

See pages 235, 942, 1203.

Ambiguity Ambiguity is a technique in which a word, phrase, or event has more than one meaning or can be interepreted in more than one way. Some writers deliberately create this effect to give richness and depth of meaning. T. S. Eliot and Robert Frost are two poets known for their use of ambiguity.

See pages 483, 937, 1061.

Analogy An analogy is a point-by-point comparison between two things for the purpose of clarifying the less familiar of the two subjects.

Example: In "My Dungeon Shook," James Baldwin draws an analogy between his nephew's probable reaction to seeing the stars shining while the sun is out and white people's reaction to black people moving out of their fixed places.

See pages 1215, 1255.

Anapest *See* **Meter.**

Anaphora Anaphora is a repetition of a word or words at the beginning of successive lines, clauses, or sentences.

> **Blackness**
> **is a title,**
> **is a preoccupation,**
> **is a commitment . . .**
>
> **—Gwendolyn Brooks, "Primer for Blacks"**

See pages 531, 1295.
See also **Repetition.**

Anecdote An anecdote is a brief story that focuses on a single episode or event in a person's life and that is used to illustrate a particular point.

Example: In "Straw into Gold," Sandra Cisneros provides an anecdote about the challenge she faced when ordered to make corn tortillas, a task she had never done before. This anecdote illustrates Cisneros's pluck in attempting the seemingly impossible.

See pages 379, 1287.

Antagonist An antagonist is usually the principal character in opposition to the **protagonist,** or hero of a narrative or drama. The antagonist can also be a force of nature.

Example: In "The Open Boat," the sea is the antagonist of the four shipwrecked men. Its powerful force is described in such detail that it seems like a character.

See pages 759, 977.
See also **Character; Protagonist.**

Antihero An antihero is a protagonist who has the qualities opposite to those of a hero; he or she may be insecure, ineffective, cowardly, sometimes dishonest or dishonorable, or—most often—a failure. A popular antihero in contemporary culture is the cartoon character Homer Simpson.

Aphorism An aphorism is a brief statement, usually one sentence long, that expresses a general principle or truth about life.

Example: Ralph Waldo Emerson's "Self-Reliance" is sprinkled with such memorable aphorisms as "A foolish consistency is the hobgoblin of little minds."

See page 275.

Archetype An archetype is a pattern in literature that is found in a variety of works from different cultures throughout the ages. An archetype can be a plot, a character, an image, or a setting. For example, the association of death and rebirth with winter and spring is an archetype common to many cultures.

Aside In drama, an aside is a short speech directed to the audience, or another character, that is not heard by the other characters on stage.

See also **Soliloquy.**

Assonance Assonance is the repetition of vowel sounds within words. Both poets and prose writers use assonance to impart a musical quality to their works, to create mood, to reinforce meaning, to emphasize particular words, and to unify lines, stanzas, or passages. Note examples of assonance in the following lines:

> **Along the window-sill, the lipstick stubs**
> **Glittered in their steel shells.**
> **—Rita Dove, "Adolescence—III"**

See also **Alliteration; Consonance; Rhyme.**

Atmosphere *See* **Mood.**

Audience Audience is the person or persons who are intended to read a piece of writing. The intended audience of a work determines its form, style, tone, and the details included. For example, Cabeza de Vaca's audience for *La Relación* was the king of Spain. Hence, *La Relación* took the form of a formal report with a patriotic tone that included details of the explorers' hardship and determination. Had the work been addressed to Cabeza de Vaca's wife, it would likely have been less formal and probably would have included details about his personal feelings.

See pages 73, 123, 1257.

Author's Perspective An author's perspective is a unique combination of ideas, values, feelings, and beliefs that influences the way the writer looks at a topic. **Tone,** or attitude, often reveals an author's perspective. For example, Jonathan Edwards was a Puritan minister whose father and grandfather were also Puritan ministers; he began his theological training at age 12. His family upbringing, his beliefs, and the time and place in which he lived all contributed to the perspective found in *Sinners in the Hands of an Angry God.*

See pages 122, 403, 769.

Author's Purpose A writer usually writes for one or more of these purposes: to inform, to entertain, to express himself or herself, or to persuade readers to believe or do something. For example, the purpose of a news report (either in a newspaper or magazine) is primarily to inform; the purpose of an news editorial is to persuade the readers or audience to do or believe something.

Examples: In *The Interesting Narrative of the Life of Olaudah Equiano,* the author's purpose is primarily to inform readers about the horrors that captured Africans endured in the holds of slave ships during the Middle Passage. Thoreau's purpose in "Civil Disobedience," on the other hand, is to persuade his audience to use nonviolent resistance to oppose unjust laws.

See pages 83, 559.

Autobiographical Essay *See* **Essay.**

Autobiography An autobiography is the story of a person's life written by that person. Generally written from the first-person point of view, autobiographies can vary in style from straightforward chronological accounts to impressionistic narratives.

Example: Both *Narrative of the Life of Frederick Douglass, an American Slave* and *Coming of Age in Mississippi* are autobiographies.

See pages 266, 558, 660.

Ballad A ballad is a narrative poem that was originally meant to be sung. Ballads often contain dialogue and repetition and suggest more than they actually state. Traditional **folk ballads,** composed by unknown authors and handed down orally, are written in four-line stanzas with regular rhythm and rhyme. A **literary ballad** is one that is modeled on the folk ballads but written by a single author—for example, Dudley Randall's "Ballad of Birmingham."

See page 1214.

See also **Narrative Poem; Rhyme; Rhythm.**

Biography A biography is a type of nonfiction in which a writer gives a factual account of someone else's life. Written in the third person, a biography may cover a person's entire life or focus on only an important part of it. The poet Carl Sandburg wrote an acclaimed six-volume biography of Abraham Lincoln. Modern biography includes a popular form called **fictionalized biography,** in which writers use their imaginations to re-create past conversations and to elaborate on some incidents.

Blank Verse A poem written in blank verse consists of unrhymed lines of iambic pentameter. In other words, each line of blank verse has five pairs of syllables. In most pairs, an unstressed syllable is followed by a stressed syllable. The most versatile of poetic forms, blank verse imitates the natural rhythms of English speech, as in the following lines:

> **She ran | on tip | toe down | the dark | ened passage**
> **To meet | him in | the door | way with | the news**
> **And put | him on | his guard. | "Silas | is back."**
> **She pushed | him out | ward with | her through |**
> **the door**
> **And shut | it aft | er her. | "Be kind," | she said.**
> **—Robert Frost, "The Death of the Hired Man"**

See pages 337, 943.
See also **Iambic Pentameter; Meter; Rhythm.**

Caesura A caesura is a pause or a break in a line of poetry. Poets use a caesura to emphasize the word or phrase that precedes it or to vary the rhythmical effects. In the following line, a caesura follows the word *die:*

> **If we must die, let it not be like hogs**
> **—Claude McKay, "If We Must Die"**

Cast of Characters The cast of characters is a list of all the characters in a play, usually in the order of appearance. This list is found at the beginning of a script.
See page 137.

Catalog A catalog is a list of people, things, or attributes. This technique, found in epics and in the Bible, also characterizes Whitman's style, as seen in the beginning of this line:

> **Kanuck, Tuckahoe, Congressman, Cuff, I give them the same, I receive them the same.**
> **—Walt Whitman, "Song of Myself"**

See page 531.

Character Characters are the people, and sometimes animals or other beings, who take part in the action of a story or novel. Events center on the lives of one or more characters, referred to as **main characters.** The other characters, called **minor characters,** interact with the main characters and help move the story along. In Kurt Vonnegut's story "Adam," Heinz Knechtmann is the main character, while the other expectant father, Mr. Sousa, is a minor character.

Characters may also be classified as either static or dynamic. **Static characters** tend to stay in a fixed position over the course of the story. They do not experience life-altering moments and seem to act the same, even though their situations may change. In contrast, **dynamic characters** evolve as individuals, learning from their experiences and growing emotionally.
See pages 717, 943, 977, 1179.
See also **Antagonist; Characterization; Foil; Motivation; Protagonist.**

Characterization Characterization refers to the techniques a writer uses to develop characters. There are four basic methods of characterization:

1. A writer may use physical description. In F. Scott Fitzgerald's "Winter Dreams," Judy Jones is described as follows:

> **She wore a blue gingham dress, rimmed at throat and shoulders with a white edging that accentuated her tan. . . . She was arrestingly beautiful. The color in her cheeks was centered like the color in a picture—it was not a "high" color, but a sort of fluctuating and feverish warmth. . . .**

2. The character's own actions, words, thoughts, and feelings might be presented. In Fitzgerald's story, after Judy Jones tries to revive the romance between herself and Dexter, she cries and says, "I'm more beautiful than anybody else, . . . why can't I be happy?"

3. The actions, words, thoughts, and feelings of other characters provide another means of developing a character. Mr. Sandwood, in Fitzgerald's story, exclaims about Judy Jones: "My God, she's good-looking!" To which Mr. Hedrick replies: "Good-looking! She always looks as if she wanted to be kissed! Turning those big cow-eyes on every calf in town!"

4. The narrator's own direct comments also serve to develop a character. The narrator of "Winter Dreams" says of Judy Jones:

> **Whatever Judy wanted, she went after with the full pressure of her charm. There was no divergence of method, no jockeying for position or premeditation of effects—there was very little mental side to any of her affairs. She simply made men conscious to the highest degree of her physical loveliness.**

See pages 691, 921, 1179.
See also **Character; Narrator.**

Chorus In the theater of ancient Greece, the chorus was a group of actors who commented on the **action** of the play. Between scenes, the chorus sang and danced to musical accompaniment, giving insights into the message of the play. The chorus is often considered a kind of ideal spectator, representing the response of ordinary citizens to the tragic events that unfold. Certain dramatists have continued to employ this classical convention as a way of representing the views of the society being depicted.
See also **Drama.**

Cliché A cliché is an overused expression that has lost its freshness, force, and appeal. The phrase "happy as a lark" is an example of a cliché.

Climax In a plot structure, the climax, or turning point, is the moment when the reader's interest and emotional intensity reach a peak. The climax usually occurs toward the end of a story and often results in a change in the characters or a solution to the conflict.
Example: In Edgar Allan Poe's "The Masque of the Red Death," the climax occurs when the Red Death arrives at the masked ball and is confronted by Prince Prospero. Shortly afterward, Prospero and all of his guests die.
See also **Falling Action; Plot; Rising Action; Resolution.**

Comedy A comedy is a dramatic work that is light and often humorous in tone, usually ending happily with a peaceful resolution of the main conflict. A comedy differs from a **farce** by having a more believable plot, more realistic characters, and less boisterous behavior.
See also **Drama; Farce.**

Comic Relief Comic relief consists of humorous scenes, incidents, or speeches that are included in a serious drama to provide a reduction in emotional intensity. Because it breaks the tension, comic relief allows an audience to prepare emotionally for events to come.

Complication A complication is an additional factor or problem introduced into the rising action of a story to make the conflict more difficult. Often, a plot complication makes it seem as though the main character is getting farther away from the thing he or she wants.

Conceit *See* **Extended Metaphor.**

Conflict A conflict is a struggle between opposing forces that is the basis of a story's plot. An **external conflict** pits a character against nature, society, or another character. An **internal conflict** is a conflict between opposing forces within a character.
Example: In "Coyote and the Buffalo," Coyote's struggle to keep Buffalo Bull from killing him is an external conflict, whereas Coyote's struggle to decide whether to kill and eat the buffalo cow is an internal conflict.
See pages 48, 759, 1195.
See also **Antagonist; Plot.**

Connotation Connotation is the emotional response evoked by a word, in contrast to its denotation, which is its literal meaning. *Kitten,* for example, is defined as "a young cat." However, the word also suggests, or connotes, images of softness, warmth, and playfulness.

Consonance Consonance is the repetition of consonant sounds within and at the ends of words.

> **Some late visitor entreating entrance at my chamber door.**
> **—Edgar Allan Poe, "The Raven"**

See also **Alliteration; Assonance.**

Couplet *See* **Sonnet.**

Creation Myth *See* **Myth.**

Critical Essay *See* **Essay.**

Cultural Hero A cultural hero is a larger-than-life figure who reflects the values of a people. Rather than being the creation of a single writer, this kind of hero evolves from the telling of folk tales from one generation to the next. The role of the cultural hero is to provide a noble image that will inspire and guide the actions of all who share that culture.

Dactyl *See* **Meter.**

Denotation *See* **Connotation.**

Dénouement *See* **Falling Action.**

Description Description is writing that helps a reader to picture scenes, events, and characters. Effective description usually relies on imagery, figurative language, and precise diction, as in the following passage:

> **I saw again the naked house on the prairie, black and grim as a wooden fortress; the black pond where I had learned to swim, its margin pitted with sun-dried cattle tracks; the rain gullied clay banks about the naked house, the four dwarf ash seedlings where the dish-cloths were always hung to dry before the kitchen door.**
> **—Willa Cather, "A Wagner Matinee"**

See pages 718, 735.
See also **Diction; Figurative Language; Imagery.**

Dialect A dialect is the distinct form of a language as it is spoken in one geographical area or by a particular social or ethnic group. A group's dialect is reflected in characteristic pronunciations, vocabulary, idioms, and grammatical constructions. When trying to reproduce a given dialect, writers often use unconventional spellings to suggest the way words actually sound. Writers use dialect to establish setting, to provide local color, and to develop characters. In the following passage, the use of dialect captures the sound and tang of frontier speech:

> **And he had a little small bull-pup, that to look at him you'd think he warn't worth a cent but to set around and look ornery and lay for a chance to steal something.**
> **—Mark Twain,**
> **"The Notorious Jumping Frog of Calaveras County"**

See pages 683, 1080.
See also **Local Color Realism.**

Dialogue Dialogue is conversation between two or more characters in either fiction or nonfiction. In drama, the story is told almost exclusively through dialogue, which moves the plot forward and reveals characters' motives.

See pages 674, 943, 1095.
See also **Drama.**

Diary A diary is a writer's personal day-to-day account of his or her experiences and impressions. Most diaries are private and not intended to be shared. Some, however, have been published because they are well written and provide useful perspectives on historical events or on the everyday life of particular eras. One important American diary found in this book is Mary Chesnut's diary of the Civil War.

Diction A writer's or speaker's choice of words is called diction. Diction includes both vocabulary (individual words) and syntax (the order or arrangement of words). Diction can be formal or informal, technical or common, abstract or concrete. In the following complex sentence, the diction is formal:

> **When, however, the mass movement repudiates violence while moving resolutely toward its goal, its opponents are revealed as the instigators and practitioners of violence if it occurs.**
> **—Martin Luther King Jr., "Stride Toward Freedom"**

See pages 259, 673, 1113.

Drama Drama is literature in which plot and character are developed through dialogue and action; in other words, drama is literature in play form. It is performed on stage and radio and in films and television. Most plays are divided into acts, with each act having an emotional peak, or climax, of its own. The acts sometimes are divided into scenes; each scene is limited to a single time and place. Most contemporary plays have two or three acts, although some have only one act.

See pages 132, 135, 1153.
See also **Act; Dialogue; Scene; Stage Directions.**

Dramatic Irony *See* **Irony.**

Dramatic Monologue A dramatic monologue is a lyric poem in which a speaker addresses a silent or absent listener in a moment of high intensity or deep emotion, as if engaged in private conversation. The speaker proceeds without interruption or argument, and the effect on the reader is that of hearing just one side of a conversation. This technique allows the poet to focus on the feelings, personality, and motivations of the speaker.

See also **Lyric Poetry; Soliloquy.**

Dynamic Character *See* **Character.**

Elegy An elegy is a poem written in tribute to a person, usually someone who has died recently. The tone of an elegy is usually formal and dignified.

Epic An epic is a long narrative poem on a serious subject presented in an elevated or formal style. An epic traces the adventures of a hero whose actions consist of courageous, even superhuman, deeds, which often represent the ideals and values of a nation or race. Epics typically address universal issues, such as good and evil, life and death, and sin and redemption. Homer's *Iliad* and *Odyssey* are famous epics from western civilization. The *Ramayana* is an epic from India.

Epic Hero An epic hero is a larger-than-life figure who embodies the ideals of a nation or race. Epic heroes take part in dangerous adventures and accomplish great deeds. Many undertake long, difficult journeys and display great courage and superhuman strength.

Epithet An epithet is a brief descriptive phrase that points out traits associated with a particular person or thing.

Example: Carl Sandburg's "Chicago" begins with a series of epithets, such as "Hog Butcher for the World."

Essay An essay is a short work of nonfiction that deals with a single subject. Essays are often informal, loosely structured, and highly personal. They can be descriptive, informative, persuasive, narrative, or any combination of these. Amy Tan's personal essay "Mother Tongue" combines all of these qualities.

An **autobiographical essay** focuses on an aspect of a writer's life. Generally, writers of autobiographical essays use the first-person point of view, combining objective description with the expression of subjective feelings. Zora Neale Hurston's "How It Feels to Be Colored Me" is an example of an autobiographical essay.

See pages 379, 910, 1114, 1263.

Exaggeration *See* **Hyperbole.**

Experimental Poetry Poetry described as experimental is often full of surprises—unusual word order, invented forms, descriptions of ordinary objects, and other distinctive elements not found in traditional verse forms. William Carlos Williams belonged to a group of experimental poets known as the Imagists. Their poems contain sharp, clear images of striking beauty, similar to the ones found in haiku. E. E. Cummings's "anyone lived in a pretty how town" reflects his unique brand of poetic experimentation, such as altering the expected presentation of words.

See page 961.

Exposition Exposition is the part of a literary work that provides the background information necessary to understand characters and their actions. Typically found at the beginning of a work, the exposition introduces the characters, describes the setting, and summarizes significant events that took place before the action begins.

Example: In the exposition to "The Devil and Tom Walker," Washington Irving introduces the main characters—a miser and his wife—who dwell in a desolate house near a swamp and take wicked glee in hoarding things from each other.

See also **Plot; Rising Action.**

Expository Essay *See* **Essay.**

Extended Metaphor Like any metaphor, an extended metaphor is a comparison between two essentially unlike things that nevertheless have something in common. It does not contain the word *like* or *as*. An extended metaphor compares two things at some length and in various ways. Sometimes the comparison is carried throughout a paragraph, a stanza, or an entire selection. In the following stanza, notice the extended metaphor in which the speaker compares himself to a loom for God's use:

Make me, O Lord, Thy spinning wheel complete.
Thy holy word my distaff make for me.
Make mine affections Thy swift flyers neat,
And make my soul Thy holy spool to be.
My conversation make to be Thy reel,
And reel the yarn thereon spun of Thy wheel.
—Edward Taylor, "Huswifery"

Like an extended metaphor, a **conceit** compares two apparently dissimilar things in several ways. The term usually implies a more elaborate, formal, and ingeniously clever comparison than the extended metaphor.

See pages 115, 897.

External Conflict *See* **Conflict.**

Eyewitness Account An eyewitness account is a firsthand report of an event written by someone who directly observed it or participated in it. As such, an eyewitness account is a primary source. Narrated from the first-person point of view, eyewitness accounts almost always include the following:

- objective facts about an event
- a chronological (time-order) pattern of organization
- vivid sensory details
- quotations from people who were present
- description of the writer's feelings and interpretations.

The excerpt from Anne Moody's autobiography, *Coming of Age in Mississippi*, is an eyewitness account of a sit-in in 1963.

See page 1239.

See also **Primary Source.**

Fable A fable is a brief tale that illustrates a clear, often directly stated, moral, or lesson. The characters in a fable are usually animals, but sometimes they are humans. The best-known fables—for example, "The Fox and the Crow" and "The Tortoise and the Hare" are those of Aesop, a Greek slave who lived about 600 B.C. Traditionally, fables are handed down from generation to generation as oral literature.

See also **Oral Literature.**

Falling Action In a plot structure, the falling action, or **resolution,** occurs after the climax to reveal the final outcome of events and to tie up any loose ends.

See also **Climax; Exposition; Plot; Rising Action.**

Farce A farce is a type of exaggerated comedy that features an absurd plot, ridiculous situations, and humorous dialogue. The main purpose of a farce is to keep an audience laughing. The characters are usually **stereotypes,** or simplified examples of different traits or qualities. Comic devices typically used in farces include mistaken identity, deception, wordplay—such as puns and double meanings—and exaggeration.

See also **Comedy; Stereotype.**

Fiction Fiction refers to works of prose that contain imaginary elements. Although fiction, like nonfiction, may be based on actual events and real people, it differs from nonfiction in that it is shaped primarily by the writer's imagination. For example, although Hemingway's "In Another Country" is based on autobiographical experiences, it cannot be classified as nonfiction because it is imbued with imaginary events and exaggeration in order to hold the reader's interest. The two major types of fiction are novels and short stories. The four basic elements of a work of fiction are **character, setting, plot,** and **theme.**

See also **Novel; Short Story.**

Figurative Language Figurative language is language that communicates ideas beyond the literal meaning of words. Figurative language can make descriptions and unfamiliar or difficult ideas easier to understand. Note the figurative language in this passage from "The Open Boat":

> **A seat in this boat was not unlike a seat upon a bucking broncho, and, by the same token, a broncho is not much smaller. The craft pranced and reared, and plunged like an animal. As each wave came, and she rose for it, she seemed like a horse making at a fence outrageously high.**
>
> **—Stephen Crane, "The Open Boat"**

The most common types of figurative language, called **figures of speech,** are **simile, metaphor, personification,** and **hyperbole.**

See pages 115, 547, 735, 893.

See also **Hyperbole; Metaphor; Personification; Simile.**

Figures of Speech *See* **Figurative Language.**

First-Person Point of View *See* **Point of View.**

Flashback A flashback is a scene that interrupts the action of a narrative to describe events that took place at an earlier time. It provides background helpful in understanding a character's present situation.

Example: William Faulkner's "A Rose for Emily" opens with Miss Emily's funeral, followed by a flashback that recounts how, when she was alive, Colonel Sartoris exempted her from paying taxes.

Foil A foil is a character whose traits contrast with those of another character. A writer might use a minor character as a foil to emphasize the positive traits of the main character.

Example: In Flannery O'Connor's "The Life You Save May Be Your Own," the innocent Lucynell Crater serves as a foil to the cunning, deceitful Mr. Shiftlet.

See page 1080.

See also **Character.**

Folk Tale A folk tale is a short, simple story that is handed down, usually by word of mouth, from generation to generation. Folk tales include legends, fairy tales, myths, and fables. Folk tales often teach family obligations or societal values. "Coyote and the Buffalo" is an Okanogan folk tale.

See also **Legend; Myth; Fable.**

Foot *See* **Meter.**

Foreshadowing Foreshadowing is a writer's use of hints or clues to indicate events that will occur in a story. Foreshadowing creates suspense and at the same time prepares the reader for what is to come.

Example: In Faulkner's "A Rose for Emily," the scene in which Miss Emily buys the rat poison foreshadows the death of Homer Barron.

See page 1066.

Form At its simplest, form refers to the physical arrangement of words in a poem—the length and placement of the lines and the grouping of lines into stanzas. The term can also be used to refer to other types of patterning in poetry—anything from rhythm and other sound patterns to the design of a traditional poetic type, such as a sonnet or dramatic monologue.
See also **Genre; Stanza.**

Frame Story A frame story exists when a story is told within a narrative setting, or "frame"; it creates a story within a story. This storytelling method has been used for over one thousand years and was employed in famous works such as *One Thousand and One Arabian Nights* and Geoffrey Chaucer's *The Canterbury Tales.* "The Notorious Jumping Frog of Calaveras County" by Mark Twain is also a frame story.
See page 691.

Free Verse Free verse is poetry that does not have regular patterns of rhyme and meter. The lines in free verse often flow more naturally than do rhymed, metrical lines and thus achieve a rhythm more like that of everyday human speech. Walt Whitman is generally credited with bringing free verse to American poetry.

And you O my soul where you stand,
Surrounded, detached, in measureless oceans of space,
Ceaselessly musing, venturing, throwing, seeking
the spheres to connect them,
Till the bridge you will need be form'd, till the
ductile anchor hold,
Till the gossamer thread you fling catch
somewhere, O my soul.
—Walt Whitman, "The Noiseless Patient Spider"

See pages 531, 953.
See also **Meter; Rhyme.**

Genre Genre refers to the distinct types into which literary works can be grouped. The four main literary genres are fiction, poetry, nonfiction, and drama.

Gothic Literature Gothic literature is characterized by grotesque characters, bizarre situations, and violent events. Originating in Europe, gothic literature was a popular form of writing in the United States during the 19th century, especially in the hands of such notables as Edgar Allan Poe and Nathaniel Hawthorne. Interest in the gothic revived in the 20th century among southern writers such as William Faulkner and Flannery O'Connor.
See pages 445, 460, 1066.

Haiku Haiku is a form of Japanese poetry in which 17 syllables are arranged in three lines of 5, 7, and 5 syllables. The rules of haiku are strict. In addition to the syllabic count, the poet must create a clear picture that will evoke a strong emotional response in the reader. Nature is a particularly important source of inspiration for Japanese haiku poets, and details from nature are often the subjects of their poems.

Hero *See* **Cultural Hero; Tragic Hero.**

Historical Context The historical context of a literary work refers to the social conditions that inspired or influenced its creation. To understand and appreciate some works, the reader must relate them to particular events in history. For example, to understand fully Lincoln's "Gettysburg Address," the reader must imaginatively re-create the scene—Lincoln addressing a war-weary crowd on the very site where a horrific battle had recently been fought.
Example: Patrick Henry's "Speech in the Virginia Convention" was inspired by the British military buildup in the American colonies prior to the American Revolution; Martin Luther King's *Stride Toward Freedom* was inspired by the civil rights struggle of the 1950s to overturn segregation laws in the South.
See pages 73, 216, 230.

Historical Narratives Historical narratives are accounts of real-life historical experiences, given either by a person who experienced those events or by someone who has studied or observed them. Cabeza de Vaca's *La Relación,* William Bradford's *Of Plymouth Plantation,* and *The Interesting Narrative of the Life of Olaudah Equiano* all are historical narratives.
See pages 70, 74, 83, 93, 104.
See also **Primary Sources; Secondary Sources.**

Horror Fiction Horror fiction contains strange, mysterious, violent, and often supernatural events that create suspense and terror in the reader. Edgar Allan Poe is an author famous for his horror fiction.

Humor Humor is a term applied to a literary work whose purpose is to entertain and to evoke laughter—for example, Twain's "The Celebrated Jumping Frog of Calaveras County." In literature, there are three basic types of humor, all of which may involve exaggeration or irony. **Humor of situation,** which is derived from the plot of a work, usually involves exaggerated events or situational irony. **Humor of character** is often based on exaggerated personalities or on characters who fail to recognize their own flaws, a form of dramatic irony. **Humor of language** may include sarcasm, exaggeration, puns, or verbal irony, which occurs when what is said is not what is meant.
See pages 659, 1106, 1113.
See also **Comedy; Farce; Irony.**

Hyperbole Hyperbole is a figure of speech in which the truth is exaggerated for emphasis or for humorous effect. The expression "I'm so hungry I could eat a horse" is hyperbole. In the following passage, Dorothy Parker uses hyperbole to describe literary critics' love for a Hemingway novel:

> **Ernest Hemingway wrote a novel called *The Sun Also Rises.* Promptly upon its publication, Ernest Hemingway was discovered, the Stars and Stripes were reverentially raised over him, eight hundred and forty-seven book reviewers formed themselves into the word "welcome," and the band played "Hail to the Chief" in three concurrent keys.**
>
> **—Dorothy Parker, "A Book of Great Short Stories"**

See also **Understatement.**

Iamb *See* ***Meter.***

Iambic Pentameter Iambic pentameter is a metrical pattern of five feet, or units, each of which is made up of two syllables, the first unstressed and the second stressed. Iambic pentameter is the most common meter used in English poetry; it is the meter used in blank verse and in the sonnet. The following lines are examples of iambic pentameter:

> **So live, | that when | thy sum | mons comes | to join**
> **The innu | mera | ble car | avan, | which moves**
> **To that | myste | rious realm, | where each | shall take**
> **His cham | ber in | the si | lent halls | of death . . .**
>
> **—William Cullen Bryant, "Thanatopsis"**

See pages 337, 887.
See also **Blank Verse; Meter; Sonnet.**

Idiom An idiom is a common figure of speech whose meaning is different from the literal meaning of its words. For example, the phrase "raining cats and dogs" does not literally mean that cats and dogs are falling from the sky; the expression means "raining heavily."

Imagery The descriptive words and phrases that a writer uses to re-create sensory experiences are called imagery. By appealing to the five senses, imagery helps a reader imagine exactly what the characters and experiences being described are like. In the following passage, the imagery lets the reader experience the miserliness of the main character and his wife:

> **They lived in a forlorn-looking house that stood alone and had an air of starvation. A few straggling savin trees, emblems of sterility, grew near it; no smoke ever curled from its chimney. . . . A miserable horse, whose ribs were as articulate as the bars of a gridiron, stalked about a field, where a thin carpet of moss . . . tantalized and balked his hunger.**
>
> **—Washington Irving, "The Devil and Tom Walker"**

The term ***synesthesia*** refers to imagery that appeals to one sense when another is being stimulated; for example, description of sounds in terms of colors, as in this passage:

> **Music. The great blobs of purple and red emotion have not touched him.**
>
> **—Zora Neale Hurston, "How It Feels to Be Colored Me"**

See page 900.
See also **Description; Kinesthetic Imagery.**

Imagists *See* **Experimental Poetry; Style.**

Interior Monologue *See* **Monologue; Stream of Consciousness.**

Internal Conflict *See* **Conflict.**

Interview An interview is a conversation conducted by a writer or reporter in which facts or statements are elicited from another person, recorded, and then broadcast or published.

Inverted Syntax Inverted syntax is a reversal in the expected order of words.
Example: In the first line of "Upon the Burning of Our House," Anne Bradstreet writes "when rest I took" rather than "when I took rest."

Irony Irony refers to a contrast between appearance and reality. **Situational irony** is a contrast between what is expected to happen and what actually does happen, as in the poem "Richard Cory," when a gentleman who is admired and envied commits suicide. **Dramatic irony** occurs when readers know more about a situation or a character in a story than the characters do. In Flannery O'Connor's "The Life You Save May Be Your Own," for example, readers find out that Mr. Shiftlet is a scoundrel before the other characters do. **Verbal irony** occurs when someone states one thing and means another, as in the following passage, when the narrator refers to honesty as an "incumbrance," or burden:

Hicks was born honest, I without that incumbrance—so some people said.
—Mark Twain, *The Autobiography of Mark Twain*

See pages 659, 922, 1079.

Kinesthetic Imagery Kinesthetic imagery re-creates the tension felt through muscles, tendons, or joints in the body. In the following passage, John Steinbeck uses kinesthetic imagery to describe a soldier's experience:

This is how you feel after a few days of constant firing. Your skin feels thick and insensitive. There is a salty taste in your mouth. A hard, painful knot is in your stomach where the food is undigested. Your eyes do not pick up much detail and the sharp outlines of objects are slightly blurred. Everything looks a little unreal.
—John Steinbeck, "Why Soldiers Don't Talk"

See page 1172.
See also **Imagery.**

Journal *See* **Diary.**

Legend A legend is a story passed down orally from generation to generation and popularly believed to have a historical basis. While some legends may be based on real people or situations, most of the events are either greatly exaggerated or fictitious. Like myths, legends may incorporate supernatural elements and magical deeds. But legends differ from myths in that they claim to be stories about real human beings and are often set in a particular time and place.

Limited Point of View *See* **Point of View.**

Line The line is the core unit of a poem. In poetry, line length is an essential element of the poem's meaning and rhythm. There are a variety of terms to describe the way a line of poetry ends or is connected to the next line. Line breaks, where a line of poetry ends, may coincide with grammatical units. However, a line break may also occur in the middle of a grammatical or syntactical unit, creating pauses or emphasis. Poets use a variety of line breaks to play with meaning, thus creating a wide range of effects.

Literary Criticism Literary criticism refers to writing that focuses on a literary work or a genre, describing some aspect of it, such as its origin, its characteristics, or its effects. Toni Morrison's "Thoughts on the African-American Novel" is an example of literary criticism.

See page 909.

Literary Letter A literary letter is a letter that has been published and read by a wider audience because it was written by a well-known public figure or provides information about the period in which it was written. Abigail Adams's "Letter to John Adams" is an example of a literary letter.

See pages 262, 1204, 1252.

Literary Nonfiction Literary nonfiction is informational text that is recognized as being of artistic value or that is about literature. Autobiographies, biographies, essays, and eloquent speeches typically fall into this category.

Local Color Realism Local color realism, especially popular in the late 18th century, is a style of writing that truthfully imitates ordinary life and brings a particular region alive by portraying the dialects, dress, mannerisms, customs, character types, and landscapes of that region. Mark Twain frequently uses local color realism in his writing for humorous effect.

See pages 684, 698.
See also **Dialect.**

Lyric Poem A lyric poem is a short poem in which a single speaker expresses thoughts and feelings. In a love lyric, a speaker expresses romantic love. In other lyrics, a speaker may meditate on nature or seek to resolve an emotional crisis. Anne Bradstreet's poem "To My Dear and Loving Husband" is a love lyric.

Magical Realism Magical realism is a style of writing that often includes exaggeration, unusual humor, magical and bizarre events, dreams that come true, and superstitions that prove warranted. Magical realism differs from pure fantasy in combining fantastic elements with realistic elements such as recognizable characters, believable dialogue, a true-to-life setting, a matter-of-fact tone, and a plot that sometimes contains historic events. This style characterizes some of the fiction of such influential South American writers as the late Jorge Luis Borges of Argentina and Gabriel García Márquez of Colombia.

Main Character *See* **Character.**

Memoir A memoir is a form of autobiographical writing in which a person recalls significant events and people in his or her life. Most memoirs share the following characteristics: (1) they usually are structured as narratives told by the writers themselves, using the first-person point of view; (2) although some names may be changed to protect privacy, memoirs are true accounts of actual events; (3) although basically personal, memoirs may deal with newsworthy events having a significance beyond the confines of the writer's life; (4) unlike strictly historical accounts, memoirs often include the writers' feelings and opinions about historical events, giving the reader insight into the impact of history on people's lives. N. Scott Momaday's *The Way to Rainy Mountain* is a memoir.

Metaphor A metaphor is a figure of speech that compares two things that have something in common. Unlike similes, metaphors do not use the words *like* or *as,* but make comparisons directly.

Example: Abigail Adams's statement "our country is . . . the first and greatest parent" is a metaphor.

See pages 115, 893, 958.
See also **Extended Metaphor; Figurative Language; Simile.**

Meter Meter is the repetition of a regular rhythmic unit in a line of poetry. Each unit, known as a **foot,** has one stressed syllable (indicated by a ˊ) and either one or two unstressed syllables (indicated by a ˇ). The four basic types of metrical feet are the **iamb,** an unstressed syllable followed by a stressed syllable; the **trochee,** a stressed syllable followed by an unstressed syllable; the **anapest,** two unstressed syllables followed by a stressed syllable; and the **dactyl,** a stressed syllable followed by two unstressed syllables.

Two words are typically used to describe the meter of a line. The first word identifies the type of metrical foot—iambic, trochaic, anapestic, or dactylic—and the second word indicates the number of feet in a line: monometer (one foot), **dimeter** (two feet), **trimeter** (three feet), **tetrameter** (four feet), **pentameter** (five feet), **hexameter** (six feet), and so forth.

Examples: In "To My Dear and Loving Husband," by Anne Bradstreet, the meter is iambic pentameter, the most common form of meter in English poetry.

> **If ev | er man | were loved | by wife | then thee.**

In the following lines from Henry Wadsworth Longfellow's "A Psalm of Life," the meter is trochaic tetrameter:

> **Tell me | not, in | mournful | numbers,**
> **Life is | but an | empty | dream!—**

See pages 343, 349, 355, 887, 921.
See also **Rhythm; Scansion.**

Minor Character *See* **Character.**

Mise-en-Scène *Mise-en-scène* is a term from the French that refers to the various physical aspects of a dramatic presentation, such as lighting, costumes, scenery, makeup, and props.

Modernism Modernism was a literary movement that roughly spanned the time period between the two world wars, 1914–1945. Modernist works are characterized by a high degree of experimentation and spare, elliptical prose. Modernist characters are most often alienated people searching unsuccessfully for meaning and love in their lives. Katherine Ann Porter's "The Jilting of Granny Weatherall" is an example of modernist writing.

See page 934, 970, 1036.

Monologue In a drama, the speech of a character who is alone on stage, voicing his or her thoughts, is known as a monologue. In a short story or a poem, the direct presentation of a character's unspoken thoughts is called an **interior monologue.** An interior monologue may jump back and forth between past and present, displaying thoughts, memories, and impressions just as they might occur in a person's mind.

See page 136.
See also **Stream of Consciousness.**

Mood Mood is the feeling or atmosphere that a writer creates for the reader. The writer's use of connotation, imagery, figurative language, sound and rhythm, and descriptive details all contribute to the mood. These elements help create a creepy, threatening mood in the following passage:

> **The swamp was thickly grown with great gloomy pines and hemlocks, . . . It was full of pits and quagmires, partly covered with weeds and mosses, where the green surface often betrayed the traveler into a gulf of black, smothering mud; . . .**
> **—Washington Irving, "The Devil and Tom Walker"**

See page 937.
See also **Connotation; Description; Diction; Figurative Language; Imagery; Style.**

Moral *See* **Fable.**

Motivation Motivation is the stated or implied reason behind a character's behavior. The grounds for a character's actions may not be obvious, but they should be comprehensible and consistent, in keeping with the character as developed by the writer.

See page 977.
See also **Character.**

Myth A myth is a traditional story, passed down through generations, that explains why the world is the way it is. Myths are essentially religious because they present supernatural events and beings and articulate the values and beliefs of a cultural group. A **creation myth** is a particular kind of myth that explains how the universe, the earth, and life on earth began. "The World on the Turtle's Back" is an Iroquois creation myth.

See page 37.

Narrative A narrative is any type of writing that is primarily concerned with relating an event or a series of events. A narrative can be imaginary, as is a short story or novel, or factual, as is a newspaper account or a work of history. The word *narration* can be used interchangeably with *narrative,* which comes from the Latin word meaning "tell."

See also **Fiction; Nonfiction; Novel; Plot; Short Story.**

Narrative Poem A narrative poem is a poem that tells a story using elements of character, setting, and plot to develop a theme. Edgar Allan Poe's "The Raven" is a narrative poem, as is Dudley Randall's "Ballad of Birmingham."

See pages 436, 943, 1214.
See also **Ballad.**

Narrator The narrator of a story is the character or voice that relates the story's events to the reader.

Example: The narrator of William Faulkner's "A Rose for Emily" is an unidentified citizen of Jefferson, Mississippi, Emily Grierson's hometown.

See pages 684, 1064.

Naturalism An offshoot of realism, naturalism was a literary movement that originated in France in the late 1800s. Like the realists, the naturalists sought to render common people and ordinary life accurately. However, the naturalists emphasized how instinct and environment affect human behavior. Strongly influenced by Charles Darwin's ideas, the naturalists believed that the fate of humans is determined by forces beyond individual control. Stephen Crane's story "The Open Boat" is an example of naturalism.

See pages 735, 769.

Nonfiction Nonfiction, or informational text, is writing about real people, places, and events. Unlike fiction, nonfiction is largely concerned with factual information, although the writer shapes the information according to his or her purpose and viewpoint. Biography, autobiography, and newspaper articles are examples of nonfiction.

See also **Autobiography; Biography; Essay.**

Novel A novel is an extended work of fiction. Like the short story, a novel is essentially the product of a writer's imagination. The most obvious difference between a novel and a short story is length. Because the novel is considerably longer, a novelist can develop a wider range of characters and a more complex plot.

Novella A novella is a work of fiction that is longer than a short story but shorter than a novel. A novella differs from a novel in that it concentrates on a limited cast of characters, a relatively short time span, and a single chain of events. The novella is an attempt to combine the compression of the short story with the development of a novel.

Octave *See* **Sonnet.**

Ode An ode is a complex lyric poem that develops a serious and dignified theme. Odes appeal to both the imagination and the intellect, and many commemorate events or praise people or elements of nature.

Off Rhyme *See* **Slant Rhyme.**

Omniscient Point of View *See* **Point of View.**

Onomatopoeia The word *onomatopoeia* literally means "name-making." It is the process of creating or using words that imitate sounds. The *buzz* of the bee, the *honk* of the car horn, the *peep* of the chick are all onomatopoetic, or echoic, words.

Onomatopoeia as a literary technique goes beyond the use of simple echoic words. Writers, particularly poets, choose words whose sounds suggest their denotative and connotative meanings: for example, *whisper, kick, gargle, gnash,* and *clatter.*

Open Letter An open letter is addressed to a specific person but published for a wider readership.

Example: James Baldwin's "My Dungeon Shook" is an open letter addressed to his nephew but intended for the general public, particularly white Americans.

See pages 1204, 1252.

Oral Literature Oral literature is literature that is passed from one generation to another by performance or word of mouth. Folk tales, fables, myths, chants, and legends are part of the oral tradition of cultures throughout the world.
See pages 38, 48.
See also **Fable; Folk Tale; Legend; Myth.**

Overstatement *See* **Hyperbole.**

Oxymoron An oxymoron is a special kind of concise paradox that brings together two contradictory terms, such as "venomous love" or "sweet bitterness."

Parable A parable is a brief story that is meant to teach a lesson or illustrate a moral truth. A parable is more than a simple story, however. Each detail of the parable corresponds to some aspect of the problem or moral dilemma to which it is directed. The story of the prodigal son in the Bible is a classic parable. In *Walden*, Thoreau's parable of the strong and beautiful bug that emerges from an old table is meant to show that, similarly, new life can awaken in human beings despite the deadness of society.

Paradox A paradox is a statement that seems to contradict itself but may nevertheless suggest an important truth.
Example: In *Walden*, Henry David Thoreau writes the paradox "I am not as wise as the day I was born." The statement suggests that civilization erases a child's innate wisdom and spiritual awareness.

A special kind of paradox is the oxymoron, which brings together two contradictory terms, as in the phrases "wise fool" and "feather of lead."
See pages 380, 1250.

Parallelism Parallelism is the use of similar grammatical constructions to express ideas that are related or equal in importance. Note that in the following passage, Whitman begins the last three lines with the name of a type of tradesman, each followed by a gerund phrase beginning with *singing:*

> **I hear America singing, the varied carols I hear,**
> **Those of mechanics, each one singing his as it should be blithe and strong,**
> **The carpenter singing his as he measures his plank or beam,**
> **The mason singing his as he makes ready for work, or leaves off work,**
> **—Walt Whitman, "I Hear America Singing"**

This parallel construction creates a rolling rhythm and emphasizes the different types of people that comprise America.
See page 531.

Parallel Plot A parallel plot is a particular type of plot in which two stories of equal importance are told simultaneously. The story moves back and forth between the two plots.

Parody Parody is writing that imitates either the style or the subject matter of a literary work for the purpose of criticism, humorous effect, or flattering tribute.
See page 443.

Persona *See* **Speaker.**

Personal Essay *See* **Essay.**

Personification Personification is a figure of speech in which an object, animal, or idea is given human characteristics.
Example: In Emily Dickinson's poem "Because I could not stop for Death," death is personified as a gentleman of kindness and civility.
See pages 547, 736.

Persuasive Writing Persuasive writing is intended to convince a reader to adopt a particular opinion or to perform a certain action. Effective persuasion usually appeals to both the reason and the emotions of an audience. Patrick Henry, Jonathan Edwards, Martin Luther King Jr., and Malcolm X all use persuasion in their writing.
See pages 230, 249, 1215.

Petrarchan Sonnet *See* **Sonnet.**

Plot The plot is the sequence of actions and events in a literary work. Generally, plots are built around a **conflict**—a problem or struggle between two or more opposing forces. Plots usually progress through stages: exposition, rising action, climax, and falling action.

The **exposition** provides important background information and introduces the setting, characters, and conflict. During the **rising action,** the conflict becomes more intense and suspense builds as the main characters struggle to resolve their problem. The **climax** is the turning point in the plot when the outcome of the conflict becomes clear, usually resulting in a change in the characters or a solution to the conflict. After the climax, the **falling action** occurs and shows the effects of the climax. As the falling action begins, the suspense is over but the results of the decision or action that caused the climax are not yet fully worked out. The **resolution,** which often blends with the falling action, reveals the final outcome of events and ties up loose ends.
See pages 783, 1066.
See also **Climax; Conflict; Exposition; Falling Action; Rising Action.**

Poetry Poetry is language arranged in lines. Like other forms of literature, poetry attempts to re-create emotions and experiences. Poetry, however, is usually more condensed and suggestive than prose.

Poems often are divided into stanzas, or paragraph-like groups of lines. The stanzas in a poem may contain the same number of lines or may vary in length. Some poems have definite patterns of meter and rhyme. Others rely more on the sounds of words and less on fixed rhythms and rhyme schemes. The use of figurative language is also common in poetry.

The form and content of a poem combine to convey meaning. The way that a poem is arranged on the page, the impact of the images, the sounds of the words and phrases, and all the other details that make up a poem work together to help the reader grasp its central idea.

See pages 528, 880, 937, 1301.
See also **Experimental Poetry; Form; Free Verse; Meter; Rhyme; Rhythm; Stanza.**

Point of View Point of view refers to the narrative perspective from which events in a story or novel are told. In the **first-person point of view,** the narrator is a character in the work who tells everything in his or her own words and uses the pronouns *I, me,* and *my.* In the **third-person point of view,** events are related by a voice outside the action, not by one of the characters. A third-person narrator uses pronouns such as *he, she,* and *they.* In the **third-person omniscient point of view,** the narrator is an all-knowing, objective observer who stands outside the action and reports what different characters are thinking. Flannery O'Connor's "The Life You Save May Be Your Own" is told from the third-person omniscient point of view. In the **third-person limited point of view,** the narrator stands outside the action and focuses on one character's thoughts, observations, and feelings. Kate Chopin's "The Story of an Hour" is told from primarily the third-person limited point of view.

In the **second-person point of view,** rarely used, the narrator addresses the reader intimately as you. Much of John Steinbeck's essay "Why Soldiers Don't Talk" is narrated from the second-person point of view.

See pages 784, 1080, 1172.

Primary Sources Materials written or created by people who were present at events are called primary sources. Letters, diaries, speeches, autobiographies, and photographs are examples of primary sources, as are certain narrative accounts written by actual participants or observers.

See also **Secondary Sources.**

Prologue A prologue is an introductory scene in a drama.

Prop Prop, an abbreviation of *property,* refers to a physical object that is used in a stage production.

Example: In Arthur Miller's *The Crucible,* an important prop is the small rag doll that Mary Warren brings from the court and gives to Elizabeth Proctor.

Prose Generally, *prose* refers to all forms of written or spoken expression that are not in verse. The term, therefore, may be used to describe very different forms of writing—short stories as well as essays, for example.

Protagonist The protagonist is the main character in a work of literature, who is involved in the central conflict of the story. Usually, the protagonist changes after the central conflict reaches a climax. He or she may be a hero and is usually the one with whom the audience tends to identify. In Kurt Vonnegut's story "Adam," Heinz Knechtmann is the protagonist.

See page 1180.
See also **Antagonist; Character; Tragic Hero.**

Purpose *See* **Author's Purpose.**

Quatrain A quatrain is a four-line stanza, as in the following example:

The snow had begun in the gloaming,
And busily all the night
Had been heaping field and highway
With a silence deep and white.
—James Russell Lowell, "The First Snowfall"

See page 354.
See also **Poetry; Stanza.**

Realism As a general term, *realism* refers to any effort to offer an accurate and detailed portrayal of actual life. Thus, critics talk about Shakespeare's realistic portrayals of his characters and praise the medieval poet Chaucer for his realistic descriptions of people from different social classes.

More specifically, realism refers to a literary method developed in the 19th century. The realists based their writing on careful observations of contemporary life, often focusing on the middle or lower classes. They attempted to present life objectively and honestly, without the sentimentality or idealism that had colored earlier literature. Typically, realists developed their settings in great detail in an effort to re-create a specific time and place for the reader. Willa Cather, Kate Chopin, and Mark Twain are all considered realists.

See pages 647, 684, 784.
See also **Local-Color Realism; Naturalism.**

Recurring Theme *See* ***Theme.***

Reflective Essay *See* ***Essay.***

Refrain In poetry, a refrain is part of a stanza, consisting of one or more lines that are repeated regularly, sometimes with changes, often at the ends of succeeding stanzas. For example, in "The Raven," the line "Quoth the Raven, 'Nevermore'" is a refrain. Refrains are often found in ballads.

Regionalism Regionalism is a literary movement that arose from an effort to accurately represent the speech, manners, habits, history, folklore, and beliefs of people in specific geographic areas. Bret Harte's "The Outcasts of Poker Flat" is a famous example of American regionalist writing.

Repetition Repetition is a technique in which a sound, word, phrase, or line is repeated for emphasis or unity. Repetition often helps to reinforce meaning and create an appealing rhythm. The term includes specific devices associated with both prose and poetry, such as **alliteration** and **parallelism.**

See pages 229, 531, 879, 1251.
See also **Alliteration; Parallelism; Sound Devices.**

Resolution *See* **Falling Action.**

Rhetorical Devices *See* **Analogy; Repetition; Rhetorical Questions,** *Glossary of Reading and Informational Terms,* page R123.

Rhyme Rhyme is the occurrence of similar or identical sounds at the end of two or more words, such as *suite, heat,* and *complete.* Rhyme that occurs within a single line of poetry, as in the following example, is called **internal rhyme**.

> **Ah, distinctly I remember it was in the bleak December;**
> **—Edgar Allan Poe, "The Raven"**

When rhyme comes at the end of a line of poetry, it is called **end rhyme.** The pattern of end rhyme in a poem is called the **rhyme scheme** and is charted by assigning a letter, beginning with the letter *a,* to each line. Lines that rhyme are given the same letter. The rhyme scheme of the following stanza is *aabbcc:*

> **In silent night when rest I took** *a*
> **For sorrow near I did not look** *a*
> **I wakened was with thund'ring noise** *b*
> **And piteous shrieks of dreadful voice.** *b*
> **That fearful sound of "Fire!" and "Fire!"** *c*
> **Let no man know is my desire.** *c*
> **—Anne Bradstreet, "Upon the Burning of Our House"**

See pages 343, 436, 887.
See also **Slant Rhyme.**

Rhyme Scheme *See* **Rhyme.**

Rhythm Rhythm refers to the pattern or flow of sound created by the arrangement of stressed and unstressed syllables, particularly in poetry. Some poems follow a regular pattern, or **meter,** of accented and unaccented syllables. Poets use rhythm to bring out the musical quality of language, to emphasize ideas, to create mood, and to reinforce subject matter.

See pages 337, 879.
See also **Meter.**

Rising Action Rising action is the stage of a plot in which the conflict develops and story events build toward a climax. During this stage, complications arise that make the conflict more intense. Tension grows as the characters struggle to resolve the conflict.

See pages 736, 783, 798.
See also **Plot.**

Romanticism Romanticism was a movement in the arts that flourished in Europe and America throughout much of the 19th century. Romantic writers glorified nature and celebrated individuality. Their treatment of subject was emotional rather than rational, intuitive rather than analytic. Washington Irving and Henry Wadsworth Longfellow were popular American romantic writers.

See pages 308, 320, 344.

Sarcasm Sarcasm, a type of verbal irony, refers to a critical remark expressed in a statement in which literal meaning is the opposite of actual meaning. Sarcasm is mocking, and its intention is to hurt.

See also **Irony.**

Satire Satire is a literary technique in which foolish ideas or customs are ridiculed for the purpose of improving society. Satire may be gently witty, mildly abrasive, or bitterly critical. Short stories, poems, novels, essays, and plays all may be vehicles for satire.

Example: In "The Devil and Tom Walker," Irving satirizes various aspects of 18th-century New England life, including religious hypocrisy and the institution of marriage.

Scansion The process of determining meter is known as scansion. When you scan a line of poetry, you mark its stressed (´) and unstressed syllables (˘) in order to identify the rhythm.

See also **Meter.**

Scene In drama, a scene is a subdivision of an act. Each scene usually establishes a different time or place.

See also **Act; Drama.**

Scenery Scenery is a painted backdrop or other structures used to create the setting for a play.

Science Fiction Science fiction is prose writing that presents the possibilities of the past or the future, using known scientific data and theories as well as the creative imagination of the writer. Most science fiction comments on present-day society through the writer's fictional conception of a past or future society. Ray Bradbury and Kurt Vonnegut Jr. are two popular writers of science fiction.

Screenplay A screenplay is a play written for film.

Script The text of a play, film, or broadcast is called a script.

Secondary Sources Accounts written by people were not directly involved in or witnesses to an event are called secondary sources. A history textbook is an example of a secondary source.

See also **Primary Sources.**

Sensory Details Sensory details are words and phrases that appeal to the reader's senses of sight, hearing, touch, taste, and smell. For example, the sensory detail "a fine film of rain" appeals to the senses of sight and touch. Sensory details stimulate the reader to create images in his or her mind.

See also **Imagery.**

Sermon A sermon is a form of religious persuasion in which a speaker exhorts the audience to behave in a more spiritual and moral fashion. "Sinners in the Hands of an Angry God" is a sermon.

Sestet *See* **Sonnet.**

Setting The setting of a literary work refers to the time and place in which the action occurs. A story can be set in an imaginary place, such as an enchanted castle, or a real place, such as New York City or Tombstone, Arizona. The time can be the past, the present, or the future. In addition to time and place, setting can include the larger historical and cultural contexts that form the background for a narrative. Setting is one of the main elements in fiction and often plays an important role in what happens and why.

Example: Willa Cather's story "A Wagner Matinee" is set in Boston around the turn of the 20th century.

See pages 135, 697, 717, 1080.

Short Story A short story is a work of fiction that centers on a single idea and can be read in one sitting. Generally, a short story has one main conflict that involves the characters, keeps the story moving, and stimulates readers' interest.

See also **Fiction.**

Simile A simile is a figure of speech that compares two things that have something in common, using a word such as *like* or *as.*

Examples: Abigail Adams's statement "power and liberty are like heat and moisture" and Thoreau's statement "we live meanly, like ants" contain similes.

See pages 262, 380, 547.
See also **Figurative Language; Metaphor.**

Situational Irony See **Irony.**

Slant Rhyme Rhyme that is not exact but only approximate is known as slant rhyme, or **off rhyme,** as in the second and fourth lines below:

I heard a Fly buzz—when I died—
The Stillness in the Room
Was like the Stillness in the Air—
Between the Heaves of Storm—

—Emily Dickinson,
"I heard a Fly buzz—when I died—"

See page 547.
See also **Rhyme.**

Slave Narrative A slave narrative is an autobiographical account written by someone who endured the miseries of slavery. Olaudah Equiano's and Frederick Douglass's autobiographies are examples of slave narratives. These writers often use sensory details to re-create their experiences. For example, to re-create the horror of confinement in the hold of a slave ship, Equiano gives the reader such details as "the galling of the chains" and "the groans of the dying."

See pages 83, 560, 574.
See also **Autobiography.**

Soliloquy *See* **Monologue.**

Sonnet A sonnet is a 14-line lyric poem, commonly written in iambic pentameter. The **Petrarchan sonnet** consists of two parts. The first eight lines, called the octave, usually have the rhyme scheme *abbaabba.* In the last six lines, called the sestet, the rhyme scheme may be *cdecde, cdcdcd,* or another variation. The **octave** generally presents a problem or raises a question, and the ***sestet*** resolves or comments on the problem. James Weldon Johnson's "My City" is a Petrarchan sonnet. A **Shakespearean sonnet** is divided into three **quatrains** (groups of four lines) and a **couplet** (two rhyming lines). Its rhyme scheme is *abab cdcd efef gg.* The couplet usually expresses a response to the important issue developed in the three quatrains. Claude McKay's "If We Must Die" is a Shakespearean sonnet.

See page 887.
See also **Meter; Quatrain; Rhyme.**

Sound Devices *See* **Alliteration; Assonance; Consonance; Meter; Onomatopoeia; Repetition; Rhyme; Rhyme Scheme; Rhythm.**

Speaker The speaker of a poem, like the narrator of a story, is the voice that talks to the reader. In some poems, the speaker can be identified with the poet. In other poems, the poet invents a fictional character, or a persona, to play the role of the speaker. *Persona* is a Latin word meaning "actor's mask."

See pages 879, 921, 970.

Speech A speech is a talk or public address. The purpose of a speech may be to entertain, to explain, to persuade, to inspire, or any combination of these aims.

Stage Directions Stage directions are the playwright's instructions for the director, performers, and stage crew. Usually set in italics, they are located at the beginning of and throughout a script. Stage directions usually tell the time and place of the action and explain how characters move and speak. They also describe scenery, props, lighting, costumes, music, or sound effects.

See pages 132, 136.
See also **Drama.**

Stanza A stanza is a group of lines that form a unit in a poem. A stanza is usually characterized by a common pattern of meter, rhyme, and number of lines. Longfellow's "A Psalm of Life" is written in four-line stanzas. During the 20th century, poets experimented more freely with stanza form than did earlier poets, sometimes writing poems without any stanza breaks.

See page 343.

Static Character *See* **Character.**

Stereotype A stereotype is an over simplified image of a person, group, or institution. Sweeping generalizations about "all Southerners" or "every used-car dealer" are stereotypes. Simplified or stock characters in literature are often called stereotypes. Such characters do not usually demonstrate the complexities of real people.

Example: In Washington Irving's "The Devil and Tom Walker," Tom Walker's wife is a stereotype of a greedy and shrewish wife.

Stream of Consciousness Stream of consciousness is a technique that was developed by modernist writers to present the flow of a character's seemingly unconnected thoughts, responses, and sensations. The term was coined by American psychologist William James to characterize the unbroken flow of thought that occurs in the waking mind.

Example: In "The Love Song of J. Alfred Prufrock," T. S. Eliot uses this technique to reveal the jumble of thoughts that flow through Prufrock's mind.

See pages 969, 1035.
See also **Modernism.**

Structure The structure of a literary work is the way in which it is put together—the arrangement of its parts. In poetry, structure refers to the arrangement of words and lines to produce a desired effect. A common structural unit in poetry is the stanza, of which there are numerous types. In prose, structure is the arrangement of larger units or parts of a selection. Paragraphs, for example, are a basic unit in prose, as are chapters in novels and acts in plays. The structure of a poem, short story, novel, play, or nonfiction selection usually emphasizes certain important aspects of content.

See pages 239, 337, 603.
See also **Form; Stanza.**

Style Style is the distinctive way in which a work of literature is written. Style refers not so much to what is said but how it is said. Word choice, sentence length, tone, imagery, and use of dialogue all contribute to a writer's style. A group of writers might exemplify common stylistic characteristics; for example, the Imagists of the early 20th century wrote in a style that employs compression and rich sensory images.

Example: E. E. Cummings's style is decidedly unconventional, breaking rules of capitalization, punctuation, diction, and syntax.

See pages 547, 559, 937, 1009.

Surprise Ending A surprise ending is an unexpected plot twist at the end of a story.

Example: "The Story of an Hour" ends with a surprise when Mrs. Mallard drops dead after her husband, presumed to be dead, reappears.

See page 783.
See also **Irony.**

Suspense Suspense is the excitement or tension that readers feel as they become involved in a story and eagerly await the outcome.

Example: In Ambrose Bierce's "An Occurrence at Owl Creek Bridge," the suspense builds as the reader awaits the outcome of Peyton Farquhar's attempted escape from hanging at the hands of Union troops.

See page 604.
See also **Rising Action.**

Symbol A symbol is a person, place, or object that has a concrete meaning in itself and also stands for something beyond itself, such as an idea or feeling.

Example: In Gilman's "The Yellow Wallpaper," the wallpaper in the narrator's bedroom comes to symbolize her growing madness.

See pages 469, 798.

Synesthesia *See* **Imagery.**

Tall Tale A tall tale is a distinctively American type of humorous story characterized by exaggeration. Tall tales and practical jokes have similar kinds of humor. In both, someone gets fooled, to the amusement of the person or persons who know the truth, as in Twain's "The Notorious Jumping Frog of Calaveras County."

See page 683.
See also **Humor; Hyperbole.**

Theme A theme is an underlying message that a writer wants the reader to understand. It is a perception about life or human nature that the writer shares with the reader. In most cases, themes are not stated directly but must be inferred.

Example: One theme of "The Masque of the Red Death" could be stated, "No one, not even the wealthiest person, has the power to escape death."

Recurring themes are themes found in a variety of works. For example, authors from varying backgrounds might convey similar themes having to do with the importance of family values. **Universal themes** are themes that are found throughout the literature of all time periods.

See pages 446, 769, 780, 1049.

Third-Person Point of View *See* **Point of View.**

Title The title of a literary work introduces readers to the piece and usually reveals something about its subject or theme. Often, a poet uses the title to provide information necessary for understanding a poem.

Example: "A Worn Path," the title of Eudora Welty's short story, suggests the main character, Phoenix, herself: the path of her life is worn with age and struggle, and her life has centered on a single routine motivated by love.

See pages 784, 1050, 1296.

Tone Tone is a writer's attitude toward his or her subject. A writer can communicate tone through diction, choice of details, and direct statements of his or her position. Unlike mood, which refers to the emotional response of the reader to a work, tone reflects the feelings of the writer. To identify the tone of a work of literature, you might find it helpful to read the work aloud, as if giving a dramatic reading before an audience. The emotions that you convey in an oral reading should give you hints as to the tone of the work.

Example: Claude McKay's tone in "If We Must Die" is proud, defiant, and urgent.

See pages 531, 735, 890, 1106.
See also **Connotation; Diction; Mood; Style.**

Tragedy A tragedy is a dramatic work that presents the downfall of a dignified character who is involved in historically, morally, or socially significant events. The main character, or **tragic hero,** has a **tragic flaw,** a quality that leads to his or her destruction. The events in a tragic plot are set in motion by a decision that is often an error in judgment caused by the tragic flaw. Succeeding events are linked in a cause-and-effect relationship and lead inevitably to a disastrous conclusion, usually death. Arthur Miller's *The Crucible* could be classified as a tragedy.

Tragic Flaw *See* **Tragedy.**

Tragic Hero The ancient Greek philosopher Aristotle defined a tragic hero as a character whose basic goodness and superiority are marred by a tragic flaw that brings about or contributes to his or her downfall. The flaw may be poor judgment, pride, weakness, or an excess of an admirable quality. The tragic hero recognizes his or her own flaw and its consequences, but only after it is too late to change the course of events.

See also **Character.**

Traits *See* **Character.**

Transcendentalism The philosophy of transcendentalism, an American offshoot of German romanticism, was based on a belief that "transcendent forms" of truth exist beyond reason and experience. Ralph Waldo Emerson, the leader of the movement, asserted that every individual is capable of discovering this higher truth through intuition. Henry David Thoreau is another well-known transcendentalist writer.

See pages 369, 380, 390.
See also **Romanticism.**

Trickster Tale A trickster tale is a folk tale about an animal or person who engages in trickery, violence, and magic. Neither all good nor all bad, a trickster may be foolish yet clever, greedy yet helpful, immoral yet moral. "Coyote and the Buffalo" is a trickster tale.

See page 47.
See also **Folk Tale.**

Trochee *See* **Meter.**

Turning Point *See* **Climax.**

Understatement Understatement is a technique of creating emphasis by saying less than is actually or literally true. It is the opposite of **hyperbole,** or overstatement. One of the primary devices of **irony,** understatement can be used to develop a humorous effect, to create satire, or to achieve a restrained tone.

Example: In "Letter to John Adams," Abigail Adams points out the tyranny of male power by gently saying, "I cannot say that I think you very generous to the ladies."

See also **Hyperbole; Irony.**

Unity of Effect When all elements of a story—plot, character, setting, imagery, and other other literary devices—work together to create a single effect, it is known as unity of effect. Edgar Allan Poe's "The Fall of the House of Usher" demonstrates the unity of effect.

See page 411.

Universal Theme *See* **Theme.**

Verbal Irony *See* **Irony.**

Voice The term *voice* refers to a writer's unique use of language that allows a reader to "hear" a human personality in his or her writing. The elements of style that determine a writer's voice include sentence structure, diction, and tone. For example, some writers are noted for their reliance on short, simple sentences, while others make use of long, complicated ones. Certain writers use concrete words, such as *lake* or *cold,* which name things that you can see, hear, feel, taste, or smell. Others prefer abstract terms such as *memory,* which name things that cannot be perceived with the senses. A writer's tone also leaves its imprint on his or her personal voice. The term can be applied to the narrator of a selection, as well as the writer.

See page 673.
See also **Diction; Tone.**

Word Choice *See* **Diction.**

Glossary of Reading & Informational Terms

Almanac *See* **Reference Works.**

Analogy *See Glossary of Literary and Nonfiction Terms, page R104.*

Appeals by Association Appeals by association imply that one will gain acceptance or prestige by taking the writer's position.
See also **Recognizing Persuasive Techniques**—*Reading Handbook, page R20.*

Appeal to Authority An appeal to authority calls upon experts or others who warrant respect.
See also **Recognizing Persuasive Techniques**—*Reading Handbook, page R20.*

Appeal to Reason *See* **Logical Appeal.**

Argument An argument is speech or writing that expresses a position on an issue or problem and supports it with reasons and evidence. An argument often takes into account other points of view, anticipating and answering objections that opponents of the position might raise.
See also **Claim; Counterargument; Evidence; General Principle.**

Assumption An assumption is an opinion or belief that is taken for granted. It can be about a specific situation, a person, or the world in general. Assumptions are often unstated. *See also* **General Principle.**

Author's Message An author's message is the main idea or theme of a particular work.
See also **Main Idea; Theme,** *Glossary of Literary and Nonfiction Terms, page R121.*

Author's Perspective *See Glossary of Literary and Nonfiction Terms, page R105.*

Author's Position An author's position is his or her opinion on an issue or topic. *See also* **Claim.**

Author's Purpose *See Glossary of Literary and Nonfiction Terms, page R105.*

Autobiography *See Glossary of Literary and Nonfiction Terms, page R105.*

Bias Bias is an inclination toward a particular judgment on a topic or issue. A writer often reveals a strongly positive or strongly negative opinion by presenting only one way of looking at an issue or by heavily weighting the evidence. Words with intensely positive or negative connotations are often a signal of a writer's bias.

Bibliography A bibliography is a list of books and other materials related to the topic of a text. Bibliographies can be good sources of works for further study on a subject.
See also **Works Consulted.**

Biography *See Glossary of Literary and Nonfiction Terms, page R105.*

Business Correspondence Business correspondence includes all written business communications, such as business letters, e-mails, and memos. Business correspondence is to the point, clear, courteous, and professional.

Cause and Effect A **cause** is an event or action that directly results in another event or action. An **effect** is the direct or logical outcome of an event or action. Basic **cause-and-effect relationships** include a single cause with a single effect, one cause with multiple effects, multiple causes with a single effect, and a chain of causes and effects. The concept of cause and effect also provides a way of organizing a piece of writing. It helps a writer show the relationships between events or ideas.
See also **False Cause**—*Reading Handbook, page R22.*

Central Idea *See* **Main Idea.**

Chronological Order Chronological order is the arrangement of events in their order of occurrence. This type of organization is used in both fictional narratives and in historical writing, biography, and autobiography.

Claim In an argument, a claim is the writer's position on an issue or problem. Although an argument focuses on supporting one claim, a writer may make more than one claim in a work.

Clarify Clarifying is a reading strategy that helps a reader to understand or make clear what he or she is reading. Readers usually clarify by rereading, reading aloud, or discussing.

Classification Classification is a pattern of organization in which objects, ideas, or information is presented in groups, or classes, based on common characteristics.

Cliché A cliché is an overused expression. "Better late than never" and "hard as nails" are common examples.

Compare and Contrast To compare and contrast is to identify similarities and differences in two or more subjects. Compare-and-contrast organization can be used to structure a piece of writing, serving as a framework for examining the similarities and differences in two or more subjects.

Conclusion A conclusion is a statement of belief based on evidence, experience, and reasoning. A **valid conclusion** is a conclusion that logically follows from the facts or statements upon which it is based. A **deductive conclusion** is one that follows from a particular generalization or premise. An **inductive conclusion** is a broad conclusion or generalization that is reached by arguing from specific facts and examples.

Connect Connecting is a reader's process of relating the content of a text to his or her own knowledge and experience.

Consumer Documents Consumer documents are printed materials that accompany products and services. They are intended for the buyers or users of the products or services and usually provide information about use, care, operation, or assembly. Some common consumer documents are applications, contracts, warranties, manuals, instructions, package inserts, labels, brochures, and schedules.

Context Clues When you encounter an unfamiliar word, you can often use context clues as aids for understanding. Context clues are the words and phrases surrounding the word that provide hints about the word's meaning.

Controlling Idea *See* **Thesis Statement.**

Counterargument A counterargument is an argument made to oppose another argument. A good argument anticipates opposing viewpoints and provides counterarguments to refute (disprove) or answer them.

Counterclaim *See* **Counterargument.**

Credibility *Credibility* refers to the believability or trustworthiness of a source and the information it contains.

Critical Review A critical review is an evaluation or critique by a reviewer or critic. Different types of reviews include film reviews, book reviews, music reviews, and art-show reviews.

Database A database is a collection of information that can be quickly and easily accessed and searched and from which information can be easily retrieved. It is frequently presented in an electronic format.

Debate A debate is an organized exchange of opinions on an issue. In academic settings, *debate* usually refers to a formal contest in which two opposing teams defend and attack a proposition.

See also **Argument; Debate**—*Speaking and Listening Handbook, pages R82–R83.*

Deductive Reasoning Deductive reasoning is a way of thinking that begins with a generalization, presents a specific situation, and then advances with facts and evidence to a logical conclusion. The following passage has a deductive argument imbedded in it: "All students in the drama class must attend the play on Thursday. Since Ava is in the class, she had better show up." This deductive argument can be broken down as follows: generalization—all students in the drama class must attend the play on Thursday; specific situation—Ava is a student in the drama class; conclusion—Ava must attend the play.

See also **Analyzing Logic and Reasoning**—*Reading Handbook, pages R20–R21.*

Dictionary *See* **Reference Works.**

Draw Conclusions To draw a conclusion is to make a judgment or arrive at a belief based on evidence, experience, and reasoning.

Editorial An editorial is an opinion piece that usually appears on the editorial page of a newspaper or as part of a news broadcast. The editorial section of a newspaper presents opinions rather than objective news reports.

See also **Op-Ed Piece.**

Either/Or Fallacy An either/or fallacy is a statement that suggests that there are only two possible ways to view a situation or only two options to choose from. In other words, it is a statement that falsely frames a dilemma, giving the impression that no options exist but the two presented—for example, "Either we stop the construction of a new airport, or the surrounding suburbs will become ghost towns."

See also **Identifying Faulty Reasoning**—*Reading Handbook, page R22.*

Emotional Appeals Emotional appeals are messages that evoke strong feelings—such as fear, pity, or vanity—in order to persuade instead of using facts and evidence to make a point. An **appeal to fear** is a message that taps into people's fear of losing their safety or security. An **appeal to pity** is a message that taps into people's sympathy and compassion for others to build support for an idea, a cause, or a proposed action. An **appeal to vanity** is a message that attempts to persuade by tapping into people's desire to feel good about themselves.

See also **Recognizing Persuasive Techniques**—*Reading Handbook, page R20.*

Encyclopedia *See* **Reference Works.**

Essay *See Glossary of Literary and Nonfiction Terms, page R109.*

Ethical Appeals Ethical appeals establish a writer's credibility and trustworthiness with an audience. When a writer links a claim to a widely accepted value, for example, the writer not only gains moral support for that claim but also establishes a connection with readers.

See also **Recognizing Persuasive Techniques**—*Reading Handbook, page R20.*

Evaluate To evaluate is to examine something carefully and judge its value or worth. Evaluating is an important skill for gaining insight into what you read. A reader can evaluate the actions of a particular character, for example, or can form an opinion about the value of an entire work.

Evidence Evidence is the specific pieces of information that support a claim. Evidence can take the form of facts, quotations, examples, statistics, or personal experiences, among others.

Expository Essay *See* **Essay,** *Glossary of Literary and Nonfiction Terms, page R109.*

Fact versus Opinion A **fact** is a statement that can be proved or verified. An **opinion,** on the other hand, is a statement that cannot be proved because it expresses a person's beliefs, feelings, or thoughts.

See also **Inference; Generalization.**

Faulty Reasoning *See* **Logical Fallacy.**

Feature Article A feature article is a main article in a newspaper or a cover story in a magazine. A feature article is focused more on entertaining than informing. Features are lighter or more general than hard news and tend to be about human interest or lifestyles.

Functional Documents *See* **Consumer Documents; Workplace Documents.**

Generalization A generalization is a broad statement about a class or category of people, ideas, or things, based on a study of only some of its members.

See also **Overgeneralization.**

General Principle In an argument, a general principle is an assumption that links the support to the claim. If one does not accept the general principle as a truth, then the support is inadequate because it is beside the point.

Government Publications Government publications are documents produced by government organizations. Pamphlets, brochures, and reports are just some of the many forms these publications may take. Government publications can be good resources for a wide variety of topics.

Graphic Aid A graphic aid is a visual tool that is printed, handwritten, or drawn. Charts, diagrams, graphs, photographs, and maps can all be graphic aids.

See also **Graphic Aids**—*Reading Handbook, pages R5–R7.*

Graphic Organizer A graphic organizer is a visual illustration of a verbal statement that helps a reader understand a text. Charts, tables, webs, and diagrams can all be graphic organizers. Graphic organizers and graphic aids can look the same. However, graphic organizers and graphic aids do differ in how they are used. Graphic aids are the visual representations that people encounter when they read informational texts. Graphic organizers are visuals that people construct to help them understand texts or organize information.

Historical Documents Historical documents are writings that have played a significant role in human events or are themselves records of such events. The Declaration of Independence, for example, is a historical document.

How-To Book A how-to book is a book that is written to explain how to do something—usually an activity, a sport, or a household project.

Implied Main Idea *See* **Main Idea.**

Index The index of a book is an alphabetized list of important topics and details covered in the book and the page numbers on which they can be found. An index can be used to quickly find specific information about a topic.

Inductive Reasoning Inductive reasoning is the process of logical reasoning from observations, examples, and facts to a general conclusion or principle.

See also **Analyzing Logic and Reasoning**—*Reading Handbook, pages R20–R21.*

Inference An inference is a logical assumption that is based on observed facts and one's own knowledge and experience.

Informational Text Informational text is a category of writing that includes exposition, argument, and functional documents. These texts normally provide factual, historical, or technical information. However, the term also covers texts that make logical or emotional arguments in defense of a position. Examples include biographies, journalism, essays, narrative histories, instruction manuals, and speeches.

Journal A journal is a periodical publication issued by a legal, medical, or other professional organization. Alternatively, the term may be used to refer to a diary or daily record.

Literary Criticism *See Glossary of Literary and Nonfiction Terms, page R113.*

Loaded Language Loaded language consists of words with strongly positive or negative connotations intended to influence a reader's or listener's attitude.

Logical Appeal A logical appeal relies on logic and facts, appealing to people's reasoning or intellect rather than to their values or emotions. Flawed logical appeals—that is, errors in reasoning—are considered logical fallacies.
See also **Logical Fallacy.**

Logical Argument A logical argument is an argument in which the logical relationship between the support and the claim is sound.

Logical Fallacy A fallacy is an error in reasoning. Typically, a fallacy is based on an incorrect inference or a misuse of evidence. Some common logical fallacies are **circular logic, either/or fallacy, oversimplification, overgeneralization,** and **stereotyping.**
See also **Either/Or Fallacy; Logical Appeal; Overgeneralization; Identifying Faulty Reasoning**—*Reading Handbook, page R22.*

Main Idea A main idea is the central or most important idea about a topic that a writer or speaker conveys. It can be the central idea of an entire work or of just a paragraph. Often, the main idea of a paragraph is expressed in a topic sentence. However, a main idea may just be implied, or suggested, by details. A main idea and supporting details can serve as a basic pattern of organization in a piece of writing, with the central idea about a topic being supported by details.

Make Inferences *See* **Inference.**

Monitor Monitoring is the strategy of checking your comprehension as you are reading and modifying the strategies you are using to suit your needs. Monitoring may include some or all of the following strategies: **questioning, clarifying, visualizing, predicting, connecting,** and **rereading.**

Narrative *See Glossary of Literary and Nonfiction Terms, page R115.*

News Article A news article is a piece of writing that reports on a recent event. In newspapers, news articles are usually written in a concise manner to report the latest news, presenting the most important facts first and then more detailed information. In magazines, news articles are usually more elaborate than those in newspapers because they are written to provide both information and analysis. Also, news articles in magazines do not necessarily present the most important facts first.

Nonfiction *See Glossary of Literary and Nonfiction Terms, page R115.*

Op-Ed Piece An op-ed piece is an opinion piece that usually appears opposite ("op") the editorial page of a newspaper. Unlike editorials, op-ed pieces are written and submitted by named writers.

Organization *See* **Pattern of Organization.**

Overgeneralization An overgeneralization is a generalization that is too broad. You can often recognize overgeneralizations by the appearance of words and phrases such as *all, everyone, every time, any, anything, no one,* and *none.* Consider, for example, this statement: "None of the sanitation workers in our city really care about keeping the environment clean." In all probability, there are many exceptions. The writer can't possibly know the feelings of every sanitation worker in the city.
See also **Identifying Faulty Reasoning**—*Reading Handbook, page R22.*

Overview An overview is a short summary of a story, a speech, or an essay. It orients the reader by providing a preview of the text to come.

Paraphrase Paraphrasing is the restating of information in one's own words.
See also **Summarize.**

Pattern of Organization A pattern of organization is a particular arrangement of ideas and information. Such a pattern may be used to organize an entire composition or a single paragraph within a longer work. The following are the most common organizational patterns: **cause-and-effect, chronological order, compare-and-contrast, classification, deductive, inductive, order of importance, problem-solution, sequential,** and **spatial.**
See also **Cause and Effect; Chronological Order; Classification; Compare and Contrast; Problem-Solution Order; Sequential Order; Patterns of Organization**—*Reading Handbook, pages R8–R12.*

Periodical A periodical is a publication that is issued at regular intervals of more than one day. For example, a periodical may be a weekly, monthly, or quarterly journal or magazine. Newspapers and other daily publications generally are not classified as periodicals.

Personal Essay *See* **Essay,** *Glossary of Literary and Nonfiction Terms, page R109.*

Persuasion Persuasion is the art of swaying others' feelings, beliefs, or actions. Persuasion normally appeals to both the intellect and the emotions of readers. **Persuasive techniques** are the methods used to influence others to adopt certain opinions or beliefs or to act in certain ways. Types of persuasive techniques include emotional appeals, ethical appeals, logical appeals, and loaded language. When used properly, persuasive techniques can add depth to writing that's meant to persuade. Persuasive techniques can, however, be misused to cloud factual information, disguise poor reasoning, or unfairly exploit people's emotions in order to shape their opinions.

See also **Appeals by Association; Appeal to Authority; Emotional Appeals; Ethical Appeals; Loaded Language; Logical Appeal; Recognizing Persuasive Techniques—** *Reading Handbook, page R20.*

Predict Predicting is a reading strategy that involves using text clues to make a reasonable guess about what will happen next in a story.

Primary Source *See* **Sources.**

Prior Knowledge Prior knowledge is the knowledge a reader already possesses about a topic. This information might come from personal experiences, expert accounts, books, films, or other sources.

Problem-Solution Order Problem-solution order is a pattern of organization in which a problem is stated and analyzed and then one or more solutions are proposed and examined. Writers use words and phrases such as *propose, conclude, reason for, problem, answer,* and *solution* to connect ideas and details when writing about problems and solutions.

Procedural Documents *See* **Consumer Documents.**

Propaganda Propaganda is a form of communication that may use distorted, false, or misleading information. It usually refers to manipulative political discourse.

Public Documents Public documents are documents that were written for the public to provide information that is of public interest or concern. They include government documents, speeches, signs, and rules and regulations.

See also **Government Publications.**

Reference Works General reference works are sources that contain facts and background information on a wide range of subjects. More specific reference works contain in-depth information on a single subject. Most reference works are good sources of reliable information because they have been reviewed by experts. The following are some common reference works: **encyclopedias, dictionaries, thesauri, almanacs, atlases, chronologies, biographical dictionaries,** and **directories.**

Review *See* **Critical Review.**

Rhetorical Devices *See Glossary of Literary and Nonfiction Terms, page R118.*

Rhetorical Questions Rhetorical questions are those that do not require a reply. Writers use them to suggest that their arguments make the answer obvious or self-evident.

Scanning Scanning is the process of searching through writing for a particular fact or piece of information. When you scan, your eyes sweep across a page, looking for key words that may lead you to the information you want.

Secondary Source *See* **Sources.**

Sequential Order A pattern of organization that shows the order in which events or actions occur is called sequential order. Writers typically use this pattern of organization to explain steps or stages in a process.

Setting a Purpose The process of establishing specific reasons for reading a text is called setting a purpose.

Sidebar A sidebar is additional information set in a box alongside or within a news or feature article. Popular magazines often make use of sidebar information.

Signal Words Signal words are words and phrases that indicate what is to come in a text. Readers can use signal words to discover a text's pattern of organization and to analyze the relationships among the ideas in the text.

Sources A source is anything that supplies information. **Primary sources** are materials written or created by people who were present at events, either as participants or as observers. Letters, diaries, autobiographies, speeches, and photographs are primary sources. **Secondary sources** are records of events that were created sometime after the events occurred; the writers were not directly involved or were not present when the events took place. Encyclopedias, textbooks, biographies, most newspaper and magazine articles, and books and articles that interpret or review research are secondary sources.

Spatial Order Spatial order is a pattern of organization that highlights the physical positions or relationships of details or objects. This pattern of organization is typically found in descriptive writing. Writers use words and phrases such as *on the left, to the right, here, over there, above, below, beyond, nearby,* and *in the distance* to indicate the arrangement of details.

Speech *See Glossary of Literary and Nonfiction Terms, page R120.*

Stereotyping Stereotyping is a dangerous type of overgeneralization. Stereotypes are broad statements made about people on the basis of their gender, ethnicity, race, or political, social, professional, or religious group.

Summarize To summarize is to briefly retell, or encapsulate, the main ideas of a piece of writing in one's own words.

See also **Paraphrase.**

Support Support is any material that serves to prove a claim. In an argument, support typically consists of reasons and evidence. In persuasive texts and speeches, however, support may include appeals to the needs and values of the audience.

See also **General Principle.**

Supporting Detail *See* **Main Idea.**

Synthesize To synthesize information is to take information, combined with other pieces of information and prior knowledge, and make logical connections to gain a better understanding of a subject or to create a new product or idea.

Text Features Text features are design elements that indicate the organizational structure of a text and help make the key ideas and the supporting information understandable. Text features include headings, boldface type, italic type, bulleted or numbered lists, sidebars, and graphic aids such as charts, tables, timelines, illustrations, and photographs.

Thesaurus *See* **Reference Works.**

Thesis Statement In an argument, a thesis statement, or controlling idea, is an expression of the claim that the writer or speaker is trying to support. In an essay, a thesis statement is an expression, in one or two sentences, of the main idea or purpose of the piece of writing.

Topic Sentence The topic sentence of a paragraph states the paragraph's main idea. All other sentences in the paragraph provide supporting details.

Transcript A transcript is a written record of words originally spoken aloud.

Visualize Visualizing is the process of forming a mental picture based on written or spoken information.

Web Site A Web site is a collection of "pages" on the World Wide Web that is usually devoted to one specific subject. Pages are linked together and are accessed by clicking hyperlinks or menus, which send the user from page to page within the site. Web sites are created by companies, organizations, educational institutions, branches of the government, the military, and individuals.

Workplace Documents Workplace documents are materials that are produced or used within a work setting, usually to aid in the functioning of the workplace. They include job applications, office memos, training manuals, job descriptions, and sales reports.

Works Cited A list of works cited lists names of all the works a writer has referred to in his or her text. This list often includes not only books and articles but also nonprint sources.

Works Consulted A list of works consulted names all the works a writer consulted in order to create his or her text. It is not limited just to those works cited in the text.

See also **Bibliography.**

Glossary of Academic Vocabulary in English & Spanish

The Glossary of Academic Vocabulary in this section is an alphabetical list of the Academic Vocabulary words found in this textbook. Use this glossary just as you would use a dictionary—to find out the meanings of words used in your literature class to talk about and write about literary and informational texts and to talk about and write about concepts and topics in your other academic classes.

For each word, the glossary includes the pronunciation, part of speech, and meaning. A Spanish version of each word and definition follows the English version. For more information about the words in the Glossary of Academic Vocabulary, please consult a dictionary.

adequate (ad'ə-kwit) *adj.* enough to meet a need; sufficient
adecuado *adj.* bastante para cubrir una necesidad; suficiente

apparent (ə-păr'ənt) *adj.* obvious; seeming, especially without deeper examination
aparente *adj.* obvio; visible, especialmente sin necesidad de un examen profundo

complex (käm'pleks) *adj.* made up of interconnected parts; hard to understand; complicated
complejo *adj.* compuesto por partes interrelacionadas; difícil de comprender; complicado

conclude (kən'klōōd) *v.* to arrive at a belief based on evidence, experience, or reasoning; to end
concluir *v.* llegar a una creencia a partir de pruebas, experiencias o razonamientos; finalizar

confine (kən-fīn') *v.* to keep within bounds; limit
confinar *v.* mantener dentro de límites; limitar

conflict (kŏn'flĭkt) *n.* a struggle or clash between people, ideas, or interests. *v.* (kən-flĭkt') to be in opposition; differ
conflicto *sust.* lucha o choque entre personas, ideas o intereses; **estar en conflicto** *loc. v.* enfrentarse; diferir

construct (kən-strŭkt') *v.* create (an argument or a sentence, for example) by systematically arranging ideas or terms; *n.* (kŏn'strŭkt) a concept or theory
construir *v.* crear (un argumento o una oración, por ejemplo) ordenando ideas o palabras de manera sistemática; **construcción** *sust.* concepto o teoría

consult (kən-sŭlt') *v.* to seek the advice or information of; to exchange views
consultar *v.* buscar consejos o información con respecto a algo; intercambiar opiniones

create (krē-āt') *v.* to make or cause; to produce through artistic effort
crear *v.* hacer o causar; producir mediante un esfuerzo artístico

criteria (krī-tîr'ē-ə) *n. pl.* set of standard or rules by which something can be evaluated
criterio *sust.* norma o estándar según el cual se puede evaluar algo

despite (dĭ-spīt') *prep.* in spite of; not stopped by
a pesar de *loc. conj.* pese a; independientemente de

document (dŏk'yə-mənt) *n.* something, such as a piece of writing, recording or a photograph, that can be used to furnish evidence or information; *v.* to support (statements in a research paper, for example) with written references or citations
documento *sust.* algo, como un escrito, una grabación o una fotografía, que se puede usar para proporcionar pruebas o información; **documentar** *v.* respaldar (afirmaciones en un trabajo de investigación, por ejemplo) con referencias o citas escritas

economic (ĕk'ə-nŏm-ĭk) *adj.* relating to the production and exchange of goods and services; efficient
económico *adj.* relacionado con la producción y el intercambio de bienes y servicios; que rinde

element (ĕl'ə-mənt) *n.* a basic or essential part of something
elemento *sust.* parte básica o esencial de algo

emphasis (ĕm'fə-sĭs) *n.* special attention or effort directed toward something; stress on a syllable, word, or words
énfasis *sust.* atención o esfuerzo especial dirigido hacia algo; acento que se da a una sílaba, una palabra o varias palabras

establish (ĭ-stăb'lĭsh) *v.* to set up or cause to happen
establecer *v.* organizar algo o causar su existencia

ethnic (ĕth'nĭk) *adj.* relating to a group of people sharing a common racial, national, religious, linguistic, or cultural heritage
étnico *adj.* relacionado con un grupo de personas que comparten un legado racial, nacional, religioso, lingüístico o cultural común

evolve (ĭ-vŏlv') *v.* to develop gradually
evolucionar *v.* desarrollarse en forma gradual

expand (ĭk-spănd') *v.* to enlarge; to express at length or in detail
extender *v.* agrandar; expresar en forma extensa o en detalle

expose (ĭk-spōz') *v.* to subject to an action, influence, or condition; to make visible; to make known, especially something negative
exponer *v.* someter a una acción, influencia o condición; hacer visible; dar a conocer, especialmente algo negativo

focus (fō'kəs) *n.* a center of interest; close attention, concentration; *v.* to direct toward a particular point or purpose
foco *sust.* centro de interés; atención, concentración; **enfocar** *v.* dirigirse hacia un punto o propósito en particular

illustrate (ĭl'ə-strāt) *v.* to clarify, or make clear, with examples
ilustrar *v.* aclarar o explicar mediante ejemplos

indicate (ĭn'dĭ-kāt) *v.* to point out; to signify
indicar *v.* señalar; significar

interpret (ĭn-tûr'prĭt) *v.* explain the meaning or significance of something
interpretar *v.* explicar el significado o la importancia de algo

investigate (ĭn-vĕs'tĭ-gāt) *v.* to observe or look at in detail; examine systematically
investigar *v.* observar o mirar en detalle; examinar de manera sistemática

justify (jŭs'tə-fī) *v.* to show or claim to be just or right; vindicate
justificar *v.* demostrar o afirmar que algo es justo o correcto; reivindicar

maintain (mān-tān') *v.* to preserve or keep up; to declare to be true
mantener *v.* preservar o conservar; declarar que algo es verdadero

objective (əb-jek'tĭv) *adj.* factual; not influenced by bias or emotion; *n.* purpose or goal
objetivo *adj.* justo; no influenciado por parcialidades o emociones; *sust.* propósito o finalidad

perceive (pər-sēv') *v.* to become aware of through the senses, especially sight or hearing; to notice; to grasp an understanding
percibir *v.* tomar conciencia de algo mediante los sentidos, en especial mediante la vista o la audición; notar; comprender una idea

perspective (pər-spĕk'tĭv) *n.* particular way of looking at something; point of view
perspectiva *sust.* manera particular de mirar algo; punto de vista

promote (prə-mōt') *v.* to help the growth of, urge the adoption of, or attempt to popularize something
promover *v.* ayudar en el crecimiento, fomentar la adopción o intentar popularizar algo

qualitative (kwŏl'ĭ-tā-tĭv) *adj.* measuring the quality, or essential nature, of something
cualitativo *adj.* que mide la calidad o naturaleza esencial de algo

reinforce (rē-ĭn-fôrs') *v.* to strengthen something by adding extra support
reforzar *v.* fortalecer algo mediante respaldo adicional

reveal (rĭ-vēl') *v.* to make known; to show
revelar *v.* dar a conocer; mostrar

role (rōl) *n.* the character or part played by a performer; the expected behavior of an individual in society; a function or position
papel *sust.* personaje o rol que representa un actor; conducta que se espera de una persona en la sociedad; función o posición

Glossary of Vocabulary in English & Spanish

The glossary that follows is an alphabetical list of words, found in the selections in this book. Use this glossary just as you would use a dictionary—to find out the meanings of unfamiliar words. (Some technical, foreign, and more obscure words in this book are not listed here but instead are defined for you in the footnotes that accompany many of the selections.)

Many words in the English language have more than one meaning. This glossary gives the meanings that apply to the words as they are used in the selections in this book. Words closely related in form and meaning are usually listed together in one entry (for instance, *cower* and *cowered*), and the definition is given for the first form.

The following abbreviations are used:

adj. adjective
adv. adverb
n. noun
v. verb

Each word's pronunciation is given in parentheses. followed by the word and definition in Spanish. For more information about the words in this glossary or for information about words not listed here, consult a dictionary.

abdicate (ăb'dĭ-kāt') *v.* to give up responsibility for
abdicar *v.* renunciar a una responsabilidad

aberration (ăb'ə-rā'shən) *n.* a disorder of the mind
aberración *s.* desorden mental

abhor (ăb-hôr') *v.* to regard with disgust
aborrecer *v.* detestar

abject (ăb'jĕkt') *adj.* low; contemptible; wretched
abyecto *adj.* vil; despreciable; desgraciado

abominable (ə-bŏm'ə-nə-bəl) *adj.* thoroughly detestable
abominable *adj.* totalmente detestable

acquiesce (ăk'wē-ĕs') *v.* to comply or give in
consentir *v.* aceptar o ceder

adamant (ăd'ə-mənt) *adj.* immovable, especially in opposing something
inflexible *adj.* inquebrantable, especialmente en oposición a algo

admonitory (ăd-mŏn'ĭ-tôr'ē) *adj.* warning
admonitorio *adj.* que da una advertencia

affiliated (ə-fĭl'ē-āt-ĭd) *adj.* joined in close association **affiliate** *v.*
afiliado *adj.* asociado **afiliar** *v.*

affinity (ə-fĭn'ĭ-tē) *n.* a kinship or likeness
afinidad *s.* cercanía o semejanza

affluence (ăf'lo͞o-əns) *n.* wealth
opulencia *s.* riqueza

alleviation (ə-lē'vē-ā'shən) *n.* relief
alivio *s.* desahogo

ambiguity (ăm'bĭ-gyo͞o'ĭ-tē) *n.* unclearness; uncertainty
ambigüedad *s.* vaguedad; incertidumbre

amethyst (ăm'ə-thĭst) *n.* purple or violet form of transparent quartz used as a gemstone
amatista *s.* cuarzo transparente púrpura o violeta usado como piedra preciosa

amicable (ăm'ĭ-kə-bəl) *adj.* characterized by friendly goodwill
amigable *adj.* caracterizado por buena voluntad

anarchy (ăn'ər-kē) *n.* condition of lawlessness and disorder, often due to lack of governmental authority
anarquía *s.* desorden y confusión por falta de gobierno

anathema (ə-năth'ə-mə) *n.* a strong denunciation; a curse
anatema *s.* fuerte rechazo; maldición

anomaly (ə-nŏm'ə-lē) *n.* departure from the normal rules
anomalía *s.* desviación de las reglas normales

apathy (ăp'ə-thē) *n.* lack of feeling or interest
apatía *s.* falta de sentimiento o de interés

appease (ə-pēz′) *v.* to bring peace, quiet, or calm to; to soothe
aplacar *v.* apaciguar; calmar; aquietar

arbitrary (är′bĭ-trĕr′ē) *adj.* based on unpredictable decisions rather than law
arbitrario *adj.* que actúa basándose sólo en la voluntad o en el capricho y no sigue las leyes

ardor (är′dər) *n.* intense enthusiasm; passion
ardor *s.* fuerte entusiasmo; pasión

artifice (är′tə-fĭs) *n.* a clever means to an end
artificio *s.* estratagema; ardid

ascribe (ə-skrīb′) *v.* to attribute to a specified cause or source
adscribir *v.* atribuir a una causa o a una fuente

assign (ə-sīn′) *n.* person to whom property is transferred in a will or other legal document
beneficiario *s.* persona a la que transfiere propiedades un testamento u otro documento jurídico

attest (ə-tĕst′) *v.* to affirm to be true; to be proof of
atestiguar *v.* dar testimonio; certificar

avarice (ăv′ə-rĭs) *n.* immoderate desire for wealth; greed
avaricia *s.* deseo desmedido de riqueza; codicia

aversion (ə-vûr′zhən) *n.* a strong dislike
aversión *s.* fuerte desagrado

blasphemous (blăs′fə-məs) *adj.* disrespectful or offensive
blasfemo *adj.* irrespetuoso u ofensivo

blatantly (blāt′nt-lē) *adv.* in an extremely obvious way; conspicuously
descaradamente *adv.* abiertamente; patentemente

cabal (kə-băl′) *n.* a group united in a secret plot
cábala *s.* grupo unido en un complot secreto

callow (kăl′ō) *adj.* lacking adult experience; immature
inmaduro *adj.* sin experiencia; inexperto

camaraderie (kä′mə-rä′də-rē) *n.* a spirit of friendly good-fellowship
camaradería *s.* espíritu de amistad y compañerismo

cauterize (kô′tə-rīz′) *v.* to burn or sear to destroy diseased tissue
cauterizar *v.* quemar o chamuscar para destruir tejido dañado

cavorting (kə-vôr′tĭng) *adj.* prancing about in a playful manner **cavort** *v.*
retozón *adj.* que hace cabriolas de modo juguetón **retozar** *v.*

celestial (sə-lĕs′chəl) *adj.* heavenly
celestial *adj.* del cielo

censurer (sĕn′shər-ər) *n.* one who expresses strong disapproval or harsh criticism
censor *s.* persona que expresa una fuerte desaprobación o crítica

cessation (sĕ-sā′shən) *n.* a coming to an end; a stopping
cesación *s.* fin; terminación

citation (sī-tā′shən) *n.* formal statement of a soldier's achievements
mención honorífica *s.* reconocimiento de los éxitos de un militar

coerce (kō-ûrs′) *v.* to force
coaccionar *v.* obligar

cognizant (kŏg′nĭ-zənt) *adj.* aware
enterado *adj.* informado

commiseration (kə-mĭz′ə-rā′shən) *n.* a feeling of sympathy or pity
conmiseración *s.* sentimiento de compasión

comport (kəm-pôrt′) *v.* to agree
concordar *v.* estar de acuerdo

congenial (kən-jēn′yəl) *adj.* suited to one's needs or nature; agreeable
compatible *adj.* que concuerda con las necesidades o la naturaleza de uno; concorde

conjecture (kən-jĕk′chər) *v.* to guess
conjeturar *v.* suponer

consternation (kŏn′stər-nā′shən) *n.* a state of paralyzing dismay; fear
consternación *s.* estado de gran intranquilidad; temor

constitute (kŏn′stĭ-to͞ot′) *v.* to amount to; equal
constituir *v.* equivaler; formar

contentious (kən-tĕn′shəs) *adj.* quarrelsome
discutidor *adj.* pendenciero

contrive (kən-trīv′) *v.* to plan skillfully; to design
ingeniarse *v.* maquinar; inventar

convolution (kŏn′və-lo͞o′shən) *n.* a form or shape that is folded into curved, complicated windings
circunvolución *s.* repliegue; enroscadura; enrollamiento

copious (kō′pē-əs) *adj.* in large amounts; abundant
copioso *adj.* en gran cantidad; abundante

corroborate (kə-rŏb′ə-rāt′) *v.* to support with evidence
corroborar *v.* comprobar con evidencia

cosmic (kŏz′mĭk) *adj.* of, or belonging to, the universe
cósmico *adj.* relativo al universo

countenance (koun′tə-nəns) *n.* appearance, especially the expression of the face
semblante *s.* apariencia, especialmente la expresión de la cara

credulity (krĭ-do͞o′lĭ-tē) *n.* an inclination to believe too readily
credulidad *s.* facilidad para creer

dastardly (dăs′tərd-lē) *adj.* characterized by underhandedness or treachery
miserable *adj.* solapado o traidor

dearth (dûrth) *n.* lack
escasez *s.* carencia

decorum (dĭ-kôr′əm) *n.* good taste in conduct or appearance
decoro *s.* buen gusto en la conducta y la apariencia

deference (dĕf′ər-əns) *n.* respect and honor due to a superior or elder
deferencia *s.* respeto y honor que se debe a un superior o mayor

deliberately (dĭ-lĭb′ər-ĭt-lē) *adv.* in an unhurried and thoughtful manner
deliberadamente *adv.* pausadamente

deliverance (dĭ-lĭv′ər-əns) *n.* rescue from danger
salvación *s.* rescate de un peligro

demeanor (dĭ-mē′nər) *n.* behavior
comportamiento *s.* conducta

depose (dĭ-pōz′) *v.* to remove from rule
deponer *v.* destituir del gobierno

despotism (dĕs′pə-tĭz′əm) *n.* government by a ruler with unlimited power
despotismo *s.* gobierno de poder ilimitado

detached (dĭ-tăcht′) *adj.* reserved; aloof **detach** *v.*
alejado *adj.* reservado; distante **alejarse** *v.*

dilapidated (dĭ-lăp′ĭ-dā′tĭd) *adj.* in a state of disrepair; rundown **dilapidate** *v.*
dilapidado *adj.* en ruinas; desmantelado **dilapidar** *v.*

disapprobation (dĭs-ăp′rə-bā′shən) *n.* disapproval
desaprobación *s.* censura

discern (dĭ-sûrn′) *v.* to perceive or recognize something
discernir *v.* percibir o reconocer algo

dominion (də-mĭn′yən) *n.* control; authority over
dominio *s.* control; soberanía

dwindle (dwĭn′dl) *v.* to become steadily less; to shrink
menguar *v.* disminuirse poco a poco; encogerse

embody (ĕm-bŏd′ē) *v.* to represent in human form
encarnar *v.* representar en forma humana

embroidered (ĕm′broi′derd) *adj.* decorated with stitched designs **embroider** *v.*
bordado *adj.* decorado con cosidos en relieve **bordar** *v.*

enmity (ĕn′mĭ-tē) *n.* hostility; hatred
enemistad *s.* hostilidad; odio

enterprising (ĕn′tər-prī′zĭng) *adj.* possessing imagination and initiative
emprendedor *adj.* que demuestra imaginación e iniciativa

entreaty (ĕn-trē′tē) *n.* plea
súplica *s.* petición

epithet (ĕp′ə-thĕt′) *n.* an abusive word or phrase
epíteto *s.* palabra o frase insultante

equanimity (ē′kwə-nĭm′ĭ-tē) *n.* evenness of temper, especially under stress
ecuanimidad *s.* serenidad y equilibrio, especialmente bajo presión

equivocal (ĭ-kwĭv'ə-kəl) *adj.* ambiguous
equívoco *adj.* ambiguo

eradicate (ĭ-răd'ĭ-kāt') *v.* to destroy completely
erradicar *v.* destruir por completo

esteem (ĭ-stēm') *v.* to set a high value on
estimar *v.* dar mucho valor

estrangement (ĭ-strānj'-mənt) *n.* separation; alienation
extrañamiento *s.* separación; desavenencia

excruciatingly (ĭk-skrōō'shē-ā'tĭng-lē) *adv.* in a way that causes great pain or distress
dolorosamente *adv.* de modo que causa mucho dolor o angustia

exhilaration (ĭg-zĭl'ə-rā'shən) *n.* a feeling of high spirits or lively joy
regocijo *s.* alborozo y gran alegría

expatriated (ĕk-spā'trē-ā'tĭd) *adj.* sent out of a country or area; banished **expatriate** *v.*
expatriado *adj.* exiliado; desterrado **expatriar** *v.*

extenuate (ĭk-stĕn'yōō-āt') *v.* to lessen the seriousness of, especially by providing partial excuses
atenuar *v.* reducir la gravedad, especialmente dando excusas parciales

extenuating (ĭk-stĕn'yōō-āt'ĭng) *adj.* lessening the severity of **extenuate** *v.*
atenuante *adj.* que reduce la gravedad **atenuar** *v.*

exultingly (ĭg-zult'ĭng-lē) *adv.* joyfully
jubilosamente *adv.* con júbilo

fatuity (fə-tōō'ĭ-tē) *n.* something foolish or stupid
fatuidad *s.* simpleza o estupidez

feigned (fānd) *adj.* not real; pretended **feign** *v.*
fingido *adj.* irrea; ficticio **fingir** *v.*

felicity (fĭ-lĭs'ĭ-tē) *n.* great happiness
felicidad *s.* dicha

flamboyant (flăm-boi'ənt) *adj.* marked by strikingly elaborate or colorful display
flameante *adj.* llamativo; ostentoso; extravagante

flux (flŭks) *n.* change
flujo *s.* fluctuación; cambio

garrulous (găr'ə-ləs) *adj.* extremely talkative
locuaz *adj.* que habla mucho

gullible (gŭl'ə-bəl) *adj.* easily deceived or tricked
crédulo *adj.* que se deja engañar

harassing (hə-răs'ĭng) *adj.* persistently annoying **harass** *v.*
molesto *adj.* que fastidia todo el tiempo **molestar** *v.*

harry (hăr'ē) *v.* to torment, often by constant attack
hostilizar *v.* acosar con ataques constantes

imbued (ĭm-byōōd') *adj.* deeply influenced by **imbue** *v.*
imbuido *adj.* profundamente influenciado **imbuir** *v.*

immaculate (ĭ-măk'yə-lĭt) *adj.* without stain; pure
inmaculado *adj.* sin mancha; puro

impede (ĭm-pēd') *v.* to interfere with or slow the progress of
impedir *v.* obstruir; dificultar

impel (ĭm-pĕl') *v.* to drive forward; force
impeler *v.* impulsar; obligar

impending (ĭm-pĕn'dĭng) *adj.* to be about to occur **impend** *v.*
amenazante *adj.* a punto de ocurrir **amenazar** *v.*

imperceptible (ĭm'pər-sĕp'tə-bəl) *adj.* extremely slight; barely noticeable
imperceptible *adj.* tenue; que casi no se nota

impertinent (ĭm-pûr'tn-ənt) *adj.* rude; ill-mannered
impertinente *adj.* grosero; mal educado

imperviousness (ĭm-pûr'vē-əs-nəs) *n.* condition of not being able to be affected or disturbed
imperturbabilidad *s.* imposibilidad de ser afectado o perturbado

impetuous (ĭm-pĕch'ōō-əs) *adj.* acting with sudden or rash energy; hasty
impetuoso *adj.* que actúa de forma precipitada o irreflexiva; impulsivo

implacable (ĭm-plăk'ə-bəl) *adj.* impossible to satisfy
implacable *adj.* que no se puede aplacar

importune (ĭm'pôr-tōōn') *v.* to ask urgently or repeatedly; to annoy or trouble
importunar *v.* preguntar con urgencia e insistencia; molestar

incense (ĭn-sĕns') *v.* to cause to be extremely angry
exasperar *v.* encolerizar; enfurecer

incorrigible (ĭn-kôr'ĭ-jə-bəl) *adj.* incapable of being reformed or corrected
incorregible *adj.* que no se puede reformar o corregir

indifferent (ĭn-dĭf'ər-ənt) *adj.* having no particular interest
indiferente *adj.* sin interés

induce (ĭn-do͞os') *v.* to succeed in persuading someone to do something
inducir *v.* persuadir; causar; producir

industry (ĭn'də-strē) *n.* hard work; diligence
aplicación *s.* diligencia; laboriosidad

ineffable (ĭn-ĕf'ə-bəl) *adj.* beyond description; inexpressible
inefable *adj.* que no se puede describir; inexpresable

inexorable (ĭn-ĕk'sər-ə-bəl) *adj.* relentless
inexorable *adj.* implacable

inextricable (ĭn-ĕk'strĭ-kə-bəl) *adj.* incapable of being disentangled or untied
inextricable *adj.* que no se puede descifrar o desenmarañar

infamous (ĭn'fə-məs) *adj.* having a very bad reputation; disgraceful
infame *adj.* de mala reputación; vergonzoso

ingenuously (ĭn-jĕn'yo͞o-əs-lē) *adv.* in a manner showing childlike innocence or simplicity
ingenuamente *adv.* con candidez infantil

ingratiate (ĭn-grā'shē-āt') *v.* to gain another's favor by deliberate effort
congraciar *v.* conseguir aprobación o afecto con un esfuerzo deliberado

inherently (ĭn-hîr'ənt-lē') *adv.* related to part of something's inmost nature
inherentemente *adv.* intrínsecamente

iniquity (ĭ-nĭk'wĭ-tē) *n.* wickedness
iniquidad *s.* maldad

inordinate (ĭn-ôr'dn-ĭt) *adj.* exceeding reasonable limits; excessive
excesivo *adj.* que sobrepasa los límites razonables; inmoderado

insidious (ĭn-sĭd'ē-əs) *adj.* treacherous
insidioso *adj.* traidor

insipid (ĭn-sĭp'ĭd) *adj.* lacking in flavor; bland
insípido *adj.* sin sabor; desabrido

interim (ĭn'tər-ĭm) *n.* period in between; interval
ínterin *s.* intermedio; intervalo

interminable (ĭn-tûr'mə-nə-bol) *adj.* endless
interminable *adj.* sin fin

interrogation (ĭn-tĕr'ə-gā'shən) *n.* a questioning
interrogación *s.* averiguación

inundate (ĭn'ŭn-dāt') *v.* to cover with water; to overwhelm
inundar *v.* cubrir de agua; anegar

invincible (ĭn-vĭn'sə-bəl) *adj.* unbeatable
invencible *adj.* inconquistable

inviolate (ĭn-vī'ə-lĭt) *adj.* not violated; intact
inviolado *adj.* íntegro; intacto

jocular (jŏk'yə-lər) *adj.* humorous
jocoso *adj.* chistoso

latent (lāt'nt) *adj.* existing in a hidden form
latente *adj.* que existe en forma oculta

limber (lĭm'bər) *adj.* bending or moving easily; supple
flexible *adj.* que se dobla o se mueve con facilidad; ágil

locomotion (lō'kə-mō'shən) *n.* the power to move from place to place
locomoción *s.* movimiento de un lugar a otro

ludicrous (lo͞o'dĭ-krəs) *adj.* laughably absurd; ridiculous
absurdo *adj.* risible; ridículo

lurch (lûrch) *v.* to lean or roll suddenly to one side; to stagger
bambolearse *v.* dar banzados; tambalearse

lurid (lo͝or'ĭd) *adj.* shocking; gruesome
escabroso *adj.* chocante; espeluznante

luxuriant (lŭg-zho͝or'ē-ənt) *adj.* characterized by abundant growth
frondoso *adj.* que tiene mucha vegetación

malign (mə-līn') *adj.* evil; harmful
maligno *adj.* malo; dañino

martial (mär'shəl) *adj.* warlike
marcial *adj.* bélico

maudlin (môd'lĭn) *adj.* excessively sentimental
sensiblero *adj.* sentimental en exceso

mediocrity (mē'dē-ŏk'rĭ-tē) *n.* lack of quality or excellence
mediocridad *s.* poca calidad o mérito

meditative (mĕd′ĭ-tā′tĭv) *adj.* engaged in serious thought or reflection
meditabundo *adj.* que medita o reflexiona en silencio

melancholy (mĕl′ən-kŏl′ē) *adj.* gloomy; sad
melancólico *adj.* triste; lúgubre

mercenary (mûr′sə-nĕr′ē) *n.* a professional soldier hired to fight in a foreign army
mercenario *s.* soldado profesional contratado para pelear en un ejército extranjero

minutest (mī-no͞o′tĭst) *adj.* smallest; most precise
el más diminuto adj. el más pequeño; minucioso

miscellany (mĭs′ə-lā′nē) *n.* a mixture of various things
miscelánea *s.* mezcla de cosas

misconstrued (mĭs′kən-stro͞od′) *adj.* misunderstood; misinterpreted **misconstrue** *v.*
malinterpretado *adj.* mal entendido **malinterpretar** *v.*

misgiving (mĭs-gĭv′ĭng) *n.* a feeling of doubt, mistrust, or uncertainty
recelo *s.* sentimiento de duda, desconfianza o temor

mitigation (mĭt-ĭ-gā′shən) *n.* lessening of something that causes suffering
mitigación *s.* moderación de algo que causa sufrimiento

mollify (mŏl′ə-fī′) *v.* to soothe; to reduce in intensity
aplacar *v.* calmar; apaciguar

moratorium (môr′a-tôr′ē-əm) *n.* temporary stoppage or waiting period
moratoria *s.* aplazamiento; período de espera

motley (mŏt′lē) *adj.* composed of diverse, often mismatched elements
abigarrado *adj.* formado por elementos diversos y dispares

multifariously (mŭl′tə-fâr′ē-əs-lē) *adv.* in many and various ways
variadamente *adv.* de modos muy variados

mundane (mŭn-dān′) *adj.* characteristic of or concerned with the ordinary
mundano *adj.* que se preocupa de lo ordinario

myriad (mîr′ē-əd) *adj.* exceedingly numerous
innumerable *adj.* en excesiva cantidad

nettled (nĕt′əld) *adj.* irritated; annoyed **nettle** *v.*
irritado *adj.* molesto; picado **irritar** *v.*

nocturnal (nŏk-tûr′nəl) *adj.* occurring at night
nocturno *adj.* que ocurre por la noche

nominal (nŏm′ə-nəl) *adj.* in name but not in reality
nominal *adj.* de palabra pero no de hecho

nonconformist (nŏn′kən-fôr′mĭst) *n.* one who does not follow generally accepted beliefs, customs, or practices
inconformista *s.* el que no sigue las creencias, costumbres y prácticas acostumbradas

obstinate (ob′stə-nĭt) *adj.* hard to control or treat
obstinado *adj.* terco; porfiado

obstreperous (ŏb-strĕp′ər-əs) *adj.* very noisy and unruly
estrepitoso *adj.* ruidoso y revoltoso

occult (ə-kŭlt′) *adj.* secret or hidden from view
oculto *adj.* secreto o escondido

opaque (ō-pāk′) *adj.* not allowing light to pass through
opaco *adj.* que no deja pasar la luz

opprobrious (ə-prō′brē-əs) *adj.* scornful; derogatory
oprobioso *adj.* despectivo; derogatorio

oscillation (ŏs′ə-lā′shən) *n.* the action of swinging back and forth
oscilación *s.* movimiento alternativo de un lado hacia otro

ostentation (ŏs′tĕn-tā′shən) *n.* display meant to impress others; boastful showiness
ostentación *s.* exhibición que se hace para impresionar; alarde

ostentatious (ŏs′tĕn-tā′shəs) *adj.* loud; overdone
ostentoso *adj.* pretencioso; aparatoso

overture (ō′vər-cho͝or′) *n.* the orchestral introduction to a musical dramatic work
obertura *s.* pieza instrumental con que empieza una obra musical extensa

paradoxical (păr′ə-dŏks′-ĭ-kəl) *adj.* self-contradictory
paradójico *adj.* que encierra una contradicción

pariah (pə-rī′ə) *n.* an outcast, someone or something looked down on by others
paria *s.* persona a la que se considera inferior

patrimony (păt′rə-mō′nē) *n.* estate or money inherited from ancestors
patrimonio *s.* propiedades o dinero heredados de los antepasados

perfidy (pûr′fĭ-dē) *n.* treachery
perfidia *s.* traición

persecution (pûr′sĭ-kyo͞o′shən) *n.* the act or practice of oppressing or harassing with ill-treatment, especially because of race, religion, gender, or beliefs
persecución *s.* acoso con malos tratos, castigos y penas, especialmente por motivo de raza, religión, género o creencias

pertinacity (pûr′tn-ăs′ĭ-tē) *n.* stubbornness; persistence
pertinacia *s.* terquedad; persistencia

perturbation (pûr′tər-bā′shən) *n.* disturbance of the emotions; agitation; uneasiness
perturbación *s.* alteración de las emociones; agitación; inquietud

pervade (pər-vād′) *v.* to spread through every part of
penetrar *v.* infiltrarse en todas las partes

pestilential (pĕs′tə-lĕn′shəl) *adj.* deadly; poisonous
pestilente *adj.* mortal; venenoso

petulance (pĕch′ə-lənsĕ) *n.* ill temper; annoyance
malhumor *s.* mal genio; disgusto

pigmentation (pĭg′mən-tā′shən) *n.* coloring
pigmentación *s.* coloración

pillage (pĭl′ĭj) *n.* the act of looting or plundering by force
pillaje *s.* saqueo o rapiña a la fuerza

plague (plāg) *v.* to annoy; harass
fastidiar *v.* molestar; acosar

poignant (poin′yənt) *adj.* physically or mentally painful
punzante *adj.* que causa dolor físico o mental

portend (pôr-tĕnd′) *v.* to serve as an omen of; to signify
augurar *v.* presagiar; significar

precarious (prĭ-kâr′ē-əs) *adj.* risky; uncertain
precario *adj.* arriesgado; inseguro

precipitate (prĭ-sĭp′ĭ-tāt′) *v.* to bring about, especially abruptly
precipitar *v.* causar, especialmente de repente

predecessor (prĕd′ĭ-sĕs′ər) *n.* person who precedes or comes before
predecesor *s.* persona que precede o viene antes

preeminently (prē-ĕm′ə-nənt-lē) *adv.* above all; most importantly
preeminentemente *adv.* por encima de todo; sobre todo

presaging (prĕs′ĭj-ĭng) *adj.* predicting **presage** *v.*
presagioso *adj.* que anuncia o presagia **presagiar** *v.*

prescience (prĕsh′əns) *n.* knowledge of events before they occur
presciencia *s.* conocimiento de un suceso antes de que ocurra

preternatural (prē′tər-năch′ər-əl) *adj.* supernatural
preternatural *adj.* sobrenatural

procure (prō-kyo͝or′) *v.* to get by special effort; to obtain
adquirir *v.* conseguir con un esfuerzo especial; obtener

profusion (prə-fyo͞o′zhən) *n.* abundance; lavishness
profusión *s.* abundancia; esplendidez

propitious (prə-pĭsh′əs) *adj.* helpful or advantageous; favorable
propicio *adj.* benéfico; favorable

propriety (prə-prī′ĭ-tē) *n.* the quality of being proper; appropriateness
corrección *s.* decoro; idoneidad

providence (prŏv′ĭ-dəns) *n.* an instance of divine care
providencia *s.* ayuda divina

prudent (pro͞od′nt) *adj.* showing caution or good judgment
prudente *adj.* que actúa con moderación y cautela

querulous (kwĕr′ə-ləs) *adj.* complaining
quejumbroso *adj.* quejicoso

rabid (răb′ĭd) *adj.* unreasonably extreme; fanatical
rabioso *adj.* inmoderamente extremo; fanático

radiation (rā′dē-ā′shən) *n.* movement of lines or rays from a center point
radiación *s.* movimiento de líneas o rayos desde un punto central

raiment (rā′ment) *n.* clothing; garments
vestimenta *s.* ropa; indumentaria

rapt (răpt) *adj.* deeply moved, delighted, or absorbed
arrebatado *adj.* profundamente conmovido, extasiado o absorto

rectitude (rĕk'tĭ-to͞od') *n.* morally correct behavior or thinking
rectitud *s.* conducta o pensamiento justo en el sentido moral

recurrent (rĭ-kûr'ənt) *adj.* occurring time after time
recurrente *adj.* que se repite una y otra vez

redress (rĭ-drĕs') *n.* the correction of a wrong; compensation
remedio *s.* reparación de un daño; compensación

relinquish (rĭ-lĭng'kwĭsh) *v.* to withdraw from; to give up
abandonar *v.* renunciar a; ceder

remonstrate (rĭ-mŏn'strāt') *v.* to object; to protest strongly
protestar *v.* reclamar; oponerse fuertemente

rendezvous (rän'dā-vo͞o) *n.* a gathering place
lugar de reunión *s.* punto de encuentro

replenish (rĭ-plĕn'ĭsh) *v.* to fill up again
reabastecer *v.* volver a llenar

repudiate (rĭ-pyo͞o'dē-āt') *v.* to reject or renounce
repudiar *v.* rechazar o renunciar

repulse (rĭ-pŭls') *v.* to drive back by force
rechazar *v.* hacer retroceder a la fuerza

resign (rĭ-zīn') *v.* to submit or adapt oneself quietly without complaint
resignarse *v.* someterse o adaptarse sin queja

respite (rĕs'pĭt) *n.* a period of rest or relief
respiro *s.* período de descanso o de alivio

retaliating (rĭ-tăl'ē-āt'ĭng) *n.* taking revenge **retaliate** *v.*
vengador *s.* el que toma venganza **vengarse** *v.*

retinue (rĕt'n-o͞o') *n.* a group of attendants or followers
séquito *s.* grupo de ayudantes o seguidores

retrospective (rĕt'rə-spĕk'tĭv) *adj.* looking back into the past
retrospectivo *adj.* que mira al pasado

reverie (rĕv'ə-rē) *n.* daydream
ensueño *s.* arrobamiento

scintillating (sĭn'tl-āt-ĭng) *adj.* sparkling **scintillate** *v.*
centelleante *adj.* chispeante **centellear** *v.*

scruple (skro͞o'pəl) *n.* feeling of uneasiness or guilt that keeps a person from doing something
escrúpulo *s.* sentimiento de duda o de culpa que impide hacer algo

slovenly (slŭv'ən-lē) *adj.* untidy in personal appearance
desaliñado *adj.* descuidado en la apariencia personal

solace (sŏl'ĭs) *n.* comfort in sorrow or distress
solaz *s.* consuelo en el dolor o angustia

solstice (sŏl'stĭs) *n.* either of two days of the year when the sun is farthest from the celestial equator; the summer solstice is the longest day of the year, and the winter solstice is the shortest.
solsticio *s.* uno de los dos días en que el Sol está más lejos del ecuador; el solsticio de verano es el día más largo del año y el solsticio de invierno es el más corto.

somnambulant (sŏm-năm'byə-lənt') *adj.* sleepwalking
sonámbulo *adj.* que camina dormido

sordid (sôr'dĭd) *adj.* wretched; dirty; morally degraded
sórdido *adj.* vil; sucio; indecente

speculating (spĕk'yə-lā'tĭng) *n.* engaging in risky business transactions on the chance of a quick or considerable profit
especulación *s.* operaciones comerciales arriesgadas con la esperanza de obtener una ganancia rápida o considerable

subjugation (sŭb'jə-gā'shən) *n.* control by conquering
subyugación *s.* sometimiento por la fuerza

subservient (səb-sûr'vē-ənt) *adj.* acting like a servant
servil *adj.* que actúa como un sirviente

substantive (sŭb'stən-tĭv) *adj.* significant; with a strong basis
sustantivo *adj.* importante, fundamental o esencial

succumb (sə-kŭm') *v.* to give in, especially to overpowering force or strength
sucumbir *v.* rendirse, especialmente a una fuerza mayor

summarily (sə-mĕr'ə-lē) *adv.* quickly and without ceremony
sumariamente *adv.* rápidamente y sin ceremonia

supinely (so͞o-pīn'lē) *adv.* in a manner with the face upward
en posición supina *adv.* boca arriba

surfeit (sûr'fĭt) *n.* a fullness beyond the point of satisfaction
hartura *s.* saciedad más allá del punto de satisfacción

synthesis (sĭn'thĭ-sĭs) *n.* union of parts or elements into a whole
síntesis *s.* composición de un todo por la unión de sus partes

tableau (tăb'lo') *n.* dramatic scene or picture
cuadro *s.* escena dramática

tacitly (tăs'ĭt-lē) *adj.* silently
tácitamente *adv.* silenciosamente

tarry (tăr'ē) *v.* to delay
demorar *v.* tardar

temerity (tə-mər'ĭ-tē) *n.* foolish boldness
temeridad *s.* imprudencia

temperament (tĕm'prə-mənt) *n.* characteristic mode of emotional response
temperamento *s.* modo característico de respuesta emocional

tender (tĕn'dər) *v.* to offer formally
ofrecer *v.* presentar de modo formal

tentatively (tĕn'tə-tĭv-lē) *adv.* in a hesitant or uncertain manner
tentativamente *adv.* de modo provisional o cauteloso

tenuous (tĕn'yo͞o-əs) *adj.* having little substance or strength; flimsy
tenue *adj.* débil o delicado; endeble

tranquil (trăng'kwəl) *adj.* undisturbed; peaceful
tranquilo *adj.* quieto; sereno

transgress (trăns-grĕs') *v.* to violate a command or law
transgredir *v.* quebrantar una orden o una ley

tremulous (trĕm'yə-ləs) *adj.* trembling; quivering
trémulo *adj.* tembloroso

truculent (trŭk'yə-lənt) *adj.* eager for a fight; fierce
belicoso *adj.* agresivo; feroz

tyranny (tĭr'ə-nē) *n.* cruel and oppressive government or rule
tiranía *s.* gobierno cruel y opresivo

unassailable (ŭn'ə-sā'lə-bəl) *adj.* impossible to dispute or disprove
inexpugnable *adj.* que no se puede refutar

undulating (ŭn'jə-lā'tĭng) *adj.* appearing to move in waves **undulate** v.
ondulado *adj.* con movimiento de olas **ondular** v.

unremitting (ŭn'rĭ-mĭt'ĭng) *adj.* constant; never stopping
perseverante *adj.* constante; incansable

usurer (yo͞o'zhər-ər) *n.* one who lends money, at interest, especially at an unusually or unlawfully high rate of interest
usurero *s.* persona que presta dinero al interés, especialmente a una tasa muy alta o ilegal

vagary (vā'gə-rē) *n.* strange idea
capricho *s.* rareza

veritable (vĕr'ĭ-tə-bəl) *adj.* true; not unreal or imaginary
verdadero *adj.* real; auténtico

vigilant (vĭj'ə-lənt) *adj.* alert; watchful
vigilante *adj.* alerta; atento

vituperative (vī-to͞o'pər-ə-tĭv) *adj.* abusively critical
injurioso *adj.* que critica de modo ofensivo

whet (hwĕt) *adj.* sharpened **whet** *v.*
afilado *adj.* agudo **afilar** *v.*

wrangling (răng'glĭng) *adj.* arguing noisily **wrangle** *v.*
discutidor *adj.* que disputa en voz alta **discutir** *v.*

zealous (zĕl'əs) *adj.* eager and enthusiastic
fervoroso *adj.* dedicado y entusiasta

Pronunciation Key

Symbol	Examples
ă	**a**t, g**a**s
ā	**a**pe, d**ay**
ä	f**a**ther, b**a**rn
âr	f**air**, d**are**
b	**b**ell, ta**b**le
ch	**ch**in, lun**ch**
d	**d**ig, bore**d**
ĕ	**e**gg, t**e**n
ē	**e**vil, s**ee**, m**ea**l
f	**f**all, lau**gh**, **ph**rase
g	**g**old, bi**g**
h	**h**it, in**h**ale
hw	**wh**ite, every**wh**ere
ĭ	**i**nch, f**i**t
ī	**i**dle, m**y**, tr**ie**d
îr	d**ear**, h**ere**
j	**j**ar, **g**em, ba**dge**
k	**k**eep, **c**at, lu**ck**
l	**l**oad, ratt**le**
m	**m**an, see**m**
n	**n**ight, mitte**n**
ng	si**ng**, ha**ng**er
ŏ	**o**dd, n**o**t
ō	**o**pen, r**oa**d, gr**ow**
ô	**aw**ful, b**ough**t, h**o**rse
oi	c**oi**n, b**oy**
o͝o	l**oo**k, f**u**ll
o͞o	r**oo**t, gl**ue**, thr**ough**
ou	**ou**t, c**ow**
p	**p**ig, ca**p**
r	**r**ose, sta**r**
s	**s**it, fa**ce**
sh	**sh**e, ma**sh**
t	**t**ap, hopp**ed**
th	**th**ing, wi**th**
th	**th**en, o**th**er
ŭ	**u**p, n**u**t
ûr	f**ur**, **ear**n, b**ir**d, w**or**m
v	**v**an, sa**ve**
w	**w**eb, t**w**ice
y	**y**ard, law**y**er
z	**z**oo, rea**s**on
zh	trea**s**ure, gara**ge**
ə	**a**wake, ev**e**n, penc**i**l, pil**o**t, foc**u**s
ər	p**er**form, lett**er**

Sounds in Foreign Words

Symbol	Examples
KH	*German* i**ch**, au**ch**; *Scottish* lo**ch**
N	*French* e**n**tre, bo**n**, fi**n**
œ	*French* f**eu**, c**œu**r; *German* sch**ö**n
ü	*French* **u**tile, r**ue**; *German* gr**ü**n

Stress Marks

ʹ This mark indicates that the preceding syllable receives the primary stress. For example, in the word *language*, the first syllable is stressed: lăngʹgwĭj.

ʹ This mark is used only in words in which more than one syllable is stressed. It indicates that the preceding syllable is stressed, but somewhat more weakly than the syllable receiving the primary stress. In the word *literature*, for example, the first syllable receives the primary stress, and the last syllable receives a weaker stress: lĭtʹər-ə-cho͝orʹ.

INDEX OF FINE ART

Index of Skills

D

E

F

G

H

J

K

L

M

Q

R

T

U

V

W

Y

INDEX OF TITLES & AUTHORS

Page numbers that appear in italics refer to biographical information.

T

U

V

W

Y

ACKNOWLEDGMENTS

INTRODUCTORY UNIT

Scribner: Excerpt from *The Great Gatsby* by F. Scott Fitzgerald. Copyright 1925 by Charles Scribner's Sons. Copyright renewed 1953 by Frances Scott Fitzgerald Lanahan. Reprinted with the permission of Scribner, a Division of Simon & Schuster, Inc.

UNIT 1

American Anthropological Association: "The World on the Turtle's Back," from *The Great Tree and the Longhouse: The Culture of the Iroquois* (pp. 12–19) by Hazel W. Hertzberg. Copyright © 1966 American Anthropological Association. Reproduced by permission of the American Anthropological Association. Not for sale or further reproduction.

University of Nebraska Press: "Coyote and the Buffalo," from *Coyote Stories* by Mourning Dove. Collected in Masterpieces of American Indian Literature. Published by the University of Nebraska Press. Reprinted by permission.

N. Scott Momaday: Excerpt from *The Way to Rainy Mountain* by N. Scott Momaday. Copyright © N. Scott Momaday. Reprinted by permission of the author.

Scribner: From *Cabeza De Vaca's Adventures in the Unknown Interior of America,* translated and annotated by Cyclone Covey. Copyright © 1961 Macmillan Publishing Company. Reprinted with the permission of Scribner, a Division of Simon & Schuster, Inc.

University of North Carolina Press: From *The Complete Works of Captain John Smith,* 1580–1631, edited by Philip L. Barbour, with a foreword by Thad W. Tate. Published for the Omohundro Institute of Early American History and Culture. Copyright © 1986 by the University of North Carolina Press. Used by permission of the publisher.

Alfred A. Knopf: From *Of Plymouth Plantation,* 1620–1647 by William Bradford, edited by Samuel Eliot Morison. Copyright 1952 by Samuel Eliot Morison and renewed 1980 by Emily M. Beck. Used by permission of Alfred A. Knopf, a division of Random House, Inc.

Viking Penguin: *The Crucible* by Arthur Miller. Copyright 1952, 1953, 1954, renewed © 1980, 1981, 1982 by Arthur Miller. Used by permission of Viking Penguin, a division of Penguin Group (USA) Inc.

Thirteen/WNET New York: "McCarthyism". Courtesy Thirteen/ WNET New York.

New York Times: From "The Demons of Salem, With Us Still" by Victor Navasky, *The New York Times,* September 8, 1996. Copyright © 1996 The New York Times Co. All rights reserved. Used by permission and protected by the Copyright Laws of the United States. The printing, copying, redistribution, or retransmission of the Material without express written permission is prohibited.

Grove/Atlantic: Excerpt from *Timebends* by Arthur Miller. Copyright © 1987 by Arthur Miller. Used by permission of Grove/Atlantic, Inc.

Rolling Stone: From "The Crucible (film review)" by Peter Travers, *Rolling Stone,* December 12, 1996. © Rolling Stone LLC 1996. All rights reserved. Reprinted by permission.

U.S. News & World Report: "50 Ways to Fix Your Life" by Carolyn Kleiner Butler, *U.S. News & World Report,* 27 December 2004. Copyright © 2004 U.S. News & World Report, L.P. Reprinted with permission.

UNIT 2

Cynthia G. La Ferle: "Thoreau Still Beckons, if I Can Take My Laptop" by Cynthia G. La Ferle, *The Christian Science Monitor,* 3 October 1997. Copyright © 1997 by Cynthia G. La Ferle. Reprinted by permission of the author.

Navajivan Trust: Excerpt from "Readiness for Satyagraha" by Mahatma Gandhi, from *The Essential Writings of Mahatma Gandhi,* edited by Raghavan Iyer. Published by Oxford University Press. Reprinted by permission of the Navajivan Trust.

Pocket Books: Excerpt from *Danse Macabre* by Stephen King. Copyright © 1981 by Stephen King. All rights reserved. Reprinted with the permission of Pocket Books, a Division of Simon & Schuster, Inc.

Persea Books: "The Daydreamer" by Magdalena Gómez, from *Working Days: Short Stories About Teenagers at Work,* edited by Anne Mazer. Reprinted by permission of Persea Books, Inc.

Veronica Chambers: "The Secret Latina" by Veronica Chambers, *Essence,* July 2000. Copyright © 2000 by Veronica Chambers. Reprinted by permission of the author.

UNIT 3

Harvard University Press: Excerpt from "My life closed twice before its close—" by Emily Dickinson. Reprinted by permission of the publishers and the Trustees of Amherst College from *The Poems of Emily Dickinson,* Thomas H. Johnson, ed., Cambridge, Mass.: The Belknap Press of Harvard University Press, Copyright 1951, 1955, 1979, 1983 by the President and Fellows of Harvard College.

Agencia Literaria Carmen Balcells and Didier Tisdel Jaén: "Ode to Walt Whitman" by Pablo Neruda, translated by Didier Tisdel Jaén. Published in *Nuevas odas elementales* and *Homage to Walt Whitman: A Collection of Poems from the Spanish.* © Fundación Pablo Neruda, 2009. Translation copyright © Didier Tisdel Jaén. Used by permission of Agencia Literaria Carmen Balcells, S. A. and Didier Tisdel Jaén.

Harvard University Press: "Because I could not stop for Death—" by Emily Dickinson. Reprinted by permission of the publishers and the Trustees of Amherst College from *The Poems of Emily Dickinson,* Thomas H. Johnson, ed., Cambridge, Mass.: The Belknap Press of Harvard University Press, Copyright © 1951, 1955, 1979, 1983 by the President and Fellows of Harvard College.

"Success is counted sweetest" by Emily Dickinson. Reprinted by permission of the publishers and the Trustees of Amherst College from *The Poems of Emily Dickinson,* Thomas H. Johnson, ed., Cambridge, Mass.: The Belknap Press of Harvard University Press, Copyright 1951, 1955, 1979, 1983 by the President and Fellows of Harvard College.

"Much Madness is divinest Sense—" by Emily Dickinson. Reprinted by permission of the publishers and the Trustees of Amherst College from *The Poems of Emily Dickinson,* Thomas H. Johnson, ed., Cambridge, Mass.: The Belknap Press of Harvard University Press, Copyright 1951, 1955, 1979, 1983 by the President and Fellows of Harvard College.

"My life closed twice before its close—" by Emily Dickinson. Reprinted by permission of the publishers and the Trustees of Amherst College from *The Poems of Emily Dickinson,* Thomas H. Johnson, ed., Cambridge, Mass.: The Belknap Press of Harvard University Press, Copyright 1951, 1955, 1979, 1983 by the President and Fellows of Harvard College.

"The Soul selects her own Society" by Emily Dickinson. Reprinted by permission of the publishers and the Trustees of Amherst College from *The Poems of Emily Dickinson,* Thomas H. Johnson, ed., Cambridge, Mass.: The Belknap Press of Harvard University Press, Copyright 1951, 1955, 1979, 1983 by the President and Fellows of Harvard College.

"I heard a Fly buzz—when I died—" by Emily Dickinson. Reprinted by permission of the publishers and the Trustees of Amherst College from *The Poems of Emily Dickinson,* Thomas H. Johnson, ed., Cambridge, Mass.: The Belknap Press of Harvard University Press, Copyright 1951, 1955, 1979, 1983 by the President and Fellows of Harvard College.

"My life had stood—a Loaded Gun" by Emily Dickinson. Reprinted by permission of the publishers and the Trustees of Amherst College from *The Poems of Emily Dickinson,* Thomas H. Johnson, ed., Cambridge, Mass.: The Belknap Press of Harvard University Press, Copyright 1951, 1955, 1979, 1983 by the President and Fellows of Harvard College.

"Letter to Thomas Wentworth Higginson, April 16, 1892" by Emily Dickinson. Reprinted by permission of the publishers and the Trustees of Amherst College from *Letters of Emily Dickinson,* Thomas H. Johnson, ed., Cambridge, Mass.: The Belknap Press of Harvard University Press, Copyright 1951, 1955, 1979, 1983 by the President and Fellows of Harvard College.

Scribner: "Letter, January 1861," from *R.E. Lee: A Biography* by Douglas Southall Freeman. Copyright © 1934, 1935 by Charles Scribner's Sons, copyright renewed © 1962, 1963 by Inez Goddin Freeman. Reprinted with the permission of Scribner, an Division of Simon & Schuster, Inc.

Basic Books: From "Letter, July 14, 1861" by Sullivan Ballou, from *For Love & Liberty: The Untold Civil War Story of Major Sullivan Ballou & His Famous Love Letter* by Robin Young. Copyright © 2005 Robin Young. Reprinted by permission of Basic Books, a member of the Perseus Books Group.

Harvard University Press: "The Wind begun to knead the Grass" by Emily Dickinson. Reprinted by permission of the publishers and the Trustees of Amherst College from *The Poems of Emily Dickinson,* Thomas H. Johnson, ed., Cambridge, Mass.: The Belknap Press of Harvard University Press, Copyright © 1951, 1955, 1979, 1983 by the President and Fellows of Harvard College.

UNIT 4

HarperCollins Publishers: From *The Autobiography of Mark Twain,* edited by Charles Neider. Copyright © 1917, 1940, 1958, 1959 by The Mark Twain Company, renewed 1987. Copyright 1924, 1945, 1952 by Clara Clemens Samossoud. Copyright © 1959 by Charles Neider, renewed 1987. Reprinted by permission of HarperCollins Publishers.

Viking Penguin: "Sumus Quod Sumus," from *Lake Wobegone Days* by Garrison Keillor. Copyright © 1985 by Garrison Keillor. Used by permission of Viking Penguin, a division of Penguin Group (USA) Inc.

Brian Doyle: "Joyas Voladoras" by Brian Doyle from *The American Scholar,* Autumn 2004. Copyright © 2004 by Brian Doyle. Reprinted by permission of the author.

Texas Monthly: Excerpt from "The Next Frontier" by S. C. Gwynne, *Texas Monthly,* August 2007. Reprinted by permission of Texas Monthly.

UNIT 5

New Directions Publishing Corporation: "The Red Wheelbarrow," from *Collected Poems,* 1909–1939, Volume I by William Carlos Williams. Copyright © 1938 by New Directions Publishing Corp. Reprinted by permission of New Directions Publishing Corp.

Alfred A. Knopf and Harold Ober Associates: "Harlem," from *The Collected Poems of Langston Hughes* by Langston Hughes, edited by Arnold Rampersad with David Roessel, Associate Editor. Copyright © 1994 by the Estate of Langston Hughes. Used by permission of Alfred A. Knopf, a division of Random House, Inc. and Harold Ober Associates Incorporated.

"The Negro Speaks of Rivers," from *The Collected Poems of Langston Hughes* by Langston Hughes, edited by Arnold Rampersad with David Roessel, Associate Editor. Copyright © 1994 by the Estate of Langston Hughes. Used by permission of Alfred A. Knopf, a division of Random House, Inc. and Harold Ober Associates Incorporated.

"I, Too," from *The Collected Poems of Langston Hughes* by Langston Hughes, edited by Arnold Rampersad with David Roessel, Associate Editor. Copyright © 1994 by the Estate of Langston Hughes. Used by permission of Alfred A. Knopf, a division of Random House, Inc. and Harold Ober Associates Incorporated.

"The Weary Blues," from *The Collected Poems of Langston Hughes* by Langston Hughes, edited by Arnold Rampersad with David Roessel, Associate Editor. Copyright © 1994 by the Estate of Langston Hughes. Used by permission of Alfred A. Knopf, a division of Random House, Inc. and Harold Ober Associates Incorporated.

Viking Penguin: "My City," from *Saint Peter Relates an Incident* by James Weldon Johnson. Copyright 1935 by James Weldon Johnson, © renewed 1963 by Grace Nail Johnson. Used by permission of Viking Penguin, a division of Penguin Group (USA) Inc.

Schomburg Center for Research in Black Culture: "If We Must Die" by Claude McKay. Courtesy of the Literary Representative for the Works of Claude McKay, Schomburg Center for Research in Black Culture, The New York Public Library, Astor, Lenox and Tilden Foundations.

Thompson and Thompson: "Any Human to Another," from *The Medea and Some Poems* by Countee Cullen. Copyrights held by The Amistad Research Center, Tulane University. Administered by Thompson and Thompson, Brooklyn, NY. Reprinted by permission.

Liveright Publishing Corporation: "Storm Ending," from *Cane* by Jean Toomer. Copyright 1923 by Boni & Liveright, renewed 1951 by Jean Toomer. Used by permission of Liveright Publishing Corporation.

Harold Ober Associates: "A Black Man Talks of Reaping," from *Personals* by Arna Bontemps. Copyright © 1963 by Arna Bontemps. Reprinted by permission of Harold Ober Associates Incorporated.

Victoria Sanders & Associates: "How It Feels to Be Colored Me" by Zora Neale Hurston. Used with the permission of the Zora Neale Hurston Trust.

International Creative Management: "Thoughts on the African-American Novel" by Toni Morrison, Copyright © 1983 by Toni Morrison. Reprinted by permission of International Creative Management, Inc.

Houghton Mifflin Harcourt: "Chicago," and "Grass," from *Chicago Poems* by Carl Sandburg. Copyright 1916 by Holt, Rinehart and Winston and renewed 1944 by Carl Sandburg. Reprinted by permission of Houghton Mifflin Harcourt Publishing Company. This material may not be reproduced in any form or by any means without the prior written permission of the publisher.

Henry Holt and Company: "Acquainted with the Night" by Robert Frost, from *The Poetry of Robert Frost,* edited by Edward Connery Lathem. Copyright 1916, 1923, 1928, 1930, 1939, 1969 by Henry Holt and Company, copyright 1944, 1951, 1956, 1958 by Robert Frost, copyright © 1967 by Lesley Frost Ballantine. Reprinted by arrangement with Henry Holt and Company, LLC.

"Nothing Gold Can Stay" by Robert Frost, from *The Poetry of Robert Frost,* edited by Edward Connery Lathem. Copyright 1916, 1923, 1928, 1930, 1939, 1969 by Henry Holt and Company, copyright 1944, 1951, 1956, 1958 by Robert Frost, copyright © 1967 by Lesley Frost Ballantine. Reprinted by arrangement with Henry Holt and Company, LLC.

"Out, Out—" by Robert Frost, from *The Poetry of Robert Frost,* edited by Edward Connery Lathem. Copyright 1916, 1923, 1928, 1930, 1939, 1969 by Henry Holt and Company, copyright 1944, 1951, 1956, 1958 by Robert Frost, copyright © 1967 by Lesley Frost Ballantine. Reprinted by arrangement with Henry Holt and Company, LLC.

"The Death of the Hired Man" by Robert Frost, from *The Poetry of Robert Frost,* edited by Edward Connery Lathem. Copyright 1916, 1923, 1928, 1930, 1939, 1969 by Henry Holt and Company, copyright 1944, 1951, 1956, 1958 by Robert Frost, copyright © 1967 by Lesley Frost Ballantine. Reprinted by arrangement with Henry Holt and Company, LLC.

New Directions Publishing Corporation: "In a Station of the Metro," from *Personae* by Ezra Pound. Copyright © 1926 by Ezra Pound. Reprinted by permission of New Directions Publishing Corp.

"Helen," from *Collected Poems, 1912–1944* by HD (Hilda Doolittle). Copyright © 1982 by The Estate of Hilda Doolittle. Reprinted by permission of New Directions Publishing Corp.

"Spring and All, Section I," and "This is Just to Say," from *Collected Poems,* 1909–1939, Volume I by William Carlos Williams. Copyright © 1938 by New Directions Publishing Corp. Reprinted by permission of New Directions Publishing Corp.

Liveright Publishing Corporation: "anyone lived in a pretty how town," from *Complete Poems: 1904–1962* by E. E. Cummings, edited by George J. Firmage. Copyright 1940, © 1968, 1991 by the Trustees for the E. E. Cummings Trust. Used by permission of Liveright Publishing Corporation.

Scribner: "Poetry," from *The Collected Poems of Marianne Moore* by Marianne Moore. Copyright © 1935 by Marianne Moore, copyright renewed © 1963 by Marianne Moore and T.S. Eliot. Reprinted with the permission of Scribner, a Division of Simon & Schuster, Inc.

Elizabeth Barnett, Literary Executor: "Recuerdo" by Edna St. Vincent Millay. From *Collected Poems,* HarperCollins. Copyright © 1922, 1950 by Edna St. Vincent Millay. All rights reserved. Used by permission of Elizabeth Barnett, Literary Executor.

Faber and Faber: "The Love Song of J. Alfred Prufrock," from *Collected Poems, 1909–1962* by T. S. Eliot. Reprinted by permission of Faber and Faber Limited.

Scribner: Excerpt from *The Great Gatsby* by F. Scott Fitzgerald. Copyright 1925 by Charles Scribner's Sons. Copyright renewed 1953 by Frances Scott Fitzgerald Lanahan. Reprinted with the permission of Scribner, a Division of Simon & Schuster, Inc.

Scribner and Random House Group Ltd: "In Another Country," from *Men Without Women* by Ernest Hemingway. Copyright 1927 Charles Scribner's Sons. Copyright renewed 1955 by Ernest Hemingway. Reprinted with the permission of Scribner, a Division of Simon & Schuster, Inc and The Random House Group Ltd.

Newsweek: Excerpt from "Healing War's Wounds" by Karen Breslau, *Newsweek,* September 11, 2006. Copyright © 2006 Newsweek, Inc. All rights reserved. Used by permission and protected by the Copyright Laws of the United States. The printing, copying, redistribution, or retransmission of the Material without express written permission is prohibited.

Viking Penguin: From *The Grapes of Wrath* by John Steinbeck. Copyright 1939, renewed © 1967 by John Steinbeck. Used by permission of Viking Penguin, a division of Penguin Group (USA) Inc.

Life: "The Grapes of Wrath: Photo Essay," *Life,* 5 June 1939. Copyright 1939 Life Inc. Reprinted with permission. All rights reserved.

Houghton Mifflin Harcourt: "The Jilting of Granny Weatherall," from *Flowering Judas and Other Stories* by Katherine Anne Porter. Copyright 1930 and renewed 1958 by Katherine Anne Porter. Reprinted by permission of Houghton Mifflin Harcourt Publishing Company. This material may not be reproduced in any form or by any means without prior written permission of the publisher.

"A Worn Path," from *A Curtain of Green and Other Stories* by Eudora Welty. Copyright 1941 and renewed 1969 by Eudora Welty. Reprinted by permission of Houghton Mifflin Harcourt Publishing Company. This material may not be reproduced in any form or by any means without prior written permission of the publisher.

Harvard University Press: Reprinted by permission of the publisher from *One Writer's Beginnings* by Eudora Welty, pp. 99–100, Cambridge, Mass: Harvard University Press, Copyright © 1983, 1984 by Eudora Welty.

Random House: "A Rose for Emily," from *Collected Stories of William Faulkner* by William Faulkner. Copyright 1930 and renewed 1958 by William Faulkner. Used by permission of Random House, Inc.

Houghton Mifflin Harcourt: "The Life You Save May Be Your Own," from *A Good Man Is Hard to Find and Other Stories* by Flannery O'Connor. Copyright 1953 by Flannery O'Connor and renewed 1981 by Regina O'Connor. Reprinted by permission of Houghton Mifflin Harcourt Publishing Company. This material may not be reproduced in any form or by any means without prior written permission of the publisher.

Scribner and HarperCollins Publishers Ltd: "A New Kind of War" by Ernest Hemingway, from *By-Line: Ernest Hemingway,* edited by William White. Copyright © 1937 by New York Times Company. Copyright © renewed 1965 by Mary Hemingway, By-Line Ernest Hemingway, Inc., and The New York Times Company. Reprinted with the permission of Scribner, a Division of Simon & Schuster, Inc. and HarperCollins Publishers Ltd.

Viking Penguin: "A Book of Great Short Stories," from *The Portable Dorothy Parker* by Dorothy Parker, edited by Marion Meade. Copyright 1927, renewed © 1955 by Dorothy Parker. Used by permission of Viking Penguin, a division of Penguin Group (USA) Inc.

Tilbury House, Publishers: Excerpt from "Salt Water Farm," from *One Man's Meat* by E. B. White. Text copyright © 1939 by E. B. White. Copyright renewed. Reprinted by permission of Tilbury House, Publishers, Gardiner, Maine.

HarperCollins Publishers: "The Sky Blue Ball," from *Small Avalanches and Other Stories* by Joyce Carol Oates. Copyright © 2003 by The Ontario Review, Inc. Used by permission of HarperCollins Publishers.

Reader's Digest: "Change of Heart" by Mary A. Fischer, from *Reader's Digest,* March 2005. Copyright © 2005 The Reader's Digest Association, Inc. Reprinted by permission of Reader's Digest.

UNIT 6

Barbara Hogenson Agency: From *Our Town* by Thornton Wilder. Copyright © 1938, 1965 Wilder Family LLC. Reprinted by arrangement with Wilder Family LLC and the Barbara Hogenson Agency.

Georges Borchardt: From *The Glass Menagerie* by Tennessee Williams. Copyright © 1945, renewed 1973 The University of the South. Reprinted by permission of Georges Borchardt, Inc. for the Estate of Tennessee Williams.

Viking Penguin: From *Death of a Salesman* by Arthur Miller. Copyright 1949, renewed © 1977 by Arthur Miller. Used by permission of Viking Penguin, a division of Penguin Group (USA) Inc.

Random House: From *A Raisin in the Sun* by Lorraine Hansberry. Copyright © 1958 by Robert Nemiroff, as an unpublished work. Copyright © 1959, 1966, 1984 by Robert Nemiroff. Copyright renewed 1986, 1987 by Robert Nemiroff. Used by permission of Random House, Inc.

Viking Penguin: "Symptoms," from *Once There Was a War* by John Steinbeck. Copyright 1943, 1958 by John Steinbeck. Renewed © 1971 by Elaine Steinbeck, John Steinbeck IV, and Thomas Steinbeck. Used by permission of Viking Penguin, a division of Penguin Group (USA) Inc.

Farrar, Straus and Giroux: "The Death of the Ball Turret Gunner," from *The Complete Poems* by Randall Jarrell. Copyright © 1969, renewed 1997 by Mary von S. Jarrell. Reprinted by permission of Farrar, Straus and Giroux, LLC. Caution: Users are warned that this work is protected under copyright laws and downloading is strictly prohibited. The right to reproduce or transfer the work via any medium must be secured with Farrar, Straus and Giroux, LLC.

Dell Publishing: "Adam," from *Welcome to the Monkey House* by Kurt Vonnegut, Jr. Copyright 1954 by Kurt Vonnegut, Jr. Used by permission of Dell Publishing, a division of Random House, Inc.

Viking Penguin: "October 1944," from *If This Is a Man (Survival in Auschwitz)* by Primo Levi, translated by Stuart Woolf. Copyright © 1959 by Orion Press, Inc., © 1958 by Guilio Einaudi editore S.P.A. Used by permission of Viking Penguin, a division of Penguin Group (USA) Inc.

Houghton Mifflin Harcourt: "Ambush," from *The Things The Carried* by Tim O'Brien. Copyright © 1990 by Tim O'Brien. Reprinted by permission of Houghton Mifflin Harcourt Publishing Company. All rights reserved.

Writers House: "Letter from Birmingham Jail" by Martin Luther King Jr. Copyright 1963 Dr. Martin Luther King Jr.; copyright renewed 1991 Coretta Scott King. Reprinted by arrangement with The Heirs to the Estate of Martin Luther King Jr., c/o Writers House as agent for the proprietor New York, NY.

Dudley Randall Literary Estate: "Ballad of Birmingham," from *Cities Burning* by Dudley Randall. Copyright © 1965 by Dudley Randall. Reprinted by permission of the Dudley Randall Literary Estate.

Writers House: From *Stride Toward Freedom* by Martin Luther King Jr. Copyright 1958 Dr. Martin Luther King Jr.; copyright renewed 1986 Coretta Scott King. Reprinted by arrangement with The Heirs to the Estate of Martin Luther King Jr., c/o Writers House as agent for the proprietor New York, NY.

Pathfinder Press: "Necessary to Protect Ourselves" by Malcolm X, from *Malcolm X: The Last Speeches,* edited by Bruce Perry. Copyright © 1989 Betty Shabazz, Bruce Perry, Pathfinder Press. All rights reserved. Reprinted by permission of Pathfinder Press.

Cesar E. Chavez Foundation: TM/© 2008 the Cesar E. Chavez Foundation. www.chavezfoundation.org

Doubleday: Excerpt from *Coming of Age in Mississippi* by Anne Moody. Copyright © 1968 by Anne Moody. Used by permission of Doubleday, a division of Random House, Inc.

HarperCollins Publishers: "Revolutionary Dreams," from *The Women and the Men* by Nikki Giovanni. Copyright © 1971, 1974, 1975 by Nikki Giovanni. Reprinted by permission of HarperCollins Publishers.

James Baldwin Estate: "My Dungeon Shook: Letter to My Nephew on the One Hundredth Anniversary of the Emancipation" by James Baldwin. Copyright © 1962 by James Baldwin. Copyright renewed. Collected in *The Fire Next Time,* published by Vintage Books. Used by arrangement with the James Baldwin Estate.

Sandra Dijkstra Literary Agency: "Mother Tongue" by Amy Tan. Copyright © 1989 by Amy Tan. First appeared in *The Threepenny Review.* Reprinted by permission of the author and the Sandra Dijkstra Literary Agency.

Houghton Mifflin Harcourt: Excerpt from "In Search of Our Mothers' Gardens," in *In Search of Our Mothers' Gardens: Womanist Prose* by Alice Walker. Copyright © 1974 by Alice Walker. Reprinted by permission of Houghton Mifflin Harcourt Publishing Company. This material may not be reproduced in any form or by any means without prior written permission of the publisher.

"Women," from *Revolutionary Petunias & Other Poems* by Alice Walker. Copyright © 1970 and renewed 1998 by Alice Walker. Reprinted by permission of Houghton Mifflin Harcourt Publishing Company. This material may not be reproduced in any form or by any means without prior written permission of the publisher.

Susan Bergholz Literary Services: "Straw Into Gold" by Sandra Cisneros. Copyright © 1987 by Sandra Cisneros. First published in *The Texas Observer,* September 1987. Reprinted by permission of Susan Bergholz Literary Services, New York, NY and Lamy, NM. All rights reserved.

Brooks Permissions: "Life for My Child Is Simple," and "Primer for Blacks" by Gwendolyn Brooks. Reprinted by consent of Brooks Permissions.

Rita Dove: "Adolescence–III," from *The Yellow House on the Corner* by Rita Dove. Carnegie Mellon University Press. Copyright © 1980 by Rita Dove. Reprinted by permission of the author.

"Testimonial," from *On the Bus with Rosa Parks* by Rita Dove. W. W. Norton and Company. First published in Poetry magazine, January 1998. Copyright © 1999 by Rita Dove. Reprinted by permission of the author.

University of Pittsburgh Press: "Forgetfulness," and "The Man in the Moon," from *Questions About Angels* by Billy Collins. Copyright © 1991, Billy Collins. Reprinted by permission of the University of Pittsburgh Press.

Barbara Hogenson Agency: Excerpt from "The Secret Life of Walter Mitty," from *My World—And Welcome To It* by James Thurber. Copyright © 1942 by James Thurber, copyright renewed 1970 by Rosemary A. Thurber. Reprinted by arrangement with Rosemary Thurber and The Barbara Hogenson Agency. All rights reserved.

Cable News Network: "Virtual Worlds" from *CNN,* August 8, 2007. Copyright © 2007 Cable News Network. Reprinted by permission of Cable News Network.

UNIT 7

Los Angeles Times: From " 'Grapes of Wrath' Author Guards Self From Threats at Moody Gulch" by Tom Cameron, *Los Angeles Times,* July 9, 1939. Los Angeles Times, Copyright © 1939. Reprinted with permission.

STUDENT RESOURCE BANK

Random House: Excerpt from "History of the National Weather Service," from the Random House Web site (http://www.randomhouse.com/features/isaacsstorm/science/history.html). Copyright © 1999 by Random House, Inc. Used by permission of Random House, Inc.

Best Friends Animal Society: Adapted from "Katrina's South American Sister," from *Best Friends Magazine,* November/December 2005. Copyright © 2005 by Best Friends Animal Society. Adapted with permission.

Houghton Mifflin Harcourt: word definition: ambasador. Copyright © 2006 Houghton Mifflin Company. Reproduced by permission from *The American Heritage Dictionary of the English Language, Fourth Edition.*

Houghton Mifflin Harcourt: word definition: community. Copyright © 2006 Houghton Mifflin Company. Reproduced by permission from *The American Heritage Dictionary of the English Language, Fourth Edition.*

ART CREDITS

CONSULTANTS

Janet Allen © Duane McCubrey; *Arthur Applebee* © Mark Schmidt; *Kylene Beers* © Sam Dudgeon/Houghton Mifflin Harcourt; *Jim Burke* © Bruce Forrester; *Douglas Carnine* © Houghton Mifflin Harcourt; *Carol Jago* Maggie's Photography, Pacific Palisades, CA; *Yvette Jackson* © Howard Gollub; *Robert Jimenez* © Tamra Stallings; *Judith Langer* © Mark Schmidt; *Robert Marzano* © Robert J. Marzano; *Donna Ogle* © Houghton Mifflin Harcourt; *Carol Booth Olson* © Dawson & Associates Photography; *Carol Tomlinson* © Gitchell's Studio; *May Lou McClosky* © Michael Romeo; *Lydia Stack* © Monica Ani; *William McBride* © William McBride; *David Considine* © Bill Caldwell; *Larkin Pauluzzi* © Gabriel Pauluzzi; *Lisa Scheffler* © Steven Scheffler.

TABLE OF CONTENTS

FM9 © Getty Images; **FM12** *left, right* The Granger Collection, New York; **FM15** © PunchStock; **FM16** *left* © 1996 Gary Kelley; *right* © Gail Mooney/Masterfile; **FM18** © PunchStock; **FM19** *left* The Granger Collection, New York; *right* © Martin Rogers/Getty Images; **FM21** © PunchStock; **FM22** *left* © Bettmann/Corbis; *right* © Juniors Bildarchiv/Age Fotostock; **FM24** © PunchStock; **FM25** *left, Autoportrait* (1925), Tamara De Lempicka. Oil on wood, 35 cm x 26 cm. Private collection. © 2008 Artists Rights Society (ARS), New York/ADAGP, Paris; *right, The Cotton Club in Harlem, New York* (1930). Black and white photograph. Private collection. © Bridgeman Art Library; **FM28** © PunchStock; **FM29** *left, Thinking* (1990), Carlton Murrell. Oil on board. Private collection. © Bridgeman Art Library; *right* The Granger Collection, New York; **FM31** © PunchStock; **FM32** *left* The Granger Collection, New York; *inset right* © Bettmann/Corbis; *right* © Design Pics, Inc./Alamy Images.

STUDENT GUIDE TO ACADEMIC SUCCESS

FM39 © Age Fotostock America, Inc.; **FM40** Maggie's Photography, Pacific Palisades, CA; **FM42** © PunchStock.

EXPLORING AMERICAN LITERATURE

Verso *top* The Granger Collection, New York; *center* © Images.com/Corbis; *bottom* Library of Congress; **1** *top left, Kindred Spirits* (1849), Asher Brown Durand. © Francis G. Mayer/Corbis; *top right* © Bettmann/Corbis; *bottom* © 20th Century Fox Film Corp. All rights reserved/Courtesy The Everett Collection; **2** *left, The Mayflower in Plymouth Harbor* (1882), William Formby Halsall. © Pilgrim Hall Museum, Plymouth, Massachusetts; *right* Library of Congress; **3** *left* © Reza Estakhrian/Getty Images; *right* © James P. Blair/National Geographic Image Collection; **4** *#1* © Bettmann/Corbis; *#2* © Richard T. Nowitz/Corbis; *#3* Detail of *The Bloody Massacre perpetrated in... Boston on March 5th, 1770* (1770), Paul Revere. Colored engraving. Private collection. Art Resource, New York; *#4* © 1995 Gary Kelley; *#5* Detail of *Wanderer Above a Sea of Fog* (1817), Casper David Friedrich. Oil on canvas, 94.8 cm x 74.8 cm. Inv.: 5161 On permanent loan from the Foundation for the Promotion of the Hamburg Art Collections. Hamburger Kunsthalle, Hamburg, Germany. Photo by Elke Walford. © Bildarchiv Preussischer Kulturbesitz/Art Resource, New York; **5** *#1* © New York Public Library, Schomburg Center; *#2* Library of Congress; *#3* © Hulton-Deutsch Collection/Corbis; *#4* Detail of *Street Shadows* (1959), Jacob Lawrence. Egg tempera on hardboard, 24" x 30". Private collection, New York. Photo © Gwendolyn Knight Lawrence/Art Resource, New York. © 2008 The Jacob and Gwendolyn Lawrence Foundation, Seattle/Artists Rights Society (ARS), New York; *#5* Detail of *The Green Machine* (1977), Frank Dahmer. Screenprint on paper, 13 1/2" x 17 1/4". © National Vietnam Veterans Art Museum; **6** *#1, #2* The Granger Collection, New York; *#3* © Culver Pictures/The Art Archive; *#4* Detail of *Autoportrait* (1925), Tamara De Lempicka. Oil on wood, 35 cm x 26 cm. Private collection. © 2008 Artists Rights Society (ARS), New York/ADAGP, Paris; **8** © Culver Pictures/The Art Archive; **14** *left* © image100/Corbis; *center* © Doug Menuez/Getty Images; *right* © Time & Life Pictures/Getty Images.

UNIT 1

19 *top* © Manuscripts, Archives and Special Collections, Washington State University Libraries, Neg No. 89–052; *bottom* The Granger Collection, New York; **20** *left* Detail of *Mandan Offering the Buffalo Skull.* Edward S. Curtis Collection. © McCormick Library of Special Collections, Northwestern University Library; *right* Detail of *Arrival of the English in Virginia* (1585–1588), Theodore de Bry. from *Admiranta Narratio*, page 47. Engraving. Service Historique de la Marine, Vincennes, France. Photo © Giraudon/Art Resource, New York; **21** *left* Detail of *Fire, allegory* (1566), Giuseppe Arcimboldo. Painted for Emperor Maximilian II. Limewood, 66.5 cm x 51 cm. Inv 1585. Kunsthistorisches Museum, Vienna. Photo © Erich Lessing/Art Resource, New York; *right* Library of Congress; **22** *The Mayflower in Plymouth Harbor* (1882), William Formby Halsall. © Pilgrim Hall Museum, Plymouth, Massachusetts; **24** *top, bottom* The Granger Collection, New York; **26** *Raven and the First Men* (1980), Bill Reid. Yellow cedar. Courtesy University of British Columbia Museum of Anthropology, Vancouver, Canada; **28** © Richard T. Nowitz/Corbis; **29** The Granger Collection, New York; **30** *Soldier of the Revolution* (1876), George Willoughby Maynard. Oil on canvas, 51" x 39". Photo © Christie's Images Ltd.; **31** *George Washington (Vaughn Portrait)* (1795), Gilbert Stuart. Oil on canvas, 28 3/4" x 23 3/4", Andrew W. Mellon Collection. © 2005 Board of Trustees, National Gallery of Art, Washington D.C.; **32** *top* Library of Congress; *center left, Whaler off the Vineyard-Outward Bound* (1859), William Bradford. Oil on Fiberboard, 16" x 24 ". Smithsonian American Art Museum, Washington, D.C. © Smithsonian American Art Museum, Washington, D.C./Art Resource, New York; *center right* The Granger Collection, New York; *bottom* © Mary Evans Picture Library; **33** *top left, top right* The Granger Collection, New York; *center left* © North Wind/North Wind Picture Archives; *center right* Courtesy American Antiquarian Society; *bottom left* © North Wind/North Wind Picture Archives; **34** © Bruce Davidson/Magnum Photos, Courtesy of Toyota; **35** *top* © National Geographic/Getty Images; *bottom* Associated Press; **36** *top* © North Wind/North Wind Picture Archives; *bottom* Fourteen foot Abnaki style birchbark canoe. © Henri Vaillancourt; **37** © ESA/PLI/Corbis; **46** *left* © Manuscripts, Archives and Special Collections, Washington State University Libraries, Neg No. 89-052; *background* © Don Pitcher/Stock Boston; **47** *The Road Runner Show*, Wile E. Coyote, Road Runner, 1966–1973. © The Everett Collection; **49** *Coyote Survivor*, John Nieto. Serigraph, 29" x 22"; **51** *Buffalo*, John Nieto. Acrylic, 30" x 40"; **54** *left* © N. Scott Momaday/Courtesy of Royce Carlton, Inc.; *background* © Sharon Maritz/Age Fotostock America, Inc.; **55** © David Alan Harvey/Magnum Photos; **57** *A Kato Woman* (about 1924), Edward S. Curtis. Edward S. Curtis Collection/The Library of Congress, Prints and Photographs Collection; **61** *Mandan Offering the Buffalo Skull.* Edward S. Curtis Collection. © McCormick Library of

Special Collections, Northwestern University Library; **65** The Granger Collection, New York; **66** *left* © NMPFT/SSPL/The Image Works, Inc.; *inset* © 2005 Peter Fasciano and Chuck Pharis Video; *background* © Nick Koudis/Getty Images; **67** *1* Excerpts and Photography from *Smoke Signals* provided courtesy of Miramax Films. All rights reserved; *2* © 2003 Classic Media, Inc. Lone Ranger TM and associated character names and images are trademarks of Classic Media, Inc. All rights reserved; *3* Footage for *Stagecoach* provided by Castle Hill Productions, Inc.; *4* Excerpts and Photography from *Smoke Signals* provided courtesy of Miramax Films. All rights reserved; **68** *top* Footage for *Stagecoach* provided by Castle Hill Productions, Inc.; *bottom* © 2003 Classic Media, Inc. Lone Ranger TM and associated character names and images are trademarks of Classic Media, Inc. All rights reserved; *background* © United Artists/The Kobal Collection; **70** *Indian Summer* (1855), Regis Francois Gignoux © Christie's Images/Corbis; **72** *left* The Granger Collection, New York; *background* © GoodShoot/SuperStock; **73, 75** Illustration by Tom McNeely; **82** *left, background* The Granger Collection, New York; **85** Detail of *The Slave Ship* (1956), Robert Riggs, N.A. Courtesy of Les Mansfield, Cincinnati, Ohio; **92** *left* The Granger Collection, New York; *background* © Richard T. Nowitz/Corbis; **95** *Arrival of the English in Virginia* (1585–1588), Theodore de Bry. from Admiranta Narratio, page 47. Engraving. Service Historique de la Marine, Vincennes, France. Photo © Giraudon/Art Resource, New York; **97** © Getty Images; **102** *left* Culver Pictures; *background* © Raymond Forbes/Age Fotostock America, Inc.; **103** The Granger Collection, New York; **113** The Granger Collection, New York; **114** *top* Detail of *Portrait of Anne Bradstreet*, LaDonna Gulley Warrick; *bottom* © Jerry and Marcy Monkman/ EcoPhotography; **115** © Pete Turner/Getty Images; **117** *Sampler* (1796), Abigail Gould. Linen plain weave embroidered with silk and wool, 25 cm. x 30 cm Gift of Miss Jeannette Woodward 41.253. Museum of Fine Arts, Boston; **118** *Silk-On-Linen Needlework Sampler* (1822). Relief Shumway. Hardwick, Massachusetts. © Christie's Images Ltd.; **120** Detail of *Needlework Sampler* (1774), Alice Mather. Norwich, Connecticut/ Christie's Images Ltd.; **122** *foreground* The Granger Collection, New York; *background* © Getty Images; **123** © Comstock Images/Alamy Images; **132** The Granger Collection, New York; **134** *foreground* © Getty Images; *background left* © Stockdisc/Getty Images; *background right* © Brand X Pictures/Jupiterimages Corporation; **135** © 20th Century Fox Film Corp. All rights reserved/Courtesy The Everett Collection; **136–137** *top* © 1996 Photofest; **139, 143** © 20th Century Fox Film Corp. All rights reserved/ Courtesy The Everett Collection; **147** © 1996 Photofest; **153** *top, bottom* © 20th Century Fox Film Corp. All rights reserved/Courtesy The Everett Collection; **155** © Twentieth Century Film Corp./Photofest; **165** © 20th Century Fox Film Corp. All rights reserved/Courtesy The Everett Collection; **172** © 1996 Photofest; **181, 189** © 20th Century Fox Film Corp. All rights reserved/Courtesy The Everett Collection; **197** *top* © Robbie Jack/Corbis; *bottom* © 20th Century Fox Film Corp. All rights reserved/Courtesy The Everett Collection; **201** © 20th Century Fox/The Kobal Collection; **209** © 20th Century Fox Film Corp. All rights reserved/Courtesy The Everett Collection; **217** © Bettmann/Corbis; **218** *top* The New York Times Company; *bottom* AP/Wide World Photos; **220** AP/Wide World Photos; **222** *top* © Barry Wetcher/20th Century Fox/ The Kobal Collection; *bottom* © Romilly Lockyer/Getty Images; **224** AP/ Wide World Photos; **225** *The Puritan* (1883–1886), Augustus Saint-Gaudens. Bronze figure. Private collection. © Art Resource, New York; **226** © akg-images; **228** *left* The Granger Collection, New York; *background* © David Muench/Corbis; **231** *Patrick Henry Before the Virginia House of Burgesses* (1851), Peter F. Rothermel. Red Hill, The Patrick Henry National Memorial, Brookneal, Virginia; **233** *The Bloody Massacre perpetrated in... Boston on March 5th, 1770* (1770), Paul Revere. Colored engraving. Private collection. © Art Resource, New York; **238** *foreground* The Granger Collection, New York; *background* © Pat and Chuck Blackley; **239** The Granger Collection, New York; **241** Library of Congress; **243** The Granger Collection, New York; **248** *foreground* The Granger Collection, New York; *background* © Joseph Sohm/Visions of America/Corbis; **249** The Granger Collection, New York; **251** *Minute Man: Liberty or Death*. Private collection. Photo © Scala/Art Resource, New York; **253** The Granger Collection, New York; **255** *Washington Crossing the Delaware* (1851), Eastman Johnson. Copy after the Emmanuel Leutze painting in the Metropolitan Museum, New York. Private collection. Photo © Art Resource, New York; **258** *center* Library of Congress; *bottom* The Granger Collection, New York; *top* © Brand X Pictures/Alamy Images; **259** © Mark Sykes/Alamy Images; **261** The Granger Collection, New York; **263** *Abigail Smith Adams* (about 1766), Benjamin Blyth. Pastel on paper, 57.3 x 44.8 cm. © Massachusetts Historical Society, Boston/Bridgeman Art Library; *John Adams* (1766), Benjamin Blyth. Pastel on paper, 57.3 cm x 44.8 cm. © Massachusetts Historical Society, Boston, Massachusetts/Bridgeman Art Library; *background* Courtesy of Adelphi Paper Hangings and the Colonial Williamsburg Foundation; *frames* © Image Farm, Inc.; **264** The Granger Collection, New York; **266** *foreground* The Granger Collection, New York; *background* Library of Congress; 267 © Erik Dreyer/Getty Images; **269** *Benjamin Franklin* (1767), David Martin. Oil on canvas. Courtesy White House Historical Association (White House Collection), Washington, D.C. [444 444]; **274** © Bettmann/Corbis; **275** © Mike Caplanis/ Luminary Graphics; **279** The Granger Collection, New York; **280** © Craig Aurness/Corbis; **291** © Michael Newman/PhotoEdit; **298–299** *bottom* © PunchStock.

UNIT 2

301 *top* Detail of *Nathaniel Hawthorne* (1840), Charles Osgood. Oil on canvas. © Peabody Essex Museum, Salem, Massachusetts /Bridgeman Art Library; *bottom* The Granger Collection, New York; **302** *left* Detail of *Lackawanna Valley* (1855), George Inness. Oil on canvas. The Granger Collection, New York; *right* The Granger Collection, New York; **303** *left* © Bettmann/Corbis; *right* Detail of *Kindred Spirits* (1849), Asher Brown Durand. © Francis G. Mayer/Corbis; **304** Detail of *Summer Afternoon On the Hudson* (1852), Jasper Francis Cropsey. © Christie's Images/ Corbis; **306** © The British Museum/HIP/The Image Works, Inc.; **307** The Granger Collection, New York; **308** *Kindred Spirits* (1849), Asher Brown Durand. © Francis G. Mayer/Corbis; **309** Photo of books by Sharon Hoogstraten; *left* Public Domain; *center* The Granger Collection, New York; *right* Public Domain; **310** © Mary Evans Picture Library; **311** © Kim Grant/Lonely Planet Images; **313** *Like an Open-Doored Marble Tomb*, George Klauba. Acrylic on panel, 18" x 14.5 ". Courtesy of Ann Nathan Gallery. Chicago, Illinois. © George Klauba; **314** *top left* Public Domain; *top right* Manuscripts, Archives and Rare Books Division, Schomburg Cener for Research in Black Culture, The New York Public Library, Astor, Lenox and Tilden Foundations; *center left*, *Map of the United States of America* (1816), John Melish. Map division. Astor, Lenox and Tilden Foundations. © New York Public Library/Art Resource, New York; *center right*, *USS Constitution in Action with HMS Guerriere, 19 August, 1812*, Michele Felice Corne © Francis G. Mayer/ Corbis; *bottom* The Granger Collection, New York; **315** *top left* Photo by Sharon Hoogstraten; *top right* © Bettmann/Corbis; *center left* © Bettmann/Corbis; *frame* © 1996 Image Farm, Inc. All rights reserved; *center* Courtesy of the California History Room, California State Library, Sacramento, California; *center right* Photo by Beth Reitmeyer; *bottom* *left* The Granger Collection, New York; **316** © James P. Blair/National Geographic Image Collection; **317** *top* Pages from *Graphic Classics: Edgar Allan Poe* edited by Tom Pomplun. *The Tell-Tale Heart* adapted and illustrated by Rick Geary. Used by permission of Eureka Productions, Mount Horeb, Wisconsin. © Rick Geary; *bottom* © Lucasfilm, Ltd. Paramount/The Kobal Collection; **318** *foreground* © Bettmann/Corbis; *background* © Jodi Cobb/National Geographic Image Collection; **319** © Stockbyte/Getty Images; **336** *left* The Granger Collection, New York; *background* © Darrell Gulin/Corbis; **337** © Kirsty McLaren/Getty Images; **341** *Forest Landscape* (1800s), Asher Brown Durand. Oil on canvas, 76.2 cm x 66 cm. © Brooklyn Museum of Art/Bridgeman Art Library; **342** *left* © Stock Montage; *background* AP/Wide World Photos; **343** © Tommy Flynn/Getty Images; **348** *left* The Granger Collection, New York; *background* © Corbis; **349** © C Squared Studios/Getty Images; **351** © iconsight/Alamy Images; **352** © David Zimmerman/ Corbis; **354** *top* The Granger Collection, New York; *center* Library of Congress; *bottom* © Joseph Sohm/Stock Connection; **357** © Reynolds Stock Photo; **363** © Swerve/Alamy Images; **365** © North Wind/ North Wind Picture Archives; **366** © Judith Jango-Cohen; **368** *left* © Bettmann/Corbis; *background* © Michele Burgess/SuperStock; **369** Photograph by Jay Fechtman; **371** *Wanderer Above a Sea of Fog* (1817), Casper David Friedrich. Oil on canvas, 94.8 cm x 74.8 cm. Inv.: 5161 On permanent loan from the Foundation for the Promotion of the Hamburg Art Collections. Hamburger Kunsthalle, Hamburg, Germany. Photo by Elke Walford. © Bildarchiv Preussischer Kulturbesitz/Art Resource, New York; **374** *Ben Lomond* (1829–1830), Thomas Doughty. Oil on canvas. © Christie's Images/SuperStock; **378** *foreground* © FPG/ Getty Images; *background* © age fotostock/SuperStock; **379** © Duane Lofton/Painet Inc.; **381** © Gail Mooney/Masterfile; **384** *top* © Corbis; *bottom* © David Muench/Corbis; **385** *top* © RubberBall Productions/ Getty Images; *bottom* © Arthur Morris/Corbis; **391** © Lynsey Addario/ Corbis; **394–395** © Bettmann/Corbis; **394** *center* © Underwood & Underwood/Corbis; *right* © Bettmann/Corbis; **395** *left* © Wally McNamee/Corbis; *right* © Reuters/Corbis; **401** Max Desfor/AP/Wide World Photos; **402** *left* © Brown Brothers, Sterling, Pennsylvania; *background* © Corbis; **405** *Portrait of Ann Cochrells* (1848), David Parr. Oil on canvas, 9" x 11". © Christie's Images Ltd.; *frame* © Image Farm, Inc.; **409** © Howard Kingsnorth/Getty Images; **410** *left* © Bettmann/ Corbis; *background* © Lake County Museum/Corbis; **411** © Bertrand Demée/Getty Images; **413, 419, 424, 427, 431** Illustrations by Shane Rebenscheid; **435** © Michael Llewellyn/Getty Images; **437** *Raven* (1996), Keith Carter. © Keith Carter Photographs; **443** © Illustration Works; **444** *top* © Bettmann/Corbis; *bottom* © Rune Hellestad/Corbis; *background* © David McLain/Aurora Photos/Corbis; **447** *foreground* © Bill Ross/Corbis; *background* Cloister (1370–1410), Gloucester Cathedral, Gloucestershire, United Kingdom © Bridgeman Art Library; **449** *background* © Roger Wright/Getty Images; *foreground* © PNC/ Getty Images; **456** © David Elliott/Getty Images; **457** © Warner Bros./ Photofest; **460** *Gargoyles.* Notre Dame, Paris. © Vanni/Art Resource, New York; **461** © Arthur Rackham/Mary Evans Picture Library; **462** © Arthur Rackham/Mary Evans Picture Library; *background* © Tim Flach/ Getty Images; **464–465** © Jupiterimages Corporation; **464** The Granger Collection, New York; **465** © Mary Evans Picture Library/The Image Works, Inc.; **466–467** © Getty Images; **466** *top, Portrait of Nathaniel Hawthorne* (about 1862), Emanuel Gottlieb Leutze. National Portrait Gallery, Smithsonian Institution, Washington D.C. Photo © National Portrait Gallery, Smithsonian Institution/Art Resource, New York; *bottom* PBS/Courtesy of Photofest; **467** Cover illustration by Troy Thomas; **468** *left* Library of Congress, Prints and Photographs Division [LC-DIG-cwpbh-01082]; *background* © S. Solum/Photolink/Getty Images; **469** © Carlos Dominguez/Corbis; **485** © Gary Kelley, 1996; **486** © Joseph Sohm/ChromoSohm Inc./Corbis; **497** © Michael Newman/PhotoEdit; **505** © G. Monteleone/Corbis; **510–511** © PunchStock.

UNIT 3

513 *top* © Getty Images; *bottom, Union Soldiers Fighting in the Field,* Albert Bierstadt. Photo © Geoffrey Clements/Corbis; **514** *left* © Corbis; *right* The Granger Collection, New York; **515** *left* The Granger Collection, New York; *right* © Mort Kunstler, Inc.; **517** *Battle for the Shenandoah.* © Mort Kunstler, Inc.; **518** The Granger Collection, New York; **519** *Abraham Lincoln Reading the Emancipation Proclamation Before His Cabinet Members,* undated color illustration after painting by Francis Bicknell Carpenter. © Bettmann/Corbis; **520** *left, The Laughing Philosopher* (1887), George C. Cox. Photograph. © Museum of the City of New York/Bridgeman Art Library; *right* © Mary Evans Picture Library/The Image Works, Inc.; *frames* © Image Farm, Inc.; **521** © Tom Gauld/Heart USA Inc.; **522** The Granger Collection, New York; **523** *Prisoners from the Front* (1866), Winslow Homer. Oil on canvas, 24" x 38". The Metropolitan Museum of Art. Gift of Mrs. Frank B. Porter, 1922 (22.207). Photo © 1995 The Metropolitan Museum of Art, New York/Art Resource, New York; **524** *top* Public Domain; *center left* The Granger Collection, New York; *center right* © Corbis; *bottom* The Granger Collection, New York; **525** *top left, The Gettysburg Address, 1863,* Jean Leon Jerome Ferris. Private collection. Photo © Bridgeman Art Library; *top right* © Bettmann/Corbis; *center left, center right* The Granger Collection, New York; *bottom* © Araldo de Luca/Corbis; **526** © Corbis Sygma; **527** *left* © Blue Man Productions, Inc.; *top right* The Granger Collection, New York; *center left* © Reuters/Corbis; *center right* AP/Wide World Photos; *bottom left* © Mitchell Gerber/Corbis; *bottom center* © Flip Schulke/Corbis; *bottom right* AP/Wide World Photos; **528** *Walt Whitman inciting the bird of freedom to soar* (1904), Max Beerbohm. Engraving. From *The Poets Corner* published by William Heinemann. © Central Saint Martins College of Art and Design, London/Bridgeman Art Library; **530** *left* National Archives; *background* © Fabio Cardoso/ zefa/Corbis; **531** © Ken Fisher/Getty Images; **540** © Getty Images; **542** © Michael Powers/Veer; **543** © Alistair Forrester Shankie/istockphoto.com; **544** © Thomas Hoepker/Magnum Photos; **545** © Getty Images; **546** *left* The Granger Collection, New York; *background* © Gail Mooney/ Masterfile; **547** © Photodisc/Veer; **549** © Carl Rosenstein/Getty Images; **550** © Martin Rogers/Getty Images; **551** © Nick Koudis/Getty Images; **552** © Todd Gipstein/Corbis; **553** © Dr. Dennis Kunkel/Getty Images; **554** © Jeremy Woodhouse/Getty Images; **555** *top* © ShutterStock; *center, bottom* © Artbeats; **557** © Mike Caplanis/www.luminarygraphics.com; **558** *foreground* © Chester County Historical Society, West Chester, Pennsylvania; *background* © William Manning/Corbis; **561** *Panel 30* from *The Frederick Douglass Series* (1938–1939), Jacob Lawrence. Hampton University Museum. © 2007 The Jacob and Gwendolyn Lawrence Foundation, Seattle/Artists Rights Society (ARS), New York; **562** *The Life of Harriet Tubman, #9* (1940), Jacob Lawrence. Casein tempera on hardboard, 12" x 17 7/8". Hampton University Museum. Photo © Gwendolyn Knight Lawrence/Art Resource, New York. © 2007 The Jacob and Gwendolyn Lawrence Foundation, Seattle/Artists Rights Society (ARS), New York; **567** *Panel #10* from *The Frederick Douglass Series of 1938–1940,* Jacob Lawrence. © 2007 The Jacob and Gwendolyn Lawrence Foundation, Seattle/Artists Rights Society (ARS), New York; **572** *left* Cabinet photograph (1894), Gilbert Studios, Washington, D.C. Gold toned albumin print; *background* © Bettmann/Corbis; **573** *Detail of The Ride for Freedom, The Fugitive Slaves* (1862), Eastman Johnson. Oil. The Granger Collection, New York; **575** © New York Public Library,

Schomburg Center; **577** Photographic History Collection, National Museum of American History, Smithsonian Institution, Washington, D.C.; **582–583** © Map Division, New York Public Library, Astor, Lenox and Tilden Foundations; **584** *foreground* Library of Congress; *background* © Joseph Sohm/ChromoSohm Inc./Corbis; **587** © Reza Estakhrian/ Getty Images; **588** National Archives; **593–596** *bottom* © Getty Images; **593** The Granger Collection, New York; *frame* © Image Farm, Inc.; *parchment* © Artbeats; **594** *top* United States Army Military History Institute; *frame* © Image Farm, Inc.; *medal* © Getty Images; **595** *left* © David Toase/Getty Images; *right, Mary Boykin Chesnut* (1856), Samuel S. Osgood. Oil on canvas adhered to masonite, 48" x 30" with frame. © Private Collection/Art Resource, New York; **596** The Granger Collection, New York; *frame* © Image Farm, Inc.; **598** The Granger Collection, New York; **600–601** © Minnesota Historical Society/Corbis; **600** © Alderman Library/University of Virginia; **601** Public Domain; **602** *left* © Bettmann/ Corbis; *background* © Corbis; **603** © Nonstock/Jupiter Images; **605** © Stephen Graham/Owl Creek Productions; **606** © Peter L. Chapman/ Index Stock Imagery, Inc.; **609** © Ionpost/Owl Creek Productions; **611** © Stephen Frink/Getty Images; **613** © Mike Zens/Corbis; **617** *Lincoln at Gettysburg II* (1939–1942), William H. Johnson. Gouache and pen and ink on paper, 19 3/4" x 17 1/16". Gift of the Harmon Foundation. Smithsonian American Art Museum, Washington, D.C. © Smithsonian American Art Museum, Washington, D.C./Art Resource, New York; **618** *top* © Stephen Graham/Owl Creek Productions; *bottom* Clip courtesy of Owl Creek Production, L.L.C. www.owlcreekproductions.com; **620** © Daryl Benson/Masterfile; **625** whitehouse.gov; **629** © Michael Newman/ PhotoEdit; **636–637** © PunchStock.

UNIT 4

639 *top* Detail of *Willa Cather* (1923–1924), Nicholai Fechin. Oil on canvas, 24" x 30". Sheldon Memorial Art Gallery and Sculpture Garden, University of Nebraska-Lincoln, UNL–Gift of Dr. Philip L. and Helen Cather Southwick through the University of Nebraska Foundation. Art © Estate of Nicolai Fechin/Fechin Art Reproductions. Photo © Sheldon Memorial Art Gallery; *bottom, The Jolly Flatboatmen* (1877–1878), George Caleb Bingham. Oil on canvas, 26 1/16" x 36 3/8". Daniel J. Terra Acquisition Endowment Fund, 1992.15. Terra Foundation for American Art, Chicago. © Terra Foundation for American Art, Chicago /Art Resource, New York; **640** *left* Detail of *Family and their Dugout* (1870s), Anonymous. Photo 11" x 14". Near McCook Nebraska. © Nebraska State Historical Society, Lincoln, Nebraska; *right* © Joel Sartore/ National Geographic Image Collection; **641** *left* Detail of *A Sketch of a Faraway Look*, Herman Jean Joseph Richir. Bonhams, London. Photo © Bridgeman Art Library/SuperStock. © 2007 Artists Rights Society (ARS), New York/ADAGP, Paris; *right* © Corbis; **642** *Country Fair, New England* (1890), Childe Hassam. 24 1/4" x 20 1/8". Private Collection; **644** *The Hatch Family* (1871), Eastman Johnson. Oil on canvas, 48" x 73 3/8". The Metropolitan Museum of Art, Gift of Frederic H. Hatch, 1926 (26.97). Photo © 1999 The Metropolitan Museum of Art/Art Resource, New York; **645** © MPI/Getty Images; **646** The Newberry Library, Chicago; **647** Photo Courtesy of the South Dakota State Historical Society, State Archives; **648–649** © Juniors Bildarchiv/Age Fotostock; **650** © Bettman/ Corbis; **651** *In the Garden* (1904), Mary Stevenson Cassatt. Pastel on paper, 66 cm. x 81.3 cm. © The Detroit Institute of Arts/Bridgeman Art Library; **652** *top left* © Comstock/Superstock; *top center* © Harry Taylor/ Dorling Kindersley; *top right* © Bettmann/Corbis; *center left* © Time & Life Pictures/Getty Images; *center right* © Corbis; *bottom* © Images. com/Corbis; **653** *top* © Bettmann/Corbis; *center* © Corbis; *bottom* Royal biscuit. Biscuit label by Carr & Co. (CT13673A). Victoria and Albert Museum, London. © Victoria and Albert Museum, London/Art Resource, New York; **654** © Scimitar/The Kobal Collection; **655** *top* © 2004 Getty Images; *bottom* © Layne Kennedy/Corbis; **656** © Bettmann/Corbis; **657** The Granger Collection, New York; **658** *foreground* Library of Congress; *background* © Stephen Alvarez/National Geographic Image Collection; **659** © Design Pics Inc./Alamy Images; **661** Library of Congress; **663** *Levitation.* © Scala/Art Resource, New York; **667** Library of Congress; **670** © Mike Caplanis/www.luminarygraphics.com; **673** © Steve Bloom/ Getty Images; **675** *background* Library of Congress; *inset* The Granger Collection, New York; *frame* © 1996 Image Farm, Inc. All rights reserved; **679** *left* © Mary Evans Picture Library/The Image Works, Inc.; *right* © The Mariners' Museum, Newport, Virginia; **680** *Champions of the Mississippi*, Currier and Ives. Lithograph. Museum of the City of New York, New York. © Scala/Art Resource, New York; **683** © Rubberball/ Age Fotostock America, Inc.; **685, 689, 690** The Granger Collection, New York; **694–695** © Kevin Horan/Getty Images; **694** © Corbis; **695** Cover of the original *The Adventures of Huckleberry Finn* by Mark Twain © 1885. Illustrated by E.W. Kemble/The Granger Collection, New York; **696** *foreground* © Thomas Morse/PlaceStockPhoto.com; *background* © Brown Brothers, Sterling, Pennsylvania; **697** © G. Brad Lewis/Getty Images; **699** The Granger Collection, New York; **702** © Bill Manns/The Art Archive; **706–707** Library of Congress; **708** Public Domain; **713** © Corbis; **716** *foreground* © Getty Images; *background* © Age Fotostock/SuperStock; **717** © Terry Evans Photography; **719** *Old Souvenirs* (about 1881–1901), John F. Peto. Oil on canvas, 26 3/4" x 22". The Metropolitan Museum of Art, Bequest of Oliver Burr Jennings, 1968 (68.205.3) Photo © 1983 The Metropolitan Museum of Art/Art Resource, New York; **720** *Family and their Dugout* (1870s), Anonymous. Photo 11" x 14". Near McCook Nebraska. © Nebraska State Historical Society, Lincoln, Nebraska; **725** *Two on the Aisle* (1927), Edward Hopper © Francis G. Mayer/Corbis. © Heirs of Josephine N. Hopper, licensed by Whitney Museum of American Art; **729** Library of Congress; **730** © Hulton-Deutsch/Corbis; **731** *left* © Geoffrey Clements/Corbis; *right* © Corbis; **732** *top left, Castle Geyser and Firehole Basin* (1871), William Henry Jackson. Courtesy National Park Service, Yellowstone National Park, YELL 36193; *bottom left, The Castle Geyser, Firehole Basin* (1872), Thomas Moran. 7 1/2" x 11". The Gilcrease Musem, Tulsa, Oklahoma. 0226.1363. © The Gilcrease Museum; *background* © Bill Ross/Corbis; **734** *foreground* The Granger Collection, New York; *background* © Nicole Duplaix/National Geographic Image Collection; **735** © Eric Nguyen/Jim Reed Photography/Corbis; **737** Image manipulated. *German shipwreck survivors*, Achille Beltrame. Engraving in Italian newspaper *La Domenica del Corriere*, February, 1941 Photo © Dagli Orti/The Art Archive; **742–743** *The Much Resounding Sea* (1884), Thomas Moran. Oil on canvas, 25" x 62" unframed. Gift of the Avalon Foundation. 1967.9.1. © National Gallery of Art, Washington D.C.; **748** *The Escape of Henri de Rochefort, March 20, 1874* (1880–1881), Edouard Manet. Oil on canvas, 80 cm x 73 cm. Musée d'Orsay, Paris. Photo © Bridgeman Art Library; **755** *Moonlit Shipwreck at Sea* (1901), Thomas Moran. 30" x 40 1/4 ". © Christie's Images Limited; **763** Public Domain; **764** Library of Congress, Rare Book and Special Collections Division; **765** *top* Library of Congress, Rare Book and Special Collections Division; *bottom* © Bettmann/Corbis; **766** Library of Congress, Rare Book and Special Collections Division; **768** *foreground* © Underwood & Underwood/Corbis; *background* © Allen Prier/Panoramic Images/ NGSImages.com; **769** © David McLain/Aurora Photos; **771** © Werner Forman/akg-images; **775** © Alamy Images; **779** © Joel Sartore/National Geographic Image Collection; **780** © Hulton-Deutsch Collection/ Corbis; **782** *left* The Granger Collection, New York; *background* © Lee Foster/Lonely Planet Images; **785** *A Sketch of a Faraway Look*, Herman

Jean Joseph Richir. Bonhams, London. Photo © Bridgeman Art Library/ SuperStock. © 2007 Artists Rights Society (ARS), New York/ADAGP, Paris; **791** © David Tipling/Stone/Getty Images; **793** © 1991 Watterson/ Distributed by Universal Press Syndicate; **796** *foreground* © Brown Brothers, Sterling, Pennsylvania; *background* © Getty Images; **797** © T. Kruesselmann/T. Hemmings/Espressokiss/zefa/Corbis; **799** *Geraniums* (1888), Childe Hassam. 18 1/4" x 12 15/16". The Hyde Collection, Glens Falls, New York. Photo by Michael Fredericks; **802** *A Woman Seated at a Table by a Window*, Carl Holsoe. Oil on canvas. © SuperStock; **806** *Portrait of Dr. Washington Epps, My Doctor* (1885), Sir Lawrence Alma-Tadema. Oil on canvas, 64.2 cm x 51 cm. Private collection. © Bridgeman Art Library; **810** *In Bed* (1878), Federico Zandomeneghi. Oil on canvas, 60.5 cm x 73.5 cm. Galleria d'Arte Moderna, Florence. © Alinari/Art Resource, New York; **814** Public Domain; **818–819** © John Churchman/ Veer; **818** The Granger Collection, New York; **820** *left, background* © Bettmann/Corbis; **821** © Gallery Stock Limited; **823** *Girl Reading* (1909), Edmund Charles Tarbell. Oil on canvas, 32 1/4" x 28 1/2". The Hayden Collection, Charles Henry Hayden Fund 09.209. © Museum of Fine Arts, Boston; **828** *In the Station Waiting Room, Boston* (1915), Edmund Charles Tarbell. Oil on canvas, 24 3/8" x 32". Gift of Dr. Joseph R. Fazzano. © Crocker Art Museum, Sacramento, California; **833** © 2005 Getty Images; **834** © Richard Sisk/Jupiter Images; **845** © José Luis Pelaez, Inc./ Age Fotostock America, Inc.; **853** © Michael Blann/Taxi/Getty Images; **858–859** © PunchStock.

UNIT 5

861 *top* Photo by Robert W. Kelley. © Time & Life Pictures/Getty Images; *bottom, The Bicycle Race* (1912), Lyonel Feininger. Collection of Mr. and Mrs. Paul Mellon. Photo © 2006 National Gallery of Art, Washington, D.C. © 2007 Artists Rights Society (ARS), New York/VG Bild-Kunst, Bonn; **862** *left* Detail of *The Shelton with Sunspots, New York* (1926), Georgia O'Keeffe. Oil on canvas, 123.2 cm x 76.8 cm. Gift of Leigh B. Block (1985.206). Reproduction, The Art Institute of Chicago. © 2007 The Georgia O'Keeffe Museum/Artists Rights Society (ARS), New York; *right* © Corbis; **863** *left* Detail of *Family* (1955), Charles H. Alston. Oil on canvas, 48 1/4" x 35 3/4". Whitney Museum of American Art, New York. Purchase, with funds from the Artists and Students Assistance Fund 55.47. © Estate of Charles H. Alston. Courtesy of Michael Rosenfeld, LLC, New York; *right* © Bettmann/Corbis; **864** *The City from Greenwich Village* (1922), John Sloan. Oil on canvas, 26" x 33 3/4". Gift of Helen Farr Sloan. Image © 2006 Board of Trustees, National Gallery of Art, Washington, D.C. 1970.1.1; **866** © Dorothea Lange/Corbis; **867** *left, right* The Granger Collection, New York; *bottom* © Bettmann/Corbis; **868** *top* Public Domain; *center* The Granger Collection, New York; *bottom* © Alfred Eisenstaedt/Pix Inc./Time & Life Pictures/Getty Images; **869** *The Red Wheelbarrow* (1992), Frank Jensen. © Frank Jensen; **870** The Granger Collection, New York; **871** *The Migration of the Negro Panel no. 1* (1940–1941), Jacob Lawrence. Casein tempera on hardboard, 12" x 18". Acquired 1942. The Phillips Collection, Washington, D.C. © 2007 The Estate of Gwendolyn Knight Lawrence/Artists Rights Society (ARS), New York; **872** © Bettmann/Corbis; **873** The Granger Collection, New York; **874** *top* © The Poetry Foundation; *center left* © Hulton-Deutsch Collection/Corbis; *center right* © Mike Caplanis/www.luminarygraphics.com; *bottom left* The Granger Collection, New York; *bottom right* © Bettmann/Corbis; **875** *top* © Hulton Archive/Getty Images; *center right, The Wizard of Oz* (1939) MGM/Courtesy of Photofest; *center* © Angelo Hornak/Corbis; *center left* © Bettmann/Corbis; **876** © Alex McLean/ Getty Images; **877** *top* © Najlah Feanny/Corbis; *bottom* Courtesy of the Federal Deposit Insurance Company; **878** *left* © Corbis; *background* Detail of *The Cotton Club in Harlem, New York* (1930). Black and white photograph. Private collection. © Bridgeman Art Library; **879** © Frank Leather/Eye Ubiquitous/Corbis; **881** *Street Shadows* (1959), Jacob Lawrence. Egg tempera on hardboard, 24" x 30". Private collection, New York. Photo © Gwendolyn Knight Lawrence/Art Resource, New York. © 2008 The Jacob and Gwendolyn Lawrence Foundation, Seattle/Artists Rights Society (ARS), New York; **882** *The Negro Speaks of Rivers* (1998), Phoebe Beasley. Silkscreen. © Phoebe Beasley; **886** *top* © Time Life Pictures/Getty Images; *center* Courtesy of Yale Collection of American Literature, Beinecke Rare Book and Manuscript Library; *bottom* © K. Hackenberg/zefa/Corbis; **887** © Corbis/Jupiter Images; **889** © Bettmann/ Corbis; **890** © Getty Images; **892** *top* Courtesy of Yale Collection of American Literature, Beinecke Rare Book and Manuscript Library; *center* © Bettmann/Corbis; *bottom* AP/Wide World Photos; *background* © Charles E. Rotkin/Corbis; **893** © Ted Dayton/Index Stock Imagery, Inc.; **895** *Field and Storm* (2003), April Gornik. Oil on linen, 74" x 95". Courtesy of the artist and Danese Gallery, New York; **896** *Sunflowers*, Charly Palmer. Mixed media collage on canvas, 48" x 24". © Charly Palmer; **898** © Corbis; **901** *Girl in a Red Dress* (1934), Charles Alston. Oil on canvas, 71" x 55.9". Photo © The Harmon and Harriet Kelley Collection of African American Art. © Estate of Charles Alston. Courtesy of Michael Rosenfeld Gallery, LLC, New York; **903** *Empress of the Blues* (1974), Romare Bearden. Collage, 36" x 48". Photo © Smithsonian American Art Museum/Art Resource, New York. © The Romare Bearden Foundation/Licensed by VAGA, New York; **908** *left* AP/Wide World Photos; *right* © Getty Images; **909** © Karl Grupe/Getty Images; **911** *Family* (1955), Charles H. Alston. Oil on canvas, 48 1/4" x 35 3/4". Whitney Museum of American Art, New York. Purchase, with funds from the Artists and Students Assistance Fund 55.47. © Estate of Charles H. Alston. Courtesy of Michael Rosenfeld, LLC, New York; **915** The Granger Collection, New York; **916** *foreground* Library of Congress, Prints and Photographs Division; *background* © Ian Cartwright/Getty Images; **917** *top* Public Domain, New York Times, July 3, 1917; *bottom, The Cotton Club in Harlem, New York* (1930). Black and white photograph. Private collection. © Bridgeman Art Library; **918** *top left* Detail of *Church-goers, Eatonville* (1940), Jules André Smith. Oil on masonite. Courtesy The Maitland Art Center; *bottom left* Courtesy Lucy Anne Hurston; *bottom* © John Springer Collection/Corbis; **920** *top* © Bettmann/Corbis; *center* © Brown Brothers, Sterling, Pennsylvania; *bottom* © MedioImages/Getty Images; **921** © Russell Illig/Getty Images; **923** *Sir Philip Sassoon* (1923), John Singer Sargent. Oil on canvas, 95.2 cm x 57.8 cm. Tate Gallery, London © Tate Gallery, London/Art Resource, New York; **924** *Reading in a Study*, Walt Louderback. Oil on plywood, 76.2 cm x 59.7 cm. Private collection. Photo © Bridgeman Art Library; **926** *Cowboy Dance* (mural study, Anson, Texas Post Office) (1941), Jenne Magafan. Oil on fiberboard. Photo © Smithsonian American Art Museum, Washington, D.C./Art Resource, New York; **928** *left, background* © Bettmann/Corbis; **929** *left* © A. Schein/zefa/Corbis; *right* © Craig Tuttle/Corbis; **931** *South of the Loop* (1936), Charles Turzak. Color woodcut, Image 10 2/3" x 11 3/4", sheet 11 1/4" x 15". Mary and Leigh Block Museum of Art, Northwestern University, 1992.73. Printed by permission from Joan Turzak Van Hees, Charles Turzak Studio/Gallery. Orlando, Florida. © Joan Turzak Van Hees; **932** *Le Plateau de Bolante* (1917), Félix Valloton. Oil on canvas. Musee d'Histoire Contemporaine, Paris. © Musée d'Histoire Contemporaine-BDIC; **934** The Granger Collection, New York; **935** *The Red Room* (1908), Henri Matisse. Oil on canvas. State Hermitage Museum, St. Petersburg, Russia. © SuperStock, Inc./ SuperStock. © 2007 Succession H. Matisse, Paris/Artists Rights Society (ARS), New York; **936** *left* National Archives; *background* © Peter Miller/

Getty Images; **937** © Brad Wilson/Getty Images; **939** *The Flatiron Building, Evening from Camera Work*, April, 1906, Edward Steichen. Photo © Réunion des Musées Nationaux/Art Resource, New York. Reprinted by permission of Joanna T. Steichen/© Carousel Research; **940** *Haystacks and Barn* (1909), George Wesley Bellows. Oil on canvas, 56.5 cm x 71.4 cm. © Museum of Fine Arts, Houston, Texas/Bridgeman Art Library; **943** © Bill Varie/Corbis; **945** Detail of *Island Hay* (1945), Thomas Hart Benton. Gift of John Nichols Estabrook and Dorothy Coogan Estabrook. 1987.41.5. Photo © 2005 National Gallery of Art, Washington, D.C. © T.H. Benton and R.P. Benton Testamentary Trusts/UMB Bank Trustee/ Licensed by VAGA, New York; **952** *top* © Time Life Pictures/Getty Images; *center* Courtesy of The Schaffner Family Foundation; *bottom* National Archives; *background* © P. Steeger/zefa/Corbis; **953** © Georgette Douwma/Getty Images; **955** © Hans Wolf/Getty Images; **956** *top, bottom* © Corbis; **957** © Elizabeth Watt Photography/StockFood America; **960** *top, center, bottom* © Bettmann/Corbis; *background* © Elly Godfroy/Alamy Images; **963** *Couple Above St. Paul*, Marc Chagall. Private collection. Photo © Scala/Art Resource, New York. © 2007 Artists Rights Society (ARS), New York/ADAGP, Paris; **965** *Rising Moon* (1965), Hans Hofmann. Private Collection. Photo © Art Resource, New York. © 2008 Estate of Hans Hofmann/Artists Rights Society (ARS), New York; **966** *Port Scene*, Paul Klee. Atheneum Museum, Helsinki, Finland. Photo © Giraudon/Art Resource, New York. © 2007 Artists Rights Society (ARS), New York/VG Bild-Kunst, Bonn; **968** *left* © Bettmann/Corbis; *background* © Corbis; **969** © Stephen Webster/Getty Images; **975** © Vernon Leach/Alamy Images; **976** *foreground* © Getty Images; *background* © Underwood & Underwood/Corbis; **979** *Homme au Chapeau* (1900s), Jean Berque. Waterhouse and Dodd, London. © Bridgeman Art Library; **983** *Portrait of Marquess Sommi* (1925), Tamara De Lempicka. Oil on canvas, 100 cm x 73 cm. Albert and Victoria Benalloul. © 2007 Artists Rights Society (ARS), New York/ADAGP, Paris; **989** *Young Woman in Green* (1927), Tamara de Lempicka. Musée National d'Art Moderne, Centre George Pompidou, Paris. Photo © CNAC/MNAM/Dist. Réunion des Musées Nationaux/Art Resource, New York © 2007 Artists Rights Society (ARS), New York/ADAGP, Paris; **993** *Autoportrait* (1925), Tamara De Lempicka. Oil on wood, 35 cm x 26 cm. Private collection. © 2008 Artists Rights Society (ARS), New York/ADAGP, Paris; **998** Detail of *The Shelton with Sunspots* (1926), Georgia O'Keeffe. Oil on canvas, 123.1 cm x 76.8 cm. The Art Institute of Chicago, gift of Leigh B. Block (1985.206). © 2007 The Georgia O'Keeffe Museum/Artists Rights Society (ARS), New York. Photo © 1994 The Art Institute of Chicago, all rights reserved; **1002–1003** © Bettmann/Corbis; **1002** © Culver Pictures/The Art Archive; **1003, 1004** The Granger Collection, New York; **1005** © Bettmann/ Corbis; **1006** *top* Courtesy the Gaslight Collection; *bottom* © Bettmann/ Corbis; **1008** *left* © Getty Images; *background* © Suhaib Salem/Reuters/ Corbis; **1009** © Zigy Kaluzny/Getty Images; **1011** © Corbis; **1019** © Getty Images; **1020** © Getty Images; **1021** Cover of *Moving a Nation to Care* by Ilona Meagher. © 2007 by Ilona Meagher. Cover design by Lisa Force. Used by permission of Ig Publishing Inc., Brooklyn, New York; **1024–1025** © Bettmann/Corbis; **1024** © Time Life Pictures/Getty Images; **1025** The Granger Collection, New York; **1027** © Horace Bristol/ Corbis; **1028** *top* © Horace Bristol; *bottom* © Horace Bristol/Corbis; **1029, 1030, 1031** © Horace Bristol; **1032** *top, bottom* © Horace Bristol/ Corbis; **1034** *left* The Granger Collection, New York; *background* © Corbis; **1035** © photocuisine/Corbis; **1037** © Images.com/Corbis; **1044** *Blue House* (2004), Philip Hershberger. Encaustic on panel, 78" x 48". © Philip Hershberger; **1048** *foreground* © Getty Images; **1049** © DiMaggio/ Kalish/Corbis; **1051** *Brooding Silence* (date unknown), John Fabian Carlson. Smithsonian American Art Museum, Washington, D.C. © Smithsonian American Art Museum, Washington, D.C./Art Resource, New York; **1054** *Snowy Woods at Dusk* (date unknown), Dennis Sheehan. Oil, 20" x 16". Courtesy of Susan Powell Fine Art, Madison, Connecticut; **1057** *Woman Peeling Apples* (1924), Archibald J. Motley, Jr. Oil on canvas, 32 1/4" x 28". Art and Artifacts Division, Schomberg Center for Research in Black Culture, The New York Public Library, Astor, Lenox and Tilden Foundations. Courtesy Valerie Gerrard Brown; **1060** © Mississippi Department of Archives Photo; **1064** *foreground* © Hulton Archive/Getty Images; *background* The Granger Collection, New York; **1065** © Saed Hindash/Star Ledger/Corbis; **1067** © Johner/Getty Images; **1071** © David Wasserman/Veer; **1078** *left* AP/Wide World Photos; *background* © Yuri Dojc/Getty Images; **1079** © Andy Sacks/Getty Images; **1081** *Light of La Grange* (1997), Billy Morrow Jackson. Watercolor, 22" x 29". © Billy Morrow Jackson; **1085** *The Interloper* (1958), Billy Morrow Jackson. Collection of Mrs. Virginia Penofsky; **1091** © Hulton-Deutsch Collection/Corbis; **1092** © Archive Photos/Getty Images; **1094** *left* © Getty Images; *background* © Hulton-Deutsch Collection/Corbis; **1095** © Chris Hondros/Getty Images; **1097** © Hulton-Deutsch Collection/ Corbis; **1099** Photo by Robert Capa. © 2001 by Cornell Capa/Magnum Photos; **1104** *left* The Granger Collection, New York; *background* © Getty Images; **1105** Photograph by Sharon Hoogstraten; **1107** *left* Image courtesy The Newberry Library; *right* The Granger Collection, New York; *bottom* © Herbert Orth/Time Life Pictures/Getty Images; **1108** *left* © Culver Pictures/The Art Archive; *right* © Getty Images; **1112** *left* © Bettmann/Corbis; *background* © PicturePress/Getty Images; **1113** *Write about dogs!*, George Booth. *The New Yorker*, April 5, 1976. © The Cartoon Bank; **1114** © Corbis; **1117** © Ron Watts/Corbis; **1118** © Daryl Benson/Masterfile; **1129** © Houghton Mifflin Harcourt; **1137** © Paul Burns/Photodisc/Alamy Ltd.; **1142–1143** © PunchStock.

UNIT 6

1145 *top* © Gene Blevins/Corbis; *bottom, Man in Red* (2003), Diana Ong. Computer graphics. © Purestock/SuperStock; **1146** *left* © K.J. Historical/ Corbis; *right* © Bettmann/Corbis; **1147** *left, Increibles Las Cosas Q'Se Ven*, 2001 Mural at Ashland Avenue and 19th Street in Chicago. © Jeffrey Zimmermann; *right* © Josef Scaylea/Corbis; **1148** © NASA/Corbis; **1150** © Jacques Langewin/Corbis Sygma; **1151** © Ellliott Erwitt/Magnum Photos; **1152** © Josef Scaylea/Corbis; **1153** © Warner Brothers/Getty Images; **1155** *left* © Wally McNamee/Corbis; *right* © K.J. Historical/ Corbis; **1156** AP/Wide World Photos; **1157** *White Cloud Over Purple* (1957), Mark Rothko. Oil on canvas, 143 cm x 138 cm. Photo © Private collection/Bridgeman Art Library. © 2007 Kate Rothko Prizel and Christopher Rothko/Artists Rights Society (ARS), New York; **1158** *top* Associated Press; *center left* The Granger Collection, New York; *center right* © Bettmann/Corbis; *bottom* © Getty Images; **1159** *top left* Photograph by Carmine Fantasia; *top right* © Getty Images; *center left* © AFP/Getty Images; *center right* © NOAA/Corbis; *bottom* Central Intelligence Agency; **1160** © Corbis; **1161** *top* © Google; *bottom* © Steven Hunt/Getty Images; **1162–1163** © Corbis; **1162** *top* AP/Wide World Photos; *bottom* Showtime/Courtesy of Photofest; **1163** Cover of *Our Town* by Thornton Wilder. © 1938, 1957 by Thornton Wilder. Cover illustration © William Low. Reprinted by permission of Harper Perennial, a Division of Harper Collins Publishers; **1164** *top* © Bettmann/Corbis; *bottom* © ArenaPal/ Topham/The Image Works, Inc.; **1165** © Playbill/Photofest; **1166–1167** © Angela Cappetta/Getty Images; **1166** *top* © Bettmann/Corbis; *bottom* Marilyn Kingwill/ArenaPAL. © ArenaPAL/Topham/The Image Works, Inc.; **1167** The Granger Collection, New York; **1168–1169** © Getty Images; **1168** *top* © Bettmann/Corbis; *bottom* © Joan Marcus; **1170** *top* National Archives; *center* AP/Wide World Photos; *bottom* Courtesy of Franklin D. Roosevelt Presidential Library and Museum; **1171** © Todd Gipstein/Corbis; **1173** © Bettmann/Corbis; **1175** © Time Life Pictures/Getty Images; **1178** *top* © Marko Shark/Corbis; *center* Photo by Bernard Gotfryd/© Getty Images; *background* © Bettmann/Corbis; **1181** *Fatherhood* (1990s), Ed Roskowski. © Ed Roskowski/Corbis; **1186** *Life Decisions* (1995), Ed Roskowski. © Ed Roskowski/Corbis; **1189** © Bruno Barbey/Magnum Photos; **1191** © Michael St. Maur Sheil/ Corbis; **1194** *left* © Marilyn Knapp Litt; *background* © Olivier Martel/ Corbis; **1195** © Bernard Annebicque/Corbis Sygma; **1197** *The Green Machine* (1977), Frank Dahmer. Screenprint on paper, 13 1/2" x 17 1/4". © National Vietnam Veterans Art Museum; **1199** *Come a Little Closer* (1997), Michael Brostowitz. Oil on board, 15 1/4" x 19 3/4". © National Vietnam Veterans Art Museum; **1201** © Time & Life Pictures/Getty Images; **1202** *left* © Time & Life Images/Getty Images; *background* © Bob Adelman/Magnum Photos; **1203** © Bob Adelman/Magnum Photos; **1205** © Bettmann/Corbis; **1210** © Bob Adelman/Magnum Photos; **1214** Photo by Dave King/© Dorling Kindersley; **1218** *left* © Bettmann/ Corbis; *background* © Michael S. Yamashita/Corbis; **1219** AP/Wide World Photos; **1221** © Bob Adelman/Magnum Photos; **1225** © Eve Arnold/Magnum Photos; **1226** © James Nubile/The Image Works, Inc.; **1231** *left* © Bettmann/Corbis; *right* © Flip Schulke/Corbis; **1234** © Paul Fusco/Magnum Photos; **1235** *top* © Courtesy of CBS News Archives; *bottom* © Richard Thornton/ShutterStock; **1236** *top* © Courtesy of CBS News Archives; *bottom* © Owen Franken/Corbis; **1238** *left* Courtesy Austin Straus; *right* © New York Times Agency; **1239** © Greenblatt Bill/ Corbis Sygma; **1241, 1245** © Bettmann/Corbis; **1247** *Love Letter I* (1971), Charles Wilbert White. Color lithograph, 30" x 22 1/2". Gift of June Wayne. Image © 2007 Board of Trustees, National Gallery of Art, Washington, D.C. 1974.99.158.(B-27792)/PR. © 1971 The Charles White Archives; **1250** *left* © Bettmann/Corbis; *background* © Corbis; **1253** *Father,* Charly Palmer. Mixed media collage on wood. 18 " x 12". © Charly Palmer; **1256** *Thinking* (1990), Carlton Murrell. Oil on board. Private collection. © Bridgeman Art Library; 1259 © Najlah Feanny/ Corbis Saba; **1260** *top* AP/Wide World Photos; center © Christopher Felver/Corbis; *bottom* © Bassouls Sophie/Corbis Sygma; **1262** *left* © Getty Images; *background* © Alex Mares-Manton/Getty Images; **1263** © E. Streichan/zefa/Corbis; **1265** *Apple* (1983), Andy Warhol. Synthetic polymer paint and silkscreen ink on canvas, 14" x 11". © 2008 The Andy Warhol Foundation for the Visual Arts/Artists Rights Society (ARS), New York. Photo © The Andy Warhol Foundation, Inc./Art Resource, New York. Courtesy Ronald Feldman Fine Arts, New York; **1273, 1276** Illustrations by Precision Graphics; **1278** *left* © Getty Images; *background* Crazy patchwork quilt (1875), unknown artist. Smithsonian Institution, Washington, D.C./Bridgeman Art Library; **1279** © Botanica/ Jupiter Images; **1281** *Washerwoman,* James Amos Porter. Oil on canvas, 18" x 13". Private collection. Reproduction rights given by the Dorothy Porter Wesley Research Center, Fort Lauderdale, Florida; **1286** *foreground* © Gene Blevins/Corbis; *background* © Randy Faris/Corbis; **1287** © Angelo Cavalli/Getty Images; **1289** © Constantine Manos/Magnum Photos; **1294** *left* Photo © Nancy Crampton; *background* © Getty Images; **1296** © Eli Reed/Magnum Photos; **1297** *Everyman,* Brenda Joysmith. 345" x 58 1/4". © Brenda Joysmith. Courtesy of Joysmith Gallery; **1300** *top* Courtesy of Pulitzer.org; *bottom* © Photograph of Rita Dove by Fred Viebahn; *background* © Jean-Claude Marlaud/Getty Images; **1301** © Veer; **1303** *Evening Thoughts* (2002), Ernest Crichlow. Lithograph (Edition 150), 25" x 18". Photo by Marureen Turci, Mojo Portfolio. Courtesy of the Ernest Crichlow Estate; **1304** *Discovery I,* Alfred Gockel. 39 1/4" x 39 1/4". © Alfred Gockel; **1306** *left* © Christopher Felver/ Corbis; *background* © Alan Schein Photography/Corbis; 1307 © Randy Faris/Corbis; 1308 © Arthur Morris/Corbis; **1311** *Increibles Las Cosas Q'Se Ven,* 2001 Mural at Ashland Avenue and 19th Street in Chicago. © Jeffrey Zimmermann; **1312** © J. David Andrews/Masterfile; **1323** © Phil Boorman/Getty Images; **1331** © Bryan Busovicki/ShutterStock; **1336–1337** © PunchStock.

UNIT 7 RESEARCH UNIT

1339 *top* © Design Pics, Inc./Alamy Images; *top inset* © Bettmann/ Corbis; *bottom* Photographer Dorothea Lange, 1935/Library of Congress; **1340** *left* © Bettmann/Corbis; *right* © Steven Hunt/Getty Images; **1341** *left* The Granger Collection, New York; *right* © NOAA/Corbis; **1344** *left* © Science Museum/SSPL/The Image Works, Inc.; *inset right* Public Domain; *right* © Jupiter Images; **1345** © Google; **1349** *Audience in recreation hall, Tulare Migrant Camp, Visalia, California* (1940). Photo by Arthur Rothstein. *Voices From the Dust Bowl* website. Courtesy of the American Folklife Center, Library of Congress; **1350** © Los Angeles Times. Reprinted with permission; **1355** *top* Library of Congress; center © United Nations; *bottom* NASA; **1358** © Jason Ernst/Age Fotostock America, Inc.; **1379** © Paul Edmondson/Corbis.

STUDENT RESOURCE BANK

R3 National Archives; **R7** © GeoNova LLC; **R13** AP/Wide World Photos; **R14** © Bettmann/Corbis; **R16** *logo* Transportation Security Administration /U.S. Department of Homeland Security; *chart* Public Domain; **R18** http://www.museumoftheamericanwest.org/explore/ exhibits/suffrage/index.html. Reprinted by permission. © 2007 Autrey National Center. All rights reserved; *inset* © Denver Public Library, Western History Collection. Photographer Underwood & Underwood. Call number F46503. Denver, Colorado; **R95** *top* © Getty Images; *foreground* © Getty Images; *background* © Alain Evrard/Getty Images.

BACK COVER

© Masterfile.

Houghton Mifflin Harcourt has made every effort to locate the copyright holders of all copyrighted material in this book and to make full acknowledgment for its use. Omissions brought to our attention will be corrected in a subsequent edition.